WHITAKER'S CON
2020

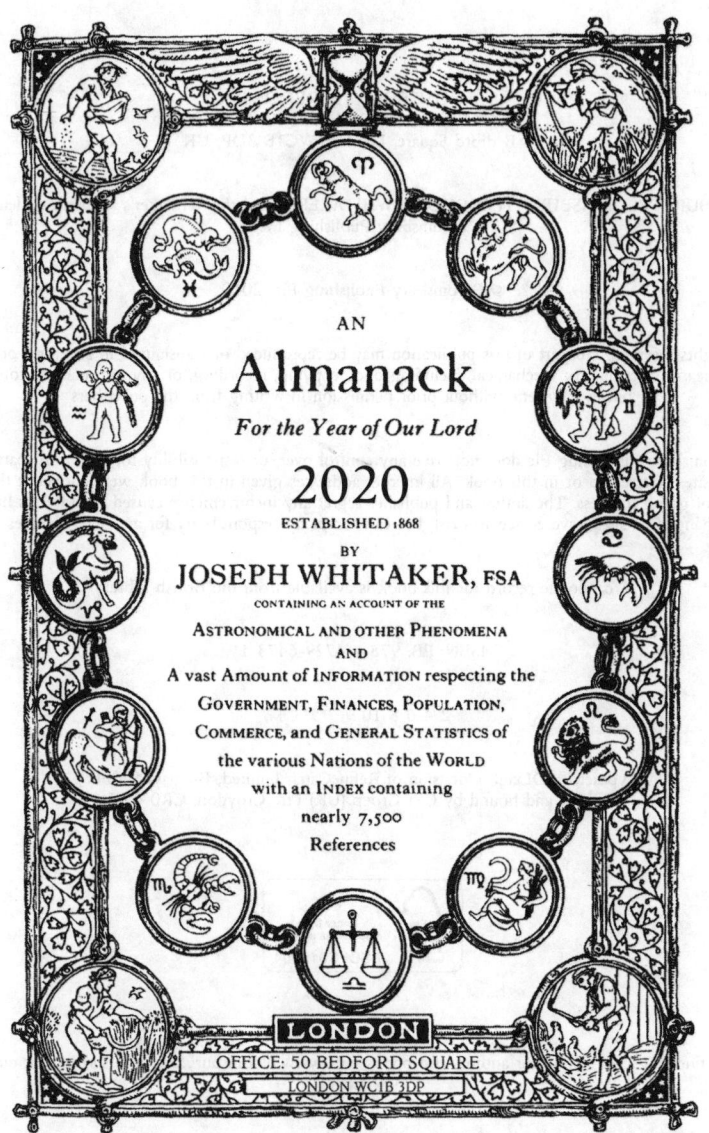

AN

Almanack

For the Year of Our Lord

2020

ESTABLISHED 1868

BY

JOSEPH WHITAKER, FSA

CONTAINING AN ACCOUNT OF THE

ASTRONOMICAL AND OTHER PHENOMENA

AND

A vast Amount of INFORMATION respecting the
GOVERNMENT, FINANCES, POPULATION,
COMMERCE, and GENERAL STATISTICS of
the various Nations of the WORLD
with an INDEX containing
nearly 7,500
References

LONDON

OFFICE: 50 BEDFORD SQUARE
LONDON WC1B 3DP

The traditional design of the title page for Whitaker's Almanack which has appeared in each edition since 1868

BLOOMSBURY YEARBOOKS

LONDON · OXFORD · NEW YORK · NEW DELHI · SYDNEY

BLOOMSBURY YEARBOOKS
Bloomsbury Publishing Plc
50 Bedford Square, London, WC1B 3DP, UK

BLOOMSBURY, BLOOMSBURY YEARBOOKS, WHITAKER'S, and the Whitaker's logo are trademarks of
Bloomsbury Publishing Plc

A catalogue record for this book is available from the British Library

ISBN: PB: 978-1-4729-6473-1

2 4 6 8 10 9 7 5 3 1

Typeset by DLxml, a division of RefineCatch Limited, Bungay, Suffolk
Printed and bound by CPI Group (UK) Ltd. Croydon, CR0 4YY

MIX
Paper from
responsible sources
FSC® C013604

To find out more about our authors and books visit www.bloomsbury.com and sign up for our
newsletters

CONTENTS

TIME AND SPACE

At the time of going to press on *Whitaker's Concise 2020,* parliament was prorogued and Prime Minister Boris Johnson had just completed his 10th September re-shuffle following Amber Rudd's departure from the cabinet.

This was just the most recent of the numerous government changes and high volume of ministerial resignations that has kept Whitaker's extraordinarily busy this year, not to mention the plethora of changes to MPs' party affiliations. Despite this, as always, the entire book has been thoroughly updated, from the arrival of Archie Mountbatten-Windsor in the Royal Family, through Defence, Law, Education and Conservation, to the UK results of the European parliament election in May.

In addition, our section on 'Human Development' in Time Measurement and Calendars has been updated in line with recent genetic discoveries, one such being the analysis of a 90,000-year-old fragment of bone, whose genetic sequence revealed the mother to be Neanderthal while the father belonged to a different hominin group altogether.

A General Election is looking increasingly likely in the near future – if, in fact, it hasn't already happened by the time this edition of Whitaker's is published. General Election results are always published in full on the Whitaker's website (www.whitakersalmanack.com). Should there be an autumn election any readers that would like a copy of the full results should contact the editorial office by email (whitakersalmanackteam@bloomsbury.com), quoting code **WhitA2020Print** and a copy will be provided at our earliest convenience.

Remember, all print purchasers can also subscribe to our entire website using the code above to receive a 30 per cent discount at checkout. An online subscription gives the benefit of access to new content as soon as it is made available, and well ahead of the next print publication. The online edition also features content not in this concise version; profiles of every country of the world and the 2018–19 year in review section, which provides a fascinating historical snapshot of the past year, covering subjects as broad as the arrival of 5G, the activities of environmental campaigners Extinction Rebellion, the past year's film blockbusters, and an amazing year of sport, culminating in the 14 July 'Super Sunday' when the Cricket World Cup and Wimbledon Men's finals, and the British Grand Prix, brought some welcome relief from the Brexit debate.

Ruth Northey
Executive Editor
whitakersalmanackteam@bloomsbury.com
www.whitakersalmanack.com

COVER PHOTOGRAPHS

Main image: New British Prime Minister Boris Johnson addresses national and international media on Downing Street in London on 24 July 2019 © Getty Images

Top, from left to right:
1. England cricketers Ben Stokes and Joe Root after winning the ICC Cricket World Cup Final against New Zealand at Lord's Cricket Ground, London on 14 July 2019 © Getty Images
2. TRH the Duke of Sussex and Duchess of Sussex, with their newborn son Archie Harrison Mountbatten-Windsor during a photocall in St George's Hall at Windsor Castle on 8 May 2019 © Getty Images
3. The Lovell Radio Telescope at Jodrell Bank, Cheshire; Jodrell Bank was made the UK's 32nd UNESCO World Heritage Site in July 2019 © Getty Images
4. HM The Queen stands with US President Donald Trump during a welcome ceremony at Buckingham Palace on 3 June 2019 at the start of the President's three-day state visit © Getty Images

SOURCES

Whitaker's Concise was compiled with the assistance of the Press Association and the UK Hydrographic Office. Crown copyright material is reproduced with the permission of the Controller of Her Majesty's Stationery Office.

EDITORIAL STAFF

Executive Editor: Ruth Northey
Project Editor: James Robinson-Prior
Editorial Assistants: Katie Amey; Kristen Mankosa; Evangeline Stanford
Head of Yearbooks: Katy McAdam

Thanks to Stephen Kershaw

CONTRIBUTORS

Sheridan Williams, Dr John Savage (Astronomy); Anthea Lipsett, Caroline Macready (Education); Clive Longhurst (Insurance); Chris Priestley, John Huxley (Legal Notes, England & Wales); Richard McMeeken (Legal Notes, Scotland); and Sarah Perkins (Taxation)

Terrestrial Magnetism data supplied by Dr Susan Macmillan of the British Geological Survey

Night Sky data supplied by John Flannery of the Irish Astronomical Society

THE YEAR 2020

THE YEAR 2020

CHRONOLOGICAL CYCLES AND ERAS

Dominical Letter	ED
Epact	5
Golden Number (Lunar Cycle)	VII
Julian Period	6733
Roman Indiction	13
Solar Cycle	13

	Beginning
*Muslim year AH 1441	31 Aug/1 Sep 2019
Japanese year Reiwa 2	1 Jan
Roman year 2773 AUC	14 Jan
Chinese year of the Rat	25 Jan
Regnal year 69	6 Feb
Sikh new year	14 Mar
Indian (Saka) year 1942	21 Mar
Hindu new year (Chaitra)	25 Mar
*Jewish year AM 5781	19 Sep

* Year begins at sunset on the previous day

RELIGIOUS CALENDARS

CHRISTIAN

Epiphany	6 Jan
Presentation of Christ in the Temple	2 Feb
Ash Wednesday	26 Feb
The Annunciation	25 Mar
Palm Sunday	5 Apr
Maundy Thursday	9 Apr
Good Friday	10 Apr
Easter Day (western churches)	12 Apr
Easter Day (Eastern Orthodox)	19 Apr
Rogation Sunday	17 May
Ascension Day	21 May
Pentecost (Whit Sunday)	31 May
Trinity Sunday	7 Jun
Corpus Christi	11 Jun
All Saints' Day	1 Nov
Advent Sunday	29 Nov
Christmas Day	25 Dec

HINDU

Makar Sankranti	14 Jan
Vasant Panchami (Sarasvati Puja)	29 Jan
Shivaratri	21 Feb
Holi	9 Mar
Chaitra (Spring new year)	25 Mar
Rama Navami	2 Apr
Raksha Bandhan	3 Aug
Krishna Janmashtami	12 Aug
Ganesh Chaturthi, first day	22 Aug
Navratri festival (Durga Puja), first day	17 Oct
Dussehra	25 Oct
Diwali (New Year festival of lights), first day	14 Nov

JEWISH

Purim	10 Mar
Pesach (Passover), first day	9 Apr
Shavuot (Feast of Weeks), first day	29 May
Rosh Hashanah (Jewish new year)	19 Sep
Yom Kippur (Day of Atonement)	28 Sep
Sukkot (Feast of Tabernacles), first day	3 Oct
Hanukkah (Festival of Lights), first day	11 Dec

MUSLIM†

Al-Hijra (Muslim new year)	1 Sep 2019
Ashura	10 Sep 2019
Ramadan, first day	25 April
Eid-ul-Fitr	25 May
Hajj, first day	30 Jul
Eid-ul-Adha	1 Aug

SIKH

Birthday of Guru Gobind Singh Ji	5 Jan
1 Chet (Sikh new year)	14 Mar
‡Hola Mohalla	10 Mar
Vaisakhi	14 Apr
Martyrdom of Guru Arjan Dev Ji	16 Jun
Martyrdom of Guru Tegh Bahadur Ji	24 Nov
‡Birthday of Guru Nanak Dev Ji	30 Nov

† The Islamic calendar is lunar so religious dates may vary by one or two days locally and according to when the new Moon is first seen
‡ Currently celebrated according to the lunar, rather than Nanakshahi, calendar, so the date varies annually

CIVIL CALENDAR

Duchess of Cambridge's birthday	9 Jan
Countess of Wessex's birthday	20 Jan
Accession of the Queen	6 Feb
Duke of York's birthday	19 Feb
St David's Day	1 Mar
Commonwealth Day	9 Mar
Earl of Wessex's birthday	10 Mar
St Patrick's Day	17 Mar
Birthday of the Queen	21 Apr
St George's Day	23 Apr
Coronation Day	2 Jun
The Queen's Official Birthday	13 Jun
Duke of Edinburgh's birthday	10 Jun
Duke of Cambridge's birthday	21 Jun
Duchess of Cornwall's birthday	17 Jul
Princess Royal's birthday	15 Aug
Remembrance Sunday	8 Nov
Prince of Wales' birthday	14 Nov
Wedding Day of the Queen	20 Nov
St Andrew's Day	30 Nov

LEGAL CALENDAR

LAW TERMS

Hilary Term	11 Jan to 8 Apr
Easter Term	21 Apr to 22 May
Trinity Term	2 Jun to 31 Jul
Michaelmas Term	1 Oct to 21 Dec

QUARTER DAYS (England, Wales & Northern Ireland)	TERM DAYS (Scotland)
Lady – 25 Mar	
Midsummer – 24 Jun	Candlemas – 28 Feb
Michaelmas – 29 Sep	Whitsunday – 28 May
Christmas – 25 Dec	Lammas – 28 Aug
	Martinmas – 28 Nov

2020

JANUARY					
Sunday		5	12	19	26
Monday		6	13	20	27
Tuesday		7	14	21	28
Wednesday	1	8	15	22	29
Thursday	2	9	16	23	30
Friday	3	10	17	24	31
Saturday	4	11	18	25	

FEBRUARY					
Sunday		2	9	16	23
Monday		3	10	17	24
Tuesday		4	11	18	25
Wednesday		5	12	19	26
Thursday		6	13	20	27
Friday		7	14	21	28
Saturday	1	8	15	22	29

MARCH					
Sunday	1	8	15	22	29
Monday	2	9	16	23	30
Tuesday	3	10	17	24	31
Wednesday	4	11	18	25	
Thursday	5	12	19	26	
Friday	6	13	20	27	
Saturday	7	14	21	28	

APRIL					
Sunday		5	12	19	26
Monday		6	13	20	27
Tuesday		7	14	21	28
Wednesday	1	8	15	22	29
Thursday	2	9	16	23	30
Friday	3	10	17	24	
Saturday	4	11	18	25	

MAY					
Sunday		3	10	17	24	31
Monday		4	11	18	25	
Tuesday		5	12	19	26	
Wednesday		6	13	20	27	
Thursday		7	14	21	28	
Friday	1	8	15	22	29	
Saturday	2	9	16	23	30	

JUNE					
Sunday		7	14	21	28
Monday	1	8	15	22	29
Tuesday	2	9	16	23	30
Wednesday	3	10	17	24	
Thursday	4	11	18	25	
Friday	5	12	19	26	
Saturday	6	13	20	27	

JULY					
Sunday		5	12	19	26
Monday		6	13	20	27
Tuesday		7	14	21	28
Wednesday	1	8	15	22	29
Thursday	2	9	16	23	30
Friday	3	10	17	24	31
Saturday	4	11	18	25	

AUGUST					
Sunday		2	9	16	23	30
Monday		3	10	17	24	31
Tuesday		4	11	18	25	
Wednesday		5	12	19	26	
Thursday		6	13	20	27	
Friday		7	14	21	28	
Saturday	1	8	15	22	29	

SEPTEMBER					
Sunday		6	13	20	27
Monday		7	14	21	28
Tuesday	1	8	15	22	29
Wednesday	2	9	16	23	30
Thursday	3	10	17	24	
Friday	4	11	18	25	
Saturday	5	12	19	26	

OCTOBER					
Sunday		4	11	18	25
Monday		5	12	19	26
Tuesday		6	13	20	27
Wednesday		7	14	21	28
Thursday	1	8	15	22	29
Friday	2	9	16	23	30
Saturday	3	10	17	24	31

NOVEMBER					
Sunday	1	8	15	22	29
Monday	2	9	16	23	30
Tuesday	3	10	17	24	
Wednesday	4	11	18	25	
Thursday	5	12	19	26	
Friday	6	13	20	27	
Saturday	7	14	21	28	

DECEMBER					
Sunday		6	13	20	27
Monday		7	14	21	28
Tuesday	1	8	15	22	29
Wednesday	2	9	16	23	30
Thursday	3	10	17	24	31
Friday	4	11	18	25	
Saturday	5	12	19	26	

PUBLIC HOLIDAYS	England and Wales	Scotland	Northern Ireland
New Year	1 January†	1, 2† January	1 January†
St Patrick's Day	—	—	17 March
*Good Friday	10 April	10 April	10 April
Easter Monday	13 April	—	13 April
Early May	8 May†	8 May	8 May†
Spring	25 May	25 May†	25 May
Battle of the Boyne	—	—	13 July‡
Summer	31 August	3 August	31 August
St Andrew's Day	—	30 November§	—
*Christmas	25, 28 December	25†, 28 December	25, 28 December

* In England, Wales and Northern Ireland, Christmas Day and Good Friday are common law holidays

† Subject to royal proclamation

‡ Subject to proclamation by the Secretary of State for Northern Ireland

§ The St Andrew's Day Holiday (Scotland) Bill was approved by parliament on 29 November 2006; it does not oblige employers to change their existing pattern of holidays but provides the legal framework in which the St Andrew's Day bank holiday could be substituted for an existing local holiday from another date in the year

Note: In the Channel Islands, Liberation Day is a bank and public holiday

2021

JANUARY						
Sunday		3	10	17	24	31
Monday		4	11	18	25	
Tuesday		5	12	19	26	
Wednesday		6	13	20	27	
Thursday		7	14	21	28	
Friday	1	8	15	22	29	
Saturday	2	9	16	23	30	

FEBRUARY						
Sunday			7	14	21	28
Monday		1	8	15	22	
Tuesday		2	9	16	23	
Wednesday		3	10	17	24	
Thursday		4	11	18	25	
Friday		5	12	19	26	
Saturday		6	13	20	27	

MARCH						
Sunday			7	14	21	28
Monday		1	8	15	22	29
Tuesday		2	9	16	23	30
Wednesday		3	10	17	24	31
Thursday		4	11	18	25	
Friday		5	12	19	26	
Saturday		6	13	20	27	

APRIL						
Sunday		4	11	18	25	
Monday		5	12	19	26	
Tuesday		6	13	20	27	
Wednesday		7	14	21	28	
Thursday	1	8	15	22	29	
Friday	2	9	16	23	30	
Saturday	3	10	17	24		

MAY						
Sunday		2	9	16	23	30
Monday		3	10	17	24	31
Tuesday		4	11	18	25	
Wednesday		5	12	19	26	
Thursday		6	13	20	27	
Friday		7	14	21	28	
Saturday	1	8	15	22	29	

JUNE						
Sunday		6	13	20	27	
Monday		7	14	21	28	
Tuesday	1	8	15	22	29	
Wednesday	2	9	16	23	30	
Thursday	3	10	17	24		
Friday	4	11	18	25		
Saturday	5	12	19	26		

JULY						
Sunday		4	11	18	25	
Monday		5	12	19	26	
Tuesday		6	13	20	27	
Wednesday		7	14	21	28	
Thursday	1	8	15	22	29	
Friday	2	9	16	23	30	
Saturday	3	10	17	24	31	

AUGUST						
Sunday	1	8	15	22	29	
Monday	2	9	16	23	30	
Tuesday	3	10	17	24	31	
Wednesday	4	11	18	25		
Thursday	5	12	19	26		
Friday	6	13	20	27		
Saturday	7	14	21	28		

SEPTEMBER						
Sunday		5	12	19	26	
Monday		6	13	20	27	
Tuesday		7	14	21	28	
Wednesday	1	8	15	22	29	
Thursday	2	9	16	23	30	
Friday	3	10	17	24		
Saturday	4	11	18	25		

OCTOBER						
Sunday		3	10	17	24	31
Monday		4	11	18	25	
Tuesday		5	12	19	26	
Wednesday		6	13	20	27	
Thursday		7	14	21	28	
Friday	1	8	15	22	29	
Saturday	2	9	16	23	30	

NOVEMBER						
Sunday			7	14	21	28
Monday		1	8	15	22	29
Tuesday		2	9	16	23	30
Wednesday		3	10	17	24	
Thursday		4	11	18	25	
Friday		5	12	19	26	
Saturday		6	13	20	27	

DECEMBER						
Sunday		5	12	19	26	
Monday		6	13	20	27	
Tuesday		7	14	21	28	
Wednesday	1	8	15	22	29	
Thursday	2	9	16	23	30	
Friday	3	10	17	24	31	
Saturday	4	11	18	25		

PUBLIC HOLIDAYS

	England and Wales	Scotland	Northern Ireland
New Year	1 January†	1, 4† January	1 January†
St Patrick's Day	—	—	17 March
*Good Friday	2 April	2 April	2 April
Easter Monday	5 April	—	5 April
Early May	3 May†	3 May	3 May†
Spring	31 May	31 May†	31 May
Battle of the Boyne	—	—	12 July‡
Summer	30 August	2 August	30 August
St Andrew's Day	—	30 November§	—
*Christmas	27, 28 December	27†, 28 December	27, 28 December

* In England, Wales and Northern Ireland, Christmas Day and Good Friday are common law holidays

† Subject to royal proclamation

‡ Subject to proclamation by the Secretary of State for Northern Ireland

§ The St Andrew's Day Holiday (Scotland) Bill was approved by parliament on 29 November 2006; it does not oblige employers to change their existing pattern of holidays but provides the legal framework in which the St Andrew's Day bank holiday could be substituted for an existing local holiday from another date in the year

Note: In the Channel Islands, Liberation Day is a bank and public holiday

FORTHCOMING EVENTS

* Provisional dates

JANUARY 2020
10–19   London Short Film Festival
16–2 Feb   Celtic Connections Music Festival, Glasgow
21–23   UK Open Dance Championships, Bournemouth
22–26   London Art Fair, Business Design Centre
* 25–27   RSPB Big Garden Birdwatch

FEBRUARY
2   World Wetlands Day
2   British Academy Film Awards, Royal Opera House, London
5– 23   Leicester Comedy Festival
9   Academy Awards, Los Angeles

MARCH
3   World Wildlife Day
5   World Book Day
5–8   Crufts Dog Show, NEC, Birmingham
6–11   Belfast Children's Festival
8   International Women's Day
*17   St Patrick's Day Parade, Piccadilly, London
18–24   BADA Antiques and Fine Art Fair, Duke of York Square, London
21   World Poetry Day
27–5 Apr   Oxford Literary Festival
27–13 Apr   Ideal Home Show, Olympia, London

APRIL
12–14   London Book Fair, Olympia, London
22   Earth Day

MAY
9–17   Stratford-upon-Avon Literary Festival
15–24   Bath Festival
19–23   RHS Chelsea Flower Show, Royal Hospital, London
21–31   Hay Festival of Literature and the Arts, Hay-on-Wye
21–30 Aug   Glyndebourne Festival

JUNE
1   Strawberry Fair, Cambridge
11–14   RHS Chatsworth Flower Show, Derbyshire
11–14   Isle of Wight Festival
13   Trooping the Colour, Horse Guards Parade, London
18–21   Royal Highland Show, Edinburgh
24–28   Glastonbury Festival of Contemporary Performing Arts, Somerset

JULY
3–12   Cheltenham Music Festival
7–12   RHS Hampton Court Palace Flower Show, Surrey
Early Jul   Pride Parade, London
Mid Jul–Early Sep   BBC Promenade Concerts, Royal Albert Hall, London
22–26   RHS Flower Show, Tatton Park, Cheshire

Late Jul   The Welsh Proms, St David's Hall, Cardiff
23–26   WOMAD Festival, Charlton Park, Wiltshire
25–1 Aug   Three Choirs Festival, Gloucester
30–2 Aug   Cambridge Folk Festival

AUGUST
Early Aug   Brighton Pride, Brighton and Hove
1–8   National Eisteddfod of Wales, Ceredigion County
7–29   Edinburgh Military Tattoo, Edinburgh Castle
*7–31   Edinburgh International Festival
30–31   Notting Hill Carnival, London
Late Aug–Early Nov   Blackpool Illuminations, Blackpool Promenade

SEPTEMBER
*5   Braemar Royal Highland Gathering, Aberdeenshire
8   International Literacy Day
*13–16   TUC Annual Congress
26–29   Liberal Democrat Party Conference
Late Sep   Labour Party Conference
Sep–Oct   Conservative Party Conference

OCTOBER
Early Oct   Frieze Art Fair, Regent's Park, London
Mid Oct   Booker Prize Awards
Mid Oct   BFI London Film Festival

NOVEMBER
14 Nov   Lord Mayor's Procession and Show, City of London
Mid Nov   CBI Annual Conference

SPORTS EVENTS

JANUARY 2020

4–12	Darts: BDO World Darts Championship, Indigo at the O2, London
10–26	Bowls: World Indoor Bowls Championships, Hopton-on-Sea
12–19	Snooker: Masters, Alexandra Palace, London
20–2 Feb	Tennis: Australian Open, Melbourne, Australia

FEBRUARY

1–14 Mar	Rugby Union: Six Nations Championship, Europe
2	American Football: Super Bowl 54, Miami, Florida, USA
12–17	Squash: British National Championships, Nottingham
21–8 Mar	Cricket: ICC T20 Women's World Cup, Australia
26–1 Mar	Cycling: UCI Track Cycling World Championships, Berlin, Germany

MARCH

1	Football: EFL Cup Final, Wembley Stadium, London
13–15	Athletics: IAAF World Indoor Championships, Nanjing, China
26–27 Sep	Baseball: Major League Baseball Season
28	Gymnastics: World Cup, Birmingham
29	Rowing: The Boat Race, Putney to Mortlake, London

APRIL

2–4	Horse Racing: Grand National, Aintree, Liverpool
9–12	Golf: Masters, Augusta, Georgia, USA
18–4 May	Snooker: World Championship, Crucible Theatre, Sheffield
22–29	Table Tennis: Team World Championships, Busan, South Korea
26	Athletics: London Marathon

MAY

1–2	Horse Racing: Kentucky Derby, Louisville, Kentucky, USA
6–10	Equestrian: Badminton Horse Trials, Badminton
9	Football: Scottish Cup Final, Hampden Park, Glasgow
11–24	Aquatics: European Championships, Budapest, Hungary
13–17	Equestrian: Royal Windsor Horse Show, Home Park, Windsor
22	Rugby Union: Challenge Cup Final, Stade de Marseille, Marseille, France
23	Rugby Union: Champions Cup Final, Stade de Marseille, Marseille, France
23	Football: FA Cup Final, Wembley Stadium, London
24	Motor Racing: Indianapolis 500, Indiana, USA

24–7 Jun	Tennis: French Open, Paris, France
27	Football: UEFA Europa League Final, Gdansk, Poland
30	Football: UEFA Champions League Final, Atatürk Olympic Stadium, Istanbul, Turkey

JUNE

6	Horse Racing: The Derby, Epsom Downs
18–21	Golf: US Open, Winged Foot Golf Club, New York, USA
*16–20	Horse Racing: Royal Ascot
27–19 Jul	Cycling: Tour de France
29–12 Jul	Tennis: Wimbledon Championships, All England Lawn Tennis Club, London

JULY

1–5	Rowing: Henley Royal Regatta, Henley-on-Thames
12–19	Golf: Open Championship, Royal St Georges, Kent
24–9 Aug	XXXII Summer Olympic Games, Tokyo, Japan
Late Jul	Horse Racing: King George VI and Queen Elizabeth Diamond Stakes, Ascot

AUGUST

12	Football: UEFA Super Cup final, Porto, Portugal
14–17	Golf: US PGA Championship, TPC Harding Park, California, USA
16–23	Rowing: World Championships, Bled, Slovenia
24–6 Sep	Tennis: US Open, New York
25–30	Athletics: European Championships, Paris, France

SEPTEMBER

2–6	Equestrian: Burghley Horse Trials, Stamford, Lincolnshire
Early Sep	Horse Racing: St Leger, Doncaster
Early Sep	Athletics: Great North Run, Newcastle
Early Sep–Late Dec	American Football: NFL Season
22–27	Golf: Ryder Cup, Whistling Straits, Wisconsin, USA

OCTOBER

18–15 Nov	Cricket: ICC T20 Men's World Cup, Australia
Late Oct–Early Nov	Baseball: World Series

NOVEMBER

1	Athletics: New York City Marathon, New York, USA
Mid Nov	Tennis: ATP World Tour Finals, O2 Arena, London
Late Nov	Tennis: Davis Cup Finals, Madrid, Spain

CENTENARIES

2019

1519
13 Mar	Conquistador Hernán Cortés landed in Mexico
2 May	Leonardo da Vinci, Italian painter, sculptor, architect and engineer, died
28 Jun	Charles V became Holy Roman Emperor
30 Nov	Michael Wolgemut, German painter, died

1619
7 Jan	Nicholas Hilliard, painter, died
18 May	Hugo de Groot was given life imprisonment
30 Jul	First elected legislative assembly in the New World convened in Jamestown, Virginia
5 Nov	Philips Koninck, Dutch painter, born
10 Nov	Rene Descartes had dreams that inspired *Meditations on First Philosophy*

1719
23 Jan	The principality of Liechtenstein was established
25 Apr	Daniel Defoe published *Robinson Crusoe*
17 Jun	Joseph Addison, essayist, poet and dramatist, died
20 Aug	Christian Mayer, astronomer, born
19 Sep	Jan Weenix, Dutch painter, buried
11 Dec	A sighting of aurora borealis was recorded for the first time

1819
19 Feb	William Smith discovered the South Shetland Islands in Antarctica
22 Feb	The USA purchased Florida from Spain
2 Mar	USA passed its first federal legislation on immigration
11 Mar	Sir Henry Tate, founder of the Tate Gallery, born
22 May	SS *Savannah* departed on the first steam propelled journey across the Atlantic Ocean
24 May	Queen Victoria, born
31 May	Walt Whitman, American poet, born
19 Aug	James Watt, developer of the steam engine, died
22 Nov	George Eliot, novelist, born
14 Dec	Alabama became the 22nd state of the Union

1919
1 Jan	Jerome Salinger, novelist, born
6 Jan	Theodore Roosevelt, 26th US President, died
21 Jan	Sinn Féin created its own parliament
25 Jan	The League of Nations was established
5 Feb	The American film and television studio United Artists was created
19 Feb	W. E. B. Du Bois convened the first Pan-African Congress in Paris
26 Feb	The United States Congress passed the act that established the Grand Canyon National Park
14 Mar	Max Brand published his first novel, *The Untamed*
17 Mar	Nat King Cole, American jazz pianist and vocalist, born
23 Mar	Benito Mussolini formed Fasci Italiani di Combattimento
13 Apr	The Amritsar massacre took place
7 May	Eva Perón, First Lady of Argentina (1946–52), born
29 May	Arthur Eddington validated Albert Einstein's theory of general relativity
28 Jun	The First World War officially ended with the signing of the Treaty of Versailles

19 Jul	The Cenotaph war monument, designed by Edwin Lutyens, was unveiled in Whitehall
20 Jul	Edmund Hillary, explorer and mountaineer, born
11 Aug	Germany established parliamentary democracy
19 Aug	Adolf Hitler joined the German Workers' Party
12 Sep	Afghanistan became independent
22 Oct	Doris Lessing, Nobel Prize winning author, born
3 Dec	Pierre-Auguste Renoir, painter, died

2020

1520
7 Jun	A summit between England and France began in the Field of the Cloth of Gold
30 Sep	Suleiman the Magnificent succeeded his father Selim I as Ottoman Sultan
21 Oct	The islands of St Pierre and Miquelon were discovered by explorer Joao Alvares Fagundes
28 Nov	Ferdinand Magellan and his fleet became the first Europeans to sail into the Pacific Ocean

1620
24 Apr	John Graunt, statistician, born
16 May	William Adams, navigator, died
7 Aug	Johannes Kepler's mother was arrested for witchcraft
20 Oct	Aelbert Cuyp, Dutch painter, baptised
8 Nov	Catholic forces were victorious in the Battle of White Mountain (Thirty Years' War 1618–48)
11 Nov	The *Mayflower* anchored at Cape Cod
31 Oct	John Evelyn, writer, born

1720
27 Jan	Samuel Foote, actor and playwright, baptised
10 Feb	Edmond Halley was appointed the second Astronomer Royal at the Greenwich Observatory
17 Feb	The War of the Quadruple Alliance ended with the Treaty of The Hague
6 Mar	Pieter van Bloemen, Flemish painter, died
6 Apr	The South Sea bill was passed in the House of Lords
25 May	The ship *Grand-Saint-Antoine* arrived in Marseille, bringing Europe's last major plague outbreak, which killed around 100,000
5 Aug	Anne Finch, Countess of Winchilsea, poet, died
15 Nov	Female pirates Anne Bonny and Mary Read are captured in Jamaica along with Captain 'Calico Jack' Rackham and his crew
29 Dec	Theatre Royal Haymarket, then called the 'Hay Market', opens with the play *La Fille à la Mode*

1820
17 Jan	Anne Brontë, novelist and poet, born
29 Jan	King George IV ascended to the throne on the death of his father George III, ending the English Regency
30 Jan	Captain Edward Bransfield became the first person to sight the Antarctic mainland
28 Feb	John Tenniel, illustrator, born
10 Mar	The Royal Astronomical Society was founded in London
15 Mar	Maine became the 23rd state of the Union, following the Missouri Compromise
11 May	HMS *Beagle,* the ship that carried Charles Darwin on his scientific voyage, was launched

12 May	Florence Nightingale, social reformer and statistician, born
19 Jun	Joseph Banks, naturalist and botanist, died
26 Jul	Union Bridge, crossing the River Tweed between England and Scotland, opened
1 Aug	The second half of the Regent's Canal in London, from Camden to Limehouse, was completed
3 Sep	Benjamin Henry Latrobe, architect, died
28 Nov	Friedrich Engels, German political philosopher, born

1920

2 Jan	Isaac Asimov, American writer and biochemist, born
6 Jan	John Maynard Smith, biologist, born
10 Jan	The Covenant of the League of Nations came into force
16 Jan	Alcohol Prohibition came into effect nationwide in the USA
23 Jan	Queen Wilhelmina of the Netherlands refused to extradite former German Kaiser Wilhelm II
24 Jan	Amedeo Modigliani, Italian painter and sculptor, died
2 Feb	Soviet Russia recognised the independence of the Republic of Estonia in the Treaty of Tartu
3 Feb	Henry Heimlich, American physician, born
14 Mar	Dorothy Tyler, Olympic high jumper, born
5 Apr	Arthur Hailey, British-Canadian novelist, born
14 Apr	John George Bartholomew, cartographer, died
9 May	Richard Adams, novelist, born
16 May	Joan of Arc (Jeanne d'Arc) was canonised by Pope Benedict XV
18 May	John Paul II, Pope of the Catholic Church (1978–2005), born
21 May	Mexican President Venustiano Carranza was executed by army generals
4 Jun	The Allied Powers defined the borders of the Kingdom of Hungary at the Treaty of Trianon
12 Jul	Soviet Russia recognised the sovereignty of Lithuania
10 Aug	The Treaty of Sèvres abolished the Ottoman Empire
11 Aug	Soviet Russia recognised Latvia's independence in the Treaty of Riga
14 Aug	The Games of the VII Olympiad opened in Antwerp, Belgium
16 Aug	Charles Bukowski, American writer, born
18 Aug	The 19th Amendment to the US Constitution was ratified, granting American women the right to vote
1 Sep	Greater Lebanon was declared a state under the French Mandate for Syria and the Lebanon
29 Sep	Peter D. Mitchell, Nobel Prize winning biochemist, born
2 Nov	Warren G. Harding was elected President of the USA
10 Dec	The Nobel Peace Prize was awarded to US president Woodrow Wilson

2021

1521

3 Jan	Pope Leo X excommunicated the German priest Martin Luther from the Roman Catholic church
28 Jan	Charles V, Holy Roman Emperor, opened the Diet of Worms
17 Mar	Portuguese navigator Ferdinand Magellan reached the Philippines
20 Apr	Zhengde, 11th Emperor of the Ming dynasty, died
23 Apr	Royalists defeated the *comuneros* at the Battle at Villalar
27 Apr	Portuguese navigator Ferdinand Magellan killed by Filipino natives
25 May	The Edict of Worms, outlawing Martin Luther, was issued
13 Aug	The Battle of Tenochtitlan ended with the capture of Cuauhtemoc, last Aztec Emperor
1 Dec	Takeda Shingen, Japanese warlord, born
13 Dec	King Manuel I of Portugal, died

1621

28 Jan	Pope Paul V, persecutor of Galileo, died
9 Feb	Alessandro Ludovisi was elected as Pope Gregory XV
31 Mar	King Philip of Spain (III) and Portugal (II), died
5 Apr	The *Mayflower* set sail from Plymouth, USA on its return voyage to England
3 May	Francis Bacon was accused of bribery
8 Jun	Anne de Xainctonge, founder of the first non-cloistered women's religious community, died
9 Oct	The Ottoman Empire and the Polish-Lithuanian Commonwealth signed the Treaty of Khotyn

1721

19 Mar	Pope Clement XI, died
3 Apr	Robert Walpole was appointed First Lord of the Treasury; *de facto* first prime minister of Great Britain
8 May	Michelangelo dei Conti was elected Pope Innocent XIII
30 Aug	Russia and Sweden signed the Treaty of Nystad, ending the Great Northern War
2 Nov	Tsar Peter I declared Emperor of All Russia
29 Dec	Madame De Pompadour, mistress of King Louis XV of France, born

1821

23 Feb	John Keats, English Romantic poet, died
5 May	Napoleon Bonaparte, military leader and Emperor of France, died
19 Jul	George IV was crowned king of the United Kingdom of Great Britain and Ireland
5 Aug	Bellingshausen's Russian Antarctic expedition, arrived back in Kronstadt
24 Aug	The Treaty of Córdoba was signed by Mexican and Spanish officials
15 Sep	Guatemala enacted the Act of Independence of Central America

1921

4 Feb	Betty Friedan, American feminist and author of *The Feminine Mystique*, born
17 Mar	Dr Marie Stopes opened Britain's first birth control clinic in London
19 Mar	Tommy Cooper, British comedian, born
7 June	The Parliament of Northern Ireland sat for the first time
23 Jul	The Communist Party of China was founded
29 Jul	Adolf Hitler assumed the leadership of the National Socialist German Workers' Party
31 Oct	The Fédération Sportive Féminine Internationale was formed
9 Nov	Benito Mussolini formed the National Fascist Party in Italy
23 Nov	US president Warren G. Harding signed the Willis-Campbell Act, prohibiting the medical prescription of beer or liquor
6 Dec	Anglo-Irish Treaty was signed, marking the end of the Irish War of Independence

THE UNITED KINGDOM

THE UK IN FIGURES

The United Kingdom comprises Great Britain (England, Wales and Scotland) and Northern Ireland. The Isle of Man and the Channel Islands are Crown dependencies with their own legislative systems and are not part of the UK.

ABBREVIATIONS
ONS   Office for National Statistics
NISRA   Northern Ireland Statistics and Research Agency

All data is for the UK unless otherwise stated.

AREA OF THE UNITED KINGDOM

	Sq. km	Sq. miles
United Kingdom	243,122	93,870
England	130,280	50,301
Wales	20,733	8,005
Scotland	77,958	30,100
Northern Ireland	14,150	5,463

Source: ONS (Crown copyright)

POPULATION

The first official census of population in England, Wales and Scotland was taken in 1801 and a census has been taken every ten years since, except in 1941 when there was no census because of the Second World War. The last official census in the UK was taken on 27 March 2011.

The first official census of population in Ireland was taken in 1841. However, all figures given below refer only to the area which is now Northern Ireland. Figures for Northern Ireland in 1921 and 1931 are estimates based on the censuses taken in 1926 and 1937 respectively.

Estimates of the population of England before 1801, calculated from the number of baptisms, burials and marriages, are:

1570	4,160,221	1670	5,773,646
1600	4,811,718	1700	6,045,008
1630	5,600,517	1750	6,517,035

Further details are available on the ONS website (W www.ons.gov.uk).

CENSUS RESULTS (THOUSANDS)

	United Kingdom			England and Wales			Scotland			Northern Ireland		
	Total	Male	Female	Total	Male	Female	Total	Male	Female	Total	Male	Female
1801	–	–	–	8,893	4,255	4,638	1,608	739	869	–	–	–
1811	13,368	6,368	7,000	10,165	4,874	5,291	1,806	826	980	–	–	–
1821	15,472	7,498	7,974	12,000	5,850	6,150	2,092	983	1,109	–	–	–
1831	17,835	8,647	9,188	13,897	6,771	7,126	2,364	1,114	1,250	–	–	–
1841	20,183	9,819	10,364	15,914	7,778	8,137	2,620	1,242	1,378	1,649	800	849
1851	22,259	10,855	11,404	17,928	8,781	9,146	2,889	1,376	1,513	1,443	698	745
1861	24,525	11,894	12,631	20,066	9,776	10,290	3,062	1,450	1,612	1,396	668	728
1871	27,431	13,309	14,122	22,712	11,059	11,653	3,360	1,603	1,757	1,359	647	712
1881	31,015	15,060	15,955	25,974	12,640	13,335	3,736	1,799	1,936	1,305	621	684
1891	34,264	16,593	17,671	29,003	14,060	14,942	4,026	1,943	2,083	1,236	590	646
1901	38,237	18,492	19,745	32,528	15,729	16,799	4,472	2,174	2,298	1,237	590	647
1911	42,082	20,357	21,725	36,070	17,446	18,625	4,761	2,309	2,452	1,251	603	648
1921	44,027	21,033	22,994	37,887	18,075	19,811	4,882	2,348	2,535	1,258	610	648
1931	46,038	22,060	23,978	39,952	19,133	20,819	4,843	2,326	2,517	1,243	601	642
1951	50,225	24,118	26,107	43,758	21,016	22,742	5,096	2,434	2,662	1,371	668	703
1961	52,709	25,481	27,228	46,105	22,304	23,801	5,179	2,483	2,697	1,425	694	731
1971	55,515	26,952	28,562	48,750	23,683	25,067	5,229	2,515	2,714	1,536	755	781
1981	55,848	27,104	28,742	49,155	23,873	25,281	5,131	2,466	2,664	*1,533	750	783
1991	56,467	27,344	29,123	49,890	24,182	25,707	4,999	2,392	2,607	1,578	769	809
2001	58,789	28,581	30,208	52,042	25,327	26,715	5,062	2,432	2,630	1,685	821	864
2011	63,182	31,028	32,153	56,076	27,574	28,502	5,295	2,567	2,728	1,810	887	923

* Figure includes 44,500 non-enumerated persons

ISLANDS

	Isle of Man			Jersey			Guernsey		
	Total	Male	Female	Total	Male	Female	Total	Male	Female
1901	54,752	25,496	29,256	52,576	23,940	28,636	40,446	19,652	20,794
1921	60,284	27,329	32,955	49,701	22,438	27,263	38,315	18,246	20,069
1951	55,123	25,749	29,464	57,296	27,282	30,014	43,652	21,221	22,431
1971	56,289	26,461	29,828	72,532	35,423	37,109	51,458	24,792	26,666
1991	69,788	33,693	36,095	84,082	40,862	43,220	58,867	28,297	30,570
2001	76,315	37,372	38,943	87,186	42,485	44,701	59,807	29,138	30,669
2006	80,058	39,523	40,535	–	–	–	–	–	–
2011	84,497	41,971	42,526	97,857	48,296	49,561	62,915	31,025	31,890

Source: Guernsey Annual Publication Bulletin, Isle of Man Government, States of Jersey Statistics Unit

RESIDENT POPULATION

ACTUAL AND PROJECTED BY COUNTRY
people, thousands

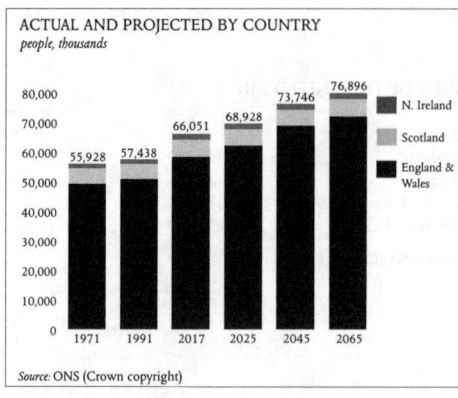

Source: ONS (Crown copyright)

PROJECTED AGE DISTRIBUTION, 2017 AND 2065
percentage

Source: ONS (Crown copyright)

NON-UK BORN RESIDENTS BY COUNTRY OF BIRTH
thousands

	2004	2018
Poland	94	832
India	505	832
Pakistan	285	535
Romania	–	392
Republic of Ireland	453	369
Germany	276	309
Italy	–	253
South Africa	181	246
Bangladesh	228	241
China	152	207

Source: ONS (Crown Copyright)

BY AGE AND SEX (UK), 2018
people, thousands

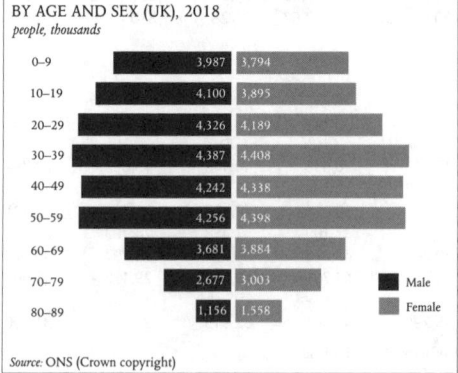

Source: ONS (Crown copyright)

ASYLUM

NATIONALITIES APPLYING FOR UK ASYLUM
in the year ending June

Top 5 Nationalities	2018	2019
1) Iran	2,432	4,208
2) Iraq	2,409	3,180
3) Albania	1,538	2,801
4) Eritrea	1,525	2,239
5) Pakistan	2,317	1,872

Source: Home Office, National Statistics: Asylum

BIRTHS

	Live births 2017	Birth rate 2017*
United Kingdom	755,042	11.4
England and Wales	679,106	11.6
Scotland	52,861	9.7
Northern Ireland	23,075	12.3

* Live births per 1,000 population
Source: ONS (Crown copyright)

FERTILITY RATES
Total fertility rate is the average number of children which would be born to a woman if she experienced the age-specific fertility rates of the period in question throughout her child-bearing life span. The figures for the years 1960–2 are estimates.

	1960–2	2000	2017
United Kingdom	3.07	1.62	1.74
England and Wales	2.77	1.65	1.76
Scotland	2.98	1.48	1.47
Northern Ireland	3.47	1.75	1.87

Source: General Register Office for Scotland, NISRA, ONS (Crown copyright)

MATERNITY RATES FOR ENGLAND AND WALES 2017

	All maternities*	Singleton	All multiple	Twins	Triplets
All ages	671,194	660,573	10,621†	10,462	154
>20	20,323	22,175	148	145	3
20–24	96,968	95,980	988	980	8
25–29	188,294	185,834	2,460	2,422	35
30–34	213,997	210,472	3,525	3,473	50
35–39	122,995	120,351	2,644	2,605	39
40–44	26,412	25,727	685	673	12
45+	2,205	2,034	171	164	7

* Includes stillbirths
† Total includes live maternities of quads and above
Source: ONS (Crown copyright)

TOP TEN BABY NAMES (ENGLAND AND WALES)

	1904 Girls	1904 Boys	2018 Girls	2018 Boys
1	Mary	William	Olivia	Oliver
2	Florence	John	Amelia	George
3	Doris	George	Ava	Harry
4	Edith	Thomas	Isla	Noah
5	Dorothy	Arthur	Emily	Jack
6	Anne	James	Mia	Leo
7	Margaret	Charles	Isabella	Arthur
8	Alice	Frederick	Sophia	Muhammad
9	Elizabeth	Albert	Ella	Oscar
10	Elsie	Ernest	Grace	Charlie

Source: ONS (Crown copyright)

LIVE BIRTHS (ENGLAND AND WALES)
by age of mother

Year	under 20	20-29	30-39	40+	All ages
1947	27,747	509,052	309,531	34,696	881,026
1957	41,228	442,219	218,883	21,051	723,381
1967	84,542	535,458	193,364	18,800	832,164
1977	54,447	382,460	126,334	5,988	569,259
1987	57,545	432,161	183,162	8,643	681,511
1997	46,372	321,381	262,428	12,914	643,095
2007	44,805	313,354	306,504	25,350	690,013
2017	20,358	287,534	341,901	29,313	679,106

Source: ONS (Crown copyright)

MARRIAGE AND DIVORCE

	Marriages 2016–17	Divorces 2016–17
England and Wales	249,793	101,669
Scotland	28,440	7,938
Northern Ireland	8,306	2,089

Source: NISRA, ONS (Crown copyright), Scottish Government

LEGAL ABORTIONS

	2005	2018
England and Wales	186,416	200,608
Scotland	12,665	13,286

Source: Department of Health, NHS Scotland

DEATHS

INFANT MORTALITY RATE 2017*

United Kingdom	3.9
England and Wales	4.0
Scotland	3.3
Northern Ireland	3.8

* Deaths of infants under one year of age per 1,000 live births
Source: NISRA, ONS (Crown copyright), Scottish Government

DEATHS IN THE UK
people

Source: ONS (Crown copyright)

EMPLOYMENT

MEDIAN FULL-TIME GROSS ANNUAL EARNINGS BY REGION (£)

Region	2005	2018
UK	22,888	29,574
England	23,280	29,005
North East	20,263	26,297
North West	21,777	27,315
Yorkshire and the Humber	21,506	26,894
East Midlands	21,494	26,749
West Midlands	21,447	27,716
East	22,883	29,128
London	29,882	38,826
South East	24,229	30,826
South West	21,279	27,969
Wales	20,634	26,346
Scotland	21,312	29,274
Northern Ireland	20,060	27,006

Source: ONS (Crown Copyright)

ANNUAL GENDER PAY GAP
percentage

Source: ONS (Crown Copyright)

OVERSEAS VISITS TO THE UK

Year	Visits (thousands)	Spending (£m)
1980	12,419	2,961
1985	14,450	5,442
1990	18,017	7,748
1995	23,538	11,762
2000	25,207	12,806
2005	29,970	14,247
2010	29,804	16,714
2011	30,798	17,998
2012	31,085	18,640
2013	32,689	21,259
2014	34,380	21,851
2015	36,115	22,072
2016	37,610	22,544
2017	39,214	24.507
2018	37,905	22,897

DEATHS BY CAUSE, 2017

	England and Wales	Scotland	N. Ireland
Total deaths	533,253	57,883	16,036
Deaths from natural causes	512,027	54,731	15,757
Certain infectious and parasitic diseases	5,368	686	212
Intestinal infectious diseases	1,259	128	24
Respiratory and other tuberculosis	153	10	3
Meningococcal infection	49	1	2
Viral hepatitis	179	28	3
Human immunodeficiency virus (HIV)	162	6	3
Neoplasms	149,652	16,558	4,581
Malignant neoplasms	146,269	16,207	4,960
Malignant neoplasm of trachea, bronchus and lung	30,131	4,069	1,058
Malignant melanoma of skin	2,106	185	71
Malignant neoplasm of breast	10,219	954	317
Malignant neoplasm of cervix uteri	730	105	19
Malignant neoplasm of prostate	10,755	986	301
Leukaemia	4,315	387	319
Diseases of the blood and blood-forming organs and certain disorders involving the immune mechanism	1,099	98	40
Endocrine, nutritional and metabolic diseases	8,435	1,330	345
Diabetes mellitus	6,046	1,016	230
Mental and behavioural disorders	50,765	4,591	1,457
Vascular and unspecified dementia	49,657	4,161	1,317
Diseases of the nervous system	33,051	3,976	1,063
Meningitis (excluding meningococcal)	154	19	3
Alzheimer's disease	17,984	2,388	583
Diseases of the circulatory system	133,511	15,114	3,780
Ischaemic heart diseases	57,923	6,727	1,825
Cerebrovascular diseases	31,713	3,927	988
Diseases of the respiratory system	73,455	136	1,973
Influenza and Pneumonia	27,635	3,535	742
Bronchitis, emphysema and other chronic obstructive pulmonary diseases	28,597	3,449	1,845
Asthma	1,320	106	38
Diseases of the digestive system	25,627	3,134	800
Gastric and duodenal ulcer	1,866	121	31
Diseases of the liver	8,450	1,063	186
Diseases of the skin and subcutaneous tissue	2,132	188	25
Diseases of the musculo-skeletal system and connective tissue	3,751	388	122
Osteoporosis	810	70	13
Diseases of the genitourinary system	9,106	957	282
Complications of pregnancy, childbirth and the puerperium	26	5	–
Certain conditions originating in the perinatal period	188	98	35
Congenital malformations, deformations and chromosomal abnormalities*	1,414	192	81
Symptoms, signs and abnormal findings not classified elsewhere	12,448	587	127
Senility	7,666	227	42
Sudden infant death syndrome	78	15	–
Deaths from external causes	21,226	3,152	773
Suicide and intentional self-harm	3,930	587	311
Assault	†269	56	20

* Excludes neonatal deaths (those at age under 28 days): for England and Wales neonatal deaths are included in the total number of deaths but excluded from the cause figures

† This will not be a true figure as registration of homicide and assault deaths in England and Wales is often delayed by adjourned inquests

Source: General Register Office for Scotland, NISRA, ONS (Crown copyright)

THE NATIONAL FLAG

The national flag of the United Kingdom is the Union Flag, generally known as the Union Jack.

The Union Flag is a combination of the cross of St George, patron saint of England, the cross of St Andrew, patron saint of Scotland and the cross of St Patrick, patron saint of Ireland.

Cross of St George: cross Gules in a field Argent (red cross on a white ground)

Cross of St Andrew: saltire Argent in a field Azure (white diagonal cross on a blue ground)

Cross of St Patrick: saltire Gules in a field Argent (red diagonal cross on a white ground)

A flag combining the cross of St George and the cross of St Andrew was first introduced by royal decree in 1606 following the conjoining of the English and Scottish crowns in 1603. In 1707 this flag became the flag of Great Britain after the parliaments of the two kingdoms were united. The cross of St Patrick was added in 1801 after the union of Great Britain and Ireland.

FLYING THE UNION FLAG

The correct orientation of the Union Flag when flying is with the broader diagonal band of white uppermost in the hoist (ie near the pole) and the narrower diagonal band of white uppermost in the fly (ie furthest from the pole).

The flying of the Union Flag on government buildings is decided by the Department for Digital Culture, Media and Sport (DCMS) at the Queen's command. There is no formal definition of a government building but it is generally accepted to mean a building owned or used by the Crown and/or predominantly occupied or used by civil servants or the Armed Forces.

The Scottish or Welsh governments are responsible for drawing up their own flag-flying guidance for their buildings. In Northern Ireland, the flying of flags is constrained by The Flags Regulations (Northern Ireland) 2000 and the Police Emblems and Flag Regulations (Northern Ireland) 2002. Individuals, local authorities and other organisations may fly the Union Flag whenever they wish, subject to compliance with any local planning requirement.

FLAGS AT HALF-MAST

Flags are flown at half-mast (ie two-thirds up between the top and bottom of the flagstaff) on the following occasions:
- from the announcement of the death of the sovereign until the funeral
- the death or funeral of a member of the royal family*
- the funerals of foreign rulers*
- the funerals of prime ministers and ex-prime ministers of the UK*
- the funerals of first ministers and ex-first ministers of Scotland, Wales and Northern Ireland (unless otherwise commanded by the sovereign, this only applies to flags in their respective countries)*
- other occasions by special command from the Queen

* By special command from the Queen in each case

DAYS FOR FLYING FLAGS

On 25 March 2008 the DCMS announced that UK government departments in England, Scotland and Wales may fly the Union Flag on their buildings whenever they choose and not just on the designated days listed below. In addition, on the patron saints' days of Scotland and Wales, the appropriate national flag may be flown alongside the Union Flag on UK government buildings in the wider Whitehall area. When flying on designated days flags are hoisted from 8am to sunset.

Duchess of Cambridge's birthday	9 Jan
Countess of Wessex's birthday	20 Jan
Accession of the Queen	6 Feb
Duke of York's birthday	19 Feb
St David's Day (in Wales only)*	1 Mar
Earl of Wessex's birthday	10 Mar
Commonwealth Day (2020)	9 Mar
St Patrick's Day (in Northern Ireland only)†	17 Mar
The Queen's birthday	21 Apr
St George's Day (in England only)*	23 Apr
Europe Day†	9 May
Coronation Day	2 Jun
The Queen's official birthday (2020)	13 Jun
Duke of Edinburgh's birthday	10 Jun
Duke of Cambridge's birthday	21 June
Duchess of Cornwall's birthday	17 Jul
Princess Royal's birthday	15 Aug
Remembrance Day (2020)	8 Nov
Prince of Wales' birthday	14 Nov
Wedding Day of the Queen	20 Nov
St Andrew's Day (in Scotland only)*	30 Nov

Opening of parliament by the Queen‡
Prorogation of parliament by the Queen‡

* The appropriate national flag, or the European flag, may be flown in addition to the Union Flag (where there are two or more flagpoles), but not in a superior position

† Only the Union Flag should be flown

‡ Only in the Greater London area, whether or not the Queen performs the ceremony in person

THE ROYAL STANDARD

The Royal Standard comprises four quarterings – two for England (three lions passant), one for Scotland* (a lion rampant) and one for Ireland (a harp).

The Royal Standard is flown when the Queen is in residence at a royal palace, on transport being used by the Queen for official journeys and from Victoria Tower when the Queen attends parliament. It may also be flown on any building (excluding ecclesiastical buildings) during a visit by the Queen. If the Queen is to be present in a building, advice on flag flying can be obtained from the DCMS.

The Royal Standard is never flown at half-mast, even after the death of the sovereign, as the new monarch immediately succeeds to the throne.

* In Scotland a version with two Scottish quarterings is used

THE ROYAL FAMILY

THE SOVEREIGN

ELIZABETH II, by the Grace of God, of the United Kingdom of Great Britain and Northern Ireland and of her other Realms and Territories Queen, Head of the Commonwealth, Defender of the Faith

Her Majesty Elizabeth Alexandra Mary of Windsor, elder daughter of King George VI and of HM Queen Elizabeth the Queen Mother

Born 21 April 1926, at 17 Bruton Street, London W1
Ascended the throne 6 February 1952
Crowned 2 June 1953, at Westminster Abbey
Married 20 November 1947, in Westminster Abbey, HRH the Prince Philip, Duke of Edinburgh
Official residences Buckingham Palace, London SW1A 1AA; Windsor Castle, Berks; Palace of Holyroodhouse, Edinburgh
Private residences Sandringham, Norfolk; Balmoral Castle, Aberdeenshire

HUSBAND OF THE QUEEN

HRH THE PRINCE PHILIP, DUKE OF EDINBURGH, KG, KT, OM, GCVO, GBE, Royal Victorian Chain, AK, QSO, PC, Ranger of Windsor Park

Born 10 June 1921, son of Prince and Princess Andrew of Greece and Denmark, naturalised a British subject 1947, created Duke of Edinburgh, Earl of Merioneth and Baron Greenwich 1947

CHILDREN OF THE QUEEN

HRH THE PRINCE OF WALES (Prince Charles Philip Arthur George), KG, KT, GCB, OM and Great Master of the Order of the Bath, AK, QSO, PC, ADC(P)

Born 14 November 1948, created Prince of Wales and Earl of Chester 1958, succeeded as Duke of Cornwall, Duke of Rothesay, Earl of Carrick and Baron Renfrew, Lord of the Isles and Great Steward of Scotland 1952

Married (1) 29 July 1981 Lady Diana Frances Spencer (Diana, Princess of Wales (1961–97), youngest daughter of the 8th Earl Spencer and the Hon. Mrs Shand Kydd), marriage dissolved 1996; (2) 9 April 2005 Mrs Camilla Rosemary Parker Bowles, now HRH the Duchess of Cornwall, GCVO, PC (*born* 17 July 1947, daughter of Major Bruce Shand and the Hon. Mrs Rosalind Shand)

Residences Clarence House, London SW1A 1BA; Highgrove, Doughton, Tetbury, Glos GL8 8TN; Birkhall, Ballater, Aberdeenshire

Issue
1. HRH the Duke of Cambridge (Prince William Arthur Philip Louis), KG, KT, PC *born* 21 June 1982, *created* Duke of Cambridge, Earl of Strathearn and Baron Carrickfergus 2011 *married* 29 April 2011 Catherine Elizabeth Middleton, now HRH the Duchess of Cambridge, GCVO (*born* 9 January 1982, elder daughter of Michael and Carole Middleton), and has issue, HRH Prince George of Cambridge (Prince George Alexander Louis), *born* 22 July 2013; HRH Princess Charlotte of Cambridge (Princess Charlotte Elizabeth Diana), *born* 2 May 2015; HRH Prince

Louis of Cambridge (Prince Louis Arthur Charles), *born* 23 April 2018 *Residences* Kensington Palace, London W8 4PU; Anmer Hall, Norfolk PE31 6RW
2. HRH the Duke of Sussex (Prince Henry Charles Albert David), KCVO *born* 15 September 1984, *created* Duke of Sussex, Earl of Dumbarton and Baron Kilkeel 2018 *married* 19 May 2018 (Rachel) Meghan Markle, now HRH the Duchess of Sussex (*born* 4 August 1981, daughter of Thomas Markle and Doria Ragland), and has issue, Archie Harrison Mountbatten-Windsor, *born* 6 May 2019 *Residence* Frogmore Cottage, Home Park, Windsor, Berks SL4 2JG

HRH THE PRINCESS ROYAL (Princess Anne Elizabeth Alice Louise), KG, KT, GCVO

Born 15 August 1950, declared the Princess Royal 1987
Married (1) 14 November 1973 Captain Mark Anthony Peter Phillips, CVO (*born* 22 September 1948); marriage dissolved 1992; (2) 12 December 1992 Vice-Adm. Sir Timothy James Hamilton Laurence, KCVO, CB, ADC (P) (*born* 1 March 1955)
Residence Gatcombe Park, Minchinhampton, Glos GL6 9AT
Issue
1. Peter Mark Andrew Phillips, *born* 15 November 1977, *married* 17 May 2008 Autumn Patricia Kelly, and has issue, Savannah Phillips, *born* 29 December 2010; Isla Elizabeth Phillips, *born* 29 March 2012
2. Zara Anne Elizabeth Tindall, MBE, *born* 15 May 1981, *married* 30 July 2011 Michael James Tindall, MBE, and has issue, Mia Grace Tindall, *born* 17 January 2014; Lena Elizabeth Tindall, *born* 18 June 2018

HRH THE DUKE OF YORK (Prince Andrew Albert Christian Edward), KG, GCVO, ADC(P)

Born 19 February 1960, created Duke of York, Earl of Inverness and Baron Killyleagh 1986
Married 23 July 1986 Sarah Margaret Ferguson, now Sarah, Duchess of York (*born* 15 October 1959, younger daughter of Major Ronald Ferguson and Mrs Hector Barrantes), marriage dissolved 1996
Residence Royal Lodge, Windsor Great Park, Berks
Issue
1. HRH Princess Beatrice of York (Princess Beatrice Elizabeth Mary), *born* 8 August 1988
2. HRH Princess Eugenie, Mrs Jack Brooksbank (Princess Eugenie Victoria Helena), *born* 23 March 1990, *married* 12 October 2018 Jack Christopher Stamp Brooksbank

HRH THE EARL OF WESSEX (Prince Edward Antony Richard Louis), KG, GCVO, ADC(P)

Born 10 March 1964, created Earl of Wessex, Viscount Severn 1999 and Earl of Forfar 2019
Married 19 June 1999 Sophie Helen Rhys-Jones, now HRH the Countess of Wessex, GCVO (*born* 20 January 1965, daughter of Mr and Mrs Christopher Rhys-Jones)
Residence Bagshot Park, Bagshot, Surrey GU19 5HS
Issue
1. Lady Louise Mountbatten-Windsor (Louise Alice Elizabeth Mary Mountbatten-Windsor), *born* 8 November 2003
2. Viscount Severn (James Alexander Philip Theo Mountbatten-Windsor), *born* 17 December 2007

NEPHEW AND NIECE OF THE QUEEN

Children of HRH the Princess Margaret, Countess of Snowdon and the Earl of Snowdon (*see* House of Windsor):
EARL OF SNOWDON (DAVID ALBERT CHARLES ARMSTRONG-JONES), *born* 3 November 1961, *married* 8 October 1993 Hon. Serena Alleyne Stanhope, and has issue, Viscount Linley (Charles Patrick Inigo Armstrong-Jones), *born* 1 July 1999; Lady Margarita Armstrong-Jones (Margarita Elizabeth Alleyne Armstrong-Jones), *born* 14 May 2002
LADY SARAH CHATTO (Sarah Frances Elizabeth), *born* 1 May 1964, *married* 14 July 1994 Daniel Chatto, and has issue, Samuel David Benedict Chatto, *born* 28 July 1996; Arthur Robert Nathaniel Chatto, *born* 5 February 1999

COUSINS OF THE QUEEN

Child of HRH the Duke of Gloucester and HRH Princess Alice, Duchess of Gloucester (*see* House of Windsor):
HRH THE DUKE OF GLOUCESTER (Prince Richard Alexander Walter George), KG, GCVO, Grand Prior of the Order of St John of Jerusalem
Born 26 August 1944
Married 8 July 1972 Birgitte Eva van Deurs, now HRH the Duchess of Gloucester, GCVO (*born* 20 June 1946, daughter of Asger Henriksen and Vivian van Deurs)
Residence Kensington Palace, London W8 4PU
Issue
1. Earl of Ulster (Alexander Patrick Gregers Richard), *born* 24 October 1974 *married* 22 June 2002 Dr Claire Alexandra Booth, and has issue, Lord Culloden (Xan Richard Anders), *born* 12 March 2007; Lady Cosima Windsor (Cosima Rose Alexandra), *born* 20 May 2010
2. Lady Davina Windsor (Davina Elizabeth Alice Benedikte), *born* 19 November 1977 *married* 31 July 2004 Gary Christie Lewis (marriage dissolved 2018), and has issue, Senna Kowhai Lewis, *born* 22 June 2010; Tane Mahuta Lewis, *born* 25 May 2012
3. Lady Rose Gilman (Rose Victoria Birgitte Louise), *born* 1 March 1980 *married* 19 July 2008 George Edward Gilman, and has issue, Lyla Beatrix Christabel Gilman, *born* 30 May 2010; Rufus Gilman, *born* 2 November 2012

Children of HRH the Duke of Kent and Princess Marina, Duchess of Kent (*see* House of Windsor):
HRH THE DUKE OF KENT (Prince Edward George Nicholas Paul Patrick), KG, GCMG, GCVO, ADC(P)
Born 9 October 1935
Married 8 June 1961 Katharine Lucy Mary Worsley, now HRH the Duchess of Kent, GCVO (*born* 22 February 1933, daughter of Sir William Worsley, Bt.)
Residence Wren House, Palace Green, London W8 4PY
Issue
1. Earl of St Andrews (George Philip Nicholas), *born* 26 June 1962, *married* 9 January 1988 Sylvana Tomaselli, and has

issue, Lord Downpatrick (Edward Edmund Maximilian George), *born* 2 December 1988; Lady Marina-Charlotte Windsor (Marina-Charlotte Alexandra Katharine Helen), *born* 30 September 1992; Lady Amelia Windsor (Amelia Sophia Theodora Mary Margaret), *born* 24 August 1995
2. Lady Helen Taylor (Helen Marina Lucy), *born* 28 April 1964, *married* 18 July 1992 Timothy Verner Taylor, and has issue, Columbus George Donald Taylor, *born* 6 August 1994; Cassius Edward Taylor, *born* 26 December 1996; Eloise Olivia Katharine Taylor, *born* 3 March 2003; Estella Olga Elizabeth Taylor, *born* 21 December 2004
3. Lord Nicholas Windsor (Nicholas Charles Edward Jonathan), *born* 25 July 1970, *married* 4 November 2006 Princess Paola Doimi de Lupis Frankopan Subic Zrinski, and has issue, Albert Louis Philip Edward Windsor, *born* 22 September 2007; Leopold Ernest Augustus Guelph Windsor, *born* 8 September 2009; Louis Arthur Nicholas Felix Windsor, *born* 27 May 2014

HRH PRINCESS ALEXANDRA, THE HON. LADY OGILVY (Princess Alexandra Helen Elizabeth Olga Christabel), KG, GCVO
Born 25 December 1936
Married 24 April 1963 the Rt. Hon. Sir Angus Ogilvy, KCVO (1928–2004), second son of 12th Earl of Airlie
Residence Thatched House Lodge, Richmond Park, Surrey TW10 5HP
Issue
1. James Robert Bruce Ogilvy, *born* 29 February 1964, *married* 30 July 1988 Julia Rawlinson, and has issue, Flora Alexandra Ogilvy, *born* 15 December 1994; Alexander Charles Ogilvy, *born* 12 November 1996
2. Marina Victoria Alexandra Ogilvy, *born* 31 July 1966, *married* 2 February 1990 Paul Julian Mowatt (marriage dissolved 1997), and has issue, Zenouska May Mowatt, *born* 26 May 1990; Christian Alexander Mowatt, *born* 4 June 1993

HRH PRINCE MICHAEL OF KENT (Prince Michael George Charles Franklin), GCVO
Born 4 July 1942
Married 30 June 1978 Baroness Marie-Christine Agnes Hedwig Ida von Reibnitz, now HRH Princess Michael of Kent (*born* 15 January 1945, daughter of Baron Gunther von Reibnitz)
Residence Kensington Palace, London W8 4PU
Issue
1. Lord Frederick Windsor (Frederick Michael George David Louis), *born* 6 April 1979, *married* 12 September 2009 Sophie Winkleman, and has issue, Maud Elizabeth Daphne Marina Windsor, *born* 15 August 2013; Isabella Alexandra May Windsor, *born* 16 January 2016
2. Lady Gabriella Kingston (Gabriella Marina Alexandra Ophelia), *born* 23 April 1981, *married* 18 May 2019 Thomas Kingston

ORDER OF SUCCESSION

The Succession to the Crown Act 2013 received royal assent on 25 April 2013 and made provision for the order of succession to the Crown not to be dependent on gender and for those members of the royal family married to a Roman Catholic to retain the right of succession to the throne. The provisions of the Act came into force on 26 March 2015, following its ratification by all 16 Realms of the Commonwealth.

On the Act's commencement HRH Prince Michael of Kent and the Earl of St Andrews were restored to the succession. In addition, all male members of the royal family born after 28 October 2011 no longer precede any elder female siblings; and their place in the order of succession changed accordingly.

The following list includes all living descendants of the sons of King George V eligible to succeed to the Crown under the current legislation. Lord Nicholas Windsor, Lord Downpatrick and Lady Marina-Charlotte Windsor renounced their rights to the throne on converting to Roman Catholicism in 2001, 2003 and 2008 respectively. Their children remain in succession provided that they are in communion with the Church of England.

1	HRH the Prince of Wales	31	Lady Davina Windsor
2	HRH the Duke of Cambridge	32	Senna Lewis
3	HRH Prince George of Cambridge	33	Tane Lewis
4	HRH Princess Charlotte of Cambridge	34	Lady Rose Gilman
5	HRH Prince Louis of Cambridge	35	Lyla Gilman
6	HRH the Duke of Sussex	36	Rufus Gilman
7	Archie Mountbatten-Windsor	37	HRH the Duke of Kent
8	HRH the Duke of York	38	Earl of St Andrews
9	HRH Princess Beatrice of York	39	Lady Amelia Windsor
10	HRH Princess Eugenie, Mrs Jack Brooksbank	40	Albert Windsor
11	HRH the Earl of Wessex	41	Leopold Windsor
12	Viscount Severn	42	Louis Windsor
13	Lady Louise Mountbatten-Windsor	43	Lady Helen Taylor
14	HRH the Princess Royal	44	Columbus Taylor
15	Peter Phillips	45	Cassius Taylor
16	Savannah Phillips	46	Eloise Taylor
17	Isla Phillips	47	Estella Taylor
18	Zara Tindall	48	HRH Prince Michael of Kent
19	Mia Tindall	49	Lord Frederick Windsor
20	Lena Tindall	50	Maud Windsor
21	Earl of Snowdon	51	Isabella Windsor
22	Viscount Linley	52	Lady Gabriella Kingston
23	Lady Margarita Armstrong-Jones	53	HRH Princess Alexandra, the Hon. Lady Ogilvy
24	Lady Sarah Chatto	54	James Ogilvy
25	Samuel Chatto	55	Alexander Ogilvy
26	Arthur Chatto	56	Flora Ogilvy
27	HRH the Duke of Gloucester	57	Marina Ogilvy
28	Earl of Ulster	58	Christian Mowatt
29	Lord Culloden	59	Zenouska Mowatt
30	Lady Cosima Windsor		

THE ROYAL HOUSEHOLD

The PRIVATE SECRETARY is responsible for:
- informing and advising the Queen on constitutional, governmental and political matters in the UK, her other Realms and the wider Commonwealth, including communications with the prime minister and government departments
- organising the Queen's domestic and overseas official programme
- the Queen's speeches, messages, patronage, photographs, portraits and official presents
- communications in connection with the role of the royal family
- dealing with correspondence to the Queen from members of the public
- royal travel policy
- coordinating and initiating research to support engagements by members of the royal family

The DIRECTOR OF ROYAL COMMUNICATIONS is in charge of Buckingham Palace's communications office and reports to the Private Secretary. The director is responsible for:
- developing communications strategies to enhance the public understanding of the role of the monarchy
- briefing the British and international media on the role and duties of the Queen and issues relating to the royal family
- responding to media enquiries
- arranging media facilities in the UK and overseas to support royal functions and engagements
- the management of the royal website

The Private Secretary is keeper of the royal archives and is responsible for the care of the records of the sovereign and the royal household from previous reigns, preserved in the royal archives at Windsor. As keeper, it is the Private Secretary's responsibility to ensure the proper management of the records of the present reign with a view to their transfer to the archives as and when appropriate. The Private Secretary is an *ex officio* trustee of the Royal Collection Trust.

The KEEPER OF THE PRIVY PURSE AND TREASURER TO THE QUEEN is responsible for:
- the Sovereign Grant, which is the money paid from the government's Consolidated Fund to meet official expenditure relating to the Queen's duties as Head of State and Head of the Commonwealth and is provided by the government in return for the net surplus from the Crown Estate and other hereditary revenues (*see also* Royal Finances)
- through the Director of Human Resources, the planning and management of personnel policy across the royal household, the allocation of employee and pensioner housing and the administration of all its pension schemes and private estates employees
- information systems and telecommunications
- property services at occupied royal palaces in England, comprising Buckingham Palace, St James's Palace, Clarence House, Marlborough House Mews, the residential and office areas of Kensington Palace, Windsor Castle and buildings in the Home and Great Parks of Windsor and Hampton Court Mews and Paddocks
- delivery of all official and approved travel operations
- audit services
- health and safety; insurance matters
- the Privy Purse, which is mainly financed by the net income of the Duchy of Lancaster, and meets both official and private expenditure incurred by the Queen
- liaison with other members of the royal family and their households on financial matters
- the Queen's private estates at Sandringham and Balmoral, the Queen's Racing Establishment and the Royal Studs and liaison with the Ascot Authority
- the Home Park at Windsor and liaison with the Crown Estate Commissioners concerning the Home Park and the Great Park at Windsor
- the Royal Philatelic Collection
- administrative aspects of the Military Knights of Windsor
- administration of the Royal Victorian Order, of which the Keeper of the Privy Purse is secretary, Long and Faithful Service Medals, and the Queen's cups, medals and prizes, and policy on commemorative medals

The Keeper of the Privy Purse is also responsible for the Royal Mews, assisted by the CROWN EQUERRY, who has day-to-day responsibility for:
- the provision of carriage processions for the state opening of parliament, state visits, Trooping of the Colour, Royal Ascot, the Garter Ceremony, the Thistle Service, the presentation of credentials to the Queen by incoming foreign ambassadors and high commissioners, and other state and ceremonial occasions
- the provision of chauffeur-driven cars
- coordinating travel arrangements by road in respect of the royal household
- supervision and administration of the Royal Mews at Buckingham Palace, Windsor Castle, Hampton Court and the Palace of Holyroodhouse

The Keeper of the Privy Purse is one of three royal trustees (in respect of his responsibilities for the Sovereign Grant) and is Receiver-General of the Duchy of Lancaster and a member of the Duchy's Council.

The Keeper of the Privy Purse has overall responsibility for the DIRECTOR OF OPERATIONS, ROYAL TRAVEL, who is responsible for the provision of travel arrangements by air and rail and is also an *ex officio* trustee of the Royal Collection Trust.

The DIRECTOR OF THE PROPERTY SECTION has day-to-day responsibility for the royal household's property section:
- fire and health and safety
- repairs and refurbishment of buildings and new building work
- utilities and telecommunications
- putting up stages, tents and other work in connection with ceremonial occasions, garden parties and other official functions

The property section is also responsible, on a sub-contract basis from the DCMS, for the maintenance of Marlborough House (which is occupied by the Commonwealth Secretariat).

The MASTER OF THE HOUSEHOLD is responsible for:
- delivering the majority of the official and private entertaining in the Queen's annual programme across all the occupied palaces and residences in the UK when required
- periodic support for entertaining by all other members of the royal family
- furnishings and internal decorative refurbishment of all the occupied palaces in the UK in conjunction with the Director, Royal Collection Trust
- all operational, domestic and kitchen staff in the royal household

The COMPTROLLER, LORD CHAMBERLAIN'S OFFICE is responsible for:

- the organisation of all ceremonial engagements, including state visits to the Queen in the UK, royal weddings and funerals, the state opening of parliament, Guards of Honour at Buckingham Palace, investitures, and the Garter and Thistle ceremonies
- garden parties at Buckingham Palace and the Palace of Holyroodhouse
- the Crown Jewels, which are part of the Royal Collection, when they are in use on state occasions
- coordination of the arrangements for the Queen to be represented at funerals and memorial services and at the arrival and departure of visiting heads of state
- advising on matters of precedence, style and titles, dress, flying of flags, gun salutes, mourning and other ceremonial issues
- supervising the applications for Royal Warrants of Appointment
- advising on the commercial use of royal emblems and contemporary royal photographs
- the ecclesiastical household, the medical household, the bodyguards and certain ceremonial appointments such as Gentlemen Ushers and Pages of Honour
- the Lords in Waiting, who represent the Queen on various occasions and escort visiting heads of state during incoming state visits
- the Queen's bargemaster and watermen and the Queen's swans
- the Royal Almonry and Royal Maundy Service

The Comptroller also has overall responsibility for the MARSHAL OF THE DIPLOMATIC CORPS, who is responsible for the relationship between the royal household and the Diplomatic Heads of Mission in London; and the SECRETARY OF THE CENTRAL CHANCERY OF THE ORDERS OF KNIGHTHOOD, who administers the Orders of Chivalry, makes arrangements for investitures and the distribution of insignia, and ensures the proper public notification of awards through The London Gazette.

The DIRECTOR, ROYAL COLLECTION TRUST is responsible for:
- the administration and custodial control of the Royal Collection in all royal residences
- the care, display, conservation and restoration of items in the collection
- initiating and assisting research into the collection and publishing catalogues and books on the collection
- making the collection accessible to the public and educating and informing the public about the collection

The Royal Collection, which contains a large number of works of art, is held by the Queen as sovereign in trust for her successors and the nation and is not owned by her as an individual. The administration, conservation and presentation of the Royal Collection are funded by the Royal Collection Trust solely from income from visitors to Windsor Castle, Buckingham Palace and the Palace of Holyroodhouse. The Royal Collection Trust is chaired by the Prince of Wales. The Lord Chamberlain, the Private Secretary and the Keeper of the Privy Purse are ex officio trustees and there are three external trustees appointed by the Queen.

The Director, Royal Collection Trust is also at present the SURVEYOR OF THE QUEEN'S WORKS OF ART, responsible for paintings, miniatures and works of art on paper, including the watercolours, prints and drawings in the Print Room at Windsor Castle, and for the books, manuscripts, coins, medals and insignia in the Royal Library.

Royal Collection Enterprises Limited is the trading subsidiary of the Royal Collection Trust. The company, whose chair is the Keeper of the Privy Purse, is responsible for:

- managing access by the public to Windsor Castle (including Frogmore House), Buckingham Palace (including the Royal Mews and the Queen's Gallery) and the Palace of Holyroodhouse (including the Queen's Gallery)
- running shops at each location
- managing the images and intellectual property rights of the Royal Collection

The Director, Royal Collection Trust is also an ex officio trustee of Historic Royal Palaces.

PRIVATE SECRETARIES

THE QUEEN
Office: Buckingham Palace, London SW1A 1AA T 020-7930 4832
Private Secretary to The Queen, Rt. Hon. Edward Young, CVO

PRINCE PHILIP, THE DUKE OF EDINBURGH
Office: Buckingham Palace, London SW1A 1AA T 020-7930 4832
Private Secretary, Brig. Archie Miller-Bakewell

THE PRINCE OF WALES AND THE DUCHESS OF CORNWALL
Office: Clarence House, London SW1A 1BA T 020-7930 4832
Principal Private Secretary, Clive Alderton, CVO

THE DUKE AND DUCHESS OF CAMBRIDGE
Office: Kensington Palace, Palace Green, London W8 4PU
T 020-7930 4832
Private Secretary to the Duke of Cambridge, Simon Case, CVO
Private Secretary to the Duchess of Cambridge, Catherine Quinn

THE DUKE AND DUCHESS OF SUSSEX
Office, Kensington Palace, Palace Green, London W8 4PU
T 020-7930 4832
Private Secretary to the Duke and Duchess of Sussex, Fiona Mcilwham

THE DUKE OF YORK
Office: Buckingham Palace, London SW1A 1AA T 020-7024 4227
Private Secretary, Amanda Thirsk, LVO

THE EARL AND COUNTESS OF WESSEX
Office: Bagshot Park, Surrey GU19 5PL T 01276-707040
Private Secretary, Capt. Andy Aspden, RN

THE PRINCESS ROYAL
Office: Buckingham Palace, London SW1A 1AA T 020-7024 4199
Private Secretary, Charles Davies, MVO

THE DUKE AND DUCHESS OF GLOUCESTER
Office: Kensington Palace, London W8 4PU T 020-7368 1000
Private Secretary, Lt.-Col. Alastair Todd

THE DUKE OF KENT
Office: York House, St James's Palace, London SW1A 1BQ
T 020-7930 4872
Private Secretary, Nicholas Turnbull, MBE, QGM

PRINCE AND PRINCESS MICHAEL OF KENT
Office: Kensington Palace, London W8 4PU
W www.princemichael.org.uk
Private Secretary, Camilla Rogers

PRINCESS ALEXANDRA, THE HON. LADY OGILVY
Office: Buckingham Palace, London SW1A 1AA
T 020-7024 4270
Private Secretary, Diane Duke, LVO

SENIOR MANAGEMENT OF THE ROYAL HOUSEHOLD

Lord Chamberlain, Earl Peel, GCVO, PC

HEADS OF DEPARTMENT
Private Secretary to The Queen, Rt. Hon. Edward Young, CVO
Keeper of the Privy Purse, Sir Michael Stevens, KCVO
Master of the Household, Vice-Adm. Tony Johnstone-Burt, CB, OBE
Comptroller, Lord Chamberlain's Office, Lt.-Col. Michael Vernon
Director of the Royal Collection, Tim Knox

NON-EXECUTIVE MEMBERS
Private Secretary to the Duke of Edinburgh, Brig. Archie Miller-Bakewell
Principal Private Secretary to the Prince of Wales and the Duchess of Cornwall, Clive Alderton, LVO

ASTRONOMER ROYAL

The post of Astronomer Royal dates back to 1675, when astronomy had many practical applications in navigation. Today the post is largely honorary, although the Astronomer Royal is expected to be available for consultation on scientific matters for as long as the holder remains a professional astronomer. The Astronomer Royal receives a stipend of £100 a year and is a member of the royal household.

Astronomer Royal, Lord Rees of Ludlow, OM, *apptd* 1995

MASTER OF THE QUEEN'S MUSIC

The office of Master of the Queen's Music is an honour conferred on a musician of great distinction. The office was first created in 1626, when the master was responsible for the court musicians. Since the reign of King George V, the position has had no fixed duties, although the Master may choose to produce compositions to mark royal or state occasions. The Master of the Queen's Music is paid an annual stipend of £15,000. In 2004 the length of appointment was changed from life tenure to a ten-year term.

Master of the Queen's Music, Judith Weir, CBE, *apptd* 2014

POET LAUREATE

The post of Poet Laureate was officially established when John Dryden was appointed by royal warrant as Poet Laureate and Historiographer Royal in 1668. The post is attached to the royal household and was originally conferred on the holder for life; in 1999 the length of appointment was changed to a ten-year term. It is customary for the Poet Laureate to write verse to mark events of national importance. The postholder currently receives an honorarium of £5,750 a year.

The Poet Laureate, Simon Armitage, *apptd* 2019

ROYAL FINANCES

Dating back to the late 17th century the Civil List was originally used by the sovereign to supplement hereditary revenues for paying the salaries of judges, ambassadors and other government officers as well as the expenses of the royal household. In 1760, on the accession of George III, it was decided that the Civil List would be provided by parliament to cover all relevant expenditure in return for the king surrendering the hereditary revenues of the Crown. At that time parliament undertook to pay the salaries of judges, ambassadors etc. In 1831 parliament agreed also to meet the costs of the royal palaces in return for a reduction in the Civil List.

Until 1 April 2012 the Civil List met the central staff costs and running expenses of the Queen's official household. Annual grants-in-aid provided for the maintenance of the occupied royal palaces (*see* Royal Household for a list of occupied palaces) and royal travel.

THE SOVEREIGN GRANT

Under the Sovereign Grant Act 2011, which came into force on 1 April 2012, the funding previously provided by the Civil List and the grants-in-aid was consolidated in the Sovereign Grant. It is provided by HM Treasury from public funds in exchange for the surrender by the Queen of the revenue of the Crown Estate.

For 2016–17 the Sovereign Grant was calculated based on 15 per cent of the income account net surplus of the Crown Estate for the financial year two years previous. From 2017–18 this increased to 25 per cent, providing for a Sovereign Grant of £82.2m in 2018–19. The additional grant generated (£32.9m in 2018–19) will be used to fund the reservicing of Buckingham Palace over a ten-year period.

Official core expenditure met by the Sovereign Grant in 2018–19 amounted to £49.6m. Royal travel accounted for £4.6m of the expenditure and property maintenance for £23.7m. The excess of core expenditure over core Sovereign Grant of £0.3m was transferred from the Sovereign Grant reserve.

The legislative requirement is for Sovereign Grant accounts to be audited by the Comptroller and Auditor-General, scrutinised by the National Audit Office, and submitted to parliament annually. They are subjected to the same scrutiny as for any other government department. The annual report for the year to 31 March 2019 was published in June 2019.

£m	2017–18	2018–19
Sovereign Grant	76.1	82.2
Core	45.7	49.3
Buckingham Palace	30.4	32.9
Transfer (to)/ from the reserve	(28.7)	(15.2)
Core	(2.4)	0.3
Buckingham Palace	(26.3)	(15.5)
Net Expenditure	47.4	67.0

PARLIAMENTARY ANNUITIES

The Civil List acts provided for other members of the royal family to receive annuities from government funds to meet the expenses of carrying out their official duties. Since 1993 these annuities the Queen reimbursed HM Treasury for all of them except those paid to the late Queen Elizabeth the Queen Mother and the Duke of Edinburgh. The Sovereign Grant Act 2011 repealed all parliamentary annuities paid to the royal family, with the exception of that paid to the Duke of Edinburgh (£359,000 in 2018–19). This is now paid directly from the Consolidated Fund.

THE PRIVY PURSE

The funds received by the Privy Purse pay for official expenses incurred by the Queen as head of state and for some of the Queen's private expenditure. The revenues of the Duchy of Lancaster are the principal source of income for the privy purse. The revenues of the Duchy were retained by George III in 1760 when the hereditary revenues were surrendered. The Duchy Council reports to the Chancellor of the Duchy of Lancaster, who is accountable directly to the sovereign rather than to parliament. However the chancellor does answer parliamentary questions on matters relating to the Duchy's responsibilities.

THE DUCHY OF LANCASTER, 1 Lancaster Place, London WC2E 7ED **W** www.duchyoflancaster.co.uk

Chancellor of the Duchy of Lancaster, Rt. Hon. Michael Gove, MP, *apptd* 2019

Chair of the Council, Sir Alan Reid, GCVO

Chief Executive and Clerk, Nathan Thompson

Receiver-General, Sir Michael Stevens, KCVO

Attorney-General, Robert Miles, QC

PERSONAL INCOME

The Queen's personal income derives mostly from investments, and is used to meet private expenditure.

PRINCE OF WALES' FUNDING

The Duchy Estate was created in 1337 by Edward III for his son Prince Edward (the Black Prince) who became the Duke of Cornwall. The Duchy's primary function is to provide an income from its assets for the Prince of Wales. Under a 1337 charter, confirmed by subsequent legislation, the Prince of Wales is not entitled to the proceeds or profit on the sale of Duchy assets but only to the annual income which is generated. The Duchy is responsible for the sustainable and commercial management of its properties, investment portfolio and 55,120 hectares of land, based mostly in the south-west of England. The Prince of Wales also uses a proportion of his Duchy income to meet the cost of his official public duties and the public, charitable and private activities of the Duchess of Cornwall, the Duke and Duchess of Cambridge and the Duke and Duchess of Sussex.

THE DUCHY OF CORNWALL, 10 Buckingham Gate, London SW1E 6LA **T** 020-7834 7346 **W** www.duchyofcornwall.org

Lord Warden of the Stannaries, Sir Nicholas Bacon, Bt., OBE

Receiver-General, Hon. Sir James Leigh-Pemberton, CVO

Attorney-General, Jonathan Crow, QC

Secretary and Keeper of the Records, Alastair Martin

TAXATION

The sovereign is not legally liable to pay income tax or capital gains tax, but since 6 April 1993 has paid both on a voluntary basis. The main provisions for the Queen and the Prince of Wales to pay tax are set out in a Memorandum of Understanding on Royal Taxation presented to parliament on 11 February 1993. The Queen pays income and capital gains tax in respect of her private income and assets, and on the proportion of the income and capital gains of the Privy Purse used for private purposes. Inheritance tax will be paid on the Queen's assets, except for those which pass to the next sovereign, whether automatically or by gift or bequest. The Prince of Wales pays income tax on income from the Duchy of Cornwall used for private purposes.

ROYAL SALUTES

ENGLAND

The basic royal salute is 21 rounds with an extra 20 rounds fired at Hyde Park because it is a royal park. At the Tower of London 62 rounds are fired on royal anniversaries (21 plus a further 20 because the Tower is a royal palace and a further 21 'for the City of London') and 41 on other occasions. When the Queen's official birthday coincides with the Duke of Edinburgh's birthday, 124 rounds are fired from the Tower (62 rounds for each birthday). Gun salutes occur on the following royal anniversaries:

• Accession Day
• The Queen's birthday
• Coronation Day
• Duke of Edinburgh's birthday
• The Queen's Official Birthday
• The Prince of Wales' birthday
• State opening of parliament

Gun salutes also occur when parliament is prorogued by the sovereign, on royal births and when a visiting head of state meets the sovereign in London, Windsor or Edinburgh.

In London, salutes are fired at Hyde Park and the Tower of London although on some occasions (state visits, state opening of parliament and the Queen's birthday parade) Green Park is used instead of Hyde Park. Other military saluting stations in England are at Colchester, Dover, Plymouth, Woolwich and York.

Constable of the Royal Palace and Fortress of London, Gen. Lord Houghton of Richmond, GCB, CBE

Lieutenant of the Tower of London, Lt.-Gen. Sir Simon Mayall, KBE, CB

Master Gunner within The Tower, Col. Hon. Mark Vincent, MBE

Resident Governor and Keeper of the Jewel House, Col. Richard Harrold, CVO, OBE

Master Gunner of St James's Park, Lt.-Gen. Sir Andrew Gregory, KBE, CB

SCOTLAND

Royal salutes are authorised at Edinburgh Castle and Stirling Castle. A salute of 21 guns is fired on the following occasions:
• the anniversaries of the birth, accession and coronation of the sovereign
• the anniversary of the birth of the Duke of Edinburgh

A salute of 21 guns is fired in Edinburgh on the occasion of the opening of the general assembly of the Church of Scotland. A salute of 21 guns may also be fired in Edinburgh on the arrival of HM The Queen or a member of the royal family who is a Royal Highness on an official visit.

Military saluting stations are also situated at Cardiff Castle in Wales, Hillsborough Castle in Northern Ireland and in Gibraltar.

MILITARY RANKS AND TITLES

THE QUEEN

ARMY
Colonel-in-Chief
The Life Guards; The Blues and Royals (Royal Horse Guards and 1st Dragoons); The Royal Scots Dragoon Guards (Carabiniers and Greys); The Royal Lancers; The Royal Tank Regiment; Corps of Royal Engineers; Grenadier Guards; Coldstream Guards; Scots Guards; Irish Guards; Welsh Guards; The Royal Regiment of Scotland; The Duke of Lancaster's Regiment (King's, Lancashire and Border); The Royal Welsh; Adjutant General's Corps; The Governor General's Horse Guards (of Canada); The King's Own Calgary Regiment (Royal Canadian Armoured Corps); Canadian Forces Military Engineering Branch; Le Royal 22e Regiment (of Canada); The Governor General's Foot Guards (of Canada); The Canadian Grenadier Guards; The Stormont, Dundas and Glengarry Highlanders; Le Régiment de la Chaudière (of Canada); The Royal New Brunswick Regiment; The North Shore (New Brunswick) Regiment; 48th Highlanders of Canada; The Argyll and Sutherland Highlanders of Canada (Princess Louise's); The Calgary Highlanders; Royal Australian Engineers; Royal Australian Infantry Corps; Royal Australian Army Ordnance Corps; Royal Australian Army Nursing Corps; The Corps of Royal New Zealand Engineers; Royal New Zealand Infantry Regiment; Malawi Rifles
Affiliated Colonel-in-Chief
The Queen's Gurkha Engineers
Captain-General
Royal Regiment of Artillery; The Honourable Artillery Company; Combined Cadet Force; Royal Regiment of Canadian Artillery; Royal Regiment of Australian Artillery; Royal Regiment of New Zealand Artillery; Royal New Zealand Armoured Corps
Royal Colonel
Balaklava Company, 5th Battalion The Royal Regiment of Scotland
Patron
Royal Army Chaplains' Department

ROYAL AIR FORCE
Air Commodore-in-Chief
Royal Auxiliary Air Force; Royal Air Force Regiment; Air Reserve (of Canada); Royal Australian Air Force Reserve; Territorial Air Force (of New Zealand)
Commandant-in-Chief
RAF College, Cranwell
Royal Honorary Air Commodore
RAF Marham; 603 (City of Edinburgh) Squadron Royal Auxiliary Air Force

TRI-SERVICE
Colonel-in-Chief
The Canadian Armed Forces Legal Branch

PRINCE PHILIP, DUKE OF EDINBURGH

ROYAL NAVY
Lord High Admiral of the United Kingdom
Admiral of the Fleet
Admiral of the Fleet, Royal Australian Navy
Admiral of the Fleet, Royal New Zealand Navy
Admiral, Royal Canadian Navy
Admiral, Royal Canadian Sea Cadets

ARMY
Field Marshal
Field Marshal, Australian Military Forces
Field Marshal, New Zealand Army
General, Royal Canadian Army
Colonel-in-Chief
The Queen's Royal Hussars (Queen's Own and Royal Irish); The Rifles; Corps of Royal Electrical and Mechanical Engineers; Intelligence Corps; Army Cadet Force Association; The Royal Canadian Regiment; The Royal Hamilton Light Infantry (Wentworth Regiment of Canada); The Cameron Highlanders of Ottawa; The Queen's Own Cameron Highlanders of Canada; The Seaforth Highlanders of Canada; The Royal Canadian Army Cadets; The Royal Australian Corps of Electrical and Mechanical Engineers; The Australian Army Cadet Corps
Royal Colonel
The Highlanders, 4th Battalion The Royal Regiment of Scotland
Honorary Colonel
The Trinidad and Tobago Regiment
Member
Honourable Artillery Company

ROYAL AIR FORCE
Marshal of the Royal Air Force
Marshal of the Royal Australian Air Force
Marshal of the Royal New Zealand Air Force
General, Royal Canadian Air Force
Air Commodore-in-Chief
Royal Canadian Air Cadets
Honorary Air Commodore
RAF Northolt

THE PRINCE OF WALES

ROYAL NAVY
Admiral of the Fleet
Admiral of the Fleet, Royal New Zealand Navy
Vice-Admiral
Royal Canadian Navy
Commodore-in-Chief
HM Naval Base Plymouth; Fleet Atlantic, Royal Canadian Navy
Honorary Commodore-in-Chief
Aircraft Carriers

ARMY
Field Marshal
Field Marshal, New Zealand Army
Lieutenant-General
Canadian Army
Colonel-in-Chief
The Royal Dragoon Guards; The Parachute Regiment; The Royal Gurkha Rifles; Army Air Corps; The Royal Canadian Dragoons; Lord Strathcona's Horse (Royal Canadians); The Royal Regiment of Canada; Royal Winnipeg Rifles; Royal Australian Armoured Corps; The Royal Pacific Islands Regiment; 1st The Queen's Dragoon Guards; The Black Watch (Royal Highland Regiment) of Canada; The Toronto Scottish Regiment (Queen Elizabeth The Queen Mother's Own); The Mercian Regiment; 2nd Battalion The Irish Regiment of Canada
Royal Colonel
The Black Watch, 3rd Battalion The Royal Regiment of Scotland; 51st Highland, 7th Battalion The Royal Regiment of Scotland

Colonel
The Welsh Guards
Royal Honorary Colonel
The Queen's Own Yeomanry

ROYAL AIR FORCE
Marshal of the RAF
Marshal of the Royal New Zealand Air Force
Lieutenant-General
Royal Canadian Air Force
Honorary Air Commodore
RAF Valley
Colonel-in-Chief
Air Reserve Canada

THE DUCHESS OF CORNWALL

ROYAL NAVY
Commodore-in-Chief
Royal Naval Medical Services; Naval Chaplaincy Services
Lady Sponsor
HMS *Astute;* HMS *Prince of Wales*

ARMY
Colonel-in-Chief
Queen's Own Rifles of Canada; Royal Australian Corps of Military Police
Royal Colonel
4th Battalion The Rifles

ROYAL AIR FORCE
Honorary Air Commodore
RAF Halton; RAF Leeming

THE DUKE OF CAMBRIDGE

ROYAL NAVY
Lieutenant Commander
Commodore-in-Chief
Scotland Command; Submarines Command

ARMY
Colonel
Irish Guards
Major
The Blues and Royals (Royal Horse Guards and 1st Dragoons)

ROYAL AIR FORCE
Squadron Leader
Honorary Air Commandant
RAF Coningsby

THE DUCHESS OF CAMBRIDGE

ROYAL AIR FORCE
Honorary Air Commandant
Air Cadets

THE DUKE OF SUSSEX

ROYAL NAVY
Lieutenant-Commander
Commodore-in-Chief
Small Ships and Diving Command

ROYAL MARINES
Captain-General

ARMY
Major
The Blues and Royals (Royal Horse Guards and 1st Dragoons)

ROYAL AIR FORCE
Squadron Leader
Honorary Air Commandant
RAF Honington

THE DUKE OF YORK

ROYAL NAVY
Vice-Admiral
Commodore-in-Chief
Fleet Air Arm
Admiral of the Sea Cadets Corps

ARMY
Colonel-in-Chief
The Royal Irish Regiment (27th (Inniskilling), 83rd, 87th and The Ulster Defence Regiment); The Yorkshire Regiment (14th/15th, 19th and 33rd/76th Foot); Small Arms School Corps; The Queen's York Rangers (First Americans); Royal New Zealand Army Logistics Regiment; The Royal Highland Fusiliers of Canada; The Princess Louise Fusiliers (Canada)
Deputy Colonel-in-Chief
The Royal Lancers (Queen Elizabeths' Own)
Colonel
Grenadier Guards
Royal Colonel
The Royal Highland Fusiliers, 2nd Battalion The Royal Regiment of Scotland

ROYAL AIR FORCE
Honorary Air Commodore
RAF Lossiemouth

THE EARL OF WESSEX

ROYAL NAVY
Commodore-in-Chief
Royal Fleet Auxiliary
Patron
Royal Fleet Auxiliary Association

ARMY
Colonel-in-Chief
Hastings and Prince Edward Regiment; Saskatchewan Dragoons; Prince Edward Island Regiment
Royal Colonel
2nd Battalion, The Rifles
Royal Honorary Colonel
Royal Wessex Yeomanry; The London Regiment

ROYAL AIR FORCE
Honorary Air Commodore
RAF Waddington

THE COUNTESS OF WESSEX

ARMY
Colonel-in-Chief
Corps of Army Music; Queen Alexandra's Royal Army Nursing Corps; The Lincoln and Welland Regiment; South Alberta Light Horse Regiment
Royal Colonel
5th Battalion, The Rifles
Patron
Queen Alexandra's Royal Army Nursing Corps Association

ROYAL AIR FORCE
Honorary Air Commodore
RAF Wittering

ROYAL NAVY
Sponsor
  HMS *Daring*

THE PRINCESS ROYAL

ROYAL NAVY
Admiral (Chief Commandant for Women in the Royal Navy)
Commodore-in-Chief
  HM Naval Base Portsmouth; Fleet Pacific Royal Canadian Navy

ARMY
Colonel-in-Chief
  The King's Royal Hussars; Royal Corps of Signals; Royal Logistic Corps; The Royal Army Veterinary Corps; 8th Canadian Hussars (Princess Louise's); Royal Newfoundland Regiment; Canadian Forces Communications and Electronics Branch; The Grey and Simcoe Foresters; The Royal Regina Rifles; Royal Canadian Medical Service; Royal Canadian Hussars; Royal Australian Corps of Signals; Royal Australian Corps of Transport; Royal New Zealand Corps of Signals; Royal New Zealand Nursing Corps
Affiliated Colonel-in-Chief
  The Queen's Gurkha Signals; The Queen's Own Gurkha Transport Regiment
Royal Colonel
  1st Battalion (Royal Scots Borderers), The Royal Regiment of Scotland; 6th Battalion (52nd Lowland Volunteers), The Royal Regiment of Scotland
Colonel
  The Blues and Royals (Royal Horse Guards and 1st Dragoons)
Honorary Colonel
  University of London Officers' Training Corps; City of Edinburgh Universities Officers' Training Corps
Commandant-in-Chief
  First Aid Nursing Yeomanry (Princess Royal's Volunteer Corps)

ROYAL AIR FORCE
Honorary Air Commodore
  RAF Brize Norton; University of London Air Squadron

THE DUKE OF GLOUCESTER

ARMY
Colonel-in-Chief
  The Royal Anglian Regiment; Royal Army Medical Corps; Royal New Zealand Army Medical Corps
Deputy Colonel-in-Chief
  The Royal Logistic Corps
Royal Colonel
  6th Battalion, The Rifles
Royal Honorary Colonel
  Royal Monmouthshire Royal Engineers (Militia)

ROYAL AIR FORCE
Honorary Air Marshal
Honorary Air Commodore
  RAF Odiham; No. 501 (County of Gloucester) Logistic Support Squadron

THE DUCHESS OF GLOUCESTER

ARMY
Colonel-in-Chief
  Royal Army Dental Corps; Royal Australian Army Educational Corps; Royal New Zealand Army Educational Corps; Royal Canadian Dental Corps; The Royal Bermuda Regiment

Deputy Colonel-in-Chief
  Adjutant General's Corps
Royal Colonel
  7th Battalion, The Rifles
Vice-Patron
  Adjutant General's Corps Regimental Association
Patron
  Royal Army Educational Corps Association; Army Families Federation

THE DUKE OF KENT

ARMY
Field Marshal
Colonel-in-Chief
  The Royal Regiment of Fusiliers; Lorne Scots (Peel, Dufferin and Hamilton Regiment)
Deputy Colonel-in-Chief
  The Royal Scots Dragoon Guards (Carabiniers and Greys)
Royal Colonel
  1st Battalion The Rifles
Colonel
  Scots Guards

ROYAL AIR FORCE
Honorary Air Chief Marshal

THE DUCHESS OF KENT

ARMY
Honorary Major-General
Deputy Colonel-in-Chief
  The Royal Dragoon Guards; Adjutant General's Corps; The Royal Logistic Corps

PRINCE MICHAEL OF KENT

ROYAL NAVY
Honorary Vice-Admiral of the Royal Naval Reserves
Commodore-in-Chief of the Maritime Reserves

ARMY
Colonel-in-Chief
  Essex and Kent Scottish Regiment (Ontario)
Royal Honorary Colonel
  Honourable Artillery Company
Senior Colonel
  King's Royal Hussars

ROYAL AIR FORCE
Honorary Air Marshal
  RAF Benson

PRINCESS ALEXANDRA, THE HON. LADY OGILVY

ROYAL NAVY
Patron
  Queen Alexandra's Royal Naval Nursing Service

ARMY
Colonel-in-Chief
  The Canadian Scottish Regiment (Princess Mary's)
Deputy Colonel-in-Chief
  The Royal Lancers
Royal Colonel
  3rd Battalion The Rifles
Royal Honorary Colonel
  The Royal Yeomanry

ROYAL AIR FORCE
Patron and Air Chief Commandant
  Princess Mary's RAF Nursing Service

KINGS AND QUEENS

ENGLISH KINGS AND QUEENS 927–1603

HOUSES OF CERDIC AND DENMARK

927–939 ÆTHELSTAN
Son of Edward the Elder, by Ecgwynn, and grandson of Alfred *acceded* to Wessex and Mercia *c.*924, established direct rule over Northumbria 927, effectively creating the Kingdom of England *reigned* 15 years

939–946 EDMUND I
born 921, son of Edward the Elder, by Eadgifu *married* (1) Ælfgifu (2) Æthelflæd *killed* aged 25 *reigned* 6 years

946–955 EADRED
Son of Edward the Elder, by Eadgifu *reigned* 9 years

955–959 EADWIG
born before 943, son of Edmund and Ælfgifu *married* Ælfgifu *reigned* 3 years

959–975 EDGAR I
born 943, son of Edmund and Ælfgifu *married* (1) Æthelflæd (2) Wulfthryth (3) Ælfthryth *died* aged 32 *reigned* 15 years

975–978 EDWARD I (the Martyr)
born c.962, son of Edgar and Æthelflæd *assassinated* aged c.16 *reigned* 2 years

978–1016 ÆTHELRED (the Unready)
born 968/969, son of Edgar and Ælfthryth *married* (1) Ælfgifu (2) Emma, daughter of Richard I, Count of Normandy, 1013–14 dispossessed of kingdom by Swegn Forkbeard (King of Denmark 987–1014) *died* aged c.47, *reigned* 38 years

1016 EDMUND II (Ironside)
(Apr–Nov) *born* before 993, son of Æthelred and Ælfgifu *married* Ealdgyth *died* aged over 23 *reigned* 7 months

1016–1035 CNUT (Canute)
born c.995, son of Swegn Forkbeard, King of Denmark, and Gunhild *married* (1) Ælfgifu (2) Emma, widow of Æthelred the Unready. Gained submission of West Saxons 1015, Northumbrians 1016, Mercia 1016, King of all England after Edmund's death, King of Denmark 1019–35, King of Norway 1028–35 *died* aged c.40 *reigned* 19 years

1035–1040 HAROLD I (Harefoot)
born 1016/17, son of Cnut and Ælfgifu *married* Ælfgifu 1035 recognised as regent for himself and his brother Harthacnut; 1037 recognised as king *died* aged c.23 *reigned* 4 years

1040–1042 HARTHACNUT (Harthacanute)
born c.1018, son of Cnut and Emma. Titular king of Denmark from 1028, acknowledged King of England 1035–7 with Harold I as regent; effective king after Harold's death *died* aged c.24 *reigned* 2 years

1042–1066 EDWARD II (the Confessor)
born between 1002 and 1005, son of Æthelred the Unready and Emma *married* Eadgyth, daughter of Godwine, Earl of Wessex *died* aged over 60 *reigned* 23 years

1066 HAROLD II (Godwinesson)
(Jan–Oct) *born* c.1020, son of Godwine, Earl of Wessex, and Gytha *married* (1) Eadgyth (2) Ealdgyth *killed* in battle aged c.46 *reigned* 10 months

THE HOUSE OF NORMANDY

1066–1087 WILLIAM I (the Conqueror)
born 1027/8, son of Robert I, Duke of Normandy; obtained the Crown by conquest *married* Matilda, daughter of Baldwin, Count of Flanders *died* aged c.60, *reigned* 20 years

1087–1100 WILLIAM II (Rufus)
born between 1056 and 1060, third son of William I; succeeded his father in England only *killed* aged c.40 *reigned* 12 years

1100–1135 HENRY I (Beauclerk)
born 1068, fourth son of William I *married* (1) Edith or Matilda, daughter of Malcolm III of Scotland (2) Adela, daughter of Godfrey, Count of Louvain *died* aged 67 *reigned* 35 years

1135–1154 STEPHEN
born not later than 1100, third son of Adela, daughter of William I, and Stephen, Count of Blois *married* Matilda, daughter of Eustace, Count of Boulogne. Feb–Nov 1141 held captive by adherents of Matilda, daughter of Henry I, who contested the Crown until 1153 *died* aged over 53 *reigned* 18 years

THE HOUSE OF ANJOU (PLANTAGENETS)

1154–1189 HENRY II (Curtmantle)
born 1133, son of Matilda, daughter of Henry I, and Geoffrey, Count of Anjou *married* Eleanor, daughter of William, Duke of Aquitaine, and divorced queen of Louis VII of France *died* aged 56 *reigned* 34 years

1189–1199 RICHARD I (Coeur de Lion)
born 1157, third son of Henry II *married* Berengaria, daughter of Sancho VI, King of Navarre *died* aged 42 *reigned* 9 years

1199–1216 JOHN (Lackland)
born 1167, fifth son of Henry II *married* (1) Isabella or Avisa, daughter of William, Earl of Gloucester (divorced) (2) Isabella, daughter of Aymer, Count of Angoulême *died* aged 48 *reigned* 17 years

1216–1272 HENRY III
born 1207, son of John and Isabella of Angoulême *married* Eleanor, daughter of Raymond, Count of Provence *died* aged 65 *reigned* 56 years

1272–1307 EDWARD I (Longshanks)
born 1239, eldest son of Henry III *married* (1) Eleanor, daughter of Ferdinand III, King of Castile (2) Margaret, daughter of Philip III of France *died* aged 68 *reigned* 34 years

1307–1327 EDWARD II
born 1284, eldest surviving son of Edward I and Eleanor *married* Isabella, daughter of Philip IV of France *deposed* Jan 1327 *killed* Sep 1327 aged 43 *reigned* 19 years

1327–1377 EDWARD III
born 1312, eldest son of Edward II *married* Philippa, daughter of William, Count of Hainault *died* aged 64 *reigned* 50 years

1377–1399 RICHARD II
born 1367, son of Edward (the Black Prince), eldest son of Edward III *married* (1) Anne, daughter of Emperor Charles IV (2) Isabelle, daughter of Charles VI of France *deposed* Sep 1399 *killed* Feb 1400 aged 33 *reigned* 22 years

THE HOUSE OF LANCASTER

1399–1413   HENRY IV
born 1366, son of John of Gaunt, fourth son of Edward III, and Blanche, daughter of Henry, Duke of Lancaster *married* (1) Mary, daughter of Humphrey, Earl of Hereford (2) Joan, daughter of Charles, King of Navarre, and widow of John, Duke of Brittany *died* aged *c.*47 *reigned* 13 years

1413–1422   HENRY V
born 1387, eldest surviving son of Henry IV and Mary *married* Catherine, daughter of Charles VI of France *died* aged 34 *reigned* 9 years

1422–1471   HENRY VI
born 1421, son of Henry V *married* Margaret, daughter of René, Duke of Anjou and Count of Provence *deposed* Mar 1461 *restored* Oct 1470 *deposed* Apr 1471 *killed* May 1471 aged 49 *reigned* 39 years

THE HOUSE OF YORK

1461–1483   EDWARD IV
born 1442, eldest son of Richard of York (grandson of Edmund, fifth son of Edward III; and son of Anne, great-granddaughter of Lionel, third son of Edward III) *married* Elizabeth Woodville, daughter of Richard, Lord Rivers, and widow of Sir John Grey *acceded* Mar 1461 *deposed* Oct 1470 *restored* Apr 1471 *died* aged 40 *reigned* 21 years

1483   EDWARD V
(Apr–Jun)   *born* 1470, eldest son of Edward IV *deposed* Jun 1483, *died* probably Jul–Sep 1483, aged 12 *reigned* 2 months

1483–1485   RICHARD III
born 1452, fourth son of Richard of York *married* Anne Neville, daughter of Richard, Earl of Warwick, and widow of Edward, Prince of Wales, son of Henry VI *killed* in battle aged 32 *reigned* 2 years

THE HOUSE OF TUDOR

1485–1509   HENRY VII
born 1457, son of Margaret Beaufort (great-granddaughter of John of Gaunt, fourth son of Edward III) and Edmund Tudor, Earl of Richmond *married* Elizabeth, daughter of Edward IV *died* aged 52 *reigned* 23 years

1509–1547   HENRY VIII
born 1491, second son of Henry VII *married* (1) Catherine, daughter of Ferdinand II, King of Aragon, and widow of his elder brother Arthur (divorced) (2) Anne, daughter of Sir Thomas Boleyn (executed) (3) Jane, daughter of Sir John Seymour (died in childbirth) (4) Anne, daughter of John, Duke of Cleves (divorced) (5) Catherine Howard, niece of the Duke of Norfolk (executed) (6) Catherine, daughter of Sir Thomas Parr and widow of Lord Latimer *died* aged 55 *reigned* 37 years

1547–1553   EDWARD VI
born 1537, son of Henry VIII and Jane Seymour *died* aged 15 *reigned* 6 years

1553   **JANE**
*(6/10–   *born* 1537, daughter of Frances (daughter of
19 Jul)   Mary Tudor, the younger daughter of Henry VII) and Henry Grey, Duke of Suffolk *married* Lord Guildford Dudley, son of the Duke of Northumberland *deposed* Jul 1553 *executed* Feb 1554 aged 16 *reigned* 13/9 days

1553–1558   MARY I
born 1516, daughter of Henry VIII and Catherine of Aragon *married* Philip II of Spain *died* aged 42 *reigned* 5 years

1558–1603   ELIZABETH I
born 1533, daughter of Henry VIII and Anne Boleyn *died* aged 69 *reigned* 44 years

* Depending on whether the date of her predecessor's death (6 July) or that of her official proclamation as Queen (10 July) is taken as the beginning of her reign

BRITISH KINGS AND QUEENS SINCE 1603

THE HOUSE OF STUART

1603–1625   JAMES I (VI OF SCOTLAND)
born 1566, son of Mary, Queen of Scots (granddaughter of Margaret Tudor, elder daughter of Henry VII), and Henry Stewart, Lord Darnley *married* Anne, daughter of Frederick II of Denmark *died* aged 58 *reigned* 22 years

1625–1649   CHARLES I
born 1600, second son of James I *married* Henrietta Maria, daughter of Henry IV of France *executed* 1649 aged 48 *reigned* 23 years

INTERREGNUM 1649–1660
1649–1653   Government by a council of state
1653–1658   Oliver Cromwell, Lord Protector
1658–1659   Richard Cromwell, Lord Protector

1660–1685   CHARLES II
born 1630, eldest son of Charles I *married* Catherine, daughter of John of Portugal *died* aged 54 *reigned* 24 years

1685–1688   JAMES II (VII OF SCOTLAND)
born 1633, second son of Charles I *married* (1) Lady Anne Hyde, daughter of Edward, Earl of Clarendon (2) Mary, daughter of Alphonso, Duke of Modena. Reign ended with flight from kingdom Dec 1688 *died* 1701 aged 67 *reigned* 3 years

INTERREGNUM 11 Dec 1688 to 12 Feb 1689

1689–1702   WILLIAM III
born 1650, son of William II, Prince of Orange, and Mary Stuart, daughter of Charles I *married* Mary, elder daughter of James II *died* aged 51 *reigned* 13 years

and
1689–1694   MARY II
born 1662, elder daughter of James II and Anne *died* aged 32 *reigned* 5 years

1702–1714   ANNE
born 1665, younger daughter of James II and Anne *married* Prince George of Denmark, son of Frederick III of Denmark *died* aged 49 *reigned* 12 years

THE HOUSE OF HANOVER

1714–1727 GEORGE I (Elector of Hanover)
born 1660, son of Sophia (daughter of Frederick, Elector Palatine, and Elizabeth Stuart, daughter of James I) and Ernest Augustus, Elector of Hanover *married* Sophia Dorothea, daughter of George William, Duke of Lüneburg-Celle *died* aged 67 *reigned* 12 years

1727–1760 GEORGE II
born 1683, son of George I *married* Caroline, daughter of John Frederick, Margrave of Brandenburg-Anspach *died* aged 76 *reigned* 33 years

1760–1820 GEORGE III
born 1738, son of Frederick, eldest son of George II *married* Charlotte, daughter of Charles Louis, Duke of Mecklenburg-Strelitz *died* aged 81 *reigned* 59 years

REGENCY 1811–1820
Prince of Wales regent owing to the insanity of George III

1820–1830 GEORGE IV
born 1762, eldest son of George III *married* Caroline, daughter of Charles, Duke of Brunswick-Wolfenbüttel *died* aged 67 *reigned* 10 years

1830–1837 WILLIAM IV
born 1765, third son of George III *married* Adelaide, daughter of George, Duke of Saxe-Meiningen *died* aged 71 *reigned* 7 years

1837–1901 VICTORIA
born 1819, daughter of Edward, fourth son of George III *married* Prince Albert of Saxe-Coburg and Gotha *died* aged 81 *reigned* 63 years

THE HOUSE OF SAXE-COBURG AND GOTHA

1901–1910 EDWARD VII
born 1841, eldest son of Victoria and Albert *married* Alexandra, daughter of Christian IX of Denmark *died* aged 68 *reigned* 9 years

THE HOUSE OF WINDSOR

1910–1936 GEORGE V
born 1865, second son of Edward VII *married* Victoria Mary, daughter of Francis, Duke of Teck *died* aged 70 *reigned* 25 years

1936 EDWARD VIII
(20 Jan–11 Dec) *born* 1894, eldest son of George V *married* (1937) Mrs Wallis Simpson *abdicated* 1936 *died* 1972 aged 77 *reigned* 10 months

1936–1952 GEORGE VI
born 1895, second son of George V *married* Lady Elizabeth Bowes-Lyon, daughter of 14th Earl of Strathmore and Kinghorne *died* aged 56 *reigned* 15 years

1952– ELIZABETH II
born 1926, elder daughter of George VI *married* Philip, son of Prince Andrew of Greece

KINGS AND QUEENS OF SCOTS 1016–1603

1016–1034 MALCOLM II
born c.954, son of Kenneth II *acceded* to Alba 1005, secured Lothian c.1016, obtained Strathclyde for his grandson Duncan c.1016, thus reigning over an area approximately the same as that governed by later rulers of Scotland *died* aged c.80 *reigned* 18 years

THE HOUSE OF ATHOLL

1034–1040 DUNCAN I
son of Bethoc, daughter of Malcolm II, and Crinan, Mormaer of Atholl *married* a cousin of Siward, Earl of Northumbria *reigned* 5 years

1040–1057 MACBETH
born c.1005, son of a daughter of Malcolm II and Finlaec, Mormaer of Moray *married* Gruoch, granddaughter of Kenneth III *killed* aged c.52 *reigned* 17 years

1057–1058 LULACH
(Aug–Mar) *born* c.1032, son of Gillacomgan, Mormaer of Moray, and Gruoch (and stepson of Macbeth) *died* aged c.26 *reigned* 7 months

1058–1093 MALCOLM III (Canmore)
born c.1031, elder son of Duncan I *married* (1) Ingibiorg (2) Margaret (St Margaret), granddaughter of Edmund II of England *killed* in battle aged c.62 *reigned* 35 years

1093–1097 DONALD III BÁN
born c.1033, second son of Duncan I *deposed* May 1094 *restored* Nov 1094 *deposed* Oct 1097 *reigned* 3 years

1094 DUNCAN II
(May–Nov) *born* c.1060, elder son of Malcolm III and Ingibiorg *married* Octreda of Dunbar *killed* aged c.34 *reigned* 6 months

1097–1107 EDGAR
born c.1074, second son of Malcolm III and Margaret *died* aged c.32 *reigned* 9 years

1107–1124 ALEXANDER I (the Fierce)
born c.1077, fifth son of Malcolm III and Margaret *married* Sybilla, illegitimate daughter of Henry I of England *died* aged c.47 *reigned* 17 years

1124–1153 DAVID I (the Saint)
born c.1085, sixth son of Malcolm III and Margaret *married* Matilda, daughter of Waltheof, Earl of Huntingdon *died* aged c.68 *reigned* 29 years

1153–1165 MALCOLM IV (the Maiden)
born c.1141, son of Henry, Earl of Huntingdon, second son of David I *died* aged c.24 *reigned* 12 years

1165–1214 WILLIAM I (the Lion)
born c.1142, brother of Malcolm IV *married* Ermengarde, daughter of Richard, Viscount of Beaumont *died* aged c.72 *reigned* 49 years

1214–1249 ALEXANDER II
born 1198, son of William I *married* (1) Joan, daughter of John, King of England (2) Marie, daughter of Ingelram de Coucy *died* aged 50 *reigned* 34 years

1249–1286 ALEXANDER III
born 1241, son of Alexander II and Marie *married* (1) Margaret, daughter of Henry III of England (2) Yolande, daughter of the Count of Dreux *killed* accidentally aged 44 *reigned* 36 years

1286–1290 MARGARET (the Maid of Norway)
born 1283, daughter of Margaret (daughter of Alexander III) and Eric II of Norway *died* aged 7 *reigned* 4 years

FIRST INTERREGNUM 1290–1292
Throne disputed by 13 competitors. Crown awarded to John Balliol by adjudication of Edward I of England

THE HOUSE OF BALLIOL

1292–1296   JOHN (Balliol)
born c.1250, son of Dervorguilla, great-great-granddaughter of David I, and John de Balliol *married* Isabella, daughter of John, Earl of Surrey *abdicated* 1296 *died* 1313 aged c.63 *reigned* 3 years

SECOND INTERREGNUM 1296–1306

Edward I of England declared John Balliol to have forfeited the throne for contumacy in 1296 and took the government of Scotland into his own hands

THE HOUSE OF BRUCE

1306–1329   ROBERT I (Bruce)
born 1274, son of Robert Bruce and Marjorie, Countess of Carrick, and great-grandson of the second daughter of David, Earl of Huntingdon, brother of William I *married* (1) Isabella, daughter of Donald, Earl of Mar (2) Elizabeth, daughter of Richard, Earl of Ulster *died* aged 54 *reigned* 23 years

1329–1371   DAVID II
born 1324, son of Robert I and Elizabeth *married* (1) Joanna, daughter of Edward II of England (2) Margaret Drummond, widow of Sir John Logie (divorced) *died* aged 46 *reigned* 41 years

1332   Edward Balliol, son of John Balliol
(Sep–Dec)
1333–1336   Edward Balliol

THE HOUSE OF STEWART

1371–1390   ROBERT II (Stewart)
born 1316, son of Marjorie (daughter of Robert I) and Walter, High Steward of Scotland *married* (1) Elizabeth, daughter of Sir Robert Mure of Rowallan (2) Euphemia, daughter of Hugh, Earl of Ross *died* aged 74 *reigned* 19 years

1390–1406   ROBERT III
born c.1337, son of Robert II and Elizabeth *married* Annabella, daughter of Sir John Drummond of Stobhall *died* aged c.69 *reigned* 16 years

1406–1437   JAMES I
born 1394, son of Robert III *married* Joan Beaufort, daughter of John, Earl of Somerset *assassinated* aged 42 *reigned* 30 years

1437–1460   JAMES II
born 1430, son of James I *married* Mary, daughter of Arnold, Duke of Gueldres *killed* accidentally aged 29 *reigned* 23 years

1460–1488   JAMES III
born 1452, son of James II *married* Margaret, daughter of Christian I of Denmark *assassinated* aged 36 *reigned* 27 years

1488–1513   JAMES IV
born 1473, son of James III *married* Margaret Tudor, daughter of Henry VII of England *killed* in battle aged 40 *reigned* 25 years

1513–1542   JAMES V
born 1512, son of James IV *married* (1) Madeleine, daughter of Francis I of France (2) Mary of Lorraine, daughter of the Duc de Guise *died* aged 30 *reigned* 29 years

1542–1567   MARY
born 1542, daughter of James V and Mary *married* (1) the Dauphin, afterwards Francis II of France (2) Henry Stewart, Lord Darnley (3) James Hepburn, Earl of Bothwell *abdicated* 1567, prisoner in England from 1568, *executed* 1587 *reigned* 24 years

1567–1625   JAMES VI (and I of England)
born 1566, son of Mary, Queen of Scots, and Henry, Lord Darnley *acceded* 1567 to the Scottish throne *reigned* 58 years *succeeded* 1603 to the English throne, so joining the English and Scottish crowns in one person. The two kingdoms remained distinct until 1707 when the parliaments of the kingdoms became conjoined

WELSH SOVEREIGNS AND PRINCES

Wales was ruled by sovereign princes from the earliest times until the death of Llywelyn in 1282. The first English Prince of Wales was the son of Edward I, who was born in Caernarvon town on 25 April 1284. According to a discredited legend, he was presented to the Welsh chieftains as their prince, in fulfilment of a promise that they should have a prince who 'could not speak a word of English' and should be native born. This son, who afterwards became Edward II, was created 'Prince of Wales and Earl of Chester' at the Lincoln Parliament on 7 February 1301.

The title Prince of Wales is borne after individual conferment and is not inherited at birth, though some Princes have been declared and styled Prince of Wales but never formally so created (s.). The title was conferred on Prince Charles by the Queen on 26 July 1958. He was invested at Caernarvon on 1 July 1969.

INDEPENDENT PRINCES AD 844 TO 1282

844–878	Rhodri the Great
878–916	Anarawd, son of Rhodri
916–950	Hywel Dda, the Good
950–979	Iago ab Idwal (or Ieuaf)
979–985	Hywel ab Ieuaf, the Bad
985–986	Cadwallon, his brother
986–999	Maredudd ab Owain ap Hywel Dda
999–1005	Cynan ap Hywel ab Ieuaf
1005–1018	Aeddan ap Blegywyrd
1018–1023	Llywelyn ap Seisyll
1023–1039	Iago ab Idwal ap Meurig
1039–1063	Gruffydd ap Llywelyn ap Seisyll
1063–1075	Bleddyn ap Cynfyn
1075–1081	Trahaern ap Caradog
1081–1137	Gruffydd ap Cynan ab Iago
1137–1170	Owain Gwynedd
1170–1194	Dafydd ab Owain Gwynedd
1194–1240	Llywelyn Fawr, the Great
1240–1246	Dafydd ap Llywelyn
1246–1282	Llywelyn ap Gruffydd ap Llywelyn

ENGLISH PRINCES SINCE 1301

1301	Edward (Edward II)
1343	Edward the Black Prince, son of Edward III
1376	Richard (Richard II), son of the Black Prince
1399	Henry of Monmouth (Henry V)
1454	Edward of Westminster, son of Henry VI
1471	Edward of Westminster (Edward V)
1483	Edward, son of Richard III (d. 1484)
1489	Arthur Tudor, son of Henry VII
1504	Henry Tudor (Henry VIII)
1610	Henry Stuart, son of James I (d. 1612)
1616	Charles Stuart (Charles I)
c.1638 (s.)	Charles Stuart (Charles II)
1688 (s.)	James Francis Edward Stuart (The Old Pretender), son of James II (d. 1766)
1714	George Augustus (George II)
1729	Frederick Lewis, son of George II (d. 1751)
1751	George William Frederick (George III)
1762	George Augustus Frederick (George IV)
1841	Albert Edward (Edward VII)
1901	George (George V)
1910	Edward (Edward VIII)
1958	Charles, son of Elizabeth II

PRINCESSES ROYAL

The style Princess Royal is conferred at the sovereign's discretion on his or her eldest daughter. It is an honorary title, held for life, and cannot be inherited or passed on. It was first conferred on Princess Mary, daughter of Charles I, in approximately 1642.

c.1642	Princess Mary (1631–60), daughter of Charles I
1727	Princess Anne (1709–59), daughter of George II
1766	Princess Charlotte (1766–1828), daughter of George III
1840	Princess Victoria (1840–1901), daughter of Victoria
1905	Princess Louise (1867–1931), daughter of Edward VII
1932	Princess Mary (1897–1965), daughter of George V
1987	Princess Anne (b. 1950), daughter of Elizabeth II

DESCENDANTS OF QUEEN VICTORIA

I. HRH Princess Victoria Adelaide Mary Louisa, Princess Royal (1840–1901) *m* Friedrich III (1831–88), later German Emperor

II. HRH Prince Albert Edward (HM KING EDWARD VII) (1841–1910) *succeeded* 22 Jan 1901 *m* HRH Princess Alexandra of Denmark (1844–1925)

III. HRH Princess Alice Maud Mary (1843–78) *m* Prince Ludwig (1837–92), later Grand Duke of Hesse

IV. HRH Prince Alfred Ernest Albert, Duke of Edinburgh (1844–1900) *succeeded* as Duke of Saxe-Coburg and Gotha 1893 *m* Grand Duchess Marie Alexandrovna of Russia (1853–1920)

I.

1. HIM Wilhelm II (1859–1941), later German Emperor *m* (1) Princess Augusta Victoria of Schleswig-Holstein-Sonderburg-Augustenburg (1858–1921) (2) Princess Hermine of Reuss (1887–1947). *Issue* Wilhelm (1882–1951); Eitel-Friedrich (1883–1942); Adalbert (1884–1948); August Wilhelm (1887–1949); Oskar (1888–1958); Joachim (1890–1920); Viktoria Luise (1892–1980)

2. Charlotte (1860–1919) *m* Bernhard, Duke of Saxe-Meiningen (1851–1928). *Issue* Feodora (1879–1945)

3. Heinrich (1862–1929) *m* Princess Irene of Hesse (*see* III.3). *Issue* Waldemar (1889–1945); Sigismund (1896–1978); Heinrich (1900–4)

4. Sigismund (1864–6)

5. Victoria (1866–1929) *m* (1) Prince Adolf of Schaumburg-Lippe (1859–1916) (2) Alexander Zubkov (1900–36)

6. Waldemar (1868–79)

7. Sophie (1870–1932) *m* Constantine I (1868–1923), later King of the Hellenes. *Issue* George II (1890–1947); Alexander I (1893–1920); Helena (1896–1982); Paul I (1901–64); Irene (1904–74); Katherine (1913–2007)

8. Margarethe (1872–1954) *m* Prince Friedrich Karl of Hesse (1868–1940). *Issue* Friedrich Wilhelm (1893–1916); Maximilian (1894–1914); Philipp (1896–1980); Wolfgang (1896–1989); Richard (1901–69); Christoph (1901–43)

II.

1. Albert Victor, Duke of Clarence and Avondale (1864–92)

2. George (HM KING GEORGE V) (1865–1936) (*see* House of Windsor)

3. Louise (1867–1931), later Princess Royal *m* 1st Duke of Fife (1849–1912). *Issue* Alexandra (1891–1959); Maud (1893–1945)

4. Victoria (1868–1935)

5. Maud (1869–1938) *m* Prince Carl of Denmark (1872–1957), later King Haakon VII of Norway. *Issue* Olav V (1903–91)

6. Alexander (6–7 Apr 1871)

III.

1. Victoria (1863–1950) *m* Prince Louis of Battenberg (1854–1921), later 1st Marquess of Milford Haven. *Issue* Alice (1885–1969); Louise (1889–1965); George (1892–1938); Louis (1900–79)

2. Elizabeth (1864–1918) *m* Grand Duke Sergius of Russia (1857–1905)

3. Irene (1866–1953) *m* Prince Heinrich of Prussia (*see* I.3)

4. Ernst Ludwig (1868–1937), Grand Duke of Hesse, *m* (1) Princess Victoria Melita of Saxe-Coburg (see IV.3) (2) Princess Eleonore of Solms-Hohensolms-Lich (1871–1937). *Issue* Elizabeth (1895–1903); George (1906–37); Ludwig (1908–68)

5. Frederick William (1870–3)

6. Alix (Tsaritsa of Russia) (1872–1918) *m* Nicholas II, Tsar of All the Russias (1868–1918). *Issue* Olga (1895–1918); Tatiana (1897–1918); Marie (1899–1918); Anastasia (1901–18); Alexis (1904–18)

7. Marie (1874–8)

QUEEN VICTORIA (Alexandrina Victoria) (1819–1901) *succeeded* 20 Jun 1837 *m* (Francis) Albert Augustus Charles Emmanuel, Duke of Saxony, Prince of Saxe-Coburg and Gotha (HRH Albert, Prince Consort) (1819–61)

VI. HRH Princess Louise Caroline Alberta (1848–1939) *m* Marquess of Lorne (1845–1914), later 9th Duke of Argyll

VII. HRH Prince Arthur William Patrick Albert, Duke of Connaught (1850–1942) *m* Princess Louisa of Prussia (1860–1917)

VIII. HRH Prince Leopold George Duncan Albert, Duke of Albany (1853–84) *m* Princess Helena of Waldeck (1861–1922)

IX. HRH Princess Beatrice Mary Victoria Feodore (1857–1944) *m* Prince Henry of Battenberg (1858–96)

1. Alfred, Prince of Saxe-Coburg (1874–99)

2. Marie (1875–1938) *m* Ferdinand (1865–1927), later King of Roumania. *Issue* Carol II (1893–1953); Elisabeth (1894–1956); Marie (1900–61); Nicolas (1903–78); Ileana (1909–91); Mircea (1913–16)

3. Victoria Melita (1876–1936) *m* (1) Grand Duke Ernst Ludwig of Hesse (*see* III.4) (2) Grand Duke Kirill of Russia (1876–1938). *Issue* Marie (1907–51); Kira (1909–67); Vladimir (1917–92)

4. Alexandra (1878–1942) *m* Ernst, Prince of Hohenlohe Langenburg (1863–1950). *Issue* Gottfried (1897–1960); Maria (1899–1967); Alexandra (1901–63); Irma (1902–86)

5. Beatrice (1884–1966) *m* Alfonso of Orleans, Infante of Spain (1886–1975). *Issue* Alvaro (1910–97); Alonso (1912–36); Ataulfo (1913–74)

1. Margaret (1882–1920) *m* Crown Prince Gustaf Adolf (1882–1973), later King of Sweden. *Issue* Gustaf Adolf (1906–47); Sigvard (1907–2002); Ingrid (1910–2000); Bertil (1912–97); Count Carl Bernadotte (1916–2012)

2. Arthur (1883–1938) *m* HH Duchess of Fife (1891–1959). *Issue* Alastair Arthur (1914–43)

3. (Victoria) Patricia (1886–1974) *m* Adm. Hon. Sir Alexander Ramsay (1881–1972). *Issue* Alexander (1919–2000)

1. Alice (1883–1981) *m* Prince Alexander of Teck (1874–1957), later 1st Earl of Athlone. *Issue* May (1906–94); Rupert (1907–28); Maurice (Mar–Sep 1910)

2. Charles Edward (1884–1954), Duke of Albany until title suspended 1917, Duke of Saxe-Coburg-Gotha *m* Princess Victoria Adelheid of Schleswig-Holstein-Sonderburg-Glücksburg (1885–1970). *Issue* Johann Leopold (1906–72); Sibylla (1908–72); Dietmar Hubertus (1909–43); Caroline (1912–83); Friedrich Josias (1918–98)

1. Alexander, 1st Marquess of Carisbrooke (1886–1960) *m* Lady Irene Denison (1890–1956). *Issue* Iris (1920–82)

2. Victoria Eugénie (1887–1969) *m* Alfonso XIII, King of Spain (1886–1941). *Issue* Alfonso (1907–38); Jaime (1908–75); Beatriz (1909–2002); Maria (1911–96); Juan (1913–93); Gonzalo (1914–34)

3. Maj. Lord Leopold Mountbatten (1889–1922)

4. Maurice (1891–1914)

V. HRH Princess Helena Augusta Victoria (1846–1923) *m* Prince Christian of Schleswig-Holstein-Sonderburg-Augustenburg (1831–1917)

1. Christian Victor (1867–1900)

2. Albert (1869–1931), later Duke of Schleswig-Holstein

3. Helena (1870–1948)

4. Marie Louise (1872–1956), *m* Prince Aribert of Anhalt (1864–1933)

5. Harold (12–20 May 1876)

THE HOUSE OF WINDSOR

King George V assumed by royal proclamation (17 July 1917) for his House and family, as well as for all descendants in the male line of Queen Victoria who are subjects of these realms, the name of Windsor.

KING GEORGE V

(George Frederick Ernest Albert), second son of King Edward VII *born* 3 June 1865 *married* 6 July 1893 HSH Princess Victoria Mary Augusta Louise Olga Pauline Claudine Agnes of Teck (Queen Mary *born* 26 May 1867 *died* 24 March 1953) *succeeded* to the throne 6 May 1910 *died* 20 January 1936. *Issue*

1. HRH PRINCE EDWARD Albert Christian George Andrew Patrick David *born* 23 June 1894 *succeeded* to the throne as King Edward VIII, 20 January 1936 *abdicated* 11 December 1936 *created* Duke of Windsor 1937 *married* 3 June 1937 Mrs Wallis Simpson (Her Grace The Duchess of Windsor *born* 19 June 1896 *died* 24 April 1986) *died* 28 May 1972

2. HRH PRINCE ALBERT Frederick Arthur George *born* 14 December 1895 *created* Duke of York 1920 *married* 26 April 1923 Lady Elizabeth Bowes-Lyon, youngest daughter of the 14th Earl of Strathmore and Kinghorne (HM Queen Elizabeth the Queen Mother *born* 4 August 1900 *died* 30 March 2002) *succeeded* to the throne as King George VI, 11 December 1936 *died* 6 February 1952. *Issue*

(1) HRH Princess Elizabeth Alexandra Mary *succeeded* to the throne as Queen Elizabeth II, 6 February 1952 (*see* Royal Family)

(2) HRH Princess Margaret Rose (later HRH The Princess Margaret, Countess of Snowdon) *born* 21 August 1930 *married* 6 May 1960 Antony Charles Robert Armstrong-Jones, GCVO *created* Earl of Snowdon 1961 (1930–2017), *marriage dissolved* 1978, *died* 9 February 2002, having had issue (*see* Royal Family)

3. HRH PRINCESS (Victoria Alexandra Alice) MARY *born* 25 April 1897 *created* Princess Royal 1932 *married* 28 February 1922 Viscount Lascelles, later the 6th Earl of Harewood (1882–1947) *died* 28 March 1965. *Issue:*

(1) George Henry Hubert Lascelles, 7th Earl of Harewood, KBE *born* 7 February 1923 *died* 11 July 2011 *married* (1) 1949 Maria (Marion) Stein (marriage dissolved 1967) *issue (a)* David Henry George, 8th Earl of Harewood *born* 1950 *(b)* James Edward *born* 1953 *(c)* (Robert) Jeremy Hugh *born* 1955 (2) 1967 Patricia Tuckwell *issue (d)* Mark Hubert *born* 1964

(2) Gerald David Lascelles *born* 21 August 1924 *died* 27 February 1998 *married* (1) 1952 Angela Dowding (marriage dissolved 1978) *issue (a)* Henry Ulick *born* 1953 (2) 1978 Elizabeth Collingwood (Elizabeth Colvin) *issue (b)* Martin David *born* 1962

4. HRH PRINCE HENRY William Frederick Albert *born* 31 March 1900 *created* Duke of Gloucester, Earl of Ulster and Baron Culloden 1928 *married* 6 November 1935 Lady Alice Christabel Montagu-Douglas-Scott, daughter of the 7th Duke of Buccleuch and Queensberry (HRH Princess Alice, Duchess of Gloucester *born* 25 December 1901 *died* 29 October 2004) *died* 10 June 1974. *Issue*

(1) HRH Prince William Henry Andrew Frederick *born* 18 December 1941 accidentally *killed* 28 August 1972

(2) HRH Prince Richard Alexander Walter George (HRH The Duke of Gloucester, *see* Royal Family)

5. HRH PRINCE GEORGE Edward Alexander Edmund *born* 20 December 1902 *created* Duke of Kent, Earl of St Andrews and Baron Downpatrick 1934 *married* 29 November 1934 HRH Princess Marina of Greece and Denmark (*born* 30 November 1906 *died* 27 August 1968) *killed* on active service 25 August 1942. *Issue*

(1) HRH Prince Edward George Nicholas Paul Patrick (HRH The Duke of Kent, *see* Royal Family)

(2) HRH Princess Alexandra Helen Elizabeth Olga Christabel (HRH Princess Alexandra, the Hon. Lady Ogilvy, *see* Royal Family)

(3) HRH Prince Michael George Charles Franklin (HRH Prince Michael of Kent, *see* Royal Family)

6. HRH PRINCE JOHN Charles Francis *born* 12 July 1905 *died* 18 January 1919

PRECEDENCE

ENGLAND AND WALES

The Sovereign
The Prince Philip, Duke of Edinburgh
The Prince of Wales
The Sovereign's younger sons
The Sovereign's grandsons
The Sovereign's cousins
Archbishop of Canterbury
Lord High Chancellor
Archbishop of York
The Prime Minister
Lord President of the Council
Speaker of the House of Commons
Speaker of the House of Lords
President of the Supreme Court
Lord Chief Justice of England and Wales
Lord Privy Seal
Ambassadors and High Commissioners
Lord Great Chamberlain
Earl Marshal
Lord Steward of the Household
Lord Chamberlain of the Household
Master of the Horse
Dukes, according to their patent of creation:
1. of England
2. of Scotland
3. of Great Britain
4. of Ireland
5. those created since the Union
Eldest sons of Dukes of the Blood Royal
Ministers, Envoys, and other important overseas visitors
Marquesses, according to their patent of creation:
1. of England
2. of Scotland
3. of Great Britain
4. of Ireland
5. those created since the Union
Dukes' eldest sons
Earls, according to their patent of creation:
1. of England
2. of Scotland
3. of Great Britain
4. of Ireland
5. those created since the Union
Younger sons of Dukes of Blood Royal

Marquesses' eldest sons
Dukes' younger sons
Viscounts, according to their patent of creation:
1. of England
2. of Scotland
3. of Great Britain
4. of Ireland
5. those created since the Union
Earls' eldest sons
Marquesses' younger sons
Bishop of London
Bishop of Durham
Bishop of Winchester
Other English Diocesan Bishops, according to seniority of consecration
Retired Church of England Diocesan Bishops, according to seniority of consecration
Suffragan Bishops, according to seniority of consecration
Secretaries of State, if of the degree of a Baron
Barons, according to their patent of creation:
1. of England
2. of Scotland (Lords of Parliament)
3. of Great Britain
4. of Ireland
5. those created since the Union, including Life Barons
Master of the Rolls
Deputy President of the Supreme Court
Justices of the Supreme Court, according to seniority of appointment
Treasurer of the Household
Comptroller of the Household
Vice-Chamberlain of the Household
Secretaries of State under the degree of Baron
Viscounts' eldest sons
Earls' younger sons
Barons' eldest sons
Knights of the Garter
Privy Counsellors
Chancellor of the Order of the Garter
Chancellor of the Exchequer
Chancellor of the Duchy of Lancaster
President of the Queen's Bench Division
President of the Family Division

Chancellor of the High Court
Lord Justices of Appeal, according to seniority of appointment
Judges of the High Court, according to seniority of appointment
Viscounts' younger sons
Barons' younger sons
Sons of Life Peers
Baronets, according to date of patent
Knights of the Thistle
Knights Grand Cross of the Bath
Knights Grand Cross of St Michael and St George
Knights Grand Cross of the Royal Victorian Order
Knights Grand Cross of the British Empire
Knights Commanders of the Bath
Knights Commanders of St Michael and St George
Knights Commanders of the Royal Victorian Order
Knights Commanders of the British Empire
Knights Bachelor
Circuit Judges, according to priority and order of their respective appointments
Master of the Court of Protection
Companions of the Bath
Companions of St Michael and St George
Commanders of the Royal Victorian Order
Commanders of the British Empire
Companions of the Distinguished Service Order
Lieutenants of the Royal Victorian Order
Officers of the British Empire
Companions of the Imperial Service Order
Eldest sons of younger sons of peers
Baronets' eldest sons
Eldest sons of knights, in the same order as their fathers
Members of the Royal Victorian Order
Members of the British Empire
Baronets' younger sons
Knights' younger sons, in the same order as their fathers
Esquires
Gentlemen

WOMEN

Women take the same rank as their husbands or as their brothers; but the daughter of a peer marrying a commoner retains her title as Lady or Honourable. Daughters of peers rank next immediately after the wives of their elder brothers, before their younger brothers' wives. Daughters of peers marrying peers of a lower degree take the same order of precedence as that of their husbands; thus the daughter of a

Duke marrying a Baron becomes of the rank of Baroness only, while her sisters married to commoners retain their rank and take precedence over the Baroness. Merely official rank on the husband's part does not give any similar precedence to the wife.
Peeresses in their own right take the same precedence as peers of the same rank, ie from their date of creation.

SCOTLAND

The Sovereign
The Prince Philip, Duke of Edinburgh
The Lord High Commissioner to the General Assembly of the Church of Scotland (while that assembly is sitting)
The Duke of Rothesay (eldest son of the Sovereign)
The Sovereign's younger sons
The Sovereign's grandsons
The Sovereign's nephews
Lord-Lieutenants
Lord Provosts, during their term of office*
Sheriffs Principal, during their term of office and within the bounds of their respective sheriffdoms
Lord Chancellor of Great Britain
Moderator of the General Assembly of the Church of Scotland
Keeper of the Great Seal of Scotland (the First Minister)
Presiding Officer
The Secretary of State for Scotland
Hereditary High Constable of Scotland
Hereditary Master of the Household in Scotland
Dukes, as in England
Eldest sons of Dukes of the Blood Royal

Marquesses, as in England
Dukes' eldest sons
Earls, as in England
Younger sons of Dukes of Blood Royal
Marquesses' eldest sons
Dukes' younger sons
Lord Justice General
Lord Clerk Register
Lord Advocate
The Advocate General
Lord Justice Clerk
Viscounts, as in England
Earls' eldest sons
Marquesses' younger sons
Lords of Parliament or Barons, as in England
Eldest sons of Viscounts
Earls' younger sons
Eldest sons of Lords of Parliament or Barons
Knights and Ladies of the Garter
Knights and Ladies of the Thistle
Privy Counsellors
Senators of the College of Justice (Lords of Session)
Viscounts' younger sons
Younger sons of Lords of Parliament or Barons
Baronets
Knights and Dames Grand Cross of orders, as in England

Knights and Dames Commanders of orders, as in England
Solicitor-General for Scotland
Lord Lyon King of Arms
Sheriffs Principal, when not within own county
Knights Bachelor
Sheriffs
Companions of Orders, as in England
Commanders of the Royal Victorian Order
Commanders of the British Empire
Lieutenants of the Royal Victorian Order
Companions of the Distinguished Service Order
Officers of the British Empire
Companions of the Imperial Service Order
Eldest sons of younger sons of peers
Eldest sons of baronets
Eldest sons of knights, as in England
Members of the Royal Victorian Order
Members of the British Empire
Baronets' younger sons
Knights' younger sons
Queen's Counsel
Esquires
Gentlemen

* The Lord Provosts of Aberdeen, Dundee, Edinburgh and Glasgow are Lord-Lieutenants for these cities *ex officio* and take precedence as such

THE PEERAGE

ABBREVIATIONS AND SYMBOLS

S.	Scottish title	§	life peer disqualified from sitting in the House of Lords as a member of the judiciary
I.	Irish title		
**	hereditary peer remaining in the House of Lords	ℂ	life peer who has resigned permanently from the House of Lords
°	there is no 'of' in the title		
b.	born	E.	life peer expelled for absenteeism under section 2 of the House of Lords Reform Act 2014 (see below)
s.	succeeded		
m.	married	F_	represents forename
c.p.	civil partnership	S_	represents surname
w.	widower or widow	†	heir not ascertained at time of going to press
M.	minor	‡	title not ascertained at time of going to press
cr.	created		

A full entry in italic type indicates that the recipient of a life peerage died within a year of it being conferred. The name is included in our list for one year for purposes of record.

The rules which govern the creation and succession of peerages are extremely complicated. There are, technically, five separate peerages, the Peerage of England, of Scotland, of Ireland, of Great Britain, and of the United Kingdom. The Peerage of Great Britain dates from 1707 when an Act of Union combined the two kingdoms of England and Scotland and separate peerages were discontinued. The Peerage of the United Kingdom dates from 1801 when Great Britain and Ireland were combined under an Act of Union. Some Scottish peers have received additional peerages of Great Britain or of the UK since 1707, and some Irish peers additional peerages of the UK since 1801.

The Peerage of Ireland was not entirely discontinued from 1801 but holders of Irish peerages, whether pre-dating or created subsequent to the Union of 1801, were not entitled to sit in the House of Lords if they had no additional English, Scottish, Great Britain or UK peerage. However, they were eligible for election to the House of Commons and to vote in parliamentary elections. An Irish peer holding a peerage of a lower grade which enabled him to sit in the House of Lords was introduced there by the title which enabled him to sit, though for all other purposes he was known by his higher title.

In the Peerage of Scotland there is no rank of Baron; the equivalent rank is Lord of Parliament, abbreviated to 'Lord' (the female equivalent is 'Lady').

All peers of England, Scotland, Great Britain or the UK who were 21 years or over, and of British, Irish or Commonwealth nationality were entitled to sit in the House of Lords until the House of Lords Act 1999, when hereditary peers lost the right to sit. However, section two of the act provided an exception for 90 hereditary peers plus the holders of the office of Earl Marshal and Lord Great Chamberlain to remain as members of the House of Lords for their lifetime or pending further reform. Of the 90 hereditary peers, 75 were elected by the hereditary peers in their political party, or Crossbench grouping, and the remaining 15 by the whole house. Until 7 November 2002 any vacancy arising due to the death of one of the 90 excepted hereditary peers was filled by the runner-up to the original election. From 7 November 2002 any vacancy due to a death – or, from 2014, a permanent retirement – has been filled by holding a by-election. By-elections are conducted in accordance with arrangements made by the Clerk of the Parliaments and have to take place within three months of a vacancy occurring. If the vacancy is among the 75, only the excepted hereditary peers in the relevant party or Crossbench grouping are entitled to vote. If

the vacancy is among the other 15, the whole house is entitled to vote.

In the list below, peers currently holding one of the 92 hereditary places in the House of Lords are indicated by **.

HEREDITARY WOMEN PEERS
Most hereditary peerages pass on death to the nearest male heir, but there are exceptions, and several are held by women.

A woman peer in her own right retains her title after marriage, and if her husband's rank is the superior she is designated by the two titles jointly, the inferior one second. Her hereditary claim still holds good in spite of any marriage whether higher or lower. No rank held by a woman can confer any title or even precedence upon her husband but the rank of a hereditary woman peer in her own right is inherited by her eldest son (or in some cases daughter).

After the Peerage Act 1963, hereditary women peers in their own right were entitled to sit in the House of Lords, subject to the same qualifications as men, until the House of Lords Act 1999.

LIFE PEERS
From 1876 to 2009 non-hereditary or life peerages were conferred on certain eminent judges to enable the judicial functions of the House of Lords to be carried out. These lords were known as Lords of Appeal in Ordinary or law lords. The judicial role of the House of Lords as the highest appeal court in the UK ended on 30 July 2009 and since 1 October 2009, under the Constitutional Reform Act 2005, any peer who holds a senior judicial office is disqualified from sitting in the House of Lords until they retire from that office. In the list of life peerages which follows, members of the judiciary who are currently disqualified from sitting and voting in the House of Lords until retirement, are marked by a '§'.

Under the Constitutional Reform and Governance Act 2010, five peers permanently resigned from the House of Lords.

Since 1958 life peerages have been conferred upon distinguished men and women from all walks of life, giving them seats in the House of Lords in the degree of Baron or Baroness. They are addressed in the same way as hereditary lords and barons, and their children have similar courtesy titles.

HOUSE OF LORDS REFORM ACT 2014
The House of Lords Reform Act 2014 makes provision for a member of the House of Lords who is a peer to retire or resign by giving notice in writing to the Clerk of Parliaments. Resignations may not be rescinded. A number of life peers and elected hereditary peers have already retired permanently

under this provision. The Act also makes provision for the expulsion of peers who do not attend the House of Lords for an entire parliamentary session which is longer than six months (indicated by an 'E.' in the following list). Peers on leave of absence or subject to a suspension or disqualification which results in absenteeism for an entire session will not be expelled. The House can also resolve that a peer should not be expelled by reason of special circumstances.

All life peers who have resigned permanently from the House of Lords are indicated by a '℄' in the following list.

PEERAGES EXTINCT SINCE 20 SEPTEMBER 2018
BARONY: Wardington (cr. 1936)
LIFE PEERAGES: Ashdown of Norton-sub-Hamdon (cr. 2001); Bell (cr. 1998); Bhattacharyya (cr. 2004); Davies of Coity (cr. 1997); Falkender (cr. 1974); Foster of Bishop Auckland (cr. 2005); Habgood (cr. 1995); Heywood of Whitehall (cr. 2018); Hollis of Heigham (cr. 1990); Lockwood (cr. 1978); Moore of Lower Marsh (cr. 1992); Patel of Blackburn (cr. 2000); Spicer (cr. 2010); Tordoff (cr. 1981); Trumpington (cr. 1980); Warnock (cr. 1985)

DISCLAIMER OF PEERAGES
The Peerage Act 1963 enables peers to disclaim their peerages for life. Peers alive in 1963 could disclaim within twelve months after the passing of the act (31 July 1963); a person subsequently succeeding to a peerage may disclaim within 12 months (one month if an MP) after the date of succession, or of reaching 21, if later. The disclaimer is irrevocable but does not affect the descent of the peerage after the disclaimant's death, and children of a disclaimed peer may, if they wish, retain their precedence and any courtesy titles and styles borne as children of a peer. The disclaimer permitted the disclaimant to sit in the House of Commons if elected as an MP. As the House of Lords Act 1999 removed the automatic right of hereditary peers to sit in the House of Lords, they are now entitled to sit in the House of Commons without having to disclaim their titles.

The following peerages are currently disclaimed:
EARLDOM: Selkirk (1994)
BARONIES: Sanderson of Ayot (1971); Silkin (2002)
PEERS WHO ARE MINORS (ie under 21 years of age)
EARLDOM: St Germans (b. 2004)
BARONY: Rodney (b. 1999)

FORMS OF ADDRESS
Forms of address are given under the style for each individual rank of the peerage. Both formal and social forms of address are given where usage differs; nowadays, the social form is generally preferred to the formal, which increasingly is used only for official documents and on very formal occasions.

ROLL OF THE PEERAGE

Crown Office, House of Lords, London SW1A 0PW
T 020-7219 4687 E hereditary.claims@gmail.com

The Roll of the Peerage is kept at the Crown Office and maintained by the Registrar and Assistant Registrar of the Peerage in accordance with the terms of a 2004 royal warrant. The roll records the names of all living life peers and hereditary peers who have proved their succession to the satisfaction of the Lord Chancellor. The Roll of the Peerage is maintained in addition to the Clerk of the Parliaments' register of hereditary peers eligible to stand for election in House of Lords' by-elections.

A person whose name is not entered on the Roll of the Peerage can not be addressed or mentioned by the title of a peer in any official document.

Registrar, Mrs Ceri King

HEREDITARY PEERS

PEERS OF THE BLOOD ROYAL

Style, His Royal Highness the Duke of _/His Royal Highness the Earl of_/His Royal Highness the Lord_
Style of address (formal) May it please your Royal Highness; *(informal)* Sir

Created	Title, order of succession, name, etc	Heir
	Dukes	
1947	Edinburgh (1st), HRH the Prince Philip, Duke of Edinburgh	The Prince of Wales *
1337	Cornwall, HRH the Prince of Wales, s. 1952	‡
1398 S.	Rothesay, HRH the Prince of Wales, s. 1952	‡
2011	Cambridge (1st), HRH Prince William of Wales	HRH Prince George of Cambridge
2018	Sussex (1st), HRH Prince Henry of Wales	Archie Mountbatten-Windsor
1986	York (1st), Prince Andrew, HRH the Duke of York	None
1928	Gloucester (2nd), Prince Richard, HRH the Duke of Gloucester, s. 1974	Earl of Ulster
1934	Kent (2nd), Prince Edward, HRH the Duke of Kent, s. 1942	Earl of St Andrews
	Earl	
1999	Wessex (1st) and Forfar (3rd) (S. 1661), Prince Edward, HRH the Earl of Wessex	Viscount Severn

* In June 1999 Buckingham Palace announced that the current Earl of Wessex will be granted the Dukedom of Edinburgh when the title reverts to the Crown. The title will only revert to the Crown on both the death of the current Duke of Edinburgh and the Prince of Wales' succession as king
‡ The title is held by the sovereign's eldest son from the moment of his birth or the sovereign's accession

DUKES

Coronet, Eight strawberry leaves

Style, His Grace the Duke of _
Envelope (formal), His Grace the Duke of _; *(social)*, The Duke of _. *Letter (formal)*, My Lord Duke; *(social)*, Dear Duke. *Spoken (formal)*, Your Grace; *(social)*, Duke
Wife's style, Her Grace the Duchess of _
Envelope (formal), Her Grace the Duchess of _; *(social)*, The Duchess of _. *Letter (formal)*, Dear Madam; *(social)*, Dear Duchess. *Spoken*, Duchess
Eldest son's style, Takes his father's second title as a courtesy title (*see* Courtesy Titles)
Younger sons' style, 'Lord' before forename (F_) and surname (S_)
Envelope, Lord F_ S_. *Letter (formal)*, My Lord; *(social)*, Dear Lord F_. *Spoken (formal)*, My Lord; *(social)*, Lord F_
Daughters' style, 'Lady' before forename (F_) and surname (S_)
Envelope, Lady F_ S_. *Letter (formal)*, Dear Madam; *(social)*, Dear Lady F_. *Spoken*, Lady F_

Created	Title, order of succession, name, etc	Heir
1868 I.	*Abercorn (5th)*, James Hamilton, KG, *b*. 1934, *s*. 1979, *w*.	Marquess of Hamilton, *b*. 1969
1701 S.	*Argyll (13th)*, Torquhil Ian Campbell, *b*. 1968, *s*. 2001, *m*.	Marquess of Lorne, *b*. 2004
1703 S.	*Atholl (12th)*, Bruce George Ronald Murray, *b*. 1960, *s*. 2012, *m*.	Marquis of Tullibardine, *b*. 1985
1682	*Beaufort (12th)*, Henry John Fitzroy Somerset, *b*. 1952, *s*. 2017, *m*.	Marquess of Worcester, *b*. 1989
1694	*Bedford (15th)*, Andrew Ian Henry Russell, *b*. 1962, *s*. 2003, *m*.	Marquess of Tavistock, *b*. 2005
1663 S.	*Buccleuch (10th) and Queensberry (12th) (S. 1684)*, Richard Walter John Montagu Douglas Scott, KT, KBE, *b*. 1954, *s*. 2007, *m*.	Earl of Dalkeith, *b*. 1984
1694	*Devonshire (12th)*, Peregrine Andrew Morny Cavendish, KCVO, CBE, *b*. 1944, *s*. 2004, *m*.	Earl of Burlington, *b*. 1969
1900	*Fife (4th)*, David Charles Carnegie, *b*. 1961, *s*. 2015, *m*.	Earl of Southesk, *b*. 1989
1675	*Grafton (12th)*, Henry Oliver Charles FitzRoy, *b*. 1978, *s*. 2011, *m*.	Earl of Euston, *b*. 2012
1643 S.	*Hamilton (16th) and Brandon (13th) (1711)*, Alexander Douglas Douglas-Hamilton, *b*. 1978, *s*. 2010, *m*. Premier Peer of Scotland	Marquess of Douglas and Clydesdale, *b*. 2012
1766 I.	*Leinster (9th)*, Maurice FitzGerald, *b*. 1948, *s*. 2004, *m*. Premier Duke, Marquess and Earl of Ireland	Edward F., *b*. 1988
1719	*Manchester (13th)*, Alexander Charles David Drogo Montagu, *b*. 1962, *s*. 2002, *m*.	Lord Kimble W. D. M., *b*. 1964
1702	*Marlborough (12th)*, Charles James Spencer-Churchill, *b*. 1955, *s*. 2014, *m*.	Marquess of Blandford, *b*. 1992
1707 S. **	*Montrose (8th)*, James Graham, *b*. 1935, *s*. 1992, *w*.	Marquis of Graham, *b*. 1973
1483 **	*Norfolk (18th)*, Edward William Fitzalan-Howard, *b*. 1956, *s*. 2002, *m*. Premier Duke and Earl Marshal	Earl of Arundel and Surrey, *b*. 1987
1766	*Northumberland (12th)*, Ralph George Algernon Percy, *b*. 1956, *s*. 1995, *m*.	Earl Percy, *b*. 1984
1675	*Richmond (11th), Gordon (6th) (1876) and Lennox (11th) (S. 1675)*, Charles Henry Gordon Lennox, *b*. 1955, *s*. 2017, *m*.	Earl of March and Kinrara, *b*. 1994
1707 S.	*Roxburghe (11th)*, Charles Robert George Innes-Ker, *b*. 1981, *s*. 2019 Premier Baronet of Scotland	Lord Edward A. G. I.-K., *b*. 1984
1703	*Rutland (11th)*, David Charles Robert Manners, *b*. 1959, *s*. 1999, *m*.	Marquess of Granby, *b*. 1999
1684	*St Albans (14th)*, Murray de Vere Beauclerk, *b*. 1939, *s*. 1988, *m*.	Earl of Burford, *b*. 1965
1547 **	*Somerset (19th)*, John Michael Edward Seymour, *b*. 1952, *s*. 1984, *m*.	Lord Seymour, *b*. 1982
1833	*Sutherland (7th)*, Francis Ronald Egerton, *b*. 1940, *s*. 2000, *m*.	Marquess of Stafford, *b*. 1975
1814 **	*Wellington (9th)*, Arthur Charles Valerian Wellesley, OBE, *b*. 1945, *s*. 2014, *m*.	Earl of Mornington, *b*. 1978
1874	*Westminster (7th) and 9th Marquess of Westminster (1831)*, Hugh Richard Louis Grosvenor, *b*. 1991, *s*. 2016	To Marquessate only, Earl of Wilton (*see* that title)

MARQUESSES

Coronet, Four strawberry leaves alternating with four silver balls

Style, The Most Hon. the Marquess (of) _ . In Scotland the spelling 'Marquis' is preferred for pre-Union creations
Envelope (formal), The Most Hon. the Marquess of _; *(social),* The Marquess of _. *Letter (formal),* My Lord; *(social),* Dear Lord _.
Spoken (formal), My Lord; *(social),* Lord _
Wife's style, The Most Hon. the Marchioness (of) _
Envelope (formal), The Most Hon. the Marchioness of _; *(social),* The Marchioness of _. *Letter (formal),* Madam; *(social),* Dear
Lady _. *Spoken,* Lady _
Eldest son's style, Takes his father's second title as a courtesy title (*see* Courtesy Titles)
Younger sons' style, 'Lord' before forename and surname, as for Duke's younger sons
Daughters' style, 'Lady' before forename and surname, as for Duke's daughter

Created	Title, order of succession, name, etc	Heir
1915	*Aberdeen and Temair (7th),* Alexander George Gordon, *b.* 1955, *s.* 2002, *m.*	Earl of Haddo, *b.* 1983
1876	*Abergavenny (6th) and 10th Earl of Abergavenny (1784),* Christopher George Charles Nevill, *b.* 1955, *s.* 2000, *m.*	To Earldom only, David M. R. N., *b.* 1941
1821	*Ailesbury (8th),* Michael Sidney Cedric Brudenell-Bruce, *b.* 1926, *s.* 1974	Earl of Cardigan, *b.* 1952
1831	*Ailsa (9th),* David Thomas Kennedy, *b.* 1958, *s.* 2015, *m.*	Earl of Cassilis, *b.* 1995
1815	*Anglesey (8th),* Charles Alexander Vaughan Paget, *b.* 1950, *s.* 2013, *m.*	Earl of Uxbridge, *b.* 1986
1789	*Bath (7th),* Alexander George Thynn, *b.* 1932, *s.* 1992, *m.*	Viscount Weymouth, *b.* 1974
1826	*Bristol (8th),* Frederick William Augustus Hervey, *b.* 1979, *s.* 1999, *m.*	Timothy H. H., *b.* 1960
1796	*Bute (7th),* John Colum Crichton-Stuart, *b.* 1958, *s.* 1993, *m.*	Earl of Dumfries, *b.* 1989
1812 °	*Camden (6th),* David George Edward Henry Pratt, *b.* 1930, *s.* 1983	Earl of Brecknock, *b.* 1965
1815 **	*Cholmondeley (7th),* David George Philip Cholmondeley, KCVO, *b.* 1960, *s.* 1990, *m. Lord Great Chamberlain*	Earl of Rocksavage, *b.* 2009
1816 I. °	*Conyngham (8th),* Henry Vivian Pierpoint Conyngham, *b.* 1951, *s.* 2009, *m.*	Earl of Mount Charles, *b.* 1975
1791 I.	*Donegall (8th),* Arthur Patrick Chichester, *b.* 1952, *s.* 2007, *m.*	Earl of Belfast, *b.* 1990
1789 I.	*Downshire (9th),* (Arthur Francis) Nicholas Wills Hill, *b.* 1959, *s.* 2003, *m.*	Earl of Hillsborough, *b.* 1996
1801 I.	*Ely (9th),* Charles John Tottenham, *b.* 1943, *s.* 2006, *m.*	Lord Timothy C. T., *b.* 1948
1801	*Exeter (8th),* (William) Michael Anthony Cecil, *b.* 1935, *s.* 1988, *m.*	Lord Burghley, *b.* 1970
1800 I.	*Headfort (7th),* Thomas Michael Ronald Christopher Taylour, *b.* 1959, *s.* 2005, *w.*	Earl of Bective, *b.* 1989
1793	*Hertford (9th),* Henry Jocelyn Seymour, *b.* 1958, *s.* 1997, *m.*	Earl of Yarmouth, *b.* 1993
1599 S.	*Huntly (13th),* Granville Charles Gomer Gordon, *b.* 1944, *s.* 1987, *m. Premier Marquess of Scotland*	Earl of Aboyne, *b.* 1973
1784	*Lansdowne (9th),* Charles Maurice Mercer Nairne Petty-Fitzmaurice, LVO, *b.* 1941, *s.* 1999, *m.*	Earl of Kerry, *b.* 1970
1902	*Linlithgow (4th),* Adrian John Charles Hope, *b.* 1946, *s.* 1987	Earl of Hopetoun, *b.* 1969
1816 I.	*Londonderry (10th),* Frederick Aubrey Vane-Tempest-Stewart, *b.* 1972, *s.* 2012	Lord Reginald A. V.-T.-S., *b.* 1977
1701 S.	*Lothian (13th) and Baron Kerr of Monteviot (life peerage, 2010),* Michael Andrew Foster Jude Kerr (Michael Ancram), PC, QC, *b.* 1945, *s.* 2004, *m.*	Lord Ralph W. F. J. K., *b.* 1957
1917	*Milford Haven (4th),* George Ivar Louis Mountbatten, *b.* 1961, *s.* 1970, *m.*	Earl of Medina, *b.* 1991
1838	*Normanby (5th),* Constantine Edmund Walter Phipps, *b.* 1954, *s.* 1994, *m.*	Earl of Mulgrave, *b.* 1994
1812	*Northampton (7th),* Spencer Douglas David Compton, *b.* 1946, *s.* 1978, *m.*	Earl Compton, *b.* 1973
1682 S.	*Queensberry (12th),* David Harrington Angus Douglas, *b.* 1929, *s.* 1954, *m.*	Viscount Drumlanrig, *b.* 1967
1926	*Reading (4th),* Simon Charles Henry Rufus Isaacs, *b.* 1942, *s.* 1980, *m.*	Viscount Erleigh, *b.* 1986
1789	*Salisbury (7th) and Baron Gascoyne-Cecil (life peerage, 1999),* Robert Michael James Gascoyne-Cecil, KG, KCVO, PC, *b.* 1946, *s.* 2003, *m.*	Viscount Cranborne, *b.* 1970
1800 I.	*Sligo (12th),* Sebastian Ulick Browne, *b.* 1964, *s.* 2014, *m.*	Earl of Altamont, *b.* 1988
1787 °	*Townshend (8th),* Charles George Townshend, *b.* 1945, *s.* 2010, *m.*	Viscount Raynham, *b.* 1977
1694 S.	*Tweeddale (14th),* Charles David Montagu Hay, *b.* 1947, *s.* 2005	(Lord) Alistair J. M. H., *b.* 1955
1789 I.	*Waterford (9th),* Henry Nicholas de la Poer Beresford, *b.* 1958, *s.* 2015, *m.*	Earl of Tyrone, *b.* 1987
1551	*Winchester (18th),* Nigel George Paulet, *b.* 1941, *s.* 1968, *m. Premier Marquess of England*	Earl of Wiltshire, *b.* 1969
1892	*Zetland (4th),* Lawrence Mark Dundas, *b.* 1937, *s.* 1989, *m.*	Earl of Ronaldshay, *b.* 1965

EARLS

Coronet, Eight silver balls on stalks alternating with eight gold strawberry leaves

Style, The Rt. Hon. the Earl (of) _
Envelope (formal), The Rt. Hon. the Earl (of) _; *(social),* The Earl (of) _. *Letter (formal),* My Lord; *(social),* Dear Lord _. *Spoken (formal),* My Lord; *(social),* Lord _.
Wife's style, The Rt. Hon. the Countess (of) _
Envelope (formal), The Rt. Hon. the Countess (of) _; *(social),* The Countess (of) _. *Letter (formal),* Madam; *(social),* Lady _. *Spoken (formal),* Madam; *(social),* Lady _.
Eldest son's style, Takes his father's second title as a courtesy title (*see* Courtesy Titles)
Younger sons' style, 'The Hon.' before forename and surname, as for Baron's children
Daughters' style, 'Lady' before forename and surname, as for Duke's daughter

Created	Title, order of succession, name, etc	Heir
1639 S.	*Airlie (13th),* David George Coke Patrick Ogilvy, KT, GCVO, PC, Royal Victorian Chain, *b.* 1926, *s.* 1968, *m.*	Lord Ogilvy, *b.* 1958
1696	*Albemarle (10th),* Rufus Arnold Alexis Keppel, *b.* 1965, *s.* 1979	Viscount Bury, *b.* 2003
1952 °	*Alexander of Tunis (2nd),* Shane William Desmond Alexander, *b.* 1935, *s.* 1969, *m.*	Hon. Brian J. A., CMG, *b.* 1939
1662 S.	*Annandale and Hartfell (11th),* Patrick Andrew Wentworth Hope Johnstone, *b.* 1941, *s.* 1983, *m.* claim established 1985	Lord Johnstone, *b.* 1971
1789 I. °	*Annesley (12th),* Michael Robert Annesley, *b.* 1933, *s.* 2011, *w.*	Viscount Glerawly, *b.* 1957
1785 I.	*Antrim (9th),* Alexander Randal Mark McDonnell, *b.* 1935, *s.* 1977, *m.*	Viscount Dunluce, *b.* 1967
1762 I. **	*Arran (9th) and 5th UK Baron Sudley (1884),* Arthur Desmond Colquhoun Gore, *b.* 1938, *s.* 1983, *m.*	To Earldom only, William H. G., *b.* 1950
1955 ° **	*Attlee (3rd),* John Richard Attlee, *b.* 1956, *s.* 1991, *m.*	None
1714	*Aylesford (12th),* Charles Heneage Finch-Knightley, *b.* 1947, *s.* 2008, *m.*	Lord Guernsey, *b.* 1985
1937 °	*Baldwin of Bewdley (4th),* Edward Alfred Alexander Baldwin, *b.* 1938, *s.* 1976, *w.*	Viscount Corvedale, *b.* 1973
1922	*Balfour (5th),* Roderick Francis Arthur Balfour, *b.* 1948, *s.* 2003, *m.*	Charles G. Y. B., *b.* 1951
1772 °	*Bathurst (9th),* Allen Christopher Bertram Bathurst, *b.* 1961, *s.* 2011, *m.*	Lord Apsley, *b.* 1990
1919 °	*Beatty (3rd),* David Beatty, *b.* 1946, *s.* 1972	Viscount Borodale, *b.* 1973
1797 I.	*Belmore (8th),* John Armar Lowry-Corry, *b.* 1951, *s.* 1960, *m.*	Viscount Corry, *b.* 1985
1739 I.	*Bessborough (12th),* Myles Fitzhugh Longfield Ponsonby, *b.* 1941, *s.* 2002, *m.*	Viscount Duncannon, *b.* 1974
1815	*Bradford (7th),* Richard Thomas Orlando Bridgeman, *b.* 1947, *s.* 1981, *m.*	Viscount Newport, *b.* 1980
1469 S.	*Buchan (17th),* Malcolm Harry Erskine, *b.* 1930, *s.* 1984, *m.*	Lord Cardross, *b.* 1960
1746	*Buckinghamshire (10th),* (George) Miles Hobart-Hampden, *b.* 1944, *s.* 1983, *m.*	Sir John V. Hobart, Bt., *b.* 1945
1800 °	*Cadogan (8th),* Charles Gerald John Cadogan, KBE, *b.* 1937, *s.* 1997, *m.*	Viscount Chelsea, *b.* 1966
1878 °	*Cairns (6th),* Simon Dallas Cairns, CVO, CBE, *b.* 1939, *s.* 1989, *m.*	Viscount Garmoyle, *b.* 1965
1455 S. **	*Caithness (20th),* Malcolm Ian Sinclair, PC, *b.* 1948, *s.* 1965	Lord Berriedale, *b.* 1981
1800 I.	*Caledon (7th),* Nicholas James Alexander, KCVO, *b.* 1955, *s.* 1980, *m.*	Viscount Alexander, *b.* 1990
1661	*Carlisle (13th),* George William Beaumont Howard, *b.* 1949, *s.* 1994	Hon. Philip C. W. H., *b.* 1963
1793	*Carnarvon (8th),* George Reginald Oliver Molyneux Herbert, *b.* 1956, *s.* 2001, *m.*	Lord Porchester, *b.* 1992
1748 I.	*Carrick (11th),* Arion Thomas Piers Hamilton Butler, *b.* 1975, *s.* 2008, *m.*	Hon. Piers E. T. L. B., *b.* 1979
1800 I.°	*Castle Stewart (8th),* Arthur Patrick Avondale Stuart, *b.* 1928, *s.* 1961, *m.*	Viscount Stuart, *b.* 1953
1814 ° **	*Cathcart (7th),* Charles Alan Andrew Cathcart, *b.* 1952, *s.* 1999, *m.*	Lord Greenock, *b.* 1986
1647 I.	*Cavan (13th),* Roger Cavan Lambart, *b.* 1944, *s.* 1988 (claim to the peerage not yet established)	Cavan C. E. L., *b.* 1957
1827 °	*Cawdor (7th),* Colin Robert Vaughan Campbell, *b.* 1962, *s.* 1993, *m.*	Viscount Emlyn, *b.* 1998
1801	*Chichester (9th),* John Nicholas Pelham, *b.* 1944, *s.* 1944, *m.*	Richard A. H. P., *b.* 1952
1803 I. **	*Clancarty (9th),* Nicholas Power Richard Le Poer Trench, *b.* 1952, *s.* 1995, *m.*	None
1776 I.	*Clanwilliam (8th),* Patrick James Meade, *b.* 1960, *s.* 2009, *m.*	Lord Gillford, *b.* 1998
1776	*Clarendon (8th),* George Edward Laurence Villiers, *b.* 1976, *s.* 2009, *m.*	Lord Hyde, *b.* 2008
1620 I. **	*Cork and Orrery (15th),* John Richard Boyle, *b.* 1945, *s.* 2003, *m.*	Viscount Dungarvan, *b.* 1978
1850	*Cottenham (9th),* Mark John Henry Pepys, *b.* 1983, *s.* 2000, *m.*	Hon. Sam R. P., *b.* 1986
1762 I. **	*Courtown (9th),* James Patrick Montagu Burgoyne Winthrop Stopford, *b.* 1954, *s.* 1975, *m.*	Viscount Stopford, *b.* 1988
1697	*Coventry (13th),* George William Coventry, *b.* 1939, *s.* 2004, *m.*	David D. S. C., *b.* 1973

1857 °	*Cowley (8th)*, Garret Graham Wellesley, *b.* 1965, *s.* 2016, *m.*	Viscount Dangan, *b.* 1991
1892	*Cranbrook (5th)*, Gathorne Gathorne-Hardy, *b.* 1933, *s.* 1978, *m.*	Lord Medway, *b.* 1968
1801	*Craven (9th)*, Benjamin Robert Joseph Craven, *b.* 1989, *s.* 1990	Rupert J. E. C., *b.* 1926
1398 S.	*Crawford (29th) and Balcarres (12th) (S. 1651) and Baron Balniel (life peerage, 1974)*, Robert Alexander Lindsay, KT, GCVO, PC, *b.* 1927, *s.* 1975, *m. Premier Earl on Union Roll*	Lord Balniel, *b.* 1958
1861	*Cromartie (5th)*, John Ruaridh Blunt Grant Mackenzie, *b.* 1948, *s.* 1989, *m.*	Viscount Tarbat, *b.* 1987
1901	*Cromer (4th)*, Evelyn Rowland Esmond Baring, *b.* 1946, *s.* 1991, *m.*	Viscount Errington, *b.* 1994
1633 S.	*Dalhousie (17th)*, James Hubert Ramsay, *b.* 1948, *s.* 1999, *m. Lord Steward*	Lord Ramsay, *b.* 1981
1725 I.	*Darnley (12th)*, Ivo Donald Stuart Bligh, *b.* 1968, *s.* 2017, *m.*	Lord Clifton, *b.* 1999
1711	*Dartmouth (10th)*, William Legge, *b.* 1949, *s.* 1997, *m.*	Hon. Rupert L., *b.* 1951
1761 °	*De La Warr (11th)*, William Herbrand Sackville, *b.* 1948, *s.* 1988, *m.*	Lord Buckhurst, *b.* 1979
1622	*Denbigh (12th) and Desmond (11th) (I. 1622)*, Alexander Stephen Rudolph Feilding, *b.* 1970, *s.* 1995, *m.*	Viscount Feilding, *b.* 2005
1485	*Derby (19th)*, Edward Richard William Stanley, *b.* 1962, *s.* 1994, *m.*	Lord Stanley, *b.* 1998
1553 **	*Devon (19th)*, Charles Peregrine Courtenay, *b.* 1975, *s.* 2015, *m.*	Lord Courtenay, *b.* 2009
1800 I.	*Donoughmore (8th)*, Richard Michael John Hely-Hutchinson, *b.* 1927, *s.* 1981, *m.*	Viscount Suirdale, *b.* 1952
1661 I.	*Drogheda (12th)*, Henry Dermot Ponsonby Moore, *b.* 1937, *s.* 1989, *m.*	Viscount Moore, *b.* 1983
1837	*Ducie (7th)*, David Leslie Moreton, *b.* 1951, *s.* 1991, *m.*	Lord Moreton, *b.* 1981
1860	*Dudley (5th)*, William Humble David Jeremy Ward, *b.* 1947, *s.* 2013	Hon. Leander G. D. W., *b.* 1971
1660 S. **	*Dundee (12th)*, Alexander Henry Scrymgeour, *b.* 1949, *s.* 1983, *w.*	Lord Scrymgeour, *b.* 1982
1669 S.	*Dundonald (15th)*, Iain Alexander Douglas Blair Cochrane, *b.* 1961, *s.* 1986	Lord Cochrane, *b.* 1991
1686 S.	*Dunmore (12th)*, Malcolm Kenneth Murray, *b.* 1946, *s.* 1995, *w.*	Hon. Geoffrey C. M., *b.* 1949
1833	*Durham (7th)*, Edward Richard Lambton, *b.* 1961, *s.* 2006, *m.*	Viscount Lambton, *b.* 1985
1643 S.	*Dysart (13th)*, John Peter Grant of Rothiemurchus, *b.* 1946, *s.* 2011, *m.*	Lord Huntingtower, *b.* 1977
1837	*Effingham (7th)*, David Mowbray Algernon Howard, *b.* 1939, *s.* 1996, *m.*	Lord Howard of Effingham, *b.* 1971
1507 S.	*Eglinton (19th) and Winton (10th) (S. 1600)*, Hugh Archibald William Montgomerie, *b.* 1966, *s.* 2018, *m.*	Lord Montgomerie, *b.* 2007
1821	*Eldon (6th)*, John Francis Thomas Marie Joseph Columba Fidelis Scott, *b.* 1962, *s.* 2017, *m.*	Viscount Encombe, *b.* 1996
1633 S.	*Elgin (11th) and Kincardine (15th) (S. 1647)*, Andrew Douglas Alexander Thomas Bruce, KT, *b.* 1924, *s.* 1968, *m.*	Lord Bruce, *b.* 1961
1789 I.	*Enniskillen (7th)*, Andrew John Galbraith Cole, *b.* 1942, *s.* 1989, *m.*	Berkeley A. C., *b.* 1949
1789 I.	*Erne (7th)*, John Henry Michael Ninian Crichton, *b.* 1971, *s.* 2016, *m.*	Charles D. B. C., *b.* 1953
1452 S. **	*Erroll (24th)*, Merlin Sereld Victor Gilbert Hay, *b.* 1948, *s.* 1978, *m. Hereditary Lord High Constable and Knight Marischal of Scotland*	Lord Hay, *b.* 1984
1661	*Essex (11th)*, Frederick Paul de Vere Capell, *b.* 1944, *s.* 2005	William J. C., *b.* 1952
1711 °	*Ferrers (14th)*, Robert William Saswalo Shirley, *b.* 1952, *s.* 2012, *m.*	Viscount Tamworth, *b.* 1984
1789 °	*Fortescue (8th)*, Charles Hugh Richard Fortescue, *b.* 1951, *s.* 1993, *m.*	John A. F. F., *b.* 1955
1841	*Gainsborough (6th)*, Anthony Baptist Noel, *b.* 1950, *s.* 2009, *m.*	Viscount Campden, *b.* 1977
1623 S.	*Galloway (13th)*, Randolph Keith Reginald Stewart, *b.* 1928, *s.* 1978, *w.*	Andrew C. S., *b.* 1949
1703 S.**	*Glasgow (10th)*, Patrick Robin Archibald Boyle, *b.* 1939, *s.* 1984, *m.*	Viscount of Kelburn, *b.* 1978
1806 I.	*Gosford (7th)*, Charles David Nicholas Alexander John Sparrow Acheson, *b.* 1942, *s.* 1966, *m.*	Nicholas H. C. A., *b.* 1947
1945	*Gowrie (2nd)*, Alexander Patrick Greysteil Hore Ruthven, PC, *b.* 1939, *s.* 1955, *m.*	Viscount Ruthven of Canberra, *b.* 1964
1684 I.	*Granard (10th)*, Peter Arthur Edward Hastings Forbes, *b.* 1957, *s.* 1992, *m.*	Viscount Forbes, *b.* 1981
1833 °	*Granville (6th)*, Granville George Fergus Leveson-Gower, *b.* 1959, *s.* 1996, *m.*	Lord Leveson, *b.* 1999
1806 °	*Grey (7th)*, Philip Kent Grey, *b.* 1940, *s.* 2013, *m.*	Viscount Howick, *b.* 1968
1752	*Guilford (10th)*, Piers Edward Brownlow North, *b.* 1971, *s.* 1999, *m.*	Lord North, *b.* 2002
1619 S.	*Haddington (14th)*, George Edmund Baldred Baillie-Hamilton, *b.* 1985, *s.* 2016	Thomas R. Hamilton-Baillie, *b.* 1948
1919 °	*Haig (3rd)*, Alexander Douglas Derrick Haig, *b.* 1961, *s.* 2009, *m.*	None
1944	*Halifax (3rd)*, Charles Edward Peter Neil Wood, *b.* 1944, *s.* 1980, *m.*	Lord Irwin, *b.* 1977
1754	*Hardwicke (10th)*, Joseph Philip Sebastian Yorke, *b.* 1971, *s.* 1974, *m.*	Viscount Royston, *b.* 2009
1812	*Harewood (8th)*, David Henry George Lascelles, *b.* 1950, *s.* 2011, *m.*	Viscount Lascelles, *b.* 1980
1742	*Harrington (12th)*, Charles Henry Leicester Stanhope, *b.* 1945, *s.* 2009, *m.*	Viscount Petersham, *b.* 1967
1809	*Harrowby (8th)*, Dudley Adrian Conroy Ryder, *b.* 1951, *s.* 2007, *m.*	Viscount Sandon, *b.* 1981
1605 S. **	*Home (15th)*, David Alexander Cospatrick Douglas-Home, KT, CVO, CBE, *b.* 1943, *s.* 1995, *m.*	Lord Dunglass, *b.* 1987
1821 ° **	*Howe (7th)*, Frederick Richard Penn Curzon, PC, *b.* 1951, *s.* 1984, *m.*	Viscount Curzon, *b.* 1994
1529	*Huntingdon (17th)*, William Edward Robin Hood Hastings-Bass, LVO, *b.* 1948, *s.* 1990	Hon. John P. R. H. H.-B., *b.* 1954
1885	*Iddesleigh (5th)*, John Stafford Northcote, *b.* 1957, *s.* 2004, *m.*	Viscount St Cyres, *b.* 1985
1756	*Ilchester (10th)*, Robin Maurice Fox-Strangways, *b.* 1942, *s.* 2006, *m.*	Paul A. F-S., *b.* 1950
1929	*Inchcape (4th)*, (Kenneth) Peter (Lyle) Mackay, *b.* 1943, *s.* 1994, *m.*	Viscount Glenapp, *b.* 1979
1919	*Iveagh (4th)*, Arthur Edward Rory Guinness, *b.* 1969, *s.* 1992, *m.*	Viscount Elveden, *b.* 2003
1925 °	*Jellicoe (3rd)*, Patrick John Bernard Jellicoe, *b.* 1950, *s.* 2007	Hon. Nicholas C. J., *b.* 1953

1697	*Jersey (10th),* George Francis William Child Villiers, *b.* 1976, *s.* 1998, *m.*	Viscount Villiers, *b.* 2015
1822 I.	*Kilmorey (6th),* Sir Richard Francis Needham, PC, *b.* 1942, *s.* 1977, *m.* (Does not use title)	Viscount Newry and Mourne, *b.* 1966
1866	*Kimberley (5th),* John Armine Wodehouse, *b.* 1951, *s.* 2002, *m.*	Lord Wodehouse, *b.* 1978
1768 I.	*Kingston (12th),* Robert Charles Henry King-Tenison, *b.* 1969, *s.* 2002	Viscount Kingsborough, *b.* 2000
1633 S. **	*Kinnoull (16th),* Charles William Harley Hay, *b.* 1962, *s.* 2013, *m.*	Viscount Dupplin, *b.* 2011
1677 S.	*Kintore (14th),* James William Falconer Keith, *b.* 1976, *s.* 2004, *m.*	Lord Inverurie, *b.* 2010
1624 S.	*Lauderdale (18th),* Ian Maitland, *b.* 1937, *s.* 2008, *m.*	Viscount Maitland, *b.* 1965
1837	*Leicester (8th),* Thomas Edward Coke, *b.* 1965, *s.* 2015, *m.*	Viscount Coke, *b.* 2003
1641 S.	*Leven (15th) and Melville (14th) (S. 1690),* Alexander Ian Leslie Melville, *b.* 1984, *s.* 2012	Hon. Archibald R. L. M., *b.* 1957
1831	*Lichfield (6th),* Thomas William Robert Hugh Anson, *b.* 1978, *s.* 2005, *m.*	Viscount Anson, *b.* 2011
1803 I.	*Limerick (7th),* Edmund Christopher Pery, *b.* 1963, *s.* 2003, *m.*	Viscount Pery, *b.* 1991
1572	*Lincoln (19th),* Robert Edward Fiennes-Clinton, *b.* 1972, *s.* 2001	Hon. William J. Howson, *b.* 1980
1633 S. **	*Lindsay (16th),* James Randolph Lindesay-Bethune, *b.* 1955, *s.* 1989, *m.*	Viscount Garnock, *b.* 1990
1626	*Lindsey (14th) and Abingdon (9th) (1682),* Richard Henry Rupert Bertie, *b.* 1931, *s.* 1963, *m.*	Lord Norreys, *b.* 1958
1776 I.	*Lisburne (9th),* David John Francis Malet Vaughan, *b.* 1945, *s.* 2014, *m.*	Hon. Michael J. W. M. V., *b.* 1948
1822 I.**	*Listowel (6th),* Francis Michael Hare, *b.* 1964, *s.* 1997	Hon. Timothy P. H., *b.* 1966
1905 **	*Liverpool (5th),* Edward Peter Bertram Savile Foljambe, *b.* 1944, *s.* 1969, *m.*	Viscount Hawkesbury, *b.* 1972
1945 °	*Lloyd George of Dwyfor (4th),* David Richard Owen Lloyd George, *b.* 1951, *s.* 2010, *m.*	Viscount Gwynedd, *b.* 1986
1785 I.	*Longford (8th),* Thomas Frank Dermot Pakenham, *b.* 1933, *s.* 2001, *m.* (Does not use title)	Edward M. P., *b.* 1970
1807	*Lonsdale (8th),* Hugh Clayton Lowther, *b.* 1949, *s.* 2006, *m.*	Hon. William J. L., *b.* 1957
1633 S.	*Loudoun (15th),* Simon Michael Abney-Hastings, *b.* 1974, *s.* 2012	Hon. Marcus W. A.-H., *b.* 1981
1795 I.	*Lucan (8th),* George Charles Bingham, *b.* 1967, *s.* 2016, *m.*	Nicholas C. B., *b.* 1943
1880 **	*Lytton (5th),* John Peter Michael Scawen Lytton, *b.* 1950, *s.* 1985, *m.*	Viscount Knebworth, *b.* 1989
1721	*Macclesfield (9th),* Richard Timothy George Mansfield Parker, *b.* 1943, *s.* 1992, *m.*	Hon. J. David G. P., *b.* 1945
1800	*Malmesbury (7th),* James Carleton Harris, *b.* 1946, *s.* 2000, *m.*	Viscount FitzHarris, *b.* 1970
1776	*Mansfield (8th) and Mansfield (9th) (1792),* Alexander David Mungo Murray, *b.* 1956, *s.* 2015, *m.*	Viscount Stormont, *b.* 1988
1565 S.	*Mar (14th) and Kellie (16th) (S. 1616) and Baron Erskine of Alloa Tower (life peerage, 2000),* James Thorne Erskine, *b.* 1949, *s.* 1994, *m.*	Hon. Alexander D. E., *b.* 1952
1785 I.	*Mayo (11th),* Charles Diarmuidh John Bourke, *b.* 1953, *s.* 2006, *m.*	Lord Naas, *b.* 1985
1627 I.	*Meath (15th),* John Anthony Brabazon, *b.* 1941, *s.* 1998, *m.*	Lord Ardee, *b.* 1977
1766 I.	*Mexborough (8th),* John Christopher George Savile, *b.* 1931, *s.* 1980, *m.*	Viscount Pollington, *b.* 1959
1813	*Minto (7th),* Gilbert Timothy George Lariston Elliot-Murray-Kynynmound, *b.* 1953, *s.* 2005, *m.*	Viscount Melgund, *b.* 1984
1562 S.	*Moray (21st),* John Douglas Stuart, *b.* 1966, *s.* 2011, *m.*	Lord Doune, *b.* 2002
1815	*Morley (7th),* Mark Lionel Parker, *b.* 1956, *s.* 2015, *m.*	Edward G. P., *b.* 1967
1458 S.	*Morton (22nd),* John Stewart Sholto Douglas, *b.* 1952, *s.* 2016, *m.*	Lord Aberdour, *b.* 1986
1789	*Mount Edgcumbe (8th),* Robert Charles Edgcumbe, *b.* 1939, *s.* 1982, *m.*	Piers V. E., *b.* 1946
1947 °	*Mountbatten of Burma (3rd),* Norton Louis Philip Knatchbull, *b.* 1947, *s.* 2017, *m.*	Lord Brabourne, *b.* 1981
1805 °	*Nelson (10th),* Simon John Horatio Nelson, *b.* 1971, *s.* 2009, *m.*	Viscount Merton, *b.* 2010
1660 S.	*Newburgh (12th),* Don Filippo Giambattista Camillo Francesco Aldo Maria Rospigliosi, *b.* 1942, *s.* 1986, *m.*	Princess Donna Benedetta F. M. R., *b.* 1974
1827 I.	*Norbury (7th),* Richard James Graham-Toler, *b.* 1967, *s.* 2000	None
1806 I.	*Normanton (7th),* James Shaun Christian Welbore Ellis Agar, *b.* 1982, *s.* 2019, *m.*	Viscount Somerton, *b.* 2016
1647 S.	*Northesk (15th),* Patrick Charles Carnegy, *b.* 1940, *s.* 2010, *m.*	Hon. Colin D. C., *b.* 1942
1801	*Onslow (8th),* Rupert Charles William Bullard Onslow, *b.* 1967, *s.* 2011, *m.*	Anthony E. E. O., *b.* 1955
1696 S.	*Orkney (9th),* (Oliver) Peter St John, *b.* 1938, *s.* 1998, *m.*	Viscount Kirkwall, *b.* 1969
1328 I.	*Ormonde and Ossory (I. 1527),* The 25th/18th Earl (7th Marquess) died in 1988	†Viscount Mountgarret *b.* 1961 (*see that title*)
1925 **	*Oxford and Asquith (3rd),* Raymond Benedict Bartholomew Michael Asquith, OBE, *b.* 1952, *s.* 2011, *m.*	Viscount Asquith, *b.* 1979
1929 ° **	*Peel (3rd),* William James Robert Peel, GCVO, PC, *b.* 1947, *s.* 1969, *m.* Lord Chamberlain	Viscount Clanfield, *b.* 1976
1551	*Pembroke (18th) and Montgomery (15th) (1605),* William Alexander Sidney Herbert, *b.* 1978, *s.* 2003, *m.*	Lord Herbert, *b.* 2012
1605 S.	*Perth (18th),* John Eric Drummond, *b.* 1935, *s.* 2002, *m.*	Viscount Strathallan, *b.* 1965
1905	*Plymouth (4th),* Ivor Edward Other Windsor-Clive, *b.* 1951, *s.* 2018, *m.*	Viscount Windsor, *b.* 1981
1785 I.	*Portarlington (7th),* George Lionel Yuill Seymour Dawson-Damer, *b.* 1938, *s.* 1959, *m.*	Viscount Carlow, *b.* 1965
1689	*Portland (12th),* Count Timothy Charles Robert Noel Bentinck, MBE, *b.* 1953, *s.* 1997, *m.*	Viscount Woodstock, *b.* 1984
1743	*Portsmouth (10th),* Quentin Gerard Carew Wallop, *b.* 1954, *s.* 1984, *m.*	Viscount Lymington, *b.* 1981
1804	*Powis (8th),* John George Herbert, *b.* 1952, *s.* 1993, *m.*	Viscount Clive, *b.* 1979

1765	*Radnor (9th)*, William Pleydell-Bouverie, *b.* 1955, *s.* 2008, *m.*	Viscount Folkestone, *b.* 1999
1831 I.	*Ranfurly (8th)*, Edward John Knox, *b.* 1957, *s.* 2018, *m.*	Viscount Northland, *b.* 1994
1771 I.	*Roden (10th)*, Robert John Jocelyn, *b.* 1938, *s.* 1993, *m.*	Viscount Jocelyn, *b.* 1989
1801	*Romney (8th)*, Julian Charles Marsham, *b.* 1948, *s.* 2004, *m.*	Viscount Marsham, *b.* 1977
1703 S.	*Rosebery (7th)*, Neil Archibald Primrose, *b.* 1929, *s.* 1974, *m.*	Lord Dalmeny, *b.* 1967
1806 I.	*Rosse (7th)*, William Brendan Parsons, *b.* 1936, *s.* 1979, *m.*	Lord Oxmantown, *b.* 1969
1801 **	*Rosslyn (7th)*, Peter St Clair-Erskine, CVO, QPM, *b.* 1958, *s.* 1977, *m.*	Lord Loughborough, *b.* 1986
1457 S.	*Rothes (22nd)*, James Malcolm David Leslie, *b.* 1958, *s.* 2005	Hon. Alexander J. L., *b.* 1962
1861 °	*Russell (7th)*, John Francis Russell, *b.* 1971, *s.* 2014, *m.*	None
1915 °	*St Aldwyn (3rd)*, Michael Henry Hicks Beach, *b.* 1950, *s.* 1992, *m.*	Hon. David S. H. B., *b.* 1955
1815 M.	*St Germans (11th)*, Albert Charger Eliot, *b.* 2004, *s.* 2016	Hon. Louis R. E., *b.* 1968
1660 **	*Sandwich (11th)*, John Edward Hollister Montagu, *b.* 1943, *s.* 1995, *m.*	Viscount Hinchingbrooke, *b.* 1969
1690	*Scarbrough (13th)*, Richard Osbert Lumley, *b.* 1973, *s.* 2004, *m.*	Hon. Thomas H. L., *b.* 1980
1701 S.	*Seafield (13th)*, Ian Derek Francis Ogilvie-Grant, *b.* 1939, *s.* 1969, *m.*	Viscount Reidhaven, *b.* 1963
1882 **	*Selborne (4th)*, John Roundell Palmer, GBE, *b.* 1940, *s.* 1971, *m.*	Viscount Wolmer, *b.* 1971
1646 S.	*Selkirk (11th)*, Disclaimed for life 1994 (*see* Lord Selkirk of Douglas, Life Peers)	Master of Selkirk, *b.* 1978
1672	*Shaftesbury (12th)*, Nicholas Edmund Anthony Ashley-Cooper, *b.* 1979, *s.* 2005, *m.*	Lord Ashley, *b.* 2011
1756 I.	*Shannon (10th)*, Richard Henry John Boyle, *b.* 1960, *s.* 2013	Robert F. B., *b.* 1930
1442 **	*Shrewsbury and Waterford (22nd)* (*I.* 1446), Charles Henry John Benedict Crofton Chetwynd Chetwynd-Talbot, *b.* 1952, *s.* 1980, *m. Premier Earl of England and Ireland*	Viscount Ingestre, *b.* 1978
1961	*Snowdon (2nd)*, David Albert Charles Armstrong-Jones, *b.* 1961, *s.* 2017, *m.*	Viscount Linley, *b.* 1999
1765 °	*Spencer (9th)*, Charles Edward Maurice Spencer, *b.* 1964, *s.* 1992, *m.*	Viscount Althorp, *b.* 1994
1703 S.**	*Stair (14th)*, John David James Dalrymple, *b.* 1961, *s.* 1996, *m.*	Viscount Dalrymple, *b.* 2008
1984	*Stockton (2nd)*, Alexander Daniel Alan Macmillan, *b.* 1943, *s.* 1986, *m.*	Viscount Macmillan of Ovenden, *b.* 1974
1821	*Stradbroke (6th)*, Robert Keith Rous, *b.* 1937, *s.* 1983, *m.*	Viscount Dunwich, *b.* 1961
1847	*Strafford (9th)*, William Robert Byng, *b.* 1964, *s.* 2016, *m.*	Viscount Enfield, *b.* 1998
1606 S.	*Strathmore and Kinghorne (19th)* (*S.* 1677), Simon Patrick Bowes Lyon, *b.* 1986, *s.* 2016	Hon. John F. B. L., *b.* 1988
1603	*Suffolk (21st) and Berkshire (14th)* (1626), Michael John James George Robert Howard, *b.* 1935, *s.* 1941, *m.*	Viscount Andover, *b.* 1974
1955	*Swinton (3rd)*, Nicholas John Cunliffe-Lister, *b.* 1939, *s.* 2006, *m.*	Lord Masham, *b.* 1970
1714	*Tankerville (10th)*, Peter Grey Bennet, *b.* 1956, *s.* 1980	Adrian G. B., *b.* 1958
1822 °	*Temple of Stowe (9th)*, James Grenville Temple-Gore-Langton, *b.* 1955, *s.* 2013, *m.*	Hon. Robert C. T.-G.-L., *b.* 1957
1815	*Verulam (7th)*, John Duncan Grimston, *b.* 1951, *s.* 1973, *m.*	Viscount Grimston, *b.* 1978
1729 °	*Waldegrave (13th)*, James Sherbrooke Waldegrave, *b.* 1940, *s.* 1995	Viscount Chewton, *b.* 1986
1759	*Warwick (9th) and Brooke (9th)* (1746), Guy David Greville, *b.* 1957, *s.* 1996, *m.*	Lord Brooke, *b.* 1982
1633 S.	*Wemyss (13th) and March (9th)* (*S.* 1697), James Donald Charteris, *b.* 1948, *s.* 2008, *m.*	Lord Elcho, *b.* 1984
1621 I.	*Westmeath (13th)*, William Anthony Nugent, *b.* 1928, *s.* 1971, *m.*	Sean C. W. N., *b.* 1965
1624	*Westmorland (16th)*, Anthony David Francis Henry Fane, *b.* 1951, *s.* 1993, *m.*	Hon. Harry St C. F., *b.* 1953
1876	*Wharncliffe (5th)*, Richard Alan Montagu Stuart Wortley, *b.* 1953, *s.* 1987, *m.*	Viscount Carlton, *b.* 1980
1801	*Wilton (8th)*, Francis Egerton Grosvenor, *b.* 1934, *s.* 1999, *w.*	Viscount Grey de Wilton, *b.* 1959
1628	*Winchilsea (17th) and Nottingham (12th)* (1681), Daniel James Hatfield Finch Hatton, *b.* 1967, *s.* 1999, *m.*	Viscount Maidstone, *b.* 1998
1766 I. °	*Winterton (8th)*, (Donald) David Turnour, *b.* 1943, *s.* 1991, *m.*	Robert C. T., *b.* 1950
1956	*Woolton (3rd)*, Simon Frederick Marquis, *b.* 1958, *s.* 1969, *m.*	None
1837	*Yarborough (8th)*, Charles John Pelham, *b.* 1963, *s.* 1991, *m.*	Lord Worsley, *b.* 1990

COUNTESSES IN THEIR OWN RIGHT

Style, The Rt. Hon. the Countess (of) _
Envelope (formal), The Rt. Hon. the Countess (of) _; *(social),* The Countess (of) _. *Letter (formal),* Madam; *(social),* Lady _. *Spoken (formal),* Madam; *(social),* Lady _.
Husband, Untitled
Children's style, As for children of an Earl
In Scotland, the heir to a Countess may be styled 'The Master/Mistress of _ (title of peer)'

Created	Title, order of succession, name, etc	Heir
c.1115 S. **	*Mar (31st),* Margaret of Mar, *b.* 1940, *s.* 1975, *m. Premier Earldom of Scotland*	Mistress of Mar, *b.* 1963
c.1235 S.	*Sutherland (24th),* Elizabeth Millicent Sutherland, *b.* 1921, *s.* 1963, *w.*	Lord Strathnaver, *b.* 1947

VISCOUNTS

Coronet, Sixteen silver balls

Style, The Rt. Hon. the Viscount _
Envelope (formal), The Rt. Hon. the Viscount _; *(social),* The Viscount _. *Letter (formal),* My Lord; *(social),* Dear Lord _. *Spoken,* Lord _.
Wife's style, The Rt. Hon. the Viscountess _
Envelope (formal), The Rt. Hon. the Viscountess _; *(social),* The Viscountess _. *Letter (formal),* Madam; *(social),* Dear Lady _. *Spoken,* Lady _.
Children's style, 'The Hon.' before forename and surname, as for Baron's children
In Scotland, the heir to a Viscount may be styled 'The Master/Mistress of _ (title of peer)'

Created	Title, order of succession, name, etc	Heir
1945	*Addison (4th),* William Matthew Wand Addison, *b.* 1945, *s.* 1992, *m.*	Hon. Paul W. A., *b.* 1973
1919	*Allenby (4th),* Henry Jaffray Hynman Allenby, *b.* 1968, *s.* 2014, *m.*	Hon. Harry M. E. A., *b.* 2000
1911	*Allendale (4th),* Wentworth Peter Ismay Beaumont, *b.* 1948, *s.* 2002, *m.*	Hon. Wentworth A. I. B., *b.* 1979
1642 S.	*of Arbuthnott (17th),* John Keith Oxley Arbuthnott, *b.* 1950, *s.* 2012, *m.*	Master of Arbuthnott, *b.* 1977
1751 I.	*Ashbrook (11th),* Michael Llowarch Warburton Flower, *b.* 1935, *s.* 1995, *m.*	Hon. Rowland F. W. F., *b.* 1975
1917 **	*Astor (4th),* William Waldorf Astor, *b.* 1951, *s.* 1966, *m.*	Hon. William W. A., *b.* 1979
1781 I.	*Bangor (8th),* William Maxwell David Ward, *b.* 1948, *s.* 1993, *m.*	Hon. E. Nicholas W., *b.* 1953
1925	*Bearsted (5th),* Nicholas Alan Samuel, *b.* 1950, *s.* 1996, *m.*	Hon. Harry R. S., *b.* 1988
1963	*Blakenham (3rd),* Caspar John Hare, *b.* 1972, *s.* 2018, *m.*	Hon. Inigo H., *b. c.*2006
1935	*Bledisloe (4th),* Rupert Edward Ludlow Bathurst, *b.* 1964, *s.* 2009, *m.*	Hon. Benjamin R. L. B., *b.* 2004
1712	*Bolingbroke (9th) and St John (10th) (1716),* Nicholas Alexander Mowbray St John, *b.* 1974, *s.* 2011, *m.*	German A. St J., *b.* 1980
1960	*Boyd of Merton (2nd),* Simon Donald Rupert Neville Lennox-Boyd, *b.* 1939, *s.* 1983, *m.*	Hon. Benjamin A. L.-B., *b.* 1964
1717 I.	*Boyne (11th),* Gustavus Michael Stucley Hamilton-Russell, *b.* 1965, *s.* 1995, *m.*	Hon. Gustavus A. E. H.-R., *b.* 1999
1929	*Brentford (4th),* Crispin William Joynson-Hicks, *b.* 1933, *s.* 1983, *m.*	Hon. Paul W. J.-H., MBE, *b.* 1971
1929 **	*Bridgeman (3rd),* Robin John Orlando Bridgeman, *b.* 1930, *s.* 1982, *m.*	Hon. Luke R. O. B., *b.* 1971
1868	*Bridport (4th) and 7th Duke, Bronte in Sicily, 1799,* Alexander Nelson Hood, *b.* 1948, *s.* 1969	Hon. Peregrine A. N. H., *b.* 1974
1952 **	*Brookeborough (3rd),* Alan Henry Brooke, KG, *b.* 1952, *s.* 1987, *m.*	Hon. Christopher A. B., *b.* 1954
1933	*Buckmaster (4th),* Adrian Charles Buckmaster, *b.* 1949, *s.* 2007, *m.*	Hon. Andrew N. B., *b.* 1980
1939	*Caldecote (3rd),* Piers James Hampden Inskip, *b.* 1947, *s.* 1999, *m.*	Hon. Thomas J. H. I., *b.* 1985
1941	*Camrose (5th),* Jonathan William Berry, *b.* 1970, *s.* 2016, *m.*	Hon. Hugo W. B., *b.* 2000
1954	*Chandos (3rd) and Baron Lyttelton of Aldershot (life peerage, 2000),* Thomas Orlando Lyttelton, *b.* 1953, *s.* 1980, *m.*	Hon. Oliver A. L., *b.* 1986

1665 I.	*Charlemont (15th)*, John Dodd Caulfeild, *b.* 1966, *s.* 2001, *m.*	Hon. Shane A. C., *b.* 1996
1921	*Chelmsford (4th)*, Frederic Corin Piers Thesiger, *b.* 1962, *s.* 1999, *m.*	Hon. Frederic T., *b.* 2006
1717 I.	*Chetwynd (11th)*, Adam Douglas Chetwynd, *b.* 1969, *s.* 2015, *m.*	Hon. Connor A. C., *b.* 2001
1911	*Chilston (4th)*, Alastair George Akers-Douglas, *b.* 1946, *s.* 1982, *m.*	Hon. Oliver I. A.-D., *b.* 1973
1718	*Cobham (12th)*, Christopher Charles Lyttelton, *b.* 1947, *s.* 2006, *m.*	Hon. Oliver C. L., *b.* 1976
1902 **	*Colville of Culross (5th)*, Charles Mark Townshend Colville, *b.* 1959, *s.* 2010	Master of Colville, *b.* 1961
1826	*Combermere (6th)*, Thomas Robert Wellington Stapleton-Cotton, *b.* 1969, *s.* 2000, *m.*	Hon. Laszlo M. W. S.-C., *b.* 2010
1917	*Cowdray (4th)*, Michael Orlando Weetman Pearson, *b.* 1944, *s.* 1995, *m.*	Hon. Peregrine J. D. P., *b.* 1994
1927 **	*Craigavon (3rd)*, Janric Fraser Craig, *b.* 1944, *s.* 1974	None
1943	*Daventry (4th)*, James Edward FitzRoy Newdegate, *b.* 1960, *s.* 2000, *m.*	Hon. Humphrey J. F. N., *b.* 1995
1937	*Davidson (3rd)*, Malcolm William Mackenzie Davidson, *b.* 1934, *s.* 2012, *w.*	Hon. John N. A. D., *b.* 1971
1956	*De L'Isle (2nd)*, Philip John Algernon Sidney, CVO, MBE, *b.* 1945, *s.* 1991, *m.*	Hon. Philip W. E. S., *b.* 1985
1776 I.	*de Vesci (7th)*, Thomas Eustace Vesey, *b.* 1955, *s.* 1983	Hon. Oliver I. V., *b.* 1991
1917	*Devonport (3rd)*, Terence Kearley, *b.* 1944, *s.* 1973, *m.*	Chester D. H. K., *b.* 1932
1964	*Dilhorne (2nd)*, John Mervyn Manningham-Buller, *b.* 1932, *s.* 1980, *m.*	Hon. James E. M.-B., *b.* 1956
1622 I.	*Dillon (22nd)*, Henry Benedict Charles Dillon, *b.* 1973, *s.* 1982, *m.*	Hon. Francis C. R. D., *b.* 2013
1785 I.	*Doneraile (10th)*, Richard Allen St Leger, *b.* 1946, *s.* 1983, *m.*	Hon. Nathaniel W. R. St J. St L., *b.* 1971
1680 I.	*Downe (12th)*, Richard Henry Dawnay, *b.* 1967, *s.* 2002	Thomas P. D., *b.* 1978
1959	*Dunrossil (3rd)*, Andrew William Reginald Morrison, *b.* 1953, *s.* 2000, *m.*	Hon. Callum A. B. M., *b.* 1994
1964 **	*Eccles (2nd)*, John Dawson Eccles, CBE, *b.* 1931, *s.* 1999, *m.*	Hon. William D. E., *b.* 1960
1897	*Esher (5th)*, Christopher Lionel Baliol Brett, *b.* 1936, *s.* 2004, *m.*	Hon. Matthew C. A. B., *b.* 1963
1816	*Exmouth (10th)*, Paul Edward Pellew, *b.* 1940, *s.* 1970	Hon. Edward F. P., *b.* 1978
1620 S.**	*of Falkland (15th)*, Lucius Edward William Plantagenet Cary, *b.* 1935, *s.* 1984, *m. Premier Scottish Viscount on the Roll*	Master of Falkland, *b.* 1963
1720	*Falmouth (9th)*, George Hugh Boscawen, *b.* 1919, *s.* 1962, *w.*	Hon. Evelyn A. H. B., *b.* 1955
1720 I.	*Gage (8th)*, (Henry) Nicolas Gage, *b.* 1934, *s.* 1993, *m.*	Hon. Henry W. G., *b.* 1975
1727 I.	*Galway (13th)*, John Philip Monckton, *b.* 1952, *s.* 2017, *m.*	Alan S. M., *b.* 1934
1478 I.	*Gormanston (17th)*, Jenico Nicholas Dudley Preston, *b.* 1939, *s.* 1940, *m. Premier Viscount of Ireland*	Hon. Jenico F. T. P., *b.* 1974
1816 I.	*Gort (9th)*, Foley Robert Standish Prendergast Vereker, *b.* 1951, *s.* 1995, *m.*	Hon. Robert F. P. V., *b.* 1993
1900 **	*Goschen (4th)*, Giles John Harry Goschen, *b.* 1965, *s.* 1977, *m.*	Hon. Alexander J. E. G., *b.* 2001
1849	*Gough (5th)*, Shane Hugh Maryon Gough, *b.* 1941, *s.* 1951	None
1929	*Hailsham (3rd) and Baron Hailsham of Kettlethorpe (life peerage, 2015)*, Douglas Martin Hogg, PC, QC, *b.* 1945, *s.* 2001, *m.*	Hon. Quintin J. N. M. H., *b.* 1973
1891	*Hambleden (5th)*, William Henry Bernard Smith, *b.* 1955, *s.* 2012, *m.*	Hon. Bernardo J. S., *b.* 1957
1884	*Hampden (7th)*, Francis Anthony Brand, *b.* 1970, *s.* 2008, *m.*	Hon. Lucian A. B., *b.* 2005
1936 **	*Hanworth (3rd)*, David Stephen Geoffrey Pollock, *b.* 1946, *s.* 1996, *m.*	Harold W. C. P., *b.* 1988
1791 I.	*Harberton (11th)*, Henry Robert Pomeroy, *b.* 1958, *s.* 2004, *m.*	Hon. Patrick C. P., *b.* 1995
1846	*Hardinge (8th)*, Thomas Henry de Montarville Hardinge, *b.* 1993, *s.* 2014	Hon. Jamie A. D. H., *b.* 1996
1791 I.	*Hawarden (9th)*, (Robert) Connan Wyndham Leslie Maude, *b.* 1961, *s.* 1991, *m.*	Hon. Varian J. C. E. M., *b.* 1997
1960	*Head (2nd)*, Richard Antony Head, *b.* 1937, *s.* 1983, *m.*	Hon. Henry J. H., *b.* 1980
1550	*Hereford (19th)*, Charles Robin de Bohun Devereux, *b.* 1975, *s.* 2004, *m. Premier Viscount of England*	Hon. Henry W. de B. D., *b.* 2015
1842	*Hill (9th)*, Peter David Raymond Charles Clegg-Hill, *b.* 1945, *s.* 2003, *m.*	Hon. Michael C. D. C.-H., *b.* 1988
1796	*Hood (8th)*, Henry Lyttelton Alexander Hood, *b.* 1958, *s.* 1999, *m.*	Hon. Archibald L. S. H., *b.* 1993
1945	*Kemsley (3rd)*, Richard Gomer Berry, *b.* 1951, *s.* 1999, *m.*	Hon. Luke G. B., *b.* 1998
1911	*Knollys (3rd)*, David Francis Dudley Knollys, *b.* 1931, *s.* 1966, *m.*	Hon. Patrick N. M. K., *b.* 1962
1895	*Knutsford (6th)*, Michael Holland-Hibbert, *b.* 1926, *s.* 1986, *w.*	Hon. Henry T. H.-H., *b.* 1959
1954	*Leathers (3rd)*, Christopher Graeme Leathers, *b.* 1941, *s.* 1996, *m.*	Hon. James F. L., *b.* 1969
1781 I.	*Lifford (9th)*, (Edward) James Wingfield Hewitt, *b.* 1949, *s.* 1987, *m.*	Hon. James T. W. H., *b.* 1979
1921	*Long (5th)*, James Richard Long, *b.* 1960, *s.* 2017	None
1957	*Mackintosh of Halifax (3rd)*, (John) Clive Mackintosh, *b.* 1958, *s.* 1980, *m.*	Hon. Thomas H. G. M., *b.* 1985
1955	*Malvern (3rd)*, Ashley Kevin Godfrey Huggins, *b.* 1949, *s.* 1978	Hon. M. James H., *b.* 1928
1945	*Marchwood (3rd)*, David George Staveley Penny, *b.* 1936, *s.* 1979, *m.*	Hon. Peter G. W. P., *b.* 1965
1942	*Margesson (3rd)*, Richard Francis David Margesson, *b.* 1960, *s.* 2014, *m.*	None
1660 I.	*Massereene (14th) and Ferrard (7th) (I. 1797)*, John David Clotworthy Whyte-Melville Foster Skeffington, *b.* 1940, *s.* 1992, *m.*	Hon. Charles J. C. W.-M. F. S., *b.* 1973
1802	*Melville (10th)*, Robert Henry Kirkpatrick Dundas, *b.* 1984, *s.* 2011, *m.*	Hon. Max D. H. M. D., *b.* 2018
1916	*Mersey (5th) and 14th Lord Nairne (S. 1681)*, Edward John Hallam Bigham, *b.* 1966, *s.* 2006, *m.*	Hon. David E. H. B., *b.* 1938 (to Viscountcy); Mistress of Nairne, *b.* 2003 (to Lordship of Nairne)
1717 I.	*Midleton (12th)*, Alan Henry Brodrick, *b.* 1949, *s.* 1988, *m.*	Hon. Ashley R. B., *b.* 1980
1962	*Mills (3rd)*, Christopher Philip Roger Mills, *b.* 1956, *s.* 1988, *m.*	None
1716 I.	*Molesworth (12th)*, Robert Bysse Kelham Molesworth, *b.* 1959, *s.* 1997	Hon. William J. C. M., *b.* 1960

1801 I.	*Monck (7th)*, Charles Stanley Monck, *b.* 1953, *s.* 1982 (Does not use title)	Hon. George S. M., *b.* 1957
1957	*Monckton of Brenchley (3rd)*, Christopher Walter Monckton, *b.* 1952, *s.* 2006, *m.*	Hon. Timothy D. R. M., *b.* 1955
1946	*Montgomery of Alamein (2nd)*, David Bernard Montgomery, CMG, CBE, *b.* 1928, *s.* 1976, *m.*	Hon. Henry D. M., *b.* 1954
1550 I.	*Mountgarret (18th)*, Piers James Richard Butler, *b.* 1961, *s.* 2004, *m.*	Hon. Theo O. S. B., *b.* 2015
1952	*Norwich (3rd)*, Jason Charles Duff Bede Cooper, *b.* 1959, *s.* 2018	None
1651 S.	*of Oxfuird (14th)*, Ian Arthur Alexander Makgill, *b.* 1969, *s.* 2003, *m.*	Master of Oxfuird, *b.* 2012
1873	*Portman (10th)*, Christopher Edward Berkeley Portman, *b.* 1958, *s.* 1999, *m.*	Hon. Luke O. B. P., *b.* 1984
1743 I.	*Powerscourt (11th) and 5th UK Baron Powerscourt (1885)*, Mervyn Anthony Wingfield, *b.* 1963, *s.* 2015, *m.*	To Viscountcy only, Richard D. N. W., *b.* 1966
1900 **	*Ridley (5th)*, Matthew White Ridley, *b.* 1958, *s.* 2012, *m.*	Hon. Matthew W. R., *b.* 1993
1960	*Rochdale (3rd)*, Jonathan Hugo Durival Kemp, *b.* 1961, *s.* 2015, *m.*	George T. K., *b.* 2001
1919	*Rothermere (4th)*, (Harold) Jonathan Esmond Vere Harmsworth, *b.* 1967, *s.* 1998, *m.*	Hon. Vere R. J. H. H., *b.* 1994
1937	*Runciman of Doxford (3rd)*, Walter Garrison (Garry) Runciman, CBE, *b.* 1934, *s.* 1989, *m.*	Hon. David W. R., *b.* 1967
1918	*St Davids (4th)*, Rhodri Colwyn Philipps, *b.* 1966, *s.* 2009, *m.*	Hon. Roland A. J. E. P., *b.* 1970
1801	*St Vincent (8th)*, Edward Robert James Jervis, *b.* 1951, *s.* 2006, *m.*	Hon. James R. A. J., *b.* 1982
1937	*Samuel (5th)*, Jonathan Herbert Samuel, *b.* 1965, *s.* 2014, *m.*	Hon. Benjamin A. S., *b.* 1983
1911	*Scarsdale (4th)*, Peter Ghislain Nathaniel Curzon, *b.* 1949, *s.* 2000, *m.*	Hon. David J. N. C., *b.* 1958
1905	*Selby (6th)*, Christopher Rolf Thomas Gully, *b.* 1993, *s.* 2001	Hon. (James) Edward H. G. G., *b.* 1945
1805	*Sidmouth (8th)*, Jeremy Francis Addington, *b.* 1947, *s.* 2005, *w.*	Hon. John A., *b.* 1990
1940 **	*Simon (3rd)*, Jan David Simon, *b.* 1940, *s.* 1993, *m.*	None
1960	*Slim (3rd)*, Mark William Rawdon Slim, *b.* 1960, *s.* 2019, *m.*	Hon. Rufus W. R. S., *b.* 1995
1954	*Soulbury (4th)*, Oliver Peter Ramsbotham, *b.* 1943, *s.* 2010, *m.*	Hon. Edward H. R., *b.* 1966
1776 I.	*Southwell (7th)*, Pyers Anthony Joseph Southwell, *b.* 1930, *s.* 1960, *m.*	Hon. Richard A. P. S., *b.* 1956
1942	*Stansgate (3rd)*, Stephen Michael Wedgwood Benn, *b.* 1951, *s.* 2014, *m.*	Hon. Daniel J. W. B., *b.* 1991
1959	*Stuart of Findhorn (3rd)*, Dominic Stuart, *b.* 1948, *s.* 1999	Hon. Andrew M. S., *b.* 1957
1957	*Tenby (3rd)*, William Lloyd George, *b.* 1927, *s.* 1983, *m.*	Hon. Timothy H. G. L. G., *b.* 1962
1952 **	*Thurso (3rd)*, John Archibald Sinclair, PC, *b.* 1953, *s.* 1995, *m.*	Hon. James A. R. S., *b.* 1984
1721	*Torrington (11th)*, Timothy Howard St George Byng, *b.* 1943, *s.* 1961, *m.*	Colin H. Cranmer-Byng, *b.* 1960
1936 **	*Trenchard (3rd)*, Hugh Trenchard, *b.* 1951, *s.* 1987, *m.*	Hon. Alexander T. T., *b.* 1978
1921 **	*Ullswater (2nd)*, Nicholas James Christopher Lowther, LVO, PC, *b.* 1942, *s.* 1949, *m.*	Hon. Benjamin J. L., *b.* 1975
1642 I.	*Valentia (16th)*, Francis William Dighton Annesley, *b.* 1959, *s.* 2005, *m.*	Hon. Peter J. A., *b.* 1967
1952 **	*Waverley (3rd)*, John Desmond Forbes Anderson, *b.* 1949, *s.* 1990, *m.*	Hon. Forbes A. R. A., *b.* 1996
1938	*Weir (3rd)*, William Kenneth James Weir, *b.* 1933, *s.* 1975, *m.*	Hon. James W. H. W., *b.* 1965
1918	*Wimborne (4th)*, Ivor Mervyn Vigors Guest, *b.* 1968, *s.* 1993, *m.*	Hon. Ivor N. G. I. G., *b.* 2016
1923 **	*Younger of Leckie (5th)*, James Edward George Younger, *b.* 1955, *s.* 2003, *m.*	Hon. Alexander W. G. Y., *b.* 1993

BARONS/LORDS

Coronet, Six silver balls

Style, The Rt. Hon. the Lord _
  Envelope (formal), The Rt. Hon. Lord _; *(social)*, The Lord _. *Letter (formal)*, My Lord; *(social)*, Dear Lord _. *Spoken*, Lord _.
In the Peerage of Scotland there is no rank of Baron; the equivalent rank is Lord of Parliament and Scottish peers should always be styled 'Lord', never 'Baron'.

Wife's style, The Rt. Hon. the Lady _
  Envelope (formal), The Rt. Hon. Lady _; *(social)*, The Lady _. *Letter (formal)*, My Lady; *(social)*, Dear Lady _. *Spoken*, Lady _
Children's style, 'The Hon.' before forename (F_) and surname (S_)
  Envelope, The Hon. F_ S_. *Letter*, Dear Mr/Miss/Mrs S_. *Spoken*, Mr/Miss/Mrs S_
In Scotland, the heir to a Lord may be styled 'The Master/Mistress of _ (title of peer)'

Created	*Title, order of succession, name, etc*	*Heir*
1911	*Aberconway (4th)*, (Henry) Charles McLaren, *b.* 1948, *s.* 2003, *m.*	Hon. Charles S. M., *b.* 1984
1873 **	*Aberdare (5th)*, Alastair John Lyndhurst Bruce, *b.* 1947, *s.* 2005, *m.*	Hon. Hector M. N. B., *b.* 1974

1835	*Abinger (9th)*, James Harry Scarlett, *b.* 1959, *s.* 2002, *m.*	Hon. Peter R. S., *b.* 1961
1869	*Acton (5th)*, John Charles Ferdinand Harold Lyon-Dalberg-Acton, *b.* 1966, *s.* 2010, *m.*	Hon. Robert P. L.-D.-A., *b.* 1946
1887 **	*Addington (6th)*, Dominic Bryce Hubbard, *b.* 1963, *s.* 1982, *m.*	Hon. Michael W. L. H., *b.* 1965
1896	*Aldenham (6th) and Hunsdon of Hunsdon (4th) (1923)*, Vicary Tyser Gibbs, *b.* 1948, *s.* 1986, *m.*	Hon. Humphrey W. F. G., *b.* 1989
1962	*Aldington (2nd)*, Charles Harold Stuart Low, *b.* 1948, *s.* 2000, *m.*	Hon. Philip T. A. L., *b.* 1990
1945	*Altrincham (3rd)*, Anthony Ulick David Dundas Grigg, *b.* 1934, *s.* 2001, *m.*	Hon. (Edward) Sebastian G., *b.* 1965
1929	*Alvingham (2nd)*, Maj.-Gen. Robert Guy Eardley Yerburgh, CBE, *b.* 1926, *s.* 1955, *m.*	Capt. Hon. Robert R. G. Y., *b.* 1956
1892	*Amherst of Hackney (5th)*, Hugh William Amherst Cecil, *b.* 1968, *s.* 2009, *m.*	Hon. Jack W. A. C., *b.* 2001
1881	*Ampthill (5th)*, David Whitney Erskine Russell, *b.* 1947, *s.* 2011, *m.*	Hon. Anthony J. M. R., *b.* 1952
1947	*Amwell (3rd)*, Keith Norman Montague, *b.* 1943, *s.* 1990, *m.*	Hon. Ian K. M., *b.* 1973
1863	*Annaly (6th)*, Luke Richard White, *b.* 1954, *s.* 1990	Hon. Luke H. W., *b.* 1990
1885	*Ashbourne (4th)*, Edward Barry Greynville Gibson, *b.* 1933, *s.* 1983, *m.*	Hon. Edward C. d'O. G., *b.* 1967
1835	*Ashburton (7th)*, John Francis Harcourt Baring, KG, KCVO, *b.* 1928, *s.* 1991, *m.*	Hon. Mark F. R. B., *b.* 1958
1892	*Ashcombe (5th)*, Mark Edward Cubitt, *b.* 1964, *s.* 2013, *m.*	Hon. Richard R. A. C., *b.* 1995
1911 **	*Ashton of Hyde (4th)*, Thomas Henry Ashton, PC, *b.* 1958, *s.* 2008, *m.*	Hon. John E. A., *b.* 1966
1800 I.	*Ashtown (8th)*, Roderick Nigel Godolphin Trench, *b.* 1944, *s.* 2010, *m.*	Hon. Timothy R. H. T., *b.* 1968
1956 **	*Astor of Hever (3rd)*, John Jacob Astor, PC, *b.* 1946, *s.* 1984, *m.*	Hon. Charles G. J. A., *b.* 1990
1789 I.	*Auckland (10th) and Auckland (10th) (1793)*, Robert Ian Burnard Eden, *b.* 1962, *s.* 1997, *m.*	Henry V. E., *b.* 1958
1313	*Audley*, Barony in abeyance between three co-heiresses since 1997	
1900	*Avebury (5th)*, Lyulph Ambrose Lubbock, *b.* 1954, *s.* 2016, *m.*	Hon. Alexander L. R. L., *b.* 1985
1718 I.	*Aylmer (14th)*, (Anthony) Julian Aylmer, *b.* 1951, *s.* 2006, *m.*	Hon. Michael H. A., *b.* 1991
1929	*Baden-Powell (3rd)*, Robert Crause Baden-Powell, *b.* 1936, *s.* 1962, *w.*	Hon. David M. B.-P., *b.* 1940
1780	*Bagot (10th)*, (Charles Hugh) Shaun Bagot, *b.* 1944, *s.* 2001, *m.*	Julian W. D'A. B., *b.* 1943
1953	*Baillieu (3rd)*, James William Latham Baillieu, *b.* 1950, *s.* 1973, *m.*	Hon. Robert L. B., *b.* 1979
1607 S.	*Balfour of Burleigh (8th)*, Robert Bruce, *b.* 1927, *s.* 1967, *m.*	Hon. Victoria B., *b.* 1973
1924	*Banbury of Southam (3rd)*, Charles William Banbury, *b.* 1953, *s.* 1981, *m.*	None
1698	*Barnard (12th)*, Henry Francis Cecil Vane, *b.* 1959, *s.* 2016, *m.*	Hon. William H. C. V., *b.* 2005
1887	*Basing (6th)*, Stuart Anthony Whitfield Sclater-Booth, *b.* 1969, *s.* 2007	Hon. Luke W. S.-B., *b.* 2000
1917	*Beaverbrook (3rd)*, Maxwell William Humphrey Aitken, *b.* 1951, *s.* 1985, *m.*	Hon. Maxwell F. A., *b.* 1977
1647 S.	*Belhaven and Stenton (13th)*, Robert Anthony Carmichael Hamilton, *b.* 1927, *s.* 1961, *m.*	Master of Belhaven, *b.* 1953
1848 I.	*Bellew (8th)*, Bryan Edward Bellew, *b.* 1943, *s.* 2010, *m.*	Hon. Anthony R. B. B., *b.* 1972
1856	*Belper (5th)*, Richard Henry Strutt, *b.* 1941, *s.* 1999, *w.*	Hon. Michael H. S., *b.* 1969
1421	*Berkeley (18th) and Gueterbock (life peerage, 2000)*, Anthony Fitzhardinge Gueterbock, OBE, *b.* 1939, *s.* 1992, *m.*	Hon. Thomas F. G., *b.* 1969
1922 **	*Bethell (5th)*, James Nicholas Bethell, *b.* 1967, *s.* 2007, *m.*	Hon. Jacob N. D. B., *b.* 2006
1938	*Bicester (5th)*, Charles James Vivian Smith, *b.* 1963, *s.* 2016, *m.*	Hon. Milo L. V. S., *b.* 2007
1903	*Biddulph (5th)*, (Anthony) Nicholas Colin Maitland Biddulph, *b.* 1959, *s.* 1988	Hon. Robert J. M. B., *b.* 1994
1958	*Birkett (3rd)*, Thomas Birkett, *b.* 1982, *s.* 2015, *m.*	None
1907	*Blyth (5th)*, James Audley Ian Blyth, *b.* 1970, *s.* 2009, *m.*	Hon. Hugo A. J. B., *b.* 2006
1797	*Bolton (8th)*, Harry Algar Nigel Orde-Powlett, *b.* 1954, *s.* 2001, *w.*	Hon. Thomas P. A. O.-P., MC, *b.* 1979
1452 S.	*Borthwick (24th)*, John Hugh Borthwick, *b.* 1940, *s.* 1996, *m.*	Hon. James H. A. B. of Glengelt, *b.* 1940
1922 **	*Borwick (5th)*, (Geoffrey Robert) James Borwick, *b.* 1955, *s.* 2007, *m.*	Hon. Edwin D. W. B., *b.* 1984
1761	*Boston (11th)*, George William Eustace Boteler Irby, *b.* 1971, *s.* 2007, *m.*	Hon. Thomas W. G. B. I., *b.* 1999
1942 **	*Brabazon of Tara (3rd)*, Ivon Anthony Moore-Brabazon, PC, *b.* 1946, *s.* 1974, *m.*	Hon. Benjamin R. M.-B., *b.* 1983
1925	*Bradbury (3rd)*, John Bradbury, *b.* 1940, *s.* 1994, *m.*	Hon. John T. B., *b.* 1973
1962	*Brain (3rd)*, Michael Cottrell Brain, *b.* 1928, *s.* 2014, *m.*	Hon. Thomas R. B., *b.* 1965
1938	*Brassey of Apethorpe (4th)*, Edward Brassey, *b.* 1964, *s.* 2015, *m.*	Hon. Christian B., *b.* 2003
1788	*Braybrooke (11th)*, Richard Ralph Neville, *b.* 1977, *s.* 2017, *m.*	Hon. Edward A. N., *b.* 2015
1957	*Bridges (3rd)*, Mark Thomas Bridges, KCVO, *b.* 1954, *s.* 2017, *m.*	Hon. Nicholas E. B., *b.* 1956
1945	*Broadbridge (4th)*, Martin Hugh Broadbridge, *b.* 1929, *s.* 2000, *w.*	Air Vice-Marshal Hon. Richard J. M. B., CB, *b.* 1959
1933	*Brocket (3rd)*, Charles Ronald George Nall-Cain, *b.* 1952, *s.* 1967, *m.*	Hon. Alexander C. C. N.-C., *b.* 1984
1860 **	*Brougham and Vaux (5th)*, Michael John Brougham, CBE, *b.* 1938, *s.* 1967	Hon. Charles W. B., *b.* 1971
1776	*Brownlow (7th)*, Edward John Peregrine Cust, *b.* 1936, *s.* 1978, *m.*	Hon. Peregrine E. Q. C., *b.* 1974
1942	*Bruntisfield (3rd)*, Michael John Victor Warrender, *b.* 1949, *s.* 2007, *m.*	Hon. John M. P. C. W., *b.* 1996
1950	*Burden (4th)*, Fraser William Elsworth Burden, *b.* 1964, *s.* 2000	Hon. Ian S. B., *b.* 1967
1529	*Burgh (8th)*, (Alexander) Gregory Disney Leith, *b.* 1958, *s.* 2001, *m.*	Hon. Alexander J. S. L., *b.* 1986
1903	*Burnham (7th)*, Harry Frederick Alan Lawson, *b.* 1968, *s.* 2005	None
1897	*Burton (4th)*, Evan Michael Ronald Baillie, *b.* 1949, *s.* 2013, *m.*	Hon. James E. B., *b.* 1975

1643	*Byron (13th)*, Robert James Byron, *b.* 1950, *s.* 1989, *m.*	Hon. Charles R. G. B., *b.* 1990
1937	*Cadman (3rd)*, John Anthony Cadman, *b.* 1938, *s.* 1966, *m.*	Hon. Nicholas A. J. C., *b.* 1977
1945	*Calverley (3rd)*, Charles Rodney Muff, *b.* 1946, *s.* 1971, *m.*	Hon. Jonathan E. Brown, *b.* 1975
1383	*Camoys (7th)*, (Ralph) Thomas Campion George Sherman Stonor, GCVO, PC, *b.* 1940, *s.* 1976, *m.*	Hon. R. William R. T. S., *b.* 1974
1715 I.	*Carbery (12th)*, Michael Peter Evans-Freke, *b.* 1942, *s.* 2012, *m.*	Hon. Dominic R. C. E.-F., *b.* 1969
1834 I.	*Carew (7th) and Carew (7th) (1838)*, Patrick Thomas Conolly-Carew, *b.* 1938, *s.* 1994, *m.*	Hon. William P. C.-C., *b.* 1973
1916	*Carnock (5th)*, Adam Nicolson, *b.* 1957, *s.* 2008, *m.*	Hon. Thomas N., *b.* 1984
1796 I.**	*Carrington (7th) and Carrington (7th) (1797)*, Rupert Francis John Carington, *b.* 1948, *s.* 2018, *m.*	Hon. Robert C., *b.* 1990
1812 I.	*Castlemaine (8th)*, Roland Thomas John Handcock, MBE, *b.* 1943, *s.* 1973, *m.*	Hon. Ronan M. E. H., *b.* 1989
1936	*Catto (3rd)*, Innes Gordon Catto, *b.* 1950, *s.* 2001, *m.*	Hon. Alexander G. C., *b.* 1952
1918	*Cawley (4th)*, John Francis Cawley, *b.* 1946, *s.* 2001, *m.*	Hon. William R. H. C., *b.* 1981
1858	*Chesham (7th)*, Charles Gray Compton Cavendish, *b.* 1974, *s.* 2009, *m.*	Hon. Oliver N. B. C., *b.* 2007
1945	*Chetwode (2nd)*, Philip Chetwode, *b.* 1937, *s.* 1950, *m.*	Hon. Roger C., *b.* 1968
1945	*Chorley (3rd)*, Nicholas Rupert Debenham Chorley, *b.* 1966, *s.* 2016, *m.*	Hon. Patrick A. C. C., *b.* 2000
1815	*Churchill (6th)*, Richard Harry Ramsay Spencer, *b.* 1926, *s.* 2017, *m.*	Hon. Michael R. de C. S., *b.* 1960
1858	*Churston (5th)*, John Francis Yarde-Buller, *b.* 1934, *s.* 1991, *m.*	Hon. Benjamin F. A. Y.-B., *b.* 1974
1800 I.	*Clanmorris (8th)*, Simon John Ward Bingham, *b.* 1937, *s.* 1988, *m.*	Robert D. de B. B., *b.* 1942
1672	*Clifford of Chudleigh (14th)*, Thomas Hugh Clifford, *b.* 1948, *s.* 1988, *m.*	Hon. Alexander T. H. C., *b.* 1985
1299	*Clinton (22nd)*, Gerard Nevile Mark Fane Trefusis, *b.* 1934, *s.* 1965, *m.*	Hon. Charles P. R. F. T., *b.* 1962
1955	*Clitheroe (2nd)*, Ralph John Assheton, *b.* 1929, *s.* 1984, *m.*	Hon. Ralph C. A., *b.* 1962
1919	*Clwyd (4th)*, (John) Murray Roberts, *b.* 1971, *s.* 2006, *m.*	Hon. John D. R., *b.* 2006
1948	*Clydesmuir (3rd)*, David Ronald Colville, *b.* 1949, *s.* 1996, *m.*	Hon. Richard C., *b.* 1980
1960	*Cobbold (2nd)*, David Antony Fromanteel Lytton Cobbold, *b.* 1937, *s.* 1987, *m.*	Hon. Henry F. L. C., *b.* 1962
1919	*Cochrane of Cults (5th)*, Thomas Hunter Vere Cochrane, *b.* 1957, *s.* 2017, *m.*	Hon. Michael C. N. C., OBE, *b.* 1959
1954	*Coleraine (2nd)*, (James) Martin (Bonar) Law, *b.* 1931, *s.* 1980, *m.*	Hon. James P. B. L., *b.* 1975
1873	*Coleridge (5th)*, William Duke Coleridge, *b.* 1937, *s.* 1984, *w.*	Hon. James D. C., *b.* 1967
1946 **	*Colgrain (4th)*, Alastair Colin Leckie Campbell, *b.* 1951, *s.* 2008, *m.*	Hon. Thomas C. D. C., *b.* 1984
1917 **	*Colwyn (3rd)*, (Ian) Anthony Hamilton-Smith, CBE, *b.* 1942, *s.* 1966, *m.*	Hon. Craig P. H.-S., *b.* 1968
1956	*Colyton (2nd)*, Alisdair John Munro Hopkinson, *b.* 1958, *s.* 1996, *m.*	Hon. James P. M. H., *b.* 1983
1841	*Congleton (9th)*, John Patrick Christian Parnell, *b.* 1959, *s.* 2015, *m.*	Hon. Christopher J. E. P., *b.* 1987
1927	*Cornwallis (4th)*, Fiennes Wykeham Jeremy Cornwallis, *b.* 1946, *s.* 2010, *m.*	Hon. Fiennes A. W. M. C., *b.* 1987
1874	*Cottesloe (6th)*, Thomas Francis Henry Fremantle, *b.* 1966, *s.* 2018	Hon. Edward W. F., *b.* 1961
1929	*Craigmyle (4th)*, Thomas Columba Shaw, *b.* 1960, *s.* 1998, *m.*	Hon. Alexander F. S., *b.* 1988
1899	*Cranworth (3rd)*, Philip Bertram Gurdon, *b.* 1940, *s.* 1964, *m.*	Hon. Sacha W. R. G., *b.* 1970
1959 **	*Crathorne (2nd)*, Charles James Dugdale, KCVO, *b.* 1939, *s.* 1977, *w.*	Hon. Thomas A. J. D., *b.* 1977
1892	*Crawshaw (5th)*, David Gerald Brooks, *b.* 1934, *s.* 1997, *m.*	Hon. John P. B., *b.* 1938
1940	*Croft (3rd)*, Bernard William Henry Page Croft, *b.* 1949, *s.* 1997, *m.*	None
1797 I.	*Crofton (8th)*, Edward Harry Piers Crofton, *b.* 1988, *s.* 2007	Hon. Charles M. G. C., *b.* 1988
1375 **	*Cromwell (7th)*, Godfrey John Bewicke-Copley, *b.* 1960, *s.* 1982, *m.*	Hon. David G. B.-C., *b.* 1997
1947	*Crook (3rd)*, Robert Douglas Edwin Crook, *b.* 1955, *s.* 2001, *m.*	Hon. Matthew R. C., *b.* 1990
1920	*Cullen of Ashbourne (4th)*, Michael John Cokayne, *b.* 1950, *s.* 2016, *m.*	None
1914	*Cunliffe (3rd)*, Roger Cunliffe, *b.* 1932, *s.* 1963, *m.*	Hon. Henry C., *b.* 1962
1332	*Darcy de Knayth (19th)*, Caspar David Ingrams, *b.* 1962, *s.* 2008	Hon. Thomas R. I., *b.* 1999
1927	*Daresbury (4th)*, Peter Gilbert Greenall, *b.* 1953, *s.* 1996, *m.*	Hon. Thomas E. G., *b.* 1984
1924	*Darling (3rd)*, (Robert) Julian Henry Darling, *b.* 1944, *s.* 2003, *m.*	Hon. Robert J. C. D., *b.* 1972
1946	*Darwen (4th)*, David Paul Cedric Davies, *b.* 1962, *s.* 2011, *m.*	Hon. Oscar K. D., *b.* 1996
1932	*Davies (3rd)*, David Davies, *b.* 1940, *s.* 1944, *m.*	Hon. David D. D., *b.* 1975
1812 I.	*Decies (7th)*, Marcus Hugh Tristram de la Poer Beresford, *b.* 1948, *s.* 1992, *m.*	Hon. Robert M. D. de la P. B., *b.* 1988
1299	*de Clifford (28th)*, Miles Edward Southwell Russell, *b.* 1966, *s.* 2018, *m.*	Hon. Edward S. R., *b.* 1998
1851	*De Freyne (8th)*, Fulke Charles Arthur John French, *b.* 1957, *s.* 2009, *m.*	Hon. Alexander J. C. F., *b.* 1988
1821	*Delamere (5th)*, Hugh George Cholmondeley, *b.* 1934, *s.* 1979, *m.*	Hugh D. C., *b.* 1998
1838 **	*de Mauley (7th)*, Rupert Charles Ponsonby, TD, *b.* 1957, *s.* 2002, *m.*	Ashley G. P., *b.* 1959
1937 **	*Denham (2nd)*, Bertram Stanley Mitford Bowyer, KBE, PC, *b.* 1927, *s.* 1948, *m.*	Hon. Richard G. G. B., *b.* 1959
1834	*Denman (6th)*, Richard Thomas Stewart Denman, *b.* 1946, *s.* 2012, *m.*	Hon. Robert J. D., *b.* 1995
1887	*De Ramsey (4th)*, John Ailwyn Fellowes, *b.* 1942, *s.* 1993, *m.*	Hon. Freddie J. F., *b.* 1978
1264	*de Ros (28th)*, Peter Trevor Maxwell, *b.* 1958, *s.* 1983, *m. Premier Baron of England*	Hon. Finbar J. M., *b.* 1988
1881	*Derwent (5th)*, Robin Evelyn Leo Vanden-Bempde-Johnstone, LVO, *b.* 1930, *s.* 1986, *m.*	Hon. Francis P. H. V.-B.-J., *b.* 1965
1831	*de Saumarez (7th)*, Eric Douglas Saumarez, *b.* 1956, *s.* 1991, *m.*	Hon. Victor T. S., *b.* 1956
1910	*de Villiers (4th)*, Alexander Charles de Villiers, *b.* 1940, *s.* 2001, *m.*	None
1930	*Dickinson (2nd)*, Richard Clavering Hyett Dickinson, *b.* 1926, *s.* 1943, *m.*	Hon. Martin H. D., *b.* 1961

1620 I.	*Digby (13th) and Digby (6th) (1765)*, Henry Noel Kenelm Digby, *b*. 1954, *s*. 2018, *m*.	Hon. Edward St V. K. D., *b*. 1985
1615	*Dormer (18th)*, William Robert Dormer, *b*. 1960, *s*. 2016, *m*.	Hon. Hugo E. G. D., *b*. 1995
1943	*Dowding (3rd)*, Piers Hugh Tremenheere Dowding, *b*. 1948, *s*. 1992, *m*.	Hon. Mark D. J. D., *b*. 1949
1439	*Dudley (15th)*, Jim Anthony Hill Wallace, *b*. 1930, *s*. 2002, *m*.	Hon. Jeremy W. G. W., *b*. 1964
1800 I.	*Dufferin and Clandeboye (11th)*, John Francis Blackwood, *b*. 1944, *s*. 1991, *m*. (claim to the peerage not yet established)	Hon. Francis S. B., *b*. 1979
1929	*Dulverton (3rd)*, (Gilbert) Michael Hamilton Wills, *b*. 1944, *s*. 1992, *m*.	Hon. Robert A. H. W., *b*. 1983
1800 I.	*Dunalley (7th)*, Henry Francis Cornelius Prittie, *b*. 1948, *s*. 1992, *m*.	Hon. Joel H. P., *b*. 1981
1324 I.	*Dunboyne (30th)*, Richard Pierce Theobald Butler, *b*. 1983, *s*. 2013, *m*.	Michael J. B., *b*. 1944
1892	*Dunleath (6th)*, Brian Henry Mulholland, *b*. 1950, *s*. 1997, *m*.	Hon. Andrew H. M., *b*. 1981
1439 I.	*Dunsany (21st)*, Randal Plunkett, *b*. 1983, *s*. 2011	Hon. Oliver P., *b*. 1985
1780	*Dynevor (10th)*, Hugo Griffith Uryan Rhys, *b*. 1966, *s*. 2008	Robert D. A. R., *b*. 1963
1963	*Egremont (2nd) and Leconfield (7th) (1859)*, John Max Henry Scawen Wyndham, *b*. 1948, *s*. 1972, *m*.	Hon. George R. V. W., *b*. 1983
1643 S.	*Elibank (15th)*, Robert Francis Alan Erskine-Murray, *b*. 1964, *s*. 2017, *m*.	Hon. Timothy A. E. E.-M., *b*. 1967
1802	*Ellenborough (9th)*, Rupert Edward Henry Law, *b*. 1955, *s*. 2013, *m*.	Hon. James R. T. L., *b*. 1983
1509 S.	*Elphinstone (19th) and Elphinstone (5th) (1885)*, Alexander Mountstuart Elphinstone, *b*. 1980, *s*. 1994, *m*.	Master of Elphinstone, *b*. 2011
1934 **	*Elton (2nd)*, Rodney Elton, TD, *b*. 1930, *s*. 1973, *m*.	Hon. Edward P. E., *b*. 1966
1627 S. **	*Fairfax of Cameron (14th)*, Nicholas John Albert Fairfax, *b*. 1956, *s*. 1964, *m*.	Hon. Edward N. T. F., *b*. 1984
1961	*Fairhaven (3rd)*, Ailwyn Henry George Broughton, *b*. 1936, *s*. 1973, *m*.	Maj. Hon. James H. A. B., *b*. 1963
1916	*Faringdon (3rd)*, Charles Michael Henderson, KCVO, *b*. 1937, *s*. 1977, *m*.	Hon. James H. H., *b*. 1961
1756 I.	*Farnham (13th)*, Simon Kenlis Maxwell, *b*. 1933, *s*. 2001, *w*.	Hon. Robin S. M., *b*. 1965
1856 I.	*Fermoy (6th)*, Maurice Burke Roche, *b*. 1967, *s*. 1984, *m*.	Hon. E. Hugh B. R., *b*. 1972
1826	*Feversham (7th)*, Jasper Orlando Slingsby Duncombe, *b*. 1968, *s*. 2009, *m*.	Hon. Orlando B. D., *b*. 2009
1798 I.	*ffrench (8th)*, Robuck John Peter Charles Mario ffrench, *b*. 1956, *s*. 1986, *m*.	None
1909	*Fisher (4th)*, Patrick Vavasseur Fisher, *b*. 1953, *s*. 2012, *m*.	Hon. Benjamin C. V. F., *b*. 1986
1295	*Fitzwalter (22nd)*, Julian Brook Plumptre, *b*. 1952, *s*. 2004, *m*.	Hon. Edward B. P., *b*. 1989
1776	*Foley (9th)*, Thomas Henry Foley, *b*. 1961, *s*. 2012	Rupert T. F., *b*. 1970
1445 S.	*Forbes (23rd)*, Malcolm Nigel Forbes, *b*. 1946, *s*. 2013, *m*. *Premier Lord of Scotland*	Master of Forbes, *b*. 2010
1821	*Forester (9th)*, Charles Richard George Weld-Forester, *b*. 1975, *s*. 2004, *m*.	Hon. Brook G. P. W.-F., *b*. 2014
1922	*Forres (4th)*, Alastair Stephen Grant Williamson, *b*. 1946, *s*. 1978, *m*.	Hon. George A. M. W., *b*. 1972
1917	*Forteviot (4th)*, John James Evelyn Dewar, *b*. 1938, *s*. 1993, *w*.	Hon. Alexander J. E. D., *b*. 1971
1951 **	*Freyberg (3rd)*, Valerian Bernard Freyberg, *b*. 1970, *s*. 1993, *m*.	Hon. Joseph J. F., *b*. 2007
1917	*Gainford (4th)*, George Pease, *b*. 1926, *s*. 2013, *w*.	Hon. Adrian C. P., *b*. 1960
1818 I.	*Garvagh (6th)*, Spencer George Stratford de Redcliffe Canning, *b*. 1953, *s*. 2013, *m*.	Hon. Stratford G. E. de R. C., *b*. 1990
1942 **	*Geddes (3rd)*, Euan Michael Ross Geddes, *b*. 1937, *s*. 1975, *m*.	Hon. James G. N. G., *b*. 1969
1876	*Gerard (5th)*, Anthony Robert Hugo Gerard, *b*. 1949, *s*. 1992	Hon. Rupert B. C. G., *b*. 1981
1824	*Gifford (6th)*, Anthony Maurice Gifford, QC, *b*. 1940, *s*. 1961, *m*.	Hon. Thomas A. G., *b*. 1967
1917	*Gisborough (3rd)*, Thomas Richard John Long Chaloner, *b*. 1927, *s*. 1951, *m*.	Hon. T. Peregrine L. C., *b*. 1961
1899	*Glanusk (5th)*, Christopher Russell Bailey, TD, *b*. 1942, *s*. 1997, *m*.	Hon. Charles H. B., *b*. 1976
1918 **	*Glenarthur (4th)*, Simon Mark Arthur, *b*. 1944, *s*. 1976, *m*.	Hon. Edward A. A., *b*. 1973
1911	*Glenconner (4th)*, Cody Charles Edward Tennant, *b*. 1994, *s*. 2010	Euan L. T., *b*. 1983
1964	*Glendevon (3rd)*, Jonathan Charles Hope, *b*. 1952, *s*. 2009	None
1922	*Glendyne (4th)*, John Nivison, *b*. 1960, *s*. 2008	None
1939	*Glentoran (3rd)*, (Thomas) Robin (Valerian) Dixon, CBE, *b*. 1935, *s*. 1995, *m*.	Hon. Daniel G. D., *b*. 1959
1909	*Gorell (5th)*, John Picton Gorell Barnes, *b*. 1959, *s*. 2007, *m*.	Hon. Oliver G. B., *b*. 1993
1953 **	*Grantchester (3rd)*, Christopher John Suenson-Taylor, *b*. 1951, *s*. 1995, *m*.	Hon. Jesse D. S.-T., *b*. 1977
1782	*Grantley (8th)*, Richard William Brinsley Norton, *b*. 1956, *s*. 1995	Hon. Francis J. H. N., *b*. 1960
1794 I.	*Graves (10th)*, Timothy Evelyn Graves, *b*. 1960, *s*. 2002, *m*.	None
1445 S.	*Gray (23rd)*, Andrew Godfrey Diarmid Stuart Campbell-Gray, *b*. 1964, *s*. 2003, *m*.	Master of Gray, *b*. 1996
1950	*Greenhill (3rd)*, Malcolm Greenhill, *b*. 1924, *s*. 1989	None
1927 **	*Greenway (4th)*, Ambrose Charles Drexel Greenway, *b*. 1941, *s*. 1975, *m*.	Nicholas W. P. G., *b*. 1988
1902	*Grenfell (3rd) and Grenfell of Kilvey (life peerage, 2000)*, Julian Pascoe Francis St Leger Grenfell, *b*. 1935, *s*. 1976, *m*.	Richard A. St L. G., *b*. 1966
1944	*Gretton (4th)*, John Lysander Gretton, *b*. 1975, *s*. 1989, *m*.	Hon. John F. B. G., *b*. 2008
1397	*Grey of Codnor (6th)*, Richard Henry Cornwall-Legh, *b*. 1936, *s*. 1996, *m*.	Hon. Richard S. C. C.-L., *b*. 1976
1955	*Gridley (3rd)*, Richard David Arnold Gridley, *b*. 1956, *s*. 1996, *m*.	Peter A. C. G., *b*. 1940
1964	*Grimston of Westbury (3rd)*, Robert John Sylvester Grimston, *b*. 1951, *s*. 2003, *m*.	Hon. Gerald C. W. G., *b*. 1953
1886	*Grimthorpe (5th)*, Edward John Beckett, *b*. 1954, *s*. 2003, *m*.	Hon. Harry M. B., *b*. 1993
1945	*Hacking (3rd)*, Douglas David Hacking, *b*. 1938, *s*. 1971, *m*.	Hon. Douglas F. H., *b*. 1968
1950	*Haden-Guest (5th)*, Christopher Haden-Guest, *b*. 1948, *s*. 1996, *m*.	Hon. Nicholas H.-G., *b*. 1951

1886	*Hamilton of Dalzell (5th)*, Gavin Goulburn Hamilton, *b.* 1968, *s.* 2006, *m.*	Hon. Francis A. J. G. H., *b.* 2009
1874	*Hampton (7th)*, John Humphrey Arnott Pakington, *b.* 1964, *s.* 2003, *m.*	Hon. Charles R. C. P., *b.* 2005
1939	*Hankey (3rd)*, Donald Robin Alers Hankey, *b.* 1938, *s.* 1996, *m.*	Hon. Alexander M. A. H., *b.* 1947
1958	*Harding of Petherton (3rd)*, William Allan John Harding, *b.* 1969, *s.* 2016, *m.*	Hon. Angus J. E. H., *b.* 2001
1910	*Hardinge of Penshurst (4th)*, Julian Alexander Hardinge, *b.* 1945, *s.* 1997, *m.*	Hon. Hugh F. H., *b.* 1948
1876	*Harlech (7th)*, Jasset David Cody Ormsby-Gore, *b.* 1986, *s.* 2016	None
1939	*Harmsworth (3rd)*, Thomas Harold Raymond Harmsworth, *b.* 1939, *s.* 1990, *m.*	Hon. Dominic M. E. H., *b.* 1973
1815	*Harris (8th)*, Anthony Harris, *b.* 1942, *s.* 1996, *w.*	Rear-Adm. Michael G. T. H., *b.* 1941
1954	*Harvey of Tasburgh (3rd)*, Charles John Giuseppe Harvey, *b.* 1951, *s.* 2010, *m.*	Hon. John C. G. H., *b.* 1993
1295	*Hastings (23rd)*, Delaval Thomas Harold Astley, *b.* 1960, *s.* 2007, *m.*	Hon. Jacob A. A., *b.* 1991
1835	*Hatherton (8th)*, Edward Charles Littleton, *b.* 1950, *s.* 1985, *m.*	Hon. Thomas E. L., *b.* 1977
1776	*Hawke (12th)*, William Martin Theodore Hawke, *b.* 1995, *s.* 2009	None
1927	*Hayter (4th)*, George William Michael Chubb, *b.* 1943, *s.* 2003, *m.*	Hon. Thomas F. F. C., *b.* 1986
1945	*Hazlerigg (3rd)*, Arthur Grey Hazlerigg, *b.* 1951, *s.* 2002, *m.*	Hon. Arthur W. G. H., *b.* 1987
1943	*Hemingford (3rd)*, (Dennis) Nicholas Herbert, *b.* 1934, *s.* 1982, *w.*	Hon. Christopher D. C. H., *b.* 1973
1906	*Hemphill (6th)*, Charles Andrew Martyn Martyn-Hemphill, *b.* 1954, *s.* 2012, *m.*	Hon. Richard P. L. M.-H., *b.* 1990
1799 I. **	*Henley (8th) and Northington (6th) (1885)*, Oliver Michael Robert Eden, PC, *b.* 1953, *s.* 1977, *m.*	Hon. John W. O. E., *b.* 1988
1800 I.	*Henniker (9th) and Hartismere (6th) (1866)*, Mark Ian Philip Chandos Henniker-Major, *b.* 1947, *s.* 2004	Hon. Edward G. M. H.-M., *b.* 1985
1461	*Herbert (19th)*, David John Seyfried Herbert, *b.* 1952, *s.* 2002, *m.* Title called out of abeyance 2002	Hon. Oliver R. S. H., *b.* 1976
1935	*Hesketh (3rd)*, Thomas Alexander Fermor-Hesketh, KBE, PC, *b.* 1950, *s.* 1955, *m.*	Hon. Frederick H. F.-H., *b.* 1988
1828	*Heytesbury (7th)*, James William Holmes à Court, *b.* 1967, *s.* 2004, *w.*	Peter M. H. H. à. C., *b.* 1968
1886	*Hindlip (6th)*, Charles Henry Allsopp, *b.* 1940, *s.* 1993, *w.*	Hon. Henry W. A., *b.* 1973
1950	*Hives (3rd)*, Matthew Peter Hives, *b.* 1971, *s.* 1997, *m.*	Robert G. H., *b.* 1953
1912	*Hollenden (4th)*, Ian Hampden Hope-Morley, *b.* 1946, *s.* 1999, *m.*	Hon. Edward H.-M., *b.* 1981
1897	*Holm Patrick (4th)*, Hans James David Hamilton, *b.* 1955, *s.* 1991, *m.*	Hon. Ion H. J. H., *b.* 1956
1797 I.	*Hotham (8th)*, Henry Durand Hotham, *b.* 1940, *s.* 1967, *m.*	Hon. William B. H., *b.* 1972
1881	*Hothfield (6th)*, Anthony Charles Sackville Tufton, *b.* 1939, *s.* 1991, *m.*	Hon. William S. T., *b.* 1977
1930	*Howard of Penrith (3rd)*, Philip Esme Howard, *b.* 1945, *s.* 1999, *m.*	Hon. Thomas P. H., *b.* 1974
1960	*Howick of Glendale (2nd)*, Charles Evelyn Baring, *b.* 1937, *s.* 1973, *m.*	Hon. David E. C. B., *b.* 1975
1796 I.	*Huntingfield (7th)*, Joshua Charles Vanneck, *b.* 1954, *s.* 1994, *w.*	Hon. Gerard C. A. V., *b.* 1985
1866 **	*Hylton (5th)*, Raymond Hervey Jolliffe, *b.* 1932, *s.* 1967, *m.*	Hon. William H. M. J., *b.* 1967
1933	*Iliffe (3rd)*, Robert Peter Richard Iliffe, *b.* 1944, *s.* 1996, *m.*	Hon. Edward R. I., *b.* 1968
1543 I.	*Inchiquin (18th)*, Conor Myles John O'Brien, *b.* 1943, *s.* 1982, *m.*	Conor J. A. O'B., *b.* 1952
1962	*Inchyra (3rd)*, Christian James Charles Hoyer Millar, *b.* 1962, *s.* 2011, *m.*	Hon. Jake C. R. M., *b.* 1996
1964 **	*Inglewood (2nd)*, (William) Richard Fletcher-Vane, *b.* 1951, *s.* 1989, *m.*	Hon. Henry W. F. F.-V., *b.* 1990
1919	*Inverforth (4th)*, Andrew Peter Weir, *b.* 1966, *s.* 1982, *m.*	Hon. Benjamin A.-W., *b.* 1997
1941	*Ironside (2nd)*, Edmund Oslac Ironside, *b.* 1924, *s.* 1959, *w.*	Hon. Charles E. G. I., *b.* 1956
1952	*Jeffreys (3rd)*, Christopher Henry Mark Jeffreys, *b.* 1957, *s.* 1986, *m.*	Hon. Arthur M. H. J., *b.* 1989
1906	*Joicey (5th)*, James Michael Joicey, *b.* 1953, *s.* 1993, *m.*	Hon. William J. J., *b.* 1990
1937	*Kenilworth (4th)*, (John) Randle Siddeley, *b.* 1954, *s.* 1981, *m.*	Hon. William R. J. S., *b.* 1992
1935	*Kennet (3rd)*, William Aldus Thoby Young, *b.* 1957, *s.* 2009	Hon. Archibald W. K. Y., *b.* 1992
1776 I.	*Kensington (9th) and Kensington (6th) (1886)*, William Owen Edwardes, *b.* 1964, *s.* 2019, *m.*	Hon. William F. I. E., *b.* 1993
1951	*Kenswood (3rd)*, Michael Christopher Whitfield, *b.* 1955, *s.* 2016, *m.*	Hon. Anthony J. W., *b.* 1957
1788	*Kenyon (7th)*, Lloyd Nicholas Tyrell-Kenyon, *b.* 1972, *s.* 2019	Hon. Alexander S. T.-K., *b.* 1975
1947	*Kershaw (4th)*, Edward John Kershaw, *b.* 1936, *s.* 1962, *m.*	Hon. John C. E. K., *b.* 1971
1943	*Keyes (3rd)*, Charles William Packe Keyes, *b.* 1951, *s.* 2005, *m.*	Hon. (Leopold R.) J. K., *b.* 1956
1909	*Kilbracken (4th)*, Christopher John Godley, *b.* 1945, *s.* 2006, *m.*	Hon. James J. G., *b.* 1972
1900	*Killanin (4th)*, (George) Redmond Fitzpatrick Morris, *b.* 1947, *s.* 1999, *m.*	Hon. Luke M. G. M., *b.* 1975
1943	*Killearn (3rd)*, Victor Miles George Aldous Lampson, *b.* 1941, *s.* 1996, *m.*	Hon. Miles H. M. L., *b.* 1977
1789 I.	*Kilmaine (8th)*, John Francis Sandford Browne, *b.* 1983, *s.* 2013	Mark Caulfield-Browne, *b.* 1966
1831	*Kilmarnock (8th)*, Dr Robin Jordan Boyd, *b.* 1941, *s.* 2009, *m.*	Hon. Simon J. B., *b.* 1978
1941	*Kindersley (4th)*, Rupert John Molesworth Kindersley, *b.* 1955, *s.* 2013, *m.*	Hon. Frederick H. M. K., *b.* 1987
1223 I.	*Kingsale (36th)*, Nevinson Mark de Courcy, *b.* 1958, *s.* 2005 *Premier Baron of Ireland*	Joseph K. C. de C., *b.* 1955
1902	*Kinross (5th)*, Christopher Patrick Balfour, *b.* 1949, *s.* 1985, *m.*	Hon. Alan I. B., *b.* 1978
1951	*Kirkwood (3rd)*, David Harvie Kirkwood, PHD, *b.* 1931, *s.* 1970, *m.*	Hon. James S. K., *b.* 1937
1800 I.	*Langford (10th)*, Owain Grenville Rowley-Conwy, *b.* 1958, *s.* 2017, *m.*	Hon. Thomas A. R.-C., *b.* 1987
1942	*Latham (2nd)*, Dominic Charles Latham, *b.* 1954, *s.* 1970	Anthony M. L., *b.* 1954
1431	*Latymer (9th)*, Crispin James Alan Nevill Money-Coutts, *b.* 1955, *s.* 2003, *m.*	Hon. Drummond W. T. M.-C., *b.* 1986

1869	*Lawrence (5th),* David John Downer Lawrence, *b.* 1937, *s.* 1968	None
1947	*Layton (4th),* Jonathan Francis Layton, *b.* 1942, *s.* 2019, *m.*	Hon. Jeremy S. L., *b.* 1978
1839	*Leigh (6th),* Christopher Dudley Piers Leigh, *b.* 1960, *s.* 2003	Hon. Rupert D. L., *b.* 1994
1962	*Leighton of St Mellons (3rd),* Robert William Henry Leighton Seager, *b.* 1955, *s.* 1998, *m.*	Hon. Simon J. L. S., *b.* 1957
1797	*Lilford (8th),* Mark Vernon Powys, *b.* 1975, *s.* 2005, *m.*	Michael J. P., *b.* 1934
1945	*Lindsay of Birker (3rd),* James Francis Lindsay, *b.* 1945, *s.* 1994, *m.*	Alexander S. L., *b.* 1940
1758 I.	*Lisle (9th),* (John) Nicholas Geoffrey Lysaght, *b.* 1960, *s.* 2003	Hon. David J. L., *b.* 1963
1850	*Londesborough (9th),* Richard John Denison, *b.* 1959, *s.* 1968, *m.*	Hon. James F. D., *b.* 1990
1541 I.	*Louth (17th),* Jonathan Oliver Plunkett, *b.* 1952, *s.* 2013	Hon. Matthew O. P., *b.* 1982
1458 S.	*Lovat (16th) and Lovat (5th) (1837),* Simon Christopher Joseph Fraser, *b.* 1977, *s.* 1995, *m.*	Hon. Jack H. F., *b.* 1984
1946	*Lucas of Chilworth (3rd),* Simon William Lucas, *b.* 1957, *s.* 2001, *m.*	Hon. John R. M. L., *b.* 1995
1663 **	*Lucas (11th) and Dingwall (8th) (S. 1609),* Ralph Matthew Palmer, *b.* 1951, *s.* 1991, *m.*	Hon. Lewis E. P., *b.* 1987
1929	*Luke (4th),* Ian James St John Lawson Johnston, *b.* 1963, *s.* 2016, *m.*	Hon. Samuel A. J. St J. L. J., *b.* 2000
1859	*Lyveden (8th),* Colin Ronald Vernon, *b.* 1967, *s.* 2017, *m.*	Hon. Robert H. V., *b.* 1942
1959	*MacAndrew (3rd),* Christopher Anthony Colin MacAndrew, *b.* 1945, *s.* 1989	Hon. Oliver C. J. M., *b.* 1983
1776 I.	*Macdonald (8th),* Godfrey James Macdonald of Macdonald, *b.* 1947, *s.* 1970, *m.*	Hon. Godfrey E. H. T. M., *b.* 1982
1937	*McGowan (4th),* Harry John Charles McGowan, *b.* 1971, *s.* 2003, *m.*	Hon. Dominic J. W. M., *b.* 1951
1922	*Maclay (3rd),* Joseph Paton Maclay, *b.* 1942, *s.* 1969, *m.*	Hon. Joseph P. M., *b.* 1977
1955	*McNair (3rd),* Duncan James McNair, *b.* 1947, *s.* 1989, *m.*	Hon. William S. A. M., *b.* 1958
1951	*Macpherson of Drumochter (3rd),* James Anthony Macpherson, *b.* 1979, *s.* 2008, *m.*	Hon. Daniel T. M., *b.* 2013
1937 **	*Mancroft (3rd),* Benjamin Lloyd Stormont Mancroft, *b.* 1957, *s.* 1987, *m.*	Hon. Arthur L. S. M., *b.* 1995
1807	*Manners (6th),* John Hugh Robert Manners, *b.* 1956, *s.* 2008, *m.*	Hon. John A. D. M., *b.* 2011
1922	*Manton (4th),* Miles Ronald Marcus Watson, *b.* 1958, *s.* 2003, *m.*	Hon. Thomas N. C. D. W., *b.* 1985
1908	*Marchamley (4th),* William Francis Whiteley, *b.* 1968, *s.* 1994, *m.*	Hon. Leon W., *b.* 2004
1965	*Margadale (3rd),* Alastair John Morrison, *b.* 1958, *s.* 2003, *m.*	Hon. Declan J. M., *b.* 1993
1961	*Marks of Broughton (3rd),* Simon Richard Marks, *b.* 1950, *s.* 1998, *m.*	Hon. Michael M., *b.* 1989
1964	*Martonmere (2nd),* John Stephen Robinson, *b.* 1963, *s.* 1989, *m.*	Hon. James I. R., *b.* 2003
1776 I.	*Massy (10th),* David Hamon Somerset Massy, *b.* 1947, *s.* 1995	Hon. John H. S. M., *b.* 1950
1935	*May (4th),* Jasper Bertram St John May, *b.* 1965, *s.* 2006, *m.*	None
1925	*Merrivale (4th),* Derek John Philip Duke, *b.* 1948, *s.* 2007, *m.*	Hon. Thomas D., *b.* 1980
1911	*Merthyr (5th),* David Trevor Lewis, *b.* 1977, *s.* 2015, *m.*	Hon. Peter H. L., *b.* 1937
1919	*Meston (3rd),* James Meston, QC, *b.* 1950, *s.* 1984, *m.*	Hon. Thomas J. D. M., *b.* 1977
1838	*Methuen (8th),* James Paul Archibald Methuen-Campbell, *b.* 1952, *s.* 2014	Thomas R. M. M.-C., *b.* 1977
1711	*Middleton (13th),* Michael Charles James Willoughby, *b.* 1948, *s.* 2011, *m.*	Hon. James W. M. W., *b.* 1976
1939	*Milford (4th),* Guy Wogan Philipps, QC, *b.* 1961, *s.* 1999, *m.*	Hon. Archie S. P., *b.* 1997
1933	*Milne (3rd),* George Alexander Milne, *b.* 1941, *s.* 2005	Hon. Iain C. L. M., *b.* 1949
1951	*Milner of Leeds (3rd),* Richard James Milner, *b.* 1959, *s.* 2003, *m.*	None
1947	*Milverton (2nd),* Revd Fraser Arthur Richard Richards, *b.* 1930, *s.* 1978, *m.*	Hon. Michael H. R., *b.* 1936
1873	*Moncreiff (6th),* Rhoderick Harry Wellwood Moncreiff, *b.* 1954, *s.* 2002, *m.*	Hon. Harry J. W. M., *b.* 1986
1884	*Monk Bretton (3rd),* John Charles Dodson, *b.* 1924, *s.* 1933, *m.*	Hon. Christopher M. D., *b.* 1958
1885	*Monkswell (5th),* Gerard Collier, *b.* 1947, *s.* 1984, *m.*	Hon. James A. C., *b.* 1977
1728	*Monson (12th),* Nicholas John Monson, *b.* 1955, *s.* 2011, *m.*	Hon. Andrew A. J. M., *b.* 1959
1885	*Montagu of Beaulieu (4th),* Ralph Douglas-Scott-Montagu, *b.* 1961, *s.* 2015, *m.*	Hon. Jonathan D. D.-S.-M., *b.* 1975
1839	*Monteagle of Brandon (7th),* Charles James Spring Rice, *b.* 1953, *s.* 2013, *m.*	Hon. Michael S. R., *b.* 1935
1943	*Moran (3rd),* James McMoran Wilson, *b.* 1952, *s.* 2014, *m.*	Hon. David A. M. W., *b.* 1990
1918	*Morris (4th),* Thomas Anthony Salmon Morris, *b.* 1982, *s.* 2011	Hon. John M. M., *b.* 1983
1950	*Morris of Kenwood (3rd),* Jonathan David Morris, *b.* 1968, *s.* 2004, *m.*	Hon. Benjamin J. M., *b.* 1998
1831	*Mostyn (7th),* Gregory Philip Roger Lloyd-Mostyn, *b.* 1984, *s.* 2011	Roger H. L.-M., *b.* 1941
1933	*Mottistone (6th),* Christopher David Peter Seely, *b.* 1974, *s.* 2013	Hon. Richard W. A. S., *b.* 1988
1945 **	*Mountevans (4th),* Jeffrey Richard de Corban Evans, *b.* 1948, *s.* 2014, *m.*	Hon. Alexander R. A. E., *b.* 1975
1283	*Mowbray (27th), Segrave (28th) (1295) and Stourton (24th) (1448),* Edward William Stephen Stourton, *b.* 1953, *s.* 2006, *m.*	Hon. James C. P. S., *b.* 1991
1932	*Moyne (3rd),* Jonathan Bryan Guinness, *b.* 1930, *s.* 1992, *m.*	Hon. Valentine G. B. G., *b.* 1959
1929 **	*Moynihan (4th),* Colin Berkeley Moynihan, *b.* 1955, *s.* 1997	Hon. Nicholas E. B. M., *b.* 1994
1781 I.	*Muskerry (9th),* Robert Fitzmaurice Deane, *b.* 1948, *s.* 1988, *m.*	Hon. Jonathan F. D., *b.* 1986
1627 S.	*Napier (15th) and Ettrick (6th) (1872),* Francis David Charles Napier, *b.* 1962, *s.* 2012, *m.*	Master of Napier, *b.* 1996
1868	*Napier of Magdala (6th),* Robert Alan Napier, *b.* 1940, *s.* 1987, *m.*	Hon. James R. N., *b.* 1966
1940	*Nathan (3rd),* Rupert Harry Bernard Nathan, *b.* 1957, *s.* 2007, *m.*	Hon. Alasdair H. St J. N., *b.* 1999
1960	*Nelson of Stafford (4th),* Alistair William Henry Nelson, *b.* 1973, *s.* 2006, *m.*	Hon. James J. N., *b.* 1947
1959	*Netherthorpe (3rd),* James Frederick Turner, *b.* 1964, *s.* 1982, *m.*	Hon. Andrew J. E. T., *b.* 1993

1946	*Newall (2nd),* Francis Storer Eaton Newall, *b.* 1930, *s.* 1963, *m.*	Hon. Richard H. E. N., *b.* 1961
1776 I.	*Newborough (8th),* Robert Vaughan Wynn, *b.* 1949, *s.* 1998, *m.*	Antony C. V. W., *b.* 1949
1892	*Newton (5th),* Richard Thomas Legh, *b.* 1950, *s.* 1992, *m.*	Hon. Piers R. L., *b.* 1979
1930	*Noel-Buxton (4th),* Charles Connal Noel-Buxton, *b.* 1975, *s.* 2013	Hon. Simon C. N.-B., *b.* 1943
1957	*Norrie (2nd),* (George) Willoughby Moke Norrie, *b.* 1936, *s.* 1977, *m.*	Hon. Mark W. J. N., *b.* 1972
1884	*Northbourne (6th),* Charles Walter Henri James, *b.* 1960, *s.* 2019, *m.*	Hon. Christopher W. J., *b.* 1988
1866 **	*Northbrook (6th),* Francis Thomas Baring, *b.* 1954, *s.* 1990, *m.*	To the Baronetcy, Peter B., *b.* 1939
1878	*Norton (8th),* James Nigel Arden Adderley, *b.* 1947, *s.* 1993, *m.*	Hon. Edward J. A. A., *b.* 1982
1906	*Nunburnholme (6th),* Stephen Charles Yanath Wilson, *b.* 1973, *s.* 2000, *m.*	Hon. Charles T. C. W., *b.* 2002
1950	*Ogmore (3rd),* Morgan Rees-Williams, *b.* 1937, *s.* 2004, *m.*	Hon. Tudor D. R.-W., *b.* 1991
1870	*O'Hagan (4th),* Charles Towneley Strachey, *b.* 1945, *s.* 1961, *m.*	Hon. Richard T. S., *b.* 1950
1868	*O'Neill (4th),* Raymond Arthur Clanaboy O'Neill, KCVO, TD, *b.* 1933, *s.* 1944, *w.*	Hon. Shane S. C. O'N., *b.* 1965
1836 I.	*Oranmore and Browne (5th) and Mereworth (3rd) (1926),* Dominick Geoffrey Thomas Browne, *b.* 1929, *s.* 2002	Shaun D. B., *b.* 1964
1933 **	*Palmer (4th),* Adrian Bailie Nottage Palmer, *b.* 1951, *s.* 1990	Hon. Hugo B. R. P., *b.* 1980
1914	*Parmoor (5th),* Michael Leonard Seddon Cripps, *b.* 1942, *s.* 2008, *m.*	Hon. Henry W. A. C., *b.* 1976
1937	*Pender (4th),* Henry John Richard Denison-Pender, *b.* 1968, *s.* 2016, *m.*	Hon. Miles J. C. D.-P., *b.* 2000
1866	*Penrhyn (7th),* Simon Douglas-Pennant, *b.* 1938, *s.* 2003, *m.*	Hon. Edward S. D.-P., *b.* 1966
1603	*Petre (18th),* John Patrick Lionel Petre, KCVO, *b.* 1942, *s.* 1989, *m.*	Hon. Dominic W. P., *b.* 1966
1918	*Phillimore (5th),* Francis Stephen Phillimore, *b.* 1944, *s.* 1994, *m.*	Hon. Tristan A. S. P., *b.* 1977
1945	*Piercy (3rd),* James William Piercy, *b.* 1946, *s.* 1981	Hon. Mark E. P. P., *b.* 1953
1827	*Plunket (9th),* Tyrone Shaun Terence Plunket, *b.* 1966, *s.* 2013, *m.*	Hon. Rory P. R. P., *b.* 2001
1831	*Poltimore (7th),* Mark Coplestone Bampfylde, *b.* 1957, *s.* 1978, *m.*	Hon. Henry A. W. B., *b.* 1985
1690 S.	*Polwarth (11th),* Andrew Walter Hepburne-Scott, *b.* 1947, *s.* 2005, *m.*	Master of Polwarth, *b.* 1973
1930	*Ponsonby of Shulbrede (4th) and Ponsonby of Roehampton (life peerage, 2000),* Frederick Matthew Thomas Ponsonby, *b.* 1958, *s.* 1990, *m.*	Hon. Cameron J. J. P., *b.* 1995
1958	*Poole (2nd),* David Charles Poole, *b.* 1945, *s.* 1993, *m.*	Hon. Oliver J. P., *b.* 1972
1852	*Raglan (6th),* Geoffrey Somerset, *b.* 1932, *s.* 2010, *w.*	Inigo A. F. S., *b.* 2004
1932	*Rankeillour (5th),* Michael Richard Hope, *b.* 1940, *s.* 2005, *w.*	Hon. James F. H., *b.* 1968
1953	*Rathcavan (3rd),* Hugh Detmar Torrens O'Neill, *b.* 1939, *s.* 1994, *m.*	Hon. François H. N. O'N., *b.* 1984
1916	*Rathcreedan (3rd),* Christopher John Norton, *b.* 1949, *s.* 1990, *m.*	Hon. Adam G. N., *b.* 1952
1868 I.	*Rathdonnell (5th),* Thomas Benjamin McClintock-Bunbury, *b.* 1938, *s.* 1959, *m.*	Hon. William L. M.-B., *b.* 1966
1911**	*Ravensdale (4th),* Daniel Nicholas Mosley, *b.* 1982, *s.* 2017, *m.*	Hon. Alexander L. M., *b.* 2012
1821	*Ravensworth (9th),* Thomas Arthur Hamish Liddell, *b.* 1954, *s.* 2004, *m.*	Hon. Henry A. T. L., *b.* 1987
1821	*Rayleigh (6th),* John Gerald Strutt, *b.* 1960, *s.* 1988, *m.*	Hon. John F. S., *b.* 1993
1937 **	*Rea (3rd),* John Nicolas Rea, MD, *b.* 1928, *s.* 1981, *m.*	Hon. Matthew J. R., *b.* 1956
1628 S.**	*Reay (15th),* Aeneas Simon Mackay, *b.* 1965, *s.* 2013, *m.*	Master of Reay, *b.* 2010
1902	*Redesdale (6th) and Mitford (life peerage, 2000),* Rupert Bertram Mitford, *b.* 1967, *s.* 1991, *m.*	Hon. Bertram D. M., *b.* 2000
1940	*Reith (3rd),* James Harry John Reith, *b.* 1971, *s.* 2016, *m.*	Hon. Harry J. J. R., *b.* 2006
1928	*Remnant (3rd),* James Wogan Remnant, CVO, *b.* 1930, *s.* 1967, *m.*	Hon. Philip J. R., CBE, *b.* 1954
1806 I.	*Rendlesham (9th),* Charles William Brooke Thellusson, *b.* 1954, *s.* 1999, *m.*	James H. T., *b.* 1961
1933	*Rennell (4th),* James Roderick David Tremayne Rodd, *b.* 1978, *s.* 2006	None
1964	*Renwick (2nd),* Harry Andrew Renwick, *b.* 1935, *s.* 1973, *m.*	Hon. Robert J. R., *b.* 1966
1885	*Revelstoke (7th),* Alexander Rupert Baring, *b.* 1970, *s.* 2012	Hon. Thomas J. B., *b.* 1971
1905	*Ritchie of Dundee (6th),* Charles Rupert Rendall Ritchie, *b.* 1958, *s.* 2008, *m.*	Hon. Sebastian R., *b.* 2004
1935	*Riverdale (3rd),* Anthony Robert Balfour, *b.* 1960, *s.* 1998	Arthur M. B., *b.* 1938
1961	*Robertson of Oakridge (3rd),* William Brian Elworthy Robertson, *b.* 1975, *s.* 2009	None
1938	*Roborough (4th),* Massey John Henry Lopes, *b.* 1969, *s.* 2015, *m.*	Hon. Henry M. P. L., *b.* 1997
1931	*Rochester (3rd),* David Charles Lamb, *b.* 1944, *s.* 2017, *m.*	Hon. Daniel L., *b.* 1971
1934	*Rockley (4th),* Anthony Robert Cecil, *b.* 1961, *s.* 2011, *m.*	Hon. William E. C., *b.* 1996
1782 M.	*Rodney (11th),* John George Brydges Rodney, *b.* 1999, *s.* 2011	Nicholas S. H. R., *b.* 1947
1651 S.	*Rollo (14th) and Dunning (5th) (1869),* David Eric Howard Rollo, *b.* 1943, *s.* 1997, *m.*	Master of Rollo, *b.* 1972
1959	*Rootes (3rd),* Nicholas Geoffrey Rootes, *b.* 1951, *s.* 1992, *m.*	William B. R., *b.* 1944
1796 I.	*Rossmore (7th) and Rossmore (6th) (1838),* William Warner Westenra, *b.* 1931, *s.* 1958, *m.*	Hon. Benedict W. W., *b.* 1983
1939 **	*Rotherwick (3rd),* (Herbert) Robin Cayzer, *b.* 1954, *s.* 1996, *m.*	Hon. H. Robin C., *b.* 1989
1885	*Rothschild (4th),* (Nathaniel Charles) Jacob Rothschild, OM, GBE, *b.* 1936, *s.* 1990, *w.*	Hon. Nathaniel P. V. J. R., *b.* 1971
1911	*Rowallan (4th),* John Polson Cameron Corbett, *b.* 1947, *s.* 1993, *m.*	Hon. Jason W. P. C. C., *b.* 1972
1947	*Rugby (3rd),* Robert Charles Maffey, *b.* 1951, *s.* 1990, *m.*	Hon. Timothy J. H. M., *b.* 1975
1919 **	*Russell of Liverpool (3rd),* Simon Gordon Jared Russell, *b.* 1952, *s.* 1981, *m.*	Hon. Edward C. S. R., *b.* 1985
1876	*Sackville (7th),* Robert Bertrand Sackville-West, *b.* 1958, *s.* 2004, *m.*	Hon. Arthur G. S.-W., *b.* 2000
1964	*St Helens (2nd),* Richard Francis Hughes-Young, *b.* 1945, *s.* 1980, *w.*	Hon. Henry T. H.-Y., *b.* 1986
1559 **	*St John of Bletso (21st),* Anthony Tudor St John, *b.* 1957, *s.* 1978, *m.*	Hon. Oliver B. St J., *b.* 1995
1887	*St Levan (5th),* James Piers Southwell St Aubyn, *b.* 1950, *s.* 2013, *m.*	Hon. Hugh J. St A., *b.* 1983

1885	St Oswald (6th), Charles Rowland Andrew Winn, b. 1959, s. 1999, m.	Hon. Rowland C. S. H. W., b. 1986
1960	Sanderson of Ayot (2nd), Alan Lindsay Sanderson, b. 1931, s. 1971, m. Disclaimed for life 1971.	Hon. Michael S., b. 1959
1945	Sandford (3rd), James John Mowbray Edmondson, b. 1949, s. 2009, w.	Hon. Devon J. E., b. 1986
1871	Sandhurst (6th), Guy Rhys John Mansfield, QC, b. 1949, s. 2002, m.	Hon. Edward J. M., b. 1982
1888	Savile (4th), John Anthony Thornhill Lumley-Savile, b. 1947, s. 2008, m.	Hon. James G. A. L.-S., b. 1975
1447	Saye and Sele (21st), Nathaniel Thomas Allen Fiennes, b. 1920, s. 1968, m.	Hon. Martin G. F., b. 1961
1826	Seaford (6th), Colin Humphrey Felton Ellis, b. 1946, s. 1999, m.	Hon. Benjamin F. T. Ellis-Goodbody, b. 1976
1932 **	Selsdon (3rd), Malcolm McEacharn Mitchell-Thomson, b. 1937, s. 1963, m.	Hon. Callum M. M. M.-T., b. 1969
1489 S.	Sempill (21st), James William Stuart Whitemore Sempill, b. 1949, s. 1995, m.	Master of Sempill, b. 1979
1916	Shaughnessy (5th), Charles George Patrick Shaughnessy, b. 1955, s. 2007, m.	David J. B. S., b. 1957
1946	Shepherd (3rd), Graeme George Shepherd, b. 1949, s. 2001, m.	Hon. Patrick M. S., b. 1980
1964	Sherfield (3rd), Dwight William Makins, b. 1951, s. 2006, m.	None
1902	Shuttleworth (5th), Charles Geoffrey Nicholas Kay-Shuttleworth, KG, KCVO, b. 1948, s. 1975, m.	Hon. Thomas E. K.-S., b. 1976
1950	Silkin (3rd), Christopher Lewis Silkin, b. 1947, s. 2001. Disclaimed for life 2002.	Rory L. S., b. 1954
1963	Silsoe (3rd), Simon Rupert Trustram Eve, b. 1966, s. 2005	Hon. Peter N. T. E., OBE, b. 1930
1947	Simon of Wythenshawe (3rd), Matthew Simon, b. 1955, s. 2002, w. In dormancy since 2016 when the 3rd baron officially reassigned his gender.	Michael B. S., b. 1970
1449 S.	Sinclair (18th), Matthew Murray Kennedy St Clair, b. 1968, s. 2004, m.	Master of Sinclair, b. 2007
1957	Sinclair of Cleeve (3rd), John Lawrence Robert Sinclair, b. 1953, s. 1985, m.	None
1919	Sinha (6th), Arup Kumar Sinha, b. 1966, s. 1999, m.	Hon. Dilip K. S., b. 1967
1828	Skelmersdale (8th), Andrew Bootle-Wilbraham, b. 1977, s. 2018, m.	Hon. Daniel P. B.-W., b. 2007
1916	Somerleyton (4th), Hugh Francis Saville Crossley, b. 1971, s. 2012, m.	Hon. John de B. T. S. C., b. 2010
1784	Somers (9th), Philip Sebastian Somers Cocks, b. 1948, s. 1995	Jonathan B. C., b. 1985
1780	Southampton (7th), Edward Charles FitzRoy, b. 1955, s. 2015, m.	Hon. Charles E. M. F., b. 1983
1959	Spens (4th), Patrick Nathaniel George Spens, b. 1968, s. 2001	Hon. Peter L. S., b. 2000
1640	Stafford (15th), Francis Melfort William Fitzherbert, b. 1954, s. 1986, m.	Hon. Benjamin J. B. F., b. 1983
1938	Stamp (4th), Trevor Charles Bosworth Stamp, MD, b. 1935, s. 1987	Hon. Nicholas C. S., b. 1978
1839	Stanley of Alderley (9th), Sheffield (9th) (I. 1738) and Eddisbury (8th) (1848), Richard Oliver Stanley, b. 1956, s. 2013, m.	Hon. Charles E. S., b. 1960
1318	Strabolgi (12th), Andrew David Whitley Kenworthy, b. 1967, s. 2010, m.	Hon. Joel B. K., b. 2004
1628	Strange (17th), Adam Humphrey Drummond of Megginch, b. 1953, s. 2005, m.	Hon. John A. H. D. of M., b. 1992
1955	Strathalmond (3rd), William Roberton Fraser, b. 1947, s. 1976, m.	Hon. William G. F., b. 1976
1936	Strathcarron (3rd), Ian David Patrick Macpherson, b. 1949, s. 2006, m.	Hon. Rory D. A. M., b. 1982
1955 **	Strathclyde (2nd), Thomas Galloway Dunlop du Roy de Blicquy Galbraith, CH, PC, b. 1960, s. 1985, m.	Hon. Charles W. du R. de B. G., b. 1962
1900	Strathcona and Mount Royal (5th), Donald Alexander Smith Howard, b. 1961, s. 2018, m.	Hon. Donald A. R. H., b. 1994
1836	Stratheden (7th) and Campbell (7th) (1841), David Anthony Campbell, b. 1963, s. 2011, m.	None
1884	Strathspey (6th), James Patrick Trevor Grant of Grant, b. 1943, s. 1992	Hon. Michael P. F. G., b. 1953
1838	Sudeley (7th), Merlin Charles Sainthill Hanbury-Tracy, b. 1939, s. 1941, m.	Nicholas E. J. H.-T., b. 1959
1786	Suffield (13th), John Edward Richard Harbord-Hamond, b. 1956, s. 2016, m.	Hon. Sam C. A. H.-H., b. 1989
1893	Swansea (5th), Richard Anthony Hussey Vivian, b. 1957, s. 2005, m.	Hon. James H. H. V., b. 1999
1907	Swaythling (5th), Charles Edgar Samuel Montagu, b. 1954, s. 1998, m.	Rupert A. S. M., b. 1965
1919 **	Swinfen (3rd), Roger Mynors Swinfen Eady, MBE, b. 1938, s. 1977, m.	Hon. Charles R. P. S. E., b. 1971
1831 I.	Talbot of Malahide (11th), Richard John Tennant Arundell, b. 1957, s. 2016, m.	Hon. John R. A., b. 1998
1946	Tedder (3rd), Robin John Tedder, b. 1955, s. 1994, m.	Hon. Benjamin J. T., b. 1985
1884	Tennyson (6th), David Harold Alexander Tennyson, b. 1960, s. 2006	Alan J. D. T., b. 1965
1918	Terrington (6th), Christopher Richard James Woodhouse, MB, b. 1946, s. 2001, m.	Hon. Jack H. L. W., b. 1978
1940	Teviot (2nd), Charles John Kerr, b. 1934, s. 1968, m.	Hon. Charles R. K., b. 1971
1616	Teynham (20th), John Christopher Ingham Roper-Curzon, b. 1928, s. 1972, m.	Hon. David J. H. I. R.-C., b. 1965
1964	Thomson of Fleet (3rd), David Kenneth Roy Thomson, b. 1957, s. 2006	Hon. Benjamin J. L. T., b. 2006
1792 **	Thurlow (9th), Roualeyn Robert Hovell-Thurlow-Cumming-Bruce, b. 1952, s. 2013, m.	Hon. Nicholas E. H.-T.-C.-B., b. 1986
1876	Tollemache (5th), Timothy John Edward Tollemache, KCVO, b. 1939, s. 1975, m.	Hon. Edward J. H. T., b. 1976
1564 S.	Torphichen (15th), James Andrew Douglas Sandilands, b. 1946, s. 1975, m.	Robert P. S., b. 1950
1947 **	Trefgarne (2nd), David Garro Trefgarne, PC, b. 1941, s. 1960, m.	Hon. George G. T., b. 1970
1921 **	Trevethin (5th) and Oaksey (3rd) (1947), Patrick John Tristram Lawrence, QC, b. 1960, s. 2012, m.	Hon. Oliver J. T. L., b. 1990

1880	Trevor (5th), Marke Charles Hill-Trevor, b. 1970, s. 1997	Hon. Iain R. H.-T., b. 1971
1461 I.	Trimlestown (21st), Raymond Charles Barnewall, b. 1930, s. 1997	None
1940	Tryon (4th), Charles George Barrington Tryon, b. 1976, s. 2018, m.	Hon. Guy A. G. T., b. 2015
1935	Tweedsmuir (4th), John William de l'Aigle (Toby) Buchan, b. 1950, s. 2008, m.	Hon. John A. G. B., b. 1986
1523 **	Vaux of Harrowden (12th), Richard Hubert Gordon Gilbey, b. 1965, s. 2014, m.	Hon. Alexander J. C. G., b. 2000
1800 I.	Ventry (8th), Andrew Wesley Daubeny de Moleyns, b. 1943, s. 1987, m.	Hon. Francis W. D. de M., b. 1965
1762	Vernon (11th), Anthony William Vernon-Harcourt, b. 1939, s. 2000, m.	Hon. Simon A. V.-H., b. 1969
1922	Vestey (3rd), Samuel George Armstrong Vestey, GCVO, b. 1941, s. 1954, m.	Hon. William G. V., b. 1983
1841	Vivian (7th), Charles Crespigny Hussey Vivian, b. 1966, s. 2004	Thomas C. B. V., b. 1971
1934	Wakehurst (3rd), (John) Christopher Loder, b. 1925, s. 1970, m.	Hon. Timothy W. L., b. 1958
1723	Walpole (10th) and Walpole of Wolterton (8th) (1756), Robert Horatio Walpole, b. 1938, s. 1989, m.	Hon. Jonathan R. H. W., b. 1967
1780	Walsingham (9th), John de Grey, MC, b. 1925, s. 1965, m.	Hon. Robert de G., b. 1969
1792 I.	Waterpark (8th), Roderick Alexander Cavendish, b. 1959, s. 2013, m.	Hon. Luke F. C., b. 1990
1942	Wedgwood (5th), Antony John Wedgwood, b. 1944, s. 2014, m.	Hon. Josiah T. A. W., b. 1978
1861	Westbury (6th), Richard Nicholas Bethell, MBE, b. 1950, s. 2001, m.	Hon. Richard A. D. B., b. 1986
1944	Westwood (4th), (William) Fergus Westwood, b. 1972, s. 2019	Hon. Alistair C. W., b. 1974
1544/5	Wharton (12th), Myles Christopher David Robertson, b. 1964, s. 2000, m.	Hon. Meghan Z. M. R., b. 2006
1935	Wigram (3rd), Andrew Francis Clive Wigram, MVO, b. 1949, s. 2017, m.	Hon. Harry R. C. W., b. 1977
1491 **	Willoughby de Broke (21st), Leopold David Verney, b. 1938, s. 1986, m.	Hon. Rupert G. V., b. 1966
1937	Windlesham (4th), James Rupert Hennessy, b. 1968, s. 2010, m.	Hon. George R. J. H., b. 2006
1951	Wise (3rd), Christopher John Clayton Wise, b. 1949, s. 2012, m.	Hon. Thomas C. C. W., b. 1989
1869	Wolverton (8th), Miles John Glyn, b. 1966, s. 2011	Jonathan C. G., b. 1990
1928	Wraxall (4th), Antony Hubert Gibbs, b. 1958, s. 2017, m.	Hon. Orlando H. G., b. 1995
1915	Wrenbury (4th), William Edward Buckley, b. 1966, s. 2014, m.	Arthur B. B., b. 1967
1838	Wrottesley (6th), Clifton Hugh Lancelot de Verdon Wrottesley, b. 1968, s. 1977, m.	Hon. Victor E. F. de V. W., b. 2004
1829	Wynford (9th), John Philip Robert Best, b. 1950, s. 2002, m.	Hon. Harry R. F. B., b. 1987
1308	Zouche (18th), James Assheton Frankland, b. 1943, s. 1965, m.	Hon. William T. A. F., b. 1984

BARONESSES/LADIES IN THEIR OWN RIGHT

Style, The Rt. Hon. the Lady _ , or The Rt. Hon. the Baroness _ , according to her preference. Either style may be used, except in the case of Scottish titles (indicated by S.), which are not baronies and whose holders are always addressed as Lady.

Envelope, may be addressed in same way as a Baron's wife or, if she prefers (formal), The Rt. Hon. the Baroness _; (social), The Baroness _. Otherwise as for a Baron's wife

Husband, Untitled

Children's style, As for children of a Baron

In Scotland, the heir to a Lady may be styled 'The Master/Mistress of _ (title of peer)'

Created	Title, order of succession, name, etc	Heir
1664	Arlington (11th), Jennifer Jane Forwood, b. 1939, s. 1999, w. Title called out of abeyance 1999	Hon. Patrick J. D. F., b. 1967
1455	Berners (16th), Pamela Vivien Kirkham, b. 1929, s. 1995, w. Title called out of abeyance 1995	Hon. Rupert W. T. K., b. 1953
1529	Braye (8th), Mary Penelope Aubrey-Fletcher, b. 1941, s. 1985, m.	Linda K. C. Fothergill, b. 1930
1321	Dacre (29th), Emily Beamish, b. 1983, s. 2014, m.	Three co-heiresses
1283	Fauconberg (10th) and Conyers (16th) (1509), Baronies in abeyance between two co-heiresses since 2013	
1490 S.	Herries of Terregles (16th), (Theresa) Jane Kerr, Marchioness of Lothian, b. 1945, s. 2017, m.	Lady Clare T. Hurd, b. 1979
1597	Howard de Walden (10th), Mary Hazel Caridwen Czernin, b. 1935, s. 2004, w. Title called out of abeyance 2004	Hon. Peter J. J. C., b. 1966
1602 S.	Kinloss (13th), Teresa Mary Nugent Freeman-Grenville, b. 1957, s. 2012	Mistress of Kinloss, b. 1960
1445 S.	Saltoun (20th), Flora Marjory Fraser, b. 1930, s. 1979, w.	Hon. Katharine I. M. I. F., b. 1957
1313	Willoughby de Eresby (27th), (Nancy) Jane Marie Heathcote-Drummond-Willoughby, b. 1934, s. 1983	Two co-heirs

LIFE PEERS

Style, The Rt. Hon. the Lord _ /The Rt. Hon. the Lady _ , or The Rt. Hon. the Baroness _ , according to her preference
Envelope (formal), The Rt. Hon. Lord _/Lady_/Baroness_; (social), The Lord _/Lady_/Baroness_ Letter (formal), My Lord/Lady; (social), Dear Lord/Lady _. Spoken, Lord/Lady _
Wife's style, The Rt. Hon. the Lady _
Husband, Untitled
Children's style, 'The Hon.' before forename (F_) and surname (S_)
Envelope, The Hon. F_ S_. Letter, Dear Mr/Miss/Mrs S_. Spoken, Mr/Miss/Mrs S_

KEY
* Hereditary peer who has been granted a life peerage. For further details, please refer to the Hereditary Peers section. For example, life peer Balniel can be found under his hereditary title Earl of Crawford and Balcarres
§ Members of the Judiciary currently disqualified from sitting or voting in the House of Lords until they retire from that office. For further information see Law Courts and Offices
‡ Title not confirmed at time of going to press
₡ Peer who has permanently resigned from the House of Lords
E. Peer who has been expelled for absenteeism, under section 2 of the House of Lords Reform Act 2014, for failing to attend a sitting of the House during a session lasting six months or longer see The Peerage, introduction

A full entry in italic type indicates that the recipient of a life peerage died within a year of it being conferred. The name is included in our list for one year for purposes of record.

NEW LIFE PEERAGES
Since 20 September 2018:

Nicola Claire Blackwood; Sir Jeremy John Heywood, GCB, CVO; Rt. Hon. Lord Reed

CREATED UNDER THE APPELLATE JURISDICTION ACT 1876 (AS AMENDED)

BARONS
Created
2004   Brown of Eaton-under-Heywood, Simon Denis Brown, PC, b. 1937, m.
2004   Carswell, Robert Douglas Carswell, PC, b. 1934, m.
2009   Collins of Mapesbury, Lawrence Antony Collins, PC, b. 1941 m.
1995   Hoffmann, Leonard Hubert Hoffmann, PC, b. 1934, m.
1997   ₡Hutton, (James) Brian (Edward) Hutton, PC, b. 1931, m.
2009   §Kerr of Tonaghmore, Brian Francis Kerr, PC, b. 1948, m.
1993   ₡Lloyd of Berwick, Anthony John Leslie Lloyd, PC, b. 1929, m.
2005   Mance, Jonathan Hugh Mance, PC, b. 1943, m.
1998   ₡Millett, Peter Julian Millett, PC, b. 1932, m.
2007   Neuberger of Abbotsbury, David Edmond Neuberger, PC, b. 1948, m.
1994   ₡Nicholls of Birkenhead, Donald James Nicholls, PC, b. 1933, m.
1999   Phillips of Worth Matravers, Nicholas Addison Phillips, KG, PC, b. 1938, m.

1997   Saville of Newdigate, Mark Oliver Saville, PC, b. 1936, m.
2000   ₡Scott of Foscote, Richard Rashleigh Folliott Scott, PC, b. 1934, m.
2003   Walker of Gestingthorpe, Robert Walker, PC, b. 1938, m.
1992   Woolf, Harry Kenneth Woolf, CH, PC, b. 1933, m.

BARONESSES
2004   §Hale of Richmond, Brenda Marjorie Hale, DBE, PC, b. 1945, m. President of the Supreme Court

CREATED UNDER THE LIFE PEERAGES ACT 1958

BARONS
Created
2001   Adebowale, Victor Olufemi Adebowale, CBE, b. 1962
2005   Adonis, Andrew Adonis, PC, b. 1963, m.
2017   Agnew of Oulton, Theodore Thomas More Agnew, b. 1961, m.
2011   Ahmad of Wimbledon, Tariq Mahmood Ahmad, b. 1968, m.
1998   Ahmed, Nazir Ahmed, b. 1957, m.
1996   Alderdice, John Thomas Alderdice, b. 1955, m.
2010   Allan of Hallam, Richard Beecroft Allan, b. 1966
2013   Allen of Kensington, Charles Lamb Allen, CBE, b. 1957
1998   Alli, Waheed Alli, b. 1964
2004   Alliance, David Alliance, CBE, b. 1932
1997   Alton of Liverpool, David Patrick Paul Alton, b. 1951, m.
2018   Anderson of Ipswich, David William Kinloch Anderson, KBE, QC, b. 1961, m.
2005   Anderson of Swansea, Donald Anderson, PC, b. 1939, m.
2015   Arbuthnot of Edrom, James Norwich Arbuthnot, PC, b. 1952, m.
1992   Archer of Weston-super-Mare, Jeffrey Howard Archer, b. 1940, m.
1988   Armstrong of Ilminster, Robert Temple Armstrong, GCB, CVO, b. 1927, m.
2000   ₡Ashcroft, Michael Anthony Ashcroft, KCMG, PC, b. 1946, m.
1998   Bach, William Stephen Goulden Bach, b. 1946, m.
1997   Baker of Dorking, Kenneth Wilfred Baker, CH, PC, b. 1934, m.
2013   Balfe, Richard Andrew Balfe, b. 1944, m.
1974   *Balniel, The Earl of Crawford and Balcarres, KT, GCVO, PC, b. 1927, m. (see Hereditary Peers)
2013   Bamford, Anthony Paul Bamford, b. 1945, m.
2015   Barker of Battle, Gregory Leonard George Barker, PC, b. 1966
1997   Bassam of Brighton, (John) Steven Bassam, PC, b. 1953
2008   Bates, Michael Walton Bates, PC, b. 1961, m.
2010   Beecham, Jeremy Hugh Beecham, b. 1944, m.
2015   Beith, Alan James Beith, PC, b. 1943, m.
2013   Berkeley of Knighton, Michael Fitzhardinge Berkeley, CBE, b. 1948, m.
2001   Best, Richard Stuart Best, OBE, b. 1945, m.
2007   Bew, Prof. Paul Anthony Elliott Bew, b. 1950, m.
2001   Bhatia, Amirali Alibhai Bhatia, OBE, b. 1932, m.
2010   Bichard, Michael George Bichard, KCB, b. 1947, m.
2006   Bilimoria, Karan Faridoon Bilimoria, CBE, b. 1961, m.
2015   Bird, John Anthony Bird, MBE, b. 1946, m.
2000   Birt, John Francis Hodgess Birt, b. 1944, m.
2010   Black of Brentwood, Guy Vaughan Black, b. 1964, m.

2001 *Black of Crossharbour,* Conrad Moffat Black, *b.* 1944, *m.*

1997 *Blackwell,* Norman Roy Blackwell, *b.* 1952, *m.*

2010 *Blair of Boughton,* Ian Warwick Blair, QPM, *b.* 1953, *m.*

2011 *Blencathra,* David John Maclean, PC, *b.* 1953

2015 *Blunkett,* David Blunkett, PC, *b.* 1947, *m.*

1995 ℭ*Blyth of Rowington,* James Blyth, *b.* 1940, *m.*

2010 *Boateng,* Paul Yaw Boateng, PC, *b.* 1951, *m.*

2010 *Boswell of Aynho,* Timothy Eric Boswell, *b.* 1942, *m.*

2013 *Bourne of Aberystwyth,* Nicholas Henry Bourne, *b.* 1952

1996 *Bowness,* Peter Spencer Bowness, CBE, *b.* 1943, *m.*

2003 *Boyce,* Michael Boyce, KG, GCB, OBE, *b.* 1943, *w.*

2006 §*Boyd of Duncansby,* Colin David Boyd, PC, *b.* 1953, *m.*

2006 *Bradley,* Keith John Charles Bradley, PC, *b.* 1950, *m.*

1999 *Bradshaw,* William Peter Bradshaw, *b.* 1936, *m.*

1998 *Bragg,* Melvyn Bragg, CH, *b.* 1939, *m.*

1987 *Bramall,* Edwin Noel Westby Bramall, KG, GCB, OBE, MC, *b.* 1923, *w.*

2000 *Brennan,* Daniel Joseph Brennan, QC, *b.* 1942, *m.*

2015 *Bridges of Headley,* James George Robert Bridges, MBE, *b.* 1970, *m.*

2004 *Broers,* Prof. Alec (Nigel) Broers, *b.* 1938, *m.*

1997 *Brooke of Alverthorpe,* Clive Brooke, *b.* 1942, *m.*

2001 ℭ*Brooke of Sutton Mandeville,* Peter Leonard Brooke, CH, PC, *b.* 1934, *m.*

1998 *Brookman,* David Keith Brookman, *b.* 1937, *m.*

2006 *Browne of Belmont,* Wallace Hamilton Browne, *b.* 1947

2010 *Browne of Ladyton,* Desmond Henry Browne, PC, *b.* 1952

2001 *Browne of Madingley,* Edmund John Phillip Browne, *b.* 1948

2015 *Bruce of Bennachie,* Malcolm Gray Bruce, PC, *b.* 1944, *m.*

2006 *Burnett,* John Patrick Aubone Burnett, *b.* 1945, *m.*

2017 §*Burnett of Maldon,* Ian Duncan Burnett, PC, *b.* 1958, *m. Lord Chief Justice of England and Wales*

1998 *Burns,* Terence Burns, GCB, *b.* 1944, *m.*

1998 *Butler of Brockwell,* (Frederick Edward) Robin Butler, KG, GCB, CVO, PC, *b.* 1938, *m.*

2016 *Caine,* Jonathan Michael Caine, *b.* 1966

2014 *Callanan,* Martin John Callanan, *b.* 1961, *m.*

2004 *Cameron of Dillington,* Ewen (James Hanning) Cameron, *b.* 1949, *m.*

1984 ℭ*Cameron of Lochbroom,* Kenneth John Cameron, PC, *b.* 1931, *m.*

2015 *Campbell of Pittenweem,* (Walter) Menzies Campbell, CH, CBE, PC, QC, *b.* 1941, *m.*

2001 *Campbell-Savours,* Dale Norman Campbell-Savours, *b.* 1943, *m.*

2002 *Carey of Clifton,* Rt. Revd George Leonard Carey, PC, Royal Victorian Chain, *b.* 1935, *m.*

1999 *Carlile of Berriew,* Alexander Charles Carlile, CBE, QC, *b.* 1948, *m.*

2013 *Carrington of Fulham,* Matthew Hadrian Marshall Carrington, *b.* 1947, *m.*

2008 *Carter of Barnes,* Stephen Andrew Carter, CBE, *b.* 1964, *m.*

2004 *Carter of Coles,* Patrick Robert Carter, *b.* 1946, *m.*

2014 *Cashman,* Michael Maurice Cashman, CBE, *b.* 1950

1990 *Cavendish of Furness,* (Richard) Hugh Cavendish, *b.* 1941, *m.*

1996 *Chadlington,* Peter Selwyn Gummer, *b.* 1942, *m.*

1964 ℭ*Chalfont,* (Alun) Arthur Gwynne Jones, OBE, MC, PC, *b.* 1919, *w.*

2017 *Chartres,* Rt. Revd Richard John Carew Chartres, GCVO, PC, *b.* 1947, *m.*

2005 *Chidgey,* David William George Chidgey, *b.* 1942, *m.*

1998 *Christopher,* Anthony Martin Grosvenor Christopher, CBE, *b.* 1925, *m.*

2001 *Clark of Windermere,* David George Clark, PC, PHD, *b.* 1939, *m.*

1998 *Clarke of Hampstead,* Anthony James Clarke, CBE, *b.* 1932, *m.*

2009 *Clarke of Stone-Cum-Ebony,* Anthony Peter Clarke, PC, *b.* 1943, *m.*

1998 *Clement-Jones,* Timothy Francis Clement-Jones, CBE, *b.* 1949, *m.*

1990 ℭ*Clinton-Davis,* Stanley Clinton Clinton-Davis, PC, *b.* 1928, *m.*

2000 *Coe,* Sebastian Newbold Coe, CH, KBE, *b.* 1956, *m.*

2011 *Collins of Highbury,* Raymond Edward Harry Collins, *b.* 1954, *m.*

2001 ℭ*Condon,* Paul Leslie Condon, QPM, *b.* 1947, *m.*

2014 *Cooper of Windrush,* Andrew Timothy Cooper, *b.* 1963, *m.*

1997 *Cope of Berkeley,* John Ambrose Cope, PC, *b.* 1937, *m.*

2010 *Cormack,* Patrick Thomas Cormack, *b.* 1939, *m.*

2006 *Cotter,* Brian Joseph Michael Cotter, *b.* 1938, *m.*

1991 *Craig of Radley,* David Brownrigg Craig, GCB, OBE, *b.* 1929, *w.*

2006 *Crisp,* (Edmund) Nigel (Ramsay) Crisp, KCB, *b.* 1952, *m.*

2003 ℭ*Cullen of Whitekirk,* William Douglas Cullen, KT, PC, *b.* 1935, *m.*

2005 *Cunningham of Felling,* John Anderson Cunningham, PC, *b.* 1939, *m.*

1996 *Currie of Marylebone,* David Anthony Currie, *b.* 1946, *m.*

2011 *Curry of Kirkharle,* Donald Thomas Younger Curry, CBE, *b.* 1944, *m.*

2011 *Dannatt,* (Francis) Richard Dannatt, GCB, CBE, MC, *b.* 1950, *m.*

2015 *Darling of Roulanish,* Alistair Maclean Darling, PC, *b.* 1953, *m.*

2007 *Darzi of Denham,* Ara Warkes Darzi, OM, KBE, PC, *b.* 1960, *m.*

2006 *Davidson of Glen Clova,* Neil Forbes Davidson, QC, *b.* 1950, *m.*

2009 *Davies of Abersoch,* Evan Mervyn Davies, CBE, *b.* 1952, *m.*

1997 *Davies of Oldham,* Bryan Davies, PC, *b.* 1939, *m.*

2010 *Davies of Stamford,* John Quentin Davies, *b.* 1944, *m.*

2006 *Dear,* Geoffrey (James) Dear, QPM, *b.* 1937, *m.*

2010 *Deben,* John Selwyn Gummer, PC, *b.* 1939, *m.*

2012 *Deighton,* Paul Clive Deighton, KBE, *b.* 1956, *m.*

1991 *Desai,* Prof. Meghnad Jagdishchandra Desai, PHD, *b.* 1940, *m.*

1997 *Dholakia,* Navnit Dholakia, OBE, PC, *b.* 1937, *m.*

1993 *Dixon-Smith,* Robert William Dixon-Smith, *b.* 1934, *m.*

2010 *Dobbs,* Michael John Dobbs, *b.* 1948, *m.*

1985 *Donoughue,* Bernard Donoughue, DPHIL, *b.* 1934, *m.*

2004 *Drayson,* Paul Rudd Drayson, PC, *b.* 1960, *m.*

1994 *Dubs,* Alfred Dubs, *b.* 1932, *m.*

2017 *Duncan of Springbank,* Ian James Duncan, *b.* 1973, *c.p.*

2015 *Dunlop,* Andrew James Dunlop, *b.* 1959, *m.*

2004 *Dykes,* Hugh John Maxwell Dykes, *b.* 1939

1995 *Eames,* Rt. Revd Robert Henry Alexander Eames, OM, PHD, *b.* 1937, *m.*

1992 *Eatwell,* John Leonard Eatwell, PHD, *b.* 1945, *m.*

1983 ℭ*Eden of Winton,* John Benedict Eden, PC, *b.* 1925, *m.*

2011 ℭ*Edmiston,* Robert Norman Edmiston, *b.* 1946, *m.*

1999 *Elder,* Thomas Murray Elder, *b.* 1950

1992 *Elis-Thomas,* Dafydd Elis Elis-Thomas, PC, *b.* 1946, *m.*

1981 *Elystan-Morgan,* Dafydd Elystan Elystan-Morgan, *b.* 1932, *w.*

2011 *Empey,* Reginald Norman Morgan Empey, OBE, *b.* 1947, *m.*

2000 ℭ*Erskine of Alloa Tower,* Earl of Mar and Kellie, *b.* 1949, *m. (see* Hereditary Peers)

1998 *Evans of Watford,* David Charles Evans, *b.* 1942, *m.*

2014 *Evans of Weardale,* Jonathan Douglas Evans, KCB, *b.* 1958

1997 *Falconer of Thoroton,* Charles Leslie Falconer, PC, QC, *b.* 1951, *m.*

2014 *Farmer,* Michael Stahel Farmer, *b.* 1944, *m.*

1999 *Faulkner of Worcester,* Richard Oliver Faulkner, *b.* 1946, *m.*

2010 *Faulks,* Edward Peter Lawless Faulks, QC, *b.* 1950, *m.*

2001 ℭ*Fearn,* Ronald Cyril Fearn, OBE, *b.* 1931, *m.*

1996 ℭ*Feldman,* Basil Feldman, *b.* 1926, *m.*

2010 *Feldman of Elstree,* Andrew Simon Feldman, PC, *b.* 1966, *m.*

1999 *Fellowes,* Robert Fellowes, GCB, GCVO, PC, *b.* 1941, *m.*

2011 *Fellowes of West Stafford,* Julian Alexander Fellowes, *b.* 1949, *m.*

1999 *Filkin,* David Geoffrey Nigel Filkin, CBE, *b.* 1944, *m.*

2011 *Fink,* Stanley Fink, *b.* 1957, *m.*

2013 *Finkelstein,* Daniel William Finkelstein, OBE, *b.* 1962, *m.*

2011 *Flight,* Howard Emerson Flight, *b.* 1948, *m.*

1999 *Forsyth of Drumlean,* Michael Bruce Forsyth, PC, *b.* 1954, *m.*

2015 *Foster of Bath,* Donald Michael Ellison Foster, PC, *b.* 1947, *m.*

1999 ℭ*Foster of Thames Bank,* Norman Robert Foster, OM, *b.* 1935, *m.*

2005 *Foulkes of Cumnock,* George Foulkes, PC, *b.* 1942, *m.*

2001 *Fowler,* (Peter) Norman Fowler, PC, *b.* 1938, *m. Lord Speaker*

2014 *Fox,* Christopher Francis Fox, *b.* 1957, *m.*

2011 *Framlingham,* Michael Nicholson Lord, *b.* 1938, *m.*

2016 *Fraser of Corriegarth,* (Alexander) Andrew (Macdonell) Fraser, *b.* 1946, *m.*

1997 *Freeman,* Roger Norman Freeman, PC, *b.* 1942, *m.*

2009 *Freud,* David Anthony Freud, PC, *b.* 1950, *m.*

2016 *Gadhia,* Jitesh Kishorekumar Gadhia, *b.* 1970, *m.*

2010 *Gardiner of Kimble,* John Gardiner, *b.* 1956, *m.*

1997 *Garel-Jones,* (William Armand Thomas) Tristan Garel-Jones, PC, *b.* 1941, *m.*

2018 *Garnier,* Edward Henry Garnier, PC, QC, *b.* 1952, *m.*

1999 ℭ*Gascoyne-Cecil,* The Marquess of Salisbury, KG, KCVO, PC, *b.* 1946, *m. (see* Hereditary Peers)

2017 *Geidt,* Christopher Edward Wollaston MacKenzie Geidt, GCB, GCVO, OBE, PC, *b.* 1961, *m.*

2010 *German,* Michael James German, OBE, *b.* 1945, *m.*

2004 *Giddens,* Prof. Anthony Giddens, *b.* 1938, *m.*

2015 *Gilbert of Panteg,* Stephen Gilbert, *b.* 1963

2011 *Glasman,* Maurice Mark Glasman, *b.* 1961, *m.*

2011 *Glendonbrook,* Michael David Bishop, CBE, *b.* 1942

2014 *Goddard of Stockport,* David Goddard, *b.* 1952

2011 *Gold,* David Laurence Gold, *b.* 1951, *m.*

1999 *Goldsmith,* Peter Henry Goldsmith, PC, QC, *b.* 1950, *m.*

2005 *Goodlad,* Alastair Robertson Goodlad, KCMG, PC, *b.* 1943, *m.*

1997 *Gordon of Strathblane,* James Stuart Gordon, CBE, *b.* 1936, *m.*

1999 *Grabiner,* Anthony Stephen Grabiner, QC, *b.* 1945, *m.*

2011 *Grade of Yarmouth,* Michael Ian Grade, CBE, *b.* 1943, *m.*

1983 *Graham of Edmonton,* (Thomas) Edward Graham, PC, *b.* 1925, *m.*

2000 *Greaves,* Anthony Robert Greaves, *b.* 1942, *m.*

2014 *Green of Deddington,* Andrew Fleming Green, KCMG, *b.* 1941, *m.*

2010 *Green of Hurstpierpoint,* Stephen Keith Green, *b.* 1948, *m.*

2000 ℭ*Grenfell of Kilvey,* Lord Grenfell, *b.* 1935, *m. (see* Hereditary Peers)

2004 *Griffiths of Burry Port,* Revd Dr Leslie John Griffiths, *b.* 1942, *m.*

1991 *Griffiths of Fforestfach,* Brian Griffiths, *b.* 1941, *m.*

2001 *Grocott,* Bruce Joseph Grocott, PC, *b.* 1940, *m.*

2000 **Gueterbock,* Lord Berkeley, OBE, *b.* 1939, *m. (see* Hereditary Peers)

2000 *Guthrie of Craigiebank,* Charles Ronald Llewelyn Guthrie, GCB, GCVO, OBE, *b.* 1938, *m.*

2015 *Hague of Richmond,* William Jefferson Hague, PC, *b.* 1961, *m.*

2015 **Hailsham of Kettlethorpe,* Viscount Hailsham, PC, QC, *b.* 1945, *m. (see* Hereditary Peers)

2015 *Hain,* Peter Gerald Hain, PC, *b.* 1950, *m.*

2010 *Hall of Birkenhead,* Anthony William Hall, CBE, *b.* 1951, *m.*

2007 *Hameed,* Dr Khalid Hameed, CBE, *b.* 1941, *m.*

2005 *Hamilton of Epsom,* Archibald Gavin Hamilton, PC, *b.* 1941, *m.*

2001 *Hannay of Chiswick,* David Hugh Alexander Hannay, GCMG, CH, *b.* 1935, *w.*

1998 *Hanningfield,* Paul Edward Winston White, *b.* 1940

1997 ℭ*Hardie,* Andrew Rutherford Hardie, PC, QC, *b.* 1946, *m.*

2006 *Harries of Pentregarth,* Rt. Revd Richard Douglas Harries, *b.* 1936, *m.*

1998 *Harris of Haringey,* (Jonathan) Toby Harris, *b.* 1953, *m.*

1996 *Harris of Peckham,* Philip Charles Harris, *b.* 1942, *m.*

1999 *Harrison,* Lyndon Henry Arthur Harrison, *b.* 1947, *m.*

2018 *Haselhurst,* Alan Gordon Barraclough Haselhurst, PC, *b.* 1937, *m.*

1993 *Haskel,* Simon Haskel, *b.* 1934, *m.*

1998 *Haskins,* Christopher Robin Haskins, *b.* 1937, *m.*

2005 *Hastings of Scarisbrick,* Michael John Hastings, CBE, *b.* 1958, *m.*

1997 ℭ*Hattersley,* Roy Sidney George Hattersley, PC, *b.* 1932, *m.*

2013 *Haughey,* William Haughey, OBE, *b.* 1956, *m.*

2004 *Haworth,* Alan Robert Haworth, *b.* 1948, *m.*

2014 *Hay of Ballyore,* William Alexander Hay, *b.* 1950, *m.*

2015 *Hayward,* Robert Antony Hayward, OBE, *b.* 1949

2010 *Hennessy of Nympsfield,* Prof. Peter John Hennessy, *b.* 1947, *m.*

2001 *Heseltine,* Michael Ray Dibdin Heseltine, CH, PC, *b.* 1933, *m.*

2018 *Heywood of Whitehall,* Jeremy John Heywood, GCB, CVO, *b.* 1961, *m., d.* 2018

1997 ℭ*Higgins,* Terence Langley Higgins, KBE, PC, *b.* 1928, *m.*

2010 *Hill of Oareford,* Jonathan Hopkin Hill, CBE, PC, *b.* 1960, *m.*

2000 *Hodgson of Astley Abbotts,* Robin Granville Hodgson, CBE, *b.* 1942, *m.*

2017 *Hogan-Howe,* Bernard Hogan-Howe, QPM, *b.* 1957, *m.*

1991 *Hollick,* Clive Richard Hollick, *b.* 1945, *m.*

2013 *Holmes of Richmond,* Christopher Holmes, MBE, *b.* 1971

2004   *McKenzie of Luton*, William David McKenzie, *b.* 1946, *m.*

1996   ❰*MacLaurin of Knebworth*, Ian Charter MacLaurin, *b.* 1937, *m.*

2001   *Maclennan of Rogart*, Robert Adam Ross Maclennan, PC, *b.* 1936, *m.*

1995   *McNally*, Tom McNally, PC, *b.* 1943, *m.*

2018   *McNicol of West Kilbride*, Iain Mackenzie McNicol, *b.* 1969, *m.*

2016   *Macpherson of Earl's Court*, Nicholas Ian Macpherson, GCB, *b.* 1959, *m.*

2011   *Magan of Castletown*, George Morgan Magan, *b.* 1945, *m.*

2001   *Maginnis of Drumglass*, Kenneth Wiggins Maginnis, *b.* 1938, *m.*

2015   *Mair*, Prof. Robert James Mair, CBE, PHD, FRS, *b.* 1950, *m.*

2007   *Malloch-Brown*, George Mark Malloch Brown, KCMG, PC, *b.* 1953, *m.*

2008   *Mandelson*, Peter Benjamin Mandelson, PC, *b.* 1953

2011   *Marks of Henley-on-Thames*, Jonathan Clive Marks, QC, *b.* 1952, *m.*

2006   *Marland*, Jonathan Peter Marland, *b.* 1956, *m.*

1991   *Marlesford*, Mark Shuldham Schreiber, *b.* 1931, *m.*

2015   *Maude of Horsham*, Francis Anthony Aylmer Maude, TD, PC, *b.* 1953, *m.*

2005   *Mawhinney*, Brian Stanley Mawhinney, PC, *b.* 1940, *m.*

2007   *Mawson*, Revd Andrew Mawson, OBE, *b.* 1954, *m.*

2004   *Maxton*, John Alston Maxton, *b.* 1936, *m.*

2001   ❰*May of Oxford*, Robert McCredie May, OM, *b.* 1936, *m.*

2013   *Mendelsohn*, Jonathan Neil Mendelsohn, *b.* 1966, *m.*

2000   *Mitchell*, Parry Andrew Mitchell, *b.* 1943, *m.*

2000   **Mitford*, Lord Redesdale, *b.* 1967, *m.* (*see* Hereditary Peers)

2008   ❰*Mogg*, John (Frederick) Mogg, KCMG, *b.* 1943, *m.*

2010   *Monks*, John Stephen Monks, *b.* 1945, *m.*

2005   *Moonie*, Dr Lewis George Moonie, *b.* 1947, *m.*

2000   *Morgan*, Kenneth Owen Morgan, *b.* 1934, *m.*

2001   *Morris of Aberavon*, John Morris, KG, PC, QC, *b.* 1931, *m.*

2006   *Morris of Handsworth*, William Manuel Morris, *b.* 1938, *w.*

2006   *Morrow*, Maurice George Morrow, *b.* 1948, *m.*

2015   *Murphy of Torfaen*, Paul Peter Murphy, PC, *b.* 1948

2008   *Myners*, Paul Myners, CBE, *b.* 1948, *m.*

1997   *Naseby*, Michael Wolfgang Laurence Morris, PC, *b.* 1936, *m.*

2013   *Nash*, John Alfred Stoddard Nash, *b.* 1949, *m.*

1997   *Newby*, Richard Mark Newby, OBE, PC, *b.* 1953, *m.*

1994   ❰*Nickson*, David Wigley Nickson, KBE, FRSE, *b.* 1929, *m.*

1998   *Norton of Louth*, Philip Norton, *b.* 1951

2000   *Oakeshott of Seagrove Bay*, Matthew Alan Oakeshott, *b.* 1947, *m.*

2015   *Oates*, Jonathan Oates, *b.* 1969, *c.p.*

2012   *O'Donnell*, Augustine Thomas (Gus) O'Donnell, GCB, *b.* 1952, *m.*

2005   *O'Neill of Clackmannan*, Martin John O'Neill, *b.* 1945, *m.*

2015   *O'Neill of Gatley*, Terence James O'Neill, *b.* 1957, *m.*

2015   *O'Shaughnessy*, James Richard O'Shaughnessy, *b.* 1976, *m.*

2001   ❰*Ouseley*, Herman George Ouseley, *b.* 1945, *m.*

1992   *Owen*, David Anthony Llewellyn Owen, CH, PC, *b.* 1938, *m.*

1999   *Oxburgh*, Ernest Ronald Oxburgh, KBE, FRS, PHD, *b.* 1934, *m.*

2013   *Paddick*, Brian Leonard Paddick, *b.* 1958, *m.*

2011   *Palmer of Childs Hill*, Monroe Edward Palmer, OBE, *b.* 1938, *m.*

1991   ❰*Palumbo*, Peter Garth Palumbo, *b.* 1935, *m.*

2013   *Palumbo of Southwark*, James Rudolph Palumbo, *b.* 1963

2008   *Pannick*, David Philip Pannick, QC, *b.* 1956, *m.*

2000   *Parekh*, Bhikhu Chhotalal Parekh, *b.* 1935, *m.*

1999   *Patel*, Narendra Babubhai Patel, KT, *b.* 1938 *m.*

2006   *Patel of Bradford*, Prof. Kamlesh Kumar Patel, OBE, *b.* 1960, *m.*

1997   *Patten*, John Haggitt Charles Patten, PC, *b.* 1945, *m.*

2005   *Patten of Barnes*, Christopher Francis Patten, CH, PC, *b.* 1944, *m.*

1996   *Paul*, Swraj Paul, PC, *b.* 1931, *m.*

1990   *Pearson of Rannoch*, Malcolm Everard MacLaren Pearson, *b.* 1942, *m.*

2001   *Pendry*, Thomas Pendry, PC, *b.* 1934, *m.*

1998   ❰*Phillips of Sudbury*, Andrew Wyndham Phillips, OBE, *b.* 1939, *m.*

2018   *Pickles*, Eric (Jack) Pickles, PC, *b.* 1952, *m.*

1992   *Plant of Highfield*, Prof. Raymond Plant, PHD, *b.* 1945, *m.*

1987   ❰*Plumb*, (Charles) Henry Plumb, *b.* 1925, *m.*

2015   *Polak*, Stuart Polak, CBE, *b.* 1961

2000   **Ponsonby of Roehampton*, Lord Ponsonby of Shulbrede, *b.* 1958, *m.* (*see* Hereditary Peers)

2010   *Popat*, Dolar Amarshi Popat, *b.* 1953, *m.*

2015   *Porter of Spalding*, Gary Andrew Porter, CBE, *b.* 1960, *m.*

2000   *Powell of Bayswater*, Charles David Powell, KCMG, *b.* 1941, *m.*

2010   *Prescott*, John Leslie Prescott, *b.* 1938, *m.*

2016   *Price*, Mark Ian Price, CVO, *b.* 1961, *m.*

2015   *Prior of Brampton*, David Gifford Leathes Prior, *b.* 1954, *m.*

2013   *Purvis of Tweed*, Jeremy Purvis, *b.* 1974

1997   *Puttnam*, David Terence Puttnam, CBE, *b.* 1941, *m.*

2001   *Radice*, Giles Heneage Radice, PC, *b.* 1936, *m.*

2005   *Ramsbotham*, David John Ramsbotham, GCB, CBE, *b.* 1934, *m.*

2004   *Rana*, Dr Diljit Singh Rana, MBE, *b.* 1938

2018   *Randall of Uxbridge*, (Alexander) John Randall, PC, *b.* 1955, *m.*

1997   *Razzall*, (Edward) Timothy Razzall, CBE, *b.* 1943

2019   ‡§*Reed*, Robert John, PC, *b.* 1956, *m.* President of the Supreme Court (*from January 2020*)

2005   *Rees of Ludlow*, Prof. Martin John Rees, OM, *b.* 1942, *m.*

2010   *Reid of Cardowan*, Dr John Reid, PC, *b.* 1947, *m.*

1991   *Renfrew of Kaimsthorn*, (Andrew) Colin Renfrew, FBA, *b.* 1937, *m.*

1999   *Rennard*, Christopher John Rennard, MBE, *b.* 1960, *m.*

1997   ❰*Renton of Mount Harry*, (Ronald) Timothy Renton, PC, *b.* 1932, *m.*

1997   ❰*Renwick of Clifton*, Robin William Renwick, KCMG, *b.* 1937, *m.*

2010   *Ribeiro*, Bernard Francisco Ribeiro, CBE, *b.* 1944, *m.*

2014   *Richards of Herstmonceux*, David Julian Richards, GCB, CBE, DSO, *b.* 1952, *m.*

2016   *Ricketts*, Peter (Forbes) Ricketts, GCMG, GCVO, *b.* 1952, *m.*

2010   *Risby*, Richard John Grenville Spring, *b.* 1946

2015   *Robathan*, Andrew Robathan, PC, *b.* 1951, *m.*

2004   *Roberts of Llandudno*, Revd John Roger Roberts, *b.* 1935, *w.*

1999   *Robertson of Port Ellen*, George Islay MacNeill Robertson, KT, GCMG, PC, *b.* 1946, *m.*

1992   *Rodgers of Quarry Bank*, William Thomas Rodgers, PC, *b.* 1928, *w.*

1999   *Rogan*, Dennis Robert David Rogan, *b.* 1942, *m.*

1996 *Rogers of Riverside,* Richard George Rogers, CH, RA, RIBA, *b.* 1933, *m.*

2001 *Rooker,* Jeffrey William Rooker, PC, *b.* 1941, *m.*

2014 *Rose of Monewden,* Stuart Alan Ransom Rose, *b.* 1949

2004 *Rosser,* Richard Andrew Rosser, *b.* 1944, *m.*

2006 *Rowe-Beddoe,* David (Sydney) Rowe-Beddoe, *b.* 1937, *m.*

2004 *Rowlands,* Edward Rowlands, CBE, *b.* 1940, *w.*

1997 *Ryder of Wensum,* Richard Andrew Ryder, OBE, PC, *b.* 1949, *m.*

1996 *Saatchi,* Maurice Saatchi, *b.* 1946, *w.*

2009 *Sacks,* Chief Rabbi Dr Jonathan Henry Sacks, *b.* 1948, *m.*

1989 *Sainsbury of Preston Candover,* John Davan Sainsbury, KG, *b.* 1927, *m.*

1997 *Sainsbury of Turville,* David John Sainsbury, *b.* 1940, *m.*

1985 ⟪*Sanderson of Bowden,* Charles Russell Sanderson, *b.* 1933, *m.*

2010 *Sassoon,* James Meyer Sassoon, *b.* 1955, *m.*

1998 *Sawyer,* Lawrence (Tom) Sawyer, *b.* 1943

2014 *Scriven,* Paul James Scriven, *b.* 1966

1997 *Selkirk of Douglas,* James Alexander Douglas-Hamilton, PC, QC, *b.* 1942, *m.*

1996 ⟪*Sewel,* John Buttifant Sewel, CBE, *b.* 1946

2010 *Sharkey,* John Kevin Sharkey, *b.* 1947, *m.*

1999 ⟪*Sharman,* Colin Morven Sharman, OBE, *b.* 1943, *m.*

1994 ⟪*Shaw of Northstead,* Michael Norman Shaw, *b.* 1920, *m.*

2006 *Sheikh,* Mohamed Iltaf Sheikh, *b.* 1941, *m.*

2001 ⟪*Sheldon,* Robert Edward Sheldon, PC, *b.* 1923, *m.*

2013 *Sherbourne of Didsbury,* Stephen Ashley Sherbourne, CBE, *b.* 1945

2015 *Shinkwin,* Kevin Joseph Maximilian Shinkwin, *b.* 1971

2010 *Shipley,* John Warren Shipley, OBE, *b.* 1946, *m.*

2000 *Shutt of Greetland,* David Trevor Shutt, OBE, PC, *b.* 1942, *m.*

1997 ⟪*Simon of Highbury,* David Alec Gwyn Simon, CBE, *b.* 1939, *m.*

1997 ⟪*Simpson of Dunkeld,* George Simpson, *b.* 1942, *m.*

2011 *Singh of Wimbledon,* Indarjit Singh, CBE, *b.* 1932, *m.*

1991 *Skidelsky,* Robert Jacob Alexander Skidelsky, DPHIL, *b.* 1939, *m.*

1997 ⟪*Smith of Clifton,* Trevor Arthur Smith, *b.* 1937, *m.*

2005 *Smith of Finsbury,* Christopher Robert Smith, PC, *b.* 1951

2015 *Smith of Hindhead,* Philip Roland Smith, CBE, *b.* 1966

2008 *Smith of Kelvin,* Robert (Haldane) Smith, KT, CH, *b.* 1944, *m.*

1999 *Smith of Leigh,* Peter Richard Charles Smith, *b.* 1945, *m.*

2004 *Snape,* Peter Charles Snape, *b.* 1942, *m.*

2005 *Soley,* Clive Stafford Soley, *b.* 1939

1997 *Steel of Aikwood,* David Martin Scott Steel, KT, KBE, PC, *b.* 1938, *m.*

2011 *Stephen,* Nicol Ross Stephen, *b.* 1960, *m.*

1991 *Sterling of Plaistow,* Jeffrey Maurice Sterling, GCVO, CBE, *b.* 1934, *m.*

2007 *Stern of Brentford,* Nicholas Herbert Stern, CH, *b.* 1946, *m.*

2005 *Stevens of Kirkwhelpington,* John Arthur Stevens, QPM, *b.* 1942, *m.*

1987 *Stevens of Ludgate,* David Robert Stevens, *b.* 1936, *m.*

2010 *Stevenson of Balmacara,* Robert Wilfrid Stevenson, *b.* 1947, *m.*

1999 *Stevenson of Coddenham,* Henry Dennistoun Stevenson, CBE, *b.* 1945, *m.*

2011 *Stirrup,* Graham Eric Stirrup, KG, GCB, AFC, *b.* 1949, *m.*

1983 *Stoddart of Swindon,* David Leonard Stoddart, *b.* 1926, *m.*

1997 *Stone of Blackheath,* Andrew Zelig Stone, *b.* 1942, *m.*

2011 *Stoneham of Droxford,* Benjamin Russell Mackintosh Stoneham, *b.* 1948, *m.*

2011 *Storey,* Michael John Storey, CBE, *b.* 1949, *m.*

2011 *Strasburger,* Paul Cline Strasburger, *b.* 1946, *m.*

2015 *Stunell,* Robert Andrew Stunell, OBE, PC, *b.* 1942, *m.*

2009 *Sugar,* Alan Michael Sugar, *b.* 1947, *m.*

2014 *Suri,* Ranbir Singh Suri, *b.* 1935

1971 ⟪*Tanlaw,* Simon Brooke Mackay, *b.* 1934, *m.*

1996 *Taverne,* Dick Taverne, QC, *b.* 1928, *m.*

2010 *Taylor of Goss Moor,* Matthew Owen John Taylor, *b.* 1963, *m.*

2006 *Taylor of Holbeach,* John Derek Taylor, CBE, PC, *b.* 1943, *m.*

1996 *Taylor of Warwick,* John David Beckett Taylor, *b.* 1952, *m.*

1992 *Tebbit,* Norman Beresford Tebbit, CH, PC, *b.* 1931, *m.*

2006 *Teverson,* Robin Teverson, *b.* 1952, *m.*

2013 *Thomas of Cwmgiedd,* Roger John Laugharne Thomas, PC, *b.* 1947, *m.*

1996 *Thomas of Gresford,* Donald Martin Thomas, OBE, QC, *b.* 1937, *m.*

1990 ⟪*Tombs,* Francis Leonard Tombs, FRENG, *b.* 1924, *w.*

1998 *Tomlinson,* John Edward Tomlinson, *b.* 1939, *m.*

1994 *Tope,* Graham Norman Tope, CBE, *b.* 1943, *m.*

2010 *Touhig,* James Donnelly Touhig, PC, *b.* 1947, *m.*

2012 *Trees,* Alexander John Trees, PHD, *b.* 1946, *m.*

2004 *Triesman,* David Maxim Triesman, *b.* 1943 *m.*

2006 *Trimble,* William David Trimble, PC, *b.* 1944, *m.*

2010 *True,* Nicholas Edward True, CBE, *b.* 1951, *m.*

2004 *Truscott,* Dr Peter Derek Truscott, *b.* 1959, *m.*

1993 *Tugendhat,* Christopher Samuel Tugendhat, *b.* 1937, *m.*

2004 *Tunnicliffe,* Denis Tunnicliffe, CBE, *b.* 1943, *m.*

2000 *Turnberg,* Leslie Arnold Turnberg, MD, *b.* 1934, *m.*

2005 *Turnbull,* Andrew Turnbull, KCB, CVO, PC, *b.* 1945, *m.*

2005 *Turner of Ecchinswell,* (Jonathan) Adair Turner, *b.* 1955, *m.*

2005 *Tyler,* Paul Archer Tyler, CBE, PC, *b.* 1941, *m.*

2018 *Tyrie,* Andrew Guy Tyrie, PC, *b.* 1957

2004 *Vallance of Tummel,* Iain (David Thomas) Vallance, *b.* 1943, *m.*

2013 *Verjee,* Rumi Verjee, CBE, *b.* 1957

1985 *Vinson,* Nigel Vinson, LVO, *b.* 1931, *m.*

1992 *Wakeham,* John Wakeham, PC, *b.* 1932, *m.*

1999 *Waldegrave of North Hill,* William Arthur Waldegrave, PC, *b.* 1946, *m.*

2007 *Walker of Aldringham,* Michael John Dawson Walker, GCB, CMG, CBE, *b.* 1944, *m.*

1995 *Wallace of Saltaire,* William John Lawrence Wallace, PC, PHD, *b.* 1941, *m.*

2007 *Wallace of Tankerness,* James Robert Wallace, PC, QC, *b.* 1954, *m.*

1998 *Warner,* Norman Reginald Warner, PC, *b.* 1940, *m.*

2011 *Wasserman,* Gordon Joshua Wasserman, *b.* 1938 *m.*

1997 *Watson of Invergowrie,* Michael Goodall Watson, *b.* 1949, *m.*

1999 *Watson of Richmond,* Alan John Watson, CBE, *b.* 1941, *m.*

2015 *Watts,* David Leonard Watts, *b.* 1951, *m.*

2010 *Wei,* Nathanael Ming-Yan Wei, *b.* 1977, *m.*

2007 *West of Spithead,* Alan William John West, GCB, DSC, PC, *b.* 1948, *m.*

2013   *Whitby,* Michael John Whitby, *b.* 1948 *m.*
1996   *Whitty,* John Lawrence (Larry) Whitty, PC, *b.* 1943, *m.*
2011   *Wigley,* Dafydd Wynne Wigley, PC, *b.* 1943, *m.*
2015   *Willetts,* David Lindsay Willetts, PC, *b.* 1956, *m.*
1985   *Williams of Elvel,* Charles Cuthbert Powell Williams, CBE, PC, *b.* 1933, *m.*
2013   *Williams of Oystermouth,* Rt. Revd Rowan Douglas Williams, PC, Royal Victorian Chain, DPHIL, *b.* 1950, *m.*
2010   *Willis of Knaresborough,* George Philip Willis, *b.* 1941, *m.*
2010   *Wills,* Michael David Wills, PC, *b.* 1952, *m.*
2002   *Wilson of Dinton,* Richard Thomas James Wilson, GCB, *b.* 1942, *m.*
1992   *Wilson of Tillyorn,* David Clive Wilson, KT, GCMG, PHD, *b.* 1935, *m.*
1995   *Winston,* Robert Maurice Lipson Winston, FRCOG, *b.* 1940, *m.*
2010   *Wolfson of Aspley Guise,* Simon Adam Wolfson, *b.* 1967, *m.*
1991   **E.** *Wolfson of Sunningdale,* David Wolfson, *b.* 1935, *m.*
2011   *Wood of Anfield,* Stewart Martin Wood, *b.* 1968, *m.*
1999   *Woolmer of Leeds,* Kenneth John Woolmer, *b.* 1940, *m.*
2013   *Wrigglesworth,* Ian William Wrigglesworth, *b.* 1939, *m.*
1994   *Wright of Richmond,* Patrick Richard Henry Wright, GCMG, *b.* 1931, *m.*
2015   *Young of Cookham,* George Samuel Knatchbull Young, CH, PC, *b.* 1941, *m.*
1984   *Young of Graffham,* David Ivor Young, CH, PC, *b.* 1932, *m.*
2004   *Young of Norwood Green,* Anthony (Ian) Young, *b.* 1942, *m.*

BARONESSES
Created
2005   *Adams of Craigielea,* Katherine Patricia Irene Adams, *b.* 1947, *w.*
2007   *Afshar,* Prof. Haleh Afshar, OBE, *b.* 1944, *m.*
2015   *Altmann,* Dr Rosalind Miriam Altmann, CBE, *b.* 1956, *m.*
1997   *Amos,* Valerie Ann Amos, CH, PC, *b.* 1954
2000   *Andrews,* Elizabeth Kay Andrews, OBE, *b.* 1943
1996   *Anelay of St Johns,* Joyce Anne Anelay, DBE, PC, *b.* 1947, *m.*
2010   *Armstrong of Hill Top,* Hilary Jane Armstrong, PC, *b.* 1945, *m.*
1999   *Ashton of Upholland,* Catherine Margaret Ashton, GCMG, PC, *b.* 1956, *m.*
2011   *Bakewell,* Joan Dawson Bakewell, DBE, *b.* 1933
2013   *Bakewell of Hardington Mandeville,* Catherine Mary Bakewell, MBE, *b.* 1949, *m.*
1999   *Barker,* Elizabeth Jean Barker, *b.* 1961, *m.*
2018   *Barran,* Diana Francesca Caroline Barran, MBE, *b.* 1959, *m.*
2010   *Benjamin,* Floella Karen Yunies Benjamin, OBE, *b.* 1949, *m.*
2011   *Berridge,* Elizabeth Rose Berridge, *b.* 1972
2016   *Bertin,* Gabrielle Louise Bertin, *b.* 1978, *m.*
2000   *Billingham,* Angela Theodora Billingham, DPHIL, *b.* 1939, *w.*
1987   *Blackstone,* Tessa Ann Vosper Blackstone, PC, PHD, *b.* 1942
2019   *Blackwood of North Oxford,* Nicola Claire Blackwood, *b.* 1979, *m.*
1999   ₵*Blood,* May Blood, MBE, *b.* 1938
2016   *Bloomfield of Hinton Waldrist,* Olivia Caroline Bloomfield, *b.* 1960, *m.*

2004   *Bonham-Carter of Yarnbury,* Jane Bonham Carter, *b.* 1957, *w.*
2000   *Boothroyd,* Betty Boothroyd, OM, PC, *b.* 1929
2005   *Bottomley of Nettlestone,* Virginia Hilda Brunette Maxwell Bottomley, PC, *b.* 1948, *m.*
2015   *Bowles of Berkhamsted,* Sharon Margaret Bowles, *b.* 1953, *m.*
2018   *Boycott,* Rosel Marie Boycott, MBE, *b.* 1951, *m.*
2014   *Brady,* Karren Rita Brady, CBE, *b.* 1969, *m.*
2011   *Brinton,* Sarah Virginia Brinton, *b.* 1955, *m.*
2015   *Brown of Cambridge,* Prof. Julia Elizabeth King, DBE, PHD, FRENG, *b.* 1954, *m.*
2010   *Browning,* Angela Frances Browning, *b.* 1946, *m.*
2018   *Bryan of Partick,* Pauline Christina Bryan
2018   *Bull,* Deborah Clare Bull, CBE, *b.* 1963
2015   *Burt of Solihull,* Lorely Jane Burt, *b.* 1954, *m.*
1998   *Buscombe,* Peta Jane Buscombe, *b.* 1954, *m.*
2006   *Butler-Sloss,* (Ann) Elizabeth (Oldfield) Butler-Sloss, GBE, PC, *b.* 1933, *m.*
1996   *Byford,* Hazel Byford, DBE, *b.* 1941, *w.*
2008   *Campbell of Loughborough,* Susan Catherine Campbell, CBE, *b.* 1948
2007   *Campbell of Surbiton,* Jane Susan Campbell, DBE, *b.* 1959, *m.*
2016   *Cavendish of Little Venice,* Hilary Camilla Cavendish, *b.* 1968, *m.*
2016   *Chakrabarti,* Sharmishta Chakrabarti, PC, CBE, *b.* 1969
1992   *Chalker of Wallasey,* Lynda Chalker, PC, *b.* 1942
2014   *Chisholm of Owlpen,* Caroline Elizabeth (Carlyn) Chisholm, *b.* 1951, *m.*
2005   §*Clark of Calton,* Dr Lynda Margaret Clark, PC, *b.* 1949
2000   *Cohen of Pimlico,* Janet Cohen, *b.* 1940, *m.*
2005   *Corston,* Jean Ann Corston, PC, *b.* 1942, *w.*
2007   *Coussins,* Jean Coussins, *b.* 1950, *m.*
2016   *Couttie,* Philippa Marion Roe, *b.* 1962, *m.*
1982   *Cox,* Caroline Anne Cox, *b.* 1937, *w.*
1998   *Crawley,* Christine Mary Crawley, *b.* 1950, *m.*
1990   *Cumberlege,* Julia Frances Cumberlege, CBE, *b.* 1943, *m.*
2005   *Deech,* Ruth Lynn Deech, DBE, *b.* 1943, *m.*
2010   *Donaghy,* Rita Margaret Donaghy, CBE, *b.* 1944, *m.*
2010   *Doocey,* Elizabeth Deirdre Doocey, OBE, *b.* 1948, *m.*
2010   *Drake,* Jean Lesley Patricia Drake, CBE, *b.* 1948, *m.*
2004   *D'Souza,* Dr Frances Gertrude Claire D'Souza, CMG, PC, *b.* 1944, *m.*
1990   ₵*Dunn,* Lydia Selina Dunn, DBE, *b.* 1940, *m.*
2010   *Eaton,* Ellen Margaret Eaton, DBE, *b.* 1942, *m.*
1990   *Eccles of Moulton,* Diana Catherine Eccles, *b.* 1933, *m.*
1997   *Emerton,* Audrey Caroline Emerton, DBE, *b.* 1935
2014   *Evans of Bowes Park,* Natalie Jessica Evans, PC, *b.* 1975, *m.*
2017   *Fairhead,* Rona Alison Fairhead, CBE, *b.* 1961, *m.*
2004   *Falkner of Margravine,* Kishwer Falkner, *b.* 1955, *m.*
2015   *Fall,* Catherine Susan Fall, *b.* 1967, *m.*
2015   *Featherstone,* Lynne Choona Featherstone, PC, *b.* 1951
2001   *Finlay of Llandaff,* Ilora Gillian Finlay, *b.* 1949, *m.*
2015   *Finn,* Simone Jari Finn, *b.* 1968, *m.*
1990   *Flather,* Shreela Flather, *b.* 1934, *w.*
1997   *Fookes,* Janet Evelyn Fookes, DBE, *b.* 1936
2006   *Ford,* Margaret Anne Ford, OBE, *b.* 1957, *m.*
2005   *Fritchie,* Irene Tordoff Fritchie, DBE, *b.* 1942, *w.*
1999   *Gale,* Anita Gale, *b.* 1940
2007   *Garden of Frognal,* Susan Elizabeth Garden, PC, *b.* 1944, *w.*
1981   *Gardner of Parkes,* (Rachel) Trixie (Anne) Gardner, *b.* 1927, *w.*
2013   *Goldie,* Annabel MacNicholl Goldie, *b.* 1950

2001   *Golding,* Llinos Golding, *b.* 1933, *w.*

1998   *Goudie,* Mary Teresa Goudie, *b.* 1946, *m.*

1993   ☾*Gould of Potternewton,* Joyce Brenda Gould, *b.* 1932, *m.*

2001   *Greenfield,* Susan Adele Greenfield, CBE, *b.* 1950

2000   *Greengross,* Sally Ralea Greengross, OBE, *b.* 1935, *w.*

2013   *Grender,* Rosalind Mary Grender, MBE, *b.* 1962 *m.*

2010   *Grey-Thompson,* Tanni Carys Davina Grey-Thompson, DBE, *b.* 1969, *m.*

1991   *Hamwee,* Sally Rachel Hamwee, *b.* 1947

1999   *Hanham,* Joan Brownlow Hanham, CBE, *b.* 1939, *m.*

2014   *Harding of Winscombe,* Diana Mary (Dido) Harding, *b.* 1967, *m.*

1999   *Harris of Richmond,* Angela Felicity Harris, *b.* 1944, *m.*

1996   *Hayman,* Helene Valerie Hayman, GBE, PC, *b.* 1949, *m.*

2010   *Hayter of Kentish Town,* Dr Dianne Hayter, *b.* 1949, *m.*

2010   *Healy of Primrose Hill,* Anna Healy, *b.* 1955, *m.*

2014   *Helic,* Arminka Helic, *b.* 1968

2004   *Henig,* Ruth Beatrice Henig, CBE, *b.* 1943, *m.*

1991   *Hilton of Eggardon,* Jennifer Hilton, QPM, *b.* 1936

2013   *Hodgson of Abinger,* Fiona Ferelith Hodgson, CBE, *b.* 1954, *m.*

1995   *Hogg,* Sarah Elizabeth Mary Hogg, *b.* 1946, *m.*

2010   *Hollins,* Prof. Sheila Clare Hollins, *b.* 1946, *m.*

1985   *Hooper,* Gloria Dorothy Hooper, CMG, *b.* 1939

2001   *Howarth of Breckland,* Valerie Georgina Howarth, OBE, *b.* 1940

2001   *Howe of Idlicote,* Elspeth Rosamond Morton Howe, CBE, *b.* 1932, *w.*

1999   ☾*Howells of St Davids,* Rosalind Patricia-Anne Howells, OBE, *b.* 1931, *m.*

2010   *Hughes of Stretford,* Beverley Hughes, PC, *b.* 1950, *m.*

2013   *Humphreys,* Christine Mary Humphreys, *b.* 1947

2010   *Hussein-Ece,* Meral Hussein Ece, OBE, *b.* 1953

2014   *Janke,* Barbara Lilian Janke, *b.* 1947, *m.*

1992   *Jay of Paddington,* Margaret Ann Jay, PC, *b.* 1939, *m.*

2011   *Jenkin of Kennington,* Anne Caroline Jenkin, *b.* 1955, *m.*

2010   *Jolly,* Judith Anne Jolly, *b.* 1951, *m.*

2013   *Jones of Moulsecoomb,* Jennifer Helen Jones, *b.* 1949

2006   *Jones of Whitchurch,* Margaret Beryl Jones, *b.* 1955

2013   *Kennedy of Cradley,* Alicia Pamela Kennedy, *b.* 1969, *m.*

1997   *Kennedy of the Shaws,* Helena Ann Kennedy, QC, *b.* 1950, *m.*

2012   *Kidron,* Beeban Tania Kidron, OBE, *b.* 1961, *m.*

2011   *King of Bow,* Oona Tamsyn King, *b.* 1967, *m.*

2006   *Kingsmill,* Denise Patricia Byrne Kingsmill, CBE, *b.* 1947, *m.*

2009   *Kinnock of Holyhead,* Glenys Elizabeth Kinnock, *b.* 1944, *m.*

1997   ☾*Knight of Collingtree,* (Joan Christabel) Jill Knight, DBE, *b.* 1927, *w.*

2010   *Kramer,* Susan Veronica Kramer, PC, *b.* 1950, *w.*

2013   *Lane-Fox of Soho,* Martha Lane Fox, CBE, *b.* 1973

2013   *Lawrence of Clarendon,* Doreen Delceita Lawrence, OBE, *b.* 1952

2010   *Liddell of Coatdyke,* Helen Lawrie Liddell, PC, *b.* 1950, *m.*

1997   ☾*Linklater of Butterstone,* Veronica Linklater, *b.* 1943, *m.*

2011   *Lister of Burtersett,* Margot Ruth Aline Lister, CBE, *b.* 1949

1997   *Ludford,* Sarah Ann Ludford, *b.* 1951, *m.*

2004   *McDonagh,* Margaret Josephine McDonagh, *b.* 1961

2015   *McGregor-Smith,* Ruby McGregor-Smith, CBE, *b.* 1963, *m.*

1999   *McIntosh of Hudnall,* Genista Mary McIntosh, *b.* 1946

2015   *McIntosh of Pickering,* Anne Caroline Ballingall McIntosh, *b.* 1954, *m.*

1997   *Maddock,* Diana Margaret Maddock, *b.* 1945, *m.*

1991   *Mallalieu,* Ann Mallalieu, QC, *b.* 1945

2008   *Manningham-Buller,* Elizabeth (Lydia) Manningham-Buller, LG, DCB, *b.* 1948, *m.*

2013   *Manzoor,* Zahida Parveen Manzoor, CBE, *b.* 1958, *m.*

1970   *Masham of Ilton,* Susan Lilian Primrose Cunliffe-Lister, *b.* 1935, *w.*

1999   *Massey of Darwen,* Doreen Elizabeth Massey, *b.* 1938, *m.*

2006   *Meacher,* Molly Christine Meacher, *b.* 1940, *m.*

2018   *Meyer,* Catherine Irene Jacqueline Meyer, CBE, *b.* 1953, *m.*

1998   *Miller of Chilthorne Domer,* Susan Elizabeth Miller, *b.* 1954, *m.*

2014   §*Mobarik,* Nosheena Shaheen Mobarik, CBE, MEP, *b.* 1957, *m.*

2015   *Mone,* Michelle Georgina Mone, OBE, *b.* 1971

2004   *Morgan of Drefelin,* Delyth Jane Morgan, *b.* 1961, *m.*

2011   *Morgan of Ely,* Mair Eluned Morgan, *b.* 1967, *m.*

2001   *Morgan of Huyton,* Sally Morgan, *b.* 1959, *m.*

2004   *Morris of Bolton,* Patricia Morris, OBE, *b.* 1953, *m.*

2005   *Morris of Yardley,* Estelle Morris, PC, *b.* 1952

2004   *Murphy,* Elaine Murphy, *b.* 1947, *m.*

2004   *Neuberger,* Rabbi Julia (Babette Sarah) Neuberger, DBE, *b.* 1950, *m.*

2007   *Neville-Jones,* (Lilian) Pauline Neville-Jones, DCMG, PC, *b.* 1939

2013   *Neville-Rolfe,* Lucy Jeanne Neville-Rolfe, DBE, CMG, *b.* 1953, *m.*

2010   *Newlove,* Helen Margaret Newlove, *b.* 1961, *w.*

1997   *Nicholson of Winterbourne,* Emma Harriet Nicholson, *b.* 1941, *w.*

2000   *Noakes,* Sheila Valerie Masters, DBE, *b.* 1949, *m.*

2000   *Northover,* Lindsay Patricia Granshaw, PC, *b.* 1954

2010   *Nye,* Susan Nye, *b.* 1955, *m.*

1991   *O'Cathain,* Detta O'Cathain, OBE, *b.* 1938, *w.*

2009   *O'Loan,* Nuala Patricia O'Loan, DBE, *b.* 1951, *m.*

1999   *O'Neill of Bengarve,* Onora Sylvia O'Neill, CH, CBE, FRS, FBA, *b.* 1941

1989   ☾*Oppenheim-Barnes,* Sally Oppenheim-Barnes, PC, *b.* 1930, *w.*

2018   *Osamor,* Martha Otito Osamor, *b.* 1940, *w.*

2006   ☾*Paisley of St George's,* Eileen Emily Paisley, *b.* 1931, *w.*

2010   *Parminter,* Kathryn Jane Parminter, *b.* 1964, *m.*

1991   ☾*Perry of Southwark,* Pauline Perry, *b.* 1931, *w.*

2015   *Pidding,* Emma Samantha Pidding, CBE, *b.* 1966

2014   *Pinnock,* Kathryn Mary Pinnock, *b.* 1946, *m.*

1997   *Pitkeathley,* Jill Elizabeth Pitkeathley, OBE, *b.* 1940, *m.*

1999   *Prashar,* Usha Kumari Prashar, CBE, PC, *b.* 1948, *m.*

2015   *Primarolo,* Dawn Primarolo, DBE, PC, *b.* 1954, *m.*

2004   *Prosser,* Margaret Theresa Prosser, OBE, *b.* 1937

2006   *Quin,* Joyce Gwendoline Quin, PC, *b.* 1944

1996   *Ramsay of Cartvale,* Margaret Mildred (Meta) Ramsay, *b.* 1936

2011   *Randerson,* Jennifer Elizabeth Randerson, *b.* 1948, *m.*

1994   *Rawlings,* Patricia Elizabeth Rawlings, *b.* 1939

2014   *Rebuck,* Gail Ruth Rebuck, DBE, *b.* 1952, *w.*

2015   *Redfern,* Elizabeth Marie Redfern, *b.* 1947, *w.*

1998   ☾*Richardson of Calow,* Kathleen Margaret Richardson, OBE, *b.* 1938, *m.*

2015   *Rock,* Kate Harriet Alexandra Rock, *b.* 1968, *m.*

2004   *Royall of Blaisdon,* Janet Anne Royall, PC, *b.* 1955, *m.*

2018	*Sater,* Amanda Jacqueline Sater, *b.* 1960, *m.*
1997	*Scotland of Asthal,* Patricia Janet Scotland, PC, QC, *b.* 1955, *m.*
2015	*Scott of Bybrook,* Jane Antoinette Scott, OBE, *b.* 1947, *m.*
2000	*Scott of Needham Market,* Rosalind Carol Scott, *b.* 1957 *m.*
1991	*Seccombe,* Joan Anna Dalziel Seccombe, DBE, *b.* 1930, *w.*
2010	*Shackleton of Belgravia,* Fiona Sara Shackleton, LVO, *b.* 1956, *m.*
1998	☾*Sharp of Guildford,* Margaret Lucy Sharp, *b.* 1938, *m.*
1973	☾*Sharples,* Pamela Sharples, *b.* 1923, *w.*
2015	*Sheehan,* Shaista Ahmad Sheehan, *b.* 1959, *m.*
2005	*Shephard of Northwold,* Gillian Patricia Shephard, PC, *b.* 1940, *m.*
2010	*Sherlock,* Maeve Christina Mary Sherlock, OBE, *b.* 1960
2014	*Shields,* Joanna Shields, OBE, *b.* 1962, *m.*
2010	*Smith of Basildon,* Angela Evans Smith, PC, *b.* 1959, *m.*
1995	*Smith of Gilmorehill,* Elizabeth Margaret Smith, *b.* 1940, *w.*
2014	*Smith of Newnham,* Dr Julie Elizabeth Smith, *b.* 1969
2010	*Stedman-Scott,* Deborah Stedman-Scott, OBE, *b.* 1955, *c.p.*
1999	*Stern,* Vivien Helen Stern, CBE, *b.* 1941
2011	*Stowell of Beeston,* Tina Wendy Stowell, MBE, PC, *b.* 1967
2015	*Stroud,* Philippa Claire Stroud, *b.* 1965, *m.*
2016	*Sugg,* Elizabeth Grace Sugg, CBE, *b.* 1977
2013	*Suttie,* Alison Mary Suttie, *b.* 1968
1996	*Symons of Vernham Dean,* Elizabeth Conway Symons, PC, *b.* 1951, *w.*
2005	*Taylor of Bolton,* Winifred Ann Taylor, PC, *b.* 1947, *m.*
1994	**E.** *Thomas of Walliswood,* Susan Petronella Thomas, OBE, *b.* 1935, *m.*
2006	*Thomas of Winchester,* Celia Marjorie Thomas, MBE, *b.* 1945
2015	*Thornhill,* Dorothy Thornhill, MBE, *b.* 1955, *m.*
1998	*Thornton,* (Dorothea) Glenys Thornton, *b.* 1952, *m.*
2005	*Tonge,* Dr Jennifer Louise Tonge, *b.* 1941, *m.*
2011	*Tyler of Enfield,* Claire Tyler, *b.* 1957
1998	*Uddin,* Manzila Pola Uddin, *b.* 1959, *m.*
2007	*Vadera,* Shriti Vadera, PC, *b.* 1962
2005	*Valentine,* Josephine Clare Valentine, *b.* 1958, *m.*
2016	*Vere of Norbiton,* Charlotte Sarah Emily Vere, *b.* 1969
2006	*Verma,* Sandip Verma, *b.* 1959, *m.*
2000	*Walmsley,* Joan Margaret Walmsley, *b.* 1943, *m.*
2007	*Warsi,* Sayeeda Hussain Warsi, PC, *b.* 1971, *m.*
1999	*Warwick of Undercliffe,* Diana Mary Warwick, *b.* 1945, *m.*
2015	*Watkins of Tavistock,* Mary Jane Watkins, PHD, *b.* 1955, *m.*
2010	*Wheatcroft,* Patience Jane Wheatcroft, *b.* 1951, *m.*
2010	*Wheeler,* Margaret Eileen Joyce Wheeler, MBE, *b.* 1949
1999	*Whitaker,* Janet Alison Whitaker, *b.* 1936, *w.*
1996	*Wilcox,* Judith Ann Wilcox, *b.* 1940, *w.*
1999	☾*Wilkins,* Rosalie Catherine Wilkins, *b.* 1946
1993	☾*Williams of Crosby,* Shirley Vivien Teresa Brittain Williams, CH, PC, *b.* 1930, *w.*
2013	*Williams of Trafford,* Susan Frances Maria Williams, *b.* 1967, *m.*
2014	*Wolf of Dulwich,* Alison Margaret Wolf, CBE, *b.* 1949, *m.*
2011	*Worthington,* Bryony Katherine Worthington, *b.* 1971, *m.*
2017	*Wyld,* Laura Lee Wyld, *b.* 1978, *m.*
2004	*Young of Hornsey,* Prof. Margaret Omolola Young, OBE, *b.* 1951, *m.*
1997	*Young of Old Scone,* Barbara Scott Young, *b.* 1948

COURTESY TITLES

The heir apparent to a Duke, Marquess or Earl uses the highest of his father's other titles as a courtesy title. For example, the Marquess of Blandford is heir to the Dukedom of Marlborough, and Viscount Amberley to the Earldom of Russell. Titles of second heirs (when in use) are also given, and the courtesy title of the father of a second heir is indicated by * eg Earl of Mornington, eldest son of *Marquess of Douro.

The holder of a courtesy title is not styled 'the Most Hon.' or 'the Rt. Hon.', and in correspondence 'the' is omitted before the title. The heir apparent to a Scottish title may use the title 'Master'.

MARQUESSES
Blandford – *Marlborough, D.*
Douglas and Clydesdale – *Hamilton and Brandon, D.*
Graham – *Montrose, D.*
Granby – *Rutland, D.*
*Hamilton – *Abercorn, D.*
Lorne – *Argyll, D.*
Stafford – *Sutherland, D.*
Tavistock – *Bedford, D.*
Tullibardine – *Atholl, D.*
Worcester – *Beaufort, D.*

EARLS
*Aboyne – *Huntly, M.*
Altamont – *Sligo, M.*
Arundel and Surrey – *Norfolk, D.*
Bective – *Headfort, M.*

Belfast – *Donegall, M.*
Brecknock – *Camden, M.*
*Burford – *St Albans, D.*
*Burlington – *Devonshire, D.*
*Cardigan – *Ailesbury, M.*
Cassilis – *Ailsa, M.*
Compton – *Northampton, M.*
Dalkeith – *Buccleuch and Queensberry, D.*
Dumfries – *Bute, M.*
Euston – *Grafton, D.*
*Haddo – *Aberdeen and Temair, M.*
Hillsborough – *Downshire, M.*
*Hopetoun – *Linlithgow, M.*
Kerry – *Lansdowne, M.*
March and Kinrara – *Richmond, Gordon and Lennox, D.*

Medina – *Milford Haven, M.*
*Mornington – *Wellington, D.*
*Mount Charles – *Conyngham, M.*
Mulgrave – *Normanby, M.*
Percy – *Northumberland, D.*
Rocksavage – *Cholmondeley, M.*
Ronaldshay – *Zetland, M.*
*St Andrews – *Kent, D.*
Southesk – *Fife, D.*
Tyrone – *Waterford, M.*
*Ulster – *Gloucester, D.*
Uxbridge – *Anglesey, M.*
*Wiltshire – *Winchester, M.*
Yarmouth – *Hertford, M.*

VISCOUNTS
Aithrie – *Hopetoun, E.*
Alexander – *Caledon, E.*
Althorp – *Spencer, E.*
Andover – *Suffolk and Berkshire, E.*
Anson – *Lichfield, E.*
Asquith – *Oxford and Asquith, E.*
Borodale – *Beatty, E.*
Bury – *Albemarle, E.*
Campden – *Gainsborough, E.*
Carlow – *Portarlington, E.*
Carlton – *Wharncliffe, E.*
Chelsea – *Cadogan, E.*
Chewton – *Waldegrave, E.*
Clanfield – *Peel, E.*
Clive – *Powis, E.*
Coke – *Leicester, E.*

Corry – *Belmore, E.*
Corvedale – *Baldwin of Bewdley, E.*
Cranborne – *Salisbury, M.*
Curzon – *Howe, E.*
Dalrymple – *Stair, E.*
Dangan – *Cowley, E.*
Drumlanrig – *Queensberry, M.*
Duncannon – *Bessborough, E.*
Dungarvan – *Cork and Orrery, E.*
Dunluce – *Antrim, E.*
Dunwich – *Stradbroke, E.*
Dupplin – *Kinnoull, E.*
Elveden – *Iveagh, E.*
Emlyn – *Cawdor, E.*
Encombe – *Eldon, E.*
Enfield – *Strafford, E.*
Erleigh – *Reading, M.*
Errington – *Cromer, E.*
Feilding – *Denbigh and Desmond, E.*
FitzHarris – *Malmesbury, E.*
Folkestone – *Radnor, E.*
Forbes – *Granard, E.*
Formartine – **Haddo, E.*
Garmoyle – *Cairns, E.*
Garnock – *Lindsay, E.*
Glenapp – *Inchcape, E.*
Glerawly – *Annesley, E.*
Grey de Wilton – *Wilton, E.*
Grimston – *Verulam, E.*
Gwynedd – *Lloyd George of Dwyfor, E.*
Hawkesbury – *Liverpool, E.*
Hinchingbrooke – *Sandwich, E.*
Howick – *Grey, E.*
Ikerrin – *Carrick, E.*
Ingestre – *Shrewsbury and Waterford, E.*

Jocelyn – *Roden, E.*
Kelburn – *Glasgow, E.*
Kingsborough – *Kingston, E.*
Kirkwall – *Orkney, E.*
Knebworth – *Lytton, E.*
Lambton – *Durham, E.*
Lascelles – *Harewood, E.*
Linley – *Snowdon, E.*
Lymington – *Portsmouth, E.*
Macmillan of Ovenden – *Stockton, E.*
Maidstone – *Winchilsea and Nottingham, E.*
Maitland – *Lauderdale, E.*
Marsham – *Romney, E.*
Melgund – *Minto, E.*
Merton – *Nelson, E.*
Moore – *Drogheda, E.*
Newport – *Bradford, E.*
Newry and Mourne – *Kilmorey, E.*
Northland – *Ranfurly, E.*
Pery – *Limerick, E.*
Petersham – *Harrington, E.*
Pollington – *Mexborough, E.*
Raynham – *Townshend, M.*
Reidhaven – *Seafield, E.*
Royston – *Hardwicke, E.*
Ruthven of Canberra – *Gowrie, E.*
St Cyres – *Iddesleigh, E.*
Sandon – *Harrowby, E.*
Savernake – **Cardigan, E.*
Severn – *Wessex, E.*
Slane – **Mount Charles, E.*
Somerton – *Normanton, E.*
Stopford – *Courtown, E.*
Stormont – *Mansfield and Mansfield, E.*
Strabane – **Hamilton, M.*

Strathallan – *Perth, E.*
Stuart – *Castle Stewart, E.*
Suirdale – *Donoughmore, E.*
Tamworth – *Ferrers, E.*
Tarbat – *Cromartie, E.*
Villiers – *Jersey, E.*
Wellesley – **Mornington, E.*
Weymouth – *Bath, M.*
Windsor – *Plymouth, E.*
Wolmer – *Selborne, E.*
Woodstock – *Portland, E.*

BARONS (LORDS)
Aberdour – *Morton, E.*
Apsley – *Bathurst, E.*
Ardee – *Meath, E.*
Ashley – *Shaftesbury, E.*
Balniel – *Crawford and Balcarres, E.*
Berriedale – *Caithness, E.*
Brabourne – *Mountbatten of Burma, E.*
Brooke – *Warwick and Brooke, E.*
Bruce – *Elgin and Kincardine, E.*
Buckhurst – *De La Warr, E.*
Burghley – *Exeter, M.*
Cardross – *Buchan, E.*
Cavendish – **Burlington, E.*
Clifton – *Darnley, E.*
Cochrane – *Dundonald, E.*
Courtenay – *Devon, E.*
Culloden – ** Ulster, E.*
Dalmeny – *Rosebery, E.*
Doune – *Moray, E.*
Downpatrick – **St Andrews, E.*
Dunglass – *Home, E.*
Elcho – *Wemyss and March, E.*
Gillford – *Clanwilliam, E.*

Greenock – *Cathcart, E.*
Guernsey – *Aylesford, E.*
Hay – *Erroll, E.*
Herbert – *Pembroke and Montgomery, E.*
Howard of Effingham – *Effingham, E.*
Huntingtower – *Dysart, E.*
Hyde – *Clarendon, E.*
Inverurie – *Kintore, E.*
Irwin – *Halifax, E.*
Johnstone – *Annandale and Hartfell, E.*
Leveson – *Granville, E.*
Loughborough – *Rosslyn, E.*
Masham – *Swinton, E.*
Medway – *Cranbrook, E.*
Montgomerie – *Eglinton and Winton, E.*
Moreton – *Ducie, E.*
Naas – *Mayo, E.*
Norreys – *Lindsey and Abingdon, E.*
North – *Guilford, E.*
Ogilvy – *Airlie, E.*
Oxmantown – *Rosse, E.*
Porchester – *Carnarvon, E.*
Ramsay – *Dalhousie, E.*
St John – **Wiltshire, E.*
Scrymgeour – *Dundee, E.*
Seymour – *Somerset, D.*
Stanley – *Derby, E.*
Strathavon – **Aboyne, E.*
Strathnaver – *Sutherland, C.*
Vere of Hanworth – **Burford, E.*
Wodehouse – *Kimberley, E.*
Worsley – *Yarborough, E.*

PEERS' SURNAMES

The following symbols indicate the rank of the peer holding each title:

C. Countess
D. Duke
E. Earl
M. Marquess
V. Viscount
*   Life Peer

Where no designation is given, the title is that of a hereditary Baron or Baroness.

Abney-Hastings – *Loudoun, E.*
Acheson – *Gosford, E.*
Adams – *A. of Craigielea**
Adderley – *Norton*
Addington – *Sidmouth, V.*
Agar – *Normanton, E.*
Agnew – *A. of Oulton**
Ahmad – *A. of Wimbledon**
Aitken – *Beaverbrook*
Akers-Douglas – *Chilston, V.*
Alexander – *A. of Tunis, E.*

Alexander – *Caledon, E.*
Allan – *A. of Hallam**
Allen – *A. of Kensington**
Allsopp – *Hindlip*
Alton – *A. of Liverpool**
Anderson – *A. of Ipswich**
Anderson – *A. of Swansea**
Anderson – *Waverley, V.*
Anelay – *A. of St Johns**
Annesley – *Valentia, V.*
Anson – *Lichfield, E.*
Arbuthnot – *A. of Edrom**
Archer – *A. of Weston-super-Mare**
Armstrong – *A. of Hill Top**
Armstrong – *A. of Ilminster**
Armstrong-Jones – *Snowdon, E.*
Arthur – *Glenarthur*
Arundell – *Talbot of Malahide*
Ashley-Cooper – *Shaftesbury, E.*
Ashton – *A. of Hyde*
Ashton – *A. of Upholland**

Asquith – *Oxford and Asquith, E.*
Assheton – *Clitheroe*
Astley – *Hastings*
Astor – *A. of Hever*
Aubrey-Fletcher – *Braye*
Bailey – *Glanusk*
Baillie – *Burton*
Baillie Hamilton – *Haddington, E.*
Baker – *B. of Dorking**
Bakewell – *B. of Hardington Mandeville**
Balchin – *Lingfield**
Baldwin – *B. of Bewdley, E.*
Balfour – *Kinross*
Balfour – *Riverdale*
Bampfylde – *Poltimore*
Banbury – *B. of Southam*
Baring – *Ashburton*
Baring – *Cromer, E.*
Baring – *Howick of Glendale*
Baring – *Northbrook*
Baring – *Revelstoke*

Barker – *B. of Battle**
Barnes – *Gorell*
Barnewall – *Trimlestown*
Bassam – *B. of Brighton**
Bathurst – *Bledisloe, V.*
Beamish – *Dacre*
Beauclerk – *St Albans, D.*
Beaumont – *Allendale, V.*
Beckett – *Grimthorpe*
Benn – *Stansgate, V.*
Bennet – *Tankerville, E.*
Bentinck – *Portland, E.*
Beresford – *Decies*
Beresford – *Waterford, M.*
Berkeley – *B. of Knighton**
Berry – *Camrose, V.*
Berry – *Kemsley, V.*
Bertie – *Lindsey and Abingdon, E.*
Best – *Wynford*
Bethell – *Westbury*
Bewicke-Copley – *Cromwell*
Bigham – *Mersey, V.*
Bingham – *Clanmorris*

Gathorne-Hardy – *Cranbrook, E.*

Gibbs – *Aldenham*

Gibbs – *Wraxall*

Gibson – *Ashbourne*

Gilbert – *G. of Panteg*

Gilbey – *Vaux of Harrowden*

Glyn – *Wolverton*

Goddard – *G. of Stockport*

Godley – *Kilbracken*

Golding – *G. of Newcastle-under-Lyme*

Gordon – *Aberdeen and Temair, M.*

Gordon – *G. of Strathblane*

Gordon – *Huntly, M.*

Gordon Lennox – *Richmond, Gordon and Lennox, D.*

Gore – *Arran, E.*

Gould – *G. of Potternewton*

Grade – *G. of Yarmouth*

Graham – *G. of Edmonton*

Graham – *Montrose, D.*

Graham-Toler – *Norbury, E.*

Granshaw – *Northover*

Grant of Grant – *Strathspey*

Grant of Rothiemurchus – *Dysart, E.*

Green – *G. of Deddington*

Green – *G. of Hurstpierpoint*

Greenall – *Daresbury*

Greville – *Warwick and Brooke, E.*

Griffiths – *G. of Burry Port*

Griffiths – *G. of Fforestfach*

Grigg – *Altrincham*

Grimston – *G. of Westbury*

Grimston – *Verulam, E.*

Grosvenor – *Westminster, D.*

Grosvenor – *Wilton, E.*

Guest – *Wimborne, V.*

Gueterbock – *Berkeley*

Guinness – *Iveagh, E.*

Guinness – *Moyne*

Gully – *Selby, V.*

Gummer – *Chadlington*

Gummer – *Deben*

Gurdon – *Cranworth*

Guthrie – *G. of Craigiebank*

Gwynne Jones – *Chalfont*

Hague – *H. of Richmond*

Hale – *H. of Richmond*

Hall – *H. of Birkenhead*

Hamilton – *Abercorn, D.*

Hamilton – *Belhaven and Stenton*

Hamilton – *H. of Dalzell*

Hamilton – *H. of Epsom*

Hamilton – *Holm Patrick*

Hamilton-Russell – *Boyne, V.*

Hamilton-Smith – *Colwyn*

Hanbury-Tracy – *Sudeley*

Handcock – *Castlemaine*

Hannay – *H. of Chiswick*

Harbord-Hamond – *Suffield*

Harding – *H. of Petherton*

Harding – *H. of Winscombe*

Hardinge – *H. of Penshurst*

Hare – *Blakenham, V.*

Hare – *Listowel, E.*

Harmsworth – *Rothermere, V.*

Harries – *H. of Pentregarth*

Harris – *H. of Haringey*

Harris – *H. of Peckham*

Harris – *H. of Richmond*

Harris – *Malmesbury, E.*

Harvey – *H. of Tasburgh*

Hastings – *H. of Scarisbrick*

Hastings Bass – *Huntingdon, E.*

Hay – *Erroll, E.*

Hay – *H. of Ballyore*

Hay – *Kinnoull, E.*

Hay – *Tweeddale, M.*

Hayter – *H. of Kentish Town*

Healy – *H. of Primrose Hill*

Heathcote-Drummond-Willoughby – *Willoughby de Eresby*

Hely-Hutchinson – *Donoughmore, E.*

Henderson – *Faringdon*

Hennessy – *H. of Nympsfield*

Hennessy – *Windlesham*

Henniker-Major – *Henniker*

Hepburne-Scott – *Polwarth*

Herbert – *Carnarvon, E.*

Herbert – *Hemingford*

Herbert – *Pembroke and Montgomery, E.*

Herbert – *Powis, E.*

Hervey – *Bristol, M.*

Hewitt – *Lifford, V.*

Heywood – *H. of Whitehall*

Hicks Beach – *St Aldwyn, E.*

Hill – *Downshire, M.*

Hill – *H. of Oareford*

Hill-Trevor – *Trevor*

Hilton – *H. of Eggardon*

Hobart-Hampden – *Buckinghamshire, E.*

Hodgson – *H. of Abinger*

Hodgson – *H. of Astley Abbotts*

Hogg – *Hailsham, V.*

Holland-Hibbert – *Knutsford, V.*

Holmes – *H. of Richmond*

Holmes à Court – *Heytesbury*

Hood – *Bridport, V.*

Hope – *Glendevon*

Hope – *H. of Craighead*

Hope – *H. of Thornes*

Hope – *Linlithgow, M.*

Hope – *Rankeillour*

Hope Johnstone – *Annandale and Hartfell, E.*

Hope-Morley – *Hollenden*

Hopkinson – *Colyton*

Hore Ruthven – *Gowrie, E.*

Houghton – *H. of Richmond*

Hovell-Thurlow-Cumming-Bruce – *Thurlow*

Howard – *Carlisle, E.*

Howard – *Effingham, E.*

Howard – *H. of Lympne*

Howard – *H. of Penrith*

Howard – *H. of Rising*

Howard – *Strathcona and Mount Royal*

Howard – *Suffolk and Berkshire, E.*

Howarth – *H. of Breckland*

Howarth – *H. of Newport*

Howe – *H. of Idlicote*

Howell – *H. of Guildford*

Howells – *H. of St. Davids*

Hubbard – *Addington*

Huggins – *Malvern, V.*

Hughes – *H. of Stretford*

Hughes – *H. of Woodside*

Hughes-Young – *St Helens*

Hunt – *H. of Chesterton*

Hunt – *H. of Kings Heath*

Hunt – *H. of Wirral*

Hurd – *H. of Westwell*

Hutton – *H. of Furness*

Ingrams – *Darcy de Knayth*

Innes-Ker – *Roxburghe, D.*

Inskip – *Caldecote, V.*

Irby – *Boston*

Irvine – *I. of Lairg*

Isaacs – *Reading, M.*

James – *J. of Blackheath*

James – *Northbourne*

Jay – *J. of Ewelme*

Jay – *J. of Paddington*

Jenkin – *J. of Kennington*

Jervis – *St Vincent, V.*

Jocelyn – *Roden, E.*

Jolliffe – *Hylton*

Jones – *J. of Birmingham*

Jones – *J. of Cheltenham*

Jones – *J. of Moulsecoomb*

Jones – *J. of Whitchurch*

Joynson-Hicks – *Brentford, V.*

Kay-Shuttleworth – *Shuttleworth*

Kearley – *Devonport, V.*

Keith – *Kintore, E.*

Kemp – *Rochdale, V.*

Kennedy – *Ailsa, M.*

Kennedy – *K. of Cradley*

Kennedy – *K. of Southwark*

Kennedy – *K. of the Shaws*

Kenworthy – *Strabolgi*

Keppel – *Albemarle, E.*

Kerr – *Herries of Terregles*

Kerr – *K. of Kinlochard*

Kerr – *K. of Tonaghmore*

Kerr – *Lothian, M. / K. of Monteviot*

Kerr – *Teviot*

King – *Brown of Cambridge*

King – *K. of Bow*

King – *K. of Lothbury*

King-Tenison – *Kingston, E.*

Kinnock – *K. of Holyhead*

Kirkham – *Berners*

Kirkhope – *K. of Harrogate*

Kirkwood – *K. of Kirkhope*

Knatchbull – *Brabourne*

Knatchbull – *Mountbatten of Burma, E.*

Knight – *K. of Collingtree*

Knight – *K. of Weymouth*

Knox – *Ranfurly, E.*

Lamb – *Rochester*

Lambart – *Cavan, E.*

Lambton – *Durham, E.*

Lamont – *L. of Lerwick*

Lampson – *Killearn*

Lane Fox – *L.-F. of Soho*

Lang – *L. of Monkton*

Lascelles – *Harewood, E.*

Law – *Coleraine*

Law – *Ellenborough*

Lawrence – *L. of Clarendon*

Lawrence – *Trevethin and Oaksey*

Lawson – *Burnham*

Lawson – *L. of Blaby*

Lawson Johnston – *Luke*

Lea – *L. of Crondall*

Lee – *L. of Trafford*

Legge – *Dartmouth, E.*

Legh – *Newton*

Leigh – *L. of Hurley*

Leith – *Burgh*

Lennox-Boyd – *Boyd of Merton, V.*

Le Poer Trench – *Clancarty, E.*

Leslie – *Rothes, E.*

Leslie Melville – *Leven and Melville, E.*

Lester – *L. of Herne Hill*

Levene – *L. of Portsoken*

Leveson-Gower – *Granville, E.*

Lewis – *Merthyr*

Liddell – *L. of Coatdyke*

Liddell – *Ravensworth*

Lindesay-Bethune – *Lindsay, E.*

Lindsay – *Crawford and Balcarres, E.*

Lindsay – *L. of Birker*

Linklater – *L. of Butterstone*

Lister – *L. of Burtersett*

Littleton – *Hatherton*

Livingston – *L. of Parkhead*

Llewellyn – *L. of Steep*

Lloyd – *L. of Berwick*

Lloyd George – *Lloyd George of Dwyfor, E.*

Lloyd George – *Tenby, V.*

Lloyd-Mostyn – *Mostyn*

Loder – *Wakehurst*

Lopes – *Roborough*

Lord – *Framlingham*

Low – *Aldington*

Low – *L. of Dalston*

Lowry-Corry – *Belmore, E.*

Lowther – *Lonsdale, E.*

Lowther – *Ullswater, V.*

Lubbock – *Avebury*

Lucas – *L. of Chilworth*

Lumley – *Scarbrough, E.*

Lumley-Savile – *Savile*

Lyon-Dalberg-Acton – *Acton*

Lysaght – *Lisle*

Lyttelton – *Chandos, V.*

Lyttelton – *Cobham, V.*

Lytton Cobbold – *Cobbold*

McClintock-Bunbury – *Rathdonnell*

McColl – *M. of Dulwich*

McConnell – *M. of Glenscorrodale**

McCrea – *M. of Magherafelt and Cookstown**

Macdonald – *M. of River Glaven**

Macdonald – *M. of Tradeston**

McDonnell – *Antrim, E.*

McFall – *M. of Alcluith**

Macfarlane – *M. of Bearsden**

MacGregor – *M. of Pulham Market**

McInnes – *M. of Kilwinning**

McIntosh – *M. of Hudnall**

McIntosh – *M. of Pickering**

Mackay – *Inchcape, E.*

Mackay – *M. of Clashfern**

Mackay – *Reay*

Mackay – *Tanlaw**

Mackenzie – *Cromartie, E.*

MacKenzie – *M. of Culkein**

Mackenzie – *M. of Framwellgate**

McKenzie – *M. of Luton**

Mackintosh – *M. of Halifax, V.*

McLaren – *Aberconway*

MacLaurin – *M. of Knebworth**

Maclean – *Blencathra**

Maclennan – *M. of Rogart**

Macmillan – *Stockton, E.*

McNicol – *M. of West Kilbride**

Macpherson – *M. of Drumochter*

Macpherson – *M. of Earl's Court**

Macpherson – *Strathcarron*

Maffey – *Rugby*

Magan – *M. of Castletown**

Maginnis – *M. of Drumglass**

Maitland – *Lauderdale, E.*

Makgill – *Oxfuird, V.*

Makins – *Sherfield*

Manners – *Rutland, D.*

Manningham-Buller – *Dilhorne, V.*

Mansfield – *Sandhurst*

Marks – *M. of Broughton*

Marks – *M. of Henley-on-Thames**

Marquis – *Woolton, E.*

Marsham – *Romney, E.*

Martyn-Hemphill – *Hemphill*

Massey – *M. of Darwen**

Masters – *Noakes**

Maude – *Hawarden, V.*

Maude – *M. of Horsham**

Maxwell – *de Ros*

Maxwell – *Farnham*

May – *M. of Oxford**

Meade – *Clanwilliam, E.*

Mercer Nairne Petty-Fitzmaurice – *Lansdowne, M.*

Methuen-Campbell – *Methuen*

Millar – *Inchyra*

Miller – *M. of Chilthorne Domer**

Milner – *M. of Leeds*

Mitchell-Thomson – *Selsdon*

Mitford – *Redesdale*

Monckton – *Galway, V.*

Monckton – *M. of Brenchley, V.*

Money-Coutts – *Latymer*

Montagu – *Manchester, D.*

Montagu – *Sandwich, E.*

Montagu – *Swaythling*

Montagu Douglas Scott – *Buccleuch and Queensberry, D.*

Montagu Stuart Wortley – *Wharncliffe, E.*

Montague – *Amwell*

Montgomerie – *Eglinton and Winton, E.*

Montgomery – *M. of Alamein, V.*

Moore – *Drogheda, E.*

Moore-Brabazon – *Brabazon of Tara*

Moreton – *Ducie, E.*

Morgan – *M. of Drefelin**

Morgan – *M. of Ely**

Morgan – *M. of Huyton**

Morris – *Killanin*

Morris – *M. of Aberavon**

Morris – *M. of Bolton**

Morris – *M. of Handsworth**

Morris – *M. of Kenwood*

Morris – *M. of Yardley**

Morris – *Naseby**

Morrison – *Dunrossil, V.*

Morrison – *Margadale*

Mosley – *Ravensdale*

Mountbatten – *Milford Haven, M.*

Muff – *Calverley*

Mulholland – *Dunleath*

Murphy – *M. of Torfaen**

Murray – *Atholl, D.*

Murray – *Dunmore, E.*

Murray – *Mansfield and Mansfield, E.*

Nall-Cain – *Brocket*

Napier – *Napier and Ettrick*

Napier – *N. of Magdala*

Needham – *Kilmorey, E.*

Nelson – *N. of Stafford*

Neuberger – *N. of Abbotsbury**

Nevill – *Abergavenny, M.*

Neville – *Braybrooke*

Nicholls – *N. of Birkenhead**

Nicolson – *Carnock*

Nicolson – *N. of Winterbourne**

Nivison – *Glendyne*

Noel – *Gainsborough, E.*

North – *Guilford, E.*

Northcote – *Iddesleigh, E.*

Norton – *Grantley*

Norton – *N. of Louth**

Norton – *Rathcreedan*

Nugent – *Westmeath, E.*

Oakeshott – *O. of Seagrove Bay**

O'Brien – *Inchiquin*

Ogilvie-Grant – *Seafield, E.*

Ogilvy – *Airlie, E.*

O'Neill – *O'N. of Bengarve**

O'Neill – *O'N. of Clackmannan**

O'Neill – *O'N. of Gatley**

O'Neill – *Rathcavan*

Orde-Powlett – *Bolton*

Ormsby-Gore – *Harlech*

Paget – *Anglesey, M.*

Paisley – *P. of St George's**

Pakenham – *Longford, E.*

Pakington – *Hampton*

Palmer – *Lucas and Dingwall*

Palmer – *P. of Childs Hill**

Palmer – *Selborne, E.*

Palumbo – *P. of Southwark**

Parker – *Macclesfield, E.*

Parker – *Morley, E.*

Parnell – *Congleton*

Parsons – *Rosse, E.*

Patel – *P. of Bradford**

Patten – *P. of Barnes**

Paulet – *Winchester, M.*

Pearson – *Cowdray, V.*

Pearson – *P. of Rannoch**

Pease – *Gainford*

Pelham – *Chichester, E.*

Pelham – *Yarborough, E.*

Pellew – *Exmouth, V.*

Penny – *Marchwood, V.*

Pepys – *Cottenham, E.*

Percy – *Northumberland, D.*

Perry – *P. of Southwark**

Pery – *Limerick, E.*

Philipps – *Milford*

Philipps – *St Davids, V.*

Phillips – *P. of Sudbury**

Phillips – *P. of Worth Matravers**

Phipps – *Normanby, M.*

Plant – *P. of Highfield**

Pleydell-Bouverie – *Radnor, E.*

Plumptre – *Fitzwalter*

Plunkett – *Dunsany*

Plunkett – *Louth*

Pollock – *Hanworth, V.*

Pomeroy – *Harberton, V.*

Ponsonby – *Bessborough, E.*

Ponsonby – *de Mauley*

Ponsonby – *P. of Shulbrede*

Porter – *P. of Spalding**

Powell – *P. of Bayswater**

Powys – *Lilford*

Pratt – *Camden, M.*

Preston – *Gormanston, V.*

Primrose – *Rosebery, E.*

Prittie – *Dunalley*

Purvis – *P. of Tweed**

Ramsay – *Dalhousie, E.*

Ramsay – *R. of Cartvale**

Ramsbotham – *Soulbury, V.*

Randall –R. of Uxbridge**

Rees – *R. of Ludlow**

Rees-Williams – *Ogmore*

Reid – *R. of Cardowan**

Renfrew – *R. of Kaimsthorn**

Renton – *R. of Mount Harry**

Renwick – *R. of Clifton**

Rhys – *Dynevor*

Richards – *Milverton*

Richards – *R. of Herstmonceux**

Richardson – *R. of Calow**

Ritchie – *R. of Dundee*

Roberts – *Clwyd*

Roberts – *R. of Llandudno**

Robertson – *R. of Oakridge*

Robertson – *R. of Port Ellen**

Robertson – *Wharton*

Robinson – *Martonmere*

Roche – *Fermoy*

Rodd – *Rennell*

Rodgers – *R. of Quarry Bank**

Roe – *Couttie**

Rogers – *Lisvane**

Rogers – *R. of Riverside**

Roper-Curzon – *Teynham*

Rose – *R. of Monewden**

Rospigliosi – *Newburgh, E.*

Rous – *Stradbroke, E.*

Rowley-Conwy – *Langford*

Royall – *R. of Blaisdon**

Runciman – *R. of Doxford, V.*

Russell – *Ampthill*

Russell – *Bedford, D.*

Russell – *de Clifford*

Russell – *R. of Liverpool*

Ryder – *Harrowby, E.*

Ryder – *R. of Wensum**

Sackville – *De La Warr, E.*

Sackville-West – *Sackville*

Sainsbury – *S. of Preston Candover**

Sainsbury – *S. of Turville**

St Aubyn – *St Levan*

St Clair – *Sinclair*

St Clair-Erskine – *Rosslyn, E.*

St John – *Bolingbroke and St John, V.*

St John – *St John of Bletso*

St Leger – *Doneraile, V.*

Samuel – *Bearsted, V.*

Sanderson – *S. of Ayot*

Sanderson – *S. of Bowden**

Sandilands – *Torphichen*

Saumarez – *de Saumarez*

Savile – *Mexborough, E.*

Saville – *S. of Newdigate**

Scarlett – *Abinger*

Schreiber – *Marlesford**

Sclater-Booth – *Basing*

Scotland – *S. of Asthal**

Scott – *Eldon, E.*

Scott – *S. of Bybrook**

Scott – *S. of Foscote**

Scott – *S. of Needham Market**

Scrymgeour – *Dundee, E.*

Seager – *Leighton of St Mellons*

Seely – *Mottistone*

Seymour – *Hertford, M.*

Seymour – *Somerset, D.*

Shackleton – *S. of Belgravia**

Sharp – *S. of Guildford**

Shaw – *Craigmyle*

Shaw – *S. of Northstead**

Shephard – *S. of Northwold**

Sherbourne – *S. of Didsbury**

Shirley – *Ferrers, E.*

Shutt – S. of Greetland*
Siddeley – Kenilworth
Sidney – De L'Isle, V.
Simon – S. of Highbury*
Simon – S. of Wythenshawe
Simpson – S. of Dunkeld*
Sinclair – Caithness, E.
Sinclair – S. of Cleeve
Sinclair – Thurso, V.
Singh – S. of Wimbledon*
Skeffington – Massereene and Ferrard, V.
Smith – Bicester
Smith – Hambleden, V.
Smith – Kirkhill*
Smith – S. of Basildon*
Smith – S. of Clifton*
Smith – S. of Finsbury*
Smith – S. of Gilmorehill*
Smith – S. of Hindhead*
Smith – S. of Kelvin*
Smith – S. of Leigh*
Smith – S. of Newnham*
Somerset – Beaufort, D.
Somerset – Raglan
Spencer – Churchill
Spencer-Churchill – Marlborough, D.
Spring – Risby*
Spring Rice – Monteagle of Brandon
Stanhope – Harrington, E.
Stanley – Derby, E.
Stanley – S. of Alderley and Sheffield
Stapleton-Cotton – Combermere, V.
Steel – S. of Aikwood*
Sterling – S. of Plaistow*
Stern – S. of Brentford*
Stevens – S. of Kirkwhelpington*

Stevens – S. of Ludgate*
Stevenson – S. of Balmacara*
Stevenson – S. of Coddenham*
Stewart – Galloway, E.
Stoddart – S. of Swindon*
Stone – S. of Blackheath*
Stoneham – S. of Droxford*
Stonor – Camoys
Stopford – Courtown, E.
Stourton – Mowbray, Segrave and S.
Stowell – S. of Beeston*
Strachey – O'Hagan
Strutt – Belper
Strutt – Rayleigh
Stuart – Castle Stewart, E.
Stuart – Moray, E.
Stuart – S. of Findhorn, V.
Suenson-Taylor – Grantchester
Symons – S. of Vernham Dean*
Taylor – Kilclooney*
Taylor – T. of Bolton*
Taylor – T. of Goss Moor*
Taylor – T. of Holbeach*
Taylor – T. of Warwick*
Taylour – Headfort, M.
Temple-Gore-Langton – Temple of Stowe, E.
Tennant – Glenconner
Thellusson – Rendlesham
Thesiger – Chelmsford, V.
Thomas – T. of Cwmgiedd*
Thomas – T. of Gresford*
Thomas – T. of Walliswood*
Thomas – T. of Winchester*
Thomson – T. of Fleet
Thynn – Bath, M.
Tottenham – Ely, M.
Trefusis – Clinton
Trench – Ashtown
Tufton – Hothfield
Turner – Netherthorpe

Turner – T. of Ecchinswell*
Turnour – Winterton, E.
Tyler – T. of Enfield*
Tyrell-Kenyon – Kenyon
Vallance – V. of Tummel*
Vanden-Bempde-Johnstone – Derwent
Vane – Barnard
Vane-Tempest-Stewart – Londonderry, M.
Vanneck – Huntingfield
Vaughan – Lisburne, E.
Vere – V. of Norbiton*
Vereker – Gort, V.
Verney – Willoughby de Broke
Vernon – Lyveden
Vesey – de Vesci, V.
Villiers – Clarendon, E.
Vivian – Swansea
Waldegrave – W. of North Hill*
Walker – W. of Aldringham*
Walker – W. of Gestingthorpe*
Wallace – Dudley
Wallace – W. of Saltaire*
Wallace – W. of Tankerness*
Wallop – Portsmouth, E.
Ward – Bangor, V.
Ward – Dudley, E.
Warrender – Bruntisfield
Warwick – W. of Undercliffe*
Watkins – W. of Tavistock*
Watson – Manton
Watson – W. of Invergowrie*
Watson – W. of Richmond*
Webber – Lloyd-Webber*
Weir – Inverforth
Weld-Forester – Forester
Wellesley – Cowley, E.
Wellesley – Wellington, D.
West – W. of Spithead*
Westenra – Rossmore

White – Annaly
White – Hanningfield*
Whiteley – Marchamley
Whitfield – Kenswood
Williams – W. of Crosby*
Williams – W. of Elvel*
Williams – W. of Oystermouth*
Williams – W. of Trafford*
Williamson – Forres
Willis – W. of Knaresborough*
Willoughby – Middleton
Wills – Dulverton
Wilson – Moran
Wilson – Nunburnholme
Wilson – W. of Dinton*
Wilson – W. of Tillyorn*
Windsor – Gloucester, D.
Windsor – Kent, D.
Windsor-Clive – Plymouth, E.
Wingfield – Powerscourt, V.
Winn – St Oswald
Wodehouse – Kimberley, E.
Wolf – W. of Dulwich*
Wolfson – W. of Aspley Guise*
Wolfson – W. of Sunningdale*
Wood – Halifax, E.
Wood – W. of Anfield*
Woodhouse – Terrington
Woolmer – W. of Leeds*
Wright – W. of Richmond*
Wyndham – Egremont and Leconfield
Wynn – Newborough
Yarde-Buller – Churston
Yerburgh – Alvingham
Yorke – Hardwicke, E.
Young – Kennet
Young – Y. of Cookham*
Young – Y. of Graffham*
Young – Y. of Hornsey*
Young – Y. of Norwood Green*
Young – Y. of Old Scone*
Younger – Y. of Leckie, V.

LORDS SPIRITUAL

The Lords Spiritual are the Archbishops of Canterbury and York and 24 other diocesan bishops of the Church of England. The Bishops of London, Durham and Winchester always have seats in the House of Lords; the other 21 seats were previously filled by the remaining diocesan bishops in order of seniority. However, the Lords Spiritual (Women) Act 2015 provides for vacancies among the remaining 21 places to be filled by any female diocesan bishop in office at the time and, only if there is no female diocesan bishop without a seat, by the longest serving male diocesan bishop. The provision will remain in place for ten years from 2015, equivalent to two fixed-term parliaments. At the end of this period, the provision under the Act will end and the previous arrangements under which vacancies are filled according to length of service as a diocesan bishop will be restored.

The Bishop of Sodor and Man and the Bishop of Gibraltar in Europe are not eligible to sit in the House of Lords.

ARCHBISHOPS

Style, The Most Revd and Rt. Hon. the Lord Archbishop of_
Addressed as Archbishop *or* Your Grace

INTRODUCED TO HOUSE OF LORDS
2012	*Canterbury* (105th), Justin Portal Welby, PC, *b.* 1956, *m., cons.* 2011, *elected* 2011, *trans.* 2013
2006	*York* (97th), John Mugabi Tucker Sentamu, PC, PHD, *b.* 1949, *m., cons.* 1996, *elected* 2002, *trans.* 2005

BISHOPS

Style, The Rt. Revd the Lord/Lady Bishop of _
Addressed as Bishop or My Lord/Lady
elected date of confirmation as diocesan bishop

INTRODUCED TO HOUSE OF LORDS
as at November 2019
2018	*London* (133rd), Dame Sarah Elisabeth Mullally, DBE, PC, *b.* 1962, *m., cons.* 2015, *elected* 2018
2014	*Durham* (74th), Paul Roger Butler, *b.* 1955, *m., cons.* 2004, *elected* 2009, *trans.* 2014
2012	*Winchester* (97th), Timothy John Dakin, *b.* 1958, *m., cons.* 2011, *cons.* 2012
2010	*Birmingham* (9th), David Andrew Urquhart, KCMG, *b.* 1952, *cons.* 2000, *elected* 2006
2012	*Worcester* (113th), John Geoffrey Inge, PHD, *b.* 1955, *m., cons.* 2003, *elected* 2007
2013	*Coventry* (9th), Christopher John Cocksworth, PHD, *b.* 1959, *m., cons.* 2008, *elected* 2008
2013	*Oxford* (44th), Stephen John Lindsey Croft, PHD, *b.* 1957, *m., cons.* 2009, *elected* 2009, *trans.* 2016
2013	*Carlisle* (66th), James William Scobie Newcome, *b.* 1953, *m., cons.* 2002, *elected* 2009
2013	*St Albans* (10th), Alan Gregory Clayton Smith, PHD, *b.* 1957, *cons.* 2001, *elected* 2009
2014	*Peterborough* (38th), Donald Spargo Allister, *b.* 1952, *m., cons.* 2010, *elected* 2010
2014	*Portsmouth* (9th), Christopher Richard James Foster, *b.* 1953, *m., cons.* 2001, *elected* 2010
2014	*Chelmsford* (10th), Stephen Geoffrey Cottrell, *b.* 1958, *m., cons.* 2004, *elected* 2010
2014	*Rochester* (107th), James Henry Langstaff, *b.* 1956, *m., cons.* 2004, *elected* 2010
2014	*Ely* (69th), Stephen David Conway, *b.* 1957, *cons.* 2006, *elected* 2010
2014	*Southwark* (10th), Christopher Thomas James Chessun, *b.* 1956, *cons.* 2005, *elected* 2011
2015	*Leeds* (1st), Nicholas Baines, *b.* 1957, *m., cons.* 2003, *elected* 2011, *trans.* 2014
2015	*Salisbury* (78th), Nicholas Roderick Holtam, *b.* 1954, *m., cons.* 2011, *elected* 2011
2015	*Gloucester* (41st), Rachel Treweek, *b.* 1963, *m., cons.* 2015, *elected* 2015
2016	*Newcastle* (12th), Christine Elizabeth Hardman, *b.* 1951, *m., cons.* 2015, *elected* 2015
2017	*Lincoln* (72nd), Christopher Lowson, *b.* 1953, *m., cons.* 2011, *elected* 2011
2018	*Chichester* (103rd), Martin Clive Warner, PHD, *b.* 1958, *cons.* 2010, *elected* 2012
2018	*Bristol* (56th), Vivienne Frances Faull, *b.* 1955, *m., cons.* 2018, *elected* 2018
2019	*Derby* (8th), Elizabeth Jane Holden Lane, *b.* 1966, *m., cons.* 2015, *elected* 2019
2019	*Blackburn* (9th), Julian Tudor Henderson, *b.* 1954, *m., cons.* 2013, *elected* 2013

BISHOPS AWAITING SEATS, in order of seniority
as at November 2019

Manchester (12th), David Stuart Walker, *b.* 1957, *m., cons.* 2000, *elected* 2013
Bath and Wells (79th), Peter Hancock, *b.* 1955, *m., cons.* 2010, *elected* 2014
Exeter (71st), Robert Ronald Atwell, *b.* 1954, *cons.* 2008, *elected* 2014
Liverpool (8th), Paul Bayes, *b.* 1953, *m., cons.* 2010, *elected* 2014
Hereford (105th), Richard Michael Cokayne Frith, *b.* 1949, *m., cons.* 1998, *elected* 2014
Guildford (10th), Andrew John Watson, *b.* 1961, *m., cons.* 2008, *elected* 2014
St Edmundsbury and Ipswich (11th), Martin Alan Seeley, *b.* 1954, *m., cons.* 2015, *elected* 2015
Southwell and Nottingham (12th), Paul Gavin Williams, *b.* 1968, *m., cons.* 2009, *elected* 2015
Leicester (7th), Martyn James Snow, *b.* 1968, *m., cons.* 2013, *elected* 2016
Lichfield (99th), Michael Geoffrey Ipgrave, OBE, PHD, *b.* 1958, *m., cons.* 2012, *elected* 2016
Sheffield (8th), Peter Jonathan Wilcox, DPHIL, *b.* 1961, *m., cons.* 2017, *elected* 2017
Truro (16th), Philip Ian Mountstephen, *b.* 1959, *m., cons.* 2018, *elected* 2018
Norwich (72nd), Graham Barham Usher, *b.* 1970, *m. cons.* 2014, *elected* 2019
Chester (41st), vacant

ORDERS OF CHIVALRY

THE MOST NOBLE ORDER OF THE GARTER (1348)

KG
Ribbon, Blue
Motto, Honi soit qui mal y pense (*Shame on him who thinks evil of it*)

The number of Knights and Ladies Companion is limited to 24

SOVEREIGN OF THE ORDER
The Queen

LADIES OF THE ORDER
HRH The Princess Royal, 1994
HRH Princess Alexandra, The Hon. Lady Ogilvy, 2003

ROYAL KNIGHTS
HRH The Prince Philip, Duke of Edinburgh, 1947
HRH The Prince of Wales, 1958
HRH The Duke of Kent, 1985
HRH The Duke of Gloucester, 1997
HRH The Duke of York, 2006
HRH The Earl of Wessex, 2006
HRH The Duke of Cambridge, 2008

EXTRA KNIGHTS COMPANION AND LADIES
HM The Queen of Denmark, 1979
HM The King of Sweden, 1983
HM King Juan Carlos, 1988
HRH Princess Beatrix of the Netherlands, 1989
HIM, Akihito, Emperor Emeritus of Japan, 1998
HM The King of Norway, 2001
HM The King of Spain, 2017
HM The King of the Netherlands, 2018

KNIGHTS AND LADIES COMPANION
Lord Bramall, 1990
Lord Sainsbury of Preston Candover, 1992
Lord Ashburton, 1994
Sir Timothy Colman, 1996
Duke of Abercorn, 1999
Lord Inge, 2001
Sir Anthony Acland, 2001
Lord Butler of Brockwell, 2003
Lord Morris of Aberavon, 2003

Sir John Major, 2005
Lord Luce, 2008
Sir Thomas Dunne, 2008
Lord Phillips of Worth Matravers, 2011
Lord Boyce, 2011
Lord Stirrup, 2013
Baroness Manningham-Buller, 2014
Lord King of Lothbury, 2014
Lord Shuttleworth, 2016
Sir David Brewer, 2016
Viscount Brookeborough, 2018
Dame Mary Fagan, 2018
Marquess of Salisbury, 2019
Dame Mary Peters, 2019

Prelate, Bishop of Winchester
Chancellor, Duke of Abercorn, KG
Register, Dean of Windsor, KCVO
Garter King of Arms, Thomas Woodcock, CVO
Lady Usher of the Black Rod, Sarah Clarke, OBE
Secretary, Patric Dickinson, LVO

THE MOST ANCIENT AND MOST NOBLE ORDER OF THE THISTLE (REVIVED 1687)

KT
Ribbon, Green
Motto, Nemo me impune lacessit (*No one provokes me with impunity*)

The number of Knights and Ladies of the Thistle is limited to 16

SOVEREIGN OF THE ORDER
The Queen

ROYAL KNIGHTS
HRH The Prince Philip, Duke of Edinburgh, 1952
HRH The Prince of Wales, Duke of Rothesay, 1977
HRH The Duke of Cambridge, Earl of Strathearn, 2012

ROYAL LADY OF THE ORDER
HRH The Princess Royal, 2000

KNIGHTS AND LADIES
Earl of Elgin and Kincardine, 1981
Earl of Airlie, 1985
Earl of Crawford and Balcarres, 1996
Lord Macfarlane of Bearsden, 1996

Lord Mackay of Clashfern, 1997
Lord Wilson of Tillyorn, 2000
Sir Eric Anderson, 2002
Lord Steel of Aikwood, 2004
Lord Robertson of Port Ellen, 2004
Lord Cullen of Whitekirk, 2007
Lord Hope of Craighead, 2009
Lord Patel, 2009
Earl of Home, 2013
Lord Smith of Kelvin, 2013
Duke of Buccleuch and Queensberry, 2017
Sir Ian Wood, 2018

Chancellor, Earl of Airlie, KT, GCVO, PC
Dean, Very Revd Prof. David Fergusson, OBE
Secretary, Mrs Christopher Roads, LVO
Lord Lyon King of Arms, Dr Joseph Morrow, CBE, QC
Gentleman Usher of the Green Rod, Rear-Adm. Christopher Layman, CB, DSO, LVO

THE MOST HONOURABLE ORDER OF THE BATH (1725)

GCB   GCB *Civil*
Military

GCB Knight (or Dame) Grand Cross
KCB Knight Commander
DCB Dame Commander
CB   Companion

Ribbon, Crimson
Motto, Tria juncta in uno (*Three joined in one*)

Remodelled 1815, and enlarged many times since. The order is divided into civil and military divisions. Women became eligible for the order from 1 January 1971.

THE SOVEREIGN

GREAT MASTER AND FIRST OR PRINCIPAL KNIGHT GRAND CROSS
HRH The Prince of Wales, KG, KT, GCB, OM

Dean of the Order, Dean of Westminster
King of Arms, Air Chief Marshal Sir Stephen Dalton, GCB
Registrar and Secretary, Rear-Adm. Iain Henderson, CB, CBE

Genealogist, Thomas Woodcock, CVO
Gentleman Usher of the Scarlet Rod, Maj.-Gen. James Gordon, CB, CBE
Deputy Secretary, Secretary of the Central Chancery of the Orders of Knighthood
Chancery, Central Chancery of the Orders of Knighthood, St James's Palace, London SW1A 1BH

THE ORDER OF MERIT (1902)

OM *Military*   OM *Civil*

OM
Ribbon, Blue and crimson

This order is designed as a special distinction for eminent men and women without conferring a knighthood upon them. The order is limited in numbers to 24, with the addition of foreign honorary members.

THE SOVEREIGN
HRH The Prince Philip, Duke of Edinburgh, 1968
Lord Foster of Thames Bank, 1997
Prof. Sir Roger Penrose, 2000
Sir Tom Stoppard, 2000
HRH The Prince of Wales, 2002
Lord May of Oxford, 2002
Lord Rothschild, 2002
Sir David Attenborough, 2005
Baroness Boothroyd, 2005
Sir Michael Howard, 2005
Sir Timothy Berners-Lee, 2007
Lord Eames, 2007
Lord Rees of Ludlow, 2007
Rt. Hon. Jean Chrétien, QC, 2009
Robert Neil MacGregor, 2010
Hon. John Howard, 2011
David Hockney, 2011
Sir Simon Rattle, 2013
Prof. Sir Magdi Yacoub, 2013
Lord Darzi of Denham, 2016
Prof. Dame Ann Dowling, 2016
Sir James Dyson, 2016

Secretary and Registrar, Lord Fellowes, GCB, GCVO, PC, QSO

Chancery, Central Chancery of the Orders of Knighthood, St James's Palace, London SW1A 1BH

THE MOST DISTINGUISHED ORDER OF ST MICHAEL AND ST GEORGE (1818)

GCMG   KCMG

GCMG Knight (or Dame) Grand Cross
KCMG Knight Commander
DCMG Dame Commander
CMG Companion

Ribbon, Saxon blue, with scarlet centre
Motto, Auspicium melioris aevi (*Token of a better age*)

THE SOVEREIGN

GRAND MASTER
HRH The Duke of Kent, KG, GCMG, GCVO, ADC

Prelate, Rt. Revd David Urquhart, KCMG
Chancellor, Lord Robertson of Port Ellen, KT, GCMG, PC
Secretary, Permanent Under-Secretary of State at the Foreign and Commonwealth Office and Head of the Diplomatic Service
Registrar, Sir David Manning, GCMG, KCVO
King of Arms, Baroness Ashton of Upholland, GCMG, PC
Lady Usher of the Blue Rod, Dame DeAnne Julius, DCMG, CBE
Dean, Dean of St Paul's
Deputy Secretary, Secretary of the Central Chancery of the Orders of Knighthood
Hon. Genealogist, Timothy Duke

Chancery, Central Chancery of the Orders of Knighthood, St James's Palace, London SW1A 1BH

THE IMPERIAL ORDER OF THE CROWN OF INDIA (1877) FOR LADIES

CI

Badge, the royal cipher of Queen Victoria in jewels within an oval, surmounted by an heraldic crown and attached to a bow of light blue watered ribbon, edged white

The honour does not confer any rank or title upon the recipient

No conferments have been made since 1947

HM The Queen, 1947

THE ROYAL VICTORIAN ORDER (1896)

GCVO   KCVO

GCVO Knight or Dame Grand Cross
KCVO Knight Commander
DCVO Dame Commander
CVO Commander
LVO Lieutenant
MVO Member

Ribbon, Blue, with red and white edges
Motto, Victoria

THE SOVEREIGN

GRAND MASTER
HRH The Princess Royal, KG, KT, GCVO, QSO

Chancellor, Lord Chamberlain
Secretary, Keeper of the Privy Purse
Registrar, Secretary of the Central Chancery of the Orders of Knighthood
Chaplain, Chaplain of the Queen's Chapel of the Savoy
Hon. Genealogist, David White

THE MOST EXCELLENT ORDER OF THE BRITISH EMPIRE (1917)

GBE   KBE

The order was divided into military and civil divisions in December 1918

GBE Knight or Dame Grand Cross
KBE Knight Commander
DBE Dame Commander
CBE Commander
OBE Officer
MBE Member

Ribbon, Rose pink edged with pearl grey with vertical pearl stripe in centre (military division); without vertical pearl stripe (civil division)
Motto, For God and the Empire

THE SOVEREIGN

GRAND MASTER
HRH The Prince Philip, Duke of Edinburgh, KG, KT, OM, GCVO, GBE, PC

Prelate, Bishop of London
King of Arms, Lt.-Gen. Sir Robert Fulton, KBE
Registrar, Secretary of the Central Chancery of the Orders of Knighthood
Secretary, Secretary of the Cabinet and Head of the Home Civil Service
Dean, Dean of St Paul's
Lady Usher of the Purple Rod, Dame Amelia Fawcett, DBE, CVO

Chancery, Central Chancery of the Orders of Knighthood, St James's Palace, London SW1A 1BH

ORDER OF THE COMPANIONS OF HONOUR (1917)

CH

Ribbon, Carmine, with gold edges

This order consists of one class only and carries with it no title. The number of awards is limited to 65 (excluding honorary members).

Amos, Baroness, 2016
Anthony, John, 1981
Attenborough, Sir David, 1995
Atwood, Margaret, 2018
Baker, Dame Janet, 1993
Baker of Dorking, Lord, 1992
Birtwistle, Sir Harrison, 2000
Bragg, Lord, 2017
Brook, Peter, 1998
Brooke of Sutton Mandeville, Lord, 1992
Campbell of Pittenweem, Lord, 2013
Clarke, Kenneth, 2014
Coe, Lord, 2012
Conran, Sir Terence, 2017
De Chastelain, Gen. John, 1998
Dench, Dame Judi, 2005
Elder, Sir Mark, 2017
Eyre, Sir Richard, 2016
Fraser, Lady Antonia, 2017
Glennie, Dame Evelyn, 2016
Grey, Dame Beryl, 2017
Hannay of Chiswick, Lord, 2003
Henderson, Prof. Richard, 2018
Heseltine, Lord, 1997
Higgs, Prof. Peter, 2012
Hockney, David, 1997
Howard, Sir Michael, 2002

Howard of Lympne, Lord, 2011
Hurd of Westwell, Lord, 1995
Jeffreys, Sir Alec, 2016
King of Bridgwater, Lord, 1992
Lovelock, Prof. James, 2002
Lynn, Dame Vera, 2016
McCartney, Sir Paul, 2017
McKellen, Sir Ian Murray, 2007
McKenzie, Prof. Dan Peter, 2003
MacMillan, Prof. Margaret, 2017
Major, Sir John, 1998
O'Neill of Bengarve, Baroness, 2013
Osborne, George, 2016
Owen, Lord, 1994
Patten of Barnes, Lord, 1998
Peters, Dame Mary, 2014
Riley, Bridget, 1998
Rogers of Riverside, Lord, 2008
Rowling, Joanne, 2017
Serota, Sir Nicholas, 2013
Shirley, Dame Stephanie, 2017
Smith, Delia, 2017
Smith, Dame Margaret (Maggie), 2014
Smith of Kelvin, Lord, 2016
Somare, Sir Michael, 1978
Stern of Brentford, Lord, 2017
Strathclyde, Lord, 2013
Strong, Sir Roy, 2015
Te Kanawa, Dame Kiri, 2018
Tebbit, Lord, 1987
Williams of Crosby, Baroness, 2016
Woolf, Lord, 2015
Young of Cookham, Lord, 2012
Young of Graffham, Lord, 2014

Honorary Members, Bernard Haitink, 2002; Prof. Amartya Sen, 2000; Most Revd Desmond Tutu, 2015
Secretary and Registrar, Secretary of the Central Chancery of the Orders of Knighthood

THE DISTINGUISHED SERVICE ORDER (1886)

DSO

Ribbon, Red, with blue edges

Bestowed in recognition of especial services in action of commissioned officers in the Navy, Army and Royal Air Force and (since 1942) Mercantile Marine. The members are Companions only. A bar may be awarded for any additional act of service.

THE IMPERIAL SERVICE ORDER (1902)

ISO

Ribbon, Crimson, with blue centre

Appointment as companion of this order is open to members of the civil services whose eligibility is determined by the grade they hold. The order consists of the sovereign and companions to a number not exceeding 1,900, of whom 1,300 may belong to the home civil services and 600 to overseas civil services. The then prime minister announced in March 1993 that he would make no further recommendations for appointments to the order.

Secretary, Head of the Home Civil Service
Registrar, Secretary of the Central Chancery of the Orders of Knighthood

THE ROYAL VICTORIAN CHAIN (1902)

It confers no precedence on its holders

HM The Queen

HM The Queen of Denmark, 1974
HM The King of Sweden, 1975
HRH Princess Beatrix of the Netherlands, 1982
Gen. Antonio Eanes, 1985
HM King Juan Carlos, 1986
HM The King of Norway, 1994
Earl of Airlie, 1997
Rt. Revd and Rt. Hon. Lord Carey of Clifton, 2002
HRH Prince Philip, Duke of Edinburgh, 2007
HM The Sultan of Oman, 2010
Rt. Revd and Rt. Hon. Lord Williams of Oystermouth, 2012

BARONETAGE AND KNIGHTAGE

BARONETS

Style, 'Sir' before forename and surname, followed by 'Bt.'
   Envelope, Sir F_ S_, Bt. *Letter (formal),* Dear Sir; *(social),* Dear Sir F_. *Spoken,* Sir F_
Wife's style, 'Lady' followed by surname
   Envelope, Lady S_. *Letter (formal),* Dear Madam; *(social),* Dear Lady S_. *Spoken,* Lady S_
Style of Baronetess, 'Dame' before forename and surname, followed by 'Btss.' *(see also* Dames)

There are five different creations of baronetcies: Baronets of England (creations dating from 1611); Baronets of Ireland (creations dating from 1619); Baronets of Scotland or Nova Scotia (creations dating from 1625); Baronets of Great Britain (creations after the Act of Union 1707 which combined the kingdoms of England and Scotland); and Baronets of the United Kingdom (creations after the union of Great Britain and Ireland in 1801).

| *Badge of Baronets of the UK* | *Badge of Baronets of Nova Scotia* | *Badge of Ulster* |

The patent of creation limits the destination of a baronetcy, usually to male descendants of the first baronet. In some cases, however, special remainders have allowed baronetcies to pass, in the absence of sons, to another relative. In the case of baronetcies of Scotland or Nova Scotia, a special remainder of 'heirs male and of tailzie' allows the baronetcy to descend to heirs general, including women. There are four existing Scottish baronetcies with such a remainder.

The Official Roll of the Baronetage is kept at the Crown Office and maintained by the Registrar and Assistant Registrar of the Baronetage. Anyone who considers that he or she is entitled to be entered on the roll may apply through the Crown Office to prove their succession. Every person succeeding to a baronetcy must exhibit proofs of succession to the Lord Chancellor. A person whose name is not entered on the official roll will not be addressed or mentioned by the title of baronet or baronetess in any official document, nor will he or she be accorded precedence as a baronet or baronetess.

The Standing Council of the Baronetage, established in 1898 as the Honourable Society of the Baronetage, is responsible for maintaining the interests of the Baronetage and for publishing the Official Roll of the Baronetage as established by royal warrant in 1910 (W www.baronetage.org/official-roll-of-the-baronets).

OFFICIAL ROLL OF THE BARONETAGE, Crown Office, House of Lords, London SW1A 0PW T 020-7219 4687
   E hereditary.claims@gmail.com
   Registrar, Mrs Ceri King
STANDING COUNCIL OF THE BARONETAGE, 1 Tarrel Farm Cottages, Portmahomack, Tain IV20 1SL
   E secretary@baronetage.org W www.baronetage.org
   Chair, Sir Nicholas Thompson, Bt.
   Secretary, Sarah Rawlings

BARONETCY IDENTIFIED AS EXTINCT SINCE SEPTEMBER 2018
Leith-Buchanan (cr. 1775)

KNIGHTS

Style, 'Sir' before forename and surname, followed by appropriate post-nominal initials if a Knight Grand Cross or Knight Commander
   Envelope, Sir F_ S_. *Letter (formal),* Dear Sir; *(social),* Dear Sir F_. *Spoken,* Sir F_
Wife's style, 'Lady' followed by surname
   Envelope, Lady S_. *Letter (formal),* Dear Madam; *(social),* Dear Lady S_. *Spoken,* Lady S_

The prefix 'Sir' is not used by knights who are clerics of the Church of England, who do not receive the accolade. Their wives are entitled to precedence as the wife of a knight but not to the style of 'Lady'.

ORDERS OF KNIGHTHOOD

Knight Grand Cross and Knight Commander are the higher classes of the Orders of Chivalry (*see* Orders of Chivalry). Honorary knighthoods of these orders may be conferred on men who are citizens of countries of which the Queen is not head of state. As a rule, the prefix 'Sir' is not used by honorary knights.

KNIGHTS BACHELOR

The Knights Bachelor do not constitute a royal order, but comprise the surviving representation of the ancient state orders of knighthood. The Register of Knights Bachelor, instituted by James I in the 17th century, lapsed, and in 1908 a voluntary association under the title of the Society of Knights (now the Imperial Society of Knights Bachelor) was formed with the primary objectives of continuing the various registers dating from 1257 and obtaining the uniform registration of every created Knight Bachelor. In 1926 a design for a badge to be worn by Knights Bachelor was approved and adopted; in 1974 a neck badge and miniature were added.

THE IMPERIAL SOCIETY OF KNIGHTS BACHELOR, Magnesia House, 6 Playhouse Yard, London EC4V 5EX
   Knight Principal, Rt. Hon. Sir Gary Hickinbottom
   Prelate, Rt. Revd and Rt. Hon. Dame Sarah Mullally, DBE
   Registrar, Sir Michael Hirst
   Hon. Treasurer, Sir Clive Thompson
   Clerk to the Council, Col. Simon Doughty

LIST OF BARONETS AND KNIGHTS

as at 31 August 2019
†   Not registered on the Official Roll of the Baronetage
( )   The date of creation of the baronetcy is given in parentheses
I   Baronet of Ireland
NS   Baronet of Nova Scotia
S   Baronet of Scotland

A full entry in italic type indicates that the recipient of a knighthood died within a year of the honour being conferred. The name is included in our list for one year for purposes of record. Peers are not included in this list.

Aaronson, Sir Michael John, Kt., CBE
†Abdy, Sir Robert Etienne Eric, Bt. (1850)
Abed, *Dr* Sir Fazle Hasan, KCMG
Abel, Sir Christopher Charles, Kt.
Acher, Sir Gerald, Kt., CBE, LVO
Ackroyd, Sir Timothy Robert Whyte, Bt. (1956)
Acland, Sir Antony Arthur, KG, GCMG, GCVO
Acland, *Lt.-Col.* Sir (Christopher) Guy (Dyke), Bt. (1890), LVO
Acland, Sir Dominic Dyke, Bt. (1678)
Adams, Sir Geoffrey Doyne, KCMG
Adams, Sir William James, KCMG
Adjaye, Sir David Frank, Kt., OBE
Adsetts, Sir William Norman, Kt., OBE
Adye, Sir John Anthony, KCMG
Aga Khan IV, HH Prince Karim, KBE
Agnew, Sir Crispin Hamlyn, Bt. (S. 1629)
Agnew, Sir George Anthony, Bt. (1895)
Agnew, Sir Rudolph Ion Joseph, Kt.
Agnew-Somerville, Sir James Lockett Charles, Bt. (1957)
Ah Koy, Sir James Michael, KBE
Aikens, *Rt. Hon.* Sir Richard John Pearson, Kt.
Ainslie, Sir Charles Benedict, Kt., CBE
†Ainsworth, Sir Anthony Thomas Hugh, Bt. (1917)
Aird, Sir (George) John, Bt. (1901)
Airy, *Maj.-Gen.* Sir Christopher John, KCVO, CBE
Aitchison, Sir Charles Walter de Lancey, Bt. (1938)
Ajegbo, Sir Keith Onyema, Kt., OBE
Akenhead, *Hon.* Sir Robert, Kt.
Akers-Jones, Sir David, KBE, CMG
Alberti, *Prof.* Sir Kurt George Matthew Mayer, Kt.
Albu, Sir George, Bt. (1912)
Alcock, *Air Chief Marshal* Sir (Robert James) Michael, GCB, KBE
Aldridge, Sir Rodney Malcolm, Kt., OBE
Alexander, *Rt. Hon.* Sir Daniel (Grian), Kt.
Alexander, Sir Douglas, Bt. (1921)
Alexander, Sir Richard, Bt. (1945)
Alghanim, Sir Kutayba Yusuf, KCMG
Allan, *Hon.* Sir Alexander Claud Stuart, KCB
Allen, Sir Errol Newton Fitzrose, KCMG

Allen, *Prof.* Sir Geoffrey, Kt., PHD, FRS
Allen, Sir Mark John Spurgeon, Kt., CMG
Allen, *Hon.* Sir Peter Austin Philip Jermyn, Kt.
Allen, Sir Thomas Boaz, Kt., CBE
Allen, *Hon.* Sir William Clifford, KCMG
Allen, Sir William Guilford, Kt.
Alleyne, Sir George Allanmoore Ogarren, Kt.
Alleyne, *Revd* John Olpherts Campbell, Bt. (1769)
Allinson, Sir (Walter) Leonard, KCVO, CMG
Allison, *Air Chief Marshal* Sir John Shakespeare, KCB, CBE
Alston, Sir Richard John William, Kt., CBE
Altman, Sir Paul Bernard, Kt.
Amess, Sir David Anthony Andrew, Kt.
Amet, *Hon.* Sir Arnold Karibone, Kt.
Amory, Sir Ian Heathcoat, Bt. (1874)
Anderson, *Dr* Sir James Iain Walker, Kt., CBE
Anderson, Sir John Anthony, KBE
Anderson, Sir Leith Reinsford Steven, Kt., CBE
Anderson, *Prof.* Sir Roy Malcolm, Kt.
Anderson, *Air Marshal* Sir Timothy Michael, KCB, DSO
Anderson, Sir (William) Eric Kinloch, KT
Anderton, Sir (Cyril) James, Kt., CBE, QPM
Andrew, Sir Robert John, KCB
Andrew, Sir Warwick, Kt.
Andrews, Sir Ian Charles Franklin, Kt., CBE, TD
Angest, Sir Henry, Kt.
Annesley, Sir Hugh Norman, Kt., QPM
Anson, Sir John, KCB
Anson, Sir Philip Roland, Bt. (1831)
Anstruther, Sir Sebastian Paten Campbell, Bt. (S. 1694 and S. 1700)
Anstruther-Gough-Calthorpe, Sir Euan Hamilton, Bt. (1929)
Antrobus, Sir Edward Philip, Bt. (1815)
Appleyard, Sir Leonard Vincent, KCMG
Arbib, Sir Martyn, Kt.

Arbuthnot, Sir Keith Robert Charles, Bt. (1823)
Arbuthnot, Sir William Reierson, Bt. (1964)
Arbuthnott, *Prof.* Sir John Peebles, Kt., PHD, FRSE
†Archdale, Sir Nicholas Edward, Bt. (1928)
Arculus, Sir Thomas David Guy, Kt.
Armitage, *Air Chief Marshal* Sir Michael John, KCB, CBE
Armitt, Sir John Alexander, Kt., CBE
Armour, *Prof.* Sir James, Kt., CBE
Armstrong, Sir Christopher John Edmund Stuart, Bt. (1841), MBE
Armstrong, Sir Richard, Kt., CBE
Armytage, Sir John Martin, Bt. (1738)
Arnold, *Hon.* Sir Richard David, Kt.
Arnold, Sir Thomas Richard, Kt.
Arnott, Sir Alexander John Maxwell, Bt. (1896)
†Arthur, Sir Benjamin Nathan, Bt. (1841)
Arthur, *Lt.-Gen.* Sir (John) Norman Stewart, KCB, CVO
Arthur, Sir Michael Anthony, KCMG
Arulkumaran, *Prof.* Sir Sabaratnam, Kt.
Asbridge, Sir Jonathan Elliott, Kt.
Ash, *Prof.* Sir Eric Albert, Kt., CBE, FRS, FRENG
Ashburnham, Sir James Fleetwood, Bt. (1661)
Ashworth, *Dr* Sir John Michael, Kt.
Aske, Sir Robert John Bingham, Bt. (1922)
Askew, Sir Bryan, Kt.
Asquith, *Hon.* Sir Dominic Anthony Gerard, KCMG
Astill, *Hon.* Sir Michael John, Kt.
Astley-Cooper, Sir Alexander Paston, Bt. (1821)
Astwood, *Hon.* Sir James Rufus, KBE
Atha, *Air Marshal* Sir Stuart David, KBE, CB, DSO
Atkins, *Rt. Hon.* Sir Robert James, Kt.
Atkinson, Sir William Samuel, Kt.
Atopare, Sir Sailas, GCMG
Attenborough, Sir David Frederick, Kt., OM, CH, CVO, CBE, FRS
Aubrey-Fletcher, Sir Henry Egerton, Bt. (1782), KCVO
Audland, Sir Christopher John, KCMG
Augier, *Prof.* Sir Fitzroy Richard, Kt.
Auld, *Rt. Hon.* Sir Robin Ernest, Kt.
Austen-Smith, *Air Marshal* Sir Roy David, KBE, CB, CVO, DFC

Austin, Sir Peter John, Bt. (1894)
Austin, *Air Marshal* Sir Roger Mark, KCB, AFC
Avei, Sir Moi, KBE
Ayaz, *Dr* Sir Iftikhar Ahmad, KBE
Ayckbourn, Sir Alan, Kt., CBE
Aykroyd, Sir Henry Robert George, Bt. (1920)
Aykroyd, Sir James Alexander Frederic, Bt. (1929)
Aylmer, Sir Richard John, Bt. (I. 1622)
Aylward, *Prof.* Sir Mansel, Kt., CB
Aynsley-Green, *Prof.* Sir Albert, Kt.

Bacha, Sir Bhinod, Kt., CMG
Backhouse, Sir Alfred James Stott, Bt. (1901)
Bacon, Sir Nicholas Hickman Ponsonby, Bt., OBE (1611 and 1627), *Premier Baronet of England*
Baddeley, Sir John Wolsey Beresford, Bt. (1922)
Badge, Sir Peter Gilmour Noto, Kt.
Bagge, Sir (John) Jeremy Picton, Bt. (1867)
Baggott, Sir Matthew David, Kt., CBE, QPM
Bagnall, *Air Chief Marshal* Sir Anthony, GBE, KCB
Bai, Sir Brown, KBE
Bailey, Sir Alan Marshall, KCB
Bailey, Sir Brian Harry, Kt., OBE
Bailey, Sir John Bilsland, KCB
Bailey, Sir John Richard, Bt. (1919)
Bailhache, Sir Philip Martin, Kt.
Bailhache, Sir William, Kt.
Baillie, Sir Adrian Louis, Bt. (1823)
Bain, *Prof.* Sir George Sayers, Kt.
Baird, Sir Charles William Stuart, Bt. (1809)
†Baird, Sir James Andrew Gardiner, Bt. (S. 1695)
Baird, *Air Marshal* Sir John Alexander, KBE
Baird, *Vice-Adm.* Sir Thomas Henry Eustace, KCB
Baker, *Hon.* Sir Andrew William, Kt.
Baker, Sir Bryan William, Kt.
Baker, *Hon.* Sir Jeremy Russell, Kt.
Baker, *Prof.* Sir John Hamilton, Kt., QC
Baker, Sir John William, Kt., CBE
Baker, *Rt. Hon.* Sir Jonathan Leslie, Kt.
Baker, *Rt. Hon.* Sir (Thomas) Scott (Gillespie), Kt.
Balasubramanian, *Prof.* Sir Shankar, Kt.
Baldry, Sir Antony Brian, Kt.
Baldwin, *Prof.* Sir Jack Edward, Kt., FRS
Ball, Sir Christopher John Elinger, Kt.
Ball, *Prof.* Sir John Macleod, Kt.
Ball, Sir Richard Bentley, Bt. (1911)
Ballantyne, *Dr* Sir Frederick Nathaniel, GCMG
Band, *Adm.* Sir Jonathon, GCB
Banham, Sir John Michael Middlecott, Kt.
Bannerman, Sir David Gordon, Bt. (S. 1682), OBE

Barber, Sir Brendan, Kt.
Barber, Sir Michael Bayldon, Kt.
Barber, Sir (Thomas) David, Bt. (1960)
Barclay, Sir David Rowat, Kt.
Barclay, Sir Frederick Hugh, Kt.
Barclay, Sir Robert Colraine, Bt. (S. 1668)
Baring, Sir John Francis, Bt. (1911)
Barker, *Hon.* Sir (Richard) Ian, Kt.
Barling, *Hon.* Sir Gerald Edward, Kt.
Barlow, Sir Christopher Hilaro, Bt. (1803)
Barlow, Sir Frank, Kt., CBE
Barlow, Sir James Alan, Bt. (1902)
Barlow, Sir John Kemp, Bt. (1907)
Barnes, Sir (James) David (Francis), Kt., CBE
Barnett, *Hon.* Sir Michael Lancelot Patrick, Kt.
Barnett, *Prof.* Sir Richard Robert, Kt.
Barnewall, Sir Peter Joseph, Bt. (I. 1623)
†Barran, Sir John Ruthven, Bt. (1895)
Barrett, Sir Stephen Jeremy, KCMG
†Barrett-Lennard, Sir Peter John, Bt. (1801)
†Barrington, Sir Benjamin, Bt. (1831)
Barrington-Ward, *Rt. Revd* Simon, KCMG
Barron, *Rt. Hon.* Sir Kevin, Kt.
Barrons, *Gen.* Sir Richard, KCB, CBE, ADC
Barrow, Sir Anthony John Grenfell, Bt. (1835)
Barrow, Sir Timothy Earle, KCMG, LVO, MBE
Barry, Sir (Lawrence) Edward (Anthony Tress), Bt. (1899)
Barter, Sir Peter Leslie Charles, Kt., OBE
†Bartlett, Sir Andrew Alan, Bt. (1913)
Barttelot, *Col.* Sir Brian Walter de Stopham, Bt. (1875), OBE
Bate, *Prof.* Sir Andrew Jonathan, Kt., CBE
Bates, Sir James Geoffrey, Bt. (1880)
Bates, Sir Richard Dawson Hoult, Bt. (1937)
Batho, Sir Peter Ghislain, Bt. (1928)
Bathurst, *Admiral of the Fleet* Sir (David) Benjamin, GCB
Battishill, Sir Anthony Michael William, GCB
Baulcombe, *Prof.* Sir David Charles, Kt., FRS
Baxendell, Sir Peter Brian, Kt., CBE, FRENG
Bayley, Sir Hugh Nigel Edward, Kt.
Bayne, Sir Nicholas Peter, KCMG
Baynes, Sir Christopher Rory, Bt. (1801)
Bazalgette, Sir Peter Lytton, Kt.
Bazley, Sir Thomas John Sebastian, Bt. (1869)
Beach, *Gen.* Sir (William Gerald) Hugh, GBE, KCB, MC
Beache, *Hon.* Sir Vincent Ian, KCMG
Beale, *Lt.-Gen.* Sir Peter John, KBE, FRCP

Beamish, Sir Adrian John, KCMG
Beamish, Sir David Richard, KCB
Bean, *Dr* Sir Charles Richard, Kt.
Bean, *Rt. Hon.* Sir David Michael, Kt.
Bear, Sir Michael David, Kt.
Beatson, *Rt. Hon.* Sir Jack, Kt.
Beaumont, Sir William Blackledge, Kt., CBE
Beavis, *Air Chief Marshal* Sir Michael Gordon, KCB, CBE, AFC
Beck, Sir Edgar Philip, Kt.
Beckett, Sir Richard Gervase, Bt. (1921), QC
Beckett, *Lt.-Gen.* Sir Thomas Anthony, KCB, CBE
Beckwith, Sir John Lionel, Kt., CBE
Beddington, *Prof.* Sir John Rex, Kt., CMG
†Beecham, Sir Robert Adrian, Bt. (1914)
Beevor, Sir Antony James, Kt.
Beevor, Sir Thomas Hugh Cunliffe, Bt. (1784)
Behan, Sir David, Kt., CBE
Beldam, *Rt. Hon.* Sir (Alexander) Roy (Asplan), Kt.
Belgrave, *HE* Sir Elliott Fitzroy, GCMG
Bell, Sir David Charles Maurice, Kt.
Bell, Sir David Robert, KCB
Bell, *Prof.* Sir John Irving, GBE
Bell, Sir John Lowthian, Bt. (1885)
Bell, *Prof.* Sir Peter Robert Frank, Kt.
Bell, *Hon.* Sir Rodger, Kt.
Bellamy, *Hon.* Sir Christopher William, Kt.
Bellingham, Sir Henry Campbell, Kt.
†Bellingham, Sir William Alexander Noel Henry, Bt. (1796)
Bender, Sir Brian Geoffrey, KCB
Benjamin, Sir George William John, Kt., CBE
Benn, Sir (James) Jonathan, Bt. (1914)
Bennett, *Air Vice-Marshal* Sir Erik Peter, KBE, CB
Bennett, *Hon.* Sir Hugh Peter Derwyn, Kt.
Bennett, *Gen.* Sir Phillip Harvey, KBE, DSO
Bennett, Sir Ronald Wilfrid Murdoch, Bt. (1929)
Benson, Sir Christopher John, Kt.
Benton-Jones, Sir James Peter Martin, Bt. (1919)
Beresford, Sir (Alexander) Paul, Kt.
Beresford-Peirse, Sir Henry Njers de la Poer, Bt. (1814)
Berghuser, *Hon.* Sir Eric, Kt., MBE
Beringer, *Prof.* Sir John Evelyn, Kt., CBE
Berman, Sir Franklin Delow, KCMG
Bernard, Sir Dallas Edmund, Bt. (1954)
Berners-Lee, Sir Timothy John, OM, KBE, FRS
Berney, Sir Julian Reedham Stuart, Bt. (1620)
Bernstein, Sir Howard, Kt.

Berragan, *Lt.-Gen.* Sir Gerald William, KBE, CB

Berridge, *Prof.* Sir Michael John, Kt., FRS

Berriman, Sir David, Kt.

Berry, *Prof.* Sir Colin Leonard, Kt., FRCPATH

Berry, *Prof.* Sir Michael Victor, Kt., FRS

Berthoud, Sir Martin Seymour, KCVO, CMG

Berwick, *Prof.* Sir George Thomas, Kt., CBE

Besley, *Prof.* Sir Timothy John, Kt., CBE

Best-Shaw, Sir Thomas Joshua, Bt. (1665)

Bethel, Sir Baltron Benjamin, KCMG

Bethlehem, Sir Daniel, KCMG

Bett, Sir Michael, Kt., CBE

Bettison, Sir Norman George, Kt., QPM

Bevan, Sir James David, KCMG

Bevan, Sir Martyn Evan Evans, Bt. (1958)

Bevan, Sir Nicolas, Kt., CB

Beverley, *Lt.-Gen.* Sir Henry York La Roche, KCB, OBE, RM

Bhadeshia, *Prof.* Sir Harshad Kumar Dharamshi, Kt., FRS

Bibby, Sir Michael James, Bt. (1959)

Biddulph, Sir Ian D'Olier, Bt. (1664)

Biggam, Sir Robin Adair, Kt.

Bilas, Sir Angmai Simon, Kt., OBE

Bill, *Lt.-Gen.* Sir David Robert, KCB

Billière, *Gen.* Sir Peter Edgar de la Cour de la, KCB, KBE, DSO, MC

Bindman, Sir Geoffrey Lionel, Kt.

Bingham, *Hon.* Sir Eardley Max, Kt.

Birch, Sir John Allan, KCVO, CMG

Birch, Sir Roger, Kt., CBE, QPM

Bird, *Prof.* Sir Adrian Peter, Kt., CBE, FRS, FRSE

Bird, Sir Richard Geoffrey Chapman, Bt. (1922)

Birkett, Sir Peter, Kt.

Birkin, Sir John Christian William, Bt. (1905)

Birkin, Sir (John) Derek, Kt., TD

Birkmyre, Sir James, Bt. (1921)

Birrell, Sir James Drake, Kt.

Birss, *Hon.* Sir Colin Ian, Kt.

Birt, Sir Michael, Kt.

Birtwistle, Sir Harrison, Kt., CH

Bischoff, Sir Winfried Franz Wilhelm, Kt.

Black, *Prof.* Sir Nicholas Andrew, Kt.

Black, Sir Robert David, Bt. (1922)

Blackburn, *Vice-Adm.* Sir David Anthony James, KCVO, CB

Blackburne, *Hon.* Sir William Anthony, Kt.

Blackett, Sir Hugh Francis, Bt. (1673)

Blackham, *Vice-Adm.* Sir Jeremy Joe, KCB

Blackman, Sir Frank Milton, KCVO, OBE

Blair, Sir Patrick David Hunter, Bt. (1786)

Blair, *Hon.* Sir William James Lynton, Kt.

†Blake, Sir Charles Valentine Bruce, Bt. (I. 1622)

Blake, Sir Francis Michael, Bt. (1907)

Blake, *Hon.* Sir Nicholas John Gorrod, Kt.

Blake, Sir Peter Thomas, Kt., CBE

Blake, Sir Quentin Saxby, Kt., CBE

Blakemore, *Prof.* Sir Colin Brian, Kt., FRS

Blaker, Sir John, Bt. (1919)

Blakiston, Sir Ferguson Arthur James, Bt. (1763)

Blanch, Sir Malcolm, KCVO

Bland, *Lt.-Col.* Sir Simon Claud Michael, KCVO

Blank, Sir Maurice Victor, Kt.

Blatchford, Sir Ian Craig, Kt.

Blatherwick, Sir David Elliott Spiby, KCMG, OBE

Blavatnik, Sir Leonard, Kt.

Blennerhassett, Sir (Marmaduke) Adrian Francis William, Bt. (1809)

Blewitt, *Maj.* Sir Shane Gabriel Basil, GCVO

Blofeld, *Hon.* Sir John Christopher Calthorpe, Kt.

Blois, Sir Charles Nicholas Gervase, Bt. (1686)

Blomefield, Sir Thomas Charles Peregrine, Bt. (1807)

Bloom, *Prof.* Sir Stephen Robert, Kt.

Bloomfield, Sir Kenneth Percy, KCB

Blundell, *Prof.* Sir Richard William, Kt., CBE, FBA

Blundell, Sir Thomas Leon, Kt., FRS

†Blunden, Sir Hubert Chisholm, Bt. (I. 1766)

Blunt, Sir David Richard Reginald Harvey, Bt. (1720)

Blyth, Sir Charles (Chay), Kt., CBE, BEM

Boardman, *Prof.* Sir John, Kt., FSA, FBA

Bodey, *Hon.* Sir David Roderick Lessiter, Kt.

Bodmer, Sir Walter Fred, Kt., PHD, FRS

Bogan, Sir Nagora, KBE

Bogle, Sir Nigel, Kt.

Boileau, Sir Nicolas Edmond George, Bt. (1838)

Boleat, Sir Mark John, Kt.

Boles, Sir Richard Fortescue, Bt. (1922)

Bollom, *Air Marshal* Sir Simon John, KBE, CB

Bona, Sir Kina, KBE

Bonallack, Sir Michael Francis, Kt., OBE

Bond, Sir John Reginald Hartnell, Kt.

Bond, *Prof.* Sir Michael Richard, Kt., FRCPSYCH, FRCPGLAS, FRCSE

Bone, *Prof.* Sir (James) Drummond, Kt., FRSE

Bone, Sir Roger Bridgland, KCMG

Bonfield, Sir Peter Leahy, Kt., CBE, FRENG

Bonham, Sir George Martin Antony, Bt. (1852)

Bonington, Sir Christian John Storey, Kt., CVO, CBE

Bonsor, Sir Nicholas Cosmo, Bt. (1925)

Boord, Sir Andrew Richard, Bt. (1896)

Boorman, *Lt.-Gen.* Sir Derek, KCB

Booth, Sir Clive, Kt.

Booth, Sir Douglas Allen, Bt. (1916)

Boothby, Sir Brooke Charles, Bt. (1660)

Bore, Sir Albert, Kt.

Boreel, Sir Stephan Gerard, Bt. (1645)

Borthwick, Sir Antony Thomas, Bt. (1908)

Borysiewicz, *Prof.* Sir Leszek Krzysztof, Kt.

Boseto, *Revd* Leslie Tanaboe, KBE

Bosher, Sir Robin, Kt.

Bossano, *Hon.* Sir Joseph John, KCMG

Bossom, Sir Bruce Charles, Bt. (1953)

Boswell, *Lt.-Gen.* Sir Alexander Crawford Simpson, KCB, CBE

Botham, Sir Ian Terence, Kt., OBE

Bottomley, Sir Peter James, Kt.

Bottoms, *Prof.* Sir Anthony Edward, Kt.

Boughey, Sir John George Fletcher, Bt. (1798)

Boulton, Sir John Gibson, Bt. (1944)

Bouraga, Sir Phillip, KBE

Bourn, Sir John Bryant, KCB

Bourne, Sir Matthew Christopher, Kt., OBE

Bowater, Sir Euan David Vansittart, Bt. (1939)

†Bowater, Sir Michael Patrick, Bt. (1914)

Bowden, Sir Andrew, Kt., MBE

Bowden, Sir Nicholas Richard, Bt. (1915)

Bowen, Sir Barry Manfield, KCMG

Bowen, Sir Geoffrey Fraser, Kt.

Bowen, Sir George Edward Michael, Bt. (1921)

Bowes Lyon, Sir Simon Alexander, KCVO

Bowlby, Sir Richard Peregrine Longstaff, Bt. (1923)

Bowman, Sir Charles Edward Beck, Kt.

Bowman, Sir Edwin Geoffrey, KCB

Bowman, Sir Jeffery Haverstock, Kt.

Bowness, Sir Alan, Kt., CBE

Bowyer-Smyth, Sir Thomas Weyland, Bt. (1661)

Boyce, Sir Graham Hugh, KCMG

Boyce, Sir Robert Charles Leslie, Bt. (1952)

Boyd, Sir Alexander Walter, Bt. (1916)

Boyd, *Prof.* Sir Ian Lamont, Kt., FRSE

Boyd, Sir John Dixon Iklé, KCMG

Boyd, Sir Michael, Kt.

Boyd, *Prof.* Sir Robert David Hugh, Kt.

Boyd-Carpenter, Sir (Marsom) Henry, KCVO

Boyd-Carpenter, *Lt.-Gen. Hon.* Sir Thomas Patrick John, KBE

Boyle, *Prof.* Sir Roger Michael, Kt., CBE

Boyle, Sir Simon Hugh Patrick, KCVO

Boyle, Sir Stephen Gurney, Bt. (1904)

Bracewell-Smith, Sir Charles, Bt. (1947)

Bradford, Sir Edward Alexander Slade, Bt. (1902)

Bradshaw, *Lt.-Gen.* Sir Adrian, KCB, OBE

Brady, Sir Graham Stuart, Kt.

Brady, *Prof.* Sir John Michael, Kt., FRS

Brailsford, Sir David John, Kt., CBE

Braithwaite, Sir Rodric Quentin, GCMG

Bramley, *Prof.* Sir Paul Anthony, Kt.

Branagh, Sir Kenneth Charles, Kt.

Branson, Sir Richard Charles Nicholas, Kt.

Bratza, *Hon.* Sir Nicolas Dušan, Kt.

Brazier, Sir Julian William Hendy, Kt., TD

Breckenridge, *Prof.* Sir Alasdair Muir, Kt., CBE

Brennan, *Hon.* Sir (Francis) Gerard, KBE

Brenton, Sir Anthony Russell, KCMG

Brewer, Sir David William, KG, CMG, CVO

Brierley, Sir Ronald Alfred, Kt.

Briggs, *Rt. Hon.* Sir Michael Townley Featherstone, Kt. (Lord Briggs of Westbourne)

Brighouse, *Prof.* Sir Timothy Robert Peter, Kt.

Bright, Sir Graham Frank James, Kt.

Bright, Sir Keith, Kt.

Brigstocke, *Adm.* Sir John Richard, KCB

Brinckman, Sir Theodore George Roderick, Bt. (1831)

†Brisco, Sir Campbell Howard, Bt. (1782)

Briscoe, Sir Brian Anthony, Kt.

Briscoe, Sir John Geoffrey James, Bt. (1910)

Bristow, Sir Laurence Stanley Charles, KCMG

Brittan, Sir Samuel, Kt.

Britton, Sir Paul John James, Kt., CB

†Broadbent, Sir Andrew George, Bt. (1893)

Broadbent, Sir Richard John, KCB

Brocklebank, Sir Aubrey Thomas, Bt. (1885)

†Brodie, Sir Benjamin David Ross, Bt. (1834)

Bromhead, Sir John Desmond Gonville, Bt. (1806)

†Bromley, Sir Charles Howard, Bt. (1757)

Bromley, Sir Michael Roger, KBE

Bromley-Davenport, Sir William Arthur, KCVO

Brook, *Prof.* Sir Richard John, Kt., OBE

Brooke, Sir Alistair Weston, Bt. (1919)

Brooke, Sir Francis George Windham, Bt. (1903)

Brooke, Sir Richard Christopher, Bt. (1662)

Brooke, Sir Rodney George, Kt., CBE

Brooking, Sir Trevor David, Kt., CBE

Brooksbank, Sir (Edward) Nicholas, Bt. (1919)

†Broughton, Sir David Delves, Bt. (1661)

Broughton, Sir Martin Faulkner, Kt.

Broun, Sir Wayne Hercules, Bt. (S. 1686)

Brown, Sir (Austen) Patrick, KCB

Brown, *Adm.* Sir Brian Thomas, KCB, CBE

Brown, Sir David, Kt.

Brown, Sir Ewan, Kt., CBE

Brown, Sir George Francis Richmond, Bt. (1863)

Brown, Sir Mervyn, KCMG, OBE

Brown, Sir Peter Randolph, Kt.

Brown, *Rt. Hon.* Sir Stephen, GBE

Brown, Sir Stephen David Reid, KCVO

†Brownrigg, Sir Michael (Gawen), Bt. (1816)

Browse, *Prof.* Sir Norman Leslie, Kt., MD, FRCS

Bruce, Sir (Francis) Michael Ian, Bt. (s. 1628)

Bruce-Clifton, Sir Hervey Hamish Peter, Bt. (1804)

Bruce-Gardner, Sir Edmund Thomas Peter, Bt. (1945)

Brunner, Sir Hugo Laurence Joseph, KCVO

Brunner, Sir Nicholas Felix Minturn, Bt. (1895)

†Brunton, Sir James Lauder, Bt. (1908)

Bryan, *Hon.* Sir Simon James, Kt.

Bryant, *Air Chief Marshal* Sir Simon, KCB, CBE, ADC

Brydon, Sir Donald Hood, Kt., CBE

Bubb, Sir Stephen John Limrick, Kt.

Buchan-Hepburn, Sir John Alistair Trant Kidd, Bt. (1815)

Buchanan, Sir Andrew George, Bt. (1878), KCVO

Buchanan-Jardine, Sir John Christopher Rupert, Bt. (1885)

Buckland, Sir Ross, Kt.

Buckley, *Dr* Sir George William, Kt.

Buckley, Sir Michael Sidney, Kt.

Buckley, *Lt.-Cdr.* Sir (Peter) Richard, KCVO

Buckley, *Hon.* Sir Roger John, Kt.

Bucknall, *Lt.-Gen.* Sir James Jeffrey Corfield, KCB, CBE

†Buckworth-Herne-Soame, Sir Richard John, Bt. (1697)

Budd, Sir Alan Peter, GBE

Budd, Sir Colin Richard, KCMG

Buffini, Sir Damon Marcus, Kt.

Bull, Sir George Jeffrey, Kt.

†Bull, Sir Stephen Louis, Bt. (1922)

Bullock, Sir Stephen Michael, Kt.

Bultin, Sir Bato, Kt., MBE

Bunbury, Sir Michael William, Bt. (1681), KCVO

Bunyard, Sir Robert Sidney, Kt., CBE, QPM

Burbidge, Sir Peter Dudley, Bt. (1916)

Burden, Sir Anthony Thomas, Kt., QPM

Burdett, Sir Crispin Peter, Bt. (1665)

Burgen, Sir Arnold Stanley Vincent, Kt., FRS

Burgess, Sir (Joseph) Stuart, Kt., CBE, PHD, FRSC

Burgess, *Prof.* Sir Robert George, Kt.

Burke, Sir James Stanley Gilbert, Bt. (I. 1797)

Burke, Sir (Thomas) Kerry, Kt.

Burn, *Prof.* Sir John, Kt.

Burnell-Nugent, *Vice-Adm.* Sir James Michael, KCB, CBE, ADC

Burnett, Sir Charles David, Bt. (1913)

Burney, Sir Nigel Dennistoun, Bt. (1921)

Burns, *Dr* Sir Henry, Kt.

Burns, Sir (Robert) Andrew, KCMG

Burns, *Rt. Hon.* Sir Simon Hugh McGuigan, Kt.

Burnton, *Rt. Hon.* Sir Stanley Jeffrey, Kt.

Burrell, Sir Charles Raymond, Bt. (1774)

Burridge, *Air Chief Marshal* Sir Brian Kevin, KCB, CBE, ADC

Burton, *Lt.-Gen.* Sir Edmund Fortescue Gerard, KBE

Burton, Sir Graham Stuart, KCMG

Burton, *Hon.* Sir Michael John, GBE

Burton, Sir Michael St Edmund, KCVO, CMG

Butcher, *Hon.* Sir Christopher John, Kt.

Butler, *Dr* Sir David Edgeworth, Kt., CBE

Butler, Sir Percy James, Kt., CBE

Butler, Sir Reginald Richard Michael, Bt. (1922)

Butler, Sir Richard Pierce, Bt. (I. 1628)

Butterfield, *Hon.* Sir Alexander Neil Logie, Kt.

Butterfill, Sir John Valentine, Kt.

Buxton, Sir Crispin Charles Gerard, Bt. (1840)

Buxton, *Rt. Hon.* Sir Richard Joseph, Kt.

Buzzard, Sir Anthony Farquhar, Bt. (1929)

Byatt, Sir Ian Charles Rayner, Kt.

Byron, *Rt. Hon.* Sir Charles Michael Dennis, Kt.

Cable, *Rt. Hon.* Sir (John) Vincent, Kt., PHD

†Cable-Alexander, Sir Patrick Desmond William, Bt. (1809)

Cadbury, Sir (Nicholas) Dominic, Kt.

Cadogan, *Prof.* Sir John Ivan George, Kt., CBE, FRS, FRSE

Cahn, Sir Albert Jonas, Bt. (1934)

Cahn, Sir Andrew Thomas, KCMG

Caine, Sir Michael (Maurice Micklewhite), Kt., CBE

Caines, Sir John, KCB

Cairns, *Very Revd* John Ballantyne, KCVO

Caldwell, Sir Edward George, KCB

Callaghan, Sir William Henry, Kt.

Callan, Sir Ivan Roy, KCVO, CMG

Callender, Sir Colin Nigel, Kt., CBE

Callman, *His Hon.* Sir Clive Vernon, Kt.

Calman, *Prof.* Sir Kenneth Charles, KCB, MD, FRCP, FRCS, FRSE

Calne, *Prof.* Sir Roy Yorke, Kt., FRS

Calvert-Smith, Sir David, Kt., QC

Cameron, Sir Hugh Roy Graham, Kt., QPM

Campbell, *Rt. Hon* Sir Alan, Kt.

Campbell, *Prof.* Sir Colin Murray, Kt.

Campbell, Sir Ian Tofts, Kt., CBE, VRD

Campbell, Sir James Alexander Moffat Bain, Bt. (S. 1668)

Campbell, Sir John Park, Kt., OBE

Campbell, Sir Lachlan Philip Kemeys, Bt. (1815)

Campbell, Sir Louis Auchinbreck, Bt. (S. 1628)

Campbell, *Dr* Sir Philip Henry Montgomery, Kt.

Campbell, Sir Roderick Duncan Hamilton, Bt. (1831)

Campbell, *Dr* Sir Simon Fraser, Kt., CBE

Campbell, *Rt. Hon.* Sir William Anthony, Kt.

†Campbell-Orde, Sir John Simon Arthur, Bt. (1790)

Cannadine, *Prof.* Sir David Nicholas, Kt.

Capewell, *Lt.-Gen.* Sir David Andrew, KCB, OBE, RM

†Carden, Sir Christopher Robert, Bt. (1887)

†Carden, Sir John Craven, Bt. (I. 1787)

Carew, Sir Rivers Verain, Bt. (1661)

Carey, Sir de Vic Graham, Kt.

Carleton-Smith, *Gen.* Sir Mark Alexander Popham, KCB, CBE, ADC

Carleton-Smith, *Maj.-Gen.* Sir Michael Edward, Kt., CBE

Carlisle, Sir James Beethoven, GCMG

Carlisle, Sir John Michael, Kt.

Carlisle, Sir Kenneth Melville, Kt.

Carnegie, Sir Roderick Howard, Kt.

Carnwath, *Rt. Hon.* Sir Robert John Anderson, Kt., CVO (Lord Carnwath of Notting Hill)

Carr, Sir Roger Martyn, Kt.

Carrick, Sir Roger John, KCMG, LVO

Carrington, Sir Nigel Martyn, Kt.

Carruthers, Sir Ian James, Kt., OBE

Carsberg, *Prof.* Sir Bryan Victor, Kt.

Carter, Sir Andrew Nicholas, Kt., OBE

Carter, Sir David Anthony, Kt.

Carter, *Prof.* Sir David Craig, Kt., FRCSE, FRCSGLAS, FRCPE

Carter, Sir Edward Charles, KCMG

Carter, Sir John Gordon Thomas, Kt.

Carter, *Gen.* Sir Nicholas Patrick, GCB, CBE, DSO, ADC

Cartledge, Sir Bryan George, KCMG

Caruna, *Hon.* Sir Peter Richard, KCMG, QC

†Cary, Sir Nicolas Robert Hugh, Bt. (1955)

Cash, Sir Andrew John, Kt., OBE

Cash, Sir William Nigel Paul, Kt.

Cass, Sir Geoffrey Arthur, Kt.

Cassel, Sir Timothy Felix Harold, Bt. (1920)

Cassidi, *Adm.* Sir (Arthur) Desmond, GCB

Castell, Sir William Martin, Kt.

Catto, *Prof.* Sir Graeme Robertson Dawson, Kt.

Caulfield, *Prof.* Sir Mark Jonathan, Kt.

Cavanagh, *Hon.* Sir John, Kt.

Cave, Sir George Charles, Bt. (1896)

Cave-Browne-Cave, Sir John Robert Charles, Bt. (1641)

Cayley, Sir Digby William David, Bt. (1661)

Cazalet, *Hon.* Sir Edward Stephen, Kt.

Cenac, *HE* Sir (Emmanuel) Neville, GCMG

Chadwick, *Rt. Hon.* Sir John Murray, Kt.

Chadwick, Sir Joshua Kenneth Burton, Bt. (1935)

Chadwyck-Healey, Sir Charles Edward, Bt. (1919)

Chakrabarti, Sir Sumantra, KCB

Chalmers, Sir Iain Geoffrey, Kt.

Chalmers, Sir Neil Robert, Kt.

Chalstrey, Sir (Leonard) John, Kt., MD, FRCS

Chamberlain, *Hon.* Sir Martin Daniel, Kt.

Chan, *Rt. Hon.* Sir Julius, GCMG, KBE

Chan, Sir Thomas Kok, Kt., OBE

Chance, Sir John Sebastian, Bt. (1900)

Chandler, Sir Colin Michael, Kt.

Chantler, *Prof.* Sir Cyril, GBE, MD, FRCP

Chaplin, Sir Malcolm Hilbery, Kt., CBE

Chapman, Sir David Robert Macgowan, Bt. (1958)

Chapman, Sir Frank, Kt.

Chapman, Sir George Alan, Kt.

Chapple, *Field Marshal* Sir John Lyon, GCB, CBE

Charles, *Hon.* Sir Arthur William Hessin, Kt.

Charlton, Sir Robert (Bobby), Kt., CBE

Charnley, Sir (William) John, Kt., CB, FRENG

Chastanet, Sir Michael Thomas, KCMG, OBE

†Chaytor, Sir Bruce Gordon, Bt. (1831)

Checketts, *Sqn. Ldr.* Sir David John, KCVO

Checkland, Sir Michael, Kt.

Cheshire, Sir Ian Michael, Kt.

Cheshire, *Air Chief Marshal* Sir John Anthony, KBE, CB

Chessells, Sir Arthur David (Tim), Kt.

†Chetwynd, Sir Peter James Talbot, Bt. (1795)

Cheyne, Sir Patrick John Lister, Bt. (1908)

Chichester, Sir James Henry Edward, Bt. (1641)

Chilcot, *Rt. Hon.* Sir John Anthony, GCB

Chilcott, Sir Dominick John, KCMG

Child, Sir (Coles John) Jeremy, Bt. (1919)

Chinn, Sir Trevor Edwin, Kt., CVO

†Chinubhai, Sir Prashant, Bt. (1913)

Chipperfield, *Prof.* Sir David Alan, Kt., CBE

Chipperfield, Sir Geoffrey Howes, KCB

Chisholm, Sir John Alexander Raymond, Kt., FRENG

†Chitty, Sir Andrew Edward Willes, Bt. (1924)

Cholmeley, Sir Hugh John Frederick Sebastian, Bt. (1806)

Chope, Sir Christopher Robert, Kt., OBE

Choudhury, *Hon.* Sir Akhlaq Ur-Rahman, Kt.

Chow, Sir Chung Kong, Kt.

Chow, Sir Henry Francis, Kt., OBE

Christopher, Sir Duncan Robin Carmichael, KBE, CMG

Chung, Sir Sze-yuen, GBE, FRENG

Clark, *Prof.* Sir Christopher Munro, Kt.

Clark, Sir Francis Drake, Bt. (1886)

Clark, Sir Jonathan George, Bt. (1917)

Clark, Sir Terence Joseph, KBE, CMG, CVO

Clark, Sir Timothy Charles, KBE

Clarke, Sir (Charles Mansfield) Tobias, Bt. (1831)

Clarke, *Rt. Hon.* Sir Christopher Simon Courtenay Stephenson, Kt.

Clarke, *Hon.* Sir David Clive, Kt.

Clarke, Sir Jonathan Dennis, Kt.

Clarke, Sir Paul Robert Virgo, KCVO

Clarke, Sir Rupert Grant Alexander, Bt. (1882)

Clary, *Prof.* Sir David Charles, Kt.

Clay, Sir Edward, KCMG

Clay, Sir Richard Henry, Bt. (1841)

Clayton, Sir David Robert, Bt. (1732)

Cleobury, *Dr* Sir Stephen John, Kt., CBE

Cleaver, Sir Anthony Brian, Kt.

Clegg, *Rt. Hon.* Sir Nicholas William Peter, Kt.

Clementi, Sir David Cecil, Kt.

Clerk, Sir Robert Maxwell, Bt. (S. 1679), OBE

Clerke, Sir Francis Ludlow Longueville, Bt. (1660)

Clifford, Sir Roger Joseph, Bt. (1887)

Clifford, Sir Timothy Peter Plint, Kt.

Clifton-Brown, Sir Geoffrey Robert, Kt.

Coates, Sir Anthony Robert Milnes, Bt. (1911)

Coates, Sir David Frederick Charlton, Bt. (1921)

†Coats, Sir Alexander James Stuart, Bt. (1905)

Cobb, *Hon.* Sir Stephen William Scott, Kt.

Cochrane, Sir (Henry) Marc (Sursock), Bt. (1903)

†Cockburn, Sir Charles Christopher, Bt. (S. 1671)

Cockburn-Campbell, Sir Alexander Thomas, Bt. (1821)

Cockell, Sir Merrick, Kt.

Cockshaw, Sir Alan, Kt., FRENG

Codrington, Sir Christopher George Wayne, Bt. (1876)

Codrington, Sir Giles Peter, Bt. (1721)

Codron, Sir Michael Victor, Kt., CBE

Coghill, Sir Patrick Kendal Farley, Bt. (1778)

Coghlin, *Rt. Hon.* Sir Patrick, Kt.

Cohen, Sir Ivor Harold, Kt., CBE, TD

Cohen, *Hon.* Sir Jonathan Lionel, Kt.

Cohen, *Prof.* Sir Philip, Kt., PHD, FRS

Cohen, Sir Robert Paul, Kt., CBE

Cohen, Sir Ronald, Kt.

Cole, Sir (Robert) William, Kt.

Coleman, Sir Robert John, KCMG

Coleridge, *Hon.* Sir Paul James Duke, Kt.

Coles, Sir (Arthur) John, GCMG

Coles, Sir Jonathan Andrew, Kt.

Colfox, Sir Philip John, Bt. (1939)

Collas, Sir Richard John, Kt.

Collett, Sir Ian Seymour, Bt. (1934)

Collier, Sir Paul, Kt., CBE

Collins, Sir Alan Stanley, KCVO, CMG

Collins, *Hon.* Sir Andrew David, Kt.

Collins, Sir Bryan Thomas Alfred, Kt., OBE, QFSM

Collins, *Dr* Sir David John, Kt., CBE

Collins, Sir John Alexander, Kt.

Collins, Sir Kenneth Darlingston, Kt.

Collins, *Dr* Sir Kevan Arthur, Kt.

Collins, *Prof.* Sir Rory Edwards, Kt.

Collyear, Sir John Gowen, Kt.

Colman, Sir Michael Jeremiah, Bt. (1907)

Colman, Sir Timothy, KG

Colquhoun of Luss, Sir Rory Malcolm, Bt. (1786)

Colt, Sir Edward William Dutton, Bt. (1694)

Colthurst, Sir Charles St John, Bt. (I. 1744)

Colton, *Hon.* Sir Adrian George Patrick, Kt.

Conant, Sir John Ernest Michael, Bt. (1954)

Conner, *Rt Revd* David John, KCVO

Connery, Sir Sean, Kt.

Connolly, Sir William (Billy), Kt., CBE

Connor, Sir William Joseph, Kt.

Conran, Sir Terence Orby, Kt., CH

Cons, *Hon.* Sir Derek, Kt.

Constantinou, Sir Kosta George, Kt., OBE

Constantinou, Sir Theophilus George, Kt., CBE

Conway, *Prof.* Sir Gordon Richard, KCMG, FRS

Cook, Sir Alastair Nathan, Kt., CBE

Cook, Sir Andrew, Kt., CBE

Cook, Sir Christopher Wymondham Rayner Herbert, Bt. (1886)

Cook, *Prof.* Sir Peter Frederic Chester, Kt.

Cooke, *Hon.* Sir Jeremy Lionel, Kt.

Cooke, *Prof.* Sir Ronald Urwick, Kt.

Cooke-Yarborough, Sir Anthony Edmund, Bt. (1661)

Cooksey, Sir David James Scott, GBE

Cooper, *Prof.* Sir Cary Lynn, Kt., CBE

Cooper, *Gen.* Sir George Leslie Conroy, GCB, MC

Cooper, Sir Richard Adrian, Bt. (1905)

Cooper, Sir Robert Francis, KCMG, MVO

Cooper, *Maj.-Gen.* Sir Simon Christie, GCVO

Cooper, Sir William Daniel Charles, Bt. (1863)

Coote, Sir Nicholas Patrick, Bt. (I. 1621), *Premier Baronet of Ireland*

Corbett, *Maj.-Gen.* Sir Robert John Swan, KCVO, CB

Corder, *Vice-Adm.* Sir Ian Fergus, KBE, CB

Cordy-Simpson, *Lt.-Gen.* Sir Roderick Alexander, KBE, CB

Corness, Sir Colin Ross, Kt.

Corry, Sir James Michael, Bt. (1885)

Cory, Sir (Clinton Charles) Donald, Bt. (1919)

Cory-Wright, Sir Richard Michael, Bt. (1903)

Cossons, Sir Neil, Kt., OBE

Cotter, Sir Patrick Laurence Delaval, Bt. (I. 1763)

Cotterell, Sir Henry Richard Geers, Bt. (1805), OBE

†Cotts, Sir Richard Crichton Mitchell, Bt. (1921)

Coulson, *Rt. Hon.* Sir Peter David William, Kt.

Couper, Sir James George, Bt. (1841)

Courtenay, Sir Thomas Daniel, Kt.

Cousins, *Air Chief Marshal* Sir David, KCB, AFC

Coville, *Air Marshal* Sir Christopher Charles Cotton, KCB

Cowan, *Gen.* Sir Samuel, KCB, CBE

Coward, *Lt.-Gen.* Sir Gary Robert, KBE, CB, OBE

Coward, *Vice-Adm.* Sir John Francis, KCB, DSO

Cowdery, Sir Clive, Kt.

Cowley, *Prof.* Sir Steven Charles, Kt., FRS, FRENG

Cowper-Coles, Sir Sherard Louis, KCMG, LVO

Cox, Sir Alan George, Kt., CBE

Cox, *Prof.* Sir David Roxbee, Kt.

Cox, Sir George Edwin, Kt.

Craft, *Prof.* Sir Alan William, Kt.

Cragg, *Prof.* Sir Anthony Douglas, Kt., CBE

Cragnolini, Sir Luciano, Kt.

Craig-Cooper, Sir (Frederick Howard) Michael, Kt., CBE, TD

Craig-Martin, Sir Michael, Kt., CBE

Crane, *Prof.* Sir Peter Robert, Kt.

Cranston, *Hon.* Sir Ross Frederick, Kt.

Craufurd, Sir Robert James, Bt. (1781)

Crausby, Sir David Anthony, Kt.

Craven, Sir John Anthony, Kt.

Craven, Sir Philip Lee, Kt., MBE

Crawford, *Prof.* Sir Frederick William, Kt., FRENG

Crawford, Sir Robert William Kenneth, Kt., CBE

Crawley-Boevey, Sir Thomas Michael Blake, Bt. (1784)

Cresswell, *Hon.* Sir Peter John, Kt.

Crew, Sir (Michael) Edward, Kt., QPM

Crewe, *Prof.* Sir Ivor Martin, Kt.

Crisp, Sir John Charles, Bt. (1913)

Critchett, Sir Charles George Montague, Bt. (1908)

Crittin, *Hon.* Sir John Luke, KBE

Croft, Sir Owen Glendower, Bt. (1671)

Croft, Sir Thomas Stephen Hutton, Bt. (1818)

Crofton, Sir Edward Morgan, Bt. (1801)

Crofton, Sir William Robert Malby, Bt. (1838)

Crombie, Sir Alexander, Kt.

Crompton, Sir Dan, Kt., CBE, QPM

Cropper, Sir James Anthony, KCVO

Crosby, Sir Lynton Keith, Kt.

Crossley, Sir Sloan Nicholas, Bt. (1909)

Crowe, Sir Brian Lee, KCMG

Cruickshank, Sir Donald Gordon, Kt.

Cubie, *Dr* Sir Andrew, Kt., CBE

Cubitt, Sir Hugh Guy, Kt., CBE

Cubitt, *Maj.-Gen.* Sir William George, KCVO, CBE

Cullen, Sir (Edward) John, Kt., FRENG

Culme-Seymour, Sir Michael Patrick, Bt. (1809)

Culpin, Sir Robert Paul, Kt.

Cummins, Sir Michael John Austin, Kt.

Cunliffe, *Prof.* Sir Barrington, Kt., CBE

Cunliffe, Sir David Ellis, Bt. (1759)

Cunliffe, Sir Jonathan Stephen, Kt., CB

Cunliffe-Owen, Sir Hugo Dudley, Bt. (1920)

Cunningham, *Lt.-Gen.* Sir Hugh Patrick, KBE

Cunningham, *Prof.* Sir John, KCVO

Cunningham, Sir Roger Keith, Kt., CBE

Cunningham, Sir Thomas Anthony, Kt.

Cunynghame, Sir Andrew David Francis, Bt. (S. 1702)

Curran, *Prof.* Sir Paul James, Kt.

Curtain, Sir Michael, KBE

Curtice, *Prof.* Sir John Kevin, Kt., FBA, FRSE

Curtis, Sir Barry John, Kt.

Curtis, Sir Edward Philip, Bt. (1802)

Curtis, *Hon.* Sir Richard Herbert, Kt.

Cuschieri, *Prof.* Sir Alfred, Kt.

Cyrus, *Dr* Sir Arthur Cecil, KCMG, OBE

Dain, Sir David John Michael, KCVO

Dales, Sir Richard Nigel, KCVO

Dalglish, Sir Kenneth, Kt., MBE

Dalrymple-Hay, Sir Malcolm John Robert, Bt. (1798)

†Dalrymple-White, Sir Jan Hew, Bt. (1926)

Dalton, Sir David Nigel, Kt.

Dalton, *Vice-Adm.* Sir Geoffrey Thomas James Oliver, GCB

Dalton, Sir Richard John, KCMG

Dalton, *Air Chief Marshal* Sir Stephen Gary George, GCB

Dalyell, Sir Gordon Wheatley, Bt. (NS 1685)

Dancer, Sir Eric, KCVO, CBE

Daniel, Sir John Sagar, Kt., DSC

Darell, Sir Guy Jeffrey Adair, Bt. (1795)

Darrington, Sir Michael John, Kt.

Darroch, Sir Nigel Kim, KCMG

Dasgupta, *Prof.* Sir Partha Sarathi, Kt.

Dashwood, *Prof.* Sir (Arthur) Alan, KCMG, CBE, QC

Dashwood, Sir Edward John Francis, Bt. (1707), *Premier Baronet of Great Britain*

Dashwood, Sir Frederick George Mahon, Bt. (1684)

Daunt, Sir Timothy Lewis Achilles, KCMG

Davey, *Rt. Hon.* Sir Edward Jonathan, Kt.

Davidson, Sir Martin Stuart, KCMG

Davies, *Prof.* Sir David Evan Naughton, Kt., CBE, FRS, FRENG

Davies, Sir David John, Kt.

Davies, Sir Frank John, Kt., CBE

Davies, *Prof.* Sir Graeme John, Kt., FRENG

Davies, Sir John Howard, Kt.

Davies, Sir John Michael, KCB

Davies, Sir Raymond Douglas, Kt.

Davies, Sir Rhys Everson, Kt., QC

Davis, Sir Andrew Frank, Kt., CBE

Davis, Sir Crispin Henry Lamert, Kt.

Davis, Sir Ian Edward Lamert, Kt.

Davis, Sir John Gilbert, Bt. (1946)

Davis, Sir Michael Lawrence, Kt.

Davis, *Rt. Hon.* Sir Nigel Anthony Lamert, Kt.

Davis, Sir Peter John, Kt.

Davis, *Hon.* Sir William Easthope, Kt.

Davis-Goff, Sir Robert (William), Bt. (1905)

Davson, Sir George Trenchard Simon, Bt. (1927)

Dawanincura, Sir John Norbert, Kt., OBE

Dawbarn, Sir Simon Yelverton, KCVO, CMG

Dawson, *Hon.* Sir Daryl Michael, KBE, CB

Dawson, Sir Nicholas Anthony Trevor, Bt. (1920)

Day, Sir Barry Stuart, Kt., OBE

Day, *Air Chief Marshal* Sir John Romney, KCB, OBE, ADC

Day, Sir Jonathan Stephen, Kt., CBE

Day, Sir (Judson) Graham, Kt.

Day, Sir Michael John, Kt., OBE

Day, Sir Simon James, Kt.

Day-Lewis, Sir Daniel Michael Blake, Kt.

Deane, *Hon.* Sir William Patrick, KBE

Dearlove, Sir Richard Billing, KCMG, OBE

Deaton, *Prof.* Sir Angus Stewart, Kt.

†Debenham, Sir Thomas Adam, Bt. (1931)

Deegan, Sir Michael, Kt., CBE

Deeny, *Rt. Hon.* Sir Donnell Justin Patrick, Kt.

De Haan, Sir Roger Michael, Kt., CBE

De Halpert, *Rear-Adm.* Sir Jeremy Michael, KCVO, CB

de Hoghton, Sir (Richard) Bernard (Cuthbert), Bt. (1611)

de la Rue, Sir Andrew George Ilay, Bt. (1898)

Dellow, Sir John Albert, Kt., CBE

Delves, *Lt.-Gen.* Sir Cedric Norman George, KBE

Denison-Smith, *Lt.-Gen.* Sir Anthony Arthur, KBE

Denny, Sir Charles Alistair Maurice, Bt. (1913)

Denny, Sir Piers Anthony de Waltham, Bt. (I. 1782)

Desmond, Sir Denis Fitzgerald, KCVO, CBE

de Trafford, Sir John Humphrey, Bt. (1841)

Devane, Sir Ciaran Gearoid, Kt.

Deverell, *Lt.-Gen.* Sir Christopher Michael, KCB, MBE

Deverell, *Gen.* Sir John Freegard, KCB, OBE

Devereux, Sir Robert, KCB

De Ville, Sir Harold Godfrey Oscar, Kt., CBE

Devine, *Prof.* Sir Thomas Martin, Kt., OBE, FRSE

Devitt, Sir James Hugh Thomas, Bt. (1916)

Dewey, Sir Rupert Grahame, Bt. (1917)

De Witt, Sir Ronald Wayne, Kt.

Diamond, *Prof.* Sir Ian David, Kt., FRSE

Dick-Lauder, Sir Piers Robert, Bt. (S. 1690)

Dilke, Revd Charles John Wentworth, Bt. (1862)

Dilley, Sir Philip Graham, Kt.

Dillon, Sir Andrew Patrick, Kt., CBE

Dillwyn-Venables-Llewelyn, Sir John Michael, Bt. (1890)

Dilnot, Sir Andrew William, Kt., CBE

Dingemans, *Hon.* Sir James Michael, Kt.

Dion, Sir Leo, KBE

Dixon, Sir Jeremy, Kt.

Dixon, Sir Jonathan Mark, Bt. (1919)

Dixon, *Dr* Sir Michael, Kt.

Dixon, Sir Peter John Bellett, Kt.

Djanogly, Sir Harry Ari Simon, Kt., CBE

Dobson, *Prof.* Sir Christopher Martin, Kt.

Dobson, *Vice-Adm.* Sir David Stuart, KBE

Dollery, Sir Colin Terence, Kt.

Don-Wauchope, Sir Roger (Hamilton), Bt. (S. 1667)

Donaldson, *Rt. Hon.* Sir Jeffrey Mark, Kt.

Donaldson, *Prof.* Sir Liam Joseph, Kt.

Donaldson, *Prof.* Sir Simon Kirwan, Kt.

Donnelly, Sir Joseph Brian, KBE, CMG

Donnelly, Sir Martin Eugene, KCB, CMG

Donnelly, *Prof.* Sir Peter James, Kt.

Donohoe, Sir Brian Harold, Kt.

Dorfman, Sir Lloyd, Kt., CBE

Dorman, Sir Philip Henry Keppel, Bt. (1923)

Douglas, *Prof.* Sir Neil James, Kt.

Douglas, *Hon.* Sir Roger Owen, Kt.

Dove, *Hon.* Sir Ian William, Kt.

Dowell, Sir Anthony James, Kt., CBE

Dowling, Sir Robert, Kt.

Downes, *Prof.* Sir Charles Peter, Kt., OBE, FRSE

Downey, Sir Gordon Stanley, KCB

Doyle, Sir Reginald Derek Henry, Kt., CBE

D'Oyly, Sir Hadley Gregory, Bt. (1663)

Drewry, *Lt.-Gen.* Sir Christopher Francis, KCB, CBE

Dryden, Sir John Stephen Gyles, Bt. (1733 and 1795)

Duberly, Sir Archibald Hugh, KCVO, CBE

Duckworth, Sir James Edward Dyce, Bt. (1909)

du Cros, Sir Julian Claude Arthur Mallet, Bt. (1916)

Dudley-Williams, Sir Alastair Edgcumbe James, Bt. (1964)

Duff, *Prof.* Sir Gordon William, Kt.

Duff-Gordon, Sir Andrew Cosmo Lewis, Bt. (1813)

Duffell, *Lt.-Gen.* Sir Peter Royson, KCB, CBE, MC

Duffy, Sir (Albert) (Edward) Patrick, Kt., PHD

Dugdale, Sir (William) Matthew Stratford, Bt. (1936)

Duggin, Sir Thomas Joseph, Kt.

Dunbar, Sir Edward Horace, Bt. (S. 1700)

Dunbar, Sir James Michael, Bt. (S. 1694)

Dunbar, Sir Robert Drummond Cospatrick, Bt. (S. 1698)

Dunbar of Hempriggs, Sir Richard Francis, Bt. (S. 1706)

Dunbar-Nasmith, *Prof.* Sir James Duncan, Kt., CBE

Duncan, *Rt. Hon.* Sir Alan James Carter, KCMG

Duncan, Sir James Blair, Kt.

Dunford, *Dr* Sir John Ernest, Kt., OBE

Dunlop, Sir Thomas, Bt. (1916)

Dunne, Sir Martin, KCVO

Dunne, Sir Thomas Raymond, KG, KCVO

Dunning, Sir Simon William Patrick, Bt. (1930)

Dunnington-Jefferson, Sir John Alexander, Bt. (1958)

Dunstone, Sir Charles William, Kt., CVO

Dunt, *Vice-Adm.* Sir John Hugh, KCB

†Duntze, Sir Daniel Evans, Bt. (1774)

Dupre, Sir Tumun, Kt., MBE

Durand, Sir Edward Alan Christopher David Percy, Bt. (1892)

Durie, Sir David Robert Campbell, KCMG

†Durrant, Sir David Alexander, Bt. (1784)

Duthie, Sir Robert Grieve (Robin), Kt., CBE

Dutton, *Lt.-Gen.* Sir James Benjamin, KCB, CBE

Dwyer, Sir Joseph Anthony, Kt.

†Dyer-Bennet, Sir David, Bt. (1678)

Dyke, Sir David William Hart, Bt. (1677)

Dymock, *Vice-Adm.* Sir Anthony Knox, KBE, CB

Dyson, Sir James, Kt., OM, CBE

Dyson, *Rt. Hon.* Sir John Anthony, Kt. (Lord Dyson)

Eadie, Sir James Raymond, Kt., QC

Eady, *Hon.* Sir David, Kt.

Eardley-Wilmot, Sir Benjamin John Assheton, Bt. (1821)

Earle, Sir (Hardman) George (Algernon), Bt. (1869)

Eastwood, *Prof.* Sir David Stephen, Kt.

Eaton, *Adm.* Sir Kenneth John, GBE, KCB

Ebdon, *Prof.* Sir Leslie Colin, Kt., CBE

Ebrahim, Sir (Mahomed) Currimbhoy, Bt. (1910)

Eddington, Sir Roderick Ian, Kt.

Eder, *Hon.* Sir Henry Bernard, Kt.

Edis, *Hon.* Sir Andrew Jeremy Coulter, Kt.

Edge, *Capt.* Sir (Philip) Malcolm, KCVO

†Edge, Sir William, Bt. (1937)

Edmonstone, Sir Archibald Bruce Charles, Bt. (1774)

Edward, *Rt. Hon.* Sir David Alexander Ogilvy, KCMG

Edwardes, Sir Michael Owen, Kt.

Edwards, Sir Christopher John Churchill, Bt. (1866)

Edwards, *Prof.* Sir Christopher Richard Watkin, Kt.

Edwards, Sir Gareth Owen, Kt., CBE

Edwards, Sir Llewellyn Roy, Kt.

Edwards, *Prof.* Sir Michael, OBE

Edwards, Sir Robert Paul, Kt.

†Edwards-Moss, Sir David John, Bt. (1868)

Edwards-Stuart, *Hon.* Sir Antony James Cobham, Kt.

Egan, Sir John Leopold, Kt.

Egerton, Sir William de Malpas, Bt. (1617)

Ehrman, Sir William Geoffrey, KCMG

Elder, Sir Mark Philip, Kt., CH, CBE

Eldon, Sir Stewart Graham, KCMG, OBE

Elias, *Rt. Hon.* Sir Patrick, Kt.

Eliott of Stobs, Sir Rodney Gilbert Charles, Bt. (S. 1666)

Elliott, Sir David Murray, KCMG, CB

†Elliott, Sir Ivo Antony Moritz, Bt. (1917)

Elliott, *Prof.* Sir John Huxtable, Kt., FBA

Ellis, Sir Vernon James, Kt.

Ellwood, Sir Peter Brian, Kt., CBE

Elphinston, Sir Alexander, Bt. (S. 1701)

Elphinstone, Sir John Howard Main, Bt. (1816)

Elton, Sir Arnold, Kt., CBE

Elton, Sir Charles Abraham Grierson, Bt. (1717)

Elvidge, Sir John, KCB

Elwes, *Dr* Sir Henry William, KCVO

Elwes, Sir Jeremy Vernon, Kt., CBE

Elwood, Sir Brian George Conway, Kt., CBE

Elworthy, *Air Cdre Hon.* Sir Timothy Charles, KCVO, CBE

Enderby, *Prof.* Sir John Edwin, Kt. CBE, FRS

English, Sir Terence Alexander Hawthorne, KBE, FRCS

Ennals, Sir Paul Martin, Kt., CBE

Epstein, *Prof.* Sir (Michael) Anthony, Kt., CBE, FRS

Errington, Sir Robin Davenport, Bt. (1963)

Erskine, Sir (Thomas) Peter Neil, Bt. (1821)

Erskine-Hill, Sir Alexander Roger, Bt. (1945)

Esmonde, Sir Thomas Francis Grattan, Bt. (I. 1629)

†Esplen, Sir William John Harry, Bt. (1921)

Esquivel, *Rt. Hon.* Sir Manuel, KCMG

Essenhigh, *Adm.* Sir Nigel Richard, GCB

Etherington, Sir Stuart James, Kt.

Etherton, *Rt. Hon.* Sir Terence Michael Elkan Barnet, Kt.

Evans, *Rt. Hon.* Sir Anthony Howell Meurig, Kt., RD

Evans, *Prof.* Sir Christopher Thomas, Kt., OBE

Evans, *Air Chief Marshal* Sir David George, GCB, CBE

Evans, *Hon.* Sir David Roderick, Kt.

Evans, Sir Harold Matthew, Kt.

Evans, Sir John Stanley, Kt., QPM

Evans, Sir Malcolm David, KCMG, OBE

Evans, *Prof.* Sir Martin John, Kt., FRS

Evans, Sir Richard Harry, Kt., CBE

Evans, *Prof.* Sir Richard John, Kt.

Evans, Sir Robert, Kt., CBE, FRENG

Evans-Lombe, *Hon.* Sir Edward Christopher, Kt.

†Evans-Tipping, Sir David Gwynne, Bt. (1913)

Evennett, *Rt. Hon.* Sir David Anthony, Kt.

Everard, Sir Henry Peter Charles, Bt. (1911)

Everard, *Lt.-Gen.* Sir James Rupert, KCB, CBE

Everington, *Dr* Sir Anthony Herbert, Kt., OBE

Every, Sir Henry John Michael, Bt. (1641)

Ewart, Sir William Michael, Bt. (1887)

Eyre, Sir Richard Charles Hastings, Kt., CH, CBE

†Fagge, Sir John Christopher Frederick, Bt. (1660)

Fahy, Sir Peter, Kt., QPM

Fairbairn, Sir Robert William, Bt. (1869)

Fairlie-Cuninghame, Sir Robert Henry, Bt. (S. 1630)

Fairweather, Sir Patrick Stanislaus, KCMG

Faldo, Sir Nicholas Alexander, Kt., MBE

†Falkiner, Sir Benjamin Simon Patrick, Bt. (I. 1778)

Fall, Sir Brian James Proetel, GCVO, KCMG

Fallon, *Rt. Hon.* Sir Michael Cathel, KCB

Fancourt, *Hon.* Sir Timothy Miles, Kt.

Fang, *Prof.* Sir Harry, Kt., CBE

Farah, Sir Mohamed (Mo) Muktar Jama, Kt., CBE

Fareed, Sir Djamil Sheik, Kt.

Farmer, Sir Thomas, Kt., CVO, CBE

Farquhar, Sir Michael Fitzroy Henry, Bt. (1796)

Farr, Sir Charles Blandford, Kt., CMG, OBE

Farrar, *Prof.* Sir Jeremy James, Kt., OBE

Farrell, Sir Terence, Kt., CBE

Farrer, Sir (Charles) Matthew, GCVO

Farrington, Sir Henry William, Bt. (1818)

Faull, Sir Jonathan Michael Howard, KCMG

Fay, Sir (Humphrey) Michael Gerard, Kt.

Feachem, *Prof.* Sir Richard George Andrew, KBE

Fean, Sir Thomas Vincent, KCVO

Feilden, Sir Henry Rudyard, Bt. (1846)

Feldmann, *Prof.* Sir Marc, Kt.

Fell, Sir David, KCB

Fender, Sir Brian Edward Frederick, Kt., CMG, PHD

Fenwick, Sir Leonard Raymond, Kt., CBE

Fergus, Sir Howard Archibald, KBE

Ferguson, *Prof.* Sir Michael Anthony John, Kt., CBE, FRS

Ferguson-Davie, Sir Michael, Bt. (1847)

Fergusson, *Rt. Hon.* Sir Alexander Charles Onslow, Kt.

Fergusson of Kilkerran, Sir Charles, Bt. (S. 1703)

Fersht, *Prof.* Sir Alan Roy, Kt., FRS

ffolkes, Sir Robert Francis Alexander, Bt. (1774), OBE

Field, Sir Malcolm David, Kt.

Field, *Hon.* Sir Richard Alan, Kt.

Fielding, Sir Leslie, KCMG

Fields, Sir Allan Clifford, KCMG

Fiennes, Sir Ranulph Twisleton-Wykeham, Bt. (1916), OBE

Figgis, Sir Anthony St John Howard, KCVO, CMG

Finlay, Sir David Ronald James Bell, Bt. (1964)

Finlayson, Sir Garet Orlando, KCMG, OBE

Fish, *Prof.* Sir David Royden, Kt.

†Fison, Sir Charles William, Bt. (1905)

Fittall, Sir William Robert, Kt.

FitzGerald, Sir Adrian James Andrew Denis, Bt. (1880)

†Fitzgerald, Sir Andrew Peter, Bt. (1903)

FitzHerbert, Sir Richard Ranulph, Bt. (1784)

Fitzpatrick, *Air Marshal* Sir John Bernard, KBE, CB

Flanagan, Sir Ronald, GBE, QPM

Flaux, *Rt. Hon.* Sir Julian Martin, Kt.

Flint, Sir Douglas Jardine, Kt., CBE

Floud, *Prof.* Sir Roderick Castle, Kt.

Floyd, *Rt. Hon.* Sir Christopher David, Kt.

Floyd, Sir Giles Henry Charles, Bt. (1816)

Foley, *Lt.-Gen.* Sir John Paul, KCB, OBE, MC

Follett, *Prof.* Sir Brian Keith, Kt., FRS

†Forbes of Craigievar, Sir Andrew Iain Ochoncar, Bt. (S. 1630)

Forbes, *Adm.* Sir Ian Andrew, KCB, CBE

Forbes, Sir James Thomas Stewart, Bt. (1823)

Forbes, *Vice-Adm.* Sir John Morrison, KCB

Forbes, *Hon.* Sir Thayne John, Kt.

Forbes Adam, Sir Nigel Colin, Bt. (1917)

Forbes-Leith, Sir George Ian David, Bt. (1923)

Ford, *Lt.-Col.* Sir Andrew Charles, KCVO

Ford, Sir Andrew Russell, Bt. (1929)

Forestier-Walker, Sir Michael Leolin, Bt. (1835)

Forrest, *Prof.* Sir (Andrew) Patrick (McEwen), Kt.

Forte, *Hon.* Sir Rocco John Vincent, Kt.

Forwood, *Hon.* Sir Nicholas James, Kt., QC

Forwood, Sir Peter Noel, Bt. (1895)

Foskett, *Hon.* Sir David Robert, Kt.

Foster, Sir Andrew William, Kt.

Foster, *Prof.* Sir Christopher David, Kt.

Foster, Sir Saxby Gregory, Bt. (1930)

Foulkes, Sir Arthur Alexander, GCMG

Fountain, *Hon.* Sir Cyril Stanley Smith, Kt.

Fowke, Sir David Frederick Gustavus, Bt. (1814)

Fowler, Sir (Edward) Michael Coulson, Kt.

Fox, Sir Christopher, Kt., QPM

Fox, Sir Paul Leonard, Kt., CBE

Francis, Sir Horace William Alexander, Kt., CBE, FRENG

Francis, *Hon.* Sir Peter Nicholas, Kt.

Francis, Sir Robert Anthony, Kt., QC

Frank, Sir Robert Andrew, Bt. (1920)

†Fraser, Sir Benjamin James, Bt. (1943)

Fraser, Sir Charles Annand, KCVO

Fraser, Sir James Murdo, KBE

Fraser, *Hon.* Sir Peter Donald, Kt.

Fraser, Sir Simon James, GCMG

Frayling, *Prof.* Sir Christopher John, Kt.

Frederick, Sir Christopher St John, Bt. (1723)

Freedman, *Hon.* Sir (Benjamin) Clive, Kt.

Freedman, *Rt. Hon. Prof.* Sir Lawrence David, KCMG, CBE

†Freeman, Sir James Robin, Bt. (1945)

French, *Air Marshal* Sir Joseph Charles, KCB, CBE

Frere, *Vice-Adm.* Sir Richard Tobias, KCB

Friend, *Prof.* Sir Richard Henry, Kt.

Froggatt, Sir Peter, Kt.

Fry, Sir Graham Holbrook, KCMG

Fry, *Lt.-Gen.* Sir Robert Allan, KCB, CBE

Fry, *Dr* Sir Roger Gordon, Kt., CBE

Fulford, *Rt. Hon.* Sir Adrian Bruce, Kt.

Fuller, Sir James Henry Fleetwood, Bt. (1910)

Fulton, *Lt.-Gen.* Sir Robert Henry Gervase, KBE

Furness, Sir Stephen Roberts, Bt. (1913)

Gage, *Rt. Hon.* Sir William Marcus, Kt, QC

Gains, Sir John Christopher, Kt.

Gainsford, Sir Ian Derek, Kt.

Gale, *Rt. Hon.* Sir Roger James, Kt.

Galsworthy, Sir Anthony Charles, KCMG

Galway, Sir James, Kt., OBE

Gamble, Sir David Hugh Norman, Bt. (1897)

Gambon, Sir Michael John, Kt., CBE

Gammell, Sir William Benjamin Bowring, Kt.

Gardiner, Sir John Eliot, Kt., CBE

Gardner, *Prof.* Sir Richard Lavenham, Kt.

Gardner, Sir Roy Alan, Kt.

Garland, *Hon.* Sir Patrick Neville, Kt.

Garland, *Hon.* Sir Ransley Victor, KBE

Garland, *Dr* Sir Trevor, KBE

Garnett, *Adm.* Sir Ian David Graham, KCB

Garnham, *Hon.* Sir Neil Stephen, Kt.

Garnier, *Rear-Adm.* Sir John, KCVO, CBE

Garrard, Sir David Eardley, Kt.

Garrett, Sir Anthony Peter, Kt., CBE

Garrick, Sir Ronald, Kt., CBE, FRENG

Garthwaite, Sir (William) Mark (Charles), Bt. (1919)

Garwood, *Air Marshal* Sir Richard Frank, KBE, CB, DFC

Gass, Sir Simon Lawrance, KCMG, CVO

Geim, *Prof.* Sir Andre Konstantin, Kt.

Geno, Sir Makena Viora, KBE

Gent, Sir Christopher Charles, Kt.

George, *Prof.* Sir Charles Frederick, Kt., MD, FRCP

Gerken, *Vice-Adm.* Sir Robert William Frank, KCB, CBE

Gershon, Sir Peter Oliver, Kt., CBE

Gethin, Sir Richard Joseph St Lawrence, Bt. (I. 1665)

Gibb, Sir Barry Alan Crompton, Kt., CBE

Gibbings, Sir Peter Walter, Kt.

Gibbons, Sir William Edward Doran, Bt. (1752)

Gibbs, *Hon.* Sir Richard John Hedley, Kt.

†Gibson, *Revd* Christopher Herbert, Bt. (1931)

Gibson, Sir Ian, Kt., CBE

Gibson, Sir Kenneth Archibald, Kt.

Gibson, *Rt. Hon.* Sir Peter Leslie, Kt.

Gibson-Craig-Carmichael, Sir David Peter William, Bt. (S. 1702 and 1831)

Gieve, Sir Edward John Watson, KCB

Giffard, Sir (Charles) Sydney (Rycroft), KCMG

Gifford, Sir Michael Roger, Kt.

Gilbert, *Air Chief Marshal* Sir Joseph Alfred, KCB, CBE

†Gilbey, Sir Walter Gavin, Bt. (1893)

Gill, Sir Robin Denys, KCVO

Gillam, Sir Patrick John, Kt.

Gillen, *Hon.* Sir John de Winter, Kt.

Gillett, Sir Nicholas Danvers Penrose, Bt. (1959)

Gillinson, Sir Clive Daniel, Kt., CBE

Gilmore, *Prof.* Sir Ian Thomas, Kt.

†Gilmour, *Hon.* Sir David Robert, Bt. (1926)

Gilmour, Sir John Nicholas, Bt. (1897)

Gina, Sir Lloyd Maepeza, KBE

Giordano, Sir Richard Vincent, KBE

Girolami, Sir Paul, Kt.

Girvan, *Rt. Hon.* Sir (Frederick) Paul, Kt.

Gladstone, Sir Charles Angus, Bt. (1846)

Glean, Sir Carlyle Arnold, GCMG

Globe, *Hon.* Sir Henry Brian, Kt.

Glover, Sir Victor Joseph Patrick, Kt.

Glyn, Sir Richard Lindsay, Bt. (1759 and 1800)

Gobbo, Sir James Augustine, Kt., AC

Godfray, *Prof.* Sir Hugh Charles Jonathan, Kt., CBE

Goldberg, *Prof.* Sir David Paul Brandes, Kt.

Goldring, *Rt. Hon.* Sir John Bernard, Kt.

Gomersall, Sir Stephen John, KCMG

Gonsalves-Sabola, *Hon.* Sir Joaquim Claudino, Kt.

Gooch, Sir Arthur Brian Sherlock Heywood, Bt. (1746)

Gooch, Sir Miles Peter, Bt. (1866)

Good, Sir John James Griffen, Kt., CBE

Goodall, *Air Marshal* Sir Roderick Harvey, KBE, CB, AFC

Goode, *Prof.* Sir Royston Miles, Kt., CBE, QC

Goodenough, Sir Anthony Michael, KCMG

Goodenough, Sir William McLernon, Bt. (1943)

Goodhart, Sir Robert Anthony Gordon, Bt. (1911)

Goodison, Sir Nicholas Proctor, Kt.

Goodson, Sir Alan Reginald, Bt. (1922)

Goodwin, Sir Frederick, KBE

Goold, Sir George William, Bt. (1801)

Goose, *Hon.* Sir Julian Nicholas, Kt.

Gordon, Sir Donald, Kt.

Gordon, Sir Gerald Henry, Kt., CBE, QC

Gordon, Sir Robert James, Bt. (S. 1706)

Gordon-Cumming, Sir Alexander Alastair Penrose, Bt. (1804)

Gore, Sir Hugh Frederick Corbet, Bt. (I. 1622)

Gore-Booth, Sir Josslyn Henry Robert, Bt. (I. 1760)

Goring, Sir William Burton Nigel, Bt. (1678)

Gormley, Sir Antony Mark David, Kt., OBE

Gormley, Sir Paul Brendan, KCMG, MBE

Goschen, Sir (Edward) Alexander, Bt. (1916)

Gosling, Sir (Frederick) Donald, KCVO

Goss, *Hon.* Sir James Richard William, Kt.

Goulden, Sir (Peter) John, GCMG

†Goulding, Sir (William) Lingard Walter, Bt. (1904)

Gourlay, Sir Simon Alexander, Kt.

Gowans, Sir James Learmonth, Kt., CBE, FRCP, FRS

Gowers, *Prof.* Sir William Timothy, Kt.

Gozney, Sir Richard Hugh Turton, KCMG

Graaff, Sir De Villiers, Bt. (1911)

Graham, Sir Alexander Michael, GBE

Graham, Sir James Bellingham, Bt. (1662)

Graham, Sir James Fergus Surtees, Bt. (1783)

Graham, Sir James Thompson, Kt., CMG

Graham, Sir John Alexander Noble, Bt. (1906), GCMG

Graham, Sir John Alistair, Kt.

Graham, Sir John Moodie, Bt. (1964)

Graham, Sir Peter, KCB, QC

Graham, *Lt.-Gen.* Sir Peter Walter, KCB, CBE

†Graham, Sir Ralph Stuart, Bt. (1629)

Graham-Moon, Sir Peter Wilfred Giles, Bt. (1855)

Graham-Smith, *Prof.* Sir Francis, Kt.

Grainge, Sir Lucian Charles, Kt., CBE

Grange, Sir Kenneth Henry, Kt., CBE

Grant, Sir Archibald, Bt. (S. 1705)

Grant, *Dr* Sir David, Kt., CBE

Grant, Sir Ian David, Kt., CBE

Grant, Sir John Douglas Kelso, KCMG

Grant, *Prof.* Sir Malcolm John, Kt., CBE

Grant, Sir Mark Justin Lyall, GCMG

Grant, Sir Patrick Alexander Benedict, Bt. (S. 1688)

Grant, Sir Paul Joseph Patrick, Kt.

Grant, *Lt.-Gen.* Sir Scott Carnegie, KCB

Grant-Suttie, Sir James Edward, Bt. (S. 1702)

Granville-Chapman, *Gen.* Sir Timothy John, GBE, KCB, ADC

Grattan-Bellew, Sir Henry Charles, Bt. (1838)

Gray, Sir Bernard Peter, Kt.

Gray, *Hon.* Sir Charles Anthony St John, Kt.

Gray, Sir Charles Ireland, Kt., CBE

Gray, *Prof.* Sir Denis John Pereira, Kt., OBE, FRCGP

Gray, *Dr* Sir John Armstrong Muir, Kt., CBE

Gray, Sir Robert McDowall (Robin), Kt.

Gray, Sir William Hume, Bt. (1917)

Graydon, *Air Chief Marshal* Sir Michael James, GCB, CBE

Grayson, Sir Jeremy Brian Vincent Harrington, Bt. (1922)

Greaves, *Prof.* Sir Melvyn Francis, Kt.

Green, Sir Allan David, KCB, QC

Green, Sir David John Mark, Kt., CB, QC

Green, Sir Edward Patrick Lycett, Bt. (1886)

Green, Sir Gregory David, KCMG

Green, *Hon.* Sir Guy Stephen Montague, KBE

Green, *Prof.* Sir Malcolm, Kt.

Green, *Rt. Hon.* Sir Nicholas Nigel, Kt.

Green, Sir Philip Green, Kt.

Green-Price, Sir Robert John, Bt. (1874)

Greenaway, *Prof.* Sir David, Kt.

Greenaway, Sir Thomas Edward Burdick, Bt. (1933)

Greener, Sir Anthony Armitage, Kt.

Greenstock, Sir Jeremy Quentin, GCMG

Greenwell, Sir Edward Bernard, Bt. (1906)

Greenwood, *Prof.* Sir Brian Mellor, Kt., CBE

Greenwood, *Prof.* Sir Christopher John, GBE, CMG

Gregory, *Lt.-Gen.* Sir Andrew Richard, KBE, CB

Gregory, *Prof.* Sir Michael John, Kt., CBE

Gregson, *Prof.* Sir Peter John Kt., FRENG

Grey, Sir Anthony Dysart, Bt. (1814)

Grice, Sir Paul Edward, Kt.

Griffiths, Sir Michael, Kt.

Grigson, *Hon.* Sir Geoffrey Douglas, Kt.

Grimshaw, Sir Nicholas Thomas, Kt., CBE

Grimstone, Sir Gerald Edgar, Kt.

Grimwade, Sir Andrew Sheppard, Kt., CBE

Grose, *Vice-Adm.* Sir Alan, KBE

Gross, *Rt. Hon.* Sir Peter Henry, Kt.

Grossart, Sir Angus McFarlane McLeod, Kt., CBE

Grotrian, Sir Philip Christian Brent, Bt. (1934)

†Grove, Sir Charles Gerald, Bt. (1874)

Grundy, Sir Mark, Kt.

Guinness, Sir John Ralph Sidney, Kt., CB

Guinness, Sir Kenelm Edward Lee, Bt. (1867)

Guise, Sir Christopher James, Bt. (1783)

Gull, Sir Rupert William Cameron, Bt. (1872)

Gunning, Sir Charles Theodore, Bt. (1778)

Gunston, Sir John Wellesley, Bt. (1938)

Gurdon, *Prof.* Sir John Bertrand, Kt., DPHIL, FRS

Guthrie, Sir Malcolm Connop, Bt. (1936)

Habgood, Sir Anthony John, Kt.

Haddacks, *Vice-Adm.* Sir Paul Kenneth, KCB

Haddon-Cave, *Rt. Hon.* Sir Charles Anthony, Kt.

Hadlee, Sir Richard John, Kt., MBE

Hagart-Alexander, Sir Claud, Bt. (1886)

Haines, *Prof.* Sir Andrew Paul, Kt.

Haji-Ioannou, Sir Stelios, Kt.

Halberg, Sir Murray Gordon, Kt., MBE

Hall, *Dr* Sir Andrew James, Kt.
†Hall, Sir David Bernard, Bt. (1919)
Hall, Sir David Christopher, Bt. (1923)
Hall, *Prof.* Sir David Michael Baldock, Kt.
Hall, Sir Ernest, Kt., OBE
Hall, Sir Geoffrey, Kt.
Hall, Sir Graham Joseph, Kt.
Hall, Sir Iain Robert, Kt.
Hall, Sir John, Kt.
Hall, Sir John Douglas Hoste, Bt. (S. 1687)
Hall, HE *Prof.* Sir Kenneth Octavius, GCMG
Hall, Sir Peter Edward, KBE, CMG
Hall, *Revd* Wesley Winfield, Kt.
Hall, Sir William Joseph, KCVO
Halliday, *Prof.* Sir Alexander Norman, Kt., FRS
Haloute, Sir Assad John, Kt.
Halpern, Sir Ralph Mark, Kt.
Halsey, *Revd* John Walter Brooke, Bt. (1920)
Halstead, Sir Ronald, Kt., CBE
Ham, *Prof.* Sir Christopher John, Kt., CBE
Hamblen, *Rt. Hon.* Sir Nicholas Archibald, Kt.
Hambling, Sir Herbert Peter Hugh, Bt. (1924)
Hamilton, Sir Andrew Caradoc, Bt. (S. 1646)
Hamilton, Sir David, Kt.
Hamilton, Sir George Ernest Craythorne, Kt., QPM
Hamilton, Sir Nigel, KCB
†Hamilton-Dalrymple, Sir Hew Richard, Bt. (S. 1698)
Hamilton-Spencer-Smith, Sir John, Bt. (1804)
Hammick, Sir Jeremy Charles, Bt. (1834)
Hammond, Sir Anthony Hilgrove, KCB, QC
Hampel, Sir Ronald Claus, Kt.
Hampson, Sir Stuart, Kt., CVO
Hampton, Sir (Leslie) Geoffrey, Kt.
Hampton, Sir Philip Roy, Kt.
Hanham, Sir William John Edward, Bt. (1667)
Hankes-Drielsma, Sir Claude Dunbar, KCVO
Hanley, *Rt. Hon.* Sir Jeremy James, KCMG
Hanmer, Sir Wyndham Richard Guy, Bt. (1774)
Hannam, Sir John Gordon, Kt.
Hanson, Sir (Charles) Rupert (Patrick), Bt. (1918)
Harcourt-Smith, *Air Chief Marshal* Sir David, GBE, KCB, DFC
Hardie Boys, *Rt. Hon.* Sir Michael, GCMG
Harding, *Marshal of the Royal Air Force* Sir Peter Robin, GCB
Hardy, Sir David William, Kt.
Hardy, Sir James Gilbert, Kt., OBE
Hare, Sir David, Kt., FRSL
Hare, Sir Nicholas Patrick, Bt. (1818)

Haren, *Dr* Sir Patrick Hugh, Kt.
Harford, Sir Mark John, Bt. (1934)
Harington, Sir David Richard, Bt. (1611)
Harkness, *Very Revd* James, KCVO, CB, OBE
Harley, *Gen.* Sir Alexander George Hamilton, KBE, CB
Harman, *Hon.* Sir Jeremiah LeRoy, Kt.
Harman, Sir John Andrew, Kt.
†Harmsworth, Sir Hildebrand Harold, Bt. (1922)
Harper, *Air Marshal* Sir Christopher Nigel, KBE
Harper, Sir Ewan William, Kt., CBE
Harper, *Prof.* Sir Peter Stanley, Kt., CBE
Harris, Sir Christopher John Ashford, Bt. (1932)
Harris, *Air Marshal* Sir John Hulme, KCB, CBE
Harris, *Prof.* Sir Martin Best, Kt., CBE
Harris, Sir Michael Frank, Kt.
Harris, Sir Thomas George, KBE, CMG
Harrison, *Prof.* Sir Brian Howard, Kt.
Harrison, Sir David, Kt., CBE, FRENG
†Harrison, Sir Edwin Michael Harwood, Bt. (1961)
Harrison, *Hon.* Sir Michael Guy Vicat, Kt.
Harrison, Sir (Robert) Colin, Bt. (1922)
Harrop, Sir Peter John, KCB
Hart, *Hon.* Sir Anthony Ronald, Kt.
Hart, Sir Graham Allan, KCB
Hartwell, Sir (Francis) Anthony Charles Peter, Bt. (1805)
Harvey, Sir Charles Richard Musgrave, Bt. (1933)
Harvey, Sir Nicholas Barton, Kt.
Harvie, Sir John Smith, Kt., CBE
Harvie-Watt, Sir James, Bt. (1945)
Harwood, Sir Ronald, Kt., CBE
Haslam, *Prof.* Sir David Antony, Kt., CBE
Hastie, *Cdre* Sir Robert Cameron, KCVO, CBE, RD
Hastings, Sir Max Macdonald, Kt.
Hastings, *Dr* Sir William George, Kt., CBE
Hatter, Sir Maurice, Kt.
Havelock-Allan, Sir (Anthony) Mark David, Bt. (1858), QC
Hawkes, Sir John Garry, Kt., CBE
Hawkhead, Sir Anthony Gerard, Kt., CBE
Hawkins, Sir Richard Caesar, Bt. (1778)
Hawley, Sir James Appleton, KCVO, TD
Haworth, Sir Philip, Bt. (1911)
Hay, Sir John Erroll Audley, Bt. (S. 1663)
†Hay, Sir Ronald Frederick Hamilton, Bt. (S. 1703)
Hayden, *Hon.* Sir Anthony Paul, Kt.
Hayes, Sir Brian, Kt., CBE, QPM
Hayes, Sir Brian David, GCB

Hayes, *Rt. Hon.* Sir John Henry, Kt., CBE
Hayman-Joyce, *Lt.-Gen.* Sir Robert John, KCB, CBE
Hayter, Sir Paul David Grenville, KCB, LVO
Hazlewood, Sir Frederick Asa, KCMG
Head, Sir Patrick, Kt.
Head, Sir Richard Douglas Somerville, Bt. (1838)
Heald, *Rt. Hon.* Sir Oliver, Kt.
Heap, Sir Peter William, KCMG
Heap, *Prof.* Sir Robert Brian, Kt., CBE, FRS
Hearne, Sir Graham James, Kt., CBE
Heathcote, Sir Simon Robert Mark, Bt. (1733), OBE
†Heathcote, Sir Timothy Gilbert, Bt. (1733)
Heaton, Sir Richard, KCB
Heber-Percy, Sir Algernon Eustace Hugh, KCVO
Hedley, *Hon.* Sir Mark, Kt.
Hegarty, Sir John Kevin, Kt.
Heiser, Sir Terence Michael, GCB
Helfgott, Sir Ben, Kt., MBE
Heller, Sir Michael Aron, Kt.
Hempleman-Adams, *Dr* Sir David Kim, KCVO, OBE
Henderson, *Rt Hon.* Sir Launcelot Dinadin James, Kt.
Henderson, *Maj.* Sir Richard Yates, KCVO
Hendrick, Sir Mark, Kt.
Hendry, *Prof.* Sir David Forbes, Kt.
Hendy, Sir Peter Gerard, Kt., CBE
Hennessy, Sir James Patrick Ivan, KBE, CMG
†Henniker, Sir Adrian Chandos, Bt. (1813)
Henniker-Heaton, Sir Yvo Robert, Bt. (1912)
Henriques, *Hon.* Sir Richard Henry Quixano, Kt.
Henry, Sir Lenworth George, Kt., CBE
†Henry, Sir Patrick Denis, Bt. (1923)
Henshaw, Sir David George, Kt.
Herbecq, Sir John Edward, KCB
Heron, Sir Conrad Frederick, KCB, OBE
†Heron-Maxwell, Sir Nigel Mellor, Bt. (S. 1683)
Hervey, Sir Roger Blaise Ramsay, KCVO, CMG
Hervey-Bathurst, Sir Frederick William John, Bt. (1818)
Heseltine, *Rt. Hon.* Sir William Frederick Payne, GCB, GCVO
Hewetson, Sir Christopher Raynor, Kt., TD
Hewett, Sir Richard Mark John, Bt. (1813)
Hewitt, Sir (Cyrus) Lenox (Simson), Kt., OBE
Hewitt, Sir Nicholas Charles Joseph, Bt. (1921)
Heygate, Sir Richard John Gage, Bt. (1831)
Heywood, Sir Peter, Bt. (1838)

Hickey, Sir John Tongri, Kt., CBE

Hickinbottom, *Rt. Hon.* Sir Gary Robert, Kt.

Hickman, Sir (Richard) Glenn, Bt. (1903)

Hicks, Sir Robert, Kt.

Hielscher, Sir Leo Arthur, Kt.

Higgins, Sir David Hartmann, Kt.

Higgins, *Rt. Hon.* Sir Malachy Joseph, Kt.

Hildyard, *Hon.* Sir Robert Henry Thoroton, Kt.

Hill, *Rt. Revd Dr* Christopher John, KCVO

Hill, Sir James Frederick, Bt. (1917), OBE

Hill, Sir John Alfred Rowley, Bt. (I. 1779)

Hill, *Vice-Adm.* Sir Robert Charles Finch, KBE, FRENG

Hill-Norton, *Vice-Adm. Hon.* Sir Nicholas John, KCB

Hill-Wood, Sir Samuel Thomas, Bt. (1921)

Hillhouse, Sir (Robert) Russell, KCB

Hillier, *Air Marshal* Sir Stephen John, KCB, CBE, DFC

Hills, Sir John Robert, Kt., CBE

Hilly, Sir Francis Billy, KCMG

Hine, *Air Chief Marshal* Sir Patrick Bardon, GCB, GBE

Hintze, Sir Michael, Kt.

Hirsch, *Prof.* Sir Peter Bernhard, Kt., PHD, FRS

Hirst, Sir Michael William, Kt.

Hitchens, Sir Timothy Mark, KCVO, CMG

Hoare, *Prof.* Sir Charles Anthony Richard, Kt., FRS

Hoare, Sir Charles James, Bt. (I. 1784)

Hoare, Sir David John, Bt. (1786)

Hobart, Sir John Vere, Bt. (1914)

Hobbs, *Maj.-Gen.* Sir Michael Frederick, KCVO, CBE

Hobhouse, Sir Charles John Spinney, Bt. (1812)

†Hodge, Sir Andrew Rowland, Bt. (1921)

Hodge, Sir James William, KCVO, CMG

Hodgkinson, Sir Michael Stewart, Kt.

Hodson, Sir Michael Robin Adderley, Bt. (I. 1789)

Hogg, Sir Christopher Anthony, Kt.

Hogg, Sir Piers Michael James, Bt. (1846)

Hohn, Sir Christopher, KCMG

Holcroft, Sir Charles Anthony Culcheth, Bt. (1921)

Holden, Sir John David, Bt. (1919)

Holden, Sir Michael Peter, Bt. (1893)

Holder, Sir John Henry, Bt. (1898)

Holderness, Sir Martin William, Bt. (1920)

Holdgate, Sir Martin Wyatt, Kt., CB, PHD

Holgate, *Hon.* Sir David John, Kt.

Holland, *Hon.* Sir Christopher John, Kt.

Holland, Sir John Anthony, Kt.

Holm, Sir Ian (Holm Cuthbert), Kt., CBE

Holman, *Hon.* Sir Edward James, Kt.

Holman, *Prof.* Sir John Stranger, Kt.

Holmes, Sir John Eaton, GCVO, KBE, CMG

Holroyd, Sir Michael De Courcy Fraser, Kt., CBE

Holroyde, *Rt. Hon.* Sir Timothy Victor, Kt.

Home, Sir William Dundas, Bt. (S. 1671)

Honywood, Sir Filmer Courtenay William, Bt. (1660)

†Hood, Sir John Joseph Harold, Bt. (1922)

Hooper, *Rt. Hon.* Sir Anthony, Kt.

Hope, Sir Alexander Archibald Douglas, Bt. (S. 1628), OBE

Hope-Dunbar, Sir David, Bt. (S. 1664)

Hopkin, *Prof.* Sir Deian Rhys, Kt.

Hopkin, Sir Royston Oliver, KCMG

Hopkins, Sir Anthony Philip, Kt., CBE

Hopkins, Sir Michael John, Kt., CBE, RA, RIBA

Hopwood, *Prof.* Sir David Alan, Kt., FRS

Hordern, *Rt. Hon.* Sir Peter Maudslay, Kt.

Horlick, *Vice-Adm.* Sir Edwin John, KBE, FRENG

Horlick, Sir James Cunliffe William, Bt. (1914)

Horn-Smith, Sir Julian Michael, Kt.

Horne, Sir Alan Gray Antony, Bt. (1929)

Horner, *Hon.* Sir Thomas Mark, Kt.

Horsbrugh-Porter, Sir Andrew Alexander Marshall, Bt. (1902)

Horsfall, Sir Edward John Wright, Bt. (1909)

Hort, Sir Andrew Edwin Fenton, Bt. (1767)

Hosker, Sir Gerald Albery, KCB, QC

Hoskins, *Prof.* Sir Brian John, Kt., CBE, FRS

Hoskyns, Sir Robin Chevallier, Bt. (1676)

Hotung, Sir Joseph Edward, Kt.

Hough, *Prof.* Sir James, Kt., OBE

Houghton, Sir John Theodore, Kt., CBE, FRS

Houghton, Sir Stephen Geoffrey, Kt., CBE

Houldsworth, Sir Richard Thomas Reginald, Bt. (1887)

Hourston, Sir Gordon Minto, Kt.

Housden, Sir Peter James, KCB

House, Sir Stephen, Kt., QPM

Houssemayne du Boulay, Sir Roger William, KCVO, CMG

Houstoun-Boswall, Sir (Thomas) Alford, Bt. (1836)

Howard, Sir David Howarth Seymour, Bt. (1955)

Howard, *Dr* Sir Laurence, KCVO, OBE

Howard, *Prof.* Sir Michael Eliot, Kt., OM, CH, CBE, MC

Howard-Lawson, Sir John Philip, Bt. (1841)

Howarth, *Rt. Hon.* Sir George Edward, Kt.

Howarth, Sir (James) Gerald Douglas, Kt.

Howells, Sir Eric Waldo Benjamin, Kt., CBE

Howes, Sir Christopher Kingston, KCVO, CB

Howlett, *Gen.* Sir Geoffrey Hugh Whitby, KBE, MC

Hoy, Sir Christopher Andrew, Kt., MBE

Hoyle, *Rt. Hon.* Sir Lindsay Harvey, Kt.

Huddleston, *Hon.* Sir Ian William, Kt.

Hudson, Sir Mark, KCVO

Hughes, *Rt. Hon.* Sir Anthony Philip Gilson, Kt. (Lord Hughes of Ombersley)

Hughes, *Rt. Hon.* Sir Simon Henry Ward, Kt.

Hughes, Sir Thomas Collingwood, Bt. (1773)

Hughes-Hallett, Sir Thomas Michael Sydney, Kt.

Hughes-Morgan, Sir (Ian) Parry David, Bt. (1925)

Hull, *Prof.* Sir David, Kt.

Hulme, Sir Philip William, Kt.

Hulse, Sir Edward Jeremy Westrow, Bt. (1739)

Hum, Sir Christopher Owen, KCMG

Humphreys, *Prof.* Sir Colin John, Kt., CBE

Hunt, *Dr* Sir Richard Timothy, Kt.

Hunte, *Hon. Dr* Sir Julian Robert, KCMG, OBE

Hunter, Sir Alistair John, KCMG

Hunter, *Prof.* Sir Laurence Colvin, Kt., CBE, FRSE

Hunter, *Dr* Sir Philip John, Kt., CBE

Hunter, Sir Thomas Blane, Kt.

†Huntington-Whiteley, Sir Leopold Maurice, Bt. (1918)

Hurn, Sir (Francis) Roger, Kt.

Hurst, Sir Geoffrey Charles, Kt., MBE

Husbands, *Prof.* Sir Christopher Roy, Kt.

†Hutchison, Sir James Colville, Bt. (1956)

Hutchison, *Rt. Hon.* Sir Michael, Kt.

Hutchison, Sir Robert, Bt. (1939)

Hutt, Sir Dexter Walter, Kt.

Hytner, Sir Nicholas, Kt.

Iacobescu, Sir George, Kt., CBE

Ibbotson, *Vice-Adm.* Sir Richard Jeffrey, KBE, CB, DSC

Ife, *Prof.* Sir Barry William, Kt., CBE

Imbert-Terry, Sir Michael Edward Stanley, Bt. (1917)

Imray, Sir Colin Henry, KBE, CMG

Ingham, Sir Bernard, Kt.

Ingilby, Sir Thomas Colvin William, Bt. (1866)

Inglis, Sir William St Clair Inglis, Bt. (S. 1687)
†Inglis of Glencorse, Sir Ian Richard, Bt. (S. 1703)
Ingram, Sir James Herbert Charles, Bt. (1893)
Innes, Sir Alastair Charles Deverell, Bt. (NS 1686)
Innes of Edingight, Sir Malcolm Rognvald, KCVO
Innes, Sir Peter Alexander Berowald, Bt. (S. 1628)
Insall, Sir Donald William, Kt., CBE
Ipatas, *Hon.* Sir Peter, KBE
Irving, *Prof.* Sir Miles Horsfall, Kt., MD, FRCS, FRCSE
Irwin, *Lt.-Gen.* Sir Alistair Stuart Hastings, KCB, CBE
Irwin, *Rt. Hon.* Sir Stephen John, Kt.
Isaacs, Sir Jeremy Israel, Kt.
Isham, Sir Norman Murray Crawford, Bt. (1627), OBE
Ishiguro, Sir Kazuo, Kt., OBE
Italeli, *HE* Sir Iakoba Taeia, GCMG
Ive, Sir Jonathan Paul, KBE
Ivory, Sir Brian Gammell, Kt., CBE

Jack, Sir Malcolm Roy, KCB
Jack, *Hon.* Sir Raymond Evan, Kt.
Jackling, Sir Roger Tustin, KCB, CBE
Jackson, Sir Barry Trevor, Kt.
Jackson, Sir Kenneth Joseph, Kt.
Jackson, *Gen.* Sir Michael David, GCB, CBE
†Jackson, Sir Neil Keith, Bt. (1815)
Jackson, Sir Nicholas Fane St George, Bt. (1913)
Jackson, *Rt. Hon.* Sir Peter Arthur Brian, Kt.
Jackson, *Rt. Hon.* Sir Rupert Matthew, Kt.
Jackson, Sir Thomas Saint Felix, Bt. (1902)
Jackson, Sir (William) Roland Cedric, Bt. (1869)
Jacob, *Rt. Hon.* Sir Robert Raphael Hayim (Robin), Kt.
Jacobi, Sir Derek George, Kt., CBE
Jacobs, Sir Cecil Albert, Kt., CBE
Jacobs, *Rt. Hon.* Sir Francis Geoffrey, KCMG, QC
Jacobs, *Dr* Sir Michael Graham, Kt.
Jacobs, *Hon.* Sir Richard David, Kt.
Jacomb, Sir Martin Wakefield, Kt.
Jaffray, Sir William Otho, Bt. (1892)
Jagger, Sir Michael Philip, Kt.
James, Sir Jeffrey Russell, KBE
James, Sir John Nigel Courtenay, KCVO, CBE
Jameson, *Brig.* Sir Melville Stewart, KCVO, CBE
Jardine, Sir Andrew Colin Douglas, Bt. (1916)
Jardine of Applegirth, Sir William Murray, Bt. (S. 1672)
Jarman, *Prof.* Sir Brian, Kt., OBE
Jarratt, Sir Alexander Anthony, Kt., CB
Jay, *Hon.* Sir Robert Maurice, Kt.
Jeewoolall, Sir Ramesh, Kt.

Jeffery, Sir Thomas Baird, Kt., CB
Jeffrey, Sir William Alexander, KCB
Jeffreys, *Prof.* Sir Alec John, Kt., CH, FRS
Jeffries, *Hon.* Sir John Francis, Kt.
Jehangir, Sir Cowasji, Bt. (1908)
Jejeebhoy, Sir Jamsetjee, Bt. (1857)
Jenkin, *Hon.* Sir Bernard Christison, Kt.
Jenkins, Sir Brian Garton, GBE
Jenkins, Sir James Christopher, KCB, QC
Jenkins, Sir John, KCMG, LVO
Jenkins, *Dr* Sir Karl William Pamp, Kt., CBE
Jenkins, Sir Michael Nicholas Howard, Kt., OBE
Jenkins, Sir Simon, Kt.
Jenkinson, Sir John Banks, Bt. (1661)
Jenks, Sir (Richard) Peter, Bt. (1932)
Jenner, *Air Marshal* Sir Timothy Ivo, KCB
Jennings, Sir John Southwood, Kt., CBE, FRSE
Jennings, Sir Peter Neville Wake, Kt., CVO
Jephcott, Sir David Welbourn, Bt. (1962)
Jessel, Sir Charles John, Bt. (1883)
Jewkes, Sir Gordon Wesley, KCMG
Jewson, Sir Richard Wilson, KCVO
Job, Sir Peter James Denton, Kt.
John, Sir David Glyndwr, KCMG
John, Sir Elton Hercules (Reginald Kenneth Dwight), Kt., CBE
Johns, *Vice-Adm.* Sir Adrian James, KCB, CBE, ADC
Johns, *Air Chief Marshal* Sir Richard Edward, GCB, KCVO, CBE
Johnson, Sir Colpoys Guy, Bt. (1755)
Johnson, *Gen.* Sir Garry Dene, KCB, OBE, MC
Johnson, *Hon.* Sir Jeremy Charles, Kt.
†Johnson, Sir Patrick Eliot, Bt. (1818)
Johnson, *Hon.* Sir Robert Lionel, Kt.
Johnson-Ferguson, Sir Mark Edward, Bt. (1906)
Johnston, *Lt.-Gen.* Sir Maurice Robert, KCB, CVO, OBE
Johnston, Sir Thomas Alexander, Bt. (S. 1626)
Johnston, Sir William Ian Ridley, Kt., CBE, QPM
Johnstone, *Vice-Adm.* Sir Clive Charles Carruthers, KBE, CB
Johnstone, Sir Geoffrey Adams Dinwiddie, KCMG
Johnstone, Sir (George) Richard Douglas, Bt. (S. 1700)
Johnstone, Sir (John) Raymond, Kt., CBE
Jolliffe, Sir Anthony Stuart, GBE
Jolly, Sir Arthur Richard, KCMG
Jonas, Sir John Peter, Kt., CBE
Jones, Sir Alan Jeffrey, Kt.
Jones, Sir Bryn Terfel, Kt., CBE
Jones, Sir Clive William, KCMG, CBE
Jones, Sir David Charles, Kt., CBE
Jones, Sir Derek William, KCB

Jones, Sir Harry George, Kt., CBE
Jones, *Rt. Revd* James Stuart, KBE
Jones, Sir John Francis, Kt.
Jones, Sir Kenneth Lloyd, Kt., QPM
Jones, Sir Lyndon, Kt.
Jones, Sir Mark Ellis Powell, Kt.
Jones, *Vice-Adm.* Sir Philip Andrew, KCB
Jones, Sir Richard Anthony Lloyd, KCB
Jones, Sir Robert Edward, Kt.
Jones, Sir Roger Spencer, Kt., OBE
†Joseph, *Hon.* Sir James Samuel, Bt. (1943)
Jowell, *Prof.* Sir Jeffrey Lionel, KCMG, QC
Jowitt, *Hon.* Sir Edwin Frank, Kt.
Jugnauth, *Rt. Hon.* Sir Anerood, KCMG
Jungius, *Vice-Adm.* Sir James George, KBE

Kaberry, *Hon.* Sir Christopher Donald, Bt. (1960)
Kabui, Sir Frank Utu Ofagioro, GCMG, OBE
Kadoorie, *Hon.* Sir Michael David, Kt.
Kakaraya, Sir Pato, KBE
Kamit, Sir Leonard Wilson, Kt., CBE
Kapoor, Sir Anish Mikhail, Kt., CBE
Kaputin, Sir John Rumet, KBE, CMG
Kavali, Sir Thomas, Kt., OBE
Kay, *Rt. Hon.* Sir Maurice Ralph, Kt.
Kay, Sir Nicholas Peter, KCMG
Kaye, Sir Paul Henry Gordon, Bt. (1923)
Keane, Sir John Charles, Bt. (1801)
Kearney, *Hon.* Sir William John Francis, Kt., CBE
Keegan, *Dr* Sir Donal Arthur John, KCVO, OBE
Keehan, *Hon.* Sir Michael Joseph, Kt.
Keene, *Rt. Hon.* Sir David Wolfe, Kt.
Keenlyside, Sir Simon John, Kt., CBE
Keith, *Hon.* Sir Brian Richard, Kt.
Keith, *Rt. Hon.* Sir Kenneth, KBE, CBE
†Kellett, Sir Stanley Charles, Bt. (1801)
Kelly, Sir Christopher William, KCB
Kelly, Sir David Robert Corbett, Kt., CBE
Kemakeza, Sir Allan, Kt.
Kemball, *Air Marshal* Sir (Richard) John, KCB, CBE
Kemp-Welch, Sir John, Kt.
Kendall, Sir Peter Ashley, Kt.
Kennaway, Sir John-Michael, Bt. (1791)
†Kennedy, Sir George Matthew Rae, Bt. (1836)
Kennedy, *Hon.* Sir Ian Alexander, Kt.
Kennedy, *Prof.* Sir Ian McColl, Kt.
Kennedy, *Rt. Hon.* Sir Paul Joseph Morrow, Kt.
Kenny, Sir Anthony John Patrick, Kt., DPHIL, DLITT, FBA
Kenny, Sir Paul Stephen, Kt.
Kentridge, Sir Sydney Woolf, KCMG, QC

Kenyon, Sir Nicholas Roger, Kt., CBE

Keogh, *Prof.* Sir Bruce Edward, KBE

Kere, *Dr* Sir Nathan, KCMG

Kerr, *Adm.* Sir John Beverley, GCB

Kerr, Sir Ronald James, Kt., CBE

Kerr, *Hon.* Sir Timothy Julian, Kt.

Kershaw, *Prof.* Sir Ian, Kt.

Keswick, Sir Henry Neville Lindley, Kt.

Keswick, Sir John Chippendale Lindley, Kt.

Kevau, *Prof.* Sir Isi Henao, Kt., CBE

Khaw, *Prof.* Sir Peng Tee, Kt.

Kikau, *Ratu* Sir Jone Latianara, KBE

Kimber, Sir Rupert Edward Watkin, Bt. (1904)

King, *Prof.* Sir David Anthony, Kt., FRS

King, Sir James Henry Rupert, Bt. (1888)

King, Sir Julian Beresford, KCVO, CMG

King, *Hon.* Sir Timothy Roger Alan, Kt.

King, Sir Wayne Alexander, Bt. (1815)

Kingman, *Prof.* Sir John Frank Charles, Kt., FRS

Kingman, Sir John Oliver Frank, KCB

Kingsley, Sir Ben, Kt.

Kinloch, Sir David, Bt. (S. 1686)

Kinloch, Sir David Oliphant, Bt. (1873)

Kipalan, Sir Albert, Kt.

Kirch, Sir David Roderick, KBE

Kirkpatrick, Sir Ivone Elliott, Bt. (S. 1685)

Kiszely, *Lt.-Gen.* Sir John Panton, KCB, MC

Kitchin, *Rt. Hon.* Sir David James Tyson, Kt. (Lord Kitchin)

Kitson, *Gen.* Sir Frank Edward, GBE, KCB, MC

Kleinwort, Sir Richard Drake, Bt. (1909)

Klenerman, *Prof.* Sir David, Kt., FRS

Knight, *Rt. Hon.* Sir Gregory, Kt.

Knight, Sir Kenneth John, Kt., CBE, QFSM

Knight, *Air Chief Marshal* Sir Michael William Patrick, KCB, AFC

Knight, *Prof.* Sir Peter, Kt.

Knill, Sir Thomas John Pugin Bartholomew, Bt. (1893)

Knowles, Sir Charles Francis, Bt. (1765)

Knowles, *Hon.* Sir Julian Bernard, Kt.

Knowles, Sir Nigel Graham, Kt.

Knowles, *Hon.* Sir Robin St John, Kt.

Knox, Sir David Laidlaw, Kt.

Knox-Johnston, Sir William Robert Patrick (Sir Robin), Kt., CBE, RD

Koraea, Sir Thomas, Kt.

Kornberg, *Prof.* Sir Hans Leo, Kt., DSc, SCD, PHD, FRS

Korowi, Sir Wiwa, GCMG

Kulukundis, Sir Elias George (Eddie), Kt., OBE

Kulunga, Sir Toami, Kt., OBE, QPM

Kumar, Sir Harpal Singh, Kt.

Kwok-Po Li, *Dr* Sir David, Kt., OBE

Lachmann, *Prof.* Sir Peter Julius, Kt.

Lacon, Sir Edmund Richard Vere, Bt. (1818)

Lacy, Sir Patrick Brian Finucane, Bt. (1921)

Laing, Sir (John) Martin (Kirby), Kt., CBE

Lake, Sir Edward Geoffrey, Bt. (1711)

Lakin, Sir Richard Anthony, Bt. (1909)

Lamb, Sir Albert Thomas, KBE, CMG, DFC

Lamb, *Lt.-Gen.* Sir Graeme Cameron Maxwell, KBE, CMG, DSO

Lamb, *Rt. Hon.* Sir Norman Peter, Kt.

Lambert, *Vice-Adm.* Sir Paul, KCB

†Lambert, Sir Peter John Biddulph, Bt. (1711)

Lambert, Sir Richard Peter, Kt.

Lampl, Sir Peter, Kt., OBE

Lamport, Sir Stephen Mark Jeffrey, GCVO

Lancashire, Sir Steve, Kt.

Landau, Sir Dennis Marcus, Kt.

Lander, Sir Stephen James, KCB

Lane, Prof. Sir David Philip, Kt.

Lane, *Hon.* Sir Peter Richard, Kt.

Langham, Sir John Stephen, Bt. (1660)

Langlands, Sir Robert Alan, Kt.

Langley, *Hon.* Sir Gordon Julian Hugh, Kt.

Langrishe, Sir James Hercules, Bt. (I. 1777)

Langstaff, *Hon.* Sir Brian Frederick James, Kt.

Lankester, Sir Timothy Patrick, KCB

Lapli, Sir John Ini, GCMG

Lapthorne, Sir Richard Douglas, Kt., CBE

Large, Sir Andrew McLeod Brooks, Kt.

Latasi, *Rt. Hon.* Sir Kamuta, KCMG, OBE

Latham, *Rt. Hon.* Sir David Nicholas Ramsey, Kt.

Latham, Sir Richard Thomas Paul, Bt. (1919)

Laughton, Sir Anthony Seymour, Kt.

Laurence, *Vice-Adm.* Sir Timothy James Hamilton, KCVO, CB, ADC

Laurie, Sir Andrew Ronald Emilius, Bt. (1834)

Lavender, *Hon.* Sir Nicholas, Kt.

†Lawrence, Sir Aubrey Lyttelton Simon, Bt. (1867)

Lawrence, Sir Clive Wyndham, Bt. (1906)

Lawrence, Sir Edmund Wickham, GCMG, OBE

Lawrence, Sir Henry Peter, Bt. (1858)

Lawrence, Sir Ivan John, Kt., QC

Lawrence-Jones, Sir Christopher, Bt. (1831)

Laws, *Rt. Hon.* Sir John Grant McKenzie, Kt.

Laws, Sir Stephen Charles, KCB

Lawson, Sir Charles John Patrick, Bt. (1900)

Lawson, *Gen.* Sir Richard George, KCB, DSO, OBE

Lawson-Tancred, Sir Andrew Peter, Bt. (1662)

Lawton, *Prof.* Sir John Hartley, Kt., CBE, FRS

Layard, *Adm.* Sir Michael Henry Gordon, KCB, CBE

Lea, Sir Thomas William, Bt. (1892)

Leahy, Sir Daniel Joseph, Kt.

Leahy, Sir Terence Patrick, Kt.

Learmont, *Gen.* Sir John Hartley, KCB, CBE

Leaver, Sir Christopher, GBE

Lechler, *Prof.* Sir Robert Ian, Kt.

Lechmere, Sir Nicholas Anthony Hungerford, Bt. (1818)

†Leeds, Sir John Charles Hildyard, Bt. (1812)

Lees, Sir Christopher James, Bt. (1897), TD

Lees, Sir David Bryan, Kt.

Lees, Sir Thomas Harcourt Ivor, Bt. (1804)

Lees, Sir (William) Antony Clare, Bt. (1937)

Leese, Sir Richard Charles, Kt., CBE

Leeson, *Air Marshal* Sir Kevin James, KCB, CBE

le Fleming, Sir David Kelland, Bt. (1705)

Legard, Sir Charles Thomas, Bt. (1660)

Legg, Sir Thomas Stuart, KCB, QC

Leggatt, *Rt. Hon.* Sir Andrew Peter, Kt.

Leggatt, *Rt. Hon.* Sir George Andrew Midsomer, Kt.

Leggett, *Prof.* Sir Anthony James, KBE

Le Grand, *Prof.* Sir Julian Ernest, Kt.

Leigh, *Rt. Hon.* Sir Edward Julian Egerton, Kt.

Leigh, Sir Geoffrey Norman, Kt.

Leigh, *Dr* Sir Michael, KCMG

Leigh, Sir Richard Henry, Bt. (1918)

Leigh-Pemberton, Sir James Henry, Kt., CVO

Leighton, Sir John Mark Nicholas, Kt.

Leighton, Sir Michael John Bryan, Bt. (1693)

Le Marchant, Sir Piers Alfred, Bt. (1841)

Lennox-Boyd, *Hon.* Sir Mark Alexander, Kt.

Leon, Sir John Ronald, Bt. (1911)

Lepani, Sir Charles Watson, KBE

†Leslie, Sir Shaun Rudolph Christopher, Bt. (1876)

Lester, Sir James Theodore, Kt.

Lethbridge, Sir Thomas Periam Hector Noel, Bt. (1804)

Letwin, *Rt. Hon.* Sir Oliver, Kt.

Lever, Sir Jeremy Frederick, KCMG, QC

Lever, Sir Paul, KCMG

Lever, Sir (Tresham) Christopher Arthur Lindsay, Bt. (1911)

Leveson, *Rt. Hon.* Sir Brian Henry, Kt.

Levi, Sir Wasangula Noel, Kt., CBE

Levinge, Sir Richard George Robin, Bt. (I. 1704)

Lewinton, Sir Christopher, Kt.

Lewis, *Hon.* Sir Clive Buckland, Kt.

Lewis, Sir David Thomas Rowell, Kt.

Lewis, Sir John Anthony, Kt., OBE

Lewis, Sir John Henry James, Kt., OBE

Lewis, Sir Leigh Warren, KCB

Lewis, Sir Martyn John Dudley, Kt., CBE

Lewis, Sir Terence Murray, Kt., OBE, GM, QPM

Lewison, *Rt. Hon.* Sir Kim Martin Jordan, Kt.

Ley, Sir Christopher Ian, Bt. (1905)

Li, Sir Ka-Shing, KBE

Lickiss, Sir Michael Gillam, Kt.

Liddington, Sir Bruce, Kt.

Lightman, *Hon.* Sir Gavin Anthony, Kt.

Lighton, Sir Thomas Hamilton, Bt. (I. 1791)

Likierman, *Prof.* Sir John Andrew, Kt.

Lilleyman, *Prof.* Sir John Stuart, Kt.

Lindblom, *Rt. Hon.* Sir Keith John, Kt.

†Lindsay, Sir James Martin Evelyn, Bt. (1962)

Lindsay, *Hon.* Sir John Edmund Frederic, Kt.

†Lindsay-Hogg, Sir Michael Edward, Bt. (1905)

Lipton, Sir Stuart Anthony, Kt.

Lipworth, Sir (Maurice) Sydney, Kt.

Lister, *Vice-Adm.* Sir Simon Robert, KCB, OBE

Lister-Kaye, Sir John Phillip Lister, Bt. (1812), OBE

Lithgow, Sir William James, Bt. (1925)

Llewellyn, Sir Roderic Victor, Bt. (1922)

Llewellyn-Smith, *Prof.* Sir Christopher Hubert, Kt.

Lloyd, *Prof.* Sir Geoffrey Ernest Richard, Kt., FBA

Lloyd, Sir Nicholas Markley, Kt.

Lloyd, *Rt. Hon.* Sir Peter Robert Cable, Kt.

Lloyd, Sir Richard Ernest Butler, Bt. (1960)

Lloyd, *Rt. Hon.* Sir Timothy Andrew Wigram, Kt.

Lloyd-Edwards, *Capt.* Sir Norman, KCVO, RD

Lloyd Jones, *Rt. Hon.* Sir David, Kt. (Lord Lloyd-Jones)

Loader, Air Marshal Sir Clive Robert, KCB, OBE

Lobban, Sir Iain Robert, KCMG, CB

Lockett, Sir Michael Vernon, KCVO

Lockhead, Sir Moir, Kt., OBE

Loder, Sir Edmund Jeune, Bt. (1887)

Logan, Sir David Brian Carleton, KCMG

Long, Sir Richard Julian, Kt., CBE

Longley, *Hon.* Sir Hartman Godfrey, Kt.

Longmore, *Rt. Hon.* Sir Andrew Centlivres, Kt.

Lorimer, *Lt.-Gen.* Sir John Gordon, KCB, MBE, DSO

Lorimer, Sir (Thomas) Desmond, Kt.

Los, *Hon.* Sir Kubulan, Kt., CBE

Loughran, Sir Gerald Finbar, KCB

Lourdenadin, Sir Ninian Mogan, KCMG, KBE

Lovegrove, Sir Stephen Augustus, KCB

Lovestone, *Prof.* Sir Simon, Kt.

Lovill, Sir John Roger, Kt., CBE

Low, *Dr* Sir John Menzies, Kt., CBE

Lowa, *Rt. Revd* Sir Samson, KBE

Lowcock, Sir Mark Andrew, KCB

Lowe, Sir Frank Budge, Kt.

Lowe, Sir Philip Martin, KCMG

Lowe, Sir Thomas William Gordon, Bt. (1918), QC

Lowson, Sir Ian Patrick, Bt. (1951)

†Lowther, Sir Patrick William, Bt. (1824)

Lowy, Sir Frank, Kt.

Loyd, Sir Julian St John, KCVO

Lu, Sir Tseng Chi, Kt.

Lucas, *Prof.* Sir Colin Renshaw, Kt.

†Lucas, Sir Thomas Edward, Bt. (1887)

Lucas-Tooth, Sir (Hugh) John, Bt. (1920)

Luff, Sir Peter James, Kt.

Lumsden, Sir David James, Kt.

Lushington, Sir John Richard Castleman, Bt. (1791)

Lyall Grant, Sir Mark Justin, KCMG

Lyle, Sir Gavin Archibald, Bt. (1929)

Lynch-Blosse, *Capt.* Sir Richard Hely, Bt. (I. 1622)

Lynch-Robinson, Sir Dominick Christopher, Bt. (1920)

Lyne, *Rt. Hon.* Sir Roderic Michael John, KBE, CMG

Lyons, Sir John, Kt.

Lyons, Sir Michael Thomas, Kt.

McAlinden, *Hon.* Sir Gerald Joseph, Kt.

McAllister, Sir Ian Gerald, Kt., CBE

McAlpine, Sir Andrew William, Bt. (1918)

McCamley, Sir Graham Edward, KBE

McCanny, *Prof.* Sir John Vincent, Kt., CBE

McCarthy, Sir Callum, Kt.

McCartney, *Rt. Hon.* Sir Ian, Kt.

McCartney, Sir (James) Paul, Kt., CH, MBE

†Macartney, Sir John Ralph, Bt. (I. 1799)

McClement, *Vice-Admiral* Sir Timothy Pentreath, KCB, OBE

Macleod, Sir Iain, KCMG

McCloskey, *Hon.* Sir John Bernard, Kt.

McColl, Sir Colin Hugh Verel, KCMG

McColl, *Gen.* Sir John Chalmers, KCB, CBE, DSO

McCollum, *Rt. Hon.* Sir William, Kt.

McCombe, *Rt. Hon.* Sir Richard George Bramwell, Kt.

McConnell, Sir Robert Shean, Bt. (1900)

†McCowan, Sir David William, Bt. (1934)

McCoy, Sir Anthony Peter, Kt., OBE

McCullin, Sir Donald, Kt., CBE

MacCulloch, *Prof.* Sir Diarmaid Ninian John, Kt.

McCulloch, *Rt. Revd* Nigel Simeon, KCVO

MacDermott, *Rt. Hon.* Sir John Clarke, Kt.

Macdonald, Sir Alasdair Uist, Kt., CBE

MacDonald, *Hon.* Sir Alistair William Orchard, Kt.

Macdonald of Sleat, Sir Ian Godfrey Bosville, Bt. (S. 1625)

McDonald, *Prof.* Sir James, Kt.

Macdonald, Sir Kenneth Carmichael, KCB

McDonald, Sir Simon Gerard, KCMG, KCVO

McDonald, Sir Trevor, Kt., OBE

McDowell, Sir Eric Wallace, Kt., CBE

MacDuff, *Hon.* Sir Alistair Geoffrey, Kt.

Mace, *Lt.-Gen.* Sir John Airth, KBE, CB

McEwen, Sir John Roderick Hugh, Bt. (1953)

MacFadyen, *Air Marshal* Sir Ian David, KCVO, CB, OBE

McFarland, Sir John Talbot, Bt. (1914)

MacFarlane, *Prof.* Sir Alistair George James, Kt., CBE, FRS

McFarlane, *Rt. Hon.* Sir Andrew Ewart, Kt.

Macfarlane, Sir (David) Neil, Kt.

McGeechan, Sir Ian Robert, Kt., OBE

McGrath, Sir Harvey Andrew, Kt.

†Macgregor, Sir Ian Grant, Bt. (1828)

MacGregor of MacGregor, Sir Malcolm Gregor Charles, Bt. (1795)

McGrigor, Sir James Angus Rhoderick Neil, Bt. (1831)

McIntosh, Sir Neil William David, Kt., CBE

McIntyre, Sir Donald Conroy, Kt., CBE

McIntyre, Sir Meredith Alister, Kt.

Mackay, *Hon.* Sir Colin Crichton, Kt.

MacKay, Sir Francis Henry, Kt.

McKay, Sir Neil Stuart, Kt., CB

McKay, Sir William Robert, KCB

Mackay-Dick, *Maj.-Gen.* Sir Iain Charles, KCVO, MBE

Mackechnie, Sir Alistair John, Kt.

McKellen, Sir Ian Murray, Kt., CH, CBE

†Mackenzie, Sir (James William) Guy, Bt. (1890)

Mackenzie, *Gen.* Sir Jeremy John George, GCB, OBE

†Mackenzie, Sir Peter Douglas, Bt. (S. 1673)

†Mackenzie, Sir Roderick McQuhae, Bt. (S. 1703)

Mackeson, Sir Rupert Henry, Bt. (1954)

Mackey, Sir Craig Thomas, Kt., QPM

Mackey, Sir James, Kt.

McKibbin, *Dr* Sir Malcolm, KCB

McKillop, Sir Thomas Fulton Wilson, Kt.

McKinnon, *Rt. Hon.* Sir Donald Charles, GCVO

McKinnon, *Hon.* Sir Stuart Neil, Kt.

Mackintosh, Sir Cameron Anthony, Kt.

†Mackworth, Sir Alan Keith, Bt. (1776)

McLaughlin, Sir Richard, Kt.

Maclean of Dunconnel, Sir Charles Edward, Bt. (1957)

Maclean, *Hon.* Sir Lachlan Hector Charles, Bt., (NS 1631), CVO

Maclean, Sir Murdo, Kt.

†McLeod, Sir James Roderick Charles, Bt. (1925)

MacLeod, *Hon.* Sir (John) Maxwell Norman, Bt. (1924)

Macleod, Sir (Nathaniel William) Hamish, KBE

McLintock, Sir Michael William, Bt. (1934)

McLoughlin, Sir Francis, Kt., CBE

McLoughlin, *Rt. Hon.* Sir Patrick Allen, Kt.

Maclure, Sir John Robert Spencer, Bt. (1898)

McMahon, Sir Brian Patrick, Bt. (1817)

McMahon, Sir Christopher William, Kt.

McMaster, Sir Brian John, Kt., CBE

McMichael, *Prof.* Sir Andrew James, Kt., FRS

MacMillan, *Very Revd* Gilleasbuig Iain, KCVO

McMillan, Sir Iain Macleod, Kt., CBE

Macmillan, *Dr* Sir James Loy, Kt., CBE

MacMillan, *Lt.-Gen.* Sir John Richard Alexander, KCB, CBE

McMurtry, Sir David, Kt., CBE

Macnaghten, Sir Malcolm Francis, Bt. (1836)

McNair-Wilson, Sir Patrick Michael Ernest David, Kt.

McNulty, Sir (Robert William) Roy, Kt., CBE

MacPhail, Sir Bruce Dugald, Kt.

Macpherson of Cluny, *Hon.* Sir William Alan, Kt., TD

MacRae, Sir (Alastair) Christopher (Donald Summerhayes), KCMG

Macready, Sir Charles Nevil, Bt. (1923)

Mactaggart, Sir John Auld, Bt. (1938)

McVicar, Sir David, Kt.

McWilliam, Sir Michael Douglas, KCMG

McWilliams, Sir Francis, GBE

Madden, Sir Charles Jonathan, Bt. (1919)

Madden, Sir David Christopher Andrew, KCMG

Maddison, *Hon.* Sir David George, Kt.

Madejski, Sir John Robert, Kt., OBE

Madel, Sir (William) David, Kt.

Magee, Sir Ian Bernard Vaughan, Kt., CB

Magnus, Sir Laurence Henry Philip, Bt. (1917)

Maguire, *Hon.* Sir Paul Richard, Kt.

Mahon, Sir William Walter, Bt. (1819), LVO

Mahoney, Sir Paul John, KCMG

Maiden, Sir Colin James, Kt., DPHIL

Maini, *Prof.* Sir Ravinder Nath, Kt.

Maino, Sir Charles, KBE

†Maitland, Sir Charles Alexander, Bt. (1818)

Major, *Rt. Hon.* Sir John, KG, CH

Malbon, *Vice-Adm.* Sir Fabian Michael, KBE

Malcolm, Sir Alexander James Elton, Bt. (S. 1665), OBE

Malcolm, *Dr* Noel Robert, Kt., FBA

Males, *Rt. Hon.* Sir Stephen Martin, Kt.

Malet, Sir Harry Douglas St Lo, Bt. (1791)

Mallaby, Sir Christopher Leslie George, GCMG, GCVO

Mallick, *Prof.* Sir Netar Prakash, Kt.

Mallinson, Sir William James, Bt. (1935)

Malpas, Sir Robert, Kt., CBE

Mander, Sir (Charles) Nicholas, Bt. (1911)

Mann, *Hon.* Sir George Anthony, Kt.

Mann, Sir Rupert Edward, Bt. (1905)

Manning, Sir David Geoffrey, GCMG, KCVO

Mano, Sir Koitaga, Kt., MBE

Mans, *Lt.-Gen.* Sir Mark Francis Noel, KCB, CBE

Mansel, Sir Philip, Bt. (1622)

Manuella, Sir Tulaga, GCMG, MBE

Mara, Sir Nambuga, KBE

Margetson, Sir John William Denys, KCMG

Margetts, Sir Robert John, Kt., CBE

Markesinis, *Prof.* Sir Basil Spyridonos, Kt., QC

Markham, *Prof.* Sir Alexander Fred, Kt.

Markham, Sir (Arthur) David, Bt. (1911)

Marling, Sir Charles William Somerset, Bt. (1882)

Marmot, Prof. Sir Michael Gideon, Kt.

Marr, Sir Leslie Lynn, Bt. (1919)

Marsden, Sir Jonathan Mark, KCVO

†Marsden, Sir Tadgh Orlando Denton, Bt. (1924)

Marshall, Sir Paul, Kt.

Marshall, Sir Peter Harold Reginald, KCMG

Marshall, *Prof. Emeritus* Sir Woodville Kemble, Kt.

Marsters, *HE* Sir Tom John, KBE

Martin, Sir Clive Haydon, Kt., OBE

Martin, Sir Gregory Michael Gerard, Kt.

Martin, *Prof.* Sir Laurence Woodward, Kt.

Masefield, Sir Charles Beech Gordon, Kt.

Mason, *Hon.* Sir Anthony Frank, KBE

Mason, *Prof.* Sir David Kean, Kt., CBE

Mason, Sir Peter James, KBE

Mason, *Prof.* Sir Ronald, KCB, FRS

Massey, *Vice-Adm.* Sir Alan, KCB, CBE, ADC

Matane, HE Sir Paulias Nguna, GCMG, OBE

Matheson of Matheson, Sir Alexander Fergus, Bt. (1882), LVO

Mathews, *Vice-Adm.* Sir Andrew David Hugh, KCB

Mathewson, Sir George Ross, Kt., CBE, PHD, FRSE

Matthews, Sir Terence Hedley, Kt., OBE

Maughan, Sir Deryck, Kt.

Mawer, Sir Philip John Courtney, Kt.

Maxwell, Sir Michael Eustace George, Bt. (S. 1681)

Maxwell Macdonald (formerly Stirling-Maxwell), Sir John Ronald, Bt. (NS 1682)

Maxwell-Scott, Sir Dominic James, Bt. (1642)

May, *Rt. Hon.* Sir Anthony Tristram Kenneth, Kt.

Mayall, *Lt.-Gen.* Sir Simon Vincent, KBE, CB

Mayfield, Sir Andrew Charles, Kt.

Meadow, *Prof.* Sir (Samuel) Roy, Kt., FRCP, FRCPE

Meale, Sir Joseph Alan, Kt.

Medlycott, Sir Mervyn Tregonwell, Bt. (1808)

Meeran, *His Hon.* Sir Goolam Hoosen Kader, Kt.

Meldrum, Sir Graham, Kt., CBE, QFSM

Melhuish, Sir Michael Ramsay, KBE, CMG

Mellars, *Prof.* Sir Paul Anthony, Kt., FBA

Mellon, Sir James, KCMG

Melmoth, Sir Graham John, Kt.

Melville, *Prof.* Sir David, Kt., CBE

Melville-Ross, Sir Timothy David, Kt., CBE

Merifield, Sir Anthony James, KCVO, CB

Messenger, *Gen.* Sir Gordon Kenneth, KCB, DSO, OBE

Metcalf, *Prof.* Sir David Harry, Kt., CBE

†Meyer, Sir (Anthony) Ashley Frank, Bt. (1910)

Meyer, Sir Christopher John Rome, KCMG

†Meyrick, Sir Timothy Thomas Charlton, Bt. (1880)

Miakwe, *Hon.* Sir Akepa, KBE

Michael, Sir Duncan, Kt.

Michael, *Dr* Sir Jonathan, Kt.

Michael, Sir Peter Colin, Kt., CBE

Michels, Sir David Michael Charles, Kt.

Middleton, Sir John Maxwell, Kt.

Middleton, Sir Peter Edward, GCB

Miers, Sir (Henry) David Alastair Capel, KBE, CMG

Milbank, Sir Edward Mark Somerset, Bt. (1882)

Milborne-Swinnerton-Pilkington, Sir Thomas Henry, Bt. (S. 1635)

Milburn, Sir Anthony Rupert, Bt.
(1905)

†Miles, Sir Philip John, Bt. (1859)

Millais, Sir Geoffroy Richard Everett,
Bt. (1885)

Millar, *Prof.* Sir Fergus Graham
Burtholme, Kt.

Miller, Sir Anthony Thomas, Bt.
(1705)

Miller, Sir Donald John, Kt., FRSE,
FRENG

Miller, *Air Marshal* Sir Graham
Anthony, KBE

Miller, Sir Jonathan Wolfe, Kt., CBE

Miller, Sir Robin Robert William, Kt.

Miller, Sir Ronald Andrew Baird, Kt.,
CBE

Miller of Glenlee, Sir Stephen William
Macdonald, Bt. (1788)

Mills, Sir Ian, Kt.

Mills, Sir Jonathan Edward Harland
(John), Kt., FRSE

Mills, Sir Keith Edward, GBE

Mills, Sir Peter Frederick Leighton, Bt.
(1921)

Milman, Sir David Patrick, Bt. (1800)

Milne-Watson, Sir Andrew Michael,
Bt. (1937)

Milner, Sir Timothy William Lycett,
Bt. (1717)

Mitchell, *Rt. Hon.* Sir James FitzAllen,
KCMG

Mitchell, *Very Revd* Patrick Reynolds,
KCVO

Mitchell, *Hon.* Sir Stephen George, Kt.

Mitting, *Hon.* Sir John Edward, Kt.

Moberly, Sir Patrick Hamilton, KCMG

Moir, Sir Christopher Ernest, Bt.
(1916)

Molesworth-St Aubyn, Sir William, Bt.
(1689)

Molony, Sir Peter John, Bt. (1925)

Moncada, *Prof.* Sir Salvador, Kt.

Montagu, Sir Nicholas Lionel John,
KCB

†Montagu-Pollock, Sir Guy
Maximilian, Bt. (1872)

Montague, Sir Adrian Alastair, Kt.,
CBE

Montgomery, Sir (Basil Henry) David,
Bt. (1801), CVO

Montgomery, *Vice-Adm.* Sir Charles
Percival Ross, KBE, ADC

Montgomery, *Prof.* Sir James Robert,
Kt.

Montgomery-Cuninghame, Sir John
Christopher Foggo, Bt. (NS 1672)

Moody-Stuart, Sir Mark, KCMG

Moollan, Sir Abdool Hamid Adam, Kt.

†Moon, Sir Humphrey, Bt. (1887)

Moor, *Hon.* Sir Philip Drury, Kt.

Moorcroft, Sir William, KBE

Moore, *Most Revd* Desmond Charles,
KBE

Moore, Sir Francis Thomas, Kt.

Moore, *Vice-Adm.* Sir Michael Antony
Claës, KBE, LVO

Moore, Sir Peter Alan Cutlack, Bt.
(1919)

Moore, Sir Richard William, Bt.
(1932)

Moore-Bick, *Rt. Hon.* Sir Martin James,
Kt.

Morauta, Sir Mekere, KCMG

Mordaunt, Sir Richard Nigel Charles,
Bt. (1611)

Moree, *Hon.* Sir Brian, Kt.

Morgan, *Vice-Adm.* Sir Charles
Christopher, KBE

Morgan, *Rt. Hon.* Sir (Charles) Declan,
Kt.

Morgan, Sir Graham, Kt.

Morgan, *Hon.* Sir Paul Hyacinth, Kt.

Morgan, Sir Terence Keith, Kt., CBE

Morison, *Hon.* Sir Thomas Richard
Atkin, Kt.

Moritz, Sir Michael Jonathan, KBE

Morland, *Hon.* Sir Michael, Kt.

Morland, Sir Robert Kenelm, Kt.

Morpurgo, Sir Michael Andrew
Bridge, Kt., OBE

†Morris, Sir Allan Lindsay, Bt. (1806)

Morris, Sir Andrew Valentine, Kt.,
OBE

Morris, *Air Marshal* Sir Arnold Alec,
KBE, CB

Morris, Sir Derek James, Kt.

Morris, Sir Keith Elliot Hedley, KBE,
CMG

Morris, *Prof.* Sir Peter John, Kt.

Morris, *Hon.* Sir Stephen Nathan, Kt.

Morris, Sir Trefor Alfred, Kt., CBE,
QPM

Morrison, Sir (Alexander) Fraser, Kt.,
CBE

Morrison, Sir George Ivan, Kt., OBE

Morrison, Sir Howard Andrew Clive,
KCMG, CBE

Morrison-Bell, Sir William Hollin
Dayrell, Bt. (1905)

Morrison-Low, Sir Richard Walter, Bt.
(1908)

Morritt, *Rt. Hon.* Sir (Robert) Andrew,
Kt., CVO

Morse, Sir Amyas Charles Edward,
KCB

Moses, *Rt. Hon.* Sir Alan George, Kt.

Moses, *Very Revd* Dr John Henry,
KCVO

Moss, Sir David Joseph, KCVO, CMG

Moss, Sir Stephen Alan, Kt.

Moss, Sir Stirling Craufurd, Kt., OBE

Mostyn, *Hon.* Sir Nicholas Anthony
Joseph Ghislain, Kt.

Mostyn, Sir William Basil John, Bt.
(1670)

Motion, Sir Andrew, Kt.

Mott, Sir David Hugh, Bt. (1930)

Mottley, Sir Elliott Deighton, KCMG,
QC

Mottram, Sir Richard Clive, GCB

†Mount, Sir (William Robert)
Ferdinand, Bt. (1921)

Mountain, Sir Edward Brian Stanford,
Bt. (1922)

Mowbray, Sir John Robert, Bt. (1880)

Moylan, *Rt. Hon.* Sir Andrew John
Gregory, Kt.

Moynihan, *Dr* Sir Daniel, Kt.

†Muir, Sir Richard James Kay, Bt.
(1892)

Muir-Mackenzie, Sir Alexander
Alwyne Henry Charles Brinton, Bt.
(1805)

Mulcahy, Sir Geoffrey John, Kt.

Mummery, *Rt. Hon.* Sir John Frank, Kt.

Munby, *Rt. Hon.* Sir James Lawrence,
Kt.

Munro, Sir Alan Gordon, KCMG

†Munro, Sir Ian Kenneth, Bt. (S.
1634)

Munro, Sir Keith Gordon, Bt. (1825)

Muria, *Hon.* Sir Gilbert John Baptist,
Kt.

Murphy, Sir Jonathan Michael, Kt.,
QPM

Murray, Sir Andrew, Kt., OBE

Murray, Sir David Edward, Kt.

Murray, *Hon.* Sir Edward Henry, Kt

Murray, Sir Nigel Andrew Digby, Bt.
(S. 1628)

Murray, Sir Patrick Ian Keith, Bt.
(S. 1673)

Murray, Sir Robert Sydney, Kt., CBE

Murray, Sir Robin MacGregor, Kt.

†Murray, Sir Rowland William, Bt. (S.
1630)

Muscatelli, *Prof.* Sir Vito Antonio, Kt.,
FRSE

Musgrave, Sir Christopher John Shane,
Bt. (I. 1782)

Musgrave, Sir Christopher Patrick
Charles, Bt. (1611)

Myers, Sir Derek John, Kt.

Myers, *Prof.* Sir Rupert Horace, KBE

Mynors, Sir Richard Baskerville, Bt.
(1964)

Nairn, Sir Michael, Bt. (1904)

Nalau, Sir Jerry Kasip, KBE

Nall, Sir Edward William Joseph, Bt.
(1954)

Namaliu, *Rt. Hon.* Sir Rabbie Langanai,
KCMG

Napier, Sir Charles Joseph, Bt. (1867)

Napier, Sir John Archibald Lennox, Bt.
(S. 1627)

Narey, Sir Martin James, Kt.

Natzler, Sir David Lionel, KCB

Naylor, Sir Robert, Kt.

Naylor-Leyland, Sir Philip Vyvian, Bt.
(1895)

Neal, Sir Eric James, Kt., CVO

Neave, Sir Paul Arundell, Bt. (1795)

†Nelson, Sir Jamie Charles Vernon
Hope, Bt. (1912)

Nelson, *Hon.* Sir Robert Franklyn, Kt.

New, *Maj.-Gen.* Sir Laurence Anthony
Wallis, Kt., CB, CBE

Newbigging, Sir David Kennedy, Kt.,
OBE

Newby, *Prof.* Sir Howard Joseph, Kt.,
CBE

Newey, *Rt. Hon.* Sir Guy Richard, Kt.

Newman, Sir Francis Hugh Cecil, Bt.
(1912)

Newman, Sir Geoffrey Robert, Bt. (1836)

Newman, Vice-Adm. Sir Roy Thomas, KCB

Newman Taylor, Prof. Sir Anthony John, Kt., CBE

Newsam, Sir Peter Anthony, Kt.

Newson-Smith, Sir Peter Frank Graham, Bt. (1944)

Newton, Revd George Peter Howgill, Bt. (1900)

Newton, Sir John Garnar, Bt. (1924)

Newton, Lt.-Gen. Sir Paul Raymond, KBE

Newton, Hon. Sir Roderick Brian, Kt.

Nice, Sir Geoffrey, Kt., QC

Nichol, Sir Duncan Kirkbride, Kt., CBE

Nicholas, Sir David, Kt., CBE

Nicholson, Sir Bryan Hubert, GBE, Kt.

Nicholson, Sir Charles Christian, Bt. (1912)

Nicholson, Sir David, KCB, CBE

Nicholson, Rt. Hon. Sir Michael, Kt.

Nicholson, Sir Paul Douglas, KCVO, Kt.

Nicholson, Sir Robin Buchanan, Kt., PHD, FRS, FRENG

Nickell, Prof. Sir Stephen John, Kt., CBE, FBA

Nicklin, Hon. Sir Matthew James, Kt.

Nicol, Hon. Sir Andrew George Lindsay, Kt.

Nightingale, Sir Charles Manners Gamaliel, Bt. (1628)

†Nixon, Sir Simon Michael Christopher, Bt. (1906)

Noble, Sir David Brunel, Bt. (1902)

Noble, Sir Timothy Peter, Bt. (1923)

Nombri, Sir Joseph Karl, Kt., ISO, BEM

Norgrove, Sir David Ronald, Kt.

Norman, Sir Nigel James, Bt. (1915)

Norman, Sir Ronald, Kt., OBE

Norman, Sir Torquil Patrick Alexander, Kt., CBE

Normington, Sir David John, GCB

Norrington, Sir Roger Arthur Carver, Kt., CBE

Norris, Hon. Sir Alastair Hubert, Kt.

Norriss, Air Marshal Sir Peter Coulson, KBE, CB, AFC

North, Air Marshal Sir Barry Mark, KCB, OBE

North, Sir Jeremy William Francis, Bt. (1920)

North, Sir Peter Machin, Kt., CBE, QC, DCL, FBA

Norton, Sir Barry, Kt.

Norton, Maj.-Gen. Sir George Pemberton Ross, KCVO, CBE

Norton-Griffiths, Sir Michael, Bt. (1922)

Nossal, Sir Gustav Joseph Victor, Kt., CBE

Nott, Rt. Hon. Sir John William Frederic, KCB

Novoselov, Prof. Sir Konstantin, Kt.

Nugee, Hon. Sir Christopher George, Kt.

Nugent, Sir Christopher George Ridley, Bt. (1806)

†Nugent, Sir Nicholas Myles John, Bt. (I. 1795)

Nugent, Sir (Walter) Richard Middleton, Bt. (1831)

Nunn, Sir Trevor Robert, Kt., CBE

Nunneley, Sir Charles Kenneth Roylance, Kt.

Nursaw, Sir James, KCB, QC

Nurse, Sir Paul Maxime, Kt.

Nuttall, Sir Harry, Bt. (1922)

Nutting, Sir John Grenfell, Bt. (1903), QC

Oakeley, Sir Robert John Atholl, Bt. (1790)

Oakes, Sir Christopher, Bt. (1939)

Oakshott, Sir Thomas Hendrie, Bt. (1959)

O'Brien, Sir Robert Stephen, Kt., CBE

O'Brien, Rt. Hon. Sir Stephen Rothwell, Kt.

†O'Brien, Sir Timothy John, Bt. (1849)

O'Brien, Sir William, Kt.

O'Connell, Sir Bernard, Kt.

O'Connell, Sir Maurice James Donagh MacCarthy, Bt. (1869)

O'Connor, Sir Denis Francis, Kt., CBE, QPM

Odell, Sir Stanley John, Kt.

Odgers, Sir Graeme David William, Kt.

O'Donnell, Sir Christopher John, Kt.

O'Donoghue, Lt.-Gen. Sir Kevin, KCB, CBE

O'Dowd, Sir David Joseph, Kt., CBE, QPM

Ogden, Dr Sir Peter James, Kt.

Ogden, Sir Robert, Kt., CBE

Ogilvy, Sir Francis Gilbert Arthur, Bt. (S. 1626)

Ogilvy-Wedderburn, Sir Andrew John Alexander, Bt. (1803)

Ognall, Hon. Sir Harry Henry, Kt.

O'Hara, Hon. Sir John Ailbe

Ohlson, Sir Peter Michael, Bt. (1920)

Oldham, Dr Sir John, Kt., OBE

Olisa, Sir Kenneth Aphunezi, Kt., OBE

Oliver, Sir Craig Stewart, Kt.

Oliver, Sir James Michael Yorrick, Kt.

Oliver, Sir Stephen John Lindsay, Kt., QC

†O'Loghlen, Sir Michael, Bt. (1838)

O'Lone, Sir Marcus James, KCVO

Olver, Sir Richard Lake, Kt.

Omand, Sir David Bruce, GCB

Ondaatje, Sir Christopher, Kt., CBE

O'Nions, Prof. Sir Robert Keith, Kt., FRS, PHD

Onslow, Sir Richard Paul Atherton, Bt. (1797)

Openshaw, Hon. Sir Charles Peter Lawford, Kt.

Oppenheimer, Sir Michael Bernard Grenville, Bt. (1921)

O'Rahilly, Prof. Sir Stephen Patrick, Kt., FRS

Ord, Sir David Charles, Kt.

Orde, Sir Hugh Stephen Roden, Kt., OBE, QPM

O'Regan, Dr Sir Stephen Gerard (Tipene), Kt.

O'Reilly, Sir Anthony John Francis, Kt.

O'Reilly, Prof. Sir John James, Kt.

Orr-Ewing, Hon. Sir (Alistair) Simon, Bt. (1963)

Orr-Ewing, Sir Archibald Donald, Bt. (1886)

Osborn, Sir Richard Henry Danvers, Bt. (1662)

Osborne, Sir Peter George, Bt. (I. 1629)

O'Shea, Prof. Sir Timothy Michael Martin, Kt.

Osmotherly, Sir Edward Benjamin Crofton, Kt., CB

Oswald, Sir (William Richard) Michael, KCVO

Ottaway, Rt. Hon. Sir Richard Geoffrey James, Kt.

Otton, Sir Geoffrey John, KCB

Otton, Rt. Hon. Sir Philip Howard, Kt.

Ouseley, Hon. Sir Duncan Brian Walter, Kt.

Outram, Sir Alan James, Bt. (1858)

Owen, Sir Geoffrey, Kt.

Owen, Prof. Sir Michael John, Kt.

Owen, Hon. Sir Robert Michael, Kt.

Owen-Jones, Sir Lindsay Harwood, KBE

Packer, Sir Richard John, KCB

Paget, Sir Henry James, Bt. (1871)

Paget, Sir Richard Herbert, Bt. (1886)

Paice, Rt. Hon. Sir James Edward Thornton, Kt.

Paine, Sir Christopher Hammon, Kt., FRCP, FRCR

Pakenham, Hon. Sir Michael Aiden, KBE, CMG

Palin, Sir Michael Edward, KCMG, CBE

Palin, Air Chief Marshal Sir Roger Hewlett, KCB, OBE

Palmer, Sir Albert Rocky, Kt.

Palmer, Sir (Charles) Mark, Bt. (1886)

Palmer, Sir Geoffrey Christopher John, Bt. (1660)

Palmer, Rt. Hon. Sir Geoffrey Winston Russell, KCMG

Palmer, Prof. Sir Godfrey Henry Oliver, Kt, OBE

†Palmer, Sir Robert John Hudson, Bt. (1791)

Panter, Sir Howard Hugh, Kt.

Pappano, Sir Antonio, Kt.

Parbo, Sir Arvi Hillar, Kt.

Park, Hon. Sir Andrew Edward Wilson, Kt.

Parker, Sir Alan, Kt.

Parker, Sir Alan William, Kt., CBE

Parker, Sir Andrew David, KCB

Parker, Rt. Hon. Sir Jonathan Frederic, Kt.

Parker, *Hon.* Sir Kenneth Blades, Kt.

Parker, *Maj.* Sir Michael John, KCVO, CBE

Parker, *Gen.* Sir Nicholas Ralph, KCB, CBE

Parker, Sir Richard (William) Hyde, Bt. (1681)

Parker, Sir (Thomas) John, GBE

Parker, Sir William Peter Brian, Bt. (1844)

Parkes, Sir Edward Walter, Kt., FRENG

Parkinson, Sir Michael, Kt., CBE

Parmley, *Dr* Sir Andrew Charles, Kt.

Parry, *Prof.* Sir Eldryd Hugh Owen, KCMG, OBE

Parry, Sir Emyr Jones, GCMG

Parry-Evans, *Air Chief Marshal* Sir David, GCB, CBE

Parsons, Sir John Christopher, KCVO

Partridge, Sir Michael John Anthony, KCB

Partridge, Sir Nicholas Wyndham, Kt., OBE

Pascoe, *Gen.* Sir Robert Alan, KCB, MBE

Pasley, Sir Robert Killigrew Sabine, Bt. (1794)

Paston-Bedingfeld, Sir Henry Edgar, Bt. (1661)

Patey, Sir William Charters, KCMG

Patten, *Rt. Hon.* Sir Nicholas John, Kt.

Pattie, *Rt. Hon.* Sir Geoffrey Edwin, Kt.

Pattison, *Prof.* Sir John Ridley, Kt., DM, FRCPATH

Pattullo, Sir (David) Bruce, Kt., CBE

Pauncefort-Duncombe, Sir David Philip Henry, Bt. (1859)

Payne, *Prof.* Sir David Neil, Kt., CBE, FRS

Peace, Sir John Wilfrid, Kt.

Peach, *Air Chief Marshal* Sir Stuart William, GBE, KCB, ADC

Pearce, Sir (Daniel Norton) Idris, Kt., CBE, TD

Pears, Sir Trevor Stephen, Kt., CMG

Pearse, Sir Brian Gerald, Kt.

Pearson, Sir David Lee, Kt., CBE

Pearson, Sir Francis Nicholas Fraser, Bt. (1964)

Pearson, Sir Keith, Kt.

Pearson, *Gen.* Sir Thomas Cecil Hook, KCB, CBE, DSO

Pease, Sir Joseph Gurney, Bt. (1882)

Pease, Sir Richard Thorn, Bt. (1920)

Peat, Sir Gerrard Charles, KCVO

Peat, Sir Michael Charles Gerrard, GCVO

Peckham, *Prof.* Sir Michael John, Kt.,

Peek, Sir Richard Grenville, Bt. (1874)

Pelgen, Sir Harry Friedrich, Kt., MBE

Pelham, *Dr* Sir Hugh Reginald Brentnall, Kt., FRS

Pelly, Sir Richard John, Bt. (1840)

Pendry, *Prof.* Sir John Brian, Kt., FRS

Penning, *Rt. Hon.* Sir Michael Allan, Kt.

Penny, *Dr* Nicholas Beaver, Kt., FBA

Penrose, *Prof.* Sir Roger, Kt., OM, FRS

Pepper, *Dr* Sir David Edwin, KCMG

Pepper, *Prof.* Sir Michael, Kt.

Pepperall, *Hon.* Sir Edward Brian, Kt

Pepys, *Prof.* Sir Mark Brian, Kt.

Perowne, *Vice-Adm.* Sir James Francis, KBE

Perring, Sir John Raymond, Bt. (1963), TD

Perris, Sir David (Arthur), Kt., MBE

Perry, Sir David Howard, KCB

Perry, Sir Michael Sydney, GBE

Pervez, Sir Mohammed Anwar, Kt., OBE

Petchey, Sir Jack, Kt., CBE

Peters, *Prof.* Sir (David) Keith, GBE, FRCP

Pethica, *Prof.* Sir John Bernard, Kt., FRS

Petit, Sir Dinshaw Manockjee, Bt. (1890)

Peto, Sir Francis Michael Morton, Bt. (1855)

Peto, Sir Henry Christopher Morton Bampfylde, Bt. (1927)

Peto, *Prof.* Sir Richard, Kt., FRS

Petrie, Sir Peter Charles, Bt. (1918), CMG

†Philipson-Stow, Sir (Robert) Matthew, Bt. (1907)

Phillips, Sir (Gerald) Hayden, GCB

Phillips, Sir John David, Kt., QPM

Phillips, Sir Jonathan, KCB

Phillips, Sir Peter John, Kt., OBE

Phillips, Sir Robin Francis, Bt. (1912)

Phillips, *Hon.* Sir Stephen Edmund, Kt.

Phillips, Sir Tom Richard Vaughan, KCMG

Pickard, Sir (John) Michael, Kt.

Picken, *Hon.* Sir Simon Derek, Kt.

Pickthorn, Sir James Francis Mann, Bt. (1959)

†Piers, Sir James Desmond, Bt. (I. 1661)

Pigot, Sir George Hugh, Bt. (1764)

Pigott, *Lt.-Gen.* Sir Anthony David, KCB, CBE

†Pigott, Sir David John Berkeley, Bt. (1808)

Pigott-Brown, Sir William Brian, Bt. (1903)

Pike, *Lt.-Gen.* Sir Hew William Royston, KCB, DSO, MBE

Pike, Sir Michael Edmund, KCVO, CMG

Pilditch, Sir John Richard, Bt. (1929)

Pile, Sir Anthony John Devereux, Bt. (1900), MBE

Pill, *Rt. Hon.* Sir Malcolm Thomas, Kt.

Pilling, Sir Joseph Grant, KCB

Pinsent, Sir Matthew Clive, Kt., CBE

Pinsent, Sir Thomas Benjamin Roy, Bt. (1938)

Pirmohamed, *Prof.* Sir Hussein Munir, Kt.

Pissarides, *Prof.* Sir Christopher Antoniou, Kt., FBA

Pitcher, Sir Desmond Henry, Kt.

Pitchers, *Hon.* Sir Christopher (John), Kt.

Pitoi, Sir Sere, Kt., CBE

Pitt, Sir Michael Edward, Kt.

Platt, Sir Martin Philip, Bt. (1959)

Pledger, *Air Chief Marshal* Sir Malcolm David, KCB, OBE, AFC

Plender, *Hon.* Sir Richard Owen, Kt.

Plumbly, Sir Derek John, KCMG

Pocock, *Dr* Sir Andrew John, KCMG

Poffley, *Lt.-Gen.* Sir Mark William, KCB, OBE

Poh, Sir Sang Chung, Kt., MBE

Pohai, Sir Timothy, Kt., MBE

Pole, Sir John Chandos, Bt. (1791)

Pole, Sir (John) Richard (Walter Reginald) Carew, Bt. (1628), OBE

Poliakoff, *Prof.* Sir Martyn, Kt., CBE

Polkinghorne, *Revd Canon* John Charlton, KBE

Pollard, Sir Charles, Kt.

†Pollen, Sir Richard John Hungerford, Bt. (1795)

Pollock, Sir David Frederick, Bt. (1866)

Pomeroy, Sir Brian Walter, Kt., CBE

Ponder, *Prof.* Sir Bruce Anthony John, Kt.

Ponsonby, Sir Charles Ashley, Bt. (1956)

Poon, Sir Dickson, Kt., CBE

†Poore, Sir Roger Ricardo, Bt. (1795)

Pope, *Lt.-Gen.* Sir Nicholas Arthur William, KCB

Popplewell, *Hon.* Sir Andrew John, Kt.

Popplewell, *Hon.* Sir Oliver Bury, Kt.

Porritt, *Hon.* Sir Jonathon Espie, Bt. (1963), CBE

Portal, Sir Jonathan Francis, Bt. (1901)

Porter, *Prof.* Sir Keith Macdonald, Kt.

Potter, *Rt. Hon.* Sir Mark Howard, Kt.

Pound, Sir John David, Bt. (1905)

Pountney, Sir David Willoughby, Kt., CBE

Povey, Sir Keith, Kt., QPM

Powell, Sir Ian Clifford, Kt.

†Powell, Sir James Richard Douglas, Bt. (1897)

Powell, Sir John Christopher, Kt.

Power, Sir Alastair John Cecil, Bt. (1924)

Pownall, Sir Michael Graham, KCB

Poya, Sir Nathaniel, Kt.

Prance, *Prof.* Sir Ghillean Tolmie, Kt., FRS

Prendergast, Sir (Walter) Kieran, KCVO, CMG

Prescott, Sir Mark, Bt. (1938)

Preston, *Prof.* Sir Paul, Kt., CBE

Preston, Sir Philip Charles Henry Hulton, Bt. (1815)

Prevost, Sir Christopher Gerald, Bt. (1805)

Price, Sir Francis Caradoc Rose, Bt. (1815)

Price, Sir Frank Leslie, Kt.

†Prichard-Jones, Sir David John Walter, Bt. (1910)

†Primrose, Sir John Ure, Bt. (1903)

Pringle, *Hon.* Sir John Kenneth, Kt.

Pringle, Sir Norman Murray Archibald Macgregor, Bt. (S. 1683)

Proby, Sir William Henry, Bt. (1952), CBE

Proctor-Beauchamp, Sir Christopher Radstock, Bt. (1745)

Prosser, Sir David John, Kt.

Prosser, Sir Ian Maurice Gray, Kt.

Pryke, Sir Christopher Dudley, Bt. (1926)

Puapua, Rt. Hon. Sir Tomasi, GCMG, KBE

Pulford, Air Chief Marshal Sir Andrew Douglas, GCB, CBE, ADC

Pullman, Sir Philip Nicholas Outram, Kt., CBE

Purves, Sir William, Kt., CBE, DSO

Purvis, Vice-Adm. Sir Neville, KCB

Quan, Sir Henry (Francis), KBE

Quilter, Sir Guy Raymond Cuthbert, Bt. (1897)

Radcliffe, Sir Sebastian Everard, Bt. (1813)

Radda, Prof. Sir George Karoly, Kt., CBE, FRS

Rae, Sir William, Kt., QPM

Raeburn, Sir Michael Edward Norman, Bt. (1923)

Rake, Sir Michael Derek Vaughan, Kt.

Ralli, Sir David Charles, Bt. (1912)

Ramakrishnan, Dr Sir Venkatraman, Kt.

Ramdanee, Sir Mookteswar Baboolall Kailash, Kt.

Ramphal, Sir Shridath Surendranath, GCMG

Ramphul, Sir Baalkhristna, Kt.

Ramphul, Sir Indurduth, Kt.

Ramsay, Sir Alexander William Burnett, Bt. (1806)

Ramsay, Sir Allan John (Hepple), KBE, CMG

Ramsay-Fairfax-Lucy, Sir Edmund John William Hugh, Bt. (1836)

Ramsden, Sir David Edward John, Kt., CBE

Ramsden, Sir John Charles Josslyn, Bt. (1689)

Ramsey, Dr Sir Frank Cuthbert, KCMG

Ramsey, Hon. Sir Vivian Arthur, Kt.

Rankin, Sir Ian Niall, Bt. (1898)

Rasch, Sir Simon Anthony Carne, Bt. (1903)

Rashleigh, Sir Richard Harry, Bt. (1831)

Ratcliffe, Sir James Arthur, Kt.

Ratcliffe, Prof. Sir Peter John, Kt., FRS

Ratford, Sir David John Edward, KCMG, CVO

Rattee, Hon. Sir Donald Keith, Kt.

Rattle, Sir Simon Dennis, Kt., OM, CBE

Rawlins, Hon. Sir Hugh Anthony, Kt.

Rawlins, Prof. Sir Michael David, GBE, FRCP, FRCPED

Rawlinson, Sir Anthony Henry John, Bt. (1891)

Rea, Prof. Sir Desmond, Kt., OBE

Read, Prof. Sir David John, Kt.

Reardon-Smith, Sir (William) Antony (John), Bt. (1920)

Reddaway, Sir David Norman, KCMG, MBE

Redgrave, Sir Steven Geoffrey, Kt., CBE

Redmayne, Sir Giles Martin, Bt. (1964)

Redmond, Sir Anthony Gerard, Kt.

Redwood, Rt. Hon. Sir John Alan, Kt.

Redwood, Sir Peter Boverton, Bt. (1911)

Reed, Prof. Sir Alec Edward, Kt., CBE

Reedie, Sir Craig Collins, GBE

Rees, Sir David Allan, Kt., PHD, DSC, FRS

Rees, Sir Richard Ellis Meuric, Kt., CBE

Reffell, Adm. Sir Derek Roy, KCB

Reich, Sir Erich Arieh, Kt.

†Reid, Sir Charles Edward James, Bt. (1897)

Reid, Sir David Edward, Kt.

Reid, Rt. Hon. Sir George, Kt.

Reid, Sir (Philip) Alan, GCVO

Reid, Sir Robert Paul, Kt.

Reid, Sir William Kennedy, KCB

Reiher, Sir Frederick Bernard Carl, KCMG, KBE

Renals, Sir Stanley, Bt. (1895)

Renouf, Sir Clement William Bailey, Kt.

Renshaw, Sir John David Bine, Bt. (1903)

Renwick, Sir Richard Eustace, Bt. (1921)

Reynolds, Sir James Francis, Bt. (1923)

Reynolds, Sir Peter William John, Kt., CBE

Rhodes, Sir John Christopher Douglas, Bt. (1919)

Ribat, Most Revd John, KBE

Rice, Prof. Sir Charles Duncan, Kt.

Rice, Maj.-Gen. Sir Desmond Hind Garrett, KCVO, CBE

Rice, Sir Timothy Miles Bindon, Kt.

Richard, Sir Cliff, Kt., OBE

Richards, Sir Brian Mansel, Kt., CBE, PHD

Richards, Rt. Hon. Sir David Anthony Stewart, Kt.

Richards, Sir David Gerald, Kt.

Richards, Sir Francis Neville, KCMG, CVO

Richards, Prof. Sir Michael Adrian, Kt., CBE

Richards, Rt. Hon. Sir Stephen Price, Kt.

Richardson, Sir Anthony Lewis, Bt. (1924)

Richardson, Sir Thomas Legh, KCMG

Richardson-Bunbury, Sir Thomas William, Bt. (I. 1787)

Richmond, Sir David Frank, KBE, CMG

Richmond, Prof. Sir Mark Henry, Kt., FRS

Ricketts, Sir Stephen Tristram, Bt. (1828)

Ricks, Prof. Sir Christopher Bruce, Kt.

Riddell, Sir Walter John Buchanan, Bt. (S. 1628)

Ridgway, Lt.-Gen. Sir Andrew Peter, KBE, CB

Ridley, Sir Adam (Nicholas), Kt.

Ridley, Sir Michael Kershaw, KCVO

Rifkind, Rt. Hon. Sir Malcolm Leslie, KCMG

Rigby, Sir Anthony John, Bt. (1929)

Rigby, Sir Peter, Kt.

Rimer, Rt. Hon. Sir Colin Percy Farquharson, Kt.

Ripley, Sir William Hugh, Bt. (1880)

Ritako, Sir Thomas Baha, Kt., MBE

Ritblat, Sir John Henry, Kt.

Ritchie, Prof. Sir Lewis Duthie, Kt., OBE

Rivett-Carnac, Sir Jonathan James, Bt. (1836)

Rix, Rt. Hon. Sir Bernard Anthony, Kt.

Robb, Sir John Weddell, Kt.

Roberts, Sir Derek Harry, Kt., CBE, FRS, FRENG

Roberts, Prof. Sir Edward Adam, KCMG

Roberts, Sir Gilbert Howland Rookehurst, Bt. (1809)

Roberts, Sir Hugh Ashley, GCVO

Roberts, Sir Ivor Anthony, KCMG

†Roberts, Sir James Elton Denby Buchanan, Bt. (1909)

Roberts, Dr Sir Richard John, Kt.

Roberts, Sir Samuel, Bt. (1919)

Roberts, Maj.-Gen. Sir Sebastian John Lechmere, KCVO, OBE

Robertson, Rt. Hon. Sir Hugh Michael, KCMG

Robertson, Sir Simon Manwaring, Kt.

Robey, Sir Simon Christopher Townsend, Kt.

Robins, Sir Ralph Harry, Kt., FRENG

Robinson, Sir Anthony, Kt.

Robinson, Sir Bruce, KCB

†Robinson, Sir Christopher Philipse, Bt. (1854)

Robinson, Sir Gerrard Jude, Kt.

Robinson, Sir Ian, Kt.

Robinson, Sir John James Michael Laud, Bt. (1660)

Robinson, Dr Sir Kenneth, Kt.

Robinson, Sir Peter Frank, Bt. (1908)

Robson, Sir Stephen Arthur, Kt., CB

Roch, Rt. Hon. Sir John Ormond, Kt.

Roche, Sir David O'Grady, Bt. (1838)

Roche, Sir Henry John, Kt.

Rodgers, Sir (Andrew) Piers (Wingate Aikin-Sneath), Bt. (1964)

Rogers, Air Chief Marshal Sir John Robson, KCB, CBE

Rogers, Sir Mark Ivan, KCMG

Rogers, Sir Peter, Kt.

Rollo, Lt.-Gen. Sir William Raoul, KCB, CBE

†Ropner, Sir Henry John William, Bt. (1952)

Ropner, Sir Robert Clinton, Bt. (1904)

Rose, Sir Arthur James, Kt., CBE

Rose, *Rt. Hon.* Sir Christopher Dudley Roger, Kt.

†Rose, Sir David Lancaster, Bt. (1874)

Rose, *Gen.* Sir (Hugh) Michael, KCB, CBE, DSO, QGM

Rose, Sir John Edward Victor, Kt.

Rose, Sir Julian Day, Bt. (1872 and 1909)

Rosenthal, Sir Norman Leon, Kt.

Ross, *Maj.* Sir Andrew Charles Paterson, Bt. (1960)

Ross, *Lt.-Gen.* Sir Robert Jeremy, KCB, OBE

Ross, *Lt.-Col.* Sir Walter Hugh Malcolm, GCVO, OBE

Ross, Sir Walter Robert Alexander, KCVO

Rossi, Sir Hugh Alexis Louis, Kt.

Roth, *Hon.* Sir Peter Marcel, Kt.

Rothschild, Sir Evelyn Robert Adrian de, Kt.

Rowe, *Rear-Adm.* Sir Patrick Barton, KCVO, CBE

Rowe-Ham, Sir David Kenneth, GBE

Rowland, Sir Geoffrey Robert, Kt.

Rowley, Sir Mark Peter, Kt., QPM

Rowley, Sir Richard Charles, Bt. (1786 and 1836)

Rowling, Sir John Reginald, Kt.

Royce, *Hon.* Sir Roger John, Kt.

Royden, Sir John Michael Joseph, Bt. (1905)

Rubin, *Prof.* Sir Peter Charles, Kt.

Rudd, Sir (Anthony) Nigel (Russell), Kt.

Ruddock, Sir Paul, Kt.

Rudge, Sir Alan Walter, Kt., CBE, FRS

†Rugge-Price, Sir James Keith Peter, Bt. (1804)

Ruggles-Brise, Sir Timothy Edward, Bt. (1935)

Rumbold, Sir Henry John Sebastian, Bt. (1779)

Rushdie, Sir (Ahmed) Salman, Kt.

Russell, Sir Charles Dominic, Bt. (1916)

Russell, Sir George, Kt., CBE

Russell, Sir Muir, KCB

Russell, Sir Robert, Kt.

†Russell, Sir Stephen (Steve) Charles, Bt. (1812)

Russell Beale, Sir Simon, Kt., CBE

Rutnam, Sir Philip McDougall, KCB

Rutter, *Prof.* Sir Michael Llewellyn, Kt., CBE, MD, FRS

Ryan, Sir Derek Gerald, Bt. (1919)

Rycroft, Sir Richard John, Bt. (1784)

Ryder, *Rt. Hon.* Sir Ernest Nigel, Kt., TD

Sacranie, Sir Iqbal Abdul Karim Mussa, Kt., OBE

Saini, *Hon.* Sir Pushpinder Singh, Kt.

Sainsbury, *Rt. Hon.* Sir Timothy Alan Davan, Kt.

St Clair-Ford, Sir William Sam, Bt. (1793)

St George, Sir John Avenel Bligh, Bt. (I. 1766)

St John, Sir Walter, KCMG, OBE

St John-Mildmay, Sir Walter John Hugh, Bt. (1772)

St Paul, Sir Lyle Kevin, KCMG

Sainty, Sir John Christopher, KCB

Sakora, *Hon.* Sir Bernard Berekia, KBE

Sales, *Rt. Hon.* Sir Philip James, Kt.

Salika, Sir Gibuna Gibbs, KBE

Salisbury, Sir Robert William, Kt.

Salt, Sir Patrick MacDonnell, Bt. (1869)

Salt, Sir (Thomas) Michael John, Bt. (1899)

Salusbury-Trelawny, Sir John William Richard, Bt. (1628)

Salz, Sir Anthony Michael Vaughan, Kt.

Samani, *Prof.* Sir Nilesh Jayantilal, Kt.

Sampson, Sir Colin, Kt., CBE, QPM

Samuel, Sir John Michael Glen, Bt. (1898)

Samuelson, Sir James Francis, Bt. (1884)

Samuelson, Sir Sydney Wylie, Kt., CBE

Samworth, Sir David Chetwode, Kt., CBE

Sanders, Sir Ronald Michael, KCMG

Sanderson, Sir Frank Linton, Bt. (1920), OBE

Sands, Sir Roger Blakemore, KCB

Sants, Sir Hector William Hepburn, Kt.

Sargent, Sir William Desmond, Kt., CBE

Satchwell, Sir Kevin Joseph, Kt.

Saumarez Smith, *Dr* Sir Charles, Kt., CBE, FBA

Saunders, Sir Bruce Joshua, KBE

Saunders, *Hon.* Sir John Henry Boulton, Kt.

Savill, *Prof.* Sir John Stewart, Kt.

Savory, Sir Michael Berry, Kt.

Sawers, Sir Robert John, GCMG

Saxby, *Prof.* Sir Robin Keith, Kt.

Scarlett, Sir John McLeod, KCMG, OBE

Schama, *Prof.* Sir Simon, Kt., CBE, FBA

Schiemann, *Rt. Hon.* Sir Konrad Hermann Theodor, Kt.

Schiff, Sir András, Kt.

Scholar, Sir Michael Charles, KCB

Scholar, Sir Thomas Whinfield, KCB

Scholey, Sir David Gerald, Kt., CBE

Scipio, Sir Hudson Rupert, Kt.

Scott, Sir Christopher James Anderson, Bt. (1909)

Scott, Sir David Richard Alexander, Kt., CBE

Scott, *Prof.* Sir George Peter, Kt.

Scott, Sir Henry Douglas Edward, Bt. (1913)

Scott, Sir James Jervoise, Bt. (1962)

Scott, Sir John Hamilton, KCVO

Scott, Sir Ridley, Kt.

Scott, Sir Robert David Hillyer, Kt.

Scott, Sir Walter John, Bt. (1907)

Scott-Lee, Sir Paul Joseph, Kt., QPM

Scruton, *Prof.* Sir Roger Vernon, Kt.

Seale, Sir Clarence David, Kt.

Seale, Sir John Robert Charters, Bt. (1838)

Sealy, Sir Austin Llewellyn, Kt.

Seaton, HE Sir Samuel Weymouth Tapley, GCMG, CVO

†Sebright, Sir Rufus Hugo Giles, Bt. (1626)

Sedley, *Rt. Hon.* Sir Stephen John, Kt.

Sedwill, Sir Mark, KCMG

†Seely, Sir William Victor Conway, Bt. (1896)

Seeto, Sir Ling James, Kt., MBE

Seeyave, Sir Rene Sow Choung, Kt., CBE

Seldon, *Dr* Sir Anthony Francis, Kt.

Semple, Sir John Laughlin, KCB

Sergeant, Sir Patrick, Kt.

Serota, *Hon.* Sir Nicholas Andrew, Kt., CH

Setchell, Sir Marcus Edward, KCVO

†Seton, Sir Charles Wallace, Bt. (S. 1683)

Seton, Sir Iain Bruce, Bt. (S. 1663)

Seymour, Sir Julian Roger, Kt., CBE

Shadbolt, *Prof.* Sir Nigel Richard, Kt.

Shakerley, Sir Nicholas Simon Adam, Bt. (1838)

Shakespeare, Sir Thomas William, Bt. (1942)

Sharp, Sir Adrian, Bt. (1922)

Sharp, Sir Fabian Alexander Sebastian, Bt. (1920)

Sharp, Sir Leslie, Kt., QPM

Sharples, Sir James, Kt., QPM

Shaw, Sir Charles De Vere, Bt. (1821)

Shaw, *Prof.* Sir John Calman, Kt., CBE

Shaw, Sir Neil McGowan, Kt.

Shaw-Stewart, Sir Ludovic Houston, Bt. (S. 1667)

Shebbeare, Sir Thomas Andrew, KCVO

Sheffield, Sir Reginald Adrian Berkeley, Bt. (1755)

Sheil, *Rt. Hon.* Sir John, Kt.

Sheinwald, Sir Nigel Elton, GCMG

Shelley, Sir John Richard, Bt. (1611)

Shepherd, Sir Colin Ryley, Kt.

Shepherd, Sir John Alan, KCVO, CMG

Shepherd, Sir Richard Charles Scrimgeour, Kt.

Sher, Sir Antony, KBE

Sherlock, Sir Nigel, KCVO, OBE

Sherston-Baker, Sir Robert George Humphrey, Bt. (1796)

†Shiffner, Sir Michael Goerge Edward, Bt. (1818)

Shinwell, Sir (Maurice) Adrian, Kt.

Shirreff, *Gen.* Sir Alexander Richard David, KCB, CBE

Shortridge, Sir Jon Deacon, KCB

Shuckburgh, Sir James Rupert Charles, Bt. (1660)

Siedentop, *Dr* Sir Larry Alan, Kt., CBE

Silber, *Rt. Hon.* Sir Stephen Robert, Kt.

Silk, Sir Evan Paul, KCB

Silverman, *Prof.* Sir Bernard Walter, Kt.

†Simeon, Sir Stephen George Barrington, Bt. (1815)

Simmonds, *Rt. Hon. Dr* Sir Kennedy Alphonse, KCMG

Simmons, *Air Marshal* Sir Michael George, KCB, AFC

Simms, Sir Neville Ian, Kt., FRENG

Simon, *Rt. Hon.* Sir Peregrine Charles Hugh, Kt.

Simonet, Sir Louis Marcel Pierre, Kt., CBE

Simpson, Sir Peter Austin, Kt., OBE

Simpson, *Dr* Sir Peter Jeffery, Kt.

Sims, Sir Roger Edward, Kt.

Sinclair, Sir Clive Marles, Kt.

Sinclair, Sir Robert John, Kt.

Sinclair, Sir William Robert Francis, Bt. (S. 1704)

Sinclair-Lockhart, Sir Simon John Edward Francis, Bt. (S. 1636)

Singh, Sir Pritpal, Kt.

Singh, *Rt. Hon.* Sir Rabinder, Kt.

Singleton, Sir Roger, Kt., CBE

Sitwell, Sir George Reresby Sacheverell, Bt. (1808)

Skeggs, Sir Clifford George, Kt.

Skehel, Sir John James, Kt., FRS

Skinner, Sir (Thomas) Keith (Hewitt), Bt. (1912)

Skipwith, Sir Alexander Sebastian Grey d'Estoteville, Bt. (1622)

Slade, *Rt. Hon.* Sir Christopher John, Kt.

Slade, Sir Julian Benjamin Alfred, Bt. (1831)

Slater, *Adm.* Sir John (Jock) Cunningham Kirkwood, GCB, LVO

Sleight, Sir Richard, Bt. (1920)

Sloman, Sir David Morgan, Kt.

Smiley, *Lt.-Col.* Sir John Philip, Bt. (1903)

Smith, *Prof.* Sir Adrian Frederick Melhuish, Kt., FRS

Smith, *Hon.* Sir Andrew Charles, Kt.

Smith, Sir Andrew Thomas, Bt. (1897)

Smith, Sir David Iser, KCVO

Smith, *Prof.* Sir Eric Brian, Kt., PHD

Smith, *Prof.* Sir James Cuthbert, Kt., FRS

Smith, Sir John Alfred, Kt., QPM

Smith, Sir Joseph William Grenville, Kt.

Smith, Sir Kevin, Kt., CBE

Smith, *Hon.* Sir Marcus Alexander, Kt.

Smith, Sir Martin Gregory, Kt.

Smith, Sir Michael John Llewellyn, KCVO, CMG

Smith, Sir (Norman) Brian, Kt., CBE, PHD

Smith, Sir Paul Brierley, Kt., CBE

Smith, *Hon.* Sir Peter Winston, Kt.

Smith, Sir Robert Courtney, Kt., CBE

Smith, Sir Robert Hill, Bt. (1945)

Smith, *Gen.* Sir Rupert Anthony, KCB, DSO, OBE, QGM

Smith, Sir Steven Murray, Kt.

Smith-Dodsworth, Sir David John, Bt. (1784)

Smith-Gordon, Sir (Lionel) Eldred (Peter), Bt. (1838)

Smith-Marriott, Sir Peter Francis, Bt. (1774)

Smurfit, *Dr* Sir Michael William Joseph, KBE

Smyth, Sir Timothy John, Bt. (1956)

Smyth-Osbourne, *Lt.-Gen.* Sir Edward Alexander, KCVO, CBE

Snowden, *Prof.* Sir Christopher Maxwell, Kt.

Snowden, *Hon.* Sir Richard Andrew, Kt.

Snyder, Sir Michael John, Kt.

Soames, *Rt. Hon.* Sir (Arthur) Nicholas Winston, Kt.

Soar, *Adm.* Sir Trevor Alan, KCB, OBE

Sobers, Sir Garfield St Auburn, Kt.

Solomon, Sir Harry, Kt.

Somare, *Rt. Hon.* Sir Michael Thomas, GCMG, CH

Songo, Sir Bernard Paul, Kt., CMG, OBE

Soole, *Hon.* Sir Michael Alexander, Kt.

Sorabji, *Prof.* Sir Richard Rustom Kharsedji, Kt., CBE

Sorrell, Sir John William, Kt., CBE

Sorrell, Sir Martin Stuart, Kt.

Sosa, Sir Manuel, Kt.

Soulsby, Sir Peter Alfred, Kt.

Souter, Sir Brian, Kt.

Southby, Sir John Richard Bilbe, Bt. (1937)

Southern, *Prof.* Sir Edwin Mellor, Kt.

Southgate, Sir Colin Grieve, Kt.

Southgate, Sir William David, Kt.

Southward, *Dr* Sir Nigel Ralph, KCVO

Sparks, *Prof.* Sir Robert Stephen John, Kt., CBE

Sparrow, Sir John, Kt.

Spearman, Sir Alexander Young Richard Mainwaring, Bt. (1840)

Spencer, Sir Derek Harold, Kt., QC

Spencer, *Hon.* Sir Martin Benedict, Kt.

Spencer, *Vice-Adm.* Sir Peter, KCB

Spencer, *Hon.* Sir Robin Godfrey, Kt.

Spencer-Nairn, Sir Robert Arnold, Bt. (1933)

Spicer, Sir Nicholas Adrian Albert, Bt. (1906)

Spiegelhalter, *Prof.* Sir David John, Kt., OBE, FRS

Spiers, Sir Donald Maurice, Kt., CB, TD

Spring, Sir Dryden Thomas, Kt.

Spurling, Sir John Damian, KCVO, OBE

Stacey, *Air Marshal* Sir Graham Edward, KBE, CB

Stadlen, *Hon.* Sir Nicholas Felix, Kt.

Stagg, Sir Charles Richard Vernon, KCMG

Staite, Sir Richard John, Kt., OBE

Stamer, Sir Peter Tomlinson, Bt. (1809)

Stanhope, *Adm.* Sir Mark, GCB, OBE, ADC

Stanier, Sir Beville Douglas, Bt. (1917)

Stanley, *Rt. Hon.* Sir John Paul, Kt.

Starkey, Sir John Philip, Bt. (1935)

Starkey, Sir Richard, Kt., MBE

Starmer, *Rt. Hon.* Sir Keir, KCB, QC

Stear, *Air Chief Marshal* Sir Michael James Douglas, KCB, CBE

Steel, *Vice-Adm.* Sir David George, KBE

Steel, *Hon.* Sir David William, Kt.

Steer, Sir Alan William, Kt.

Stephens, Sir (Edwin) Barrie, Kt.

Stephens, Sir Jonathan Andrew de Sievrac, KCB

Stephens, *Rt. Hon.* Sir (William) Benjamin Synge, Kt.

†Stephenson, Sir Henry Upton, Bt. (1936)

Stephenson, Sir Paul Robert, Kt., QPM

Stephenson, *Prof.* Sir Terence John, Kt.

Sterling, Sir Michael John Howard, Kt.

Stevens, Sir Michael John, KCVO

Stevenson, Sir Hugh Alexander, Kt.

Stewart, Sir Alan d'Arcy, Bt. (I. 1623)

Stewart, Sir Alastair Robin, Bt. (1960)

Stewart, Sir Brian John, Kt., CBE

Stewart, Sir David James Henderson, Bt. (1957)

Stewart, Sir David John Christopher, Bt. (1803)

Stewart, Sir James Moray, KCB

Stewart, Sir (John) Simon (Watson), Bt. (1920)

Stewart, Sir John Young, Kt., OBE

Stewart, Sir Patrick, Kt., OBE

Stewart, *Lt.-Col.* Sir Robert Christie, KCVO, CBE, TD

Stewart, Sir Roderick David, Kt., CBE

Stewart, *Hon.* Sir Stephen Paul, Kt.

Stewart, *Prof.* Sir William Duncan Paterson, Kt., FRS, FRSE

Stewart-Clark, Sir John, Bt. (1918)

Stewart-Richardson, Sir Simon Alaisdair Ian Neile, Bt. (S. 1630)

Stheeman, Sir Robert Alexander Talma, Kt., CB

Stilgoe, Sir Richard Henry Simpson, Kt., OBE

Stirling, Sir Angus Duncan Aeneas, Kt.

Stirling of Garden, *Col.* Sir James, KCVO, CBE, TD

Stirling-Hamilton, Sir Malcolm William Bruce, Bt. (S. 1673)

Stockdale, Sir Thomas Minshull, Bt. (1960)

Stoddart, *Prof.* Sir James Fraser, Kt.

Stoller, Sir Norman Kelvin, Kt., CBE

Stone, Sir Christopher, Kt.

Stone, Sir Roy Alexander, Kt., CBE

Stonhouse, *Revd* Michael Philip, Bt. (1628 and 1670)

Stonor, *Air Marshal* Sir Thomas Henry, KCB

Stoppard, Sir Thomas, Kt., OM, CBE

Storey, *Hon.* Sir Richard, Bt., CBE (1960)

Stothard, Sir Peter Michael, Kt.

Stott, Sir Adrian George Ellingham, Bt. (1920)

Stoute, Sir Michael Ronald, Kt.

Stoutzker, Sir Ian Isaac, Kt., CBE

Stracey, Sir John Simon, Bt. (1818)

Strachan, Sir Curtis Victor, Kt., CVO

Strachan, Sir Hew Francis Anthony, Kt.

†Strachey, Sir Henry Leofric Benvenuto, Bt. (1801)

Straker, Sir Louis Hilton, KCMG

Strang, *Prof.* Sir John Stanley, Kt.

Strang Steel, Sir (Fiennes) Michael, Bt. (1938), CBE

Stratton, *Prof.* Sir Michael Rudolf, Kt., FRS

Streeter, Sir Gary Nicholas, Kt.

Strickland-Constable, Sir Frederic, Bt. (1641)

Stringer, Sir Donald Edgar, Kt., CBE

Stringer, Sir Howard, Kt.

Strong, Sir Roy Colin, Kt., CH, PHD, FSA

†Stronge, Sir James Anselan Maxwell, Bt. (1803)

†Stuart, Sir Geoffrey Phillip, Bt. (1660)

Stuart, Sir James Keith, Kt.

†Stuart-Forbes, Sir William Daniel, Bt. (S. 1626)

Stuart-Menteth, Sir Charles Greaves, Bt. (1838)

Stuart-Paul, *Air Marshal* Sir Ronald Ian, KBE

Stuart-Smith, *Hon.* Sir Jeremy Hugh, Kt

Stuart-Smith, *Rt. Hon.* Sir Murray, KCMG

Stubbs, Sir William Hamilton, Kt., PHD

Stucley, *Lt.* Sir Hugh George Coplestone Bampfylde, Bt. (1859)

Studd, Sir Edward Fairfax, Bt. (1929)

Studholme, Sir Henry William, Bt. (1956)

Sturridge, Sir Nicholas Anthony, KCVO

Stuttard, Sir John Boothman, Kt.

†Style, Sir William Frederick, Bt. (1627)

Sullivan, *Rt. Hon.* Sir Jeremy Mirth, Kt.

Sullivan, Sir Richard Arthur, Bt. (1804)

Sunderland, Sir John Michael, Kt.

Supperstone, *Hon.* Sir Michael Alan, Kt.

Sutherland, Sir John Brewer, Bt. (1921)

Sutherland, Sir William George MacKenzie, Kt.

Sutton, Sir Richard Lexington, Bt. (1772)

Swan, Sir John William David, KBE

Swann, Sir Michael Christopher, Bt. (1906), TD

Swayne, *Rt. Hon.* Sir Desmond, Kt., TD

Sweeney, Sir George, Kt.

Sweeney, *Hon.* Sir Nigel Hamilton, Kt.

Sweeting, *Prof.* Sir Martin Nicholas, Kt., OBE, FRS

Swift, *Hon.* Sir Jonathan Mark, Kt

Swire, *Rt. Hon.* Sir Hugo George William, KCMG

Sykes, Sir David Michael, Bt. (1921)

Sykes, Sir Francis John Badcock, Bt. (1781)

Sykes, Sir Hugh Ridley, Kt.

Sykes, *Prof.* Sir (Malcolm) Keith, Kt.

Sykes, Sir Richard, Kt.

Sykes, Sir Tatton Christopher Mark, Bt. (1783)

Symons, *Vice-Adm.* Sir Patrick Jeremy, KBE

Syms, *Rt. Hon.* Sir Robert Andrew Raymond, Kt.

†Synge, Sir Allen James Edward, Bt. (1801)

Tanner, Sir David Whitlock, Kt., CBE

Tantum, Sir Geoffrey Alan, Kt., CMG, OBE

Tapps-Gervis-Meyrick, Sir George Christopher Cadafael, Bt. (1791)

Tate, Sir Edward Nicolas, Bt. (1898)

Taureka, *Dr* Sir Reubeh, KBE

Tauvasa, Sir Joseph James, KBE

Taylor, Sir Hugh Henderson, KCB

Taylor, *Dr* Sir John Michael, Kt., OBE

Taylor, Sir Jonathan McLeod Grigor, KCMG

Taylor, *Prof.* Sir Martin John, Kt., FRS

Taylor, Sir Nicholas Richard Stuart, Bt. (1917)

Taylor, *Prof.* Sir William, Kt., CBE

Taylor, Sir William George, Kt.

Teagle, *Vice-Adm.* Sir Somerford Francis, KBE

Teare, *Hon.* Sir Nigel John Martin, Kt.

Teasdale, *Prof.* Sir Graham Michael, Kt.

Tebbit, Sir Kevin Reginald, KCB, CMG

Temple, *Prof.* Sir John Graham, Kt.

Temple, Sir Richard Carnac Chartier, Bt. (1876)

Temu, *Hon. Dr* Sir Puka, KBE, CMG

Tennyson-D'Eyncourt, Sir Mark Gervais, Bt. (1930)

Terry, *Air Marshal* Sir Colin George, KBE, CB

Thatcher, *Hon.* Sir Mark, Bt. (1990)

Thomas, Sir David John Godfrey, Bt. (1694)

Thomas, Sir Derek Morison David, KCMG

Thomas, *Prof.* Sir Eric Jackson, Kt.

Thomas, Sir Gilbert Stanley, Kt., OBE

Thomas, Sir Jeremy Cashel, KCMG

Thomas, *Prof.* Sir John Meurig, Kt., FRS

Thomas, Sir Keith Vivian, Kt.

Thomas, *Dr* Sir Leton Felix, KCMG, CBE

Thomas, Sir Philip Lloyd, KCVO, CMG

Thomas, Sir Quentin Jeremy, Kt., CB

Thomas, Sir William Michael, Bt. (1919)

Thompson, Sir Christopher Peile, Bt. (1890)

Thompson, Sir Clive Malcolm, Kt.

Thompson, Sir David Albert, KCMG

Thompson, Sir Jonathan Michael, KCB

Thompson, *Prof.* Sir Michael Warwick, Kt., DSc

Thompson, Sir Nicholas Annesley, Bt. (1963)

Thompson, Sir Nigel Cooper, KCMG, CBE

Thompson, Sir Paul Anthony, Bt. (1963)

Thompson, Sir Peter Anthony, Kt.

Thompson, *Dr* Sir Richard Paul Hepworth, KCVO

Thompson, Sir Thomas d'Eyncourt John, Bt. (1806)

Thomson, Sir Adam McClure, KCMG

Thomson, Sir (Frederick Douglas) David, Bt. (1929)

Thomson, Sir Mark Wilfrid Home, Bt. (1925)

Thorne, Sir Neil Gordon, Kt., OBE, TD

Thornicroft, *Prof.* Sir Graham John, Kt.

Thornton, *Air Marshal* Sir Barry Michael, KCB

Thornton, Sir (George) Malcolm, Kt.

Thornton, Sir Peter Ribblesdale, Kt.

†Thorold, Sir (Anthony) Oliver, Bt. (1642)

Thorpe, *Rt. Hon.* Sir Mathew Alexander, Kt.

Thrift, *Prof.* Sir Nigel John, Kt.

Thurecht, Sir Ramon Richard, Kt., OBE

Thwaites, Sir Bryan, Kt., PHD

Tickell, Sir Crispin Charles Cervantes, GCMG, KCVO

Tidmarsh, Sir James Napier, KCVO, MBE

Tilt, Sir Robin Richard, Kt.

Tiltman, Sir John Hessell, KCVO

Timmins, *Col.* Sir John Bradford, KCVO, OBE, TD

Timpson, Sir William John Anthony, Kt., CBE

Tims, Sir Michael David, KCVO

Tindle, Sir Ray Stanley, Kt., CBE

Tirvengadum, Sir Harry Krishnan, Kt.

Tod, *Vice-Adm.* Sir Jonathan James Richard, KCB, CBE

Togolo, Sir Melchior Pesa, Kt.

Toka, Sir Mahuru Dadi, Kt., MBE

Tollemache, Sir Lyonel Humphry John, Bt. (1793)

Tomkys, Sir (William) Roger, KCMG

Tomlinson, Sir John Rowland, Kt., CBE

Tomlinson, Sir Michael John, Kt., CBE

Tomlinson, *Rt. Hon.* Sir Stephen Miles, Kt.

Tooke, *Prof.* Sir John Edward, Kt.

Tooley, Sir John, Kt.

ToRobert, Sir Henry Thomas, KBE

Torpy, *Air Chief Marshal* Sir Glenn Lester, GCB, CBE, DSO

Torrance, *Very Revd Prof.* Iain Richard, KCVO, TD

Torry, Sir Peter James, GCVO, KCMG

†Touche, Sir Eric MacLellan, Bt. (1962)

Touche, Sir William George, Bt. (1920)

Tovadek, Sir Martin, Kt. CMG

Tovua, Sir Paul Joshua, KCMG

ToVue, Sir Ronald, Kt., OBE

Towneley, Sir Simon Peter Edmund Cosmo William, KCVO

Townsley, Sir John Arthur, Kt.

Traill, Sir Alan Towers, GBE

Trainor, *Prof.* Sir Richard Hughes, KBE

Trawen, Sir Andrew Sean, Kt., CMG, MBE

Treacy, *Rt. Hon.* Sir Colman Maurice, Kt.

Treacy, *Hon.* Sir (James Mary) Seamus, Kt.

Treisman, Sir Richard Henry, Kt., FRS

Trescowthick, Sir Donald Henry, KBE

†Trevelyan, Sir Peter John, Bt. (1662 and 1874)

Trezise, Sir Kenneth Bruce, Kt., OBE

Trippier, Sir David Austin, Kt., RD

Tritton, Sir Jeremy Ernest, Bt. (1905)

Trollope, Sir Anthony Simon, Bt. (1642)

Trotter, Sir Neville Guthrie, Kt.

Troubridge, Sir Thomas Richard, Bt. (1799)

Troup, Sir Edward Astley (John), Kt.

Trousdell, *Lt.-Gen.* Sir Philip Charles Cornwallis, KBE, CB

†Truscott, Sir Ralph Eric Nicholson, Bt. (1909)

Tsang, Sir Donald Yam-keun, KBE

Tuck, Sir Bruce Adolph Reginald, Bt. (1910)

Tucker, Sir Paul, Kt.

Tucker, *Hon.* Sir Richard Howard, Kt.

Tuckett, *Prof.* Sir Alan John, Kt., OBE

Tuckey, *Rt. Hon.* Sir Simon Lane, Kt.

Tugendhat, *Hon.* Sir Michael George, Kt.

Tuite, Sir Christopher Hugh, Bt. (I. 1622), PHD

Tully, Sir William Mark, KBE

Tunnock, Sir Archibald Boyd, Kt., CBE

Tunstall, Sir Craig, Kt.

†Tupper, Sir Charles Hibbert, Bt. (1888)

Turing, Sir John Dermot, Bt. (S. 1638)

Turnbull, *Prof.* Sir Douglass Matthew, Kt.

Turner, *Hon.* Sir Mark George, Kt.

Turnquest, Sir Orville Alton, GCMG, QC

Tusa, Sir John, Kt.

Tweedie, *Prof.* Sir David Philip, Kt.

Tyrwhitt, Sir Reginald Thomas Newman, Bt. (1919)

Udny-Lister, Sir Edward Julian, Kt.

Ullmann, Sir Anthony James, Kt.

Underhill, *Rt. Hon.* Sir Nicholas Edward, Kt.

Underwood, *Prof.* Sir James Cressee Elphinstone, Kt.

Unwin, Sir (James) Brian, KCB

Ure, Sir John Burns, KCMG, LVO

Urquhart, Sir Brian Edward, KCMG, MBE

Urquhart, *Rt. Revd* David Andrew, KCMG

Usher, Sir Andrew John, Bt. (1899)

Utting, Sir William Benjamin, Kt., CB

Vallance, *Dr* Sir Patrick John Thompson, Kt.

Vardy, Sir Peter, Kt.

Varney, Sir David Robert, Kt.

Vassar-Smith, Sir John Rathbone, Bt. (1917)

Vavasour, Sir Eric Michael Joseph Marmaduke, Bt. (1828)

Veness, Sir David, Kt., CBE, QPM

Vereker, Sir John Michael Medlicott, KCB

Verey, Sir David John, Kt., CBE

Verity, Sir Gary Keith, Kt.

Verney, Sir Edmund Ralph, Bt. (1818)

†Verney, Sir John Sebastian, Bt. (1946)

Vernon, Sir James William, Bt. (1914)

Vestey, Sir Paul Edmund, Bt. (1921)

Vickers, *Prof.* Sir Brian William, Kt.

Vickers, Sir John Stuart, Kt.

Vickers, *Lt.-Gen.* Sir Richard Maurice Hilton, KCB, CVO, OBE

Vickers, Sir Roger Henry, KCVO

Viggers, *Lt.-Gen.* Sir Frederick Richard, KCB, CMG, MBE

Viggers, Sir Peter John, Kt.

Vincent, Sir William Percy Maxwell, Bt. (1936)

Vineall, Sir Anthony John Patrick, Kt.

Virdee, *Prof.* Sir Tejinder Singh, Kt.

von Friesendorff, Sir Rickard Fredrik Knut, Bt. (1661)

Vos, *Rt. Hon.* Sir Geoffrey Charles, Kt.

Vuatha, Sir Tipo, Kt., LVO, MBE

†Vyvyan, Sir Ralph Ferrers Alexander, Bt. (1645)

Waena, Sir Nathaniel Rahumaea, GCMG

Waine, *Rt. Revd* John, KCVO

Wainwright, Sir Robert Mark, KCMG

Waite, *Rt. Hon.* Sir John Douglas, Kt.

Waka, Sir Lucas Joseph, Kt., OBE

Wake, Sir Hereward Charles, Bt. (1621)

Wakefield, Sir (Edward) Humphry (Tyrrell), Bt. (1962)

Wakefield, Sir Norman Edward, Kt.

Wakeford, Sir Geoffrey Michael Montgomery, Kt., OBE

Wakeham, *Prof.* Sir William Arnot, Kt.

†Wakeley, Sir Nicholas Jeremy, Bt. (1952)

Waksman, *Hon.* Sir David Michael, Kt.

Wald, *Prof.* Sir Nicholas John, Kt.

Wales, Sir Robert Andrew, Kt.

Waley-Cohen, Sir Stephen Harry, Bt. (1961)

Walker, *Gen.* Sir Antony Kenneth Frederick, KCB

Walker, Sir Christopher Robert Baldwin, Bt. (1856)

Walker, Sir David Alan, Kt.

Walker, *Air Vice-Marshal* Sir David Allan, KCVO, OBE

Walker, Sir Harold Berners, KCMG

Walker, Sir John Ernest, Kt., DPHIL, FRS

Walker, *Air Marshal* Sir John Robert, KCB, CBE, AFC

Walker, Sir Malcolm Conrad, Kt., CBE

Walker, Sir Miles Rawstron, Kt., CBE

Walker, Sir Patrick Jeremy, KCB

Walker, *Hon.* Sir Paul James, Kt.

Walker, Sir Rodney Myerscough, Kt.

Walker, Sir Roy Edward, Bt. (1906)

Walker, *Hon.* Sir Timothy Edward, Kt.

Walker, Sir Victor Stewart Heron, Bt. (1868)

Walker-Okeover, Sir Andrew Peter Monro, Bt. (1886)

Walker-Smith, *Hon.* Sir John Jonah, Bt. (1960)

Wall, Sir (John) Stephen, GCMG, LVO

Wall, *Gen.* Sir Peter Anthony, GCB, CBE, ADC

Wallace, *Prof.* Sir David James, Kt., CBE, FRS

Waller, *Rt. Hon.* Sir (George) Mark, Kt.

Waller, Sir John Michael, Bt. (I. 1780)

Waller, *Revd Dr* Sir Ralph, KBE

Wallis, Sir Peter Gordon, KCVO

Wallis, Sir Timothy William, Kt.

Walmsley, *Vice-Adm.* Sir Robert, KCB

Walport, *Dr* Sir Mark Jeremy, Kt.

†Walsham, Sir Gerald Percy Robert, Bt. (1831)

Walters, Sir Dennis Murray, Kt., MBE

Walters, Sir Frederick Donald, Kt.

Walters, Sir Peter Ingram, Kt.

Wamiri, Sir Akapite, KBE

Warby, *Hon.* Sir Mark David John, Kt.

Ward, *Rt. Hon.* Sir Alan Hylton, Kt.

Ward, Sir Austin, Kt., QC

Ward, *Hon.* Sir (Frederik) Gordon (Roy), Kt., OBE

Ward, *Prof.* Sir John MacQueen, Kt., CBE

Ward, Sir Joseph James Laffey, Bt. (1911)

Ward, Sir Timothy James, Kt.

†Wardlaw, Sir Henry Justin, Bt. (NS. 1631)

Waring, Sir (Alfred) Holburt, Bt. (1935)

Warmington, Sir Rupert Marshall, Bt. (1908)

Warner, Sir Gerald Chierici, KCMG

Warner, Sir Philip Courtenay Thomas, Bt. (1910)

Warren, Sir David Alexander, KCMG

Warren, Sir (Frederick) Miles, KBE

Warren, *Hon.* Sir Nicholas Roger, Kt.

Waterlow, Sir Christopher Rupert, Bt. (1873)

Waterlow, Sir (Thomas) James, Bt. (1930)

Waters, *Gen.* Sir (Charles) John, GCB, CBE

Waters, Sir David Mark Rylance (Mark Rylance), Kt.

Waterstone, Sir Timothy, Kt.

Wates, Sir Christopher Stephen, Kt.

Wates, Sir James Garwood Michael, Kt., CBE

Watson, Sir Graham Robert, Kt.

Watson, Sir (James) Andrew, Bt. (1866)

Watson, *Prof.* Sir Robert Tony, Kt., CMG

Watson, Sir Ronald Matthew, Kt., CBE

Watt, *Gen.* Sir Charles Redmond, KCB, KCVO, CBE, ADC

Watts, Sir Philip Beverley, KCMG

Weatherup, *Hon.* Sir Ronald Eccles, Kt.

Webb, *Prof.* Sir Adrian Leonard, Kt.

Webb, *Rt. Hon.* Sir Steven John, Kt.

Webb-Carter, *Maj.-Gen.* Sir Evelyn John, KCVO, OBE

Webster, *Vice-Adm.* Sir John Morrison, KCB

Wedgwood, Sir Ralph Nicholas, Bt. (1942)

Weekes, Sir Everton DeCourcey, KCMG, OBE

Weinberg, Sir Mark Aubrey, Kt.

Weir, *Hon.* Sir Reginald George, Kt.

Weir, Sir Roderick Bignell, Kt.

Welby, Sir (Richard) Bruno Gregory, Bt. (1801)

Welch, Sir John Reader, Bt. (1957)

Weldon, Sir Anthony William, Bt. (I. 1723)

Wellend, *Prof.* Sir Mark Edward, Kt.

Weller, *Prof.* Sir Ian Vincent Derrick, Kt.

Weller, Sir Nicholas John, Kt.

†Wells, Sir Christopher Charles, Bt. (1944)

Wells, *Prof.* Sir Stanley William, Kt., CBE

Wells, Sir William Henry Weston, Kt., FRICS

Wenge, *Rt. Revd* Girege, KBE

Wessely, *Prof.* Sir Simon Charles, Kt.

Westmacott, Sir Peter John, GCMG, LVO

Weston, Sir Michael Charles Swift, KCMG, CVO

Weston, Sir (Philip) John, KCMG

Whalen, Sir Geoffrey Henry, Kt., CBE

Wheeler, *Rt. Hon.* Sir John Daniel, Kt.

Wheeler, Sir John Frederick, Bt. (1920)

Wheeler, *Gen.* Sir Roger Neil, GCB, CBE

Wheler, Sir Trevor Woodford, Bt. (1660)

Whitaker, Sir John James Ingham (Jack), Bt. (1936)

Whitbread, Sir Samuel Charles, KCVO

Whitchurch, Sir Graeme Ian, Kt., OBE

White, Sir Adrian Edwin, Kt., CBE

White, *Prof.* Sir Christopher John, Kt., CVO

White, Sir David (David Jason), Kt., OBE

White, Sir David Harry, Kt.

White, Sir George Stanley James, Bt. (1904)

White, Sir John Woolmer, Bt. (1922)

White, *Maj.-Gen.* Sir Martin, KCVO, CB, CBE

White, *Prof.* Sir Nicholas John, KCMG, OBE

White, Sir Nicholas Peter Archibald, Bt. (1802)

White, Sir Willard Wentworth, Kt., CBE

White-Spunner, *Lt.-Gen.* Sir Barnabas William Benjamin, KCB, CBE

Whitehead, Sir Philip Henry Rathbone, Bt. (1889)

Whitmore, Sir Clive Anthony, GCB, CVO

Whitmore, Sir Jason Kevin, Bt. (1954)

Whitson, Sir Keith Roderick, Kt.

Whittam Smith, Sir Andreas, Kt., CBE

Wickerson, Sir John Michael, Kt.

Wicks, Sir Nigel Leonard, GCB, CVO, CBE

Wigan, Sir Michael Iain, Bt. (1898)

Wiggin, Sir Richard Edward John, Bt. (1892)

Wiggins, Sir Bradley Marc, Kt., CBE

Wigram, Sir John Woolmore, Bt. (1805)

Wilbraham, Sir Richard Baker, Bt. (1776)

Wild, Sir John Ralston, Kt., CBE

Wiles, *Prof.* Sir Andrew John, KBE

Wilkie, *Hon.* Sir Alan Fraser, Kt.

Wilkins, Sir Michael, Kt.

Wilkinson, Sir (David) Graham (Brook), Bt. (1941)

Willcocks, *Lt.-Gen.* Sir Michael Alan, KCB, CVO

Williams, Sir Anthony Geraint, Bt. (1953)

Williams, Sir (Arthur) Gareth Ludovic Emrys Rhys, Bt. (1918)

Williams, Sir Charles Othniel, Kt.

Williams, Sir Daniel Charles, GCMG, QC

Williams, *Hon.* Sir David Basil, Kt.

Williams, Sir David Reeve, Kt., CBE

Williams, Sir Donald Mark, Bt. (1866)

Williams, *Prof.* Sir (Edward) Dillwyn, Kt., FRCP

Williams, Sir Francis Owen Garbett, Kt., CBE

Williams, *Hon.* Sir (John) Griffith, Kt.

Williams, Sir Nicholas Stephen, Kt.

Williams, *Prof.* Sir Norman Stanley, Kt.

Williams, Sir Paul Michael, Kt., OBE

Williams, Sir Peter Michael, Kt.

Williams, *Prof.* Sir Robert Hughes, Kt.

Williams, Sir (Robert) Philip Nathaniel, Bt. (1915)

Williams, *HE Dr* Sir Rodney Errey Lawrence, GCMG

Williams, *Prof.* Sir Roger, Kt.

Williams, Sir (William) Maxwell (Harries), Kt.

Williams, *Hon.* Sir Wyn Lewis, Kt.

Williams-Bulkeley, Sir Richard Thomas, Bt. (1661)

Williams-Wynn, Sir David Watkin, Bt. (1688)

Williamson, Sir George Malcolm, Kt.

Williamson, Sir Robert Brian, Kt., CBE

Willink, Sir Edward Daniel, Bt. (1957)

Wills, Sir David James Vernon, Bt. (1923)

Wills, Sir David Seton, Bt. (1904)

Wilmot, Sir Henry Robert, Bt. (1759)

Wilmut, *Prof.* Sir Ian, Kt., OBE

Wilsey, *Gen.* Sir John Finlay Willasey, GCB, CBE

Wilshaw, Sir Michael, Kt.

Wilson, *Prof.* Sir Alan Geoffrey, Kt.

Wilson, Sir David Mackenzie, Kt.

Wilson, Sir Franklyn Roosevelt, KCMG

Wilson, Sir James William Douglas, Bt. (1906)

Wilson, *Brig.* Sir Mathew John Anthony, Bt. (1874), OBE, MC

Wilson, *Rt. Hon.* Sir Nicholas Allan Roy, Kt. (Lord Wilson of Culworth)

Wilson, *Prof.* Sir Robert James Timothy, Kt.

Wilson, Sir Robert Peter, KCMG

Wilson, *Air Chief Marshal* Sir (Ronald) Andrew (Fellowes), KCB, AFC

Wilson, Sir Thomas David, Bt. (1920)

Winkley, Sir David Ross, Kt.

Winnington, Sir Anthony Edward, Bt. (1755)

Winship, Sir Peter James Joseph, Kt., CBE

Winsor, Sir Thomas Philip, Kt.

Winter, *Dr* Sir Gregory Winter, Kt., CBE

Winterton, Sir Nicholas Raymond, Kt.

Wiseman, Sir John William, Bt. (1628)

Witty, Sir Andrew, Kt.

Wolfendale, *Prof.* Sir Arnold Whittaker, Kt., FRS

†Wolseley, Sir James Douglas, Bt. (I. 1745)

†Wolseley, Sir Stephen Garnet Hugo Charles, Bt. (1628)

†Wombwell, Sir George Philip Frederick, Bt. (1778)

Womersley, Sir Peter John Walter, Bt. (1945)

Woo, Sir Leo Joseph, Kt., MBE

Woo, Sir Po-Shing, Kt.

Wood, Sir Alan Thorpe Richard, Kt., CBE

Wood, Sir Andrew Marley, GCMG

Wood, Sir Anthony John Page, Bt. (1837)

Wood, Sir Ian Clark, KT, GBE

Wood, Sir James Sebastian Lamin, KCMG

Wood, Sir Martin Francis, Kt., OBE

Wood, Sir Michael Charles, KCMG
Wood, Sir Peter John, Kt., CBE
Wood, *Hon.* Sir Roderic Lionel James, Kt.
Woodard, *Rear Adm.* Sir Robert Nathaniel, KCVO
Woodcock, *Vice-Adm.* Sir (Simon) Jonathan, KCB, OBE
Woodhead, *Vice-Adm.* Sir (Anthony) Peter, KCB
Woods, *Prof.* Sir Kent Linton, Kt.
Woods, Sir Robert Kynnersley, Kt., CBE
Woodward, Sir Clive Ronald, Kt., OBE
Woodward, Sir Thomas Jones (Tom Jones), Kt., OBE
Woolley, Sir Simon, Kt.
Wootton, Sir David Hugh, Kt.
Wormald, Sir Christopher Stephen, KCB
Worsley, Sir William Ralph, Bt. (1838)
Worsthorne, Sir Peregrine Gerard, Kt.
Worthington, Sir Mark, Kt., OBE
Wratten, *Air Chief Marshal* Sir William John, GBE, CB, AFC
Wraxall, Sir Charles Frederick Lascelles, Bt. (1813)
Wrey, Sir George Richard Bourchier, Bt. (1628)

Wright, Sir Allan Frederick, KBE
Wright, Sir David John, GCMG, LVO
Wright, *Hon.* Sir (John) Michael, Kt.
Wright, *Prof.* Sir Nicholas Alcwyn, Kt.
Wright, Sir Peter Robert, Kt., CBE
Wright, *Air Marshal* Sir Robert Alfred, KBE, AFC
Wright, Sir Stephen John Leadbetter, KCMG
Wright, *Dr* Sir William Thompson, Kt., CBE
Wrightson, Sir Charles Mark Garmondsway, Bt. (1900)
Wrigley, *Prof.* Sir Edward Anthony (Sir Tony), Kt., PHD, PBA
Wrixon-Becher, Sir John William Michael, Bt. (1831)
Wroughton, Sir Philip Lavallin, KCVO
Wu, Sir Gordon Ying Sheung, KCMG
Wynne, Sir Graham Robert, Kt., CBE

Yacoub, *Prof.* Sir Magdi Habib, Kt., OM, FRCS
Yaki, Sir Roy, KBE
Yang, *Hon.* Sir Ti Liang, Kt.
Yarrow, Sir Alan Colin Drake, Kt.
Yarrow, Sir Ross William Grant, Bt. (1916)
Yassaie, *Dr* Sir Hossein, Kt.

Yoo Foo, Sir (François) Henri, Kt.
Young, Sir Colville Norbert, GCMG, MBE
Young, Sir Dennis Charles, KCMG
Young, Sir John Kenyon Roe, Bt. (1821)
Young, Sir John Robertson, GCMG
Young, Sir Nicholas Charles, Kt.
Young, Sir Robin Urquhart, KCB
Young, Sir Stephen Stewart Templeton, Bt. (1945), QC
Young, Sir William Neil, Bt. (1769)
Younger, Sir Alexander, KCMG
Younger, *Capt.* Sir John David Bingham, KCVO
Younger Thieriot, Sir Andrew William, Bt. (1911)
Yuwi, Sir Matiabe, KBE

Zacaroli, *Hon.* Sir Antony James, Kt.
Zacca, *Rt. Hon.* Sir Edward, KCMG
Zahedi, *Prof.* Sir Mir Saeed, Kt., OBE
Zambellas, *Adm.* Sir George Michael, GCB, DSC, ADC
Zissman, Sir Bernard Philip, Kt.
Zumla, *Prof.* Sir Alimuddin, Kt.
Zurenuoc, Sir Manasupe Zure, Kt., OBE
Zurenuoc, Sir Zibang, KBE

THE ORDER OF ST JOHN

THE MOST VENERABLE ORDER OF THE HOSPITAL OF ST JOHN OF JERUSALEM (1888)

GCStJ	Bailiff/Dame Grand Cross
KStJ	Knight of Justice/Grace
DStJ	Dame of Justice/Grace
CStJ	Commander
OStJ	Officer
SBStJ	Serving Brother
SSStJ	Serving Sister

Motto, Pro Fide, Pro Utilitate Hominum
(For the faith and in the service of humanity)

The Order of St John, founded in the early 12th century in Jerusalem, was a religious order with a particular duty to care for the sick. In Britain the order was dissolved by Henry VIII in 1540 but the British branch was revived in the early 19th century. The branch was not accepted by the Grand Magistracy of the Order in Rome but its search for a role in the tradition of the hospitallers led to the founding of the St John Ambulance Association in 1877 and later the St John Ambulance Brigade; in 1882 the St John Ophthalmic Hospital was founded in Jerusalem. A royal charter was granted in 1888 establishing the Order of St John as a British Order of Chivalry with the sovereign as its head.

Since October 1999 the whole order worldwide has been governed by a Grand Council which includes a representative from each of the 11 priories (England, Scotland, Wales, Hong Kong, Kenya, Singapore, South Africa, New Zealand, Canada, Australia and the USA). In addition there are also five commanderies in Northern Ireland, Jersey, Guernsey, the Isle of Man and Western Australia. There are also branches in about 30 other Commonwealth countries. Apart from St John Ambulance, the Order is also responsible for the Eye Hospital in Jerusalem. Admission to the order is usually conferred in recognition of service to either one of these institutions. Membership does not confer any rank, style, title or precedence on a recipient.

SOVEREIGN HEAD OF THE ORDER
HM The Queen

GRAND PRIOR
HRH The Duke of Gloucester, KG, GCVO

Lord Prior, Prof. Mark Compton
Prelate, Rt. Revd Timothy Stevens, CBE
Chancellor, Patrick Burgess, OBE
Sub-Prior, John Mah, QC
Secretary-General, Vice-Adm. Sir Paul Lambert, KCB

International Office, 3 Charterhouse Mews, London EC1M 6BB
T 020-7251 3292 **W** www.stjohninternational.org

DAMES

Style, 'Dame' before forename and surname, followed by appropriate post-nominal initials. Where such an award is made to a lady already in possession of a higher title, the appropriate initials follow her name
Envelope, Dame F_ S_, followed by appropriate post-nominal letters. *Letter (formal),* Dear Madam; *(social),* Dear Dame F_. *Spoken,* Dame F_
Husband, Untitled

Dame Grand Cross and Dame Commander are the higher classes for women of the Order of the Bath, the Order of St Michael and St George, the Royal Victorian Order, and the Order of the British Empire. Dames Grand Cross rank after the wives of Baronets and before the wives of Knights Grand Cross. Dames Commanders rank after the wives of Knights Grand Cross and before the wives of Knights Commanders.

Honorary damehoods may be conferred on women who are citizens of countries of which the Queen is not head of state.

LIST OF DAMES *as at 31 August 2019*
Women peers in their own right and life peers are not included in this list. Female members of the royal family are not included in this list; details of the orders they hold can be found within the Royal Family section.

If a dame has a double barrelled or hyphenated surname, she is listed under the first element of the name.

Abaijah, Dame Josephine, DBE
Abramsky, Dame Jennifer Gita, DBE
Acland Hood Gass, Lady (Elizabeth Periam), DCVO
Airlie, The Countess of, DCVO
Allen, *Hon.* Dame Anita Mildred, DBE
Allen, *Prof.* Dame Ingrid Victoria, DBE
Andrews, *Hon.* Dame Geraldine Mary, DBE
Andrews, Dame Julie, DBE
Angiolini, *Rt. Hon.* Dame Elish, DBE, QC
Anionwu, *Prof.* Dame Elizabeth Nneka, DBE
Anson, Lady (Elizabeth Audrey), DBE
Archer, Dame Mary Doreen, DBE
Arden, *Rt. Hon.* Dame Mary Howarth (Mrs Mance), DBE (Lady Arden of Heswall)
Ashcroft, *Prof.* Dame Frances Mary, DBE, FRS
Asplin, *Rt. Hon.* Dame Sarah Jane (Mrs Sherwin), DBE
Atkins, Dame Eileen, DBE
Atkins, *Prof.* Dame Madeleine Julia, DBE
August, Dame Kathryn, DBE
Bacon, Dame Patricia Anne, DBE
Bailey, Dame Glenda Adrianne, DBE
Bailey, *Prof.* Dame Susan Mary, DBE
Baird, Dame Vera, DBE
Baker, Dame Janet Abbott (Mrs Shelley), CH, DBE
Barbour, Dame Margaret (Mrs Ash), DBE
Barker, Dame Katharine Mary, DBE
Barker-Welch, *Hon.* Dame Maizie Irene, DBE
Barrow, Dame Jocelyn Anita (Mrs Downer), DBE
Barstow, Dame Josephine Clare (Mrs Anderson), DBE
Bassey, Dame Shirley, DBE
Beale, Dame Inga Kristine, DBE
Beard, *Prof.* Dame (Winifred) Mary, DBE
Beasley, *Prof.* Dame Christine Joan, DBE
Beaurepaire, Dame Beryl Edith, DBE
Beckett, *Rt. Hon.* Dame Margaret Mary, DBE
Beer, *Prof.* Dame Gillian Patricia Kempster, DBE, FBA
Beer, *Prof.* Dame Janet Patricia, DBE
Begg, Dame Anne, DBE
Beral, *Prof.* Dame Valerie, DBE
Bertschinger, *Dr* Dame Claire, DBE
Bevan, Dame Yasmin, DBE
Bibby, Dame Enid, DBE

Black, *Prof.* Dame Carol Mary, DBE
Black, *Rt. Hon.* Dame Jill Margaret, DBE (Lady Black of Derwent)
Black, *Prof.* Dame Susan Margaret, DBE, FRSE
Blackadder, Dame Elizabeth Violet, DBE
Blaize, Dame Venetia Ursula, DBE
Blaxland, Dame Helen Frances, DBE
Blume, Dame Hilary Sharon Braverman, DBE
Booth, *Hon.* Dame Margaret Myfanwy Wood, DBE
Bostwick, *Hon.* Dame Janet Gwennett, DBE
Boulding, Dame Hilary, DBE
Bourne, Dame Susan Mary (Mrs Bourne), DBE
Bowe, *Dr* Dame (Mary) Colette, DBE
Bowtell, Dame Ann Elizabeth, DCB
Braddock, *Dr* Dame Christine, DBE
Brain, Dame Margaret Anne (Mrs Wheeler), DBE
Breakwell, *Prof.* Dame Glynis Marie, DBE
Brennan, Dame Maureen, DBE
Brennan, Dame Ursula, DCB
Brewer, *Dr* Dame Nicola Mary, DCMG
Bridges, Dame Mary Patricia, DBE
Brindley, Dame Lynne Janie, DBE
Brittan, Dame Diana (Lady Brittan of Spennithorne), DBE
Brooke, *Rt. Hon.* Dame Annette (Lesley), DBE
Bruce, Dame Susan Margaret, DBE
Bruce, *Prof.* Dame Victoria Geraldine, DBE, FBA, FRSE
Buckland, Dame Yvonne Helen Elaine, DBE
Burnell, *Prof.* Dame Susan Jocelyn Bell, DBE
Burslem, Dame Alexandra Vivien, DBE
Bussell, Dame Darcey Andrea, DBE
Butler, Dame Rosemary Janet Mair, DBE
Byatt, Dame Antonia Susan, DBE, FRSL
Cairncross, Dame Frances Anne, DBE, FRSE
Caldicott, Dame Fiona, DBE, FRCP, FRCPSYCH
Callil, Dame Carmen Thérèse, DBE
Cameron, *Prof.* Dame Averil Millicent, DBE
Campbell-Preston, Dame Frances Olivia, DCVO
Carew Pole, Lady Mary, DCVO
Carnall, Dame Ruth, DBE
Carnwath, Dame Alison Jane, DBE
Carr, *Hon.* Dame Sue Lascelles (Mrs Birch), DBE
Cartwright, Dame Silvia Rose, DBE
Casey, Dame Louise, DBE, CB
Chapman, *Prof.* Dame Hilary Anne, DBE
Cheema-Grubb, *Hon.* Dame Bobbie, DBE
Clancy, Dame Claire Elizabeth, DCB
Clark, *Prof.* Dame Jill MacLeod, DBE
Clark, *Prof.* Dame (Margaret) June, DBE, PHD
Cleverdon, Dame Julia Charity, DCVO, CBE
Coates, Dame Sally, DBE
Cockerill, *Hon.* Dame Sara Elizabeth, DBE
Coia, *Dr* Dame Denise Assunta, DBE
Collarbone, Dame Patricia, DBE
Collins, Dame Joan Henrietta, DBE
Connolly, Dame Sarah Patricia, DBE
Contreras, *Prof.* Dame Marcela, DBE
Corley, Dame Elizabeth Pauline Lucy, DBE
Corner, *Prof.* Dame Jessica Lois, DBE
Corsar, *Hon.* Dame Mary Drummond, DBE
Courtice, Dame Veronica Anne (Polly), DBE, LVO
Coward, Dame Pamela Sarah, DBE
Cowley, *Prof.* Dame Sarah Ann, DBE
Cox, *Hon.* Dame Laura Mary, DBE
Cramp, *Prof.* Dame Rosemary Jean, DBE
Cullum, *Prof.* Dame Nicola Anne, DBE
Cunliffe-Lister *Hon.* Dame (Elizabeth) Susan, DCVO
Cutts, *Hon.* Dame Johannah, DBE

Dacon, Dame Monica Jessie, DBE, CMG
Dacre, *Prof.* Dame Jane Elizabeth, DBE
Daniel, Dame Jacqueline Lesley, DBE
Davies, *Prof.* Dame Kay Elizabeth, DBE
Davies, Dame Laura Jane, DBE
Davies, *Rt. Hon.* Dame Nicola Velfor, DBE
Davies, *Prof.* Dame Sally Claire, DBE
Davies, Dame Wendy Patricia, DBE
Davis, Dame Karlene Cecile, DBE
Dawson, *Prof.* Dame Sandra Jane Noble, DBE
de Havilland, Dame Olivia Mary, DBE
De Souza, Dame Rachel Mary, DBE
Dean, *Prof.* Dame Caroline, DBE, FRS
Dell, Dame Miriam Patricia, DBE
Dench, Dame Judith Olivia (Mrs Williams), CH, DBE
Descartes, Dame Marie Selipha Sesenne, DBE, BEM
Dethridge, Dame Kate, DBE
Digby, The Lady, DBE
Dobbs, *Hon.* Dame Linda Penelope, DBE
Docherty, Dame Jacqueline, DBE
Dominiczak, *Prof.* Dame Anna Felicja, DBE, FRSE
Donald, *Prof.* Dame Athene Margaret, DBE, FRS
Dowling, *Prof.* Dame Ann Patricia, OM, DBE
Duffield, Dame Vivien Louise, DBE
Duffy, Dame Carol Ann, DBE
Dumont, Dame Ivy Leona, DCMG
Dunnell, Dame Karen, DCB
Dyche, Dame Rachael Mary, DBE
Eady, *Hon.* Dame Jennifer, DBE
Elcoat, Dame Catherine Elizabeth, DBE
Ellison, Dame Jill, DBE
Ellman, Dame Louise Joyce, DBE
Elton, Dame Susan Richenda (Lady Elton), DCVO
Ennis-Hill, Dame Jessica, DBE
Esteve-Coll, Dame Elizabeth Anne Loosemore, DBE
Evans, Dame Anne Elizabeth Jane, DBE
Evans, Dame Madeline Glynne Dervel, DBE, CMG
Evans, Dame Oremi, DBE
Fagan, Dame (Florence) Mary, LG, DCVO
Fairbairn, Dame Carolyn Julie, DBE
Falk, *Hon.* Dame Sarah, DBE
Fallowfield, *Prof.* Dame Lesley Jean, DBE
Farbey, *Hon.* Dame Judith Sarah, DBE
Farnham, Dame Marion (Lady Farnham), DCVO
Fawcett, Dame Amelia Chilcott, DBE
Fielding, Dame Pauline, DBE
Finch, *Prof.* Dame Janet Valerie, DBE
Fisher, *Prof.* Dame Amanda Gray, DBE
Fisher, Dame Jacqueline, DBE
Forgan, Dame Elizabeth Anne Lucy, DBE
Foster, *Hon.* Dame Alison Lee Caroline, DBE
Foster, Dame Jacqueline, DBE
Fradd, Dame Elizabeth, DBE
Francis, *Prof.* Dame Jane Elizabeth, DCMG
Fraser, Lady Antonia, CH, DBE
Fraser, Dame Helen Jean Sutherland, DBE
Frost, Dame Barbara May, DBE
Fry, Dame Margaret Louise, DBE
Furse, Dame Clara Hedwig Frances, DBE
Gadhia, Dame Jayne-Anne, DBE
Gai, *Prof.* Dame Pratibha Laxman (Mrs Gai-Boyes), DBE
Gaymer, Dame Janet Marion, DBE, QC
Ghosh, Dame Helen Frances, DCB
Gibb, Dame Moira Margaret, DBE
Gillian, *Rt. Hon.* Dame Cheryl Elise Kendall, DBE
Glenn, *Prof.* Dame Hazel Gillian, DBE
Glennie, *Dr* Dame Evelyn Elizabeth Ann, CH, DBE
Gloag, Dame Ann Heron, DBE
Gloster, *Rt. Hon.* Dame Elizabeth (Lady Popplewell), DBE
Glover, Dame Audrey Frances, DBE, CMG
Glover, *Prof.* Dame Lesley Anne, DBE, FRSE
Goad, Dame Sarah Jane Frances, DCVO

Goodall, *Dr* Dame (Valerie) Jane, DBE
Goodfellow, *Prof.* Dame Julia Mary, DBE
Gordon, Dame Minita Elmira, GCMG, GCVO
Gordon, *Hon.* Dame Pamela Felicity, DBE
Gow, Dame Jane Elizabeth (Mrs Whiteley), DBE
Grafton, Ann, The Duchess of, GCVO
Grainger, *Dr* Dame Katherine Jane, DBE
Grant, Dame Mavis, DBE
Green, Dame Moya Marguerite, DBE
Green, Dame Pauline, DBE
Gretton, Lady Jennifer Ann, DCVO
Grey, Dame Beryl Elizabeth (Mrs Svenson), CH, DBE
Griffiths, Dame Marianne, DBE
Grimthorpe, Elizabeth, The Lady, DCVO
Guilfoyle, Dame Margaret Georgina Constance, DBE
Guthardt, *Revd Dr* Dame Phyllis Myra, DBE
Hackitt, Dame Judith Elizabeth, DBE
Hakin, *Dr* Dame Barbara Ann, DBE
Hall, *Prof.* Dame Wendy, DBE
Hallett, *Rt. Hon.* Dame Heather Carol, DBE
Hallett, Dame Nancy Karen, DBE
Hamilton, *Prof.* Dame Carolyn Paula, DBE
Harbison, Dame Joan Irene, DBE
Harper, Dame Elizabeth Margaret Way, DBE
Harris, Dame Pauline (Lady Harris of Peckham), DBE
Harris, Dame Philippa Jill Olivier, DBE
Hassan, Dame Anna Patricia Lucy, DBE
Hay, Dame Barbara Logan, DCMG, MBE
Henderson, Dame Fiona Douglas, DCVO
Hercus, *Hon.* Dame (Margaret) Ann, DCMG
Higgins, *Prof.* Dame Joan Margaret, DBE
Higgins, *Prof.* Dame Julia Stretton, DBE, FRS
Higgins, *Prof.* Dame Rosalyn, GBE, QC
Hill, *Prof.* Dame Judith Eileen, DBE
Hill, *Prof.* Dame Susan Lesley, DBE
Hine, Dame Deirdre Joan, DBE, FRCP
Hodge, *Rt. Hon.* Dame Margaret (Eve), DBE
Hodgson, Dame Patricia Anne, DBE
Hogg, *Hon.* Dame Mary Claire (Mrs Koops), DBE
Hollows, Dame Sharon, DBE
Holmes, Dame Kelly, DBE
Holroyd, Lady (Margaret Drabble), DBE
Holt, Dame Denise Mary, DCMG
Homer, Dame Linda Margaret, DCB
Hoodless, Dame Elisabeth Anne, DBE
Hoyles, *Prof.* Dame Celia Mary, DBE
Hudson, Dame Alice, DBE
Hufton, *Prof.* Dame Olwen, DBE
Humphrey, *Prof.* Dame Caroline (Lady Rees of Ludlow), DBE
Hunt, Dame Vivian, DBE
Husband, *Prof.* Dame Janet Elizabeth Siarey, DBE
Hussey, Dame Susan Katharine (Lady Hussey of North Bradley), GCVO
Hutton, Dame Deirdre Mary, DBE
Hyde, Dame Helen, DBE
Imison, Dame Tamsyn, DBE
Ion, *Dr* Dame Susan Elizabeth, DBE
Isaacs, Dame Albertha Madeline, DBE
James, Dame Naomi Christine (Mrs Haythorne), DBE
Jefford, *Hon.* Dame Nerys Angharad, DBE
Jiang, *Prof.* Dame Xiangqian (Jane), DBE
John, Dame Susan, DBE
Johnson, *Prof.* Dame Anne Mandall, DBE
Johnston, Dame Rotha Geraldine Diane, DBE
Jones, Dame Gwyneth (Mrs Haberfeld-Jones), DBE
Jordan, *Prof.* Dame Carole, DBE
Joseph, Dame Monica Theresa, DBE
Jowett, Dame Clara, DBE
Judd, *Hon.* Dame Frances, DBE
Julius, *Dr* Dame DeAnne Shirley, DCMG, CBE
Karika, Dame Pauline Margaret Rakera George (Mrs Taripo), DBE

Keeble, *Dr* Dame Reena, DBE
Keegan, Dame Elizabeth Mary, DBE
Keegan, Dame Geraldine Mary Marcella, DBE
Keegan, *Hon.* Dame Siobhan Roisin, DBE
Keith, Dame Penelope Anne Constance (Mrs Timson), DBE
Kekedo, Dame Rosalina Violet, DBE
Kelly, Dame Barbara Mary, DBE
Kelly, Dame Lorna May Boreland, DBE
Kendrick, Dame Fiona Marie, DBE
Kenny, Dame Julie Ann, DBE
Kershaw, Dame Janet Elizabeth Murray (Dame Betty), DBE
Kharas, Dame Zarine, DBE
Khemka, Dame Asha, DBE
Kidu, Lady, DBE
King, *Rt. Hon.* Dame Eleanor Warwick, DBE
Kinnair, Dame Donna, DBE
Kirby, Dame Georgina Kamiria, DBE
Kirkby, Dame (Carolyn) Emma, DBE
Kirwan, *Prof.* Dame Frances Clare, DBE, FRS
Knowles, *Hon.* Dame Gwynneth Frances Dietinde, DBE
Kumar, *Prof.* Dame Parveen June (Mrs Leaver), DBE
La Grenade, *HE* Dame Cécile Ellen Fleurette, GCMG, OBE
Laine, Dame Cleo (Clementine) Dinah (Lady Dankworth), DBE
Laing, *Rt. Hon.* Dame Eleanor Fulton, DBE
Laing, *Hon.* Dame Elisabeth Mary Caroline, DBE
Lake-Tack, *HE* Dame Louise Agnetha, GCMG
Lamb, Dame Dawn Ruth, DBE
Lambert, *Hon.* Dame Christina Caroline, DBE
Lang, *Hon.* Dame Beverley Ann Mcnaughton, DBE
Lannon, *Dr* Dame Frances, DBE
Lansbury Shaw, Dame Angela Brigid, DBE
Lavender, *Prof.* Dame Tina, DBE
Lawson, Dame Lesley (Twiggy), DBE
Leather, Dame Susan Catherine, DBE
Lee, *Prof.* Dame Hermione, DBE
Lee, Dame Laura Elizabeth, DBE
Legge-Bourke, *Hon.* Dame Elizabeth Shân Josephine, DCVO
Lenehan, Dame Christine, DBE
Leslie, Dame Alison Mariot, DCMG
Leslie, Dame Ann Elizabeth Mary, DBE
Lewis, Dame Edna Leofrida (Lady Lewis), DBE
Leyser Day, *Prof.* Dame Henrietta Miriam Ottoline, DBE
Lieven, *Hon.* Dame Nathalie Maria Daniella, DBE
Lively, Dame Penelope Margaret, DBE
Lott, Dame Felicity Ann Emwhyla (Mrs Woolf), DBE
Louisy, Dame (Calliopa) Pearlette, GCMG
Lynn, Dame Vera (Mrs Lewis), CH, DBE
MacArthur, Dame Ellen Patricia, DBE
McBride, *Hon.* Dame Denise Anne, DBE
McCall, Dame Carolyn Julia, DBE
McLean, *Prof.* Dame Angela Ruth, DBE
Macdonald, Dame Mary Beaton, DBE
McDonald, Dame Mavis, DCB
Mace, *Prof.* Dame Georgina, DBE
McGowan, *Hon.* Dame Maura Patricia, DBE
Macgregor, Dame Judith Anne, DCMG, LVO
McGuire, *Rt. Hon.* Dame Anne Catherine, DBE
MacIntyre, *Prof.* Dame Sarah Jane, DBE
Macur, *Rt. Hon.* Dame Julia Wendy, DBE
McVittie, Dame Joan Christine, DBE
Major, Dame Malvina Lorraine (Mrs Fleming), DBE
Major, Dame Norma Christina Elizabeth, DBE
Makin, *Dr* Dame Pamela Louise, DBE
Mantel, *Dr* Dame Hilary Mary, DBE
Manzie, Dame Stella Gordon, DBE
Marsden, *Dr* Dame Rosalind Mary, DCMG
Marsh, Dame Mary Elizabeth, DBE
Marteau, *Prof.* Dame Theresa Mary, DBE
Martin, Dame Louise Livingstone, DBE
Marx, Dame Clare Lucy, DBE
Mason, Dame Monica Margaret, DBE

Mason, *HE* Dame Sandra Prunella, DCMG
Massenet, Dame Natalie Sara, DBE
Matheson, Dame Jilian Norma, DCB
May, *Hon.* Dame Juliet Mary May, DBE
Mayhew Jonas, Dame Judith, DBE
Mellor, Dame Julie Thérèse, DBE
Metge, *Dr* Dame (Alice) Joan, DBE
Middleton, Dame Elaine Madoline, DCMG, MBE
Milburn, Dame Martina Jane, DCVO, CBE
Mills, *Prof.* Dame Anne Jane, DCMG, CBE
Mirren, Dame Helen, DBE
Mitcham, Dame Constance Viola, DBE
Monroe, *Prof.* Dame Barbara, DBE
Moore, Dame Henrietta Louise, DBE, FBA
Moore, Dame Julie, DBE
Moores, Dame Yvonne, DBE
Morgan, *Dr* Dame Gillian Margaret, DBE
Morgan, Dame Shan Elizabeth, DCMG
Morris, Dame Sylvia Ann, DBE
Morrison, *Hon.* Dame Mary Anne, GCVO
Morrissey, Dame Helena Louise, DBE
Moulder, *Hon.* Dame Jane Clare, DBE
Muirhead, Dame Lorna Elizabeth Fox, DCVO, DBE
Mullally, *Rt. Revd* Dame Sarah Elisabeth, DBE
Murray, Dame Jennifer Susan, DBE
Nelson, *Prof.* Dame Janet Laughland, DBE
Nelson-Taylor, Dame Nicola Jane, DBE
Neville, Dame Elizabeth, DBE, QPM
Newell, Dame Priscilla Jane, DBE
Ney, Dame Mary Thérèse, DBE
Nimmo Dame Alison, DBE
O'Brien, Dame Una, DCB
O'Farrell, *Hon.* Dame Finola Mary, DBE
Ogilvie, Dame Bridget Margaret, DBE, PHD, DSc
Oliver, Dame Gillian Frances, DBE
Owen, Dame Susan Jane, DCB
Owers, Dame Anne Elizabeth (Mrs Cook), DBE
Oxenbury, Dame Shirley Ann, DBE
Palmer, Dame Felicity Joan, DBE
Paraskeva, *Rt. Hon.* Dame Janet, DBE
Park, Dame Merle Florence (Mrs Bloch), DBE
Parker, *Hon.* Dame Judith Mary Frances, DBE
Partridge, *Prof.* Dame Linda, DBE
Patel, Dame Indira, DBE
Paterson, Dame Vicki, DBE
Pauffley, *Hon.* Dame Anna Evelyn Hamilton, DBE
Peacock, Dame Alison Margaret, DBE
Pearce, *Prof.* Dame Shirley, DBE
Pedder, Dame Angela Mary, DBE
Penhaligon, Dame Annette (Mrs Egerton), DBE
Pereira, *Hon.* Dame Janice Mesadis, DBE
Perkins, Dame Mary Lesley, DBE
Peters, Dame Mary Elizabeth, KG, CH, DBE
Peyton-Jones, Dame Julia, DBE
Phillips, Dame Jane Elizabeth Ailwen (Sian), DBE
Pienaar, Dame Erica, DBE
Pierce, Dame Karen Elizabeth, DCMG
Pindling, Lady (Marguerite Matilda), GCMG
Platt, Dame Denise, DBE
Plotnikoff, Dame Joyce Evelyn, DBE
Plowright, Dame Joan Ann, DBE
Plunket Greene, Dame Barbara Mary, DBE
Poole, Dame Avril Anne Barker, DBE
Porter, Dame Shirley (Lady Porter), DBE
Powell, Dame Sally Ann Vickers, DBE
Pringle, Dame Anne Fyfe, DCMG
Proudman, *Hon.* Dame Sonia Rosemary Susan, DBE
Pugh, *Dr* Dame Gillian Mary, DBE
Rabbatts, Dame Heather Victoria, DBE
Rafferty, *Rt. Hon.* Dame Anne Judith, DBE
Rantzen, Dame Esther Louise (Mrs Wilcox), DBE
Rawson, *Prof.* Dame Jessica Mary, DBE

Rees, *Prof.* Dame Judith Anne, DBE
Rees, *Prof.* Dame Lesley Howard, DBE
Rees, *Prof.* Dame Teresa Lesley, DBE
Reeves, Dame Helen May, DBE
Refson, Dame Benita, DBE
Rego, Dame Paula Figueiroa, DBE
Reid, Dame Seona Elizabeth, DBE
Reynolds, Dame Fiona Claire, DBE
Rhodes, Dame Zandra Lindsey, DBE
Rice, Lady Susan Ilene, DBE
Richard, Dame Alison (Fettes), DBE
Richardson, Dame Mary, DBE
Rigg, Dame Diana, DBE
Rimington, Dame Stella, DCB
Ritterman, Dame Janet, DBE
Roberts, Dame Jane Elisabeth, DBE
Roberts, *Hon.* Dame Jennifer Mary, DBE
Roberts, *Hon.* Dame Priscilla Jane Stephanie (Lady Roberts), DCVO
Robins, Dame Ruth Laura, DBE
Robinson, *Prof.* Dame Ann Louise
Robinson, *Prof.* Dame Carol Vivien, DBE
Robottom, Dame Marlene, DBE
Roe, Dame Marion Audrey, DBE
Roe, Dame Raigh Edith, DBE
Ronson, Dame Gail, DBE
Roscoe, *Dr* Dame Ingrid Mary, DCVO
Rose, *Rt. Hon.* Dame Vivien Judith, DBE
Ross-Wawrzynski, Dame Dana (Mrs Ross-Wawrzynski), DBE
Rothwell, *Prof.* Dame Nancy Jane, DBE
Routledge, Dame Katherine Patricia, DBE
Ruddock, *Rt. Hon.* Dame Joan Mary, DBE
Runciman of Doxford, The Viscountess, DBE
Russell, *Hon.* Dame Alison Hunter, DBE
Russell, *Dr* Dame Philippa Margaret, DBE
Ryan, Dame Christine, DBE
Sackler, Dame Theresa, DBE
Salmond, *Prof.* Dame Mary Anne, DBE
Saunders, *Dr* Dame Frances Carolyn, DBE, CB
Savill, Dame Rosalind Joy, DBE
Sawyer, *Rt. Hon.* Dame Joan Augusta, DBE
Scardino, Dame Marjorie, DBE
Scott, Dame Catherine Margaret (Mrs Denton), DBE
Scott Thomas, Dame Kristin, DBE
Seward, Dame Margaret Helen Elizabeth, DBE
Shafik, *Dr* Dame Nemat Talaat, DBE
Sharp, *Rt. Hon.* Dame Victoria Madeleine, DBE
Shaw, *Prof.* Dame Pamela Jean, DBE
Shirley, Dame Stephanie, CH, DBE
Shovelton, Dame Helena, DBE
Sibley, Dame Antoinette (Mrs Corbett), DBE
Sills, *Prof.* Dame Eileen, DBE
Silver, *Dr* Dame Ruth Muldoon, DBE
Simler, *Rt. Hon.* Dame Ingrid Ann (Mrs Bernstein), DBE
Slade, *Hon.* Dame Elizabeth Ann, DBE
Slingo, *Prof.* Dame Julia Mary, DBE
Smith, Dame Dela, DBE
Smith, *Rt. Hon.* Dame Janet Hilary (Mrs Mathieson), DBE
Smith, *Hon.* Dame Jennifer Meredith, DBE
Smith, Dame Margaret Natalie (Maggie) (Mrs Cross), CH, DBE
Snowball, Dame Priscilla (Cilla) Deborah, DBE
Southgate, *Prof.* Dame Lesley Jill, DBE
Spelman, *Rt. Hon.* Dame Caroline Alice, DBE
Spencer, Dame Rosemary Jane, DCMG
Squire, Dame Rosemary Anne, DBE
Stacey, Dame Glenys Jean (Mrs Kyle), DBE
Steel, *Hon.* Dame (Anne) Heather (Mrs Beattie), DBE
Stephens, *Prof.* Dame Elan Cross, DBE
Stocking, Dame Barbara Mary, DBE

Storey, Dame Sarah Joanne, DBE
Strachan, Dame Valerie Patricia Marie, DCB
Strank, *Dr* Dame Angela Rosemary Emily, DBE
Strathern, *Prof.* Dame Anne Marilyn, DBE
Street, Dame Susan Ruth, DCB
Stringer, *Prof.* Dame Joan Kathleen, DBE
Sutherland, Dame Veronica Evelyn, DBE, CMG
Suzman, Dame Janet, DBE
Swift, *Hon.* Dame Caroline Jane (Mrs Openshaw), DBE
Symmonds, Dame Olga Patricia, DBE
Tanner, *Dr* Dame Mary Elizabeth, DBE
Taylor, Dame Meg, DBE
Te Kanawa, Dame Kiri Janette, CH, DBE
Theis, *Hon.* Dame Lucy Morgan, DBE
Thirlwall, *Rt. Hon.* Dame Kathryn Mary, DBE
Thomas, *Prof.* Dame Jean Olwen, DBE
Thomas, Dame Kathrin Elizabeth, DCVO
Thomas, Dame Maureen Elizabeth (Lady Thomas), DBE
Thompson, Dame Emma, DBE
Thompson, Dame Ila Dianne, DBE
Thornton, *Prof.* Dame Janet Maureen, DBE
Thornton, *Hon.* Dame Justine, DBE
Thornton, Dame Sara Joanne, DBE, QPM
Tickell, Dame Clare Oriana, DBE
Tinson, Dame Sue, DBE
Tizard, Dame Catherine Anne, GCMG, GCVO, DBE
Tokiel, Dame Rosa, DBE
Trotter, Dame Janet Olive, DBE
Twelftree, Dame Marcia, DBE
Uchida, Dame Mitsuko, DBE
Uprichard, Dame Mary Elizabeth, DBE
Vitmayer, Dame Janet Mary, DBE
Wagner, Dame Gillian Mary Millicent (Lady Wagner), DBE
Wallace, *Prof.* Dame Helen Sarah, DBE, CMG
Wallis, Dame Sheila Ann, DBE
Walter, Dame Harriet Mary, DBE
Walters, Dame Julie Mary, DBE
Warburton, Dame Arabella, DBE
Warner, *Prof.* Dame Marina Sarah, DBE, FBA
Warwick, Dame Catherine Lilian, DBE
Waterhouse, *Dr* Dame Rachel Elizabeth, DBE
Waterman, *Dr* Dame Fanny, DBE
Watkins, *Prof.* Dame Caroline Leigh, DBE
Watkinson, Dame Angela Eileen, DBE
Webb, *Prof.* Dame Patricia, DBE
Weir, Dame Gillian Constance (Mrs Phelps), DBE
Weller, Dame Rita, DBE
Wells, Dame Rachel Anne, DCVO
Weston, Dame Margaret Kate, DBE
Westwood, Dame Vivienne Isabel, DBE
Whipple, *Hon.* Dame Philippa Jane Edwards, DBE
Whitehead, *Hon.* Dame Annabel Alice Hoyer, DCVO
Whitehead, *Prof.* Dame Margaret McRae, DBE
Whiteread, Dame Rachel, DBE
Wigley, Dame Susan Louise, DCVO
Williams, Dame Josephine, DBE
Willmot, Dame Glenis, DBE
Wilson, Dame Jacqueline, DBE
Wilson-Barnett, *Prof.* Dame Jenifer, DBE
Wilton, Dame Penelope Alice, DBE
Windsor, Dame Barbara, DBE
Winterton, *Rt. Hon.* Dame Rosalie, DBE
Wintour, Dame Anna, DBE
Wolfson de Botton, Dame Janet (Mrs Wolfson de Botton), DBE
Wong Yick-ming, Dame Rosanna, DBE
Woodward, Dame Barbara Janet, DCMG, OBE
Woolf, Dame Catherine Fiona, DBE
Wykes, *Prof.* Dame Til Hilary Margaret, DBE
Yip, *Hon.* Dame Amanda Louise, DBE
Zaffar, Dame Naila, DBE

DECORATIONS AND MEDALS

PRINCIPAL DECORATIONS AND MEDALS IN ORDER OF WEAR

VICTORIA CROSS (VC), 1856 (*see* below)
GEORGE CROSS (GC), 1940 (*see* below)

BRITISH ORDERS OF KNIGHTHOOD
(*see also* Orders of Chivalry)

Order of the Garter
Order of the Thistle
Order of St Patrick
Order of the Bath
Order of Merit
Order of the Star of India
Order of St Michael and George
Order of the Indian Empire
Order of the Crown of India
Royal Victorian Order (Classes I, II and III)
Order of the British Empire (Classes I, II and III)
Order of the Companions of Honour
Distinguished Service Order
Royal Victorian Order (Class IV)
Order of the British Empire (Class IV)
Imperial Service Order
Royal Victorian Order (Class V)
Order of the British Empire (Class V)

BARONET'S BADGE

KNIGHT BACHELOR'S BADGE

INDIAN ORDER OF MERIT (MILITARY)

DECORATIONS, MEDALS FOR GALLANTRY AND DISTINGUISHED CONDUCT
Conspicuous Gallantry Cross (CGC), 1995
Distinguished Conduct Medal (DCM), 1854
Conspicuous Gallantry Medal (CGM), 1874
Conspicuous Gallantry Medal (Flying)
George Medal (GM), 1940
Royal West African Field Force Distinguished Conduct Medal (DCM)
Queen's Police Medal for Gallantry
Queen's Fire Service Medal for Gallantry
Royal Red Cross Class I (RRC), 1883
Distinguished Service Cross (DSC), 1914
Military Cross (MC), December 1914
Distinguished Flying Cross (DFC), 1918
Air Force Cross (AFC), 1918
Royal Red Cross Class II (ARRC)
Order of British India (OBI)
Kaisar-i-Hind Medal
Order of St John
Union of South Africa Queen's Medal for Bravery (Gold)
King's African Rifles Distinguished Conduct Medal
Indian Distinguished Service Medal (IDSM)
Union of South Africa Queen's Medal for Bravery (Silver)
Distinguished Service Medal (DSM), 1914
Military Medal (MM)
Distinguished Flying Medal (DFM)
Air Force Medal (AFM)
Constabulary Medal (Ireland)
Medal for Saving Life at Sea (Sea Gallantry Medal)

Indian Order of Merit (Civil)
Indian Police Medal for Gallantry
Ceylon Police Medal for Gallantry
Sierra Leone Police Medal for Gallantry
Sierra Leone Fire Brigades Medal for Gallantry
Colonial Police Medal for Gallantry
Overseas Territories Police Medal for Gallantry
Queen's Gallantry Medal (QGM), 1974
Royal Victorian Medal (RVM) (Gold, Silver and Bronze)
British Empire Medal (BEM)
Canada Medal
Queen's Police Medal for Distinguished Service (QPM)
Queen's Fire Service Medal for Distinguished Service (QFSM)
Queen's Ambulance Service Medal
Queen's Volunteer Reserves Medal
Queen's Medal for Chiefs

BADGE OF HONOUR

CAMPAIGN MEDALS AND STARS
Including any authorised UN, European Community/Union and NATO medals (in order of date of campaign for which awarded).
World War medals are worn in the following order:
First World War, 1914 Star; 1914–15 Star; British War Medal; Mercantile Marine War Medal; Victory Medal; Territorial Force War Medal
Second World War, 1939–45 Star; Atlantic Star; Arctic Star; Air Crew Europe Star; Africa Star; Pacific Star; Burma Star; Italy Star; France & Germany Star; Defence Medal; Canadian/Newfoundland Volunteer Service Medal; War Medal; Africa Service Medal; India Service Medal; New Zealand War Service Medal; Southern Rhodesia Service Medal; Australian Service Medal

POLAR MEDALS *in order of date*

IMPERIAL SERVICE MEDAL

POLICE MEDALS FOR VALUABLE SERVICE
Indian Police Medal for Meritorious Service
Ceylon Police Medal for Merit
Sierra Leone Police Medal for Meritorious Service
Sierra Leone Fire Brigades Medal for Meritorious Service
Colonial Police Medal for Meritorious Service
Overseas Territories Police Medal for Meritorious Service

JUBILEE, CORONATION AND DURBAR MEDALS
Queen Victoria, King Edward VII, King George V, King George VI, Queen Elizabeth II, Visit Commemoration and Long and Faithful Service Medals

EFFICIENCY AND LONG SERVICE DECORATIONS AND MEDALS
Meritorious Service Medal
Accumulated Campaign Service Medal
Accumulated Campaign Service Medal (2011)
Army Long Service and Good Conduct Medal
Naval Long Service and Good Conduct Medal
Medal for Meritorious Service (Royal Navy 1918–28)
Indian Long Service and Good Conduct Medal
Indian Meritorious Service Medal
Royal Marines Meritorious Service Medal (1849–1947)
Royal Air Force Meritorious Service Medal (1918–1928)

Royal Air Force Long Service and Good Conduct Medal
Medal for Long Service and Good Conduct (Ulster Defence Regiment)
Indian Long Service and Good Conduct Medal
Royal West African Frontier Force Long Service and Good Conduct Medal
Royal Sierra Leone Military Forces Long Service and Good Conduct Medal
King's African Rifles Long Service and Good Conduct Medal
Indian Meritorious Service Medal
Police Long Service and Good Conduct Medal
Fire Brigade Long Service and Good Conduct Medal
African Police Medal for Meritorious Service
Royal Canadian Mounted Police Long Service Medal
Ceylon Police Long Service Medal
Ceylon Fire Services Long Service Medal
Sierra Leone Police Long Service Medal
Colonial Police Long Service Medal
Overseas Territories Police Long Service Medal
Sierra Leone Fire Brigades Long Service Medal
Mauritius Police Long Service and Good Conduct Medal
Mauritius Fire Services Long Service and Good Conduct Medal
Mauritius Prisons Service Long Service and Good Conduct Medal
Colonial Fire Brigades Long Service Medal
Overseas Territories Fire Brigades Long Service Medal
Colonial Prison Service Medal
Overseas Territories Prison Service Medal
Hong Kong Disciplined Services Medal
Army Emergency Reserve Decoration (ERD)
Volunteer Officers' Decoration (VD)
Volunteer Long Service Medal
Volunteer Officers' Decoration (for India and the Colonies)
Volunteer Long Service Medal (for India and the Colonies)
Colonial Auxiliary Forces Officers' Decoration
Colonial Auxiliary Forces Long Service Medal
Medal for Good Shooting (Naval)
Militia Long Service Medal
Imperial Yeomanry Long Service Medal
Territorial Decoration (TD), 1908
Ceylon Armed Services Long Service Medal
Efficiency Decoration (ED)
Territorial Efficiency Medal
Efficiency Medal
Special Reserve Long Service and Good Conduct Medal
Decoration for Officers of the Royal Navy Reserve
Decoration for Officers of the Royal Naval Volunteer Reserve
Royal Naval Reserve Long Service Medal
Royal Naval Volunteer Reserve Long Service Medal
Royal Naval Auxiliary Sick Berth Reserve Long Service and Good Conduct Medal
Royal Fleet Reserve Long Service and Good Conduct Medal
Royal Naval Wireless Auxiliary Reserve Long Service and Good Conduct Medal
Royal Naval Auxiliary Service Medal
Air Efficiency Award (AE), 1942
Volunteer Reserves Service Medal
Ulster Defence Regiment Medal
Northern Ireland Home Service Medal
Queen's Medal (for Champion Shots of the RN and RM)
Queen's Medal (for Champion Shots of the New Zealand Naval Forces)
Queen's Medal (for Champion Shots in the Military Forces)
Queen's Medal (for Champion Shots of the Air Forces)
Cadet Forces Medal, 1950
Coastguard Auxiliary Service Long Service Medal
Special Constabulary Long Service Medal
Canadian Forces Decoration
Royal Observer Corps Medal
Civil Defence Long Service Medal

Ambulance Service (Emergency Duties) Long Service and Good Conduct Medal
Royal Fleet Auxiliary Service Medal
Prison Services (Operational Duties) Long Service and Good Conduct Medal
Jersey Honorary Police Long Service and Good Conduct Medal
Merchant Navy Medal for Meritorious Service
Ebola Medal for Service in West Africa
National Crime Agency Long Service and Good Conduct Medal
Rhodesia Medal (1980)
Royal Ulster Constabulary Service Medal
Northern Ireland Prison Service Medal
Union of South Africa Commemoration Medal
Indian Independence Medal
Pakistan Medal
Ceylon Armed Services Inauguration Medal
Ceylon Police Independence Medal (1948)
Sierra Leone Independence Medal
Jamaica Independence Medal
Uganda Independence Medal
Malawi Independence Medal
Fiji Independence Medal
Papua New Guinea Independence Medal
Solomon Islands Independence Medal
Service Medal of the Order of St John
Badge of the Order of the League of Mercy
Voluntary Medical Service Medal
Women's Royal Voluntary Service Medal
South African Medal for War Services
Overseas Territories Special Constabulary Medal
Colonial Special Constabulary Medal

COMMONWEALTH REALM'S ORDERS, DECORATIONS AND MEDALS *in order of date*

OTHER COMMONWEALTH MEMBER'S ORDERS, DECORATIONS AND MEDALS *in order of date*

FOREIGN ORDERS, FOREIGN DECORATIONS AND FOREIGN MEDALS *in order of date*

THE VICTORIA CROSS (1856)

FOR CONSPICUOUS BRAVERY

VC

Ribbon, Crimson, for all Services (until 1918 it was blue for the Royal Navy)

Instituted on 29 January 1856, the Victoria Cross was awarded retrospectively to 1854, the first being held by Lt. C. D. Lucas, RN, for bravery in the Baltic Sea on 21 June 1854 (gazetted 24 February 1857). The first 62 crosses were presented by Queen Victoria in Hyde Park, London, on 26 June 1857.
   The Victoria Cross is worn before all other decorations, on the left breast, and consists of a cross-pattée of bronze, 3.8cm in diameter, with the royal crown surmounted by a lion in the centre, and beneath there is the inscription *For Valour.* In July 2015 the tax-free annuity given to holders of the VC, irrespective of need or other conditions, was increased to £10,000. At the same time, further annual increases to the annuity were linked to the CPI rate of inflation. In 1911, the right to receive the cross was extended to Indian soldiers, and in 1920 to matrons, sisters and nurses, the staff of the nursing

services and other services pertaining to hospitals and nursing, and to civilians of either sex regularly or temporarily under the orders, direction or supervision of the naval, military, or air forces of the crown.

SURVIVING RECIPIENTS OF THE VICTORIA CROSS
as at 31 August 2019

Apiata, *Cpl.* B. H., VC (New Zealand Special Air Service)
 2004 *Afghanistan*
Beharry, *LSgt* J. G., VC (Princess of Wales's Royal Regiment)
 2005 *Iraq*
Cruickshank, *Flt Lt.* J. A., VC (RAFVR)
 1944 *World War*
Donaldson, *Cpl.* M. G. S., VC (Australian Special Air Service)
 2008 *Afghanistan*
Keighran, *Cpl.* D. A., VC (Royal Australian Regiment)
 2012 *Afghanistan*
Leakey, *Lance Cpl.* J. M., VC (Parachute Regiment)
 2015 *Afghanistan*
Payne, *WO* K., VC, DSC (USA) (Australian Army Training Team)
 1969 *Vietnam*
Rambahadur Limbu, *Capt.,* VC, MVO (10th Princess Mary's Gurkha Rifles)
 1965 *Sarawak*
Roberts-Smith, *Cpl.* B., VC (Australian Special Air Service)
 2010 *Afghanistan*

THE GEORGE CROSS (1940)

FOR GALLANTRY

GC

Ribbon, Dark blue, threaded through a bar adorned with
 laurel leaves
Instituted 24 September 1940 (with amendments,
 3 November 1942)

The George Cross is worn before all other decorations (except the VC) on the left breast (when worn by a woman it may be worn on the left shoulder from a ribbon of the same width and colour fashioned into a bow). It consists of a plain silver cross with four equal limbs, the cross having in the centre a circular medallion bearing a design showing St George and the Dragon. The inscription *For Gallantry* appears round the medallion and in the angle of each limb of the cross is the royal cypher 'G VI' forming a circle concentric with the medallion. The reverse is plain and bears the name of the recipient and the date of the award. The cross is suspended by a ring from a bar adorned with laurel leaves on dark blue ribbon 3.8cm wide.

The cross is intended primarily for civilians; awards to the fighting services are confined to actions for which purely military honours are not normally granted. It is awarded only for acts of the greatest heroism or of the most conspicuous courage in circumstances of extreme danger. In July 2015 the tax-free annuity given to holders of the GC, irrespective of need or other conditions, was increased to £10,000. At the same time, further annual increases to the annuity were linked to the CPI rate of inflation. The cross has twice been awarded collectively rather than to an individual: to the island of Malta (1942) and the Royal Ulster Constabulary (1999).

In October 1971 all surviving holders of the Albert Medal and the Edward Medal had their awards translated to the George Cross.

SURVIVING RECIPIENTS OF THE GEORGE CROSS
as at 31 August 2019

If the recipient originally received the Albert Medal (AM) or the Edward Medal (EM), this is indicated by the initials in parentheses.

Bamford, J., GC, 1952
Beaton, J., GC, CVO, 1974
Croucher, *Lance Cpl.* M., GC, 2008
Finney, C., GC, 2003
Flintoff, H. H., GC (EM), 1944
Gledhill, A. J., GC, 1967
Haberfield, *CSgt.* K. H., GC, 2005
Hughes, *WO2* K. S., GC, 2010
Johnson, *WO1* (*SSM*) B., GC, 1990
Lowe, A. R., GC (AM), 1949
Norton, *Maj.* P. A., GC, 2006
Pratt, M. K., GC, 1978
Purves, Mrs M., GC (AM), 1949
Raweng, Awang anak, GC, 1951
Shephard, S. J., GC, 2014
Troulan, D., GC, QGM, 2017
Walker, C., GC, 1972

THE ELIZABETH CROSS (2009)

EC

Instituted 1 July 2009

The Elizabeth Cross consists of a silver cross with a laurel wreath passing between the arms, which bear the floral symbols of England (rose), Scotland (thistle), Ireland (shamrock) and Wales (daffodil). The centre of the cross bears the royal cypher and the reverse is inscribed with the name of the person for whom it is in honour. The cross is accompanied by a memorial scroll and a miniature.

The cross was created to commemorate UK armed forces personnel who have died on operations or as a result of an act of terrorism. It may be granted to and worn by the next of kin of any eligible personnel who died from 1 January 1948 to date. It offers the wearer no precedence. Those that are eligible include the next of kin of personnel who died while serving on a medal earning operation, as a result of an act of terrorism, or on a non-medal earning operation where death was caused by the inherent high risk of the task.

The Elizabeth Cross is not intended as a posthumous medal for the fallen but as an emblem of national recognition of the loss and sacrifice made by the personnel and their families.

CHIEFS OF CLANS IN SCOTLAND

Only chiefs of whole Names or Clans are included, except certain special instances (marked *) who, though not chiefs of a whole Name, were or are for some reason (eg the Macdonald forfeiture) independent. Under decision (*Campbell-Gray*, 1950) that a bearer of a 'double or triple-barrelled' surname cannot be held chief of a part of such, several others cannot be included in the list at present.

THE ROYAL HOUSE: HM The Queen

AGNEW: Sir Crispin Agnew of Lochnaw, Bt., QC
ANSTRUTHER: Tobias Anstruther of Anstruther and Balcaskie
ARBUTHNOTT: Viscount of Arbuthnott
BANNERMAN: Sir David Bannerman of Elsick, Bt.
BARCLAY: Peter C. Barclay of Towie Barclay and of that Ilk
BORTHWICK: Lord Borthwick
BOYLE: Earl of Glasgow
BRODIE: Alexander Brodie of Brodie
BROUN OF COLSTOUN: Sir Wayne Broun of Colstoun, Bt.
BRUCE: Earl of Elgin and Kincardine, KT
BUCHAN: Charles Buchan of Auchmacoy
BURNETT: James C. A. Burnett of Leys
CAMERON: Donald Cameron of Lochiel, CVO
CAMPBELL: Duke of Argyll
CARMICHAEL: Richard Carmichael of Carmichael
CARNEGIE: Duke of Fife
CATHCART: Earl Cathcart
CHARTERIS: Earl of Wemyss and March
CLAN CHATTAN: K. Mackintosh of Clan Chattan
CHISHOLM: Hamish Chisholm of Chisholm (*The Chisholm*)
COCHRANE: Earl of Dundonald
COLQUHOUN: Sir Malcolm Rory Colquhoun of Luss, Bt.
CRANSTOUN: David Cranstoun of that Ilk
CUMMING: Sir Alastair Cumming of Altyre, Bt.
DARROCH: Duncan Darroch of Gourock
DAVIDSON OF DAVIDSTON: Grant Davidson of Davidston
DEWAR: Michael Dewar of that Ilk and Vogrie
DRUMMOND: Earl of Perth
DUNBAR: Sir James Dunbar of Mochrum, Bt.
DUNDAS: David Dundas of Dundas
DURIE: Andrew Durie of Durie, CBE
ELIOTT: Mrs Margaret Eliott of Redheugh
ERSKINE: Earl of Mar and Kellie
FARQUHARSON: Capt. Alwyne Farquharson of Invercauld, MC
FERGUSSON: Sir Charles Fergusson of Kilkerran, Bt.
FORBES: Lord Forbes
FORSYTH: Alistair Forsyth of that Ilk
FRASER: Lady Saltoun
*FRASER (OF LOVAT): Lord Lovat
GAYRE: Reinold Gayre of Gayre and Nigg
GORDON: Marquess of Huntly
GRAHAM: Duke of Montrose
GRANT: Lord Strathspey
GUNN: Iain Gunn of Gunn
GUTHRIE: Alexander Guthrie of Guthrie
HAIG: Earl Haig
HALDANE: Martin Haldane of Gleneagles
HANNAY: David Hannay of Kirkdale and of that Ilk
HAY: Earl of Erroll

HENDERSON: Alistair Henderson of Fordell
HUNTER: Pauline Hunter of Hunterston
IRVINE OF DRUM: Alexander H. R. Irvine of Drum
JARDINE: Sir William Jardine of Applegirth, Bt.
JOHNSTONE: Earl of Annandale and Hartfell
KEITH: Earl of Kintore
KENNEDY: Marquess of Ailsa
KERR: Marquess of Lothian, PC
KINCAID: Madam Arabella Kincaid of Kincaid
LAMONT: Revd Peter Lamont of that Ilk
LEASK: Jonathan Leask of that Ilk
LENNOX: Edward Lennox of that Ilk
LESLIE: Earl of Rothes
LINDSAY: Earl of Crawford and Balcarres, KT, GCVO, PC
LIVINGSTONE (or MACLEA): Niall Livingstone of the Bachuil
LOCKHART: Ranald Lockhart of the Lee
LUMSDEN: Gillem Lumsden of that Ilk and Blanerne
MACALESTER: William St J. McAlester of Loup and Kennox
MACARTHUR; John MacArthur of that Ilk
MCBAIN: James H. McBain of McBain
MACDONALD: Lord Macdonald (*The Macdonald of Macdonald*)
*MACDONALD OF CLANRANALD: Ranald Macdonald of Clanranald
*MACDONALD OF KEPPOCH: Ranald MacDonald of Keppoch
*MACDONALD OF SLEAT (CLAN HUSTEAIN): Sir Ian Macdonald of Sleat, Bt.
*MACDONELL OF GLENGARRY: Ranald MacDonell of Glengarry
MACDOUGALL: Morag MacDougall of MacDougall
MACDOWALL: Fergus Macdowall of Garthland
MACGREGOR: Sir Malcolm MacGregor of MacGregor, Bt.
MACINTYRE: Donald MacIntyre of Glenoe
MACKAY: Lord Reay
MACKENZIE: Earl of Cromartie
MACKINNON: Anne Mackinnon of Mackinnon
MACKINTOSH: John Mackintosh of Mackintosh (*The Mackintosh of Mackintosh*)
MACLACHLAN: Euan MacLachlan of MacLachlan
MACLAINE: Lorne Maclaine of Lochbuie
MACLAREN: Donald MacLaren of MacLaren and Achleskine
MACLEAN: Hon. Sir Lachlan Maclean of Duart, Bt., CVO
MACLENNAN: Ruaraidh MacLennan of MacLennan
MACLEOD: Hugh MacLeod of MacLeod
MACMILLAN: George MacMillan of MacMillan
MACNAB: James W. A. Macnab of Macnab (*The Macnab*)
MACNAGHTEN: Sir Malcolm Macnaghten of Macnaghten and Dundarave, Bt.
MACNEACAIL: John Macneacail of Macneacail and Scorrybreac
MACNEIL OF BARRA: Rory Macneil of Barra (*The Macneil of Barra*)
MACPHERSON: Hon. Sir William Macpherson of Cluny, TD
MACTAVISH: Steven MacTavish of Dunardry
MACTHOMAS: Andrew MacThomas of Finegand
MAITLAND: Earl of Lauderdale
MAKGILL: Viscount of Oxfuird
MALCOLM (MACCALLUM): Robin N. L. Malcolm of Poltalloch

MAR: Countess of Mar
MARJORIBANKS: Andrew Marjoribanks of that Ilk
MATHESON: Sir Alexander Matheson of Matheson, Bt.
MENZIES: David Menzies of Menzies
MOFFAT: Madam Moffat of that Ilk
MONCREIFFE: Hon. Peregrine Moncreiffe of that Ilk
MONTGOMERIE: Earl of Eglinton and Winton
MORRISON: Dr John Ruairidh Morrison of Ruchdi
MUNRO: Hector Munro of Foulis
MURRAY: Duke of Atholl
NESBITT (or NISBET): Mark Nesbitt of that Ilk
OGILVY: Earl of Airlie, KT, GCVO, PC
OLIPHANT: Richard Oliphant of that Ilk
RAMSAY: Earl of Dalhousie
RIDDELL: Sir Walter Riddell of Riddell, Bt.
ROBERTSON: Alexander Robertson of Struan *(Struan-Robertson)*
ROLLO: Lord Rollo

ROSS: David Ross of that Ilk and Balnagowan
RUTHVEN: Earl of Gowrie, PC
SCOTT: Duke of Buccleuch and Queensberry, KT, KBE
SCRYMGEOUR: Earl of Dundee
SEMPILL: Lord Sempill
SHAW: Iain Shaw of Tordarroch
SINCLAIR: Earl of Caithness, PC
SKENE: Dugald Skene of Skene
STIRLING: Fraser Stirling of Cader
STRANGE: Maj. Timothy Strange of Balcaskie
SUTHERLAND: Countess of Sutherland
SWINTON: John Swinton of that Ilk
TROTTER: Alexander Trotter of Mortonhall, CVO
URQUHART: Wilkins F. Urquhart of Urquhart
WALLACE: Andrew Wallace of that Ilk
WEDDERBURN: The Master of Dundee
WEMYSS: Michael Wemyss of that Ilk

THE PRIVY COUNCIL

The sovereign in council, or Privy Council, was the chief source of executive power until the system of cabinet government developed in the 18th century. Now the Privy Council's main functions are to advise the sovereign and to exercise its own statutory responsibilities independent of the sovereign in council.

Membership of the Privy Council is automatic upon appointment to certain government and judicial positions in the UK, eg cabinet ministers must be Privy Counsellors and are sworn in on first assuming office. Membership is also accorded by the Queen to eminent people in the UK and independent countries of the Commonwealth of which she is Queen, on the recommendation of the prime minister. Membership of the council is retained for life, except for very occasional removals.

The administrative functions of the Privy Council are carried out by the Privy Council Office under the direction of the president of the council, who is always a member of the cabinet. (*see also* Parliament)

President of the Council, Rt. Hon. Jacob Rees-Mogg, MP

Clerk of the Council, Richard Tilbrook

Style The Right (or Rt.) Hon._

Envelope, The Right (or Rt.) Hon. F_ S_. *Letter,* Dear Mr/Miss/Mrs S_. *Spoken,* Mr/Miss/Mrs S_

It is incorrect to use the letters PC after the name in conjunction with the prefix The Right Hon., unless the Privy Counsellor is a peer below the rank of Marquess and so is styled The Right Hon. because of his/her rank.

MEMBERS *as at 31 August 2019*

HRH The Duke of Edinburgh, 1951
HRH The Prince of Wales, 1977
HRH The Duke of Cambridge, 2016
HRH The Duchess of Cornwall, 2016

Abbott, Diane, 2017
Abernethy, *Hon.* Lord (Alastair Cameron), 2005
Adonis, Lord, 2009
Aikens, Sir Richard, 2008
Ainsworth, Robert, 2005
Airlie, Earl of, 1984
Alebua, Ezekiel, 1988
Alexander, Sir Danny, 2010
Alexander, Douglas, 2005
Amos, Baroness, 2003
Anderson of Swansea, Lord, 2000
Anelay of St Johns, Baroness, 2009
Angiolini, Dame Elish, 2006
Anthony, Douglas, 1971
Arbuthnot of Edrom, Lord, 1998
Arden of Heswall, Lady, 2000
Armstrong of Hill Top, Baroness, 1999
Arthur, *Hon.* Owen, 1995
Ashcroft, Lord, 2012
Ashton of Hyde, Lord, 2019
Ashton of Upholland, Baroness, 2006
Asplin, Dame Sarah, 2017
Astor of Hever, Lord, 2015
Atkins, Sir Robert, 1995
Auld, Sir Robin, 1995
Baker, Sir Jonathan, 2018
Baker, Norman, 2014
Baker, Sir Thomas, 2002
Baker of Dorking, Lord, 1984
Baldry, Sir Tony, 2013
Balls, Ed, 2007
Barclay, Stephen, 2018
Barker of Battle, Lord, 2012
Barron, Sir Kevin, 2001
Barrow, Dean, 2016
Barwell, Gavin, 2017
Bassam of Brighton, Lord, 2009
Bates, Lord, 2015
Battle, John, 2002

Bean, Sir David, 2014
Beatson, Sir Jack, 2013
Beckett, Dame Margaret, 1993
Beith, Lord, 1992
Beldam, Sir Roy, 1989
Benn, Hilary, 2003
Benyon, Richard, 2017
Bercow, John, 2009
Berry, Jake, 2019
Birch, Sir William, 1992
Black of Derwent, Lady, 2010
Blackford, Ian, 2017
Blackstone, Baroness, 2001
Blair, Anthony, 1994
Blanchard, Peter, 1998
Blears, Hazel, 2005
Blencathra, Lord, 1995
Blunkett, Lord, 1997
Boateng, Lord, 1999
Bolger, James, 1991
Bonomy, *Hon.* Lord (Iain Bonomy), 2010
Boothroyd, Baroness, 1992
Bottomley of Nettlestone, Baroness, 1992
Boyd of Duncansby, Lord, 2000
Brabazon of Tara, Lord, 2013
Bracadale, *Hon.* Lord (Alistair Campbell), 2013
Bradley, Karen, 2016
Bradley, Lord, 2001
Bradshaw, Ben, 2009
Brake, Thomas, 2011
Briggs of Westbourne, Lord, 2013
Brodie, *Hon.* Lord (Philip Brodie), 2013
Brokenshire, James, 2015
Brooke, Dame Annette, 2014
Brooke of Sutton Mandeville, Lord, 1988
Brown, Gordon, 1996
Brown, Nicholas, 1997
Brown, Sir Stephen, 1983
Brown of Eaton-under-Heywood, Lord, 1992
Browne of Ladyton, Lord, 2005

Bruce of Bennachie, Lord, 2006
Buckland, Robert, 2019
Burnett of Maldon, Lord, 2014
Burnham, Andy, 2007
Burns, Sir Simon, 2011
Burnton, Sir Stanley, 2008
Burstow, Paul, 2012
Burt, Alistair, 2013
Butler of Brockwell, Lord, 2004
Butler-Sloss, Baroness, 1988
Buxton, Sir Richard, 1997
Byers, Stephen, 1998
Byrne, Liam, 2008
Byron, Sir Dennis, 2004
Cable, Sir Vincent, 2010
Caborn, Richard, 1999
Cairns, Alun, 2016
Caithness, Earl of, 1990
Cameron, David, 2005
Cameron of Lochbroom, Lord, 1984
Camoys, Lord, 1997
Campbell, Sir Alan, 2014
Campbell, Sir William, 1999
Campbell of Pittenweem, Lord, 1999
Canterbury, Archbishop of, 2013
Carey of Clifton, Lord, 1991
Carloway, *Hon.* Lord (Colin Sutherland), 2008
Carmichael, Alistair, 2010
Carnwath of Notting Hill, Lord, 2002
Carswell, Lord, 1993
Chadwick, Sir John, 1997
Chakrabarti, Baroness, 2018
Chalfont, Lord, 1964
Chalker of Wallasey, Baroness, 1987
Chan, Sir Julius, 1981
Chartres, Rt. Revd Lord, 1995
Chilcot, Sir John, 2004
Christie, Perry, 2004
Clark, Greg, 2010
Clark, Helen, 1990
Clark of Calton, Baroness, 2013
Clark of Windermere, Lord, 1997
Clarke, Charles, 2001
Clarke, Sir Christopher, 2013
Clarke, Kenneth, 1984

Clarke, *Hon.* Lord (Matthew Clarke), 2008
Clarke, Thomas, 1997
Clarke of Stone-Cum-Ebony, Lord, 1998
Clegg, Sir Nicholas, 2008
Cleverly, James, 2019
Clinton-Davis, Lord, 1998
Clwyd, Ann, 2004
Coffey, Thérèse, 2019
Coghlin, Sir Patrick, 2009
Collins of Mapesbury, Lord, 2007
Cooper, Yvette, 2007
Cope of Berkeley, Lord, 1988
Corbyn, Jeremy, 2015
Corston, Baroness, 2003
Cosgrove, *Hon.* Lady (Hazel Cosgrove), 2003
Coulson, Sir Peter, 2018
Cox, Geoffrey, 2018
Crabb, Stephen, 2014
Crawford and Balcarres, Earl of, 1972
Creech, *Hon.* Wyatt, 1999
Cullen of Whitekirk, Lord, 1997
Cunningham of Felling, Lord, 1993
Curry, David, 1996
Darling of Roulanish, Lord, 1997
Darzi of Denham, Lord, 2009
Davey, Sir Edward, 2012
Davidson, Ruth, 2016
Davies, Dame Nicola, 2018
Davies, Ronald, 1997
Davies of Oldham, Lord, 2006
Davis, David, 1997
Davis, Sir Nigel, 2011
Davis, Terence, 1999
de la Bastide, Michael, 2004
Deben, Lord, 1985
Deeny, Sir Donnell, 2017
Denham, John, 2000
Denham, Lord, 1981
Dholakia, Lord, 2010
Dobson, Frank, 1997
Dodds, Nigel, 2010
Donaldson, Sir Jeffrey, 2007
Dorrell, Stephen, 1994
Dorrian, *Hon.* Lady (Leona Dorrian), 2013
Douglas, *Dr* Denzil, 2011
Dowden, Oliver, 2019
Drakeford, Mark, 2019
Drayson, Lord, 2008
Drummond Young, *Hon.* Lord (James Drummond Young), 2013
D'Souza, Baroness, 2009
Duncan, Sir Alan, 2010
Duncan Smith, Iain, 2001
Dunne, Philip, 2019
Dyson, Lord, 2001
Eassie, *Hon.* Lord (Ronald Mackay), 2006
East, Paul, 1998
Eden of Winton, Lord, 1972
Edward, Sir David, 2005
Eggar, Timothy, 1995
Elias, Sir Patrick, 2009
Elias, *Hon.* Dame Sian, 1999
Elis-Thomas, Lord, 2004
Ellwood, Tobias, 2017
Emslie, *Hon.* Lord (George Emslie), 2011

Esquivel, Manuel, 1986
Etherton, Sir Terence, 2008
Evans, Sir Anthony, 1992
Evans of Bowes Park, Baroness, 2016
Evennett, Sir David, 2015
Falconer of Thoroton, Lord, 2003
Fallon, Sir Michael, 2012
Featherstone, Baroness, 2014
Feldman of Elstree, Lord, 2015
Fellowes, Lord, 1990
Field, Frank, 1997
Field, Mark, 2015
Flaux, Sir Julian, 2017
Flint, Caroline, 2008
Floyd, Sir Christopher, 2013
Forsyth of Drumlean, Lord, 1995
Foster, Arlene, 2016
Foster of Bath, Lord, 2010
Foulkes of Cumnock, Lord, 2002
Fowler, Lord, 1979
Fox, Liam, 2010
Francois, Mark, 2010
Freedman, Sir Lawrence, 2009
Freeman, Lord, 1993
Freud, Lord, 2015
Fulford, Sir Adrian, 2013
Gage, Sir William, 2004
Gale, Sir Roger, 2019
Garden of Frognal, Baroness, 2015
Garel-Jones, Lord, 1992
Garnier, Lord, 2015
Gauke, David, 2016
Geidt, Lord, 2007
George, Bruce, 2000
Gibb, Nicolas, 2016
Gibson, Sir Peter, 1993
Gill, *Hon.* Lord (Brian Gill), 2002
Gillan, Dame Cheryl, 2010
Gillen, Sir John, 2014
Girvan, Sir (Frederick) Paul, 2007
Glennie, *Hon.* Lord (Angus Glennie), 2016
Gloster, Dame Elizabeth, 2013
Goldring, Sir John, 2008
Goldsmith, Lord, 2002
Goodlad, Lord, 1992
Goodwill, Robert, 2018
Gove, Michael, 2010
Gowrie, Earl of, 1984
Graham, Sir Douglas, 1998
Graham of Edmonton, Lord, 1998
Grayling, Chris, 2010
Green, Damian, 2012
Green, Sir Nicholas, 2018
Greening, Justine, 2011
Grieve, Dominic, 2010
Grocott, Lord, 2002
Gross, Sir Peter, 2010
Gummer, Ben, 2016
Haddon-Cave, Sir Charles, 2018
Hague of Richmond, Lord, 1995
Hailsham, Viscount, 1992
Hain, Lord, 2001
Hale of Richmond, Baroness, 1999
Halfon, Robert, 2015
Hallett, Dame Heather, 2005
Hamblen, Sir Nicholas, 2016
Hamilton, *Hon.* Lord (Arthur Hamilton), 2002
Hamilton of Epsom, Lord, 1991

Hammond, Philip, 2010
Hancock, Matthew, 2014
Hands, Gregory, 2014
Hanley, Sir Jeremy, 1994
Hanson, David, 2007
Hardie, Lord, 1997
Hardie Boys, Sir Michael, 1989
Harman, Harriet, 1997
Harper, Mark, 2015
Haselhurst, Lord, 1999
Hattersley, Lord, 1975
Hayes, Sir John, 2013
Hayman, Baroness, 2000
Heald, Sir Oliver, 2016
Healey, John, 2008
Heath, David, 2015
Heathcoat-Amory, David, 1996
Henderson, Sir Launcelot, 2016
Hendry, Charles, 2015
Henley, Lord, 2013
Henry, John, 1996
Herbert, Nick, 2010
Heseltine, Lord, 1979
Heseltine, Sir William, 1986
Hesketh, Lord, 1991
Hewitt, Patricia, 2001
Hickinbottom, Sir Gary, 2017
Higgins, Lord, 1979
Higgins, Sir Malachy, 2007
Hill, Keith, 2003
Hill of Oareford, Lord, 2013
Hinds, Damian, 2018
Hodge, Dame Margaret, 2003
Hodge, Lord, 2013
Hoffmann, Lord, 1992
Holroyde, Sir Timothy, 2017
Hoon, Geoffrey, 1999
Hooper, Sir Anthony, 2004
Hope of Craighead, Lord, 1989
Hope of Thornes, Lord, 1991
Hordern, Sir Peter, 1993
Howard of Lympne, Lord, 1990
Howarth, Sir George, 2005
Howarth of Newport, Lord, 2000
Howe, Earl, 2013
Howell of Guildford, Lord, 1979
Howells, Kim, 2009
Hoyle, Sir Lindsay, 2013
Hughes, Sir Simon, 2010
Hughes of Ombersley, Lord, 2006
Hughes of Stretford, Baroness, 2004
Hunt, Jeremy, 2010
Hunt, Jonathon, 1989
Hunt of Kings Heath, Lord, 2009
Hunt of Wirral, Lord, 1990
Hurd, Nicholas, 2017
Hurd of Westwell, Lord, 1982
Hutchison, Sir Michael, 1995
Hutton, Lord, 1988
Hutton of Furness, Lord, 2001
Inge, Lord, 2004
Ingraham, Hubert, 1993
Ingram, Adam, 1999
Irvine of Lairg, Lord, 1997
Irwin, Sir Stephen, 2016
Jack, Alister, 2019
Jack, Michael, 1997
Jackson, Sir Peter, 2017
Jackson, Sir Rupert, 2008
Jacob, Sir Robert, 2004

Jacobs, Francis, 2005
Janvrin, Lord, 1998
Javid, Sajid, 2014
Jay of Paddington, Baroness, 1998
Jenrick, Robert, 2019
Johnson, Alan, 2003
Johnson, Boris, 2016
Johnson, Joseph, 2019
Jones, Carwyn, 2010
Jones, David, 2012
Jones, Kevan, 2018
Jones, Lord, 1999
Jopling, Lord, 1979
Judge, Lord, 1996
Jugnauth, Sir Anerood, 1987
Kakkar, Lord, 2014
Kay, Sir Maurice, 2004
Keen of Elie, Lord, 2017
Keene, Sir David, 2000
Keith, Sir Kenneth, 1998
Kelly, Ruth, 2004
Kennedy, Jane, 2003
Kennedy, Sir Paul, 1992
Kerr of Tonaghmore, Lord, 2004
Khan, Sadiq, 2009
King, Dame Eleanor, 2014
King of Bridgwater, Lord, 1979
Kingarth, Hon. Lord (Derek Emslie), 2006
Kinnock, Lord, 1983
Kitchin, Lord, 2011
Knight, Sir Gregory, 1995
Knight of Weymouth, Lord, 2008
Kramer, Baroness, 2014
Kwarteng, Kwasi, 2019
Laing, Dame Eleanor, 2017
Lamb, Sir Norman, 2014
Laming, Lord, 2014
Lammy, David, 2008
Lamont of Lerwick, Lord, 1986
Lancaster, Mark, 2017
Lang of Monkton, Lord, 1990
Lansley, Lord, 2010
Latasi, Sir Kamuta, 1996
Latham, Sir David, 2000
Laws, David, 2010
Laws, Sir John, 1999
Lawson of Blaby, Lord, 1981
Leadsom, Andrea, 2016
Leggatt, Sir Andrew, 1990
Leggatt, Sir George, 2018
Leigh, Sir Edward, 2019
Letwin, Sir Oliver, 2002
Leveson, Sir Brian, 2006
Lewis, Brandon, 2016
Lewis, Dr Julian, 2015
Lewison, Sir Kim, 2011
Liddell of Coatdyke, Baroness, 1998
Lidington, David, 2010
Lilley, Lord, 1990
Lindblom, Sir Keith, 2015
Llewellyn of Steep, Lord, 2015
Lloyd, Sir Peter, 1994
Lloyd, Sir Timothy, 2005
Lloyd of Berwick, Lord, 1984
Lloyd-Jones, Lord, 2012
Llwyd, Elfyn, 2011
Longmore, Sir Andrew, 2001
Lothian, Marquess of, 1996
Luce, Lord, 1986

Lyne, Sir Roderic, 2009
McAvoy, Lord, 2003
McCartney, Sir Ian, 1999
McCloskey, Sir Bernard, 2019
McCollum, Sir Liam, 1997
McCombe, Sir Richard, 2012
McConnell of Glenscorrodale, Lord, 2001
MacDermott, Sir John, 1987
McDonnell, John, 2016
Macdonald of Tradeston, Lord, 1999
McFadden, Patrick, 2008
McFall of Alcluith, Lord, 2004
McFarlane, Sir Andrew, 2011
MacGregor of Pulham Market, Lord, 1985
McGuire, Dame Anne, 2008
Macintosh, Kenneth, 2016
Mackay, Andrew, 1998
Mackay of Clashfern, Lord, 1979
McKinnon, Sir Donald, 1992
Maclean, Hon. Lord (Ranald MacLean), 2001
McLeish, Henry, 2000
Maclennan of Rogart, Lord, 1997
McLoughlin, Sir Patrick, 2005
McNally, Lord, 2005
McNulty, Anthony, 2007
Mactaggart, Fiona, 2015
Macur, Dame Julia, 2013
McVey, Esther, 2014
Major, Sir John, 1987
Malcolm, Hon. Lord (Colin Campbell), 2015
Males, Sir Stephen, 2019
Malloch-Brown, Lord, 2007
Mance, Lord, 1999
Mandelson, Lord, 1998
Marnoch, Hon. Lord (Michael Marnoch), 2001
Marwick, Tricia, 2012
Mates, Michael, 2004
Maude of Horsham, Lord, 1992
Mawhinney, Lord, 1994
May, Sir Anthony, 1998
May, Theresa, 2003
Mellor, David, 1990
Menzies, Hon. Lord (Duncan Menzies), 2012
Michael, Alun, 1998
Milburn, Alan, 1998
Miliband, David, 2005
Miliband, Ed, 2007
Miller, Maria, 2012
Millett, Lord, 1994
Milton, Anne, 2015
Mitchell, Andrew, 2010
Mitchell, Sir James, 1985
Mitchell, Dr Keith, 2004
Moore, Michael, 1990
Moore, Michael, 2010
Moore-Bick, Sir Martin, 2005
Morauta, Sir Mekere, 2001
Mordaunt, Penny, 2017
Morgan, Sir Declan, 2009
Morgan, Nicky, 2014
Morris of Aberavon, Lord, 1970
Morris of Yardley, Baroness, 1999
Morritt, Sir Robert, 1994
Moses, Sir Alan, 2005

Moylan, Sir Andrew, 2017
Mulholland, Frank, 2011
Mullally, Rt. Revd Dame Sarah, 2018
Mummery, Sir John, 1996
Munby, Sir James, 2009
Mundell, David, 2010
Murphy, James, 2008
Murphy of Torfaen, Lord, 1999
Murrison, Dr Andrew, 2019
Musa, Wilbert, 2005
Namaliu, Sir Rabbie, 1989
Naseby, Lord, 1994
Needham, Sir Richard, 1994
Neuberger of Abbotsbury, Lord, 2004
Neville-Jones, Baroness, 2010
Newby, Lord, 2014
Newey, Sir Guy, 2017
Nicholls of Birkenhead, Lord, 1995
Nicholson, Sir Michael, 1995
Nimmo Smith, Hon. Lord (William Nimmo Smith), 2005
Nokes, Caroline, 2018
Northover, Baroness, 2015
Nott, Sir John, 1979
O'Brien, Mike, 2009
O'Brien, Sir Stephen, 2013
Oppenheim-Barnes, Baroness, 1979
Osborne, George, 2010
Osborne, Hon. Lord (Kenneth Osborne), 2001
Ottaway, Sir Richard, 2013
Otton, Sir Philip, 1995
Owen, Lord, 1976
Paeniu, Bikenibeu, 1991
Paice, Sir James, 2010
Palmer, Sir Geoffrey, 1986
Paraskeva, Dame Janet, 2010
Parker, Sir Jonathan, 2000
Patel, Priti, 2015
Paterson, Owen, 2010
Paton, Hon. Lady (Ann Paton), 2007
Patten, Lord, 1990
Patten, Sir Nicholas, 2009
Patten of Barnes, Lord, 1989
Patterson, Percival, 1993
Pattie, Sir Geoffrey, 1987
Paul, Lord, 2009
Peel, Earl, 2006
Pendry, Lord, 2000
Penning, Sir Mike, 2014
Penrose, Hon. Lord (George Penrose), 2000
Perry, Claire, 2018
Peters, Winston, 1998
Philip, Hon. Lord (Alexander Philip), 2005
Phillips of Worth Matravers, Lord, 1995
Pickles, Lord, 2010
Pill, Sir Malcolm, 1995
Pincher, Christopher, 2018
Portillo, Michael, 1992
Potter, Sir Mark, 1996
Prashar, Baroness, 2009
Primarolo, Baroness, 2002
Puapua, Sir Tomasi, 1982
Purnell, James, 2007
Quin, Baroness, 1998
Raab, Dominic, 2018
Radice, Lord, 1999

Rafferty, Dame Anne, 2011
Ramsden, James, 1963
Randall of Uxbridge, Lord, 2010
Raynsford, Nick, 2001
Redwood, Sir John, 1993
Reed, Lord, 2008
Rees-Mogg, Jacob, 2019
Reid, Sir George, 2004
Reid of Cardowan, Lord, 1998
Renton of Mount Harry, Lord, 1989
Richards, Sir David, 2016
Richards, Sir Stephen, 2005
Riddell, Peter, 2010
Rifkind, Sir Malcolm, 1986
Rimer, Sir Colin, 2007
Rix, Sir Bernard, 2000
Robathan, Lord, 2010
Robertson, Angus, 2015
Robertson, Sir Hugh, 2012
Robertson of Port Ellen, Lord, 1997
Robinson, Peter, 2007
Roch, Sir John, 1993
Rodgers of Quarry Bank, Lord, 1975
Rooker, Lord, 1999
Rose, Sir Christopher, 1992
Rose, Dame Vivien, 2019
Ross, *Hon.* Lord (Donald MacArthur), 1985
Royall of Blaisdon, Baroness, 2008
Rudd, Amber, 2015
Ruddock, Dame Joan, 2010
Ryan, Joan, 2007
Ryder, Sir Ernest, 2013
Ryder of Wensum, Lord, 1990
Sainsbury, Sir Timothy, 1992
Sales, Sir Philip, 2014
Salisbury, Marquess of, 1994
Salmond, Alex, 2007
Sandiford, Lloyd Erskine, 1989
Saville of Newdigate, Lord, 1994
Saville Roberts, Elizabeth, 2019
Sawyer, Dame Joan, 2004
Schiemann, Sir Konrad, 1995
Scotland of Asthal, Baroness, 2001
Scott of Foscote, Lord, 1991
Sedley, Sir Stephen, 1999
Selkirk of Douglas, Lord, 1996
Shapps, Grant, 2010
Sharma, Alok, 2019
Sharp, Dame Victoria, 2013
Sheil, Sir John, 2005
Sheldon, Lord, 1977
Shephard of Northwold, Baroness, 1992
Shipley, Jennifer, 1998
Short, Clare, 1997
Shutt of Greetland, Lord, 2009
Simler, Dame Ingrid, 2019
Simmonds, Sir Kennedy, 1984

Simmonds, Mark, 2014
Simon, Sir Peregrine, 2015
Simpson, Keith, 2015
Sinclair, Ian, 1977
Singh, Sir Rabinder, 2017
Slade, Sir Christopher, 1982
Smith, Andrew, 1997
Smith, *Hon.* Lady (Anne Smith), 2013
Smith, Jacqueline, 2003
Smith, Dame Janet, 2002
Smith, Julian, 2017
Smith of Basildon, Baroness, 2009
Smith of Finsbury, Lord, 1997
Soames, Sir Nicholas, 2011
Somare, Sir Michael, 1977
Sopoaga, Enele, 2018
Soubry, Anna, 2015
Spellar, John, 2001
Spelman, Dame Caroline, 2010
Spencer, Mark, 2019
Stanley, Sir John, 1984
Starmer, Sir Keir, 2017
Steel of Aikwood, Lord, 1977
Stephens, Sir Benjamin, 2017
Stewart, Rory, 2019
Stowell of Beeston, Baroness, 2014
Strang, Gavin, 1997
Strathclyde, Lord, 1995
Straw, Jack, 1997
Stride, Melvyn, 2017
Stuart, Freundel, 2013
Stuart, Gisela, 2015
Stuart-Smith, Sir Murray, 1988
Stunell, Lord, 2012
Sturgeon, Nicola, 2014
Sullivan, Sir Jeremy, 2009
Sumption, Lord, 2011
Sunak, Rishi, 2019
Sutherland, *Hon.* Lord (Ranald Sutherland), 2000
Swayne, Sir Desmond, 2011
Swire, Sir Hugo, 2010
Symons of Vernham Dean, Baroness, 2001
Tami, Mark, 2018
Taylor of Bolton, Baroness, 1997
Taylor of Holbeach, Lord, 2014
Tebbit, Lord, 1981
Thirlwall, Dame Kathryn, 2017
Thomas, Edmund, 1996
Thomas of Cwmgiedd, Lord, 2003
Thornberry, Emily, 2017
Thorpe, Sir Matthew, 1995
Thurso, Viscount, 2014
Timms, Stephen, 2006
Tipping, Andrew, 1998
Tomlinson, Sir Stephen, 2010
Touhig, Lord, 2006
Treacy, Sir Colman, 2012

Trefgarne, Lord, 1989
Trimble, Lord, 1997
Truss, Elizabeth, 2014
Tuckey, Sir Simon, 1998
Turnbull, Lord, 2016
Tyler, Lord, 2014
Tyrie, Lord, 2015
Ullswater, Viscount, 1994
Underhill, Sir Nicholas, 2013
Upton, Simon, 1999
Vadera, Baroness, 2009
Vaizey, Ed, 2016
Vaz, Keith, 2006
Villiers, Theresa, 2010
Vos, Sir Geoffrey, 2013
Waite, Sir John, 1993
Wakeham, Lord, 1983
Waldegrave of North Hill, Lord, 1990
Walker of Gestingthorpe, Lord, 1997
Wallace, Ben, 2017
Wallace of Saltaire, Lord, 2012
Wallace of Tankerness, Lord, 2000
Waller, Sir Mark, 1996
Ward, Sir Alan, 1995
Warner, Lord, 2006
Warsi, Baroness, 2010
Weatherup, Sir Ronald, 2016
Webb, Sir Steven, 2014
Weir, Sir Reginald, 2016
West of Spithead, Lord, 2010
Wheatley, *Hon.* Lord (John Wheatley), 2007
Wheeler, Sir John, 1993
Whittingdale, John, 2015
Whitty, Lord, 2005
Widdecombe, Ann, 1997
Wigley, Lord, 1997
Willetts, Lord, 2010
Williams of Crosby, Baroness, 1974
Williams of Elvel, Lord, 2013
Williams of Oystermouth, Lord, 2002
Williamson, Gavin, 2015
Willott, Jennifer, 2014
Wills, Lord, 2008
Wilson, Brian, 2003
Wilson, Sammy, 2017
Wilson of Culworth, Lord, 2005
Wingti, Paias, 1987
Winterton, Dame Rosie, 2006
Wolffe, James, 2016
Woodward, Shaun, 2007
Woolf, Lord, 1986
Wright, Jeremy, 2014
York, Archbishop of, 2005
Young, Edward, 2017
Young of Cookham, Lord, 1993
Young of Graffham, Lord, 1984
Zacca, Sir Edward, 1992

PRIVY COUNCIL OF NORTHERN IRELAND

The Privy Council of Northern Ireland had responsibilities in Northern Ireland similar to those of the Privy Council in Great Britain until the Northern Ireland Act 1974. Membership of the Privy Council of Northern Ireland is retained for life. Since the Northern Ireland Constitution Act 1973 no further appointments have been made. The post-nominal initials PC (NI) are used to differentiate its members from those of the Privy Council.

MEMBERS *as at 10 September 2019*
Bailie, Robin, 1971
Dobson, John, 1969
Kilclooney, Lord, 1970

PARLIAMENT

The UK constitution is not contained in any single document but has evolved over time, formed by statute, common law and convention. A constitutional monarchy, the UK is governed by ministers of the crown in the name of the sovereign, who is head both of the state and of the government.

The organs of government are the legislature (parliament), the executive and the judiciary. The executive comprises HM government (the cabinet and other ministers), government departments and local authorities (see the Government, Public Bodies and Local Government). The judiciary (see Law Courts and Offices) pronounces on the law, both written and unwritten, interprets statutes and is responsible for the enforcement of the law; the judiciary is independent of both the legislature and the executive.

THE MONARCHY

The sovereign personifies the state and is, in law, an integral part of the legislature, head of the executive, head of the judiciary, commander-in-chief of all armed forces of the crown and supreme governor of the Church of England. In the Channel Islands and the Isle of Man, which are crown dependencies, the sovereign is represented by a lieutenant-governor. In the member states of the Commonwealth of which the sovereign is head of state, her representative is a governor-general; in UK overseas territories the sovereign is usually represented by a governor, who is responsible to the British government.

Although in practice the powers of the monarchy are now very limited, and restricted mainly to the advisory and ceremonial, there are important acts of government which require the participation of the sovereign. These include summoning, proroguing and dissolving parliament, giving royal assent to bills passed by parliament, appointing important office-holders, eg government ministers, judges, bishops and governors, conferring peerages, knighthoods and other honours, and granting pardon to a person wrongly convicted of a crime. The sovereign appoints the prime minister; by convention this office is held by the leader of the political party which enjoys, or can secure, a majority of votes in the House of Commons. In international affairs the sovereign, as head of state, has the power to declare war and make peace, to recognise foreign states and governments, to conclude treaties and to annex or cede territory. However, as the sovereign entrusts executive power to ministers of the crown and acts on the advice of her ministers, which she cannot ignore, royal prerogative powers are in practice exercised by ministers, who are responsible to parliament.

Ministerial responsibility does not diminish the sovereign's importance to the smooth working of government. She holds meetings of the Privy Council (see below), gives audiences to her ministers and other officials at home and overseas, receives accounts of cabinet decisions, reads dispatches and signs state papers; she must be informed and consulted on every aspect of national life; and she must show complete impartiality.

COUNSELLORS OF STATE

If the sovereign travels abroad for more than a few days or suffers from a temporary illness, it is necessary to appoint members of the royal family, known as counsellors of state, under letters patent to carry out the chief functions of the monarch, including the holding of Privy Councils and giving royal assent to acts passed by parliament. The normal procedure is to appoint two or more members of the royal family remaining in the UK from among the sovereign's spouse and the four adults next in succession, provided they have reached the age of 21. There are currently four members of the royal family from which the counsellors of state are appointed: the Prince of Wales, the Duke of Cambridge, the Duke of Sussex and the Duke of York.

In the event of the sovereign on accession being under the age of 18 years, or by infirmity of mind or body, rendered incapable of performing the royal functions, provision is made for a regency.

THE PRIVY COUNCIL

The sovereign in council, or Privy Council, was the chief source of executive power until the system of cabinet government developed. Its main function today is to advise the sovereign on the approval of various statutory functions and acts of the royal prerogative. These powers are exercised through orders in council and royal proclamations, approved by the Queen at meetings of the Privy Council. The council is also able to exercise a number of statutory duties without approval from the sovereign, including powers of supervision over the registering bodies for the medical and allied professions. These duties are exercised through orders of council.

Although appointment as a privy counsellor is for life, only those who are currently government ministers are involved in the day-to-day business of the council. A full council is summoned only on the death of the sovereign or when the sovereign announces his or her intention to marry. (For a full list of privy counsellors, see the Privy Council section.)

There are a number of advisory Privy Council committees whose meetings the sovereign does not attend. Some are prerogative committees, such as those dealing with legislative matters submitted by the legislatures of the Channel Islands and the Isle of Man or with applications for charters of incorporation; and some are provided for by statute, eg those for the universities of Oxford and Cambridge and some Scottish universities.

Administrative work is carried out by the Privy Council Office under the direction of the Lord President of the Council, a cabinet minister.

JUDICIAL COMMITTEE OF THE PRIVY COUNCIL
Supreme Court Building, Parliament Square, London SW1P 3BD
T 020-7960 1500 W www.jcpc.uk

The Judicial Committee of the Privy Council is the court of final appeal from courts of the UK dependencies, courts of independent Commonwealth countries which have retained the right of appeal and courts of the Channel Islands and the Isle of Man. It also hears very occasional appeals from a number of ancient and ecclesiastical courts.

The committee is composed of privy counsellors who hold, or have held, high judicial office. Only three or five judges hear each case, and these are usually justices of the supreme court.

Chief Executive, Mark Ormerod, CB

PARLIAMENT

Parliament is the supreme law-making authority and can legislate for the UK as a whole or for any parts of it separately (the Channel Islands and the Isle of Man are crown dependencies and not part of the UK). The main functions of parliament are to pass laws, to enable the government to raise taxes and to scrutinise government policy and administration, particularly proposals for expenditure. International treaties and agreements are customarily presented to parliament before ratification.

Parliament can trace its roots to two characteristics of Anglo-Saxon rule: the *witan* (a meeting of the king, nobles and advisors) and the *moot* (county meetings where local matters were discussed). However, it was the parliament that Simon de Montfort called in 1265 that is accepted as the forerunner to modern parliament, as it included non-noble representatives from counties, cities and towns alongside the nobility. The nucleus of early parliaments at the beginning of the 14th century were the officers of the king's household and the king's judges, joined by such ecclesiastical and lay magnates as the king might summon to form a prototype 'House of Lords', and occasionally by the knights of the shires, burgesses and proctors of the lower clergy. By the end of Edward III's reign a 'House of Commons' was beginning to appear; the first known Speaker was elected in 1377.

Parliamentary procedure is based on custom and precedent, partly formulated in the standing orders of both houses of parliament. Each house has the right to control its own internal proceedings and to commit for contempt. The system of debate in the two houses is similar; when a motion has been moved, the Speaker proposes the question as the subject of a debate. Members speak from wherever they have been sitting. Questions are decided by a vote on a simple majority. Draft legislation is introduced, in either house, as a bill. Bills can be introduced by a government minister or a private member, but in practice the majority of bills which become law are introduced by the government. To become law, a bill must be passed by each house (for parliamentary stages, *see* Parliamentary Information) and then sent to the sovereign for the royal assent, after which it becomes an act of parliament.

Proceedings of both houses are public, except on extremely rare occasions. The minutes (called *Votes and Proceedings,* in the Commons and *House of Lords Minutes of Proceedings* in the Lords) and the speeches *(The Official Report of Parliamentary Debates,* Hansard) are published daily. Proceedings are also recorded for transmission on radio and television and stored in the Parliamentary Recording Unit before transfer to the British Library Sound Archive. Television cameras have been allowed into the House of Lords since 1985 and into the House of Commons since 1989; committee meetings may also be televised.

The Fixed Term Parliament Act 2011 fixed the duration of a parliament at five years in normal circumstances, the term being reckoned from the date given on the writs for the new parliament. The term of a parliament has been prolonged by legislation in such rare circumstances as the two World Wars (31 January 1911 to 25 November 1918; 26 November 1935 to 15 June 1945). The life of a parliament is divided into sessions, usually of one year in length, beginning and ending most often in May.

DEVOLUTION

The Scottish parliament and the National Assembly for Wales have legislative power over all devolved matters, ie matters not reserved to Westminster or otherwise outside its powers. The Northern Ireland Assembly has legislative authority in the fields previously administered by the Northern Ireland departments. The assembly was suspended in October 2002 and dissolved in April 2003, before being reinstated on 8 May 2007. Following a snap election in March 2017, negotiations to form an executive have failed and the Northern Ireland Assembly remains suspended. For further information, *see* Devolved Government

THE HOUSE OF LORDS

London SW1A 0PW
T 020-7219 3107
E hlinfo@parliament.uk W www.parliament.uk

The House of Lords is the second chamber, or 'Upper House', of the UK's bicameral parliament. Until the beginning of the 20th century, the House of Lords had considerable power, being able to veto any bill submitted to it by the House of Commons. Since the introduction of the Parliament Acts 1911 and 1949, however, it has no powers over money bills and its power of veto over public legislation has been reduced over time to the power to delay bills for up to one session of parliament (usually one year). Today the main functions of the House of Lords are to contribute to the legislative process, to act as a check on the government, and to provide a forum of expertise. Its judicial role as final court of appeal ended in 2009 with the establishment of a new UK Supreme Court (*see* Law Courts and Offices section).

The House of Lords has a number of select committees. Some relate to the internal affairs of the house – such as its House of Lords Commission – while others carry out important investigative work on matters of public interest. The main committees are: the Communications Committee; the Constitution Committee; the Economic Affairs Committee; the European Union Committee; and the Science and Technology Committee. House of Lords' investigative committees look at broad issues and do not mirror government departments as the select committees in the House of Commons do.

The Constitutional Reform Act 2005 significantly altered the judicial function of the House of Lords and the role of the Lord Chancellor as a judge and its presiding officer. The Lord Chancellor is no longer the presiding officer of the House of Lords nor head of the judiciary in England and Wales, but remains a cabinet minister (the Lord Chancellor and Secretary of State for Justice), and is currently a member of the House of Commons. The function of the presiding officer of the House of Lords was devolved to the newly created post of the Speaker of the House of Lords, commonly known as Lord Speaker. The first Lord Speaker elected by the House was the Rt. Hon. Baroness Hayman on 4 July 2006.

Membership of the House of Lords comprises mainly of life peers created under the Life Peerages Act 1958, along with 92 hereditary peers and a small number of Lords of Appeal in Ordinary, ie law lords, who were created under the Appellate Jurisdiction Act 1876*. The Archbishops of Canterbury and York, the Bishops of London, Durham and Winchester, and the 21 senior diocesan bishops of the Church of England are also members.

The House of Lords Act 1999 provides for 92 hereditary peers to remain in the House of Lords until further reform of the House has been carried out. Of these, 75 (42 Conservative, 28 crossbench, three Liberal Democrat and two Labour) were elected by hereditary peers in their political party or crossbench grouping. In addition, 15 office holders were elected by the whole house. Two hereditary peers with royal duties, the Earl Marshal and the Lord Great Chamberlain, have also remained members. Since November 2002, by-elections have been held to replace elected hereditary peers who have died, and since 2014 to replace those who retire permanently from the House. By-elections are held under the Alternative Vote System, and must take place within three months of a vacancy occurring. (*see also* The Peerage).

Peers are disqualified from sitting in the house if they are:
• absent for an entire parliamentary session which is longer than six months (under the House of Lords Reform Act 2014), unless they are on leave of absence (*see* below)

- aliens, ie any peer who is not a British citizen, a Commonwealth citizen (under the British Nationality Act 1981) or a citizen of the Republic of Ireland
- under the age of 21
- undischarged bankrupts or, in Scotland, those whose estate is sequestered
- holders of a disqualifying judicial office
- members of the European parliament
- convicted of treason

Bishops cease to be members of the house when they retire.

Members who do not wish to attend sittings of the House of Lords may apply for leave of absence for the duration of a parliament. Since the passage of the House of Lords Reform Act 2014, members of the House may also retire permanently by giving notice in writing to the Clerk of the Parliaments.

Members of the House of Lords, who are not paid a salary, may claim a daily allowance of £305 (or may elect to claim a reduced daily allowance of £153) per sitting day – but only if they attend a sitting of the House and/or committee proceedings.

* Although the office of Lord of Appeal in Ordinary no longer exists, law lords created under the Appellate Jurisdiction Act 1876 remain members of the House. Those in office at the time of the establishment of the Supreme Court became justices of the UK Supreme Court and are not permitted to sit or vote in the House of Lords until they retire.

COMPOSITION *as at 10 September 2019*

Archbishops and bishops	26
Life peers under the Appellate Jurisdiction Act 1876 and the Life Peerages Act 1958*	658
Peers under the House of Lords Act 1999†	91
Total	775

* Excluding 15 peers on leave of absence
† Excluding one peer on leave of absence

STATE OF THE PARTIES* *as at 10 September 2019*

Conservative	234
Crossbench	182
Labour	179
Liberal Democrats	94
Non-affiliated	44
Archbishops and bishops	26
Other parties	15
Lord Speaker	1
Total	775

* Excluding peers on leave of absence

HOUSE OF LORDS PAY FOR SENIOR STAFF 2018–19

Senior staff are placed in the following pay bands according to their level of responsibility and taking account of other factors such as experience and marketability.

Judicial group 4	£185,197
Senior band 3	£111,500–£158,805
Senior band 2	£90,500–£119,850
Senior band 1A	£75,956–£105,560
Senior band 1	£69,000–£93,380

OFFICERS AND OFFICIALS

The house is presided over by the Lord Speaker, whose powers differ from those of the Speaker of the House of Commons. The Lord Speaker has no power to rule on matters of order because the House of Lords is self-regulating. The maintenance of the rules of debate is the responsibility of all the members who are present.

A panel of deputy speakers is appointed by Royal Commission. The first deputy speaker is the Chair of Committees, a salaried officer of the house appointed at the beginning of each session. He or she chairs a number of 'domestic' committees relating to the internal affairs of the house. The first deputy speaker is assisted by a panel of deputy chairs, headed by the salaried Principal Deputy Chair of Committees, who is also chair of the European Union Committee of the house.

The Clerk of the Parliaments is the accounting officer and the chief permanent official responsible for the administration of the house. The Lady Usher of the Black Rod is responsible for security and other services and also has royal duties as secretary to the Lord Great Chamberlain.

Lord Speaker, Rt. Hon. Lord Fowler
Senior Deputy Speaker of the House of Lords, Rt. Hon. Lord McFall of Alcluith
Principal Deputy Chair, Lord Boswell of Aynho
Clerk of the Parliaments, Edward Ollard
Clerk Assistant, Simon Burton
Reading Clerk and Clerk of the Overseas Office, Jake Vaughan
Lady Usher of the Black Rod, Sarah Clarke, OBE
Yeoman Usher of the Black Rod, Brig. Neil Baverstock
Commissioner for Lords' Standards, Lucy Scott-Moncrieff, CBE
Counsel to the Chair of Committees, J. Cooper
Registrar of Lords' Interests, Tom Wilson
Clerk of Committees, Dr Philippa Tudor
Legal Adviser to the Human Rights Committee, Eleanor Hourigan
Director of Library Services, Patrick Vollmer
Director of Facilities, Carl Woodall
Finance Director, vacant
Director of Parliamentary Digital Service, Tracey Jessup
Director of Human Resources, Nigel Sully
Clerk of Legislation, Andrew Makower
Principal Clerk of Select Committees, Christopher Johnson, DPHIL
Director of Parliamentary Archives, Adrian Brown

LORD GREAT CHAMBERLAIN'S OFFICE
Lord Great Chamberlain, 7th Marquess of Cholmondeley, KCVO

SELECT COMMITTEES
The main House of Lords select committees, as at September 2019, are as follows:

Bribery Act 2010 – Chair, Rt. Hon. Lord Saville of Newdigate; *Clerk,* Michael Collon
Communications – Chair, Lord Gilbert of Panteg; *Clerk,* Theodore Pembroke
Conduct – Chair, Rt. Hon. Lord Mance; *Clerk,* Kate Lawrence
Constitution – Chair, Rt. Hon. Baroness Taylor of Bolton; *Clerk,* Matt Korris
Delegated Powers and Regulatory Reform – Chair, Rt. Hon. Lord Blencathra
Democracy and Digital Technologies – Chair, Lord Black of Brentwood
Economic Affairs – Chair, Rt. Hon. Lord Forsyth of Drumlean; *Clerk,* Sam Newhouse
Economic Affairs Finance Bill – Chair, Rt. Hon.Lord Forsyth of Drumlean; *Clerk,* Sam Newhouse
Electoral Registration Act 2013 – Chair, Baroness Adams of Craigielea
European Union – Chair, Lord Boswell of Aynho; *Principal Clerk,* Christopher Johnson; *Clerk,* Stuart Stoner
European Union – Sub-committees:
  Energy and Environment – Chair, Lord Teverson; *Clerk,* Jennifer Mills
  External Affairs – Chair, Baroness Verma; *Clerk,* Jennifer Martin-Kohlmorgen

Financial Affairs – *Chair,* Lord Sharkey; *Clerk,* Matthew Manning
Home Affairs – *Chair,* Lord Jay of Ewelme, GCMG; *Clerk,* Phillipa Patterson
Internal Market – *Chair,* Baroness Donaghy, CBE; *Clerk,* Rosanna Barry
Justice – *Chair,* Rt. Hon. Lord Morris of Aberavon, KG, QC; *Clerk,* Alexandra McMillan
Finance – *Chair,* Baroness Doocey, OBE; *Clerk,* Gabby Longdin
Food, Poverty, Health and Environment – *Chair,* Baroness Boycott
Gambling Industry – *Chair,* Rt. Hon. Baroness Armstrong of Hill Top
House – *Chair,* Rt. Hon. Lord Fowler; *Clerk,* Patrick Milner
Hybrid Instruments – *Chair,* Rt. Hon. Lord McFall of Alcluith
Intergenerational Fairness and Provision – *Chair,* Lord True, CBE; *Clerk,* Olivia Crabtree
International Relations – *Chair,* Rt. Hon. Baroness Anelay of St Johns, DBE; *Clerk,* Eva George
Liaison – *Chair,* Rt. Hon. Lord McFall of Alcluith; *Clerk,* Philippa Tudor
Lords' Conduct – *Chair,* Rt. Hon. Lord Brown of Eaton-under-Heywood
Privileges and Conduct – *Chair,* Rt. Hon. Lord McFall of Alcluith; *Clerk,* Chloe Mawson
Procedure – *Chair,* Rt. Hon. Lord McFall of Alcluith; *Clerk,* Chloe Mawson
Regenerating Seaside Towns – *Chair,* Rt. Hon. Lord Bassam of Brighton; *Clerk,* Chris Clarke
Rural Economy – *Chair,* Rt. Hon. Lord Foster of Bath; *Clerk,* Simon Keal
Science and Technology – *Chair,* Lord Patel, KT; *Clerk,* Simon Cran-McGreehin
Secondary Legislation Scrutiny – *Chair,* Lord Hodgson of Astley Abbotts, CBE
Selection – *Chair,* Rt. Hon. Lord McFall of Alcluith
Services – *Chair,* Rt. Hon. Lord Laming, CBE; *Clerk,* Gabby Longdin
Standing Orders (Private Bills) – *Chair,* Rt. Hon. Lord McFall of Alcluith

THE HOUSE OF COMMONS
London SW1A 0AA
T 020-7219 3000 W www.parliament.uk

HOUSE OF COMMONS ENQUIRY SERVICE
14 Tothill Street, London SW1H 9NB
T 020-7219 4272 E hcinfo@parliament.uk

The members of the House of Commons are elected by universal adult suffrage. For electoral purposes, the UK is divided into constituencies, each of which returns one member to the House of Commons, the member being the candidate who obtains the largest number of votes cast in the constituency. To ensure equitable representation, the four Boundary Commissions keep constituency boundaries under review and recommend any redistribution of seats which may seem necessary because of population movements etc. At the 2010 general election the number of seats increased from 646 to 650. Of the present 650 seats, there are 533 for England, 40 for Wales, 59 for Scotland and 18 for Northern Ireland.

NUMBER OF SEATS IN THE HOUSE OF COMMONS BY COUNTRY

	2005	2017
England	529	533
Wales	40	40
Scotland	59	59
Northern Ireland	18	18
Total	646	650

ELECTIONS
Elections are by secret ballot, each elector casting one vote; voting is not compulsory. (For entitlement to vote in parliamentary elections, *see* Legal Notes.) When a seat becomes vacant between general elections, a by-election is held.

British subjects and citizens of the Irish Republic can stand for election as MPs provided they are 18 or over and not subject to disqualification. Those disqualified from sitting in the house include:

- undischarged bankrupts
- people sentenced to more than one year's imprisonment
- members of the House of Lords (but hereditary peers not sitting in the Lords are eligible)
- holders of certain offices listed in the House of Commons Disqualification Act 1975, eg members of the judiciary, civil service, regular armed forces, police forces, some local government officers and some members of public corporations and government commissions

A candidate does not require any party backing but his or her nomination for election must be supported by the signatures of ten people registered in the constituency. A candidate must also deposit £500 with the returning officer, which is forfeit if the candidate does not receive more than 5 per cent of the votes cast. All election expenses at a general election, except the candidate's personal expenses, are subject to a statutory limit of £8,700, plus six pence for each elector in a borough constituency or nine pence for each elector in a county constituency.

See also members of parliament for a current alphabetical list.

STATE OF THE PARTIES *as at 10 September 2019*

Party	Seats
Conservative*	288
Labour	247
Scottish National Party	35
Independent	35
Liberal Democrats	17
Democratic Unionist Party	10
Sinn Fein (have not taken their seats)	7
The Independent Group for Change	5
Plaid Cymru	4
Green	1
The Speaker	1
Total	650

* The Conservative Party have formed a minority government and have signed a 'confidence and supply' agreement with the Democratic Unionist Party

BUSINESS
The week's business of the house is outlined each Thursday by the leader of the house, after consultation between the chief government whip and the chief opposition whip. A quarter to a third of the time will be taken up by the government's legislative programme and the rest by other business. As a rule, bills likely to raise political controversy are introduced in the Commons before going on to the Lords, and the Commons claims exclusive control in respect of national taxation and expenditure. Bills such as the finance bill, which imposes taxation, and the consolidated fund bills, which authorise expenditure, must begin in the Commons. A bill of which the financial provisions are subsidiary may begin in the Lords, and the Commons may waive its rights in regard to Lords' amendments affecting finance.

The Commons has a public register of MPs' financial and certain other interests; this is published annually as a House of Commons paper. Members must also disclose any relevant financial interest or benefit in a matter before the house when taking part in a debate, in certain other proceedings of the house, or in consultations with other MPs, with ministers or with civil servants.

MEMBERS' PAY AND ALLOWANCES

Since 1911 members of the House of Commons have received salary payments; facilities for free travel were introduced in 1924. Salary rates for the last 30 years are as follows:

1988 Jan – £22,548	2003 Apr – £56,358
1989 Jan – £24,107	2004 Apr – £57,485
1990 Jan – £26,701	2005 Apr – £59,095
1991 Jan – £29,970	2006 Apr – £59,686
1992 Jan – £30,854	2007 Apr – £61,181
1993 Jan – £30,854	2008 Apr – £63,291
1994 Jan – £31,687	2009 Apr – £64,766
1995 Jan – £33,189	2010 Apr – £65,738
1995 Jan – £33,189	2011 Apr – £65,738
1996 Jan – £34,085	2012 Apr – £65,738
1996 Jul – £43,000	2013 Apr – £66,396
1997 Apr – £43,860	2014 Apr – £67,060
1998 Apr – £45,066	2015 May – £74,000
1999 Apr – £47,008	2016 Apr – £74,962
2000 Apr – £48,371	2017 Apr – £76,011
2001 Apr – £49,822	2018 Apr – £77,379
2002 Apr – £55,118	2019 Apr – £79,468

The Independent Parliamentary Standards Authority (IPSA) was established under the Parliamentary Standards Act 2009 and is responsible for the independent regulation and administration of the MPs' Scheme of Business Costs and Expenses, as well as for paying the salaries of MPs and their staff members. Since May 2011, the IPSA has also been responsible for determining MPs' pay and setting the level of any increase to their salary.

For 2019–20, the office costs expenditure budget is £28,270 for London area MPs and £25,450 for non-London area MPs. The maximum annual staff budget for London area MPs is £166,950 and £155,930 for non-London area MPs.

Since 1972 MPs have been able to claim reimbursement for the additional cost of staying overnight away from their main residence while on parliamentary business. This is not payable to London area MPs and those MPs who reside in 'grace and favour' accommodation. Accommodation expenses for MPs claiming rental payments in the London area is capped at £22,920 a year; outside of the London area each constituency is banded according to rental values in the area and capped at £16,010. For MPs who own their own homes, mortgage interest and associated expenses up to £5,270 are payable.

For ministerial salaries see Government Departments.

MEMBERS' PENSIONS

Pension arrangements for MPs were first introduced in 1964. Under the Parliamentary Contributory Pension Fund CARE (career-averaged revalued earnings) scheme, MPs receive a pension on retirement based upon their salary in their final year, and upon accumulating proportions of pensionable earnings over each year of membership. MPs contributions are payable at a rate of 11.09 per cent of pay. Exchequer contributions are paid at a rate recommended by the Government Actuary and meet the balance of the cost of providing MP's retirement benefits. Pensions are normally payable upon retirement at age 65 to those who are no longer MPs. Abated pensions may be payable to members aged 55 or over. Pensions are also payable to spouses and other qualifying partners of deceased scheme members at the rate of three-eighths of the deceased member's pension. In the case of members who die in service, an enhanced spouse's or partner's pension and a lump sum equal to two times pensionable salary is payable. There are also provisions in place for dependants and MPs of any age who retire due to ill health. All pensions are CPI index-linked.

The House of Commons Members' Fund provides for annual or lump sum grants to ex-MPs, their widows or widowers, and children of those who either ceased to serve as an MP prior to the PCPF being established or who are experiencing hardship. Historically, income to the Fund has been derived from individual contributions from MPs (£24 per annum), an Exchequer contribution (a maximum of £215,000 per annum) and the return on investments. Under the provision of the House of Commons Members Fund Act 2016 the trustees can suspend or increase MP contributions up to a maximum of 0.2 per cent of an member's ordinary salary. The 2016 Act also removed the Exchequer contribution.

HOUSE OF COMMONS PAY BANDS FOR SENIOR STAFF

Senior Staff are placed in the following Senior Civil Service pay bands. These pay bands are for 2018–19 and apply to the most senior staff in departments and agencies.

Pay Band 1	£68,000–£117,800
Pay Band 1A*	£68,000–£128,900
Pay Band 2	£90,500–£162,500
Pay Band 3	£111,500–£208,100
Permanent Secretaries	£150,000–£200,000

* Pay Band 1A is now effectively a closed grade, although existing staff will remain on this grade

OFFICERS AND OFFICIALS

The House of Commons is presided over by the Speaker, who has considerable powers to maintain order. A deputy speaker, called the Chairman of Ways and Means, and two deputy chairs may preside over sittings of the House of Commons; they are elected by the house, and, like the Speaker, neither speak nor vote other than in their official capacity.

The staff of the house are employed by a commission chaired by the Speaker. The heads of the six House of Commons departments are permanent officers of the house, not MPs. The Clerk of the House is the principal adviser to the Speaker on the privileges and procedures of the house, the conduct of the business of the house, and committees. The Serjeant-at-Arms is responsible for security and ceremonial functions of the house.

Speaker, Rt. Hon. John Bercow, MP
Chairman of Ways and Means, Rt. Hon. Sir Lindsay Hoyle, MP
First Deputy Chairman of Ways and Means, Rt. Hon. Dame Eleanor Laing, DBE, MP
Second Deputy Chairman of Ways and Means, Rt. Hon. Dame Rosie Winterton, DBE, MP
House of Commons Commission, Rt, Hon. John Bercow, MP *(chair);* Ian Ailles *(Director-General of the House of Commons);* Dr John Benger *(Clerk of the House);* Sir Paul Beresford, MP; Rt. Hon. Tom Brake, MP; Jane McCall *(external member);* Dr Rima Makarem *(external member);* Rt Hon. Jacob Rees-Mogg, MP *(Leader of the House);* Valerie Vaz, MP *(Shadow Leader of the House);* Rt. Hon. Dame Rosie Winterton, DBE, MP; Pete Wishart, MP
Secretary of the Commission, Marianne Cwynarski
Assistant Secretary, Robert Cope

OFFICE OF THE SPEAKER

Speaker's Secretary, Peter Barratt
Trainbearer, Jim Davey
Speaker's Counsel, Saira Salimi
Chaplain to the Speaker, Revd Rose Hudson-Wilkin

OFFICE OF THE CLERK OF THE HOUSE
Clerk of the House, Dr John Benger

PARLIAMENTARY COMMISSIONER FOR STANDARDS
Parliamentary Commissioner for Standards, Kathryn Stone, OBE
Registrar of Members' Financial Interests, Heather Wood

PARLIAMENTARY SECURITY DIRECTOR
Parliamentary Security Director, Eric Hepburn, CBE

GOVERNANCE OFFICE
Head of Office, Marianne Cwynarski
Corporate Risk Management Facilitator, Rachel Harrison
Head of Central Communications, Lee Bridges
Head of Internal Audit and Risk,, Richard Stammers

DEPARTMENT OF CHAMBER AND COMMITTEE SERVICES
Clerk Assistant and Managing Director, Sarah Davies

OVERSEAS OFFICE
Principal Clerk, Dr Lynn Gardner
Delegation Secretary, Nick Wright
Inward Visits Manager, Dawn Amey
National Parliament Representative (Brussels), Fraser McIntosh

COMMITTEE OFFICE
Clerk of Committees, Paul Evans
Principal Clerks of Select Committees, Tom Healey; Chris Stanton

DEPARTMENTAL SELECT COMMITTEES *as at 10 September 2019*
Administration – Chair, Sir Paul Beresford, MP; *Clerk,* Kevin Candy
Backbench Business – Chair, Ian Mearns, MP; *Clerk,* Sarah Hartwell-Naguib
Business, Energy and Industrial Strategy – Chair, Rachel Reeves, MP; *Clerk,* Chris Shaw
Defence – Chair, Rt. Hon. Dr Julian Lewis, MP; *Clerk,* Mark Etherton
Digital, Culture, Media and Sport – Chair, Damian Collins. MP; *Clerk,* Chloe Challender
Education – Chair, Robert Halfon, MP; *Clerk,* Richard Ward
Environment, Food and Rural Affairs – Chair, Neil Parish, MP; *Clerk,* Ian Bradshaw
Environmental Audit – Chair, Mary Creagh, MP; *Clerk,* Lloyd Owen
European Scrutiny – Chair, Sir William Cash, MP; *Clerk,* Jessica Mulley
European Statutory Instruments – Chair, Rt. Hon. Sir Patrick McLoughlin, MP; *Clerk,* Yohanna Sallberg
Exiting the European Union – Chair, Rt. Hon. Hilary Benn, MP; *Clerk,* James Rhys
Finance – Chair, Chris Bryant, MP; *Clerk,* Rob Cope
Foreign Affairs – Chair, Tom Tugendhat, MP; *Clerk,* Tom Goldsmith
Health and Social Care – Chair, Dr Sarah Wollaston, MP; *Clerk,* Huw Yardley
High Speed Rail (West Midlands – Crewe) Bill – Chair, James Duddridge, MP
Home Affairs – Chair, Rt. Hon. Yvette Cooper, MP; *Clerk,* Elizabeth Hunt
Housing, Communities and Local Government, Chair, Clive Betts, MP, *Clerk* Mike Winter
International Development – Chair, Stephen Twigg, MP; *Clerk,* Fergus Reid
International Trade – Chair, Angus Brendan MacNeil, MP; *Clerk,* Joanna Welham
Justice – Chair, Robert Neill, MP; *Clerk,* David Weir

Liaison – Chair, Dr Sarah Wollaston, MP; *Clerk,* Lucinda Maer
Northern Ireland Affairs – Chair, Simon Hoare, MP; *Clerk,* Margaret McKinnon
Petitions – Chair, Helen Jones, MP
Privileges – Chair, Kate Green, MP; *Clerk,* Robin James
Procedure – Chair, Charles Walker, MP; *Clerk,* Martyn Atkins
Public Accounts – Chair, Meg Hillier, MP; *Clerk,* Richard Cooke
Public Administration and Constitutional Affairs – Chair, Hon. Sir Bernard Jenkin, MP; *Clerks,* Libby Kurien; Dr Sarah Thatcher
Regulatory Reform – Chair, Stephen McPartland, MP; *Clerk,* Alison Groves
Science and Technology – Chair, Rt. Hon. Sir Norman Lamb, MP; *Clerk,* Danielle Nash
Scottish Affairs – Chair, Pete Wishart, MP; *Clerk,* Ben Williams
Selection – Chair, Bill Wiggin, MP; *Clerks,* Anwen Rees; Yohanna Sallberg
Standards – Chair, Kate Green, MP; *Clerk,* Robin James
Standing Orders (Private Bills) – Chair, Rt. Hon. Sir Lindsay Hoyle, MP
Statutory Instruments – Chair, Jessica Morden, MP; *Clerk,* Yohanna Sallberg
Transport – Chair, Lillian Greenwood, MP; *Clerk,* Gordon Clarke
Treasury – Chair, Stephen Hammond, MP; *Clerk,* Gosia McBride
Welsh Affairs – Chair, David T. C. Davies, MP; *Clerk,* Kevin Maddison
Women and Equalities – Chair, Rt. Hon. Maria Miller, MP; *Clerk,* Jyoti Chandola
Work and Pensions – Chair, Rt. Hon. Frank Field, MP; *Clerk,* Anne-Marie Griffiths

SCRUTINY UNIT
Heads of Unit, Elizabeth Flood; David Lloyd
Head of Financial Scrutiny, Larry Honeysett

VOTE OFFICE
Deliverer of the Vote, Tom McVeagh
Head of Procedural Publishing, vacant
Procedural Publishing Operations Manager, Stuart Miller

CHAMBER BUSINESS DIRECTORATE
Clerk of Legislation, Liam Laurence Smyth
Acting Clerk of Bills, Kenneth Fox
Principal Clerks: Colin Lee *(Table Office);* Mark Hutton (Journals)

OFFICIAL REPORT DIRECTORATE
Editor, Alex Newton
Deputy Editor, Jack Homer
Managing Editors, Adele Dodd; David Hampton; Jonathan Hoare; Deborah Jones; Emma Kirby; Tony Minichiello; Jez Oates; Ian Oakhill; Ann Street; Vivien Wilson
Director of Parliamentary Audio and Video, John Angeli

SERJEANT-AT-ARMS DIRECTORATE
Serjeant-at-Arms, Kamal El-Hajji
Operations Manager, Chris Rust
Principal Doorkeeper, Phil Howse

DEPARTMENT OF PARLIAMENTARY MAINTENANCE AND CATERING SERVICES
Director of Parliamentary Maintenance, Tim Killip
Head of Parliamentary Maintenance Mike McCann
Reactive and Ceremonial Maintenance, Steve Jaggs
Operations Manager (Maintenance), Phil Sturgeon
Director of Catering Services, Richard Tapner-Evans
Executive Chef, Mark Hill, MBE

Private Dining and Events Manager, Lee Holt
Operations Manager (Catering Services), Robert Gibbs

DEPARTMENT OF FINANCE
Head of Finance, Ebenezer Oduwole

DEPARTMENT OF HUMAN RESOURCES AND DIVERSITY
Director-General of HR and Diversity, Mandy Eddolls
Head of HR Shared Services, Deborah Macaly
Heads of Diversity and Inclusion, Jennifer Crook; Maxine Albert
Head of Parliamentary Health and Wellbeing, Anne Mossop
Director-General of Participation, Dr Edge Watchorn

DEPARTMENT OF INFORMATION SERVICES
Director-General and Librarian, Penny Young
Curator of Works of Art, Melissa Hamnett
Deputy Curator, Melanie Unwin
Assistant Curators, Emma Gormley; Sileas Wood
Keeper of Historic Collections, Mary-Jane Tsang
Collections Care Manager, Caroline Babington
Collections Information Manager, Natasha Walsh

PARLIAMENTARY DIGITAL SERVICE (PDS)
Director of Parliamentary Digital Service, Tracey Jessup
Deputy Director, David Smith
Chief Technology and Security Officer, Mark Harbord
Digital Portfolio Director, Dan Cook
Director of Cyber Security, Steven Mark
Director of Resources, Tim Youngs

OTHER PRINCIPAL OFFICERS
Clerk of the Crown in Chancery, Sir Richard Heaton, KCB
Parliamentary and Health Service Ombudsman, Robert Behrens, CBE

NATIONAL AUDIT OFFICE
157–197 Buckingham Palace Road, London SW1W 9SP
T 020-7798 7000
E enquiries@nao.gsi.gov.uk W www.nao.org.uk

The National Audit Office came into existence under the National Audit Act 1983 to replace and continue the work of the former Exchequer and Audit Department. The act reinforced the office's total financial and operational independence from the government and brought its head, the Comptroller and Auditor-General, into a closer relationship with parliament as an officer of the House of Commons.

The National Audit Office (NAO) scrutinises public spending on behalf of parliament, helping it to hold government departments to account and helping public service managers improve performance and service delivery. The NAO audits the financial statements of all government departments and a wide range of other public bodies. It regularly publishes 'value for money' reports on the efficiency and effectiveness of how public resources are used.

Chair, Lord Bichard, KCB
Comptroller and Auditor-General, Gareth Davies
Executive Leaders, Abdool Kara; Daniel Lambauer; Kate Mathers; Rebecca Sheeran; Stephen Smith; Max Tse; John Thorpe

PARLIAMENTARY INFORMATION

The following is a short glossary of aspects of the work of parliament. Unless otherwise stated, references are to House of Commons procedures.

BILL – Proposed legislation is termed a bill. The stages of a public bill (for private bills, *see* below) in the House of Commons are as follows:

First reading: This stage introduces the legislation to the house and, for government bills, merely constitutes an order to have the bill printed.

Second reading: The debate on the principles of the bill.

Committee stage: The detailed examination of a bill, clause by clause. In most cases this takes place in a public bill committee, or the whole house may act as a committee. Public bill committees may take evidence before embarking on detailed scrutiny of the bill. Very rarely, a bill may be examined by a select committee.

Report stage: Detailed review of a bill as amended in committee, on the floor of the house, and an opportunity to make further changes.

Third reading: Final debate on the full bill in the Commons.

Public bills go through the same stages in the House of Lords, but with important differences: the committee stage is taken in committee of the whole house or in a grand committee, in which any peer may participate. There are no time limits, all amendments are debated, and further amendments can be made at third reading.

A bill may start in either house, and has to pass through both houses to become law. Both houses have to agree the final text of a bill, so that amendments made by the second house are then considered in the originating house, and if not agreed, sent back or themselves amended, until agreement is reached.

CHILTERN HUNDREDS – A nominal office of profit under the crown, the acceptance of which requires an MP to vacate his/her seat. The Manor of Northstead is similar. These are the only means by which an MP may resign.

CONSOLIDATED FUND BILL – A bill to authorise the issue of money to maintain government services. The bill is dealt with without debate.

EARLY DAY MOTION – A motion put on the notice paper by an MP without, in general, the real prospect of its being debated. Such motions are expressions of back-bench opinion.

FATHER OF THE HOUSE – The MP whose continuous service in the House of Commons is the longest. The present Father of the House is the Rt. Hon. Kenneth Clarke, CH, QC, MP.

GRAND COMMITTEES – There are three grand committees in the House of Commons, one each for Northern Ireland, Scotland and Wales; they consider matters relating specifically to that country. In the House of Lords, bills may be sent to a grand committee instead of a committee of the whole house (*see also* Bill).

HOURS OF MEETING – The House of Commons normally meets on Mondays at 2.30pm, Tuesdays and Wednesdays at 11.30am, Thursdays at 9.30am and some Fridays at 9.30am. (*See also* Westminster Hall Sittings, below.) The House of Lords normally meets at 2.30pm Mondays and Tuesdays, 3pm on Wednesdays and at 11am on Thursdays. The House of Lords occasionally sits on Fridays at 10am.

LEADER OF THE OPPOSITION – In 1937 the office of leader of the opposition was recognised and a salary was assigned to the post. In 2019–20 this is £143,497 (including a parliamentary salary of £79,468). The present leader of the opposition is the Rt. Hon. Jeremy Corbyn, MP.

THE LORD CHANCELLOR – The office of Lord High Chancellor of Great Britain was significantly altered by the Constitutional Reform Act 2005. Previously, the Lord Chancellor was (*ex officio*) the Speaker of the House of Lords, and took part in debates and voted in divisions in the House of Lords. The Department for Constitutional Affairs was created in 2003, and became the Ministry of Justice in 2007, incorporating most of the responsibilities of the Lord Chancellor's department. The role of Speaker has been transferred to the post of Lord Speaker. The Constitutional Reform Act 2005 also brought to an end the Lord

Chancellor's role as head of the judiciary. A Judicial Appointments Commission was created in April 2006, and a supreme court (separate from the House of Lords) was established in 2009.

THE LORD GREAT CHAMBERLAIN – The Lord Great Chamberlain is a Great Officer of State, the office being hereditary since the grant of Henry I to the family of De Vere, Earls of Oxford. It is now a joint hereditary office rotating on the death of the sovereign between the Cholmondeley, Carington and Ancaster families.

The Lord Great Chamberlain, currently the 7th Marquess of Cholmondeley, is responsible for the royal apartments in the Palace of Westminster, the Royal Gallery, the administration of the Chapel of St Mary Undercroft and, in conjunction with the Lord Speaker and the Speaker of the House of Commons, Westminster Hall. The Lord Great Chamberlain has the right to perform specific services at a coronation and has particular responsibility for the internal administrative arrangements within the House of Lords for state openings of parliament.

THE LORD SPEAKER – The first Lord Speaker of the House of Lords, the Rt. Hon. Baroness Hayman, took up office on 4 July 2006. The Lord Speaker is independent of the government and elected by members of the House of Lords rather than appointed by the prime minister. Although the Lord Speaker's primary role is to preside over proceedings in the House of Lords, she does not have the same powers as the Speaker of the House of Commons. For example, the Lord Speaker is not responsible for maintaining order during debates, as this is the responsibility of the house as a whole. The Lord Speaker sits in the Lords on one of the woolsacks, which are couches covered in red cloth and stuffed with wool.

MOTHER OF THE HOUSE – Introduced by Theresa May in 2017, the Mother of the House is the female MP whose continuous service is the longest. The inaugural and present Mother of the House is Rt. Hon. Harriet Harman, QC, MP.

OPPOSITION DAY – A day on which the topic for debate is chosen by the opposition. There are 20 such days in a normal session. On 17 days, subjects are chosen by the leader of the opposition; on the remaining three days by the leader of the next largest opposition party.

PARLIAMENT ACTS 1911 AND 1949 – Under these acts, bills may become law without the consent of the Lords, though the House of Lords has the power to delay a public bill for a parliamentary session.

PRIME MINISTER'S QUESTIONS – The prime minister answers questions from 12 to 12.30pm on Wednesdays.

PRIVATE BILL – A bill promoted by a body or an individual to give powers additional to, or in conflict with, the general law, and to which a special procedure applies to enable people affected to object.

PRIVATE MEMBER'S BILL – A public bill promoted by an MP or peer who is not a member of the government.

PRIVATE NOTICE QUESTION – A question adjudged of urgent importance on submission to the Speaker (in the Lords, the Lord Speaker), answered at the end of oral questions.

PRIVILEGE – The House of Commons has rights and immunities to protect it from obstruction in carrying out its duties. These are known as parliamentary privilege and enable Members of Parliament to debate freely. The most important privilege is that of freedom of speech. MPs cannot be prosecuted for sedition or sued for libel or slander over anything said during proceedings in the house. This enables them to raise in the house questions affecting the public good which might be difficult to raise outside owing to the possibility of legal action against them. The House of Lords has similar privileges.

QUESTION TIME – Oral questions are answered by ministers in the Commons from 2.30 to 3.30pm on Mondays, 11.30am to 12.30pm on Tuesdays and Wednesdays, and 9.30 to 10.30am on Thursdays. Questions are also taken for half an hour at the start of the Lords sittings.

ROYAL ASSENT – The royal assent is signified by letters patent to such bills and measures as have passed both Houses of Parliament (or bills which have been passed under the Parliament Acts 1911 and 1949). The sovereign has not given royal assent in person since 1854. On occasion, for instance in the prorogation of parliament, royal assent may be pronounced to the two houses by Lords Commissioners. More usually royal assent is notified to each house sitting separately in accordance with the Royal Assent Act 1967. The old French formulae for royal assent are then endorsed on the acts by the Clerk of the Parliaments.

The power to withhold assent resides with the sovereign but has not been exercised in the UK since 1707.

SELECT COMMITTEES – Consisting usually of 10 to 15 members of all parties, select committees are a means used by both houses in order to investigate certain matters.

Most select committees in the House of Commons are tied to departments: each committee investigates subjects within a government department's remit. There are other select committees dealing with matters such as public accounts (ie the spending by the government of money voted by parliament) and European legislation, and also committees advising on procedures and domestic administration of the house. Major select committees usually take evidence in public; their evidence and reports are published on the parliament website and in hard copy by The Stationery Office (TSO). House of Commons select committees are reconstituted after a general election.

In the House of Lords, select committees do not mirror government departments but cover broader issues. There is a select committee on the European Union (EU), which has six sub-committees dealing with specific areas of EU policy, a select committee on science and technology, a select committee on economic affairs and also one on the constitution. There is also a select committee on delegated powers and regulatory reform and one on privileges and conduct. In addition, *ad hoc* select committees have been set up from time to time to investigate specific subjects. There are also joint committees of the two houses, eg the committees on statutory instruments and on human rights.

THE SPEAKER – The Speaker of the House of Commons is the spokesperson and chair of the Chamber. He or she is elected by the house at the beginning of each parliament or when the previous Speaker retires or dies. The Speaker neither speaks in debates nor votes in divisions except when the voting is equal.

VACANT SEATS – When a vacancy occurs in the House of Commons during a session of parliament, the writ for the by-election is moved by a whip of the party to which the member whose seat has been vacated belonged. If the house is in recess, the Speaker can issue a warrant for a writ, should two members certify to him that a seat is vacant.

WESTMINSTER HALL SITTINGS – Following a report by the Modernisation of the House of Commons Select Committee, the Commons decided in May 1999 to set up a second debating forum. It is known as 'Westminster Hall' and sittings are in the Grand Committee Room on some Mondays from 4.30pm to 7.30pm, Tuesdays and Wednesdays from 9.30am to 11.30am and from 2.30pm to 5.30pm, and Thursdays from 1.30pm to 4.30pm. Sittings are open to the public at the times indicated.

WHIPS – In order to secure the attendance of members of a particular party in parliament, particularly on the occasion of an important vote, whips (originally known as 'whippers-in') are appointed. The written appeal or circular letter issued by them is also known as a 'whip', its urgency being denoted by the number of times it is underlined. Failure to respond to a three-line whip is tantamount in the Commons to secession (at any rate temporarily) from the party. Whips are provided with office accommodation in both houses, and government and some opposition whips receive salaries from public funds.

PARLIAMENTARY ARCHIVES
Houses of Parliament, London SW1A 0PW
T 020-7219 3074 E archives@parliament.uk W www.parliament.uk/archives

Since 1497, the records of parliament have been kept within the Palace of Westminster. They are in the custody of the Clerk of Parliaments. In 1946 the House of Lords Record Office, which became the Parliamentary Archives in 2006, was established to supervise their preservation and their availability to the public. Some 3 million documents are preserved, including acts of parliament from 1497, journals of the House of Lords from 1510, minutes and committee proceedings from 1610, and papers laid before parliament from 1531. Among the records are the Petition of Right, the death warrant of Charles I, the Declaration of Breda, and the Bill of Rights. Records are made available through a public search room.
Director of the Parliamentary Archives, Adrian Brown

GOVERNMENT OFFICE

The government is the body of ministers responsible for the administration of national affairs, determining policy and introducing into parliament any legislation necessary to give effect to government policy. The majority of ministers are members of the House of Commons but members of the House of Lords, or of neither house, may also hold ministerial responsibility. The prime minister is, by current convention, always a member of the House of Commons.

THE PRIME MINISTER
The office of prime minister, which had been in existence for nearly 200 years, was officially recognised in 1905 and its holder was granted a place in the table of precedence. The prime minister, by tradition also First Lord of the Treasury and Minister for the Civil Service, is appointed by the sovereign and is usually the leader of the party which enjoys, or can secure, a majority in the House of Commons. Other ministers are appointed by the sovereign on the recommendation of the prime minister, who also allocates functions among ministers and has the power to dismiss ministers from their posts.

The prime minister informs the sovereign on state and political matters, advises on the dissolution of parliament, and makes recommendations for important crown appointments, ie the award of honours, etc.

As the chair of cabinet meetings and leader of a political party, the prime minister is responsible for translating party policy into government activity. As leader of the government, the prime minister is responsible to parliament and to the electorate for the policies and their implementation.

The prime minister also represents the nation in international affairs, eg summit conferences.

THE CABINET
The cabinet developed during the 18th century as an inner committee of the Privy Council, which was the chief source of executive power until that time. The cabinet is composed of about 20 ministers chosen by the prime minister, usually the heads of government departments (generally known as secretaries of state unless they have a special title, eg Chancellor of the Exchequer), the leaders of the two houses of parliament, and the holders of various traditional offices.

The cabinet's functions are the final determination of policy, control of government and coordination of government departments. The exercise of its functions is dependent upon

the incumbent party's (or parties') majority support in the House of Commons. Cabinet meetings are held in private, taking place once or twice a week during parliamentary sittings and less often during a recess. Proceedings are confidential, the members being bound by their oath as privy counsellors not to disclose information about the proceedings.

The convention of collective responsibility means that the cabinet acts unanimously even when cabinet ministers do not all agree on a subject. The policies of departmental ministers must be consistent with the policies of the government as a whole, and once the government's policy has been decided, each minister is expected to support it or resign.

The convention of ministerial responsibility holds a minister, as the political head of his or her department, accountable to parliament for the department's work. Departmental ministers usually decide all matters within their responsibility, although on matters of political importance they normally consult their colleagues collectively. A decision by a departmental minister is binding on the government as a whole.

POLITICAL PARTIES

Before the reign of William and Mary, the principal officers of state were chosen by and were responsible to the sovereign alone, and not to parliament or the nation at large. Such officers acted sometimes in concert with one another but more often independently, and the fall of one did not, of necessity, involve that of others, although all were liable to be dismissed at any moment.

In 1693 the Earl of Sunderland recommended to William III the advisability of selecting a ministry from the political party which enjoyed a majority in the House of Commons, and the first united ministry was drawn in 1696 from the Whigs, to which party the king owed his throne. This group became known as the 'junto' and was regarded with suspicion as a novelty in the political life of the nation, being a small section meeting in secret apart from the main body of ministers. It may be regarded as the forerunner of the cabinet and in the course of time it led to the establishment of the principle of joint responsibility of ministers, so that internal disagreement caused a change of personnel or resignation of the whole body of ministers.

The accession of George I, who was unfamiliar with the English language, led to a disinclination on the part of the sovereign to preside at meetings of his ministers and caused the emergence of a prime minister, a position first acquired by Robert Walpole in 1721 and retained by him without interruption for 20 years and 326 days. The office of prime minister was formally recognised in 1905 when it was established by royal warrant.

DEVELOPMENT OF PARTIES
In 1828 the Whigs became known as Liberals, a name originally given by opponents to imply laxity of principles, but gradually accepted by the party to indicate its claim to be pioneers and champions of political reform and progressive legislation. In 1861 a Liberal Registration Association was founded and Liberal Associations became widespread. In 1877 a National Liberal Federation was formed, with its headquarters in London. The Liberal Party was in power for long periods during the second half of the 19th century and for several years during the first quarter of the 20th century, but after a split in the party in 1931, the numbers elected remained small. In 1988 a majority of the Liberals agreed on a merger with the Social Democratic Party under the title Social and Liberal Democrats; since 1989 they have been known as the Liberal Democrats. A minority continue separately as the Liberal Party.

Soon after the change from Whig to Liberal, the Tory Party became known as Conservative, a name believed to have been invented by John Wilson Croker in 1830 and to have been generally adopted around the time of the passing of the Reform Act of 1832 – to indicate that the preservation of national institutions was the leading principle of the party. After the Home Rule crisis of 1886 the dissentient Liberals entered into a compact with the Conservatives, under which the latter undertook not to contest their seats, but a separate Liberal Unionist organisation was maintained until 1912, when it was united with the Conservatives.

Labour candidates for parliament made their first appearance at the general election of 1892, when there were 27 standing as Labour or Liberal-Labour. In 1900 the Labour Representation Committee (LRC) was set up in order to establish a distinct Labour group in parliament, with its own whips, its own policy, and a readiness to cooperate with any party which might be engaged in promoting legislation in the direct interests of labour. In 1906 the LRC became known as the Labour Party.

The Green Party was founded in 1973 and campaigns for social and environmental justice. The party began as 'People', was renamed the Ecology Party, and became the Green Party in 1985.

The Independent Group for Change (ChangeUK) was founded in 2019 after a group of Labour and Conservative MP's left their parties due to disagreement over the handling of Brexit and a perceived shift in both parties away from the centre ground towards the political left and right respectively. ChangeUK are a centrist, pro-European party who champion rational, evidence-based policy over ideology who believe in holding a second referendum on leaving the EU.

Plaid Cymru was founded in 1926 to provide an independent political voice for Wales and to campaign for self-government in Wales.

The Scottish National Party (SNP) was founded in 1934 to campaign for independence for Scotland and a referendum on the subject was held in September 2014 which culminated in a 'no' to independence result.

The Democratic Unionist Party (DUP) was founded in 1971 to resist moves by the Ulster Unionist Party which were considered a threat to the Union. Its aim is to maintain Northern Ireland as an integral part of the UK.

Sinn Fein first emerged in the 1900s as a federation of nationalist clubs. It is a left-wing republican party who rejects British Sovereignity following a policy of abstentionism at Westminster and strives for a united Ireland.

GOVERNMENT AND OPPOSITION

The government is formed by the party which wins the largest number of seats in the House of Commons at a general election, or which has the support of a majority of members in the House of Commons. By tradition, the leader of the majority party is asked by the sovereign to form a government, while the largest minority party becomes the official opposition with its own leader and a shadow cabinet. Leaders of the government and opposition sit on the front benches of the Commons with their supporters (the back-benchers) sitting behind them.

FINANCIAL SUPPORT

Financial support for opposition parties in the House of Commons was introduced in 1975 and is commonly known as Short Money, after Edward Short, the leader of the house at that time, who introduced the scheme. Short Money is only payable to those parties that secured at least two seats, or one seat and more than 150,000 votes, at the previous general election and is only intended to provide assistance for parliamentary duties. The amount payable is around £17,674 for every seat won at the most recent general election plus £35.30 for every 200 votes gained by the party (the figures are uprated annually in line with CPI). Short Money allocations for 2018–19 were:

DUP	£233,368
Green	£112,889
Labour	£7,879,790
Liberal Democrats	£644,680
Plaid Cymru	£101,920
SNP	£808,615

The sum paid to Sinn Fein and any other party that may choose not to take their seats in the House of Commons is calculated on the same basis as Short Money, but is known as Representative Money. Sinn Fein's allocation in 2018–19 was £165,539.

For the financial year which commenced on 1 April 2018, the leader of the opposition's office was allocated £823,420 for running costs.

Financial support for opposition parties in the House of Lords was introduced in 1996 and is commonly known as Cranborne Money, after former leader of the house, Viscount Cranborne.

The following list of political parties are those with at least one MP or sitting member of the House of Lords in the present parliament.

CONSERVATIVE PARTY

Conservative Campaign Headquarters, 4 Matthew Parker Street, London SW1H 9HQ
T 020-7222 9000 W www.conservatives.com

Parliamentary Party Leader, Rt. Hon. Boris Johnson, MP
Leader in the Lords, Rt. Hon. Baroness Evans of Bowes Park
Leader in the Commons and Lord President of the Council, Rt. Hon. Jacob Rees-Mogg, MP
Co-Chairs, Rt. Hon. James Cleverly, MP; Ben Elliot
Chief Executive (interim), Mike Chattey, OBE
Party Treasurer, Ehud Sheleg

GREEN PARTY

The Biscuit Factory, Unit 201 A Block, 100 Clements Road, London SE16 4DG
T 020-3691 9400 E office@greenparty.org.uk
W www.greenparty.org.uk

Party Leaders, Sian Berry, AM and Jonathan Bartley
Deputy Leader, Amelia Womack
Chair, Liz Reason
Finance Coordinator, Jon Nott

THE INDEPENDENT GROUP FOR CHANGE

52 Grosvenor Gardens, London SW1W OAU
W www.voteforchange.uk

Party Leader, Rt. Hon. Anna Soubry, MP
Deputy Leader, Chris Leslie, MP
Group Business Manager, Rt. Hon. Joan Ryan, MP

LABOUR PARTY

Labour Central, Kings Manor, Newcastle upon Tyne NE1 6PA
T 0845-092 2299 W www.labour.org.uk

General Secretary, Jennie Formby
General Secretary, Welsh Labour, Louise Magee
General Secretary (interim), Scottish Labour Party, Lorna Finlayson

SHADOW CABINET
Leader of the Opposition, Rt. Hon. Jeremy Corbyn, MP
Deputy Leader and Secretary of State for Digital, Culture, Media and Sport, Tom Watson, MP
Chancellor of the Exchequer, Rt. Hon. John McDonnell, MP
Foreign Secretary, Rt. Hon. Emily Thornberry, MP
Home Secretary, Rt. Hon. Diane Abbot, MP

Secretary of State for Business, Energy and Industrial Strategy, Rebecca Long-Bailey, MP
Secretary of State for Environment, Food and Rural Affairs, Sue Hayman, MP
Secretary of State for Communities and Local Government, Andrew Gwynne, MP
Secretary of State for Defence, Nia Griffith, MP
Secretary of State for Education, Angela Rayner, MP
Secretary of State for Exiting the European Union, Rt. Hon. Sir Keir Starmer, KCB, QC, MP
Secretary of State for Health, Jonathan Ashworth, MP
Secretary of State for Housing, Rt. Hon. John Healey, MP
Secretary of State for International Development, Dan Carden, MP
Secretary of State for International Trade, Barry Gardiner, MP
Lord Chancellor and Secretary of State for Justice, Richard Burgon, MP
Secretary of State for Scotland, Lesley Laird, MP
Secretary of State for Transport, Andy McDonald, MP
Chief Secretary to the Treasury, Peter Dowd, MP
Secretary of State for Wales, Christina Rees, MP
Secretary of State for Northern Ireland, Tony Lloyd, MP
Secretary of State for Work and Pensions, Margaret Greenwood, MP
Ministers for Mental Health and Social Care, Barbara Keeley, MP; Paula Sherriff, MP
Minister for Voter Engagement and Youth Affairs, Cat Smith, MP
Minister for Women and Equalities, Dawn Butler, MP
Chair and Co-National Campaign Co-ordinator, Ian Lavery, MP
Lord President of the Council and Minister for the Cabinet Office, Jon Trickett, MP
Leader of the House of Commons, Valerie Vaz, MP
Leader of the House of Lords, Rt. Hon. Baroness Smith of Basildon
Attorney General, Baroness Chakrabarti, CBE

LABOUR WHIPS
Chief Whip (Commons), Rt. Hon. Nick Brown, MP
Chief Whip (Lords), Rt. Hon. Lord McAvoy

LIBERAL DEMOCRATS
8–10 Great George Street, London SW1P 3AE
T 020-7022 0988 E info@libdems.org.uk W www.libdems.org.uk

Parliamentary Party Leader, Jo Swinson, CBE, MP
Deputy Party Leader, Rt. Hon. Sir Ed Davey, MP
Leader in the Lords, Rt. Hon. Lord Newby, OBE
President, Baroness Brinton

NORTHERN IRELAND DEMOCRATIC UNIONIST PARTY
91 Dundela Avenue, Belfast BT4 3BU
T 028-9047 1155
E info@mydup.com W www.mydup.com

Parliamentary Party Leader, Rt. Hon. Arlene Foster, MLA
Deputy Leader & House of Commons Group Leader, Rt. Hon. Nigel Dodds, OBE, MP
Chair, Lord Morrow, MLA

PLAID CYMRU – THE PARTY OF WALES
Ty Gwynfor, Anson Court, Atlantic Wharf, Caerdydd CF10 4AL
T 029-2047 2272 E post@plaidcymru.org W www.partyof.wales

Party Leader, Adam Price, AM
Hon. Party President, Rt. Hon. Lord Wigley
Parliamentary Group Leader, Liz Saville Roberts, MP
Chair, Alun Ffred Jones
Chief Executive, Gareth Clubb

SCOTTISH NATIONAL PARTY
Gordon Lamb House, 3 Jackson's Entry, Edinburgh EH8 8PJ
T 0800-633 5432 E info@snp.org W www.snp.org

Westminster Parliamentary Party Leader, Rt. Hon. Ian Blackford, MP
Westminster Parliamentary Party Chief Whip, Patrick Grady, MP
First Minister of Scotland and Leader of the SNP, Rt. Hon. Nicola Sturgeon, MSP
Deputy Leader, Keith Brown, MSP
Party President, Ian Hudghton
National Treasurer, Colin Beattie, MSP
Chief Executive, Peter Murrell

SINN FEIN
53 Falls Road, Belfast BT12 4PD
T 028-9034 7350 E admin@sinnfein.ie W www.sinnfein.ie

Party President, Mary Lou McDonald, TD
Vice-President, Michelle O'Neill, MLA
Chair, Declan Kearney, MLA

MEMBERS OF PARLIAMENT *as at 10 September 2019*

KEY

* Previously an MP for this seat in the 2015–17 parliament

† Previously an MP for this seat in any parliament prior to the 2015–17 parliament

‡ Previously an MP for a different seat in any previous parliament

** Elected via a by-election after the 2017 General Election

* **Abbott**, Rt. Hon. Diane (*b.* 1953) *Lab., Hackney North & Stoke Newington*, Maj. 35,139

* **Abrahams**, Debbie (*b.* 1960) *Lab., Oldham East & Saddleworth*, Maj. 8,182

* **Adams**, Nigel (*b.* 1966) *C., Selby & Ainsty*, Maj. 13,772

Afolami, Bim (*b.* 1986) *C., Hitchin & Harpenden*, Maj. 12,031

* **Afriyie**, Adam (*b.* 1965) *C., Windsor*, Maj. 22,384

* **Aldous**, Peter (*b.* 1961) *C., Waveney*, Maj. 9,215

* **Ali**, Rushanara (*b.* 1975) *Lab., Bethnal Green & Bow*, Maj. 35,393

* **Allan**, Lucy (*b.* 1964) *C., Telford*, Maj. 720

* **Allen**, Heidi (*b.* 1975) *Ind., Cambridgeshire South*, Maj. 15,952

* **Allin-Khan**, Dr Rosena (*b.* 1977) *Lab., Tooting*, Maj. 15,458

Amesbury, Mike (*b.* 1969) *Lab., Weaver Vale*, Maj. 3,928

*‡ **Amess**, Sir David (*b.* 1952) *C., Southend West*, Maj. 10,000

* **Andrew**, Stuart (*b.* 1971) *C., Pudsey*, Maj. 331

Antoniazzi, Tonia (*b.* 1971) *Lab., Gower*, Maj. 3,269

* **Argar**, Edward (*b.* 1977) *C., Charnwood*, Maj. 16,341

* **Ashworth**, Jon (*b.* 1978) *Lab. Co-op, Leicester South*, Maj. 26,261

* **Atkins**, Victoria (*b.* 1976) *C., Louth & Horncastle*, Maj. 19,641

* **Austin**, Ian (*b.* 1965) *Ind., Dudley North*, Maj. 22

* **Bacon**, Richard (*b.* 1962) *C., Norfolk South*, Maj. 16,678

Badenoch, Kemi (*b.* 1980) *C., Saffron Walden*, Maj. 24,966

* **Bailey**, Adrian (*b.* 1945) *Lab. Co-op, West Bromwich West*, Maj. 4,460

* **Baker**, Steve (*b.* 1971) *C., Wycombe*, Maj. 6,578

* **Baldwin**, Harriett (*b.* 1960) *C., Worcestershire West*, Maj. 21,328

* **Barclay**, Rt. Hon. Stephen (*b.* 1972) *C., Cambridgeshire North East*, Maj. 21,270

* **Bardell**, Hannah (*b.* 1984) *SNP, Livingston*, Maj. 3,878

* **Baron**, John (*b.* 1959) *C., Basildon & Billericay*, Maj. 13,400

* **Barron**, Rt. Hon. Sir Kevin (*b.* 1946) *Lab., Rother Valley*, Maj. 3,882

* **Bebb**, Guto (*b.* 1968) *Ind., Aberconwy*, Maj. 635

*‡ **Beckett**, Rt. Hon. Dame Margaret, DBE (*b.* 1943) *Lab., Derby South*, Maj. 11,248

** **Begley**, Órfhlaith (*b.* 1992) *SF, Tyrone West*, Maj. 7,956

* **Bellingham**, Sir Henry (*b.* 1955) *C., Norfolk North West*, Maj. 13,788

* **Benn**, Rt. Hon. Hilary (*b.* 1953) *Lab., Leeds Central*, Maj. 23,698

* **Benyon**, Rt. Hon. Richard (*b.* 1960) *Ind., Newbury*, Maj. 24,380

* **Bercow**, Rt. Hon. John (*b.* 1963) *Speaker, Buckingham*, Maj. 25,725

* **Beresford**, Sir Paul (*b.* 1946) *C., Mole Valley*, Maj. 24,137

* **Berger**, Luciana (*b.* 1981) *LD, Liverpool Wavertree*, Maj. 29,466

* **Berry**, Rt. Hon. Jake (*b.* 1978) *C., Rossendale & Darwen*, Maj. 3,216

* **Betts**, Clive (*b.* 1950) *Lab., Sheffield South East*, Maj. 11,798

* **Black**, Mhairi (*b.* 1994) *SNP, Paisley & Renfrewshire South*, Maj. 2,541

* **Blackford**, Rt. Hon. Ian (*b.* 1961) *SNP, Ross, Skye & Lochaber*, Maj. 5,919

* **Blackman**, Bob (*b.* 1956) *C., Harrow East*, Maj. 1,757

* **Blackman**, Kirsty (*b.* 1986) *SNP, Aberdeen North*, Maj. 4,139

* **Blackman-Woods**, Roberta, PHD (*b.* 1957) *Lab., Durham, City of*, Maj. 12,364

* **Blomfield**, Paul (*b.* 1953) *Lab., Sheffield Central*, Maj. 27,748

* **Blunt**, Crispin (*b.* 1960) *C., Reigate*, Maj. 17,614

* **Boles**, Nick (*b.* 1965) *Ind., Grantham & Stamford*, Maj. 20,094

* **Bone**, Peter (*b.* 1952) *C., Wellingborough*, Maj. 12,460

*‡ **Bottomley**, Sir Peter (*b.* 1944) *C., Worthing West*, Maj. 12,090

Bowie, Andrew (*b.* 1988) *C., Aberdeenshire West & Kincardine*, Maj. 7,950

* **Brabin**, Tracy (*b.* 1961) *Lab. Co-op, Batley & Spen*, Maj. 8,961

Bradley, Ben (*b.* 1989) *C., Mansfield*, Maj. 1,057

* **Bradley**, Rt. Hon. Karen (*b.* 1970) *C., Staffordshire Moorlands*, Maj. 10,830

* **Bradshaw**, Rt. Hon. Ben (*b.* 1960) *Lab., Exeter*, Maj. 16,117

* **Brady**, Sir Graham (*b.* 1967) *C., Altrincham & Sale West*, Maj. 6,426

* **Brady**, Mickey (*b.* 1950) *SF, Newry & Armagh*, Maj. 12,489

* **Brake**, Rt. Hon. Tom (*b.* 1962) *LD, Carshalton & Wallington*, Maj. 1,369

* **Braverman**, Suella (*b.* 1980) *C., Fareham*, Maj. 21,555

* **Brennan**, Kevin (*b.* 1959) *Lab., Cardiff West*, Maj. 12,551

Brereton, Jack (*b.* 1991) *C., Stoke-on-Trent South*, Maj. 663

* **Bridgen**, Andrew (*b.* 1964) *C., Leicestershire North West*, Maj. 13,286

* **Brine**, Steve (*b.* 1974) *Ind., Winchester*, Maj. 9,999

* **Brock**, Deidre (*b.* 1961) *SNP, Edinburgh North & Leith*, Maj. 1,625

*‡ **Brokenshire**, Rt. Hon. James (*b.* 1968) *C., Old Bexley & Sidcup*, Maj. 15,466

* **Brown**, Alan (*b.* 1970) *SNP, Kilmarnock & Loudoun*, Maj. 6,269

* **Brown**, Lyn (*b.* 1960) *Lab., West Ham*, Maj. 36,754

* **Brown**, Rt. Hon. Nick (*b.* 1950) *Lab., Newcastle upon Tyne East*, Maj. 19,261

* **Bruce**, Fiona (*b.* 1957) *C., Congleton*, Maj. 12,619

* **Bryant**, Chris (*b.* 1962) *Lab., Rhondda*, Maj. 13,746

* **Buck**, Karen (*b.* 1958) *Lab., Westminster North*, Maj. 11,512

* **Buckland**, Rt. Hon. Robert (*b.* 1968) *C., Swindon South*, Maj. 2,464

* **Burden**, Richard (*b.* 1954) *Lab., Birmingham Northfield*, Maj. 4,667

Burghart, Alex (*b.* 1977) *C., Brentwood & Ongar*, Maj. 24,002

* **Burgon**, Richard (*b.* 1980) *Lab., Leeds East*, Maj. 12,752

* **Burns**, Conor (*b.* 1972) *C., Bournemouth West*, Maj. 7,711

*‡ **Burt**, Rt. Hon. Alistair (*b.* 1955) *Ind., Bedfordshire North East*, Maj. 20,862

*‡ **Butler**, Dawn (*b.* 1969) *Lab., Brent Central*, Maj. 27,997

* **Byrne**, Rt. Hon. Liam (*b.* 1970) *Lab., Birmingham Hodge Hill*, Maj. 31,026

† **Cable**, Rt. Hon. Sir Vince, PHD (*b.* 1943) *LD, Twickenham*, Maj. 9,762

* **Cadbury**, Ruth (*b.* 1959) *Lab., Brentford & Isleworth*, Maj. 12,182

* **Cairns**, Rt. Hon. Alun (*b.* 1970) *C., Vale of Glamorgan*, Maj. 2,190

* **Cameron**, Dr Lisa (*b.* 1972) *SNP, East Kilbride, Strathaven & Lesmahagow*, Maj. 3,866

* **Campbell**, Rt. Hon. Sir Alan (*b.* 1957) *Lab., Tynemouth*, Maj. 11,666

* **Campbell**, Gregory (*b.* 1953) *DUP, Londonderry East*, Maj. 8,842

* **Campbell**, Ronnie (*b.* 1943) *Lab., Blyth Valley*, Maj. 7,915

Carden, Dan (b. 1987) Lab., Liverpool Walton, Maj. 32,551
* Carmichael, Rt. Hon. Alistair (b. 1965) LD, Orkney & Shetland, Maj. 4,563
* Cartlidge, James (b. 1974) C., Suffolk South, Maj. 17,749
* Cash, Sir William (b. 1940) C., Stone, Maj. 17,495
* Caulfield, Maria (b. 1974) C., Lewes, Maj. 5,508
* Chalk, Alex (b. 1977) C., Cheltenham, Maj. 2,569
* Champion, Sarah (b. 1969) Lab., Rotherham, Maj. 11,387
* Chapman, Douglas (b. 1955) SNP, Dunfermline & Fife West, Maj. 844
* Chapman, Jenny (b. 1973) Lab., Darlington, Maj. 3,280
Charalambous, Bambos (b. 1967) Lab., Enfield Southgate, Maj. 4,355
* Cherry, Joanna (b. 1966) SNP, Edinburgh South West, Maj. 1,097
* Chishti, Rehman (b. 1978) C., Gillingham & Rainham, Maj. 9,430
*‡ Chope, Sir Christopher, OBE (b. 1947) C., Christchurch, Maj. 25,171
* Churchill, Jo (b. 1964) C., Bury St Edmunds, Maj. 18,441
Clark, Colin (b. 1968) C., Gordon, Maj. 2,607
* Clark, Rt. Hon. Greg, PHD (b. 1967) Ind., Tunbridge Wells, Maj. 16,465
* Clarke, Rt. Hon. Kenneth, CH (b. 1940) Ind., Rushcliffe, Maj. 8,010
Clarke, Simon (b. 1984) C., Middlesbrough South & Cleveland East, Maj. 1,020
* Cleverly, Rt. Hon. James (b. 1969) C., Braintree, Maj. 18,422
* Clifton-Brown, Sir Geoffrey (b. 1953) C., Cotswolds, The, Maj. 25,499
* Clwyd, Rt. Hon. Ann (b. 1937) Lab., Cynon Valley, Maj. 13,238
* Coaker, Vernon (b. 1953) Lab., Gedling, Maj. 4,694
* Coffey, Ann (b. 1946) ChangeUK, Stockport, Maj. 14,477
* Coffey, Rt. Hon. Thérèse, PHD (b. 1971) C., Suffolk Coastal, Maj. 16,012
* Collins, Damian (b. 1974) C., Folkestone & Hythe, Maj. 15,411
* Cooper, Julie (b. 1960) Lab., Burnley, Maj. 6,353
* Cooper, Rosie (b. 1950) Lab., Lancashire West, Maj. 11,689
* Cooper, Rt. Hon. Yvette (b. 1969) Lab., Normanton, Pontefract & Castleford, Maj. 14,499
* Corbyn, Rt. Hon. Jeremy (b. 1949) Lab., Islington North, Maj. 33,215
* Costa, Alberto (b. 1971) C., Leicestershire South, Maj. 18,631
* Courts, Robert (b. 1978) C., Witney, Maj. 21,241
* Cowan, Ronnie (b. 1959) SNP, Inverclyde, Maj. 384
* Cox, Rt. Hon. Geoffrey (b. 1960) C., Devon West & Torridge, Maj. 20,686
* Coyle, Neil (b. 1978) Lab., Bermondsey & Old Southwark, Maj. 12,972
* Crabb, Rt. Hon. Stephen (b. 1973) C., Preseli Pembrokeshire, Maj. 314
* Crausby, Sir David (b. 1946) Lab., Bolton North East, Maj. 3,797
* Crawley, Angela (b. 1987) SNP, Lanark & Hamilton East, Maj. 266
* Creagh, Mary (b. 1967) Lab., Wakefield, Maj. 2,176
* Creasy, Stella, PHD (b. 1977) Lab. Co-op, Walthamstow, Maj. 32,017
* Crouch, Tracey (b. 1975) C., Chatham & Aylesford, Maj. 10,458
* Cruddas, Jon (b. 1962) Lab., Dagenham & Rainham, Maj. 4,652
*‡ Cryer, John (b. 1964) Lab., Leyton & Wanstead, Maj. 22,607
* Cummins, Judith (b. 1967) Lab., Bradford South, Maj. 6,700
* Cunningham, Alex (b. 1955) Lab., Stockton North, Maj. 8,715
* Cunningham, Jim (b. 1941) Lab., Coventry South, Maj. 7,947
** Daby, Janet (b. 1972) Lab., Lewisham East, Maj. 5,629

* Dakin, Nic (b. 1955) Lab., Scunthorpe, Maj. 3,431
† Davey, Rt. Hon. Sir Edward (b. 1965) LD, Kingston & Surbiton, Maj. 4,124
* David, Wayne (b. 1957) Lab., Caerphilly, Maj. 12,078
* Davies, David (b. 1970) C., Monmouth, Maj. 8,206
*‡ Davies, Geraint (b. 1960) Lab. Co-op, Swansea West, Maj. 10,598
* Davies, Glyn (b. 1944) C., Montgomeryshire, Maj. 9,285
* Davies, Mims (b. 1975) C., Eastleigh, Maj. 14,179
* Davies, Philip (b. 1972) C., Shipley, Maj. 4,681
* Davis, Rt. Hon. David (b. 1948) C., Haltemprice & Howden, Maj. 15,405
* Day, Martyn (b. 1971) SNP, Linlithgow & Falkirk East, Maj. 2,919
De Cordova, Marsha (b. 1976) Lab., Battersea, Maj. 2,416
* De Piero, Gloria (b. 1972) Lab., Ashfield, Maj. 441
* Debbonaire, Thangam (b. 1966) Lab., Bristol West, Maj. 37,336
Dent Coad, Emma (b. 1954) Lab., Kensington, Maj. 20
Dhesi, Tanmanjeet (b. 1978) Lab., Slough, Maj. 16,998
* Dinenage, Caroline (b. 1971) C., Gosport, Maj. 17,211
* Djanogly, Jonathan (b. 1965) C., Huntingdon, Maj. 14,475
Docherty, Leo (b. 1976) C., Aldershot, Maj. 11,478
* Docherty-Hughes, Martin (b. 1971) SNP, Dunbartonshire West, Maj. 2,288
Dodds, Anneliese, PHD (b. 1978) Lab. Co-op, Oxford East, Maj. 23,284
** Dodds, Jane (b. 1963) LD, Brecon & Radnorshire, Maj. 1,425
* Dodds, Rt. Hon. Nigel, OBE (b. 1958) DUP, Belfast North, Maj. 2,081
* Donaldson, Rt. Hon. Sir Jeffrey (b. 1962) DUP, Lagan Valley, Maj. 19,229
* Donelan, Michelle (b. 1984) C., Chippenham, Maj. 16,630
* Dorries, Nadine (b. 1957) C., Bedfordshire Mid, Maj. 20,983
* Double, Steve (b. 1966) C., St Austell & Newquay, Maj. 11,142
* Doughty, Stephen (b. 1980) Lab. Co-op, Cardiff South & Penarth, Maj. 14,864
* Dowd, Peter (b. 1957) Lab., Bootle, Maj. 36,200
* Dowden, Rt. Hon. Oliver, CBE (b. 1978) C., Hertsmere, Maj. 16,951
* Doyle-Price, Jackie (b. 1969) C., Thurrock, Maj. 345
* Drax, Richard (b. 1958) C., Dorset South, Maj. 11,695
† Drew, David (b. 1952) Lab. Co-op, Stroud, Maj. 687
* Dromey, Jack (b. 1948) Lab., Birmingham Erdington, Maj. 7,285
* Duddridge, James (b. 1971) C., Rochford & Southend East, Maj. 5,548
Duffield, Rosie (b. 1971) Lab., Canterbury, Maj. 187
Duguid, David (b. 1970) C., Banff & Buchan, Maj. 3,693
* Duncan, Rt. Hon. Sir Alan, KCMG (b. 1957) C., Rutland & Melton, Maj. 23,104
* Duncan Smith, Rt. Hon. Iain (b. 1954) C., Chingford & Woodford Green, Maj. 2,438
* Dunne, Rt. Hon. Philip (b. 1958) C., Ludlow, Maj. 19,286
* Eagle, Angela (b. 1961) Lab., Wallasey, Maj. 23,320
* Eagle, Maria (b. 1961) Lab., Garston & Halewood, Maj. 32,149
* Edwards, Jonathan (b. 1976) PC, Carmarthen East & Dinefwr, Maj. 3,908
* Efford, Clive (b. 1958) Lab., Eltham, Maj. 6,296
* Elliott, Julie (b. 1963) Lab., Sunderland Central, Maj. 9,997
* Ellis, Michael (b. 1967) C., Northampton North, Maj. 807
* Ellman, Dame Louise, DBE (b. 1945) Lab. Co-op, Liverpool Riverside, Maj. 35,947
* Ellwood, Rt. Hon. Tobias (b. 1966) C., Bournemouth East, Maj. 7,937
* Elmore, Chris (b. 1983) Lab., Ogmore, Maj. 13,871
* Elphicke, Charlie (b. 1971) C., Dover, Maj. 6,437

* **Esterson**, Bill (b. 1966) Lab., Sefton Central, Maj. 15,618
* **Eustice**, George (b. 1971) C., Camborne & Redruth, Maj. 1,577
* **Evans**, Chris (b. 1976) Lab. Co-op, Islwyn, Maj. 11,412
* **Evans**, Nigel (b. 1957) C., Ribble Valley, Maj. 13,199
* **Evennett**, Rt. Hon. Sir David (b. 1949) C., Bexleyheath & Crayford, Maj. 9,073
* **Fabricant**, Michael (b. 1950) C., Lichfield, Maj. 18,581
*‡ **Fallon**, Rt. Hon. Sir Michael, KCB (b. 1952) C., Sevenoaks, Maj. 21,917
* **Farrelly**, Paul (b. 1962) Lab., Newcastle-under-Lyme, Maj. 30
* **Farron**, Tim (b. 1970) LD, Westmorland & Lonsdale, Maj. 777
* **Fellows**, Marion (b. 1949) SNP, Motherwell & Wishaw, Maj. 318
* **Field**, Rt. Hon. Frank (b. 1942) Ind., Birkenhead, Maj. 25,514
* **Field**, Rt. Hon. Mark (b. 1964) C., Cities of London & Westminster, Maj. 3,148
* **Fitzpatrick**, Jim (b. 1952) Lab., Poplar & Limehouse, Maj. 27,712
* **Fletcher**, Colleen (b. 1954) Lab., Coventry North East, Maj. 15,580
* **Flint**, Rt. Hon. Caroline (b. 1961) Lab., Don Valley, Maj. 5,169
** **Forbes**, Lisa (b. 1969) Lab., Peterborough, Maj. 683
Ford, Vicky (b. 1967) C., Chelmsford, Maj. 13,572
* **Foster**, Kevin (b. 1978) C., Torbay, Maj. 14,283
* **Fovargue**, Yvonne (b. 1956) Lab., Makerfield, Maj. 13,542
* **Fox**, Rt. Hon. Dr Liam (b. 1961) C., Somerset North, Maj. 17,103
* **Foxcroft**, Vicky (b. 1977) Lab., Lewisham Deptford, Maj. 34,899
* **Francois**, Rt. Hon. Mark (b. 1965) C., Rayleigh & Wickford, Maj. 23,450
* **Frazer**, Lucy (b. 1972) C., Cambridgeshire South East, Maj. 16,158
* **Freeman**, George (b. 1967) C., Norfolk Mid, Maj. 16,086
* **Freer**, Mike (b. 1960) C., Finchley & Golders Green, Maj. 1,657
Frith, James (b. 1977) Lab., Bury North, Maj. 4,375
* **Furniss**, Gill (b. 1957) Lab., Sheffield Brightside & Hillsborough, Maj. 19,143
* **Fysh**, Marcus (b. 1970) C., Yeovil, Maj. 14,723
Gaffney, Hugh (b. 1963) Lab., Coatbridge, Chryston & Bellshill, Maj. 1,586
* **Gale**, Rt. Hon. Sir Roger (b. 1943) C., Thanet North, Maj. 10,738
* **Gapes**, Mike (b. 1952) ChangeUK, Ilford South, Maj. 31,647
* **Gardiner**, Barry (b. 1957) Lab., Brent North, Maj. 17,061
* **Garnier**, Mark (b. 1963) C., Wyre Forest, Maj. 13,334
* **Gauke**, Rt. Hon. David (b. 1971) Ind., Hertfordshire South West, Maj. 19,550
George, Ruth (b. 1969) Lab., High Peak, Maj. 2,322
* **Gethins**, Stephen (b. 1976) SNP, Fife North East, Maj. 2
* **Ghani**, Nusrat (b. 1972) C., Wealden, Maj. 23,628
* **Gibb**, Rt. Hon. Nick (b. 1960) C., Bognor Regis & Littlehampton, Maj. 17,494
* **Gibson**, Patricia (b. 1968) SNP, Ayrshire North & Arran, Maj. 3,633
† **Gildernew**, Michelle (b. 1970) SF, Fermanagh & South Tyrone, Maj. 875
Gill, Preet (b. 1972) Lab. Co-op, Birmingham Edgbaston, Maj. 6,917
* **Gillan**, Rt. Hon. Dame Cheryl, DBE (b. 1952) C., Chesham & Amersham, Maj. 22,140
Girvan, Paul (b. 1963) DUP, Antrim South, Maj. 3,208
* **Glen**, John (b. 1974) C., Salisbury, Maj. 17,333
* **Glindon**, Mary (b. 1957) Lab., Tyneside North, Maj. 19,284
* **Godsiff**, Roger (b. 1946) Lab., Birmingham Hall Green, Maj. 33,944

* **Goldsmith**, Rt. Hon. Zac (b. 1975) C., Richmond Park, Maj. 45
* **Goodman**, Helen (b. 1958) Lab., Bishop Auckland, Maj. 502
* **Goodwill**, Rt. Hon. Robert (b. 1956) C., Scarborough & Whitby, Maj. 3,435
* **Gove**, Rt. Hon. Michael (b. 1967) C., Surrey Heath, Maj. 24,943
* **Grady**, Patrick (b. 1980) SNP, Glasgow North, Maj. 1,060
Graham, Luke (b. 1985) C., Ochil & Perthshire South, Maj. 3,359
* **Graham**, Richard (b. 1958) C., Gloucester, Maj. 5,520
Grant, Bill (b. 1951) C., Ayr, Carrick & Cumnock, Maj. 2,774
* **Grant**, Helen (b. 1961) C., Maidstone & The Weald, Maj. 17,704
* **Grant**, Peter (b. 1961) SNP, Glenrothes, Maj. 3,267
* **Gray**, James (b. 1954) C., Wiltshire North, Maj. 22,877
* **Gray**, Neil (b. 1986) SNP, Airdrie & Shotts, Maj. 195
* **Grayling**, Rt. Hon. Chris (b. 1962) C., Epsom & Ewell, Maj. 20,475
* **Green**, Chris (b. 1973) C., Bolton West, Maj. 936
* **Green**, Rt. Hon. Damian (b. 1956) C., Ashford, Maj. 17,478
* **Green**, Kate (b. 1960) Lab., Stretford & Urmston, Maj. 19,705
* **Greening**, Rt. Hon. Justine (b. 1969) Ind., Putney, Maj. 1,554
* **Greenwood**, Lilian (b. 1966) Lab., Nottingham South, Maj. 15,162
* **Greenwood**, Margaret (b. 1959) Lab., Wirral West, Maj. 5,365
* **Grieve**, Rt. Hon. Dominic (b. 1956) Ind., Beaconsfield, Maj. 24,543
* **Griffith**, Nia (b. 1956) Lab., Llanelli, Maj. 12,024
* **Griffiths**, Andrew (b. 1970) C., Burton, Maj. 10,047
‡ **Grogan**, John (b. 1956) Lab., Keighley, Maj. 249
* **Gwynne**, Andrew (b. 1974) Lab., Denton & Reddish, Maj. 14,077
* **Gyimah**, Sam (b. 1976) Ind., Surrey East, Maj. 23,914
* **Haigh**, Louise (b. 1987) Lab., Sheffield Heeley, Maj. 13,828
Hair, Kirstene (b. 1989) C., Angus, Maj. 2,645
* **Halfon**, Rt. Hon. Robert (b. 1969) C., Harlow, Maj. 7,031
* **Hall**, Luke (b. 1986) C., Thornbury & Yate, Maj. 12,071
* **Hamilton**, Fabian (b. 1955) Lab., Leeds North East, Maj. 16,991
* **Hammond**, Rt. Hon. Philip (b. 1955) Ind., Runnymede & Weybridge, Maj. 18,050
* **Hammond**, Stephen (b. 1962) Ind., Wimbledon, Maj. 5,622
* **Hancock**, Rt. Hon. Matt (b. 1978) C., Suffolk West, Maj. 17,063
* **Hands**, Rt. Hon. Greg (b. 1965) C., Chelsea & Fulham, Maj. 8,188
* **Hanson**, Rt. Hon. David (b. 1957) Lab., Delyn, Maj. 4,240
Hardy, Emma (b. 1980) Lab., Hull West & Hessle, Maj. 8,025
* **Harman**, Rt. Hon. Harriet (b. 1950) Lab., Camberwell & Peckham, Maj. 37,316
* **Harper**, Rt. Hon. Mark (b. 1970) C., Forest of Dean, Maj. 9,502
* **Harrington**, Richard (b. 1957) Ind., Watford, Maj. 2,092
* **Harris**, Carolyn (b. 1960) Lab., Swansea East, Maj. 13,168
* **Harris**, Rebecca (b. 1967) C., Castle Point, Maj. 18,872
* **Harrison**, Trudy (b. 1976) C., Copeland, Maj. 1,695
* **Hart**, Simon (b. 1963) C., Carmarthen West & Pembrokeshire South, Maj. 3,110
* **Hayes**, Helen (b. 1974) Lab., Dulwich & West Norwood, Maj. 28,156
* **Hayes**, Rt. Hon. Sir John, CBE (b. 1958) C., South Holland & The Deepings, Maj. 24,897
* **Hayman**, Sue (b. 1962) Lab., Workington, Maj. 3,925
Hazzard, Chris (b. 1984) SF, Down South, Maj. 2,446
* **Heald**, Sir Oliver (b. 1954) C., Hertfordshire North East, Maj. 16,835
* **Healey**, Rt. Hon. John (b. 1960) Lab., Wentworth & Dearne, Maj. 14,803

* **Heappey**, James (*b.* 1981) *C., Wells,* Maj. 7,582
* **Heaton-Harris**, Chris (*b.* 1967) *C., Daventry,* Maj. 21,734
* **Heaton-Jones**, Peter (*b.* 1963) *C., Devon North,* Maj. 4,332
* **Henderson**, Gordon (*b.* 1948) *C., Sittingbourne & Sheppey,* Maj. 15,211
* **Hendrick**, Sir Mark (*b.* 1958) *Lab. Co-op, Preston,* Maj. 15,723
* **Hendry**, Drew (*b.* 1964) *SNP, Inverness, Nairn, Badenoch & Strathspey,* Maj. 4,924
* **Hepburn**, Stephen (*b.* 1959) *Lab., Jarrow,* Maj. 17,263
* **Herbert**, Rt. Hon. Nick, CBE (*b.* 1963) *C., Arundel & South Downs,* Maj. 23,883
* **Hermon**, Lady (Sylvia) (*b.* 1955) *Ind., Down North,* Maj. 1,208
Hill, Mike (*b.* 1963) *Lab., Hartlepool,* Maj. 7,650
* **Hillier**, Meg (*b.* 1969) *Lab. Co-op, Hackney South & Shoreditch,* Maj. 37,931
* **Hinds**, Rt. Hon. Damian (*b.* 1969) *C., Hampshire East,* Maj. 25,852
* **Hoare**, Simon (*b.* 1969) *C., Dorset North,* Maj. 25,777
Hobhouse, Wera (*b.* 1960) *LD, Bath,* Maj. 5,694
* **Hodge**, Rt. Hon. Dame Margaret, DBE (*b.* 1944) *Lab., Barking,* Maj. 21,608
* **Hodgson**, Sharon (*b.* 1966) *Lab., Washington & Sunderland West,* Maj. 12,940
* **Hoey**, Kate (*b.* 1946) *Lab., Vauxhall,* Maj. 20,250
* **Hollern**, Kate (*b.* 1955) *Lab., Blackburn,* Maj. 20,368
* **Hollingbery**, George (*b.* 1963) *C., Meon Valley,* Maj. 25,692
* **Hollinrake**, Kevin (*b.* 1963) *C., Thirsk & Malton,* Maj. 19,001
* **Hollobone**, Philip (*b.* 1964) *C., Kettering,* Maj. 10,562
* **Holloway**, Adam (*b.* 1965) *C., Gravesham,* Maj. 9,347
* **Hopkins**, Kelvin (*b.* 1941) *Ind., Luton North,* Maj. 14,364
* **Hosie**, Stewart (*b.* 1963) *SNP, Dundee East,* Maj. 6,645
* **Howarth**, Rt. Hon. Sir George (*b.* 1949) *Lab., Knowsley,* Maj. 42,214
* **Howell**, John (*b.* 1955) *C., Henley,* Maj. 22,294
* **Hoyle**, Rt. Hon. Sir Lindsay (*b.* 1957) *Lab., Chorley,* Maj. 7,512
* **Huddleston**, Nigel (*b.* 1970) *C., Worcestershire Mid,* Maj. 23,326
Hughes, Eddie (*b.* 1968) *C., Walsall North,* Maj. 2,601
* **Hunt**, Rt. Hon. Jeremy (*b.* 1966) *C., Surrey South West,* Maj. 21,590
* **Huq**, Dr Rupa (*b.* 1972) *Lab., Ealing Central & Acton,* Maj. 13,807
* **Hurd**, Rt. Hon. Nick (*b.* 1962) *C., Ruislip, Northwood & Pinner,* Maj. 13,980
* **Hussain**, Imran (*b.* 1978) *Lab., Bradford East,* Maj. 20,540
Jack, Rt. Hon. Alister (*b.* 1964) *C., Dumfries & Galloway,* Maj. 5,643
* **James**, Margot (*b.* 1957) *Ind., Stourbridge,* Maj. 7,654
Jardine, Christine (*b.* 1960) *LD, Edinburgh West,* Maj. 2,988
* **Jarvis**, Dan (*b.* 1972) *Lab., Barnsley Central,* Maj. 15,546
* **Javid**, Rt. Hon. Sajid (*b.* 1969) *C., Bromsgrove,* Maj. 16,573
* **Jayawardena**, Ranil (*b.* 1986) *C., Hampshire North East,* Maj. 27,772
* **Jenkin**, Hon. Sir Bernard (*b.* 1959) *C., Harwich & Essex North,* Maj. 14,356
* **Jenkyns**, Andrea (*b.* 1974) *C., Morley & Outwood,* Maj. 2,104
* **Jenrick**, Rt. Hon. Robert (*b.* 1982) *C., Newark,* Maj. 18,149
*‡ **Johnson**, Rt. Hon. Boris (*b.* 1964) *C., Uxbridge & Ruislip South,* Maj. 5,034
* **Johnson**, Caroline (*b.* 1977) *C., Sleaford & North Hykeham,* Maj. 25,237
* **Johnson**, Diana (*b.* 1966) *Lab., Hull North,* Maj. 14,262
* **Johnson**, Gareth (*b.* 1969) *C., Dartford,* Maj. 13,186
* **Johnson**, Rt. Hon. Jo (*b.* 1971) *C., Orpington,* Maj. 19,461

* **Jones**, Andrew (*b.* 1963) *C., Harrogate & Knaresborough,* Maj. 18,168
Jones, Darren (*b.* 1986) *Lab., Bristol North West,* Maj. 4,761
* **Jones**, Rt. Hon. David (*b.* 1952) *C., Clwyd West,* Maj. 3,437
* **Jones**, Gerald (*b.* 1970) *Lab., Merthyr Tydfil & Rhymney,* Maj. 16,334
* **Jones**, Graham (*b.* 1966) *Lab., Hyndburn,* Maj. 5,815
* **Jones**, Helen (*b.* 1954) *Lab., Warrington North,* Maj. 9,582
* **Jones**, Rt. Hon. Kevan (*b.* 1964) *Lab., Durham North,* Maj. 12,939
* **Jones**, Marcus (*b.* 1974) *C., Nuneaton,* Maj. 4,739
** **Jones**, Ruth, (*b.* 1962) *Lab., Newport West* Maj. 1,951
Jones, Sarah (*b.* 1972) *Lab., Croydon Central,* Maj. 5,652
* **Jones**, Susan Elan (*b.* 1968) *Lab., Clwyd South,* Maj. 4,356
* **Kane**, Mike (*b.* 1969) *Lab., Wythenshawe & Sale East,* Maj. 14,944
* **Kawczynski**, Daniel (*b.* 1972) *C., Shrewsbury & Atcham,* Maj. 6,627
Keegan, Gillian (*b.* 1968) *C., Chichester,* Maj. 22,621
* **Keeley**, Barbara (*b.* 1952) *Lab., Worsley & Eccles South,* Maj. 8,379
* **Kendall**, Liz (*b.* 1971) *Lab., Leicester West,* Maj. 11,060
* **Kennedy**, Seema (*b.* 1974) *C., South Ribble,* Maj. 7,421
Kerr, Stephen (*b.* 1960) *C., Stirling,* Maj. 148
Khan, Afzal, CBE (*b.* 1958) *Lab., Manchester Gorton,* Maj. 31,730
Killen, Ged (*b.* 1986) *Lab. Co-op, Rutherglen & Hamilton West,* Maj. 265
* **Kinnock**, Stephen (*b.* 1970) *Lab., Aberavon,* Maj. 16,761
*‡ **Knight**, Rt. Hon. Sir Greg (*b.* 1949) *C., Yorkshire East,* Maj. 15,006
* **Knight**, Julian (*b.* 1972) *C., Solihull,* Maj. 20,571
* **Kwarteng**, Rt. Hon. Kwasi, PHD (*b.* 1975) *C., Spelthorne,* Maj. 13,425
* **Kyle**, Peter, DPHIL (*b.* 1970) *Lab., Hove,* Maj. 18,757
* **Laing**, Rt. Hon. Dame Eleanor, DBE (*b.* 1958) *C., Epping Forest,* Maj. 18,243
Laird, Lesley (*b.* 1958) *Lab., Kirkcaldy & Cowdenbeath,* Maj. 259
Lake, Ben (*b.* 1993) *PC, Ceredigion,* Maj. 104
* **Lamb**, Rt. Hon. Sir Norman (*b.* 1957) *LD, Norfolk North,* Maj. 3,512
* **Lammy**, Rt. Hon. David (*b.* 1972) *Lab., Tottenham,* Maj. 34,584
Lamont, John (*b.* 1976) *C., Berwickshire, Roxburgh & Selkirk,* Maj. 11,060
* **Lancaster**, Rt. Hon. Mark (*b.* 1970) *C., Milton Keynes North,* Maj. 1,915
* **Latham**, Pauline, OBE (*b.* 1948) *C., Derbyshire Mid,* Maj. 11,616
* **Lavery**, Ian (*b.* 1963) *Lab., Wansbeck,* Maj. 10,435
* **Law**, Chris (*b.* 1969) *SNP, Dundee West,* Maj. 5,262
* **Leadsom**, Rt. Hon. Andrea, CBE (*b.* 1963) *C., Northamptonshire South,* Maj. 22,840
Lee, Karen (*b.* 1961) *Lab., Lincoln,* Maj. 1,538
* **Lee**, Dr Phillip (*b.* 1970) *LD, Bracknell,* Maj. 16,016
* **Lefroy**, Jeremy (*b.* 1959) *C., Stafford,* Maj. 7,729
* **Leigh**, Rt. Hon. Sir Edward (*b.* 1950) *C., Gainsborough,* Maj. 17,023
* **Leslie**, Chris (*b.* 1972) *ChangeUK, Nottingham East,* Maj. 19,590
* **Letwin**, Rt. Hon. Sir Oliver, PHD (*b.* 1956) *Ind., Dorset West,* Maj. 19,091
* **Lewell-Buck**, Emma (*b.* 1978) *Lab., South Shields,* Maj. 14,508
Lewer, Andrew (*b.* 1971) *C., Northampton South,* Maj. 1,159
* **Lewis**, Rt. Hon. Brandon (*b.* 1971) *C., Great Yarmouth,* Maj. 7,973
* **Lewis**, Clive (*b.* 1971) *Lab., Norwich South,* Maj. 15,596

* **Lewis**, Ivan (b. 1967) Ind., Bury South, Maj. 5,965
* **Lewis**, Rt. Hon. Julian, DPHIL (b. 1951) C., New Forest East, Maj. 21,995
* **Liddell-Grainger**, Ian (b. 1959) C., Bridgwater & Somerset West, Maj. 15,448
* **Lidington**, Rt. Hon. David, CBE (b. 1956) C., Aylesbury, Maj. 14,696
  Linden, David (b. 1990) SNP, Glasgow East, Maj. 75
  Little Pengelly, Emma (b. 1979) DUP, Belfast South, Maj. 1,996
† **Lloyd**, Stephen (b. 1957) Ind., Eastbourne, Maj. 1,609
‡ **Lloyd**, Tony (b. 1950) Lab., Rochdale, Maj. 14,819
* **Long Bailey**, Rebecca (b. 1979) Lab., Salford & Eccles, Maj. 19,132
  Lopez, Julia (b. 1984) C., Hornchurch & Upminster, Maj. 17,723
* **Lopresti**, Jack (b. 1969) C., Filton & Bradley Stoke, Maj. 4,182
* **Lord**, Jonathan (b. 1962) C., Woking, Maj. 16,724
* **Loughton**, Tim (b. 1962) C., Worthing East & Shoreham, Maj. 5,106
* **Lucas**, Caroline, PHD (b. 1960) Green, Brighton Pavilion, Maj. 14,689
* **Lucas**, Ian (b. 1960) Lab., Wrexham, Maj. 1,832
* **Lynch**, Holly (b. 1986) Lab., Halifax, Maj. 5,376
* **McCabe**, Steve (b. 1955) Lab., Birmingham Selly Oak, Maj. 15,207
  McCallion, Elisha (b. 1982) SF, Foyle, Maj. 169
* **McCarthy**, Kerry (b. 1965) Lab., Bristol East, Maj. 13,394
* **McDonagh**, Siobhain (b. 1960) Lab., Mitcham & Morden, Maj. 21,375
* **McDonald**, Andy (b. 1958) Lab., Middlesbrough, Maj. 13,873
* **McDonald**, Stewart (b. 1986) SNP, Glasgow South, Maj. 2,027
* **McDonald**, Stuart (b. 1978) SNP, Cumbernauld, Kilsyth & Kirkintilloch East, Maj. 4,264
* **McDonnell**, Rt. Hon. John (b. 1951) Lab., Hayes & Harlington, Maj. 18,115
* **McFadden**, Rt. Hon. Pat (b. 1965) Lab., Wolverhampton South East, Maj. 8,514
* **McGinn**, Conor (b. 1984) Lab., St Helens North, Maj. 18,406
* **McGovern**, Alison (b. 1980) Lab., Wirral South, Maj. 8,323
* **McInnes**, Liz (b. 1959) Lab., Heywood & Middleton, Maj. 7,617
* **Mackinlay**, Craig (b. 1966) C., Thanet South, Maj. 6,387
* **McKinnell**, Catherine (b. 1976) Lab., Newcastle upon Tyne North, Maj. 10,349
  Maclean, Rachel (b. 1965) C., Redditch, Maj. 7,363
* **McLoughlin**, Rt. Hon. Sir Patrick (b. 1957) C., Derbyshire Dales, Maj. 14,327
* **McMahon**, Jim (b. 1980) Lab. Co-op, Oldham West & Royton, Maj. 17,198
  McMorrin, Anna (b. 1971) Lab., Cardiff North, Maj. 4,174
* **McNally**, John (b. 1951) SNP, Falkirk, Maj. 4,923
* **MacNeil**, Angus (b. 1970) SNP, Na h-Eileanan an Iar, Maj. 1,007
* **McPartland**, Stephen (b. 1976) C., Stevenage, Maj. 3,384
‡ **McVey**, Rt. Hon. Esther (b. 1967) C., Tatton, Maj. 14,787
* **Madders**, Justin (b. 1972) Lab., Ellesmere Port & Neston, Maj. 11,390
* **Mahmood**, Khalid (b. 1961) Lab., Birmingham Perry Barr, Maj. 18,383
* **Mahmood**, Shabana (b. 1980) Lab., Birmingham Ladywood, Maj. 28,714
* **Main**, Anne (b. 1957) C., St Albans, Maj. 6,109
* **Mak**, Alan (b. 1983) C., Havant, Maj. 15,956
* **Malhotra**, Seema (b. 1972) Lab. Co-op, Feltham & Heston, Maj. 15,603
* **Malthouse**, Kit (b. 1966) C., Hampshire North West, Maj. 22,679
* **Mann**, John (b. 1960) Lab., Bassetlaw, Maj. 4,852

* **Mann**, Scott (b. 1977) C., Cornwall North, Maj. 7,200
* **Marsden**, Gordon (b. 1953) Lab., Blackpool South, Maj. 2,523
  Martin, Sandy (b. 1957) Lab., Ipswich, Maj. 831
* **Maskell**, Rachael (b. 1972) Lab. Co-op, York Central, Maj. 18,575
* **Maskey**, Paul (b. 1967) SF, Belfast West, Maj. 21,652
  Masterton, Paul (b. 1985) C., Renfrewshire East, Maj. 4,712
* **Matheson**, Chris (b. 1968) Lab., Chester, City of, Maj. 9,176
* **May**, Rt. Hon. Theresa (b. 1956) C., Maidenhead, Maj. 26,457
* **Maynard**, Paul (b. 1975) C., Blackpool North & Cleveleys, Maj. 2,023
* **Mearns**, Ian (b. 1957) Lab., Gateshead, Maj. 17,350
* **Menzies**, Mark (b. 1971) C., Fylde, Maj. 11,805
* **Mercer**, Johnny (b. 1981) C., Plymouth Moor View, Maj. 5,019
* **Merriman**, Huw (b. 1973) C., Bexhill & Battle, Maj. 22,165
* **Metcalfe**, Stephen (b. 1966) C., Basildon South & Thurrock East, Maj. 11,490
* **Miliband**, Rt. Hon. Edward (b. 1969) Lab., Doncaster North, Maj. 14,024
* **Miller**, Rt. Hon. Maria (b. 1964) C., Basingstoke, Maj. 9,466
* **Milling**, Amanda (b. 1975) C., Cannock Chase, Maj. 8,391
* **Mills**, Nigel (b. 1974) C., Amber Valley, Maj. 8,300
* **Milton**, Rt. Hon. Anne (b. 1955) Ind., Guildford, Maj. 17,040
*‡ **Mitchell**, Rt. Hon. Andrew (b. 1956) C., Sutton Coldfield, Maj. 15,339
* **Molloy**, Francie (b. 1950) SF, Ulster Mid, Maj. 12,890
* **Monaghan**, Carol (b. 1972) SNP, Glasgow North West, Maj. 2,561
* **Moon**, Madeleine (b. 1950) Lab., Bridgend, Maj. 4,700
  Moore, Damien (b. 1980) C., Southport, Maj. 2,914
  Moran, Layla (b. 1982) LD, Oxford West & Abingdon, Maj. 816
* **Mordaunt**, Rt. Hon. Penny (b. 1973) C., Portsmouth North, Maj. 9,965
* **Morden**, Jessica (b. 1968) Lab., Newport East, Maj. 8,003
* **Morgan**, Rt. Hon. Nicky (b. 1972) C., Loughborough, Maj. 4,269
  Morgan, Stephen (b. 1981) Lab., Portsmouth South, Maj. 1,554
* **Morris**, Anne Marie (b. 1957) C., Newton Abbot, Maj. 17,160
* **Morris**, David (b. 1966) C., Morecambe & Lunesdale, Maj. 1,399
* **Morris**, Grahame (b. 1961) Lab., Easington, Maj. 14,892
* **Morris**, James (b. 1967) C., Halesowen & Rowley Regis, Maj. 5,253
* **Morton**, Wendy (b. 1967) C., Aldridge-Brownhills, Maj. 14,307
* **Mundell**, Rt. Hon. David (b. 1962) C., Dumfriesshire, Clydesdale & Tweeddale, Maj. 9,441
* **Murray**, Ian (b. 1976) Lab., Edinburgh South, Maj. 15,514
* **Murray**, Sheryll (b. 1956) C., Cornwall South East, Maj. 17,443
* **Murrison**, Rt. Hon. Dr Andrew (b. 1961) C., Wiltshire South West, Maj. 18,326
* **Nandy**, Lisa (b. 1979) Lab., Wigan, Maj. 16,027
* **Neill**, Robert (b. 1952) C., Bromley & Chislehurst, Maj. 9,590
* **Newlands**, Gavin (b. 1980) SNP, Paisley & Renfrewshire North, Maj. 2,613
* **Newton**, Sarah (b. 1962) C., Truro & Falmouth, Maj. 3,792
* **Nokes**, Rt. Hon. Caroline (b. 1972) Ind., Romsey & Southampton North, Maj. 18,006
* **Norman**, Jesse (b. 1962) C., Hereford & Herefordshire South, Maj. 15,013
  Norris, Alex (b. 1984) Lab. Co-op, Nottingham North, Maj. 11,160
  O'Brien, Neil (b. 1978) C., Harborough, Maj. 12,429
* **Offord**, Matthew, PHD (b. 1969) C., Hendon, Maj. 1,072
* **O'Hara**, Brendan (b. 1963) SNP, Argyll & Bute, Maj. 1,328
* **Onn**, Melanie (b. 1979) Lab., Great Grimsby, Maj. 2,565
* **Onwurah**, Chi (b. 1965) Lab., Newcastle upon Tyne Central, Maj. 14,937

* **Opperman**, Guy (*b.* 1965) *C., Hexham,* Maj. 9,236
* **Osamor**, Kate (*b.* 1968) *Lab. Co-op, Edmonton,* Maj. 21,115
* **Owen**, Albert (*b.* 1959) *Lab., Ynys Mon,* Maj. 5,259
* **Paisley**, Hon. Ian (*b.* 1960) *DUP, Antrim North,* Maj. 20,643
* **Parish**, Neil (*b.* 1956) *C., Tiverton & Honiton,* Maj. 19,801
* **Patel**, Rt. Hon. Priti (*b.* 1972) *C., Witham,* Maj. 18,646
* **Paterson**, Rt. Hon. Owen (*b.* 1956) *C., Shropshire North,* Maj. 16,355
* **Pawsey**, Mark (*b.* 1957) *C., Rugby,* Maj. 8,212
Peacock, Stephanie (*b.* 1986) *Lab., Barnsley East,* Maj. 13,283
* **Pearce**, Teresa (*b.* 1955) *Lab., Erith & Thamesmead,* Maj. 10,014
* **Penning**, Rt. Hon. Sir Mike (*b.* 1957) *C., Hemel Hempstead,* Maj. 9,445
* **Pennycook**, Matthew (*b.* 1982) *Lab., Greenwich & Woolwich,* Maj. 20,714
* **Penrose**, John (*b.* 1964) *C., Weston-Super-Mare,* Maj. 11,544
* **Percy**, Andrew (*b.* 1977) *C., Brigg & Goole,* Maj. 12,363
* **Perkins**, Toby (*b.* 1970) *Lab., Chesterfield,* Maj. 9,605
* **Perry**, Rt. Hon. Claire (*b.* 1964) *C., Devizes,* Maj. 21,136
* **Phillips**, Jess (*b.* 1981) *Lab., Birmingham Yardley,* Maj. 16,574
* **Phillipson**, Bridget (*b.* 1983) *Lab., Houghton & Sunderland South,* Maj. 12,341
* **Philp**, Chris (*b.* 1976) *C., Croydon South,* Maj. 11,406
Pidcock, Laura (*b.* 1988) *Lab., Durham North West,* Maj. 8,792
* **Pincher**, *Rt. Hon.* Christopher (*b.* 1969) *C., Tamworth,* Maj. 12,347
Platt, Jo (*b.* 1968) *Lab. Co-op, Leigh,* Maj. 9,554
Pollard, Luke (*b.* 1980) *Lab. Co-op, Plymouth Sutton & Devonport,* Maj. 6,002
* **Poulter**, Dr Dan (*b.* 1978) *C., Suffolk Central & Ipswich North,* Maj. 17,185
* **Pound**, Stephen (*b.* 1948) *Lab., Ealing North,* Maj. 19,693
* **Pow**, Rebecca (*b.* 1960) *C., Taunton Deane,* Maj. 15,887
* **Powell**, Lucy (*b.* 1974) *Lab. Co-op, Manchester Central,* Maj. 31,445
* **Prentis**, Hon. Victoria (*b.* 1971) *C., Banbury,* Maj. 12,399
* **Prisk**, Mark (*b.* 1962) *C., Hertford & Stortford,* Maj. 19,035
* **Pritchard**, Mark (*b.* 1966) *C., Wrekin, The,* Maj. 9,564
* **Pursglove**, Tom (*b.* 1988) *C., Corby,* Maj. 2,690
* **Quin**, Jeremy (*b.* 1968) *C., Horsham,* Maj. 23,484
* **Quince**, Will (*b.* 1982) *C., Colchester,* Maj. 5,677
* **Qureshi**, Yasmin (*b.* 1963) *Lab., Bolton South East,* Maj. 13,126
* **Raab**, Rt. Hon. Dominic (*b.* 1974) *C., Esher & Walton,* Maj. 23,298
Rashid, Faisal (*b.* 1972) *Lab., Warrington South,* Maj. 2,549
* **Rayner**, Angela (*b.* 1980) *Lab., Ashton Under Lyne,* Maj. 11,295
* **Redwood**, Rt. Hon. Sir John, DPHIL (*b.* 1951) *C., Wokingham,* Maj. 18,798
* **Reed**, Steve (*b.* 1963) *Lab. Co-op, Croydon North,* Maj. 32,365
* **Rees**, Christina (*b.* 1954) *Lab. Co-op, Neath,* Maj. 12,631
* **Rees-Mogg**, Rt. Hon. Jacob (*b.* 1969) *C., Somerset North East,* Maj. 10,235
Reeves, Ellie (*b.* 1980) *Lab., Lewisham West & Penge,* Maj. 23,162
* **Reeves**, Rachel (*b.* 1979) *Lab., Leeds West,* Maj. 15,965
* **Reynolds**, Emma (*b.* 1977) *Lab., Wolverhampton North East,* Maj. 4,587
* **Reynolds**, Jonathan (*b.* 1980) *Lab. Co-op, Stalybridge & Hyde,* Maj. 8,084
* **Rimmer**, Marie (*b.* 1947) *Lab., St Helens South & Whiston,* Maj. 24,343
* **Robertson**, Laurence (*b.* 1958) *C., Tewkesbury,* Maj. 22,574
* **Robinson**, Gavin (*b.* 1984) *DUP, Belfast East,* Maj. 8,474
* **Robinson**, Geoffrey (*b.* 1938) *Lab., Coventry North West,* Maj. 8,580
* **Robinson**, Mary (*b.* 1955) *C., Cheadle,* Maj. 4,507

Rodda, Matt (*b.* 1966) *Lab., Reading East,* Maj. 3,749
* **Rosindell**, Andrew (*b.* 1966) *C., Romford,* Maj. 13,778
Ross, Douglas (*b.* 1983) *C., Moray,* Maj. 4,159
Rowley, Danielle (*b.* 1990) *Lab., Midlothian,* Maj. 885
Rowley, Lee (*b.* 1980) *C., Derbyshire North East,* Maj. 2,861
† **Ruane**, Chris (*b.* 1958) *Lab., Vale of Clwyd,* Maj. 2,379
* **Rudd**, Rt. Hon. Amber (*b.* 1963) *Ind., Hastings & Rye,* Maj. 346
Russell-Moyle, Lloyd (*b.* 1986) *Lab. Co-op, Brighton Kemptown,* Maj. 9,868
* **Rutley**, David (*b.* 1961) *C., Macclesfield,* Maj. 8,608
* **Ryan**, Rt. Hon. Joan (*b.* 1955) *ChangeUK, Enfield North,* Maj. 10,247
* **Sandbach**, Antoinette (*b.* 1969) *Ind., Eddisbury,* Maj. 11,942
* **Saville Roberts**, Rt. Hon. Liz (*b.* 1964) *PC, Dwyfor Meirionnydd,* Maj. 4,850
* **Scully**, Paul (*b.* 1968) *C., Sutton & Cheam,* Maj. 12,698
Seely, Bob (*b.* 1966) *C., Isle of Wight,* Maj. 21,069
* **Selous**, Andrew (*b.* 1962) *C., Bedfordshire South West,* Maj. 14,168
* **Shah**, Naz (*b.* 1973) *Lab., Bradford West,* Maj. 21,902
* **Shannon**, Jim (*b.* 1955) *DUP, Strangford,* Maj. 18,343
* **Shapps**, Rt. Hon. Grant (*b.* 1968) *C., Welwyn Hatfield,* Maj. 7,369
* **Sharma**, Rt. Hon. Alok (*b.* 1967) *C., Reading West,* Maj. 2,876
* **Sharma**, Virendra (*b.* 1947) *Lab., Ealing Southall,* Maj. 22,090
* **Sheerman**, Barry (*b.* 1940) *Lab. Co-op, Huddersfield,* Maj. 12,005
* **Shelbrooke**, Alec (*b.* 1976) *C., Elmet & Rothwell,* Maj. 9,805
* **Sheppard**, Tommy (*b.* 1959) *SNP, Edinburgh East,* Maj. 3,425
* **Sherriff**, Paula (*b.* 1975) *Lab., Dewsbury,* Maj. 3,321
* **Shuker**, Gavin (*b.* 1981) *Ind., Luton South,* Maj. 13,925
* **Siddiq**, Tulip (*b.* 1982) *Lab., Hampstead & Kilburn,* Maj. 15,560
* **Simpson**, David (*b.* 1959) *DUP, Upper Bann,* Maj. 7,992
* **Simpson**, Rt. Hon. Keith (*b.* 1949) *C., Broadland,* Maj. 15,816
* **Skidmore**, Chris (*b.* 1981) *C., Kingswood,* Maj. 7,500
* **Skinner**, Dennis (*b.* 1932) *Lab., Bolsover,* Maj. 5,288
* **Slaughter**, Andy (*b.* 1960) *Lab., Hammersmith,* Maj. 18,651
* **Smeeth**, Ruth (*b.* 1979) *Lab., Stoke-on-Trent North,* Maj. 2,359
* **Smith**, Angela (*b.* 1961) *LD., Penistone & Stocksbridge,* Maj. 1,322
* **Smith**, Cat (*b.* 1985) *Lab., Lancaster & Fleetwood,* Maj. 6,661
* **Smith**, Chloe (*b.* 1982) *C., Norwich North,* Maj. 507
Smith, Eleanor (*b.* 1957) *Lab., Wolverhampton South West,* Maj. 2,185
* **Smith**, Henry (*b.* 1969) *C., Crawley,* Maj. 2,457
* **Smith**, Jeff (*b.* 1963) *Lab., Manchester Withington,* Maj. 29,875
* **Smith**, Rt. Hon. Julian (*b.* 1971) *C., Skipton & Ripon,* Maj. 19,985
Smith, Laura (*b.* 1985) *Lab., Crewe & Nantwich,* Maj. 48
* **Smith**, Nick (*b.* 1960) *Lab., Blaenau Gwent,* Maj. 11,907
* **Smith**, Owen (*b.* 1970) *Lab., Pontypridd,* Maj. 11,448
* **Smith**, Royston (*b.* 1964) *C., Southampton Itchen,* Maj. 31
* **Smyth**, Karin (*b.* 1964) *Lab., Bristol South,* Maj. 15,987
* **Snell**, Gareth (*b.* 1986) *Lab. Co-op, Stoke-on-Trent Central,* Maj. 3,897
* **Soames**, Rt. Hon. Sir Nicholas (*b.* 1948) *Ind., Sussex Mid,* Maj. 19,673
Sobel, Alex (*b.* 1975) *Lab. Co-op, Leeds North West,* Maj. 4,224
* **Soubry**, Rt. Hon. Anna (*b.* 1956) *ChangeUK, Broxtowe,* Maj. 863
*‡ **Spellar**, Rt. Hon. John (*b.* 1947) *Lab., Warley,* Maj. 16,483
* **Spelman**, Rt. Hon. Dame Caroline, DBE (*b.* 1958) *C., Meriden,* Maj. 19,198
* **Spencer**, Rt. Hon. Mark (*b.* 1970) *C., Sherwood,* Maj. 5,198

GENERAL ELECTION 2017 RESULTS

UK Turnout

Electorate (E.) 46,843,896 Turnout (T.). 32,181,757 (68.7%)

The results of voting in each of the 650 parliamentary constituencies at the general election on 8 June 2017 are given below.

KEY

* Previously an MP for this seat in the 2015–17 parliament

† Previously an MP for this seat in any parliament prior to the 2015–17 parliament

‡ Previously an MP for a different seat in any previous parliament

℃ By-election held since the 2017 General Election

swing N/A indicates a constituency for which the swing data cannot be calculated because one of the top two parties in the 2015 General Election did not field a candidate in the seat in 2017.

ABBREVIATIONS OF POLITICAL PARTIES

Active Dem.	Movement for Active Democracy
AD	Apolitical Democrats
Alliance	Alliance Party of Northern Ireland
AP	All People's Party
APNI	APNI Party
AWAP	Abolish the Welsh Assembly Party
AWP	Animal Welfare Party
BA	Brexit Alliance
Blue	Blue Revolution
BNP	British National Party
Bournemouth	Bournemouth Independent Alliance
BPE	Bus-Pass Elvis Party
Bradford	Better for Bradford
Brexit	The Brexit Party
Bristol	Independents for Bristol
C.	Conservative
Change	Alter Change
ChangeUK	The Independent Group for Change
Ch. P.	The Christian Party
CISTA	Cannabis is Safer than Alcohol
Citizens	Citizens Independent Social Thought Alliance
Co. Gd	Common Good
Comm.	Communist Party of Britain
Comm. Lge	Communist League
Community	Communities United Party
Compass	Compass Party
Concordia	Concordia
CPA	Christian Peoples Alliance
Croydon	Putting Croydon First
CSP	Common Sense Party
DDI	Demos Direct Initiative
Digital	Digital Democracy
DUP	Democratic Unionist Party
DVP	Democrats and Veterans Party
Eccentric	The Eccentric Party of Great Britain
Elmo	Give Me Back Elmo
Elvis	Church of the Militant Elvis
Eng. Dem.	English Democrats
Eng. Ind.	English Independence

For Britain	The For Britain Movement
Friends	Friends Party
GM Homeless	Greater Manchester Homeless Voice
Good	The Common Good
Green	Green Party
Green Soc.	Alliance for Green Socialism
Guildford	Guildford Greenbelt Group
Humanity	Humanity
Ind.	Independent
IPP	Immigrants Political Party
JACP	Justice & Anti-Corruption Party
Just	The Just Political Party
Lab.	Labour
Lab. Alt	Labour Alternative
Lab. Co-op	Labour and Co-operative
LD	Liberal Democrat
Lib.	The Liberal Party
Lib. GB	Liberty Great Britain
Libertarian	Libertarian Party
Lincs Ind.	Lincolnshire Independents
Loony	Monster Raving Loony Party
Love	One Love Party
MC	The Magna Carta Party
Money	Money Free Party
ND	No description
NE	The North East Party
NF	National Front
NHAP	National Health Action Party
North	Putting North of England People First
Northern	Northern Party
Open	Open Borders Party
Patria	Patria
PBP	People Before Profit Alliance
PC	Plaid Cymru
Peace	Peace Party
PF	People First
Pilgrim	The Pilgrim Party
Pirate	Pirate Party UK
Poole	The Party for Poole People Ltd
Populist	Populist Party
PUP	Progressive Unionist Party
Radical	The Radical Party

Realist	The Realists' Party
Rebooting	Rebooting Democracy
Referendum	Scotland's Independence Referendum Party
Renew	Renew Party
Respect	The Respect Party
Rochdale	Rochdale First Party
Roman	The Roman Party
S. New	Something New
SCP	Scottish Christian Party
SDLP	Social Democratic and Labour Party
SF	Sinn Fein
SNP	Scottish National Party
Soc.	Socialist Party
Soc. Dem.	Social Democratic Party
Soc. Lab.	Socialist Labour Party
Southampton	Southampton Independents
Southend	Southend Independent Association
Southport	The Southport Party
Sovereign	Independent Sovereign Democratic Britain
Space	Space Navies Party
Speaker	The Speaker
SPGB	The Socialist Party of Great Britain
SSP	Scottish Socialist Party
Thanet	Party for a United Thanet
TUSC	Trade Unionist and Socialist Coalition
TUV	Traditional Unionist Voice
UKEUP	UK European Union Party
UKIP	UK Independence Party
UUP	Ulster Unionist Party
Wessex Reg.	Wessex Regionalists
Wigan	Wigan Independents
Women	Women's Equality Party
Worth	The New Society of Worth
WP	Workers' Party
WRP	Workers' Revolutionary Party
WVPTFP	War Veteran's Pro-Traditional Family Party
Yorks	Yorkshire First
Yorkshire	The Yorkshire Party
Young	Young People's Party UK

ENGLAND

ALDERSHOT
E. 76,205   T. 48,955 (64.24%)   C. hold
Leo Docherty, C. — 26,955
Gary Puffett, Lab. — 15,477
Alan Hilliar, LD — 3,637
Roy Swales, UKIP — 1,796
Donna Wallace, Green — 1,090
C. majority 11,478 (23.45%)
4.41% swing C. to Lab.
(2015: C. majority 14,901 (32.26%))

ALDRIDGE-BROWNHILLS
E. 60,363   T. 40,235 (66.66%)   C. hold
*Wendy Morton, C. — 26,317
John Fisher, Lab. — 12,010
Ian Garrett, LD — 1,343
Mark Beech, Loony — 565
C. majority 14,307 (35.56%)
2.94% swing Lab. to C.
(2015: C. majority 11,723 (29.68%))

ALTRINCHAM & SALE WEST
E. 73,220   T. 52,790 (72.10%)   C. hold
*Graham Brady, C. — 26,933
Andrew Western, Lab. — 20,507
Jane Brophy, LD — 4,051
Geraldine Coggins, Green — 1,000
Neil Taylor, Lib. — 299
C. majority 6,426 (12.17%)
7.07% swing C. to Lab.
(2015: C. majority 13,290 (26.31%))

AMBER VALLEY
E. 68,065   T. 45,811 (67.30%)   C. hold
*Nigel Mills, C. — 25,905
James Dawson, Lab. — 17,605
Kate Smith, LD — 1,100
Matt McGuinness, Green — 650
Daniel Bamford, Ind. — 551
C. majority 8,300 (18.12%)
4.46% swing Lab. to C.
(2015: C. majority 4,205 (9.20%))

ARUNDEL & SOUTH DOWNS
E. 80,766   T. 60,256 (74.61%)   C. hold
*Nick Herbert, C. — 37,573
Caroline Fife, Lab. — 13,690
Shweta Kapadia, LD — 4,783
Jo Prior, Green — 2,542
John Wallace, UKIP — 1,668
C. majority 23,883 (39.64%)
4.98% swing C. to Lab.
(2015: C. majority 26,177 (46.35%))

ASHFIELD
E. 78,099   T. 49,993 (64.01%)   Lab. hold
*Gloria De Piero, Lab. — 21,285
Tony Harper, C. — 20,844
Gail Turner, Ind. — 4,612
Ray Young, UKIP — 1,885
Bob Charlesworth, LD — 969
Arran Rangi, Green — 398
Lab. majority 441 (0.88%)
8.86% swing Lab. to C.
(2015: Lab. majority 8,820 (18.60%))

ASHFORD
E. 87,396   T. 59,879 (68.51%)   C. hold
*Damian Green, C. — 35,318
Sally Gathern, Lab. — 17,840
Adrian Gee-Turner, LD — 3,101
Gerald O'Brien, UKIP — 2,218
Mandy Rossi, Green — 1,402
C. majority 17,478 (29.19%)
2.41% swing C. to Lab.
(2015: C. majority 19,296 (33.63%))

ASHTON-UNDER-LYNE
E. 67,674   T. 39,773 (58.77%)   Lab. hold
*Angela Rayner, Lab. — 24,005
Jack Rankin, C. — 12,710
Maurice Jackson, UKIP — 1,878
Carly Hicks, LD — 646
Andy Hunter-Rossall, Green — 534
Lab. majority 11,295 (28.40%)
0.38% swing C. to Lab.
(2015: Lab. majority 10,756 (27.64%))

AYLESBURY
E. 82,546   T. 58,743 (71.16%)   C. hold
*David Lidington, C. — 32,313
Mark Bateman, Lab. — 17,617
Steven Lambert, LD — 5,660
Vijay Srao, UKIP — 1,296
Coral Simpson, Green — 1,237
Kyle Michael, Ind. — 620
C. majority 14,696 (25.02%)
5.26% swing C. to Lab.
(2015: C. majority 17,158 (30.96%))

BANBURY
E. 83,818   T. 61,562 (73.45%)   C. hold
*Victoria Prentis, C. — 33,388
Sean Woodcock, Lab. — 20,989
John Howson, LD — 3,452
Dickie Bird, UKIP — 1,581
Ian Middleton, Green — 1,225
Roseanne Edwards, Ind. — 927
C. majority 12,399 (20.14%)
5.79% swing C. to Lab.
(2015: C. majority 18,395 (31.71%))

BARKING
E. 77,020   T. 47,679 (61.90%)   Lab. hold
*Margaret Hodge, Lab. — 32,319
Minesh Talati, C. — 10,711
Roger Gravett, UKIP — 3,031
Shannon Butterfield, Green — 724
Pauline Pearce, LD — 599
Noel Falvey, Ind. — 295
Lab. majority 21,608 (45.32%)
1.97% swing C. to Lab.
(2015: Lab. majority 15,272 (35.50%))

BARNSLEY CENTRAL
E. 64,204   T. 39,089 (60.88%)   Lab. hold
*Dan Jarvis, Lab. — 24,982
Amanda Ford, C. — 9,436
Gavin Felton, UKIP — 3,339
Richard Trotman, Green — 572
David Ridgway, LD — 549
Stephen Morris, Eng. Dem. — 211
Lab. majority 15,546 (39.77%)
0.48% swing Lab. to C.
(2015: Lab. majority 12,435 (34.01%))

BARNSLEY EAST
E. 69,204   T. 40,776 (58.92%)   Lab. hold
Stephanie Peacock, Lab. — 24,280
Andrew Lloyd, C. — 10,997
James Dalton, UKIP — 3,247
Tony Devoy, Yorkshire — 1,215
Nicola Turner, LD — 750
Kevin Riddiough, Eng. Dem. — 287
Lab. majority 13,283 (32.58%)
3.78% swing Lab. to C.
(2015: Lab. majority 12,034 (31.24%))

BARROW & FURNESS
E. 69,474   T. 47,590 (68.50%)   Lab. Co-op hold
*John Woodcock,
Lab. Co-op — 22,592
Simon Fell, C. — 22,383
Loraine Birchall, LD — 1,278
Alan Piper, UKIP — 962
Rob O'Hara, Green — 375
Lab. Co-op majority 209 (0.44%)
0.70% swing Lab. to C.
(2015: Lab. Co-op majority 795 (1.84%))

BASILDON & BILLERICAY
E. 69,149   T. 44,918 (64.96%)   C. hold
*John Baron, C. — 27,381
Kayte Block, Lab. — 13,981
Tina Hughes, UKIP — 2,008
Antonia Harrison, LD — 1,548
C. majority 13,400 (29.83%)
0.41% swing Lab. to C.
(2015: C. majority 12,482 (29.01%))

BASILDON SOUTH & THURROCK EAST
E. 73,541   T. 47,120 (64.07%)   C. hold
*Stephen Metcalfe, C. — 26,811
Byron Taylor, Lab. — 15,321
Peter Whittle, UKIP — 3,193
Reetendra Banerji, LD — 732
Sim Harman, Green — 680
Paul Borg, BNP — 383
C. majority 11,490 (24.38%)
3.10% swing Lab. to C.
(2015: C. majority 7,691 (16.87%))

BASINGSTOKE
E. 81,873   T. 55,960 (68.35%)   C. hold
*Maria Miller, C. — 29,510
Terry Bridgeman, Lab. — 20,044
John Shaw, LD — 3,406
Alan Stone, UKIP — 1,681
Richard Winter, Green — 1,106
Scott Neville, Libertarian — 213
C. majority 9,466 (16.92%)
1.96% swing C. to Lab.
(2015: C. majority 11,063 (20.84%))

BASSETLAW
E. 78,535   T. 52,250 (66.53%)   Lab. hold
*John Mann, Lab. — 27,467
Annette Simpson, C. — 22,615
Leon Duveen, LD — 1,154
Nigel Turner, Ind. — 1,014
Lab. majority 4,852 (9.29%)
4.33% swing Lab. to C.
(2015: Lab. majority 8,843 (17.94%))

BATH
E. 66,769   T. 49,582 (74.26%)   LD gain
Wera Hobhouse, LD	23,436
*Ben Howlett, C.	17,742
Joe Rayment, Lab.	7,279
Eleanor Field, Green	1,125

LD majority 5,694 (11.48%)
9.81% swing C. to LD
(2015: C. majority 3,833 (8.13%))

BATLEY & SPEN
E. 80,153   T. 53,780 (67.10%)
	Lab. Co-op hold
*Tracy Brabin, Lab. Co-op	29,844
Ann Myatt, C.	20,883
John Lawson, LD	1,224
Aleks Lukic, Ind.	1,076
Alan Freeman, Green	695
Mohammed Hanif, Ind.	58

Lab. Co-op majority 8,961 (16.66%)
2.33% swing C. to Lab.
(2015: Lab. majority 6,057 (12.00%))
(2016: Lab. majority 16,537 (81.09%))

BATTERSEA
E. 77,572   T. 55,058 (70.98%)   Lab. gain
Marsha De Cordova, Lab.	25,292
*Jane Ellison, C.	22,876
Richard Davis, LD	4,401
Chris Coghlan, Ind.	1,234
Lois Davis, Green	866
Eugene Power, UKIP	357
Daniel Lambert, SPGB	32

Lab. majority 2,416 (4.39%)
9.97% swing C. to Lab.
(2015: C. majority 7,938 (15.56%))

BEACONSFIELD
E. 77,534   T. 56,028 (72.26%)   C. hold
*Dominic Grieve, C.	36,559
James English, Lab.	12,016
Peter Chapman, LD	4,448
Jon Conway, UKIP	1,609
Russell Secker, Green	1,396

C. majority 24,543 (43.80%)
4.01% swing C. to Lab.
(2015: C. majority 26,311 (49.49%))

BECKENHAM
E. 67,928   T. 51,630 (76.01%)   C. hold
*Bob Stewart, C.	30,632
Marina Ahmad, Lab.	15,545
Julie Ireland, LD	4,073
Ruth Fabricant, Green	1,380

C. majority 15,087 (29.22%)
4.31% swing C. to Lab.
(2015: C. majority 18,471 (37.85%))

BEDFORD
E. 71,829   T. 48,480 (67.49%)   Lab. gain
Mohammad Yasin, Lab.	22,712
*Richard Fuller, C.	21,923
Henry Vann, LD	2,837
Lucy Bywater, Green	1,008

Lab. majority 789 (1.63%)
2.00% swing C. to Lab.
(2015: C. majority 1,097 (2.38%))

BEDFORDSHIRE MID
E. 83,800   T. 63,148 (75.36%)   C. hold
*Nadine Dorries, C.	38,936
Rhiannon Meades, Lab.	17,953
Lisa French, LD	3,798
Gareth Ellis, Green	1,794
Ann Kelly, Loony	667

C. majority 20,983 (33.23%)
3.47% swing C. to Lab.
(2015: C. majority 23,327 (40.18%))

BEDFORDSHIRE NORTH EAST
E. 86,988   T. 64,220 (73.83%)   C. hold
*Alistair Burt, C.	39,139
Julian Vaughan, Lab.	18,277
Stephen Rutherford, LD	3,693
Duncan Strachan, UKIP	1,896
Philippa Fleming, Green	1,215

C. majority 20,862 (32.49%)
5.61% swing C. to Lab.
(2015: C. majority 25,644 (43.71%))

BEDFORDSHIRE SOUTH WEST
E. 79,670   T. 55,635 (69.83%)   C. hold
*Andrew Selous, C.	32,961
Daniel Scott, Lab.	18,793
Daniel Norton, LD	2,630
Morvern Rennie, Green	950
Morenike Mafoh, CPA	301

C. majority 14,168 (25.47%)
4.63% swing C. to Lab.
(2015: C. majority 17,813 (34.72%))

BERMONDSEY & OLD SOUTHWARK
E. 87,227   T. 58,521 (67.09%)   Lab. hold
*Neil Coyle, Lab.	31,161
Simon Hughes, LD	18,189
Siobhan Baillie, C.	7,581
Elizabeth Jones, UKIP	838
John Tyson, Green	639
James Clarke, Ind.	113

Lab. majority 12,972 (22.17%)
6.72% swing LD to Lab.
(2015: Lab. majority 4,489 (8.73%))

BERWICK-UPON-TWEED
E. 58,774   T. 42,212 (71.82%)   C. hold
*Anne-Marie Trevelyan, C.	22,145
Scott Dickinson, Lab.	10,364
Julie Porksen, LD	8,916
Thomas Stewart, Green	787

C. majority 11,781 (27.91%)
0.89% swing Lab. to C.
(2015: C. majority 4,914 (12.16%))

BETHNAL GREEN & BOW
E. 86,071   T. 59,825 (69.51%)   Lab. hold
*Rushanara Ali, Lab.	42,969
Charlie Chirico, C.	7,576
Ajmal Masroor, Ind.	3,888
William Dyer, LD	2,982
Alistair Polson, Green	1,516
Ian de Wulverton, UKIP	894

Lab. majority 35,393 (59.16%)
6.61% swing C. to Lab.
(2015: Lab. majority 24,317 (45.95%))

BEVERLEY & HOLDERNESS
E. 80,657   T. 55,678 (69.03%)   C. hold
*Graham Stuart, C.	32,499
Johanna Boal, Lab.	18,457
Denis Healy, LD	2,808
Lee Walton, Yorkshire	1,158
Richard Howarth, Green	756

C. majority 14,042 (25.22%)
1.03% swing Lab. to C.
(2015: C. majority 12,203 (23.17%))

BEXHILL & BATTLE
E. 78,512   T. 59,472 (75.75%)   C. hold
*Huw Merriman, C.	36,854
Christine Bayliss, Lab.	14,689
Joel Kemp, LD	4,485
Geoffrey Bastin, UKIP	2,006
Jonathan Kent, Green	1,438

C. majority 22,165 (37.27%)
1.69% swing C. to Lab.
(2015: C. majority 20,075 (36.36%))

BEXLEYHEATH & CRAYFORD
E. 65,315   T. 45,189 (69.19%)   C. hold
*David Evennett, C.	25,113
Stef Borella, Lab.	16,040
Mike Ferro, UKIP	1,944
Simone Reynolds, LD	1,201
Ivor Lobo, Green	601
Peter Finch, BNP	290

C. majority 9,073 (20.08%)
0.48% swing C. to Lab.
(2015: C. majority 9,192 (21.04%))

BIRKENHEAD
E. 64,484   T. 43,663 (67.71%)   Lab. hold
*Frank Field, Lab.	33,558
Stewart Gardiner, C.	8,044
Allan Brame, LD	1,118
Jayne Clough, Green	943

Lab. majority 25,514 (58.43%)
1.81% swing C. to Lab.
(2015: Lab. majority 20,652 (54.81%))

BIRMINGHAM EDGBASTON
E. 68,091   T. 43,612 (64.05%)
	Lab. Co-op hold
Preet Gill, Lab. Co-op	24,124
Caroline Squire, C.	17,207
Colin Green, LD	1,564
Alice Kiff, Green	562
Dick Rodgers, Good	155

Lab. Co-op majority 6,917 (15.86%)
4.65% swing C. to Lab.
(2015: Lab. majority 2,706 (6.55%))

BIRMINGHAM ERDINGTON
E. 65,067   T. 37,217 (57.20%)   Lab. hold
*Jack Dromey, Lab.	21,571
Robert Alden, C.	14,286
Ann Holtom, LD	750
James Lovatt, Green	610

Lab. majority 7,285 (19.57%)
2.39% swing C. to Lab.
(2015: Lab. majority 5,129 (14.79%))

BIRMINGHAM HALL GREEN
E. 78,271 T. 54,310 (69.39%) Lab. hold
*Roger Godsiff, Lab. 42,143
Reena Ranger, C. 8,199
Jerry Evans, LD 3,137
Patrick Cox, Green 831
Lab. majority 33,944 (62.50%)
10.19% swing C. to Lab.
(2015: Lab. majority 19,818 (42.12%))

BIRMINGHAM HODGE HILL
E. 75,698 T. 46,394 (61.29%) Lab. hold
*Liam Byrne, Lab. 37,606
Ahmereen Reza, C. 6,580
Mohammed Khan, UKIP 1,016
Phil Bennion, LD 805
Clare Thomas, Green 387
Lab. majority 31,026 (66.88%)
4.97% swing C. to Lab.
(2015: Lab. majority 23,362 (56.93%))

BIRMINGHAM LADYWOOD
E. 70,023 T. 41,307 (58.99%) Lab. hold
*Shabana Mahmood, Lab. 34,166
Andrew Browning, C. 5,452
Lee Dargue, LD 1,156
Kefentse Dennis, Green 533
Lab. majority 28,714 (69.51%)
4.31% swing C. to Lab.
(2015: Lab. majority 21,868 (60.89%))

BIRMINGHAM NORTHFIELD
E. 72,322 T. 44,348 (61.32%) Lab. hold
*Richard Burden, Lab. 23,596
Meg Powell-Chandler, C. 18,929
Roger Harmer, LD 959
Eleanor Masters, Green 864
Lab. majority 4,667 (10.52%)
2.31% swing C. to Lab.
(2015: Lab. majority 2,509 (5.91%))

BIRMINGHAM PERRY BARR
E. 70,106 T. 44,197 (63.04%) Lab. hold
*Khalid Mahmood, Lab. 30,109
Charlotte Hodivala, C. 11,726
Harjun Singh, LD 1,080
Shangara Bhatoe, Soc. Lab. 592
Vijay Rana, Green 591
Harjinder Singh, Open 99
Lab. majority 18,383 (41.59%)
2.83% swing C. to Lab.
(2015: Lab. majority 14,828 (35.94%))

BIRMINGHAM SELLY OAK
E. 74,370 T. 48,985 (65.87%) Lab. hold
*Steve McCabe, Lab. 30,836
Sophie Shrubsole, C. 15,629
David Radcliffe, LD 1,644
Julien Pritchard, Green 876
Lab. majority 15,207 (31.04%)
6.20% swing C. to Lab.
(2015: Lab. majority 8,447 (18.65%))

BIRMINGHAM YARDLEY
E. 72,581 T. 44,502 (61.31%) Lab. hold
*Jess Phillips, Lab. 25,398
Mohammed Afzal, C. 8,824
John Hemming, LD 7,984
Paul Clayton, UKIP 1,916
Christopher Garghan, Green 280
Abu Nowshed, Ind. 100
Lab. majority 16,574 (37.24%)
4.81% swing C. to Lab.
(2015: Lab. majority 6,595 (16.03%))

BISHOP AUCKLAND
E. 67,661 T. 43,281 (63.97%) Lab. hold
*Helen Goodman, Lab. 20,808
Christopher Adams, C. 20,306
Ciaran Morrissey, LD 1,176
Adam Walker, BNP 991
Lab. majority 502 (1.16%)
3.87% swing Lab. to C.
(2015: Lab. majority 3,508 (8.91%))

BLACKBURN
E. 70,657 T. 47,512 (67.24%) Lab. hold
*Kate Hollern, Lab. 33,148
Bob Eastwood, C. 12,780
Duncan Miller, Ind. 875
Irfan Ahmed, LD 709
Lab. majority 20,368 (42.87%)
6.93% swing C. to Lab.
(2015: Lab. majority 12,760 (29.00%))

BLACKLEY & BROUGHTON
E. 71,648 T. 40,113 (55.99%) Lab. hold
*Graham Stringer, Lab. 28,258
David Goss, C. 8,657
Martin Power, UKIP 1,825
Charles Gadsden, LD 737
David Jones, Green 462
Abi Ajoku, CPA 174
Lab. majority 19,601 (48.86%)
0.99% swing C. to Lab.
(2015: Lab. majority 16,874 (45.47%))

BLACKPOOL NORTH &
CLEVELEYS
E. 63,967 T. 41,007 (64.11%) C. hold
*Paul Maynard, C. 20,255
Chris Webb, Lab. 18,232
Paul White, UKIP 1,392
Sue Close, LD 747
Duncan Royle, Green 381
C. majority 2,023 (4.93%)
1.77% swing C. to Lab.
(2015: C. majority 3,340 (8.48%))

BLACKPOOL SOUTH
E. 58,450 T. 34,953 (59.80%) Lab. hold
*Gordon Marsden, Lab. 17,581
Peter Anthony, C. 15,058
Noel Matthews, UKIP 1,339
Bill Greene, LD 634
John Peter Warnock, Green 341
Lab. majority 2,523 (7.22%)
0.38% swing Lab. to C.
(2015: Lab. majority 2,585 (7.97%))

BLAYDON
E. 68,459 T. 48,084 (70.24%) Lab. hold
Liz Twist, Lab. 26,979
Thomas Smith, C. 13,502
Jonathan Wallace, LD 4,366
Ray Tolley, UKIP 2,459
Paul McNally, Green 583
Michael Marchetti,
Libertarian 114
Lisabela Marschild, Space 81
Lab. majority 13,477 (28.03%)
1.84% swing Lab. to C.
(2015: Lab. majority 14,227 (31.66%))

BLYTH VALLEY
E. 63,371 T. 42,490 (67.05%) Lab. hold
*Ronnie Campbell, Lab. 23,770
Ian Levy, C. 15,855
Jeff Reid, LD 1,947
Dawn Furness, Green 918
Lab. majority 7,915 (18.63%)
2.99% swing Lab. to C.
(2015: Lab. majority 9,229 (24.00%))

BOGNOR REGIS &
LITTLEHAMPTON
E. 75,827 T. 51,352 (67.72%) C. hold
*Nick Gibb, C. 30,276
Alan Butcher, Lab. 12,782
Francis Oppler, LD 3,352
Paul Sanderson, Ind. 2,088
Patrick Lowe, UKIP 1,861
Andrew Bishop, Green 993
C. majority 17,494 (34.07%)
1.73% swing C. to Lab.
(2015: C. majority 13,944 (29.60%))

BOLSOVER
E. 73,429 T. 46,519 (63.35%) Lab. hold
*Dennis Skinner, Lab. 24,153
Helen Harrison, C. 18,865
Philip Rose, UKIP 2,129
Ross Shipman, LD 1,372
Lab. majority 5,288 (11.37%)
7.70% swing Lab. to C.
(2015: Lab. majority 11,778 (26.77%))

BOLTON NORTH EAST
E. 67,233 T. 45,183 (67.20%) Lab. hold
*David Crausby, Lab. 22,870
James Daly, C. 19,073
Harry Lamb, UKIP 1,567
Warren Fox, LD 1,316
Liz Spencer, Green 357
Lab. majority 3,797 (8.40%)
0.87% swing Lab. to C.
(2015: Lab. majority 4,377 (10.14%))

BOLTON SOUTH EAST
E. 68,886 T. 42,323 (61.44%) Lab. hold
*Yasmin Qureshi, Lab. 25,676
Sarah Pochin, C. 12,550
Jeff Armstrong, UKIP 2,779
Frank Harasiwka, LD 781
Alan Johnson, Green 537
Lab. majority 13,126 (31.01%)
0.45% swing C. to Lab.
(2015: Lab. majority 10,928 (26.82%))

BOLTON WEST
E. 72,797 T. 51,054 (70.13%) C. hold
*Chris Green, C. 24,459
Julie Hilling, Lab. 23,523
Martin Tighe, UKIP 1,587
Rebecca Forrest, LD 1,485
C. majority 936 (1.83%)
0.09% swing Lab. to C.
(2015: C. majority 801 (1.65%))

BOOTLE
E. 72,872   T. 50,288 (69.01%)   Lab. hold
*Peter Dowd, Lab.   42,259
Charles Fifield, C.   6,059
David Newman, LD   837
Alison Gibbon, Green   709
Kim Bryan, Soc. Lab.   424
Lab. majority 36,200 (71.99%)
2.79% swing C. to Lab.
(2015: Lab. majority 28,704 (63.57%))

BOSTON & SKEGNESS
E. 68,391   T. 42,879 (62.70%)   C. hold
*Matt Warman, C.   27,271
Paul Kenny, Lab.   10,699
Paul Nuttall, UKIP   3,308
Philip Smith, LD   771
Victoria Percival, Green   547
Mike Gilbert, Blue   283
C. majority 16,572 (38.65%)
5.67% swing Lab. to C.
(2015: C. majority 4,336 (10.00%))

BOSWORTH
E. 80,633   T. 56,168 (69.66%)   C. hold
*David Tredinnick, C.   31,864
Chris Kealey, Lab.   13,513
Michael Mullaney, LD   9,744
Mick Gregg, Green   1,047
C. majority 18,351 (32.67%)
3.66% swing Lab. to C.
(2015: C. majority 10,988 (20.51%))

BOURNEMOUTH EAST
E. 74,591   T. 48,618 (65.18%)   C. hold
*Tobias Ellwood, C.   25,221
Mel Semple, Lab.   17,284
Jon Nicholas, LD   3,168
David Hughes, UKIP   1,405
Alasdair Keddie, Green   1,236
Kieron Wilson, Ind.   304
C. majority 7,937 (16.33%)
8.14% swing C. to Lab.
(2015: C. majority 14,612 (32.60%))

BOURNEMOUTH WEST
E. 73,195   T. 44,507 (60.81%)   C. hold
*Conor Burns, C.   23,812
David Stokes, Lab.   16,101
Phil Dunn, LD   2,929
Simon Bull, Green   1,247
Jason Halsey, Pirate   418
C. majority 7,711 (17.33%)
6.62% swing C. to Lab.
(2015: C. majority 12,410 (29.71%))

BRACKNELL
E. 79,199   T. 55,892 (70.57%)   C. hold
*Phillip Lee, C.   32,882
Paul Bidwell, Lab.   16,866
Patrick Smith, LD   4,186
Len Amos, UKIP   1,521
Olivio Barreto, Ind.   437
C. majority 16,016 (28.66%)
5.12% swing C. to Lab.
(2015: C. majority 20,650 (38.90%))

BRADFORD EAST
E. 70,389   T. 45,622 (64.81%)   Lab. hold
*Imran Hussain, Lab.   29,831
Mark Trafford, C.   9,291
David Ward, Ind.   3,576
Jonathan Barras, UKIP   1,372
Mark Jewell, LD   843
Paul Parkins, Bradford   420
Andy Stanford, Green   289
Lab. majority 20,540 (45.02%)
4.84% swing C. to Lab.
(2015: Lab. majority 7,084 (17.11%))

BRADFORD SOUTH
E. 67,752   T. 41,049 (60.59%)   Lab. hold
*Judith Cummins, Lab.   22,364
Tanya Graham, C.   15,664
Stephen Place, UKIP   1,758
Stuart Thomas, LD   516
Therese Hirst, Eng. Dem.   377
Darren Parkinson, Green   370
Lab. majority 6,700 (16.32%)
0.42% swing Lab. to C.
(2015: Lab. majority 6,450 (17.15%))

BRADFORD WEST
E. 67,568   T. 45,528 (67.38%)   Lab. hold
*Naz Shah, Lab.   29,444
George Grant, C.   7,542
Salma Yaqoob, ND   6,345
Derrick Hodgson, UKIP   885
Alun Griffiths, LD   712
Celia Hickson, Green   481
Hussain Khadim, ND   65
Muhammad Hijazi, Ind.   54
Lab. majority 21,902 (48.11%)
swing N/A
(2015: Lab. majority 11,420 (28.34%))

BRAINTREE
E. 75,316   T. 52,326 (69.48%)   C. hold
*James Cleverly, C.   32,873
Malcolm Fincken, Lab.   14,451
Peter Turner, LD   2,251
Richard Bingley, UKIP   1,835
Thomas Pashby, Green   916
C. majority 18,422 (35.21%)
0.07% swing C. to Lab.
(2015: C. majority 17,610 (35.02%))

BRENT CENTRAL
E. 80,845   T. 52,296 (64.69%)   Lab. hold
*Dawn Butler, Lab.   38,208
Rahoul Bhansali, C.   10,211
Anton Georgiou, LD   2,519
Shaka Lish, Green   802
Janice North, UKIP   556
Lab. majority 27,997 (53.54%)
5.88% swing C. to Lab.
(2015: Lab. majority 19,649 (41.78%))

BRENT NORTH
E. 82,556   T. 56,444 (68.37%)   Lab. hold
*Barry Gardiner, Lab.   35,496
Ameet Jogia, C.   18,435
Paul Lorber, LD   1,614
Michaela Lichten, Green   660
Elcena Jeffers, Ind.   239
Lab. majority 17,061 (30.23%)
4.74% swing C. to Lab.
(2015: Lab. majority 10,834 (20.74%))

BRENTFORD & ISLEWORTH
E. 85,151   T. 61,629 (72.38%)   Lab. hold
*Ruth Cadbury, Lab.   35,364
Mary Macleod, C.   23,182
Joe Bourke, LD   3,083
Lab. majority 12,182 (19.77%)
9.48% swing C. to Lab.
(2015: Lab. majority 465 (0.81%))

BRENTWOOD & ONGAR
E. 74,911   T. 52,910 (70.63%)   C. hold
Alex Burghart, C.   34,811
Gareth Barrett, Lab.   10,809
Karen Chilvers, LD   4,426
Michael McGough, UKIP   1,845
Paul Jeater, Green   915
Louca Kousoulou, Ind.   104
C. majority 24,002 (45.36%)
0.48% swing C. to Lab.
(2015: C. majority 21,810 (42.03%))

BRIDGWATER & SOMERSET WEST
E. 89,294   T. 58,267 (65.25%)   C. hold
*Ian Liddell-Grainger, C.   32,111
Wes Hinckes, Lab.   16,663
Marcus Kravis, LD   6,332
Simon Smedley, UKIP   2,102
Kay Powell, Green   1,059
C. majority 15,448 (26.51%)
0.91% swing C. to Lab.
(2015: C. majority 14,583 (26.78%))

BRIGG & GOOLE
E. 66,069   T. 45,057 (68.20%)   C. hold
*Andrew Percy, C.   27,219
Terence Smith, Lab.   14,856
David Jeffreys, UKIP   1,596
Jerry Lonsdale, LD   836
Isabel Pires, Green   550
C. majority 12,363 (27.44%)
0.81% swing Lab. to C.
(2015: C. majority 11,176 (25.83%))

BRIGHTON KEMPTOWN
E. 67,893   T. 49,207 (72.48%)
                                 Lab. Co-op gain
Lloyd Russell-Moyle,   28,703
Lab. Co-op
*Simon Kirby, C.   18,835
Emily Tester, LD   1,457
Doktor Haze, ND   212
Lab. Co-op majority 9,868 (20.05%)
10.79% swing C. to Lab.
(2015: C. majority 690 (1.52%))

BRIGHTON PAVILION
E. 75,486   T. 57,677 (76.41%)
                                     Green hold
*Caroline Lucas, Green   30,139
Solomon Curtis, Lab.   15,450
Emma Warman, C.   11,082
Ian Buchanan, UKIP   630
Nick Yeomans, Ind.   376
Green majority 14,689 (25.47%)
5.45% swing Lab. to Green
(2015: Green majority 7,967 (14.57%))

BRISTOL EAST
E. 72,414 T. 50,799 (70.15%) Lab. hold
*Kerry McCarthy, Lab.	30,847
Theo Clarke, C.	17,453
Chris Lucas, LD	1,389
Lorraine Francis, Green	1,110

Lab. majority 13,394 (26.37%)
8.88% swing C. to Lab.
(2015: Lab. majority 3,980 (8.61%))

BRISTOL NORTH WEST
E. 75,431 T. 54,096 (71.72%) Lab. gain
Darren Jones, Lab.	27,400
*Charlotte Leslie, C.	22,639
Celia Downie, LD	2,814
Sharmila Bousa, Green	1,243

Lab. majority 4,761 (8.80%)
9.17% swing C. to Lab.
(2015: C. majority 4,944 (9.54%))

BRISTOL SOUTH
E. 83,009 T. 54,382 (65.51%) Lab. hold
Karin Smyth, Lab.	32,666
Mark Weston, C.	16,679
Benjamin Nutland, LD	1,821
Ian Kealey, UKIP	1,672
Tony Dyer, Green	1,428
John Langley, Ind.	116

Lab. majority 15,987 (29.40%)
7.69% swing C. to Lab.
(2015: Lab. majority 7,128 (14.02%))

BRISTOL WEST
E. 92,986 T. 71,608 (77.01%) Lab. hold
*Thangam Debbonaire, Lab.	47,213
Annabel Tall, C.	9,877
Molly Scott Cato, Green	9,216
Stephen Williams, LD	5,201
Jodian Rodgers, Money	101

Lab. majority 37,336 (52.14%)
15.83% swing C. to Lab.
(2015: Lab. majority 5,673 (8.83%))

BROADLAND
E. 77,334 T. 55,971 (72.38%) C. hold
*Keith Simpson, C.	32,406
Iain Simpson, Lab.	16,590
Steve Riley, LD	4,449
David Moreland, UKIP	1,594
Andrew Boswell, Green	932

C. majority 15,816 (28.26%)
1.73% swing C. to Lab.
(2015: C. majority 16,838 (31.72%))

BROMLEY & CHISLEHURST
E. 65,113 T. 46,662 (71.66%) C. hold
*Robert Neill, C.	25,175
Sara Hyde, Lab.	15,585
Sam Webber, LD	3,369
Emmett Jenner, UKIP	1,383
Roisin Robertson, Green	1,150

C. majority 9,590 (20.55%)
5.11% swing C. to Lab.
(2015: C. majority 13,564 (30.78%))

BROMSGROVE
E. 73,571 T. 54,040 (73.45%) C. hold
*Sajid Javid, C.	33,493
Michael Thompson, Lab.	16,920
Neil Lewis, LD	2,488
Spoz Esposito, Green	1,139

C. majority 16,573 (30.67%)
0.48% swing C. to Lab.
(2015: C. majority 16,529 (31.64%))

BROXBOURNE
E. 73,502 T. 47,485 (64.60%) C. hold
*Charles Walker, C.	29,515
Selina Norgrove, Lab.	13,723
Tony Faulkner, UKIP	1,918
Andy Graham, LD	1,481
Tabitha Evans, Green	848

C. majority 15,792 (33.26%)
2.20% swing C. to Lab.
(2015: C. majority 16,723 (36.34%))

BROXTOWE
E. 74,017 T. 55,508 (74.99%) C. hold
*Anna Soubry, C.	25,983
Greg Marshall, Lab.	25,120
Tim Hallam, LD	2,247
Fran Loi, UKIP	1,477
Pat Morton, Green	681

C. majority 863 (1.55%)
3.23% swing C. to Lab.
(2015: C. majority 4,287 (8.02%))

BUCKINGHAM
E. 79,616 T. 52,679 (66.17%)
		Speaker hold
*John Bercow, Speaker		34,299
Michael Sheppard, Green		8,574
Scott Raven, Ind.		5,638
Brian Mapletoft, UKIP		4,168

Speaker majority 25,725 (48.83%)
0.93% swing C. to Green
(2015: Speaker majority 22,942 (42.73%))

BURNLEY
E. 64,714 T. 40,290 (62.26%) Lab. hold
*Julie Cooper, Lab.	18,832
Paul White, C.	12,479
Gordon Birtwistle, LD	6,046
Tom Commis, UKIP	2,472
Laura Fisk, Green	461

Lab. majority 6,353 (15.77%)
4.16% swing Lab. to C.
(2015: Lab. majority 3,244 (8.16%))

BURTON
E. 73,954 T. 49,911 (67.49%) C. hold
*Andrew Griffiths, C.	28,936
John McKiernan, Lab.	18,889
Dominic Hardwick, LD	1,262
Simon Hales, Green	824

C. majority 10,047 (20.13%)
1.34% swing C. to Lab.
(2015: C. majority 11,252 (22.81%))

BURY NORTH
E. 67,587 T. 47,903 (70.88%) Lab. gain
James Frith, Lab.	25,683
*David Nuttall, C.	21,308
Richard Baum, LD	912

Lab. majority 4,375 (9.13%)
4.98% swing C. to Lab.
(2015: C. majority 378 (0.84%))

BURY ST EDMUNDS
E. 87,758 T. 62,160 (70.83%) C. hold
*Jo Churchill, C.	36,794
Bill Edwards, Lab.	18,353
Helen Korfanty, LD	3,565
Helen Geake, Green	2,596
Liam Byrne, Ind.	852

C. majority 18,441 (29.67%)
3.11% swing C. to Lab.
(2015: C. majority 21,301 (35.90%))

BURY SOUTH
E. 73,723 T. 50,990 (69.16%) Lab. hold
*Ivan Lewis, Lab.	27,165
Robert Largan, C.	21,200
Ian Henderson, UKIP	1,316
Andrew Page, LD	1,065
Peter Wright, Ind.	244

Lab. majority 5,965 (11.70%)
0.64% swing C. to Lab.
(2015: Lab. majority 4,922 (10.42%))

CALDER VALLEY
E. 79,045 T. 58,054 (73.44%) C. hold
*Craig Whittaker, C.	26,790
Josh Fenton-Glynn, Lab.	26,181
Janet Battye, LD	1,952
Paul Rogan, UKIP	1,466
Robert Holden, Ind.	1,034
Kieran Turner, Green	631

C. majority 609 (1.05%)
3.61% swing C. to Lab.
(2015: C. majority 4,427 (8.27%))

CAMBERWELL & PECKHAM
E. 85,586 T. 57,412 (67.08%) Lab. hold
*Harriet Harman, Lab.	44,665
Ben Spencer, C.	7,349
Michael Bukola, LD	3,413
Eleanor Margolies, Green	1,627
Ray Towey, CPA	227
Sellu Aminata, WRP	131

Lab. majority 37,316 (65.00%)
7.46% swing C. to Lab.
(2015: Lab. majority 25,824 (50.08%))

CAMBORNE & REDRUTH
E. 67,462 T. 48,456 (71.83%) C. hold
*George Eustice, C.	23,001
Graham Winter, Lab.	21,424
Geoff Williams, LD	2,979
Geoff Garbett, Green	1,052

C. majority 1,577 (3.25%)
6.01% swing C. to Lab.
(2015: C. majority 7,004 (15.27%))

CAMBRIDGE
E. 78,003 T. 55,934 (71.71%) Lab. hold
*Daniel Zeichner, Lab.	29,032
Julian Huppert, LD	16,371
John Hayward, C.	9,133
Stuart Tuckwood, Green	1,265
Keith Garrett, Reboot	133

Lab. majority 12,661 (22.64%)
10.74% swing LD to Lab.
(2015: Lab. majority 599 (1.16%))

CAMBRIDGESHIRE NORTH EAST
E. 84,404 T. 53,284 (63.13%) C. hold
*Stephen Barclay, C.	34,340
Ken Rustidge, Lab.	13,070
Darren Fower, LD	2,383
Robin Talbot, UKIP	2,174
Ruth Johnson, Green	1,024
Stephen Goldspink, Eng. Dem.	293

C. majority 21,270 (39.92%)
0.37% swing C. to Lab.
(2015: C. majority 16,874 (32.59%))

CAMBRIDGESHIRE NORTH WEST
E. 93,223   T. 63,991 (68.64%)   C. hold
*Shailesh Vara, C.   37,529
Iain Ramsbottom, Lab.   19,521
Bridget Smith, LD   3,168
John Whitby, UKIP   2,518
Greg Guthrie, Green   1,255
C. majority 18,008 (28.14%)
3.23% swing C. to Lab.
(2015: C. majority 19,795 (32.40%))

CAMBRIDGESHIRE SOUTH
E. 85,257   T. 64,924 (76.15%)   C. hold
*Heidi Allen, C.   33,631
Dan Greef, Lab.   17,679
Susan van de Ven, LD   12,102
Simon Saggers, Green   1,512
C. majority 15,952 (24.57%)
4.45% swing C. to Lab.
(2015: C. majority 20,594 (33.46%))

CAMBRIDGESHIRE SOUTH EAST
E. 86,121   T. 63,002 (73.16%)   C. hold
*Lucy Frazer, C.   33,601
Huw Jones, Lab.   17,443
Lucy Nethsingha, LD   11,958
C. majority 16,158 (25.65%)
3.84% swing C. to Lab.
(2015: C. majority 16,837 (28.29%))

CANNOCK CHASE
E. 74,540   T. 47,872 (64.22%)   C. hold
*Amanda Milling, C.   26,318
Paul Dadge, Lab.   17,927
Paul Allen, UKIP   2,018
Paul Woodhead, Green   815
Nat Green, LD   794
C. majority 8,391 (17.53%)
3.54% swing Lab. to C.
(2015: C. majority 4,923 (10.45%))

CANTERBURY
E. 78,137   T. 56,800 (72.69%)   Lab. gain
Rosie Duffield, Lab.   25,572
*Julian Brazier, C.   25,385
James Flanagan, LD   4,561
Henry Stanton, Green   1,282
Lab. majority 187 (0.33%)
9.33% swing C. to Lab.
(2015: C. majority 9,798 (18.33%))

CARLISLE
E. 62,294   T. 43,056 (69.12%)   C. hold
*John Stevenson, C.   21,472
Ruth Alcroft, Lab.   18,873
Fiona Mills, UKIP   1,455
Peter Thornton, LD   1,256
C. majority 2,599 (6.04%)
0.24% swing C. to Lab.
(2015: C. majority 2,774 (6.51%))

CARSHALTON & WALLINGTON
E. 70,849   T. 50,753 (71.64%)   LD hold
*Tom Brake, LD   20,819
Matthew Maxwell Scott, C.   19,450
Emina Ibrahim, Lab.   9,360
Shasha Khan, Green   501
Nick Mattey, Ind.   434
Ashley Dickenson, CPA   189
LD majority 1,369 (2.70%)
0.24% swing LD to C.
(2015: LD majority 1,510 (3.17%))

CASTLE POINT
E. 69,470   T. 44,710 (64.36%)   C. hold
*Rebecca Harris, C.   30,076
Joe Cooke, Lab.   11,204
David Kurten, UKIP   2,381
Tom Holder, LD   1,049
C. majority 18,872 (42.21%)
2.59% swing Lab. to C.
(2015: C. majority 8,934 (19.66%))

CHARNWOOD
E. 78,071   T. 55,176 (70.67%)   C. hold
*Edward Argar, C.   33,318
Sean Kelly-Walsh, Lab.   16,977
Simon Sansome, LD   2,052
Victoria Connor, UKIP   1,471
Nick Cox, Green   1,036
Stephen Denham, BNP   322
C. majority 16,341 (29.62%)
1.39% swing C. to Lab.
(2015: C. majority 16,931 (32.40%))

CHATHAM & AYLESFORD
E. 70,419   T. 44,890 (63.75%)   C. hold
*Tracey Crouch, C.   25,587
Vince Maple, Lab.   15,129
Nicole Bushill, UKIP   2,225
Thomas Quinton, LD   1,116
Bernard Hyde, Green   573
John Gibson, CPA   260
C. majority 10,458 (23.30%)
1.65% swing C. to Lab.
(2015: C. majority 11,455 (26.59%))

CHEADLE
E. 72,780   T. 54,572 (74.98%)   C. hold
*Mary Robinson, C.   24,331
Mark Hunter, LD   19,824
Martin Miller, Lab.   10,417
C. majority 4,507 (8.26%)
1.95% swing C. to LD
(2015: C. majority 6,453 (12.15%))

CHELMSFORD
E. 81,045   T. 56,860 (70.16%)   C. hold
Vicky Ford, C.   30,525
Chris Vince, Lab.   16,953
Stephen Robinson, LD   6,916
Nigel Carter, UKIP   1,645
Hossain Reza, Green   821
C. majority 13,572 (23.87%)
5.02% swing C. to Lab.
(2015: C. majority 18,250 (33.91%))

CHELSEA & FULHAM
E. 63,728   T. 42,128 (66.11%)   C. hold
*Greg Hands, C.   22,179
Alan De'Ath, Lab.   13,991
Louise Rowntree, LD   4,627
Bill Cashmore, Green   807
Alasdair Seton-   524
Marsden, UKIP
C. majority 8,188 (19.44%)
10.20% swing C. to Lab.
(2015: C. majority 16,022 (39.83%))

CHELTENHAM
E. 78,875   T. 57,012 (72.28%)   C. hold
*Alex Chalk, C.   26,615
Martin Horwood, LD   24,046
Keith White, Lab.   5,408
Adam Van   943
Coevorden, Green
C. majority 2,569 (4.51%)
3.81% swing C. to LD
(2015: C. majority 6,516 (12.13%))

CHESHAM & AMERSHAM
E. 71,645   T. 55,252 (77.12%)   C. hold
*Cheryl Gillan, C.   33,514
Nina Dluzewska, Lab.   11,374
Peter Jones, LD   7,179
Alan Booth, Green   1,660
David Meacock, UKIP   1,525
C. majority 22,140 (40.07%)
3.13% swing C. to Lab.
(2015: C. majority 23,920 (45.36%))

CHESTER, CITY OF
E. 72,859   T. 56,421 (77.44%)   Lab. hold
*Chris Matheson, Lab.   32,023
Will Gallagher, C.   22,847
Lizzie Jewkes, LD   1,551
Lab. majority 9,176 (16.26%)
8.04% swing C. to Lab.
(2015: Lab. majority 93 (0.18%))

CHESTERFIELD
E. 72,063   T. 47,927 (66.51%)   Lab. hold
*Toby Perkins, Lab.   26,266
Spencer Pitfield, C.   16,661
Tom Snowdon, LD   2,612
Stuart Bent, UKIP   1,611
David Wadsworth, Green   777
Lab. majority 9,605 (20.04%)
4.90% swing Lab. to C.
(2015: Lab. majority 13,598 (29.84%))

CHICHESTER
E. 84,996   T. 59,918 (70.50%)   C. hold
Gillian Keegan, C.   36,032
Mark Farwell, Lab.   13,411
Jonathan Brown, LD   6,749
Heather Barrie, Green   1,992
Andrew Moncreiff, UKIP   1,650
Andrew Emerson, Patria   84
C. majority 22,621 (37.75%)
3.89% swing C. to Lab.
(2015: C. majority 24,413 (42.73%))

CHINGFORD & WOODFORD
GREEN
E. 66,078   T. 46,961 (71.07%)   C. hold
*Iain Duncan Smith, C.   23,076
Bilal Mahmood, Lab.   20,638
Deborah Unger, LD   2,043
Sinead King, Green   1,204
C. majority 2,438 (5.19%)
6.98% swing C. to Lab.
(2015: C. majority 8,386 (19.14%))

CHIPPENHAM
E. 76,432   T. 57,140 (74.76%)   C. hold
*Michelle Donelan, C.   31,267
Helen Belcher, LD   14,637
Andrew Newman, Lab.   11,236
C. majority 16,630 (29.10%)
5.46% swing LD to C.
(2015: C. majority 10,076 (18.19%))

CHIPPING BARNET
E. 77,020 T. 55,423 (71.96%) C. hold
*Theresa Villiers, C. 25,679
Emma Whysall, Lab. 25,326
Marisha Ray, LD 3,012
Phil Fletcher, Green 1,406
C. majority 353 (0.64%)
6.90% swing C. to Lab.
(2015: C. majority 7,656 (14.44%))

CHORLEY
E. 76,404 T. 55,634 (72.82%) Lab. hold
*Lindsay Hoyle, Lab. 30,745
Caroline Moon, C. 23,233
Stephen Fenn, LD 1,126
Peter Lageard, Green 530
Lab. majority 7,512 (13.50%)
2.37% swing C. to Lab.
(2015: Lab. majority 4,530 (8.76%))

CHRISTCHURCH
E. 70,329 T. 50,633 (71.99%) C. hold
*Christopher Chope, C. 35,230
Patrick Canavan, Lab. 10,059
Michael Cox, LD 4,020
Chris Rigby, Green 1,324
C. majority 25,171 (49.71%)
0.57% swing Lab. to C.
(2015: C. majority 18,224 (36.66%))

CITIES OF LONDON & WESTMINSTER
E. 61,533 T. 38,654 (62.82%) C. hold
*Mark Field, C. 18,005
Ibrahim Dogus, Lab. 14,857
Bridget Fox, LD 4,270
Lawrence McNally, Green 821
Anil Bhatti, UKIP 426
Tim Lord, ND 173
Ankit Love The Maharaja of Kashmir, Ind. 59
Benjamin Weenen, Young 43
C. majority 3,148 (8.14%)
9.29% swing C. to Lab.
(2015: C. majority 9,671 (26.73%))

CLACTON
E. 69,263 T. 44,145 (63.74%) C. gain
Giles Watling, C. 27,031
Tasha Osben, Lab. 11,203
Paul Oakley, UKIP 3,357
David Grace, LD 887
Chris Southall, Green 719
Caroline Shearer, Ind. 449
Robin Tilbrook, Eng. Dem. 289
Nick Martin, Ind. 210
C. majority 15,828 (35.85%)
30.70% swing UKIP to C.
(2015: UKIP majority 3,437 (7.77%))

CLEETHORPES
E. 73,047 T. 47,844 (65.50%) C. hold
*Martin Vickers, C. 27,321
Peter Keith, Lab. 16,921
Tony Blake, UKIP 2,022
Roy Horobin, LD 1,110
Loyd Emmerson, Green 470
C. majority 10,400 (21.74%)
2.12% swing Lab. to C.
(2015: C. majority 7,893 (17.51%))

COLCHESTER
E. 79,996 T. 53,545 (66.93%) C. hold
*Will Quince, C. 24,565
Tim Young, Lab. 18,888
Bob Russell, LD 9,087
Mark Goacher, Green 828
Robin Rennie, CPA 177
C. majority 5,677 (10.60%)
6.09% swing C. to Lab.
(2015: C. majority 5,575 (11.47%))

COLNE VALLEY
E. 84,381 T. 60,420 (71.60%) Lab. gain
Thelma Walker, Lab. 28,818
*Jason McCartney, C. 27,903
Cahal Burke, LD 2,494
Sonia King, Green 892
Patricia Sadio, Ind. 313
Lab. majority 915 (1.51%)
5.49% swing C. to Lab.
(2015: C. majority 5,378 (9.47%))

CONGLETON
E. 76,694 T. 56,231 (73.32%) C. hold
*Fiona Bruce, C. 31,830
Sam Corcoran, Lab. 19,211
Peter Hirst, LD 2,902
Mark Davies, UKIP 1,289
Alexander Heath, Green 999
C. majority 12,619 (22.44%)
5.23% swing C. to Lab.
(2015: C. majority 16,773 (32.90%))

COPELAND
E. 61,751 T. 42,927 (69.52%) C. hold
*Trudy Harrison, C. 21,062
Gillian Troughton, Lab. 19,367
Rebecca Hanson, LD 1,404
Herbert Crossman, UKIP 1,094
C. majority 1,695 (3.95%)
5.21% swing Lab. to C.
(2015: Lab. majority 2,564 (6.47%))
(2017: C. majority 2,147 (6.91%))

CORBY
E. 82,439 T. 59,997 (72.78%) C. hold
*Tom Pursglove, C. 29,534
Beth Miller, Lab. 26,844
Chris Stanbra, LD 1,545
Sam Watts, UKIP 1,495
Steven Scrutton, Green 579
C. majority 2,690 (4.48%)
0.09% swing Lab. to C.
(2015: C. majority 2,412 (4.29%))

CORNWALL NORTH
E. 68,850 T. 50,944 (73.99%) C. hold
*Scott Mann, C. 25,835
Daniel Rogerson, LD 18,635
Joy Bassett, Lab. 6,151
John Allman, CPA 185
Robert Hawkins, Soc. Lab. 138
C. majority 7,200 (14.13%)
0.20% swing LD to C.
(2015: C. majority 6,621 (13.72%))

CORNWALL SOUTH EAST
E. 71,896 T. 53,214 (74.02%) C. hold
*Sheryll Murray, C. 29,493
Gareth Derrick, Lab. 12,050
Phil Hutty, LD 10,336
Martin Corney, Green 1,335
C. majority 17,443 (32.78%)
4.23% swing C. to Lab.
(2015: C. majority 16,995 (33.65%))

COTSWOLDS, THE
E. 80,446 T. 59,702 (74.21%) C. hold
*Geoffrey Clifton-Brown, C. 36,201
Mark Huband, Lab. 10,702
Andrew Gant, LD 9,748
Sabrina Poole, Green 1,747
Chris Harlow, UKIP 1,197
Sandy Steel, ND 107
C. majority 25,499 (42.71%)
2.30% swing C. to Lab.
(2015: C. majority 21,477 (37.90%))

COVENTRY NORTH EAST
E. 75,792 T. 46,508 (61.36%) Lab. hold
*Colleen Fletcher, Lab. 29,499
Timothy Mayer, C. 13,919
Avtar Taggar, UKIP 1,350
Russell Field, LD 1,157
Matthew Handley, Green 502
Afzal Mahmood, Ind. 81
Lab. majority 15,580 (33.50%)
2.22% swing C. to Lab.
(2015: Lab. majority 12,274 (29.06%))

COVENTRY NORTH WEST
E. 75,214 T. 49,849 (66.28%) Lab. hold
*Geoffrey Robinson, Lab. 26,894
Resham Kotecha, C. 18,314
Michael Gee, UKIP 1,525
Andrew Hilton, LD 1,286
Ciaran Norris, Ind. 1,164
Stephen Gray, Green 666
Lab. majority 8,580 (17.21%)
3.62% swing C. to Lab.
(2015: Lab. majority 4,509 (9.97%))

COVENTRY SOUTH
E. 70,754 T. 47,009 (66.44%) Lab. hold
*Jim Cunningham, Lab. 25,874
Michelle Lowe, C. 17,927
Greg Judge, LD 1,343
Ian Rogers, UKIP 1,037
Aimee Challenor, Green 604
Sandra Findlay, Ind. 224
Lab. majority 7,947 (16.91%)
4.80% swing C. to Lab.
(2015: Lab. majority 3,188 (7.30%))

CRAWLEY
E. 73,424 T. 50,273 (68.47%) C. hold
*Henry Smith, C. 25,426
Tim Lunnon, Lab. 22,969
Marko Scepanovic, LD 1,878
C. majority 2,457 (4.89%)
4.28% swing C. to Lab.
(2015: C. majority 6,526 (13.44%))

CREWE & NANTWICH
E. 78,895   T. 55,027 (69.75%)   Lab. gain

Laura Smith, Lab.	25,928
*Edward Timpson, C.	25,880
Michael Stanley, UKIP	1,885
David Crowther, LD	1,334

Lab. majority 48 (0.09%)
3.67% swing C. to Lab.
(2015: C. majority 3,620 (7.26%))

CROYDON CENTRAL
E. 80,045   T. 57,091 (71.32%)   Lab. gain

Sarah Jones, Lab.	29,873
*Gavin Barwell, C.	24,221
Gill Hickson, LD	1,083
Peter Staveley, UKIP	1,040
Tracey Hague, Green	626
John Boadu, CPA	177
Don Locke, Ind.	71

Lab. majority 5,652 (9.90%)
5.11% swing C. to Lab.
(2015: C. majority 165 (0.31%))

CROYDON NORTH
E. 87,461   T. 59,623 (68.17%)
Lab. Co-op hold

*Steve Reed, Lab. Co-op	44,213
Samuel Kasumu, C.	11,848
Maltby Pindar, LD	1,656
Peter Underwood, Green	983
Michael Swadling, UKIP	753
Lee Berks, Ind.	170

Lab. Co-op majority 32,365 (54.28%)
7.18% swing C. to Lab.
(2015: Lab. Co-op majority 21,364 (39.92%))

CROYDON SOUTH
E. 83,518   T. 61,257 (73.35%)   C. hold

*Chris Philp, C.	33,334
Jennifer Brathwaite, Lab.	21,928
Anna Jones, LD	3,541
Catherine Shelley, Green	1,125
Kathleen Garner, UKIP	1,116
David Omamogho, CPA	213

C. majority 11,406 (18.62%)
5.54% swing C. to Lab.
(2015: C. majority 17,140 (29.70%))

DAGENHAM & RAINHAM
E. 70,620   T. 45,843 (64.92%)   Lab. hold

*Jon Cruddas, Lab.	22,958
Julie Marson, C.	18,306
Peter Harris, UKIP	3,246
Denis Breading, Green	544
Jonathan Fryer, LD	465
Paul Sturdy, BNP	239
Terence London, Concordia	85

Lab. majority 4,652 (10.15%)
3.45% swing Lab. to C.
(2015: Lab. majority 4,980 (11.57%))

DARLINGTON
E. 66,341   T. 44,817 (67.56%)   Lab. hold

*Jenny Chapman, Lab.	22,681
Peter Cuthbertson, C.	19,401
Kevin Brack, UKIP	1,180
Anne-Marie Curry, LD	1,031
Matthew Snedker, Green	524

Lab. majority 3,280 (7.32%)
0.18% swing Lab. to C.
(2015: Lab. majority 3,158 (7.68%))

DARTFORD
E. 78,506   T. 54,224 (69.07%)   C. hold

*Gareth Johnson, C.	31,210
Bachchu Kaini, Lab.	18,024
Ben Fryer, UKIP	2,544
Simon Beard, LD	1,428
Andrew Blatchford, Green	807
Ola Adewunmi, Ind.	211

C. majority 13,186 (24.32%)
0.38% swing Lab. to C.
(2015: C. majority 12,345 (23.55%))

DAVENTRY
E. 75,335   T. 55,663 (73.89%)   C. hold

*Chris Heaton-Harris, C.	35,464
Aiden Ramsey, Lab.	13,730
Andrew Simpson, LD	4,015
Ian Gibbins, UKIP	1,497
Jamie Wildman, Green	957

C. majority 21,734 (39.05%)
0.53% swing C. to Lab.
(2015: C. majority 21,059 (40.10%))

DENTON & REDDISH
E. 65,751   T. 39,599 (60.23%)   Lab. hold

*Andrew Gwynne, Lab.	25,161
Rozila Kana, C.	11,084
Josh Seddon, UKIP	1,798
Catherine Ankers, LD	853
Gareth Hayes, Green	486
Farmin Lord Dave, Loony	217

Lab. majority 14,077 (35.55%)
4.19% swing C. to Lab.
(2015: Lab. majority 10,511 (27.17%))

DERBY NORTH
E. 69,919   T. 48,672 (69.61%)   Lab. gain

†Chris Williamson, Lab.	23,622
*Amanda Solloway, C.	21,607
Lucy Care, LD	2,262
Bill Piper, UKIP	1,181

Lab. majority 2,015 (4.14%)
2.12% swing C. to Lab.
(2015: C. majority 41 (0.09%))

DERBY SOUTH
E. 69,918   T. 45,306 (64.80%)   Lab. hold

*Margaret Beckett, Lab.	26,430
Evonne Williams, C.	15,182
Alan Graves, UKIP	2,011
Joe Naitta, LD	1,229
Ian Sleeman, Green	454

Lab. majority 11,248 (24.83%)
1.60% swing C. to Lab.
(2015: Lab. majority 8,828 (21.63%))

DERBYSHIRE DALES
E. 64,418   T. 49,571 (76.95%)   C. hold

*Patrick McLoughlin, C.	29,744
Andy Botham, Lab.	15,417
Andrew Hollyer, LD	3,126
Matthew Buckler, Green	1,002
Robin Greenwood, Humanity	282

C. majority 14,327 (28.90%)
0.38% swing C. to Lab.
(2015: C. majority 14,044 (29.65%))

DERBYSHIRE MID
E. 67,466   T. 50,371 (74.66%)   C. hold

*Pauline Latham, C.	29,513
Alison Martin, Lab.	17,897
Adam Wain, LD	1,793
Sue Macfarlane, Green	1,168

C. majority 11,616 (23.06%)
1.85% swing C. to Lab.
(2015: C. majority 12,774 (26.76%))

DERBYSHIRE NORTH EAST
E. 72,097   T. 50,381 (69.88%)   C. gain

Lee Rowley, C.	24,784
*Natascha Engel, Lab.	21,923
James Bush, UKIP	1,565
David Lomax, LD	1,390
David Kesteven, Green	719

C. majority 2,861 (5.68%)
4.80% swing Lab. to C.
(2015: Lab. majority 1,883 (3.93%))

DERBYSHIRE SOUTH
E. 76,341   T. 52,631 (68.94%)   C. hold

*Heather Wheeler, C.	30,907
Robert Pearson, Lab.	18,937
Lorraine Johnson, LD	1,870
Marten Kats, Green	917

C. majority 11,970 (22.74%)
0.07% swing Lab. to C.
(2015: C. majority 11,471 (22.60%))

DEVIZES
E. 72,184   T. 50,593 (70.09%)   C. hold

*Claire Perry, C.	31,744
Imtiyaz Shaikh, Lab.	10,608
Christopher Coleman, LD	4,706
Timothy Page, UKIP	1,706
Emma Dawnay, Green	1,606
Jim Gunter, Wessex Reg.	223

C. majority 21,136 (41.78%)
1.49% swing C. to Lab.
(2015: C. majority 20,751 (42.34%))

DEVON CENTRAL
E. 74,370   T. 57,844 (77.78%)   C. hold

*Mel Stride, C.	31,278
Lisa Robillard Webb, Lab.	15,598
Alex White, LD	6,770
Andy Williamson, Green	1,531
Tim Matthews, UKIP	1,326
John Dean, NHAP	871
Lloyd Knight, Lib.	470

C. majority 15,680 (27.11%)
6.14% swing C. to Lab.
(2015: C. majority 21,265 (39.06%))

DEVON EAST
E. 82,382   T. 60,382 (73.30%)   C. hold

*Hugo Swire, C.	29,306
Claire Wright, Ind.	21,270
Jan Ross, Lab.	6,857
Alison Eden, LD	1,468
Brigitte Graham, UKIP	1,203
Peter Faithfull, Ind.	150
Michael Val Davies, Ind.	128

C. majority 8,036 (13.31%)
4.55% swing C. to Ind.
(2015: C. majority 12,261 (22.41%))

DEVON NORTH
E. 75,784   T. 55,705 (73.50%)   C. hold
*Peter Heaton-Jones, C.   25,517
Nick Harvey, LD   21,185
Mark Cann, Lab.   7,063
Stephen Crowther, UKIP   1,187
Ricky Knight, Green   753
C. majority 4,332 (7.78%)
2.74% swing C. to LD
(2015: C. majority 6,936 (13.26%))

DEVON SOUTH WEST
E. 71,262   T. 52,857 (74.17%)   C. hold
*Gary Streeter, C.   31,634
Philippa Davey, Lab. Co-op   15,818
Caroline Voaden, LD   2,732
Ian Ross, UKIP   1,540
Win Scutt, Green   1,133
C. majority 15,816 (29.92%)
5.00% swing C. to Lab.
(2015: C. majority 20,109 (39.92%))

DEVON WEST & TORRIDGE
E. 80,527   T. 59,480 (73.86%)   C. hold
*Geoffrey Cox, C.   33,612
Vince Barry, Lab. Co-op   12,926
David Chalmers, LD   10,526
Chris Jordan, Green   1,622
Robin Julian, Ind.   794
C. majority 20,686 (34.78%)
2.72% swing C. to Lab.
(2015: C. majority 18,403 (32.52%))

DEWSBURY
E. 81,338   T. 56,545 (69.52%)   Lab. hold
*Paula Sherriff, Lab.   28,814
Beth Prescott, C.   25,493
Ednan Hussain, LD   1,214
Simon Cope, Green   1,024
Lab. majority 3,321 (5.87%)
1.58% swing C. to Lab.
(2015: Lab. majority 1,451 (2.71%))

DON VALLEY
E. 73,988   T. 45,988 (62.16%)   Lab. hold
*Caroline Flint, Lab.   24,351
Aaron Bell, C.   19,182
Stevie Manion, Yorkshire   1,599
Anthony Smith, LD   856
Lab. majority 5,169 (11.24%)
4.84% swing Lab. to C.
(2015: Lab. majority 8,885 (20.91%))

DONCASTER CENTRAL
E. 71,716   T. 43,024 (59.99%)   Lab. hold
*Rosie Winterton, Lab.   24,915
Tom Hunt, C.   14,784
Chris Whitwood, Yorkshire   1,346
Eddie Todd, Ind.   1,006
Alison Brelsford, LD   973
Lab. majority 10,131 (23.55%)
2.40% swing Lab. to C.
(2015: Lab. majority 10,093 (24.97%))

DONCASTER NORTH
E. 72,372   T. 42,312 (58.46%)   Lab. hold
*Ed Miliband, Lab.   25,711
Shade Adoh, C.   11,687
Kim Parkinson, UKIP   2,738
Charlie Bridges, Yorkshire   741
Robert Adamson, LD   706
Frank Calladine, Ind.   366
David Allen, Eng. Dem.   363
Lab. majority 14,024 (33.14%)
0.48% swing Lab. to C.
(2015: Lab. majority 11,780 (29.82%))

DORSET MID & POOLE NORTH
E. 65,054   T. 48,254 (74.18%)   C. hold
*Michael Tomlinson, C.   28,585
Vikki Slade, LD   13,246
Steve Brew, Lab.   6,423
C. majority 15,339 (31.79%)
4.57% swing LD to C.
(2015: C. majority 10,530 (22.65%))

DORSET NORTH
E. 76,385   T. 55,724 (72.95%)   C. hold
*Simon Hoare, C.   36,169
Pat Osborne, Lab.   10,392
Thomas Panton, LD   7,556
John Tutton, Green   1,607
C. majority 25,777 (46.26%)
0.70% swing C. to Lab.
(2015: C. majority 21,118 (39.56%))

DORSET SOUTH
E. 72,323   T. 51,906 (71.77%)   C. hold
*Richard Drax, C.   29,135
Tashi Warr, Lab.   17,440
Howard Legg, LD   3,053
Jon Orrell, Green   2,278
C. majority 11,695 (22.53%)
1.07% swing C. to Lab.
(2015: C. majority 11,994 (24.68%))

DORSET WEST
E. 79,043   T. 59,598 (75.40%)   C. hold
*Oliver Letwin, C.   33,081
Andy Canning, LD   13,990
Lee Rhodes, Lab.   10,896
Kelvin Clayton, Green   1,631
C. majority 19,091 (32.03%)
1.73% swing LD to C.
(2015: C. majority 16,130 (28.57%))

DOVER
E. 74,564   T. 51,966 (69.69%)   C. hold
*Charlie Elphicke, C.   27,211
Stacey Blair, Lab.   20,774
Piers Wauchope, UKIP   1,722
Simon Dodd, LD   1,336
Beccy Sawbridge, Green   923
C. majority 6,437 (12.39%)
0.07% swing C. to Lab.
(2015: C. majority 6,294 (12.53%))

DUDLEY NORTH
E. 62,043   T. 38,910 (62.71%)   Lab. hold
*Ian Austin, Lab.   18,090
Les Jones, C.   18,068
Bill Etheridge, UKIP   2,144
Ben France, LD   368
Andrew Nixon, Green   240
Lab. majority 22 (0.06%)
5.47% swing Lab. to C.
(2015: Lab. majority 4,181 (11.00%))

DUDLEY SOUTH
E. 61,323   T. 38,244 (62.36%)   C. hold
*Mike Wood, C.   21,588
Natasha Millward, Lab.   13,858
Mitch Bolton, UKIP   1,791
Jon Bramall, LD   625
Jenny Maxwell, Green   382
C. majority 7,730 (20.21%)
4.52% swing Lab. to C.
(2015: C. majority 4,270 (11.18%))

DULWICH & WEST NORWOOD
E. 77,947   T. 56,143 (72.03%)   Lab. hold
*Helen Hayes, Lab.   39,096
Rachel Wolf, C.   10,940
Gail Kent, LD   4,475
Rashid Nix, Green   1,408
Robin Lambert, Ind.   121
Yen Lin Chong, Ind.   103
Lab. majority 28,156 (50.15%)
9.38% swing C. to Lab.
(2015: Lab. majority 16,122 (31.39%))

DURHAM, CITY OF
E. 71,132   T. 48,324 (67.94%)   Lab. hold
*Roberta Blackman-Woods,
Lab.   26,772
Richard Lawrie, C.   14,408
Amanda Hopgood, LD   4,787
Malcolm Bint, UKIP   1,116
Jonathan Elmer, Green   797
Jim Clark, Ind.   399
Jon Collings, Young   45
Lab. majority 12,364 (25.59%)
0.27% swing C. to Lab.
(2015: Lab. majority 11,439 (25.05%))

DURHAM NORTH
E. 66,970   T. 43,284 (64.63%)   Lab. hold
*Kevan Jones, Lab.   25,917
Laetitia Glossop, C.   12,978
Kenneth Rollings, UKIP   2,408
Craig Martin, LD   1,981
Lab. majority 12,939 (29.89%)
2.05% swing Lab. to C.
(2015: Lab. majority 13,644 (33.99%))

DURHAM NORTH WEST
E. 71,982   T. 47,902 (66.55%)   Lab. hold
Laura Pidcock, Lab.   25,308
Sally-Ann Hart, C.   16,516
Owen Temple, LD   3,398
Alan Breeze, UKIP   2,150
Dominic Horsman, Green   530
Lab. majority 8,792 (18.35%)
2.57% swing Lab. to C.
(2015: Lab. majority 10,056 (23.49%))

EALING CENTRAL & ACTON
E. 74,200   T. 55,342 (74.58%)   Lab. hold
*Rupa Huq, Lab.   33,037
Joy Morrissey, C.   19,230
Jon Ball, LD   3,075
Lab. majority 13,807 (24.95%)
12.21% swing C. to Lab.
(2015: Lab. majority 274 (0.54%))

EALING NORTH
E. 74,764   T. 52,516 (70.24%)   Lab. hold
*Stephen Pound, Lab.   34,635
Isobel Grant, C.   14,942
Humaira Sanders, LD   1,275
Peter McIlvenna, UKIP   921
Meena Hans, Green   743
Lab. majority 19,693 (37.50%)
6.04% swing C. to Lab.
(2015: Lab. majority 12,326 (25.41%))

EALING SOUTHALL
E. 65,188   T. 45,145 (69.25%)   Lab. hold
*Virendra Sharma, Lab.   31,720
Fabio Conti, C.   9,630
Nigel Bakhai, LD   1,892
Peter Ward, Green   1,037
John Poynton, UKIP   504
Arjinder Thiara, WRP   362
Lab. majority 22,090 (48.93%)
2.81% swing C. to Lab.
(2015: Lab. majority 18,760 (43.30%))

EASINGTON
E. 62,385   T. 36,364 (58.29%)   Lab. hold
*Grahame Morris, Lab.   23,152
Barney Campbell, C.   8,260
Susan McDonnell, NE   2,355
Allyn Roberts, UKIP   1,727
Tom Hancock, LD   460
Martie Warin, Green   410
Lab. majority 14,892 (40.95%)
3.57% swing Lab. to C.
(2015: Lab. majority 14,641 (42.29%))

EAST HAM
E. 83,827   T. 56,633 (67.56%)   Lab. hold
*Stephen Timms, Lab.   47,124
Kirsty Finlayson, C.   7,241
Daniel Oxley, UKIP   697
Glanville Williams, LD   656
Chidi Oti-Obihara, Green   474
Choudhry Afzal, Friends   311
Mirza Rahman, Ind.   130
Lab. majority 39,883 (70.42%)
2.46% swing C. to Lab.
(2015: Lab. majority 34,252 (65.50%))

EASTBOURNE
E. 78,754   T. 57,420 (72.91%)   LD gain
†Stephen Lloyd, LD   26,924
*Caroline Ansell, C.   25,315
Jake Lambert, Lab.   4,671
Alex Hough, Green   510
LD majority 1,609 (2.80%)
2.09% swing C. to LD
(2015: C. majority 733 (1.39%))

EASTLEIGH
E. 81,213   T. 57,280 (70.53%)   C. hold
*Mims Davies, C.   28,889
Mike Thornton, LD   14,710
Jill Payne, Lab.   11,454
Malcolm Jones, UKIP   1,477
Ron Meldrum, Green   750
C. majority 14,179 (24.75%)
4.14% swing LD to C.
(2015: C. majority 9,147 (16.48%))

EDDISBURY
E. 70,272   T. 51,319 (73.03%)   C. hold
*Antoinette Sandbach, C.   29,192
Cathy Reynolds, Lab.   17,250
Ian Priestner, LD   2,804
John Bickley, UKIP   1,109
Mark Green, Green   785
Morgan Hill, Pirate   179
C. majority 11,942 (23.27%)
2.06% swing C. to Lab.
(2015: C. majority 12,974 (27.40%))

EDMONTON
E. 65,705   T. 43,678 (66.48%)
                          Lab. Co-op hold
*Kate Osamor, Lab. Co-op   31,221
Gonul Daniels, C.   10,106
Nigel Sussman, UKIP   860
David Schmitz, LD   858
Benjamin Gill, Green   633
Lab. Co-op majority 21,115 (48.34%)
5.52% swing C. to Lab.
(2015: Lab. Co-op majority 15,419
(37.30%))

ELLESMERE PORT & NESTON
E. 68,666   T. 50,939 (74.18%)   Lab. hold
*Justin Madders, Lab.   30,137
Nigel Jones, C.   18,747
Ed Gough, LD   892
Fred Fricker, UKIP   821
Steven Baker, Green   342
Lab. majority 11,390 (22.36%)
4.47% swing C. to Lab.
(2015: Lab. majority 6,275 (13.43%))

ELMET & ROTHWELL
E. 80,291   T. 59,542 (74.16%)   C. hold
*Alec Shelbrooke, C.   32,352
David Nagle, Lab.   22,547
Stewart Golton, LD   2,606
Matthew Clover, Yorkshire   1,042
Dylan Brown, Green   995
C. majority 9,805 (16.47%)
0.89% swing Lab. to C.
(2015: C. majority 8,490 (14.69%))

ELTHAM
E. 64,474   T. 46,155 (71.59%)   Lab. hold
*Clive Efford, Lab.   25,128
Matt Hartley, C.   18,832
David Hall-Matthews, LD   1,457
John Clarke, BNP   738
Lab. majority 6,296 (13.64%)
3.70% swing C. to Lab.
(2015: Lab. majority 2,693 (6.24%))

ENFIELD NORTH
E. 68,454   T. 48,565 (70.95%)   Lab. hold
*Joan Ryan, Lab.   28,177
Nick de Bois, C.   17,930
Nicholas da Costa, LD   1,036
Deborah Cairns, UKIP   848
Bill Linton, Green   574
Lab. majority 10,247 (21.10%)
9.37% swing C. to Lab.
(2015: Lab. majority 1,086 (2.35%))

ENFIELD SOUTHGATE
E. 65,137   T. 48,328 (74.19%)   Lab. gain
Bambos Charalambous, Lab.   24,989
*David Burrowes, C.   20,634
Pippa Morgan, LD   1,925
David Flint, Green   780
Lab. majority 4,355 (9.01%)
9.69% swing C. to Lab.
(2015: C. majority 4,753 (10.38%))

EPPING FOREST
E. 74,737   T. 50,779 (67.94%)   C. hold
*Eleanor Laing, C.   31,462
Liam Preston, Lab.   13,219
Jon Whitehouse, LD   2,884
Patrick O'Flynn, UKIP   1,871
Simon Heap, Green   1,233
Thomas Hall, Young   110
C. majority 18,243 (35.93%)
1.35% swing C. to Lab.
(2015: C. majority 17,978 (36.43%))

EPSOM & EWELL
E. 80,029   T. 59,266 (74.06%)   C. hold
*Chris Grayling, C.   35,313
Ed Mayne, Lab.   14,838
Steve Gee, LD   7,401
Janice Baker, Green   1,714
C. majority 20,475 (34.55%)
4.11% swing C. to Lab.
(2015: C. majority 24,443 (42.78%))

EREWASH
E. 72,991   T. 49,781 (68.20%)   C. hold
*Maggie Throup, C.   25,939
Catherine Atkinson, Lab.   21,405
Martin Garnett, LD   1,243
Ralph Hierons, Green   675
Roy Dunn, Ind.   519
C. majority 4,534 (9.11%)
0.85% swing Lab. to C.
(2015: C. majority 3,584 (7.42%))

ERITH & THAMESMEAD
E. 69,724   T. 44,464 (63.77%)   Lab. hold
*Teresa Pearce, Lab.   25,585
Edward Baxter, C.   15,571
Ronie Johnson, UKIP   1,728
Simon Waddington, LD   750
Claudine Letsae, Green   507
Temi Olodu, CPA   243
Doro Oddiri, Ind.   80
Lab. majority 10,014 (22.52%)
0.09% swing C. to Lab.
(2015: Lab. majority 9,525 (22.35%))

ESHER & WALTON
E. 80,938   T. 59,842 (73.94%)   C. hold
*Dominic Raab, C.   35,071
Lana Hylands, Lab.   11,773
Andrew Davis, LD   10,374
Olivia Palmer, Green   1,074
David Ions, UKIP   1,034
Baron Badger, Loony   318
Della Reynolds, Ind.   198
C. majority 23,298 (38.93%)
5.65% swing C. to Lab.
(2015: C. majority 28,616 (50.22%))

EXETER
E. 77,329   T. 55,423 (71.67%)   Lab. hold
*Ben Bradshaw, Lab.	34,336
James Taghdissian, C.	18,219
Vanessa Newcombe, LD	1,562
Joe Levy, Green	1,027
Jonathan West, Ind.	212
Jonathan Bishop, ND	67

Lab. majority 16,117 (29.08%)
7.89% swing C. to Lab.
(2015: Lab. majority 7,183 (13.30%))

FAREHAM
E. 79,495   T. 57,014 (71.72%)   C. hold
*Suella Fernandes, C.	35,915
Matthew Randall, Lab.	14,360
Matthew Winnington, LD	3,896
Tony Blewett, UKIP	1,541
Miles Grindey, Green	1,302

C. majority 21,555 (37.81%)
2.02% swing C. to Lab.
(2015: C. majority 22,262 (40.70%))

FAVERSHAM & KENT MID
E. 76,008   T. 49,749 (65.45%)   C. hold
*Helen Whately, C.	30,390
Michael Desmond, Lab.	12,977
David Naghi, LD	3,249
Mark McGiffin, UKIP	1,702
Alastair Gould, Green	1,431

C. majority 17,413 (35.00%)
1.59% swing C. to Lab.
(2015: C. majority 16,652 (36.36%))

FELTHAM & HESTON
E. 81,707   T. 53,027 (64.90%)
Lab. Co-op hold
*Seema Malhotra, Lab. Co-op	32,462
Samir Jassal, C.	16,859
Stuart Agnew, UKIP	1,510
Hina Malik, LD	1,387
Tony Firkins, Green	809

Lab. Co-op majority 15,603 (29.42%)
3.11% swing C. to Lab.
(2015: Lab. Co-op majority 11,463 (23.20%))

FILTON & BRADLEY STOKE
E. 72,569   T. 50,694 (69.86%)   C. hold
*Jack Lopresti, C.	25,331
Naomi Rylatt, Lab.	21,149
Eva Fielding, LD	3,052
Diana Warner, Green	1,162

C. majority 4,182 (8.25%)
5.89% swing C. to Lab.
(2015: C. majority 9,838 (20.04%))

FINCHLEY & GOLDERS GREEN
E. 73,138   T. 52,385 (71.62%)   C. hold
*Mike Freer, C.	24,599
Jeremy Newmark, Lab.	22,942
Jonathan Davies, LD	3,463
Adele Ward, Green	919
Andrew Price, UKIP	462

C. majority 1,657 (3.16%)
4.00% swing C. to Lab.
(2015: C. majority 5,662 (11.15%))

FOLKESTONE & HYTHE
E. 84,090   T. 58,875 (70.01%)   C. hold
*Damian Collins, C.	32,197
Laura Davison, Lab.	16,786
Lynne Beaumont, LD	4,222
Stephen Priestley, UKIP	2,565
Martin Whybrow, Green	2,498
David Plumstead, Ind.	493
Naomi Slade, Ind.	114

C. majority 15,411 (26.18%)
3.62% swing C. to Lab.
(2015: C. majority 13,797 (25.08%))

FOREST OF DEAN
E. 70,898   T. 51,767 (73.02%)   C. hold
*Mark Harper, C.	28,096
Shaun Stammers, Lab.	18,594
Janet Ellard, LD	2,029
James Greenwood, Green	1,241
Ernie Warrender, UKIP	1,237
Julian Burrett, Ind.	570

C. majority 9,502 (18.36%)
1.92% swing C. to Lab.
(2015: C. majority 10,987 (22.19%))

FYLDE
E. 65,937   T. 46,467 (70.47%)   C. hold
*Mark Menzies, C.	27,334
Jed Sullivan, Lab.	15,529
Freddie van Mierlo, LD	2,341
Tina Rothery, Green	1,263

C. majority 11,805 (25.41%)
2.48% swing C. to Lab.
(2015: C. majority 13,224 (30.36%))

GAINSBOROUGH
E. 75,893   T. 51,425 (67.76%)
*Edward Leigh, C.	31,790
Catherine Tite, Lab.	14,767
Lesley Rollings, LD	3,630
Vicky Pearson, Green	1,238

C. majority 17,023 (33.10%)
0.87% swing Lab. to C.
(2015: C. majority 15,449 (31.36%))

GARSTON & HALEWOOD
E. 75,248   T. 53,522 (71.13%)   Lab. hold
*Maria Eagle, Lab.	41,599
Adam Marsden, C.	9,450
Anna Martin, LD	1,723
Lawrence Brown, Green	750

Lab. majority 32,149 (60.07%)
2.32% swing C. to Lab.
(2015: Lab. majority 27,146 (55.42%))

GATESHEAD
E. 65,186   T. 42,103 (64.59%)   Lab. hold
*Ian Mearns, Lab.	27,426
Lauren Hankinson, C.	10,076
Mark Bell, UKIP	2,281
Frank Hindle, LD	1,709
Andy Redfern, Green	611

Lab. majority 17,350 (41.21%)
0.43% swing Lab. to C.
(2015: Lab. majority 14,784 (38.90%))

GEDLING
E. 71,221   T. 51,682 (72.57%)   Lab. hold
*Vernon Coaker, Lab.	26,833
Carolyn Abbott, C.	22,139
Lee Waters, UKIP	1,143
Robert Swift, LD	1,052
Rebecca Connick, Green	515

Lab. majority 4,694 (9.08%)
1.43% swing C. to Lab.
(2015: Lab. majority 2,986 (6.22%))

GILLINGHAM & RAINHAM
E. 72,903   T. 48,868 (67.03%)   C. hold
*Rehman Chishti, C.	27,091
Andrew Stamp, Lab.	17,661
Martin Cook, UKIP	2,097
Paul Chaplin, LD	1,372
Clive Gregory, Green	520
Roger Peacock, CPA	127

C. majority 9,430 (19.30%)
1.54% swing C. to Lab.
(2015: C. majority 10,530 (22.37%))

GLOUCESTER
E. 82,963   T. 54,071 (65.17%)   C. hold
*Richard Graham, C.	27,208
Barry Kirby, Lab.	21,688
Jeremy Hilton, LD	2,716
Daniel Woolf, UKIP	1,495
Gerald Hartley, Green	754
George Ridgeon, Loony	210

C. majority 5,520 (10.21%)
1.79% swing C. to Lab.
(2015: C. majority 7,251 (13.79%))

GOSPORT
E. 73,886   T. 49,481 (66.97%)   C. hold
*Caroline Dinenage, C.	30,647
Alan Durrant, Lab.	13,436
Bruce Tennent, LD	2,328
Chloe Palmer, UKIP	1,790
Monica Cassidy, Green	1,024
Jeffrey Roberts, Ind.	256

C. majority 17,211 (34.78%)
3.00% swing C. to Lab.
(2015: C. majority 17,098 (35.87%))

GRANTHAM & STAMFORD
E. 81,762   T. 56,593 (69.22%)   C. hold
*Nick Boles, C.	35,090
Barrie Fairbairn, Lab.	14,996
Anita Day, LD	3,120
Marietta King, UKIP	1,745
Tariq Mahmood, Ind.	860
Becca Thackray, Green	782

C. majority 20,094 (35.51%)
0.23% swing C. to Lab.
(2015: C. majority 18,989 (35.33%))

GRAVESHAM
E. 72,948   T. 48,997 (67.17%)   C. hold
*Adam Holloway, C.	27,237
Mandy Garford, Lab.	17,890
Emmanuel Feyisetan, UKIP	1,742
James Willis, LD	1,210
Marna Gilligan, Green	723
Michael Rogan, Ind.	195

C. majority 9,347 (19.08%)
1.18% swing Lab. to C.
(2015: C. majority 8,370 (16.71%))

GREAT GRIMSBY
E. 61,743   T. 35,521 (57.53%)   Lab. hold
*Melanie Onn, Lab.   17,545
Jo Gideon, C.   14,980
Mike Hookem, UKIP   1,648
Steve Beasant, LD   954
Christina
McGilligan-Fell, Ind.   394
Lab. majority 2,565 (7.22%)
3.12% swing Lab. to C.
(2015: Lab. majority 4,540 (13.46%))

GREAT YARMOUTH
E. 71,408   T. 44,146 (61.82%)   C. hold
*Brandon Lewis, C.   23,901
Mike Smith-Clare, Lab.   15,928
Catherine Blaiklock, UKIP   2,767
James Joyce, LD   987
Harry Webb, Green   563
C. majority 7,973 (18.06%)
2.11% swing Lab. to C.
(2015: C. majority 6,154 (13.84%))

GREENWICH & WOOLWICH
E. 77,190   T. 53,106 (68.80%)   Lab. hold
*Matthew Pennycook, Lab.   34,215
Caroline Attfield, C.   13,501
Chris Adams, LD   3,785
Daniel Garrun, Green   1,605
Lab. majority 20,714 (39.01%)
6.72% swing C. to Lab.
(2015: Lab. majority 11,946 (25.57%))

GUILDFORD
E. 75,454   T. 55,509 (73.57%)   C. hold
*Anne Milton, C.   30,295
Zoe Franklin, LD   13,255
Howard Smith, Lab.   10,545
Mark Bray-Parry, Green   1,152
John Morris, Peace   205
Semi Essessi, ND   57
C. majority 17,040 (30.70%)
5.44% swing C. to LD
(2015: C. majority 22,448 (41.58%))

HACKNEY NORTH & STOKE
NEWINGTON
E. 83,955   T. 56,298 (67.06%)   Lab. hold
*Diane Abbott, Lab.   42,265
Amy Gray, C.   7,126
Joe Richards, LD   3,817
Alastair Binnie-   2,606
Lubbock, Green
Jonathan Homan, AWP   222
Abraham Spielmann, Ind.   203
Coraline Corlis-   59
Khan, Friends
Lab. majority 35,139 (62.42%)
7.15% swing C. to Lab.
(2015: Lab. majority 24,008 (48.12%))

HACKNEY SOUTH & SHOREDITCH
E. 82,004   T. 55,354 (67.50%)
                              Lab. Co-op hold
*Meg Hillier, Lab. Co-op   43,974
Luke Parker, C.   6,043
Dave Raval, LD   3,168
Rebecca Johnson, Green   1,522
Vanessa Hudson, AWP   226
Russell Higgs, Ind.   143
Angel Watt, CPA   113
Jonty Leff, WRP   86
Hugo Sugg, Ind.   50
Dale Kalamazad, Ind.   29
Lab. Co-op majority 37,931 (68.52%)
8.80% swing C. to Lab.
(2015: Lab. Co-op majority 24,243
(50.92%))

HALESOWEN & ROWLEY REGIS
E. 68,856   T. 44,379 (64.45%)   C. hold
*James Morris, C.   23,012
Ian Cooper, Lab.   17,759
Stuart Henley, UKIP   2,126
Jamie Scott, LD   859
James Robertson, Green   440
Tim Weller, Ind.   183
C. majority 5,253 (11.84%)
2.40% swing Lab. to C.
(2015: C. majority 3,082 (7.03%))

HALIFAX
E. 71,224   T. 48,276 (67.78%)   Lab. hold
*Holly Lynch, Lab.   25,507
Chris Pearson, C.   20,131
Mark Weedon, UKIP   1,568
James Baker, LD   1,070
Lab. majority 5,376 (11.14%)
5.08% swing Lab. to C.
(2015: Lab. majority 428 (0.98%))

HALTEMPRICE & HOWDEN
E. 71,520   T. 51,440 (71.92%)   C. hold
*David Davis, C.   31,355
Hollie Devanney, Lab.   15,950
David Nolan, LD   2,482
Diana Wallis, Yorkshire   942
Carole Needham, Green   711
C. majority 15,405 (29.95%)
1.63% swing C. to Lab.
(2015: C. majority 16,195 (33.22%))

HALTON
E. 73,457   T. 49,518 (67.41%)   Lab. hold
*Derek Twigg, Lab.   36,115
Matthew Lloyd, C.   10,710
Glyn Redican, UKIP   1,488
Ryan Bate, LD   896
Vic Turton, Ind.   309
Lab. majority 25,405 (51.30%)
3.12% swing Lab. to C.
(2015: Lab. majority 20,285 (45.05%))

HAMMERSMITH
E. 72,803   T. 52,252 (71.77%)   Lab. hold
*Andy Slaughter, Lab.   33,375
Charlie Dewhirst, C.   14,724
Joyce Onstad, LD   2,802
Alex Horn, Green   800
Jack Bovill, UKIP   507
Jagdeosingh Hauzaree, Ind.   44
Lab. majority 18,651 (35.69%)
11.05% swing C. to Lab.
(2015: Lab. majority 6,518 (13.59%))

HAMPSHIRE EAST
E. 74,148   T. 55,408 (74.73%)   C. hold
*Damian Hinds, C.   35,263
Rohit Dasgupta, Lab.   9,411
Richard Robinson, LD   8,403
Richard Knight, Green   1,760
Susan Jerrard, JACP   571
C. majority 25,852 (46.66%)
1.95% swing C. to Lab.
(2015: C. majority 25,147 (48.69%))

HAMPSHIRE NORTH EAST
E. 75,476   T. 57,627 (76.35%)   C. hold
*Ranil Jayawardena, C.   37,754
Barry Jones, Lab.   9,982
Graham Cockarill, LD   6,987
Chas Spradbery, Green   1,476
Mike Gascoigne, UKIP   1,061
Robert Blay, Ind.   367
C. majority 27,772 (48.19%)
3.94% swing C. to Lab.
(2015: C. majority 29,916 (55.40%))

HAMPSHIRE NORTH WEST
E. 81,430   T. 58,772 (72.17%)   C. hold
*Kit Malthouse, C.   36,471
Andy Fitchet, Lab.   13,792
Alex Payton, LD   5,708
Roger Clark, UKIP   1,467
Dan Hill, Green   1,334
C. majority 22,679 (38.59%)
3.09% swing C. to Lab.
(2015: C. majority 23,943 (43.38%))

HAMPSTEAD & KILBURN
E. 82,957   T. 58,407 (70.41%)   Lab. hold
*Tulip Siddiq, Lab.   34,464
Claire-Louise Leyland, C.   18,904
Kirsty Allan, LD   4,100
John Mansook, Green   742
Hugh Easterbrook, Ind.   136
Rainbow George Weiss, Ind.   61
Lab. majority 15,560 (26.64%)
12.27% swing C. to Lab.
(2015: Lab. majority 1,138 (2.11%))

HARBOROUGH
E. 78,647   T. 57,598 (73.24%)   C. hold
Neil O'Brien, C.   30,135
Andy Thomas, Lab.   17,706
Zuffar Haq, LD   7,286
Teck Khong, UKIP   1,361
Darren Woodiwiss, Green   1,110
C. majority 12,429 (21.58%)
7.92% swing Lab. to C.
(2015: C. majority 19,632 (37.41%))

HARLOW
E. 67,697   T. 44,846 (66.25%)   C. hold
*Robert Halfon, C.   24,230
Phil Waite, Lab.   17,199
Mark Gough, UKIP   1,787
Geoffrey Seeff, LD   970
Hannah Clare, Green   660
C. majority 7,031 (15.68%)
1.60% swing Lab. to C.
(2015: C. majority 8,350 (18.87%))

HARROGATE & KNARESBOROUGH

E. 77,265   T. 56,740 (73.44%)   C. hold

*Andrew Jones, C.	31,477
Helen Flynn, LD	13,309
Mark Sewards, Lab.	11,395
Donald Fraser, Ind.	559

C. majority 18,168 (32.02%)
0.67% swing LD to C.
(2015: C. majority 16,371 (30.67%))

HARROW EAST

E. 71,757   T. 50,845 (70.86%)   C. hold

*Bob Blackman, C.	25,129
Navin Shah, Lab.	23,372
Adam Bernard, LD	1,573
Emma Wallace, Green	771

C. majority 1,757 (3.46%)
3.13% swing C. to Lab.
(2015: C. majority 4,757 (9.71%))

HARROW WEST

E. 69,798   T. 50,355 (72.14%)
Lab. Co-op hold

*Gareth Thomas, Lab. Co-op	30,640
Hannah David, C.	17,326
Christopher Noyce, LD	1,267
Rowan Langley, Green	652
Rathy Alagaratnam, UKIP	470

Lab. Co-op majority 13,314 (26.44%)
10.85% swing C. to Lab.
(2015: Lab. Co-op majority 2,208 (4.74%))

HARTLEPOOL

E. 70,718   T. 41,835 (59.16%)   Lab. hold

Mike Hill, Lab.	21,969
Carl Jackson, C.	14,319
Phillip Broughton, UKIP	4,801
Andy Hagon, LD	746

Lab. majority 7,650 (18.29%)
1.77% swing C. to Lab.
(2015: Lab. majority 3,024 (7.66%))

HARWICH & ESSEX NORTH

E. 71,294   T. 51,141 (71.73%)   C. hold

*Bernard Jenkin, C.	29,921
Rosalind Scott, Lab.	15,565
Dominic Graham, LD	2,787
Aaron Hammond, UKIP	1,685
Blake Roberts, Green	1,042
Stephen Todd, CPA	141

C. majority 14,356 (28.07%)
1.63% swing C. to Lab.
(2015: C. majority 15,174 (31.33%))

HASTINGS & RYE

E. 78,298   T. 54,766 (69.95%)   C. hold

*Amber Rudd, C.	25,668
Peter Chowney, Lab.	25,322
Nicholas Perry, LD	1,885
Michael Phillips, UKIP	1,479
Nicholas Wilson, Ind.	412

C. majority 346 (0.63%)
4.39% swing C. to Lab.
(2015: C. majority 4,796 (9.42%))

HAVANT

E. 72,464   T. 46,314 (63.91%)   C. hold

*Alan Mak, C.	27,676
Graham Giles, Lab.	11,720
Paul Gray, LD	2,801
John Perry, UKIP	2,011
Tim Dawes, Green	1,122
Ann Buckley, Ind.	984

C. majority 15,956 (34.45%)
0.63% swing C. to Lab.
(2015: C. majority 13,920 (31.05%))

HAYES & HARLINGTON

E. 73,268   T. 47,802 (65.24%)   Lab. hold

*John McDonnell, Lab.	31,796
Greg Smith, C.	13,681
Cliff Dixon, UKIP	1,153
Bill Newton Dunn, LD	601
John Bowman, Green	571

Lab. majority 18,115 (37.90%)
1.53% swing C. to Lab.
(2015: Lab. majority 15,700 (34.85%))

HAZEL GROVE

E. 62,684   T. 44,132 (70.40%)   C. hold

*William Wragg, C.	20,047
Lisa Smart, LD	14,533
Nav Mishra, Lab.	9,036
Robbie Lee, Green	516

C. majority 5,514 (12.49%)
1.33% swing C. to LD
(2015: C. majority 6,552 (15.16%))

HEMEL HEMPSTEAD

E. 75,011   T. 52,282 (69.70%)   C. hold

*Mike Penning, C.	28,735
Mandi Tattershall, Lab.	19,290
Sally Symington, LD	3,233
Sherief Hassan, Green	1,024

C. majority 9,445 (18.07%)
5.49% swing C. to Lab.
(2015: C. majority 14,420 (29.05%))

HEMSWORTH

E. 71,870   T. 45,944 (63.93%)   Lab. hold

*Jon Trickett, Lab.	25,740
Mike Jordan, C.	15,566
David Dews, UKIP	2,591
Martin Roberts, Yorkshire	1,135
Joan MacQueen, LD	912

Lab. majority 10,174 (22.14%)
3.17% swing Lab. to C.
(2015: Lab. majority 12,078 (28.48%))

HENDON

E. 76,329   T. 52,215 (68.41%)   C. hold

*Matthew Offord, C.	25,078
Mike Katz, Lab.	24,006
Alasdair Hill, LD	1,985
Carmen Legarda, Green	578
Sabriye Warsame, UKIP	568

C. majority 1,072 (2.05%)
2.73% swing C. to Lab.
(2015: C. majority 3,724 (7.50%))

HENLEY

E. 74,987   T. 57,099 (76.15%)   C. hold

*John Howell, C.	33,749
Oliver Kavanagh, Lab.	11,455
Laura Coyle, LD	8,485
Robin Bennett, Green	1,864
Tim Scott, UKIP	1,154
Patrick Gray, Radical	392

C. majority 22,294 (39.04%)
3.45% swing C. to Lab.
(2015: C. majority 25,375 (45.94%))

HEREFORD & HEREFORDSHIRE SOUTH

E. 71,088   T. 50,484 (71.02%)   C. hold

*Jesse Norman, C.	27,004
Anna Coda, Lab.	11,991
Jim Kenyon, Ind.	5,560
Lucy Hurds, LD	3,556
Diana Toynbee, Green	1,220
Gwyn Price, UKIP	1,153

C. majority 15,013 (29.74%)
5.02% swing C. to Lab.
(2015: C. majority 16,890 (35.74%))

HEREFORDSHIRE NORTH

E. 67,751   T. 50,177 (74.06%)   C. hold

*Bill Wiggin, C.	31,097
Roger Page, Lab.	9,495
Jeanie Falconer, LD	5,874
Ellie Chowns, Green	2,771
Sasha Norris, Ind.	577
Arthur Devine, Ind.	363

C. majority 21,602 (43.05%)
0.59% swing C. to Lab.
(2015: C. majority 19,996 (41.64%))

HERTFORD & STORTFORD

E. 82,429   T. 59,992 (72.78%)   C. hold

*Mark Prisk, C.	36,184
Katherine Chibah, Lab.	17,149
Mark Argent, LD	4,845
David Woollcombe, Green	1,814

C. majority 19,035 (31.73%)
3.25% swing C. to Lab.
(2015: C. majority 21,509 (38.22%))

HERTFORDSHIRE NORTH EAST

E. 75,967   T. 55,580 (73.16%)   C. hold

*Oliver Heald, C.	32,587
Doug Swanney, Lab.	15,752
Nicky Shepard, LD	4,276
Tim Lee, Green	2,965

C. majority 16,835 (30.29%)
3.10% swing C. to Lab.
(2015: C. majority 19,080 (36.49%))

HERTFORDSHIRE SOUTH WEST

E. 80,293   T. 60,653 (75.54%)   C. hold

*David Gauke, C.	35,128
Robert Wakely, Lab.	15,578
Christopher Townsend, LD	7,078
Paul De Hoest, Green	1,576
Mark Anderson, UKIP	1,293

C. majority 19,550 (32.23%)
4.19% swing C. to Lab.
(2015: C. majority 23,263 (40.62%))

HERTSMERE

E. 73,554 T. 52,253 (71.04%)   C. hold
*Oliver Dowden, C.   31,928
Fiona Smith, Lab.   14,977
Joe Jordan, LD   2,794
David Hoy, UKIP   1,564
Sophie Summerhayes, Green   990
C. majority 16,951 (32.44%)
2.21% swing C. to Lab.
(2015: C. majority 18,461 (36.85%))

HEXHAM

E. 61,012 T. 46,224 (75.76%)   C. hold
*Guy Opperman, C.   24,996
Stephen Powers, Lab.   15,760
Fiona Hall, LD   3,285
Wesley Foot, Green   1,253
Francis Miles, UKIP   930
C. majority 9,236 (19.98%)
3.89% swing C. to Lab.
(2015: C. majority 12,031 (27.76%))

HEYWOOD & MIDDLETON

E. 79,901 T. 49,865 (62.41%)   Lab. hold
*Liz McInnes, Lab.   26,578
Chris Clarkson, C.   18,961
Lee Seville, UKIP   3,239
Bill Winlow, LD   1,087
Lab. majority 7,617 (15.28%)
4.37% swing Lab. to C.
(2015: Lab. majority 5,299 (10.92%))

HIGH PEAK

E. 73,254 T. 53,853 (73.52%)   Lab. gain
Ruth George, Lab.   26,753
*Andrew Bingham, C.   24,431
Charles Lawley, LD   2,669
Lab. majority 2,322 (4.31%)
6.97% swing C. to Lab.
(2015: C. majority 4,894 (9.64%))

HITCHIN & HARPENDEN

E. 75,916 T. 58,783 (77.43%)   C. hold
Bim Afolami, C.   31,189
John Hayes, Lab.   19,158
Hugh Annand, LD   6,236
Richard Cano, Green   1,329
Ray Blake, Ind.   629
Sid Cordle, CPA   242
C. majority 12,031 (20.47%)
7.87% swing C. to Lab.
(2015: C. majority 20,055 (36.22%))

HOLBORN & ST PANCRAS

E. 88,088 T. 58,997 (66.98%)   Lab. hold
*Keir Starmer, Lab.   41,343
Tim Barnes, C.   10,834
Stephen Crosher, LD   4,020
Sian Berry, Green   1,980
Giles Game, UKIP   727
Janus Polenceus, Eng. Dem.   93
Lab. majority 30,509 (51.71%)
10.33% swing C. to Lab.
(2015: Lab. majority 17,048 (31.04%))

HORNCHURCH & UPMINSTER

E. 80,821 T. 56,107 (69.42%)   C. hold
Julia Dockerill, C.   33,750
Rocky Gill, Lab.   16,027
Lawrence Webb, UKIP   3,502
Jonathan Mitchell, LD   1,371
Peter Caton, Green   1,077
David Furness, BNP   380
C. majority 17,723 (31.59%)
1.36% swing Lab. to C.
(2015: C. majority 13,074 (23.67%))

HORNSEY & WOOD GREEN

E. 79,944 T. 62,293 (77.92%)   Lab. hold
*Catherine West, Lab.   40,738
Dawn Barnes, LD   10,000
Emma Lane, C.   9,246
Sam Hall, Green   1,181
Nimco Ali, Women   551
Ruth Price, UKIP   429
Helen Spiby-Vann, CPA   93
Anna Athow, WRP   55
Lab. majority 30,738 (49.34%)
15.10% swing LD to Lab.
(2015: Lab. majority 11,058 (19.14%))

HORSHAM

E. 82,773 T. 61,987 (74.89%)   C. hold
*Jeremy Quin, C.   36,906
Susannah Brady, Lab.   13,422
Morwen Millson, LD   7,644
Catherine Ross, Green   1,844
Roger Arthur, UKIP   1,533
James Smith, S. New   375
Jim Duggan, Peace   263
C. majority 23,484 (37.89%)
4.01% swing C. to Lab.
(2015: C. majority 24,658 (43.32%))

HOUGHTON & SUNDERLAND SOUTH

E. 68,123 T. 41,480 (60.89%)   Lab. hold
*Bridget Phillipson, Lab.   24,665
Paul Howell, C.   12,324
Michael Joyce, UKIP   2,379
Paul Edgeworth, LD   908
Richard Bradley, Green   725
Mick Watson, Ind.   479
Lab. majority 12,341 (29.75%)
3.46% swing Lab. to C.
(2015: Lab. majority 12,938 (33.61%))

HOVE

E. 74,236 T. 57,596 (77.58%)   Lab. hold
*Peter Kyle, Lab.   36,942
Kristy Adams, C.   18,185
Caroline Hynds, LD   1,311
Phelim Mac Cafferty, Green   971
Charley Sabel, Ind.   187
Lab. majority 18,757 (32.57%)
15.10% swing C. to Lab.
(2015: Lab. majority 1,236 (2.37%))

HUDDERSFIELD

E. 67,033 T. 43,834 (65.39%)
                                Lab. Co-op hold
*Barry Sheerman,
Lab. Co-op   26,470
Scott Benton, C.   14,465
Andrew Cooper, Green   1,395
Zulfiqar Ali, LD   1,155
Bikatshi Katenga, Yorkshire   274
Marteen
Thokkudubiyyapu, Ind.   75
Lab. Co-op majority 12,005 (27.39%)
4.62% swing C. to Lab.
(2015: Lab. Co-op majority 7,345
(18.15%))

HULL EAST

E. 65,959 T. 36,638 (55.55%)   Lab. hold
*Karl Turner, Lab.   21,355
Simon Burton, C.   10,959
Mark Fox, UKIP   2,573
Andrew Marchington, LD   1,258
Julia Brown, Green   493
Lab. majority 10,396 (28.37%)
3.72% swing Lab. to C.
(2015: Lab. majority 10,319 (29.36%))

HULL NORTH

E. 64,666 T. 37,102 (57.37%)   Lab. hold
*Diana Johnson, Lab.   23,625
Lia Nici-Townend, C.   9,363
Mike Ross, LD   1,869
John Kitchener, UKIP   1,601
Martin Deane, Green   644
Lab. majority 14,262 (38.44%)
0.32% swing C. to Lab.
(2015: Lab. majority 12,899 (36.50%))

HULL WEST & HESSLE

E. 60,181 T. 34,565 (57.44%)   Lab. hold
Emma Hardy, Lab.   18,342
Christine Mackay, C.   10,317
Claire Thomas, LD   2,210
Michelle Dewberry, Ind.   1,898
Gary Shores, UKIP   1,399
Mike Lammiman, Green   332
Will Taylor, Libertarian   67
Lab. majority 8,025 (23.22%)
4.25% swing Lab. to C.
(2015: Lab. majority 9,333 (29.35%))

HUNTINGDON

E. 84,320 T. 59,720 (70.83%)   C. hold
*Jonathan Djanogly, C.   32,915
Nik Johnson, Lab.   18,440
Rod Cantrill, LD   5,090
Paul Bullen, UKIP   2,180
Tom MacLennan, Green   1,095
C. majority 14,475 (24.24%)
5.23% swing C. to Lab.
(2015: C. majority 19,404 (34.70%))

HYNDBURN

E. 73,110 T. 45,202 (61.83%)   Lab. hold
*Graham Jones, Lab.   24,120
Kevin Horkin, C.   18,305
Janet Brown, UKIP   1,953
Les Jones, LD   824
Lab. majority 5,815 (12.86%)
1.30% swing C. to Lab.
(2015: Lab. majority 4,400 (10.26%))

ILFORD NORTH
E. 72,997 T. 52,941 (72.52%) Lab. hold
*Wes Streeting, Lab.   30,589
Lee Scott, C.   20,950
Richard Clare, LD   1,034
Doris Osen, Ind.   368
Lab. majority 9,639 (18.21%)
8.50% swing C. to Lab.
(2015: Lab. majority 589 (1.20%))

ILFORD SOUTH
E. 85,358 T. 57,657 (67.55%)
                         Lab. Co-op hold
*Mike Gapes, Lab. Co-op   43,724
Chris Chapman, C.   12,077
Farid Ahmed, LD   772
Rosemary
Warrington, Green   542
Tariq Saeed, UKIP   477
Kane Khan, Friends   65
Lab. Co-op majority 31,647 (54.89%)
8.40% swing C. to Lab.
(2015: Lab. Co-op majority 19,777
(38.10%))

IPSWICH
E. 74,799 T. 51,137 (68.37%) Lab. gain
Sandy Martin, Lab.   24,224
*Ben Gummer, C.   23,393
Tony Gould, UKIP   1,372
Adrian Hyyrylainen-Trett,
LD   1,187
Charlotte Armstrong, Green   840
David Tabane, Ind.   121
Lab. majority 831 (1.63%)
4.65% swing C. to Lab.
(2015: C. majority 3,733 (7.67%))

ISLE OF WIGHT
E. 110,697 T. 74,479 (67.28%)   C. hold
Bob Seely, C.   38,190
Julian Critchley, Lab.   17,121
Vix Lowthion, Green   12,915
Nick Belfitt, LD   2,740
Daryll Pitcher, UKIP   1,921
Julie Jones-Evans, Ind.   1,592
C. majority 21,069 (28.29%)
0.20% swing Lab. to C.
(2015: C. majority 13,703 (19.49%))

ISLINGTON NORTH
E. 74,831 T. 54,928 (73.40%) Lab. hold
*Jeremy Corbyn, Lab.   40,086
James Clark, C.   6,871
Keith Angus, LD   4,946
Caroline Russell, Green   2,229
Keith Fraser, UKIP   413
Michael Foster, ND   208
Knigel Knapp, Loony   106
Susanne Cameron-Blackie,
Ind.   41
Bill Martin, SPGB   21
Andres Mendoza,
Comm. Lge   7
Lab. majority 33,215 (60.47%)
8.71% swing C. to Lab.
(2015: Lab. majority 21,194 (43.05%))

ISLINGTON SOUTH & FINSBURY
E. 69,534 T. 48,049 (69.10%) Lab. hold
*Emily Thornberry, Lab.   30,188
Jason Charalambous, C.   9,925
Alain Desmier, LD   5,809
Benali Hamdache, Green   1,198
Pete Muswell, UKIP   929
Lab. majority 20,263 (42.17%)
6.73% swing C. to Lab.
(2015: Lab. majority 12,708 (28.71%))

JARROW
E. 64,828 T. 43,023 (66.36%) Lab. hold
*Stephen Hepburn, Lab.   28,020
Robin Gwynn, C.   10,757
James Askwith, UKIP   2,338
Peter Maughan, LD   1,163
David Herbert, Green   745
Lab. majority 17,263 (40.13%)
0.77% swing C. to Lab.
(2015: Lab. majority 13,881 (35.99%))

KEIGHLEY
E. 71,429 T. 51,724 (72.41%) Lab. gain
‡John Grogan, Lab.   24,066
*Kris Hopkins, C.   23,817
Paul Latham, UKIP   1,291
Matt Walker, LD   1,226
Ros Brown, Green   790
David Crabtree, Ind.   534
Lab. majority 249 (0.48%)
3.35% swing C. to Lab.
(2015: C. majority 3,053 (6.22%))

KENILWORTH & SOUTHAM
E. 66,323 T. 51,311 (77.37%)   C. hold
*Jeremy Wright, C.   31,207
Bally Singh, Lab.   13,121
Richard Dickson, LD   4,921
Rob Ballantyne, Green   1,133
Harry Cottam, UKIP   929
C. majority 18,086 (35.25%)
3.90% swing C. to Lab.
(2015: C. majority 21,002 (43.04%))

KENSINGTON
E. 60,594 T. 38,677 (63.83%) Lab. gain
Emma Dent Coad, Lab.   16,333
*Lady (Victoria) Borwick, C.   16,313
Annabel Mullin, LD   4,724
Jennifer Nadel, Green   767
James Torrance, Ind.   393
Peter Marshall, Ind.   98
John Lloyd, Green Soc.   49
Lab. majority 20 (0.05%)
10.59% swing C. to Lab.
(2015: C. majority 7,361 (21.14%))

KETTERING
E. 71,523 T. 49,404 (69.07%)   C. hold
*Philip Hollobone, C.   28,616
Mick Scrimshaw, Lab.   18,054
Suzanna Austin, LD   1,618
Rob Reeves, Green   1,116
C. majority 10,562 (21.38%)
2.64% swing C. to Lab.
(2015: C. majority 12,590 (26.66%))

KINGSTON & SURBITON
E. 81,584 T. 62,178 (76.21%)   LD gain
†Edward Davey, LD   27,810
*James Berry, C.   23,686
Laurie South, Lab.   9,203
Graham Matthews, UKIP   675
Chris Walker, Green   536
Jason Chinnery, Loony   168
Michael Basman, Ind.   100
LD majority 4,124 (6.63%)
5.71% swing C. to LD
(2015: C. majority 2,834 (4.78%))

KINGSWOOD
E. 69,426 T. 48,741 (70.21%)   C. hold
*Chris Skidmore, C.   26,754
Mhairi Threlfall, Lab.   19,254
Karen Wilkinson, LD   1,749
Matt Furey-King, Green   984
C. majority 7,500 (15.39%)
1.66% swing C. to Lab.
(2015: C. majority 9,006 (18.71%))

KNOWSLEY
E. 81,751 T. 55,483 (67.87%) Lab. hold
*George Howarth, Lab.   47,351
James Spencer, C.   5,137
Neil Miney, UKIP   1,285
Carl Cashman, LD   1,189
Steve Baines, Green   521
Lab. majority 42,214 (76.08%)
2.30% swing C. to Lab.
(2015: Lab. majority 34,655 (68.32%))

LANCASHIRE WEST
E. 73,258 T. 54,389 (74.24%) Lab. hold
*Rosie Cooper, Lab.   32,030
Sam Currie, C.   20,341
Jo Barton, LD   1,069
Nate Higgins, Green   680
David Braid, WVPTFP   269
Lab. majority 11,689 (21.49%)
2.33% swing C. to Lab.
(2015: Lab. majority 8,360 (16.83%))

LANCASTER & FLEETWOOD
E. 67,171 T. 45,989 (68.47%) Lab. hold
*Cat Smith, Lab.   25,342
Eric Ollerenshaw, C.   18,681
Robin Long, LD   1,170
Rebecca Novell, Green   796
Lab. majority 6,661 (14.48%)
5.73% swing C. to Lab.
(2015: Lab. majority 1,265 (3.03%))

LEEDS CENTRAL
E. 89,537 T. 47,673 (53.24%) Lab. hold
*Hilary Benn, Lab.   33,453
Gareth Davies, C.   9,755
Bill Palfreman, UKIP   2,056
Ed Carlisle, Green   1,189
Andy Nash, LD   1,063
Alex Coetzee, CPA   157
Lab. majority 23,698 (49.71%)
6.02% swing C. to Lab.
(2015: Lab. majority 16,967 (37.66%))

LEEDS EAST
E. 65,950   T. 41,441 (62.84%) Lab. hold
*Richard Burgon, Lab.   25,428
Matthew Robinson, C.   12,676
Paul Spivey, UKIP   1,742
Ed Sanderson, LD   739
Jaimes Moran, Green   434
John Otley, Yorkshire   422
Lab. majority 12,752 (30.77%)
1.02% swing Lab. to C.
(2015: Lab. majority 12,533 (32.81%))

LEEDS NORTH EAST
E. 70,112   T. 52,999 (75.59%) Lab. hold
*Fabian Hamilton, Lab.   33,436
Ryan Stephenson, C.   16,445
Jon Hannah, LD   1,952
Ann Forsaith, Green   680
Tess Seddon, Yorkshire   303
Celia Foote, Green Soc.   116
Tim Mutamiri, CPA   67
Lab. majority 16,991 (32.06%)
8.52% swing C. to Lab.
(2015: Lab. majority 7,250 (15.01%))

LEEDS NORTH WEST
E. 68,152   T. 46,287 (67.92%)
                              Lab. Co-op gain
Alex Sobel, Lab. Co-op   20,416
*Greg Mulholland, LD   16,192
Alan Lamb, C.   9,097
Martin Hemingway, Green   582
Lab. Co-op majority 4,224 (9.13%)
7.92% swing LD to Lab.
(2015: LD majority 2,907 (6.70%))

LEEDS WEST
E. 67,955   T. 42,229 (62.14%) Lab. hold
*Rachel Reeves, Lab.   27,013
Zoe Metcalfe, C.   11,048
Mark Thackray, UKIP   1,815
Andrew Pointon, Green   1,023
Alisdair McGregor, LD   905
Ed Jones, Yorkshire   378
Mike Davies, Green Soc.   47
Lab. majority 15,965 (37.81%)
4.94% swing C. to Lab.
(2015: Lab. majority 10,727 (27.92%))

LEICESTER EAST
E. 77,788   T. 52,424 (67.39%) Lab. hold
*Keith Vaz, Lab.   35,116
Edward He, C.   12,688
Sujata Barot, Ind.   1,753
Nitesh Dave, LD   1,343
Melanie Wakley, Green   1,070
Ian Fox, Ind.   454
Lab. majority 22,428 (42.78%)
2.30% swing C. to Lab.
(2015: Lab. majority 18,352 (38.18%))

LEICESTER SOUTH
E. 75,534   T. 50,517 (66.88%)
                              Lab. Co-op hold
*Jon Ashworth, Lab. Co-op   37,157
Meera Sonecha, C.   10,896
Harrish Bisnauthsing, LD   1,287
Mags Lewis, Green   1,177
Lab. Co-op majority 26,261 (51.98%)
6.56% swing C. to Lab.
(2015: Lab. Co-op majority 17,845
(38.87%))

LEICESTER WEST
E. 64,834   T. 37,512 (57.86%) Lab. hold
*Liz Kendall, Lab.   22,823
Jack Hickey, C.   11,763
Stuart Young, UKIP   1,406
Ian Bradwell, LD   792
Mel Gould, Green   607
David Bowley, Ind.   121
Lab. majority 11,060 (29.48%)
4.31% swing C. to Lab.
(2015: Lab. majority 7,203 (20.86%))

LEICESTERSHIRE NORTH WEST
E. 75,362   T. 53,541 (71.05%)   C. hold
*Andrew Bridgen, C.   31,153
Sean Sheahan, Lab.   17,867
Michael Wyatt, LD   3,420
Mia Woolley, Green   1,101
C. majority 13,286 (24.81%)
1.38% swing Lab. to C.
(2015: C. majority 11,373 (22.06%))

LEICESTERSHIRE SOUTH
E. 78,985   T. 56,689 (71.77%)   C. hold
*Alberto Costa, C.   34,795
Shabbir Aslam, Lab.   16,164
Gregory Webb, LD   2,403
Roger Helmer, UKIP   2,235
Mary Morgan, Green   1,092
C. majority 18,631 (32.87%)
0.83% swing Lab. to C.
(2015: C. majority 16,824 (31.20%))

LEIGH
E. 76,211   T. 46,874 (61.51%)
                              Lab. Co-op hold
Jo Platt, Lab. Co-op   26,347
James Grundy, C.   16,793
Mark Bradley, UKIP   2,783
Richard Kilpatrick, LD   951
Lab. Co-op majority 9,554 (20.38%)
5.43% swing Lab. to C.
(2015: Lab. majority 14,096 (31.24%))

LEWES
E. 70,947   T. 54,192 (76.38%)   C. hold
*Maria Caulfield, C.   26,820
Kelly-Marie Blundell, LD   21,312
Daniel Chapman, Lab.   6,060
C. majority 5,508 (10.16%)
4.01% swing LD to C.
(2015: C. majority 1,083 (2.14%))

LEWISHAM DEPTFORD
E. 78,472   T. 55,112 (70.23%) Lab. hold
*Vicky Foxcroft, Lab.   42,461
Melanie McLean, C.   7,562
Bobby Dean, LD   2,911
John Coughlin, Green   1,640
Malcolm Martin, CPA   252
Laura McAnea, AWP   225
Jane Lawrence, Realist   61
Lab. majority 34,899 (63.32%)
8.98% swing C. to Lab.
(2015: Lab. majority 21,516 (45.37%))

LEWISHAM EAST ℭ
E. 68,126   T. 47,201 (69.28%) Lab. hold
*Heidi Alexander, Lab.   32,072
Peter Fortune, C.   10,859
Emily Frith, LD   2,086
Storm Poorun, Green   803
Keith Forster, UKIP   798
Willow Winston, Ind.   355
Maureen Martin, CPA   228
Lab. majority 21,213 (44.94%)
5.77% swing C. to Lab.
(2015: Lab. majority 14,333 (33.39%))

LEWISHAM WEST & PENGE
E. 72,902   T. 53,196 (72.97%) Lab. hold
Ellie Reeves, Lab.   35,411
Shaun Bailey, C.   12,249
John Russell, LD   3,317
Karen Wheller, Green   1,144
Hoong-Wai Cheah, UKIP   700
Katherine Hortense, CPA   325
Russell White, Populist   50
Lab. majority 23,162 (43.54%)
8.56% swing C. to Lab.
(2015: Lab. majority 12,714 (26.42%))

LEYTON & WANSTEAD
E. 65,285   T. 46,173 (70.73%) Lab. hold
*John Cryer, Lab.   32,234
Laura Farris, C.   9,627
Ben Sims, LD   2,961
Ashley Gunstock, Green   1,351
Lab. majority 22,607 (48.96%)
6.15% swing C. to Lab.
(2015: Lab. majority 14,919 (36.65%))

LICHFIELD
E. 74,430   T. 53,524 (71.91%)   C. hold
*Michael Fabricant, C.   34,018
Chris Worsey, Lab.   15,437
Paul Ray, LD   2,653
Robert Pass, Green   1,416
C. majority 18,581 (34.72%)
0.31% swing C. to Lab.
(2015: C. majority 18,189 (35.34%))

LINCOLN
E. 73,111   T. 48,718 (66.64%) Lab. gain
Karen Lee, Lab.   23,333
*Karl McCartney, C.   21,795
Nick Smith, UKIP   1,287
Caroline Kenyon, LD   1,284
Benjamin Loryman, Green   583
Phil Gray, Ind.   312
Iain Scott-Burdon, Ind.   124
Lab. majority 1,538 (3.16%)
3.12% swing C. to Lab.
(2015: C. majority 1,443 (3.08%))

LIVERPOOL RIVERSIDE
E. 76,332   T. 48,020 (62.91%)
                              Lab. Co-op hold
*Louise Ellman, Lab. Co-op   40,599
Pamela Hall, C.   4,652
Stephanie Pitchers, Green   1,582
Tom Sebire, LD   1,187
Lab. Co-op majority 35,947 (74.86%)
8.52% swing C. to Lab.
(2015: Lab. Co-op majority 24,463
(55.27%))

LIVERPOOL WALTON
E. 62,738   T. 42,197 (67.26%)   Lab. hold
Dan Carden, Lab.   36,175
Laura Evans, C.   3,624
Terry May, Ind.   1,237
Kris Brown, LD   638
Colm Feeley, Green   523
Lab. majority 32,551 (77.14%)
0.27% swing C. to Lab.
(2015: Lab. majority 27,777 (72.33%))

LIVERPOOL WAVERTREE
E. 62,411   T. 43,640 (69.92%)
                              Lab. Co-op hold
*Luciana Berger, Lab. Co-op   34,717
Denise Haddad, C.   5,251
Richard Kemp, LD   2,858
Ted Grant, Green   598
Adam Heatherington, ND   216
Lab. Co-op majority 29,466 (67.52%)
4.10% swing C. to Lab.
(2015: Lab. Co-op majority 24,303
(59.31%))

LIVERPOOL WEST DERBY
E. 65,164   T. 45,163 (69.31%)
                              Lab. Co-op hold
*Stephen Twigg, Lab. Co-op   37,371
Paul Richardson, C.   4,463
Steve Radford, Lib.   2,150
Paul Parr, LD   545
Will Ward, Green   329
Graham Hughes, Ind.   305
Lab. Co-op majority 32,908 (72.86%)
2.15% swing C. to Lab.
(2015: Lab. Co-op majority 27,367
(66.70%))

LOUGHBOROUGH
E. 79,607   T. 54,148 (68.02%)   C. hold
*Nicky Morgan, C.   27,022
Jewel Miah, Lab.   22,753
David Walker, LD   1,937
Andy McWilliam, UKIP   1,465
Philip Leicester, Green   971
C. majority 4,269 (7.88%)
4.88% swing C. to Lab.
(2015: C. majority 9,183 (17.65%))

LOUTH & HORNCASTLE
E. 79,006   T. 52,771 (66.79%)   C. hold
*Victoria Atkins, C.   33,733
Julie Speed, Lab.   14,092
Jonathan Noble, UKIP   2,460
Lisa Gabriel, LD   1,990
The Iconic Arty-Pole, Loony   496
C. majority 19,641 (37.22%)
2.04% swing Lab. to C.
(2015: C. majority 14,977 (29.75%))

LUDLOW
E. 68,034   T. 49,970 (73.45%)   C. hold
*Philip Dunne, C.   31,433
Julia Buckley, Lab.   12,147
Heather Kidd, LD   5,336
Hilary Wendt, Green   1,054
C. majority 19,286 (38.60%)
1.71% swing C. to Lab.
(2015: C. majority 18,929 (39.38%))

LUTON NORTH
E. 66,811   T. 46,622 (69.78%)   Lab. hold
*Kelvin Hopkins, Lab.   29,765
Caroline Kerswell, C.   15,401
Rabi Martins, LD   808
Simon Hall, Green   648
Lab. majority 14,364 (30.81%)
4.24% swing C. to Lab.
(2015: Lab. majority 9,504 (22.33%))

LUTON SOUTH
E. 67,188   T. 46,133 (68.66%)
                              Lab. Co-op hold
*Gavin Shuker, Lab. Co-op   28,804
Dean Russell, C.   14,879
Andrew Strange, LD   1,056
Ujjawal Ub, UKIP   795
Marc Scheimann, Green   439
Abid Ali, Ind.   160
Lab. Co-op majority 13,925 (30.18%)
8.33% swing C. to Lab.
(2015: Lab. Co-op majority 5,711
(13.53%))

MACCLESFIELD
E. 75,228   T. 54,307 (72.19%)   C. hold
*David Rutley, C.   28,595
Neil Puttick, Lab.   19,987
Richard Flowers, LD   3,350
James Booth, Green   1,213
Mark Johnson, Ind.   1,162
C. majority 8,608 (15.85%)
7.01% swing C. to Lab.
(2015: C. majority 14,811 (29.86%))

MAIDENHEAD
E. 76,276   T. 58,239 (76.35%)   C. hold
*Theresa May, C.   37,718
Pat McDonald, Lab.   11,261
Tony Hill, LD   6,540
Derek Wall, Green   907
Gerard Batten, UKIP   871
Andrew Knight, AWP   282
Lord Buckethead, ND   249
Grant Smith, Ind.   152
Howling 'Laud'
Hope, Loony   119
Edmonds Victor, CPA   69
Julian Reid, Just   52
Yemi Hailemariam, Ind.   16
Bobby Smith, ND   3
C. majority 26,457 (45.43%)
4.26% swing C. to Lab.
(2015: C. majority 29,059 (53.96%))

MAIDSTONE & THE WEALD
E. 75,334   T. 51,696 (68.62%)   C. hold
*Helen Grant, C.   29,136
Allen Simpson, Lab.   11,432
Emily Fermor, LD   8,455
Pamela Watts, UKIP   1,613
Stuart Jeffery, Green   888
Yolande Kenward, Ind.   172
C. majority 17,704 (34.25%)
0.35% swing C. to Lab.
(2015: C. majority 10,709 (21.41%))

MAKERFIELD
E. 74,259   T. 46,933 (63.20%)   Lab. hold
*Yvonne Fovargue, Lab.   28,245
Adam Carney, C.   14,703
Bob Brierley, Ind.   2,663
John Skipworth, LD   1,322
Lab. majority 13,542 (28.85%)
1.71% swing Lab. to C.
(2015: Lab. majority 13,155 (29.37%))

MALDON
E. 66,960   T. 50,202 (74.97%)   C. hold
*John Whittingdale, C.   34,111
Peter Edwards, Lab.   10,681
Zoe O'Connell, LD   2,181
Jesse Pryke, UKIP   1,899
Steven Betteridge, Green   1,073
Richard Perry, BNP   257
C. majority 23,430 (46.67%)
1.04% swing C. to Lab.
(2015: C. majority 22,070 (45.94%))

MANCHESTER CENTRAL
E. 90,261   T. 49,720 (55.08%)
                              Lab. Co-op hold
*Lucy Powell, Lab. Co-op   38,490
Xingang Wang, C.   7,045
John Bridges, LD   1,678
Kalvin Chapman, UKIP   1,469
Rachael Shah, Green   846
Neil Blackburn, Pirate   192
Lab. Co-op majority 31,445 (63.24%)
7.75% swing C. to Lab.
(2015: Lab. Co-op majority 21,639
(47.74%))

MANCHESTER GORTON
E. 75,362   T. 45,953 (60.98%)   Lab. hold
Afzal Khan, Lab.   35,085
Shaden Jaradat, C.   3,355
George Galloway, Ind.   2,615
Jackie Pearcey, LD   2,597
Jess Mayo, Green   1,038
Phil Eckersley, UKIP   952
Kemi Abidogun, CPA   233
David Hopkins, Ind.   51
Peter Clifford, Comm. Lge   27
Lab. majority 31,730 (69.05%)
5.82% swing C. to Lab.
(2015: Lab. majority 24,079 (57.31%))

MANCHESTER WITHINGTON
E. 74,553   T. 53,602 (71.90%)   Lab. hold
*Jeff Smith, Lab.   38,424
John Leech, LD   8,549
Sarah Heald, C.   5,530
Laura Bannister, Green   865
Sally Carr, Women   234
Lab. majority 29,875 (55.73%)
12.98% swing LD to Lab.
(2015: Lab. majority 14,873 (29.77%))

MANSFIELD
E. 77,811   T. 50,157 (64.46%)   C. gain
Ben Bradley, C.   23,392
*Sir Alan Meale, Lab.   22,335
Sid Pepper, UKIP   2,654
Philip Shields, Ind.   1,079
Anita Prabhakar, LD   697
C. majority 1,057 (2.11%)
6.68% swing Lab. to C.
(2015: Lab. majority 5,315 (11.26%))

MEON VALLEY
E. 74,246   T. 54,192 (72.99%)   C. hold
*George Hollingbery, C.   35,624
Sheena King, Lab.   9,932
Martin Tod, LD   5,900
Paul Bailey, UKIP   1,435
Andrew Hayward, Green   1,301
C. majority 25,692 (47.41%)
1.36% swing C. to Lab.
(2015: C. majority 23,913 (46.24%))

MERIDEN
E. 81,437   T. 54,643 (67.10%)   C. hold
*Caroline Spelman, C.   33,873
Tom McNeil, Lab.   14,675
Antony Rogers, LD   2,663
Leslie Kaye, UKIP   2,016
Alison Gavin, Green   1,416
C. majority 19,198 (35.13%)
0.30% swing C. to Lab.
(2015: C. majority 18,795 (35.73%))

MIDDLESBROUGH
E. 61,114   T. 35,637 (58.31%) Lab. hold
*Andy McDonald, Lab.   23,404
Jacob Young, C.   9,531
David Hodgson, UKIP   1,452
Terry Lawton, Ind.   632
Dawud Islam, LD   368
Carl Martinez, Green   250
Lab. majority 13,873 (38.93%)
0.71% swing Lab. to C.
(2015: Lab. majority 12,477 (38.15%))

MIDDLESBROUGH SOUTH &
CLEVELAND EAST
E. 72,336   T. 47,620 (65.83%)   C. gain
Simon Clarke, C.   23,643
Tracy Harvey, Lab.   22,623
Chris Foote-Wood, LD   1,354
C. majority 1,020 (2.14%)
3.55% swing Lab. to C.
(2015: Lab. majority 2,268 (4.97%))

MILTON KEYNES NORTH
E. 89,272   T. 63,864 (71.54%)   C. hold
*Mark Lancaster, C.   30,307
Charlynne Pullen, Lab.   28,392
Imogen Shepherd-   2,499
Dubey, LD
Jeff Wyatt, UKIP   1,390
Alan Francis, Green   1,107
Venetia Sams, CPA   169
C. majority 1,915 (3.00%)
6.95% swing C. to Lab.
(2015: C. majority 9,753 (16.91%))

MILTON KEYNES SOUTH
E. 92,494   T. 64,486 (69.72%)   C. hold
*Iain Stewart, C.   30,652
Hannah O'Neill, Lab.   28,927
Tahir Maher, LD   1,895
Vince Peddle, UKIP   1,833
Graham Findlay, Green   1,179
C. majority 1,725 (2.67%)
6.07% swing C. to Lab.
(2015: C. majority 8,742 (14.81%))

MITCHAM & MORDEN
E. 68,705   T. 48,118 (70.04%) Lab. hold
*Siobhain McDonagh, Lab.   33,039
Alicia Kearns, C.   11,664
Claire Mathys, LD   1,494
Richard Hilton, UKIP   1,054
Laura Collins, Green   644
Des Coke, CPA   223
Lab. majority 21,375 (44.42%)
3.47% swing C. to Lab.
(2015: Lab. majority 16,922 (37.49%))

MOLE VALLEY
E. 74,545   T. 56,726 (76.10%)   C. hold
*Paul Beresford, C.   35,092
Paul Kennedy, LD   10,955
Marc Green, Lab.   7,864
Jacquetta Fewster, Green   1,463
Judy Moore, UKIP   1,352
C. majority 24,137 (42.55%)
1.81% swing C. to LD
(2015: C. majority 25,453 (46.16%))

MORECAMBE & LUNESDALE
E. 66,838   T. 45,657 (68.31%)   C. hold
*David Morris, C.   21,773
Vikki Singleton, Lab.   20,374
Matthew Severn, LD   1,699
Robert Gillespie, UKIP   1,333
Cait Sinclair, Green   478
C. majority 1,399 (3.06%)
3.78% swing C. to Lab.
(2015: C. majority 4,590 (10.61%))

MORLEY & OUTWOOD
E. 76,495   T. 52,357 (68.44%)   C. hold
*Andrea Jenkyns, C.   26,550
Neil Dawson, Lab. Co-op   24,446
Craig Dobson, LD   1,361
C. majority 2,104 (4.02%)
1.57% swing Lab. to C.
(2015: C. majority 422 (0.87%))

NEW FOREST EAST
E. 72,602   T. 51,366 (70.75%)   C. hold
*Julian Lewis, C.   32,162
Julie Renyard, Lab.   10,167
David Harrison, LD   7,786
Henry Mellor, Green   1,251
C. majority 21,995 (42.82%)
0.63% swing C. to Lab.
(2015: C. majority 19,162 (38.75%))

NEW FOREST WEST
E. 68,787   T. 49,627 (72.15%)   C. hold
*Desmond Swayne, C.   33,170
Jo Graham, Lab.   9,739
Terry Scriven, LD   4,781
Janet Richards, Green   1,454
Des Hjerling, Pirate   483
C. majority 23,431 (47.21%)
0.95% swing C. to Lab.
(2015: C. majority 20,604 (43.46%))

NEWARK
E. 75,526   T. 55,042 (72.88%)   C. hold
*Robert Jenrick, C.   34,493
Chantal Lee, Lab.   16,344
David Watts, LD   2,786
Xandra Arundel, UKIP   1,419
C. majority 18,149 (32.97%)
1.17% swing C. to Lab.
(2015: C. majority 18,474 (35.32%))

NEWBURY
E. 82,923   T. 60,849 (73.38%)   C. hold
*Richard Benyon, C.   37,399
Judith Bunting, LD   13,019
Alex Skirvin, Lab.   8,596
Paul Field, Green   1,531
Dave Yates, AD   304
C. majority 24,380 (40.07%)
2.98% swing C. to LD
(2015: C. majority 26,368 (46.02%))

NEWCASTLE-UNDER-LYME
E. 65,540   T. 43,842 (66.89%) Lab. hold
*Paul Farrelly, Lab.   21,124
Owen Meredith, C.   21,094
Nigel Jones, LD   1,624
Lab. majority 30 (0.07%)
0.72% swing Lab. to C.
(2015: Lab. majority 650 (1.51%))

NEWCASTLE UPON TYNE
CENTRAL
E. 55,571   T. 37,094 (66.75%) Lab. hold
*Chi Onwurah, Lab.   24,071
Steve Kyte, C.   9,134
Nick Cott, LD   1,812
David Muat, UKIP   1,482
Peter Thomson, Green   595
Lab. majority 14,937 (40.27%)
2.07% swing C. to Lab.
(2015: Lab. majority 12,673 (36.12%))

NEWCASTLE UPON TYNE EAST
E. 62,333   T. 41,637 (66.80%) Lab. hold
*Nick Brown, Lab.   28,127
Simon Kitchen, C.   8,866
Wendy Taylor, LD   2,574
Tony Sanderson, UKIP   1,315
Alistair Ford, Green   755
Lab. majority 19,261 (46.26%)
7.20% swing C. to Lab.
(2015: Lab. majority 12,494 (31.85%))

NEWCASTLE UPON TYNE NORTH
E. 66,312   T. 48,288 (72.82%) Lab. hold
*Catherine McKinnell, Lab.   26,729
Duncan Crute, C.   16,380
Anita Lower, LD   2,533
Timothy Marron, UKIP   1,780
Alison Whalley, Green   513
Brian Moore, North   353
Lab. majority 10,349 (21.43%)
0.59% swing Lab. to C.
(2015: Lab. majority 10,153 (22.62%))

NEWTON ABBOT
E. 71,722   T. 51,637 (72.00%)   C. hold
*Anne Marie Morris, C.   28,635
James Osben, Lab.   11,475
Marie Chadwick, LD   10,601
Kathryn Driscoll, Green   926
C. majority 17,160 (33.23%)
2.12% swing C. to Lab.
(2015: C. majority 11,288 (23.42%))

NORFOLK MID

E. 80,026 T. 55,668 (69.56%)	
*George Freeman, C.	32,828
Sarah Simpson, Lab.	16,742
Fionna Tod, LD	2,848
Tracy Knowles, UKIP	2,092
Hannah Lester, Green	1,158

C. majority 16,086 (28.90%)
2.43% swing C. to Lab.
(2015: C. majority 17,276 (33.09%))

NORFOLK NORTH

E. 69,263 T. 52,188 (75.35%)		LD hold
*Norman Lamb, LD	25,260	
James Wild, C.	21,748	
Stephen Burke, Lab.	5,180	

LD majority 3,512 (6.73%)
0.73% swing LD to C.
(2015: LD majority 4,043 (8.18%))

NORFOLK NORTH WEST

E. 72,062 T. 48,811 (67.73%)		C. hold
*Henry Bellingham, C.	29,408	
Jo Rust, Lab.	15,620	
Michael Stone, UKIP	1,539	
Rupert Moss-Eccardt, LD	1,393	
Andrew de Whalley, Green	851	

C. majority 13,788 (28.25%)
0.60% swing C. to Lab.
(2015: C. majority 13,948 (29.44%))

NORFOLK SOUTH

E. 83,056 T. 61,111 (73.58%)		C. hold
*Richard Bacon, C.	35,580	
Danielle Glavin, Lab.	18,902	
Christopher Brown, LD	5,074	
Catherine Rowett, Green	1,555	

C. majority 16,678 (27.29%)
4.29% swing C. to Lab.
(2015: C. majority 20,493 (35.88%))

NORFOLK SOUTH WEST

E. 77,874 T. 52,416 (67.31%)		C. hold
*Elizabeth Truss, C.	32,894	
Peter Smith, Lab.	14,582	
David Williams, UKIP	2,575	
Stephen Gordon, LD	2,365	

C. majority 18,312 (34.94%)
0.64% swing Lab. to C.
(2015: C. majority 13,861 (27.66%))

NORMANTON, PONTEFRACT & CASTLEFORD

E. 81,641 T. 49,191 (60.25%)		Lab. hold
*Yvette Cooper, Lab.	29,268	
Andrew Lee, C.	14,769	
Lewis Thompson, UKIP	3,030	
Daniel Gascoigne, Yorkshire	1,431	
Clarke Roberts, LD	693	

Lab. majority 14,499 (29.47%)
2.31% swing Lab. to C.
(2015: Lab. majority 15,428 (33.61%))

NORTHAMPTON NORTH

E. 58,183 T. 40,378 (69.40%)		C. hold
*Michael Ellis, C.	19,065	
Sally Keeble, Lab.	18,258	
Jonathan Bullock, UKIP	1,404	
George Smid, LD	1,015	
Steve Miller, Green	636	

C. majority 807 (2.00%)
3.12% swing C. to Lab.
(2015: C. majority 3,245 (8.23%))

NORTHAMPTON SOUTH

E. 60,993 T. 41,034 (67.28%)		C. hold
Andrew Lewer, C.	19,231	
Kevin McKeever, Lab.	18,072	
Rose Gibbins, UKIP	1,630	
Jill Hope, LD	1,405	
Scott Mabbutt, Green	696	

C. majority 1,159 (2.82%)
3.47% swing C. to Lab.
(2015: C. majority 3,793 (9.75%))

NORTHAMPTONSHIRE SOUTH

E. 85,756 T. 64,998 (75.79%)		C. hold
*Andrea Leadsom, C.	40,599	
Sophie Johnson, Lab.	17,759	
Chris Lofts, LD	3,623	
Nigel Wickens, UKIP	1,363	
Denise Donaldson, Green	1,357	
Josh Phillips, Ind.	297	

C. majority 22,840 (35.14%)
4.13% swing C. to Lab.
(2015: C. majority 26,416 (43.40%))

NORWICH NORTH

E. 66,924 T. 45,895 (68.58%)		C. hold
*Chloe Smith, C.	21,900	
Chris Jones, Lab.	21,393	
Hugh Lanham, LD	1,480	
Adrian Holmes, Green	782	
Liam Matthews, Pirate	340	

C. majority 507 (1.10%)
4.57% swing C. to Lab.
(2015: C. majority 4,463 (10.24%))

NORWICH SOUTH

E. 74,182 T. 51,359 (69.23%)		Lab. hold
*Clive Lewis, Lab.	31,311	
Lana Hempsall, C.	15,715	
James Wright, LD	2,841	
Richard Bearman, Green	1,492	

Lab. majority 15,596 (30.37%)
7.29% swing C. to Lab.
(2015: Lab. majority 7,654 (15.79%))

NOTTINGHAM EAST

E. 61,762 T. 39,327 (63.68%)		
		Lab. Co-op hold
*Chris Leslie, Lab. Co-op	28,102	
Simon Murray, C.	8,512	
Barry Holliday, LD	1,003	
Robert Hall-Palmer, UKIP	817	
Kat Boettge, Green	698	
David Bishop, Elvis	195	

Lab. Co-op majority 19,590 (49.81%)
8.02% swing C. to Lab.
(2015: Lab. Co-op majority 11,894 (33.78%))

NOTTINGHAM NORTH

E. 66,894 T. 38,319 (57.28%)		
		Lab. Co-op hold
Alex Norris, Lab. Co-op	23,067	
Jack Tinley, C.	11,907	
Stephen Crosby, UKIP	2,133	
Tad Jones, LD	674	
Kirsty Jones, Green	538	

Lab. Co-op majority 11,160 (29.12%)
2.22% swing Lab. to C.
(2015: Lab. majority 11,860 (33.56%))

NOTTINGHAM SOUTH

E. 71,178 T. 48,129 (67.62%)		Lab. hold
*Lilian Greenwood, Lab.	30,013	
Jane Hunt, C.	14,851	
Tony Sutton, LD	1,564	
David Hollas, UKIP	1,103	
Adam McGregor, Green	598	

Lab. majority 15,162 (31.50%)
7.77% swing C. to Lab.
(2015: Lab. majority 6,936 (15.96%))

NUNEATON

E. 69,201 T. 46,067 (66.57%)		C. hold
*Marcus Jones, C.	23,755	
Philip Johnson, Lab.	19,016	
Craig Carpenter, UKIP	1,619	
Richard Brighton-Knight, LD	914	
Chris Brookes, Green	763	

C. majority 4,739 (10.29%)
0.19% swing C. to Lab.
(2015: C. majority 4,882 (10.67%))

OLD BEXLEY & SIDCUP

E. 66,005 T. 48,042 (72.79%)		C. hold
*James Brokenshire, C.	29,545	
Danny Hackett, Lab.	14,079	
Freddy Vachha, UKIP	1,619	
Drew Heffernan, LD	1,572	
Derek Moran, Green	820	
Michael Jones, BNP	324	
Chinwe Nwadikeduruibe, CPA	83	

C. majority 15,466 (32.19%)
0.81% swing C. to Lab.
(2015: C. majority 15,803 (33.80%))

OLDHAM EAST & SADDLEWORTH

E. 72,223 T. 47,037 (65.13%)		Lab. hold
*Debbie Abrahams, Lab.	25,629	
Kashif Ali, C.	17,447	
Ian Bond, UKIP	2,278	
Jonathan Smith, LD	1,683	

Lab. majority 8,182 (17.39%)
1.95% swing C. to Lab.
(2015: Lab. majority 6,002 (13.49%))

OLDHAM WEST & ROYTON

E. 72,418 T. 45,788 (63.23%)		
		Lab. Co-op hold
*Jim McMahon, Lab. Co-op	29,846	
Christopher Glenny, C.	12,648	
Ruth Keating, UKIP	1,899	
Garth Harkness, LD	956	
Adam King, Green	439	

Lab. Co-op majority 17,198 (37.56%)
0.88% swing Lab. to C.
(2015: Lab. majority 14,738 (34.17%))
(2015: Lab. majority 10,722 (38.70%))

ORPINGTON

E. 67,906 T. 50,461 (74.31%)		C. hold
*Joseph Johnson, C.	31,762	
Nigel de Gruchy, Lab.	12,301	
Alex Feakes, LD	3,315	
Brian Philp, UKIP	2,023	
Tamara Galloway, Green	1,060	

C. majority 19,461 (38.57%)
1.63% swing C. to Lab.
(2015: C. majority 19,979 (40.75%))

OXFORD EAST
E. 78,360 T. 53,896 (68.78%)
Lab. Co-op hold
Anneliese Dodds,
Lab. Co-op   35,118
Suzanne Bartington, C.   11,834
Kirsten Johnson, LD   4,904
Larry Sanders, Green   1,785
Chaka Artwell, Ind.   255
Lab. Co-op majority 23,284 (43.20%)
6.53% swing C. to Lab.
(2015: Lab. majority 15,280 (30.14%))

OXFORD WEST & ABINGDON
E. 79,289 T. 60,020 (75.70%)   LD gain
Layla Moran, LD   26,256
*Nicola Blackwood, C.   25,440
Marie Tidball, Lab.   7,573
Alan Harris, UKIP   751
LD majority 816 (1.36%)
9.05% swing C. to LD
(2015: C. majority 9,582 (16.74%))

PENDLE
E. 64,963 T. 44,854 (69.05%)   C. hold
*Andrew Stephenson, C.   21,986
Wayne Blackburn, Lab.   20,707
Gordon Lishman, LD   941
Brian Parker, BNP   718
Ian Barnett, Green   502
C. majority 1,279 (2.85%)
4.71% swing C. to Lab.
(2015: C. majority 5,453 (12.27%))

PENISTONE & STOCKSBRIDGE
E. 71,293 T. 49,787 (69.83%) Lab. hold
*Angela Smith, Lab.   22,807
Nicola Wilson, C.   21,485
John Booker, UKIP   3,453
Penny Baker, LD   2,042
Lab. majority 1,322 (2.66%)
5.85% swing Lab. to C.
(2015: Lab. majority 6,723 (14.35%))

PENRITH & THE BORDER
E. 65,139 T. 46,470 (71.34%)   C. hold
*Rory Stewart, C.   28,078
Lola McEvoy, Lab.   12,168
Neil Hughes, LD   3,641
Kerryanne Wilde, UKIP   1,142
Douglas Lawson, Green   1,029
Jonathan Davies, Ind.   412
C. majority 15,910 (34.24%)
5.53% swing C. to Lab.
(2015: C. majority 19,894 (45.29%))

PETERBOROUGH ℂ
E. 71,522 T. 47,738 (66.75%) Lab. gain
Fiona Onasanya, Lab.   22,950
*Stewart Jackson, C.   22,343
Beki Sellick, LD   1,597
Fiona Radic, Green   848
Lab. majority 607 (1.27%)
2.68% swing C. to Lab.
(2015: C. majority 1,925 (4.09%))

PLYMOUTH MOOR VIEW
E. 69,342 T. 45,417 (65.50%)   C. hold
*Johnny Mercer, C.   23,567
Sue Dann, Lab.   18,548
Wendy Noble, UKIP   1,849
Graham Reed, LD   917
Joshua Pope, Green   536
C. majority 5,019 (11.05%)
4.32% swing Lab. to C.
(2015: C. majority 1,026 (2.41%))

PLYMOUTH SUTTON &
DEVONPORT
E. 76,584 T. 44,621 (58.26%)
Lab. Co-op gain
Luke Pollard, Lab. Co-op   23,808
*Oliver Colvile, C.   17,806
Richard Ellison, UKIP   1,148
Henrietta Bewley, LD   1,106
Daniel Sheaff, Green   540
Danny Bamping, Ind.   213
Lab. Co-op majority 6,002 (13.45%)
7.27% swing C. to Lab.
(2015: C. majority 523 (1.09%))

POOLE
E. 73,811 T. 49,850 (67.54%)   C. hold
*Robert Syms, C.   28,888
Katie Taylor, Lab.   14,679
Mike Plummer, LD   4,433
Adrian Oliver, Green   1,299
Marty Caine, DDI   551
C. majority 14,209 (28.50%)
4.36% swing C. to Lab.
(2015: C. majority 15,789 (33.32%))

POPLAR & LIMEHOUSE
E. 87,274 T. 58,814 (67.39%) Lab. hold
*Jim Fitzpatrick, Lab.   39,558
Christopher Wilford, C.   11,846
Elaine Bagshaw, LD   3,959
Oliur Rahman, Ind.   1,477
Bethan Lant, Green   989
Nicholas McQueen, UKIP   849
David Barker, ND   136
Lab. majority 27,712 (47.12%)
6.98% swing C. to Lab.
(2015: Lab. majority 16,924 (33.16%))

PORTSMOUTH NORTH
E. 71,374 T. 47,210 (66.14%)   C. hold
*Penny Mordaunt, C.   25,860
Rumal Khan, Lab.   15,895
Darren Sanders, LD   2,608
Mike Fitzgerald, UKIP   1,926
Ken Hawkins, Green   791
Joe Jenkins, Libertarian   130
C. majority 9,965 (21.11%)
1.05% swing C. to Lab.
(2015: C. majority 10,537 (23.21%))

PORTSMOUTH SOUTH
E. 69,785 T. 44,566 (63.86%) Lab. gain
Stephen Morgan, Lab.   18,290
*Flick Drummond, C.   16,736
Robert Vernon-Jackson, LD   7,699
Kevan Chippindall-Higgin,
UKIP   1,129
Ian McCulloch, Green   712
Lab. majority 1,554 (3.49%)
9.38% swing C. to Lab.
(2015: C. majority 5,241 (12.51%))

PRESTON
E. 57,791 T. 35,597 (61.60%)
Lab. Co-op hold
*Mark Hendrick, Lab. Co-op   24,210
Kevin Beaty, C.   8,487
Simon Platt, UKIP   1,348
Neil Darby, LD   1,204
Anne Power, Green   348
Lab. Co-op majority 15,723 (44.17%)
4.06% swing C. to Lab.
(2015: Lab. Co-op majority 12,067
(36.05%))

PUDSEY
E. 72,622 T. 53,959 (74.30%)   C. hold
*Stuart Andrew, C.   25,550
Ian McCargo, Lab. Co-op   25,219
Allen Nixon, LD   1,761
Bob Buxton, Yorkshire   1,138
Michael Wharton, Ind.   291
C. majority 331 (0.61%)
4.11% swing C. to Lab.
(2015: C. majority 4,501 (8.84%))

PUTNEY
E. 65,026 T. 46,894 (72.12%)   C. hold
*Justine Greening, C.   20,679
Neeraj Patil, Lab.   19,125
Ryan Mercer, LD   5,448
Ben Fletcher, Green   1,107
Patricia Ward, UKIP   477
Lotta Quizeen, Ind.   58
C. majority 1,554 (3.31%)
10.23% swing C. to Lab.
(2015: C. majority 10,180 (23.78%))

RAYLEIGH & WICKFORD
E. 78,556 T. 55,323 (70.42%)   C. hold
*Mark Francois, C.   36,914
Mark Daniels, Lab.   13,464
Peter Smith, UKIP   2,326
Ron Tindall, LD   1,557
Paul Hill, Green   1,062
C. majority 23,450 (42.39%)
0.16% swing Lab. to C.
(2015: C. majority 17,230 (32.38%))

READING EAST
E. 75,522 T. 55,238 (73.14%) Lab. gain
Matt Rodda, Lab.   27,093
*Rob Wilson, C.   23,344
Jenny Woods, LD   3,378
Kizzi Johannessen, Green   1,093
Michael Turberville, Ind.   188
Andy Kirkwood,
Active Dem.   142
Lab. majority 3,749 (6.79%)
9.85% swing C. to Lab.
(2015: C. majority 6,520 (12.91%))

READING WEST
E. 74,518 T. 51,766 (69.47%)   C. hold
*Alok Sharma, C.   25,311
Olivia Bailey, Lab.   22,435
Meri O'Connell, LD   3,041
Jamie Whitham, Green   979
C. majority 2,876 (5.56%)
4.09% swing C. to Lab.
(2015: C. majority 6,650 (13.74%))

REDCAR
E. 66,836   T. 42,560 (63.68%)
Lab. Co-op hold
*Anna Turley, Lab. Co-op   23,623
Peter Gibson, C.   14,138
Josh Mason, LD   2,849
Chris Gallacher, UKIP   1,950
Lab. Co-op majority 9,485 (22.29%)
2.68% swing Lab. to C.
(2015: Lab. Co-op majority 10,388
(25.39%))

REDDITCH
E. 64,334   T. 45,203 (70.26%)   C. hold
Rachel Maclean, C.   23,652
Rebecca Blake, Lab.   16,289
Neal Stote, NHAP   2,239
Paul Swansborough, UKIP   1,371
Susan Juned, LD   1,173
Kevin White, Green   380
Sally Woodhall, Ind.   99
C. majority 7,363 (16.29%)
0.15% swing Lab. to C.
(2015: C. majority 7,054 (16.00%))

REIGATE
E. 74,628   T. 53,823 (72.12%)   C. hold
*Crispin Blunt, C.   30,896
Toby Brampton, Lab.   13,282
Anna Tarrant, LD   5,889
Jonathan Essex, Green   2,214
Joseph Fox, UKIP   1,542
C. majority 17,614 (32.73%)
5.62% swing C. to Lab.
(2015: C. majority 22,334 (43.49%))

RIBBLE VALLEY
E. 77,968   T. 55,200 (70.80%)   C. hold
*Nigel Evans, C.   31,919
David Hinder, Lab.   18,720
Allan Knox, LD   3,247
Graham Sowter, Green   1,314
C. majority 13,199 (23.91%)
1.07% swing C. to Lab.
(2015: C. majority 13,606 (26.04%))

RICHMOND (YORKS)
E. 80,920   T. 57,013 (70.46%)   C. hold
*Rishi Sunak, C.   36,458
Dan Perry, Lab.   13,350
Tobie Abel, LD   3,360
Chris Pearson, Yorkshire   2,106
Fiona Yorke, Green   1,739
C. majority 23,108 (40.53%)
1.17% swing Lab. to C.
(2015: C. majority 19,550 (36.20%))

RICHMOND PARK
E. 80,025   T. 63,330 (79.14%)   C. gain
*Zac Goldsmith, C.   28,588
*Sarah Olney, LD   28,543
Cate Tuitt, Lab.   5,773
Peter Jewell, UKIP   426
C. majority 45 (0.07%)
19.44% swing C. to LD
(2015: C. majority 23,015 (38.94%))
(2016: LD majority 1,872 (4.53%))

ROCHDALE
E. 78,064   T. 50,044 (64.11%) Lab. gain
‡Tony Lloyd, Lab.   29,035
Jane Howard, C.   14,216
Andy Kelly, LD   4,027
Christopher Baksa, UKIP   1,641
*Simon Danczuk, ND   883
Andy Littlewood,
GM Homeless   242
Lab. majority 14,819 (29.61%)
0.26% swing C. to Lab.
(2015: Lab. majority 12,442 (27.39%))

ROCHESTER & STROOD
E. 82,702   T. 53,769 (65.02%)   C. hold
*Kelly Tolhurst, C.   29,232
Teresa Murray, Lab.   19,382
David Allen, UKIP   2,893
Bart Ricketts, LD   1,189
Sonia Hyner, Green   781
Steve Benson, CPA   163
Primerose Chiguri, Ind.   129
C. majority 9,850 (18.32%)
2.98% swing C. to Lab.
(2015: C. majority 7,133 (13.58%))

ROCHFORD & SOUTHEND EAST
E. 73,501   T. 47,248 (64.28%)   C. hold
*James Duddridge, C.   23,013
Ashley Dalton, Lab.   17,465
Ron Woodley, Ind.   2,924
Neil Hookway, UKIP   1,777
Peter Gwizdala, LD   1,265
Simon Cross, Green   804
C. majority 5,548 (11.74%)
4.99% swing C. to Lab.
(2015: C. majority 9,476 (21.73%))

ROMFORD
E. 73,516   T. 49,944 (67.94%)   C. hold
*Andrew Rosindell, C.   29,671
Angelina
Leatherbarrow, Lab.   15,893
Andrew Beadle, UKIP   2,350
Ian Sanderson, LD   1,215
David Hughes, Green   815
C. majority 13,778 (27.59%)
1.25% swing C. to Lab.
(2015: C. majority 13,859 (28.18%))

ROMSEY & SOUTHAMPTON
NORTH
E. 67,186   T. 50,168 (74.67%)   C. hold
*Caroline Nokes, C.   28,668
Catherine Royce, LD   10,662
Darren Paffey, Lab.   9,614
Ian Callaghan, Green   953
Don Jerrard, JACP   271
C. majority 18,006 (35.89%)
0.35% swing C. to LD
(2015: C. majority 17,712 (36.60%))

ROSSENDALE & DARWEN
E. 72,495   T. 50,156 (69.19%)   C. hold
*Jake Berry, C.   25,499
Alyson Barnes, Lab.   22,283
Sean Bonner, LD   1,550
John Payne, Green   824
C. majority 3,216 (6.41%)
2.56% swing C. to Lab.
(2015: C. majority 5,654 (11.53%))

ROTHER VALLEY
E. 75,230   T. 49,488 (65.78%) Lab. hold
*Kevin Barron, Lab.   23,821
Bethan Eddy, C.   19,939
Lee Hunter, UKIP   3,704
Katie Pruszynski, LD   1,155
Paul Martin, Green   869
Lab. majority 3,882 (7.84%)
6.24% swing Lab. to C.
(2015: Lab. majority 7,297 (15.52%))

ROTHERHAM
E. 63,237   T. 37,923 (59.97%) Lab. hold
*Sarah Champion, Lab.   21,404
James Bellis, C.   10,017
Allen Cowles, UKIP   3,316
Adam Carter, LD   1,754
Mick Bower, Yorkshire   1,432
Lab. majority 11,387 (30.03%)
5.09% swing Lab. to C.
(2015: Lab. majority 8,446 (22.33%))

RUGBY
E. 72,175   T. 51,336 (71.13%)   C. hold
*Mark Pawsey, C.   27,872
Claire Edwards, Lab.   19,660
Jerry Roodhouse, LD   2,851
Graham Bliss, Green   953
C. majority 8,212 (16.00%)
2.56% swing C. to Lab.
(2015: C. majority 10,345 (21.11%))

RUISLIP, NORTHWOOD & PINNER
E. 73,425   T. 53,382 (72.70%)   C. hold
*Nick Hurd, C.   30,555
Rebecca Lury, Lab.   16,575
Alex Cunliffe, LD   3,813
Sarah Green, Green   1,268
Richard Braine, UKIP   1,171
C. majority 13,980 (26.19%)
6.65% swing C. to Lab.
(2015: C. majority 20,224 (39.48%))

RUNNYMEDE & WEYBRIDGE
E. 74,887   T. 51,609 (68.92%)   C. hold
*Philip Hammond, C.   31,436
Fiona Dent, Lab.   13,386
John Vincent, LD   3,765
Nicholas Wood, UKIP   1,675
Lee-Anne Lawrance, Green   1,347
C. majority 18,050 (34.97%)
4.62% swing C. to Lab.
(2015: C. majority 22,134 (44.22%))

RUSHCLIFFE
E. 74,740   T. 58,311 (78.02%)   C. hold
*Kenneth Clarke, C.   30,223
David Mellen, Lab.   22,213
Jayne Phoenix, LD   2,759
George Mallender, Green   1,626
Matthew Faithfull, UKIP   1,490
C. majority 8,010 (13.74%)
5.67% swing C. to Lab.
(2015: C. majority 13,829 (25.07%))

RUTLAND & MELTON
E. 78,463   T. 57,569 (73.37%)   C. hold
*Alan Duncan, C.   36,169
Heather Peto, Lab.   13,065
Ed Reynolds, LD   4,711
John Scutter, UKIP   1,869
Alastair McQuillan, Green   1,755
C. majority 23,104 (40.13%)
0.08% swing C. to Lab.
(2015: C. majority 21,705 (39.75%))

SAFFRON WALDEN
E. 83,690   T. 60,911 (72.78%)   C. hold
Kemi Badenoch, C.   37,629
Jane Berney, Lab.   12,663
Mike Hibbs, LD   8,528
Lorna Howe, UKIP   2,091
C. majority 24,966 (40.99%)
2.21% swing C. to Lab.
(2015: C. majority 24,991 (43.42%))

ST ALBANS
E. 72,811   T. 56,998 (78.28%)   C. hold
*Anne Main, C.   24,571
Daisy Cooper, LD   18,462
Kerry Pollard, Lab.   13,137
Jack Easton, Green   828
C. majority 6,109 (10.72%)
8.71% swing C. to LD
(2015: C. majority 12,732 (23.39%))

ST AUSTELL & NEWQUAY
E. 78,618   T. 54,212 (68.96%)   C. hold
*Steve Double, C.   26,856
Kevin Neil, Lab.   15,714
Stephen Gilbert, LD   11,642
C. majority 11,142 (20.55%)
4.72% swing C. to Lab.
(2015: C. majority 8,173 (16.23%))

ST HELENS NORTH
E. 76,088   T. 50,222 (66.01%)   Lab. hold
*Conor McGinn, Lab.   32,012
Jackson Ng, C.   13,606
Peter Peers, UKIP   2,097
Tom Morrison, LD   1,287
Rachel Parkinson, Green   1,220
Lab. majority 18,406 (36.65%)
0.37% swing Lab. to C.
(2015: Lab. majority 17,291 (37.38%))

ST HELENS SOUTH & WHISTON
E. 79,036   T. 52,886 (66.91%)   Lab. hold
*Marie Rimmer, Lab.   35,879
Ed McRandal, C.   11,536
Brian Spencer, LD   2,101
Mark Hitchen, UKIP   1,953
Jess Northey, Green   1,417
Lab. majority 24,343 (46.03%)
1.07% swing C. to Lab.
(2015: Lab. majority 21,243 (43.89%))

ST IVES
E. 67,462   T. 51,226 (75.93%)   C. hold
*Derek Thomas, C.   22,120
Andrew George, LD   21,808
Christopher Drew, Lab.   7,298
C. majority 312 (0.61%)
2.25% swing C. to LD
(2015: C. majority 2,469 (5.11%))

SALFORD & ECCLES
E. 78,082   T. 47,619 (60.99%)   Lab. hold
*Rebecca Long Bailey, Lab.   31,168
Jason Sugarman, C.   12,036
Christopher Barnes, UKIP   2,320
John Reid, LD   1,286
Wendy Olsen, Green   809
Lab. majority 19,132 (40.18%)
5.59% swing C. to Lab.
(2015: Lab. majority 12,541 (28.99%))

SALISBURY
E. 72,892   T. 53,311 (73.14%)   C. hold
*John Glen, C.   30,952
Tom Corbin, Lab.   13,619
Paul Sample, LD   5,982
Dean Palethorpe, UKIP   1,191
Brig Oubridge, Green   1,152
King Arthur Pendragon, Ind.   415
C. majority 17,333 (32.51%)
3.88% swing C. to Lab.
(2015: C. majority 20,421 (40.27%))

SCARBOROUGH & WHITBY
E. 73,593   T. 50,449 (68.55%)   C. hold
*Robert Goodwill, C.   24,401
Eric Broadbent, Lab.   20,966
Sam Cross, UKIP   1,682
Robert Lockwood, LD   1,354
David Malone, Green   915
John Freeman, Ind.   680
Bill Black, Yorkshire   369
Gordon Johnson, Ind.   82
C. majority 3,435 (6.81%)
3.09% swing C. to Lab.
(2015: C. majority 6,200 (12.99%))

SCUNTHORPE
E. 61,578   T. 40,202 (65.29%)   Lab. hold
*Nic Dakin, Lab.   20,916
Holly Mumby-Croft, C.   17,485
Andy Talliss, UKIP   1,247
Ryk Downes, LD   554
Lab. majority 3,431 (8.53%)
0.03% swing C. to Lab.
(2015: Lab. majority 3,134 (8.48%))

SEDGEFIELD
E. 63,890   T. 41,591 (65.10%)   Lab. hold
*Phil Wilson, Lab.   22,202
Dehenna Davison, C.   16,143
John Grant, UKIP   1,763
Stephen Psallidas, LD   797
Melissa Wilson, Green   686
Lab. majority 6,059 (14.57%)
1.55% swing Lab. to C.
(2015: Lab. majority 6,843 (17.67%))

SEFTON CENTRAL
E. 69,019   T. 52,079 (75.46%)   Lab. hold
*Bill Esterson, Lab.   32,830
Jade Marsden, C.   17,212
Daniel Lewis, LD   1,381
Mike Carter, Green   656
Lab. majority 15,618 (29.99%)
2.91% swing C. to Lab.
(2015: Lab. majority 11,846 (24.17%))

SELBY & AINSTY
E. 75,765   T. 56,076 (74.01%)   C. hold
*Nigel Adams, C.   32,921
David Bowgett, Lab.   19,149
Callum Delhoy, LD   2,293
Tony Pycroft, UKIP   1,713
C. majority 13,772 (24.56%)
0.56% swing C. to Lab.
(2015: C. majority 13,557 (25.67%))

SEVENOAKS
E. 71,061   T. 51,218 (72.08%)   C. hold
*Michael Fallon, C.   32,644
Chris Clark, Lab.   10,727
Alan Bullion, LD   4,280
Graham Cushway, UKIP   1,894
Philip Dodd, Green   1,673
C. majority 21,917 (42.79%)
0.63% swing C. to Lab.
(2015: C. majority 19,561 (39.03%))

SHEFFIELD BRIGHTSIDE & HILLSBOROUGH
E. 70,344   T. 41,870 (59.52%)   Lab. hold
*Gill Furniss, Lab.   28,193
Michael Naughton, C.   9,050
Shane Harper, UKIP   2,645
Simon Clement-Jones, LD   1,061
Christine Gilligan
Kubo, Green   737
Mike Driver, WRP   137
Muzafar Rahman, Soc. Dem.   47
Lab. majority 19,143 (45.72%)
0.07% swing C. to Lab.
(2015: Lab. majority 13,807 (34.47%))
(2016: Lab. majority 9,590 (42.47%))

SHEFFIELD CENTRAL
E. 77,560   T. 47,877 (61.73%)   Lab. hold
*Paul Blomfield, Lab.   33,963
Stephanie Roe, C.   6,215
Natalie Bennett, Green   3,848
Shaffaq Mohammed, LD   2,465
Dominic Cook, UKIP   1,060
Jack Carrington, Yorkshire   197
Robert Moran, Pirate   91
Joe Westridge, Soc. Dem.   38
Lab. majority 27,748 (57.96%)
7.03% swing C. to Lab.
(2015: Lab. majority 17,309 (39.18%))

SHEFFIELD HALLAM
E. 73,455   T. 57,020 (77.63%)   Lab. gain
Jared O'Mara, Lab.   21,881
*Nick Clegg, LD   19,756
Ian Walker, C.   13,561
John Thurley, UKIP   929
Logan Robin, Green   823
Steven Winstone, Soc. Dem.   70
Lab. majority 2,125 (3.73%)
3.98% swing LD to Lab.
(2015: LD majority 2,353 (4.24%))

SHEFFIELD HEELEY
E. 68,040   T. 44,226 (65.00%)   Lab. hold
*Louise Haigh, Lab.   26,524
Gordon Gregory, C.   12,696
Joe Otten, LD   2,022
Howard Denby, UKIP   1,977
Declan Walsh, Green   943
Jaspreet Oberoi, Soc. Dem.   64
Lab. majority 13,828 (31.27%)
0.39% swing Lab. to C.
(2015: Lab. majority 12,954 (30.81%))

SHEFFIELD SOUTH EAST
E. 68,945   T. 43,596 (63.23%)   Lab. hold
*Clive Betts, Lab.   25,520
Lindsey Cawrey, C.   13,722
Dennise Dawson, UKIP   2,820
Colin Ross, LD   1,432
Ishleen Oberoi, Soc. Dem.   102
Lab. majority 11,798 (27.06%)
3.50% swing Lab. to C.
(2015: Lab. majority 12,311 (29.53%))

SHERWOOD
E. 76,196   T. 53,364 (70.04%)   C. hold
*Mark Spencer, C.   27,492
Mike Pringle, Lab.   22,294
Stuart Bestwick, UKIP   1,801
Becky Thomas, LD   1,113
Morris Findley, Green   664
C. majority 5,198 (9.74%)
0.29% swing Lab. to C.
(2015: C. majority 4,647 (9.17%))

SHIPLEY
E. 73,133   T. 53,395 (73.01%)   C. hold
*Philip Davies, C.   27,417
Steve Clapcote, Lab.   22,736
Caroline Jones, LD   2,202
Sophie Walker, Women   1,040
C. majority 4,681 (8.77%)
5.14% swing C. to Lab.
(2015: C. majority 9,624 (19.04%))

SHREWSBURY & ATCHAM
E. 79,043   T. 58,203 (73.63%)   C. hold
*Daniel Kawczynski, C.   29,073
Laura Davies, Lab.   22,446
Hannah Fraser, LD   4,254
Edward   1,363
Higginbottom, UKIP
Emma Bullard, Green   1,067
C. majority 6,627 (11.39%)
3.15% swing C. to Lab.
(2015: C. majority 9,565 (17.68%))

SHROPSHIRE NORTH
E. 80,535   T. 55,599 (69.04%)   C. hold
*Owen Paterson, C.   33,642
Graeme Currie, Lab.   17,287
Tom Thornhill, LD   2,948
Duncan Kerr, Green   1,722
C. majority 16,355 (29.42%)
0.98% swing C. to Lab.
(2015: C. majority 16,494 (31.37%))

SITTINGBOURNE & SHEPPEY
E. 81,715   T. 51,389 (62.89%)   C. hold
*Gordon Henderson, C.   30,911
Mike Rolfe, Lab.   15,700
Mike Baldock, Ind.   2,133
Keith Nevols, LD   1,392
Mark Lindop, Green   558
Mad Mike Young, Loony   403
Lee McCall, Ind.   292
C. majority 15,211 (29.60%)
0.14% swing C. to Lab.
(2015: C. majority 12,168 (24.64%))

SKIPTON & RIPON
E. 78,108   T. 58,138 (74.43%)   C. hold
*Julian Smith, C.   36,425
Alan Woodhead, Lab.   16,440
Andy Brown, Green   3,734
Jack Render, Yorkshire   1,539
C. majority 19,985 (34.38%)
1.84% swing C. to Lab.
(2015: C. majority 20,761 (38.05%))

SLEAFORD & NORTH HYKEHAM
E. 90,925   T. 65,797 (72.36%)   C. hold
*Caroline Johnson, C.   42,245
Jim Clarke, Lab.   17,008
Ross Pepper, LD   2,722
Sally Chadd, UKIP   1,954
Fiona McKenna, Green   968
Paul Coyne, Ind.   900
C. majority 25,237 (38.36%)
0.29% swing C. to Lab.
(2015: C. majority 24,115 (38.93%))
(2016: C. majority 13,144 (40.03%))

SLOUGH
E. 83,272   T. 54,295 (65.20%)   Lab. hold
Tan Dhesi, Lab.   34,170
Mark Vivis, C.   17,172
Tom McCann, LD   1,308
Karen Perez, UKIP   1,228
Paul Janik, Ind.   417
Lab. majority 16,998 (31.31%)
8.06% swing C. to Lab.
(2015: Lab. majority 7,336 (15.20%))

SOLIHULL
E. 77,784   T. 56,748 (72.96%)   C. hold
*Julian Knight, C.   32,985
Nigel Knowles, Lab.   12,414
Ade Adeyemo, LD   8,901
Andrew Garcarz, UKIP   1,291
Max McLoughlin, Green   1,157
C. majority 20,571 (36.25%)
1.28% swing C. to Lab.
(2015: C. majority 12,902 (23.55%))

SOMERSET NORTH
E. 80,538   T. 61,994 (76.97%)   C. hold
*Liam Fox, C.   33,605
Greg Chambers, Lab.   16,502
Richard Foord, LD   5,982
Donald Davies, Ind.   3,929
Charley Pattison, Green   1,976
C. majority 17,103 (27.59%)
5.80% swing C. to Lab.
(2015: C. majority 23,099 (39.19%))

SOMERSET NORTH EAST
E. 71,350   T. 54,043 (75.74%)   C. hold
*Jacob Rees-Mogg, C.   28,992
Robin Moss, Lab.   18,757
Manda Rigby, LD   4,461
Sally Calverley, Green   1,245
Shaun Hughes, Ind.   588
C. majority 10,235 (18.94%)
3.00% swing C. to Lab.
(2015: C. majority 12,749 (24.94%))

SOMERTON & FROME
E. 84,435   T. 63,592 (75.31%)   C. hold
*David Warburton, C.   36,231
Mark Blackburn, LD   13,325
Sean Dromgoole, Lab.   10,998
Theo Simon, Green   2,047
Richard Hadwin, Ind.   991
C. majority 22,906 (36.02%)
1.21% swing LD to C.
(2015: C. majority 20,268 (33.61%))

SOUTH HOLLAND & THE
DEEPINGS
E. 76,381   T. 50,315 (65.87%)   C. hold
*John Hayes, C.   35,179
Voyteck Kowalewski, Lab.   10,282
Nicola Smith, UKIP   2,185
Julia Cambridge, LD   1,433
Daniel Wilshire, Green   894
Rick Stringer, Ind.   342
C. majority 24,897 (49.48%)
1.19% swing Lab. to C.
(2015: C. majority 18,567 (37.73%))

SOUTH RIBBLE
E. 75,752   T. 54,834 (72.39%)   C. hold
*Seema Kennedy, C.   28,980
Julie Gibson, Lab.   21,559
John Wright, LD   2,073
Mark Smith, UKIP   1,387
Andrew Wight, Green   494
Mark Jarnell, NHAP   341
C. majority 7,421 (13.53%)
1.09% swing Lab. to C.
(2015: C. majority 5,945 (11.35%))

SOUTH SHIELDS
E. 63,449   T. 40,772 (64.26%)   Lab. hold
*Emma Lewell-Buck, Lab.   25,078
Felicity Buchan, C.   10,570
Richard Elvin, UKIP   3,006
Shirley Ford, Green   1,437
Gita Gordon, LD   681
Lab. majority 14,508 (35.58%)
0.46% swing Lab. to C.
(2015: Lab. majority 10,614 (29.27%))

SOUTHAMPTON ITCHEN
E. 71,716   T. 46,783 (65.23%)   C. hold
*Royston Smith, C.   21,773
Simon Letts, Lab.   21,742
Eleanor Bell, LD   1,421
Kim Rose, UKIP   1,122
Rosie Pearce, Green   725
C. majority 31 (0.07%)
2.56% swing C. to Lab.
(2015: C. majority 2,316 (5.18%))

SOUTHAMPTON TEST
E. 70,194   T. 46,903 (66.82%)   Lab. hold
*Alan Whitehead, Lab.   27,509
Paul Holmes, C.   16,006
Thomas Gravatt, LD   1,892
Andrew Pope, Southampton   816
Keith Morrell, Ind.   680
Lab. majority 11,503 (24.53%)
7.90% swing C. to Lab.
(2015: Lab. majority 3,810 (8.73%))

SOUTHEND WEST
E. 67,677   T. 47,191 (69.73%)   C. hold
*David Amess, C.	26,046
Julian Ware-Lane, Lab.	16,046
Lucy Salek, LD	2,110
John Stansfield, UKIP	1,666
Dominic Ellis, Green	831
Tino Callaghan, Southend	305
Jason Pilley, Ind.	187

C. majority 10,000 (21.19%)
5.16% swing C. to Lab.
(2015: C. majority 14,021 (31.50%))

SOUTHPORT
E. 69,400   T. 47,956 (69.10%)   C. gain
Damien Moore, C.	18,541
Liz Savage, Lab.	15,627
Sue McGuire, LD	12,661
Terry Durrance, UKIP	1,127

C. majority 2,914 (6.08%)
7.63% swing LD to C.
(2015: LD majority 1,322 (3.00%))

SPELTHORNE
E. 72,641   T. 50,115 (68.99%)   C. hold
*Kwasi Kwarteng, C.	28,692
Rebecca Geach, Lab.	15,267
Rosamund Shimell, LD	2,755
Redvers Cunningham, UKIP	2,296
Paul Jacobs, Green	1,105

C. majority 13,425 (26.79%)
2.16% swing C. to Lab.
(2015: C. majority 14,152 (28.84%))

STAFFORD
E. 68,445   T. 51,924 (75.86%)   C. hold
*Jeremy Lefroy, C.	28,424
David Williams, Lab.	20,695
Christine Tinker, LD	1,540
Tony Pearce, Green	1,265

C. majority 7,729 (14.89%)
1.97% swing C. to Lab.
(2015: C. majority 9,177 (18.82%))

STAFFORDSHIRE MOORLANDS
E. 66,009   T. 44,655 (67.65%)   C. hold
*Karen Bradley, C.	25,963
Dave Jones, Lab.	15,133
Nicholas Sheldon, ND	1,524
Henry Jebb, LD	1,494
Mike Shone, Green	541

C. majority 10,830 (24.25%)
0.18% swing Lab. to C.
(2015: C. majority 10,174 (23.89%))

STAFFORDSHIRE SOUTH
E. 73,453   T. 51,109 (69.58%)   C. hold
*Gavin Williamson, C.	35,656
Adam Freeman, Lab.	12,923
Hilary Myers, LD	1,348
Claire McIlvenna, Green	1,182

C. majority 22,733 (44.48%)
1.70% swing Lab. to C.
(2015: C. majority 20,371 (41.07%))

STALYBRIDGE & HYDE
E. 71,409   T. 42,457 (59.46%)
	Lab. Co-op hold
*Jonathan Reynolds,	
Lab. Co-op	24,277
Tom Dowse, C.	16,193
Paul Ankers, LD	996
Julie Wood, Green	991

Lab. Co-op majority 8,084 (19.04%)
1.37% swing C. to Lab.
(2015: Lab. Co-op majority 6,686 (16.29%))

STEVENAGE
E. 70,765   T. 49,329 (69.71%)   C. hold
*Stephen McPartland, C.	24,798
Sharon Taylor, Lab. Co-op	21,414
Barbara Gibson, LD	2,032
Victoria Snelling, Green	1,085

C. majority 3,384 (6.86%)
1.75% swing C. to Lab.
(2015: C. majority 4,955 (10.37%))

STOCKPORT
E. 63,425   T. 41,544 (65.50%)   Lab. hold
*Ann Coffey, Lab.	26,282
Daniel Hamilton, C.	11,805
Daniel Hawthorne, LD	1,778
John Kelly, UKIP	1,088
Gary Lawson, Green	591

Lab. majority 14,477 (34.85%)
4.74% swing C. to Lab.
(2015: Lab. majority 10,061 (25.38%))

STOCKTON NORTH
E. 66,279   T. 42,731 (64.47%)   Lab. hold
*Alex Cunningham, Lab.	24,304
Mark Fletcher, C.	15,589
Ted Strike, UKIP	1,834
Sarah Brown, LD	646
Emma Robson, Green	358

Lab. majority 8,715 (20.40%)
0.37% swing Lab. to C.
(2015: Lab. majority 8,367 (21.14%))

STOCKTON SOUTH
E. 75,619   T. 53,824 (71.18%)   Lab. gain
Paul Williams, Lab.	26,102
*James Wharton, C.	25,214
David Outterside, UKIP	1,186
Drew Durning, LD	951
Jo Fitzgerald, Green	371

Lab. majority 888 (1.65%)
5.70% swing C. to Lab.
(2015: C. majority 5,046 (9.74%))

STOKE-ON-TRENT CENTRAL
E. 58,196   T. 33,145 (56.95%)
	Lab. Co-op hold
*Gareth Snell, Lab. Co-op	17,083
Daniel Jellyman, C.	13,186
Mick Harold, UKIP	1,608
Peter Andras, LD	680
Adam Colclough, Green	378
Barbara Fielding, Ind.	210

Lab. Co-op majority 3,897 (11.76%)
2.51% swing Lab. to C.
(2015: Lab. majority 5,179 (16.66%))
(2017: Lab. majority 2,620 (12.38%))

STOKE-ON-TRENT NORTH
E. 72,368   T. 41,786 (57.74%)   Lab. hold
*Ruth Smeeth, Lab.	21,272
Ben Adams, C.	18,913
Richard Whelan, LD	916
Douglas Rouxel, Green	685

Lab. majority 2,359 (5.65%)
3.43% swing Lab. to C.
(2015: Lab. majority 4,836 (12.51%))

STOKE-ON-TRENT SOUTH
E. 66,046   T. 41,690 (63.12%)   C. gain
Jack Brereton, C.	20,451
*Rob Flello, Lab.	19,788
Ian Wilkes, LD	808
Jan Zablocki, Green	643

C. majority 663 (1.59%)
4.04% swing Lab. to C.
(2015: Lab. majority 2,539 (6.49%))

STONE
E. 67,824   T. 50,032 (73.77%)   C. hold
*William Cash, C.	31,614
Sam Hale, Lab. Co-op	14,119
Martin Lewis, LD	2,222
Edward Whitfield, UKIP	1,370
Samantha Pancheri, Green	707

C. majority 17,495 (34.97%)
0.21% swing Lab. to C.
(2015: C. majority 16,250 (34.55%))

STOURBRIDGE
E. 70,215   T. 47,135 (67.13%)   C. hold
*Margot James, C.	25,706
Pete Lowe, Lab.	18,052
Glen Wilson, UKIP	1,801
Christoper Bramall, LD	1,083
Andi Mohr, Green	493

C. majority 7,654 (16.24%)
0.85% swing Lab. to C.
(2015: C. majority 6,694 (14.54%))

STRATFORD-ON-AVON
E. 72,609   T. 52,532 (72.35%)   C. hold
*Nadhim Zahawi, C.	32,657
Jeff Kenner, Lab.	11,699
Elizabeth Adams, LD	6,357
Dominic Giles, Green	1,345
Jandy Spurway, Ind.	255
Tom Darwood, Ind.	219

C. majority 20,958 (39.90%)
2.40% swing Lab. to C.
(2015: C. majority 22,876 (44.45%))

STREATHAM
E. 78,532   T. 55,795 (71.05%)   Lab. hold
*Chuka Umunna, Lab.	38,212
Kim Caddy, C.	11,927
Alex Davies, LD	3,611
Nicole Griffiths, Green	1,696
Robert Stephenson, UKIP	349

Lab. majority 26,285 (47.11%)
9.60% swing C. to Lab.
(2015: Lab. majority 13,934 (27.91%))

STRETFORD & URMSTON
E. 71,840 T. 50,191 (69.86%) Lab. hold
*Kate Green, Lab. 33,519
Lisa Cooke, C. 13,814
Andrew Beaumont, UKIP 1,094
Anna Fryer, LD 1,001
Michael Ingleson, Green 641
Rose Doman, CPA 122
Lab. majority 19,705 (39.26%)
7.03% swing C. to Lab.
(2015: Lab. majority 11,685 (25.19%))

STROUD
E. 82,849 T. 63,816 (77.03%)
                              Lab. Co-op gain
†David Drew, Lab. Co-op 29,994
*Neil Carmichael, C. 29,307
Max Wilkinson, LD 2,053
Sarah Lunnon, Green 1,423
Glenville Gogerly, UKIP 1,039
Lab. Co-op majority 687 (1.08%)
4.54% swing C. to Lab.
(2015: C. majority 4,866 (8.00%))

SUFFOLK CENTRAL & IPSWICH
NORTH
E. 78,116 T. 56,524 (72.36%) C. hold
*Dan Poulter, C. 33,992
Elizabeth Hughes, Lab. 16,807
Aidan Van de Weyer, LD 2,431
Regan Scott, Green 1,659
Stephen Searle, UKIP 1,635
C. majority 17,185 (30.40%)
3.42% swing C. to Lab.
(2015: C. majority 20,144 (37.24%))

SUFFOLK COASTAL
E. 79,366 T. 58,074 (73.17%) C. hold
*Therese Coffey, C. 33,713
Cameron Matthews, Lab. 17,701
James Sandbach, LD 4,048
Eamonn O'Nolan, Green 1,802
Philip Young, Ind. 810
C. majority 16,012 (27.57%)
3.16% swing C. to Lab.
(2015: C. majority 18,842 (33.89%))

SUFFOLK SOUTH
E. 75,967 T. 54,235 (71.39%) C. hold
*James Cartlidge, C. 32,829
Emma Bishton, Lab. 15,080
Andrew
Aalders-Dunthorne, LD 3,154
Robert Lindsay, Green 1,723
Aidan Powlesland, UKIP 1,449
C. majority 17,749 (32.73%)
0.54% swing C. to Lab.
(2015: C. majority 17,545 (33.80%))

SUFFOLK WEST
E. 76,984 T. 51,746 (67.22%) C. hold
*Matt Hancock, C. 31,649
Michael Jefferys, Lab. 14,586
Julian Flood, UKIP 2,396
Elfreda Tealby-Watson, LD 2,180
Donald Allwright, Green 935
C. majority 17,063 (32.97%)
0.86% swing C. to Lab.
(2015: C. majority 14,984 (30.44%))

SUNDERLAND CENTRAL
E. 72,728 T. 45,111 (62.03%) Lab. hold
*Julie Elliott, Lab. 25,056
Robert Oliver, C. 15,059
Gary Leighton, UKIP 2,209
Niall Hodson, LD 1,777
Rachel Featherstone, Green 705
Sean Cockburn, Ind. 305
Lab. majority 9,997 (22.16%)
2.30% swing Lab. to C.
(2015: Lab. majority 11,179 (26.77%))

SURREY EAST
E. 82,004 T. 59,203 (72.20%) C. hold
*Sam Gyimah, C. 35,310
Hitesh Tailor, Lab. 11,396
David Lee, LD 6,197
Andy Parr, Ind. 2,973
Helena Windsor, UKIP 2,227
Benedict Southworth, Green 1,100
C. majority 23,914 (40.39%)
2.60% swing C. to Lab.
(2015: C. majority 22,658 (40.39%))

SURREY HEATH
E. 80,537 T. 57,822 (71.80%) C. hold
*Michael Gove, C. 37,118
Laween Atroshi, Lab. 12,175
Anne-Marie Barker, LD 6,271
Sharon Galliford, Green 2,258
C. majority 24,943 (43.14%)
2.76% swing C. to Lab.
(2015: C. majority 24,804 (45.57%))

SURREY SOUTH WEST
E. 78,042 T. 60,432 (77.44%) C. hold
*Jeremy Hunt, C. 33,683
Louise Irvine, NHAP 12,093
David Black, Lab. 7,606
Ollie Purkiss, LD 5,967
Mark Webber, UKIP 1,083
C. majority 21,590 (35.73%)
7.83% swing C. to NHAP
(2015: C. majority 28,556 (49.99%))

SUSSEX MID
E. 83,747 T. 61,632 (73.59%) C. hold
*Nicholas Soames, C. 35,082
Greg Mountain, Lab. 15,409
Sarah Osborne, LD 7,855
Chris Jerrey, Green 1,571
Toby Brothers, UKIP 1,251
Baron Von
Thunderclap, Loony 464
C. majority 19,673 (31.92%)
5.16% swing C. to Lab.
(2015: C. majority 24,286 (42.24%))

SUTTON & CHEAM
E. 70,404 T. 51,970 (73.82%) C. hold
*Paul Scully, C. 26,567
Amna Ahmad, LD 13,869
Bonnie Craven, Lab. 10,663
Claire Jackson-Prior, Green 871
C. majority 12,698 (24.43%)
8.29% swing LD to C.
(2015: C. majority 3,921 (7.86%))

SUTTON COLDFIELD
E. 75,652 T. 52,858 (69.87%) C. hold
*Andrew Mitchell, C. 32,224
Rob Pocock, Lab. 16,885
Jennifer Wilkinson, LD 2,302
David Ratcliff, Green 965
Hannah Sophia, ND 482
C. majority 15,339 (29.02%)
1.63% swing C. to Lab.
(2015: C. majority 16,417 (32.28%))

SWINDON NORTH
E. 80,194 T. 54,911 (68.47%) C. hold
*Justin Tomlinson, C. 29,431
Mark Dempsey, Lab. 21,096
Liz Webster, LD 1,962
Steve Halden, UKIP 1,564
Andy Bentley, Green 858
C. majority 8,335 (15.18%)
3.69% swing C. to Lab.
(2015: C. majority 11,786 (22.56%))

SWINDON SOUTH
E. 72,391 T. 51,271 (70.83%) C. hold
*Robert Buckland, C. 24,809
Sarah Church, Lab. Co-op 22,345
Stan Pajak, LD 2,079
Martin Costello, UKIP 1,291
Talis Kimberley-Fairbourn,
Green 747
C. majority 2,464 (4.81%)
3.47% swing C. to Lab.
(2015: C. majority 5,785 (11.74%))

TAMWORTH
E. 71,319 T. 47,110 (66.06%) C. hold
*Christopher Pincher, C. 28,748
Andrew Hammond, Lab. 16,401
Jenny Pinkett, LD 1,961
C. majority 12,347 (26.21%)
1.13% swing Lab. to C.
(2015: C. majority 11,302 (23.96%))

TATTON
E. 67,874 T. 49,116 (72.36%) C. hold
‡Esther McVey, C. 28,764
Sam Rushworth, Lab. 13,977
Gareth Wilson, LD 4,431
Nigel Hennerley, Green 1,024
Quentin Abel, Ind. 920
C. majority 14,787 (30.11%)
5.08% swing C. to Lab.
(2015: C. majority 18,241 (40.27%))

TAUNTON DEANE
E. 85,466 T. 63,053 (73.78%) C. hold
*Rebecca Pow, C. 33,333
Gideon Amos, LD 17,446
Martin Jevon, Lab. 9,689
Alan Dimmick, UKIP 1,434
Clive Martin, Green 1,151
C. majority 15,887 (25.20%)
0.78% swing C. to LD
(2015: C. majority 15,491 (26.76%))

TELFORD
E. 68,164 T. 44,686 (65.56%) C. hold
*Lucy Allan, C. 21,777
Kuldip Sahota, Lab. 21,057
Susan King, LD 954
Luke Shirley, Green 898
C. majority 720 (1.61%)
0.09% swing C. to Lab.
(2015: C. majority 730 (1.80%))

TEWKESBURY
E. 81,442   T. 59,084 (72.55%)   C. hold
*Laurence Robertson, C.   35,448
Manjinder Kang, Lab.   12,874
Cait Clucas, LD   7,981
Cate Cody, Green   1,576
Simon Collins, UKIP   1,205
C. majority 22,574 (38.21%)
0.75% swing C. to Lab.
(2015: C. majority 21,972 (39.70%))

THANET NORTH
E. 72,657   T. 48,325 (66.51%)   C. hold
*Roger Gale, C.   27,163
Frances Rehal, Lab.   16,425
Clive Egan, UKIP   2,198
Martyn Pennington, LD   1,586
Ed Targett, Green   825
Iris White, CPA   128
C. majority 10,738 (22.22%)
4.44% swing C. to Lab.
(2015: C. majority 10,948 (23.27%))

THANET SOUTH
E. 72,342   T. 49,753 (68.77%)   C. hold
*Craig Mackinlay, C.   25,262
Raushan Ara, Lab.   18,875
Stuart Piper, UKIP   2,997
Jordan Williams, LD   1,514
Trevor Roper, Green   809
Tim Garbutt, Ind.   181
Faith Fisher, CPA   115
C. majority 6,387 (12.84%)
0.77% swing C. to Lab.
(2015: C. majority 2,812 (5.69%))

THIRSK & MALTON
E. 78,670   T. 55,929 (71.09%)   C. hold
*Kevin Hollinrake, C.   33,572
Alan Avery, Lab.   14,571
Dinah Keal, LD   3,859
Toby Horton, UKIP   1,532
Martin Brampton, Green   1,100
John Clark, Lib.   753
Philip Tate, Ind.   542
C. majority 19,001 (33.97%)
1.59% swing C. to Lab.
(2015: C. majority 19,456 (37.15%))

THORNBURY & YATE
E. 67,927   T. 50,690 (74.62%)   C. hold
*Luke Hall, C.   28,008
Claire Young, LD   15,937
Brian Mead, Lab.   6,112
Iain Hamilton, Green   633
C. majority 12,071 (23.81%)
10.37% swing LD to C.
(2015: C. majority 1,495 (3.08%))

THURROCK
E. 78,153   T. 50,325 (64.39%)   C. hold
*Jackie Doyle-Price, C.   19,880
John Kent, Lab.   19,535
Tim Aker, UKIP   10,112
Kevin McNamara, LD   798
C. majority 345 (0.69%)
0.20% swing C. to Lab.
(2015: C. majority 536 (1.08%))

TIVERTON & HONITON
E. 80,731   T. 57,815 (71.61%)   C. hold
*Neil Parish, C.   35,471
Caroline Kolek, Lab.   15,670
Matthew Wilson, LD   4,639
Gill Westcott, Green   2,035
C. majority 19,801 (34.25%)
3.52% swing C. to Lab.
(2015: C. majority 20,173 (37.52%))

TONBRIDGE & MALLING
E. 77,234   T. 56,907 (73.68%)   C. hold
*Tom Tugendhat, C.   36,218
Dylan Jones, Lab.   12,710
Keith Miller, LD   3,787
April Clark, Green   2,335
Colin Bullen, UKIP   1,857
C. majority 23,508 (41.31%)
1.97% swing C. to Lab.
(2015: C. majority 23,734 (44.22%))

TOOTING
E. 77,960   T. 58,171 (74.62%)   Lab. hold
*Rosena Allin-Khan, Lab.   34,694
Dan Watkins, C.   19,236
Alexander Glassbrook, LD   3,057
Esther Obiri-Darko, Green   845
Ryan Coshall, UKIP   339
Lab. majority 15,458 (26.57%)
10.63% swing C. to Lab.
(2015: Lab. majority 2,842 (5.31%))
(2016: Lab. majority 6,357 (19.87%))

TORBAY
E. 75,936   T. 51,174 (67.39%)   C. hold
*Kevin Foster, C.   27,141
Deborah Brewer, LD   12,858
Paul Raybould, Lab.   9,310
Tony McIntyre, UKIP   1,213
Sam Moss, Green   652
C. majority 14,283 (27.91%)
10.54% swing LD to C.
(2015: C. majority 3,286 (6.83%))

TOTNES
E. 68,913   T. 50,270 (72.95%)   C. hold
*Sarah Wollaston, C.   26,972
Gerrie Messer, Lab.   13,495
Julian Brazil, LD   6,466
Jacqi Hodgson, Green   2,097
Steven Harvey, UKIP   1,240
C. majority 13,477 (26.81%)
6.72% swing C. to Lab.
(2015: C. majority 18,285 (38.82%))

TOTTENHAM
E. 72,883   T. 49,339 (67.70%)   Lab. hold
*David Lammy, Lab.   40,249
Myles Stacey, C.   5,665
Brian Haley, LD   1,687
Jarelle Francis, Green   1,276
Patricia Rumble, UKIP   462
Lab. majority 34,584 (70.09%)
7.36% swing C. to Lab.
(2015: Lab. majority 23,564 (55.37%))

TRURO & FALMOUTH
E. 74,691   T. 56,647 (75.84%)   C. hold
*Sarah Newton, C.   25,123
Jayne Kirkham, Lab.   21,331
Rob Nolan, LD   8,465
Duncan Odgers, UKIP   897
Amanda Pennington, Green   831
C. majority 3,792 (6.69%)
11.07% swing C. to Lab.
(2015: C. majority 14,000 (27.16%))

TUNBRIDGE WELLS
E. 75,138   T. 54,209 (72.15%)   C. hold
*Greg Clark, C.   30,856
Charles Woodgate, Lab.   14,391
Rachel Sadler, LD   5,355
Chris Hoare, UKIP   1,464
Trevor Bisdee, Green   1,441
Celine Thomas, Women   702
C. majority 16,465 (30.37%)
7.05% swing C. to Lab.
(2015: C. majority 22,874 (44.48%))

TWICKENHAM
E. 83,362   T. 66,290 (79.52%)   LD gain
†Vince Cable, LD   34,969
*Tania Mathias, C.   25,207
Katherine Dunne, Lab.   6,114
LD majority 9,762 (14.73%)
8.99% swing C. to LD
(2015: C. majority 2,017 (3.25%))

TYNEMOUTH
E. 77,434   T. 56,858 (73.43%)   Lab. hold
*Alan Campbell, Lab.   32,395
Nick Varley, C.   20,729
John Appleby, LD   1,724
Stuart Houghton, UKIP   1,257
Julia Erskine, Green   629
Anthony The Durham
   Cobbler Jull, ND   124
Lab. majority 11,666 (20.52%)
2.56% swing C. to Lab.
(2015: Lab. majority 8,240 (15.40%))

TYNESIDE NORTH
E. 78,914   T. 51,892 (65.76%)   Lab. hold
*Mary Glindon, Lab.   33,456
Henry Newman, C.   14,172
Gary Legg, UKIP   2,101
Greg Stone, LD   1,494
Martin Collins, Green   669
Lab. majority 19,284 (37.16%)
0.22% swing C. to Lab.
(2015: Lab. majority 17,194 (36.73%))

UXBRIDGE & RUISLIP SOUTH
E. 69,938   T. 46,694 (66.76%)
*Boris Johnson, C.   23,716
Vincent Lo, Lab.   18,682
Rosina Robson, LD   1,835
Elizabeth Kemp, UKIP   1,577
Mark Keir, Green   884
C. majority 5,034 (10.78%)
6.54% swing C. to Lab.
(2015: C. majority 10,695 (23.87%))

VAUXHALL
E. 81,907   T. 55,042 (67.20%)   Lab. hold
*Kate Hoey, Lab.   31,576
George Turner, LD   11,326
Dolly Theis, C.   10,277
Gulnar Hasnain, Green   1,152
Harini Iyengar, Women   539
Mark Chapman, Pirate   172
Lab. majority 20,250 (36.79%)
5.04% swing Lab. to LD
(2015: Lab. majority 12,708 (26.51%))

WAKEFIELD
E. 70,340   T. 46,284 (65.80%)   Lab. hold
*Mary Creagh, Lab.   22,987
Antony Calvert, C.   20,811
Lucy Brown, Yorkshire   1,176
Denis Cronin, LD   943
Waj Ali, Ind.   367
Lab. majority 2,176 (4.70%)
0.69% swing Lab. to C.
(2015: Lab. majority 2,613 (6.08%))

WALLASEY
E. 67,454   T. 48,353 (71.68%)   Lab. hold
*Angela Eagle, Lab.   34,552
Andy Livsey, C.   11,232
Debbie Caplin, UKIP   1,160
Paul Childs, LD   772
Lily Clough, Green   637
Lab. majority 23,320 (48.23%)
5.27% swing C. to Lab.
(2015: Lab. majority 16,348 (37.70%))

WALSALL NORTH
E. 67,309   T. 38,118 (56.63%)   C. gain
Eddie Hughes, C.   18,919
*David Winnick, Lab.   16,318
Liz Hazell, UKIP   2,295
Isabelle Parasram, LD   586
C. majority 2,601 (6.82%)
6.04% swing Lab. to C.
(2015: Lab. majority 1,937 (5.25%))

WALSALL SOUTH
E. 67,417   T. 44,072 (65.37%)   Lab. hold
*Valerie Vaz, Lab.   25,286
James Bird, C.   16,394
Derek Bennett, UKIP   1,805
Anna Wellings Purvis, LD   587
Lab. majority 8,892 (20.18%)
2.91% swing C. to Lab.
(2015: Lab. majority 6,007 (14.36%))

WALTHAMSTOW
E. 68,144   T. 48,143 (70.65%)
                          Lab. Co-op hold
*Stella Creasy, Lab. Co-op   38,793
Molly Samuel, C.   6,776
Ukonu Obasi, LD   1,384
Andrew Johns, Green   1,190
Lab. Co-op majority 32,017 (66.50%)
5.50% swing C. to Lab.
(2015: Lab. Co-op majority 23,195
(55.50%))

WANSBECK
E. 62,099   T. 42,454 (68.37%)   Lab. hold
*Ian Lavery, Lab.   24,338
Chris Galley, C.   13,903
Joan Tebbutt, LD   2,015
Melanie Hurst, UKIP   1,483
Steven Leyland, Green   715
Lab. majority 10,435 (24.58%)
1.83% swing Lab. to C.
(2015: Lab. majority 10,881 (28.24%))

WANTAGE
E. 87,735   T. 63,602 (72.49%)   C. hold
*Edward Vaizey, C.   34,459
Rachel Eden, Lab. Co-op   17,079
Chris Carrigan, LD   9,234
Sue Ap-Roberts, Green   1,546
David McLeod, UKIP   1,284
C. majority 17,380 (27.33%)
4.98% swing C. to Lab.
(2015: C. majority 21,749 (37.29%))

WARLEY
E. 63,724   T. 40,206 (63.09%)   Lab. hold
*John Spellar, Lab.   27,004
Anthony Mangnall, C.   10,521
Darryl Magher, UKIP   1,349
Bryan Manley-Green, LD   777
Mark Redding, Green   555
Lab. majority 16,483 (41.00%)
1.07% swing C. to Lab.
(2015: Lab. majority 14,702 (38.86%))

WARRINGTON NORTH
E. 72,015   T. 48,517 (67.37%)   Lab. hold
*Helen Jones, Lab.   27,356
Val Allen, C.   17,774
James Ashington, UKIP   1,561
Stefan Krizanac, LD   1,207
Lyndsay McAteer, Green   619
Lab. majority 9,582 (19.75%)
0.05% swing C. to Lab.
(2015: Lab. majority 8,923 (19.65%))

WARRINGTON SOUTH
E. 85,755   T. 61,995 (72.29%)   Lab. gain
Faisal Rashid, Lab.   29,994
*David Mowat, C.   27,445
Bob Barr, LD   3,339
John Boulton, Ind.   1,217
Lab. majority 2,549 (4.11%)
4.37% swing C. to Lab.
(2015: C. majority 2,750 (4.63%))

WARWICK & LEAMINGTON
E. 74,237   T. 54,055 (72.81%)   Lab. gain
Matt Western, Lab.   25,227
*Chris White, C.   24,021
Nick Solman, LD   2,810
Jonathan Chilvers, Green   1,198
Bob Dhillon, UKIP   799
Lab. majority 1,206 (2.23%)
7.65% swing C. to Lab.
(2015: C. majority 6,606 (13.06%))

WARWICKSHIRE NORTH
E. 72,277   T. 47,178 (65.27%)   C. hold
*Craig Tracey, C.   26,860
Julie Jackson, Lab.   18,350
James Cox, LD   1,028
Keith Kondakor, Green   940
C. majority 8,510 (18.04%)
5.88% swing Lab. to C.
(2015: C. majority 2,973 (6.28%))

WASHINGTON & SUNDERLAND
WEST
E. 67,280   T. 40,574 (60.31%)   Lab. hold
*Sharon Hodgson, Lab.   24,639
Jonathan Gullis, C.   11,699
Bryan Foster, UKIP   2,761
Tom Appleby, LD   961
Michal Chantkowski, Green   514
Lab. majority 12,940 (31.89%)
2.10% swing Lab. to C.
(2015: Lab. majority 13,157 (35.31%))

WATFORD
E. 86,507   T. 58,610 (67.75%)   C. hold
*Richard Harrington, C.   26,731
Chris Ostrowski, Lab.   24,639
Ian Stotesbury, LD   5,335
Ian Green, UKIP   1,184
Alex Murray, Green   721
C. majority 2,092 (3.57%)
6.94% swing C. to Lab.
(2015: C. majority 9,794 (17.44%))

WAVENEY
E. 80,784   T. 52,674 (65.20%)   C. hold
*Peter Aldous, C.   28,643
Sonia Barker, Lab.   19,428
Bert Poole, UKIP   1,933
Elfrede Brambley-Crawshaw,
Green   1,332
Jacky Howe, LD   1,012
Allyson Barron, Ind.   326
C. majority 9,215 (17.49%)
6.44% swing Lab. to C.
(2015: C. majority 2,408 (4.61%))

WEALDEN
E. 81,425   T. 60,464 (74.26%)   C. hold
*Nus Ghani, C.   37,027
Angela Smith, Lab.   13,399
Chris Bowers, LD   6,281
Colin Stocks, Green   1,959
Nicola Burton, UKIP   1,798
C. majority 23,628 (39.08%)
3.56% swing C. to Lab.
(2015: C. majority 22,967 (40.28%))

WEAVER VALE
E. 69,016   T. 50,613 (73.34%)   Lab. gain
Mike Amesbury, Lab.   26,066
*Graham Evans, C.   22,138
Paul Roberts, LD   1,623
Christopher
Copeman, Green   786
Lab. majority 3,928 (7.76%)
4.74% swing C. to Lab.
(2015: C. majority 806 (1.72%))

WELLINGBOROUGH
E. 79,258   T. 53,240 (67.17%)   C. hold
*Peter Bone, C.   30,579
Andrea Watts, Lab.   18,119
Allan Shipham, UKIP   1,804
Chris Nelson, LD   1,782
Jonathan Hornett, Green   956
C. majority 12,460 (23.40%)
4.58% swing C. to Lab.
(2015: C. majority 16,397 (32.51%))

WELLS
E. 82,449 T. 60,843 (73.79%) C. hold
*James Heappey, C.   30,488
Tessa Munt, LD   22,906
Andy Merryfield, Lab.   7,129
Lorna Corke, CPA   320
C. majority 7,582 (12.46%)
0.43% swing C. to LD
(2015: C. majority 7,585 (13.33%))

WELWYN HATFIELD
E. 72,888 T. 51,669 (70.89%) C. hold
*Grant Shapps, C.   26,374
Anawar Miah, Lab.   19,005
Nigel Quinton, LD   3,836
Dean Milliken, UKIP   1,441
Christianne Sayers, Green   835
Melvyn Jones, Ind.   178
C. majority 7,369 (14.26%)
4.97% swing C. to Lab.
(2015: C. majority 12,153 (24.21%))

WENTWORTH & DEARNE
E. 74,890 T. 43,947 (58.68%) Lab. hold
*John Healey, Lab.   28,547
Steven Jackson, C.   13,744
Janice Middleton, LD   1,656
Lab. majority 14,803 (33.68%)
4.15% swing Lab. to C.
(2015: Lab. majority 13,838 (32.04%))

WEST BROMWICH EAST
E. 63,833 T. 39,098 (61.25%) Lab. hold
*Tom Watson, Lab.   22,664
Emma Crane, C.   14,951
Karen Trench, LD   625
John Macefield, Green   533
Colin Rankine, Ind.   325
Lab. majority 7,713 (19.73%)
2.77% swing Lab. to C.
(2015: Lab. majority 9,470 (25.26%))

WEST BROMWICH WEST
E. 65,956 T. 36,094 (54.72%)
                      Lab. Co-op hold
*Adrian Bailey, Lab. Co-op   18,789
Andrew Hardie, C.   14,329
Star Anderton, UKIP   2,320
Flo Clucas, LD   333
Robert Buckman, Green   323
Lab. Co-op majority 4,460 (12.36%)
5.55% swing Lab. to C.
(2015: Lab. Co-op majority 7,742
(22.10%))

WEST HAM
E. 92,243 T. 60,708 (65.81%) Lab. hold
*Lyn Brown, Lab.   46,591
Patrick Spencer, C.   9,837
Paul Reynolds, LD   1,836
Rosamund Beattie, UKIP   1,134
Michael Spracklin, Green   957
Kayode Shedowo, CPA   353
Lab. majority 36,754 (60.54%)
3.77% swing C. to Lab.
(2015: Lab. majority 27,986 (53.01%))

WESTMINSTER NORTH
E. 63,846 T. 43,295 (67.81%) Lab. hold
*Karen Buck, Lab.   25,934
Lindsey Hall, C.   14,422
Alex Harding, LD   2,253
Emmanuelle Tandy, Green   595
Abby Dharamsey, ND   91
Lab. majority 11,512 (26.59%)
10.79% swing C. to Lab.
(2015: Lab. majority 1,977 (5.00%))

WESTMORLAND & LONSDALE
E. 66,391 T. 51,687 (77.85%) LD hold
*Tim Farron, LD   23,686
James Airey, C.   22,909
Eli Aldridge, Lab.   4,783
Mr Fishfinger, Ind.   309
LD majority 777 (1.50%)
8.39% swing LD to C.
(2015: LD majority 8,949 (18.29%))

WESTON-SUPER-MARE
E. 82,160 T. 56,415 (68.66%) C. hold
*John Penrose, C.   29,982
Timothy Taylor, Lab.   18,438
Mike Bell, LD   5,175
Helen Hims, UKIP   1,932
Suneil Basu, Green   888
C. majority 11,544 (20.46%)
4.62% swing C. to Lab.
(2015: C. majority 15,609 (29.70%))

WIGAN
E. 75,359 T. 47,542 (63.09%) Lab. hold
*Lisa Nandy, Lab.   29,575
Alexander Williams, C.   13,548
Nathan Ryding, UKIP   2,750
Mark Clayton, LD   916
William Patterson, Green   753
Lab. majority 16,027 (33.71%)
1.14% swing C. to Lab.
(2015: Lab. majority 14,236 (31.43%))

WILTSHIRE NORTH
E. 71,408 T. 53,706 (75.21%) C. hold
*James Gray, C.   32,398
Brian Mathew, LD   9,521
Peter Baldrey, Lab.   9,399
Phil Chamberlain, Green   1,141
Paddy Singh, UKIP   871
Lisa Tweedie, Ind.   376
C. majority 22,877 (42.60%)
0.48% swing LD to C.
(2015: C. majority 21,046 (41.63%))

WILTSHIRE SOUTH WEST
E. 76,898 T. 54,751 (71.20%) C. hold
*Andrew Murrison, C.   32,841
Laura Pictor, Lab.   14,515
Trevor Carbin, LD   5,360
Christopher Walford, Green   1,445
Liam Silcocks, Ind.   590
C. majority 18,326 (33.47%)
2.87% swing C. to Lab.
(2015: C. majority 18,168 (35.18%))

WIMBLEDON
E. 66,771 T. 51,526 (77.17%) C. hold
*Stephen Hammond, C.   23,946
Imran Uddin, Lab.   18,324
Carl Quilliam, LD   7,472
Charles Barraball, Green   1,231
Strachan McDonald, UKIP   553
C. majority 5,622 (10.91%)
7.57% swing C. to Lab.
(2015: C. majority 12,619 (26.06%))

WINCHESTER
E. 72,497 T. 57,156 (78.84%) C. hold
*Steve Brine, C.   29,729
Jackie Porter, LD   19,730
Mark Chaloner, Lab.   6,007
Andrew Wainwright, Green   846
Martin Lyon, UKIP   695
Teresa Skelton, JACP   149
C. majority 9,999 (17.49%)
6.54% swing C. to LD
(2015: C. majority 16,914 (30.58%))

WINDSOR
E. 73,595 T. 53,921 (73.27%) C. hold
*Adam Afriyie, C.   34,718
Peter Shearman, Lab.   12,334
Julian Tisi, LD   5,434
Fintan McKeown, Green   1,435
C. majority 22,384 (41.51%)
4.25% swing C. to Lab.
(2015: C. majority 25,083 (50.01%))

WIRRAL SOUTH
E. 57,670 T. 45,195 (78.37%) Lab. hold
*Alison McGovern, Lab.   25,871
Adam Sykes, C.   17,548
Chris Carubia, LD   1,322
Mandi Roberts, Green   454
Lab. majority 8,323 (18.42%)
3.71% swing C. to Lab.
(2015: Lab. majority 4,599 (10.99%))

WIRRAL WEST
E. 55,995 T. 43,951 (78.49%) Lab. hold
*Margaret Greenwood, Lab.   23,866
Tony Caldeira, C.   18,501
Peter Reisdorf, LD   1,155
John Coyne, Green   429
Lab. majority 5,365 (12.21%)
5.61% swing C. to Lab.
(2015: Lab. majority 417 (1.00%))

WITHAM
E. 69,137 T. 49,241 (71.22%) C. hold
*Priti Patel, C.   31,670
Phil Barlow, Lab.   13,024
Jo Hayes, LD   2,715
James Abbott, Green   1,832
C. majority 18,646 (37.87%)
1.90% swing C. to Lab.
(2015: C. majority 19,554 (41.46%))

WITNEY
E. 82,727 T. 60,927 (73.65%) C. hold
*Robert Courts, C.   33,839
Laetisia Carter, Lab.   12,598
Liz Leffman, LD   12,457
Claire Lasko, Green   1,053
Alexander Craig, UKIP   980
C. majority 21,241 (34.86%)
4.08% swing C. to Lab.
(2015: C. majority 25,155 (43.01%))
(2016: C. majority 5,702 (14.83%))

WOKING
E. 76,167 T. 55,246 (72.53%)   C. hold
*Jonathan Lord, C.   29,903
Fiona Colley, Lab.   13,179
Will Forster, LD   9,711
Troy De Leon, UKIP   1,161
James Brierley, Green   1,092
Hassan Akbarali, Ind.   200
C. majority 16,724 (30.27%)
4.89% swing C. to Lab.
(2015: C. majority 20,810 (40.05%))

WOKINGHAM
E. 79,879 T. 59,690 (74.73%)   C. hold
*John Redwood, C.   33,806
Andy Croy, Lab.   15,008
Clive Jones, LD   9,512
Russell Seymour, Green   1,364
C. majority 18,798 (31.49%)
5.86% swing C. to Lab.
(2015: C. majority 24,197 (43.21%))

WOLVERHAMPTON NORTH EAST
E. 60,799 T. 36,508 (60.05%) Lab. hold
*Emma Reynolds, Lab.   19,282
Sarah Macken, C.   14,695
Graham Eardley, UKIP   1,479
Ian Jenkins, LD   570
Clive Wood, Green   482
Lab. majority 4,587 (12.56%)
1.80% swing Lab. to C.
(2015: Lab. majority 5,495 (16.16%))

WOLVERHAMPTON SOUTH EAST
E. 69,951 T. 36,304 (51.90%) Lab. hold
*Pat McFadden, Lab.   21,137
Kieran Mullan, C.   12,623
Barry Hodgson, UKIP   1,675
Ben Mathis, LD   448
Amy Bertaut, Green   421
Lab. majority 8,514 (23.45%)
3.78% swing Lab. to C.
(2015: Lab. majority 10,778 (31.00%))

WOLVERHAMPTON SOUTH WEST
E. 60,003 T. 42,346 (70.57%) Lab. hold
Eleanor Smith, Lab.   20,899
Paul Uppal, C.   18,714
Rob Jones, UKIP   1,012
Sarah Quarmby, LD   784
Andrea Cantrill, Green   579
Jagmeet Singh, Ind.   358
Lab. majority 2,185 (5.16%)
1.58% swing C. to Lab.
(2015: Lab. majority 801 (1.99%))

WORCESTER
E. 72,815 T. 51,423 (70.62%)   C. hold
*Robin Walker, C.   24,731
Joy Squires, Lab.   22,223
Stephen Kearney, LD   1,757
Paul Hickling, UKIP   1,354
Louis Stephen, Green   1,211
Alex Rugg, Ind.   109
Mark Shuker, Compass   38
C. majority 2,508 (4.88%)
3.24% swing C. to Lab.
(2015: C. majority 5,646 (11.35%))

WORCESTERSHIRE MID
E. 76,065 T. 55,089 (72.42%)   C. hold
*Nigel Huddleston, C.   35,967
Fred Grindrod, Lab.   12,641
Margaret Rowley, LD   3,450
David Greenwood, UKIP   1,660
Fay Whitfield, Green   1,371
C. majority 23,326 (42.34%)
0.10% swing C. to Lab.
(2015: C. majority 20,532 (39.31%))

WORCESTERSHIRE WEST
E. 74,385 T. 56,471 (75.92%)   C. hold
*Harriett Baldwin, C.   34,703
Samantha Charles, Lab.   13,375
Edward McMillan-Scott, LD   5,307
Natalie McVey, Green   1,605
Mike Savage, UKIP   1,481
C. majority 21,328 (37.77%)
2.46% swing C. to Lab.
(2015: C. majority 22,578 (41.73%))

WORKINGTON
E. 60,256 T. 41,676 (69.16%) Lab. hold
*Sue Hayman, Lab.   21,317
Clark Vasey, C.   17,392
George Kemp, UKIP   1,556
Phill Roberts, LD   1,133
Roy Ivinson, Ind.   278
Lab. majority 3,925 (9.42%)
1.38% swing Lab. to C.
(2015: Lab. majority 4,686 (12.18%))

WORSLEY & ECCLES SOUTH
E. 73,692 T. 45,642 (61.94%) Lab. hold
*Barbara Keeley, Lab.   26,046
Iain Lindley, C.   17,667
Kate Clarkson, LD   1,087
Tom Dylan, Green   842
Lab. majority 8,379 (18.36%)
2.11% swing C. to Lab.
(2015: Lab. majority 5,946 (14.14%))

WORTHING EAST & SHOREHAM
E. 75,543 T. 53,117 (70.31%)   C. hold
*Tim Loughton, C.   25,988
Sophie Cook, Lab.   20,882
Oli Henman, LD   2,523
Mike Glennon, UKIP   1,444
Leslie Groves   1,273
Williams, Green
Carl Walker, NHAP   575
Andy Lutwyche, Ind.   432
C. majority 5,106 (9.61%)
10.17% swing C. to Lab.
(2015: C. majority 14,949 (29.96%))

WORTHING WEST
E. 77,777 T. 54,503 (70.08%)   C. hold
*Peter Bottomley, C.   30,181
Beccy Cooper, Lab.   18,091
Hazel Thorpe, LD   2,982
Mark Withers, UKIP   1,635
Benjamin Cornish, Green   1,614
C. majority 12,090 (22.18%)
6.80% swing C. to Lab.
(2015: C. majority 16,855 (33.20%))

WREKIN, THE
E. 68,642 T. 49,523 (72.15%)   C. hold
*Mark Pritchard, C.   27,451
Dylan Harrison, Lab.   17,887
Denis Allen, UKIP   1,656
Rod Keyes, LD   1,345
Pat McCarthy, Green   804
Fay Easton, Ind.   380
C. majority 9,564 (19.31%)
2.17% swing C. to Lab.
(2015: C. majority 10,743 (23.64%))

WYCOMBE
E. 77,089 T. 53,493 (69.39%)   C. hold
*Steve Baker, C.   26,766
Rafiq Raja, Lab.   20,188
Steve Guy, LD   4,147
Richard Phoenix, UKIP   1,210
Peter Sims, Green   1,182
C. majority 6,578 (12.30%)
8.29% swing C. to Lab.
(2015: C. majority 14,856 (28.88%))

WYRE & PRESTON NORTH
E. 72,319 T. 52,646 (72.80%)   C. hold
*Ben Wallace, C.   30,684
Michelle Heaton-Bentley,
Lab.   18,438
John Potter, LD   2,551
Ruth Norbury, Green   973
C. majority 12,246 (23.26%)
2.55% swing C. to Lab.
(2015: C. majority 14,151 (28.36%))

WYRE FOREST
E. 77,734 T. 51,129 (65.77%)   C. hold
*Mark Garnier, C.   29,859
Matthew Lamb, Lab.   16,525
Shazu Miah, LD   1,943
George Connolly, UKIP   1,777
Brett Caulfield, Green   1,025
C. majority 13,334 (26.08%)
0.02% swing Lab. to C.
(2015: C. majority 12,871 (26.03%))

WYTHENSHAWE & SALE EAST
E. 76,361 T. 45,846 (60.04%) Lab. hold
*Mike Kane, Lab.   28,525
Fiona Green, C.   13,581
William Jones, LD   1,504
Mike Bayley-Sanderson,
UKIP   1,475
Dan Jerrome, Green   576
Luckson Francis
Augustine, Ind.   185
Lab. majority 14,944 (32.60%)
4.08% swing C. to Lab.
(2015: Lab. majority 10,569 (24.43%))

YEOVIL
E. 82,911 T. 59,404 (71.65%)   C. hold
*Marcus Fysh, C.   32,369
Jo Roundell Greene, LD   17,646
Ian Martin, Lab.   7,418
Robert Wood, Green   1,052
Katy Pritchard, Ind.   919
C. majority 14,723 (24.78%)
7.73% swing LD to C.
(2015: C. majority 5,313 (9.33%))

YORK CENTRAL

E. 77,315   T. 53,088 (68.66%)

	Lab. Co-op hold
*Rachael Maskell, Lab. Co-op	34,594
Ed Young, C.	16,019
Nick Love, LD	2,475

Lab. Co-op majority 18,575 (34.99%)
10.45% swing C. to Lab.
(2015: Lab. Co-op majority 6,716 (14.09%))

YORK OUTER

E. 75,856   T. 57,427 (75.71%)   C. hold

*Julian Sturdy, C.	29,356
Luke Charters-Reid, Lab.	21,067
James Blanchard, LD	5,910
Bethan Vincent, Green	1,094

C. majority 8,289 (14.43%)
4.96% swing C. to Lab.
(2015: C. majority 13,129 (24.36%))

YORKSHIRE EAST

E. 81,065   T. 53,956 (66.56%)   C. hold

*Greg Knight, C.	31,442
Alan Clark, Lab.	16,436
Carl Minns, LD	2,134
Andrew Dennis, UKIP	1,986
Timothy Norman, Yorkshire	1,015
Michael Jackson, Green	943

C. majority 15,006 (27.81%)
1.03% swing C. to Lab.
(2015: C. majority 14,933 (29.87%))

WALES

ABERAVON

E. 49,891   T. 33,268 (66.68%)   Lab. hold

*Stephen Kinnock, Lab.	22,662
Sadie Vidal, C.	5,901
Andrew Bennison, PC	2,761
Caroline Jones, UKIP	1,345
Cen Phillips, LD	599

Lab. majority 16,761 (50.38%)
6.67% swing C. to Lab.
(2015: Lab. majority 10,445 (33.13%))

ABERCONWY

E. 45,251   T. 32,150 (71.05%)   C. hold

*Guto Bebb, C.	14,337
Emily Owen, Lab.	13,702
Wyn Jones, PC	3,170
Sarah Lesiter-Burgess, LD	941

C. majority 635 (1.98%)
5.64% swing C. to Lab.
(2015: C. majority 3,999 (13.26%))

ALYN & DEESIDE

E. 63,041   T. 44,760 (71.00%)   Lab. hold

*Mark Tami, Lab.	23,315
Laura Knightly, C.	18,080
Jacqui Hurst, PC	1,171
David Griffiths, UKIP	1,117
Pete Williams, LD	1,077

Lab. majority 5,235 (11.70%)
1.80% swing C. to Lab.
(2015: Lab. majority 3,343 (8.09%))

ARFON

E. 41,367   T. 28,208 (68.19%)   PC hold

*Hywel Williams, PC	11,519
Mary Griffiths Clarke, Lab.	11,427
Phillippa Parry, C.	4,614
Calum Davies, LD	648

PC majority 92 (0.33%)
6.67% swing PC to Lab.
(2015: PC majority 3,668 (13.67%))

BLAENAU GWENT

E. 51,227   T. 32,384 (63.22%)   Lab. hold

*Nick Smith, Lab.	18,787
Nigel Copner, PC	6,880
Tracey West, C.	4,783
Dennis May, UKIP	973
Vicki Browning, Ind.	666
Cameron Sullivan, LD	295

Lab. majority 11,907 (36.77%)
6.13% swing Lab. to PC
(2015: Lab. majority 12,703 (40.09%))

BRECON & RADNORSHIRE ℂ

E. 56,010   T. 41,334 (73.80%)   C. hold

*Chris Davies, C.	20,081
James Gibson-Watt, LD	12,043
Dan Lodge, Lab.	7,335
Kate Heneghan, PC	1,299
Peter Gilbert, UKIP	576

C. majority 8,038 (19.45%)
3.36% swing LD to C.
(2015: C. majority 5,102 (12.73%))

BRIDGEND

E. 62,185   T. 43,255 (69.56%)   Lab. hold

*Madeleine Moon, Lab.	21,913
Karen Robson, C.	17,213
Rhys Watkins, PC	1,783
Jonathan Pratt, LD	919
Alun Williams, UKIP	781
Isabel Robson, Ind.	646

Lab. majority 4,700 (10.87%)
2.99% swing C. to Lab.
(2015: Lab. majority 1,927 (4.88%))

CAERPHILLY

E. 64,381   T. 41,297 (64.14%)   Lab. hold

*Wayne David, Lab.	22,491
Jane Pratt, LD	10,413
Lindsay Whittle, PC	5,962
Liz Wilks, UKIP	1,259
Kay David, LD	725
Andrew Creak, Green	447

Lab. majority 12,078 (29.25%)
0.75% swing C. to Lab.
(2015: Lab. majority 10,073 (25.01%))

CARDIFF CENTRAL

E. 59,288   T. 40,367 (68.09%)   Lab. hold

*Jo Stevens, Lab.	25,193
Gregory Stafford, C.	7,997
Eluned Parrott, LD	5,415
Mark Hooper, PC	999
Benjamin Smith, Green	420
Sarul-Islam Mohammed, UKIP	343

Lab. majority 17,196 (42.60%)
8.64% swing C. to Lab.
(2015: Lab. majority 4,981 (12.89%))

CARDIFF NORTH

E. 67,221   T. 52,022 (77.39%)   Lab. gain

Anna McMorrin, Lab.	26,081
*Craig Williams, C.	21,907
Steffan Webb, PC	1,738
Matthew Hemsley, LD	1,714
Gary Oldfield, UKIP	582

Lab. majority 4,174 (8.02%)
6.10% swing C. to Lab.
(2015: C. majority 2,137 (4.18%))

CARDIFF SOUTH & PENARTH

E. 76,499   T. 50,736 (66.32%)

	Lab. Co-op hold
*Stephen Doughty, Lab. Co-op	30,182
Bill Rees, C.	15,318
Ian Titherington, PC	2,162
Emma Sands, LD	1,430
Andrew Bevan, UKIP	942
Anthony Slaughter, Green	532
Jeb Hedges, Pirate	170

Lab. Co-op majority 14,864 (29.30%)
6.66% swing C. to Lab.
(2015: Lab. Co-op majority 7,453 (15.97%))

CARDIFF WEST

E. 67,221   T. 46,629 (69.37%)   Lab. hold

*Kevin Brennan, Lab.	26,425
Matt Smith, C.	13,874
Michael Deem, PC	4,418
Alex Meredith, LD	1,214
Richard Lewis, UKIP	698

Lab. majority 12,551 (26.92%)
5.71% swing C. to Lab.
(2015: Lab. majority 6,789 (15.50%))

CARMARTHEN EAST & DINEFWR

E. 55,976   T. 41,029 (73.30%)   PC hold

*Jonathan Edwards, PC	16,127
David Darkin, Lab.	12,219
Havard Hughes, C.	10,778
Neil Hamilton, UKIP	985
Lesley Prosser, LD	920

PC majority 3,908 (9.52%)
2.34% swing PC to Lab.
(2015: PC majority 5,599 (14.21%))

CARMARTHEN WEST & PEMBROKESHIRE SOUTH

E. 58,548   T. 42,226 (72.12%)   C. hold

*Simon Hart, C.	19,771
Marc Tierney, Lab.	16,661
Abi Thomas, PC	3,933
Alistair Cameron, LD	956
Phil Edwards, UKIP	905

C. majority 3,110 (7.37%)
3.82% swing C. to Lab.
(2015: C. majority 6,054 (15.00%))

CEREDIGION

E. 52,889   T. 39,767 (75.19%)   PC gain

Ben Lake, PC	11,623
*Mark Williams, LD	11,519
Dinah Mulholland, Lab.	8,017
Ruth Davis, C.	7,307
Tom Harrison, UKIP	602
Grenville Ham, Green	542
Crazed Sir Dudley, Loony	157

PC majority 104 (0.26%)
4.23% swing LD to PC
(2015: LD majority 3,067 (8.20%))

CLWYD SOUTH

E. 54,341   T. 37,474 (68.96%)   Lab. hold

*Susan Elan Jones, Lab.	19,002
Simon Baynes, C.	14,646
Christopher Allen, PC	2,293
Jeanette Bassford-Barton, UKIP	802
Bruce Roberts, LD	731

Lab. majority 4,356 (11.62%)
2.39% swing C. to Lab.
(2015: Lab. majority 2,402 (6.85%))

CLWYD WEST

E. 58,263   T. 40,654 (69.78%)   C. hold

*David Jones, C.	19,541
Gareth Thomas, Lab.	16,104
Dilwyn Roberts, PC	3,918
Victor Babu, LD	1,091

C. majority 3,437 (8.45%)
4.62% swing C. to Lab.
(2015: C. majority 6,730 (17.70%))

CYNON VALLEY

E. 51,332   T. 31,802 (61.95%)   Lab. hold

*Ann Clwyd, Lab.	19,404
Keith Dewhurst, C.	6,166
Liz Walters, PC	4,376
Ian McLean, UKIP	1,271
Nicola Knight, LD	585

Lab. majority 13,238 (41.63%)
3.00% swing C. to Lab.
(2015: Lab. majority 9,406 (30.87%))

DELYN

E. 54,116   T. 39,418 (72.84%)   Lab. hold

*David Hanson, Lab.	20,573
Matt Wright, C.	16,333
Paul Rowlinson, PC	1,481
Tom Rippeth, LD	1,031

Lab. majority 4,240 (10.76%)
1.47% swing C. to Lab.
(2015: Lab. majority 2,930 (7.82%))

DWYFOR MEIRIONNYDD

E. 44,699   T. 30,348 (67.89%)   PC hold

*Liz Saville Roberts, PC	13,687
Neil Fairlamb, C.	8,837
Mathew Norman, Lab.	6,273
Stephen Churchman, LD	937
Frank Wykes, UKIP	614

PC majority 4,850 (15.98%)
1.11% swing PC to C.
(2015: PC majority 5,261 (18.20%))

GOWER

E. 62,163   T. 45,576 (73.32%)   Lab. gain

Tonia Antoniazzi, Lab.	22,727
*Byron Davies, C.	19,458
Harri Roberts, PC	1,669
Howard Evans, LD	931
Ross Ford, UKIP	642
Jason Winstanley, Pirate	149

Lab. majority 3,269 (7.17%)
3.62% swing C. to Lab.
(2015: C. majority 27 (0.06%))

ISLWYN

E. 56,256   T. 36,093 (64.16%)   Lab. Co-op hold

*Chris Evans, Lab. Co-op	21,238
Dan Thomas, C.	9,826
Darren Jones, PC	2,739
Joe Smyth, UKIP	1,605
Matthew Kidner, LD	685

Lab. Co-op majority 11,412 (31.62%)
1.10% swing Lab. to C.
(2015: Lab. Co-op majority 10,404 (29.39%))

LLANELLI

E. 59,434   T. 40,342 (67.88%)   Lab. hold

*Nia Griffith, Lab.	21,568
Stephen Davies, C.	9,544
Mari Arthur, PC	7,351
Ken Rees, UKIP	1,331
Rory Daniels, LD	548

Lab. majority 12,024 (29.81%)
1.40% swing C. to Lab.
(2015: Lab. majority 7,095 (18.39%))

MERTHYR TYDFIL & RHYMNEY

E. 55,463   T. 33,545 (60.48%)   Lab. hold

*Gerald Jones, Lab.	22,407
Pauline Jorgensen, C.	6,073
Amy Kitcher, PC	2,740
David Rowlands, UKIP	1,484
Bob Griffin, LD	841

Lab. majority 16,334 (48.69%)
2.45% swing C. to Lab.
(2015: Lab. majority 11,513 (35.19%))

MONMOUTH

E. 64,909   T. 49,734 (76.62%)   C. hold

*David Davies, C.	26,411
Ruth Jones, Lab.	18,205
Veronica German, LD	2,064
Carole Damon, PC	1,338
Ian Chandler, Green	954
Roy Neale, UKIP	762

C. majority 8,206 (16.50%)
3.32% swing C. to Lab.
(2015: C. majority 10,982 (23.14%))

MONTGOMERYSHIRE

E. 50,755   T. 34,891 (68.74%)   C. hold

*Glyn Davies, C.	18,075
Jane Dodds, LD	8,790
Iwan Jones, Lab.	5,542
Aled Hughes, PC	1,960
Richard Chaloner, Green	524

C. majority 9,285 (26.61%)
5.42% swing LD to C.
(2015: C. majority 5,325 (15.77%))

NEATH

E. 55,859   T. 38,285 (68.54%)   Lab. Co-op hold

*Christina Rees, Lab. Co-op	21,713
Orla Lowe, C.	9,082
Daniel Williams, PC	5,339
Richard Pritchard, UKIP	1,419
Frank Little, LD	732

Lab. Co-op majority 12,631 (32.99%)
2.25% swing C. to Lab.
(2015: Lab. majority 9,548 (25.71%))

NEWPORT EAST

E. 57,233   T. 36,820 (64.33%)   Lab. hold

*Jessica Morden, Lab.	20,804
Natasha Asghar, C.	12,801
Ian Gorman, UKIP	1,180
Pete Brown, LD	966
Cameron Wixcey, PC	881
Nadeem Ahmed, ND	188

Lab. majority 8,003 (21.74%)
4.17% swing C. to Lab.
(2015: Lab. majority 4,705 (13.40%))

NEWPORT WEST C

E. 64,399   T. 43,438 (67.45%)   Lab. hold

*Paul Flynn, Lab.	22,723
Angela Jones-Evans, C.	17,065
Stan Edwards, UKIP	1,100
Morgan Bowler-Brown, PC	1,077
Sarah Lockyer, LD	976
Pippa Bartolotti, Green	497

Lab. majority 5,658 (13.03%)
2.16% swing C. to Lab.
(2015: Lab. majority 3,510 (8.70%))

OGMORE

E. 56,661   T. 37,204 (65.66%)   Lab. hold

*Chris Elmore, Lab.	23,225
Jamie Wallis, C.	9,354
Huw Marshall, PC	2,796
Glenda Davies, UKIP	1,235
Gerald Francis, LD	594

Lab. majority 13,871 (37.28%)
0.14% swing C. to Lab.
(2015: Lab. majority 13,043 (37.00%))
(2016: Lab. majority 8,575 (36.44%))

PONTYPRIDD

E. 60,566   T. 39,894 (65.87%)   Lab. hold

*Owen Smith, Lab.	22,103
Juliette Ash, C.	10,655
Fflur Elin, PC	4,102
Michael Powell, LD	1,963
Robin Hunter-Clarke, UKIP	1,071

Lab. majority 11,448 (28.70%)
2.49% swing C. to Lab.
(2015: Lab. majority 8,985 (23.72%))

PRESELI PEMBROKESHIRE

E. 58,540   T. 42,197 (72.08%)   C. hold

*Stephen Crabb, C.	18,302
Philippa Thompson, Lab.	17,988
Owain Williams, PC	2,711
Chris Overton, Ind.	1,209
Bob Kilmister, LD	1,106
Susan Bale, UKIP	850
Rodney Maile, Worth	31

C. majority 314 (0.74%)
5.75% swing C. to Lab.
(2015: C. majority 4,969 (12.25%))

RHONDDA
E. 50,513   T. 32,936 (65.20%)   Lab. hold
*Chris Bryant, Lab.   21,096
Branwen Cennard, PC   7,350
Virginia·Crosbie, C.   3,333
Janet Kenrick, UKIP   880
Karen Roberts, LD   277
Lab. majority 13,746 (41.74%)
9.05% swing PC to Lab.
(2015: Lab. majority 7,455 (23.64%))

SWANSEA EAST
E. 58,521   T. 35,159 (60.08%)   Lab. hold
*Carolyn Harris, Lab.   22,307
Dan Boucher, C.   9,139
Steffan Phillips, PC   1,689
Clifford Johnson, UKIP   1,040
Charley Hasted, LD   625
Chris Evans, Green   359
Lab. majority 13,168 (37.45%)
0.11% swing Lab. to C.
(2015: Lab. majority 12,028 (35.78%))

SWANSEA WEST
E. 56,892   T. 37,282 (65.53%)
                              Lab. Co-op hold
*Geraint Davies, Lab. Co-op   22,278
Craig Lawton, C.   11,680
Rhydian Fitter, PC   1,529
Michael O'Carroll, LD   1,269
Mike Whittall, Green   434
Brian Johnson, SPGB   92
Lab. Co-op majority 10,598 (28.43%)
4.21% swing C. to Lab.
(2015: Lab. Co-op majority 7,036
(20.01%))

TORFAEN
E. 61,839   T. 38,429 (62.14%)   Lab. hold
*Nick Thomas-Symonds,   22,134
Lab.
Graham Smith, C.   11,894
Jeff Rees, PC   2,059
Ian Williams, UKIP   1,490
Andrew Best, LD   852
Lab. majority 10,240 (26.65%)
2.56% swing C. to Lab.
(2015: Lab. majority 8,169 (21.53%))

VALE OF CLWYD
E. 56,890   T. 38,684 (68.00%)   Lab. gain
†Chris Ruane, Lab.   19,423
*James Davies, C.   17,044
David Wyatt, PC   1,551
Gwyn Williams, LD   666
Lab. majority 2,379 (6.15%)
3.41% swing C. to Lab.
(2015: C. majority 237 (0.67%))

VALE OF GLAMORGAN
E. 73,958   T. 53,718 (72.63%)   C. hold
*Alun Cairns, C.   25,501
Camilla Beaven, Lab.   23,311
Ian Johnson, PC   2,295
Jennifer Geroni, LD   1,020
Melanie Hunter-   868
Clarke, UKIP
Stephen Davis-Barker, Green   419
Sharon Lovell, Women   177
David Elston, Pirate   127
C. majority 2,190 (4.08%)
4.67% swing C. to Lab.
(2015: C. majority 6,880 (13.41%))

WREXHAM
E. 50,422   T. 35,092 (69.60%)   Lab. hold
*Ian Lucas, Lab.   17,153
Andrew Atkinson, C.   15,321
Carrie Harper, PC   1,753
Carole O'Toole, LD   865
Lab. majority 1,832 (5.22%)
0.19% swing Lab. to C.
(2015: Lab. majority 1,831 (5.60%))

YNYS MON
E. 52,448   T. 37,367 (71.25%)   Lab. hold
*Albert Owen, Lab.   15,643
Tomos Davies, C.   10,384
Ieuan Wyn Jones, PC   10,237
James Turner, UKIP   624
Sarah Jackson, LD   479
Lab. majority 5,259 (14.07%)
2.06% swing C. to Lab.
(2015: Lab. majority 229 (0.66%))

SCOTLAND

ABERDEEN NORTH
E. 62,130   T. 36,757 (59.16%)
                                    SNP hold
*Kirsty Blackman, SNP   15,170
Orr Vinegold, Lab.   11,031
Grace O'Keeffe, C.   8,341
Isobel Davidson, LD   1,693
Richard Durkin, Ind.   522
SNP majority 4,139 (11.26%)
9.61% swing SNP to Lab.
(2015: SNP majority 13,396 (30.49%))

ABERDEEN SOUTH
E. 64,964   T. 44,483 (68.47%)   C. gain
Ross Thomson, C.   18,746
*Callum McCaig, SNP   13,994
Callum O'Dwyer, Lab.   9,143
Jenny Wilson, LD   2,600
C. majority 4,752 (10.68%)
14.75% swing SNP to C.
(2015: SNP majority 7,230 (14.89%))

ABERDEENSHIRE WEST &
KINCARDINE
E. 72,477   T. 51,625 (71.23%)   C. gain
Andrew Bowie, C.   24,704
*Stuart Donaldson, SNP   16,754
Barry Black, Lab.   5,706
John Waddell, LD   4,461
C. majority 7,950 (15.40%)
14.07% swing SNP to C.
(2015: SNP majority 7,033 (12.74%))

AIRDRIE & SHOTTS
E. 64,146   T. 38,002 (59.24%)
                                    SNP hold
*Neil Gray, SNP   14,291
Helen McFarlane, Lab.   14,096
Jennifer Donnellan, C.   8,813
Ewan McRobert, LD   802
SNP majority 195 (0.51%)
9.66% swing SNP to Lab.
(2015: SNP majority 8,779 (19.82%))

ANGUS
E. 63,840   T. 40,192 (62.96%)   C. gain
Kirstene Hair, C.   18,148
*Mike Weir, SNP   15,503
William Campbell, Lab.   5,233
Clive Sneddon, LD   1,308
C. majority 2,645 (6.58%)
15.91% swing SNP to C.
(2015: SNP majority 11,230 (25.24%))

ARGYLL & BUTE
E. 67,230   T. 48,069 (71.50%)
                                    SNP hold
*Brendan O'Hara, SNP   17,304
Gary Mulvaney, C.   15,976
Alan Reid, LD   8,745
Michael Kelly, Lab.   6,044
SNP majority 1,328 (2.76%)
13.29% swing SNP to C.
(2015: SNP majority 8,473 (16.33%))

AYR, CARRICK & CUMNOCK
E. 71,241   T. 46,222 (64.88%)   C. gain
Bill Grant, C.   18,550
*Corri Wilson, SNP   15,776
Carol Mochan, Lab.   11,024
Callum Leslie, LD   872
C. majority 2,774 (6.00%)
17.50% swing SNP to C.
(2015: SNP majority 11,265 (21.58%))

AYRSHIRE CENTRAL
E. 68,997   T. 45,087 (65.35%)
                                    SNP hold
*Philippa Whitford, SNP   16,771
Caroline Hollins Martin, C.   15,504
Nairn McDonald, Lab.   11,762
Tom Inglis, LD   1,050
SNP majority 1,267 (2.81%)
16.51% swing SNP to C.
(2015: SNP majority 13,589 (26.76%))

AYRSHIRE NORTH & ARRAN
E. 73,174   T. 47,433 (64.82%)
                                    SNP hold
*Patricia Gibson, SNP   18,451
David Rocks, C.   14,818
Chris Rimicans, Lab.   13,040
Mark Dickson, LD   1,124
SNP majority 3,633 (7.66%)
15.36% swing SNP to C.
(2015: SNP majority 13,573 (25.20%))

BANFF & BUCHAN
E. 67,601   T. 41,643 (61.60%)   C. gain
David Duguid, C. 19,976
*Eilidh Whiteford, SNP 16,283
Caitlin Stott, Lab. 3,936
Galen Milne, LD 1,448
C. majority 3,693 (8.87%)
20.15% swing SNP to C.
(2015: SNP majority 14,339 (31.43%))

BERWICKSHIRE, ROXBURGH & SELKIRK
E. 73,191   T. 52,367 (71.55%)   C. gain
John Lamont, C. 28,213
*Calum Kerr, SNP 17,153
Ian Davidson, Lab. Co-op 4,519
Caroline Burgess, LD 2,482
C. majority 11,060 (21.12%)
10.86% swing SNP to C.
(2015: SNP majority 328 (0.60%))

CAITHNESS, SUTHERLAND & EASTER ROSS
E. 46,868   T. 30,901 (65.93%)   LD gain
Jamie Stone, LD 11,061
*Paul Monaghan, SNP 9,017
Struan Mackie, C. 6,990
Olivia Bell, Lab. 3,833
LD majority 2,044 (6.61%)
8.93% swing SNP to LD
(2015: SNP majority 3,844 (11.24%))

COATBRIDGE, CHRYSTON & BELLSHILL
E. 71,198   T. 45,040 (63.26%)   Lab. gain
Hugh Gaffney, Lab. 19,193
*Phil Boswell, SNP 17,607
Robyn Halbert, C. 7,318
David Bennie, LD 922
Lab. majority 1,586 (3.52%)
13.10% swing SNP to Lab.
(2015: SNP majority 11,501 (22.69%))

CUMBERNAULD, KILSYTH & KIRKINTILLOCH EAST
E. 66,554   T. 43,833 (65.86%)
SNP hold
*Stuart McDonald, SNP 19,122
Elisha Fisher, Lab. 14,858
Stephen Johnston, C. 8,010
Rod Ackland, LD 1,238
Carl Pearson, UKIP 605
SNP majority 4,264 (9.73%)
10.07% swing SNP to Lab.
(2015: SNP majority 14,752 (29.87%))

DUMFRIES & GALLOWAY
E. 74,206   T. 51,599 (69.53%)   C. gain
Alister Jack, C. 22,344
*Richard Arkless, SNP 16,701
Daniel Goodare, Lab. 10,775
Joan Mitchell, LD 1,241
Yen Hongmei Jin, ND 538
C. majority 5,643 (10.94%)
11.22% swing SNP to C.
(2015: SNP majority 6,514 (11.51%))

DUMFRIESSHIRE, CLYDESDALE & TWEEDDALE
E. 67,672   T. 48,964 (72.35%)   C. hold
*David Mundell, C. 24,177
Mairi McAllan, SNP 14,736
Douglas Beattie, Lab. 8,102
John Ferry, LD 1,949
C. majority 9,441 (19.28%)
8.88% swing SNP to C.
(2015: C. majority 798 (1.53%))

DUNBARTONSHIRE EAST
E. 66,300   T. 51,801 (78.13%)   LD gain
†Jo Swinson, LD 21,023
*John Nicolson, SNP 15,684
Sheila Mechan, C. 7,563
Callum McNally, Lab. 7,531
LD majority 5,339 (10.31%)
7.13% swing SNP to LD
(2015: SNP majority 2,167 (3.95%))

DUNBARTONSHIRE WEST
E. 67,602   T. 44,083 (65.21%)
SNP hold
*Martin Docherty, SNP 18,890
Jean Anne Mitchell, Lab. 16,602
Penny Hutton, C. 7,582
Rebecca Plenderleith, LD 1,009
SNP majority 2,288 (5.19%)
11.26% swing SNP to Lab.
(2015: SNP majority 14,171 (27.71%))

DUNDEE EAST
E. 65,854   T. 42,928 (65.19%)
SNP hold
*Stewart Hosie, SNP 18,391
Eleanor Price, C. 11,746
Lesley Brennan, Lab. 11,176
Christopher McIntyre, LD 1,615
SNP majority 6,645 (15.48%)
14.63% swing SNP to C.
(2015: SNP majority 19,162 (39.77%))

DUNDEE WEST
E. 62,644   T. 38,677 (61.74%)
SNP hold
*Chris Law, SNP 18,045
Alan Cowan, Lab. 12,783
Darren Cormack, C. 6,257
Jenny Blain, LD 1,189
Sean Dobson, Ind. 403
SNP majority 5,262 (13.60%)
12.31% swing SNP to Lab.
(2015: SNP majority 17,092 (38.23%))

DUNFERMLINE & FIFE WEST
E. 75,672   T. 51,010 (67.41%)
SNP hold
*Douglas Chapman, SNP 18,121
Cara Hilton, Lab. Co-op 17,277
Belinda Hacking, C. 12,593
James Calder, LD 3,019
SNP majority 844 (1.65%)
8.43% swing SNP to Lab.
(2015: SNP majority 10,352 (18.52%))

EAST KILBRIDE, STRATHAVEN & LESMAHAGOW
E. 80,442   T. 54,102 (67.26%)
SNP hold
*Lisa Cameron, SNP 21,023
Monique McAdams, Lab. 17,157
Mark McGeever, C. 13,704
Paul McGarry, LD 1,590
Janice MacKay, UKIP 628
SNP majority 3,866 (7.15%)
10.08% swing SNP to Lab.
(2015: SNP majority 16,527 (27.30%))

EAST LOTHIAN
E. 79,093   T. 55,878 (70.65%)   Lab. gain
Martin Whitfield, Lab. 20,158
*George Kerevan, SNP 17,075
Sheila Low, C. 16,540
Elisabeth Wilson, LD 1,738
Mike Allan, Ind. 367
Lab. majority 3,083 (5.52%)
8.52% swing SNP to Lab.
(2015: SNP majority 6,803 (11.53%))

EDINBURGH EAST
E. 65,896   T. 43,523 (66.05%)
SNP hold
*Tommy Sheppard, SNP 18,509
Patsy King, Lab. 15,084
Katie Mackie, C. 8,081
Tristan Gray, LD 1,849
SNP majority 3,425 (7.87%)
5.73% swing SNP to Lab.
(2015: SNP majority 9,106 (19.34%))

EDINBURGH NORTH & LEITH
E. 79,473   T. 56,552 (71.16%)
SNP hold
*Deidre Brock, SNP 19,243
Gordon Munro, Lab. Co-op 17,618
Iain McGill, C. 15,385
Martin Veart, LD 2,579
Lorna Slater, Green 1,727
SNP majority 1,625 (2.87%)
3.39% swing SNP to Lab.
(2015: SNP majority 5,597 (9.65%))

EDINBURGH SOUTH
E. 64,553   T. 47,840 (74.11%)   Lab. hold
*Ian Murray, Lab. 26,269
Jim Eadie, SNP 10,755
Stephanie Smith, C. 9,428
Alan Beal, LD 1,388
Lab. majority 15,514 (32.43%)
13.54% swing SNP to Lab.
(2015: Lab. majority 2,637 (5.35%))

EDINBURGH SOUTH WEST
E. 71,178   T. 49,390 (69.39%)
SNP hold
*Joanna Cherry, SNP 17,575
Miles Briggs, C. 16,478
Foysol Choudhury, Lab. 13,213
Aisha Mir, LD 2,124
SNP majority 1,097 (2.22%)
10.25% swing SNP to C.
(2015: SNP majority 8,135 (15.76%))

EDINBURGH WEST
E. 71,500 T. 52,795 (73.84%) LD gain
Christine Jardine, LD   18,108
Toni Giugliano, SNP   15,120
Sandy Batho, C.   11,559
Mandy Telford, Lab.   7,876
Mark Whittet, Referendum   132
LD majority 2,988 (5.66%)
5.76% swing SNP to LD
(2015: SNP majority 3,210 (5.85%))

FALKIRK
E. 82,240 T. 53,809 (65.43%)
                                    SNP hold
*John McNally, SNP   20,952
Craig Martin, Lab.   16,029
Callum Laidlaw, C.   14,088
Austin Reid, LD   1,120
Debra Pickering, Green   908
Stuart Martin, UKIP   712
SNP majority 4,923 (9.15%)
11.75% swing SNP to Lab.
(2015: SNP majority 19,701 (32.65%))

FIFE NORTH EAST
E. 58,685 T. 41,822 (71.27%)
                                    SNP hold
*Stephen Gethins, SNP   13,743
Janet Riches, LD   13,741
Tony Miklinski, C.   10,088
Rosalind Garton, Lab.   4,026
Mike Scott-Hayward,   224
Sovereign
SNP majority 2 (0.00%)
4.80% swing SNP to LD
(2015: SNP majority 4,344 (9.60%))

GLASGOW CENTRAL
E. 64,346 T. 35,984 (55.92%)
                                    SNP hold
*Alison Thewliss, SNP   16,096
Faten Hameed, Lab.   13,829
Charlotte Fairbanks, C.   5,014
Isabel Nelson, LD   1,045
SNP majority 2,267 (6.30%)
6.59% swing SNP to Lab.
(2015: SNP majority 7,662 (19.49%))

GLASGOW EAST
E. 66,242 T. 36,175 (54.61%)
                                    SNP hold
David Linden, SNP   14,024
Kate Watson, Lab.   13,949
Thomas Kerr, C.   6,816
Matthew Clark, LD   576
John Ferguson, UKIP   504
Karin Finegan, Ind.   158
Steven Marshall, Soc. Dem.   148
SNP majority 75 (0.21%)
12.14% swing SNP to Lab.
(2015: SNP majority 10,387 (24.49%))

GLASGOW NORTH
E. 53,863 T. 33,473 (62.14%)
                                    SNP hold
*Patrick Grady, SNP   12,597
Pam Duncan-Glancy, Lab.   11,537
Stuart Cullen, C.   4,935
Patrick Harvie, Green   3,251
Calum Shepherd, LD   1,153
SNP majority 1,060 (3.17%)
11.00% swing SNP to Lab.
(2015: SNP majority 9,295 (25.17%))

GLASGOW NORTH EAST
E. 59,932 T. 31,775 (53.02%)
                                Lab. Co-op gain
Paul Sweeney, Lab. Co-op   13,637
*Anne McLaughlin, SNP   13,395
Jack Wylie, C.   4,106
Daniel Donaldson, LD   637
Lab. Co-op majority 242 (0.76%)
12.56% swing SNP to Lab.
(2015: SNP majority 9,222 (24.36%))

GLASGOW NORTH WEST
E. 63,773 T. 38,844 (60.91%)
                                    SNP hold
*Carol Monaghan, SNP   16,508
Michael Shanks, Lab.   13,947
Christopher Land, C.   7,002
James Speirs, LD   1,387
SNP majority 2,561 (6.59%)
8.52% swing SNP to Lab.
(2015: SNP majority 10,364 (23.63%))

GLASGOW SOUTH
E. 69,126 T. 44,550 (64.45%)
                                    SNP hold
*Stewart McDonald, SNP   18,312
Eileen Dinning, Lab.   16,285
Taylor Muir, C.   8,506
Ewan Hoyle, LD   1,447
SNP majority 2,027 (4.55%)
10.30% swing SNP to Lab.
(2015: SNP majority 12,269 (25.15%))

GLASGOW SOUTH WEST
E. 62,991 T. 35,378 (56.16%)
                                    SNP hold
*Chris Stephens, SNP   14,386
Matt Kerr, Lab. Co-op   14,326
Thomas Haddow, C.   5,524
Ben Denton-Cardew, LD   661
Sarah Hemy, UKIP   481
SNP majority 60 (0.17%)
12.07% swing SNP to Lab.
(2015: SNP majority 9,950 (24.32%))

GLENROTHES
E. 66,378 T. 40,399 (60.86%)
                                    SNP hold
*Peter Grant, SNP   17,291
Altany Craik, Lab.   14,024
Andrew Brown, C.   7,876
Rebecca Bell, LD   1,208
SNP majority 3,267 (8.09%)
10.55% swing SNP to Lab.
(2015: SNP majority 13,897 (29.20%))

GORDON
E. 78,531 T. 53,685 (68.36%) C. gain
Colin Clark, C.   21,861
*Alex Salmond, SNP   19,254
Kirsten Muat, Lab.   6,340
David Evans, LD   6,230
C. majority 2,607 (4.86%)
20.40% swing SNP to C.
(2015: SNP majority 8,687 (14.94%))

INVERCLYDE
E. 58,853 T. 39,093 (66.42%)
                                    SNP hold
*Ronnie Cowan, SNP   15,050
Martin McCluskey, Lab.   14,666
David Wilson, C.   8,399
David Stevens, LD   978
SNP majority 384 (0.98%)
11.91% swing SNP to Lab.
(2015: SNP majority 11,063 (24.80%))

INVERNESS, NAIRN, BADENOCH & STRATHSPEY
E. 76,844 T. 52,801 (68.71%)
                                    SNP hold
*Drew Hendry, SNP   21,042
Nicholas Tulloch, C.   16,118
Mike Robb, Lab.   8,552
Ritchie Cunningham, LD   6,477
Donald Boyd, SCP   612
SNP majority 4,924 (9.33%)
17.41% swing SNP to C.
(2015: SNP majority 10,809 (18.76%))

KILMARNOCK & LOUDOUN
E. 73,327 T. 46,509 (63.43%)
                                    SNP hold
*Alan Brown, SNP   19,690
Laura Dover, Lab.   13,421
Alison Harper, C.   12,404
Irene Lang, LD   994
SNP majority 6,269 (13.48%)
5.91% swing SNP to Lab.
(2015: SNP majority 13,638 (25.30%))

KIRKCALDY & COWDENBEATH
E. 72,721 T. 46,193 (63.52%) Lab. gain
Lesley Laird, Lab.   17,016
*Roger Mullin, SNP   16,757
Dave Dempsey, C.   10,762
Malcolm Wood, LD   1,118
David Coburn, UKIP   540
Lab. majority 259 (0.56%)
9.71% swing SNP to Lab.
(2015: SNP majority 9,974 (18.86%))

LANARK & HAMILTON EAST
E. 77,313 T. 50,470 (65.28%)
                                    SNP hold
*Angela Crawley, SNP   16,444
Poppy Corbett, C.   16,178
Andrew Hilland, Lab.   16,084
Colin Robb, LD   1,214
Donald Mackay, UKIP   550
SNP majority 266 (0.53%)
16.21% swing SNP to C.
(2015: SNP majority 10,100 (18.28%))

LINLITHGOW & FALKIRK EAST
E. 86,186 T. 56,094 (65.08%)
                                    SNP hold
*Martyn Day, SNP   20,388
Joan Coombes, Lab.   17,469
Charles Kennedy, C.   16,311
Sally Pattle, LD   1,926
SNP majority 2,919 (5.20%)
7.90% swing SNP to Lab.
(2015: SNP majority 12,934 (21.00%))

LIVINGSTON
E. 81,208   T. 52,505 (64.65%)

	SNP hold
*Hannah Bardell, SNP	21,036
Rhea Wolfson, Lab.	17,158
Damian Timson, C.	12,799
Charles Dundas, LD	1,512

SNP majority 3,878 (7.39%)
10.94% swing SNP to Lab.
(2015: SNP majority 16,843 (29.27%))

MIDLOTHIAN
E. 68,328   T. 45,273 (66.26%)   Lab. gain

Danielle Rowley, Lab.	16,458
*Owen Thompson, SNP	15,573
Chris Donnelly, C.	11,521
Ross Laird, LD	1,721

Lab. majority 885 (1.95%)
11.18% swing SNP to Lab.
(2015: SNP majority 9,859 (20.40%))

MORAY
E. 70,649   T. 47,605 (67.38%)   C. gain

Douglas Ross, C.	22,637
*Angus Robertson, SNP	18,478
Jo Kirby, Lab.	5,208
Alex Linklater, LD	1,078
Anne Glen, Ind.	204

C. majority 4,159 (8.74%)
13.57% swing SNP to C.
(2015: SNP majority 9,065 (18.39%))

MOTHERWELL & WISHAW
E. 68,215   T. 41,926 (61.46%)

	SNP hold
*Marion Fellows, SNP	16,150
Angela Feeney, Lab.	15,832
Meghan Gallacher, C.	8,490
Yvonne Finlayson, LD	920
Neil Wilson, UKIP	534

SNP majority 318 (0.76%)
11.95% swing SNP to Lab.
(2015: SNP majority 11,898 (24.67%))

NA H-EILEANAN AN IAR
E. 21,301   T. 14,818 (69.56%)

	SNP hold
*Angus MacNeil, SNP	6,013
Ealasaid MacDonald, Lab.	5,006
Dan McCroskrie, C.	2,441
John Cormack, SCP	1,108
James Paterson, LD	250

SNP majority 1,007 (6.80%)
9.47% swing SNP to Lab.
(2015: SNP majority 4,102 (25.74%))

OCHIL & PERTHSHIRE SOUTH
E. 76,767   T. 54,168 (70.56%)   C. gain

Luke Graham, C.	22,469
*Tasmina Ahmed-Sheikh, SNP	19,110
Joanne Ross, Lab.	10,847
Iliyan Stefanov, LD	1,742

C. majority 3,359 (6.20%)
15.74% swing SNP to C.
(2015: SNP majority 10,168 (17.57%))

ORKNEY & SHETLAND
E. 34,164   T. 23,277 (68.13%)   LD hold

*Alistair Carmichael, LD	11,312
Miriam Brett, SNP	6,749
Robina Barton, Lab.	2,664
Jamie Halcro Johnston, C.	2,024
Robert Smith, UKIP	283
Stuart Hill, Ind.	245

LD majority 4,563 (19.60%)
8.00% swing SNP to LD
(2015: LD majority 817 (3.59%))

PAISLEY & RENFREWSHIRE NORTH
E. 67,436   T. 46,615 (69.12%)

	SNP hold
*Gavin Newlands, SNP	17,455
Alison Taylor, Lab.	14,842
David Gardiner, C.	12,842
John Boyd, LD	1,476

SNP majority 2,613 (5.61%)
6.19% swing SNP to Lab.
(2015: SNP majority 9,076 (17.99%))

PAISLEY & RENFREWSHIRE SOUTH
E. 61,344   T. 41,712 (68.00%)

	SNP hold
*Mhairi Black, SNP	16,964
Alison Dowling, Lab.	14,423
Amy Thomson, C.	8,122
Eileen McCartin, LD	1,327
Paul Mack, Ind.	876

SNP majority 2,541 (6.09%)
3.10% swing SNP to Lab.
(2015: SNP majority 5,684 (12.30%))

PERTH & PERTHSHIRE NORTH
E. 71,743   T. 51,525 (71.82%)

	SNP hold
*Pete Wishart, SNP	21,804
Ian Duncan, C.	21,783
David Roemmele, Lab.	5,349
Peter Barrett, LD	2,589

SNP majority 21 (0.04%)
8.87% swing SNP to C.
(2015: SNP majority 9,641 (17.79%))

RENFREWSHIRE EAST
E. 70,067   T. 53,738 (76.70%)   C. gain

Paul Masterton, C.	21,496
*Kirsten Oswald, SNP	16,784
Blair McDougall, Lab.	14,346
Aileen Morton, LD	1,112

C. majority 4,712 (8.77%)
13.68% swing SNP to C.
(2015: SNP majority 3,718 (6.55%))

ROSS, SKYE & LOCHABER
E. 53,638   T. 38,454 (71.69%)

	SNP hold
*Ian Blackford, SNP	15,480
Robert Mackenzie, C.	9,561
Jean Davis, LD	8,042
Peter O'Donnghaile, Lab.	4,695
Ronnie the Crofter	499
Campbell, Ind.	
Stick Sturrock, S New	177

SNP majority 5,919 (15.39%)
13.26% swing SNP to C.
(2015: SNP majority 5,124 (12.26%))

RUTHERGLEN & HAMILTON WEST
E. 80,098   T. 50,872 (63.51%)

	Lab. Co-op gain
Ged Killen, Lab. Co-op	19,101
*Margaret Ferrier, SNP	18,836
Ann Le Blond, C.	9,941
Robert Brown, LD	2,158
Caroline Santos, UKIP	465
Andy Dixon, Ind.	371

Lab. Co-op majority 265 (0.52%)
8.92% swing SNP to Lab.
(2015: SNP majority 9,975 (17.31%))

STIRLING
E. 66,415   T. 49,356 (74.31%)   C. gain

Stephen Kerr, C.	18,291
*Steven Paterson, SNP	18,143
Chris Kane, Lab.	10,902
Wendy Chamberlain, LD	1,683
Kirstein Rummery, Women	337

C. majority 148 (0.30%)
11.40% swing SNP to C.
(2015: SNP majority 10,480 (20.10%))

NORTHERN IRELAND

ANTRIM EAST
E. 62,908   T. 38,143 (60.63%)

	DUP hold
*Sammy Wilson, DUP	21,873
Stewart Dickson, Alliance	5,950
John Stewart, UUP	4,524
Oliver McMullan, SF	3,555
Margaret McKillop, SDLP	1,278
Mark Logan, C.	963

DUP majority 15,923 (41.75%)
10.30% swing Alliance to DUP
(2015: DUP majority 5,795 (17.30%))

ANTRIM NORTH
E. 75,657   T. 48,460 (64.05%)

	DUP hold
*Ian Paisley, DUP	28,521
Cara McShane, SF	7,878
Jackson Minford, UUP	3,482
Timothy Gaston, TUV	3,282
Patricia O'Lynn, Alliance	2,723
Declan O'Loan, SDLP	2,574

DUP majority 20,643 (42.60%)
5.83% swing SF to DUP
(2015: DUP majority 11,546 (27.55%))

ANTRIM SOUTH
E. 68,244   T. 43,170 (63.26%)

	DUP gain
Paul Girvan, DUP	16,508
*Danny Kinahan, UUP	13,300
Declan Kearney, SF	7,797
Neil Kelly, Alliance	3,203
Roisin Lynch, SDLP	2,362

DUP majority 3,208 (7.43%)
5.01% swing UUP to DUP
(2015: UUP majority 949 (2.60%))

BELFAST EAST

E. 63,495   T. 42,890 (67.55%)

	DUP hold
*Gavin Robinson, DUP	23,917
Naomi Long, Alliance	15,443
Hazel Legge, UUP	1,408
Mairead O'Donnell, SF	894
Georgina Milne, Green	561
Sheila Bodel, C.	446
Seamas de Faoite, SDLP	167
Bobby Beck, Ind.	54

DUP majority 8,474 (19.76%)
6.61% swing Alliance to DUP
(2015: DUP majority 2,597 (6.54%))

BELFAST NORTH

E. 68,249   T. 45,936 (67.31%)

	DUP hold
*Nigel Dodds, DUP	21,240
John Finucane, SF	19,159
Sam Nelson, Alliance	2,475
Martin McAuley, SDLP	2,058
Malachai O'Hara, Green	644
Gemma Weir, WP	360

DUP majority 2,081 (4.53%)
4.30% swing DUP to SF
(2015: DUP majority 5,326 (13.12%))

BELFAST SOUTH

E. 66,105   T. 43,705 (66.11%)

	DUP gain
Emma Little Pengelly, DUP	13,299
*Alasdair McDonnell, SDLP	11,303
Paula Bradshaw, Alliance	7,946
Mairtin O Muilleoir, SF	7,143
Clare Bailey, Green	2,241
Michael Henderson, UUP	1,527
Clare Salier, C.	246

DUP majority 1,996 (4.57%)
3.45% swing SDLP to DUP
(2015: SDLP majority 906 (2.33%))

BELFAST WEST

E. 62,423   T. 40,633 (65.09%)   SF hold

*Paul Maskey, SF	27,107
Frank McCoubrey, DUP	5,455
Gerry Carroll, PBP	4,132
Tim Attwood, SDLP	2,860
Sorcha Eastwood, Alliance	731
Conor Campbell, WP	348

SF majority 21,652 (53.29%)
3.45% swing DUP to SF
(2015: SF majority 12,365 (35.00%))

DOWN NORTH

E. 64,334   T. 39,185 (60.91%)   Ind. hold

*Lady (Sylvia) Hermon, Ind.	16,148
Alex Easton, DUP	14,940
Andrew Muir, Alliance	3,639
Steven Agnew, Green	2,549
Frank Shivers, C.	941
Therese McCartney, SF	531
Caoimhe McNeill, SDLP	400
Gavan Reynolds, Ind.	37

Ind. majority 1,208 (3.08%)
20.56% swing Ind. to Ind.
(2015: Ind. majority 9,202 (25.60%))

DOWN SOUTH

E. 75,685   T. 50,893 (67.24%)   SF gain

Chris Hazzard, SF	20,328
*Margaret Ritchie, SDLP	17,882
Diane Forsythe, DUP	8,867
Harold McKee, UUP	2,002
Andrew McMurray, Alliance	1,814

SF majority 2,446 (4.81%)
9.30% swing SDLP to SF
(2015: SDLP majority 5,891 (13.80%))

FERMANAGH & SOUTH TYRONE

E. 70,601   T. 53,481 (75.75%)   SF gain

†Michelle Gildernew, SF	25,230
*Tom Elliott, UUP	24,355
Mary Garrity, SDLP	2,587
Noreen Campbell, Alliance	886
Tanya Jones, Green	423

SF majority 875 (1.64%)
1.34% swing UUP to SF
(2015: UUP majority 530 (1.04%))

FOYLE

E. 70,324   T. 45,965 (65.36%)   SF gain

Elisha McCallion, SF	18,256
*Mark Durkan, SDLP	18,087
Gary Middleton, DUP	7,398
Shaun Harkin, PBP	1,377
John Doherty, Alliance	847

SF majority 169 (0.37%)
8.35% swing SDLP to SF
(2015: SDLP majority 6,046 (16.34%))

LAGAN VALLEY

E. 72,380   T. 44,926 (62.07%)

	DUP hold
*Jeffrey Donaldson, DUP	26,762
Robbie Butler, UUP	7,533
Aaron McIntyre, Alliance	4,996
Pat Catney, SDLP	3,384
Jacqui Russell, SF	1,567
Ian Nickels, C.	462
Jonny Orr, ND	222

DUP majority 19,229 (42.80%)
5.07% swing UUP to DUP
(2015: DUP majority 13,000 (32.67%))

LONDONDERRY EAST

E. 67,038   T. 41,030 (61.20%)

	DUP hold
*Gregory Campbell, DUP	19,723
Dermot Nicholl, SF	10,881
Stephanie Quigley, SDLP	4,423
Richard Holmes, UUP	3,135
Chris McCaw, Alliance	2,538
Liz St Clair-Legge, C.	330

DUP majority 8,842 (21.55%)
0.47% swing DUP to SF
(2015: DUP majority 7,804 (22.48%))

NEWRY & ARMAGH

E. 78,266   T. 53,579 (68.46%)   SF hold

*Mickey Brady, SF	25,666
William Irwin, DUP	13,177
Justin McNulty, SDLP	9,055
Sam Nicholson, UUP	4,425
Jackie Coade, Alliance	1,256

SF majority 12,489 (23.31%)
swing N/A
(2015: SF majority 4,176 (8.37%))

STRANGFORD

E. 64,327   T. 38,749 (60.24%)

	DUP hold
*Jim Shannon, DUP	24,036
Kellie Armstrong, Alliance	5,693
Mike Nesbitt, UUP	4,419
Joe Boyle, SDLP	2,404
Carole Murphy, SF	1,083
Ricky Bamford, Green	607
Claire Hiscott, C.	507

DUP majority 18,343 (47.34%)
8.39% swing Alliance to DUP
(2015: DUP majority 10,185 (30.02%))

TYRONE WEST

E. 64,009   T. 43,486 (67.94%)   SF hold

Barry McElduff, SF	22,060
Thomas Buchanan, DUP	11,718
Daniel McCrossan, SDLP	5,635
Alicia Clarke, UUP	2,253
Stephen Donnelly, Alliance	1,000
Ciaran McClean, Green	427
Barry Brown, Citizens	393

SF majority 10,342 (23.78%)
1.12% swing SF to DUP
(2015: SF majority 10,060 (26.03%))

ULSTER MID

E. 68,485   T. 46,694 (68.18%)   SF hold

*Francie Molloy, SF	25,455
Keith Buchanan, DUP	12,565
Malachy Quinn, SDLP	4,563
Mark Glasgow, UUP	3,017
Fay Watson, Alliance	1,094

SF majority 12,890 (27.61%)
3.88% swing SF to DUP
(2015: SF majority 13,617 (33.28%))

UPPER BANN

E. 80,168   T. 51,258 (63.94%)

	DUP hold
*David Simpson, DUP	22,317
John O'Dowd, SF	14,325
Doug Beattie, UUP	7,900
Declan McAlinden, SDLP	4,397
Tara Doyle, Alliance	2,319

DUP majority 7,992 (15.59%)
3.73% swing SF to DUP
(2015: DUP majority 2,264 (4.79%))

BY-ELECTIONS 2017–19

All UK parliament by-elections since the 2017 General Election. For a full list of party abbreviations see General Election 2017 results.

BRECON AND RADNORSHIRE
1 August 2019

E. 53,032	T. 31,814 (59.72%)	LD gain

Jane Dodds, LD	13,826
Chris Davies, C	12,401
Des Parkinson, Brexit	3,331
Tom Davies, Lab.	1,680
Lady Lily the Pink, Loony	334
Liz Phillips, UKIP	242

LD majority 1,425 (4.48%)
12% swing C. to LD
(2017: C. majority 8,038 (19.45%))

LEWISHAM EAST
14 June 2018

E. 66,140	T. 22,056 (33.35%)	Lab. hold

Janet Daby, Lab.	11,033
Lucy Salek, LD	5,404
Ross Archer, C.	3,161
Rosamund Adoo-Kissi-Debrah, Green	788
Mandu Reid, Women	506
David Kurten, UKIP	380
Anne Marie Waters, For Britain	266
Maureen Martin, CPA	168
Howling Laud Hope, Loony	93
Massimo DiMambro, DVP	67
Sean Finch, Libertarian	38
Charles Carey, Ind.	37
Patrick Gray, Radical	20
Thomas Hall, Young	18

Lab majority 5,629 (25.61%)
19% swing Lab to LD
(2017: Lab. majority 21,123 (44.94%))

NEWPORT WEST
4 April 2019

E. 63,623	T. 23,515 (37.1%)	Lab. hold

Ruth Jones, Lab.	9,308
Matthew Evans, C.	7,357
Neil Hamilton, UKIP	2,023
Jonathan Clarke, PC	1,185
Ryan Jones, LD	1,088
Amelia Womack, Green	924
June Davies, Renew	879
Richard Suchorzewski, AWAP	205
Ian McLean, Soc. Dem.	202
Philip Taylor, DVP	185
Hugh Nicklin, For Britain	159

Lab majority 1,951 (8.3%)
2.4% swing Lab. to C.
(2017: Lab. majority 5,658 (13.03%))

PETERBOROUGH
6 June 2019

E. 70,083	T. 33,920 (48.4%)	Lab. hold

Lisa Forbes, Lab.	10,484
Mike Green, Brexit	9,801
Paul Bristow, C.	7,243
Beki Sellick, LD	4,159
Joseph Wells, Green	1,035
John Whitby, UKIP	400
Tom Rogers, CPA	162
Stephen Goldspink, Eng. Dem.	153
Patrick O'Flynn, Soc. Dem.	135
Howling Laud Hope, Loony	112
Andrew Moore, Ind.	101
Dick Rodgers, Co. Gd	60
Peter Ward, Renew	45
Pierre Kirk, UKEUP	25
Bobby Smith, Ind.	5

Lab majority 683 (2.0%)
swing N/A
(2017: Lab. majority 607 (1.27%))

TYRONE WEST
3 May 2018

E. 64,178	T. 35,029 (54.58%)	SF hold

Órfhlaith Begley, SF	16,346
Thomas Buchanan, DUP	8,390
Daniel McCrossan, SDLP	6,254
Chris Smyth, UUP	2,909
Stephen Donnelly, Alliance	1,130

SF majority 7,956 (22.71%)
0.53% swing SF to DUP
(2017: SF. majority 10,342 (23.78%))

THE GOVERNMENT

As at 10 September 2019

THE CABINET

Prime Minister, First Lord of the Treasury and Minister for the Civil Service
Rt. Hon. Boris Johnson, MP
Chancellor of the Exchequer
Rt. Hon. Sajid Javid, MP
Secretary of State for Foreign and Commonwealth Affairs and First Secretary of State
Rt. Hon. Dominic Raab, MP
Secretary of State for the Home Department
Rt. Hon. Priti Patel, MP
Chancellor of the Duchy of Lancaster
Rt. Hon. Michael Gove, MP
Lord Chancellor and Secretary of State for Justice
Rt. Hon. Robert Buckland, QC, MP
Secretary of State for Exiting the European Union
Rt. Hon. Stephen Barclay, MP
Secretary of State for Defence
Rt. Hon. Ben Wallace, MP
Secretary of State for Health and Social Care
Rt. Hon. Matt Hancock, MP
Secretary of State for Business, Energy and Industrial Strategy
Rt. Hon. Andrea Leadsom, MP
Secretary of State for International Trade and President of the Board of Trade
Rt. Hon. Elizabeth Truss, MP*
Secretary of State for Work and Pensions
Rt. Hon. Thérèse Coffey, MP
Secretary of State for Education
Rt. Hon. Gavin Williamson, CBE, MP
Secretary of State for Environment, Food and Rural Affairs
Rt. Hon. Theresa Villiers, MP
Secretary of State for Housing, Communities and Local Government
Rt. Hon. Robert Jenrick, MP
Secretary of State for Transport
Rt. Hon. Grant Shapps, MP
Secretary of State for Northern Ireland
Rt. Hon. Julian Smith, MP
Secretary of State for Scotland
Rt. Hon. Alister Jack, MP
Secretary of State for Wales
Rt. Hon. Alun Cairns, MP
Leader of the House of Lords and Lord Privy Seal
Rt. Hon. Baroness Evans of Bowes Park
Secretary of State for Digital, Culture, Media and Sport
Rt. Hon. Nicky Morgan, MP
Secretary of State for International Development
Rt. Hon. Alok Sharma, MP
Minister without Portfolio
Rt. Hon. James Cleverly, MP

* Alongside role as Minister for Women and Equalities

ALSO ATTENDING CABINET MEETINGS
Chief Secretary to the Treasury
Rt. Hon. Rishi Sunak, MP
Lord President of the Council and Leader of the House of Commons
Rt. Hon. Jacob Rees-Mogg, MP
Parliamentary Secretary to the Treasury and Chief Whip
Rt. Hon. Mark Spencer, MP
Attorney-General
Rt. Hon. Geoffrey Cox, QC, MP
Minister for Business, Energy and Clean Growth
Rt. Hon. Kwasi Kwarteng, MP

Minister for the Cabinet Office and Paymaster-General
Rt. Hon. Oliver Dowden, CBE, MP
Minister of State for the Northern Powerhouse and Local Growth
Rt. Hon. Jake Berry, MP
Minister of State for Housing
Rt. Hon. Esther McVey, MP
Minister for Security
Rt. Hon. Brandon Lewis, MP
Minister of State for Environment and International Development
Rt. Hon. Zac Goldsmith, MP

LAW OFFICERS

Attorney-General
Rt. Hon. Geoffrey Cox, QC, MP
Solicitor-General
Michael Ellis, QC, MP
Advocate-General for Scotland
Rt. Hon. Lord Keen of Elie, QC

MINISTERS OF STATE

Business, Energy and Industrial Strategy
Rt. Hon. Kwasi Kwarteng, MP
Chris Skidmore, MP*
Cabinet Office
Rt. Hon. Jake Berry, MP†
Rt. Hon. Oliver Dowden, CBE, MP
Defence
Baroness Goldie
Rt. Hon. Mark Lancaster, TD, MP
Digital, Culture, Media and Sport
Nigel Adams, MP
Education
Rt. Hon. Nick Gibb, MP
Chris Skidmore, MP‡
Environment, Food and Rural Affairs
George Eustice, MP
Rt. Hon. Zac Goldsmith, MP§
Exiting the European Union
Lord Callanan
Foreign and Commonwealth Office
Lord Ahmad of Wimbledon
Rt. Hon. Dr Andrew Murrison, MP§
Rt. Hon. Christopher Pincher, MP
Andrew Stephenson, MP§
Health and Social Care
Edward Argar, MP
Caroline Dinenage, MP
Home Office
Rt. Hon. Brandon Lewis, MP
Kit Malthouse, MP
Baroness Williams of Trafford℄
Housing, Communities and Local Government
Rt. Hon. Jake Berry, MP**
Rt. Hon. Esther McVey, MP
International Development
Rt. Hon. Zac Goldsmith, MP‡‡
Rt. Hon. Dr Andrew Murrison, MP††
Andrew Stephenson, MP††
International Trade
Conor Burns, MP
Justice
Lucy Frazer, QC, MP

Northern Ireland Office
  Rt. Hon. Nick Hurd, MP
Transport
  George Freeman, MP
  Chris Heaton-Harris, MP
Work and Pensions
  Justin Tomlinson, MP
  Baroness Williams of Trafford §§

* Jointly held with the DfE
† Jointly held with the MHCLG
‡ Jointly held with the DBEIS
§ Jointly held with the DFID
℄ Alongside role as Minister for Equalities at the DWP
** Jointly held with the Cabinet Office
†† Jointly held with the FCO
‡‡ Jointly held with DEFRA
§§ Alongside role at the Home Office

UNDER-SECRETARIES OF STATE

Business, Energy and Industrial Strategy
  Lord Duncan of Springbank*
  Kelly Tolhurst, MP
  Nadhim Zahawi, MP
Cabinet Office
  Johnny Mercer, MP†
Defence
  Johnny Mercer, MP‡
  Anne-Marie Trevelyan, MP
Digital, Culture, Media and Sport
  Baroness Barran, MBE
  Matt Warman, MP
  Helen Whately, MP
Education
  Lord Agnew of Oulton
  Kemi Badenoch, MP
Environment, Food and Rural Affairs
  Lord Gardiner of Kimble
  Rebecca Pow, MP
Exiting the European Union
  James Duddridge, MP
Foreign and Commonwealth Office
  Heather Wheeler, MP
Health and Social Care
  Baroness Blackwood of North Oxford
  Jo Churchill, MP
  Nadine Dorries, MP
Home Office
  Victoria Atkins, MP §
  Seema Kennedy, MP
Housing, Communities and Local Government
  Luke Hall, MP
  Viscount Younger of Leckie
International Development
  Baroness Sugg, CBE
International Trade
  Graham Stuart, MP
Justice
  Wendy Morton, MP
  Chris Philp, MP
Northern Ireland Office
  Lord Duncan of Springbank℄
  Robin Walker, MP**
Office of the Secretary of State for Scotland
  Colin Clark, MP††
  Robin Walker, MP*
Transport
  Nusrat Ghani, MP††
  Paul Maynard, MP
  Baroness Vere of Norbiton

Office of the Secretary of State for Wales
  Kevin Foster, MP††
Work and Pensions
  Victoria Atkins, MP‡‡
  Mims Davies, MP
  Guy Opperman, MP
  Will Quince, MP
  Baroness Stedman-Scott, OBE

* Alongside role at the Northern Ireland Office
† Alongside role at MoD
‡ Alongside role at the Cabinet Office
§ Alongside role as Under-Secretary of State (Minister for Women) at DWP
℄ Alongside role at DBEIS
** Alongside role at the Scottish Office
†† Alongside role as government Whip
‡‡ Alongside role at the Home Office

OTHER MINISTERS

Cabinet Office
  Rt. Hon. Oliver Dowden, CBE, MP *(Minister for the Cabinet Office and Paymaster-General)*
  Kevin Foster, MP* *(Interim Minister for the Constitution and Parliamentary Secretary)*
  Simon Hart, MP *(Minister for Implementation)*
Office of the Leader of the House of Lords
  Rt. Hon. Earl Howe *(Deputy Leader of the House of Lords)*
Treasury
  Jesse Norman, MP *(Financial Secretary)*
  John Glen, MP *(Economic Secretary)*
  Simon Clarke, MP *(Exchequer Secretary)*
  * Alongside roles as Under-Secretary of State at the Wales Office and a government Whip

GOVERNMENT WHIPS

HOUSE OF LORDS

Lords Chief Whip and Captain of the Honourable Corps of Gentlemen-at-Arms
  Rt. Hon. Lord Ashton of Hyde
Deputy Chief Whip and Captain of the Queen's Bodyguard of the Yeomen of the Guard
  Earl of Courtown
Lord-in-Waiting
  Lord Bethell
Baronesses-in-Waiting
  Baroness Berridge
  Baroness Bloomfield of Hinton Waldrist
  Baroness Chisholm of Owlpen

HOUSE OF COMMONS

Chief Whip and Parliamentary Secretary to the Treasury
  Rt. Hon. Mark Spencer, MP
Deputy Chief Whip and Treasurer of HM Household
  Amanda Milling, MP
Government Whip and Comptroller of HM Household
  Jeremy Quin, MP
Government Whip and Vice-Chamberlain of HM Household
  Stuart Andrew, MP
Lords Commissioners of HM Treasury (Whips)
  Colin Clark, MP*; Michele Donelan, MP; Mike Freer, MP; Nusrat Ghani, MP†; Rebecca Harris, MP; David Rutley, MP
Assistant Whips
  Leo Docherty, MP; Kevin Foster, MP‡; Nigel Huddleston, MP; Marcus Jones, MP; James Morris, MP; Tom Pursglove, MP; Iain Stewart, MP

*Alongside role as Under-Secretary of State at the Scottish Office
† Alongside role as Under-Secretary of State at DfT
‡ Alongside role as Under-Secretary of State at the Wales Office

GOVERNMENT DEPARTMENTS

THE CIVIL SERVICE

The civil service helps the government develop and deliver its policies as effectively as possible. It works in three types of organisations – departments, executive agencies, and non-departmental government bodies (NDPBs). Under the Next Steps programme, launched in 1988, many semi-autonomous executive agencies were established to carry out much of the work of the civil service. Executive agencies operate within a framework set by the responsible minister which specifies policies, objectives and available resources. All executive agencies are set annual performance targets by their minister. Each agency has a chief executive, who is responsible for the day-to-day operations of the agency and who is accountable to the minister for the use of resources and for meeting the agency's targets. The minister accounts to parliament for the work of the agency.

There are currently 414,390 civil servants on a full-time equivalent (FTE) basis and 435,520 on a headcount basis. FTE is a measure that counts staff according to the proportion of full-time hours that they work. Almost three-quarters of all civil servants work outside London and the south-east. All government departments and executive agencies are responsible for their own pay and grading systems for civil servants outside the senior civil service.

SALARIES 2019–20

MINISTERIAL SALARIES
Ministers who are members of the House of Commons receive a parliamentary salary of £79,468 in addition to the ministerial salary.

Prime minister	£79,286
Cabinet minister (Commons)	£71,090
Cabinet minister (Lords)	£104,360
Minister of state (Commons)	£34,087
Minister of state (Lords)	£81,485
Parliamentary under-secretary (Commons)	£24,477
Parliamentary under-secretary (Lords)	£70,969

SPECIAL ADVISERS' SALARIES
Special advisers to government ministers are paid out of public funds; their salaries are negotiated individually, but are usually in the range of £53,000 to £142,000.

CIVIL SERVICE SALARIES	
Senior Civil Servants	
Permanent secretary	£150,000–£200,000
Band 3	£111,500–£208,100
Band 2	£90,500–£162,500
Band 1	£68,000–£117,800

Staff are placed in pay bands according to their level of responsibility and taking account of other factors such as experience and marketability. Movement within and between bands is based on performance.

GOVERNMENT DEPARTMENTS

As at 10 September 2019

For more information on government departments, *see* W www.gov.uk/government/organisations

ATTORNEY-GENERAL'S OFFICE
Attorney-General's Office, 5–8 The Sanctuary, London SW1P 3JS
T 020-7271 2492 E correspondence@attorneygeneral.gov.uk
W www.gov.uk/government/organisations/attorney-generals-office

The law officers of the crown for England and Wales are the Attorney-General and the Solicitor-General. The Attorney-General, assisted by the Solicitor-General, is the chief legal adviser to the government and is also ultimately responsible for all crown litigation. He has overall responsibility for the work of the Law Officers' Departments (the Treasury Solicitor's Department, the Crown Prosecution Service – incorporating the Revenue and Customs Prosecutions Office – and the Serious Fraud Office, and HM Crown Prosecution Service Inspectorate). The Attorney-General also oversees the armed forces' prosecuting authority and the government legal service. He has a specific statutory duty to superintend the discharge of their duties by the Director of Public Prosecutions (who heads the Crown Prosecution Service) and the Director of the Serious Fraud Office. The Attorney-General has specific responsibilities for the enforcement of the criminal law and also performs certain public interest functions, eg protecting charities and appealing unduly lenient sentences. He also deals with questions of law arising in bills and with issues of legal policy.

Following the devolution of power to the Northern Ireland Assembly on 12 April 2010, the assembly now appoints the Attorney-General for Northern Ireland. The Attorney-General for England and Wales holds the office of Advocate-General for Northern Ireland, with significantly reduced responsibilities in Northern Ireland. The Attorney-General's Office is supported by four executive agencies and public bodies.

Attorney-General, Rt. Hon. Geoffrey Cox, QC, MP
Parliamentary Private Secretary, vacant
Principal Private Secretary, Josh Dodd
Deputy Principal Private Secretary, Samuel Chivers
Assistant Private Secretary, Leeann Thayalanayagam
Solicitor-General, Michael Ellis, QC, MP

MANAGEMENT BOARD
Director-General, Rowena Collins Rice
Deputy Legal Secretary and Head of Operations, Michelle Crotty

DEPARTMENT FOR BUSINESS, ENERGY AND INDUSTRIAL STRATEGY
1 Victoria Street, London SW1H 0ET
T 020-7215 5000 E enquiries@beis.gov.uk W www.gov.uk/government/organisations/department-for-business-energy-and-industrial-strategy

The Department for Business, Energy and Industrial Strategy (DBEIS) was established in July 2016 following the appointment of Theresa May as prime minister. It merged the Department of Business, Innovation and Skills and the Department of Energy and Climate Change. BEIS brings together responsibilities for business, industrial strategy, science, innovation, energy and climate change, and is supported by 45 executive agencies and public bodies. It is responsible for: developing and delivering a comprehensive industrial strategy and leading the government's relationship with business; ensuring that the UK has secure, reliable, affordable and clean energy supplies; ensuring the UK remains at the forefront of science, research and innovation; and tackling climate change.

Secretary of State for Business, Energy and Industrial Strategy, Rt. Hon. Andrea Leadsom, MP
Parliamentary Private Secretary, Craig Tracey, MP
Special Advisers, Samantha Magnus; Marc Pooler
Minister of State, Rt. Hon. Kwasi Kwarteng, MP
Minister of State, Rt. Hon. Chris Skidmore, MP*
Parliamentary Private Secretary, David Duguid, MP
Parliamentary Under-Secretary of State, Nadim Zahawi, MP
Parliamentary Under-Secretary of State, Kelly Tolhurst, MP
   (Small Business, Consumers and Corporate Responsibility)
Parliamentary Under-Secretary of State, Rt. Hon. Lord Duncan of Springbank† *(Lords)*
* Jointly held with the DfE
† Alongside role at the Northern Ireland Office

MANAGEMENT BOARD
Permanent Secretary, Alex Chisholm
Members, Sam Beckett *(EU Exit and Analysis);* Nick Chism *(Chief Business Adviser);* Julian Critchlow *(Energy Transformation and Clean Growth);* Sarah Harrison, MBE *(Corporate Services);* Prof. John Loughhead, CB, OBE *(BEIS Chief Scientific Adviser);* Sarah Munby *(Business Sectors);* Jaee Samant *(Market Frameworks);* Jo Shanmugalingam *(Industrial Strategy, Science and Innovation);* Joanna Whittington *(Energy and Security)*
Non-Executive Members, Archie Norman *(Lead);* Nigel Boardman; Stephen Carter; Dame Carolyn McCall, DBE; Leena Nair; Kathryn Parsons; Stuart Quickenden

BETTER REGULATION EXECUTIVE
1 Victoria Street, London SW1 0ET
T 020-7215 5000 E enquiries@beis.gov.uk
W www.gov.uk/government/policy-teams/better-regulation-executive

The Better Regulation Executive (BRE) is a joint BEIS/Cabinet Office unit which leads on delivering the government's manifesto commitment to reduce the overall burden on business, in order to increase growth and create jobs. Each government department is, however, responsible for delivering its part of the deregulation agenda within the framework put in place by the BRE.

Non-Executive Chair, Lord Curry of Kirkharle, CBE
Chief Executive, Graham Turnock

CABINET OFFICE
70 Whitehall, London SW1A 2AS
T 020-7276 1234
W www.gov.uk/government/organisations/cabinet-office

The Cabinet Office, alongside the Treasury, sits at the centre of the government, with an overarching purpose of making government work better. It supports the prime minister and the cabinet, helping to ensure effective development, coordination and implementation of policy and operations across all government departments. The Cabinet Office also leads work to ensure that the Civil Service provides the most effective and efficient support to the government to meet its objectives. The department is headed by the Minister for the Cabinet Office. The Cabinet Office is responsible for: supporting collective government; supporting the National

Security Council and the Joint Intelligence Organisation, coordinating the government's response to crises and managing the UK's cyber security; promoting efficiency and reform across government through innovation, better procurement and project management, and by transforming the delivery of services; promoting the release of government data, and making the way government works more transparent; improving the capability and effectiveness of the Civil Service; and political constitution and reform.

The priorities of the Cabinet Office include: supporting the prime minister and cabinet to deliver the government's programme; driving efficiencies and reforms to improve the government's performance; creating a more united democracy; and strengthening and securing the UK at home and abroad. The Cabinet Office employs around 2,050 staff and is supported by 22 executive agencies and public bodies.

Prime Minister, First Lord of the Treasury and Minister for the Civil Service, Rt. Hon. Boris Johnson, MP
Parliamentary Private Secretaries, Alex Burghart, MP; James Heappey, MP
Principal Private Secretary, Peter Hill
Special Advisers, David Beckingham; Alex Crowley; Dominic Cummings; Danny Kruger; Diana Varley; Rupert Yorke
Special Adviser (Europe), David Frost
Special Adviser (Business), Andrew Griffiths
Special Adviser (Union), Elliot Roy
Chancellor of the Duchy of Lancaster and Minister for the Cabinet Office, Rt. Hon. Michael Gove, MP
Parliamentary Private Secretary, Damien Moore, MP
Special Advisers, Henry Cook; Josh Grimstone; Henry Newman; Charlie Rowley
Lord President of the Council, Rt. Hon. Jacob Rees-Mogg, MP
Parliamentary Private Secretary, Michael Tomlinson, MP
Special Advisers, Hugh Bennett; Beatrice Timpson
Minister without Portfolio, Rt. Hon. James Cleverly, MP
Parliamentary Private Secretary, vacant
Special Advisers, Jess Pestridge; Hudson Roe
Minister of State and Paymaster-General, Rt. Hon. Oliver Dowden, CBE, MP
Minister of State, Rt. Hon. Jake Berry, MP *(The Northern Powerhouse and Local Growth)**
Parliamentary Under-Secretary of State, Johnny Mercer, MP *(Minister for Defence, People and Veterans)†*
Parliamentary Secretary (interim), Kevin Foster, MP *(Constitution)*
Parliamentary Secretary, Simon Hart, MP *(implementation)*
*Jointly held with the MHCLG
† Jointly held with the MoD

MANAGEMENT BOARD
Permanent Secretary and Chief Executive of the Civil Service, John Manzoni
Cabinet Secretary and Head of the Civil Service, Sir Mark Sedwill, KCMG
First Parliamentary Counsel, Elizabeth Gardiner
Executive Director, Implementation Group, James Quinault
Chief People Officer, Rupert McNeil
Director-General, Propriety and Ethics Team and Head of Private Offices Group, Helen MacNamara
National Security Adviser, Dominic Fortescue
Deputy National Security Adviser, David Quarrey
Director of the Constitution Group, Peter Lee
Director of Hostile State Activity & Cyber Unit and National Security Secretariat, Rosemary Pratt
Chair of the Joint Intelligence Committee, Sir Simon Gass, KCMG, CVO
Director-General, Prime Minister's Office, Peter Hill

Government Chief Commercial Officer, Gareth Rhys Williams
Finance Director, Guy Lester
Human Resources Director, Carol Bernard, CBE
Executive Director, Government Communications, Alex Aiken
Interim Director-General, Government Digital Service, Alison
    Pritchard
Director-General, Government Property, Mike Parsons
Director-General, UK Governance, Lucy Smith
Lead Non-Executive Director, Sir Ian Cheshire
Non-Executive Board Member, Catherine Brown

SPECIAL REPRESENTATIVE
Kevin Cunnington (Digital Envoy for the UK)

HONOURS AND APPOINTMENTS BOARD
Room G-39, Horse Guards Road, London SW1A 2HQ
T 020-7276 2777
Chair, Sir Jonathan Stephens, KCB

OFFICE OF THE LEADER OF THE HOUSE OF
COMMONS
1 Horse Guards Road, London SW1A 2HQ
T 020-7276 1005 E commonsleader@cabinetoffice.gov.uk
W www.gov.uk/government/organisations/
the-office-of-the-leader-of-the-house-of-commons

The Office of the Leader of the House of Commons is
responsible for the arrangement of government business in
the House of Commons and for planning and supervising the
government's legislative programme. The Leader of the House
of Commons upholds the rights and privileges of the house
and acts as a spokesperson for the government as a whole.
    The leader reports regularly to the cabinet on parliamentary
business and the legislative programme. In their capacity as
leader of the house, they are a member of the House of
Commons Commission. They also chair the cabinet committee
on the legislative programme. As Lord President of the
Council, they are a member of the cabinet and in charge of
the Office of the Privy Council.
    The Deputy Leader of the House of Commons supports the
leader in handling the government's business in the house.
They are responsible for monitoring MPs' and peers'
correspondence.

Lord President of the Privy Council and Leader of the House of
    Commons, Rt. Hon. Jacob Rees-Mogg, MP
Parliamentary Private Secretary, Michael Tomlinson, MP
Special Advisers, Hugh Bennett; Beatrice Timpson

OFFICE OF THE LEADER OF THE HOUSE OF LORDS
House of Lords, London SW1A 0PW
T 020-7219 3200 E pslseaderofthelords@cabinet-office.x.gsi.gov.uk
W www.gov.uk/government/organisations/
office-of-the-leader-of-the-house-of-lords

The Office of the Leader of the House of Lords provides
support to the leader in their parliamentary and ministerial
duties, which include leading the government benches in the
House of Lords; the delivery of the government's business in
the Lords; taking part in formal ceremonies such as the state
opening of parliament; and giving guidance to the House of
Lords on matters of procedure and order.

Lord Privy Seal and Leader of the House of Lords, Rt. Hon.
    Baroness Evans of Bowes Park
Parliamentary Private Secretary, Stephen Kerr, MP
Special Advisers, Annabelle Eyre; Katharine Howell; Tom
    Kennedy, James Price
Deputy Leader of the House of Lords, Rt. Hon. Earl Howe

PRIME MINISTER'S OFFICE
10 Downing Street, London SW1A 2AA
T 020-7930 4433
W www.number10.gov.uk

Prime Minister, Rt. Hon. Boris Johnson, MP
Parliamentary Private Secretaries, Alex Burghart, MP; James
    Heappey, MP
Special Advisers,David Beckingham; Alex Crowley; Dominic
    Cummings; Danny Kruger; Diana Varley; Rupert Yorke
Special Adviser (Europe), David Frost
Special Adviser (Business), Andrew Griffiths
Special Adviser, (Union), Elliot Roy
Principal Private Secretary, Peter Hill
Director of Communications, Lee Cain
Director of Policy, Munira Mirza
Prime Minister's Official Spokesman, James Slack
Prime Minister's Official Speech Writer, Alex Marklew
Chief of Staff, Sir Edward Lister
Deputy Chiefs of Staff, Liam Booth-Smith; Ben Gascoigne;
    Cleo Watson
Press Secretary, James Slack
Head of Grid, Meg Powell-Chandler
Head of Legislation, Nikki Da Costa
Head of Operations, Shelley Williams-Walker
Head of Research and Information, Will Karani
Head of Implementation Unit, Jonathan Nancekivell-Smith

IMPLEMENTATION GROUP
Executive Director, James Quinault

PRIVATE OFFICES GROUP
Director-General, Propriety and Ethics and Head of Private Offices
    Group, Helen MacNamara

UK GOVERNANCE GROUP
Head of UK Governance, Lucy Smith

CABINET OFFICE CORPORATE SERVICES
Executive Director, Government Communications, Alex Aiken
Finance Director, Guy Lester
Human Resources Director, Carol Bernard, CBE

NATIONAL SECURITY
Comprises the National Security Secretariat and the Joint
Intelligence Organisation. The National Security Secretariat
is responsible for providing policy advice to the National
Security Council, where ministers discuss national security
issues at a strategic level; coordinating and developing foreign
and defence policy across government; coordinating policy,
ethical and legal issues across the intelligence community,
managing its funding and priorities, and dealing with the
Intelligence and Security Committee which calls it to account;
developing effective protective security policies and
capabilities for government; improving the UK's resilience to
respond to and recover from emergencies, and maintaining
facilities for the effective coordination of government response
to crises; and providing strategic leadership for cyber security
in the UK, in line with the National Cyber Security Strategy.

NATIONAL SECURITY SECRETARIAT
National Security Adviser, Sir Mark Sedwill, KCMG
Deputy National Security Adviser, Madeleine Alessandri

JOINT INTELLIGENCE ORGANISATION
Chair of the Joint Intelligence Committee, Sir Simon Gass, KCMG,
    CVO

INDEPENDENT OFFICES

CIVIL SERVICE COMMISSION
1 Horse Guards Road, London SW1A 2HQ
T 020-7271 0831
W www.civilservicecommission.independent.gov.uk

The Civil Service Commission regulates the requirement that
selection for appointment to the Civil Service must be on

merit on the basis of fair and open competition; the commission publishes its recruitment principles and audit departments and agencies' performance against these. Commissioners personally chair competitions for the most senior jobs in the civil service. In addition, the commission hears complaints from civil servants under the Civil Service Code.

The commission was established as a statutory body in November 2010 under the provisions of the Constitutional Reform and Governance Act 2010.

Commissioners, Jane Burgess; Jan Cameron; Natalie Campbell; Isabel Doverty; Margaret Edwards; Andrew Flanagan; Rosie Glazebrook; Sarah Laessig; June Milligan; Joe Montgomery; Ian Watmore; Kevin Woods

THE COMMISSIONER FOR PUBLIC APPOINTMENTS

G/8, 1 Horse Guards Road, London SW1A 2HQ
T 020-7271 0833 E publicappointments@csc.gov.uk
W http://publicappointmentscommissioner.independent.gov.uk

The Commissioner for Public Appointments is responsible for monitoring, regulating and reporting on ministerial appointments (including those made by Welsh government ministers) to public bodies. The commissioner can investigate complaints about the way in which appointments were made.

Commissioner for Public Appointments, Peter Riddell
Chief Executive Commission Secretariat, Peter Lawrence, OBE

OFFICE OF THE PARLIAMENTARY COUNSEL

1 Horse Guards Road, London SW1A 2HQ
T 02-7276 6586 E good.law@cabinetoffice.gov.uk W www.gov.uk/government/organisations/office-of-the-parliamentary-counsel

The Office of the Parliamentary Counsel is a group of government lawyers who specialise in drafting government bills; advising departments on the rules and procedures of Parliament; reviewing orders and regulations which amend Acts of Parliament; and assisting the government on a range of legal and constitutional issues.

First Parliamentary Counsel, Elizabeth Gardiner

GOVERNMENT EQUALITIES OFFICE

Sanctuary Buildings, 16–20 Great Smith Street, London SW1P 3BT
T 0300-020 0229 W www.gov.uk/government/organisations/government-equalities-office

The Government Equalities Office (GEO) is responsible for the government's overall strategy on equality. Its work includes leading the development of a more integrated approach on equality across government with the aim of improving equality and reducing discrimination and disadvantage for all. The office is also responsible for leading policy on gender equality, sexual orientation and transgender equality matters.

Minister for Women and Equalities, Rt. Hon. Elizabeth Truss, MP*
Parliamentary Under-Secretary of State, Victoria Atkins, MP *(Women)†*
Parliamentary Under-Secretary of State, Baroness Williams of Trafford *(Equalities)†*
Director, Hilary Spencer

* Alongside role as Secretary of State for International Trade and President of the Board of Trade
† Jointly held with the Home Office

MINISTRY OF DEFENCE

Main Building, Whitehall, London SW1A 2HB
T 020-7218 9000 W www.gov.uk/government/organisations/ministry-of-defence

For further information on the responsibilities and remit of the MoD *see* the Defence Chapter.

Secretary of State for Defence, Rt. Hon. Ben Wallace, MP

Parliamentary Private Secretary, James Cartlidge, MP
Special Adviser, Lynn Davidson, MP
Minister of State, Rt. Hon. Mark Lancaster, TD, MP *(Armed Forces)*
Minister of State, Baroness Goldie *(Lords)*
Parliamentary Under-Secretary of State and Minister for Defence Procurement, Anne-Marie Trevelyan, MP
Parliamentary Under-Secretary of State and Minister for Defence People and Veterans, Johnny Mercer, MP*
*Jointly held with the Cabinet Office

SENIOR MILITARY OFFICIALS

Chief of the Defence Staff, Gen. Sir Nick Carter, GCB, CBE, DSO, ADC
Vice-Chief of the Defence Staff, Adm. Tim Fraser, CB
Chief of Naval Staff and First Sea Lord, Adm. Tony Radakin, CB, ADC
Chief of the General Staff, Gen. Sir Mark Carleton-Smith, KCB, CBE, ADC
Chief of the Air Staff, Air Chief Marshal Mike Wigston, CBE
Commander of Joint Forces Command, Gen. Patrick Sanders, CBE, DSO, ADC

MANAGEMENT BOARD

Permanent Secretary, Sir Stephen Lovegrove, KCB
Members,
Members, Lt.-Gen. Doug Chalmers *(Deputy Chief of Defence Staff (Military Strategy and Operations));* Charlie Forte *(Chief Information Officer);* David Goldstone *(Chief Operating Officer);* Prof. Robin Grimes, FRS, FRENG *(Chief Scientific Adviser (Nuclear));* Air Marshal Richard Knighton *(Deputy Chief of the Defence Staff (Financial and Military Capability));* Angus Lapsley *(Strategy and International);* Cat Little *(Finance);* Prof. Dame Angela McLean, DBE *(Chief Scientific Adviser);* Vanessa Nicholls *(Nuclear);* Lt.-Gen. Richard Nugee, CVO, CBE *(Chief of Defence People);* Dominic Wilson *(Security Policy)*
Non-Executive Members, Sir Gerry Grimstone *(Lead);* Simon Henry; Danuta Gray

DEPARTMENT FOR DIGITAL, CULTURE, MEDIA AND SPORT

100 Parliament Street, London SW1A 2BQ
T 020-7211 6000 E enquiries@culture.gov.uk W www.gov.uk/government/organisations/department-for-digital-culture-media-sport

The Department for Digital, Culture, Media and Sport (DCMS) was established in July 1997 (as the Department for Culture, Media and Sport) and aims to improve the quality of life for all those in the UK through cultural and sporting activities while championing the tourism, creative and leisure industries. It is responsible for government policy relating to the arts, sport, the National Lottery, tourism, libraries, museums and galleries, broadcasting, creative industries – including film and the music industry – press freedom and regulation, licensing, gambling, the historic environment, telecommunications and online and media ownership and mergers. In July 2017, the department was rebranded to reflect its growing commitment and responsibility regarding digital infrastructure, communication and cyber security.

The department is also responsible for 45 agencies and public bodies that help deliver the department's strategic aims and objectives, the listing of historic buildings and scheduling of ancient monuments, the export licensing of cultural goods, and the management of the Government Art Collection and the Royal Parks (its sole executive agency). It has the responsibility for humanitarian assistance in the event of a disaster, as well as for the organisation of the annual Remembrance Day ceremony at the Cenotaph. In September

2012, the Government Equalities Office became part of DCMS, having previously been part of the Home Office.

Secretary of State for Digital, Culture, Media and Sport, Rt. Hon. Nicky Morgan, MP

Special Adviser, Sophia True

Minister of State, Nigel Adams, MP *(Sport, Media and Creative Industries)*

Parliamentary Under-Secretary of State, Baroness Barran, MBE *(Civil Society)*

Parliamentary Under-Secretary of State, Helen Whately, MP *(Arts, Heritage and Tourism)*

Parliamentary Under-Secretary of State, Matt Warman, MP *(Digital and Broadband)*

MANAGEMENT BOARD

Permanent Secretary, Sarah Healey

Members, Clare Dove, OBE *(Voluntary, Community and Social Enterprise Representative);* Helen Judge *(Performance and Strategy);* Prof. Tom Rodden *(Chief Scientific Adviser);* Tim Sparrow *(Finance Director)*

Non-Executive Members, Charles Alexander *(Lead);* Matthew Campbell-Hill; Sherry Coutu, CBE; Neil Mendoza; Fields Wicker-Miurin, OBE

DEPARTMENT FOR EDUCATION

Piccadilly Gate, Store Street, Manchester M1 2WD
T 0370-000 2288 W www.gov.uk/government/organisations/department-for-education

The Department for Education (DfE) was established in May 2010 in place of the Department for Children, Schools and Families (DCSF), in order to refocus the department on its core purpose of supporting teaching and learning. The department is responsible for education and children's services, while the Department for Business, Energy and Industrial Strategy is responsible for higher education. The DfE is supported by 17 executive agencies and public bodies.

The department's objectives include the expansion of the academies programme, to allow schools to apply to become independent of their local authority, and the introduction of the free schools programme, to allow any suitable proposers, such as parents, businesses or charities, to set up their own school.

Secretary of State for Education, Rt. Hon. Gavin Williamson, CBE, MP

Parliamentary Private Secretary, Chris Green, MP

Special Adviser, Rick Holden

Minister of State, Rt. Hon. Nick Gibb, MP *(School Standards)*

Minister of State, Chris Skidmore, MP* *(Universities, Science, Research and Innovation)*

Parliamentary Under-Secretary of State, Lord Agnew of Oulton *(School System)*

Parliamentary Under-Secretary of State, Kemi Badenoch, MP *(Children and Families)*

*Jointly held with the DBEIS

MANAGEMENT BOARD

Permanent Secretary, Jonathan Slater

Members, Mike Green *(Chief Operating Officer, Operations Group);* Paul Kett *(Higher and Further Education Group);* Andrew McCully, CB, CBE *(Early Years and Schools);* Emran Mian *(Strategy and International);* Elaine Milner *(ex officio);* Indra Morris *(Social Care, Mobility and Disadvantage)*

Non-Executive Members, Richard Pennycook *(Lead);* Ian Ferguson, CBE; Irene Lucas; Baroness Ruby McGregor-Smith, CBE; Toby Peyton-Jones

DEPARTMENT FOR ENVIRONMENT, FOOD AND RURAL AFFAIRS

Nobel House, 17 Smith Square, London SW1P 3JR
T 03459-335577 E defra.helpline@defra.gsi.gov.uk
W www.gov.uk/government/organisations/department-for-environment-food-rural-affairs

The Department for Environment, Food and Rural Affairs (DEFRA) is responsible for government policy on the environment, rural matters and farming and food production. In association with the agriculture departments of the Scottish government, the National Assembly for Wales and the Northern Ireland Office, the department is responsible for negotiations in the EU on the common agricultural and fisheries policies, and for single European market questions relating to its responsibilities. Its remit includes international agricultural and food trade policy.

The department's five strategic priorities are climate change adaptation; sustainable consumption and production; the protection of natural resources and the countryside; sustainable rural communities; and sustainable farming and food, including animal health and welfare. DEFRA, which is supported by 33 executive agencies and public bodies, is also the lead government department for emergencies in animal and plant diseases, flooding, food and water supply, dealing with the consequences of a chemical, biological, radiological or nuclear incident, and other threats to the environment.

Secretary of State for Environment, Food and Rural Affairs, Rt. Hon. Theresa Villiers, MP

Parliamentary Private Secretary, Robert Courts, MP

Special Advisers, Sara Rajeswaran; Robert Rams

Minister of State, George Eustice, MP

Minister of State, Rt. Hon. Zac Goldsmith, MP*

Parliamentary Under-Secretary of State, Lord Gardiner of Kimble *(Rural Affairs and Biosecurity)*

Parliamentary Under-Secretary of State, Rebecca Pow, MP

* Alongside role at DFID

MANAGEMENT BOARD

Permanent Secretary, Tamara Finkelstein

Members, Prof. Sir Ian Boyd, FRSE *(Chief Scientific Adviser);* Shaun Gallagher *(Strategy Delivery);* Sarah Homer *(Chief Operating Officer);* Emma Howard Boyd *(ex officio);* David Kennedy *(Food, Farming and Biosecurity);* Emily Miles *(EU Exit Delivery);* Sonia Phippard *(Environment, Rural and Marine);* John Seglias *(Chief Digital and Information Officer);* Andrew Sells *(ex officio)*

Non-Executive Members, Henry Dimbleby *(Lead);* Elizabeth Buchanan; Colin Day; Ben Goldsmith; Lizzie Noel

DEPARTMENT FOR EXITING THE EUROPEAN UNION

9 Downing Street, London SW1A 2AG
T 020-7276 0432 W www.gov.uk/government/organisations/department-for-exiting-the-european-union

The Department for Exiting the European Union (DEEU) was formed by the prime minister Theresa May in July 2016 after the UK voted to leave the European Union in a referendum on 23 June 2016. The DEEU is responsible for overseeing negotiations to leave the EU and establishing the future relationship of the UK with the EU.

The department has four main responsibilities: to support the UK's negotiations to leave the EU and to establish the future relationship between the UK and the EU; to work closely with the UK's devolved administrations, Parliament, and a range of other interested parties on the approach to the negotiations; to conduct the negotiations in support of the prime minister including supporting bilateral discussions on exiting the EU with other European countries; and to lead and coordinate cross-government work to seize the opportunities and ensure a smooth process of exit on positive terms.

Secretary of State for Exiting the European Union, Rt. Hon. Stephen Barclay, MP
Parliamentary Private Secretary, Jack Brereton, MP
Special Advisers, Stephanie Lis; Craig Williams
Minister of State, Lord Callanan
Parliamentary Under-Secretary of State, James Duddridge, MP

MANAGEMENT BOARD
Permanent Secretary, Clare Moriarty
Members, Matt Baugh *(Strategy and Coordination)*; Rhys Bowen *(International Agreements and Trade)*; Anna Clunes *(Security, Territories and Ongoing Business)*; Alex Ellis, *(Director-General)*; Olivia Evans *(Communications and Stakeholders)*; Chris Hobley *(Market Access and Budget)*; Chris Jones *(Justice, Security and Migration)*; Joanna Key *(Legislation and Constitution)*; Helen Mills *(Corporate Centre)*; Eoin Parker *(Market Access and Budget Directorate & Chief Scientific Adviser)*; Nathan Phillips *(Planning and Analysis)*; Tom Shinner *(Policy and Delivery Coordination)*; Susannah Storey *(Director-General)*
Non-Executive Members, Susan Hooper; Margaret Stephens

FOREIGN AND COMMONWEALTH OFFICE
King Charles Street, London SW1A 2AH
T 020-7008 1500 E fcocorrespondence@fco.gov.uk
W www.gov.uk/government/organisations/foreign-commonwealth-office

The Foreign and Commonwealth Office (FCO) provides the means of communication between the British government and other governments – and international governmental organisations – on all matters falling within the field of international relations. The FCO employs over 14,000 people in nearly 270 places across the world through a network of embassies and consulates, which help to protect and promote national interests. FCO diplomats are skilled in understanding and influencing what is happening abroad, supporting British citizens who are travelling and living overseas, helping to manage migration into Britain, promoting British trade and other interests abroad and encouraging foreign investment in the UK. The FCO is supported by ten executive agencies and public bodies.

Secretary of State for Foreign and Commonwealth Affairs, Rt. Hon. Dominic Raab, MP
Parliamentary Private Secretary, Alex Chalk, MP
Special Advisers, Beth Armstrong; Simon Finkelstien; Simon Jupp
Minister of State, Lord Ahmad of Wimbledon *(Commonwealth, the UN and South Asia)*
Minister of State, Rt. Hon. Dr Andrew Murrison, MP *(Middle East and North Africa)**
Minister of State, Rt. Hon. Christopher Pincher, MP *(Europe and the Americas)*
Minister of State, Andrew Stephenson, MP *(Africa)**
Parliamentary Under-Secretary of State, Heather Wheeler, MP *(Asia and the Pacific)*
* Alongside role as Minister of State at DFID

SPECIAL REPRESENTATIVES
Lord Ahmad of Wimbledon *(Prime Minister's Special Representative on Preventing Sexual Violence in Conflict & Special Envoy on Freedom of Religion or Belief)*; Gareth Bayley *(Afghanistan and Pakistan)*; Nick Bridge *(Climate Change)*; Amal Clooney *(Special Envoy on Media Freedom)*; Robert Fairweather, OBE *(Sudan and South Sudan)*; Matthew Johnson *(Migration Envoy)*; Prof. Carole Mundell *(Chief*

Scientific Adviser); Simon Mustard *(Special Envoy for the African Great Lakes and Head of the Southern and Central African Department)*; Philip Parham *(Commonweath)*; Rt. Hon. Lord Pickles *(UK Special Envoy for Post-Holocaust Issues)*; Joanna Roper, CMG *(Special Envoy for Gender Equality)*

MANAGEMENT BOARD
Permanent Under-Secretary and Head of the Diplomatic Service, Sir Simon McDonald, KCMG, KCVO
Members, Philip Barton, CMG *(Consular and Security)*; Helen Bower-Easton, CBE *(Communications)*; Lindsay Croisdale-Appleby *(EU Exit)*; Peter Jones *(Chief Operating Officer)*; Sir Iain Macleod, KCMG *(Legal)*; Richard Moore *(Political)*; David Quarrey *(International Affairs Adviser and Deputy National Security Adviser)*; Meena Rawlings, CMG *(Economic and Global Issues)*; Andrew Sanderson *(Finance)*; Liane Saunders *(Strategy and Strategic Programmes Coordinator)*; Jonathan Sinclair, LVO *(Human Resources)*
Non-Executive Members, Miranda Curtis *(Lead)*; Gaenor Bagley; Sir Edward Lister; Warren Tucker

DEPARTMENT OF HEALTH AND SOCIAL CARE
39 Victoria Street, London SW1H 0EU
T 020-7210 4850 W www.gov.uk/government/organisations/department-of-health-and-social-care

The Department of Health and Social Care (DHSC) leads, shapes and funds health and social care in England, making sure people have the support, care and treatment they need and that this is delivered in a compassionate, respectful and dignified manner.

The DHSC leads across health and care by creating national policies and legislation to meet current and future challenges. It provides funding, assures the delivery and continuity of services and accounts to parliament in a way that represents the best interests of patients, the public and the taxpayer. The DHSC is supported by 28 executive agencies and public bodies.

Secretary of State for Health and Social Care, Rt. Hon. Matthew Hancock, MP
Parliamentary Private Secretary, Maggie Throup, MP
Special Advisers, Emma Dean; Allan Nixon; James Njoku-Goodwin
Minister of State, Edward Argar, MP *(Health)*
Minister of State, Caroline Dinenage, MP *(Care)*
Parliamentary Private Secretary, David Duguid, MP
Parliamentary Under-Secretary of State, Jo Churchill, MP
Parliamentary Under-Secretary of State, Nadine Dorries, MP
Parliamentary Under-Secretary of State (Lords), Baroness Blackwood of North Oxford *(Innovation)*

DEPARTMENTAL BOARD
Permanent Secretary, Sir Chris Wormald, KCB
Members, Prof. Dame Sally Davies, DBE *(Chief Medical Officer)*; Jonathan Marron *(Community and Social Care)*; Lee McDonough *(Acute Care and Workforce)*; Clara Swinson *(Global and Public Health)*; Prof. Chris Whitty *(Chief Scientific Adviser)*; David Williams *(Finance and Group Operations)*

HOME OFFICE
2 Marsham Street, London SW1P 4DF
T 020-7035 4848 E public.enquiries@homeoffice.gsi.gov.uk
W www.gov.uk/government/organisations/home-office

The Home Office deals with those internal affairs in England and Wales which have not been assigned to other government departments. The Secretary of State for the Home Department is the link between the Queen and the public, and exercises certain powers on her behalf, including that of the royal pardon.

The Home Office aims to build a safe, just and tolerant society and to maintain and enhance public security and protection; to support and mobilise communities so that they are able to shape policy and improvement for their locality, overcome nuisance and anti-social behaviour, maintain and enhance social cohesion and enjoy their homes and public spaces peacefully; to deliver departmental policies and responsibilities fairly, effectively and efficiently; and to make the best use of resources. These objectives reflect the priorities of the government and the home secretary in areas of crime, citizenship and communities, namely to work on the problems caused by illegal drug use; shape the alcohol strategy, policy and licensing conditions; keep the UK safe from the threat of terrorism; reduce and prevent crime, and ensure people feel safe in their homes and communities; secure the UK border and control immigration; consider applications to enter and stay in the UK; issue passports and visas; and to support visible, responsible and accountable policing by empowering the public and freeing up the police to fight crime.

The Home Office delivers these aims through its immigration services, its 30 executive agencies and non-departmental public bodies, and by working with partners in private, public and voluntary sectors, individuals and communities. The home secretary is also the link between UK government and the governments of the Channel Islands and the Isle of Man.

Secretary of State for the Home Department, Rt. Hon. Priti Patel, MP
Parliamentary Private Secretary, Mike Wood, MP
Special Advisers, Hannah Guerin; Charlotte Miller; James Starkie; Alex Wild
Minister of State, Rt. Hon. Brandon Lewis, MP
Minister of State, Kit Malthouse, MP
Minister of State, Baroness Williams of Trafford *(Countering Terrorism)**
Parliamentary Under-Secretary of State, Victoria Atkins, MP *(Crime, Safeguarding and Vulnerability)†*
Parliamentary Under-Secretary of State, Seema Kennedy, MP
*Alongside role as Minister for State (Minister for Equalities) at the DWP
† Alongside role as Under-Secretary of State (Minister for Women) at the DWP

MANAGEMENT BOARD
Permanent Secretary, Sir Philip Rutnam, KCB
Second Permanent Secretary, Shona Dunn
Members, Joanna Davinson *(Chief Digital, Data and Technology Officer)*; Peter Fish *(Legal)*; Charu Gorasia *(Capabilities and Resources)*; Jill Hatcher *(Chief People Officer)*; Tyson Hepple *(Immigration Enforcement)*; Tom Hurd *(Security and Counter-Terrorism)*; Julia Kinniburgh *(Serious and Organised Crime Group)*; Paul Lincoln *(Border Force)*; Scott McPherson *(Crime, Policing and Fire Group)*; Mark Thomson *(UK Visas and Immigration; Director-General HM Passport Office)*; Andy Tighe *(Communications)*; Glyn Williams, CB *(Borders, Immigration and Citizenship)*
Non-Executive Members, Sue Langley, OBE *(Lead)*; Adrian Joseph; Suzy Levy; Nicholas Shott; John Studzinski, CBE

MINISTRY OF HOUSING, COMMUNITIES AND LOCAL GOVERNMENT

2 Marsham Street, London SW1P 4DF
T 0303-444 0000 W www.gov.uk/government/organisations/ministry-of-housing-communities-and-local-government

The Ministry of Housing, Communities and Local Government was formed in January 2018 uniting housing, communities and civil renewal functions with responsibility for regeneration,

neighbourhood renewal and local government. The ministry ensures that the Fire and Rescue services have the resources they need to reduce the number of deaths from fire, promote fire prevention activity and respond swiftly to national emergencies. The ministry is supported by 13 executive agencies and public bodies.

Secretary of State for Housing, Communities and Local Government, Rt. Hon. Robert Jenrick, MP
Parliamentary Private Secretary, Ben Bradley, MP
Special Advisers, Olivia Oates
Minister of State, Rt. Hon. Esther McVey, MP *(Housing)*
Minister of State, Rt. Hon. Jake Berry, MP *(The Northern Powerhouse and Local Growth)**
Parliamentary Under-Secretary of State, Luke Hall, MP *(Local Government and Homelessness)*
Parliamentary Under-Secretary of State, Viscount Younger of Leckie *(Faith and Communities)*
* Jointly held with the Cabinet Office

MANAGEMENT BOARD
Permanent Secretary, Melanie Dawes, CB
Members, Ruth Bailey *(People Capability and Change)*; Lise-Anne Boissiere *(Strategy, Communications and Private Office)*; Catherine Frances *(Local Government and Public Services)*; Rachel McLean *(Chief Financial Officer)*; Jeremy Pocklington *(Housing)*; Simon Ridley *(Decentralisation and Growth)*
Non-Executive Members, Michael Jary *(Lead)*; Pam Chesters, CBE; Daniel Morley; Dame Mary Ney, DBE

SPECIAL REPRESENTATIVES
UK Special Envoy for post-Holocaust Issues, Rt. Hon. Lord Pickles

DEPARTMENT FOR INTERNATIONAL DEVELOPMENT

22 Whitehall, London SW1A 2EG T 020-7023 0000
Abercrombie House, Eaglesham Road, East Kilbride, Glasgow G75 8EA T 01355-844000
Public Enquiries 0300-200 3343 E enquiry@dfid.gov.uk
W www.gov.uk/government/organisations/department-for-international-development

The Department for International Development (DFID) is responsible for promoting sustainable development and reducing poverty. The central focus of the government's policy is to honour the UK's international commitments and take action to achieve the United Nations' Global Goals. The DFID seeks to make British aid more effective by improving transparency, openness and value for money; target British international development policy on economic growth and wealth creation; improve the coherence and performance of British international development policy in fragile and conflict-affected countries; improve the lives of girls and women through better education and a greater choice on family planning; prevent violence against girls and women in the developing world; and help to prevent climate change and encourage adaptation and low-carbon growth in developing countries.

The DFID works in countries across Africa, Asia and the Middle East. It also has regional programmes in Africa, Asia and the Caribbean, and development relationships with 3 aid dependent UK Overseas Territories – St Helena, the Pitcairn Islands and Montserrat. In addition to working directly in countries, DFID also gives UK Aid through multi-country global programmes and core contributions to multilateral institutions, including the World Bank, United Nations agencies and the European Commission. The department, which is supported by three agencies and public bodies, has headquarters in London and East Kilbride, offices in many developing countries, and staff based in British embassies and high commissions around the world.

Secretary of State for International Development, Rt. Hon. Alok Sharma, MP
Parliamentary Private Secretary, Vicky Ford, MP
Special Advisers, Natasha Adkins; Will Holloway
Minister of State, Rt. Hon. Dr Andrew Murrison, MP*
Minister of State, Andrew Stephenson, MP*
Minister of State, Rt. Hon. Zac Goldsmith, MP†
Parliamentary Under-Secretary of State, Baroness Sugg, CBE

* Jointly held with the FCO
† Alongside role at DEFRA

MANAGEMENT BOARD
Permanent Secretary, Matthew Rycroft, CBE
Members, Juliet Chua *(Finance and Corporate Performance);* Richard Clarke *(Policy, Research and Humanitarian);* Nick Dyer *(Economic Development and International);* Rachel Glennerster *(Chief Economist);* George Turkington, CBE *(Country Programmes)*
Non-Executive Members, Marc Bolland *(Lead);* Alan Johnson; Sally Jones-Evans; Tim Robinson

CDC GROUP
123 Victoria Street, London SW1E 6DE
T 020-7963 4700 E enquiries@cdcgroup.com
W www.cdcgroup.com

Founded in 1948, CDC is the UK's Development Finance Institution wholly owned by the UK government. It invests to create jobs and build businesses in developing countries in Africa and South Asia. In 2017 CDC's new investment commitments totalled £1.4bn to 715 businesses in Africa and 338 businesses in South Asia, helping to create new jobs across these regions. CDC is a public limited company with net assets of £5.3bn.

Chair, Graham Wrigley
Chief Executive, Nick O'Donohoe

DEPARTMENT FOR INTERNATIONAL TRADE
King Charles Street, Whitehall, London SW1A 2AH
T 020-7215 5000 W www.gov.uk/government/organisations/department-for-international-trade

The Department for International Trade was formed in July 2016 following the UK referendum to leave the European Union. The department is responsible for promoting British trade around the world, striking and extending trade agreements between the UK and non-EU states. It is supported by two executive agencies and public bodies.

Secretary of State for International Trade and President of the Board of Trade, Rt. Hon. Elizabeth Truss, MP
Parliamentary Private Secretary, vacant
Special Advisers, James Caldecourt; Nerissa Chesterfield; Sophie Jarvis
Minister of State, Conor Burns, MP
Parliamentary Under-Secretary of State, Graham Stuart, MP *(Investment)*

MANAGEMENT BOARD
Permanent Secretary, Antonia Romeo
Second Permanent Secretary and Chief Trade Negotiation Adviser, Crawford Falconer
Members, John Alty *(Trade Policy);* John Mahon *(Exports);* Mark Slaughter *(Investment);* Louis Taylor *(UK Export Finance);* Catherine Vaughan *(Chief Operating Officer)*
Non-Executive Members, Simon Walker *(Lead);* Julie Currie, Noel Harwerth, Sir Stephen O'Brien

MINISTRY OF JUSTICE
102 Petty France, London SW1H 9AJ
T 020-3334 3555
W www.gov.uk/government/organisations/ministry-of-justice

The Ministry of Justice (MoJ) was established in May 2007. MoJ is headed by the Lord Chancellor and Secretary of State for Justice who is responsible for improvements to the justice system so that it better serves the public. He is also responsible for some areas of constitutional policy.

The MoJ's key priorities are to reduce reoffending by using the skills of the public, private and voluntary sectors; reduce youth crime by putting education at the centre of youth justice; build a prison system that delivers maximum value for money; reduce the cost of legal aid and ensure it helps those cases that genuinely require it; and to improve the way the courts are run and put the needs of victims first. The MoJ has a budget of around £9bn and is supported by 33 executive agencies and public bodies to achieve its targets.

The Lord Chancellor and Secretary of State for Justice is the government minister responsible to parliament for the judiciary, the court system and prisons and probation. The Lord Chief Justice has been the head of the judiciary since 2006.

MoJ incorporates HM Prison and Probation Service; HM Courts and Tribunals Service; the Legal Aid Agency; and the Youth Justice Board.

Lord Chancellor and Secretary of State for Justice, Rt. Hon. Robert Buckland, QC, MP
Parliamentary Private Secretary, Neil O'Brien, MP
Special Advisers, Peter Cardwell; Rajiv Shah
Minister of State, Lucy Frazer, QC, MP
Parliamentary Under-Secretary of State, Wendy Morton, MP
Parliamentary Under-Secretary of State, Chris Philp, MP
HM Advocate-General for Scotland and MoJ Spokesperson for the Lords, Rt. Hon. Lord Keen of Elie, QC

MANAGEMENT BOARD
Permanent Secretary, Sir Richard Heaton, KCB
Members, Susan Acland-Hood *(Chief Executive and Board member, HM Courts and Tribunals Service);* Phil Copple *(Prisons);* Mike Driver *(Chief Financial Officer and Head of the Government Finance Function);* Jo Farrar *(Chief Executive Officer, HM Prison & Probation Service);* Naomi Mallick *(Legal);* Amy Rees *(HMPPS Wales & Strategy);* Mark Sweeney *(Communication and Analysis Group);* Dr Neil Wooding *(Chief People Officer)*
Non-Executive Members, Mark Rawlinson *(Lead);* Nick Campsie; Shirley Cooper; Liz Doherty

NORTHERN IRELAND OFFICE
1 Horse Guards Road, London SW1A 2HQ
Stormont House, Stormont Estate, Belfast BT4 3SH
T 028-9052 0700 E comms@nio.gov.uk
W www.gov.uk/government/organisations/northern-ireland-office

The Northern Ireland Office was established in 1972, when the Northern Ireland (Temporary Provisions) Act transferred the legislative and executive powers of the Northern Ireland parliament and government to the UK parliament and a secretary of state. Under the terms of the 1998 Good Friday Agreement, power was devolved to the Northern Ireland Assembly in 1999. The assembly took on responsibility for the relevant areas of work previously undertaken by the departments of the Northern Ireland Office, covering agriculture and rural development, the environment, regional development, social development, education, higher education, training and employment, enterprise, trade and investment, culture, arts and leisure, health, social services, public safety and finance and personnel. In October 2002 the Northern Ireland Assembly was suspended and Northern Ireland returned to direct rule, but despite repeated setbacks, devolution was restored on 8 May 2007. On 9 January 2017 Martin McGuinness resigned as Deputy First Minister of Northern Ireland. Under the joint protocols that govern the power-sharing agreement, if either the first minister or the deputy resigns and a replacement is not nominated by the relevant party within seven days, then a snap election must be called. The assembly was formerly dissolved at midnight on 25 January 2017 and the most recent assembly elections were held on 2 March 2017. The assembly failed to appoint the executive committee of ministers in charge of the nine government departments within the three-week deadline following the election and, to date, the devolved government in Northern Ireland has yet to be restored. For further details, *see* Devolved Government.

The Northern Ireland Office is supported by three executive agencies and public bodies and is currently responsible for overseeing the devolution settlement; representing Northern Ireland interests within the UK government and similarly representing the UK government in Northern Ireland; working in partnership with the Northern Ireland Executive for a stable, prosperous Northern Ireland; and supporting and implementing political agreements to increase stability.

Secretary of State for Northern Ireland, Rt. Hon. Julian Smith, MP
Parliamentary Private Secretary, Andrew Lewer, MBE, MP
Special Advisers, Ross Easton; Lilah Howson-Smith
Minister of State, Rt. Hon. Nick Hurd, MP
Parliamentary Under-Secretary of State, Robin Walker, MP*
Parliamentary Under-Secretary of State, Lord Duncan of Springbank *(Lords)*†
Permanent Secretary, Sir Jonathan Stephens
* Jointly held with the Scottish Office
† Alongside role at the DBEIS

OFFICE OF THE ADVOCATE-GENERAL FOR SCOTLAND

Dover House, Whitehall, London SW1A 2AU
T 020-7270 6770
Office of the Solicitor to the Advocate-General, Victoria Quay, Edinburgh EH6 6QQ T 0131-244 0359
E enquiries@advocategeneral.gsi.gov.uk
W www.gov.uk/government/organisations/
office-of-the-advocate-general-for-scotland

The Advocate-General for Scotland is one of the three law officers of the crown, alongside the Attorney-General and the Solicitor-General for England and Wales. He is the legal adviser to the UK government on Scottish law and is supported by staff in the Office of the Advocate-General for Scotland. The office is divided into the Legal Secretariat, based mainly in London, and the Office of the Solicitor to the Advocate-General, based in Edinburgh.

The post was created as a consequence of the constitutional changes set out in the Scotland Act 1998, which created a devolved Scottish parliament. The Lord Advocate and the Solicitor-General for Scotland then became part of the Scottish government and the Advocate-General took over their previous role as legal adviser to the UK government on Scots law. *See also* Devolved Government *and* Ministry of Justice.

HM Advocate-General for Scotland and MoJ Spokesperson for the Lords, Rt. Hon. Lord Keen of Elie, QC
Private Secretary, Nathan Lappin

MANAGEMENT BOARD
Director and Solicitor to the Advocate-General, Neil Taylor
Legal Secretary to the Advocate General, Chris Stephen

Members, Jim Logie *(Head of HMRC Division);* Fiona Robertson *(Head of Litigation Division)*

OFFICE OF THE SECRETARY OF STATE FOR SCOTLAND

Dover House, Whitehall, London SW1A 2AU
1 Melville Crescent, Edinburgh EH3 7HW
T 0131-244 9010 E enquiries@scotlandoffice.gsi.gov.uk
W www.gov.uk/government/organisations/
office-of-the-secretary-of-state-for-scotland

The Office of the Secretary of State for Scotland represents Scottish interests within the UK government in matters reserved to the UK parliament. The Secretary of State for Scotland maintains the stability of the devolution settlement for Scotland; delivers secondary legislation under the Scotland Act 1998; is responsible for the conduct and funding of the Scottish parliament elections; manages the Scottish vote provision and authorises the monthly payment of funds from the UK consolidated fund to the Scottish consolidated fund; and publishes regular information on the state of the Scottish economy.

Matters reserved to the UK parliament include the constitution, foreign affairs, defence, international development, the civil service, financial and economic matters, national security, immigration and nationality, misuse of drugs, trade and industry, various aspects of energy regulation (eg coal, electricity, oil, gas and nuclear energy), various aspects of transport, social security, employment, abortion, genetics, surrogacy, medicines, broadcasting and equal opportunities. Devolved matters include health and social work, education and training, local government and housing, justice and police, agriculture, forestry, fisheries, the environment, tourism, sports, heritage, economic development and internal transport. It is supported by one public body. *See also* Devolved Government *and* Ministry of Justice.

Secretary of State for Scotland, Rt. Hon. Alister Jack, MP
Special Advisers, Magnus Gardham; William Saunders
Principal Private Secretary, Victoria Jones
Parliamentary Under-Secretary of State, Colin Clark, MP
Parliamentary Under-Secretary of State, Robin Walker, MP*
* Jointly with the Office of the Secretary of State for Northern Ireland

MANAGEMENT BOARD
Director, Gillian McGregor, CBE
Members, Victoria Bowman, *(Corporate Services);* Laura Crawforth *(Constitutional Policy);* Rebecca Hackett *(Policy Delivery, Relationship Management);* Rachel Irvine *(Constitutional Policy);* Nick Leake *(Policy Delivery and Relationship Management);* Anna Macmillan *(Communications)*

DEPARTMENT FOR TRANSPORT

Great Minster House, 33 Horseferry Road, London SW1P 4DR
T 0300-330 3000 W www.gov.uk/government/organisations/
department-for-transport

The Department for Transport (DfT) works with its agencies and partners to support the transport network that helps the UK's businesses and gets people and goods travelling around the country. The DfT plans and invests in transport infrastructure and is supported by 23 executive agencies and public bodies.

Secretary of State for Transport, Rt. Hon. Grant Shapps, MP
Parliamentary Private Secretary, Maria Caulfield, MP
Special Advisers, Emma Barr; Rupert Oldham-Reid
Minister of State, George Freeman, MP
Minister of State, Chris Heaton-Harris, MP
Parliamentary Under-Secretary of State, Nusrat Ghani, MP*
Parliamentary Under-Secretary of State, Paul Maynard, MP

Parliamentary Under-Secretary of State, Baroness Vere of Norbiton
* Alongside role as government Whip

MANAGEMENT BOARD
Permanent Secretary, Bernadette Kelly, CB
Members, Prof. Phil Blythe *(Chief Scientific Adviser);* Gareth Davies, *(International and Security Group);* Ruth Hannant *(Rail Group);* Tricia Hayes *(Roads, Devolution and Motoring Group);* Nick Joyce *(Resources and Strategy Group);* Clive Maxwell *(High Speed Rail and Major Projects);* Polly Payne *(Rail Group);* Brett Welch *(Legal Director)*
Non-Executive Members, Ian King *(Lead);* Richard Aitken-Davies; Richard Keys; Tony Poulter; Tracy Westall

HM TREASURY
1 Horse Guards Road, London SW1A 2HQ
T 020-7270 5000 E public.enquiries@hmtreasury.gov.uk
W www.gov.uk/government/organisations/hm-treasury

HM Treasury is the country's economics and finance ministry, and is responsible for formulating and implementing the government's financial and economic policy. It aims to raise the rate of sustainable growth, boost prosperity, and provide the conditions necessary for universal economic and employment opportunities. The Office of the Lord High Treasurer has been continuously in commission for over 200 years. The Lord High Commissioners of HM Treasury are the First Lord of the Treasury (who is also the prime minister), the Chancellor of the Exchequer and five junior lords. This board of commissioners is assisted at present by the chief secretary, the parliamentary secretary (who is also the government chief whip in the House of Commons), the financial secretary, the economic secretary, the exchequer secretary and the commercial secretary. The prime minister as first lord is not primarily concerned with the day-to-day aspects of Treasury business; neither are the parliamentary secretary and the junior lords as government whips. Treasury business is managed by the Chancellor of the Exchequer and the other Treasury ministers, assisted by the permanent secretary.

The chief secretary is responsible for public expenditure, including spending reviews and strategic planning; in-year control; public-sector pay and pensions; Annually Managed Expenditure and welfare reform; efficiency in public services; procurement and capital investment. He also has responsibility for the Treasury's interest in devolution.

The financial secretary has responsibility for financial services policy including banking and financial services reform and regulation; financial stability; city competitiveness; wholesale and retail markets in the UK, Europe and internationally; and the Financial Services Authority. His other responsibilities include banking support; bank lending; UK Financial Investments; Equitable Life; and personal savings and pensions policy. He also provides support to the chancellor on EU and wider international finance issues.

The exchequer secretary is a title only used occasionally, normally when the post of paymaster-general is allocated to a minister outside of the Treasury. The exchequer secretary's responsibilities include strategic oversight of the UK tax system; corporate and small business taxation, with input from the commercial secretary; departmental minister for HM Revenue and Customs and the Valuation Office Agency; and lead minister on European and international tax issues.

The economic secretary's responsibilities include environmental issues such as taxation of transport, international climate change and energy; North Sea oil taxation; tax credits and child poverty; assisting the chief secretary on welfare reform; charities and the voluntary sector; excise duties and gambling; stamp duty land tax; EU Budget; the Royal Mint; and departmental minister for HM Treasury Group.

HM Treasury is supported by 14 executive agencies and public bodies.

Prime Minister and First Lord of the Treasury, Rt. Hon. Boris Johnson, MP
Parliamentary Private Secretaries, Alex Burghart, MP; James Heappey, MP
Chancellor of the Exchequer, Rt. Hon. Sajid Javid, MP
Parliamentary Private Secretary, vacant
Special Advisers, Samuel Coates; James Hedgeland; Adam Memon; Mats Persson; Jennifer Powell
Chief Secretary to the Treasury, Rt. Hon. Rishi Sunak, MP
Special Adviser, Claire Coutinho
Financial Secretary to the Treasury, Jesse Norman, MP
Economic Secretary to the Treasury, John Glen, MP
Exchequer Secretary to the Treasury, Simon Clarke, MP
Parliamentary Private Secretary, vacant
Parliamentary Secretary to the Treasury (Chief Whip), Rt. Hon. Mark Spencer, MP
Special Advisers, Sophie Bolsover; Simon Burton
Lords Commissioners of HM Treasury (Whips), Colin Clark, MP*; Michelle Donelan, MP; Mike Freer, MP; Nusrat Ghani, MP†; Rebecca Harris, MP; David Rutley, MP
Assistant Whips, Leo Docherty, MP; Kevin Foster, MP‡; Nigel Huddleston, MP; Marcus Jones, MP; James Morris, MP; Tom Pursglove, MP; Iain Stewart, MP
* Along role at the Scottish Office
† Alongside role at the DfT
‡ Alongside roles at the Wales Office

MANAGEMENT BOARD
Permanent Secretary, Sir Tom Scholar, KCB
Second Permanent Secretary, Charles Roxburgh
Executive Members, James Bowler *(Public Spending);* Mark Bowman *(International and EU);* Katharine Braddick *(Financial Services);* Mike Driver *(Chief Financial Officer and Head of the Government Finance Function);* Clare Lombardelli *(Chief Economic Adviser);* Beth Russell *(Tax and Welfare)*
Non-Executive Member, Rt. Hon. Lord Hill, CBE *(Lead);* Gay Huey Evans, OBE; Tim Score

UK GOVERNMENT INVESTMENTS
1 Victoria Street, London SW1H 0ET
T 020-7638 9571 E ukgi@citigatedr.co.uk
W www.ukgi.org.uk/

UK Government Investments (UKGI) is the government's centre of expertise in corporate finance and corporate governance. UKGI Limited began operating on 1 April 2016 as a government company, wholly owned by HM Treasury, which brought together the functions of the Shareholder Executive (formerly part of the Department for Business, Energy and Industrial Strategy) and UK Financial Investments. UKGI's principle investments are to: prepare and execute all significant corporate asset sales by the UK government; advise on all major UK government financial interventions into corporate structures; act as shareholder for those arm's length bodies of the UK government that are structured to allow a meaningful shareholder function and for other UK government assets facing complex transformations; and to advise on major UK government negotiations with corporates.

Chief Executive, Mark Russell, CBE

Chair, Robert Swannell, CBE
Board, Alex Chisholm; Andrew Duff; Lord Gardia; Jane Guyett; Clare Hollingsworth; Robin Lawther; Hon. Sir James Leigh-Pemberton *(Deputy Chair);* Charles Roxburgh; Caroline Thompson

OFFICE OF TAX SIMPLIFICATION
HM Treasury, 1 Horse Guards Road, London SW1A 2HQ
T 0300-0585 028 E ots@ots.gsi.gov.uk
W www.gov.uk/government/organisations/
office-of-tax-simplification

The chancellor and exchequer secretary to HM Treasury launched the Office of Tax Simplification (OTS) on 20 July 2010 to provide the government with independent advice on simplifying the UK tax system. The OTS is part of HM Treasury and provides the government with independent advice on simplifying the UK tax system. It carries out projects investigating complex areas of the tax system and makes recommendations to the chancellor in reports which are published on its website.

Chair, Kathryn Cearns, OBE
Tax Director, Bill Dodwell

ROYAL MINT LTD
PO Box 500, Llantrisant, Pontyclun CF72 8YT
T 01443-222111 W www.royalmint.com

From 1975 the Royal Mint operated as a trading fund and was established as an executive agency in 1990. Since 2010 it has operated as Royal Mint Ltd, a company 100 per cent owned by HM Treasury, with an exclusive contract to supply all coinage for the UK.

The Royal Mint actively competes in world markets for a share of the available circulating coin business and about half of the coins and blanks it produces annually are exported. It is the leading export mint, accounting for around 15 per cent of the world market. The Royal Mint also manufactures special proof and uncirculated quality coins in gold, silver and other metals; military and civil decorations and medals; commemorative and prize medals; and royal and official seals.

Master of the Mint, Chancellor of the Exchequer *(ex officio)*
Chair, Graham Love
Chief Executive, Anne Jessopp

UK EXPORT FINANCE
1 Horse Guards Road, London SW1A 2HQ
T 020-7271 8010 E customer.service@ukexportfinance.gov.uk
W www.gov.uk/government/organisations/uk-export-finance

UK Export Finance is the UK's export credit agency. It helps UK exporters by providing insurance to them and guarantees to banks to share the risks of providing export finance. Additionally, it can make loans to overseas buyers of goods and services from the UK. UK Export Finance is the operating name of the Export Credits Guarantee Department.

The priorities of UK Export Finance are to fulfil its statutory remit to support exports; operate within the policy and financial objectives established by the government, which includes international obligations; and to recover the maximum amount of debt in respect of claims paid, taking account of the government's policy on debt forgiveness. It is a ministerial department supported by one public body, the Export Guarantees Advisory Council.

Secretary of State for International Trade and President of the Board of Trade, Rt. Hon. Elizabeth Truss, MP
Special Advisers, James Caldecourt; Nerissa Chesterfield; Sophie Jarvis

MANAGEMENT BOARD
Chief Executive, Louis Taylor
Chair, Noel Harwerth
Members, Cameron Fox *(Chief Finance and Operating Officer);* Shane Lynch *(Resources);* Davinder Mann *(Head of Legal Division);* Madelaine McTernan *(UK Government*

Investments); Samir Parkash *(Chief Risk Officer);* Richard Simon-Lewis *(Origination, Client Coverage, Marketing and Communications);* Gordon Welsh *(Head of the Business Group)*
Non-Executive Members, Shalini Khemka; John Mahon; Oliver Peterken; Lawrence Weiss; Kimberly Wiehl

OFFICE OF THE SECRETARY OF STATE FOR WALES
Gwydyr House, Whitehall, London SW1A 2NP
T 029-2092 4228 E correspondence@walesoffice.gsi.gov.uk
W www.gov.uk/government/organisations/
office-of-the-secretary-of-state-for-wales

The Office of the Secretary of State for Wales, informally known as the Wales Office, was established in 1999 when most of the powers of the Welsh Office were handed over to the National Assembly for Wales. It is the department of the Secretary of State for Wales, who is the key government figure liaising with the devolved government in Wales and who represents Welsh interests in the cabinet and parliament. The secretary of state has the right to attend and speak at sessions of the National Assembly (and must consult the assembly on the government's legislative programme). *See also* Devolved Government *and* Ministry of Justice.

Secretary of State for Wales, Rt. Hon. Alun Cairns, MP
Parliamentary Private Secretary, Glyn Davies, MP
Special Adviser, Geraint Evans
Principal Private Secretary, Michael Dynan-Oakley
Parliamentary Under-Secretary of State, Kevin Foster, MP*
* Alongside role as government Whip

MANAGEMENT BOARD
Director, Glynne Jones
Members, Ashok Ahir *(Communications);* Michael Dynan-Oakley *(Principal Private Secretary);* Louise Parry *(Policy);* Kate Starkey *(Policy);* Geth Williams *(Constitution and Policy)*
Non-Executive Members, Alison White *(Lead);* Peter Umbleja

DEPARTMENT FOR WORK AND PENSIONS
Caxton House, Tothill Street, London SW1H 9NA
T 020-3267 5144 E ministers@dwp.gsi.gov.uk
W www.gov.uk/government/organisations/
department-for-work-pensions

The Department for Work and Pensions was formed in June 2001 from parts of the former Department of Social Security, the Department for Education and Employment and the Employment Service. The department helps unemployed people of working age into work, helps employers to fill their vacancies and provides financial support to people unable to help themselves, through back-to-work programmes. The department also administers the child support system, social security benefits and the social fund. In addition, the department has reciprocal social security arrangements with other countries. The department is supported by 15 executive agencies and public bodies.

Secretary of State for Work and Pensions, Rt. Hon. Thérèse Coffey, MP, MP
Parliamentary Private Secretary, Rachel Maclean, MP
Special Advisers, Alex Hitchcock; Jean-Andre Prager; Eleanor Shawcross Wolfson; Jason Stein
Minister of State, Justin Tomlinson, MP *(Disabled People, Health and Work)*
Minister of State, Rt. Hon. Elizabeth Truss, MP *(Minister for Women and Equalities)**
Minister of State, Baroness Williams of Trafford *(Minister for Equalities)†*

Parliamentary Under-Secretary of State, Victoria Atkins, MP
   (Minister for Women)†
Parliamentary Under-Secretary of State, Mims Davies, MP
   (Employment)
Parliamentary Under-Secretary of State, Guy Opperman, MP
   (Pensions and Financial Inclusion)
Parliamentary Under-Secretary of State, Will Quince, MP *(Family Support, Housing and Child Maintenance)*
Parliamentary Under-Secretary of State, Baroness Stedman-Scott, OBE *(Lords)*
* Alongside role as Secretary of State for International Trade and President of the Board of Trade
† Alongside role at the Home Office

MANAGEMENT BOARD
Permanent Secretary, Peter Schofield
Members, Debbie Alder, CB *(Human Resources);* Neil Couling, CBE *(Universal Credit Programme);* Emma Haddad *(Service Excellence);* Nick Joicey *(Finance);* John-Paul Marks *(Work and Health Services);* Jonathan Mills *(Policy Group);* Simon McKinnon *(Digital and Information Officer)*

EXECUTIVE AGENCIES

Executive agencies are well-defined business units that carry out services with a clear focus on delivering specific outputs within a framework of accountability to ministers. They can be set up or disbanded without legislation, and they are organisationally independent from the department they are answerable to. In the following list the agencies are shown in the accounts of their sponsor departments. Legally they act on behalf of the relevant secretary of state. Their chief executives also perform the role of accounting officers, which means they are responsible for the money spent by their organisations. Staff employed by agencies are civil servants.

DEPARTMENT FOR BUSINESS, ENERGY AND INDUSTRIAL STRATEGY

COMPANIES HOUSE
Crown Way, Cardiff CF14 3UZ
T 0303-123 4500 E enquiries@companies-house.gov.uk
W www.gov.uk/government/organisations/companies-house

Companies House incorporates and dissolves limited companies, examines and stores company information delivered under the Companies Act and related legislation; and makes this information available to the public.

Chief Executive, Louise Smyth

THE INSOLVENCY SERVICE
4 Abbey Orchard Street, London SW1P 2HT
T 020-7637 1110
E redundancypaymentsonline@insolvency.gsi.gov.uk
W www.gov.uk/government/organisations/insolvency-service

The role of the service includes administration and investigation of the affairs of bankrupts, individuals subject to debt relief orders, partnerships and companies in compulsory liquidation; dealing with the disqualification of directors in all corporate failures; authorising and regulating the insolvency profession; providing banking and investment services for bankruptcy and liquidation estate funds; assessing and paying statutory entitlement to redundancy payments when an employer cannot, or will not, pay its employees; and advising ministers on insolvency, redundancy and related issues. The service has around 1,700 staff, operating from 22 locations across Great Britain.

Inspector-General and Chief Executive, Sarah Albon

INTELLECTUAL PROPERTY OFFICE
Concept House, Cardiff Road, Newport NP10 8QQ
T 0300-300 2000 E information@ipo.gov.uk
W www.gov.uk/government/organisations/
intellectual-property-office

The Intellectual Property Office (an operating name of the Patent Office) was set up in 1852 to act as the UK's sole office for the granting of patents. It was established as an executive agency in 1990 and became a trading fund in 1991. The office is responsible for the granting of intellectual property (IP) rights, which include patents, trade marks, designs and copyright.

Comptroller-General and Chief Executive, Tim Moss

MET OFFICE
FitzRoy Road, Exeter, Devon EX1 3PB
T 0370-900 0100 E enquiries@metoffice.gov.uk
W www.metoffice.gov.uk

The Met Office is the UK's National Weather Service, operating as an executive agency of BEIS, having transferred from the MoD to the Department for Business, Energy and Industrial Strategy in July 2011. It is a world leader in providing weather and climate services, using over 10 million weather observations a day, and employs more than 1,700 people at 60 locations throughout the world.

Chief Executive, Prof. Penelope Endersby
Chief Scientist, Prof. Stephen Belcher

UK SPACE AGENCY
Polaris House, North Star Avenue, Swindon, Wiltshire SN2 1SZ
T 020-7215 5000 E uk@ukspaceagency.gov.uk
W www.gov.uk/government/organisations/uk-space-agency

The UK Space Agency was established on 23 March 2010 and became an executive agency on 1 April 2011. It was created to provide a single voice for UK space ambitions, and is responsible for all strategic decisions on the UK civil space programme. Responsibilities of the UK Space Agency include coordinating UK civil space activity; supporting academic research; nurturing the UK space industry; raising the profile of UK space activities at home and abroad; working to increase understanding of space science and its practical benefits; and inspiring the next generation of UK scientists and engineers. It aims to capture 10 per cent of the global market for space by 2030.

Chief Executive, Dr Graham Turnock

CABINET OFFICE

CROWN COMMERCIAL SERVICE
Floor 9, The Capital Building, Old Hall Street, Liverpool L3 9PP
T 0345-410 2222 E info@crowncommercial.gov.uk
W www.gov.uk/government/organisations/
crown-commercial-service

The Crown Commercial Service (CCS) is an executive agency of the Cabinet Office, bringing together policy, advice and direct buying; providing commercial services to the public sector; and saving money for the taxpayer. The CCS works with over 17,000 customer organisations in the public sector.

Chief Executive, Simon Tse

MINISTRY OF HOUSING, COMMUNITIES AND LOCAL GOVERNMENT

PLANNING INSPECTORATE
Temple Quay House, 2 The Square, Temple Quay, Bristol BS1 6PN
T 0303-444 5000 E enquiries@pins.gsi.gov.uk
W www.gov.uk/government/organisations/planning-inspectorate

The main work of the inspectorate consists of national infrastructure planning under the Planning Act 2008 as amended by the Localism Act 2011, the processing of planning and enforcement appeals, and holding examinations into development plan documents. It also deals with listed building consent appeals; advertisement appeals; rights of way cases; cases arising from the Environmental Protection and Water acts, the Transport and Works Act 1992 and other highways legislation; and reporting on planning applications called in for decision by the Ministry of Housing, Communities and Local Government and the Welsh government.

Chief Executive, Sarah Richards

THE QUEEN ELIZABETH II CONFERENCE CENTRE
Broad Sanctuary, London SW1P 3EE
T 020-7798 4000 W www.qeiicentre.london

The centre provides secure conference facilities for national and international government and private sector use.

Chief Executive, Mark Taylor

MINISTRY OF DEFENCE
See also Defence Chapter.

DEFENCE ELECTRONICS AND COMPONENTS AGENCY
Welsh Road, Deeside, Flintshire CH5 2LS T 01244-847694
E decainfo@deca.mod.uk
W www.gov.uk/deca

The Defence Electronics and Components Agency (DECA) provides maintenance, repair, overhaul, upgrade and procurement in avionics, electronics and components fields to support the MoD. As a 'trading' executive agency DECA is run along commercial lines, with funding for DECA's activities being generated entirely by payments for delivery of services provided to the MoD and other private sector customers. DECA currently has an annual turnover of around £25m and employs over 400 staff across its head office and main operating centre in North Wales, a site in Stafford and various deployed locations across the UK.

Chief Executive, Geraint Spearing

DEFENCE SCIENCE AND TECHNOLOGY LABORATORY
Porton Down, Salisbury, Wiltshire SP4 0JQ
T 01980-950000 E centralenquiries@dstl.gov.uk
W www.gov.uk/dstl

The Defence Science and Technology Laboratory (DSTL) supplies specialist science and technology services to the MoD and wider government.

Chief Executive, Gary Aitkenhead

UK HYDROGRAPHIC OFFICE
Admiralty Way, Taunton, Somerset TA1 2DN
T 01823-484444 E customerservices@ukho.gov.uk
W www.gov.uk/ukho

The UK Hydrographic Office (UKHO) collects and supplies hydrographic and geospatial data for the Royal Navy and merchant shipping to protect lives at sea. Working with other national hydrographic offices, UKHO sets and raises global standards of hydrography, cartography and navigation.

Chief Executive, Rear-Adm. Tim Lowe, CBE

DEPARTMENT FOR EDUCATION

THE EDUCATION AND SKILLS FUNDING AGENCY
Sanctuary Buildings, 20 Great Smith Street, London SW1P 3BT
T 0370-000 2288 W www.gov.uk/government/organisations/education-and-skills-funding-agency

Formed on 1 April 2017 after a merger of the Education Funding Agency (EFA) and the Skills Funding Agency (SFA), the Education and Skills Funding Agency (ESFA) is the DfE's delivery agency for funding and compliance. It manages £58bn of funding each year to support all state-provided education and training for children and young people aged 3 to 19. The ESFA also supports the delivery of building and maintenance programmes for schools, academies, free schools and sixth-form colleges. It also administers the National Careers Service, the National Apprenticeship Service and the Learning Records Service.

Chief Executive, Eileen Milner

STANDARDS AND TESTING AGENCY
Ground Floor, South Building, Cheylesmore House, 5 Quinton Road, Coventry CV1 2WT
T 0300-303 3013 E assessments@education.gov.uk
W www.gov.uk/government/organisations/standards-and-testing-agency

The Standards and Testing Agency (STA) opened on 1 October 2011 and is responsible for the development and delivery of all statutory assessments from early years to the end of Key Stage 2.

Chief Executive, Una Bennett

TEACHING REGULATION AGENCY
Ground Floor, South Building, Cheylesmore House, 5 Quinton Road, Coventry CV1 2WT
T 0207-593 5394 E qts.enquiries@education.gov.uk
W www.gov.uk/government/organisations/teaching-regulation-agency

On 1 April 2018 the Teaching Regulation Agency became operational. It is responsible for maintaining the database of qualified teachers in England and is the awarding body for Qualified Teacher Status (QTS).

Chief Executive, Alan Meyrick

DEPARTMENT FOR ENVIRONMENT, FOOD AND RURAL AFFAIRS

ANIMAL AND PLANT HEALTH AGENCY
Woodham Lane, New Haw, Addlestone, Surrey KT15 3NB
T 020-8225 7611 E enquiries@apha.gov.uk
W www.gov.uk/government/organisations/animal-and-plant-health-agency

The Animal and Plant Health Agency (APHA) was launched on 1 October 2014. It merged the former Animal Health and Veterinary Laboratories Agency with parts of the Food and Environment Research Agency responsible for plant and bee health to create a single agency responsible for animal, plant and bee health.

APHA is responsible for identifying and controlling endemic and exotic diseases and pests in animals, plants and bees, and surveillance of new and emerging pests and diseases; scientific research in areas such as bacterial, viral, prion and parasitic diseases, vaccines and food safety and act as an international reference laboratory for many farm animal diseases; facilitating international trade in animals, products of animal origin, and plants; protecting endangered wildlife through licensing and registration; managing a programme of apiary inspections, diagnostics, research and development, training and advice; and regulating the safe disposal of animal by-products to reduce the risk of potentially dangerous substances entering the food chain.

The agency provides all or some of these services to DEFRA and the Scottish and Welsh governments.

Chief Executive, Chris Hadkiss

CENTRE FOR ENVIRONMENT, FISHERIES AND AQUACULTURE SCIENCE (CEFAS)

Pakefield Road, Lowestoft, Suffolk NR33 0HT
T 01502-562244 W www.gov.uk/government/organisations/centre-for-environment-fisheries-and-aquaculture-science

Established in April 1997, the agency provides research and consultancy services in fisheries science and management, aquaculture, fish health and hygiene, environmental impact assessment, and environmental quality assessment.

Chief Executive, Tom Karsten

RURAL PAYMENTS AGENCY

PO Box 69, Reading RG1 3YD
T 0300-0200 301 E ruralpayments@defra.gov.uk
W www.gov.uk/government/organisations/rural-payments-agency

The RPA was established in 2001. It pays out over £2bn each year to support the farming and food sector and is responsible for Common Agricultural Policy (CAP) schemes in England. In addition it manages over 40 other rural economy and community schemes. It is also responsible for operating cattle tracing services across Great Britain; conducting inspections of farms, processing plants and fresh produce markets in England; and managing the Rural Land Register.

Chief Executive, Paul Caldwell

VETERINARY MEDICINES DIRECTORATE

Woodham Lane, New Haw, Addlestone, Surrey KT15 3LS
T 01932-336911 E postmaster@vmd.defra.gsi.gov.uk
W www.gov.uk/government/organisations/veterinary-medicines-directorate

The Veterinary Medicines Directorate is responsible for all aspects of the authorisation and control of veterinary medicines, including post-authorisation surveillance of residues in animals and animal products. It is also responsible for the development and enforcement of legislation concerning veterinary medicines and the provision of policy advice to ministers.

Chief Executive, Prof. Peter Borriello

FOREIGN AND COMMONWEALTH OFFICE

FCO SERVICES

Hanslope Park, Milton Keynes MK19 7BH
T 01908-515789 W www.fcoservices.gov.uk

FCO Services was established as an executive agency in April 2006 and became a trading fund in April 2008. It operates as the service delivery arm of the FCO, keeping their people, assets and information across the globe safe and secure from the threats they face. FCO Services also works with central government departments, law enforcement, HM government abroad, local government and the UK's critical national infrastructure.

Chief Executive, Danny Payne

WILTON PARK CONFERENCE CENTRE

Wiston House, Steyning, W. Sussex BN44 3DZ
T 01903-815020 W www.wiltonpark.org.uk

Wilton Park organises international affairs conferences and is hired out to government departments and commercial users.

Chair, Gisela Stuart
Chief Executive, Sharmila Nebhrajani, OBE

DEPARTMENT OF HEALTH AND SOCIAL CARE

MEDICINES AND HEALTHCARE PRODUCTS REGULATORY AGENCY (MHRA)

10 South Colonnade, London E14 4PU
T 020-3080 6000 E info@mhra.gov.uk W www.gov.uk/government/organisations/medicines-and-healthcare-products-regulatory-agency

The MHRA is a centre of the Medicines and Healthcare Products Regulatory Agency which also includes the National Institute for Biological Standards and Control (NIBSC) and the Clinical Practice Research Datalink (CPRD). The MHRA is responsible for regulating all medicines and medical devices in the UK by ensuring they work and are acceptably safe.

Chair, Prof. Sir Michael Rawlins, GBE
Chief Executive, Dr Ian Hudson

PUBLIC HEALTH ENGLAND

Wellington House, 133–155 Waterloo Road, London SE1 8UG
T 020-7654 8000 E enquiries@phe.gov.uk
W www.gov.uk/government/organisations/public-health-england

Public Health England (PHE) began operating on 1 April 2013 with a remit to protect and improve the health and wellbeing of people within the UK, and reducing health inequalities. PHE employs 5,500 staff who are mostly scientists, researchers and public health professionals. It has eight local centres and four regions in England and works closely with public health professionals in Wales, Scotland, Northern Ireland and internationally.

Chief Executive, Duncan Selbie

MINISTRY OF JUSTICE

CRIMINAL INJURIES COMPENSATION AUTHORITY (CICA)

Alexander Bain House, Atlantic Quay, 15 York Street, Glasgow G2 8JQ T 0300-003 3601
W www.gov.uk/government/organisations/criminal-injuries-compensation-authority

CICA is the executive agency responsible for administering the Criminal Injuries Compensation Scheme in England, Scotland and Wales (separate arrangements apply in Northern Ireland). CICA handles up to 40,000 applications for compensation each year, covering every aspect of compensation under the 1996, 2001 and 2008 Criminal Injuries Compensation Schemes. Appeals against decisions made by CICA can be put to the First-tier Tribunal (Criminal Injuries Compensation) *see* Tribunals.

Chief Executive, Linda Brown

HM COURTS AND TRIBUNALS SERVICE

102 Petty France, London SW1H 9AJ
W www.gov.uk/government/organisations/hm-courts-and-tribunals-service

HM Courts Service and the Tribunals Service merged on 1 April 2011 to form HM Courts and Tribunals Service, an integrated agency providing support for the administration of justice in courts and tribunals. As an agency within the MoJ it operates as a partnership between the Lord Chancellor, the Lord Chief Justice and the Senior President of Tribunals. It is responsible for the administration of the criminal, civil and family courts and tribunals in England and Wales and non-devolved tribunals in Scotland and Northern Ireland. The agency's work is overseen by a board headed by an independent chair working with non-executive, executive and judicial members.

Chief Executive, Susan Acland-Hood

HM PRISON AND PROBATION SERVICE
102 Petty France, London SW1H 9EX
T 01633-630941 E public.enquiries@noms.gsi.gov.uk
W www.gov.uk/government/organisations/
her-majestys-prison-and-probation-service

HM Prison and Probation Service (HMPPS) was established on 1 April 2017, responsible for the roll out of government policies concerning the welfare of offenders and communities, and for reducing levels of reoffending by the rehabilitation of offenders through education and training schemes. Through HM Prison Service, HMPPS manages public sector prisons and the contracts for private prisons in England and Wales.

Chief Executive, Jo Farrar

HM PRISON SERVICE
Clive House, 70 Petty France, London SW1H 9EX
T 0300-047 6325 E public.enquiries@noms.gsi.gov.uk
W www.gov.uk/government/organisations/hm-prison-service

As an executive agency of HM Prison and Probation Service, HM Prison Service is responsible for keeping those sentenced to prison in custody, helping them lead law-abiding and useful lives, both while they are in prison and after they have been released. HM Prison Service works alongside courts, police and local councils, in addition to voluntary organisations to achieve their aims. The agency runs 109 of the 120 prisons in England and Wales. HM Prison Service is further responsible for managing prison and probation services, and supporting effective offender management.

Executive Director, Prisons, Phil Copple

LEGAL AID AGENCY
Berkley Way, Viking Business Park, Jarrow, South Tyneside NE31 1SF
T 0300-200 2020 E contactcivil@justice.gov.uk
W www.gov.uk/government/organisations/legal-aid-agency

The Legal Aid Agency provides civil and criminal legal aid and advice in England and Wales. Formed on 1 April 2013 as part of the Legal Aid, Sentencing and Punishment of Offenders Act 2012, the agency replaced the Legal Services Commission, a non-departmental public body of the MoJ.

Chief Executive, Shaun McNally, CBE

OFFICE OF THE PUBLIC GUARDIAN
PO Box 16185, Birmingham B2 2WH
T 0300-456 0300 E customerservices@publicguardian.gsi.gov.uk
W www.gov.uk/government/organisations/
office-of-the-public-guardian

The Office of the Public Guardian (OPG) works within the Mental Capacity Act 2005 to support and protect those who lack the mental capacity to make decisions for themselves. It supports the Public Guardian in the registration of Enduring Powers of Attorney (EPA) and Lasting Powers of Attorney (LPA), and the supervision of deputies appointed by the Court of Protection. The OPG also has responsibility for investigating and acting on allegations of abuse by attorneys and deputies. The OPG's responsibility extends across England and Wales.

Chief Executive and Public Guardian, Alan Eccles, CBE

DEPARTMENT FOR TRANSPORT

DRIVER AND VEHICLE LICENSING AGENCY (DVLA)
Longview Road, Swansea SA6 7JL
W www.gov.uk/government/organisations/
driver-and-vehicle-licensing-agency

The DVLA, established as an executive agency in 1990, maintains registers of drivers and vehicles in Great Britain. The information collated by the DVLA helps to improve road safety, reduce vehicle related crime, support environmental initiatives and limit vehicle tax evasion. The DVLA maintains over 48 million driver records and over 40 million vehicle records and collects over £6bn a year in vehicle tax.

Chief Executive, Julie Lennard

DRIVER AND VEHICLE STANDARDS AGENCY
Berkeley House, Croydon Street, Bristol BS5 0DA
T 0300-123 9000
W www.gov.uk/government/organisations/
driver-and-vehicle-standards-agency

Formed by the merger of the Driving Standards Agency and the Vehicle and Operator Services Agency in 2014, the Driver and Vehicle Standards Agency (DVSA) is responsible for improving road safety in the UK by setting standards for driving and motorcycling, and ensuring drivers, vehicle operators and MOT garages understand and comply with roadworthiness standards. It additionally provides a range of licensing, testing, education and enforcement services.

Chief Executive, Gareth Llewellyn

MARITIME AND COASTGUARD AGENCY
Spring Place, 105 Commercial Road, Southampton SO15 1EG
T 020-3817 2000 W www.gov.uk/government/organisations/
maritime-and-coastguard-agency

The agency's aims are to prevent loss of life, continuously improve maritime safety and protect the marine environment.

Chief Executive, Brian Johnson

VEHICLE CERTIFICATION AGENCY
1 Eastgate Office Centre, Eastgate Road, Bristol BS5 6XX
T 0300-330 5797 E enquiries@vca.gov.uk
W www.vehicle-certification-agency.gov.uk

The agency is the UK authority responsible for ensuring that new road vehicles, agricultural tractors, off-road vehicles and vehicle parts have been designed and constructed to meet internationally agreed standards of safety and environmental protection.

Chief Executive, Pia Wilkes

HM TREASURY

GOVERNMENT INTERNAL AUDIT AGENCY
1 Horse Guards Road, London SW1A 2HQ
E Correspondence@giaa.gov.uk W www.gov.uk/government/
organisations/government-internal-audit-agency

Launched on 1 April 2015, the Government Internal Audit Agency (GIAA) helps ensure government and the wider public sector provide services effectively. GIAA offers quality assurance on organisation's systems and processes, based on an objective assessment of the governance, risk management and control arrangements in place.

Chief Executive, Elizabeth Honer

UK DEBT MANAGEMENT OFFICE
Eastcheap Court, 11 Philpot Lane, London EC3M 8UD
T 020-7862 6500 W www.dmo.gov.uk

The UK Debt Management Office (DMO) was launched as an executive agency of HM Treasury in April 1998. The Chancellor of the Exchequer determines the policy and financial framework within which the DMO operates, but delegates operational decisions on debt and cash management and the day-to-day running of the office to the chief executive. The DMO's remit is to carry out the government's debt management policy of minimising financing costs over the long term, and to minimise the cost of offsetting the government's net cash flows over time, while operating at a level of risk approved by ministers in both cases. The DMO is also responsible for providing loans to local authorities through the Public Works Loan Board, and for managing the assets of certain public-sector bodies through the Commissioners for the Reduction of the National Debt.

Chief Executive, Sir Robert Stheeman, CB

NON-MINISTERIAL GOVERNMENT DEPARTMENTS

Non-ministerial government departments are part of central government but are not headed by a minister and are not funded by a sponsor department. They are created to implement specific legislation, but do not have the ability to change it. Departments may have links to a minister, but the minister is not responsible for the department's overall performance. Staff employed by non-ministerial departments are civil servants.

CHARITY COMMISSION
PO Box 1227, Liverpool L69 3UG
T 0300-066 9197 W www.gov.uk/government/organisations/charity-commission

The Charity Commission is established by law as the independent regulator and registrar of charities in England and Wales. Its aim is to provide the best possible regulation of these charities in order to ensure their legal compliance and increase their efficiency, accountability and effectiveness, as well as to encourage public trust and confidence in them. The commission maintains a register of 168,186 charities. It is accountable to both parliament and the First-tier Tribunal (Charity), and the chamber of the Upper Tribunal or high court for decisions made in exercising the commission's legal powers. The Charity Commission has offices in London, Liverpool, Taunton and Newport.

Chair, Rt. Hon. Baroness Stowell of Beeston, MBE
Chief Executive, Helen Stephenson, CBE

COMPETITION AND MARKETS AUTHORITY
Victoria House, Southampton Row, London WC1B 4AD
T 020-3738 6000 E general.enquiries@cma.gov.uk
W www.gov.uk/government/organisations/competition-and-markets-authority

The Competition and Markets Authority (CMA) is the UK's primary competition and consumer authority. It is an independent non-ministerial government department with responsibility for carrying out investigations into mergers, markets and the regulated industries and enforcing competition and consumer law. From 1 April 2014 it took over the functions of the Competition Commission and the competition and certain consumer functions of the Office of Fair Trading under the Enterprise Act 2002, as amended by the Enterprise and Regulatory Reform Act 2013.

Chair, Rt. Hon. Lord Tyrie
Chief Executive, Dr Andrea Coscelli

CROWN PROSECUTION SERVICE
Rose Court, 2 Southwark Bridge Road, London SE1 9HS
T 020-3357 0899 E enquiries@cps.gsi.gov.uk W www.cps.gov.uk

The Crown Prosecution Service (CPS) is the independent body responsible for prosecuting people in England and Wales. The CPS was established as a result of the Prosecution of Offences Act 1985. It works closely with the police to advise on lines of inquiry and to decide on appropriate charges and other disposals in all but minor cases. *See also* Law Courts and Offices.

Director of Public Prosecutions, Max Hill, QC
Interim Chief Executive, Paul Staff

FOOD STANDARDS AGENCY
Floor 6 & 7, Clive House, 70 Petty France, London SW1H 9EX
T 020-7276 8829 E helpline@food.gov.uk
W www.food.gov.uk

Established in April 2000, the FSA is a UK-wide non-ministerial government body responsible for food safety and hygiene. The agency has the general function of developing policy in these areas and provides information and advice to the government, other public bodies and consumers. The FSA also works with local authorities to enforce food safety regulations and has staff working in UK meat plants to check that the requirements of the regulations are being met.

Chair, Heather Hancock
Chief Executive, Jason Feeney

FOOD STANDARDS AGENCY NORTHERN IRELAND,
   10C Clarendon Road, Belfast BT1 3BG T 028-9041 7700
   E infosani@food.gov.uk
FOOD STANDARDS AGENCY WALES, 11th Floor, South
   Gate House, Wood Street, Cardiff CF10 1EW T 029-2067 8999
   E walesadminteam@food.gov.uk

FORESTRY COMMISSION
620 Bristol Business Park, Coldharbour Lane, Bristol BS16 1EJ
T 0300-067 4000 E nationalenquiries@forestrycommission.gov.uk
W www.gov.uk/government/organisations/forestry-commission

The Forestry Commission is the non-ministerial government department responsible for forestry policy in England. It is supported by two executive agencies: Forest Research, which carries out scientific research and technical development relevant to forestry, and Forestry England, responsible for managing around 20 per cent of the country's woodland.

On 1 April 2013 the functions of its Welsh division, Forestry Commission Wales, were subsumed into Natural Resources Wales, a new body established by the Welsh government to regulate and manage natural resources in Wales.

On 1 April 2019 responsibility for forestry in Scotland was devolved to two new Scottish government agencies: Forestry and Land Scotland and Scottish Forestry, who are accountable to the Scottish ministers.

The commission's principal objectives are to protect and expand England's forests and woodlands; enhance the economic value of forest resources; conserve and improve the biodiversity, landscape and cultural heritage of forests and woodlands; develop opportunities for woodland recreation; and increase public understanding of, and community participation in, forestry. It does this by managing public forests in its care to implement these objectives; by supporting other woodland owners with grants, regulation, advice and tree felling licences; and, through its Forest Research agency, by carrying out scientific research and technical development in support of these objectives.

Chair (2014–20), Sir Harry Studholme, Bt.
Chief Executive, Forest Research, Prof. James Pendlebury
Chief Executive, Forestry England, vacant

GOVERNMENT ACTUARY'S DEPARTMENT
Finlaison House, 15–17 Furnival Street, London EC4A 1AB
T 020-7211 2601 E enquiries@gad.gov.uk
Elgin House, Haymarket Yards, Edinburgh EH12 5WN
T 0131-467 0324 E scottish-enquiries@gad.gov.uk
W www.gov.uk/government/organisations/government-actuarys-department

The Government Actuary's Department (GAD) was established in 1919 and provides actuarial advice to the public sector in the UK and overseas, and also to the private sector, where consistent with government policy. The GAD provides advice on occupational pension schemes, social security and National Insurance, investment and strategic risk management, insurance analysis and advice, financial risk management, and healthcare financing.

Government Actuary, Martin Clarke
Deputy Government Actuary, Colin Wilson

GOVERNMENT LEGAL DEPARTMENT
1 Kemble Street, London WC2B 4TS
T 020-7210 3000 E thetreasurysolicitor@governmentlegal.gov.uk
W www.gov.uk/government/organisations/
government-legal-department

The Treasury Solicitor's Department became the Government Legal Department (GLD) on 1 April 2015. The department provides legal advice to government on the development, design and implementation of government policies and decisions, and represents the government in court. It is superintended by the Attorney-General. The permanent secretary of the GLD, the Treasury Solicitor, is also the Queen's Proctor, and is responsible for collecting ownerless goods *(bona vacantia)* on behalf of the crown.

HM Procurator-General and Treasury Solicitor, Jonathan Jones
Directors-General, Stephen Braviner-Roman; Peter Fish, CB; Susanna McGibbon
Head of Bona Vacantia, Caroline Harold

HM LAND REGISTRY
Trafalgar House, 1 Bedford Park, Croydon CR0 2AQ
T 0300-006 0411
W www.gov.uk/government/organisations/land-registry

A government department and trading fund of BEIS, HM Land Registry maintains the Land Register – the definitive source of information for more than 25 million property titles in England and Wales. The Land Register has been open to public inspection since 1990.

Chief Land Registrar and Chief Executive, Mike Harlow (acting)

HM REVENUE AND CUSTOMS (HMRC)
100 Parliament Street, London SW1A 2BQ
Income Tax Enquiries 0300-200 3300
National Insurance Enquiries 0300-200 3500
VAT Enquiries 0300-200 3700
W www.gov.uk/government/organisations/hm-revenue-customs

HMRC was formed following the integration of the Inland Revenue and HM Customs and Excise, which was made formal by parliament in April 2005. It collects and administers direct taxes (capital gains tax, corporation tax, income tax, inheritance tax and national insurance contributions) and indirect taxes (excise duties, insurance premium tax, petroleum revenue tax, stamp duty, stamp duty land tax, stamp duty reserve tax and value-added tax). HMRC also pays and administers child benefit, tax credits and the Child Trust Fund, in addition to being responsible for environmental taxes, national minimum wage enforcement, recovery of student loans, the climate change levy and landfill tax. HMRC also administers the Government Banking Service.

Chief Executive and Permanent Secretary, Sir Jonathan Thompson, KCB
Second Permanent Secretary and Tax Assurance Commissioner, Jim Harra, CB

VALUATION OFFICE AGENCY
Wingate House, 93–107 Shaftesbury Avenue, London W1D 5BU
T 0300-050 1501 W www.gov.uk/government/organisations/
valuation-office-agency

Established in 1991, the Valuation Office is an executive agency of HM Revenue and Customs. It is responsible for compiling and maintaining the business rating and council tax valuation lists for England and Wales; valuing property throughout Great Britain for the purposes of taxes administered by HMRC; providing statutory and non-statutory property valuation services in England, Wales and Scotland; and giving policy advice to ministers on property valuation matters. In April 2009 the VOA assumed responsibility for the functions of The Rent Service, which provided a rental valuation service to local authorities in England, and fair rent determinations for landlords and tenants.

Chief Executive, Melissa Tatton

NATIONAL ARCHIVES
NATIONAL ARCHIVES
Kew, Richmond, Surrey TW9 4DU
T 020-8876 3444 W www.nationalarchives.gov.uk

The National Archives is a non-ministerial government department of the Ministry of Justice. It incorporates the Public Record Office, Historical Manuscripts Commission, Office of Public Sector Information and Her Majesty's Stationery Office. As the official archive of the UK government, it preserves, protects and makes accessible the historical collection of official records.

The National Archives also manages digital information including the UK government web archive which contains over one billion digital documents, and devises solutions for keeping government records readable now and in the future.

The organisation administers the UK's public records system under the Public Records Acts of 1958 and 1967. The records it holds span 1,000 years – from the Domesday Book to the latest government papers to be released – and fill more than 167km (104 miles) of shelving.

Chief Executive and Keeper, Jeff James

NATIONAL CRIME AGENCY
Units 1–6 Citadel Place, Tinworth Street, London SE11 5EF
T 0370-496 7622 E communication@nca.gov.uk
W www.nationalcrimeagency.gov.uk

The National Crime Agency (NCA) is an operational crime fighting agency introduced under the Crime and Courts Act 2013, which became fully operational in October 2013. The NCA's remit is to fight organised crime, strengthen UK borders, tackle fraud and cyber crime and protect children and young people. The agency provides leadership through its organised crime, border policing, economic crime and Child Exploitation and Online Protection Centre commands, the National Cyber Crime Unit and specialist capability teams.

Director-General, Lynne Owens, CBE, QPM

NATIONAL SAVINGS AND INVESTMENTS
Glasgow G58 1SB
T 08085-007007 W www.nsandi.com

NS&I (National Savings and Investments) came into being in 1861 when the Palmerston government set up the Post Office Savings Bank, a savings scheme which aimed to encourage ordinary wage earners 'to provide for themselves against adversity and ill health'. NS&I was established as a government department in 1969. It is responsible for the design, marketing and administration of savings and investment products for personal savers and investors. It has over 25 million customers and around £157bn invested. *See also* Banking and Finance, National Savings.

Chief Executive, Ian Ackerley

OFFICE OF GAS AND ELECTRICITY MARKETS (OFGEM)

10 South Colonnade, Canary Wharf, London E14 4PU
T 020-7901 7000 W www.ofgem.gov.uk

OFGEM is the regulator for Britain's gas and electricity industries. Its role is to protect and advance the interests of consumers by promoting competition where possible, and through regulation only where necessary. OFGEM operates under the direction and governance of the Gas and Electricity Markets Authority, which makes all major decisions and sets policy priorities for OFGEM. OFGEM's powers are provided for under the Gas Act 1986 and the Electricity Act 1989, as amended by the Utilities Act 2000. It also has enforcement powers under the Competition Act 1998 and the Enterprise Act 2002.

Chair, Martin Cave
Chief Executive, Dermot Nolan

OFFICE OF RAIL AND ROAD

1 Kemble Street, London WC2B 4AN
T 020-7282 2000 E contact.cct@orr.gov.uk W www.orr.gov.uk

The Office of the Rail and Road (ORR) is the operating name of the Office of Rail Regulation. The Office of Rail Regulation was established on 5 July 2004 under the Railways and Transport Safety Act 2003. It replaced the Office of the Rail Regulator.

On 1 April 2006, ORR assumed new responsibilities as a combined safety and economic regulator under the Railways Act 2005. It also has concurrent jurisdiction with the Competition and Market Authority under the Competition Act 1998 as the competition authority for the railways.

As the railway industry's independent health and safety and economic regulator, its principal functions are to: ensure that Network Rail and HS1 manage the national network efficiently and in a way that meets the needs of its users; encourage continuous health and safety performance; secure compliance with relevant health and safety law, including taking enforcement action as necessary; develop policy and enhance relevant railway health and safety legislation; and license operators of railway assets, setting the terms for access by operators to the network and other railway facilities, and enforce competition and consumer law in the rail sector.

On 1 April 2015, under the Infrastructure Act 2015, ORR assumed responsibility for monitoring Highways England's management and development of the strategic road network – the motorways and main 'A' roads in England. In this role ORR ensures that the network is managed efficiently, safely and sustainably, for the benefit of road users and the public.

On 16 March 2015, ORR signed an agreement with the French rail regulator ARAF to establish a collaborative regulatory approach for consistent independent regulation across the Channel tunnel network.

ORR is led by a board appointed by the Secretary of State for Transport.

Chair, Declan Collier
Chief Executive, John Larkinson (interim)

OFFICE OF QUALIFICATIONS AND EXAMINATIONS REGULATION (OFQUAL)

Earlsdon Park, 53–55 Butts Road, Coventry CV1 3BH
T 0300-303 3344 E public.enquiries@ofqual.gov.uk
W www.gov.uk/government/organisations/ofqual

OFQUAL became the independent regulator of qualifications, examinations and assessments on 1 April 2010. It is responsible for maintaining standards, improving confidence and distributing information about qualifications and examinations, as well as regulating general and vocational qualifications in England.

Chief Regulator, Sally Collier
Chair, Roger Taylor

OFFICE FOR STANDARDS IN EDUCATION, CHILDREN'S SERVICES AND SKILLS (OFSTED)

Aviation House, 125 Kingsway, London WC2B 6SE
T 0300-123 1231 E enquiries@ofsted.gov.uk
W www.gov.uk/government/organisations/ofsted

Ofsted was established under the Education (Schools Act) 1992 and was relaunched on 1 April 2007 with a wider remit, bringing together four formerly separate inspectorates. It works to raise standards in services through the inspection and regulation of care for children and young people, and inspects education and training for children of all ages. *See also* Education.

HM Chief Inspector, Amanda Spielman
Chair, Prof. Julius Weinburg

ORDNANCE SURVEY

Adanac Drive, Southampton SO16 0AS
T 0345-605 0505 E customerservices@os.uk
W www.ordnancesurvey.co.uk

Ordnance Survey is the national mapping agency for Great Britain. It is a government department and executive agency operating as a trading fund since 1999.

Director-General and Chief Executive, Nigel Clifford

SERIOUS FRAUD OFFICE

2–4 Cockspur Street, London SW1Y 5BS
T 020-7239 7272 E public.enquiries@sfo.gov.uk
W www.sfo.gov.uk

The Serious Fraud Office is an independent government department that investigates and, where appropriate, prosecutes serious or complex fraud, bribery and corruption. It is part of the UK criminal justice system with jurisdiction over England, Wales and Northern Ireland but not Scotland, the Isle of Man or the Channel Islands. The office is headed by a director who is superintended by the Attorney-General.

Director, David Green, CB, QC

SUPREME COURT OF THE UNITED KINGDOM

Parliament Square, London SW1P 3BD
T 020-7960 1900 E enquiries@supremecourt.uk
W www.supremecourt.uk

The Supreme Court of the United Kingdom is the highest domestic judicial authority; it replaced the appellate committee of the House of Lords (the house functioning in its judicial capacity) on 1 October 2009. It is the final court of appeal for cases heard in Great Britain and Northern Ireland (except for criminal cases from Scotland). Cases concerning the interpretation and application of European Union law, including preliminary rulings requested by British courts and tribunals, are decided by the Court of Justice of the European Union (CJEU), and the supreme court can make a reference to the CJEU in appropriate cases. Additionally, in giving effect to rights contained in the European Convention on Human Rights, the supreme court must take account of any decision of the European Court of Human Rights.

The supreme court also assumed jurisdiction in relation to devolution matters under the Scotland Act 1998 (now partly superseded by the Scotland Act 2012), the Northern Ireland Act 1988 and the Government of Wales Act 2006; these powers were transferred from the Judicial Committee of the Privy Council. Ten of the 12 Lords of Appeal in Ordinary (Law Lords) from the House of Lords transferred to the 12-member supreme court when it came into operation (at the same time one law lord retired and another was appointed Master of the Rolls). All new justices of the supreme court are now appointed by an independent selection commission, and, although styled Rt. Hon. Lord, are not members of the House of Lords. Peers who are members of the judiciary are disqualified from sitting or voting in the House of Lords until they retire from their judicial office.

Chief Executive, Mark Ormerod, CB

UK STATISTICS AUTHORITY

1 Drummond Gate, London SW1V 2QQ
T 0845-604 1857 E authority.enquiries@statistics.gov.uk
W www.statisticsauthority.gov.uk

The UK Statistics Authority was established on 1 April 2008 by the Statistics and Registration Service Act 2007 as an independent body operating at arm's length from government, reporting to the UK parliament and the devolved legislatures. Its overall objective is to promote and safeguard the production and publication of official statistics and ensure their quality and comprehensiveness. The authority's main functions are the oversight of the Office for National Statistics (ONS); monitoring and reporting on all UK official statistics, which includes around 30 central government departments and the devolved administrations; and the production of a code of practice for statistics and the assessment of official statistics against the code.

BOARD
Chair, Sir David Norgrove
Board Members, Sian Jones *(Deputy Chair);* Jonathan Athow *(Deputy National Statistician for Economic Statistics);* Iain Bell *(Deputy National Statistician for Population and Public Policy);* Heather Boaden; Prof. Sir Ian Diamond, FBA, FRSE,

FACSS; Prof. David Hand, OBE, FBA; Prof. Jonathan Haskel; Ed Humpherson; Nora Nanayakkara; John Pullinger *(National Statistician);* Heather Savory *(Deputy National Statistician for Data Capability);* Prof. Sir Adrian Smith, FRS; Prof. Anne Trefethen, FBCS, FRENG

OFFICE FOR NATIONAL STATISTICS (ONS)
Cardiff Road, Newport NP10 8XG
T 0845-601 3034 E info@ons.gsi.gov.uk W www.ons.gov.uk

The ONS was created in 1996 by the merger of the Central Statistical Office and the Office of Population Censuses and Surveys. On 1 April 2008 it became the executive office of the UK Statistics Authority. As part of these changes, the office's responsibility for the General Register Office transferred to HM Passport Office of the Home Office.

The ONS is responsible for preparing, interpreting and publishing key statistics on the government, economy and society of the UK. Its key responsibilities include designing, managing and running the Census and providing statistics on health and other demographic matters in England and Wales; the production of the UK National Accounts and other economic indicators; the organisation of population censuses in England and Wales and surveys for government departments and public bodies.

National Statistician, John Pullinger
Director-Generals, Jonathan Athow; Iain Bell; Heather Savory

WATER SERVICES REGULATION AUTHORITY (OFWAT)

Centre City Tower, 7 Hill Street, Birmingham B5 4UA
T 0121-644 7500 E mailbox@ofwat.gov.uk
W www.ofwat.gov.uk

OFWAT is the independent economic regulator of the water and sewerage companies in England and Wales. It is responsible for ensuring that the water industry in England and Wales provides household and business customers with a good quality service and value for money. This is done by ensuring that the companies provide customers with a good quality, efficient service at a fair price; limiting the prices companies can charge; monitoring the companies' performance and taking action, including enforcement, to protect customers' interests; setting the companies efficiency targets; making sure the companies deliver the best for consumers and the environment in the long term; and encouraging competition where it benefits consumers.

Chair, Jonson Cox
Chief Executive, Rachel Fletcher

PUBLIC BODIES

The following section is a listing of public bodies and other civil service organisations: it is not a complete list of these organisations.

Whereas executive agencies are either part of a government department or are one in their own right (*see* Government Departments), public bodies carry out their functions to a greater or lesser extent at arm's length from central government. Ministers are ultimately responsible to parliament for the activities of the public bodies sponsored by their department and in almost all cases (except where there is separate statutory provision) ministers make the appointments to their boards. Departments are responsible for funding and ensuring good governance of their public bodies.

The term 'public body' is a general one which includes public corporations, such as the BBC; NHS bodies; and non-departmental public bodies (NDPBs).

ADJUDICATOR'S OFFICE
PO Box 10280, Nottingham NG2 9PF
T 0300-057 1111 W www.adjudicatorsoffice.gov.uk

The Adjudicator's Office investigates complaints from individuals and businesses about the way that HM Revenue and Customs and the Valuation Office Agency have handled a person's affairs. The Adjudicator's Office will only consider a complaint after the respective organisation's internal complaints procedure has been exhausted.

The Adjudicator, Helen Megarry

ADVISORY, CONCILIATION AND ARBITRATION SERVICE (ACAS)
22nd Floor, Euston Tower, 286 Euston Road, London NW1 3JJ
T 0300-123 1100 W www.acas.org.uk

The Advisory, Conciliation and Arbitration Service was set up under the Employment Protection Act 1975 (the provisions now being found in the Trade Union and Labour Relations (Consolidation) Act 1992).

ACAS is largely funded by the Department for Business, Energy and Industrial Strategy. A council sets its strategic direction, policies and priorities, and ensures that the agreed strategic objectives and targets are met. It consists of a chair and 11 employer, trade union and independent members, appointed by the Secretary of State for Business, Energy and Industrial Strategy.

ACAS aims to improve organisations and working life through better employment relations, to provide up-to-date information, independent advice and high-quality training, and to work with employers and employees to solve problems and improve performance.

ACAS has regional offices in Birmingham, Bristol, Bury St Edmunds, Cardiff, Fleet, Glasgow, Leeds, Manchester, Newcastle upon Tyne and Nottingham. The head office is in London.

Chair, Sir Brendan Barber
Chief Executive, Susan Clews

ADVISORY COUNCIL ON NATIONAL RECORDS AND ARCHIVES
The National Archives, Kew, Surrey TW9 4DU
T 020-8392 5337
E advisorycouncilsecretary@nationalarchives.gov.uk
W http://www.nationalarchives.gov.uk/about/our-role/advisory-council

The Advisory Council on National Records and Archives advises the Secretary of State for Digital, Culture, Media and Sport on issues relating to public records that are over 20 years old including public access to them. The council meets four times a year, and its main task is to consider requests for the extended closure of public records; it also reaches decisions regarding government departments that want to keep records.

The Forum on Historical Manuscripts and Academic Research, a sub-committee of the Advisory Council, provides advice to the Chief Executive of The National Archives and Keeper of Public Records on matters relating to historical manuscripts, records and archives, other than public records.

Chair, Rt. Hon. Sir Terence Etherton *(Master of the Rolls)*

AGRICULTURE AND HORTICULTURE DEVELOPMENT BOARD
Stoneleigh Park, Kenilworth, Warwickshire CV8 2TL
T 024-7669 2051 E info@ahdb.org.uk W www.ahdb.org.uk

The Agriculture and Horticulture Development Board (AHDB) is funded by the agriculture and horticulture industries through statutory levies, with the duty to improve efficiency and competitiveness within six sectors: beef and lamb in England; cereals and oilseeds in the UK; commercial horticulture in Great Britain; milk in Great Britain; pigs in England; and potatoes in Great Britain. The AHDB represents around 70 per cent of total UK agricultural output. Levies raised from the six sectors are ring-fenced to ensure that they can only be used to the benefit of the sectors from which they were raised.

Chair, Sir Peter Kendall
Independent members, Will Lifford; George Lyon; Janet Swadling
Sector members, Hayley Campbell-Gibbons *(Horticulture);* Sophie Churchill *(Potatoes);* Gwyn Jones *(Dairy);* Mike Sheldon *(Pork);* Paul Temple *(Cereals and Oilseeds);* Adam Quinney *(Beef and Lamb)*
Chief Executive, Jane King

ARCHITECTURE AND DESIGN SCOTLAND
9 Bakehouse Close, 146 Canongate, Edinburgh EH8 8DD
T 0131-556 6699 E info@ads.org.uk W www.ads.org.uk

Architecture and Design Scotland (A&DS) was established in 2005 by the Scottish government as the national champion for good architecture, urban design and planning in the built environment; it works with a wide range of organisations at national, regional and local levels.

Chair, Ann Allen
Chief Executive, Jim MacDonald

ARMED FORCES' PAY REVIEW BODY
8th Floor, Fleetbank House, 2–6 Salisbury Square, London EC4Y 8JX
T 020-7211 8315 W www.gov.uk/government/organisations/armed-forces-pay-review-body

The Armed Forces' Pay Review Body was appointed in 1971. It advises the prime minister and the Secretary of State for Defence on the pay and allowances of members of naval, military and air forces of the Crown.

Chair, Peter Maddison, QPM
Members, Brendan Connor; Tim Flesher, CB; Kerry Holden; Prof. Ken Mayhew; Lesley Mercer; Vilma Patterson, MBE; Rear-Admiral (retd) Jon Westbrook, CBE

ARTS COUNCIL ENGLAND
21 Bloomsbury Street, London WC1B 3HF
T 0161-934 4317 W www.artscouncil.org.uk

Arts Council England is the national development agency for the arts in England. Using public money from government and the National Lottery, it supports a range of artistic activities, including theatre, music, literature, dance, photography, digital art, carnival and crafts. Between 2018 and 2022, Arts Council England is investing £408m a year in 829 arts organisations, museums and libraries within its national portfolio, this includes £340m of grant-in-aid and £68m of National Lottery funding; £97.3m of National Lottery funding a year in Arts Council National Lottery project grants, its open-access funding programme; and £72.2m a year in its Arts Council development funds.

The governing body, the national council, comprises 14 members, who are appointed by the Secretary of State for Digital, Culture, Media and Sport usually for a term of four years. There are also five councils, responsible for the agreement of area strategies, plans and priorities for action within the national framework.

National Council Chair, Sir Nicholas Serota, CH
National Council Members, Helen Birchenough; Prof. Roni Brown; Michael Eakin; Ciara Eastell, OBE; Sukhy Johal, MBE; David Joseph; Ruth Mackenzie, CBE; Catherine Mallyon; Andrew Miller; George Mpanga; Elisabeth Murdoch; Paul Roberts, OBE; Tessa Ross; Kate Willard
Chief Executive, Darren Henley, OBE

ARTS COUNCIL OF NORTHERN IRELAND
1 The Sidings, Antrim Road, Lisburn BT28 3AJ
T 028-9262 3555 E info@artscouncil-ni.org
W www.artscouncil-ni.org

The Arts Council of Northern Ireland is the prime distributor of government funds in support of the arts in Northern Ireland. It is funded by the Department for Communities and from National Lottery funds.

Chair, John Edmund
Members, David Alderdice; Anna Carragher; Roisin Erskine; Dr Siún Hanrahan; Dr Leon Litvack; Noelle McAlinden; Katherine McCloskey; Paul Mullan; Dr Katy Radford, MBE *(Vice-Chair);* Cian Smyth
Chief Executive, Roisin McDonough

ARTS COUNCIL OF WALES
Bute Place, Cardiff CF10 5AL
T 029-2044 1300 E comms@arts.wales W www.arts.wales

The Arts Council of Wales was established in 1994 by royal charter and is the development body for the arts in Wales. It funds arts organisations with funding from the Welsh government and is the distributor of National Lottery funds to the arts in Wales.

Chair, Phil George
Members, Iwan Bala; Andy Eagle; Kate Eden; Michael Griffiths; Melanie Hawthorne; Andrew Miller; Rachel O'Riordan; Dafydd Rhys; Richard Turner; Alan Watkin; Marian Wyn Jones
Chief Executive, Nick Capaldi

AUDIT SCOTLAND
102 West Port, Edinburgh EH3 9DN
T 0131-625 1500 E info@audit-scotland.gov.uk
W www.audit-scotland.gov.uk

Audit Scotland was set up in 2000 to provide services to the Accounts Commission and the Auditor-General for Scotland. Together they help to ensure that public-sector bodies in Scotland are held accountable for the proper, efficient and effective use of public funds.

Audit Scotland's is responsible for auditing 224 public bodies, including: 75 Scottish government bodies (including the police, fire and Scottish Water) and the Scottish parliament; 23 NHS bodies; 32 councils; 73 joint boards and committees (including 30 health integration boards); and 21 further education colleges.

Audit Scotland carries out financial and regularity audits to ensure that public-sector bodies adhere to the highest standards of financial management and governance. It also carries out performance audits to ensure that these bodies achieve the best value for money. All of Audit Scotland's work in connection with local authorities is carried out for the Accounts Commission; its other work is undertaken for the Auditor-General.

Chair, Ian Leitch, CBE
Auditor-General, Caroline Gardner
Chair of the Accounts Commission, Dr Graham Sharp

BANK OF ENGLAND
Threadneedle Street, London EC2R 8AH
T 020-3461 4444 E enquiries@bankofengland.co.uk
W www.bankofengland.co.uk

The Bank of England was incorporated in 1694 under royal charter. It was nationalised in 1946 under the Bank of England Act of that year which gave HM Treasury statutory powers over the bank. It is the banker of the government and it manages the issue of banknotes. Since 1998 it has been operationally independent and its Monetary Policy Committee has been responsible for setting short-term interest rates to meet the government's inflation target. Its responsibility for banking supervision was transferred to the Financial Services Authority in the same year. As the central reserve bank of the country, the Bank of England keeps the accounts of British banks, and of most overseas central banks; the larger banks and building societies are required to maintain with it a proportion of their cash resources. The bank's core purposes are monetary stability and financial stability. The Banking Act 2009 increased the responsibilities of the bank, including giving it a new financial stability objective and creating a special resolution regime for dealing with failing banks.

In 2013, through the Prudential Regulation Authority (PRA), the bank became responsible for the prudential regulation and supervision of banks, building societies, credit unions, insurers and major investment firms.

COURT OF DIRECTORS
Governor, Mark Carney
Deputy Governors, Dr Ben Broadbent *(Monetary Policy);* Sir Jon Cunliffe, CB *(Financial Stability);* Sir Dave Ramsden
    Markets and Banking; Sam Woods *(Prudential Regulation)*
Non-Executive Members, Bradley Fried *(Chair, Court of Directors);* Anne Glover, CBE; Baroness Harding of Winscombe; Ron Kalifa, OBE; Diana Noble, CBE; Frances O'Grady; Hanneke Smits; Dorothy Thompson

FINANCIAL POLICY COMMITTEE
Members, Andrew Bailey; Alex Brazier; Dr Ben Broadbent; Mark Carney; Sir Jon Cunliffe, CB; Anil Kashyap; Donald Kohn; Sir Dave Ramsden; Charles Roxburgh; Elisabeth Stheeman; Martin Taylor; Sam Woods

MONETARY POLICY COMMITTEE
Members, Dr Ben Broadbent; Mark Carney; Sir Jon Cunliffe, CB; Andy Haldane; Jonathan Haskel; Sir Dave Ramsden; Michael Saunders; Silvana Tenreyro; Dr Gertjan Vlieghe

Chief Operating Officer, Joanna Place
General Counsel, Sonya Branch
Chief Cashier and Director of Notes, Sarah John

BOUNDARY COMMISSIONS

The commissions, established in 1944, are constituted under the Parliamentary Constituencies Act 1986 (as amended). The Speaker of the House of Commons is the *ex officio* chair of all four commissions in the UK.

The last reviews of UK parliament constituencies were undertaken using the electoral register from 1 December 2015; these reviews were submitted by the commissions in September 2018.

ENGLAND
2nd Floor, 35 Great Smith Street, London SW1P 3BQ
T 020-7276 1102
E information@boundarycommissionengland.gov.uk
W http://boundarycommissionforengland.independent.gov.uk

Deputy Chair, Hon. Mr Justice Nicol

WALES
Hastings House, Fitzalan Court, Cardiff CF24 0BL
T 029-2046 4819 E enquiries@boundaries.wales
W www.bcomm-wales.gov.uk

Deputy Chair, Hon. Mr Justice Lewis

SCOTLAND
Thistle House, 91 Haymarket Terrace, Edinburgh EH12 5HD
T 0131-244 2001 E bcs@scottishboundaries.gov.uk
W www.bcomm-scotland.independent.gov.uk

Deputy Chair, Hon. Lord Matthews

NORTHERN IRELAND
The Bungalow, Stormont House, Stormont Estate, Belfast BT4 3SH
T 028-9052 7821 E contact@boundarycommission.org.uk
W www.boundarycommission.org.uk

Deputy Chair, Hon. Ms Justice McBride, DBE

BRITISH BROADCASTING CORPORATION (BBC)
BBC Broadcasting House, Portland Place, London W1A 1AA
W www.bbc.co.uk

The BBC was incorporated under royal charter in 1926 as successor to the British Broadcasting Company Ltd. The BBC's current charter, which came into force on 1 January 2017 and extends to 31 December 2027, recognises the BBC's editorial independence and sets out its public purposes. The BBC Board was formed under the new charter and is responsible for ensuring that the Corporation fulfils its mission and public purposes by setting the strategic direction of the BBC, establishing its creative remit, setting the budget and determining the framework for assessing performance. As part of the new charter, The Office of Communications (OFCOM) was awarded sole regulatory responsibility for the BBC. The BBC is financed by television licence revenue to ensure it remains independent from political control.

BBC BOARD
Chair, Sir David Clementi
Director-General, Lord Hall of Birkenhead, CBE
National Members, Steve Morrison *(Scotland)*; Dr Ashley Steel *(England)*; Dame Elan Closs Stephens, DBE *(Wales)*
Members, Simon Burke *(Senior Independent Director)*; Tim Davie *(CEO BBC Studios)*; Ken MacQuarrie *(Nations and Regions)*; Francesca Unsworth *(News and Current Affairs)*
Non-Executive Members, Baroness Grey-Thompson, DBE; Ian Hargreaves, CBE; Tom Ilube; Sir Nicholas Serota, CH

EXECUTIVE COMMITTEE
Director-General, Lord Hall of Birkenhead, CBE
Directors, Kerris Bright *(Chief Customer Officer)*; Tim Davie *(CEO, BBC Studios)*; Valerie Hughes-D'Aeth *(Human*

Resources); Glyn Isherwood *(Chief Financial Officer)*; David Jordan *(Editorial Policy and Standards)*; Ken MacQuarrie *(Nations and Regions)*; Charlotte Moore *(Content)*; Matthew Postgate *(Chief Technology and Product Officer)*; James Purnell *(Radio and Education)*; Gautam Rangarajan *(Strategy)*; John Sheild *(Communications and Corporate Affairs)*; Clare Sumner *(Policy)*; Francesca Unsworth *(News and Current Affairs)*

CHANNEL AND PLATFORM HEADS
Director of BBC Content and BBC One, Charlotte Moore
Controller BBC Two, Patrick Holland
Controller BBC Three, Fiona Campbell
Editor BBC Four, Cassian Harrison
Controller of Programming and Daytime, Dan McGolpin
Director of Sport, Barbara Slater
Head of Content BBC Children's, Cheryl Taylor

GENRE CONTROLLERS
Entertainment, Kate Phillips
Factual, Alison Kirkham
Drama, Piers Wenger
Comedy, Shane Allen

Director of BBC Radio and BBC Music, Bob Shennan

BRITISH COUNCIL
Bridgewater House, 58 Whitworth Street, Manchester M1 6BB
T 0161-957 7755 E general.enquiries@britishcouncil.org
W www.britishcouncil.org

The British Council was established in 1934, incorporated by royal charter in 1940 and granted a supplemental charter in 1993. It is an independent, non-political organisation which promotes Britain abroad and is the UK's international organisation for educational and cultural relations. The British Council is represented in over 100 countries.

Chair, Christopher Rodrigues, CBE
Chief Executive, Sir Ciarán Devane

BRITISH FILM INSTITUTE
21 Stephen Street, London W1T 1LN
T 020-7255 1444 W www.bfi.org.uk

The BFI, established in 1933, offers opportunities for people throughout the UK to experience, learn and discover more about the world of film and moving image culture. It incorporates the BFI National Archive, the BFI Reuben Library, BFI Southbank, BFI Distribution, the annual BFI London Film Festival as well as the BFI FLARE: London LGBT Film Festival, and the BFI IMAX cinema. It also publishes the monthly *Sight and Sound* magazine and provides advice and support for regional cinemas and film festivals across the UK.

Following the closure of the UK Film Council in April 2011, the BFI became the lead body for film in the UK, in charge of allocating lottery money for the development and production of new British films.

Chair, Josh Berger, CBE
Chief Executive, Amanda Nevill

BRITISH LIBRARY
96 Euston Road, London NW1 2DB
T 020-7412 7676 E customer-services@bl.uk W www.bl.uk

The British Library was established in 1973. It is the UK's national library and one of the world's greatest research libraries. It aims to serve scholarship, research, industry, commerce and all other major users of information. The Library's collection has developed over 250 years and exceeds 170 million items, including books, journals, manuscripts, maps, stamps, music, patents, newspapers and sound recordings in all written and spoken languages. The library is now based at two sites: London St Pancras and Boston Spa, W.

Yorks. The library's sponsoring department is the Department for Digital, Culture, Media and Sport. Up to 3 million digitised items are added to the collection each year.

BRITISH LIBRARY BOARD

Chair, Dame Carol Black, DBE, FRCP
Members, Dr Robert Black, CBE, FRSE; Jonathan Callaway; Tracy Chevalier, FRSL; Martin Dickson; Lord Janvrin, GCB, GCVO, QSO, PC; Roly Keating; Patrick Plant; Sir John Ritblat; Dr Simon Thurley, CBE; Prof. Dame Helen Wallace, DBE, CMG, FBA

EXECUTIVE
Chief Executive, Roly Keating
Chief Librarian, Liz Jolly
Chief Operating Officer, Phil Spence

BRITISH LIBRARY, BOSTON SPA
Boston Spa, Wetherby, W. Yorks LS23 7BQ
T 01937-546070

BRITISH MUSEUM
Great Russell Street, London WC1B 3DG
T 020-7323 8000 E info@britishmuseum.org
W www.britishmuseum.org

The British Museum houses the national collection of antiquities, ethnography, coins and paper money, medals, prints and drawings. The British Museum dates from 7 June 1753, when parliament approved the holding of a public lottery to raise funds for the purchase of the collections of Sir Hans Sloane and the Harleian manuscripts, and for their proper housing and maintenance. The building (Montagu House) was opened in 1759. The existing buildings were erected between 1823 and the present day, and the original collection has increased to its current dimensions by gifts and purchases. Total government grant-in-aid for 2017–18 was £53.6m.

Chair, Sir Richard Lambert
Trustees, Hon. Nigel Boardman; Cheryl Carolus; Elizabeth Corley, CBE; Patricia Cumper, MBE; Clarissa Farr; Prof. Chris Gosden; Muriel Gray; Prof. Nicola Lacey, FBA; Sir Richard Lambert; Sir Deryck Maughan; Sir Charles Mayfield; John Micklethwait, CBE; Sir Paul Nurse, FRS; Gavin Patterson; Mark Pears, CBE; Grayson Perry, CBE, RA; Sir Paul Ruddock; Lord Sassoon; Dame Nemat (Minouche) Shafik; Ahdaf Soueif; Lord Turner of Ecchinswell, FRS

OFFICERS
Director, Dr Hartwig Fischer
Deputy Directors, Joanna Mackle; Jonathan Williams; Christopher Yates

KEEPERS
Keeper of Africa, Oceania and the Americas, Lissant Bolton
Keeper of Ancient Egypt and Sudan, Neal Spencer
Keeper of Asia, Jane Portal
Deputy Keeper of Britain, Europe and Prehistory, Jill Cook
Keeper of Coins and Medals, Philip Attwood
Keeper of Greece and Rome, J. Lesley Fitton
Keeper of the Middle East, Jonathan N. Tubb
Keeper of Portable Antiquities and Treasure, Roger Bland
Keeper of Prints and Drawings, Hugo Chapman

BRITISH PHARMACOPOEIA COMMISSION
151 Buckingham Palace Road, London SW1W 9SZ
T 020-3080 6561 E bpcom@mhra.gov.uk
W www.pharmacopoeia.com

The British Pharmacopoeia Commission sets standards for medicinal products used in human and veterinary medicines and is responsible for publication of *British Pharmacopoeia* (a publicly available statement of the standard that a medicinal substance or product must meet throughout its shelf-life),

British Pharmacopoeia (Veterinary) and *British Approved Names.* It has 17 members, including two lay members, who are appointed on behalf of the Secretary of State for Health and Social Care by the Department of Health and Social Care.

Chair, Prof. Kevin Taylor
Vice-Chair, Prof. Alastair Davidson

CARE QUALITY COMMISSION
Citygate, Gallowgate, Newcastle upon Tyne NE1 4PA
T 0300-061 6161 E enquiries@cqc.org.uk W www.cqc.org.uk

The Care Quality Commission (CQC) is the independent regulator of health and adult social care services in England, ensuring health and social care services provide people with safe, effective, compassionate, high-quality care and encouraging them to improve. CQC monitors, inspects and regulates services to make sure they meet fundamental standards of quality and safety and publishes performance ratings to help people choose care.

Chair, Peter Wyman, CBE
Board Members, Prof. Louis Appleby, CBE; Prof. Ted Baker; Rosie Benneyworth; Paul Corrigan, CBE; Sir Robert Francis, QC; Dr Malte Gerhold; Jora Gill; Sir John Oldham; Paul Rew; Mark Saxton; Liz Sayce, OBE; Kirsty Shaw; Debbie Westhead
Chief Executive, Ian Trenholm

CENTRAL ARBITRATION COMMITTEE
Fleetbank House, 2-6 Salisbury Square, London EC4Y 8JX
T 0330-109 3610 E enquiries@cac.gov.uk
W www.gov.uk/government/organisations/
central-arbitration-committee

The Central Arbitration Committee (CAC) is a permanent independent body with statutory powers whose main function is to adjudicate on applications relating to the statutory recognition and de-recognition of trade unions for collective bargaining purposes, where such recognition or de-recognition cannot be agreed voluntarily. In addition, the CAC has a statutory role in determining disputes between trade unions and employers over the disclosure of information for collective bargaining purposes, and in resolving applications and complaints under the information and consultation regulations, and performs a similar role in relation to the legislation on the European Works Council, European companies, European cooperative societies and cross-border mergers. The CAC and its predecessors have also provided voluntary arbitration in collective disputes.

Chair, Stephen Redmond
Chief Executive, James Jacob

CERTIFICATION OFFICE FOR TRADE UNIONS AND EMPLOYERS' ASSOCIATIONS
Lower Ground Floor, Fleetbank House, 2-6 Salisbury Square, London EC4Y 8JX
T 0330-109 3602 E info@certoffice.org
W www.gov.uk/government/organisations/certification-officer

The Certification Office is an independent statutory authority. The Certification Officer is appointed by the Secretary of State for Business, Energy and Industrial Strategy and is responsible for maintaining a list of trade unions and employers' associations; ensuring compliance with statutory requirements and keeping available for public inspection annual returns from trade unions and employers' associations; determining complaints concerning trade union elections, certain ballots and certain breaches of trade union rules; ensuring observance of statutory requirements governing mergers between trade unions and between employers' associations; overseeing the political funds and finances of trade unions and employers' associations; and for certifying the independence of trade unions.

Certification Officer, Sarah Bedwell

CHURCH COMMISSIONERS

Church House, Great Smith Street, London SW1P 3AZ
T 020-7898 1000 E commissioners.enquiry@churchofengland.org
W www.churchofengland.org/about/leadership-and-governance/
church-commissioners

The Church Commissioners were established in 1948 by the amalgamation of Queen Anne's Bounty (established 1704) and the Ecclesiastical Commissioners (established 1836). They are responsible for the management of some of the Church of England's assets, the income from which is predominantly used to help pay for the stipend and pension of the clergy and to support the church's work throughout the country. The commissioners own UK and global company shares, over 120,000 acres of forestry estate, a residential estate in central London, and commercial property across Great Britain, plus an interest in overseas property via managed funds. They also carry out administrative duties in connection with pastoral reorganisation and closed churches.

The 33 commissioners are: the Archbishops of Canterbury and of York; eleven people elected by the General Synod, comprising four bishops, three clergy and four lay persons; three Church Estates Commissioners; two cathedral deans; nine people appointed by the crown and the archbishops; six holders of state office, comprising the Prime Minister, the Lord Chancellor, the Lord President of the Council, the Secretary of State for Digital, Culture, Media and Sport, the Speaker of the House of Commons and the Lord Speaker.

CHURCH ESTATES COMMISSIONERS
First, Loretta Minghella, OBE
Second, Rt. Hon. Dame Caroline Spelman, DBE, MP
Third, Dr Eve Poole

OFFICERS
Chief Executive, Andrew Brown
Official Solicitor, Revd Alexander McGregor

COAL AUTHORITY

200 Lichfield Lane, Mansfield, Notts NG18 4RG
T 0345-762 6848 E thecoalauthority@coal.gov.uk
W www.gov.uk/government/organisations/the-coal-authority

The Coal Authority was established under the Coal Industry Act 1994 to manage certain functions previously undertaken by British Coal, including ownership of unworked coal. It is responsible for licensing coal mining operations and for providing information on coal reserves and past and future coal mining. It settles subsidence damage claims which are not the responsibility of licensed coal mining operators. It deals with the management and disposal of property, and with surface hazards such as abandoned coal mine entries and mine water discharges. The Coal Authority's powers were extended alongside the Energy Act 2011 to enable it to deal with metal mine subsidence issues and deliver a metal mine water treatment programme.

Chair, Stephen Dingle
Chief Executive, Lisa Pinney, MBE

COMMITTEE ON STANDARDS IN PUBLIC LIFE

1 Horse Guards Road, London SW1A 2HQ
T 020-7271 2948 E public@public-standards.gov.uk
W www.gov.uk/government/organisations/
the-committee-on-standards-in-public-life

The Committee on Standards in Public Life (CSPL) was set up in October 1994. It is formed of 8 people appointed by the prime minister, comprising the chair, three political members nominated by the leaders of the three main political parties and four independent members. The CSPL advises the prime minister on ethical standards across the whole of public life in the UK. It monitors and reports on issues relating to the standards of conduct of all public office holders. It is responsible for promoting the seven principles of public life, being: selflessness; integrity; objectivity; accountability; openness; honesty; and leadership.

Chair, Lord Evans of Weardale, KCB
Members, Dame Margaret Beckett, DBE, PC, MP; Simon Hart, MP; Dr Jane Martin, CBE; Dame Shirley Pearce, DBE; Jane Ramsey; Monisha Shah; Lord Stunell, OBE, PC

COMMONWEALTH WAR GRAVES COMMISSION

2 Marlow Road, Maidenhead, Berks SL6 7DX
T 01628-634221 E enquiries@cwgc.org W www.cwgc.org

The Commonwealth War Graves Commission (formerly Imperial War Graves Commission) was founded by royal charter in 1917. It is responsible for the commemoration of around 1.7 million members of the forces of the Commonwealth who lost their lives in the two world wars. More than one million graves are maintained in over 23,000 burial grounds across 154 countries. Over three-quarters of a million men and women who have no known grave or who were cremated are commemorated by name on memorials built by the commission.

The funds of the commission are derived from the six participating governments: the UK, Canada, Australia, New Zealand, South Africa and India.

President, HRH the Duke of Kent, KG, GCMG, GCVO, ADC
Chair, Secretary of State for Defence
Vice-Chair, Vice-Adm. Sir Tim Laurence, KCVO, CB, ADC(P)
Members, High Commissioners in London for Australia, Canada, India, New Zealand and South Africa; Edward Chaplin, CMG, OBE; Rt. Hon. Philip Dunne, MP; Diana Johnson, MP; Dame Judith Mayhew Jonas, DBE; Hon. Ros Kelly; Lt.-Gen. Sir William Rollo, KCB, CBE; Vasuki Shastry; Air Marshal David Walker, CB, CBE, AFC
Director-General and Secretary to the Commission, Victoria Wallace

COMPETITION SERVICE

Victoria House, Bloomsbury Place, London WC1A 2EB
T 020-7979 7979 W www.catribunal.org.uk

The Competition Service is the financial corporate body by which the Competition Appeal Tribunal is administered and through which it receives funding for the performance of its judicial functions.

Registrar, Charles Dhanowa, OBE, QC

CONSUMER COUNCIL FOR WATER

Victoria Square House, Victoria Square, Birmingham, B2 4AJ
T 0300-034 2222 E enquiries@ccwater.org.uk
W www.ccwater.org.uk

The Consumer Council for Water was established in 2005 under the Water Act 2003 to represent consumers' interests in respect of price, service and value for money from their water and sewerage services, and to investigate complaints from customers about their water company. There are four regional committees in England and one in Wales.

Chair, Alan Lovell
Chief Executive, Tony Smith

CORPORATION OF TRINITY HOUSE

Trinity House, Tower Hill, London EC3N 4DH
T 020-7481 6900 E enquiries@trinityhouse.co.uk
W www.trinityhouse.co.uk

The Corporation of Trinity House of Deptford Strond is the UK's largest-endowed maritime charity, established formally by royal charter by Henry VIII in 1514, with statutory duties as the General Lighthouse Authority (GLA) for England, Wales, the Channel Islands and Gibraltar. Its remit is to assist the safe passage of a variety of vessels through some of the busiest sea-lanes in the world; it does this by inspecting and auditing almost 11,000 local aids to navigation, ranging from lighthouses to a satellite navigation service. The corporation also has certain statutory jurisdiction over aids to navigation maintained by local harbour authorities and is responsible for marking or dispersing wrecks dangerous to navigation, except those occurring within port limits or wrecks of HM ships.

The statutory duties of Trinity House are funded by the General Lighthouse Fund, which is provided from light dues levied on commercial vessels calling at ports in the British Isles, based on the net registered tonnage of the vessel. Light Dues are paid into the General Lighthouse Fund under the stewardship of the Department for Transport. The fund finances the work of Trinity House and the Northern Lighthouse Board (Scotland and the Isle of Man). The corporation is a deep-sea pilotage authority, authorised by the Secretary of State for Transport to license deep-sea pilots. In addition, Trinity House is a charitable organisation that maintains a number of retirement homes for mariners and their dependants, funds a four-year training scheme for those seeking a career in the merchant navy, and also dispenses grants to a wide range of maritime charities. Trinity House's maritime and corporate charities are entirely self-funded by incomes derived from endowed funds.

The corporation is controlled by a court of 31 elected Elder Brethren, who oversee the corporate and lighthouse boards. The Elder Brethren also act as nautical assessors in marine cases in the Admiralty Division of the High Court.

ELDER BRETHREN

Master, HRH the Princess Royal, KG, KT, GCVO
Deputy Master, Capt. Ian McNaught, CVO
Wardens, Capt. Nigel Palmer, OBE *(Rental);* Rear-Adm. David Snelson, CB *(Nether)*
Elder Brethren, HRH the Duke of Edinburgh, KG, KT, OM, GBE; HRH the Prince of Wales, KG, KT, GCB; HRH the Duke of York, KG, GCVO, ADC; Capt. Roger Barker; Adm. Lord Boyce, KG, GCB, OBE; Capt. Lord Browne of Madingley, FRS, FRENG; Capt. John Burton-Hall, RD, RNR; Viscount Cobham; Cdre Robert Dorey, RFA; Capt. Sir Malcolm Edge, KCVO; Capt. Ian Gibb, MBE; Malcolm Glaister; Capt. Duncan Glass, OBE; Capt. Stephen Gobbi; Lord Greenway, Bt.; Rear-Adm. Sir Jeremy de Halpert, KCVO, CB; Capt. Nigel Hope, RD, RNR; Lord Mackay of Clashfern, KT, PC; Sir John Major, KG, CH, PC; Capt. Peter Mason, CBE; Cdre Peter Melson, CVO, CBE, RN; Capt. David Orr; Sir John Parker, GBE; Douglas Potter; Capt. Nigel Pryke; Richard Sadler; Lord Robertson of Port Ellen, KT, GCMG, PC; Rear-Adm. Sir Patrick Rowe, KCVO, CBE; Cdre James Scorer, RN; Simon Sherrard; Adm. Sir Jock Slater, GCB, LVO; Cdre David Squire, CBE, RFA; Vice-Adm. Lord Sterling of Plaistow, GCVO, CBE, RNR; Capt. Colin Stewart, LVO; Capt. Thomas Woodfield, OBE; Capt. Richard Woodman, LVO; Cdre William Walworth, CBE; Adm. Sir George Zambellas, GCB, DSC

OFFICERS
Secretary, Thomas Arculus
Director of Business Services, Ton Damen, RA
Director of Navigational Requirements, Capt. Roger Barker
Director of Operations, Cdre Rob Dorey

CREATIVE SCOTLAND
Waverley Gate, 2–4 Waterloo Place, Edinburgh EH1 3EG
T 0330-333 2000 E enquiries@creativescotland.com
W www.creativescotland.com

Creative Scotland is the organisation tasked with leading the development of the arts, creative and screen industries across Scotland. It was created in 2010 as an amalgamation of the Scottish Arts Council and Scottish Screen, and it encourages and sustains the arts through investment in the form of grants, bursaries, loans and equity. It aims to invest in talent; artistic production; audiences, access and participation; and the cultural economy. Total Scottish government grant-in-aid funding for 2019–20 is £62m.

Chair, Robert Wilson
Board, Ian Aitchison; Ewan Angus; David Brew; Karen Forbes; Erin Forster; Sheila Murray, FRSA; Cate Nelson-Shaw; Elizabeth Partyka; David Strachan; Karthik Subramanya
Chief Executive, Iain Munro *(acting)*

CRIMINAL CASES REVIEW COMMISSION
5 St Philip's Place, Birmingham B3 2PW
T 0121-233 1473 E info@ccrc.gov.uk W www.ccrc.gov.uk

The Criminal Cases Review Commission is the independent body set up under the Criminal Appeal Act 1995. It is a non-departmental public body reporting to parliament via the Lord Chancellor and Secretary of State for Justice. It is responsible for investigating possible miscarriages of justice in England, Wales and Northern Ireland, and deciding whether or not to refer cases back to an appeal court. Members of the commission are appointed in accordance with the Office of the Commissioner for Public Appointments' code of practice.

Chair, Helen Pitcher, OBE
Members, David Brown, QFSM; Cindy Butts; Ian Comfort; Rachel Ellis; Jill Gramann; Johanna Higgins; Celia Hughes; Sukhvinder Kaur; Stephen Leach, CB; Linda Lee; Jennifer Portway; Christine Smith, QC; Robert Ward, CBE
Chief Executive, Karen Kneller

CROFTING COMMISSION
Great Glen House, Leachkin Road, Inverness IV3 8NW
T 01463-663439 E info@crofting.gov.scot
W www.crofting.scotland.gov.uk

The Crofting Commission was established on 1 April 2012, taking over the regulation of crofting from the Crofters Commission. The aim of the Crofting Commission is to regulate crofting, to promote the occupancy of crofts, active land use, and shared management of the land by crofters, as a means of sustaining and enhancing rural communities in Scotland.

Chief Executive, Bill Barron

CROWN ESTATE
St James's Market, London SW1Y 4AH
T 020-7851 5000 E enquiries@thecrownestate.co.uk
W www.thecrownestate.co.uk

The Crown Estate is part of the hereditary possessions of the sovereign 'in right of the crown', managed under the provisions of the Crown Estate Act 1961. It had a capital value of £14.1bn in 2018 , and includes substantial blocks of urban property, primarily in London, almost 95,000 hectares of rural land, around half of the foreshore, and the seabed out to the 12 nautical mile territorial limit throughout the UK. The Crown Estate has a duty to maintain and enhance the capital value of estate and the income obtained from it. Under the terms of the act, the estate pays its revenue surplus to the Treasury every year.

Chair and First Commissioner, Robin Budenberg, CBE
Chief Executive and Second Commissioner, Dame Alison Nimmo, DBE, FRICS

DISCLOSURE AND BARRING SERVICE
PO Box 3961, Royal Wootton Bassett SN4 4HF
T 0300-020 0190 E customerservices@dbs.gsi.gov.uk
W www.gov.uk/government/organisations/
disclosure-and-barring-service

The Disclosure and Barring Service (DBS) is an executive non-departmental public body of the Home Office. It helps employers make safer recruitment decisions and prevent unsuitable people from working with vulnerable groups, including children. It was formed on 1 December 2012 and replaced the Criminal Records Bureau (CRB) and Independent Safeguarding Authority (ISA). The DBS is responsible for the children's barred list and adults' barred list for England, Wales and Northern Ireland.

Chair, Dr Gillian Fairfield
Chief Executive, Adele Downey

ENVIRONMENT AGENCY
PO Box 544, Rotherham S60 1BY
T 0370-850 6506 E enquiries@environment-agency.gov.uk
Incident Hotline 0800-807060
W www.gov.uk/government/organisations/environment-agency

Established in 1996 under the Environment Act 1995, the Environment Agency is a non-departmental public body sponsored by the Department for Environment, Food and Rural Affairs. On 1 April 2013, Natural Resources Wales took over the Environment Agency's responsibilities in Wales. Around 68 per cent of the agency's funding is from the government, with the rest raised from various charging schemes. The agency is responsible for pollution prevention and control in England and for the management and use of water resources, including flood defences, fisheries and navigation. Its remit also includes: scrutinising potentially hazardous business operations; helping businesses to use resources more efficiently; taking action against those who do not take environmental responsibilities seriously; looking after wildlife; working with farmers; helping people get the most out of their environment; and improving the quality of inner city areas and parks by restoring rivers and lakes.

The Environment Agency has head offices in Bristol and London, as well as offices across England, divided into 14 regions. Its total grant-in-aid for 2017–18 was £850m.

Chair, Emma Howard Boyd
Deputy Chair, Richard Macdonald
Board Members, Maria Adebowale-Schwarte; Judith Batchelar, OBE; Lynne Frostick; Robert Gould; John Lelliott, OBE; Caroline Mason, CBE; John Varley, OBE; Gill Weeks, OBE
Chief Executive, Sir James Bevan

EQUALITY AND HUMAN RIGHTS COMMISSION
Arndale House, The Arndale Centre, Manchester M4 3AQ
T 0161-829 8100 E correspondence@equalityhumanrights.com
W www.equalityhumanrights.com

The Equality and Human Rights Commission (EHRC) is a statutory body, established under the Equality Act 2006 and launched in October 2007. It inherited the responsibilities of the Commission for Racial Equality, the Disability Rights Commission and the Equal Opportunities Commission. The EHRC's purpose is to reduce inequality, eliminate discrimination, strengthen relations between people, and promote and protect human rights. It enforces equality legislation on age, disability, gender reassignment, marriage and civil partnership, pregnancy and maternity, race, religion or belief, sex and sexual orientation, and encourages compliance with the Human Rights Act 1998 throughout England, Wales and Scotland.

Chair, David Isaac, CBE
Deputy Chair, Caroline Waters, OBE
Commissioners, Suzanne Baxter; Pavita Cooper; Alasdair Hendersonsan Johnson, OBE; Mark McLane; Helen Mahy, CBE; June Milligan *(Wales Commissioner);* Dr Lesley Sawers, OBE *(Scotland Commissioner);* Prof. Swaran Singh
Chief Executive, Rebecca Hilsenrath

EQUALITY COMMISSION FOR NORTHERN IRELAND
Equality House, 7–9 Shaftesbury Square, Belfast BT2 7DP
T 028-9050 0600Textphone 028-9050 0589
E information@equalityni.org W www.equalityni.org

The Equality Commission was set up in 1999 under the Northern Ireland Act 1998 and is responsible for promoting equality, keeping the relevant legislation under review, eliminating discrimination on the grounds of age, race, disability, sex and sexual orientation, gender (including marital and civil partner status, gender reassignment, pregnancy and maternity), religion and political opinion, and for overseeing the statutory duties on public authorities to promote equality of opportunity and good relations.

Chief Commissioner, Dr Michael Wardlow
Deputy Chief Commissioner, Revd Dr Lesley Carroll
Chief Executive, Dr Evelyn Collins, CBE

GAMBLING COMMISSION
Victoria Square House, Victoria Square, Birmingham B2 4BP
T 0121-230 6666 E info@gamblingcommission.gov.uk
W www.gamblingcommission.gov.uk

The Gambling Commission was established under the Gambling Act 2005, and took over the role previously occupied by the Gaming Board for Great Britain in regulating and licensing all commercial gambling – apart from spread betting and the National Lottery – ie casinos, bingo, betting, remote gambling, gaming machines and lotteries. It also advises local and central government on related issues, and is responsible for the protection of children and the vulnerable from being harmed by gambling. In October 2013, the Gambling Commission took over all the responsibilities of the National Lottery Commission in regulating the National Lottery. The commission is sponsored by the Department for Digital, Culture, Media and Sport, with its work funded by licence fees paid by the gambling industry.

Chair, Dr Bill Moyes
Commissioners, John Baillie; Carol Brady; Stephen Cohen; Alison Hastings; Sarika Patel; Trevor Pearce, CBE, QPM; Simone Pennie; Jonathan Scott; Catharine Seddon
Chief Executive, Neil McArthur, MBE

HEALTH AND SAFETY EXECUTIVE
Redgrave Court, Merton Road, Bootle, Merseyside L20 7HS
T 0300-003 1747 W www.hse.gov.uk

The Health and Safety Commission (HSC) and the Health and Safety Executive (HSE) merged on 1 April 2008 to form a single national regulatory body – the HSE – responsible for promoting the cause of better health and safety at work. The HSE is sponsored by the Department for Work and Pensions. HSE regulates all industrial and commercial sectors except operations in the air and at sea. This includes agriculture, construction, manufacturing, services, transport, mines, offshore oil and gas, quarries and major hazard sites in chemicals and petrochemicals.

HSE is responsible for developing and enforcing health and safety law; providing guidance and advice; commissioning research; conducting inspections and accident and ill-health investigations; developing standards; and licensing or approving some work activities such as asbestos removal.

Chair, Martin Temple, CBE
Board Members, Jonathan Baume; George Brechin; Janice Crawford; Martin Esom; Susan Johnson, OBE; Sir Paul Kenny; Sarah Pinch; Ken Robertson; Kevin Rowan; Martyn Thomas
Chief Executive, Sarah Albon

HER MAJESTY'S OFFICERS OF ARMS

COLLEGE OF ARMS (HERALDS' COLLEGE)
130 Queen Victoria Street, London EC4V 4BT
T 020-7248 2762 W www.college-of-arms.gov.uk

The Sovereign's Officers of Arms (King's, Heralds and Pursuivants of Arms) were first incorporated by Richard III in 1484. The powers vested by the crown in the Earl Marshal (the Duke of Norfolk) with regard to state ceremonial are largely exercised through the college. The college is also the official repository of the arms and pedigrees of English, Welsh, Northern Irish and Commonwealth (except Canadian) families and their descendants, and its records include official copies of the records of the Ulster King of Arms, the originals of which remain in Dublin. The 13 officers of the college specialise in genealogical and heraldic work for their respective clients.
   Arms have long been, and still are, granted by letters patent from the Kings of Arms. A right to arms can only be established by the registration in the official records of the College of Arms of a pedigree showing direct male line descent from an ancestor already appearing therein as being entitled to arms, or by making application through the College of Arms for a grant of arms. Grants are made to corporations as well as to individuals.

Earl Marshal, the Duke of Norfolk

KINGS OF ARMS
Garter, Thomas Woodcock, CVO, FSA
Clarenceux, Patric Dickinson, LVO
Norroy and Ulster, Timothy Duke, FSA

HERALDS
Lancaster, Robert Noel
Somerset, David White
Richmond, Clive Cheesman, FSA
York, Peter O'Donoghue, FSA
Chester, Hon. Christopher Fletcher-Vane
Windsor, John Allen-Petrie

PURSUIVANTS
Rouge Dragon, Adam Tuck
Bluemantle, Mark Scott
Portcullis, vacant
Rouge Croix, vacant

COURT OF THE LORD LYON
HM New Register House, Edinburgh EH1 3YT
T 0131-556 7255 E lyonoffice@gov.scot
W www.courtofthelordlyon.scot

Her Majesty's Officers of Arms in Scotland perform ceremonial duties and, in addition, may be consulted by members of the public on heraldic and genealogical matters in a professional capacity.

KING OF ARMS
Lord Lyon King of Arms, Dr Joseph Morrow, CBE, QC

HERALDS
Rothesay, Sir Crispin Agnew of Lochnaw, Bt., QC
Snawdoun, Elizabeth Roads, LVO, FSA, FSA SCOT
Marchmont, Hon. Adam Bruce, WS

PURSUIVANTS
Dingwall, Yvonne Holton
Unicorn, Liam Devlin
Carrick, George Way of Plean

EXTRAORDINARY OFFICERS
Orkney Herald Extraordinary, Sir Malcolm Innes of Edingight, KCVO, WS
Angus Herald Extraordinary, Robin Blair, CVO, WS
Ross Herald Extraordinary, Mark Dennis
Islay Herald Extraordinary, vacant
Linlithgow Pursuivant Extraordinary, John Stirling, WS
Falkland Pursuivant Extraordinary, Roderick Macpherson

HIGHLANDS AND ISLANDS ENTERPRISE
An Lòchran, 10 Inverness Campus, Inverness IV2 5NA
T 01463-245245 E info@hient.co.uk W www.hie.co.uk

Highlands and Islands Enterprise (HIE) was set up under the Enterprise and New Towns (Scotland) Act 1991. Its role is to deliver community and economic development in line with the Scottish government economic strategy. It focuses on four priorities: supporting businesses and social enterprises; strengthening communities and fragile areas; developing growth sectors; and creating the conditions for a competitive and low carbon region. HIE's draft budget for 2019–20 is £61m.

Chair, Prof. Lorne Crerar
Chief Executive, Charlotte Wright

HISTORIC ENGLAND
Cannon Bridge House, 25 Dowgate Hill, London EC4R 2YA
T 020-7973 3700 E customers@historicengland.org.uk
W www.historicengland.org.uk

Established under the National Heritage Act 1983, Historic England, officially the Historic Buildings and Monuments Commission for England, has three statutory purposes: to secure the preservation of ancient monuments and historic buildings; to promote the preservation and enhancement of the character and appearance of conservation areas; and to promote the public's enjoyment of, and advance their knowledge of, ancient monuments and historic buildings. In 2018–19 Historic England received £91.6m grant-in-aid from the Department for Digital, Culture, Media and Sport.

Chair, Sir Laurie Magnus
Commissioners, Alex Balfour; Nicholas Boys Smith; Prof. Martin Daunton; Sandra Dinneen; Paul Farmer; Prof. Michael Fulford, CBE; Victoria Harley; Rosemarie MacQueen, MBE; Neil Mendoza; Michael Morrison; Patrick Newberry; Charles O'Brien; Susie Thornberry; Richard Upton
Chief Executive, Duncan Wilson, OBE

HISTORIC ENVIRONMENT SCOTLAND
Longmore House, Salisbury Place, Edinburgh EH9 1SH
T 0131-668 8600 W www.historicenvironment.scot

Historic Environment Scotland is the lead public body established to investigate, care for and promote Scotland's historic environment. It is the result of the bringing together of two of Scotland's leading heritage bodies, Historic Scotland and the Royal Commission on Ancient and Historical Monuments Scotland, and has been formed to help deliver the Our Place in Time strategy. It is responsible for more than 300 properties of national importance, including Edinburgh Castle, Skara Brae and Fort George, and for collections that include more than 5 million drawings, photographs, negatives and manuscripts, along with Scotland's National Collection of

Aerial Photography, containing more than 26 million aerial images. The Historic Environment Scotland's draft budget from the Scottish government for 2019–20 is £39.8m.

Chair, Jane Ryder, OBE
Trustees, Ian Brennan; Dr Janet Brennan; Trudi Craggs; Andrew Holmes; Amanda Livingstone; Dr Coinneach Maclean; Dr Fiona McLean; Ian Robertson; Dr Paul Stollard; Dr Ken Thomson
Chief Executive, Alex Paterson

HISTORIC ROYAL PALACES
Apartment 39A, Hampton Court Palace, Surrey KT8 9AU
T 020-3166 6000 E operators@hrp.org.uk W www.hrp.org.uk

Historic Royal Palaces was established in 1998 as a royal charter body with charitable status and is contracted by the Secretary of State for Digital, Culture, Media and Sport to manage the palaces on his behalf. The palaces – the Tower of London, Hampton Court Palace, the Banqueting House, Kensington Palace and Kew Palace – are owned by the Queen on behalf of the nation. Since 1 April 2014, Historic Royal Palaces is also responsible for the management of Hillsborough Castle in Northern Ireland under contract with the Secretary of State for Northern Ireland.

The organisation is governed by a board comprising a chair and 11 non-executive trustees. The chief executive is accountable to the board of trustees and ultimately to parliament. Historic Royal Palaces receives no funding from the government or the Crown.

TRUSTEES

Chair, Rupert Gavin
Appointed by the Queen, Zeinab Badawi; Ajay Chowdhury; Tim Knox (ex officio, Director of the Royal Collection Trust); Sir Michael Stevens, KCVO (ex officio, the Keeper of the Privy Purse)
Appointed by the Secretary of State, Bruce Carnegie-Brown (ex officio, the Chair of Historic Royal Palaces' Campaign Board); Gen. Lord Houghton of Richmond, GCB, CBE (ex officio, the Constable of the Tower of London); Jane Kennedy; Carole Souter, CBE; Sue Wilkinson, MBE; Louise Wilson, FRSA; Prof. Michael Wood

OFFICER
Chief Executive, John Barnes

HOMES ENGLAND
50 Victoria Street, Westminster, London SW1H 0TL
T 0300-123 4500 E enquiries@homesengland.gov.uk
W www.gov.uk/government/organisations/homes-england

Homes England is an executive non-departmental public body, sponsored by the Ministry of Housing, Communities and Local Government to facilitate delivery of sufficient new homes by bringing together land, money, expertise, planning and compulsory purchase powers. It replaced the Homes and Communities Agency in January 2018, adopting the new trading name Homes England. Along with it, its regulation directorate, which undertakes the functions of the Regulation Committee, refers to itself as the Regulator of Social Housing. Homes England invests mostly in building new homes, but also in creating employment floorspace nationwide, as well as bringing forward public land for development and increasing the speed with which it is made available.

Chair, Simon Dudley
Chief Executive, Nick Walkley

HUMAN TISSUE AUTHORITY (HTA)
151 Buckingham Palace Road, London SW1W 9SZ
T 020-7269 1900 E enquiries@hta.gov.uk W www.hta.gov.uk

The Human Tissue Authority (HTA) was established on 1 April 2005 under the Human Tissue Act 2004, and is sponsored and part-funded by the Department of Health and Social Care. It regulates organisations that remove, store and use tissue for research, medical treatment, post-mortem examination, teaching and display in public. The HTA also gives approval for organ and bone marrow donations from living people. Under the EU tissues and cells directives, the HTA is one of the two designated competent authorities for the UK responsible for regulating tissues and cells. The HTA is also the sole competent authority for the UK under the EU organ donation directive.

Chair, Bill Horne (interim)
Chief Executive, Allan Marriott-Smith

IMPERIAL WAR MUSEUMS (IWM)
Lambeth Road, London SE1 6HZ
T 020-7416 5000 E contact@iwm.org.uk W www.iwm.org.uk

IWM is the world's leading authority on conflict and its impact, focusing on Britain, its former empire and the Commonwealth from the First World War to the present. IWM aims to enrich people's understanding of the causes, course and consequences of war and conflict.

IWM comprises the organisation's flagship, IWM London; IWM North in Trafford, Manchester; IWM Duxford in Cambridgeshire; the Churchill War Rooms in Whitehall; and HMS Belfast in the Pool of London.

The total grant-in-aid for 2019–20 is £19.74m.

President, HRH the Duke of Kent, KG, GCMG, GCVO, ADC
Chair, Air Chief Marshal Sir Stuart Peach, GBE, KCB, ADC
Trustees, Desmond Bowen, CB, CMG; HE Hon. George Brandis, QC; Hugh Bullock; HE Janice Charette; Elizabeth Cleaver; Lt.-Gen. Andrew Figgures, CB, CBE; HE Ruchi Ghanashyam; HE Manisha Gunasekera; Rear-Adm. Amjad Hussain, CB; Margaret Macmillan, CH; Tim Marlow; HE Rt. Hon. Sir Jerry Mateparae; HE Mohammad Nafees Zakaria; Suzanne Nicholas; HE Nomatemba Tambo; Tamsin Todd; Mark Urban; Peter Watkins, CBE; Matthew Westerman
Director-General, Diane Lees, CBE
Directors, John Brown (Commercial Services and Operations); Jon Card (Collections and Governance); Graeme Etheridge (Change); Gill Webber (Content and Public Programmes)

INFORMATION COMMISSIONER'S OFFICE
Wycliffe House, Water Lane, Wilmslow, Cheshire SK9 5AF
T 0303-123 1113 W www.ico.org.uk

The Information Commissioner's Office (ICO) oversees and enforces the Freedom of Information Act 2000 and the Data Protection Act 1998, with the objective of promoting public access to official information and protecting personal information.

The Data Protection Act 1998 sets out rules for the processing of personal information and applies to records held on computers and some paper files. The Freedom of Information Act 2000 is designed to help end the culture of unnecessary secrecy and open up the inner workings of the public sector to citizens and businesses.

The ICO also enforces and oversees the privacy and electronic communications regulations 2003 and the environmental regulations 2004. It also has limited responsibilities under the INSPIRE regulations 2009 and DRR regulations 2014.

The Information Commissioner reports annually to parliament on the performance of his/her functions under the acts and has obligations to assess breaches of the acts. Since April 2010, the ICO has been able to fine organisations up to £500,000 for serious breaches of the Data Protection Act.

Information Commissioner, Elizabeth Denham, CBE

INDUSTRIAL INJURIES ADVISORY COUNCIL
First Floor, Caxton House, Tothill Street, London SW1H 9NA
T 020-7449 5618 E iiac@dwp.gsi.gov.uk
W www.gov.uk/government/organisations/
industrial-injuries-advisory-council

The Industrial Injuries Advisory Council was established under the National Insurance (Industrial Injuries) Act 1946, which came into effect on 5 July 1948. Statutory provisions governing its work are set out in the Social Security Administration Act 1992 and corresponding Northern Ireland legislation. The council usually consists of 17 members, including a chair, appointed by the Secretary of State for Work and Pensions, and has three roles: to advise on the prescription of diseases; to consider and advise on draft regulations and proposals concerning the industrial injuries disablement benefit scheme referred to the council by the Secretary of State for Work and Pensions or the Department for Communities in Northern Ireland; and to advise on any other matter concerning the scheme or its administration.

Chair, Dr Leslie Rushton, OBE

JOINT NATURE CONSERVATION COMMITTEE
Monkstone House, City Road, Peterborough PE1 1JY
T 01733-562626 E comment@jncc.gov.uk
W www.jncc.defra.gov.uk

The committee was established under the Environmental Protection Act 1990 and was reconstituted by the Natural Environment and Rural Communities Act 2006. It advises the government and devolved administrations on UK and international nature conservation issues. Its work contributes to maintaining and enriching biological diversity, conserving geological features and sustaining natural systems.

Chair, Prof. Chris Gilligan, CBE
Chief Executive, Marcus Yeo

LAW COMMISSION
1st Floor, Tower, 52 Queen Anne's Gate, London SW1H 9AG
T 020-3334 0200 E enquiries@lawcommission.gsi.gov.uk
W www.lawcom.gov.uk

The Law Commission was set up under the Law Commissions Act 1965 to make proposals to the government for the examination of the law in England and Wales and for its revision where it is unsuited for modern requirements, obscure or otherwise unsatisfactory. It recommends to the lord chancellor programmes for the examination of different branches of the law and suggests whether the examination should be carried out by the commission itself or by some other body. The commission is also responsible for the preparation of Consolidation and Statute Law (Repeals) Bills.

Chair, Sir Nicholas Green
Commissioners, Prof. Nicholas Hopkins; Stephen Lewis; Prof. David Ormerod, QC; Nicholas Paines, QC
Chief Executive, Phil Golding

NATIONAL ARMY MUSEUM
Royal Hospital Road, Chelsea, London SW3 4HT
T 020-7730 0717 E info@nam.ac.uk W www.nam.ac.uk

The National Army Museum shares the stories of the British Army and its soldiers. It was established by royal charter in 1960 and moved to its current site in Chelsea in 1971. The museum re-opened in spring 2017 following a major redevelopment project. The new museum features five state-of-the-art galleries, housing a wide array of artefacts, paintings, photographs, uniforms and equipment; a café; a shop; and learning and research facilities.

Chair, Gen. Sir Richard Shirreff, KCB, CBE
Council Members, Patrick Aylmer; Dr Jonathan Boff; Judith Donovan, CBE; John Duncan; Rt. Hon. Lord Hamilton of Epsom, PC; Lt.-Gen. Sir Simon Mayall, KBE, CB; Guy Perricone; Paul Schreier; Jessica Spungin; Sabine Vandenbroucke; William Wells
Director-General, Justin Maciejewski, DSO, MBE

NATIONAL GALLERIES OF SCOTLAND
73 Belford Road, Edinburgh EH4 3DS
T 0131-624 6200 E enquiries@nationalgalleries.org
W www.nationalgalleries.org

The National Galleries of Scotland comprise three galleries in Edinburgh: the National Gallery of Scotland, the Scottish National Portrait Gallery and the Scottish National Gallery of Modern Art. There are also partner galleries at Paxton House, Berwickshire, and Duff House, Banffshire. It also owns the Granton Centre for Art, a purpose built storage facility.

TRUSTEES
Chair, Benny Higgins
Trustees, Tricia Bey; Audrey Carlin; Alistair Dodds; Edward Green; Tari Lang; Catherine Muirden; Prof. Nicholas Pearce; Dr Hannah Rudman; Willie Watt

OFFICERS
Director-General, Sir John Leighton
Directors, Prof. Christopher Breward *(Collection and Research);* Jo Coomber *(Public Engagement);* Jacqueline Ridge *(Conservation and Collection Management);* Bryan Robertson *(Chief Operating Officer)*

NATIONAL GALLERY
Trafalgar Square, London WC2N 5DN
T 020-7747 2885 E information@ng-london.org.uk
W www.nationalgallery.org.uk

The National Gallery, which houses a collection of paintings in the western European tradition from the 13th to the 20th century, was founded in 1824, following a parliamentary grant of £57,000 for the purchase of the Angerstein collection of pictures. The present site was first occupied in 1838; an extension to the north of the building with a public entrance in Orange Street was opened in 1975; the Sainsbury Wing was opened in 1991; and the Getty Entrance opened off Trafalgar Square at the east end of the main building in 2004. Total government grant-in-aid for 2017–18 was £24.1m.

BOARD OF TRUSTEES
Chair, Hannah Rothschild, CBE
Trustees, Prof. Dexter Dalwood; Dame Moya Greene, DBE; Doug Gurr; Katrin Henkel; Sir John Kingman; Rosemary Leith; David Marks; Tonya Nelson; Charles Sebag-Montefiore; John Singer; Molly Stevens

OFFICERS
Director of the National Gallery, Dr Gabriele Finaldi
Deputy Director, Dr Susan Foister *(Public Programmes and Partnerships)*

Directors, Dr Caroline Campbell *(Collections and Research);* Andy Hibbert *(Finance (interim);* Chris Michaels *(Digital)*

NATIONAL HERITAGE MEMORIAL FUND

7 Holbein Place, London SW1W 8NR
T 020-7591 6044 E NHMF_Enquiries@nhmf.org.uk
W www.nhmf.org.uk

The National Heritage Memorial Fund was set up under the National Heritage Act 1980 in memory of people who have given their lives for the United Kingdom. The fund provides grants to organisations based in the UK, mainly so that they can buy items of outstanding interest and of importance to the national heritage. These must either be at risk or have a memorial character. The fund is administered by a chair and trustees who are appointed by the prime minister.

The National Heritage Memorial Fund receives an annual grant from the Department for Digital, Culture, Media and Sport. Under the National Lottery etc. Act 1993, the trustees of the fund became responsible for the distribution of funds for both the National Heritage Memorial Fund and the Heritage Lottery Fund. Total annual government grant-in-aid is £5m.

Chair, Sir Peter Luff
Trustees, Maria Adebowale-Schwarte; Baroness Andrews, OBE, FSA; Anna Carragher; Sir Neil Cossons, OBE; Dr Angela Dean; Jim Dixon; Dr Claire Feehily; Sarah Flannigan; Perdita Hunt, OBE; Steve Miller; René Olivieri; Dame Seona Reid, DBE; David Stocker; Dr Tom Tew
Chief Executive, Ros Kerslake, OBE

NATIONAL LIBRARY OF SCOTLAND

George IV Bridge, Edinburgh EH1 1EW
T 0131-623 3700 E enquiries@nls.uk W www.nls.uk

The library, which was formally opened as the Advocates' Library in 1689, became the National Library of Scotland in 1925. It contains over 24 million printed items in multiple formats including: books, manuscripts, archives, websites, newspapers, maps, music, moving images and sound, along with the John Murray Archive. One of only six legal deposit libraries, it receives more than 4,000 new items a week. It has an unrivalled Scottish collection as well as online catalogues and digital resources which can be accessed through the Library's website. Material can be consulted in the library branches in Edinburgh and Glasgow, which are open to anyone with a valid library card.

The National Library of Scotland Act 2012 modernised the composition and responsibilities of the board. Board members are appointed by the Scottish ministers.

Chair, Sir Kenneth Calman
Board members, Noreen Adams; Elizabeth Carmichal, CBE; Ruth Crawford, QC; Helen Durndell; Dianne Haley; Alan Horn; Simon Learoyd; Lesley McPherson; Iain Marley; Prof. Adrienne Scullion; Amina Shah; Prof. Melissa Terras; Robert Wallen
National Librarian and Chief Executive, Dr John Scally
Heads of Department, John Coll *(Access);* Jackie Cromarty *(External Relations and Governance (interim));* Graeme Forbes *(Collections Management);* Anthony Gillespie *(Business Support);* Stuart Lewis *(Digital);* Robin Smith *(Collections and Research)*

NATIONAL LIBRARY OF WALES/ LLYFRGELL GENEDLAETHOL CYMRU

Aberystwyth, Ceredigion, Wales SY23 3BU
T 01970-632800 E gofyn@llgc.org.uk W www.library.wales

The National Library of Wales was founded by royal charter in 1907, and is funded by the Welsh government. It contains about six million books and newspapers, 40,000 manuscripts, four million deeds and documents, numerous maps, prints and drawings, and a sound and moving image collection. It specialises in manuscripts and books relating to Wales and the Celtic peoples. It is the repository for pre-1858 Welsh probate records, manorial records and tithe documents, and certain legal records. Admission to the reading rooms is by reader's ticket, but entry to the exhibition programme is free.

The draft budget from the Welsh government was 2018–19 is £10.8m.

President, Rhodi Thomas

Trustees, Lord Aberdare; Eleri Twynog Davies; Iwan Davies; Richard Houdmont; Dyfrig Jones; Gwilym Dyfri Jones; Elizabeth Siberry; Hugh Thomas; Steve Williams; Lee Yale-Helms *(Treasurer)*
Chief Executive and Librarian, Pedr ap Llwyd

NATIONAL MUSEUM OF THE ROYAL NAVY

HM Naval Base (PP66), Portsmouth PO1 3NH
T 023-9289 1370 W www.nmrn.org.uk

The National Museum of the Royal Navy comprises nine museums: HMS *Victory,* HMS *Caroline,* HMS *M.33,* the National Museum of the Royal Navy Portsmouth, the National Museum of the Royal Navy Hartlepool, the Fleet Air Arm Museum, the Royal Navy Submarine Museum, the Royal Marines Museum and Explosion! Museum of Naval Firepower. The Fleet Air Museum is located at RNAS Yeovilton, Somerset, and HMS Caroline is located at Alexandra Dock, Belfast, while the other five are situated in Portsmouth and Gosport.

Chair, Adm. Sir Jonathon Band, GCB
Trustees, Michael Bedingfield; Prof. John Davidson; Helen Jackson; Cllr Donna Jones; Mike Gambazzi; Vice-Adm. Sir Adrian Johns, KCB, CBE, ADC; Maj.-Gen. Jeffrey Mason, MBE; Hon. Mary Montagu-Scott; Tim Schadla-Hall; Prof. Sara Selwood, PHD; Rear-Adm. Robert Stevens; Gavin Whitter; Dr Caroline Williams; Charles Wilson
Director-General, Prof. Dominic Tweddle

NATIONAL LOTTERY COMMUNITY FUND

1 Plough Place, London EC4A 1DE
T 0345-410 2030
E general.enquiries@tnlcommunityfund.org.uk
W www.tnlcommunityfund.org.uk

The National Lottery Community Fund, formerly the Big Lottery Fund, awarded over £500m of National Lottery funds in 2017–18; 90 per cent in grants under £10,000. The Fund supports health, education, environmental and charitable projects.

Chair, Peter Ainsworth
Vice-Chair, Tony Burton, CBE
Regional Chairs, Julie Harrison *(Northern Ireland);* Maureen McGinn *(Scotland);* Nat Sloane, CBE *(England);* Sir Adrian Webb *(Wales)*
Chief Executive, Dawn Austwick, OBE

NATIONAL MUSEUM WALES/ AMGUEDDFA CYMRU

Cathays Park, Cardiff CF10 3NP
T 0300-111 2333 W https://museum.wales

National Museum Wales *(Amgueddfa Cymru)* is the body that runs Wales' seven national museums. It comprises National Museum Cardiff; St Fagans: National History Museum; Big Pit: National Coal Museum, Blaenafon; National Roman Legion Museum, Caerleon; National Slate Museum, Llanberis; National Wool Museum, Dre-fach Felindre; National Waterfront Museum, Swansea; and National Collections

Centre, Nantgarw. The draft budget from the Welsh government for 2018–19 was £22.7m.

President, vacant
Vice-President, Dr Carol Bell
Trustees, Laurence Pavelin, CBE *(Treasurer);* Baroness Andrews, OBE; Dr Caroline Duigan; Carys Howell; Rachel Hughes; Hywel John; Dr Glenda Jones; Dr Hywel Jones, CMG; Prof. Robert Pickard; Michael Prior; Victoria Provis; Jessica Seaton
Director-General, David Anderson, OBE

NATIONAL MUSEUMS LIVERPOOL
127 Dale Street, Liverpool L2 2JH
T 0151-207 0001 W www.liverpoolmuseums.org.uk

Regulated by the Department of Digital, Culture, Media and Sport, National Museums Liverpool is a group of museums and collections, comprising eight venues: International Slavery Museum, Lady Lever Art Gallery, Merseyside Maritime Museum, Museum of Liverpool, Seized! (UK Border Force National Museum), Sudley House, Walker Art Gallery and World Museum.

Chair, Sir David Henshaw
Trustees, Carmel Booth; Laura Carstensen; James Chapman; Sarah Dean; David Fleming; Heather Lauder; Andrew McCluskey; Philip Price; Ian Rosenblatt, OBE; Max Steinberg, CBE; Virginia Tandy; Dr Nicola Thorp
Director National Museums Liverpool, Laura Pye
Directors, Janet Dugdale *(Museums);* Andrew Evans *(Development);* Stacey Hammond *(Business Development);* Mairi Johnson *(Estates);* Melanie Lewis *(Commercial and Business Development);* Tracey McGeagh *(Marketing and Communications);* Karen O'Connor *(Commercial Enterprises);* Louise Parnell *(Business Support);* Sandra Penketh *(Galleries and Collections Management);* Fiona Philpott *(Exhibitions);* Carol Rogers *(Engagement);* David Spilsbury *(Finance)*

NATIONAL MUSEUMS NORTHERN IRELAND
Cultra, Holywood, Northern Ireland BT18 0EU
T 0845-608 0000 E info@nmni.com W www.nmni.com

Across three unique sites National Museums Northern Ireland cares for and presents inspirational collections reflecting the creativity, innovation, history, culture and people of Northern Ireland and beyond.

Together the Ulster Museum, Ulster Folk and Transport Museum and Ulster American Folk Park offer a unique opportunity to experience the heritage and way of life of Northern Ireland.

Chair, Miceal McCoy
Vice-Chair, Dr Leon Litvack
Trustees, Michael Catto; Prof. Garth Earls; Prof. Karen Fleming; Hazel Francey; Daphne Harshaw; Dr Rosemary Kelly, OBE; Alan McFarland; Dr George McIlroy; Catherine Molloy; Annette Moor; Joseph Rice; Dr Margaret Ward
Chief Executive, Kathryn Thomson

NATIONAL MUSEUMS SCOTLAND
Chambers Street, Edinburgh EH1 1JF
T 0300-123 6789 E info@nms.ac.uk W www.nms.ac.uk

National Museums Scotland provides advice, expertise and support to the museums community across Scotland, and undertakes fieldwork that often involves collaboration at local, national and international levels. National Museums Scotland comprises the National Museum of Scotland, the National War Museum, the National Museum of Rural Life, the National

Museum of Flight and the National Museums Collection Centre. Its collections represent more than two centuries of collecting and include Scottish and classical archaeology, decorative and applied arts, world cultures and social history and science, technology and the natural world.

Up to 15 trustees can be appointed by the Minister for Culture, Tourism and External Affairs for a term of four years, and may serve a second term.

Chair, Bruce Minto, OBE
Trustees, Ann Allen; Prof. Mary Bownes, OBE, FRSE; Adam Bruce; Gordon Drummond; Chris Fletcher; Dr Brian Lang, CBE, FRSE; Lynda Logan; Dr Catriona Macdonald; Prof. Walter Nimmo, CBE, MD, FRCP; Ian Russell, CBE; Janet Stevenson; Eilidh Wiseman; Dr Laura Young, MBE
Director, Dr Gordon Rintoul, CBE, FRSE

NATIONAL PORTRAIT GALLERY
St Martin's Place, London WC2H 0HE
T 020-7306 0055 W www.npg.org.uk

The National Portrait Gallery was established in 1856. Today the Gallery collects portraits of those who have made, or are making, a significant contribution to British history and culture. The Collection is free to visit, and includes works across all media, from painting and sculpture to photography and digital portraits. To complement the Collection, the Gallery stages exhibitions, displays, talks and events throughout the year which explore the nature of portraiture. The Gallery loans exhibitions, displays and individual portraits to organisations across the UK and internationally as part of its ongoing commitment to sharing the Collection as widely as possible.

Chair of the Board of Trustees, David Ross
Director, Dr Nicholas Cullinan

NATURAL ENGLAND
County Hall, Spetchley Road, Worcester WR5 2NP
T 0300-060 3900 E enquiries@naturalengland.org.uk
W www.gov.uk/government/organisations/natural-england

Natural England is the government's adviser on the natural environment, providing practical scientific advice on how to look after England's landscapes and wildlife.

The organisation's remit is to ensure sustainable stewardship of the land and sea so that people and nature can thrive.

Natural England works with farmers and land managers; business and industry; planners and developers; national and local government; charities and conservationists; interest groups and local communities to help them improve their local environment.

Chair, Tony Juniper, CBE
Chief Executive, Marian Spain *(interim)*

NATURAL HISTORY MUSEUM
Cromwell Road, London SW7 5BD
T 020-7942 5000 W www.nhm.ac.uk

The Natural History Museum, which houses 80 million natural history specimens, originates from the natural history departments of the British Museum, which grew extensively during the 19th century; in 1860 it was agreed that the natural history collections should be separated from the British Museum's collections of books, manuscripts and antiquities. Part of the site of the 1862 International Exhibition in South Kensington was acquired for the new museum, and the museum opened to the public in 1881. In 1963 the Natural History Museum became completely independent with its own board of trustees. The Natural History Museum at Tring, bequeathed by the second Lord Rothschild, has formed part of the museum since 1937. The Geological Museum merged with the Natural History Museum in 1986. In September 2009 the Natural History Museum opened the Darwin Centre, which contains public galleries, a high-tech interactive area known as the Attenborough Studio and scientific research facilities. Total budgeted government grant-in-aid for 2019–20 is £41.8m.

Chair, Lord Green of Hurstpierpoint
Trustees, Prof. Sir John Beddington, CMG, FRS; Dame Frances Cairncross, DBE, FRSE; Prof. Christopher Gilligan, CBE; Prof. Sir John Holman; Anand Mahindra; Hilary Newiss; Robert Noel; Simon Patterson; Prof. Stephen Sparks, CMG, FRS, CBE; Prof. Dame Janet Thornton, DBE, FRS, FMEDSCI; Dr Kim Winser, OBE
Museum Director, Sir Michael Dixon
Directors, Neil Greenwood *(Finance and Corporate Services);* Fiona McWilliams *(Development and Communications);* Clare Matterson, CBE *(Engagement);* Prof. Ian Owens *(Science)*

NATURAL RESOURCES WALES
Ty Cambria, 29 Newport Road, Cardiff CF24 0TP
T 0300-065 3000 E enquiries@naturalresourceswales.gov.uk
W www.naturalresources.wales

Natural Resources Wales is the principal adviser to the Welsh government on the environment. It became operational on 1 April 2013 following a merger of the Countryside Council for Wales, Environment Agency Wales and the Forestry Commission Wales. It is responsible for ensuring that the natural resources of Wales are sustainably maintained, enhanced and used; now and in the future.

Chair, Sir David Henshaw *(interim)*
Board Members, Karen Balmer; Chris Blake; Catherine Brown; Julia Cherrett; Geraint Davies; Howard Davies; Dr Elizabeth Haywood; Zoë Henderson; Prof. Steve Ormerod, FCIEEM; Dr Rosie Plummer; Prof. Peter Rigby, FRS, FMEDSCI
Chief Executive, Clare Pillman

NHS PAY REVIEW BODY
8th Floor, Fleetbank House, 2-6 Salisbury Square, London EC4Y 8JX
T 020-7211 8295 W www.gov.uk/government/organisations/nhs-pay-review-body

The NHS Pay Review Body (NHSPRB) advises the prime minister, Secretary of State for Health and ministers in Scotland, Wales and Northern Ireland on the remuneration of all paid staff under agenda for change and employed in the NHS. The review body was established in 1983 for nurses and allied health professionals. Its remit has since expanded to cover just under 1.5 million staff, ie almost all staff in the NHS, with the exception of dentists, doctors and very senior managers.

Chair, Philippa Hird
Members, Richard Cooper; Patricia Gordon; Neville Hounsome; Stephanie Marston; Prof. David Ulph, CBE; Prof. Jonathan Wadsworth

NORTHERN IRELAND HUMAN RIGHTS COMMISSION
Temple Court, 39 North Street, Belfast BT1 1NA
T 028-9024 3987 E info@nihrc.org W www.nihrc.org

The Northern Ireland Human Rights Commission is a non-departmental public body, established by the Northern Ireland Act 1998 and set up in March 1999. Its purpose is to protect and promote human rights in Northern Ireland. Its main functions include reviewing the law and practice relating to human rights, advising government and the Northern Ireland Assembly, and promoting an awareness of human rights. It can

also investigate human rights violations and take cases to court. The members of the commission are appointed by the Secretary of State for Northern Ireland.

Chief Commissioner, Les Allamby
Commissioners, Helen Ferguson; Helena Macormac; Paul Mageean; John McCallister; Eddie Rooney; Graham Shields, OBE
Chief Executive, Dr David Russell

NORTHERN LIGHTHOUSE BOARD
84 George Street, Edinburgh EH2 3DA
T 0131-473 3100 E enquiries@nlb.org.uk W www.nlb.org.uk

The Northern Lighthouse Board is the general lighthouse authority for Scotland and the Isle of Man and owes its origin to an act of parliament passed in 1786. At present there are 19 commissioners who operate under the Merchant Shipping Act 1995.

The commissioners control 206 lighthouses, 165 lighted and unlighted buoys, 26 beacons, 35 AIS (automatic identification system) stations, 29 radar beacons, four DGPS (differential global positioning system) stations and an ELORAN (long-range navigation) system. *See also* Transport.

Chair, Capt. Michael Brew
Vice-Chair, Capt. Alastair Beveridge
Commissioners, Lord Advocate; Solicitor-General for Scotland; Lord Provosts of Edinburgh, Glasgow and Aberdeen; Convener of Highland Council; Provost of Argyll and Bute Council; Sheriffs-Principal of South Strathclyde, Dumfries and Galloway, Tayside, Central and Fife, North Strathclyde, Grampian, Highlands and Islands, Lothian and Borders, and Glasgow and Strathkelvin; Graham Crerar; Hugh Shaw, OBE; Elaine Wilkinson; Rob Woodward
Chief Executive, Mike Bullock, MBE

NUCLEAR DECOMMISSIONING AUTHORITY
Herdus House, Westlakes Science and Technology Park, Moor Row, Cumbria CA24 3HU
T 01925-802001 E enquiries@nda.gov.uk
W www.gov.uk/government/organisations/nuclear-decommissioning-authority

The Nuclear Decommissioning Authority (NDA) was created under the Energy Act 2004. It is a strategic authority that owns 17 sites plus associated civil nuclear liabilities and assets of the public sector, previously under the control of the UK Energy Authority and British Nuclear Fuels. The NDA's responsibilities include decommissioning and cleaning up civil nuclear facilities; ensuring the safe management of waste products, both radioactive and non-radioactive; implementing government policy on the long-term management of nuclear waste; and developing UK-wide low-level waste strategy plans.

Total planned expenditure for 2018–19 is £3.146bn, with total grant-in-aid standing at £2.269bn. The remaining £0.877bn will come from commercial operations.

Chair, Tom Smith
Chief Executive, David Peattie

OFFICE FOR BUDGET RESPONSIBILITY
14T, 102 Petty France, London SW1H 9AJ
T 020-3334 6117 E OBR.Enquiries@obr.uk W www.obr.uk

The Office for Budget Responsibility (OBR) was created in 2010 to provide independent and authoritative analysis of the UK's public finances. It has five main roles: producing forecasts for the economy and public finances; judging progress towards the government's fiscal targets; evaluating fiscal risks; assessing the long-term sustainability of the public finances; and scrutinising HM Treasury's costing of tax and welfare spending measures.

Chair, Robert Chote
Committee Members, Prof. Sir Charles Bean; Andy King

OFFICE OF COMMUNICATIONS (OFCOM)
Riverside House, 2A Southwark Bridge Road, London SE1 9HA
T 0300-123 3000 W www.ofcom.org.uk

OFCOM was established in 2003 under the Office of Communications Act 2002 as the independent regulator and competition authority for the UK communications industries with responsibility, for television, video-on-demand, radio, telecommunications and wireless communications services.

Following the passing of the Postal Services Act 2011, OFCOM also assumed regulatory responsibility for postal services.

Chair, Lord Burns
Deputy Chair, Maggie Carver
Board Members, Angela Dean *(Audit and Risk);* Bob Downes *(Scotland);* Graham Mather; Jonathan Oxley; Tim Suter; Ben Verwaayen
Chief Executive, Sharon White

OFFICE OF MANPOWER ECONOMICS (OME)
8th Floor, Fleetbank House, 2–6 Salisbury Square, London EC4Y 8JX
T 020-7211 8165 W www.gov.uk/government/organisations/office-of-manpower-economics

The Office of Manpower Economics (OME) was established in 1971. It is an independent non-statutory organisation responsible for providing an independent secretariat to eight independent review bodies: the Armed Forces' Pay Review Body (AFPRB); the Review Body on Doctors' and Dentists' Remuneration (DDRB); the NHS Pay Review Body (NHSPRB); the Prison Service Pay Review Body (PSPRB); the School Teachers' Review Body (STRB); the Senior Salaries Review Body (SSRB); the Police Remuneration Review Body (PRRB); and the National Crime Agency Remuneration Review Body (NCARRB). In total these pay bodies make recommendations impacting 2.5 million workers – around 45 per cent of public sector staff – and with a total pay bill of £100bn.

OME Director, Martin Williams
Directors, Heidi Grainger *(Chief Economist and Research and Analysis Group);* Ffiona Hesketh *(SSRB);* Stuart Sarson *(PSPRB; AFPRB; STRB);* Edmund Quilty *(NHSPRB; DDRB; NCARRB; PRRB)*

PARADES COMMISSION
2nd Floor, Andras House, 60 Great Victoria Street, Belfast BT2 7BB
T 028-9089 5900 E info@paradescommissionni.org
W www.paradescommission.org

The Parades Commission was set up under the Public Processions (Northern Ireland) Act 1998. Its function is to encourage and facilitate local accommodation of contentious parades; where this is not possible, the commission is empowered to make legal determinations about such parades, which may include imposing conditions on aspects of the notified parade (such as restrictions on routes/areas and exclusion of certain groups with a record of bad behaviour).

The chair and members are appointed by the Secretary of State for Northern Ireland; the membership must, as far as is practicable, be representative of the community in Northern Ireland.

Chair, Anne Henderson
Members, Joelle Black; Sarah Havlin; Paul Hutchinson; Colin Kennedy; Anne Marshall; Geraldine McGahey

PAROLE BOARD FOR ENGLAND AND WALES
3rd Floor, 10 South Colonnade, Canary Wharf, London E14 4PU
T 020-3880 0885 E info@paroleboard.gov.uk
W www.gov.uk/government/organisations/parole-board

The Parole Board was established in 1968 under the Criminal Justice Act 1967 and became an independent executive non-departmental public body on 1 July 1996 under the Criminal Justice and Public Order Act 1994. It is the body that protects the public by making risk assessments about prisoners to decide who may safely be released into the community and who must remain in, or be returned to, custody. Board decisions are taken at two main types of panels of up to three members: 'paper panels' for the majority of cases, or oral hearings for decisions concerning prisoners serving life or indeterminate sentences for public protection. The budget for 2017–18 was £19.2m.

Chair, Caroline Corby
Chief Executive, Martin Jones

PAROLE BOARD FOR SCOTLAND
Saughton House, Broomhouse Drive, Edinburgh EH11 3XD
T 0131-244 8373 E paroleboardforscotland@gov.scot
W www.scottishparoleboard.gov.uk

The board directs and advises the Scottish ministers on the release of prisoners on licence, and related matters.

Chair, John Watt

PENSION PROTECTION FUND (PPF)
Renaissance, 12 Dingwall Road, Croydon CR0 2NA
T 0345-600 2541 E information@ppf.co.uk
W www.pensionprotectionfund.org.uk

The PPF became operational in 2005. It was established to pay compensation to members of eligible defined-benefit pension schemes, when a qualifying insolvency event in relation to the employer occurs and where there is a lack of sufficient assets in the pension scheme. The PPF also administers the Financial Assistance Scheme, which helps members whose schemes wound-up before 2005. It is also responsible for the Fraud Compensation Fund (which provides compensation to occupational pension schemes that suffer a loss that can be attributed to dishonesty). The chair and board of the PPF are appointed by, and accountable to, the Secretary of State for Work and Pensions, and are responsible for paying compensation, calculating annual levies (which help fund the PPF), and setting and overseeing investment strategy.

Chair, Arnold Wagner, OBE
Chief Executive, Oliver Morley, CBE

PENSIONS REGULATOR
Napier House, Trafalgar Place, Brighton BN1 4DW
T 0345-600 0707 E customersupport@tpr.gov.uk
W www.thepensionsregulator.gov.uk

The Pensions Regulator was established in 2005 as the regulator of workplace pension schemes in the UK, replacing the Occupational Pensions Regulatory Authority (OPRA). It aims to make sure employers put their staff into a pension scheme and pay money into it (automatic enrolment) and to protect the benefits of occupational and personal pension scheme members by working with trustees, employers, pension providers and advisers. The regulator's work focuses on encouraging better management and administration of schemes, ensuring that final salary schemes have a sensible funding plan, and encouraging money purchase schemes to provide members with the information that they need to make informed choices about their pension fund. The Pensions Act 2004 and the Pensions Act 2008 gave the regulator a range of powers which can be used to protect scheme members, but a strong emphasis is placed on educating and enabling those responsible for managing pension schemes, and powers are used only where necessary. The regulator offers free online resources to help trustees, employers, professionals and advisers understand their role, duties and obligations.

Chair, Mark Boyle
Chief Executive, Charles Counsell

POLICE ADVISORY BOARD FOR ENGLAND AND WALES
Home Office, 6th Floor Fry, 2 Marsham Street, London SW1P 4DF
E pabewsecretariat@homeoffice.gov.uk
W www.gov.uk/government/organisations/
police-advisory-board-for-england-and-wales

The Police Advisory Board for England and Wales was established in 1965 by section 46 of the Police Act 1964 and provides advice to the home secretary on general questions affecting the police in England and Wales. It also considers draft regulations under the Police Act 1996 about matters such as recruitment, diversity and collaboration between forces.

Independent Chair, Elizabeth France

PRISON SERVICE PAY REVIEW BODY
8th Floor, Fleetbank House, 2-6 Salisbury Square, London EC4Y 8JX
T 020-7211 8259 W www.gov.uk/government/organisations/
prison-services-pay-review-body

The Prison Service Pay Review Body was set up in 2001. It makes independent recommendations on the pay of prison governors, operational managers, prison officers and related grades for the Prison Service in England and Wales, and for the Northern Ireland Prison Service.

Chair, Tim Flesher, CB
Members, Roberta Brownlee; Mary Carter; Nicholas Caton; Prof. Andy Dickerson; Leslie Manasseh, MBE; Paul West, QPM

PRIVY COUNCIL OFFICE
Room G/04, 1 Horse Guards Road, London SW1A 2HQ
T 020-7271 3292 E enquiries@pco.gov.uk
W https://privycouncil.independent.gov.uk

The primary function of the office is to act as the secretariat to the Privy Council. It is responsible for the arrangements leading to the making of all royal proclamations and orders in council; for certain formalities connected with ministerial changes; for considering applications for the granting (or amendment) of royal charters; for the scrutiny and approval of by-laws and statutes of chartered institutions and of the governing instruments of universities and colleges; and for the appointment of high sheriffs and Privy Council appointments to governing bodies. Under the relevant acts, the office is responsible for the approval of certain regulations and rules made by the regulatory bodies of the medical and certain allied professions.

The Lord President of the Council is the ministerial head of the office and presides at meetings of the Privy Council. The Clerk of the Council is the administrative head of the Privy Council office.

Lord President of the Council and Leader of the House of Commons, Rt. Hon. Andrea Leadsom
Clerk of the Council, Richard Tilbrook
Head of Secretariat and Deputy Clerk, Ceri King
Deputy Clerk, Christopher Berry

REVIEW BODY ON DOCTORS' AND DENTISTS' REMUNERATION
8th Floor, Fleetbank House, 2-6 Salisbury Square, London EC4Y 8JX
T 020-7211 8809 W www.gov.uk/government/organisations/
review-body-on-doctors-and-dentists-remuneration

The Review Body on Doctors' and Dentists' Remuneration was set up in 1971. It advises the prime minister, the secretary of state for health and social care, first ministers in Scotland, Wales and Northern Ireland, and the ministers for Health and Social Care, in England, Scotland, Wales and Northern Ireland on the remuneration of doctors and dentists taking any part in the National Health Service.

Chair, Prof. Sir Paul Curran
Members, David Bingham; Prof. Peter Kopelman, MD, FRCP, FFPH; Prof. Kevin Lee; Prof. James Malcomson; John Matheson, CBE; Jane Williams

ROYAL AIR FORCE MUSEUM
Grahame Park Way, London NW9 5LL
T 020-8205 2266 E london@rafmuseum.org
W www.rafmuseum.org.uk

The museum has two sites, one at the former airfield at Colindale, in North London, and the second at Cosford, in the West Midlands, both of which illustrate the development of aviation from before the Wright brothers to the present-day RAF. The museum's collection across both sites consists of over 170 aircraft, as well as artefacts, aviation memorabilia, fine art and photographs.

Chair, Air Chief Marshal Sir Andrew Pulford, GCB, CBE
Trustees, Peter Bateson; Laurie Benson; Dr Carol Cole; Dr Rodney Eastwood, MBE; Richard Holman; Catriona Lougher Julie McGarvey; Andrew Reid; Nick Sanders; Michael Schindler
Chief Executive, Maggie Appleton, MBE

ROYAL BOTANIC GARDEN EDINBURGH
20A Inverleith Row, Edinburgh EH3 5LR
T 0131-552 7171 E info@rbge.org.uk W www.rbge.org.uk

The Royal Botanic Garden Edinburgh (RBGE) originated as the Physic Garden, established in 1670 beside the Palace of Holyroodhouse. The garden moved to its present 28ha site at Inverleith, Edinburgh, in 1820. There are also three regional gardens: Benmore Botanic Garden, near Dunoon, Argyll; Logan Botanic Garden, near Stranraer, Wigtownshire; and Dawyck Botanic Garden, near Stobo, Peeblesshire. Since 1986 RBGE has been administered by a board of trustees established under the National Heritage (Scotland) Act 1985. It receives an annual grant from the Scottish government's Environment and Forestry Directorate.

The RBGE is an international centre for scientific research on plant diversity and for horticulture education and conservation. It has an extensive library, a herbarium with almost three million preserved plant specimens, and over 13,500 species in the living collections.

Chair, Sir Muir Russell, KCB, FRSE
Trustees, Prof. Beverley Glover; Dr David Hamilton; Prof. Thomas Meagher; Diana Murray; Prof. Ian Wall, FRSE; Chris Wallace
Regius Keeper and Queen's Botanist in Scotland, Simon Milne, MBE

ROYAL BOTANIC GARDENS, KEW

Kew Gardens, Richmond, London TW9 3AB
T 020-8332 5655 E info@kew.org
Wakehurst, Ardingly, W. Sussex RH17 6TN
T 01444-894066 E wakehurst@kew.org
W www.kew.org

Kew Gardens was originally laid out as a private garden for the now demolished White House for George III's mother, Princess Augusta, in 1759. The gardens were much enlarged in the 19th century, notably by the inclusion of the grounds of the former Richmond Lodge. In 1965 Kew acquired the gardens at Wakehurst on a long lease from the National Trust. Under the National Heritage Act 1983 a board of trustees was set up to administer the gardens, which in 1984 became an independent body supported by grant-in-aid from the Department for Environment, Food and Rural Affairs. Total grant in aid for 2017–18 was £40.8m.

The functions of RBG, Kew are to carry out research into plant sciences, to disseminate knowledge about plants and to provide the public with the opportunity to gain knowledge and enjoyment from the gardens' collections. There are extensive national reference collections of living and preserved plants and a comprehensive library and archive. The main emphasis is on plant conservation and biodiversity; Wakehurst houses the Millennium Seed Bank Partnership, which is the largest *ex situ* conservation project in the world – its aim is to bank seeds from 25 per cent of the earth's wild plant species by 2020.

Chair, Marcus Agius
Trustees, Nick Baird; Prof. Liam Dolan; Catherine Dugmore; Sarah Flannigan; Valerie Gooding; Krishnan Guru-Murthy; Prof. Sue Hartley; Ian Karet; Jantiene Klein Roseboom van der Veer; Michael Lear; Sir Derek Myers; Prof. Malcolm Press
Director, Richard Deverell

ROYAL COMMISSION ON THE ANCIENT AND HISTORICAL MONUMENTS OF WALES

Ffordd Penglais, Aberystwyth SY23 3BU
T 01970-621200 E nmr.wales@rcahmw.gov.uk
W www.rcahmw.gov.uk

The Royal Commission on the Ancient and Historical Monuments of Wales, established in 1908, is the investigation body and national archive for the historic environment of Wales. It has the lead role in ensuring that Wales's archaeological, built and maritime heritage is authoritatively recorded, and seeks to promote the understanding and appreciation of this heritage nationally and internationally. The commission is funded by the Welsh government.

Chair, Prof. Nancy Edwards, FSA
Vice-Chair, Catherine Hardman, FSA
Commissioners, Neil Beagrie, FRSA; Chris Brayne; Caroline Crewe-Read, FRSA; Dr Louise Emanuel; Thomas Lloyd, OBE, FSA; Dr Hayley Roberts; Jonathan Vining
Secretary, Christopher Catling

ROYAL MUSEUMS GREENWICH

National Maritime Museum, Greenwich, London SE10 9NF
T 020-8312 6565 E RMGenquiries@rmg.co.uk
W www.rmg.co.uk

Royal Museums Greenwich comprises the National Maritime Museum, the Queen's House and the Royal Observatory Greenwich. It also works in collaboration with the Cutty Sark Trust. The National Maritime Museum provides information on the maritime history of Great Britain and is the largest institution of its kind in the world, with over 2.5 million items in its collections related to seafaring, navigation and astronomy. Originally the home of Charles I's Queen, Henrietta Maria, the Queen's House was designed by Inigo Jones and built between 1616–18, although it was structurally altered between 1629–35. It now contains a fine-art collection. The Royal Observatory, Greenwich is the home of Greenwich Mean Time and the prime meridian of the world. It also contains London's only planetarium, Harrison's timekeepers and the UK's largest refracting telescope.

Chair, Sir Charles Dunstone, CVO
Trustees, Joyce Bridges, CBE; Dr Fiona Butcher; Dr Helen Czerski; Prof. Julian Dowdeswell; Dr Aminul Hoque, MBE; Carol Marlow; Alastair Marsh; Jeremy Penn; Eric Reynolds; Gerald Russell; Adm. Sir Mark Stanhope, GCB, OBE
Director, Kevin Fewster, FRSA

SCHOOL TEACHERS' REVIEW BODY

8th Floor, Fleetbank House, 2-6 Salisbury Square, London EC4Y 8JX
T 020-7211 8463 W www.gov.uk/government/organisations/school-teachers-review-body

The School Teachers' Review Body was set up under the School Teachers' Pay and Conditions Act 1991. It is required to examine and make recommendations on such matters relating to the statutory conditions of employment of school teachers in England and Wales. It reports to the education secretary and the prime minister.

Chair, Dr Patricia Rice
Members, Peter Batley; Sir Robert Burgess; Ken Clark; Harriet Kemp; John Lakin; Mike Redhouse; Dr Andrew Walker; Jeanne Watson

SCIENCE MUSEUM GROUP

W https://group.sciencemuseum.org.uk

SCIENCE MUSEUM
Exhibition Road, London SW7 2DD
T 020-7942 4000 E info@sciencemuseum.ac.uk
W www.sciencemuseum.org.uk

MUSEUM OF SCIENCE AND INDUSTRY
Liverpool Road, Castlefield, Manchester M3 4FP
T 0161-832 2244 E contact@scienceandindustrymuseum.org.uk
W www.scienceandindustrymuseum.org.uk

NATIONAL RAILWAY MUSEUM AND LOCOMOTION
NRM York, Leeman Road, York YO26 4XJ
T 0333-016 1010 E info@railwaymuseum.org.uk
W www.railwaymuseum.org.uk
Locomotion, Shildon, Co. Durham DL4 2RE
T 01904-685780 E info@locomotion.org.uk
W www.locomotion.org.uk

NATIONAL SCIENCE AND MEDIA MUSEUM
Pictureville, Bradford BD1 1NQ
T 0844-856 3797 E talk.nsmm@scienceandmediamuseum.org.uk
W www.scienceandmediamuseum.org.uk

The Science Museum Group (SMG) consists of the Science Museum; the Museum of Science and Industry, Manchester; the National Railway Museum, York; the National Science and Media Museum, Bradford; and Locomotion at Shildon. The Science Museum houses the national collections of science, technology, industry and medicine and attracts around 3.2 million visits annually. The museum began as the science collection of the South Kensington Museum and first opened in 1857. In 1883 it acquired the collections of the Patent Museum and in 1909 the science collections were transferred to the new Science Museum, leaving the art collections with the Victoria and Albert Museum. The Wellcome Wing was opened in July 2000.

The Trustees of the Science Museum Group have statutory duties under the National Heritage Act 1983 for the general management and control of SMG.

Total government grant-in-aid for 2017–18 was £45.2m.

Chair, Dame Mary Archer, DBE
Trustees, Matthew D'Ancona; Prof. Brian Cantor; Judith Donovan, CBE; Dr Sarah Dry; Sharon Flood; Prof. Russell Foster, CBE, FRS, FMEDSCI; Andreas Goss; Lord Grade of Yarmouth, CBE; Prof. Ludmilla Jordanova, FRHS, FRSM; Prof. Ajit Lalvani; Iain McIntosh; Lopa Patel; Prof. David Phoenix, OBE; Sarah Staniforth; Steven Underwood; Anton Valk, CBE; Rt. Hon. Lord Willetts; Dame Fiona Woolf, CBE
Director of Science Museum, Sir Ian Blatchford
Director of Museum of Science & Industry, Sally MacDonald
Director of National Science and Media Museum, Jo Quinton-Tulloch
Director of National Railway Museum, Judith McNicol

SCOTTISH CRIMINAL CASES REVIEW COMMISSION

5th Floor, Portland House, 17 Renfield Street, Glasgow G2 5AH
T 0141-270 7030 E info@sccrc.org.uk W www.sccrc.org.uk

The commission is a non-departmental public body, funded by the Scottish Government Justice Directorate, and established under the Criminal Procedure (Scotland) Act 1995 in April 1999. It assumed the role previously performed by the Secretary of State for Scotland to consider alleged miscarriages of justice in Scotland and refer cases meeting the relevant criteria to the high court for determination. Members are appointed by the Queen on the recommendation of the first minister; senior executive staff are appointed by the commission.

Chair, Bill Matthews
Members, Dr Rajan Darjee; Colin Dunipace; Peter Ferguson, QC; Prof. Jim Fraser; Frances McMenamin, QC; Raymond McMenamin; Elaine Noad
Chief Executive, Gerard Sinclair

SCOTTISH ENTERPRISE

Atrium Court, 50 Waterloo Street, Glasgow G2 6HQ
T 0300-013 3385 E enquiries@scotent.co.uk
W www.scottish-enterprise.com

Scottish Enterprise was established in 1991 and its purpose is to stimulate the sustainable growth of Scotland's economy. It is mainly funded by the Scottish government and is responsible to the Scottish ministers. Working in partnership with the private and public sectors, Scottish Enterprise plan to invest £358.5m in 2018–19 to further the development of Scotland's economy by helping ambitious and innovative businesses grow and become more successful. Scottish Enterprise is particularly interested in supporting companies that provide renewable energy, encourage trade overseas, increase innovation, and those that will help Scotland become a low-carbon economy. Its anticipated grant-in-aid allocation (capital and resource allocation) for 2018–19 was £179.3m.

Chair, Lord Smith of Kelvin, KT, CH
Chief Executive, Steve Dunlop

SCOTTISH ENVIRONMENT PROTECTION AGENCY (SEPA)

Erskine Court, Castle Business Park, Stirling FK9 4TZ
T 0300-099 6699 W www.sepa.org.uk

SEPA was established in 1996 and is the public body responsible for environmental protection in Scotland. It regulates potential pollution to land, air and water; the storage, transport and disposal of controlled waste; and the safekeeping and disposal of radioactive materials. It does this within a complex legislative framework of acts of parliament, EU directives and regulations, granting licences to operations of industrial processes and waste disposal. SEPA also operates Floodline (T 0345-988 1188), a public service providing information on the possible risk of flooding 24 hours a day, 365 days a year.

Chair, Bob Downes
Members, Franceska van Dijk; Dr Richard Dixon; Michelle Francis; Nicola Gordon; Martin Hill; Nick Martin; Prof. Bill McKelvey, OBE; Prof. Keith Nicholson; Dr Lesley Sawers
Chief Executive, Terry A'Hearn

SCOTTISH LAW COMMISSION

140 Causewayside, Edinburgh EH9 1PR
T 0131-668 2131 E info@scotlawcom.gsi.gov.uk
W www.scotlawcom.gov.uk

The Scottish Law Commission, established in 1965, keeps the law in Scotland under review and makes proposals for its development and reform. It is responsible to the Scottish ministers through the Scottish government constitution, law and courts directorate.

Chair, Rt. Hon. Lady Paton
Commissioners, Kate Dowdalls, QC; Caroline Drummond; David Johnston, QC; Dr Andrew Steven
Chief Executive, Malcolm McMillan

SCOTTISH LEGAL AID BOARD

Thistle House, 91 Haymarket Terrace, Edinburgh EH12 5HE
T 0131-226 7061 E general@slab.org.uk W www.slab.org.uk

The Scottish Legal Aid Board was set up under the Legal Aid (Scotland) Act 1986 to manage legal aid in Scotland. It is designed to help individuals on low or modest incomes gain access to the legal system. It reports to the Scottish government. Board members are appointed by Scottish ministers.

Chair, Ray MacFarlane
Members, Brian Baverstock; Rani Dhir; Marieke Dwarshuis; Stephen Humphreys; Tim McKay; Raymond McMenamin; Sheriff John Morris; Sarah O'Neill; Paul Reid; David Sheldon, QC; Lesley Ward
Chief Executive, Colin Lancaster

SCOTTISH NATURAL HERITAGE (SNH)

Great Glen House, Leachkin Road, Inverness IV3 8NW
T 01463-725000 E enquiries@nature.scot W www.nature.scot

SNH was established in 1992 under the Natural Heritage (Scotland) Act 1991. It is the government's adviser on all aspects of nature and landscape across Scotland and its role is to help the public understand, value and enjoy Scotland's nature, as well as to support those people and organisations that manage it.

Chair, Dr Mike Cantlay, OBE
Chief Executive and Accountable Officer, Francesca Osowska
Directors, Nick Halfhide *(Sustainable Growth);* Jane Macdonald *(Business Services and Transformation);* Sally Thomas *(People and Nature)*

SEAFISH

18 Logie Mill, Logie Green Road, Edinburgh EH7 4HS
T 0131-558 3331 E seafish@seafish.co.uk W www.seafish.org

Established under the Fisheries Act 1981, Seafish works with all sectors of the UK seafood industry to satisfy consumers, raise standards, improve efficiency and secure a sustainable and profitable future. Services range from research and development, economic consulting, market research and training and accreditation through to legislative advice for the seafood industry. It is sponsored by the four UK fisheries departments, which appoint the board, and receives 80 per cent of its funding through a levy on seafood.

Chair, Brian Young
Chief Executive, Marcus Coleman

SECURITY AND INTELLIGENCE SERVICES

GOVERNMENT COMMUNICATIONS HEADQUARTERS (GCHQ)

Hubble Road, Cheltenham GL51 0EX
T 01242-221491 W www.gchq.gov.uk

GCHQ produces signals intelligence in support of national security and the UK's economic wellbeing, and in the prevention or detection of serious crime. . It is the national authority for cyber security and provides advice and assistance to government departments, the armed forces and other national infrastructure bodies on the security of their communications and information systems. GCHQ was placed on a statutory footing by the Intelligence Services Act 1994 and is headed by a director who is directly accountable to the foreign secretary.

Director, Jeremy Fleming

SECRET INTELLIGENCE SERVICE (MI6)

PO Box 1300, London SE1 1BD
Anti-Terrorist Hotline 0800-789 321 W www.sis.gov.uk

Established in 1909 as the Foreign Section of the Secret Service Bureau, the Secret Intelligence Service produces secret intelligence in support of the government's security, defence, foreign and economic policies. It was placed on a statutory footing by the Intelligence Services Act 1994 and is headed by a chief, known as 'C', who is directly accountable to the foreign secretary.

Chief, Sir Alex Younger, KCMG

SECURITY SERVICE (MI5)

PO Box 3255, London SW1P 1AE
T 0800-111 4645Anti-Terrorist Hotline 0800-789 321
W www.mi5.gov.uk

The Security Service is responsible for security intelligence work against covertly organised threats to the UK. It is organised into ten branches, each with dedicated areas of responsibility, which include countering terrorism, espionage and the proliferation of weapons of mass destruction. The Security Service also provides security advice to a wide range of organisations to help reduce vulnerability to threats from individuals, groups or countries hostile to UK interests. The home secretary has parliamentary accountability for the Security Service. There is a network of regional offices around the UK, plus a Northern Ireland headquarters.

Director-General, Sir Andrew Parker, KCB

SENIOR SALARIES REVIEW BODY

8th Floor, Fleetbank House, 2-6 Salisbury Square, London EC4Y 8JX
T 020-7211 8315 E SSRB@BEIS.gov.uk W www.gov.uk/ government/organisations/review-body-on-senior-salaries

The Senior Salaries Review Body (formerly the Top Salaries Review Body) was set up in 1971 and advises the prime minister, the Lord Chancellor, the defence secretary, the health secretary and the home secretary on the remuneration of the judiciary, senior civil servants, senior officers of the armed forces, certain senior managers in the NHS, police and crime commissioners and chief police officers. In 1993 its remit was extended to cover the pay, pensions and allowances of MPs, ministers and others whose pay is determined by the Ministerial and Other Salaries Act 1975, and also the allowances of peers. If asked, it advises on the pay of officers and members of the devolved parliament and assemblies.

Chair, Dr Martin Read, CBE
Members, Sir Adrian Johns, KCB, CBE; Pippa Lambert; Peter Maddison, QPM; Dr Peter Westaway; Sharon Witherspoon

STUDENT LOANS COMPANY LTD

100 Bothwell Street, Glasgow G2 7JD
T 0300-100 0607 (England); 0300-200 4050 (Wales); 0300-555 0505 (Scotland); 0300-100 0077 (Northern Ireland)
W www.slc.co.uk

The Student Loans Company (SLC) is owned by the Department for Education. It processes and administers financial assistance, in the form of grants and loans, for undergraduates who have secured a place at university or college. The SLC also provides loans for tuition fees, which are paid directly to the university or college. In 2016 the SLC introduced the provision of loans to postgraduates in accordance with government policy. The SLC supports around 1.8 million students per year.

Chair, Christian Brodie
Chief Executive, Paula Sussex

TATE

W www.tate.org.uk

TATE BRITAIN
Millbank, London SW1P 4RG
T 020-7887 8888 E information@tate.org.uk

TATE MODERN
Bankside, London SE1 9TG
T 020-7887 8888 E information@tate.org.uk

TATE LIVERPOOL
Royal Albert Dock, Liverpool L3 4BB
T 015-1702 7400 E visiting.liverpool@tate.org.uk

TATE ST IVES
Porthmeor Beach, St Ives, Cornwall TR26 1TG
T 01736-796226 E visiting.stives@tate.org.uk

Tate comprises four art galleries: Tate Britain and Tate Modern in London, Tate Liverpool and Tate St Ives.
   Tate Britain, which opened in 1897, displays the national collection of British art from 1500 to the present day – with special attention and dedicated space given to Blake, Turner and Constable.
   Opened in May 2000, Tate Modern displays the Tate collection of international modern art dating from 1900 to the present day. It includes works by Dalí, Picasso, and Matisse, as well as many contemporary works. It is housed in the former Bankside Power Station in London, which was redesigned by

the Swiss architects Herzog and de Meuron, and in the neighbouring and purpose-built Switch House, which was designed by Herzog and de Meuron and opened in 2016.

Tate Liverpool opened in 1988 and houses mainly 20th-century art, and Tate St Ives, which features work by artists from and working in St Ives and includes the Barbara Hepworth Museum and Sculpture Garden, opened in 1993.

BOARD OF TRUSTEES
Chair, Lionel Barber
Trustees, John Akomfrah, CBE; John Booth; Tim Davie, CBE; Dame Jayne-Anne Gadhia, DBE; Dame Moya Greene, DBE; Michael Lynton; Dame Seona Reid, DBE; Roland Rudd; James Timpson, OBE; Jane Wilson; Stephen Witherford

OFFICERS
Director, Tate, Maria Balshaw, CBE
Directors, Anne Barlow *(Tate St Ives);* Anna Cutler *(Learning and Research);* Alex Farquharson *(Tate Britain);* Helen Legg *(Tate Liverpool);* Rosemary Lynch *(Collection Care);* Kerstin Mogull *(Managing Director);* Frances Morris *(Tate Modern);* Stephen Wingfield *(Finance and Estates)*

TOURISM BODIES

Visit Britain, Visit Scotland, Visit Wales and the Northern Ireland Tourist Board are responsible for developing and marketing the tourist industry in their respective regions. Visit Wales is not listed here as it is part of the Welsh government, within the Department for Heritage, and not a public body.

VISITBRITAIN
151 Buckingham Palace Road, London SW1W 9SZ
T 020-7578 1000 W www.visitbritain.org
Chair, Steve Ridgway, CBE
Chief Executive, Sally Balcombe

VISITSCOTLAND
Ocean Point One, 94 Ocean Drive Edinburgh EH6 6JH
T 0131-472 2222 E info@visitscotland.com
W www.visitscotland.com
Chair, Lord Thurso
Chief Executive, Malcolm Roughead, OBE

NORTHERN IRELAND TOURIST BOARD
Floors 10–12, Linum Chambers, Bedford Square, Bedford Street, Belfast BT2 7ES T 028-9023 1221
E info@tourismni.com W www.tourismni.com
Chair, Terence Brannigan
Chief Executive, John McGrillen

TRANSPORT FOR LONDON (TFL)

4th Floor, 14 Pier Walk, London SE10 0ES
T 0343-222 1234 W www.tfl.gov.uk

TfL was created in July 2000 and is the integrated body responsible for the capital's transport system. Its role is to implement the Mayor of London's transport strategy and manage the transport services across London, for which the mayor has responsibility. These services include TfL Rail, London's buses, London Underground, London Overground, the Docklands Light Railway (DLR), London Trams, London River Services and Victoria Coach Station. TfL also runs the Emirates Air Line and the London Transport Museum. In a joint venture with the Department for Transport, TfL is responsible for the construction of Crossrail – a new railway linking Reading and Heathrow in the west, to Shenfield and Abbey Wood in the east. The 73-mile section through London, which was due to open in December 2018, is expected to be operational in 2020. In 2017 TfL announced plans for

Crossrail 2, a railway running between Surrey and Hertfordshire.

TfL is responsible for managing the Congestion Charging scheme and the Transport for London road network, London's 'red routes', which make up 5 per cent of the city's roads, but carry around 30 per cent of the traffic. It manages, maintains and operates London's 6,000+ traffic lights and regulates the city's taxis and private hire vehicles. TfL runs the Santander Cycle Hire scheme, allowing customers to hire a bicycle from £2, and the Dial-a-ride scheme, a door-to-door service for disabled people unable to use buses, trams or the London Underground.

Chair, Rt. Hon. Sadiq Khan
Members, Heidi Alexander *(Deputy Chair);* Kay Carberry, CBE; Prof. Greg Clark, CBE; Bronwen Handyside; Ron Kalifa; Anne McMeel; Dr Alice Maynard, CBE; Dr Mee Ling Ng, OBE; Dr Nelson Ogunshakin, OBE; Mark Phillips; Val Shawcross, CBE; Dr Nina Skorupska, CBE; Dr Lynn Sloman; Ben Story
Commissioner, Mike Brown, MVO

UK ATOMIC ENERGY AUTHORITY

Culham Science Centre, Abingdon, Oxfordshire OX14 3DB
T 01235-528822 W www.gov.uk/government/organisations/
uk-atomic-energy-authority

The UK Atomic Energy Authority (UKAEA) was established by the Atomic Energy Authority Act 1954 and took over responsibility for the research and development of the civil nuclear power programme. The UKAEA reports to the Department for Business, Energy and Industrial Strategy and is responsible for managing UK fusion research, including operating the Joint European Torus (JET) on behalf of the UKAEA's European partners at its site in Culham, Oxfordshire. Culham also houses the facilities for Materials Research, Remote Access in Challenging Environments and Oxford Advanced Skills. In October 2009, as part of the government's Operation Efficiency Programme, the authority sold its commercial arm, UKAEA Limited; as a result, the UKAEA no longer provides nuclear decommissioning services.

Chair, Prof. David Gann, CBE
Chief Executive, Prof. Ian Chapman

UK SPORT

21 Bloomsbury Street, London WC1B 3HF
T 020-7211 5100 E info@uksport.gov.uk W www.uksport.gov.uk

UK Sport was established by royal charter in 1997 and is accountable to parliament through the Department for Digital, Culture, Media and Sport. Its mission is to lead sport in the UK to world-class success. This means working with partner organisations to deliver medals at the Olympic and Paralympic Games and organising, bidding for and staging major sporting events in the UK; increasing the UK's sporting activity and influence overseas; and promoting sporting conduct, ethics and diversity in society. UK Sport is funded by a mix of grant-in-aid and National Lottery income.

Chair, Dame Katherine Grainger, DBE
Chief Executive, Liz Nicholl, OBE

VICTORIA AND ALBERT MUSEUM

Cromwell Road, London SW7 2RL
T 020-7942 2000 E hello@vam.ac.uk W www.vam.ac.uk

The Victoria and Albert Museum (V&A) is the national museum of art, design and performance. It descends directly from the Museum of Manufactures, which opened in Marlborough House in 1852 after the Great Exhibition of 1851. The museum was moved in 1857 to become part of the South

Kensington Museum. It was renamed the Victoria and Albert Museum in 1899. It also houses the National Art Library and Print Room.

The museum's collections span over 5,000 years of human creativity, including paintings, sculpture, architecture, ceramics, furniture, fashion and textiles, theatre and performance, photography, glass, jewellery, book arts, Asian art and design and metalwork. Materials relating to childhood are displayed at the V&A Museum of Childhood at Bethnal Green, which opened in 1872 and is the most important surviving example of the type of glass and iron construction used by Joseph Paxton for the Great Exhibition. The V&A also houses the National Art Library, which holds over 950,000 books dedicated to the study of fine and decorative arts from around the world.

Chair, Nicholas Coleridge, CBE
Trustees, Jonathan Anderson; Benjamin Elliot; Robert Glick; Andrew Hochhauser, QC; Nick Hoffman; Steven Murphy; Prof. Lynda Nead; Kavita Puri; Dame Theresa Sackler, DBE; Marc St John; Caroline Silver; Sir John Sorrell; Dr Paul Thompson; Edmund de Waal, OBE; Nigel Webb
Director, Dr Tristram Hunt

WALLACE COLLECTION
Hertford House, Manchester Square, London W1U 3BN
T 020-7563 9500 E collection@wallacecollection.org
W www.wallacecollection.org

The Wallace Collection was bequeathed to the nation by the widow of Sir Richard Wallace, in 1897, and Hertford House was subsequently acquired by the government. The collection contains works by Titian and Rembrandt, and includes porcelain, furniture and an array of arms and armour.

Chair, António Horta-Osório
Trustees, Marilyn Berk; Jennifer Eady, QC; Eric Ellul; Dounia Nadar; Jessica Pulay; Jemima Rellie; Kate de Rothschild-Agius; Dr Ashok Roy; Timothy Schroder
Director, Dr Xavier Bray

DEVOLVED GOVERNMENT

WALES

NATIONAL ASSEMBLY FOR WALES
Cardiff Bay, Cardiff CF99 1NA
T 0300-200 6565 W www.assemblywales.org

The National Assembly for Wales has been in existence since 1999, following a 'yes' vote in the 1997 referendum. However, the way the assembly is structured and its powers have changed over time.

The UK Act that created the assembly was the Government of Wales Act 1998. This stated that the Assembly was a 'corporate body' which meant that the Welsh government and the assembly were a single organisation. Also, it could not pass its own acts. It could, however make orders and regulations, known as secondary legislation.

The Government of Wales Act 2006 created a formal legal separation between:
- the legislative branch: the National Assembly for Wales, made up of 60 assembly members, and
- the executive branch: the Welsh government, made up of the First Minister, Welsh cabinet secretaries and the Counsel General

The act allowed the assembly to seek the power to make laws from the UK parliament. The laws were known as 'measures' of the National Assembly for Wales ('assembly measures'). The power to make laws ('legislative competence') was granted through clauses in Westminster bills or through legislative competence orders. These had to be approved by parliament and by the assembly. This is how the third assembly operated between 2007 and 2011.

The Government of Wales Act 2006 also contained provision for the assembly to make its own lawns without the permission of the UK parliament. These provisions could only be triggered by:
- two-thirds of all assembly members voting in favour of a referendum
- the approval of the UK government and parliament to hold a referendum
- a 'yes' vote in a referendum of the Welsh public

A referendum held on 3 March 2011 resulted in a 'yes' vote in favour of bringing into force part four of the Government of Wales Act 2006. This has meant that since the 2011 National Assembly of Wales election the assembly has been able to pass laws on all subjects in the devolved areas without first needing the agreement of the UK parliament.

During an assembly election, the people of Wales have two votes. One vote is for their constituency assembly member who represents local areas. Wales is divided into 40 constituencies and each is represented by one assembly member (AM).

The other vote is for a party or independent candidate to represent the voter's region. Wales is divided into five regions – North Wales, Mid and West Wales, South Wales West, South Wales East and South Wales Central.

This system means that the overall number of seats held by each political party more closely reflects the share of the vote that the party receives.

The 60 assembly members who are elected make decisions regarding many things that affect life in Wales – health, education, housing and transport. Their job is to make sure that the Welsh government's decisions are in the best interests of Wales and its people.

The National Assembly for Wales does this by:

- scrutinising the policies the Welsh government sets and the decisions it makes
- scrutinising suggestions for laws, proposing changes and voting on whether they should be passed
- asking questions to Welsh government and making suggestions about policies
- voting on how the Welsh government spends its budget every year

The assembly also makes laws for Wales. A law can be put forward by the Welsh government, an individual assembly member, or an assembly committee or the Assembly Commission. The majority of laws are put forward by the Welsh government.

The assembly operates in both Welsh and English and all its legislation is made bilingually.

In July 2018 the National Assembly of Wales Commission announced plans to lower the minimum voting age for assembly elections to 16 years. They also announced plans to change the name of the assembly to Welsh Parliament/Senedd Cymru. The assembly intends to legislate both changes prior to the next assembly elections in 2021.

ASSEMBLY COMMISSION
The Assembly Commission was created under the Government of Wales Act 2006 to ensure that the assembly is provided with the property, staff and services required for it to carry out its functions. The commission also sets the National Assembly's strategic aims, objectives, standards and values. The Assembly Commission consists of the presiding officer, plus four other assembly members, one nominated by each of the four party groups. The five commissioners are accountable to the National Assembly.

Presiding Officer, Elin Jones, AM
Deputy Presiding Officer, Ann Jones, AM
Commissioners, Suzy Davies, AM; Siân Gwenllian, AM, David Rowlands, AM, Joyce Watson, AM
Chief Executive and Clerk of the Assembly, Manon Antoniazzi

ASSEMBLY COMMITTEES
The Business Committee, chaired by the Presiding Officer and established on 24 May 2016, is responsible for facilitating the effective organisation of assembly proceedings. The rest of the assembly committees *as at* August 2019 are:

Children, Young People and Education
Chair, Lynne Neagle, AM
Climate Change, Environment and Rural Affairs
Chair, Mike Hedges, AM
Constitutional and Legislative Affairs
Chair, Mick Antoniw, AM
Culture, Welsh Language and Communications
Chair, Bethan Sayed, AM
Economy, Infrastructure and Skills
Chair, Russell George, AM
Equality, Local Government and Communities
Chair, John Griffiths, AM
External Affairs and Additional Legislation
Chair, David Rees, AM
Finance
Chair, Llyr Gruffydd, AM
Health, Social Care and Sport
Chair, Dai Lloyd, AM
Petitions
Chair, Janet Finch-Saunders, AM

Public Accounts
Chair, Nick Ramsay, AM
Scrutiny of the First Minister
Chair, Ann Jones, AM
Standards of Conduct
Chair, Jayne Bryant, AM

SALARIES* *2019–20*

First Minister	£147,983
Presiding Officer	£110,987
Cabinet Secretary	£105,701
Minister/Deputy Presiding Officer	£89,846
Assembly Commissioners	£81,390
Assembly Member (AM)	£67,649

* All salaries include the AM salary

MEMBERS OF THE NATIONAL ASSEMBLY FOR WALES *as at 31 August 2019*

KEY
* Elected via a by-election since the 2016 National Assembly election
† Replacement from the party list since the 2016 National Assembly election
‡ Previously AM for PC
§ Previously AM for UKIP
ℂ Previously an Ind. AM
** Previously an AM for C.

Antoniw, Mick, *Lab., Pontypridd,* Maj. 5,327
ap Iorwerth, Rhun, *PC, Ynys Môn,* Maj. 9,510
Asghar, Mohammad, *C., South Wales East region*
Bennett, Gareth, *UKIP, South Wales Central region*
Blythyn, Hannah, *Lab., Delyn,* Maj. 3,582
Bowden, Dawn, *Lab., Merthyr Tydfil and Rhymney,* Maj. 5,486
§ **Brown**, Michelle, *Ind., North Wales region*
Bryant, Jayne, *Lab., Newport West,* Maj. 4,115
Burns, Angela, *C., Carmarthen West and South Pembrokeshire,* Maj. 3,373
David, Hefin, *Lab., Caerphilly,* Maj. 1,575
Davies, Alun, *Lab., Blaenau Gwent,* Maj. 650
Davies, Andrew R. T., *C., South Wales Central region*
Davies, Paul, *C., Preseli Pembrokeshire,* Maj. 3,930
Davies, Suzy, *C., South Wales West region*
Drakeford, Rt. Hon. Mark, *Lab., Cardiff West,* Maj. 1,176
‡ **Elis-Thomas**, Rt. Hon. Lord, *Ind., Dwyfor Meirionnydd,* Maj. 6,406
Evans, Rebecca, *Lab., Gower,* Maj. 1,829
Finch-Saunders, Janet, *C., Aberconwy,* Maj. 754
George, Russell, *C., Montgomeryshire,* Maj. 3,339
Gething, Vaughan, *Lab., Cardiff South and Penarth,* Maj. 6,921
Griffiths, John, *Lab., Newport East,* Maj. 4,896
Griffiths, Lesley, *Lab., Wrexham,* Maj. 1,325
Gruffydd, Llyr, *PC, North Wales region*
Gwenllian, Siân, *PC, Arfon,* Maj. 4,162
Hamilton, Neil, *UKIP, Mid and West Wales region*
Hedges, Mike, *Lab., Swansea East,* Maj. 7,452
Howells, Vikki, *Lab., Cynon Valley,* Maj. 5, 994
Hutt, Jane, *Lab., Vale of Glamorgan,* Maj. 777
Irranca-Davies, Huw, *Lab., Ogmore,* Maj. 9,468
Isherwood, Mark, *C., North Wales region*
James, Julie, *Lab., Swansea West,* Maj. 5,080
† **Jewell**, Delyth, *PC, South Wales East region*
Jones, Ann, *Lab., Vale of Clwyd,* Maj. 768
§ **Jones**, Caroline, *Brexit, South Wales West region*
Jones, Rt. Hon. Carwyn, *Lab., Bridgend,* Maj. 5,623
Jones, Elin, *PC, Ceredigion,* Maj. 2,408

Jones, Helen Mary, *PC, Mid and West Wales region*
ℂ **Jones**, Mandy, *Brexit, North Wales region*
Lloyd, Dai, *PC, South Wales West region*
‡ **McEvoy**, Neil, *Ind., South Wales Central region*
Melding, David, *C. South Wales Central region*
Miles, Jeremy, *Lab. Neath,* Maj. 2,923
Millar, Darren, *C., Clwyd West,* Maj. 5,063
Morgan, Eluned *Lab., Mid and West Wales region*
Morgan, Julie, *Lab., Cardiff North,* Maj. 3,667
Neagle, Lynne, *Lab., Torfaen,* Maj. 4,498
Passmore, Rhianon, *Lab., Islwyn,* Maj. 5,106
Price, Adam, *PC, Carmarthen East and Dinefwr,* Maj. 8,700
Ramsay, Nick, *C., Monmouth,* Maj. 5,147
Rathbone, Jenny, *Lab., Cardiff Central,* Maj. 817
§ ** **Reckless**, Mark, *Brexit, South Wales East*
Rees, David, *Lab, Aberavon,* Maj. 6,402
§ **Rowlands**, David J., *Brexit, South Wales East region*
* **Sargeant**, Jack, *Lab., Alyn and Deeside* Maj. 6,545
Sayed, Bethan, *PC, South Wales West region*
Skates, Ken, *Lab., Clwyd South,* Maj. 3,016
Waters, Lee, *Lab., Llanelli,* Maj. 382
Watson, Joyce, *Lab., Mid and West Wales region*
Williams, Kirsty, *LD, Brecon and Radnorshire,* Maj. 8,170
Wood, Leanne, *PC, Rhondda,* Maj. 3,359

STATE OF THE PARTIES *as at 31 August 2019*

	Constituency AMs	Regional AMs	AM total
Labour (Lab.)	*27	2	29
Conservative (C.)	6	5	11
Plaid Cymru (PC)	†5	5	10
Brexit Party (Brexit)	0	4	4
UKIP	0	2	2
Independent (Ind.)	1	2	3
Liberal Democrats (LD)	1	0	1
Total	40	20	60

* Includes the Deputy Presiding Officer
† Includes the Presiding Officer

WELSH GOVERNMENT
Cathays Park, Cardiff CF10 3NQ
T 0300-060 4400 W www.gov.wales

The Welsh government is the devolved government of Wales. It is accountable to the National Assembly for Wales, the Welsh legislature which represents the interests of the people of Wales, and makes laws for Wales. The Welsh government and the National Assembly for Wales were established as separate institutions under the Government of Wales Act 2006.

The Welsh government comprises the first minister, who is usually the leader of the largest party in the National Assembly for Wales; up to 14 cabinet secretaries and ministers and deputy ministers; and a counsel-general (the chief legal adviser).

Following the referendum on 3 March 2011 on granting further law-making powers to the National Assembly, the Welsh government's functions now include the ability to propose bills to the National Assembly on subjects within 20 set areas of policy. Subject to limitations prescribed by the Government of Wales Act 2006, acts of the National Assembly may make any provision that could be made by act of parliament. The 20 areas of responsibility devolved to the National Assembly for Wales (and within which Welsh ministers exercise executive functions) are: agriculture, fisheries, forestry and rural development; ancient monuments and historic buildings; culture; economic development; education and training; environment; fire and rescue services and promotion of fire safety; food; health and health services; highways and transport; housing; local government; the National Assembly for Wales; public administration; social welfare; sport and recreation; tourism; town and county planning; water and flood defence; and the Welsh language.

CABINET

Ministers
First Minister of Wales, Rt. Hon. Mark Drakeford, AM
Economy and Transport, Ken Skates, AM
Education, Kirsty Williams, AM
Environment, Energy and Rural Affairs, Lesley Griffiths, AM
Finance and Trefnydd (Leader of the House), Rebecca Evans, AM
Health and Social Services, Vaughan Gething, AM
Housing and Local Government, Julie James, AM
International Relations and the Welsh Language, Eluned Morgan, AM
Counsel-General and Brexit Minister, Jeremy Miles, AM

Deputy Ministers
Culture, Sport and Tourism, Rt. Hon. Lord Elis-Thomas, AM
Economy and Transport, Lee Waters, AM
Health and Social Services, Julie Morgan, AM
Housing and Local Government, Hannah Blythyn, AM

Chief Whip, Jane Hutt, AM

MANAGEMENT BOARD
Permanent Secretary, Dame Shan Morgan, DCMG
Director-Generals, Tracey Burke *(Education and Public Services);* Desmond Clifford *(Office of the First Minister and Brexit);* Dr Andrew Goodall, CBE *(Health and Social Services);* Andrew Slade *(Economy, Skills and Natural Resources)*
Directors, Jeff Godfrey *(Legal Services);* Peter Kennedy *(HR);* David Richards *(Governance and Ethics)*
Head of Organisational Development and Engagement, Natalie Pearson
Board Equality and Diversity Champion, Gillian Baranski
Finance Director, Gawain Evans
Non-Executive Directors, Ellen Donovan; Jeff Farrar; Ann Keane; Gareth Lynn

DEPARTMENTS
Permanent Secretary's Group – Welsh Treasury, Finance, Governance and HR

DIRECTORATES
Office of the First Minister and Brexit
Education and Public Services
Health and Social Services
Economy, Skills and Natural Resources

NATIONAL ASSEMBLY ELECTION RESULTS *as at 5 May 2016*

Electorate (E.) 2,248,050 Turnout (T.) 45.3%
See General Election Results for a list of party abbreviations

ABERAVON (S. WALES WEST)
E. 49,074 T. 20,852 (42.49%)
David Rees, Lab.	10,578
Bethan Jenkins, PC	4,176
Glenda Davies, UKIP	3,119
David Jenkins, C.	1,342
Helen Ceri Clarke, LD	1,248
Jonathan Tier, Green	389

Lab. majority 6,402 (30.70%)
9.31% swing Lab. to PC

ABERCONWY (WALES N.)
E. 44,960 T. 22,038 (49.02%)
Janet Finch-Saunders, C.	7,646
Trystan Lewis, PC	6,892
Mike Priestley, Lab.	6,039
Sarah Lesiter-Burgess, LD	781
Petra Haig, Green	680

C. majority 754 (3.42%)
2.15% swing C. to PC

ALYN AND DEESIDE (WALES N.)
E. 62,697 T. 21,696 (34.60%)
Carl Sargeant, Lab.	9,922
Mike Gibbs, C.	4,558
Michelle Brown, UKIP	3,765
Jacqui Hurst, PC	1,944
Pete Williams, LD	980
Martin Bennewith, Green	527

Lab. majority 5,364 (24.72%)
0.11% swing C. to Lab.

ARFON (WALES N.)
E. 39,269 T. 19,994 (50.92%)
Sian Gwenllian, PC	10,962
Sion Jones, Lab.	6,800
Martin Peet, C.	1,655
Sara Lloyd Williams, LD	577

PC majority 4,162 (20.82%)
4.86% swing PC to Lab.

BLAENAU GWENT (S. WALES EAST)
E. 50,574 T. 21,291 (42.10%)
Alun Davies, Lab.	8,442
Nigel Copner, PC	7,792
Kevin Boucher, UKIP	3,423
Tracey West, C.	1,334
Brendan D'Cruz, LD	300

Lab. majority 650 (3.05%)
27.73% swing Lab. to PC

BRECON AND RADNORSHIRE (WALES MID AND W.)
E. 53,793 T. 30,367 (56.45%)
Kirsty Williams, LD	15,898
Gary Price, C.	7,728
Alex Thomas, Lab.	2,703
Thomas Turton, UKIP	2,161
Freddy Greaves, PC	1,180
Grenville Ham, Green	697

LD majority 8,170 (26.90%)
8.59% swing C. to LD

BRIDGEND (S. WALES WEST)
E. 60,195 T. 26,851 (44.61%)
Carwyn Jones, Lab.	12,166
George Jabbour, C.	6,543
Caroline Jones, UKIP	3,919
James Radcliffe, PC	2,569
Jonathan Pratt, LD	1,087
Charlie Barlow, Green	567

Lab. majority 5,623 (20.94%)
3.62% swing Lab. to C.

CAERPHILLY (S. WALES EAST)
E. 62,449 T. 27,115 (43.42%)
Hefin David, Lab.	9,584
Lindsay Whittle, PC	8,009
Sam Gould, UKIP	5,954
Jane Pratt, C.	2,412
Andrew Creak, Green	770
Aladdin Ayesh, LD	386

Lab. majority 1,575 (5.81%)
6.72% swing Lab. to PC

CARDIFF CENTRAL (S. WALES CENTRAL)
E. 57,177 T. 26,068 (45.59%)
Jenny Rathbone, Lab.	10,016
Eluned Parrott, LD	9,199
Joel Williams, C.	2,317
Glyn Wise, PC	1,951
Mohammed Islam, UKIP	1,223
Amelia Womack, Green	1,150
Jane Croad, Ind.	212

Lab. majority 817 (3.13%)
1.49% swing LD to Lab.

CARDIFF NORTH (S. WALES CENTRAL)
E. 65,927 T. 37,452 (56.81%)
Julie Morgan, Lab.	16,766
Jayne Cowan, C.	13,099
Haydn Rushworth, UKIP	2,509
Elin Walker Jones, PC	2,278
John Dixon, LD	1,130
Fiona Burt, Ind.	846
Chris von Ruhland, Green	824

Lab. majority 3,667 (9.79%)
2.31% swing C. to Lab.

CARDIFF SOUTH AND PENARTH (S. WALES CENTRAL)
E. 76,110 T. 30,276 (39.78%)

Vaughan Gething, Lab.	13,274
Ben Gray, C.	6,353
Dafydd Davies, PC	4,320
Hugh Moelwyn Hughes, UKIP	3,716
Nigel Howells, LD	1,345
Anthony Slaughter, Green	1,268

Lab. majority 6,921 (22.86%)
0.04% swing C. to Lab.

CARDIFF WEST (S. WALES CENTRAL)
E. 66,040 T. 31,960 (48.39%)

Mark Drakeford, Lab.	11,381
Neil McEvoy, PC	10,205
Sean Driscoll, C.	5,617
Gareth Bennett, UKIP	2,629
Hannah Pudner, Green	1,032
Cadan ap Tomos, LD	868
Eliot Freedman, Ind.	132
Lee Woolls, FTC	96

Lab. majority 1,176 (3.68%)
11.71% swing Lab. to PC

CARMARTHEN EAST AND DINEFWR (WALES MID AND W.)
E. 55,395 T. 29,751 (53.71%)

Adam Price, PC	14,427
Stephen Jeacock, Lab.	5,727
Matthew Paul, C.	4,489
Neil Hamilton, UKIP	3,474
William Powell, LD	837
Freya Amsbury, Green	797

PC majority 8,700 (29.24%)
7.17% swing Lab. to PC

CARMARTHEN WEST AND SOUTH PEMBROKESHIRE (WALES MID AND W.)
E. 56,886 T. 29,237 (51.40%)

Angela Burns, C.	10,355
Marc Tierney, Lab.	6,982
Simon Thomas, PC	5,459
Allan Brookes, UKIP	3,300
Chris Overton, Ind.	1,638
Val Bradley, Green	804
Alistair Cameron, LD	699

C. majority 3,373 (11.54%)
3.10% swing Lab. to C.

CEREDIGION (WALES MID AND W.)
E. 51,230 T. 29,485 (57.55%)

Elin T Jones, PC	12,014
Elizabeth Evans, LD	9,606
Gethin James, UKIP	2,665
Felix Aubel, C.	2,075
Iwan Wyn Jones, Lab.	1,902
Brian Williams, Green	1,223

PC majority 2,408 (8.17%)
1.03% swing LD to PC

CLWYD SOUTH (WALES N.)
E. 54,185 T. 22,159 (40.90%)

Ken Skates, Lab.	7,862
Simon Baynes, C.	4,846
Mabon ap Gwynfor, PC	3,861
Mandy Jones, UKIP	2,827
Aled Roberts, LD	2,289
Duncan Rees, Green	474

Lab. majority 3,016 (13.61%)
0.17% swing C. to Lab.

CLWYD WEST (WALES N.)
E. 57,657 T. 26,226 (45.49%)

Darren Millar, C.	10,831
Llyr Gruffydd, PC	5,768
Jo Thomas, Lab.	5,246
David Edwards, UKIP	2,985
Victor Babu, LD	831
Julian Mahy, Green	565

C. majority 5,063 (19.31%)
0.52% swing C. to PC

CYNON VALLEY (S. WALES CENTRAL)
E. 50,292 T. 19,236 (38.25%)

Vikki Howells, Lab.	9,830
Cerith Griffiths, PC	3,836
Liz Wilks, UKIP	3,460
Lyn Hudson, C.	1,177
John Matthews, Green	598
Michael Wallace, LD	335

Lab. majority 5,994 (31.16%)
1.78% swing Lab. to PC

DELYN (WALES N.)
E. 53,490 T. 23,159 (43.30%)

Hannah Blythyn, Lab.	9,480
Huw Williams, C.	5,898
Nigel Williams, UKIP	3,794
Paul Rowlinson, PC	2,269
Tom Rippeth, LD	1,718

Lab. majority 3,582 (15.47%)
1.52% swing C. to Lab.

DWYFOR MEIRIONNYDD (WALES MID AND W.)
E. 43,304 T. 20,236 (46.73%)

Dafydd Elis-Thomas, PC	9,566
Neil Fairlamb, C.	3,160
Ian MacIntyre, Lab.	2,443
Frank Wykes, UKIP	2,149
Louise Hughes, Ind.	1,259
Steve Churchman, LD	916
Alice Hooker-Stroud, Green	743

PC majority 6,406 (31.66%)
2.77% swing C. to PC

GOWER (S. WALES WEST)
E. 60,631 T. 30,187 (49.79%)

Rebecca Evans, Lab.	11,982
Lyndon Jones, C.	10,153
Colin Beckett, UKIP	3,300
Harri Roberts, PC	2,982
Sheila Kingston-Jones, LD	1,033
Abi Cherry-Hamer, Green	737

Lab. majority 1,829 (6.06%)
6.05% swing Lab. to C.

ISLWYN (S. WALES EAST)
E. 54,465 T. 22,309 (40.96%)

Rhianon Passmore, Lab.	10,050
Joe Smyth, UKIP	4,944
Lyn Ackerman, PC	4,349
Paul Williams, C.	1,775
Matthew Kidner, LD	597
Katy Beddoe, Green	594

Lab. majority 5,106 (22.89%)

LLANELLI (WALES MID AND W.)
E. 59,651 T. 28,116 (47.13%)

Lee Waters, Lab.	10,267
Helen Mary Jones, PC	9,885
Ken Rees, UKIP	4,132
Stefan Ryszewski, C.	1,937
Sian Caiach, PF	1,113
Guy Smith, Green	427
Gemma Bowker, LD	355

Lab. majority 382 (1.36%)
0.53% swing PC to Lab.

MERTHYR TYDFIL AND RHYMNEY (S. WALES EAST)
E. 53,754 T. 20,683 (38.48%)

Dawn Bowden, Lab.	9,763
David Rowlands, UKIP	4,277
Brian Thomas, PC	3,721
Elizabeth Simon, C.	1,331
Bob Griffin, LD	1,122
Julie Colbran, Green	469

Lab. majority 5,486 (26.52%)

MONMOUTH (S. WALES EAST)
E. 64,197 T. 31,401 (48.91%)

Nick Ramsay, C.	13,585
Catherine Fookes, Lab.	8,438
Tim Price, UKIP	3,092
Debby Blakebrough, Ind.	1,932
Jonathan Clark, PC	1,824
Veronica German, LD	1,474
Chris Were, Green	910
Stephen Morris, Eng Dem	146

C. majority 5,147 (16.39%)
2.00% swing C. to Lab.

MONTGOMERYSHIRE (WALES MID AND W.)
E. 48,682 T. 23,600 (48.48%)

Russell George, C.	9,875
Jane Dodds, LD	6,536
Des Parkinson, UKIP	2,458
Aled Morgan Hughes, PC	2,410
Martyn Singleton, Lab.	1,389
Richard Chaloner, Green	932

C. majority 3,339 (14.15%)
2.01% swing LD to C.

NEATH (S. WALES WEST)
E. 55,395 T. 25,363 (45.79%)

Jeremy Miles, Lab.	9,468
Alun Llewelyn, PC	6,545
Richard Pritchard, UKIP	3,780
Peter Crocker-Jaques, C.	2,179
Steve Hunt, Ind.	2,056
Frank Little, LD	746
Lisa Rapado, Green	589

Lab. majority 2,923 (11.52%)
7.63% swing Lab. to PC

NEWPORT EAST (S. WALES EAST)
E. 55,499 T. 20,688 (37.28%)

John Griffiths, Lab.	9,229
James Peterson, UKIP	4,333
Munawar Mughal, C.	3,768
Paul Halliday, LD	1,481
Tony Salkeld, PC	1,386
Peter Varley, Green	491

Lab. majority 4,896 (23.67%)

NEWPORT WEST (S. WALES EAST)
E. 62,169 T. 27,751 (44.64%)

Jayne Bryant, Lab.	12,157
Matthew Evans, C.	8,042
Michael Ford, UKIP	3,842
Simon Coopey, PC	1,645
Liz Newton, LD	880
Pippa Bartolotti, Green	814
Bill Fearnley-Whittingstall, Ind.	333
Gruff Meredith, WSov	38

Lab. majority 4,115 (14.83%)
1.75% swing Lab. to C.

OGMORE (S. WALES WEST)
E. 54,502 T. 23,356 (42.85%)

Huw Irranca-Davies, Lab.	12,895
Tim Thomas, PC	3,427
Elizabeth Kendall, UKIP	3,233
Jamie Wallis, C.	2,587
Anita Davies, LD	698
Laurie Brophy, Green	516

Lab. majority 9,468 (40.54%)
3.36% swing Lab. to PC

PONTYPRIDD (S. WALES CENTRAL)
E. 58,277 T. 25,338 (43.48%)

Mick Antoniw, Lab.	9,986
Chad Rickard, PC	4,659
Joel James, C.	3,884
Edwin Allen, UKIP	3,322
Mike Powell, LD	2,979
Ken Barker, Green	508

Lab. majority 5,327 (21.02%)
8.18% swing Lab. to PC

PRESELI PEMBROKESHIRE (WALES MID AND W.)
E. 56,414 T. 28,397 (50.34%)

Paul Davies, C.	11,123
Dan Lodge, Lab.	7,193
John Osmond, PC	3,957
Howard Lillyman, UKIP	3,286
Bob Kilmister, LD	1,677
Frances Bryant, Green	1,161

C. majority 3,930 (13.84%)
2.92% swing Lab. to C.

RHONDDA (S. WALES CENTRAL)
E. 49,758 T. 23,486 (47.20%)

Leanne Wood, PC	11,891
Leighton Andrews, Lab.	8,432
Stephen Clee, UKIP	2,203
Maria Hill, C.	528
Pat Matthews, Green	259
Rhys Taylor, LD	173

PC majority 3,459 (14.73%)
24.19% swing Lab. to PC

SWANSEA EAST (S. WALES WEST)
E. 57,589 T. 20,576 (35.73%)

Mike Hedges, Lab.	10,726
Clifford Johnson, UKIP	3,274
Dic Jones, PC	2,744
Sadie Vidal, C.	1,729
Charlene Webster, LD	1,574
Tony Young, Green	529

Lab. majority 7,452 (36.22%)

SWANSEA WEST (S. WALES WEST)
E. 54,593 T. 22,202 (40.67%)

Julie James, Lab.	9,014
Craig Lawton, C.	3,934
Dai Lloyd, PC	3,225
Rosie Irwin, UKIP	3,058
Chris Holley, LD	2,012
Gareth Tucker, Green	883
Brian Johnson, SPGB	76

Lab. majority 5,080 (22.88%)
0.77% swing C. to Lab.

TORFAEN (S. WALES EAST)
E. 60,246 T. 22,978 (38.14%)

Lynne Neagle, Lab.	9,688
Susan Boucher, UKIP	5,190
Graham Smith, C.	3,931
Matthew Woolfall-Jones, PC	2,860
Steve Jenkins, Green	681
Alison Willott, LD	628

Lab. majority 4,498 (19.58%)

VALE OF CLWYD (WALES N.)
E. 56,322 T. 24,183 (42.94%)

Ann Jones, Lab.	9,560
Sam Rowlands, C.	8,792
Paul Davies-Cooke, UKIP	2,975
Mair Rowlands, PC	2,098
Gwyn Williams, LD	758

Lab. majority 768 (3.18%)
7.11% swing Lab. to C.

VALE OF GLAMORGAN (S. WALES CENTRAL)
E. 71,177 T. 37,798 (53.10%)

Jane Hutt, Lab.	14,655
Ross England, C.	13,878
Ian Johnson, PC	3,871
Lawrence Andrews, UKIP	3,662
Denis Campbell, LD	938
Alison Haden, Green	794

Lab. majority 777 (2.06%)
4.65% swing Lab. to C.

WREXHAM (WALES N.)
E. 51,567 T. 20,354 (39.47%)

Lesley Griffiths, Lab.	7,552
Andrew Atkinson, C.	6,227
Carrie Harper, PC	2,631
Jeanette Bassford-Barton, UKIP	2,393
Beryl Blackmore, LD	1,140
Alan Butterworth, Green	411

Lab. majority 1,325 (6.51%)
5.67% swing Lab. to C.

YNYS MON (WALES N.)
E. 50,345 T. 25,167 (49.99%)

Rhun ap Iorwerth, PC	13,788
Julia Dobson, Lab.	4,278
Simon Wall, UKIP	3,212
Clay Theakston, C.	2,904
Gerry Wolff, Green	389
Thomas Crofts, LD	334
Daniel ap Eifion Jones, Ind.	262

PC majority 9,510 (37.79%)
11.29% swing Lab. to PC

REGIONS *as at 5 May 2016*
E. 2,248,050 T. 45.3%

MID AND WEST WALES
E. 425,355 T. 215,840 (50.74%)

PC	56,754	(26.29%)
C.	44,461	(20.60%)
Lab.	41,975	(19.45%)
UKIP	25,042	(11.60%)
LD	23,554	(10.91%)
Abolish	10,707	(4.96%)
Green	8,222	(3.81%)
PF	1,496	(0.69%)
Ch. P.	1,103	(0.51%)
Loony	1,071	(0.50%)
Loc. Ind.	1,032	(0.48%)
Welsh Comm	423	(0.20%)

PC majority 12,293 (5.70%)
2.02% swing C. to PC (2011 PC majority 3,479)

ADDITIONAL MEMBERS
Joyce Watson, *Lab.*
Eluned Morgan, *Lab.*
Simon Thomas, *PC*
Neil Hamilton, *UKIP*

NORTH WALES
E. 470,492 T. 204,490 (43.46%)

Lab.	57,528	(28.13%)
PC	47,701	(23.33%)
C	45,468	(22.23%)
UKIP	25,518	(12.48%)
Abolish	9,409	(4.60%)
LD	9,345	(4.57%)
Green	4,789	(2.34%)
Loc Ind.	1,865	(0.91%)
Loony	1,355	(0.66%)
Ind.	926	(0.45%)
Welsh Comm	586	(0.29%)

Lab. majority 9,827 (4.81%)
2.98% swing Lab. to PC (2011 Lab. majority 10,476)

ADDITIONAL MEMBERS
Mark Isherwood, *C.*
Llyr Gruffydd, *PC*
Nathan Gill, *UKIP*
Michelle Brown, *UKIP*

SOUTH WALES CENTRAL
E. 494,758 T. 231,133 (46.72%)

Lab.	78,366	(33.91%)
PC	48,357	(20.92%)
C.	42,185	(18.25%)
UKIP	23,958	(10.37%)
LD	14,875	(6.44%)
Abolish	9,163	(3.96%)
Green	7,949	(3.44%)
Women	2,807	(1.21%)
Loony	1,096	(0.47%)
TUSC	736	(0.32%)
Ind.	651	(0.28%)
Comm	520	(0.22%)
FTC	470	(0.20%)

Lab. majority 30,009 (12.98%)
7.24% swing Lab. to PC (2011 Lab. majority 39,694)

ADDITIONAL MEMBERS
Andrew Davies, *C.*
David Melding, *C.*
Neil McEvoy, *PC*
Gareth Bennett, *UKIP*

SOUTH WALES EAST
E. 463,353 T. 194,091 (41.89%)

Lab.	74,424	(38.34%)
UKIP	34,524	(17.79%)
C.	33,318	(17.17%)
PC	29,686	(15.29%)
Abolish	7,870	(4.05%)
LD	6,784	(3.50%)
Green	4,831	(2.49%)
Loony	1,115	(0.57%)
TUSC	618	(0.32%)
Welsh Comm	492	(0.25%)
NF	429	(0.22%)

Lab. majority 39,900 (20.56%)
9.93% swing Lab. to UKIP (2011 Lab. majority 47,240)

ADDITIONAL MEMBERS
Oscar Asghar, *C.*
Steffan Lewis, *PC*
Mark Reckless, *UKIP*
David Rowlands, *UKIP*

SOUTH WALES WEST
E. 391,979 T. 169,189 (43.16%)

Lab.	66,903	(39.54%)
PC	29,050	(17.17%)
C.	25,414	(15.02%)
UKIP	23,096	(13.65%)
LD	10,946	(6.47%)
Abolish	7,137	(4.22%)
Green	4,420	(2.61%)
Loony	1,106	(0.65%)
TUSC	686	(0.41%)
Welsh Comm	431	(0.25%)

Lab. majority 37,853 (22.37%)
5.17% swing Lab. to PC (2011 Lab. majority 44,309)

ADDITIONAL MEMBERS
Suzy Davies, *C.*
Bethan Jenkins, *PC*
Dai Lloyd, *PC*
Caroline Jones, *UKIP*

SCOTLAND

SCOTTISH PARLIAMENT
Edinburgh EH99 1SP
T 0131-348 5000/ 0800-092 7500
E info@parliament.scot
W www.parliament.scot

In July 1997 the government announced plans to establish a Scottish parliament. In a referendum on 11 September 1997 about 60 per cent of the electorate voted. Of those who voted, 74.3 per cent voted in favour of the parliament and 63.5 per cent voted in support of granting the parliament having tax-raising powers. Elections are normally held every four years, but the current session is scheduled to last for five years. The first elections were held on 6 May 1999, when around 59 per cent of the electorate voted. The first meeting was held on 12 May 1999 and the Scottish parliament was officially opened on 1 July 1999 at the Assembly Hall, Edinburgh. A new building to house the parliament was opened, in the presence of the Queen, at Holyrood on 9 October 2004. On 5 May 2016 the fifth elections to the Scottish parliament took place.

The Scottish parliament has 129 members (including the presiding officer), comprising 73 constituency members and 56 additional regional members, drawn from the party lists. It can introduce primary legislation and has the power to set rates and bands for income tax on non-savings and non-dividend income for Scottish taxpayers.

Members of the Scottish parliament are elected using the additional member system, the same system used to elect London Assembly and Welsh Assembly members. Under the additional member system the electorate has two votes; the first to elect their constituency member via the 'first past the post' method of voting and the second to elect their regional members. The 56 regional seats are filled proportionally from the parties' lists according to their share of the vote on the second ballot paper. By-elections are held for constituency seat vacancies but not for regional seat vacancies which are filled by the next candidate on the list from the same political party in which the vacancy arose.

The areas for which the Scottish parliament is responsible include: civil and criminal justice; education; health; environment; economic development; local government; housing; police; fire services; planning; financial assistance to industry; tourism; heritage and the arts; agriculture; social work; sports; public registers and records; forestry; food standards; some aspects of transport; and some areas of welfare.

SALARIES* *as at 1 April 2019*

First Minister	£155,680
Cabinet Secretary/ Presiding Officer	£111,359
Minister/ Deputy Presiding Officer	£93,510
MSP†	£63,579
Lord Advocate	£126,000
Solicitor-General for Scotland	£108,718

* All salaries include the MSP salary
† Reduced by two-thirds if the member is also an MP or MEP

The Presiding Officer, Ken Macintosh, MSP
Deputy Presiding Officers, Linda Fabiani, MSP; Christine Grahame, MSP

MEMBERS OF THE SCOTTISH PARLIAMENT *as at August 2019*

KEY
* Elected via a by-election since the 2016 Scottish parliament election
† Replacement from the party list since the 2016 Scottish parliament election under the additional member system
‡ The Presiding Officer was elected as a regional member for Labour but has no party affiliation while in post

Adam, George, *SNP, Paisley,* Maj. 5,199
Adamson, Clare, *SNP, Motherwell and Wishaw,* Maj. 6,223
Allan, Alasdair, *SNP, Na h-Eileanan an Iar,* Maj. 3,496
Arthur, Tom, *SNP, Renfrewshire South,* Maj. 4,408
Baillie, Jackie, *Lab., Dumbarton,* Maj. 109
Baker, Claire, *Lab., Mid Scotland and Fife region*
Balfour, Jeremy, *C., Lothian region*
† **Ballantyne**, Michelle, *C., South Scotland region*
Beamish, Claudia, *Lab., South Scotland region*
Beattie, Colin, *SNP, Midlothian North and Musselburgh,* Maj. 7,035
Bibby, Neil, *Lab., West Scotland region*
† **Bowman**, Bill, *C., North East Scotland region*
† **Boyack**, Sarah, *Lab., Lothian region*
Briggs, Miles, *C. Lothian region*
Brown, Keith, *SNP, Clackmannanshire and Dunblane,* Maj. 6,721
Burnett, Alexander, *C., Aberdeenshire West,* Maj. 900
Cameron, Donald, *C., Highlands and Islands region*
Campbell, Aileen, *SNP, Clydesdale,* Maj. 5,979
Carlaw, Jackson, *C., Eastwood,* Maj. 1.610
Carson, Finlay, *C., Galloway and West Dumfries,* Maj. 1,514
Chapman, Peter, *C., North East Scotland region*
Coffey, Willie, *SNP, Kilmarnock and Irvine Valley,* Maj. 11,194
Cole-Hamilton, Alex, *LD, Edinburgh Western,* Maj. 2,960
Constance, Angela, *SNP, Almond Valley,* Maj. 8,393
Corry, Maurice, *C., West Scotland region*
Crawford, Bruce, *SNP, Stirling,* Maj. 6,718
Cunningham, Roseanna, *SNP, Perthshire South and Kinross-shire,* Maj. 1,422
Davidson, Ruth, *C., Edinburgh Central,* Maj. 610
Denham, Ash, *SNP, Edinburgh Eastern,* Maj. 5,087
Dey, Graeme, *SNP, Angus South,* Maj. 4,304
Doris, Bob, *SNP, Glasgow Maryhill and Springburn,* Maj. 5,602
Dornan, James, *SNP, Glasgow Cathcart,* Maj. 9,390
Ewing, Annabelle, *SNP, Cowdenbeath,* Maj. 3,041
Ewing, Fergus, *SNP, Inverness and Nairn,* Maj. 10,857
Fabiani, Linda, *SNP, East Kilbride,* Maj. 10,979
Fee, Mary, *Lab., West Scotland region*
Findlay, Neil, *Lab., Lothian region*
Finnie, John, *Green, Highlands and Islands region*
FitzPatrick, Joe, *SNP, Dundee City West,* Maj. 8,828
Forbes, Kate, *SNP, Skye, Lochaber and Badenoch,* Maj. 9,043
Fraser, Murdo, *C., Mid Scotland and Fife region*
Freeman, Jeane, *SNP, Carrick, Cumnock and Doon Valley,* Maj. 6,006
Gibson, Kenneth, *SNP, Cunninghame North,* Maj. 8,724
Gilruth, Jenny, *SNP, Mid Fife and Glenrothes,* Maj. 8,276
Golden, Maurice, *C., West Scotland region*
Gougeon, Mairi, *SNP, Angus North and Mearns,* Maj. 2,472
Grahame, Christine, *SNP, Midlothian South, Tweeddale and Lauderdale,* Maj. 5,868
Grant, Rhoda, *Lab., Highlands and Islands region*
Gray, Iain, *Lab., East Lothian,* Maj. 1,127
Greene, Jamie, *C., West Scotland region*

Greer, Ross, *Green, West Scotland region*
Griffin, Mark, *Lab., Central Scotland region*
† Halcro Johnston, Jamie, *C., Highlands and Islands region*
* Hamilton, Rachael, *C., Ettrick, Roxburgh and Berwickshire,* Maj. 9,338
Harper, Emma, *SNP, South Scotland region*
Harris, Alison, *C., Central Scotland region*
Harvie, Patrick, *Green, Glasgow region*
Haughey, Clare, *SNP, Rutherglen,* Maj. 3,743
Hepburn, Jamie, *SNP, Cumbernauld and Kilsyth,* Maj. 9,478
Hyslop, Fiona, *SNP, Linlithgow,* Maj. 9,335
Johnson, Daniel, *Lab., Edinburgh Southern,* Maj. 1,123
Johnstone, Alison, *Green, Lothian region*
Kelly, James, *Lab., Glasgow region*
Kerr, Liam, *C., North East Scotland region*
Kidd, Bill, *SNP, Glasgow Anniesland,* Maj. 6,153
Lamont, Johann, *Lab., Glasgow region*
Lennon, Monica, *Lab., Central Scotland region*
Leonard, Richard, *Lab., Central Scotland region*
Lindhurst, Gordon, *C., Lothian region*
Lochhead, Richard, *SNP, Moray,* Maj. 2,875
Lockhart, Dean, *C., Mid Scotland and Fife region*
Lyle, Richard, *SNP, Uddingston and Bellshill,* Maj. 4,809
McAlpine, Joan, *SNP, South Scotland region*
McArthur, Liam, *LD, Orkney Islands,* Maj. 4,534
MacDonald, Angus, *SNP, Falkirk East,* Maj. 8,312
MacDonald, Gordon, *SNP, Edinburgh Pentlands,* Maj. 2,456
Macdonald, Lewis, *Lab., North East Scotland region*
McDonald, Mark, *Ind., Aberdeen Donside,* Maj. 11,630
MacGregor, Fulton, *SNP, Coatbridge and Chryston,* Maj. 3,779
‡ Macintosh, Ken, *no party affiliation, West Scotland region*
Mackay, Derek, *SNP, Renfrewshire North and West,* Maj. 7,373
Mackay, Rona, *SNP, Strathkelvin and Bearsden,* Maj. 8,100
McKee, Ivan, *SNP, Glasgow Provan,* Maj. 4,783
McKelvie, Christina, *SNP, Hamilton, Larkhall and Stonehouse,* Maj. 5,437
McMillan, Stuart, *SNP, Greenock and Inverclyde,* Maj. 8,230
McNeill, Pauline, *Lab., Glasgow region*
Macpherson, Ben, *SNP, Edinburgh Northern and Leith,* Maj. 6,746
Maguire, Ruth, *SNP, Cunninghame South,* Maj. 5,693
Marra, Jenny, *Lab., North East Scotland region*
Martin, Gillian, *SNP, Aberdeenshire East,* Maj. 5,837
Mason, John, *SNP, Glasgow Shettleston,* Maj. 7,323
† Mason, Tom, *C., North East Scotland region*
Matheson, Michael, *SNP, Falkirk West,* Maj. 11,280
Mitchell, Margaret, *C., Central Scotland region*
Mountain, Edward, *C., Highlands and Islands region*
Mundell, Oliver, *C., Dumfriesshire,* Maj. 1,230
Neil, Alex, *SNP, Airdrie and Shotts,* Maj. 6,192
Paterson, Gil, *SNP, Clydebank and Milngavie,* Maj. 8,432
Rennie, Willie, *LD, North East Fife,* Maj. 3,465
Robison, Shona, *SNP, Dundee City East,* Maj. 10,898
Ross, Gail, *SNP, Caithness, Sutherland and Ross,* Maj. 3,913
Rowley, Alex, *Lab., Mid Scotland and Fife region*
Rumbles, Mike, *LD, North East Scotland region*
Ruskell, Mark, *Green, Mid Scotland and Fife region*
Russell, Michael, *SNP, Argyll and Bute,* Maj. 5,978
Sarwar, Anas, *Lab., Glasgow region*
Scott, John, *C., Ayr,* Maj. 750
Simpson, Graham, *C., Central Scotland region*
Smith, Elaine, *Lab., Central Scotland region*
Smith, Liz, *C., Mid Scotland and Fife region*
Smyth, Colin, *Lab., South Scotland region*
Somerville, Shirley-Anne, *SNP, Dunfermline,* Maj. 4,558
Stevenson, Stewart, *SNP, Banffshire and Buchan Coast,* Maj. 6,583

Stewart, Alexander, *C., Mid Scotland and Fife region*
Stewart, David, *Lab., Highlands and Islands region*
Stewart, Kevin, *SNP, Aberdeen Central,* Maj. 4,349
Sturgeon, Nicola, *SNP, Glasgow Southside,* Maj. 9,593
Swinney, John, *SNP, Perthshire North,* Maj. 3,336
Todd, Maree, *SNP, Highlands and Islands region*
Tomkins, Adam, *C., Glasgow region*
Torrance, David, *SNP, Kirkcaldy,* Maj. 7,395
Watt, Maureen, *SNP, Aberdeen South and North Kincardine,* Maj. 2,755
Wells, Annie, *C., Glasgow region*
Wheelhouse, Paul, *SNP, South Scotland region*
White, Sandra, *SNP, Glasgow Kelvin,* Maj. 4,048
Whittle, Brian, *C., South Scotland region*
Wightman, Andy, *Green, Lothian region*
* Wishart, Beatrice, *LD, Shetland Islands,* Maj. 1,837
Yousaf, Humza, *SNP, Glasgow Pollok,* Maj. 6,482

STATE OF THE PARTIES *as at August 2019*

	Constituency MSPs	Regional MSPs	Total
Scottish National Party (SNP)	58	4	62
Scottish Conservative and Unionist Party (C.)	7	24	31
Scottish Labour Party (Lab.)	3	20	23
Scottish Green Party (Green)	0	6	6
Scottish Liberal Democrats (LD)	4	1	4
Independent (Ind.)	1	–	1
*Presiding Officer	–	1	1
Total	73	56	129

SCOTTISH GOVERNMENT

St Andrew's House, Regent Road, Edinburgh EH1 3DG
T 0300-244 4000
E ceu@gov.scot W www.gov.scot

The devolved government for Scotland is responsible for most of the issues of day-to-day concern to the people of Scotland, including health, education, justice, rural affairs and transport.

The Scottish government was known as the Scottish executive when it was established in 1999, following the first elections to the Scottish parliament. There has been a majority Scottish National Party administration since the elections in May 2011.

The government is led by a first minister who is nominated by the parliament and in turn appoints the other Scottish ministers who make up the cabinet.

Civil servants in Scotland are accountable to Scottish ministers, who are themselves accountable to the Scottish parliament.

CABINET

First Minister, Rt. Hon. Nicola Sturgeon, MSP
Deputy First Minister and Cabinet Secretary for Education and Skills, John Swinney, MSP

Cabinet Secretaries
Communities and Local Government, Aileen Campbell, MSP
Culture, Tourism and External Affairs, Fiona Hyslop, MSP
Environment, Climate Change and Land Reform, Roseanna Cunningham, MSP
Finance, Economy and Fair Work, Derek Mackay, MSP
Government Business and Constitutional Relations, Michael Russell, MSP
Health and Sport, Jeane Freeman, MSP
Justice, Humza Yousaf, MSP
Rural Economy, Fergus Ewing, MSP
Social Security and Older People, Shirley-Anne Somerville, MSP

Transport, Infrastructure and Connectivity, Michael Matheson, MSP

Ministers
Business, Fair Work and Skills, Jamie Hepburn, MSP
Childcare and Early Years, Maree Todd, MSP
Community Safety, Ash Denham, MSP
Energy, Connectivity and the Islands, Paul Wheelhouse, MSP
Europe, Migration and International Development, Ben Macpherson, MSP
Further Education, Higher Education and Science, Richard Lochhead, MSP
Local Government, Housing and Planning, Kevin Stewart, MSP
Mental Health, Clare Haughey, MSP
Older People and Equalities, Christina McKelvie, MSP
Parliamentary Business and Veterans, Graeme Dey, MSP
Public Finance and Digital Economy, Kate Forbes
Public Health, Sport and Wellbeing, Joe FitzPatrick, MSP
Rural Affairs and the Natural Environment, Mairi Gougeon, MSP
Trade, Investment and Innovation, Ivan McKee, MSP

LAW OFFICERS
Lord Advocate, James Wolffe, QC
Solicitor-General for Scotland, Alison di Rollo

STRATEGIC BOARD
Permanent Secretary, Leslie Evans
Director-General Constitution and External Affairs, Ken Thomson
Director-General, Economy, Liz Ditchburn
Director-General, Education, Communities and Justice, Paul Johnston
Director-General, Scottish Exchequer, Alyson Stafford
Director-General, Health and Social Care, Malcolm Wright
Director-General, Organisational Development and Operations, Lesley Fraser

GOVERNMENT DEPARTMENTS

CONSTITUTION AND EXTERNAL AFFAIRS
St Andrew's House, Regent Road, Edinburgh EH1 3DG
Director-General, Ken Thomson
Directorates: Constitution and Cabinet; EU Directorate; EU Exit and Transition; External Affairs; Legal Services (Solicitor to the Scottish Government); Parliamentary Counsel

ECONOMY
St Andrew's House, Regent Road, Edinburgh EH1 3DG
Director-General, Liz Ditchburn
Directorates: Agriculture and Rural Economy; Chief Economist; Culture, Tourism and Major Events; Economic Development; Economic Policy and Capability; Energy and Climate Change; Environment and Forestry; Fair Work, Employability and Skills; International Trade and Investment; Marine Scotland; Scottish Development International; Scottish National Investment Bank
Executive Agencies: Accountant in Bankruptcy; Drinking Water Quality Regulator; Forestry and Land Scotland; James Hutton Institute; Moredun Research Institute; National Records of Scotland; Scottish Agricultural College; Scottish Forestry; Transport Scotland; Waterwatch Scotland

EDUCATION, COMMUNITIES AND JUSTICE
St Andrew's House, Regent Road, Edinburgh EH1 3DG
Director-General Paul Johnston
Directorates: Advance Learning and Science; Children and Families; Early Learning and Childcare Programme; Education Analytical Services; Housing and Social Justice;

Justice; Learning; Local Government and Communities; Safer Communities
Executive Agencies: Disclosure Scotland; Education Scotland; HM Chief Inspector of Prosecution in Scotland; HM Inspectorate of Constabulary; HM Inspectorate of Prisons; Inspectorate of Prosecution in Scotland; Justice of the Peace Advisory Committee; Scottish Prison Service; Student Awards Agency for Scotland; Visiting Committees for Scottish Penal Establishments

SCOTTISH EXCHEQUER
Victoria Quay, Edinburgh, EH6 6QQ
Director-General, Alyson Stafford
Directorates: Budget and Sustainability; Internal Audit and Assurance; Performance and Outcomes; Taxation
Executive Agency: Audit Scotland

HEALTH AND SOCIAL CARE
St Andrew's House, Regent Road, Edinburgh EH1 3DG
Director-General Health and Social Care and Chief Executive NHS Scotland, Malcolm Wright
Directorates: Chief Medical Officer; Chief Nursing Officer; Community Health and Social Care; Corporate Governance and Value; Health Finance; Health Performance and Delivery; Health Workforce, Leadership and Service Reform; Healthcare Quality and Improvement; Mental Health; Office of the Chief Executive NHS Scotland; Performance and Delivery; Population Health
Executive Agency: Scottish Children's Reporters Administration

ORGANISATIONAL DEVELOPMENT AND OPERATIONS
St Andrew's House, Regent Road, Edinburgh EH1 3DG
Directorates: Communications, Ministerial Support and Facilities; Digital; Financial Management; People; Social Security; Scottish Procurement and Commercial
Executive Agencies: Scottish Public Pensions Agency; Social Security Scotland

NON-MINISTERIAL DEPARTMENTS

FOOD STANDARDS SCOTLAND
Pilgrim House, Old Ford Road, Aberdeen AB11 5RL T 01224-285100
W www.foodstandards.gov.scot
Chief Executive, Geoff Ogle
NATIONAL RECORDS OF SCOTLAND
General Register House, 2 Princes Street, Edinburgh EH1 3YY
T 0131-334 0380 W www.nrscotland.gov.uk
Registrar General and Keeper of the Records of Scotland, Paul Lowe
OFFICE OF THE SCOTTISH CHARITY REGULATOR
2nd Floor, Quadrant House, 9 Riverside Drive, Dundee DD1 4NY
T 01382-220446 W www.oscr.org.uk
Chief Executive, Maureen Mallon *(interim)*
REGISTERS OF SCOTLAND
Meadowbank House, 153 London Road, Edinburgh, Midlothian EH8 7AU T 0800-169 9391 W www.ros.gov.uk
Keeper, Jennifer Henderson
REVENUE SCOTLAND
PO Box 24068, Victoria Quay, Edinburgh EH6 9BR T 0300-020 0310
W www.revenue.scot
Chief Executive, Dr Keith Nicholson
SCOTTISH COURTS AND TRIBUNALS SERVICE
Saughton House, Broomhouse Drive, Edinburgh EH11 3XD
T 0131-444 3300 W www.scotcourts.gov.uk
Chief Executive, Eric McQueen
SCOTTISH HOUSING REGULATOR
Buchanan House, 58 Port Dundas Road, Glasgow G4 0HF
T 0141-242 5642 W www.scottishhousingregulator.gov.uk
Chief Executive, George Walker

SCOTTISH PARLIAMENT ELECTION RESULTS *as at 5 May 2016*

Electorate (E.) 4,099,407 Turnout (T.) 55.6%
See General Election Results for a list of party abbreviations

ABERDEEN CENTRAL
(Scotland North East Region)
E. 57,195 T. 26,704 (46.69%)

Kevin Stewart, SNP	11,648
Lewis Macdonald, Lab.	7,299
Tom Mason, C.	6,022
Ken McLeod, LD	1,735

SNP majority 4,349 (16.29%)
6.92% swing Lab. to SNP

ABERDEEN DONSIDE
(Scotland North East Region)
E. 61,200 T. 30,981 (50.62%)

Mark McDonald, SNP	17,339
Liam Kerr, C.	5,709
Greg Williams, Lab.	5,672
Isobel Davidson, LD	2,261

SNP majority 11,630 (37.54%)
4.82% swing SNP to C.

ABERDEEN SOUTH &
KINCARDINE NORTH
(Scotland North East Region)
E. 59,710 T. 32,340 (54.16%)

Maureen Watt, SNP	13,604
Ross Thomson, C.	10,849
Alison Evison, Lab.	5,603
John Waddell, LD	2,284

SNP majority 2,755 (8.52%)
9.49% swing SNP to C.

ABERDEENSHIRE EAST
(Scotland North East Region)
E. 62,844 T. 34,753 (55.30%)

Gillian Martin, SNP	15,912
Colin Clark, C.	10,075
Christine Jardine, LD	6,611
Sarah Flavell, Lab.	2,155

SNP majority 5,837 (16.80%)
16.90% swing SNP to C.

ABERDEENSHIRE WEST
(Scotland North East Region)
E. 59,576 T. 35,198 (59.08%)

Alexander Burnett, C.	13,400
Dennis Robertson, SNP	12,500
Mike Rumbles, LD	7,262
Sarah Christina Duncan, Lab.	2,036

C. majority 900 (2.56%)
12.03% swing SNP to C.

AIRDRIE & SHOTTS
(Scotland Central Region)
E. 53,899 T. 26,573 (49.30%)

Alex Neil, SNP	13,954
Richard Leonard, Lab.	7,762
Eric Holford, C.	4,164
Louise Young, LD	693

SNP majority 6,192 (23.30%)
7.46% swing Lab. to SNP

ALMOND VALLEY
(Lothian Region)
E. 64,901 T. 34,872 (53.73%)

Angela Constance, SNP	18,475
Neil Findlay, Lab.	10,082
Stephanie Smith, C.	5,308
Charles Dundas, LD	1,007

SNP majority 8,393 (24.07%)
3.02% swing Lab. to SNP

ANGUS NORTH & MEARNS
(Scotland North East Region)
E. 54,268 T. 29,379 (54.14%)

Mairi Evans, SNP	13,417
Alex Johnstone, C.	10,945
John Ruddy, Lab.	2,752
Euan Davidson, LD	2,265

SNP majority 2,472 (8.41%)
10.41% swing SNP to C.

ANGUS SOUTH
(Scotland North East Region)
E. 56,278 T. 31,929 (56.73%)

Graeme Dey, SNP	15,622
Kirstene Hair, C.	11,318
Joanne McFadden, Lab.	3,773
Clive Sneddon, LD	1,216

SNP majority 4,304 (13.48%)
12.40% swing SNP to C.

ARGYLL & BUTE
(Highlands and Islands Region)
E. 48,804 T. 29,476 (60.40%)

Michael Russell, SNP	13,561
Alan Reid, LD	7,583
Donald Cameron, C.	5,840
Mick Rice, Lab.	2,492

SNP majority 5,978 (20.28%)
9.07% swing SNP to LD

AYR
(Scotland South Region)
E. 61,558 T. 37,615 (61.10%)

John Scott, C.	16,183
Jennifer Dunn, SNP	15,433
Brian McGinley, Lab.	5,283
Robbie Simpson, LD	716

C. majority 750 (1.99%)
0.67% swing C. to SNP

BANFFSHIRE & BUCHAN COAST
(Scotland North East Region)
E. 59,155 T. 28,683 (48.49%)

Stewart Stevenson, SNP	15,802
Peter Chapman, C.	9,219
Nathan Morrison, Lab.	2,372
David Evans, LD	1,290

SNP majority 6,583 (22.95%)
12.96% swing SNP to C.

CAITHNESS, SUTHERLAND & ROSS
(Highlands and Islands Region)
E. 55,176 T. 32,207 (58.37%)

Gail Ross, SNP	13,937
Jamie Stone, LD	10,024
Struan Mackie, C.	4,912
Leah Franchetti, Lab.	3,334

SNP majority 3,913 (12.15%)
6.96% swing SNP to LD

**CARRICK, CUMNOCK & DOON
VALLEY**
(Scotland South Region)
E. 58,548 T. 31,680 (54.11%)

Jeane Freeman, SNP	14,690
Carol Mochan, Lab.	8,684
Lee Lyons, C.	7,666
Dawud Islam, LD	640

SNP majority 6,006 (18.96%)
4.98% swing Lab. to SNP

**CLACKMANNANSHIRE &
DUNBLANE**
(Mid Scotland and Fife Region)
E. 50,557 T. 29,746 (58.84%)

Keith Brown, SNP	14,147
Craig Miller, Lab.	7,426
Alexander Stewart, C.	6,915
Christopher McKinlay, LD	1,258

SNP majority 6,721 (22.59%)
4.72% swing Lab. to SNP

CLYDEBANK & MILNGAVIE
(Scotland West Region)
E. 54,761 T. 32,838 (59.97%)

Gil Paterson, SNP	16,158
Gail Casey, Lab.	7,726
Maurice Golden, C.	6,029
Frank Bowles, LD	2,925

SNP majority 8,432 (25.68%)
11.58% swing Lab. to SNP

CLYDESDALE
(Scotland South Region)
E. 58,471 T. 33,619 (57.50%)

Aileen Campbell, SNP	14,821
Alex Allison, C.	8,842
Claudia Beamish, Lab.	6,895
Danny Meikle, Ind.	1,332
Bev Gauld, CSSInd.	909
Jennifer Jamieson Ball, LD	820

SNP majority 5,979 (17.78%)
8.88% swing SNP to C.

COATBRIDGE & CHRYSTON
(Scotland Central Region)
E. 54,169 T. 28,334 (52.31%)

Fulton MacGregor, SNP	13,605
Elaine Smith, Lab.	9,826
Robyn Halbert, C.	2,868
John Wilson, Green	1,612
Jenni Lang, LD	423

SNP majority 3,779 (13.34%)
12.56% swing Lab. to SNP

COWDENBEATH
(Mid Scotland and Fife Region)
E. 54,596 T. 29,734 (54.46%)

Annabelle Ewing, SNP	13,715
Alex Rowley, Lab.	10,674
Dave Dempsey, C.	4,251
Bryn Jones, LD	1,094

SNP majority 3,041 (10.23%)
7.54% swing Lab. to SNP

CUMBERNAULD & KILSYTH
(Scotland Central Region)
E. 49,964 T. 28,308 (56.66%)

Jamie Hepburn, SNP	17,015
Mark Griffin, Lab.	7,537
Anthony Newman, C.	3,068
Irene Lang, LD	688

SNP majority 9,478 (33.48%)
9.89% swing Lab. to SNP

CUNNINGHAME NORTH
(Scotland West Region)
E. 55,647 T. 31,965 (57.44%)

Kenneth Gibson, SNP	16,587
Jamie Greene, C.	7,863
Johanna Baxter, Lab.	6,735
Charity Pierce, LD	780

SNP majority 8,724 (27.29%)
5.83% swing SNP to C.

CUNNINGHAME SOUTH
(Scotland South Region)
E. 50,215 T. 25,695 (51.17%)

Ruth Maguire, SNP	13,416
Joe Cullinane, Lab.	7,723
Billy McClure, C.	3,940
Ruby Kirkwood, LD	616

SNP majority 5,693 (22.16%)
5.76% swing Lab. to SNP

DUMBARTON
(Scotland West Region)
E. 55,098 T. 33,598 (60.98%)

Jackie Baillie, Lab.	13,522
Gail Robertson, SNP	13,413
Maurice Corry, C.	4,891
Aileen Morton, LD	1,131
Andrew Muir, Ind.	641

Lab. majority 109 (0.32%)
2.71% swing Lab. to SNP

DUMFRIESSHIRE
(Scotland South Region)
E. 60,698 T. 36,260 (59.74%)

Oliver Mundell, C.	13,536
Joan McAlpine, SNP	12,306
Elaine Murray, Lab.	9,151
Richard Brodie, LD	1,267

C. majority 1,230 (3.39%)
10.99% swing Lab. to C.

DUNDEE EAST
(Scotland North East Region)
E. 55,261 T. 28,437 (51.46%)

Shona Robison, SNP	16,509
Richard McCready, Lab.	5,611
Bill Bowman, C.	4,969
Craig Duncan, LD	911
Leah Ganley, TUSC	437

SNP majority 10,898 (38.32%)
1.57% swing SNP to Lab.

DUNDEE WEST
(Scotland North East Region)
E. 53,830 T. 27,788 (51.62%)

Joe FitzPatrick, SNP	16,070
Jenny Marra, Lab.	7,242
Nicola Ross, C.	2,826
Daniel Coleman, LD	1,008
Jim McFarlane, TUSC	642

SNP majority 8,828 (31.77%)
2.79% swing Lab. to SNP

DUNFERMLINE
(Scotland Mid and Fife Region)
E. 57,740 T. 32,909 (57.00%)

Shirley-Anne Somerville, SNP	14,257
Cara Hilton, Lab.	9,699
James Reekie, C.	5,797
James Calder, LD	3,156

SNP majority 4,558 (13.85%)
5.92% swing Lab. to SNP

EAST KILBRIDE
(Scotland Central Region)
E. 61,134 T. 34,629 (56.64%)

Linda Fabiani, SNP	19,371
LizAnne Handibode, Lab.	8,392
Graham Simpson, C.	5,857
Paul McGarry, LD	1,009

SNP majority 10,979 (31.70%)
12.59% swing Lab. to SNP

EAST LOTHIAN
(Scotland South Region)
E. 60,848 T. 37,913 (62.31%)

Iain Gray, Lab.	14,329
DJ Johnston-Smith, SNP	13,202
Rachael Hamilton, C.	9,045
Ettie Spencer, LD	1,337

Lab. majority 1,127 (2.97%)
1.25% swing SNP to Lab.

EASTWOOD
(Scotland West Region)
E. 53,085 T. 36,255 (68.30%)

Jackson Carlaw, C.	12,932
Stewart Maxwell, SNP	11,321
Ken Macintosh, Lab.	11,081
John Duncan, LD	921

C. majority 1,611 (4.44%)
5.70% swing Lab. to C.

EDINBURGH CENTRAL
(Lothian Region)
E. 59,581 T. 34,169 (57.35%)

Ruth Davidson, C.	10,399
Alison Dickie, SNP	9,789
Sarah Boyack, Lab.	7,546
Alison Johnstone, Green	4,644
Hannah Bettsworth, LD	1,672
Tom Laird, SLP	119

C. majority 610 (1.79%)
9.73% swing SNP to C.

EDINBURGH EASTERN
(Lothian Region)
E. 62,817 T. 35,397 (56.35%)

Ash Denham, SNP	16,760
Kezia Dugdale, Lab.	11,673
Nick Cook, C.	5,700
Cospatric D'Inverno, LD	1,264

SNP majority 5,087 (14.37%)
3.55% swing Lab. to SNP

EDINBURGH NORTHERN & LEITH
(Lothian Region)
E. 67,273 T. 37,102 (55.15%)

Ben Macpherson, SNP	17,322
Lesley Hinds, Lab.	10,576
Iain McGill, C.	6,081
Martin Veart, LD	1,779
Jack Caldwell, Ind.	1,344

SNP majority 6,746 (18.18%)
10.05% swing Lab. to SNP

EDINBURGH PENTLANDS
(Lothian Region)
E. 55,241 T. 33,353 (60.38%)

Gordon MacDonald, SNP	13,181
Gordon Lindhurst, C.	10,725
Blair Heary, Lab.	7,811
Emma Farthing-Sykes, LD	1,636

SNP majority 2,456 (7.36%)
0.76% swing C. to SNP

EDINBURGH SOUTHERN
(Lothian Region)
E. 59,587 T. 38,259 (64.21%)

Daniel Johnson, Lab.	13,597
Jim Eadie, SNP	12,474
Miles Briggs, C.	9,972
Pramod Subbaraman, LD	2,216

Lab. majority 1,123 (2.94%)
2.49% swing SNP to Lab.

EDINBURGH WESTERN
(Lothian Region)
E. 61,666 T. 39,766 (64.49%)

Alex Cole-Hamilton, LD	16,645
Toni Giugliano, SNP	13,685
Sandy Batho, C.	5,686
Cat Headley, Lab.	3,750

LD majority 2,960 (7.44%)
7.74% swing SNP to LD

ETTRICK, ROXBURGH & BERWICKSHIRE
(Scotland South Region)
E. 54,506 T. 33,095 (60.72%)

John Lamont, C.	18,257
Paul Wheelhouse, SNP	10,521
Jim Hume, LD	2,551
Barrie Cunning, Lab.	1,766

C. majority 7,736 (23.38%)
2.43% swing SNP to C.

FALKIRK EAST
(Scotland Central Region)
E. 60,271 T. 32,524 (53.96%)

Angus MacDonald, SNP	16,720
Craig Martin, Lab.	8,408
Callum Laidlaw, C.	6,342
James Munro, LD	1,054

SNP majority 8,312 (25.56%)
6.50% swing Lab. to SNP

FALKIRK WEST
(Scotland Central Region)
E. 59,812 T. 32,083 (53.64%)

Michael Matheson, SNP	18,260
Mandy Telford, Lab.	6,980
Alison Harris, C.	5,877
Gillian Cole-Hamilton, LD	966

SNP majority 11,280 (35.16%)
7.39% swing Lab. to SNP

FIFE MID & GLENROTHES
(Scotland Mid and Fife Region)
E. 53,241 T. 28,547 (53.62%)

Jenny Gilruth, SNP	15,555
Kay Morrison, Lab.	7,279
Alex Stewart-Clark, C.	4,427
Jane-Ann Liston, LD	1,286

SNP majority 8,276 (28.99%)
6.54% swing Lab. to SNP

FIFE NORTH EAST
(Scotland Mid and Fife Region)
E. 54,052 T. 34,063 (63.02%)

Willie Rennie, LD	14,928
Roderick Campbell, SNP	11,463
Huw Bell, C.	5,646
Rosalind Garton, Lab.	2,026

LD majority 3,465 (10.17%)
9.45% swing SNP to LD

GALLOWAY & WEST DUMFRIES
(Scotland South Region)
E. 56,321 T. 33,363 (59.24%)

Finlay Carson, C.	14,527
Aileen McLeod, SNP	13,013
Fiona O'Donnell, Lab.	4,876
Andrew Metcalf, LD	947

C. majority 1,514 (4.54%)
0.83% swing SNP to C.

GLASGOW ANNIESLAND
(Glasgow Region)
E. 57,884 T. 29,016 (50.13%)

Bill Kidd, SNP	15,007
Bill Butler, Lab.	8,854
Adam Tomkins, C.	4,057
James Speirs, LD	1,098

SNP majority 6,153 (21.21%)
10.59% swing Lab. to SNP

GLASGOW CATHCART
(Glasgow Region)
E. 60,871 T. 30,637 (50.33%)

James Dornan, SNP	16,200
Soryia Siddique, Lab.	6,810
Kyle Thornton, C.	4,514
Margot Clark, LD	1,703
Brian Smith, TUSC	909
Chris Creighton, Ind.	501

SNP majority 9,390 (30.65%)
12.29% swing Lab. to SNP

GLASGOW KELVIN
(Glasgow Region)
E. 62,203 T. 28,442 (45.72%)

Sandra White, SNP	10,964
Patrick Harvie, Green	6,916
Michael Shanks, Lab.	5,968
Sheila Mechan, C.	3,346
Carole Ford, LD	1,050
Tom Muirhead, Ind.	198

SNP majority 4,048 (14.23%)

GLASGOW MARYHILL & SPRINGBURN
(Glasgow Region)
E. 53,647 T. 23,612 (44.01%)

Bob Doris, SNP	13,109
Patricia Ferguson, Lab.	7,507
John Anderson, C.	2,305
James Harrison, LD	691

SNP majority 5,602 (23.73%)
15.01% swing Lab. to SNP

GLASGOW POLLOK
(Glasgow Region)
E. 61,350 T. 27,943 (45.55%)

Humza Yousaf, SNP	15,316
Johann Lamont, Lab.	8,834
Thomas Haddow, C.	2,653
Isabel Nelson, LD	585
Ian Leech, TUSC	555

SNP majority 6,482 (23.20%)
12.96% swing Lab. to SNP

GLASGOW PROVAN
(Glasgow Region)
E. 56,169 T. 24,077 (42.87%)

Ivan McKee, SNP	13,140
Paul Martin, Lab.	8,357
Annie Wells, C.	2,062
Tom Coleman, LD	518

SNP majority 4,783 (19.87%)
15.35% swing Lab. to SNP

GLASGOW SHETTLESTON
(Glasgow Region)
E. 58,021 T. 25,375 (43.73%)

John Mason, SNP	14,198
Thomas Rannachan, Lab.	6,875
Thomas Kerr, C.	3,151
Jamie Cocozza, TUSC	583
Giovanni Caccavello, LD	568

SNP majority 7,323 (28.86%)
13.05% swing Lab. to SNP

GLASGOW SOUTHSIDE
(Glasgow Region)
E. 52,141 T. 24,903 (47.76%)

Nicola Sturgeon, SNP	15,287
Fariha Thomas, Lab.	5,694
Graham Hutchison, C.	3,100
Kevin Lewsey, LD	822

SNP majority 9,593 (38.52%)
9.64% swing Lab. to SNP

GREENOCK & INVERCLYDE
(Scotland West Region)
E. 55,171 T. 31,725 (57.50%)

Stuart McMillan, SNP	17,032
Siobhan McCready, Lab.	8,802
Graeme Brooks, C.	4,487
John Watson, LD	1,404

SNP majority 8,230 (25.94%)
13.88% swing Lab. to SNP

HAMILTON, LARKHALL & STONEHOUSE
(Scotland Central Region)
E. 57,656 T. 28,885 (50.10%)

Christina McKelvie, SNP	13,945
Margaret McCulloch, Lab.	8,508
Margaret Mitchell, C.	5,596
Eileen Baxendale, LD	836

SNP majority 5,437 (18.82%)
5.05% swing Lab. to SNP

INVERNESS & NAIRN
(Highlands and Islands Region)
E. 66,619 T. 38,317 (57.52%)

Fergus Ewing, SNP	18,505
Edward Mountain, C.	7,648
David Stewart, Lab.	6,719
Carolyn Caddick, LD	5,445

SNP majority 10,857 (28.33%)
5.80% swing SNP to C.

KILMARNOCK & IRVINE VALLEY
(Scotland South Region)
E. 62,620 T. 34,385 (54.91%)

Willie Coffey, SNP	19,047
Dave Meechan, Lab.	7,853
Brian Whittle, C.	6,597
Rebecca Plenderleith, LD	888

SNP majority 11,194 (32.55%)
6.87% swing Lab. to SNP

KIRKCALDY
(Scotland Mid and Fife Region)
E. 59,533 T. 31,108 (52.25%)

David Torrance, SNP	16,358
Claire Baker, Lab.	8,963
Martin Laidlaw, C.	4,568
Lauren Jones, LD	1,219

SNP majority 7,395 (23.77%)
11.56% swing Lab. to SNP

LINLITHGOW
(Lothian Region)
E. 71,434 T. 38,407 (53.77%)

Fiona Hyslop, SNP	19,362
Angela Moohan, Lab.	10,027
Charles Kennedy, C.	7,699
Dan Farthing-Sykes, LD	1,319

SNP majority 9,335 (24.31%)
6.17% swing Lab. to SNP

MIDLOTHIAN NORTH &
MUSSELBURGH
(Lothian Region)
E. 63,360 T. 34,685 (54.74%)

Colin Beattie, SNP	16,948
Bernard Harkins, Lab.	9,913
Jeremy Balfour, C.	6,267
Jacquie Bell, LD	1,557

SNP majority 7,035 (20.28%)
5.12% swing Lab. to SNP

MIDLOTHIAN SOUTH,
TWEEDDALE & LAUDERDALE
(Scotland South Region)
E. 60,204 T. 35,581 (59.10%)

Christine Grahame, SNP	16,031
Michelle Ballantyne, C.	10,163
Fiona Dugdale, Lab.	5,701
Kris Chapman, LD	3,686

SNP majority 5,868 (16.49%)
7.63% swing SNP to C.

MORAY
(Highlands and Islands Region)
E. 61,969 T. 33,421 (53.93%)

Richard Lochhead, SNP	15,742
Douglas Ross, C.	12,867
Sean Morton, Lab.	3,547
Jamie Paterson, LD	1,265

SNP majority 2,875 (8.60%)
14.83% swing SNP to C.

MOTHERWELL & WISHAW
(Scotland Central Region)
E. 57,045 T. 29,111 (51.03%)

Clare Adamson, SNP	15,291
John Pentland, Lab.	9,068
Meghan Gallacher, C.	3,991
Yvonne Finlayson, LD	761

SNP majority 6,223 (21.38%)
11.89% swing Lab. to SNP

NA H-EILEANAN AN IAR
(Highlands and Islands Region)
E. 21,695 T. 13,206 (60.87%)

Alasdair Allan, SNP	6,874
Rhoda Grant, Lab.	3,378
Ranald Fraser, C.	1,499
John Cormack, SCP	1,162
Ken MacLeod, LD	293

SNP majority 3,496 (26.47%)
5.10% swing SNP to Lab.

ORKNEY
(Highlands and Islands Region)
E. 16,997 T. 10,534 (61.98%)

Liam McArthur, LD	7,096
Donna Heddle, SNP	2,562
Jamie Halcro Johnston, C.	435
Gerry McGarvey, Lab.	304
Paul Dawson, Ind.	137

LD majority 4,534 (43.04%)
16.20% swing SNP to LD

PAISLEY
(Scotland West Region)
E. 51,673 T. 29,464 (57.02%)

George Adam, SNP	14,682
Neil Bibby, Lab.	9,483
Paul Masterton, C.	3,533
Eileen McCartin, LD	1,766

SNP majority 5,199 (17.65%)
8.34% swing Lab. to SNP

PERTHSHIRE NORTH
(Scotland and Mid Fife Region)
E. 54,255 T. 34,025 (62.71%)

John Swinney, SNP	16,526
Murdo Fraser, C.	13,190
Anna McEwan, Lab.	2,604
Peter Barrett, LD	1,705

SNP majority 3,336 (9.80%)
12.38% swing SNP to C.

PERTHSHIRE SOUTH & KINROSS-
SHIRE
(Scotland and Mid Fife Region)
E. 59,397 T. 36,149 (60.86%)

Roseanna Cunningham, SNP	15,315
Liz Smith, C.	13,893
Scott Nicholson, Lab.	3,389
Willie Robertson, LD	3,008
Craig Finlay, Community	544

SNP majority 1,422 (3.93%)
9.51% swing SNP to C.

RENFREWSHIRE NORTH & WEST
(Scotland West Region)
E. 50,555 T. 30,807 (60.94%)

Derek Mackay, SNP	14,718
David Wilson, C.	7,345
Mary Fee, Lab.	7,244
Rod Ackland, LD	888
Jim Halfpenny, TUSC	414
Peter Morton, Ind.	198

SNP majority 7,373 (23.93%)
1.02% swing C. to SNP

RENFREWSHIRE SOUTH
(Scotland West Region)
E. 49,422 T. 29,681 (60.06%)

Thomas Arthur, SNP	14,272
Paul O'Kane, Lab.	9,864
Ann Le Blond, C.	4,752
Tristan Gray, LD	793

SNP majority 4,408 (14.85%)
12.21% swing Lab. to SNP

RUTHERGLEN
(Glasgow Region)
E. 60,702 T. 32,952 (54.28%)

Clare Haughey, SNP	15,222
James Kelly, Lab.	11,479
Taylor Muir, C.	3,718
Robert Brown, LD	2,533

SNP majority 3,743 (11.36%)
8.96% swing Lab. to SNP

SHETLAND ISLANDS
(Highlands and Islands Region)
E. 17,784 T. 11,041 (62.08%)

Tavish Scott, LD	7,440
Danus Skene, SNP	2,545
Robina Barton, Lab.	651
Cameron Smith, C.	405

LD majority 4,895 (44.33%)
4.45% swing SNP to LD

SKYE, LOCHABER & BADENOCH
(Highlands and Islands Region)
E. 59,537 T. 36,505 (61.31%)

Kate Forbes, SNP	17,362
Angela MacLean, LD	8,319
Robbie Munro, C.	5,887
Linda Stewart, Lab.	3,821
Ronnie Campbell, Ind.	1,116

SNP majority 9,043 (24.77%)
4.56% swing LD to SNP

STIRLING
(Scotland and Mid Fife Region)
E. 55,785 T. 34,189 (61.29%)

Bruce Crawford, SNP	16,303
Dean Lockhart, C.	9,585
Rebecca Bell, Lab.	6,885
Elisabeth Wilson, LD	1,416

SNP majority 6,718 (19.65%)
7.03% swing SNP to C.

STRATHKELVIN & BEARSDEN
(Scotland West Region)
E. 62,598 T. 39,188 (62.60%)

Rona Mackay, SNP	17,060
Andrew Polson, C.	8,960
Margaret McCarthy, Lab.	8,288
Katy Gordon, LD	4,880

SNP majority 8,100 (20.67%)
4.21% swing SNP to C.

UDDINGSTON & BELLSHILL
(Central Scotland Region)
E. 57,556 T. 29,543 (51.33%)

Richard Lyle, SNP	14,424
Michael McMahon, Lab.	9,615
Andrew Morrison, C.	4,693
Kaitey Blair, LD	811

SNP majority 4,809 (16.28%)
9.57% swing Lab. to SNP

REGIONS *as at 5 May 2016*
E. 4,099,407 T. 55.6%

GLASGOW
E. 522,988 T. 248,109 (47.44%)

SNP	111,101	(44.78%)
Lab.	59,151	(23.84%)
C.	29,533	(11.90%)
Green	23,398	(9.43%)
LD	5,850	(2.36%)
UKIP	4,889	(1.97%)
Solidarity	3,593	(1.45%)
RISE	2,454	(0.99%)
UP	2,453	(0.99%)
Women	2,091	(0.84%)
Animal	1,819	(0.73%)
SCP	1,506	(0.61%)
Ind.	271	(0.11%)

SNP majority 51,950 (20.94%)
8.05% swing Lab. to SNP (2011 SNP majority 10,078)
ADDITIONAL MEMBERS

Adam Tomkins, *C.*	James Kelly, *Lab.*
Annie Wells, *C.*	Pauline McNeill, *Lab.*
Anas Sarwar, *Lab.*	Patrick Harvie, *Green*
Johann Lamont, *Lab.*	

HIGHLANDS AND ISLANDS
E. 348,581 T. 205,313 (58.90%)

SNP	81,600	(39.74%)
C.	44,693	(21.77%)
LD	27,223	(13.26%)
Lab.	22,894	(11.15%)
Green	14,781	(7.20%)
UKIP	5,344	(2.60%)
Ind.	3,689	(1.80%)
SCP	3,407	(1.66%)
RISE	889	(0.43%)
Solidarity	793	(0.39%)

SNP majority 36,907 (17.98%)
8.95% swing SNP to C. (2011 SNP majority 59,198)
ADDITIONAL MEMBERS

Douglas Ross, *C.*	David Steward, *Lab.*
Edward Mountain, *C.*	Maree Todd, *SNP*
Donald Cameron, *C.*	John Finnie, *Green*
Rhoda Grant, *Lab.*	

LOTHIAN
E. 565,860 T. 327,178 (57.82%)

SNP	118,546	(36.23%)
C.	74,972	(22.91%)
Lab.	67,991	(20.78%)
Green	34,551	(10.56%)
LD	18,479	(5.65%)
UKIP	5,802	(1.77%)
Women	3,877	(1.18%)
RISE	1,641	(0.50%)
Solidarity	1,319	(0.40%)

SNP majority 43,574 (13.32%)
7.10% swing SNP to C. (2011 SNP majority 40,409)
ADDITIONAL MEMBERS

Miles Briggs, *C.*	Neil Findlay, *Lab.*
Gordon Lindhurst, *C.*	Alison Johnstone, *Green*
Jeremy Balfour, *C.*	Andy Wightman, *Green*
Kezia Dugdale, *Lab.*	

SCOTLAND CENTRAL
E. 511,506 T. 270,706 (52.92%)

SNP	129,082	(47.68%)
Lab.	67,103	(24.79%)
C.	43,602	(16.11%)
Green	12,722	(4.70%)
UKIP	6,088	(2.25%)
LD	5,015	(1.85%)
Solidarity	2,684	(0.99%)
SCP	2,314	(0.85%)
RISE	1,636	(0.60%)
Ind.	460	(0.17%)

SNP majority 61,979 (22.90%)
5.92% swing Lab. to SNP (2011 SNP majority 25,802)
ADDITIONAL MEMBERS

Margaret Mitchell, *C.*	Monica Lennon, *Lab.*
Graham Simpson, *C.*	Mark Griffin, *Lab.*
Alison Harris, *C.*	Elaine Smith, *Lab.*
Richard Leonard, *Lab.*	

SCOTLAND MID AND FIFE

E. 499,156 T. 291,172 (58.33%)

SNP	120,128	(41.26%)
C.	73,293	(25.17%)
Lab.	51,373	(17.64%)
LD	20,401	(7.01%)
Green	17,860	(6.13%)
UKIP	5,345	(1.84%)
RISE	1,073	(0.37%)
Solidarity	1,049	(0.36%)
SLP	650	(0.22%)

SNP majority 46,835 (16.08%)
7.50% swing SNP to C. (2011 SNP majority 52,068)
ADDITIONAL MEMBERS

Murdo Fraser, C.	Alex Rowley, Lab.
Liz Smith, C.	Claire Baker, Lab.
Dean Lockhart, C.	Mark Ruskell, Green
Alexander Stewart, C.	

SCOTLAND NORTH EAST

E. 579,317 T. 307,006 (52.99%)

SNP	137,086	(44.65%)
C.	85,848	(27.96%)
Lab.	38,791	(12.64%)
LD	18,444	(6.01%)
Green	15,123	(4.93%)
UKIP	6,376	(2.08%)
SCP	2,068	(0.67%)
Solidarity	992	(0.32%)
Nat Front	617	(0.20%)
RISE	599	(0.20%)
SLP	552	(0.18%)
Comm Brit	510	(0.17%)

SNP majority 51,238 (16.69%)
10.95% swing SNP to C. (2011 SNP majority 96,856)
ADDITIONAL MEMBERS

Alex Johnstone, C.	Jenny Marra, Lab.
Ross Thomson, C.	Lewis Macdonald, Lab.
Peter Chapman, C.	Mike Rumbles, LD
Liam Kerr, C.	

SCOTLAND SOUTH

E. 533,774 T. 314,192 (58.86%)

SNP	120,217	(38.26%)
C.	100,753	(32.07%)
Lab.	56,072	(17.85%)
Green	14,773	(4.70%)
LD	11,775	(3.75%)
UKIP	6,726	(2.14%)
CSSInd.	1,485	(0.47%)
Solidarity	1,294	(0.41%)
RISE	1,097	(0.35%)

SNP majority 19,464 (6.19%)
7.65% swing SNP to C. (2011 SNP majority 43,675)
ADDITIONAL MEMBERS

Rachel Hamilton, C.	Joan McAlpine, SNP
Brian Whittle, C.	Emma Harper, SNP
Claudia Beamish, Lab.	Paul Wheelhouse, SNP
Colin Smyth, Lab.	

SCOTLAND WEST

E. 538,225 T. 322,076 (59.84%)

SNP	135,827	(42.17%)
Lab.	72,544	(22.52%)
C.	71,528	(22.21%)
Green	17,218	(5.35%)
LD	12,097	(3.76%)
UKIP	5,856	(1.82%)
Solidarity	2,609	(0.81%)
SCP	2,391	(0.74%)
RISE	1,522	(0.47%)
SLP	484	(0.15%)

SNP majority 63,283 (19.65%)
5.44% swing Lab. to SNP (2011 SNP majority 24,776)
ADDITIONAL MEMBERS

Jamie Green, C.	Mary Fee, Lab.
Maurice Golden, C.	Ken Macintosh, Lab.
Maurice Corry, C.	Ross Greer, Green
Neil Bibby, Lab.	

NORTHERN IRELAND

NORTHERN IRELAND ASSEMBLY
Parliament Buildings, Stormont, Belfast BT4 3XX
T 028-9052 1137 E info@niassembly.gov.uk
W www.niassembly.gov.uk

The Northern Ireland Assembly was established as a result of the Belfast Agreement (also known as the Good Friday Agreement) in April 1998. The agreement was endorsed through a referendum held in May 1998 and subsequently given legal force through the Northern Ireland Act 1998.

The Northern Ireland Assembly has full legislative and executive authority for all matters that are the responsibility of the government's Northern Ireland departments – known as transferred matters. Excepted and reserved matters are defined in schedules 2 and 3 of the Northern Ireland Act 1998 and remain the responsibility of UK parliament.

The first assembly election occurred on 25 June 1998 and the 108 members elected met for the first time on 1 July 1998.

On 29 November 1999 the assembly appointed ten ministers as well as the chairs and deputy chairs for the ten statutory departmental committees. Devolution of powers to the Northern Ireland Assembly occurred on 2 December 1999, following several delays concerned with Sinn Fein's inclusion in the executive while Irish Republican Army (IRA) weapons were yet to be decommissioned.

Since the devolution of powers, the assembly has been suspended by the Secretary of State for Northern Ireland on four occasions. The first was between 11 February and 30 May 2000, with two 24-hour suspensions on 10 August and 22 September 2001 – all owing to a lack of progress in decommissioning. The final suspension took place on 14 October 2002 after unionists walked out of the executive following a police raid on Sinn Fein's office investigating alleged intelligence gathering.

The assembly was formally dissolved in April 2003 in anticipation of an election, which eventually took place on 26 November 2003. The results of the election changed the balance of power between the political parties, with an increase in the number of seats held by the Democratic Unionist Party (DUP) and Sinn Fein (SF), so that they became the largest parties. The assembly was restored to a state of suspension following the November election while political parties engaged in a review of the Belfast Agreement aimed at fully restoring the devolved institutions.

In July 2005 the leadership of the IRA formally ordered an end to its armed campaign; it authorised a representative to engage with the Independent International Commission on Decommissioning in order to verifiably put the arms beyond use. On 26 September 2005 General John de Chastelain, the chair of the commission, along with two independent church witnesses confirmed that the IRA's entire arsenal of weapons had been decommissioned.

Following the passing of the Northern Ireland Act 2006 the secretary of state created a non-legislative fixed-term assembly, whose membership consisted of the 108 members elected in the 2003 election. It first met on 15 May 2006 with the remit of making preparations for the restoration of devolved government; its discussions informed the next round of talks called by the British and Irish governments held at St Andrews. The St Andrews agreement of 13 October 2006 led to the establishment of the transitional assembly.

The Northern Ireland (St Andrews Agreement) Act 2006 set out a timetable to restore devolution, and also set the date for the third election to the assembly as 7 March 2007. The DUP and SF again had the largest number of Members of the Legislative Assembly (MLAs) elected, and although the initial restoration deadline of 26 March was missed, the leaders of

the DUP and SF (Revd Dr Ian Paisley and Gerry Adams respectively) took part in a historic meeting and made a joint commitment to establish an executive committee in the assembly to which devolved powers were restored on 8 May 2007.

RECENT DEVELOPMENTS
Assembly elections took place on 5 May 2016 to elect the 108 members of the legislative assembly for a fifth term. The fifth assembly collapsed on 9 January 2017 when Martin McGuinness resigned as Deputy First Minister. Under the joint protocols that govern the power-sharing agreement, if either the first minister or the deputy resigns and a replacement is not nominated by the relevant party within seven days, then a snap election must be called. The assembly was formally dissolved at midnight on 25 January 2017 and the most recent assembly elections were held on 2 March 2017 to elect the 90 members of the legislative assembly. Under the Assembly Members (Reduction of Numbers) Act Northern Ireland 2016, the number of assembly members was reduced from 108 to 90 – five members to be elected by each constituency, rather than six.

Following the March 2017 election, negotiations to form an executive missed both the normal three week deadline and an extended deadline of 29 June 2017 set by the Secretary of State for Northern Ireland. The sixth assembly remains suspended until an executive is formed.

THE SINGLE TRANSFERABLE VOTE SYSTEM
Members of the Northern Ireland Assembly are elected by the single transferable vote system from 18 constituencies – five per constituency. Under the single transferable vote system every voter has a single vote that can be transferred from one candidate to another. Voters number their candidates in order of preference. Where candidates reach their quota of votes and are elected, surplus votes are transferred to other candidates according to the next preference on each voter's ballot slip. The candidate in each round with the fewest votes is eliminated and their surplus votes are redistributed according to the voter's next preference. The process is repeated until the required number of members are elected.

SALARIES*

	From 1 January 2019
Speaker	£55,848
Deputy Speaker	£37,388
Commission member	£40,688
MLA	£35,888

* MLA salaries were reduced on 1 November 2018 and further reduced on 1 January 2019 for the present period while there is no executive

NORTHERN IRELAND ASSEMBLY
MEMBERS *as at August 2019*
KEY
* Replacement from the party list since the 2 March 2017 Northern Ireland Assembly election

Agnew, Steven, *Green, Down North*
Aiken, Dr Steve, OBE, *UUP, Antrim South*
Allen, Andy, *UUP, Belfast East*
Allister, Jim, *TUV, Antrim North*
Archibald, Caoimhe, *SF, Londonderry East*
Armstrong, Kellie, *Alliance, Strangford*
Bailey, Clare, *Green, Belfast South*
Barton, Rosemary, *UUP, Fermanagh and South Tyrone*
Beattie, Doug, MC, *UUP, Upper Bann*
Beggs, Roy, *UUP, Antrim East*
* **Blair**, John, *Alliance, Antrim South*

Boylan, Cathal, *SF, Newry and Armagh*
Bradley, Maurice, *DUP, Londonderry East*
Bradley, Paula, *DUP, Belfast North*
Bradley, Sinéad, *SDLP, Down South*
Bradshaw, Paula, *Alliance, Belfast South*
Buchanan, Keith, *DUP, Ulster Mid*
Buchanan, Thomas, *DUP, Tyrone West*
Buckley, Jonathan, *DUP, Upper Bann*
Bunting, Joanne, *DUP, Belfast East*
Butler, Robbie, *UUP, Lagan Valley*
Cameron, Pam, *DUP, Antrim South*
Carroll, Gerry, *PBP, Belfast West*
Catney, Pat, *SDLP, Lagan Valley*
Chambers, Alan, *UUP, Down North*
* Clarke, Trevor, *DUP, Antrim South*
Dallat, John, *SDLP, Londonderry East*
Dickson, Stewart, *Alliance, Antrim East*
Dillon, Linda, *SF, Ulster Mid*
Dolan, Jemma, *SF, Fermanagh and South Tyrone*
Dunne, Gordon, *DUP, Down North*
Durkan, Mark, *SDLP, Foyle*
Easton, Alex, *DUP, Down North*
Eastwood, Colum, *SDLP, Foyle*
Ennis, Sinéad, *SF, Down South*
Farry, Dr Stephen, *Alliance, Down North*
Fearon, Megan, *SF, Newry and Armagh*
Flynn, Órlaithí, *SF, Belfast West*
Foster, Arlene, *DUP, Fermanagh and South Tyrone*
Frew, Paul, *DUP, Antrim North*
* Gildernew, Colm, *SF, Fermanagh and South Tyrone*
Givan, Paul, *DUP, Lagan Valley*
Hamilton, Simon, *DUP, Strangford*
Hanna, Claire, *SDLP, Belfast South*
* Hendron, Máire, *Alliance, Belfast East*
Hilditch, David, *DUP, Antrim East*
Humphrey, William, *DUP, Belfast North*
Irwin, William, *DUP, Newry and Armagh*
Kearney, Declan, *SF, Antrim South*
* Kelly, Catherine, *SF, Tyrone West*
Kelly, Dolores, *SDLP, Upper Bann*
Kelly, Gerry, *SF, Belfast North*
Lockhart, Carla, *DUP, Upper Bann*
Long, Naomi, *Alliance, Belfast East*
Lunn, Trevor, *Alliance, Lagan Valley*
Lynch, Seán, *SF, Fermanagh and South Tyrone*
Lyons, Gordon, *DUP, Antrim East*
Lyttle, Chris, *Alliance, Belfast East*
McAleer, Declan, *SF, Tyrone West*
McCann, Fra, *SF, Belfast West*
McCartney, Raymond, *SF, Foyle*
McCrossan, Daniel, *SDLP, Tyrone West*
McGlone, Patsy, *SDLP, Ulster Mid*
McGrath, Colin, *SDLP, Down South*
McGuigan, Philip, *SF, Antrim North*
* McHugh, Maoliosa, *SF, Tyrone West*
McIlveen, Michelle, *DUP, Strangford*
McNulty, Justin, *SDLP, Newry and Armagh*
Mallon, Nichola, *SDLP, Belfast North*
Maskey, Alex, *SF, Belfast West*
Middleton, Gary, *DUP, Foyle*
* Mullan, Karen, *SF, Foyle*
Murphy, Conor, *SF, Newry and Armagh*
Nesbitt, Mike, *UUP, Strangford*
Newton, Robin, *DUP, Belfast East*
Ní Chuilín, Carál, *SF, Belfast North*
O'Dowd, John, *SF, Upper Bann*
O'Neill, Michelle, *SF, Ulster Mid*
Ó Muilleoir, Máirtín, *SF, Belfast South*
Poots, Edwin, *DUP, Lagan Valley*

Robinson, George, *DUP, Londonderry East*
* Rogan, Emma, *SF, Down South*
Sheehan, Pat, *SF, Belfast West*
* Sheerin, Emma, *SF, Ulster Mid*
Stalford, Christopher, *DUP, Belfast South*
Stewart, John, *UUP, Antrim East*
Storey, Mervyn, *DUP, Antrim North*
Sugden, Claire, *Ind., Londonderry East*
Swann, Robin, *UUP, Antrim North*
Weir, Peter, *DUP, Down North*
Wells, Jim, *DUP, Down South*

STATE OF THE PARTIES *as at 2 March 2017 election*

Party	Seats
Democratic Unionist Party (DUP)	28
Sinn Fein (SF)	27
Social Democratic and Labour Party (SDLP)	12
Ulster Unionist Party (UUP)	10
Alliance Party of Northern Ireland (Alliance)	8
Green Party (Green)	2
People Before Profit Alliance (PBP)	1
Traditional Unionist Voice (TUV)	1
Independents (Ind.)	1
Total	90

NORTHERN IRELAND EXECUTIVE
Stormont Castle, Stormont, Belfast BT4 3TT
T 028-9052 8400
W www.northernireland.gov.uk

The Northern Ireland Executive comprises the first minister, deputy first minister, two junior ministers and eight departmental ministers.

The executive exercises authority on behalf of the Northern Ireland Assembly, and takes decisions on significant issues and matters which cut across the responsibility of two or more ministers.

The executive also agrees proposals put forward by ministers for new legislation in the form of 'executive bills' for consideration by the assembly. It is also responsible for drawing up a programme for government and an agreed budget for approval by the assembly. Ministers of the executive are nominated by the political parties in the Northern Ireland Assembly. The number of ministers which a party can nominate is determined by its share of seats in the assembly. The first minister and deputy first minister are nominated by the largest and second largest parties respectively and act as chairs of the executive. Each executive minister has responsibility for a specific Northern Ireland government department.

EXECUTIVE COMMITTEE OF MINISTERS
There are currently no executive ministers in post since the most recent assembly elections which took place on 2 March 2017. Negotiations to appoint the executive committee of ministers in charge of the nine government departments failed to meet both the three-week deadline following the election and an extended deadline of 29 June 2017 set by the Secretary of State for Northern Ireland. The assembly remains suspended until an executive is formed.

NORTHERN IRELAND EXECUTIVE DEPARTMENTS
THE EXECUTIVE OFFICE, Stormont Castle, Stormont, Belfast BT4 3TT T 028-9052 8400 W www.executiveoffice-ni.gov.uk
DEPARTMENT OF AGRICULTURE, ENVIRONMENT AND RURAL AFFAIRS, Dundonald House, Upper Newtownards Road, Belfast BT4 3SB T 0300-200 7850 W www.daera-ni.gov.uk

DEPARTMENT FOR COMMUNITIES, Causeway Exchange, 1–7 Bedford Street, Belfast BT2 7EG T 028-9082 9000 W www.communities-ni.gov.uk
DEPARTMENT FOR THE ECONOMY, Netherleigh, Massey Avenue, Belfast BT4 2JP T 028-9052 9900 W www.economy-ni.gov.uk
DEPARTMENT OF EDUCATION, Rathgael House, Balloo Road, Bangor, Co. Down BT19 7PR T 028-9127 9279 W www.education-ni.gov.uk
DEPARTMENT OF FINANCE, Clare House, 303 Airport Road, Belfast BT3 9ED T 028-9185 8111 W www.finance-ni.gov.uk
DEPARTMENT OF HEALTH, Castle Buildings, Stormont, Belfast BT4 3SQ T 028-9052 0500 W www.health-ni.gov.uk
DEPARTMENT FOR INFRASTRUCTURE, Clarence Court, 10–18 Adelaide Street, Belfast BT2 8GB T 028-9054 0540 W www.infrastructure-ni.gov.uk
DEPARTMENT OF JUSTICE, Block B, Castle Buildings, Stormont Estate, Belfast BT4 3SG T 028-9076 3000 W www.justice-ni.gov.uk

NORTHERN IRELAND AUDIT OFFICE
106 University Street, Belfast BT7 1EU
T 028-9025 1000 E info@niauditoffice.gov.uk
W www.niauditoffice.gov.uk

The Northern Ireland Audit Office supports the Comptroller and Auditor-General in fulfilling his responsibilities. He is responsible for authorising the issue of money from central government funds to Northern Ireland departments and for both financial and value for money audits of central government bodies in Northern Ireland, including, Northern Ireland departments, executive agencies, executive non-departmental public bodies and health and social care bodies.

Comptroller and Auditor-General, Kieran Donnelly, CB

OFFICE OF THE ATTORNEY-GENERAL FOR NORTHERN IRELAND
PO Box 1272, Belfast BT1 9LU
T 028-9072 5333 E contact@attorneygeneralni.gov.uk
W www.attorneygeneralni.gov.uk

With the devolution of justice responsibilities on 12 April 2010, the Justice (Northern Ireland) Act 2002 was enacted which established a new post of Attorney-General for Northern Ireland. The Attorney-General acts as the chief legal adviser to the Northern Ireland executive for both civil and criminal matters that fall within the devolved powers of the assembly. He is the executive's most senior representative in the courts and responsible for protecting the public interest in matters of law; overseeing the legal work of the in-house advisers to the executive and its departments; and for the appointment of the director and deputy director of the Public Prosecution Service for Northern Ireland. The Attorney-General participates in the assembly proceedings to the extent permitted by its standing orders, but does not vote in the assembly.

The post of Attorney-General is statutorily independent of the first minister, deputy first minister, the executive and executive departments.

Attorney-General for Northern Ireland, John Larkin, QC

NORTHERN IRELAND ASSEMBLY ELECTION RESULTS *as at 2 March 2017*

Electorate (E.) 1,254,709 Turnout (T.) 64.8%
First = number of first-preference votes
See General Election Results for a list of party abbreviations

ANTRIM EAST
E. 62,933 T. 37,836 (60.12%)

	First	Round Elected
David Hilditch, DUP	6,000	3
Roy Beggs, UUP	5,121	6
Stewart Dickson, Alliance, DUP	4,179	6
Gordon Lyons, DUP	3,851	8
Oliver McMullan, SF	3,701	
John Stewart, UUP	3,377	9
Stephen Ross, DUP	3,313	
Danny Donnelly, Alliance	1,817	
Noel Jordan, UKIP	1,579	
Ruth Wilson, TUV	1,534	
Margaret McKillop, SDLP	1,524	
Dawn Patterson, Green	777	
Conor Sheridan, Lab. Alt	393	
Alan Dunlop, Lab. C	152	
Ricky Best, Ind.	106	

ANTRIM NORTH
E. 76,739 T. 48,518 (63.22%)

	First	Round Elected
Philip McGuigan, SF	7,600	6
Paul Frew, DUP	6,975	7
Mervyn Storey, DUP	6,857	7
Jim Allister, TUV	6,214	7
Robin Swann, UUP	6,022	6
Phillip Logan, DUP	5,708	
Connor Duncan, SDLP	3,519	
Patricia O'Lynn, Alliance	2,616	
Timothy Gaston, TUV	1,505	
Mark Bailey, Green	530	
Monica Digney, Ind.	435	
Adam McBride, Ind.	113	

ANTRIM SOUTH
E. 68,475 T. 42,726 (62.40%)

	First	Round Elected
Declan Kearney, SF	6,891	4
Steve Aiken, UUP	6,287	5
David Ford, Alliance	5,278	7
Paul Girvan, DUP	5,152	8
Pam Cameron, DUP	4,604	8
Trevor Clarke, DUP	4,522	
Roisin Lynch, SDLP	4,024	
Adrian Cochrane-Watson, UUP	2,505	
Richard Cairns, TUV	1,353	
Ivanka Antova, PBP	530	
David McMaster, Ind.	503	
Eleanor Bailey, Green	501	
Mark Logan, C.	194	

BELFAST EAST
E. 64,788 T. 40,828 (63.02%)

	First	Round Elected
Naomi Long, Alliance	7,610	1
Joanne Bunting, DUP	6,007	9
Andy Allen, UUP	5,275	9
Chris Lyttle, Alliance	5,059	8
Robin Newton, DUP	4,729	11
David Douglas, DUP	4,431	
John Kyle, PUP	2,658	
Georgina Milne, Green	1,447	
Mairead O'Donnell, SF	1,173	
Andrew Girvin, TUV.	917	
Courtney Robinson, CCLA	442	
Sheila Bodel, C.	275	
Séamas de Faoite, SDLP	250	
Jordy McKeag, Ind.	84	

BELFAST NORTH
E. 68,187 T. 42,119 (61.77%)

	First	Round Elected
Gerry Kelly, SF	6,275	7
Caral Ni Chuilin, SF	5,929	7
Nichola Mallon, SDLP	5,431	7
Paula Bradley, DUP	4,835	6
William Humphrey, DUP	4,418	6
Nelson McCausland, DUP	4,056	
Nuala McAllister, Alliance	3,487	
Robert Foster, UUP	2,418	
Julie-Anne Corr-Johnston, PUP	2,053	
Fiona Ferguson, PBP	1,559	
Malachai O'Hara, Green	711	
Gemma Weir, WP	248	
Adam Millar, Ind.	66	

BELFAST SOUTH
E. 61,309 T. 43,465 (70.89%)

	First	Round Elected
Máirtín Ó Muilleoir, SF	7,610	1
Claire Hanna, SDLP	6,559	6
Paula Bradshaw, Alliance	5,595	6
Christopher Stalford, DUP	4,529	9
Emma Little-Pengelly, DUP	4,446	
Clare Bailey, Green	4,247	9
Michael Henderson, UUP	3,863	
Emmet McDonough-Brown, Alliance	2,053	
Naomh Gallagher, SDLP	1,794	
Padraigin Mervyn, PBP	760	
John Hiddleston, TUV	703	
Sean Burns, Lab. Alt	531	
George Jabbour, C.	200	
Lily Kerr, WP	163	

BELFAST WEST
E. 61,309 T. 40,930 (66.76%)

	First	Round Elected
Orlaithi Flynn, SF	6,918	1
Alex Maskey, SF	6,346	3
Fra McCann, SF	6,201	4
Pat Sheehan, SF	5,466	4
Gerry Carroll, PBP	4,903	3
Frank McCoubrey, DUP	4,063	
Alex Attwood, SDLP	3,452	
Michael Collins, PBP	1,096	
Sorcha Eastwood, Alliance	747	
Fred Rodgers, UUP	486	
Connor Campbell, WP	415	
Ellen Murray, Green	251	

DOWN NORTH
E. 64,461 T. 38,174 (59.22%)

	First	Round Elected
Alex Easton, DUP	8,034	1
Alan Chambers, UUP	7,151	1
Stephen Farry, Alliance	7,014	1
Gordon Dunne, DUP	6,118	2
Steven Agnew, Green	5,178	7
Melanie Kennedy, Ind.	1,246	
William Cudworth, UUP	964	
Caoimhe McNeill, SDLP	679	
Frank Shivers, C.	641	
Kieran Maxwell, SF	591	
Chris Carter, Ind.	92	
Gavan Reynolds, Ind.	31	

DOWN SOUTH
E. 75,415 T. 49,934 (66.21%)

	First	Round Elected
Sinéad Ennis, SF	10,256	1
Chris Hazzard, SF	8,827	1
Jim Wells, DUP	7,786	5
Sinéad Bradley, SDLP	7,323	3
Colin McGrath, SDLP	5,110	7
Patrick Brown, Alliance	4,535	
Harold McKee, UUP	4,172	
Lyle Rea, TUV	630	
Hannah George, Green	483	
Patrick Clarke, Ind.	192	
Gary Hynds, C.	85	

FERMANAGH AND SOUTH TYRONE
E. 73,100 T. 53,075 (72.61%)

	First	Round Elected
Arlene Foster, DUP	8,479	2
Michelle Gildernew, SF	7,987	3
Jemma Dolan, SF	7,767	3
Maurice Morrow, DUP	7,102	
Sean Lynch, SF	6,254	4
Rosemary Barton, UUP	6,060	4
Richie McPhillips, SDLP	5,134	
Noreen Campbell, Alliance	1,437	
Alex Elliott, TUV	780	
Donal O'Cofaigh, Lab. Alt	643	
Tanya Jones, Green	550	
Richard Dunn, C.	70	

FOYLE
E. 69,718 T. 45,317 (65.00%)

	First	Round Elected
Elisha McCallion, SF	9,205	1
Colum Eastwood, SDLP	7,240	3
Raymond McCartney, SF	7,145	2
Mark H. Durkan, SDLP	6,948	5
Gary Middleton, DUP	5,975	6
Eamon McCann, PBP	4,760	
Julia Kee, UUP	1,660	
Colm Cavanagh, Alliance	1,124	
Shannon Downey, Green	242	
John Lindsay, CISTA	196	
Stuart Canning, C.	77	
Arthur McGuinness, Ind.	44	

LAGAN VALLEY
E. 72,621 T. 45,440 (62.50%)

	First	Round Elected
Paul Givan, DUP	8,035	1
Robbie Butler, UUP	6,846	7
Trevor Lunn, Alliance	6,105	7
Edwin Poots, DUP	6,013	8
Brenda Hale, DUP	4,566	
Jenny Palmer, UUP	4,492	
Pat Catney, SDLP	3,795	8
Peter Doran, SF	1,801	
Samuel Morrison, TUV	1,389	
Dan Barrios-O'Neill, Green	912	
Jonny Orr, Ind.	856	
Matthew Robinson, C.	183	
Keith John Gray, Ind.	76	

LONDONDERRY EAST
E. 67,392 T. 42,248 (62.69%)

	First	Round Elected
Caoimhe Archibald, SF	5,851	12
Maurice Bradley, DUP	5,444	9
Cathal ohOisin, SF	4,953	
Claire Sugden, Ind.	4,918	8
George Robinson, DUP	4,715	9
Adrian McQuillan, DUP	3,881	
John Dallat, SDLP	3,319	12
William McCandless, UUP	2,814	
Chris McCaw, Alliance	1,841	
Gerry Mullan, Ind.	1,204	
Jordan Armstrong, TUV	1,038	
Russell Watton, PUP	879	
Gavin Campbell, PBP	492	
Anthony Flynn, Green	305	
David Harding, C.	219	

NEWRY AND ARMAGH
E. 80,140 T. 55,625 (69.41%)

	First	Round Elected
William Irwin, DUP	9,760	1
Cathal Boylan, SF	9,197	1
Justin McNulty, SDLP	8,983	2
Megan Fearon, SF	8,881	2
Conor Murphy, SF	8,454	3
Danny Kennedy, UUP	7,256	
Jackie Coade, Alliance	1,418	
Emmet Crossan, CISTA	704	
Rowan Tunnicliffe, Green	265	

STRANGFORD
E. 64,393 T. 39,239 (60.94%)

	First	Round Elected
Simon Hamilton, DUP	6,221	5
Kellie Armstrong, Alliance	5,813	4
Michelle McIlveen, DUP	5,728	9
Mike Nesbitt, UUP	5,323	9
Peter Weir, DUP	3,543	11
Joe Boyle, SDLP	3,045	
Philip Smith, UUP	2,453	
Jimmy Menagh, Ind.	1,627	
Jonathan Bell, Ind.	1,479	
Stephen Cooper, TUV	1,330	
Dermot Kennedy, SF	1,110	
Ricky Bamford, Green	918	
Scott Benton, C.	195	

TYRONE WEST
E. 64,258 T. 44,907 (69.89%)

	First	Round Elected
Thomas Buchanan, DUP	9,064	1
Michaela Boyle, SF	7,714	1
Barry McElduff, SF	7,573	1
Daniel McCrossan, SDLP	6,283	5
Declan McAleer, SF	6,034	5
Alicia Clarke, UUP	3,654	
Stephen Donnelly, Alliance	1,252	
Sorcha McAnespy, Ind.	864	
Charlie Chittick, TUV	851	
Ciaran McClean, Green	412	
Barry Brown, CISTA	373	
Corey French, Ind.	98	
Roisin McMackin, Ind.	85	
Susan-Anne White, Ind.	41	
Roger Lomas, C.	27	

ULSTER MID
E. 69,396 T. 50,228 (72.38%)

	First	Round Elected
Michelle, O'Neill, SF	10,258	1
Keith Buchanan, DUP	9,568	1
Ian Milne, SF	8,143	2
Linda Dillon, SF	7,806	2
Patsy McGlone, SDLP	6,419	5
Sandra Overend, UUP	4,516	
Hannah Loughrin, TUV	1,244	
Fay Watson, Alliance	1,017	
Hugh McCloy, Ind.	247	
Stefan Taylor, Green	243	
Hugh Scullion, WP	217	

UPPER BANN
E. 83,431 T. 52,174 (62.54%)

	First	Round Elected
Carla Lockhart, DUP	9,140	1
John O'Dowd, SF	8,220	5
Jonathan Buckley, DUP	7,745	4
Nuala Toman, SF	6,108	
Doug Beattie, UUP	5,467	5
Jo-Anne Dobson, UUP	5,132	
Dolores Kelly, SDLP	5,127	6
Tara Doyle, Alliance	2,720	
Roy Ferguson, TUV	1,035	
Simon Lee, Green	555	
Colin Craig, WP	218	
Ian Nickels, C.	81	

REGIONAL GOVERNMENT

LONDON

GREATER LONDON AUTHORITY (GLA)

City Hall, The Queen's Walk, London SE1 2AA
T 020-7983 4000 E mayor@london.gov.uk W www.london.gov.uk

On 7 May 1998 London voted in favour of the formation of the Greater London Authority (GLA). The first elections to the GLA took place on 4 May 2000 and the new authority took over its responsibilities on 3 July 2000. In July 2002 the GLA moved to one of London's most spectacular buildings, newly built on a brownfield site on the south bank of the Thames, adjacent to Tower Bridge. The fifth and most recent election to the GLA took place on 5 May 2016.

The structure and objectives of the GLA stem from its main areas of responsibility: transport, policing, fire and emergency planning, economic development, planning, culture and health. There are four functional bodies which form part of the wider GLA group and report to the GLA: the Mayor's Office for Policing and Crime (MOPAC), Transport for London (TfL), the London Fire Commissioner and the London Legacy Development Corporation.

The GLA consists of a directly elected mayor, the Mayor of London, and a separately elected assembly, the London Assembly. The mayor has the key role in decision making, with the assembly responsible for regulating and scrutinising these decisions, and investigating issues of importance to Londoners. In addition, the GLA has around 800 permanent staff to support the activities of the mayor and the assembly, which are overseen by a head of paid service. The mayor may appoint two political advisers and not more than ten other members of staff, though he does not necessarily exercise this power, but he does not appoint the chief executive, the monitoring officer or the chief finance officer. These must be appointed jointly by the assembly and the mayor.

Every aspect of the assembly and its activities must be open to public scrutiny and therefore accountable. The assembly holds the mayor to account through scrutiny of his strategies, decisions and actions. Mayor's Question Time, conducted on ten occasions a year at City Hall, is carried out by direct questioning at assembly meetings and by conducting detailed investigations in committee.

People's Question Time, held twice a year, and Talk London (W www.london.gov.uk/talk-london) give Londoners the chance to question and express their opinions to the mayor and the assembly about plans, priorities and policies for London.

The role of the mayor can be broken down into a number of key areas:

- to represent and promote London at home and abroad and speak up for Londoners
- to devise strategies and plans to tackle London-wide issues, such as crime, transport, housing, planning, economic development and regeneration, environment, public services, society and culture, sport and health; and to set budgets for TfL, MOPAC, London Fire Commissioner and the London Legacy Development Corporation
- the mayor is chair of TfL, and is responsible for the Metropolitan Police's priorities and performance

The role of the assembly can be broken down into a number of key areas:

- to hold the mayor to account by examining his decisions and actions
- to have the power to amend the mayor's budget by a majority of two-thirds

- to have the power to summon the mayor, senior staff of the GLA and functional bodies
- to investigate issues of London-wide significance and make proposals to appropriate stakeholders
- to examine the work of MOPAC and to review the police and crime plan for London through the Police and Crime Committee

MAYORAL TEAM

Mayor, Sadiq Khan
Deputy Mayors, Rajesh Agrawal *(Business);* Sophie Linden *(Policing and Crime);* Joanne McCartney, AM *(Education and Childcare);* James Murray *(Housing and Residential Development);* Jules Pipe, CBE *(Planning, Regeneration and Skills);* Shirley Rodrigues *(Environment and Energy);* Heidi Alexander *(Transport);* Justine Simons, OBE *(Culture and the Creative Industries);* Dr Fiona Twycross, AM *(Fire and Resilience);* Debbie Weekes-Bernard *(Social Integration, Social Mobility and Community Engagement)*
Chief of Staff, David Bellamy
Directors, Nick Bowes *(Policy);* Patrick Hennessy *(Communications);* Leah Kreitzman *(External and International Affairs);* Jack Stenner *(Political and Public Affairs)*
Special Appointments, Theo Blackwell, MBE *(Chief Digital Officer);* Dr Tom Coffey, OBE *(Health Adviser);* Amy Lamé *(Night Czar);* Dr Will Norman *(Walking and Cycling Commissioner);* Claire Waxman *(Victims Commissioner)*

ELECTIONS AND VOTING SYSTEMS

The assembly is elected every four years at the same time as the mayor, and consists of 25 members. There is one member from each of the 14 GLA constituencies topped up with 11 London-wide members who are either representatives of political parties or individuals standing as independent candidates. The last election was on 5 May 2016.

Two distinct voting systems are used to appoint the existing mayor and the assembly. The mayor is elected using the supplementary vote system (SVS). With SVS, electors have two votes: one to give a first choice for mayor and one to give a second choice; they cannot vote twice for the same candidate. If one candidate gets more than half of all the first-choice votes, he or she becomes mayor. If no candidate gets more than half of the first-choice votes, the two candidates with the most first-choice votes remain in the election and all the other candidates drop out. The second-choice votes on the ballot papers are then counted. Where these second-choice votes are for the two remaining candidates, they are added to the first-choice votes these candidates already have. The candidate with the most first- and second-choice votes combined becomes the Mayor of London.

The assembly is appointed using the additional member system (AMS). Under AMS, electors have two votes. The first vote is for a constituency candidate. The second vote is for a party list or individual candidate contesting the London-wide assembly seats. The 14 constituency members are elected under the first-past-the-post system, the same system used in general and local elections. Electors vote for one candidate and the candidate with the most votes wins. The additional members are drawn from party lists or are independent candidates who stand as London members; they are chosen using a form of proportional representation.

The Greater London Returning Officer (GLRO) is the independent official responsible for running the election in London. He is supported in this by returning officers in each of the 14 London constituencies.
GLRO for 2016 Election, Jeff Jacobs

TRANSPORT FOR LONDON (TFL)

TfL is the integrated body responsible for London's transport system. Its role is to implement the mayor's transport strategy for London and manage transport services across the capital for which the mayor has responsibility. TfL is directed by a management board whose members are chosen for their understanding of transport matters and are appointed by the mayor, who chairs the board. TfL's role is:

- to manage the London Underground, buses, Croydon Tramlink, London Overground and the Docklands Light Railway (DLR)
- to manage a 580km network of main roads and all 6,000 of London's traffic lights
- to regulate taxis and minicabs
- to run the London River Services, Victoria Coach Station and London Transport Museum
- to help to coordinate the Dial-a-Ride, Capital Call and Taxicard schemes for door-to-door services for transport users with mobility problems

The London Borough Councils maintain the role of highway and traffic authorities for 95 per cent of London's roads. A congestion charge for motorists driving into central London between the hours of 7am and 6.30pm, Monday to Friday (excluding public holidays) was introduced on 17 February 2003. On 19 February 2007, the charge zone roughly doubled in size after a westward expansion and the charging hours were shortened, to finish at 6pm. On 4 January 2011, the westward expansion was removed from the charging zone and an automated payment system was introduced. As at September 2019 the daily congestion charge is £11.50. (W www.tfl.gov.uk/modes/driving/congestion-charge).

TfL introduced a low emission zone (LEZ) for London on 4 February 2008; the LEZ covers most of Greater London and is in constant operation for larger vans, minibuses, lorries, buses and other heavy vehicles that do not meet the LEZ emissions standards (cars and motorcycles are exempt). The daily charge is £100 for larger vans, minibuses and other specialist vehicles and £200 for lorries, buses and coaches. (W www.tfl.gov.uk/modes/driving/low-emission-zone).

Since 8 April 2019 a new ultra low emission zone (ULEZ) has operated constantly in central London and covers the same area of central London as the congestion charge. Most vehicles, including cars and vans, need to meet the ULEZ emissions standards or their drivers must pay a daily charge, in addition to the congestion charge and, if applicable, the LEZ, to drive within the zone. As at September 2019 the charge is £12.50 for most vehicle types, including cars, motorcycles and vans (up to and including 3.5 tonnes) and £100 for heavier vehicles, including lorries (over 3.5 tonnes) and buses/coaches (over 5 tonnes). (W www.tfl.gov.uk/modes/driving/ultra-low-emission-zone).

Since 2 January 2009, Londoners over pensionable age (or over 60 if born before 1950) and those with eligible disabilities are entitled to free travel on the capital's transport network at any time. War veterans who are receiving ongoing payments under the war pensions scheme, or those receiving guaranteed income payments under the armed forces compensation scheme can travel free at any time on bus, underground, DLR, tram and London Overground services and at certain times on National Rail services.

In the summer of 2010, the London cycle hire scheme launched with 6,000 new bicycles for hire from 400 docking stations across eight boroughs, the City and the Royal parks. The scheme has been expanded and there are now around 11,500 bicycles available and over 750 docking stations.

Commissioner of TfL, Mike Brown, MVO

MAYOR'S OFFICE FOR POLICING AND CRIME (MOPAC)

The Mayor's Office for Policing and Crime (MOPAC) was set up in response to the Police Reform and Social Responsibility Act 2011, replacing the Metropolitan Police Authority. MOPAC is headed by the mayor, or the appointed statutory deputy mayor for policing and crime. Operational responsibility for policing in London belongs to the Metropolitan Police Commissioner. The major areas of focus of MOPAC are:

- operational policing and crime reduction including counter terrorism
- ensuring the Metropolitan Police effectively reduce gang crime and violence in London and coordinating support for communities and local organisations to prevent gang activities
- criminal justice, including preventing reoffending, reducing crime and decreasing demand within the criminal justice system in addition to reducing alcohol and drug abuse.

The Police and Crime Committee consisting of nine elected members of the London Assembly scrutinises the work of MOPAC and meets regularly to hold to account the Deputy Mayor for Policing and Crime.

Deputy Mayor for Policing and Crime, Sophie Linden

LONDON FIRE COMMISSIONER

Under the Policing and Crime Act 2017, the London Fire Commissioner replaced the London Fire and Emergency Planning Authority (LFEPA) and was tasked with overseeing the London Fire Brigade, the fire and rescue authority for London. It consists of three main structural bodies: operational staff and firefighters, control staff and emergency responders, and a non-uniformed support team. Operational staff provide the only full-time fire service in the UK.

The Mayor of London sets its budget, approves its London Safety Plan, and can direct it to act. The London Fire Commissioner is further scrutinised by the Fire, Resilience and Emergency Planning (FREP) Committee of the London Assembly.

Commissioner, Dany Cotton, QFSM

LONDON LEGACY DEVELOPMENT CORPORATION

Following the London 2012 Olympic Games, the London Legacy Development Corporation was made responsible for the long-term planning, development, management and maintenance of the Queen Elizabeth Olympic Park (formerly the Olympic Park) and its facilities. The organisation is tasked with transforming the area into a thriving neighbourhood.

Chair, Sir Peter Hendy, CBE

SALARIES *as at September 2019*

Mayor	£146,804
Chief of Staff	£137,243
Deputy Mayors	
Housing and Residential Development	£130,063
Business	£130,063
Culture and the Creative Industries	£130,063
Transport	£130,063
Policing and Crime	£130,063
Fire and Resilience	£106,140
Stautory Deputy Mayor (Education and Childcare)	£101,182
Chair of the Assembly	£67,498
Assembly Member	£56,270

LONDON ASSEMBLY COMMITTEES

Chair, Audit Panel, Unmesh Desai, AM
Chair, Budget and Performance Committee, Gareth Bacon, AM

Chair, Budget Monitoring Sub-Committee, Gareth Bacon, AM
Chair, Confirmation Hearings Committee, Andrew Boff, AM
Chair, Economy Committee, Leonie Cooper, AM
Chair, Environment Committee, Caroline Russell, AM
Chair, Fire, Resilience and Emergency Planning Committee, Andrew Dismore, AM
Chair, GLA Oversight Committee, Len Duvall, OBE, AM
Chair, Health Committee, Dr Onkar Sahota, AM
Chair, Housing Committee, Tom Copley, AM
Chair, Planning Committee, Andrew Boff, AM
Chair, Police and Crime Committee, Unmesh Desai, AM
Chair, Regeneration Committee, Tony Deverish, AM
Chair, Transport Committee, Florence Eshalomi, AM

LONDON ASSEMBLY MEMBERS

as at September 2019

Arbour, Tony, C., South West, Maj. 21,444
Arnold, Jennette, OBE, Lab., North East, Maj. 101,742
Bacon, Gareth, C., Bexley and Bromley, Maj. 41,669
Bailey, Shaun, C., London-wide
Berry, Sian, Green, London-wide
Boff, Andrew, C., London-wide
Cooper, Leonie, Lab., Merton and Wandsworth, Maj. 4,301
Copley, Tom, Lab., London-wide
Desai, Unmesh, Lab., City and East, Maj. 89,629
Devenish, Tony, C., West Central, Maj. 14,564
Dismore, Andrew, Lab., Barnet and Camden, Maj. 16,240
Duvall, Len, OBE, Lab., Greenwich and Lewisham, Maj. 54,895
Eshalomi, Florence, Lab., Lambeth and Southwark, Maj. 62,243
Gavron, Nicky, Lab., London-wide
Hall, Susan, C., London-wide
Kurten, David, BA, London-wide
McCartney, Joanne, Lab., Enfield and Haringey, Maj. 51,152
O'Connell, Steve, C., Croydon and Sutton, Maj. 11,614
Pidgeon, Caroline, MBE, LD, London-wide
Prince, Keith, C. Havering and Redbridge, Maj. 1,438
Russell, Caroline, Green, London-wide
Sahota, Dr Onkar, Lab., Ealing and Hillingdon, Maj. 15,933
Shah, Navin, Lab., Brent and Harrow, Maj. 20,755
Twycross, Dr Fiona, Lab., London-wide
Whittle, Peter, BA, London-wide

Chair of the London Assembly, Jennette Arnold, OBE, AM

STATE OF THE PARTIES as at September 2019

Party	Seats
Labour (Lab.)	12
Conservative (C.)	8
Green	2
Brexit Alliance (BA)	2
Liberal Democrats (LD)	1

MAYORAL ELECTION RESULTS

as at 5 May 2016

Electorate 5,739,011 Turnout 45.6%

First	Party	Votes	%
Sadiq Khan	Lab.	1,148,716	44.2
Zac Goldsmith	C.	909,755	35.0
Siân Berry	Green	150,673	5.8
Caroline Pidgeon	LD	120,005	4.6
Peter Whittle	UKIP	94,373	3.6
Sophie Walker	Women	53,055	2.0
George Galloway	Respect	37,007	1.4
Paul Golding	Brit. First	31,372	1.2
Lee Harris	CISTA	20,537	0.8
David Furness	BNP	13,325	0.5
Prince Zylinski	Ind.	13,202	0.5
Ankit Love	One Love	4,941	0.2

Second	Party	Votes	%
Sadiq Khan	Lab.	161,427	65.5
Zac Goldsmith	C.	84,859	34.5

LONDON ASSEMBLY ELECTION RESULTS *as at 5 May 2016*

E. Electorate T. Turnout
See General Election Results for a list of party abbreviations

CONSTITUENCIES
E. 5,739,011 T 45.6%

BARNET AND CAMDEN
E. 387,844 T. 47.44%

Andrew Dismore, Lab.	81,482
Daniel Thomas, C.	65,242
Stephen Taylor, Green	16,996
Zack Polanski, LD	11,204
Joseph Langton, UKIP	9,057

Lab. majority 16,240

BEXLEY AND BROMLEY
E. 404,342 T. 46.94%

Gareth Bacon, C.	87,460
Sam Russell, Lab.	45,791
Frank Gould, UKIP	30,485
Roisin Robertson, Green	12,685
Julie Ireland, LD	12,145
Veronica Obadara, APP	1,243

C. majority 41,669

BRENT AND HARROW
E. 381,778 T. 45.76%

Navin Shah, Lab.	79,902
Joel Davidson, C.	59,147
Anton Georgiou, LD	11,534
Jafar Hassan, Green	9,874
Rathy Alagaratnam, UKIP	9,074
Akib Mahmood, Respect GG	5,170

Lab. majority 20,755

CITY AND EAST
E. 503,301 T. 42.01%

Unmesh Desai, Lab.	122,175
Chris Chapman, C.	32,546
Rachel Collinson, Green	18,766
Peter Harris, UKIP	18,071
Elaine Bagshaw, LD	10,714
Rayne Mickail, Respect GG	6,772
Amina Gichinga, TBTC	1,368
Aaron D'Souza, APP	1,009

Lab. majority 89,629

CROYDON AND SUTTON
E. 401,660 T. 45.29%

Steve O'Connell, C.	70,156
Marina Ahmad, Lab.	58,542
Amna Ahmad, LD	18,859
Peter Staveley, UKIP	18,338
Tracey Hague, Green	13,513
Madonna Lewis, APP	1,386
Richard Edmonds, NF	1,106

C. majority 11,614

EALING AND HILLINGDON
E. 444,168 T. 45.25%

Onkar Sahota, Lab.	86,088
Dominic Gilham, C.	70,155
Alex Nieora, UKIP	15,832
Meena Hans, Green	15,758
Francesco Fruzza, LD	13,154

Lab. majority 15,933

ENFIELD AND HARINGEY
E. 377,060 T. 44.73%

Joanne McCartney, Lab.	91,075
Linda Kelly, C.	39,923
Ronald Stewart, Green	15,409
Nicholas da Costa, LD	12,038
Neville Watson, UKIP	9,042
Godson Azu, APP	1,172

Lab. majority 51,152

GREENWICH AND LEWISHAM
E. 362,376 T. 45.08%

Len Duvall, Lab.	85,735
Adam Thomas, C.	30,840
Imogen Solly, Green	20,520
Paul Oakley, UKIP	13,686
Julia Fletcher, LD	11,303
Ajaratu Bangura, APP	1,275

Lab. majority 54,895

HAVERING AND REDBRIDGE
E. 383,234 T. 44.63%

Keith Prince, C.	64,483
Ivana Bartoletti, Lab.	63,045
Lawrence Webb, UKIP	26,788
Lee Burkwood, Green	9,617
Ian Sanderson, LD	7,105

C. majority 1,438

LAMBETH AND SOUTHWARK
E. 426,966 T. 43.98%

Florence Eshalomi, Lab.	96,946
Robert Flint, C.	34,703
Rashid Nix, Green	25,793
Michael Bukola, LD	21,489
Idham Ramadi, UKIP	6,591
Kevin Parkin, SPGB	1,333
Amadu Kanumansa, APP	906

Lab. majority 62,243

MERTON AND WANDSWORTH
E. 374,126 T. 49.56%

Leonie Cooper, Lab.	77,340
David Dean, C.	73,039
Esther Obiri-Darko, Green	14,682
Adrian Hyyrylainen-Trett, LD	10,732
Elizabeth Jones, UKIP	8,478
Thamilini Kulendran, Ind.	1,142

Lab. majority 4,301

NORTH EAST
E. 500,432 T. 45.72%

Jennette Arnold, Lab.	134,307
Sam Malik, C.	32,565
Samir Jeraj, Green	29,401
Terry Stacy, LD	14,312
Freddy Vachha, UKIP	11,315
Tim Allen, Respect GG	5,068
Bill Martin, SPGB	1,293
Jonathan Silberman, Comm L	536

Lab. majority 101,742

SOUTH WEST
E. 435,877 T. 49.04%

Tony Arbour, C.	84,381
Martin Whelton, Lab.	62,937
Rosina Robson, LD	30,654
Andree Frieze, Green	19,745
Alexander Craig, UKIP	14,983
Adam Buick, SPGB	1,065

C. majority 21,444

WEST CENTRAL
E. 348,740 T. 43.96%

Tony Devenish, C.	67,775
Mandy Richards, Lab.	53,211
Jennifer Nadel, Green	14,050
Annabel Mullin, LD	10,577
Clive Egan, UKIP	7,708

C. majority 14,564

LONDON-WIDE MEMBERS

Conservative Party	*Labour Party*
Kemi Badenoch	Fiona Twycross
Andrew Boff	Tom Copley
Shaun Bailey	Nicky Gavron

Green Party	*UKIP*
Sian Berry	Peter Whittle
Caroline Russell	David Kurten

Liberal Democrats
Caroline Pidgeon

EUROPEAN PARLIAMENT

European parliament elections take place at five-yearly intervals. The last European parliament elections took place 23–26 May 2019. UK MEPs will cease their mandates at such time when the UK officially withdraws from the EU. Following the UK's withdrawal, the total number of seats in the European parliament will be reduced from 751 to 705. with 27 of the current 73 UK seats redistributed among the 27 remaining member states. France and Spain will gain the most seats at five each, increasing from 74 to 79 and 54 to 59 respectively. Italy and the Netherlands will each gain three seats, from 73 to 76 and 26 to 29, and Ireland will gain two seats. Austria, Croatia, Denmark, Estonia, Finland, Poland, Romania, Slovakia, and Sweden will all be allocated one additional seat. The remaining 13 countries will keep their current allocation.

The first direct elections to the parliament were held in 1979. In mainland Britain, members of the European parliament (MEPs) were elected in all constituencies on a first-past-the-post basis until 1999, when a regional system of proportional representation was introduced; in Northern Ireland three MEPs have been elected by the single transferable vote system of proportional representation since 1979. Under the terms of the Lisbon Treaty, the UK gained an extra seat in December 2011, taking the total to 73. This seat was added to the West Midlands region and filled by the highest-ranked losing candidate standing for the region in the 2009 European parliament elections.

At the 2019 European parliament elections all MEPs for England, Wales and Scotland were elected under a 'closed-list' regional system of proportional representation, with England being divided into nine regions (residents of Gibraltar vote in the South West region) and Wales and Scotland each constituting a single region. Parties submitted a list of candidates for each region in their own order of preference. Votes were cast for a party or an independent candidate, and the first seat in each region was allocated to the party or candidate with the highest number of votes. The rest of the seats in each region were then allocated broadly in proportion to each party's share of the vote. Each region returned the following number of members: East Midlands, 5; Eastern, 7; London, 8; North East, 3; North West, 8; South East, 10; South West, 6; West Midlands, 7; Yorkshire and the Humber, 6; Wales, 4; Scotland, 6. In Northern Ireland the single transferable vote system is used to return three members.

If a vacancy occurs due to the resignation or death of an MEP, it is filled by the next available person on that party's list. If an independent MEP resigns or dies, a by-election is held. Where an MEP leaves a party on whose list he/she was elected, there is no requirement to resign the post of MEP.

Nationals of member states of the European Union are eligible for election to the European parliament provided they are aged 18 or over and not subject to disqualification. Since 1994, eligible citizens have had the right to vote in elections to the European parliament in the UK as long as they were entered on the electoral register.

In July 2009 an MEP statute introduced a uniform salary for all MEPs, set at a rate of 38.5 per cent of the basic salary of a European court of justice judge. This currently equates to an annual pre-tax salary of €105,092 (approximately £95,800, depending on the monthly exchange rate). The salary comes from European parliament's budget and is subject to EU tax and insurance contributions. Member states can also subject the salary to national taxes. In the UK the salary is taxed by HM Revenue and Customs in order to bring the total tax paid up to the level of taxation payable by a UK resident.

For further information visit the UK's European parliament website (W www.europarl.europa.eu/unitedkingdom).

UK MEMBERS *as at 23 May 2019 Election*

KEY
* Denotes membership of the last European parliament

Ainslie, Scott (*b.* 1968), *Green, London*
Allard, Christian (*b.* 1964), *SNP, Scotland*
*****Anderson**, Martina (*b.* 1962), *SF, Northern Ireland*
*****Bearder**, Catherine (*b.* 1949), *LD, South East*
Bennion, Phil (*b.* 1954), *LD, West Midlands*
Brophy, Jane (*b.* 1963), *LD, North West*
Bull, David (*b.* 1969), *Brexit, North West*
*****Bullock**, Jonathan (*b.* 1963), *Brexit, East Midlands*
Bunting, Judith, *LD, South East*
Chowns, Ellie, (*b.* 1975), *Green, West Midlands*
*****Corbett**, Richard (*b.* 1955), *Lab., Yorkshire and the Humber*
*****Dance**, Seb (*b.* 1981), *Lab., London*
Daubney, Martin (*b.* 1970), *Brexit, West Midlands*
Davies, Chris (*b.* 1954), *LD, North West*
De Camborne Lucy, Belinda, (*b.* 1976), *Brexit, South East*
Dhamija, Dinesh (*b.* 1950), *LD, London*
*****Dodds**, Diane (*b.* 1958), *DUP, Northern Ireland*
Dowding, Gina (*b.* 1958), *Green, North West*
England Kerr, Andrew (*b.* 1958), *Brexit, West Midlands*
*****Evans**, Jill (*b.* 1959), *PC, Wales*
*****Farage**, Nigel (*b.* 1964), *Brexit, South East*
Forman, Lance, (*b.* 1962), *Brexit, London*
Fox, Claire (*b.* 1960), *Brexit, North West*
Gibson, Barbara, *LD, Eastern*
*****Gill**, Nathan (*b.* 1973), *Brexit, Wales*
*****Gill**, Neena, CBE (*b.* 1957), *Lab., West Midlands*
Glancy, James, *Brexit, South West*
*****Griffin**, Theresa (*b.* 1962), *Lab., North West*
Habib, Benyamin (*b.* 1965), *Brexit, London*
*****Hannan**, Daniel (*b.* 1971), *C., South East*
Harris, Lucy (*b.* 1990), *Brexit, Yorkshire and the Humber*
Heaver, Michael (*b.* 1989), *Brexit, Eastern*
Hook, Antony (*b.* 1980), *LD, South East*
Horwood, Martin (*b.* 1962), *LD, South West*
*****Howarth**, John (*b.* 1958), *Lab., South East*
Jones, Jackie, *Lab., Wales*
Jordan, Christina, *Brexit, South West*
*****Kirton-Darling**, Judith (*b.* 1977), *Lab., North East*
Long, Naomi (*b.* 1971), *Alliance, Northern Ireland*
Longworth, John (*b.* 1958), *Brexit, Yorkshire and the Humber*
Lowe, Rupert (*b.* 1959), *Brexit, West Midlands*
Magid, Magid (*b.* 1989), *Green, Yorkshire and the Humber*
*****McIntyre**, Anthea (*b.* 1954), *C., West Midlands*
McLeod, Aileen (*b.* 1971), *SNP, Scotland*
*****Mobarik**, Baroness, CBE (*b.* 1957), *C., Scotland*
Mohammed Shaffaq, MBE (*b.* 1972), *LD, Yorkshire and the Humber*
Monteith, Brian (*b.* 1958), *Brexit, North East*
*****Moraes**, Claude (*b.* 1965), *Lab., London*
Mummery, June *Brexit, Eastern*
Nethsingha, Lucy (*b.* 1973), *LD, Eastern*
Newton Dunn, Bill (*b.* 1941), *LD, East Midlands*
Overgaard-Nielsen, Henrik (*b.* 1959), *Brexit, North West*
*****Palmer,** Rory (*b.* 1981), *Lab, East Midlands*
Patten, Matthew (*b.* 1962), *Brexit, East Midlands*
Phillips, Alexandra (*b.* 1985), *Green, South East*

Phillips, Alexandra (*b.* 1983), *Brexit, South East*
Porritt, Luisa (*b.* 1987), *LD, London*
Pugh, Jake (*b.* 1960), *Brexit, Yorkshire and the Humber*
Rees-Mogg, Annunziata (*b.* 1979), *Brexit, East Midlands*
Ritchie, Sheila (*b.* 1967), *LD, Scotland*
Rowett, Catherine (*b.* 1956), *Green, Eastern*
Rowland, Robert (*b.* 1966), *Brexit, South East*
*****Scott Cato**, Molly (*b.* 1963), *Green, South West*
*****Smith**, Alyn (*b.* 1973), *SNP, Scotland*
Stedman-Bryce, Louis, *Brexit, Scotland*
Tennant, John (*b.* 1986), *Brexit, North East*
Tice, Richard (*b.* 1964), *Brexit, Eastern*
*****Van Orden**, Geoffrey (*b.* 1945), *C., Eastern*
Voaden, Caroline, *LD, South West*
Von Wiese, Irina (*b.* 1967), *LD, London*

*****Ward**, Julie (*b.* 1957), *Lab., North West*
Wells, James, *Brexit, Wales*
Widdecombe, Ann (*b.* 1947), *Brexit, South West*

STATE OF THE PARTIES *as at 23 May 2019 Election*

Party	No. of Seats
Brexit Party (Brexit)	29
Liberal Democrats (LD)	16
Labour (Lab.)	10
Green Party (Green)	7
Conservative (C.)	4
Scottish National Party (SNP)	3
Others*	4
Total	**73**

* The Alliance Party of Northern Ireland, the Democratic Unionist Party (DUP), Plaid Cymru (PC) and Sinn Fein (SF) have one seat each.

UK REGIONS AS AT 23 MAY 2019 ELECTION

Abbreviations
EDP　European Democratic Party
Network Independent Network
For all other abbreviations, *see* UK General Election Results.

E. 46,611,656 T. 36.9%

EASTERN
(Bedfordshire, Cambridgeshire, Essex, Hertfordshire, Luton, Norfolk, Peterborough, Southend-on-Sea, Suffolk, Thurrock)
E. 4,407,975 T. 36.26%

Brexit	604,715 (37.83%)
LD	361,563 (22.62%)
Green	202,460 (12.67%)
C.	163,830 (10.25%)
Lab.	139,490 (8.73%)
ChangeUK	58,274 (3.65%)
UKIP	54,676 (3.42%)
EDP	10,217 (0.64%)
Ind. Csordas	3,230 (0.20%)
Brexit majority	243,152

(May 2014, UKIP maj. 96,243)
MEMBERS ELECTED
1. *G. Van Orden, *C.* 2. B. Gibson, *LD* 3. L. Nethsingha, *LD* 4. R. Tice, *Brexit* 5. M. Heaver, *Brexit* 6. J. Mummery, *Brexit* 7. C. Rowett, *Green*

EAST MIDLANDS
(Derby, Derbyshire, Leicester, Leicestershire, Lincolnshire, Northamptonshire, Nottingham, Nottinghamshire, Rutland)
E. 3,411,045 T. 34.69%

Brexit	452,321 (38.23%)
LD	203,989 (17.24%)
Lab.	164,682 (13.92%)
C.	126,138 (10.66%)
Green	124,630 (10.53%)
UKIP	58,198 (4.92%)
ChangeUK	41,117 (3.47%)
Network	7,641 (0.65%)
Ind. Rood	4,511 (0.38%)
Brexit majority	248,332

(May 2014, UKIP maj. 77,464)
MEMBERS ELECTED
1. *R. Palmer, *Lab.* 2. B. Newton Dunn, *LD* 3. A. Rees-Mogg, *Brexit* 4. *J. Bullock, *Brexit* 5. M. Patten, *Brexit*

LONDON
E. 5,476,515 T. 40.93%

LD	608,725 (27.15%)
Lab.	536,810 (23.95%)
Brexit	400,257 (17.86%)
Green	278,957 (12.44%)
C.	177,964 (7.94%)
ChangeUK	117,635 (5.25%)
UKIP	46,497 (2.07%)
AWP	25,232 (1.13%)
Women	23,766 (1.06%)
UKEUP	18,806 (0.84%)
Ind. Mcdowell	1,036 (0.05%)
Ind. Aghaji	1,018 (0.05%)
Ind. Hallam	924 (0.04%)
Ind. Klu	869 (0.04%)
ND	731 (0.03%)
Ind. Shad	707 (0.03%)
Ind. Lafferty	436 (0.02%)
Ind. Medhurst	430 (0.02%)
Ind. Kirkby	401 (0.02%)
Ind. Sowden	254 (0.01%)
Ind. Muss	226 (0.01%)
LD majority	71,915

(May 2014, Lab. maj. 311,320)

MEMBERS ELECTED
1. *C. Moraes, *Lab.* 2. *S. Dance, *Lab.* 3. I. Von Wiese, *LD* 4. D. Dhamija, *LD* 5. L. Porritt, *LD* 6. B. Habib, *Brexit* 7. L. Forman, *Brexit* 8. S. Ainslie, *Green*

NORTH EAST
(Co. Durham, Darlington, Hartlepool, Middlesbrough, Northumberland, Redcar and Cleveland, Stockton-on-Tees, Tyne and Wear)
E. 1,905,534 T. 32.53%

Brexit	240,056 (38.73%)
Lab.	119,931 (19.35%)
LD	104,330 (16.83%)
Green	49,905 (8.05%)
C.	42,395 (6.84%)
UKIP	38,269 (6.17%)
ChangeUK	24,968 (4.03%)
Brexit majority	120,125

(May 2014, Lab. maj. 44,328)

MEMBERS ELECTED
1. *J. Kirton-Darling, *Lab.* 2. B. Monteith, *Brexit* 3. J. Tennant, *Brexit*

NORTHERN IRELAND
(Northern Ireland forms a three-member seat with a single transferable vote system)
E. 1,278,951 T. 45.14%

	Total votes
Martina Anderson, *SF*	152,436.5
Diane Dodds, *DUP*	155,422
Naomi Long, *Alliance*	170,370
Colum Eastwood, *SDLP*	82,413.5
Jim Allister, *TUV*	90,079
Danny Kennedy, *UUP*	54,736
Clare Bailey, *Green*	12,471
Robert Hill, *UKIP*	5,115
Jane Morrice, *Ind.*	1,719
Neil McCann, *Ind.*	948
Amandeep Singh Bhogal *C.*	662

MEMBERS ELECTED
1. *M. Anderson, *SF* 2. *D. Dodds, *DUP* 3. N. Long, *Alliance*

NORTH WEST
(Blackburn-with-Darwen, Blackpool, Cheshire, Cumbria, Greater Manchester, Halton, Lancashire, Merseyside, Warrington)
E. 5,276,907 T. 32.88%

Brexit	541,843 (31.23%)
Lab.	380,193 (21.91%)
LD	297,507 (17.15%)
Green	216,581 (12.48%)
C.	131,002 (7.55%)
UKIP	62,464 (3.60%)
ChangeUK	47,237 (2.72%)
Ind. Robinson	38,908 (2.24%)
EDP	10,045 (0.58%)
UKEUP	7,125 (0.41%)
Ind. Aslam	2,002 (0.12%)
Brexit majority	161,650

(May 2014, Lab. maj. 112,131)

MEMBERS ELECTED
1. *T. Griffin, *Lab.* 2. *J. Ward, *Lab.* 3. C. Davies, *LD* 4. J. Brophy, *LD* 5. C. Fox, *Brexit* 6. H. Overgaard Nielsen, *Brexit* 7. D. Bull, *Brexit* 8. G. Dowding, *Green*

SCOTLAND

E. 3,953,289 T. 39.75%

SNP	594,553 (37.84%)
Brexit	233,006 (14.83%)
LD	218,285 (13.89%)
C.	182,476 (11.61%)
Lab.	146,724 (9.34%)
Green	129,603 (8.25%)
ChangeUK	30,004 (1.91%)
UKIP	28,418 (1.81%)
Ind. Edgar	6,128 (0.39%)
Ind. Parke	2,049 (0.13%)
SNP majority	361,547

(May 2014, SNP maj. 41,284)

MEMBERS ELECTED

1. *N. Mobarik, C. 2. S. Ritchie, LD 3. *A. Smith, SNP 4. C. Allard, SNP 5. A. McLeod, SNP 6. L. Stedman-Bruce, Brexit

SOUTH EAST

(Bracknell Forest, Brighton and Hove, Buckinghamshire, East Sussex, Hampshire, Isle of Wight, Kent, Medway, Milton Keynes, Newbury, Oxfordshire, Portsmouth, Reading, Slough, Southampton, Surrey, West Sussex, Windsor and Maidenhead, Wokingham)

E. 6,496,429 T. 39.08%

Brexit	915,686 (36.07%)
LD	653,743 (25.75%)
Green	343,249 (13.52%)
C.	260,277 (10.25%)
Lab.	184,678 (7.27%)
ChangeUK	105,832 (4.17%)
UKIP	56,487 (2.22%)
UKEUP	7,645 (0.30%)
Ind. McMahon	3,650 (0.14%)
SPGB	3,505 (0.14%)
Ind. Round	2,606 (0.10%)
Ind. Turberville	1,587 (0.06%)
Brexit majority	261,943

(May 2014, UKIP maj. 27,868)

MEMBERS ELECTED

1. *D. Hannan, C. 2. *J. Howarth, Lab. 3. *C. Bearder, LD 4. A. Hook, LD 5. J. Bunting, LD 6. *N. Farage, Brexit 7. A. Phillips, Brexit 8. R. Rowland, Brexit 9. B. De Camborne Lucy, Brexit 10. A. Phillips, Green

SOUTH WEST

(Bath and North East Somerset, Bournemouth, Bristol, Cornwall, Devon, Dorset, Gloucestershire, North Somerset, Plymouth, Poole, Somerset, South Gloucestershire, Swindon, Torbay, Wiltshire, Isles of Scilly, Gibraltar)

E. 4,143,765 T. 40.22%

Brexit	611,742 (36.71%)
LD	385,095 (23.11%)
Green	302,364 (18.14%)
C.	144,674 (8.68%)
Lab.	108,100 (6.49%)
UKIP	53,739 (3.22%)
ChangeUK	46,612 (2.80%)
EDP	8,393 (0.50%)
Ind. Seed	3,383 (0.20%)
Ind. Maxey	1,772 (0.11%)
Ind. Rahman	755 (0.05%)
Brexit majority	226,647

(May 2014, UKIP maj. 51,033)

MEMBERS ELECTED

1. C. Voaden, LD 2. M. Horwood, LD 3. A. Widdecombe, Brexit 4. J. Glancy, Brexit 5. C. Jordan, Brexit 6. *M. Scott Cato, Green

WALES

E. 2,256,607 T. 37.06%

Brexit	271,404 (32.46%)
PC	163,928 (19.60%)
Lab.	127,833 (15.29%)
LD	113,885 (13.62%)
C.	54,587 (6.53%)
Green	52,660 (6.30%)
UKIP	27,566 (3.30%)
ChangeUK	24,332 (2.91%)
Brexit majority	107,476

(May 2014, Lab. maj. 4,349)

MEMBERS ELECTED

1. J. Jones, Lab. 2. *J. Evans, PC 3. *N. Gill, Brexit 4. J. Wells, Brexit

WEST MIDLANDS

(Herefordshire, Shropshire, Staffordshire, Stoke-on-Trent, Telford and Wrekin, Warwickshire, West Midlands Metropolitan area, Worcestershire)

E. 4,094,226 T. 32.90%

Brexit	507,152 (37.66%)
Lab.	228,298 (16.95%)
LD	219,982 (16.33%)
Green	143,520 (10.66%)
C.	135,279 (10.04%)
UKIP	66,934 (4.97%)
ChangeUK	45,673 (3.39%)
Brexit majority	278,854

(May 2014, UKIP maj. 64,977)

MEMBERS ELECTED

1. *A. McIntyre, C. 2. *N. Gill, Lab. 3. P. Bennion, LD 4. R. Lowe, Brexit 5. M. Daubney, Brexit 6. A. England Kerr, Brexit 7. E. Chowns, Green

YORKSHIRE AND THE HUMBER

(East Riding of Yorkshire, Kingston-upon-Hull, North East Lincolnshire, North Lincolnshire, North Yorkshire, South Yorkshire, West Yorkshire, York)

E. 3,867,792 T. 33.33%

Brexit	470,351 (36.48%)
Lab.	210,516 (16.33%)
LD	200,180 (15.53%)
Green	166,980 (12.95%)
C.	92,863 (7.20%)
UKIP	56,100 (4.35%)
Yorks	50,842 (3.94%)
ChangeUK	30,162 (2.34%)
EDP	11,283 (0.88%)
Brexit majority	259,835

(May 2014, UKIP maj. 23,441)

MEMBERS ELECTED

1. *R. Corbett, Lab. 2. S. Mohammed, LD 3. J. Longworth, Brexit 4. L. Harris, Brexit 5. J. Pugh, Brexit 6. M. Magid, Green

LOCAL GOVERNMENT

Major changes in local government were introduced in England and Wales in 1974 and in Scotland in 1975 by the Local Government Act 1972 and the Local Government (Scotland) Act 1973. Further significant alterations were made in England by the Local Government Acts of 1985, 1992 and 2000.

The structure in England was based on two tiers of local authorities (county councils and district councils) in the non-metropolitan areas; and a single tier of metropolitan councils in the six metropolitan areas of England and London borough councils in London.

Following reviews of the structure of local government in England by the Local Government Commission (now the Boundary Commission for England), 46 unitary (all-purpose) authorities were created between April 1995 and April 1998 to cover certain areas in the non-metropolitan counties. The remaining county areas continue to have two tiers of local authorities. The county and district councils in the Isle of Wight were replaced by a single unitary authority on 1 April 1995; the former counties of Avon, Cleveland, Humberside and Berkshire were replaced by unitary authorities; and Hereford & Worcester was replaced by a new county council for Worcestershire (with district councils) and a unitary authority for Herefordshire. On 1 April 2009 the county areas of Cornwall, Durham, Northumberland, Shropshire and Wiltshire were given unitary status and two new unitary authorities were created for Bedfordshire (Bedford and Central Bedfordshire) and Cheshire (Cheshire East and Cheshire West & Chester) replacing the two-tier county/district system in these areas.

In April 2019 Dorset's nine councils to merged into two unitary authorities. Bournemouth and Poole unitary authorities merged with Christchurch district council to become Bournemouth, Christchurch and Poole (BCP) unitary authority, while Dorset unitary authority was formed from Dorset County Council together with East Dorset, North Dorset, Purbeck, Weymouth & Portland and West Dorset district councils. Also in April 2019, in what is expected to be a continuing trend in order to share resources and make substantial financial savings, a total of six district councils merged into three new district authorities. The three councils, East Suffolk, West Suffolk and Somerset West and Taunton, continue to operate at district level.

The Local Government (Wales) Act 1994 and the Local Government etc (Scotland) Act 1994 abolished the two-tier structure in Wales and Scotland with effect from 1 April 1996, replacing it with a single tier of unitary authorities.

In Northern Ireland a reform programme to reduce the number of local authorities from 26 to 11 began in 2012 when legislation finalising the boundaries of the new 11 local government district authorities was approved by the Northern Ireland Assembly. The Local Government Act (Northern Ireland) 2014 received royal assent on 12 May 2014, providing the legislative framework for the 11 new councils. On 1 April 2015 additional functions, previously the responsibility of the Northern Ireland executive, fully transferred to the new district authorities.

ELECTIONS

Local elections are normally held on the first Thursday in May. Generally, all citizens of the UK, the Republic of Ireland, Commonwealth and other European Union citizens who are 18 years or over and resident on the qualifying date in the area

for which the election is being held, are entitled to vote at local government elections. A register of electors is prepared and published annually by local electoral registration officers.

A returning officer has the overall responsibility for an election. Voting takes place at polling stations, arranged by the local authority and under the supervision of a presiding officer specially appointed for the purpose. Candidates, who are subject to various statutory qualifications and disqualifications designed to ensure that they are suitable to hold office, must be nominated by electors for the electoral area concerned.

In England, the Local Government Boundary Commission for England is responsible for carrying out periodic reviews of electoral arrangements, to consider whether the boundaries of wards or divisions within a local authority need to be altered to take account of changes in electorate; structural reviews, to consider whether a single, unitary authority should be established in an area instead of an existing two-tier system; and administrative boundary reviews of district or county authorities.

The Local Democracy and Boundary Commission for Wales, the Local Government Boundary Commission for Scotland and the local government boundary commissioner for Northern Ireland (appointed when required by the Boundary Commission for Northern Ireland) are responsible for reviewing the electoral arrangements and boundaries of local authorities within their respective regions.

The Local Government Act 2000 provided for the secretary of state to change the frequency and phasing of elections in England and Wales.

LOCAL GOVERNMENT BOUNDARY COMMISSION FOR ENGLAND, SW1H 0TL1st Floor, Windsor House, 50 Victoria Street, London SW1H 0TL **T** 0330-500 1525
E reviews@lgbce.org.uk **W** www.lgbce.org.uk
LOCAL DEMOCRACY AND BOUNDARY COMMISSION FOR WALES, Ground Floor, Hastings House, Fitzalan Court, Cardiff CF24 0BL **T** 029-2046 4819
E enquiries@boundaries.wales **W** www.ldbc.gov.wales
LOCAL GOVERNMENT BOUNDARY COMMISSION FOR SCOTLAND, Thistle House, 91 Haymarket Terrace, Edinburgh EH12 5HD **T** 0131-244 2001
E lgbcs@scottishboundaries.gov.uk
W www.lgbc-scotland.gov.uk
BOUNDARY COMMISSION FOR NORTHERN IRELAND, The Bungalow, Stormont House, Stormont Estate, Belfast BT4 3SH **T** 028-9052 7821
E contact@boundarycommission.org.uk
W www.boundarycommission.org.uk

LOCAL GOVERNMENT DEVOLUTION

Local government is a devolved matter in Scotland, Wales and Northern Ireland.

In England, under the Cities and Local Government Devolution Act 2016, multiple local authorities can combine and take on more functions, over and above those they were allowed to take on under previous legislation. In order for a combined or 'regional' authority to be given these extra powers a mayor must be elected for the region by the electorate in the combined-authority area. The first six combined authority mayoral elections took place in May 2017. The exact functions the combined authority and mayor manage varies depending on the devolution agreement reached with central government, but the directly-elected 'metro' mayor does have powers and responsibilities to make strategic decisions across whole city regions. This is in contrast to existing city mayors (which are also directly elected) or local council leaders that only make decisions for, and on behalf of, their local authority (*see* Internal Organisation). To date, nine combined authorities have been established, seven of which have a mayor and a devolution agreement with national government (*see* Combined Authorities for a complete list).

INTERNAL ORGANISATION

The council as a whole is the final decision-making body within any authority. Councils are free to a great extent to make their own internal organisational arrangements. The Local Government Act, given royal assent on 28 July 2000, allows councils to adopt one of three broad categories of constitution which include a separate executive:

- A directly elected mayor with a cabinet selected by that mayor
- A cabinet, either elected by the council or appointed by its leader
- A directly elected mayor and council manager

Normally, questions of policy are settled by the full council, while the administration of the various services is the responsibility of committees of councillors. Day-to-day decisions are delegated to the council's officers, who act within the policies laid down by the councillors.

FINANCE

Local government in England, Wales and Scotland is financed from four sources: council tax, non-domestic rates, government grants and income from fees and charges for services.

COUNCIL TAX

Council tax is a local tax levied by each local council. Liability for the council tax bill usually falls on the owner-occupier or tenant of a dwelling which is their sole or main residence. Council tax bills may be reduced because of the personal circumstances of people resident in a property and there are discounts in the case of dwellings occupied by fewer than two adults.

In England, unitary and metropolitan authorities are responsible for collecting their own council tax. In areas where there are two tiers of local authority, each county and district authority sets its own council tax rate; the district authorities collect the combined council tax and the county councils claim their share from the district councils' collection funds. In Wales and Scotland each unitary authority sets its own council tax rate and is responsible for collection.

The tax relates to the value of the dwelling. In England and Scotland each dwelling is placed in one of eight valuation bands, ranging from A to H, based on the property's estimated market value as at 1 April 1991. In Wales there are nine bands, ranging from A to I, based on the estimated market value of property as at 1 April 2003.

The valuation bands and ranges of values in England, Wales and Scotland are:

England

A	Up to £40,000	E	£88,001–£120,000
B	£40,001–£52,000	F	£120,001–£160,000
C	£52,001–£68,000	G	£160,001–£320,000
D	£68,001–£88,000	H	Over £320,001

Wales

A	Up to £44,000	F	£162,001–£223,000
B	£44,001–£65,000	G	£223,001–£324,000
C	£65,001–£91,000	H	£324,001–£424,000
D	£91,001–£123,000	I	Over £424,001
E	£123,001–£162,000		

Scotland

A	Up to £27,000	E	£58,001–£80,000
B	£27,001–£35,000	F	£80,001–£106,000
C	£35,001–£45,000	G	£106,001–£212,000
D	£45,001–£58,000	H	Over £212,001

The council tax within a local area varies between the different bands according to proportions laid down by law. The charge attributable to each band as a proportion of the Band D charge set by the council is:

A	67%	F	144%
B	78%	G	167%
C	89%	H	200%
D	100%	I*	233%
E	122%		

* Wales only

The Band D council tax bill for 2018–19, inclusive of adult social care and parish precepts, for each authority area is given in the complete lists of local authorities for England, London, Wales and Scotland which follow. There may be variations from the given figure within each district council area because of different parish or community precepts being levied, the personal circumstances of the residents in a property or in the case of dwellings occupied by fewer than two adults.

Domestic property in Northern Ireland is subjected to a rateable system based on the capital value of a property as at 1 January 2005 *see* Northern Ireland, Finance for further information.

NON-DOMESTIC RATES

Non-domestic (business) rates are collected by billing authorities; these are the district councils in those areas of England with two tiers of local government and unitary authorities in other parts of England, in Wales and in Scotland. In respect of England and Wales, the Local Government Finance Act 1988 provides for liability for rates to be assessed on the basis of a poundage (multiplier) tax on the rateable value of property (hereditaments). Separate multipliers are set by the Ministry of Housing, Communities and Local Government (MHCLG) in England, the Welsh government and the Scottish government. Rates are collected by the billing authority for the area where a property is located. Rate income collected by billing authorities is paid into a national non-domestic rating (NNDR) pool and redistributed to individual authorities on the basis of the adult population figure as prescribed by MHCLG, the Welsh government or the Scottish government. The rates pools are maintained separately in England, Wales and Scotland. Actual payment of rates in certain cases is subject to transitional arrangements, to phase in the larger increases and reductions in rates resulting from the effects of the latest revaluation.

The most recent rating lists for England, Wales and Scotland came into effect on 1 April 2017. The rateable values on these lists are derived from the rental value of property as at 1 April 2015 and determined on certain statutory assumptions by the Valuation Office Agency in England and Wales, and by local area assessors in Scotland. New property which is added to the list, and significant changes to existing property, necessitate amendments to the rateable value on the same basis. Rating lists (valuation rolls in Scotland) remain in force until the next general revaluation, which usually takes place every five years to reflect changes in the property market.

A revaluation of non-domestic properties in Northern Ireland was completed at the start of 2015 and since 1 April 2015 the rateable value of all non-domestic properties in Northern Ireland is based on the rental value of the property as at 1 April 2013. The next revaluation is currently underway with a view to new valuation lists being ready from April 2020.

Certain types of property are exempt from rates, eg agricultural land and buildings, buildings used for the training or welfare of disabled people and buildings registered for public religious worship. Charities and other non-profit-making organisations may receive full or partial relief and relief schemes for small businesses are available in England, Wales, Scotland and Northern Ireland. Empty commercial property in England and Wales is exempt from business rates for the first three months that the property is vacant, empty industrial property for six months and listed buildings are exempt until re-occupied; after which full business rates are normally payable. In Scotland empty commercial property is entitled to a 50 per cent discount on business rates for the first three months and a 10 per cent discount thereafter, empty industrial buildings are entitled to full relief for six months and a 10 per cent discount thereafter and empty listed buildings and properties with a rateable value of less than £1,700 are entirely exempt. In Northern Ireland all vacant non-domestic property, which has been previously occupied for at least six weeks, is entirely exempt from rates for three months, after this period, rates are billed at 50 per cent of the normal occupied amount.

COMPLAINTS

In England the Local Government and Social Care Ombudsman investigates complaints of injustice arising from maladministration by local authorities about most council services, including planning, some housing issues, social care, some education and schools issues, children's services, housing benefit, council tax, transport and highways, environment and waste, neighbour nuisance and antisocial behaviour and service failure by local authorities, schools and all registered social care providers, including all adult social care complaints. The Local Government Ombudsman will not usually consider a complaint unless the local authority concerned has had an opportunity to investigate and reply to a complainant.

The functions of the Local Government Ombudsman for Wales were subsumed into the office of Public Services Ombudsman for Wales on 1 April 2006 and the Scottish Public Services Ombudsman is responsible for complaints regarding the maladministration of local government in Scotland.

The Office of Northern Ireland Public Services Ombudsman (NIPSO) was established in April 2016, replacing and expanding the functions of the Northern Ireland Assembly Ombudsman and Commissioner for Complaints. NIPSO provides an independent review of complaints of members of the public, where they believe they have sustained an injustice or hardship as a result or inaction of a public service provider. NIPSO additionally ensures that public services improve as a result of the complaints brought to them by the public. The professional, independent and impartial service is provided free of charge to the citizens of Northern Ireland.

LOCAL GOVERNMENT AND SOCIAL CARE
OMBUDSMAN, PO Box 4771, Coventry CV4 0EH
T 0300-061 0614 W www.lgo.org.uk
Ombudsman, Michael King
PUBLIC SERVICES OMBUDSMAN FOR WALES, 1 Ffordd
yr Hen Gae, Pencoed CF35 5LJ T 0300-790 0203
W www.ombudsman-wales.org.uk
Ombudsman, Nick Bennett

SCOTTISH PUBLIC SERVICES OMBUDSMAN, Bridgeside
House, 99 McDonald Road, Edinburgh EH7 4NS
T 0800-377 7330 W www.spso.org.uk
Ombudsman, Rosemary Agnew
NORTHERN IRELAND PUBLIC SERVICES
OMBUDSMAN, Progressive House, 33 Wellington Place,
Belfast BT1 6HN T 028-9023 3821 E nipso@nipso.org.uk
W www.nipso.org.uk
Ombudsman, Marie Anderson

THE QUEEN'S REPRESENTATIVES

The lord-lieutenant of a county is the permanent local representative of the Crown in that county. The appointment of lord-lieutenants is now regulated by the Lieutenancies Act 1997. They are appointed by the sovereign on the recommendation of the prime minister. The retirement age is 75. The office of lord-lieutenant dates from 1551, and its holder was originally responsible for maintaining order and for local defence in the county. The duties of the post include attending on royalty during official visits to the county, performing certain duties in connection with the armed forces (and in particular the reserve forces), and making presentations of honours and awards on behalf of the Crown. In England, Wales and Northern Ireland, the lord-lieutenant usually also holds the office of *Custos Rotulorum.* As such, he or she acts as head of the county's commission of the peace (which recommends the appointment of magistrates).

The office of sheriff (from the Old English *shire-reeve*) of a county was created in the tenth century. The sheriff was the special nominee of the sovereign, and the office reached its peak of its influence under the Norman kings. The Provisions of Oxford (1258) laid down a yearly tenure of office. Since the mid-16th century the office has been purely civil, with military duties taken over by the lord-lieutenant of the county. The sheriff (commonly known as 'high sheriff') attends on royalty during official visits to the county, acts as the returning officer during parliamentary elections in county constituencies, attends the opening ceremony when a high court judge goes on circuit, executes high court writs, and appoints under-sheriffs to act as deputies. The appointments and duties of the sheriffs in England and Wales are laid down by the Sheriffs Act 1887.

The serving high sheriff submits a list of names of possible future sheriffs to a tribunal, which chooses three names to put to the sovereign. The tribunal nominates the high sheriff annually on 12 November and the sovereign picks the name of the sheriff to succeed in the following year. The term of office runs from 25 March to the following 24 March (the civil and legal year before 1752). No person may be chosen twice in three years if there is any other suitable person in the county.

CIVIC DIGNITIES

District councils in England and local councils in Wales may petition for a royal charter granting borough or 'city' status to the council.

In England and Wales the chair of a borough or county borough council may be called a mayor, and the chair of a city council may be called a lord mayor (if lord mayoralty has been conferred on that city). Parish councils in England and community councils in Wales may call themselves 'town councils', in which case their chair is the town mayor.

In Scotland the chair of a local council may be known as a convenor; a provost is the mayoral equivalent. The chair of the councils for the cities of Aberdeen, Dundee, Edinburgh and Glasgow are lord provosts.

ENGLAND

The country of England lies between 55° 46' and 49° 57' 30" N. latitude (from a few miles north of the mouth of the Tweed to the Lizard), and between 1° 46' E. and 5° 43' W. longitude (from Lowestoft to Land's End). England is bounded on the north by the Cheviot Hills; on the south by the English Channel; on the east by the Straits of Dover (Pas de Calais) and the North Sea; and on the west by the Atlantic Ocean, Wales and the Irish Sea. It has a total area of 130,309 sq. km (50,313 sq. miles).

There are currently 26 counties, divided into 201 districts, 56 unitary authorities (including the Isles of Scilly), 36 metropolitan boroughs and 32 London Boroughs (including the Corporation of London). See Local Government, London for information on London Borough councils and the Corporation of London.

POPULATION
The population at the mid-2018 estimate was 55,977,178 (men 27,667,942; women 28,309,236). The average density of the population at the mid-2018 estimate was 430 persons per sq. km (1,113 per sq. mile).

The populations of most of the unitary authorities are in the range of 100,000 to 500,000. The district councils have populations broadly in the range of 60,000 to 200,000; some, however, have larger populations, because of the need to avoid dividing large towns, or because they were formed from the merger of multiple district councils, and some in mainly rural areas have smaller populations.

The main conurbations outside Greater London – Tyne and Wear, West Midlands, Merseyside, Greater Manchester, West Yorkshire and South Yorkshire – are divided into 36 metropolitan boroughs, most of which have a population of over 200,000.

ELECTIONS
For districts, counties and for around 9,000 towns and parishes, there are elected councils, consisting of directly elected councillors. The councillors elect one of their number as chair annually.

In general, councils can have whole council elections, elections by thirds or elections by halves. However all metropolitan authorities must hold elections by thirds. The electoral cycle of any new unitary authority is specified in the appropriate statutory order under which it is established.

COMBINED AUTHORITIES
Under the Cities and Local Government Devolution Act 2016, multiple local authorities can combine and take on more functions, over and above those they were allowed to take on under previous legislation. In order for a combined or 'regional' authority to be given these extra powers a mayor must be elected for the region by the electorate in the combined-authority area. The first six combined authority mayoral elections took place in May 2017.

The exact functions the combined authority and mayor manage varies depending on the devolution agreement reached with central government, but the directly-elected 'metro' mayor does have powers and responsibilities to make strategic decisions across whole city regions. This is in contrast to existing city mayors (which are also directly elected) or local council leaders that only make decisions for, and on behalf of, their local authority.

On 2 November 2018, the North East combined authority was divided into two. The boundaries of the re-constituted North East combined authority now cover the local authorities of Durham, Gateshead, South Tyneside and Sunderland, while the boundaries of the newly created North of Tyne combined authority cover the local authorities of Newcastle, North Tyneside and Northumberland. As at July 2019, ten combined authorities had been established, eight of which have a mayor and a devolution agreement with national government. The combined authorities comprise constituent and non-constituent councils and other local authorities. Constituent councils have full voting rights and cannot be a member of another combined authority. Non-constituent councils usually have restricted voting rights, although this decision rests with the combined authority. In addition, non-constituent councils can be a member of more than one combined authority, as long as this is also on a non-constituent basis. See the list of Combined Authorities for details of the devolved regions, their mayors and constituent councils.

COUNCIL FUNCTIONS
In areas with a two-tier system of local governance, functions are divided between the district and county authorities, with those functions affecting the larger area or population generally being the responsibility of the county council. A few functions continue to be exercised over the larger area by joint bodies, made up of councillors from each authority within the area.

Generally the allocation of functions is as follows:
County councils: education; strategic planning; traffic, transport and highways; fire service; consumer protection; refuse disposal; smallholdings; social care; libraries
District councils: local planning; housing; highways (maintenance of certain urban roads and off-street car parks); building regulations; environmental health; refuse collection; cemeteries and crematoria; collection of council tax and non-domestic rates
Unitary and metropolitan councils: their functions are all those listed above, except that the fire service is exercised by a joint body
Concurrently by county and district councils: recreation (parks, playing fields, swimming pools); museums; encouragement of the arts, tourism and industry

PARISH COUNCILS
Parish or town councils are the most local tier of government in England. There are currently 10,219 parishes in England, of which 8,859 have councils. Since 15 February 2008 local councils have been able to create new parish councils without seeking approval from the government. Around 80 per cent of parish councils represent populations of less than 2,500; parishes with no parish council can be grouped with neighbouring parishes under a common parish council. A parish council comprises at least five members, the number being fixed by the district council. Elections are held every four years, at the time of the election of the district councillor for the ward including the parish. Full parish councils must be formed for those parishes with more than 999 electors – below this number, parish meetings comprising the electors of the parish must be held at least twice a year.

Parish council functions include: allotments; encouragement of arts and crafts; community halls, recreational facilities (eg open spaces, swimming pools), cemeteries and crematoria; and many minor functions. They must also be given an opportunity to comment on planning applications. They may, like county and district councils, spend limited sums for the general benefit of the parish. They levy a precept on the district councils for their funds. Parish precepts for 2019–20 total £552m, an increase of 6.6 per cent on 2018–19.

FINANCE

Total revenue expenditure by all local authorities in England is budgeted to be £99.2bn in 2019–20; of this £31.5bn is to be raised through council tax, £17.1bn from the business rate retention scheme and £49bn from government grants. The remainder will be drawn down from local authority reserves.

Since April 2013 local authorities retain a share of business rates and keep the growth on that share (the 'rate retention scheme'). Revenue support grant is paid to local authorities to enable all authorities in the same class to broadly set the same council tax; in 2019–20 revenue support grant totals £653m. In addition central government pays specific grants in support of revenue expenditure on particular services. Police grant totals £7.5bn in 2019–20. In 2019–20, local authorities with adult social care responsibilities, who had not already utilised all of their precept flexibilty for 2017/18–2019/20 (capped at six percentage points for the period) were able to increase council tax by up to 2 per cent to fund adult social care; this is in addition to the usual funding of adult social care through council tax. Adult social care precepts total £200m in 2019–20.

In England, the average council tax per dwelling for 2019–20 is £1,327, an increase of 5.5 per cent from 2018–19. The average council tax bill for a Band D dwelling (occupied by two adults, including adult social care and parish precepts) for 2019–20 is £1,750, an increase of 4.7 per cent from 2018–19. The average Band D council tax is £1,826 in shire districts, £1,739 in metropolitan areas, £1,814 in unitary authority areas and £1,477 in London.

The non-domestic rating multiplier for England for 2019–20 is 50.4p (49.1p for small businesses). The City of London is able to set a different multiplier from the rest of England; for 2019–20 this is 51.00p (49.7p for small businesses).

Under the Local Government and Housing Act 1989, local authorities have four main ways of paying for capital expenditure: borrowing and other forms of extended credit; capital grants from central government towards some types of capital expenditure; 'usable' capital receipts from the sale of land, houses and other assets; and revenue.

The amount of capital expenditure which a local authority can finance by borrowing (or other forms of credit) is effectively limited by the credit approvals issued to it by central government. Most credit approvals can be used for any kind of local authority capital expenditure; these are known as basic credit approvals. Others (supplementary credit approvals) can be used only for the kind of expenditure specified in the approval, and so are often given to fund particular projects or services.

Local authorities can use all capital receipts from the sale of property or assets for capital spending, except in the case of sales of council houses. Generally, the 'usable' part of a local authority's capital receipts consists of 25 per cent of receipts from the sale of council houses and 50 per cent of other housing assets such as shops or vacant land. The balance has to be set aside as provision for repaying debt and meeting other credit liabilities.

EXPENDITURE

Budgeted revenue expenditure for 2019–20 is:

Service	£ million
Education	34,296
Highways and transport	4,864
Children's social care	9,105
Adult social care	16,787
Public health	3,242
Housing (excluding HRA)	1,680
Cultural	2,128
Environmental	5,172
Planning & development	1,251
Police	12,130
Fire and rescue	2,188
Central	2,969
Other	340
Total Service Expenditure	96,152
*Housing benefits	17,828
Parish precepts	552
†Levies & trading account and other adjustments	(462)
Total Net Current Expenditure	112,022
Non-current Expenditure and External Receipts	
Capital expenditure charged to revenue account	1,288
Housing benefits subsidies	(17,627)
Community infrastructure levy	(132)
Capital financing and debt servicing	4,548
REVENUE EXPENDITURE	99,191

HRA = Housing Revenue Account
* Includes all mandatory and non-mandatory housing benefits
† Includes Integrated Transport Authority levy, Waste Disposal Authority levy, London Pensions Fund Authority levy and other levies

RELIEF

There is a marked division between the upland and lowland areas of England. In the extreme north the Cheviot Hills (highest point, the Cheviot, 815m/2,674ft) form a natural boundary with Scotland. Running south from the Cheviots, though divided from them by the Tyne Gap, is the Pennine range (highest point, Cross Fell, 893m/2,930ft), the main orological feature of the country. The Pennines culminate in the Peak District of Derbyshire (Kinder Scout, 636m/2,088ft). West of the Pennines are the Cumbrian mountains, which include Scafell Pike (978m/3,210ft), the highest peak in England, and to the east are the Yorkshire Moors, their highest point being Urra Moor (454m/1,490ft).

In the west, the foothills of the Welsh mountains extend into the bordering English counties of Shropshire (the Wrekin, 407m/1,334ft; Long Mynd, 516m/1,694ft) and Hereford and Worcester (the Malvern Hills – Worcestershire Beacon, 425m/1,394ft). Extensive areas of highland and moorland are also to be found in the south-western peninsula formed by Somerset, Devon and Cornwall, principally Exmoor (Dunkery Beacon, 519m/1,704ft), Dartmoor (High Willhays, 621m/2,038ft) and Bodmin Moor (Brown Willy, 420m/1,377ft). Ranges of low, undulating hills run across the south of the country, including the Cotswolds in the Midlands and south-west, the Chilterns to the north of London, and the North (Kent) and South (Sussex) Downs of the south-east coastal areas.

The lowlands of England lie in the Vale of York, East Anglia and the area around the Wash. The lowest-lying are the Cambridgeshire Fens in the valleys of the Great Ouse and the river Nene, which are below sea-level in places. Since the 17th century extensive drainage has brought much of the Fens under cultivation. The North Sea coast between the Thames and the Humber, low-lying and formed of sand and shingle for the most part, is subject to erosion and defences against further incursion have been built along many stretches.

HYDROGRAPHY

The Severn is the longest river in Great Britain, rising on the north-eastern slopes of Plynlimon (Wales) and entering England in Shropshire, with a total length of 354km (220 miles) from its source to its outflow into the Bristol Channel, where it receives the Bristol Avon on the east and the Wye on the west; its other tributaries are the Vyrnwy, Tern, Stour, Teme and Upper (or Warwickshire) Avon. The Severn is tidal below Gloucester, and a high bore or tidal wave sometimes reverses the flow as high as Tewkesbury (21.75km/13.5 miles above Gloucester). The Severn Tunnel was begun in 1873 and completed in 1886 at a cost of £2m and after many difficulties caused by flooding. It is 7km (4 miles 628 yards) in length (of which 3.67km/2.25 miles are under the river). The Severn road bridge between Haysgate, Gwent, and Almondsbury, Glos, with a centre span of 988m (3,240ft), was opened in 1966.

The longest river wholly in England is the Thames, with a total length of 346km (215 miles) from its source in the Cotswold hills to the Nore. The Thames is tidal to Teddington (111km/69 miles from its mouth) and forms county boundaries almost throughout its course; on its banks are situated London, Windsor Castle, Eton College and Oxford University. Of the remaining English rivers, those flowing into the North Sea are the Tyne, Wear, Tees, Ouse and Trent from the Pennine Range, the Great Ouse (257km/ 160 miles), which rises in Northamptonshire, and the Orwell and Stour from the hills of East Anglia. Flowing into the English Channel are the Sussex Ouse from the Weald, the Itchen from the Hampshire hills, and the Axe, Teign, Dart, Tamar and Exe from the Devonian hills. Flowing into the Irish Sea are the Mersey, Ribble and Eden from the western slopes of the Pennines and the Derwent from the Cumbrian mountains.

The English Lakes, notable for their picturesque scenery and poetic associations, lie in Cumbria's Lake District, designated a UNESCO World Heritage Site in 2017 for its cultural significance. The largest lakes are Windermere (14.7 sq. km/ 5.7 sq. miles), Ullswater (8.8 sq. km/3.4 sq. miles) and Derwent Water (5.3 sq. km/2.0 sq. miles).

FLAG
The flag of England is the cross of St George, a red cross on a white field (cross gules in a field argent). The cross of St George, the patron saint of England, has been used since the 13th century.

ISLANDS
The Isle of Wight is separated from Hampshire by the Solent. The capital, Newport, stands at the head of the estuary of the Medina, and Cowes (at the mouth) is the chief port. Other centres are Ryde, Sandown, Shanklin, Ventnor, Freshwater, Yarmouth, Totland Bay, Seaview and Bembridge.

Lundy (the name is derived from the Old Norse for 'puffin island'), 18km (11 miles) north-west of Hartland Point, Devon, is around 5km (3 miles) long and almost 1km (half a mile) wide on average, with a total area of around 452 hectares (1,116 acres), and a population of 28. It became the property of the National Trust in 1969 and is financed, administered and maintained by the Landmark Trust. Lundy is principally a bird sanctuary; the waters around the island were formerly designated as a marine conservation zone in 2013.

The Isles of Scilly comprise around 140 islands and skerries (total area, 10 sq. km/6 sq. miles) situated 45 km (28 miles) south-west of Land's End in Cornwall. Only five are inhabited: St Mary's, St Agnes, Bryher, Tresco and St Martin's. The 2018 mid-year population estimate was 2,242. The entire group has been designated an Area of Outstanding Natural Beauty because of its unique flora and fauna. Tourism and the winter/spring flower trade for the home market form the basis of the economy of the islands.

EARLY HISTORY
Archaeological evidence suggests that England has been inhabited since at least the Palaeolithic period, though the extent of the various Palaeolithic cultures was dependent upon the degree of glaciation. The succeeding Neolithic and

Bronze Age cultures have left abundant remains throughout the country; the best-known of these are the henges and stone circles of Stonehenge (ten miles north of Salisbury, Wilts) and Avebury (Wilts). In the latter part of the Bronze Age the Goidels, a people of the Celtic race, invaded the country and brought with them Celtic civilisation and dialects; as a result place names in England bear witness to the spread of the invasion across the whole region.

THE ROMAN CONQUEST
The Roman conquest of Gaul (57–50 BC) brought Britain into close contact with Roman civilisation, but although Julius Caesar raided the south of Britain in 55 and 54 BC, conquest was not undertaken until nearly 100 years later. In AD 43 the Emperor Claudius dispatched Aulus Plautius, with a well-equipped force of 40,000, and himself followed with reinforcements in the same year. Success was delayed by the resistance of Caratacus (Caractacus), the British leader from AD 48–51, who was finally captured and sent to Rome, and by a great revolt in AD 61 led by Boudicca (Boadicea), Queen of the Iceni, but the south of Britain was secured by AD 70, and Wales and the area north to the Tyne by about AD 80.

In AD 122, the Emperor Hadrian visited Britain and built a continuous rampart, since known as Hadrian's Wall, from Wallsend to Bowness (Tyne to Solway). The work was entrusted by the Emperor Hadrian to Aulus Platorius Nepos, legate of Britain from AD 122 to 126, and it was intended to form the northern frontier of the Roman Empire.

The Romans administered Britain as a province under a governor, with a well-defined system of local government, each Roman municipality ruling itself and its surrounding territory, while London was the centre of the road system and the seat of the financial officials of the Province of Britain. Colchester, Lincoln, York, Gloucester and St Albans stand on the sites of five Roman municipalities, and Wroxeter, Caerleon, Chester, Lincoln and York were at various times the sites of legionary fortresses. Well-preserved Roman towns have been uncovered at or near Silchester *(Calleva Atrebatum),* ten miles south of Reading, Wroxeter *(Viroconium Cornoviorum),* near Shrewsbury and St Albans *(Verulamium)* in Hertfordshire.

Four main groups of roads radiated from London, and a fifth (the Fosse) ran obliquely from Lincoln through Leicester, Cirencester and Bath to Exeter. Of the four groups radiating from London, one ran south-east to Canterbury and the coast of Kent, a second to Silchester and thence to parts of western Britain and south Wales, a third (later known as Watling Street) ran through St Albans to Chester, with various branches, and the fourth reached Colchester, Lincoln, York and the eastern counties.

In the fourth century Britain was subjected to raids along the east coast by Saxon pirates, which led to the establishment of a system of coastal defences from the Wash to Southampton Water, with forts at Brancaster, Burgh Castle (Yarmouth), Walton (Felixstowe), Bradwell, Reculver, Richborough, Dover, Lympne, Pevensey and Porchester (Portsmouth). The Irish (Scoti) and Picts in the north were also becoming more aggressive and from around AD 350 incursions became more frequent and more formidable. As the Roman Empire came increasingly under attack towards the end of the fourth century, many troops were removed from Britain for service in other parts of the empire. The island was eventually cut off from Rome by the Teutonic conquest of Gaul, and with the withdrawal of the last Roman garrison early in the fifth century, the Romano-British were left to themselves.

SAXON SETTLEMENT
According to legend, the British King Vortigern called in the Saxons to defend his lands against the Picts. The Saxon chieftains Hengist and Horsa landed at Ebbsfleet, Kent, and

established themselves in the Isle of Thanet, but the events during the one-and-a-half centuries between the final break with Rome and the re-establishment of Christianity are unclear. However, it would appear that over the course of this period the raids turned into large-scale settlement by invaders traditionally known as Angles (England north of the Wash and East Anglia), Saxons (Essex and southern England) and Jutes (Kent and the Weald), which pushed the Romano-British into the mountainous areas of the north and west. Celtic culture outside Wales and Cornwall survives only in topographical names. Various kingdoms established at this time attempted to claim overlordship of the whole country, hegemony finally being achieved by Wessex (with the capital at Winchester) in the ninth century. This century also saw the beginning of raids by the Vikings (Danes), which were resisted by Alfred the Great (871–899), who fixed a limit on the advance of Danish settlement by the Treaty of Wedmore (878), giving them the area north and east of Watling Street on the condition that they adopt Christianity.

In the tenth century the kings of Wessex recovered the whole of England from the Danes, but subsequent rulers were unable to resist a second wave of invaders. England paid tribute (Danegeld) for many years, and was invaded in 1013 by the Danes and ruled by Danish kings (including Cnut) from 1016 until 1042, when Edward the Confessor was recalled from exile in Normandy. On Edward's death in 1066 Harold Godwinson (brother-in-law of Edward and son of Earl Godwin of Wessex) was chosen to be King of England. After defeating (at Stamford Bridge, Yorkshire, 25 September 1066) an invading army under Harald Hadraada, King of Norway (aided by the outlawed Earl Tostig of Northumbria, Harold's brother), Harold was himself defeated at the Battle of Hastings on 14 October 1066, and the Norman conquest secured the throne of England for Duke William of Normandy, a cousin of Edward the Confessor.

CHRISTIANITY

Christianity reached the Roman province of Britain from Gaul in the third century (or possibly earlier). Alban, traditionally Britain's first martyr, was put to death as a Christian during the persecution of Diocletian (22 June 303) at his native town Verulamium, and the bishops of Londinium, Eboracum (York), and Lindum (Lincoln) attended the Council of Arles in 314. However, the Anglo-Saxon invasions submerged the Christian religion in England until the sixth century: conversion was undertaken in the north from 563 by Celtic missionaries from Ireland led by St Columba, and in the south by a mission sent from Rome in 597 which was led by St Augustine, who became the first archbishop of Canterbury. England appears to have been converted again by the end of the seventh century and followed, after the Council of Whitby in 663, the practices of the Roman Church, which brought the kingdom into the mainstream of European thought and culture.

PRINCIPAL CITIES

There are 51 cities in England and space constraints prevent us from including profiles of them all. Below is a selection of England's principal cities with the date on which city status was conferred in parentheses. Other cities are Bradford (pre-1900), Chelmsford (2012), Chichester (pre-1900), Coventry (pre-1900), Derby (1977), Ely (pre-1900), Exeter (pre-1900), Gloucester (pre-1900), Hereford (pre-1900), Kingston-upon-Hull (pre-1900), Lancaster (1937), Lichfield (pre-1900), London (pre-1900), Peterborough (pre-1900), Plymouth (1928), Portsmouth (1926), Preston (2002), Ripon (pre-1900), Salford (1926), Stoke-on-Trent (1925), Sunderland (1992), Truro (pre-1900), Wakefield (pre-1900), Wells (pre-

1900), Westminster (pre-1900), Wolverhampton (2000) and Worcester (pre-1900).

Certain cities have also been granted a lord mayoralty – this grant confers no additional powers or functions and is purely honorific. Cities with lord mayors are Birmingham, Bradford, Bristol, Canterbury, Chester, Coventry, Exeter, Kingston-upon-Hull, Leeds, Leicester, Liverpool, London, Manchester, Newcastle-upon-Tyne, Norwich, Nottingham, Oxford, Plymouth, Portsmouth, Sheffield, Stoke-on-Trent, Westminster and York.

BATH (PRE-1900)

Bath stands on the river Avon between the Cotswold Hills to the north and the Mendips to the south, and was originally a small roman town (Aquae Sulis) with a baths and temple complex built around naturally occurring hot springs. In the early 18th century Bath became England's premier spa town where the rich and celebrated members of fashionable society gathered to 'take the waters' and enjoy the town's theatres and concert rooms. During this period the architect John Wood laid the foundations of a new Georgian city built using the honey-coloured stone for which Bath is famous today. Since 1987 the city has been listed as a UNESCO World Heritage Site.

Contemporary Bath is a thriving tourist destination and remains a leading cultural, religious and historical centre with many art galleries and historic sites including the Pump Room (1790); the Royal Crescent (1767); the Circus (1754); the 18th-century Assembly Rooms (housing the Museum of Costume); Pulteney Bridge (1771); the Guildhall and the Abbey, now over 500 years old, which is built on the site of a Saxon monastery. In 2006 the Bath Thermae Spa was completed and the hot springs reopened to the public for the first time since 1978.

BIRMINGHAM (PRE-1900)

Birmingham is Britain's second largest city, with a population of over one million. The generally accepted derivation of 'Birmingham' is the ham (dwelling-place) of the ing (family) of Beorma, presumed to have been Saxon. During the Industrial Revolution the town grew into a major manufacturing centre, known as the 'city of a thousand trades', and in 1889 was granted city status. By the 18th century, Birmingham was the main European producer of items such as buckles, medals and coins. Today, around 40 per cent of all the UK's handmade jewellery is produced in Birmingham's Jewellery Quarter. Another product of the Industrial Revolution are the city's 34 miles (56km) of canals.

Recent developments include Millennium Point, which houses Thinktank, the Birmingham science museum, and Brindleyplace, a development of shops, offices and leisure facilities clustered around canals. In 2003 the Bullring shopping centre was officially opened as part of the city's urban regeneration programme.

The principal buildings are the Town Hall (1834–50), the Council House (1879), Victoria Law Courts (1891), the University of Birmingham (1906–9), the 13th-century church of St Martin in the Bull Ring (rebuilt 1873), the cathedral (formerly St Philip's Church) (1711), the Roman Catholic cathedral of St Chad (1839–41), the Assay Office (1773), the Rotunda (1964) and the National Exhibition Centre (1976).

BRIGHTON AND HOVE (2000)

Brighton and Hove is situated on the south coast of England, around 96km (60 miles) south of London. Originally a fishing village called Brighthelmstone, it was transformed into a fashionable seaside resort in the 18th century when Dr Richard Russell popularised the benefits of his 'sea-water cure'; as one of the closest beaches to London, Brighton began to attract wealthy visitors. One of these was the Prince Regent (the future King George IV), who first visited in 1783 and became so fond of the city that in 1807 he bought the former farmhouse he had been renting, and gradually turned it into Brighton's most recognisable building, the Royal Pavilion. The Pavilion is renowned for its Indo-Saracenic exterior, featuring minarets and an enormous central dome designed by John Nash, combined with the lavish chinoiserie of Frederick Crace's and Robert Jones' interiors. Queen Victoria sold the Pavilion to Brighton's municipal authority in 1850.

Brighton and Hove's Regency heritage can also be seen in the numerous elegant squares and crescents designed by Amon Wilds and Augustin Busby that dominate the seafront.

BRISTOL (PRE-1900)

Bristol was a royal borough before the Norman conquest. The earliest form of the name is *Bricgstow*. Due to the city's position close to the mouth of the River Avon, it was an important location for marine trade for centuries and prospered greatly from the transatlantic slave trade during the 18th century.

The principal buildings include the 12th-century cathedral with Norman chapter house and gateway; the 14th-century church of St Mary Redcliffe; Wesley's Chapel, Broadmead; the Merchant Venturers' Almshouses; the Council House (1956); the Guildhall; the Exchange (erected from the designs of John Wood in 1743); Cabot Tower; the university and Clifton College.

The Clifton Suspension Bridge, with a span of 214m (702ft) over the Avon, was projected by Isambard Kingdom Brunel in 1836 but was not completed until 1864. Brunel's SS *Great Britain*, the first ocean-going propeller-driven ship, now forms a museum at the western dockyard, from where she was originally launched in 1843. The docks themselves have been extensively restored and redeveloped; the 19th-century two-storey former tea warehouse is now the Arnolfini Centre for Contemporary Arts, and an 18th-century sail-loft houses the Architecture Centre. On Princes Wharf, 1950s transit sheds have been renovated and converted into the museum of Bristol, M Shed, which opened in 2011.

CAMBRIDGE (1951)

Cambridge, a settlement far older than its ancient university, lies on the River Cam (or Granta). Its industries include technology research and development, and biotechnology. Among its open spaces are Jesus Green, Sheep's Green, Coe Fen, Parker's Piece, Christ's Pieces, the University Botanic Garden, and the 'Backs' – lawns and gardens through which the Cam winds behind the principal line of college buildings. Historical sites east of the Cam include King's Parade, Great St Mary's Church, Gibbs' Senate House and King's College Chapel.

University and college buildings provide the outstanding features of Cambridge's architecture but several churches (especially St Benet's, the oldest building in the city, and Holy Sepulchre or the Round Church) are also notable. The Guildhall (1937) stands on a site of which at least part has held municipal buildings since 1224. In 2009 the University of Cambridge celebrated its 800th anniversary.

CANTERBURY (PRE-1900)

Canterbury, seat of the Archbishop of Canterbury, the primate of the Church of England, dates back to prehistoric times. It was the Roman *Durovernum Cantiacorum* and the Saxon *Cant-wara-byrig* (stronghold of the men of Kent). It was here in 597 that St Augustine began the conversion of the English to Christianity, when Ethelbert, King of Kent, was baptised.

Of the Benedictine St Augustine's Abbey, burial place of the Jutish kings of Kent, only ruins remain. According to Bede, St Martin's Church, on the eastern outskirts of the city, was the place of worship of Queen Bertha, the Christian wife of King Ethelbert, before the advent of St Augustine. In 1170 the rivalry of Church and State culminated in the murder of Archbishop Thomas Becket in Canterbury Cathedral, by Henry II's knights. His shrine became a great centre of pilgrimage, as described in Chaucer's *Canterbury Tales*. After the Reformation pilgrimages ceased, the prosperity of the city was strengthened by an influx of Huguenot refugees, who introduced weaving. The poet and playwright Christopher Marlowe was born and raised in Canterbury and the city is home to the 1,200-seat Marlowe Theatre, which reopened to the public in 2011, following an extensive £25m rebuild.

The cathedral, with its architecture ranging from the 11th to the 15th centuries, is famous worldwide. Visitors are attracted particularly to the Martyrdom, the Black Prince's Tomb and the Warriors' Chapel.

The medieval city walls are built on Roman foundations and the 14th-century West Gate is one of the finest buildings of its kind in the country.

CHESTER (PRE-1900)

Chester is situated on the River Dee. Its recorded history dates from the first century when the Romans founded the fortress of *Deva*. The city's name is derived from the latin *Castra* (a camp or encampment). During the middle ages, Chester was the principal port of north-west England but declined with the silting of the Dee estuary and competition from Liverpool. The city was also an important military centre, notably during Edward I's Welsh campaigns and the Elizabethan Irish campaigns. During the Civil War, Chester supported the king and was besieged from 1643 to 1646. Chester's first charter was granted c.1175 and the city was incorporated in 1506. The office of sheriff is the earliest created in the country (1120s), and in 1992 the mayor, who also enjoys the title 'Admiral of the Dee', was made a lord mayor.

The city's architectural features include the city walls (an almost complete two-mile circuit), the unique 13th-century Rows (covered galleries above the street-level shops), the Victorian Gothic town hall (1869), the castle (rebuilt 1788 and 1822) and numerous half-timbered buildings. The cathedral was a Benedictine abbey until the dissolution of the monasteries. Chester racecourse is the oldest racecourse in Britain, believed to have origins in the 13th century. The first recorded horserace was in 1539 during the reign of Henry VIII. Chester also houses the ruins of a Roman amphitheatre, built in the late first century AD.

DURHAM (PRE-1900)

The city of Durham's prominent Norman cathedral and castle are set high on a wooded peninsula overlooking the River Wear. The cathedral was founded as a shrine for the body of St Cuthbert in 995. The present building dates from 1093 and among its many treasures is the tomb of the Venerable Bede (673–735). Durham's prince bishops had unique powers up to 1836, being lay rulers as well as religious leaders. As a palatinate, Durham could have its own army, nobility, coinage and courts. The castle was the main seat of the prince bishops for nearly 800 years; it is now used as a college by the University of Durham. The university, founded in the early 19th century on the initiative of Bishop William Van Mildert, is England's third oldest.

Annual events include Durham's regatta in June (claimed to be the oldest rowing event in Britain) and the annual Durham Miners' Gala in July. Durham County Cricket Club was established in 1882.

LEEDS (PRE-1900)

Leeds, situated in the lower Aire valley, was first incorporated by Charles I in 1626. The earliest forms of the name are *Loidis* or *Ledes,* the origins of which are obscure.

The principal buildings are the Civic Hall (1933), the Town Hall (1858), the Municipal Buildings and Art Gallery (1884) with the Henry Moore Gallery (1982), the Corn Exchange (1863) and the university. The parish church of St Peter was rebuilt in 1841 and granted minister status in 2012. The 17th-century St John's Church has a fine interior with a famous English Renaissance screen; the last remaining 18th-century church in the city is Holy Trinity in Boar Lane (1727). Kirkstall Abbey (about three miles from the centre of the city), founded by Henry de Lacy in 1152, is one of the most complete examples of a Cistercian house now remaining. The Royal Armouries Museum forms part of a group of museums that house the national collection of antique arms and armour. The Grand Theatre and Opera House is home to Northern Ballet and Opera North.

LEICESTER (1919)

Leicester is situated in central England. The city was an important Roman settlement and also one of the five 'burghs' or boroughs of the Danelaw. In 1485 Richard III was buried in Leicester following his death at the nearby Battle of Bosworth. In 1589 Queen Elizabeth I granted a charter to the city and the ancient title was confirmed by letters patent in 1919.

The textile industry was responsible for Leicester's early expansion and the city still maintains a strong manufacturing base. Cotton mills and factories are now undergoing extensive regeneration and are being converted into offices, apartments, bars and restaurants. The principal buildings include the two universities (the University of Leicester and De Montfort University), as well as the Town Hall, the 13th-century Guildhall, De Montfort Hall, Leicester Cathedral, the Jewry Wall (the UK's highest standing Roman wall), St Nicholas Church and St Mary de Castro church. The motte and Great Hall of Leicester can be seen from the castle gardens, situated next to the River Soar.

LINCOLN (PRE-1900)

Situated 64km (40 miles) inland on the river Witham, Lincoln derives its name from a contraction of *Lindum Colonia,* the settlement founded in AD 48 by the Romans to command the crossing of Ermine Street and Fosse Way. Sections of the third-century Roman city wall can be seen, including an extant gateway (Newport Arch). The Romans also drained the surrounding fenland and created a canal system, laying the foundations of Lincoln's agricultural prosperity and also the city's importance in the medieval wool trade as a port and staple town.

As one of the five 'burghs' or boroughs of the Danelaw, Lincoln was an important trading centre in the ninth and tenth centuries and prosperity from the wool trade lasted until the 14th century. This wealth enabled local merchants to build parish churches, of which three survive, and there are also remains of a 12th-century Jewish community. However, the removal of the staple to Boston in 1369 heralded a decline, from which the city only recovered fully in the 19th century, when improved fen drainage made Lincoln agriculturally important. Improved canal and rail links led to industrial development, mainly in the manufacture of machinery and engineering products.

The castle was built shortly after the Norman Conquest and is unusual in having two mounds; on one motte stands a keep (Lucy's Tower) added in the 12th century. It currently houses one of the four surviving copies of the Magna Carta. The cathedral was begun c.1073 but was mostly destroyed by fire and earthquake in the 12th century. Rebuilding was begun by St Hugh and completed over a century later. Other notable architectural features are the 12th-century High Bridge, the oldest in Britain still to carry buildings, and the Guildhall, situated above the 15th-century Stonebow gateway.

LIVERPOOL (PRE-1900)

Liverpool, on the north bank of the river Mersey, 5km (3 miles) from the Irish Sea, is the UK's foremost port for Atlantic trade. There are 2,100 acres of dockland on both sides of the river and the Gladstone and Royal Seaforth Docks can accommodate tanker-sized vessels. Liverpool Free Port was opened in 1984.

Liverpool was created a free borough in 1207 and was given city status in 1880. From the early 18th century it expanded rapidly with the growth of industrialisation and the transatlantic slave trade. Surviving buildings from this period include the Bluecoat Chambers (1717, formerly the Bluecoat School), and the Town Hall (1754, rebuilt to the original design 1795). Notable from the 19th and 20th centuries are the Anglican cathedral (built from the designs of Sir Giles Gilbert Scott, it took 74 years to construct), and the Catholic Metropolitan Cathedral (designed by Sir Frederick Gibberd, consecrated 1967). Both of these cathedrals are situated on Hope Street, named after the merchant William Hope, which is the only street in the UK with a cathedral at either end. The refurbished Albert Dock (designed by Jesse Hartley) contains the Merseyside Maritime Museum, the International Slavery Museum, the Beatles Story and the Tate Liverpool art gallery. The Museum of Liverpool opened in 2011.

MANCHESTER (PRE-1900)

Manchester (the *Mamucium* of the Romans, who occupied it in AD 79) is a commercial and industrial centre connected with the sea by the Manchester Ship Canal, 57km (35.5 miles) long, opened in 1894 and accommodating ships up to 15,000 tons. During the Industrial Revolution the city had a thriving cotton industry and by 1853 there were over 100 cotton mills, which dominated the city's landscape.

The principal buildings are the Town Hall, erected in 1877 from the designs of Alfred Waterhouse, with a large extension of 1938; the Royal Exchange (1869, enlarged 1921); the Central Library (1934); Heaton Hall; the 17th-century Chetham Library; the Rylands Library (1900), which includes the Althorp collection; the university precinct; the 15th-century cathedral (formerly the parish church); the Manchester Central conference and exhibition centre and the Bridgewater Hall (1996) concert venue. Manchester is the home of the Hallé Orchestra, the Royal Northern College of Music, the Royal Exchange Theatre and numerous public art galleries.

The town received its first charter of incorporation in 1838 and was created a city in 1853.

NEWCASTLE UPON TYNE (PRE-1900)

Newcastle upon Tyne, on the north bank of the River Tyne, is 13km (8 miles) from the North Sea. A cathedral and university city, it is the administrative, commercial and cultural centre for north-east England and the principal port.

The principal buildings include the Castle Keep (12th century), Black Gate (13th century), Blackfriars (13th century), West Walls (13th century), St Nicholas Cathedral (15th century, fine lantern tower), St Andrew's Church (12th–14th century), St John's (14th–15th century), All Saints (1786 by Stephenson), St Mary's Roman Catholic Cathedral (1844), Trinity House (17th century), Sandhill (16th-century houses), Guildhall (Georgian), Grey Street (1834–9), Central Station (1846–50) and the Central Library (1969). Open spaces include the Town Moor (927 acres).

Numerous bridges span the Tyne at Newcastle, including the Tyne Bridge (1928) and the Tilting Millennium Bridge (2001) which links the city with Gateshead to the south.

The city's name is derived from the 'new castle' (1080) erected as a defence against the Scots. In 1265 defensive walls over two miles in length were built around the city as further protection; parts of these walls remain today and can be found to the west of the city centre.

NORWICH (PRE-1900)

Norwich grew from an early Anglo-Saxon settlement near the confluence of the rivers Yare and Wensum, and now serves as the provincial capital for the predominantly agricultural region of East Anglia. The name is thought to relate to the most northerly of a group of Anglo-Saxon villages or *wics*. The city's first known charter was granted in 1158 by Henry II.

Norwich serves its surrounding area as a market town and commercial centre. From the 14th century until the Industrial Revolution, Norwich was the regional centre of the woollen industry. Now the biggest single industry is financial services and principal trades are engineering, printing and shoemaking. The University of East Anglia is on the city's western boundary and admitted its first students in 1963. Norwich is accessible to seagoing vessels by means of the river Yare, entered at Great Yarmouth, 32km (20 miles) to the east.

Among many historic buildings are the cathedral (completed in the 12th century and surmounted by a 15th-century spire 96m (315ft) in height); the keep of the Norman castle (now a museum and art gallery); the 15th-century flint-walled Guildhall; some 30 medieval parish churches; St Andrew's and Blackfriars' Halls; the Tudor houses preserved in Elm Hill and the Georgian Assembly House.

NOTTINGHAM (PRE-1900)

Nottingham stands on the river Trent. *Snotingaham* or *Notingeham,* the 'homestead of the people of Snot', is the Anglo-Saxon name for the Celtic settlement of *Tigguocobauc,* or the house of caves. In 878, Nottingham became one of the five 'burghs' or boroughs of the Danelaw. William the Conqueror ordered the construction of Nottingham Castle, while the town itself developed rapidly under Norman rule. Its laws and rights were formally recognised by Henry II's charter in 1155. The castle became a favoured residence of King John. In 1642 Charles I raised his personal standard at Nottingham Castle at the start of the Civil War.

Architecturally, Nottingham has a wealth of notable buildings, particularly those designed in the Victorian era by T. C. Hine and Watson Fothergill. The city council owns the castle (of Norman origin but restored in 1878), Wollaton Hall (1580–8), Newstead Abbey (once the home of Lord Byron), the Guildhall (1888) and the Council House (1929). St Mary's, St Peter's and St Nicholas' churches are of interest, as is the Roman Catholic cathedral (Pugin, 1842–4). Nottingham was granted city status in 1897.

OXFORD (PRE-1900)

Oxford is a university city, an important industrial centre and a market town.

Oxford is known for its architecture, its oldest specimens being the reputedly Saxon tower of St Michael's Church, the remains of the Norman castle and city walls, and the Norman church at Iffley. It also has many Gothic buildings, such as the Divinity Schools, the Old Library at Merton College, William of Wykeham's New College, Magdalen and Christ Church colleges and many other college buildings. Later centuries are represented by the Laudian Quadrangle at St John's College, the Renaissance Sheldonian Theatre by Sir Christopher Wren, Trinity College Chapel, All Saints Church, Hawksmoor's mock-Gothic at All Souls College, and the 18th-century Queen's College. In addition to individual buildings, High Street and Radcliffe Square both form interesting architectural compositions. Most of the colleges have gardens, those of Magdalen, New College, St John's and Worcester being the largest.

The Oxford University Museum of Natural History, renowned for its spectacular neo-Gothic architecture, houses the university's scientific collections of zoological, entomological and geological specimens and is attached to the neighbouring Pitt Rivers Museum, which houses ethnographic and archaeological objects from around the world. The Ashmolean is the city's museum of art and archaeology and Modern Art Oxford hosts a programme of contemporary art exhibitions.

ST ALBANS (PRE-1900)

The origins of St Albans, situated on the river Ver, stem from the Roman town of *Verulamium.* Named after the first Christian martyr in Britain, who was executed there, St Albans has developed around the Norman abbey and the cathedral church (consecrated 1115), which was built partly of materials from the old Roman city. The museums house Iron Age and Roman artefacts and the Roman theatre, unique in Britain, has a stage as opposed to an amphitheatre. Archaeological excavations in the city centre have revealed evidence of pre-Roman, Saxon and medieval occupation.

The town's significance grew to the extent that it was a signatory and venue for the drafting of the Magna Carta. It was also the scene of riots during the Peasants' Revolt, the French King John was imprisoned there after the Battle of Poitiers, and heavy fighting took place there during the Wars of the Roses.

Previously controlled by the Abbot, the town achieved a charter in 1553 and city status in 1877. The street market, first established in 1553, is still an important feature of the city, as are many hotels and inns, surviving from the days when St Albans was an important coach stop. St Albans is also noted for its clock tower, built between 1403 and 1412, the only remaining medieval town belfry in England.

SALISBURY (PRE-1900)

The history of Salisbury centres around the cathedral and cathedral close. The city evolved from an Iron Age camp a mile to the north of its current position which was strengthened by the Romans and called *Serviodunum.* The Normans built a castle and cathedral on the site and renamed it Sarum. In 1220 Bishop Richard Poore and the architect Elias de Derham decided to build a new Gothic-style cathedral. The cathedral was completed 38 years later and a community known as New Sarum, now called Salisbury, grew around it. Originally the cathedral had a squat tower; the 123m (404ft) spire that makes the cathedral the tallest medieval structure in the world was added c.1315. A walled close with houses for the clergy was built around the cathedral; the Medieval Hall still stands today, alongside buildings dating from the 13th to the 20th century, including some designed by Sir Christopher Wren.

A prosperous wool and cloth trade allowed Salisbury to flourish until the 17th century. When the wool trade declined new crafts were established, including cutlery, leather and basket work, saddlery, lacemaking, joinery and malting. By 1750 it had become an important road junction and coaching centre and in the Victorian era the railways enabled a new age of expansion and prosperity.

SHEFFIELD (PRE-1900)

Sheffield is situated at the confluence of the rivers Sheaf, Porter, Rivelin and Loxley with the river Don and was created a city in 1893.

The parish church of St Peter and St Paul, founded in the 12th century, became the cathedral church of the diocese of Sheffield in 1914. The Roman Catholic Cathedral Church of St Marie (founded 1847) was made a cathedral for the new diocese of Hallam in 1980; parts of the present building date from c.1435. The principal buildings are the Town Hall (1897), the Cutlers' Hall (1832), City Hall (1932), Graves Art Gallery (1934) and the Millennium Gallery (2001). The City Museum and Mappin Art Gallery (1874) reopened to the public as the Weston Park Museum in 2006 after undergoing a major £19m redevelopment, housing Sheffield's archaeology, natural history, art and social history collections, it underwent further refurbishment in 2016. The restored Lyceum Theatre, which dates from 1897, reopened in 1990 and The Crucible Theatre (1971), famous for hosting the World Snooker Championship, was refurbished between 2007 and 2009 and officially reopened in 2010. Three major sporting and entertainment venues were opened between 1990 and 1991: Sheffield Arena, now FlyDSA Arena, and Ponds Forge, which houses an Olympic sized swimming pool and the UK's deepest diving pool, home to the GB Diving Squad. The Don Valley Stadium, completed in 1990, was demolished in 2013 and the site redeveloped as the Olympic Legacy Park, which includes a research centre, sport centre and educational facilities for local universities, opened in 2018. The Leadmill, Sheffield's longest-running independent live music venue, opened in 1980.

SOUTHAMPTON (1964)

Southampton is a major seaport on the south coast of England, situated between the mouths of the Test and Itchen rivers. Southampton's natural deep-water harbour has made the area an important settlement since the Romans built the first port (known as *Clausentum*) in the first century, and Southampton's port has witnessed several important departures, including those of Henry V in 1415 for the Battle of Agincourt, the *Mayflower* in 1620, and the RMS *Titanic* in 1912.

The city's strategic importance, not only as a seaport but also as a centre for aircraft production, meant that it was heavily bombed during the Second World War. However, many historically significant structures remain, including the Wool House, dating from 1417 and now used as the Maritime Museum; parts of the Norman city walls, which are among the most complete in the UK; the Bargate, which was originally the main gateway into the city; God's House Tower, now the Museum of Archaeology; St Michael's, the city's oldest church; and the Tudor Merchants Hall.

WINCHESTER (PRE-1900)

Winchester, the ancient capital of England, is situated on the river Itchen. The city is rich in architecture of all types, and especially notable is the cathedral. Built in 1079–93 the cathedral exhibits examples of Norman, early English and Perpendicular styles and is the burial place of author Jane Austen. Winchester College, founded in 1382, is one of the country's most famous public schools, and the original

building (1393) remains largely unaltered. St Cross Hospital, another great medieval foundation, lies one mile south of the city. The almshouses were founded in 1136 by Bishop Henry de Blois, and Cardinal Henry Beaufort added a new almshouse of 'Noble Poverty' in 1446. The chapel and dwellings are of great architectural interest, and visitors may still receive the 'Wayfarer's Dole' of bread and ale, a tradition now 900 years old.

Excavations have done much to clarify the origins and development of Winchester. Part of the forum and several of the streets from the Roman town have been discovered. Excavations in the cathedral close have uncovered the entire site of the Anglo-Saxon cathedral (known as the Old Minster) and parts of the New Minster which was built by Alfred the Great's son, Edward the Elder, and is the burial place of the Alfredian dynasty. The original burial place of St Swithun, before his remains were translated to a site in the present cathedral, was also uncovered.

Excavations in other parts of the city have cast much light on Norman Winchester, notably on the site of the Royal Castle (adjacent to which the new Law Courts have been built) and in the grounds of Wolvesey Castle, where the great house built by bishops Giffard and Henry de Blois in the 12th century has been uncovered. The Great Hall, built by Henry III between 1222 and 1236, survives and houses the Arthurian Round Table.

YORK (PRE-1900)

The city of York is an archiepiscopal seat. Its recorded history dates from AD 71, when the Roman Ninth Legion established a base under Petilius Cerealis that would later become the fortress of *Eburacum*, or *Eboracum*. In Anglo-Saxon times the city was the royal and ecclesiastical centre of Northumbria, and after capture by a Viking army in AD 866 it became the capital of the Viking kingdom of Jorvik. By the 14th century the city had become a great mercantile centre, mainly because of its control of the wool trade, and was used as the chief base against the Scots. Under the Tudors its fortunes declined, although Henry VIII made it the headquarters of the Council of the North. Excavations on many sites, including Coppergate, have greatly expanded knowledge of Roman, Viking and medieval urban life. The JORVIK Viking Centre (reopened in 2017) takes visitors on a journey through a reconstructed 10th century Viking-age York.

The city is rich in examples of architecture of all periods. The earliest church was built in AD 627 and, from the 12th to 15th centuries, the present Minster was built in a succession of styles.

LORD-LIEUTENANTS AND HIGH SHERIFFS

Area	Lord-Lieutenant	High Sheriff (2019–20)
Bedfordshire	Helen Nellis	Cora Dolling
Berkshire	James Puxley	Lucy Zeal
Bristol	Peaches Golding, OBE	Charles Wyld
Buckinghamshire	Sir Henry Aubrey-Fletcher, Bt., KCVO	Julia Upton, MBE
Cambridgeshire	Julie Spence, OBE, QPM	His Hon. Neil McKittrick
Cheshire	David Briggs, MBE	Mark Mitchell
Cornwall	Col. Edward Bolitho, OBE	John Willis
Cumbria	Claire Hensman	Marcia Fotheringham
Derbyshire	William Tucker, CVO	Earl of Burlington
Devon	David Fursdon	Capt. Simon Martin, LVO, OBE, RN
Dorset	Angus Campbell	Philip Warr
Durham	Susan Snowden	Peter Candler
East Riding of Yorkshire	James Dick, OBE	Susan Stephenson
East Sussex	Peter Field	Violet Hancock
Essex	Jennifer Tolhurst	Dr Francis Bettley
Gloucestershire	Edward Gillespie, OBE	Robert Berkeley
Greater London	Sir Kenneth Olisa, OBE	Iqbal Wahhab, OBE
Greater Manchester	Warren Smith	Mark Adlestone, OBE
Hampshire	Nigel Atkinson	Catherine Le May
Herefordshire	Countess of Darnley, CVO	James Hervey-Bathurst, CBE
Hertfordshire	Robert Voss, CBE	Sarah Beazley
Isle of Wight	Susan Sheldon	Geoffrey Underwood
Kent	Viscount De L'Isle, CVO, MBE	Paul Barrett
Lancashire	Lord Shuttleworth, KG, KCVO	Hon. Ralph Assheton, TD
Leicestershire	Michael Kapur, OBE	Timothy Hercock
Lincolnshire	Toby Dennis	Robert Day
Merseyside	Mark Blundell	David Steer, QC
Norfolk	Lady Dannatt, MBE	Lady Agnew
North Yorkshire	Johanna Ropner	Linda Fenwick
Northamptonshire	David Laing	Nicholas Robertson
Northumberland	Duchess of Northumberland	Lady Joicey
Nottinghamshire	Sir John Peace	His Hon. Jonathan Teare
Oxfordshire	Tim Stevenson, OBE	Lady Jay of Ewelme, CBE
Rutland	Dr Sarah Furness	Margaret Miles
Shropshire	Anna Turner	Dr Jeremy Dixey
Somerset	Anne Maw	Jonathan Halliday
South Yorkshire	Andrew Coombe	John Pickering
Staffordshire	Ian Dudson, CBE	Ashley Brough
Suffolk	Clare, Countess of Euston	Rosalind Eminson
Surrey	Michael More-Molyneux	Bridget Biddell
Tyne and Wear	Susan Winfield, OBE	Catherine Moran, OBE
Warwickshire	Timothy Cox	Simon Miesegaes
West Midlands	John Crabtree, OBE	Michael Kuo
West Sussex	Susan Pyper	Davina Irwin-Clark
West Yorkshire	Edmund Anderson	Paul Lawrence
Wiltshire	Sarah Troughton	David Scott
Worcestershire	Lt.-Col. Patrick Holcroft, LVO, OBE	Edward Holloway

COMBINED AUTHORITIES

Authority	Constituent Councils*	Pop. †	Mayor, Political Party
Cambridgeshire & Peterborough	Cambridge, Cambridgeshire, E. Cambridgeshire, Fenland, Huntingdonshire, Peterborough, S. Cambridgeshire	852,523	James Palmer, C.
Greater Manchester	Bolton, Bury, Manchester, Oldham, Rochdale, Salford, Stockport, Tameside, Trafford, Wigan	2,812,569	Andy Burnham, Lab.
Liverpool City Region	Halton, Knowsley, Liverpool, St Helens, Sefton, Wirral	1,551,497	Steve Rotheram, Lab.
North East	Durham, Gateshead, S. Tyneside, Sunderland	1,157,170	None
North of Tyne	Newcastle Upon Tyne, N. Tyneside, Northumberland	826,455	Jamie Driscoll, Lab.
Sheffield City Region	Barnsley, Doncaster, Rotherham, Sheffield	1,402,918	Dan Jarvis, Lab.
Tees Valley	Darlington, Hartlepool, Middlesbrough, Redcar & Cleveland, Stockton-On-Tees	674,284	Ben Houchen, C.
West of England	Bath & N. E. Somerset, Bristol, S. Gloucestershire	938,155	Tim Bowles, C.
West Midlands	Birmingham, Coventry, Dudley, Sandwell, Solihull, Walsall, Wolverhampton	2,916,458	Andy Street, C.
West Yorkshire	Bradford, Calderdale, Kirklees, Leeds, Wakefield	2,320,214	None

COUNTY COUNCILS

Council & Administrative HQ	Telephone	Population†	Council Tax‡	Chief Executive§
Buckinghamshire, Aylesbury	01296-395000	540,059	£1,330	Rachael Shimmin, OBE
Cambridgeshire, Cambridge	0345-045 5200	651,482	£1,312	Gillian Beasley
Cumbria, Carlisle	01228-606060	498,888	£1,385	Katherine Fairclough
Derbyshire, Matlock	01629-580000	796,142	£1,323	E. Alexander; M. Ashworth; J. Parfrement; S. Stevens
Devon, Exeter	0345-155 1015	795,286	£1,384	Dr Phil Norrey
East Sussex, Lewes	0345-608 0190	554,590	£1,435	Becky Shaw
Essex, Chelmsford	0845-7430 430	1,477,764	£1,270	Gavin Jones
Gloucestershire, Gloucester	01452-425000	633,558	£1,294	Peter Bungard
Hampshire, Winchester	0300-555 1375	1,376,316	£1,237	John Coughlan, CBE
Hertfordshire, Hertford	0300-123 4040	1,184,365	£1,360	Owen Mapley
Kent, Maidstone	0300-041 4141	1,568,623	£1,299	David Cockburn
Lancashire, Preston	0300-123 6701	1,210,053	£1,347	Angie Ridgwell
Leicestershire, Leicester	0116-232 3232	698,268	£1,292	John Sinnott
Lincolnshire, Lincoln	01522-552222	755,833	£1,292	Keith Ireland
Norfolk, Norwich	0344-800 8020	903,680	£1,362	Dr Wendy Thomson, CBE
North Yorkshire, Northallerton	01609-780780	614,505	£1,311	Richard Flinton
Northamptonshire, Northampton	0300-126 1000	747,622	£1,236	Theresa Grant
Nottinghamshire, Nottingham	0115-982 3823	823,126	£1,476	Anthony May
Oxfordshire, Oxford	01865-792422	687,524	£1,469	Yvonne Rees
Somerset, Taunton	0300-123 2224	559,399	£1,240	Patrick Flaherty
Staffordshire, Stafford	0300-111 8000	875,219	£1,246	John Henderson, CB
Suffolk, Ipswich	03456-606 6067	758,556	£1,292	Nicola Beach
Surrey, Kingston upon Thames	0345-600 9009	1,189,934	£1,454	Joanna Killian
Warwickshire, Warwick	01926-410410	571,010	£1,432	Monica Fogarty
West Sussex, Chichester	01243-777100	858,852	£1,384	Nathan Elvery
Worcestershire, Worcester	01905-763763	592,057	£1,261	Paul Robinson

*See the following pages for information on individual constituent councils
† Source: Office for National Statistics – Mid-2018 Population Estimates (Crown copyright)
‡ Average 2019–20 Band D council tax in the county area inclusive of the adult social care precept, but exclusive of precepts for fire authorities and Police and Crime Commissioners. County councils claim their share of the combined council tax from the collection funds of the district authorities within their area. Band D council tax bills for the billing authority are given on the following pages
§ Or equivalent postholder

DISTRICT COUNCILS

District Council	Telephone	Pop.*	Council Tax†	Chief Executive‡
Adur	01273-263000	63,869	£1,892	Alex Bailey
Allerdale	01900-702702	97,527	£1,887	Ian Frost
Amber Valley	01773-570222	126,678	£1,833	Sylvia Delahay & Julian Townsend
Arun	01903-737500	159,827	£1,829	Nigel Lynn
Ashfield	01623-450000	127,151	£1,969	Robert Mitchell
Ashford	01233-331111	129,281	£1,777	Tracey Kerly
Aylesbury Vale	01296-585858	199,448	£1,850	Tracey Aldworth & Andrew Small
Babergh	01473-822801	91,401	£1,751	Arthur Charvonia
Barrow-in-Furness	01229-876543	67,137	£1,884	Sam Plum
Basildon	01268-533333	185,862	£1,822	Scott Logan
Basingstoke and Deane	01256-844844	175,729	£1,648	Melbourne Barrett
Bassetlaw	01909-533333	116,839	£1,982	Neil Taylor
Blaby	0116-275 0555	100,421	£1,847	Jane Toman
Bolsover	01246-242424	79,530	£1,924	Daniel Swaine
Boston	01205-314200	69,366	£1,780	Phil Drury
Braintree	01376-552525	151,561	£1,758	Andy Wright
Breckland	01362-656870	139,329	£1,798	Anna Graves
Brentwood	01277-312500	76,550	£1,741	vacant
Broadland	01603-431133	129,464	£1,817	Trevor Holden
Bromsgrove	01527-881288	98,662	£1,810	Kevin Dicks
Broxbourne	01992-785555	96,876	£1,681	Jeff Stack
Broxtowe	0115-917 7777	113,272	£1,963	Ruth Hyde, OBE
Burnley	01282-425011	88,527	£1,924	Mick Cartledge
CAMBRIDGE	01223-457000	125,758	£1,803	Antoinette Jackson
Cannock Chase	01543-462621	100,109	£1,779	Tony McGovern
CANTERBURY	01227-862000	164,553	£1,797	Colin Carmichael
CARLISLE	01228-817000	108,387	£1,873	Dr Jason Gooding
Castle Point	01268-882200	90,070	£1,802	David Marchant
Charnwood	01509-263151	182,643	£1,791	Geoffrey Parker
CHELMSFORD	01245-606606	177,079	£1,768	Nick Eveleigh
Cheltenham	01242-262626	117,090	£1,760	Jan Britton (Publica Group)
Cherwell	01295-227001	149,161	£1,899	Yvonne Rees
Chesterfield	01246-345345	104,628	£1,796	Huw Bowen
Chichester	01243-785166	120,750	£1,794	Diane Shepherd
Chiltern	01494-729000	95,927	£1,858	Bob Smith
Chorley	01257-515151	116,821	£1,828	Gary Hall
Colchester	01206-282222	192,523	£1,756	Adrian Pritchard
Copeland	01946-598300	68,424	£1,901	Pat Graham
Corby	01536-464000	70,827	£1,740	Norman Stronach
Cotswold	01285-623000	89,022	£1,749	Jan Britton (Publica Group)
Craven	01756-700600	56,832	£1,873	Paul Shevlin
Crawley	01293-438000	112,448	£1,777	Natalie Brahma-Pearl
Dacorum	01442-228000	154,280	£1,764	Sally Marshall
Dartford	01322-343434	109,709	£1,779	Graham Harris
Daventry	01327-871100	84,484	£1,789	Ian Vincent
Derbyshire Dales	01629-761100	71,977	£1,881	Paul Wilson
Dover	01304-821199	116,969	£1,823	Nadeem Aziz
East Cambridgeshire	01353-665555	89,362	£1,824	John Hill
East Devon	01395-516551	144,317	£1,893	Mark Williams
East Hampshire	01730-266551	120,681	£1,714	Gill Kneller
East Hertfordshire	01279-655261	148,105	£1,786	Richard Cassidy
East Lindsey	01507-601111	140,741	£1,736	Rob Barlow
East Northamptonshire	01832-742000	93,906	£1,802	David Oliver
East Staffordshire	01283-508000	118,574	£1,754	Andy O'Brien
East Suffolk	03330-162000	248,249	£1,741	Stephen Baker
Eastbourne	01323-410000	103,160	£1,965	Robert Cottrill
Eastleigh	023-8068 8000	131,819	£1,705	Nick Tustian
Eden	01768-817817	52,881	£1,886	Rose Rouse
Elmbridge	01372-474474	136,626	£1,936	Robert Moran
Epping Forest	01992-564000	131,137	£1,756	Georgina Blakemore
Epsom and Ewell	01372-732000	79,928	£1,912	Kathryn Beldon
Erewash	0115-907 2244	115,490	£1,813	Jeremy Jaroszek
EXETER	01392-277888	130,428	£1,838	Karime Hassan
Fareham	01329-236100	116,339	£1,666	Peter Grimwood
Fenland	01354-654321	101,491	£1,912	Paul Medd
Folkestone and Hythe	01303-853000	112.578	£1,893	Dr Susan Priest

Forest of Dean	01594-810000	86,543	£1,804	Jan Britton (Publica Group)
Fylde	01253-658658	79,770	£1,857	Allan Oldfield
Gedling	0115-901 3901	117,786	£1,958	Karen Bradford
GLOUCESTER	01452-396396	129,285	£1,753	John McGinty
Gosport	023-9258 4242	85,283	£1,732	David Williams
Gravesham	01474-564422	106,385	£1,783	David Hughes
Great Yarmouth	01493-856100	99,370	£1,792	Sheila Oxtoby
Guildford	01483-505050	147,889	£1,917	James Whiteman
Hambleton	01619-779977	91,134	£1,788	Dr Justin Ives
Harborough	01858-828282	92,499	£1,800	Beverley Jolly & Norman Proudfoot
Harlow	01279-446655	86,594	£1,814	Brian Keane
Harrogate	01423-500600	160,533	£1,896	Wallace Sampson
Hart	01252-622122	96,293	£1,757	Patricia Hughes & Daryl Phillips
Hastings	01424-451066	92,855	£1,984	Jane Hartnell & Simon Hubbard
Havant	023-9244 6019	125,813	£1,711	Gill Kneller
Hertsmere	020-8207 2277	104,205	£1,755	Dr Donald Graham
High Peak	0345-129 7777	92,211	£1,827	Simon Baker
Hinckley and Bosworth	01455-238141	112,423	£1,768	Bill Cullen
Horsham	01403-215100	142,217	£1,786	Glen Chip
Huntingdonshire	01480-388388	177,352	£1,855	Jo Lancaster
Hyndburn	01254-388111	80,815	£1,864	David Welsby
Ipswich	01473-432000	137,532	£1,867	Russell Williams
Kettering	01536-410333	101,266	£1,762	Graham Soulsby
King's Lynn and West Norfolk	01553-616200	151,811	£1,805	Ray Harding
LANCASTER	01524-582000	144,246	£1,860	Kieran Keane
Lewes	01273-471600	102,744	£2,024	Robert Cottrill
Lichfield	01543-308000	103,965	£1,763	Diane Tilley
LINCOLN	01522-881188	99,039	£1,809	Angela Andrews
Maidstone	01622-602000	169,955	£1,862	Alison Broom
Maldon	01621-854477	64,425	£1,793	P. Dodson, E. Foy & R. Holmes
Malvern Hills	01684-862151	78,113	£1,791	Jack Hegarty
Mansfield	01623-463463	108,841	£1,963	Hayley Barsby
Melton	01664-502502	51,100	£1,819	Edd de Coverly
Mendip	0300-3038588	114,881	£1,800	Stuart Brown
Mid Devon	01884-255255	81,695	£1,947	Stephen Walford
Mid Suffolk	01449-720711	102,493	£1,744	Arthur Charvonia
Mid Sussex	01444-458166	149,716	£1,808	Kathryn Hall
Mole Valley	01306-885001	87,253	£1,901	Karen Brimacombe
New Forest	023-8028 5000	179,753	£1,765	Bob Jackson
Newark and Sherwood	01636-650000	121,566	£2,024	John Robinson
Newcastle-under-Lyme	01782-717717	129,490	£1,750	Martin Hamilton
North Devon	01271-327711	96,110	£1,927	Ken Miles
North East Derbyshire	01246-231111	101,125	£1,907	Daniel Swaine
North Hertfordshire	01462-474000	133,214	£1,802	David Scholes
North Kesteven	01529-414155	115,985	£1,788	Ian Fytche
North Norfolk	01263-513811	104,552	£1,823	Nick Baker & Steve Blatch
North Warwickshire	01827-715341	64,850	£1,916	Steve Maxey (acting)
North West Leicestershire	01530-454545	102,126	£1,817	Beverley Smith
Northampton	0300-330 7000	225,146	£1,785	George Candler
NORWICH	0344-980 3333	141,137	£1,879	Laura McGillivray
Nuneaton and Bedworth	024-7637 6376	128,902	£1,893	Brent Davis & Simone Hines
Oadby and Wigston	0116-288 8961	57,056	£1,807	Mark Hall
OXFORD	01865-249811	154,327	£1,989	Gordon Mitchell
Pendle	01282-661661	91,405	£1,965	Dean Langton & Philip Mousdale
PRESTON	01772-906900	141,818	£1,941	Adrian Phillips
Redditch	01527-64252	84,989	£1,801	Kevin Dicks
Reigate and Banstead	01737-276000	147,757	£1,948	John Jory
Ribble Valley	01200-425111	60,075	£1,788	Marshal Scott
Richmondshire	01748-829100	53,244	£1,885	Tony Clark
Rochford	01702-318111	86,981	£1,815	Angela Hutchings & Shaun Scrutton
Rossendale	01706-217777	70,895	£1,892	Stuart Sugarman
Rother	01424-787000	95,656	£1,959	Malcolm Johnston & Dr Anthony Leonard
Rugby	01788-533533	107,194	£1,871	Adam Norburn
Runnymede	01932-838383	88,000	£1,879	Paul Turrell
Rushcliffe	0115-981 9911	117,671	£1,979	Allen Graham
Rushmoor	01252-398398	95,142	£1,710	Kath Marriott
Ryedale	01653-600666	54,920	£1,865	Stacey Burlet
ST ALBANS	01727-866100	147,373	£1,769	Amanda Foley
Scarborough	01723-232323	108,736	£1,896	Michael Greene

Sedgemoor	0845-408 2540	122,791	£1,765	Allison Griffin
Selby	01757-705101	89,106	£1,875	Janet Waggott
Sevenoaks	01732-227000	120,293	£1,872	Dr Pav Ramewal
Somerset West and Taunton	0300-304 8000	153,866	£1,741	James Hassett
South Bucks	01895-837200	70,043	£1,844	Bob Smith
South Cambridgeshire	0345-045 0500	157,519	£1,841	Liz Watts
South Derbyshire	01283-595795	104,493	£1,802	Frank McArdle
South Hams	01803-861234	86,221	£1,913	Sophie Hosking
South Holland	01775-761161	93,980	£1,747	Anna Graves
South Kesteven	01476-406080	141,853	£1,729	Paul Thomas (acting)
South Lakeland	01539-733333	104,532	£1,875	Lawrence Conway
South Norfolk	01508-533633	138,017	£1,844	Trevor Holden
South Northamptonshire	01327-322322	92,515	£1,819	Richard Ellis
South Oxfordshire	01235-520202	140,504	£1,887	David Hill
South Ribble	01772-421491	110,527	£1,848	Heather McManus
South Somerset	01935-462462	167,861	£1,802	Alex Parmley
South Staffordshire	01902-696000	112,126	£1,710	Dave Heywood
Spelthorne	01784-451499	99,334	£1,917	Daniel Mouawad
Stafford	01785-619000	135,880	£1,717	Tim Clegg
Staffordshire Moorlands	0345-605 3010	98,397	£1,740	Simon Baker
Stevenage	01438-242242	87,754	£1,759	Matt Partridge
Stratford-on-Avon	01789-267575	127,580	£1,860	Dave Buckland (interim)
Stroud	01453-766321	119,019	£1,840	Joanna Killian
Surrey Heath	01276-707100	88,874	£1,953	Karen Whelan
Swale	01795-417850	148,519	£1,774	Mark Radford
Tamworth	01827-709709	76,678	£1,715	Anthony Goodwin
Tandridge	01883-722000	87,496	£1,955	Louise Round
Teignbridge	01626-361101	132,844	£1,923	Phil Shears
Tendring	01255-686868	145,803	£1,743	Ian Davidson
Test Valley	01264-368000	125,169	£1,687	Roger Tetstall
Tewkesbury	01684-295010	92,599	£1,723	Mike Dawson
Thanet	01843-577000	141,819	£1,846	Madeline Homer
Three Rivers	01923-776611	93,045	£1,772	vacant
Tonbridge and Malling	01732-844522	130,508	£1,837	Julie Beilby
Torridge	01237-428700	68,143	£1,910	Jenny Wallace
Tunbridge Wells	01892-526121	118,054	£1,805	William Benson
Uttlesford	01799-510510	89,179	£1,779	Dawn French
Vale of White Horse	01235-520202	133,732	£1,883	Mark Stone
Warwick	01926-410410	142,484	£1,856	Chris Elliott
Watford	01923-226400	96,767	£1,816	Manny Lewis
Waverley	01483-523333	125,610	£1,956	Tom Horwood
Wealden	01323-443322	160,175	£2,012	Trevor Scott
Wellingborough	01933-229777	79,479	£1,716	Liz Elliott
Welwyn & Hatfield	01707-357000	122,746	£1,800	Rob Bridge
West Devon	01822-813600	55,528	£1,987	Sophie Hosking
West Lancashire	01695-577177	113,949	£1,838	Kim Webber
West Lindsey	01427-676676	94,869	£1,816	E. Fawcett-Moralee, I. Knowles, M. Sturgess
West Oxfordshire	01993-861000	109,800	£1,857	Jan Britton (Publica Group)
West Suffolk	01284-763233	178,881	£1,749	Ian Gallin
WINCHESTER	01962-840222	124,295	£1,730	Laura Taylor
Woking	01483-755855	101,167	£1,955	Ray Morgan, OBE
WORCESTER	01905-722233	101,891	£1,752	David Blake
Worthing	01903-239999	110,025	£1,811	Alex Bailey
Wychavon	01386-565000	127,340	£1,730	Jack Hegarty
Wycombe	01494-461000	174,641	£1,781	John East (acting)
Wyre	01253-891000	111,223	£1,836	Garry Payne
Wyre Forest	01562-732928	101,062	£1,812	Ian Miller

* *Source:* Office for National Statistics – *Mid-2018 Population Estimates* (Crown copyright)
† Band D council tax bill for 2019–20 inclusive of adult social care and parish precepts
‡ Or equivalent postholder
Councils in CAPITAL LETTERS have city status

METROPOLITAN BOROUGH COUNCILS

Metropolitan Borough Council	Telephone	Pop.*	Council Tax†	Chief Executive‡
Barnsley	01226-770770	245,199	£1,757	Sarah Norman
BIRMINGHAM	0121-303 1111	1,141,374	£1,601	Dawn Baxendale
Bolton	01204-333333	285,372	£1,767	Tony Oakman
BRADFORD	01274-432001	537,173	£1,640	Kersten England
Bury	0161-253 5000	190,108	£1,826	Geoff Little, OBE
Calderdale	01422-288001	210,082	£1,750	Robin Tuddenham
COVENTRY	0500-834 333	366,785	£1,834	Dr Martin Reeves
Doncaster	01302-736000	310,542	£1,647	Damian Allen
Dudley	0300-555 2345	320,626	£1,542	Kevin O'Keefe
Gateshead	0191-433 3000	202,508	£1,971	Sheena Ramsey
Kirklees	01484-221000	438,727	£1,768	Jacqui Gedman
Knowsley	0151-489 6000	149,571	£1,818	Mike Harden
LEEDS	0113-222 4444	789,194	£1,654	Tom Riordan
LIVERPOOL	0151-233 3000	494,814	£1,950	Tony Reeves
MANCHESTER	0161-234 5000	547,627	£1,646	Joanne Roney, OBE
NEWCASTLE UPON TYNE	0191-278 7878	300,196	£1,861	Pat Ritchie
North Tyneside	0191-643 5991	205,985	£1,785	Paul Hanson
Oldham	0161-770 3000	235,623	£1,905	Dr Carolyn Wilkins, OBE
Rochdale	01706-647474	220,001	£1,857	Steve Rumbelow
Rotherham	01709-382121	264,671	£1,832	Sharon Kemp
St Helens	01744-676789	180,049	£1,752	Mike Palin
SALFORD	0161-794 4711	254,408	£1,853	Jim Taylor
Sandwell	0121-569 2200	327,378	£1,615	David Stevens (acting)
Sefton	0345 140 0845	275,396	£1,883	Dwayne Johnson
SHEFFIELD	0114-273 4567	582,506	£1,830	John Mothersole
Solihull	0121-704 8001	214,909	£1,589	Nick Page
South Tyneside	0191-427 7000	150,265	£1,784	Martin Swales
Stockport	0161-480 4949	291,775	£1,917	Pam Smith
SUNDERLAND	0191-520 5555	277,417	£1,631	Patrick Melia
Tameside	0161-342 8355	225,197	£1,745	Steven Pleasant. MBE
Trafford	0161-912 2000	236,370	£1,568	Sara Todd
WAKEFIELD	0845-850 6506	345,038	£1,669	Merran McRae
Walsall	01922-650000	283,378	£1,928	Dr Helen Paterson
Wigan	01942-244991	326,088	£1,566	Alison McKenzie-Folan
Wirral	0151-606 2000	323,235	£1,823	Paul Satoor (interim)
WOLVERHAMPTON	01902-551155	262,008	£1,830	Tim Johnson

* Source: Office for National Statistics – Mid-2018 Population Estimates (Crown copyright)
† Band D council tax bill for 2019–20 inclusive of adult social care and parish precepts
‡ Or equivalent postholder
Councils in CAPITAL LETTERS have city status

UNITARY COUNCILS

Unitary Council	Telephone	Pop.*	Council Tax†	Chief Executive‡
Bath and North East Somerset	01225-477000	192,106	£1,734	vacant
Bedford	01234-267422	171,623	£1,837	Philip Simpkins
Blackburn with Darwen	01254-585585	148,942	£1,785	Denise Park
Blackpool	01253-477477	139,305	£1,827	Neil Jack
Bournemouth, Christchurch and Poole (BCP)	01202-451451	395,784	£1,788	Graham Farrant
Bracknell Forest	01344-352000	121,676	£1,650	Timothy Wheadon
BRIGHTON AND HOVE	01273-290000	290,395	£1,880	Geoff Raw
BRISTOL	0117-922 2000	463,405	£1,982	M. Jackson; J. Jensen; C. Molton
Central Bedfordshire	0300-300 8000	283,606	£1,921	Richard Carr
Cheshire East	0300-123 5500	380,790	£1,777	Kath O'Dwyer *(acting)*
Cheshire West and Chester	0300-123 8123	340,502	£1,829	Andrew Lewis
Cornwall	0300-123 4100	565,968	£1,864	Kate Kennally
Darlington	01325-380651	106,566	£1,820	Paul Wildsmith
DERBY	01332-293111	257,174	£1,710	Carole Mills
Dorset	01305-221000	376,484	£2,038	Matt Prosser
DURHAM	0300-026000	526,980	£1,993	Terry Collins
East Riding of Yorkshire	01482-393939	339,614	£1,808	Caroline Lacey
Halton	0303-333 4300	128,432	£1,720	David Parr
Hartlepool	01429-266522	93,242	£2,015	Gill Alexander
Herefordshire	01432-260000	192,107	£1,883	Alistair Neill
Isle of Wight	01983-821000	141,538	£1,889	John Metcalfe
Isles of Scilly§	01720-424000	2,242	£1,489	Mark Boden *(interim)*
KINGSTON-UPON-HULL	01482-609100	260,645	£1,680	Matt Jukes
LEICESTER	0116-254 1000	355,218	£1,842	Andy Keeling
Luton	01582-546000	214,109	£1,779	Robin Porter
Medway	01634-333333	277,855	£1,692	Neil Davies
Middlesbrough	01642-245432	140,545	£1,973	Tony Parkinson
Milton Keynes	01908-691691	268,607	£1,747	Michael Bracey
North East Lincolnshire	01472-313131	159,821	£1,855	Rob Walsh
North Lincolnshire	01724-296296	172,005	£1,811	Denise Hyde
North Somerset	01934-888888	213,919	£1,731	Jo Walker
Northumberland	0345-600 6400	320,274	£1,915	Daljit Lally, OBE
NOTTINGHAM	0115-915 5555	331,069	£2,038	Ian Curryer
PETERBOROUGH	01733-747474	201,041	£1,649	Gillian Beasley
PLYMOUTH	01752-668000	263,100	£1,813	Tracey Lee
PORTSMOUTH	023-9282 2251	215,133	£1,666	David Williams
Reading	0118-937 3787	163,203	£1,900	Peter Sloman
Redcar and Cleveland	0164-277 4774	136,718	£1,920	Amanda Skelton, CBE
Rutland	01572-722577	39,697	£2,043	Helen Briggs
Shropshire	0345-678 9000	320,274	£1,779	Clive Wright
Slough	01753-475111	149,112	£1,642	Josie Wragg
South Gloucestershire	01454-868009	279,027	£1,853	Dave Perry
SOUTHAMPTON	023-8083 3000	282,644	£1,805	Sandy Hopkins
Southend-on-Sea	01702-215000	182,463	£1,655	Alison Griffin
Stockton-on-Tees	01642-393939	197,213	£1,932	Neil Schneider
STOKE-ON-TRENT	01782-234567	255,833	£1,598	David Sidaway
Swindon	01793-463000	221,996	£1,755	Susie Kemp
Telford and Wrekin	01952-380000	177,799	£1,704	Richard Partington
Thurrock	01375-652652	172,525	£1,553	Lyn Carpenter
Torbay	01803-201201	135,780	£1,809	Steve Parrock
Warrington	01925-443322	209,547	£1,747	Prof. Steven Broomhead
West Berkshire	01635-42400	158,527	£1,843	Nick Carter
Wiltshire	0300-456 0100	498,064	£1,855	C. Brand; A. Cunningham; T. Herbert
Windsor and Maidenhead	01628-683800	150,906	£1,330	Duncan Sharkey
Wokingham	0118-974 6000	167,979	£1,819	Susan Parsonage
YORK	01904-551550	209,893	£1,668	Mary Weastell

* *Source:* Office for National Statistics – *Mid-2018 Population Estimates* (Crown copyright)

† Band D council tax bill for 2019–20 inclusive of adult social care and parish precepts

‡ Or equivalent postholder

§ Under the Isles of Scilly Clause the council has additional functions to other unitary authorities

Councils in CAPITAL LETTERS have city status

SINGLE-TIER & COUNTY COUNCIL AREAS IN ENGLAND

1 Stockton-on-Tees
2 Middlesbrough
3 Blackpool
4 Blackburn
  with Darwen
5 Bolton
6 Bury
7 Rochdale
8 Salford
9 Oldham
10 Liverpool
11 Knowsley
12 St Helens
13 Halton
14 Warrington
15 Trafford
16 Manchester
17 Tameside
18 Stockport
19 Nottingham
20 Telford and
  Wrekin
21 Wolverhampton

22 Walsall
23 Sandwell
24 Dudley
25 Birmingham
26 Solihull
27 Coventry
28 Peterborough
29 South Glos
30 Bristol
31 Bath and
  NE Somerset
32 Windsor and
  Maidenhead
33 Slough
34 Reading
35 Wokingham
36 Bracknell Forest
37 Thurrock
38 Southend
39 Medway
40 Plymouth
41 Torbay

LONDON

1 Hillingdon
2 Harrow
3 Barnet
4 Enfield
5 Waltham Forest
6 Redbridge
7 Barking and Dagenham
8 Havering
9 Ealing
10 Brent
11 Camden
12 Haringey
13 Islington
14 Hackney
15 Newham
16 Hounslow
17 Hammersmith and Fulham

18 Kensington and Chelsea
19 City of Westminster
20 City of London
21 Tower Hamlets
22 Richmond upon Thames
23 Wandsworth
24 Lambeth
25 Southwark
26 Lewisham
27 Greenwich
28 Bexley
29 Kingston upon Thames
30 Merton
31 Sutton
32 Croydon
33 Bromley

LONDON

The Greater London Council was abolished in 1986 and London was divided into 32 borough councils, which have a status similar to the metropolitan borough councils in the rest of England, and the City of London Corporation.

In March 1998 the government announced proposals for a Greater London Authority (GLA) covering the area of the 32 London boroughs and the City of London, which would comprise a directly elected mayor and a 25-member assembly. A referendum was held in London on 7 May 1998 and 72 per cent of voters balloted in favour of the GLA. A London mayor was elected on 4 May 2000 and the authority assumed its responsibilities on 3 July 2000 (see also Regional Government).

LONDON BOROUGH COUNCILS

The London boroughs have whole council elections every four years, in the year immediately following the county council election year. The most recent elections took place on 3 May 2018.

The borough councils have responsibility for the following functions: building regulations, cemeteries and crematoria, consumer protection, education, youth employment, environmental health, electoral registration, food, drugs, housing, leisure services, libraries, local planning, local roads, museums, parking, recreation (parks, playing fields, swimming pools), refuse collection and street cleaning, social services, town planning and traffic management.

LONDON BOROUGH COUNCILS

Council	Telephone	Pop.*	Council Tax†	Chief Executive‡
Barking and Dagenham	020-8592 4500	211,998	£1,556	Chris Naylor
Barnet	020-8359 2000	392,140	£1,545	John Hooton
Bexley	020-8303 7777	247,258	£1,679	Jackie Belton
Brent	020-8937 1234	330,795	£1,583	Carolyn Downs
Bromley	020-8464 3333	331,096	£1,537	Ade Adetosoye, OBE (interim)
Camden	020-7974 4444	262,226	£1,563	Jenny Rowlands
CITY OF LONDON CORPORATION	020-7606 3030	8,706	£973	John Barradell, OBE
Croydon	020-8726 6000	385,346	£1,717	Jo Negrini
Ealing	020-8825 5000	341,982	£1,512	Paul Najsarek
Enfield	020-8379 1000	333,869	£1,632	Ian Davis
Greenwich	020-8854 8888	286,186	£1,490	Debbie Warren
Hackney	020-8356 5000	279,665	£1,455	Tim Shields
Hammersmith and Fulham	020-8748 3020	185,426	£1,083	Kim Dero
Haringey	020-8489 0000	270,624	£1,640	Zina Etheridge
Harrow	020-8863 5611	250,149	£1,785	Sean Harriss
Havering	01708-434343	257,810	£1,729	Andrew Blake-Herbert
Hillingdon	01895-250111	304,824	£1,460	Fran Beasley
Hounslow	020-8583 2000	270,782	£1,547	Niall Bolger
Islington	020-7527 2000	239,142	£1,490	Lesley Seary
Kensington and Chelsea	020-7361 3000	156,197	£1,208	Barry Quirk, CBE
Kingston upon Thames	020-8547 5000	175,470	£1,872	Ian Thomas, CBE
Lambeth	020-7926 1000	325,917	£1,445	Andrew Travers
Lewisham	020-8314 6000	303,536	£1,584	vacant
Merton	020-8274 4901	206,186	£1,553	Ged Curran
Newham	020-8430 2000	352,005	£1,331	Althea Loderick
Redbridge	020-8554 5000	303,858	£1,626	Andy Donald
Richmond upon Thames	020-8891 1411	196,904	£1,804	Paul Martin
Southwark	020-7525 5000	317,256	£1,387	Eleanor Kelly
Sutton	020-8770 5000	204,525	£1,694	Helen Bailey
Tower Hamlets	020-7364 5000	317,705	£1,340	Will Tuckley
Waltham Forest	020-8496 3000	276,700	£1,694	Martin Esom
Wandsworth	020-8871 6000	326,474	£770	Paul Martin
WESTMINSTER	020-7641 6000	255,324	£755	Stuart Love

* Source: Office for National Statistics – Mid-2018 Population Estimates (Crown copyright)
† Band D council tax bill for 2019–20 inclusive of adult social care and parish precepts
‡ Or equivalent postholder
Councils in CAPITAL LETTERS have city status

CITY OF LONDON CORPORATION

The City of London Corporation is the local authority for the City of London. Its legal definition is the 'Mayor and Commonalty and Citizens of the City of London'. It is governed by the court of common council, which consists of the lord mayor, 24 other aldermen and 100 common councilmen. The lord mayor and two sheriffs are nominated annually by the City guilds (the livery companies) and elected by the court of aldermen. Aldermen and councilmen are elected from the 25 wards into which the City is divided; councilmen must stand for re-election every four years. The council is a legislative assembly, and there are no political parties.

The corporation has the same functions as the London borough councils. In addition, it runs the City of London Police; is the health authority for the Port of London; has health control of animal imports throughout Greater London, including at Heathrow airport; owns and manages public open spaces throughout Greater London; runs the central criminal court; and runs Billingsgate, New Spitalfields and Smithfield markets.

The City of London is the historic centre at the heart of London known as 'the square mile', around which the vast metropolis has grown over the centuries. The City's residential population was 8,706 at the mid-2018 estimate and in addition, around 400,000 people work in the City. The City is an international financial and business centre, generating about £30bn a year for the British economy. It includes the head offices of the principal banks, insurance companies and mercantile houses, in addition to buildings ranging from the historic Roman Wall and the 15th-century Guildhall, to the massive splendour of St Paul's Cathedral and the architectural beauty of Wren's spires.

The City of London was described by Tacitus in AD 62 as 'a busy emporium for trade and traders'. Under the Romans it became an important administration centre and hub of the road system. Little is known of London in Saxon times, when it formed part of the kingdom of the East Saxons. In 886 Alfred recovered London from the Danes and reconstituted it a burgh under his son-in-law. In 1066 the citizens submitted to William the Conqueror who in 1067 granted them a charter, which is still preserved, establishing them in the rights and privileges they had hitherto enjoyed.

THE MAYORALTY

The mayoralty was probably established about 1189, the first mayor being Henry Fitz Ailwyn who filled the office for 23 years and was succeeded by Fitz Alan (1212–14). A new charter was granted by King John in 1215, directing the mayor to be chosen annually, which has been done ever since, though in early times the same individual often held the office more than once. A familiar instance is that of 'Whittington, thrice Lord Mayor of London' (in reality four times: 1397, 1398, 1406 and 1419); and many modern cases have occurred. The earliest instance of the phrase 'lord mayor' in English is in 1414. It was used more generally in the latter part of the 15th century and became invariable from 1535 onwards. At Michaelmas the liverymen in Common Hall choose two aldermen who have served the office of sheriff for presentation to the Court of Aldermen, and one is chosen to be lord mayor for the following mayoral year.

LORD MAYOR'S DAY

The lord mayor of London was previously elected on the feast of St Simon and St Jude (28 October), and from the time of Edward I, at least, was presented to the King or to the Barons of the Exchequer on the following day, unless that day was a Sunday. The day of election was altered to 16 October in 1346, and after some further changes was fixed for

Michaelmas Day in 1546, but the ceremonies of admittance and swearing-in of the lord mayor continued to take place on 28 and 29 October respectively until 1751. In 1752, at the reform of the calendar, the lord mayor was continued in office until 8 November, the 'new style' equivalent of 28 October. The lord mayor is now presented to the lord chief justice at the royal courts of justice on the second Saturday in November to make the final declaration of office, having been sworn in at Guildhall on the preceding day. The procession to the royal courts of justice is popularly known as the Lord Mayor's Show.

REPRESENTATIVES

Aldermen are mentioned in the 11th century and their office is of Saxon origin. They were elected annually between 1377 and 1394, when an act of parliament of Richard II directed them to be chosen for life. Aldermen now serve a six-year term of office before submitting themselves for re-election.

The Common Council was, at an early date, substituted for a popular assembly called the *Folkmote*. At first only two representatives were sent from each ward, but now each of the City's 25 wards is represented by an alderman and at least two Common Councilmen (the number depending on the size of the ward). Common Councilmen are elected every four years at all-out ward elections.

OFFICERS

Sheriffs were Saxon officers; their predecessors were the *wicreeves* and *portreeves* of London and Middlesex. At first they were officers of the Crown, and were named by the Barons of the Exchequer; but Henry I (in 1132) gave the citizens permission to choose their own sheriffs, and the annual election of sheriffs became fully operative under King John's charter of 1199. The citizens lost this privilege, as far as the election of the sheriff of Middlesex was concerned, by the Local Government Act 1888; but the liverymen continue to choose two sheriffs of the City of London, who are appointed on Midsummer Day and take office at Michaelmas.

The office of chamberlain is an ancient one, the first contemporary record of which is 1237. The town clerk (or common clerk) is first mentioned in 1274.

ACTIVITIES

The work of the City of London Corporation is assigned to a number of committees which make decisions on behalf of the Court of Common Council or which make recommendations for decisions by the court. The committees are extensive given the diverse services delivered by the City Corporation and include: Audit and Risk Management; Barbican Centre; Barbican Residential; Board of Governors of the City of London Freeman's School, City of London School, City of London School for Girls and the Guildhall School of Music and Drama; City Bridge Trust; Community and Children's Services; Culture, Heritage and Libraries; Education; Epping Forest and Commons; Establishment; Finance; Freedom Applications; Gresham (City Side); Hampstead Heath; Highgate Wood and Queen's Park; Health and Wellbeing; Investment; Licensing; Markets; Open Spaces and City Gardens; Pensions Board; Planning and Transportation; Police; Policy and Resources; Port Health and Environmental Services; Standards; and West Ham Park. There are numerous other sub-committees which report to the City of London Corporation's committees.

The City's estate, in the possession of which the City of London Corporation differs from other municipalities, is largely managed by the property investment board.

The Honourable the Irish Society, which manages the City Corporation's estates in Ulster, consists of a governor, two other aldermen and 12 common councilmen.

THE LORD MAYOR 2019–20

The Rt. Hon. the Lord Mayor, William Russell*
*Executive Director of Mansion House and the Central Criminal
Court,* Vic Annells

* Provisional

THE SHERIFFS 2019–20

Alderman Michael Mainelli (Broad Street); Christopher
Hayward

OFFICERS, ETC

Town Clerk, John Barradell
Chamberlain, Peter Kane
Chief Commoner (2019), Tom Hoffman
Clerk, The Honourable the Irish Society, H. E. J. Montgomery,
MBE

THE ALDERMEN

with office held and date of appointment to that office

Name and Ward	Common Councilman	Alderman	Sheriff	Lord Mayor
Ian Luder, *Castle Baynard*	1998	2005	2007	2008
Nicholas Anstee, *Aldersgate*	1987	1996	2003	2009
Sir David Wootton, *Langbourn*	2002	2005	2009	2011
Sir Roger Gifford, *Cordwainer*	–	2004	2008	2012
Sir Alan Yarrow, *Bridge & Bridge Wt.*	–	2007	2011	2014
Dr Sir Andrew Parmley, *Vintry*	1992	2001	2014	2016
Sir Charles Bowman, *Lime Street*	–	2013	2015	2017
Peter Estlin, *Coleman Street*	–	2013	2016	2018
William Russell, *Bread Street*	–	2013	2016	2019

All the above have passed the Civic Chair

	Common Councilman	Alderman	Sheriff
Alison Gowman, *Dowgate*	1991	2002	–
David Graves, *Cripplegate*	–	2008	–
John Garbutt, *Walbrook*	–	2009	–
Timothy Hailes, *Bassishaw*	–	2013	2017
Prof. Michael Mainelli, *Broad Street*	–	2013	2019
Vincent Keaveny, *Farringdon Wn.*	–	2013	2018
Baroness Scotland of Asthal, QC, *Bishopsgate*	–	2015	–
Robert Howard, *Cornhill*	2011	2015	–
Alistair King, *Queenhithe*	–	2016	–
Gregory Jones, QC, *Farringdon Wt.*	2013	2017	–
Prem Goyal, *Portsoken*	2017	2017	–
Nicholas Lyons, *Tower*	2017	2017	–
Emma Edhem, *Candlewick*	2018	2018	–
Robert Hughes-Penney, *Cheap*	–	2018	–
Susan Langley, Aldgate	–	2018	–
Bronek Masojada, Billingsgate	–	2019	–

THE COMMON COUNCIL

Deputy: each common councilman so described serves as
deputy to the alderman of her/his ward.

Abrahams, G. C. (2000)	*Farringdon Wt.*
Absalom, *Deputy* J. D. (1994)	*Farringdon Wt.*
Addy, C. K. (2017)	*Farringdon Wt.*
Ali, M. (2017)	*Portsoken*
Ameer, R. B. (2017)	*Vintry*
Anderson, R. K. (2013)	*Aldersgate*
Barr, A. R. M. (2017)	*Cordwainer*
Barrow, *Deputy* D. G. F. (2007)	*Aldgate*
Bastow, A. M. (2017)	*Aldersgate*
Bell, M. (2017)	*Farringdon Wn.*
Bennett, *Deputy* J. A. (2005)	*Broad Street*
Bennett, P. G. (2016)	*Walbrook*
Bensted-Smith, N. M. (2014)	*Cheap*
Boden, C. P. (2013)	*Castle Baynard*
Bostock, R. M. (2017)	*Cripplegate*
Bottomley, *Deputy* K. D. F. (2015)	*Bridge & Bridge Wt.*
Bradshaw, *Deputy* D. J. (1991)	*Cripplegate Wn.*
Broeke, T. (2017)	*Cheap*
Cassidy, *Deputy* M. J., CBE (1980)	*Coleman Street*
Chadwick, *Deputy* R. A. H., OBE (1994)	*Tower*
Chapman, *Deputy* J. D. (2006)	*Langbourn*
Christian, D. G. (2016)	*Lime Street*
Clementi, T. C. (2017)	*Lime Street*
Colthurst, H. N. A. (2013)	*Lime Street*
Crossan, R. P. (2017)	*Aldersgate*
Dostalova, K. H. (2013)	*Farringdon Wn.*
Duckworth, S. D., OBE (2000)	*Bishopsgate Wn.*
Dunphy, P. G. (2009)	*Cornhill*
Durcan, J. M. (2017)	*Cripplegate*
Edwards, J. E. (2019)	*Farringdon Wn.*
Everett, *Deputy* K. M. (1984)	*Candlewick*
Fairweather, A. H. (2016)	*Tower*
Fernandes, S. A. (2009)	*Coleman Street*
Fletcher, J. W. (2011)	*Portsoken*
Fredericks, M. B. (2008)	*Tower*
Graham, T. (2019)	*Cordwainer*
Haines, C. W. (2017)	*Queenhithe*
Haines, *Deputy* Revd S. D. (2005)	*Cornhill*
Harrower, G. G. (2015)	*Bassishaw*
Hayward, C. M. (2013)	*Broad Street*
Hill, C. (2017)	*Farringdon Wn.*
Hoffman, *Deputy* T. D. D. (2002)	*Vintry*
Holmes, A. (2013)	*Farringdon Wn.*
Hudson, M. (2007)	*Castle Baynard*
Hyde, *Deputy* W. (2011)	*Bishopsgate Wt.*
Ingham Clark, *Deputy* J. (2013)	*Billingsgate*
James, *Deputy* C. (2008)	*Farringdon Wn.*
Jones, *Deputy* H. L. M. (2004)	*Portsoken*
Joshi, S. J. (2018)	*Bishopsgate*
Knowles-Cutler, A. (2017)	*Castle Baynard*
Lawrence, G. A. (2002)	*Farringdon Wt.*
Levene, T. C. (2017)	*Bridge and Bridge Wt.*
Littlechild, V. (2009)	*Cripplegate Wn.*
Lloyd-Owen, N. M. C. (2018)	*Castle Baynard*
Lodge, O. A. W., TD (2009)	*Bread Street*
Lord, *Deputy* C. E., OBE (2001)	*Farringdon Wt.*
Martinelli, P. N. (2013)	*Farringdon Wt.*
Mayer, A. P. (2017)	*Bishopsgate*
Mayhew, J. P. (1996)	*Aldersgate*
McGuinness, *Deputy* C. S. (1997)	*Castle Baynard*
McMurtie, A. S. (2013)	*Coleman Street*
Mead, W., OBE (1997)	*Farringdon Wt.*
Merrett, *Deputy* R. A. (2009)	*Bassishaw*
Meyers, A. G. D. (2017)	*Aldgate*
Mooney, *Deputy* B. D. F. (1998)	*Queenhithe*
Morris, H. F. (2008)	*Aldgate*
Moss, *Deputy* A. M. (2013)	*Cheap*
Moys, S. D. (2001)	*Aldgate*
Murphy, B. D. (2017)	*Bishopsgate*
Nash, *Deputy* J. C., OBE (1983)	*Aldersgate*
Newman, B. P., CBE (1989)	*Aldersgate*
Packham, G. D. (2013)	*Castle Baynard*
Patel, D. (2013)	*Aldgate*
Pearson, S. J. (2017)	*Cripplegate*
Petrie, J. (2018)	*Billingsgate*
Pimlott, W. (2017)	*Cripplegate*
Pleasance, J. L. (2013)	*Langbourn*
Pollard, *Deputy* J. H. G. (2002)	*Dowgate*
Priest, H. J. S. (2009)	*Castle Baynard*

Pritchard, J. P. (2017) — *Portsoken*
Quilter, S. D. (1998) — *Cripplegate Wt.*
Regan, *Deputy* R. D., OBE (1998) — *Farringdon Wn.*
Rogula, *Deputy* E. (2008) — *Lime Street*
de Sausmarez, H. J. (2015) — *Candlewick*
Sayed, R. (2017) — *Farringdon Wt.*
Scott, (Chief Commoner) J. G. S. (1999) — *Broad Street*
Seaton, I. C. N. (2009) — *Cornhill*
Sells, O. M., QC (2017) — *Farringdon Wt.*
Shilson, *Deputy*, G. R. E. (2009) — *Bread Street*
Simons, J. L. (2004) — *Castle Baynard*
Sleigh, *Deputy* T. C. C. (2013) — *Bishopsgate Wt.*
Smith, G. M. (2013) — *Farringdon Wn.*
Snyder, *Deputy* Sir Michael (1986) — *Cordwainer*
Thompson, D. J. (2004) — *Aldgate*
Tomlinson, *Deputy* J. (2004) — *Cripplegate Wt.*
Tumbridge, J. R. (2009) — *Tower*
Upton, J. W. D. (2017) — *Farringdon Wt.*
Wheatley, M. R. P. H. D. (2013) — *Dowgate*
Woodhouse, *Deputy* P. J. (2013) — *Langbourn*
Wright, D. L. (2019) — *Coleman Street*

THE CITY GUILDS (LIVERY COMPANIES)

The livery companies of the City of London grew out of early medieval religious fraternities and began to emerge as trade and craft guilds, retaining their religious aspect, in the 12th century. From the early 14th century, only members of the trade and craft guilds could call themselves citizens of the City of London. The guilds began to be called livery companies, because of the distinctive livery worn by the most prosperous guild members on ceremonial occasions, in the late 15th century.

By the early 19th century the power of the companies within their trades had begun to wane, but those wearing the livery of a company continued to play an important role in the government of the City of London. Liverymen still have the right to nominate the Lord Mayor and sheriffs, and most members of the Court of Common Council are liverymen.

The constitution of the livery companies has been unchanged for centuries. There are three ranks of membership: freemen, liverymen and assistants. A person can become a freeman by patrimony (through a parent having been a freeman); by servitude (through having served an apprenticeship to a freeman); or by redemption (by purchase).

Election to the livery is the prerogative of the company, who can elect any of its freemen as liverymen. Assistants are usually elected from the livery and form a court of assistants which is the governing body of the company. The master (in some companies called the prime warden) is elected annually from the assistants.

The register for 2019–20 lists 26,001 liverymen of the guilds entitled to vote at elections at common hall.

The order of precedence, omitting extinct companies, is given in parentheses after the name of each company in the list below. In certain companies the election of master or prime warden for the year does not take place until the autumn. In such cases the master or prime warden for 2018–19, rather than 2019–20, is given.

The Twelve Great Companies are given in order of civic precedence and appear first in the list below; the remaining guilds are listed in alphabetical order. Parish clerks and watermen and lightermen have requested to remain with no livery and are marked with a '*'

MERCERS (1). *Hall*, Mercers' Hall, 6 Frederick's Place, London EC2R 8AB *Livery*, 245.
Clerk, Rob Abernethy *Master*, Mark Aspinall

GROCERS (2). *Hall*, Grocers' Hall, Princes Street, London EC2R 8AD *Livery*, 370.
Clerk, Brig. Greville Bibby, CBE *Master*, Rupert Uloth
DRAPERS (3). *Hall*, Drapers' Hall, Throgmorton Avenue, London EC2N 2DQ *Livery*, 300.
Clerk, Col. Richard Winstanley, OBE *Master*, Timothy Orchard
FISHMONGERS (4). *Hall*, Fishmongers' Hall, London Bridge, London EC4R 9EL *Livery*, 369.
Clerk, Cdre Toby Williamson, MVO, RN
Prime Warden, David Jones
GOLDSMITHS (5). *Hall*, Goldsmiths' Hall, Foster Lane, London EC2V 6BN *Livery*, 285.
Clerk, Sir David Reddaway, KCMG, MBE
Prime Warden, Dr Timothy Schroder, FSA
MERCHANT TAYLORS (6/7). *Hall*, Merchant Taylors' Hall, 30 Threadneedle Street, London EC2R 8JB *Livery*, 356.
Clerk, Rear-Adm. John Clink, CBE
Master, Nicholas Hunter Jones
SKINNERS (6/7). *Hall*, Skinners' Hall, 8 Dowgate Hill, London EC4R 2SP *Livery*, 400.
Clerk, Maj.-Gen. Andrew Kennett, CB, CBE
Master, Johnny Aisher
HABERDASHERS (8). *Hall*, Haberdashers' Hall, 18 West Smithfield, London EC1A 9HQ *Livery*, 320.
Clerk, Cdre Philip Thicknesse, RN *Master*, Caroline Davis
SALTERS (9). *Hall*, Salters' Hall, 4 London Wall Place, London EC2Y 5DE *Livery*, 176.
Clerk, vacant *Master*, Alan Wordie
IRONMONGERS (10). *Hall*, Ironmongers' Hall, Shaftesbury Place, London EC2Y 8AA *Livery*, 150.
Clerk, Col. Charlie Knaggs, OBE *Master*, John Biles
VINTNERS (11). *Hall*, Vintners' Hall, Upper Thames Street, London EC4V 3BG *Livery*, 398.
Clerk, Brig. Jonathan Bourne-May *Master*, Christopher Davey
CLOTHWORKERS (12). *Hall*, Clothworkers' Hall, Dunster Court, London EC3R 7AH *Livery*, 255.
Clerk, Joss Stuart-Grumbar *Master*, Sir Jonathan Portal, Bt
ACTUARIES (91). 2nd Floor, 2 London Wall Place, London EC2Y 5AU *Livery*, 220.
Clerk, Lyndon Jones *Master*, Fiona Morrison
AIR PILOTS AND AIR NAVIGATORS (81). Air Pilots House, 52A Borough High Street, London SE1 1XN *Livery*, 600.
Clerk, Paul Tacon *Master*, Malcolm White, OBE
APOTHECARIES (58). *Hall*, Apothecaries' Hall, 14 Black Friars Lane, London EC4V 6EJ *Livery*, 1,215.
Clerk, Nick Royle *Master*, Prof. Martin Rossor
ARBITRATORS (93). 28 The Meadway, Cuffley EN6 4ES *Livery*, 180.
Clerk, Biagio Fraulo *Master*, Rt. Hon. Sir Gary Hickinbottom
ARMOURERS AND BRASIERS (22). *Hall*, Armourers' Hall, 81 Coleman Street, London EC2R 5BJ *Livery*, 135.
Clerk, Peter Bateman *Master*, Mike Goulette
ARTS SCHOLARS (110). 5 Queen Anne's Gate, White House Walk, Farnham GU9 9AN *Livery*, 85.
Clerk, Lt.-Col. Chris Booth *Master*, Georgina Gough
BAKERS (19). *Hall*, Bakers' Hall, 9 Harp Lane, London EC3R 6DP *Livery*, 250.
Clerk, Lance Whitehouse *Master*, Christopher Freeman
BARBERS (17). *Hall*, Barber-Surgeons' Hall, Monkwell Square, London EC2Y 5BL *Livery*, 230.
Clerk, Col. Malachy Doran *Master*, Malcolm Roberts
BASKETMAKERS (52). 30 Cadgwith Place, Port Solent, Portsmouth PO6 4TD *Livery*, 300.
Clerk, Fiona Janczur *Prime Warden*, Christopher Hipkins, FCSI
BLACKSMITHS (40). Painters' Hall, 9 Little Trinity Lane, London EC4V 2AD *Livery*, 246.
Clerk, Jill Moffatt *Prime Warden*, Dr Robin McNeill Love
BOWYERS (38). Fosters Lodge, Duck Street, Warminster BA12 7AL *Livery*, 99.
Clerk, Lt.-Col. Tony Marinos *Master*, Ian Spring
BREWERS (14). *Hall*, Brewers' Hall, Aldermanbury Square, London EC2V 7HR *Livery*, 200.
Clerk, Col. Michael O'Dwyer, OBE *Master*, Simon Theakston

BRODERERS (48). Orchard House, Vicarage Lane, Steeple Ashton BA14 6HH *Livery*, 118.
Clerk, Bill Aldridge *Master*, Michael Stevens
BUILDERS MERCHANTS (88). 4 College Hill, London EC4R 2RB *Livery*, 210.
Clerk, Virginia Rounding *Master*, Dame Fiona Woolf, DBE
BUTCHERS (24). 4th Floor, 14 Charterhouse Square, London EC1M 6AX *Livery*, 635.
Clerk, Maj.-Gen. Jeff Mason, MBE, RM *Master*, Graham Baker
CARMEN (77). Plaisterers' Hall, 1 London Wall, London EC2Y 5JU *Livery*, 500.
Clerk, Walter Gill *Master*, Stephen Britt
CARPENTERS (26). *Hall*, Carpenters' Hall, 1 Throgmorton Avenue, London EC2N 2JJ *Livery*, 150.
Clerk, Brig. Tim Gregson, MBE
Master, His Hon. Peter Birts, QC
CHARTERED ACCOUNTANTS (86). 35 Ascot Way, Bicester OX26 1AG *Livery*, 365.
Clerk, Jonathan Grosvenor *Master*, John Cardnell
CHARTERED ARCHITECTS (98). 53 Lychgate Drive, Horndean PO8 9QE *Livery*, 159.
Clerk, Phil Gibbs *Master*, Barry Munday
CHARTERED SECRETARIES AND ADMINISTRATORS (87). 3rd Floor, Saddlers' Hall, 40 Gutter Lane, London EC2V 6BR *Livery*, 220.
Clerk, Keith Povey *Master*, Christina Parry, OBE
CHARTERED SURVEYORS (85). 75 Meadway Drive, Horsell, Woking GU21 4TF *Livery*, 340.
Clerk, Amanda Jackson *Master*, John Woodman
CLOCKMAKERS (61). 1 Throgmorton Avenue, London EC2N 2BY *Livery*, 270.
Clerk, Lt.-Col. Oliver Bartrum, MBE *Master*, Joanna Migdal
COACHMAKERS AND COACH-HARNESS MAKERS (72). The Old Barn, Church Lane, Glentham LN8 2EL *Livery*, 500.
Clerk, Cdr Mark Leaning, RN *Master*, Graham Cole, CBE
CONSTRUCTORS (99). 5 Delft Close, Southampton SO31 7TQ *Livery*, 170.
Clerk, Kim Tyrrell *Master*, Mike Parrett
COOKS (35). 18 Solent Drive, Warsash SO31 9HB *Livery*, 75.
Clerk, Vice-Adm. Peter Wilkinson, CB, CVO
Master, Cdre David Smith, MBE, RN
COOPERS (36). *Hall*, Coopers' Hall, 13 Devonshire Square, London EC2M 4TH *Livery*, 260.
Clerk, Cdr Stephen White,, RN *Master*, Perry Bousfield
CORDWAINERS (27). Clothworkers' Hall, Dunster Court, London EC3R 7AH *Livery*, 188.
Clerk, Penny Graham *Master*, Col. Nigel Easton, QVRM, TD
CURRIERS (29). Oak Lodge, 4 Greenhill Lane, Wimborne BH21 2RN *Livery*, 112.
Clerk, Adrian Rafferty *Master*, Mary McNeill
CUTLERS (18). *Hall*, Cutlers' Hall, Warwick Lane, London EC4M 7BR *Livery*, 100.
Clerk, Rupert Meacher
Master, His Hon. Peter Beaumont, CBE, QC
DISTILLERS (69). 1 The Sanctuary, London SW1P 3JT *Livery*, 260.
Clerk, Edward Macey-Dare *Master*, Martin Riley
DYERS (13). *Hall*, Dyers' Hall, 10 Dowgate Hill, London EC4R 2ST *Livery*, 140.
Clerk, Russell Vaizey, FCA *Prime Warden*, A. Crockatt
EDUCATORS (109). 8 Little Trinity Lane, London EC4V 2AN *Livery*, 200.
Clerk, Christian Jensen *Master*, Dr Elisabeth Goodwin, OBE
ENGINEERS (94). Saddlers' House, 44 Gutter Lane, London EC2V 6BR *Livery*, 312.
Clerk, Col. David Swann, CBE *Master*, Cdre Barry Brooks, RN
ENVIRONMENTAL CLEANERS (97). 94 Coniston Road, BR1 4JB *Livery*, 189.
Clerk, Matthew Johnson *Master*, Barrie Torbett
FAN MAKERS (76). Skinners' Hall, 8 Dowgate Hill, London EC4R 2SP *Livery*, 188.
Clerk, Martin Davies *Master*, Dr Jeffrey Bines

FARMERS (80). *Hall*, The Farmers' and Fletchers' Hall, 3 Cloth Street, London EC1A 7LD *Livery*, 350.
Clerk, Graham Bamford *Master*, Rosemary Carne, DSc
FARRIERS (55). 19 Queen Street, Chipperfield, Kings Langley WD4 9BT *Livery*, 324.
Clerk, Charlotte Clifford *Master*, Steven Wilson
FELTMAKERS (63). Post Cottage, Hook RG29 1DA *Livery*, 190.
Clerk, Maj. Jollyon Coombs *Master*, William Gammell
FIREFIGHTERS (103). 3rd Floor, Wax Chandlers' Hall, 6 Gresham Street, London EC2V 7AD *Livery*, 210.
Clerk, Steven Tamcken *Master*, Andrew Mayes
FLETCHERS (39). *Hall*, The Farmers' and Fletchers' Hall, 3 Cloth Street, London EC1A 7LD *Livery*, 150.
Clerk, Kate Pink *Master*, Duncan Garland
FOUNDERS (33). *Hall*, Founders' Hall, 1 Cloth Fair, London EC1A 7JQ *Livery*, 170.
Clerk, Andrew Bell *Master*, Martin Shenton
FRAMEWORK KNITTERS (64). The Grange, Walton Road, Lutterworth LE17 5RU *Livery*, 185.
Clerk, Shaun Mackaness *Master*, Ian Grundy
FRUITERERS (45). The Old Bakery, Bull Lane, Ketton PE9 3TB *Livery*, 283.
Clerk, John Grant *Master*, Cheryl Roux
FUELLERS (95). Skinners' Hall, 8 Dowgate Hill, London EC4R 2SP *Livery*, 164.
Clerk, Bill Walworth, CBE *Master*, Shravan Joshi
FURNITURE MAKERS (83). *Hall*, Furniture Makers' Hall, 12 Austin Friars, London EC2N 2HE *Livery*, 230.
Clerk, Jonny Westbrooke *Master*, Dids Macdonald, OBE
GARDENERS (66). Ingrams, Ingram's Green, Midhurst GU29 0LJ *Livery*, 287.
Clerk, Maj. Jeremy Herrtage *Master*, Margaret Holland Prior
GIRDLERS (23). *Hall*, Girdlers' Hall, Basinghall Avenue, London EC2V 5DD *Livery*, 80.
Clerk, Brig. Murray Whiteside, OBE
Master, Charlie Crowther-Smith
GLASS SELLERS (71). 238 Nelson Road, Whitton *Livery*, 179.
Clerk, Paul Wenham *Master*, Richard Katz
GLAZIERS AND PAINTERS OF GLASS (53). *Hall*, Glaziers' Hall, 9 Montague Close, London SE1 9DD *Livery*, 164.
Clerk, Alison Evans *Master*, Andy Lane
GLOVERS (62). Seniors Farmhouse, Semley, Shaftesbury SP7 9AX *Livery*, 260.
Clerk, Mark Butler *Master*, Roger De Courcey
GOLD AND SILVER WYRE DRAWERS (74). Lye Green Forge, Lye Green, Crowborough TN6 1UU *Livery*, 276.
Clerk, Cdr Mark Dickens *Master*, Malcolm Craig
GUNMAKERS (73). The Proof House, 48–50 Commercial Road, London E1 1LP *Livery*, 358.
Clerk, Adrian Mundin, MVO
Master, Roderick Richmond-Watson
HACKNEY CARRIAGE DRIVERS (104). London, PO Box 75581, London SW11 9LU *Livery*, 105.
Clerk, Belinda Tregear *Master*, Phillip Davis
HORNERS (54). 12 Coltsfoot Close, Ixworth IP31 2NJ *Livery*, 225.
Clerk, Jonathan Mead, FRSA
Master, Dr David Giachardi, FRSC
INFORMATION TECHNOLOGISTS (100). *Hall*, Information Technologists' Hall, 39A Bartholomew Close, London EC1A 7JN *Livery*, 365.
Clerk, Susan Hoefling *Master*, Lady Wendy Parmley
INNHOLDERS (32). *Hall*, Innholders' Hall, 30 College Street, London EC4R 2RH *Livery*, 180.
Clerk, Charles Henty *Master*, Revd Canon Bill Christianson
INSURERS (92). First Floor, 21 Lombard Street, London EC3V 9AH *Livery*, 260.
Clerk, Sarah Clark *Master*, Terry Masters
INTERNATIONAL BANKERS (106). 12 Austin Friars, London EC2N 2HE *Livery*, 210.
Clerk, Nicholas Westgarth *Master*, Mark Sismey-Durrant

JOINERS AND CEILERS (41). 75 Meadway Drive, Horsell, Woking GU21 4TF *Livery*, 135.
Clerk, Amanda Jackson *Master*, Chris Chivers

LAUNDERERS (89). 9 Montague Close, London SE1 9DD *Livery*, 175.
Clerk, Margaret Campbell *Master*, Jack Strachan, MBE

LEATHERSELLERS (15). 7 St Helen's Place, London EC3A 6AB *Livery*, 150.
Clerk, David Santa-Olalla, DSO, MC *Master*, Christopher Barrow

LIGHTMONGERS (96). 1 Manor House Garden, E11 2RU *Livery*, 148.
Clerk, Phillip Hyde *Master*, Stephen Thomas

LORINERS (57). 30 Elm Park, Royal Wootton Bassett SN4 7TA *Livery*, 400.
Clerk, Honor Page *Master*, Peter English

MAKERS OF PLAYING CARDS (75). 256 St David's Square, London E14 3WE *Livery*, 150.
Clerk, David Barrett *Master*, Mark Winston

MANAGEMENT CONSULTANTS (105). Skinners' Hall, 8 Dowgate Hill, London EC4R 2SP *Livery*, 180.
Clerk, Julie Fox *Master*, John Corneille

MARKETORS (90). Plaisterers' Hall, One London Wall, London EC2Y 5JU *Livery*, 257.
Clerk, John Hammond *Master*, Richard Christou

MASONS (30). 8 Little Trinity Lane, London EC4V 2AN *Livery*, 163.
Clerk, Maj. Giles Clapp *Master*, Christopher Radmore

MASTER MARINERS (78). *Hall*, HQS Wellington, Temple Stairs, London WC2R 2PN *Livery*, 188.
Clerk, Cdre Angus Menzies, RN *Master*, Capt. Robert Booth

MUSICIANS (50). 1 Speed Highwalk, Barbican EC2Y BDX *Livery*, 420.
Clerk, Hugh Lloyd *Master*, Michael Lewin

NEEDLEMAKERS (65). PO Box 73635, London SW14 9BY *Livery*, 200.
Clerk, Fiona Sedgwick *Master*, Anthony de Lacey

PAINTER-STAINERS (28). *Hall*, Painters' Hall, 9 Little Trinity Lane, London EC4V 2AD *Livery*, 250.
Clerk, Christopher Twyman *Master*, Julian Briant

PATTENMAKERS (70). 3 The High Street, Sutton Valence ME17 3AG *Livery*, 203.
Clerk, Col. R. W. Murfin, TD *Master*, Dr David Best

PAVIORS (56). Paviors' House, Charterhouse, London EC1M 6AN *Livery*, 285.
Clerk, John Freestone *Master*, Sue Illman

PEWTERERS (16). *Hall*, Pewterers' Hall, Oat Lane, London EC2V 7DE *Livery*, 140.
Clerk, Capt. Paddy Watson, RN *Master*, Richard Parsons

PLAISTERERS (46). *Hall*, Plaisterers' Hall, 1 London Wall, London EC2Y 5JU *Livery*, 230.
Clerk, Nigel Bamping *Master*, Alderman Alison Gowman

PLUMBERS (31). Carpenters' Hall, 1 Throgmorton Avenue, London EC2N 2JJ *Livery*, 350.
Clerk, Adrian Mumford *Master*, Dr Peter Rumley

POULTERS (34). 20 Waltham Road, Woodford Green 1G8 8DN *Livery*, 160.
Clerk, Julie Pearce *Master*, David Walker

SADDLERS (25). *Hall*, Saddlers' Hall, 40 Gutter Lane, London EC2V 6BR *Livery*, 83.
Clerk, Brig. Philip Napier, OBE *Prime Warden*, Nicholas Mason

SCIENTIFIC INSTRUMENT MAKERS (84). Glaziers' Hall, 9 Montague Close, London SE1 9DD *Livery*, 185.
Clerk, Dr Misha Hebel *Master*, Kenneth Sanders

SCRIVENERS (44). HQS Wellington, Temple Stairs, Victoria Embankment, London WC2R 2PN *Livery*, 196.
Clerk, Giles Cole *Master*, David Philip

SECURITY PROFESSIONALS (108). 4 Holmere Farm Cottages, Goose Green, Ashill IP25 7AS *Livery*, 178.
Clerk, Patricia Boswell *Master*, Michael Barley

SHIPWRIGHTS (59). Ironmonger's Hall, Shaftesbury Place, London EC2Y 8AA *Livery*, 435.
Clerk, Lt.-Col. Richard Cole-Mackintosh *Prime Warden*, John Denholm

SOLICITORS (79). 4 College Hill, London EC4R 2RB *Livery*, 350.
Clerk, Linzi James *Master*, John Wotton

SPECTACLE MAKERS (60). Apothecaries' Hall, Black Friars Lane, London EC4V 6EL *Livery*, 380.
Clerk, Helen Perkins *Master*, Huntly Taylor

STATIONERS AND NEWSPAPER MAKERS (47). *Hall*, Stationers' Hall, Ave Maria Lane, London EC4M 7DD *Livery*, 540.
Clerk, William Alden, MBE *Master*, Trevor Fenwick

TALLOW CHANDLERS (21). *Hall*, Tallow Chandlers' Hall, 4 Dowgate Hill, London EC4R 2SH *Livery*, 180.
Clerk, Brig. David Homer, MBE *Master*, Anthony Green

TAX ADVISERS (107). 10 Deena Close, Queen's Drive W3 0HR *Livery*, 158.
Clerk, Stephen Henderson *Master*, Marcus Fincham

TIN PLATE WORKERS (ALIAS WIRE WORKERS) (67). PO Box 71002, London W4 9FH *Livery*, 180.
Clerk, Dr Piers Baker *Master*, Laurence Mutkin

TOBACCO PIPE MAKERS AND TOBACCO BLENDERS (82). 14 Montpelier Road, Sutton SM1 4QE *Livery*, 133.
Clerk, Sandra Stocker *Master*, Andrew Golding

TURNERS (51). Skinner's Hall, 8 Dowgate Hill, London EC4R 2SP *Livery*, 200.
Clerk, Alex Robertson *Master*, Andrew Sindall

TYLERS AND BRICKLAYERS (37). 3 Farmers Way, Seer Green HP9 2YY *Livery*, 200.
Clerk, John Brooks *Master*, Dr Michel Saminaden

UPHOLDERS (49). Pembroke Lodge, 162 Tonbridge Road, Hildenborough TN11 9HP *Livery*, 160.
Clerk, Susan Nevard *Master*, Anthony Demby

WATER CONSERVATORS (102). The Lark, 2 Bell Lane, Worlington, Bury St Edmunds IP28 8SE *Livery*, 201.
Clerk, Ralph Riley *Master*, Mark Lane

WAX CHANDLERS (20). *Hall*, Wax Chandlers' Hall, 6 Gresham Street, London EC2V 7AD *Livery*, 216.
Clerk, Richard Moule *Master*, Joan Beavington

WEAVERS (42). Saddlers' House, Gutter Lane, London EC2V 6BR *Livery*, 128.
Clerk, John Snowdon *Upper Bailiff*, Peter Towler

WHEELWRIGHTS (68). 90 Fernside Road, London SW12 8LJ *Livery*, 218.
Clerk, Susie Morris *Master*, James Tucker

WOOLMEN (43). 153 Leathwaite Road, SW11 6RW *Livery*, 160.
Clerk, Duncan Crole *Master*, Mark Johnson

WORLD TRADERS (101). 13 Hall Gardens, Colney Heath, St. Albans AL4 0QF *Livery*, 216.
Clerk, Gaye Duffy *Master*, Dr Edwina Moreton, OBE

PARISH CLERKS (No Livery*). Acreholt, 33 Medstead Road, Beech, Alton GU34 4AD *Members*, 88.
Clerk, Alana Coombes *Master*, Nick Hull

WATERMEN AND LIGHTERMEN (No Livery*). *Hall*, Watermen's Hall, 16–18 St Mary at Hill, London EC3R 8EF *Craft Owning Freemen*, 380.
Clerk, Colin Middlemiss *Master*, Tony Maynard

WALES
Cymru

The principality of Wales (Cymru) occupies the extreme west of the central southern portion of the island of Great Britain, with a total area of 20,736 sq. km (8,006 sq. miles). It is bordered in the north by the Irish Sea, in the south by the Bristol Channel, in the east by the English counties of Cheshire West and Chester, Shropshire, Herefordshire and Gloucestershire, and in the west by St George's Channel.

Across the Menai Straits is Ynys Mon (Isle of Anglesey) (715 sq. km/276 sq. miles), communication with which is facilitated by the Menai Suspension Bridge (305m/1,000ft long) built by Telford in 1826, and by the Britannia Bridge (351m/1,151ft), a two-tier road and rail truss arch design, rebuilt in 1972 after a fire destroyed the original tubular railway bridge built by Stephenson in 1850. Holyhead harbour, on Holy Isle (north-west of Anglesey), provides ferry services to Dublin (113km/70 miles).

The Local Government (Wales) Act 1994 abolished the two-tier structure of eight county and 37 district councils which had existed since 1974, and replaced it, from 1 April 1996, with 22 unitary authorities. The new authorities were elected in May 1995. Each unitary authority inherited all the functions of the previous county and district councils, except fire services (which are provided by three combined fire authorities, composed of representatives from the unitary authorities) and national parks (which are the responsibility of three independent national park authorities).

POPULATION
The population at the mid-2018 estimate was 3,138,631 (men 1,547,309; women 1,591,322). The average density of the population at the mid-2018 estimate was 151 persons per sq. km (392 per sq. mile).

COMMUNITY COUNCILS
In Wales communities are the equivalent of parishes in England. Unlike England, where many areas are not in any parish, communities have been established for the whole of Wales, 870 communities in all. Community meetings may be convened as and when desired.

Community or town councils exist in around 730 of the communities and further councils may be established at the request of a community meeting. Community councils have broadly the same range of powers as English parish councils. Community councillors are elected for a term of four years.

ELECTIONS
Elections usually take place every four years; the last elections took place on 4 May 2017.

FINANCE
Total budgeted revenue expenditure for 2019–20 is £8.3bn, an increase of 2.4 per cent on 2018–19. Total budget requirement, which excludes expenditure financed by specific and special government grants and any use of reserves, is £6.5bn. This comprises revenue support grant of £3.3bn, support from the national non-domestic rate pool of £1.1bn, police grant of £214m and £1.9bn to be raised through council tax. The non-domestic rating multiplier for Wales for 2019–20 is 52.6p. The average Band D council tax levied in Wales for 2019–20 is £1,591, comprising unitary authorities £1,294, police and crime commissioners £260 and community councils £36.

EXPENDITURE
Local authority budgeted revenue expenditure for 2019–20 is:

Service	£ million
Education	2,719.2
Social services	1,918.1
Housing*	1,094.3
Local environmental services	378.5
Roads and transport	270.2
Libraries, culture, heritage, sport & recreation	191.2
Planning, economic & community development	76.8
Council tax collection	29.8
Debt financing	295.5
Central administrative & other revenue expenditure	383.0
Police	774.0
Fire	158.1
National parks	18.5
Gross revenue expenditure	8,307.2
Less specific & special government grants	(1,899.0)
Net revenue expenditure	6,408.2
Less appropriations from reserves	(140.7)
Council tax reduction scheme	269.9
BUDGET REQUIREMENT	6,537.4

* Includes housing benefit and provision for the homeless, not council owned housing

RELIEF
Wales is a country of extensive tracts of high plateau and shorter stretches of mountain ranges deeply dissected by river valleys. Lower-lying ground is largely confined to the coastal belt and the lower parts of the valleys. The highest mountains are those of Snowdonia in the north-west (Snowdon, 1,085m/3,559ft and Aran Fawddwy, 906m/2,971ft). Snowdonia is also home to Cader Idris (Pen y Gadair, 892m/2,928ft). Other high peaks are to be found in the Cambrian range (Plynlimon, 752m/2,467ft), and the Black Mountains, Brecon Beacons and Black Forest ranges in the south-east (Pen y Fan, 886m/2,906ft; Waun Fâch, 811m/2,660ft; Carmarthen Van, 802m/2,630ft).

HYDROGRAPHY
The principal river in Wales is the Severn, which flows from the slopes of Plynlimon to the English border. The Wye (209km/130 miles) also rises on the slopes of Plynlimon. The Usk (90km/56 miles) flows into the Bristol Channel through Gwent. The Dee (113km/70 miles) rises in Bala Lake and flows through the Vale of Llangollen, where an aqueduct (built by Telford in 1805) carries the Pontcysyllte branch of the Shropshire Union Canal across the valley. The estuary of the Dee is the navigable portion; it is 23km (14 miles) in length and about 8km (5 miles) in breadth. The Towy (109km/68 miles), Teifi (80km/50 miles), Taff (64km/40 miles), Dovey (48km/30 miles), Taf (40km/25 miles) and Conway (39km/24 miles) are wholly Welsh rivers.

The largest natural lake is Bala (Llyn Tegid) in Gwynedd, nearly 7km (4 miles) long and 1.6km (1 mile) wide. Lake Vyrnwy is an artificial reservoir, about the size of Bala, and forms the water supply of Liverpool; Birmingham's water is supplied from reservoirs in the Elan and Claerwen valleys.

FLAG
The flag of Wales, the Red Dragon *(Y Ddraig Goch)*, is a red dragon on a field divided by white over green *(per fess argent and vert a dragon passant gules)*. The flag was augmented in 1953 by a royal badge on a shield encircled with a riband

bearing the words *Ddraig Goch Ddyry Cychwyn* and imperially crowned, but this augmented flag is rarely used.

WELSH LANGUAGE

At the 2011 census the percentage of people, aged three years and over, recorded as able to speak Welsh was:

Blaenau Gwent	7.8	Neath Port Talbot	15.3
Bridgend	9.7	Newport	9.3
Caerphilly	11.2	Pembrokeshire	19.2
Cardiff	11.1	Powys	18.6
Carmarthenshire	43.9	Rhondda Cynon Taf	12.3
Ceredigion	47.3	Swansea	11.4
Conwy	27.4	Torfaen	9.8
Denbighshire	24.6	Vale of Glamorgan	10.8
Flintshire	13.2	Wrexham	12.9
Gwynedd	65.4	Ynys Mon	
Merthyr Tydfil	8.9	(Isle of Anglesey)	57.2
Monmouthshire	9.9	*Total in Wales*	19.0

EARLY HISTORY

The earliest inhabitants of whom there is any record appear to have been subdued or exterminated by the Goidels (a people of Celtic race) in the Bronze Age. A further invasion of Celtic Brythons and Belgae followed in the ensuing Iron Age. The Roman conquest of southern Britain and Wales was for some time successfully opposed by Caratacus (Caractacus or Caradog), chieftain of the Catuvellauni and son of Cunobelinus (Cymbeline). South-east Wales was subjugated and the legionary fortress at Caerleon-on-Usk established by around AD 75–7; the conquest of Wales was completed by Agricola around AD 78. Communications were opened up by the construction of military roads from Chester to Caerleon-on-Usk and Caerwent, and from Chester to Conwy (and thence to Carmarthen and Neath). Christianity was introduced in the fourth century, during the Roman occupation.

ANGLO-SAXON ATTACKS

The Anglo-Saxon invaders of southern Britain drove the Celts into the mountain stronghold of Wales, and into Strathclyde (Cumberland and south-west Scotland) and Cornwall, giving them the name of *Waelisc* (Welsh), meaning 'foreign'. The West Saxons' victory of Deorham (AD 577) isolated Wales from Cornwall and the battle of Chester (AD 613) cut off communication with Strathclyde and northern Britain. In the eighth century the boundaries of the Welsh were further restricted by the annexations of Offa, King of Mercia, and counter-attacks were largely prevented by the construction of an artificial boundary from the Dee to the Wye (Offa's Dyke).

In the ninth century Rhodri Mawr (844–878) united the country and successfully resisted further incursions of the Saxons by land and raids of Norse and Danish pirates by sea, but at his death his three provinces of Gwynedd (north), Powys (central) and Deheubarth (south) were divided among his three sons, Anarawd, Mervyn and Cadell. Cadell's son Hywel Dda ruled a large part of Wales and codified its laws but the provinces were not united again until the rule of Llewelyn ap Seisyllt (husband of the heiress of Gwynedd) from 1018 to 1023.

THE NORMAN CONQUEST

After the Norman conquest of England, William I created palatine counties along the Welsh frontier, and the Norman barons began to make encroachments into Welsh territory. The Welsh princes recovered many of their losses during the civil wars of Stephen's reign (1135–54), and in the early 13th

century Owen Gruffydd, prince of Gwynedd, was the dominant figure in Wales. Under Llywelyn ap Iorwerth (1194–1240) the Welsh united in powerful resistance to English incursions and Llywelyn's privileges and *de facto* independence were recognised in the Magna Carta. His grandson, Llywelyn ap Gruffydd, was the last native prince; he was killed in 1282 during hostilities between the Welsh and English, allowing Edward I of England to establish his authority over the country. On 7 February 1301, Edward of Caernarvon, son of Edward I, was created Prince of Wales, a title subsequently borne by the eldest son of the sovereign.

Strong Welsh national feeling continued, expressed in the early 15th century in the rising led by Owain Glyndwr, the situation was altered by the accession to the English throne in 1485 of Henry VII of the Welsh House of Tudor. Wales was politically annexed by England under the Act of Union of 1535, which extended English laws to the principality and gave it parliamentary representation for the first time.

EISTEDDFOD

The Welsh are a distinct nation, with a language and literature of their own; the national bardic festival (Eisteddfod), instituted by Prince Rhys ap Griffith in 1176, is still held annually.

PRINCIPAL CITIES

There are six cities in Wales (with date city status conferred): Bangor (pre-1900), Cardiff (1905), Newport (2002), St Asaph (2012), St David's (1994) and Swansea (1969).

Cardiff and Swansea have also been granted lord mayoralties.

CARDIFF

Cardiff *(Caerdydd)*, at the mouth of the rivers Taff, Rhymney and Ely, is the capital city of Wales. The city has changed dramatically in recent years following the regeneration of Cardiff Bay and construction of a barrage, which has created a permanent freshwater lake and waterfront for the city. As the capital city, Cardiff is home to the National Assembly for Wales and is a major administrative, retail, business and cultural centre.

The city is home to many fine buildings, including the City Hall, Cardiff Castle, Llandaff Cathedral, the National Museum of Wales, university buildings, law courts and the Temple of Peace and Health. The Millennium Stadium opened in 1999 and has hosted high-profile events since 2001.

SWANSEA

Swansea *(Abertawe)* is a seaport with a population of 239,023 at the 2011 census. The Gower peninsula was brought within the city boundary under local government reform in 1974.

The principal buildings are the Norman castle (rebuilt *c.*1330), the Royal Institution of South Wales, founded in 1835 (including library), the University of Swansea at Singleton and the Guildhall, containing Frank Brangwyn's British Empire panels. The Dylan Thomas Centre, formerly the old Guildhall, was restored in 1995. More recent buildings include the County Hall, the Maritime Quarter Marina, the Wales National Pool and the National Waterfront Museum.

Swansea was chartered by the Earl of Warwick (1158–84), and further charters were granted by King John, Henry III, Edward II, Edward III and James II, Oliver Cromwell and the Marcher Lord William de Breos. It was formally invested with city status in 1969.

LORD-LIEUTENANTS AND HIGH SHERIFFS

Area	Lord-Lieutenant	High Sheriff (2019–20)
Clwyd	Henry Fetherstonhaugh, OBE	Stephanie Catherall
Dyfed	Sara Edwards	Anne Lewis
Gwent	Brig. Robert Aiken, CBE	Dame Claire Clancy, DBE
Gwynedd	Edmund Bailey	Susan Jones
Mid Glamorgan	Prof. Peter Vaughan, QPM	Col. (retd) Wilma Donnelly, CBE, TD
Powys	Tia Jones	David Lloyd Peate
S. Glamorgan	Morfudd Meredith	Dr Isabel Graham
W. Glamorgan	D. Byron Lewis, CVO	Sally Goldstone

LOCAL COUNCILS

Council	Administrative HQ	Telephone	Pop.*	Council Tax†	Chief Executive
Blaenau Gwent	Ebbw Vale	01495-311556	69,713	£1,928	Michelle Morris
Bridgend	Bridgend	01656-643643	144,876	£1,777	Mark Shephard
Caerphilly	Hengoed	01443-815588	181,019	£1,400	Christina Harrhy (interim)
CARDIFF	Cardiff	029-2087 2087	364,248	£1,471	Paul Orders
Carmarthenshire	Carmarthen	01267-234567	187,568	£1,588	Wendy Walters
Ceredigion	Aberaeron	01545-570881	72,992	£1,596	Eifion Evans
Conwy	Conwy	01492-574000	117,181	£1,603	Iwan Davies
Denbighshire	Ruthin	01824-706101	95,330	£1,657	Judith Greenhalgh
Flintshire	Mold	01352-752121	155,593	£1,604	Colin Everett
Gwynedd	Caernarfon	01766-771000	124,178	£1,699	Dilwyn Williams
Merthyr Tydfil	Merthyr Tydfil	01685-725000	60,183	£1,849	Gareth Chapman
Monmouthshire	Cwmbran	01633-644644	94,142	£1,630	Paul Matthews
Neath Port Talbot	Port Talbot	01639-686868	142,906	£1,857	Stephen Phillips
NEWPORT	Newport	01633-656656	153,302	£1,382	Will Godfrey
Pembrokeshire	Haverfordwest	01437-764551	125,055	£1,377	Ian Westley
Powys	Llandrindod Wells	01597-827460	132,447	£1,613	Dr Caroline Turner
Rhondda Cynon Taff	Tonypandy	01443-425005	240,131	£1,741	Chris Bradshaw
SWANSEA	Swansea	01792-636000	246,466	£1,618	Phil Roberts
Torfaen	Pontypool	01495-762200	93,049	£1,620	Alison Ward
Vale of Glamorgan	Barry	01446-700111	132,165	£1,552	Rob Thomas
Wrexham	Wrexham	01978-292000	136,126	£1,481	Ian Barncroft
Ynys Mon (Isle of Anglesey)	Ynys Mon	01248-750057	69,961	£1,572	Dr Gwynne Jones

* Source: Office for National Statistics – Mid-2018 Population Estimates (Crown copyright)
† Band D council tax bill for 2019–20.
Councils in CAPITAL LETTERS have city status

Key	Council	Key	Council
1	Anglesey (Ynys Mon)	12	Merthyr Tydfil
2	Blaenau Gwent	13	Monmouthshire
3	Bridgend	14	Neath Port Talbot
4	Caerphilly	15	NEWPORT
5	CARDIFF	16	Pembrokeshire
6	Carmarthenshire	17	Powys
7	Ceredigion	18	Rhondda Cynon Taff
8	Conwy	19	SWANSEA
9	Denbighshire	20	Torfaen
10	Flintshire	21	Vale of Glamorgan
11	Gwynedd	22	Wrexham

SCOTLAND

Scotland occupies the northern portion of the main island of Great Britain and includes the Inner and Outer Hebrides, Orkney, Shetland and many other islands. It lies between 60° 51′ 30″ and 54° 38′ N. latitude and between 1° 45′ 32″ and 6° 14′ W. longitude, with England to the south-east, the North Channel and the Irish Sea to the south-west, the Atlantic Ocean on the north and west, and the North Sea on the east.

The greatest length of the mainland (Cape Wrath to the Mull of Galloway) is 441km (274 miles), and the greatest breadth (Buchan Ness to Applecross) is 248km (154 miles). The customary measurement of the island of Great Britain is from the site of John o' Groats house, near Duncansby Head, Caithness, to Land's End, Cornwall, a total distance of 970km (603 miles) in a straight line and approximately 1,448km (900 miles) by road.

The Local Government etc (Scotland) Act 1994 abolished the two-tier structure of nine regional and 53 district councils which had existed since 1975 and replaced it, from 1 April 1996, with 29 unitary authorities on the mainland; the three islands councils remained. The new authorities were elected in April 1995.

In July 1999 the Scottish parliament assumed responsibility for legislation on local government.

The total area of Scotland is 77,911 sq. km (30,081 sq. miles).

POPULATION

The population at the mid-2018 estimate was 5,438,100 (men 2,648,751; women 2,789,349). The average density of the population at the mid-2018 estimate was 70 persons per sq. km (181 per sq. mile).

ELECTIONS

The unitary authorities consist of directly elected councillors. The Scottish Local Government (Elections) Act 2002 moved elections from a three-year to a four-year cycle. The last local authority elections took place in May 2017.

FUNCTIONS

The functions of the councils and islands councils are: education; social work; strategic planning; the provision of infrastructure such as roads; consumer protection; flood prevention; coast protection; valuation and rating; the police and fire services; civil defence; electoral registration; public transport; registration of births, deaths and marriages; housing; leisure and recreation; development and building control; environmental health; licensing; allotments; public conveniences; and the administration of district courts.

COMMUNITY COUNCILS

Scottish community councils differ from those in England and Wales. Their purpose as defined in statute is to ascertain and express the views of the communities they represent, and to take in the interests of their communities such action as appears to be expedient or practicable. Around 1,200 community councils have been established under schemes drawn up by local authorities in Scotland.

FINANCE

For 2019–20 Scotland's local authorities set a net revenue expenditure budget of £12.6bn for spending on all services, a 4.1 per cent increase compared with 2018–19; education accounted for 44 per cent of the total budget and social work 27 per cent.

The budgeted net revenue expenditure for 2019–20 of £12.6bn was financed by Scottish government grants (£7.2bn), non-domestic rates (£2.9bn) and council tax (£2.5bn). The remaining £114m was funded from local authority reserves.

The non-domestic rate multiplier or poundage for 2019–20 is 49p. Larger businesses in 2019–20 (rateable value in excess of £51,000) pay a poundage supplement of 2.6p, which contributes towards the cost of the small business bonus scheme. Non-domestic properties with a rateable value of £15,000 or less do not have to pay business rates in 2019–20. The average Band D council tax for 2019–20 is £1,251.

EXPENDITURE

Local authority budgeted net revenue expenditure for 2019–20 is:

Service	£ million
Education	5,557
Social work	3,414
Environmental services	699
Culture & related service	554
Roads & transport	377
Planning & development	221
All other services	698
Non-service expenditure	1,114
TOTAL	12,635

RELIEF

There are three natural orographic divisions of Scotland. The southern uplands have their highest points in Merrick (843m/2,766ft), Rhinns of Kells (814m/2,669ft) and Cairnsmuir of Carsphairn (797m/2,614ft), in the west; and the Tweedsmuir Hills in the east (Broad Law 840m/2,756ft; Dollar Law 817m/2,682ft; Hartfell 808m/2,651ft).

The central lowlands, formed by the valleys of the Clyde, Forth and Tay, divide the southern uplands from the Highlands, which extend from close to the extreme north of the mainland to the central lowlands, and are divided into a northern and a southern system by the Great Glen.

The Grampian Mountains, the southern Highland system, include in the west Ben Nevis (1,345m/4,412ft), the highest point in the British Isles, and in the east the Cairngorm Mountains (Ben Macdui 1,309m/4,296ft; Braeriach 1,295m/4,248ft; Cairn Gorm 1,245m/4,084ft). The north-west Highlands contain the mountains of Wester and Easter Ross (Carn Eige 1,183m/3,880ft; Sgurr na Lapaich 1,151m/3,775ft).

Created, like the central lowlands, by a major geological fault, the Great Glen (97km/60 miles long) runs between Inverness and Fort William, and contains Loch Ness, Loch Oich and Loch Lochy. These are linked to each other and to the north-east and south-west coasts of Scotland by the Caledonian Canal, providing a navigable passage between Moray Firth and the Inner Hebrides.

HYDROGRAPHY

The western coast is fragmented by peninsulas and islands, and indented by fjords (sea-lochs), the longest of which is Loch Fyne (68km/42 miles long) in Argyll. Although the east coast tends to be less fractured and lower, there are several great drowned inlets (firths), including the Firth of Forth, Firth of Tay and the Moray Firth, as well as the Firth of Clyde in the west.

The lochs are the principal hydrographic feature. The largest in Scotland and in Britain is Loch Lomond (70 sq. km/27 sq.

miles), in the Grampian valleys, and the longest and deepest is Loch Ness (39km/24 miles long and 244m/800ft deep), in the Great Glen.

The longest river is the Tay (188km/117 miles), noted for its salmon. It flows into the North Sea, with Dundee on the estuary, which is spanned by the Tay Bridge (3,136m/10,289ft) opened in 1887 and the Tay Road Bridge (2,245m/7,365ft) opened in 1966. Other noted salmon rivers are the Dee (145km/90 miles) which flows into the North Sea at Aberdeen, and the Spey (177km/110 miles), the swiftest flowing river in the British Isles, which flows into the Moray Firth. The Tweed, which gave its name to the woollen cloth produced along its banks, marks in the lower stretches of its 154km (96 mile) course the border between Scotland and England.

The most important river commercially is the Clyde (171km/106 miles), formed by the junction of the Daer and Portrail water, which flows through the city of Glasgow to the Firth of Clyde. During its course it passes over the picturesque Falls of Clyde, Bonnington Linn (9m/30ft), Corra Linn (26m/84ft), Dundaff Linn (3m/10ft) and Stonebyres Linn (24m/80ft), above and below Lanark. The Forth (106km/66 miles), upon which stands Edinburgh, the capital, is spanned by the Forth Railway Bridge (1890), which is 1,625m (5,330ft) long, and the Forth Road Bridge (1964), which has a total length of 1,876m (6,156ft) (over water) and a single span of 914m (3,000ft).

The highest waterfall in Scotland, and the British Isles, is Eas a'Chùal Aluinn with a total height of 201m (658ft), which falls from Glas Bheinn in Sutherland. The Falls of Glomach, on a head-stream of the Elchaig in Wester Ross, have a drop of 113m (370ft).

GAELIC LANGUAGE
According to the 2011 census, 1.1 per cent (58,000 people) of the population of Scotland aged three and over were able to speak the Scottish form of Gaelic. This was a slight decrease from the 1.2 per cent recorded at the 2001 census.

LOWLAND SCOTTISH LANGUAGE
Several regional lowland Scottish dialects, known variously as Scots, Lallans or Doric, are widely spoken. According to the 2011 census, 43 per cent of the population of Scotland aged three and over stated they could do one or a combination of read, write, speak or understand Scots. A question on Scots was not included in the 2001 census.

FLAG
The flag of Scotland is known as the Saltire. It is a white diagonal cross on a blue field (saltire argent in a field azure) and represents St Andrew, the patron saint of Scotland.

THE SCOTTISH ISLANDS

ORKNEY
The Orkney Islands (total area 972 sq. km/376 sq. miles) lie about 10km (six miles) north of the mainland, separated from it by the Pentland Firth. Of the 90 islands and islets (holms and skerries) in the group, about one-third are inhabited.

The total population at the 2011 census was 21,349; the 2011 populations of the islands shown here include those of smaller islands forming part of the same council district.

Mainland, 17,162	Inner Holm, 1
Auskerry, 4	Norh Ronaldsay, 72
Burray, 409	Papa Westray, 90
Eday, 160	Rousay, 216
Egilsay, 26	Sanday, 494
Flotta, 8	Shapinsay, 307
Gairsay, 3	South Ronaldsay, 909
Graemsay, 28	Stronsay, 349

Holm of Grimbister, 3	Westray, 588
Hoy, 419	Wyre, 29

The islands are rich in prehistoric and Scandinavian remains, the most notable being the Stone Age village of Skara Brae, the burial chamber of Maes Howe, the many brochs (towers) and the 12th-century St Magnus Cathedral. Scapa Flow, between the Mainland and Hoy, was the war station of the British Grand Fleet from 1914 to 1919 and the scene of the scuttling of the surrendered German High Seas Fleet (21 June 1919).

Most of the islands are low-lying and fertile, and farming (principally beef cattle) is the main industry. Flotta, to the south of Scapa Flow, is the site of the oil terminal for the Piper, Claymore and Tartan fields in the North Sea.

The capital is Kirkwall (population 7,045) situated on Mainland.

SHETLAND
The Shetland Islands have a total area of 1,427 sq. km (551 sq. miles) and had a population at the 2011 census of 23,167. They lie about 80km (50 miles) north of the Orkneys, with Fair Isle about half way between the two groups. Out Stack, off Muckle Flugga, 1.6km (one mile) north of Unst, is the most northerly part of the British Isles (60° 51′ 30″ N. lat.).

There are over 100 islands, of which 16 are inhabited. Populations at the 2011 census were:

Mainland, 18,765	Muckle Roe, 130
Bressay, 368	Papa Stour, 15
Bruray, 24	Trondra, 135
East Burra, 76	Unst, 632
Fair Isle, 68	Vaila, 2
Fetlar, 61	West Burra, 776
Foula, 38	Whalsay, 1,061
Housay, 50	Yell, 966

Shetland's many archaeological sites include Jarlshof, Mousa and Clickhimin, and its long connection with Scandinavia has resulted in a strong Norse influence on its place names and dialect.

Industries include fishing, knitwear and farming. In addition to the fishing fleet there are fish processing factories, and the traditional handknitting of Fair Isle and Unst is now supplemented with machine-knitted garments. Farming is mainly crofting, with sheep being raised on the moorland and hills of the islands. Since 1970s the islands have been at the centre of the North Sea oil industry, with pipelines from the Brent and Ninian fields running to the terminal at Sullom Voe, one of the largest in Europe. Although much quieter than at the height of oil production in the late 1990s, the terminal marked a milestone 40-year anniversary since first oil in November 2018.

The capital is Lerwick (population 6,958) situated on Mainland. Lerwick is the main centre for supply services for offshore oil exploration and development.

THE HEBRIDES
Until the late 13th century the Hebrides included other Scottish islands in the Firth of Clyde, the peninsula of Kintyre (Argyll), the Isle of Man and the (Irish) Isle of Rathlin. The origin of the name is probably the Greek *Eboudai*, latinised as *Hebudes* by Pliny, and corrupted to its present form. The Norwegian name *Sudreyjar* (Southern Islands) was latinised as *Sodorenses*, a name that survives in the Anglican bishopric of Sodor and Man.

There are over 500 islands and islets, of which about 100 are inhabited, though mountainous terrain and extensive peat bogs mean that only a fraction of the total area is under cultivation. Stone, Bronze and Iron Age settlement has left many remains, including those at Callanish on Lewis, and

Norse colonisation influenced language, customs and place names. Occupations include farming (mostly crofting and stock-raising), fishing and the manufacture of tweeds and other woollens. Tourism is an important part of the economy.

The Inner Hebrides lie off the west coast of Scotland and are relatively close to the mainland. The largest and best-known is Skye (area 1,665 sq. km/643 sq. miles; pop. 10,008; chief town, Portree), which contains the Cuillin Hills (Sgurr Alasdair, 993m/3,257ft), Bla Bheinn (928m/3,046ft), the Storr (719m/2,358ft) and the Red Hills (Beinn na Caillich, 732m/2,403ft). Other islands in the Highland council area include Raasay (pop. 161), Eigg (pop. 83), Muck (pop. 27) and Rhum (pop. 22).

Further south the Inner Hebridean islands include Arran (pop. 4,629), containing Goat Fell (874m/2,868ft); Coll (pop. 195) and Tiree (pop. 653); Colonsay (pop. 124) and Oronsay (pop. 8); Easdale (pop. 59); Gigha (pop. 163); Islay (area 608 sq. km/235 sq. miles; pop. 3,228); Jura (area 414 sq. km/160 sq. miles; pop. 196), with a range of hills culminating in the Paps of Jura (Beinn-an-Oir, 785m/2,576ft, and Beinn Chaolais, 755m/2,477ft); Lismore (pop. 192); Luing (pop. 195); and Mull (area 950 sq. km/367 sq. miles; pop. 2,800; chief town Tobermory), containing Ben More (1,174m/3,852 ft).

The Outer Hebrides, separated from the mainland by the Minch, now form the Eilean Siar (Western Isles) council (area 2,897 sq. km/1,119 sq. miles; pop. 27,684). The main islands are Lewis with Harris (area 1,994 sq. km/770 sq. miles, pop. 21,031), whose chief town, Stornoway, is the administrative seat; North Uist (pop. 1,254); South Uist (pop. 1,754); Benbecula (pop. 1,303) and Barra (pop. 1,174). Other inhabited islands include Great Bernera (252), Berneray (138), Eriskay (143), Grimsay (169), Scalpay (291) and Vatersay (90).

EARLY HISTORY

There is evidence of human settlement in Scotland dating from the third millennium BC, the earliest settlers being Mesolithic hunters and fishermen. Early in the second millennium BC, Neolithic farmers began to cultivate crops and rear livestock; their settlements were on the west coast and in the north, and included Skara Brae and Maeshowe (Orkney). Settlement by the early Bronze Age 'Beaker Folk', so-called from the shape of their drinking vessels, in eastern Scotland dates from about 1800 BC. Further settlement is believed to have occurred from 700 BC onwards, as tribes were displaced from further south by new incursions from the Continent and the Roman invasions from AD 43.

Julius Agricola, the Roman governor of Britain AD 77–84, extended the Roman conquests in Britain by advancing into Caledonia, culminating with a victory at Mons Graupius, probably in AD 84; he was recalled to Rome shortly after and his forward policy was not pursued. Hadrian's Wall, mostly completed by AD 30, marked the northern frontier of the Roman empire except for the period between about AD 144 and 190 when the frontier moved north to the Forth-Clyde isthmus and a turf wall, the Antonine Wall, was manned.

After the Roman withdrawal from Britain, there were centuries of warfare between the Picts, Scots, Britons, Angles and Vikings. The Picts, generally accepted to be descended from the indigenous Iron Age people of northern Scotland, occupied the area north of the Forth. The Scots, a Gaelic-speaking people of northern Ireland, colonised the area of Argyll and Bute (the kingdom of Dalriada) in the fifth century AD and then expanded eastwards and northwards. The Britons, speaking a Brythonic Celtic language, colonised Scotland from the south from the first century BC; they lost control of south-eastern Scotland (incorporated into the kingdom of Northumbria) to the Angles in the early seventh century but retained Strathclyde (south-western Scotland and Cumbria). Viking raids from the late eighth century were followed by Norse settlement in the western and northern isles, Argyll, Caithness and Sutherland from the mid-ninth century onwards.

UNIFICATION

The union of the areas which now comprise Scotland began in AD 843 when Kenneth MacAlpin, king of the Scots from c.834, also became king of the Picts, joining the two lands to form the kingdom of Alba (comprising Scotland north of a line between the Forth and Clyde rivers). Lothian, the eastern part of the area between the Forth and the Tweed, seems to have been leased to Kenneth II of Alba (reigned 971–995) by Edgar of England c.973, and Scottish possession was confirmed by Malcolm II's victory over a Northumbrian army at Carham c.1016. At about this time Malcolm II (reigned 1005–34) placed his grandson Duncan on the throne of the British kingdom of Strathclyde, bringing under Scots rule virtually all of what is now Scotland.

The Norse possessions were incorporated into the kingdom of Scotland from the 12th century onwards. An uprising in the mid-12th century drove the Norse from most of mainland Argyll. The Hebrides were ceded to Scotland by the Treaty of Perth in 1266 after a Norwegian expedition in 1263 failed to maintain Norse authority over the islands. Orkney and Shetland fell to Scotland in 1468–9 as a pledge for the unpaid dowry of Margaret of Denmark, wife of James III, although Danish claims of suzerainty were relinquished only with the marriage of Anne of Denmark to James VI in 1590.

From the 11th century, there were frequent wars between Scotland and England over territory and the extent of England's political influence. The failure of the Scottish royal line with the death of Margaret of Norway in 1290 led to disputes over the throne which were resolved by the adjudication of Edward I of England. He awarded the throne to John Balliol in 1292 but Balliol's refusal to be a puppet king led to war. Balliol surrendered to Edward I in 1296 and Edward attempted to rule Scotland himself. Resistance to Scotland's loss of independence was led by William Wallace, who defeated the English at Stirling Bridge (1297), and Robert Bruce, crowned in 1306, who held most of Scotland by 1311 and routed Edward II's army at Bannockburn (1314). England recognised the independence of Scotland in the Treaty of Northampton in 1328. Subsequent clashes include the disastrous battle of Flodden (1513) in which James IV and many of his nobles fell.

THE UNION

In 1603 James VI of Scotland succeeded Elizabeth I on the throne of England (his mother, Mary Queen of Scots, was the great-granddaughter of Henry VII), his successors reigning as sovereigns of Great Britain. Political union of the two countries did not occur until 1707.

THE JACOBITE REVOLTS

After the abdication (by flight) in 1688 of James VII and II, the crown devolved upon William III (grandson of Charles I) and Mary II (elder daughter of James VII and II). In 1689 Graham of Claverhouse roused the Highlands on behalf of James VII and II, but died after a military success at Killiecrankie. After the death of Anne (younger daughter of James VII and II), the throne devolved upon George I (great-grandson of James VI and I). In 1715, armed risings on behalf of James Stuart (the Old Pretender, son of James VII and II) led to the indecisive battle of Sheriffmuir, and the Jacobite movement died down until 1745, when Charles Stuart (the Young Pretender) defeated the Royalist troops at Prestonpans and advanced to Derby (1746). From Derby, Charles Stuart's forces fell back on the defensive and were finally crushed at Culloden (16 April 1746) by an army led by the Duke of Cumberland, son of George II.

PRINCIPAL CITIES

ABERDEEN

Aberdeen, 209km (130 miles) north-east of Edinburgh, received its charter as a Royal Burgh in 1124. Scotland's third largest city, Aberdeen lies between two rivers, the Dee and the Don, facing the North Sea; the city has a strong maritime history and is today a major centre for offshore oil exploration and production. It is also an ancient university town and distinguished research centre.

Places of interest include King's College, St Machar's Cathedral, Brig o' Balgownie, Duthie Park and Winter Gardens, Hazlehead Park, Kirk of St Nicholas, Mercat Cross, Marischal College and Marischal Museum, Provost Skene's House, Gordon Highlanders Museum, Aberdeen Science Centre (formerly Satrosphere), and Aberdeen Maritime Museum. Closed in 2015 for a major £30m redevelopment, Aberdeen Art Gallery, which first opened in 1885 and comprises the Cowdray Hall concert venue and the city's Remembrance Hall will reopen in November 2019.

DUNDEE

The Royal Burgh of Dundee is situated on the north bank of the Tay estuary. The city's port and dock installations are important to the offshore oil industry and the airport also provides servicing facilities.

The unique City Churches – three churches under one roof, together with the 15th-century St Mary's Tower – are the most prominent architectural feature. Dundee is home to two historic ships: the Dundee-built RRS *Discovery* which took Capt. Scott to the Antarctic lies alongside Discovery Quay, and the frigate *Unicorn*, the only British-built wooden warship still afloat, is moored in Victoria Dock. Places of interest include Mills Observatory, the Tay road and rail bridges, Dundee Contemporary Arts centre, The McManus (Dundee's art gallery and museum), Claypotts Castle, Broughty Castle, Verdant Works (textile heritage centre) and the Dundee Science Centre (formerly Sensation).

EDINBURGH

Edinburgh is the capital city and seat of government in Scotland. The new Scottish parliament building designed by Enric Miralles was completed in 2004 and is open to visitors. The city is built on a group of hills and both the Old and New Towns are inscribed on the UNESCO World Cultural and Natural Heritage List for their cultural significance.

Other places of interest include the castle, which houses the Stone of Scone and also includes St Margaret's Chapel, the oldest building in Edinburgh, and near it, the Scottish National War Memorial; the Palace of Holyroodhouse, the Queen's official residence in Scotland; Parliament House, the present seat of the judicature; Princes Street; three universities (Edinburgh, Heriot-Watt, Napier); St Giles' Cathedral; St Mary's (Scottish Episcopal) Cathedral (Sir George Gilbert Scott); General Register House (Robert Adam); the National Library of Scotland, the Signet Library; the Royal Scottish Academy and National Galleries Scotland – comprising the Scottish National Gallery, the Scottish National Portrait Gallery and the Scottish National Gallery of Modern Art.

GLASGOW

Glasgow, a Royal Burgh, is Scotland's largest city and its principal commercial and industrial centre. The city occupies the north and south banks of the Clyde, formerly one of the chief commercial estuaries in the world.

The chief buildings are the 13th-century Gothic cathedral, the university (Sir George Gilbert Scott), the City Chambers, the Royal Concert Hall, St Mungo Museum of Religious Life and Art, Pollok House, Kelvingrove Art Gallery and Museum, the Gallery of Modern Art, the Riverside Museum: Scotland's Museum of Transport and Travel (Zaha Hadid), Mitchell Library and the Burrell Collection museum, which is currently undergoing a major refurbishment and is due to re-open in Spring 2021. The iconic School of Art designed by Charles Rennie Mackintosh (first half completed 1899; second half, 1909) is being rebuilt after it was devastated by two fires; the first in 2014 and the second in 2018, which left only the shell remaining. The city is home to the Royal Scottish National Orchestra, Scottish Opera, Scottish Ballet, BBC Scotland and Scottish Television (STV).

Inverness was granted city status in 2000, Sterling in 2002 and Perth in 2012. Aberdeen, Dundee, Edinburgh and Glasgow have also been granted lord mayoralty/lord provostship.

LORD-LIEUTENANTS

Title	Name
Aberdeen City*	Lord Provost Barney Crockett
Aberdeenshire	James Ingleby, CVO
Angus	Georgiana Osborne, CVO
Argyll and Bute	Patrick Stewart, MBE
Ayrshire & Arran	Iona McDonald
Banffshire	Clare Russell, CVO
Berwickshire	Jeannna Swan
Caithness	Viscount Thurso, PC
Clackmannanshire	Lt.-Col. Johnny Stewart
Dumfries	Lady Fiona MacGregor of MacGregor (Fiona Armstrong)
Dunbartonshire	Rear-Adm. Michael Gregory, OBE
Dundee City*	Lord Provost Ian Borthwick
East Lothian	Maj. Michael Williams, MBE
Edinburgh City*	Rt. Hon. Lord Provost Frank Ross
Eilean Siar (Western Isles)	Donald Martin
Fife	Robert Balfour
Glasgow City*	Rt. Hon. Lord Provost Eva Bolander
Inverness-shire	Donald Cameron of Lochiel, CVO
Kincardineshire	Carol Kinghorn
Lanarkshire	Lady Susan Haughey, CBE
Midlothian	Sir Robert Clerk, Bt., OBE
Moray	Lt.-Col. Grenville Johnston, CVO, OBE, TD
Nairn	George Asher
Orkney	William Spence
Perth & Kinross	Brig. Sir Melville Jameson, KCVO, CBE
Renfrewshire	Col. Peter McCarthy
Ross & Cromarty	Joanie Whiteford
Roxburgh, Ettrick & Lauderdale	Duke of Buccleuch and Queensberry, KT, KBE, FRSE
Shetland	Robert Hunter
Stirling & Falkirk	Alan Simpson, OBE
Sutherland	Dr Monica Main
The Stewartry of Kirkcudbright	Elizabeth Gilroy
Tweeddale	Prof. Sir Hew Strachan
West Lothian	Moira Niven, MBE
Wigtown	John Ross, CBE

* The Lord Provosts of the four cities of Aberdeen, Dundee, Edinburgh and Glasgow are Lord-Lieutenants *ex officio* for those districts

LOCAL COUNCILS

Council	Administrative Headquarters	Telephone	Pop.*	Council Tax†	Chief Executive
ABERDEEN	Aberdeen	0300-020 0291	227,560	£1,324	Angela Scott
Aberdeenshire	Aberdeen	0845-608 1207	261,470	£1,241	Jim Savege
Angus	Forfar	0345-277 7778	116,040	£1,171	Margo Williamson
Argyll and Bute	Lochgilphead	01546-602127	86,260	£1,309	Cleland Sneddon
Clackmannanshire	Alloa	01259-450000	51,400	£1,267	Nikki Bridle
Dumfries and Galloway	Dumfries	030-3333 3000	148,790	£1,166	Gavin Stevenson
DUNDEE	Dundee	01382-434000	148,750	£1,316	David Martin
East Ayrshire	Kilmarnock	01563-576000	121,840	£1,312	Fiona Lees
East Dunbartonshire	Kirkintilloch	0300-123 4510	108,330	£1,259	Gerry Cornes
East Lothian	Haddington	01620-827827	105,790	£1,242	Angela Leitch
East Renfrewshire	Giffnock	0141-577 3000	95,170	£1,230	Lorraine McMillan
EDINBURGH	Edinburgh	0131-200 2000	518,500	£1,277	Andrew Kerr
Eilean Siar (Western Isles)	Stornoway	01851-703773	26,830	£1,138	Malcolm Burr
Falkirk	Falkirk	01324-506070	160,340	£1,169	Kenneth Lawrie
Fife	Glenrothes	0345-155 0000	371,910	£1,222	Steve Grimmond
GLASGOW	Glasgow	0141-287 2000	626,410	£1,325	Annemarie O'Donnell
Highland	Inverness	01349-886606	235,540	£1,271	Donna Manson
Inverclyde	Greenock	01475-717171	78,150	£1,293	Aubrey Fawcett
Midlothian	Dalkeith	0131-270 7500	91,340	£1,344	Dr Grace Vickers
Moray	Elgin	01343-543451	95,520	£1,262	Roddy Burns
North Ayrshire	Irvine	01294-310000	135,280	£1,281	Craig Hatton
North Lanarkshire	Motherwell	01698-403200	340,180	£1,165	Des Murray
Orkney	Kirkwall	01856-873535	22,190	£1,153	Alistair Buchan
Perth and Kinross	Perth	01738-475000	151,290	£1,264	Karen Reid
Renfrewshire	Paisley	0300-300 0300	177,790	£1,257	Sandra Black
Scottish Borders	Melrose	01835-824000	115,270	£1,196	Tracey Logan
Shetland	Lerwick	01595-693535	22,990	£1,151	Maggie Sandison
South Ayrshire	Ayr	0300-123 0900	112,550	£1,283	Eileen Howat
South Lanarkshire	Hamilton	0303-123 1015	319,020	£1,168	Lindsay Freeland
STIRLING	Stirling	0845-277 7000	94,330	£1,282	Carol Beattie
West Dunbartonshire	Dumbarton	01389-737000	89,130	£1,234	Joyce White
West Lothian	Livingston	01506-280000	182,140	£1,217	Graham Hope

* Source: Office for National Statistics – Mid-2018 Population Estimates (Crown copyright)
† Average Band D council tax bill 2019–20.
Councils in CAPITAL LETTERS have city status

Key	Council	Key	Council
1	Aberdeen City	17	Inverclyde
2	Aberdeenshire	18	Midlothian
3	Angus	19	Moray
4	Argyll and Bute	20	North Ayrshire
5	City of Edinburgh	21	North Lanarkshire
6	Clackmannanshire	22	Orkney
7	Dumfries and Galloway	23	Perth and Kinross
8	Dundee City	24	Renfrewshire
9	East Ayrshire	25	Scottish Borders
10	East Dunbartonshire	26	Shetland
11	East Lothian	27	South Ayrshire
12	East Renfrewshire	28	South Lanarkshire
13	Falkirk	29	Stirling
14	Fife	30	West Dunbartonshire
15	Glasgow City	31	Western Isles (Eilean Siar)
16	Highland	32	West Lothian

NORTHERN IRELAND

Northern Ireland has a total area of 13,793 sq. km (5,326 sq. miles).

In 2012 a reform programme began to reduce the number of district councils from 26 to 11. The Local Government Act (Northern Ireland) received royal assent on 12 May 2014 providing new governance arrangements for local councils and made transitional provisions for the transfer of staff, assets and liabilities etc to the new 11 councils. On 1 April 2015 additional functions, that were previously the responsibility of the Northern Ireland executive, fully transferred to the new district authorities.

POPULATION
The population of Northern Ireland at the mid-2018 estimate was 1,881,641 (men 926,200; women 955,441). The estimated average density of population at mid-2018 was 136 persons per sq. km (353 per sq. mile).

ELECTIONS
Elections to the 11 councils took place on 22 May 2014.

FUNCTIONS
The councils are responsible for approving business and financial plans, setting domestic and non-domestic rates. Since April 2016 councils have also been responsible for urban regeneration and community development.

The district councils are responsible for:
Direct Service Provision of a wide range of local services, including: building control-inspection and the regulation of new buildings; byelaw enforcement; cemeteries; community centres; cultural facilities; dog control; environmental health; food safety; health and safety; local economic development; local planning; off-street parking (except park and ride schemes); parks, open spaces and playgrounds; public conveniences; recycling and waste management; registration of births, deaths and marriages; sport, leisure and recreational facilities; and street cleaning. District councils also have a role in community development and safety; sports development; summer schemes; and tourism.
Representation: nominating representatives to sit as members of the various statutory bodies responsible for the administration of regional services such as education, health and social services, libraries and road safety committees

FINANCE
Government in Northern Ireland is part-funded by a system of rates, which supplement the Northern Ireland budget from the UK government. The ratepayer receives a combined tax bill consisting of the regional rate, set by the Northern Ireland executive, and the district rate, which is set by each district council. The regional and district rates are both collected by Land and Property Services (part of the Department of Finance). The product of the district rates is paid over to each council while the product of the regional rate supports expenditure by the departments of the executive and assembly.

Since April 2007 domestic rates bills have been based on the capital value of a property, rather than the rental value. The capital value is defined as the price the property might reasonably be expected to realise had it been sold on the open market on 1 January 2005. Non-domestic rates bills are based on the rental value of the property as at 1 April 2013.

Rate bills are calculated by multiplying the property's net annual rental value (in the case of non-domestic property), or capital value (in the case of domestic property), by the regional and district rate poundages respectively.

For 2019–20 the overall average domestic poundage is 0.8302p compared to 0.8016p in 2018–19. The overall average non-domestic rate poundage in 2019–20 is 59.53p compared to 58.40p in 2018–19.

FLAG
The official national flag of Northern Ireland is the Union Flag.

PRINCIPAL CITIES

In addition to Belfast and Londonderry, three other places in Northern Ireland have been granted city status: Armagh (1994), Lisburn (2002) and Newry (2002).

BELFAST
Belfast, the administrative centre of Northern Ireland, is situated at the mouth of the River Lagan at its entrance to Belfast Lough. The city grew to be a great industrial centre, owing to its easy access by sea to Scottish coal and iron.

The principal buildings are of a relatively young age and include the parliament buildings at Stormont, the City Hall, Waterfront Hall, the Law Courts, the Public Library and the Ulster Museum, situated in the botanic gardens. The Metropolitan Arts Centre (MAC), an award-winning arts venue designed by Belfast-based architectural practice Hall McKnight, which is situated opposite St Anne's Cathedral was completed in February 2012 and in March 2012 Titanic Belfast, opened on the banks of the Lagan River on the site of the shipyard where RMS *Titanic* was built and launched. The museum forms the centrepiece of a new mixed-use maritime quarter.

Belfast received its first charter of incorporation in 1613 and was created a city in 1888; the title of lord mayor was conferred in 1892.

LONDONDERRY
Londonderry (originally Derry) is situated on the River Foyle, and has important associations with the City of London. The Irish Society was created by the City of London in 1610, and under its royal charter of 1613 it fortified the city and was for a long time closely associated with its administration. Because of this connection the city was incorporated in 1613 under the new name of Londonderry.

The city is famous for the great siege of 1688–9, when for 105 days the town held out against the forces of James II. The city walls are still intact and form a circuit of 1.6 km (one mile) around the old city.

Interesting buildings are the Protestant cathedral of St Columb's (1633) and the Guildhall, reconstructed in 1912 and containing a number of beautiful stained glass windows, many of which were presented by the livery companies of London.

CONSTITUTIONAL HISTORY

Northern Ireland is subject to the same fundamental constitutional provisions which apply to the rest of the UK. It had its own parliament and government from 1921 to 1972, but after increasing civil unrest the Northern Ireland (Temporary Provisions) Act 1972 transferred the legislative and executive powers of the Northern Ireland parliament and government to the UK parliament and a secretary of state. The

Northern Ireland Constitution Act 1973 provided for devolution in Northern Ireland through an assembly and executive, but a power-sharing executive formed by the Northern Ireland political parties in January 1974 collapsed in May 1974 and Northern Ireland returned to direct rule governance under the provisions of the Northern Ireland Act 1974, placing the Northern Ireland department under the direction and control of the Northern Ireland secretary.

In December 1993 the British and Irish governments published the Joint Declaration, complementing their political talks and making clear that any settlement would need to be founded on principles of democracy and consent.

On 12 January 1998 the British and Irish governments issued a joint document, *Propositions on Heads of Agreement*, proposing the establishment of various new cross-border bodies; further proposals were presented on 27 January. A draft peace settlement was issued by the talks' chair, US Senator George Mitchell, on 6 April 1998 but was rejected by the Unionists the following day. On 10 April agreement was reached between the British and Irish governments and the eight Northern Ireland political parties still involved in the talks (the Good Friday Agreement). The agreement provided for an elected Northern Ireland Assembly, a North/South Ministerial Council, and a British-Irish Council comprising representatives of the British, Irish, Channel Islands and Isle of Man governments and members of the new assemblies for Scotland, Wales and Northern Ireland. Further points included the abandonment of the Republic of Ireland's constitutional claim to Northern Ireland, the decommissioning of weapons, the release of paramilitary prisoners and changes in policing.

The agreement was ratified in referendums held in Northern Ireland and the Republic of Ireland on 22 May 1998. In the UK, the Northern Ireland Act received royal assent in November 1998.

On 28 April 2003 the secretary of state again assumed responsibility for the direction of the Northern Ireland departments on the dissolution of the Northern Ireland Assembly, following its initial suspension from midnight on 14 October 2002. In 2006, following the passing of the Northern Ireland Act, the secretary of state created a non-legislative fixed-term assembly which would cease to operate either when the political parties agreed to restore devolution, or on 24 November 2006 (whichever occurred first). In October 2006 a timetable to restore devolution was drawn up (St Andrews Agreement) and a transitional Northern Ireland Assembly was formed on 24 November. The transitional assembly was dissolved in January 2007 in preparation for elections to be held on 7 March; following the elections a power-sharing executive was formed and the new 108-member Northern Ireland Assembly became operational on 8 May 2007.

A breakdown of trust between the parties following the Renewable Heat Incentive scandal resulted in the dissolution of the 5th assembly and executive on 26 January 2017 and a new election took place in March 2017. Following this election negotiations to form an executive missed both the normal three week deadline and an extended deadline of 29 June 2017 and the sixth assembly currently remains suspended. For further information *see* Devolved Government.

LORD-LIEUTENANTS AND HIGH SHERIFFS

County	Lord-Lieutenant	High Sheriff (2019)
Antrim	David McCorkell	James Hassard
Armagh	Earl of Caledon, KCVO	Ian Chapman
Belfast City	Fionnuala Mary Jay-O'Boyle, CBE	Alderman Thomas Sandford
Down	David Lindsay	Henry Shields
Fermanagh	Viscount Brookeborough, KG	Mary Doherty, OBE
Londonderry	Alison Millar	Samuel Mawhinney
Londonderry City	Dr Angela Garvey	Julia Kee
Tyrone	Robert Scott, OBE	Samuel Atchison

LOCAL COUNCILS

Council	Telephone	Population*	Chief Executive
Antrim & Newtownabbey	028-9448 1311	142,492	Jacqui Dixon
Ards & North Down	0300-013 3333	160,864	Stephen Reid
Armagh City, Banbridge & Craigavon	0300-030 0900	214,090	Roger Wilson
Belfast City	028-9027 0549	341,877	Suzanne Wylie
Causeway Coast & Glens	028-7034 7034	144,246	David Jackson, MBE
Derry City & Strabane	028-7138 2204	150,679	John Kelpie
Fermanagh & Omagh	0300-303 1777	116,835	Brendan Hegarty
Lisburn & Castlereagh	028-9250 9250	144,381	David Burns
Mid & East Antrim	028-9335 8000	138,773	Anne Donaghy
Mid Ulster	0300-013 2132	147,392	Anthony Tohill
Newry, Mourne & Down	028-3031 3037	180,012	Marie Ward

* *Source: Office for National Statistics – Mid-2018 Population Estimates* (Crown copyright)

POLITICAL COMPOSITION OF COUNCILS

Following the local elections held on 2 May 2019

Abbreviations

All.	Alliance
BNP	British National Party
C.	Conservative
DUP	Democratic Unionist Party
Green	Green
Ind.	Independent
Lab.	Labour
LD	Liberal Democrat
Lib.	Liberal
O.	Other
PBP	People Before Profit
PC	Plaid Cymru
PUP	Progressive Unionist Party of Northern Ireland
R.	Residents Associations/Ratepayers
SD	Social Democrat
SDLP	Social Democratic and Labour Party
SF	Sinn Fein
SNP	Scottish National Party
Soc.	Socialist
TUV	Traditional Unionist Voice
UKIP	UK Independence Party
UUP	Ulster Unionist Party
v.	vacant

Total number of seats is given in parentheses after the council name.

ENGLAND

COUNTY COUNCILS

Buckinghamshire (49)	C. 41; LD 4; Ind. 3; Lab. 1
Cambridgeshire (61)	C. 36; LD 15; Lab. 7; Ind. 3
Cumbria (84)	C. 37; Lab. 26; LD 16; Ind. 5
Derbyshire (64)	C. 37; Lab. 24; LD 3
Devon (60)	C. 42; Lab. 7; LD 7; Ind. 3; Green 1
East Sussex (50)	C. 30; LD 11; Ind. 5; Lab. 4
Essex (75)	C. 56; LD 7; Lab. 6; Ind. 4; R 1; Green 1
Gloucestershire (53)	C. 31; LD 14; Lab. 5; Green 2; Ind. 1
Hampshire (78)	C. 56; LD 19; Lab. 2; Ind. 1
Hertfordshire (78)	C. 51; LD 18; Lab. 9
Kent (81)	C. 67; LD 7; Lab. 5; Green 1; R 1
Lancashire (84)	C. 46; Lab. 30; LD 4; Ind. 2; Green 1; UKIP 1
Leicestershire (55)	C. 36; LD 13; Lab. 6
Lincolnshire (70)	C. 58; Lab. 6; Ind. 5; LD 1
Norfolk (84)	C. 55; Lab. 17; LD 11; Ind. 1
North Yorkshire (72)	C. 55; Ind. 10; Lab. 4; LD 3
Northamptonshire (57)	C. 43; Lab. 12; LD 2
Nottinghamshire (66)	C. 31; Lab. 23; Ind. 11; LD 1
Oxfordshire (63)	C. 31; Lab. 14; LD 13; Ind. 4; R 1
Somerset (55)	C. 35; LD 12; Ind. 3; Lab. 3; Green 2
Staffordshire (62)	C. 51; Lab. 10; Ind. 1
Suffolk (75)	C. 52; Lab. 11; LD 5; Ind. 4; Green 3
Surrey (81)	C. 60; LD 9; R 8; Ind. 2; Lab. 1; Green 1
Warwickshire (57)	C. 36; Lab. 10; LD 7; Ind. 2; Green 2
West Sussex (70)	C. 56; LD 9; Lab. 5
Worcestershire (57)	C. 40; Lab. 10; LD 3; Green 2; Ind. 1; O. 1

DISTRICT COUNCILS

Adur (29)	C. 16; Lab. 7; UKIP 4; Ind. 2
Allerdale (49)	Ind. 20; C. 15; Lab. 14
Amber Valley (45)	Lab. 25; C. 19; Green 1
Arun (54)	LD 22; C. 21; Ind. 8; Green 2; Lab. 1
Ashfield (35)	Ind. 30; C. 3; Lab. 2
Ashford (47)	C. 26; Ind. 12; Lab. 7; Green 2
Aylesbury Vale (59)	C. 43; LD 9; UKIP 4; Lab. 2; Ind. 1
Babergh (32)	C. 15; Ind. 8; Green 4; LD 3; Lab. 2
Barrow-in-Furness (36)	Lab. 24; C. 12
Basildon (42)	C. 20; Lab. 15; Ind. 6; UKIP 1
Basingstoke and Deane (60)	C. 31; Lab. 21; LD 7; Ind. 1
Bassetlaw (48)	Lab. 37; C. 5; Ind. 5; LD 1
Blaby (39)	C. 25; Lab. 6; LD 6; Green 1; Ind. 1
Bolsover (37)	Lab. 18; Ind. 16; C. 2; LD 1
Boston (30)	C. 16; Ind. 11; Lab. 2; UKIP 1
Braintree (49)	C. 34; Green 6; R 4; Ind. 3; Lab. 2
Breckland (49)	C. 37; Lab. 6; Ind. 4; Green 2
Brentwood (37)	C. 21; LD 12; Lab. 3; Ind. 1
Broadland (47)	C. 32; LD 12; Lab. 2; Ind. 1
Bromsgrove (31)	C. 17; Lab. 5; Ind. 5; LD 3; R 1
Broxbourne (30)	C. 27; Lab. 2; Ind. 1
Broxtowe (44)	C. 20; Lab. 14; LD 5; Ind. 3; v. 2
Burnley (45)	Lab. 22; LD 8; Ind. 6; C. 4; UKIP 3; Green 2
Cambridge (42)	Lab. 26; LD 15; Ind. 1
Cannock Chase (41)	Lab. 18; C. 15; Green 5; LD 2; Ind. 1
Canterbury (39)	C. 23; Lab. 10; LD 6
Carlisle (39)	C. 17; Lab. 15; Ind. 4; LD 1; UKIP 1; Green 1
Castle Point (41)	C. 25; Ind. 16
Charnwood (52)	C. 37; Lab. 13; Ind. 1; Green 1
Chelmsford (57)	LD 31; C. 21; Ind. 5
Cheltenham (40)	LD 32; C. 6; Ind. 2
Cherwell (48)	C. 32; Lab. 9; Ind. 4; LD 2; Green 1
Chesterfield (48)	Lab. 28; LD 17; Ind. 3
Chichester (36)	C. 18; LD 11; Ind. 3; Lab. 2; Green 2
Chiltern (40)	C. 35; LD 3; Ind. 2
Chorley (47)	Lab. 37; C. 8; Ind. 2
Colchester (51)	C. 23; LD 13; Lab. 11; Ind. 3; Green 1
Copeland (33)	Lab. 19; C. 10; Ind. 4
Corby (29)	Lab. 24; C. 5
Cotswolds (34)	C. 24; LD 10
Craven (30)	C. 15; Ind. 9; Lab. 3; Green 2; LD 1
Crawley (36)	Lab. 19; C. 17
Dacorum (51)	C. 31; LD 19; Ind. 1
Dartford (42)	C. 29; Lab. 10; R 3
Daventry (36)	C. 30; Lab. 5; LD 1
Derbyshire Dales (39)	C. 20; LD 8; Lab. 6; Ind. 3; Green 2
Dover (32)	C. 19; Lab. 12; Ind. 1
East Cambridgeshire (28)	C. 15; LD 13
East Devon (60)	Ind. 31; C. 19; LD 8; Green 2
East Hampshire (43)	C. 32; LD 7; Lab. 2; Ind. 2
East Hertfordshire (50)	C. 40; LD 6; Lab. 2; Green 2
East Lindsey (55)	C. 29; Ind. 18; Lab. 7; LD 1
East Northamptonshire (40)	C. 37; Ind. 2; LD 1
East Staffordshire (39)	C. 25; Lab. 10; Ind. 3; LD 1

East Suffolk (55)   C. 39; Lab. 7; Green 4; LD 3; Ind. 2
Eastbourne (27)   LD 18; C. 9
Eastleigh (39)   LD 34; Ind. 3; C. 2
Eden (38)   C. 14; LD 10; Ind. 10; Lab. 2; Green 2
Elmbridge (48)   C. 21; R 17; LD 10
Epping Forest (58)   C. 37; R 13; Green 3; LD 3; Ind. 2
Epsom and Ewell (38)   R 32; Lab. 3; LD 2; C. 1
Erewash (47)   C. 27; Lab. 19; LD 1
Exeter (39)   Lab. 29; C. 6; LD 2; Ind. 1; Green 1
Fareham (31)   C. 24; LD 5; Ind. 1; UKIP 1
Fenland (39)   C. 26; Ind. 10; LD 2; Green 1
Folkestone and Hythe (30)   C. 13; Lab. 6; Green 6; LD 2; UKIP 2; Ind. 1
Forest of Dean (38)   Ind. 14; C. 10; Green 6; Lab. 5; v. 3
Fylde (51)   C. 31; Ind. 19; LD 1
Gedling (41)   Lab. 29; C. 8; Ind. 2; LD 2
Gloucester (39)   C. 22; Lab. 10; LD 7
Gosport (34)   C. 18; LD 14; Lab. 2
Gravesham (44)   Lab. 24; C. 18; Ind. 2
Great Yarmouth (39)   C. 20; Lab. 15; Ind. 3; UKIP 1
Guildford (48)   Ind. 19; LD 17; C. 9; Lab. 2; Green 1
Hambleton (28)   C. 24; Ind. 2; LD 1; Lab. 1
Harborough (34)   C. 22; LD 11; Lab. 1
Harlow (33)   Lab. 20; C. 13
Harrogate (40)   C. 31; LD 7; Ind. 2
Hart (33)   R 11; C. 11; LD 10; Ind. 1
Hastings (32)   Lab. 24; C. 8
Havant (38)   C. 33; Lab. 2; UKIP 2; LD 1
Hertsmere (39)   C. 29; Lab. 7; LD 3
High Peak (43)   Lab. 22; C. 16; LD 3; Green 2
Hinckley and Bosworth (34)   LD 21; C. 11; Lab. 2
Horsham (48)   C. 32; LD 13; Green 2; Ind. 1
Huntingdonshire (52)   C. 30; Ind. 11; LD 7; Lab. 4
Hyndburn (35)   Lab. 26; C. 9
Ipswich (48)   Lab. 36; C. 9; LD 3
Kettering (36)   C. 25; Lab. 7; Ind. 1; v. 3
King's Lynn and West Norfolk (55)   C. 28; Ind. 15; Lab. 10; LD 1; Green 1
Lancaster (60)   Lab. 21; Ind. 14; C. 12; Green 10; LD 3
Lewes (41)   C. 19; Green 9; LD 8; Lab. 3; Ind. 2
Lichfield (47)   C. 34; Lab. 10; Ind. 2; LD 1
Lincoln City (33)   Lab. 24; C. 9
Maidstone (55)   C. 24; LD 20; Ind. 7; Lab. 4
Maldon (31)   C. 17; Ind. 14
Malvern Hills (38)   C. 13; Ind. 10; LD 9; Green 5; Lab. 1
Mansfield (36)   Ind. 19; Lab. 15; C. 2
Melton (28)   C. 22; Ind. 5; Green 1
Mendip (36)   LD 22; C. 10; Green 10; Ind. 5
Mid Devon (42)   C. 18; LD 12; Ind. 10; Green 2
Mid Suffolk (34)   C. 16; Green 12; LD 5; Ind. 1
Mid Sussex (54)   C. 34; LD 13; Ind. 4; Green 3
Mole Valley (41)   LD 22; C. 12; Ind. 7
New Forest (60)   C. 46; LD 13; Ind. 1
Newark and Sherwood (39)   C. 27; Lab. 7; Ind. 3; LD 2
Newcastle-under-Lyme (44)   Lab. 20; C. 18; Ind. 3; LD 3
North Devon (42)   LD 21; C. 11; Ind. 7; Green 2; v. 1
North East Derbyshire (53)   C. 30; Lab. 18; LD 3; Ind. 2
North Hertfordshire (49)   C. 22; Lab. 16; LD 11
North Kesteven (43)   Ind. 22; C. 20; v. 1
North Norfolk (40)   LD 30; C. 6; Ind. 4
North Warwickshire (35)   C. 21; Lab. 14

North West Leicestershire (38)   C. 20; Lab. 10; LD 4; Ind. 3; Green 1
Northampton (45)   C. 26; Lab. 17; LD 2
Norwich (39)   Lab. 27; Green 9; LD 3
Nuneaton and Bedworth (34)   Lab. 17; C. 16; Green 1
Oadby and Wigston (26)   LD 24; C. 2
Oxford (48)   Lab. 36; LD 9; Green 2; Ind. 1
Pendle (49)   C. 23; Lab. 16; LD 10
Preston (48)   Lab. 30; C. 9; LD 9
Redditch (29)   C. 18; Lab. 11
Reigate and Banstead (45)   C. 29; Green 6; R 6; LD 3; Ind. 1
Ribble Valley (40)   C. 28; LD 10; Ind. 2
Richmondshire (24)   C. 10; Ind. 10; LD 3; Green 1
Rochford (39)   C. 26; R 4; Green 3; LD 3; Ind. 3
Rossendale (36)   Lab. 20; C. 13; Ind. 3
Rother (38)   C. 14; Ind. 13; LD 7; Lab. 3; Green 1
Rugby (42)   C. 24; LD 9; Lab. 9
Runnymede (42)   C. 26; Ind. 9; LD 3; Lab. 2; Green 2
Rushcliffe (44)   C. 29; Lab. 7; Ind. 3; LD 3; Green 2
Rushmoor (39)   C. 26; Lab. 11; LD 2
Ryedale (30)   C. 12; Ind. 11; Lib. 5; LD 2
St Albans (58)   LD 25; C. 23; Lab. 6; Ind. 3; Green 1
Scarborough (46)   C. 16; Ind. 14; Lab. 13; Green 2; UKIP 1
Sedgemoor (48)   C. 28; Lab. 12; LD 7; Ind. 1
Selby (31)   C. 16; Lab. 8; Ind. 7
Sevenoaks (54)   C. 46; Ind. 4; LD 3; Lab. 1
Somerset West and Taunton (59)   LD 30; Ind. 14; C. 10; Lab. 3; Green 2
South Bucks (28)   C. 27; Ind. 1
South Cambridgeshire (45)   LD 30; C. 11; Ind. 2; Lab. 2
South Derbyshire (36)   C. 22; Lab. 14
South Hams (31)   C. 16; LD 10; Green 3; Ind. 2
South Holland (37)   C. 24; Ind. 13
South Kesteven (56)   C. 40; Ind. 11; Lab. 3; LD 2
South Lakeland (51)   LD 32; C. 15; Lab. 3; Green 1
South Norfolk (46)   C. 35; LD 10; Lab. 1
South Northamptonshire (42)   C. 35; Lab. 4; LD 3
South Oxfordshire (36)   LD 12; C. 10; Green 5; Ind. 3; Lab. 3; R 3
South Ribble (50)   Lab. 22; C. 21; LD 5; v. 2
South Somerset (60)   LD 41; C. 15; Ind. 4
South Staffordshire (49)   C. 35; Ind. 7; Green 3; v. 2; UKIP 1; Lab. 1
Spelthorne (39)   C. 23; LD 8; Lab. 4; Green 2; Ind. 2
Stafford (40)   C. 22; Lab. 10; Ind. 7; Green 1
Staffordshire Moorlands (56)   C. 25; Ind. 17; Lab. 13; LD 1
Stevenage (39)   Lab. 27; C. 7; LD 5
Stratford-on-Avon (36)   C. 20; LD 11; Ind. 4; Green 1
Stroud (51)   C. 23; Lab. 18; Green 8; LD 2
Surrey Heath (35)   C. 18; LD 10; Ind. 4; Green 2; Lab. 1
Swale (47)   C. 16; Ind. 12; Lab. 11; LD 5; Green 2; UKIP 1
Tamworth (30)   C. 22; Lab. 5; UKIP 2; Ind. 1
Tandridge (42)   C. 16; LD 11; Ind. 8; R 7
Teignbridge (47)   LD 26; C. 12; Ind. 9
Tendring (48)   Ind. 17; C. 16; Lab. 6; UKIP 5; v. 2; LD 2
Test Valley (43)   C. 24; LD 12; Ind. 7
Tewkesbury (38)   C. 23; LD 8; Ind. 6; Green 1
Thanet (56)   C. 25; Lab. 20; Ind. 8; Green 3
Three Rivers (39)   LD 24; C. 12; Lab. 3

Tonbridge and Malling (54) — C. 39; LD 9; Ind. 3; Green 2; Lab. 1

Torridge (36) — Ind. 18; C. 11; Lab. 3; LD 2; Green 2

Tunbridge Wells (48) — C. 28; LD 9; Ind. 7; Lab. 4

Uttlesford (39) — R 26; LD 7; C. 4; Ind. 2

Vale of White Horse (38) — LD 31; C. 6; Green 1

Warwick (44) — C. 19; LD 9; Green 8; Lab. 5; R 3

Watford (36) — LD 26; Lab. 10

Waverley (57) — C. 23; R 15; LD 14; Green 2; Lab. 2; Ind. 1

Wealden (45) — C. 34; Ind. 5; LD 4; Green 2

Wellingborough (36) — C. 27; Lab. 9

Welwyn and Hatfield (48) — C. 23; Lab. 13; LD 12

West Devon (31) — C. 16; Ind. 11; LD 2; Green 2

West Lancashire (54) — Lab. 29; C. 19; Ind. 6

West Lindsey (36) — C. 19; LD 12; Ind. 5

West Oxfordshire (49) — C. 28; LD 10; Lab. 9; Ind. 2

West Suffolk (64) — C. 36; Ind. 22; Lab. 5; Green 1

Winchester (45) — LD 27; C. 18

Woking (30) — C. 14; LD 10; Ind. 3; Lab. 3

Worcester (35) — C. 17; Lab. 15; Green 3

Worthing (37) — C. 21; Lab. 10; LD 3; Ind. 2; UKIP 1

Wychavon (45) — C. 36; LD 6; Green 2; Ind. 1

Wycombe (60) — C. 47; Lab. 6; O. 3; Ind. 2; LD 1; UKIP 1

Wyre (50) — C. 37; Lab. 9; UKIP 4

Wyre Forest (33) — C. 14; Ind CHC 8; Ind. 5; LD 3; Lab. 2; Green 1

LONDON BOROUGH COUNCILS

Barking and Dagenham (51) — Lab. 51

Barnet (63) — C. 38; Lab. 25

Bexley (45) — C. 34; Lab. 11

Brent (63) — Lab. 57; C. 3; v. 3

Bromley (60) — C. 50; Lab. 8; Ind. 2

Camden (54) — Lab. 43; C. 7; LD 3; Green 1

Croydon (70) — Lab. 41; C. 29

Ealing (69) — Lab. 57; C. 8; LD 4

Enfield (63) — Lab. 46; C. 17

Greenwich (51) — Lab. 42; C. 9

Hackney (57) — Lab. 52; C. 5

Hammersmith and Fulham (46) — Lab. 35; C. 11

Haringey (57) — Lab. 42; LD 15

Harrow (63) — Lab. 35; C. 28

Havering (54) — C. 25; R 23; Lab. 5; Ind. 1

Hillingdon (65) — C. 44; Lab. 21

Hounslow (60) — Lab. 51; C. 9

Islington (48) — Lab. 47; Green 1

Kensington and Chelsea (50) — C. 36; Lab. 13; LD 1

Kingston upon Thames (48) — C. 28; LD 18; Lab. 2

Lambeth (63) — Lab. 57; Green 5; C. 1

Lewisham (54) — Lab. 54

Merton (60) — Lab. 34; C. 17; LD 6; R 3

Newham (60) — Lab. 60

Redbridge (63) — Lab. 51; C. 12

Richmond upon Thames (54) — C. 39; LD 15

Southwark (63) — Lab. 49; LD 11; v. 3

Sutton (54) — LD 33; C. 18; Ind. 3

Tower Hamlets (45) — Lab. 42; C. 2; Ind. 1

Waltham Forest (60) — Lab. 46; C. 14

Wandsworth (60) — C. 33; Lab. 26; Ind. 1

Westminster (60) — C. 41; Lab. 19

METROPOLITAN BOROUGHS

Barnsley (63) — Lab. 49; Ind. 7; LD 4; C. 3

Birmingham (101) — Lab. 67; C. 25; LD 8; Green 1

Bolton (60) — Lab. 23; C. 20; Ind. 8; LD 6; UKIP 3

Bradford (90) — Lab. 52; C. 22; LD 9; Ind. 5; Green 2

Bury (51) — Lab. 29; C. 16; LD 4; Ind. 2

Calderdale (51) — Lab. 28; C. 14; LD 7; Ind. 2

Coventry (54) — Lab. 40; C. 13; Ind. 1

Doncaster (55) — Lab. 43; C. 7; Ind. 5

Dudley (72) — Lab. 36; C. 36

Gateshead (66) — Lab. 52; LD 14

Kirklees (69) — Lab. 36; C. 16; LD 10; Ind. 4; Green 3

Knowsley (45) — Lab. 37; LD 3; Green 3; Ind. 2

Leeds (99) — Lab. 58; C. 23; LD 8; Ind. 7; Green 3

Liverpool (90) — Lab. 72; LD 10; Green 4; Lib. 3; Ind. 1

Manchester (96) — Lab. 93; LD 3

Newcastle-upon-Tyne (78) — Lab. 54; LD 20; Ind. 4

North Tyneside (60) — Lab. 51; C. 7; Ind. 1; LD 1

Oldham (60) — Lab. 45; LD 8; C. 4; Ind. 3

Rochdale (60) — Lab. 47; C. 9; LD 4

Rotherham (63) — Lab. 48; UKIP 14; Ind. 1

St Helens (48) — Lab. 37; LD 4; C. 3; Green 2; Ind. 2

Salford (60) — Lab. 50; C. 8; Ind. 1; v. 1

Sandwell (72) — Lab. 72

Sefton (66) — Lab. 43; LD 12; C. 6; Ind. 5

Sheffield (84) — Lab. 49; LD 26; Green 8; UKIP 1

Solihull (51) — C. 26; Green 14; LD 6; Lab. 3; Ind. 2

South Tyneside (54) — Lab. 48; Ind. 5; Green 1

Stockport (63) — Lab. 26; LD 26; C. 8; Ind. 2; R 1

Sunderland (75) — Lab. 51; C. 12; LD 8; UKIP 3; Green 1

Tameside (57) — Lab. 51; C. 5; Green 1

Trafford (63) — Lab. 36; C. 20; LD 4; Green 3

Wakefield (63) — Lab. 49; C. 11; Ind. 2; LD 1

Walsall (60) — C. 32; Lab. 26; LD 2

Wigan (75) — Lab. 57; Ind. 10; C. 8

Wirral (66) — Lab. 32; C. 22; LD 6; Green 3; Ind. 3

Wolverhampton (60) — Lab. 50; C. 10

UNITARY COUNCILS

Bath and North East Somerset (59) — LD 37; C. 11; Ind. 6; Lab. 5

Bedford (40) — LD 15; Lab. 11; C. 11; Green 2; Ind. 1

Blackburn with Darwen (51) — Lab. 36; C. 13; LD 2

Blackpool (42) — Lab. 23; C. 15; Ind. 4

Bournemouth, Christchurch & Poole (BCP) (76) — C. 36; Ind. 19; LD 15; Lab. 3; Green 2; UKIP 1

Bracknell Forest (42) — C. 38; Lab. 3; LD 1

Brighton and Hove (54) — Lab. 20; Green 19; C. 14; Ind. 1

Bristol (70) — Lab. 37; C. 14; Green 11; LD 8

Central Bedfordshire (59) — C. 41; Ind. 13; LD 3; Lab. 1; UKIP 1

Cheshire East (82) — C. 34; Lab. 25; Ind. 14; R 5; LD 4

Cheshire West and Chester (70) — Lab. 35; C. 28; Ind. 4; LD 2; Green 1

Cornwall (123) — C. 46; LD 37; Ind. 30; Lab. 5; O. 4; v. 1

Darlington (50) — C. 22; Lab. 20; LD 3; Ind. 3; Green 2

Derby (51) — C. 20; Lab. 16; LD 7; UKIP 5; Ind. 3

Dorset (82) — C. 43; LD 29; Green 4; Ind. 4; Lab. 2

Durham (126) — Lab. 74; Ind. 28; LD. 14; C. 10

East Riding of Yorkshire (67) — C. 49; Ind. 10; LD 8

Halton (56)	Lab. 51; LD 3; C. 2
Hartlepool (33)	Ind. 16; Lab. 13; C. 3; UKIP 1
Herefordshire (53)	Ind. 26; C. 13; Green 7; LD 6; v. 1
Isle of Wight (40)	C. 25; Ind. 11; LD 2; Green 1; Lab. 1
*Isles of Scilly (16)	Ind. 9; O. 7
Kingston-upon-Hull (57)	Lab. 31; LD 24; C. 2
Leicester (54)	Lab. 53; LD 1
Luton (48)	Lab. 32; LD 12; C. 4
Medway (55)	C. 33; Lab. 20; Ind. 2
Middlesbrough (46)	Ind. 23; Lab. 20; C. 3
Milton Keynes (57)	Lab. 23; C. 19; LD 15
North East Lincolnshire (42)	C. 23; Lab. 14; LD 4; UKIP 1
North Lincolnshire (43)	C. 27; Lab. 16
North Somerset (50)	Ind. 17; C. 13; LD 11; Lab. 6; Green 3
Northumberland (67)	C. 33; Lab. 24; Ind. 7; LD. 3
Nottingham (55)	Lab. 50; Ind. 3; C. 2
Peterborough (60)	C. 28; Lab. 17; LD 9; Ind. 3; Green 2; Lib. 1
Plymouth (57)	Lab. 31; C. 25; Ind. 1
Portsmouth (42)	LD 18; C. 16; Lab. 6; Ind. 2
Reading (46)	Lab. 30; C. 10; Green 4; LD 2
Redcar and Cleveland (59)	Ind. 18; Lab. 15; LD 13; C. 11; UKIP 2
Rutland (27)	C. 15; Ind. 8; LD 3; Green 1
Shropshire (74)	C. 49; LD. 12; Lab. 8; Ind. 3; Green 1, O. 1
Slough (42)	Lab. 37; C. 5
South Gloucestershire (61)	C. 33; LD 17; Lab. 11
Southampton (48)	Lab. 29; C. 18; Ind. 1
Southend-on-Sea (51)	C. 20; Lab. 14; Ind. 12; LD 5
Stockton-on-Tees (56)	Lab. 24; Ind. 16; C. 14; LD 2
Stoke-on-Trent (44)	Lab. 16; C. 15; Ind. 13
Swindon (57)	C. 31; Lab. 24; LD 2
Telford and Wrekin (54)	Lab. 36; C. 13; LD 4; Ind. 1
Thurrock (49)	C. 22; Lab. 18; Ind. 9
Torbay (36)	C. 15; LD 13; Ind. 8
Warrington (58)	Lab. 45; LD 11; C. 2
West Berkshire (43)	C. 24; LD 16; Green 3
Wiltshire (98)	C. 69; LD. 19; Ind. 7; Lab. 3
Windsor and Maidenhead (41)	C. 23; LD 9; R. 5; Ind. 4
Wokingham (54)	C. 31; LD 16; Lab. 4; Ind. 3
York (47)	LD 21; Lab. 17; Green 4; Ind. 3; C. 2

* Twelve councillors are elected by the residents of the isle of St Mary's and one councillor each are elected by the residents of the four other islands (Bryher, St Agnes, St Martin's and Tresco)

WALES

Blaenau Gwent (42)	Ind. 28; Lab. 13; PC 1
Bridgend (54)	Lab. 26; Ind. 13; C. 11; PC 3; LD 1
Caerphilly (73)	Lab. 50; PC 18; Ind. 5
Cardiff (75)	Lab. 40; C. 20; LD 11; PC 3; Ind. 1
Carmarthenshire (74)	PC 36; Lab. 22; Ind. 16
Ceredigion (42)	PC 19; Ind. 13; LD 8; v. 1; Lab. 1
Conwy (59)	Ind. 21; C. 16; PC 10; Lab. 8; LD 4
Denbighshire (47)	C. 16; Lab. 13; PC 9; Ind. 8; LD 1
Flintshire (70)	Lab. 34; Ind. 25; C. 6; LD 5

Gwynedd (75)	PC 41; Ind. 26; O. 6; Lab. 1; LD 1
Merthyr Tydfil (33)	Ind. 16; Lab. 14; v. 3
Monmouthshire (43)	C. 25; Lab. 10; Ind. 5; LD 3
Neath Port Talbot (64)	Lab. 43; PC 15; Ind. 5; LD 1
Newport (50)	Lab. 31; C. 12; Ind. 5; LD 2
Pembrokeshire (60)	Ind. 35; C. 11; Lab. 7; PC 6; LD 1
Powys (73)	Ind. 30; C. 19; LD 13; Lab. 7; PC 2; v. 1; Green 1
Rhondda Cynon Taff (75)	Lab. 47; PC 18; Ind. 5; C. 4; LD 1
Swansea (72)	Lab. 48; Ind. 9; C. 8; LD 7
Torfaen (44)	Lab. 29; Ind. 11; C. 4
Vale of Glamorgan (47)	C. 23; Lab. 14; Ind. 6; PC 4
Wrexham (52)	Ind. 26; Lab. 12; C. 9; PC 3; LD 2
Ynys Mon (Isle of Anglesey) (30)	PC 14; Ind. 13; Lab. 2; LD 1

SCOTLAND

Aberdeen (45)	SNP 19; C. 11; Lab. 9; LD 4; Ind. 2
Aberdeenshire (70)	C. 23; SNP 21; LD 14; Ind. 10; Green 1; Lab. 1
Angus (28)	Ind. 9; SNP 9; C. 8; LD 2
Argyll and Bute (36)	SNP 11; Ind. 10; C. 9; LD 6
Clackmannanshire (18)	SNP 8; Lab. 5; C. 5
Dumfries and Galloway (43)	C. 16; Lab. 11; SNP 11; Ind. 4; LD 1
Dundee (29)	SNP 14; Lab. 9; C. 3; LD 2; Ind. 1
East Ayrshire (32)	SNP 14; Lab. 9; C. 6; Ind. 3
East Dunbartonshire (22)	SNP 7; C. 6; LD 6; Lab. 2; Ind. 1
East Lothian (22)	Lab. 9; C. 7; SNP 6
East Renfrewshire (18)	C. 7; SNP 5; Lab. 4; Ind. 2
Edinburgh (63)	SNP 19; C. 18; Lab. 12; Green 8; LD 6
Eilean Siar (Western Isles) (31)	Ind. 23; SNP 7; C. 1
Falkirk (30)	SNP 12; Lab. 9; C. 7; Ind. 2
Fife (75)	SNP 29; Lab. 24; C. 15; LD 7
Glasgow (85)	SNP 39; Lab. 31; C. 8; Green 7
Highland (74)	Ind. 28; SNP 22; LD 10; C. 10; Lab. 3; Green 1
Inverclyde (22)	Lab. 8; SNP 7; Ind. 4; C. 2; LD 1
Midlothian (18)	Lab. 7; SNP 6; C. 5
Moray (26)	SNP 9; Ind. 8; C. 8; Lab. 1
North Ayrshire (32)	Lab. 11; SNP 11; C. 7; Ind. 4
North Lanarkshire (77)	SNP 33; Lab. 32; C. 10; Ind. 2
Orkney Islands (21)	Ind. 20; Green 1
Perth and Kinross (40)	C. 17; SNP 15; LD 4; Ind. 3; Lab. 1
Renfrewshire (43)	SNP 19; Lab. 13; C. 8; Ind. 2; LD 1
Scottish Borders (34)	C. 15; SNP 9; Ind. 8; LD 2
Shetland Islands (22)	Ind. 21; SNP 1
South Ayrshire (28)	C. 12; SNP 9; Lab. 5; Ind. 2
South Lanarkshire (64)	SNP 27; Lab. 22; C. 14; LD 1
Stirling (23)	C. 9; SNP 9; Lab. 4; Green 1
West Dunbartonshire (22)	SNP 10; Lab. 8; Ind. 2; C. 2
West Lothian (33)	SNP 13; Lab. 12; C. 7; Ind. 1

NORTHERN IRELAND

Antrim & Newtownabbey (40)	DUP 14; UUP 9; All. 7; SF 5; SDLP 4; Ind. 1
Ards & North Down (40)	DUP 14; All. 10; UUP 8; Green 3; Ind. 3; SDLP 1; TUV 1
Armagh City, Banbridge & Craigavon (41)	DUP 11; UUP 10; SF 10; SDLP 6; All. 3; Ind. 1
Belfast City (60)	SF 18; DUP 15; All. 10; SDLP 6; Green 4; PBP 3; PUP 2; UUP 2
Causeway Coast & Glens (40)	DUP 14; SF 9; UUP 7; SDLP 6; All. 2; Ind. 1; PUP 1
Derry City & Strabane (40)	SF 11; SDLP 11; DUP 7; Ind. 4; All. 2; PBP 2; UUP 2; O. 1
Fermanagh & Omagh (40)	SF 15; UUP 9; SDLP 5; DUP 5; Ind. 4; All. 1; O. 1
Lisburn & Castlereagh (40)	DUP 15; UUP 11; All. 9; SDLP 2; SF 2; Green 1
Mid & East Antrim (40)	DUP 15; UUP 7; All. 7; TUV 5; SF 2; Ind. 3; SDLP 1
Mid Ulster (40)	SF 17; DUP 9; UUP 6; SDLP 6; Ind. 2
Newry, Mourne & Down (41)	SF 16; SDLP 11; Ind. 5; UUP 4; DUP 3; All. 2

THE ISLE OF MAN

Ellan Vannin

The Isle of Man is an island situated in the Irish Sea, at latitude 54° 3′–54° 25′ N. and longitude 4° 18′–4° 47′ W., nearly equidistant from England, Scotland and Ireland. Although the early inhabitants were of Celtic origin, the Isle of Man was part of the Norwegian Kingdom of the Hebrides until 1266, when this was ceded to Scotland. Subsequently granted to the Stanleys (Earls of Derby) in the 15th century and later to the Dukes of Atholl, it was brought under the administration of the Crown in 1765. The island forms the bishopric of Sodor and Man.

The total land area is 572 sq. km (221 sq. miles). The 2016 census showed a resident population of 83,314 (men, 41,269; women, 42,045). The main language in use is English. Around 1,660 people are able to speak the Manx Gaelic language.

CAPITAL – ΨDouglas; population, 26,997 (2016). ΨCastletown (3,216) is the ancient capital; the other towns are ΨPeel (5,374) and ΨRamsey (7,845)

FLAG – A red flag charged with three conjoined armoured legs in white and gold

NATIONAL DAY – 5 July (Tynwald Day)

GOVERNMENT
The Isle of Man is a self-governing Crown dependency, with its own parliamentary, legal and administrative system. The British government is responsible for international relations and defence. Under the UK Act of Accession, Protocol 3, the island's relationship with the European Union is limited to trade alone and does not extend to financial aid. The Lieutenant-Governor is the Queen's personal representative on the island.

The legislature, Tynwald, is the oldest parliament in the world in continuous existence. It has two branches: the Legislative Council and the House of Keys. The council consists of the President of Tynwald, the Bishop of Sodor and Man, the Attorney-General (who does not have a vote) and eight members elected by the House of Keys. The House of Keys has 24 members, elected by universal adult suffrage. The branches sit separately to consider legislation and sit together, as Tynwald Court, for most other parliamentary purposes.

The presiding officer of Tynwald Court is the President of Tynwald, elected by the members, who also presides over sittings of the Legislative Council. The presiding officer of the House of Keys is the Speaker, who is elected by members of the house.

The principal members of the Manx government are the chief minister and eight departmental ministers, who comprise the Council of Ministers.

Lieutenant-Governor, HE Sir Richard Gozney, KCMG, CVO

President of Tynwald, Hon. Steve Rodan, OBE
Speaker, House of Keys, Hon. Juan Paul Watterson, SHK
Deputy Speaker, House of Keys, Chris Robertshaw, MHK
The First Deemster and Clerk of the Rolls, His Hon. Andrew Corlett
Clerk of Tynwald, Secretary to the House of Keys and Counsel to the Speaker, Roger Phillips
Clerk of the Legislative Council and Deputy Clerk of Tynwald, Jonathan King
HM Attorney-General, John Quinn, QC
Chief Minister, Hon. Howard Quayle, MHK
Chief Secretary, Will Greenhow

ECONOMY
Much of the income generated in the island is earned in the services sector with financial and professional services accounting for 42.3 per cent of the national income. Two other significant sectors are e-gaming and ICT, contributing 18.4 per cent and 10 per cent respectively, to the national income. Under the terms of protocol 3, the island has tariff-free access to EU markets for the products of its engineering, farming and fishing industries.

In July 2019 the island's unemployment rate was 0.8 per cent and the CPI rate of inflation was 2.1 per cent.

FINANCE
The budget for 2019–20 provides for gross revenue expenditure of £1,040m. The principal sources of government revenue are direct and indirect taxes. Income tax is payable at a rate of 10 per cent on the first £6,500 of taxable income for single resident individuals and 20 per cent on the balance, after personal allowances of £14,000. These bands are doubled for married couples. The rate of income tax for trading companies is zero per cent except for income from banking and major retail operations which is taxed at 10 per cent, and income from land and property which is taxed at 20 per cent. By agreement with the British government, the island keeps most of its rates of indirect taxation (VAT and duties) the same as those in the UK. However, VAT on tourist accommodation, property, repairs and renovations is charged at 5 per cent. Taxes are also charged on property (rates), but these are comparatively low.

The major government expenditure items are social security payments, health and education. The island makes an annual contribution to the UK for defence and other external services.

The island has a special relationship with the European Union and neither contributes money to nor receives funds from the EU budget.

Ψ = sea port

THE CHANNEL ISLANDS

The Channel Islands, situated off the north-west coast of France (at a distance of 16km (10 miles) at their closest point), are the only portions of the Dukedom of Normandy still belonging to the Crown, to which they have been attached since the Norman Conquest of 1066. They were the only British territory to come under German occupation during the Second World War, following invasion on 30 June and 1 July 1940. Guernsey and Jersey were relieved by British forces on 9 May 1945, Sark on 10 May 1945 and Alderney on 16 May 1945; 9 May (Liberation Day) is now observed as a bank and public holiday in Guernsey and Jersey.

The islands consist of Jersey (11,630ha/28,717 acres), Guernsey (6,340ha/15,654 acres), and the dependencies of Guernsey: Alderney (795ha/1,962 acres), Brecqhou (30ha/74 acres), Great Sark (419ha/1,035 acres), Little Sark (97ha/239 acres), Herm (130ha/320 acres), Jethou (18ha/44 acres) and Lihou (15ha/38 acres) – a total of 19,474ha/48,083 acres, or 195 sq. km/75 sq. miles.

Official figures estimated the population of Jersey as 106,800 at the end of 2018. Guernsey uses a rolling electronic census system and the most recent figures (March 2018) showed the populations of Guernsey and Alderney to be 62,297 and 2,019 respectively. Sark's population is estimated to be around 600. The official language is English but French is often used for ceremonial purposes. A Norman-French *patois* is also spoken by a few in Jersey, Guernsey and Sark.

GOVERNMENT
The islands are Crown dependencies with their own legislative assemblies (the States of Jersey, the States of Alderney, the States of Deliberation in Guernsey and the Chief Pleas in Sark), systems of local administration and law, and their own courts. *Projets de Loi* (Acts) passed by the States require the sanction of the Queen-in-council. The UK government is responsible for defence and international relations, although the islands are increasingly entering into agreements with other countries in their own right. The Channel Islands are not members of the European Union but, under protocol 3 of the UK's Treaty of Accession, have trading rights with the free movement of goods within the EU. A common customs tariff, levies and agricultural and import measures apply to trade between the islands and non-member countries.

In both Jersey and Guernsey bailiwicks the Lieutenant-Governor and Commander-in-Chief, who is appointed by the Crown, is the personal representative of the Queen and the official channel of communication between the Crown (via the Privy Council) and the islands' governments.

The head of government in both Jersey and Guernsey is the Chief Minister. Jersey has a ministerial system of government; the executive comprises the Council of Ministers and consists of a chief minister and eleven other ministers. The ministers are assisted by up to nine assistant ministers. Members of the States who are not in the executive are able to sit on a number of scrutiny panels and the Public Accounts Committee to examine the policy of the executive and hold ministers to account. Guernsey is administered by a number of committees. The Policy and Resources committee is the senior committee responsible for leadership and coordination of the work of the States and is presided over by the Chief Minister, in addition there are six principal committees with mandated responsibilities. The States of Deliberation is the island's

parliamentary assembly. Alderney has a legislature comprising a President and ten members elected by universal suffrage. Sark has a directly elected legislature of 28 members *(conseillers)* who serve on a number of committees.

Justice is administered by the royal courts of Jersey and Guernsey, each consisting of the bailiff and 12 elected jurats. The bailiffs of Jersey and Guernsey, appointed by the Crown, are presidents of the royal courts of their respective islands. Each bailiff is the *ex-officio* presiding officer in their respective parliaments and, by convention, the civic head.

The Church of England in each bailiwick is under the jurisdiction of the Dean of Jersey and the Dean of Guernsey respectively. The Bishop of Dover (Diocese of Canterbury) has episcopal oversight of the Channel Islands.

ECONOMY
A mild climate and good soil have led to the development of intensive systems of agriculture and horticulture, which form a significant part of the economy. Equally important are earnings from tourism and banking and finance: the low rates of income and corporation tax and the absence of death duties make the islands an important offshore financial centre. The financial services sector contributes over 50 per cent of GDP in Jersey and 44 per cent of GVA in Guernsey. In addition, there is no VAT or equivalent tax in Guernsey and only small goods and services tax in Jersey (5 per cent since 1 June 2011). The international stock exchange is located in Guernsey, which also has a thriving e-gaming sector.

Principal exports are agricultural produce and flowers; imports are chiefly machinery, manufactured goods, food, fuel and chemicals. Trade with the UK is regarded as internal.

British currency is legal tender in the Channel Islands but each bailiwick issues its own coins and notes (*see* Currency section). They also issue their own postage stamps; UK stamps are not valid.

JERSEY
Lieutenant-Governor and Commander-in-Chief of Jersey, HE Air Chief Marshal Sir Stephen Dalton, GCB, *from* 2017
Chief of Staff, Maj. Justin Oldridge
Bailiff of Jersey, Sir William J. Bailhache
Deputy Bailiff, Timothy J. Le Cocq
Attorney-General, Robert J. MacRae, QC
Receiver-General, David Pett
Solicitor-General, Mark Temple, QC
Greffier of the States, Mark Egan
States Treasurer, Richard Bell
Chief Minister, Senator John Le Fondré

FINANCE
	2017	2018
Revenue income	£767,300,000	£799,205,000
Revenue expenditure	£703,800,000	£759.303,000
Capital expenditure	£47,600,000	£18,077,000*

* Much reduced on the 2017 figure due to a major new hospital project being postponed.

CHIEF TOWN – ΨSt Helier, on the south coast
FLAG – A white field charged with a red saltire cross, and the arms of Jersey in the upper centre

GUERNSEY AND DEPENDENCIES

Lieutenant-Governor and Commander-in-Chief of the Bailiwick of Guernsey and its Dependencies, Vice-Adm. Sir Ian Corder, KBE, CB

Presiding Officer of the Royal Court and of the States of Deliberation, Bailiff Sir Richard Collas

Deputy Presiding Officer of the Royal Court and States of Deliberation, Deputy Bailiff Richard McMahon, QC

HM Procureur and Receiver-General (Attorney-General), Megan Pullum, QC

HM Comptroller (Solicitor-General), Robert Titterington, QC

GUERNSEY

President of the Policy and Resources Committee, Deputy Gavin St Pier

Chief Executive, Paul Whitfield

FINANCE

	2017	2018
Revenue income	£438,536,000	£452,438,000
Other income	£144,958,000	£48,812,000
Revenue expenditure	£437,311,000	£458,988,000
Capital expenditure	£15,103,000	£37,057,000
Other expenditure	£17,022,000	£21,424,000

CHIEF TOWNS – ΨSt Peter Port, on the east coast of Guernsey; St Anne on Alderney

FLAG – White, bearing a red cross of St George, with a gold cross of Normandy overall in the centre

ALDERNEY

President of the States, Stuart Trought

Chief Executive, Andrew Muter

Greffier, Jonathan Anderson

SARK

Sark was the last European territory to abolish feudal parliamentary representation. Elections for a democratic legislative assembly took place in December 2008, with the *conseillers* taking their seats in the newly constituted Chief Pleas in January 2009.

Seigneur of Sark, Maj. Christopher Beaumont

Seneschal, Jeremy la Trobe-Bateman

President, Arthur Rolfe

Greffier, Trevor Hamon

OTHER DEPENDENCIES

Herm and Lihou are owned by the States of Guernsey; Herm is leased, Lihou is uninhabited. Jethou is leased by the Crown to the States of Guernsey and is sub-let by the States. Brecqhou is within the legislative and judicial territory of Sark.

Ψ = seaport

LAW COURTS AND OFFICES

SUPREME COURT OF THE UNITED KINGDOM

The Supreme Court of the United Kingdom is the highest domestic judicial authority; it replaced the appellate committee of the House of Lords (the house functioning in its judicial capacity) on 1 October 2009. It is the final court of appeal for cases heard in Great Britain and Northern Ireland (except for criminal cases from Scotland). Cases concerning the interpretation and application of European Union law, including preliminary rulings requested by British courts and tribunals, which are decided by the Court of Justice of the European Union (CJEU) (*see* European Union), and the supreme court can make a reference to the CJEU in appropriate cases. Additionally, in giving effect to rights contained in the European Convention on Human Rights, the supreme court must take account of any decision of the European Court of Human Rights.

The supreme court also assumed jurisdiction in relation to devolution matters under the Scotland Act 1998 (now partly superseded by the Scotland Act 2012), the Northern Ireland Act 1988 and the Government of Wales Act 2006; these powers were transferred from the Judicial Committee of the Privy Council. Ten of the 12 Lords of Appeal in Ordinary (Law Lords) from the House of Lords transferred to the 12-member supreme court when it came into operation (at the same time one law lord retired and another was appointed Master of the Rolls). All new justices of the supreme court are now appointed by an independent selection commission, and, although styled *Rt. Hon. Lord,* are not members of the House of Lords. Peers who are members of the judiciary are disqualified from sitting or voting in the House of Lords until they retire from their judicial office. *See* Life Peers for a list of such peers (§).

President of the Supreme Court (£234,184), Rt. Hon. Lord Reed born 1956, *apptd* 2019 (from January 2020)
Deputy President of the Supreme Court (£226,193), vacant

JUSTICES OF THE SUPREME COURT *as at November 2019* (each £226,193)
Style, The Rt. Hon. Lord/Lady–

Rt. Hon. Lord Kerr of Tonaghmore, *born* 1948, *apptd* 2009
Rt. Hon. Lord Wilson of Culworth, *born* 1945, *apptd* 2011
Rt. Hon. Lord Carnwath of Notting Hill, CVO, *born* 1945, *apptd* 2012
Rt. Hon. Lord Hodge, *born* 1953, *apptd* 2013
Rt. Hon. Lady Black of Derwent, DBE, *born* 1954, *apptd* 2017
Rt. Hon. Lord Lloyd-Jones, *born* 1952, *apptd* 2017
Rt. Hon. Lord Briggs of Westbourne, *born* 1954, *apptd* 2017
Rt. Hon. Lady Arden of Heswall, DBE, *born* 1947, *apptd* 2018
Rt. Hon. Lord Kitchin, *born* 1955, *apptd* 2018
Rt. Hon. Lord Sales, *born* 1962, *apptd* 2019

UNITED KINGDOM SUPREME COURT
Parliament Square, London SW1P 3BD T 020-7960 1900
Chief Executive, Mark Ormerod, CB

JUDICATURE OF ENGLAND AND WALES

The legal system in England and Wales is divided into criminal law and civil law. Criminal law is concerned with acts harmful to the community and the rules laid down by the state for the benefit of citizens, whereas civil law governs the relationships and transactions between individuals. Administrative law is a kind of civil law usually concerning the interaction of individuals and the state, and most cases are heard in tribunals specific to the subject (*see* Tribunals section). Scotland and Northern Ireland possess legal systems that differ from the system in England and Wales in law, judicial procedure and court structure, but retain the distinction between criminal and civil law.

Under the provisions of the Criminal Appeal Act 1995, a commission was set up to direct and supervise investigations into possible miscarriages of justice and to refer cases to the appeal courts on the grounds of conviction and sentence; these functions were formerly the responsibility of the home secretary.

HIERARCHY OF ENGLISH AND WELSH COURTS

SENIOR COURTS OF ENGLAND AND WALES

The senior courts of England and Wales (until September 2009 known as the supreme court of judicature of England and Wales) comprise the high court, the crown court and the court of appeal. The President of the Courts of England and Wales, a new title given to the Lord Chief Justice under the Constitutional Reform Act 2005, is the head of the judiciary.

The high court was created in 1875 and combined many previously separate courts. Sittings are held at the royal courts of justice in London or at around 120 district registries outside the capital. It is the superior civil court and is split into three divisions – the chancery division, the Queen's bench division and the family division – each of which is further divided. The chancery division is headed by the Chancellor of the High Court and is concerned mainly with equity, trusts, tax and bankruptcy, while also including two specialist courts, the patents court and the companies court. The Queen's bench division (QBD) is the largest of the three divisions, and is headed by its own president. It deals with common law (ie tort, contract, debt and personal injuries), some tax law, eg VAT tribunal appeals, and encompasses the admiralty court and the commercial court. The QBD also administers the technology and construction court. The family division was created in 1970 and is headed by its own president, who is also Head of Family Justice, and hears cases concerning divorce, access to and custody of children, and other family matters. The divisional court of the high court sits in the family and chancery divisions, and hears appeals from the magistrates' courts and county courts.

The crown court was set up in 1972 and sits at 77 centres throughout England and Wales. It deals with more serious (indictable) criminal offences, which are triable before a judge and jury, including treason, murder, rape, kidnapping, armed robbery and Official Secrets Act offences. It also handles cases transferred from the magistrates' courts where the magistrate decides his or her own power of sentence is inadequate, or where someone appeals against a magistrate's decision, or in a case that is triable 'either way' where the accused has chosen a jury trial. The crown court centres are divided into three tiers: high court judges, circuit judges and sometimes recorders (part-time circuit judges), sit in first-tier centres, hearing the most serious criminal offences (eg murder, treason, rape, manslaughter) and some civil high court cases. The second-tier centres are presided over by high court judges, circuit judges or recorders and also deal with the most serious criminal cases. Third-tier courts deal with the remaining criminal offences, with circuit judges or recorders presiding.

The court of appeal hears appeals against both fact and law, and was last restructured in 1966 when it replaced the court of criminal appeal. It is split into the civil division (which hears appeals from the high court, tribunals and in certain cases, the county courts) and the criminal division (which hears appeals from the crown court). Cases are heard by Lords Justices of Appeal and high court judges if deemed suitable for reconsideration.

The Constitutional Reform Act 2005 instigated several key changes to the judiciary in England and Wales. These included the establishment of the independent supreme court, which opened in October 2009; the reform of the post of Lord Chancellor, transferring its judicial functions to the President of the Courts of England and Wales; a duty on government ministers to uphold the independence of the judiciary by barring them from trying to influence judicial decisions through any special access to judges; the formation of a fully transparent and independent Judicial Appointments Commission that is responsible for selecting candidates to recommend for judicial appointment to the Lord Chancellor and Secretary of State for Justice; and the creation of the post of Judicial Appointments and Conduct Ombudsman.

CRIMINAL CASES

In criminal matters the decision to prosecute (in the majority of cases) rests with the Crown Prosecution Service (CPS), which is the independent prosecuting body in England and Wales. The CPS is headed by the director of public prosecutions, who works under the superintendence of the Attorney-General. Certain categories of offence continue to require the Attorney-General's consent for prosecution.

Most minor criminal cases (summary offences) are dealt with in magistrates' courts, usually by a bench of three unpaid lay magistrates (justices of the peace) sitting without a jury and assisted on points of law and procedure by a legally trained clerk. There are approximately 23,000 justices of the peace. In some courts a full-time, salaried and legally qualified district judge (magistrates' court) – formerly known as a stipendiary judge – presides alone. There are 140 district judges and 170 deputy district judges operating in around 330 magistrates' courts in England and Wales. Magistrates' courts deal with 95 per cent of all criminal cases. Magistrates' courts also house some family proceedings courts (which deal with relationship breakdown and childcare cases) and youth courts. Cases of medium seriousness (known as 'offences triable either way') where the defendant pleads not guilty can be heard in the crown court for a trial by jury, if the defendant so chooses. Preliminary proceedings in a serious case to decide whether there is evidence to justify committal for trial in the crown court are dealt with in the magistrates' courts.

The 77 centres that the crown court sits in are divided into seven regions. There are over 600 circuit judges and 1,000 recorders (part-time circuit judges); expected to sit for 30 days a year. A jury is present in all trials that are contested.

Appeals from magistrates' courts against sentence or conviction are made to the crown court, and appeals upon a point of law are made to the high court, which may ultimately be appealed to the supreme court. Appeals from the crown court, either against sentence or conviction, are made to the court of appeal (criminal division). Again, these appeals may be brought to the supreme court if a point of law is contested, and if the house considers it is of sufficient importance.

CIVIL CASES

Most minor civil cases – including contract, tort (especially personal injuries), property, divorce and other family matters, bankruptcy etc – are dealt with by the county courts, of which there are around 200 (see W www.justice.gov.uk for further details). Cases are heard by circuit judges, recorders or district judges. For cases involving small claims (with certain exceptions, where the amount claimed is £5,000 or less) there are informal and simplified procedures designed to enable parties to present their cases themselves without recourse to lawyers. Where there are financial limits on county court jurisdiction, claims that exceed those limits may be tried in the county courts with the consent of the parties, subject to the court's agreement, or in certain circumstances on transfer from the high court. Outside London, bankruptcy proceedings can be heard in designated county courts. Magistrates' courts also deal with certain classes of civil case, and committees of magistrates license public houses, clubs and betting shops. For the implementation of the Children Act 1989, a new structure of hearing centres was set up in 1991 for family proceedings cases, involving magistrates' courts (family proceedings courts), divorce county courts, family hearing centres and care centres.

Appeals in certain family matters heard in the family proceedings courts go to the family division of the high court. Appeals from county courts may be heard in the court of appeal (civil division) or the high court, and may go on to the supreme court.

CORONERS' COURTS

Unlike the unified courts system, administered by HM Courts and Tribunals Service, there are 92 separate coroners' jurisdictions in England and Wales. Each jurisdiction is locally funded and resourced by local authorities. Coroners are barristers, solicitors or medical practitioners of not less than five years standing, who continue in their legal or medical practices when not sitting as coroners. Some 32 coroners are 'full-time' coroners and are paid an annual salary regardless of their caseload. The remainder are paid according to the number of cases referred to them. The coroner's jurisdiction is territorial – it is the location of the dead body which dictates which coroner has jurisdiction in any particular case.

The coroners' courts investigate violent and unnatural deaths or sudden deaths where the cause is unknown. Doctors, the police, various public authorities or members of the public may bring cases before a coroner. Where a death is sudden and the cause is unknown, the coroner may order a post-mortem examination to determine the cause of death rather than hold an inquest in court. An inquest must be held, however, if a person died in a violent or unnatural way, or died in prison or other unusual circumstances. If the coroner suspects murder, manslaughter or infanticide, then they must summon a jury.

Coroners are required to appoint a deputy or assistant deputy to act in their stead if they are out of the district or otherwise unable to act. Deputies and assistant deputies have the same professional qualifications as the coroner. In exceptionally high-profile or complex cases, a serving judge may be appointed as a deputy coroner.

SENIOR JUDICIARY OF ENGLAND AND WALES

Lord Chief Justice of England and Wales and Head of Criminal Justice (£262,264), Rt. Hon. Lord Burnett of Maldon, *born* 1958, *apptd* 2017

Master of the Rolls and Head of Civil Justice (£234,184), Rt. Hon. Sir Terence Etherton, *born* 1951, *apptd* 2016

President of the Queen's Bench Division (£226,193), Rt. Hon. Dame Victoria Sharp, DBE, *born* 1956, *apptd* 2019

President of the Family Division and Head of Family Justice (£226,193), Rt. Hon. Sir Andrew McFarlane, *born* 1954, *apptd* 2018

Chancellor of the High Court (£226,193), Rt. Hon. Sir Geoffrey Vos, *born* 1955, *apptd* 2016

SENIOR COURTS OF ENGLAND AND WALES

COURT OF APPEAL

Presiding Judge, Criminal Division, Lord Chief Justice of England and Wales

Presiding Judge, Civil Division, Master of the Rolls

Vice-President, Civil Division (£215,094), Rt. Hon. Sir Nicholas Underhill *born* 1952, *apptd* 2018

Vice-President, Criminal Division (£215,094), Rt. Hon. Dame Heather Hallett, DBE, *born* 1949, *apptd* 2013

LORD JUSTICES OF APPEAL *as at September 2019* (each £215,094)

Style, The Rt. Hon. Lord/Lady Justice [surname]

Rt. Hon. Sir Andrew Longmore, *born* 1944, *apptd* 2001
Rt. Hon. Dame Heather Hallett, DBE, *born* 1949, *apptd* 2005
Rt. Hon. Sir Nicholas Patten, *born* 1950, *apptd* 2009
Rt. Hon. Sir Peter Gross, *born* 1952, *apptd* 2010
Rt. Hon. Dame Anne Rafferty, DBE, *born* 1950, *apptd* 2011
Rt. Hon. Sir Nigel Davis, *born* 1951, *apptd* 2011
Rt. Hon. Sir Kim Lewison, *born* 1952, *apptd* 2011
Rt. Hon. Sir Colman Treacy, *born* 1949, *apptd* 2012
Rt. Hon. Sir Richard McCombe, *born* 1952, *apptd* 2012

Rt. Hon. Sir Ernest Ryder, TD, *born* 1957, *apptd* 2013
Rt. Hon. Sir Nicholas Underhill, *born* 1952, *apptd* 2013
Rt. Hon. Sir Christopher Floyd, *born* 1951, *apptd* 2013
Rt. Hon. Sir Adrian Fulford, *born* 1953, *apptd* 2013
Rt. Hon. Dame Julia Macur, DBE, *born* 1957, *apptd* 2013
Rt. Hon. Sir David Bean, *born* 1954, *apptd* 2014
Rt. Hon. Dame Eleanor King, DBE, *born* 1957, *apptd* 2014
Rt. Hon. Sir Peregrine Simon, *born* 1950, *apptd* 2015
Rt. Hon. Sir Keith Lindblom, *born* 1956, *apptd* 2015
Rt. Hon. Sir David Richards, *born* 1951, *apptd* 2015
Rt. Hon. Sir Nicholas Hamblen, *born* 1957, *apptd* 2016
Rt. Hon. Sir Stephen Irwin, *born* 1953, *apptd* 2016
Rt. Hon. Sir Launcelot Henderson, *born* 1951, *apptd* 2016
Rt. Hon. Sir Julian Flaux, *born* 1955, *apptd* 2016
Rt. Hon. Dame Kathryn Thirlwall, DBE, *born* 1957, *apptd* 2017
Rt. Hon. Sir Gary Hickinbottom, *born* 1955, *apptd* 2017
Rt. Hon. Sir Andrew Moylan, *born* 1953, *apptd* 2017
Rt. Hon. Sir Timothy Holroyde, *born* 1955, *apptd* 2017
Rt. Hon. Sir Peter Jackson, *born* 1955, *apptd* 2017
Rt. Hon Sir Guy Newey, *born* 1959, *apptd* 2017
Rt. Hon Sir Rabinder Singh, *born* 1964, *apptd* 2017
Rt. Hon. Dame Sarah Asplin, DBE, *born* 1959, *apptd* 2017
Rt. Hon. Sir George Leggatt, *born* 1957, *apptd* 2018
Rt. Hon. Sir Peter Coulson, *born* 1958, *apptd* 2018
Rt. Hon. Sir Jonathan Baker, *born* 1955, *apptd* 2018
Rt. Hon. Sir Charles Haddon-Cave, *born* 1956, *apptd* 2018
Rt. Hon. Sir Nicholas Green, *born* 1958, *apptd* 2018
Rt. Hon. Dame Nicola Davies, DBE, *born* 1953, *apptd* 2018
Rt. Hon. Sir Stephen Males, *born* 1955, *apptd* 2019
Rt. Hon. Dame Vivien Rose, DBE, *born* 1960, *apptd* 2019
Rt. Hon. Dame Ingrid Simler, DBE, *born* 1963, *apptd* 2019

Ex Officio Judges, Lord Chief Justice of England and Wales; Master of the Rolls; President of the Queen's Bench Division; President of the Family Division; Chancellor of the High Court

COURTS-MARTIAL APPEAL COURT

Judges, Lord Chief Justice of England and Wales; Master of the Rolls; Lord Justices of Appeal; Judges of the High Court of Justice

HIGH COURT

CHANCERY DIVISION

Chancellor of the High Court (£226,193), Rt. Hon. Sir Geoffrey Vos, *born* 1955, *apptd* 2016
Clerk, Natalie Ford
Legal Secretary, Vannina Ettori

JUDGES *as at September 2019* (each £188,901)
Style, The Hon. Mr/Mrs/Ms Justice [surname]

Hon. Sir George Mann, *born* 1951, *apptd* 2004
Hon. Sir Paul Morgan, *born* 1952, *apptd* 2007
Hon. Sir Alastair Norris, *born* 1950, *apptd* 2007
Hon. Sir Gerald Barling, *born* 1949, *apptd* 2007
Hon. Sir Richard Arnold, *born* 1961, *apptd* 2008
Hon. Sir Peter Roth, *born* 1952, *apptd* 2009
Hon. Sir Robert Hildyard, *born* 1952, *apptd* 2011
Hon. Sir Colin Birss, *born* 1964, *apptd* 2013
Hon. Sir Christopher Nugee, *born* 1959, *apptd* 2013
Hon. Sir Richard Snowden, *born* 1962, *apptd* 2015
Hon. Sir Marcus Smith, *born* 1967, *apptd* 2017
Hon. Sir Antony Zacaroli, *born* 1963, *apptd* 2017
Hon. Sir Timothy Fancourt, *born* 1964, *apptd* 2018
Hon. Dame Sarah Falk, DBE, *born* 1962, *apptd* 2018
The Chancery Division also includes three specialist courts: the Companies Court, the Patents Court and the Bankruptcy Court.

QUEEN'S BENCH DIVISION
President (£226,193), Rt. Hon. Dame Victoria Sharp, DBE, *born* 1956, *apptd* 2019
Vice-President (£215,094), vacant

JUDGES *as at September 2019* (each £188,901)
Style, The Hon. Mr/Mrs/Ms Justice [surname]

Hon. Sir Paul Walker, *born* 1954, *apptd* 2004
Hon. Sir Nigel Teare, *born* 1952, *apptd* 2006
Hon. Sir Nigel Sweeney, *born* 1954, *apptd* 2008
Hon. Sir Andrew Nicol, *born* 1951, *apptd* 2009
Hon. Sir Michael Supperstone, *born* 1950, *apptd* 2010
Hon. Sir Robin Spencer, *born* 1955, *apptd* 2010
Hon. Sir Andrew Popplewell, *born* 1959, *apptd* 2011
Hon. Dame Beverley Lang, DBE, *born* 1955, *apptd* 2011
Hon. Sir Jeremy Stuart-Smith, *born* 1955, *apptd* 2012
Hon. Sir Mark Turner, *born* 1959, *apptd* 2013
Hon. Sir Jeremy Baker, *born* 1958, *apptd* 2013
Hon. Sir Stephen Stewart, *born* 1953, *apptd* 2013
Hon. Sir Robert Jay, *born* 1959, *apptd* 2013
Hon. Sir James Dingemans, *born* 1964, *apptd* 2013
Hon. Sir Clive Lewis, *born* 1960, *apptd* 2013
Hon. Dame Sue Carr, DBE, *born* 1964, *apptd* 2013
Hon. Sir Stephen Phillips, *born* 1961, *apptd* 2013
Hon. Dame Geraldine Andrews, DBE, *born* 1959, *apptd* 2013
Hon. Dame Elisabeth Laing, DBE, *born* 1956, *apptd* 2014
Hon. Sir William Davis, *born* 1954, *apptd* 2014
Hon. Sir Mark Warby, *born* 1958, *apptd* 2014
Hon. Sir Andrew Edis, *born* 1957, *apptd* 2014
Hon. Sir James Goss, *born* 1953, *apptd* 2014
Hon. Dame Maura McGowan, DBE, *born* 1957, *apptd* 2014
Hon. Sir Robin Knowles, *born* 1960, *apptd* 2014
Hon. Sir Ian Dove, *born* 1963, *apptd* 2014
Hon. Sir David Holgate, *born* 1956, *apptd* 2014
Hon. Sir Timothy Kerr, *born* 1958, *apptd* 2015
Hon. Sir Simon Picken, *born* 1966, *apptd* 2015
Hon. Dame Philippa Whipple, DBE, *born* 1966, *apptd* 2015
Hon. Sir Peter Fraser, *born* 1963, *apptd* 2015
Hon. Sir Neil Garnham, *born* 1959, *apptd* 2015
Hon. Dame Bobbie Cheema-Grubb, DBE *born* 1966, *apptd* 2015
Hon. Sir Michael Soole, *born* 1954, *apptd* 2015
Hon. Dame Juliet May, DBE, *born* 1961, *apptd* 2015
Hon. Sir Stephen Morris, *born* 1957, *apptd* 2016
Hon. Dame Nerys Jefford, DBE, *born* 1962, *apptd* 2016
Hon. Sir Nicholas Lavender, *born* 1964, *apptd* 2016
Hon. Dame Finola O'Farrell, DBE, *born* 1960, *apptd* 2016
Hon. Sir Andrew Baker, *born* 1965, *apptd* 2016
Hon. Sir Julian Goose, *born* 1961, *apptd* 2017
Hon. Sir Peter Lane, *born* 1953, *apptd* 2017
Hon. Sir Simon Bryan, *born* 1965, *apptd* 2017
Hon. Dame Jane Moulder, DBE, *born* 1960, *apptd* 2017
Hon. Sir Martin Spencer, *born* 1956, *apptd* 2017
Hon. Sir Julian Knowles, *born* 1969, *apptd* 2017
Hon. Dame Amanda Yip, DBE, *born* 1969, *apptd* 2017
Hon. Sir Matthew Nicklin, *born* 1970, *apptd* 2017
Hon. Sir Akhlaq Choudhury, *born* 1967, *apptd* 2017
Hon. Dame Sara Cockerill, DBE, *born* 1968, *apptd* 2017
Hon. Dame Christina Lambert, DBE, *born* 1963, *apptd* 2018
Hon. Sir Christopher Butcher, *born* 1962, *apptd* 2018
Hon. Sir Richard Jacobs, *born* 1956, *apptd* 2018
Hon. Sir David Waksman, *born* 1957, *apptd* 2018
Hon. Dame Johannah Cutts, DBE, *born* 1964, *apptd* 2018
Hon. Sir Jonathan Swift, *born* 1964, *apptd* 2018
Hon. Sir Edward Pepperall, *born* 1966, *apptd* 2018
Hon. Sir Edward Murray, *born* 1958, *apptd* 2018
Hon. Dame Judith Farbey, DBE, *born* 1965, *apptd* 2018
Hon. Clive Freedman, *born* 1955, *apptd* 2018

Hon. Dame Justine Thornton, *born* 1970, *apptd* 2019
Hon. Dame Jennifer Eady, DBE, *born* 1965, *apptd* 2019
Hon. Sir John Cavanagh, *born* 1960, *apptd* 2019
Hon. Dame Alison Foster, *born* 1957, *apptd* 2019
Hon. Sir Pushpinder Saini, *born* 1968, *apptd* 2019
Hon. Sir Jeremy Johnson, *born* 1971, *apptd* 2019
Hon. Sir Martin Chamberlain, *born* 1974, *apptd* 2019

The Queen's Bench Division also includes the Divisional Court, the Admiralty Court, Commercial Court and Technology and Construction Court.

FAMILY DIVISION
President (£226,193), Rt. Hon. Sir Andrew McFarlane, *born* 1954, *apptd* 2018

JUDGES *as at September 2019* (each £188,901)
Style, The Hon. Mr/Mrs/Ms Justice [surname]

Hon. Sir Edward Holman, *born* 1947, *apptd* 1995
Hon. Sir Nicholas Mostyn, *born* 1957, *apptd* 2010
Hon. Dame Lucy Theis, DBE, *born* 1960, *apptd* 2010
Hon. Sir Philip Moor, *born* 1959, *apptd* 2011
Hon. Sir Stephen Cobb, *born* 1962, *apptd* 2013
Hon. Sir Michael Keehan, *born* 1960, *apptd* 2013
Hon. Sir Anthony Hayden, *born* 1961, *apptd* 2013
Hon. Dame Alison Russell, DBE, *born* 1958, *apptd* 2014
Hon. Sir Roderick Newton, *born* 1958, *apptd* 2014
Hon. Dame Jennifer Roberts, DBE, *born* 1953, *apptd* 2014
Hon. Sir Alistair MacDonald, *born* 1970, *apptd* 2015
Hon. Sir Peter Francis, *born* 1958, *apptd* 2016
Hon. Dame Gwynneth Knowles, DBE *born* 1962, *apptd* 2017
Hon. Sir Jonathan Cohen, *born* 1951, *apptd* 2017
Hon. Sir David Williams, *born* 1961, *apptd* 2017
Hon. Dame Nathalie Lieven, DBE, *born* 1964, *apptd* 2019
Hon. Dame Frances Judd, DBE, *born* 1961, *apptd* 2019

COURTS, DIVISIONS AND OFFICES OF THE HIGH COURT OF ENGLAND AND WALES

ADMINISTRATIVE COURT
Royal Courts of Justice, London WC2A 2LL
T 020-7947 6655
Judge in charge of the Administrative Court (£188,901), Hon. Mr Justice Supperstone
Registrar of Criminal Appeals, Master of the Crown Office and Queen's Coroner and Attorney (£140,289), Master Beldam

ADMIRALTY COURT
Ground Floor, 7 Rolls Building, Fetter Lane, London EC4A 1NL
T 020-7947 6112
Admiralty Judge (£188,901), Hon. Mr Justice Teare
Clerk, Paul Doerr
Registrar (£112,542), vacant

CIRCUIT COMMERCIAL COURT (formerly Mercantile Court)
Ground Floor, 7 Rolls Building, Fetter Lane, London EC4A 1NL
T 020-7947 6112

CHANCERY DIVISION
7 Rolls Building, Fetter Lane, London EC4A 1NL T 020-7947 7391
Chief Chancery Master (£140,289), Chief Master Marsh *apptd* 2014
Masters of Chancery (£112,542), Master Clark *apptd* 2015; Master Kaye *apptd* 2019; Master Matthews *apptd* 2015; Master Shuman *apptd* 2017; Master Teverson *apptd* 2005

COMMERCIAL COURT
Ground Floor, 7 Rolls Building, Fetter Lane, London EC4A 1NL
T 020-7947 7501
Judge in charge of the Commercial Court (£188,901), Hon. Mr
Justice Teare
Clerk, Paul Doerr

COURT OF APPEAL CIVIL DIVISION
Royal Courts of Justice, London WC2A 2LL T 020-7947 6916

COURT OF APPEAL CRIMINAL DIVISION
Royal Courts of Justice, London WC2A 2LL T 020-7947 6011

COURT OF PROTECTION
First Avenue House, 42–49 High Holborn, London WC1V 6NP
T 0300-456 4600
Senior Judge and Master of the Court of Protection (£140,289),
Her Hon. Judge Hilder, *apptd* 2017

FAMILY DIVISION
Royal Courts of Justice, London WC2A 2LL T 020-7947 6000

INSOLVENCY AND COMPANIES LIST
7 Rolls Building, Fetter Lane, London EC4A 1NL
T 020-7947 6294
Chief Registrar (140,289), Nicholas Briggs *apptd* 2017
Insolvency and Companies Court Judges (£112,542), Judge
Barber *apptd* 2009; Judge Burton *apptd* 2018; Judge Jones
apptd 2012; Judge Mullen *apptd* 2018; Judge Prentis *apptd*
2018

INTELLECTUAL PROPERTY ENTERPRISE COURT
7 Rolls Building, Fetter Lane, London EC4A 1NL
T 020-7947 7783 E ipec@hmcts.gsi.gov.uk
Judge in Charge, His Hon. Judge Hacon
Clerk, Irram Khan

PATENTS COURT
7 Rolls Building, Fetter Lane, London EC4A 1NL
T 020-7073 1789
Judge in Charge, Hon. Mr Justice Arnold
Clerk, Pauline Drewett

PLANNING COURT
Royal Courts of Justice, London WC2A 2LL
T 020-7947 6655

QUEEN'S BENCH DIVISION
Judge in Charge of the Queen's Bench Civil List, Hon. Mr Justice
Stewart
Senior Master and Queen's Remembrancer (£140,289), Senior
Master Fontaine *apptd* 2014
Masters of the Queen's Bench Division (£112,542), Master Cook
apptd 2011; Master Davison *apptd* 2016; Master Eastman
apptd 2009; Master Gidden *apptd* 2012; Master McCloud
apptd 2010; Master Thornett *apptd* 2016; Master Yoxall
apptd 2002

SENIOR COURT COSTS OFFICE
Thomas More Building, Royal Courts of Justice, London WC2A 2LL
T 020-7947 6000
Senior Costs Judge (Chief Taxing Master) (£140,289), Chief
Master Gordon-Saker *apptd* 2014
Cost Judges (Taxing Masters) (£112,542), Master Brown *apptd*
2016; Master Haworth *apptd* 2006; Master James *apptd*
2015; Master Leonard *apptd* 2010; Master Nagalingam
apptd 2017; Master Rowley *apptd* 2013; Master Whalan
apptd 2015

TECHNOLOGY AND CONSTRUCTION COURT (TCC)
Ground Floor, 7 Rolls Building, Fetter Lane, London EC4A 1NL
T 020-7947 7156
Judge in charge of the TCC (£188,901), Hon. Mr Justice Fraser

COURT FUNDS OFFICE

Sunderland SR43 3AB T 0300-020 0199 E enquiries@cfo.gsi.gov.uk

The Court Funds Office (CFO), established in 1726, provides
a banking and administration service for the civil courts
throughout England and Wales, including the High Court.

ELECTION PETITIONS OFFICE

Room E113, Royal Courts of Justice, Strand, London WC2A 2LL
T 020-7947 6877

The office accepts petitions and deals with all matters relating
to the questioning of parliamentary, European parliament,
local government and parish elections, and with applications
for relief under the 'representation of the people' legislation.

Prescribed Officer, The Senior Master and Senior Remembrancer
(£140,289), B. Fontaine

EXAMINERS OF THE COURT

A panel of 18 advocates and solicitor advocates, of at least three
years standing, is empowered to take examination of witnesses
in all divisions of the High Court.

Examiners, Tony Baumgartner; Naomi Candlin; Angharad
Davies; Judy Dawson; Alison Green; Nicholas Hill; Mathias
Kelly; John Leslie; Simon Lewis; Josh Lewison; Susan Lindsey;
Andrew McLoughlin; Christopher McNall; Michael Salter;
Ashley Serr; Frederico Singarajah; Lara Spencer; John
Hamilton

OFFICIAL SOLICITOR AND PUBLIC TRUSTEE

Victory House, 30–34 Kingsway, London WC2B 6EX
E enquiries@ospt.gov.uk

The Official Solicitor and the Public Trustee are independent
statutory office holders. Their office (OSPT) is an arms-length
body of the Ministry of Justice that exists to support their work.
The Official Solicitor provides access to the justice system to
those who are vulnerable by virtue of minority or lack of mental
capacity. The Public Trustee acts as executor or administrator
of estates and as the appointed trustee of settlements, providing
an effective executor and trustee service of last resort.

Official Solicitor to the Senior Courts and the Public Trustee, Sarah
Castle
Deputy Public Trustee, Janet Peel
Deputy Official Solicitors, Brid Breathnach; Elaine Brown; Janet
Ilett

PROBATE REGISTRIES

London Probate Department, 7th Floor, First Avenue House, 42–49
High Holborn, London WC1V 6NP T 020-7421 8509

Probate registries issue grants of probate and grants of letters
of administration. The principal probate registry is situated in
central London and there are 11 district probate registries in
Birmingham, Brighton, Bristol, Cardiff, Ipswich, Leeds,
Liverpool, Manchester, Newcastle, Oxford and Winchester,
and a further 18 probate sub-registries. Probate registries are
administered by HM Courts and Tribunals Service.

JUDGE ADVOCATES GENERAL

The Judge Advocate General is the judicial head of the Service justice system, and the leader of the judges who preside over trials in the court martial and other Service courts. The defendants are service personnel from the Royal Navy, the army and the Royal Air Force, and civilians accompanying them overseas.

JUDGE ADVOCATE GENERAL OF THE FORCES
9th Floor, Thomas More Building, Royal Courts of Justice, Strand, London WC2A 2LL T 020-7218 8095

Judge Advocate General (£151,497), His Hon. Judge Blackett
Vice-Judge Advocate General (£132,075), Judge Hunter
Assistant Judge Advocates General (£112,542), J. P. Camp; R. D. Hill; A. M. Large; A. J. B. McGrigor
Style, Judge [surname]

CROWN COURT CENTRES

The crown court sits in 77 court centres across England and Wales. It deals with serious criminal cases which include:
* cases sent for trial by magistrates' courts because the offences are 'indictable only' (ie those which can only be heard by the crown court)
* 'either way' offences (which can be heard in a magistrates' court, but can also be sent to the crown court if the defendant chooses a jury trial)
* defendants convicted in magistrates' courts, but sent to the Crown Court for sentencing due to the seriousness of the offence
* appeals against decisions of magistrates' courts

First-tier centres deal with both civil and criminal cases and are served by high court and circuit judges. Second-tier centres deal with criminal cases only and are served by high court and circuit judges. Third-tier centres deal with criminal cases only and are served only by circuit judges.

In London, the high court acts as the first-tier centre, sitting at the Royal Courts of Justice, and the second-tier is the Central Criminal Court.

CIRCUIT JUDGES

Circuit judges are barristers of at least seven years' standing or recorders of at least five years' standing. Circuit judges serve in the county courts and the crown court.

Style, His/Her Hon. Judge [surname]
Senior Presiding Judge, Rt. Hon. Lady Justice Macur, DBE
Deputy Senior Presiding Judge, Rt. Hon Lady Justice Thirlwall, DBE
Senior Circuit Judges, each £151,497
Circuit Judges at the Central Criminal Court, London (Old Bailey Judges), each £151,497
Circuit Judges, each £140,289

MIDLAND CIRCUIT
Presiding Judges, Hon. Mrs Justice Carr; Hon. Mr Justice Jeremy Baker
NORTH-EASTERN CIRCUIT
Presiding Judges, Hon. Mr Justice Goss; Hon. Mr Justice Lavender
NORTHERN CIRCUIT
Presiding Judges, Hon. Mr Justice William Davis; Hon. Mr Justice Dove
SOUTH-EASTERN CIRCUIT
Presiding Judges, Hon. Mrs Justice McGowan; Hon. Mr Justice Edis; Hon. Mrs Justice Whipple; Hon. Mrs Justice Cheema-Grubb
WALES CIRCUIT
Presiding Judges, Hon. Mr Justice Lewis; Hon. Mr Justice Picken

WESTERN CIRCUIT
Presiding Judges, Hon. Mrs Justice May; Hon. Mr Justice Garnham

DISTRICT JUDGES

District judges, formerly known as registrars of the court, are solicitors of at least seven years' standing and serve in county courts.
District Judges, each £112,542

DISTRICT JUDGES (MAGISTRATES' COURTS)

District judges (magistrates' courts), formerly known as stipendiary magistrates, serve in magistrates courts where they hear criminal cases, youth cases and some civil proceedings. Many also hear family cases in the single family court. Some may be authorised to handle extradition proceedings and terrorist cases. District judges (magistrates' courts) are appointed following competition conducted by the Judicial Appointments Commission.
District Judges (Magistrates' Courts), each £112,542

OFFICE OF THE CHIEF MAGISTRATE
181 Marylebone Road, London NW1 5BR
T 020-3126 3100

The Chief Magistrate (senior district judge) is responsible for hearing many of the sensitive or complex cases – extradition and special jurisdiction cases in particular – in the magistrates' courts. The Chief Magistrate also supports and guides district judges (magistrates' courts), and liaises with the senior judiciary and presiding judges on matters pertaining to magistrates' courts.

The Office of the Chief Magistrate provides administration support to both the Chief Magistrate and to all the district judges sitting at magistrates' courts in England and Wales.

Chief Magistrate, Emma Arbuthnot
Deputy Chief Magistrate, Tanweer Ikram

CROWN PROSECUTION SERVICE

102 Petty France, London SW1H 9EA
T 020-3357 0899 E enquiries@cps.gov.uk W www.cps.gov.uk

The Crown Prosecution Service (CPS) is responsible for prosecuting cases investigated by the police in England and Wales, with the exception of cases conducted by the Serious Fraud Office and certain minor offences.

The CPS is headed by the director of public prosecutions (DPP), who works under the superintendence of the attorney-general. The service is divided into 14 regional teams across England and Wales, with each area led by a chief crown prosecutor.

Director of Public Prosecutions, Max Hill, QC
Chief Executive, Rebecca Lawrence
Directors, Jean Ashton, OBE *(Business Services);* Sue Hemming *(Legal Services);* Gregor McGill *(Legal Services)*

CPS AREAS
EAST MIDLANDS, 2 King Edward Court, King Edward Street, Nottingham NG1 1EL T 0115-852 3300
Chief Crown Prosecutor, Janine Smith
EAST OF ENGLAND, County House, 100 New London Road, Chelmsford, Essex CM2 0RG T 01245-455800
Chief Crown Prosecutor, Chris Long
LONDON, 1st Floor, Zone A, 102 Petty France, London SW1H 9EA T 020-3357 7000
Chief Crown Prosecutor London North, Ed Beltrami, CBE
Chief Crown Prosecutor London South, Claire Lindley

MERSEY–CHESHIRE, 2nd Floor, Walker House, Exchange Flags, Liverpool L2 3YL T 0151-239 6400
Chief Crown Prosecutor, Siobhan Blake

NORTH EAST, St Ann's Quay, 112 Quayside, Newcastle Upon Tyne, NE1 3BD T 0191-260 4200
Chief Crown Prosecutor, Andrew Penhale

NORTH WEST, 1st Floor, Stocklund House, Castle Street, Carlisle CA3 8SY T 01228-882900
Chief Crown Prosecutor, Martin Goldman

SOUTH EAST, Riding Gate House, 37 Old Dover Road, Canterbury, Kent CT1 3JG T 01227-866000
Chief Crown Prosecutor, Frank Ferguson

SOUTH WEST, 5th Floor, Kite Wing, Temple Quay House, 2 The Square, Bristol BS1 6PN T 0117-930 2800
Chief Crown Prosecutor, Victoria Cook

THAMES AND CHILTERN, Eaton Court, 112 Oxford Road, Reading, Berks RG1 7LL T 01727-798700
Chief Crown Prosecutor, Jaswant Kaur Narwal

WALES, 20th Floor, Capital Tower, Greyfriars Road, Cardiff CF10 3PL T 029-2080 3800
Chief Crown Prosecutor, Barry Hughes

WESSEX, 3rd Floor, Black Horse House, 8–10 Leigh Road, Eastleigh, Hants SO50 9FH T 0238-067 3800
Chief Crown Prosecutor, Joanne Jakymec

WEST MIDLANDS, Colmore Gate, 2 Colmore Row, Birmingham B3 2QA T 0121-262 1300
Chief Crown Prosecutor, Grace Ononiwu, OBE

YORKSHIRE AND HUMBERSIDE, 27 Park Place, Leeds LS1 2SZ T 0113-290 2700
Chief Crown Prosecutor, Gerry Wareham

HER MAJESTY'S COURTS AND TRIBUNALS SERVICE

1st Floor, 102 Petty France, London SW1H 9AJ
W www.gov.uk/government/organisations/hm-courts-and-tribunals-service

Her Majesty's Courts Service and the Tribunals Service merged on 1 April 2011 to form HM Courts and Tribunals Service. It is an agency of the Ministry of Justice, operating as a partnership between the Lord Chancellor, the Lord Chief Justice and the Senior President of Tribunals. It is responsible for administering the criminal, civil and family courts and tribunals in England and Wales and non-devolved tribunals in Scotland and Northern Ireland.

Chief Executive, Susan Acland-Hood

JUDICIAL APPOINTMENTS COMMISSION

5th Floor, Clive House, 70 Petty France, London SW1H 9EX
T 020-3334 0123 E jaas@judicialappointments.gov.uk
W www.judicialappointments.gov.uk

The Judicial Appointments Commission was established as an independent non-departmental public body in April 2006 by the Constitutional Reform Act 2005. Its role is to select judicial office holders independently of government (a responsibility previously held by the Lord Chancellor) for courts and tribunals in England and Wales, and for some tribunals whose jurisdiction extends to Scotland or Northern Ireland. It has a statutory duty to encourage diversity in the range of persons available for selection and is sponsored by the Ministry of Justice and accountable to parliament through the Lord Chancellor. It is made up of a total of 15 commissioners: seven judicial (including one non-legal), two professional, five lay and the chair.

Chair, Rt. Hon. Prof. Lord Kakkar
Vice-Chair, Rt. Hon. Dame Anne Rafferty, DBE
Commissioners, Judge Mathu Asokan; Her Hon. Judge Anuja Dhir; Emir Khan Feisal; Jane Furness, CBE; Sue Hoyle;

Andrew Kennon; Sarah Lee; Judge Fiona Monk; Brie Stevens-Hoare, QC; His Hon. Judge Phillip Sycamore; Sir Simon Wessely; Dame Philippa Whipple, DBE
Chief Executive, Richard Jarvis

JUDICIAL OFFICE

The Judicial Office was established in April 2006 to support the judiciary in discharging its responsibilities under the Constitutional Reform Act 2005. It is led by a chief executive, who reports to the Lord Chief Justice and Senior President of Tribunals rather than to ministers, and its work is directed by the judiciary rather than by the administration of the day. The Judicial Office incorporates the Judicial College, sponsorship of the Family and Civil Justice Councils, the Office for Judicial Complaints and Office of the Chief Coroner.

Chief Executive, Andrew Key

JUDICIAL COMMITTEE OF THE PRIVY COUNCIL

The Judicial Committee of the Privy Council is the final court of appeal for the United Kingdom overseas territories (*see* UK Overseas Territories section), crown dependencies and those independent Commonwealth countries which have retained this avenue of appeal and the sovereign base areas of Akrotiri and Dhekelia in Cyprus. The committee also hears appeals against pastoral schemes under the Pastoral Measure 1983, and deals with appeals from veterinary disciplinary bodies.

Until October 2009, the Judicial Committee of the Privy Council was the final arbiter in disputes as to the legal competence of matters done or proposed by the devolved legislative and executive authorities in Scotland, Wales and Northern Ireland. This is now the responsibility of the UK Supreme Court.

The members of the Judicial Committee are the justices of the supreme court, and Privy Counsellors who hold or have held high judicial office in the United Kingdom or in certain designated courts of Commonwealth countries from which appeals are taken to committee.

JUDICIAL COMMITTEE OF THE PRIVY COUNCIL
Parliament Square, London SW1P 3BD T 020-7960 1500
W www.jcpc.uk
Chief Executive, Mark Ormerod
Registrar of the Privy Council, Louise di Mambro

SCOTTISH JUDICATURE

Scotland has a legal system separate from, and differing greatly from, the English legal system in enacted law, judicial procedure and the structure of courts.

In Scotland the system of public prosecution is headed by the Lord Advocate and is independent of the police, who have no say in the decision to prosecute. The Lord Advocate, discharging his functions through the Crown Office in Edinburgh, is responsible for prosecutions in the high court, sheriff courts and justice of the peace courts. Prosecutions in the high court are prepared by the Crown Office and conducted in court by one of the law officers, by an advocate-depute, or by a solicitor advocate. In the inferior courts the decision to prosecute is made and prosecution is preferred by procurators fiscal, who are lawyers and full-time civil servants subject to the directions of the Crown Office. A permanent legally qualified civil servant, known as the crown agent, is responsible for the running of the Crown Office and the organisation of the Procurator Fiscal Service, of which he or she is the head.

Scotland is divided into six sheriffdoms, each with a full-time sheriff principal. The sheriffdoms are further divided into sheriff court districts, each of which has a legally qualified resident sheriff or sheriffs, who are the judges of the court.

In criminal cases sheriffs principal and sheriffs have the same powers; sitting with a jury of 15 members, they may try more serious cases on indictment, or, sitting alone, may try lesser cases under summary procedure. Minor summary offences are dealt with in justice of the peace courts, which replaced district courts formerly operated by local authorities, and presided over by lay justices of the peace (of whom some 500 regularly sit in court) and, in Glasgow only, by stipendiary magistrates. Juvenile offenders (children under 16) may be brought before an informal children's hearing comprising three local lay people. The superior criminal court is the high court of justiciary which is both a trial and an appeal court. Cases on indictment are tried by a high court judge, sitting with a jury of 15, in Edinburgh and on circuit in other towns. Appeals from the lower courts against conviction or sentence are also heard by the high court, which sits as an appeal court only in Edinburgh. There is no further appeal to the UK supreme court in criminal cases.

In civil cases the jurisdiction of the sheriff court extends to most kinds of action. Appeals against decisions of the sheriff may be made to the sheriff principal and thence to the court of session, or direct to the court of session, which sits only in Edinburgh. The court of session is divided into the inner and the outer house. The outer house is a court of first instance in which cases are heard by judges sitting singly, sometimes with a jury of 12. The inner house, itself subdivided into two divisions of equal status, is mainly an appeal court. Appeals may be made to the inner house from the outer house as well as from the sheriff court. An appeal may be made from the inner house to the UK supreme court.

The judges of the court of session are the same as those of the high court of justiciary, with the Lord President of the court of session also holding the office of Lord Justice General in the high court. Senators of the College of Justice are Lords Commissioners of Justiciary as well as judges of the court of session. On appointment, a senator takes a judicial title, which is retained for life. Although styled The Hon./Rt. Hon. Lord, the senator is not a peer, although some judges are peers in their own right.

The office of coroner does not exist in Scotland. The local procurator fiscal inquires privately into sudden or suspicious deaths and may report findings to the crown agent. In some cases a fatal accident inquiry may be held before the sheriff.

COURT OF SESSION AND HIGH COURT OF JUSTICIARY

The Lord President and Lord Justice General (£234,184), Rt. Hon. Lord Carloway, *born* 1954, *apptd* 2015
Private Secretary, Paul Gilmour

INNER HOUSE
Lords of Session (each £215,094)

FIRST DIVISION
The Lord President

Rt. Hon. Lord Menzies (Duncan Menzies), *born* 1953, *apptd* 2012
Rt. Hon. Lady Smith (Anne Smith), *born* 1955, *apptd* 2012
Rt. Hon. Lord Brodie (Philip Brodie), *born* 1950, *apptd* 2012
Rt. Hon. Lady Clark of Calton (Lynda Clark), *born* 1949, *apptd* 2013
Rt. Hon. Lord Glennie (Angus Glennie), *born* 1950, *apptd* 2016

SECOND DIVISION
Lord Justice Clerk (£226,193), Rt. Hon. Lady Dorrian (Leeona Dorrian), *born* 1957, *apptd* 2016

Rt. Hon. Lady Paton (Ann Paton), *born* 1952, *apptd* 2007
Rt. Hon. Lord Drummond Young (James Drummond Young), *born* 1950, *apptd* 2013
Rt. Hon. Lord Malcolm (Colin M. Campbell), *born* 1953, *apptd* 2015
Hon. Lord Turnbull (Alan Turnbull), *born* 1958, *apptd* 2016

OUTER HOUSE
Lords of Session (each £188,901)

Hon. Lord Kinclaven (Alexander F. Wylie, OBE), *born* 1951, *apptd* 2005
Hon. Lord Brailsford (S. Neil Brailsford), *born* 1954, *apptd* 2006
Hon. Lord Uist (Roderick Macdonald), *born* 1951, *apptd* 2006
Hon. Lord Matthews (Hugh Matthews), *born* 1953, *apptd* 2007
Hon. Lord Woolman (Stephen Woolman), *born* 1953, *apptd* 2008
Hon. Lord Pentland (Paul Cullen), *born* 1957, *apptd* 2008
Hon. Lord Bannatyne (Iain Peebles, QC), *born* 1954, *apptd* 2008
Hon. Lady Stacey (Valerie E. Stacey), *born* 1954, *apptd* 2009
Hon. Lord Tyre (Colin Tyre, CBE), *born* 1956, *apptd* 2010
Hon. Lord Doherty (J. Raymond Doherty), *born* 1958, *apptd* 2010
Rt. Hon. Lord Boyd of Duncansby (Colin Boyd), *born* 1953, *apptd* 2012
Hon. Lord Burns (David Burns), *born* 1952, *apptd* 2012
Hon. Lady Scott (Margaret Scott), *born* 1960, *apptd* 2012
Hon. Lady Wise (Morag Wise), *born* 1963, *apptd* 2013
Hon. Lord Armstrong (Iain Armstrong), *born* 1956, *apptd* 2013
Hon. Lady Rae (Rita Rae), *born* 1950, *apptd* 2014
Hon. Lady Wolffe (Sarah Wolffe, QC), *born* 1964, *apptd* 2014
Hon. Lord Beckett (John Beckett, QC), *apptd* 2016
Hon. Lord Clark (Alistair Clark, QC), *born* 1955, *apptd* 2016
Hon. Lord Ericht (Andrew Stewart, QC), *born* 1963, *apptd* 2016
Hon. Lady Carmichael (Ailsa Carmichael, QC), *born* 1969, *apptd* 2016
Rt. Hon. Lord Mulholland (Frank Mulholland, QC), *born* 1959, *apptd* 2016
Hon. Lord Summers (Alan Summers, QC), *born* 1964, *apptd* 2017
Hon. Lord Arthurson (Paul Arthurson, QC), *born* 1964, *apptd* 2017

COURT OF SESSION AND HIGH COURT OF JUSTICIARY
Parliament House, Parliament Square, Edinburgh EH1 1RQ
T 0131-225 2595

Director and Principal Clerk of Session and Justiciary, Gillian Prentice
Deputy Principal Clerk of Session, Diane Machin
Deputy Principal Clerk of Justiciary, Joe Moyes
Depute in Charge of the Court of Session Office, Christina Bardsley
Officer in Charge of the Justiciary Office, Ross Martin
Keeper of the Rolls, Trish Fiddes
Assistant Keeper of the Rolls, Grahame Simpson
Appeals Manager, Alex McKay
Clerking Services Manager, Chris Fyffe
Court Manager, Zac Conway

JUDICIAL APPOINTMENTS BOARD FOR SCOTLAND
Thistle House, 91 Haymarket Terrace, Edinburgh EH12 5HE
T 0131-528 5101 W www.judicialappointments.scot

The board's remit is to provide the first minister with the names of candidates recommended for appointment to the court posts of senator of the college of justice, chair of the Scottish Land Court, sheriff principal, sheriff and part-time sheriff. It is also responsible for recommending individuals to the office of vice-president of the Upper Tribunal; chamber and deputy chamber presidents of the First-tier Tribunal; and members of the Upper Tribunal and First-tier Tribunal.

Chair, Nicola Gordon
Chief Executive, John Craig

JUDICIAL OFFICE FOR SCOTLAND
Parliament House, Edinburgh EH1 1RQ
T 0131-240 6677 W www.scotland-judiciary.org.uk

The Judicial Office for Scotland came into being on 1 April 2010 as part of the changes introduced by the Judiciary and Courts (Scotland) Act 2008. It provides support for the Lord President in his role as head of the Scottish judiciary with responsibility for the training, welfare, deployment and conduct of judges and the efficient disposal of business in the courts.

Executive Director, Tim Barraclough

SCOTTISH COURTS AND TRIBUNALS SERVICE
Saughton House, Broomhouse Drive, Edinburgh EH11 3XD
T 0131-444 3300 W www.scotcourts.gov.uk

The Scottish Courts and Tribunals Service (SCTS) is an independent body which was established on 1 April 2010 under the Judiciary and Courts (Scotland) Act 2008. Its function is to provide administrative support to Scottish courts and tribunals and to the judiciary of courts, including the High Court of Justiciary, Court of Session, sheriff courts and justice of the peace courts, and to the Office of the Public Guardian and Accountant of Court.

Chief Executive, Eric McQueen

SCOTTISH GOVERNMENT JUSTICE DIRECTORATE
St Andrew's House, Edinburgh EH1 3DG
T 0131-244 4000

The Justice Directorate is responsible for the appointment of judges and sheriffs to meet the needs of the business of the supreme and sheriffs court in Scotland. It is also responsible for providing resources for the efficient administration of certain specialist courts and tribunals.

Director (Justice), Neil Rennick

SCOTTISH LAND COURT
126 George Street, Edinburgh EH2 4HH
T 0131-271 4360 W www.scottish-land-court.org.uk

The court deals with disputes relating to agricultural and crofting land in Scotland.

Chair (£151,497), Hon. Lord Miningish (Roderick John MacLeod, QC)
Deputy Chair, Iain Maclean
Members, Tom Campbell; John Smith
Principal Clerk, Barbara Brown

SHERIFF COURTS
The majority of cases in Scotland are handled by one of the 39 sheriff courts. Criminal cases are heard by a sheriff and a jury (solemn procedure) but can be heard by a sheriff alone (summary procedure). Civil cases are heard by a single sheriff. Scotland is split into six sheriffdoms, each headed by a sheriff principal.

SALARIES
Sheriff Principal, £151,497
Sheriff, £140,289

SHERIFFDOMS

GLASGOW AND STRATHKELVIN
Sheriff Principal, Craig Turnbull
GRAMPIAN, HIGHLAND AND ISLANDS
Sheriff Principal, Derek Pyle
LOTHIAN AND BORDERS
Sheriff Principal, Mhairi Stephen, QC
NORTH STRATHCLYDE
Sheriff Principal, Duncan Murray
SOUTH STRATHCLYDE, DUMFRIES AND GALLOWAY
Sheriff Principal, Ian Abercrombie, QC
TAYSIDE, CENTRAL AND FIFE
Sheriff Principal, Marysia Lewis

JUSTICE OF THE PEACE COURTS
Justice of the peace courts replaced district courts and are a unique feature of Scotland's judicial system. Justices of the peace are lay magistrates who either sit alone, or in a bench of three, and deal with summary crimes such as speeding and careless driving. In court, justices have access to solicitors, who fulfil the role of legal advisers or clerks of court.

A justice of the peace court can be presided over by a stipendiary magistrate – a legally qualified solicitor or advocate who sits alone. They deal with more serious summary business similar to sheriffs, such as drink driving and assault. All sheriffs principal have powers to appoint stipendiary magistrates, but at present there are no justice of the peace courts in the sheriff court districts of Lerwick, Kirkwall, Wick, Stornoway, Lochmaddy and Portree.

CROWN OFFICE AND PROCURATOR FISCAL SERVICE
25 Chambers Street, Edinburgh EH1 1LA
T 0300-020 3000 W www.copfs.gov.uk

The Crown Office and Procurator Fiscal Service (COPFS) is Scotland's prosecution service. COPFS receive reports about crimes from the police and other reporting agencies and then decide what action to take, including whether to prosecute someone. It is also responsible for looking into deaths that need further explanation and investigating allegations of criminal conduct against police officers.

Lord Advocate, Rt. Hon. James Wolffe, QC
Solicitor-General, Alison Di Rollo, QC
Crown Agent, David Harvie

COURT OF THE LORD LYON
HM New Register House, Edinburgh EH1 3YT
T 0131-556 7255 W www.courtofthelordlyon.scot

The Court of the Lord Lyon is the Scottish Court of Chivalry (including the genealogical jurisdiction of the *Ri-Sennachie* of Scotland's Celtic kings). The Lord Lyon King of Arms has jurisdiction, subject to appeal to the Court of Session and the House of Lords, in questions of heraldry and the right to bear arms. The court also administers the Public Register of All Arms and Bearings and the Public Register of All Genealogies in Scotland. Pedigrees are established by decrees of Lyon Court and by letters patent. As Royal Commissioner in Armory, the Lord Lyon grants patents of arms to virtuous and well-deserving Scots and to petitioners (personal or corporate) in the Queen's overseas realms of Scottish connection, and also issues birthbrieves. For information on Her Majesty's Officers of Arms in Scotland, *see* the Court of the Lord Lyon in the Public Bodies section.

Lord Lyon King of Arms, Dr Joseph Morrow, CBE, QC
Lyon Clerk and Keeper of the Records, Russell Hunter
Procurator Fiscal, Alexander Green

NORTHERN IRELAND JUDICATURE

In Northern Ireland the legal system and the structure of courts closely resemble those of England and Wales; there are, however, often differences in enacted law.

The court of judicature of Northern Ireland comprises the court of appeal, the high court of justice and the crown court. The practice and procedure of these courts is similar to that in England. The superior civil court is the high court of justice, from which an appeal lies to the Northern Ireland court of appeal; the UK supreme court is the final civil appeal court.

The crown court, served by high court and county court judges, deals with criminal trials on indictment. Cases are heard before a judge and, except those certified by the Director of Public Prosecutions under the Justice and Security Act 2007, a jury. Appeals from the crown court against conviction or sentence are heard by the Northern Ireland court of appeal; the UK supreme court is the final court of appeal.

The decision to prosecute in criminal cases in Northern Ireland rests with the Director of Public Prosecutions.

Minor criminal offences are dealt with in magistrates' courts by a legally qualified district judge (magistrates' courts) and, where an offender is under the age of 18, by youth courts each consisting of a district judge (magistrates' courts) and two lay magistrates (at least one of whom must be a woman). There are approximately 200 lay magistrates in Northern Ireland. Appeals from magistrates' courts are heard by the county court, or by the court of appeal on a point of law or an issue as to jurisdiction.

Magistrates' courts in Northern Ireland can deal with certain classes of civil case but most minor civil cases are dealt with in county courts. Judgments of all civil courts are enforceable through a centralised procedure administered by the Enforcement of Judgments Office.

COURT OF JUDICATURE

The Royal Courts of Justice, Chichester Street, Belfast BT1 3JF
T 0300-200 7812 W www.courtsni.gov.uk

Lord Chief Justice of Northern Ireland (£234,184), Rt. Hon. Sir Declan Morgan, *born* 1952, *apptd* 2009

LORDS JUSTICES OF APPEAL (£215,094)
Style, The Rt. Hon. Lord/Lady Justice [surname]

Rt. Hon. Sir Benjamin Stephens, *born* 1954, *apptd* 2017
Hon. Sir Seamus Treacy, *born* 1956, *apptd* 2017

Hon. Sir Bernard McCloskey, *born* 1956, *apptd* 2019

HIGH COURT JUDGES (£188,901)
Style, The Hon. Mr/Mrs/Ms Justice [surname]

Hon. Sir Paul Maguire, *born* 1952, *apptd* 2012
Hon. Sir Mark Horner, *born* 1956, *apptd* 2012
Hon. Sir John O'Hara, *born* 1956, *apptd* 2013
Hon. Sir Adrian Colton, *born* 1959, *apptd* 2015
Hon. Dame Denise McBride, DBE, *apptd* 2015
Hon. Dame Siobhan Keegan, DBE, *apptd* 2015
Hon. Sir Gerry McAlinden, *apptd* 2018
Hon. Sir Ian Huddleston, *apptd* 2019

MASTERS OF THE HIGH COURT (£112,542)
Presiding Master, Master McCorry, *apptd* 2001
Masters, Master Bell *apptd* 2006; Master Hardstaff, *apptd* 2014; Master Kelly, *apptd* 2005; Master McGivern *apptd* 2015; Master Sweeney, *apptd* 2015; Master Wells, *apptd* 2005

COUNTY COURTS

JUDGES (£151,498†)
Style, His/Her Hon. Judge [surname]

Judge Babington *apptd* 2004; Judge Crawford *apptd* 2015; Judge Devlin *apptd* 2011; Judge Fowler, QC *apptd* 2011; Judge Gilpin *apptd* 2019; Judge Kerr, QC *apptd* 2012; Judge Kinney *apptd* 2012; Judge Lynch, QC *apptd* 2004; Judge McCaffrey *apptd* 2016; Judge McColgan, QC *apptd* 2013; Judge McCormick *apptd* 2018; Judge McFarland *apptd* 1998; Judge McReynolds *apptd* 2004; Judge Miller, QC *apptd* 2009; Judge Rafferty, QC *apptd* 2016; Judge Ramsay, QC *apptd* 2014; Judge Sherrard *apptd* 2012; Judge Smyth *apptd* 2010

† County court judges are paid £151,498 so long as they are required to carry out significantly different work from their counterparts elsewhere in the UK

RECORDERS
Belfast (£163,617), Judge McFarland
Londonderry (£151,497), Judge Babington

DISTRICT JUDGES (£112,542)
Only barristers and solicitors with ten years' standing are eligible to become district judges. There are usually four district judges in Northern Ireland:

Presiding District Judge Brownlie *apptd* 1997; District Judge Collins *apptd* 2000; District Judge Duncan *apptd* 2014

MAGISTRATES' COURTS

DISTRICT JUDGES (MAGISTRATES' COURTS) (£112,542)
There are usually 21 district judges (magistrates' courts) in Northern Ireland:

Presiding District Judge Bagnall *apptd* 2003; District Judge Brady *apptd* 2016; District Judge Broderick *apptd* 2013; District Judge Conner *apptd* 1999; District Judge Copeland *apptd* 1993; District Judge Hamill *apptd* 1999; District Judge Henderson *apptd* 2005; District Judge Kelly *apptd* 1997; District Judge Keown *apptd* 2018; District Judge E. King *apptd* 2005; District Judge P. King *apptd* 2013; District Judge McElholm *apptd* 1998; District Judge McGarrity *apptd* 2019; District Judge McNally *apptd* 2003; District Judge P. Magill *apptd* 2018; District Judge Meehan *apptd* 2002; District Judge Mullan *apptd* 2016; District Judge Prytherch *apptd* 2005; District Judge Ranaghan *apptd* 2017; District Judge Watters *apptd* 1998

NORTHERN IRELAND COURTS AND TRIBUNALS SERVICE

23–27 Oxford Street, Belfast BT1 3LA
T 0300-200 7812 W www.justice-ni.gov.uk/topics/courts-and-tribunals
Chief Executive (acting), Peter Luney

CROWN SOLICITOR'S OFFICE

Royal Courts of Justice, Chichester Street, Belfast BT1 3JE
T 028-9054 2555
Crown Solicitor, Fiona Chamberlain

PUBLIC PROSECUTION SERVICE

Belfast Chambers, 93 Chichester Street, Belfast BT1 3JR
T 028-9089 7100 W www.ppsni.gov.uk
Director of Public Prosecutions, Stephen Herron

TRIBUNALS

Information on all the tribunals listed here, with the exception of the independent tribunals and the tribunals based in Scotland, Wales and Northern Ireland, can be found online (W www.gov.uk/government/organisations/hm-courts-and-tribunals-service).

HM COURTS AND TRIBUNALS SERVICE

102 Petty France, London SW1H 9AJ
W www.gov.uk/government/organisations/hm-courts-and-tribunals-service
W www.gov.uk/find-court-tribunal

HM Courts Service and the Tribunals Service merged on 1 April 2011 to form HM Courts and Tribunals Service, an integrated agency providing support for the administration of justice in courts and tribunals. It is an agency within the Ministry of Justice, operating as a partnership between the Lord Chancellor, the Lord Chief Justice and the Senior President of Tribunals. It is responsible for the administration of the criminal, civil and family courts and tribunals in England and Wales and non-devolved tribunals in Scotland

and Northern Ireland. The agency's work is overseen by a board headed by an independent chair working with non-executive, executive and judicial members.

A two-tier tribunal system, comprising the First-tier Tribunal and Upper Tribunal, was established on 3 November 2008 as a result of radical reform under the Tribunals, Courts and Enforcement Act 2007. Both of these tiers are split into a number of separate chambers. These chambers group together individual tribunals (also known as 'jurisdictions') which deal with similar work or require similar skills. Cases start in the First-tier Tribunal and there is a right of appeal to the Upper Tribunal. Some tribunals transferred to the new two-tier system immediately, with more transferring between 2009 and 2011. The exception is employment tribunals, which remain outside this structure. The Act also allowed legally qualified tribunal chairs and adjudicators to swear the judicial oath and become judges.

Senior President, Rt. Hon. Sir Ernest Ryder, TD
Vice-President of the Unified Tribunals, Hon. Sir Keith Lindblom
Chief Executive, Susan Acland-Hood

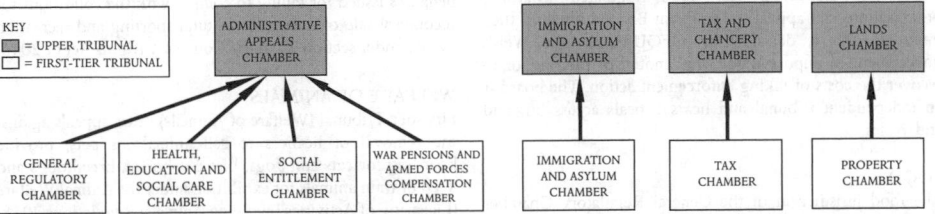

FIRST-TIER TRIBUNAL

The main function of the First-tier Tribunal is to hear appeals by citizens against decisions of the government. In most cases appeals are heard by a panel made up of one judge and two specialists in their relevant field, known as 'members'. Both judges and members are appointed through the Independent Judicial Appointments Commission. Most of the tribunals administered by central government are part of the First-tier Tribunal, which is split into seven separate chambers.

GENERAL REGULATORY CHAMBER

For all jurisdictions: General Regulatory Chamber, HMCTS, PO Box 9300, Leicester LE1 8DJ T 0300-123 4504
E grc@justice.gov.uk
Chamber President, Judge McKenna

CHARITY

Under the Charities Act 2011 (only applicable to England and Wales), First-tier Tribunal (Charity) hears appeals against the decisions of the Charity Commission, applications for the review of decisions made by the Charity Commission and considers references from the Attorney-General or the Charity Commission on points of law.

COMMUNITY RIGHT TO BID

The Community Right to Bid jurisdiction of the General Regulatory Chamber was established in January 2013 and hears appeals against review decisions made by local authorities to list your property as a community asset and

give local communities the right to bid for it if you decide to sell. Individuals have the right to appeal against a listing decision under the Localism Act 2011 and the assets of community value (England) regulations 2012.

CONSULTANT LOBBYISTS

First-tier Tribunal (Consultant Lobbyists) hears appeals against penalties imposed for an offence under section 12 of the Transparency of Lobbying, Non-Party Campaigning and Trade Union Administration Act 2014 by the Office of the Registrar of Consultant Lobbyists.

CONVEYANCING

The professional regulation jurisdiction hears appeals against decisions made by the Council for Licensed Conveyancers under the Legal Services Act 2007.

COPYRIGHT LICENSING

Under the copyright (regulation of relevant licensing bodies) regulations 2014 a copyright licensing body may appeal to a First-tier Tribunal (Copyright Licensing) against a government decision to fine or impose a code of conduct on their organisation.

DRIVING INSTRUCTORS

First-tier Tribunal (Driving Instructors) hears appeals against decisions made by the Registrar of Approved Driving Instructors under the Road Traffic Act 1988, Transport Act 2000 and the Motor Cars (Driving Instruction) Regulations 2005. Its jurisdiction covers England, Scotland and Wales.

ELECTRONIC COMMUNICATIONS AND POSTAL SERVICES
Hears appeals against decisions made by the Interception of Communications Commissioner under the Regulation of Investigatory Powers (Monetary Penalty Notices and Consents for Interceptions) Regulations 2011.

ENVIRONMENT
First-tier Tribunal (Environment) was created to decide appeals regarding civil sanctions made by environmental regulators. Established in April 2010, the jurisdiction of the tribunal extends to England and Wales.

ESTATE AGENTS
First-tier Tribunal (Estate Agents) hears appeals, under the Estate Agents Act 1979, against decisions made by the Office of Fair Trading pertaining to orders prohibiting a person from being employed as an estate agent when that person has been, for example, convicted of fraud or another offence involving dishonesty. The tribunal also hears appeals relating to decisions refusing to revoke or vary a prohibition order or warning order, as well as appeals regarding the issuing of a warning order when a person has not fulfilled their obligations under the Act.

EXAM BOARDS
Under the Education Act 1997 regulated awarding organisations can appeal to the Exam Board tribunal if they disagree with a decision by OFQUAL or the Welsh government to impose a fine, the amount of the fine, or to recover the costs of taking enforcement action. The board is an independent tribunal and hears appeals across England and Wales.

FOOD
The food jurisdiction of the General Regulatory Chamber was established in January 2013 and hears appeals against some of the decisions taken by the Food Standards Agency, Department for Environment, Food and Rural Affairs and local authority trading standards departments. It also deals with appeals against decisions under the Fish Labelling (England) Regulations.

GAMBLING
First-tier Tribunal (Gambling) hears and decides appeals against decisions made by the Gambling Commission under the Gambling Act 2005.

IMMIGRATION SERVICES
First-tier Tribunal (Welfare of Animals) hears appeals against the removal of licences to sell animals as pets, provide boarding for cats and dogs, hire out horses, breed dogs and keep or train animals for exhibition under the Animal Welfare (Licensing of Activities Involving Animals) Regulations 2018.

INFORMATION RIGHTS
First-tier Tribunal (Information Rights) determines appeals against notices issued by the Information Commissioner under the Freedom of Information Act 2000 and other regulations.
  When a minister of the crown issues a certificate on the grounds of national security, the appeal must be transferred to the Administrative Appeals Chamber of the Upper Tribunal on receipt.

LETTING AND MANAGING AGENTS
First-tier Tribunal (Letting and Managing Agents) hears appeals against a decision by a local authority or the Trading Standards Office to impose a fine on an agent for not being a member of an approved complaints scheme or for not clearly publicising fees under The Redress Schemes for Lettings Agency Work and Property Management Work (Requirements to Belong to a Scheme etc) (England) Order 2014 and schedule 9 of the Consumer Rights Act 2015.

MICROCHIPPING DOGS
Established under the Microchipping of Dogs (England) Regulations 2015, appeals can be made to First-Tier Tribunal (Microchipping Dogs) against a decision by the Department for the Environment and Rural Affairs to ban or stop an individual from microchipping dogs or from running a database on microchipped dogs. Dog owners can also appeal against a notice to microchip their dog served by the police or local authority.

PENSIONS REGULATION
First-tier Tribunal (Pensions) hears appeals against decisions made by the Pensions Regulator under section 44 of the Pensions Act 2008. Appeals under section 102 of the Act are heard by the Tax and Chancery Chamber of the Upper Tribunal.

SECONDARY TICKETING
First-tier Tribunal (Secondary Ticketing) hears appeals against penalties issued for failing to comply with the conditions for secondary sale of tickets for cultural sporting and recreation events under section 90 of the Consumer Rights Act of 2015.

WELFARE OF ANIMALS
First-tier Tribunal (Welfare of Animals) hears appeals against the removal of licences to sell animals as pets, provide boarding for cats and dogs, hire out horses, breed dogs and keep or train animals for exhibition under the Animal Welfare (Licensing of Activities Involving Animals) Regulations 2018.

HEALTH, EDUCATION AND SOCIAL CARE CHAMBER
Chamber President, His Hon. Judge Sycamore

CARE STANDARDS
First-tier Tribunal (Care Standards), 1st Floor Darlington Magistrates' Court, Parkgate DL1 1RU
T 01325-289350 E cst@justice.gov.uk

First-tier Tribunal (Care Standards) was established under the Protection of Children Act 1999 and considers appeals in relation to decisions made by the Secretary of State for Education, the Secretary of State for Health, the Care Quality Commission, Ofsted or the Care Council for Wales about the inclusion of individuals' names on the list of those considered unsuitable to work with children or vulnerable adults, restrictions from teaching and employment in schools/further education institutions, and the registration of independent schools. It also deals with general registration decisions made about care homes, children's homes, childcare providers, nurses' agencies, social workers, residential family centres, independent hospitals and fostering agencies.

MENTAL HEALTH
PO Box 8793, 5th Floor, Leicester LE1 8BN
T 0300-123 2201 E MHRTEnquiries@justice.gov.uk

The First-tier Tribunal (Mental Health) hears applications and references for people detained under the Mental Health Act 1983 (as amended by the Mental Health Act 2007). There are separate mental health tribunals for Wales and Scotland.

PRIMARY HEALTH LISTS

First-tier Tribunal (Primary Health Lists), 1st Floor Darlington Magistrates' Court, Parkgate DL1 1RU T 01325-289350

First-tier Tribunal (Primary Health Lists) hears appeals against decisions made by the NHS Commissioning Board to not include, to remove or to change the conditions of inclusion for medical practitioners and providers on the NHS medical, dental, ophthalmic or pharmaceutical lists.

SPECIAL EDUCATIONAL NEEDS AND DISABILITY

First-tier Tribunal (SEND), 1st Floor Darlington Magistrates' Court, Parkgate DL1 1RU
T 01325-289350 E send@justice.gov.uk

First-tier Tribunal (Special Educational Needs and Disability) considers parents' appeals against the decisions of local authorities about children's special educational needs if parents cannot reach agreement with the local authority. It also considers claims of disability discrimination in schools.

IMMIGRATION AND ASYLUM CHAMBER

Chamber President, Judge Clements
PO Box 6987, Leicester LE1 6ZX
T 0300-123 1711 E customer.service@justice.gov.uk

The Immigration and Asylum Chamber is an independent tribunal dealing with appeals against decisions made by the Home Office concerning immigration, asylum and nationality matters.

PROPERTY CHAMBER

Chamber President, Judge McGrath
10 Alfred Place, London WC1E 7LR
T 020-7291 7250 E alr@justice.gov.uk

The First-tier Tribunal (Property Chamber) handles applications, appeals and references relating to disputes over property and land. It serves the private-rented and leasehold property market in England regarding rent increases, leasehold disputes, improvement notices under the Housing Act 2004, land registration matters and agricultural land and drainage matters.

SOCIAL ENTITLEMENT CHAMBER

Chamber President, His Hon. Judge Aitken

ASYLUM SUPPORT

2nd Floor, Anchorage House, 2 Clove Crescent, London E14 2BE
T 0800-681 6509

First-tier Tribunal (Asylum Support) deals with appeals against decisions made by the Home Office. The Home Office decides whether asylum seekers, failed asylum seekers and/or their dependants are entitled to support and accommodation on the grounds of destitution, as provided by the Immigration and Asylum Act 1999. The tribunal can only consider appeals against a refusal or termination of support. It can, if appropriate, require the Secretary of State for the Home Department to reconsider the original decision, substitute the original decision with the tribunal's own decision or dismiss the appeal.

CRIMINAL INJURIES COMPENSATION

20 York Street, Glasgow G2 8GT T 0300-790 6234
E cic.enquiries@justice.gov.uk

First-tier Tribunal (Criminal Injuries Compensation) determines appeals against review decisions made by the Criminal Injuries Compensation Authority on applications for compensation made by victims of violent crime.

SOCIAL SECURITY AND CHILD SUPPORT

England and Wales T 0300-123 1142
Scotland T 0300-790 6234

First-tier Tribunal (Social Security and Child Support) arranges and hears appeals against decisions made by the Department for Work and Pensions and HM Revenue and Customs regarding social security benefits. Appeals considered include those concerned with: attendance, bereavement and carer's allowances; child benefit; child support; the compensation recovery scheme (including NHS recovery claims); diffuse mesotheliomia and the industrial injuries disablement benefit payment schemes; income support; jobseeker's allowance; tax credits; universal credit; and vaccine damage payment.

TAX CHAMBER

Chamber President, Judge Sinfield
PO Box 16972, Birmingham B16 6TZ
T 0300-123 1024 E taxappeals@justice.gov.uk

First-tier Tribunal Tax Chamber hears most appeals against decisions made by HM Revenue and Customs in relation to income tax, corporation tax, capital gains tax, inheritance tax, stamp duty land tax, statutory sick and maternity pay, national insurance contributions and VAT or duties. The tribunal also hears some appeals relating to goods seized by HM Revenue and Customs or Border Force and against some decisions made by the National Crime Agency. Appeals can be made by individuals or organisations, single taxpayers or large multinational companies. First-tier Tribunal (Tax) also hears appeals against certain decisions made by a compliance officer, an independent office holder appointed by the Independent Parliamentary Standards Authority, the organisation responsible for determining and paying MP expenses. Appeals can be made by current or former MPs under the Parliamentary Standards Act 2009. The jurisdiction is UK-wide.

WAR PENSIONS AND ARMED FORCES COMPENSATION CHAMBER

Acting Chamber President, Judge Sehba Storey
5th Floor, Fox Court, 14 Gray's Inn Road, London WC1X 8HN
T 020-3206 0701 E armedforces.chamber@justice.gov.uk

The War Pensions and Armed Forces Compensation Chamber of the First-tier Tribunal hears appeals brought by ex-servicemen and women against decisions by Veterans UK regarding pensions, compensation and other amounts under the war pensions legislation for injuries sustained before 5 April 2005, and under the armed forces compensation scheme for injuries after that date.

UPPER TRIBUNAL

Comprising four separate chambers, the Upper Tribunal deals mostly with appeals from, and enforcement of, decisions taken by the First-tier Tribunal, but it also handles some cases that do not go through the First-tier Tribunal. Additionally, it has assumed some of the supervisory powers of the courts to deal with the actions of tribunals, government departments and some other public authorities. All the decision-makers of the Upper Tribunal are judges or expert members sitting in a panel chaired by a judge, and are specialists in the areas of law they handle. Over time their decisions are expected to build comprehensive case law for each area covered by the tribunals.

ADMINISTRATIVE APPEALS CHAMBER

Chamber President, Hon. Dame Judith Farbey, DBE
England and Wales, 5th Floor, 7 Rolls Building, Fetter Lane,
London EC4A 1NL T 020-7071 5662
E adminappeals@justice.gov.uk

Scotland, George House, 126 George Street, Edinburgh EH2 4HH
T 0131-271 4310 E UTAACmailbox@gov.scot

Northern Ireland, Tribunal Hearing Centre, 2nd Floor, Royal
Courts of Justice, Chichester Street, Belfast BT1 3JF
T 028-9072 4883 E tribunalsunit@courtsni.gov.uk

The Administrative Appeals Chamber appeals against
decisions made by certain lower tribunals and organisations
including: social security and child support, war pensions and
armed forces compensation, mental health, special education
needs or disabilities, disputes heard by the General Regulatory
Chamber, decisions made by the Disclosure and Barring
Service, decisions made by the Traffic Commissioner (or the
Transport Regulation Unit in Northern Ireland), Special
Education Needs Tribunal for Wales, Mental Health Review
Tribunal for Wales and the Pensions Appeal Tribunal in
Northern Ireland (only for assessment appeals under the War
Pensions Scheme). It also handles applications for judicial
review of decisions made by: First-tier Tribunal (Criminal
Injuries Compensation) and other first-tier tribunals where
there is no right of appeal.

IMMIGRATION AND ASYLUM CHAMBER

Chamber President, Hon. Sir Peter Lane
1A Field House, 15–25 Bream's Buildings, London EC4A 1DZ
T 0300-123 1711 E FieldHouseCorrespondence@justice.gov.uk

The Immigration and Asylum Chamber hears appeals against
decisions made by the First-tier Tribunal (Immigration and
Asylum) relating to visa and asylum applications and the right
to enter or stay in the UK. The chamber also deals with
applications for judicial review of certain decisions made by
the Home Office relating to immigration, asylum and human
rights claims.

LANDS CHAMBER

Chamber President, Hon. Sir David Holgate
5th Floor, 7 Rolls Buildings, London EC4A 1NL
T 020-7612 9710 E lands@justice.gov.uk

The Lands Chamber is responsible for handling appeals
against decisions made by the First-tier Tribunal (Property
Chamber) (except decisions about land registration), the
Residential Property Tribunal in Wales and the Leasehold
Valuation Tribunal in Wales, It is also responsible for
handling applications for cases regarding decisions about
rates made by the Valuation Tribunal in England or Wales,
compensation for the compulsory purchase of land, discharge
or modification of land affected by a 'restrictive covenant',
compensation for the effect on land affected by public works,
a tree preservation order, compensation for damage to land
damaged by subsidence from mining, the valuation of land or
buildings for Capital Gains Tax or Inheritance Tax purposes
and compensation for blighted land.

TAX AND CHANCERY CHAMBER

Chamber President, Hon. Sir Antony Zacaroli
5th Floor, 7 Rolls Buildings, London EC4A 1NL
T 020-7612 9730 E uttc@justice.gov.uk

The Tax and Chancery Chamber hears appeals against
decisions made by the First-tier Tribunal (Tax), the land
registration division of the First-tier Tribunal (Property
Chamber) and the General Regulatory Chamber in cases
relating to charities. The chamber also hears appeals against

decisions issued by the Financial Conduct Authority, the
Prudential Regulation Authority, the Pensions Regulator, the
Bank of England, HM Treasury and OFGEM.

SPECIAL IMMIGRATION APPEALS COMMISSION

15–25 Bream's Buildings, London EC4A 1DZ
T 0300-123 1711

The commission was set up under the Special Immigration
Appeals Commission Act 1997. It remains separate from the
First-tier and Upper Tribunal structure but is part of HM
Courts and Tribunals Service. Its main function is to consider
appeals against orders for deportation or exclusion, or orders
withdrawing or refusing British nationality, in cases which
involve considerations of national security.

Chair, Hon. Dame Elisabeth Laing, DBE

EMPLOYMENT TRIBUNALS

Employment Tribunal Central Office England and Wales, PO
Box 10218, Leicester LE1 8EG T 0300-123 1024
Employment Tribunal Central Office Scotland, PO Box 27105,
Glasgow G2 9JR T 0300-790 6234

Employment tribunals hear claims regarding matters of
employment law, redundancy, dismissal, contract disputes,
sexual, racial and disability discrimination and related areas
of dispute which may arise in the workplace.

President (England and Wales), Judge Doyle
President (Scotland), Judge Simon

EMPLOYMENT APPEAL TRIBUNAL

Employment Appeal Tribunal England and Wales, 5th Floor, 7 Rolls
Buildings, Fetter Lane, London EC4A 1NL T 020-7273 1041
E londoneat@justice.gov.uk
Employment Appeal Tribunal Scotland, George House, 126 George
Street, Edinburgh, EH2 4HH T 0131-225 3963
E edinburgheat@justice.gov.uk

The Employment Appeal Tribunal hears appeals (on points of
law only) arising from decisions made by employment
tribunals.

President, Hon. Mr Justice Choudhury

SCOTTISH COURTS AND TRIBUNALS SERVICE

Saughton House, Broomhouse Drive, Edinburgh EH11 3XD
T 0131-444 3300
W www.scotcourts.gov.uk E enquiries@scotcourts.gov.uk

The Tribunals (Scotland) Act 2014 created a new, simplified
statutory framework for tribunals in Scotland, bringing
existing jurisdictions together and providing a structure for
new ones. The Act created two new tribunals, the First-tier
Tribunal for Scotland and the Upper Tribunal for Scotland.

The Lord President is the head of the Scottish Courts and
Tribunals Service and has delegated various functions to the
President of Scottish Tribunals.

President of Scottish Tribunals, Rt. Hon. Lady Smith (Anne
Smith)

UPPER TRIBUNAL FOR SCOTLAND

The Glasgow Tribunals Centre, 20 York Street, Glasgow G2 8GT
T 0141-302 5880
E uppertribunalforscotland@scotcourtstribunals.gov.uk

The Upper Tribunal hears appeals on decisions of the chambers of the First-tier Tribunal.

FIRST-TIER TRIBUNAL

The First-tier Tribunal is organised into five chambers.

GENERAL REGULATORY CHAMBER

George House, 126 George Street, Edinburgh EH2 4HH
T 0131-271 4340 E Charityappeals@scotcourtstribunals.gov.uk

HEALTH AND EDUCATION CHAMBER

20 York Street, Glasgow G2 8GT
T 0141-302 5860

HOUSING AND PROPERTY CHAMBER

20 York Street, Glasgow G2 8GT
T 0141-302 5900

SOCIAL SECURITY CHAMBER

20 York Street, Glasgow G2 8GT
T 0141-302 5858

TAX CHAMBER

George House, 126 George Street, Edinburgh EH2 4HH
T 0131-271 4385 E taxchamber@scotcourtstribunals.gov.uk

The Scottish Courts and Tribunals Service currently provides administrative support for the following Scottish tribunals:

COUNCIL TAX REDUCTION REVIEW PANEL, 20 York
  Street, Glasgow G2 8GT T 0141-302 5840
  E ctrrpadmin@scotcourtstribunals.gov.uk
  W www.counciltaxreductionreview.scotland.gov.uk
THE LANDS TRIBUNAL FOR SCOTLAND, George House,
  126 George Street, Edinburgh EH2 4HH T 0131-271 4350
  E LTS_mailbox@scotcourtstribunals.gov.uk
  W www.lands-tribunal-scotland.org.uk
  President, Hon. Lord Minginish (Roderick MacLeod)
THE MENTAL HEALTH TRIBUNAL FOR SCOTLAND,
  Bothwell House, First Floor, Hamilton Business Park, Caird Park,
  Hamilton ML3 0QA T 0800-345 7060
  E mhtsTeam1@scotcourtstribunals.gov.uk
  W www.mhtscotland.gov.uk
  President, Dr Joe Morrow, CBE
THE PENSIONS APPEAL TRIBUNAL SCOTLAND,
  126 George Street, Edinburgh EH2 4HH T 0131-271 4340
  E PAT_Info_Mailbox@scotcourtstribunals.gov.uk
  W www.patscotland.org.uk
  President, Marion Caldwell, QC

NORTHERN IRELAND COURTS AND TRIBUNALS SERVICE

Department of Justice, Block B, Castle Buildings, Stormont Estate,
Belfast BT4 3SG
T 028-9076 3000 W www.justice-ni.gov.uk/topics/
courts-and-tribunals
Lord Chief Justice of Northern Ireland, Rt. Hon. Sir Declan
  Morgan

The Northern Ireland Courts and Tribunals Service currently provides administrative support for the following Northern Ireland tribunals. All the tribunals below, unless otherwise specified, can be contacted at: 2nd Floor, Royal Courts of Justice, Chichester Street, Belfast BT1 3JF T 0300-200 7812
E tribunalsunit@courtsni.gov.uk

THE APPEALS SERVICE, 6th Floor, Oyster House, 12
  Wellington Place, Belfast BT1 6GE T 028-9054 4000
  E appeals.service.belfast@dsdni.gov.uk
THE CARE TRIBUNAL
  Chairs, Diane Drennan, Stephen Quinn
THE CHARITY TRIBUNAL
CRIMINAL INJURIES COMPENSATION APPEALS
  PANEL NORTHERN IRELAND,
  E cicapnicustomer@courtsni.gov.uk
  Chair, Patricia McKaigue
LANDS TRIBUNAL
MENTAL HEALTH REVIEW TRIBUNAL
NORTHERN IRELAND HEALTH AND SAFETY
  TRIBUNAL
NORTHERN IRELAND TRAFFIC PENALTY TRIBUNAL
NORTHERN IRELAND VALUATION TRIBUNAL
OFFICE OF SOCIAL SECURITY COMMISSIONERS AND
  CHILD SUPPORT COMMISSIONERS
  Chief Commissioner, Kenneth Mullan
PAROLE COMMISSIONERS FOR NORTHERN
  IRELAND, Laganside Court, Mezzanine 1st Floor,
  Oxford Street, Belfast BT1 3LL T 028-9041 2969
  E info@parolecomni.org.uk
  Chief Commissioner, Christine Glenn
PENSIONS APPEAL COMMISSIONERS
PENSIONS APPEAL TRIBUNALS
RENT ASSESSMENT PANEL, Cleaver House, 3 Donegall
  Square North, Belfast BT1 5GA T 028-9051 8518
  E appeals.service.belfast@dsdni.gov.uk
SPECIAL EDUCATIONAL NEEDS AND DISABILITY
  TRIBUNAL

INDEPENDENT TRIBUNALS

The following represents a selection of tribunals not administered by HM Courts and Tribunals Service.

CIVIL AVIATION AUTHORITY

Aviation House, Beehive Ringroad, Crawley, W. Sussex RH6 0YR
T 0330-022 1500 W www.caa.co.uk

The Civil Aviation Authority (CAA) does not have a separate tribunal department as such, but for certain purposes the CAA must conform to tribunal requirements, for example, to deal with appeals against the refusal or revocation of aviation licences and certificates issued by the CAA, and the allocation of routes outside of the EU to airlines.

The chair and non-executive members who may sit on panels for tribunal purposes are appointed by the Secretary of State for Transport.

Chair, Dame Deirdre Hutton, DBE

COMPETITION APPEAL TRIBUNAL

Victoria House, Bloomsbury Place, London WC1A 2EB
T 020-7979 7979 W www.catribunal.org.uk

The Competition Appeal Tribunal (CAT) is a specialist tribunal established to hear certain cases in the sphere of UK competition and economic regulatory law. It hears appeals against decisions of the Competition and Markets Authority (CMA) and the sectoral regulators in respect of infringements of competition law and with respect to mergers and markets. The CAT also has jurisdiction to award damages in respect of infringements of EU or UK competition law and to hear appeals against decisions of the Office of Communications (OFCOM) in telecommunications matters.

President, Hon. Sir Peter Roth

COPYRIGHT TRIBUNAL
4 Abbey Orchard Street, London SW1P 2HT
T 020-7034 2836 E copyright.tribunal@ipo.gov.uk
W www.gov.uk/government/organisations/copyright-tribunal

The Copyright Tribunal resolves disputes over the terms and conditions of licences offered by, or licensing schemes operated by, collective management organisations in the copyright and related rights area. Its decisions are appealable to the high court on points of law only.

Chair, His Hon. Judge Hacon

INDUSTRIAL TRIBUNALS AND THE FAIR EMPLOYMENT TRIBUNAL (NORTHERN IRELAND)
Killymeal House, 2 Cromac Quay, Ormeau Road, Belfast BT7 2JD
T 028-9032 7666 E mail@employmenttribunalsni.org
W www.employmenttribunalsni.org

The industrial tribunal system in Northern Ireland was set up in 1965 and has a similar remit to the employment tribunals in the rest of the UK. There is also a Fair Employment Tribunal, which hears and determines individual cases of alleged religious or political discrimination in employment. Employers can appeal to the Fair Employment Tribunal if they consider the directions of the Equality Commission to be unreasonable, inappropriate or unnecessary, and the Equality Commission can make application to the tribunal for the enforcement of undertakings or directions with which an employer has not complied.

President, Eileen McBride, CBE

INVESTIGATORY POWERS TRIBUNAL
PO Box 33220, London SW1H 9ZQ
T 020-7035 3711 E info@ipt-uk.com W www.ipt-uk.com

The Investigatory Powers Tribunal replaced the Interception of Communications Tribunal, the Intelligence Services Tribunal, the Security Services Tribunal and the complaints function of the commissioner appointed under the Police Act 1997.

The Regulation of Investigatory Powers Act 2000 (RIPA) provides for a tribunal made up of senior members of the legal profession, independent of the government and appointed by the Queen, to consider all complaints against the intelligence services and those against public authorities in respect of powers covered by RIPA; and to consider proceedings brought under section 7 of the Human Rights Act 1998 against the intelligence services and law enforcement agencies in respect of these powers.

President, Rt. Hon, Sir Rabinder Singh

SOLICITORS' DISCIPLINARY TRIBUNAL
3rd Floor, Gate House, 1 Farringdon Street, London EC4M 7LG
T 020-7329 4808 E enquiries@solicitorsdt.com
W www.solicitorstribunal.org.uk

The Solicitors' Disciplinary Tribunal is an independent statutory body whose members are appointed by the Master of the Rolls. The tribunal adjudicates upon alleged breaches of the rules and regulations applicable to solicitors and their firms, including the Solicitors' Code of Conduct 2007. It also decides applications by former solicitors for restoration to the Roll.

Chair, Edward Nally

SCOTTISH SOLICITORS' DISCIPLINE TRIBUNAL
Unit 3.5, The Granary Business Centre, Coal Road, Cupar, Fife KY15 5YQ
T 01334-659099 E enquiries@ssdt.org.uk W www.ssdt.org.uk

The Scottish Solicitors' Discipline Tribunal is an independent statutory body with a panel of 24 members, 12 of whom are solicitors appointed by the Lord President of the Court of Session. Its principal function is to consider complaints of misconduct against solicitors in Scotland.

Chair, Nicholas Whyte

TRAFFIC PENALTY TRIBUNAL
Springfield House, Water Lane, Wilmslow, Cheshire SK9 5BG
T 0800-160 1999 E help@trafficpenaltytribunal.gov.uk
W www.trafficpenaltytribunal.gov.uk

The Traffic Penalty Tribunal adjudicators consider appeals in relation to penalty charge notices issued by local authorities in England (outside London) and Wales for parking and bus lane contraventions and, additionally in Wales, moving traffic contraventions. The tribunal also considers appeals in relation to penalties issued by the Secretary of State for Transport for failing to pay a charge at the Dartford river crossing, the Durham peninsular congestion charging zone and the Mersey Gateway bridge crossings.

Chief Adjudicator, Caroline Sheppard, OBE

VALUATION TRIBUNAL FOR ENGLAND
2nd Floor, 120 Leman Street, London E1 8EU
T 020-7246 3900 W www.valuationtribunal.gov.uk

The Valuation Tribunal for England (VTE) came into being on 1 October 2009, replacing 56 valuation tribunals in England. Provision for the VTE was made in the Local Government and Public Involvement in Health Act 2007. The VTE hears appeals concerning council tax and non-domestic (business) rates, as well as a small number of appeals against drainage boards' assessments of drainage rates. A separate panel is constituted for each hearing, and consists of a chair and usually one or two other members.

The Valuation Tribunal Service (VTS) was created as a corporate body by the Local Government Act 2003, and is responsible for providing or arranging the services required for the operation of the Valuation Tribunal for England. The VTS board consists of a chair and members appointed by the secretary of state. The VTS is sponsored by the Ministry of Housing, Communities and Local Government.

President (VTE), Gary Garland
Chair (VTS), Robin Evans

VALUATION TRIBUNAL FOR WALES
W www.valuationtribunal.wales

The Valuation Tribunal for Wales (VTW) was established by the Valuation Tribunal for Wales Regulations 2010, and hears and determines appeals concerning council tax, non-domestic rating and drainage rates in Wales. The governing council, comprising the president, four regional representatives and one member who is appointed by the Welsh government, performs the management functions on behalf of the tribunal. There are a number of VTW offices across Wales and contact details for these can be found on the website listed above.

President, Carol Cobert

OMBUDSMAN SERVICES

The following section is a listing of selected ombudsman services. Ombudsmen are a free, independent and impartial means of resolving certain disputes outside of the courts. These disputes are, in the majority of cases, concerned with whether something has been badly or unfairly handled (for example owing to delay, neglect, inefficiency or failure to follow proper procedures). Most ombudsman schemes are established by statute; they cover various public and private bodies and generally examine matters only after the relevant body has been given a reasonable opportunity to deal with the complaint.

After conducting an investigation an ombudsman will usually issue a written report, which normally suggests a resolution to the dispute and often includes recommendations concerning the improvement of procedures.

OMBUDSMAN ASSOCIATION

PO Box 343, Carshalton, Surrey SM5 9BX
E secretary@ombudsmanassociation.org
W www.ombudsmanassociation.org

The Ombudsman Association was established in 1994 and exists to provide information to the government, public bodies and the public about ombudsmen and other complaint-handling services in the UK and Ireland. An ombudsman scheme must meet four criteria in order to attain full Ombudsman Association membership: independence from the organisations the ombudsman has the power to investigate, fairness, effectiveness and public accountability. Complaint Handler membership is open to complaint-handling bodies that do not meet these criteria in full. Ombudsmen schemes from the UK, Ireland, British crown dependencies and overseas territories may apply to the Ombudsman Association for membership. The Ombudsman Association publishes a quarterly magazine containing news about ombudsmen and complaint-handling services in the UK, Ireland and overseas, along with topical articles of interest to members of the Association.

Chair, Nick Bennett

The following is a selection of organisations that are members of the Ombudsman Association.

FINANCIAL OMBUDSMAN SERVICE

Exchange Tower, London E14 9SR
T 020-7964 1000 E complaint.info@financial-ombudsman.org.uk
W www.financial-ombudsman.org.uk

The Financial Ombudsman Service settles individual disputes between businesses providing financial services and their customers. The service examines complaints about most financial matters, including banking, insurance, mortgages, pensions, savings, loans and credit cards. *See also* Banking and Finance.

Chief Ombudsman and Chief Executive, Caroline Wayman

HOUSING OMBUDSMAN SERVICE

Exchange Tower, London E14 9GE
T 0300-111 3000 E info@housing-ombudsman.org.uk
W www.housing-ombudsman.org.uk

The Housing Ombudsman Service was established in 1997 to deal with complaints and disputes involving tenants and housing associations and social landlords, certain private-

sector landlords and managing agents. The ombudsman has a statutory jurisdiction over all registered social landlords in England. Private and other landlords can join the service on a voluntary basis. On 1 April 2013 a new Housing Ombudsman Service was launched with an extended jurisdiction covering all housing associations and local authorities.

Ombudsman, Andrea Keenoy *(interim)*

INDEPENDENT OFFICE FOR POLICE CONDUCT

90 High Holborn, London WC1V 6BH
T 0300-020 0096 E enquiries@policeconduct.gov.uk
W www.policeconduct.gov.uk

Established under the Policing and Crime Act 2017, the Independent Office for Police Conduct (IOPC) succeeded the Independent Police Complaints Commission (IPCC) in January 2018. The IOPC is responsible for carrying out independent investigations into serious incidents or allegations of misconduct by those serving with the police forces in England and Wales, as well as Police and Crime Commissioners in England and Wales and the London Mayor's Office for Policing and Crime (MOPAC). The IOPC's director-general and its regional directors must not have worked for police in any capacity prior to their appointment. It has the power to initiate, undertake and oversee investigations and is also responsible for the way in which complaints are handled by local police forces. The IOPC is also responsible for serious complaints and conduct matters relating to staff at the National Crime Agency (NCA), Her Majesty's Revenue and Customs (HMRC), and the Gangmasters and Labour Abuse Authority.

Director-General, Michael Lockwood

LEGAL OMBUDSMAN

PO Box 6806, Wolverhampton WV1 9WJ
T 0300-555 0333 E enquiries@legalombudsman.org.uk
W www.legalombudsman.org.uk

The Legal Ombudsman was set up by the Office for Legal Complaints under the Legal Services Act 2007 and is the single body for all consumer legal complaints in England and Wales. It replaced the Office of the Legal Services Ombudsman in 2010. The Legal Ombudsman aims to resolve disputes between individuals and authorised legal practitioners, including barristers, law cost draftsmen, legal executives, licensed conveyancers, notaries, patent attorneys, probate practitioners, registered European lawyers, solicitors and trade mark attorneys. The Legal Ombudsman is an independent and impartial organisation and deals with various types of complaints against legal services, such as wills, family issues, personal injury and buying or selling a house.

Chief Ombudsman, Rebecca Marsh

LOCAL GOVERNMENT AND SOCIAL CARE OMBUDSMAN

PO Box 4771, Coventry CV4 0EH
T 0300-061 0614 W www.lgo.org.uk

The Local Government and Social Care Ombudsman deals with complaints about most council services, including planning, some housing issues, social care, some education and schools issues, children's services, housing benefit, council tax, transport and highways, environment and waste, neighbour nuisance and antisocial behaviour and service failure by local authorities, schools and all registered social care providers, including all adult social care complaints. The Ombudsman's powers to investigate include complaints about publicly and privately funded social care.

If a complaint is about both health and social care services, a joint investigation with the Health Service Ombudsman can be carried out with the Social Care Ombudsman as the single point of contact.

Local Government and Social Care Ombudsman, Michael King

NORTHERN IRELAND PUBLIC SERVICES OMBUDSMAN
33 Wellington Place, Belfast BT1 6HN
T 028-9023 3821 E nipso@nipso.org.uk
W www.nipso.org.uk

The Office of Northern Ireland Public Services Ombudsman (NIPSO) was established in April 2016, replacing and expanding the functions of the Northern Ireland Assembly Ombudsman and Commissioner for Complaints. NIPSO provides an independent review of complaints of members of the public, where they believe they have sustained an injustice or hardship as a result or inaction of a public service provider. NIPSO additionally ensures that public services improve as a result of the complaints brought to them by the public. The professional, independent and impartial service is provided free of charge to the citizens of Northern Ireland.

Ombudsman, Marie Anderson

OFFICE OF THE PENSIONS OMBUDSMAN
10 South Colonnade, Canary Wharf, London E14 4PU
T 0800-917 4487 E enquiries@pensions-ombudsman.org.uk
W www.pensions-ombudsman.org.uk

The Pensions Ombudsman can investigate and decide complaints and disputes regarding the way occupational and personal pension schemes are administered and managed. Unless there are special circumstances, this only usually includes issues and disputes that have arisen within the past three years. The Pensions Ombudsman is also the Ombudsman for the Pension Protection Fund (PPF) and the Financial Assistance Scheme (which offers help to those who were a member of an under-funded defined benefit pension scheme that started to wind-up in specific financial circumstances between 1 January 1997 and 5 April 2005).

Pensions Ombudsman, Anthony Arter
Deputy Pensions Ombudsman, Karen Johnston

OMBUDSMAN SERVICES
3300 Daresbury Park, Warrington WA4 4HS
W www.ombudsman-services.org

Ombudsman Services was founded in 2002 and provides independent dispute resolution for the communications, copyright licensing and energy sectors. Ombudsman Services ceased dealing with complaints concerning the property sector in 2018.

Ombudsman Services: Communications investigates complaints from consumers about companies which provide communication services to the public.

Ombudsman Services: Copyright Licensing helps to resolve complaints about bodies that either own or administer, on behalf of third parties, the licensing of copyright materials.

Ombudsman Services: Energy helps to resolve complaints from consumers about energy (gas and electricity companies). This service is also responsible for handling investigations concerning the government's Green Deal policy, which launched in 2013, and offers long-term loans towards energy-saving home improvements.

Chair, Lord Tim Clement-Jones, CBE
Chief Ombudsman, Matthew Vickers

OMBUDSMAN SERVICES: COMMUNICATIONS
PO Box 730, Warrington WA4 6WU
T 0330-440 1614

OMBUDSMAN SERVICES: COPYRIGHT LICENSING
PO Box 1124, Warrington WA4 9GH
T 0330-440 1601

OMBUDSMAN SERVICES: ENERGY
PO Box 966, Warrington WA4 9DF
T 0330-440 1624

PARLIAMENTARY AND HEALTH SERVICE OMBUDSMAN
Millbank Tower, Millbank, London SW1P 4QP
T 0345-015 4033
W www.ombudsman.org.uk

The Parliamentary Commissioner for Administration (commonly known as the Parliamentary Ombudsman) is independent of government and is an officer of parliament. He is responsible for investigating complaints referred to him by MPs from members of the public who claim to have sustained injustice in consequence of maladministration by or on behalf of government departments and certain non-departmental public bodies in the UK. Certain types of action by government departments or bodies are excluded from investigation.

The Health Service Ombudsman is responsible for investigating complaints about services funded by the National Health Service in England that have not been dealt with by the service providers to the satisfaction of the complainant. This includes complaints about doctors, dentists, pharmacists and opticians. Complaints can be referred directly by the member of the public who claims to have sustained injustice or hardship in consequence of the failure in a service provided by a relevant organisation.

The two offices of the Parliamentary and Health Service Ombudsman are traditionally held by the same person.

Parliamentary Ombudsman and Health Service Ombudsman, Robert Behrens, CBE

PRISONS AND PROBATION OMBUDSMAN
Third Floor, 10 South Colonnade, London E14 4PU
T 020-7633 4100 E mail@ppo.gov.uk
W www.ppo.gov.uk

The Prisons and Probation Ombudsman investigates complaints from prisoners, people on probation and immigration detainees, deaths of prisoners, residents of probation-service approved premises and those held in immigration removal centres. The ombudsman is appointed by the Secretary of State for Justice and works closely with the Ministry of Justice. All deaths that occur in prison are investigated and an anonymised fatal incident report is written after each investigation.

Ombudsman, Sue McAllister, CB

PROPERTY OMBUDSMAN
Milford House, 43–55 Milford Street, Salisbury SP1 2BP
T 01722-333306
W www.tpos.co.uk

The Property Ombudsman (TPO) scheme was established in 1998 and provides a free, impartial and independent service for dealing with unresolved disputes between property agents and buyers, sellers, tenants and landlords of property in the UK.

The ombudsman's role is to consider complaints against the agents' obligation to act in accordance with the TPO codes of practice and to propose a full and final resolution to the dispute. Consumers are not bound by the Ombudsman's decision, but registered agents are.

TPO is the primary dispute-resolution service for the property industry.

Ombudsman, Katrine Sporle, CBE

PUBLIC SERVICES OMBUDSMAN FOR WALES

1 Ffordd yr Hen Gae, Pencoed CF35 5LJ
T 0300-790 0203 E ask@ombudsman-wales.org.uk
W www.ombudsman.wales

The office of Public Services Ombudsman for Wales was established, with effect from 1 April 2006, by the Public Services Ombudsman (Wales) Act 2005. The ombudsman, who is appointed by the Queen, investigates complaints of injustice caused by maladministration or service failure by public services such as the Assembly Commission (and public bodies sponsored by the assembly); Welsh government; National Health Service bodies, including GPs, family health service providers and hospitals; registered social landlords; local authorities, including community councils; fire and rescue authorities; police authorities; the Arts Council of Wales; national park authorities; and countryside and environmental organisations.

Ombudsman, Nick Bennett

REMOVALS INDUSTRY OMBUDSMAN SCHEME

PO Box 1535, High Wycombe HP12 9EE
T 020-8144 3790 E ombudsman@removalsombudsman.co.uk
W www.removalsombudsman.co.uk

The Removals Industry Ombudsman Scheme was established to resolve disputes between removal companies that are members of the scheme and their clients, both domestic and commercial. It comprises a board of four members, only one of whom has any connection with the removals industry. The ombudsman investigates complaints such as breaches of contract, unprofessional conduct, delays, excessive charges or breaches in the code of practice. The National Guild of Removers and Storers is currently the principal member.

Ombudsman, Tony Kaye

SCOTTISH PUBLIC SERVICES OMBUDSMAN

Bridgeside House, 99 McDonald Road, Edinburgh EH7 4NS
T 0800-377 7330
W www.spso.org.uk

The Scottish Public Services Ombudsman (SPSO) was established in 2002. The SPSO is the final stage for complaints about public services in Scotland. Its service is free and independent. SPSO investigates complaints about the Scottish government, its agencies and departments; the Scottish Parliamentary Corporate Body; colleges and universities; councils; housing associations; NHS Scotland; prisons; some water and sewerage service providers; and most other Scottish public bodies. The ombudsman looks at complaints regarding poor service or administrative failure and can usually only look at those that have been through the formal complaints process of the organisation concerned. It also has a statutory function in improving complaints handling in public services, which it carries out through its Complaints Standards Authority.

Scottish Public Services Ombudsman, Rosemary Agnew

WATERWAYS OMBUDSMAN

PO Box 854, Altrincham WA15 5JS
T 0161-980 4858 E enquiries@waterways-ombudsman.org
W www.waterways-ombudsman.org

Since July 2012, the Waterways Ombudsman has investigated complaints about the Canal and River Trust and its subsidiaries (such as British Waterways Marinas Limited). The ombudsman does not consider complaints about canals in Scotland, which are the responsibility of the Scottish Public Services Ombudsman.

Ombudsman, Sarah Daniel

THE POLICE SERVICE

There are 45 police forces in the United Kingdom: 43 in England and Wales, including the Metropolitan Police and the City of London Police, Police Scotland and the Police Service of Northern Ireland. The Isle of Man, Jersey and Guernsey have their own forces responsible for policing in their respective islands and bailiwicks. The National Crime Agency, which became operational in October 2013, is responsible for preventing organised crime and strengthening UK borders.

Since 1964, police authorities – separate independent bodies for each police force – were responsible for the supervision of local policing in England and Wales. Following the government's white paper *Policing in the 21st Century* it was concluded that, in order to make the police more accountable, police authorities should be replaced with a directly elected commissioner for each force, supported by a police and crime panel made up of representatives from each local authority in a police force area. In November 2012, following the enactment of the Police Reform and Social Responsibility Act 2011, the first elections to install police and crime commissioners (PCCs) were held in November 2012 across England and Wales; the most recent elections took place in May 2016. The PCCs are responsible for appointing the chief constable of their force, establishing local priorities and setting budgets. The PCCs are not in place to run their local force but rather to hold them to account. The Mayor of London, through the Deputy Mayor for Policing and Crime and supported by the Mayor's Office for Policing and Crime (MOPAC), acts as the PCC for the Metropolitan Police. Since 2017 the Mayor of Greater Manchester fulfils the PCC responsibilities for this area's force. The City of London Corporation acts as the police authority for the City of London Police.

Under the Police and Fire Reform (Scotland) Act 2012, Police Scotland was established on 1 April 2013, merging the eight separate territorial police forces, the Scottish Crime and Drug Enforcement Agency and the Association of Chief Police Officers in Scotland. Responsible for policing the whole of Scotland, Police Scotland is the second largest force in the UK after the Metropolitan Police. The service is led by a chief constable who is supported by a team of four deputy constables, assistant chief constables and three directors. The Scottish Police Authority, established in October 2012, is responsible for maintaining policing, promoting policing principles, the continuous improvement of policing and holds the Chief Constable to account. In Northern Ireland, the Northern Ireland Policing Board, an independent public body consisting of 19 political and independent members, fulfils a similar role.

Police forces in England, Scotland and Wales are financed by central and local government grants and a precept on the council tax. The Police Service of Northern Ireland is wholly funded by central government.

The home secretary, the Scottish government and the Northern Ireland Minister of Justice are responsible for the organisation, administration and operation of the police service. They regulate police ranks, discipline, hours of duty and pay and allowances. All police forces are subject to inspection by HM Inspectorate of Constabulary, which reports to the home secretary and the Northern Ireland Minister of Justice. Police forces in Scotland are inspected by HM Inspectorate of Constabulary for Scotland which operates independently of the Scottish government.

COMPLAINTS

Established under the Policing and Crime Act 2017, the Independent Office for Police Conduct (IOPC) succeeded the Independent Police Complaints Commission (IPCC) in January 2018. The IOPC is responsible for carrying out independent investigations into serious incidents or allegations of misconduct by those serving with the police forces in England and Wales, as well as Police and Crime Commissioners in England and Wales and the London Mayor's Office for Policing and Crime (MOPAC). The IOPC's director-general and its regional directors must not have worked for the police in any capacity prior to their appointment. It has the power to initiate, undertake and oversee investigations and is also responsible for the way in which complaints are handled by local police forces. The IOPC is also responsible for serious complaints and conduct matters relating to staff at the National Crime Agency (NCA).

Complaints about the police must first be recorded with the relevant police force and the local force will attempt to resolve the matter internally. Certain serious complaints are automatically referred to the IOPC. The IOPC or police force may refer the case to the Crown Prosecution Service, which will decide whether to bring criminal charges against the officer/s involved.

On 1 April 2013, under the Police and Fire Reform (Scotland) Act 2012 which brought together Scotland's eight police services into the single Police Service of Scotland, the remit of the Police Complaints Commissioner for Scotland (PCCS) was expanded to include investigations into the most serious incidents concerning the police. To reflect this change, the PCCS was renamed the Police Investigations and Review Commissioner (PIRC).

The Police Ombudsman for Northern Ireland provides an independent police complaints system for Northern Ireland, dealing with all stages of the complaints procedure. Complaints that cannot be resolved informally are investigated and the ombudsman recommends a suitable course of action to the Chief Constable of the Police Service of Northern Ireland or the Northern Ireland Policing Board based on the investigation's findings. The ombudsman may recommend that a police officer be prosecuted, but the decision to prosecute a police officer rests with the Director of Public Prosecutions.

INDEPENDENT OFFICE FOR POLICE CONDUCT, PO Box 473, Sale M33 0BW T 0300-020 0096
E enquiries@policeconduct.gov.uk
W www.policeconduct.gov.uk
Director-General, Michael Lockwood

POLICE INVESTIGATIONS AND REVIEW COMMISSIONER, Hamilton House, Hamilton Business Park, Caird Park, Hamilton ML3 0QA T 01698-542900
E enquiries@pirc.gov.scot W www.pirc.scotland.gov.uk
Police Investigations and Review Commissioner, Kate Frame

POLICE OMBUDSMAN FOR NORTHERN IRELAND, New Cathedral Buildings, Writers' Square, 11 Church Street, Belfast BT1 1PG T 028-9082 8600 E info@policeombudsman.org
W www.policeombudsman.org
Police Ombudsman, Dr Michael Maguire

POLICE SERVICES

COLLEGE OF POLICING

Leamington Road, Ryton-on-Dunsmore, Coventry CV8 3EN
T 0800-496 3322 E contactus@college.pnn.police.uk
W www.college.police.uk

The College of Policing was established in December 2012 as the first professional body set up for policing. It works on behalf of the public to raise professional standards in policing and to assist forces to reduce crime and protect the public. It engages with the public through the Police and Crime Commissioners to ensure that it is responsive to the issues of greatest concern.

The government has designated the college as a centre for reviewing and testing practices and interventions to identify which are effective in reducing crime. It makes this information accessible for all in policing, particularly frontline practitioners. The college also supports continuous professional development and sets national standards for promotion and progression.

Chief Executive, Mike Cunningham, QPM
Chair, Millie Banerjee, CBE

NATIONAL CRIME AGENCY

Units 1–6 Citadel Place, Tinworth Street, London SE11 5EF
T 0370-496 7622
E communication@nca.gov.uk
W www.nationalcrimeagency.gov.uk

Established under the Crime and Courts Act 2013 the National Crime Agency (NCA) became fully operational in October 2013. The NCA is a non-ministerial government department.

The NCA's remit is to fight organised crime, including child sexual exploitation, modern slavery and human trafficking, illegal firearms, cyber crime and money laundering.

The director-general has independent operational direction and control over the NCA's activities and, through the home secretary, is accountable to parliament.

Director-General, Lynne Owens, CBE, QPM

UK MISSING PERSONS UNIT

PO Box 58358, London NW1W 9LA T 0800-234 6034
E ukmpu@nca.gov.uk
W www.missingpersons.police.uk

The UK Missing Persons Unit, part of the National Crime Agency, acts as the centre for the exchange of information connected with the search for missing persons nationally and internationally alongside the police and other related organisations. The unit focuses on cross-matching missing persons with unidentified persons or bodies by maintaining records, including a dental index of ante-mortem chartings of long-term missing persons and post-mortem chartings from unidentified bodies.

Information is supplied and collected for all persons who have been missing in the UK for over 72 hours (or fewer where police deem appropriate), foreign nationals reported missing in the UK, UK nationals reported missing abroad and all unidentified bodies and persons found within the UK.

SPECIALIST FORCES

BRITISH TRANSPORT POLICE

25 Camden Road, London NW1 9LN T 0800-405040
E first_contact@btp.pnn.police.uk
W www.btp.police.uk
Strength (August 2019), 3,069

British Transport Police is the national police force for the railways in England, Wales and Scotland, including the London Underground system, Docklands Light Railway, Glasgow Subway, Midland Metro tram system, Sunderland Metro, London Tramlink and the Emirates Air Line cable car.

The chief constable reports to the British Transport Police Authority. The members of the authority are appointed by the transport secretary and include representatives from the rail industry as well as independent members. Officers are paid the same salary as those in other police forces.

Chief Constable, Paul Crowther, OBE

CIVIL NUCLEAR CONSTABULARY

Building F6, Culham Science Centre, Abingdon,
Oxfordshire OX14 3DB T 0300-313 5400
W www.gov.uk/government/organisations/civil-nuclear-constabulary
*Strength, c.*1,500

The Civil Nuclear Constabulary (CNC) is overseen by the Civil Nuclear Police Authority, an executive non-departmental public body sponsored by the Department for Business, Energy and Industrial Strategy. The CNC is a specialised armed force that protects civil nuclear sites and nuclear materials. The constabulary is responsible for policing UK civil nuclear industry facilities and for escorting nuclear material between establishments within the UK and worldwide.

Chief Constable, Simon Chesterman, QPM
Deputy Chief Constable, Chris Armitt, QPM

MINISTRY OF DEFENCE POLICE

Ministry of Defence Police HQ, Wethersfield, Braintree, Essex
CM7 4AZ T 01371-854000
W www.mod.police.uk
Strength (July 2018), 2,733

Part of the Ministry of Defence Police and Guarding Agency, the Ministry of Defence Police is a statutory civil police force with particular responsibility for the security and policing of the MoD environment. It contributes to the physical protection of property and personnel within its jurisdiction and provides a comprehensive police service to the MoD as a whole.

Chief Constable, Andy Adams
Deputy Chief Constable, Gareth Wilson

THE SPECIAL CONSTABULARY

Strength (March 2019), 10,640

The Special Constabulary is a force of trained volunteers who support and work with their local police force, usually for a minimum of 16 hours a month. Special constables are thoroughly grounded in the basic aspects of police work, such as self-defence, powers of arrest, common crimes and preparing evidence for court, before they can begin to carry out any police duties. Once they have completed their training, they have the same powers as a regular officer and wear a similar uniform. The Metropolitan Police Service have further information on their website.

POLICE FORCES

The telephone number for each local police force in England, Wales, Scotland and Northern Ireland is T 101

Force	Strength†	Chief Constable	Police and Crime Commissioner
ENGLAND			
Avon and Somerset	2,676	Andy Marsh, QPM	Sue Mountstevens
Bedfordshire	1,164	Jon Boutcher, QPM	Kathryn Holloway
Cambridgeshire	1,447	Nick Dean	Jason Ablewhite
Cheshire	2,006	Darren Martland	David Keane
Cleveland	1,198	Richard Lewis	Barry Coppinger
Cumbria	1,160	Michelle Skeer, QPM	Peter McCall
Derbyshire	1,767	Peter Goodman	Hardyal Dhindsa
Devon and Cornwall	3,000	Shaun Sawyer, QPM	Alison Hernandez
Dorset	1,223	James Vaughan, QPM	Martyn Underhill
Durham	1,118	Jo Farrell	Ron Hogg
Essex	3,071	Ben-Julian Harrington	Roger Hirst
Gloucestershire	1,073	Rod Hansen	Martin Surl
Greater Manchester	6,444	Ian Hopkins, QPM	Mayor of Greater Manchester
Hampshire	2,697	Olivia Pinkney	Michael Lane
Hertfordshire	2,009	Charlie Hall, QPM	David Lloyd
Humberside	1,889	Lee Freeman	Keith Hunter
Kent	3,553	Alan Pughsley, QPM	Matthew Scott
Lancashire	2,895	Andy Rhodes	Clive Grunshaw
Leicestershire	1,829	Simon Cole, QPM	Lord Bach
Lincolnshire	1,096	Bill Skelly	Marc Jones
Merseyside	3,396	Andy Cooke, QPM	Jane Kennedy
Norfolk	1,609	Simon Bailey, QPM	Lorne Green
North Yorkshire	1,377	Lisa Winward	Julia Mulligan
Northamptonshire	1,187	Nick Adderley	Stephen Mold
Northumbria	3,081	Winton Keenen	Kim McGuiness
Nottinghamshire	1,936	Craig Guilford	Paddy Tipping
South Yorkshire	2,370	Stephen Watson, QPM	Dr Alan Billings
Staffordshire	1,567	Gareth Morgan	Matthew Ellis
Suffolk	1,172	Steve Jupp	Tim Passmore
Surrey	1,882	Nick Ephgrave	David Munro
Sussex	2,629	Giles York, QPM	Katy Bourne
Thames Valley	4,149	Francis Habgood, QPM	Anthony Stansfeld
Warwickshire	817	Martin Jelley, QPM	Philip Seccombe
West Mercia	1,989	Anthony Bangham	John-Paul Campion
West Midlands	6,495	Dave Thompson, QPM	David Jamieson
West Yorkshire	5,137	John Robins, QPM	Mark Burns-Williamson, OBE
Wiltshire	992	Kier Pritchard	Angus Macpherson
WALES			
Dyfed-Powys	1,145	Mark Collins	Dafydd Llywelyn
Gwent	1,308	Pam Kelly *(acting)*	Jeff Cuthbert
North Wales	1,458	Carl Foulkes	Arfon Jones
South Wales	2,986	Matt Jukes	Rt. Hon. Alun Michael
POLICE SCOTLAND	17,251	Iain Livingstone, QPM	–
POLICE SERVICE OF NORTHERN IRELAND	6,716	Simon Byrne	–

ISLANDS	Strength†	Chief Constable	Telephone
Isle of Man	236	Gary Roberts	01624-631212
States of Jersey	189	Rob Bastable	01534-612612
Guernsey	146	Rauri Hardy	01481-725111

† Size of force (full-time equivalent; excluding long-term absentees) as at 31 March 2019

LONDON FORCES

CITY OF LONDON POLICE

182 Bishopsgate, London EC2M 4NP T 020-7601 2222
W www.cityoflondon.police.uk
Strength (June 2019), 756

The City of London has one of the most important financial centres in the world and the force has particular expertise in fraud investigation. The force concentrates on: economic crime, counter terrorism and community policing. It has a wholly elected police authority, the police committee of the City of London Corporation, which appoints the commissioner.

Commissioner, Ian Dyson, QPM
Assistant Commissioner, Alistair Sutherland, QPM
Commander, Karen Baxter *(Economic Crime)*

METROPOLITAN POLICE SERVICE

New Scotland Yard, Broadway, London SW1H 0BG
T 020-7230 1212 W www.met.police.uk
*Strength (June 2019),*30,059

Commissioner, Cressida Dick, CBE, QPM
Deputy Commissioner, Sir Stephen House, QPM

The Metropolitan Police Service (MPS) is divided into four main areas for operational purposes:

FRONTLINE POLICING
Most of the day-to-day policing of London is carried out by 32 borough operational command units operating within the same boundaries as the London borough councils.

Assistant Commissioner, Mark Simmons

SPECIALIST OPERATIONS
Counter Terrorism Command is responsible for the prevention and disruption of terrorist activity, domestic extremism and related offences within London and nationally. It provides an explosives disposal and chemical, biological, radiological and nuclear capability in London, assists the security services in fulfilling their roles and provides a point of contact for international partners.
Protection Command is responsible for the protection and security of high-profile persons, such as the royal family, prime minister and visiting heads of state.
Security Command works with authorities at the Houses of Parliament to provide security for peers, MPs, employees and visitors to the Palace of Westminster.

Assistant Commissioner & National Coordinator for Counter Terrorism Policing, Neil Basu

MET OPERATIONS
Met Operations provides two main services: reducing the harm caused by serious crime and criminal networks and providing specialist policing services across London.

Assistant Commissioner, Nick Ephgrave

PROFESSIONALISM
The Directorate of Professionalism's key aims are to uphold and improve professional standards across the MPS. It works with the IOPC to establish good practice, reduce bureaucracy and review decision making. It also works with the CPS to ensure timely investigations of complaints and conduct matters.

Assistant Commissioner, Helen Ball

STAFF ASSOCIATIONS

Police officers are not permitted to join a trade union or to take strike action. All ranks have their own staff associations.
NATIONAL POLICE CHIEFS' COUNCIL (NPCC), 10 Victoria Street, London SW1H 0NN T 020-3276 3795
W www.npcc.police.uk
Chair, Barbara Scott

ENGLAND AND WALES
POLICE FEDERATION OF ENGLAND AND WALES, Federation House, Highbury Drive, Leatherhead, Surrey KT22 7UY T 01372-352050 W www.polfed.org
National Secretary, Alex Duncan
POLICE SUPERINTENDENTS' ASSOCIATION OF ENGLAND AND WALES, 67A Reading Road, Pangbourne, Reading RG8 7JD T 0118-984 4005 W www.policesupers.com
National Secretary, Chief Supt. Dan Murphy

SCOTLAND
ASSOCIATION OF SCOTTISH POLICE SUPERINTENDENTS, Scottish Police College, Kincardine, Fife FK10 4BE T 01259-732122
W www.scottishpolicesupers.org.uk
General Secretary, Craig Suttie
SCOTTISH POLICE FEDERATION, 5 Woodside Place, Glasgow G3 7QF T 0300-303 0027 W www.spf.org.uk
General Secretary, Calum Steele

NORTHERN IRELAND
POLICE FEDERATION FOR NORTHERN IRELAND, 77–79 Garnerville Road, Belfast BT4 2NX T 028-9076 4200
W www.policefed-ni.org.uk
Chair, Mark Lindsay
SUPERINTENDENTS' ASSOCIATION OF NORTHERN IRELAND, T 028-9092 2201
E SuptAssociation@psni.pnn.police.uk

RATES OF PAY *as at 1 September 2019*

Chief Constable of Greater Manchester or W. Midlands*	£199,386
Chief Constable	£142,896–£186,099
Deputy Chief Constable	£119,637–£152,871
Assistant Chief Constable/ Commander	£103,023–£116,313
Chief Superintendent	£84,849–£89,511
Superintendent	
in rank on or after 1 April 2014	£68,460–£80,859
in rank before 1 April 2014	£68,460–£79,758
Chief Inspector†	£56,910 (£59,175)–£60,219 (£62,469)
Inspector†	£51,414 (£53,664)–£55,767 (£58,038)
Sergeant	£41,499–£45,099
Constable	
apptd on or after 1 April 2013	£20,880–£40,128
apptd before 1 April 2013	£25,560–£40,128
Metropolitan Police	
Commissioner	£285,792
Deputy Commissioner	£235,944
City of London Police	
Commissioner	£176,802
Assistant Commissioner	£145,830
Police Scotland	
Chief Constable	£214,404
Deputy Chief Constable	£174,741
Assistant Chief Constable	£118,485
Police Service of Northern Ireland	
Chief Constable	£207,489
Deputy Chief Constable	£168,582

* Also applicable to the four Assistant Commissioners of the MPS
† London salary in parentheses. All other officers (not MPS or City of London Commissioners) working in London receive an additional payment of £2,505 per annum

THE PRISON SERVICE

The prison services in the UK are the responsibility of the Secretary of State for Justice, the Scottish Secretary for Justice and the Minister of Justice in Northern Ireland. The chief executive (director-general in Northern Ireland), officers of HM Prison and Probation Service (HMPPS), the Scottish Prison Service (SPS) and the Northern Ireland Prison Service are responsible for the day-to-day running of the system.

There are 122 prison establishments in England and Wales, 15 in Scotland and three in Northern Ireland. Convicted prisoners are classified according to their assessed security risk and are housed in establishments appropriate to that level of security. There are no open prisons in Northern Ireland. Female prisoners are housed in women's establishments or in separate wings of mixed prisons. Remand prisoners are, where possible, housed separately from convicted prisoners. Offenders under the age of 21 are usually detained in a Young Offender Institution, which may be a separate establishment or part of a prison. Appellant and failed asylum seekers are held in Immigration Removal Centres, or in separate units of other prisons.

Fifteen prisons are now run by the private sector in England and Wales, and in England, Wales and Scotland all escort services have been contracted out to private companies. In Scotland, two prisons (Kilmarnock and Addiewell) were built and financed by the private sector and are being operated by private contractors.

There are independent prison inspectorates in England, Wales and Scotland which report annually on conditions and the treatment of prisoners. The Chief Inspector of Criminal Justice in Northern Ireland and HM Inspectorate of Prisons for England and Wales perform an inspectorate role for prisons in Northern Ireland. Every prison establishment also has an independent monitoring board made up of local volunteers.

Any prisoner whose complaint is not satisfied by the internal complaints procedures may complain to the prisons and probation ombudsman for England and Wales, the Scottish public services ombudsman or the prisoner ombudsman for Northern Ireland. The prisons and probation inspectors, the prisons ombudsman and the independent monitoring boards report to the home secretary and to the Minister of Justice in Northern Ireland.

PRISON STATISTICS

The current projections forecast that the prison population in England and Wales will grow to 85,800 by June 2022.

PRISON POPULATION 2019 (UK)

	Remand	Sentenced	Other
ENGLAND AND WALES	8,957	72,860	817
Male	8,437	69,576	739
Female	520	3,284	28
SCOTLAND	1,808	6,416	–
Male	1,697	6,125	–
Female	111	291	–
N. IRELAND*	436	987	–
Male	414	944	–
Female	22	43	–
UK TOTAL	11,201	80,263	1,584

* Figures from September 2018
Sources: MoJ; Scottish Prison Service; NI Prison Service

PRISON CAPACITY (ENGLAND AND WALES)
as at July 2019

Male prisoners	79,211
Female prisoners	3,831
Total	83,042
Useable operational capacity	85,131
Under home detention curfew supervision	2,884

Source: MoJ – Prisons and Probation Statistics

SENTENCED PRISON POPULATION BY SEX AND OFFENCE (ENGLAND AND WALES) as at 31 March 2019

	Male	Female
Violence against the person	18,342	948
Sexual offences	13,234	125
Robbery	6,840	324
Theft offences	8,494	590
Criminal damage and arson	1,052	95
Drugs offences	10,579	436
Possession of weapons	2,854	113
Public order offences	1,148	41
Miscellaneous crimes against society	2,820	177
Fraud offences	1,079	169
Summary non-motoring	2,502	224
Summary motoring	350	10
Offence not recorded	233	26
Total	69,527	3,278

Source: MoJ – Prisons and Probation Statistics

SENTENCED POPULATION BY LENGTH OF SENTENCE (ENGLAND AND WALES)
as at 31 March 2019

	British	Other Nationalities or Not Recorded
Less than 12 months	4,432	522
12 months to less than 4 years	14,140	1,628
4 years to less than life	31,285	3,441
Indeterminate	8,561	875
Total*	58,418	6,466

* Figures do not include civil (non-criminal) prisoners or fine defaulters
Source: MoJ – Prisons and Probation Statistics

AVERAGE DAILY POPULATION BY TYPE OF CUSTODY 2019 (SCOTLAND)

Remand	1,489
Convicted awaiting sentence	319
Sentenced	6,416
Total	8,224

Source: SPS

SUICIDES IN PRISON (ENGLAND AND WALES)
Dec. 2017–Dec. 2018

Total	92

Source: MoJ

THE PRISON SERVICES

HM PRISON AND PROBATION SERVICE

102 Petty France, London SW1H 9AJ
T 0163-363 0941 E public.enquiries@noms.gsi.gov.uk
W www.gov.uk/government/organisations/
her-majestys-prison-and-probation-service

HM Prison and Probation Service (HMPPS) was formed on 1 April 2017, incorporating the National Offender Management Service (NOMS) and HM Prisons. HMPPS is responsible for implementing government policy concerning the welfare of prison populations and local communities, working closely with HM Prison Service to oversee the management of public sector prisons in England and Wales.

SALARIES (ENGLAND AND WALES)
from 1 April 2019

All salary ranges given are for the average across England and Wales (includes inner and outer London salaries) and are based on a 37-hour-week inclusive of the required hours allowance (Governors, Deputy Governors and Heads of Function) or the additional 17 per cent unsocial hours payment for all other grades.

Governor	£68,604–£97,859
Deputy Governor	£48,656–£79,520
Head of Function	£43,545–£54,810
Custodial Manager	£31,615–£40,319
Supervising/Specialist Officer	£28,101–£35,988
Prison Officer	£22,293–£29,518
Operational Support Grade	£20,095–£24,829

HM PRISON AND PROBATION SERVICE BOARD
Chief Executive, Jo Farrar
Executive Directors, Ian Blakeman *(Performance)*; Phil Copple *(Prisons)*; Amy Rees *(HMPPS Wales and Strategy)*; Adrian Scott *(Electronic Monitoring Programme and Procurement)*; Helga Swindenbank *(Youth Custody Service)*

OPERATING COSTS OF HM PRISON AND PROBATION SERVICE 2018–19

Operating income	(£245,575,000)
Total operating expenditure	£5,072,722,000
Staff costs	£2,146,359,000
Net operating expenditure	£4,827,147,000

Source: HM Prison and Probation Service – *Annual Report and Accounts 2018–19*

SCOTTISH PRISON SERVICE (SPS)

Calton House, 5 Redheughs Rigg, Edinburgh EH12 9HW
T 0131-330 3500 E gaolinfo@sps.pnn.gov.uk
W www.sps.gov.uk

SALARIES
from 1 April 2018

Governor in Charge	£64,771–£73,365
Deputy Governor	£52,361–£60,790
Head of Operations	£42,301–£50,547
Unit Manager	£34,440–£42,941
First Line Manager	£28,071–£36,175
Residential Officer	£23,564–£30,356
Operations Officer	£18,871–£23,372

SPS BOARD
Chief Executive, Colin McConnell
Directors, Caroline Johnston *(Strategy and Stakeholder Engagement, interim)*; James Kerr *(Operations)*; Ruth Sutherland *(Corporate Services, interim)*
Non-Executive Directors, K. Hampton; R. Molan; H. Monro; G. Scott; G. Stillie

OPERATING COSTS OF SPS 2017–18

Staff costs	£170,437,000
Total income	(£7,389,000)
Total operating expenditure	£331,518,000
Net operating expenditure	£324,129,000

Source: SPS – *Annual Report and Accounts 2017–18*

NORTHERN IRELAND PRISON SERVICE

Dundonald House, Upper Newtownards Road, Belfast BT4 3SU
T 028-9052 2922 E niprisonservice@nics.gov.uk
W www.justice-ni.gov.uk/topics/prisons

SALARIES
from 1 April 2018

Governor in Charge (Maghaberry)	£75,875–£82,375
Governor in Charge	£68,535–£75,035
Head of Function	£54,350–£58,775
Head of Unit	£48,750–£52,600
Senior Prison Officer	£37,680–£42,276
Main Grade Prison Officer	£34,121–£38,688
Custody Prison Officer	£23,950–£29,470
Operational Support Grade	£23,950
Prisoner Custody Officer (PCO)*	£20,026–£21,798

* 35-hour/week

MANAGEMENT BOARD
Director-General (Chair), Ronnie Armour
Permanent Secretary, Peter May
Directors, Louise Blair *(Finance)*; Paul Doran *(Rehabilitation)*; Brendan Giffen *(Strategy and Governance)*; Austin Treacy, OBE *(Prisons)*; Jacqui Wallace *(HR)*
Non-Executive Directors, Dale Ashford; Claire Keatinge

OPERATING COSTS OF NORTHERN IRELAND PRISON SERVICE 2016–17

Staff costs	£61,606,000
Operating income	£2,732,000
Total operating expenditure	£106,602,000
Net operating expenditure	£103,870,000

Source: NI Prison Service – *Annual Report and Accounts 2017–18*

PRISON ESTABLISHMENTS

ENGLAND AND WALES *as at June 2019*

Prison	Address	Capacity	Prisoners	Governor/Director
†‡ ALTCOURSE	Liverpool L9 7LH	1,164	1,147	Steve Williams
ASHFIELD	Bristol BS16 9QJ	400	398	Martin Booth
*‡ ASKHAM GRANGE	York YO23 3FT	128	112	Natalie McKee
‡ AYLESBURY	Bucks HP20 1EH	209	200	Laura Sapwell
BEDFORD	Bedford MK40 1HG	411	347	Patrick Butler
BELMARSH	London SE28 0EB	906	806	Rob Davis, OBE
BERWYN	Wrexham, LL13 9QE	1,400	1,361	Nick Leader
BIRMINGHAM	Birmingham B18 4AS	977	925	Paul Newton
BLANTYRE HOUSE	Kent TN17 2NH	–	–	James Bourke
†‡ BRINSFORD	Wolverhampton WV10 7PY	577	554	Heather Whitehead
†‡ BRISTOL	Bristol BS7 8PS	520	463	Steve Cross
BRIXTON	London SW2 5XF	798	737	Dave Bamford
* BRONZEFIELD	Middlesex TW15 3JZ	567	530	Ian Whiteside
BUCKLEY HALL	Lancs OL12 9DP	459	'449	Rob Knight
BULLINGDON	Oxon OX25 1PZ	1,114	1,055	Ian Blakeman
BURE	Norfolk NR10 5GB	656	653	Simon Rhoden
† CARDIFF	Cardiff CF24 0UG	779	722	Helen Ryder
CHANNINGS WOOD	Devon TQ12 6DW	724	690	Richard Luscombe
‡ CHELMSFORD	Essex CM2 6LQ	700	665	Penny Bartlett
COLDINGLEY	Surrey GU24 9EX	426	421	Jo Sims
‡ COOKHAM WOOD	Kent ME1 3LU	188	164	Paul Durham
DARTMOOR	Devon PL20 6RR	640	628	Bridie Oakes-Richards
‡ DEERBOLT	Co. Durham DL12 9BG	387	354	Gavin O'Malley
DONCASTER (private prison)	Doncaster DN5 8UX	1,145	1,081	Jerry Spencer
† DOVEGATE (private prison)	Staffs ST14 8XR	1,160	1,150	John Hewitson
* DOWNVIEW	Surrey SM2 5PD	293	273	Natasha Wilson
* DRAKE HALL	Staffs ST21 6LQ	340	333	Carl Hardwick
† DURHAM	Durham DH1 3HU	996	918	Phil Husband (*acting*)
* EAST SUTTON PARK	Kent ME17 3DF	101	96	Robin Eldridge
* EASTWOOD PARK	Glos GL12 8DB	432	396	Suzy Dymond-White
† ELMLEY	Kent ME12 4DZ	1,212	1,159	Paul Woods
ERLESTOKE	Wilts SN10 5TU	524	507	Tim Knight
†‡ EXETER	Devon EX4 4EX	545	488	Dave Atkinson
FEATHERSTONE	Wolverhampton WV10 7PU	637	611	Babafemi Dada
†‡ FELTHAM	Middx TW13 4ND	568	470	Emily Martin
FORD	W. Sussex BN18 0BX	544	538	Stephen Fradley
‡ FOREST BANK	Salford M27 8FB	1,460	1,430	Matt Spencer
* FOSTON HALL	Derby DE65 5DN	336	286	Andrea Black
FRANKLAND	Durham DH1 5YD	852	838	Gavin O'Malley
FULL SUTTON	York YO41 1PS	574	521	Gareth Sands
GARTH	Preston PR26 8NE	845	817	Steve Pearson
GARTREE	Leics LE16 7RP	'708	678	Ali Barker
GRENDON	Bucks HP18 0TL	568	538	Jamie Bennett
GUYS MARSH	Dorset SP7 0AH	396	387	Jamie Lucas
HATFIELD (AND MOORLAND)	S. Yorks DN7 6EL	1,384	1,328	Julie Spence
HAVERIGG	Cumbria LA18 4NA	269	264	Tony Corcoran
HEWELL	Worcs B97 6QS	1,115	1,094	Clare Pearson
HIGH DOWN	Surrey SM2 5PJ	1,203	1,107	Sally Hill
HIGHPOINT	Suffolk CB8 9YG	1,325	1,279	Nigel Smith
‡ HINDLEY	Lancs WN2 5TH	578	547	Mark Livingston
‡ HOLLESLEY BAY	Suffolk IP12 3JW	485	481	Gary Newnes
HOLME HOUSE	Stockton-on-Tees TS18 2QU	1,210	1,199	Chris Dyer
HULL	Hull HU9 5LS	1,036	989	Anthony Oliver
HUMBER	E. Yorks HU15 2JZ	1,062	937	Marcella Goligher
§ HUNTERCOMBE	Oxon RG9 5SB	480	464	David Redhouse
‡ ISIS	Thamesmead SE28 0NZ	628	622	Emily Thomas
ISLE OF WIGHT	Isle of Wight PO30 5RS	1,053	1,016	Doug Graham
KIRKHAM	Lancs PR4 2RN	657	644	Dan Cooper
KIRKLEVINGTON GRANGE	Cleveland TS15 9PA	283	279	Angie Petit
†‡ LANCASTER FARMS	Lancaster LA1 3QZ	560	551	Peter Francis
LEEDS	Leeds LS12 2TJ	1,212	1,066	Steven Robson
LEICESTER	Leicester LE2 7AJ	411	302	Jim Donaldson
‡ LEWES	E. Sussex BN7 1EA	606	514	Stephen Fradley
LEYHILL	Glos GL12 8BT	515	511	Neil Lavis
† LINCOLN	Lincoln LN2 4BD	629	514	Paul Yates
LINDHOLME	Doncaster DN7 6EE	945	938	Simon Walters
LITTLEHEY	Cambs PE28 0SR	1,220	1,205	Stephen Ruddy
LIVERPOOL	Liverpool L9 3DF	700	670	Pia Sinha
LONG LARTIN	Worcs WR11 8TZ	602	584	Jamie Bennett
* LOW NEWTON	Durham DH1 5YA	352	314	Gabrielle Lee
LOWDHAM GRANGE (private prison)	Notts NG14 7DA	888	878	Mark Hanson

Prison	Address	Average Daily	Max. Number	Governor/Director
§ MAIDSTONE	Kent ME14 1UZ	600	585	Dave Atkinson
† MANCHESTER	Manchester M60 9AH	1,072	918	Rob Young
§ MORTON HALL	Lincoln LN6 9PT	392	254	Karen Head
The MOUNT	Herts HP3 0NZ	1,028	990	Kevin Leggett
*‡ NEW HALL	W. Yorks WF4 4XX	425	358	Natalie McKee
NORTH SEA CAMP	Lincs PE22 0QX	420	411	Michelle Quirke
NORTHUMBERLAND	Northumberland NE65 9XG	1,348	1,342	Nick Leader
† NORWICH	Norfolk NR1 4LU	773	719	Declan Moore
NOTTINGHAM	Notts NG5 3AG	800	787	Phil Novis
OAKWOOD	W. Midlands WV10 7QD	2,106	2,080	John McLaughlin
ONLEY	Warks CV23 8AP	734	730	Matthew Tilt
‡ PARC	Bridgend CF35 6AP	1,699	1,631	Janet Wallsgrove
PENTONVILLE	London N7 8TT	1,098	1,065	Darren Hughes
* PETERBOROUGH	Peterborough PE3 7PD	1,240	1,149	Damian Evans
‡ PORTLAND	Dorset DT5 1DL	530	518	Steve Hodson
PRESTON	Lancs PR1 5AB	811	697	Steve Lawrence
RANBY	Notts DN22 8EU	1,038	1,014	Nigel Hirst
RISLEY	Cheshire WA3 6BP	1,014	1,066	Nicki Smith
‡ ROCHESTER	Kent ME1 3QS	695	680	Dean Gardiner
RYE HILL	Warks CV23 8SZ	664	660	Pete Small
* SEND	Surrey GU23 7LJ	282	268	Carlene Dixon
STAFFORD	Stafford ST16 3AW	751	750	Ralph Lubkowski
STANDFORD HILL	Kent ME12 4AA	464	459	Dawn Mauldon
STOCKEN	Rutland LE15 7RD	913	864	Neil Thomas
† STOKE HEATH	Shropshire TF9 2JL	782	755	John Huntington
* STYAL	Cheshire SK9 4HR	486	461	Kate Robinson
‡ SUDBURY	Derbys DE6 5HW	581	579	Adrian Turner
SWALESIDE	Kent ME12 4AX	1,112	1,064	Mark Icke
SWANSEA	Swansea SA1 3SR	497	419	Graham Barrett
‡ SWINFEN HALL	Staffs WS14 9QS	594	574	Ian West
THAMESIDE	London SE28 0FJ	1,232	1,200	Craig Thomson
THORN CROSS	Cheshire WA4 4RL	385	384	Mick Povall
USK/PRESCOED	Monmouthshire NP15 1XP	526	519	Giles Mason
VERNE	Dorset DT5 1EQ	580	480	David Bourne
WAKEFIELD	W. Yorks WF2 9AG	750	723	Tom Wheatley
WANDSWORTH	London SW18 3HU	1,540	1,496	Jeanne Bryant
WARREN HILL	Suffolk IP12 3BF	258	240	Dave Nickolson
WAYLAND	Norfolk IP25 6RL	940	931	Sonia Walsh
WEALSTUN	W. Yorks LS23 7AZ	832	804	Diane Lewis
‡ WERRINGTON	Stoke-on-Trent ST9 0DX	118	116	Ian Darlington
‡ WETHERBY	W. Yorks LS22 5ED	336	223	Andrew Dickinson
WHATTON	Nottingham NG13 9FQ	841	836	Lynn Saunders, OBE
WHITEMOOR	Cambs PE15 0PR	458	451	Will Styles
WINCHESTER	Winchester SO22 5DF	500	474	James Bourke
WOODHILL	Bucks MK4 4DA	622	571	Nicola Marfleet
WORMWOOD SCRUBS	London W12 0AE	1,096	1,039	Sarah Pennington
WYMOTT	Preston PR26 8LW	1,169	1,149	Graham Beck

SCOTLAND *as at June 2019*

Prison	Address	Average Daily	Max. Number	Governor/Director
ADDIEWELL	West Lothian EH55 8QA	696	702	Ian Whitehead
†‡ BARLINNIE	Glasgow G33 2QX	1,127	1,195	Michael Stoney
CASTLE HUNTLY (Open Estate)	Dundee DD2 5HL	189	X	Gerry Michie
*†‡ CORNTON VALE	Stirling FK9 5NU	86	96	Jacqueline Clinton
† DUMFRIES	Dumfries DG2 9AX	172	180	Linda Dorward
*† EDINBURGH	Edinburgh EH11 3LN	872	913	David Abernethy
GLENOCHIL	Tullibody FK10 3AD	641	667	Andrew Hodge
*‡ GRAMPIAN	Peterhead AB42 2YY	449	474	Mike Hebden (*acting*)
*† GREENOCK	Greenock PA16 9AJ	248	257	Karen Smith
† INVERNESS	Inverness IV2 3HH	110	137	Stephen Coyle
† KILMARNOCK (private prison)	Kilmarnock KA1 5AA	499	509	Michael Guy
LOW MOSS	Glasgow G64 2PZ	757	778	James Farish
† PERTH	Perth PH2 8AT	617	654	Fraser Munro
*†‡ POLMONT	Falkirk FK2 0AB	470	522	Brenda Stewart
SHOTTS	Lanarkshire ML7 4LE	531	540	Allister Purdie

NORTHERN IRELAND *as at June 2019*

Prison	Address	Prisoners	Governor/Director
* HYDEBANK WOOD	Belfast BT8 8NA	152	Richard Taylor
†§ MAGHABERRY	Co. Antrim BT28 2NF	857	David Kennedy
MAGILLIGAN	Co. Londonderry BT49 0LR	430	Richard Taylor

* Women's establishment or establishment with units for women
† Remand Centre or establishment with units for remand prisoners
‡ Young Offender Institution or establishment with units for young offenders
§ Immigration Removal Centre or establishment with units for immigration detainees

DEFENCE

The armed forces of the UK comprise the Royal Navy, the Army and the Royal Air Force (RAF). The Queen is Commander-in-Chief of all the armed forces. The Secretary of State for Defence is responsible for the formulation and content of defence policy and for providing the means by which it is conducted. The formal legal basis for the conduct of defence in the UK rests on a range of powers vested by statute and letters patent in the Defence Council, chaired by the Secretary of State for Defence. Beneath the ministers lies the top management of the Ministry of Defence (MoD), headed jointly by the Permanent Secretary and the Chief of the Defence Staff. The Permanent Secretary is the government's principal civilian adviser on defence and has the primary responsibility for policy, finance, management and administration. The Permanent Secretary is also personally accountable to parliament for the expenditure of all public money allocated to defence purposes. The Chief of the Defence Staff is the professional head of the armed forces in the UK and the principal military adviser to the secretary of state and the government.

The Defence Board is the executive of the Defence Council. Chaired by the Permanent Secretary, it acts as the main executive board of the Ministry of Defence, providing senior level leadership and strategic management of defence.

The Central Staff, headed by the Vice-Chief of the Defence Staff and the Second Permanent Under-Secretary of State, is the policy core of the department. Defence Equipment and Support, headed by the Chief of Defence Materiel, is responsible for purchasing defence equipment and providing logistical support to the armed forces.

A permanent Joint Headquarters for the conduct of joint operations was set up at Northwood in 1996. The Joint Headquarters connects the policy and strategic functions of the MoD head office with the conduct of operations and is intended to strengthen the policy/executive division.

The UK pursues its defence and security policies through its membership of NATO (to which most of its armed forces are committed), the European Union, the Organisation for Security and Cooperation in Europe and the UN (see International Organisations section).

STRENGTH OF THE REGULAR ARMED FORCES

	Royal Navy	Army	RAF	All Services
1975 strength	76,200	167,100	95,000	338,300
2000 strength	42,850	110,050	54,720	207,620
2005 strength	39,940	109,290	51,870	201,100
2010 strength	38,730	108,920	44,050	191,700
2011 strength	37,660	106,240	42,460	186,360
2012 strength	35,540	104,250	40,000	179,800
2013 strength	33,960	99,730	37,030	170,710
2014 strength	33,330	91,070	35,230	159,630
2015 strength	32,740	87,060	33,930	153,720
2016 strength	32,502	85,038	33,456	150,966
2017 strength	32,544	83,561	33,261	149,366
2018 strength	32,483	81,116	32,957	146,556
2019 strength	32,537	79,029	32,862	144,428

Source: MoD – Defence Statistics (Tri-Service)

UK REGULAR ARMED FORCES BY RANK 2019

Officers	27,500
Other Ranks	116,928

Source: MoD – Defence Statistics (Tri-Service)

UK regular forces include trained and untrained personnel and nursing services, but exclude Gurkhas, full-time reserve service personnel, mobilised reservists and naval activated reservists. As at 1 April 2019 these groups numbered:

All Gurkhas	3,429
Full-time reserve service	5,099
Mobilised reservists	372
Army	196
RAF	102
Royal Navy	74

Source: MoD – Defence Statistics (Tri-Service)

CIVILIAN PERSONNEL

2000 level	121,300
2005 level	107,680
2006 level	102,970
2007 level	95,790
2008 level	89,499
2009 level	86,621
2010 level	85,850
2011 level	83,063
2012 level	71,008
2013 level	65,400
2014 level	62,501
2015 level	58,161
2016 level	56,243
2017 level	56,675
2018 level	56,865
2019 level	57,760

Source: MoD – Defence Statistics (Tri-Service)

UK REGULAR FORCES: DEATHS

In 2018 there were a total of 61 deaths among the UK regular armed forces, of which 12 were serving in the Royal Navy and Royal Marines, 38 in the Army and 11 in the RAF. The largest single cause of death was cancers, which accounted for 10 deaths (16 per cent of the total) in 2018. Land transport accidents accounted for 10 deaths (16 per cent) and other accidents provisionally accounted for a further 22 deaths (36 per cent). There was one death as a result of hostile action. Suicides and open verdicts accounted for five deaths.

NUMBER OF DEATHS AND MORTALITY RATES

	2014	2015	2016	2017	2018
Total number	68	60	72	63	61
Royal Navy	12	11	17	12	12
Army	40	39	41	40	38
RAF	16	10	14	11	11
Mortality rates per thousand					
Tri-service rate	0.42	0.39	0.47	0.42	0.41
Navy	0.35	0.32	0.52	0.36	0.34
Army	0.42	0.45	0.47	0.49	0.46
RAF	0.40	0.28	0.36	0.27	0.29

Source: MoD National Statistics

NUCLEAR FORCES

The Vanguard Class SSBN (ship submersible ballistic nuclear) provides the UK's strategic nuclear deterrent. Each Vanguard Class submarine is capable of carrying 16 Trident D5 missiles equipped with nuclear warheads.

There is a ballistic missile early warning system station at RAF Fylingdales in North Yorkshire.

ARMS CONTROL

The 1990 Conventional Armed Forces in Europe (CFE) Treaty, which commits all NATO and former Warsaw Pact members to limiting their holdings of five major classes of conventional weapons, has been adapted to reflect the changed geo-strategic environment and negotiations continue for its implementation. The Open Skies Treaty, which the UK signed in 1992 and entered into force in 2002, allows for the overflight of states parties by other states parties using unarmed observation aircraft.

The UN Convention on Certain Conventional Weapons (as amended 2001), which bans or restricts the use of specific types of weapons that are considered to cause unnecessary or unjustifiable suffering to combatants, or to affect civilians indiscriminately, was ratified by the UK in 1995. In 1968 the UK signed and ratified the Nuclear Non-Proliferation Treaty, which came into force in 1970 and was indefinitely and unconditionally extended in 1995. In 1996 the UK signed the Comprehensive Nuclear Test Ban Treaty and ratified it in 1998. The UK is a party to the 1972 Biological and Toxin Weapons Convention, which provides for a worldwide ban on biological weapons, and the 1993 Chemical Weapons Convention, which came into force in 1997 and provides for a verifiable worldwide ban on chemical weapons.

DEFENCE BUDGET

DEPARTMENTAL EXPENDITURE LIMITS

£ billion

	2019–20
Resource DEL	29.0
Capital DEL	9.8
Total	38.8

Source: HM Treasury – The Budget 2018 (Crown copyright)

MINISTRY OF DEFENCE

Main Building, Whitehall, London SW1A 2HB
T 020-7218 9000
W www.gov.uk/government/organisations/ministry-of-defence

For further information on the responsibilities and remit of the MoD see the Defence Chapter.

Secretary of State for Defence, Rt. Hon. Ben Wallace, MP
Parliamentary Private Secretary, James Cartlidge, MP
Special Adviser, Lynn Davidson
Minister of State, Rt. Hon. Mark Lancaster, TD, MP (Armed Forces)
Minister of State, Baroness Goldie (Lords)
Parliamentary Under-Secretary of State and Minister for Defence Procurement, Anne-Marie Trevelyan, MP
Parliamentary Under-Secretary of State and Minister for Defence People and Veterans, Johnny Mercer, MP

CHIEFS OF STAFF

Chief of the Defence Staff, Gen. Sir Nick Carter, GCB, CBE, DSO, ADC
Vice-Chief of the Defence Staff, Adm. Tim Fraser, CB
Chief of Naval Staff and First Sea Lord, Adm. Tony Radakin, CB, ADC
Second Sea Lord and Deputy Chief of Naval Staff, Vice-Adm. Nicholas Hine, CB

Chief of the General Staff, Gen. Sir Mark Carleton-Smith, KCB, CBE, ADC
Deputy Chief of the General Staff, Lt.-Gen. Christopher Tickell, CBE
Chief of the Air Staff, Air Chief Marshal Mike Wigston, CBE
Assistant Chief of the Air Staff, Air Vice-Marshal Ian Gale, MBE
Commander of Joint Forces Command, Gen. Patrick Sanders, CBE, DSO, ADC

SENIOR OFFICIALS

Permanent Secretary, Sir Stephen Lovegrove, KCB
Chief Scientific Adviser, Prof. Dame Angela McLean, DBE
Chief Scientific Adviser (Nuclear), Prof. Robin Grimes, FRS, FRENG
Director-General Finance, Cat Little

THE DEFENCE COUNCIL

The Defence Council is chaired by the Secretary of State, and comprises the other ministers, the Permanent Under-Secretary, the Chief of Defence Staff and senior service officers and officials who head the armed services and the department's major corporate functions. It provides the formal legal basis for the conduct of UK defence through a range of powers vested in it by statute and letters patent.

THE DEFENCE BOARD

The Defence Board is the main corporate board of the MoD, providing senior level leadership and strategic management of defence. The Defence Board is the highest committee in the MoD, responsible for the full range of defence business, other than the conduct of operations.

MANAGEMENT BOARD

Permanent Secretary, Sir Stephen Lovegrove, KCB
Members, Lt.-Gen. Doug Chalmers (Deputy Chief of Defence Staff (Military Strategy and Operations)); Charlie Forte (Chief Information Officer); David Goldstone (Chief Operating Officer); Prof. Robin Grimes, FRS, FRENG (Chief Scientific Adviser (Nuclear)); Air Marshal Richard Knighton (Deputy Chief of the Defence Staff (Financial and Military Capability)); Angus Lapsley (Strategy and International); Cat Little (Finance); Prof. Dame Angela McLean, DBE (Chief Scientific Adviser); Vanessa Nicholls (Nuclear); Lt.-Gen. Richard Nugee, CVO, CBE (Chief of Defence People); Dominic Wilson (Security Policy)
Non-Executive Members, Sir Gerry Grimstone (Lead); Simon Henry; Danuta Gray

CENTRAL STAFF

Vice-Chief of the Defence Staff, Adm. Tim Fraser, CB

JOINT FORCES COMMAND

Commander Joint Forces Command, Gen. Patrick Sanders, CBE, DSO, ADC
Chief of Joint Operations, Vice-Adm. Benjamin Key, CB
Chief of Staff, Air Vice-Marshal Johnny Stringer, CBE

FLEET COMMAND

First Sea Lord, Adm. Tony Radakin, CB, ADC
Fleet Commander and Chief Naval Warfare Officer, Vice-Adm. Jeremy Kyd, CBE

NAVAL HOME COMMAND

Second Sea Lord, Vice-Adm. Nicholas Hine, CB

LAND FORCES

Commander Field Army, Lt.-Gen. Ivan Jones, CB
Deputy Commander Field Army, Maj.-Gen. William O'Leary, QVRM, TD, VR/ Maj.-Gen. Celia Harvey, OBE, QVRM, TD, VR (from March 2020)

AIR COMMAND

Deputy Commander Operations and Air Member for Operations, Air Marshal Gerry Mayhew, CBE

Deputy Commander Capability and Air Member for Personnel and Capability, Air Marshal Andrew Turner, CB, CBE

DEFENCE EQUIPMENT AND SUPPORT

Chief Executive, Sir Simon Bollom
Chief of Materiel (Ships), Vice-Adm. Chris Gardner, CBE
Chief of Materiel (Land), Lt.-Gen. Paul Jacques, CBE
Chief of Materiel (Air), Air Marshal Julian Young, CB, OBE

EXECUTIVE AGENCIES

DEFENCE ELECTRONICS AND COMPONENTS AGENCY

Welsh Road, Deeside, Flintshire CH5 2LS T 01244-847694
E decainfo@deca.mod.uk
W www.gov.uk/deca

The Defence Electronics and Components Agency (DECA) provides maintenance, repair, overhaul, upgrade and procurement in avionics, electronics and components fields to support the MoD. As a 'trading' executive agency DECA is run along commercial lines with funding for DECA's activities being generated entirely by payments for delivery of services provided to the MoD and other private sector customers. DECA currently has an annual turnover of around £25m and employs over 400 staff across its head office and main operating centre in North Wales, a site in Stafford and various deployed locations across the UK.

Chief Executive, Geraint Spearing

DEFENCE SCIENCE AND TECHNOLOGY LABORATORY

Porton Down, Salisbury, Wiltshire SP4 0JQ T 01980-950000
E centralenquiries@dstl.gov.uk
W www.gov.uk/dstl

The Defence Science and Technology Laboratory (DSTL) supplies specialist science and technology services to the MoD and wider government.

Chief Executive, Gary Aitkenhead

UK HYDROGRAPHIC OFFICE

Admiralty Way, Taunton, Somerset TA1 2DN
T 01823-484444
E customerservices@ukho.gov.uk
W www.gov.uk/ukho

The UK Hydrographic Office (UKHO) collects and supplies hydrographic and geospatial data for the Royal Navy and merchant shipping, to protect lives at sea. Working with other national hydrographic offices, UKHO sets and raises global standards of hydrography, cartography and navigation.

Chief Executive, Rear-Adm. Tim Lowe, CBE

ARMED FORCES TRAINING AND RECRUITMENT

From Naval Bases at Plymouth, the Clyde in Scotland and a small team at Northwood in Middlesex, Flag Officer Sea Training (FOST) provides Operational Sea Training for all surface ships, submarines and Royal Fleet Auxiliaries of the Royal Navy. All aspects of naval training are offered by FOST including new entry, officer, Royal Marine, submarine, surface and aviation training. FOST also offers specialist training in a number of areas including hydrography, meteorology, oceanography, marine engineering and diving.

The Army Recruiting and Training Division (ARTD) is responsible for the four key areas of army training: soldier initial training, at the School of Infantry or at one of the army's four other facilities; officer initial training at the Royal Military Academy Sandhurst; trade training at one of the army's specialist facilities; and resettlement training for those about to leave the army. Trade training facilities include: the Armour Centre; the Infantry Battle School; the Infantry Training Centre, Catterick; the Royal School of Military Engineering and the Army Aviation Centre.

The Royal Air Force No. 22 (Training) Group is responsible for the recruitment, selection, initial and professional training of RAF personnel as well as providing trained specialist personnel to the armed forces as a whole, such as providing the army air corps with trained helicopter pilots. The group is split into five areas: RAF College Cranwell; the Air Cadet Organisation (ACO); the Directorate of Flying Training (DFT); the Directorate of Ground Training; and the Defence College of Technical Training.

The Defence College of Technical Training provides technical training to all three services and includes the Defence School of Communications Information Systems (DSCIS); the Defence School of Electronic and Mechanical Engineering (DSEME); and the Defence School of Marine Engineering (DSMarE).

USEFUL WEBSITES

W www.royalnavy.mod.uk
W www.army.mod.uk
W www.raf.mod.uk

THE ROYAL NAVY

In Order of Seniority as at November 2019

LORD HIGH ADMIRAL OF THE UNITED KINGDOM
HRH The Prince Philip, Duke of Edinburgh, KG, KT, OM, GBE, AK, QSO, PC, *apptd* 2011

ADMIRALS OF THE FLEET
HRH The Prince Philip, Duke of Edinburgh, KG, KT, OM, GBE, AC, QSO, PC, *apptd* 1953
Sir Benjamin Bathurst, GCB, *apptd* 1995
HRH The Prince of Wales, KG, KT, GCB, OM, AK, QSO, PC, ADC, *apptd* 2012
Lord Boyce, KG, GCB, OBE, *apptd* 2014

ADMIRALS
(Former Chiefs or Vice Chiefs of Defence Staff and First Sea Lords who remain on the active list)
Slater, Sir Jock, GCB, LVO, *apptd* 1991
Essenhigh, Sir Nigel, GCB, *apptd* 1998
West of Spithead, Lord, GCB, DSC, PC, *apptd* 2000
Band, Sir Jonathon, GCB, *apptd* 2002
Stanhope, Sir Mark, GCB, OBE, *apptd* 2004
Zambellas, Sir George, GCB, DSC, *apptd* 2012
Jones, Sir Philip, KCB, ADC, *apptd* 2016

ADMIRALS
HRH The Princess Royal, KG, KT, GCVO, QSO *(Cdre-in-Chief Portsmouth)*
Radakin, Antony, CB, ADC *(First Sea Lord and Chief of Naval Staff)*
Fraser, Tim, CB *(Vice-Chief of the Defence Staff)*

VICE-ADMIRALS
HRH The Duke of York, KG, GCVO, ADC *(Adm. of the Sea Cadet Corps and Cdre-in-Chief Fleet Air Arm)*
Lister, Sir Simon, KCB, OBE *(career intermission)*
Blount, Keith, CB, OBE *(Cdr Maritime Command)*
Kyd, Jeremy, CBE *(Fleet Cdr and Chief Naval Warfare Officer)*
Key, Benjamin, CBE *(Chief of Joint Operations)*
Hine, Nicholas, CB *(Second Sea Lord and Deputy Chief of Naval Staff)*
Bennett, Paul, CB, OBE *(Chief of Staff, Supreme Allied Cdr Transformation)*
Gardner, Chris, CBE *(Chief of Materiel (Ships))*

REAR-ADMIRALS
Lowe, Timothy, CBE *(National Hydrographer and Deputy Chief Executive (Hydrography))*
Kingwell, John, CBE *(Deputy Commandant Royal College of Defence Studies)*
Beckett, Keith, CBE *(Chief Strategic Systems Executive)*
Weale, John, CB, OBE *(Flag Officer Scotland & Northern Ireland, Assistant Chief of Naval Staff (Submarines) and Rear-Adm. Submarines (Head of Fighting Arm))*
Connell, Martin *(Assistant Chief of Naval Staff (Aviation, Amphibious Capability and Carriers))*
Higham, Jim, OBE *(Assistant Chief of Naval Staff (Ships))*
Chivers, Paul, CBE *(Director Military Aviation Authority)*
Hodgson, Timothy, MBE *(Director Submarine Capability)*
Thompson, Richard, CBE *(secondment)*
Methven, Paul *(Director Submarines Acquisition)*
Pentreath, Jonathan, CB, OBE *(Cdr Joint Helicopter Command)*
Halton, Paul, OBE *(Cdr Operations)*
Robinson, Guy, OBE *(Deputy Cdr Strike Force NATO)*
Briers, Matthew *(Director Carrier Strike)*

Morley, James *(Director Capability Joint Forces Command)*
Warrender, William, CBE *(Flag Officer Sea Training and Assistant Chief of Naval Staff (Training))*
Bath, Michael *(Naval Secretary, Assistant Chief of Naval Staff (Personnel) and Flag Officer Reserves)*
Toy, Malcolm *(Director (Technical) Military Aviation Authority)*
Burns, Andrew, OBE *(Cdr UK Maritime Forces)*
Kyte, Andrew *(Assistant Chief of the Defence Staff (Logistics Operations) and Chief Naval Logistics Officer)*
Beard, Hugh *(Assistant Chief of Naval Staff (Capability))*
Marshall, Paul, CBE *(Assistant Chief of Naval Staff (Ships Acquisition))*
Hally, Philip *(Assistant Chief of Naval Staff (People Transformation))*
Macleod, James *(Assistant Chief of the Defence Staff (Personnel Capability) and Defence Services Secretary)*

ROYAL MARINES

CAPTAIN-GENERAL
HRH the Duke of Sussex, KCVO

GENERAL
Messenger, Sir Gordon, KCB, DSO*, OBE, ADC

MAJOR-GENERALS
Bevis, Timothy, CBE *(Director Operations and Plans, International Military Staff)*
Magowan, Robert, CB, CBE *(Assistant Chief of the Defence Staff (Capability and Force Design))*
Holmes, Matthew, CBE, DSO *(Cdr UK Amphibious Forces and Commandant-General Royal Marines)*
Jenkins, Gwyn, OBE *(Assistant Chief of Naval Staff (Policy))*
Stickland, Charles, CB, OBE *(Assistant Chief of the Defence Staff (Commitments))*
Morris, Jim, DSO *(Director of Joint Warfare)*

The Royal Marines were formed in 1664 and are part of the Naval Service. Their primary purpose is to conduct amphibious and land warfare. The principal operational units are:
• Three Commando Brigade, an amphibious all-arms brigade trained to operate in arduous environments (a core element of the UK's Joint Rapid Reaction Force). The commando units, 40 Commando, 42 Commando and 45 Commando each have a strength of around 700 and are based in Taunton, Plymouth and Arbroath, respectively. 43 Commando Fleet Protection Group is around 550 strong and is based at HM Naval Base Clyde on the west coast of Scotland.
• 1 Assault Group, which has its headquarters located in Devonport, Plymouth is responsible for ten landing craft training squadron at Poole, Dorset and 11 amphibious trials and training squadron at Instow, Devon
The Royal Marines also provide detachments for warships and land-based naval parties as required.

ROYAL MARINES RESERVES (RMR)
The Royal Marines Reserve is a commando-trained volunteer force with the principal role, when mobilised, of supporting the Royal Marines. The RMR consists of approximately 600 trained ranks who are distributed between the four RMR centres in the UK. Approximately 10 per cent of the RMR are working with the regular corps on long-term attachments within all of the Royal Marines regular units.

OTHER PARTS OF THE NAVAL SERVICE

FLEET AIR ARM

The Fleet Air Arm (FAA) provides the Royal Navy with a multi-role aviation combat capability able to operate autonomously at short notice worldwide in all environments, over the sea and land. The FAA numbers some 6,200 people, which comprises 11.5 per cent of the total Royal Naval strength. It operates some 200 combat aircraft and more than 50 support/training aircraft.

ROYAL FLEET AUXILIARY (RFA)

The Royal Fleet Auxiliary is a 1,620-strong civilian-manned flotilla of 13 ships owned by the MoD. Its primary role is to supply the Royal Navy and host nations while at sea with fuel, ammunition, food and spares, enabling them to maintain operations away from their home ports. It also provides amphibious support and secure sea transport for military units and their equipment. The ships routinely support and embark Royal Naval Air Squadrons.

ROYAL NAVAL RESERVE (RNR)

The Royal Naval Reserve is an integral part of the Naval Service. It is a part-time force of around 3,000 trained men and women who are deployed with the Royal Navy in times of tension, humanitarian crisis or conflict.

The Royal Naval Reserve has 18 units throughout the UK; 17 of these provide initial training while one other specialist unit, HMS Ferret, Bedford provides intelligence training. Basic training is provided at HMS Raleigh, Torpoint in Cornwall for ratings and at the Britannia Royal Naval College, Dartmouth in Devon for officers.

Reservists serve part-time unless mobilised for an operational tour of duty and are expected to fulfil a commitment of 24 days a year, comprising 12 days continuous training and 12 days non-continuous training.

QUEEN ALEXANDRA'S ROYAL NAVAL NURSING SERVICE

The first nursing sisters were appointed to naval hospitals in 1884 and the Queen Alexandra's Royal Naval Nursing Service (QARNNS) gained its current title in 1902. Today QARNNS is a branch of the Royal Naval Medical Service that is committed to supporting the medical component of Royal Naval operational capability. QARNNS trains and employs nurses in a wide variety of specialities including emergency nursing, intensive care, burns and plastics, trauma and orthopaedics, surgical, medical and ophthalmology.

QARNNS is ready to deploy anywhere in the world to support global naval operations; recent deployments have included fighting the Ebola outbreak in Sierra Leone and helping to save lives in the Mediterranean.

Patron, HRH Princess Alexandra, the Hon. Lady Ogilvy, KG, GCVO
Head of the Naval Nursing Service, Capt. Alison Hofman

HM FLEET

as at September 2019

Submarines	
Vanguard Class	Vanguard, Vengeance, Victorious, Vigilant
Trafalgar Class	Talent, Trenchant, Triumph
Astute Class	Artful, Astute, Ambush, Audacious
Aircraft Carrier	Queen Elizabeth, Prince of Wales
Landing Platform Dock	Albion, Bulwark
Destroyers	
Type 45	Daring, Dauntless, Defender, Diamond, Dragon, Duncan
Frigates	
Type 23	Argyll, Iron Duke, Kent, Lancaster, Monmouth, Montrose, Northumberland, Portland, Richmond, St Albans, Somerset, Sutherland, Westminster
Mine Warfare Vessels	
Hunt Class	Atherstone, Brocklesby, Cattistock, Chiddingfold, Hurworth, Ledbury, Middleton, Quorn
Sandown Class	Bangor, Blyth, Grimsby, Pembroke, Penzance, Ramsey, Shoreham
Patrol Vessels	
Archer Class P2000 Training Boats	Archer, Biter, Blazer, Charger, Dasher, Example, Exploit, Explorer, Express, Puncher, Pursuer, Raider, Ranger, Smiter, Tracker, Trumpeter
Gibraltar Squadron 16m Fast Patrol Boats	Sabre, Scimitar
River Class	Clyde, Forth, Medway, Mersey, Tyne
Survey Vessels	
Ice Patrol Ship	Protector
Ocean Survey Vessel	Scott
Coastal Survey Vessel	Magpie
Multi-Role Survey Vessels	Echo, Enterprise

ROYAL FLEET AUXILIARY

Landing Ship Dock (Auxiliary)	RFA Cardigan Bay, RFA Mounts Bay, RFA Lyme Bay
Tide Class	RFS Tideforce, RFA Tiderace, RFA Tidespring, RFA Tidesurge
Wave Class	RFA Wave Knight, RFA Wave Ruler
Fort Class	RFA Fort Austin, RFA Fort Rosalie, RFA Fort Victoria
Casualty Receiving Ship/ Aviation Training Facilities	RFA Argus

THE ARMY

In Order of Seniority as at November 2019

THE QUEEN

FIELD MARSHALS
HRH The Prince Philip, Duke of Edinburgh, KG, KT, OM, GBE, AK, QSO, PC, *apptd* 1953
Lord Bramall, KG, GCB, OBE, MC, *apptd* 1982
Sir John Chapple, GCB, CBE, *apptd* 1992
HRH The Duke of Kent, KG, GCMG, GCVO, ADC, *apptd* 1993
Lord Inge, KG, GCB, PC, *apptd* 1994
HRH The Prince of Wales, KG, KT, GCB, OM, AK, QSO, PC, ADC, *apptd* 2012
Lord Guthrie of Craigiebank, GCB, GCVO, OBE, *apptd* 2012
Lord Walker of Aldringham, GCB, CMG, CBE, *apptd* 2014

FORMER CHIEFS OF STAFF
Gen. Sir Roger Wheeler, GCB, CBE, *apptd* 1997
Gen. Sir Mike Jackson, GCB, CBE, DSO, *apptd* 2003
Gen. Sir Timothy Granville-Chapman, GBE, KCB, *apptd* 2005
Gen. Lord Dannatt, GCB, CBE, MC, *apptd* 2006
Gen. Lord Richards of Herstmonceux, GCB, CBE, DSO, *apptd* 2009
Gen. Lord Houghton of Richmond, GCB, CBE, *apptd* 2009
Gen. Sir Peter Wall, GCB, CBE, *apptd* 2010
Gen. Sir Richard Barrons, KCB, CBE, *apptd* 2013
Gen. Sir Christopher Deverell, KCB, MBE, *apptd* 2016

GENERALS
Carter, Sir Nicholas, KCB, CBE, DSO, ADC *(Chief of the Defence Staff)*
Everard, Sir James, KCB, CBE *(Deputy Supreme Allied Cdr Europe)*
Carleton-Smith, Sir Mark, KCB, CBE, ADC *(Chief of the General Staff)*
Sanders, P., CBE, DSO, ADC *(Cdr Joint Forces Command)*

LIEUTENANT-GENERALS
Lorimer, Sir John, KCB, DSO, MBE *(Defence Senior Adviser to the Middle East)*
Radford, T., CB, DSO, OBE *(Deputy Supreme Allied Cdr Europe designate (from April 2020))*
Pope, Sir Nicholas, KCB, CBE *(pending retirement)*
Jaques, P., CB, CBE *(pending retirement)*
Nugee, R., CVO, CBE *(Chief of Defence People)*
Norton, Sir George, KCVO, CBE *(UK National Military Representative to NATO and the EU)*
Cripwell, R., CB, CBE *(Deputy Cdr NATO Land Command Izmir)*
Urch T., CBE *(Cdr Home Command)*
Chalmers, D., DSO, OBE *(Deputy Chief of the Defence Staff (Military Strategy and Operations))*
Hooper, I., CB *(pending retirement)*
Hockenhull, J., OBE *(Chief of Defence Intelligence)*
Skeates, S., CBE *(Deputy Cdr Joint Force Command Brunssum)*
Jones, I., CB *(Cdr Field Army)*
Smyth-Osbourne, Sir Edward, KCVO, CBE *(Cdr Allied Rapid Reaction Corps)*
Tickell, C., OBE *(Deputy Chief of the General Staff)*
Hill, G., CBE *(Deputy Cdr Resolute Support)*

MAJOR-GENERALS
Munro, R., CBE, TD, VR *(Army Reserve Reinforcement Group)*
Bathurst, B., CBE *(pending appointment)*
Fay, A., CB *(Director Defence Support Transformation)*
Bruce, R., CBE, DSO *(pending appointment)*
Gaunt, M., CB *(pending appointment)*
Stanford, R., MBE *(Senior British Loan Service Officer – Oman)*
Bramble, W., CBE *(Deputy Cdr NATO Rapid Deployable Corps – Italy)*
Cave, I., *(Chief of Staff, Field Army)*
Nanson, P., CBE *(GOC Army Recruiting and Initial Training)*
Wardlaw, R., OBE *(Director Army Basing and Infrastructure)*
Brooks-Ward, S., CVO, OBE, TD, VR *(Assistant Chief of the Defence Staff (Reserves and Cadets))*
Swift, J., OBE *(GOC 3rd (UK) Division)*
Mitchell, G., MBE *(Director Development, Concepts and Doctrine Centre)*
Cavanagh, N., CB *(Director Strategy and Planning, Defence Infrastructure Organisation)*
Jones, R., CBE *(Standing Joint Force Cdr, Standing Joint Force HQ)*
Hyams, T., OBE *(Military Secretary and General Officer Scotland)*
Borton, N., DSO, MBE *(Chief of Staff (Operations), Permanent Joint HQ)*
Illingworth, J., OBE *(Director Land Warfare)*
Gedney, F., OBE *(pending assignment)*
Wooddisse, R., CBE, MC *(Assistant Chief of the General Staff)*
Capps, D., CBE *(GOC Regional Command)*
Herbert, C., OBE *(pending retirement)*
Ford, K., CBE *(Deputy Chief of Staff Plans, Joint Forces Command Brunssum; Director Policy and Capabilities Division, International Military Staff, HQ NATO (Brussels) designate (from March 2020))*
McClean, C., CBE *(Director Land Equipment, Defence Equipment and Support)*
Copinger-Symes, T., CBE *(pending assignment)*
O'Leary, W., QVRM, TD, VR *(Deputy Cdr Field Army)*
Walker, C., DSO *(MoD)*
Cole, J., OBE *(Director Information)*
Deakin, G., CBE *(Deputy Chief of Staff Plans, Joint Force Command Naples)*
Cain, P., QHP *(Director Defence Healthcare)*
Ghika, C., CBE *(GOC London District and Maj.-Gen. The Household Division)*
Potter, S., QVRM, TD, VR *(Director Reserves)*
Sexton, N. *(Director Engagement and Communications)*
Weir, C., DSO, MBE *(GOC 1st (UK) Division)*
Bennett, J., CBE *(Chief of Staff, HQ Allied Rapid Reaction Corps)*
Langston, C., QHC, CF *(Chaplain-General)*
Nesmith, S. *(Director Personnel)*
Hamilton, S., CBE *(Director Support)*
Humphrey, S., OBE *(Senior British Military Adviser, USA Central Command)*
Roe, A. *(Chief Executive Defence Academy and Commandant Joint Service Command and Staff College)*
Strickland, G., DSO, MBE *(Deputy to the Commanding General – Support HQ III (USA) Corps and Fort Hood)*
Harrison, A., DSO, MBE *(Deputy Adviser Ministry of Interior Kabul, Resolute Support)*
McMahon, S., CBE *(Assistant Chief of the Defence Staff (Defence Engagement))*
Bruce of Crionaich, A., OBE, VR *(Governor of Edinburgh Castle)*
Taylor A. *(Director Army Legal Services)*

Bowder, J., OBE *(GOC 6th Division)*
Thomson, R., CBE. DSO *(Cdr British Forces Cyprus and Adminstrator of the Sovereign Base Areas)*
Eastman, D., MBE *(GOC Regional Command designate (from February 2020))*
Harvey, C. OBE, QVRM, TD, VR *(Deputy Cdr Field Army designate (from March 2020))*
Amison, D., CBE *(Director Development, Concepts and Doctrine Centre designate (from April 2020))*
Ridge, J., CBE *(GOC Army Recruiting and Initial Training Command designate (from April 2020))*

CONSTITUTION OF THE ARMY

The army consists of the Regular Army, the Regular Reserve and the Army Reserve. It is commanded by the Chief of the General Staff, who is the professional Head of Service and Chair of the Executive Committee of the Army Board, which provides overall strategic policy and direction to the Commander Land Forces (formerly Commander-in-Chief, Land Forces). There are four subordinate commands that report to the Commander Land Forces: the Field Army; Support Command, headed by the Adjutant General; Force Development and Capability Command and the Joint Helicopter Command. The army is divided into functional arms and services, subdivided into regiments and corps (listed below in order of precedence).

During 2008, as part of the Future Army Structure (FAS) reform programme, the infantry was re-structured into large multi-battalion regiments, which involved amalgamations and changes in title for some regiments. The main changes at divisional, brigade and unit level occurred largely between mid-2014 and mid-2015. As at April 2018 there were 31 Regular Army battalions in the infantry and 15 Army Reserves battalions. The 2010 Strategic Defence and Security Review laid out the commitments expected of the UK Armed Forces, and, as a result, Army 2020 was created to replace FAS.

All enquiries with regard to records of serving personnel (Regular and Reserve) should be directed to: The Army Personnel Centre Help Desk, Kentigern House, 65 Brown Street, Glasgow G2 8EX T 0345-600 9663. Enquirers should note that the Army is governed in the release of personal information by various acts of parliament.

ORDER OF PRECEDENCE OF CORPS AND REGIMENTS OF THE BRITISH ARMY

ARMS

HOUSEHOLD CAVALRY
The Life Guards
The Blues and Royals (Royal Horse Guards and 1st Dragoons)

ROYAL HORSE ARTILLERY
(when on parade, the Royal Horse Artillery take precedence over the Household Cavalry)

ROYAL ARMOURED CORPS
1st the Queen's Dragoon Guards
The Royal Scots Dragoon Guards (Carabiniers and Greys)
The Royal Dragoon Guards
The Queen's Royal Hussars (The Queen's Own and Royal Irish)
The Royal Lancers
The King's Royal Hussars
The Light Dragoons
Royal Tank Regiment

ROYAL REGIMENT OF ARTILLERY
(with the exception of the Royal Horse Artillery (*see* above))

CORPS OF ROYAL ENGINEERS

ROYAL CORPS OF SIGNALS

REGIMENTS OF FOOT GUARDS
Grenadier Guards
Coldstream Guards
Scots Guards
Irish Guards
Welsh Guards

REGIMENTS OF INFANTRY
The Royal Regiment of Scotland
The Princess of Wales's Royal Regiment (Queen and Royal Hampshire's)
The Duke of Lancaster's Regiment (King's, Lancashire and Border)
The Royal Regiment of Fusiliers
The Royal Anglian Regiment
The Rifles
The Yorkshire Regiment
The Mercian Regiment
The Royal Welsh
The Royal Irish Regiment
The Parachute Regiment
The Royal Gurkha Rifles

SPECIAL AIR SERVICE

ARMY AIR CORPS

SERVICES

ROYAL ARMY CHAPLAINS' DEPARTMENT

THE ROYAL LOGISTIC CORPS

ROYAL ARMY MEDICAL CORPS

CORPS OF ROYAL ELECTRICAL AND MECHANICAL ENGINEERS

ADJUTANT-GENERAL'S CORPS

ROYAL ARMY VETERINARY CORPS

SMALL ARMS SCHOOL CORPS

ROYAL ARMY DENTAL CORPS

INTELLIGENCE CORPS

ROYAL ARMY PHYSICAL TRAINING CORPS

QUEEN ALEXANDRA'S ROYAL ARMY NURSING CORPS

CORPS OF ARMY MUSIC

THE ROYAL MONMOUTHSHIRE ROYAL ENGINEERS (MILITIA) (THE ARMY RESERVE)

THE HONOURABLE ARTILLERY COMPANY (THE ARMY RESERVE)

REST OF THE ARMY RESERVE

EQUIPMENT

VEHICLES

Combat Vehicles	Bulldog, Challenger 2, Stormer, Warrior
Reconnaissance Vehicles	Coyote, Jackal 2, Scimitar, Spartan
Protected Patrol Vehicles	Foxhound, Husky, Mastiff, Panther, Ridgback, Wolfhound

THE ARMY RESERVE

The Army Reserve (formerly the Territorial Army (TA)) is part of the UK's reserve land forces and provides support to the regular army at home and overseas. The Army Reserve is divided into three types of unit: national, regional, and sponsored. Army Reserve soldiers serving in regional units complete a minimum of 27 days training a year, comprising some evenings, weekends and an annual two-week camp. National units normally specialise in a specific role or trade, such as logistics, IT, communications or medical services. Members of national units have a lower level of training commitment and complete 19 days training a year. Sponsored reserves are individuals who will serve, as members of the workforce of a company contracted to the MoD, in a military capacity and have agreed to accept a reserve liability to be called up for active service in a crisis. In 2012 the Secretary of State for Defence issued a consultation paper *Future Reserves 2020: Delivering the Nation's Security Together*, which outlined plans to invest an additional £1.8bn in the Reserve Forces over a ten-year period, for the Reserve Forces to be more integrated with the regular forces and to have a more significant role within the armed forces as a whole.

QUEEN ALEXANDRA'S ROYAL ARMY NURSING CORPS

The Queen Alexandra's Royal Army Nursing Corps (QARANC) was founded in 1902 as Queen Alexandra's Imperial Military Nursing Service and gained its present title in 1949. The QARANC has trained nurses for the register since 1950 and also trains and employs healthcare assistants. Nursing officers, Nursing soldiers, healthcare assistants and student nurses of the QARANC deliver a high quality, adaptable and dedicated nursing care wherever the Army needs it and can find themselves working in a variety of settings. These can vary from NHS hospitals with military units, to ground based environments such as medical regiments and field hospitals. QARANC personnel deal with a wide range of medical situations, with civilian and military patients in the UK, to military casualties of war and conflict. Work locations vary between clinical roles and instructional positions at training bases. Currently, Army nurses are based and deployed in the UK, Germany, Cyprus, Canada, Poland, Brunei, Nepal, Kenya and Sierra Leone.

Colonel-in-Chief, HRH The Countess of Wessex, GCVO
Colonels Commandant, Col. Jane Davis, OBE, QVRM, TD; Col. Carol Kefford

THE ROYAL AIR FORCE

In Order of Seniority as at November 2019

THE QUEEN

MARSHALS OF THE ROYAL AIR FORCE
HRH The Prince Philip, Duke of Edinburgh, KG, KT, OM,
GBE, AK, QSO, PC, *apptd* 1953
HRH The Prince of Wales, KG, KT, GCB, OM, AK, QSO,
PC, ADC, *apptd* 2012

FORMER CHIEFS OF THE AIR STAFF

MARSHALS OF THE ROYAL AIR FORCE
Lord Craig of Radley, GCB, OBE, *apptd* 1988
Lord Stirrup, KG, GCB, AFC, *apptd* 2014

AIR CHIEF MARSHALS
Sir Michael Graydon, GCB, CBE, *apptd* 1991
Sir Richard Johns, GCB, KCVO, *apptd* 1994
Sir Glenn Torpy, GCB, CBE, DSO, *apptd* 2006
Sir Stephen Dalton, GCB, *apptd* 2009
Sir Andrew Pulford, GCB, CBE, *apptd* 2013

AIR RANK LIST

AIR CHIEF MARSHALS
Peach, Sir Stuart, GBE, KCB *(Chair of the Military Committee, NATO)*
Hillier, Sir Stephen, KCB, CBE, DFC, ADC *(pending retirement)*
Wigston, M., CBE, ADC *(Chief of the Air Staff)*

AIR MARSHALS
Young, J., CB, OBE *(Chief of Materiel (Air) and Air Member for Materiel)*
Evans, S., CB, CBE *(pending retirement)*
Stringer, E., CB, CBE *(Director-General Joint Force Development and Director Defence Academy)*
Knighton, R., CB *(Deputy Chief of the Defence Staff, Military Capability)*
Gray, S., CB, OBE *(Director-General Defence Safety Authority)*
Turner, A., CB, CBE *(Deputy Cdr Capability and Air Member for Personnel and Capability)*
Mayhew, G., CBE *(Deputy Cdr Operations and AIr Member for Operations)*

AIR VICE-MARSHALS
Waterfall, G., CBE *(Chief of Staff (Operations), Permanent Joint HQ)*
Parker, G., CB, OBE *(Head of British Forces (USA) and Defence Attaché, Washington)*
Hedley, B., MBE *(pending appointment)*
Tunnicliffe, G., CVO *(Deputy Commandant Royal College of Defence Studies)*
Bethell, K., CBE *(Director Combat Air, Defence Equipment and Support)*
Elliot, C., CBE *(Chief of Staff Personnel and Air Secretary)*
Russell, G., CB *(Director Helicopters, Defence Equipment and Support)*

Shell, S., OBE *(Director Military Aviation Authority)*
Rochelle, S., OBE, DFC *(Chief of Staff Capability, Air Command)*
James, W., CBE *(Air Officer Commanding No. 22 (Training) Group and Chief of Staff Training)*
Cooper, D., CBE *(pending appointment)*
Hart, M., CBE *(Head of Joint Terrorism Analysis Centre)*
Sampson, M., CBE, DSO *(Director Saudi Armed Forces Project)*
Vallely, I., OBE *(Cdr Cyber, Intelligence, Surveillance and Reconnaissance, Joint Forces Command)*
Moore, C. *(Director Service Operations, Information Services and Solutions)*
Stringer, J., CBE *(Chief of Staff, Joint Forces Command)*
Reid, A. *(Defence Medical Director, Joint Forces Command)*
Smyth, H., OBE, DFC *(Air Officer Commanding No. 1 Group)*
Ellis, J., *(Chaplain-in-Chief and Director-General Chaplaincy Service (RAF))*
Jennings, T., OBE *(Director Legal Services (RAF))*
Duguid, I., OBE *(Air Officer Commanding No. 11 Group)*
Ellard, S. *(Air Officer Commanding No. 38 Group)*
Gale, I., MBE *(Assistant Chief of the Air Staff)*
Gillespie, A., CBE *(Air Officer Commanding No. 2 Group)*

CONSTITUTION OF THE RAF

The RAF consists of a single command, Air Command, based at RAF High Wycombe. RAF Air Command was formed on 1 April 2007 from the amalgamation of Strike Command and Personnel and Training Command.

Air Command consists of three groups, each organised around specific operational duties. No. 1 Group is the coordinating organisation for the tactical fast-jet forces responsible for attack, offensive support and air defence operations. No. 2 Group provides air combat support including air transport and air-to-air refuelling; intelligence surveillance; targeting and reconnaissance; and force protection. No. 22 (Training) Group recruits personnel and provides trained specialist personnel to the RAF, as well as to the Royal Navy and the Army (*see also* Armed Forces Training and Recruitment).

RAF EQUIPMENT

AIRCRAFT

Combat	Lightening II, Typhoon FGR4
Training	Embraer Phenom 100, Hawk T1, Hawk T2, 120TP Prefect, Texan T, Tucano T1, Tutor T1, Viking T1
Surveillance	P-8A Poseidon, MQ-9 Reaper, RC-135W Rivet Joint, Sentinel R1, E-3D Sentry AEW1, Shadow R1
Transport	Atlas, BAe146, C17 Globemaster III, C-130J Hercules, C17

HELICOPTERS

Helicopters	Chinook, Griffin HAR2, Puma HC2
Training	Airbus H135 Juno, Airbus H145 Jupiter
Transport	Leonardo GrandNew

ROYAL AUXILIARY AIR FORCE

The Auxiliary Air Force was formed in 1924 to train an elite corps of civilians to serve their country in flying squadrons in their spare time. In 1947 the force was awarded the prefix 'royal' in recognition of its distinguished war service and the Sovereign's Colour for the RAuxAF was presented in 1989. The RAuxAF continues to recruit civilians who undertake military training in their spare time, with a standard minimum commitment of 27 days a year. With the amendments to the reserve service made under the Defence Reform Act 2014, reservists can now be employed to support the RAF across the full spectrum of military tasks. There are currently 27 squadrons with the RAuxAF, with a total establishment of just under 3,200 posts, with reservist posts being available in the majority of trades.

Air Commodore-in-Chief, HM The Queen
Commandant General, Air Vice-Marshal Lord Beaverbrook, ADC
Inspector, Gp Capt. Gavin Hellard, ADC

PRINCESS MARY'S ROYAL AIR FORCE NURSING SERVICE

The Princess Mary's Royal Air Force Nursing Service (PMRAFNS) was formed on 1 June 1918 as the Royal Air Force Nursing Service. In June 1923, His Majesty King George V gave his royal assent for the Royal Air Force Nursing Service to be known as the Princess Mary's Royal Air Force Nursing Service. The Princess Mary's Royal Air Force Nursing Service (PMRAFNS) is committed to providing a skilled, knowledgeable and able nursing workforce to deliver high quality care, whilst being responsive to the dynamic nature of RAF Nursing in peacetime and on operations.

Patron and Air Chief Commandant, HRH Princess Alexandra, The Hon. Lady Ogilvy, KG, GCVO
Matron-in-Chief, Gp Capt. Fionnuala Bradley

SERVICE SALARIES

Pay 16 was introduced on 1 April 2016, replacing the previous Pay 2000 scheme for all regular and reserve personnel on the main pay spines up to and including the rank of Commodore/ Brigadier/ Air Commodore (*see* following page for table of relative rank). Compared with Pay 2000 the total number of increments has been reduced and personnel, with the exception of Lieutenants, remain on the same salary for the first two years in rank.

The following rates of pay apply from 1 April 2019 and are rounded to the nearest pound.

The pay rates shown are for army personnel. The rates also apply to personnel of equivalent rank and pay band in the other services.

Rank	Annual Salary
Second Lieutenant	£27,273

LIEUTENANT	
On appointment	£32,781
After 1 year in rank	£33,932
After 2 years in rank	£35,082
After 3 years in rank	£36,234

CAPTAIN	
On appointment	£42,009
After 2 years in rank	£43,334
After 3 years in rank	£44,659
After 4 years in rank	£45,984
After 5 years in rank	£47,309
After 6 years in rank	£48,634
After 7 years in rank	£49,958

MAJOR	
On appointment	£52,917
After 2 years in rank	£54,660
After 3 years in rank	£56,403
After 4 years in rank	£58,146
After 5 years in rank	£59,889
After 6 years in rank	£61,632
After 7 years in rank	£63,375

LIEUTENANT-COLONEL	
On appointment	£74,268
After 2 years in rank	£76,229
After 3 years in rank	£78,178
After 4 years in rank	£80,133
After 5 years in rank	£82,087
After 6 years in rank	£84,042
After 7 years in rank	£85,997

COLONEL	
On appointment	£89,977
After 2 years in rank	£91,466
After 3 years in rank	£92,955
After 4 years in rank	£94,443
After 5 years in rank	£95,932
After 6 years in rank	£97,421
After 7 years in rank	£98,910

BRIGADIER	
On appointment	£107,224
After 2 years in rank	£108,309
After 3 years in rank	£109,393
After 4 years in rank	£110,478
After 5 years in rank	£111,563

PAY SYSTEM FOR SENIOR MILITARY OFFICERS

Pay rates effective as at 1 April 2019 for all military officers of 2* rank and above (excluding medical and dental officers). All pay rates are rounded to the nearest pound.

Rank	Annual Salary
MAJOR-GENERAL (2*)	
Scale 1	£118,658
Scale 2	£120,977
Scale 3	£123,342
Scale 4	£125,755
Scale 5	£128,215
Scale 6	£130,724
LIEUTENANT-GENERAL (3*)	
Scale 1	£138,058
Scale 2	£144,825
Scale 3	£151,930
Scale 4	£157,898
Scale 5	£162,553
Scale 6	£167,349
GENERAL (4*)	
Scale 1	£181,088
Scale 2	£185,615
Scale 3	£190,256
Scale 4	£195,012
Scale 5	£198,912
Scale 6	£202,890

Field Marshal – appointments to this rank will not usually be made in peacetime. The salary for holders of the rank is equivalent to the salary of a 5-star General, a salary created only in times of war. In peacetime, the equivalent rank to Field Marshal is the Chief of the Defence Staff. As at 1 April 2019, the annual salary range for the Chief of the Defence Staff is £260,891–£276,860.

OFFICERS COMMISSIONED FROM THE SENIOR RANKS

Rank	Annual salary
Level 15	£56,151
Level 14	£55,784
Level 13	£55,398
Level 12	£54,650
Level 11	£53,906
Level 10	£53,153
Level 9	£52,404
Level 8	£51,655
Level 7*	£50,721
Level 6	£50,144
Level 5	£49,559
Level 4†	£48,402
Level 3	£47,826
Level 2	£47,236
Level 1‡	£46,084

* Officers commissioned from the ranks with more than 15 years' service enter on level 7

† Officers commissioned from the ranks with between 12 and 15 years' service enter on level 4

‡ Officers commissioned from the ranks with less than 12 years' service enter on level 1

SOLDIERS' SALARIES

Pay16 was introduced on 1 April 2016, replacing the previous Pay 2000 scheme for all regular and reserve personnel on the main pay spines up to and including the rank of Commodore/ Brigadier/ Air Commodore (*see* below for table of relative rank). Rank remains the key determinant of pay, but the 'high' and 'low' bands under the Pay 2000 scheme were removed and replaced with 4 supplements *(Supp.)* under which trades are allocated. All ranks in a particular trade are treated the same for pay supplement purposes. Compared with Pay 2000 the total number of increments has been reduced and personnel remain on increment Level 1 for the first two years in rank, with the exception of Privates who remain on increment Level 2 for two years.

Rates of pay effective from 1 April 2019 (rounded to the nearest pound) are:

Rank	Supp. 1	Supp. 2	Supp. 3	Supp 4
PRIVATE				
Level 1	20,000	–	–	–
Level 2	20,814	–	–	–
Level 3	22,197	22,459	22,731	22,731
Level 4	23,358	23,619	23,971	24,299
Level 5	24,491	25,843	25,284	25,612
Level 6	25,625	26,133	26,669	27,009
LANCE CORPORAL				
(levels 7 to 9 also applicable to Privates)				
Level 7	26,791	27,413	27,948	28,435
Level 8	28,032	28,767	29,329	29,848
Level 9	29,335	30,145	30,781	31,382

CORPORAL				
Level 1	31,245	32,154	33,038	33,858
Level 2	32,080	33,008	33,918	34,737
Level 3	32,555	33,664	34,681	35,552
Level 4	33,000	34,125	35,412	36,404
Level 5	33,469	34,594	36,054	37,132
SERGEANT				
Level 1	35,151	36,335	37,870	39,114
Level 2	36,026	37,297	38,838	40,244
Level 3	36,933	38,305	39,792	41,306
Level 4	37,852	39,412	40,785	42,379
Level 5	38,780	40,413	41,829	43,495
STAFF SERGEANT				
Level 1	39,567	41,232	42,727	44,451
Level 2	40,190	41,950	43,491	45,174
Level 3	40,836	42,597	44,257	45,938
Level 4	41,459	43,220	45,042	46,725
Level 5	42,111	43,871	45,947	47,458
WARRANT OFFICER CLASS II				
(also applicable to Staff Sergeants)				
Level 1	43,035	45,030	47,246	48,787
Level 2	43,957	45,951	47,922	49,303
Level 3	44,828	46,588	48,265	49,671
Level 4	45,588	47,221	48,574	49,980
Level 5	46,366	47,836	48,864	50,270
WARRANT OFFICER CLASS I				
Level 1	49,842	–	–	51,288
Level 2	50,130	–	–	51,727
Level 3	50,703	–	–	52,223
Level 4	51,276	–	–	52,725
Level 5	51,801	–	–	53,198

RELATIVE RANK – ARMED FORCES

Royal Navy	*Army*	*Royal Air Force*
1 Admiral of the Fleet	1 Field Marshal	1 Marshal of the RAF
2 Admiral (Adm.)	2 General (Gen.)	2 Air Chief Marshal
3 Vice-Admiral (Vice-Adm.)	3 Lieutenant-General (Lt.-Gen.)	3 Air Marshal
4 Rear-Admiral (Rear-Adm.)	4 Major-General (Maj.-Gen.)	4 Air Vice-Marshal
5 Commodore (Cdre)	5 Brigadier (Brig.)	5 Air Commodore (Air Cdre)
6 Captain (Capt.)	6 Colonel (Col.)	6 Group Captain (Gp Capt.)
7 Commander (Cdr)	7 Lieutenant-Colonel (Lt.-Col.)	7 Wing Commander (Wg Cdr)
8 Lieutenant-Commander (Lt.-Cdr)	8 Major (Maj.)	8 Squadron Leader (Sqn Ldr)
9 Lieutenant (Lt.)	9 Captain (Capt.)	9 Flight Lieutenant (Flt Lt)
10 Sub-Lieutenant (Sub-Lt.)	10 Lieutenant (Lt.)	10 Flying Officer (FO)
11 Midshipman	11 Second Lieutenant (2nd Lt.)	11 Pilot Officer (PO)

EDUCATION

THE UK EDUCATION SYSTEM

The structure of the education system in the UK is a devolved matter with each of the countries of the UK having separate systems under separate governments. The school systems differ as regards curriculum, examinations and final qualifications; at university level, there are differences in the nature of some degrees and in tuition fees. The systems in England, Wales and Northern Ireland have more in common with each other than with the Scottish system.

Education in England is overseen by the Department for Education (DfE), with university research covered by the Department for Business, Energy and Industrial Strategy (DfBEIS).

Responsibility for education in Wales lies with the Department for Education and Skills (DfES) within the Welsh government. Ministers in the Scottish government are responsible for education in Scotland, led by the directorates of Learning and Lifelong Learning, while in Northern Ireland responsibility lies with the Department of Education (DfE) and the Department for the Economy (DE) within the Northern Ireland government.

DEPARTMENT FOR EDUCATION T 0370-000 2288
  W www.gov.uk/government/organisations/
  department-for-education
DEPARTMENT FOR EDUCATION AND SKILLS (DFES)
  T 0300-060 4400 W www.gov.wales/topics/educationandskills
SCOTTISH GOVERNMENT – EDUCATION
  T 0300-244 4000 W www.gov.scot/education
DEPARTMENT OF EDUCATION (NI) T 028-9127 9279
  W www.education-ni.gov.uk
DEPARTMENT FOR THE ECONOMY T 028-9052 9900
  W www.economy-ni.gov.uk

RECENT DEVELOPMENTS

England saw a change of ministerial responsibility for education and gave more detail on T-levels, while Wales began consulting on changes to curriculum, qualifications, assessment and inspection as part of its wide-ranging future education reforms. Scotland boosted early years support and outlined plans to help teaching careers. All countries set out new student finance packages ahead of the UK leaving the EU.

ENGLAND
- The government issued final guidance ahead of the September 2020 introduction of compulsory relationships education for primary-age pupils, relationships and sex education for secondary-age pupils, and health education for all pupils in state-funded schools
- A £6.5m Early Outcomes Fund was announced, to help local authorities improve early language outcomes. A further £24m will go to maintained nursery schools in 2019–20
- A new online test to check how well 8- and 9-year-olds know their multiplication tables has been trialled. All primary pupils will take the test from summer 2020, but results will not be published at school level or used to compare schools' performance
- Nearly 10,000 primary schools (more than half) signed up to trial a new 20-minute Reception Baseline Assessment (RBA) in 2019, for national roll-out in 2020. By providing a snapshot of pupils' development when they start school, the RBA will set the baseline for assessing their progress throughout primary schooling

- New T-level qualifications launched from September 2020: the government published more details of the further education providers who will deliver them from 2021, and provided an extra £3.75 million for 2019–20 to cover roll-out costs. These technical alternatives to A-levels for 16- to 19-year-olds combine classroom theory, practical learning and an industry placement (of at least 315 hours)
- To help children with special educational needs £250m was allocated to local authorities to fund 37 new special free schools and two alternative provision schools. New mental health support teams will be based in or near schools and colleges in 25 areas from 2019
- To improve music education, an expert panel will devise a model music curriculum to help schools deliver world-class teaching
- £4.8m was pledged to a centre for excellence at the University of York, to boost modern foreign language (MFL) skills and coordinate the work of nine MFL hub schools
- Improved support and guidance for primary schools to ensure all children can swim confidently by the end of primary school
- Ofsted issued a new inspection handbook from September 2019. Future inspections will focus more on what children actually learn, as opposed to test results and will give do more to support underperforming schools
- The Timpson review of exclusions proposed 30 recommendations, including making schools accountable for the pupils they exclude
- Following an independent review of the Teachers' Pension Scheme recommending increased employer contributions, the government gave £940m to state-funded schools and colleges to cover their increased costs in 2019–20
- Some 80 new expert teachers are to be recruited from industry into further education through the £5m Taking Teaching Further programme; new teachers will have guidance and support from the Early Career Framework expert panel and a reduced timetable; and £10.7m over the next two years will go to programmes to recruit experienced professionals into teaching
- New Essential Digital Skills and Digital Functional Skills Qualifications will be launched free to anyone over the age of 19 from 2020
- An £18.5m investment will drive up artificial intelligence (AI) skills in the technology sector, supporting adults to retrain in data science and AI. The Adult Learning Technology Innovation Fund will encourage tech companies to develop ways of improving the quality of online learning for adults
- The government told universities to halt 'unethical' admissions practices (such as 'conditional unconditional offers' by which a student is guaranteed a place regardless of A-level results but only if they make that institution their first choice) and grade inflation (unexplained increases in first-class and 2:1 degrees awarded). The Office for Students (OfS) is reviewing universities' recruitment and degree-awarding practices and will be challenging them where dubious
- The government's International Education Strategy, published in March 2019, plans to boost international student numbers to 600,000 and generate £35bn income through international education exports by 2030
- Parliament approved legislation to support the expansion of two-year and other accelerated degrees, giving students starting university from September 2019 more choice

- The government's Higher Education Principles of March 2019 ask universities – especially the most selective and best-resourced – to do more for young people leaving care by providing them with personal support and money for course materials and a full student experience
- The government-commissioned Augur review recommended in May 2019 that England's maximum university tuition fees should be cut from £9,250 to £7,500, repayments should be extended from 30 to 40 years and maintenance grants should be reinstated. EU students starting courses in England in 2019–20 should continue to be charged the same tuition fees as UK students and should access existing financial support for the duration of their course
- Several recent developments affect university research. The Teaching Excellence Framework's ratings process has been reviewed. The first Future Leaders Fellowships have been awarded, a total of £40m, to 41 early-career researchers
- Universities won £279m of government funding for 28 new international research projects to tackle global issues such as ocean pollution and infectious diseases; the UK and Japanese governments launched a £30m research partnership to tackle degenerative and incurable diseases

WALES

- Wellbeing will form part of the new syllabus from September 2019. New guidance on keeping pupils healthy and happy is due at the end of 2019. The Universities Council for the Education of Teachers Cymru is developing materials for use from September 2020
- A new code for students with Additional Learning Needs is due late in 2019, and a new system will be implemented over three years from September 2020
- The Welsh government announced £36m to reduce infant class sizes and measures to manage workload and reduce bureaucracy
- The second phase of the flagship school investment programme, 21st Century Schools and Colleges, sees a further investment of £2.3bn to transform schools and colleges into hubs for wider learning and local activities
- New regulations on Welsh language in schools opened to consultation in May 2019. The government will agree targets aimed at achieving a million Welsh speakers by 2050. Some £51m for 41 projects was announced to support Welsh-medium education in 2019
- A refined Curriculum for Wales will be available in January 2020 for use in September 2022 in primary schools and Year 7. The new curriculum will then be rolled out yearly in secondary schools until it includes Year 11 by 2026
- Revised evaluation, improvement, accountability and inspection arrangements are under consultation. The arrangements should be fair, coherent, proportionate and transparent. Inspections will be suspended in 2020–21 to allow Estyn to help schools make the curriculum changes. Consultation on school target-setting at key stage 4 will be included in this set of reforms
- Qualifications will be adapted to reflect the curriculum on the following timetable: stakeholder discussions on the purposes of future qualifications in 2019; Qualifications Wales and the Welsh government confirm the qualifications offer in 2020; consultation on the detailed design of qualifications in 2021; new qualifications approved, training and resources available in 2023; new qualifications taught in schools in 2025. Further information can be found at W https://hwb.gov.wales
- A £36m fund to help local authorities recruit additional teachers and build 54 new classrooms will be available for the schools with the largest infant class sizes and highest levels of deprivation and/or additional needs
- Some £3.2m was allocated in 2018–19 to make up the shortfall in government funding for the 3.5 per cent increase in teachers' pay, with £4.8m to follow in 2019–20. A further £8m will help to increase pay for support staff in FE colleges
- Funding for Pupil Development Grant (PDG) – Access will be doubled from £1.7m in 2018–19 to £3.5m in 2019–20, offering parents up to £125 and equipment for activities within the curriculum, such as design and technology. The grant gives greater support to learners eligible for free school meals and to Looked After Children
- Since September 2018, the £8.2m Trio Sci Cymru project has helped increase take up and grades in STEM subjects among 11- to 19-year-olds in west and north Wales and the south Wales valleys, while a £2.3m EU project will support 35 graduates into financial services and 25 graduates into a data sciences programme
- In response to an Estyn report on A-levels in sixth forms and FE colleges, the Welsh government is developing its approach to measuring the outcomes of post-16 learning programmes
- Digital 2030, a strategic framework for post-16 digital learning in Wales, was launched in June 2019. It sets out a strategy for digital learning over the next ten years, including FE, work-based learning, apprenticeships and employability programmes and adult and community learning
- The assembly decided that the Welsh Baccalaureate will be funded as a separate qualification equivalent to an A-level from September 2019
- A £20m government-funded university-run degree apprenticeship scheme started in 2019–20. Subjects include software engineering, cyber security and data analytics, with further courses being developed
- Funding of £2m was announced to improve wellbeing and mental health support for students and staff in higher education
- A new bursary scheme was introduced, at a cost of £1.3m in 2019–20, to increase the number of Welsh graduates who remain in or return to Wales to undertake a master's degree in science, technology, engineering, mathematics, medicine or Welsh. Welsh students starting such a postgraduate course in autumn 2019 can receive up to £17,000 towards their studies and living costs. EU nationals intending to study in Wales in 2020–21 will be eligible to pay the same tuition fees and receive the same student support as Welsh students
- Welsh universities secured €100m of EU Horizon 2020 research and innovation funding, while Swansea University is leading a £35m project, SUSTAIN, to research and innovate steel-making

SCOTLAND

- The Scottish government is almost doubling entitlement to early learning and childcare from August 2020 to 1,140 hours a year, while the new £250 School Age Payment benefits poor families with a child old enough to start primary school in August 2019
- An action plan to make it easier for schools to cover important global issues, such as climate change and a sustainable economy. Teachers are encouraged to take advantage of training opportunities to deliver a sustainable curriculum, backed by £650,000 of Scottish government grant funding.
- New ways for teachers and headteachers to advance their careers are to be adopted by August 2021, including the creation of specialist 'Lead Teacher' roles focussed on areas such as: curriculum, best practice in teaching and provision for

pupils with Additional Support Needs; better access to coaching, mentoring and sabbaticals; and enabling all teachers to complete a Masters degree through Initial Teacher Education
- The government published national guidance on healthy relationships and consent so that advice and information will be consistent and age-appropriate
- The government issued new guidance on mainstreaming pupils with additional support needs
- The Scottish government promised to invest a further £1bn in rebuilding and refurbishing schools from 2021, when the current school building programme ends
- Scotland aims to have lesbian, gay, bisexual, transgender and intersex (LGBTI) inclusive education embedded in the curriculum by 2021. All state schools will be supported to teach LGBTI equality and inclusion across different age groups and subjects, grouped under various themes, including terminology and identities; tackling homophobia, biphobia and transphobia; prejudice; and promoting awareness of LGBTI history
- Changes to national assessments to reduce workloads will be introduced in 2019. The interim measure of 'Recognising Positive Achievement' – the automatic fallback to National 4 for young people unsuccessful at National 5 level – ends from academic year 2019–20
- A review of the first year of standardised assessments, which take place in P1, P4, P7 and S3 to help teachers judge progress on a child's learning, found them to be 'accessible and stimulating' and 'very helpful'. All children will be asked to rate their experience at the end of each assessment, while teachers can provide feedback at any time
- The first ever national action plan to encourage and support all parents to be fully involved in their child's education was announced in August 2018. With 50 recommendations, the strategy is supported by £350,000 from the Scottish government to help address barriers some parents may face
- In June 2018, the assembly agreed to fast-track reform of education in Scotland following a joint agreement with local councils, including giving headteachers more control over decisions to raise standards and improve attainment. A £46m three-year funding package was confirmed
- A new National School Library Strategy includes 20 action points to support the improvement of literacy and numeracy, boost attainment across the curriculum and enable opportunities for family learning
- The new Youth Work and Schools Partnership programme will offer young people the opportunity to develop relationships with trusted adults and provide learning opportunities outside the home and school environment. As part of the wider £750m Scottish Attainment Challenge, it will be delivered by YouthLink Scotland, with up to £324,000 Scottish government funding over three years
- The government set a target of 29,000 Modern Apprenticeship opportunities in 2019–20 as part of a commitment to 30,000 new apprenticeship starts each year by 2020
- EU citizens on a Further or Higher education course in Scotland in the 2020–21 academic year will be charged the same tuition fees and get the same fee support as Scottish students throughout their courses. Funding for students on research Masters courses will be available for the first time in 2019, including tuition fee loans of up to £5,500 and living cost loan support of up to £4,500
- Scotland's academic research and £2.63m funding will be shared between Scotland's four science centres in 2019–20

NORTHERN IRELAND
- The Department of Education launched a consultation on the existing 2009 policy for supporting 'newcomer' pupils who speak a difference language at home from that used in their school
- Statistics published in May 2019 showed that 1,267 more pupils will transfer into post-primary education in 2019–20 than in 2018–19, following on from an increase of 952 the year before
- In February 2019, the £24m Foyle College opened and the Department of Education announced the second call for bids under the £40m School Enhancement Programme, which supports school refurbishment or extension projects valued between £500,000 and £4m

STATE SCHOOL SYSTEM

PRE-SCHOOL
Pre-school education is not compulsory.

In England, a free place is available for every 3- and 4-year-old whose parents want one, although parents may use as little or as much of their entitlement as they choose. All 3- and 4-year-olds, and disadvantaged 2-year-olds, are entitled to 15 hours a week of free early education over 38 weeks of the year until they reach compulsory school age (the term following their fifth birthday). Working parents of 3- and 4-year-old children may be eligible for up to 30 hours free childcare. Free places are funded by local authorities and are delivered by a range of approved providers in the maintained and non-maintained sectors: nursery schools, nursery classes in primary schools, private schools, private day nurseries, voluntary playgroups, pre-schools and registered childminders. In order to receive funding, providers must be working towards the early learning goals and the Early Years Foundation Stage curriculum, must be inspected on a regular basis by Ofsted and must meet any conditions set by the local authority.

In Wales, every child is entitled to receive free Foundation Phase education for a minimum of two hours a day from the term following their third birthday. The Flying Start scheme allows disadvantaged 2- to 3-year-olds 2.5 hours childcare a week for 39 weeks. The government is testing offering 30 hours free childcare to working parents of 3- to 4-year-olds in seven local authorities, before extending the offer across Wales by 2020. All children in Wales are entitled to a minimum of 10 hours of free, part-time Foundation Phase education in a school or funded nursery, in the term following their third birthday.

In Scotland, councils have a duty to provide a pre-school education for all 3- and 4-year-olds, and some disadvantaged 2- to 3-year-olds, whose parents request one. Education authorities must offer each child at least 600 hours of free pre-school education a year, although they may provide more if they choose. From August 2020 entitlement will increase to 1,140 hours a year (see Recent Developments).

In Northern Ireland, the Department of Education aims to provide a funded place for all 3- and 4-year-old children in their final pre-school year. All places offer 2.5 hours a day, five days a week for at least 38 weeks a year.

PRIMARY AND SECONDARY SCHOOLS
By law, full-time education starts at the age of five for children in England, Scotland and Wales and at the age of four in Northern Ireland. In practice, most children in the UK start school before their fifth birthday: in England all children are entitled to a primary school place from the September after their fourth birthday.

Children in England are required to stay in education or training until the end of the academic year in which they turn 18. In all other parts of the UK, compulsory schooling ends at age 16, but children born between certain dates may leave school before their 16th birthday; most young people stay in some form of education until 17 or 18.

Primary education consists mainly of infant schools for children aged 5 to 7, junior schools for those aged 7 to 11, and combined infant and junior schools for both age groups. Scotland has only primary schools with no infant/junior division.

In a few parts of England there are schools catering for ages 5 to 10 as the first stage of a three-tier system of first (lower), middle and secondary (upper) schools.

Children usually leave primary school and move on to secondary school at the age of 11 (or 12 in Scotland). In the few areas of England that have a three-tier system, middle schools cater for children for three to four years between the ages of 8 and 14, depending on the local authority.

Secondary schools cater for children aged 11 to 16 and, if they have a sixth form, for those who choose to stay on to the age of 18. From the age of 16, students may move instead to further education colleges or work-based training.

Most UK secondary schools are co-educational. The largest secondary schools have more than 1,700 pupils and around 60 per cent of secondary pupils in the UK are in schools that take more than 1,000 pupils.

Most state-maintained secondary schools in England, Wales and Scotland are comprehensive schools, which admit pupils without reference to ability. In England there remain some areas with grammar schools, catering for pupils aged 11 to 18, which select pupils on the basis of high academic ability. Two-thirds of state secondary schools in England (2,315 out of 3,448) are now academies; academies are funded directly by the state rather than being maintained by local authorities. Northern Ireland still had 67 grammar schools in 2019; the 11-plus has been officially discontinued but schools, or consortia of schools, use their own unregulated entry tests.

More than 90 per cent of pupils in the UK attend publicly funded schools and receive free education. The rest (6.6 per cent) attend privately funded 'independent' schools which charge fees, or are educated at home.

The bulk of the UK government's expenditure on school education is through local authorities (Education and Library Boards (ELBs) in Northern Ireland), which pass on state funding to schools and other educational institutions.

SPECIAL EDUCATION

Schools and local authorities in England and Wales, Education and Library Boards (ELBs) in Northern Ireland and education authorities in Scotland are required to identify and secure provision for children with special educational needs and to involve parents in decisions. The majority of children with special educational needs are educated in ordinary mainstream schools, sometimes with supplementary help from outside specialists. Parents of children with special educational needs (referred to as additional support needs in Scotland and additional learning needs in Wales) have a right of appeal to independent tribunals if their wishes are not met.

Special educational needs provision may be made in maintained special schools, in special units attached to mainstream schools or in mainstream classes, all funded by local authorities. There are also non-maintained special schools run by voluntary bodies, mainly charities, who may receive grants from central government for capital expenditure and equipment but whose other costs are met primarily from the fees charged to local authorities for pupils placed in the schools. Some independent schools also provide education wholly or mainly for children with special educational needs.

ADDITIONAL SUPPORT NEEDS TRIBUNALS FOR SCOTLAND T 0141-302 5860
W www.healthandeducationchamber.scot

FIRST-TIER TRIBUNAL (SPECIAL EDUCATIONAL NEEDS AND DISABILITY) T 01325-289350
W www.gov.uk/special-educational-needs-disability-tribunal

INFORMATION ADVICE AND SUPPORT SERVICES NETWORK FOR SEND E iassn@ncb.org.uk
W https://councilfordisabledchildren.org.uk/
information-advice-and-support-services-network

SPECIAL EDUCATIONAL NEEDS TRIBUNAL FOR WALES T 01597-829800 W www.sentw.gov.uk

HOME EDUCATION

In England and Wales parents have the right to educate their children at home and do not have to be qualified teachers to do so. Home-educated children do not have to follow the National Curriculum or take national tests. Nor do they need a fixed timetable, formal lessons or to observe school hours, days or terms. However, by law parents must ensure that the home education provided is full-time and suitable for the child's age, ability and aptitude and, if appropriate, for any special educational needs. Parents have no legal obligation to notify the local authority that a child is being educated at home, but if they take a child out of school, they must notify the school in writing and the school must report this to the local authority. Local authorities can make informal enquiries of parents to establish that a suitable education is being provided. For children in special schools, parents must seek the consent of the local authority before taking steps to educate them at home.

In Northern Ireland, ELBs monitor the quality of home provision and provide general guidance on appropriate materials and exam types through regular home visits.

The home schooling law in Scotland is similar to that of England. One difference, however, is that if parents wish to take a child out of school they must have permission from the local education authority.

HOME EDUCATION ADVISORY SERVICE
T 01707-371854 W www.heas.org.uk

HOME EDUCATION IN NORTHERN IRELAND
W www.hedni.org

SCHOOLHOUSE HOME EDUCATION ASSOCIATION (SCOTLAND) T 01307-463120
E contact@schoolhouse.org.uk W www.schoolhouse.org.uk

EDUCATION OTHERWISE T 0845-4786345
W www.educationotherwise.org

FURTHER EDUCATION

In the UK, further education (FE) is generally understood as post-secondary education, ie any education undertaken after an individual leaves school that is below higher education level. FE therefore embraces a wide range of general and vocational study, full-time or part-time, undertaken by people of all ages from 16 upwards who may be self-funded, employer-funded or state-funded.

There are three types of technical and applied qualifications for 16- to 19-year-olds: level 3 tech levels which equip people to specialise in specific technical jobs; level 2 technical certificates to help them get employment or progress to another tech level; and applied general qualifications which prepare them to continue general education at advanced level through applied learning.

FE in the UK is often undertaken at further education colleges, although some takes place on employers' premises. Many of these colleges offer some courses at higher education level; some FE colleges teach certain subjects to 14- to 16-year-olds under collaborative arrangements with schools.

Colleges' income comes from public funding, student fees and work for and with employers.

HIGHER EDUCATION

Higher education (HE) in the UK describes courses of study, provided in universities, specialist colleges of higher education and in some FE colleges, where the level of instruction is above that of A-level or equivalent exams.

All UK universities and colleges that provide HE are autonomous bodies with their own internal systems of governance. They are not owned by the state. However, most receive a portion of their income from state funds distributed by the Office for Students in England, the Higher Education Funding Council for Wales, the Scottish Funding Council or the Department for the Economy in Northern Ireland. The rest of their income comes from a number of sources including fees from home and overseas students, government funding for research, endowments and work with or for business.

EXPENDITURE

PUBLIC SECTOR EXPENDITURE ON EDUCATION
(Real terms adjusted to 2018–19 price levels) £bn

2013–14	91.9
2014–15	91.1
2015–16	90.2
2016–17	88.2
2017–18	87.5
2018–19	89.4

Source: HM Treasury – *Public Expenditure Statistical Analyses (PESA)* July 2019

SCHOOLS

UK SCHOOLS BY CATEGORY

	England	Wales
*Maintained nursery schools	391	9
†Maintained primary and secondary schools	12,275	1,444
Community	6,669	–
Voluntary-aided	3,019	–
Voluntary-controlled	1,831	–
Foundation	756	–
Pupil Referral Units	352	–
Maintained Special schools	986	41
‡Non-maintained Special schools	58	–
‡Academies	7,942	–
Independent schools	2,319	75
Total	24,323	1,569

* Includes one direct grant school in England
† Includes 13 middle schools in Wales
‡ Includes City Technology Colleges, University Technology Colleges, studio schools and free schools; excludes voluntary and private pre-school education centres and academies and free schools alternative provision
Source: DfE & Welsh government, January 2019

SCOTLAND

Maintained schools	5,046
Nursery	2,532
Primary	2,019
Secondary	360
Special	135
Independent schools	92
Total	5,138

Source: Education and Training Statistics for the UK 2017–18

NORTHERN IRELAND

State-maintained nursery schools	95
State-maintained primary and secondary schools	1,009
Controlled	430
Voluntary	61
Catholic maintained	423
Other maintained	30
Integrated	65
*Special schools	39
Independent schools	14
Total	1,157

* Includes one hospital school
Source: DENI

ENGLAND AND WALES

In England and Wales, publicly funded schools are referred to as 'state schools'. Local authorities have a duty to ensure there is a suitable place for every school-age child resident in their area. Local authorities maintain four categories of state school – Community, Foundation, Voluntary-aided and Voluntary-controlled. Each school has a governing body – made up of volunteers elected or appointed by parents, staff, the community and the local authority – which is responsible for strategic management, ensuring accountability, monitoring school performance, setting budgets and appointing the headteacher and senior staff. The headteacher is responsible for the school's day-to-day management and operations and for decisions requiring professional teaching expertise.

In *Community schools,* which are non-denominational, local authorities are the employers of the staff, own the land and buildings and set the admissions criteria.

In *Foundation schools,* the governing body employs the staff and sets the admissions criteria. The land and buildings are usually owned by the governing body or a charitable foundation. A Foundation school may have a religious character, although most do not.

Most *Voluntary-aided schools* are religious schools founded by Christian denominations or other faiths. As with Foundation schools, the governing body employs the staff and sets the admissions criteria, which may include priority for members of the faith or denomination. The school buildings and land are normally owned and provided by a charitable foundation, often a religious organisation, which appoints a majority of the school's governors and makes a small contribution to major building costs.

Voluntary-controlled schools are similar to Voluntary-aided schools in that they often have a particular religious ethos, commonly Church of England, and the school land and buildings are normally owned by a charity. However, as with Community schools, the local authority employs the school's staff, sets the admissions criteria and bears all the costs.

Among the local authority-maintained schools are some with particular characteristics:

- *Community and Foundation Special schools* cater for children with specific special educational needs, which may include physical disabilities or learning difficulties
- *Grammar schools* are secondary schools catering for pupils aged 11 to 18 that select all of their pupils based on academic ability. In England there are 164 grammar schools, concentrated in certain local authority areas. Wales has none
- *Maintained boarding schools* are state-funded and offer free tuition but charge fees for board and lodging

In Wales, Welsh-medium primary and secondary schools were first established in the 1950s and 1960s, originally in response to the wishes of Welsh-speaking parents who wanted their children to be educated through the medium of the Welsh language. Now, many children who are not from Welsh-speaking homes also attend Welsh-medium and bilingual schools throughout Wales. In 2017–18 there are 404 Welsh-medium primary schools where instruction is mainly or solely in the Welsh language, eight Welsh-medium middle schools and 47 Welsh-medium secondary schools, where more than half of foundation subjects (other than English and Welsh) and religious education are taught wholly or partly in Welsh.

England now has increasing numbers of *Academies*. Those set up before the Academies Act 2010 were sponsored by business, faith or voluntary groups who contributed to funding their land and buildings, while the government covered the running costs at a level comparable to other local schools. The Academies Act 2010 streamlined the process of becoming an academy, enabled high-performing schools to convert without a sponsor and allowed primary and special schools to become academies. All academies now receive funding from central government at the level they would have received if still maintained by their local authority, with extra funding only to cover those services the local authority no longer provides. Academies have greater freedoms over how they use their budgets, set staff pay and conditions and deliver the curriculum. In March 2019 there were 8,269 open academies (including special schools and alternative provision), 40.4 per cent of all state-funded schools.

SCOTLAND

Most schools in Scotland, known as 'publicly funded' schools, are state-funded and charge no fees. Funding is met from resources raised by the Scottish local authorities and from an annual grant from the Scottish government. Scotland does not have school governing bodies like the rest of the UK: local authorities retain greater responsibility for the management and performance of publicly funded schools. Headteachers manage at least 80 per cent of a school's budget, covering staffing, furnishings, repairs, supplies, services and energy costs. Spending on new buildings, modernisation projects and equipment is financed by the local authority within the limits set by the Scottish government.

Scotland has 370 state-funded *faith schools*, the majority of which are Catholic. It has no grammar schools.

Integrated community schools form part of the Scottish government's strategy to promote social inclusion and to raise educational standards. They encourage closer and better joint working among education, health and social work agencies and professionals, greater pupil and parental involvement in schools, and improved support and service provision for vulnerable children and young people.

Scotland has eight *grant-aided schools* that are independent of local authorities but are supported financially by the Scottish government. These schools are managed by boards and most of them provide education for children and young people with special educational needs.

NORTHERN IRELAND

Most schools in Northern Ireland are maintained by the state and generally charge no fees, though fees may be charged in preparatory departments of some grammar schools. There are different types of state-funded schools, each under the control of management committees, which also employ the teachers.

Controlled schools (nursery, primary, special, secondary and grammar schools) are managed by Northern Ireland's five ELBs through boards of governors consisting of teachers, parents, members of the ELB and transferor representatives (mainly from the Protestant churches).

Catholic maintained schools (nursery, primary, special and secondary) are under the management of boards of governors consisting of teachers, parents and members nominated by the employing authority, the Council for Catholic Maintained Schools (CCMS).

Other maintained schools (primary, special and secondary) are, in the main, Irish-medium schools that provide education in an Irish-speaking environment. The Department of Education has a duty to encourage and facilitate the development of Irish-medium education. Northern Ireland has 29 standalone Irish-medium schools, most of them primary schools, and ten Irish-medium units attached to English-medium host schools.

Voluntary schools are mainly grammar schools (66 in 2018–19), which select most pupils according to academic ability. They are managed by boards of governors consisting of teachers, parents and, in most cases, representatives from the Department of Education and the ELB.

Integrated schools (primary and secondary) educate pupils from both the Protestant and Catholic communities as well as those of other faiths and no faith; each school is managed by a board of governors. There are at present 62 integrated schools maintained by the state, 24 of which are controlled schools.

Since 2013 all pupils are guaranteed access to a wide range of courses, with a minimum of 24 courses at Key Stage 4, and 27 at post-16. At least one-third of the courses on offer will be academic and another third will be vocational. Schools work with other schools, FE colleges and other providers to widen the range of courses on offer.

INDEPENDENT SCHOOLS

Between 6 and 7 per cent of UK schoolchildren are educated by privately funded 'independent' schools that charge fees and set their own admissions policies. Independent schools are required to meet certain minimum standards but need not teach the National Curriculum. *See also* Independent Schools.

INSPECTION

ENGLAND

The Office for Standards in Education, Children's Services and Skills (Ofsted) is the main body responsible for inspecting education in English schools. As well as inspecting all publicly funded and some independent schools, Ofsted inspects a range of other services in England, including childcare, children's homes, pupil referral units, local authority children's services, further education, initial teacher training and publicly funded adult skills training. Inspection reports, recommendations and statistical information are published on Ofsted's website.

Ofsted is an independent, non-ministerial government department that reports directly to parliament, headed by Her Majesty's Chief Inspector (HMCI). Ofsted is required to promote improvement in the public services that it inspects; ensure that these services focus on the interests of their users – children, parents, learners and employers; and see that these services are efficient, effective and promote value for money.

From September 2019, Ofsted will adopt a revised inspection framework that focuses less on exam and test results, more on the quality, breadth and depth of the education provided and on supporting underperforming schools. Inspectors' view of an education provider's overall effectiveness will be based on four other judgements: on quality of education; students' behaviour and attitudes; their personal development; and leadership and management. Judgements will still be expressed using the current 4-point grading scale: outstanding, good, requires improvement or inadequate. (*See also* Recent Developments).

OFFICE FOR STANDARDS IN EDUCATION, CHILDREN'S SERVICES AND SKILLS T 0300-123 1231 W www.gov.uk/government/organisations/ofsted

WALES

Estyn is the office of Her Majesty's Inspectorate for Education and Training in Wales. It is independent of, but funded by the, Welsh government and is led by Her Majesty's Chief Inspector of Education and Training in Wales.

Estyn's role is to inspect quality and standards in education and training in Wales, including in primary, secondary, special and independent schools, pupil referral units, publicly funded nursery schools and settings, further education, adult community-based and work-based learning, local authorities and teacher education and training.

Estyn also provides advice on quality and standards in education and training to the Welsh government and others and its remit includes making public good practice based on inspection evidence. Estyn publishes on its website the findings of its inspection reports, its recommendations and statistical information.

Since September 2017, the inspection regime changed to focus on: standards; wellbeing and attitudes to learning; teaching and learning experiences; care, support and guidance; leadership and management; and a thematic area. Reports are now shorter and no longer feature an overall judgement on current performance or prospects for improvement. Many aspects previously covered in reports are only included by exception, in particularly strong or weak cases. The notice period for inspections was reduced to 15 days, with inspections typically taking four days rather than five.

Estyn announced changes to evaluation and improvement arrangements in line with the education reforms in Wales in 2019. A partial suspension of inspection for maintained schools from September 2020 to August 2021 will allow Estyn to help schools get to grips with curriculum reforms. Changes to inspection arrangements – all under consultation – are expected to take place in three phases.

HER MAJESTY'S INSPECTORATE FOR EDUCATION AND TRAINING IN WALES T 029-2044 6446 W www.estyn.gov.uk

SCOTLAND

HM Inspectorate of Education (HMIE) merged with Learning and Teaching Scotland in July 2011 to become Education Scotland, an executive agency of the Scottish government. Education Scotland operates independently and impartially while being directly accountable to Scottish ministers for the standards of its work. The agency's core business is inspection and review. It is responsible for delivering measurable year-on-year improvements, with maximum efficiency, by promoting excellence, building on strengths, and identifying and addressing underperformance. Since August 2015, inspections take account of national expectations of progress in implementing Curriculum for Excellence.

Inspection reports and reviews, recommendations, examples of good practice and statistical information are published on Education Scotland's website.

EDUCATION SCOTLAND T 0131-244 4330 W https:// education.gov.scot

NORTHERN IRELAND

The Education and Training Inspectorate (ETINI) provides inspection services for the Department of Education and the Department for the Economy in Northern Ireland.

ETINI carries out inspections of all schools, pre-school services, special education, further education colleges, initial teacher training, training organisations, and curriculum advisory and support services. Since September 2013 regional colleges of further education have received four weeks' notice of inspection, while all other organisations have received two weeks' notice.

The inspectorate's role is to improve services and provide ministers with evidence-based advice to assist in policy formulation. It publishes the findings of its inspection reports, its recommendations and statistical information on its website.

EDUCATION AND TRAINING INSPECTORATE T 028-9127 9726 W www.etini.gov.uk

THE NATIONAL CURRICULUM

ENGLAND

The National Curriculum, first introduced in 1988, is mandatory in all state schools for children from age five onwards.

Until age five, or the end of Reception Year in primary school, children are in the Early Years Foundation Stage (EYFS), which has its own learning and development requirements for children in nursery and primary schools. Changes to the EYFS came into effect in 2012, 2014 and 2017. These included simplifying the statutory assessment of children's development at age five; reducing the number of early learning goals from 69 to 17; focusing on seven areas of learning and development (communication and language; physical development; personal, social and emotional development; literacy; mathematics; understanding the world; and expressive arts and design) and, for parents, a new progress check on their child's development between the ages of two and three.

After the Foundation Stage the National Curriculum is organised into 'Key Stages', and sets out the core subjects that must be taught and the standards or attainment targets for each subject at each Key Stage.

- Key Stage 1 covers Years 1 and 2 of primary school, for children aged 5–7
- Key Stage 2 covers Years 3 to 6 of primary school, for children aged 7–11
- Key Stage 3 covers Years 7 to 9 of secondary school, for children aged 11–14
- Key Stage 4 covers Years 10 and 11 of secondary school, for children aged 14–16

Within the framework of the National Curriculum, schools may plan and organise teaching and learning in the way that best meets the needs of their pupils, but maintained schools are expected to follow the programmes of study associated with particular subjects. The programmes of study describe the subject knowledge, skills and understanding that pupils are expected to have developed by the end of each Key Stage.

The government brought in a new National Curriculum for England for maintained primary and secondary schools from September 2014. From September 2017 schools have taught the new programmes of study to all pupils in all Key Stages.

COMPULSORY SUBJECTS IN KEY STAGES 1 AND 2	
English	Design and technology
Mathematics	Geography
Science	History
Art and design	Music
Computing	Physical education (incl. swimming)

Foreign languages are compulsory in Key Stage 2, but not Key Stage 1: schools can choose from French, German, Italian, Mandarin, Spanish, Latin and Ancient Greek.

In Key Stage 3, compulsory subjects include those compulsory for Key Stage 2 (though the language taught should be a modern foreign language) plus citizenship.

Pupils in Key Stage 4 study a mix of compulsory and optional subjects in preparation for national examinations such as GCSEs. The compulsory subjects are English, mathematics, science, citizenship, computing and physical education. Key Stage 4 pupils also have to undertake careers education and work-related learning. In addition, schools must offer at least one subject from each of four 'entitlement' areas: arts (art and design, music, dance, drama and media arts); design and technology; humanities (history and geography); and modern foreign languages. To meet the entitlement requirements, schools must ensure that courses in these areas lead to approved qualifications, and must allow pupils to take courses in all four areas if they wish to do so. Schools must teach religious education (RE) at all key stages, although parents have the right to withdraw children from all or part of the subject. Secondary schools must provide sex and relationship education.

ASSESSMENT

Statutory assessment must be undertaken for all pupils in publicly funded schools in the relevant years. It first takes place towards the end of the Early Years Foundation Stage, when children's level of development is compared to and recorded against a Foundation Stage Profile. This will continue to be statutory until the end of the 2017–18 academic year. Pupils receive a phonics screening check at the end of the first year in Key Stage 1, repeated the following year if necessary. Teacher assessments in English, mathematics and science take place at the end of Key Stage 1 (Year 2) and Key Stage 2 (Year 6); at the end of Key Stage 3 (Year 9) teachers assess progress in all subjects being studied. National tests in English and mathematics take place in Year 6. At Key Stage 4, national examinations are the main form of assessment.

The assessment process for English at the end of Key Stage 2 now involves the following elements: English reading; English grammar, punctuation and spelling.

Key stage 2 results no longer use the previous system of levels. Instead, test results are converted into 'scaled scores', with a score of 100 being the expected standard. Any score below 100 means the pupil is working 'towards the expected standard'; any score above 100 means the pupil is working 'above the expected standard'. Previously the expected standard was a level 4.

Each year the Department for Education publishes on its website performance tables covering every school, college and local authority. The primary school tables are based mainly on the results of the tests taken by children at the end of Key Stage 2 when they are usually aged 11; since 2010 teacher assessment results are also included.

Headline indicators in the secondary school tables are: pupils' average progress and attainment across eight specified subjects; percentages of pupils achieving passes and strong passes (grades 5 and above) in English and maths; percentages of pupils entering and achieving strong passes in the English Baccalaureate (the EBacc is made up of English, maths, two sciences, a language and history or geography); and the percentage of pupils staying in education or employment for at least two terms after Key Stage 4.

DEPARTMENT FOR EDUCATION T 0370-000 2288
W www.gov.uk/government/organisations/
department-for-education

WALES

A new curriculum for 3- to 16-year-olds in Wales is expected to be in use by 2022 (see below). For now, a Foundation Phase curriculum for 3- to 7-year-olds, introduced in September 2008, places emphasis on learning by doing. Children's skills and knowledge are planned across seven areas of learning. They are:

• Personal and social development, wellbeing and cultural diversity
• Language, literacy and communication skills
• Mathematical development
• Welsh language development
• Knowledge and understanding of the world
• Physical development
• Creative development

Full details of the Foundation Phase can be found in *Framework for Children's Learning for 3- to 7-year-olds in Wales*, available on the Welsh government website (see below).

Currently the National Curriculum is for 7- to 16-year-olds. Originally it was similar to that of England, with distinctive characteristics for Wales reflected in the programmes of study. From September 2008 a revised school curriculum was implemented, consisting of the National Curriculum subjects together with non-statutory frameworks for personal and social education, the world of work, religious education and skills.

The National Curriculum in Wales includes the following subjects:

• *Key Stage 2* – English, Welsh, mathematics, science, design and technology, ICT, history, geography, art and design, music, and physical education
• *Key Stage 3* – as Key Stage 2, plus a modern foreign language
• *Key Stage 4* – English, Welsh, mathematics, science and physical education

Welsh is compulsory for pupils at all key stages, as either a first or second language. In 2010, 16.5 per cent of pupils were taught Welsh as a first language. In April 2012, the Minister for Education and Skills approved an action plan to raise standards and attainment in Welsh second language education.

Qualified for Life, the new curriculum for Wales from age 3 to 16, is being developed and was tested in 106 Pioneer schools in 2016 with the aim of making it available to all settings and schools, originally by September 2018, now by 2019. The purpose of the curriculum in Wales is to develop children and young people as: ambitious, capable learners, ready to learn throughout their lives; enterprising, creative contributors, ready to play a full part in life and work; ethical, informed citizens of Wales and the world; and healthy, confident individuals, ready to lead fulfilling lives as valued members of society.

The new curriculum will include:

• Six areas of learning and experience from age 3 to 16 years
• Three cross-curriculum responsibilities: literacy, numeracy and digital competence
• Progression reference points at ages 5, 8, 11, 14 and 16
• Achievement outcomes which describe expected achievements at each progression reference point

The six Areas of Learning and Experience will be:

• Expressive arts
• Health and well-being
• Humanities (including RE which should remain compulsory to age 16)
• Languages, literacy and communication (including Welsh, which should remain compulsory to age 16, and modern foreign languages)
• Mathematics and numeracy
• Science and technology (including computer science)

All teachers should be responsible for developing literacy, numeracy and digital competence across the curriculum.

The Pioneer schools had developed individual action plans and the Digital Competence Framework was available from September 2016. From 2017 to 2021 the Welsh Assembly will help schools and teachers to prepare for the new curriculum. Final curriculum and assessment arrangements will be available by January 2020. First teaching of all year groups from primary school to Year 7 will begin in September 2022 and the new curriculum will roll out from this point.

ASSESSMENT

Statutory testing at the end of Key Stage 2 was removed for pupils in Wales from 2004–5, leaving only statutory teacher assessment. This takes place at the end of Key Stage 1 (the Foundation Phase) and Key Stage 3, and is being strengthened by moderation and accreditation arrangements.

A National Literacy and Numeracy Framework (LNF), outlining the skills 5- to 15-year-olds are expected to acquire, became statutory from September 2013. For literacy, this means children should become accomplished in reading for information, writing for information and expressing themselves fluently and grammatically in speech. In numeracy, children are expected to develop numerical reasoning and use number skills, measuring skills and data skills.

National reading and numeracy tests for pupils in Years 2 to 9 started in Wales in May 2013. The tests are designed to give teachers a clearer insight into a learner's development and progress, to allow them to intervene at an earlier stage if learners are falling behind.

The reading test includes a statutory 'core' test, and a set of optional test materials to help teachers investigate learners' strengths and development needs in more depth.

The numeracy test is split into two papers: numerical procedures and numerical reasoning. The procedural paper consists of a set of questions designed to assess the basic, essential numeracy skills such as addition, multiplication and division.

A numerical reasoning paper was introduced in May 2014. It assesses learners' ability to find the most effective ways to solve everyday numeracy problems.

Learners in Welsh-medium schools take a reading test in Welsh only in Years 2 and 3, but in both English and Welsh from Year 4 onwards. Schools have the option to use both tests in Year 3. Learners take the numeracy test in either English or Welsh.

THE WELSH GOVERNMENT – EDUCATION AND SKILLS W https://curriculumforwales.gov.wales
W www.learning.wales.gov.uk

SCOTLAND

The curriculum in Scotland is not prescribed by statute but is the responsibility of education authorities and individual schools. However, schools and authorities are expected to follow the Scottish government's guidance on management and delivery of the curriculum, which is primarily through Education Scotland.

Scotland is now implementing *Curriculum for Excellence*, which aims to provide more autonomy for teachers, greater choice and opportunity for pupils and a single coherent curriculum for all children and young people aged 3 to 18.

The purpose of Curriculum for Excellence is encapsulated in 'the four capacities': to enable each child or young person to be a successful learner, a confident individual, a responsible citizen and an effective contributor. It focuses on providing a broad curriculum that develops skills for learning, skills for life and skills for work, with a sustained focus on literacy and numeracy. The period of education from pre-school through to the end of secondary stage 3, when pupils reach 14, aims to provide every young person in Scotland with this broad general education.

Curriculum for Excellence sets out 'experiences and outcomes', which describe broad areas of learning and what is to be achieved within them. They are:
- Expressive arts (including art and design, dance, drama, music)
- Health and well-being (including physical education, food and health, relationships and sexual health and mental, physical and social well-being)
- Languages
- Mathematics
- Religious and moral education
- Sciences
- Social studies (including history, geography, society and economy)
- Technologies (including business, computing, food and textiles, craft, design, engineering and graphics)

The experiences and outcomes are written at five levels with progression to examinations and qualifications during the senior phase, which covers secondary stages 4 to 6 when students are generally aged 14 to 17. The framework is designed to be flexible so that pupils can progress at their own pace.

Level	Stage
Early	The pre-school years and primary 1 (ages 3–5), or later for some
First	To the end of primary 4 (age 8), but earlier or later for some
Second	To the end of primary 7 (age 11), but earlier or later for some
Third and Fourth	Secondary 1 to secondary 3 (ages 12–14), but earlier for some. The fourth level experiences and outcomes are intended to allow choice, and young people's programmes will not include all of the fourth level outcomes
Senior phase	Secondary 4 to secondary 6 (ages 15–18), and college or other studies

Under the new curriculum, assessment of students' progress and achievements from ages 3 to 15 is carried out by teachers who base their assessment judgments on a range of evidence rather than single assessment instruments such as tests. Teachers have access to an online National Assessment Resource, which provides a range of assessment material and national exemplars across the curriculum areas.

In the senior phase, young people aged 16 to 18, including those studying outside school, build up a portfolio of national qualifications, awarded by the Scottish Qualifications Authority (SQA).

Provision is made for teaching in Gaelic in many parts of Scotland and the number of pupils in Gaelic-medium education, from nursery to secondary, is growing.

EDUCATION SCOTLAND T 0113-1244 4330 W https://education.gov.scot

SCOTTISH QUALIFICATIONS AUTHORITY
T 0345-279 1000 W www.sqa.org.uk

NORTHERN IRELAND

Children aged four to 16 in all grant-aided schools in Northern Ireland must be taught the curriculum put in place in September 2009. The statutory curriculum for Years 1 to 12 places greater emphasis on developing skills and preparing young people for life and work.

This curriculum includes a Foundation Stage to cover Years 1 and 2 of primary school, to allow a more appropriate learning style for the youngest pupils and to ease the transition from pre-school. Key Stage 1 covers primary Years 3 and 4, until children are 8, and Key Stage 2 covers primary Years 5, 6 and 7, until children are 11. Post-primary, Key Stage 3 covers Years 8, 9 and 10 and Key Stage 4 covers Years 11 and 12.

The primary curriculum is made up of the following areas of learning:

- Language and literacy
- Mathematics and numeracy
- The arts
- The world around us
- Personal development and mutual understanding
- Physical education
- Religious education

The post-primary curriculum includes a new area of learning for life and work, made up of employability, personal development, local and global citizenship and home economics (at Key Stage 3). It is also made up of RE and the following areas of learning:

- Language and literacy
- Mathematics and numeracy
- Modern languages
- The arts
- Environment and society
- Physical education
- Science and technology

At Key Stage 4, there are nine areas of learning, but statutory requirements are reduced to learning for life and work, physical education and RE. The aim is to provide greater choice and flexibility for pupils and allow them access to a wider range of academic and vocational courses provided under the revised curriculum's 'Entitlement Framework' (EF).

Since September 2013, schools have been required to provide pupils with access to at least 18 courses at Key Stage 4 and 21 courses at post-16. This increased to 24 and 27 courses respectively in September 2015. At least one third of the courses must be 'general' with one third 'applied'. The remaining third is at the discretion of each school. Individual pupils decide on the number and mix of courses they wish to follow.

RE is a compulsory part of the Northern Ireland curriculum, although parents have the right to withdraw their children from part or all of RE or collective worship. Schools have to provide RE in accordance with a core syllabus drawn up by the province's four main churches (Church of Ireland, Presbyterian, Methodist and Roman Catholic) and specified by the Department of Education.

Revised assessment and reporting arrangements were introduced when the curriculum was revised. The focus from Foundation to Key Stage 3 is on 'Assessment for Learning'. This programme includes classroom-based teacher assessment, computer-based assessment of literacy and numeracy and pupils deciding on their strengths and weaknesses and how they might progress to achieve their potential. Assessment information is given to parents in an annual report. Pupils at Key Stage 4 and beyond continue to be assessed through public examinations.

The Council for the Curriculum, Examinations and Assessment (CCEA), a non-departmental public body reporting to the Department of Education in Northern Ireland, is unique in the UK in combining the functions of a curriculum advisory body, an awarding body and a qualifications regulatory body. It advises the government on what should be taught in Northern Ireland's schools and colleges, ensures that the qualifications and examinations offered by awarding bodies in Northern Ireland are of an appropriate quality and standard and, as the leading awarding body itself, offers a range of qualifications including GCSEs, A-levels and AS-levels.

The CCEA hosts a dedicated curriculum website covering all aspects of the revised curriculum, assessment and reporting.

COUNCIL FOR THE CURRICULUM, EXAMINATIONS AND ASSESSMENT T 028-9026 1200 W www.ccea.org.uk

QUALIFICATIONS

ENGLAND, WALES AND NORTHERN IRELAND

There is a very wide range of public examinations and qualifications available, accredited by the Office of Qualifications and Examinations Regulation (OFQUAL) in England, Qualifications Wales in Wales and the Council for the Curriculum, Examinations and Assessment (CCEA) in Northern Ireland. Up-to-date information on all accredited qualifications and awarding bodies is available online at the Register of Regulated Qualifications website.

The qualifications frameworks group all accredited qualifications into levels. All the qualifications within a level place similar demands on individuals as learners. Entry level, for example, covers basic knowledge and skills in English, maths and ICT not geared towards specific occupations, level 3 includes qualifications such as A-levels which are appropriate for those wishing to go on to higher education, level 7 covers Master's degrees and vocational qualifications appropriate for senior professionals and managers and level 8 is equivalent to a doctorate.

Young people aged 14 to 19 in schools or (post-16) colleges or apprenticeships may gain academic qualifications such as GCSEs, AS-levels and A-levels; qualifications linked to particular career fields, like diplomas; vocational qualifications such as BTECs and NVQs; and functional key or basic skills qualifications.

In October 2015, both the National Qualifications Framework (NQF) formerly used in England, Wales and Northern Ireland and its successor the Qualifications and Credit Framework (QCF) for England and Northern Ireland were replaced by the Regulated Qualifications Framework (RQF) for England and the Credit and Qualifications Framework for Wales (CQFW). In Northern Ireland the Council for the Curriculum, Examinations and Assessment (CCEA) regulates qualifications. There is also a Framework for Higher Education Qualifications (FHEQ) for England, Wales and Northern Ireland.

In England, Wales and Northern Ireland there are nine qualification levels:

Entry level – each entry-level qualification is available at three sub-levels: 1, 2 and 3, with level 3 the most difficult. Entry-level qualifications are: entry-level award; entry-level certificate (ELC); entry-level diploma; entry-level English for speakers of other languages (ESOL); entry-level essential skills; entry-level functional skills; Skills for Life.

Level 1 qualifications are: first certificate; GCSE – grade D, E, F or G (3, 2 or 1 in the new grading structure); level 1 award; level 1 certificate; level 1 diploma; level 1 ESOL; level 1 essential skills; level 1 functional skills; level 1 national vocational qualification (NVQ); music grades 1, 2 and 3.

Level 2 qualifications are: CSE – grade 1; GCSE – grade A*, A, B or C (4 or above in the new grading structure); intermediate apprenticeship; level 2 award; level 2 certificate; level 2 diploma; level 2 ESOL; level 2 essential skills; level 2 functional skills; level 2 national certificate; level 2 national diploma; level 2 NVQ; music grades 4 and 5; O level – grade A, B or C.

Level 3 qualifications are: A level – grade A*, A, B, C, D or E; access to higher education; diploma; advanced apprenticeship; applied general; AS level; international Baccalaureate diploma; level 3 award; level 3 certificate; level 3 diploma; level 3 ESOL; level 3 national certificate; level 3 national diploma; level 3 NVQ; music grades 6, 7 and 8; tech level.

Level 4 qualifications are: certificate of higher education (CertHE); higher apprenticeship; higher national certificate (HNC); level 4 award; level 4 certificate; level 4 diploma; level 4 NVQ.

Level 5 qualifications are: diploma of higher education (DipHE); foundation degree; higher national diploma (HND); level 5 award; level 5 certificate; level 5 diploma; level 5 NVQ.

Level 6 qualifications are: degree apprenticeship; degree with honours – for example bachelor of arts (BA) with honours, bachelor of science (BSc) with honours; graduate certificate; graduate diploma; level 6 award; level 6 certificate; level 6 diploma; level 6 NVQ; ordinary degree without honours.

Level 7 qualifications are: integrated master's degree, for example master of engineering (MEng); level 7 award; level 7 certificate; level 7 diploma; level 7 NVQ; master's degree, for example master of arts (MA), master of science (MSc); postgraduate certificate; postgraduate certificate in education (PGCE); postgraduate diploma.

Level 8 qualifications are: doctorate, for example doctor of philosophy (PHD or DPHIL); level 8 award; level 8 certificate; level 8 diploma.

FRAMEWORK FOR HIGHER EDUCATION QUALIFICATIONS (FHEQ)

This framework applies to degrees, diplomas, certificates and other academic awards (other than honorary degrees and higher doctorates) granted by a higher education provider in the exercise of its degree awarding powers. It starts at RQF level 4 and goes up to level 8 and includes the following qualifications: Certificate of Higher Education; Diploma of Higher Education; Bachelor's degrees; Master's degrees; and Doctoral degrees.

COUNCIL FOR THE CURRICULUM, EXAMINATIONS AND ASSESSMENT (NORTHERN IRELAND)
T 028-9026 1200 W www.ccea.org.uk

QUALIFICATIONS WALES T 01633-373222
W www.qualificationswales.org

REGISTER OF REGULATED QUALIFICATIONS
W http://register.ofqual.gov.uk

OFFICE OF QUALIFICATIONS AND EXAMINATIONS REGULATION (OFQUAL) T 0300-303 3344
W www.ofqual.gov.uk

GCSE

The vast majority of pupils in their last year of compulsory schooling in England, Wales and Northern Ireland take at least one General Certificate of Secondary Education (GCSE) exam, though GCSEs may be taken at any age. GCSEs assess the performance of pupils on a subject-specific basis and are mostly taken after a two-year course. They are available in more than 50 subjects, most of them academic subjects, though some, known as vocational or applied GCSEs, involve the study of a particular area of employment and the development of work-related skills. Some subjects are also offered as short-course qualifications, equivalent to half a standard GCSE, or as double awards, equivalent to two GCSEs.

For many years GCSEs were assessed on coursework completed by students during the course as well as exams at the end, and GCSE certificates were awarded on an eight-point scale from A* to G. In most subjects two different papers, higher tier and foundation tier, were provided for different ranges of ability, with grades A*–D available to students taking the higher paper and grades C–G available from the foundation paper.

In England, all traditional GCSEs have been replaced by new GCSEs or, in some subjects, withdrawn. The new GCSEs no longer involve modules and coursework, just exam assessment at the end of the two-year course; a very few subjects (such as music technology) may include an element of non-exam assessment. Only maths, science and foreign language GCSEs will be tiered. New GCSEs are graded 9 to 1, rather than A* to G.

The changeover to new GCSEs was phased in. In September 2015 schools began teaching revised GCSEs in English language, English literature and mathematics, for exams in 2017. Teaching of revised GCSEs in ancient and modern foreign languages, art and design, biology, chemistry, citizenship, computer science, double science, dance, drama, food preparation and nutrition, geography, history, music, physics, physical education and religious studies started in September 2016 for exams in 2018. Teaching in 14 other subjects started in September 2017 for exams in 2019.

In 2017 English language, English literature and maths were the first subjects to be graded from 9 to 1. Another 20 subjects were graded 9 to 1 in 2018, with most others following in 2019. During this transition, students received a mixture of letter and number grades. It will take until summer 2020 for all reformed GCSEs to be graded on the new scale.

In Northern Ireland, new CCEA GCSEs were introduced for first teaching in 2017, with first awards in 2019 (W   www.gov.uk/government/collections/gcse-subject-content). They are graded on a 9 grade system from A*-G with a new C* grade.

All GCSE specifications, assessments and grading procedures are monitored by OFQUAL, QW and the CCEA.

Since September 2010 state schools have been allowed to offer pupils International GCSE (iGCSE) qualifications in key subjects including English, mathematics, science and ICT. Though iGCSEs were considered more rigorous than traditional GCSEs, the government regards the new GCSEs in these subjects as superior, and iGCSE results no longer count in school performance tables from 2017, or later, depending on the subject.

GCE A-LEVEL AND AS-LEVEL

GCE (General Certificate of Education) Advanced levels (A-levels) are the qualifications used by most young people in England, Wales and Northern Ireland to gain entry to university.

A-levels are subject-based qualifications. They are mostly taken by UK students aged 16 to 19 over a two-year course in school sixth forms or at college, but can be taken at any age. They are available in more than 45, mostly academic, subjects, though there are some A-levels in vocational areas, often termed 'applied A-levels'.

Traditionally, A-level qualifications consisted of two parts: advanced subsidiary (AS) and A2 units. The AS was a qualification assessed at the standard expected of a learner half way through an A-level course, normally consisting of two units that together contributed 50 per cent towards the full A-level. The A2 was the second half of a full A-level qualification. It was assessed at the standard expected of a learner at the end of a full A-level course, and normally consisted of two units that together made up the remaining 50 per cent of the full A-level qualification. Each unit was graded A–E, with an A* grade available to exceptional candidates since 2010.

An extended project was introduced in September 2008 as a separate qualification. It is a single piece of work on a topic of the student's own choosing that requires a high degree of planning, preparation, research and autonomous working. Awards are graded A–E and the extended project is accredited as half an A-level.

Since September 2013, students in England in their first or second year of A-level studies have not been allowed to sit A-level exams in January. A-levels are still examined unit by unit, but all exams are taken in the summer.

Revised AS and A-levels were introduced in phases from 2015 to 2017. All assessment of the new A-levels now takes place at the end of the two-year course and the AS has become a standalone qualification rather than contributing to a full A-level qualification.

Since September 2015, students have been taught the new-style AS-levels and A-levels in art and design, biology, business, chemistry, computer science, economics, English language, English language and literature, English literature, history, physics, psychology and sociology. New AS and A-levels in ancient languages, dance, drama and theatre, geography, modern foreign languages (French, German and Spanish), music, physical education and religious studies started to be taught in September 2016.

From September 2017, new-style A-levels were introduced in: accounting, ancient history, archaeology, classical civilisation, design and technology, electronics, film studies, geology, government and politics, history of art, law, maths and further maths, media studies, music technology, philosophy and statistics.
W www.gov.uk/government/collections/gce-as-and-a-level-subject-content

INTERNATIONAL BACCALAUREATE

The International Baccalaureate (IB) offers four educational programmes for students aged 3 to 19: IB primary years programme, IB middle years programme, IB diploma programme, IB career-related certificate.

Some 155 'IB World Schools' in the UK offer at least one IB programme.

The IB diploma programme for students aged 16 to 19 is based around detailed academic study of a wide range of subjects, including languages, the arts, science, maths, history and geography, leading to a single qualification recognised by UK universities.

The IB diploma is made up of a compulsory 'core' plus six separate subjects where individuals have some choice over what they study. The compulsory core contains three elements: theory of knowledge; creativity, action and service; and a 4,000-word extended essay.

The IB diploma normally takes two years to complete and most of the assessment is done through externally marked examinations. Candidates are awarded points for each part of the programme, up to a maximum of 45. A candidate must score 24 points or more to achieve a full diploma.

Successfully completing the diploma earns points on the 'UCAS tariff', the UK system for allocating points to qualifications used for entry to higher education. An IB diploma total of 24 points is worth 260 UCAS points – the same as a B and two C grades at A-level. The maximum of 45 points earns 720 UCAS points – equivalent to six A-levels at grade A.

WELSH BACCALAUREATE

The Welsh Baccalaureate Qualification (WBQ), available for 14- to 19-year-olds in Wales, combines a compulsory core, which incorporates personal development skills, with options from existing academic and vocational qualifications, such as A-levels, GCSEs and NVQs, to make one broader award. The WBQ can be studied in English or Welsh, or a combination of the two. Candidates who meet the requirements of the compulsory core and options relevant to each level of the qualification are awarded the Welsh Baccalaureate Foundation, Intermediate or Advanced Diploma as appropriate.

WJEC (Welsh Joint Education Committee), which administers the WBQ, has also developed two new WBQs at level 1 and level 2 suitable for delivery over one year and with a particular focus on employability.

A revised and more rigorous Welsh Baccalaureate has been taught since September 2015. It is based on a graded Skills Challenge Certificate and supporting qualifications. The aim is to enable learners to develop and demonstrate an understanding of, and proficiency in, essential and employability skills: communication, numeracy, digital literacy, planning and organisation, creativity and innovation, critical thinking and problem solving, and personal effectiveness. The emphasis is on applied and purposeful learning and opportunities for assessment in a range of real life contexts through three 'challenge briefs' and an individual project.

APPLIED GENERAL AND TECH LEVEL QUALIFICATIONS

Tech levels, first taught in schools from September 2014, are a new advanced qualification for students aged 16-19 who wish to specialise in a technical occupation. They take as long as A-levels to complete and, like A-levels, are at level 3; they lead to recognised occupations in, for example, engineering, IT, accounting or hospitality. They must be recognised by a relevant trade or professional body or at least five employers representative of the industry sector or occupation. Many higher education institutions have pledged support for Tech levels.

Tech levels have counted towards the TechBacc (Technical Baccalaureate) performance measure in the post-16 school and college performance tables since 2016. To achieve the TechBacc, students need an approved level 3 Tech level qualification, an approved level 3 mathematics qualification and the extended project qualification. Additional funding is provided for students who successfully complete a large TechBacc programme (960 guided learning hours or more).

From 2017, post-16 performance tables have also recognised Applied General Qualifications, which take the same time to complete as AS-levels and focus on broader study of a technical area. These are advanced (level 3) qualifications that allow 16 to 19 year old students to develop transferable knowledge and skills. They allow entry to a range of higher education courses, either by meeting the entry requirements in their own right or by adding value to other qualifications such as A-levels.

New 'T-level' qualifications in Digital, Construction and Education and Childcare are due to be taught from 2020 (*see also* Recent Developments).

BTECS, OCR NATIONALS AND OTHER VOCATIONAL QUALIFICATIONS

Vocational qualifications can range from general qualifications where a person learns skills relevant to a variety of jobs, to specialist qualifications designed for a particular sector. They are available from several awarding bodies, such as City & Guilds, Edexcel and OCR, and can be taken at many different levels. All vocational and work-related qualifications fit into the Regulated Qualifications Framework (RQF).

BTEC qualifications and OCR Nationals are particular types of work-related qualifications, available in a wide range of subjects, including: art and design, business, health and social care, information technology, media, public services, science and sport. The qualifications offer a mix of theory and practice, can include work experience and can be part of an Apprenticeship. They can be studied full-time at college or school, or part-time at college.

Learners complete a range of assignments, case studies and practical activities, as well as a portfolio of evidence that shows what work has been completed.

Since 2016, the quality and assessment of all vocational courses offered by schools and colleges to 14- to 19-year-olds has been strengthened. The standards of reformed BTECs, along with Cambridge OCR National Certificates and Vocational Certificates (V-Certs), equal those of GCSE A*–C grades. All vocational qualifications are graded (previously many were simply pass/fail) and all have a 25 per cent externally examined component. New Substantial Vocational Qualifications at level 2 provide 16- to 19-year-old students seeking entry at a more basic level to a skilled trade or occupation with qualifications that are valued by employers.

NVQs

A National Vocational Qualification (NVQ) is a 'competence-based' qualification that is recognised by employers. Individuals learn practical, work-related tasks designed to help them develop the skills and knowledge to do a particular job effectively. NVQs can be taken in school, at college or by people already in work. There are more than 1,300 different NVQs available from the vast majority of business sectors. NVQs exist at levels 1 to 5 on the RQF. An NVQ qualification at level 2 or 3 can also be taken as part of an Apprenticeship.

Functional Skills

Functional skills qualifications were launched during 2010, for all learners aged 14 and above. They test practical skills that allow people to work confidently, effectively and independently in life, and are available only in England. Wales and Northern Ireland have literacy and numeracy qualifications known as 'Essential Skills'.

In England, the government is reforming functional skills qualifications in English and mathematics. The reformed qualifications will be available for teaching from September 2019.

Apprenticeships

Apprenticeships combine on-the-job training with nationally recognised qualifications, allowing individuals to gain skills and qualifications while working and earning a wage. More than 200 different types of apprenticeships are available, offering over 1,500 job roles; they take between one and five years to complete. There are four levels available:

- Intermediate Apprenticeships – at level 2 on the Regulated Qualifications Framework (RQF), they are equivalent to five good GCSE passes (9–4)
- Advanced Apprenticeships – at level 3 on the RQF, they are equivalent to two A-level passes/Level 3 Diploma/International Baccalaureate
- Higher Apprenticeships – levels 4, 5, 6 and 7 equivalent to Foundation degree and above
- Degree Apprenticeships – added in 2015 (RQF level 6 and 7) equivalent to a bachelor's or master's degree

In England, the National Apprenticeship Service (NAS), launched in 2009, is responsible for the delivery of apprenticeships and provides an online vacancy matching system. The way in which the government funds the training and assessment costs of apprenticeships was revised in May 2017, when the apprenticeship levy was introduced. In 2017–18, there were 814,800 people participating in an apprenticeship in England, with 375,800 apprenticeship starts and 276,200 apprenticeship achievements. Some 18 groups of universities have developed new degree apprenticeships, which began in September 2017. The Welsh government and the Department for the Economy are responsible for the apprenticeship programmes in Wales and Northern Ireland respectively.

NATIONAL APPRENTICESHIP SERVICE (NAS)
T 0800-015 0400 W www.gov.uk/apply-apprenticeship

REGISTER OF APPRENTICESHIP TRAINING PROVIDERS
W www.gov.uk/guidance/register-of-apprenticeship-training-providers

SCOTLAND

Scotland has its own system of public examinations and qualifications. The Scottish Qualifications Authority (SQA) is Scotland's national body for qualifications, responsible for developing, accrediting, assessing and certificating all Scottish qualifications apart from university degrees and some professional body qualifications.

There are qualifications at all levels of attainment. Almost all school candidates gain SQA qualifications in the fourth year of secondary school and most obtain further qualifications in the fifth or sixth year or in further education colleges. Increasingly, people also take qualifications in the workplace.

SQA, with partners such as Universities Scotland, has introduced the Scottish Credit and Qualifications Framework (SCQF) as a way of comparing and understanding Scottish qualifications. It includes qualifications across academic and vocational sectors and compares them by giving a level and credit points. There are 12 levels in the SCQF, level 1 being the least difficult and level 12 the most difficult. The number of SCQF credit points shows how much learning has to be done to achieve the qualification. For instance, one SCQF credit point equals about 10 hours of learning including assessment.

Since reforms introduced in 2013, qualifications in Scotland are divided into academic National Qualifications and more practical-based Qualifications for Work.

National Qualifications

- National 1 units are assessed as a pass or fail by a teacher or lecturer. They could lead to National 2 courses or awards at SCQF level 1 or 2
- National 2 courses are made up of units assessed as pass or fail by a teacher or lecturer. Learners need to pass all units to achieve the qualification. They could lead to National 3 courses or awards at SCQF level 2 or 3
- National 3 courses comprise three National Units assessed as pass or fail by a teacher or lecturer. They could lead to related courses at National 4, awards at SQCF level 3 or 4, National Certificates or National Progression Awards or employment opportunities
- National 4 courses are made up of units, including an added value unit, which assesses learners' performance across the course. They could lead to National 5 courses, units or awards at SCQF level 4 or 5, National Certificate or National Progression Awards, or Modern Apprenticeships or other employment opportunities
- National 5 courses are assessed through exams, coursework or both, most of which is marked by the Scottish Qualifications Authority. Courses are graded A to D or 'no award'. They could lead to Higher courses, units or awards at SCQF level 5 or 6, National Certificate or National Progression Awards, Foundation Apprenticeships or a Modern Apprenticeship at SCQF level 6
- Higher courses are made up of exams or coursework (units will be removed from 2018–19) or both, marked by the SQA, or teachers or lecturers in some cases. They could lead to Advanced Higher courses, units or awards at SCQF level 6 or 7, National Certificate or National Progression Awards, Higher National Certificate or Higher National Diplomas, or Modern Apprenticeships at SCQF level 7
- Advanced Higher courses are made up of exams or coursework (units will be removed from 2019–20) or both,

marked by the SQA, or teachers or lecturers in some cases. They could lead to a Higher National Diploma, undergraduate degree or a Technical Apprenticeship at SCQF level 8

- Skills for Work courses encourage learners to become familiar with the world of work. They are available in a variety of areas such as construction, hairdressing and hospitality (W www.sqa.org.uk/skillsforwork)
- Scottish Baccalaureates are qualifications at SCQF level 7, and are available for learners in S5 and S6. They exist in Expressive Arts, Languages, Science, and Social Sciences and are awarded as a pass or distinction. Learners undertake an interdisciplinary project, which allows them to develop and show evidence of initiative, responsibility, and independent working – skills of value in the world of higher education (W www.sqa.org.uk/baccalaureates)

Qualifications For Work
- Introduction to Work Place Skills qualification is designed to help 'can do' learners to develop core and employability skills. It comprises an employer-assessed work experience placement of a minimum of 150 hours. Successful completion allows learners to go to Certificate of Work Readiness, further training, education or employment (W www.sqa.org.uk/introtowork)
- Certificate of Work Readiness award includes an employer-assessed work experience placement and is available through colleges and training providers working in partnership with employers (W www.sqa.org.uk/workready).
- Foundation Apprenticeships are new, work-based learning qualifications for secondary school pupils and allow pupils in S4 to S6 to complete elements of a Modern Apprenticeship while still at school. Depending on their subject, pupils study towards Foundation Apprenticeships alongside their other subjects and spend part of their school week at college or with a local employer. By December 2017, some 18,700 young people had started apprenticeships. (W www.apprenticeships.scot/foundation-apprenticeships).
- Modern Apprenticeships offer anyone aged over 16 paid employment combined with the opportunity to train for jobs at craft, technician and management level. They are developed by the industry or sector in which they will be implemented. (W www.sqa.org.uk/modernapprenticeships or W www.apprenticeships.scot)
- SQA Awards are flexible and nationally recognised. They provide learners with opportunities to acquire skills, recognise achievement and promote confidence
- Wider Achievement qualifications provide young people with the opportunity to have learning and skills formally recognised, whether developed in or outside the classroom. Available at a number of levels in subjects including Employability, Leadership and Enterprise, these qualifications help schools deliver skills for learning, life and work
- Scottish Vocational Qualifications are based on national standards drawn up by people from industry, commerce and education covering a wide range of occupations
- Professional Development Awards develop the skills of those already in professional employment and can be embedded within another qualification such as a Higher National Certificate or Diploma
- National Certificates prepare people for employment, development or progression to advanced study. They are aimed at 16-18 year olds and are at SCQF levels 2 to 6
- National Progression Awards assess a defined set of skills and knowledge in specialist vocational areas, linking to National Occupational Standards, which are the basis of SVQs

- Higher National qualifications are offered by colleges, universities and other training centres. Higher National Certificates, Higher National Diplomas and Professional Development Awards are designed to meet employers' needs and can give candidates access to second or third year entry at university

As part of the Curriculum for Excellence programme SQA developed revised National qualifications that became available in schools from August 2013, replacing Standard Grade, Intermediate and Access qualifications at all levels. New Higher qualifications became available from August 2014 and Advanced Higher qualifications from August 2015:

SCQF level	National qualifications
1 & 2	National 1 & 2
3	National 3
4	National 4
5	National 5
6	Higher
7	Advanced Higher

Since 2017–18 mandatory unit assessments have been removed from the National 5 qualification to reduce teacher and pupil workload. Course assessments for National 5 – a combination of exam and coursework – were strengthened to maintain their integrity, breadth and standards.

Mandatory unit assessment was removed for Higher courses from 2018–19 and will be removed from Advanced Higher courses from 2019–20.

THE SCOTTISH QUALIFICATIONS AUTHORITY (SQA)
T 0345-279 1000 W www.sqa.org.uk

SCOTTISH CREDIT AND QUALIFICATIONS FRAMEWORK (SCQF) T 0845-270 7371
W www.scqf.org.uk

SKILLS DEVELOPMENT SCOTLAND (SDS)
T 0800-917 8000 W www.skillsdevelopmentscotland.co.uk

FURTHER EDUCATION AND LIFELONG LEARNING

ENGLAND

The further education (FE) system in England provides a wide range of education and training opportunities for young people and adults. From the age of 16, young people who wish to remain in education, but not in a school setting, can undertake further education (including skills training) in an FE college. There are two main types of college in the FE sector: sixth form colleges and general further education (GFE) colleges. Some FE colleges focus on a particular area, such as art and design or agriculture and horticulture. Each institution decides its own range of subjects and courses. Students at FE colleges can study for a wide and growing range of academic and/or work-related qualifications, from entry level to higher education level.

The Department for Business, Innovation and Skills was responsible for the FE sector and for funding adult FE until July 2016, when these responsibilities passed to the Department for Education, which already funded all education and training for 16- to 18-year-olds.

The proportion of 16- to 18-year-olds in education or training has risen steadily over recent years, driven by increases in state-funded schools and in higher education. The 'September Guarantee', introduced in 2007, offers a place in post-16 education or training to all 16- and 17-year-olds who want one. The latest statistics, for 2018, show 81.3 per cent of young people in full-time education and apprenticeships, with only 6.3 per cent not in education, employment or training.

The Education and Skills Funding Agency (ESFA) replaced the Skills Funding Agency and the Education Funding Agency in April 2017. The ESFA is accountable for £59bn of funding for the education and training sector, regulating academies, FE colleges, employers and training providers, intervening where there is risk of failure or where there is evidence of mismanagement of public funds, and delivering major projects in the education and skills sector, such as school capital programmes, the National Careers Service, the digital Apprenticeship Service and National Apprenticeship Service.

There are currently 12 centres of training excellence called National Skills Academies, led, funded and designed by employers, in various stages of development. Each academy offers specialist training in a key sector of the economy, working in partnership with colleges, schools and independent training providers.

Among the many voluntary bodies providing adult education, the Workers' Educational Association (WEA) is the UK's largest, operating throughout England and Scotland. It provides part-time courses to adults in response to local need in community centres, village halls, schools, pubs or workplaces. Similar but separate WEA organisations operate in Wales and Northern Ireland.

In 2016, the National Institute of Adult Continuing Education (NIACE), a charitable non-governmental organisation, merged with the Centre for Economic and Social Inclusion to form the Learning and Work Institute, which promotes lifelong learning opportunities for adults in England and Wales.

LEARNING AND WORK INSTITUTE T 0116-204 4200
    W www.learningandwork.org.uk
THE EDUCATION AND SKILLS FUNDING AGENCY
    W www.gov.uk/government/organisations/
    education-and-skills-funding-agency
WORKERS' EDUCATIONAL ASSOCIATION (WEA)
    T 0300-303346 W www.wea.org.uk
EDUCATION AND TRAINING FOUNDATION
    T 020-3740 8280 W www.et-foundation.co.uk

WALES

In Wales, the aims and makeup of the FE system are similar to those outlined for England. The Welsh government funds a wide range of learning programmes for young people through its 15 FE colleges, local authorities and private organisations. The Welsh government has set out plans to improve learning opportunities for all post-16 learners in the shortest possible time, to increase the engagement of disadvantaged young people in the learning process, and to transform the learning network to increase learner choice, reduce duplication of provision and encourage higher-quality learning and teaching in all post-16 provision.

Responsibility for adult and continuing education lies with the Department for Education and Skills (DfES) within the Welsh government. Wales operates a range of programmes to support skills development, including subsidised work-based training courses for employees and the Workforce Development Programme, where employers can use the free services of experienced skills advisers to develop staff training plans.

COLLEGES WALES T 029-2052 2500
    W www.collegeswales.ac.uk
ADULT LEARNING WALES T 029-2023 5277
    W www.adultlearning.wales
LEARNING AND WORK INSTITUTE T 029-2037 0900
    W www.learningandwork.wales
WEA SOUTH WALES T 029-2023 5277
    W www.swales.wea.org.uk

SCOTLAND

Following a series of mergers, Scotland now has 27 FE colleges (known simply as colleges), which are at the forefront of lifelong learning, education, training and skills in Scotland. Colleges cater for the needs of learners both in and out of employment and at all stages in their lives. Colleges' courses span much of the range of learning needs, from specialised vocational education and training through to general educational programmes. The level of provision ranges from essential life skills and provision for students with learning difficulties to HNCs and HNDs. Some colleges, notably those in the Highlands and Islands, also deliver degrees and postgraduate qualifications.

A shift in study patterns is taking place within the college sector as colleges concentrate on full-time courses aimed at helping people gain employment and no longer fund short courses lasting less than ten hours. Overall figures are stable, but this change has led to a decline in part-time study and an increase in full-time study.

The Scottish Funding Council (SFC) is the statutory body responsible for funding teaching and learning provision, research and other activities in Scotland's colleges. Overall strategic direction for the sector is provided by the Lifelong Learning Directorate of the Scottish government, which provides annual guidance to the SFC and liaises closely with bodies such as Colleges Scotland, the Scottish Qualifications Authority and the FE colleges themselves to ensure that policies remain relevant and practical.

The Scottish government takes responsibility for community learning and development in Scotland while Skills Development Scotland, a non-departmental public body, is charged with improving Scotland's skills performance by linking skills supply and demand and helping people and organisations to learn, develop and make use of these skills to greater effect.

ILA SCOTLAND T 0800-917 8000
    W www.myworldofwork.co.uk/learn-and-train/funding
COLLEGES SCOTLAND T 01786-892100
    W www.collegesscotland.ac.uk
SCOTTISH FUNDING COUNCIL T 0131-313 6500
    W www.sfc.ac.uk
SKILLS DEVELOPMENT SCOTLAND T 0800-917 8000
    W www.skillsdevelopmentscotland.co.uk

NORTHERN IRELAND

FE in Northern Ireland is provided through six regional multi-campus colleges and the College of Agriculture, Food and Rural Affairs. Most secondary schools also have a sixth form which students may attend for two additional years to complete their AS-levels and A-levels.

Colleges Northern Ireland acts as the representative body for the six FE colleges which, like their counterparts in the rest of the UK, are independent corporate bodies each managed by their own governing body. The range of courses that they offer spans essential skills, a wide choice of vocational and academic programmes and higher education programmes. Most full-time students in the six colleges are aged 16 to 19, while most part-time students are over 19.

The Department for the Economy is responsible for the policy, strategic development and financing of the statutory FE sector and for lifelong learning, and also provides support to a small number of non-statutory FE providers. The Educational Guidance Service for Adults, an independent, not-for-profit organisation, has a network of local offices based across Northern Ireland that provide services to adult learners, learning advisers, providers, employers and others interested in improving access to learning for adults.

THE EDUCATIONAL GUIDANCE SERVICE FOR
ADULTS E info@egsa.org.uk W www.egsa.org.uk

NI DIRECT FE COLLEGES
W www.nidirect.gov.uk/contacts/further-education-fe-colleges

FINANCIAL SUPPORT

England has a bursary scheme of up to £1,200 a year for full-time 16- to 19-year-old students facing financial hardship. Two types of bursary exist: vulnerable student bursary and discretionary bursary. Help with transport costs is also possible for some students. This scheme replaced the Education Maintenance Allowance (EMA), which gave 16- to 19-year-olds from low-income families a weekly allowance to continue in education.

There are EMA schemes in Scotland, Wales and Northern Ireland, but with slightly different eligibility conditions. Students must apply to the EMA scheme for the part of the UK where they intend to study.

Colleges and learning providers award learner support funds directly to new students aged 19 and over.

Care to Learn is available in England to help young parents under the age of 20, caring for their own child or children while they are in some form of publicly funded learning (below higher education level), with the costs of childcare and travel. The scheme is not income-assessed and pays up to £160 a week (£175 in London) to cover costs.

Dance and Drama Awards (DaDA) are state-funded scholarships for students aged 16 to 23 enrolled at one of 19 private dance and drama schools in England, who are taking specified courses at National Certificate or National Diploma level. Awards, based on household income, cover some of students' tuition fees and from £1,350 to £5,185 of maintenance in 2019–20.

Young people studying away from home because their chosen course is not available locally may qualify for the *Residential Support Scheme* (up to £3,458 outside London and £4,079 in London for household incomes of less than £21,000).

Information and advice on funding support and applications are available from the Learner Support helpline (T 0800-121 8989) or on the GOV.UK website (*see* below).

Discretionary Support Funds (DSF) are available in colleges and school sixth forms to help students who have trouble meeting the costs of participating in further education.

In Wales, students aged 19 or over on FE courses may be eligible for the *Welsh Government Learning Grant FE* (previously the Assembly Learning Grant for Further Education). This is a means-tested payment of up to £1,500 for full-time students and up to £750 for those studying part-time. *Discretionary Assistance Funds* are also available to all students in Wales suffering hardship.

In Scotland, FE students can apply to their college for discretionary support in the form of *Further Education Bursaries,* which can include allowances for maintenance, travel, study, childcare and additional support needs. *Individual Training Accounts,* which replaced *Individual Learning Accounts* from October 2017, allow eligible students up to £200 towards a single course or training episode per year.

In Northern Ireland, FE students with annual household incomes below £21,330 may be eligible for a *Further Education Grant* of up to £2,092, non-refundable assistance, administered on behalf of the five Education and Library Boards by the Western Education and Library Board.

EDUCATION AUTHORITY W www.eani.org.uk

GOV.UK W www.gov.uk/further-education-courses/financial-help
MY WORLD OF WORK W www.myworldofwork.co.uk
STUDENT FINANCE WALES T 0300-200 4050
W www.studentfinancewales.co.uk

HIGHER EDUCATION

Publicly funded higher education (HE) in the UK is provided in universities, higher education colleges and other specialist HE institutions, and in a significant number of FE colleges offering higher education courses.

Since the closure of the Higher Education Funding Council for England (HEFCE) in March 2018, universities and university colleges are funded through UK Research and Innovation (UKRI).

The Higher Education Funding Council for Wales (HEFCW) distributes funding for HE in Wales through Wales' 8 HEIs, the Open University in Wales and some FE colleges.

The Scottish Funding Council (SFC) – which is also responsible for FE in Scotland – is the national strategic body responsible for funding HE teaching and research in Scotland's 19 HEIs and 26 colleges.

In Northern Ireland, HE is provided by two universities, two university colleges, six regional institutes of further and higher education and the Open University (OU), which operates UK-wide. Northern Ireland has no higher education funding body; the Department for the Economy fulfils that role.

All UK universities and a number of HE colleges award their own degrees and other HE qualifications. HE providers who do not have their own degree-awarding powers offer degrees under 'validation arrangements' with other institutions that do have those powers. The OU, for example, runs a validation service which enables a number of other institutions to award OU degrees, after the OU has assured itself that the academic standards of their courses are as high as the OU's own standards.

Each HE institution is responsible for the standards of the awards it makes and the quality of the education it provides to its students, and each has its own internal quality assurance procedures. External quality assurance for HE institutions throughout the UK is provided by the Quality Assurance Agency for Higher Education (QAA).

The QAA is independent of government, funded by subscriptions from all publicly funded UK universities and colleges of HE. Its main role is to safeguard the standards of HE qualifications. It does this by defining standards for HE through a framework known as the academic infrastructure. QAA carries out reviews of the quality of UK HE institutions via a system known as 'institutional audits', advises on a range of HE quality issues and publishes reports on its website.

DEPARTMENT FOR THE ECONOMY (NI)
T 028-9052 9900 W www.economy-ni.gov.uk

HIGHER EDUCATION FUNDING COUNCIL FOR WALES T 029-2085 9698 W www.hefcw.ac.uk

RESEARCH ENGLAND T 0117-905 7600 W https://re.ukri.org

SCOTTISH FUNDING COUNCIL T 0131-313 6500
W www.sfc.ac.uk

THE QUALITY ASSURANCE AGENCY FOR HIGHER EDUCATION T 01452-557000 W www.qaa.ac.uk

STUDENTS APPLYING TO UNIVERSITY			
	2018	2019	Difference
Total applicants by 15 Jan*	559,030	561,420	0%
* Deadline for 2019 cycle			
Source: UCAS			

STUDENTS IN HIGHER EDUCATION 2017–18*		
	Full-time	Part-time
HE students	1,844,545	489,550
Postgraduate students	339,480	227,075
Undergraduate students	1,505,480	271,475
* Includes UK, EU and non-EU students		
Source: Higher Education Statistics Authority (HESA) 2019		

UK HIGHER EDUCATION QUALIFICATIONS AWARDED 2017–18		
	Full-time	Part-time
First degrees	391,390	27,510
Other undergraduate qualifications	45,610	27,880
Postgraduate Certificate in Education	19,665	895
Other postgraduate research and taught qualifications	190,070	73,985
Total qualifications awarded	646,735	130,270

Source: HESA 2019

COURSES

HE institutions in the UK mainly offer courses leading to the following qualifications. These qualifications go from levels 4 to 8 on England's Regulated Qualifications Framework, levels 7 to 12 on Scotland's Credit and Qualifications Framework. Individual HEIs may not offer all of these.

Certificates of Higher Education (CertHE) are awarded after one year's full-time study (or equivalent). If available to students on longer courses, they certify that students have reached a minimum standard in their first year.

Diplomas of Higher Education (DipHE) and other *Higher Diplomas* are awarded after two to three years' full-time study (or equivalent). They certify that a student has achieved a minimum standard in first- and second-year courses and, in the case of nursing, third-year courses. They can often be used for entry to the third year of a related degree course.

Foundation degrees are awarded after two years of full-time study (or equivalent). These degrees combine academic study with work-based learning, and have been designed jointly by universities, colleges and employers with a particular area of work in mind. They are usually accepted as a basis for entry to the third year of a related degree course.

Bachelor's degrees, also referred to as *first degrees,* have different titles, Bachelor of Arts (BA) and Bachelor of Science (BSc) being the most common. In England, Wales and Northern Ireland most Bachelor's degree courses are 'with Honours' and awarded after three years of full-time study, although in some subjects the courses last longer. In Scotland, where young people may leave school and go to university a year younger, HE institutions typically offer Ordinary Bachelor's degrees after three years' study and Bachelor's degrees with Honours after four years. Honours degrees are graded as first, upper second (2:1), lower second (2:2), or third. HEIs in England, Wales and Northern Ireland may allow students who fail the first year of an Honours degree by a small margin to transfer to an Ordinary degree course, if they have one. Ordinary degrees may also be awarded to Honours degree students who do not finish an Honours degree course but complete enough of it to earn a pass.

Postgraduate or *Higher degrees.* Graduates may go on to take *Master's degrees,* which involve one or two years' work and can be taught or research-based. They may also take one-year postgraduate diplomas and certificates, often linked to a specific profession, such as the *Postgraduate Certificate in Education* (PGCE) required to become a state school teacher. A *doctorate,* leading to a qualification such as Doctor of Philosophy – a PHD or DPHIL – usually involves at least three years of full-time research.

The framework for HE qualifications in England, Wales and Northern Ireland (FHEQ) and the framework for qualifications of HE institutions in Scotland can both be found on the QAA website, which describes the achievement represented by HE qualifications.

ADMISSIONS

When preparing to apply to a university or other HE college, individuals can compare facts and figures on institutions and courses using the government's Unistats website. This includes details of students' views from the annual National Student Survey. They can also consult the results of the Teaching Excellence Framework, which is an official survey of teaching quality in universities listed on the Office for Students' website (*see also* Recent Developments).

For the vast majority of full-time undergraduate courses, individuals need to apply online through UCAS, the organisation responsible for managing applications to HE courses in the UK. More than half a million people wanting to study at a university or college each year use this UCAS service, which has useful online tools to help students find the right course.

UCAS also provides two specialist applications services used by more than 50,000 people each year: the Conservatoires UK Admissions Service (CUKAS), for those applying to UK music conservatoires, and the Graduate Teacher Training Registry (GTTR), for postgraduate applications for initial teacher training courses in England and Wales and some in Scotland. Details of initial teacher training courses in Scotland can also be obtained from Universities Scotland and from Teach in Scotland, the website created by the Scottish government to promote teaching.

Each university or college sets its own entry requirements. These can be in terms of particular exam grades or total points on the 'UCAS tariff' (UCAS's system for allocating points to different qualifications on a common basis), or be non-academic, like having a health check. HE institutions will make 'firm offers' to candidates who have already gained the qualifications they present for entry, and 'conditional offers' to those who have yet to take their exams or obtain their results. Conditional offers often require a minimum level of achievement in a specified subject, for example '300 points to include grade A at A-level Chemistry'. If candidates' achievements are lower than specified in their conditional offers, the university or college may not accept them; then, if they still wish to go into HE, they need to find another institution through the UCAS 'clearing' process.

The Open University conducts its own admissions. It is the UK's only university dedicated to distance learning and the UK's largest for part-time HE. Because it is designed to be 'open' to all, no qualifications are needed for entry to the majority of its courses.

Individuals can search thousands of UK postgraduate courses and research opportunities on UK graduate careers website Prospects. The application process for postgraduate places can vary between institutions. Most universities and colleges accept direct applications and many accept applications through UKPASS, a free, centralised online service run by UCAS that allows individuals to submit up to ten different applications, track their progress and attach supporting material, such as references.

UNISTATS W http://unistats.direct.gov.uk

TEACHING EXCELLENCE FRAMEWORK
    W www.officeforstudents.org.uk/advice-and-guidance/teaching
UCAS T 0371-468 0468 W www.ucas.com
UNIVERSITIES SCOTLAND T 0131-226 1111
    W www.universities-scotland.ac.uk
TEACH IN SCOTLAND T 0845-345 4745
    W https://teachinscotland.scot
PROSPECTS T 0161-277 5200 W www.prospects.ac.uk
UKPASS T 0371-334 4447 W http://ukpass.ac.uk

TUITION FEES AND STUDENT SUPPORT

TUITION FEES

Higher Education institutions (HEIs) in England, Wales and Northern Ireland charge tuition fees for full-time HE courses. Although students from outside the EU can be charged the full cost of their courses, the tuition fees that universities may charge undergraduate degree students from the UK and other EU countries is capped at £9,250 for 2019–20. In Scotland, tuition fees for 2019–20 are £1,820 for full-time Scottish-domiciled or EU students and capped at £9,250 for full-time students from the rest of the UK (England, Wales and Northern Ireland). In Wales, maximum tuition fees are £9,000, while in Northern Ireland fees are £4,275 for resident and EU students, otherwise £9,250.

Full-time students do not have to pay their fees themselves before or during their course, as tuition fee loans are available to cover the full cost; these do not have to be repaid until the student is working and earning more than a specified amount (see Student Loans, Grants and Bursaries).

STUDENT LOANS, GRANTS AND BURSARIES

England

Students starting their first full-time HE course in 2019–20 can apply through Student Finance England for financial support. Two student loans are available from the government: a *tuition fee loan* of up to £9,250 for 2019–20, or up to £6,165 for a private university or college, or £11,100 for an accelerated degree course; and a *maintenance loan* (for students aged under 60) to help with living expenses of up to £8,944 for those living away from home (£11,672 if studying away from home in London), or up to £7,529 for those living with their parents during term time, or up to £10,242 if living and studying abroad for a year.

The tuition fee loan is not affected by household income and is paid directly to the relevant HE institution. A proportion (currently 65 per cent) of the maximum maintenance loan is available irrespective of household income while the rest depends on an income assessment. Student Finance England usually pays the money into the student's own bank account in three instalments, one at the start of each term.

Repayment of both loans does not start until the April after the student has left university or college, or before they are earning £25,725 a year, £2,143 a month or £494 a week in the UK (£21,000 for postgraduate loans).

At this point the individual's employer will deduct 9 per cent of any salary above the starting limit through the Pay As You Earn (PAYE) system (6 per cent for postgraduate loans). The self-employed make repayments through their tax returns. Student loans accrue interest from the date they are paid out, until they are repaid in full. Generally, the interest rate for student loans is set in September each year. The latest rate can be found online (W www.studentloanrepayment.co.uk).

For all new full-time students starting HE since September 2016, maintenance grants have been replaced by loans. Students whose family income is up to £42,620 can apply in 2019–20 for maintenance loans of up to £8,944 a year (£11,672 in London) – the maximum amount applying only to students with a household income of less than £25,000 a year. Special support grants are also being replaced by maintenance loans.

Students needing extra help may also be entitled to receive disabled students' allowance, adult dependants' grant, childcare grant or parents' learning allowance.

Part-time Higher Education Students are entitled to tuition fee loans (which replaced grants) of up to £6,935 in 2019–20.

Details are available on the Student Finance England website (W www.gov.uk/student-finance/loans-and-grants). There is a

student finance calculator on the website to work out what financial support is available.

Universities and other higher education providers offer their own grants and bursaries, with differing criteria. Bursaries do not have to be repaid. Students should always check with the institution they are planning to attend to find out what extra financial support may be available.

If the student's chosen HE institution runs the *additional fee support scheme*, it could provide extra financial help if the student is on a low income and in certain other circumstances. For students in financial difficulty help may also be available through the institution's *access to learning fund.*

Wales

Welsh students starting a full-time HE course in 2019–20 can apply through Student Finance Wales for the forms of financial support described below.

The system of tuition fee and maintenance loans and grants in Wales is similar to England's, particularly for new students, but continuing Welsh students can also receive a substantial tuition *fee grant*. Maximum maintenance loans are: up to £9,225 for students living away from home (£11,530 if studying away from home in London) and up to £7,840 for those living with their parents during term time.

Welsh-domiciled students may apply for a *Welsh government learning grant* of up to £10,124 to help meet general living costs. This is paid in three instalments, one at the start of each term, like the student maintenance loan. The amount that a student gets depends on household income. The maximum grant is available to those with a household income of £18,370 or under. Those with an income of £59,200 or over will receive £1,000.

There is also a *special support grant* for single parents, student parents or those with disabilities, which is worth up to £5,161 a year in 2019–20. It is paid directly to students and is not offset against student loan borrowing.

Students can use the student finance calculator on the Student Finance Wales website to work out what financial support they may be entitled to.

Welsh HE institutions also hold financial contingency funds to provide discretionary assistance to students experiencing financial difficulties.

For 2019–20 part-time undergraduate higher education students and continuing students studying at least 25 per cent of an equivalent full-time course are entitled to receive a fee loan of £2,625 (£6,935 for a course at a publicly funded university or college elsewhere in the UK, or £4,625 at a private university or college). The maximum amount of grants and loans available is £5,111.75 depending on household income and course intensity.

Childcare Grants, Parents' Learning Allowance, Adult Dependants' Grant, and Disabled Students' Allowances are also available.

STUDENT FINANCE WALES T 0300-200 4050
  W www.studentfinancewales.co.uk

Scotland

Students starting a full-time HE course in 2019–20 can apply through the Student Awards Agency for Scotland for financial support. Full-time Scottish-domiciled or EU students enrolling on a course in 2019 will be eligible to have their tuition fees (£1,285 for a HND/HNC or £1,820 for a degree or equivalent) paid for the duration of their studies through the Student Awards Agency for Scotland (applications for tuition fee payment should be made annually). Tuition fees for full-time students from the rest of the UK (England, Wales and Northern Ireland) are capped at £9,250 for 2019–20, for which loans are available from the relevant body (Student Finance England, Student Finance Wales or Student Finance

Northern Ireland). Living cost support is mainly provided through a *student loan*, the majority of which is income-assessed. The maximum loan for 2019–20 is £7,625.

The *young students' bursary* (YSB) is available to young students from low-income backgrounds and is non-repayable. Eligible students receive this bursary instead of part of the student loan, thus reducing their level of repayable debt. In 2019–20 the maximum annual support provided through YSB is £2,000 if household income is £20,999 or less a year.

The *independent students' bursary* (ISB) similarly replaces part of the loan and reduces repayable debt for low-income students independent of parental support. The maximum paid is £1,000 a year to those whose household income is £20,999 or less a year.

In 2019–20, students who have come from a care setting will be eligible to apply for a non-means-tested bursary of £8,100 and a grant of £105 a week for accommodation costs. This new bursary replaces the current income-assessed living cost loan and bursary (ISB/YSB) package.

Travel expenses are included within the student loan. There are *supplementary grants* available to certain categories of students such as lone parents (£1,305) and those with dependants (£2,640). Extra help is also available to those who have a disability, learning difficulty or mental health problem.

STUDENT AWARDS AGENCY FOR SCOTLAND
T 0300-555 0505 W www.saas.gov.uk

Northern Ireland
Students starting a full-time HE course in 2019–20 can apply through Student Finance Northern Ireland for financial support. The arrangements for both full-time and part-time students are similar to those for England. The main difference is that the income-assessed *maintenance grant* (or *special support grant* for students on certain income-assessed benefits) for new full-time students studying at UK universities and colleges is worth up to £3,475 (for household incomes of £19,203 or less).

Universities and colleges in Northern Ireland can charge up to £4,275 for tuition fees in academic year 2019–20, and students can get a loan for up to this amount. There are tuition fee loans of up to £9,250 for students studying in England, Scotland and Wales.

Loans are available for living costs: £3,750 for study in Northern Ireland, £4,840 for study elsewhere in the UK (£6,780 in London), £4,840 for study in the Republic of Ireland or £5,770 for study overseas.

STUDENT FINANCE NORTHERN IRELAND
T 0300-100 0077 W www.studentfinanceni.co.uk

Disabled Students' Allowances
Disabled Students' Allowances (DSAs) are grants available throughout the UK to help meet the extra course costs that full-time, part-time and postgraduate (taught or research) students can face as a direct result of a disability, ongoing health condition, mental health condition or specific learning difficulty. They help disabled people to study in HE on an equal basis with other students. They are paid on top of the standard student finance package and do not have to be repaid. The amount that an individual gets depends on the type of extra help needed, not on household income.

In all parts of the UK, the following three allowances are available: a specialist equipment or large items allowance for the entire course (2019–20 maximum rates vary from £5,266 in Northern Ireland to £5,684 in England); an annual non-medical helper allowance (2019–20 maximum rates for full-time students vary from £20,938 in Northern Ireland to £22,603 in England); and an annual general or basic allowance (2019–20 maximum rates for full-time students vary from £1,759 in Northern Ireland to £1,899 in England).

Reasonable spending on extra disability-related travel costs can also be reimbursed. Eligible individuals should apply as early as possible to the relevant UK awarding authority.

POSTGRADUATE AWARDS
In England, postgraduate loans for a master's course of £10,906 and doctoral loans of up to £25,700 are available to cover tuition and living costs for the duration of study, dependent on course, age and nationality or residency as well as other factors. Some courses such as a Postgraduate Certificate in Education (PGCE) allow students to qualify for the finance package usually available only to undergraduates. There are also bursaries available for social work and some medical students.

In Wales, Masters loans of up to £16,000 and doctoral loans of up to £25,000 are available, while in Northern Ireland up to £5,500 is available to cover course fees only. In Scotland, student support reforms now enable eligible students to receive a loan of up to £10,000 in any taught postgraduate course up to full Masters level, at any Scottish higher education institute.

A new bursary scheme has been introduced to increase the number of Welsh graduates who remain in or return to Wales to undertake a Masters degree in science, technology, engineering, mathematics, medicine, or Welsh. Welsh students starting a postgraduate course in autumn 2019 can receive up to £17,000 towards their studies and living costs. All eligible students receive a non-repayable universal grant of £1,000, a means-tested grant of up to £5,885 (for students with a household income of up to £18,370) and a loan. Part-time students are entitled to the equivalent support pro-rata. Repayments are only made once the student has finished or left their course and is earning over £21,000.

There is heavy competition for other postgraduate funding. Individuals can search for postgraduate awards and scholarships on two websites: Hot Courses and Prospects. They can also search for grants available from educational trusts, often reserved for students from poorer backgrounds or for those who have achieved academic excellence, on W www.gov.uk/grant-bursary-adult-learners or the Family Action website.

DEPARTMENT FOR THE ECONOMY (DE),
NORTHERN IRELAND T 028-9052 9900
W www.nidirect.gov.uk/articles/postgraduate-awards
FAMILY ACTION T 020-7254 6251
W www.family-action.org.uk
HOT COURSES W www.hotcourses.com
POSTGRADUATE SEARCH W www.postgraduatesearch.com
PROSPECTS W www.prospects.ac.uk
STUDENT AWARDS AGENCY FOR SCOTLAND (SAAS)
T 0300-555 0505 W www.saas.gov.uk

TEACHER TRAINING
See Professional Education/Teaching.

EMPLOYEES AND SALARIES

QUALIFIED TEACHERS IN MAINTAINED SCHOOLS
Full-time equivalent, thousands (2017–18)

	England	Wales	Scotland	NI	UK
Nursery and primary schools	*214.7	12.1	25.7	8.4	260.9
Secondary schools	*193.1	10.5	23.3	9.1	236.0
Special schools	†23.0	0.7	1.9	0.9	26.5
Total	430.8	23.3	†50.9	18.4	523.4

* Includes academies and city technology colleges in England
† Includes all centrally employed teachers

SUPPORT STAFF IN MAINTAINED SCHOOLS, ENGLAND AND WALES (2017–18)
Full-time equivalent, thousands

	England	Wales
Teaching assistants	262.8	–
Other support staff	*145.3	–
Total	*408.1	23.8

* Includes academies and city technology colleges in England

ACADEMIC STAFF IN UK HIGHER EDUCATION INSTITUTIONS (2017–18)

	Full-time	Part-time	Total
Professors	16,440	4,500	20,940
Non-professors	124,280	66,755	191,035
Teaching only	17,300	43,750	61,050
Teaching and research	81,915	18,205	100,120
Research only	40,665	8,850	49,515
Neither teaching nor research	845	445	1,290

Source: HESA 2018

SALARIES

State school teachers in England and Wales are employed by local authorities or the governing bodies of their schools. All teachers are eligible for membership of the Teachers' Pension Scheme.

There are teaching and learning responsibility payments for specific posts, special needs work and recruitment and retention factors which may be awarded at the discretion of the school governing body or the local authority. There are separate pay ranges for Headteachers and other school leaders. Academies are free to set their own salaries.

In 2013 every school was required to revise its pay and appraisal policies, setting out how pay progression would, in future, be linked to a teacher's performance. From September 2014, school governing bodies were given more flexibility, within the national pay ranges, to determine the pay of headteachers and other school leaders.

In July 2019 the Education Secretary accepted in full recommendations from the School Teachers' Review Body to raise the upper and lower boundaries of all pay ranges by 2.75 per cent from September 2019. From that date, after completing initial teacher training and achieving qualified teacher status (QTS), newly qualified teachers (NQTs) in maintained schools can expect to start on a salary of £24,373 a year in England and Wales (or £30,480 in inner London).

The pay ranges for teachers in England and Wales from September 2019 are:

Main pay range (including NQTs)	
London fringe	£25,543–£37,152
Outer London	£28,355–£40,035
Inner London	£30,480–£41,483
Rest of England and Wales	£24,373–£35,971

Upper pay range	
London fringe	£38,797–£41,635
Outer London	£41,419–£44,541
Inner London	£45,713–£49,571
Rest of England and Wales	£37,654–£40,490

The pay of school leaders in England and Wales from September 2019 ranges from £41,065 to £114,060 (Headteachers: £46,457 to £114,060) a year outside London and from £48,824 to £121,749 (Headteachers: £54,223 to £121,749) a year in inner London.

Teachers in Scotland are paid on a six-point scale where the entry point is for newly qualified teachers undertaking their probationary year. Experienced teachers who reach the top of the main pay scale are eligible to become chartered teachers and earn more on a separate pay scale. However, to do so they must study for further professional qualifications. Headteachers and deputies have a separate pay scale as do 'principals' or heads of department. Additional allowances are payable to teachers in circumstances such as working in distant islands and remote schools. The Scottish Negotiating Committee for Teachers reached agreement on a three-year pay deal (2018–21) on 25 April 2019: 3 per cent increase from April 2018, 7 per cent from April 2019 and a further 3 per cent from April 2020. Teachers received back pay for the months they worked since the beginning of the pay settlement date (ie April 2018). Salary scales for teachers in Scotland from April 2019 are:

Headteacher/deputy headteacher	£49,716–£95,931
Principal teacher	£43,836–£56,571
Chartered teacher	£41,451–£49,293
Main grade	£26,694–£40,205

Teachers in Northern Ireland have broadly similar pay scales to teachers in England and Wales. Classroom teachers who take on teaching and learning responsibilities outside their normal classroom duties may be awarded one of five teaching allowances. In July 2015 a 1 per cent increase to salary scales was announced; this increase was backdated to September 2014. A further 1 per cent pay increase was awarded from September 2016. As at 1 September 2019, salary scales in Northern Ireland remained at:

Principal (headteacher)	£43,664–£108,282
School leaders	£38,597–£42,596
Classroom teacher (upper pay scale)	£35,217–£37,870
Classroom teacher (main pay scale)	£22,243–£32,509
Unqualified teacher	£14,151
Teaching allowances	£1,903–£12,272

Since 2007, most academic staff in HE across the UK are paid on a single national pay scale as a result of a national framework agreement negotiated by the HE unions and HE institutions. Staff are paid according to rates on a 51-point national pay scale and academic and academic-related staff are graded according to a national grading structure. As HE institutions are autonomous employers, precise job grades and salaries may vary, but the following table outlines salaries that typically tally with certain job roles in HE. In 2018–19, the pay scale was as follows:

Principal lecturer	£50,132–£58,089
Senior lecturer	£39,609–£48,677
Lecturer	£33,199–£38,460
Junior researcher	£26,243–£32,236

UNIVERSITIES

The following is a list of universities, which are those institutions that have been granted degree-awarding powers by either a royal charter or an act of parliament, or have been permitted to use the word 'university' (or 'university college') by the Privy Council. There are other recognised bodies in the UK with degree-awarding powers, as well as institutions offering courses leading to a degree from a recognised body. Further information is available at W www.gov.uk/recognised-uk-degrees

Student figures represent the number of undergraduate (UG) and postgraduate (PG) students based on information available at July 2019.

Higher Education institutions in England, Wales and Northern Ireland charge tuition fees for full-time HE courses. Although students from outside the EU can be charged the full cost of their courses, the tuition fees that universities may charge undergraduate degree students from the UK and other EU countries is capped at £9,250 for 2019–20. In Scotland, tuition fees for 2019–20 are £1,820 for full-time Scottish-domiciled or EU students and capped at £9,250 for full-time students from the rest of the UK (England, Wales and Northern Ireland). In Wales, maximum tuition fees are £9,000, while in Northern Ireland they are £4,275 for resident and EU students, otherwise £9,250. For detailed information on tuition fees and student loans, including for the devolved administrations, *see* Education, Higher Education, Tuition Fees and Student Support.

RESEARCH EXCELLENCE FRAMEWORK
The research excellence framework (REF) is the system for assessing the quality of research in UK higher education institutions. The next REF assessment will be published in 2021, further information on this and the existing 2014 REF assessment can be found at W www.ref.ac.uk.

TEACHING EXCELLENCE FRAMEWORK
The teaching excellence framework (TEF) rates teaching in universities and colleges and provides information about teaching provision and student outcomes. Participation for institutions is voluntary and open to universities and colleges in England, Wales, Scotland and Northern Ireland. A list of participating institutions and their current ratings (gold, silver, bronze or provisional) can be found on the Office for Students website (W www.officeforstudents.org.uk/advice-and-guidance/teaching/tef-outcomes).

UNIVERSITY OF ABERDEEN (1495)
King's College, Aberdeen AB24 3FX T 01224-272000
W www.abdn.ac.uk
Students: 10,255 UG; 4,115 PG
Chancellor, HRH the Duchess of Rothesay, GCVO, PC
Vice-Chancellor, Prof. George Boyne
University Secretary, Caroline Inglis

UNIVERSITY OF ABERTAY DUNDEE (1994)
Bell Street, Dundee DD1 1HG T 01382-308000
W www.abertay.ac.uk
Students: 3,605 UG; 450 PG
Chancellor, Lord Cullen of Whitekirk, KT, PC, FRSE
Vice-Chancellor, Prof. Nigel Seaton, FRENG
University Secretary, Sheena Stewart

ABERYSTWYTH UNIVERSITY (1872)
Penglais, Aberystwyth SY23 3FL T 01970-62311 1
W www.aber.ac.uk
Students: 7,035 UG; 1,150 PG
Chancellor, Lord Thomas of Cwmgiedd, PC, QC
Vice-Chancellor, Prof. Elizabeth Treasure
University Secretary, Geraint Pugh

ANGLIA RUSKIN UNIVERSITY (1992)
Chelmsford Campus, Bishop Hall Lane, Chelmsford CM1 1SQ
T 01245-493131 E answers@anglia.ac.uk W www.aru.ac.uk
Students: 19,010 UG; 4,490 PG
Chancellor, Lord Ashcroft, KCMG, PC
Vice-Chancellor, Prof. Roderick Watkins
Secretary and Clerk, Paul Bogle

ARTS UNIVERSITY BOURNEMOUTH (2012)
Wallisdown BH12 5HH T 01202-533011 W www.aub.ac.uk
Students: 3,365 UG; 125 PG
Chancellor, Prof. Sir Christopher Frayling
Vice-Chancellor, Prof. Paul Gough, CBE
University Secretary, Jon Reynard

UNIVERSITY OF THE ARTS LONDON (2003 (Formerly The London Institute (1986), renamed 2004))
272 High Holborn, London WC1V 7EY T 020-7514 6000
W www.arts.ac.uk
Students: 15,120 UG; 3,850 PG
Chancellor, Grayson Perry, CBE, RA
Vice-Chancellor, Sir Nigel Carrington
Secretary and Registrar, Stephen Marshall

COLLEGES
CAMBERWELL COLLEGE OF ARTS (1898)
45–65 Peckham Road, London SE5 8UF
T 020-7514 6301
W www.arts.ac.uk/camberwell
Head of College, Prof. David Crow
CENTRAL SAINT MARTINS COLLEGE OF ART AND DESIGN (1854)
Granary Building, 1 Granary Square, London N1C 4AA
T 020-7514 7444
W www.arts.ac.uk/csm
Head of College, Prof. Jeremy Till
CHELSEA COLLEGE OF ARTS (1895)
16 John Islip Street, London SW1P 4JU
T 020-7514 7751
W www.arts.ac.uk/chelsea
Head of College, Prof. David Crow
LONDON COLLEGE OF COMMUNICATION (1894)
Elephant and Castle, London SE1 6SB
T 020-7514 6500
W www.arts.ac.uk/cc
Head of College, Natalie Brett
LONDON COLLEGE OF FASHION (1963)
20 John Prince's Street, London W1G 0BJ
T 020-7514 7400
W www.arts.ac.uk/fashion
Head of College, Prof. Frances Corner, OBE
WIMBLEDON COLLEGE OF ART (1930)
Merton Hall Road, London SW19 3QA
T 020-7514 9641
W www.arts.ac.uk/wimbledon
Head of College, Prof. David Crow

ASTON UNIVERSITY (1966)
Aston Triangle, Birmingham B4 7ET **T** 0121-204 3000
W www2.aston.ac.uk
Students: 11,850 UG; 2,765 PG
Chancellor, Sir John Sunderland
Vice-Chancellor, Prof. Alec Cameron
Chief Operating Officer, Neil Scott

BANGOR UNIVERSITY (1884)
Gwynedd LL57 2DG **T** 01248-3511 51 **W** www.bangor.ac.uk
Students: 8,455 UG; 2,700 PG
Chancellor, George Meyrick
Vice-Chancellor, Prof. Graham Upton (interim)
University Secretary, Dr Kevin Mundy

UNIVERSITY OF BATH (1966)
Bath BA2 7AY **T** 01225-388388 **W** www.bath.ac.uk
Students: 13,275 UG; 4,275 PG
Chancellor, HRH the Earl of Wessex, KG, GCVO
Vice-Chancellor, Prof. Ian White, FRENG
University Secretary, Mark Humphriss

BATH SPA UNIVERSITY (2005)
Newton Park, Bath BA2 9BN **T** 01225-875875
E enquiries@bathspa.ac.uk **W** www.bathspa.ac.uk
Students: 6,320 UG; 1,670 PG
Chancellor, Jeremy Irons
Vice-Chancellor, Prof. Sue Rigby
Registrar, Christopher Ellicott

UNIVERSITY OF BEDFORDSHIRE (1993)
University Square, Luton LU1 3JU **T** 01234-400400
W www.beds.ac.uk
Students: 10,475 UG; 2,325 PG
Chancellor, Rt. Hon. John Bercow, MP
Vice-Chancellor, Bill Rammell
Registrar, Jenny Jenkin

UNIVERSITY OF BIRMINGHAM (1900)
Edgbaston, Birmingham B15 2TT **T** 0121-414 3344
W www.birmingham.ac.uk
Students: 22,710 UG; 12,205 PG
Chancellor, Lord Bilimoria, CBE
Vice-Chancellor and Principal, Prof. Sir David Eastwood
Registrar and Secretary, Lee Sanders

BIRMINGHAM CITY UNIVERSITY (1992)
University House, 15 Bartholemew Row, Birmingham B5 5JU
T 0121-331 5000 **W** www.bcu.ac.uk
Students: 19,790 UG; 4,785 PG
Chancellor, Sir Lenny Henry, CBE
Vice-Chancellor, Prof. Philip Plowden
University Secretary, Karen Stephenson

UNIVERSITY COLLEGE BIRMINGHAM (2012)
Summer Rowe, Birmingham B3 1JB **T** 0121-604 1000
E admissions@ucb.ac.uk **W** www.ucb.ac.uk
Students: 4,425 UG; 520 PG
Vice-Chancellor and Principal, Prof. Ray Linforth, OBE

BISHOP GROSSETESTE UNIVERSITY (2013)
Longdales Road, Lincoln LN1 3DY **T** 01522-527347
E enquiries@bishopg.ac.uk **W** www.bishopg.ac.uk
Students: 1,705 UG; 550 PG
Chancellor, Dame Judith Mayhew-Jonas, DBE
Vice-Chancellor, Revd. Canon Prof. Peter Neil
Registrar and University Secretary, Dr Anne Craven

UNIVERSITY OF BOLTON (2005)
Deane Road, Bolton BL3 5AB **T** 01204-900600
E enquiries@bolton.ac.uk **W** www.bolton.ac.uk
Students: 5,340 UG; 1,205 PG
Chancellor, Earl of St Andrews
Vice-Chancellor, Prof. George E. Holmes
Registrar and Secretary, Sue Duncan, LLD

BOURNEMOUTH UNIVERSITY (1992)
Fern Barrow, Poole BH12 5BB **T** 01202-961916
E enquiries@bournemouth.ac.uk **W** www.bournemouth.ac.uk
Students: 15,420 UG; 3,265 PG
Chancellor, Kate Adie, CBE
Vice-Chancellor, Prof. John Vinney
Chief Operating Officer, Jim Andrews

UNIVERSITY OF BRADFORD (1966)
Richmond Road, Bradford BD7 1DP **T** 01274-232323
W www.bradford.ac.uk
Students: 7,695 UG; 2,420 PG
Chancellor, Kate Swann
Vice-Chancellor and Principal, Prof. Brian Cantor, CBE
University Secretary, Riley Power

UNIVERSITY OF BRIGHTON (1992)
Mithras House, Lewes Road, Brighton BN2 4AT **T** 01273-600900
W www.brighton.ac.uk
Students: 17,700 UG; 3,855 PG
Vice-Chancellor, Prof. Debra Humphris, FRCP
Secretary and Registrar, Stephen Dudderidge

UNIVERSITY OF BRISTOL (1909)
Beacon House, Queens Road, Bristol BS8 1QU **T** 0117-928 9000
W www.bristol.ac.uk
Students: 18,270 UG; 6,585 PG
Chancellor, Sir Paul Nurse, FRS, FMEDSCI
Vice-Chancellor, Prof. Hugh Brady
Registrar, Lucinda Parr

BRUNEL UNIVERSITY LONDON (1966)
Kingston Lane, Uxbridge UB8 3PH **T** 01895-274000
E admissions@brunel.ac.uk **W** www.brunel.ac.uk
Students: 10,545 UG; 3,365 PG
Chancellor, Sir Richard Sykes
Vice-Chancellor, Prof. Julia Buckingham, CBE, PHD, DSc, FRSA
Chief Operating Officer, Paul Thomas, CBE

UNIVERSITY OF BUCKINGHAM (1983)
Buckingham MK18 1EG **T** 01280-814080
E info@buckingham.ac.uk **W** www.buckingham.ac.uk
Students: 1,465 UG; 1,395 PG
Chancellor, The Hon. Lady Keswick
Vice-Chancellor, Sir Anthony Seldon, PHD, FRSA
University Secretary, Emma Potts

BUCKS NEW UNIVERSITY (2007)
High Wycombe Campus, Queen Alexandra Road, High Wycombe
HP11 2JZ **T** 01494-522141 **E** advice@bucks.ac.uk
W www.bucks.ac.uk
Students: 8,030 UG; 1,060 PG
Vice-Chancellor, Prof. Nick Braisby
Academic Registrar and Secretary, Ellie Smith

UNIVERSITY OF CAMBRIDGE (1209)
The Old Schools, Trinity Lane, Cambridge CB2 1TN
T 01223-337733 W www.cam.ac.uk
Students: 12,540 UG; 7,970 PG
Chancellor, Lord Sainsbury of Turville, FRS (King's)
Vice-Chancellor, Prof. Stephen J. Toope (Clare Hall)
High Steward, Lord Watson of Richmond, CBE (Jesus)
Deputy High Steward, Mrs A. Lonsdale, CBE (Murray
    Edwards)
Commissary, Lord Judge, PC (Magdalene)
Pro-Vice-Chancellors, Prof. G. Virgo, QC (Downing); Prof. E.
    Ferran, FBA (St Catharine's); Prof. C. Abell, FRS,
    FMEDSCI (Christ's); Prof. A. Neely (Sidney Sussex); Prof.
    D. Cardwell, FRENG (Fitzwilliam)
Proctors (2019–20), Dr Timothy Dickens (Peterhouse);
    Francis Knights (Fitzwilliam)
Deputy Proctors (2019–20), Dr Gemma Burgess (Newnham);
    Gordon Chesterman (St Edmund's)
Orator, Dr R. Thompson (Selwyn)
Registrary, E. Rampton (Sidney Sussex)
Librarian, Dr J. Gardner (Selwyn)
Director of the Fitzwilliam Museum, L. Syson
Interim Academic Secretary, Dr. R. Coupe
Director of Finance, J. Hughes (Wolfson)
Executive Director of Development, Ms A. Traub
Esquire Bedells, Mrs N. Hardy (Jesus); Ms S. Scarlett (Lucy
    Cavendish)
*University Advocate,*Dr R. Thornton (Emmanuel)
Deputy University Advocate, Dr J. Seymour (Sidney Sussex)

COLLEGES AND HALLS
(with dates of foundation)
CHRIST'S (1505)
Master, Prof. J. Stapleton, FBA
CHURCHILL (1960)
Master, Prof. Dame Athene Donald, DBE, FRS
CLARE (1326)
Master, Lord Grabiner, QC
CLARE HALL (1966)
President, Prof. D. Ibbetson, FBA
CORPUS CHRISTI (1352)
Master, Prof. C. Kelly
DARWIN (1964)
*Master,*Prof. C. Fowler, FRAS, FGS
DOWNING (1800)
Master, A. Bookbinder
EMMANUEL (1584)
Master, Dame Fiona Reynolds, DBE
FITZWILLIAM (1966)
Master, Baroness Morgan of Huyton
GIRTON (1869)
Mistress, Prof. S. Smith, FRSE FBA
GONVILLE AND CAIUS (1348)
Master, Dr. P. Rogerson
HOMERTON (1976)
Principal, Prof. G. Ward, FRSA
HUGHES HALL (1885)
President, Dr A. Freeling
JESUS (1496)
Master, Ms S. Alleyne, OBE, FRSA
KING'S (1441)
Provost, Prof. M. R. E. Proctor, FRS
LUCY CAVENDISH (1965)
President, Dame Madeleine Atkins, DBE, FACSS
MAGDALENE (1542)
Master, Rt. Revd Lord Williams of Oystermouth, PC, FBA
MURRAY EDWARDS (1954)
President, Dame Barbara Stocking, DBE

NEWNHAM (1871)
Principal, Ms A. Rose
PEMBROKE (1347)
Master, Lord Smith of Finsbury, PC
PETERHOUSE (1284)
Master, Ms Bridget Kendall, MBE
QUEENS' (1448)
President, Prof. Lord Eatwell
ROBINSON (1977)
Warden, Prof. A. D. Yates
ST CATHARINE'S (1473)
Master, Prof. Sir Mark Welland, FRS, FRENG
ST EDMUND'S (1896)
Master, Ms C. Arnold, OBE
ST JOHN'S (1511)
Master, Prof. Sir Christopher Dobson, FRS, FMEDSCI
SELWYN (1882)
Master, R. Mosey
SIDNEY SUSSEX (1596)
Master, Prof. R. V. Penty, FRENG
TRINITY (1546)
Master, Dame Sally Davies, DBE, FRS
TRINITY HALL (1350)
Master, Revd. Canon Dr J. Morris, FRHISTS
WOLFSON (1965)
President, Prof. J. Clarke, FRS, FMEDSCI

CANTERBURY CHRIST CHURCH UNIVERSITY (2005)
North Holmes Road, Canterbury CT1 1QU T 01227-767700
E admissions@canterbury.co.uk W www.canterbury.ac.uk
Students: 11,765 UG; 2,690 PG
Chancellor, Most Revd and Rt. Hon. Archbishop of Canterbury
Vice-Chancellor, Prof. Rama Thirunamachandran
Director of Academic Administration, Cathy Lambert

CARDIFF UNIVERSITY (1883)
Cardiff CF10 3AT T 029-2087 4000 W www.cardiff.ac.uk
Students: 23,480 UG; 8,455 PG
Chancellor, Baroness Randerson
Vice-Chancellor, Prof. Colin Riordan
Chief Operating Officer, Deborah Collins

CARDIFF METROPOLITAN UNIVERSITY (1865)
Western Avenue, Cardiff CF5 2YB T 029-2041 6070
W www.cardiffmet.ac.uk
Students: 8,330 UG; 2,100 PG
President and Vice-Chancellor, Prof. Cara Carmichael Aitchison,
    FACSS, FRGS, FHEA
Chief Operating Officer, John Cappock

UNIVERSITY OF CENTRAL LANCASHIRE (1992)
Preston PR1 2HE T 01772-201201 E cenquiries@uclan.ac.uk
W www.uclan.ac.uk
Students: 18,020 UG; 4,980 PG
Chancellor, Ranvir Singh
Vice-Chancellor, Lynne Livesey (interim)
University Secretary, Ian Fisher

UNIVERSITY OF CHESTER (Founded in 1839 as Chester
Diocesan Training College; gained University status in
2005)
Parkgate Road, Chester CH1 4BJ T 01244-511000
E enquiries@chester.ac.uk W www.chester.ac.uk
Students: 10,945 UG; 4,465 PG
Chancellor, Gyles Brandreth
Vice-Chancellor, Canon Prof. Tim Wheeler
University Secretary, Adrian Lee

UNIVERSITY OF CHICHESTER (2005)
College Lane, Chichester PO19 6PE T 01243-816000
E help@chi.ac.uk W www.chi.ac.uk
Students: 4,465 UG; 1,055 PG
Vice-Chancellor, Prof. Jane Longmore
University Secretary, Sophie Egleton

COVENTRY UNIVERSITY (1992)
Priory Street, Coventry CV1 5FB T 024-7688 7688
W www.coventry.ac.uk
Students: 27,895 UG; 6,230 PG
Chancellor, Margaret Casely-Hayford
Vice-Chancellor, Prof. John Latham
Academic Registrar, Kate Quantrell

CRANFIELD UNIVERSITY (1969)
Cranfield MK43 0AL T 01234-750111 E info@cranfield.ac.uk
W www.cranfield.ac.uk
Students: 4,355 PG (postgraduate only)
Chancellor, Baroness Young of Old Scone
Vice-Chancellor, Prof. Sir Peter Gregson
University Secretary, Gregor Douglas

UNIVERSITY FOR THE CREATIVE ARTS (2008)
Falkner Road, Farnham GU9 7DS T 01252-722441
W www.uca.ac.uk
Students: 6,260 UG; 360 PG
Chancellor, Prof. Magdalene Odundo, OBE
Vice-Chancellor, Prof. Bashir Makhoul
University Secretary, Marion Wilks

UNIVERSITY OF CUMBRIA (2007)
Fusehill Street, Carlisle CA1 2HH T 01228-616234
W www.cumbria.ac.uk
Students: 5,860 UG; 1,720 PG
Chancellor, Most Revd and Rt. Hon. Archbishop of York
Vice-Chancellor, Prof. Julie Mennell
Registrar and Secretary, Jean Brown

DE MONTFORT UNIVERSITY (1992)
The Gateway, Leicester LE1 9BH T 0116-255 1551
E enquiry@dmu.ac.uk W www.dmu.ac.uk
Students: 20,855 UG; 4,845 PG
Chancellor, Baroness Lawrence of Clarendon, OBE
Vice-Chancellor, Prof. Andy Collop (interim)

UNIVERSITY OF DERBY (1992)
Kedleston Road, Derby DE22 1GB T 01332-590500
E askadmissions@derby.ac.uk W www.derby.ac.uk
Students: 14,595 UG; 3,895 PG
Chancellor, Earl of Burlington
Vice-Chancellor and Principal, Prof. Kathryn Mitchell
Registrar, June Hughes

UNIVERSITY OF DUNDEE (1967)
Nethergate, Dundee DD1 4HN T 01382-383000
W www.dundee.ac.uk
Students: 10,715 UG; 4,390 PG
Chancellor, Dame Jocelyn Bell Burnell, DBE, FRS, FRSE, FRAS
Vice-Chancellor and Principal, Prof. Andrew Atherton
University Secretary, Dr James McGeorge

DURHAM UNIVERSITY (1832)
The Palatine Centre, Stockton Road, Durham DH1 3LE
T 0191-334 2000 W www.dur.ac.uk
Students: 13,835 UG; 4,495 PG
Chancellor, Sir Thomas Allen, CBE
Vice-Chancellor, Prof. Stuart Corbridge
University Secretary, Jennifer Sewel

COLLEGES
COLLINGWOOD (1972)
Principal, Prof. J. Elliott

GREY (1959)
Master, Prof. T. Allen
HATFIELD (1846)
Master, Prof. A. M. MacLarnon
JOHN SNOW (2001)
Principal, Prof. C. Summerbell
JOSEPHINE BUTLER (2006)
Principal, A. Simpson
ST AIDAN'S (1947)
Principal, S. F. Frenk
ST CHAD'S (1904)
Principal, M. Masson
ST CUTHBERT'S SOCIETY (1888)
Principal, Prof. E. Archibald
ST HILD AND ST BEDE (1839)
Principal, Prof. S. Forrest
ST JOHN'S (1909)
Principal, Revd Dr D. Wilkinson
ST MARY'S (1899)
Principal, Prof. M. Dawn
SOUTH (2020)
Principal, Prof. T. Luckhurst
STEPHENSON (2001)
Principal, Prof. R. Lynes
TREVELYAN (1966)
Principal, Prof. A. Adeyeye
UNIVERSITY (1832)
Master, Dr R. Lawrie (acting)
USTINOV (2003)
Principal, S. Prescott (acting)
VAN MILDERT (1965)
Principal, Prof. D. Harper

UNIVERSITY OF EAST ANGLIA (1963)
Norwich Research Park, Norwich NR4 7TJ T 01603-456161
E admissions@uea.ac.uk W www.uea.ac.uk
Students: 12,985 UG; 4,970 PG
Chancellor, Karen Jones, CBE
Vice-Chancellor, Prof. David Richardson

UNIVERSITY OF EAST LONDON (1898)
University Way, London E16 2RD T 020-8223 3000
E study@uel.ac.uk W www.uel.ac.uk
Students: 9,695 UG; 3,390 PG
Chancellor, Shabir Randeree, CBE
Vice-Chancellor, Prof. Amanda Broderick
University Secretary, Tristan Foote (acting)

EDGE HILL UNIVERSITY (2006)
St Helens Road, Ormskirk L39 4QP T 01695-575171
W www.edgehill.ac.uk
Students: 11,050 UG; 3,205 PG
Chancellor, Prof. Tanya Byron
Vice-Chancellor, Dr John Cater, CBE
University Secretary, Lynda Brady

UNIVERSITY OF EDINBURGH (1583)
Old College, South Bridge, Edinburgh EH8 9YL T 0131-650 1000
E communications.office@ed.ac.uk W www.ed.ac.uk
Students: 22,095 UG; 10,795 PG
Chancellor, HRH the Princess Royal, KG, KT, GCVO
Vice-Chancellor and Principal, Prof. Peter Mathieson, FRCP, FRCPE
University Secretary, Sarah Smith

EDINBURGH NAPIER UNIVERSITY (1992)
Sighthill Campus, Edinburgh EH11 4BN T 0333-900 6040
W www.napier.ac.uk
Students: 10,280 UG; 2,830 PG
Chancellor, David Eustace
Vice-Chancellor, Prof. Andrea Nolan, OBE
Secretary, David Cloy

UNIVERSITY OF ESSEX (1965)
Wivenhoe Park, Colchester CO4 3SQ **T** 01206-873333
E admit@essex.ac.uk **W** www.essex.ac.uk
Students: 11,370 UG; 3,390 PG
Chancellor, Rt. Hon. John Bercow, MP
Vice-Chancellor, Prof. Anthony Forster, DPHIL
Registrar, Bryn Morris

UNIVERSITY OF EXETER (1955)
Stocker Road, Exeter EX4 4PY **T** 01392-661000
W www.exeter.ac.uk
Students: 18,480 UG; 5,565 PG
Chancellor, Lord Myners, CBE
Vice-Chancellor, Prof. Sir Steve Smith, FACSS
Registrar and Secretary, Mike Shore-Nye

FALMOUTH UNIVERSITY (2012)
Falmouth Campus, Woodlane, Falmouth TR11 4RH
T 01326-211077 **W** www.falmouth.ac.uk
Students: 5,605 UG; 400 PG
Chancellor, Dawn French
Vice-Chancellor, Prof. Anne Carlisle, OBE

UNIVERSITY OF GLASGOW (1451)
University Avenue, Glasgow G12 8QQ **T** 0141-330 2000
E student.recruitment@glasgow.ac.uk **W** www.gla.ac.uk
Students: 20,805 UG; 8,920 PG
Chancellor, Prof. Sir Kenneth Calman, KCB, FRCS, FRSE
Vice-Chancellor, Prof. Sir Anton Muscatelli, FRSE, FACSS
Registrar, David Bennion

GLASGOW CALEDONIAN UNIVERSITY (1993)
City Campus, Cowcaddens Road, Glasgow G4 0BA
T 0141-331 3000 **E** ukroenquiries@gcu.ac.uk **W** www.gcu.ac.uk
Students: 13,575 UG; 2,875 PG
Chancellor, Annie Lennox, OBE
Vice-Chancellor, Prof. Pamela Gillies, CBE, FRSE
University Secretary, Jan Hulme

UNIVERSITY OF GLOUCESTERSHIRE (2001)
The Park, Cheltenham GL50 2RH **T** 03330-141414
E admissions@glos.ac.uk **W** www.glos.ac.uk
Students: 7,080 UG; 1,415 PG
Chancellor, Baroness Fritchie, DBE
Vice-Chancellor, Stephen Marston
Secretary and Registrar, Dr Matthew Andrews

UNIVERSITY OF GREENWICH (1992)
Old Royal Naval College, Park Row, London SE10 9LS
T 020-8331 8000 **E** courseinfo@gre.ac.uk **W** www.gre.ac.uk
Students: 14,740 UG; 4,065 PG
Chancellor, Lord Boateng, PC, QC
Vice-Chancellor, Prof. David Maguire
Secretary, Peter Garrod

HARPER ADAMS UNIVERSITY (2012)
Newport TF10 8NB **T** 01952-820280
E admissions@harper-adams.ac.uk **W** www.harper-adams.ac.uk
Students: 4,805 UG; 505 PG
Chancellor, HRH the Princess Royal, KG, KT, GCVO
Vice-Chancellor, David Llewellyn
University Secretary, Dr Catherine Baxter

HARTPURY UNIVERSITY AND COLLEGE (2017)
Hartpury House, Gloucester GL19 3BE **T** 0
E admissions@hartpury.ac.uk **W** www.hartpury.ac.uk
Students: 1,800
Vice-Chancellor and Chief Executive, Russell Marchant
Vice-Principal and Deputy Chief Executive, Lynn Forrester-Walker

HERIOT-WATT UNIVERSITY (1966)
Edinburgh EH14 4AS **T** 0131-449 5111 **E** enquiries@hw.ac.uk
W www.hw.ac.uk
Students: 7660 UG; 3,250 PG
Chancellor, Dr Robert Buchan
Vice-Chancellor, Prof. Richard A. Williams, OBE, FRSE, FRENG
University Secretary, Ann Marie Dalton-Pillay

UNIVERSITY OF HERTFORDSHIRE (1992)
Hatfield AL10 9AB **T** 01707-284000 **W** www.herts.ac.uk
Students: 18,840 UG; 5,565 PG
Chancellor, Marquess of Salisbury, KG, KCVO, PC
Vice-Chancellor, Prof. Quintin McKellar, CBE
Secretary and Registrar, Sue Grant

UNIVERSITY OF THE HIGHLANDS AND ISLANDS (2011)
Ness Walk, Inverness IV3 5SQ **T** 01463-279190 **W** www.uhi.ac.uk
Students: 8,470 UG; 850 PG
Chancellor, HRH the Princess Royal, KG, KT, GCVO
Vice-Chancellor, Prof. Crichton Lang (interim)
Chief Operating Officer, Fiona Larg

UNIVERSITY OF HUDDERSFIELD (1992)
Queensgate, Huddersfield HD1 3DH **T** 01484-422288
W www.hud.ac.uk
Students: 14,165 UG; 4,080 PG
Chancellor, HRH the Duke of York, KG, GCVO, ADC(P)
Vice-Chancellor, Prof. Bob Cryan, CBE, DL, FRENG
University Secretary, Michaela Boryslawskyj

UNIVERSITY OF HULL (1927)
Cottingham Road, Hull HU6 7RX **T** 01482-346311
W www.hull.ac.uk
Students: 13,390 UG; 2,200 PG
Chancellor, Baroness Bottomley of Nettlestone, PC
Vice-Chancellor, Prof. Susan Lea, PHD
Registrar, Jeanette Strachan

IMPERIAL COLLEGE LONDON (1907)
South Kensington SW7 2AZ **T** 020-7589 5111
W www.imperial.ac.uk
Students: 9,730 UG; 8,645 PG
President, Prof. Alice Gast
Provost, Prof. Ian Walmsley, FRS
Secretary and Registrar, David Ashton

KEELE UNIVERSITY (1962)
Keele ST5 5BG **T** 01782-732000 **E** admissions@keele.ac.uk
W www.keele.ac.uk
Students: 8,510 UG; 2,360 PG
Chancellor, Sir Jonathon Porritt, CBE
Vice-Chancellor, Prof. Trevor McMillan
Academic Registrar, Dr Helen Galbraith

UNIVERSITY OF KENT (1965)
Canterbury CT2 7NZ **T** 01227-764000 **E** information@kent.ac.uk
W www.kent.ac.uk
Students: 15,905 UG; 3,920 PG
Chancellor, Gavin Esler
Vice-Chancellor & Principal, Prof. Karen Cox
Provost, David Nightingale

KINGSTON UNIVERSITY (1992)
River House, 53–57 High Street, Kingston upon Thames KT1 1LQ
T 020-8417 9000 **E** admissionsops@kingston.ac.uk
W www.kingston.ac.uk
Students: 13,625 UG; 4,010 PG
Chancellor, Bonnie Greer, OBE
Vice-Chancellor, Prof. Stephen Spier
University Secretary, Keith Brennan

UNIVERSITY OF LANCASTER (1964)
Bailrigg, Lancaster LA1 4YW T 01524-65201
W www.lancaster.ac.uk
Students: 10,220 UG; 3,990 PG
Chancellor, Rt. Hon. Alan Milburn
Vice-Chancellor, Prof. Mark E. Smith, PHD
University Secretary, Nicola Owen

UNIVERSITY OF LEEDS (1904)
Leeds LS2 9JT T 0113-243 1751 W www.leeds.ac.uk
Students: 25,430 UG; 8,990 PG
Chancellor, Prof. Dame Jane Francis, DCMG
Vice-Chancellor, Sir Alan Langlands
University Secretary, Roger Gair

LEEDS ARTS UNIVERSITY (2017)
Blenheim Walk, Leeds LS2 9AQ T 0113-202 8000
W www.leeds-art.ac.uk
Students: 1,570 UG; 35 PG
Vice-Chancellor, Prof. Simone Wonnacott

LEEDS BECKETT UNIVERSITY (1992)
City Campus, Leeds LS1 3HE T 0113-812 0000
W www.leedsbeckett.ac.uk
Students: 18,615 UG; 4,955 PG
Chancellor, Sir Bob Murray, CBE
Vice-Chancellor, Prof. Peter Slee
Secretary and Registrar, Jenny Share

LEEDS TRINITY UNIVERSITY (2012)
Brownberrie Lane, Leeds LS18 5HD T 0113-283 7100
E hello@leedstrinity.ac.uk W www.leedstrinity.ac.uk
Students: 2,725 UG; 640 PG
Chancellor, Deborah McAndrew
Vice-Chancellor, Prof. Margaret House, OBE
Chief Operating Officer, Phill Dixon

UNIVERSITY OF LEICESTER (1957)
University Road, Leicester LE1 7RH T 0116-252 2522
W www.le.ac.uk
Students: 12,555 UG; 4,855 PG
Chancellor, Lord Willets, PC
Vice-Chancellor, Prof. E Burke (acting)
Registrar, David Hall

UNIVERSITY OF LINCOLN (1992)
Brayford Pool, Lincoln LN6 7TS T 01522-882000
E enquiries@lincoln.ac.uk W www.lincoln.ac.uk
Students: 12,645 UG; 2,325 PG
Chancellor, Lord Adebowale, CBE
Vice-Chancellor, Prof. Mary Stuart, CBE
Registrar, Chris Spendlove

UNIVERSITY OF LIVERPOOL (1903)
Brownlow Hill, Liverpool L69 7ZX T 0151-794 2000
W www.liverpool.ac.uk
Students: 22,070 UG; 6,725 PG
Chancellor, Colm Tóibín
Vice-Chancellor, Prof. Dame Janet Beer, DBE

LIVERPOOL HOPE UNIVERSITY (2005)
Hope Park, Liverpool L16 9JD T 0151-291 3000
E enquiry@hope.ac.uk W www.hope.ac.uk
Students: 3,910 UG; 1,290 PG
Chancellor, Lord Guthrie of Craigiebank, GCB, LVO, OBE
Vice-Chancellor and Rector, Prof. Gerald Pillay
University Secretary, Graham Donelan

LIVERPOOL JOHN MOORES UNIVERSITY (1992)
Kingsway House, 2nd Floor, Hatton Garden, Liverpool L3 2QP
T 0151-231 2121 E courses@ljmu.ac.uk W www.ljmu.ac.uk
Students: 18,875 UG; 4,350 PG
Chancellor, Rt. Hon. Sir Brian Leveson
Vice-Chancellor, Mark Power
Registrar, Liz McGough

UNIVERSITY OF LONDON (1836)
Senate House, Malet Street, London WC1E 7HU T 020-7862 8000
W www.london.ac.uk
Chancellor, HRH the Princess Royal, KG, KT, GCVO
Vice-Chancellor, Prof. Wendy Thomson, CBE
University Secretary, Chris Cobb

COLLEGES
BIRKBECK
Malet Street, London WC1E 7HX
Students: 7,155 UG; 4,785 PG
President, Baroness Bakewell, DBE
Master, Prof. David Latchman, CBE
CITY
Northampton Square, London EC1V 0HB
Students: 10,640 UG; 9,140 PG
President, Prof. Sir Paul Curran
COURTAULD INSTITUTE OF ART
Somerset House, Strand, London WC2R 0RN
Students: 205 UG; 300 PG
Director, Prof. Deborah Swallow
GOLDSMITHS
New Cross, London SE14 6NW
Students, 6,545 UG; 3,455 PG
Warden, Patrick Loughrey
INSTITUTE OF CANCER RESEARCH
15 Cotswold Road, Sutton, Surrey SM2 5NG
Students: 290 PG (postgraduate only)
Chief Executive, Prof. Paul Workman
KING'S COLLEGE LONDON
(includes Guy's, King's and St Thomas's Schools of
Medicine, Dentistry and Biomedical Sciences)
Strand, London WC2R 2LS
Students: 18,925 UG; 13,345 PG
Principal, Prof. Edward Byrne
LONDON BUSINESS SCHOOL
Regent's Park, London NW1 4SA
Students: 1,915 PG (postgraduate only)
Dean, François Ortalo-Magné
LONDON SCHOOL OF ECONOMICS AND POLITICAL
SCIENCE
Houghton Street, London WC2A 2AE
Students: 4,835 UG; 6,790 PG
Director, Dame Minouche Shafik, DBE
LONDON SCHOOL OF HYGIENE AND TROPICAL
MEDICINE
Keppel Street, London WC1E 7HT
Students: 1,085 PG (postgraduate only)
Director, Prof. Baron Peter Piot, KCMG, MD, PHD
QUEEN MARY'S
(incorporating St Bartholomew's and the London School of
Medicine and Dentistry)
Mile End Road, London E1 4NS
Students: 13,935 UG; 6,135 PG
Principal, Prof. Colin Bailey
ROYAL ACADEMY OF MUSIC
Marylebone Road, London NW1 5HT
Students: 415 UG; 430 PG
Principal, Prof. Jonathan Freeman-Attwood, CBE
ROYAL CENTRAL SCHOOL OF SPEECH AND DRAMA
Eton Avenue, London NW3 3HY
Students: 685 UG; 405 PG
Principal, Prof. Gavin Henderson, CBE
ROYAL HOLLOWAY
Egham Hill, Egham, Surrey TW20 0EX
Students: 7,725 UG; 2,835 PG
Principal, Prof. Paul Layzell

ROYAL VETERINARY COLLEGE
Royal College Street, London NW1 0TU
Students: 1,995 UG; 545 PG
Principal, Prof. Stuart Reid
SOAS
Thornhaugh Street, Russell Square, London WC1H 0XG
Students: 3,155 UG; 3,115 PG
Director, Baroness Amos, CH, PC
ST GEORGE'S
Cranmer Terrace, London SW17 0RE
Students: 3,935 UG; 1,035 PG
Principal, Prof. Jenny Higham
UCL
(including the Institute of Neurology, Eastman Dental
Institute, School of Pharmacy and Institute of Education)
Gower Street, London WC1E 6BT
Students: 19,705 UG; 20,310 PG
Provost and President, Prof. Michael Arthur, FRCP, FMEDSCI
UNIVERSITY OF LONDON INSTITUTE IN PARIS
9–11 rue de Constantine, 75340 Paris Cedex 07, France
Chief Executive, Dr Tim Gore, OBE

INSTITUTES
SCHOOL OF ADVANCED STUDY
Senate House, Malet Street, London WC1H 0XG
Dean and Chief Executive, Prof. Rick Rylance
The school consists of nine institutes:
INSTITUTE OF ADVANCED LEGAL STUDIES
Charles Clore House, 17 Russell Square, London WC1B 5DR
Director, Prof. Carl Stychin
INSTITUTE OF CLASSICAL STUDIES
Senate House, Malet Street, London WC1E 7HU
Director, Prof. Greg Woolf, FSA
INSTITUTE OF COMMONWEALTH STUDIES
Senate House, Malet Street, London WC1E 7HU
Director, Prof. Philip Murphy
INSTITUTE OF ENGLISH STUDIES
Senate House, Malet Street, London WC1E 7HU
Director, Prof. Clare A. Lees
INSTITUTE OF HISTORICAL RESEARCH
Senate House, Malet Street, London WC1E 7HU
Director, Prof. Jo Fox
INSTITUTE OF LATIN AMERICAN STUDIES
Senate House, Malet Street, London WC1E 7HU
Director, Prof. Linda Newson, OBE
INSTITUTE OF MODERN LANGUAGES RESEARCH
Senate House, Malet Street, London WC1E 7HU
Director, Prof. Catherine Davies
INSTITUTE OF PHILOSOPHY
Senate House, Malet Street, London WC1E 7HU
Director, Prof. Barry Smith
THE WARBURG INSTITUTE
Woburn Square, London WC1H 0AB
Director, Prof. Bill Sherman

LONDON METROPOLITAN UNIVERSITY (2002)
166–220 Holloway Road, London N7 8DB **T** 020-7423 0000
W www.londonmet.ac.uk
Students: 7,920 UG; 2,375 PG
Patron, HRH the Duke of York, KG, GCVO, ADC(P)
Vice-Chancellor, Prof. Lynn Dobbs
University Secretary, Chris Ince

LONDON SOUTH BANK UNIVERSITY (1992)
103 Borough Road, London SE1 0AA **T** 020-7815 7815
E course.enquiry@lsbu.ac.uk **W** www.lsbu.ac.uk
Students: 12,320 UG; 4,810 PG
Chancellor, Sir Simon Hughes, PC
Vice-Chancellor, Prof. David Phoenix
University Secretary, James Stevenson

LOUGHBOROUGH UNIVERSITY (1966)
Epinal Way, Loughborough LE11 3TU **T** 01509-222222
W www.lboro.ac.uk
Students: 13,110 UG; 4,205 PG
Chancellor, Lord Coe, CH, OBE
Vice-Chancellor, Prof. Robert Allison
Chief Operating Officer, Richard Taylor

UNIVERSITY OF MANCHESTER (2004. Formed by the
amalgamation of Victoria University of Manchester (1851;
reorganised 1880 and 1903) and the University of
Manchester Institute of Science and Technology (1824))
Oxford Road, Manchester M13 9PL **T** 0161-306 6000
W www.manchester.ac.uk
Students: 27,505 UG; 12,640 PG
Chancellor, Lemn Sissay, MBE
Vice-Chancellor, Prof. Dame Nancy Rothwell, DBE, FRS
Secretary and Registrar, Patrick Hackett

MANCHESTER METROPOLITAN UNIVERSITY (1992)
All Saints, Manchester M15 6BH **T** 0161-247 2000
W www2.mmu.ac.uk
Students: 26,605 UG; 6,475 PG
Chancellor, Lord Mandelson, PC
Vice-Chancellor, Prof. Malcolm Press
Chief Operating Officer, Prof. Karen Moore

MIDDLESEX UNIVERSITY (1992)
Hendon Campus, London NW4 4BT **T** 020-8411 5555
W www.mdx.ac.uk
Students: 14,920 UG; 4,770 PG
Chancellor, Dame Janet Ritterman, DBE
Vice-Chancellor, Prof. Tim Blackman
Chief Operating Officer, Sophie Bowen, PHD

NEWCASTLE UNIVERSITY (1963)
Newcastle upon Tyne NE1 7RU **T** 0191-208 6000
W www.ncl.ac.uk
Students: 19,860 UG; 6,615 PG
Chancellor, Prof. Sir Liam Donaldson
Vice-Chancellor, Prof. Chris Day, FRS, DPHIL
Registrar, Dr. John Hogan

NEWMAN UNIVERSITY, BIRMINGHAM (2013)
Genners Lane, Birmingham B32 3NT **T** 0121-476 1181
E admissions@newman.ac.uk **W** www.newman.ac.uk
Students: 2,220 UG; 540 PG
Vice-Chancellor, Prof. Scott Davidson
Secretary and Registrar, Andrea Bolshaw

UNIVERSITY OF NORTHAMPTON (2005)
Waterside Campus, University Drive, Northampton NN1 5PH
T 01604-735500 **E** bc.applicationservices@northumbria.ac.uk
W www.northampton.ac.uk
Students: 9,655 UG; 2,310 PG
Chancellor, Revd Richard Coles
Vice-Chancellor, Prof. Nick Petford, PHD, DSc
Chief Operating Officer, Terry Neville, OBE

NORTHUMBRIA UNIVERSITY AT NEWCASTLE (1992)
Ellison Building, Ellison Place, Newcastle upon Tyne NE1 8ST
T 0191-232 6002 **E** course.enquiries@northumbria.ac.uk
W www.northumbria.ac.uk
Students: 21,150 UG; 5,495 PG
Chancellor, Baroness Grey-Thompson, DBE
Vice-Chancellor, Prof. Andrew Wathey, CBE, DPHIL

NORWICH UNIVERSITY OF THE ARTS (2012)
Francis House, 3–7 Redwell Street, Norwich NR2 4SN
T 01603-610561 **E** info@nua.ac.uk **W** www.nua.ac.uk
Students: 2,115 UG; 105 PG
Vice-Chancellor, Prof. John Last, OBE, FRSA
Academic Registrar, Angela Tubb

UNIVERSITY OF NOTTINGHAM (1948)
University Park, Nottingham NG7 2RD T 0115-951 5151
W www.nottingham.ac.uk
Students: 24,605 UG; 8,495 PG
Chancellor, Sir Andrew Witty
Vice-Chancellor, Prof. Shearer West
Registrar, Dr Paul Greatrix

NOTTINGHAM TRENT UNIVERSITY (1992)
50 Shakespeare Street, Nottingham NG1 4FQ T 0115-941 8418
W www.ntu.ac.uk
Students: 24,520 UG; 6,370 PG
Chancellor, Sir John Peace
Vice-Chancellor, Prof. Edward Peck
Chief Operating Officer, Steve Denton

OPEN UNIVERSITY (1969)
Walton Hall, Milton Keynes MK7 6AA T 0300-303 5303
W www.open.ac.uk
Students: 108,990 UG; 8,945 PG
Chancellor, Baroness Lane-Fox of Soho, CBE
Acting Vice-Chancellor, Prof. Mary Kellett
University Secretary, Dr Jonathan Nicholls

UNIVERSITY OF OXFORD (c.12th century)
University Offices, Wellington Square, Oxford OX1 2JD
T 01865-270000 E information.office@admin.ox.ac.uk
W www.ox.ac.uk
Students: 14,640 UG; 10,275 PG
Chancellor, Lord Patten of Barnes, CH, PC (Balliol, St Antony's)
Vice-Chancellor, Prof. Louise Richardson, FRSE
Pro-Vice-Chancellors, Dr D. Prout, CB (Queen's); Prof. M.
    Williams (New College); Dr R. Easton (New College);
    Prof. A. Trefethen (St Cross); Prof. Chas Bountra
    (Merton); Prof. P.S. Grant (St Catherine's)
Registrar, G. Aitken
Academic Registrar, Dr S. Shaikh
Public Orator, Dr J. Katz (All Souls)
Director of University Library Services and Bodley's Librarian, R.
    Ovenden (Balliol)
Director of the Ashmolean Museum, Dr A. Sturgis (Worcester)
Director of the Museum of the History of Science, Dr S.
    Ackermann (Linacre)
Director of the Pitt Rivers Museum, Dr L. Van Broekhoven
    (Linacre)
Director of the University Museum of Natural History, Prof. P.
    Smith (Kellogg)
Chief Executive of Oxford University Press, N. Portwood (Exeter)
Keeper of Archives, S. Bailey (Linacre)
Director of Estates, P. Goffin (Jesus)
Director of Finance, L. Pearson (New College)

COLLEGES AND HALLS *(with dates of foundation)*
ALL SOULS (1438)
Warden, Prof. Sir John Vickers, FBA
BALLIOL (1263)
Master, Dame Helen Ghosh, DCB
BLACKFRIARS HALL (1221)
Regent, Very Revd Dr Simon Gaine, OP
BRASENOSE (1509)
Principal, John Bowers, QC
CAMPION HALL (1896)
Master, Revd James Hanvey
CHRIST CHURCH (1546)
Dean, Very Revd Prof. Martyn Percy
CORPUS CHRISTI (1517)
President, Dr Helen Moore
EXETER (1314)
Rector, Prof. Sir Rick Trainor, KBE
GREEN TEMPLETON (2008)
Principal, Prof. Denise Lievesley, CBE

HARRIS MANCHESTER (1889)
Principal, Very Revd Prof. Jane Shaw
HERTFORD (1740)
Principal, Will Hutton
JESUS (1571)
Principal, Prof. Sir Nigel Shadbolt, FRS, FREng
KEBLE (1870)
Warden, Sir Jonathan Phillips, KCB
KELLOGG (1990)
President, Prof. Jonathan M. Michie
LADY MARGARET HALL (1878)
Principal, Alan Rusbridger
LINACRE (1962)
Principal, Dr Nick Brown
LINCOLN (1427)
Rector, Prof. Henry Woudhuysen, FBA
MAGDALEN (1458)
President, Prof. Sir David Clary, FRS
MANSFIELD (1886)
Principal, Helen Mountfield, QC
MERTON (1264)
Warden, Prof. Irene Tracey, FMedSci
NEW COLLEGE (1379)
Warden, Miles Young
NUFFIELD (1958)
Warden, Sir Andrew Dilnot, CBE
ORIEL (1326)
Provost, Neil Mendoza
PEMBROKE (1624)
Master, Dame Lynne Brindley, DBE, FRSA
QUEEN'S (1341)
Provost, Prof. Paul Madden, FRS, FRSE
REGENT'S PARK COLLEGE (1810)
Principal, Revd Dr Robert Ellis
ST ANNE'S (1878)
Principal, Helen King, QPM
ST ANTONY'S (1953)
Warden, Prof. Roger Goodman
ST BENET'S HALL (1897)
Master, Prof. Richard Cooper
ST CATHERINE'S (1963)
Master, Prof. Peter Battle
ST CROSS (1965)
Master, Carole Souter, CBE
ST EDMUND HALL (C. 1278)
Principal, Prof. Katherine Willis, CBE
ST HILDA'S (1893)
Principal, Prof. Sir Gordon Duff, FRCP, FRSE, FMedSci
ST HUGH'S (1886)
Principal, Dame Elish Angiolini, PC, DBE, QC
ST JOHN'S (1555)
President, Prof. Margaret J. Snowling, FBA, CBE
ST PETER'S (1929)
Principal, Mark Damazer, CBE
ST STEPHEN'S HOUSE (1876)
Principal, Revd Canon Dr Robin Ward
SOMERVILLE (1879)
Principal, Baroness Royall of Blaisdon, PC
TRINITY (1554)
President, Dame Hilary Boulding, DBE
UNIVERSITY (1249)
Master, Sir Ivor Crewe
WADHAM (1610)
Warden, Lord Macdonald of River Glaven, QC
WOLFSON (1981)
President, Sir Tim Hitchens, KCVO, CMG

WORCESTER (1714)
Provost, Prof. Sir Jonathan Bate, CBE, FBA, FRSL

WYCLIFFE HALL (1877)
Principal, Revd Michael Lloyd

OXFORD BROOKES UNIVERSITY (1992)
Gipsy Lane, Oxford OX3 0BP **T** 01865-741111
E query@brookes.ac.uk **W** www.brookes.ac.uk
Students: 13,120 UG; 4,055 PG
Chancellor, Dame Dr Katherine Grainger, DBE
Vice-Chancellor, Prof. Alistair Fitt
Registrar, Brendan Casey

UNIVERSITY OF PLYMOUTH (1992)
Drake Circus, Plymouth PL4 8AA **T** 01752-600600
E admissions@plymouth.ac.uk **W** www.plymouth.ac.uk
Students: 17,740 UG; 3,030 PG
Chancellor, Lord Kestenbaum
Vice-Chancellor, Prof. Judith Petts, CBE
University Secretary, Gordon Stewart

PLYMOUTH MARJON UNIVERSITY (2012)
Derriford Road, Plymouth PL6 8BH **T** 01752-636700
E admissions@marjon.ac.uk **W** www.marjon.ac.uk
Students: 2,140 UG; 495 PG
Vice-Chancellor, Prof. Rob Warner
Registrar, Stephen Plant

UNIVERSITY OF PORTSMOUTH (1992)
University House, Winston Churchill Avenue, Portsmouth PO1 2UP
T 023-9284 8484 **E** info@port.ac.uk **W** www.port.ac.uk
Students: 20,305 UG; 4,090 PG
Chancellor, Karen Blackett, OBE
Vice-Chancellor, Prof. Graham Galbraith, PHD
Chief Operating Officer, Bernie Topham

QUEEN MARGARET UNIVERSITY (2007)
Edinburgh EH21 6UU **T** 0131-474 0000 **W** www.qmu.ac.uk
Students: 3,430 UG; 1,745 PG
Chancellor, Prue Leith, CBE
Vice-Chancellor, Sir Paul Grice, FRSE
Secretary, Prof. Irene Hynd

QUEEN'S UNIVERSITY BELFAST (1908)
University Road, Belfast BT7 1NN **T** 028-9024 5133
E comms.office@qub.ac.uk **W** www.qub.ac.uk
Students: 18,630 UG; 5,855 PG
Chancellor, vacant
Vice-Chancellor, Prof. Ian Greer, FRCP,
Registrar, Joanne Clague

RAVENSBOURNE UNIVERSITY LONDON (2018)
Greenwich Peninsula, 6 Penrose Way, London SE10 0EW
T 020-3040 3500 **W** www.ravensbourne.ac.uk
Students: 2,475 UG; 55 PG
Interim Director and Chief Operating Officer, Andy Cook

UNIVERSITY OF READING (1926)
Whiteknights, PO Box 217, Reading RG6 6AH **T** 0118-987 5123
W www.reading.ac.uk
Students: 12,380 UG; 4,620 PG
Chancellor, Lord Waldegrave of North Hill, PC
Vice-Chancellor, Prof. Robert Van de Noort
University Secretary, Dr Richard Messer

RICHMOND, AMERICAN INTERNATIONAL
UNIVERSITY (1972 (obtained UK degree awarding powers
2018))
Queens Road, Richmond-upon-Thames TW10 6JP
T 0208 322 8200 **W** www.richmond.ac.uk
Students: 1,600
Principal and Vice-Chancellor, Prof. Lawrence S. Abeln
Provost, Phil Davies

ROBERT GORDON UNIVERSITY (1992)
Garthdee House, Garthdee Road, Aberdeen AB10 7QB
T 01224-262000 **E** admissions@rgu.ac.uk **W** www.rgu.ac.uk
Students: 9,175 UG; 3,355 PG
Chancellor, Sir Ian Wood, KT, GBE
Vice-Chancellor, Prof. John Harper
Academic Registrar, Hilary Douglas

ROEHAMPTON UNIVERSITY (2004)
Erasmus House, Roehampton Lane, London SW15 5PU
T 020-8392 3000 **E** Info@roehampton.ac.uk
W www.roehampton.ac.uk
Students: 10,155 UG; 1,750 PG
Chancellor, Dame Jacqueline Wilson, DBE, FRSL
Vice-Chancellor, Prof. Jean-Noël Ezingeard
University Secretary, Mark Ellul

ROYAL AGRICULTURAL UNIVERSITY (2013)
Stroud Road, Cirencester GL7 6JS **T** 01285-652531
E admissions@rau.ac.uk **W** www.rau.ac.uk
Students: 1,045 UG; 145 PG
Vice-Chancellor, Prof. Joanna Price
Chief Operating Officer, Susan O'Neill

ROYAL COLLEGE OF ART (1967)
Kensington Gore, London SW7 2EU **T** 020-7590 4444
E info@rca.ac.uk **W** www.rca.ac.uk
Students: 2,105 PG (postgraduate only)
Chancellor, Sir Jonathan Ive, KBE
Vice-Chancellor, Dr Paul Thompson
Chief Operating Officer (interim), Jocelyn Prudence

UNIVERSITY OF ST ANDREWS (1413)
St Andrews KY16 9AJ **T** 01334-476161 **W** www.st-andrews.ac.uk
Students: 8,625 UG; 2,110 PG
Chancellor, Lord Campbell of Pittenweem, CH, CBE, PC, QC
Vice-Chancellor, Prof. Sally Mapstone, FRSE
Academic Registrar, Marie-Noël Earley

ST MARY'S UNIVERSITY (2014)
Waldegrave Road, Strawberry Hill, Twickenham TW1 4SX
T 020-8240 4000 **W** www.stmarys.ac.uk
Students: 3,860 UG; 1,450 PG
Chancellor, Cardinal Vincent Nichols
Vice-Chancellor, Prof. Francis Campbell
University Secretary, Andrew Bogg

UNIVERSITY OF SALFORD (1967)
The Crescent, Salford M5 4WT **T** 0161-295 5000
W www.salford.ac.uk
Students: 15,985 UG; 4,305 PG
Chancellor, Jackie Kay, MBE
Vice-Chancellor, Prof. Helen Marshall
University Secretary, Alison Blackburn

UNIVERSITY OF SHEFFIELD (1905)
Western Bank, Sheffield S10 2TN **T** 0114-222 2000
E study@sheffield.ac.uk **W** www.sheffield.ac.uk
Students: 19,760 UG; 9,915 PG
Chancellor, Lady Justice Rafferty, DBE, PC
President and Vice-Chancellor, Prof. Koen Lamberts

SHEFFIELD HALLAM UNIVERSITY (1992)
City Campus, Howard Street, Sheffield S1 1WB **T** 011 4-225 5555
E enquiries@shu.ac.uk **W** www.shu.ac.uk
Students: 24,320 UG; 6,410 PG
Chancellor, Baroness Kennedy of The Shaws, FRSA, QC
Vice-Chancellor, Prof. Sir Chris Husbands
Chief Operating Officer, Richard Calvert

UNIVERSITY OF SOUTHAMPTON (1952)
University Road, Southampton SO17 1BJ T 023-8059 5000
W www.southampton.ac.uk
Students: 17,000 UG; 7,620 PG
Chancellor, Ruby Wax, OBE
Vice-Chancellor (interim), Prof. Mark Spearing
Chief Operating Officer, Ian Dunn

SOUTHAMPTON SOLENT UNIVERSITY (2005)
East Park Terrace, Southampton SO14 0YN T 023-8201 3000
E ask@solent.ac.uk W www.solent.ac.uk
Students: 10,015 UG; 560 PG
Chancellor, Theo Paphitis
Vice-Chancellor, Prof. Graham Baldwin
University Secretary, Caroline Carpenter

UNIVERSITY OF SOUTH WALES (1992)
Pontypridd CF37 1DL T 0345-576 0101 W www.southwales.ac.uk
Students: 18,360 UG; 4,500 PG
Chancellor, Rt. Revd Lord Williams of Oystermouth, PC, DPHIL
Vice-Chancellor, Prof. Julie Lydon, OBE
Academic Registrar, Sara Moggridge

STAFFORDSHIRE UNIVERSITY (1992)
College Road, Stoke-on-Trent ST4 2DE T 01782-294000
W www.staffs.ac.uk
Students: 12,305 UG; 2,045 PG
Chancellor, Lord Stafford
Vice-Chancellor, Prof. Liz Barnes
Chief Operating Officer, Ian Blachford

UNIVERSITY OF STIRLING (1967)
Stirling FK9 4LA T 01786-473171 W www.stir.ac.uk
Students: 8,745 UG; 3,835 PG
Chancellor, Lord McConnell of Glenscorrodale, PC
Vice-Chancellor, Prof. Gerry McCormac, FRSE
University Secretary, Eileen Schofield

UNIVERSITY OF STRATHCLYDE (1964)
16 Richmond Street, Glasgow G1 1XQ T 0141-552 4400
E corporatecomms@strath.ac.uk W www.strath.ac.uk
Students: 14,860 UG; 7,435 PG
Chancellor, Lord Smith of Kelvin, KT, CH
Vice-Chancellor, Prof. Sir Jim McDonald, FRSE, FRENG
Academic Registrar, Dr Veena O'Halloran

UNIVERSITY OF SUFFOLK (2016)
Waterfront Building, Neptune Quay, Ipswich IP4 1QJ
T 01473-338000 W www.uos.ac.uk
Students: 4,910 UG; 465 PG
Chancellor, Dr Helen Pankhurst
Vice-Chancellor, Prof. Helen Langton
Secretary and Registrar, Tim Greenacre

UNIVERSITY OF SUNDERLAND (1992)
Edinburgh Building, Chester Road, Sunderland SR1 3SD
T 0191-515 2000 E student.helpline@sunderland.ac.uk
W www.sunderland.ac.uk
Students: 11,320 UG; 2,750 PG
Chancellor, Emeli Sandé, MBE
Vice-Chancellor, Sir David Bell, KCB
Chief Operating Officer, Steve Knight

UNIVERSITY OF SURREY (1966)
Guildford GU2 7XH T 01483-300800 E admissions@surrey.ac.uk
W www.surrey.ac.uk
Students: 13,225 UG; 3,720 PG
Chancellor, HRH the Duke of Kent, KG, GCMG, GCVO
Vice-Chancellor, Prof. G. Q. Max Lu
Registrar, Sarah Litchfield

UNIVERSITY OF SUSSEX (1961)
Sussex House, Brighton BN1 9RH T 01273-606755
E information@sussex.ac.uk W www.sussex.ac.uk
Students: 13,000 UG; 4,800 PG
Chancellor, Sanjeev Bhaskar, OBE
Vice-Chancellor, Prof. Adam Tickell
Chief Operating Officer, Dr Tim Westlake

SWANSEA UNIVERSITY (1920)
Singleton Park, Swansea SA2 8PP T 01792-205678
W www.swansea.ac.uk
Students: 16,850 UG; 3,565 PG
Chancellor, Prof. Dame Jean Thomas, DBE, FMEDSCI, FLSW, FRS
Vice-Chancellor, Prof. Paul Boyle
Registrar, Andrew Rhodes

TEESIDE UNIVERSITY (1992)
Middlesbrough TS1 3BX T 01642-218121 E enquiries@tees.ac.uk
W www.tees.ac.uk
Students: 15,830 UG; 2,545 PG
Chancellor, Paul Drechsler, CBE
Vice-Chancellor, Prof. Paul Croney, CBE
Chief Operating Officer, Malcolm Page

UNIVERSITY OF ULSTER (1984)
Cromore Road, Coleraine BT52 1SA T 028-7012 3456
W www.ulster.ac.uk
Students: 18,365 UG; 5,350 PG
Chancellor, James Nesbitt, OBE
Vice-Chancellor, Prof. Paddy Nixon
University Secretary, Eamon Mullan

UNIVERSITY OF WALES, TRINITY SAINT DAVID (1828)
Carmarthen Campus, SA31 3EP T 01267-676767
W www.uwtsd.ac.uk
Students: 8,495 UG; 1,785 PG
Vice-Chancellor, Prof. Medwin Hughes, FRSA

UNIVERSITY OF WARWICK (1965)
Coventry CV4 7AL T 024-7652 3523 W www.warwick.ac.uk
Students: 16,520 UG; 9,185 PG
Chancellor, Baroness Ashton of Upholland, GCMG, PC
Vice-Chancellor, Prof. Stuart Croft
Registrar, Rachel Sandby Thomas, CB

UNIVERSITY OF WEST LONDON (1992)
St Mary's Road, London W5 5RF T 0800-036 8888
W www.uwl.ac.uk
Students: 8,985 UG; 1,785 PG
Chancellor, Laurence S. Geller, CBE
Vice-Chancellor, Prof. Peter John
University Secretary, Marion Lowe

UNIVERSITY OF WESTMINSTER (1992)
309 Regent Street, London W1B 2HW T 020-7911 5000
E course-enquiries@westminster.ac.uk W www.westminster.ac.uk
Students: 14,890 UG; 4,350 PG
Chancellor, Lady Sorrell, OBE
Vice-Chancellor and Rector, Dr Peter Bonfield
University Secretary, John Cappock

UNIVERSITY OF THE WEST OF ENGLAND (1992)
Frenchay Campus, Coldharbour Lane, Bristol BS16 1QY
T 0117-965 6261 E infopoint@uwe.ac.uk W www.uwe.ac.uk
Students: 21,520 UG; 7,270 PG
Chancellor, Sir Ian Carruthers, OBE
Vice-Chancellor, Prof. Steve West, CBE
Registrar, Rachel Cowie

UNIVERSITY OF THE WEST OF SCOTLAND (2007)
Paisley PA1 2BE T 0141-848 3000 E ask@uws.ac.uk
W www.uws.ac.uk
Students: 13,465 UG; 2,970 PG
Chancellor, Rt. Hon. Dame Elish Angiolini, DBE, QC
Vice-Chancellor and Principal, Prof. Craig Mahoney
Chief Operating Officer, Susan Mitchell

UNIVERSITY OF WINCHESTER (2005)
Winchester SO22 4NR T 01962-841515
E enquiries@winchester.ac.uk W www.winchester.ac.uk
Students: 6,290 UG; 1,290 PG
Chancellor, Alan Titchmarsh, MBE
Vice-Chancellor, Prof. Joy Carter, CBE
Registrar, Dee Povey

UNIVERSITY OF WOLVERHAMPTON (1992)
Wulfruna Street, Wolverhampton WV1 1LY T 01902-321000
E enquiries@wlv.ac.uk W www.wlv.ac.uk
Students: 16,055 UG; 3,575 PG
Chancellor, Lord Paul, PC
Vice-Chancellor, Prof. Geoff Layer, OBE
Academic Registrar, Dr Jo Wright

UNIVERSITY OF WORCESTER (1946)
Henwick Grove, Worcester WR2 6AJ T 01905-855000
E study@worc.ac.uk W www.worcester.ac.uk
Students: 8,945 UG; 1,855 PG
Chancellor, HRH the Duke of Gloucester, KG, GCVO
Vice Chancellor, Prof. David Green, CBE
Registrar, Kevin Pickess

WREXHAM GLYNDWR UNIVERSITY (2008)
Mold Road, Wrexham LL11 2AW T 01978-290666
E enquiries@glyndwr.ac.uk W www.glyndwr.ac.uk
Students: 5,130 UG; 610 PG
Chancellor, Colin Jackson, CBE
Vice-Chancellor, Maria Hinfelaar

WRITTLE UNIVERSITY COLLEGE (2015)
Lordship Road, Writtle, Chelmsford CM1 3RR T 01245-424200
E info@writtle.ac.uk W www.writtle.ac.uk
Students: 720 UG; 90 PG
Chancellor, Baroness Jenkin of Kennington
Vice-Chancellor, Prof. Tim Middleton
University Secretary, Andrew Williamson

UNIVERSITY OF YORK (1963)
York YO10 5DD T 01904-320000 W www.york.ac.uk
Students: 13,810 UG; 5,010 PG
Chancellor, Prof. Sir Malcolm Grant, CBE
Vice-Chancellor (acting), Prof. Saul Tendler, PHD
Registrar and Secretary, Jo Horsburgh, PHD

YORK ST JOHN UNIVERSITY (2006)
Lord Mayor's Walk, York YO31 7EX T 01904-624624
E admissions@yorksj.ac.uk W www.yorksj.ac.uk
Students: 5,460 UG; 785 PG
Chancellor, Most Revd and Rt. Hon. Archbishop of York
Vice-Chancellor, Prof. Karen Stanton
University Secretary, Dr Amanda Wilcox

PROFESSIONAL EDUCATION

The organisations selected below provide specialist training, conduct examinations or are responsible for maintaining a register of those with professional qualifications in their sector, thereby controlling entry into a profession.

EU RECOGNITION

It is possible for those with professional qualifications obtained in the UK to have these recognised in other European countries. Further information can be obtained from:

UK NARIC, Suffolk House, 68–70 Suffolk Road, Cheltenham GL50 2ED **T** 0871-330 7033 **W** www.naric.org.uk/naric

ACCOUNTANCY

Salary range for chartered accountants: Certified £25,000 (starting), rising to £26,000–£45,000+ (qualified); £40,000–£100,000+ at senior levels Management £28,000 (starting); £32,000 (CIMA student); £62,000 (average); £46,000–£129,000+ at senior levels Public finance £12,000–£35,000 (starting); £35,000–£50,000 (qualified); £50,000–£70,000 (5 years post-qualification experience); £80,000+ at senior levels

Chartered Accountancy trainees can be school-leavers or graduates. They usually undertake a three-year training contract with an approved employer culminating in professional exams provided by ICAEW, ICAS or CAI. Success in the exams and membership of one of the professional bodies, which offers continuous professional development and regulation, allows the use of the designation 'chartered accountant' and the letters ACA, FCA or CA.

The Association of Chartered Certified Accountants (ACCA) is the global body for professional accountants. The ACCA aims to offer business-relevant qualifications to students in a range of business sectors and countries seeking a career in accountancy, finance and management. The ACCA Qualification consists of up to 13 examinations, practical experiences and a professional ethics module. Chartered certified accountants can use the designatory letters ACCA.

Chartered global management accountants focus on accounting for businesses, and most do not work in accountancy practices but in industry, commerce, not-for-profit and public-sector organisations. Graduates who have not studied a business or accounting degree must complete the Chartered Institute of Management Accountants (CIMA) Certificate in Business Accounting before progressing to the CIMA Professional Qualification, which requires three years of practical experience and 12 examinations. In May 2011, CIMA and the American Institute of Certified Public Accountants (AICPA) agreed on the creation of a new professional designation, the Chartered Global Management Accountant (CGMA), which represents a worldwide standard in management accounting.

The Chartered Institute of Public Finance and Accountancy (CIPFA) is the professional body for people working in public finance. Chartered public finance accountants usually work for public bodies, but they can also work in the private sector. To gain chartered public finance accountant status (CPFA), trainees must complete a professional qualification in public sector accountancy. CIPFA also offers a postgraduate diploma for those already working in leadership positions.

ASSOCIATION OF CHARTERED CERTIFIED ACCOUNTANTS (ACCA), The Adelphi, 1–11 John Adam Street, London WC2N 6AU **T** 0141-582 2000 **E** info@accaglobal.com **W** www.accaglobal.com *Chief Executive,* Helen Brand, OBE

CHARTERED ACCOUNTANTS IRELAND (CAI), 47–49 Pearse Street, Dublin 2 **T** 0353-1637 7200 **W** www.charteredaccountants.ie *Chief Executive,* Barry Dempsey

CHARTERED INSTITUTE OF MANAGEMENT ACCOUNTANTS (CIMA), The Helicon, One South Place, London EC2M 2RB **T** 020-8849 2251 **E** cima.contact@aicpa-cima.com **W** www.cimaglobal.com *Chief Executive,* Andrew Harding

CHARTERED INSTITUTE OF PUBLIC FINANCE AND ACCOUNTANCY (CIPFA), 77 Mansell Street, London E1 8AN **T** 020-7543 5600 **E** customerservices@cipfa.org **W** www.cipfa.org *Chief Executive,* Rob Whiteman

INSTITUTE OF CHARTERED ACCOUNTANTS IN ENGLAND AND WALES (ICAEW), Chartered Accountants' Hall, Moorgate Place, London EC2R 6EA **T** 020-7920 8100 **E** general.enquiries@icaew.com **W** www.icaew.com *Chief Executive,* Michael Izza

INSTITUTE OF CHARTERED ACCOUNTANTS OF SCOTLAND (ICAS), CA House, 21 Haymarket Yards, Edinburgh EH12 5BH **T** 0131-347 0100 **E** enquiries@icas.com **W** www.icas.com *Chief Executive,* Bruce Cartwright

ACTUARIAL SCIENCE

Salary range: £25,000–£35,000 for graduate trainees; £40,000–£55,000 after qualification; £60,000+ for senior roles; £200,000+ for senior directors

Actuaries apply financial and statistical theories to solve business problems. These problems usually involve analysing future financial events in order to assess investment risks. To qualify, graduate trainees must complete 15 exams and three years worth of actuarial work-based training; most graduate trainees take between three and six years to qualify. Students can become Associate members of the Institute and Faculty of Actuaries (IFoA) and gain the right to describe themselves as an actuary and to use the letters AIA or AFA. Members of the profession who wish to continue their studies to an advanced level, or who specialise in a particular actuarial field, may take further specialist exams to qualify as a Fellow and bear the designations FIA or FFA.

The IFoA is the UK's chartered professional body dedicated to educating, developing and regulating actuaries based both in the UK and internationally. As at June 2019, the IFoA represent and regulate 32,938 members and oversee their education at all stages of qualification and development throughout their careers.

The Financial Reporting Council (FRC) is the unified independent regulator for corporate reporting, auditing, actuarial practice, corporate governance and the professionalism of accountants and actuaries. In 2012, the FRC assumed responsibility for setting and maintaining technical actuarial standards independently of the profession, as well as overseeing the regulation of the accountancy and actuarial professions by their respective professional bodies.

FINANCIAL REPORTING COUNCIL (FRC), 8th Floor, 125 London Wall, London EC2Y 5AS T 020-7492 2300 E enquiries@frc.org.uk W www.frc.org.uk
Chief Executive, Stephen Haddrill

INSTITUTE AND FACULTY OF ACTUARIES (IFoA), 7th Floor, Holborn Gate, 326–330 High Holborn, London WC1V 7PP T 020-7632 2100 E careers@actuaries.org.uk W www.actuaries.org.uk
Executive Director, Des Hudson

ARCHITECTURE

Salary range: architectural assistant (part I) £18,000–£22,000; (part II) £22,000–£35,000; fully qualified £32,000–£45,000; senior associate, partner or director £45,000–£70,000

It takes a minimum of seven years to become an architect, involving three stages: a three-year first degree, a two-year second degree or diploma and two years of professional experience followed by the successful completion of a professional practice examination.

The Architects Registration Board (ARB) is the independent regulator for the profession. It was set up by an act of parliament in 1997 and is responsible for maintaining the register of UK architects, prescribing qualifications that lead to registration as an architect, investigating complaints about the conduct and competence of architects and ensuring that only those who are registered offer their services as an architect. Following registration with ARB an architect can apply for chartered membership of the Royal Institute of British Architects (RIBA). RIBA, the UK body for architecture and the architectural profession, received its royal charter in 1837 and validates courses at over 50 schools of architecture in the UK; it also validates overseas courses. RIBA provides support and guidance for its members in the form of training, technical services and events and sets standards for the education of architects.

The Chartered Institute of Architectural Technologists is the international qualifying body for Chartered Architectural Technologists and Architectural Technicians.

ARCHITECTS REGISTRATION BOARD (ARB) 8 Weymouth Street, London W1W 5BU T 020-7580 5861 E info@arb.org.uk W www.arb.org.uk
Registrar and Chief Executive, Karen Holmes

CHARTERED INSTITUTE OF ARCHITECTURAL TECHNOLOGISTS 397 City Road, London EC1V 1NH T 020-7278 2206 E info@ciat.org.uk W www.ciat.org.uk
Chief Executive, Francesca Berriman, MBE

ROYAL INCORPORATION OF ARCHITECTS IN SCOTLAND 15 Rutland Square, Edinburgh EH1 2BE T 0131-229 7545 E info@rias.org.uk W www.rias.org.uk
President, Prof. Robin Webster, OBE

ROYAL INSTITUTE OF BRITISH ARCHITECTS (RIBA) 66 Portland Place, London W1B 1AD T 020-7580 5533 E info@riba.org W www.architecture.com
Chief Executive, Alan Vallance

ENGINEERING

Salary range:
Civil/structural £22,000–£30,000 (graduate); £50,000 (members of the Institution of Civil Engineers (ICE)); £81,447 (fellows of ICE)
Chemical £28,600 average (graduate); £78,500+ (chartered)
Electrical £26,000 (graduate); £35,000–£60,000 with experience; £60,000+ (chartered)

The Engineering Council holds the national registers of Engineering Technicians (EngTech), Incorporated Engineers (IEng), Chartered Engineers (CEng) and Information and Communication Technology Technicians (ICTTech). It also sets and maintains the internationally recognised standards of competence and ethics that govern the award and retention of these titles.

To apply for the EngTech, IEng, CEng or ICTTech titles, an individual must be a member of one of the 36 engineering institutions and societies (listed below) currently licensed by the Engineering Council to assess candidates. Applicants must demonstrate that they possess a range of technical and personal competences and are committed to keeping these up-to-date.

ENGINEERING COUNCIL, 5th Floor, Woolgate Exchange, 25 Basinghall Street, London EC2V 5HA T 020-3206 0500 W www.engc.org.uk
Chief Executive, Alasdair Coates

LICENSED MEMBERS

BCS – The Chartered Institute for IT W www.bcs.org
British Institute of Non-Destructive Testing W www.bindt.org
Chartered Institute of Plumbing and Heating Engineering W www.ciphe.org.uk
Chartered Institution of Building Services Engineers W www.cibse.org
Chartered Institution of Highways and Transportation W www.ciht.org.uk
Chartered Institution of Water and Environmental Management W www.ciwem.org
Energy Institute W www.energyinst.org
Institute of Acoustics W www.ioa.org.uk
Institute of Cast Metals Engineers W www.icme.org.uk
Institute of Healthcare Engineering and Estate Management W www.iheem.org.uk
Institute of Highway Engineers W www.theihe.org
Institute of Marine Engineering, Science and Technology W www.imarest.org
Institute of Materials, Minerals and Mining W www.iom3.org
Institute of Measurement and Control W www.instmc.org
Institute of Physics W www.iop.org
Institute of Physics and Engineering in Medicine W www.ipem.ac.uk
Institute of Water W www.instituteofwater.org.uk
Institution of Agricultural Engineers W www.iagre.org
Institution of Chemical Engineers W www.icheme.org
Institution of Civil Engineers W www.ice.org.uk
Institution of Engineering Designers W www.institution-engineering-designers.org.uk
Institution of Engineering and Technology W www.theiet.org
Institution of Fire Engineers W www.ife.org.uk
Institution of Gas Engineers and Managers W www.igem.org.uk
Institution of Lighting Professionals W www.theilp.org.uk
Institution of Mechanical Engineers W www.imeche.org
Institution of Railway Signal Engineers W www.irse.org
Institution of Royal Engineers W www.instre.org
Institution of Structural Engineers W www.istructe.org
Nuclear Institute W www.nuclearinst.com
Permanent Way Institution W www.thepwi.org
Royal Aeronautical Society W www.aerosociety.com
Royal Institution of Naval Architects W www.rina.org.uk
Society of Environmental Engineers W www.environmental.org.uk
Society of Operations Engineers W www.soe.org.uk
The Welding Institute W www.theweldinginstitute.com

HEALTHCARE

CHIROPRACTIC

Salary range: £30,000–£50,000 starting salary; with own practice £50,000–£100,000 (depending on experience and size of practice)

Chiropractors diagnose and treat conditions caused by problems with joints, ligaments, tendons and nerves of the body. The General Chiropractic Council (GCC) is the independent statutory regulatory body for chiropractors and its role and remit is defined in the Chiropractors Act 1994. The GCC sets the criteria for the recognition of chiropractic degrees and for standards of proficiency and conduct. Details of the institutions offering degree programmes are available on the GCC website (*see* below). It is illegal for anyone in the UK to use the title 'chiropractor' unless registered with the GCC.

The British Chiropractic Association, Scottish Chiropractic Association, McTimoney Chiropractic Association and United Chiropractic Association are the representative bodies for the profession and are sources of further information.

BRITISH CHIROPRACTIC ASSOCIATION, 59 Castle Street, Reading RG1 7SN T 0150-663 9607
E enquiries@chiropractic-uk.co.uk W www.chiropractic-uk.co.uk
Executive Director, Tom Mullarkey, MBE

GENERAL CHIROPRACTIC COUNCIL (GCC), Park House, 186 Kennington Park Road, London SE11 4BT
T 020-7713 5155 E enquiries@gcc-uk.org W www.gcc-uk.org
Chief Executive and Registrar, Nick Jones

SCOTTISH CHIROPRACTIC ASSOCIATION, The Old Barn, Houston Road, Houston, Renfrewshire PA6 7BH
T 0141-404 0260 E admin@sca-chiropractic.org
W www.sca-chiropractic.org
Administrator, Morag Cairns

DENTISTRY

Salary range: see Health: Employees and Salaries

The General Dental Council (GDC) is the organisation that regulates dental professionals in the UK. All dentists, dental hygienists, dental therapists, dental technicians, clinical dental technicians, dental nurses and orthodontic therapists must be registered with the GDC to work in the UK.

There are various different routes to qualify for registration as a dentist, including holding a degree from a UK university, completing the GDC's qualifying examination or holding a relevant European Economic Area or overseas diploma. The GDC's purpose is to protect the public through the regulation of UK dental professionals. It keeps up-to-date registers of dental professionals and works to set standards of dental practice, behaviour and education.

Founded in 1880, the British Dental Association (BDA) is the professional association and trade union for dentists in the UK. It represents dentists working in general practice, community and hospital settings, in academia, research and the armed forces, and includes dental students.

BRITISH DENTAL ASSOCIATION (BDA), 64 Wimpole Street, London W1G 8YS T 020-7935 0875 E enquiries@bda.org
W www.bda.org
Chief Executive, Martin Woodrow *(acting)*

GENERAL DENTAL COUNCIL (GDC), 37 Wimpole Street, London W1G 8DQ T 020-7167 6000 E information@gdc-uk.org
W www.gdc-uk.org
Chief Executive, Ian Brack

MEDICINE

Salary range: see Health: Employees and Salaries

The General Medical Council (GMC) regulates medical education and training in the UK. This covers undergraduate study (usually five years), the two-year foundation programme taken by doctors directly after graduation and all subsequent postgraduate study, including speciality and GP training.

All doctors must be registered with the GMC, which is responsible for protecting the public. It does this by promoting high standards of medical education and training, fostering good medical practice, keeping a register of qualified doctors and taking action where a doctor's fitness to practise is in doubt. Doctors are eligible for full registration upon successful completion of the first year of training after graduation.

Following the foundation programme, many doctors undertake specialist training (provided by the colleges and faculties listed below) to become either a consultant or a GP. Once specialist training has been completed, doctors are awarded the Certificate of Completion of Training (CCT) and are eligible to be placed on either the GMC's specialist register or its GP register.

The British Medical Association (BMA) is a trade union and professional body for doctors in the UK, providing individual and collective representation, as well as information and professional guidance and support.

BRITISH MEDICAL ASSOCIATION (BMA), BMA House, Tavistock Square, London WC1H 9JP T 020-7387 4499
E info.public@bma.org.uk W www.bma.org.uk
President, Prof. Dinesh Bhugra, CBE

GENERAL MEDICAL COUNCIL (GMC), Regent's Place, 350 Euston Road, London NW1 3JN T 0161-923 6602
E gmc@gmc-uk.org W www.gmc-uk.org
Chief Executive, Charlie Massey

WORSHIPFUL SOCIETY OF APOTHECARIES OF LONDON, Black Friars Lane, London EC4V 6EJ
T 020-7236 1189 E clerksec@apothecaries.org
W www.apothecaries.org
Master, Prof. Martin Rossor

SPECIALIST TRAINING COLLEGES AND FACULTIES

Faculty of Occupational Medicine W www.facoccmed.ac.uk
Faculty of Public Health W www.fph.org.uk
Joint Committee on Surgical Training W www.jcst.org
Joint Royal Colleges of Physicians Training Board
W www.jrcptb.org.uk
Royal College of Anaesthetists W www.rcoa.ac.uk
Royal College of Emergency Medicine www.rcem.ac.uk
Royal College of General Practitioners W www.rcgp.org.uk
Royal College of Obstetricians and Gynaecologists
W www.rcog.org.uk
Royal College of Ophthalmologists W www.rcophth.ac.uk
Royal College of Paediatrics and Child Health
W www.rcpch.ac.uk
Royal College of Pathologists W www.rcpath.org
Royal College of Physicians, London W www.rcplondon.ac.uk
Royal College of Psychiatrists W www.rcpsych.ac.uk
Royal College of Radiologists W www.rcr.ac.uk

MEDICINE, SUPPLEMENTARY PROFESSIONS

The standard of professional education for arts therapists, biomedical scientists, chiropodists and podiatrists, clinical scientists, dietitians, hearing aid dispensers, occupational therapists, operating department practitioners, orthoptists, paramedics, physiotherapists, practitioner psychologists, prosthetists and orthotists, radiographers, social workers in England and speech and language therapists are regulated by the Health and Care Professions Council (HCPC), which only registers those practitioners who meet certain standards of training, professional skills, behaviour and health. The HCPC can take action against professionals who do not meet these standards or falsely declare they are registered. Each profession regulated by the HCPC has at least one professional title that is protected by law.

HEALTH AND CARE PROFESSIONS COUNCIL (HCPC),
Park House, 184–186 Kennington Park Road, London SE11 4BU
T 0300-500 6184 E registration@hcpc-uk.org
W www.hcpc-uk.org
Chief Executive and Registrar, Marc Seale

ART, DRAMA AND MUSIC THERAPIES
Salary range: £26,000–£37,000 (starting); £31,000–£43,000 with experience; £40,000–£50,000 (senior and principal therapists)

An art, drama or music therapist encourages people to express their feelings and emotions through art, such as painting and drawing, drama or music. A postgraduate qualification in the relevant therapy is required. Details of accredited training programmes in the UK can be obtained from the following organisations:

BRITISH ASSOCIATION FOR MUSIC THERAPY, 24–27
White Lion Street, London N1 9PD T 020-7837 6100
E info@bamt.org W www.bamt.org
Chair, Ben Saul

BRITISH ASSOCIATION OF ART THERAPISTS, 24–27
White Lion Street, London N1 9PD T 020-7686 4216
E info@baat.org W www.baat.org
Chief Executive, Dr Val Huet

BRITISH ASSOCIATION OF DRAMATHERAPISTS, PO
Box 1257, Cheltenham, Gloucestershire GL50 9YX
T 01242-235515 E info@badth.org.uk W www.badth.org.uk
Chair, Madeline Anderson-Warren *(acting)*

BIOMEDICAL SCIENCES
Salary range: £22,128–£28,746 (starting); £26,565–£35,577 with experience; £31,696–£48,514 for senior roles

The Institute of Biomedical Science (IBMS) is the professional body for biomedical scientists in the UK. Biomedical scientists carry out investigations on tissue and body fluid samples to diagnose disease and monitor the progress of a patient's treatment. The IBMS sets quality standards for the profession through training, education, assessments, examinations and continuous professional development.

INSTITUTE OF BIOMEDICAL SCIENCE (IBMS), 12
Coldbath Square, London EC1R 5HL T 020-7713 0214
E mail@ibms.org W www.ibms.org
Chief Executive, Jill Rodney

CHIROPODY AND PODIATRY
Salary range: £23,000–£4; £42,000–£85,000 (consultant podiatrist or specialist registrar in practice)

Chiropodists and podiatrists assess, diagnose and treat problems of the lower leg and foot. The College of Podiatry (formerly Society of Chiropodists and Podiatrists) is the professional body and trade union for the profession. Qualifications granted and degrees recognised by the society are approved by the HCPC. HCPC registration is required in order to use the titles chiropodist and podiatrist.

COLLEGE OF PODIATRY, Quartz House, 207 Providence
Square, Mill Street, London SE1 2EW T 020-7234 8620
E reception@scpod.org W www.cop.org.uk
Chief Executive, Steve Jamieson

CLINICAL SCIENCE
Salary range: £25,000–£99,000

Clinical scientists conduct tests in laboratories in order to diagnose and manage disease. The Association of Clinical Scientists is responsible for setting the criteria for competence of applicants to the HCPC's register and for presenting a Certificate of Attainment to candidates following a successful assessment. This certificate will allow direct registration with the HCPC.

ASSOCIATION OF CLINICAL SCIENTISTS, 130–132
Tooley Street, London SE1 2TU T 020-7940 8960
E info@assclinsci.org W www.assclinsci.org
Chair, Prof. Richard Lerski

DIETETICS
Salary range: £23,000–£43,000

Dietitians advise patients on how to improve their health and counter specific health problems through diet. The British Dietetic Association, established in 1936, is the professional association for dietitians. Full membership is open to UK-registered dietitians, who must also be registered with the HCPC.

BRITISH DIETETIC ASSOCIATION, 5th Floor, Charles
House, 148–149 Great Charles Street Queensway, Birmingham B3 3HT T 0121-200 8080 E info@bda.uk.com
W www.bda.uk.com
Chief Executive, Andy Burman

MENTAL HEALTH
Salary range: Clinical psychologist £26,000, rising to £31,000+ after qualification; £48,000–£83,000 at senior levels
Counselling psychologist £26,000–£35,000 (starting), rising to £31,500–£41,500 (qualified) and up to £82,000 at senior levels
Educational psychologist £22,000, rising to £48,211 (fully qualified) and up to £66,000 at senior levels
Psychotherapist £26,250–£35,250 (starting), rising to £55,000 with experience

Psychologists and counsellors are mental health professionals who can work in a range of settings including prisons, schools and hospitals. The British Psychological Society (BPS) is the representative body for psychology and psychologists in the UK. The BPS is responsible for the development, promotion and application of psychology for the public good. The Association of Educational Psychologists (AEP) represents the interests of educational psychologists. The British Association for Counselling and Psychotherapy (BACP) sets educational standards and provides professional support to counsellors, psychotherapists and others working in counselling, psychotherapy or counselling-related roles. The BPS website provides more information on the different specialisations that may be pursued by psychologists.

ASSOCIATION OF EDUCATIONAL PSYCHOLOGISTS
(AEP), 4 The Riverside Centre, Frankland Lane, Durham DH1 5TA T 0191-384 9512 E enquiries@aep.org.uk
W www.aep.org.uk
President, Lisa O'Connor

BRITISH ASSOCIATION FOR COUNSELLING AND
PSYCHOTHERAPY (BACP), BACP House, 15 St John's Business Park, Lutterworth, Leicestershire LE17 4HB
T 01455-883300 E bacp@bacp.co.uk W www.bacp.co.uk
President, David Weaver

BRITISH PSYCHOLOGICAL SOCIETY (BPS), St Andrews
House, 48 Princess Road East, Leicester LE1 7DR
T 0116-254 9568 E info@bps.org.uk W www.bps.org.uk
President, Kate Bullen

OCCUPATIONAL THERAPY
Salary range: £22,000–£41,500; £40,000–£58,000 for consultancy roles

Occupational therapists work with people who have physical, mental and/or social problems, either from birth or as a result of accident, illness or ageing, and aim to make them as independent as possible. The professional qualification and eligibility for registration may be obtained upon successful completion of a validated course in any of the educational institutions approved by the College of Occupational Therapists, which is the professional body for occupational therapy in the UK. The courses are normally degree-level and based in higher education institutions.

COLLEGE OF OCCUPATIONAL THERAPISTS, 106–114 Borough High Street, London SE1 1LB T 020-7357 6480 E hello@rcot.co.uk W www.rcot.co.uk
Chief Executive, Julia Scott

ORTHOPTICS
Salary range: £24,200 (graduate), rising to £30,000–£86,600 in senior posts

Orthoptists undertake the diagnosis and treatment of all types of squint and other anomalies of binocular vision, working in close collaboration with ophthalmologists. The all-graduate workforce comes from three universities: the University of Liverpool, the University of Sheffield and Glasgow Caledonian University.

BRITISH AND IRISH ORTHOPTIC SOCIETY, 5th Floor, Charles House, 148–9 Great Street Queensway, Birmingham B3 3HT T 0344-209 0754 E bios@orthoptics.org.uk W www.orthoptics.org.uk
Chair, Rowena McNamara

PARAMEDICAL SERVICES
Salary range: £23,000–£36,600; £59,000–£71,000 for consultancy roles

Paramedics deal with accidents and emergencies, assessing patients and carrying out any specialist treatment and care needed in the first instance. The body that represents ambulance professionals is the College of Paramedics.

COLLEGE OF PARAMEDICS, The Exchange, Express Park, Bristol Road, Bridgwater TA6 4RR T 01278-420014 E membership@collegeofparamedics.co.uk W www.collegeofparamedics.co.uk
Chief Executive, Gerry Egan

PHYSIOTHERAPY
Salary range: £23,000–£49,000; £60,000 (management roles)

Physiotherapists are concerned with movement and function and deal with problems arising from injury, illness and ageing. Full-time three- or four-year degree courses are available at around 40 higher education institutions in the UK. Information about courses leading to state registration is available from the Chartered Society of Physiotherapy.

CHARTERED SOCIETY OF PHYSIOTHERAPY, 14 Bedford Row, London WC1R 4ED T 020-7306 6666 W www.csp.org.uk
Chief Executive, Karen Middleton, CBE

PROSTHETICS AND ORTHOTICS
Salary range: £21,000 on qualification, up to £67,000 as a consultant

Prosthetists provide artificial limbs, while orthotists provide devices to support or control a part of the body. It is necessary to obtain an honours degree to become a prosthetist or orthotist. Training is centred at the University of Salford and the University of Strathclyde.

BRITISH ASSOCIATION OF PROSTHETISTS AND ORTHOTISTS, Unit 3010, Mile End Mill, Abbey Mill Business Centre, Paisley PA1 1JS T 0141-561 7217 E enquiries@bapo.com W www.bapo.com
Chair, Lynne Rowley

RADIOGRAPHY
Salary range: £22,000–£43,000, rising to £69,100 in consultancy posts

In order to practise both diagnostic and therapeutic radiography in the UK, it is necessary to have successfully completed a course of education and training recognised by the HCPC. Such courses are offered by around 24 universities throughout the UK and lead to the award of a degree in radiography. Further information is available from the Society of Radiographers, the trade union and professional body which represents the whole of the radiographic workforce in the UK.

SOCIETY OF RADIOGRAPHERS, 207 Providence Square, Mill Street, London SE1 2EW T 020-7740 7200 W www.sor.org
Chief Executive, Richard Evans, OBE

SPEECH AND LANGUAGE THERAPY
Salary range: £23,000–£43,000

Speech and language therapists (SLTs) work with people with communication, swallowing, eating and drinking problems. The Royal College of Speech and Language Therapists is the professional body for speech and language therapists and support workers. Alongside the HCPC, it accredits education and training courses leading to qualification.

ROYAL COLLEGE OF SPEECH AND LANGUAGE THERAPISTS, 2 White Hart Yard, London SE1 1NX T 020-7378 1200 W www.rcslt.org
Chief Executive, Kamini Gadhok, MBE

NURSING
Salary range: see Health: Employees and Salaries

In order to practise in the UK, all nurses and midwives must be registered with the Nursing and Midwifery Council (NMC). The NMC is a statutory regulatory body that establishes and maintains standards of education, training, conduct and performance for nursing and midwifery. Courses leading to registration are currently at a minimum of degree level. All take a minimum of three years if undertaken full-time. The NMC approves programmes run jointly by higher education institutions with their healthcare service partners who offer clinical placements. The nursing part of the register has four fields of practice: adult, children's (paediatric), learning disability and mental health nursing. In most cases students must select one specific field to study before applying to an institution. Some universities run courses which offer the simultaneous study of two nursing fields. In addition, those studying to become adult nurses gain experience of nursing in relation to medicine, surgery, maternity care and nursing in the home. The NMC also sets standards for programmes leading to registration as a midwife and a range of post-registration courses including specialist practice programmes, nurse prescribing and those for teachers of nursing and midwifery. The NMC has a part of the register for specialist community public health nurses and approves programmes for health visitors, occupational health nurses and school nurses.
  The Royal College of Nursing is the largest professional union for nursing in the UK, representing qualified nurses, midwives, healthcare assistants and nursing students in the NHS and the independent sector.

NURSING AND MIDWIFERY COUNCIL (NMC), 23 Portland Place, London W1B 1PZ T 020-7637 7181 E ukenquiries@nmc-uk.org W www.nmc.org.uk
Chief Executive and Registrar, Andrea Sutcliffe, CBE

ROYAL COLLEGE OF NURSING, 20 Cavendish Square, London W1G 0RN T 020-7409 3333 W www.rcn.org.uk
Chief Executive and General Secretary, Dame Donna Kinnair, DBE

OPTOMETRY AND DISPENSING OPTICS

Salary range: Optometrist £20,000–£85,000 (NHS); £14,000–£65,000+ (private)
Dispensing Optician £14,000–£45,000+

There are various routes to qualification as a dispensing optician. Qualification takes three years in total, and can be completed by combining a distance learning course or day release while working as a trainee under the supervision of a qualified and registered optician. Alternatively, students can do a two-year full-time course followed by one year of supervised practice with a qualified and registered optician. Training must be done at a training establishment approved by the regulatory body – the General Optical Council (GOC). There are six training establishments which are approved by the GOC: ABDO (Association of British Dispensing Opticians) College, Anglia Ruskin University, Bradford College, City and Islington College, City University and Glasgow Caledonian University. After the completion of training to fit contact lenses and attaining the ABDO Level 6 certificate in contact lens practice qualification, a Contact Lens Optician may apply to be included in the GOC Speciality Register. Students are also able to complete a Foundation or Undergraduate degree in Ophthalmic Dispensing, offered by ABDO in conjunction with Canterbury Christ Church University. All routes are concluded by professional qualifying examinations, successful completion of which leads to the awarding of the Level 6 Fellowship Diploma of the Association of British Dispensing Opticians (FBDO) by ABDO. FBDO holders are able to register with the GOC following the awarding of their diploma, with registration being compulsory for all practising dispensing opticians.

Continuing Education and Training (CET) is a statutory requirement for all registered dispensing opticians and contact lens opticians to retain GOC registration.

ASSOCIATION OF BRITISH DISPENSING OPTICIANS (ABDO), Godmersham Park, Godmersham, Canterbury, Kent CT4 7DT T 01227-733905 E general@abdo.org.uk W www.abdo.org.uk
General Secretary, Sir Anthony Garrett, CBE

COLLEGE OF OPTOMETRISTS, 42 Craven Street, London WC2N 5NG T 020-7839 6000 W www.college-optometrists.org
Chief Executive, Ian Humphreys

GENERAL OPTICAL COUNCIL (GOC), 10 Old Bailey, London EC4M 7NG T 020-7580 3898 E goc@optical.org W www.optical.org
Chief Executive and Registrar, Lesley Longstone, CB

OSTEOPATHY

Salary Range: £20,000–£100,000+

Osteopathy is a system of diagnosis and treatment for a wide range of conditions. It works with the structure and function of the body, and is based on the principle that the well-being of an individual depends on the skeleton, muscles, ligaments and connective tissues functioning smoothly together. The General Osteopathic Council (GOsC) regulates the practice of osteopathy in the UK and maintains a register of those entitled to practise. It is a criminal offence for anyone to describe

themselves as an osteopath unless they are registered with the GOsC.

To gain entry to the register, applicants must hold a recognised qualification from an osteopathic education institute accredited by the GOsC; this involves a four- to five-year honours degree programme combined with clinical training.

GENERAL OSTEOPATHIC COUNCIL (GOsC), Osteopathy House, 176 Tower Bridge Road, London SE1 3LU T 020-7357 6655 E info@osteopathy.org.uk W www.osteopathy.org.uk
Chief Executive and Registrar, Leonie Milliner

PHARMACY

Salary range: £30,000–£70,000 (community); £26,500–£100,000 (hospital)

Pharmacists are involved in the preparation and use of medicines, from the discovery of their active ingredients to their use by patients. Pharmacists also monitor the effects of medicines, both for patient care and for research purposes.

The General Pharmaceutical Council (GPhC) is the independent regulatory body for pharmacists in England, Scotland and Wales, having taken over the regulating function of the Royal Pharmaceutical Society in 2010. The GPhC maintains the register of pharmacists, pharmacy technicians and pharmacy premises; it also sets national standards for training, ethics, proficiency and continuing professional development. The Pharmaceutical Society of Northern Ireland (PSNI) performs the same role in Northern Ireland. In order to register, students must complete a four-year degree in pharmacy that is accredited by either the GPhC or the PSNI, followed by one year of pre-registration training at an approved pharmacy; they must then pass an entrance examination.

GENERAL PHARMACEUTICAL COUNCIL (GPhC), 25 Canada Square, London, E14 5LQ T 020-3713 8000 E info@pharmacyregulation.org W www.pharmacyregulation.org
Chief Executive and Registrar, Duncan Rudkin

PHARMACEUTICAL SOCIETY OF NORTHERN IRELAND (PSNI), 73 University Street, Belfast BT7 1HL T 028-9032 6927 E info@psni.org.uk W www.psni.org.uk
Chief Executive, Trevor Patterson

ROYAL PHARMACEUTICAL SOCIETY, 66 East Smithfield, London, E1W 1AW T 020-7572 2737 E support@rpharms.com W www.rpharms.com
Chief Executive, Paul Bennett

INFORMATION MANAGEMENT

Salary range: Archivist £22,443 (newly qualified); £25,000–£45,000 (with experience); £55,000 in senior posts
Information Officer £18,000–£31,000 (starting); £21,000–£28,000 (newly qualified); £26,000–£50,000+ in senior and chartered posts
Librarian £16,000–£20,000 (trainee); £22,500–£29,500 (assistant librarian); £30,000–£40,000 (experienced); £43,000–£70,000 (chief/head librarian)

The Chartered Institute of Library and Information Professionals (CILIP) is the leading professional body for librarians, information specialists and knowledge managers. The Archives and Records Association is the professional body for archivists and record managers.

ARCHIVES AND RECORDS ASSOCIATION, Prioryfield House, 20 Canon Street, Taunton, Somerset TA1 1SW T 01823-327077 E ara@archives.org.uk W www.archives.org.uk
Chief Executive, John Chambers

CHARTERED INSTITUTE OF LIBRARY AND INFORMATION PROFESSIONALS (CILIP), 7 Ridgmount Street, London WC1E 7AE T 020-7255 0500 E info@cilip.org.uk W www.cilip.org.uk
Chief Executive, Nick Poole

JOURNALISM

Salary range: £12,000–£18,000 (trainee); £25,000 for established journalists, rising to £35,000–£65,000+ for those with over a decade's experience in print media, as high as £80,000+ for top/high-profile broadcast journalists.

The National Council for the Training of Journalists (NCTJ) accredits courses for journalists run by a number of different education providers throughout the United Kingdom; it also provides professional support to journalists.

The Broadcast Journalism Training Council (BJTC) is an association of the UK's main broadcast journalism employers and accredits courses in broadcast journalism.

BROADCAST JOURNALISM TRAINING COUNCIL (BJTC), Sterling House, 20 Station Road, Gerard's Cross, Buckinghamshire, SL9 8EL T 0845-600 8789 E sec@bjtc.org.uk W www.bjtc.org.uk
Chief Executive, Jon Godel

NATIONAL COUNCIL FOR THE TRAINING OF JOURNALISTS (NCTJ), The New Granary, Station Road, Newport, Saffron Walden, Essex CB11 3PL T 01799-544014 E info@nctj.com W www.nctj.com
Chief Executive, Joanne Butcher

LAW

There are three types of practising lawyers: barristers, notaries and solicitors. Solicitors tend to work as a group in firms, and can be approached directly by individuals. They advise on a variety of legal issues and must decide the most appropriate course of action, if any. Notaries have all the powers of a solicitor other than the conduct of litigation. Most of them are primarily concerned with the preparation and authentication of documents for use abroad. Barristers are usually self-employed. If a solicitor believes that a barrister is required, he or she will instruct one on behalf of the client; the client will not have contact with the barrister without the solicitor being present.

When specialist expertise is needed, barristers give opinions on complex matters of law, and when clients require representation in the higher courts (crown courts, the high court, the court of appeal and the supreme court), barristers provide a specialist advocacy service. However, solicitors – who represent their clients in the lower courts such as magistrates' courts and county courts – can also apply for advocacy rights in the higher courts instead of briefing a barrister.

THE BAR

Salary range: £12,000–£50,000 (pupillage); £50,000–£200,000 (qualified); £65,000–£1,000,000+ with ten years experience

The governing body of the Bar of England and Wales is the General Council of the Bar, also known as the Bar Council. Since January 2006, the regulatory functions of the Bar Council (including regulating the education and training requirements for those wishing to enter the profession) have been undertaken by the Bar Standards Board.

In the first (or 'academic') stage of training, aspiring barristers must obtain a law degree of a good standard (at least second class). Alternatively, those with a non-law degree (at least second class) may complete a one-year full-time or two-year part-time Common Professional Examination (CPE) or Graduate Diploma in Law (GDL).

The second (vocational) stage is the completion of the Bar Professional Training Course (BPTC), which is available at a number of validated institutions in the UK and must be applied for one year in advance. All barristers must join one of the four Inns of Court prior to commencing the BPTC.

Students are 'called to the Bar' by their Inn after completion of the vocational stage, but cannot practise as a barrister until completion of the third stage, which is called 'pupillage'. Being called to the Bar does not entitle a person to practise as a barrister – successful completion of pupillage is now a prerequisite. Pupillage lasts for two six-month periods: the 'first six' and the 'second six'. The former consists of shadowing an experienced barrister, while the latter involves appearing in court as a barrister. Chambers can then offer a long term 'tenancy' to students. Students who are not given 'tenancy' may take a 'third six'.

In Northern Ireland admission to the Bar is controlled by the Bar of Northern Ireland; admission as an Advocate to the Scottish Bar is through the Faculty of Advocates.

BAR STANDARDS BOARD 289-293 High Holborn, London, WC1V 7HZ T 020-7611 1444 E contactus@barstandardsboard.org.uk W www.barstandardsboard.org.uk
Chair of the Bar Council, Rt. Hon. Baroness Blackstone

FACULTY OF ADVOCATES, Parliament Square, Edinburgh EH1 1RF T 0131-226 5071 E info@advocates.org.uk W www.advocates.org.uk
Dean, Gordon Jackson, QC

GENERAL COUNCIL OF THE BAR (THE BAR COUNCIL), 289–293 High Holborn, London WC1V 7HZ T 020-7242 0082 E contactus@barcouncil.org.uk W www.barcouncil.org.uk
Chief Executive, Malcolm Cree, CBE

THE BAR OF NORTHERN IRELAND, 91 Chichester Street, Belfast BT1 3JQ T 028-9024 1523 W www.barofni.com
Chief Executive, David Mulholland

THE INNS OF COURT

HONOURABLE SOCIETY OF GRAY'S INN, 8 South Square, London WC1R 5ET T 020-7458 7900 W www.graysinn.org.uk
Under-Treasurer, Brig. Anthony Harking, OBE

HONOURABLE SOCIETY OF LINCOLN'S INN, Treasury Office, Lincoln's Inn, London WC2A 3TL T 020-7405 1393 E mail@lincolnsinn.org.uk W www.lincolnsinn.org.uk
Treasurer, Rt. Hon. Lord Justice McCombe

HONOURABLE SOCIETY OF THE INNER TEMPLE, Treasury Office, Inner Temple, 1 Mitre Court, London EC4Y 7BS T 020-7797 8250 E enquiries@innertemple.org.uk W www.innertemple.org.uk
Treasurer, Rt. Hon. Lord Hughes of Ombersley

HONOURABLE SOCIETY OF THE MIDDLE TEMPLE, Treasury Office, Ashley Building, Middle Temple Lane, London EC4Y 9BT T 020-7427 4800 E education@middletemple.org.uk W www.middletemple.org.uk
Chief Executive, Guy Perricone

NOTARIES PUBLIC

Notaries are qualified lawyers with a postgraduate diploma in notarial practice. Once a potential notary has passed the postgraduate diploma, they can petition the Court of Faculties for a 'faculty'. After the faculty is granted, the notary is able to practise; however, for the first two years this must be under the supervision of an experienced notary. The admission and regulation of notaries in England and Wales is a statutory function of the Faculty Office. This jurisdiction was confirmed by the Courts and Legal Services Act 1990. The Notaries Society of England and Wales is the representative body for practising notaries.

THE FACULTY OFFICE, 1 The Sanctuary, Westminster, London SW1P 3JT T 020-7222 5381
E faculty.office@1thesanctuary.com W www.facultyoffice.org.uk
Registrar, Howard Dellar

THE NOTARIES SOCIETY OF ENGLAND AND WALES, PO Box 1023, Ipswich IP1 9XB
E admin@thenotariessociety.org.uk
W www.thenotariessociety.org.uk
Secretary, Christopher Vaughan

SOLICITORS

Salary range: Trainee solicitors paid at least the national minimum wage; £25,000–£65,000 after qualification; £100,000+ (associate or partner)

Graduates from any discipline can train to be a solicitor; however, if the undergraduate degree is not in law, a one-year conversion course – either the Common Professional Examination (CPE) or the Graduate Diploma in Law (GDL) – must be completed. The next stage, and the beginning of the vocational phase, is the Legal Practice Course (LPC), which takes one year and is obligatory for both law and non-law graduates. The LPC provides professional instruction for prospective solicitors and can be completed on a full-time or part-time basis. Trainee solicitors then enter the final stage, which is a paid period of supervised work that lasts two years for full-time contracts. The employer that provides the training contract must be authorised by the Solicitors Regulation Authority (SRA) (the regulatory body of the Law Society of England and Wales), the Law Society of Scotland or the Law Society of Northern Ireland. The SRA also monitors the training contract to ensure that it provides the trainee with the expertise to qualify as a solicitor.

Conveyancers are specialist property lawyers, dealing with the legal processes involved in transferring buildings, land and associated finances from one owner to another. This was the sole responsibility of solicitors until 1987 but under current legislation it is now possible for others to train as conveyancers.

COUNCIL FOR LICENSED CONVEYANCERS (CLC), WeWork, 131 Finsbury Pavement, London EC2A 1NT
T 020-3859 0904 E clc@clc-uk.org W www.clc-uk.org
Chief Executive, Sheila Kumar

THE LAW SOCIETY OF ENGLAND AND WALES, The Law Society's Hall, 113 Chancery Lane, London WC2A 1PL
T 020-7242 1222 W www.lawsociety.org.uk
Chief Executive, Paul Tennant, OBE

LAW SOCIETY OF NORTHERN IRELAND, 96 Victoria Street, Belfast BT1 3GN T 028-9023 1614W www.lawsoc-ni.org
Chief Executive, Alan Hunter

LAW SOCIETY OF SCOTLAND, Atria One, 144 Morrison Street, Edinburgh EH3 8EX T 0131-226 7411
E lawscot@lawscot.org.uk W www.lawscot.org.uk
Chief Executive, Lorna Jack

SOLICITORS REGULATION AUTHORITY (SRA), The Cube, 199 Wharfside Street, Birmingham B1 1RN
T 0370-606 2555 W www.sra.org.uk
Chief Executive, Paul Philip

SOCIAL WORK

Salary range: £22,000 (newly qualified); £40,000 (with experience); £26,565–£35,577 (NHS)

Social workers tend to specialise in either adult or children's services. Social Work England obtains regulatory responsibility from the Health and Care Professions Council (HCPC) on 2 December 2019, taking on responsibility for setting standards of conduct and practice for social care workers and their employers, regulating the workforce and social work education and training. A degree or postgraduate qualification is needed in order to become a social worker.

SOCIAL WORK ENGLAND, 1 North Bank, Blonk Street, Sheffield S3 8JY W www.socialworkengland.org.uk
Chief Executive, Colum Conway

SURVEYING

Salary range: £20,000–£25,000 (starting); £50,000 (senior); up to £100,000+ (partners and directors)

The Royal Institution of Chartered Surveyors (RICS) is the professional body that represents and regulates property professionals including land surveyors, valuers, auctioneers, quantity surveyors and project managers. Entry to the institution, following completion of a RICS-accredited degree, is through completion of the Assessment of Professional Competence (APC), which involves a period of practical training concluded by a final assessment of competence. Entry as a technical surveyor requires completion of the Assessment of Technical Competence (ATC), which mirrors the format of the APC. The different levels of RICS membership are MRICS (member) or FRICS (fellow) for chartered surveyors, and AssocRICS for associate members.

Relevant courses can also be accredited by the Chartered Institute of Building (CIOB), which represents managers working in a range of construction disciplines. The CIOB offers four levels of membership to those who satisfy its requirements: FCIOB (fellow), MCIOB (member), ICIOB (incorporated) and ACIOB (associate).

CHARTERED INSTITUTE OF BUILDING (CIOB), 1 Arlington Square, Downshire Way, Bracknell RG12 1WA T 01344-630700 E reception@ciob.org.uk W www.ciob.org
Chief Executive, Caroline Gumble

ROYAL INSTITUTION OF CHARTERED SURVEYORS (RICS), Parliament Square, London SW1P 3AD T 024-7686 8555 E contactrics@rics.org W www.rics.org
Chief Executive, Sean Tompkins

TEACHING

Salary range: school teachers £24,373–£49,571; school leaders £41,065–£121,749 (for more detailed information see Education: Employees and Salaries)

Since 1 April 2018, the Teaching Regulation Agency, an executive agency sponsored by the Department for Education, is responsible for maintaining the register of qualified teachers in England and is the awarding body for Qualified Teacher Status (QTS). The Education Workforce Council in Wales and the General Teaching Council for Scotland fulfil this responsibility in their respective administrations. In Northern Ireland teacher registration is the responsibility of the General Teaching Council for Northern Ireland. Registration is a legal requirement in order to teach in local authority maintained schools. UCAS Teacher Training is the body through which to apply for postgraduate teacher training in the UK. To become a qualified teacher in a state school, all entrants must have a degree and gain QTS, which includes a minimum of 24 weeks in at least two different schools and academic study of teaching. QTS is not required to teach in independent schools, academies or free schools, but it is a definite advantage. Another route is through School-centred Initial Teacher Training (SCITT), where practical, hands-on teacher training is delivered by experienced, practising teachers in their own government-approved school.

Many courses also award an academic qualification known as the Postgraduate Certificate in Education (PGCE) in England and Wales and the Professional Graduate Diploma in Education (PGDE) in Scotland. Once training is completed, applicants spend a year in school as a newly qualified teacher (NQT).

Teachers in Further Education (FE) need not have QTS, though new entrants to FE may be required to work towards a specified FE qualification by employers. A range of courses are offered and usually require one year of study in addition to 100 hours of teaching experience. Similarly, academic staff in Higher Education require no formal teaching qualification, but are expected to obtain a qualification that meets standards set by the Higher Education Academy.

Details of routes to gaining QTS in England are available from the Department for Education, the Teaching Regulation Agency and UCAS. In the devolved administrations information is available from the Welsh government, Teach in Scotland and from the Department of Education in Northern Ireland.

In July 2017, the College of Teaching became the Chartered College of Teaching. Under the terms of its royal charter, it provides professional qualifications and membership to teachers and those involved in education in the UK and overseas.

ADVANCE HE Innovation Way, York Science Park, Heslington, York YO10 5BR T 0330-041 6201
E enquiries@advance-he.ac.uk W www.advance-he.ac.uk
Chief Executive, Alison Johns

CHARTERED COLLEGE OF TEACHING, 9–11 Endsleigh Gardens, London WC1H 0EH T 020-7911 5589
E hello@chartered.college W www.chartered.college
Chief Executive, Prof. Dame Alison Peacock, DBE

DEPARTMENT OF EDUCATION NORTHERN IRELAND, Rathgael House, Balloo Road, Rathgill, Bangor BT19 7PR T 028-9127 9279 E DE.DEWebMail@education-ni.gov.uk
W www.education-ni.gov.uk

EDUCATION WORKFORCE COUNCIL, 9th Floor, Eastgate House, 35–43 Newport Road, Cardiff CF24 0AB
T 029-2046 0099 E information@ewc.wales W www.ewc.wales
Chief Executive, Hayden Llewellyn

GENERAL TEACHING COUNCIL FOR NORTHERN IRELAND, 3rd Floor, Albany House, 73–75 Great Victoria Street, Belfast BT2 7AF T 028-9033 3390 E info@gtcni.org.uk
W www.gtcni.org.uk
Chair, David Canning, OBE

GENERAL TEACHING COUNCIL FOR SCOTLAND, Clerwood House, 96 Clermiston Road, Edinburgh EH12 6UT
T 0131-314 6000 E gtcs@gtcs.org.uk W www.gtcs.org.uk
Chief Executive, Ken Muir

TEACHING REGULATION AGENCY, Ground Floor South, Cheylesmore House, 5 Quinton Road, Coventry CV1 2WT
T 0207 593 5394 E qts.enquiries@education.gov.uk
W www.gov.uk/government/organisations/teaching-regulation-agency
Chief Executive, Alan Meyrick

UCAS TEACHER TRAINING, Rosehill, New Barn Lane, Cheltenham GL52 3LZ T 0371-468 0469
W www.ucas.com/teaching-in-the-uk
Chief Executive, Clare Marchant

VETERINARY MEDICINE

Salary range: £30,000 (newly qualified); £43,200–£64,870 (with experience); £72,360 (20+ years experience)

The regulatory body for veterinary surgeons in the UK is the Royal College of Veterinary Surgeons (RCVS), which keeps the register of those entitled to practise veterinary medicine, the register of veterinary nurses and veterinary practice premises (on behalf of the Veterinary Medicines Directorate). Holders of recognised degrees from any of the seven UK university veterinary schools that have been approved by the RCVS or from certain EU or overseas universities are entitled to be registered, and holders of certain other degrees may take a statutory membership examination. The UK's RCVS-approved veterinary schools are located at the University of Bristol, the University of Cambridge, the University of Edinburgh, the University of Glasgow, the University of Liverpool, University of Nottingham and the Royal Veterinary College in London; all veterinary degrees last for five years except that offered at Cambridge, which lasts for six.

The British Veterinary Association is the national representative body for the UK veterinary profession. The British Veterinary Nursing Association is the professional body representing veterinary nurses.

BRITISH VETERINARY ASSOCIATION, 7 Mansfield Street, London W1G 9NQ T 020-7636 6541 E bvahq@bva.co.uk
W www.bva.co.uk
Chief Executive, David Calpin

BRITISH VETERINARY NURSING ASSOCIATION, 79 Greenway Business Centre, Harlow Business Park, Harlow, Essex CM19 5QE T 01279-408644 E bvna@bvna.co.uk
W www.bvna.org.uk
Honorary Treasurer, Erika Feilberg

ROYAL COLLEGE OF VETERINARY SURGEONS (RCVS), Belgravia House, 62–64 Horseferry Road, London SW1P 2AF T 020-7222 2001 E info@rcvs.org.uk
W www.rcvs.org.uk
Chief Executive, Lizzie Lockett

INDEPENDENT SCHOOLS

Independent schools (non-maintained mainstream schools) charge fees and are owned privately or managed under special trusts, with profits being used for the benefit of the schools concerned. As at January 2019 there were 2,486 non-maintained mainstream schools in the UK, educating 580,955 pupils; 6.6 per cent of the total school-age population.

The Independent Schools Council (ISC), formed in 1974, acts on behalf of the seven independent schools' associations which constitute it. These associations are:

Association of Governing Bodies of Independent Schools (AGBIS)
Girls' Schools Association (GSA)
Headmasters' & Headmistresses' Conference (HMC)
Independent Association of Prep Schools (IAPS)
Independent Schools Association (ISA)
Independent Schools' Bursars Association (ISBA)
The Society of Heads

In January 2019 there were 536,109 pupils being educated in 1,364 schools in membership of associations within the Independent Schools Council (ISC). Most schools not in membership of an ISC association are likely to be privately owned. The Independent Schools Inspectorate (ISI) was demerged from ISC with effect from 1 January 2008 and is legally and operationally independent of ISC. ISI works as an accredited inspectorate of schools in membership of the ISC associations under a framework agreed with the Department for Education (DfE). A school must pass an ISI accreditation inspection to qualify for membership of an association within ISC.

In 2019 at GCSE 23.1 per cent of all exams taken by candidates in ISC associations' member schools were awarded a grade 9 (compared to the national average of 4.5 per cent), and at A-level 17.2 per cent of entries were awarded an A* grade (national average, 8 per cent). In 2019 a total of 176,633 pupils (34 per cent) at schools in ISC associations were receiving help with their fees, mainly in the form of bursaries and scholarships from the schools. ISC schools provided £864m of assistance with fees.

INDEPENDENT SCHOOLS COUNCIL, First Floor, 27 Queen Anne's Gate, London SW1H 9BU T 020-7766 7070
W www.isc.co.uk

The list of schools below was compiled from the *Independent Schools Yearbook 2018–19* (ed. Judy Mott, published by Bloomsbury Publishing) which includes schools whose heads are members of one of the ISC's five Heads' Associations. Further details are available online (W www.isyb.co.uk).

The fees shown below represent the upper limit payable for the year 2018–19.

School	Web Address	Termly Fees		Head
		Day	Board	
ENGLAND				
Abbey Gate College, Cheshire	www.abbeygatecollege.co.uk	£4,280	–	Mrs T. Pollard
Abbot's Hill School, Herts	www.abbotshill.herts.sch.uk	£6,172	–	Mrs E. Thomas
Abbotsholme School, Derbys, Staffs	www.abbotsholme.co.uk	£7,495	£10,995	R. Barnes
Abingdon School, Oxon	www.abingdon.org.uk	£6,650	£11,070	M. Windsor
Adcote School, Shrops	www.adcoteschool.org.uk	£4,946	£9,032	Mrs D. Browne
AKS Lytham, Lancs	www.akslytham.com	£3,929	–	M. Walton
Aldenham School, Herts	www.aldenham.com	£7,538	£11,078	J. Fowler
Alderley Edge School for Girls, Cheshire	www.aesg.co.uk	£4,150	–	Mrs H. Jeys
Alleyn's School, London, SE22	www.alleyns.org.uk	£6,617	–	Dr G. Savage
Ampleforth College, N. Yorks	www.ampleforth.org.uk/college	£8,212	£11,808	Miss D. Rowe
Ardingly College, W. Sussex	www.ardingly.com	£7,870	£11,470	B. Figgis
Ashford School, Kent	www.ashfordschool.co.uk	£5,600	£12,000	M. Hall
Austin Friars, Cumbria	www.austinfriars.co.uk	£4,880	–	M. Harris
Bablake School, W. Midlands	www.bablake.com	£3,898	–	A. Wright
Badminton School, Bristol	www.badmintonschool.co.uk	£5,475	£12,525	Mrs R. Tear
Bancroft's School, Essex	www.bancrofts.org	£6,041	–	S. Marshall
Barnard Castle School, Durham	www.barnardcastleschool.org.uk	£4,650	£8,400	A. Jackson
Bedales School, Hants	www.bedales.org.uk	£12,095	£9,505	M. Bashaarat
Bede's Senior School, E. Sussex	www.bedes.org	£11,720	£7,370	P. Goodyer
Bedford Girls' School, Beds	www.bedfordgirlsschool.co.uk	£4,468	–	Miss J. MacKenzie
Bedford Modern School, Beds	www.bedmod.co.uk	£4,468	–	A. Tate
Bedford School, Beds	www.bedfordschool.org.uk	£6,344	£10,730	J. Hodgson
Bedstone College, Shrops	www.bedstone.org	£4,885	£8,840	D. Gajadharsingh
Beechwood Sacred Heart School, Kent	www.beechwood.org.uk	£5,375	£9,950	Mrs H. Rowe
Benenden School, Kent	www.benenden.kent.sch.uk	–	£12,650	Mrs S. Price
Berkhamsted, Herts	www.berkhamsted.com	£6,880	£11,530	R. Backhouse
Bethany School, Kent	www.bethanyschool.org.uk	£6,155	£10,500	F. Healy
Birkdale School, S. Yorks	www.birkdaleschool.org.uk	£4,330	–	P. Harris
Birkenhead School, Merseyside	www.birkenheadschool.co.uk	£3,998	–	P. Vicars
Bishop's Stortford College, Herts	www.bishopsstortfordcollege.org	£6,613	£10,237	J. Gladwin
Blackheath High School, London, SE3	www.blackheathhighschool.gdst.net	£5,498	–	Mrs C. Chandler-Thompson
Blundell's School, Devon	www.blundells.org	£7,470	£11,735	B. Wielenga
Bolton School Boys' Division, Lancs	www.boltonschool.org/seniorboys	£3,992	–	P. Britton

School	Website	Fee 1	Fee 2	Head
Bolton School Girls' Division, Lancs	www.boltonschool.org/seniorgirls	£3,992	–	Miss S. Hincks
Bootham School, N. Yorks	www.boothamschool.com	£5,995	£10,155	C. Jeffrey
Bournemouth Collegiate School, Dorset	www.bournemouthcollegiateschool.co.uk	£4,810	£9,890	R. Slatford
Box Hill School, Surrey	www.boxhillschool.com	£6,570	£13,310	C. Lowde
Bradfield College, Berks	www.bradfieldcollege.org.uk	£9,975	£12,468	Dr C. Stevens
Bradford Grammar School, W. Yorks	www.bradfordgrammar.com	£4,223	–	Dr S. Hinchliffe
Bredon School, Glos	www.bredonschool.org	£7,315	£11,715	K. Claeys
Brentwood School, Essex	www.brentwoodschool.co.uk	£6,315	£12,376	D. Davies
Brighton & Hove High School, E. Sussex	www.bhhs.gdst.net	£4,807	–	Ms J. Smith
Brighton College, E. Sussex	www.brightoncollege.org.uk	–	£13,190	R. Cairns
Bristol Grammar School, Bristol	www.bristolgrammarschool.co.uk	£4,870	–	J. Barot
Bromley High School, Kent	www.bromleyhigh.gdst.net	£5,697	–	Mrs A. Drew
Bromsgrove School, Worcs	www.bromsgrove-school.co.uk	£5,555	£12,430	P. Clague
Bruton School for Girls, Somerset	www.brutonschool.co.uk	£5,935	£10,110	Mrs N. Botterill
Bryanston School, Dorset	www.bryanston.co.uk	£10,438	£12,728	Ms S. Thomas
Burgess Hill Girls, W. Sussex	www.burgesshillgirls.com	£6,400	£11,400	Mrs L. Laybourn
Bury Grammar School Boys, Lancs	www.burygrammar.com	£3,585	–	Mrs J. Anderson
Bury Grammar School Girls, Lancs	www.burygrammar.com	£3,585	–	Mrs J. Anderson
Caterham School, Surrey	www.caterhamschool.co.uk	£6,300	£12,190	C. Jones
Channing School, London, N6	www.channing.co.uk	£6,470	–	Mrs B. Elliott
Charterhouse, Surrey	www.charterhouse.org.uk	–	£13,055	Dr A. Peterken
Cheltenham College, Glos	www.cheltenhamcollege.org	£9,195	£12,260	Mrs N. Huggett
Cheltenham Ladies' College, Glos	www.cheltladiescollege.org	£8,270	£12,315	Ms E. Jardine-Young
Chetham's School of Music, Greater Manchester	www.chethams.com	–	–	A. Jones
Chigwell School, Essex	www.chigwell-school.org	£5,995	£10,011	M. Punt
Christ's Hospital, W. Sussex	www.christs-hospital.org.uk	£5,930	£11,480	S. Reid
Churcher's College, Hants	www.churcherscollege.com	£5,140	–	S. Williams
City of London Freemen's School, Surrey	www.freemens.org	£6,081	£10,260	R. Martin
City of London School, London, EC4	www.cityoflondonschool.org.uk	£5,967	–	A. Bird
City of London School for Girls, London, EC2	www.clsg.org.uk	£6,128	–	Mrs E. Harrop
Claremont Fan Court School, Surrey	www.claremontfancourt.co.uk	£5,890	–	W. Brierly
Clayesmore School, Dorset	www.clayesmore.com	£8,740	£11,910	Mrs J. Thomson
Clifton College, Bristol	www.cliftoncollege.com	£8,230	£12,390	Dr T. Greene
Clifton High School, Bristol	www.cliftonhigh.co.uk	£4,985	–	Dr A. Neill
Cobham Hall, Kent	www.cobhamhall.com	£7,401	£11,517	Ms M. Roberts
Cokethorpe School, Oxon	www.cokethorpe.org.uk	£6,400	–	D. Ettinger
Colfe's School, London, SE12	www.colfes.com	£5,643	–	R. Russell
Colston's, Bristol	www.colstons.org	£4,650	–	J. McCullough
Concord College, Shrops	www.concordcollegeuk.com	£4,903	£13,967	N. Hawkins
Cranford House, Oxon	www.cranfordhouse.net	£5,680	–	Dr J. Raymond
Cranleigh School, Surrey	www.cranleigh.org	£10,390	£12,635	M. Reader
Croydon High School, Surrey	www.croydonhigh.gdst.net	£5,552	–	Mrs E. Pattison
Culford School, Suffolk	www.culford.co.uk	£6,500	£10,580	J. Johnson-Munday
Dauntsey's School, Wilts	www.dauntseys.org	£6,330	£10,480	M. Lascelles
Dean Close School, Glos	www.deanclose.org.uk	£8,200	£11,939	Mrs E. Taylor
Denstone College, Staffs	www.denstonecollege.org	£5,293	£8,407	M. Norris
Derby Grammar School, Derbys	www.derbygrammar.org	£4,483	–	Dr R. Norris
Derby High School, Derbys	www.derbyhigh.derby.sch.uk	£4,290	–	Mrs A. Chapman
Dover College, Kent	www.dovercollege.org.uk	£5,350	£10,500	G. Doodes
d'Overbroeck's, Oxon	www.doverbroecks.com	£7,950	£12,900	J. Cuff
Downe House, Berks	www.downehouse.net	£9,165	£12,510	Mrs E. McKendrick
Downside School, Somerset	www.downside.co.uk	£6,417	£11,287	A. Hobbs
Dulwich College, London, SE21	www.dulwich.org.uk	£6,816	£14,227	Dr J. Spence
Dunottar School, Surrey	www.dunottarschool.com	£5,345	–	M. Tottman
Durham High School for Girls, Durham	www.dhsfg.org.uk	£4,375	–	Mrs S. Niblock
Eastbourne College, E. Sussex	www.eastbourne-college.co.uk	£7,710	£11,750	T. Lawson
Edgbaston High School, W. Midlands	www.edgbastonhigh.co.uk	£4,258	–	Dr R. Weeks
Ellesmere College, Shrops	www.ellesmere.com	£6,123	£10,977	B. Wignall
Eltham College, London, SE9	www.elthamcollege.london	£5,925	–	G. Sanderson
Emanuel School, London, SW11	www.emanuel.org.uk	£6,194	–	R. Milne
Epsom College, Surrey	www.epsomcollege.org.uk	£8,422	£12,421	J. Piggot
Eton College, Berks	www.etoncollege.com	–	£13,556	S. Henderson
Ewell Castle School, Surrey	www.ewellcastle.co.uk	£5,564	–	S. Edmonds
Exeter School, Devon	www.exeterschool.org.uk	£4,410	–	B. Griffin
Farnborough Hill, Hants	www.farnborough-hill.org.uk	£4,932	–	Mrs A. Neil

Farringtons School, Kent	www.farringtons.org.uk	£4,870	£10,560	Mrs D. Nancekievill
Felsted School, Essex	www.felsted.org	£7,850	£11,995	C. Townsend
Forest School, London, E17	www.forest.org.uk	£6,227	–	M. Hodges
Framlingham College, Suffolk	www.framcollege.co.uk	£6,642	£10,328	P. Taylor
Francis Holland School, London, NW1	www.fhs-nw1.org.uk	£6,680	–	C. Fillingham
Francis Holland School, London, SW1	www.fhs-sw1.org.uk	£6,970	–	Mrs L. Elphinstone
Frensham Heights, Surrey	www.frensham.org	£6,410	£9,890	R. Clarke
Fulneck School, W. Yorks	www.fulneckschool.co.uk	£4,375	£8,485	P. Taylor
Gateways School, W. Yorks	www.gatewaysschool.co.uk	£4,538	–	Dr T. Johnson
Giggleswick School, N. Yorks	www.giggleswick.org.uk	£6,475	£10,715	M. Turnbull
The Godolphin and Latymer School, London, W6	www.godolphinandlatymer.com	£7,205	–	Dr F. Ramsey
Godolphin School, Wilts	www.godolphin.org	£7,030	£10,675	Mrs E. Hattersley
The Grange School, Cheshire	www.grange.org.uk	£3,835	–	Mrs D. Leonard
Gresham's School, Norfolk	www.greshams.com	£8,140	£11,660	D. Robb
Guildford High School – Senior School, Surrey	www.guildfordhigh.co.uk	£5,664	–	Mrs F. Boulton
The Haberdashers' Aske's Boys' School, Herts	www.habsboys.org.uk	£6,782	–	G. Lock
Haberdashers' Aske's School for Girls, Herts	www.habsgirls.org.uk	£6,131	–	Miss B. O'Connor
Halliford School, Middx	www.hallifordschool.co.uk	£5,320	–	J. Davies
Hampshire Collegiate School, Hants	www.hampshirecs.org.uk	£5,253	£8,925	C. Canning
Hampton School, Middx	hamptonschool.org.uk	£6,685	–	K. Knibbs
Harrogate Ladies' College, N. Yorks	www.hlc.org.uk	£5,345	£12,170	Mrs S. Brett
Harrow School, Middx	www.harrowschool.org.uk	–	£13,350	A. Land
Headington School, Oxon	www.headington.org	£6,417	£12,762	Mrs C. Jordan
Heathfield School, Berks	www.heathfieldschool.net	£7,600	£12,210	Mrs M. Legge
Hereford Cathedral School, Herefords	www.herefordcs.com	£4,627	–	P. Smith
Hethersett Old Hall School, Norfolk	www.hohs.co.uk	£5,210	£8,020	S. Crump
Highclare School, W. Midlands	www.highclareschool.co.uk	£4,215	–	Dr R. Luker
Highgate School, London, N6	www.highgateschool.org.uk	£6,990	–	A. Pettitt
Hill House School, S. Yorks	www.hillhouse.doncaster.sch.uk	£4,400	–	D. Holland
Hurstpierpoint College, W. Sussex	www.hppc.org.uk	£7,950	£9,985	T. Manly
Hymers College, E. Yorks	www.hymerscollege.co.uk	£3,786	–	D. Elstone
Ibstock Place School, London, SW15	www.ibstockplaceschool.co.uk	£6,960	–	Mrs A. Sylvester-Johnson
Immanuel College, Herts	www.immanuelcollege.co.uk	£5,890	–	G. Griffin
Ipswich High School, Suffolk	www.ipswichhighschool.co.uk	£4,708	–	Ms O. Carlin
Ipswich School, Suffolk	www.ipswich.school	£5,193	£10,057	N. Weaver
James Allen's Girls' School (JAGS), London, SE22	www.jags.org.uk	£5,997	–	Mrs S. Huang
The John Lyon School, Middx	www.johnlyon.org	£6,194	–	Miss K. Haynes
Kent College, Kent	www.kentcollege.com	£6,105	£11,497	Dr D. Lamper
Kimbolton School, Cambs	www.kimbolton.cambs.sch.uk	£5,265	£8,760	J. Belbin
King Edward VI High School for Girls, W. Midlands	www.kehs.org.uk	£4,296	–	Mrs A. Clark
King Edward VI School, Hants	www.kes.hants.sch.uk	£5,350	–	J. Thould
King Edward's School, Somerset	www.kesbath.com	£4,825	–	M. Boden
King Edward's School, W. Midlands	www.kes.org.uk	£4,410	–	K. Phillips
King Edward's Witley, Surrey	www.kesw.org	£6,820	£10,665	J. Attwater
King Henry VIII School, W. Midlands	www.khviii.com	£3,898	–	J. Slack
King William's College, Isle of Man	www.kwc.im	£6,520	£9,882	J. Buchanan
King's College School, London, SW19	www.kcs.org.uk	£7,200	–	A. Halls
King's College, Taunton, Somerset	www.kings-taunton.co.uk	£7,460	£11,055	R. Biggs
King's Ely, Cambs	www.kingsely.org	£7,153	£10,355	Mrs S. Freestone
King's High School, Warwicks	www.kingshighwarwick.co.uk	£4,325	–	R. Nicholson
The King's School, Kent	www.kings-school.co.uk	£9,165	£12,485	P. Roberts
The King's School, Cheshire	www.kingschester.co.uk	£4,505	–	G. Hartley
The King's School, Cheshire	www.kingsmac.co.uk	£4,330	–	Dr S. Hyde
King's Rochester, Kent	www.kings-rochester.co.uk	£6,440	£10,530	B. Charles
The King's School, Worcs	www.ksw.org.uk	£4,663	–	M. Armstrong
The Kingsley School, Warwicks	www.thekingsleyschool.com	£4,418	–	Ms H. Owens
Kingsley School, Devon	www.kingsleyschoolbideford.co.uk	£4,460	£8,945	P. Last
Kingston Grammar School, Surrey	www.kgs.org.uk	£6,410	–	S. Lehec
Kingswood School, Somerset	www.kingswood.bath.sch.uk	£5,061	£10,909	S. Morris
Kirkham Grammar School, Lancs	www.kirkhamgrammar.co.uk	£3,875	£7,355	D. Berry
Lady Eleanor Holles, Middx	www.lehs.org.uk	£5,576	–	Mrs H. Hanbury

School	Website	Fee 1	Fee 2	Head
Lancing College, W. Sussex	www.lancingcollege.co.uk	£8,190	£11,995	D. Oliver
Latymer Upper School, London, W6	www.latymer-upper.org	£6,710	–	D. Goodhew
The Grammar School at Leeds, W. Yorks	www.gsal.org.uk	£4,596	–	Mrs S. Woodroofe
Leicester Grammar School, Leics	www.lgs-senior.org.uk	£4,343	–	?J. Watson
Leicester High School for Girls, Leics	www.leicesterhigh.co.uk	£4,065	–	A. Whelpdale
Leighton Park School, Berks	www.leightonpark.com	£7,326	£11,915	M. Judd
Leweston School, Dorset	www.leweston.co.uk	£5,140	£10,185	Mrs K. Reynolds
The Leys, Cambs	www.theleys.net	£7,345	£10,975	M. Priestley
Lichfield Cathedral School, Staffs	www.lichfieldcathedralschool.com	£4,605	–	Mrs S. Hannam
Lincoln Minster School, Lincolns	www.lincolnminsterschool.co.uk	£4,608	£9,022	M. Wallace
Lingfield College, Surrey	www.lingfieldcollege.co.uk	£5,104	–	R. Bool
Longridge Towers School, Northumberland	www.lts.org.uk	£4,550	£9,250	J. Lee
Lord Wandsworth College, Hants	www.lordwandsworth.org	£10,600	£11,100	A. Williams
Loughborough Grammar School, Leics	www.lsf.org/grammar	£4,183	£9,584	D. Byrne
Loughborough High School, Leics	www.lsf.org/high	£4,183	–	Dr F. Miles
Luckley House School, Berks	www.luckleyhouseschool.org	£5,540	£9,694	Mrs J. Tudor
LVS Ascot, Berks	www.lvs.ascot.sch.uk	£5,657	£10,077	Mrs C. Cunniffe
Magdalen College School, Oxon	www.mcsoxford.org	£6,159	–	Miss H. Pike
Malvern College, Worcs	www.malverncollege.org.uk	£8,485	£13,153	K. Metcalfe
The Manchester Grammar School, Greater Manchester	www.mgs.org	£4,190	–	Dr M. Boulton
Manchester High School for Girls, Greater Manchester	www.manchesterhigh.co.uk	£3,958	–	Mrs C. Hewitt
Manor House School, Bookham, Surrey	www.manorhouseschool.org	£5,801	–	Ms T. Fantham
The Marist School – Senior Phase, Berks	www.themarist.com	£4,870	–	K. McCloskey
Marlborough College, Wilts	www.marlboroughcollege.org	–	£12,605	Mrs L. Moelwyn-Hughes
Marymount International School, Surrey	www.marymountlondon.com	£7,925	£13,475	Mrs M. Frazier
Mayfield School, E. Sussex	www.mayfieldgirls.org	£7,000	£11,300	Miss A. Beary
The Maynard School, Devon	www.maynard.co.uk	£4,416	–	Miss S. Dunn
Merchant Taylors' Boys' School, Merseyside	www.merchanttaylors.com	£3,798	–	D. Wickes
Merchant Taylors' Girls' School, Merseyside	www.merchanttaylors.com	£3,798	–	Mrs C. Tao
Merchant Taylors' School, Middx	www.mtsn.org.uk	£6,899	–	S. Everson
Mill Hill School, London, NW7	millhill.org	£7,047	£11,239	Mrs J. Sanchez
Millfield, Somerset	millfieldschool.com	£8,535	£12,870	G. Horgan
Milton Abbey School, Dorset	www.miltonabbey.co.uk	£6,750	£12,850	Mrs J. Fremont-Barnes
Monkton Combe School, Somerset	www.monktoncombeschool.com	£6,970	£11,115	C. Wheeler
More House School, London, SW1	www.morehouse.org.uk	£6,650	–	Mrs A. Leach
Moreton Hall, Shrops	www.moretonhall.org	£9,575	£11,625	J. Forster
Mount House School, Herts	www.mounthouse.org.uk	£5,010	–	T. Mullins
Mount Kelly, Devon	www.mountkelly.com	£5,840	£10,190	G. Ayling
Mount St Mary's College, Derbys	www.msmcollege.com	£4,695	£9,995	Dr N. Cuddihy
New Hall School, Essex	www.newhallschool.co.uk	£6,626	£10,002	Mrs K. Jeffrey
Newcastle High School for Girls, Tyne and Wear	www.newcastlehigh.gdst.net	£4,341	–	M. Tippett
Newcastle School for Boys, Tyne and Wear	www.newcastleschool.co.uk	£4,161	–	D. Tickner
Newcastle-under-Lyme School, Staffs	www.nuls.org.uk	£3,993	–	M. Getty
North London Collegiate School, Middx	www.nlcs.org.uk	£6,676	–	Mrs S. Clark
Norwich High School, Norfolk	www.norwichhigh.gdst.net	£4,854	–	Mrs K. Malaisé
Norwich School, Norfolk	www.norwich-school.org.uk	£5,404	–	S. Griffiths
Notre Dame School, Surrey	www.notredame.co.uk	£5,590	–	Mrs A. King
Notting Hill and Ealing High School, London, W13	www.nhehs.gdst.net	£6,187	–	M. Shoults
Nottingham Girls' High School, Notts	www.nottinghamgirlshigh.gdst.net	£4,527	–	Miss J. Keller
Nottingham High School, Notts	www.nottinghamhigh.co.uk	£4,955	–	K. Fear
Oakham School, Rutland	www.oakham.rutland.sch.uk	£6,845	£11,220	N. Lashbrook
Ockbrook School, Derbys	www.ockbrooksch.co.uk	£4,390	–	T. Brooksby
Oldham Hulme Grammar School, Lancs	www.ohgs.co.uk	£3,745	–	C. Mairs
The Oratory School, Oxon	www.oratory.co.uk	£8,322	£11,433	J. Smith
Oundle School, Northants	www.oundleschool.org.uk	£7,935	£12,230	Mrs S. Kerr-Dineen
Our Lady's Abingdon Senior School, Oxon	www.olab.org.uk	£5,350	–	S. Oliver
Oxford High School, Oxon	www.oxfordhigh.gdst.net	£5,182	–	Dr P. Hills
Palmers Green High School, London, N21	www.pghs.co.uk	£5,310	–	Mrs W. Kempster
Pangbourne College, Berks	www.pangbourne.com	£8,295	£11,730	T. Garnier
The Perse Upper School, Cambs	www.perse.co.uk	£5,774	–	E. Elliott
The Peterborough School, Cambs	www.thepeterboroughschool.co.uk	£4,956	–	A. Meadows
Pipers Corner School, Bucks	www.piperscorner.co.uk	£6,130	–	Mrs H. Ness-Gifford

Pitsford School, Northants	www.pitsfordschool.com	£4,902	–	Dr C. Walker
Plymouth College, Devon	www.plymouthcollege.com	£5,225	£9,995	J. Cohen
Pocklington School, E. Yorks	www.pocklingtonschool.com	£4,873	£9,497	T. Seth
Portland Place School, London, W1B	www.portland-place.co.uk	£7,040	–	D. Bradbury
The Portsmouth Grammar School, Hants	www.pgs.org.uk	£5,317	–	Dr A. Cotton
Portsmouth High School, Hants	www.portsmouthhigh.co.uk	£4,662	–	Mrs J. Prescott
Princess Helena College, Herts	www.princesshelenacollege.co.uk	£6,741	£9,800	Mrs S. Davis
Princethorpe College, Warwicks	www.princethorpe.co.uk	£4,231	–	E. Hester
Prior Park College, Somerset	www.priorparkschools.com	£5,585	£10,315	J. Murphy-O'Connor
The Purcell School, Herts	www.purcell-school.org	£8,656	£11,025	P. Bambrough
Putney High School, London, SW15	www.putneyhigh.gdst.net	£6,300	–	Mrs S. Longstaff
Queen Anne's School, Berks	www.qas.org.uk	£8,045	£11,860	Mrs J. Harrington
Queen Elizabeth's Hospital (QEH), Bristol	www.qehbristol.co.uk	£4,802	–	S. Holliday
Queen Mary's School, N. Yorks	www.queenmarys.org	£6,325	£8,630	Mrs C. Cameron
Queen's College, London, London, W1G	www.qcl.org.uk	£6,375	–	R. Tillett
Queen's College, Somerset	www.queenscollege.org.uk	£6,150	£10,660	Dr L. Earps
Queen's Gate School, London, SW7	www.queensgate.org.uk	£6,850	–	Mrs R. Kamaryc
Queenswood School, Herts	www.queenswood.org	£8,125	£10,900	Mrs J. Cameron
Radley College, Oxon	www.radley.org.uk	–	£12,775	J. Moule
Ratcliffe College, Leics	www.ratcliffecollege.com	£5,429	£8,653	J. Reddin
The Read School, N. Yorks	www.readschool.co.uk	£4,132	£9,482	Mrs R. Ainley
Reading Blue Coat School, Berks	www.rbcs.org.uk	£5,565	–	J. Elzinga
Reddam House Berkshire, Berks	www.reddamhouse.org.uk	£5,760	£10,935	Mrs T. Howard
Redmaids' High School, Bristol	www.redmaidshigh.co.uk	£5,025	–	Mrs I. Tobias
Reed's School, Surrey	www.reeds.surrey.sch.uk	£8,225	£10,600	M. Hoskins
Reigate Grammar School, Surrey	www.reigategrammar.org	£6,240	–	S. Fenton
Rendcomb College, Glos	www.rendcombcollege.org.uk	£7,775	£10,500	R. Jones
Repton School, Derbys	www.repton.org.uk	£8,831	£11,904	M. Semmence
RGS Worcester, Worcs	www.rgsw.org.uk	£4,360	–	J. Pitt
Rishworth School, W. Yorks	www.rishworth-school.co.uk	£4,220	£9,995	Dr P. Silverwood
Roedean Moira House Girls School, E. Sussex	www.roedeanmoirahouse.co.uk	£6,020	£11,140	A. Wood
Roedean School, E. Sussex	www.roedean.co.uk	£7,165	£12,855	O. Blond
Rossall School, Lancs	www.rossall.org.uk	£4,360	£12,450	J. Quartermain
Royal Grammar School, Surrey	www.rgsg.co.uk	£6,095	–	Dr J. Cox
Royal Grammar School, Tyne and Wear	www.rgs.newcastle.sch.uk	£4,388	–	J. Fern
Royal Hospital School, Suffolk	www.royalhospitalschool.org	£5,830	£10,865	S. Lockyer
The Royal Masonic School for Girls, Herts	www.rmsforgirls.org.uk	£5,825	£9,945	K. Carson
Royal Russell School, Surrey	www.royalrussell.co.uk	£6,160	£12,175	C. Hutchinson
Rugby School, Warwicks	www.rugbyschool.co.uk	£7,479	£11,920	P. Green
Ryde School with Upper Chine, Isle of Wight	www.rydeschool.org.uk	£4,410	–	M. Waldron
Rye St Antony, Oxon	www.ryestantony.co.uk	£5,110	£8,645	Mrs S. Ryan
St Albans High School for Girls, Herts	www.stahs.org.uk	£6,265	–	Mrs J. Brown
St Albans School, Herts	www.st-albans.herts.sch.uk	£6,200	–	J. Gillespie
St Augustine's Priory School, London, W5	www.sapriory.com	£5,231	–	Mrs S. Raffray
St Bede's College, Greater Manchester	www.sbcm.co.uk	£3,775	–	L. d'Arcy
St Benedict's School, London, W5	www.stbenedicts.org.uk	£5,615	–	A. Johnson
St Catherine's School, Surrey	www.stcatherines.info	£6,125	£10,095	Mrs A. Phillips
St Catherine's School, Middx	www.stcatherineschool.co.uk	£4,970	–	Mrs J. McPherson
St Christopher School, Herts	www.stchris.co.uk	£6,025	£10,550	R. Palmer
St Columba's College, Herts	www.stcolumbascollege.org	£5,233	–	D. Buxton
St Dominic's Grammar School, Staffs	www.stdominicsgrammarschool.co.uk	£4,404	–	P. McNabb
St Dunstan's College, London, SE6	www.stdunstans.org	£5,732	–	N. Hewlett
St Edmund's College, Herts	www.stedmundscollege.org	£5,935	£10,305	P. Durán
St Edmund's School Canterbury, Kent	www.stedmunds.org.uk	£6,822	£11,656	E. O'Connor
St Edward's, Oxford, Oxon	www.stedwardsoxford.org	£10,095	£12,615	S. Jones
St Edward's School, Glos	www.stedwards.co.uk	£5,920	–	Mrs P. Clayfield
St Gabriel's, Berks	www.stgabriels.co.uk	£5,806	–	R. Smith
St George's College, Weybridge, Surrey	www.stgeorgesweybridge.com	£6,395	–	Mrs R. Owens
St George's, Ascot, Berks	www.stgeorges-ascot.org.uk	£7,600	£11,820	Mrs E. Hewer
St Helen & St Katharine, Oxon	www.shsk.org.uk	£5,490	–	Mrs R. Dougall
St Helen's School, Middx	www.sthelens.london	£5,816	–	Dr M. Short
St James Senior Boys' School, Surrey	www.stjamesboys.co.uk	£6,310	–	D. Brazier
St James Senior Girls' School, London, W14	www.stjamesgirls.co.uk	£6,700	–	Mrs S. Labram
St John's College, Hants	www.stjohnscollege.co.uk	£4,030	£8,695	Mrs M. Maguire
St Joseph's College, Suffolk	www.stjos.co.uk	£5,050	£11,590	Mrs D. Clarke
St Lawrence College, Kent	www.slcuk.com	£5,333	£11,945	A. Spencer
St Mary's School Ascot, Berks	www.st-marys-ascot.co.uk	£9,210	£12,930	Mrs M. Breen

School	Website	Fee 1	Fee 2	Head
St Mary's Calne, Wilts	www.stmaryscalne.org	£9,675	£12,975	Dr F. Kirk
St Mary's School, Essex	www.stmaryscolchester.org.uk	£4,995	–	Mrs H. Vipond
St Mary's College, Merseyside	www.stmarys.ac	£3,720	–	M. Kennedy
St Mary's School, Bucks	www.stmarysschool.co.uk	£5,660	–	Mrs P. Adams
St Mary's School, Dorset	www.stmarys.eu	£6,950	£10,490	Mrs M. Young
St Nicholas' School, Hants	www.st-nicholas.hants.sch.uk	£4,786	–	Dr O. Wright
St Paul's Girls' School, London, W6	www.spgs.org	£8,297	–	Mrs S. Fletcher
St Paul's School, London, SW13	www.stpaulsschool.org.uk	£8,344	£12,537	Professor Mark Bailey
St Peter's School, York, N. Yorks	www.stpetersyork.org.uk	£6,025	£10,010	J. Walker
St Swithun's School, Hants	www.stswithuns.com	£6,855	£11,200	Ms J. Gandee
Scarborough College, N. Yorks	www.scarboroughcollege.co.uk	£4,898	£8,267	G. Emmett
Seaford College, W. Sussex	www.seaford.org	£7,130	£11,030	J. Green
Sevenoaks School, Kent	www.sevenoaksschool.org	£7,785	£12,432	Dr K. Ricks
Shebbear College, Devon	www.shebbearcollege.co.uk	£4,325	£8,775	S. Weale
Sheffield High School for Girls, S. Yorks	www.sheffieldhighschool.org.uk	£4,325	–	Mrs N. Gunson
Sherborne Girls, Dorset	www.sherborne.com	£7,095	£11,960	Dr R. Sullivan
Sherborne School, Dorset	www.sherborne.org	£10,125	£12,500	D. Luckett
Shiplake College, Oxon	www.shiplake.org.uk	£7,410	£11,025	A. Davies
Shrewsbury School, Shrops	www.shrewsbury.org.uk	£8,745	£13,040	L. Winkley
Sibford School, Oxon	www.sibfordschool.co.uk	£4,913	£9,548	T. Spence
Solihull School, W. Midlands	www.solsch.org.uk	£4,331	–	D. Lloyd
South Hampstead High School, London, NW3	www.shhs.gdst.net	£6,218	–	Mrs V. Bingham
Stafford Grammar School, Staffs	www.staffordgrammar.co.uk	£4,260	–	M. Darley
Stamford High School, Lincolns	www.ses.lincs.sch.uk	£5,106	£9,482	W. Phelan
Stamford School, Lincolns	www.ses.lincs.sch.uk	£5,106	£9,482	W. Phelan
The Stephen Perse Foundation, Cambs	www.stephenperse.com	£5,850	–	Miss P. Kelleher
Stockport Grammar School, Cheshire	www.stockportgrammar.co.uk	£3,900	–	Dr P. Owen
Stonar, Wilts	www.stonarschool.com	£5,500	£10,135	Dr S. Divall
Stonyhurst College, Lancs	www.stonyhurst.ac.uk	£6,650	£12,100	J. Browne
Stover School, Devon	www.stover.co.uk	£4,260	£8,730	R. Notman
Stowe School, Bucks	www.stowe.co.uk	£6,330	£12,220	Dr A. Wallersteiner
Streatham & Clapham High School, London, SW16	www.schs.gdst.net	£5,874	–	Dr M. Sachania
Sutton Valence School, Kent	www.svs.org.uk	£7,135	£11,115	B. Grindlay
Sydenham High School, London, SE26	www.sydenhamhighschool.gdst.net	£5,579	–	Mrs K. Woodcock
Talbot Heath, Dorset	www.talbotheath.org	£4,801	£8,364	Mrs A. Holloway
Tettenhall College, W. Midlands	www.tettenhallcollege.co.uk	£4,627	£10,533	D. Williams
Thetford Grammar School, Norfolk	www.thetfordgrammar.co.uk	£4,555	–	M. Brewer
Tonbridge School, Kent	www.tonbridge-school.co.uk	£10,114	£13,482	J. Priory
Tormead School, Surrey	www.tormeadschool.org.uk	£5,150	–	Mrs C. Foord
Tring Park School for the Performing Arts, Herts	www.tringpark.com	£7,125	£11,135	S. Anderson
Trinity School, Surrey	www.trinity-school.org	£5,816	–	A. Kennedy
Trinity School, Devon	www.trinityschool.co.uk	£4,100	£9,259	L. Coen
Truro School, Cornwall	www.truroschool.com	£4,690	£9,355	A. Gordon-Brown
Tudor Hall, Oxon	www.tudorhallschool.com	£7,365	£11,870	Miss W. Griffiths
University College School, London, NW3	www.ucs.org.uk	£6,776	–	M. Beard
Uppingham School, Rutland	www.uppingham.co.uk	£8,771	£12,530	Dr R. Maloney
Walthamstow Hall, Kent	www.walthamstow-hall.co.uk	£6,690	–	Miss S. Ferro
Warminster School, Wilts	www.warminsterschool.org.uk	£5,110	£10,880	M. Mortimer
Warwick School, Warwicks	www.warwickschool.org	£4,398	£9,586	Dr D. Smith
Welbeck – The Defence Sixth Form College, Leics	www.dsfc.ac.uk	£6,666	–	J. Middleton
Wellingborough School, Northants	www.wellingboroughschool.org	£5,330	–	A. Holman
Wellington College, Berks	www.wellingtoncollege.org.uk	£9,680	£13,250	J. Thomas
Wellington School, Somerset	www.wellington-school.org.uk	£5,075	£10,270	H. Price
Wells Cathedral School, Somerset	www.wells-cathedral-school.com	£6,124	£10,255	A. Tighe
West Buckland School, Devon	www.westbuckland.com	£5,020	£10,240	P. Stapleton
Westfield School, Tyne and Wear	www.westfield.newcastle.sch.uk	£4,530	–	N. Walker
Westholme School, Lancs	www.westholmeschool.com	£3,760	–	Mrs L. Horner
Westminster School, London, SW1	www.westminster.org.uk	£9,058	£13,084	P. Derham
Westonbirt School, Glos	www.westonbirt.org	£4,995	£9,750	Mrs N. Dangerfield
Wimbledon High School, London, SW19	www.wimbledonhigh.gdst.net	£6,270	–	Mrs J. Lunnon
Winchester College, Hants	www.winchestercollege.org	–	£13,304	Dr T. Hands

Windermere School, Cumbria	www.windermereschool.co.uk	£5,820	£9,950	I. Lavender
Wisbech Grammar School, Cambs	www.wisbechgrammar.com	£4,449	–	C. Staley
Withington Girls' School, Greater Manchester	www.wgs.org	£4,084	–	Mrs S. Haslam
Woldingham School, Surrey	www.woldinghamschool.co.uk	£7,480	£12,180	Mrs A. Hutchinson
Wolverhampton Grammar School, W. Midlands	www.wgs.org.uk	£4,554	–	Mrs K. Crewe-Read
Woodbridge School, Suffolk	www.woodbridgeschool.org.uk	£5,500	£10,295	Dr R. Robson
Woodhouse Grove School, W. Yorks	www.woodhousegrove.co.uk	£4,525	£9,340	J. Lockwood
Worth School, W. Sussex	www.worthschool.org.uk	£7,910	£11,230	S. McPherson
Wrekin College, Shrops	www.wrekincollege.com	£5,975	£8,440	T. Firth
Wychwood School, Oxon	www.wychwoodschool.org	£5,300	£9,300	Mrs A. Johnson
Wycliffe College, Glos	www.wycliffe.co.uk	£6,995	£11,740	N. Gregory
Wycombe Abbey, Bucks	www.wycombeabbey.com	–	£12,980	Mrs R. Wilkinson
The Yehudi Menuhin School, Surrey	www.menuhinschool.co.uk	–	–	Mrs K. Clanchy

WALES

The Cathedral School Llandaff, Cardiff	www.cathedral-school.co.uk	£4,238	–	Mrs C. Sherwood
Christ College, Brecon	www.christcollegebrecon.com	£5,892	£9,217	G. Pearson
Howell's School Llandaff, Cardiff	www.howells-cardiff.gdst.net	£4,461	–	Mrs S. Davis
Monmouth School for Boys, Monmouth	www.habsmonmouth.org	£5,272	£10,687	Dr A. Daniel
Monmouth School for Girls, Monmouth	www.habsmonmouth.org	£4,926	£10,687	Mrs J. Miles
Myddelton College, Denbigh	www.myddeltoncollege.com	£4,000	£9,366	M. Roberts
Rougemont School, Newport	www.rougemontschool.co.uk	£4,512	–	R. Carnevale
Ruthin School, Ruthin	www.ruthinschool.co.uk	£4,666	£11,500	T. Belfield

SCOTLAND

The High School of Dundee, Dundee	www.highschoolofdundee.org.uk	£4,333	–	Dr J. Halliday
The Edinburgh Academy, Edinburgh	www.edinburghacademy.org.uk	£3,792	–	B. Welsh
Fettes College, Edinburgh	www.fettes.com	£9,400	£11,600	G. Stanford
George Heriot's School, Edinburgh	www.george-heriots.com	£4,174	–	Mrs L. Franklin
The Glasgow Academy, Glasgow	www.theglasgowacademy.org.uk	£4,128	–	P. Brodie
The High School of Glasgow, Glasgow	www.highschoolofglasgow.co.uk	£4,256	–	J. O'Neill
Glenalmond College, Perth	www.glenalmondcollege.co.uk	£8,617	£11,502	H. Ouston
Gordonstoun, Elgin	www.gordonstoun.org.uk	£9,445	£12,765	Mrs L. Kerr
Kelvinside Academy, Glasgow	www.kelvinsideacademy.org.uk	£4,220	–	I. Munro
Kilgraston School, Bridge of Earn	www.kilgraston.com	£5,880	£10,045	Mrs D. MacGinty
Lomond School, Helensburgh	www.lomondschool.com	£3,990	£9,250	Mrs J. Urquhart
Loretto School, Musselburgh	www.loretto.com	£7,775	£11,420	G. Hawley
Merchiston Castle School, Edinburgh	www.merchiston.co.uk	£8,070	£10,970	J. Anderson
Morrison's Academy, Crieff	www.morrisonsacademy.org	£4,332	–	G. Warren
Robert Gordon's College, Aberdeen	www.rgc.aberdeen.sch.uk	£4,377	–	S. Mills
St Aloysius' College, Glasgow	www.staloysius.org	£4,275	–	M. Bartlett
St Columba's School, Kilmacolm	www.st-columbas.org	£4,032	–	Mrs A. Angus
St Leonards School, St Andrews	www.stleonards-fife.org	£4,736	£11,551	Dr M. Carslaw
St Margaret's School for Girls, Aberdeen	www.st-margaret.aberdeen.sch.uk	£5,292	–	Miss A. Tomlinson
Strathallan School, Perth	www.strathallan.co.uk	£7,470	£11,000	M. Lauder

NORTHERN IRELAND

Campbell College, Belfast	www.campbellcollege.co.uk	£930	£4,915	R. Robinson
The Royal School Dungannon, Dungannon	www.royaldungannon.com	£50	£3,550	D. Burnett

CHANNEL ISLANDS

Elizabeth College, Guernsey	www.elizabethcollege.gg	£3,995	–	Mrs J. Palmer
Victoria College, Jersey	www.victoriacollege.je	£1,916	–	A. Watkins

NATIONAL ACADEMIES OF SCHOLARSHIP

The national academies are self-governing bodies whose members are elected as a result of achievement and distinction in the academy's field. Within their discipline, the academies provide advice, support education and exceptional scholars, stimulate debate, promote UK research worldwide and collaborate with international counterparts.

The UK's four national academies – the Royal Society, the British Academy, the Royal Academy of Engineering and the Academy of Medical Sciences – receive funding from the Department for Business, Energy and Industrial Strategy (BEIS) for key programmes that help deliver government priorities. The total amount of resource funding allocated by BEIS to the four national academies for 2019–20 is £195m. The Royal Society of Edinburgh is aided by funds provided by the Scottish government. In addition to government funding, the national academies generate additional income from donations, membership contributions, trading and investments.

ACADEMY OF MEDICAL SCIENCES (1998)

41 Portland Place, London W1B 1QH
T 020-3141 3200 W www.acmedsci.ac.uk

Founded in 1998, the Academy of Medical Sciences is the independent body in the UK representing the diversity of medical science. The Academy seeks to improve health through research, as well as to promote medical science and its translation into benefits for society.

The academy is self-governing and receives funding from a variety of sources, including the fellowship, charitable donations, government and industry.

Fellows are elected from a broad range of medical sciences: biomedical, clinical and population based. The academy includes in its remit veterinary medicine, dentistry, nursing, medical law, economics, sociology and ethics. Elections are from nominations put forward by existing fellows.

There are around 1,200 fellows and 42 honorary fellows.

President, Prof. Sir Robert Lechler, PMEDSCI
Executive Director, Dr Rachel Quinn *(interim)*

BRITISH ACADEMY (1902)

10–11 Carlton House Terrace, London SW1Y 5AH
T 020-7969 5200 W www.thebritishacademy.ac.uk

The British Academy is an independent, self-governing learned society for the promotion of the humanities and social sciences. It was founded in 1901 and granted a royal charter in 1902. The British Academy supports advanced academic research and is a channel for the government's support of research in those disciplines.

The fellows are scholars who have attained distinction in one of the branches of study that the academy exists to promote. Candidates must be nominated by existing fellows. There are just over 1,000 fellows, around 30 honorary fellows and 300 corresponding fellows overseas.

President, Prof. Sir David Cannadine
Chief Executive, Dr Robin Jackson *(interim)*

ROYAL ACADEMY OF ENGINEERING (1976)

3 Carlton House Terrace, London SW1Y 5DG
T 020-7766 0600 W www.raeng.org.uk

The Royal Academy of Engineering was established as the Fellowship of Engineering in 1976. It was granted a royal charter in 1983 and its present title in 1992. It is an independent, self-governing body whose object is the pursuit, encouragement and maintenance of excellence in the whole field of engineering, in order to promote the advancement of the science, art and practice of engineering for the benefit of the public.

Election to the fellowship is by invitation only, from nominations supported by the body of fellows. There are around 1,500 fellows, 40 honorary fellows and 100 international fellows. The Duke of Edinburgh is the senior fellow and the Princess Royal and the Duke of Kent are both royal fellows.

President, Prof. Dame Ann Dowling, OM, DBE, FRENG, FRS
Chief Executive, Dr Hayaatun Sillem

ROYAL SOCIETY (1660)

6–9 Carlton House Terrace, London SW1Y 5AG
T 020-7451 2500 W www.royalsociety.org

The Royal Society is an independent academy promoting the natural and applied sciences. Founded in 1660 and granted a royal charter in 1662, the society has three roles: as the UK academy of science, as a learned society and as a funding agency. It is an independent, self-governing body under a royal charter, promoting and advancing all fields of physical and biological sciences, of mathematics and engineering, medical and agricultural sciences and their application.

Fellows are elected for their contributions to science, both in fundamental research resulting in greater understanding, and also in leading and directing scientific and technological progress in industry and research establishments. Each year up to 52 new fellows, who must be citizens or residents of the Commonwealth or Ireland, and up to ten foreign members may be elected. In addition one honorary fellow may also be elected annually from those not eligible for election as fellows or foreign members. There are around 1,700 fellows and foreign members and eight honorary members covering all scientific disciplines. The Queen is the patron of the Royal Society, and there are also five royal fellows.

President, Sir Venki Ramakrishnan, PRS
Executive Director, Dr Julie Maxton, CBE

ROYAL SOCIETY OF EDINBURGH (1783)

22–26 George Street, Edinburgh EH2 2PQ
T 0131-240 5000 W www.rse.org.uk

The Royal Society of Edinburgh (RSE) is an educational charity and Scotland's national academy. An independent body with charitable status, its multidisciplinary membership represents a knowledge resource for the people of Scotland. Granted its royal charter in 1783 for the 'advancement of learning and useful knowledge', the society organises conferences, debates and lectures; conducts independent inquiries; facilitates international collaboration and showcases the country's research and development capabilities; provides educational activities for primary and secondary school students; and awards prizes and medals. The society also awards over £2m annually to Scotland's top researchers and entrepreneurs working in Scotland.

There are over 1,750 fellows, including honorary fellows and corresponding fellows overseas.

President, Prof. Dame Anne Glover
Chief Executive, Dr Rebekah Widdowfield

PRIVATELY FUNDED ARTS ACADEMIES

The Royal Academy and the Royal Scottish Academy support the visual arts community in the UK, hold educational events and promote interest in the arts. They are entirely privately funded through contributions by 'friends' (regular donors who receive benefits such as free entry, previews and magazines), bequests, corporate donations and exhibitions.

ROYAL ACADEMY OF ARTS (1768)

Burlington House, Piccadilly, London W1J 0BD
T 020-7300 8000 W www.royalacademy.org.uk

Founded by George III in 1768, the Royal Academy of Arts is an independent, self-governing society devoted to the encouragement and promotion of the fine arts.

Membership of the academy is limited to 100 academicians, all of whom are either painters, engravers, printmakers, draughtsmen, sculptors or architects. There must always be at least 14 sculptors, 12 architects and eight printmakers among the academicians. Candidates must be professionally active in the UK and are nominated and elected by the existing academicians. The members are known as royal academicians (RAs) and are responsible for both the governance and direction of the academy. When RAs reach the age of 75, they become senior academicians and can no longer serve as officers or on the committees.

The title of honorary academician is awarded to a small number of distinguished artists who are not resident in the UK; as at July 2019, there were 34 honorary academicians. Unlike the RAs, they do not take part in the governance of the academy and are unable to vote.

President, Christopher Le Brun, PRA
Secretary and Chief Executive, Axel Rüger

ROYAL SCOTTISH ACADEMY (1838)

The Mound, Edinburgh EH2 2EL
T 0131-225 6671 W www.royalscottishacademy.org

Founded in 1826 and led by a body of academicians comprising eminent artists and architects, the Royal Scottish Academy (RSA) is an independent voice for cultural advocacy and one of the largest supporters of artists in Scotland. The Academy administers a number of scholarships, awards and residencies and has a historic collection of Scottish artworks, recognised by the Scottish government as being of national significance. The Academy is independent from local or national government funding, relying instead on bequests, legacies, sponsorship and earned income.

Academicians have to be Scots by birth or domicile, and are elected from the disciplines of art and architecture following nominations put forward by the existing membership. There are also a small number of honorary academicians – distinguished artists and architects, writers, historians and musicians – who do not have to be Scottish. As at July 2019 there were 135 academicians and 41 honorary academicians.

President, Joyce W. Cairns, PRSA
Secretary, Robbie Bushe, RSA
Treasurer, Robin Webster, RSA

RESEARCH COUNCILS

The government funds research through nine research councils, supported by the Department for Business, Energy and Industrial Strategy (BEIS) through UK Research and Innovation (for further information see W www.ukri.org). The councils support research and training in universities and other higher education and research facilities.

Under the Higher Education and Research Act 2017, the existing seven research councils, Innovate UK and the research and knowledge exchange functions of the former Higher Education Funding Council for England (HEFCE) were subsumed into a new single funding body, UK Research and Innovation (UKRI), which became operational in April 2018. Research England is a new council within UKRI, taking forward the England-only responsibilities of HEFCE in relation to research and knowledge exchange. Innovate UK is a non-departmental public body which works with companies and partner organisations to facilitate scientific and technological development for the UK economy.

Quality-related research funding is administered through UKRI. Additional funds may also be provided by other government departments, devolved administrations and other international bodies. The councils also receive income for research specifically commissioned by government departments and the private sector, and income from charitable sources.

ARTS AND HUMANITIES RESEARCH COUNCIL

Polaris House, North Star Avenue, Swindon SN2 1FL
T 01793-416000 W www.ahrc.ukri.org

The AHRC is the successor organisation to the Arts and Humanities Research Board and was incorporated by royal charter and established in 2005. It provides funding for postgraduate training and research in the arts and humanities; in any one year, the AHRC makes approximately 700 research awards and around 2,000 postgraduate scholarships. Awards are made after a rigorous peer review system, which ensures the quality of applications.

Executive Chair, Prof. Andrew Thompson, DPHIL

BIOTECHNOLOGY AND BIOLOGICAL SCIENCES RESEARCH COUNCIL

Polaris House, North Star Avenue, Swindon SN2 1UH
T 01793-413200 W www.bbsrc.ukri.org

Established by royal charter in 1994, the BBSRC is the UK funding agency for research in the non-clinical life sciences. It funds research into how all living organisms function and behave, benefiting the agriculture, food, health, pharmaceutical and chemical sectors. To deliver its mission, the BBSRC supports research and training in universities and research centres throughout the UK, including providing strategic research grants to the eight institutes listed below. In June 2015, the institutes founded the National Institutes of Bioscience (NIB) partnership in order to increase the impact of bioscience research and to strengthen the UK's reputation in the field.

Chair, Prof. Melanie Welham

INSTITUTES

BABRAHAM INSTITUTE, Babraham Hall, Cambridge CB22 3AT T 01223-496000
Director, Prof. Michael Wakelam

INSTITUTE FOR BIOLOGICAL, ENVIRONMENTAL AND RURAL SCIENCES (ABERYSTWYTH UNIVERSITY), Penglais, Aberystwyth SY23 3DA
T 01970-621986
Director, Prof. Mike Gooding
EARLHAM INSTITUTE, Norwich Research Park, Colney, Norwich NR4 7UZ T 01603-450001
Director, Prof. Neil Hall
JOHN INNES CENTRE, Norwich Research Park, Colney, Norwich NR4 7UH T 01603-450000
Director, Prof. Dale Sanders
PIRBRIGHT INSTITUTE, Ash Road, Woking, Surrey GU24 0NF
T 01483-232441
Director, Dr Bryan Charleston
QUADRAM INSTITUTE, Norwich Research Park, Norwich, Norfolk NR4 7UA T 01603-255000
Director, Prof. Ian Charles
ROSLIN INSTITUTE (UNIVERSITY OF EDINBURGH), Easter Bush, Midlothian EH25 9RG T 0131-651 9100
Director, Prof. Eleanor Riley
ROTHAMSTED RESEARCH, Harpenden, Herts AL5 2JQ
T 01582-763133
Director, Prof. Achim Dobermann

ECONOMIC AND SOCIAL RESEARCH COUNCIL

Polaris House, North Star Avenue, Swindon SN2 1UJ
T 01793-413000 W www.esrc.ukri.org

The ESRC was established by royal charter in 1965 as an organisation for funding and promoting research and postgraduate training in the social sciences. It supports independent research which has an impact on business, the public sector and civil society and also provides advice, disseminates knowledge and promotes public understanding in these areas.

The ESRC has a total budget of around £202m and provides funding to over 4,000 researchers and postgraduate students in academic institutions and independent research institutes.

Executive Chair, Prof. Jennifer Rubin

ENGINEERING AND PHYSICAL SCIENCES RESEARCH COUNCIL

Polaris House, North Star Avenue, Swindon SN2 1ET
T 01793-444000 W www.epsrc.ukri.org

Formed in 1994 by royal charter, the EPSRC is the UK government's main agency for funding research and training in engineering and the physical sciences in universities and other organisations throughout the UK. The EPSRC invests around £800m a year in a broad range of subjects – from mathematics to materials science, and from information technology to structural engineering. It also provides advice, disseminates knowledge and promotes public understanding in these areas.

Executive Chair, Prof. Lynn Gladden, CBE

MEDICAL RESEARCH COUNCIL

Polaris House, North Star Avenue, Swindon SN2 1FL
T 01793-416200 W www.mrc.ukri.org

The MRC is a publicly funded organisation dedicated to improving human health. The MRC supports research across the entire spectrum of medical sciences, in universities, hospitals, centres and institutes.

Chair, Prof. Fiona Watt
Chair, Infections and Immunity Board, Prof. Paul Kaye
Chair, Molecular and Cellular Medicine Board, Prof. Anne Ferguson-Smith
Chair, Neurosciences and Mental Health Board, Prof. Patrick Chinnery
Chair, Population and Systems Medicine Board, Prof. Paul Elliott
Chair, Regenerative Medicine Research Board, Prof. Martin Wilkins

NATURAL ENVIRONMENT RESEARCH COUNCIL

Polaris House, North Star Avenue, Swindon SN2 1EU
T 01793-411500 W www.nerc.ukri.org

NERC is the leading funder of independent research, training and innovation in environmental science in the UK. Its work covers the full range of atmospheric, earth, biological, terrestrial and aquatic sciences. NERC invests around £330m a year in research exploring how we can sustainably benefit from our natural resources, predict and respond to natural hazards and understand environmental change. NERC works closely with policymakers and industry to support sustainable economic growth in the UK and around the world.
Executive Chair, Prof. Duncan Wingham

RESEARCH CENTRES

BRITISH ANTARCTIC SURVEY, High Cross, Madingley Road, Cambridge CB3 OET T 01223-221400
Director, Prof. Dame Jane Francis, DCMG
BRITISH GEOLOGICAL SURVEY, Kingsley Dunham Centre, Keyworth, Nottingham NG12 5GG T 0115-936 3100
Executive Director, Prof. John Ludden
CENTRE FOR ECOLOGY AND HYDROLOGY, Maclean Building, Benson Lane, Crowmarsh Gifford, Wallingford OX10 8BB T 01491-838800
Director, Prof. Mark Bailey
NATIONAL CENTRE FOR ATMOSPHERIC SCIENCE, NCAS Headquarters, School of Earth and Environment, University of Leeds, Leeds LS2 9JT T 0113-343 6408
Director, Prof. Stephen Mobbs

NATIONAL CENTRE FOR EARTH OBSERVATION, Michael Atiyah Building, University of Leicester, University Road, Leicester LE1 7RH T 0116-252 2016
Director, Prof. John Remedios
NATIONAL OCEANOGRAPHY CENTRE, University of Southampton Waterfront Campus, European Way, Southampton SO14 3ZH T 0238-059 6666
Director, Prof. Ed Hill, OBE

SCIENCE AND TECHNOLOGY FACILITIES COUNCIL

Polaris House, North Star Avenue, Swindon SN2 1SZ
T 01793-442000 W www.stfc.ukri.org

Formed by royal charter in 2007, through the merger of the Council for the Central Laboratory of the Research Councils and the Particle Physics and Astronomy Research Council, the STFC is a non-departmental public body reporting to BEIS.
The STFC invests in large national and international research facilities, while delivering science and technology expertise for the UK. The council is involved in research projects such as the Diamond Light Source Synchrotron and the Large Hadron Collider, and develops new areas of science and technology. The EPSRC has transferred its responsibility for nuclear physics to the STFC.

Executive Chair, Prof. Mark Thompson

RESEARCH CENTRES

BOULBY UNDERGROUND SCIENCE FACILITY, Boulby Mine, Loftus, Saltburn-by-the-Sea, Cleveland TS13 4UZ T 01287-646300
CHILBOLTON OBSERVATORY, Chilbolton, Stockbridge, Hampshire SO20 6BJ T 01264-860391
DARESBURY LABORATORY, SciTech Daresbury, Keckwick Lane, Warrington WA4 4AD T 01925-603000
RUTHERFORD APPLETON LABORATORY, Harwell Campus, Didcot OX11 0QX T 01235-445000
UK ASTRONOMY TECHNOLOGY CENTRE, Royal Observatory Edinburgh, Blackford Hill, Edinburgh EH9 3HJ T 0131-668 8100

HEALTH

NATIONAL HEALTH SERVICE

The National Health Service (NHS) came into being on 5 July 1948 under the National Health Service Act 1946, covering England and Wales and, under separate legislation, Scotland and Northern Ireland. The NHS is now administered by the Secretary of State for Health (in England), the Welsh government, the Scottish government and the Northern Ireland Executive.

The function of the NHS is to provide a comprehensive health service designed to secure improvement in the physical and mental health of the people and to prevent, diagnose and treat illness. It was founded on the principle that treatment should be provided according to clinical need rather than ability to pay, and should be free at the point of delivery.

Hospital, mental, dental, nursing, ophthalmic and ambulance services and facilities for the care of expectant and nursing mothers and young children are provided by the NHS to meet all reasonable requirements. Rehabilitation services such as occupational therapy, physiotherapy, speech therapy and surgical and medical appliances are supplied where appropriate. Specialists and consultants who work in NHS hospitals can also engage in private practice, including the treatment of their private patients in NHS hospitals.

STRUCTURE

The structure of the NHS remained relatively stable for the first 30 years of its existence. In 1974, a three-tier management structure comprising regional health authorities, area health authorities and district management teams was introduced in England, and the NHS became responsible for community health services. In 1979, area health authorities were abolished and district management teams were replaced by district health authorities.

The National Health Service and Community Care Act 1990 provided for more streamlined regional health authorities and district health authorities, and for the establishment of family health services authorities (FHSAs) and NHS trusts. The concept of the 'internal market' was introduced into health care, whereby care was provided through NHS contracts where health authorities or boards and GP fundholders (the purchasers) were responsible for buying health care from hospitals, non-fundholding GPs, community services and ambulance services (the providers). The Act also paved the way for the community care reforms, which were introduced in April 1993, and changed the way care is administered for older people, the mentally ill, the physically disabled and people with learning disabilities.

ENGLAND

Under the Health and Social Care Act 2012, which gained royal assent in March 2012, The NHS in England underwent a complete operational and budgetary restructure at a cost of approximately £1.4bn.

Hospitals were extensively affected by the overhaul, with the cap on income from private hospital patients increased from 1.5 per cent to 49 per cent. All hospitals will become foundation trusts, competing for treatment contracts from clinical commissioning groups (CCGs).

On 1 April 2013 the new commissioning board, NHS England, took on full statutory responsibilities; at the same time, strategic health authorities (SHAs) and primary care trusts (PCTs) which, alongside the Department of Health, had been responsible for NHS planning and delivery, were abolished. NHS England is an executive non-departmental public body of the Department of Health and Social Care (DHSC) with a remit to:

- provide national leadership to improve the quality of care
- oversee the operation of clinical commissioning groups
- allocate resources to clinical commissioning groups
- commission primary care and specialist services

The secretary of state has ultimate responsibility for the provision of a comprehensive health service in England and for ensuring the system works to its optimum capacity to meet the needs of its patients. The DHSC is responsible for strategic leadership of the health and social care systems, but is not the headquarters of the NHS, nor does it directly manage any NHS organisations.

In October 2014, NHS England published *Five Year Forward View* which committed the organisation to further change, including additional decentralisation and a greater emphasis on out-of-hospital care and preventative medicine. In January 2019 the *NHS Long Term Plan* was published outlining NHS England's healthcare plans for the next ten years.

NHS ENGLAND, PO Box 16738, Redditch B97 9PT
T 0300-311 2233 W www.england.nhs.uk
Chief Executive, Simon Stevens

CLINICAL COMMISSIONING GROUPS (CCGS)

On 1 April 2013, PCTs, which controlled 80 per cent of the NHS budget and commissioned most NHS services, were abolished. They were replaced with CCGs which took on many of the functions of the PCTs in addition to some functions previously assumed by the Department of Health. All GP practices now belong to a CCG which also includes other health professionals, such as nurses. CCGs commission most services, including:

- mental health and learning disability services
- planned hospital care
- rehabilitative care
- urgent and emergency care (including out-of-hours)
- most community health services

CCGs can commission any service provider that meets NHS standards and costs. These can be NHS hospitals, social enterprises, charities, or private-sector providers. There are around 190 CCGs, which together are responsible for around two-thirds of the NHS budget, around £79.9bn in 2019–20. In April 2015, 64 CCGs were approved to take on additional responsibility for commissioning GP services within their area.

HEALTH AND WELLBEING BOARDS

Every upper-tier local authority has established a health and wellbeing board to act as a forum for local commissioners across the NHS, social care, public health and other services. There are more than 150 health and wellbeing boards in England, which are intended to:

- encourage integrated commissioning of health and social care services
- increase democratic input into strategic decisions about health and wellbeing services
- strengthen working relationships between health and social care

PUBLIC HEALTH ENGLAND (PHE)

Established on 1 April 2013, PHE provides national leadership and expert services to support public health and also works with local government and the NHS to respond to emergencies. PHE's responsibilities are to:

- coordinate a national public health service
- support the public to make healthier choices
- provide leadership to the public health delivery system
- support the development of the public health workforce

REGULATION

Since the restructuring of the NHS in England began in April 2013, some elements of the regulation system have changed. Responsibility for the regulation of particular aspects of care is shared across a number of different bodies, including the Care Quality Commission (CQC), and individual professional regulatory bodies, such as the General Medical Council, Nursing and Midwifery Council, General Dental Council and the Health and Care Professions Council.

CARE QUALITY COMMISSION (CQC)

The CQC regulates all health and social care services in England, including those provided by the NHS, local authorities, private companies or voluntary organisations. In addition it protects the interests of people detained under the Mental Health Act. The CQC ensures that all essential standards of quality and safety are met where care is provided, from hospitals to private care homes. By law all NHS providers (such as hospitals and ambulance services) must register with the CQC to show they are protecting people from the risk of infection. The CQC possesses a range of legal powers and duties and will take action if providers do not meet essential standards of quality or safety.

NHS IMPROVEMENT

NHS Improvement is responsible for overseeing NHS foundation trusts, NHS trusts and independent providers, helping them give patients consistently high quality, safe and compassionate care within local health systems that are financially sustainable. In April 2019, It was announced that NHS Improvement would fully integrate into NHS England to act as a single organisation as part of the *NHS Long Term Plan*.

HEALTHWATCH

Healthwatch England was established in October 2012 following the restructuring of the NHS. The organisation functions at a national and local level as an independent consumer body, gathering and representing the views of the public about health and social care services in England.

CARE QUALITY COMMISSION, 151 Buckingham Palace Road, London SW1W 9SZ T 03000-616161 W www.cqc.org.uk
Chief Executive, Ian Trenholm

NHS IMPROVEMENT, Wellington House, 133–155 Waterloo Road, London SE1 8UG T 0300-123 2257
W https://improvement.nhs.uk
Chief Executive, Ian Dalton, CBE

HEALTHWATCH, 151 Buckingham Palace Road, London SW1W 9SZ T 0300-068 3000 W www.healthwatch.co.uk
National Director, Imelda Redmond, CBE

AUTHORITIES AND TRUSTS

REGIONS

In April 2019, as outlined in the *NHS Long Term Plan*, all NHS trusts were re-organised into seven integrated regional teams to ensure the commissioning of high quality primary care and specialised services at a local level across England.

ACUTE TRUSTS

Hospitals in England are managed by acute trusts. There were around 135 acute non-specialist trusts, of which 84 have foundation trust status and 17 acute specialist trusts, of which 16 have foundation trust status. Acute trusts ensure hospitals provide high-quality healthcare and spend money efficiently. They employ a large sector of the NHS workforce, including doctors, nurses, pharmacists, midwives and health visitors. Acute trusts also employ those in supplementary medical professions, such as physiotherapists, radiographers and podiatrists, in addition to many other non-medical staff.

AMBULANCE TRUSTS

There are 10 ambulance services (five foundation trusts) in England, providing emergency services to healthcare.

CLINICAL SENATES AND STRATEGIC CLINICAL NETWORKS

Clinical senates are advisory groups of experts from across health and social care. There are 12 senates covering England comprising clinical leaders from across the healthcare system, in addition to members from social care and public health.

There are 12 strategic clinical networks across England, comprising groups of clinical experts covering a particular disease, patient or professional group. They offer advice to CCGs and NHS England.

Neither organisation is a statutory body, and although they comment on CCG plans to NHS England, they are unable to veto them.

FOUNDATION TRUSTS

NHS foundation trusts are independent legal entities with unique governance arrangements. Each NHS foundation trust has a duty to consult and involve a board of governors in the strategic planning of its organisation. They have financial freedoms and can raise capital from both the public and private sectors within borrowing limits determined by projected cash flows and based on affordability.

MENTAL HEALTH TRUSTS

There are 69 mental health trusts in England, 42 of which have foundation trust status.

WALES

The NHS Wales was reorganised according to Welsh Assembly commitments laid out in the *One Wales* strategy which came into effect in October 2009. There are now seven local health boards (LHBs) that are responsible for delivering all health care services within a geographical area, rather than the trust and local health board system that existed previously. Community health councils (CHCs) are statutory lay bodies that represent the public for the health service in their region. There are currently eight CHCs.

NHS TRUSTS

There are three NHS trusts in Wales. The Welsh Ambulance Services NHS Trust is for emergency services; the Velindre NHS Trust offers specialist services in cancer care; while Public Health Wales serves as a unified public health organisation for Wales.

LOCAL HEALTH BOARDS

The websites of the seven LHBs, and contact details for community health councils and NHS trusts, are available in the *NHS Wales Directory* (W www.wales.nhs.uk).

ABERTAWE BRO MORGANNWG UNIVERSITY, One Talbot Gateway, Baglan Energy Park, Baglan, Port Talbot SA12 7BR T 01656-752752
Chief Executive, Tracy Myhill

ANEURIN BEVAN, Headquarters, Lodge Road, Caerleon, Newport NP18 3XQ T 01495-745656
Chief Executive, Judith Paget, CBE

BETSI CADWALADR UNIVERSITY, Ysbyty Gwynedd, Penrhosgarnedd, Bangor, Gwynedd LL57 2PW T 01248-384384
Chief Executive, Gary Doherty

CARDIFF AND VALE UNIVERSITY, Cardigan House, University Hospital of Wales, Heath Park, Cardiff CF14 4XW
T 029-2074 7747
Chief Executive, Len Richards

CWM TAF MORGANNWG UNIVERSITY, Ynysmeurig House, Navigation Park, Abercynon CF45 4SN T 01443-744800
Chief Executive, Dr Sharon Hopkins *(interim)*

HYWEL DDA, Corporate Offices, Ystwyth Building, Hafan Derwen, Jobswell Road, Carmarthen SA31 3BB T 01267-235151
Chief Executive, Steve Moore

POWYS TEACHING, Glasbury House, Bronllys Hospital, Bronllys, Brecon, Powys LD3 0LS T 01874-771661
Chief Executive, Carol Shillabeer

SCOTLAND

The Scottish government Health and Social Care directorates are responsible both for NHS Scotland and for the development and implementation of health and community care policy. The chief executive of NHS Scotland leads the central management of the NHS, is accountable to ministers for the efficiency and performance of the service and heads the Health Department which oversees the work of the 14 regional health boards. These boards provide strategic management for the entire local NHS system and are responsible for ensuring that services are delivered effectively and efficiently.

In addition to the 14 regional health boards there are a further seven special boards and one public health body, which provide national services, such as the Scottish ambulance service and NHS Health Scotland. Healthcare Improvement Scotland, was formed on 1 April 2011 by the Public Services Reform Act 2010 to improve the quality of Scottish healthcare.

REGIONAL HEALTH BOARDS

AYRSHIRE AND ARRAN, Eglinton House, Ailsa Hospital, Dalmellington Road, Ayr KA6 6AB T 0800-169 1441
W www.nhsaaa.net
Chief Executive, John Burns

BORDERS, Borders General Hospital, Melrose, Roxburghshire TD6 9BS T 01896-826000 W www.nhsborders.scot.nhs.uk
Chief Executive, Jane Davidson

DUMFRIES AND GALLOWAY, Crichton Hall, Dumfries DG1 4TG T 01387-246246 W www.nhsdg.scot.nhs.uk
Chief Executive, Jeff Ace

EILEAN SIAR (WESTERN ISLES), 37 South Beach Street, Stornoway, Isle of Lewis HS1 2BB T 01851-702997
W www.wihb.scot.nhs.uk
Chief Executive, Gordon Jamieson

FIFE, Hayfield House, Hayfield Road, Kirkcaldy, Fife KY2 5AH T 01592-643355 W www.nhsfife.org
Chief Executive, Paul Hawkins

FORTH VALLEY, Carseview House, Castle Business Park, Stirling FK9 4SW T 01786-463031 W www.nhsforthvalley.com
Chief Executive, Cathie Cowan

GRAMPIAN, Summerfield House, 2 Eday Road, Aberdeen AB15 6RE T 0345-456 6000 W www.nhsgrampian.org
Chief Executive, Prof. Amanda Croft

GREATER GLASGOW AND CLYDE, J. B. Russell House, Gartnavel Royal Hospital Campus, 1055 Great Western Road, Glasgow G12 0XH T 0141-201 4444 W www.nhsggc.org.uk
Chief Executive, Jane Grant

HIGHLAND, Assynt House, Beechwood Park, Inverness IV2 3BW T 01463 705150 W www.nhshighland.scot.nhs.uk
Chief Executive, Iain Stewart

LANARKSHIRE, Kirklands, Fallside Road, Bothwell G71 8BB T 0300-3030 243 W www.nhslanarkshire.org.uk
Chief Executive, Calum Campbell

LOTHIAN, Waverley Gate, 2–4 Waterloo Place, Edinburgh EH1 3EG T 0131-536 9000 W www.nhslothian.scot.nhs.uk
Chief Executive, Tim Davison

ORKNEY, The Balfour, Foreland Road, Kirkwall, Orkney KW15 1NZ T 01856-888100 W www.ohb.scot.nhs.uk
Chief Executive, Gerry O'Brien

SHETLAND, Upper Floor Montfield, Burgh Road, Lerwick ZE1 0LA T 01595-743060 W www.shb.scot.nhs.uk
Chief Executive, Simon Bokor-Ingram *(interim)*

TAYSIDE, Ninewells Hospital & Medical School, Dundee DD1 9SY T 01382-660111 W www.nhstayside.scot.nhs.uk
Chief Executive, Grant Archibald

NORTHERN IRELAND

On 1 April 2009 the four health and social services boards in Northern Ireland were replaced by a single health and social care board for the whole of Northern Ireland. The new board together with its local commissioning groups (whose boundaries are subject to review pending the outcome of local government reform) are responsible for improving the health and social wellbeing of people in the area for which they are responsible, planning and commissioning services, and coordinating the delivery of services in a cost-effective manner. In March 2016, the health minister announced plans to abolish the health and social care board, with all commissioning powers to be transferred to the Department of Health and a new group being established to hold the five Northern Ireland trusts to account. As at July 2019, no further decision regarding the future of the board had been taken and the board remains operational.

HEALTH AND SOCIAL CARE BOARD, 12–22 Linenhall Street, Belfast BT2 8BS T 030-0555 0115
W www.hscboard.hscni.net
Chief Executive, Valerie Watts

FINANCE

The NHS is still funded mainly through general taxation, although in recent years more reliance has been placed on the NHS element of national insurance contributions, patient charges and other sources of income.

Funding for NHS England was set at £121bn for 2019–20. Expenditure for the NHS in Wales, Scotland and Northern Ireland is set by the devolved governments.

EMPLOYEES AND SALARIES

NHS ENGLAND HEALTH SERVICE STAFF 2019
Full-time equivalent

All hospital, community and dental staff	1,238,061
Consultants	51,043
Ambulance staff	22,924
Qualified nursing and midwifery staff	351,301
Qualified scientific, therapeutic and technical staff	161,877

Source: NHS Digital

SALARIES

Many general practitioners (GPs) are self-employed and hold contracts, either on their own or as part of a Clinical Commissioning Group (CCG). The profit of GPs varies according to the services they provide for their patients and the way they choose to provide these services. Salaried GPs who are part of a CCG earn between £58,808 and £88,743. Most NHS dentists are self-employed contractors. A contract for dentists was introduced on 1 April 2006 which provides dentists with an annual income in return for carrying out an agreed amount, or units, of work. A salaried dentist employed by the NHS, who works mainly with community dental services earns between £40,629 and £86,900.

BASIC SALARIES FOR HOSPITAL MEDICAL AND DENTAL STAFF 2019–20

Consultant (2003 contract)	£79,860–£107,668
Associate specialist	£56,681–£93,302
Speciality doctor	£40,428–£75,389
Core/higher training year 3+	£48,310
Core training year 1 & 2	£38,120
Foundation doctor year 2	£32,207
Foundation doctor year 1	£27,825

NURSES

From 1 December 2004 the *Agenda for Change* pay system was introduced throughout the UK for all NHS staff with the exception of medical and dental staff, doctors in public health medicine and the community health service. Nurses' salaries are incorporated in the *Agenda for Change* nine band pay structure, which provides additional payments for flexible working such as providing out-of-hours services, working weekends and nights and being on-call. There is also additional payments for those staff who work in high-cost areas such as London.

SALARIES FOR NURSES AND MIDWIVES 2019–20

Nurse/Midwife consultant	£41,486–£72,597
Modern matron	£41,486–£50,819
Nurse advanced/team manager	£32,525–£43,772
Midwife higher level	£32,525–£43,772
Nurse specialist/team leader	£27,260–£37,267
Hospital/community midwife	£27,260–£37,267
Registered nurse/entry level midwife*	£24,214–£30,112

*The starting salary in Wales is currently the same as in England. The starting salary is £24,670 in Scotland and £22,795 in Northern Ireland.

HEALTH SERVICES

PRIMARY CARE

Primary care comprises the services provided by general practitioners, community health centres, pharmacies, dental practices and opticians. Primary nursing care includes the work carried out by practice nurses, community nurses, community midwives and health visitors.

PRIMARY MEDICAL SERVICES

In England, primary medical services (PMS) are provided by 44,847 registered GPs, working in around 6,900 GP practices, with 59.8 million registered patients.

In Wales, responsibility for primary medical services rests with local health boards (LHBs), in Scotland with the 14 regional health boards and in Northern Ireland with the Health and Social Care Board.

Any vocationally trained doctor may provide general or personal medical services. GPs may also have private fee-paying patients, but not if that patient is already an NHS patient on that doctor's patient list.

A person who is ordinarily resident in the UK is eligible to register with a GP (or PMS provider) for free primary care treatment. Should a patient have difficulty in registering with a doctor, he or she should contact the local CCG for help. When a person is away from home he/she can still access primary care treatment from a GP if they ask to be treated as a temporary resident. In an emergency any doctor in the service will give treatment and advice.

GPs or CCGs are responsible for the care of their patients 24 hours a day, seven days a week, but can fulfil the terms of their contract by delegating or transferring responsibility for out-of-hours care to an accredited provider.

In addition, NHS walk-in centres (WICs) throughout England are usually open seven days a week, from early in the morning until late in the evening. They are nurse-led and provide treatment for minor illnesses and injuries, health information and self-help advice. Some WICs are not able to treat young children.

HEALTH COSTS

Some people are exempt from, or entitled to help with, health costs such as prescription charges, ophthalmic and dental costs, and in some cases help towards travel costs to and from hospital.

The following list is intended as a general guide to those who may be entitled to help, or who are exempt from some of the charges relating to the above:

• children under 16 and young people in full-time education who are under 19
• people aged 60 or over
• pregnant women and women who have had a baby in the last 12 months and have a valid maternity exemption certificate (MatEx)
• people, or their partners, who are in receipt of income support, income-based jobseeker's allowance and/or income-based employment and support allowance
• people in receipt of the pension credit
• diagnosed glaucoma patients, people who have been advised by an ophthalmologist that they are at risk of glaucoma and people aged 40 or over who have an immediate family member who is a diagnosed glaucoma patient
• NHS in-patients
• NHS out-patients for all prescribed contraceptives, medication given at a hospital, NHS walk-in centre, personally administered by a GP or supplied at a hospital or primary care trust clinic for the treatment of tuberculosis or a sexually transmissible infection
• out-patients of the NHS Hospital Dental Service
• people registered blind or partially sighted
• people who need complex lenses
• war pensioners whose treatment/prescription is for their accepted disablement and who have a valid exemption certificate
• people who are entitled to, or named on, a valid NHS tax credit exemption or HC2 certificate
• people who have a medical exemption (MedEx) certificate, including those with cancer or diabetes

People in other circumstances may also be eligible for help; *see* www.nhs.uk/using-the-nhs/help-with-health-costs for further information.

WALES

On 1 April 2007 all prescription charges (including those for medical supports and appliances and wigs) for people living in Wales were abolished. The above guide still applies for NHS dental and optical charges although all people aged under 25 living in Wales are also entitled to free dental examinations.

SCOTLAND

On 1 April 2011 all prescription charges in Scotland were abolished. Those entitled to free prescriptions in Scotland include patients registered with a Scottish GP and receiving a prescription from a Scottish pharmacy, and Scottish patients who have an English GP and an entitlement card.

NORTHERN IRELAND

On 1 April 2010 all prescription charges in Northern Ireland were abolished. All prescriptions dispensed in Northern Ireland are free, even for patients visiting from England, Wales or Scotland.

PHARMACEUTICAL SERVICES

Patients may obtain medicines and appliances under the NHS from any pharmacy whose owner has entered into arrangements with the CCG to provide this service. There are also some suppliers who only provide special appliances. In rural areas, where access to a pharmacy may be difficult, patients may be able to obtain medicines, etc, from a dispensing doctor.

In England, a charge of £9.00 is payable for each item supplied (except for contraceptives for which there is no charge), unless the patient is exempt and the declaration on the back of the prescription form is completed. Prescription prepayment certificates (£29.10 valid for three months, £104.00 valid for a year) may be purchased by those patients not entitled to exemption who require frequent prescriptions.

DENTAL SERVICES

Dentists, like doctors, may take part in the NHS and also have private patients. Dentists are responsible to the local health provider in whose areas they provide services. Patients may go to any dentist who is taking part in the NHS and is willing to accept them. There is a three-tier payment system based on the individual course of treatment required.

NHS DENTAL CHARGES from 1 April 2019	
	England/Wales
Band 1* – Examination, diagnosis, preventive care (eg x-rays, scale and polish)	£22.70/£14.30
Band 2 – Band 1 + basic additional treatment (eg fillings and extractions)	£62.10/£46.00
Band 3 – Bands 1 and 2 + all other treatment (eg crowns, dentures and bridges)	£269.30/£199.10
* Urgent and out-of-hours treatment is also charged at this tier	

The cost of individual treatment plans should be known prior to treatment and some dental practices may require payment in advance. There is no charge for writing a prescription or removing stitches and only one charge is payable for each course of treatment even if more than one visit to the dentist is required. If additional treatment is required within two months of visiting the dentist and this is covered by the course of treatment most recently paid for (eg payment was made for the second tier of treatment but an additional filling is required) then this will be provided free of charge.

SCOTLAND AND NORTHERN IRELAND

Scotland and Northern Ireland have yet to simplify their charging systems. NHS dental patients pay 80 per cent of the cost of the individual items of treatment provided up to a maximum of £384. An NHS dental examination in Scotland is free of charge for everyone.

GENERAL OPHTHALMIC SERVICES

General ophthalmic services are administered by local health providers. Testing of sight may be carried out by any ophthalmic medical practitioner or ophthalmic optician (optometrist). The optician must give the prescription to the patient, who can take this to any supplier of glasses to have them dispensed. Only registered opticians can supply glasses to children and to people registered as blind or partially sighted.

Free eyesight tests and help towards the cost are available to people in certain circumstances. Help is also available for the purchase of glasses or contact lenses (see Health Costs). In Scotland eye examinations, which include a sight test, are free to all UK residents. Help is also available for the purchase of glasses or contact lenses to those entitled to help with health costs in the same way it is available to those in England and Wales.

CHILD HEALTH SERVICES

Pre-school services at GP surgeries or child health clinics provide regular monitoring of children's physical, mental and emotional health and development and advise parents on their children's health and welfare.

NHS 111, NHS DIRECT AND NHS 24

NHS Direct Wales is a website and 24-hour nurse-led advice telephone service for Wales. It provides medical advice as well as directing people to the appropriate part of the NHS for treatment if necessary. (T 0845 46 47 W www.nhsdirect.wales.nhs.uk). NHS Direct had also operated in England but closed on 31 March 2014. Non-urgent 24-hour nurse-led advice in England can be accessed via the NHS 111 service (T 111).

NHS 24 provides an equivalent service for Scotland (T 111 W www.nhs24.scot).

SECONDARY CARE AND OTHER SERVICES

HOSPITALS

NHS hospitals provide acute and specialist care services, treating conditions which normally cannot be dealt with by primary care specialists, and provide for medical emergencies.

NUMBER OF BEDS 2018–19

	Average daily	
	available beds	occupation of beds
England	142,745	126,758
Wales	10,564	9,170
Scotland	12,981	11,293
Northern Ireland*	5,902	4,934

* Figures are for 2017–18
Sources: NHS England, Welsh government, ISD Scotland, Northern Ireland Executive

HOSPITAL CHARGES

Acute or foundation trusts can provide hospital accommodation in single rooms or small wards, if not required for patients who need privacy for medical reasons. The patient is still an NHS patient, but there may be a charge for these additional facilities. Acute or foundation trusts can charge for certain patient services that are considered to be additional treatments over and above the normal hospital service provision. There is no blanket policy to cover this and each case is considered in the light of the patient's clinical need. However, if an item or service is considered to be an integral part of a patient's treatment by their clinician, then a charge should not be made.

In some NHS hospitals, accommodation and services are available for the treatment of private patients where it does not interfere with care for NHS patients. Income generated by treating private patients is then put back into local NHS services. Private patients undertake to pay the full costs of medical treatment, accommodation, medication and other related services. Charges for private patients are set locally.

WAITING LISTS

England

During February 2019, 284,212 patients started admitted treatment and 1,033,312 started non-admitted treatment. At the end of February, 87 per cent of patients had been treated within 18 weeks of referral, below the 92 per cent standard; the median waiting time was 6.7 weeks.

Wales

During April 2019, 80 per cent of 393,703 patients were treated within 26 weeks and 94.7 per cent were treated within 36 weeks of the date the referral letter was received by the hospital.

Scotland

In the quarter ending March 2019, 77.3 per cent of patients were seen within the 18 week referral to treatment (RTT) standard. In the same month, 90 per cent of patients waiting for a new outpatient appointment were seen within 12 weeks.

Northern Ireland

By March 2019 the aim was for at least 55 per cent of patients to wait no longer than 13 weeks for a first out-patient appointment, with no patient waiting longer than 52 weeks. The total number of people waiting for a first out-patient appointment at the end of March 2019 was 87,450, of these, 65 per cent had been waiting over 13 weeks. The number of people waiting to be admitted to hospital in Northern Ireland at the end of March 2019 was 50,248 – 62.3 per cent had been waiting for more than 13 weeks.

AMBULANCE SERVICE

The NHS provides emergency ambulance services free of charge via the 999 emergency telephone service. Air ambulances, provided through local charities and partially funded by the NHS, are used throughout the UK. They assist with cases where access may be difficult or heavy traffic could hinder road progress. Non-emergency ambulance services are provided free to patients who are deemed to require them on medical grounds.

Since 1 April 2001 all services have had a system of call prioritisation. Since 2017, ambulances have been expected to reach Red 1 – calls requiring a defibrillator – and Red 2 emergency calls within seven minutes, at least 75 per cent of the time. Non-emergency calls are categorised as Green 1, 2, 3 or 4, with category Green 4 calls being the least serious. Green calls are generally responded to between 20 minutes and one hour.

In 2016 it was agreed that all ambulance staff were to be re-banded from a band 5 to a band 6 under the *Agenda for Change* pay scale. In 2019, the NHS employed 22,924 qualified ambulance staff in England earning between £18,813 (emergency care assistant) and £37,267 (senior paramedic).

BLOOD AND TRANSPLANT SERVICES

There are four national bodies which coordinate the blood donor programme and transplant and related services in the UK. Donors give blood at local centres on a voluntary basis.

NHS BLOOD AND TRANSPLANT, Oak House, Reeds Crescent, Watford, Herts WD24 4QN T 0300-123 2323 W www.nhsbt.nhs.uk

WELSH BLOOD SERVICE, Ely Valley Road, Talbot Green, Pontyclun CF72 9WB T 0800-252 2266 W www.welsh-blood.org.uk

SCOTTISH NATIONAL BLOOD TRANSFUSION SERVICE, The Jack Copland Centre, 52 Research Avenue North, Herriot-Watt Research Park, Edinburgh EH14 4BE T 0131-314536 5510 W www.scotblood.co.uk

NORTHERN IRELAND BLOOD TRANSFUSION SERVICE, Lisburn Road, Belfast BT9 7TS T 028-9032 1414 W www.nibts.org

HOSPICES

Hospice or palliative care may be available for patients with life-threatening illnesses. It may be provided at the patient's home, in a voluntary or NHS hospice or at hospital, and is intended to ensure the best possible quality of life for the patient, and to provide help and support to both the patient and the patient's family. Hospice UK coordinates NHS and voluntary services in England, Wales and Northern Ireland; the Scottish Partnership for Palliative Care performs the same function in Scotland.

HOSPICE UK, Hospice House, 34–44 Britannia Street, London WC1X 9JG T 020-7520 8200 W www.hospiceUK.org

SCOTTISH PARTNERSHIP FOR PALLIATIVE CARE, CBC House, 24 Canning Street, Edinburgh EH3 8EG T 0131-272 2735 W www.palliativecarescotland.org.uk

COMPLAINTS

Patient advice and liaison services (PALS) have been established for every NHS and PCT in England. PALS can give advice on local complaints procedure, or resolve concerns informally. If the case is not resolved locally or the complainant is not satisfied with the way a local NHS body or practice has dealt with their complaint, they may approach the Parliamentary and Health Service Ombudsman in England, the Scottish Public Services Ombudsman, Public Services Ombudsman for Wales or the Northern Ireland Public Services Ombudsman. *See* Ombudsman Services.

HEALTH ADVICE AND MEDICAL TREATMENT ABROAD

IMMUNISATION

Country-by-country guidance is set out on the website W www.fitfortravel.nhs.uk

RECIPROCAL ARRANGEMENTS

The European Health Insurance Card (EHIC) allows UK residents access to state-provided healthcare while temporarily travelling in all European Economic Area countries and Switzerland either free or at a reduced cost. A card is free, valid for up to five years and should be obtained before travelling. Applications can be made by telephone (T 0300-330 1350) or online (W www.ehic.org.uk). At such time as the UK leaves the European Union the EHIC may no longer be valid and/ or be dependent on arrangements made with individual countries; further information is available online (W www.ehic.org.uk).

The UK also has bilateral agreements with several other countries, including Australia and New Zealand, for the free provision of urgent medical treatment.

European Economic Area nationals visiting the UK and visitors from other countries with which the UK has bilateral health care agreements are currently able to receive emergency health care on the NHS on the same terms as is available to UK residents. After the UK has left the EU, European Economic Area nationals may lose this entitlement or it will be dependent on arrangements made with individual countries.

SOCIAL WELFARE

SOCIAL SERVICES

The Secretary of State for Health (in England), the Welsh government, the Scottish government and the Secretary of State for Northern Ireland are responsible, under the Local Authority Social Services Act 1970, for the provision of social services for older people, disabled people, families and children, and those with mental disorders. Personal social services are administered by local authorities according to policies, with standards set by central and devolved government. Each authority has a director and a committee responsible for the social services functions placed upon them. Local authorities provide, enable and commission care after assessing the needs of their population. The private and voluntary sectors also play an important role in the delivery of social services, and an estimated 7 million people in the UK provide substantial regular care for a member of their family.

The Care Quality Commission (CQC) was established in April 2009, bringing together the independent regulation of health, mental health and adult social care. Prior to 1 April 2009 this work was carried out by three separate organisations: the Healthcare Commission, the Mental Health Act Commission and the Commission for Social Care Inspection. The CQC is responsible for the registration of health and social care providers, the monitoring and inspection of all health and adult social care, issuing fines, public warnings or closures if standards are not met and for undertaking regular performance reviews. Since April 2007 the Office for Standards in Education, Children's Services and Skills (Ofsted) has been responsible for inspecting and regulating all care services for children and young people in England. Both Ofsted and CQC collate information on local care services and make this information available to the public.

The Care Inspectorate Wales, an operationally independent part of the Welsh government, is responsible for the regulation and inspection of all social care services in Wales.

In Scotland, the Care Inspectorate, is the independent care services regulator for Scotland.

The Department of Health is responsible for social care in Northern Ireland.

CARE QUALITY COMMISSION (CQC), Citygate, Gallowgate, Newcastle upon Tyne NE1 4PA T 0300-061 6161 W www.cqc.org.uk

OFFICE FOR STANDARDS IN EDUCATION, CHILDREN'S SERVICES AND SKILLS (Ofsted), Piccadilly Gate, Store Street, Manchester M1 2WD T 0300-123 1231 E enquiries@ofsted.gov.uk W www.gov.uk/government/organisations/ofsted

CARE INSPECTORATE WALES (CIW), Welsh Government Office, Sarn Mynach, Llandudno Junction LL31 9RZ T 0300-790 0126 E ciw@gov.wales W www.careinspectorate.wales

CARE INSPECTORATE, Compass House, 11 Riverside Drive, Dundee DD1 4NY T 0345 600 9527 E enquiries@careinspectorate.com W www.careinspectorate.com

DEPARTMENT OF HEALTH, Castle Buildings, Stormont, Belfast BT4 3SQ T 028-9052 0500 E webmaster@health-ni.gov.uk W www.health-ni.gov.uk

ADULT SOCIAL CARE WORKFORCE ESTIMATES (ENGLAND)

Total: all job roles	1,600,000
Managerial	119,000
Regulated professional	83,000
Direct care	1,220,000
Other	180,000

Source: Skills for Care, 2018

OLDER PEOPLE

Services for older people are designed to enable them to remain living in their own homes for as long as possible. Local authority services include advice, domestic help, meals in the home, alterations to the home to aid mobility, emergency alarm systems, day and/or night attendants, laundry services and the provision of day centres and recreational facilities. Charges may be made for these services. Respite care may also be provided in order to allow carers temporary relief from their responsibilities.

Local authorities and the private sector also provide 'sheltered housing' for older people, sometimes with resident wardens.

If an older person is admitted to a residential home, charges are made according to a means test; if the person cannot afford to pay, the costs are met by the local authority.

DISABLED PEOPLE

Services for disabled people are designed to enable them to remain living in their own homes wherever possible. Local authority services include advice, adaptations to the home, meals in the home, help with personal care, occupational therapy, educational facilities and recreational facilities. Respite care may also be provided in order to allow carers temporary relief from their responsibilities.

Special housing may be available for disabled people who can live independently, and residential accommodation for those who cannot.

FAMILIES AND CHILDREN

Local authorities are required to provide services aimed at safeguarding the welfare of children in need and, wherever possible, allowing them to be brought up by their families. Services include advice, counselling, help in the home and the provision of family centres. Many authorities also provide short-term refuge accommodation for women and children.

DAY CARE

In allocating day care places to children, local authorities give priority to children with special needs, whether in terms of their health, learning abilities or social needs. Since September 2001, Ofsted has been responsible for the regulation and registration of all early years childcare and education provision in England (previously the responsibility of the local authorities). All day care and childminding services that care for children under eight years of age for more than two hours a day must register with Ofsted and are inspected at least every two years. In 2018 there were an estimated 81,500 childcare providers in England.

CHILD PROTECTION

Children considered to be at risk of physical injury, neglect or sexual abuse are placed on the local authority's child protection register. Local authority social services staff, schools, health visitors and other agencies work together to prevent and detect cases of abuse. As at 31 March 2018, there was a total of 61,500 children on child protection registers or subject to a child protection plan in the UK. In England, there were 53,790 children on child protection registers, of these, 25,820 were at risk of neglect, 4,120 of physical abuse, 2,180 of sexual abuse and 18,860 of emotional abuse. At 31 March (July in Scotland) 2018 there were 2,960 children on child protection registers in Wales, 2,668 in Scotland and 2,082 in Northern Ireland.

LOCAL AUTHORITY CARE
Local authorities are required to provide accommodation for children who have no parents or guardians or whose parents or guardians are unable or unwilling to care for them. A family proceedings court may also issue a care order where a child is being neglected or abused, or is not attending school; the court must be satisfied that this would positively contribute to the well-being of the child.

The welfare of children in local authority care must be properly safeguarded. Children may be placed with foster families, who receive payments to cover the expenses of caring for the child or children, or in residential care.

Children's homes may be run by the local authority or by the private or voluntary sectors; all homes are subject to inspection procedures. As at 31 March 2018, 75,420 children in England were in the care of local authorities, of these, 55,200 were in foster placements and 8,530 were in children's homes, hostels or secure units.

ADOPTION
Local authorities are required to provide an adoption service, either directly or via approved voluntary societies. In the year to 31 March 2018, 2,230 children in local authority care in England were placed for adoption.

PEOPLE WITH LEARNING DISABILITIES
Services for people with learning disabilities are designed to enable them to remain living in the community wherever possible. Local authority services include short-term care, support in the home, the provision of day care centres, and help with other activities outside the home. Residential care is provided for the severely or profoundly disabled.

MENTALLY ILL PEOPLE
Under the care programme approach, mentally ill people should be assessed by specialist services and receive a care plan. A key worker should be appointed for each patient and regular reviews of the person's progress should be conducted. Local authorities provide help and advice to mentally ill people and their families, and places in day centres and social centres. Social workers can apply for a mentally disturbed person to be compulsorily detained in hospital. Where appropriate, mentally ill people are provided with accommodation in special hospitals, local authority accommodation, or at homes run by private or voluntary organisations. Patients who have been discharged from hospitals may be placed on a supervision register.

NATIONAL INSURANCE

The National Insurance (NI) scheme operates under the Social Security Contributions and Benefits Act 1992 and the Social Security Administration Act 1992, and orders and regulations made thereunder. The scheme is financed by contributions payable by earners, employers and others (see below). Money collected under the scheme is used to finance the National Insurance Fund (from which contributory benefits are paid) and to contribute to the cost of the National Health Service.

NATIONAL INSURANCE FUND
Estimated receipts, payments and statement of balances of the National Insurance Fund for 2019–20:

Receipts	£ million
Net national insurance contributions	108,706
Compensation from the Consolidated Fund for statutory payments recoveries	2,760
Income from investments	305
State scheme premiums	0
Other receipts	0
TOTAL RECEIPTS	111,771

Payments	£ million
Benefits	
At present rates	102,008
Increase due to proposed rate changes	2,515
Administration costs	743
Redundancy fund payments	295
Transfer to Northern Ireland	737
Other payments	188
TOTAL PAYMENTS	106,486

Balances	£ million
Balance at the beginning of the year	27,337
Excess of receipts over payments	5,285
BALANCE AT END OF YEAR	32,622

CONTRIBUTIONS
There are six classes of National Insurance contributions (NICs):

Class 1	paid by employees and their employers
Class 1A	paid by employers who provide employees with certain benefits in kind for private use, such as company cars
Class 1B	paid by employers who enter into a pay as you earn (PAYE) settlement agreement (PSA) with HM Revenue and Customs
Class 2	paid by self-employed people
Class 3	voluntary contributions paid to protect entitlement to the state pension for those who do not pay enough NI contributions in another class
Class 4	paid by the self-employed on their taxable profits over a set limit. These are normally paid by self-employed people in addition to class 2 contributions. Class 4 contributions do not count towards benefits.

The lower and upper earnings limits and the percentage rates referred to below apply from April 2019 to April 2020.

CLASS 1
Class 1 primary (employee) contributions are paid where a person:
• is an employed earner (employee), office holder (eg company director) or employed under a contract of service in Great Britain or Northern Ireland
• is 16 or over and under state pension age
• earns at or above the earnings threshold of £166.00 per week (including overtime pay, bonus, commission, etc, without deduction of superannuation contributions)

Class 1 contributions are made up of primary and secondary contributions. Primary contributions are those paid by the employee and these are deducted from earnings by the employer. Since 6 April 2001 the employee's and employer's earnings thresholds have been the same. Primary contributions are not paid on earnings below the earnings threshold of £166.00 per week. However, between the lower earnings limit of £118.00 per week and the earnings threshold of £166.00 per week, NI contributions are treated as having been paid to protect the benefit entitlement position of lower earners. Contributions are payable at the rate of 12 per cent on earnings between the earnings threshold and the upper earnings limit of £962.00 per week. Above the upper earnings limit 2 per cent is payable.

Some married women or widows pay a reduced rate of 5.85 per cent on earnings between the earnings threshold and upper earnings limits and 2 per cent above this. It is no longer possible to elect to pay the reduced rate but those who had reduced liability before 12 May 1977 may retain it for as long as certain conditions are met.

Secondary contributions are paid by employers of employed earners at the rate of 13.8 per cent on all earnings above the earnings threshold of £166.00 per week. There is a zero rate between the earnings threshold and the upper threshold of £962 per week for employers of relevant apprentices and employed earners under the age of 21.

CLASS 2
Class 2 contributions are paid where a person is self-employed and is 16 or over and under state pension age. Contributions are paid at a flat rate of £3.00 per week regardless of the amount earned. However, those with profits of less than £6,365 a year can apply for small profits exception. Those granted exemption from class 2 contributions may pay class 2 or class 3 contributions voluntarily. Self-employed earners (whether or not they pay class 2 contributions) may also be liable to pay class 4 contributions based on profits. There are special rules for those who are concurrently employed and self-employed.

Married women and widows can no longer choose not to pay class 2 contributions but those who elected not to pay class 2 contributions before 12 May 1977 may retain the right for as long as certain conditions are met.

Class 2 contributions are assessed and collected annually by HM Revenue and Customs (HMRC) as part of the self-assessment tax bill. For self-employed people that do not pay tax through self-assessment, a bill is issued by HMRC by the end of October.

CLASS 3
Class 3 contributions are voluntary flat-rate contributions of £15.00 per week payable by persons over the age of 16 who would otherwise be unable to qualify for retirement pension and certain other benefits because they have an insufficient record of class 1 or class 2 contributions. This may include those who are not working, those not liable for class 1 or class 2 contributions, or those excepted from class 2 contributions. Married women and widows who on or before 11 May 1977 elected not to pay class 1 (full rate) or class 2 contributions cannot pay class 3 contributions while they retain this right. Class 3 contributions are collected by HMRC by quarterly bills or monthly direct debit. One-off payments can also be made.

CLASS 4
Self-employed people whose profits and gains are over £8,632 a year pay class 4 contributions in addition to class 2 contributions. This applies to self-employed earners over 16 and under the state pension age. Class 4 contributions are calculated at 9 per cent of annual profits or gains between £8,632 and £50,000 and 2 per cent above. Class 4 contributions are assessed and collected annually by HMRC as part of the self-assessment tax bill. It is possible, in some circumstances, to apply for exceptions from liability to pay class 4 contributions or to have the amount of contribution reduced.

PENSIONS
Many people will qualify for a state pension; however, there are further pension choices available, such as workplace, personal and stakeholder pensions. There are also other non-pension savings and investment options.

STATE PENSION
From 6 April 2016, the system of basic and additional state pension was replaced with a new scheme for people reaching state pension age after that date (ie men born on or after 6 April 1951, and women born on or after 6 April 1953).

Those that reached state pension age before this date continue to receive their state pension in line with the old rules.

The earliest state pension can be claimed is at state pension age, people can delay claiming it to earn weekly state pension or a lump sum payment.

NEW STATE PENSION
The full rate of the new state pension, for people reaching state pension age on or after 6 April 2016, is £168.60 per week for a single person in 2019–20. The amount received is based on the individual's national insurance record.

An individual's 'starting amount', part of the new state pension, is based on NI contributions and credits made before 6 April 2016 and will be the higher of either:
- the amount received under the old state pension rules (including basic state pension and additional state pension)
- the amount received if the new state pension had been in place from the start of their working life

A deduction may be made to these amounts for periods an individual was contracted out of the additional state pension because they were in a certain type of workplace, personal or stakeholder pension.

If the individual's starting amount is less than the full new state pension (£168.60 per week) more qualifying years can be added to their national insurance record after 5 April 2016 until the individual reaches the full rate of new state pension or reaches state pension age – whichever is first. If the individual's starting amount is more than the full new state pension of £168.60 per week, then the amount above the full new state pension (the 'protected payment') is paid on top of the full new state pension.

If an individual did not make NI contributions or get NI credits prior to 6 April 2016 than their state pension will be calculated entirely under the new state pension rules.

Further information about the new state pension can be found online (www.gov.uk/new-state-pension).

CATEGORY A OR B STATE PENSION
The category A or B state pension scheme is paid to individuals who reached state pension age before 6 April 2016 and is based on their own contributions or those made by a deceased spouse or civil partner. The full weekly rate in 2019–20 is £129.20.

For further information see Benefits, State Pension: Categories A and B.

WORKING LIFE
The working life is from the start of the tax year (6 April) in which a person reaches 16 to the end of the tax year (5 April) before the one in which they reach state pension age (see State Pension Age).

QUALIFYING YEARS
A 'qualifying year' is a tax year in which a person has sufficient earnings upon which they have paid, are treated as having paid, or have been credited with national insurance (NI) contributions (see National Insurance Credits).

For people reaching state pension age on or after 6 April 2016 a full new state pension (£168.60 per week in 2019–20) is payable to those individuals who have 35 qualifying years on their national insurance record. Individuals usually need at least ten qualifying years and will receive a proportion of the new state pension if they have between ten and 35 qualifying years.

For people who reached state pension age between 6 April 2010 and 5 April 2016 a full category A or B pension (£129.20 per week in 2019–20) is payable to those individuals who have 30 qualifying years on their national insurance record. Someone with less than 30 qualifying years will be entitled to a proportion of the full category A or B pension based on the number of qualifying years they have. Just one qualifying year, achieved through paid or credited contributions, will give entitlement to the basic state pension worth one-thirtieth of the full basic state pension.

For people who reached state pension age before 6 April 2010, women normally needed 39 qualifying years for a full basic state pension (£129.20 per week in 2019–20) and men normally needed 44 qualifying years. A reduced-rate basic state pension was payable if the number of qualifying years was less than 90 per cent of the individual's working life, but to receive any state pension at all, a person must have had enough qualifying years, normally ten or 11, to receive a basic state pension of at least 25 per cent of the full rate.

The state pension of transgender people may be affected for those that changed their gender or started claiming state pension before 4 April 2005; claims for those who legally changed their gender and started claiming state pension on or after 4 April 2005 are based on the individual's legal gender.

NATIONAL INSURANCE CREDITS
Those in receipt of carer's allowance, working tax credit (with a disability premium), jobseeker's allowance, employment and support allowance, unemployability supplement, statutory sick pay, maternity allowance, statutory maternity, paternity or statutory adoption pay may have class 1 NI contributions credited to them each week. People may also get credits if they are unemployed and looking for work or too sick to work, even if they are not in receipt of any benefit, although the credits must be applied for in these circumstances. Since April 2010, spouses and civil partners of members of HM forces may get credits if they are on an accompanied assignment outside the UK. Those who reach state pension age on or after 6 April 2016 can apply for NI credits for periods before April 2010 during which they were married to, or in a civil partnership with, a member of HM forces and accompanied them on a posting outside the UK. Persons undertaking certain training courses or jury service or who have been wrongly imprisoned for a conviction which is quashed on appeal may also get class 1 NI credits for each week they fulfil certain conditions. Class 1 credits may also be available to men approaching state pension age, born before 6 October 1953 who live in the UK for at least 183 days a year and who don't work, earn enough to make a qualifying year or are self-employed with profits of less than £6,365. Class 1 NI credits count toward all future contributory benefits.

A class 3 NI credit for basic state pension and bereavement benefit purposes is awarded, where required, for each week universal credit, working tax credit (without a disability premium) or child benefit, for a child under 12, has been received. Class 3 credits may also be awarded, on application, to approved foster carers and people caring for others for at least 20 hours a week. Since 6 April 2011, class 3 credits have been available to adults under state pension age who care for a family member under 12. Further information regarding eligibility for NI credits is available online (www.gov.uk/national-insurance-credits/eligibility)

STATE PENSION AGE
From 6 November 2018 state pension age is 65 for both men and women and this will increase to age 66 for both men and women by October 2020. The Pensions Act 2014 makes provision for a regular review of state pension age. Reviews will take place at least once every six years and will take into account up-to-date life expectancy data and the findings of an independently led review, which will consider wider factors such as variation in life expectancy and employment opportunities for older workers. Further information can be obtained from the online state pension calculator (W www.gov.uk/state-pension-age).

USING THE NI CONTRIBUTION RECORD OF ANOTHER TO CLAIM A STATE PENSION
Married people or civil partners who reached state pension age before 6 April 2016 whose own NI record is incomplete may get a lower-rate basic state pension calculated using their partner's NI contribution record. This can be up to £77.45 a week in 2019–20.

People who reached state pension age before 6 April 2016 will continue to be able to use these provisions, even if their spouse or civil partner reaches state pension age on or after that date. However, contributions their spouse or civil partner pays, or is credited with, following implementation of the new system will only count towards their own state pension. This means that only the NI record of the spouse or civil partner up to and including 2015–16 will be used to calculate any derived entitlement.

People who reached state pension age on or after 6 April 2016 will not be able to claim state pension on their spouse's or civil partner's NI record. There will be special arrangements for women who had opted to pay the married women's and widows reduced rate contributions before May 1977.

NON-CONTRIBUTORY STATE PENSIONS
A non-contributory state pension may be payable to those aged 80 or over who live in England, Scotland or Wales, and have done so for a total of ten years or more for any continuous period in the 20 years after their 60th birthday, if they are not entitled to another category of state pension, or are entitled to one below the rate of £77.45 a week in 2019–20 (see also Benefits, State Pension for people aged 80 and over).

GRADUATED RETIREMENT BENEFIT
Graduated Retirement Benefit (GRB) is based on the amount of graduated NI contributions paid into the GRB scheme between April 1961 and April 1975 (see also Benefits, Graduated Retirement Benefit). It is normally paid as an increase to a main state pension. For those reaching state pension age under the new state pension rules, it will be included in the calculation of their basic amount.

HOME RESPONSIBILITIES PROTECTION
From 6 April 1978 until 5 April 2010, it was possible for people who had low income or were unable to work because they cared for children or a sick or disabled person at home to reduce the number of qualifying years required for basic state pension. This was called home responsibilities protection (HRP); the number of years for which HRP was given was deducted from the number of qualifying years needed. HRP could, in some cases, also qualify the recipient for additional state pension. From April 2003 to April 2010 HRP was also available to approved foster carers.

From 6 April 2010, HRP was replaced by weekly credits for parents and carers. A class 3 national insurance credit is also given, where eligible, towards state pension and bereavement benefits for spouses and civil partners. An earnings factor credit towards additional state pension was also awarded. Any years of HRP accrued before 6 April 2010 were converted into qualifying years of credits for people reaching state pension age after that date, up to a maximum of 22 years for state pension purposes.

ADDITIONAL STATE PENSION

The additional state pension is an extra sum paid on top of a basic state pension to men born before 6 April 1951 or women born before 1953. Individuals born after these dates will get the new state pension instead and won't qualify for the additional state pension, although they might still be able to inherit additional state pension from their partner. Additional state pension is paid automatically if an individual is eligible for it, unless they contracted out of it. There is no fixed amount for the additional state pension, the amount paid depends on the amount of earnings a person has, or is treated as having, between the lower and upper earnings limits for each complete tax year between 6 April 1978 and the tax year before they reach state pension age. The additional state pension is paid with the basic state pension.

From 1978 to 2002, additional state pension was called the State Earnings-Related Pension Scheme (SERPS). SERPS covered all earnings by employees from 6 April 1978 to 5 April 1997 on which standard rate class 1 NI contributions had been paid, and earnings between 6 April 1997 and 5 April 2002 if the standard rate class 1 NI contributions had been contracted-in.

In 2002, SERPS was reformed through the state second pension, by improving the pension available to low and moderate earners and extending access to certain carers and people with long-term illness or disability. If earnings on which class 1 NI contributions have been paid or can be treated as paid are above the annual NI lower earnings limit (£6,136 for 2019–2020) but below the primary threshold (£8,632 for 2019–2020), the state second pension regards this as earnings of £8,632 and it is treated as equivalent. Certain carers and people with long-term illness and disability will be considered as having earned at the primary threshold for each complete tax year since 2002–3 even if they do not work at all, or earn less than the annual NI lower earnings limit.

The amount of additional state pension paid also depends on when a person reaches state pension age; changes phased in from 6 April 1999 mean that pensions are calculated differently from that date.

ADDITIONAL STATE PENSION INHERITANCE

Men or women widowed before 6 October 2002 may inherit all of their late spouse's SERPS pension. Since 6 October 2002, the maximum percentage of SERPS pension that a person can inherit from a late spouse or civil partner depends on their late spouse's or civil partner's date of birth:

Maximum SERPS entitlement	d.o.b. (men)	d.o.b. (women)
100%	5/10/37 or earlier	5/10/42 or earlier
90%	6/10/37 to 5/10/39	6/10/42 to 5/10/44
80%	6/10/39 to 5/10/41	6/10/44 to 5/10/46
70%	6/10/41 to 5/10/43	6/10/46 to 5/10/48
60%	6/10/43 to 5/10/45	6/10/48 to 5/7/50
50%	6/10/45 or later	6/7/50 or later

The maximum state second pension a person can inherit from a spouse or civil partner is 50 per cent. If a person is bereaved before they have reached their state pension age, inherited SERPS or state second pension can be paid as part of widowed parent's allowance (in the case of a person who has dependent children) or otherwise only from state pension age. If they remarry or form a new civil partnership before state pension age they lose the right to inherit any state pension.

NEW STATE PENSION INHERITANCE

A person who reached state pension age before 6 April 2016 will still be able to inherit additional state pension under the existing rules. However, if their late spouse or civil partner reaches state pension age on or after that date, the amount they can inherit will be based on the deceased's contributions up to 5 April 2016 only.

A person reaching state pension age on or after 6 April 2016 whose deceased spouse or civil partner reached state pension age or died before that date will be able to inherit additional state pension under the current rules. If the deceased spouse or civil partner is also in the new state pension the survivor may inherit half of any 'protected payment'. A person will have a protected payment if their state pension calculated under current rules is more than the full rate of new state pension at April 2016. The protected payment is the amount of the excess.

In order for a person reaching state pension age on or after 6 April 2016 to qualify for an inherited amount the marriage or civil partnership must have begun before that date; and, in the case of a person widowed under state pension age, they must not remarry or form a new civil partnership before state pension age.

STATE PENSION STATEMENTS

The Department for Work and Pensions provide state pension statements. These statements give an estimate of the state pension an individual may get based on their current NI contribution record.

There is also an online state pension calculator (W www.gov.uk/check-state-pension).

PRIVATE PENSIONS

CONTRACTED-OUT PENSIONS

From 6 April 2012, employees have not been able to contract-out of the state second pension through a money purchase (defined contribution) occupational pension scheme or a personal or stakeholder pension. Anyone contracted-out via these schemes, from that date, was automatically contracted back into the additional state pension. Although those rights built up before the abolition date can be used to provide pension benefits. These changes did not affect contracting-out via a salary-related occupational pension scheme (also known as contracted-out defined benefit (DB) or final salary schemes), which provide a pension related to earnings and the length of pensionable service. However, the introduction of the single-tier pension scheme in April 2016 closed the additional state pension for those reaching state pension age after this date, and contracting out on a DB basis ended.

STAKEHOLDER PENSION SCHEMES

Introduced in 2001, stakeholder pensions are available to everyone but are principally for moderate earners who do not have access to a good value company pension scheme. Stakeholder pensions must meet minimum standards to make sure they are flexible, portable and annual management charges are capped. The minimum contribution is £20.

AUTOMATIC ENROLMENT INTO WORKPLACE PENSIONS

Under the Pensions Act 2008 automatic enrolment into workplace pensions was phased in between October 2012 and February 2018, from when all employers must automatically enrol their workers who meet the age and earnings criteria into a workplace pension. This applies to people who are not already in a qualifying workplace pension scheme and who:

- earn at least £10,000 per annum
- are aged 22 or over
- are under state pension age
- ordinarily work in the UK

Employees who meet the above requirements are entitled to opt out of the scheme at any time if they wish to do so; if they opt out within one calendar month of enrolment they will get back any money already paid in, otherwise payments will usually stay in the pension until retirement. Employees can opt back in at any time by writing to their employer, although they do not have to accept the employer back into their workplace scheme if they they have opted in and opted out within the past 12 months. Employers will automatically re-enrol those that have opted out every three years (from the date they were first enrolled) and will write to the employee when they do this. Employees can leave the scheme again, but only once they have been re-enrolled.

Additionally certain employees can also choose to opt in to the scheme. Currently, employees can opt in if they are:
- aged 16 to 21, or state pension age to 74
- earning above £6,032 up to and including £10,000 per annum

If they remain in the scheme, they, together with their employer, will pay into it every month. The government will also contribute through tax relief. Further information is available at W www.gov.uk/workplace-pensions

COMPLAINTS

The Pensions Advisory Service provides information and guidance to members of the public, on state, company, personal and stakeholder schemes. They also help any member of the public who has a problem, complaint or dispute with their occupational or personal pensions.

There are two bodies for pension complaints. The Financial Ombudsman Service deals with complaints which predominantly concern the sale and/or marketing of occupational, stakeholder and personal pensions. The Pensions Ombudsman deals with complaints regarding the management (after sale or marketing) of occupational, stakeholder and personal pensions.

The Pensions Regulator is the UK regulator for work-based pension schemes; it concentrates its resources on schemes where there is the greatest risk to the security of members' benefits, promotes good administration practice for all work-based schemes and works with trustees, employers and professional advisers to put things right when necessary.

WAR PENSIONS AND THE ARMED FORCES COMPENSATION SCHEME

Veterans UK is part of the Ministry of Defence. It was formed on 1 April 2007 to provide services to both serving personnel and veterans.

Veterans UK is responsible for the administration of the war pensions scheme and the armed forces compensation scheme (AFCS) to members of the armed forces in respect of disablement or death due to service. They are also responsible for the administration of the armed forces pension scheme (AFPS), which provides occupational pensions for ex-service personnel.

THE WAR PENSIONS SCHEME

War disablement pension is awarded for the disabling effects of any injury, wound or disease which was the result of, or was aggravated by, service in the armed forces prior to 6 April 2005. Claims are only considered once the person has left the armed forces. The amount of pension paid depends on the severity of disablement, which is assessed by comparing the health of the claimant with that of a healthy person of the same age and sex. The person's earning capacity or occupation are not taken into account in this assessment. A pension is awarded if the person has a disablement of 20 per cent or more and a lump sum is usually payable to those with a disablement of less than 20 per cent. No award is made for noise-induced sensorineural hearing loss where the assessment of disablement is less than 20 per cent. Where an assessment of disablement is at 40 per cent or more, an age addition is automatically given when the pensioner reaches 65.

A pension is payable to war widows, widowers and surviving civil partners where the spouse's or civil partner's death was due to, or hastened by, service in the armed forces prior to 6 April 2005 or where the spouse or civil partner was in receipt of a war disablement pension constant attendance allowance (or would have been if not in hospital) at the time of death. A pension is also payable to widows, widowers or surviving civil partners if the spouse or civil partner was receiving the war disablement pension at the 80 per cent rate or higher in conjunction with unemployability supplement at the time of death. War widows, widowers and surviving civil partners receive a standard rank-related rate, but a lower weekly rate is payable to war widows, widowers and surviving civil partners of personnel of the rank of Major or below who are under the age of 40, without children and capable of maintaining themselves. This is increased to the standard rate at age 40. Allowances are paid for children and adult dependants. An age allowance is automatically given when the widow, widower or surviving civil partner reaches 65 and increased at ages 70 and 80.

Pensioners living overseas receive the same pension rates as those living in the UK. All war disablement pensions and allowances and pensions for war widows, widowers and surviving civil partners are tax-free in the UK; this does not always apply in overseas countries due to different tax laws.

SUPPLEMENTARY ALLOWANCES

A number of supplementary allowances may be awarded to a war pensioner and are intended to meet various needs. The principal supplementary allowances are unemployability supplement, allowance for lowered standard of occupation, constant attendance allowance and war pensions mobility supplement. Others include exceptionally severe disablement allowance, severe disablement occupational allowance, treatment allowance, comforts allowance, clothing allowance, age allowance and widow/widower/surviving civil partner's age allowance. Rent and children's allowances are also available with pensions for war widows, widowers and surviving civil partners.

ARMED FORCES COMPENSATION SCHEME

The armed forces compensation scheme (AFCS) became effective on 6 April 2005 and covers all regular (including Gurkhas) and reserve personnel whose injury, ill health or death is caused predominantly by service on or after 6 April 2005. There are time limits under this scheme and generally claims must be made within seven years of the injury occurring or from first seeking medical advice about an illness. There are some exceptions to this time limit, the main one being for a late-onset illness. Claims for a late-onset illness can be made, after discharge, at any time after the event to which it relates, providing the claim is made within three years of medical advice being sought.

The AFCS provides compensation where service in the armed forces is the only or predominant cause of injury, illness or death. Any other personal accident cover held by the individual is not taken into account when determining an AFCS award. Under the terms of the scheme a tax-free lump sum is payable to service or ex-service personnel based on a 15-level tariff, graduated according to the seriousness of the injury. If multiple injuries are sustained in the same incident compensation for each injury, up to the scheme maximum, is awarded. For those with the most serious injuries and illness a tax-free, index-linked monthly payment – a guaranteed income payment or GIP – is paid for life from the point of discharge. A taxable survivor's GIP (SGIP) will also be paid to surviving spouses, civil partners and unmarried partners who meet certain criteria. GIP and SGIP are calculated by multiplying the pensionable pay of the service person by a factor that depends on the age at the person's last birthday. The younger the person, the higher the factor, because there are more years to normal retirement age.

ARMED FORCES INDEPENDENCE PAYMENT

Armed forces independence payment (AFIP) is designed to provide financial support for service personnel and veterans who have been seriously injured to cover the extra costs they may incur as a result of their injury. It is administered by Veterans UK as part of AFCS although payments are made by the Department for Work and Pensions (DWP). It is non-taxable and non-means-tested.

Service personnel and veterans awarded a GIP of 50 per cent or higher under the AFCS are eligible. Those eligible for AFIP are not required to undergo an assessment and will keep the payment for as long as they are entitled to receive a GIP of 50 per cent or higher.

DEPARTMENT FOR WORK AND PENSIONS BENEFITS

Payments under the AFCS and the war pensions scheme may affect income related benefits from the DWP. In particular any supplementary allowances in payment with war pensions. Any state pension for which a war widow, widower or surviving civil partner qualifies for on their own NI contribution record can be paid in addition to monies received under the war pensions scheme.

CLAIMS AND QUESTIONS

Further information on the war pensions scheme, the AFCS and contact details for Veterans Welfare Service centres can be obtained from Veterans UK (T 0808-191 4218, if calling from the UK or, if living overseas, T (+44) (1253) 866-043).

VETERANS UK, Norcross Lane, Thornton-Cleveleys FY5 3WP
E veterans-uk@mod.gov.uk W www.gov.uk/government/organisations/veterans-uk

TAX CREDITS

Tax credits are administered by HM Revenue and Customs (HMRC). They are based on an individual's or couple's household income and current circumstances. Adjustments can be made during the year to reflect changes in income and/or circumstances. Tax credits are being replaced by universal credit. Further information regarding the qualifying conditions for tax credits, how to claim and the rates payable is available online at (W www.gov.uk/browse/benefits/tax-credits).

WORKING TAX CREDIT

Working tax credit is a payment from the government to support people on low incomes. New claims may only be made by those who are in receipt of a severe disability premium. Those who do not meet this criteria may be eligible for universal credit if they are of working age, or pension credits if they are of qualifying age.

For those in receipt of working tax credit (where this has not been replaced by universal credit) the amount received depends on individual circumstances and income. The basic amount is up to £1,960 per annum and extra 'elements' are paid on top of this:

Element	Amount per annum
Couple applying together	up to £2,010
Single parent	up to £2,010
An individual working at least 30 hours a week	up to £810
An individual with a disability	up to £3,165
An individual with a severe disability	up to £1,365*

* Usually in addition to the disability payment

Childcare Element

Those already in receipt of tax credits, may still be able to claim for the childcare element. In families with children where a lone parent works at least 16 hours a week, or couples who work at least 24 hours a week between them with one partner working at least 16 hours a week, or where one partner works at least 16 hours a week and the other is disabled, an in-patient in hospital, or in prison, the family is entitled to the childcare element of working tax credit. Depending on circumstances this payment can contribute up to £122.50 a week towards childcare costs for one child and up to £210.00 a week for two or more children. Families can only claim if they use an approved childcare provider.

CHILD TAX CREDIT

Child tax credit has been replaced by universal credit for most people. The credit is made up of a main 'family' element of up to £545 a year with an additional 'child' payment of up to £2,780 a year for each child in a household born before 6 April 2017. For children born after this date, only the 'child' element of child tax credit will apply for the first two children in a household with no 'family element', however there are exceptions to this two-child rule. An additional payment is paid for children with a disability, plus a further payment for children who are severely disabled. New child tax credit claims are still possible for individuals who are eligible for a severe disability premium and have legal responsibility and care for any child who is 16 years and younger.

BENEFITS

The following is intended as a general guide to the benefits system. Conditions of entitlement and benefit rates change annually and all prospective claimants should check exact entitlements and rates of benefit directly with their local Jobcentre Plus office, pension centre or online (W www.gov.uk/browse/benefits). Leaflets relating to the various benefits and contribution conditions for different benefits are available from local Jobcentre Plus offices.

UNIVERSAL CREDIT

Universal credit (UC) is a single benefit which combines benefits for in and out of work support, housing and childcare costs, with additional payments for people who have disabilities or caring responsibilities. UC is gradually being rolled out to all new and existing claimants in all local authority areas in the country, replacing six means-tested benefits with a single monthly payment. The six benefits being replaced by UC are:

- Income-based jobseeker's allowance (JSA)
- Income-related employment and support allowance (ESA)
- Income support
- Child tax credit
- Working tax credit
- Housing benefit

The UC full service completed its roll-out for all new claimants in December 2018 and is available in all parts of the UK. It is expected that existing claimants of the above six benefits will be moved to UC between November 2020 and December 2023. This will follow a pilot involving up to 10,000 people moved between July 2019 and July 2020.

The amount of UC awarded is determined by the circumstances of the claimant, this includes income and number of dependants in the household. It consists of a basic 'standard allowance' and additional payments as applicable to the claimant's circumstances. UC can be claimed while working, but the monthly payment will reduce gradually as the claimant earns more.

Standard monthly allowance from April 2019

Single, under 25	£251.77
Single, over 25	£317.82
Couple, both under 25	£395.20
Couple, one or both over 25	£498.89

Additional monthly payments from April 2019

Disability or health condition	£336.20
Carer allowance	£160.20
First child born before 6 April 2017	£277.08
First child born after 6 April 2017	£231.67
Second child	£231.67
Childcare for one child (max.)	£646.35
Childcare for two or more children (max.)	£1,108.04
Child with a disability	
Lower rate addition	£126.11
Higher rate addition	£392.08

For more information and to check eligibility visit W www.gov.uk/universal-credit

CONTRIBUTORY BENEFITS

Entitlement to contributory benefits depends on national insurance contribution conditions being satisfied either by the claimant or by someone on the claimant's behalf (depending on the kind of benefit). The class or classes of national insurance contribution relevant to each benefit are:

Jobseeker's allowance (contribution-based)	Class 1
Employment and Support Allowance (contributory)	Class 1 or 2
Widow's benefit and bereavement benefit	Class 1, 2 or 3
State pensions, categories A and B	Class 1, 2 or 3

The system of contribution conditions relates to yearly levels of earnings on which national insurance (NI) contributions have been paid.

JOBSEEKER'S ALLOWANCE

Jobseeker's allowance (JSA) replaced unemployment benefit and income support for unemployed people under state pension age from 7 October 1996. There are three different types of JSA: 'new style' JSA, contribution-based JSA and income-based JSA. Following the roll out of universal credit (UC) new claimants can only claim contribution-based JSA if they are entitled to the severe disability premium, existing claimants will transfer to 'new style' JSA in line with UC roll-out in their area. JSA is paid at a personal rate (ie additional benefit for dependants is not paid) to those who have made sufficient Class 1 NI contributions in the previous two or three tax years. Savings and partner's earnings are not taken into account and payment can be made for up to six months. Rates of JSA correspond to income support rates.

Claims are made through Jobcentre Plus. A person wishing to claim JSA must generally be unemployed or working on average less than 16 hours a week, capable of work and available for any work which he or she can reasonably be expected to do, usually for at least 40 hours a week. The claimant must agree and sign a 'jobseeker's agreement', which will set out his or her plans to find work, and must actively seek work. If the claimant refuses work or training the benefit may be sanctioned for between one and 26 weeks. On successfully claiming the 'new style' JSA, UC payments will be reduced.

A person will be sanctioned from JSA for up to 26 weeks if he or she has left a job voluntarily without just cause or through misconduct. In these circumstances, it may be possible to receive hardship payments, particularly where the claimant or the claimant's family is vulnerable, eg if sick or pregnant, or with children or caring responsibilities.

Weekly Rates from April 2019

Person aged under 25	£57.90
Person aged 25 or over	£73.10

EMPLOYMENT AND SUPPORT ALLOWANCE

From 27 October 2008, employment and support allowance (ESA) replaced incapacity benefit and income support paid on the grounds of incapacity or disability. There are three different types of ESA: 'new style' ESA, contribution-based ESA and income-related ESA. Those eligible for UC may be able to get UC at the same time or instead of 'new style' ESA. Contributory ESA is available to those who have limited capability for work but cannot get statutory sick pay from their employer; new claimants must be in receipt of the severe disability premium otherwise they can only apply for 'new style' ESA. Those over pensionable age are not entitled to ESA. Apart from those who qualify under the special provisions for people incapacitated in youth, entitlement to contributory ESA is based on a person's NI contribution record. The amount of contributory ESA payable may be reduced where the person receives more than a specified amount of occupational or personal pension. Contributory ESA is paid only in respect of the person claiming the benefit – there are no additional amounts for dependants.

Those with the most severe health conditions or disabilities will receive the support component, which is more than the work-related activity component. Claimants in receipt of the support component are not required to engage in work-related activities, although they can volunteer to do so or undertake permitted work if their condition allows.

Weekly Rates from April 2019

ESA plus work-related activity component	up to £102.15
ESA plus support component	up to £111.65

BEREAVEMENT SUPPORT PAYMENT

Bereavement support payment replaced bereavement payment, widowed parent's allowance and bereavement allowance for those whose spouse or civil partner died on or after 6 April 2017. It may be paid to those under state pension age at the time of their spouse or civil partner's death and whose spouse or civil partner had paid National Insurance contributions for at least 25 weeks or died because of an accident at work or a disease caused by work.

It consists of an initial one-off payment followed by up to 18 monthly payments. There are two rates: those in receipt of, or entitled to, child benefit or those who were pregnant when their spouse or civil partner died receive the higher rate. In order to receive the full amount claims must be made within three months of the death of the spouse or civil partner. After three months, claims can still be made up to 21 months after the spouse or civil partner's death but the payments will be less.

Rates from April 2019

Standard rate	
lump sum	£2,500.00
monthly payment	£100.00
Higher rate	
lump sum	£3,500.00
monthly payment	£350.00

NEW STATE PENSION

The new state pension is payable to men and women who reach state pension age on or after 6 April 2016 (ie men born on or after 6 April 1951 or women born on or after 6 April

1953). Those that reached state pension age before this date continue to receive state pension under the old rules.

The full new state pension of £168.60 a week in 2019–20 is payable to those individuals who have 35 qualifying years on their national insurance record. Individuals usually need at least ten qualifying years and will receive a proportion of the new state pension if they have between ten and 35 qualifying years. The starting amount is the higher of the amount receivable under the old state pension rules (category A and B) and the amount the individual would receive had the new state pension been in place at the start of their working life. The amount received includes a deduction for those who were contracted out of the additional state pension.

Each qualifying year on an individual's national insurance record after 5 April 2016 adds £4.82 a week to the new state pension. The exact amount can be calculated by dividing £168.60 by 35 and then multiplying by the number of qualifying years after 5 April 2016. Additional qualifying years can be added to a person's national insurance record until the person reaches the full new state pension amount or the state pension age – whichever is first.

Those individuals who have accrued an amount, before 5 April 2016, which is above the new full state pension – a 'protected payment' – have this paid on top of the full new state pension.

The new state pension increases each year by whichever is the highest:

• earnings – the average percentage growth in wages (in Great Britain)
• prices – the percentage growth in prices in the UK as measured by the Consumer Prices Index (CPI)
• 3 per cent

Any protected payment increases each year in line with CPI.

The new state pension can be deferred beyond state pension age and will increase by 1 per cent for every nine weeks it is deferred, as long as it is deferred for at least nine weeks. This equates to just under 5.8 per cent for every full year a new state pension is deferred.The new state pension can only be deferred once and for a period of at least nine weeks (there is no upper limit).

Weekly Rate from April 2019	
Full new state pension	£168.60

STATE PENSION: CATEGORIES A AND B

Category A pension is payable for life to men and women who reach state pension age, who satisfy the contributions conditions and who claim for it. Category B pension may be payable to married women, married men and civil partners who are not entitled to a basic state pension on their own NI contributions or whose own basic state pension entitlement is less than £77.45 a week in 2019–20. It is based on their spouse or civil partner's NI contributions and is payable when both members of the couple have reached state pension age. Married men and civil partners may only be able to qualify for a category B pension if their wife or civil partner was born on or after 6 April 1950. Category B pension is also payable to widows, widowers and surviving civil partners who are bereaved before state pension age if they were previously entitled to widowed parent's allowance or bereavement allowance based on their late spouse's or civil partner's NI contributions. If they were receiving widowed parent's allowance on reaching state pension age, they could qualify for a category B pension payable at the same rate as their widowed parent's allowance comprising a basic pension, plus, if applicable, the appropriate share of their late spouse's or late civil partner's additional state pension. If their widowed

parent's allowance had stopped before they reached state pension age, or they had been getting bereavement allowance at any time before state pension age, their category B pension will consist of inheritable additional state pension only. No basic state pension is included, although they may qualify for a basic state pension or have their own basic state pension improved by substituting their late spouse's or late civil partner's NI records for their own.

Widows who are bereaved when over state pension age can qualify for a category B pension regardless of the age of their husband when he died. This is payable at the same rate as the basic state pension the widow's late husband was entitled to (or would have been entitled to) at the time of his death. It can also be paid to widowers and civil partners who are bereaved when over state pension age if their wife or civil partner had reached state pension age when they died. Widowers and surviving civil partners who reached state pension age on or after 6 April 2010 and bereaved when over state pension age can qualify for a category B pension regardless of the age of their wife or civil partner when they died.

Where a person is entitled to both a category A and category B pension then they can be combined to give a composite pension, but this cannot be more than the full rate pension. Where a person is entitled to more than one category A or category B pension then only one can be paid. In such cases the person can choose which to get; if no choice is made, the most favourable one is paid.

A person may defer claiming their pension beyond state pension age. In doing so they may earn increments which will increase the weekly amount paid by 1 per cent per five weeks of deferral (equivalent to 10.4 per cent/year) when they claim their state pension. If a person delays claiming for at least 12 months they are given the option of a one-off taxable lump sum, instead of a pension increase, based on the weekly pension deferred, plus interest of at least 2 per cent above the Bank of England base rate. Since 6 April 2010, a category B pension has been treated independently of the spouse's or partner's pension. It is possible to take a category B pension even if the spouse or partner has deferred theirs.

It is no longer possible to claim an increase on a state pension for another adult (known as adult dependency increase). Those who received the increase before April 2010 can keep receiving it until the conditions are no longer met or until 5 April 2020, whichever is first.

Provision for children is made through universal credit. An age addition of 25p a week is payable with a state pension if a pensioner is aged 80 or over.

Since 1989 pensioners have been allowed to have unlimited earnings without affecting their state pension. *See also* Pensions.

Weekly Rates from April 2019	
Category A or B pension for a single person	£129.20
Category B pension based on spouse or civil partner's NI contributions	£77.45

GRADUATED RETIREMENT BENEFIT

Graduated retirement benefit (GRB) is based on the amount of graduated NI contributions paid into the GRB scheme between April 1961 and April 1975; however, it is still paid in addition to any state pension to those who made the relevant contributions. A person will receive graduated retirement benefit based on their own contributions, even if not entitled to a basic state pension. Widows, widowers and surviving civil partners may inherit half of their deceased spouse's or civil partner's entitlement, but none that the deceased spouse or civil partner may have been eligible for from a former spouse or civil partner. If a person defers making a claim beyond state pension age, they may earn an increase or a one-off lump sum payment in respect of their deferred graduated retirement benefit; calculated in the same way as for a category A or B state pension.

NON-CONTRIBUTORY BENEFITS

These benefits are paid from general taxation and are not dependent on NI contributions.

JOBSEEKER'S ALLOWANCE (INCOME-BASED)

Those who do not qualify for contribution-based jobseeker's allowance (JSA) and those who have exhausted their entitlement to contribution-based JSA may qualify for income-based JSA. Universal credit and 'new style' Jobseeker's Allowance (JSA) has replaced income-based JSA for most people, only those in receipt of, or eligible for, a benefit with a severe disability premium and those who recently stopped getting a benefit with a severe disability premium and still meet the eligibility requirements can make a new claim for income-based JSA.

The amount paid depends on age, whether they are single or a couple and amount of income and savings. To get income-based JSA the claimant must usually be aged 18 or over but below state pension age, although there are some exceptions for 16- or 17-year-olds. The rules of entitlement are the same as for contribution-based JSA.

Weekly Rates from April 2019	
Person aged under 25	£57.90
Person aged 25 or over	£73.10
Couple, both aged 18 or over	£114.85

MATERNITY ALLOWANCE

Maternity allowance (MA) is a benefit available for pregnant women who cannot get statutory maternity pay (SMP) from their employer or have been employed/self-employed during or close to their pregnancy. In order to qualify for payment, a woman must have been employed and/or self-employed for at least 26 weeks in the 66-week period up to and including the week before the baby is due (test period). These weeks do not have to be in a row and any part weeks worked will count towards the 26 weeks. She must also have an average weekly earning of at least £30 (maternity allowance threshold) over any 13 weeks of the woman's choice within the test period.

Self-employed women who pay class 2 NI contributions or who hold a small earnings exception certificate are deemed to have enough earnings to qualify for MA.

A woman can choose to start receiving MA from the 11th week before the week in which the baby is due (if she stops work before then) up to the day following the day of birth. The exact date MA starts will depend on when the woman stops work to have her baby or if the baby is born before she stops work. However, where the woman is absent from work wholly or partly due to her pregnancy in the four weeks before the week the baby is due to be born, MA will start the day following the first day of absence from work. MA is paid for a maximum of 39 weeks.

Women who are not eligible for statutory maternity pay or the higher amount of MA may be eligible for a reduced rate of MA for either a 39-week or a 14-week period. For example, women who have not made enough Class 2 NI contributions or who take part in the business of their self-employed spouse or civil partner, for at least 26 weeks in the 66 weeks before their baby is due, and the work they do is unpaid.

Weekly Rates from April 2019	
Standard rate	£148.68 or 90 per cent of the woman's average weekly earnings if less than £148.68
39-week reduced rate	£27.00
14-week reduced rate	£27.00

CHILD BENEFIT

A person responsible for one or more children under 16 (or under 20 if they stay in approved education or training) is entitled to claim child benefit. There's no limit to the number of children that can be claimed for, but only one person can receive child benefit for a child. Child benefit is taxable if the claimant or their partner's individual income is over £50,000. An individual can choose not to receive child benefit payments, but they should still fill in the claim form in order to get National Insurance credits and to ensure the child is registered to get a National Insurance number when they become 16-years-old

Weekly Rates from April 2019	
Eldest/only child	£20.70
Each subsequent child	£13.70

GUARDIAN'S ALLOWANCE

Guardian's allowance is payable to a person who is bringing up a child or young person because the child's parents have died, or in some circumstances, where only one parent has died. To receive the allowance the person must be in receipt of child benefit for the child or young person, although they do not have to be the child's legal guardian.

Weekly Rate (in addition to child benefit) from April 2019	
Each child	£17.60

CARER'S ALLOWANCE

Carer's allowance (CA) is a benefit payable to people who spend at least 35 hours a week caring for a severely disabled person. To qualify for CA a person must be caring for someone in receipt of one of the following benefits:
• attendance allowance
• disability living allowance (middle or highest care rate)
• personal independence payment (daily living component)
• constant attendance allowance, paid at not less than the normal maximum rate with an industrial injuries disablement benefit or at the basic (full-day) rate with a war disablement pension
• armed forces independence payment

Weekly Rate from April 2019	
Carer's allowance	£66.15

ATTENDANCE ALLOWANCE

This may be payable to people aged 65 or over who need help with personal care because they are physically or mentally disabled, and who have needed help for a period of at least six months. Attendance allowance has two rates: the lower rate is for day or night care, and the higher rate is for day and night care. People not expected to live for more than six months because of a progressive disease can receive the highest rate of attendance allowance straight away.

Weekly Rates from April 2019	
Higher rate	£87.65
Lower rate	£58.70

PERSONAL INDEPENDENCE PAYMENT (PIP)

Personal independence payment (PIP) replaced disability living allowance (DLA) for people aged 16 to 64 on 8 April 2013. PIP has two components: the daily living component and the mobility component, with each offering two different benefit rates: standard and enhanced. Whether one or both components are claimed depends on the requirements of the individual. Claimants are assessed on their ability to carry out everyday activities, with the majority of claims evaluated via an interview. Claimants with a terminal illness automatically receive the enhanced daily living component.

Weekly Rates from April 2019	
Daily living component	
Standard	£58.70
Enhanced	£87.65
Mobility component	
Standard	£23.20
Enhanced	£61.20

STATE PENSION FOR PEOPLE AGED 80 AND OVER

A state pension, referred to as category D pension, is provided for people aged 80 and over if they are not entitled to another category of state pension or are entitled to a state pension that is less than £77.45 a week. The person must live in Great Britain and have done so for a period of ten years or more in any continuous 20-year period since their 60th birthday.

Weekly Rate from April 2019	
Single person	£77.45
Age addition	£0.25

INCOME SUPPORT

Broadly speaking income support is a benefit for those aged between 16 and pension credit qualifying age, whose income is below a certain level, work on average less than 16 hours a week and are:
- bringing up children alone
- registered sick or disabled
- a student who is also a lone parent or disabled
- caring for someone who is sick or elderly

Income support is being replaced by universal credit, new claims for income support can only be made by those entitled to the severe disability premium or those in receipt of it in the last month and who are still eligible.

Income support is not payable if the claimant, or claimant and partner, have capital or savings in excess of £16,000 – and deductions are made for capital and savings in excess of £6,000. For people permanently in residential care and nursing homes, deductions apply for capital over £10,000. A permanent address is not needed to claim income support.

Sums payable depend on fixed allowances laid down by law for people in different circumstances. If both partners are eligible for income support, either may claim it for the couple. People receiving income support may be able to receive housing benefit and help with healthcare. They may also be eligible for help with exceptional expenses from the Social Fund. Special rates may apply to some people living in residential care or nursing homes.

INCOME SUPPORT PREMIUMS

Income support premiums are extra weekly payments for those with additional needs. People qualifying for more than one premium will normally only receive the highest single premium for which they qualify. However, family premium, disabled child premium, severe disability premium and carer premium are payable in addition to other premiums.

Child tax credit replaced premiums for people with children for all new income support claims from 6 April 2004. People with children who were already in receipt of income support in April 2004 and have not claimed child tax credit may qualify for:
- the family premium if they have at least one child
- the disabled child premium if they have a child who receives disability living allowance or is registered blind
- the enhanced disability child premium if they have a child in receipt of the higher rate disability living allowance care component

Carers may qualify for the carer premium if they or their partner are in receipt of carer's allowance and Long-term sick or disabled people may qualify for the disability premium, the severe disability premium or the enhanced disability premium. People with a partner at state pension age may qualify for the pensioner premium.

WEEKLY RATES OF INCOME SUPPORT

from April 2019

Single person	
Aged under 18	£57.90
aged 25+	£73.10
Aged under 18 and a single parent	£57.90
Aged 18+ and a single parent	£73.10

Couples	
Both under 18	£57.90
Both under 18, in certain circumstances	£87.50
One under 18, one under 25	£57.90
One under 18, one aged 25+	£73.10
Both aged 18+	£114.85

Premiums	
Carer premium	£36.85
Severe disability premium	£65.85
Enhanced disability premium	
Single person	£16.80
Couples	£24.10
Pensioner premium (couple)	£140.40

PENSION CREDIT

To qualify for pension credit you must have reached state pension age. Since 15 May 2019 only couples where both parties have both reached state pension age, or one party is in receipt of housing benefit for people aged over state pension age, are eligible for pension credit. Couples not in receipt of pension credit could backdate their claim until 13 August 2019. Those already in receipt of pension credit under the old rules on 15 May 2019 will continue to receive it while they remain eligible. If their entitlement stops for any reason they can not start getting it again until they are eligible under the new rules. Those not entitled to pension credit can apply for universal credit instead.

Income from state pension, private pensions, earnings and most benefits are taken into account when calculating the pension credit. For savings and capital in excess of £10,000, £1 for every £500 or part of £500 held is taken into account as income when working out entitlement to pension credit.

There are two elements to pension credit:

THE GUARANTEE CREDIT

The guarantee credit guarantees a minimum income of £167.25 for single people and £255.25 for couples, with additional elements for people who have severe disabilities and caring responsibilities.

Weekly Rates from April 2019	
Additional amount for severe disability	
Single person	£65.85
Couple (one qualifies)	£65.85
Couple (both qualify)	£131.70
Additional amount for carers	£36.85

THE SAVINGS CREDIT
Savings Credit is only available to individuals and couples that reached state pension age before 6 April 2016. Those that have been in receipt of savings credit since before 6 April 2016, will continue to receive it as long as there are no breaks in their entitlement. If eligibility ceases the individual or couple will not be able to claim it again.

The savings credit is calculated by taking into account any qualifying income above the savings credit threshold. For 2019–20 the threshold is £144.38 for single people and £229.67 for couples. The maximum savings credit is £13.73 a week (£15.35 a week for couples).

HOUSING BENEFIT
Housing benefit is designed to help people with rent (including rent for accommodation in guesthouses, lodgings or hostels), but does not cover mortgage payments. This benefit is being replaced by universal credit (UC). Since May 2019, only new claimants in receipt of a severe disability premium, who have reached state pension age or who live in temporary accommodation or sheltered housing are eligible to make a claim for housing benefit. Couples are only eligible if both have reached state pension age or one party has reached state pension age and started claiming housing benefit or pension credit (as a couple) before 15 May 2019.

The amount of benefit paid depends on:
- the income of the claimant, and partner if there is one, including earned income, unearned income (any other income including some other benefits) and savings
- number of dependants
- certain extra needs of the claimant, partner or any dependants
- number and gross income of people sharing the home who are not dependent on the claimant
- how much rent is paid

Housing benefit is not payable if the claimant, or claimant and partner, have savings in excess of £16,000. The amount of benefit is affected if savings held exceed £6,000 (£10,000 for people living in residential care and nursing homes). Housing benefit is not paid for meals, fuel or certain service charges that may be included in the rent. Deductions are also made for most non-dependants who live in the same accommodation as the claimant (and their partner). If the claimant is living with a partner or civil partner there can only be one claim.

The maximum amount of benefit (which is not necessarily the same as the amount of rent paid) may be paid where the claimant is in receipt of income support, income-based jobseeker's allowance, the guarantee element of pension credit or where the claimant's income is less than the amount allowed for their needs. Any income over that allowed for their needs will mean that their benefit is reduced.

LOCAL HOUSING ALLOWANCE
Local Housing Allowance (LHA) is the name given to housing benefit for private renters. LHA rates are calculated for every local area based on local rents. The maximum amount of support a household can claim will depend on where they live, the minimum number of bedrooms they need and their income.

COUNCIL TAX REDUCTION
From April 2013, council tax benefit was replaced by council tax reduction. Nearly all the rules that apply to housing benefit apply to council tax reduction, which helps people on low incomes to pay council tax bills. The amount payable depends on how much council tax is paid and who lives with the claimant. The benefit may be available to those receiving income support, income-based jobseeker's allowance, the guarantee element of pension credit or to those whose income is less than that allowed for their needs. Any income over that allowed for their needs will mean that they will receive less help with their council tax reduction. Deductions are made for non-dependants.

A full council tax bill is based on at least two adults living in a home. Residents may receive a 25 per cent reduction on their bill if they count as an adult for council tax and live on their own. If the property is the resident's main home and there is no-one who counts as an adult, the reduction is 50 per cent.

THE SOCIAL FUND

REGULATED PAYMENTS

Sure Start Maternity Grant
Sure start maternity grant (SSMG) is a one-off payment of £500 (or £1,000 for multiple births of three or more) to help people in England, Wales and Northern Ireland on low incomes pay for essential items for new babies that are expected, born, adopted, the subject of a parental order (following a surrogate birth) or, in certain circumstances, the subject of a residency order. SSMG can be claimed any time within 11 weeks of the expected birth and up to six months after the birth, adoption or date of parental or residency order. Those eligible are people in receipt of universal credit, income support, income-based jobseeker's allowance, pension credit, child tax credit at a rate higher than the family element or working tax credit where a disability or severe disability element is in payment. SSMG is only available if there are no other children under 16 in the family, unless the claimant is expecting a multiple birth. There are also exceptions for those who have taken on responsibility for another's child (eg through adoption, legal guardianship or a parental order). Expectant parents in Scotland may be eligible for a pregnancy and baby payment as part of the 'best start' grant. See www.mygov.scot/best-start-grant for further information.

Funeral Expenses Payment
Payable to help cover the necessary cost of burial or cremation, a new burial plot, moving the body, the purchase of official documents and certificates and certain other expenses plus an additional payment of up to £700 for any other funeral expenses, such as the funeral director's fees, the coffin or flowers. Those eligible are people receiving universal credit, income support, income-based jobseeker's allowance, pension credit, child tax credit at a higher rate than the family element, working tax credit where a disability or severe disability element is in payment, council tax benefit or housing benefit who have good reason for taking responsibility for the funeral expenses, such as partner, child or parent of the deceased. These payments are recoverable from any estate of the deceased.

Cold Weather Payments
A payment of £25 per seven-day period between 1 November and 31 March when the average temperature is recorded at or forecast to be 0°C or below over seven consecutive days in the qualifying person's area. Payments are made to people on universal credit, pension credit or child tax credit with a disability element, those on income support whose benefit includes a pensioner or disability premium, and those on

income-based jobseeker's allowance or employment and support allowance who have a child who is disabled or under the age of five. Payments are made automatically and do not have to be repaid.

Winter Fuel Payments
For 2019–20 the winter fuel payment is £200 for households with someone born on or before 5 April 1954 and £300 for households with someone aged 80 or over. The rate paid is based on the person's age and circumstances in the 'qualifying week' between 16 and 22 September 2019. The majority of eligible people are paid automatically between November and December, although a few need to claim. Payments do not have to be repaid.

Christmas Bonus
The Christmas bonus is a one-off tax-free £10 payment made before Christmas to those people in receipt of a qualifying benefit in the qualifying week (usually the first full week of December).

DISCRETIONARY PAYMENTS

Finance Support – Northern Ireland
The Northern Ireland (Welfare Reform) Act 2016 introduced Finance Support to replace Crisis Loans and Community Care Grants on 31 October 2016. Since 31 October 2016, people suffering a financial crisis are able to apply for a discretionary support loan or short term benefit advance from the Finance Support Service (W www.nidirect.gov.uk/contacts/contacts-az/finance-support-service-times-crisis-and-need). To receive discretionary support, the applicant must have a crisis which places themselves or their family's health, safety or wellbeing at significant risk. Applicants must be a resident of Northern Ireland and be over 18-years-old (16-years-old if they do not have any parental support) and be earning less than the national living wage. If eligible, the applicant may be offered a discretionary support loan or grant; usually no more than three loans and one grant can be awarded within a 12-month period.

Short-term benefit advances are available to those that have an urgent financial need that may impact the applicant or their family's health, safety or wellbeing. The applicant must be able to afford to repay the advance within 12 weeks.

If an applicant's combined discretionary support and short-term benefit advance debt is £1,000 or more they will not be able to get further support until their debt falls below this limit.

Budgeting Loans
These are interest-free loans to people who have been receiving universal credit, income support, income-based jobseeker's allowance or income-related employment and support allowance or pension credit for the past six months, for intermittent expenses that may be difficult to budget for. Those claiming universal credit can apply for a budgeting advance instead. The smallest borrowable amount is £100.

SAVINGS
Savings of £1,000 (£2,000 if the applicant or their partner is aged 63 or over) are taken into account for budgeting loans. Savings are not taken into account for sure start maternity grant, funeral payments, cold weather payments, winter fuel payments or the Christmas bonus.

INDUSTRIAL INJURIES AND DISABLEMENT BENEFITS
The Industrial Injuries Scheme, administered under the Social Security Contributions and Benefits Act 1992, provides a range of benefits designed to compensate for disablement resulting from an industrial accident (ie an accident arising out of and in the course of an earner's employment) or from a prescribed disease due to the nature of a person's employment. Those who are self-employed are not covered by this scheme.

INDUSTRIAL INJURIES DISABLEMENT BENEFIT
A person may be able to claim industrial injuries disablement benefit if they are ill or disabled due to an accident or incident that happened at work or in connection with work in England, Scotland or Wales. The amount of benefit awarded depends on the person's age and the degree of disability as assessed by a doctor.

The benefit is payable whether the person works or not and those who are incapable of work are entitled to draw other benefits, such as statutory sick pay or incapacity benefit, in addition to industrial injuries disablement benefit. It may also be possible to claim the following allowances:
- reduced earnings allowance for those who are unable to return to their regular work or work of the same standard and who had their accident (or whose disease started) before 1 October 1990. At state pension age this is converted to retirement allowance
- constant attendance allowance for those with a disablement of 100 per cent who need constant care. There are four rates of allowance depending on how much care the person needs
- exceptionally severe disablement allowance can be claimed in addition to constant care attendance allowance at one of the higher rates for those who need constant care permanently

Weekly Rates from April 2019

Degree of disablement	Aged 18+ or with dependants
100 per cent	£179.00
90	£161.10
80	£143.20
70	£125.30
60	£107.40
50	£89.50
40	£71.60
30	£53.70
20	£35.80
Unemployability supplement	£110.65
Reduced earnings allowance (max)	£71.60
Retirement allowance (max)	£17.90
Constant attendance allowance (normal max rate)	£71.60
Exceptionally severe disablement allowance	£71.60

OTHER BENEFITS
People who are disabled because of an accident or disease that was the result of work that they did before 5 July 1948 are not entitled to industrial injuries disablement benefit. They may, however, be entitled under the Workmen's Compensation Scheme or the Pneumoconiosis, Byssinosis and Miscellaneous Diseases Benefit Scheme. People who suffer from certain industrial diseases caused by dust can make a claim for an additional payment under the Pneumoconiosis Act 1979 if they are unable to get damages from the employer responsible.

Diffuse Mesothelioma Payments (2008 Scheme)
Since 1 October 2008 any person suffering from the asbestos-related disease, diffuse mesothelioma, who is unable to make a claim under the Pneumoconiosis Act 1979, have not received payment in respect of the disease from an employer, via a civil claim or elsewhere, and are not entitled to compensation from a MoD scheme, can claim a one-off lump sum payment. The scheme covers people whose exposure to asbestos occurred in the UK and was not as a result of their work (ie they lived near a factory using asbestos). The amount paid depends on the age of the person when the disease was diagnosed, or the date of the claim if the diagnosis date is not

known. The current rate is £92,259 for those who were diagnosed aged 37 and under to £14,334 for persons aged 77 and over at the time of diagnosis. Since 1 October 2009 claims must be received within 12 months of the date of diagnosis. If the sufferer has died, their dependants may be able to claim, but must do so within 12 months of the date of death.

CLAIMS AND QUESTIONS

Entitlement to benefit and regulated Social Fund payments is determined by a decision maker on behalf of the Secretary of State for the Department for Work and Pensions. A claimant who is dissatisfied with that decision can ask for an explanation. He or she can dispute the decision by applying to have it revised or, in particular circumstances, superseded. The claimant can appeal to the First-tier Tribunal (Social Security and Child Support). There is a further right of appeal to the Administrative Appeals Chamber of the Upper Tribunal (see Tribunals).

Decisions on claims and applications for housing benefit and council tax benefit are made by local authorities. The explanation, dispute and appeals process is the same as for other benefits.

All decisions on applications to the discretionary Social Fund are made by Jobcentre Plus Social Fund decision makers. Applicants can ask for a review of the decision within 28 days of the date on the decision letter. As above, the claimant has a right of appeal to the First-tier Tribunal (Social Security and Child Support).

EMPLOYER PAYMENTS

STATUTORY MATERNITY PAY

Employers pay statutory maternity pay (SMP) to pregnant women who have been employed by them, full or part-time, continuously for at least 26 weeks into the 15th week before the week the baby is due, and whose earnings on average at least equal the lower earnings limit applied to NI contributions (£118 a week if the end of the qualifying week is in the 2019–20 tax year). SMP can be paid for a period of up to 39 weeks. If the qualifying conditions are met women will receive a payment of 90 per cent of their average earnings for the first six weeks, followed by 33 weeks at £148.68 or 90 per cent of the woman's average weekly earnings if this is less than £148.68. SMP can be paid, at the earliest, 11 weeks before the week in which the baby is due, up to the day following the birth. Women can decide when they wish their maternity leave and pay to start and can work until the baby is born. However, where the woman is absent from work wholly or partly due to her pregnancy in the four weeks before the week the baby is due to be born, SMP will start the day following the first day of absence from work.

Employers are reimbursed for 92 per cent of the SMP they pay. Small employers with annual gross NI payments of £45,000 or less recover 103 per cent of the SMP paid out.

STATUTORY PATERNITY PAY

Employers pay statutory paternity pay (SPP) to employees who are taking leave when a child is born or placed for adoption. To qualify the employee must:
- be the father or the intended parent (ie in a surrogacy arrangement)
- be the husband or partner of the mother (or adopter) – this includes same-sex partners
- be the child's adopter
- have been employed continuously by the same employer for at least 26 weeks ending with the 15th week before the baby is due (or the week in which the adopter is notified of having been matched with a child)

- continue working for the employer up to the child's birth (or placement for adoption) and give the correct notice
- be earning an average of at least £118 a week (before tax)

Employees who meet these conditions receive payment of £148.68 or 90 per cent of the employee's average weekly earnings if this is less than £148.68. The employee can choose to be paid for one or two consecutive weeks. The SPP period can not start before the birth of the child or date of placement for adoption and must be completed within eight weeks of that date. SPP is not payable for any week in which the employee works. Employers are reimbursed in the same way as for statutory maternity pay.

STATUTORY ADOPTION PAY

Employers pay statutory adoption pay (SAP) to employees taking adoption leave from their employers. To qualify for SAP the employee must:
- have been continuously employed by the same employer for at least 26 weeks ending up to any day in the week in which they were matched with a child
- be earning an average of at least £118 a week (before tax) during the 'relevant' eight week period
- have given the correct notice and provided proof of the adoption or surrogacy
- have permission from a UK authority, in cases where the child is being adopted from abroad

Employees who meet these conditions receive payment of £148.68 or 90 per cent of their average weekly earnings if this is less than £148.68 for up to 39 weeks. The earliest SAP can be paid from is two weeks before the expected date of placement (UK adoptions), on the date the employee is matched with a child (UK adoptions), on arrival of the child in the UK or within 28 days of this date (overseas adoptions) or the day or day after the child's birth in surrogacy arrangements. Where a couple adopt a child, only one of them may receive SAP, the other may be able to receive statutory paternity pay if they meet the eligibility criteria. Employers are reimbursed in the same way as for statutory maternity pay.

STATUTORY SHARED PARENTAL PAY

The Children and Families Act 2014 provided parents greater flexibility to maternity and paternity provisions. Shared parental leave (SPL) provides up to 50 weeks of leave and 37 weeks of pay for couples having a baby or adopting a child. The leave and pay is shared between the couple in the first year after the birth or, in the case of adoption, placement of the child. SPL is flexible and can be used in blocks separated by periods of work, or taken all in one go. Couples can also choose to be off work together or to stagger the leave and pay. There are different eligibility criteria for birth and adoptive parents. For further information see W www.gov.uk/shared-parental-leave-and-pay

The current rate of statutory shared parental pay is £148.68 a week or 90 per cent of the employee's average weekly earnings if this is less than £148.68. The earnings threshold is the same as for SMP and SPP (£118 a week (before tax)).

STATUTORY SICK PAY

Employers pay statutory sick pay (SSP) for up to 28 weeks, to any employee incapable of work for four or more consecutive days (including non-working days). Employees must have done some work under their contract of service, have average weekly earnings of at least £118 a week (before tax) and inform their employer they are sick before their employer's deadline, or within seven days if their employer does not have a deadline. SSP is a daily payment and is usually paid for the days that an employee would normally work. SSP is paid at £94.25 a week and is subject to PAYE and NI contributions.

THE WATER INDUSTRY

In the UK, the water industry provides clean and safe drinking water to over 60 million homes and has an annual turnover of around £10bn. It supplies around 15 billion litres of water a day to domestic and commercial customers and collects and treats more than 16 billion litres of wastewater a day. It also manages assets that include around 1,400 water treatment and 9,350 wastewater treatment works, 550 impounding reservoirs, over 6,500 service reservoirs/water towers and 800,000km of water mains and sewers.

Water services in England and Wales are provided by private companies. In Scotland and Northern Ireland there are single authorities, Scottish Water and Northern Ireland Water, that are publicly owned companies answerable to their respective governments. In drinking water quality tests carried out in 2018 by the Drinking Water Inspectorate, the water industry in England and Wales achieved 99.96 per cent compliance with the standards required by the EU Drinking Water Directive; Scotland achieved 99.91 per cent and Northern Ireland 99.88 per cent.

In 2016, the Drinking Water Inspectorate (DWI) introduced the Compliance Risk Index (CRI) to illustrate the risk arising from failing to meet water safety standards and the proportion of consumers potentially at risk. In 2018, the CRI for England, Wales and Scotland was 3.86.

Water UK is the industry association that represents all UK water and wastewater service suppliers at national and European level and is funded directly by its members, the service suppliers for England, Scotland, Wales and Northern Ireland, of which each has a seat on the Water UK Council.

WATER UK, 3rd Floor, 36 Broadway, London SW1H 0BH
T 020-7344 1844 W www.water.org.uk
Chief Executive, Michael Roberts

ENGLAND AND WALES

In England and Wales, the Secretary of State for Environment, Food and Rural Affairs and the Welsh government have overall responsibility for water policy and oversee environmental standards for the water industry.

The statutory consumer representative body for water services is the Consumer Council for Water.

CONSUMER COUNCIL FOR WATER, 1st Floor, Victoria Square House, Victoria Square, Birmingham B2 4AJ
T 0300-034 2222 E enquiries@ccwater.org.uk
W www.ccwater.org.uk

REGULATORY BODIES

The Water Services Regulation Authority (OFWAT) was established in 1989 when the water and sewerage industry in England and Wales was privatised. Its statutory role and duties are laid out under the Water Industry Act 1991 and it is the independent economic regulator of the water and sewerage companies in England and Wales. OFWAT's main duties are to ensure that the companies can finance and carry out their statutory functions and to protect the interests of water customers. OFWAT is a non-ministerial government department headed by a board following a change in legislation introduced by the Water Act 2003.

Under the Competition Act 1998, from 1 March 2000 the Competition Appeal Tribunal has heard appeals against the regulator's decisions regarding anti-competitive agreements and abuse of a dominant position in the marketplace. The Water Act 2003 placed a new duty on OFWAT to contribute to the achievement of sustainable development.

The Environment Agency has statutory duties and powers in relation to water resources, pollution control, flood defence, fisheries, recreation, conservation and navigation in England and Wales. It is also responsible for issuing permits, licences, consents and registrations such as industrial licences to extract water and fishing licences.

The DWI is the drinking water quality regulator for England and Wales, responsible for assessing the quality of drinking water supplied by the water companies and investigating any incidents affecting drinking water quality, initiating prosecution where necessary. The DWI science and strategy group provides scientific advice on drinking water policy to DEFRA and the Welsh government.

OFWAT, Centre City Tower, 7 Hill Street, Birmingham B5 4UA
T 0121-644 7500 E mailbox@ofwat.gov.uk
W www.ofwat.gov.uk
Chair, Jonson Cox
Chief Executive, Rachel Fletcher

METHODS OF CHARGING

In England and Wales, most domestic customers still pay for domestic water supply and sewerage services through charges based on the rateable value of their property. Currently around half of household customers in England and Wales have a metered supply. Nearly all non-household customers are charged according to consumption.

Under the Water Industry Act 1999, water companies can continue basing their charges on the old rateable value of the property. Domestic customers can continue paying on an unmeasured basis unless they choose to pay according to consumption. After having a meter installed (which is free of charge), a customer can revert to unmeasured charging within 12 months. However, water companies may charge by meter for new homes, or homes where there is a high discretionary use of water. Domestic, school and hospital customers cannot be disconnected for non-payment.

In December 2014, OFWAT finalised its 2014 price review decisions for household water bills for the five-year period to 2020. This meant that average bills for water and wastewater customers in England and Wales decreased by around 5 per cent, before adjustments for inflation, between 2015 and 2020; an average household bill decrease of around £20, from £396 to £376 per annum, compared with the previous period. In January 2019, OFWAT published their initial assessment of all water and sewage companies for its 2019 price review for the five-year period to 2025. The 2019 price review decisions will be finalised in December 2019.

AVERAGE HOUSEHOLD BILLS 2017–20 (£)
WATER AND SEWERAGE COMPANIES

	2017–18 (£)	2018–19 (£)	2019–20 (£)
Anglian	427	429	440
Dwr Cymru	434	447	444
Hafren Dyfrdwy	–	311	312
Northumbrian	390	401	409
Severn Trent	334	348	354
South West	496	500	491
Southern	420	437	438
Thames	373	386	398
United Utilities	415	432	441
Wessex	480	488	485
Yorkshire	374	385	401

WATER ONLY COMPANIES

	2017–18 (£)	2018–19 (£)	2019–20 (£)
Affinity*	188	193	188
Bournmouth	144	146	144
Bristol	177	183	189
Cambridge	137	140	139
Essex and Suffolk	245	251	255
Portsmouth	102	103	106
South East	201	210	211
South Staffs	141	147	146
SES	190	197	202

* Average figures from central, east and south-east regions
Source: OFWAT

SCOTLAND

In 2002 the three existing water authorities in Scotland (East of Scotland Water, North of Scotland Water and West of Scotland Water) merged to form Scottish Water. Scottish Water, which serves more than 2.2 million households and provides 2.3 billion litres of water per day while removing almost one billion litres of waste water, is a public sector company, structured and managed like a private company, but remains answerable to the Scottish parliament. Scottish Water is regulated by the Water Industry Commission for Scotland (established under the Water Services (Scotland) Act 2005), the Scottish Environment Protection Agency (SEPA) and the Drinking Water Quality Regulator for Scotland. The Water Industry Commissioner is responsible for regulating all aspects of economic and customer service performance, including water and sewerage charges. SEPA, created under the Environment Act 1995, is responsible for environmental issues, including controlling pollution and promoting the cleanliness of Scotland's rivers, lochs and coastal waters. The Public Services Reform (Scotland) Act 2010 transferred the complaints handling function of Waterwatch Scotland regarding Scottish Water, to the Scottish Public Services Ombudsman. Consumer Futures represented the views and interests of Scottish Water customers but became part of Citizens Advice Scotland in 2014.

METHODS OF CHARGING
Scottish Water sets charges for domestic and non-domestic water and sewerage provision through charges schemes which are regulated by the Water Industry Commission for Scotland. In February 2004 the harmonisation of all household charges across the country was completed following the merger of the separate authorities under Scottish Water. In November 2014 the Water Industry Commission for Scotland published *The Strategic Review of Charges 2015–2021*, stating that annual price rises would not increase at a rate higher than that of consumer price inflation during this six-year period. For the year 2019–20, the combined service charge, covering the water supply and waste water collection, increased by a maximum of 1.6 per cent on the previous year; resulting in an annual average household bill of £369.

CITIZENS ADVICE SCOTLAND, T 0808-800 9060
W www.cas.org.uk

DRINKING WATER QUALITY REGULATOR FOR SCOTLAND, Area 3-J South, Victoria Quay, Edinburgh EH6 6QQ T 0131-244 0190 W www.dwqr.scot

SCOTTISH ENVIRONMENT PROTECTION AGENCY, Third Floor, Silvan House, 231 Corstorphine Road, Edinburgh EH12 7AT T 0131-449 7296 W www.sepa.org.uk

SCOTTISH PUBLIC SERVICES OMBUDSMAN, Bridgewater House, 99 McDonald Rd, Edinburgh EH7 4NS T 0800-377 7330 W www.spso.org.uk

SCOTTISH WATER, Castle House, 6 Castle Drive, Dunfermline KY11 8GG T 0800-077 8778 W www.scottishwater.co.uk
Chief Executive, Douglas Millican

WATER INDUSTRY COMMISSION FOR SCOTLAND, First Floor, Moray House, Forthside Way, Stirling FK8 1QZ T 01786-430200 W www.watercommission.co.uk

NORTHERN IRELAND

Formerly an executive agency of the Department for Regional Development, Northern Ireland Water is a government-owned company but with substantial independence from government. Northern Ireland Water was set up as a result of government reform of water and sewerage services in April 2007. It is responsible for policy and coordination with regard to the supply, distribution and cleanliness of water, and the provision and maintenance of sewerage services. It supplies 560 million litres of clean water a day to just over 1.8 million people and treats 320 million litres of waste water each day. The Northern Ireland Authority for Utility Regulation (known as the Utility Regulator) is responsible for regulating the water services provided by Northern Ireland Water. The Drinking Water Inspectorate, a unit in the Northern Ireland Environment Agency (NIEA), regulates drinking water quality. Another NIEA unit, the Water Management Unit, has responsibility for the protection of the aquatic environment. The Consumer Council for Northern Ireland is the consumer representative body for water services.

METHODS OF CHARGING
The water and sewerage used by metered domestic customers in Northern Ireland is currently paid for by the Department for Infrastructure (un-metered domestic customers pay 50 per cent of the full charge), however the future of the subsidy system is uncertain. Non-domestic customers in Northern Ireland became subject to water and sewerage charges and trade effluent charges where applicable in April 2008.

CONSUMER COUNCIL FOR NORTHERN IRELAND, Seatem House, 28–32 Alfred Street, Belfast BT2 8EN T 028-9025 1600 W www.consumercouncil.org.uk

NORTHERN IRELAND AUTHORITY FOR UTILITY REGULATION, Queens House, 14 Queen Street, Belfast BT1 6ED T 028-9031 1575 W www.uregni.gov.uk

NORTHERN IRELAND WATER, Westland House, 40 Old Westland Road, Belfast BT14 6TE T 0345-744 0088 W www.niwater.com
Chief Executive, Sara Venning

WATER SERVICE COMPANIES

WATER UK MEMBERS

AFFINITY WATER, Tamblin Way, Hatfield, Herts AL10 9EZ T 0345-357 2407 W www.affinitywater.co.uk

ALBION WATER, Harpenden Hall, Southdown Road, Harpenden, Herts AL5 1TE T 01582-767720 W www.albionwater.co.uk

ANGLIAN WATER SERVICES LTD, Lancaster House, Lancaster Way, Huntington PE29 6YJ T 01480-32300 W www.anglianwater.co.uk

BOURNEMOUTH WATER, George Jessel House, Francis Avenue, Bournemouth, Dorset BH11 8NX T 01202-590059 W www.bournemouthwater.co.uk

BRISTOL WATER PLC, Bridgwater Road, Bristol BS13 7AX T 0345-702 3797 W www.bristolwater.co.uk

CAMBRIDGE WATER COMPANY, 90 Fulborn Road, Cambridge CB1 9JN T 01223-706050 W www.cambridge-water.co.uk

CHOLDERTON AND DISTRICT WATER COMPANY, Cholderton Estate Office, Cholderton, Wiltshire, SP4 0DR T 01980-629203 W www.choldertonwater.co.uk

DWR CYMRU (WELSH WATER), Pentwyn Road, Nelson, Treharris, Mid Glamorgan CF46 6LY T 0800-052 0145 W www.dwrcymru.co.uk

ESSEX & SUFFOLK WATER PLC (subsidiary of Northumbrian Water Ltd), Sandon Valley House, Cannon Barnes Road, Chelmsford CM3 8BD T 0845-609 4638 W www.eswater.co.uk

HAFREN DYFRDWY WATER Packsaddle/ Wrexham Road, Rhostyllen, Wrexham, Clwyd LL14 4EH T 0330-678 0679 W www.hdcymru.co.uk

ICOSA WATER LTD, Sophia House, 28 Cathedral Road, Cardiff CF11 9LI T 0330-111 0780 W www.icosawater.co.uk

INDEPENDENT WATER NETWORKS, Driscoll 2, Ellen Street, Cardiff CF10 4BP T 029-2002 8711 W www.iwnl.co.uk

LEEP UTILITIES, The Greenhouse, MediaCityUK, Salford M50 2EQ T 0345-122 6786 W www.leeputilities.co.uk

NORTHERN IRELAND WATER, Westland House, Old Westland Road, Belfast BT14 6TE T 0345-744 0088 W www.niwater.com

NORTHUMBRIAN WATER LTD, Abbey Road, Pity Me, Durham DH1 5FJ T 0845-604 7468 W www.nwl.co.uk

THE PEEL GROUP, The Trafford Centre, Manchester M17 8PL T 0161-6298200 W www.peel.co.uk

PORTSMOUTH WATER PLC, PO Box 99, West Street, Havant, Hants PO9 1LG T 023-9249 9888 W www.portsmouthwater.co.uk

SCOTTISH WATER, Castle House, 6 Castle Drive, Carnegie Campus, Dunfermline KY11 8GG T 0345-601 8855 W www.scottishwater.co.uk

SEVERN TRENT WATER PLC, 2 St Johns Street, Coventry CV1 2LZ T 024-7771 5000 W www.stwater.co.uk

SOUTH EAST WATER LTD, Rocfort Road, Snodland, Kent ME6 5AH T 0333-000 0001 W www.southeastwater.co.uk

SOUTH STAFFS WATER PLC, Green Lane, Walsall WS2 7PD T 0845-607 0456 W www.south-staffs-water.co.uk

SOUTH WEST WATER LTD, Peninsula House, Rydon Lane, Exeter EX2 7HR T 01392-443020 W www.southwestwater.co.uk

SOUTHERN WATER SERVICES LTD, PO Box 41, Worthing BN13 3NZ T 01903-264444 W www.southernwater.co.uk

SES WATER PLC, London Road, Redhill, Surrey RH1 1LJ T 01737-772000 W www.waterplc.com

THAMES WATER UTILITIES LTD, Clearwater Court, Vastern Road, Reading RG1 8DB T 0800-980 8800 W www.thameswater.co.uk

UNITED UTILITIES WATER PLC, Haweswater House, Lingley Mere Business Park, Great Sankey, Warrington WA5 3LP T 0845-746 2200 W www.unitedutilities.com

VEOLIA WATER PROJECTS, 210 Pentonville Road, London N1 9JYT 020-7812 5000 W www.veoliawater.co.uk

WESSEX WATER SERVICES LTD, Claverton Down, Bath BA2 7WW T 01225-526000 W www.wessexwater.co.uk

YORKSHIRE WATER SERVICES LTD, Western House, Western Way, Bradford BD6 2LZ T 0345-124 2424 W www.yorkshirewater.com

ASSOCIATE MEMBERS
(not members of Water UK)

GUERNSEY WATER, PO Box 30, Brickfield House, St Andrew, Guernsey GY1 3AS T 01481-239500 W www.water.gg

IRISH WATER (UISCE EIREANN), Colvill House, 24–26 Talbot Street, Dublin 1 T (+353) (1) 707 2828 W www.water.ie

JERSEY WATER, Mulcaster House, Westmount Road, St Helier, Jersey JE1 1DG T 01534-707300 W www.jerseywater.je

ENERGY

The main primary sources of energy in Britain are coal, oil, natural gas, renewables and nuclear power. The main secondary sources are electricity, coke and smokeless fuels and petroleum products. The UK was a net importer of fuels in the 1970s, however as a result of growth in oil and gas production from the North Sea, the UK became a net exporter of energy for most of the 1980s. Output decreased in the late 1980s following the Piper Alpha disaster until the mid-1990s, after which the UK again became a net exporter. Since 2004, the UK has reverted back to become a net importer of energy. In 2018, the UK net import gap decreased for the fifth consecutive year – from the 2013 peak of 104 million tonnes of oil equivalent to 73 million tonnes of oil equivalent – accounting for 36 per cent of the total energy used in the UK.

The Department for Business, Energy and Industrial Strategy (DBEIS) is responsible for promoting energy efficiency.

INDIGENOUS PRODUCTION OF PRIMARY FUELS
Million tonnes of oil equivalent

	2017	2018
Primary oils	51.1	55.7
Natural gas	40.0	38.7
Primary electricity	20.9	20.5
Coal	2.0	1.7
Bioenergy and waste	12.4	13.4
Total	126.4	130.0
Source: DBEIS		

INLAND ENERGY CONSUMPTION BY PRIMARY FUEL
Million tonnes of oil equivalent

	2017	2018
Natural gas	74.4	75.0
Petroleum	69.4	68.5
Coal	10.2	8.5
Nuclear electricity	15.1	14.1
Bioenergy and waste	15.4	17.3
Wind and hydro electricity	5.8	6.5
Net Imports	1.3	1.6
Total	191.6	191.5
Source: DBEIS		

TRADE IN FUELS AND RELATED MATERIALS (2018)

	Quantity, million tonnes of oil equivalent	Value £m
Imports		
Crude oil	57.4	20,580
Petroleum products	38.7	17,630
Natural gas	44.5	10,825
Coal and other solid fuel	11.7	1,535
Electricity	1.8	1,295
Total	154.1	51,865
Exports		
Crude oil	48.8	18,605
Petroleum products	24.4	12,865
Natural gas	7.2	1,815
Coal and other solid fuel	0.7	85
Electricity	0.2	130
Total	81.3	33,500
Source: DBEIS, ONS		

OIL

Until the 1960s Britain imported almost all its oil supplies. In 1969 oil was discovered in the Arbroath field in the North Sea. The first oilfield to be brought into production was Argyll in 1975, and since the mid-1970s Britain has been a major producer of crude oil.

To date, the UK has produced around 3.7 billion tonnes of oil. It is estimated that there are around 501 million tonnes remaining to be produced. Licences for exploration and production are granted to companies by the Oil and Gas Authority. As at July 2018, 435 offshore production licences and 181 onshore petroleum exploration and development licences had been awarded and there was a total of 294 offshore oil and gas (208 oil, 86 gas). Total UK oil production peaked in 1999 but is now declining. Production stood at 51.2 million tonnes in 2018, just under a third of the 1999 level. Profits from oil production are subject to a special tax regime with different taxes applying depending on the date of approval of each field.

INDIGENOUS PRODUCTION AND REFINERY RECEIPTS
Thousand tonnes

	2017	2018
Indigenous production	47,049	51,246
Crude oil	43,185	47,550
*NGLs	3,446	3,320
Refinery receipts	60,244	58,684

* Natural Gas Liquids: condensates and petroleum gases derived at onshore treatment plants
Source: DBEIS

DELIVERIES OF PETROLEUM PRODUCTS FOR INLAND CONSUMPTION BY ENERGY USE
Thousand tonnes

	2017	2018
Transport	50,434	50,065
Industry	4,052	4,014
Domestic	2,223	2,223
Other	5,731	5,461
Total	62,440	61,763
Source: DBEIS		

COAL

Mines were in private ownership until 1947 when they were nationalised and came under the management of the National Coal Board, later the British Coal Corporation. The corporation held a near monopoly on coal production until 1994 when the industry was restructured. Under the Coal Industry Act 1994, the Coal Authority was established to take over ownership of coal reserves and to issue licences to private mining companies. The Coal Authority is also responsible for the physical legacy of mining, eg subsidence damage claims that are not the responsibility of licensees, and for holding and making available all existing records. It also publishes current data on the coal industry on its website (W www.gov.uk/government/organisations/the-coal-authority).

The mines owned by the British Coal Corporation were sold as five separate businesses in 1994 and coal production is now undertaken entirely in the private sector. Coal output was around 50 million tonnes a year in 1994 but has since declined. In 2018, coal output stood at a record low of 2.6 million tonnes, a decrease of 15 per cent on 2017 and less than a tenth of the value recorded at the start of the century. The decrease was mainly due to a decrease in demand for coal fired electricity and one of the large surface mines not producing coal since April 2017, as it was under 'care and maintenance'. Deep mine production of coal virtually ceased in 2018, accounting for less than one per cent of production, while surface production has decreased by 15 per cent. As at 31 December 2018, there were seven deep mines and nine surface mines in production in the UK, with a further two deep mines and one surface mine in 'care and maintenance'.

The main consumer of coal in the UK is the electricity supply industry. Coal supplies 5.1 per cent of the UK's electricity needs but as indigenous production has declined, imports have continued to make up the shortfall and now represent around 80 per cent of UK coal supply, 46 per cent of which is currently supplied from Russia.

UK government policy is to meet the long-term challenges posed by climate change while continuing to ensure secure, clean and affordable energy. Coal's availability, flexibility and reliability compared to other sources mean that it is expected to continue to play an important role in the future generating mix, but its carbon emissions will need to be managed through the introduction of abatement technologies including carbon capture and storage (CCS).

CCS attempts to mitigate the effects of global warming by capturing the carbon dioxide emissions from power stations that burn fossil fuels, preventing the gas from being released into the atmosphere, and storing it in underground geological formations. CCS is still in its infancy and only through its successful demonstration and development will it be possible for coal to remain a part of a low-carbon UK energy mix. The government is committed to public sector investment in CCS technology on four power stations and has made it clear that there can be no new coal power stations in England and Wales without CCS on a defined amount of capacity. As part of a wider package of reforms to the electricity market, the government will also be introducing an Emissions Performance Standard, which will limit the emissions from new fossil fuel power stations.

INLAND COAL USE
Thousand tonnes

	2017	2018
Fuel producers		
Electricity generators	8,716	6,655
Coke manufacture	1888	1,767
Blast furnaces	1,301	1,156
Heat generation	6	6
Patent fuel manufacture	207	194
Final consumption		
Industry	1,732	1,581
Transport	15	15
Domestic	536	518
Public administration	26	26
Commercial	5	5
Agriculture	0	0
Miscellaneous	7	7

Source: DBEIS

COAL PRODUCTION AND FOREIGN TRADE
Thousand tonnes

	2017	2018
Surface mining	3,021	2,556
Deep-mined	20	25
Imports	8,498	10,144
Exports	(495)	(634)
*Total supply	14,422	11,933
Total demand	14,439	11,929

* Includes stock change

Source: DBEIS

GAS

From the late 18th century gas in Britain was produced from coal. In the 1960s town gas began to be produced from oil-based feedstocks using imported oil. In 1965 gas was discovered in the North Sea in the West Sole field, which became the first gasfield in production in 1967, and from the late 1960s natural gas began to replace town gas. From October 1998 Britain was connected to the continental European gas system via a pipeline from Bacton, Norfolk to Zeebrugge, Belgium. Gas is transported through 278,000km of mains pipeline including 7,600km of high-pressure gas pipelines owned and operated in the UK by National Grid Gas plc.

The gas industry in Britain was nationalised in 1949 and operated as the Gas Council. The Gas Council was replaced by the British Gas Corporation in 1972 and the industry became more centralised. The British Gas Corporation was privatised in 1986 as British Gas plc. In 1993 the Monopolies and Mergers Commission found that British Gas's integrated business in Great Britain as a gas trader and the owner of the gas transportation system could operate against the public interest. In February 1997, British Gas demerged its trading arm to become two separate companies, BG plc and Centrica plc. In February 2016, Royal Dutch Shell announced that it had acquired BG Group, whose principal business was finding and developing gas reserves and building gas markets. Its core operations are located in the UK, South America, Egypt, Trinidad and Tobago, Kazakhstan and India. Centrica runs the trading and services operations under the British Gas brand name in Great Britain. In October 2000 BG demerged its pipeline business, Transco, which became part of Lattice Group, finally merging with the National Grid Group in 2002 to become National Grid Transco plc.

In July 2005 National Grid Transco plc changed its name to National Grid plc and Transco plc became National Grid Gas plc. In the same year National Grid Gas also completed the sale of four of its eight gas distribution networks. The distribution networks transport gas at lower pressures, which eventually supply the consumers such as domestic customers. The Scotland and south-east of England networks were sold to Scotia Gas Networks. The Wales and south-west network was sold to Wales & West Utilities and the network in the north-east to Northern Gas Networks. This was the biggest change in the corporate structure of gas infrastructure since privatisation in 1986.

Competition was gradually introduced into the industrial gas market from 1986. Supply of gas to the domestic market was opened to companies other than British Gas, starting in April 1996 with a pilot project in the West Country and Wales, with the rest of the UK following soon after.

Declines in UK indigenous gas production and increasing demand led to the UK becoming a net importer of gas once more in 2004. With the depletion of the UK Continental Shelf reserves, UK gas production has seen growing rates of decline. As part of the Energy Act 2008, the government planned to strengthen regulation of the offshore gas supply infrastructure, to allow private sector investment to help maintain UK energy supplies.

In 2012, it was estimated that there could be over 200 trillion cubic feet of untapped gas underneath Lincolnshire. Trapped inside rock formations, the gas is known as shale gas and the process to release the gas is called hydraulic fracturing or fracking, whereby water, chemicals and sand are pumped into a drilled well at high pressure. A further investigation by the British Geological Survey in 2012 claimed that there could in fact be up to 1,300 trillion cubic feet of gas but opponents to the process raised concerns that fracking results in more greenhouse gas emissions than conventional gas, damages the environment significantly and that it may cause seismic tremors.

CENTRICA PLC, Millstream, Maidenhead Road, Windsor, Berkshire SL4 5GD T 01753-494000 W www.centrica.com
Chair, Charles Berry
Chief Executive, Iain Conn

NATIONAL GRID PLC, 1–3 Strand, London WC2N 5EH
T 0207-0043 000 W www.nationalgrid.com
Chair, Sir Peter Gershon, CBE
Chief Executive, John Pettigrew

UK GAS CONSUMPTION BY INDUSTRY
GWh

	2017	2018
Domestic	295,077	309,170
Industry	103,292	105,409
Public administration	35,566	36,989
Commercial	44,631	45,904
Agriculture	1,020	1,043
Non-energy use	4,956	4,807
Miscellaneous	10,497	10,726
Total gas consumption	495,039	514,048

Source: DBEIS

ELECTRICITY

The first power station in Britain generating electricity for public supply began operating in 1882. In the 1930s a national transmission grid was developed and it was reconstructed and extended in the 1950s and 1960s. Power stations were operated by the Central Electricity Generating Board.

Under the Electricity Act 1989, 12 regional electricity companies, responsible for the distribution of electricity from the national grid to consumers, were formed from the former area electricity boards in England and Wales. Four companies were formed from the Central Electricity Generating Board: three generating companies (National Power plc, Nuclear Electric plc and Powergen plc) and the National Grid Company plc, which owned and operated the transmission system in England and Wales. National Power and Powergen were floated on the stock market in 1991.

National Power was demerged in October 2000 to form two separate companies: International Power plc and Innogy plc, which manages the bulk of National Power's UK assets. Nuclear Electric was split into two parts in 1996.

The National Grid Company was floated on the stock market in 1995 and formed a new holding company, National Grid Group. National Grid Group completed a merger with Lattice in 2002 to form National Grid Transco, a public limited company (*see* Gas).

Following privatisation, generators and suppliers in England and Wales traded via the Electricity Pool. A competitive wholesale trading market known as NETA (New Electricity Trading Arrangements) replaced the Electricity Pool in March 2001, and was extended to include Scotland via the British Electricity Transmissions and Trading Arrangements (BETTA) in 2005. As part of BETTA, National Grid became the system operator for all transmission. The introduction of competition into the domestic electricity market was completed in May 1999.

In Scotland, three new companies were formed under the Electricity Act 1989: Scottish Power plc and Scottish Hydro-Electric plc, which were responsible for generation, transmission, distribution and supply; and Scottish Nuclear Ltd. Scottish Power and Scottish Hydro-Electric were floated on the stock market in 1991. Scottish Hydro-Electric merged with Southern Electric in 1998 to become Scottish and Southern Energy plc. Scottish Nuclear was incorporated into British Energy in 1996.

In Northern Ireland, Northern Ireland Electricity plc (NIE) was set up in 1993 under a 1991 Order in Council. In 1993 it was floated on the stock market and in 1998 it became part of the Viridian Group and was responsible for distribution and supply until NIE was sold to ESB Independent Energy in December 2010. In June 2010, Airtricity became the first new electricity supplier since the Northern Ireland electricity market was opened to competition in 2007.

On 12 July 2011, the government published *Planning Our Electric Future: a White Paper for Secure, Affordable and Low-carbon Electricity* in response to the challenges set by increasing electricity demands. It was agreed that extensive investment is needed to update the grid and build new power stations. Currently, 19.5 per cent of the UK electricity generation comes from nuclear reactors, a process by which uranium atoms are split to produce heat through a chemical process known as fission. While the existing nuclear power stations will close gradually over the next decade, with only one expected to produce power beyond 2030, there are plans in place for a new generation of reactors to be built, the first of which is expected to be running by 2025. A significant proportion of the UK's electricity still comes from burning fossil fuels and, in 2018, natural gas provided 39.5 per cent of electricity production, coal provided 5.1 per cent – a record low – and 0.3 per cent was provided from oil. However, the picture is changing; renewables provided 33 per cent of the UK's electricity in 2018, up from 29.2 per cent in 2017.

Interconnecting cables import and export electricity to Europe. These link the UK to the grids of France, the Netherlands and Ireland. A new interconnector was launched in January 2019, connecting the UK to the Belgian grid. In 2018, the UK was a net importer of electricity via these cables, totalling 19.1TWh (terawatt hours), or 5.4 per cent of electricity supplied to the UK grid.

On 30 September 2003 the Electricity Association, the industry's main trade association, was replaced with three separate trade bodies: the Association of Electricity Producers; the Energy Networks Association; and the Energy Retail Association. In April 2012, following a merger between the Association of Electricity Producers, the Energy Retail Association and the UK Business Council for Sustainable Energy, Energy UK – the new trade association for the gas and electricity sector – was established.

ENERGY NETWORKS ASSOCIATION, 4 More London Riverside, London SE1 2AU T 020-7706 5100
W www.energynetworks.org
Chief Executive, David Smith

ENERGY UK, 1st Floor, 26 Finsbury Square, London EC2A 1DS
T 020-7930 9390 W www.energy-uk.org.uk
Chief Executive, Lawrence Slade

ELECTRICITY PRODUCTION, SUPPLY AND CONSUMPTION
GWh

	2017	2018
Electricity produced		
Nuclear	70,336	65,064
Hydro	5,902	5,490
Wind, wave and solar photovoltaics	61,113	69,771
Coal	22,530	16,831
Oil	1,615	1,063
Gas	136,746	131,490
Other renewables	31,778	34,758
Other	5,281	5,927
Total	335,300	330,394
Electricity supplied		
Production	335,300	330,394
*Other sources	2,872	2,498
Imports	18,167	21,332
Exports	(3,407)	(2,225)
Total	352,932	352,000
Electricity consumed		
Industry	92,308	93,020
Transport	4,833	4,984
Other	202,508	201,641
Domestic	105,368	105,065
Public administration	19,746	18,259
Commercial	73,046	73,998
Agriculture	4,348	4,320
Total	299,649	299.645

* Pumped storage production
Source: DBEIS

GAS AND ELECTRICITY SUPPLIERS

With the gas and electricity markets open, most suppliers offer their customers both services. The majority of gas/electricity companies have become part of larger multi-utility companies, often operating internationally.

As part of measures to reduce the UK's carbon output, the government has outlined plans to introduce 'smart meters' to all UK homes. Smart meters perform the traditional meter function of measuring energy consumption, in addition to more advanced functions such as allowing energy suppliers to communicate directly with their customers and removing the need for meter readings and bill estimates. The meters also allow domestic customers to have direct access to energy consumption information.

The following list comprises a selection of suppliers offering gas and electricity. After E.ON absorbed Npower, one of its major competitors, in April 2019, the 'Big Six' energy suppliers in the UK became the 'Big Five', providing gas and electricity to around 50 million homes and businesses, a combined market share of around 75 per cent. Organisations in italics are subsidiaries of the companies listed in capital letters directly above.

ENGLAND, SCOTLAND AND WALES

CENTRICA PLC, Millstream, Maidenhead Road, Windsor, Berkshire SL4 5GD T 01753-494000 W www.centrica.com
British Gas, PO Box 227, Rotherham S98 1PD T 0800-072 8625 W www.britishgas.co.uk
EDF ENERGY, 90 Whitfield Street, London W1T 4EZ T 0333-200 5100 W www.edfenergy.com
E.ON UK, Westward Way Business Park, Coventry, CV4 8LG T 024-7642 4000 W www.eonenergy.com
Npower, Windmill Business Park, Whitehall Way, Swindon SN5 6PB T 0800-073 3000 W www.npower.com

SCOTTISH POWER, 320 St Vincent Street, Glasgow G2 5AD T 0800-027 0072 W www.scottishpower.co.uk
SSE PLC, Inveralmond House, 200 Dunkeld Road, Perth PH1 3AQ T 0345-026 2658 W www.sse.co.uk

NORTHERN IRELAND

AIRTRICITY (a member of SSE plc), 3rd Floor, Millennium House, 17–25 Great Victoria Street, Belfast BT2 7AQ T 0345-600 9093 W www.sseairtricity.com/uk
ELECTRIC IRELAND, The Gasworks, 1 Cromac Place, Belfast BT7 2JD T 0345-643 643 W www.electricireland.com
ENERGIA GROUP PLC, Greenwood House, 64 Newforge Lane, Belfast BT9 5NF T 0345-073 0099 W www.energiagroup.com
PowerNI, 120 Malone Road, Belfast BT9 5HT T 0345-745 5455 W www.powerni.co.uk

REGULATION OF THE GAS AND ELECTRICITY INDUSTRIES

The Office of Gas and Electricity Markets (OFGEM) regulates the gas and electricity industries in Great Britain. It was formed in 1999 by the merger of the Office of Gas Supply and the Office of Electricity Regulation. OFGEM's overriding aim is to protect and promote the interests of all gas and electricity customers by promoting competition and regulating monopolies. It is governed by an authority and its powers are provided for under the Gas Act 1986, the Electricity Act 1989, the Competition Act 1998, the Utilities Act 2000 and the Enterprise Act 2002.

THE OFFICE OF GAS AND ELECTRICITY MARKETS (OFGEM), 10 South Colonnade, Canary Wharf, London E14 4PU T 020-7901 7000 W www.ofgem.gov.uk

NUCLEAR POWER

Nuclear reactors began to supply electricity to the national grid in 1956. There are presently 15 reactors at eight sites which supply approximately 19.5 per cent of the UK's electricity generation. Approximately half of this capacity is due to end by 2025. In December 2015, the final magnox reactor (Wylfa 1) was shut down after 44 years of operation, which left seven advanced gas-cooled reactors (AGR) and one pressurised water reactor (PWR), Sizewell 'B' in Suffolk. The AGRs and PWR are owned by a private company, EDF Energy. Apart from Sizewell B, which first produced power in 1995, the seven other sites are expected to be shut down by 2035, however in June 2011, eight new sites across the UK were selected for locations of new nuclear power stations. The eight sites, which stemmed from the 2008 Energy bill, are: Bradwell, Hartlepool, Heysham, Hinkley Point, Oldbury, Sellafield, Sizewell and Wylfa. EDF Energy plan to construct four new European Pressurised Reactors, two of which are scheduled to be established at Hinkley Point, with the other two at Sizewell. The four new reactors could supply 10 million homes with energy by 2025. Each year, EDF Energy spends around £600m upgrading its eight sites.

Hinkley Point, which was designated as the first new nuclear power plant to be built in 20 years, was scheduled to be given the green light in the summer of 2016, but the Secretary of State for Business, Energy and Industrial Strategy delayed the decision. The French firm EDF Energy, which is set to finance two-thirds of the £18bn site (the other £6bn being funded by China), had approved the funding but critics of the planned nuclear site warned of environmental damage, increasing costs and concern over the implications of nuclear sites being built in the UK by foreign investors. However, in September 2016, the prime minister gave the go ahead for the nuclear power station at Hinkley Point after the government imposed significant new safeguards for future projects.

In April 2005 the responsibility for the decommissioning of civil nuclear reactors and other nuclear facilities used in research and development was handed to the Nuclear Decommissioning Authority (NDA). The NDA is a non-departmental public body, funded mainly by the DBEIS. The total planned expenditure for the NDA in 2018–19 was £3.1bn. Until April 2007, UK Nirex was responsible for the disposal of intermediate and some low-level nuclear waste. After this date Nirex was integrated into the NDA and renamed the Radioactive Waste Management directorate.

There are currently 17 nuclear sites owned by the NDA that are in various stages of decommissioning, including the world's first commercial power station at Calder Hall on the Sellafield site in Cumbria and Windscale, which produced plutonium in the 1950s to be used for military purposes. The responsibilities of the NDA include: decommissioning and cleaning up nuclear facilities; ensuring that all waste, including radioactive and non-radioactive products, are safely managed; developing nationwide strategies and plans for Low Level Waste; implementing a long-term plan for the management of nuclear waste; and scrutinising EDF Energy's decommissioning plans, which includes the fleet of AGR nuclear stations.

In 2018 electricity supplied from nuclear sources accounted for 65TWh, or 19.5 per cent of total electricity generation (7.3 per cent of total energy supplied). A number of factors have led to government backing for nuclear power: domestic gas supplies are running low; oil and gas prices are high; and carbon emissions must be cut to comply with EU legislation and meet global climate change targets.

Nuclear power has its advantages: reactors emit virtually no carbon dioxide and uranium prices remain relatively steady. However, the advantages of low emissions are countered by the high costs of construction and difficulties in disposing of nuclear waste. Currently, the only method is to store it securely until it has slowly decayed to safe levels. Public distrust persists despite the advances in safety technology. Following the tsunami which struck Japan in March 2011 and the level 7 meltdowns of three reactors in the Fukushima Daiichi Nuclear Plant, the safety of nuclear reactors was brought further into public interest and became a government priority.

SAFETY AND REGULATION

The Office for Nuclear Regulation (ONR) is responsible for regulation of nuclear safety and security across the UK. The Civil Nuclear Constabulary, a specialised armed force created in April 2005, is responsible for policing the industry.

RENEWABLE SOURCES

Progress was made towards the UK's target of consuming 15 per cent of energy from renewable sources by 2020, introduced in the 2009 EU Renewable Directive, as 11 per cent of energy consumption came from renewable sources in 2018, up from 9.9 per cent in 2017. Renewable sources provided 33 per cent of the electricity generated in the UK in 2018, up from 29.2 per cent in 2017, with record annual generations for wind, solar and bioenergy. This increase is attributed to a 10 per cent increase in capacity.

In 2018 onshore wind was the leading technology in terms of capacity at 30.6 per cent, closely followed by solar photovoltaics (30 per cent), which had been the leading technology in 2015 and 2016.. The capacity of onshore wind increased by 7.6 per cent from 2017, although this was offset with slightly lower wind speeds, a 5.2 per cent increase in onshore wind generation was still achieved between 2017

and 2018. Generation from offshore wind also increased by 28 per cent in 2018, however lower than average rainfall resulted in a 7 per cent reduction in hydro generation. Meanwhile, heat generation from renewable sources increased by 11 per cent and solar photovoltaic generation grew by 12 per cent, aided by both an increase in capacity and longer sunlight hours.

The government's principal mechanism for developing renewable energy sources is the Contracts for Difference (CfD) scheme. The CfD scheme recently replaced the Renewables Obligation (RO) which had been in place since 2002. It aims to increase the contribution of electricity from renewables in the UK by offering long-term contracts to new low carbon electricity generators. These guarantee a certain price for their generated electricity, which helps to tackle the risks and uncertainties associated with investing in renewables. The RO closed to new capacity in March 2017, but will continue to provide support to existing generators for 20 years.

The Feed-in Tariff (FIT) scheme has run alongside CfDs and the RO, providing incentives to encourage the uptake of small-scale low carbon electricity generation technologies, principally renewables such as solar photovoltaics, wind and hydro-electricity. The scheme was hugely successful in attracting investment; however, the scheme closed to new registrations at the end of March 2019. Following this, the government laid legislation on 10 June 2019 to introduce a new supplier-led smart export guarantee (SEG) in Great Britain from 1 January 2020. Under the SEG, licensed electricity suppliers (with 150,000 domestic customers or more) are required to offer small-scale low-carbon generators a price per kWh for electricity exported to the grid.

In addition to these schemes, the Renewable Heat Incentive (RHI) aims to promote the use of renewable heating systems. The RHI was originally introduced in November 2011 to provide a long-term financial incentive to support the uptake of renewable heat in the non-domestic sector. In April 2014, the RHI was extended to cover the domestic sector replacing the renewable heat premium payment scheme which closed in March 2013. Participants of the scheme receive tariff payments for the heat generated from an eligible renewable heating system which is heating a single dwelling.

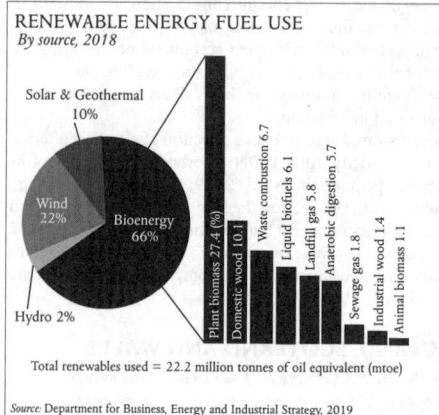

RENEWABLE ENERGY FUEL USE
By source, 2018

Solar & Geothermal 10%

Wind 22%

Bioenergy 66%

Hydro 2%

Plant biomass 27.4 (%)
Domestic wood 10.1
Waste combustion 6.7
Liquid biofuels 6.1
Landfill gas 5.8
Anaerobic digestion 5.7
Sewage gas 1.8
Industrial wood 1.4
Animal biomass 1.1

Total renewables used = 22.2 million tonnes of oil equivalent (mtoe)

Source: Department for Business, Energy and Industrial Strategy, 2019

TRANSPORT

CIVIL AVIATION

Since the privatisation of British Airways in 1987, UK airlines have been operated entirely by the private sector. In 2018, total capacity of British airlines amounted to 54 billion tonne-km.. UK airlines carried around 176 million passengers; 165 million on scheduled services and 11 million on charter flights. Passenger traffic through UK airports increased by 3 per cent in 2018. Traffic at the six main London area airports (Gatwick, Heathrow, London City, Luton, Southend and Stansted) increased by 4 per cent over 2017 and other UK regional airports saw an increase of 1 per cent.

Leading British airlines include British Airways, EasyJet, Thomas Cook Airlines, Thomson Airways and Virgin Atlantic. Irish airline Ryanair also operates frequent flights from the UK.

There are around 126 licensed civil aerodromes in Britain, with Heathrow and Gatwick handling the highest volume of passengers.

The Civil Aviation Authority (CAA), an independent statutory body, is responsible for the regulation of UK airlines. This includes economic and airspace regulation, air safety, consumer protection and environmental research and consultancy. All commercial airline companies must be granted an air operator's certificate, which is issued by the CAA to operators meeting the required safety standards. The CAA issues airport safety licences, which must be obtained by any airport used for public transport and training flights. All British-registered aircraft must be granted an airworthiness certificate, and the CAA issues professional licences to pilots, flight crew, ground engineers and air traffic controllers. The CAA also manages the Air Travel Organiser's Licence (ATOL), the UK's principal travel protection scheme. The CAA's costs are met entirely from charges on those whom it regulates; there is no direct government funding of the CAA's work.

The Transport Act 2000 separated the CAA from its subsidiary, National Air Traffic Services (NATS), which provides air traffic control services to aircraft flying in UK airspace and over the eastern part of the North Atlantic. NATS is a public private partnership (PPP) between the Airline Group (a consortium of UK airlines), which holds 42 per cent of the shares; NATS staff, who hold 5 per cent; UK airport operator LHR Airports Limited, which holds 4 per cent, and the government, which holds 49 per cent and a golden share. In 2018 NATS handled 2.54m flights, an increase of 1.2 per cent on 2017.

AIR PASSENGERS 2018

All UK Airports: Total	292,359,234
Aberdeen	3,056,018
Barra	14,706
Belfast City	2,511,261
Belfast International	6,268,960
Benbecula	35,417
Birmingham	12,457,051
Blackpool	19,321
Bournemouth	674,972
Bristol	8,699,529
Cambridge	–
Campbeltown	8,532
Cardiff	1,581,131
City of Derry (Eglinton)	185,843
Doncaster Sheffield	1,222,347
Dundee	21,185
Durham Tees Valley	142,080
East Midlands	4,873,831
Edinburgh	14,294,305
Exeter	931,265
Gatwick	46,086,089
Glasgow	9,656,227
Gloucestershire	–
Heathrow	80,124,537
Humberside	192,526
Inverness	894,360
Islay	32,775
Isle of Man	836,656
Isles of Scilly (St Mary's)	92,195
Kirkwall	181,562
Lands End (St Just)	64,216
Leeds Bradford	4,038,889
Lerwick (Tingwall)	3,881
Liverpool	5,046,995
London City	4,820,292
Luton	16,769,634
Lydd	284
Manchester	28,292,797
Newcastle	5,334,095
Newquay	456,888
Norwich	536,578
Oxford (Kidlington)	100
Prestwick	681,715
Scatsta	174,934
Shoreham	–
Southampton	1,991,014
Southend	1,480,139
Stansted	27,996,116
Stornoway	135,700
Sumburgh	245,868
Tiree	12,625
Wick	16,775
Channel Islands Airports	2,555,133
Alderney	53,343
Guernsey	837,615
Jersey	1,664,175

Source: Civil Aviation Authority

CAA, CAA House, 45–59 Kingsway, London WC2B 6TE
T 020-7379 7311 W www.caa.co.uk

Heathrow Airport	T 0844-335 1801
Gatwick Airport	T 0344-892 0322
Manchester Airport	T 0800-042 0213
Stansted Airport	T 0844-335 1803

BRITISH AIRLINES

BRITISH AIRWAYS, PO Box 365, Waterside, Harmondsworth UB7 0GB T 0844-493 0787 W www.britishairways.com

EASYJET, Hangar 89, London Luton Airport LU2 9PF T 0330-365 5000 W www.easyjet.com

THOMAS COOK AIRLINES, 3rd Floor, South Building, 200 Aldersgate, London, EC1A 4HD T 01733-244330 W www.thomascookairlines.com

TUI AIRWAYS, Wigmore House, Wigmore Place, Wigmore Lane, Luton, Beds LU2 9TN T 0203-451 2688 W www.tui.co.uk

VIRGIN ATLANTIC, Fleming Way, Crawley, W. Sussex RH10 9DF T 0344-874 7747 W www.virginatlantic.com

RAILWAYS

The railway network in Britain was developed by private companies in the 19th century. In 1948 the main railway companies were nationalised and were run by a public authority, the British Transport Commission. The commission was replaced by the British Railways Board in 1963, operating as British Rail. On 1 April 1994, responsibility for managing the track and railway infrastructure passed to a newly formed company, Railtrack plc. In October 2001 Railtrack was put into administration under the Railways Act 1993. In October 2002 Railtrack was taken out of administration and replaced by the not-for-profit company Network Rail. The British Railways Board continued as operator of all train services until 1996–7, when they were sold or franchised to the private sector.

The Strategic Rail Authority (SRA) was created to provide strategic leadership to the rail industry and formally came into being on 1 February 2001 following the passing of the Transport Act 2000. In January 2002 it published its first strategic plan, setting out the strategic priorities for Britain's railways over the next ten years. In addition to its coordinating role, the SRA was responsible for allocating government funding to the railways and awarding and monitoring the franchises for operating rail services.

On 15 July 2004 the transport secretary announced a new structure for the rail industry in the white paper *The Future of Rail*. These proposals were implemented under the Railways Act 2005, which abolished the SRA, passing most of its functions to the Department for Transport; established the Rail Passengers Council as a single national body, dissolving the regional committees; and gave devolved governments in Scotland and Wales more say in decisions at a local level. In addition, responsibility for railway safety regulation was transferred to the Office of Rail Regulation from the Health and Safety Executive.

OFFICE OF RAIL AND ROAD

The Office of Rail and Road (ORR), previously known as the Office of Rail Regulation, was established on 5 July 2004 by the Railways and Transport Safety Act 2003, replacing the Office of the Rail Regulator. In April 2015 it acquired responsibility for monitoring Highways England in addition to its existing role as the railway industry's economic and safety regulator and changed its name to better reflect its functions. The ORR regulates Network Rail's stewardship of the national network, licenses operators, approves network access agreements, and enforces domestic competition law. The ORR is led by a board appointed by the Secretary of State for Transport and chaired by Declan Collier.

SERVICES

For privatisation, under the Railways Act 1993, domestic passenger services were divided into 25 train operating units, which were franchised to private sector operators via a competitive tendering process. The train operators formed the Association of Train Operating Companies (ATOC) to act as the official voice of the passenger rail industry and provide its members with a range of services enabling them to comply with conditions imposed on them through their franchise agreements and operating licences.

As at August 2019 there were 31 passenger train operating companies: c2c, Caledonian Sleeper, Chiltern Railways, CrossCountry, East Midlands Railway, Eurostar, Gatwick Express, Grand Central, Great Northern, Great Western Railway, Greater Anglia, Heathrow Express, Hull Trains, Island Line, London North Eastern Railway, London Northwestern Railway, London Overground, London Underground, Merseyrail, Northern, ScotRail, South Western Railway, Southeastern, Southern, Stansted Express, TfL Rail, Thameslink, TransPennine Express, Transport for Wales, Virgin Trains, West Midlands Railway.

Network Rail publishes a national timetable which contains details of rail services operated over the UK network and sea ferry services which provide connections with Ireland, the Isle of Man, the Isle of Wight, the Channel Islands and some European destinations.

The national rail enquiries service offers information about train times and fares for any part of the country, Transport for London (TfL) provides London-specific travel information for all modes of travel and Eurostar provides information for international channel tunnel rail services:

NATIONAL RAIL ENQUIRIES
T 0345-748 4950 W www.nationalrail.co.uk

TRANSPORT FOR LONDON
T 0343-222 1234 W www.tfl.gov.uk

EUROSTAR
T 0343-186186 W www.eurostar.com

CONSUMER WATCHDOGS

Previously known as Passenger Focus, Transport Focus is the national consumer watchdog for bus, tram, coach and rail passengers in England. Under The Transport Act 2015 Transport Focus's role was expanded to also represent users of the strategic road network. The entity is funded by the Department for Transport and is an executive non-departmental public body.

Established in July 2000, London TravelWatch is the operating name of the official watchdog organisation representing the interests of transport users in and around the capital. Officially known as the London Transport Users' Committee, it is sponsored and funded by the London Assembly and is independent of the transport operators. London TravelWatch represents users of buses, Underground, river and rail services in and around London, including Eurostar and Heathrow Express, Croydon Tramlink and the Docklands Light Railway. The interests of pedestrians, cyclists and motorists are also represented, as are those of taxi users.

FREIGHT

On privatisation in 1996, British Rail's bulk freight operations were sold to North and South Railways – subsequently called English, Welsh and Scottish Railways (EWS). In 2007, EWS was bought by Deutsche Bahn and is now DB Cargo UK. The other major companies in the rail freight sector are: Colas Rail, Direct Rail Services, Freightliner and GB Railfreight (GBRf). In 2018–19 total volume of freight moved by rail amounted to 17.4 billion net tonne-kilometres, a 3 per cent decrease from 2017–18.

NETWORK RAIL

Network Rail is responsible for the tracks, bridges, tunnels, level crossings, viaducts and main stations that form Britain's rail network. In addition to providing the timetables for the passenger and freight operators, Network Rail is also responsible for all the signalling and electrical control equipment needed to operate the rail network and for monitoring and reporting performance across the industry.

In September 2014, Network Rail was reclassified as a public body after being privately run since 2002 as a commercial business which was directly accountable to its members. The members had similar rights to those of shareholders in a public company except they did not receive dividends or share capital and thereby had no financial interest in Network Rail. On 1 July 2015, the 46 public members were dismissed and the company is now accountable directly to parliament through the Secretary of State for Transport. Network Rail is regulated by the ORR and all of its profits are reinvested into maintaining and upgrading the rail infrastructure. In 2018–19 a total of 1.76 billion passenger journeys were made on the rail network.

LONDON TRAVELWATCH, Europoint 5–11, Lavington Street, London SE1 0NZ T 020-3176 2999
W www.londontravelwatch.org.uk

NETWORK RAIL, 1 Eversholt Street, London NW1 2DN
T 020-7557 8000 W www.networkrail.co.uk

OFFICE OF RAIL AND ROAD, 1 Kemble Street, London WC2B 4AN T 020-7282 2000 W www.orr.gov.uk

TRANSPORT FOCUS, Fleetbank House, 2–6 Salisbury Square, London EC4Y 8AE T 0300-123 2350
W www.transportfocus.org.uk

RAIL SAFETY

On 1 April 2006 responsibility for health and safety policy and enforcement on the railways transferred from the Health and Safety Executive to the Office of Rail Regulation (ORR).

In 2017–18 a total of 49 passengers, railway staff and other members of the public were fatally injured in all rail incidents (excluding suicides).

ACCIDENTS ON RAILWAYS

	2016–17	2017–18
Rail incident fatalities	40	49
Passengers	5	4
Railway employees	1	1
Public	34	44
Rail incident major injuries	466	526
Passengers	264	318
Railway employees	165	164
Public	37	44

SUICIDES AND ATTEMPTED SUICIDES 2017–18

Fatalities	242

Source: RSSB – *Annual Safety Performance Report 2017–18*

OTHER RAIL SYSTEMS

Responsibility for the London Underground passed from the government to the Mayor and Transport for London on 15 July 2003, with a public-private partnership already in place. Plans for a public-private partnership for London Underground were pushed through by the government in February 2002 despite opposition from the Mayor of London and a range of transport organisations. Under the PPP, long-term contracts with private companies were estimated to enable around £16bn to be invested in renewing and upgrading the London Underground's infrastructure over 15 years. In July 2007, Metronet, which was responsible for two of three PPP contracts, went into administration; TfL took over both contracts. Responsibility for stations, trains, operations, signalling and safety remains in the public sector. In 2018–19 there were 930 million passenger journeys on the London Underground.

In addition to Glasgow Subway (12.7 million passenger journeys in 2017–18) and Edinburgh Trams (6.8 million passenger journeys in 2017–18), Britain has eight other light rail and tram systems: Blackpool Tramway, Docklands Light Railway (DLR), London Tramlink, Manchester Metrolink, Midland Metro, Nottingham Express Transit (NET), Sheffield Supertram and Tyne and Wear Metro. These eight accounted for 272.4 million passenger journeys in 2018–19; an increase of 1.9 per cent on 2017–18 figures.

THE CHANNEL TUNNEL

The earliest recorded scheme for a submarine transport connection between Britain and France was in 1802.

Tunnelling began simultaneously on both sides of the Channel three times: in 1881, in the early 1970s, and on 1 December 1987, when construction workers bored the first of the three tunnels which form the Channel Tunnel. Engineers 'holed through' the first tunnel (the service tunnel) on 1 December 1990 and tunnelling was completed in June 1991. The tunnel was officially inaugurated by the Queen and President Mitterrand of France on 6 May 1994.

The submarine link comprises two rail tunnels, each carrying trains in one direction, which measure 7.6m (24.93ft) in diameter. Between them lies a smaller service tunnel, measuring 4.8m (15.75ft) in diameter. The service tunnel is linked to the rail tunnels by 130 cross-passages for maintenance and safety purposes. The tunnels are 50km (31 miles) long, 38km (24 miles) of which is under the seabed at an average depth of 40m (132ft). The rail terminals are situated at Folkestone and Calais, and the tunnels go underground at Shakespeare Cliff, Dover and Sangatte, west of Calais.

HIGH SPEED 1

The Channel Tunnel rail link, High Speed 1, runs from Folkestone to St Pancras station, London, with intermediate stations at Ashford and Ebbsfleet in Kent.

Construction of the rail link was financed by the private sector with a substantial government contribution. A private sector consortium, London and Continental Railways Ltd (LCR), comprising Union Railways and the UK operator of Eurostar, owns the rail link and was responsible for its design and construction. The rail link was constructed in two phases: phase one, from the Channel Tunnel to Fawkham Junction, Kent, began in October 1998 and opened to fare-paying passengers on 28 September 2003; phase two, from Southfleet Junction to St Pancras, was completed in November 2007.

Eurostar provides direct services from the UK (London) to Avignon (5 hours 49 minutes), Calais (55 minutes), Disneyland Paris (2 hours 49 minutes), Lille (1 hour 22 minutes), Lyon (4 hours 41 minutes), Marseille (6 hours 26 minutes) and Paris (2 hours 16 minutes) in France; Brussels (1 hour 53 minutes) in Belgium; and Amsterdam (3 hours 52 minutes) and Rotterdam (3 hours 13 minutes) in the Netherlands.

ROADS

HIGHWAY AUTHORITIES

The powers and responsibilities of highway authorities in England and Wales are set out in the Highways Act 1980; for Scotland there is separate legislation.

Responsibility for motorways and other trunk roads in Great Britain rests in England with the Secretary of State for Transport, in Scotland with the Scottish government, and in Wales with the Welsh government. The highway authority for non-trunk roads in England, Wales and Scotland is, in general, the local authority in whose area the roads lie. With the establishment of the Greater London Authority in July 2000, Transport for London became the highway authority for roads in London.

In Northern Ireland the Department for Infrastructure is responsible for public roads and their maintenance and construction.

FINANCE

In England all aspects of trunk road and motorway funding are provided directly by the government to Highways England, which operates, maintains and improves a network of motorways and trunk roads around 6,920km (4,300 miles) long, on behalf of the secretary of state. Since 2001 the length of the network that the Highways England is responsible for has been decreasing owing to a policy of de-trunking, which transfers responsibility for non-core roads to local authorities. For the financial year 2019–20 Highways England's total capital and resource budget is £4,306m. This includes maintenance, major schemes, traffic management, technology improvements, other programmes and administration costs.

Government support for local authority capital expenditure on roads and other transport infrastructure is provided through grant and credit approvals as part of the Local Transport Plan (LTP). Local authorities bid for resources on the basis of a five-year programme built around delivering integrated transport strategies. As well as covering the structural maintenance of local roads and the construction of major new road schemes, LTP funding also includes smaller-scale safety and traffic management measures with associated improvements for public transport, cyclists and pedestrians.

In Northern Ireland all roads, some 26,000km (16,160 miles) are managed by the Department for Infrastructure (DfI) for Northern Ireland as the sole road authority. The road network is made up of some 300km (185 miles) of motorway, 1,300km (810 miles) of trunk roads and 24,500km (15,225miles) of other roads. The department is also responsible for maintaining some 10,000km (6,210 miles) of footpaths and 5,900 bridges.

For the financial year 2018–19 DfI Roads gross expenditure, excluding depreciation, was £416m. This included maintenance, capital schemes, traffic management and technology improvements. Planned gross expenditure for 2019–20 is £395m, excluding depreciation.

The Transport Act 2000 gave English and Welsh local authorities (outside London) powers to introduce road-user charging or workplace parking levy schemes. The act requires that the net revenue raised is used to improve local transport services and facilities for at least ten years. The aim is to reduce congestion and encourage greater use of alternative modes of transport. Schemes developed by local authorities require government approval. The UK's first toll road, the M6 Toll, opened in December 2003 and runs for 43.5km (27 miles) around Birmingham from junction 3a to junction 11a on the M6.

Charging schemes in London are allowed under the 1999 Greater London Authority Act. The Central London Congestion Charge Scheme began on 17 February 2003 (see also Regional Government London).

ROAD LENGTHS 2018
Miles

	England	Wales	Scotland	Great Britain
Major Roads	22,333	2,715	6,706	31,754
Motorways	1,929	88	296	2,313
Minor Roads	166,496	18,306	30,142	214,943
Total	188,829	21,020	36,848	246,697
Source: Department for Transport				

BUSES
The majority of bus services outside London are provided on a commercial basis by private operators. Local authorities have powers to subsidise services where needs are not being met by a commercial service.

Since April 2008 men and women who have attained the state pension age and disabled people who qualify under the categories listed in the Transport Act 2000 have been able to travel for free on any local bus across England between 9.30am and 11pm Monday to Friday and all day on weekends and bank holidays. Local authorities recompense operators for the reduced fare revenue. The age of eligibility

for concessionary travel is the female state pension age, regardless of your gender. A similar scheme from age 60 operates in Wales and within London, although there is no time restriction. In Scotland, people aged 60 and over and disabled people have been able to travel for free on any local or long-distance bus since April 2006.

In London, Transport for London (TfL) has overall responsibility for setting routes, service standards and fares for the bus network. Almost all routes are competitively tendered to commercial operators.

In Northern Ireland, passenger transport services are provided by Ulsterbus, Metro (formerly Citybus) and Glider, a new service added in 2018, three wholly owned subsidiaries of the Northern Ireland Transport Holding Company. Along with Northern Ireland Railways, Ulsterbus, Metro and Glider operate under the brand name of Translink and are publicly owned. Ulsterbus is responsible for virtually all bus services in Northern Ireland except Belfast city services, which are operated by Metro and Glider, which connects East Belfast, West Belfast and the Titanic Quarter through the city centre. People living in Northern Ireland aged 60 and over can travel on buses and trains for free once they have obtained a SmartPass from Translink.

LOCAL BUS PASSENGER JOURNEYS 2017–18
No. of journeys (millions)

England	4,356
London	2,225
Scotland	388
Wales	100
Total	4,844
Source: Department for Transport	

TAXIS AND PRIVATE HIRE VEHICLES
A taxi is a public transport vehicle with fewer than nine passenger seats, which is licensed to 'ply for hire'. This distinguishes taxis from private hire vehicles (PHVs) which must be booked in advance through an operator. In London, taxis and private hire vehicles are licensed by the Public Carriage Office (PCO), part of TfL. At the end of March 2018 there were 21,000 taxis and 87,900 PHVs licensed in London. Outside London, local authorities are responsible for the licensing of taxis and private hire vehicles operational in their respective administrative areas. At the end of March 2018 there were 73,100 licensed taxis and 212,300 licensed PHVs in England.

ROAD TRAFFIC BY VEHICLE TYPE (UK) 2018

	Million vehicle miles
All motor vehicles	328,000
Cars & taxis	255,000
Light goods vehicles	51,000
Heavy goods vehicles	17,100
Motorcycles	2,700
Buses & coaches	2,300
Source: Department for Transport	

ROAD SAFETY
The key findings from the Department for Transport's 2018 annual road casualty report found that, despite a 0.3 per cent rise in traffic volume, the total number of reported casualties of all severities in Great Britain in 2018 was 160,378; a 6 per cent decrease from 2017. Of these a total of 1,782 people were killed in 2018; a decrease of 1 per cent from 2017. Serious injuries accounted for 25,484 of the casualties and slight injuries for 133,112. Total reported child casualties (0–15 years) decreased by 9 per cent to 14,254 in 2018.

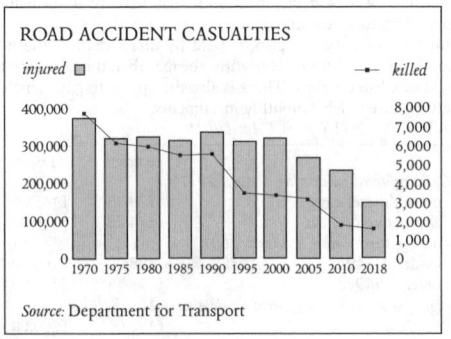

ROAD ACCIDENT CASUALTIES

injured □ —•— killed

Source: Department for Transport

Exchanging
a paper licence for a photocard licence‡	£20/£20
a full Northern Ireland licence for a full GB licence	Free
a full GB licence for a full EU/EEA or other designated foreign licence	Free
a full EU/EEA or other designated foreign licence for a full GB licence	£43

Changing
name or address	Free
photo	£14/£17

* Not all services are available online; in these instances just the postal fee is shown. Licence fees differ in Northern Ireland (W www.nidirect.gov.uk/the-cost-of-a-driving-licence).
† For an alcohol-related offence where the DVLA need to arrange medical enquiries
‡ If a paper licence is exchanged for a photocard at the same time as name or address details are changed there is no charge

DRIVING LICENCES

It is necessary to hold a valid full licence in order to drive unaccompanied on public roads in the UK. Learner drivers must obtain a provisional driving licence before starting to learn to drive and must then pass theory and practical tests to obtain a full driving licence.

There are separate tests for driving motorcycles, cars, passenger-carrying vehicles (PCVs) and large goods vehicles (LGVs). Drivers must hold full car entitlement before they can apply for PCV or LGV entitlements.

The Driver and Vehicle Licensing Agency (DVLA) ceased the issue of paper licences in March 2000, but those currently in circulation will remain valid until they expire or the details on them change. The photocard driving licence was introduced to comply with the second EC directive on driving licences. This requires a photograph of the driver to be included on all UK licences issued from July 2001. The photocard licence must be renewed every ten years, with fines of up to £1,000 for failure to do so.

To apply for a first photocard driving licence, individuals are required to either apply online or complete the form *Application for a Driving Licence* (D1) and submit by post.

The minimum age for driving motor cars, light goods vehicles up to 3.5 tonnes and motorcycles is 17 (moped, 16). Since June 1997, drivers who collect six or more penalty points within two years of qualifying lose their licence and are required to take another test. Forms and leaflets are available from post offices and online (W www.gov.uk/dvlaforms or W www.gov.uk/government/organisations/driver-and-vehicle-licensing-agency).

The DVLA is responsible for issuing driving licences, registering and licensing vehicles, and collecting excise duty in Great Britain. The Driver and Vehicle Agency (DVA), has similar responsibilities in Northern Ireland.

DRIVING LICENCE FEES *as at August 2019*

	online*/postal
Provisional licence	
Car, motorcycle or moped	£34/£43
Bus or lorry	Free
Changing a provisional licence to a full licence	Free
Renewal	
Renewing an expired licence (must be renewed every 10 years)	£14/£17
At age 70 and over	Free
For medical reasons	Free
Bus or lorry driver entitlement	Free
After disqualification	£65
After disqualification for some drink driving offences†	£90
After revocation (under the New Drivers Act)	£50
Replacing a lost, stolen, defaced or destroyed licence	£20/£20
Adding an entitlement to a full licence	Free

DRIVING TESTS

The Driver and Vehicle Standards Agency (DVSA) is responsible for improving road safety in Great Britain by setting standards for driving and motorcycling and making sure drivers, vehicle operators and MOT garages understand and follow roadworthiness standards. The agency also provides a range of licensing, testing, education and enforcement services.

DRIVING TESTS TAKEN AND PASSED
2018–2019

	Number Taken	Percentage Passed
Practical Test		
Car	1,664,219	45.8
Motorcycle Module 1	55,263	72.2
Motorcycle Module 2	54,264	70.8
PCV	7,353	59.8
LGV	73,895	58.3
Theory Test		
Car	1,787,773	47.3
Motorcycle	67,283	71.6
PCV		
Multiple choice	8,525	60.6
Hazard perception	6,801	81.7
Driver CPC*	5,722	49.5
LGV		
Multiple choice	57,549	60.9
Hazard perception	45,853	81.7
Driver CPC*	36,118	67.8

LGV = Large goods vehicle; PCV = Passenger-carrying vehicle
* Driver Certificate of Professional Competence – legal requirement for all professional bus, coach and lorry drivers
Source: DVSA

The theory and practical driving tests can be booked online (W www.gov.uk/book-driving-test) or by phone (T 0300-200 1122).

DRIVING TEST FEES *as at August 2019*

	Weekday/evening* and weekend
Theory tests	
Car and motorcycle	£23.00/£23.00
Bus and lorry	
Multiple choice	£26.00/£26.00
Hazard perception	£11.00/£11.00
Driver CPC†	£23.00/£23.00
Practical tests	
Car	£62.00/£75.00
Tractor and other specialist vehicles	£62.00/£75.00
Motorcycle	
Module 1 (off-road)	£15.50/£15.50
Module 2 (on-road)	£75.00/£88.50
Lorry and bus	£115.00/£141.00
Driver CPC†	£55.00/£63.00
Car and trailer	£115.00/£141.00
Extended tests for disqualified drivers	
Car	£124.00/£150.00
Motorcycle Module 1 (on-road)	£150.00/£177.00

* After 4.30pm
† Driver Certificate of Professional Competence – legal requirement for all professional bus, coach and lorry drivers

VEHICLE LICENCES

Registration and first licensing of vehicles is through local offices of the DVLA in Swansea. Local facilities for relicensing are available at any post office which deals with vehicle licensing. Applicants will need to take their vehicle registration document (V55/5) or, if this is not available, the applicant must complete form V62. Forms are available at post offices and online (W www.gov.uk/dvlaforms)

MOTOR VEHICLES LICENSED (UK)
As at 31 March 2019

	Thousands
All cars	32,670
Light goods vehicles	4,171.6
Motorcycles	1,279.8
Heavy goods vehicles	522.7
Buses and coaches	159.3
Other vehicles*	791.6
Total	39,594.8

* Includes rear diggers, lift trucks, rollers, ambulances, Hackney Carriages, three-wheelers and agricultural vehicles
Source: Department for Transport

VEHICLE EXCISE DUTY
Details of the present duties chargeable on motor vehicles are available at post offices and online (W www.gov.uk/government/publications/rates-of-vehicle-tax-v149). The Vehicle Excise and Registration Act 1994 provides *inter alia* that any vehicle kept on a public road but not used on roads is chargeable to excise duty as if it were in use. All non-commercial vehicles constructed before 1 January 1973 are exempt from vehicle excise duty. Any vehicle licensed on or after 31 January 1998, not in use and not kept on public roads must be registered as SORN (Statutory Off Road Notification) to be exempted from vehicle excise duty. From 1 January 2004 the registered keeper of a vehicle remains responsible for taxing a vehicle or making a SORN declaration until that liability is formally transferred to a new keeper.

All rates of duty can also be paid by direct debit – the 6-month direct debit rate is slightly cheaper than the non-direct debit rate listed below. There is also the option to pay vehicle duty by direct debit monthly instalments.

RATES OF DUTY *from 1 April 2019*

	6 months	12 months
Cars registered on or after 1 April 2017*†		
petrol/diesel car	£79.75	£145.00
alternative fuel car	£74.25	£135.00
Cars registered before 1 March 2001		
Under 1,549cc	£88.00	£160.00
Over 1,549cc	£145.75	£265.00
Light goods vehicles registered on or after 1 March 2001		
	£143.00	£260.00
Euro 4 light goods vehicles registered between 1 March 2003 and 31 December 2006		
	£77.00	£140.00
Euro 5 light goods vehicles registered between 1 January 2009 and 31 December 2010		
	£77.00	£140.00
Motorcycles (with or without sidecar)		
Not over 150cc	–	£20.00
151–400cc	–	£43.00
401–600cc	£36.30	£66.00
600cc+	£50.05	£91.00
Tricycles		
Not over 150cc	–	£20.00
All others	£50.05	£91.00

* Different first year licence rates based on CO_2 emissions are payable at first registration
† Cars with a list price of over £40,000 at first registration pay an additional £320 on the standard 12-month rate above for five years from the start of the second tax payment

RATES OF DUTY FOR CARS REGISTERED BETWEEN 1 MARCH 2001 AND 1 APRIL 2017
from 1 April 2019

	CO_2 Emissions	Petrol and Diesel Car		Alternative Fuel Car	
	(g/km)	6 months	12 months	6 months	12 months
A	Up to 100	–	£0.00	–	£0.00
B	101–110	–	£20.00	–	£10.00
C	111–120	–	£30.00	–	£20.00
D	121–130	£68,75	£125.00	£63.25	£115.00
E	131–140	£79.75	£145.00	£74.25	£135.00
F	141–150	£88.00	£160.00	£82.50	£150.00
G	151–165	£110.00	£200.00	£104.50	£190.00
H	166–175	£129.25	£235.00	£123.75	£225.00
I	176–185	£143.00	£260.00	£137.50	£250.00
J	186–200	£165.00	£300.00	£159.50	£290.00
K*	201–255	£178.75	£325.00	£173.25	£315.00
L	226–255	£305.25	£555.00	£299.75	£545.00
M	255+	£313.50	£570.00	£308.00	£560.00

* Includes cars that have a CO_2 emission figure over 225g/km but were registered before 23 March 2006

MOT TESTING
Cars, motorcycles, motor caravans, light goods and dual-purpose vehicles more than three years old must be covered by a current MOT test certificate. However, some vehicles (ie minibuses, ambulances and taxis) may require a certificate at one year old. All certificates must be renewed annually. Only MOT testing stations showing a blue sign with three triangles and an official 'MOT: Test: Fees and Appeals' poster may carry out an approved MOT. The MOT testing scheme is administered by the Driver and Vehicle Standards Agency (DVSA) on behalf of the Secretary of State for Transport.

A fee is payable to MOT testing stations. The current maximum fees are:

For cars, private hire and public service vehicles, motor caravans, dual purpose vehicles, ambulances and taxis (all up to eight passenger seats)	£54.85
For motorcycles	£29.65
For motorcycles with sidecar	£37.80
For three-wheeled vehicles (up to 450kg unladen weight)	£37.80
*Private passenger vehicles and ambulances with:	
9–12 passenger seats	£57.30 (£64.00)
13–16 passenger seats	£59.55 (£80.50)
16+ passenger seats	£80.65 (£124.50)
Goods vehicles (3,000–3,500kg)	£58.60

* Figures in parentheses include seatbelt installation check

SHIPPING AND PORTS

Sea trade has always played a central role in Britain's economy. By the 17th century Britain had built up a substantial merchant fleet and by the early 20th century it dominated the world shipping industry. In 2018 the UK registered trading fleet decreased by 1 per cent in gross tonnage (GT), to 16 million GT, and is now 16 per cent higher than the recent low in 2014. At the end of 2018, the number of UK registered trading vessels was 1,306, broadly unchanged since 2014 (1,327). The UK registered share of the world fleet has been broadly stable in recent years – 0.8 per cent of the world fleet on a deadweight tonnage basis and 1.1 per cent when measured using GT. The UK registered trading fleet was 18th largest in the world by deadweight tonnage at the end of 2018.

Freight is carried by liner and bulk services, almost all scheduled liner services being containerised. About 95 per cent by weight of Britain's overseas trade is carried by sea. Passengers and vehicles are carried by roll-on, roll-off ferries, hovercraft, cruise ships and high-speed catamarans. In 2018 the number of international short-sea route passengers increased by 1 per cent to 19.6 million after three years of steady decline.

Lloyd's of London provides the most comprehensive shipping intelligence service in the world. *Lloyd's List* (www.lloydslistintelligence.com) lists 120,000 ocean-going vessels and gives the latest known report of each.

PORTS

There are 51 major ports in the UK. Total freight tonnage handled by UK ports in 2018 was 483.3 million tonnes, broadly level with 2017 (481.8 million tonnes). The largest ports in terms of freight tonnage in 2018 were Grimsby and Immingham (55.6 million tonnes), London (53.2 million tonnes), Southampton (34.5 million tonnes), Liverpool (32.6 million tonnes) and Milford Haven (30.9 million tonnes). Belfast (18.9 million tonnes) is the principal freight port in Northern Ireland.

Broadly speaking, ports are owned and operated by private companies, local authorities or self-owning bodies, known as trust ports. The largest operator is Associated British Ports which owns 21 ports.

MARINE SAFETY

The Maritime and Coastguard Agency (MCA) is an executive agency of the Department for Transport responsible for implementing the government's maritime safety policy in the UK and works to prevent the loss of life on the coast and at sea.

HM Coastguard maintains a 24-hour search and rescue response and coordination capability for the whole of the UK coast and the internationally agreed search and rescue region. HM Coastguard is responsible for mobilising and organising resources in response to people in distress at sea, or at risk of injury or death on the UK's cliffs or shoreline.

The MCA also inspects and surveys ships to ensure that they are meeting UK and international safety rules, provides certification to seafarers, registers vessels and responds to pollution from shipping and offshore installations.

Locations hazardous to shipping in coastal waters are marked by lighthouses and other lights and buoys. The lighthouse authorities are the Corporation of Trinity House (for England, Wales and the Channel Islands), the Northern Lighthouse Board (for Scotland and the Isle of Man), and the Commissioners of Irish Lights (for Northern Ireland and the Republic of Ireland). Trinity House maintains 66 lighthouses, nine light vessels/floats, 544 buoys, 18 beacons, 52 radar beacons, seven DGPS (differential global positioning system) stations* and three AIS (automatic identification system) stations. The Northern Lighthouse Board maintains 206 lighthouses, 170 buoys, 25 beacons, 29 radar beacons, 49 AIS stations and four DGPS stations.; and Irish Lights looks after 67 lighthouses, 136 buoys, 21 beacons, and three DGPS stations, with AIS in operation on 48 lighthouses.

Harbour authorities are responsible for pilotage within their harbour areas; and the Ports Act 1991 provides for the transfer of lights and buoys to harbour authorities where these are used mainly for local navigation.

* DGPS is a satellite-based navigation system

UK-OWNED TRADING VESSELS
500 gross tons and over, as at end 2018

Type of vessel	No.	Gross tonnage
Tankers	102	3,130,000
Fully cellular container	72	3,219,000
Dry bulk carriers	70	2,626,000
Ro-Ro (passenger & cargo)	82	1,168,000
Passenger (incl cruise)	33	2,044,000
Other general cargo	103	327,000
Specialised carriers	12	413,000
All vessels	474	12,926,000

Source: Department for Transport

UK SEA PASSENGER* MOVEMENTS 2017

Type of journey	No. of passenger movements
Short-sea routes	19,461,000
Cruises beginning or ending at a UK port*	1,919,000
Long sea journeys	87,000
Total	21,467,000

* Passengers are included at both departure and arrival if their journeys begin and end at a UK seaport
Source: Department for Transport

UK SHIPPING FORECAST AREAS

Weather bulletins for shipping are broadcast daily on BBC Radio 4 at 00h 48m, 05h 20m and 17h 54m. All transmissions are broadcast on long wave at 198kHz and the 00h 48m and 05h 20m transmissions are also broadcast on FM 92–95. The bulletins consist of a gale warning summary, general synopsis, sea-area forecasts and coastal station reports. In addition, gale warnings are broadcast at the first available programme break after receipt. If this does not coincide with a news bulletin, the warning is repeated after the next news bulletin. Shipping forecasts and gale warnings are also available on the Met Office and BBC Weather websites.

KEY

BR   Bridlington
C   Chanel Light-Vessel (automatic)
F   Fife Ness
G   Greenwich Light-Vessel (automatic)
J   Jersey
L   Lerwick
M   Malin Head
R   Ronaldsway
S   Sandettie Light-Vessel (automatic)
Sc   Scilly (automatic)
St   Stornoway
T   Tiree
V   Valentia

RELIGION IN THE UK

The 2011 census in England and Wales included a voluntary question on religion; 92.8 per cent of the population chose to answer the question. Christianity remained the largest religion, despite a decrease of 4 million people from the 2001 census, to 33.2 million adherents, or 59.3 per cent of the population. The second largest religious group were Muslims with 2.7 million people identifying themselves as such, an increase of 1.2 million since 2001. The number of people reporting that they had 'no religion' was 14.1 million, around a quarter of the population. Of those reporting that they had no religion, the majority identified themselves as white (93 per cent) and born in the UK (also 93 per cent); in terms of age, the largest demographic were those aged 20 to 24 (1.4 million or 10 per cent). More than 240,000 people listed 'other religion' on the census, which included, among many others, 176,632 Jedi Knights, 56,620 Pagans and 39,061 Spiritualists. Norwich remained the city with the highest proportion reporting no religion (42.5 per cent), while London was the most diverse region with the largest proportion of people classifying themselves as Buddhist, Hindu, Jewish and Muslim. Knowsley, in Merseyside, was the local authority with the highest proportion of Christians at 80.9 per cent, while Tower Hamlets in London had the highest population of Muslims at 34.5 per cent.

In Northern Ireland, the religion question was phrased differently; 738,033 (41 per cent) identified themselves as Roman Catholic, 752,555 (42 per cent) as 'Protestant and other Christian', 14,859 (0.8 per cent) belonged to an 'other religion' and 183,164 (10 per cent) stated they had no religion.

CENSUS 2011 RESULTS – RELIGION IN ENGLAND, WALES AND SCOTLAND*

	thousands	per cent
Christian	36,093	58.8
Buddhist	261	0.4
Hindu	833	1.4
Jewish	269	0.4
Muslim	2,783	4.5
Sikh	432	0.7
Other religion	256	0.4
All religions	40,927	66.6
No religion	16,038	26.1
Not stated	4,406	7.2
All no religion/not stated	20,444	33.3
TOTAL	61,371	100

* Figures from the 2011 census for Northern Ireland did not contain a full breakdown of each major religion
Source: Census 2011

INTER-CHURCH AND INTER-FAITH COOPERATION

The main umbrella body for the Christian churches in the UK is Churches Together in Britain and Ireland. There are also ecumenical bodies in each of the constituent countries of the UK: Churches Together in England, Action of Churches Together in Scotland, CYTUN (Churches Together in Wales), and the Irish Council of Churches. The Free Churches Group (formerly the Free Churches Council), which is closely associated with Churches Together in England, represents most of the free churches in England and Wales, and the Evangelical Alliance represents evangelical Christians.

The Inter Faith Network for the United Kingdom promotes cooperation between faiths, and the Council of Christians and Jews works to improve relations between the two religions. Churches Together in Britain and Ireland also has a commission on inter-faith relations.

ACTION OF CHURCHES TOGETHER IN SCOTLAND, Jubilee House, Forthside Way, Stirling FK8 1QZ T 01259-216980 W www.acts-scotland.org
General Secretary (interim), Revd Ian Boa

CHURCHES TOGETHER IN BRITAIN AND IRELAND, Interchurch House, 35 Lower Marsh, London SE1 7RL T 020-3794 2288 E info@ctbi.org.uk W www.ctbi.org.uk
General Secretary, Bob Fyffe

CHURCHES TOGETHER IN ENGLAND, 27 Tavistock Square, London WC1H 9HH T 020-7529 8131 E office@cte.org.uk W www.cte.org.uk
General Secretary, Revd Dr Paul Goodliff

COUNCIL OF CHRISTIANS AND JEWS, Mary Sumner House, 24 Tufton Street, London SW1P 3RB T 020-3515 3003 E cjrelations@ccj.org.uk W www.ccj.org.uk
Director, Elizabeth Harris-Sawczenko

CYTUN (CHURCHES TOGETHER IN WALES), 58 Richmond Road, Cardiff CF24 3AT T 029-2046 4204 E post@cytun.cymru W www.cytun.co.uk
Chief Executive, Revd Aled Edwards, OBE

EVANGELICAL ALLIANCE, 176 Copenhagen Street, London N1 0ST T 020-7520 3830 E info@eauk.org W www.eauk.org
General Director, Steve Clifford

FREE CHURCHES GROUP, 27 Tavistock Square, London WC1H 9HH T 020-3651 8334 E info@freechurches.org.uk W www.freechurches.org.uk
General Secretary, Revd Paul Rochester

INTERFAITH NETWORK FOR THE UK, 2 Grosvenor Gardens, London SW1W 0DH T 020-7730 0410 W www.interfaith.org.uk
Director, Dr Harriet Crabtree, OBE

IRISH COUNCIL OF CHURCHES, 48 Elmwood Avenue, Belfast BT9 6AZ T 028-9066 3145 E info@irishchurches.org W www.irishchurches.org
General Secretary, Dr Nicola Brady

RELIGIONS AND BELIEFS

BAHA'I FAITH

Baha'u'llah ('Glory of God'), the founder of the Baha'i faith, was born in Iran in 1817. He was imprisoned in 1852 for advocating the teachings of the Bab ('Gate'), a prophet who was martyred in 1850. Baha'u'llah was persecuted and sent into successive stages of exile, first to Baghdad – where in 1863 he announced that he was the 'promised one' foretold by the Bab – and then to Constantinople, Adrianople and eventually Acre, in present day Israel. He died in 1892 and was succeeded by his son, Abdu'l-Baha, as head of the Baha'i faith, under whose guidance the faith spread to Europe and North America. He was in turn succeeded by Shoghi Effendi, his grandson, who oversaw the establishment of the administrative order and the spread of the faith around the world until his death in 1957. The Universal House of Justice, an elected international governing council, was formed in 1963 in accordance with Baha'u'llah's teachings.

The Baha'i faith espouses the oneness of humanity and of religion and teaches that there is only one God, whose will has been revealed to mankind by a series of messengers, such as Zoroaster, Abraham, Moses, Buddha, Krishna, Christ, Muhammad, the Bab and Baha'u'llah, who were seen as the founders of separate religions, but whose common purpose was to bring God's message to mankind. The Baha'i faith attributes the differences in teachings between religions to humanity's changing needs. Baha'i teachings include that all races and both sexes are equal and deserving of equal opportunities and treatment, that education is a fundamental right and that extremes of wealth and poverty should be eliminated. In addition, the faith exhorts mankind to establish a world federal system to promote peace and unity.

In an effort to translate these principles into action, Baha'is have initiated an educational process across the world that seeks to raise the capacity of people of all ages and from all backgrounds to contribute towards the betterment of society. There is no clergy; each local community elects a local spiritual assembly to tend to its administrative needs. A national spiritual assembly is elected annually by locally elected delegates, and every five years the national spiritual assemblies meet together to elect the Universal House of Justice, the supreme international governing body of the Baha'i Faith. Worldwide there are over 13,000 local spiritual assemblies and nearly 7 million followers, with around 7,000 in the UK.

BAHA'I COMMUNITY OF THE UK, 27 Rutland Gate, London SW7 1PD T 020-7584 2566 E opa@bahai.org.uk
W www.bahai.org.uk
Director, Office of Public Affairs, Padideh Sabeti

BUDDHISM

Buddhism originated in what is now the Bihar area of northern India in the teachings of Siddhartha Gautama, who became the *Buddha* ('Enlightened One'). In the Thai or Suriyakati calendar the beginning of the Buddhist era is dated from the death of Buddha; the year 2020 is therefore 2563 by the Thai Buddhist reckoning.

Fundamental to Buddhism is the concept of rebirth, whereby each life carries with it the consequences of the conduct of earlier lives (known as the law of *karma*) and this cycle of death and rebirth is broken only when the state of *nirvana* has been reached. Buddhism steers a middle path between belief in personal continuity and the belief that death results in total extinction.

While doctrine does not have a pivotal position in Buddhism, a statement of four 'Noble Truths' is common to all its schools and varieties. These are: suffering is inescapable in even the most fortunate of existences; craving is the root cause of suffering; abandonment of the selfish mindset is the way to end suffering; and bodily and mental discipline, accompanied by the cultivation of wisdom and compassion, provides the spiritual path ('Noble Eightfold Path') to accomplish this. Buddhists deny the idea of a creator and prefer to emphasise the practical aspects of moral and spiritual development.

The schools of Buddhism can be broadly divided into three: *Theravada,* the generally monastic-led tradition practised in Sri Lanka and South East Asia; *Mahayana,* the philosophical and popular traditions of the Far East; and *Esoteric,* the Tantric-derived traditions found in Tibet and Mongolia and, to a lesser extent, China and Japan. The extensive Theravada scriptures are contained in the *Pali Canon,* which dates in its written form from the first century BC. Mahayana and Esoteric schools have Sanskrit-derived translations of these plus many more additional scriptures as well as exegetical material.

In the East the new and full moons and the lunar quarter days were (and to a certain extent, still are) significant in determining the religious calendar. Most private homes contain a shrine where offerings, worship and other spiritual practices (such as meditation, chanting or mantra recitation)

take place on a daily basis. Buddhist festivals vary according to local traditions within the different schools and there is little uniformity – even in commemorating the birth, enlightenment and death of the Buddha.

There is no governing authority for Buddhism in the UK. Communities representing all schools of Buddhism operate independently. The Buddhist Society was established in 1924; it runs courses, lectures and meditation groups, and publishes books about Buddhism. The Network of Buddhist Organisations was founded in 1993 to promote fellowship and dialogue between Buddhist organisations and to facilitate cooperation in matters of common interest.

There are estimated to be at least 490 million Buddhists worldwide. Of the 248,000 Buddhists in England and Wales (according to the 2011 census), 72,000 are white British (the majority are converts), 49,000 Chinese, 93,000 'other Asian' and 36,000 are 'other ethnic'.

THE BUDDHIST SOCIETY, 58 Eccleston Square, London SW1V 1PH T 020-7834 5858 E info@thebuddhistsociety.org
W www.thebuddhistsociety.org
President, Dr Desmond Biddulph, CBE

LONDON BUDDHIST CENTRE, 51 Roman Road, London E2 0HU T 020-8981 1225 E contact@lbc.org.uk
W www.lbc.org.uk
Chair, Dharmachari Subhuti

THE NETWORK OF BUDDHIST ORGANISATIONS, PO Box 4147, Maidenhead SL60 1DN T 0845-345 8978 E nboadmin@nbo.org.uk W www.nbo.org.uk
Chair, Juliet Hackney

SOKA GAKKAI UK, Taplow Court Grand Cultural Centre, Cliveden Road, Taplow, Berkshire SL6 0ER T 01628-773163 W www.sgi-uk.org
General Director, Robert Harrap

TIBET HOUSE TRUST, Tibet House, 1 Culworth Street, London NW8 7AF T 020-7722 5378
E secretary@tibet-house-trust.co.uk
W www.tibet-house-trust.co.uk
Chair, Sonam Tsering Frasi

CHRISTIANITY

Christianity is a monotheistic faith based on the person and teachings of Jesus Christ, and all Christian denominations claim his authority. Central to its teaching is the concept of God and his son Jesus Christ, who was crucified and resurrected in order to enable mankind to attain salvation.

The Jewish scriptures predicted the coming of a *Messiah,* an 'anointed one', who would bring salvation. To Christians, Jesus of Nazareth, a Jewish rabbi (teacher) who was born in Palestine, was the promised Messiah. Jesus' birth, teachings, crucifixion and subsequent resurrection are recorded in the *Gospels,* which, together with other scriptures that summarise Christian belief, form the *New Testament.* This, together with the Hebrew scriptures – entitled the *Old Testament* by Christians – makes up the Bible, the sacred texts of Christianity.

Christians believe that sin distanced mankind from God, and that Jesus was the son of God, sent to redeem mankind from sin by his death. In addition, many believe that Jesus will return again at some future date, triumph over evil and establish a kingdom on earth, thus inaugurating a new age. The Gospel assures Christians that those who believe in Jesus and obey his teachings will be forgiven their sins and will be resurrected from the dead.

The Apostles were Jesus' first converts and are recognised by Christians as the founders of the Christian community. Early Christianity spread rapidly throughout the eastern provinces of the Roman Empire but was subjected to great persecution until AD 313, when Emperor Constantine's Edict of Toleration confirmed its right to exist. Christianity was established as the religion of the Roman Empire in AD 381.

Between AD 325 and 787 there were seven Oecumenical Councils at which bishops from the entire Christian world assembled to resolve various doctrinal disputes. The estrangement between East and West began after Constantine moved the centre of the Roman Empire from Rome to Constantinople, and it grew after the division of the Roman Empire into eastern and western halves. Linguistic and cultural differences between Greek East and Latin West served to encourage separate ecclesiastical developments which became pronounced in the tenth and early 11th centuries. Administration of the church was divided between five ancient patriarchates: Rome and all the West, Constantinople (the imperial city – the 'New Rome'), Jerusalem and all of Palestine, Antioch and all the East, and Alexandria and all of Africa. Of these, only Rome was in the Latin West and after the schism in 1054, Rome developed a structure of authority centralised on the Papacy, while the Orthodox East maintained the style of localised administration. Papal authority over the doctrine and jurisdiction of the church in Western Europe was unrivalled after the split with the Eastern Orthodox Church until the Protestant Reformation in the 16th century.

Christian practices vary widely between different Christian churches, but prayer, charity and giving (for the maintenance of the church buildings, for the work of the church, and to those in need) are common to all. In addition, certain days of observance, ie the Sabbath, Easter and Christmas, are celebrated by most Christians. The Orthodox, Roman Catholic and Anglican churches celebrate many more days of observance, based on saints and significant events in the life of Jesus. The belief in sacraments, physical signs believed to have been ordained by Jesus Christ to symbolise and convey spiritual gifts, varies greatly between Christian denominations; baptism and the Eucharist are practised by most Christians. Baptism, symbolising repentance and faith in Jesus, is an act marking entry into the Christian community; the Eucharist, the ritual re-enactment of the Last Supper, Jesus' final meal with his disciples, is also practised by most denominations. Other sacraments, such as anointing the sick, the laying on of hands to symbolise the passing on of the office of priesthood or to heal the sick, and speaking in tongues, where it is believed that the person is possessed by the Holy Spirit, are less common. In denominations where infant baptism is practised, confirmation (where the person confirms the commitments made on their behalf in infancy) is common. Matrimony and the ordination of priests are also widely believed to be sacraments. Many Protestants regard only baptism and the Eucharist to be sacraments; the Quakers and the Salvation Army reject the use of sacraments.

See Churches for contact details of the Church of England, the Roman Catholic Church and other Christian churches in the UK.

HINDUISM

Hinduism has no historical founder but had become highly developed in India by c.2500 BC. Its adherents originally called themselves Aryans; Muslim invaders first called the Aryans 'Hindus' (derived from 'Sindhu', the name of the river Indus) in the eighth century.

Most Hindus hold that satya (truthfulness), honesty, sincerity and devotion to God are essential for good living. They believe in one supreme spirit *(Brahman)*, and in the transmigration of atman (the soul). Most Hindus accept the doctrine of karma (consequences of actions), the concept of samsara (successive lives) and the possibility of all atmans achieving moksha (liberation from samsara) through jnana (knowledge), yoga (meditation), karma (work or action) and bhakti (devotion).

Most Hindus offer worship to murtis (images of deities) representing different incarnations or aspects of Brahman, and follow their dharma (religious and social duty) according to the traditions of their varna (social class), ashrama (stage in life), jaiti (caste) and kula (family).

Hinduism's sacred texts are divided into shruti ('that which is heard'), including the Vedas, and smriti ('that which is remembered'), including the Ramayana, the Mahabharata, the Puranas (ancient myths), and the sacred law books. Most Hindus recognise the authority of the Vedas, the oldest holy books, and accept the philosophical teachings of the Upanishads, the Vedanta Sutras and the Bhagavad-Gita.

Hindus believe Brahman to be omniscient, omnipotent, limitless and all-pervading. Brahman is usually worshipped in its deity form. Brahma, Vishnu and Shiva are the most important deities or aspects of Brahman worshipped by Hindus; their respective consorts are Saraswati, Lakshmi and Durga or Parvati, also known as Shakti. There are believed to have been ten avatars (incarnations) of Vishnu, of whom the most important are Rama and Krishna. Other popular gods are Ganesha, Hanuman and Subrahmanyam. All Hindu gods are seen as aspects of the supreme spirit (Brahman), not as competing deities.

Orthodox Hindus revere all gods and goddesses equally, but there are many denominations, including the Hare-Krishna movement (ISKCon), the Arya Samaj and the Swaminarayan Hindu mission, in which worship is concentrated on one deity. The guru (spiritual teacher) is seen as the source of spiritual guidance.

Hinduism does not have a centrally trained and ordained priesthood. The pronouncements of the shankaracharyas (heads of monasteries) of Shringeri, Puri, Dwarka and Badrinath are heeded by the orthodox but may be ignored by the various sects.

The commonest form of worship is puja, in which water, flowers, food, fruit, incense and light are offered to the deity. Puja may be done either in a home shrine or a mandir (temple). Many British Hindus celebrate samskars (purification rites), to name a baby, for the sacred thread (an initiation ceremony), marriage and cremation.

The largest communities of Hindus in Britain are in Leicester, London, Birmingham and Bradford, and developed as a result of immigration from India, eastern Africa and Sri Lanka.

There are an estimated 800 million Hindus worldwide; there are around 817,000 adherents, according to the 2011 census in England and Wales, and around 135 temples in the UK.

ARYA SAMAJ LONDON, 69 Argyle Road, London W13 0LY
  T 020-8991 1732 E aryasamajlondon@yahoo.co.uk
  W www.aryasamajlondon.org.uk
  General Secretary, Amrit Lal Bhardwaj

BHARATIYA VIDYA BHAVAN, 4A Castletown Road, London W14 9HE T 020-7381 3086 E info@bhavan.net
  W www.bhavan.net
  Executive Director, Dr N. M Nandakumara

BHAKTIVEDANTA MANOR: INTERNATIONAL SOCIETY FOR KRISHNA CONSCIOUSNESS
  (ISKCON), Bhaktivedanta Manor, Dharam Marg, Hilfield Lane, Aldenham, Watford, Herts WD25 8EZ T 01923-851000
  E info@krishnatemple.com W www.bhaktivedantamanor.co.uk
  Temple President, Gauri Das

NATIONAL COUNCIL OF HINDU TEMPLES (UK), c/o Shree Sanatan Mandir, 84 Weymouth Street, Leicester LE4 6FQ
  T 0771-781 4357 E info@nchtuk.org W www.nchtuk.org
  General Secretary, Satish K. Sharma

SWAMINARAYAN HINDU MISSION (SHRI SWAMINARAYAN MANDIR), 105–119 Brentfield Road, London NW10 8 LD T 020-8965 2651
  E info@londonmandir.baps.org W www.londonmandir.baps.org

HUMANISM

Humanism traces its roots back to ancient times, with Chinese, Greek, Indian and Roman philosophers expressing Humanist ideas some 2,500 years ago. Confucius, the Chinese philosopher who lived c.500 BC, believed that religious observances should be replaced with moral values as the basis of social and political order and that 'the true way' is based on reason and humanity. He also stressed the importance of benevolence and respect for others, and believed that the individual situation should be considered rather than the global application of traditional rules.

Humanists believe that there is no God or other supernatural being, that humans have only one life (Humanists do not believe in an afterlife or reincarnation) and that humans can live ethical and fulfilling lives without religious beliefs through a moral code derived from a shared history, personal experience and thought. There are no sacred Humanist texts. Particular emphasis is placed on science as the only reliable source of knowledge of the universe. Many Humanists recognise a need for ceremonies to mark important occasions in life and the British Humanist Association has a network of celebrants who are trained and accredited to conduct baby namings, weddings and funerals. The British Humanist Association's campaigns for a secular state (a state based on freedom of religious or non-religious belief with no privileges for any particular set of beliefs) are based on equality and human rights. The association also campaigns for inclusive schools that meet the needs of all parents and pupils, regardless of their religious or non-religious beliefs. According to figures from the 2011 census, there are just over 15,000 Humanists in England and Wales.

BRITISH HUMANIST ASSOCIATION, 39 Moreland Street, London EC1V 8BB T 020-7324 3060 E info@humanism.org.uk W www.humanism.org.uk
Chief Executive, Andrew Copson

ISLAM

Islam (which means 'peace arising from submission to the will of Allah' in Arabic) is a monotheistic religion which was taught in Arabia by the Prophet Muhammad, who was born in Mecca (Al-Makkah) in 570 AD. Islam spread to Egypt, north Africa, Spain and the borders of China in the century following the Prophet's death, and is now the predominant religion in Indonesia, the near and Middle East, northern and parts of western Africa, Pakistan, Bangladesh, Malaysia and some of the former Soviet republics. There are also large Muslim communities in other countries.

For Muslims (adherents of Islam), there is one God *(Allah)*, who holds absolute power. Muslims believe that Allah's commands were revealed to mankind through the prophets, who include Abraham, Moses and Jesus, but that Allah's message was gradually corrupted until revealed finally and in perfect form to Muhammad through the angel *Jibril* (Gabriel) over a period of 23 years. This last, incorruptible message is said to have been recorded in the *Qur'an* (Koran), which contains 114 divisions called *surahs,* each made up of *ayahs* of various lengths, and is held to be the essence of all previous scriptures. The *Ahadith* are the records of the Prophet Muhammad's deeds and sayings (the *Sunnah*) as practised and recounted by his immediate followers. A culture and a system of law and theology gradually developed to form a distinctive Islamic civilisation. Islam makes no distinction between sacred and worldly affairs and provides rules for every aspect of human life. The *Shariah* is the sacred law of Islam based primarily upon prescriptions derived from the *Qur'an* and the *Sunnah* of the Prophet.

The 'five pillars of Islam' are *shahadah* (a declaration of faith in the oneness and supremacy of Allah and the messengership of Muhammad); *salat* (formal prayer, to be performed five times a day facing the *Ka'bah* (the most sacred shrine in the holy city of Mecca)); *zakat* (welfare due, paid annually on all savings at the rate of 2.5 per cent); *sawm* (fasting during the month of Ramadan from dawn until sunset); and *hajj* (pilgrimage to Mecca made once in a lifetime if the believer is financially and physically able). Some Muslims would add *jihad* as the sixth pillar (striving for the cause of good and resistance to evil).

Two main groups developed among Muslims. *Sunni* Muslims accept the legitimacy of Muhammad's first four *caliphs* (successors as head of the Muslim community) and of the authority of the Muslim community as a whole. About 90 per cent of Muslims are Sunni Muslims.

Shi'ites recognise only Muhammad's son-in-law Ali as his rightful successor and the *Imams* (descendants of Ali, not to be confused with *imams,* who are prayer leaders or religious teachers) as the principal legitimate religious authority. The largest group within Shi'ism is *Twelver Shi'ism,* which has been the official school of law and theology in Iran since the 16th century; other subsects include the *Ismailis,* the *Druze* and the *Alawis,* the latter two differing considerably from the main body of Muslims. The *Ibadis* of Oman are neither Sunni nor Shia, deriving from the strictly observant *Khariji* (Seceders). There is no organised priesthood, but learned men such as imams, *ulama,* and *ayatollahs* are accorded great respect. The *Sufis* are the mystics of Islam. Mosques are centres for worship and teaching and also for social and welfare activities.

Islam was first recorded in western Europe in the eighth century AD when 800 years of Muslim rule began in Spain. Later, Islam spread to eastern Europe. More recently, Muslims came to Europe from Africa, the Middle East and Asia in the late 19th century. Both the Sunni and Shia traditions are represented in Britain, but the majority of Muslims in Britain adhere to Sunni Islam. Efforts to establish a representative national body for Muslims in Britain resulted in the founding, in 1997, of the Muslim Council of Britain. In addition, there are many other Muslim organisations in the UK. There are around 1.6 billion Muslims worldwide, with around 2.8 million adherents in England, Wales and Scotland and about 1,500 mosques in the UK.

ISLAMIC CULTURAL CENTRE – THE LONDON CENTRAL MOSQUE, 146 Park Road, London NW8 7RG T 020-7724 3363 E info@iccuk.org W www.iccuk.org
Director-General, Dr Ahmad Al-Dubayan

MUSLIM COUNCIL OF BRITAIN, PO Box 57330, London E1 2WJ T 0845-262 6786 E admin@mcb.org.uk W www.mcb.org.uk
Secretary-General, Harun Rashid Khan

MUSLIM LAW (SHARIAH) COUNCIL UK, 20–22 Creffield Road, London W5 3RP T 0208-992 6636 E info@shariahcouncil.org W www.shariahcouncil.org
Chair, Dr Mohamed Benotman

MUSLIM WORLD LEAGUE LONDON, 46 Goodge Street, London W1T 4LU T 020-7636 7568 E info@mwllo.org.uk W www.mwllo.org.uk
Director, Dr Ahmed Makhdoom

JAINISM

Jainism traces its history to Vardhamana Jnatriputra, known as *Tirthankara Mahavira* ('the Great Hero') whose traditional dates were 599–527 BC. Jains believe he was the last of the current era in a series of 24 *Jinas* (those who overcome all passions and desires) or *Tirthankaras* (those who show a way across the ocean of life) stretching back to remote antiquity. Born to a noble family in north-eastern India (presently the state of Bihar), he renounced the world for the life of a wandering ascetic and after 12 years of austerity and meditation he attained enlightenment. He then preached his message until, at the age of 72, he left the mortal world and achieved total liberation *(moksha)* from the cycle of death and rebirth.

Jains declare that the Hindu rituals of transferring merit are not acceptable as each living being is responsible for its own actions. They recognise some of the minor deities of the Hindu pantheon, but the supreme objects of worship are the Tirthankaras. The pious Jain does not ask favours from the Tirthankaras, but seeks to emulate their example in his or her own life.

Jains believe that the universe is eternal and self-subsisting, that there is no omnipotent creator God ruling it and the destiny of the individual is in his or her own hands. *Karma,* the fruit of past actions, is believed to determine the place of every living being and rebirth may be in the heavens, on earth as a human, an animal or other lower being, or in the hells. The ultimate goal of existence for Jains is *moksha,* a state of perfect knowledge and tranquillity for each individual soul, which can be achieved only by gaining enlightenment.

The Jainist path to liberation is defined by the three jewels: *Samyak Darshan* (right perception), *Samyak Jnana* (right knowledge) and *Samyak Charitra* (right conduct). Of the five fundamental precepts of the Jains, *Ahimsa* (non-injury to any form of being, in any mode: thought, speech or action) is the first and foremost, and was popularised by Gandhi as *Ahimsa paramo dharma* (non-violence is the supreme religion).

The largest population of Jains can be found in India but there are approximately 30,000 Jains in Britain, with sizeable communities in North America, East Africa, Australia and smaller groups in many other countries.

INSTITUTE OF JAINOLOGY, Unit 18, Silicon Business Centre, 28 Wadsworth Road, Perivale, Greenford, Middx UB6 7JZ T 020-8997 2300 E info@jainology.org W www.jainology.org
Chair, Nemu Chandaria, OBE

JUDAISM

Judaism is the oldest monotheistic faith. The primary text of Judaism is the Hebrew bible or *Tanakh,* which records how the descendants of Abraham were led by Moses out of their slavery in Egypt to Mount Sinai where God's law *(Torah)* was revealed to them as the chosen people. The *Talmud,* which consists of commentaries on the *Mishnah* (the first text of rabbinical Judaism), is also held to be authoritative, and may be divided into two main categories: the *halakeh* dealing with legal and ritual matters) and the *aggadah* (dealing with theological and ethical matters not directly concerned with the regulation of conduct). The *midrash* comprises rabbinic writings containing biblical interpretations in the spirit of the aggadah. The halakah has become a source of division: orthodox Jews regard Jewish law as derived from God and therefore unalterable; progressive Jews seek to interpret it in the light of contemporary considerations; and conservative Jews aim to maintain most of the traditional rituals but to allow changes in accordance with tradition. Reconstructionist Judaism, a 20th-century movement, regards Judaism as a culture rather than a theological system and accepts all forms of Jewish practice.

The family is the basic unit of Jewish ritual, with the synagogue playing an important role as the centre for public worship and religious study. A synagogue is led by a group of laymen who are elected to office. The Rabbi is primarily a teacher and spiritual guide. The *Sabbath* is the central religious observance. Most British Jews are descendants of either the *Ashkenazim* of central and eastern Europe or the *Sephardim* of Spain, Portugal and the Middle East.

The Chief Rabbi of the United Hebrew Congregations of the Commonwealth is appointed by a Chief Rabbinate Conference, and is the rabbinical authority of the mainstream Orthodox sector of the Ashkenazi Jewish community, the largest body of which is the United Synagogue. His formal ecclesiastical authority is not recognised by the Reform Synagogues of Great Britain (the largest progressive group), the Union of Liberal and Progressive Synagogues, the Spanish and Portuguese Jews' Congregation or the Assembly of Masorti Synagogues. He is, however, generally recognised both outside the Jewish community and within it as the public religious representative of the totality of British Jewry. The Chief Rabbi is President of the London *Beth Din* (Court of Judgment), a rabbinic court. The *Dayanim* (Judges) adjudicate in disputes or on matters of Jewish law and tradition; they also oversee dietary law administration, marriage, divorce and issues of personal status.

The Board of Deputies of British Jews, established in 1760, is the representative body of British Jewry. The basis of representation is through the election of deputies by synagogues and communal organisations. It protects and promotes the interests of British Jewry, acts as the central voice of the community and seeks to counter anti-Jewish discrimination and anti-Semitic activities.

There are approximately 13.9 million Jews worldwide; in the UK there are an estimated 290,000 adherents and over 400 synagogues.

OFFICE OF THE CHIEF RABBI, 305 Ballards Lane, London N12 8GB T 020-8343 6301 E info@chiefrabbi.org
W www.chiefrabbi.org
Chief Rabbi, Ephraim Mirvis

BETH DIN (THE UNITED SYNAGOGUE), 305 Ballards Lane, London N12 8GB T 020-8343 6270 E info@bethdin.org.uk
W www.theus.org.uk
President, Michael Goldstein
Dayanim, Menachem Gelley *(Rosh Beth Din);* Ivan Binstock; Shmuel Simons

MASORTI JUDAISM, Alexander House, 3 Shakespeare Road, London N3 1XE T 020-8349 6650 E enquiries@masorti.org.uk
W www.masorti.org.uk
Executive Director, Matt Plen

BOARD OF DEPUTIES OF BRITISH JEWS, 1 Torriano Mews, London NW5 2RZ T 020-7543 5400 E info@bod.org.uk
W www.bod.org.uk
Chief Executive, Gillian Merron

FEDERATION OF SYNAGOGUES, 65 Watford Way, London NW4 3AQ T 020-8202 2263
E info@federationofsynagogues.com
W www.federationofsynagogues.com
Chief Executive, Rabbi Ari Lazarus

LIBERAL JUDAISM, The Montagu Centre, 21 Maple Street, London W1T 4BE T 020-7580 1663
E montagu@liberaljudaism.org W www.liberaljudaism.org
Chief Executive, Rabbi Danny Rich

THE MOVEMENT FOR REFORM JUDAISM, The Sternberg Centre for Judaism, 80 East End Road, London N3 2SY
T 020-8349 5640 E admin@reformjudaism.org.uk
W www.reformjudaism.org.uk
Senior Rabbi, Laura Janner-Klausner

THE SEPHARDI COMMUNITY, 119–121 Brent Street, London NW4 2DX T 020-7289 2573 E admin@spsyn.org.uk
W www.sephardi.org.uk
Executive Director, David Arden

UNITED SYNAGOGUE HEAD OFFICE, Adler House, 735 High Road, London N12 0US T 020-8343 8989
W www.theus.org.uk
Chief Executive, Dr Stephen Wilson

PAGANISM

Paganism draws on the ideas of the Celtic people of pre-Roman Europe and is closely linked to Druidism. The first historical record of Druidry comes from classical Greek and Roman writers of the third century BC, who noted the existence of Druids among a people called the Keltoi who inhabited central and southern Europe. The word druid may derive from the Indo-European 'dreo-vid', meaning 'one who knows the truth'. In practice it was probably understood to mean something like 'wise-one' or 'philosopher-priest'.

Paganism is a pantheistic nature-worshipping religion which incorporates beliefs and ritual practices from ancient times. Pagans place much emphasis on the natural world and the ongoing cycle of life and death is central to their beliefs. Most Pagans believe that they are part of nature and not separate from, or superior to it, and seek to live in a way that minimises harm to the natural environment (the word Pagan derives from the Latin *Paganus*, meaning 'rural'). Paganism strongly emphasises the equality of the sexes, with women playing a prominent role in the modern Pagan movement and goddess worship featuring in most ceremonies. Paganism cannot be defined by any principal beliefs because it is shaped by each individual's experiences.

The Pagan Federation was founded in 1971 to provide information on Paganism, campaigns on issues which affect Paganism and provides support to members of the Pagan community. Within the UK the Pagan Federation is divided into 12 districts each with a district manager and a regional coordinator. Local meetings are called 'moots' and take place in private homes, pubs or coffee bars. The Pagan Federation publishes a quarterly journal, *Pagan Dawn*, formerly *The Wiccan* (founded in 1968). The federation also publishes other material, arranges members-only and public events and maintains personal contact by letter with individual members and the wider Pagan community. Regional gatherings and conferences are held throughout the year.

THE PAGAN FEDERATION, Suite 1, The Werks, 45 Church Road, Hove BN3 2BE E info@paganfederation.co.uk
W www.paganfed.org
President, Robin Taylor

SIKHISM

The Sikh religion dates from the birth of Guru Nanak in the Punjab in 1469. 'Guru' means teacher but in Sikh tradition has come to represent the divine presence of God giving inner spiritual guidance. Nanak's role as the human vessel of the divine guru was passed on to nine successors, the last of whom (Guru Gobind Singh) died in 1708. The immortal guru is now held to reside in the sacred scripture, *Guru Granth Sahib,* and so to be present in all Sikh gatherings.

Guru Nanak taught that there is one God and that different religions are like different roads leading to the same destination. He condemned religious conflict, ritualism and caste prejudices. The fifth Guru, Guru Arjan Dev, largely compiled the Sikh Holy scripture, a collection of hymns *(gurbani)* known as the *Adi Granth.* It includes the writings of the first five gurus and the ninth guru, and selected writings of Hindu and Muslim saints whose views are in accord with the gurus' teachings. Guru Arjan Dev also built the Golden Temple at Amritsar, the centre of Sikhism. The tenth guru, Guru Gobind Singh, passed on the guruship to the sacred scripture, Guru Granth Sahib, and founded the *Khalsa,* an order intended to fight against tyranny and injustice. Male initiates to the order added 'Singh' to their given names and women added 'Kaur'. Guru Gobind Singh also made the wearing of five symbols obligatory: *kaccha* (a special undergarment), *kara* (a steel bangle), *kirpan* (a small sword),

kesh (long unshorn hair, and consequently the wearing of a turban) and *kangha* (a comb). These practices are still compulsory for those Sikhs who are initiated into the Khalsa (the *Amritdharis*). Those who do not seek initiation are known as *Sehajdharis.*

There are no professional priests in Sikhism; anyone with a reasonable proficiency in the Punjabi language can conduct a service. Worship can be offered individually or communally, and in a private house or a *gurdwara* (temple). Sikhs are forbidden to eat meat prepared by ritual slaughter; they are also asked to abstain from smoking, alcohol and other intoxicants. Such abstention is compulsory for the Amritdharis.

There are about 24 million Sikhs worldwide and, according to the 2011 census, there are 432,000 adherents in England, Wales and Scotland. Every gurdwara manages its own affairs; there is no central body in the UK. The Sikh Missionary Society provides an information service.

SIKH MISSIONARY SOCIETY UK, 10 Featherstone Road, Southall, Middx UB2 5AA T 020-8574 1902
E info@sikhmissionarysociety.org
W www.sikhmissionarysociety.org

ZOROASTRIANISM

Zoroastrians are followers of the Iranian prophet Spitaman Zarathushtra (or Zoroaster in its hellenised form) who lived *c.*1200–1500 BC. Zoroastrians were persecuted in Iran following the Arab invasion of Persia in the seventh century AD and a group (who are known as Parsis) migrated to India in the ninth century AD to avoid harassment and persecution. Zarathushtra's words are recorded in 17 hymns called the *Gathas,* which, together with other scriptures, form the *Avesta.*

Zoroastrianism teaches that there is one God, *Ahura Mazda* ('Wise Lord'), and that all creation stems ultimately from God; the Gathas teach that human beings have free will, are responsible for their own actions and can choose between good and evil. It is believed that choosing *Asha* (truth or righteousness), with the aid of *Vohu Manah* (good mind), leads to happiness for the individual and society, whereas choosing evil leads to unhappiness and conflict. The *Gathas* also encourage hard work, good deeds and charitable acts. Zoroastrians believe that after death the immortal soul is judged by God, and is then sent to paradise or hell, where it will stay until the end of time to be resurrected for the final judgment.

In Zoroastrian places of worship, an urn containing fire is the central feature; the fire symbolises purity, light and truth and is a visible symbol of the *Fravashi* or *Farohar* (spirit), the presence of Ahura Mazda in every human being. Zoroastrians respect nature and much importance is attached to cultivating land and protecting air, earth and water.

The Zoroastrian Trust Funds of Europe is the main body for Zoroastrians in the UK. Founded in 1861 as the Religious Funds of the Zoroastrians of Europe, it disseminates information on the Zoroastrian faith, provides a place of worship and maintains separate burial grounds for Zoroastrians. It also holds religious and social functions and provides assistance to Zoroastrians as considered necessary, including the provision of loans and grants to students of Zoroastrianism, and participates in inter-faith educational activities.

There are approximately 150,000 Zoroastrians worldwide, of which around 4,000 reside in England and Wales, mainly in London and the South East.

ZOROASTRIAN TRUST FUNDS OF EUROPE, Zoroastrian Centre, 440 Alexandra Avenue, Harrow, Middx HA2 9TL
T 020-8866 0765 E secretary@ztfe.com W www.ztfe.com
President, Malcolm Deboo

CHURCHES

There are two established (ie state) churches in the UK: the Church of England and the Church of Scotland. There are no established churches in Wales or Northern Ireland, though the Church in Wales, the Scottish Episcopal Church and the Church of Ireland are members of the Anglican Communion.

THE CHURCH OF ENGLAND

The Church of England is divided into the two provinces of Canterbury and York, each under an archbishop. The two provinces are subdivided into 42 dioceses, the newest of which came into existence on 20 April 2014. The new Diocese of Leeds was formed from the amalgamation of the former dioceses of Bradford, Ripon and Leeds and Wakefield.

Legislative provision for the Church of England is made by the General Synod, established in 1970. It also discusses and expresses opinion on any other matter of religious or public interest. The General Synod has 483 members in total, divided between three houses: the House of Bishops, the House of Clergy and the House of Laity. It is presided over jointly by the Archbishops of Canterbury and York and normally meets twice a year. The synod has the power, delegated by parliament, to frame statute law (known as a 'measure') on any matter concerning the Church of England. A measure must be laid before both houses of parliament, who may accept or reject it but cannot amend it. Once accepted the measure is submitted for royal assent and then has the full force of law. In addition to the General Synod, there are synods at diocesan level. The entire General Synod is re-elected once every five years. The tenth General Synod was inaugurated by the Queen on 23 November 2015.

THE ARCHBISHOPS' COUNCIL

The Archbishops' Council was established in January 1999. Its creation was the result of changes to the Church of England's national structure proposed in 1995 and subsequently approved by the synod and parliament. The council's purpose, set out in the National Institutions Measure 1998, is 'to coordinate, promote and further the work and mission of the Church of England'. It reports to the General Synod. The Archbishops' Council comprises the Archbishops of Canterbury and York, ex officio, the prolocutors elected by the convocations of Canterbury and York, the chair and vice-chair of the House of Laity, two bishops and two lay persons elected by their respective houses of the General Synod, the Church Estates Commissioner, and up to six persons appointed jointly by the two archbishops.

There are also a number of national boards, councils and other bodies working on matters such as social responsibility, mission, Christian unity and education, which report to the General Synod through the Archbishops' Council.

GENERAL SYNOD OF THE CHURCH OF ENGLAND/ ARCHBISHOPS' COUNCIL, Church House, Great Smith Street, London SW1P 3AZ T 020-7898 1000
Secretary-General, William Nye, LVO

THE ORDINATION AND CONSECRATION OF WOMEN

The canon making it possible for women to be ordained to the priesthood was promulgated in the General Synod in February 1994 and the first 32 women priests were ordained on 12 March 1994.

On 14 July 2014 the General Synod approved the Bishops and Priests (Consecration and Ordination of Women) Measure which made provision for the consecration of women as bishops and for the continuation of provision for the ordination of women. The Revd Elizabeth Lane was consecrated as the first female bishop on 26 January 2015 when she became Bishop Suffragan of Stockport in the diocese of Chester. The first female diocesan bishop, Rachel Treweek, was consecrated as the 41st Bishop of Gloucester on 22 July 2015.

PORVOO DECLARATION

The Porvoo Declaration was approved by the General Synod of the Church of England in July 1995. Churches that approve the declaration regard baptised members of each other's churches as members of their own, and allow free interchange of episcopally ordained ministers within the rules of each church.

MEMBERSHIP AND MINISTRY

	Full-time Diocesan Clergy 2017		Electoral Roll Membership 2017
	Male	Female	
Bath and Wells	132	52	29,800
Birmingham	108	42	15,800
Blackburn	132	24	28,200
Bristol	70	29	14,700
Canterbury	97	27	20,700
Carlisle	72	16	17,600
Chelmsford	222	85	40,800
Chester	138	53	38,900
Chichester	217	31	47,000
Coventry	79	29	15,300
Derby	94	38	15,000
Durham	95	43	18,900
Ely	75	41	17,500
Europe	63	5	11,600
Exeter	154	33	26,000
Gloucester	77	40	21,400
Guildford	119	48	26,300
Hereford	58	25	14,700
Leeds	218	89	38,900
Leicester	79	37	15,900
Lichfield	179	56	38,200
Lincoln	102	53	21,300
Liverpool	119	60	23,800
London	427	86	76,100
Manchester	135	63	28,000
Newcastle	86	32	13,800
Norwich	125	45	17,800
Oxford	264	96	51,800
Peterborough	94	47	17,900
Portsmouth	64	27	14,300
Rochester	145	40	25,900
St Albans	163	70	31,800
St Edmundsbury and Ipswich	79	36	19,000
Salisbury	132	60	35,200
Sheffield	94	32	15,500
Sodor and Man	15	3	2,000
Southwark	231	87	43,600
Southwell and Nottingham	76	31	17,500
Truro	48	34	13,200
Winchester	119	33	28,200
Worcester	74	34	14,500
York	139	54	28,600
Channel Islands	26	4	–
Total	5,235	1,870	1,053,000

In 2017, 102,250 people were baptised, 38,420 people were married in parish churches, the Church of England had an electoral roll membership of 1.05 million, and each week an average 895,300 people (all ages) attended services. There were 15,583 churches; 377 senior clergy (including bishops, archdeacons and cathedral clergy); 7,270 parochial stipendiary clergy; 100 non-parochial stipendiary clergy; 3,060 self-supporting ministers; 1,070 ordained chaplains; 5,180 readers or licensed lay ministers in active ministry; and 3,310 readers or licensed lay ministers with permission to officiate (active emeriti).

STIPENDS
The stipends below are for those appointed on or after 1 April 2004; transitional arrangements are in place for those appointed prior to this date. The national minimum stipend from 1 April 2019 is £24,770; under common tenure all full-time office-holders must receive stipend, or stipend together with other income related to their office, of at least this amount.

	2019–20
Archbishop of Canterbury	£83,400
Archbishop of York	£71,470
Bishop of London	£65,510
Diocesan bishops	£45,270
Suffragan bishops	£36,930
Deans	£36,930
Archdeacons	£35,400
Residentiary canons	*£28,580
Incumbents and clergy of similar status	*£26,470

* National stipend benchmark: adjusted regionally to reflect variations in the cost of living

CANTERBURY

105TH ARCHBISHOP AND PRIMATE OF ALL ENGLAND
Most Revd and Rt. Hon. Justin Welby, *cons.* 2011, *apptd* 2013; Lambeth Palace, London SE1 7JU
Signs Justin Cantuar:

BISHOPS SUFFRAGAN
Dover, vacant

Ebbsfleet, Rt. Revd Jonathan Goodall, *cons.* 2013, *apptd* 2013; Hill House, Treetops, The Mount, Caversham, Reading RG4 7RE
Richborough, Rt. Revd Norman Banks, *cons.* 2011, *apptd* 2011; Parkside House, Abbey Mill Lane, St Albans AL3 4HE
Maidstone, Rt. Revd Roderick Thomas, *cons.* 2015, *apptd* 2015; The Bishop's Lodge, Church Road, Worth, Crawley RH10 7RT

DEAN
Very Revd Robert Willis, *apptd* 2001

Dean of Jersey (A Peculiar), Very Revd Mike Keirle, *apptd* 2017
Dean of Guernsey (A Peculiar), Very Revd Tim Barker, *apptd* 2015

Organist (Canterbury Cathedral), David Flood, FRCO, *apptd* 1988

ARCHDEACONS
Ashford, Ven. Darren Miller, *apptd* 2018
Canterbury, Ven. Jo Kelly Moore *apptd* 2017
Maidstone, Ven. Stephen Taylor, *apptd* 2011

Vicar-General of Province and Diocese, Chancellor Sheila Cameron, QC
Commissary-General, Morag Ellis, QC
Joint Registrars of the Province, Canon John Rees; Stephen Slack

Diocesan Registrar and Legal Adviser, Owen Carew Jones
Diocesan Secretary, Julian Hills, Diocesan House, Lady Wootton's Green, Canterbury CT1 1NQ T 01227-459401

YORK

97TH ARCHBISHOP AND PRIMATE OF ENGLAND
Most Revd and Rt. Hon. Dr John Sentamu, *cons.* 1996, *trans.* 2005; Bishopthorpe, York YO23 2GE
Signs Sentamu Ebor:

BISHOPS SUFFRAGAN
Hull, Rt. Revd Alison White, *cons.* 2015, *apptd* 2015; Hullen House, Woodfield Lane, Hessle, Hull HU13 0ES
Selby, Rt. Revd John Thomson, *cons.* 2014, *apptd* 2014; 6 Pinfold Garth, Malton YO17 7XQ
Whitby, Rt. Revd Paul Fergson, *cons.* 2014, *apptd* 2014; 21 Thornton Road, Stainton TS8 9DS

PRINCIPAL EPISCOPAL VISITOR
Beverley, Rt. Revd Glyn Webster, *cons.* 2013, *apptd* 2013; Holy Trinity Rectory, Micklegate, York YO1 6LE

DEAN
Very Revd Jonathan Frost, *apptd* 2019

Director of Music, Robert Sharpe, *apptd* 2008

ARCHDEACONS
Cleveland, Ven. Samantha Rushton, *apptd* 2015
East Riding, Ven. Andy Broom, *apptd* 2014
York, vacant

Chancellor of the Diocese, His Hon. Judge Collier, QC, *apptd* 2006
Acting Registrar and Legal Secretary, Louise Connacher
Diocesan Secretary, Canon Peter Warry, Diocesan House, Amy Johnson Way, York YO30 4XT T 01904-699500

LONDON (CANTERBURY)

133RD BISHOP
Rt. Revd Dame Sarah Mullally, DBE, *cons.* 2015, *apptd* 2017; Bishop of London's Office, St Michael Paternoster Royal, College Hill, London EC4R 2RL
Signs Sarah Londin:

AREA BISHOPS
Edmonton, Rt. Revd Robert Wickham, *cons.* 2015, *apptd* 2015; 27 Thurlow Road, London NW3 5PP
Kensington, Rt. Revd Graham Tomlin, *cons.* 2015, *apptd* 2015; Dial House, Riverside, Twickenham TW1 3DT
Stepney, Rt. Revd Joanne Grenfell, *cons.* 2019, *apptd* 2019; 63 Coburn Road, London E3 2DB
Willesden, Rt. Revd Peter Broadbent, *cons.* 2001, *apptd* 2001; 173 Willesden Lane, London NW6 7YN

BISHOP SUFFRAGAN
Islington, Rt. Revd Ric Thorpe, *cons.* 2015, *apptd* 2015; St Edmund the King, Lombard Street, London, EC3V 9EA
Fulham, Rt. Revd Jonathan Baker, *cons.* 2011, *apptd* 2013; The Vicarage, 5 St Andrew Street, London EC4A 3AF

DEAN OF ST PAUL'S
Very Revd Dr David Ison, PHD, *apptd* 2012

Director of Music, Andrew Carwood, *apptd* 2007

ARCHDEACONS
Hackney, Ven. Liz Adekunle, *apptd* 2016
Hampstead, Ven. John Hawkins, *apptd* 2015
London, Ven. Luke Miller, *apptd* 2016
Middlesex, Ven. Stephan Welch, *apptd* 2006

Northolt, Ven. Duncan Green, *apptd* 2013
Two Cities, vacant

Chancellor, Nigel Seed, QC, *apptd* 2002
Registrar and Legal Secretary, Paul Morris
Diocesan Secretary, Richard Gough, London Diocesan House,
36 Causton Street, London SW1P 4AU **T** 020-7932 1100

DURHAM (YORK)

74TH BISHOP

Rt. Revd Paul Butler, *cons.* 2004, *trans.* 2013; Auckland Castle,
Bishop Auckland DL14 7NR
Signs Paul Dunelm:

BISHOP SUFFRAGAN

Jarrow, Rt. Revd Sarah Clark, *cons.* 2019, *apptd* 2019;
Bishop's House, 25 Ivy Lane, Low Fell, Gateshead NE9 6QD

DEAN

Very Revd Andrew Tremlett, *apptd* 2015

Organist, Daniel Cook, *apptd* 2017

ARCHDEACONS

Auckland, Ven. Rick Simpson, *apptd* 2017
Durham, Ven. Ian Jagger, *apptd* 2006
Sunderland, Ven. Bob Cooper, *apptd* 2018

Chancellor, Adrian Iles, *apptd* 2017
Registrar and Legal Secretary, Philip Wills, *apptd* 2018
Diocesan Secretary, Andrew Thurston, Diocesan Office, Cuthbert
House, Stonebridge, Durham DH1 3RY **T** 01388-660010

WINCHESTER (CANTERBURY)

97TH BISHOP

Rt. Revd Tim Dakin, cons. 2012, *apptd* 2011; Bishop's Office,
Wolvesey, Winchester SO23 9ND
Signs Tim Winton:

BISHOPS SUFFRAGAN

Basingstoke, Rt. Revd David Williams, *cons.* 2014, *apptd* 2014;
Diocesan Office, Old Alresford Place, Alresford, Hants SO24 9DH
Southampton, Rt. Revd Deborah Sellin, *cons.* 2019, *apptd*
2019; Diocesan Office, Old Alresford Place, Alresford, Hants
SO24 9DH

DEAN

Very Revd Catherine Ogle, *apptd* 2017

Director of Music, Andrew Lumsden, *apptd* 2002

ARCHDEACONS

Bournemouth, Ven. Dr Peter Rouch, *apptd* 2011
Winchester, Ven. Richard Brand, *apptd* 2016
For Mission Development, Ven. Paul Moore, *apptd* 2014

Chancellor, Cain Ormondroyd, *apptd* 2017
Registrar and Legal Secretary, Sue de Candole
Chief Executive, Andrew Robinson, Old Alresford Place,
Alresford, Hants SO24 9DH **T** 01962-737300

BATH AND WELLS (CANTERBURY)

79TH BISHOP

Rt. Revd Peter Hancock, *cons.* 2010, *apptd* 2014; The Bishop's
Palace, Wells, Somerset BA5 2PD
Signs Peter Bath & Wells:

BISHOP SUFFRAGAN

Taunton, Rt. Revd Ruth Worsley, *cons.* 2015, *apptd* 2015;
The Bishop's Palace, Market Place, Wells BA5 2PD

DEAN

Very Revd John Davies, *apptd* 2016

Organist, Matthew Owens, *apptd* 2005

ARCHDEACONS

Bath, Ven. Dr Adrian Youings, *apptd* 2017
Taunton, Ven. Simon Hill, *apptd* 2016
Wells, Ven. Anne Gell, *apptd* 2017

Chancellor, Timothy Briden, *apptd* 1993
Registrar and Legal Secretary, Roland Callaby
Diocesan Secretary, Nick May, The Old Deanery, St Andrew's
Street, Wells, Somerset BA5 2UG **T** 01749-670777

BIRMINGHAM (CANTERBURY)

9TH BISHOP

Rt. Revd David Urquhart, KCMG *cons.* 2000, *apptd* 2006;
Bishop's Croft, Old Church Road, Harborne, Birmingham
B17 0BG
Signs David Birmingham:

BISHOP SUFFRAGAN

Aston, Anne Hollinghurst, *cons.* 2015, *apptd* 2015, Bishop's
Lodge, 16 Coleshill Street, Sutton Coldfield B72 1SH

DEAN

Very Revd Matt Thompson, *apptd* 2017

Director of Music, David Hardie, *apptd* 2018

ARCHDEACONS

Aston, Ven. Simon Heathfield, *apptd* 2014
Birmingham, Ven. Jenny Tomlinson, *apptd* 2019

Chancellor, Mark Powell, QC, *apptd* 2012
Registrar and Legal Secretary, Vicki Simpson
Diocesan Secretary, Andrew Halstead, 1 Colmore Row,
Birmingham B3 2BJ **T** 0121-426 0400

BLACKBURN (YORK)

9TH BISHOP

Rt. Revd Julian Henderson, *cons.* 2013, *apptd* 2013; Bishop's
House, Ribchester Road, Blackburn BB1 9EF
Signs Julian Blackburn

BISHOPS SUFFRAGAN

Burnley, Rt. Revd Philip North, *cons.* 2015, *apptd* 2015; Dean
House, 449 Padiham Road, Burnley BB12 6TE
Lancaster, Rt. Revd Dr Jill Duff, *cons.* 2018, *apptd* 2018;
Shireshead Vicarage, Whinney Brow, Forton, Preston PR3 0AE

DEAN

Very Revd Peter Howell-Jones, *apptd* 2016

Organist and Director of Music, John Robinson, *apptd* 2019

ARCHDEACON

Blackburn, Ven. Mark Ireland, *apptd* 2015
Lancaster, vacant

Chancellor, His Hon. Judge Bullimore, *apptd* 1990
Registrar and Legal Secretary, Revd Paul Benfield
Diocesan Secretary, Graeme Pollard, Diocesan Office, Clayton
House, Walker Office Park, Blackburn BB1 2QE **T** 01254-503070

BRISTOL (CANTERBURY)

56TH BISHOP

Rt. Revd Vivienne Faull, *cons.* 2018, *apptd* 2018; 58A High
Street, Winterbourne, Bristol BS36 1JQ
Signs Vivienne Bristol

BISHOP SUFFRAGAN
Swindon, Rt. Revd Dr Lee Rayfield, *cons.* 2005, *apptd* 2005; Mark House, Field Rise, Swindon, Wiltshire SN1 4HP

DEAN
Very Revd David Hoyle, *apptd* 2010

Organist and Director of Music, Mark Lee, *apptd* 1998

ARCHDEACONS
Bristol, Ven. Neil Warwick, *apptd* 2019
Malmesbury, Ven. Christopher Bryan, *apptd* 2019

Chancellor, Revd Justin Gau
Registrar and Legal Secretary, Roland Callaby

Diocesan Secretary, Oliver Home, First Floor, Hillside House, 1500 Parkway North, Stoke Gifford, Bristol BS34 8YU T 0117-9060100

CARLISLE (YORK)
67TH BISHOP
Rt. Revd James Newcome, *cons.* 2002, *apptd* 2009; Bishop's House, Ambleside Road, Keswick CA12 4DD
Signs James Carliol

BISHOP SUFFRAGAN
Penrith, Revd Dr Emma Ineson, *cons.* 2019, *apptd* 2018; Holm Croft, 13 Castle Road, Kendal, Cumbria LA9 7AU

DEAN
Very Revd Mark Boyling, *apptd* 2004

Director of Music, Mark Duthie, *apptd* 2017

ARCHDEACONS
Carlisle, Ven. Lee Townend, *apptd* 2017
West Cumberland, Ven. Dr Richard Pratt, *apptd* 2009
Westmorland and Furness, Ven. Vernon Ross, *apptd* 2017

Chancellor, Geoffrey Tattersall, QC, *apptd* 2003
Registrar and Legal Secretary, Jane Lowdon

Diocesan Secretary, Derek Hurton, Church House, 19–24 Friargate, Penrith, Cumbria CA11 7XR T 01768-807777

CHELMSFORD (CANTERBURY)
10TH BISHOP
Rt. Revd Stephen Cottrell, *cons.* 2004, *apptd* 2010; Bishopscourt, Main Road, Margaretting, Ingatestone, Essex CM4 0HD
Signs Stephen Chelmsford

BISHOPS SUFFRAGAN
Barking, Rt. Revd Peter Hill, *cons.* 2014, *apptd* 2014; Barking Lodge, Verulam Avenue, London E17 8ES
Bradwell, Rt. Revd Dr John Perumbalath, *cons.* 2018, *apptd* 2018; Bishop's House. Orsett Road, Horndon-on-the-Hill, Essex SS17 8NS
Colchester, Rt. Revd Roger Morris, *cons.* 2014, *apptd* 2014; 1 Fitzwater Road, Colchester, Essex CO3 3SS

DEAN
Very Revd Nicholas Henshall, *apptd* 2013

Director of Music, James Davy, *apptd* 2012

ARCHDEACONS
Barking, Ven. Christopher Burke, *apptd* 2019
Chelmsford, Ven. Elizabeth Snowden, *apptd* 2016
Colchester, Ven. Ruth Patten, *apptd* 2019
Harlow, Ven. Vanessa Herrick, *apptd* 2017
Southend, Ven. Mike Lodge, *apptd* 2017
Stansted, Ven. Robin King, *apptd* 2013
West Ham, Ven. Elwin Cockett, *apptd* 2007

Chancellor, George Pulman, QC, *apptd* 2001
Registrar and Legal Secretary, Aiden Hargreaves-Smith
Chief Executive, Joel Gowen, 53 New Street, Chelmsford, Essex CM1 1AT T 01245-294400

CHESTER (YORK)
41ST BISHOP
vacant

BISHOPS SUFFRAGAN
Birkenhead, Rt. Revd Keith Sinclair, *cons.* 2007, *apptd* 2007; Bishop's Lodge, 67 Bidston Road, Prenton CH43 6TR
Stockport, vacant; Bishop's Lodge, Back Lane, Dunham, Altrincham WA14 4SG

DEAN
Very Revd Dr Timothy Stratford, *apptd* 2018

Organist and Director of Music, Philip Rushforth, FRCO, *apptd* 2008

ARCHDEACONS
Chester, Ven. Dr Michael Gilbertson, *apptd* 2010
Macclesfield, Ven. Ian Bishop, *apptd* 2011

Chancellor, His Hon. Judge Turner, QC, *apptd* 1998
Registrar and Legal Secretary, Lisa Moncur

Diocesan Secretary, George Colville, Church House, 5500 Daresbury Park, Daresbury, Warrington WA4 4GE T 01928-718834

CHICHESTER (CANTERBURY)
103RD BISHOP
Rt. Revd Dr Martin Warner, *cons.* 2010, *apptd* 2012; The Palace, Chichester PO19 1PY
Signs Martin Cicestr:

BISHOPS SUFFRAGAN
Horsham, vacant

Lewes, Rt. Revd Richard Jackson, *cons.* 2014, *apptd* 2014; Ebenezer House, Kingston Ridge, Kingston, Lewes BN7 3JU

DEAN
Very Revd Stephen Waine, *apptd* 2015

Organist, Charles Harrison, *apptd* 2014

ARCHDEACONS
Brighton and Lewes, Ven. Martin Lloyd Williams, *apptd* 2015
Chichester, Ven. Luke Irvine-Capel, *apptd* 2019
Horsham, Ven. Fiona Windsor, *apptd* 2014
Hastings, Ven. Edward Dowler, *apptd* 2016

Chancellor, Prof. Mark Hill, QC
Deputy Registrar and Legal Secretary, Darren Oliver
Diocesan Secretary, Gabrielle Higgins, Diocesan Church House, 211 New Church Road, Hove, E. Sussex BN3 4ED T 01273-421021

COVENTRY (CANTERBURY)
9TH BISHOP
Rt. Revd Dr Christopher Cocksworth, *cons.* 2008, *apptd* 2008; The Bishop's House, 23 Davenport Road, Coventry CV5 6PW
Signs Christopher Coventry

BISHOP SUFFRAGAN
Warwick, Rt. Revd John Stroyan, *cons.* 2005, *apptd* 2005; Warwick House, School Hill, Offchurch, Leamington Spa CV33 9AL

DEAN
Very Revd John Witcombe, *apptd* 2013

Director of Music, Mr Kerry Beaumont, *apptd* 2006

ARCHDEACONS
Archdeacon Missioner, Ven. Barry Dugmore, *apptd* 2019
Archdeacon Pastor, Ven. Sue Field *apptd* 2017

Chancellor, His Hon. Judge Eyre, *apptd* 2009
Registrar and Legal Secretary, Mary Allanson

Diocesan Secretary, Ruth Marlow, Cathedral & Diocesan Offices, 1 Hilltop, Coventry CV1 5AB **T** 024-7652 1200

DERBY (CANTERBURY)

8TH BISHOP
Rt. Revd. Elizabeth Lane, *cons.* 2015, *apptd* 2019; The Bishop's Office, 6 King Street, Duffield DE56 4EU
Signs Elizabeth Derby

BISHOP SUFFRAGAN
Repton, Rt. Revd Jan McFarlane, *cons.* 2016, *apptd* 2016; Repton House, 39 Hickton Road, Swanwick, Alfreton DE55 1AF

DEAN
Very Revd Dr Stephen Hance, *apptd* 2017

Director of Music, Alexander Binns, *apptd* 2019

ARCHDEACONS
Chesterfield, Ven. Carol Coslett, *apptd* 2018
Derby, Ven. Dr Christopher Cunliffe, *apptd* 2006

Chancellor, His Hon. Judge Bullimore, *apptd* 1981
Registrar and Legal Secretary, Nadine Waldron

Diocesan Secretary, Rachel Morris, Derby Church House, Full Street, Derby DE1 3DR **T** 01332-388650

ELY (CANTERBURY)

69TH BISHOP
Rt. Revd Stephen Conway, *cons.* 2006, *apptd* 2011; The Bishop's House, Ely CB7 4DW
Signs Stephen Ely

BISHOP SUFFRAGAN
Huntingdon, Rt. Revd Dr Dagmar Winter, *cons.* 2019, *apptd* 2019; 14 Lynn Road, Ely, Cambs CB6 1DA

DEAN
Very Revd Mark Bonney, *apptd* 2012

Director of Music, Edmund Aldhouse, *apptd* 2018

ARCHDEACONS
Cambridge, Ven. Dr Alex Hughes, *apptd* 2014
Huntingdon and Wisbech, Ven. Hugh McCurdy, *apptd* 2005

Chancellor, His Hon. Judge Leonard, QC
Registrar, Howard Dellar

Diocesan Secretary, Paul Evans, Bishop Woodford House, Barton Road, Ely, Cambs CB7 4DX **T** 01353-652701

EXETER (CANTERBURY)

71ST BISHOP
Rt. Revd Robert Atwell, *cons.* 2008, *apptd* 2014; The Palace, Exeter EX1 1HY
Signs Robert Exon:

BISHOPS SUFFRAGAN
Crediton, Rt. Revd Jackie Searle, *cons.* 2018, *apptd* 2018; 32 The Avenue, Tiverton EX16 4HW

Plymouth, Rt. Revd Nick McKinnel, *cons.* 2012, *trans.* 2015; 108 Molesworth Road, Stoke, Plymouth PL3 4AQ

DEAN
Very Revd Jonathan Greener, *apptd* 2017

Director of Music, Timothy Noon, *apptd* 2016

ARCHDEACONS
Barnstaple, Ven. Mark Butchers, *apptd* 2015
Exeter, Ven. Andrew Beane, *apptd* 2019
Plymouth, Ven. Nick Shutt, *apptd* 2019
Totnes, Ven. Douglas Dettmer, *apptd* 2015

Chancellor, Hon. Sir Andrew McFarlane
Registrar and Legal Secretary, Alison Stock

Diocesan Secretary, Stephen Hancock, The Old Deanery, The Cloisters, Exeter EX1 1HS **T** 01392-272686

GIBRALTAR IN EUROPE (CANTERBURY)

4TH BISHOP
Rt. Revd Robert Innes, PHD, *cons.* 2014, *apptd* 2014; Office of the Bishop in Europe, 47, rue Capitaine Crespel – boite 49, 1050 Brussels, Belgium

BISHOP SUFFRAGAN
In Europe, Rt. Revd David Hamid, *cons.* 2002, *apptd* 2002; 14 Tufton Street, London SW1P 3QZ

Dean, Cathedral Church of the Holy Trinity, Gibraltar, vacant

Chancellor, Pro-Cathedral of St Paul, Valletta, Malta, Canon Simon Godfrey
Chancellor, Pro-Cathedral of the Holy Trinity, Brussels, Belgium, Ven. Dr Paul Vrolijk

ARCHDEACONS
Eastern, Canon Adèle Kelham *(acting)*
France, Ven. Meurig Williams
Germany and Northern Europe, Canon John Newsome *(acting)*
Gibraltar, Ven. Geoffrey Johnston *(interim)*
Italy and Malta, Ven. Geoffrey Johnston *(acting)*
North-West Europe, Ven. Dr Paul Vrolijk
Switzerland, Canon Adèle Kelham

Chancellor, Prof. Mark Hill, QC
Registrar and Legal Secretary, Aiden Hargreaves-Smith

Diocesan Secretary, Andrew Caspari 14 Tufton Street, London SW1P 3QZ **T** 020-7898 1155

GLOUCESTER (CANTERBURY)

41ST BISHOP
Rt. Revd Rachel Treweek, *cons.* 2015, *apptd* 2015; 2 College Green, Gloucester GL1 2LR
Signs Rachel Gloucestr

BISHOP SUFFRAGAN
Tewkesbury, Rt. Revd Robert Springett, *cons.* 2016, *apptd* 2016; 2 College Green, Gloucester GL1 2LR

DEAN
Very Revd Stephen Lake, *apptd* 2011

Director of Music, Adrian Partington, *apptd* 2007

ARCHDEACONS
Cheltenham, Ven. Phil Andrew, *apptd* 2017
Gloucester, Ven. Hilary Dawson, *apptd* 2019

Chancellor and Vicar-General, June Rodgers, *apptd* 1990
Registrar and Legal Secretary, Jos Moule

Diocesan Secretary, Ben Preece Smith, Church House, College Green, Gloucester GL1 2LY **T** 01452-410022

GUILDFORD (CANTERBURY)

10TH BISHOP
Rt. Revd Andrew Watson, *cons.* 2008, *apptd* 2014; Willow Grange, Woking Road, Guildford, Surrey GU4 7QS
Signs Andrew Guildford

BISHOP SUFFRAGAN
Dorking, Rt Revd Jo Wells, *cons.* 2016, *apptd* 2016; Dayspring, 13 Pilgrim's Way, Guildford, Surrey GU4 8AD

DEAN
Very Revd Dianna Gwilliams, *apptd* 2013

Organist, Katherine Dienes-Williams, *apptd* 2007

ARCHDEACONS
Dorking, vacant
Surrey, Ven. Paul Davies, *apptd* 2017

Chancellor, Andrew Jordan
Registrar and Legal Secretary, Howard Dellar
Diocesan Secretary, Peter Coles, Church House, 20 Alan Turing Road, Guildford GU2 7YF **T** 01483-790300

HEREFORD (CANTERBURY)

105TH BISHOP
Rt. Revd Richard Frith, cons. 1998, apptd 2014; Bishop's House, The Palace, Hereford HR4 9BN
Signs Richard Hereford

BISHOP SUFFRAGAN
Ludlow, Rt. Revd Alistair Magowan, *cons.* 2009, *apptd* 2009; Bishop's House, Corvedale Road, Craven Arms, Shropshire SY7 9BT

DEAN
Very Revd Michael Tavinor, *apptd* 2002

Organist and Director of Music, Geraint Bowen, FRCO, *apptd* 2001

ARCHDEACONS
Hereford, Ven. Derek Chedzey, *apptd* 2018
Ludlow, Rt. Revd Alistair Magowan, *apptd* 2009

Chancellor, His Hon. Judge Kaye, QC
Registrar and Legal Secretary, Howard Dellar
Diocesan Secretary, Sam Pratley, The Palace, Hereford HR4 9BL **T** 01432-373300

LEEDS (YORK)

1ST BISHOP OF LEEDS
Rt. Revd Nicholas Baines, *cons.* 2003, *apptd* 2014; Hollin House, Weetwood Avenue, Leeds LS16 5NG
Signs Nicholas Leeds

AREA BISHOPS
Bradford, Rt. Revd Dr Toby Howarth, *cons.* 2014, *apptd* 2014; 47 Kirkgate, Shipley BD18 3EH
Huddersfield, Rt. Revd Jonathan Gibbs, *cons.* 2014, *apptd* 2014; University of Huddersfield, Ground Floor, Sir John Ramsden Court, Huddersfield HD1 3AQ
Ripon, Rt. Revd Dr Helen-Ann Hartley, *cons.* 2014, *apptd* 2018; The Bishop's Office, Redwood, New Road, Sharow, Ripon HG4 5BS
Wakefield, Rt. Revd Anthony Robinson, *cons.* 2002, *apptd* 2014; Pontefract House 181A Manygates Lane, Sandal, Wakefield WF2 7DR

SUFFRAGAN BISHOP
Richmond, Rt. Revd Paul Slater, *cons.* 2015, apptd 2015; Church House, 17–19 York Place, Leeds LS1 2EX

DEANS
Bradford, Very Revd Jerry Lepine, *apptd* 2013
Ripon, Very Revd John Dobson, *apptd* 2014
Wakefield, Very Revd Simon Cowling, *apptd* 2018

Directors of Music, Alexander Berry (Bradford), *apptd* 2017; Andrew Bryden (Ripon), *apptd* 2003; Thomas Moore (Wakefield), *apptd* 2010

ARCHDEACONS
Bradford, Ven. Andrew Jolley, *apptd* 2016
Halifax, Ven. Dr Anne Dawtry, *apptd* 2011
Leeds, Ven. Paul Ayers, *apptd* 2017
Richmond and Craven, Ven. Jonathan Gough, *apptd* 2019
Pontefract, Ven. Peter Townley, *apptd* 2008

Chancellor, Prof. Mark Hill, QC
Registrar and Legal Secretary, Peter Foskett
Diocesan Secretary, Debbie Child; Church House, 17–19 York Place, Leeds LS1 2EX **T** 0113-200 0540

LEICESTER (CANTERBURY)

7TH BISHOP
Rt Revd Martyn Snow, *cons.* 2013, *apptd* 2016; Bishop's Lodge, 10 Springfield Road, Leicester LE2 3BD
Signs Martyn Leicester

SUFFRAGAN BISHOP
Loughborough, Rt. Revd Guli Francis-Dehqani, *cons.* 2017, *apptd* 2017; c/o Bishop's Lodge, 10 Springfield Road, Leicester LE2 3BD

DEAN
Very Revd David Monteith, *apptd* 2013

Director of Music, Dr Christopher Ouvry-Johns

ARCHDEACONS
Leicester, Ven. Richard Worsfold, *apptd* 2018
Loughborough, Ven. Claire Wood, *apptd* 2017

Chancellor, Mark Blackett-Ord
Registrar and Legal Secretary, Lee Coley
Diocesan Secretary, Jonathan Kerry, St Martin's House, 7 Peacock Lane, Leicester LE1 5PZ **T** 0116-261 5200

LICHFIELD (CANTERBURY)

99TH BISHOP
Rt. Revd Dr Michael Ipgrave, OBE, *cons.* 2012, *apptd* 2016; 22 The Close, Lichfield, WS13 7LG
Signs Michael Lich:

AREA BISHOPS
Shrewsbury, Rt. Revd Sarah Bullock, *cons.* 2019, *apptd* 2019; Athlone House, 68 London Road, Shrewsbury SY2 6PG
Stafford, Rt. Revd Geoffrey Annas, *cons.* 2010, *apptd* 2010; Ash Garth, Broughton Crescent, Barlaston, Stoke-on-Trent ST12 9DD
Wolverhampton, Rt. Revd Clive Gregory, *cons.* 2007, *apptd* 2007; 61 Richmond Road, Wolverhampton WV3 9JH

DEAN
Very Revd Adrian Dorber, *apptd* 2005

Director of Music, Ben Lamb, *apptd* 2010
Organist, Martyn Rawles, *apptd* 2010

ARCHDEACONS
Lichfield, vacant
Salop, Ven. Paul Thomas, *apptd* 2011
Stoke-on-Trent, Ven. Matthew Parker, *apptd* 2013
Walsall, Ven. Julian Francis, *apptd* 2019

Chancellor, His Hon. Judge Eyre, *apptd* 2012
Joint Registrars and Legal Secretaries, Niall Blackie; Andrew Wynne

Diocesan Secretary, Julie Jones, St Mary's House, The Close, Lichfield, Staffs WS13 7LD T 01543-306030

LINCOLN (CANTERBURY)

72ND BISHOP
Rt. Revd Christopher Lowson, *cons.* 2011, *apptd* 2011; Bishop's Office, The Old Palace, Minster Yard, Lincoln LN2 1PU
Signs Christopher Lincoln

BISHOPS SUFFRAGAN
Grantham, Rt. Revd Dr Nicholas Chamberlain, *cons.* 2015, *apptd* 2015; The Old Palace, Minster Yard, Lincoln LN2 1PU
Grimsby, Rt. Revd Dr David Court (acting diocesan bishop), *cons.* 2014, *apptd* 2014; The Old Palace, Minster Yard, Lincoln LN2 1PU

DEAN
Very Revd Christine Wilson, *apptd* 2016 (currently on leave of absence)

Director of Music, Aric Prentice, *apptd* 2003

ARCHDEACONS
Boston, Ven. Dr Justine Allain Chapman, *apptd* 2013
Lincoln, Ven. Gavin Kirk, *apptd* 2016
Stow and Lindsey, Ven. Mark Steadman, *apptd* 2015

Chancellor, His Hon. Judge Bishop
Registrar and Legal Secretary, Ian Blaney
Diocesan Secretary, Revd David Dadswell, Edward King House, Minster Yard, Lincoln LN2 1PU T 01522-504050

LIVERPOOL (YORK)

8TH BISHOP
Rt. Revd Paul Bayes, *cons.* 2010, *apptd* 2014; Bishop's Lodge, Woolton Park, Liverpool L25 6DT
Signs Paul Liverpool

BISHOP SUFFRAGAN
Warrington, Rt. Revd Bev Mason, *cons.* 2018, *apptd* 2018; 34 Central Avenue, Eccleston Park, Prescot L34 2QP

DEAN
Very Revd Susan Jones, PHD, *apptd* 2018

Director of Music, Lee Ward, *apptd* 2017

ARCHDEACONS
Liverpool, Ven. Mike McGurk, *apptd* 2017
Knowlsey & Sefton, Ven. Pete Spiers *apptd* 2015
St Helens & Warrington, Ven. Peter Preece, *apptd* 2015
Wigan & West Lancashire, Ven. Jennifer McKenzie, *apptd* 2015

Chancellor, His Hon. Judge Wood, QC
Registrar and Legal Secretary, Howard Dellar
Diocesan Secretary, Mike Eastwood, St James House, 20 St James Street, Liverpool L1 7BY T 0151-709 9722

MANCHESTER (YORK)

12TH BISHOP
Rt. Revd Dr David Walker, *cons.* 2000, *apptd* 2013; Bishopscourt, Bury New Road, Salford M7 4LE
Signs David Manchester

BISHOPS SUFFRAGAN
Bolton, Rt. Revd Mark Ashcroft, *cons.* 2016, *apptd* 2016; Bishop's Lodge, Walkenden Road, Walkenden M28 2WH
Middleton, Rt. Revd Mark Davies, *cons.* 2008, *apptd* 2008; The Hollies, Manchester Road, Rochdale OL11 3QY

DEAN
Very Revd Rogers Govender, *apptd* 2006

Organist, Christopher Stokes, *apptd* 1992

ARCHDEACONS
Bolton, Ven. Jean Burgess, *apptd* 2018
Manchester, Ven. Karen Lund, *apptd* 2017
Rochdale, Ven. Cherry Vann, *apptd* 2008
Salford, Ven. David Sharples, *apptd* 2009

Chancellor, Canon Geoffrey Tattersall, QC
Registrar and Legal Secretary, Jane Monks
Diocesan Secretary, Helen Platts, Diocesan Church House, 90 Deansgate, Manchester M3 2GH T 0161-828 1400

NEWCASTLE (YORK)

12TH BISHOP
Rt. Revd Christine Elizabeth Hardman, *cons.* 2015, apptd 2015; Bishop's House, 29 Moor Road South, Gosforth, Newcastle upon Tyne NE3 1PA
Signs Christine Newcastle

SUFFRAGAN BISHOP
Berwick Rt. Revd Mark Tanner, *cons.* 2016, *apptd* 2016; Berwick House, Longhirst Road, Pegswood, Morpeth NE61 6XF

DEAN
Very Revd Geoff Miller, *apptd* 2018

Director of Music, Ian Roberts, *apptd* 2016

ARCHDEACONS
Lindisfarne, Ven. Dr Peter Robinson, *apptd* 2008
Northumberland, Ven. Mark Wroe, *apptd* 2019

Chancellor, Euan Duff, *apptd* 2013
Registrar and Legal Secretary, Jane Lowdon
Diocesan Secretary, Canon Shane Waddle, Church House, St John's Terrace, North Shields NE29 6HS T 0191-270 4100

NORWICH (CANTERBURY)

72ND BISHOP
Rt. Revd Graham Usher, *cons.* 2014, *apptd* 2019; Bishop's House, Norwich NR3 1SB
Signs Graham Norvic:

BISHOPS SUFFRAGAN
Lynn, Rt. Revd Jonathan Meyrick, *cons.* 2011, *apptd* 2011; The Old Vicarage, Castle Acre, King's Lynn PE32 2AA
Thetford, Rt. Revd Alan Winton, PHD, *cons.* 2009, *apptd* 2009; The Red House, 53 Norwich Road, Stoke Holy Cross, Norwich NR14 8AB

DEAN
Very Revd Jane Hedges, *apptd* 2014

Master of Music, Ashley Grote, *apptd* 2012

ARCHDEACONS
Lynn, Ven. Ian Bentley, *apptd* 2018
Norfolk, Ven. Steven Betts, *apptd* 2012
Norwich, Ven. Karen Hutchinson, *apptd* 2016

Chancellor, Ruth Arlow, *apptd* 2012
Registrar and Legal Secretary, Stuart Jones
Diocesan Secretary, Richard Butler, Diocesan House, 109
Dereham Road, Easton, Norwich, Norfolk NR9 5ES T 01603-880853

OXFORD (CANTERBURY)

44TH BISHOP
Rt. Revd Steven Croft, *cons.* 2009, *apptd* 2016; Church House
Oxford, Langford Locks, Kidlington, Oxford OX5 1GF
Signs Steven Oxon:

AREA BISHOPS
Buckingham, Rt. Revd Dr Alan Wilson, *cons.* 2003, *apptd*
2003; Sheridan, Grimms Hill, Great Missenden, Bucks HP16 9BD
Dorchester, Rt. Revd Colin Fletcher, *cons.* 2000, *apptd* 2000;
Arran House, Sandy Lane, Yarnton, Oxon OX5 1PB
Reading, vacant; Bishop's House, Tidmarsh Lane, Tidmarsh,
Reading RG8 8HA

DEAN OF CHRIST CHURCH
Very Revd Martyn Percy, PHD, *apptd* 2014

Organist, Steven Grahl, *apptd* 2018

ARCHDEACONS
Berkshire, Ven. Olivia Graham, *apptd* 2013
Buckingham, Ven. Guy Elsmore, *apptd* 2016
Dorchester, Ven. Judy French, *apptd* 2014
Oxford, Ven. Martin Gorick, *apptd* 2013

Chancellor, His Hon. Judge Hodge, QC, *apptd* 2019
Joint Registrars and Legal Secretaries, Darren Oliver; Revd
Canon John Rees
Diocesan Secretary, Mark Humphriss, Church House Oxford,
Langford Locks, Kidlington, Oxford OX5 1GF T 01865-208200

PETERBOROUGH (CANTERBURY)

38TH BISHOP
Rt. Revd Donald Allister, *cons.* 2010, *apptd* 2009; Bishop's
Lodging, The Palace, Peterborough PE1 1YA
Signs Donald Petriburg:

BISHOP SUFFRAGAN
Brixworth, Rt. Revd John Holbrook, *cons.* 2011, *apptd* 2011;
Orchard Acre, 11 North Street, Mears Ashby, Northants NN6
0DW

DEAN
Very Revd Christopher Dalliston, *apptd* 2018

Director of Music, Tansy Castledine, *apptd* 2018

ARCHDEACONS
Northampton, Ven. Richard Ormston, *apptd* 2014
Oakham, Ven. Gordon Steele, *apptd* 2012

Chancellor, David Pittaway, QC, *apptd* 2005
Registrar and Legal Secretary, Anna Spriggs
Diocesan Secretary, Andrew Roberts, Diocesan Office, The Palace,
Peterborough PE1 1YB T 01733-887000

PORTSMOUTH (CANTERBURY)

9TH BISHOP
Rt. Revd Christopher Foster, *cons.* 2010, *apptd* 2010;
Bishopsgrove, 26 Osborn Road, Fareham, Hants PO16 7DQ
Signs Christopher Portsmouth

DEAN
Very Revd Anthony Cane, *apptd* 2019

Organist, David Price, *apptd* 1996

ARCHDEACONS
Isle of Wight, Ven. Peter Leonard, *apptd* 2019
Portsdown, vacant
The Meon, Ven. Gavin Collins, *apptd* 2011

Chancellor, His Hon. Judge Waller, CBE
Registrar and Legal Secretary, Hilary Tyler
Diocesan Secretary, Victoria James, Diocesan Offices, 1st Floor,
Peninsular House, Wharf Road, Portsmouth PO2 8HB
T 023-9289 9664

ROCHESTER (CANTERBURY)

107TH BISHOP
Rt. Revd James Langstaff, *cons.* 2004, *apptd* 2010;
Bishopscourt, 24 St Margaret's Street, Rochester ME1 1TS
Signs, James Roffen:

BISHOP SUFFRAGAN
Tonbridge, Rt. Revd Simon Burton-Jones, *cons.* 2018, *apptd*
2018; 25 Shoesmith Lane, Kings Hill, Kent ME19 4FF

DEAN
Very Revd Dr Philip Hesketh, *apptd* 2016

Interim Director of Music, Adrian Bawtree, *apptd* 2018

ARCHDEACONS
Bromley & Bexley, Ven. Dr Paul Wright, *apptd* 2003
*Rochester,*Ven. Andrew Wooding Jones, *apptd* 2018
Tonbridge, Ven. Julie Conalty *apptd* 2017

Chancellor, The Worshipful John Gallagher
Registrar and Legal Secretary, Owen Carew-Jones
Diocesan Secretary, vacant, St Nicholas Church, Boley Hill,
Rochester ME1 1SL T 01634-560000

ST ALBANS (CANTERBURY)

10TH BISHOP
Rt. Revd Dr Alan Smith, *cons.* 2001, *apptd* 2009, *trans.* 2009;
Abbey Gate House, St Albans AL3 4HD
Signs Alan St Albans

BISHOPS SUFFRAGAN
Bedford, Rt. Revd Richard Atkinson, OBE, *cons.* 2012, *apptd*
2012; Bishop's Lodge, Bedford Road, Cardington, Bedford
MK44 3SS
Hertford, Rt. Revd Dr Michael Beasley, *cons.* 2015, *apptd*
2015; Bishopswood, 3 Stobarts Close, Knebworth SG3 6ND

DEAN
Very Revd Dr Jeffrey John, *apptd* 2004

Organist, Andrew Lucas, *apptd* 1998

ARCHDEACONS
Bedford, Ven. Dave Middlebrook, *apptd* 2019
Hertford, Ven. Janet Mackenzie, *apptd* 2016
St Albans, Ven. Jonathan Smith, *apptd* 2008

Chancellor, Lyndsey de Mestre, QC
Deputy Registrars, Jonathan Baldwin; Owen Carew-Jones
Diocesan Secretary, Susan Pope, Holywell Lodge, 41 Holywell Hill,
St Albans AL1 1HE T 01727-854532

ST EDMUNDSBURY AND IPSWICH (CANTERBURY)

11TH BISHOP

Rt. Revd Martin Seeley, *cons.* 2015, *apptd* 2015; The Bishop's House, 4 Park Road, Ipswich IP1 3ST
Signs Martin St Edmundsbury and Ipswich

BISHOP SUFFRAGAN

Dunwich, Rt. Revd Michael Harrison, PHD, *cons.* 2016, *apptd* 2015; Robin Hall, Chapel Lane, Mendlesham, Stowmarket IP14 5SQ

DEAN

Very Revd Joe Hawes, *apptd* 2018

Director of Music, James Thomas, *apptd* 1997

ARCHDEACONS

Ipswich, Ven. Rhiannon King, *apptd* 2019
Sudbury, Ven. Dr David Jenkins, *apptd* 2010
Suffolk, Ven. Ian Morgan, *apptd* 2012
Rural Mission, Ven. Sally Gaze, *apptd* 2019

Chancellor, David Etherington, QC
Registrar and Legal Secretary, James Hall

Diocesan Secretary, Anna Hughes, Diocesan Office, St Nicholas Centre, 4 Cutler Street, Ipswich IP1 1UQ T 01473-298500

SALISBURY (CANTERBURY)

78TH BISHOP

Rt. Revd Nicholas Holtam, *cons.* 2011, *apptd* 2011; South Canonry, 71 The Close, Salisbury SP1 2ER
Signs Nicholas Sarum

BISHOPS SUFFRAGAN

Ramsbury, Rt. Revd Dr Andrew Rumsey, *cons.* 2019, *apptd* 2018; Church House, Crane Street, Salisbury SP1 2QB
Sherborne, Rt. Revd Karen Gorham, *cons.* 2016, *apptd* 2015; The Sherborne Office, St Nicholas' Church Centre, 30 Wareham Road, Corfe Mullen BH21 3LE

DEAN

Very Revd Nicholas Papadopulos *apptd* 2018

Director of Music, David Halls, *apptd* 2005

ARCHDEACONS

Dorset, Ven. Antony MacRow-Wood, *apptd* 2015
Sarum, Ven. Alan Jeans, *apptd* 2003
Sherborne, Ven. Penny Sayer, *apptd* 2018
Wilts, Ven. Sue Groom, *apptd* 2016

Chancellor, Canon Ruth Arlow, *apptd* 2016
Registrar and Legal Secretary, Sue de Candole

Diocesan Secretary, David Pain, Church House, Crane Street, Salisbury SP1 2QB T 01722-411922

SHEFFIELD (YORK)

8TH BISHOP

Rt. Revd Dr Peter Wilcox, *cons.* 2017, *apptd* 2017; Bishopscroft, Snaithing Lane, Sheffield S10 3LG
Signs Peter Sheffield

BISHOP SUFFRAGAN

Doncaster, vacant

DEAN

Very Revd Peter Bradley, *apptd* 2003

Director of Music, Thomas Corns, *apptd* 2017

ARCHDEACONS

Doncaster, Ven. Steve Wilcockson, *apptd* 2012
Sheffield and Rotherham, Ven. Malcolm Chamberlain, *apptd* 2013

Chancellor, Her Hon. Judge Sarah Singleton, QC, *apptd* 2014
Registrar and Legal Secretary, Andrew Vidler

Diocesan Secretary, Heidi Adcock, Church House, 95–99 Effingham Street, Rotherham S65 1BL T 01709-309100

SODOR AND MAN (YORK)

82ND BISHOP

Rt. Revd Peter Eagles, *cons.* 2017, *apptd* 2017; Thie yn Aspick, 4 The Falls, Douglas, Isle of Man IM4 4PZ
Signs Peter Sodor as Mannin

ARCHDEACON OF MAN

Ven. Andrew Brown, *apptd* 2011

Vicar-General and Chancellor, Howard Connell
Registrar, Louise Connacher

Diocesan Secretary, Andrew Swithinbank, c/o Thie yn Aspick, 4 The Falls, Douglas, Isle of Man IM4 4PZ T 07624-314590

SOUTHWARK (CANTERBURY)

10TH BISHOP

Rt. Revd Christopher Chessun, *cons.* 2005, *apptd* 2011; Trinity House, 4 Chapel Court, Borough High Street, London SE1 1HW
Signs Christopher Southwark

AREA BISHOPS

Croydon, Rt. Revd Jonathan Clark, *cons.* 2012, *apptd* 2012; St Matthew's House, 100 George Street, London CR0 1PE
Kingston upon Thames, Rt. Revd Dr Richard Cheetham, *cons.* 2002, *apptd* 2002; 620 Kingston Road, Raynes Park, London SW20 8DN
Woolwich, Rt. Revd Dr Karowei Dorgu, *cons.* 2017, *apptd* 2017; Trinity House, 4 Chapel Court, Borough High Street, London SE1 1HW

DEAN

Very Revd Andrew Nunn, *apptd* 2011

Director of Music, Ian Keatley, *apptd* 2019

ARCHDEACONS

Croydon, Ven. Christopher Skilton, *apptd* 2013
Lambeth, Ven. Simon Gates, *apptd* 2013
Lewisham & Greenwich, Ven. Alastair Cutting, *apptd* 2013
Reigate, Ven. Moira Astin, *apptd* 2016
Southwark, Ven. Dr Jane Steen, *apptd* 2013
Wandsworth, Ven. John Kiddle, *apptd* 2015

Chancellor, Philip Petchey
Registrar and Legal Secretary, Paul Morris

Diocesan Secretary, Ruth Martin, Trinity House, 4 Chapel Court, Borough High Street, London SE1 1HW T 020-7939 9400

SOUTHWELL AND NOTTINGHAM (YORK)

12TH BISHOP

Rt. Revd Paul Williams, *cons.* 2009, *trans.* 2015; Jubilee House, Westgate, Southwell NG25 0JH
Signs Paul Southwell and Nottingham

BISHOP SUFFRAGAN

Sherwood, Rt. Revd Anthony Porter, *cons.* 2006, *apptd* 2006; Jubilee House, Westgate, Southwell NG25 0JH

DEAN
Very Revd Nicola Sullivan, *apptd* 2016

Rector Chori, Paul Provost, *apptd* 2017

ARCHDEACONS
Newark, Ven. David Picken, *apptd* 2012
Nottingham, Ven. Phil Williams, *apptd* 2019

Chancellor, His Hon. Judge Ockelton
Registrar and Legal Secretary, Amanda Redgate

Chief Executive, Nigel Spraggins, Jubilee House, Westgate, Southwell, Notts NG25 0JH **T** 01636-814331

TRURO (CANTERBURY)

16TH BISHOP
Rt. Revd Philip Mounstephen, *cons.* 2018, *apptd* 2018; Lis Escop, Feock, Truro TR3 6QQ
Signs Philip Truro

BISHOP SUFFRAGAN
St Germans, Rt. Revd Christopher Goldsmith, DPHIL, *cons.* 2013, *apptd* 2013; Lis Escop, Feock, Truro TR3 6QQ

DEAN
Very Revd Roger Bush, *apptd* 2012

Organist and Director of Music, Chris Gray, *apptd* 2008

ARCHDEACONS
Bodmin, Ven. Audrey Elkington, *apptd* 2011
Cornwall, Ven. Paul Bryer, *apptd* 2019

Chancellor, Timothy Briden, *apptd* 1998
Registrar and Legal Secretary, Jos Moule
Diocesan Secretary, Esther Pollard, Church House, Woodlands Court, Truro Business Park, Threemilestone, Truro TR4 9NH **T** 01872-274351

WORCESTER (CANTERBURY)

113TH BISHOP
Rt. Revd Dr John Inge, *cons.* 2003, *apptd* 2007; The Bishop's Office, The Old Palace, Deansway, Worcester WR1 2JE
Signs John Wigorn

SUFFRAGAN BISHOP
Dudley, vacant; Bishop's House, 60 Bishop's Walk, Cradley Heath, West Midlands B64 7RH

DEAN
Very Revd Dr Peter Atkinson, *apptd* 2006

Director of Music, Samuel Hudson, *apptd* 2018

ARCHDEACONS
Dudley, Ven. Nikki Groarke, *apptd* 2014
Worcester, Ven. Robert Jones, *apptd* 2014

Chancellor, Charles Mynors, *apptd* 1999
Registrar and Legal Secretary, Stuart Ness
Diocesan Secretary, John Preston, The Old Palace, Deansway, Worcester WR1 2JE **T** 01905-20537

ROYAL PECULIARS

WESTMINSTER
The Collegiate Church of St Peter

Dean, vacant
Canon Steward, Revd Anthony Ball

Chapter Clerk, Receiver-General and Registrar, Paul Baumann, CBE; Chapter Office, 20 Dean's Yard, London SW1P 3PA
Organist, James O'Donnell, *apptd* 2000

Legal Secretary, Christopher Vyse, *apptd* 2000

WINDSOR
The Queen's Free Chapel of St George within Her Castle of Windsor

Dean, Rt. Revd David Conner, KCVO, *apptd* 1998
Chapter Clerk, Charlotte Manley, CVO, OBE, *apptd* 2003; Chapter Office, The Cloisters, Windsor Castle, Windsor, Berks SL4 1NJ
Director of Music, James Vivian, *apptd* 2013

OTHER ANGLICAN CHURCHES

THE CHURCH IN WALES

The Anglican Church was the established church in Wales from the 16th century until 1920, when the estrangement of the majority of Welsh people from Anglicanism resulted in disestablishment. Since then the Church in Wales has been an autonomous province consisting of six sees. The bishops are elected by an electoral college comprising elected lay and clerical members, who also elect one of the diocesan bishops as Archbishop of Wales.

The legislative body of the Church in Wales is the Governing Body, which has 138 members divided between the three orders of bishops, clergy and laity. Its president is the Archbishop of Wales and it meets twice annually. Its decisions are binding upon all members of the church. The church's property and finances are the responsibility of the Representative Body. There are 44,875 members of the Church in Wales, with 410 stipendiary clergy and 563 parishes.

THE REPRESENTATIVE BODY OF THE CHURCH IN WALES, 2 Callaghan Square, Cardiff CF10 5BT
T 029-2034 8200 *Secretary,* Simon Lloyd
13TH ARCHBISHOP OF WALES, Most Revd John Davies (Bishop of Swansea and Brecon), *elected* 2017
Signs John Cambrensis

BISHOPS
Bangor (81st), Rt. Revd Andrew John, *b.* 1964, *cons.* 2008, *elected* 2008; Ty'r Esgob, Bangor, Gwynedd LL57 2SS
Signs Andrew Bangor. *Stipendiary clergy,* 45
Llandaff (103rd), Rt. Revd June Osborne, *b.* 1953, *cons.* 2017, *elected* 2017; Llys Esgob, The Cathedral Green, Llandaff, Cardiff CF5 2YE
Signs June Landav. *Stipendiary clergy,* 107
Monmouth (11th), vacant; Bishopstow, Stow Hill, Newport NP20 4EA
Stipendiary clergy, 45
St Asaph (76th), Rt. Revd Gregory Cameron, *b.* 1959, *cons.* 2009, *elected* 2009; Esgobty, Upper Denbigh Road, St Asaph, Denbighshire LL17 0TW
Signs Gregory Llanelwy. *Stipendiary clergy,* 76
St David's (129th), Rt. Revd Joanna Penberthy, *b.* 1960, *cons.* 2017, *elected* 2016; Llys Esgob, Abergwili, Carmarthen SA31 2JG
Signs Joanna Tyddewi. *Stipendiary clergy,* 82
Swansea and Brecon (9th), Most Revd John Davies (also Archbishop of Wales), *b.* 1953, *cons.* 2008, *trans.* 2017; Ely Tower, Castle Square, Brecon, Powys LD3 9DJ
Signs John Cambrensis. *Stipendiary clergy,* 55

The stipend for a diocesan bishop of the Church in Wales is £45,956 a year for 2019–20.

SCOTTISH EPISCOPAL CHURCH

The Scottish Episcopal Church was founded after the Act of Settlement (1690) established the presbyterian nature of the Church of Scotland. The Scottish Episcopal Church is a member of the worldwide Anglican Communion. The governing authority is the General Synod, which consists of the Church's seven bishops, the conveners of the provincial Standing Committee, the conveners of the boards, the Church's representatives on the Anglican Consultative Council and 124 elected members (62 from the clergy and 62 from the laity). The General Synod meets once a year. The bishop who convenes and presides at meetings of the General Synod is called the 'primus' and is elected by his fellow bishops.

As at December 2018 there were 28,647 members of the Scottish Episcopal Church, seven bishops, around 500 serving clergy and 300 churches and places of worship.

THE GENERAL SYNOD OF THE SCOTTISH EPISCOPAL CHURCH, 21 Grosvenor Crescent, Edinburgh EH12 5EE T 0131-225 6357 W www.scotland.anglican.org
Secretary-General, John Stuart

PRIMUS OF THE SCOTTISH EPISCOPAL CHURCH, Most Revd Mark Strange (Bishop of Moray, Ross and Caithness), *elected* 2017

BISHOPS
Aberdeen and Orkney, Rt. Revd Anne Dyer, *b.* 1957, *cons.* 2018, *elected* 2017. *Clergy,* 50
Argyll and the Isles, Rt. Revd Kevin Pearson, *b.* 1954, *cons.* 2011, *elected* 2010. *Clergy,* 25
Brechin, Rt. Revd Andrew Swift, *b.* 1968, *cons.* 2018, *elected* 2018. *Clergy,* 36
Edinburgh, Rt. Revd Dr John Armes, *b.* 1955, *cons.* 2012, *elected* 2012. *Clergy,* 160
Glasgow and Galloway, vacant. *Clergy,* 110
Moray, Ross and Caithness, Most Revd Mark Strange, *b.* 1961, *cons.* 2007, *elected* 2007. *Clergy,* 60
St Andrews, Dunkeld and Dunblane, Rt. Revd Ian Paton, *elected* 2018. *Clergy,* 75
The minimum stipend of a diocesan bishop of the Scottish Episcopal Church for 2019 is £39,705 (ie 1.5 times the standard clergy stipend of £26,470).

CHURCH OF IRELAND

The Anglican Church was the established church in Ireland from the 16th century but never secured the allegiance of the majority and was disestablished in 1871. The Church of Ireland is divided into the provinces of Armagh and Dublin, each under an archbishop. The provinces are subdivided into 12 dioceses.

The legislative body is the General Synod, which has 660 members in total, divided between the House of Bishops (12 members) and the House of Representatives (216 clergy and 432 laity). The Archbishop of Armagh is elected by the House of Bishops; other episcopal elections are made by an electoral college.

There are around 375,000 members of the Church of Ireland, 249,000 in Northern Ireland and 126,000 in the Republic of Ireland. There are two archbishops, ten bishops and 441 stipendiary clergy.

CENTRAL OFFICE, Church of Ireland House, Church Avenue, Rathmines, Dublin D06 CF67 T (+353) (1) 497 8422
Chief Officer and Secretary-General of the Representative Church Body, David Ritchie

PROVINCE OF ARMAGH
Archbishop of Armagh, Primate of all Ireland and Metropolitan, Most Revd Richard Clarke, PHD, *b.* 1949, *cons.* 1996, *trans.* 2012. *Clergy,* 42

BISHOPS
Clogher, Rt. Revd John McDowell, *b.* 1956, *cons.* 2011, *elected* 2011. *Clergy,* 23

Connor, Rt. Revd Alan Abernethy, *b.* 1957, *cons.* 2007, *elected* 2007. *Clergy,* 70
Derry and Raphoe, vacant. *Clergy,* 46
Down and Dromore, Rt. Revd Harold Miller, *b.* 1950, *cons.* 1997, *elected* 1997. *Clergy,* 79
Kilmore, Elphin and Ardagh, Rt. Revd Ferran Glenfield, PHD *b.* 1954, *cons.* 2013, *elected* 2013. *Clergy,* 22
Tuam, Killala and Achonry, Rt. Revd Patrick Rooke, *b.* 1955, *cons.* 2011, *elected* 2011. *Clergy,* 10

PROVINCE OF DUBLIN
Archbishop of Dublin, Bishop of Glendalough, Primate of Ireland and Metropolitan, Most Revd Michael Jackson, PHD, DPHIL, *b.* 1956, *cons.* 2002, *trans.* 2011. *Clergy,* 61

BISHOPS
Cashel, Ferns and Ossory, Rt. Revd Michael Burrows, *b.* 1961, *cons.* 2006, *elected* 2006. *Clergy,* 32
Cork, Cloyne and Ross, Rt. Revd Paul Colton, PHD, *b.* 1960, *cons.* 1999, *elected* 1999. *Clergy,* 25
Limerick, Killaloe and Ardfert, Rt. Revd Kenneth Kearon, *b.* 1953, *cons.* 2015, *elected* 2014. *Clergy,* 16
Meath and Kildare, Most Revd Patricia Storey, *b.* 1960, *cons.* 2013, *elected* 2013. *Clergy,* 15

OVERSEAS

PRIMATES
Primates and Archbishops of Aotearoa, New Zealand and Polynesia, Most Revd Philip Richardson; Most Revd Don Tamihere
Primate of Australia, Most Revd Phillip Freier
Primate of Brazil, Most Revd Naudal Alves Gomes
Archbishop of the Province of Burundi, Most Revd Martin Nyaboho
Primate of Canada, Most Revd Linda Nicholls
Archbishop of the Province of Central Africa, Most Revd Albert Chama
Primate of the Central Region of America, Rt. Revd Julio Thompson
Primate of Chile, Most Revd Héctor Zavala Muñoz
Archbishop of the Province of Congo, Most Revd Zacharie Masimango Katanda
Archbishop of Hong Kong Sheng Kung Hui, Most Revd Paul Kwong
Archbishop of the Province of the Indian Ocean, Most Revd James Wong Yin Song
Primate of Japan (Nippon Sei Ko Kai), Most Revd Nathaniel Makoto Uematsu
Archbishop of Jerusalem and the Middle East, Most Revd Suheil Dawani
Primate and Archbishop of All Kenya, Most Revd Jackson Ole Sapit
Primate of Korea, Most Revd Moses Nagjun Yoo
Archbishop of Melanesia, Most Revd George Takeli
Presiding Bishop of Mexico, Most Revd Francisco Moreno
Archbishop of the Province of Myanmar (Burma), Most Revd Stephen Oo
Metropolitan and Primate of All Nigeria, Most Revd Nicholas Okoh
Archbishop of Papua New Guinea, Rt. Revd Allan Migi
Prime Bishop of the Philippines, Most Revd Joel Atiwag Pachao
Archbishop of the Province of Rwanda, Most Revd Laurent Mbanda
Archbishop of the Province of South East Asia, Most Revd Ng Moon Hing
Primate of Southern Africa, Most Revd Dr Thabo Makgoba
Presiding Bishop of South America, Most Revd Gregory Venables
Primate of the Province of South Sudan, Most Revd Justin Badi Arama

Archbishop of the Province of Sudan, Most Revd Ezekiel Kumir Kondo
Archbishop of Tanzania, Most Revd Maimbo Mndolwa
Archbishop of the Province of Uganda, Most Revd Stanley Ntagali
Presiding Bishop of the USA, Most Revd Michael Curry
Primate and Metropolitan of the Province of West Africa, Most Revd Dr Daniel Sarfo
Archbishop of the Province of the West Indies, Most Revd Howard Gregory

OTHER CHURCHES AND EXTRA-PROVINCIAL DIOCESES

Anglican Church of Bermuda, extra-provincial to Canterbury
Bishop, Rt. Revd Nicholas Dill
Church of Ceylon, extra-provincial to Canterbury
Bishop of Colombo, Rt. Revd Dhiloraj Canagasabey
Bishop of Kurunegala, Rt. Revd Keerthisiri Fernando
Episcopal Church of Cuba, Rt. Revd Griselda Del Carpio
Falkland Islands, extra-provincial to Canterbury
Bishop, Rt. Revd Timothy Thornton (Bishop to the Forces)
Lusitanian Church (Portuguese Episcopal Church), extra-provincial to Canterbury
Bishop, Rt. Revd Jose Cabral
Reformed Episcopal Church of Spain, extra-provincial to Canterbury
Bishop, Rt. Revd Carlos López-Lozano

MODERATION OF CHURCHES IN FULL COMMUNION WITH THE ANGLICAN COMMUNION

Church of Bangladesh, Most Revd Samuel Mankhin
Church of North India, Most Revd Dr Prem Chand Singh
Church of South India, Most Revd Thomas Oommen
Church of Pakistan, Most Revd Humphrey Peters

CHURCH OF SCOTLAND

The Church of Scotland is the national church of Scotland. The church is reformed in doctrine, and presbyterian in constitution; ie based on a hierarchy of courts of ministers and elders and, since 1990, of members of a diaconate. At local level the Kirk Session consists of the parish minister and ruling elders. At district level the presbyteries, of which there are 44 in Britain, consist of all the ministers in the district, one ruling elder from each congregation, and those members of the diaconate who qualify for membership. The General Assembly is the supreme authority, and is presided over by a Moderator chosen annually by the Assembly. The sovereign, if not present in person, is represented by a Lord High Commissioner who is appointed each year by the Crown. In May 2019 the General Assembly voted in favour of replacing the Council of Assembly with a new 12-person body, the Assembly Trustees, from June 2019. The Assembly Trustees appoint a chief officer, who has oversight of budgets and staff, and other office bearers.

The Church of Scotland has around 360,000 members, 780 parish ministers and 30,000 elders. The majority of parishes are in Scotland, but there are also churches in England, Europe and overseas.

Lord High Commissioner (2019–20), Duke of Buccleuch and Queensberry, KT, KBE
Moderator of the General Assembly (2019–20), Rt. Revd Colin Sinclair
Principal Clerk, Revd Dr George Whyte
Procurator, James McNeill, QC
Law Agent and Solicitor of the Church, Mary Macleod
Parliamentary Officer, Chloe Clemmons
General Treasurer, Anne Macintosh
Convener to the Assembly Trustees, Very Revd D John Chalmers

CHURCH OFFICE, 121 George Street, Edinburgh EH2 4YN
T 0131-225 5722

PRESBYTERIES AND CLERKS
Aberdeen, Revd Dr John Ferguson
Abernethy, Revd James MacEwan
Angus, Revd Dr Ian McLean
Annandale and Eskdale, Revd Adam Dillon
Ardrossan, Jean Hunter
Argyll, Dr Christopher Brett
Ayr, Revd Kenneth Elliott
Buchan, Revd Sheila Kirk
Caithness, Revd Ronald Johnstone
Dumbarton, David Sinclair
Dumfries and Kirkcudbright, Revd Donald Campbell
Dundee, Revd James Wilson
Dunfermline, Revd Iain Greenshields
Dunkeld and Meigle, Revd John Russell
Duns, David Philp
Edinburgh, Revd Marjory McPherson
England, Revd Alistair Cumming
Falkirk, Revd Andrew Sarle
Glasgow, Revd George Cowie
Gordon, Revd Euan Glen
Greenock and Paisley, Revd Dr Peter McEnhill
Hamilton, Revd Dr Gordon McCracken
International, Revd Jim Sharp
Inverness, Revd Trevor Hunt
Irvine and Kilmarnock, Steuart Dey
Jedburgh, Revd Lisa-Jane Rankin
Jerusalem, Revd Joanna Oakley-Levstein
Kincardine and Deeside, Revd Hugh Conkey
Kirkcaldy, Revd Alan Kimmitt
Lanark, Revd Bryan Kerr
Lewis, John Cunningham
Lochaber, Revd Donald McCorkindale
Lochcarron-Skye, Revd John Murray
Lothian, John McCulloch
Melrose and Peebles, Revd Victoria Linford
Moray, Revd Alastair Gray
Orkney, Dr Mike Partridge
Perth, Revd Colin Caskie
Ross, Cath Chambers
St Andrews, Revd Nigel Robb
Shetland, Revd Deborah Dobby
Stirling, Revd Alan Miller
Sutherland, Revd Ian McCree
Uist, Revd Gavin Elliott
West Lothian, Revd Duncan Shaw
Wigtown and Stranraer, Sam Scobie

The stipends for ministers in the Church of Scotland in 2019 range from £27,585–£33,899, depending on length of service.

ROMAN CATHOLIC CHURCH

The Roman Catholic Church is a worldwide Christian church acknowledging as its head the Bishop of Rome, known as the Pope (father). Despite its widespread usage, 'Pope' is actually an unofficial term. The Annuario Pontificio, (Pontifical Yearbook) lists eight official titles: Bishop of Rome, Vicar of Jesus Christ, Successor of the Prince of the Apostles, Supreme Pontiff of the Universal Church, Primate of Italy, Archbishop and Metropolitan of the Roman Province, Sovereign of the State of the Vatican City and Servant of the Servants of God.

The Pope leads a communion of followers of Christ, who believe they continue His presence in the world as servants of faith, hope and love to all society. The Pope is held to be the successor of St Peter and thus invested with the power which was entrusted to St Peter by Jesus Christ. A direct line of succession is therefore claimed from the earliest Christian communities. With the fall of the Roman Empire the Pope also became an important political leader. His territory is now limited to the 0.44 sq. km (0.17 sq. miles) of the Vatican City State, created to provide some independence to the Pope from Italy and other nations. The episcopal jurisdiction of the Roman Catholic Church is called the Holy See.

The Pope exercises spiritual authority over the church with the advice and assistance of the Sacred College of Cardinals, the supreme council of the church. The number of cardinals was fixed at 70 by Pope Sixtus V in 1586 but has increased steadily since the pontificate of John XXIII. On 28 February 2013, the date of Pope Benedict XVI's resignation, there were 207 cardinals.

Following the death or resignation of the Pope, the members of the College of Cardinals under the age of 80 are called to the Vatican to elect a successor. They are known as cardinal electors and form an assembly called the conclave. The conclave, which comprised 115 cardinal electors when it convened in March 2013, conducts a secret ballot in complete seclusion to elect the next Pope. A two-thirds majority is necessary before the vote can be accepted as final. When a cardinal receives the necessary number of votes, the Dean of the Sacred College formally asks him if he will accept election and the name by which he wishes to be known. On his acceptance of the office of Supreme Pontiff, the conclave is dissolved and the first Cardinal Deacon announces the election to the assembled crowd in St Peter's Square.

The Pope has full legislative, judicial and administrative power over the whole Roman Catholic Church. He is aided in his administration by the curia, which is made up of a number of departments. The Secretariat of State is the central office for carrying out the Pope's instructions and is presided over by the Cardinal Secretary of State. It maintains relations with the departments of the curia, with the episcopate, with the representatives of the Holy See in various countries, governments and private persons. The congregations and pontifical councils are the Pope's ministries and include departments such as the Congregation for the Doctrine of Faith, whose field of competence concerns faith and morals; the Congregation for the Clergy and the Congregation for the Evangelisation of Peoples, the Pontifical Council for the Family and the Pontifical Council for the Promotion of Christian Unity.

The Holy See, composed of the Pope and those who help him in his mission for the church, is recognised by the Conventions of Vienna as an international moral body. Apostolic nuncios are the Pope's diplomatic representatives; in countries where no formal diplomatic relations exist between the Holy See and that country, the papal representative is known as an apostolic delegate.

According to the 2019 Pontifical Yearbook the number of baptised Roman Catholics worldwide was 1,313 million in 2017 and there were 414,582 priests.

SUPREME PONTIFF

His Holiness Pope Francis (Jorge Mario Bergoglio), *born* Buenos Aires, Argentina, 17 December 1936; *ordained priest* 13 December 1969; *appointed Archbishop* (of Buenos Aires), 28 February 1998; *created Cardinal* 21 February 2001; *assumed pontificate* 13 March 2013

PONTIFF EMERITUS

His Holiness Pope Benedict XVI (Joseph Ratzinger), *born* Bavaria, Germany, 16 April 1927; *ordained priest* 29 June 1951; *appointed Archbishop* (of Munich), 24 March 1977; *created Cardinal* 27 June 1977; *assumed pontificate* 19 April 2005; *resigned pontificate* 28 February 2013

SECRETARIAT OF STATE

Secretary of State, His Eminence Cardinal Pietro Parolin
First Section (General Affairs), Most Revd Edgar Peña Parra (Titular Archbishop of Thélepte)
Second Section (Relations with Other States), Most Revd Paul Gallagher (Titular Archbishop of Hodelm)

BISHOPS' CONFERENCE

The Catholic Bishops' Conference of England and Wales is the permanent assembly of Catholic Bishops and Ordinaries in the two member countries. The membership of the Conference comprises the Archbishops, Bishops and Auxiliary Bishops of the 22 Dioceses within England and Wales, the Bishop of the Forces (Military Ordinariate), the Apostolic Eparchs of the Ukrainian Church and Syro-Malabar Catholics in Great Britain, the Ordinary of the Personal Ordinariate of Our Lady of Walsingham, and the Apostolic Prefect of the Falkland Islands. The Conference is headed by a president and vice-president. There are six departments, each with an episcopal chair: Christian Life and Worship, Dialogue and Unity, Education and Formation, Evangelisation and Catechesis, International Affairs, and Social Justice.

The Bishops' Conference Standing Committee is made up of two directly elected bishops in addition to the Metropolitan Archbishops and chairs from each of the above departments. The committee has general responsibility for continuity of policy between the plenary sessions of the conference, preparing the conference agenda and implementing its decisions.

The administration of the Bishops' Conference is funded by a levy on each diocese, according to income. A general secretariat in London coordinates and supervises the Bishops' Conference administration activities. There are also other agencies and consultative bodies affiliated to the conference.

The Bishops' Conference of Scotland is the permanently constituted assembly of the eight bishops of Scotland. The conference is headed by the president (Rt. Revd. Hugh Gilbert, Bishop of Aberdeen). The conference establishes various agencies which perform advisory functions in relation to the conference. The more important of these agencies are called commissions; each one is headed by a bishop president who, with the other members of the commissions, are appointed by the conference.

The Irish Catholic Bishops' Conference (also known as the Irish Episcopal Conference) has as its president the Most Revd Eamon Martin (Archbishop of Armagh and Primate of All Ireland). Its membership comprises all the archbishops and bishops of Ireland. It appoints various commissions and agencies to assist with the work of the Catholic Church in Ireland.

The Catholic Church in the UK has over 900,000 mass attendees, 5,500 priests and 4,550 churches.

Bishops' Conferences secretariats:
ENGLAND AND WALES, 39 Eccleston Square, London SW1V 1BX T 020-7630 8220 W www.cbcew.org.uk
General Secretary, Revd Christopher Thomas
SCOTLAND, 64 Aitken Street, Airdrie ML6 6LT T 01236-764061 W www.bcos.org.uk
General Secretary, Fr James Grant
IRELAND, Columba Centre, Maynooth, County Kildare W23 P6D3 T (+353) (1) 505 3000 E info@catholicbishops.ie W www.catholicbishops.ie
Episcopal Secretary, Most Revd Kieran O'Reilly (Archbishop of Cashel and Emly)
Executive Secretary, Mgr Gearóid Dullea

GREAT BRITAIN

APOSTOLIC NUNCIO TO GREAT BRITAIN

HE Most Revd Edward Joseph Adams (Titular Archbishop of Scala), *apptd* 2017. *Apostolic Nunciature*, 54 Parkside, London SW19 5NE T 020-8944 7189

ENGLAND AND WALES

THE MOST REVD ARCHBISHOPS

Westminster, HE Cardinal Vincent Nichols, *cons.* 1992, *apptd* 2009 *Auxiliaries*, John Sherrington, *cons.* 2011; Nicholas Hudson, *cons.* 2014; Paul McAleenan, *cons.* 2016; John Sherrington, *cons.* 2011. *Clergy*, 318. *Archbishop's House*, Ambrosden Avenue, London SW1P 1QJ T 020-7798 9033

Birmingham, Bernard Longley, *cons.* 2003, *apptd* 2009 *Auxiliaries*, William Kenney, *cons.* 1987; David McGough, *cons.* 2005; Robert Byrne, *cons.* 2014. *Clergy*, 430. *Archbishop's House*, 8 Shadwell Street, Birmingham B4 6EY T 0121-236 9090

Cardiff, George Stack, *cons.* 2001, *apptd* 2011. *Clergy*, 47. *Archbishop's House*, 41–43 Cathedral Road, Cardiff CF11 9HD T 029-2022 0411

Liverpool, Malcolm McMahon, *cons.* 2000, *apptd* 2014 *Auxiliary*, Tom Williams, *cons.* 2003. *Clergy*, 402. *Archbishop's House*, 19 Salisbury Road, Cressington Park, Liverpool L19 0PH T 0151-494 0686

Southwark, John Wilson, *cons.* 2016, *apptd* 2019 *Auxiliaries*, Patrick Lynch, *cons.* 2006; Paul Hendricks, *cons.* 2006. *Clergy*, 366. *Archbishop's House*, 150 St George's Road, London SE1 6HX T 020-7928 2495

THE RT. REVD BISHOPS

Arundel and Brighton, Richard Moth, *cons.* 2009, *apptd* 2015. *Clergy*, 95. *Bishop's House*, High Oaks, Old Brighton Road North, Pease Pottage RH11 9AJ T 01293-526428

Brentwood, Alan Williams, *cons.* 2014, *apptd* 2014. *Clergy*, 170. *Bishop's Office*, Cathedral House, Ingrave Road, Brentwood, Essex CM15 8AT T 01277-232266

Clifton, Declan Lang, *cons.* 2001, *apptd* 2001. *Clergy*, 153. *Bishop's House*, St Ambrose, North Road, Leigh Woods, Bristol BS8 3PW T 0117-973 3072

East Anglia, Alan Hopes, *cons.* 2003, *apptd* 2013. *Clergy*, 129. *Diocesan Curia*, The White House, 21 Upgate, Poringland, Norwich NR14 7SH T 01508-492202

Hallam, Ralph Heskett, *cons.* 2010, *apptd* 2014. *Clergy*, 71. *Bishop's House*, 75 Norfolk Road, Sheffield S2 2SZ T 0114-278 7988

Hexham and Newcastle, Robert Byrne, *cons.* 2014, *apptd* 2019. *Clergy*, 164. *Bishop's House*, 800 West Road, Newcastle upon Tyne NE5 2BJ T 0191-228 0003

Lancaster, Paul Swarbrick, *cons.* 2018, *apptd* 2018. *Clergy*, 97. *Bishop's Office*, The Pastoral Centre, Balmoral Road, Lancaster LA1 3BT T 01524-596050

Leeds, Marcus Stock, *cons.* 2014, *apptd* 2014. *Clergy*, 193. *Diocesan Curia*, Hinsley Hall, 62 Headingley Lane, Leeds LS6 2BX T 0113-230 4533

Menevia (Wales), vacant. *Clergy*, 60. *Diocesan Office*, 27 Convent Street, Swansea SA1 2BX T 01792-644017

Middlesbrough, Terence Drainey, *cons.* 2008, *apptd* 2007. *Clergy*, 50. *Diocesan Curia*, 16 Cambridge Road, Middlesbrough TS5 5NN T 01642-850505

Northampton, Peter Doyle, *cons.* 2005, *apptd* 2005. *Clergy*, 116. *Bishop's House*, Marriott Street, Northampton NN2 6AW T 01604-715635

Nottingham, Patrick McKinney, *cons.* 2015, *apptd* 2015. *Clergy*, 166. *Diocesan Curia*, 27 Cavendish Road East, The Park, Nottingham NG7 1BB T 0115-947 4786

Plymouth, Mark O'Toole, *cons.* 2014, *apptd* 2013. *Clergy*, 50. *Bishop's House*, 45 Cecil Street, Plymouth PL1 5HW T 01752-224414

Portsmouth, Philip Egan, *cons.* 2012, *apptd* 2012. *Clergy*, 214. *Bishop's House*, Bishop Crispian Way, Portsmouth, Hants PO1 3HG T 023-9282 0894

Salford, John Arnold, *cons.* 2006, *apptd* 2014. *Clergy*, 218. *Diocesan Curia*, Wardley Hall, Worsley, Manchester M28 2ND T 0161-794 2825

Shrewsbury, Mark Davies, *cons.* 2010, *apptd* 2010. *Clergy* 112. *Diocesan Curia*, 2 Park Road South, Prenton, Wirral CH43 4UX T 0151-652 9855

Wrexham (Wales), Peter Brignall, *cons.* 2012, *apptd* 2012. *Clergy*, 16. *Bishop's House*, Sontley Road, Wrexham LL13 7EW T 01978-262726

SCOTLAND

THE MOST REVD ARCHBISHOPS

St Andrews and Edinburgh, Leo Cushley, *cons.* 2013, *apptd* 2013. *Clergy*, 50. *Archdiocese Offices*, 100 Strathearn Road, Edinburgh EH9 1BB T 0131-623 8900

Glasgow, Philip Tartaglia, *cons.* 2005, *apptd* 2012. *Clergy*, 198. *Diocesan Curia*, 196 Clyde Street, Glasgow G1 4JY T 0141-226 5898

THE RT. REVD BISHOPS

Aberdeen, Hugh Gilbert, *cons.* 2011, *apptd* 2011. *Clergy*, 47. *Bishop's House*, 3 Queen's Cross, Aberdeen AB15 4XU T 01224-319154

Argyll and the Isles, Brian McGee, *cons.* 2016, *apptd* 2015. *Clergy*, 32. *Diocesan Office* Bishop's House, Esplanade, Oban, Argyll PA34 5AB T 01631-567436

Dunkeld, Stephen Robson, *cons.* 2012, *apptd* 2013. *Clergy*, 43. *Diocesan Curia*, 24–28 Lawside Road, Dundee DD3 6XY T 01382-225453

Galloway, William Nolan, *cons.* 2015, *apptd* 2014. *Clergy*, 19. *Diocesan Office*, 8 Corsehill Road, Ayr KA7 2ST T 01292-266750

Motherwell, Joseph Toal, *cons.* 2008, *trans.* 2014. *Clergy*, 123. *Diocesan Curia*, Coursington Road, Motherwell ML1 1PP T 01698-269114

Paisley, John Keenan, *cons.* 2014, *apptd* 2014. *Clergy*, 75. *Diocesan Curia*, Cathedral Precincts, Incle Street, Paisley PA1 1HR T 0141-847 6131

BISHOPRIC OF THE FORCES

Rt. Revd Paul Mason, *cons.* 2016, *apptd* 2018. *Administration*, RC Bishopric of the Forces, Wellington House, St Omer Barracks, Thornhill Road, Aldershot, Hants GU11 2BG T 01252-348234

IRELAND

There is one hierarchy for the whole of Ireland. Several of the dioceses have territory partly in the Republic of Ireland and partly in Northern Ireland.

APOSTOLIC NUNCIO TO IRELAND

Most Revd Jude Thaddeus Okolo (Titular Archbishop of Novica), *apptd* 2017. *Apostolic Nunciature*, 183 Navan Road, Dublin 7 T (+353) (1) 838 0577

THE MOST REVD ARCHBISHOPS

Armagh, Eamon Martin (*also* Primate of All Ireland), *cons.* 2013, *apptd* 2014. *Archbishop Emeritus*, HE Cardinal Seán Brady *cons.* 1995, *elevated* 2007. *Auxiliary*, Michael Router, *cons.* 2019. *Clergy*, 135. *Bishop's Residence*, Ara Coeli, Cathedral Road, Armagh BT61 7QY T 028-3752 2045

Cashel and Emly, Kieran O'Reilly, *cons.* 2010, *apptd* 2015. *Clergy*, 83. *Archbishop's House*, Thurles, Co. Tipperary T (+353) (504) 21512

Dublin, Diarmuid Martin (*also* Primate of Ireland), *cons.* 1999, *apptd Coadjutor Archbishop* 2003, *succeeded as Archbishop* 2004. *Auxiliary*, Éamonn Walsh, *cons.* 1990. *Clergy*, 389. *Archbishop's House*, Drumcondra, Dublin 9 T (+353) (1) 837 3732

Tuam, Dr Michael Neary, *cons.* 1992, *apptd* 1995. *Clergy*, 110. *Archbishop's House*, Tuam, Co. Galway T (+353) (93) 24166

THE MOST REVD BISHOPS

Achonry, vacant. *Clergy*, 50. *Bishop's House*, Edmondstown, Ballaghaderreen, Co. Roscommon T (+353) (94) 986 0034
Ardagh and Clonmacnois, Francis Duffy, *cons.* 2013, *apptd* 2013. *Clergy*, 60. *Diocesan Office*, St Mel's, Longford T (+353) (43) 334 6432
Clogher, Lawrence Duffy, *cons.* 2019, *apptd* 2019. *Clergy*, 74. *Bishop's House*, Monaghan T (+353) (47) 81019
Clonfert, John Kirby, *cons.* 1988, *apptd* 1988. *Clergy*, 37. *Bishop's House*, Coorheen, Loughrea, Co. Galway T (+353) (91) 841560
Cloyne, William Crean, *cons.* 2013, *apptd* 2013. *Clergy*, 126. *Diocesan Office*, Cobh, Co. Cork T (+353) (21) 481 1430
Cork and Ross, Fintan Gavin, *cons.* 2019, *apptd* 2019. *Clergy*, 133. *Diocesan Office*, Cork and Ross Offices, Redemption Road, Cork T (+353) (21) 430 1717
Derry, Dónal McKeown, *cons.* 2001, *apptd* 2014. *Clergy*, 108. *Bishop's House*, PO Box 227, Derry BT48 9YG T 028-7126 2302
Down and Connor, Noël Treanor, *cons.* 2008, *apptd* 2008. *Clergy*, 199. *Bishop's Residence*, Lisbreen, 73 Somerton Road, Belfast, Co. Antrim BT15 4DE T 028-9077 6185
Dromore, vacant. *Clergy*, 364. *Bishop's House*, 44 Armagh Road, Newry, Co. Down BT35 6PN T 028-3026 2444
Elphin, Kevin Doran, *cons.* 2014, *apptd* 2014. *Clergy*, 66. *Bishop's House*, Temple St, St Mary's, Sligo T (+353) (71) 915 0106
Ferns, Denis Brennan, *cons.* 2006, *apptd* 2006. *Clergy*, 88. *Bishop's House*, Summerhill, Wexford T (+353) (53) 912 2177
Galway, Kilmacduagh and Kilfenora, Brendan Kelly, *cons.* 2008, *apptd* 2018. *Clergy*, 57. *Diocesan Office*, The Cathedral, Galway T (+353) (91) 563566
Kerry, Ray Browne, *cons.* 2013, *apptd* 2013. *Clergy*, 88. *Bishop's House*, Killarney, Co. Kerry T (+353) (64) 663 1168
Kildare and Leighlin, Denis Nulty, *cons.* 2013, *apptd* 2013. *Clergy*, 72. *Bishop's House*, Old Dublin Road, Carlow Town T (+353) (59) 917 6725
Killala, John Fleming, *cons.* 2002, *apptd* 2002. *Clergy*, 40. *Bishop's House*, Ballina, Co. Mayo T (+353) (96) 21518
Killaloe, Fintan Monahan, *cons.* 2016, *apptd* 2016. *Clergy*, 95. *Diocesan Office*, Westbourne, Ennis, Co. Clare T (+353) (65) 682 8638
Kilmore, vacant. *Clergy*, 67. *Bishop's House*, Cullies, Cavan, Co. Cavan T (+353) (49) 433 1496
Limerick, Brendan Leahy, *cons.* 2013, *apptd* 2013. *Clergy*, 109. *Diocesan Office*, Social Service Centre, Henry Street, Limerick T (+353) (61) 315856
Meath, Thomas Deenihan, *cons.* 2018, *apptd* 2018. *Clergy*, 120. *Bishop's House*, Dublin Road, Mullingar, Co. Westmeath T (+353) (44) 934 8841
Ossory, Dermot Farrell, *cons.* 2018, *apptd* 2018. *Clergy*, 81. *Diocesan Office*, James's Street, Kilkenny T (+353) (56) 776 2448
Raphoe, Alan McGuckian, *cons.* 2017, *apptd* 2017. *Clergy*, 80. *Bishop's House*, Ard Adhamhnáin, Letterkenny, Co. Donegal T (+353) (74) 912 1208
Waterford and Lismore, Alphonsus Cullinan, *cons.* 2015, *apptd* 2015. *Clergy*, 114. *Bishop's House*, John's Hill, Waterford T (+353) (51) 874463

OTHER CHURCHES IN THE UK

ASSOCIATED PRESBYTERIAN CHURCHES OF SCOTLAND

The Associated Presbyterian Churches came into being in 1989 as a result of a division within the Free Presbyterian Church of Scotland. The Associated Presbyterian Churches is reformed and evangelistic in nature and emphasises the importance of doctrine based primarily on the Bible and secondly on the Westminster Confession of Faith. There are an estimated 500 members, 8 ministers and 18 congregations in Scotland. There are also congregations in Canada.

ASSOCIATED PRESBYTERIAN CHURCHES OF SCOTLAND, Bruach Taibh, 2 Borve, Arnisort, Isle of Skye IV51 9PS T 01470-582264 W www.apchurches.org
Presbytery Clerk, Revd J.R. Ross Macaskill

BAPTIST CHURCH

Baptists trace their origins to John Smyth, who in 1609 in Amsterdam reinstituted the baptism of conscious believers as the basis of the fellowship of a gathered church. Members of Smyth's church established the first Baptist church in England in 1612. They came to be known as 'General' Baptists and their theology was Arminian, whereas a later group of Calvinists who adopted the baptism of believers came to be known as 'Particular' Baptists. The two sections of the Baptists were united into one body in 1891: the Baptist Union of Great Britain and Ireland (renamed the Baptist Union of Great Britain in 1988).

Baptists emphasise the complete autonomy of the local church, although individual churches are linked in various kinds of associations. There are international bodies (such as the Baptist World Alliance) and national bodies, but some Baptist churches belong to neither. However, in Great Britain the majority of churches and associations belong to the Baptist Union of Great Britain. There are also Baptist unions in Wales, Scotland and Ireland and there is some overlap of membership.

There are currently around 135,000 members, 2,500 ministers and 2,080 churches associated with the Baptist Union of Great Britain. The Baptist Union of Great Britain is one of the founder members of the European Baptist Federation (1948) and the Baptist World Alliance (1905); the latter represents 42 million members worldwide.

In the Baptist Union of Wales (Undeb Bedyddwyr Cymru) there are 11,355 members, 88 pastors and 386 churches, including those in England.

In the Baptist Union of Scotland there are 11,500 members and 161 churches.

BAPTIST UNION OF GREAT BRITAIN, Baptist House, PO Box 44, 129 Broadway, Didcot, Oxon OX11 8RT T 01235-517700 W www.baptist.org.uk
President (2019–20), Revd Ken Benjamin
General Secretary, Lynn Green

BAPTIST UNION OF WALES, Y Llwyfan, College Road, Carmarthen SA31 3EQ T 01267-245660 E mennajones@ubc.cymru W www.buw.org.uk
President of the Welsh Assembly (2019–20), David Peregrine
President of the English Assembly (2019–20), Janet Matthews
General Secretary of the Baptist Union of Wales, Revd Judith Morris

BAPTIST UNION OF SCOTLAND, 48 Speirs Wharf, Glasgow G4 9TH T 0141-423 6169 E admin@scottishbaptist.org.uk W www.scottishbaptist.com
General Director, Revd Martin Hodson

THE BRETHREN

The Brethren was founded in Dublin in 1827–8, basing itself on the structures and practices of the early church and rejecting denominationalism and clericalism. Many groups sprang up; the group at Plymouth became the best known, resulting in its designation by others as the 'Plymouth Brethren'. Early worship had a prescribed form but quickly assumed an unstructured, non-liturgical format.

There are services devoted to worship, usually involving the breaking of bread, and separate preaching meetings. There is no salaried ministry.

A theological dispute led in 1848 to schism between the Open Brethren and the Closed or Exclusive Brethren, each branch later suffering further divisions.

Open Brethren churches are run by appointed elders and are completely independent, but freely cooperate with each other. Exclusive Brethren churches believe in a universal fellowship between congregations. They do not have appointed elders, but use respected members of their congregation to perform certain administrative functions.

There are a number of publishing houses that publish Brethren-related literature. Chapter Two is the main supplier of such literature in the UK; it also has a Brethren history archive which is available for use by appointment.

CHAPTER TWO, 3 Conduit Mews, London SE18 7AP
T 020-8316 5389 E info@chaptertwobooks.org.uk
W www.chaptertwobooks.org.uk

CONGREGATIONAL FEDERATION

The Congregational Federation was founded by members of Congregational churches in England and Wales who did not join the United Reformed Church in 1972. There are also churches in Scotland and France affiliated to the federation. The federation exists to encourage congregations of believers to worship in free assembly, but it has no authority over them and emphasises their right to independence and self-governance.

The federation has around 7,000 members, 187 accredited ministers and 265 churches in England, Wales and Scotland.

CONGREGATIONAL FEDERATION, 8 Castle Gate,
Nottingham NG1 7AS T 0115-911 1460
E admin@congregational.org.uk W www.congregational.org.uk
President of the Federation (2019–20), Revd Dr Janet Wootton
General Secretary, Yvonne Campbell

FELLOWSHIP OF INDEPENDENT EVANGELICAL CHURCHES

The Fellowship of Independent Evangelical Churches (FIEC) was founded by Revd E. J. Poole-Connor (1872–1962) in 1922. In 1923 the fellowship published its first register of non-denominational pastors, evangelists and congregations who had accepted the doctrinal basis for the fellowship.

Members of the fellowship have two primary convictions: firstly to defend the evangelical faith, and secondly that evangelicalism is the bond that unites the fellowship, rather than forms of worship or church government.

The FIEC exists to promote the welfare of non-denominational Bible churches and to give expression to the fundamental doctrines of evangelical Christianity. It supports individual churches by providing resources and advising churches on current theological, moral, social and practical issues.

There are currently around 600 churches affiliated to the fellowship.

FELLOWSHIP OF INDEPENDENT EVANGELICAL
CHURCHES, 39 The Point, Market Harborough, Leics LE16
7QU T 01858-434540 E admin@fiec.org.uk W www.fiec.org.uk
National Director, John Stevens

FREE CHURCH OF ENGLAND

The Free Church of England, otherwise called the Reformed Episcopal Church, is an independent episcopal church, constituted according to the historic faith, tradition and practice of the Church of England. Its roots lie in the 18th century, but it started to grow significantly from the 1840s onwards, as clergy and congregations joined it from the established church in protest against the Oxford Movement. The historic episcopate was conferred on the English church in 1876 through bishops of the Reformed Episcopal Church (which had broken away from the Protestant Episcopal Church in the USA in 1873). A branch of the Reformed Episcopal Church was founded in the UK and this merged with the Free Church of England in 1927 to create the present church. The Orders of the Free Church of England are recognised by the Church of England.

Worship is according to the Book of Common Prayer and some modern liturgy is permissible. Only men are ordained to the orders of deacon, presbyter and bishop.

The Free Church of England has two dioceses, 19 congregations and around 900 members in England. There is one congregation in St Petersburg, Russia and three congregations and six missions in Brazil.

THE FREE CHURCH OF ENGLAND, 329 Wolverhampton
Road West, Willenhall, W. Midlands WV13 2RL T 01902-607335
W www.fcofe.org.uk
Bishop Primus, Rt. Revd Dr John Fenwick (Bishop of the Northern Diocese)
General Secretary, Rt. Revd Paul Hunt (Bishop of the Southern Diocese)

FREE CHURCH OF SCOTLAND

The Free Church of Scotland was formed in 1843 when over 400 ministers withdrew from the Church of Scotland as a result of interference in the internal affairs of the church by the civil authorities. In 1900, all but 26 ministers joined with others to form the United Free Church (most of which rejoined the Church of Scotland in 1929). In 1904 the remaining 26 ministers were recognised by the House of Lords as continuing the Free Church of Scotland.

The church maintains strict adherence to the Westminster Confession of Faith (1648) and accepts the Bible as the sole rule of faith and conduct. Its general assembly meets annually. It also has links with reformed churches overseas. The Free Church of Scotland has about 13,000 members, 90 ministers and 100 congregations.

FREE CHURCH OF SCOTLAND, 15 North Bank Street,
The Mound, Edinburgh EH1 2LS T 0131-226 5286
E offices@freechurchofscotland.org.uk W www.freechurch.org
Chief Executive, Scott Matheson

FREE PRESBYTERIAN CHURCH OF SCOTLAND

The Free Presbyterian Church of Scotland was formed in 1893 by two ministers of the Free Church of Scotland who refused to accept a Declaratory Act passed by the Free Church General Assembly in 1892. The Free Presbyterian Church of Scotland is Calvinistic in doctrine and emphasises observance of the Sabbath. It adheres strictly to the Westminster Confession of Faith (1648).

The church has about 700 members in Scotland. It has 17 ministers and 40 churches in the UK.

FREE PRESBYTERIAN CHURCH OF SCOTLAND,
133 Woodlands Road, Glasgow G3 6LE
E outreach@fpchurch.org.uk W www.fpchurch.org.uk
Moderator (2019–20), Revd Roderick McLeod
Clerk of the Synod, Revd Keith Watkins

HOLY APOSTOLIC CATHOLIC ASSYRIAN CHURCH OF THE EAST

The Holy Apostolic Catholic Assyrian Church of the East traces its beginnings to the middle of the first century. It spread from Upper Mesopotamia throughout the territories of the Persian Empire. The Assyrian Church of the East became theologically separated from the rest of the Christian community following the Council of Ephesus in 431. The church is headed by the Catholicos Patriarch and is episcopal in government. The liturgical language is Syriac (Aramaic). The Assyrian Church of the East and the Roman Catholic Church agreed a common Christological declaration in 1994, and a process of dialogue between the Assyrian Church of the East and the Chaldean Catholic Church, which is in communion with Rome but shares the Syriac liturgy, was instituted in 1996.

The church has around 325,000 members in the Middle East, India, Russia, Europe, North America and Australasia. In Great Britain there is one parish, which is situated in London. The church in Great Britain forms part of the Diocese of Europe under HG Mar Odisho Oraham.

HOLY APOSTOLIC CATHOLIC ASSYRIAN CHURCH OF THE EAST, St Mary's Church Hall, 62 Greenford Avenue, Hanwell, London W7 3QP **T** 0786-873 7112

INDEPENDENT METHODIST CHURCHES

The Independent Methodist Churches were formed in 1805 and remained independent when the Methodist Church in Great Britain was formed in 1932. They are mainly concentrated in the industrial areas of the north of England.

The churches are Methodist in doctrine but their organisation is congregational. All the churches are members of the Independent Methodist Connexion of Churches. The controlling body of the Connexion is the Annual Meeting, to which churches send delegates. The Connexional President is elected every two years. Between annual meetings the affairs of the Connexion are handled by the Connexional Committee and departmental committees. Ministers are appointed by the churches and trained through the Connexion. The ministry is open to both men and women.

There are 1,600 members, 70 ministers and 74 churches in Great Britain.

INDEPENDENT METHODIST RESOURCE CENTRE, The Resource Centre, Fleet Street, Wigan WN5 0DS **T** 01942-223526 **E** resourcecentre@imchurches.org.uk **W** www.imchurches.org.uk
General Secretary, Brian Rowney

LUTHERAN CHURCH

Lutheranism is based on the teachings of Martin Luther, the German leader of the Protestant Reformation. The authority of the scriptures is held to be supreme over church tradition. The teachings of Lutheranism are explained in detail in 16th-century confessional writings, particularly the Augsburg Confession. Lutheranism is one of the largest Protestant denominations and it is particularly strong in northern Europe and the USA. Some Lutheran churches are episcopal, while others have a synodal form of organisation; unity is based on doctrine rather than structure. Most Lutheran churches are members of the Lutheran World Federation, based in Geneva.

Lutheran services in Great Britain are held in 15 languages to serve members of different nationalities. Services usually follow ancient liturgies. English-language congregations are members either of the Lutheran Church in Great Britain or of the Evangelical Lutheran Church of England. The Lutheran Church in Great Britain and other Lutheran churches in Britain are members of the Lutheran Council of Great Britain, which represents them and coordinates their common work.

There are around 70 million Lutherans worldwide, with around 180,000 members in Great Britain.

THE LUTHERAN COUNCIL OF GREAT BRITAIN, 30 Thanet Street, London WC1H 9QH **T** 020-7554 9753 **E** enquiries@lutheran.org.uk **W** www.lutheran.org.uk
Chair, Revd Torbjorn Holt
General Secretary, Malcolm Bruce

METHODIST CHURCH

The Methodist movement started in England in 1729 when the Revd John Wesley, an Anglican priest, and his brother Charles met with others in Oxford and resolved to conduct their lives by 'rule and method'. In 1739 the Wesleys began evangelistic preaching and the first Methodist chapel was founded in Bristol in the same year. In 1744 the first annual conference was held, at which the Articles of Religion were drawn up. Doctrinal emphases included repentance, faith, the assurance of salvation, social concern and the priesthood of all believers. After John Wesley's death in 1791 the Methodists withdrew from the established church to form the Methodist Church. Methodists gradually drifted into many groups, but in 1932 the Wesleyan Methodist Church, the United Methodist Church and the Primitive Methodist Church united to form the Methodist Church in Britain.

The governing body is the Conference. The Conference meets annually and consists of two parts: the ministerial and representative sessions. The Methodist Church is structured as a 'Connexion' of churches, circuits and districts. The local churches in a defined area form a circuit, and a number of these 368 circuits make up each of the 31 districts. The latest 2019 *Statistics for Mission* show that as at October 2018 the Methodist Church in Britain had 173,000 members, 1,600 active ministers and 4,271 local churches.

THE METHODIST CHURCH IN BRITAIN, Methodist Church House, 25 Marylebone Road, London NW1 5JR **T** 020-7486 5502 **E** enquiries@methodistchurch.org.uk **W** www.methodist.org.uk
Conference President (2019–20), Revd Barbara Glasson
Conference Vice-President (2019–20), Clive Marsh
Conference Secretary, Doug Swanney

THE METHODIST CHURCH IN IRELAND

The Methodist Church in Ireland is autonomous but has close links with British Methodism. As at December 2014 it had 45,828 members, 121 active ministers and 270 lay preachers.

METHODIST CHURCH IN IRELAND, 1 Fountainville Avenue, Belfast BT9 6AN **T** 028-9032 4554 **E** secretary@irishmethodist.org **W** www.irishmethodist.org
President of the Conference (2019–20), Revd Sam McGuffin
Lay Leader of the Conference (2019–20), Lynda Neilands
Secretary, Revd Tom McKnight

ORTHODOX CHURCHES

EASTERN ORTHODOX CHURCH

The Eastern (or Byzantine) Orthodox Church is a communion of self-governing Christian churches that recognises the honorary primacy of the Ecumenical Patriarch of Constantinople.

The position of Orthodox Christians is that the faith was fully defined during the period of the Oecumenical Councils. In doctrine it is strongly trinitarian, and stresses the mystery and importance of the sacraments. It is episcopal in government. The structure of the Orthodox Christian year differs from that of western churches.

Orthodox Christians throughout the world are estimated to number about 300 million; there are around 300,000 in the UK.

GREEK ORTHODOX CHURCH (PATRIARCHATE OF ANTIOCH)

The church is led by John X, Patriarch of Antioch, who was enthroned in February 2013. The Archdiocese of the British Isles and Ireland has 18 parishes, including St George's Cathedral in London, and 27 clergy.

ANTIOCHIAN ORTHODOX ARCHDIOCESE OF THE BRITISH ISLES AND IRELAND, St George's Cathedral, 1A Redhill Street, London NW1 4BG **T** 020-7383 0403 **E** fr.s.gholam@antiochianorth.co.uk **W** www.antiochian-orthodox.co.uk *Archbishop,* Metropolitan Silouan Oner

GREEK ORTHODOX CHURCH (PATRIARCHATE OF CONSTANTINOPLE)

The presence of Greek Orthodox Christians in Britain dates back at least to 1677 when Archbishop Joseph Geogirenes of Samos fled from Turkish persecution and came to London. The present Greek cathedral in Moscow Road, Bayswater, was opened for public worship in 1879, and the Diocese of Thyateira and Great Britain was established in 1922. There are now around 100 parishes and one monastery in the UK, served by one archbishop, three bishops and around 120 clergy.

THE PATRIARCHATE OF CONSTANTINOPLE IN GREAT BRITAIN, Archdiocese of Thyateira and Great Britain, Thyateira House, 5 Craven Hill, London W2 3EN **T** 020-7723 4787 **E** mail@thyateira.org.uk **W** www.thyateira.org.uk *Archbishop,* Nikitas of Thyateira and Great Britain

THE RUSSIAN ORTHODOX CHURCH (PATRIARCHATE OF MOSCOW)

The records of Russian Orthodox Church activities in Britain date from the visit to England of Tsar Peter I in the early 18th century. Clergy were sent from Russia to serve the chapel established to minister to the staff of the Imperial Russian Embassy in London.

In 2007, after an 80-year division, the Russian Orthodox Church Outside Russia agreed to become an autonomous part of the Russian Orthodox Church, Patriarchate of Moscow. The reunification agreement was signed by Patriarch Alexy II, 15th Patriarch of Moscow and All Russia and Metropolitan Laurus, leader of the Russian Orthodox Church Outside Russia on 17 May at a ceremony at Christ the Saviour Cathedral in Moscow. Patriarch Alexy II died on 5 December 2008. Metropolitan Kirill of Smolensk and Kaliningrad was enthroned as the 16th Patriarch of Moscow and All Russia on 1 February 2009, having been elected by a secret ballot of clergy on 27 January 2009.

The diocese of Sourozh is the diocese of the Russian Orthodox Church in Great Britain and Ireland and is led by Bishop Matthew of Sourozh.

DIOCESE OF SOUROZH, Diocesan Office, Cathedral of the Dormition of the Mother of God and All Saints, 67 Ennismore Gardens, London SW7 1NH **T** 020-7584 0096 **W** www.sourozh.org *Diocesan Hierarch,* Bishop Matthew of Sourozh

SERBIAN ORTHODOX CHURCH (PATRIARCHATE OF SERBIA)

There are seven parishes in Great Britain and around 4,000 members. Great Britain is part of the Diocese of Great Britain and Scandinavia, which is led by Bishop Dositey. The church can be contacted via the church of St Sava in London.

SERBIAN ORTHODOX CHURCH IN GREAT BRITAIN, Church of Saint Sava, 89 Lancaster Road, London W11 1QQ **T** 020-7727 8367 **E** crkva@spclondon.org.uk **W** www.spclondon.org.uk *Archpriest,* Very Revd Goran Spaic

OTHER NATIONALITIES

The Patriarchates of Romania and Bulgaria (Diocese of Western Europe) have memberships estimated at 20,000 and 2,000 respectively, while the Georgian Orthodox Church has around 500 members. The Belarusian (membership estimated at 2,400) and Latvian (membership of around 100).

ORIENTAL ORTHODOX CHURCHES

The term 'Oriental Orthodox Churches' is now generally used to describe a group of six ancient eastern churches (Armenian, Coptic, Eritrean, Ethiopian, Indian (Malankara) and Syrian) which rejected the Christological definition of the Council of Chalcedon (AD 451). There are around 50 million members worldwide of the Oriental Orthodox Churches and over 20,000 in the UK.

ARMENIAN ORTHODOX CHURCH (CATHOLICOSATE OF ETCHMIADZIN)

The Armenian Orthodox Church is led by HH Karekin II, Catholicos of All Armenians. HG Bishop Hovakim Manukyan was appointed Primate of the Armenian Church in the UK and Ireland in 2015.

ARMENIAN CHURCH IN THE UK AND IRELAND, The Armenian Vicarage, 27 Haven Green, London W5 2NZ **T** 020-8998 9210 **W** www.armeniandiocese.org.uk *Primate,* HG Bishop Hovakim Manukyan

COPTIC ORTHODOX CHURCH

The Coptic Orthodox Church is headed by Pope Tawadros II, who was appointed in November 2012. There are three dioceses in the UK: the Midlands, led by HG Bishop Missael; Ireland, Scotland and north-east England, led by HG Bishop Antony; and the Papal Diocese which is led by HG Bishop Angaelos and covers all the remaining parishes in the UK.

CATHEDRAL OF ST GEORGE AT THE COPTIC ORTHODOX CHURCH CENTRE, Shephalbury Manor, Broadhall Way, Stevenage, Herts SG2 8NP **T** 020-7993 9001 **W** www.copticcentre.com *Bishop,* HG Bishop Angaelos

BRITISH ORTHODOX CHURCH

The British Orthodox Church is a small autonomous Orthodox jurisdiction, originally deriving from the Syrian Orthodox Church. It was canonically part of the Coptic Orthodox Patriarchate of Alexandria from 1994–2015. As it ministers to British people, all of its services are in English.

THE BRITISH ORTHODOX CHURCH, 10 Heathwood Gardens, Charlton, London SE7 8EP **T** 020-8854 3090 **E** info@britishorthodox.org **W** www.britishorthodox.org *Metropolitan,* Abba Seraphim

ERITREAN ORTHODOX TEWAHEDO CHURCH

The Eritrean Orthodox Church was granted independence in 1994 by Pope Shenouda III, following the declaration of Eritrea's independence from Ethiopia in 1993. In 2006, the Eritrean government removed the third patriarch, Abune Antonios, from office and imprisoned him; the government replaced him with Abune Dioskoros in 2007, although the Oriental Orthodox Churches continue to recognise Antonios as the rightful patriarch. The diocesan bishop for North America, Europe and the Middle East is HG Abune Makarios.

ETHIOPIAN ORTHODOX TAWAHEDO CHURCH

The Ethiopian Orthodox Church was administratively part of the Coptic Orthodox Church of Alexandria until 1959, when it was granted its own patriarch by the Coptic Orthodox Pope of Alexandria and Patriarch of All Africa, Cyril VI. The current patriarch is HH Abune Mathias. The church in London was established in 1976.

ETHIOPIAN ORTHODOX TAWAHEDO CHURCH, St
Mary of Zion, PO Box 56856, London N13 5US T 020-8807 5885
E pc@tserhasion.org.uk W www.stmaryofzion.co.uk
Priest-in-Charge, Melake Sion Habte Mariam

INDIAN ORTHODOX CHURCH
The Indian Orthodox Church, also known as the Malankara
Orthodox Church, traces its origins to the first century. The
head of the Malankara Orthodox Church is HH Baselios
Marthoma Paulose II. The mother church of all the parishes
in the UK and the Republic of Ireland is St Gregorios Church
in London. The London parish has around 280 families as
practising members.

INDIAN ORTHODOX CHURCH, St Gregorios Indian
Orthodox Church, Cranfield Road, Brockley, London SE4 1UF
T 020-8691 9456 E ioclondon@gmail.com
W www.ioclondon.co.uk
Diocesan Metropolitan, HG Dr Mathews Mar Thimothios
Vicar, Revd Fr Aby P Varghese

SYRIAN ORTHODOX CHURCH
The Syrian (Syriac) Orthodox Church of Antioch is an
Oriental Orthodox Church based in the Eastern Mediterranean
headed by HH Moran Mor Ignatius Aphrem II. The
Patriarchate Vicariate in the UK is represented by HE
Archbishop Mor Athanasius Toma Dawod.

SYRIAN ORTHODOX CHURCH IN THE UK, St Thomas
Cathedral, 7–11 Armstrong Road, London W3 7JL
T 020-8749 5834 E enquiry-uk@syrianorthodoxchurch.net
W www.syrianorthodoxchurch.net
Archbishop, HE Mor Athanasius Toma Dawod

PENTECOSTAL CHURCHES
Pentecostalism is inspired by the descent of the Holy Spirit
upon the apostles at Pentecost. The movement began in Los
Angeles, USA, in 1906 and is characterised by baptism with
the Holy Spirit, divine healing, speaking in tongues
(glossolalia) and a literal interpretation of the scriptures.
The Pentecostal movement in Britain dates from 1907.
Initially, groups of Pentecostalists were led by laymen and
did not organise formally. However, in 1915 the Elim
Foursquare Gospel Alliance (more commonly called the Elim
Pentecostal Church) was founded in Ireland by George
Jeffreys and currently has about 550 churches, 68,500
adherents and 650 accredited ministers. In 1924 about 70
independent assemblies formed a fellowship called Assemblies
of God in Great Britain and Ireland, which now incorporates
around 600 churches, around 75,000 adherents and 1,000
ministers.
The Apostolic Church grew out of the 1904–5 Christian
revivals in South Wales and was established in 1916. The
Apostolic Church has around 90 churches, 7,000 adherents
and 100 ministers in the UK. The New Testament Church of
God was established in England in 1953 and has over 130
congregations, 11,000 members and over 300 ministers
across England and Wales.
There are about 105 million Pentecostalists worldwide, with
over 350,000 adherents in the UK.

THE APOSTOLIC CHURCH, Suite 105, Crystal House, New
Bedford Road, Luton LU1 1HS T 020-7587 1802
E admin@apostolic-church.org W www.apostolic-church.org
National Leader, Tim Jack

ASSEMBLIES OF GOD, National Ministry Centre, Mattersey,
Doncaster DN10 5HD T 017-7781 7663 E info@aog.org.uk
W www.aog.org.uk

THE ELIM PENTECOSTAL CHURCH, Elim International
Centre, De Walden Road, Malvern WR14 4DF T 0345-302 6750
W www.elim.org.uk
General Superintendent, Chris Cartwright

THE NEW TESTAMENT CHURCH OF GOD, 3 Cheyne
Walk, Northampton NN1 5PT T 01604-824222
E mmcc@ntcg.org.uk W www.ntcg.org.uk
Administrative Bishop, Donald Bolt

PRESBYTERIAN CHURCH IN IRELAND
Irish Presbyterianism traces its origins back to the Plantation
of Ulster in 1606, when English and Scottish Protestants
began to settle on the land confiscated from the Irish
chieftains. The first presbytery was established in Ulster in
1642 by chaplains of a Scottish army that had been sent to
crush a Catholic rebellion in 1641.
The Presbyterian Church in Ireland is reformed in doctrine
and belongs to the World Alliance of Reformed Churches.
Structurally, the 536 congregations are grouped in 19
presbyteries under the General Assembly. This body meets
annually and is presided over by a moderator who is elected
for one year. The ongoing work of the church is undertaken
by boards under which there are specialist committees.
There are over 225,000 members and 326 active ministers
of Irish presbyterian churches in Ireland and Northern
Ireland.

THE PRESBYTERIAN CHURCH IN IRELAND, Assembly
Buildings, 2–10 Fisherwick Place, Belfast BT1 6DW
T 028-9032 2284 E info@presbyterianireland.org
W www.presbyterianireland.org
Moderator (2019–20), Rt. Revd Dr William Henry
Clerk of Assembly and General Secretary, Revd Trevor Gribben

PRESBYTERIAN CHURCH OF WALES
The Presbyterian Church of Wales or Calvinistic Methodist
Church of Wales is Calvinistic in doctrine and presbyterian in
constitution. It was formed in 1811 when Welsh Calvinists
severed the relationship with the established church by
ordaining their own ministers. It secured its own confession
of faith in 1823 and a Constitutional Deed in 1826, and
since 1864 the General Assembly has met annually, presided
over by a moderator elected for a year. The doctrine and
constitutional structure of the Presbyterian Church of Wales
was confirmed by act of parliament in 1931–2.
The Church has 20,000 members, 55 ministers and 600
congregations.

THE PRESBYTERIAN CHURCH OF WALES, Tabernacle
Chapel, 81 Merthyr Road, Whitchurch, Cardiff CF14 1DD
T 029-2062 7465 E swyddfa.office@ebcpcw.org.uk
W www.ebcpcw.cymru
Moderator (2019–20), Revd Brian Matthews
General Secretary, Revd Meirion Morris

RELIGIOUS SOCIETY OF FRIENDS (QUAKERS)
Quakerism is a religious denomination which was founded in
the 17th century by George Fox and others in an attempt to
revive what they saw as the original 'primitive Christianity'.
The movement, at first called Friends of the Truth, started in
the Midlands, Yorkshire and north-west England, but there
are now Quakers all over the UK and in 36 countries around
the world. The colony of Pennsylvania, founded by William
Penn, was originally a Quaker settlement.
Quakers place an emphasis on the experience of God in
daily life rather than on sacraments or religious occasions.
There is no church calendar. Worship is largely silent and
there are no appointed ministers; the responsibility for
conducting a meeting is shared equally among those present.
Religious tolerance and social reform have always been
important to Quakers, together with a commitment to peace
and non-violence in resolving disputes.
There are more than 23,000 'friends' or Quakers in Great
Britain. There are around 475 places where Quaker meetings
are held, many of them Quaker-owned Friends Meeting

Houses. The Britain Yearly Meeting is the name given to the central organisation of Quakers in Britain.

THE RELIGIOUS SOCIETY OF FRIENDS (QUAKERS) IN BRITAIN, Friends House, 173–177 Euston Road, London NW1 2BJ **T** 020-7663 1000 **E** enquiries@quaker.org.uk
W www.quaker.org.uk
General Secretary, Oliver Robertson

SALVATION ARMY

The Salvation Army is an international Christian organisation working in 126 countries worldwide. As a church and registered charity, The Salvation Army is funded through donations from its members, the general public and, where appropriate, government grants.

The Salvation Army was founded by Methodists William and Catherine Booth in the East End of London in 1865 and marked its 150th anniversary on 2 July 2015. It now has around 40,000 members and 1,067 Salvation Army Officers (full-time ministers) in the UK. There are over 700 local church and community centres, 62 residential support centres for homeless people, 16 care homes for older people and six substance-misuse centres. It also runs a clothing recycling programme, charity shops, foodbanks, a prison-visiting service and a family-tracing service. In 1878 it adopted a quasi-military command structure intended to inspire and regulate its endeavours and to reflect its view that the church was engaged in spiritual warfare.

UK TERRITORIAL HEADQUARTERS, 101 Newington Causeway, London SE1 6BN **T** 020-7367 4500
E info@salvationarmy.org.uk **W** www.salvationarmy.org.uk
UK Territorial Leaders, Commissioners Anthony and Gillian Cotterill

SEVENTH-DAY ADVENTIST CHURCH

The Seventh-day Adventist Church is a worldwide Christian church marked by its observance of Saturday as the Sabbath and by its emphasis on the imminent second coming of Jesus Christ. Adventists summarise their faith in '28 fundamental beliefs'.

The church grew out of the Millerite movement in the USA during the mid-19th century and was formally established in 1863. The church has a worldwide membership of over 17 million. In the UK and Ireland there are 37,917 members worshipping in around 300 churches and companies.

SEVENTH-DAY ADVENTIST CHURCH HQ, Stanborough Park, Watford WD25 9JZ **T** 01923-672251
E info@adventist.org.uk **W** www.adventist.org.uk
President, Pastor Ian Sweeney
Executive Secretary, John Sturridge

THE (SWEDENBORGIAN) NEW CHURCH

The New Church is based on the teachings of the 18th-century Swedish scientist and theologian Emanuel Swedenborg (1688–1772), who believed that Jesus Christ appeared to him and instructed him to reveal the spiritual meaning of the Bible. He claimed to have visions of the spiritual world, including heaven and hell, and conversations with angels and spirits. He published several theological works, including descriptions of the spiritual world and a Bible commentary.

Swedenborgians believe that the second coming of Jesus Christ is taking place, being not an actual physical reappearance of Christ, but rather his return in spirit. It is also believed that concurrent with our life on earth is life in a parallel spiritual world, of which we are usually unconscious until death. There are around 30,000 Swedenborgians worldwide, with around 600 members, 18 churches and five ministers in the UK.

THE GENERAL CONFERENCE OF THE NEW CHURCH, Purley Chase Centre, Purley Chase Lane, Mancetter, Atherstone CV9 2RQ **T** 01827-712370
W www.generalconference.org.uk

UNDEB YR ANNIBYNWYR CYMRAEG

Undeb Yr Annibynwyr Cymraeg (the Union of Welsh Independents) was formed in 1872 and is a voluntary association of Welsh Congregational churches and personal members. It is mainly Welsh-speaking. Congregationalism in Wales dates back to 1639 when the first Welsh Congregational church was opened in Gwent.

Member churches are traditionally congregationalist in organisation and Calvinistic in doctrine, although a wide range of interpretations are permitted. Each church has complete independence in the governance and administration of its affairs.

The Union has around 24,000 members, 80 ministers and 400 member churches.

UNDEB YR ANNIBYNWYR CYMRAEG, 5 Axis Court, Riverside Business Park, Swansea Vale, Swansea SA7 0AJ
T 01792-795888 **E** undeb@annibynwyr.org
W www.annibynwyr.org
President , Revd Jill-Hailey Harries
President Elect, Revd Beti-Wyn James
General Secretary, Revd Dyfrig Rees

UNITED REFORMED CHURCH

The United Reformed Church (URC) was first formed by the union of most of the Congregational churches in England and Wales with the Presbyterian Church of England in 1972. It is Calvinistic in doctrine, and its followers form independent self-governing congregations bound under God by covenant, a principle laid down in the writings of Robert Browne (1550–1633). From the late 16th century the movement was driven underground by persecution, but the cause was defended at the Westminster Assembly in 1643 and the Savoy Declaration of 1658 laid down its principles. Congregational churches formed county associations and in 1832 these associations merged to form the Congregational Union of England and Wales.

In the 1960s there was close cooperation locally and nationally between congregational and presbyterian churches. This led to union negotiations and a Scheme of Union, supported by an act of parliament in 1972. In 1981 a further unification took place, with the Reformed Association of Churches of Christ becoming part of the URC. In 2000 a third union took place, with the Congregational Union of Scotland. At its basis the URC reflects local church initiative and responsibility with a conciliar pattern of oversight.

The URC is divided into 13 synods, each with a synod moderator. There are 1,406 churches which serve 49,517 members. There are 401 stipendiary ministers.

The General Assembly is the central body, and comprises around 400 representatives, mainly appointed by the synods, of which half are lay persons and half are ministers. Since 2010 the General Assembly has met biennially to elect two moderators (one lay and one ordained), who then become the public representatives of the URC.

UNITED REFORMED CHURCH, 86 Tavistock Place, London WC1H 9RT **T** 020-7916 2020 **E** urc@urc.org.uk
W www.urc.org.uk
Moderators of the General Assembly 2018–20, Revd Nigel Uden; Derek Estill
General Secretary, Revd John Proctor

WESLEYAN REFORM UNION

The Wesleyan Reform Union was founded by Methodists who left or were expelled from Wesleyan Methodism in 1849 following a period of internal conflict. Its doctrine is conservative evangelical and its organisation is congregational, each church having complete independence in the government and administration of its affairs. The union has around 1,250 members, 20 ministers and 96 churches.

THE WESLEYAN REFORM UNION, Church Street, Jump, Barnsley S74 0HZ T 01226-891608 E admin@thewru.co.uk W www.thewru.com
President, Revd Colin Braithwaite

NON-TRINITARIAN CHURCHES

CHRISTADELPHIAN

Christadelphians believe that the Bible is the word of God and that it reveals both God's dealings with mankind in the past and his plans for the future. These plans centre on the work of Jesus Christ, who it is believed will return to Earth to establish God's kingdom. The Christadelphian group was founded in the USA in the 1850s by Englishman Dr John Thomas.

THE CHRISTADELPHIAN MAGAZINE AND PUBLISHING ASSOCIATION, 404 Shaftmoor Lane, Hall Green, Birmingham B28 8SZ T 0121-777 6328 W www.thechristadelphian.com

CHURCH OF CHRIST, SCIENTIST

The Church of Christ, Scientist was founded by Mary Baker Eddy in the USA in 1879 to 'reinstate primitive Christianity and its lost element of healing'. Christian Science teaches the need for spiritual regeneration and salvation from sin, but it is best known for its reliance on prayer alone in the healing of sickness. Adherents believe that such healing is the result of divine laws, or divine science, and is in direct line with that practised by Jesus Christ (revered, not as God, but as the son of God) and by the early Christian church.

The denomination consists of The First Church of Christ, Scientist, in Boston, Massachusetts, USA ('The Mother Church') and its branch churches in almost 80 countries worldwide. The Bible and Mary Baker Eddy's book, *Science and Health with Key to the Scriptures*, are used for daily spiritual guidance and healing by all members and are read at services. There are no clergy; those engaged in full-time healing are called Christian Science practitioners, of whom there are around 1,500 worldwide.

No membership figures are available, since Mary Baker Eddy felt that numbers are no measure of spiritual vitality and ruled that such statistics should not be published. There are almost 2,000 branch churches worldwide, including 100 in the UK.

CHRISTIAN SCIENCE COMMITTEE ON PUBLICATION UK AND IRELAND, Golden Cross House, 8 Duncannon Street, London WC2N 4JF T 020-8150 0245 E londoncs@csps.com W http://ukchristianscience.com
District Manager for the UK and Ireland, Robin Harragin Hussey

CHURCH OF JESUS CHRIST OF LATTER-DAY SAINTS

The Church of Jesus Christ of Latter-day Saints ('Mormons') was founded in New York State, USA, in 1830, and came to Britain in 1837.

Mormons are Christians who claim to belong to the 'restored church' of Jesus Christ. They believe that true Christianity died when the last original apostle died, but that it was given back to the world by God and Jesus Christ through Joseph Smith, the church's founder and first president. They accept and use the Bible as scripture, but believe in continuing revelation from God; Mormons also use additional scriptures, including *The Book of Mormon: Another Testament of Jesus Christ*. The importance of the family is central to the church's beliefs and practices. Polygamy was formally discontinued in 1890.

The church has no paid ministry: local congregations are headed by a leader chosen from among their number. The world governing body, based in Utah, USA, is led by a president, believed to be the chosen prophet, and his two counsellors. There are over 15 million members worldwide, with 185,848 members and 333 congregations in the UK.

THE CHURCH OF JESUS CHRIST OF LATTER-DAY SAINTS, London Temple Visitors' Centre, West Park Road, Newchapel, Surrey RH7 6HW T 01342-831400 W www.lds.org.uk

JEHOVAH'S WITNESSES

The movement now known as Jehovah's Witnesses grew from a Bible study group formed by Charles Taze Russell in 1872 in Pennsylvania, USA. In 1896 it adopted the name of the Watch Tower Bible and Tract Society, and in 1931 its members became known as Jehovah's Witnesses.

Jehovah's Witnesses believe in the Bible as the word of God, and consider it to be inspired and historically accurate. They take the scriptures literally, except where there are obvious indications that they are figurative or symbolic, and reject the doctrine of the Trinity. Witnesses also believe that all those approved of by Jehovah will have eternal life on a cleansed and beautified earth; only 144,000 will go to heaven to rule with Jesus Christ. They believe that the second coming of Christ began in 1914, that his thousand-year reign over the earth is imminent, and that armageddon (a final battle in which evil will be defeated) will precede Christ's rule of peace. Jehovah's Witnesses refuse to take part in military service and do not accept blood transfusions.

The world governing body is based in New York, USA. There is no paid ministry, but each congregation has elders assigned to look after various duties and every Witness takes part in the public ministry in their neighbourhood. There are 8.3 million Jehovah's Witnesses worldwide, with around 136,000 Witnesses in Great Britain organised into around 1,500 congregations.

BRITISH HEADQUARTERS, The Ridgeway, London NW7 1RN T 020-8906 2211 W www.jw.org/en

UNITARIAN AND FREE CHRISTIAN CHURCHES

Unitarianism has its historical roots in the Judaeo-Christian tradition but rejects the deity of Christ and the doctrine of the Trinity. There is no fixed creed and it allows the individual to take insights from all of the world's faiths and philosophies. It is accepted that beliefs may evolve in the light of personal experience.

Unitarian communities first became established in Poland and Transylvania in the 16th century. The first avowedly Unitarian place of worship in Britain opened in London in 1774. The General Assembly of Unitarian and Free Christian Churches came into existence in 1928 as the result of the amalgamation of two earlier organisations.

There are around 3,400 Unitarians in Great Britain in 170 self-governing congregations and fellowship groups.

GENERAL ASSEMBLY OF UNITARIAN AND FREE CHRISTIAN CHURCHES, Essex Hall, 1–6 Essex Street, London WC2R 3HY T 020-7240 2384 E info@unitarian.org.uk W www.unitarian.org.uk
President (2019–20), Revd Celia Cartwright
Chief Officer, Liz Slade

COMMUNICATIONS

POSTAL SERVICES

On 15 October 2013, under the Postal Services Act 2011, Royal Mail was privatised when it was listed on the London Stock Exchange. The government initially retained a 30 per cent stake in Royal Mail, however it sold its remaining shares in 2015. Royal Mail Group ltd operates Royal Mail, Parcelforce Worldwide and General Logistics Systems (GLS). Under the same 2011 Act, the Post Office became independent of Royal Mail Group on 1 April 2012. The government, through the Department for Business, Energy and Industrial Strategy (BEIS), holds a special share in Post Office ltd. The Post Office has a strategic agreement in place to continue to supply Royal Mail products and services through its network and also has the same group holding company (Royal Mail Holdings plc), which holds shares in both Post Office ltd and Royal Mail Group ltd. Neither Royal Mail Holdings plc, nor BEIS, have any involvement in the day-to-day operations of the Post Office.

Royal Mail is the sole provider of the 'universal service': postal products and associated minimum service standards that must be available to all addresses in the UK.

Following the passing of the Postal Services Act 2011, the Office of Communications (OFCOM) assumed regulatory responsibility for postal services. OFCOM's primary responsibility is to secure the provision of a universal postal service with regard to its financial sustainability.

ROYAL MAIL GROUP LTD, 100 Victoria Embankment, London EC4Y 0HQ T 0345-774 0740
  W www.royalmailgroup.com
OFCOM, Riverside House, 2A Southwark Bridge Road, London SE1 9HA T 0207-981 3000
  W www.ofcom.org.uk

PRICING IN PROPORTION

Since 2006 Royal Mail has priced mail according to its size as well as its weight. The system is intended to reflect the fact that larger, bulkier items cost more to handle than smaller, lighter ones. There are five basic categories of correspondence:

LETTER: *Length* up to 240mm, *width* up to 165mm, *thickness* up to 5mm, *weight* up to 100g; eg most cards and postcards
LARGE LETTER: *Length* up to 353mm, *width* up to 250mm, *thickness* up to 25mm, *weight* up to 750g; eg most A4 documents and magazines
SMALL PARCEL: *Length* up to 450mm, *width* up to 350mm, *depth* up to 160mm, *weight* up to 2kg; eg books, clothes and gifts
MEDIUM PARCEL: *Length* up to 610mm, *width* up to 460mm, *depth* up to 460mm, *weight* up to 20kg; eg gifts, shoes, heavy or bulky items
ROLLED OR CYLINDER SHAPED PARCEL: The length of the item plus twice the diameter must not exceed 104cm, with the greatest dimension being no more than 90cm; eg posters and prints

Items larger than those listed above can only be sent via Parcelforce:

STANDARD PARCELFORCE: *Length* up to 150cm, with a combined length and girth of less than 300cm, *weight* up to 30kg
LARGE PARCELFORCE*: *Length* up to 250cm, with a combined length and girth of less than 500cm, *weight* up to 30kg

* Only available at selected Post Office branches

INLAND POSTAL SERVICES

Following are the details of a number of popular postal services along with prices correct as at April 2019. For a full list of prices *see* W www.royalmail.com

FIRST AND SECOND CLASS

Format	Maximum weight	First class	Second class
Letter/postcard	100g	£0.70	£0.61
Large letter	100g	£1.06	£0.83
	250g	£1.50	£1.32
	500g	£1.97	£1.72
	750g	£2.72	£2.33
Small parcel	1,000g	£3.55	£3.00
	2,000g	£5.50	£3.00
Medium parcel	1,000g	£5.80	£5.10
	2,000g	£8.95	£5.10
	5,000g	£15.85	£13.75
	10,000g	£21.90	£20.25
	20,000g	£33.40	£28.55

First class post is normally delivered on the following working day and second class within three working days. Prices are exempt from VAT.

STANDARD PARCELFORCE

Maximum weight	Lowest tariff*
2kg	£12.12
5kg	£13.14
10kg	£16.62
15kg	£23.40
20kg	£28.80
25kg	£40.08
30kg	£44.22

* The rate listed includes VAT, compensation up to £100 and is for delivery within 48 hours

OVERSEAS POSTAL SERVICES

For charging purposes Royal Mail divides the world into four zones: UK, Europe, World Zone 1 (including the Americas, Africa, the Middle East, the Far East and S. E. Asia) and World Zone 2 (including Australia, British Indian Ocean Territory, Fiji, New Zealand, Papua New Guinea, Singapore and Samoa). There is a complete listing on the Royal Mail website (W www.royalmail.com/international-zones)

INTERNATIONAL ECONOMY MAIL RATES*

Maximum weight		Standard tariff
Letters up to 100g†		
10g		£1.20
20g		£1.20
100g		£1.50

	Large letters	Small parcels/ printed papers
100g	£2.75	£4.25
250g	£3.95	£4.55
500g	£4.55	£6.55
750g	£5.45	£7.65
1,000g	–	£8.85
2,000g	–	£12.05

* Formerly Surface Mail
† Can only be sent by International Economy to destinations outside of Europe

Printed papers only add £1.15 for each additional 250g, or part thereof, up to 5,000g

INTERNATIONAL STANDARD MAIL RATES*

Weight up to and including	Europe	World Zone 1	World Zone 2
Letters			
10g	£1.35	£1.35	£1.35
20g	£1.35	£1.55	£1.55
100g	£1.60	£2.30	£2.30
Large letters			
100g	£2.80	£3.45	£3.60
250g	£4.00	£5.00	£5.30
500g	£4.60	£6.80	£7.20
750g	£5.50	£8.70	£9.25
Small parcels and printed papers			
100g	£4.50	£5.25	£5.65
250g	£4.80	£6.00	£6.50
500g	£6.65	£9.10	£9.80
750g	£7.95	£11.65	£12.40
1,000g	£8.95	£13.80	£14.55
2,000g	£12.10	£18.30	£20.05

Printed papers only add £1.15 for Europe, £1.70 for World Zone 1 or £1.90 for World Zone 2 for each additional 250g, or part thereof, up to 5,000g

* Formerly Airmail

SPECIAL DELIVERY SERVICES

INTERNATIONAL TRACKED AND SIGNED FOR SERVICES

There are various services available: *International Tracked & Signed* provides full end-to-end tracking, signature on delivery and online delivery confirmation to over 60 destinations; *International Tracked* provides the same, but without a signature on delivery, to over 50 destinations; and *International Signed* is tracked within the UK, a signature is taken on delivery and is available to over 155 destinations. All Tracked and Signed For services deliver to Europe within 3–5 working days, and worldwide within 5–7 working days. Proof of posting and compensation up to £50 is provided as standard. Additional compensation up to £250 can be provided for an extra fee.

SAME DAY

A courier service which provides same day delivery of urgent items in most places in the UK. With collection within the hour of booking, satellite tracking, delivery confirmation and automatic compensation up to £2,500, and for an additional fee, up to £10,000, the service is charged on a loaded mile basis T 0330-088 5522

SIGNED FOR

A service which offers proof of delivery including a signature from the receiver and compensation cover up to £50. The first class service is delivered the next working day and prices vary from £1.90 to £34.40 depending on the size and weight of the item. The second class service allows two to three working days for delivery with charges of £1.81 to £29.55.

SPECIAL DELIVERY GUARANTEED

A guaranteed next working day delivery service by 9am or 1pm with a refund option guaranteed for late delivery. With many options available, Royal Mail offers a full list of prices online W www.royalmail.com/personal/uk-delivery/special-delivery

OTHER SERVICES

KEEPSAFE

Mail is held for up to 100 days while the addressee is away, and is delivered when the addressee returns. Prices start at £15.00 for 10 days up to £75.00 for 100 days.

PASSPORT CHECK & SEND

For a fee of £9.75 paper and child passport applications are checked to ensure they meet the requirements set by HM Passport Office and are dispatched to HM Passport Office by secure post.

In November 2018 a digital check and send passport service, available at over 700 branches, was launched for the renewal of adult passports. For a fee of £15.40, and on submission of the old passport, counter staff will take photographs, submit an electronic application and dispatch the old passport to HM Passport Office by special delivery. The new passport will be received from HM Passport Office within three weeks. W www.postoffice.co.uk/passport-check-send.

POST OFFICE BOX

A Post Office (PO) Box provides a short and memorable alternative address. Mail is held at a local delivery office until the addressee is ready to collect it, or delivered to a street address for an extra fee. Prices start at £31.50 for one month or £156.00 for six months or £270.00 for a year.

POSTCODE FINDER

Customers can search an online database to find UK postcodes and addresses. For more information *see* Royal Mail's postcode finder W www.royalmail.com/postcode-finder

REDELIVERY

Customers can request a redelivery of an item for up to 18 days if it was unable to be delivered and the person is unable to collect from the address on the delivery notification card. A 48-hour notice period is required for redelivery. Redelivery can be arranged to the customer's house, an alternative local address or, for a fee of £0.70 payable on collection, to a local post office branch.

REDIRECTION

Customers may arrange the redirection of their mail via post, at the Post Office or online, subject to verification of their identity. The service is available for three months, six months or 12 months. Prices start at £33.99 for redirection to a UK destination for a single applicant; a full price list is available at W www.royalmail.com/personal/receiving-mail/redirection

TRACK AND TRACE

An online service for customers to track the progress of items sent using any special delivery tracked and signed for service. It is accessible from W www.royalmail.com/track-your-item

CONTACTS

PARCELFORCE T 0344-800 4466 W www.parcelforce.com
POST OFFICE T 0345-722 3355 W www.postoffice.co.uk

TELECOMMUNICATIONS

4G AND 5G

Mobile network technology has improved dramatically since the launch in 1985 of the first-generation global system for mobile communications (GSM), which offered little or no data capability. In 1992 Vodafone launched a new GSM network, usually referred to as 2G or second generation, which used digital encoding and allowed voice and low-speed data communications. This technology was extended, via the enhanced data transfer rate of 2.5G, to 3G – a family of mobile standards that provide high bandwidth support to applications such as voice- and video-calling, data transfer, television streaming and full internet access.

EE was the first operator to launch 4G in late 2012 and by April 2013 the service was available in ten cities where the broadband speed was doubled to more than 20 megabits per second (Mbps). O2 and Vodafone subsequently launched their 4G networks in late August 2013 while 3 began their service in December 2013.

By the end of 2017, there were 58.4 million 4G subscribers, an increase of 6 million (11.5 per cent) from the previous year. The number of 4G subscribers at the end of 2017 comprised 63.5 per cent of the total number of all active mobile subscribers in the UK. 4G coverage improved in 2017, with 58 per cent of all indoor premises covered by all four networks, up from 40 per cent in 2016. Geographic areas covered by all four networks increased from 21 per cent in 2016 to 43 per cent in 2017 and geographic areas with no coverage from any network decreased from 37 per cent in 2016 to 22 per cent in 2017. The ability to connect to a good 4G service continues to vary according to location; in urban areas, good 4G data services of a least 2Mbps is available at 83 per cent of premises, in contrast, only 41 per cent of premises can access good quality data services in rural areas.

In February 2015, OFCOM stated that 5G data connections could be available in the UK by 2020 and in December 2017, the organisation that governs cellular standards, The 3rd Generation Partnership Project (3GPP), signed off on a universal standard, called 5G NR. EE officially switched on its 5G services in Belfast, Birmingham, Cardiff, Edinburgh, London and Manchester on 30 May 2019, becoming the first company to launch 5G in the UK. EE planned to extend 5G to a further ten cities in the UK by the end of 2019 and launched a 5G home broadband service in June 2019. O2 launched 5G in the UK's four capital cities in 2019 and Vodafone launched in 19 cities in 2019, starting with seven cities in July. 3 launched its 5G services in the second half of 2019. All four mobile network providers have 5G-capable devices on the market.

The headline benefit of 5G is speed. 5G is expected to reach speeds in excess of 1,000Mbps or 1Gbps (1 gigabit per second). In comparison maximum download speeds are 384Kbps (kilobits per second) for 3G, 100Mbps for 4G and 300Mbps for 4G+. However, actual download speeds depend on a variety of factors, such as distance from a base station and how many other people are using the network at the same time. As at April 2019 EE provided the fastest 4G connection with an average download speed of 29.6 Mbps; Vodafone, 3 and O2 offered average download speeds of 21.0Mbps, 18.0Mbps and 14.1Mbps respectively. So, although 5G is targeting a download speed of over 1Gbps, average mobile download speeds are expected to be in the region of 80 to 100 Mbps.

FIXED-LINE SERVICES

The total number of fixed-line services in the UK declined for the first time in 2017; from a total of 33.6 million connections in 2016 to 33.1 million in 2017. The decrease in landlines was as a result of businesses switching to mobile and voice over internet protocol (VoIP) services, such as Skype. Fixed voice call minutes continued to decline, from 65 billion minutes in 2016, to 54 billion in 2017; part of a steady decline from the 103 billion minutes recorded in 2012.

The decrease in business lines was partly offset by a 1 per cent increase in the number of residential landlines, attributed to growing fixed broadband take-up – most households in the UK need a landline to be able to access fixed broadband services. Fixed broadband connections totalled 26.0 million in 2017, compared to 25.4 million in 2016.

MOBILE PHONE USAGE

At the end of 2017 the total number of mobile subscriptions in the UK had increased by 0.5 million to 92 million since the previous year. The volume of SMS and MMS messages sent continued to decline for the fifth year in a row, decreasing to 77.3 billion; a further decline from 90 billion in 2016. The decline in text messaging is likely to be a result of the increasing number of smartphones being used for communication, with social media platforms and instant messaging services such as Whatsapp and iMessenger providing alternatives to SMS. Total outgoing mobile calls decreased by 3 billion minutes to 149 billion minutes in 2017, compared with an increase from 143 to 151 billion minutes from 2015 to 2016. Average monthly data use per mobile connection further increased from 1.3 gigabytes in 2016 to 1.9 gigabytes in 2017 and from just 0.9 gigabytes in 2015.

UK adults spent most of their time online on the smartphone in March 2018. Of the total minutes spent online by the entire UK digital population in March 2018, 62 per cent was via the smartphone, followed by the desktop/ laptop (25 per cent) and tablet (13 per cent). In 2018, nearly half (48 per cent) of UK internet users stated that smartphones were their most important device for accessing the internet. This was higher for younger adults, with 72 per cent regarding their smartphones as their most important device for accessing the internet. In contrast, only 17 per cent of those aged over 54 perceived the smartphone as the most important device.

SMARTPHONE USAGE

Average time online, hours per day, by age and gender – March 2018

Source: OFCOM – Communications Market Report 2018

HEALTH

In 1999 the Independent Expert Group on Mobile Phones (IEGMP) was established to examine the possible effects on health of mobile phones, base stations and transmitters. The main findings of the IEGMP's report *Mobile Phones and Health*, published in May 2000, were:

- exposure to radio frequency radiation below guideline levels did not cause adverse health effects to the general population
- the use of mobile phones by drivers of any vehicle can increase the chance of accidents
- the widespread use of mobile phones by children for non-essential calls should be discouraged as if there are unrecognised adverse health effects children may be more vulnerable
- there is no general risk to the health of people living near to base stations on the basis that exposures are expected to be much lower than guidelines set by the International Commission on Non-Ionising Radiation Protection

The government set up the Mobile Telecommunications Health and Research (MTHR) programme in 2001 to undertake independent research into the possible health risks from mobile telephone technology. The MTHR programme published its report in September 2007 concluding that, in the short term, neither mobile phones nor base stations have been found to be associated with any biological or adverse health effects. An international cohort study into the possible long-term health effects of mobile phone use was launched by the MTHR in April 2010. The study is known as COSMOS and aims to follow the health of 250,000 mobile phone users from five countries over 20 to 30 years. Details of the study can be found on the COSMOS website (W www.thecosmosproject.org).

A national measurement programme to ensure that emissions from mobile phone base stations do not exceed the ICNIRP guideline levels is overseen by OFCOM and annual audits of these levels can be found on the sitefinder part of its website. Public Health England is responsible for providing information and advice on the health effects of electromagnetic fields, including those emitted from mobile phones and base stations. In April 2012, the HPA's independent Advisory Group on Non-ionising Radiation published a report concluding that there was no convincing evidence that mobile phone technologies cause adverse effects on human health.

In 2014, the Department of Health and Social Care commissioned the world's biggest study into the effects of mobile phone usage on children and adolescents, known as the Study of Cognition, Adolescents and Mobile Phones (SCAMP). The first round of follow-up data collection ended in July 2018. Details of this study can be found on the SCAMP website (W www.scampstudy.org).

SAFETY WHILE DRIVING

Under legislation that came into effect in December 2003 it is illegal for drivers to use a hand-held mobile phone while driving. Since March 2017 the fixed penalty for using a hand-held mobile device while driving is £200 and six penalty points. If the driver passed their driving test in the last two years, they will lose their licence. Three penalty points can also be issued to a driver for not having proper control of a vehicle while using a hands-free device or if the device blocks the driver's view of the road and traffic ahead. If the police or driver chooses to take the case to court rather than issue or accept a fixed penalty notice, the driver may be disqualified from driving in addition to a maximum fine of £1,000 for car drivers and £2,500 for drivers of buses, coaches or heavy goods vehicles. The only exceptions for using a mobile phone while driving are to call the emergency services, when it is unsafe or impractical to stop, or when the driver is safely parked.

REGULATION

Under the Communications Act 2003, OFCOM is the independent regulator and competition authority for the UK communications industries, with responsibilities across television, radio, telecommunications and wireless communications services. Competition in the communications market is also regulated by the Competition and Markets Authority, although OFCOM takes the lead in competition investigations in the UK market. The Competition Appeal Tribunal hears appeals against OFCOM's decisions.

CONTACTS

OFCOM, Riverside House, 2A Southwark Bridge Road, London SE1 9HA T 020-7981 3000
W www.ofcom.org.uk

INTERNET

The UK ranks 31st in the world for broadband speed with an average speed of 16.51Mbps. At May 2017, OFCOM reported 100 per cent coverage in the UK at a download speed of 44Mbps, up from 37Mbps in 2016. Superfast broadband is now available in 91 per cent of the UK at a speed of 77Mbps and OFCOM are continually working to boost superfast and ultrafast connections. There were 26 million fixed broadband connections in the UK at the end of 2017, 49 per cent of which were superfast connections.

In 2018 87 per cent of UK adults (aged 16+) had broadband internet access at home. The most frequently cited reason for not having internet access was that they did not need it (45 per cent). Of adults without home internet access, 14 per cent said they were likely to get it in the next year. Home internet access varies significantly according to age group. At the beginning of 2019, 95 per cent of those aged 16 to 24 reported they had home internet access, as opposed to only 75 per cent of those aged over 55+.

In 2018 the most popular internet activity was general browsing, with 69 per cent of adults having browsed the internet in the past week. Sending emails was the second most common activity, with 66 per cent of adults reporting to have done this in the last week. Just under half of adults (44 per cent) reported they had shopped online in the last week, a reduction from 76 per cent in 2017, and around half of UK adults had used online banking and social media in the last week. In 2016, 42 per cent of internet users claimed to use the same password for most, if not all websites and in 2018, a quarter of internet users said they did not carry out appropriate checks before entering their personal or financial information online.

In the UK 77 per cent of internet users had a profile or account on a social media or messaging site or app in 2018, unchanged since 2016. Facebook remained the most-visited social platform, reaching 41 million internet users aged 13+ in 2018 (90 per cent of the total UK internet audience). However Facebook began to see a downward trend in the number of people aged under 35 accessing the platform; with the number of people aged 18 to 24 decreasing by 4 per cent in the year to March 2018, in contrast, visitors among those aged over 54 increased to 24 per cent (2.2 million people) in the same period. Snapchat and Facebook-owned Instagram saw an increase in online audiences, with 22.7 million adults visiting Snapchat in March 2018, fractionally less than Instagram with 23.1 million. However, Snapchat had much larger year-on-year growth than Instagram (122 per cent, compared with 22 per cent). Much of the growth was driven by an increased number of adults aged 25+ visiting the platform.

In March 2018 the organisation with the largest online audience in the UK was Google (41.9 million unique visitors aged 18+), closely followed by Facebook and BBC (40.2 million and 39.5 million respectively) and Amazon (37.7 million), pushing Microsoft down to fifth place with 37 million unique visitors. Within the Google portfolio, YouTube was the most popular platform (40 million), followed by Google Search (37 million), Google Maps (25 million) and Gmail (23 million).

GLOSSARY OF TERMS

The following is a list of selected internet terms. It is by no means exhaustive but is intended to cover those that the average computer user might encounter.

BANNER AD: An advertisement on a web page that links to a corresponding website when clicked.

BLOG: Short for 'web log' – an online personal journal that is frequently updated and intended to be read by the public. Blogs are kept by 'bloggers' and are commonly available as RSS feeds.

BOOKMARKS: A method of storing links or automatic pathways within web browsers which allow a user to quickly return to a webpage. Referred to as 'Favourites' in Internet Explorer.

BROWSER: Typically refers to a 'web browser' program that allows a computer user to view web page content on their computer, eg Firefox, Internet Explorer or Safari.

CLICK-THROUGH: The number of times a web user 'clicks through' a paid advertisement link to the corresponding website.

CLOUD COMPUTING: The use of IT resources as an on-demand service across a network; through cloud computing, software, advanced computation and archived information can be accessed remotely, without the user needing local dedicated hardware.

COOKIE: A piece of information placed on a user's hard disk by a web server. Cookies contain data about the user's activity on a website, and are returned to the server whenever a browser makes further requests. They are important for remembering information such as login and registration details, 'shopping cart' data, user preferences etc, and are often set to expire after a fixed period.

DOMAIN: A set of words or letters, separated by dots, used to identify an internet server, eg www.whitakersalmanack.com, where 'www' denotes a web (http) server, 'whitakersalmanack' denotes the organisation name and 'com' denotes that the organisation is a company.

ENCRYPTION: The conversion of information or data into a code in order to prevent unauthorised access.

FIREWALL: A protection system designed to prevent unauthorised access to or from a private network.

FTP: File Transfer Protocol – a set of network rules enabling a user to exchange files with a remote server.

HACKER: A person who attempts to break or 'hack' into websites. Motives typically involve the desire to procure personal information such as addresses, passwords or credit card details. Hackers may also delete code or incorporate traces of malicious code to damage the functionality of a website.

HIT: A single request from a web browser for a single item from a web server. In order for a web browser to display a page that contains three graphics, four 'hits' would occur at the server: one for the HTML page and one for each of the three graphics. Therefore the number of hits on a website is not synonymous with the number of visitors.

HTML: HyperText Mark-up Language – a programming language used to denote or mark up how an internet page should be presented to a user from an HTTP server via a web browser.

HTTP: HyperText Transfer Protocol – an internet protocol whereby a web server sends web pages, images and files to a web browser.

HYPERLINK: A piece of specially coded text that users can click on to navigate to the web page, or element of a web page, associated with that link's code. Links are typically distinguished through the use of bold, underlined or differently coloured text.

JAVA: A programming language used widely on the internet.

MALWARE: A combination of the words 'malicious' and 'software'. Malware is software designed with the intention of infiltrating a computer and damaging its system.

OPEN-SOURCE: Describes a computer program that has its source code (the instructions that make up a program) freely available for viewing and modification.

PAGERANK: A link analysis algorithm used by search engines that assigns a numerical value based on a website's relevance and reputation. In general, a site with a higher pagerank has more traffic than a site with a lower one.

PHISHING: The fraudulent practice of sending emails to acquire personal information by masquerading as a legitimate company.

PODCAST: A form of audio and video broadcasting using the internet. Although the word is a portmanteau of 'iPod' and broadcasting, podcasting does not require the use of an iPod. A podcaster creates a list of files and makes it available in the RSS 2.0 format. The list can then be obtained using podcast 'retriever' software which makes the files available to digital devices (including iPods); users may then listen or watch at their convenience.

RSS FEED: Rich Site Summary or RDF Site Summary or Real Simple Syndication – a commonly used protocol for syndication and sharing of content, originally developed to facilitate the syndication of news articles, now widely used to share the content of blogs.

SEO: Search engine optimisation – the process of optimising the content of a web page to ensure that it is indexed by search engines.

SERVER: A node on a network that provides service to the terminals on the network. These computers have higher hardware specifications, ie more resources and greater speed, in order to handle large amounts of data.

SOCIAL NETWORKING: The practice of using a web-hosted service such as Facebook or Twitter to upload and share content and build friendship networks.

SPAM: A term used for unsolicited, generally junk, email.

TRAFFIC: The number of visitors to a website.

TWITTER: An online microblogging service that allows users to stay connected through the exchange of 140-character posts, known as 'tweets'.

URL: Uniform Resource Locator – address of a file accessible on the internet, eg http://www.whitakersalmanack.com

USER-GENERATED CONTENT (UGC): Refers to various media content produced or primarily influenced by end-users, as opposed to traditional media producers such as licensed broadcasters and production companies. These forms of media include digital video, blogging, podcasting, mobile phone photography and wikis.

WIKI: A website or database developed collaboratively by a community of users, allowing any user to add or edit content.

CONSERVATION AND HERITAGE

NATIONAL PARKS

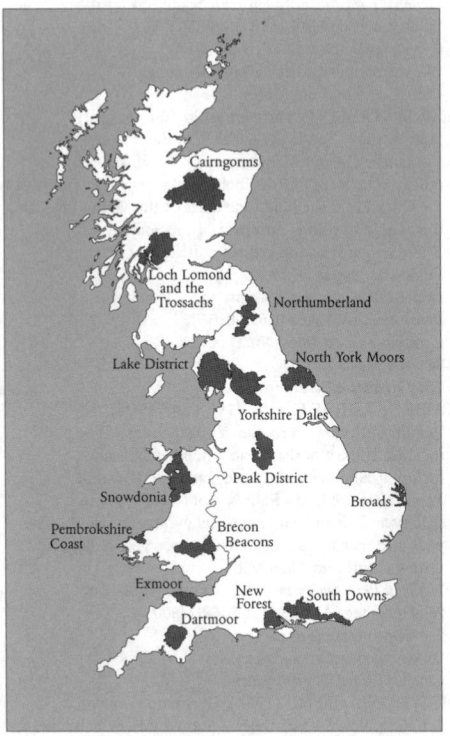

ENGLAND AND WALES

There are nine national parks in England, and three in Wales. In addition, the Norfolk and Suffolk Broads are considered to have equivalent status to a national park. Under the National Parks and Access to the Countryside Act 1949, as clarified by the Natural Environment and Rural Communities Act 2006, the two purposes of the national parks are to conserve and enhance the parks' natural beauty, wildlife and cultural heritage, and to promote opportunities for the understanding and enjoyment of the special qualities of national parks by the public. If there is a conflict between the two purposes, then conservation takes precedence.

Natural England is the statutory body that has the power to designate national parks in England, and Natural Resources Wales (formerly Countryside Council for Wales) is responsible for national parks in Wales. Designations in England are confirmed by the Secretary of State for Environment, Food and Rural Affairs and those in Wales by the Welsh government. The designation of a national park does not affect the ownership of the land or remove the rights of the local community. The majority of the land in the national parks is owned by private landowners (around 75 per cent) or by bodies such as the National Trust and the Forestry Commission. The national park authorities own only a small percentage of the land themselves.

The Environment Act 1995 replaced the existing national park boards and committees with free-standing national park authorities (NPAs). NPAs are the sole local planning authorities for their areas and as such influence land use and development, and deal with planning applications. NPAs are responsible for carrying out the statutory purposes of national parks stated above.

In pursuing these purposes they have a statutory duty to seek to foster the economic and social well-being of the communities within national parks. The NPAs publish management plans setting out overarching policies for their area and appoint their own officers and staff.

The Broads Authority was established under the Norfolk and Suffolk Broads Act 1988 and meets the requirement for the authority to have a navigation function in addition to a regard for the needs of agriculture, forestry and the economic and social interests of those who live or work in the Broads.

MEMBERSHIP

Membership of English NPAs comprises local authority appointees, members directly appointed by the Secretary of State for Environment, Food and Rural Affairs and members appointed by the secretary after consultation with local parishes. Under the Natural Environment and Rural Communities Act 2006 every district, county or unitary authority with land in a national park is entitled to appoint at least one member unless it chooses to opt out. The total number of local authority and parish members must exceed the number of national members.

Northumberland, Pembrokeshire Coast and Snowdonia NPAs have 18 members; Dartmoor has 19; the Lake District and North York Moors have 20; the Broads has 21; Exmoor, the New Forest 22; Brecon Beacons 24; Yorkshire Dales 25; South Downs 27; and the Peak District 30.

In Wales, two-thirds of NPA members are appointed by the constituent local authorities and one-third by the Welsh government, advised by Natural Resources Wales.

FUNDING

Core funding for the English NPAs and the Broads Authority is provided by central government through the Department for Environment, Food and Rural Affairs (DEFRA) National Park Grant.

In Wales, the three national parks are funded by the Welsh government; for 2019–20 budgeted gross revenue expenditure totals £18.5m and capital expenditure £3.7m.

All NPAs and the Broads Authority can take advantage of grants from other bodies including lottery and European grants.

The national parks (with date that designation was confirmed) are:

BRECON BEACONS (1957), Powys (66 per cent)/ Carmarthenshire/Rhondda, Cynon and Taff/Merthyr Tydfil/Blaenau Gwent/Monmouthshire, 1,344 sq. km/ 519 sq. miles – The park is centred on the Brecon Beacons mountain range, which includes the three highest mountains in southern Britain (Pen y Fan, Corn Du and Cribyn), but also includes the valleys of the rivers Usk and Wye, the Black Mountains to the east and the Black Mountain to the west. There is a visitor centre at Libanus, a tourist information centre at Abergavenny and community run information centres in Llandovery and Brecon.

National Park Authority, Plas y Ffynnon, Cambrian Way, Brecon, Powys LD3 7HP T 01874-624437 W www.beacons-npa.gov.uk
Chief Executive, Julian Atkins

BROADS (1989), Norfolk/Suffolk, 303 sq. km/117 sq. miles – The Broads is located between Norwich and Great Yarmouth on the flood plains of the six rivers flowing through the area to the sea. The area is one of fens, winding waterways, woodland and marsh. The 60 or so broads are man-made, and many are connected to the rivers by dykes, providing over 200km (125 miles) of navigable waterways. There are information centres at Hoveton, Whitlingham Country Park and How Hill National Nature Reserve. There are yacht stations at Norwich, Reedham and Great Yarmouth.

Broads Authority, Yare House, 62–64 Thorpe Road, Norwich NR1 1RY T 01603-610734 W www.broads-authority.gov.uk

Chief Executive, Dr John Packman

DARTMOOR (1951), Devon, 953 sq. km/368 sq. miles – The park consists of moorland and rocky granite tors, and is rich in prehistoric remains. There are visitor centres at Haytor, Princetown (main visitor centre) and Postbridge.

National Park Authority, Parke, Bovey Tracey, Devon TQ13 9JQ T 01626-832093 E hq@dartmoor.gov.uk

W www.dartmoor.gov.uk

Chief Executive, Kevin Bishop

EXMOOR (1954), Somerset (71 per cent)/Devon (29 per cent), 694 sq. km/268 sq. miles – Exmoor is a moorland plateau, with steep wooded slopes that extend along the coastline and is inhabited by wild Exmoor ponies and red deer. There are many ancient remains and burial mounds. There are national park centres at Dunster, Dulverton and Lynmouth.

National Park Authority, Exmoor House, Dulverton, Somerset TA22 9HL T 01398-323665 E info@exmoor-nationalpark.gov.uk

W www.exmoor-nationalpark.gov.uk

Chief Executive, Sarah Bryan

LAKE DISTRICT (1951), Cumbria, 2,362 sq. km/912 sq. miles – The Lake District includes England's highest mountains (Scafell Pike, Helvellyn and Skiddaw) but it is most famous for its glaciated lakes. In 2017 the Lake District was inscribed as a UNESCO World Heritage Site for its cultural significance *see also* World Heritage Sites. There are national park information centres at Bowness-on-Windermere, Keswick, Ullswater and a visitor centre at Brockhole, Windermere.

National Park Authority, Murley Moss, Oxenholme Road, Kendal, Cumbria LA9 7RL T 01539-724555

E hq@lakedistrict.gov.uk W www.lakedistrict.gov.uk

Chief Executive, Richard Leafe

NEW FOREST (2005), Hampshire, 570 sq. km/220 sq. miles – The forest has been protected since 1079 when it was declared a royal hunting forest. The area consists of forest, ancient woodland, heathland, farmland, coastal saltmarsh and mudflats. Managed by the ancient system of commoning, the landscape is shaped by grazing animals and contains a range of rare plants and animals.

National Park Authority, Town Hall, Avenue Road, Lymington, Hants SO41 9ZG T 01590-646600

E enquiries@newforestnpa.gov.uk W www.newforestnpa.gov.uk

Chief Executive, Alison Barnes

NORTH YORK MOORS (1952), North Yorkshire (96 per cent)/Redcar and Cleveland, 1,434 sq. km/554 sq. miles – The park consists of dales woodland, moorland and coast, and includes the Hambleton Hills and the Cleveland Way national trail. There are national park centres at Danby and Sutton Bank.

National Park Authority, The Old Vicarage, Bondgate, Helmsley, York YO62 5BP T 01439-772700

E general@northyorkmoors.org.uk

W www.northyorkmoors.org.uk

Chief Executive, Andy Wilson

NORTHUMBERLAND (1956), Northumberland, 1,049 sq. km/405 sq. miles – The park is an area of hill country, comprising open moorland, blanket bogs and very small patches of ancient woodland, stretching from Hadrian's Wall to the Scottish border. Visitor information is available from the Sill National Landscape Discovery Centre on Hadrian's Wall.

National Park Authority, Eastburn, South Park, Hexham, Northumberland NE46 1BS T 01434-605555

E enquiries@nnpa.org.uk

W www.northumberlandnationalpark.org.uk

Chief Executive, Tony Gates

PEAK DISTRICT (1951), Derbyshire (64 per cent)/Staffordshire/South Yorkshire/Cheshire/West Yorkshire/Greater Manchester, 1,437 sq. km/555 sq. miles – The Peak District includes the gritstone moors of the Dark Peak, the limestone dales of the White Peak and the crags and rolling farmland of the South West Peak. There are information centres at Bakewell, Castleton, Edale and Upper Derwent.

National Park Authority, Aldern House, Baslow Road, Bakewell, Derbyshire DE45 1AE T 01629-816200

E customer.service@peakdistrict.gov.uk

W www.peakdistrict.gov.uk

Chief Executive, Sarah Fowler

PEMBROKESHIRE COAST (1952 and 1995), Pembrokeshire, 615 sq. km/240 sq. miles – The park includes cliffs, moorland and a number of islands, including Skomer and Ramsey, and the 186-mile Pembrokeshire Coast Path National Trail. There is a gallery and visitor centre at Oriel y Parc, St Davids. The park also manages Castell Henllys Iron Age Village and Carew Castle and Tidal Mill.

National Park Authority, Llanion Park, Pembroke Dock, Pembrokeshire SA72 6DY T 01646-624800

E info@pembrokeshirecoast.org.uk

W www.pembrokeshirecoast.wales

Chief Executive, Tegryn Jones

SNOWDONIA/ERYRI (1951), Gwynedd/Conwy, 2,176 sq. km/840 sq. miles – Snowdonia, which takes its name from Snowdon, is an area of deep valleys and rugged mountains. There are information centres at Aberdyfi, Beddgelert and Betws y Coed.

National Park Authority, Penrhyndeudraeth, Gwynedd LL48 6LF T 01766-770274 E park@snowdonia.gov.wales

W www.snowdonia.gov.wales

Chief Executive, Emyr Williams

THE SOUTH DOWNS (2010), West Sussex/Hampshire, 1,624 sq. km/627 sq. miles – The South Downs contains a diversity of natural habitats, including flower-studded chalk grassland, ancient woodland, flood meadow, lowland heath and rare chalk heathland. There are visitor centres at Beachy Head, Queen Elizabeth Country Park in Hampshire and Seven Sisters Country Park in East Sussex.

National Park Authority, North Street, Midhurst, W. Sussex GU29 9DH T 01730-814810 W www.southdowns.gov.uk

Chief Executive, Trevor Beattie

YORKSHIRE DALES (1954), North Yorkshire (71 per cent)/Cumbria (28 per cent)/Lancashire (1 per cent), 2,179 sq. km/841 sq. miles – The Yorkshire Dales is composed primarily of limestone overlaid in places by millstone grit. The three peaks of Ingleborough, Whernside and Pen-y-ghent are within the park. There are information centres at Grassington, Hawes, Aysgarth Falls, Malham and Reeth.

National Park Authority, Yoredale, Bainbridge, Leyburn, N. Yorks DL8 3EL T 0300-456 0030 E info@yorkshiredales.org.uk

W www.yorkshiredales.org.uk

Chief Executive, David Butterworth

SCOTLAND

On 9 August 2000 the national parks (Scotland) bill received royal assent, giving parliament the ability to create national parks in Scotland. The Act gives Scottish parks wider powers than in England and Wales, including statutory responsibilities for the local economy and rural communities. The board of the Cairngorms NPA comprises 19 members; seven appointed by the Scottish ministers, a further seven nominated to the board by the five local authorities in the park area and five locally elected members. The board of Loch Lomond and the Trossachs NPA comprises 17 members; five elected by the community and 12 appointed by Scottish Ministers, six of whom are nominated by local authorities. In Scotland, the national parks are central government bodies and are wholly funded by the Scottish government. The budget for 2019–20 totals £13.4m.

CAIRNGORMS (2003), North-East Scotland, 4,528 sq. km/1,748 sq. miles – The Cairngorms national park is the largest in the UK, covering around 6 per cent of Scotland. It displays a vast collection of landforms, including five of the six highest mountains in the UK and contains 25 per cent of Britain's threatened species. The near natural woodlands contain remnants of the original ancient Caledonian pine forest. There are 13 visitor centres within the park.
National Park Authority, 14 The Square, Grantown-on-Spey, Morayshire PH26 3HG T 01479-873535
E enquiries@cairngorms.co.uk W www.cairngorms.co.uk
Chief Executive, Grant Moir

LOCH LOMOND AND THE TROSSACHS (2002), Argyll and Bute/Perth and Kinross/Stirling/West Dunbartonshire, 1,865 sq. km/720 sq. miles – The park boundaries encompass lochs, rivers, forests, 21 mountains above 914m (3,000ft) including Ben More, the highest at 1,174m (3,852ft) and a further 20 mountains between 762m (2,500ft) and 914m (3,000ft). There is a national park centre in Balmaha and several other visitor centres across the park which are administered by VisitScotland.
National Park Authority, Carrochan, Carrochan Road, Balloch G83 8EG T 01389-722600 E info@lochlomond-trossachs.org
W www.lochlomond-trossachs.org
Chief Executive, Gordon Watson

NORTHERN IRELAND

There is a power to designate national parks in Northern Ireland under the Nature Conservation and Amenity Lands Order (Northern Ireland) 1985, but there are currently no national parks in Northern Ireland.

AREAS OF OUTSTANDING NATURAL BEAUTY

ENGLAND AND WALES

Under the National Parks and Access to the Countryside Act 1949, provision was made for the designation of areas of outstanding natural beauty (AONBs). Natural England is responsible for designating AONBs in England and Natural Resources Wales for the Welsh AONBs. Designations in England are confirmed by the Secretary of State for Environment, Food and Rural Affairs and those in Wales by the Welsh government. The Countryside and Rights of Way (CROW) Act 2000 placed greater responsibility on local authorities to protect AONBs and made it a statutory duty for relevant authorities to produce a management plan for their AONB area. The CROW Act also provided for the creation of conservation boards for larger and more complex AONBs.

The primary objective of the AONB designation is to conserve and enhance the natural beauty of the area. Where an AONB has a conservation board, it has the additional purpose of increasing public understanding and enjoyment of the special qualities of the area; the board has greater weight should there be a conflict of interests between the two. In addition, the board is also required to foster the economic and social well-being of the local communities but without incurring significant expenditure in doing so. Overall responsibility for AONBs lies with the relevant local authorities or conservation board. To coordinate planning and management responsibilities between local authorities in whose area they fall, AONBs are overseen by a joint advisory committee (or similar body) which includes representatives from the local authorities, landowners, farmers, residents and conservation and recreation groups. Core funding for AONBs is provided by central government through DEFRA, local authorities and Natural Resources Wales.

The 38 AONBs (with date designation confirmed) are:

ARNSIDE AND SILVERDALE (1972), Cumbria/Lancashire, 75 sq. km/29 sq. miles
BLACKDOWN HILLS (1991), Devon/Somerset, 370 sq. km/143 sq. miles
CANNOCK CHASE (1958), Staffordshire, 68 sq. km/26 sq. miles
CHICHESTER HARBOUR (1964), Hampshire/West Sussex, 74 sq. km/29 sq. miles
CHILTERNS (1965; extended 1990), Bedfordshire/Buckinghamshire/Hertfordshire/Oxfordshire, 839 sq. km/324 sq. miles
CLWYDIAN RANGE AND DEE VALLEY (1985; extended 2011), Denbighshire/Flintshire, 389 sq. km/150 sq. miles
CORNWALL (1959; Camel Estuary 1983), 958 sq. km/370 sq. miles
COTSWOLDS (1966; extended 1990), Gloucestershire/Oxfordshire/Warwickshire/Wiltshire/Worcestershire, 2,046 sq. km/790 sq. miles
CRANBORNE CHASE AND WEST WILTSHIRE DOWNS (1983), Dorset/Hampshire/Somerset/Wiltshire, 983 sq. km/380 sq. miles
DEDHAM VALE (1970; extended 1978, 1991), Essex/Suffolk, 90 sq. km/35 sq. miles
DORSET (1959), Dorset/Somerset, 1,129 sq. km/436 sq. miles
EAST DEVON (1963), 268 sq. km/103 sq. miles
FOREST OF BOWLAND (1964), Lancashire/North Yorkshire, 803 sq. km/310 sq. miles
GOWER (1956), Swansea, 188 sq. km/73 sq. miles
HIGH WEALD (1983), East Sussex/Kent/Surrey/West Sussex, 1,461 sq. km/564 sq. miles
HOWARDIAN HILLS (1987), North Yorkshire, 204 sq. km/79 sq. miles
ISLE OF WIGHT (1963), 189 sq. km/73 sq. miles
ISLES OF SCILLY (1976), 16 sq. km/6 sq. miles
KENT DOWNS (1968), 878 sq. km/339 sq. miles
LINCOLNSHIRE WOLDS (1973), 558 sq. km/215 sq. miles
LLYN (1957), Gwynedd, 155 sq. km/60 sq. miles
MALVERN HILLS (1959), Gloucestershire/Worcestershire, 105 sq. km/41 sq. miles
MENDIP HILLS (1972; extended 1989), Somerset, 198 sq. km/76 sq. miles
NIDDERDALE (1994), North Yorkshire, 603 sq. km/233 sq. miles
NORFOLK COAST (1968), 451 sq. km/174 sq. miles
NORTH DEVON (1960), 171 sq. km/66 sq. miles
NORTH PENNINES (1988), Cumbria/Durham/North Yorkshire/Northumberland, 1,983 sq. km/766 sq. miles
NORTH WESSEX DOWNS (1972), Hampshire/Oxfordshire/Wiltshire, 1,730 sq. km/668 sq. miles

NORTHUMBERLAND COAST (1958), 138 sq. km/64 sq. miles
QUANTOCK HILLS (1957), Somerset, 99 sq. km/38 sq. miles
SHROPSHIRE HILLS (1959), 804 sq. km/310 sq. miles
SOLWAY COAST (1964), Cumbria, 115 sq. km/44 sq. miles
SOUTH DEVON (1960), 337 sq. km/130 sq. miles
SUFFOLK COAST AND HEATHS (1970), 403 sq. km/156 sq. miles
SURREY HILLS (1958), 419 sq. km/162 sq. miles
TAMAR VALLEY (1995), Cornwall/Devon, 190 sq. km/73 sq. miles
WYE VALLEY (1971), Gloucestershire/Herefordshire/Monmouthshire, 326 sq. km/126 sq. miles
YNYS MON (ISLE OF ANGLESEY) (1967), 221 sq. km/85 sq. miles

NORTHERN IRELAND

The Department of Agriculture, Environment and Rural Affairs (Northern Ireland), with advice from the Council for Nature Conservation and the Countryside, designates AONBs in Northern Ireland. Dates given are those of designation.

ANTRIM COAST AND GLENS (1988), Co. Antrim, 725 sq. km/280 sq. miles
BINEVENAGH (2006), Co. Londonderry, 166 sq. km/64 sq. miles
CAUSEWAY COAST (1989), Co. Antrim, 42 sq. km/ 16 sq. miles
LAGAN VALLEY (1965), Co. Down, 39 sq. km/15 sq. miles
MOURNE (1986), Co. Down, 580 sq. km/224 sq. miles
RING OF GULLION (1991), Co. Armagh, 153 sq. km/59 sq. miles
SPERRIN (1968; extended 2008), Co. Tyrone/Co. Londonderry, 1,182 sq. km/456 sq. miles
STRANGFORD LOUGH (2010), Co. Down, 528 sq. km/204 sq. miles

NATIONAL SCENIC AREAS

In Scotland, national scenic areas have a broadly equivalent status to AONBs. Scottish Natural Heritage recognises areas of national scenic significance. As at June 2019, there were 40, covering a land area of 1,021,600 hectares (2,524,400 acres) and a marine area of 359,500 hectares (888,300 acres).

Development within national scenic areas is dealt with by local authorities, who are required to consult Scottish Natural Heritage concerning certain categories of development. Disagreements between Scottish Natural Heritage and local authorities are referred to the Scottish government. Land management uses can also be modified in the interest of scenic conservation.

ASSYNT-COIGACH, Highland, 90,200ha/222,884 acres
BEN NEVIS AND GLEN COE, Highland, 101,600ha/251,053 acres
CAIRNGORM MOUNTAINS, Highland/Aberdeenshire/Moray, 67,200ha/166,051 acres
CUILLIN HILLS, Highland, 21,900ha/54,115 acres
DEESIDE AND LOCHNAGAR, Aberdeenshire, 40,000ha/98,840 acres
DORNOCH FIRTH, Highland, 7,500ha/18,532 acres
EAST STEWARTRY COAST, Dumfries and Galloway, 4,500ha/11,119 acres
EILDON AND LEADERFOOT, Borders, 3,600ha/8,896 acres

FLEET VALLEY, Dumfries and Galloway, 5,300ha/13,096 acres
GLEN AFFRIC, Highland, 19,300ha/47,690 acres
GLEN STRATHFARRAR, Highland, 3,800ha/9,390 acres
HOY AND WEST MAINLAND, Orkney Islands, 14,800ha/36,571 acres
JURA, Argyll and Bute, 21,800ha/53,868 acres
KINTAIL, Highland, 15,500ha/38,300 acres
KNAPDALE, Argyll and Bute, 19,800ha/48,926 acres
KNOYDART, Highland, 39,500ha/97,604 acres
KYLE OF TONGUE, Highland, 18,500ha/45,713 acres
KYLES OF BUTE, Argyll and Bute, 4,400ha/10,872 acres
LOCH LOMOND, Argyll and Bute, 27,400ha/67,705 acres
LOCH NA KEAL, Mull, Argyll and Bute, 12,700ha/31,382 acres
LOCH RANNOCH AND GLEN LYON, Perthshire and Kinross, 48,400ha/119,596 acres
LOCH SHIEL, Highland, 13,400ha/33,111 acres
LOCH TUMMEL, Perthshire and Kinross, 9,200ha/22,733 acres
LYNN OF LORN, Argyll and Bute, 4,800ha/11,861 acres
MORAR, MOIDART AND ARDNAMURCHAN, Highland, 13,500ha/33,358 acres
NITH ESTUARY, Dumfries and Galloway, 9,300ha/22,980 acres
NORTH ARRAN, North Ayrshire, 23,800ha/58,810 acres
NORTH-WEST SUTHERLAND, Highland, 20,500ha/50,655 acres
RIVER EARN, Perthshire and Kinross, 3,000ha/7,413 acres
RIVER TAY, Perthshire and Kinross, 5,600ha/13,838 acres
ST KILDA, Eilean Siar (Western Isles), 900ha/2,224 acres
SCARBA, LUNGA AND THE GARVELLACHS, Argyll and Bute, 1,900ha/4,695 acres
SHETLAND, Shetland Isles, 11,600ha/28,664 acres
SMALL ISLANDS, Highland, 15,500ha/38,300 acres
SOUTH LEWIS, HARRIS AND NORTH UIST, Eilean Siar (Western Isles), 109,600ha/270,822 acres
SOUTH UIST MACHAIR, Eilean Siar (Western Isles), 6,100ha/15,073 acres
THE TROSSACHS, Stirling, 4,600ha/11,367 acres
TROTTERNISH, Highland, 5,000ha/12,355 acres
UPPER TWEEDDALE, Borders, 10,500ha/25,945 acres
WESTER ROSS, Highland, 145,300ha/359,036 acres

THE NATIONAL FOREST

The National Forest is one of the UK's biggest environmental projects, creating a forest across 518.5 sq. km (200.2 sq. miles) of Derbyshire, Leicestershire and Staffordshire. Since the early 1990s, more than 8.9 million trees have been planted to create over 7,000ha of new woodland landscapes. Forest cover has increased from 6 per cent to 20 per cent, with the aim of eventually covering approximately one-third of the designated area.

Since its establishment in 1995, the National Forest Company leads the project and is responsible for delivery of the government-approved National Forest Strategy, sponsored by DEFRA. Priorities include continued forest creation and management, economic development of the area for recreation and tourism, and engaging local communities in the forest to improve quality of life.

NATIONAL FOREST COMPANY, Enterprise Glade, Bath Yard, Moira, Swadlincote, Derbyshire DE12 6BA
T 01283-551211 E enquiries@nationalforest.org
W www.nationalforest.org
Chief Executive, John Everitt

SITES OF SPECIAL SCIENTIFIC INTEREST

A site of special scientific interest (SSSI) is a legal notification applied to land in England, Scotland or Wales which Natural England (NE), Scottish Natural Heritage (SNH) or Natural Resources Wales (NRW) identifies as being of special interest because of its flora, fauna, geological or physiographical features. In some cases, SSSIs are managed as nature reserves.

NE, SNH and NRW must notify the designation of an SSSI to the local planning authority, every owner/occupier of the land, and the environment secretary, the Scottish ministers or the Welsh government. The Environment Agency (in England), water companies and internal drainage authorities and a number of other interested parties are also formally notified.

Objections to the notification of an SSSI can be made and ultimately considered at a full meeting of the board of NE or, in Wales, a subgroup committee of the NRW board. In Scotland an objection will be dealt with by the main board of SNH or an appropriate subgroup.

The protection of these sites depends on the cooperation of individual landowners and occupiers. Owner/occupiers must consult NE, SNH or NRW and gain written consent before they can undertake certain listed activities on the site. Funds are available through management agreements and grants to assist owners and occupiers in conserving sites' interests. Sites can also be protected by management schemes, management notices and other enforcement mechanisms. As a last resort a site can be purchased.

SSSIs in Britain as at June 2019:

	Number	Hectares	Acres
England	4,125	1,096,608	2,709,777
Scotland	1,423	1,022,883	2,527,599
Wales	1,077	262,233	647,993

Sources: Natural England; © Natural Resources Wales and database right (all rights reserved); Scottish Natural Heritage

NORTHERN IRELAND

In Northern Ireland areas of special scientific interest (ASSIs) are designated by the Department of Agriculture, Environment and Rural Affairs (Northern Ireland).

NATIONAL NATURE RESERVES

National Nature Reserves are defined in the National Parks and Access to the Countryside Act 1949 as modified by the Natural Environment and Rural Communities Act 2006. National Nature Reserves may be managed solely for the purpose of conservation, or for both the purposes of conservation and recreation, providing this does not compromise the conservation purpose.

NE, SNH or NRW can declare as a national nature reserve land which is held and managed as a nature reserve under an agreement; land held and managed by NE, SNH or NRW; or land held and managed as a nature reserve by an approved body. NE, SNH or NRW can make by-laws to protect reserves from undesirable activities; these are subject to confirmation by the Secretary of State for Environment, Food and Rural Affairs, the Welsh government or the Scottish ministers.

National nature reserves in Britain as at June 2019:

	Number	Hectares	Acres
England	224	93,912	232,062
Scotland	43	154,262	381,190
Wales	76	26,362	65,143

Sources: Natural England; © Natural Resources Wales and database right (all rights reserved); Scottish Natural Heritage

NORTHERN IRELAND

Nature reserves are established and managed by the Department of Agriculture, Environment and Rural Affairs (Northern Ireland), with advice from the Council for Nature Conservation and the Countryside. Nature reserves are declared under the Nature Conservation and Amenity Lands (Northern Ireland) Order 1985.

LOCAL NATURE RESERVES

Local Nature Reserves are defined in the National Parks and Access to the Countryside Act 1949 (as amended by the Natural Environment and Rural Communities Act 2006) as land designated for the study and preservation of flora and fauna, or of geological or physiographical features. Local Nature Reserves also have a statutory obligation to provide opportunities for the enjoyment of nature or open air recreation, providing this does not compromise the conservation purpose of the reserve. Local authorities in England, Scotland and Wales have the power to acquire, declare and manage reserves in consultation with NE, SNH and NRW. There is similar legislation in Northern Ireland, where the consulting organisation is the Environment Agency.

Any organisation, such as water companies, educational trusts, local amenity groups and charitable nature conservation bodies, such as wildlife trusts, may manage local nature reserves, provided that a local authority has a legal interest in the land. This means that the local authority must either own it, lease it or have a management agreement with the landowner.

Designated local nature reserves in Britain as at June 2019:

	Number	Hectares	Acres
England	1,622	41,954	103,671
Scotland	75	10,780	26,638
Wales	95	6,187	15,289

Sources: Natural England; © Natural Resources Wales and database right (all rights reserved); Scottish Natural Heritage

There are also local nature reserves in Northern Ireland.

FOREST RESERVES

The Forestry Commission is the government department responsible for forestry policy throughout Great Britain. Forestry is a devolved matter, with the separate Forestry Commissions for England, Scotland and Wales reporting directly to their appropriate minister. The equivalent body in Northern Ireland is the Forest Service, an agency of the Department of Agriculture and Rural Development for Northern Ireland. The Forestry Commission in each country is led by a director who is also a member of the GB Board of Commissioners. As at March 2018, UK woodland certified by the Forestry Commission (including Forestry Commission-managed woodland) amounted to around 1,388,000ha (3,429,823 acres): 337,000ha (832,745 acres) in England, 145,000ha (358,303 acres) in Wales, 841,000ha (2,078,156 acres) in Scotland and 65,000ha (160,619 acres) in Northern Ireland.

There are forest nature reserves in Northern Ireland, designated and administered by the Forest Service.

MARINE NATURE RESERVES

Marine protected areas provide protection for marine flora and fauna, and geological and physiographical features on land covered by tidal waters or parts of the sea in or adjacent to the UK. These areas also provide opportunities for study and research.

ENGLAND AND WALES

The Marine and Coastal Access Act 2009 created a new kind of statutory protection for marine protected areas in England and Wales, marine conservation zones (MCZs), which are designed to increase the protection of species and habitats deemed to be of national importance. The Secretary of State for Environment, Food and Rural Affairs and the Welsh ministers have the power to designate MCZs. Individual MCZs can have varying levels of protection: some include specific activities that are appropriately managed, while others prohibit all damaging and disturbing activities. The act converted the waters around Lundy Island, a former marine protected area, to MCZ status in 2010 and this was formerly designated as such in 2013. Similarly, the marine nature reserve in the waters around Skomer was reclassified and designated an MCZ in 2014; forming the only MCZ solely in Welsh waters.

In 2009, Natural England and the Joint Nature Conservation Committee (JNCC) gave sea-users and stakeholders the ability to recommend potential MCZs to the UK government by establishing four regional projects. On 21 November 2013, the government announced the creation of 27 MCZs, covering an area of around 9,700 sq. km, to protect wildlife including seahorses, coral reefs and oyster beds from dredging and bottom-trawling. In January 2016, 23 additional MCZs were designated and in May 2019, a further 41 sites were added to the list, bringing the total to 91. The new MCZ designations means that around 30 per cent of English waters are considered protected. Information on all 91 MCZs (with date designation confirmed) can be found online
W   www.gov.uk/government/collections/marine-conservation-zone-designations-in-england

SCOTLAND

In July 2014, under the Marine (Scotland) Act 2010, the Scottish government designated 17 marine protected areas (MPAs) in Scottish inshore territorial waters (Clyde Sea Sill; East Caithness Cliffs; Fetlar to Haroldswick; Loch Creran; Loch Sunart; Loch Sunart to the Sound of Jura; Loch Sween; Lochs Duich, Long and Alsh; Monarch Isles; Mousa to Boddam; Noss Head; Papa Westray; Small Isles; South Arran; Upper Loch Fyne and Loch Goil; Wester Ross; and Wyre and Rousay Sounds). In 2017 Loch Carron was designated an inshore MPA.

A further 13, also in July 2014, were designated in offshore waters under the UK Marine and Coastal Access Act 2009. These are: Central Fladen; East of Gannet and Montrose Fields; Faroe–Shetland Sponge Belt; Firth of Forth Banks Complex; Geikie Slide and Hebridean Slope; Hatton–Rockall Basin; North-east Faroe Shetland Channel; North-west Orkney; Norwegian Boundary Sediment Plain; Rosemary Bank Seamount; The Barra Fan and Hebrides Terrace Seamount; Turbot Bank; and West Shetland Shelf.

NORTHERN IRELAND

The Marine Act (Northern Ireland) 2013 includes provisions for establishing Marine Conservation Zones (MCZs), as well as a system of marine planning, fisheries management and marine licensing. MCZs may be designated for various purposes including the conservation of marine species and habitats, taking fully into account any economic, cultural or social consequences of doing so. The Act also allows the NI Department of Agriculture, Environment and Rural Affairs to make byelaws to protect MCZs from damage caused by unregulated activities such as anchoring, kite surfing or jet skiing. It is an offence to intentionally or recklessly destroy or damage a protected feature of an MCZ.

As at June 2019 there were five MCZs in Northern Ireland. Strangford Lough was Northern Ireland's only marine nature reserve, established in 1995 under the Nature Conservation and Amenity Lands Order (Northern Ireland) 1985, but it was redesignated as Northern Ireland's first MCZ on the introduction of the Marine Act (Northern Ireland) 2013. After a consultation period, the NI Department of Agriculture, Environment and Rural Affairs announced four new MCZ's in December 2016; Carlingford Lough, Outer Belfast Lough, Rathlin and Waterfoot.

INTERNATIONAL CONVENTIONS

The UK is party to a number of international conventions.

BERN CONVENTION

The 1979 Bern Convention on the Conservation of European Wildlife and Natural Habitats came into force in the UK in June 1982. There are 51 contracting parties and a number of other states attend meetings as observers.

The aims are to conserve wild flora and fauna and their habitats, especially where this requires the cooperation of several countries, and to promote such cooperation. The convention imposes legal obligations on contracting parties, protecting over 500 wild plant species and more than 1,000 wild animal species.

All parties to the convention must promote national conservation policies and take account of the conservation of wild flora and fauna when setting planning and development policies. The contracting parties are invited to submit reports to the standing committee every four years.

SECRETARIAT OF THE BERN CONVENTION STANDING COMMITTEE, Council of Europe, Avenue de l'Europe, F-67075 Strasbourg Cedex, France
W www.coe.int/bernconvention

BIOLOGICAL DIVERSITY

The UK ratified the Convention on Biological Diversity (CBD) in June 1994. As at June 2019 there were 196 parties to the convention.

There are seven programmes addressing agricultural biodiversity, marine and coastal biodiversity and the biodiversity of inland waters, dry and sub-humid lands, islands, mountains and forests. On 29 January 2000 the Conference of the Parties adopted a supplementary agreement to the convention known as the Cartagena Protocol on Biosafety. The protocol seeks to protect biological diversity from potential risks that may be posed by introducing modified living organisms, resulting from biotechnology, into the environment. As at June 2019, 171 countries were party to the protocol; the UK joined on 17 February 2004. The Nagoya Protocol on Access and Benefit-sharing was adopted in October 2010 and entered into force on 12 October 2014. It provides international rules and procedure on liability and redress for damage to biodiversity resulting from living modified organisms. As at June 2019, 117 countries were party to the protocol; the UK became party on 22 May 2016. The Nagoya-Kuala Lumpur Supplementary Protocol on Liability and Redress was adopted as a supplementary agreement to the Cartagena Protocol on Biosafety. It aims to contribute to the conservation and sustainable use of biodiversity by providing international rules and procedures in the field of liability and redress relating to living modified organisms; requiring that response measures are taken in the event of damage resulting from living modified organisms, or where there is sufficient likelihood that damage will result if timely response measures are not taken. The Nagoya-Kuala Lumpur Supplementary Protocol entered into force on 5 March 2018; as at June 2019 44 countries, including the UK, were party to the protocol.

The UK Biodiversity Action Plan (UKBAP), published in 1994, was the UK government's response to the CBD at the 1992 Rio Earth Summit. The UK Post-2010 Biodiversity Framework replaced UKBAP when it was published in 2012 by DEFRA and the devolved administrations. The framework covers the period 2011–20 and forms the UK government's response to the strategic plan of the CBD. It includes five internationally agreed strategic goals to be achieved by 2020: to address the underlying causes of biodiversity loss by making biodiversity a mainstream issue across government and society; to reduce the direct pressures on biodiversity and promote sustainable use; to safeguard ecosystems, species and genetic diversity; to enhance the benefits to all from biodiversity and ecosystem services; and to enhance implementation through participatory planning, knowledge management and capacity building. The list of priority species and habitats under the biodiversity framework covers 1,150 species and 65 habitats and is administered by the Joint Nature Conservation Committee (JNCC).

SECRETARIAT OF THE CONVENTION ON BIOLOGICAL DIVERSITY, 413, Saint Jacques Street, suite 800, Montreal, QC H2Y 1N9 Canada
T +1514-288 2220 E secretariat@cbd.int W www.cbd.int
JNCC, Monkstone House, City Road, Peterborough PE1 1JY
T 01733-562626 W www.jncc.defra.gov.uk

BONN CONVENTION

The 1979 Convention on Conservation of Migratory Species of Wild Animals (also known as the CMS or Bonn Convention) came into force in the UK in October 1985. As at June 2019, 128 countries were party to the convention.

It requires the protection of listed endangered migratory species and encourages international agreements covering these and other threatened species.

Seven agreements have been concluded to date under the convention. They aim to conserve African-Eurasian migratory waterbirds; albatrosses and petrels; European bats; cetaceans of the Black Sea, Mediterranean and contiguous Atlantic area; small cetaceans in the Baltic, north-east Atlantic, Irish and North Seas; gorillas and their habitats; and seals in the Wadden Sea. A further 19 memorandums of understanding have been agreed for West-African populations of the African elephant, aquatic warbler, bukhara deer, cetaceans of the Pacific Islands, dugongs (large marine mammals), middle-European population of the great bustard, high Andean flamingos, huemuls (Andean deer). manatee and small cetaceans of Western Africa and Macaronesia, marine turtles of the Atlantic coast of Africa, Indian Ocean and South East Asia, migratory birds of prey in Africa and Eurasia, migratory grassland birds of southern South America, migratory sharks, eastern-Atlantic populations of the Mediterranean monk seal, ruddy-headed goose, saiga antelope, Siberian crane and the slender-billed curlew. In addition, there are four special species initiatives for: African carnivores, central Asian mammals, Sahelo–Saharan megafauna and the central Asian flyway.

UNEP/CMS SECRETARIAT, Platz der Vereinten Nationen 1, 53113 Bonn, Germany T (+49) (228) 815 2401
E cms.secretariat@cms.int W www.cms.int

CITES

The 1973 Convention on International Trade in Endangered Species of Wild Fauna and Flora (CITES), which entered into force in 1975, is an agreement between governments to ensure that international trade in specimens of wild animals and plants does not threaten their survival. The convention came into force in the UK in October 1976 and there are currently 183 member countries. Countries party to the convention ban commercial international trade in an agreed list of endangered species and regulate and monitor trade in other species that might become endangered. The convention accords varying degrees of protection to approximately 30,000 species of plants and 5,800 species of animals, whether they are traded as live specimens or as products derived from them.

The Conference of the Parties to CITES meets every two to three years to review the convention's implementation. The Animal and Plant Health Agency at the Department for Environment, Food and Rural Affairs carries out the government's responsibilities under CITES.

CITES is implemented in the EU through a series of EC regulations known as the Wildlife Trade Regulations.

CITES SECRETARIAT, Palais des Nations, Avenue de la Paix 8-14, 1211 Genève 10, Switzerland T (+41) (22) 917 8139/40
E info@cites.org W www.cites.org

INTERNATIONAL CONVENTION FOR THE REGULATION OF WHALING

The International Convention for the Regulation of Whaling was signed in Washington DC in 1946 and currently has 88 member countries.

The measures in the convention provide for the complete protection of certain species; designate specified areas as whale sanctuaries; set limits on the numbers and size of whales which may be taken; prescribe open and closed seasons and areas for whaling; and prohibit the capture of suckling calves and female whales accompanied by calves. The International Whaling Commission meets biennially to review and revise these measures.

INTERNATIONAL WHALING COMMISSION, The Red House, 135 Station Road, Impington, Cambridge CB24 9NP
T 01223-233971 W www.iwc.int

OSPAR

The Convention for the Protection of the Marine Environment of the North-East Atlantic (the OSPAR Convention) was adopted in Paris, France in September 1992 and entered into force in March 1998. The OSPAR Convention replaced both the Oslo Convention (1972) and the Paris Convention (1974), with the intention of providing a comprehensive approach to addressing all sources of pollution which may affect the maritime area, and matters relating to the protection of the maritime environment. An annex on biodiversity and ecosystems was adopted in 1998 to cover non-polluting human activities that can adversely affect the sea.

Fifteen countries plus the European Union are party to the convention; the UK ratified OSPAR in 1998. The OSPAR Commission makes decisions and recommendations and sets out actions to be taken by the contracting parties. The OSPAR Secretariat administers the work under the convention, coordinates the work of the contracting parties and runs the formal meeting schedule of OSPAR.

OSPAR COMMISSION, The Aspect, 12 Finsbury Square, London EC2A 1AS T 020-7430 5200 E secretariat@ospar.org
W www.ospar.org

RAMSAR CONVENTION

The 1971 Convention on Wetlands of National Importance, called the Ramsar Convention, is an inter-governmental treaty that provides for the conservation and sustainable use of wetlands and their resources. The Convention entered into force in the UK in 1976.

Governments that are contracting parties to the convention must designate wetlands for inclusion in the List of Wetlands of International Importance (the 'Ramsar List') and include wetland conservation considerations in their land-use planning. As at June 2019, the Convention's 170 contracting parties had designated 2,354 wetland sites, covering 252,537,889 hectares. The UK currently has 175 designated sites covering 1,283,040 hectares.

The contracting parties meet every three years to assess progress. The 13th Meeting of the Conference of the Contracting Parties to the Ramsar Convention on Wetlands took place in Dubai, UAE in October 2018.

RAMSAR CONVENTION SECRETARIAT, Rue Mauverney 28, CH-1196 Gland, Switzerland T (+41) (22) 999 0170 E ramsar@ramsar.org W https://www.ramsar.org

UK LEGISLATION

The Wildlife and Countryside Act 1981 gives legal protection to a wide range of wild animals and plants. Every five years the statutory nature conservation agencies (Natural England, Natural Resources Wales and Scottish Natural Heritage), working jointly through the Joint Nature Conservation Committee, are required to review schedules 5 (animals, other than birds) and 8 (plants) of the Wildlife and Countryside Act 1981. They make recommendations to the Secretary of State for Environment, Food and Rural Affairs, the Welsh ministers and the Scottish government for changes to these schedules. The most recent variations of schedules 5 and 8 for England came into effect on 1 October 2011, following the fifth quinquennial review. The sixth review was submitted to DEFRA, the Welsh government and the Scottish government in April 2014; once these governments have considered the review, they will respond formally and publish amendments to the Wildlife and Countryside Act (1981).

Under section 9 of the act it is an offence to kill, injure, take, possess or sell (whether alive or dead) any wild animal included in schedule 5 of the act and to disturb its place of shelter and protection or to destroy that place. However certain species listed on schedule 5 are protected against some, but not all, of these activities.

Under section 13 of the act it is illegal without a licence to pick, uproot, sell or destroy plants listed in schedule 8. Since January 2001, under the Countryside and Rights of Way Act 2000, persons found guilty of an offence under part 1 of the Wildlife and Countryside Act 1981 face a maximum penalty of up to £5,000 and/or up to a six-month custodial sentence per specimen.

BIRDS

The act lays down a close season for birds (listed on Schedule 2, part 1) from 1 February to 31 August inclusive, each year. Variations to these dates are made for:
Black grouse – 10 December to 20 August (10 December – 1 September for Somerset, Devon and New Forest)
Capercaillie – 1 February to 30 September (England and Wales only)
Grey partridge – 1 February to 1 September
Pheasant – 1 February to 1 October
Ptarmigan and Red grouse – 10 December to 12 August
Red-legged partridge – 1 February to 1 September
Snipe – 1 February to 11 August
Woodcock – 1 February to 30 September (England and Wales); 1 February to 31 August (Scotland)
Birds listed on schedule 2, part 1 (below high water mark) (see below) – 21 February to 31 August
Wild duck and wild geese, in or over any area below the high-water mark of ordinary spring tides – 21 February to 31 August
Sundays and Christmas Day in Scotland, and Sundays for any area of England or Wales prescribed by the Secretary of State.

Birds listed on schedule 2, part 1, which may be killed or taken outside the close season are: capercaillie (England and Wales only); coot; certain wild duck (gadwall, goldeneye, mallard, Northern pintail, common pochard, Northern shoveler, teal, tufted duck, Eurasian wigeon); certain wild geese (Canada, greylag, pink-footed, white-fronted (in England and Wales only); golden plover; moorhen; snipe; and woodcock.

Section 16 of the 1981 act allows licences to be issued on either an individual or general basis, to allow the killing, taking and sale of certain birds for specified reasons such as public health and safety. All other wild birds are fully protected by law throughout the year.

ANIMALS PROTECTED BY SCHEDULE 5

Adder *(Vipera berus)*
Anemone, Ivell's Sea *(Edwardsia ivelli)*
Anemone, Starlet Sea *(Nematostella vectensis)*
Bat, Horseshoe, all species *(Rhinolophidae)*
Bat, Typical, all species *(Vespertilionidae)*
Beetle *(Hypebaeus flavipes)*
Beetle, Bembridge Water *(Paracymus aeneus)*
Beetle, Lesser Silver Water *(Hydrochara caraboides)*
Beetle, Mire Pill *(Curimopsis nigrita)*
Beetle, Moccas *(Hypebaeus flavipes)*
Beetle, Rainbow Leaf *(Chrysolina cerealis)*
Beetle, Spangled Water *(Graphoderus zonatus)*
Beetle, Stag *(Lucanus cervus)*
Beetle, Violet Click *(Limoniscus violaceus)*
Beetle, Water *(Paracymus aeneus)*
Burbot *(Lota lota)*
Butterfly, Adonis Blue *(Lysandra bellargus)*
Butterfly, Black Hairstreak *(Strymonidia pruni)*
Butterfly, Brown Hairstreak *(Thecla betulae)*
Butterfly, Chalkhill Blue *(Lysandra coridon)*
Butterfly, Chequered Skipper *(Carterocephalus palaemon)*
Butterfly, Duke of Burgundy Fritillary *(Hamearis lucina)*
Butterfly, Glanville Fritillary *(Melitaea cinxia)*
Butterfly, Heath Fritillary *(Mellicta athalia or Melitaea athalia)*
Butterfly, High Brown Fritillary *(Argynnis adippe)*
Butterfly, Large Blue *(Maculinea arion)*
Butterfly, Large Copper *(Lycaena dispar)*
Butterfly, Large Heath *(Coenonympha tullia)*
Butterfly, Large Tortoiseshell *(Nymphalis polychloros)*
Butterfly, Lulworth Skipper *(Thymelicus acteon)*
Butterfly, Marsh Fritillary *(Eurodryas aurinia)*
Butterfly, Mountain Ringlet *(Erebia epiphron)*
Butterfly, Northern Brown Argus *(Aricia artaxerxes)*
Butterfly, Pearl-bordered Fritillary *(Boloria euphrosyne)*
Butterfly, Purple Emperor *(Apatura iris)*
Butterfly, Silver Spotted Skipper *(Hesperia comma)*
Butterfly, Silver-studded Blue *(Plebejus argus)*
Butterfly, Small Blue *(Cupido minimus)*
Butterfly, Swallowtail *(Papilio machaon)*
Butterfly, White Letter Hairstreak *(Stymonida w-album)*
Butterfly, Wood White *(Leptidea sinapis)*
Cat, Wild *(Felis silvestris)*
Cicada, New Forest *(Cicadetta montana)*
Crayfish, Atlantic Stream *(Austropotamobius pallipes)*
Cricket, Field *(Gryllus campestris)*
Cricket, Mole *(Gryllotalpa gryllotalpa)*

Damselfly, Southern *(Coenagrion mercuriale)*
Dolphin, all species *(Cetacea)*
Dormouse *(Muscardinus avellanarius)*
Dragonfly, Norfolk Aeshna *(Aeshna isosceles)*
Frog, Common *(Rana temporaria)*
Frog, Pool, Northern Clade *(Pelophylax lessonae)*
Goby, Couch's *(Gobius couchii)*
Goby, Giant *(Gobius cobitis)*

Grasshopper, Wart-biter *Decticus verrucivorus*
Hatchet Shell, Northern *(Thyasira gouldi)*
Hydroid, Marine *(Clavopsella navis)*
Lagoon Snail, De Folin's *(Caecum armoricum)*
Lagoon Worm, Tentacled *(Alkmaria romijni)*
Leech, Medicinal *(Hirudo medicinalis)*
Lizard, Sand *(Lacerta agilis)*
Lizard, Viviparous *(Lacerta vivipara)*
Marten, Pine *(Martes martes)*
Moth, Barberry Carpet *(Pareulype berberata)*
Moth, Black-veined *(Siona lineata* or *Idaea lineata)*
Moth, Fiery Clearwing *(Bembecia chrysidiformis)*
Moth, Fisher's Estuarine *(Gortyna borelii)*
Moth, New Forest Burnet *(Zygaena viciae)*
Moth, Reddish Buff *(Acosmetia caliginosa)*
Moth, Slender Scotch Burnet *(Zygaena loti)*
Moth, Sussex Emerald *(Thalera fimbrialis)*
Moth, Talisker Burnet *(Zygaena lonicerae)*
Mussel, Fan *(Atrina fragilis)*
Mussel, Freshwater Pearl *(Margaritifera margaritifera)*
Newt, Great Crested (or Warty) *(Triturus cristatus)*
Newt, Palmate *(Triturus helveticus)*
Newt, Smooth *(Triturus vulgaris)*
Otter, Common *(Lutra lutra)*
Porpoise, all species *(Cetacea)*
Sandworm, Lagoon *(Armandia cirrhosa)*
Sea Fan, Pink *(Eunicella verrucosa)*
Sea Slug, Lagoon *(Tenellia adspersa)*
Sea-mat, Trembling *(Victorella pavida)*
Seahorse, Short Snouted (England only)
(Hippocampus hippocampus)
Seahorse, Spiny (England only) *(Hippocampus guttulatus)*
Shad, Allis *(Alosa alosa)*
Shad, Twaite *(Alosa fallax)*
Shark, Angel (England only) *(Squatina squatina)*
Shark, Basking *(Cetorhinus maximus)*
Shrimp, Fairy *(Chirocephalus diaphanus)*
Shrimp, Lagoon Sand *(Gammarus insensibilis)*
Shrimp, Tadpole (Apus) *(Triops cancriformis)*
Skate, White *(Rostroraja alba)*
Slow-worm *(Anguis fragilis)*
Snail, Glutinous *(Myxas glutinosa)*
Snail, Roman (England only) *(Helix pomatia)*
Snail, Sandbowl *(Catinella arenaria)*
Snake, Grass *(Natrix natrix* or *Natrix helvetica)*
Snake, Smooth *(Coronella austriaca)*
Spider, Fen Raft *(Dolomedes plantarius)*
Spider, Ladybird *(Eresus niger)*
Squirrel, Red *(Sciurus vulgaris)*
Sturgeon *(Acipenser sturio)*
Toad, Common *(Bufo bufo)*
Toad, Natterjack *(Bufo calamita)*
Turtle, Flatback *(Cheloniidae/Natator Depressus)*
Turtle, Green Sea *(Chelonia mydas)*
Turtle, Hawksbill *(Eretmochelys imbricate)*
Turtle, Kemp's Ridley Sea *(Lepidochelys kempii)*
Turtle, Leatherback Sea *(Dermo chelys coriacea)*
Turtle, Loggerhead Sea *(Caretta caretta)*
Turtle, Olive Ridley *(Lepidochelys olivacea)*
Vendace *(Coregonus albula)*
Vole, Water *(Arvicola terrestris)*
Walrus *(Odobenus rosmarus)*
Whale, all species *(Cetacea)*
Whitefish *(Coregonus lavaretus)*

PLANTS PROTECTED BY SCHEDULE 8
Adder's Tongue, Least *(Ophioglossum lusitanicum)*
Alison, Small *(Alyssum alyssoides)*
Anomodon, Long-leaved *(Anomodon longifolius)*

Beech-lichen, New Forest *(Enterographa elaborata)*
Blackwort *(Southbya nigrella)*
Bluebell *(Hyacinthoides non-scripta)*
Bolete, Royal *(Boletus regius)*
Broomrape, Bedstraw *(Orobanche caryophyllacea)*
Broomrape, Oxtongue *(Orobanche loricata)*
Broomrape, Thistle *(Orobanche reticulata)*
Cabbage, Lundy *(Rhynchosinapis wrightii)*
Calamint, Wood *(Calamintha sylvatica)*
Caloplaca, Snow *(Caloplaca nivalis)*
Catapyrenium, Tree *(Catapyrenium psoromoides)*
Catchfly, Alpine *(Lychnis alpina)*
Catillaria, Laurer's *(Catellaria laureri)*
Centaury, Slender *(Centaurium tenuiflorum)*
Cinquefoil, Rock *(Potentilla rupestris)*
Cladonia, Convoluted *(Cladonia convoluta)*
Cladonia, Upright Mountain *(Cladonia stricta)*
Clary, Meadow *(Salvia pratensis)*
Club-rush, Triangular *(Scirpus triquetrus)*
Colt's-foot, Purple *(Homogyne alpina)*
Cotoneaster, Wild *(Cotoneaster integerrimus)*
Cottongrass, Slender *(Eriophorum gracile)*
Cow-wheat, Field *(Melampyrum arvense)*
Crocus, Sand *(Romulea columnae)*
Crystalwort, Lizard *(Riccia bifurca)*
Cudweed, Broad-leaved *(Filago pyramidata)*
Cudweed, Jersey *(Gnaphalium luteoalbum)*
Cudweed, Red-tipped *(Filago lutescens)*
Cut-grass *(Leersia oryzoides)*
Diapensia *(Diapensia lapponica)*
Earwort, Marsh *(Jamesoniella undulifolia)*
Eryngo, Field *(Eryngium campestre)*
Fern, Dickie's Bladder *(Cystopteris dickieana)*
Flapwort, Norfolk *(Leiocolea rutheana)*
Fleabane, Alpine *(Erigeron borealis)*
Fleabane, Small *(Pulicaria vulgaris)*
Fleawort, South Stack *(Tephroseris integrifolia ssp maritima)*
Frostwort, Pointed *(Gymnomitrion apiculatum)*
Fungus, Hedgehog *(Hericium erinaceum)*
Galingale, Brown *(Cyperus fuscus)*
Gentian, Alpine *(Gentiana nivalis)*
Gentian, Dune *(Gentianella uliginosa)*
Gentian, Fringed *(Gentianella ciliata)*
Gentian, Spring *(Gentiana verna)*
Germander, Cut-leaved *(Teucrium botrys)*
Germander, Water *(Teucrium scordium)*
Gladiolus, Wild *(Gladiolus illyricus)*
Goblin Lights *(Catolechia wahlenbergii)*
Goosefoot, Stinking *(Chenopodium vulvaria)*
Grass-poly *(Lythrum hyssopifolia)*
Grimmia, Blunt-leaved *(Grimmia unicolor)*
Gyalecta, Elm *(Gyalecta ulmi)*
Hare's-ear, Sickle-leaved *(Bupleurum falcatum)*
Hare's-ear, Small *(Bupleurum baldense)*
Hawk's-beard, Stinking *(Crepis foetida)*
Hawkweed, Northroe *(Hieracium northroense)*
Hawkweed, Shetland *(Hieracium zetlandicum)*
Hawkweed, Weak-leaved *(Hieracium attenuatifolium)*
Heath, Blue *(Phyllodoce caerulea)*
Helleborine, Red *(Cephalanthera rubra)*
Horsetail, Branched *(Equisetum ramosissimum)*
Hound's-tongue, Green *(Cynoglossum germanicum)*
Knawel, Perennial *(Scleranthus perennis)*
Knotgrass, Sea *(Polygonum maritimum)*
Lecanora, Tarn *(Lecanora archariana)*
Lecidea, Copper *(Lecidea inops)*
Leek, Round-headed *(Allium sphaerocephalon)*
Lettuce, Least *(Lactuca saligna)*
Lichen, Arctic Kidney *(Nephroma arcticum)*

Lichen, Ciliate Strap *(Heterodermia leucomelos)*
Lichen, Coralloid Rosette *(Heterodermia propagulifera)*
Lichen, Ear-lobed Dog *(Peltigera lepidophora)*
Lichen, Forked Hair *(Bryoria furcellata)*
Lichen, Golden Hair *(Teloschistes flavicans)*
Lichen, Orange-fruited Elm *(Caloplaca luteoalba)*
Lichen, River Jelly *(Collema dichotomum)*
Lichen, Scaly Breck *(Squamarina lentigera)*
Lichen, Starry Breck *(Buellia asterella)*
Lily, Snowdon *(Lloydia serotina)*
Liverwort *(Petallophyllum ralfsi)*
Liverwort, Lindenberg's Leafy *(Adelanthus lindenbergianus)*
Lungwort, Tree *(Lobaria pulmonaria)*
Marsh-mallow, Rough *(Althaea hirsuta)*
Milk-parsley, Cambridge *(Selinum carvifolia)*
Moss *(Drepanocladius vernicosus)*
Moss, Alpine Copper *(Mielichoferia mielichoferi)*
Moss, Baltic Bog *(Sphagnum balticum)*
Moss, Blue Dew *(Saelania glaucescens)*
Moss, Blunt-leaved Bristle *(Orthotrichum obtusifolium)*
Moss, Bright Green Cave *(Cyclodictyon laetevirens)*
Moss, Cordate Beard *(Barbula cordata)*
Moss, Cornish Path *(Ditrichum cornubicum)*
Moss, Derbyshire Feather *(Thamnobryum angustifolium)*
Moss, Flamingo *(Desmatodon cernuus)*
Moss, Glaucous Beard *(Barbula glauca)*
Moss, Green Shield *(Buxbaumia viridis)*
Moss, Hair Silk *(Plagiothecium piliferum)*
Moss, Knothole *(Zygodon forsteri)*
Moss, Large Yellow Feather *(Scorpidium turgescens)*
Moss, Millimetre *(Micromitrium tenerum)*
Moss, Multi-fruited River *(Cryphaea lamyana)*
Moss, Nowell's Limestone *(Zygodon gracilis)*
Moss, Polar Feather *(Hygrohypnum polare)*
Moss, Rigid Apple *(Bartramia stricta)*
Moss, Round-leaved Feather *(Rhyncostegium rotundifolium)*
Moss, Schleicher's Thread *(Bryum schleicheri)*
Moss, Triangular Pygmy *(Acaulon triquetrum)*
Moss, Vaucher's Feather *(Hypnum vaucheri)*
Mudwort, Welsh *(Limosella australis)*
Naiad, Holly-leaved *(Najas marina)*
Nail, Rock *(Calicium corynellum)*
Orache, Stalked *(Halimione pedunculata)*
Orchid, Early Spider *(Ophrys sphegodes)*
Orchid, Ghost *(Epipogium aphyllum)*
Orchid, Lapland Marsh *(Dactylorhiza lapponica)*
Orchid, Late Spider *(Ophrys fuciflora)*
Orchid, Lizard *(Himantoglossum hircinum)*
Orchid, Military *(Orchis militaris)*
Orchid, Monkey *(Orchis simia)*
Pannaria, Caledonia *(Panneria ignobilis)*

Parmelia, New Forest *(Parmelia minarum)*
Parmentaria, Oil Stain *(Parmentaria chilensis)*
Pear, Plymouth *(Pyrus cordata)*
Penny-cress, Perfoliate *(Thlaspi perfoliatum)*
Pennyroyal *(Mentha pulegium)*
Pertusaria, Alpine Moss *(Pertusaria bryontha)*
Physcia, Southern Grey *(Physcia tribacioides)*
Pigmyweed *(Crassula aquatica)*
Pine, Ground *(Ajuga chamaepitys)*
Pink, Cheddar *(Dianthus gratianopolitanus)*
Pink, Childing *(Petrorhagia nanteuilii)*
Pink, Deptford (England and Wales only) *(Dianthus armeria)*
Polypore, Oak *(Buglossoporus pulvinus)*
Pseudocyphellaria, Ragged *(Pseudocyphellaria lacerata)*
Psora, Rusty Alpine *(Psora rubiformis)*
Puffball, Sandy Stilt *(Battarraea phalloides)*
Ragwort, Fen *(Senecio paludosus)*
Ramping-fumitory, Martin's *(Fumaria martinii)*
Rampion, Spiked *(Phyteuma spicatum)*
Restharrow, Small *(Ononis reclinata)*
Rock-cress, Alpine *(Arabis alpina)*
Rock-cress, Bristol *(Arabis stricta)*
Rustwort, Western *(Marsupella profunda)*
Sandwort, Norwegian *(Arenaria norvegica)*
Sandwort, Teesdale *(Minuartia stricta)*
Saxifrage, Drooping *(Saxifraga cernua)*
Saxifrage, Tufted *(Saxifraga cespitosa)*
Solenopsora, Serpentine *(Solenopsora liparina)*
Solomon's-seal, Whorled *(Polygonatum verticillatum)*
Sow-thistle, Alpine *(Cicerbita alpina)*
Spearwort, Adder's-tongue *(Ranunculus ophioglossifolius)*
Speedwell, Fingered *(Veronica triphyllos)*
Speedwell, Spiked *(Veronica spicata)*
Spike-rush, Dwarf *(Eleocharis parvula)*
Star-of-Bethlehem, Early *(Gagea bohemica)*
Starfruit *(Damasonium alisma)*
Stonewort, Bearded *(Chara canescens)*
Stonewort, Foxtail *(Lamprothamnium papulosum)*
Strapwort *(Corrigiola litoralis)*
Sulphur-tresses, Alpine *(Alectoria ochroleuca)*
Turpswort *(Geocalyx graveolens)*
Violet, Fen *(Viola persicifolia)*
Viper's-grass *(Scorzonera humilis)*
Water-plantain, Ribbon-leaved *(Alisma gramineum)*
Wood-sedge, Starved *(Carex depauperata)*
Woodsia, Alpine *(Woodsia alpina)*
Woodsia, Oblong *(Woodsia ilvenis)*
Wormwood, Field *(Artemisia campestris)*
Woundwort, Downy *(Stachys germanica)*
Woundwort, Limestone *(Stachys alpina)*
Yellow-rattle, Greater *(Rhinanthus serotinus)*

WORLD HERITAGE SITES

The Convention Concerning the Protection of the World Cultural and Natural Heritage was adopted by the United Nations Educational, Scientific and Cultural Organization (UNESCO) in 1972 and ratified by the UK in 1984. As at July 2019, 193 states were party to the convention. The convention provides for the identification, protection and conservation of cultural and natural sites of outstanding universal value.

Cultural sites may be:
- an extraordinary exponent of human creative genius
- sites representing architectural and technological innovation or cultural interchange
- sites of artistic, historic, aesthetic, archaeological, scientific, ethnologic or anthropologic value
- 'cultural landscapes', ie sites whose characteristics are marked by significant interactions between human populations and their natural environment
- exceptional examples of a traditional settlement or land- or sea-use, especially those threatened by irreversible changes.
- unique or exceptional examples of a cultural tradition or a civilisation either still present or extinct

Natural sites may be:
- those displaying critical periods of earth's history
- superlative examples of on-going ecological and biological processes in the evolution of ecosystems
- those exhibiting remarkable natural beauty and aesthetic significance or those where extraordinary natural phenomena are witnessed
- the habitat of threatened species and plants

Governments which are party to the convention nominate sites in their country for inclusion in the World Heritage List. Nominations are considered by the World Heritage Committee, an inter-governmental committee composed of 21 representatives of the parties to the convention. The committee is advised by the International Council on Monuments and Sites (ICOMOS), the International Centre for the Study of the Preservation and Restoration of Cultural Property (ICCROM) and the International Union for the Conservation of Nature (IUCN). ICOMOS evaluates and reports on proposed cultural and mixed sites, ICCROM provides expert advice and training on how to conserve and restore cultural property and IUCN provides technical evaluations of natural heritage sites and reports on the state of conservation of listed sites.

A prerequisite for inclusion in the World Heritage List is the existence of an effective legal protection system in the country in which the site is situated and a detailed management plan to ensure the conservation of the site. Inclusion in the list does not confer any greater degree of protection on the site than that offered by the national protection framework.

If a site is considered to be in serious danger of decay or damage, the committee may add it to the World Heritage in Danger List. Sites on this list may benefit from particular attention or emergency measures to allay threats and allow them to retain their world heritage status, or in extreme cases of damage or neglect they may lose their world heritage status completely. A total of 53 sites are currently inscribed on the World Heritage in Danger List.

Financial support for the conservation of sites on the World Heritage List is provided by the World Heritage Fund, administered by the World Heritage Committee. The fund's income is derived from compulsory and voluntary contributions from the states party to the convention and from private donations.

WORLD HERITAGE CENTRE, UNESCO, 7 Place de Fontenoy, 75352 Paris 07 SP, France **W** https://whc.unesco.org

DESIGNATED SITES

As at 10 July 2019, following the 43rd session of the World Heritage Committee, 1,121 sites across 167 countries were on the World Heritage List. Of these, 28 are in the UK and four in UK overseas territories; 27 are listed for their cultural significance (†), four for their natural significance (*) and one for both cultural and natural significance. Liverpool's Maritime Mercantile City is the only UK site on the List of World Heritage in Danger. The year in which sites were designated appears in the first set of parentheses. The number in the second set of parentheses denotes the position of each site on the map below.

WORLD HERITAGE SITES IN THE UK

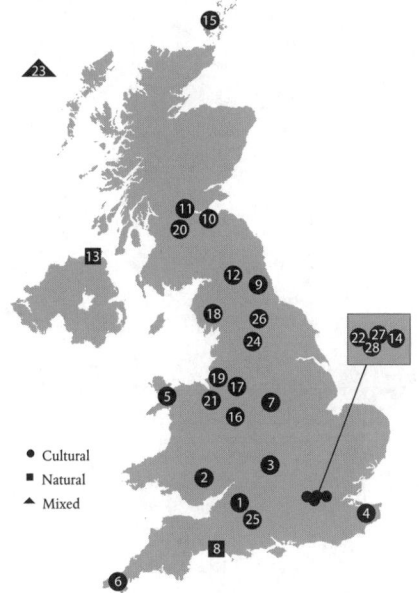

- Cultural
- Natural
- Mixed

UNITED KINGDOM

†Bath – the city (1987). (1)

†Blaenavon industrial landscape, Wales (2000). (2)

†Blenheim Palace and Park, Oxfordshire (1987). (3)

†Canterbury Cathedral, St Augustine's Abbey, St Martin's Church, Kent (1988). (4)

†Castle and town walls of King Edward I, north Wales – Beaumaris, Caernarfon Castle, Conwy Castle, Harlech Castle (1986). (5)

†Cornwall and west Devon mining landscape (2006). (6)

†Derwent Valley Mills, Derbyshire (2001). (7)

*Dorset and east Devon coast (2001). (8)

†Durham Cathedral and Castle (1986). (9)

†Edinburgh old and new towns (1995). (10)

†Forth Bridge, Firth of Forth, Scotland (2015). (11)

†Frontiers of the Roman Empire – Hadrian's Wall, northern England; Antonine Wall, central Scotland (1987, 2005, 2008). (12)

*Giant's Causeway and Causeway coast, Co. Antrim (1986). (13)

†Greenwich, London – maritime Greenwich, including the Royal Naval College, Old Royal Observatory, Queen's House, town centre (1997). (14)

†Heart of Neolithic Orkney (1999). (15)

†Ironbridge Gorge, Shropshire – the world's first iron bridge and other early industrial sites (1986). (16)

†Jodrell Bank Observatory, Cheshire (2019). (17)

†Lake District, Cumbria (2017). (18)

†Liverpool – six areas of the maritime mercantile city (2004). (19)

†New Lanark, South Lanarkshire, Scotland (2001). (20)

†Pontcysyllte Aqueduct and Canal, Wrexham, Wales (2009). (21)

†Royal Botanic Gardens, Kew (2003). (22)

†*St Kilda, Eilean Siar (Western Isles) (1986). (23)

†Saltaire, West Yorkshire (2001). (24)

†Stonehenge, Avebury and related megalithic sites, Wiltshire (1986). (25)

†Studley Royal Park, Fountains Abbey, St Mary's Church, N. Yorkshire (1986). (26)

†Tower of London (1988). (27)

†Westminster Abbey, Palace of Westminster, St Margaret's Church, London (1987). (28)

UK OVERSEAS TERRITORIES

*Henderson Island, Pitcairn Islands, South Pacific Ocean (1988)

*Gough Island and Inaccessible Island (part of Tristan da Cunha), South Atlantic Ocean (1995)

†Historic town of St George and related fortifications, Bermuda (2000)

†Gorham's Cave Complex, Gibraltar (2016)

HISTORIC BUILDINGS AND MONUMENTS

ENGLAND

Under the Planning (Listed Buildings and Conservation Areas) Act 1990, the Secretary of State for Digital, Culture, Media and Sport has a statutory duty to approve buildings or groups of buildings in England that are of special architectural or historic interest. Since April 2015 the list of such buildings is maintained by Historic England who are also responsible for making recommendations to the secretary of state for additions, removals and amendments to the list. Under the Ancient Monuments and Archaeological Areas Act 1979 as amended by the National Heritage Act 1983, the secretary of state is also responsible for compiling a schedule of ancient monuments. Decisions are taken on the advice of Historic England. A searchable database of all nationally designated heritage assets, The National Heritage List for England (NHLE), is available online: W www.historicengland.org.uk/listing/the-list.

LISTED BUILDINGS

Listed buildings are classified into Grade I, Grade II* and Grade II. As at April 2019, there were 378,570 listed buildings in England, of which approximately 90 per cent are Grade II listed. Almost all pre-1700 buildings are listed, as are most buildings of 1700 to 1850. Historic England surveys particular types of buildings with a view to making recommendations for listing. The main purpose of listing is to ensure that care is taken in deciding the future of a building. No changes which affect the architectural or historic character of a listed building can be made without listed building consent (in addition to planning permission where relevant). Applications for consent are normally dealt with by the local planning authority, although Historic England is always consulted about proposals affecting Grade I and Grade II* properties. It is a criminal offence to demolish a listed building, or alter it in such a way as to affect its character, without consent.

SCHEDULED MONUMENTS

As at April 2019, there were 19,862 scheduled monuments in England. All monuments proposed for scheduling are considered to be of national importance. Where buildings are both scheduled and listed, ancient monuments legislation takes precedence. The main purpose of scheduling a monument is to preserve it for the future and to protect it from damage, destruction or any unnecessary interference. Once a monument has been scheduled, scheduled monument consent is required before any works can be carried out. The scope of the control is more extensive and more detailed than that applied to listed buildings, but certain minor works, as detailed in the Ancient Monuments (Class Consents) Order 1994, may be carried out without consent. It is a criminal offence to carry out unauthorised work to scheduled monuments.

WALES

Under the Planning (Listed Buildings and Conservation Areas) Act 1990 and the Ancient Monuments and Archaeological Areas Act 1979, the National Assembly for Wales is responsible for listing buildings and scheduling monuments in Wales on the advice of Cadw (the Welsh government's historic environment division) and the Royal Commission on the Ancient and Historical Monuments of Wales (RCAHMW). The criteria for evaluating buildings are similar to those in England and the same listing system is used. As at April 2019, there were 30,017 listed buildings and 4,203 scheduled monuments in

Wales. A list of National Historic Assets of Wales is available online: W https://cadw.gov.wales/historicenvironment/recordsv1.

SCOTLAND

Under the Planning (Listed Buildings and Conservation Areas) (Scotland) Act 1997 and the Ancient Monuments and Archaeological Areas Act 1979, Scottish ministers are responsible for listing buildings and scheduling monuments in Scotland on the advice of Historic Environment Scotland. The Historic Environment Scotland Act 2014 sets out Historic Environment Scotland's role and legal status. The criteria for evaluating buildings are similar to those in England but an A, B, C categorisation is used. As at April 2019, there were 47,497 listed buildings and 8,283 scheduled monuments in Scotland. A list of historic buildings and monuments in Scotland is available online: W https://portal.historicenvironment.scot/search.

NORTHERN IRELAND

Under the Planning (Northern Ireland) Act 2011 and the Historic Monuments and Archaeological Objects (Northern Ireland) Order 1995, the Historic Environment Division (part of the Department for Communities, Northern Ireland) is responsible for listing buildings and scheduling monuments. The Historic Buildings Council for Northern Ireland and the relevant district council must be consulted on listing proposals, and the Historic Monuments Council for Northern Ireland must be consulted on scheduling proposals. The criteria for evaluating buildings are similar to those in England but an A, B+, B1 and B2 categorisation is used. As at As at May 2019 the most up to date figure was recorded as 8,916 listed buildings and 1,994 scheduled monuments in Norther Ireland.

ENGLAND

English Heritage cares for over 400 historic monuments, buildings and places. For more information on English Heritage properties, including those listed below, the official website is W www.english-heritage.org.uk

For more information on National Trust properties in England, including those listed below, the official website is W www.nationaltrust.org.uk

KEY
(EH) English Heritage property
(NT) National Trust property
* UNESCO World Heritage Site (*see also* World Heritage Sites)

A LA RONDE (NT), Exmouth, Devon EX8 5BD T 01395-265514
   Unique 16-sided house completed c.1796
ALNWICK CASTLE, Alnwick, Northumberland NE66 1NG
   T 01665-511100 W www.alnwickcastle.com
   Seat of the Dukes of Northumberland since 1309; Italian Renaissance-style interior; gardens with spectacular water features
ALTHORP, Northants NN7 4HQ T 01604-770006
   W www.spencerofalthorp.com
   Spencer family seat built in 1508; home to the annual Althorp Literary Festival and Althorp Food and Drink Festival
ANGLESEY ABBEY (NT), Lode, Cambs CB25 9EJ
   T 01223-810080
   Jacobean house (c.1600) with gardens and a working watermill (Lode Mill) on the site of a 12th-century priory; fine furnishings and a unique clock collection

APSLEY HOUSE (EH), London W1J 7NT T 020-7499 5676
Built by Robert Adam 1771–8; home of the Dukes of
Wellington since 1817 and known as 'No. 1 London';
collection of fine and decorative arts

ARUNDEL CASTLE, Arundel, W. Sussex BN18 9AB
T 01903-882173 W www.arundelcastle.org
Castle dating from the Norman Conquest; seat of the
Dukes of Norfolk

AVEBURY (EH/NT), Wilts SN8 1RF T 01672-539250
Remains of stone circles constructed 4,000 years ago
enclosing part of the later village of Avebury

BANQUETING HOUSE, Whitehall, London SW1A 2ER
T 020-3166 6000 W www.hrp.org.uk/banquetinghouse
Designed by Inigo Jones in 1619; ceiling paintings by
Rubens; site of the execution of Charles I

BASILDON PARK (NT), Reading, Berks RG8 9NR
T 01491-672382
Palladian mansion built in 1776–83 by John Carr

BATTLE ABBEY (EH), Battle, E. Sussex TN33 0AD
T 01424-775705
Remains of the abbey founded by William the Conqueror
on the site of the Battle of Hastings

BEESTON CASTLE (EH), Cheshire CW6 9TX T 01829-260464
Built in the 13th century by Ranulf, sixth Earl of Chester,
on the site of an Iron Age hillfort

BELVOIR CASTLE, Grantham, Lincs NG32 1PE
T 01476-871001 W www.belvoircastle.com
Seat of the Dukes of Rutland; 19th-century Gothic-style
castle; notable art collection

BERKELEY CASTLE, Glos GL13 9BQ T 01453-810303
W www.berkeley-castle.com
Completed late 12th century; site of the murder of
Edward II (1327)

BIRDOSWALD ROMAN FORT (EH), Brampton, Cumbria
CA8 7DD T 01697-747602
Stretch of Hadrian's Wall with Roman wall fort, turret
and milecastle

*BLENHEIM PALACE, Woodstock, Oxon OX20 1UL
T 01993-810530 W www.blenheimpalace.com
Seat of the Dukes of Marlborough and Winston
Churchill's birthplace; house designed by Vanbrugh;
landscaped parkland by Capability Brown

BLICKLING ESTATE (NT), Blickling, Norfolk NR11 6NF
T 01263-738030
Jacobean house with state rooms; extensive gardens,
temple and 18th-century orangery

BODIAM CASTLE (NT), Bodiam, E. Sussex TN32 5UA
T 01580-830196
Well-preserved medieval moated castle built in 1385

BOLSOVER CASTLE (EH), Bolsover, Derbys S44 6PR
T 01246-822844
17th-century castle on site of medieval fortress

BOSCOBEL HOUSE (EH), Bishops Wood, Shrops ST19 9AR
T 01902-850244
Timber-framed 17th-century hunting lodge; refuge of
fugitive Charles II from parliamentary troops

BOUGHTON HOUSE, Kettering, Northants NN14 1BJ
T 01536-515731 W www.boughtonhouse.org.uk
17th-century house with French-style additions; home of
the Dukes of Buccleuch and Queensbury

BOWOOD HOUSE, Calne, Wilts SN11 0LZ T 01249-812102
W www.bowood.org/bowood-house-gardens/house/
18th-century house in Capability Brown park, featuring
Robert Adam orangery and renowned pinetum and
arboretum

BUCKFAST ABBEY, Buckfastleigh, Devon TQ11 0EE
T 01364-645500 W www.buckfast.org.uk
Benedictine monastery on medieval foundations

BUCKINGHAM PALACE, London SW1A 1AA
T 030-3123 7300 W www.royalcollection.org.uk
Purchased by George III in 1761, and the Sovereign's
official London residence since 1837; 19 state rooms,
including the Throne Room, and Queen's Gallery

BUCKLAND ABBEY (NT), Yelverton, Devon PL20 6EY
T 01822-853607
13th-century Cistercian monastery; home of Sir Francis
Drake

BURGHLEY HOUSE, Stamford, Lincs PE9 3JY T 01780-752451
W www.burghley.co.uk
Late Elizabethan house built by William Cecil, first Lord
Burghley

CARISBROOKE CASTLE (EH), Newport, Isle of Wight PO30
1XY T 01983-522107
Norman castle; museum; prison of Charles I 1647–8

CARLISLE CASTLE (EH), Carlisle, Cumbria CA3 8UR
T 01228-591922
Medieval castle; prison of Mary, Queen of Scots

CASTLE ACRE PRIORY (EH), King's Lynn, Norfolk PE32 2XD
T 01760-755394
Remains include 12th-century church and prior's lodgings

CASTLE DROGO (NT), Drewsteignton, Devon EX6 6PB
T 01647-433306
Granite castle designed by Lutyens in 1911

CASTLE HOWARD, N. Yorks YO60 7DA T 01653-648333
W www.castlehoward.co.uk
Designed by Vanbrugh 1699–1726; mausoleum designed
by Hawksmoor

CASTLE RISING CASTLE (EH), King's Lynn, Norfolk PE31
6AH T 01553-631330 W www.castlerising.co.uk
12th-century keep with gatehouse and bridge, surrounded
by 20 acres of defensive earthworks

CHARLES DARWIN'S HOME (DOWN HOUSE) (EH),
Downe, Kent BR6 7JT T 01689-859119
The family home where Darwin wrote *On the Origin of
Species*

CHARTWELL (NT), Westerham, Kent TN16 1PS
T 01732-868381
Home and studio of Sir Winston Churchill

CHATSWORTH, Bakewell, Derbys DE45 1PP T 01246-565300
W www.chatsworth.org
Tudor mansion set in magnificent parkland; seat of the
Dukes of Devonshire

CHESTERS ROMAN FORT (EH), Chollerford,
Northumberland NE46 4EU T 01434-681379
Roman cavalry fort built to guard Hadrian's Wall

CHYSAUSTER ANCIENT VILLAGE (EH), Penzance,
Cornwall TR20 8XA T 07831-757934
Remains of nearly 2,000-year-old Celtic settlement; eight
stone-walled homesteads

CLANDON PARK (NT), Guildford, Surrey GU4 7RQ
T 01483-222482 W www.clandonpark.co.uk
18th-century Palladian mansion and gardens, with an
original Maori meeting house, brought back from New
Zealand in 1892

CLIFFORD'S TOWER (EH), York YO1 9SA T 01904-646940
13th-century keep built on a mound; remains of a castle
built by William the Conqueror

CORBRIDGE ROMAN TOWN (EH), Corbridge,
Northumberland NE45 5NT T 01434-632349
Excavated central area of a Roman garrison town

CORFE CASTLE (NT), Wareham, Dorset BH20 5EZ
T 01929-481294
Former royal castle, dating from the 11th century and
partially ruined during the English Civil War

CROFT CASTLE AND PARKLAND (NT), Yarpole,
Herefordshire HR6 9PW T 01568-780246
17th-century quadrangular manor house with Georgian-
Gothic interior; built close to the ruin of pre-Conquest
border castle

DEAL CASTLE (EH), Deal, Kent CT14 7BA T 01304-372762
Largest of the coastal defence forts built by Henry VIII;
shaped like a rose with six inner and outer bastions

*DERWENT VALLEY MILLS, Belper, Derbyshire DE56 1YD
T 01773-880474 W www.derwentvalleymills.org
Series of 18th- and 19th-century cotton mills; birthplace
of the modern factory

DOVER CASTLE (EH), Dover, Kent CT16 1HU T 01304-211067
Castle with Roman, Saxon and Norman features; tunnels
used as secret wartime operations rooms

DR JOHNSON'S HOUSE, London EC4A 3DE T 020-7353 3745
W www.drjohnsonshouse.org
300-year-old townhouseme of Samuel Johnson 1748–59

DUNSTANBURGH CASTLE (EH/NT), Alnwick,
Northumberland NE66 3TT T 01665-576231
14th-century castle ruins on a headland, with a substantial
twin-towered gatehouse-keep

ELTHAM PALACE (EH), Greenwich, London SE9 5QE
T 020-8294 2548
Art Deco mansion next to remains of medieval palace once
occupied by Henry VIII; moated gardens

FARLEIGH HUNGERFORD CASTLE (EH), Bath, Somerset
BA2 7RS T 01225-754026
Late 14th-century castle with inner and outer courts;
chapel with rare medieval wall paintings

FARNHAM CASTLE KEEP (EH), Farnham, Surrey GU9 0AG
T 01252-721194 W www.farnhamcastle.com
Large 12th-century castle keep with motte and bailey wall

FISHBOURNE ROMAN PALACE,Chichester, W. Sussex PO19
3QR T 01243-785859 W http://sussexpast.co.uk
Excavated Roman palace with largest collection of in situ
mosaics in the UK

*FOUNTAINS ABBEY (NT), Ripon, N. Yorks HG4 3DY
T 01765-608888
Ruined Cistercian monastery and corn mill; site includes
Studley Royal, a Georgian water garden and deer park

FRAMLINGHAM CASTLE (EH), Framlingham, Suffolk IP13
9BP T 01728-724922
Castle (c.1200) with high curtain walls enclosing an
almshouse (1639); once the refuge of Mary I

FURNESS ABBEY (EH), Barrow-in-Furness, Cumbria LA13 0PJ
T 01229-823420
Remains of an abbey founded in 1124 by Stephen, later
king of England

GLASTONBURY ABBEY, Glastonbury, Somerset BA6 9EL
T 01458-832267 W www.glastonburyabbey.com
12th-century abbey, destroyed by fire in 1184 and later
rebuilt; site of early Christian settlement; ruined in 1539
during dissolution of monasteries

GOODRICH CASTLE (EH), Ross-on-Wye, Herefordshire HR9
6HY T 01600-890538
Remains of 12th- and 13th-century castle; contains a
famous mortar that ruined the castle in 1646

GREENWAY (NT), Brixham, Devon TQ5 0ES T 01803-842382
Large woodland; walled garden; location of Agatha
Christie's holiday home and inspiration for several
settings in her books, including the murder in *Dead Man's
Folly*

*GREENWICH, London SE10 9NF T 020-8305 5235
W www.visitgreenwich.org.uk
Former Royal Observatory (founded 1675) home to the
Meridian Line, *Cutty Sark* and National Maritime Museum;
the Queen's House, designed for Queen Anne, wife of

James I, by Inigo Jones; Painted Hall and neoclassical
Chapel (Old Royal Naval College)

GRIME'S GRAVES (EH), Thetford, Norfolk IP26 5DE
T 01842-810656
Neolithic flint mines, dug over 5,000 years ago; one shaft
has been been excavated

GUILDHALL, London EC2V 7HH T 020-7332 1313
W www.guildhall.cityoflondon.gov.uk
Centre of civic government of the City of London built
c.1441; facade built 1788–9

HADDON HALL, Bakewell, Derbys DE45 1LA T 01629-812855
W www.haddonhall.co.uk
Well-preserved 12th-century manor house

HAILES ABBEY (EH), Cheltenham, Glos GL54 5PB
T 01242-602398
Ruins of a 13th-century Cistercian monastery

HAM HOUSE AND GARDEN (NT), Richmond, Surrey TW10
7RS T 020-8940 1950
Grand Stuart house with lavish interiors and formal
gardens

HAMPTON COURT PALACE, East Molesey, Surrey KT8 9AU
T 020-3166 6000 W www.hrp.org.uk/hampton-court-palace
Palace originally built for Cardinal Wolsey in the early
16th-century, famous as the home of Henry VIII, his
wives and children, with a 17th-century Baroque palace
by Wren commissioned by William III and Mary II in
1689; Royal Tennis Court and world-renowned maze

HARDWICK HALL (NT), Chesterfield, Derbys S44 5QJ
T 01246-850430
Elizabethan house built for Bess of Hardwick

HARDY'S COTTAGE (NT), Higher Bockhampton, Dorset DT2
8QJ T 01305-262366
Birthplace and home of Thomas Hardy

HAREWOOD HOUSE, Leeds, W. Yorks LS17 9LG
T 0113-218 1010 W https://harewood.org
18th-century house designed by John Carr and Robert
Adam; park by Capability Brown

HATFIELD HOUSE, Hatfield, Herts AL9 5NB T 01707-287010
W www.hatfield-house.co.uk
Jacobean house built by Robert Cecil; features surviving
wing of Royal Palace of Hatfield (c.1485), the childhood
home of Elizabeth I

HELMSLEY CASTLE (EH), Helmsley, N. Yorks YO62 5AB
T 01439-770442
12th-century keep and curtain wall with 16th-century
buildings; spectacular earthwork defences

HEVER CASTLE, Edenbridge, Kent TN8 7NG T 01732-865224
W www.hevercastle.co.uk
13th-century double-moated castle; childhood home of
Anne Boleyn

HOLKHAM HALL, Wells-next-the-Sea, Norfolk NR23 1AB
T 01328-710227 W www.holkham.co.uk
Palladian mansion; notable fine art collection

HOUSESTEADS ROMAN FORT (EH), Hexham,
Northumberland NE47 6NN T 01434-344363
Excavated Roman infantry fort on Hadrian's Wall with
museum

*IRONBRIDGE GORGE, Ironbridge, Shropshire
T 01952-433424 W www.ironbridge.org.uk
Important Industrial Revolution site, featuring the world's
first iron bridge

KEDLESTON HALL (NT), Derbys DE22 5JH T 01332-842191
Palladian mansion built 1759–65; complete Robert Adam
interiors; museum of Asian artefacts

KELMSCOTT MANOR, Lechlade, Glos GL7 3HU
T 01367-252486 W www.sal.org.uk/kelmscott-manor/
Built c.1600; summer home of William Morris, with
products of Morris and Co.

KENILWORTH CASTLE (EH), Kenilworth, Warks CV8 1NG
T 01926-852078
Largest castle ruin in England; Norman keep with 13th-
century outer walls; once home to Robert Dudley

KENSINGTON PALACE, Kensington Gardens, London W8 4PX
T 020-3166 6000 W www.hrp.org.uk/kensington-palace
Built in 1605 and enlarged by Wren; birthplace of Queen
Victoria

KENWOOD HOUSE (EH), Hampstead , London NW3 7JR
T 020-8348 1286
Neoclassical villa on the edge of Hampstead Heath,
housing the Iveagh bequest of paintings and furniture

KEW PALACE, Richmond, Surrey TW9 3AE T 020-3166 6000
W www.hrp.org.uk/kew-palace
Red-brick mansion (c.1631); includes Queen Charlotte's
Cottage, used by King George III and family as a
summerhouse

KINGSTON LACY (NT), Wimborne Minster, Dorset BH21 4EA
T 01202-883402
17th-century mansion with 19th-century alterations;
important art collection

KNEBWORTH HOUSE, Knebworth, Herts SG3 6HQ
T 01438-812661 W www.knebworthhouse.com
Tudor manor house concealed by 19th-century Gothic
decoration; Lutyens gardens

KNOLE (NT), Sevenoaks, Kent TN15 0RP T 01732-462100
House built in 1456, set in 1,000-acre deer park; fine art
and furniture collection; birthplace of Vita Sackville-West

LAMBETH PALACE, London SE1 7JU T 020-7898 1200
W www.archbishopofcanterbury.org/about-lambeth-palace
Official residence of the Archbishop of Canterbury since
the 13th century

LANERCOST PRIORY (EH), nr Brampton, Cumbria CA8 2HQ
T 01697-73030 W www.lanercostpriory.org.uk
The nave of the Augustinian priory's church, c.1166, is
still used; remains of other claustral buildings and
beautifully preserved cloisters

LANHYDROCK (NT), Bodmin, Cornwall PL30 5AD
T 01208-265950
House dating from the 17th century; 50 rooms, including
kitchen and nursery

LEEDS CASTLE, Maidstone, Kent ME17 1PL T 01622-765400
W www.leeds-castle.com
Castle dating from the 12th century, situated in 500 acres
of parkland and gardens; used as a royal palace by Henry
VIII

LEVENS HALL, nr Kendal, Cumbria LA8 0PD T 01539-560321
W www.levenshall.co.uk
Elizabethan house with unique topiary garden (1694);
steam engine collection

LINCOLN CASTLE, Lincoln, Lincs LN1 3AA T 01522-554559
W www.lincolncastle.com
Built by William the Conqueror in 1068 on a Roman site;
one of only two double-motted castles in Britain

LINDISFARNE PRIORY (EH), Holy Island, Northumberland
TD15 2RX T 01289-389200
Founded in AD 635; re-established in the 12th century as
a Benedictine priory, now ruined

LITTLE MORETON HALL (NT), Congleton, Cheshire CW12
4SD T 01260-272018
Iconic timber-framed moated Tudor manor house with
knot garden

LONGLEAT HOUSE, Warminster, Wilts BA12 7NW
T 01985-844400 W www.longleat.co.uk
Elizabethan house in Italian Renaissance style; Capability
Brown parkland with lakes; safari park

LULLINGSTONE ROMAN VILLA (EH), Eynsford, Kent DA4
0JA T 01322-863467
Large villa occupied for much of the Roman period;
collection of Roman artefacts and unique Christian
paintings

MIDDLEHAM CASTLE (EH), Middleham, N. Yorks DL8 4QG
T 01969-623899
12th-century keep within later fortifications; childhood
home of Richard III

MONTACUTE HOUSE (NT), Montacute, Somerset TA15 6XP
T 01935-823289
Elizabethan Renaissance mansion, with collection of
portraits from the period

MOUNT GRACE PRIORY (EH), Northallerton, N. Yorks DL6
3JG T 01609-883494
Well-preserved Carthusian priory with remains of
monastic buildings

OLD SARUM (EH), Salisbury, Wilts SP1 3SD T 01722-335398
Iron Age hill fort enclosing remains of Norman castle and
cathedral

ORFORD CASTLE (EH), Orford, Suffolk IP12 2ND
T 01394-450472
Polygonal tower keep c.1170 and remains of coastal
defence castle built by Henry II

OSBORNE HOUSE (EH), East Cowes, Isle of Wight PO32 6JT
T 01983-200022
Queen Victoria's seaside residence; built by Thomas
Cubitt in Italian Renaissance style; summer house, Swiss
Cottage and museum

OSTERLEY PARK AND HOUSE (NT), Isleworth, Middx TW7
4RB T 020-8232 5050
18th-century neoclassical mansion with Tudor stable
block

PENDENNIS CASTLE (EH), Falmouth, Cornwall TR11 4LP
T 01326-316594
Well-preserved 16th-century coastal defence castle

PENSHURST PLACE, Penshurst, Kent TN11 8DG
T 01892-870307 W www.penshurstplace.com
Medieval house featuring Baron's Hall (1341) and
gardens (1346); toy museum

PETWORTH HOUSE (NT), Petworth, W. Sussex GU28
9LRT 01798-342207
Late 17th-century house set in Capability Brown
landscaped deer park; fine art collection

PEVENSEY CASTLE (EH), Pevensey, E. Sussex BN24 5LE
T 01323-762604
Walls of a fourth-century Roman fort; remains of an 11th-
century castle

POLESDEN LACEY (NT), nr Dorking, Surrey RH5 6BD
T 01372-452048
Regency villa remodelled in the Edwardian era; fine
paintings and furnishings; walled rose garden

PORTCHESTER CASTLE (EH), Portchester, Hants PO16 9QW
T 02392-378291
Walls of a late Roman fort enclosing a Norman keep and
an Augustinian priory church

POWDERHAM CASTLE, Kenton, Devon EX6 8JQ
T 01626-890243 W www.powderham.co.uk
Medieval castle with 18th- and 19th-century alterations,
including James Wyatt music room

RABY CASTLE, Staindrop, Co. Durham DL2 3AH
T 01833-660202 W www.rabycastle.com
14th-century castle with walled gardens

RAGLEY HALL, Alcester, Warks B49 5NJ T 01789-762090
W www.ragley.co.uk
17th-century Palladian house with gardens and lake

RICHBOROUGH ROMAN FORT (EH), Sandwich, Kent
CT13 9JW T 01304-612013
Remains of a Roman Saxon Shore fortress; landing-site of
the Claudian invasion in AD 43

RICHMOND CASTLE (EH), Richmond, N. Yorks DL10 4QW
T 01748-822493
12th-century keep with 11th-century curtain wall

RIEVAULX ABBEY (EH), nr Helmsley, N. Yorks YO62 5LB
T 01439-798228
Remains of a Cistercian abbey founded c.1132

ROCHESTER CASTLE (EH), Rochester, Kent ME1 1SW
T 01634-335882
11th-century castle partly on the Roman city wall, with a
well-preserved square keep of c.1127

ROCKINGHAM CASTLE, Market Harborough, Leics LE16 8TH
T 01536-770240 W www.rockinghamcastle.com
Built by William the Conqueror; formal gardens and 400-
year-old 'elephant' hedge

ROMAN BATHS, Abbey Church Yard, Bath BA1 1LZ
T 01225-477785 W www.romanbaths.co.uk
Extensive remains of a Roman temple and bathing
complex which still flows with natural thermal water;
museum

ROYAL PAVILION, Brighton BN1 1EE T 03000-290900
W https://brightonmuseums.org.uk/royalpavilion
Unique palace of George IV, in Indo-gothic style with
chinoiserie interiors and Regency gardens

ST AUGUSTINE'S ABBEY (EH), Canterbury, Kent CT1 1PF
T 01227-767345
Remains of Benedictine monastery founded in 598

ST MAWES CASTLE (EH), St Mawes, Cornwall TR2 5DE
T 01326-270526
Coastal defence castle built by Henry VIII

ST MICHAEL'S MOUNT (NT), Marazion, Cornwall TR17 0HS
T 01736-710507 W www.stmichaelsmount.co.uk
12th-century church and castle with later additions,
situated on an iconic rocky island

*SALTAIRE VILLAGE, nr Shipley, W. Yorks T 01274-437942
W www.saltairevillage.info
Victorian industrial village founded by mill owner Titus
Salt for his workers; see also World Heritage Sites

SANDRINGHAM, Norfolk PE35 6EN T 01485-545400
W www.sandringhamestate.co.uk
The Queen's private residence; neo-Jacobean house built
in 1870 with gardens and country park

SCARBOROUGH CASTLE (EH), Scarborough, N. Yorks YO11
1HY T 01723-372451
Remains of 12th-century keep and curtain walls

SHERBORNE CASTLE, Sherborne, Dorset DT9 5NR
T 01935-812072 W www.sherbornecastle.com
16th-century castle built by Sir Walter Raleigh set in
Capability Brown landscaped gardens

SHUGBOROUGH ESTATE (NT), Milford, Staffs ST17 0XB
T 01889-880160
Late 17th century house in 18th-century park with
monuments, temples and pavilions in the Greek Revival
style; seat of the Earls of Lichfield

SISSINGHURST CASTLE GARDEN (NT), Nr Cranbrook,
Kent TN17 2AB T 01580-710700
Early 14th century site, purchased by Vita Sackville-West
in the 1930s where the writer, poet and Bloomsbury
Group member created the famous gardens

SKIPTON CASTLE, Skipton, N. Yorks BD23 1AW
T 01756-792442 W www.skiptoncastle.co.uk
Well-preserved D-shaped medieval castle with six round
towers and inner courtyard

SMALLHYTHE PLACE (NT), Tenterden, Kent TN30 7NG
T 01580-762334
Half-timbered 16th-century house

*STONEHENGE (EH), nr Amesbury, Wilts SP4 7DE
T 0370-333 1181
World-famous prehistoric monument comprising
concentric stone circles surrounded by a ditch and bank

STONOR PARK, Henley-on-Thames, Oxon RG9 6HF
T 01491-638587 W www.stonor.com
Medieval house with Georgian facade; refuge for Catholic
recusants after the Reformation

STOURHEAD (NT), Nr Mere, Wilts BA12 6QD T 01747-841152
18th-century Palladian mansion with world-renowned
landscape gardens; King Alfred's Tower

STRATFIELD SAYE HOUSE, Hants RG7 2BT T 01256-882694
W www.wellingtonestates.co.uk/stratfield-saye-house
House built 1630–40; home of the Dukes of Wellington
since 1817

STRATFORD-UPON-AVON, Warks T 01789-868191
W www.stratford-upon-avon.co.uk
Shakespeare's Birthplace Trust with Shakespeare Centre;
Anne Hathaway's Cottage; Holy Trinity Church, where
Shakespeare is buried

STRAWBERRY HILL HOUSE, Twickenham TW1 4ST
T 020-8744 1241 W www.strawberryhillhouse.org.uk
Early Gothic Revival villa built between 1749 and 1776
for Horace Walpole (1717–97)

SUDELEY CASTLE, Winchcombe, Glos GL54 5JD
T 01242-604244 W www.sudeleycastle.co.uk
Castle built in 1442; once owned by Richard III and
former home of Catherine Parr, sixth wife of Henry VIII;
restored in the 19th century

SULGRAVE MANOR, nr Banbury, Oxon OX17 2SD
T 01295-760205 W www.sulgravemanor.org.uk
Tudor and Georgian house; home of George
Washington's family

SUTTON HOUSE (NT), Hackney, London E9 6JQ
T 020-8986 2264
Tudor house, built in 1535 by Sir Ralph Sadleir

SYON HOUSE, Brentford, Middx TW8 8JF T 020-8560 0882
W www.syonpark.co.uk
Built on the site of a former monastery; Robert Adam
interior; Capability Brown park

TINTAGEL CASTLE (EH), Tintagel, Cornwall PL34 0HE
T 01840-770328
13th-century cliff-top castle and 5th–6th-century Celtic
settlement; linked with Arthurian legend

TOWER OF LONDON, London EC3N 4AB T 020-3166 6000
W www.hrp.org.uk/tower-of-london
Royal palace and fortress begun by William the
Conqueror in 1078; houses the Crown Jewels

TYNEMOUTH PRIORY AND CASTLE (EH), Tyne and Wear
NE30 4BZ T 01912-571090
Remains of a Benedictine priory, founded c.1090, moated
castle-towers, a gatehouse and keep on Saxon monastic
site

UPPARK (NT), Petersfield, W. Sussex GU31 5QR
T 01730-825415
17th-century house, restored after fire; Fetherstonhaugh
art collection; 18th-century dolls' house

WALMER CASTLE (EH), Deal, Kent CT14 7LJ T 01304-364288
One of Henry VIII's coastal defence castles, now the
residence of the Lord Warden of the Cinque Ports

WARKWORTH CASTLE (EH), Warkworth, Northumberland
NE65 0UJ T 01665-711423
14th-century keep amid earlier ruins, with hermitage
upstream

WHITBY ABBEY (EH), Whitby, N. Yorks YO22 4JT
T 01947-603568
Remains of Norman church on the site of a monastery
founded in AD 657

WILTON HOUSE, nr Salisbury, Wilts SP2 0BJ T 01722-746700
W www.wiltonhouse.com
17th-century house on the site of a Tudor house and
ninth-century nunnery; Palladian bridge

WINDSOR CASTLE, Windsor, Berks SL4 1NJ T 030-3123 7304
W www.royalcollection.org.uk
Official residence of the Queen; oldest royal residence still
in regular use; largest inhabited castle in the world. Also
St George's Chapel; Queen Mary's Dolls' House

WOBURN ABBEY, Woburn, Beds MK17 9WA T 01525-290333
W www.woburn.co.uk
Built on the site of a Cistercian abbey; seat of the Dukes
of Bedford; art collection

WROXETER ROMAN CITY (EH), nr Shrewsbury, Shropshire
SY5 6PH T 01743-761330
Second-century public baths and part of the forum of the
Roman town of *Viroconium*

WALES

For more information on Cadw properties, including those
listed below, the official website is W www.cadw.wales.gov.uk
For more information on National Trust properties in Wales,
including those listed below, the official website is
W www.nationaltrust.org.uk

KEY
(C) Property of Cadw: Welsh Historic Monuments
(NT) National Trust property
* UNESCO World Heritage Site (*see also* World Heritage Sites)

*BEAUMARIS CASTLE (C), Anglesey LL58 8AP
T 01248-810361
Concentrically planned 13th-century castle, still virtually
intact

*BLAENAVON, Blaenavon NP4 9AS T 01495-742333
W www.visitblaenavon.co.uk
18th- and 19th-century industrial landscape associated
with coal and iron production

CAERLEON ROMAN BATHS AND AMPHITHEATRE
(C), Newport NP18 1AE T 01633-422518
Rare example of a legionary bath-house and late first-
century arena surrounded by bank for spectators

*CAERNARFON CASTLE (C), Gwynedd LL55 2AY
T 01286-677617 W www.caernarfon-castle.co.uk
Huge fortress with polygonal towers built between 1283
and 1330, initially for King Edward I of England; setting
for the investiture of Prince Charles in 1969

CAERPHILLY CASTLE (C), Caerphilly CF83 1JD
T 029-2088 3143
Concentrically planned castle (*c.*1270) notable for its scale
and use of water defences

CARDIFF CASTLE, Cardiff CF10 3RB T 029-2087 8100
W www.cardiffcastle.com
Norman keep built on site of Roman fort; 'fairytale'
gothic-revival mansion added in the 19th century

CASTELL COCH (C), Tongwynlais, Cardiff CF15 7JS
T 029-2081 0101
'Fairytale'-style castle, rebuilt 1872–91 on medieval
foundations

CHEPSTOW CASTLE (C), Monmouthshire NP16 5EY
T 01291-624065
Rectangular keep amid extensive fortifications; developed
throughout the Middle Ages

*CONWY CASTLE (C), Gwynedd LL32 8AY T 01492-592358
Built for Edward I in 1283–9 on narrow rocky outcrop;
features eight towers and two barbicans

CRICCIETH CASTLE (C), Gwynedd LL52 0DP
T 01766-522227
Native Welsh 13th-century castle, taken and altered by
Edward I and Edward II

DENBIGH CASTLE (C), Denbighshire LL16 3NB
T 01745-813385
Remains of the castle (begun 1282), including triple-
towered gatehouses

DYFFRYN GARDENS (NT), St Nicholas, Cardiff CF5 6SU
T 029-2059 3328
Edwardian gardens designed by Thomas Mawson,
overlooked by a grand Edwardian mansion

*HARLECH CASTLE (C), Gwynedd LL46 2YH T 01766-780552
Well-preserved castle, constructed 1283–95, on an
outcrop above the former shoreline; withstood seven-year
siege 1461–8

PEMBROKE CASTLE, Pembrokeshire SA71 4LA
T 01646-681510 W https://pembrokecastle.co.uk
Castle founded in 1093; Great Tower built in late 12th
century; birthplace of King Henry VII

PENRHYN CASTLE (NT), Bangor, Gwynedd LL57 4HT
T 01248-353084
Neo-Norman castle built in the 19th century; railway and
dolls' museums; private art collection

*PONTCYSYLLTE AQUEDUCT AND CANAL, Trevor,
Wrexham LL20 7TY T 01978-822912
W www.pontcysyllte-aqueduct.co.uk
Longest and highest aqueduct in Great Britain; designed
by Thomas Telford and finished in 1805

POWIS CASTLE (NT), Welshpool, Powys SY21 8RF
T 01938-551944
Medieval castle with interior in variety of styles; 17th-
century gardens; Clive of India museum

RAGLAN CASTLE (C), Monmouthshire NP15 2BT
T 01291-690228
Remains of 15th-century castle with moated hexagonal
keep

ST DAVIDS BISHOP'S PALACE (C), Pembrokeshire SA62 6PE
T 01437-720517
Remains of residence of Bishops of St Davids built 1328–
47

TINTERN ABBEY (C), Tintern, Monmouthshire NP16 6SE
T 01291-689251
Remains of 13th-century church and conventual buildings
of a 12th-century Cistercian monastery

TRETOWER COURT AND CASTLE (C), Nr Crickhowell,
Powys NP8 1RD T 01874-730279
Medieval manor house rebuilt in the 15th century, with
remains of 12th-century castle nearby

SCOTLAND

For more information on Historic Environment Scotland
properties, including those listed below, the official website is
W www.historicenvironment.scot
For more information on National Trust for Scotland
properties, including those listed below, the official website is
W www.nts.org.uk

KEY
(HES) Historic Environment Scotland property
(NTS) National Trust for Scotland property
* Part of the Heart of Neolithic Orkney UNESCO World
Heritage Site

ABBOTSFORD HOUSE, Melrose, Roxburghshire TD6 9BQ
T 01896-752043 W www.scottsabbotsford.co.uk
Home of Sir Walter Scott; features historic Scottish relics
and formal gardens

BALMORAL CASTLE, Ballater, Aberdeenshire AB35 5TB
T 01339-742534 W www.balmoralcastle.com
Baronial-style castle built for Victoria and Albert; the
Queen's private residence

BLACKHOUSE, ARNOL (HES), Lewis, Western Isles HS2 9DB
T 01851-710395
Traditional Lewis thatched house
BLAIR CASTLE, Blair Atholl, Perthshire PH18 5TL
T 01796-481207 W www.blair-castle.co.uk
Mid-18th-century mansion with 13th-century tower; seat
of the Dukes and Earls of Atholl
BOWHILL, Selkirk, Scottish Borders TD7 5ET T 01750-22204
W www.bowhillhouse.co.uk
Present house dates mainly from 1812; Seat of the Dukes
of Buccleuch and Queensberry; fine collection of paintings
BROUGH OF BIRSAY (HES), Orkney KW17 2LX
T 01856-841815
Remains of Norse and Pictish village on the tidal island of
Birsay
CAERLAVEROCK CASTLE (HES), Glencaple, Dumfries and
Galloway DG1 4RU T 01387-770244
Unique triangular 13th-century moated castle with
classical Renaissance additions
CAIRNPAPPLE HILL (HES), Torphichen, West Lothian
T 01506-634622
Neolithic ceremonial site and Bronze Age burial chambers
CALANAIS STANDING STONES (HES), Lewis, Western Isles
HS2 9DY T 01851-621422
Standing stones in a cross-shaped setting, dating from
between 2900 and 2600 BC
CATERTHUNS (BROWN AND WHITE) (HES), Menmuir,
nr Brechin, Angus
Two large Iron Age hill forts
CAWDOR CASTLE, Nairn, Moray IV12 5RD T 01667-404401
W www.cawdorcastle.com
14th-century keep with 15th- and 17th-century additions
CLAVA CAIRNS (HES), nr Inverness, Inverness-shire IV2 5EU
T 0131-668 8600
Bronze Age cemetery complex of cairns and standing
stones
CRATHES CASTLE (NTS), nr Banchory, Aberdeenshire AB31
5QJ T 01330-844525
16th-century baronial castle in woodland, fields and
gardens
CULZEAN CASTLE (NTS), Maybole, Ayrshire KA19 8LE
T 01655-884455
18th-century Robert Adam castle with oval staircase and
circular saloon
DRYBURGH ABBEY (HES), nr Melrose, Roxburghshire TD6
0RQ T 01835-822381
12th-century abbey containing the tomb of Sir Walter
Scott
DUNVEGAN CASTLE, Skye IV55 8WF T 01470-521206
W www.dunvegancastle.com
13th-century castle with later additions; home of the
chiefs of the Clan MacLeod
EDINBURGH CASTLE (HES), Edinburgh EH1 2NG
T 0131-225 9846 W www.edinburghcastle.scot
Fortress perched on extinct volcano; houses the Scottish
Crown Jewels, Scottish National War Memorial, Scottish
United Services Museum
EDZELL CASTLE (HES), nr Brechin, Angus DD9 7UE
T 01356-648631
Ruined 16th-century tower house on medieval
foundations; early 17th-century walled garden
EILEAN DONAN CASTLE, Dornie, Ross and Cromarty IV40
8DX T 01599-555202 W www.eileandonancastle.com
13th-century castle situated at the meeting point of three
sea lochs; Jacobite relics
ELGIN CATHEDRAL (HES), Moray IV30 1HU T 01343-547171
13th-century cathedral and octagonal chapterhouse

FLOORS CASTLE, Kelso, Roxburghshire TD5 7SF
T 01573-223333 W www.floorscastle.com
Largest inhabited castle in Scotland; seat of the Dukes of
Roxburghe; built in the 1720s by William Adam
FORT GEORGE (HES), Ardersier, Inverness-shire IV2 7TD
T 01667-460232
18th-century fort; still a working army barracks
GLAMIS CASTLE, Forfar, Angus DD8 1RJ T 01307-840393
W www.glamis-castle.co.uk
Seat of the Lyon family (later Earls of Strathmore and
Kinghorne) since 1372; the setting for Shakespeare's
Macbeth
GLASGOW CATHEDRAL (HES), Lanarkshire G4 0QZ
T 0141-552 8198 W www.glasgowcathedral.org.uk
Late 12th-century cathedral with vaulted crypt
GLENELG BROCHS (HES), Glenelg, Ross and Cromarty
T 0131-668 8600
Two 2,000-year-old broch towers (Dun Telve and Dun
Troddan) with well-preserved structural features
HOPETOUN HOUSE, South Queensferry, West Lothian EH30
9RW T 0131-331 2451 W www.hopetoun.co.uk
Designed by Sir William Bruce in 1699 and enlarged by
William Adam 1721–48
HUNTLY CASTLE (HES), Aberdeenshire AB54 4SH
T 01466-793191
Ruin of a 16th- and 17th-century baronial residence
INVERARAY CASTLE, Argyll PA32 8XE T 01499-302203
W www.inveraray-castle.com
Gothic-style 18th-century castle designed by William
Adam and Roger Morris; seat of the Dukes of Argyll
IONA ABBEY (HES), Iona, Argyll PA76 6SQ T 01681-700512
Monastery founded by St Columba in AD 563; remains a
popular Christian pilgrimage site
JARLSHOF (HES), Sumburgh Head, Shetland ZE3 9JN
T 01950-460112
Prehistoric settlement with later ninth-century Norse
additions
JEDBURGH ABBEY (HES), Roxburghshire TD8 6JQ
T 01835-863925
Ruined Augustinian abbey founded c.1138; display of
early Christian artefacts
KISIMUL CASTLE (HES), Castlebay, Barra, Western Isles HS9
5UZ T 01871-810313
Medieval island home of the Clan MacNeil
LINLITHGOW PALACE (HES), Kirkgate, Linlithgow, West
Lothian EH49 7AL T 01506-842896
Ruined royal palace, founded in 1424, set in park;
birthplace of James V and Mary, Queen of Scots
*MAESHOWE (HES), Stenness, Orkney KW16 3LB
T 01856-851266
Neolithic chambered tomb with Viking runes
MEIGLE SCULPTURED STONES (HES), Meigle, Perthshire
PH12 8SB T 01828-640612
Twenty-six carved Pictish stones dating from the late
eighth to the late tenth centuries
MELROSE ABBEY (HES), Roxburghshire TD6 9LG
T 01896-822562
Ruin of Cistercian abbey founded c.1136 by David I;
museum of medieval objects
MOUSA BROCH (HES), Island of Mousa, Shetland ZE2 9HP
Finest surviving Iron Age broch tower c.100 BC
NEW ABBEY CORN MILL (HES), Dumfriesshire DG2 8BX
T 01387-850260
Working water-powered mill built in the late 18th
century
*NEW LANARK, South Lanarkshire ML11 9DB T 01555-661345
W www.newlanark.org
18th-century village built around a cotton mill

PALACE OF HOLYROODHOUSE, Edinburgh EH8 8DX
T 0303-123 7306 W www.royalcollection.org.uk
The Queen's official Scottish residence; home to Mary,
Queen of Scots; main part of the palace built 1671–9
close to ruined 12th-century Augustinian abbey

*RING OF BRODGAR (HES), Stenness, Orkney
T 01856-841815
Neolithic circle of upright stones surrounded by circular
ditch

ROSSLYN CHAPEL, Roslin, Midlothian EH25 9PU
T 0131-440 2159 W www.rosslynchapel.com
Historic church built between 1446 and 1484 with
unique stone carvings

ST ANDREWS CASTLE AND CATHEDRAL (HES), Fife
KY16 9AR (castle); 9QL (cathedral) T 01334-477196 (castle);
01334-472563 (cathedral)
Ruins of 13th-century castle, the former residence of
bishops of St Andrews, and remains of the largest
cathedral in Scotland; museum

SCONE PALACE, Perth, Perthshire PH2 6BD T 01738-552300
W www.scone-palace.co.uk
Georgian-Gothic house built 1802–12; originally the site
of a 12th-century church

*SKARA BRAE (HES), Sandwick, Orkney KW16 3LR
T 01856-841815
Neolithic village with adjacent replica house

SMAILHOLM TOWER (HES), nr Kelso, Roxburghshire TD5
7PG T 01573-460365
Well-preserved 15th-century tower-house

STIRLING CASTLE (HES), Stirlingshire FK8 1EJ
T 01786-450000 W www.stirlingcastle.gov.uk
Great Hall and gatehouse built for James IV c.1500;
palace built for James V in 1538; site of coronations
including Mary, Queen of Scots

*STONES OF STENNESS (HES), Stenness, Orkney KW16 3JZ
T 0131-668 8600
Four surviving Neolithic standing stones and the uprights
of a three-stone dolmen

TANTALLON CASTLE (HES), North Berwick, East Lothian
EH39 5PN T 01620-892727
Ruined 14th-century curtain wall with towers

THREAVE CASTLE (HES), Dumfries, Kirkcudbrightshire DG7
1TJ T 07711-223101
Ruined late 14th-century tower on an island; accessible
only by boat

URQUHART CASTLE (HES), Drumnadrochit, Inverness-shire
IV63 6XJ T 01456-450551
13th-century castle remains on the banks of Loch Ness

NORTHERN IRELAND

For the Northern Ireland Department for Communities, the
official website is W www.discovernorthernireland.com
For more information on National Trust properties in Northern
Ireland, including those listed below, the official website is
W www.nationaltrust.org.uk

KEY
(NIDC) Property in the care of the Northern Ireland
Department for Communities
(NT) National Trust property

CARRICKFERGUS CASTLE (NIDC), Carrickfergus, Co.
Antrim BT38 7BG T 028-9335 1273
Castle built in 1177 and taken by King John in 1210;
garrisoned until 1928. From March 2019 the Inner Ward
and Great Tower are closed to the public for renovation

CASTLE COOLE (NT), Enniskillen, Co. Fermanagh BT74 6JY
T 028-6632 2690
18th-century neoclassical mansion in parkland; designed
by James Wyatt

CASTLE WARD (NT), Strangford, Co. Down BT30 7BA
T 028-4488 1204
18th-century house with Classical and Gothic facades

DEVENISH MONASTIC SITE (NIDC), nr Enniskillen, Co.
Fermanagh T 028-9082 3207
Island monastery founded in the sixth century by St
Molaise; church dating from 13th century

DOWNHILL DEMESNE AND HEZLETT HOUSE (NT),
Castlerock, Co. Londonderry BT51 4RP T 028-7084 8728
Ruins of 18th-century mansion and a 17th-century
cottage in landscaped estate including Mussenden Temple

DUNLUCE CASTLE (NIDC), Bushmills, Co. Antrim BT57 8UY
T 028-2073 1938
Ruins of 16th-century stronghold of the McDonnells

FLORENCE COURT (NT), Enniskillen, Co. Fermanagh BT92
1DB T 028-6634 8249
Mid-18th-century house with Rococo decoration

GREY ABBEY (NIDC), Greyabbey, Co. Down BT22 2NQ
T 028-9082 3207
Substantial remains of a Cistercian abbey founded in
1193 set in landscaped parkland

MOUNT STEWART (NT), Newtownards, Co. Down BT22 2AD
T 028-4278 8387
19th-century neoclassical house; octagonal Temple of the
Winds

NENDRUM MONASTIC SITE (NIDC), Mahee Island, Co.
Down T 028-9082 3207
Pre-Norman island monastery founded in the fifth century
by St Machaoi; has links to St. Patrick

PATTERSON'S SPADE MILL (NT), Templepatrick, Co. Antrim
BT39 0AP T 028-9443 3619
Last working water-driven spade mill in the UK

TULLY CASTLE (NIDC), Derrygonnelly, Co. Fermanagh
T 028-9082 3207
Remains of a fortified house and bawn built c.1619

MUSEUMS AND GALLERIES

There are approximately 2,500 museums and galleries in the UK. As at February 2019, 1,569 of these were fully accredited by Arts Council England and a further 171 museums held provisional accreditation. Accreditation indicates that the museum or gallery has an appropriate constitution, is soundly financed, has adequate collection management standards and public services and has access to professional curatorial advice. These applications are assessed by either Arts Council England; the Museums, Archives and Libraries division of the Welsh government; Museums Galleries Scotland or the Northern Ireland Museums Council.

The following is a selection of museums and art galleries in the UK. Opening hours and admission charges vary. Further information about museums and galleries in the UK is available from the Museums Association (T 020-7566 7800 W www.museumsassociation.org).

W www.weareculture24.org.uk includes a database of all the museums and galleries in the UK.

ENGLAND
* England's national museums and galleries, which receive funding from a government department, such as the DCMS or MoD. These institutions are deemed to have collections of national importance, and the government is able to call upon their staff for expert advice.

ALTON
Jane Austen's House Museum, Chawton, Hants GU34 1SD
T 01420-83262 W www.jane-austens-house-museum.org.uk
17th-century house which tells the author's story
BARNARD CASTLE
The Bowes Museum, Co. Durham DL12 8NP T 01833-690606
W www.thebowesmuseum.org.uk
Public gallery in a French châteaux style featuring archaeology, fashion and ceramics. Houses one of the largest collections of Spanish art in the country
BATH
American Museum, Claverton Manor BA2 7BD T 01225-460503
W www.americanmuseum.org
American decorative arts from the 17th to 20th centuries
Fashion Museum, Bennett Street BA1 2QH T 01225-477789
W www.fashionmuseum.co.uk
Fashion from the 17th century to the present day
Victoria Art Gallery, Bridge Street BA2 4AT T 01225-477233
W www.victoriagal.org.uk
European Old Masters and British art since the 15th century
BEAMISH
Beamish Museum, Co. Durham DH9 0RG T 0191-370 4000
W www.beamish.org.uk
Living working museum of a northern industrial town during Georgian, Victorian and Edwardian times
BEAULIEU
National Motor Museum, Hants SO42 7ZN T 01590-612345
W www.beaulieu.co.uk
Former royal estate within the New Forest national park home to Beaulieu Abbey, Palace House and the National Motor Museum
BIRMINGHAM
Aston Hall, Trinity Road B6 6JD T 0121-348 8100
W www.birminghammuseums.org.uk/aston
Jacobean House containing paintings, furniture and tapestries from the 17th to 19th centuries

Barber Institute of Fine Arts, University of Birmingham, Edgbaston B15 2TS T 0121-414 7333 W www.barber.org.uk
Extensive coin collection; fine arts, including Old Masters
Birmingham Museum and Art Gallery, Chamberlain Square B3 3DH
T 0121-348 8000 W www.birminghammuseums.org.uk/bmag
Includes notable collection of Pre-Raphaelite art
Museum of the Jewellery Quarter, Vyse Street, B18 6HA
T 0121-348 8140
W www.birminghammuseums.org.uk/jewellery
Preserved jewellery workshop
Sarehole Mill, Cole Bank Road, B13 0BD T 0121-348 8160
W www.birminghammuseums.org.uk/sarehole
A 250-year-old watermill renowned for its association with author J. R. R. Tolkien
Thinktank, Curzon Street B4 7XG T 0121-348 8000
W www.birminghammuseums.org.uk/thinktank
Science museum featuring over 200 hands-on displays and a Planetarium
BOURNEMOUTH
Russell-Cotes Art Gallery and Museum, East Cliff Promenade BH1 3AA T 01202-451858 W www.russellcotes.com
Seaside villa housing 19th- and 20th-century art and sculptures from around the world
BOVINGTON
Tank Museum, Dorset BH20 6JG T 01929-405096
W www.tankmuseum.org
Collection of 300 tanks from their invention in 1915 to the modern conflict in Afghanistan
BRADFORD
Bradford Industrial Museum, Moorside Mills, Moorside Road, Eccleshill BD2 3HP T 01274-435900
W www.bradfordmuseums.org
Steam power, machinery and motor vehicle exhibits
Cartwright Hall Art Gallery, Lister Park BD9 4NS T 01274-431212
W www.bradfordmuseums.org
British 19th- and 20th-century fine art, contemporary prints and south Asian art
National Science and Media Museum, BD1 1NQ T 0844-856 3797
W www.scienceandmediamuseum.org.uk
The science and culture of image and sound technologies, film and television with interactive exhibits and experiments; features an IMAX cinema and the only permanent Cinerama screen in Europe
BRIGHTON
Booth Museum of Natural History, Dyke Road BN1 5AA
T 03000-290900 W www.brightonmuseums.org.uk/booth
Zoology, botany and geology collections; British birds in recreated habitats
Brighton Museum and Art Gallery, Royal Pavilion Gardens BN1 1EE
T 03000-290900 W www.brightonmuseums.org.uk/brighton
Includes fine art and design, fashion, world art; Sussex history
Royal Pavilion, 4/5 Pavilion Buildings BN1 1EE T 0300-0290900
W https://brightonmuseums.org.uk/royalpavilion
Regency seaside pleasure palace for George IV built in the visual style of India and China; includes the Prince Regent and Indian Military Hospital galleries
BRISTOL
Arnolfini, Narrow Quay BS1 4QA T 0117-917 2300
W www.arnolfini.org.uk
Experimental contemporary visual arts, dance, performance, music; talks and workshops

Blaise Castle House Museum, Henbury Road BS10 7QS
T 0117-903 9818
W www.bristolmuseums.org.uk/blaise-castle-house-museum
18th-century mansion; social history collections
Bristol Museum and Art Gallery, Queen's Road BS8 1RL
T 0117-922 3571
W www.bristolmuseums.org.uk/bristol-museum-and-art-gallery
Includes Victorian, Edwardian and French fine art;
archaeology, local history and natural sciences
M Shed, Prince's Wharf BS1 4RN T 0117-352 6600
W www.bristolmuseums.org.uk/m-shed
The story of Bristol's heritage of engineering, transport,
music and industry
Red Lodge Museum, Park Row BS1 5LJ T 0117-921 1360
W www.bristolmuseums.org.uk/red-lodge-museum
House museum showcasing original historical interiors
from the Tudor to Victorian periods
CAMBRIDGE
Fitzwilliam Museum, Trumpington Street CB2 1RB
T 01223-332900 W www.fitzmuseum.cam.ac.uk
Antiquities, fine and applied arts, clocks, ceramics,
manuscripts, furniture, sculpture, coins and medals
*Imperial War Museum Duxford, Duxford CB22 4QR
T 01223-835000 W www.iwm.org.uk/visits/iwm-duxford
Displays of military and civil aircraft, tanks and naval
exhibits
Museum of Archaeology and Anthropology, Downing Street CB2
3DZ T 01223-333516 W www.maa.cam.ac.uk
Global archaeological and anthropological collections;
photography and modern art collections
Museum of Zoology, Downing Street CB2 3EJ T 01223-336650
W www.museum.zoo.cam.ac.uk
Extensive assortment of zoological specimens; includes the
collections of Charles Darwin and Alfred Russel Wallace
Sedgwick Museum of Earth Sciences, Downing Street CB2 3EQ
T 01223-333456 W www.sedgwickmuseum.org
Extensive geological collection
Whipple Museum of the History of Science, Free School Lane CB2
3RH T 01223-330906 W www.hps.cam.ac.uk/whipple
Scientific instruments from the 14th century to the present
CARLISLE
Tullie House Museum and Art Gallery, Castle Street CA3 8TP
T 01228-618718 W www.tulliehouse.co.uk
Jacobean house with fine art, local social history,
prehistoric archaeology and natural sciences including
Hadrian's Wall exhibit
CHATHAM
The Historic Dockyard, ME4 4TE T 01634-823800
W www.thedockyard.co.uk
Maritime attractions including HMS *Cavalier,* the UK's last
Second World War destroyer
Royal Engineers Museum, Prince Arthur Road, Gillingham ME7 1UR
T 01634-822312 W www.re-museum.co.uk
Regimental history, ethnography, decorative art and
photography
CHELTENHAM
The Wilson Art Gallery and Museum, Clarence Street GL50 3JT
T 01242-387488 W www.cheltenhammuseum.org.uk
Arts and crafts, local heroes, fine art and natural history
CHESTER
Grosvenor Museum, Grosvenor Street CH1 2DD T 01244-972197
W www.grosvenormuseum.westcheshiremuseums.co.uk
Roman collections, natural history, art, Chester silver,
local history and costume
CHICHESTER
Weald and Downland Open Air Museum, Singleton PO18 0EU
T 01243-811363 W www.wealddown.co.uk
Rebuilt vernacular buildings from south-east England;
includes medieval houses and a working watermill; craft
demonstrations, Tudor kitchen and cooking

COLCHESTER
Colchester Castle Museum, Castle Park CO1 1TJ T 01206-282939
W www.colchestercastlepark.co.uk/colchester-castle
Largest Norman keep in Europe standing on foundations
of the Roman Temple of Claudius
COVENTRY
Coventry Transport Museum, Hales Street CV1 1JD
T 024-7623 4270 W www.transport-museum.com
Extensive collection of motor vehicles and bicycles; land
speed record-holding car
Herbert Art Gallery and Museum, Jordan Well CV1 5QP
T 024-7623 7521 W www.theherbert.org
Local history, archaeology, industry and visual arts
DERBY
Derby Museum and Art Gallery, The Strand DE1 1BS
T 01332-641901 W www.derbymuseums.org/museumartgallery
Includes paintings by Joseph Wright of Derby, origins of
Derby and military history
Pickford's House Museum, Friar Gate DE1 1DA T 01332-641901
W www.derbymuseums.org/pickfords-house
Georgian town house designed by architect Joseph
Pickford; museum of Georgian life and costume
DEVIZES
Wiltshire Museum, Library and Gallery, Long Street SN10 1NS
T 01380-727369 W www.wiltshiremuseum.org.uk
Natural and local history; art gallery; archaeological finds
from prehistoric, Roman and Saxon sites
DOVER
Dover Museum, Market Square CT16 1PH T 01304-201066
W www.dovermuseum.co.uk
Contains the Dover Bronze Age Boat Gallery and
archaeological finds from Bronze Age, Roman and Saxon
sites
EXETER
Royal Albert Memorial Museum and Art Gallery, Queen Street EX4
3RX T 01392-265858 W www.rammuseum.org.uk
Natural history; archaeology; worldwide fine and
decorative art including Exeter silver
GATESHEAD
BALTIC Centre for Contemporary Art, NE8 3BA T 0191-478 1810
W www.baltic.art
Contemporary art exhibitions and events
Shipley Art Gallery, Prince Consort Road NE8 4JB T 0191-477 1495
W www.shipleyartgallery.org.uk
Contemporary crafts
GAYDON
British Motor Museum, Banbury Road, Warks CV35 0BJ
T 01926-641188 W www.britishmotormuseum.co.uk
The world's largest collection of British cars with nearly
300 vehicles spanning the classic, vintage and veteran eras
GLOUCESTER
Gloucester Waterways Museum, Gloucester Docks GL1 2EH
T 01452-318200 W www.gloucesterwaterwaysmuseum.org.uk
200-year history of Britain's canals and inland waterways
GOSPORT
Royal Navy Submarine Museum, Haslar Jetty Road, Hants PO12 2AS
T 023-9251 0354 W www.nmrn.org.uk/submarine-museum
Underwater warfare exhibition, including submarines
HMS *Alliance* and HMS *Holland 1* – the Royal Navy's first
submarine
GRASMERE
Dove Cottage and the *Wordsworth Museum,* Cumbria LA22 9SH
T 015394-35544 W www.wordsworth.org.uk
William Wordsworth's manuscripts, home and garden
HOVE
Hove Museum and Art Gallery, New Church Road BN3 4AB
T 03000-290900 W www.brightonmuseums.org.uk/hove
Toys, cinema, local history and fine art collections

HULL

Ferens Art Gallery, Queen Victoria Square HU1 3RA
T 01482-300300 W www.hcandl.co.uk/ferens-art-gallery
European Old Masters, Victorian, Edwardian and
contemporary British art

Hull and East Riding Museum of Archaeology, High Street, HU1
1NQ T 01482-300300
W www.hcandl.co.uk/hull-and-east-riding-museum
Local history from the pre-historic to the present day

Hull Maritime Museum, Queen Victoria Square HU1 3DX
T 01482-300300 W www.hcandl.co.uk/maritime-museum
Hull's maritime heritage including whaling, fishing,
navigation and merchant trade

Wilberforce House, 23–25 High Street HU1 1NQ T 01482-300300
W www.hcandl.co.uk/wilberforce-house
Birthplace of abolitionist William Wilberforce; history of
the transatlantic slave trade

HUNTINGDON

The Cromwell Museum, Grammar School Walk PE29 3LF
T 01480-708008 W www.cromwellmuseum.org
Portraits and memorabilia relating to Oliver Cromwell

IPSWICH

Christchurch Mansion and Wolsey Art Gallery, Christchurch Park
IP4 2BE T 01473-433554 W www.cimuseums.org.uk
Tudor house with paintings by Gainsborough, Constable
and other Suffolk artists; furniture and 18th-century
ceramics; temporary exhibitions

KEIGHLEY

The Brontë Parsonage Museum, Haworth, W. Yorks BD22 8DR
T 01535-642323 W www.bronte.org.uk
The former home of the literary Brontë family

KESWICK

Derwent Pencil Museum, Southey Works CA12 5NG
T 01768-773626 W www.derwentart.com
500-year history of the pencil; demonstration events and
workshops throughout the year

LEEDS

Armley Mills, Leeds Industrial Museum, Canal Road, Armley
LS12 2QF T 0113-378 3173 W www.leeds.gov.uk/armleymills
Once the world's largest woollen mill, now a museum for
textiles and Leeds' industrial heritage

Leeds Art Gallery, The Headrow LS1 3AA T 0113-378 5350
W www.leeds.gov.uk/artgallery
Includes English watercolours, sculpture, contemporary
art and prints from the region's artists

*Royal Armouries Museum, Armouries Drive LS10 1LT
T 0113-220 1999 W www.royalarmouries.org
National collection of over 8,500 items of arms and
armour from BC to present over five galleries: War,
Tournament, Oriental, Self Defence and Hunting

LEICESTER

New Walk Museum and Art Gallery, 53 New Walk LE1 7EA
T 0116-255 4900
W www.leicester.gov.uk/leisure-and-culture/
museums-and-galleries
Natural and cultural history; ancient Egypt gallery;
European art including works by the German
expressionists and ceramics by Picasso

LINCOLN

The Collection, Danes Terrace LN2 1LP T 01522-782040
W www.thecollectionmuseum.com
Artefacts from the Stone Age to the Roman, Viking and
Medieval eras; adjacent art gallery; collections of
contemporary art and craft, sculpture, porcelain, clocks
and watches

Museum of Lincolnshire Life, Burton Road LN1 3LY
T 01522-782040
W www.lincolnshire.gov.uk/museumoflincolnshirelife
Social history; agricultural, industrial, military and
commercial exhibits

LIVERPOOL

*International Slavery Museum, Albert Dock L3 4AX
T 0151-478 4499 W www.liverpoolmuseums.org.uk/ism
Explores historical and contemporary aspects of slavery

*Lady Lever Art Gallery, Wirral CH62 5EQ T 0151-478 4136
W www.liverpoolmuseums.org.uk/ladylever
Paintings, furniture and porcelain

*Merseyside Maritime Museum, Albert Dock L3 4AQ
T 0151-478 4499 W www.liverpoolmuseums.org.uk/maritime
Floating exhibits, working displays and craft
demonstrations; incorporates the UK Border Agency
National Museum

*Museum of Liverpool, Pier Head L3 1DG T 0151-478 4545
W www.liverpoolmuseums.org.uk/mol
Explores the significance of the city's geography, history
and culture

* Sudley House, Mossley Hill Road L18 8BX T 0151-478 4016
W www.liverpoolmuseums.org.uk/sudley
Late 18th- and 19th-century paintings in former
shipowner's home

*Tate Liverpool, Albert Dock L3 4BB T 0151-1702 7400
W www.tate.org.uk/liverpool
20th-century paintings and sculpture

*Walker Art Gallery, William Brown Street L3 8EL
T 0151-478 4199 W www.liverpoolmuseums.org.uk/walker
Paintings and decorative arts from the 13th century to the
present day

*World Museum Liverpool, William Brown Street L3 8EN
T 0151-478 4393 W www.liverpoolmuseums.org.uk/wml
Includes Egyptian mummies, weapons and classical
sculpture; planetarium, aquarium, vivarium and natural
history centre

LONDON: GALLERIES

Barbican Art Gallery, Barbican Centre, Silk Street EC2Y 8DS
T 020-7638 4141 W www.barbican.org.uk
Art, music, theatre, dance and film exhibitions

Courtauld Institute of Art Gallery, Somerset House, Strand
WC2R 0RN T 020-3947 7673 W www.courtauld.ac.uk
Fine art from the early renaissance to the 20th century,
including impressionist and post-impressionist paintings

Dennis Severs' House, 18 Folgate Street E1 6BX T 020-7247 4013
W www.dennissevershouse.co.uk
Candlelit recreation of a Huguenot silk weaver's home

Dulwich Picture Gallery, Gallery Road SE21 7AD T 020-8693 5254
W www.dulwichpicturegallery.org.uk
England's first public art gallery; designed by Sir John
Soane to house 17th- and 18th-century paintings

Estorick Collection of Modern Italian Art, Canonbury Square
N1 2AN T 020-7704 9522 W www.estorickcollection.com
Early 20th-century Italian drawings, paintings, sculptures
and etchings, with an emphasis on Futurism

Hayward Gallery, Belvedere Road SE1 8XX T 020-7960 4200
W www.southbankcentre.co.uk
Temporary exhibitions

*National Gallery, Trafalgar Square WC2N 5DN T 020-7747 2885
W www.nationalgallery.org.uk
Western painting from the 13th to 19th centuries; early
Renaissance collection in the Sainsbury Wing

*National Portrait Gallery, St Martin's Place WC2H 0HE
T 020-7306 0055 W www.npg.org.uk
Portraits of eminent people in British history

Photographers' Gallery, Ramillies Street W1F 7LW **T** 020-7087 9300
W www.thephotographersgallery.org.uk
Temporary exhibitions; permanent camera obscura

The Queen's Gallery, Buckingham Palace SW1A 1AA
T 020-7766 7300 **W** www.royalcollection.org.uk
Art from the Royal Collection

Royal Academy of Arts, Burlington House, Piccadilly W1J 0BD
T 020-7300 8000 **W** www.royalacademy.org.uk
British art since 1768 and temporary exhibitions; annual
Summer Exhibition

Saatchi Gallery, Duke of York's HQ, King's Road SW3 4RY
T 020-7823 2363 **W** www.saatchigallery.com
Contemporary art including paintings, photographs,
sculpture and installations

Serpentine Gallery, Kensington Gardens W2 3XA **T** 020-7402 6075
W www.serpentinegallery.org
Temporary exhibitions of British and international
contemporary art

*Tate Britain, Millbank SW1P 4RG **T** 020-7887 8888
W www.tate.org.uk/britain
British art from the 16th century to the present;
international modern art

*Tate Modern, Bankside SE1 9TG **T** 020-7887 8888
W www.tate.org.uk/modern
International modern art from 1900 to the present

*Wallace Collection, Manchester Square W1U 3BN
T 020-7563 9500 **W** www.wallacecollection.org
Old Masters; French 18th-century paintings, furniture,
armour, porcelain, clocks and sculpture

Whitechapel Art Gallery, Whitechapel High Street E1 7QX
T 020-7522 7888 **W** www.whitechapelgallery.org
Temporary exhibitions of modern art

LONDON: MUSEUMS

Bank of England Museum, Bartholomew Lane EC2R 8AH
T 020-7601 5545 **W** www.bankofengland.co.uk/museum
History of the Bank of England since 1694

*British Museum, Great Russell Street WC1B 3DG **T** 020-7323 8000
W www.britishmuseum.org
Collection of art and antiquities spanning 2 million years
of human history; temporary exhibitions; houses the Elgin
Marbles from the Parthenon

Brunel Museum, Rotherhithe SE16 4LF **T** 020-7231 3840
W www.brunel-museum.org.uk
Explores the engineering achievements of Isambard
Kingdom Brunel and his father, Marc Brunel

Charles Dickens Museum, Doughty Street WC1N 2LX
T 020-7405 2127 **W** www.dickensmuseum.com
Dickens's home from 1837–9; manuscripts, personal
items and paintings

*Churchill War Rooms, King Charles Street SW1A 2AQ
T 020-7416 5000 **W** www.iwm.org.uk/visits/churchill-war-rooms
Underground rooms used by Churchill and the
government during the Second World War

Cutty Sark, King William Walk SE10 9HT **T** 020-8858 4422
W www.rmg.co.uk/cuttysark
The world's last remaining tea clipper; re-opened in April
2012 following extensive restoration

Design Museum, Kensington High Street W8 6AG **T** 020-3862 5900
W www.designmuseum.org
The development of design and the mass-production of
consumer objects

Garden Museum, Lambeth Palace Road SE1 7LB **T** 020-7401 8865
W www.gardenmuseum.org.uk
History and development of gardens and gardening;
temporary exhibitions, symposia and events

*HMS Belfast, The Queen's Walk SE1 2JH **T** 020-7940 6300
W www.iwm.org.uk/hms-belfast
Life and work on board a Second World War cruiser

*Horniman Museum and Gardens, London Road SE23 3PQ
T 020-8699 1872 **W** www.horniman.ac.uk
Museum of anthropology, musical instruments and natural
history; aquarium; reference library; gardens

*Imperial War Museum, Lambeth Road SE1 6HZ **T** 020-7416 5000
W www.iwm.org.uk
All aspects of the two World Wars and other military
operations involving Britain and the Commonwealth since
1914

Jewish Museum, Albert Street NW1 7NB **T** 020-7284 7384
W www.jewishmuseum.org.uk
Jewish life, history, art and religion

London Metropolitan Archives, Northampton Road EC1R 0HB
T 020-7332 3820 **W** www.cityoflondon.gov.uk/lma
Material on the history of London and its people dating
from 1067 to the present day

London Museum of Water and Steam, Green Dragon Lane TW8 0EN
T 020-8568 4757 **W** www.waterandsteam.org.uk
Large collection of steam engines; reopened in 2014 after
refurbishment

London Transport Museum, Covent Garden Piazza WC2E 7BB
T 020-7379 6344 **W** www.ltmuseum.co.uk
Vehicles, photographs and graphic art relating to the
history of transport in London

MCC Museum, Lord's Cricket Ground, St John's Wood NW8 8QN
T 020-7616 8656 **W** www.lords.org/tours-and-museum
Cricket exhibits including the Ashes Urn, kits, paintings
and W. G. Grace exhibit

Migration Museum, Lambeth High Street SE1 7AG
E info@migrationmuseum.org **W** www.migrationmuseum.org
Opened in 2017, tells the story of migration through the
ages and how it has affected and transformed Britain

*Museum of Childhood (V&A), Cambridge Heath Road E2 9PA
T 020-8983 5200 **W** www.vam.ac.uk/moc
Toys, games and exhibits relating to the social history of
childhood from the 17th century to the present

*Museum of London, London Wall EC2Y 5HN **T** 020-7001 9844
W www.museumoflondon.org.uk
History of London from prehistoric times to the present
day; Galleries of Modern London

Museum of London Docklands, West India Quay, Canary Wharf
E14 4AL **T** 020-7001 9844
W www.museumoflondon.org.uk/docklands
Explores the story of London's river, port and people over
2,000 years; includes the London Sugar Slavery Gallery

National Archives Museum, Kew TW9 4DU **T** 020-8876 3444
W www.nationalarchives.gov.uk/museum
Displays treasures from the archives, including the
Domesday Book and Magna Carta

*National Army Museum, Royal Hospital Road SW3 4HT
T 020-7730 0717 **W** www.nam.ac.uk
Five-hundred-year history of the British soldier; exhibits
include model of the Battle of Waterloo and recreated
First World War trench

*National Maritime Museum, Romney Road SE10 9NF
T 020-8858 4422
W www.rmg.co.uk/national-maritime-museum
Maritime history of Britain; collections include globes,
clocks, telescopes and paintings; comprises the main
building, the Royal Observatory and the Queen's House

*Natural History Museum, Cromwell Road SW7 5BD
T 020-7942 5000 **W** www.nhm.ac.uk
Natural history collections and interactive Darwin Centre

Petrie Museum of Egyptian Archaeology, University College London,
Malet Place WC1E 6BT **T** 020-7679 2884
W www.ucl.ac.uk/museums/petrie
Egyptian and Sudanese archaeology featuring around
80,000 objects

Postal Museum, 15–20 Phoenix Place, WC1X 0DL T 0300-030 0700 W www.postalmuseum.org
British postal service and communications from Tudor times to the present; interactive galleries, archives and subterranean mail train ride

Royal Air Force Museum, Grahame Park Way NW9 5LL T 020-8205 2266 W www.rafmuseum.org.uk
Aviation from before the Wright brothers to the present

Royal Mews, Buckingham Palace SW1W 0QH T 020-7766 7302 W www.rct.uk/visit/royalmews
State vehicles, including the Queen's gold state coach; home to the Queen's horses; guided tours

Science Museum, Exhibition Road SW7 2DD T 020-7942 4000 W www.sciencemuseum.org.uk
Science, technology, industry and medicine exhibitions; children's interactive gallery; IMAX cinema

Shakespeare's Globe Exhibition, New Globe Walk, Bankside SE1 9DT T 020-7902 1400 W www.shakespearesglobe.com
Recreation of Elizabethan theatre using 16th-century techniques; includes a tour of the theatre

Sir John Soane's Museum, Lincoln's Inn Fields WC2A 3BP T 020-7405 2107 W www.soane.org
Art and antiquities collected by Soane throughout his lifetime; authentic Georgian and Victorian interior

Tower Bridge Exhibition, SE1 2UP T 020-7403 3761 W www.towerbridge.org.uk
History of the bridge and display of Victorian steam machinery; panoramic views from walkways

Victoria and Albert Museum, Cromwell Road SW7 2RL T 020-7942 2000 W www.vam.ac.uk
Includes the National Art Library and the Gilbert Collection; fine and applied art and design; furniture, glass, textiles, theatre and dress collections; temporary exhibitions

Wellcome Collection, Euston Road NW1 2BE T 020-7611 2222 W www.wellcomecollection.org
Contemporary and historic exhibitions and collections including the Wellcome Library

Wimbledon Lawn Tennis Museum, Church Road SW19 5AE T 020-8944 1066 W www.wimbledon.com/museum
Tennis trophies, fashion and memorabilia; view of Centre Court

MALTON
Eden Camp, N. Yorks YO17 6RT T 01653-697777 W www.edencamp.co.uk
Restored POW camp and Second World War memorabilia

MANCHESTER
Gallery of Costume, Platt Hall, Rusholme M14 5LL T 0161-245 7245 W www.manchesterartgallery.org
Exhibits from the 17th century to the present day

Imperial War Museum North, Trafford Wharf Road M17 1TZ T 0161-836 4000 W www.iwm.org.uk/north
History of war from the 20th century to the present

Manchester Art Gallery, Mosley Street M2 3JL T 0161-235 8888 W www.manchesterartgallery.org
European fine and decorative art from the 17th to 20th centuries

Manchester Museum, Oxford Road M13 9PL T 0161-275 2648 W www.museum.manchester.ac.uk
Collections include decorative arts, natural history and zoology; three Ancient Worlds galleries

Museum of Science and Industry, Liverpool Road M3 4FP T 0161-832 2244 W www.scienceandindustrymuseum.org.uk
On site of world's oldest passenger railway station; galleries relating to space, energy, power, transport, aviation, textiles and social history

National Football Museum, Cathedral Gardens M4 3BG T 0161-605 8200 W www.nationalfootballmuseum.com
Home to the FIFA, FA and Football League collections including the 1966 World Cup final ball

People's History Museum, Left Bank, Spinningfields M3 3ER T 0161-838 9190 W www.phm.org.uk
History of British political and working life

The Whitworth, Oxford Road M15 6ER T 0161-275 7450 W www.whitworth.manchester.ac.uk
Fine and modern art, wallpapers, prints, textiles and sculptures

MILTON KEYNES
Bletchley Park National Codes Centre, Bucks MK3 6EB T 01908-640404 W www.bletchleypark.org.uk
Home of British codebreaking during the Second World War; Enigma machine; computer museum and Alan Turing gallery

The National Museum of Computing Block H, Bletchley Park, MK3 6EB T 01908-374708 W www.tnmoc.org
Charts the development of computing from the 1940s onwards and houses the world's largest collection of functional historical computers, including the Colossus and the WITCH

NEWCASTLE UPON TYNE
Discovery Museum, Blandford Square NE1 4JA T 0191-232 6789 W www.discoverymuseum.org.uk
Science and industry, local history, fashion; Tyneside's maritime history; digital jukebox of 2,000 film and TV titles from the BFI National Archive

Great North Museum: Hancock, Barras Bridge NE2 4PT T 0191-222 6765 W www.greatnorthmuseum.org.uk
Natural and ancient history; planetarium; Living Planet display incorporates live animal tanks and aquaria

Laing Art Gallery, New Bridge Street NE1 8AG T 0191-278 1611 W www.laingartgallery.org.uk
19th and 20th century art including local painters; ceramics, glass, Japanese decorative arts and prints

NEWMARKET
Palace House: National Heritage Centre for Horseracing and Sporting Art, Palace Street CB8 8EP T 01638-667314 W www.palacehousenewmarket.co.uk
Collection of horseracing memorabilia, British Sporting Art from around the UK and home of the retraining of racehorses

NORTH SHIELDS
Stephenson Railway Museum, Middle Engine Lane NE29 8DX T 0191-200 7146 W www.stephensonrailwaymuseum.org.uk
Locomotive engines and rolling stock; open April through November and school holidays outside this period

NOTTINGHAM
Natural History Museum, Wollaton Hall, Wollaton NG8 2AE T 0115-876 3100 W www.wallatonhall.org.uk
Geology, botany and zoology specimens housed in an Elizabethan mansion

OXFORD
Ashmolean Museum, Beaumont Street OX1 2PH T 01865-278000 W www.ashmolean.org
Art and archaeology including Egyptian, Minoan, Anglo-Saxon and Chinese exhibits; largest collection of Raphael drawings in the world

Modern Art Oxford, Pembroke Street OX1 1BP T 01865-722733 W www.modernartoxford.org.uk
Temporary exhibitions

Museum of the History of Science, Broad Street OX1 3AZ T 01865-277293 W www.mhs.ox.ac.uk
Displays include early scientific instruments, chemical apparatus, clocks and watches

Oxford University Museum of Natural History, Parks Road OX1 3PW **T** 01865-272950 **W** www.oumnh.ox.ac.uk
Entomology, geology, mineralogy and petrology, and zoology

Pitt Rivers Museum, South Parks Road OX1 3PP **T** 01865-613000 **W** www.prm.ox.ac.uk
Anthropological and archaeological artefacts

PLYMOUTH

City Museum and Art Gallery, Drake Circus PL4 8AJ
T 01752-304774 **W** www.plymhearts.org
Local and natural history; ceramics; silver; Old Masters; world artefacts; temporary exhibitions

PORTSMOUTH

Charles Dickens Birthplace, Old Commercial Road PO1 4QL
T 023-9282 1879 **W** www.charlesdickensbirthplace.co.uk
Reproduction Regency house; Dickens memorabilia

The D-Day Story, Clarence Esplanade, Southsea PO5 3NT
T 023-9288 2555 **W** www.theddaystory.com
The evacuation of Dunkirk, the D-Day landings and the Battle of Normandy exhibitions with over 10,000 objects and artefacts including the Overlord embroidery

Portsmouth Historic Dockyard, HM Naval Base PO1 3LJ
T 023-9283 9766 **W** www.historicdockyard.co.uk
Incorporates the *National Museum of the Royal Navy** (PO1 3NH **T** 023-9272 7574 **W** www.nmrn.org.uk), HMS *Victory* (PO1 3NH **T** 023-9283 9766 **W** www.hms-victory.com), HMS *Warrior* (PO1 3QX **T** 023-9277 8600 **W** www.hmswarrior.org), *Mary Rose* (PO1 3LX **T** 023-9281 2931 **W** www.maryrose.org) and *Action Stations* (PO1 3LJ **T** 023-9289 3338 **W** www.actionstations.org)
History of the Royal Navy and of the dockyard; warships and technology spanning 500 years

PRESTON

Harris Museum and Art Gallery, Market Square PR1 2PP
T 01772-258248 **W** www.harrismuseum.org.uk
British art since the 18th century; ceramics, glass, costume and local history; contemporary exhibitions

ST ALBANS

Verulamium Museum, St Michael's Street AL3 4SW
T 01727-751810 **W** www.stalbansmuseums.org.uk
Remains of Iron Age settlement and the third-largest city in Roman Britain

ST IVES

*Tate St Ives, Porthmeor Beach, Cornwall TR26 1TG
T 01736-796226 **W** www.tate.org.uk/stives
Modern art, much by artists associated with St Ives; includes the Barbara Hepworth Museum and Sculpture Garden; open after 2014 part closure

SALISBURY

Salisbury & South Wiltshire Museum, The Close SP1 2EN
T 01722-332151 **W** www.salisburymuseum.org.uk
Local history and archaeology; Stonehenge exhibits

SHEFFIELD

Graves Gallery, Surrey Street S1 1XZ **T** 0114-278 2600
W www.museums-sheffield.org.uk
Twentieth-century British art; European art spanning four centuries

Millennium Galleries, Arundel Gate S1 2PP **T** 0114-278 2600
W www.museums-sheffield.org.uk
Incorporates four different galleries: the Special Exhibition Gallery, the Craft and Design Gallery, the Metalwork Gallery and the Ruskin Gallery, which houses John Ruskin's collection of paintings, drawings, books and medieval manuscripts

Weston Park Museum, Western Bank S10 2TP **T** 0114-278 2600
W www.museums-sheffield.org.uk
World and local history; art and temporary exhibitions

SOUTHAMPTON

City Art Gallery, Commercial Road SO14 7LP **T** 023-8083 3007
W www.southamptoncityartgallery.com
Western art from the Renaissance to the present

SeaCity Museum, Havelock Road SO14 7FY **T** 023-8083 3007
W www.seacitymuseum.co.uk
Opened in 2012, the museum tells the story of the city's maritime past and present

SOUTH SHIELDS

Arbeia Roman Fort, Baring Street NE33 2BB **T** 0191-277 2170
W www.arbeiaromanfort.org.uk
Excavated ruins; reconstructions of original buildings

South Shields Museum and Art Gallery, Ocean Road NE33 2JA
T 0191-211 5599 **W** www.southshieldsmuseum.org.uk
South Tyneside history; interactive art gallery

STOKE-ON-TRENT

Etruria Industrial Museum, Lower Bedford Street ST4 7AF
T 07900-267711 **W** www.etruriamuseum.org.uk
Britain's sole surviving steam-powered potter's mill

Gladstone Pottery Museum, Uttoxeter Road, Longton ST3 1PQ
T 01782-237777 **W** www.stokemuseums.org.uk/gpm
The last complete Victorian pottery factory in Britain

Potteries Museum and Art Gallery, Bethesda Street ST1 3DW
T 01782-232323 **W** www.stokemuseums.org.uk/pmag
Pottery, china and porcelain collections and a Mark XVI Spitfire

The Wedgwood Museum, Barlaston ST12 9ER **T** 01782-371900
W www.wedgwoodmuseum.org.uk
The story of Josiah Wedgwood and the company he founded

SUNDERLAND

Sunderland Museum and Winter Gardens, Burdon Road SR1 1PP
T 0191-553 2323
W www.seeitdoitsunderland.co.uk/
sunderland-museum-winter-gardens
Fine and decorative art, local history and gardens

TELFORD

Ironbridge Gorge Museums, TF8 7DQ **T** 01952-433424
W www.ironbridge.org.uk
Ten museums including The Museum of the Gorge; The Iron Bridge and Tollhouse; Blists Hill (late Victorian working town); Brosely Pipeworks; Coalbrookdale Museum of Iron; Coalport China Museum; Jackfield Tile Museum; Tar Tunnel; Darby Houses

WAKEFIELD

Hepworth Wakefield, Gallery Walk WF1 5AW **T** 01924-247360
W www.hepworthwakefield.org
Historic and modern art; temporary exhibitions of contemporary art

National Coal Mining Museum for England, New Road, Overton WF4 4RH **T** 01924-848806 **W** www.ncm.org.uk
Includes underground tours of one of Britain's oldest working mines

Yorkshire Sculpture Park, West Bretton WF4 4LG **T** 01924-832631
W www.ysp.co.uk
Open-air sculpture gallery including works by Henry Moore, Barbara Hepworth and others in 500 acres of parkland

WEYBRIDGE

Brooklands Museum, Brooklands Road KT13 0QN **T** 01932-857381
W www.brooklandsmuseum.com
Birthplace of British motorsport; world's first purpose-built motor racing circuit

WILMSLOW

Quarry Bank Mill and Styal Estate, Wilmslow SK9 4LA
T 01625-527468 **W** www.nationaltrust.org.uk/quarry-bank
Europe's most powerful working waterwheel owned by the National Trust illustrating history of cotton industry; costumed guides at restored Apprentice House

WINCHESTER
Winchester Science Centre and Planetarium, Telegraph Way, Hants
SO21 1HZ T 01962-863791
W www.winchestersciencecentre.org
Interactive science centre and planetarium
WORCESTER
City Art Gallery and Museum, Foregate Street WR1 1DT
T 01905-25371
W www.museumsworcestershire.org.uk/museums/
worcester-city-art-gallery-museum
Includes the Regimental museum, 19th-century chemist
shop and changing art exhibitions
Museum of Royal Worcester, Severn Street WR1 2ND
T 01905-21247 W www.museumofroyalworcester.org
Worcester porcelain from 1751 to the present day
YEOVIL
Fleet Air Arm Museum, RNAS Yeovilton, Somerset BA22 8HT
T 01935-840565 W www.fleetairarm.com
History of naval aviation; historic aircraft, including
Concorde 002
YORK
Beningbrough Hall, Beningbrough YO30 1DD T 01904-472027
W www.nationaltrust.org.uk/beningbrough-hall
18th-century house with portraits from the National
Portrait Gallery; parklands and gardens
JORVIK Viking Centre, Coppergate YO1 9WT T 01904-615505
W www.jorvikvikingcentre.co.uk
Reconstruction of Viking York based on archaeological
evidence
National Railway Museum, Leeman Road YO26 4XJ
T 0333-016 1010 W www.nrm.org.uk
Includes locomotives, rolling stock and carriages
York Art Gallery, Exhibition Square, YO1 7EW T 01904 687687
W www.yorkartgallery.org.uk
600 years of British and European painting; ceramics and
sculpture
York Castle Museum, Eye of York YO1 9RY T 01904-687687
W www.yorkcastlemuseum.org.uk
Includes Kirkgate, a reconstructed Victorian street;
costume and military collections
Yorkshire Museum, Museum Gardens YO1 7FR T 01904-687687
W www.yorkshiremuseum.org.uk
Yorkshire life from Roman to medieval times; geology
and biology; York observatory

WALES
* Members of National Museum Wales, a public body that
receives its core funding from the Welsh government

ABERYSTWYTH
Ceredigion Museum, Terrace Road SY23 2AQ T 01970-633088
W www.ceredigionmuseum.wales
Local history, housed in a restored Edwardian theatre
Silver Mountain Experience, Ponterwyd SY23 3AB T 01970-890620
W www.silvermountainexperience.co.uk
Tours of an 18th-century silver mine, with interactive
challenges and games for children
BLAENAFON
*Big Pit National Coal Museum, Torfaen NP4 9XP
T 030-0111 2333 W www.museum.wales/bigpit
Colliery with an underground tour and exhibitions of
modern mining equipment
BODELWYDDAN
Bodelwyddan Castle, Denbighshire LL18 5YA T 01745-584060
W www.bodelwyddan-castle.co.uk
Art gallery within an historic house; features temporary art
exhibits

CAERLEON
*National Roman Legion Museum, NP18 1AE T 030-0111 2333
W www.museum.wales/roman
Features the oldest recorded piece of writing in Wales;
pottery, Roman era gemstones
CARDIFF
*National Museum Cardiff, Cathays Park CF10 3NP
T 030-0111 2333 W www.museum.wales/cardiff
Houses Wales's national art, archaeology and natural
history collections
*St Fagans: National History Museum, St Fagans CF5 6XB
T 030-0111 2333 W www.museum.wales/stfagans
Open-air museum with re-erected buildings, agricultural
equipment and costume
TECHNIQUEST, Stuart Street CF10 5BW T 029-2047 5475
W www.techniquest.org
Interactive science exhibits, planetarium and science
theatre
CRICCIETH
Lloyd George Museum, Llanystumdwy LL52 0SH T 01766-522071
W www.gwynedd.llyw.cymru
Childhood home of David Lloyd George
DRE-FACH FELINDRE
*National Wool Museum, Llandysul SA44 5UP T 030-0111 2333
W www.museum.wales/wool
Exhibitions, a working woollen mill and craft workshops
LLANBERIS
*National Slate Museum, Gwynedd LL55 4TY T 030-0111 2333
W www.museum.wales/slate
Former slate quarry with original machinery and plant;
slate crafts demonstrations; working waterwheel
LLANDRINDOD WELLS
National Cycle Collection, Automobile Palace, Temple Street
LD1 5DL T 01597-825531 W www.cyclemuseum.org.uk
Approximately 250 bicycles on display, from 1819 to the
present
PRESTEIGNE
Judge's Lodging Museum, Broad Street LD8 2AD T 01544-260650
W www.judgeslodging.org.uk
Restored apartments, courtroom, cells and servants'
quarters
SWANSEA
Glynn Vivian Art Gallery, Alexandra Road SA1 5DZ
T 01792-516900 W www.swansea.gov.uk/glynnvivian
Fine art and ceramics from 1700 to the present
*National Waterfront Museum, Oystermouth Road SA1 3RD
T 030-0111 2333 W www.museum.wales/swansea
Wales during the Industrial Revolution
Swansea Museum, Victoria Road SA1 1SN T 01792-653763
W www.swansea.gov.uk/swanseamuseum
Paintings, Egyptian artifacts, transport and nautical
collections; war time Swansea
TENBY
Tenby Museum and Art Gallery, Castle Hill SA70 7BP T 01834-
842809 W www.tenbymuseum.org.uk
Local archaeology, history, geology and art

SCOTLAND
* Members of National Museums Scotland or National
Galleries of Scotland, which are non-departmental public
bodies funded by, and accountable to, the Scottish government

ABERDEEN
Aberdeen Art Gallery, Schoolhill AB10 1FQ T 0300-020 0293
W www.aagm.co.uk
Paintings, sculptures and graphics; temporary exhibitions
Aberdeen Maritime Museum, Shiprow AB11 5BY T 01224-337700
W www.aagm.co.uk
Maritime history, including shipbuilding and North Sea
oil

AYR

Robert Burns Birthplace Museum, Murdoch's Lone, Alloway
KA7 4PQ T 0129-244 3700 W www.burnsmuseum.org.uk
Comprises Burns Cottage, birthplace of the poet, gardens
and a museum

EDINBURGH

Britannia, Leith EH6 6JJ T 0131-555 5566
W www.royalyachtbritannia.co.uk
Former royal yacht with royal barge and royal family
picture gallery

City Art Centre, Market Street EH1 1DE T 0131-529 3993
W www.edinburghmuseums.org.uk
Rolling programme of exhibitions including historic and
modern photography; contemporary art, design and
architecture

Museum of Childhood, High Street EH1 1TG T 0131-529 4142
W www.edinburghmuseums.org.uk
Toys, games, clothes and exhibits relating to the social
history of childhood

Museum of Edinburgh, Canongate, Royal Mile EH8 8DD
T 0131-529 4143 W www.edinburghmuseums.org.uk
Local history, silver, glass and Scottish pottery

National Museum of Flight, East Fortune Airfield, East Lothian
EH39 5LF T 0300-123 6789 W www.nms.ac.uk/flight
Aviation from the early 20th century to the present

National Museum of Scotland, Chambers Street EH1 1JF
T 0300-123 6789 W www.nms.ac.uk/scotland
Scottish history; world cultures; natural world; art and
design; science and technology

National War Museum of Scotland, Edinburgh Castle EH1 2NG
T 0300-123 6789 W www.nms.ac.uk/war
Scotland's military history housed within Edinburgh
Castle

Scottish National Gallery, The Mound EH2 2EL T 0131-624 6200
W www.nationalgalleries.org
Fine art from the early Renaissance to the end of the 19th
century

Scottish National Gallery of Modern Art, Belford Road EH4 3DR
T 0131-624 6200 W www.nationalgalleries.org
Contemporary art featuring British, French and Russian
collections; outdoor sculpture park

Scottish National Portrait Gallery, Queen Street EH2 1JD
T 0131-624 6200 W www.nationalgalleries.org/portraitgallery
Portraits of eminent people in Scottish history;
Photography Gallery; Victorian Library

The Writers' Museum, Lady Stair's Close EH1 2PA
T 0131-529 4901 W www.edinburghmuseums.org.uk
Exhibitions relating to Robert Burns, Sir Walter Scott and
Robert Louis Stevenson

FORT WILLIAM

West Highland Museum, Cameron Square PH33 6AJ
T 01397-702169 W www.westhighlandmuseum.org.uk
Highland life; Military, Victorian and Jacobite collections

GLASGOW

Burrell Collection, Pollokshaws Road G43 1AT T 0141-287 2550
W www.glasgowlife.org.uk/museums
Paintings by major artists; medieval art, Chinese and
Islamic art

Gallery of Modern Art, Royal Exchange Square G1 3AH
T 0141-287 3005 W www.glasgowlife.org.uk/museums
Collection of contemporary Scottish and world art

Hunterian, University of Glasgow G12 8QQ T 0141-330 4221
W www.gla.ac.uk/hunterian
Rennie Mackintosh and Whistler collections; coins;
Scottish paintings; Pacific ethnographic collection;
archaeology; medicine

Kelvingrove Art Gallery & Museum, Argyle Street G3 8AG
T 0141-276 9599 W www.glasgowlife.org.uk/museums
Includes Old Masters; natural history; arms and armour

Museum of Piping, McPhater Street G4 0HW T 0141-353 0220
W www.thepipingcentre.co.uk
The history and origins of bagpiping

Museum of Rural Life, Philipshill Road, East Kilbride G76 9HR
T 0300-123 6789 W www.nms.ac.uk/rural
History of rural life and work

People's Palace and Winter Gardens, Glasgow Green G40 1AT
T 0141-276 0788 W www.glasgowlife.org.uk/museums
Social history of Glasgow since 1750

Riverside Museum, 100 Pointhouse Place G3 8RS T 0141-287 2720
W www.glasgowlife.org.uk/museums
Scotland's museum of transport and travel; the Tall Ship
Glenlee, a Clyde-built sailing ship, is berthed alongside

St Mungo Museum of Religious Art and Life, Castle Street G4 0RH
T 0141-276 1625 W www.glasgowlife.org.uk/museums
Exhibits detailing the world's major religions; oldest Zen
garden in Britain

NORTHERN IRELAND

* Members of National Museums Northern Ireland, a public
body sponsored by the Department for Communities,
Northern Ireland executive.

ARMAGH

Armagh County Museum, The Mall East BT61 9BE
T 028-3752 3070 W www.nimc.co.uk
Local history; fine art; archaeology; crafts

BANGOR

North Down Museum, Town Hall BT20 4BT T 028-9127 1200
W www.northdownmuseum.com
Local history from the Bronze age to the present

BELFAST

Titanic Belfast, Queen's Road, Titanic Quarter BT3 9EP
T 028-9076 6386 W www.titanicbelfast.com
The story of RMS *Titanic* from her conception to demise;
Shipyard ride and ocean exploration centre

Ulster Museum, Botanic Gardens BT9 5AB T 0289-044 0000
W www.nmni.com/um
Irish antiquities; natural and local history; fine and applied
arts

W5, Queen's Quay BT3 9QQ T 028-9046 7700
W www.w5online.co.uk
Interactive science and technology centre

HOLYWOOD

Ulster Folk and Transport Museum, Cultra BT18 0EU
T 028-9042 8428 W www.nmni.com/uftm
Open-air museum with original buildings from Ulster
town and rural life c.1900; indoor galleries including Irish
rail and road transport

LONDONDERRY

The Tower Museum, Union Hall Place BT48 6LU T 028-7137 2411
W www.derrystrabane.com/towermuseum
Tells the story of Ireland through the history of
Londonderry

NEWTOWNARDS

The Somme Heritage Centre, Bangor Road BT23 7PH
T 028-9182 3202 W www.sommeassociation.com
Commemorates the part played by Irish forces in the First
World War

OMAGH

Ulster American Folk Park, Castletown, Co. Tyrone BT78 5QU
T 028-8224 3292 W www.nmni.com/uafp
Open-air museum telling the story of Ulster's emigrants to
America; restored or recreated dwellings and workshops;
ship and dockside gallery

SIGHTS OF LONDON

For historic buildings, museums and galleries in London, *see* the Historic Buildings and Monuments, and Museums and Galleries sections.

BRIDGES

The bridges over the Thames in London, from east to west, are:

Tower Bridge (268m/880ft by 18m/60ft), architect: Horace Jones, engineer: John Wolfe Barry, opened 1894

London Bridge (262m/860ft by 32m/105ft), original 13th-century stone bridge rebuilt and opened 1831 (engineer: John Rennie), reconstructed in Arizona when current London Bridge opened 1973 (architect: Lord Holford, engineer: Mott, Hay and Anderson)

Cannon Street Railway Bridge (261m/855ft), engineers: John Hawkshaw and John Wolfe Barry, originally named Alexandra Bridge, opened 1866; renovated 1979–82

Southwark Bridge (244m/800ft by 17m/56ft), engineer: John Rennie, originally named Queen Street Bridge, opened 1819; rebuilt 1912–21 (architect: Ernest George, engineer: Mott, Hay and Anderson)

Millennium Bridge (325m/1,066ft by 4m/13ft), architect: Foster and Partners, engineer: Ove Arup and Partners, opened 2000; reopened after modification 2002

Blackfriars Railway Bridge (284m/933ft), engineers: John Wolfe Barry and Henri Marc Brunel, originally named St Paul's Railway Bridge, opened 1886

Blackfriars Bridge (294m/963ft by 32m/105ft), engineer: Robert Mylne, opened 1769; rebuilt 1869 (engineer: Joseph Cubitt); widened 1909

Waterloo Bridge (366m/1,200ft by 24m/80ft), engineer: John Rennie, opened 1817; rebuilt 1945 (architect: Sir Giles Gilbert Scott, engineer: Rendel, Palmer and Triton)

Golden Jubilee Bridges (325m/1,066ft by 4.7m/15ft), architect: Lifschutz Davidson, engineer: WSP Group, opened 2002; commonly known as the Hungerford Footbridges

Hungerford Railway Bridge (366m/1,200ft), engineer: Isambard Kingdom Brunel, suspension bridge opened 1845; present railway bridge opened 1864 (engineer: John Hawkshaw); widened in 1886

Westminster Bridge (228m/748ft by 26m/85ft), engineer: Charles Labelye, opened 1750; rebuilt 1862 (architect: Charles Barry, engineer: Thomas Page)

Lambeth Bridge (237m/776ft by 18m/60ft), engineer: Peter W. Barlow, original suspension bridge opened 1862; current structure opened 1932 (architect: Reginald Blomfield, engineer: George W. Humphreys)

Vauxhall Bridge (231m/759ft by 24m/80ft), engineer: James Walker, opened 1816; redesigned and opened 1906 (architect: William Edward Riley, engineers: Alexander Binnie and Maurice Fitzmaurice)

Grosvenor Railway Bridge (213m/699ft), engineer: John Fowler, opened 1860; rebuilt 1965; also known as the Victoria Railway Bridge

Chelsea Bridge (213m/699ft by 25m/83ft), original suspension bridge opened 1858 (engineer: Thomas Page); rebuilt 1937 (architects: George Topham Forrest and E. P. Wheeler, engineer: Rendel, Palmer and Triton)

Albert Bridge (216m/710ft by 12m/40ft), engineer: Rowland M. Ordish, opened 1873; restructured 1884 (engineer: Joseph Bazalgette); strengthened 1971–3

Battersea Bridge (204m/670ft by 17m/56ft), engineer: Henry Holland, opened 1771; rebuilt 1890 (engineer: Joseph Bazalgette)

Battersea Railway Bridge (204m/670ft), engineer: William Baker, opened 1863; also known as Cremorne Bridge

Wandsworth Bridge (189m/619ft by 18m/60ft), engineer: Julian Tolmé, opened 1873; rebuilt 1940 (architect: E. P. Wheeler, engineer: T. Pierson Frank)

Putney Railway Bridge (229m/750ft), engineers: W. H. Thomas and William Jacomb, opened 1889; also known as the Fulham Railway Bridge or the Iron Bridge – it has no official name

Putney Bridge (213m/699ft by 23m/74ft), architect: Jacob Ackworth, original wooden bridge opened 1729; current granite structure completed in 1886 (engineer: Joseph Bazalgette). The starting point of the Boat Race

Hammersmith Bridge (210m/688ft by 10m/33ft), engineer: William Tierney Clarke; the first suspension bridge in London, originally built 1827; rebuilt 1887 (engineer: Joseph Bazalgette)

Barnes Railway Bridge (also footbridge, 110m/360ft), engineer: Joseph Locke, opened 1849; rebuilt 1895 (engineers: London and South Western Railway); the original structure stands unused

Chiswick Bridge (137m/450ft by 21m/70ft), architect: Herbert Baker, engineer: Alfred Dryland, opened 1933. The bridge marks the end point of the Boat Race

Kew Railway Bridge (175m/575ft), engineer: W. R. Galbraith, opened 1869

Kew Bridge (110m/360ft by 17m/56ft), engineer: Robert Tunstall, original timber bridge built 1759; replaced by a Portland stone structure in 1789 (engineer: James Paine); current granite bridge renamed King Edward VII Bridge in 1903, but still known as Kew Bridge (engineers: John Wolfe Barry and Cuthbert Brereton)

Richmond Lock (91m/300ft by 11m/36ft), engineer: F. G. M. Stoney, lock and footbridge opened 1894

Twickenham Bridge (85m/280ft by 21m/70ft), architect: Maxwell Ayrton, engineer: Alfred Dryland, opened 1933

Richmond Railway Bridge (91m/300ft), engineer: Joseph Locke, opened 1848; rebuilt 1906–8 (engineer: J. W. Jacomb-Hood)

Richmond Bridge (85m/280ft by 10m/33ft), architect: James Paine, engineer: Kenton Couse, built 1777; widened 1939

Teddington Lock (198m/650ft), engineer: G. Pooley, two footbridges opened 1889; marks the end of the tidal reach of the Thames

Kingston Railway Bridge architects: J. E. Errington and W. R. Galbraith, engineer: Thomas Brassey, opened 1863

Kingston Bridge (116m/382ft), engineer: Edward Lapidge, built 1825–8; widened 1911–14 (engineers: Basil Mott and David Hay) and 1999–2001

Hampton Court Bridge, engineers: Samuel Stevens and Benjamin Ludgator, built 1753; replaced by iron bridge 1865; present bridge opened 1933 (architect: Edwin Lutyens, engineer: W. P. Robinson)

CEMETERIES

In 1832, in response to the overcrowding of burial grounds in London, the government authorised the establishment of seven non-denominational cemeteries that would encircle the city. These large cemeteries, known as the 'magnificent seven', were seen by many Victorian families as places in which to demonstrate their wealth and stature, and as a result there are some highly ornate graves and tombs.

THE MAGNIFICENT SEVEN

Abney Park, Stoke Newington, N16 (13ha/32 acres), established 1840; tomb of William and Catherine Booth, founders of the Salvation Army, and memorials to many nonconformists and dissenters

Brompton, Old Brompton Road, SW10 (16.5ha/40 acres), established 1840; graves of Sir Henry Cole, Emmeline Pankhurst, John Wisden

Highgate, Swains Lane, N6 (15ha/38 acres), established 1839; graves of Douglas Adams, George Eliot, Eric Hobsbawm, Michael Faraday, Karl Marx, Ralph Miliband and Christina Rossetti

Kensal Green, Harrow Road, W10 (29ha/72 acres), established 1833; tombs of Charles Babbage, Isambard Kingdom Brunel, Wilkie Collins, George Cruikshank, Tom Hood, Leigh Hunt, Harold Pinter, William Makepeace Thackeray, Anthony Trollope

Nunhead, Linden Grove, SE15 (21ha/52 acres), established 1840; closed in 1969, restored and opened for burials

Tower Hamlets, Southern Grove, E3 (11ha/27 acres), established 1841, 350,000 interments; bombed heavily during the Second World War and closed to burials in 1966; now a nature reserve

West Norwood Cemetery and Crematorium, Norwood High Street, SE27 (17ha/42 acres), established 1837; tombs of C. W. Alcock, Mrs Beeton, Sir Henry Tate and Joseph Whitaker (*Whitaker's Almanack*)

OTHER CEMETERIES

Bunhill Fields, City Road, EC1 (1.6ha/4 acres), 17th-century nonconformist burial ground containing the graves of William Blake, John Bunyan and Daniel Defoe

City of London Cemetery and Crematorium, Aldersbrook Road, E12 (81ha/200 acres), established 1856; grave of Bobby Moore

Golders Green Crematorium, Hoop Lane, NW11 (5ha/12 acres), established 1902; retains the ashes of Kingsley Amis, Lionel Bart, Enid Blyton, Marc Bolan, Sigmund Freud, Keith Moon, Ivor Novello, Bram Stoker and H. G. Wells

Hampstead, Fortune Green Road, NW6 (10.5ha/26 acres), established 1876; graves of Alan Coren, Kate Greenaway, Joseph Lister and Marie Lloyd

MARKETS

Billingsgate, Trafalgar Way, E14 (fish), a market site for over 1,000 years, with the Lower Thames Street site dating from 1876; moved to the Isle of Dogs in 1982; owned and run by the City of London Corporation

Borough, Southwark Street, SE1 (vegetables, fruit, meat, dairy, bread), established on present site in 1756; privately owned and run

Brick Lane, E1 (jewellery, vintage clothes, bric-a-brac, food), open Saturday and Sunday

Brixton, SW9 (African-Caribbean food, music, clothing), open Monday to Saturday

Broadway, E8 (food, fashion, crafts), re-established in 2004, open Saturday

Camden Lock, NW1 (second-hand clothing, jewellery, alternative fashion, crafts), established in 1973

Columbia Road, E2 (flowers), dates from 19th century; became dedicated flower market in the 20th century

Covent Garden, WC2 (antiques, handicrafts, jewellery, clothing, food), originally a fruit and vegetable market (*see* New Covent Garden market); it has been trading in its current form since 1980

Grays, Davies Street, W1K (antiques), indoor market in listed building, established 1977

Greenwich, SE10 (crafts, fashion, food), market revived in the 1980s

Leadenhall, Gracechurch Street, EC3V (meat, poultry, cheese, clothing), site of market since 14th century; present hall built 1881; owned and run by the City of London Corporation

New Covent Garden, SW8 (wholesale vegetables, fruit, flowers), established in 1670 under a charter of Charles II; relocated from central London in 1974

New Spitalfields, E10 (vegetables, fruit), established 1682, modernised 1928, moved out of the City to Leyton in 1991, open Monday to Saturday

Old Spitalfields, E1 (arts, crafts, books, clothes, organic food, antiques), continues to trade on the original Spitalfields site on Commercial Street

Petticoat Lane, Middlesex Street, E1, a market has existed on the site for over 500 years, now a Sunday morning market selling almost anything

Portobello Road, W11, originally for herbs and horse-trading from 1870; became famous for antiques after the closure of the Caledonian Market in 1948

Smithfield, EC1 (meat, poultry), built 1866–8, refurbished 1993–4; the site of St Bartholomew's Fair from 12th to 19th century; owned and run by the City of London Corporation, open Monday to Friday

MONUMENTS

CENOTAPH

Whitehall, SW1. The Cenotaph (from the Greek meaning 'empty tomb') was built to commemorate 'The Glorious Dead' and is a memorial to all ranks of the sea, land and air forces who gave their lives in the service of the Empire during the First World War. Designed by Sir Edwin Lutyens and constructed in plaster as a temporary memorial in 1919, it was replaced by a permanent structure of Portland stone and unveiled by George V on 11 November 1920, Armistice Day. An additional inscription was made in 1946 to commemorate those who gave their lives in the Second World War

FOURTH PLINTH

Trafalgar Square, WC2. The fourth plinth (1841) was designed for an equestrian statue that was never built due to lack of funds. From 1999 temporary works have been displayed on the plinth including *Ecce Homo* (Mark Wallinger), *Monument* (Rachel Whiteread), *Alison Lapper Pregnant* (Marc Quinn) and *One & Other* (Antony Gormley). Since March 2018 *The Invisible Enemy Should Not Exist* (Michael Rakowitz) a recreation of the Lamassu, a winged bull and protective deity that stood at the entrance to the Nergal Gate of Nineveh from c.700 BC until it was destroyed by Islamic State in 2015, has occupied the plinth. The Lamassu is made from 10,500 empty Iraqi date syrup cans, representing a once-renowned industry now decimated by war. In 2020 it will be replaced by *The End* (Heather Phillipson); a sculpture portraying a giant dollop of cream upon which sits a fly, a cherry and a drone that will film Trafalgar Square from above

LONDON MONUMENT

(Commonly called the Monument), Monument Street, EC3. Built to designs by Sir Christopher Wren and Robert Hooke between 1671 and 1677, the Monument commemorates the Great Fire of London, which broke out in Pudding Lane on 2 September 1666. The fluted Doric column is 36.6m

(120ft) high, the moulded cylinder above the balcony supporting a flaming vase of gilt bronze is an additional 12.8m (42ft), and the column is based on a square plinth 12.2m (40ft) high (with fine carvings on the west face), making a total height of 61.6m (202ft) – the tallest isolated stone column in the world, with views of London from a gallery at the top (311 steps)

OTHER MONUMENTS

(sculptor's name in parentheses):

7 July Memorial (Carmody Groarke), Hyde Park
Afghanistan and Iraq War Memorial (Day), Victoria Embankment
African and Caribbean War Memorial, Windrush Square, Brixton
Viscount Alanbrooke (Roberts-Jones), Whitehall
Albert Memorial (Scott), Kensington Gore
Battle of Britain (Day), Victoria Embankment
Beatty (Wheeler), Trafalgar Square
Belgian Gratitude (setting by Blomfield, statue by Rousseau), Victoria Embankment
Boadicea (or Boudicca), *Queen of the Iceni* (Thornycroft), Westminster Bridge
Brunel (Marochetti), Victoria Embankment
Burghers of Calais (Rodin), Victoria Tower Gardens, Westminster
Burns (Steell), Embankment Gardens
Canada Memorial (Granche), Green Park
Carlyle (Boehm), Chelsea Embankment
Cavalry (Jones), Hyde Park
Edith Cavell (Frampton), St Martin's Place
Charles I (Le Sueur), Trafalgar Square
Charles II (Gibbons), Royal Hospital, Chelsea
Churchill (Roberts-Jones), Parliament Square
Cleopatra's Needle (20.9m/68.5ft high, c.1500 BC, erected in London in 1878; the sphinxes are Victorian), Thames Embankment
Clive (Tweed), King Charles Street
Captain Cook (Brock), The Mall
Oliver Cromwell (Thornycroft), outside Westminster Hall
Cunningham (Belsky), Trafalgar Square
Gen. Charles de Gaulle (Conner), Carlton Gardens
Diana, Princess of Wales Memorial Fountain (Gustafson Porter), Hyde Park
Disraeli, Earl of Beaconsfield (Raggi), Parliament Square
Duke of Cambridge (Jones), Whitehall
Duke of York (37.8m/124ft column, with statue by Westmacott), Carlton House Terrace
Edward VII (Mackennal), Waterloo Place
Elizabeth I (Kerwin, 1586, oldest outdoor statue in London; from Ludgate), Fleet Street
Eros (Shaftesbury Memorial) (Gilbert), Piccadilly Circus
Lord Dowding (Winter), Strand
Millicent Fawcett (Wearing), Parliament Square
Marechal/Marshall Foch (Mallisard, copy of one in Cassel, France), Grosvenor Gardens
Charles James Fox (Westmacott), Bloomsbury Square
Yuri Gagarin (Novikov, copy of Russian statue), The Mall
Mahatma Gandhi (Jackson), Parliament Square
George III (Cotes Wyatt), Cockspur Street
George IV (Chantrey), Trafalgar Square
George V (Reid Dick and Scott), Old Palace Yard
George VI (McMillan), Carlton Gardens
Gladstone (Thornycroft), Strand
Guards' (Crimea; Bell), Waterloo Place
Guards Division (Ledward, figures, Bradshaw, cenotaph), Horse Guards' Parade
Haig (Hardiman), Whitehall
Sir Arthur (Bomber) Harris (Winter), Strand
Gen. Henry Havelock (Behnes), Trafalgar Square
International Brigades Memorial (Spanish Civil War) (Ian Walters), Jubilee Gardens, South Bank

Irving (Brock), north side of National Portrait Gallery
Isis (Gudgeon), Hyde Park
James II (Gibbons), Trafalgar Square
Jellicoe (McMillan), Trafalgar Square
Samuel Johnson (Fitzgerald), opposite St Clement Danes
Kitchener (Tweed), Horse Guards Parade
Abraham Lincoln (Saint-Gaudens, copy of one in Chicago), Parliament Square
Mandela (Walters), Parliament Square
Milton (Montford), St Giles, Cripplegate
Mountbatten (Belsky), Foreign Office Green
Gen. Charles James Napier (Adams), Trafalgar Square
Nelson (Railton), Trafalgar Square, with Landseer's lions (cast from guns recovered from the wreck of the *Royal George)*
Florence Nightingale (Walker), Waterloo Place
Palmerston (Woolner), Parliament Square
Sir Keith Park (Johnson), Waterloo Place
Peel (Noble), Parliament Square
Pitt (Chantrey), Hanover Square
Portal (Nemon), Embankment Gardens
Prince Albert (Bacon), Holborn Circus
Queen Elizabeth Gate (Lund and Wynne), Hyde Park Corner
Queen Mother (Jackson), Carlton Gardens
Raleigh (McMillan), Greenwich
Richard I (Coeur de Lion) (Marochetti), Old Palace Yard
Roberts (Bates), Horse Guards' Parade
Franklin D. Roosevelt (Reid Dick), Grosvenor Square
Royal Air Force (Blomfield), Victoria Embankment
Royal Air Force Bomber Command Memorial (O'Connor), Green Park
Royal Artillery (Great War) (Jagger and Pearson), Hyde Park Corner
Royal Artillery (South Africa) (Colton), The Mall
Captain Scott (Lady Scott), Waterloo Place
Shackleton (Jagger), Kensington Gore
Shakespeare (Fontana, copy of one by Scheemakers in Westminster Abbey), Leicester Square
Smuts (Epstein), Parliament Square
Sullivan (Goscombe John), Victoria Embankment
Trenchard (McMillan), Victoria Embankment
Victoria Memorial (Webb and Brock), in front of Buckingham Palace
Raoul Wallenberg (Jackson), Great Cumberland Place
George Washington (Houdon copy), Trafalgar Square
Wellington (Boehm), Hyde Park Corner
Wellington (Chantrey), outside Royal Exchange
John Wesley (Adams Acton), City Road
Westminster School (Crimea) (Scott), Broad Sanctuary
William III (Bacon), St James's Square
Wolseley (Goscombe John), Horse Guards' Parade

PARKS, GARDENS AND OPEN SPACES

CITY OF LONDON CORPORATION OPEN SPACES

W www.cityoflondon.gov.uk

Ashtead Common (202ha/500 acres), Surrey
Burnham Beeches and *Fleet Wood* (220ha/540 acres), Bucks. Acquired by the City of London for the benefit of the public in 1880, Fleet Wood (26ha/65 acres) being presented in 1921
Coulsdon Common (51ha/127 acres), Surrey
Epping Forest (2,476ha/6,118 acres), Essex. Acquired by the City of London in 1878 and opened to the public in 1882. The Queen Elizabeth Hunting Lodge, built for Henry VIII in 1543, lies at the edge of the forest. The present forest is 19.3km (12 miles) long by around 3km (2 miles) wide, approximately one-tenth of its original area
*Epping Forest Buffer Land (735ha/1,816 acres), Waltham Abbey/Epping

Farthing Downs and New Hill (95ha/235 acres), Surrey
Hampstead Heath (275ha/680 acres), NW3. Including Golders Hill (15ha/36 acres) and Parliament Hill (110ha/271 acres)
Highgate Wood (28ha/70 acres), N6/N10
Kenley Common (56ha/139 acres), Surrey
Queen's Park (12ha/30 acres), NW6
Riddlesdown (43ha/104 acres), Surrey
Spring Park (20ha/50 acres), Kent
Stoke Common (80ha/198 acres), Bucks. Ownership was transferred to the City of London in 2007
West Ham Park (31ha/77 acres), E15
West Wickham Common (10ha/26 acres), Kent
Also over 150 smaller open spaces within the City of London, including *Finsbury Circus* and *St Dunstan-in-the-East*
* Includes Copped Hall Park, Woodredon Estate and Warlies Park

OTHER PARKS AND GARDENS
CHELSEA PHYSIC GARDEN, 66 Royal Hospital Road SW3 4HS T 020-7352 5646 W www.chelseaphysicgarden.co.uk
A garden of general botanical research and education, maintaining a wide range of rare and unusual plants; established in 1673 by the Society of Apothecaries
HAMPTON COURT PARK AND GARDENS (328ha/810 acres), Surrey KT8 9AU T 0844-482 7777 W www.hrp.org.uk
Also known as Home Park, the park lies beyond the palace's formal gardens. It contains a herd of deer and a 750-year-old oak tree from the original park
HOLLAND PARK (22.5ha/54 acres), Ilchester Place W8 T 020-7361 3000 W www.rbkc.gov.uk
The largest park in the Royal Borough of Kensington and Chelsea, includes the Kyoto Garden
KEW, ROYAL BOTANIC GARDENS (120ha/300 acres), Richmond, Surrey TW9 3AB T 020-8332 5655 W www.kew.org
Founded in 1759 and declared a UNESCO World Heritage Site in 2003
THAMES BARRIER PARK (9ha/22acres), North Woolwich Road E16 2HP T 020-7476 3741 Opened in 2000, landscaped gardens with spectacular views of the Thames Barrier

ROYAL PARKS
W www.royalparks.org.uk
Bushy Park (450ha/1,099 acres), Middx. Adjoins Hampton Court; contains an avenue of horse-chestnuts enclosed in a fourfold avenue of limes planted by William III
Green Park (19ha/47 acres), W1. Between Piccadilly and St James's Park, with Constitution Hill leading to Hyde Park Corner
Greenwich Park (74ha/183 acres), SE10. Enclosed by Humphrey, Duke of Gloucester, and laid out by Charles II from the designs of Le Nôtre. On a hill in Greenwich Park is the Royal Observatory (founded 1675). Its buildings are now managed by the National Maritime Museum (T 020-8858 4422 W www.rmg.co.uk
) and the earliest building is named Flamsteed House, after John Flamsteed (1646–1719), the first astronomer royal
Hyde Park (142ha/350 acres), W1/W2. From Park Lane to Kensington Gardens and incorporating the Serpentine lake, Apsley House, the Achilles Statue, Rotten Row and the Ladies' Mile; fine gateway at Hyde Park Corner. To the north-east is Marble Arch, originally erected by George IV at the entrance to Buckingham Palace and re-erected in the present position in 1851. At Hyde Park Corner stands Wellington Arch, built in 1825–7, it opened to the public in 2012 following major renovation
Kensington Gardens (107ha/265 acres), W2/W8. From the western boundary of Hyde Park to Kensington Palace; contains the Albert Memorial, Serpentine Gallery, Diana, Princess of Wales' Memorial Playground and the Peter Pan statue

The Regent's Park and *Primrose Hill* (197ha/487 acres), NW1. From Marylebone Road to Primrose Hill surrounded by the Outer Circle; divided by the Broad Walk leading to the Zoological Gardens
Richmond Park (1,000ha/2,500 acres), Surrey. Designated a National Nature Reserve, a Site of Special Scientific Interest and a Special Area of Conservation
St James's Park (23ha/57 acres), SW1. From Whitehall to Buckingham Palace; ornamental lake of 4.9ha (12 acres); the Mall leads from Admiralty Arch to Buckingham Palace

PLACES OF HISTORICAL AND CULTURAL INTEREST
1 Canada Square
Canary Wharf E14 5AB T 020-7418 2000
W www.canarywharf.com
Also known as 'Canary Wharf', the steel and glass skyscraper is designed to sway 35cm in the strongest winds
20 Fenchurch Street
W https://skygarden.london
Designed by architect Rafael Viñoly the skyscraper was completed in March 2014. The top three storeys are home to the Sky Garden, London's highest public garden with viewing platforms, bars, restaurants and an open air terrace. Access to the Sky Garden is free, but tickets must be booked in advance
30 St Mary Axe
EC3A 8BF W www.30stmaryaxe.com
Completed in 2004 and commonly known as the 'Gherkin', each of the floors rotates five degrees from the one below
122 Leadenhall Street
EC3V 4AB T 020-7220 8950 W www.theleadenhallbuilding.com
The distinctive 225m (737ft) asymmetrical Leadenhall Building, designed by architects Rogers Stirk Harbour & Partners, was completed in 2014
Alexandra Palace
Alexandra Palace Way N22 7AY T 020-8365 2121
W www.alexandrapalace.com
The Victorian palace was severely damaged by fire in 1980 but was restored, and reopened in 1988. Alexandra Palace now provides modern facilities for exhibitions, conferences, banquets and leisure activities. There is a winter ice rink, a boating lake and a conservation area. Restoration of the east wing and Victorian theatre was completed in 2018
Barbican Centre
Silk Street EC2Y 8DS T 020-7638 4141 W www.barbican.org.uk
Owned, funded and managed by the City of London Corporation, the Barbican Centre opened in 1982 and houses the Barbican Theatre, a studio theatre called The Pit and the Barbican Hall; it is also home to the London Symphony Orchestra. There are three cinemas, six conference rooms, two art galleries, a sculpture court, a lending library, trade and banqueting facilities and a conservatory
British Library
St Pancras, 96 Euston Road NW1 2DB T 0330-333 1144
W www.bl.uk
The largest building constructed in the UK in the 20th century with basements extending 24.5m underground. Holdings include the *Magna Carta,* the Gutenburg Bible, Shakespeare's First Folio, Beatles manuscripts and the first edition of *The Times* from 1788. Holds temporary exhibitions on a range of topics

Central Criminal Court
Old Bailey EC4M 7EH **T** 020-7192 2739
W www.cityoflondon.gov.uk
The highest criminal court in the UK, the 'Old Bailey' is located on the site of the old Newgate Prison. Trials held here have included those of Oscar Wilde, Dr Crippen and the Yorkshire Ripper. The courthouse has been rebuilt several times since 1674; Edward VII officially opened the current neo-baroque building in 1907

Charterhouse
Charterhouse Square EC1M 6AN **T** 020-7253 9503
W www.thecharterhouse.org
A Carthusian monastery from 1371 to 1538, purchased in 1611 by Thomas Sutton, who endowed it as a residence for aged men 'of gentle birth' and a school for poor scholars (removed to Godalming in 1872)

Downing Street
SW1A 2AA **W** www.number10.gov.uk
Number 10 Downing Street is the official town residence of the prime minister and number 11 of the Chancellor of the Exchequer. The street was named after Sir George Downing, Bt., soldier and diplomat, who was MP for Morpeth 1660–84

George Inn
The George Inn Yard SE1 1NH **T** 020-7407 2056
W www.nationaltrust.org.uk/george-inn
The last galleried inn in London, built in 1677. Now owned by the National Trust and run as an ordinary public house

Horse Guards
Whitehall SW1
Archway and offices built about 1753. The changing of the guard takes place daily at 11am (10am on Sundays) and the inspection is at 4pm. Only those with the Queen's permission may drive through the gates and archway into *Horse Guards Parade*, where the colour is 'trooped' on the Queen's official birthday

HOUSES OF PARLIAMENT
T 020-7219 3000 **W** www.parliament.uk
House of Commons, Westminster SW1A 0AA
House of Lords, Westminster SW1A 0PW
The royal palace of Westminster, originally built by Edward the Confessor, was the normal meeting place of Parliament from about 1340. St Stephen's Chapel was used from about 1550 for the meetings of the House of Commons, which had previously been held in the Chapter House or Refectory of Westminster Abbey. The House of Lords met in an apartment of the royal palace. The fire of 1834 destroyed much of the palace, and the present Houses of Parliament were erected on the site from the designs of Sir Charles Barry and Augustus Welby Pugin between 1840 and 1867. The chamber of the House of Commons was destroyed by bombing in 1941, and a new chamber designed by Sir Giles Gilbert Scott was used for the first time in 1950. *Westminster Hall and the Crypt Chapel* was the only part of the old palace of Westminster to survive the fire of 1834. It was built by William II from 1097 to 1099 and altered by Richard II between 1394 and 1399. The hammerbeam roof of carved oak dates from 1396–8. The Hall was the scene of the trial of Charles I. *The Victoria Tower* of the House of Lords is 98.5m (323ft) high and *The Elizabeth Tower* of the House of Commons is 96.3m (316ft) high and contains 'Big Ben', the hour bell said to be named after Sir Benjamin Hall, First Commissioner of Works when the original bell was cast in 1856. This bell, which weighed 16 tons 11 cwt, was found to be cracked in 1857. The present bell (13.5 tons) is a recasting of the original and was first brought into use in 1859. The dials of the clock are 7m (23ft) in diameter, the hands being 2.7m (9ft) and 4.3m (14ft) long (including balance piece).
During session, tours of the Houses of Parliament are only available to UK residents who have made advance arrangements through an MP or peer. Overseas visitors are no longer provided with permits to tour the Houses of Parliament during session, although they can tour on Saturdays and during the summer opening and attend debates for both houses in the Strangers' Galleries. During the summer recess, tickets for tours of the Houses of Parliament can be booked online, by telephone (**T** 020-7219 4114) or bought on site at the ticket office located at the front of Portcullis House SW1A 2LW. The Strangers' Gallery of the House of Commons is open to the public when the house is sitting. To acquire tickets in advance, UK residents should write to their local MP and overseas visitors should apply to their embassy or high commission in the UK for a permit. If none of these arrangements has been made, visitors should join the public queue outside St Stephen's Entrance, where there is also a queue for entry to the House of Lords Gallery

INNS OF COURT
The Inns of Court are ancient unincorporated bodies of lawyers which for more than five centuries have had the power to call to the Bar those of their members who have qualified for the rank or degree of Barrister-at-Law. There are four Inns of Court as well as many lesser inns:
Lincoln's Inn, WC2A 3TL **T** 020-7405 1393
W www.lincolnsinn.org.uk
The most ancient of the inns with records dating back to 1422. The hall and library buildings are from 1845, although the library is first mentioned in 1474; the old hall (late 15th century) and the chapel were rebuilt c.1619–23
Inner Temple, King's Bench Walk EC4Y 7HL **T** 020-7797 8250
W www.innertemple.org.uk
Middle Temple, Middle Temple Lane EC4Y 9BT
T 020-7427 4800 **W** www.middletemple.org.uk
Records for the Inner and Middle Temple date back to the beginning of the 16th century. The site was originally occupied by the Order of Knights Templar c.1160–1312. The two inns have separate halls thought to have been formed c.1350. The division between the two societies was formalised in 1732 with Temple Church and the Masters House remaining in common. The Inner Temple Garden is normally open to the public on weekdays between 12.30pm and 3pm
Temple Church, EC4Y 7BB **T** 020-7353 8559
W www.templechurch.com
The nave forms one of five remaining round churches in England
Gray's Inn, South Square WC1R 5ET **T** 020-7458 7800
W www.graysinn.info
Founded early 14th century; hall 1556–8
No other 'Inns' are active, but there are remains of *Staple Inn*, a gabled front on Holborn (opposite Gray's Inn Road). *Clement's Inn* (near St Clement Danes Church), *Clifford's Inn*, Fleet Street, and *Thavies Inn*, Holborn Circus, are all rebuilt. *Serjeants' Inn*, Fleet Street, and another (demolished 1910) of the same name in Chancery Lane, were composed of Serjeants-at-Law, the last of whom died in 1922

Institute of Contemporary Arts
The Mall SW1Y 5AH **T** 020-7930 3647 **W** www.ica.art
Exhibitions of modern art in the fields of film, theatre, new media and the visual arts

Lloyd's
Lime Street EC3M 7HA **T** 020-7327 1000 **W** www.lloyds.com
International insurance market which evolved during the 17th century from Lloyd's Coffee House. The present

building was opened for business in May 1986, and houses the Lutine Bell. Underwriting is on three floors with a total area of 10,591 sq. m (114,000 sq. ft). The Lloyd's building is not open to the general public

London Central Mosque and the Islamic Cultural Centre
Park Road NW8 7RG T 020-7724 3363 W www.iccuk.org
The focus for London's Muslims; established in 1944 but not completed until 1977, the mosque can accommodate about 5,000 worshippers; guided tours are available

London Eye
South Bank SE1 7PB W www.londoneye.com
Opened in March 2000 as London's millennium landmark, this 137m (450ft) observation wheel is the tallest cantilevered observation wheel in the world. The wheel provides a 30-minute ride offering panoramic views of the capital

London Zoo
Regent's Park NW1 4RY T 0344-225 1826 W www.zsl.org
Opened in 1828 by the Zoological Society of London (ZSL) to house an array of exotic and endangered animals with an emphasis on scientific research and conservation

Madame Tussauds
Marylebone Road NW1 5LR T 0871-894 3000
W www.madametussauds.com
Waxwork exhibition

Mansion House
Cannon Street EC4N 8BH T 020-7626 2500
W www.cityoflondon.gov.uk
The official residence of the Lord Mayor. Built in the 18th century in the Palladian style. Open to groups by appointment only

Marlborough House
Pall Mall SW1Y 5HX T 020-7747 6500
W www.thecommonwealth.org
Built by Wren for the first Duke of Marlborough and completed in 1711, the house reverted to the Crown in 1835. In 1863 it became the London house of the Prince of Wales and was the London home of Queen Mary until her death in 1953. In 1959 Marlborough House was given by the Queen as the headquarters for the Commonwealth Secretariat and it was opened as such in 1965. The Queen's Chapel, Marlborough Gate, was begun in 1623 from the designs of Inigo Jones for the Infanta Maria of Spain, and completed for Queen Henrietta Maria. Marlborough House is not open to the public

Neasden Temple
BAPS Shri Swaminarayan Mandir, Brentfield Road, Neasden NW10 8LD T 020-8965 2651 W http://londonmandir.baps.org
When built, it was the first and largest traditional Hindu Mandir outside of India; opened in 1995

Port of London
Port of London Authority, Royal Pier Road, Kent DA12 2BG T 01474-562200 W www.pla.co.uk
The Port of London covers the tidal section of the river Thames from Teddington to the seaward limit (the outer Tongue buoy and the Sunk light vessel), a distance of 153km (95 miles). The governing body is the Port of London Authority (PLA). Cargo is handled at privately operated riverside terminals between Fulham and Canvey Island, including the enclosed dock at Tilbury, 40km (25 miles) below London Bridge. Passenger vessels and cruise liners can be handled at moorings at Greenwich, Tower Bridge and Tilbury

Queen Elizabeth Olympic Park
Stratford E20 T 0203-288 1800
W www.queenelizabetholympicpark.co.uk
Built for the London 2012 Olympic and Paralympic Games, the park, which included the Olympic Stadium, Velodrome and Aquatics Centre has been redeveloped to provide 227ha (560 acres) of parkland with play areas, outside arts and theatre spaces, waterways and wetlands. The north of the park, which includes the Copper Box Arena sport venue, re-opened to the public in 2013. The south of the park, which re-opened in April 2014, incorporates three venues for arts and sports events and the *ArcelorMittal Orbit*, designed by Sir Anish Kapoor and Cecil Balmond; it is the UK's tallest sculpture (114.5m/376ft) and has two accessible observation floors

Roman Remains
The city wall of Roman *Londinium* was largely rebuilt during the medieval period but sections may be seen near the White Tower in the Tower of London; at Tower Hill; at Coopers' Row; at All Hallows, London Wall, its vestry being built on the remains of a semi-circular Roman bastion; at St Alphage, London Wall, showing a succession of building repairs from the Roman until the late medieval period; and at St Giles, Cripplegate. Sections of the great forum and basilica, more than 165 sq. m (1,776 sq. ft), have been encountered during excavations in the area of Leadenhall, Gracechurch Street and Lombard Street. Traces of Roman activity along the river include a massive riverside wall built in the late Roman period, and a succession of Roman timber quays along Lower and Upper Thames Street. Finds from these sites can be seen at the Museum of London.
Other major buildings are the amphitheatre at Guildhall, remains of bath-buildings in Upper and Lower Thames Street, and the temple of Mithras in Walbrook

Royal Albert Hall
Kensington Gore SW7 2AP T 020-7589 3203
W www.royalalberthall.com
The elliptical hall, one of the largest in the world, was completed in 1871; since 1941 it has been the venue each summer for the Promenade Concerts founded in 1895 by Sir Henry Wood. Other events include pop and classical music concerts, dance, opera, sporting events, conferences and banquets

Royal Courts of Justice
Strand WC2A 2LL T 020-7947 6000 W www.justice.gov.uk
Victorian Gothic building that is home to the high court. Visitors are free to watch proceedings

Royal Hospital, Chelsea
Royal Hospital Road SW3 4SR T 020-7881 5200
W www.chelsea-pensioners.co.uk
Founded by Charles II in 1682, and built by Wren; opened in 1692 for old and disabled soldiers. The extensive grounds include the former Ranelagh Gardens and are the venue for the Chelsea Flower Show each May

Royal Naval College
Greenwich SE10 9NN T 020-8269 4747 W www.ornc.org
The building was the Greenwich Hospital until 1869. It was built by Charles II, largely from designs by John Webb, and by Queen Mary II and William III, from designs by Wren. It stands on the site of an ancient abbey, a royal house and Greenwich Palace, which was constructed by Henry VII. Henry VIII, Mary I and Elizabeth I were born in the royal palace and Edward VI died there. The Painted Hall, designed by Wren, reopened in March 2019 after a major two-year conservation project to restore its vividly painted interior by Sir James Thornhill

Royal Opera House
Covent Garden WC2E 9DD T 020-7240 1200 W www.roh.org.uk
Home of The Royal Ballet (1931) and The Royal Opera (1946). The Royal Opera House is the third theatre to be built on the site, opening 1858; the first was opened in 1732

St James's Palace

Pall Mall SW1A 1BQ **W** www.royal.uk

Built by Henry VIII, only the Gatehouse and Presence Chamber remain; later alterations were made by Wren and Kent. Representatives of foreign powers are still accredited 'to the Court of St James's'. *Clarence House* (1825), the official London residence of the Prince of Wales, stands within the St James's Palace estate

St Paul's Cathedral

St Paul's Churchyard EC4M 8AD **T** 020-7246 8350
W www.stpauls.co.uk

Built 1675–1710. The cross on the dome is 111m (365ft) above ground level, the inner cupola 66.4m (218ft) above the floor. 'Great Paul' in the south-west tower weighs nearly 17 tons. The organ by Father Smith (enlarged by Willis and rebuilt by Mander) is in a case carved by Grinling Gibbons, who also carved the choir stalls

Shakespeare's Globe

New Globe Walk SE1 9DT **T** 020-7902 1500
W www.shakespearesglobe.com

Reconstructed in 1997, the open-air playhouse is a unique resource for the works of William Shakespeare through performance and education; a new indoor replica Jacobean theatre staged its first public performance in January 2014

Shard

London Bridge SE1 **T** 0344 449-7222 **W** www.the-shard.com

Completed in May 2012, the skyscraper stands at 310m (1,016ft) and possesses a unique facade of 11,000 glass panels and a 360-degree viewing gallery

Somerset House

Strand WC2R 1LA **T** 020-7845 4600
W www.somersethouse.org.uk

The river facade (183m/600ft long) was built in 1776–1801 from the designs of Sir William Chambers; the eastern extension, which houses part of King's College, was built by Smirke in 1829–35. Somerset House was the property of Lord Protector Somerset, at whose attainder in 1552 the palace passed to the Crown, and it was a royal residence until 1692. Somerset House has recently undergone extensive renovation and is home to the Embankment Galleries and the Courtauld Gallery. Open-air concerts and ice-skating (Nov–Jan) are held in the courtyard

SOUTH BANK, SE1

Arts complex on the south bank of the river Thames which consists of:

BFI Southbank T 020-7928 3232 **W** www.bfi.org.uk

Opened in 1952 and administered by the British Film Institute, has four auditoria of varying capacities. Venue for the annual London Film Festival

The *Royal Festival Hall* **T** 020-7960 4200
W www.southbankcentre.co.uk

Opened in 1951 for the Festival of Britain, adjacent are the *Queen Elizabeth Hall,* the *Purcell Room* and the *Hayward Gallery*

The *Royal National Theatre,* **T** 020-7452 3000
W www.nationaltheatre.org.uk

Opened in 1976; comprises the Olivier, the Lyttelton and Dorfman theatres. The Cottesloe Theatre closed in February 2013 and, following refurbishment reopened in 2014 as the Dorfman Theatre

Southwark Cathedral

London Bridge SE1 9DA **T** 020-7367 6700
W www.cathedral.southwark.anglican.org

Mainly 13th century, but the nave is largely rebuilt. The tomb of John Gower (1330–1408) is between the Bunyan and Chaucer memorial windows in the north aisle; Shakespeare's effigy, backed by a view of Southwark and the Globe Theatre, is in the south aisle; the tomb of Bishop Andrewes (*d.* 1626) is near the screen. The Lady Chapel was the scene of the consistory courts of the reign of Mary (Gardiner and Bonner) and is still used as a consistory court. John Harvard, after whom Harvard University is named, was baptised here in 1607, and the chapel by the north choir aisle is his memorial chapel

Thames Embankments

Sir Joseph Bazalgette (1819–91) constructed the *Victoria Embankment,* on the north side from Westminster to Blackfriars for the Metropolitan Board of Works, 1864–70 (the seats, of which the supports of some are a kneeling camel, laden with spicery, and of others a winged sphinx, were presented by the Grocers' Company and by W. H. Smith, MP, in 1874); the *Albert Embankment,* on the south side from Westminster Bridge to Vauxhall, 1866–9, and the Chelsea Embankment, 1871–4. The total cost exceeded £2m. Bazalgette also inaugurated the London main drainage system, 1858–65. A medallion *(Flumini vincula posuit)* has been placed on a pier of the *Victoria Embankment* to commemorate the engineer

Thames Flood Barrier

W www.environment-agency.gov.uk

Officially opened in May 1984, though first used in February 1983, the barrier consists of ten rising sector gates which span approximately 520m from bank to bank of the Thames at Woolwich Reach. When not in use the gates lie horizontally, allowing shipping to navigate the river normally; when the barrier is closed, the gates turn through 90 degrees to stand vertically more than 50 feet above the river bed. The barrier took eight years to complete and can be raised within about 90 minutes

Trafalgar Tavern

Park Row, Greenwich SE10 9NW **T** 020-3887 9886
W www.trafalgartavern.co.uk

Regency-period riverside public house built in 1837. Charles Dickens and William Gladstone were patrons

Wembley Stadium

Wembley HA9 0WS **W** www.wembleystadium.com

The second largest stadium in Europe; hosts major sporting events and music concerts

Westminster Abbey

SW1P 3PA **T** 020-7222 5152 **W** www.westminster-abbey.org

Founded as a Benedictine monastery over 1,000 years ago, the church was rebuilt by Edward the Confessor in 1065 and again by Henry III in the 13th century. The abbey is the resting place for monarchs including Edward I, Henry III, Henry V, Henry VII, Elizabeth I, Mary I and Mary, Queen of Scots, and has been the setting of coronations since that of William the Conqueror in 1066. In Poets' Corner there are memorials to many literary figures, and many scientists and musicians are also remembered here. The grave of the Unknown Warrior is to be found in the nave

Westminster Cathedral

Francis Street SW1P 1QW **T** 020-7798 9055
W www.westminstercathedral.org.uk

Roman Catholic cathedral built 1895–1903 from the designs of John Francis Bentley. The campanile is 83m (273ft) high

Wimbledon All England Lawn Tennis Club

Church Road SW19 5AE **T** 020-8944 1066
W www.wimbledon.com

Venue for the Wimbledon Championships. Includes the Wimbledon Lawn Tennis Museum

HALLMARKS

Hallmarks are the symbols stamped on gold, silver, palladium or platinum articles to indicate that they have been tested at an official Assay Office and that they conform to one of the legal standards. The marking of gold and silver articles to identify the maker was instituted in England in 1363 under a statute of Edward III. In 1478 the Assay Office in Goldsmiths' Hall was established and all gold and silversmiths were required to bring their wares to be date-marked by the Hall, hence the term 'hallmarked'.

With certain exceptions, all gold, silver, palladium or platinum articles are required by law to be hallmarked before they are offered for sale. Current hallmarking requirements come under the UK Hallmarking Act 1973 and subsequent amendments. The act is built around the principle of description, where it is an offence for any person to apply to an unhallmarked article a description indicating that it is wholly or partly made of gold, silver, palladium or platinum. There is an exemption by weight: compulsory hallmarks are not needed on gold and palladium under 1g, silver under 7.78g and platinum under 0.5g. Also, some descriptions, such as rolled gold and gold plate, are permissible. The British Hallmarking Council is a statutory body created as a result of the Hallmarking Act. It ensures adequate provision for assaying and hallmarking, supervises the assay offices and ensures the enforcement of hallmarking legislation. The four assay offices at London, Birmingham, Sheffield and Edinburgh operate under the act.

BRITISH HALLMARKING COUNCIL Secretariat, c/o Shakespeare Martineau, 60 Gracechurch Street, London EC3V OHR W www.gov.uk/government/organisations/british-hallmarking-council

COMPULSORY MARKS

Since January 1999 UK hallmarks have consisted of three compulsory symbols – the sponsor's mark, the millesimal fineness (purity) mark and the assay office mark. The distinction between UK and foreign articles has been removed, and more finenesses are now legal, reflecting the more common finenesses elsewhere in Europe.

SPONSOR'S MARK

Formerly known as the maker's mark, the sponsor's mark was instituted in England in 1363. Originally a device such as a bird or fleur-de-lis, now it consists of a combination of at least two initials (usually a shortened form of the manufacturer's name) and a shield design. The London Assay Office offers 45 standard shield designs but other designs are possible by arrangement.

MILLESIMAL FINENESS MARK

The millesimal fineness (purity) mark indicates the number of parts per thousand of pure metal in the alloy. The current finenesses allowed in the UK are:

Gold	999; 990; 916 (22 carat); 750 (18 carat); 585 (14 carat); 375 (9 carat)
Silver	999; 958 (Britannia); 925 (sterling); 800
Palladium	999; 950; 500
Platinum	999; 950; 900; 850

ASSAY OFFICE MARK

This mark identifies the particular assay office at which the article was tested and marked. The British assay offices are:

 LONDON, Goldsmiths' Hall, Gutter Lane, London EC2V 8AQ T 020-7606 8971 W www.assayofficelondon.co.uk

 BIRMINGHAM, 1 Moreton Street, Birmingham B1 3AX T 0121-236 6951 W www.theassayoffice.co.uk

 SHEFFIELD, Guardians' Hall, Beulah Road, Hillsborough, Sheffield S6 2AN T 0114-231 2121 W www.assayoffice.co.uk

 EDINBURGH, Goldsmiths' Hall, 24 Broughton Street, Edinburgh EH1 3RH T 0131-556 1144 W www.edinburghassayoffice.co.uk

Assay offices formerly existed in other towns, eg Chester, Exeter, Glasgow, Newcastle, Norwich and York, each having its own distinguishing mark.

OPTIONAL MARKS

Since 1999 traditional pictorial marks such as a crown for gold, the Britannia for 958 silver, the lion passant for 925 Sterling silver (lion rampant in Scotland) and the orb for 950 platinum may be added voluntarily to the millesimal mark. In 2010 a pictorial mark of the Greek goddess Pallas Athene was introduced for 950 palladium.

 Gold – a crown

 Sterling silver (Scotland)

 Britannia silver

 Platinum – an orb

 Sterling silver (England)

 Palladium – the Greek goddess Pallas Athene

DATE LETTER

The date letter shows the year in which an article was assayed and hallmarked. Each alphabetical cycle has a distinctive style of lettering or shape of shield. The date letters were different at the various assay offices and the particular office must be established from the assay office mark before reference is made to tables of date letters. Date letter marks became voluntary from 1 January 1999.

The table which follows shows one specimen shield and letter used by the London Assay Office on silver articles for each alphabetical cycle from 1498. The same letters are found on gold articles but the surrounding shield may differ. Until 1 January 1975, each hallmark covered two calendar years as the letter changed annually in May on St Dunstan's Day (the patron saint of silversmiths). Since 1 January 1975, each date letter has indicated a calendar year from January to December and each office has used the same style of date letter and shield for all articles.

LONDON (GOLDSMITHS' HALL) DATE LETTERS

	from	to		from	to
	1498–9	1517–18		1756–7	1775–6
	1518–19	1537–8		1776–7	1795–6
	1538–9	1557–8		1796–7	1815–16
	1558–9	1577–8		1816–17	1835–6
	1578–9	1597–8		1836–7	1855–6
	1598–9	1617–18		1856–7	1875–6
	1618–19	1637–8		1876–7 (A to M square shield, N to Z as shown)	1895–6
	1638–9	1657–8		1896–7	1915–16
	1658–9	1677–8		1916–17	1935–6
	1678–9	1696–7		1936–7	1955–6
	1697 (from March, 1697 only)	1715–16		1956–7	1974
	1716–17	1735–6		1975	1999
	1736–7	1738–9		2000	
	1739–40	1755–6			

OTHER MARKS

FOREIGN GOODS

Foreign goods imported into the UK are required to be hallmarked before sale, unless they already bear a convention mark or a hallmark struck by an independent assay office in the European Economic Area which is deemed to be equivalent to a UK hallmark.

The following are the assay office marks used for gold imported articles until the end of 1998. For silver and platinum the symbols remain the same but the shields differ in shape.

   London   *Sheffield*

   Birmingham   *Edinburgh*

CONVENTION HALLMARKS

The UK has been a signatory to the International Convention on Hallmarks since 1972. A convention hallmark struck by the UK assay offices is recognised by all member countries in the convention and, similarly, convention marks from member countries are legally recognised in the UK. There are currently 20 members of the hallmarking convention: Austria, Croatia, Cyprus, Czech Republic, Denmark, Finland, Hungary, Ireland, Israel, Latvia, Lithuania, the Netherlands, Norway, Poland, Portugal, Slovakia, Slovenia, Sweden, Switzerland, and the UK.

A convention hallmark comprises four marks: a sponsor's mark, a common control mark, a fineness mark, and an assay office mark.

Examples of common control marks (figures differ according to fineness, but the style of each mark remains the same for each article):

| GOLD | SILVER | PALLADIUM | PLATINUM |

COMMEMORATIVE MARKS

There are other marks to commemorate special events: the silver jubilee of King George V and Queen Mary in 1935, the coronation of Queen Elizabeth II in 1953, her silver jubilee in 1977, and her golden jubilee in 2002. During 1999 and 2000 there was a voluntary additional Millennium Mark. A mark to commemorate the Queen's diamond jubilee in 2012 was available from July 2011 to October 2012:

BANKING AND FINANCE

BRITISH CURRENCY

The unit of currency is the pound sterling (£) of 100 pence. The decimal system was introduced on 15 February 1971.

COIN

Gold Coins	Nickel-Brass Coins
One hundred pounds £100*	Two pounds £2 (pre-1997)℃
Fifty pounds £50*	One pound £1
Twenty-five pounds £25*	
Ten pounds £10*	Cupro-Nickel Coins
Five pounds £5	Crown £5 (since 1990)℃
Two pounds £2	50 pence 50p
Sovereign £1	Crown 25p (pre-1990)℃
Half-sovereign 50p	20 pence 20p
Silver Coins	Nickel-plated Steel Coins**
(Britannia coins*)	10 pence 10p
Two pounds £2	5 pence 5p
One pound £1	
50 pence 50p	Bronze Coins
Twenty pence 20p	2 pence 2p
	1 penny 1p
Maundy Money†	
Fourpence 4p	Copper-plated Steel Coins††
Threepence 3p	2 pence 2p
Twopence 2p	1 penny 1p
Penny 1p	
Bi-colour Coins‡	
Two pounds £2	
One pound £1§	

* Britannia coins: gold bullion introduced 1987; silver, 1997
† Ceremonial money given annually by the sovereign on Maundy Thursday to as many elderly men and women as there are years in the sovereign's age
‡ Cupro-nickel centre and nickel-brass outer ring
§ The 12-sided £1 entered circulation on 28 March 2017
℃ Commemorative coins; not intended for general circulation
** Since September 1992; in 1998 the 2p was additionally struck in bronze
†† Pre-2012 the 10p and 5p coins were struck in cupro-nickel

GOLD COIN

Gold ceased to circulate during the First World War. Since then controls on buying, selling and holding gold coin have been imposed at various times but have subsequently been revoked. Under the Exchange Control (Gold Coins Exemption) Order 1979, gold coins may now be imported and exported without restriction, except gold coins which are more than 50 years old and valued at a sum in excess of £8,000.

Value Added Taxation on the sale of gold coins was revoked in 2000.

SILVER COIN

Prior to 1920 silver coins were struck from sterling silver, an alloy of which 925 parts in 1,000 were silver. In 1920 the proportion of silver was reduced to 500 parts. Since 1947 all 'silver' coins, except Maundy money, have been struck from cupro-nickel, an alloy of 75 parts copper and 25 parts nickel, except for the 20p, composed of 84 parts copper, 16 parts nickel. Maundy coins continue to be struck from sterling silver.

BRONZE COIN

Bronze, introduced in 1860 to replace copper, is an alloy consisting mainly of copper with small amounts of zinc and tin. Bronze was replaced by copper-plated steel in September 1992 with the exception of 1998 when the 2p was made in both copper-plated steel and bronze.

LEGAL TENDER *as at May 2019*

	Legal up to
Gold*	any amount
£2	any amount
£1	any amount
50p	£10
20p	£10
10p	£5
5p	£5
2p	20p
1p	20p

* Dated 1838 onwards, if not below least current weight

£5 (Crown since 1990) and 25p (Crown pre-1990) up to £10 are also legal tender under the Coinage Act 1971 but, as for all commemorative coins, are not designed for general circulation and are unlikely to be accepted by banks and shops.

The following coins have ceased to be legal tender:

Farthing	31 Dec 1960
Halfpenny (½d)	31 Jul 1969
Half-crown	31 Dec 1969
Threepence	31 Aug 1971
Penny (1d)	31 Aug 1971
Sixpence	30 Jun 1980
Halfpenny (½p)	31 Dec 1984
Old 5 pence	31 Dec 1990
Old 10 pence	30 Jun 1993
Old 50 pence	28 Feb 1998
Old £1 (nickel-brass/round)	15 Oct 2017

The Channel Islands and the Isle of Man issue their own coinage, which is legal tender only in the island of issue.

COIN STANDARDS

	Metal	Standard weight (g)	Standard diameter (mm)
1p	bronze	3.56	20.30
1p	copper-plated steel	3.56	20.30
2p	bronze	7.12	25.90
2p	copper-plated steel	7.12	25.90
5p	cupro-nickel	3.25	18.00
5p	nickel-plated steel	3.25	18.00
10p	nickel-plated steel	6.50	24.50
20p	cupro-nickel	5.00	21.40
25p Crown	cupro-nickel	28.28	38.61
50p	cupro-nickel	8.00	27.30
£1	nickel-brass, nickel-plated brass alloy	8.75	23.43
£2	nickel-brass	15.98	28.40
£2	nickel-brass, cupro-nickel	12.00	28.40
£5 Crown	cupro-nickel	28.28	38.61

The 'remedy' is the amount of variation from standard permitted in weight and fineness of coins when first issued from the Royal Mint.

THE TRIAL OF THE PYX

The Trial of the Pyx is the examination by a jury to ascertain that coins made by the Royal Mint, which have been set aside in the pyx (or box), are of the proper weight, diameter and composition required by law. The trial is held annually, presided over by the Queen's Remembrancer, with a jury of freemen of the Company of Goldsmiths.

BANKNOTES

Bank of England notes are issued in denominations of £5, £10, £20 and £50 for the amount of the fiduciary note issue, and are legal tender in England and Wales.

LEGAL TENDER

A new-style £20 note, the first in series F, was introduced in March 2007. A £50 note, the second in the F series, and the first banknote issued by the Bank of England to feature two portraits on the reverse, was issued in November 2011. The first polymer G series banknote, a £5 note featuring Sir Winston Churchill, was issued in September 2016, a £10 polymer note featuring Jane Austen followed in September 2017 and a £20 polymer note featuring the artist J. M. W. Turner will be issued in 2020.

The historical figures portrayed in the F and G series are:

£5	Sep 2016–date	Sir Winston Churchill
£10	Sep 2017–date	Jane Austen
£20	Mar 2007–date	Adam Smith
£50	Nov 2011–date	Matthew Boulton and James Watt

NOTE CIRCULATION

Note circulation is highest at the two peak spending periods of the year: around Christmas and during the summer holiday period.

The Bank of England measures the value of notes in circulation on the last day of February each year. The value of notes in circulation (£ million) at the end of February 2018 and 2019 was:

	2018	2019
£5	1,910	1,979
£10	7,789	10,524
£20	42,692	40,129
£50	16,508	17,210
Other notes*	4,351	4,330
Total	73,250	74,171

* Includes higher value notes used as backing for the note issues of authorised banks in Scotland and Northern Ireland

WITHDRAWN BANKNOTES

Banknotes which are no longer legal tender are payable when presented at the head office of the Bank of England in London.

The white notes for £10, £20, £50, £100, £500 and £1,000, which were issued until April 1943, ceased to be legal tender in May 1945, and the white £5 note in March 1946.

The white £5 note issued between October 1945 and September 1956, the £5 notes issued between 1957 and 1963 (bearing a portrait of Britannia) and the first series to bear a portrait of the Queen, issued between 1963 and 1971, ceased to be legal tender in March 1961, June 1967 and September 1973 respectively.

The series of £1 notes issued during the years 1928 to 1960 and the 10 shilling notes issued from 1928 to 1961 (those without the royal portrait) ceased to be legal tender in May and October 1962 respectively. The £1 note first issued in March 1960 (bearing on the back a representation of Britannia) and the £10 note first issued in February 1964 (bearing a lion on the back), both bearing a portrait of the

Queen on the front, ceased to be legal tender in June 1979. The £1 note first issued in 1978 ceased to be legal tender on 11 March 1988. The 10 shilling note was replaced by the 50p coin in October 1969, and ceased to be legal tender on 21 November 1970.

The D series of banknotes was introduced from 1970 and ceased to be legal tender from the dates shown below. The predominant identifying feature of each note was the portrayal on the back of a prominent figure from British history:

£1	Feb 1978–Mar 1988	Sir Isaac Newton
£5	Nov 1971–Nov 1991	Duke of Wellington
£10	Feb 1975–May 1994	Florence Nightingale
£20	Jul 1970–Mar 1993	William Shakespeare
£50	Mar 1981–Sep 1996	Sir Christopher Wren

The £1 coin was introduced on 21 April 1983 to replace the £1 note. No £1 notes have been issued since 1984 and in March 1998 the outstanding notes were written off in accordance with the provision of the Currency Act 1983.

The E series of notes was introduced from June 1990, replacing the D series. E series notes were withdrawn from circulation on the dates shown below:

£5	Jun 1990–Nov 2003	George Stephenson
£5	May 2002–May 2017	Elizabeth Fry
£10	Apr 1992–Jul 2003	Charles Dickens
£10	Nov 2000–Mar 2018	Charles Darwin
£20	Jun 1991–Feb 2001	Michael Faraday
£20	Jun 1999–Jun 2010	Sir Edward Elgar
£50	Apr 1994–Apr 2014	Sir John Houblon

OTHER BANKNOTES

Scotland – Banknotes are issued by three Scottish banks. The Royal Bank of Scotland issues notes for £1, £5, £10, £20, £50 and £100. Bank of Scotland and the Clydesdale Bank issue notes for £5, £10, £20, £50 and £100. All three banks have replaced paper £5 and £10 with polymer notes. Scottish notes are not legal tender in the UK but they are an authorised currency.

Northern Ireland – Banknotes are issued by four banks in Northern Ireland. The Bank of Ireland and the Ulster Bank issue notes for £5 (polymer), £10 (polymer), £20, £50 and £100. The First Trust Bank retains the right to issue notes for £10, £20, £50 and £100 until midnight on 30 June 2020, when it will cease to do so. Danske Bank (formerly Northern Bank) issue notes for £10 (polymer) and £20. Northern Ireland notes are not legal tender in the UK but they are an authorised currency.

Channel Islands – The States of Guernsey issues its own currency notes and coinage. The notes are for £1, £5, £10, £20 and £50, and the coins are for 1p, 2p, 5p, 10p, 20p, 50p and £2. The Guernsey round £1 coin was withdrawn from circulation in October 2017 with the introduction of the UK 12-sided coin, which is used alongside the £1 note.

The States of Jersey issues its own currency notes and coinage. The notes are for £1, £5, £10, £20, £50 and £100, and the coins are for 1p, 2p, 5p, 10p, 20p, 50p and £2. The Jersey round £1 coin was withdrawn from circulation in October 2017 with the introduction of the UK 12-sided coin, which is used alongside the £1 note.

The Isle of Man – The Isle of Man government issues notes for £1, £5, £10, £20 and £50. Although these notes are only legal tender in the Isle of Man, they may be exchanged at face value at certain UK banks at their discretion. The Isle of Man issues coins for 1p, 2p, 5p, 10p, 20p, 50p, £1, £2 and £5.

Although none of the series of notes specified above is legal tender in the UK, they are generally accepted by banks irrespective of their place of issue.

BANKING AND PERSONAL FINANCE

There are two main types of deposit-taking institutions: banks and building societies, although National Savings and Investments also provides savings products. Banks and building societies are regulated by the Prudential Regulation Authority, part of the Bank of England (*see* Financial Services Regulation), and National Savings and Investments is accountable to HM Treasury.

The main institutions within the British banking system are the Bank of England (the central bank), retail banks, investment banks and overseas banks. In its role as the central bank, the Bank of England acts as banker to the government and as a note-issuing authority; it also oversees the efficient functioning of payment and settlement systems.

Since May 1997, the Bank of England has had operational responsibility for monetary policy. At monthly meetings of its monetary policy committee the Bank sets the interest rate at which it will lend to the money markets.

OFFICIAL INTEREST RATES 2006–19	
3 August 2006	4.75%
9 November 2006	5.00%
11 January 2007	5.25%
10 May 2007	5.50%
5 July 2007	5.75%
6 December 2007	5.50%
7 February 2008	5.25%
10 April 2008	5.00%
8 October 2008	4.50%
6 November 2008	3.00%
4 December 2008	2.00%
8 January 2009	1.50%
5 February 2009	1.00%
5 March 2009	0.50%
4 August 2016	0.25%
2 November 2017	0.50%
2 August 2018	0.75%

RETAIL BANKING

Retail banks offer a wide variety of financial services to individuals and companies, including current and deposit accounts, loan and overdraft facilities, credit and debit cards, investment services, pensions, insurance and mortgages. All banks offer internet and telephone banking facilities and the majority also offer traditional branch services.

The Financial Ombudsman Service provides independent and impartial arbitration in disputes between banks and their customers (*see* Financial Services Regulation).

PAYMENT CLEARINGS

The Payment Systems Regulator (PSR), a subsidiary of the Financial Conduct Authority (*see* Financial Services Regulation), is the economic regulator for the £81 trillion payment systems industry in the UK. Funded by an annual levy on the firms it regulates, it was established on 1 April 2015. The PSR's statutory objectives are:

- to ensure that payment systems are operated and developed in a way that considers and promotes the interests of all the businesses and consumers that use them
- to promote effective competition in the markets for payment systems and services – between operators, payment service providers and infrastructure providers
- to promote development and innovation in payment systems, in particular the infrastructure used to operate these systems

DESIGNATED PAYMENT SYSTEMS
The PSR can only use its regulatory powers in relation to payment systems designated by HM Treasury, which regularly reviews this list. The current designated payment systems are: BACS, C&C (Cheque & Credit), CHAPS, Faster Payments Scheme (FPS), LINK, Northern Ireland Cheque Clearing (NICC), MasterCard, Visa Europe (Visa).

PSR, 12 Endeavour Square, Stratford, London E20 1JN
T 020-7066 1000 E contactus@psr.org.uk W www.psr.org.uk
Chair, Charles Randell, CBE

MAJOR RETAIL BANKS' FINANCIAL RESULTS 2018

Bank group	Profit/(loss) before taxation £ million	Profit/(loss) after taxation £ million	Total assets £ million
Barclays Bank	3,494	2,372	1,133,283
Cooperative Bank	(141)	(69)	23,103
HSBC UK Bank	1,064	763	238,939
Lloyds Banking Group	5,960	4,400	797,598
RBS Group	3,359	2,084	694,235
Santander UK	1,545	1,104	283,372
TSB Banking Group	(105)	(63)	41,124
Virgin Money Group	119	81	45,116

GLOSSARY OF FINANCIAL TERMS

The following provides a glossary of a selection of financial terms currently in general use and does not constitute any sort of financial advice which should always be sort from a regulated provider *see also* Financial Services Regulation.

ACCIDENT, SICKNESS AND UNEMPLOYMENT (ASU) INSURANCE – Is a short-term income protection policy that replaces an individual's income for a pre-defined amount of time, should they become unable to work due to accident, sickness or involuntary redundancy. Unemployment protection insurance can also be brought as a standalone product, as can accident and sickness protection. *See also* PPI.

AER (ANNUAL EQUIVALENT RATE) – A notional rate quoted on savings and investment products which demonstrates the return on interest, when compounded and paid annually.

APR (ANNUAL PERCENTAGE RATE) – Calculates the total amount of interest payable over the whole term of a product (such as an investment or loan), allowing consumers to compare rival products on a like-for-like basis. Companies offering loans, credit cards, mortgages or overdrafts are required by law to provide the APR rate. Where typical APR is shown, it refers to the company's typical borrower and so is given as a best example; rate and costs may vary depending on individual circumstances.

ANNUITY – A type of insurance policy that provides regular income in exchange for a lump sum. The annuity can be bought from a company other than the existing pension provider.

ATM (AUTOMATED TELLER MACHINES) – Commonly referred to as cash machines. Users can access their bank accounts using a card for simple transactions such as withdrawing money and viewing an account balance. Some banks and independent ATM deployers charge for transactions.

BANKER'S DRAFT – A cheque drawn on a bank against a cash deposit. Considered to be a secure way of receiving money in instances where a cheque could 'bounce' or where it is not desirable to receive cash.

BASE RATE – The interest rate set by the Bank of England at which it will lend to financial institutions. This acts as a benchmark for all other interest rates.

BASIS POINT – Unit of measure (usually one-hundredth of a percentage point) used to express movements in interest rates, foreign rates or bond yields.

BUY-TO-LET – The purchase of a residential property for the sole purpose of letting to a tenant. Not all lenders provide mortgage finance for this purpose. Buy-to-let lenders assess projected rental income (typical expectations are between 125 and 130 per cent of the monthly interest payment) in addition to, or instead of, the borrower's income. Buy-to-let mortgages are available as either interest only or repayment.

CAPITAL GAIN/LOSS – Increase/decrease in the value of a capital asset when it is sold or transferred compared to its initial worth.

CAPPED RATE MORTGAGE – The interest rate applied to a loan is guaranteed not to rise above a certain rate for a set period of time; the rate can therefore fall but will not rise above the capped rate. The level at which the cap is fixed is usually higher than for a fixed rate mortgage for a comparable period of time. The lender normally imposes early redemption penalties within the first few years.

CASH CARD – Issued by banks and building societies for withdrawing cash from ATMs.

CHARGE CARD – Charge cards, eg American Express and Diners Club, can be used in a similar way to credit cards but the debt must be settled in full each month.

CHIP AND PIN CARD – A credit/debit card which incorporates an embedded chip containing unique owner details. When used with a PIN, such cards offer greater security as they are less prone to fraud.

CONTACTLESS PAYMENT – A system that uses radio-frequency identification (RFID) or near-field communication (NFC) for making secure payments via a credit, debit or smart card or another device, such as a smartphone, with an embedded chip and antenna which need to be in close proximity to a reader at the point of sale. Occasional PIN verification is required to authenticate the user and purchases are typically limited to small value sales.

CREDIT CARD – Normally issued with a credit limit, credit cards can be used for purchases until the limit is reached. There is normally an interest-free period on the outstanding balance of up to 56 days. Charges can be avoided if the balance is paid off in full within the interest-free period. Alternatively part of the balance can be paid and in most cases there is a minimum amount set by the issuer (normally a percentage of the outstanding balance) which must be paid on a monthly basis. Some card issuers charge an annual fee and most issuers belong to at least one major credit card network, eg Mastercard or Visa.

CREDIT RATING – Overall credit worthiness of a borrower based on information from a credit reference agency, such as Experian or Equifax, which holds details of credit agreements, payment records, county court judgments etc for all adults in the UK. This information is supplied to lenders who use it in their credit scoring or underwriting systems to calculate the risk of granting a loan to an individual and the probability that it will be repaid. Each lender sets their own criteria for credit worthiness and may accept or reject a credit application based on an individual's credit rating.

CRITICAL ILLNESS COVER – Insurance that covers borrowers against critical illnesses such as stroke, heart attack or cancer and is designed to protect mortgage or other loan payments.

DEBIT CARD – Debit cards were introduced on a large scale in the UK in the mid-1980s, replacing cash and cheques to purchase goods and services. Funds are automatically withdrawn from an individual's bank account after making a purchase and no interest is charged. They can also be used to withdraw cash from ATMs in the UK and abroad.

DIRECT DEBIT – An instruction from a customer to their bank, which authorises the payee to charge costs to the customer's bank account.

DISCOUNTED MORTGAGE – Discounted mortgages guarantee an interest rate set at a margin below the standard variable rate for a period of time. The discounted rate will move up or down with the standard variable rate, but the payment rate will retain the agreed differential below the standard variable rate. The lender normally imposes early redemption penalties within the first few years.

EARLY REDEMPTION PENALTY – *see* Redemption Penalty

ENDOWMENT MORTGAGE – Refers to a mortgage loan arranged on an interest-only basis where the capital is intended to be repaid by one or more endowment policies. The borrower has two distinct arrangements: one with the lender for the mortgage and one with the insurer for the endowment policy. The borrower can change either arrangement if they wish.

EQUITY – When applied to real estate, equity is the difference between the value of a property and the amount outstanding on any loan secured against it. Negative equity occurs when the loan is greater than the market value of the property.

FIXED RATE MORTGAGE – A repayment mortgage where the interest rate on the loan is fixed for a set amount of time, normally a period of between one and ten years. The interest rate does not vary with changes to the base rate resulting in the monthly mortgage payment remaining the same for the duration of the fixed period. The lender normally imposes early redemption penalties within the first few years.

ISA (INDIVIDUAL SAVINGS ACCOUNT) – A means by which investors can save (in a cash ISA) and invest (in a stocks and shares ISA) without paying any tax on the proceeds. There are limits on the amount that can be invested during any given tax year (see Taxation).

INTEREST ONLY MORTGAGE – Only interest is paid by the borrower and capital remains constant for the term of the loan. The onus is on the borrower to make provision to repay the capital at the end of the term. This is usually achieved through an investment vehicle such as an endowment policy or pension.

LOAN TO VALUE (LTV) – This is the ratio between the size of a mortgage loan sought and the mortgage lender's valuation. On a loan of £55,000, for example, on a property valued at £100,000, the loan to value is 55 per cent. This means that there is sufficient equity in the property for the lender to be reassured that if interest or capital repayments were stopped, it could sell the property and recoup the money owed. Fewer options are available to borrowers requiring high LTV.

LONDON INTERBANK OFFERED RATE (LIBOR) – Is the interest rate that London banks charge when lending to one another on the wholesale money market. LIBOR is set by supply and demand of money as banks lend to each other in order to balance their books on a daily basis.

MIG (MORTGAGE INDEMNITY GUARANTEE) – An insurance for the lender paid by the borrower on high LTV mortgages (typically more than 90 per cent). It is a policy designed to protect the lender against loss in the event of the borrower defaulting or ceasing to repay a mortgage and is usually paid as a one-off premium or can be added to the value of the loan. It offers no protection to the borrower. Not all lenders charge MIG premiums.

OVERDRAFT – An 'authorised' overdraft is an arrangement made between customer and bank allowing the balance of the customer's account to go below zero; interest is normally charged at an agreed rate and sometimes an arrangement fee is charged. If the negative balance exceeds the agreed terms or a prior arrangement for an overdraft facility has not been made (an 'unauthorised' overdraft) then additional penalty fees may be charged and higher interest rates may apply. Interest-free overdrafts are available for customers in certain circumstances, such as full-time higher education students and recent graduates.

PERSONAL PENSION SCHEME (PPS) – A tax-privileged individual investment vehicle, with the primary purpose of building a capital sum to provide retirement benefits,

although it will usually also provide death benefits. Contributions can be made to a PPS by both the individual and, if they are not self-employed, their employer. Contributions are exempt from tax and the retirement age may be selected at any time, usually from age 55. Up to 25 per cent of the pension fund may be taken as a tax-free cash sum on retirement. See also Social Welfare, Pensions.

PHISHING – A fraudulent attempt to obtain bank account details and security codes through an email. The email purports to come from a bona fide organisation, such as a bank or building society, and attempts to steer the recipient, usually under the pretext that the institution is updating its security arrangements, to a website which requests personal details.

PIN (PERSONAL IDENTIFICATION NUMBER) – A PIN is issued alongside a cash card to allow the user to access a bank account via an ATM. PINs are also issued with smart, credit and debit cards and, since 14 February 2006, have been compulsory as a security measure in the majority of purchases.

PORTABLE MORTGAGE – A mortgage product that can be transferred to a different property in the event of a house move. Preferable where early redemption penalties are charged.

PPI (PAYMENT PROTECTION INSURANCE) – A credit protection, or loan repayment, insurance taken out by a borrower to cover repayment of credit in the event of illness, disablement, redundancy, death or another circumstance that could prevent the borrower from earning income to service the debt.

REDEMPTION PENALTY – A charge levied for paying off a loan, debt balance or mortgage before a date agreed with the lender.

REPAYMENT MORTGAGE – In contrast to the interest only mortgage, the monthly repayment includes an element of the capital sum borrowed in addition to the interest charged.

SHARE – A share is a divided-up unit of the value of a company. If a company is worth £100m, and there are 50 million shares in issue, then each share is worth £2 (usually listed as pence). As the overall value of the company fluctuates so does the share price.

STANDING ORDER – An instruction made by the customer to their bank, which allows the transfer of a set amount to a payee at regular intervals.

UNIT TRUST – A 'pooled' fund of assets, usually shares, owned by a number of individuals. Managed by professional, authorised fund-management groups, unit trusts have traditionally delivered better than average cash deposits, but do rise and fall in value as their underlying investment varies in value.

VARIABLE RATE MORTGAGE – Repayment mortgages where the interest rate set by the lender increases or decreases in relation to the base interest rate which can result in fluctuating monthly repayments.

WITH-PROFITS – Usually applies to pensions, endowments, savings schemes or bonds. The intention is to smooth out the rises and falls in the stock market for the benefit of the investor. Actuaries working for the insurance company, or fund managers, hold back some profits in good years in order to make up the difference in years when shares perform badly.

BANK FAMILY TREE

Includes the major retail banks operating in the UK as at April 2019. For financial results for these banks *see* Banking and Personal Finance. Building societies are only included in instances where they demutualised to become a bank.

FINANCIAL SERVICES REGULATION

Under the Financial Services and Markets Act 2000, as amended by the Financial Services Act (2012), the Financial Conduct Authority and the Prudential Regulation Authority are responsible for financial regulation in the UK.

FINANCIAL CONDUCT AUTHORITY

The Financial Conduct Authority (FCA) is responsible for supervising the conduct of over 58,000 financial services firms and financial markets in the UK and for regulating the prudential standards of those firms – over 18,000 – not regulated by the Prudential Regulation authority. The FCA has three statutory objectives:

- to secure an appropriate degree of protection for consumers
- to protect and enhance the integrity of the UK financial system
- to promote effective market competition in the interests of consumers

The FCA is accountable to HM Treasury and therefore to parliament, but is operationally independent of the government and is funded entirely by the firms which it regulates. The FCA is governed by a board appointed by HM Treasury, but day-to-day decisions and staff management are the responsibility of the executive committee.

The FCA's annual budget for ongoing regulatory activity (ORA) in 2019–20 is £537.7m, a 2 per cent increase from 2018–19. The 2019–20 annual funding requirement totals £558.5m, an increase of 2.7 per cent due to the increase in the ORA budget and an additional £5m allocated for the costs associated with withdrawing from the European Union.

THE FINANCIAL SERVICES REGISTER

The Financial Services Register lists financial services firms and individuals in the UK who are authorised by the FCA and PRA (see Prudential Regulation Authority) to do business and specifies which activity each firm or individual is regulated to undertake and what products or services each is approved to provide.

FINANCIAL CONDUCT AUTHORITY, 12 Endeavour Square, London E20 1JN T 020-7066 1000 W www.fca.org.uk
Chair, Charles Randell, CBE
Chief Executive, Andrew Bailey

PRUDENTIAL REGULATION AUTHORITY

The Prudential Regulation Authority (PRA), part of the Bank of England, works alongside the FCA and is responsible for the prudential regulation and supervision of around 1,500 banks, building societies, credit unions, insurers and major investment firms. The PRA has three statutory objectives:

- to promote the safety and soundness of the firms it regulates
- to contribute to securing an appropriate degree of protection for those who are, or may become, insurance policyholders
- to facilitate effective competition

The members of the PRA's committee are: the Governor of the Bank of England (chair); the three Deputy Governors for Financial Stability, Markets and Banking, and Prudential Regulation; the chief executive of the FCA; a member appointed by the Governor with the approval of the chancellor; and six other external members appointed by the chancellor.

The PRA's budget for 2019–20 is £273m.

PRUDENTIAL REGULATION AUTHORITY, 20 Moorgate, London EC2R 6DA T 020-3461 4444
E enquiries@bankofengland.co.uk
W www.bankofengland.co.uk/prudential-regulation
Chief Executive, Sam Woods

COMPENSATION

Created under the Financial Services and Markets Act (2000), the Financial Services Compensation Scheme (FSCS) is the UK's statutory fund of last resort for customers of authorised financial services firms. It provides compensation if a firm authorised by the FCA or PRA is unable, or likely to be unable, to pay claims against it. In general this is when a firm has stopped trading and has insufficient assets to meet claims, or is in insolvency. This includes, banks, building societies and credit unions; firms providing debt management, mortgage and endowment advice; insurance firms; insurance brokers; investment firms; payment protection insurance firms and pension companies. The FSCS is independent of the UK regulators (FCA and PRA), with separate staff and premises. However, the FCA and PRA appoint the directors. The chair's appointment (and removal) is subject to HM Treasury approval. The FSCS is funded by an annual levy on every firm authorised by the UK regulators.

The Pension Protection Fund (PPF) is a statutory fund established under the Pensions Act 2004 and became operational on 6 April 2005. The fund was set up to pay compensation to members of eligible defined benefit pension schemes, where there is a qualifying insolvency event in relation to the employer and where there are insufficient assets in the pension scheme to cover PPF levels of compensation. Compulsory annual levies are charged on all eligible schemes to help fund the PPF, in addition to investment of PPF assets. The PPF is also responsible for the Fraud Compensation Fund – a fund that will provide compensation to occupational pension schemes that suffer a loss attributable to dishonesty.

FINANCIAL SERVICES COMPENSATION SCHEME, Beaufort House, 15 St Botolph Street, 10th Floor, London EC3A 7QU T 0800-678 1100 W www.fscs.org.uk
Chair, Marshall Bailey
Chief Executive, Caroline Rainbird

PENSION PROTECTION FUND, Renaissance, 12 Dingwall Road, Croydon CR0 2NA T 0345-600 2541
E information@ppf.co.uk W www.ppf.co.uk
Chair, Arnold Wagner, OBE
Chief Executive, Oliver Morley, CBE

DESIGNATED PROFESSIONAL BODIES

Professional firms are exempt from requiring direct regulation by the FCA if they carry out only certain restricted activities that arise out of, or are complementary to, the provision of professional services, such as arranging the sale of shares on the instructions of executors or trustees, or providing services to small, private companies. These firms are, however, supervised by designated professional bodies (DPBs). There are a number of safeguards to protect consumers dealing with firms that do not require direct regulation. These arrangements include:

- the FCA's power to ban a specific firm from taking advantage of the exemption and to restrict the regulated activities permitted to the firms

- rules which require professional firms to ensure that their clients are aware that they are not authorised persons
- a requirement for the DPBs to supervise and regulate the firms and inform the FCA on how the professional firms carry on their regulated activities

See Professional Education section for contact details of the following DPBs:

Association of Chartered Certified Accountants
Council for Licensed Conveyancers
Institute of Actuaries
Institute of Chartered Accountants in England and Wales
Institute of Chartered Accountants in Ireland
Institute of Chartered Accountants of Scotland
Law Society of England and Wales
Law Society of Northern Ireland
Law Society of Scotland
Royal Institution of Chartered Surveyors

RECOGNISED INVESTMENT EXCHANGES

The FCA currently supervises seven recognised investment exchanges (RIEs) in the UK; recognition confers an exemption from the need to be authorised to carry out regulated activities in the UK. The RIEs are organised markets on which member firms can trade investments such as equities and derivatives. The RIEs are listed with their year of recognition in parentheses:

CBOE EUROPE (2013), 5th Floor, The Monument Building, 11 Monument Street, London EC3R 8AF T 020-7012 8900 W https://markets.cboe.com

EURONEXT LONDON (2014), 10th Floor, 110 Cannon Street, London EC4N 6EU T 020-7076 0900 W www.euronext.com/en

ICE FUTURES EUROPE (2001), 5th Floor Milton Gate, 60 Chiswell Street, London EC1Y 4SA T 020-7065 7700 W www.theice.com

INTERNATIONAL PROPERTY SECURITIES EXCHANGE (IPSX) UK (2019), 8–10 Hill Street, London W1J 5NG T 020-3931 8800 W www.ipsx.com

LONDON METAL EXCHANGE (2001), 10 Finsbury Square, London EC2A 1AJ T 020-7113 8888 W www.lme.com

LONDON STOCK EXCHANGE (2001), 10 Paternoster Square, London EC4M 7LS T 020-7797 1000 W www.londonstockexchange.com

NEX EXCHANGE (2007), London Fruit and Wool Exchange, 1 Duval Square, London E1 6PW T 020-7818 9774 W www.nexexchange.com

RECOGNISED CLEARING HOUSES AND CENTRAL COUNTERPARTIES

The Bank of England is responsible for recognising and supervising central counterparties (CCPs) and clearing houses (RCHs). CCPs and RCHs provide clearing and settlement services for transactions in foreign exchange, securities, options and derivatives on recognised investment exchanges. There are currently three UK CCPs authorised under the European Market Infrastructure regulation (EMIR) and one recognised RCH (dates of authorisation and recognition are given in parentheses):

EUROCLEAR UK AND IRELAND (RCH, 2001), 33 Cannon Street, London EC4M 5SB T 020-7849 0000 W www.euroclear.com

ICE CLEAR EUROPE (CCP, 2016), 5th Floor, Milton Gate, 60 Chiswell Street, London EC1Y 4SA T 020-7065 7600 W www.theice.com/clear-europe

LCH (LONDON CLEARING HOUSE) (CCP, 2014), Aldgate House, 33 Aldgate High Street, London EC3N 1EA T 020-7426 7000 W www.lch.com

LME (LONDON METAL EXCHANGE) CLEAR (CCP, 2014), 10 Finsbury Square, London EC2A 1AJ T 020-7113 8888 W www.lme.com/LME-Clear

OMBUDSMAN SCHEMES

The Financial Ombudsman Service was set up by the Financial Services and Markets Act 2000 to provide consumers with a free, independent service for resolving disputes with authorised financial firms. It can consider complaints about most financial matters including: banking; credit cards and store cards; financial advice; hire purchase and pawnbroking; insurance; loans and credit; money transfer; mortgages; payday lending and debt collecting; payment protection insurance; pensions; savings and investments; stocks, shares, unit trusts and bonds.

Complainants must first complain to the firm involved. They do not have to accept the ombudsman's decision and are free to go to court if they wish, but if a decision is accepted, it is binding for both the complainant and the firm.

The Pensions Ombudsman can investigate and decide complaints and disputes regarding the way occupational and personal pension schemes are administered and managed. Unless there are special circumstances, this only usually includes issues and disputes that have arisen within the past three years. The Pensions Ombudsman is also the Ombudsman for the Pension Protection Fund (PPF) and the Financial Assistance Scheme (which offers help to those who were a member of an under-funded defined benefit pension scheme that started to wind-up in specific financial circumstances between 1 January 1997 and 5 April 2005).

FINANCIAL OMBUDSMAN SERVICE, Exchange Tower, Harbour Exchange, London E14 9SR **Helpline** 0800-023 4567 T 020-7964 1000 W www.financial-ombudsman.org.uk
Chief Ombudsman, Caroline Wayman

PENSIONS OMBUDSMAN, 10 South Colonnade, Canary Wharf, London E14 4PU T 0800-917 4487 E enquiries@pensions-ombudsman.org.uk W www.pensions-ombudsman.org.uk
Pensions Ombudsman, Anthony Arter
Deputy Pensions Ombudsman, Karen Johnston

THE TAKEOVER PANEL

The Panel on Takeovers and Mergers is an independent body, established in 1968, whose main functions are to issue and administer the City code and to ensure equality of treatment and opportunity for all shareholders in takeover bids and mergers. The panel's statutory functions are set out in the Companies Act 2006.

The panel comprises up to 36 members representing a spread of expertise in takeovers, securities markets, industry and commerce. The chair, at least one deputy chair and up to 20 other members are nominated by the panel's own nomination committee. The remaining 12 members are nominated by professional bodies representing the accountancy, financial advice, insurance, investment and pension industries; the Association for Financial Markets in Europe; the Confederation of British Industry; the Quoted Companies Alliance; and UK Finance.

THE TAKEOVER PANEL, One Angel Court, London EC2R 7HJ T 020-7382 9026 E supportgroup@thetakeoverpanel.org.uk W www.thetakeoverpanel.org.uk
Chair, Michael Crane, QC

NATIONAL SAVINGS AND INVESTMENTS

NS&I (National Savings and Investments) is both a non-ministerial government department and an executive agency of the Chancellor of the Exchequer. It is one of the UK's largest savings organisations, with 25 million customers and around £157bn invested. When people invest in NS&I they are lending money to the government which pays them interest or prizes in return. All deposits are 100 per cent financially secure because they are guaranteed by HM Treasury.

TAX-FREE PRODUCTS

PREMIUM BONDS
Introduced in 1956, premium bonds enable savers to enter a regular draw for tax-free prizes, while retaining the right to get their money back. A sum equivalent to interest on each bond is put into a prize fund and distributed by monthly prize draws. The prizes are drawn by ERNIE (electronic random number indicator equipment) and are free of all UK income tax and capital gains tax. Two £1m jackpots are drawn each month in addition to other tax-free prizes ranging in value from £25 to £100,000.

Bonds are in units of £1, with a minimum purchase of £25, up to a maximum holding limit of £50,000 per person. Bonds become eligible for prizes once they have been held for one clear calendar month following the month of purchase. Each £1 unit can win only one prize per draw, but it will be awarded the highest for which it is drawn. Bonds remain eligible for prizes until they are repaid.

The scheme offers a facility to reinvest prize wins automatically. Upon completion of an automatic prize reinvestment mandate, holders receive new bonds which are immediately eligible for future prize draws. Bonds can only be held in the name of an individual and not by organisations.

INDIVIDUAL SAVINGS ACCOUNTS
Since April 1999 NS&I has offered cash individual savings accounts (ISAs). Its Direct ISA, launched in April 2006, can be opened and managed online and by telephone with a minimum investment of £1 and a maximum investment of £20,000 in the 2019–20 tax year. Interest for the Direct ISA is calculated daily, added to the account annually on 6 April and is free of tax.

Its Junior ISA, launched in August 2017 as a successor to children's bonds, can be opened for children under 18 by those with parental responsibility or, by a young person aged 16 or 17 for themselves. There is a minimum investment of £1 and a maximum investment of £4,368 in the 2019–20 tax year. It can only be opened and managed online and there are no withdrawals allowed until the young person reaches 18. Interest is accrued daily, added to the account annually on 6 April and is free of tax.

OTHER PRODUCTS

INCOME BONDS
NS&I income bonds were introduced in 1982. They are suitable for those who want to receive regular monthly payments of interest while preserving the full cash value of their capital. The minimum holding for each investment is £500 and the maximum £1m per person. A variable rate of interest is calculated on a day-to-day basis and paid monthly. Interest is taxable but is paid gross without deduction of tax at source.

GUARANTEED GROWTH AND GUARANTEED INCOME BONDS
Guaranteed growth and guaranteed income bonds, re-launched in December 2017, offer a lump sum investment that earns a fixed rate of interest over either a one-year term or a three-year term. The minimum holding is £500 to a maximum of £10,000 per person or trust per issue. For the guaranteed growth bond interest is calculated daily and added to the bond on each anniversary of the investment. The guaranteed income bond has interest paid monthly. Interest on both bonds is taxable but is paid gross without deduction of tax at source.

SAVINGS AND INVESTMENT ACCOUNTS
The direct saver account was launched in March 2010. Accounts can be opened by an individual aged at least 16, or jointly. Customers are able to invest between £1 and £2m per person. The account can be managed online or by telephone and funds can be withdrawn at any time. Interest is paid gross without deduction of tax at source.

The investment account can be opened with a minimum balance of £20 and has a maximum limit of £1m. The interest is paid gross without deduction of tax at source.

FURTHER INFORMATION
Further information regarding products and their current availability can be obtained online (W www.nsandi.com), by telephone (T 0808-500 7007) or by writing to: NS&I, Glasgow G58 1SB.

THE NATIONAL DEBT

HISTORY

The early 1700s saw the meteoric rise of the banking and financial markets in Great Britain, with the emerging stock market revolving around government funds. The ability to raise money by means of creating debt through the issue of bills and bonds heralded the beginning of the national debt.

The war years of 1914–18 saw an increase in the national debt from £650m at the start of the war to £7,500m by 1919. The Treasury developed new expertise in foreign exchange, currency, credit and price control in order to manage the post-war economy. The slump of the 1930s necessitated the restructuring of the UK economy following the Second World War (the national debt stood at £21bn by its end) and the emphasis was placed on economic planning and financial relations.

The relatively high period of inflation in the 1970s and 1980s led to the rise of the national debt in nominal terms from £36bn in 1972 to £197bn in 1987 and then to £419bn in March 1998. Although in nominal terms the national debt has risen sharply in recent years, as a percentage of GDP it has decreased dramatically since the end of the Second World War, when it stood at 250 per cent of GDP (for current figures, *see* table below).

THE UK DEBT MANAGEMENT OFFICE

The decision in 1997 to transfer monetary policy to the Bank of England, while the Treasury retained control of fiscal policy, led to the creation of the UK Debt Management Office (DMO) as an executive agency of HM Treasury in April 1998. Initially the DMO was responsible only for the management of government marketable debt and for issuing gilts. In April 2000 responsibility for exchequer cash management and for issuing Treasury bills (short-dated securities with maturities of less than one year) was transferred from the Bank of England to the DMO. The national debt also includes the (non-marketable) liabilities of National Savings and Investments and other public sector and foreign currency debt.

In 2002 the operations of the long-standing statutory functions of the Public Works Loan Board, which lends capital to local authorities, and the Commissioners for the Reduction of the National Debt, which manages the investment portfolios of certain public funds, were integrated within the DMO.

UK PUBLIC SECTOR NET DEBT

	£ billion	per cent of GDP
2017–18 (outturn)	1,779	85.0
2018–19 (forecast)	1,810	83.7
2019–20 (forecast)	1,851	82.8

Source: HM Treasury – *The Budget 2018* (Crown copyright)

THE LONDON STOCK EXCHANGE

The London Stock Exchange Group (LSEG) serves the needs of companies by providing facilities for raising capital. It also operates marketplaces for members to trade financial instruments. including equities, bonds and derivatives, on behalf of investors and institutions such as pension funds and insurers.

LSEG's key subsidiary companies are the London Stock Exchange, Borsa Italiana, MTS (a trading platform for European government and corporate bonds), Turquoise (a trading platform for European equities) and FTSE (a global index provider).

Headquartered in London, with significant operations in Italy, France, North America and Sri Lanka, the group employs around 4,500 people.

HISTORY

The London Stock Exchange is one of the world's oldest stock exchanges, dating back more than 300 years to its origins in the coffee houses of 17th-century London. It was formally established as a membership organisation in 1801.

MAJOR DEVELOPMENTS

'BIG BANG'
In 1986 a package of reforms which are now known as 'Big Bang' transformed the London Stock Exchange and the City of London, liberalising the way in which banks and stockbroking firms operated and facilitating greater foreign investment. The London Stock Exchange ceased granting voting rights to individual members and became a private company. The 'Big Bang' also saw the start of a move towards fully electronic trading and the closure of the trading floor.

INTRODUCTION OF SETS
In October 1997, the Exchange introduced SETS, its electronic order book. The system enhanced the efficiency and transparency of trading on the Exchange, allowing trades to be executed automatically and anonymously rather than negotiated by telephone.

DEMUTUALISATION AND LISTING
The London Stock Exchange demutualised in 2000 and listed on its own main market in 2001.

MERGER WITH BORSA ITALIANA
In October 2007 the London Stock Exchange merged with the Italian stock exchange, Borsa Italiana, creating London Stock Exchange Group (LSEG).

DIVERSIFICATION
Since 2009 LSEG has diversified its business beyond the listing and trading of UK and Italian equities:
• In 2009 LSEG purchased Sri Lankan technology company MillenniumIT which provides technology to stock

exchanges, brokerages and regulators around the world. It also supplies the trading technology to LSEG's own markets
• In 2010 LSEG acquired a majority stake in Turquoise, a platform facilitating the trading of stocks listed in 19 European countries and the USA
• In 2011 LSEG became the owner of FTSE, the international business which creates and manages financial indices
• In 2013 LSEG purchased a majority stake in LCH (London Clearing House) (see also Financial Services Regulation, Recognised Clearing Houses and Central Counterparties)

UK EQUITY MARKETS

LSEG offers a range of listing options for companies, according to their size, history and requirements:
• The Main Market has the highest standards of regulation and disclosure obligations and is overseen by the UK Listing Authority (UKLA), a division of the Financial Conduct Authority (FCA). A Main Market listing enables established companies to raise capital, widen their investor base and have their shares traded alongside global peers. They are also eligible for inclusion in key indices, such as the FTSE 100 and the FTSE 250
• The Alternative Investment Market (AIM), established in June 1995, is specially designed to meet the needs of small and growing companies. It enables them to raise capital and broaden their investor base in a more flexible regulatory environment, while still being traded on an internationally recognised market. AIM companies retain an experienced Nominated Adviser (or 'Nomad') firm, which is responsible for ensuring the company's suitability for the market
• The Professional Securities Market (PSM), established in July 2005, allows companies to target professional investors only, on a market that offers greater flexibility in accounting standards
• The Specialist Fund Segment (SFS), established as the Specialist Fund Market (SFM) in November 2007, is a part of the London Stock Exchange's regulated Main Market designed for highly specialised investment entities, such as hedge funds or private equity funds, that wish to target institutional, professional, professionally advised and knowledgeable investors

As at 30 April 2019 there were 5,739 companies listed on LSEG's primary markets, with a combined market value of £2,052,073m: 1,770 on the Main Market (1,431 on the UK main market and 398 on the international main market), 3,852 on the AIM, 16 on the PSM and 35 entities on the SFS.

LONDON STOCK EXCHANGE, 10 Paternoster Square,
London EC4M 7LS T 020-7797 1000
W www.londonstockexchange.com
Chair, Don Robert
Chief Executive, David Schwimmer

THE BUDGET 2018

ABBREVIATIONS

AME = Annually Managed Expenditure
DEL = Departmental Expenditure Limits
ETS = Emissions Trading System
NI = National Insurance
OBR = Office for Budget Responsibility
Source: HM Treasury – *Budget 2018* (Crown copyright)

GOVERNMENT EXPENDITURE

DEPARTMENTAL EXPENDITURE LIMITS *(£bn)*

	Plans 2019–20
Resource DEL	
Defence	29.0
Single Intelligence Account	2.0
Home Office	10.7
Foreign and Commonwealth Office	1.2
International Development	8.2
Health (incl. NHS)	129.6
Work and Pensions	5.4
Education	63.5
Business, Energy and Industrial Strategy	1.8
Transport	2.9
Exiting the European Union	0.1
Digital, Culture, Media and Sport	1.5
MHCLG Housing and Communities	2.3
MHCLG Local Government	5.9
Scotland	15.7
Wales	11.6
Northern Ireland	10.3
Justice	6.0
Law Officers Departments	0.6
Environment, Food and Rural Affairs	1.5
HM Revenue and Customs	3.2
HM Treasury	0.2
Cabinet Office	0.3
International Trade	0.3
Small and Independent bodies	1.3
Reserves	12.3
Adjustment for budget exchange	(0.4)
TOTAL RESOURCE DEL	327.0
*OBR Allowance for shortfall	(1.7)
OBR Resource DEL	325.4
Capital DEL	
Defence	9.8
Single Intelligence Account	0.7
Home Office	0.5
Foreign and Commonwealth Office	0.1
International Development	3.7
Health (incl. NHS)	6.7
Work and Pensions	0.2
Education	5.1
Business, Energy and Industrial Strategy	11.5
†Transport	15.8
Exiting the European Union	0.0
Digital, Culture, Media and Sport	0.6
MHCLG Housing and Communities	10.8
MHCLG Local Government	0.0
Scotland	4.5
Wales	2.1
Northern Ireland	1.5
Justice	0.4
Law Officers Departments	0.0
Environment, Food and Rural Affairs	0.6
HM Revenue and Customs	0.2
HM Treasury	0.3
Cabinet Office	0.0
International Trade	0.0
Small and Independent bodies	0.4
Reserves	2.2
Adjustment for budget exchange	0.0
TOTAL CAPITAL DEL	77.7
*OBR Allowance for shortfall	(2.7)
OBR Capital DEL	75.0
TOTAL DEL	400.4

† Includes funding for Network Rail expenditure, formerly part of the DfT's AME budget

ANNUALLY MANAGED EXPENDITURE *(£bn)*

	2018–19	2019–20	2020–21
Current Expenditure			
Resource AME	397.8	403.1	412.3
Resource DEL	310.8	325.4	336.8
Ring-fenced depreciation	23.0	23.4	24.6
Current Expenditure	731.5	751.9	773.6
Capital Expenditure			
Capital AME	19.8	14.7	15.8
Capital DEL	61.5	75.0	77.6
Gross Investment	81.3	89.7	93.5
TOTAL AME	812.8	841.6	867.1
as % of GDP	38.2	38.3	38.1

GOVERNMENT RECEIPTS *(£bn)*

	Outturn 2017–18	Forecast 2018–19	Forecast 2019–20
Income tax[1]	180.7	190.2	192.9
Pay as you earn	154.9	161.7	162.0
Self assessment	28.3	30.5	32.9
NI contributions	132.5	136.9	141.9
Value added tax	125.3	132.2	137.2
Corporation tax	55.9	59.5	60.0
Petroleum revenue tax	(0.6)	(0.6)	(0.7)
Fuel duties	27.9	28.3	28.3
Business rates	30.2	30.7	30.9
Council tax	32.1	34.2	35.9
VAT refunds	17.1	17.8	18.4
Capital gains tax	7.8	8.7	9.1
Inheritance tax	5.2	5.5	5.7
Property transaction taxes[2]	13.6	12.8	13.3
Stamp taxes on shares	3.5	3.7	3.8
Tobacco duties	8.8	9.3	9.2
Alcohol duties	11.6	12.3	12.7
Air passenger duty	3.4	3.7	3.8
Insurance premium tax	5.9	6.3	6.3
Climate change levy	1.9	2.0	2.2
Bank levy	2.6	2.5	2.3
Bank surcharge	1.9	1.9	2.0
Apprenticeship levy	2.7	2.8	2.9
Diverted profits tax	0.2	0.1	0.1
Soft drinks industry levy	0.0	0.3	0.3
Other HMRC taxes[3]	7.5	7.4	7.4
Vehicle excise duties	6.2	6.4	6.4
Licence fee receipts	3.2	3.3	3.3
Environmental levies	6.5	10.2	11.2
EU ETS auction receipts	0.4	0.6	1.6
Other taxes	6.9	7.2	7.5
Total	700.7	736.1	755.8
Less own resources			
contribution to EU	(3.4)	(3.3)	(3.3)
Interest and dividends	7.1	8.8	10.7
Gross operating surplus	46.4	42.1	42.9
Other receipts	3.2	3.6	3.7
CURRENT RECEIPTS	754.0	787.3	809.8
UK oil and gas revenues[4]	1.2	1.5	1.9

[1] PAYE and Self Assessment receipts, tax on savings income and other minor income tax components
[2] UK annual tax on enveloped dwellings (ATED), stamp duty land tax (SDLT) for England and property transaction taxes of the devolved administrations
[3] Landfill tax (excl. Scotland and Wales from 2018–19), aggregates levy, betting and gaming duties and customs duties
[4] Offshore corporation tax and petroleum revenue tax

Source: OBR – *Economic and Fiscal Outlook*, October 2018

ECONOMIC STATISTICS

TRADE

TRADE IN GOODS
£ million

	Exports	Imports	Balance
2014	293,116	415,187	(122,071)
2015	286,752	404,562	(117,810)
2016	299,073	431,725	(132,652)
2017	338,739	475,774	(137,035)
2018	350,651	488,744	(138,093)

Source: ONS (Crown copyright)

BALANCE OF PAYMENTS, 2018

Current Account	£ million
Trade in goods and services	
Trade in goods	(138,093)
Trade in services	107,124
Total trade in goods and services	(30,969)
Income	
Compensation of employees	(171)
Investment income	(25,376)
Other	(1,103)
Total income	(26,650)
Total secondary income	(24,025)
TOTAL (CURRENT BALANCE)	(81,644)

Source: ONS (Crown copyright)

UK GDP GROWTH
% change on previous quarter at current market prices

Source: ONS

UK EMPLOYMENT

DISTRIBUTION OF THE WORKFORCE

	Mar 2018	Mar 2019
Workforce jobs	34,949,000	35,537,000
HM forces	154,000	152,000
Self-employment jobs	4,496,000	4,657,000
Employees jobs	30,271,000	30,701,000
Government-supported trainees	28,000	27,000

Source: ONS – Labour Market Statistics 2019 (Crown copyright)

EMPLOYED AND UNEMPLOYED
thousands, all aged 16+

	Apr–Jun 2018		Apr–Jun 2019	
	Number	Rate (%)	Number	Rate (%)
Employed	32,386	61.1	32,811	61.6
Unemployed	1,362	4.0	1,329	3.9

Source: ONS – Labour Market Statistics 2019 (Crown copyright)

DURATION OF UNEMPLOYMENT, APR–JUN 2019

All unemployed	1,329,000
Less than 6 months	793,000
6 months–1 year	194,000
1 year +	342,000
2 years +	169,000

Source: ONS – Labour Market Statistics 2019 (Crown copyright)

MEDIAN EARNINGS, 2018
full-time, £

	All	Male	Female
Gross annual	24,006.00	29,425.00	18,735.00
Gross weekly	460.00	555.00	369.90
Hourly	12.78	14.10	11.50

Source: ONS (Crown copyright)

LABOUR STOPPAGES BY DURATION, 2018

1 day	12
2–3 days	22
4 days	6
5–10 days	23
11+ days	18
All stoppages	81

Source: ONS (Crown copyright)

LABOUR DISPUTES BY INDUSTRY, 2018

Industry Group	Working Days Lost
Mining, quarrying, electricity, gas, air con.	100
Manufacturing	3,000
Sewage, waste management, water supply	4,600
Construction	5,800
Wholesale & retail, motor vehicles, accommodation, food	900
Transport & storage	42,600
Information & Communication	10,600
Financial, professional, scientific, administration	4,000
Public administration & defence	15,900
Education	179,400
Human health and social work	4,900
Other	800
All industries & services	272,600

Source: ONS (Crown copyright)

TRADE UNIONS

Year	No. of unions	Total membership
2013–14	166	7,086,116
2014–15	160	7,010,527
2015–16	160	6,948,725
2016–17	151	6,865,056
2017–18	146	6,875,231

Source: Annual Report of the Certification Officer 2017–18

COST OF LIVING AND INFLATION RATES

The first cost of living index to be calculated took July 1914 as 100 and was based on the pattern of expenditure of working-class families in 1914. The cost of living index was superseded in 1947 by the general index of retail prices (RPI), although the older term is still popularly applied.

The Harmonised Index of Consumer Prices (HICP) was introduced in 1997 to enable comparisons within the European Union using an agreed methodology. In 2003 the National Statistician renamed the HICP the Consumer Prices Index (CPI) to reflect its role as the main target measure of inflation for macroeconomic purposes. In March 2013 CPIH, an additional index which includes owner-occupiers' housing costs, was introduced.

The RPI and indices based on it continue to be published alongside the CPI. Private-sector pensions and index-linked gilts continue to be calculated with reference to RPI or its derivatives.

CPI AND RPI

The CPI and RPI measure the changes month by month in the average level of prices of goods and services purchased by households in the UK. The indices are compiled using a selection of around 700 goods and services, and the prices charged for these items are collected at regular intervals at about 140 locations throughout the country, from the internet and over the phone. The Office for National Statistics (ONS) reviews the components of the indices once a year to reflect changes in consumer preferences and the establishment of new products. The table below shows changes made by the ONS to the CPI 'shopping basket' in 2019.

The CPI excludes a number of items that are included in the RPI, mainly related to housing, such as council tax, and a range of owner-occupier housing costs, such as mortgage payments. The CPI covers all private households, whereas the RPI excludes the top 4 per cent by income and pensioner households which derive at least three-quarters of their income from state benefits. The two indices use different methodologies to combine the prices of goods and services, which means that since 1996 the CPI inflation measure is less than the RPI inflation measure.

CHANGES TO THE 'SHOPPING BASKET' OF GOODS AND SERVICES IN 2019

The table below shows changes to the CPI* basket of goods and services made by the ONS in 2019 in order to reflect changes in consumer preferences and the establishment of new products.

Goods and services group	Removed items	New items
Food	–	popcorn; peanut butter
Non-alcoholic beverages	cola flavoured drink	flavoured tea (eg herbal/ fruit); regular cola drink (bottle); diet/ sugar-free cola drink (bottle)
Clothing	–	adult hat/ cap
Furniture, furnishings & carpets	three-piece non-leather suite	non-leather settee
Glassware, tableware & household utensils	crockery set	bakeware (baking tray or roasting tin); dinner plate
Non-durable household goods	washing powder	washing liquid/ gel
Operation of personal transport equipment	brake fitting in fast-fit auto centre	wheel alignment
Audio-visual equipment & related products	hi-fi	portable speaker (eg Bluetooth speaker); smart speaker
Recreational items, gardens & pets	complete dry dog food	dog treats
Books, newspapers & stationery	envelopes	child's fiction book, 6–12-years-old
Catering services	staff restaurant soft drink	–
Personal care	–	electric toothbrush
Financial services	unit trust initial charge	–

* RPI goods and services are grouped together under different classifications

INFLATION RATE

The 12-monthly percentage change in the 'all items' index of the RPI or CPI is referred to as the rate of inflation. As the most familiar measure of inflation, the RPI is often referred to as the 'headline rate of inflation'. The CPI is the main measure of inflation for macroeconomic purposes and forms the basis of the government's inflation target, which is currently 2 per cent. The percentage change in prices between any two months/years can be obtained using this formula:

$$\frac{\text{Later date RPI/CPI} - \text{Earlier date RPI/CPI}}{\text{Earlier date RPI/CPI}} \times 100$$

For example, to find the CPI rate of inflation for 2006, using the annual averages for 2005 and 2006:

$$\frac{79.9 - 78.1}{78.1} \times 100 = 2.3$$

On 16 February 2016 the reference year for all CPI indices was re-based to 2015=100, replacing the 2005=100 series. The change of reference period does not apply to the RPI, which remains unchanged. The CPI rate of inflation figure given in the Annual Indices table may differ by plus or minus 0.1 percentage points from the figure calculated by the above equation.

The RPI and CPI figures are published around the the middle of each month in an indices bulletin on the ONS website (W www.ons.gov.uk/economy/inflationandpriceindices).

PURCHASING POWER OF THE POUND

Changes in the internal purchasing power of the pound may be defined as the 'inverse' of changes in the level of prices: when prices go up, the amount which can be purchased with a given sum of money goes down. To find the purchasing power of the pound in one month or year, given that it was 100p in a previous month or year, the calculation would be:

$$100p \times \frac{\text{Earlier month/year RPI}}{\text{Later month/year RPI}}$$

Thus, if the purchasing power of the pound is taken to be 100p in 1975, the comparable purchasing power in 2000 would be:

$$100p \times \frac{34.2}{170.3} = 20.1p$$

For longer term comparisons, it has been the practice to use an index which has been constructed by linking together the RPI for the period 1962 to date; an index derived from the consumers' expenditure deflator for the period from 1938 to 1962; and the pre-war 'cost of living' index for the period 1914 to 1938. This long-term index enables the internal purchasing power of the pound to be calculated for any year from 1914 onwards. It should be noted that these figures can only be approximate.

ANNUAL INDICES

	Annual average RPI (1987 = 100)	Purchasing power of £ (1998 = 1.00)	Annual average CPI (2015 = 100)*	Annual average CPIH† (2015=100)*	Rate of inflation (RPI/ CPI/ CPIH)†
1914	2.8	58.18			
1915	3.5	46.54			
1920	7.0	23.27			
1925	5.0	32.58			
1930	4.5	36.20			
1935	4.0	40.72			
1938	4.4	37.02			
There are no official figures for 1939–45					
1946	7.4	22.01			
1950	9.0	18.10			
1955	11.2	14.54			
1960	12.6	12.93			
1965	14.8	11.00			
1970	18.5	8.80			
1975	34.2	4.76			
1980	66.8	2.44			
1985	94.6	1.72			
1990	126.1	1.29			9.5/ 7.0
1995	149.1	1.09			3.5/ 2.6
1998	162.9	1.00	71.2		3.4/ 1.6
2000	170.3	0.96	72.7		3.0/ 0.8
2005	192.0	0.85	78.1	79.4	2.8/ 2.1
2006	198.1	0.82	79.9	81.4	3.2/ 2.3/ 2.5
2007	206.6	0.79	81.8	83.3	4.3/ 2.3/ 2.4
2008	214.8	0.76	84.7	86.2	4.0/ 3.6/ 3.5
2009	213.7	0.76	86.6	87.9	−0.5/ 2.2/ 2.0
2010	223.6	0.73	89.4	90.1	4.6/ 3.3/ 2.5
2011	235.2	0.69	93.4	93.6	5.2/ 4.5/ 3.8
2012	242.7	0.67	96.1	96.0	3.2/ 2.8/ 2.6
2013	250.1	0.65	98.5	98.2	3.0/ 2.6/ 2.3
2014	256.0	0.64	100.0	99.6	2.4/ 1.5/ 1.5
2015	258.5	0.63	100.0	100.0	1.0/ 0.0/ 0.4
2016	263.1	0.62	100.7	101.0	1.8/ 0.7/ 1.0
2017	272.5	0.60	103.4	103.6	3.6/ 2.7/ 2.6
2018	281.6	0.58	105.9	106.0	3.3/ 2.5/ 2.3

INSURANCE

AUTHORISATION AND REGULATION OF INSURANCE COMPANIES

Since 1 April 2013, under the Financial Services Act 2012, the prudential supervision of banks and insurers is the responsibility of the Prudential Regulation Authority (PRA), an operationally independent subsidiary of the Bank of England. The Financial Conduct Authority (FCA) is responsible for consumer protection and markets oversight. All life insurers, general insurers, reinsurers, insurance and reinsurance brokers, financial advisers and composite firms are statutorily regulated. See also Financial Services Regulation.

Firms wishing to effect or carry out contracts of insurance must be granted authorisation to do so. The PRA assesses applicant insurers from a prudential perspective, using the same framework that is employed for supervision of existing insurers. The FCA then assesses applicants from a conduct perspective. Although the PRA manages the authorisation process, an insurer will be granted authorisation only where both the FCA and the PRA are satisfied that they meet their relevant requirements.

There are around 700 insurance organisations and friendly societies with authorisation to transact one or more class of insurance business in the UK. Until the UK leaves the EU, it remains part of the single European insurance market. This permits insurers authorised in any EU state automatic authorisation to transact business in all other EU countries without further formality. The number of insurers currently operating within this market is over 3,500. See also Brexit.

COMPLAINTS

Disputes between consumers and financial businesses can be referred to the Financial Ombudsman Service (FOS). Consumers with a complaint about any form of money matter, including bank accounts, insurance, mortgages, savings and credit, must first take the matter to the highest level within the provider. The provider has to provide a 'final response' within eight weeks. If the complaint remains unresolved consumers can refer the complaint, free of charge, to the FOS. Since 1 April 2019 the FOS compensation limits are £350,000 for acts or omissions by firms on or after 1 April 2019 and £160,000 for acts or omissions by firms before 1 April 2019, even if the complaint is referred to the FOS after this date. From 1 April 2020 both award limits will be automatically adjusted each year in line with inflation as measured by the Consumer Prices Index (CPI).

Businesses falling under the EU definition of a micro enterprise (businesses with a turnover of up to €2m and fewer than ten employees) may also refer a matter to the FOS. In 2017–18, 55 per cent of new complaints about financial services companies related to payment protection insurance. Other types of insurance, such as motor, buildings and life insurance, accounted for just 11 per cent of the total number of 1.5 million complaints received. See also Financial Services Regulation.

ASSOCIATION OF BRITISH INSURERS

Over 80 per cent of the domestic business of UK insurance companies is transacted by the 250 members of the Association of British Insurers (ABI). The ABI is a trade association which protects and promotes the interests of all its insurance company members. Only insurers authorised in the EU are eligible for membership. Brokers, intermediaries, financial advisers and claims handlers may not join the ABI, but may have their own trade associations. Legal firms, consultants, price comparison websites and other firms which help insurers deliver their services may join the ABI as associate members.

ASSOCIATION OF BRITISH INSURERS (ABI), One America Square, 17 Crosswall, London EC3N 2LB
T 020-7600 3333 W www.abi.org.uk
Chair, Amanda Blanc (Chief Executive Zurich EMEA)
Director-General, Huw Evans

BALANCE OF PAYMENTS

In 2017, financial and insurance services contributed £119.1bn to the UK economy, 6.5 per cent of the total. The UK trade surplus for insurance and pensions was around £51bn.

WORLDWIDE MARKET

In 2018 the UK insurance industry was the largest in Europe and the fourth largest in the world behind the USA, China and Japan. China is the biggest growth area, moving from eighth largest in 2006 to second in 2018.

Market	Premium income ($bn)
USA	1,377
China	541
Japan	422
UK	283

TAKEOVERS AND MERGERS

Cheap finance, regulatory pressures and an increasing desire for scale led to a busy year of mergers and acquisitions in financial services. Internationally, this was led by the year-long process which finally ended in November 2018 with US pharmacy group CVS acquiring health insurer Aetna in a deal which valued the company at $69bn.

In the UK, uncertainty over Brexit did not suppress merger and acquisition activity. Allianz were among the most active. During the year they were linked with approaches for Swiss giant Zurich Insurance and UK companies AVIVA and RSA. Although there was no firm movement on any of these deals, Allianz did complete the the the purchase of the general insurance arms of Liverpool Victoria (known as LV=) at a total cost of around £1bn and Legal and General £240m. Allianz were, however, beaten by French insurer, AXA in the race to acquire XL Group. This $16bn deal was completed in March 2018.

Other major general insurance deals included US investment firm Bain Capital's purchase of esure for £1.2bn; China Re's purchase of speciality insurer Chaucer and motor insurer Markerstudy beating off competition from the AA, Aviva, RSA Insurance and Saga to land the general insurance arm of Co-operative Insurance.

On the life Insurance side, Phoenix Group, who specialise in 'zombie' life funds (closed funds that operate without taking on new clients or policies) doubled its size by acquiring Standard Life Assurance in a deal worth £3bn. A month after the Standard Life deal the UK's largest life insurer Prudential announced it was splitting into two operations and sold its annuity business to specialist provider Rothesay Life. It is expected that other life groups may also look very carefully at their annuity business following the implementation of Solvency II. Under Solvency II, annuities and products promising guaranteed returns have become less attractive for insurers as the new rules require that they hold significant funds to match liability risks.

BREXIT

The Insurance and financial services sector are very important to the UK and its economy. The UK is the fourth largest insurance and long-term savings industry in the world and the largest in the EU. Certainly, the insurance industry made no secret of being firmly in the 'remain' camp in the Brexit debate, with the ABI, British Insurance Brokers' Association (BIBA) and Lloyd's all stressing the volatility and uncertainty they believed a 'leave' vote would create. But the result in June 2016 proved that their lobbying had not persuaded enough voters.

While leaving the EU may present opportunities to expand global markets and the demand for insurance products will certainly not reduce, the result left the industry with a number of concerns, not least the need for the UK government to negotiate a very complicated trade agreement, or at least interim measures, in a short space of time. As a result, in the run up to the initial 29 March 2019 deadline ABI was strongly in favour of a delay to Brexit if a no deal exit was the alternative. On 25 February 2019 Huw Evans, Director-General of ABI, said a no-deal Brexit 'would be an unforgivable act of economic and social self-harm that the UK would live to regret'. Subsequently the votes in parliament, which ruled out a no-deal Brexit under any circumstances, and the delay until 31 October 2019 were warmly welcomed.

One of the main issues of concern was that after Brexit it would be illegal for EU-based clients of UK insurers to be paid pensions or claims and EU insurers would no longer be able to renew UK based policies without UK government authorisation. To alleviate this problem the Bank of England announced in July 2018 that there would be a temporary recognition regime which would allow EU firms wishing to continue carrying out business in the UK, to operate for a limited period after withdrawal while they seek authorisation or recognition from UK regulators.

The issue for EU-based clients of UK insurers has not yet been fully resolved. In November 2018 the European Insurance and Occupational Pensions Authority (EIOPA) confirmed that 124 firms from the UK and Gibraltar with cross-border business in European Economic Area (EEA) countries, had insufficient contingency plans in place to ensure service continuity in the event of a no-deal Brexit. This would leave around 9 million EU policyholders unclear about their future insurance cover. The position was partially clarified in February 2019 when EIOPA confirmed that insurance contracts for EU-based clients of UK insurers taken out before the Brexit date would remain in force but renewals and future contracts would require authorisation from the country concerned.

The ongoing political uncertainty over Brexit shows no sign of abating but despite this, the UK insurance industry continues to maintain that its financial stability, adaptability and expertise will enable it to cope with whatever the future brings.

GENERAL INSURANCE

2018 began with news of the serious fire in the Liverpool Echo Arena car park on New Year's Eve. No-one was injured but more than 1,300 vehicles were badly damaged. As well as getting the money to replace their vehicles, depending on their cover, some customers received compensation for the value of belongings that were inside their vehicle and even alternative transport costs. The ABI estimated the total cost of claims to be in the region of £20m.

At the same time, trade credit insurers were busy with claims from companies in the supply chain after the collapse of construction giant Carillion. This came after other high profile collapses including Monarch Airways, Palmer & Harvey and computer re-seller, Misco. The figures for the first quarter of 2018 suggested a 50 per cent increase in reported cases, with the Carillion insolvency alone generating claims of over £30m.

Weather related events also gave rise to heavy claims with snow and freezing temperatures dubbed the 'Beast from the East' hitting in late February and early March 2018. In total, £1.25bn was paid by insurers under domestic and commercial property insurance policies in the first quarter of 2018 a 290 per cent increase over the previous quarter.

In the latter half of 2018, the UK climate had gone to the other extreme with a prolonged period of hot weather and drought from July through to September. This, in turn, led to further headaches for insurers, with the highest level of subsidence claims for 15 years recorded in the third quarter of 2018. Claims jumped from 2,500 in the second quarter to 10,000 in quarter three, with an increase in value from £14m to £64m; 350 per cent.

Unsurprisingly, these various extreme weather events have led to speculation that above inflation premium increases for household insurance may follow. The current average premium for household buildings insurance in the UK is £258 a year with an additional £127 a year for home contents cover.

The October Budget saw general insurers breathing a sigh of relief as the chancellor chose not to increase Insurance Premium Tax (IPT) still further. IPT was introduced in 1994 at a rate of 2.5 per cent, raised in 1997 to 4 per cent and in 1999 to 5 per cent. Further increases were then made in each successive budget between 2015 and 2017 resulting in the 12 per cent now being added to most general insurance premiums and 20 per cent to travel insurance, mechanical/ electrical appliances insurance and some other motor insurances including cover for motor vehicles used for people with disabilities. The industry has repeatedly opposed further IPT increases highlighting 'the absurdity of punishing people who are doing the right thing'. This was supported by research from the Centre for Economics and Business Research which showed that around 200,000 people had moved away from health insurance towards NHS care because of recent IPT increases. In the 2019 Spring Statement the chancellor announced a review of IPT to ensure the tax operates 'fairly and efficiently'. At the time of writing no further details of the review had been announced.

On 31 October the Financial Conduct Authority (FCA) published the results of a piece of supervisory work on insurance pricing practices. As a result of this initial work, the FCA announced it would look into the way insurers price their products and whether they were fair, particularly for what it calls 'vulnerable consumers.' One area to be examined was the different price quoted to new customers compared to existing clients for the same product. The FCA aimed to publish an interim market study report in summer 2019 setting out preliminary conclusions, including a discussion of potential solutions. It aimed to publish its final report by the end of 2019.

TOP FIVE GENERAL INSURANCE COMPANIES IN
THE UK 2017

Insurance Company	Net written premium (£bn)
1. AVIVA	4.2
2. AIG	3.8
3. RSA Insurance Group	3.1
4. UK Insurance (Direct Line)	3.1
5. Chubb	3.0

LONDON INSURANCE MARKET

In recent years it has become increasingly difficult to define
the London Insurance Market business. Many businesses
operate in London as branch offices of parent companies
located elsewhere in the world and may no longer separately
identify as London Market premiums. What is acknowledged
is that, despite the growth of other international centres,
London remains the world's leading market for
internationally traded insurance and reinsurance, its business
comprising mainly overseas non-life large and high-exposure
risks. The market is centred on the square mile of the City of
London, which provides the required financial, banking, legal
and other support services. Around 56 per cent of London
market business is transacted at Lloyd's of London, the
remainder through insurance companies and protection and
indemnity clubs. In 2017 the market had a written gross
premium income of around £60bn. Around 200 Lloyd's
brokers service the market.

The trade association for the international insurers and
reinsurers writing primarily non-marine insurance and all
classes of reinsurance business in the London market is the
International Underwriting Association (IUA).

INTERNATIONAL UNDERWRITING ASSOCIATION,
1 Minster Court, Mincing Lane, London EC3R 7AA
T 020-7617 4444 W www.iua.co.uk
Chair, Malcolm Newman
Chief Executive, Dave Matcham

LLOYD'S OF LONDON

Lloyd's of London is an international market for almost all
types of general insurance. Lloyd's currently has the capacity
to accept insurance premiums of around £28bn. Much of this
business comes from outside the UK and makes a valuable
contribution to the balance of payments.

A policy is underwritten at Lloyd's by a mixture of private
and corporate members. Specialist underwriters accept
insurance risks at Lloyd's on behalf of members (referred to as
'names') grouped in syndicates. There are currently 84
syndicates of varying sizes, each managed by one of the 55
underwriting agents approved by the Council of Lloyd's.

Members divide into three categories: corporate
organisations, individuals who have no limit to their liability
for losses, and those who have an agreed limit (known as
NameCos). Currently there are around 2,000 members of
which around 200 are individuals.

Lloyd's is incorporated by an act of parliament (Lloyd's Acts
1871 onwards) and is governed by an 18-person council,
made up of six working, six external and six nominated
members. The structure immediately below this changed
when, in 2002, Lloyd's members voted at an extraordinary
general meeting to implement a new franchise system for the
market with the aim of improving profitability. The first move
was the introduction of a new governance structure, replacing

the Lloyd's Market Board and the Lloyd's Regulatory Board
with an 11-person Lloyd's Franchise Board. Four main
committees report to this board.

The corporation is a non-profit making body chiefly
financed by its members' subscriptions. It provides the
premises, administrative staff and services for Lloyd's
underwriting syndicates. It does not, however, assume
corporate liability for the risks accepted by its members.
Individual members are responsible to the full extent of their
personal means for their underwriting affairs unless they have
converted to limited liability companies.

Lloyd's syndicates have no direct contact with the public. All
business is transacted through insurance brokers accredited by
the Corporation of Lloyd's. In addition, non-Lloyd's brokers
in the UK, when guaranteed by Lloyd's brokers, are able to
deal directly with Lloyd's motor syndicates, a facility that has
made the Lloyd's market more accessible to the insuring
public.

Under the Financial Services and Markets Act 2000, Lloyd's
is regulated by the FCA and the PRA. However, in situations
where Lloyd's internal regulatory and compensation
arrangements are more far-reaching – as for example with the
Lloyd's Central Fund which safeguards claim payments to
policyholders – the regulatory role is delegated to the Council
of Lloyd's.

DEVELOPMENTS IN 2018

Global macro-economic instability, continuing uncertainty in
the UK over Brexit, a difficult underwriting environment and
a prolonged period of poor investment returns all contributed
to another poor result for the Lloyd's market. The aggregated
market result was a loss of just over £1bn which, although it
was substantial, was a considerable improvement on the 2017
loss (£2.01bn).

Major catastrophes in 2018 that contributed to the £19.7bn
total claims bill included Hurricane Florence which hit the
East Coast of the USA in August/ September; Hurricane
Michael which hit southeastern and eastern USA in October;
Typhoon Jebi, a category 5 super typhoon which caused an
estimated $3.4bn (£2.7bn) of damage in Taiwan, Japan,
Russia and the Far East in August/ September and the
California wildfires, in July/ August.

Most classes of business continued to record underwriting
losses. The total loss was £1.6bn but, in all but one class
(Aviation), these were reduced compared to the 2017 results.
Motor insurance (£12m), the energy sector (£113m) and the
very small life account (£16m) were the profit-making
exceptions.

After the £2bn losses of 2017 premium increases in 2018
were inevitable but these only averaged out at around 3.9 per
cent which reflects the continuing over-capacity and very
competitive nature of the market. The same problems are
likely to be faced by underwriters in 2019.

In November 2018 Lloyd's announced the opening of its
first Europe-wide operation, Lloyd's Brussels. The company,
(Lloyd's Insurance Company SA) is a subsidiary of Lloyd's
with 19 European branches, working with over 400
coverholders and 40 Lloyd's brokers spread across Europe. It
was established as part of Lloyd's Brexit preparations, with an
executive committee and board and 50 staff based in the
Belgian capital as well as 45 staff across the continent.

LLOYD'S OF LONDON, One Lime Street, London EC3M 7HA
T 020-7327 1000 W www.lloyds.com
Chair, Bruce Carnegie-Brown
Chief Executive, John Neal

LLOYD'S SEGMENTAL RESULTS 2018 *(£m)*

	Gross written premiums	Net earned premiums	Underwriting result
Reinsurance	11,070	7,650	(456)
Casualty	9,094	6,363	(183)
Property	9,687	6,692	(700)
Marine	2,603	2,154	(343)
Motor	1,037	940	12
Energy	1,404	897	113
Aviation	549	410	(49)
Life	83	72	16
Total from syndicate operations	35,527	25,178	(1,590)

BRITISH INSURANCE COMPANIES

The following insurance company figures refer to members and certain non-members of the ABI.

DOMESTIC PROPERTY CLAIMS STATISTICS 2017

Type	Payment (£m)
Theft	346
Fire	369
Weather	184
Escape of water	784
Domestic subsidence	92
Accidental damage	277
other domestic claims	253
Total	2,305

WORLDWIDE GENERAL BUSINESS TRADING RESULTS *(£m)*

	2016	2017
Net written premiums	39,082	45,461
Underwriting results	1,402	1,558
Investment income	2,146	3,549
Overall trading profit	3,549	3,695
Profit as percentage of premium income	9%	8%

LIFE AND LONG-TERM INSURANCE AND PENSIONS

In October 2018, the Pensions Policy Institute (PPI) published the results of the largest ever study into lost pension pots. These are pensions contributions where the owner has either lost all information about them or forgotten they have them. It was estimated that around 1.6 million pots worth nearly £250bn could remain unclaimed. More frequent job changes and home moves are thought to be the main reasons why their owners lose track of them. An average person will have around 11 different jobs over their lifetime and move house eight times. This had led the UK government to predict that there could be as many as 50 million dormant and lost pensions by 2050. Consumer groups, MPs and insurers believe more should be done and called for a central database known as the Pensions Dashboard – a digital record of all the pension accounts held by an individual together with details of the providers. A prototype system was established in 2017 by ABI but the final decisions on privacy precautions, data collection, regulation and other safeguards remain with the UK government. It is hoped that, if approved, the system will be available by late 2019.

In November 2018 the government launched a consultation on delivering collective defined contribution schemes. At present, there are defined benefit (DB) pension schemes, usually a workplace pension based on salary and how long the employee has worked for the employer, and defined contribution (DC) pension schemes where the pension pot is based solely on how much has been paid in. Just before the General Election in 2015 the government began the process to introduce legislation to allow a third type of pension, collective defined contribution (CDC) schemes, but they ran out of time. CDCs are risk sharing plans widely used in several other countries including Canada and the Netherlands, but are not currently legal in the UK.

2018 also saw an update to the 2001 agreement between insurers and the government on genetic testing and how insurers use test results. Insurers are not permitted to request genetic tests under any circumstances and will only ask to see test results obtained for other reasons if a policy is worth more than £500,000 and the applicant has tested positive for Huntingdon's Disease.

PROTECTION INSURANCE CLAIMS 2018

Type of product	No. of claims paid*	% of new claims paid	Total value paid (£ thousand)	Average claim paid (£)
Critical illness	16,452	91.60	1,166,872	70,925.83
Life	35,470	97.40	2,882,604	81,268.78
Total permanent disability	476	70.20	36,781	77,271.01
Whole of life	121,822	99.98	577,453	4,740.14
Income protection	25,843	88.10	648,815	25,106.02
All protection products	200,063	97.60	5,312,524	26,554.26

* Figures are for new claims, as well as all income protection claims in payment

UK LONG-TERM INSURANCE NET PREMIUM INCOME

Year	Life & annuities	Individual pensions	Occupational pensions	Income protection & other business	Total
2007	49,866	35,252	98,575	1,660	185,353
2008	36,300	30,523	62,820	1,541	131,183
2009	20,336	27,725	68,988	1,473	118,521
2010	19,241	28,218	64,033	1,482	112,975
2011	16,008	27,401	71,680	1,456	116,545
2012	14,893	33,219	71,148	1,862	121,122
2013	9,944	25,119	80,192	1,457	116,712
2014	9,985	23,721	70,826	1,290	105,822
2015	10,461	35,194	76,188	1,290	123,133
2016	12,679	29,684	75,634	1,553	119,551
2017	11,685	60,562	91,020	2,511	165,778

TAXATION

The government raises money to pay for public services such as education, health and the social welfare system through tax. Each year the Chancellor of the Exchequer's Budget sets out how much it will cost to provide these services and how much tax is therefore needed to pay for them. The tax is collected by HM Revenue and Customs (HMRC). There are several different types of tax:

- income tax payable on earnings, pensions, state benefits, savings and investments
- capital gains tax (CGT) payable on the disposal of certain assets
- inheritance tax (IHT) payable on estates upon death and certain lifetime gifts
- stamp duty payable when purchasing property and shares
- value added tax (VAT) payable on goods and services
- certain other duties such as fuel duty on petrol and excise duty on alcohol and tobacco

Corporation tax raises funds from companies and small businesses.

New taxation measures and changes to the administration of the taxation system are normally announced by the incumbent Chancellor of the Exchequer in the government's annual Budget in the autumn, with a spring statement on government spending forecasts.

The government has a stated policy of investing resources into reducing tax evasion and avoidance by both individuals and companies. Information and updates on the latest measures can be found on the government's website: www.gov.uk/government/policies/tax-evasion-and-avoidance).

The government also has an ongoing drive to simplify the UK tax system via the Office of Tax Simplification (OTS). Details of the OTS and its work can also be found on the government's website (W www.gov.uk/government/organisations/office-of-tax-simplification). The OTS welcomes views from individuals and can be contacted via email (E ots@ots.gov.uk).

HELP AND INFORMATION ON TAXATION

For information and help on any aspect of personal taxation, call the HMRC helpline (T 0300-200 3300). The lines are open 8am to 8pm from Monday to Friday, 8am to 4pm on Saturday, and 9am to 5pm on Sunday. For general queries (not specific cases) you can also use Twitter, starting your query with @HMRCcustomers.

HMRC no longer has a network of enquiry centres, because visitor numbers had dropped dramatically.

The HMRC website (W www.gov.uk/government/organisations/hm-revenue-customs) provides wide-ranging information.

INCOME TAX

Income tax is assessed on different sorts of income. Not all types of income are taxable and individuals are entitled to certain reliefs and allowances which reduce or, in some cases, cancel out their income tax bill.

An individual's taxable income is assessed each tax year, starting on 6 April and ending on 5 April the following year. The information below relates specifically to the year of assessment 2019–20, ending on 5 April 2020, and has only limited application to earlier years. Changes due to come into operation at a later date are briefly mentioned where information is available. Types of income that are taxable include:

- earnings from employment or profits from self-employment
- most pensions income, including state, company and personal pensions

- interest over the savings allowance
- income (dividends) from shares
- income from property
- income received from a trust
- certain state benefits
- an individual's share of any joint income

There are certain sorts of income on which individuals never pay tax. These are ignored altogether when working out how much income tax an individual may need to pay. Types of income that are not taxable include:

- certain state benefits and tax credits, such as child benefit, working tax credit, child tax credit, pension credit, attendance allowance, personal independence payment, housing benefit and maternity allowance
- winter fuel payments
- income from National Savings and Investments savings certificates
- interest, dividends and other income from various tax-free investments, notably individual savings accounts (ISAs)
- premium bond and national lottery prizes

PERSONAL ALLOWANCE

Every individual resident in the UK has a 'personal allowance' for tax purposes. This is the amount of taxable income that an individual can earn or receive each year tax-free. This tax year (2019–20) the basic personal allowance or tax-free amount is £12,500, an increase of £650 from the 2018–19 figure of £11,850. The personal allowance is for all taxpayers regardless of age.

Income tax is only due on an individual's taxable income that is above his or her tax-free allowance. Spouses and civil partners are taxed separately, with each entitled to his or her personal allowance. Each spouse or civil partner may obtain other allowances and reliefs where the required conditions are satisfied.

The personal allowance is available for all individuals with income up to £100,000. Those individuals with an 'adjusted net income' above the £100,000 limit have their personal allowance reduced by half the excess (£1 for every £2) they have over that limit until their personal allowance is reduced to nil.

An individual's 'adjusted net income' is calculated in a series of steps. The starting point is 'net income', which is the total of the individual's income subject to income tax less specified deductions such as payments made gross to pension schemes or trading losses. This net income is then reduced by the grossed-up amount of the individual's Gift Aid contributions to charities and the grossed-up amount of the individual's pension contributions that have received tax relief at source. The final step is to add back any relief for payments to trade unions or police organisations deducted in arriving at the individual's net income. The result is the individual's adjusted net income.

MARRIAGE ALLOWANCE

Some married couples and civil partners, made up of one non-taxpayer and one basic rate taxpayer, are eligible for a marriage allowance, which lets them share some of the non-taxpayer's unused annual income tax allowance. In the 2019–20 tax year, the allowance allows a spouse or civil partner with an income less than £12,500 to transfer up to £1,250 of their unused personal allowance to their higher-income partner. So long as the person receiving the transfer is a basic rate taxpayer, which, in most cases, means having an income of between £12,500 and £50,000 (£43,430 in Scotland), this transferable tax allowance is worth up to £250 in 2019–20.

BLIND PERSON'S ALLOWANCE

If an individual is registered blind or is unable to perform any work for which eyesight is essential, he or she can claim blind person's allowance, an extra amount of tax-free income added to the personal allowance. In 2019–20 the blind person's allowance is £2,450, irrespective of age or income. If an individual is married or in a civil partnership and cannot use all of the allowance because of insufficient income, the unused part of the allowance can be passed to the spouse or civil partner.

PROPERTY AND TRADING ALLOWANCES

These allowances benefit 'micro-entrepreneurs' who use one or more of a wide range of money-making activities to supplement their income. Individuals with property or trading income do not need to declare or pay tax on the first £1,000 they earn from each source per year. Should they earn more than that amount they will have to declare it to HMRC, but they can still take advantage of the allowance.

Property income qualifying for relief under the property allowance could be any income that an individual makes from renting out a residence, home, building, property or land – even from renting out a driveway as a parking space, for example, or renting out a room via websites like Airbnb.

Trading income qualifying for the allowance can be income from any sale of goods or services. An individual could do tasks such as cleaning or odd jobs, hiring out their own equipment such as power tools, or selling goods through websites like eBay or Etsy.

INCOME TAX ALLOWANCES

	2018–19	2019–20
Personal allowance	£11,850	£12,500
Income limit for personal allowance	£100,000	£100,000
Marriage allowance	£1,190	£1,250
Blind person's allowance	£2,390	£2,450
Property allowance	£1,000	£1,000
Trading allowance	£1,000	£1,000

CALCULATING INCOME TAX DUE

Individuals' liability to pay income tax is determined by establishing their level of taxable income for the year. For married couples and civil partners, income must be allocated between the couple by reference to the individual who is beneficially entitled to that income. Where income arises from jointly held assets, it is normally apportioned equally between the partners. If, however, the beneficial interests in jointly held assets are not equal, in most cases couples can make a special declaration to have income apportioned by reference to the actual interests in that income.

To work out an individual's liability for tax, his or her taxable income must be allocated between three different types:

- earned income (excluding income from savings and dividends)
- income from savings
- company dividends from shares and other equity-based investments

After the tax-free personal allowance plus any deductible allowances and reliefs have been taken into account, the amount of tax an individual pays is calculated using different tax rates and a series of tax bands. Each tax band applies to a slice of an individual's income after tax allowances and any reliefs have been taken into account.

SCOTLAND

Since the start of the tax year 2017–18, the Scottish government has been able to set the rates and bands for tax on income from earnings, pensions and most other taxable income in Scotland. The tax raised is paid to the Scottish government.

Income from savings and dividends continues to be taxed at the same rate as in the rest of the UK.

UK INCOME TAX BANDS AND RATES 2018–19

England, Wales & NI	Band*	Rate
Basic rate	£0–37,500	20%
Higher rate	£37,501–150,000	40%
Additional rate	£150,000+	45%
Scotland		
Starter rate	£0–2,049	19%
Basic rate	£2,050–12,444	20%
Intermediate rate	£12,445–30,930	21%
Higher rate	£30,931–150,000	40%
Top rate	£150,000+	46%

The first calculation is applied to earned income, which includes income from employment or self-employment, most pension income and rental income, plus the value of a wide range of employee 'benefits in kind' such as company cars, living accommodation and private medical insurance (for more information on benefits in kind, see later section on Payment of Income Tax). In working out the amount of an individual's net taxable earnings, all expenses incurred 'wholly, exclusively and necessarily' in the performance of his or her employment duties, together with the cost of business travel, may be deducted. Fees and subscriptions to certain professional bodies may also be deducted. Redundancy payments and other sums paid on the termination of an employment are assessable income, but the first £30,000 is normally tax-free provided the payment is not linked with the recipient's retirement or performance.

For UK taxpayers other than Scottish residents, the first £37,500 of taxable income remaining after the tax-free allowance and any deductible allowances and reliefs have been taken into account is taxed at the basic rate of 20 per cent. Taxable income between £37,501 and £150,000 is taxed at the higher rate of 40 per cent. Taxable income above £150,001 is taxed at the additional rate of 45 per cent.

Savings and dividend income is added to an individual's other taxable income and taxed last. This means that tax on such sorts of income is based on an individual's highest income tax band.

SAVINGS INCOME

The second calculation is applied to any income from savings received by an individual. Savings income includes interest paid on bank and building society accounts, interest paid on accounts from providers like credit unions or National Savings and Investments, interest distributions (but not dividend distributions) from authorised unit trusts, open-ended investment companies and investment trusts, interest from peer-to-peer lending, government or company bonds and life annuity payments.

The appropriate rate at which savings income must be taxed is determined by adding income from savings to an individual's other taxable income (excluding dividends). Savings interest may be set against the personal allowance (if that is not used up on income from employment or pension), the starting rate for savings income and the personal savings allowance.

The starting rate of tax for savings income allows an individual to earn up to £5,000 of interest tax-free in 2019–20, but this amount is reduced by £1 for every £1 of their non-savings income above the personal allowance threshold. For example, a person earning £16,000 from their employment:

- their personal allowance of £12,500 is set against their income, leaving £3,500 taxable
- this taxable amount reduces their starting rate for savings, but they can still receive up to £1,500 (£5,000 less £3,500) of tax-free interest on their savings

In addition, the personal savings allowance (PSA) allows a basic rate taxpayer to earn their first £1,000 of savings income tax-free. A higher rate taxpayer may earn their first £500 of savings income tax-free. Additional rate taxpayers do not get a PSA. Interest from ISAs (see Tax-Free Savings) do not count towards this limit.

It is an individual's responsibility to inform HMRC if they earn savings income above the PSA on which tax is payable; any tax owed will normally be collected via the individual's tax code.

Tax on interest over the allowance is paid at the individual's usual rate of income tax, that is for a taxpayer not resident in Scotland 20 per cent for basic rate taxpayers, 40 per cent for higher rate taxpayers and 45 per cent for additional rate taxpayers. If savings income falls on both sides of a tax band, the relevant amounts are taxed at the rates for each tax band.

DIVIDEND INCOME

The third and final income tax calculation is on UK dividends, which means income from shares in UK companies and other share-based investments.

All taxpayers now have a £2,000 tax-free dividend allowance. This means that individuals do not have to pay tax on the first £2,000 of their dividend income, no matter what non-dividend income they have. The allowance is available to anyone who has dividend income.

Dividends received that exceed the £2,000 allowance are treated as the top band of income. This means that if an individual's divided income takes them from one income tax band into the next, they will then pay the higher dividend rate on that portion of income.

TAX RATES ON DIVIDENDS OVER £2,000

Band	2019–20
Basic rate	7.5%
Higher rate	32.5%
Additional rate	38.1%

If there is significant change to an individual's savings or other income, whatever his or her current tax bracket, it is the individual's responsibility to contact HMRC immediately, even if he or she does not normally complete a tax return. This enables HMRC to work out whether more tax should be paid, or if a refund is due.

TAX-FREE SAVINGS

There is a small selection of savings and investment products that are tax-free. This means that there is no tax to pay on any income generated in the form of interest or dividends, nor on any increase in the value of the capital invested. Their tax-efficient status has been granted by the government in order to give people an incentive to save more. For this reason there are usually limits and restrictions on the amount of money an individual may invest in such savings and investments.

Individual savings accounts (ISAs) are the best known among tax-efficient savings and investments. There are four types: cash ISAs, stocks and shares ISAs, innovative finance ISAs (earning interest and capital gains free of tax on loans made via peer-to-peer lending platforms) and lifetime ISAs. Money may be invested in one of each type of ISA each tax year, up to an overall annual subscription limit, which is £20,000 in 2019–20. This may be paid into one ISA or split between some or all of the other types, although no more than £4,000 may be paid into a lifetime ISA in one tax year.

To be eligible to invest in ISAs and receive all profits free of tax, individuals must be:

- aged 16 or over to hold a cash ISA
- aged 18 or over for a stocks and shares or innovative finance ISA
- aged 18 or over but under 40 for a lifetime ISA
- resident in the UK or, if not resident in the UK, a Crown servant or their spouse or civil partner

An ISA must be in an individual's name and cannot be held jointly with another person, but spouses and civil partners may inherit their partner's ISA allowance after death.

The lifetime ISA introduced in April 2017 may be opened by UK residents between the ages of 18 and 40, and allows individuals to save up to £4,000 a year between the ages of 18 and 50. Savings put into the account before their 50th birthday will qualify for a government bonus of 25 per cent, up to £1,000 a year. An individual may use their savings and bonus towards the purchase of a first-time home worth up to £450,000. Alternatively, they may choose to keep the account as retirement savings until their 60th birthday, after which date they can withdraw all the money tax-free.

There are also long-term, tax-free savings accounts for children called Junior ISAs. The investment limit for these in 2019–20 is £4,368 per child. Parents or guardians with parental responsibility can open Junior ISAs for children aged under 18 who live in the UK. However, while parents can open and manage Junior ISAs for their children, the invested money belongs to the child, who can take control of their account when they are 16 and withdraw the money when they are 18. Children aged 16 and 17 can open their own Junior ISA as well as an adult cash ISA. Junior ISAs automatically turn into an adult ISA when the child turns 18.

The Help to Buy ISA is one of a number of government measures to help individuals save towards buying their first home. Aspiring first-time buyers aged 16 or over who open a Help to Buy ISA before 30 November 2019 may continue to save up to £200 a month and the government boosts their savings by 25 per cent, up to a maximum of £3,000 per person. If, therefore, an individual saves £12,000, the government bonus boosts their total savings to £15,000. The minimum government bonus is £400, meaning that the individual must save at least £1,600 to qualify for the scheme. There is no monthly minimum investment.

Savings held in a Help to Buy ISA can be accessed at any time, but the government payment is only added if and when the savings are used as a deposit on a first and only home in the UK. The bonus is available on home purchases of up to £450,000 in London and up to £250,000 outside London. Qualifying properties must be purchased with a mortgage and must be lived in by the purchaser and not rented out.

Those who hold an account may continue saving into their account, but must claim their bonus by 1 December 2030.

Further details about ISAs are available via the HMRC's savings helpline (T 0300-200 3300).

DEDUCTIBLE ALLOWANCES AND RELIEF

Income taxpayers may be entitled to certain tax-deductible allowances and reliefs as well as their personal allowances. Examples include the married couple's allowance and maintenance payments relief, see below. Unlike the tax-free allowances, these are not amounts of income that an individual can receive tax-free but amounts by which their tax bill can be reduced.

MARRIED COUPLE'S ALLOWANCE

A married couple's allowance (MCA) is available to taxpayers who are married or are in a civil partnership where at least one partner was born before 6 April 1935 and they usually live together. Eligible couples can start to claim the MCA from the year of marriage or civil partnership registration.

The MCA is restricted to give relief at a fixed rate of 10 per cent, which means that – unlike the personal allowance – it is not income that can be received without paying tax. Instead, it reduces an individual's tax bill by up to a fixed amount of 10 per cent of the amount of the allowance to which they are entitled.

In 2019–20, the maximum MCA is £8,915 and is therefore worth £891.50 off a couple's tax bill. In 2019–20 this maximum is reduced by £1 for every £2 the highest earner's income exceeds £29,600, to a minimum MCA of £3,450. The minimum always applies, regardless of the level of the highest earner's income.

For marriages before 5 December 2005, the allowance is based on the husband's income; for marriages and civil partnerships after that date, the allowance is based on the income of the highest earner. A couple can decide to have the minimum amount of the allowance split equally between them, or transfer the whole of the minimum MCA from one to the other. If an individual does not have enough income to use all of his or her share of the MCA, the unused part of it can be transferred to his or her spouse or civil partner. A couple must inform HMRC of their decision before the start of the new tax year in which they want the decision to take effect.

MAINTENANCE PAYMENTS RELIEF

An allowance is available to reduce an individual's tax bill for maintenance payments he or she makes to his or her ex-spouse or former civil partner in certain circumstances. To be eligible:
* one or other partner must have been born before 6 April 1935
* the couple must be legally separated or divorced
* the maintenance payments being made must be under a court order
* the payments must be for the maintenance of an ex-spouse or former civil partner (provided he or she is not now remarried or in a new civil partnership) or for children who are under 21.

For the tax year 2019–20, this allowance can reduce an individual's tax bill by:
* 10 per cent of £3,260 (maximum £326) – this applies where an individual makes maintenance payments of £3,260 or more a year
* 10 per cent of the amount the individual has actually paid – this applies where an individual makes maintenance payments of less than £3,260 a year

An individual cannot claim a tax reduction for any voluntary payments he or she makes for a child, ex-spouse or former civil partner. To claim maintenance payments relief, individuals should call the HMRC helpline (T 0300-200 3300).

TAX RELIEF FOR LANDLORDS

Up to April 2017 individual landlords were able to deduct all their costs, including mortgage interest, from their profits before they paid tax. Wealthier landlords received tax relief at 40 per cent and 45 per cent.

This calculation has been changing for properties other than furnished holiday lettings. From April 2020, tax relief on financing costs will only be at the basic rate. Property profits (excluding interest costs) and other income will be assessed, and then amount of tax due will be reduced by the amount of the interest multiplied by the basic rate of income tax. This change only applies to landlords who are individuals, including where they operate through a partnership. It does not apply to companies who rent out property. See W www.gov.uk/government/news/changes-to-tax-relief-for-residential-landlords.

CHARITABLE DONATIONS

A number of charitable donations qualify for tax relief. Individuals can increase the value of regular or one-off charitable gifts of money, however small, by using the Gift Aid scheme that allows charities or community amateur sports clubs (CASCs) to reclaim 20 per cent basic rate tax relief on donations they receive. If a taxpayer gives £10 using Gift Aid, for example, the donation is worth £12.50 to the charity or CASC.

Individuals who pay 40 per cent higher rate income tax can claim back the difference between the 40 per cent and the 20 per cent basic rate of income tax on the total (gross) value of their donations. For example, a 40 per cent tax payer donates £100; the total value of this donation to the charity or CASC is £125, of which the individual can claim back 20 per cent (£25) for themselves. Similarly, those who pay 45 per cent additional rate income tax can claim back the difference between the 45 per cent and the 20 per cent basic rate on the total (gross) value of their donations. On a £100 donation, this means they can claim back £31.25. Scottish taxpayers who pay tax at rates higher than the basic 20 per cent rate can claim extra tax relief.

In order to make a Gift Aid donation, individuals need to make a Gift Aid declaration. The charity or CASC will normally ask an individual to complete a simple form. One form can cover every gift made to the same charity or CASC for whatever period chosen, including both gifts made in the past and in the future. Charities are able to claim a Gift Aid-type tax refund on small donations in various circumstances, see W www.gov.uk/claim-gift-aid/small-donations-scheme.

Individuals can use Gift Aid provided the amount of income tax and/or capital gains tax they have paid in the tax year in which their donations are made is at least equal to the amount of basic rate tax the charity or CASC is reclaiming on their gifts. It is the responsibility of the individual to make sure this is the case. If an individual makes Gift Aid donations and has not paid sufficient tax, they may have to pay the shortfall to HMRC. The Gift Aid scheme is not available for non-taxpayers.

Individuals who complete a tax return and are due a tax refund can ask HMRC to treat all or part of it as a Gift Aid donation.

For employees or those in receipt of an occupational pension, a tax-efficient way of making regular donations to charities is to use the payroll giving scheme. It allows the donations to be paid from a salary or pension before income tax is deducted. This effectively reduces the cost of giving for donors, which may allow them to give more.

For example, it costs a basic rate taxpayer only £8 in take-home pay to give £10 to charity from their pre-tax pay. Where a donor pays 40 per cent higher rate tax, that same £10 donation costs the taxpayer £6, and for donors who pay the additional 45 per cent rate tax, it costs £5.50.

Anyone who pays tax through the pay as you earn (PAYE) system (see Payment of Income Tax) can give to any charity of their choosing in this way, providing their employer or pension provider offers the payroll giving scheme. There is no limit to the amount individuals can donate.

Details of tax-efficient charitable giving methods can be found at W www.gov.uk/donating-to-charity.

TAX RELIEF ON PENSION CONTRIBUTIONS

Pensions are long-term investments designed to help ensure that people have enough income in retirement. The government encourages individuals to save towards a pension by offering tax relief on their contributions. Tax relief reduces an individual's tax bill or increases their pension fund.

The way tax relief is given on pension contributions depends on whether an individual pays into a company, public service or personal pension scheme.

For employees who pay into a company or public service pension scheme, most employers take the pension contributions from the employee's pay before deducting tax, which means that the individual – whether they pay income tax at the basic or higher rate – gets full tax relief straight away. Some employers, however, use the same method of paying pension contributions as that used by personal pension scheme payers described below.

Individuals who pay into a personal pension scheme normally make contributions from their net salary; that is, after tax has been deducted. For each pound that individuals contribute to their pension from net salary, the pension provider claims tax back from the government at the basic rate of 20 per cent and reinvests it on behalf of the individual into the scheme. In practice this means that for every £80 an individual pays into their pension, they receive £100 in their pension fund.

Subject to certain income related limits (*see* below) higher rate taxpayers currently get 40 per cent tax relief on money they put into a pension. On contributions made from net salary, the first 20 per cent is claimed back from HMRC by the pension scheme in the same way as for a lower rate taxpayer. It is then up to individuals to claim back the other 20 per cent from HMRC. In a similar fashion, individuals subject to the 45 per cent additional rate of income tax can get 45 per cent tax relief on their pension contributions.

Non-taxpayers can still pay into a personal pension scheme and benefit from 20 per cent basic rate relief on the first £2,880 a year they contribute. In practice this means that the government tops up their £2,880 contribution to make it £3,600, which is the current universal pension allowance. Such pension contributions may be made on behalf of a non-taxpayer by another individual. An individual may, for example, contribute to a pension on behalf of a husband, wife, civil partner, child or grandchild. Tax relief will be added to their contribution at the basic rate, again on up to £2,880 a year benefiting the recipient, but their own tax bill will not be affected.

In any one tax year, individuals can get tax relief on pension contributions made into any number and type of registered pension schemes of up to 100 per cent of their annual earnings, irrespective of age, up to a maximum 'annual allowance'. For the tax year 2019–20 the annual allowance for most individuals is £40,000. This £40,000 annual allowance is reduced by £1 for every £2 of income between £150,000 and £210,000, so that those earning £210,000 and over have a £10,000 annual allowance.

Everyone also has a 'lifetime allowance' which defines the total amount a taxpayer can save in their pension fund and still get tax relief at their highest rate of income tax on all their contributions. The lifetime allowance is £1.055m in 2019–20, increased from £1.03m in 2018–19.

For information on pensions and tax relief visit W www.gov.uk/browse/working/workplace-personal-pensions. Another useful source of information and advice is the Pensions Advisory Service (TPAS), an independent voluntary organisation grant-aided by the government, at W www.pensionsadvisoryservice.org.uk; or the pensions helpline is on T 0300-123 1047.

PAYMENT OF INCOME TAX

Employees have their income tax deducted from their wages throughout the year by their employer, who sends it on to HMRC. Those in receipt of a company pension have their tax deducted in the same way by their pension provider. This system of collecting income tax is known as 'pay as you earn' (PAYE).

BENEFITS IN KIND

The PAYE system is also used to collect tax on certain employee benefits or 'benefits in kind' that employees or directors receive from their employer as part of their remuneration package. These include company cars, living accommodation, private medical insurance paid for by the employer or cheap or free loans from the employer. Some of these benefits are tax-free, including employer-paid contributions into an employee's pension fund, cheap or free canteen meals, works buses, in-house sports facilities, reasonable relocation expenses, provision of a mobile phone and workplace nursery places provided for the children of employees. Tax is paid on the 'taxable value' of any taxable benefit.

Employers submit returns for individual employees to HMRC on form P11D, with details of any benefits they have been given. Employees should get a copy of this form by 6 July following the end of the tax year and must enter the value of the benefits they have received on their tax return for the relevant year, even if tax has already been paid on them under PAYE. Benefits in kind may be taxed under PAYE by being offset against personal tax allowances in an individual's PAYE code. Otherwise tax will be collected after the end of the tax year by the issue of an assessment on the value of the benefits.

SELF ASSESSMENT

Individuals who are not on PAYE, notably the self-employed, need to complete a self assessment tax return each year online (W www.gov.uk/log-in-file-self-assessment-tax-return), and pay any income tax owed in twice-yearly instalments. Some individuals with more complex tax affairs, such as those who earn money from rents or investments above a certain level, may also need to make a self assessment return even if they are on PAYE. HMRC uses the figures supplied on the tax return to work out the individual's tax bill, or they can choose to work it out themselves. It is called self assessment because individuals are responsible for making sure the details they provide are correct.

Some people still prefer to file a paper tax return. The forms can be downloaded from W www.gov.uk/government/publications/self-assessment-tax-return-sa100, but it should be noted that the deadline for returning a paper form is earlier than the online version.

Central to the self assessment system is the requirement for individuals to register online if they should complete a self assessment return. Individuals have six months from when the tax year ends to report any new income. The registration process is online (W www.gov.uk/log-in-file-self-assessment-tax-return), but it is important to allow enough time for the process – HMRC recommend allowing up to 20 working days extra for a first online return.

TAX RETURN FILING AND PAYMENT DEADLINES

There are also key deadlines for filing (sending in) completed tax returns and paying the tax due. Failure to do so can incur penalties, interest charges and surcharges.

KEY FILING DATES FOR SELF ASSESSMENT RETURNS

Date	Why the date is important
31 Oct*	Deadline for filing paper returns* for tax year ending the previous 5 April
30 Dec	Deadline for online filing where the amount owed for tax year ending the previous 5 April is less than £3,000 and the taxpayer wants HMRC to collect any tax due through their PAYE tax code
31 Jan†	Deadline for online filing of returns for tax year ending the previous 5 April

* Or three months from the date the return was requested if this was after 31 July

† Or three months from the date the return was requested if this was after 31 October

KEY SELF ASSESSMENT PAYMENT DATES

Date   *What payment is due?*

31 Jan   Deadline for paying the balance of any tax owed – the 'balancing payment' – for the tax year ending the previous 5 April. It is also the date by which a taxpayer must make any first 'payment on account' (advance payment) for the current tax year. For example, on 31 January 2020 a taxpayer may have to pay both the balancing payment for the year 2018–19 and the first payment on account for 2019–20.

31 Jul   Deadline for making a second payment on account for the current tax year

LATE FILING AND PAYMENT PENALTIES

Late filing of tax returns incurs an automatic £100 penalty, although individuals may appeal against the penalty if they have a reasonable excuse.

- Over three months late – £10 each day, up to a maximum of £900, in addition to the penalty above
- Over six months late – an additional £300 or 5 per cent of the tax due, whichever is the higher, in addition to the penalty above
- Over 12 months late – a further £300 or 5 per cent of the tax due, whichever is the higher. In serious cases HMRC reserve the right to ask for 100 per cent of the tax due instead. In both instances this is in addition to the penalty above

Late payment of tax owing incurs interest at 3.25 per cent.

Interest is due on all outstanding amounts, including any unpaid penalties, until payment is received in full. Individuals may calculate the penalties they owe for late self assessment tax returns and payments online (W www.gov.uk/estimate-self-assessment-penalties).

TAX CREDITS

Child tax credit, working tax credit and the new universal credit are paid to qualifying individuals. Although the titles of these credits incorporate the word 'tax', they do not affect the amount of income tax payable or repayable. They are forms of social security benefits. *See* Social Welfare.

CAPITAL GAINS TAX

Capital gains tax (CGT) is a tax on the gain or profit that an individual makes when they sell, give away or otherwise dispose of certain assets, for example shares, land or buildings. An individual potentially has to pay CGT on gains they make from any disposal of taxable assets during a tax year. There is a tax-free allowance and some additional reliefs that may reduce an individual's CGT bill. The following information relates to the tax year 2019–20 ending on 5 April 2020.

CGT is paid by individuals who are either resident or ordinarily resident in the UK for the tax year, executors or administrators – 'personal representatives' – responsible for a deceased person's financial affairs and trustees of a settlement. Non-residents are not usually liable to CGT unless they carry on a business in the UK through a branch or agency. However, from April 2015, the government introduced a CGT charge on gains made by non-residents disposing of UK residential property. Special CGT rules apply to individuals who used to live and work in the UK but have since left the country.

CAPITAL GAINS CHARGEABLE TO CGT

Typically, individuals have made a gain if they sell an asset for more than they paid for it. It is the gain that is taxed, not the

amount the individual receives for the asset. For example, a man buys shares for £1,000 and later sells them for £3,000. He has made a gain of £2,000 (£3,000 less £1,000). If someone gives an asset away, the gain will be based on the difference between what the asset was worth when originally acquired and its worth at the time of disposal. The same is true when an asset is sold for less than its full worth in order to give away part of the value. For example, a woman buys a property for £120,000 and three years later, when the property's market value has risen to £180,000, she gives it to her son. The son may pay nothing for the property, or pay less than its true worth, for example £100,000. Either way, she has made a gain of £60,000 (£180,000 less £120,000).

If an individual disposes of an asset he or she received as a gift, the gain is worked out according to the market value of the asset when it was received. For example, a man gives his sister a painting worth £8,000. She pays nothing for it. Later she sells the painting for £10,000. For CGT purposes, she is treated as making a gain of £2,000 (£10,000 less £8,000). If an individual inherits an asset, the estate of the person who died does not pay CGT at the time. If the inheritor later disposes of the asset, the gain is worked out by looking at the market value at the time of the death (the probate value). For example, a woman acquires some shares for £5,000 and leaves them to her niece when she dies. No CGT is payable at the time of death when the shares are worth £8,000. Later the niece sells the shares for £10,000. She has made a gain of £2,000 (£10,000 less £8,000).

Individuals may also have to pay CGT if they dispose of part of an asset or exchange one asset for another. Similarly, CGT may be payable if an individual receives a capital sum of money from an asset without disposing of it, for example where he or she receives compensation when an asset is damaged.

Assets that may lead to a CGT charge when they are disposed of include:

- shares in a company that are not held in an ISA or PEP
- units in a unit trust
- land and buildings (though not normally an individual's main home – *see* 'Disposal of a home' section for details)
- personal possessions, including jewellery, paintings, antiques and other personal effects, individually worth £6,000 or more
- business assets

EXEMPT GAINS

Certain kinds of assets do not give rise to a chargeable gain when they are disposed of. Assets exempt from CGT include:

- a car
- an individual's main home, if certain conditions are met
- tax-free investments such as assets held in an ISA or PEP
- UK government gilts or 'bonds' (including premium bonds)
- personal belongings, including jewellery, paintings and antiques, individually worth £6,000 or less
- betting, lottery or pools winnings

DISPOSAL OF A HOME: PRIVATE RESIDENCE RELIEF

When an individual sells their own home they automatically qualify for private residence relief, which means they do not have to pay any CGT provided that:

- the property has been their only home or main residence since they bought it, and
- they have used it as their home and for no other purpose

Even if an individual has not lived in the property for all of the time that they owned it, they may still be entitled to the full relief.

Under the relief rules, the final 18 months of ownership are always treated as if the individual lived in the property even if they did not. This means that if an individual moves out of one home and into a new one, they have up to 18 months in which to sell their former home without incurring any CGT on the sale proceeds.

Full relief is granted to individuals when they sell their home if they could not live in it for periods because they were working abroad. Full relief is also granted if an individual is prevented from living in the home for periods totalling a maximum of four years because their job required them to work elsewhere in the UK. In both cases, however, for the property to qualify for full relief, the general rule is that it must have been the individual's only or main home both before and after they worked away.

Individuals can also get full relief when they sell their home if they have lived away from it for reasons other than working away, provided all of the following apply:

- they were not living away from the home for more than three years in total during the time they owned the property
- they were not entitled to private residence relief on any other property during that time
- the property was their only or main home both before and after they lived elsewhere

There are instances when individuals may not get the full amount of private residence relief when they sell their home. These include if:

- the grounds, including all buildings, are larger than 5,000 square metres
- any part of the home has been used exclusively for business purposes
- all or part of the home has been let out (or more than one lodger has been taken in at a time). The owner may, however, be entitled to another form of CGT relief – letting relief – instead
- the main reason the property was bought was to make a profit from a quick sale

If an individual lives in – not just owns – more than one property, they can 'nominate' which should be treated as their main home for private residence relief purposes. Married couples or those in a civil partnership must make such a nomination jointly as they are only entitled to private residence relief on one house between them.

There is a calculator to help individuals work out how much private residence relief they may be entitled to when selling their main residence at W www.gov.uk/tax-relief-selling-home.

OTHER TRANSACTIONS NOT CHARGEABLE TO CGT

Certain other kinds of disposal similarly do not give rise to a chargeable gain. For example, individuals who are married or in a civil partnership and live together may sell or give assets to their spouse or civil partner without having to pay CGT. Individuals may not, however, give or sell assets cheaply to their children without having to consider CGT. There is no CGT to pay on assets given to a registered charity.

CALCULATING CGT

CGT is worked out for each tax year and is charged on the total of an individual's taxable gains after taking into account certain costs and reliefs that can reduce or defer chargeable gains, allowable losses made on assets to which CGT normally applies and an annual exempt (tax-free) amount that applies to every individual. If the total of an individual's net gains in a tax year is less than the annual exempt amount (AEA), the individual will not have to pay CGT. For the tax year 2019–20 the AEA is £12,000. If an individual's net gains are more than the AEA, they pay CGT on the excess. Should any part of the exemption remain unused, this cannot be carried forward to a future year.

There are certain reliefs available that may eliminate, reduce or defer CGT. Some reliefs are available to many people while others are available only in special circumstances. Some reliefs are given automatically while others are given only if they are claimed. Some of the costs of buying, selling and improving assets may be deducted from total gains when working out an individual's chargeable gain.

RATES OF TAX

The net gains remaining, if any, calculated after subtracting the AEA, deducting costs and taking into account all CGT reliefs, incur liability to capital gains tax. Individuals pay CGT at a rate of 10 per cent on gains up to the unused amount of the basic rate income tax band (if any) and at 20 per cent on gains above that amount. Rates for individuals for gains on residential property not eligible for private residence relief (see above) are charged at a rate of 18 per cent up to any unused amount of the basic rate income tax band and at 28 per cent on gains above that amount. The CGT rate charged to trustees and personal representatives is 28 per cent on residential property and 20 per cent on other chargeable assets.

An individual can report any CGT they need to pay (see below):

- straight away using the 'real time' Capital Gains Tax service
  W www.gov.uk/capital-gains-tax/report-and-pay-capital-gains-tax*
- annually in a self assessment tax return

* It should be noted that if the 'real time' service is used but the individual needs to submit a tax return for another reason, then their gains have to be reported again through self assessment

VALUATION OF ASSETS

The disposal proceeds (the amount received as consideration for the disposal of an asset) are the sum used to establish the gain or loss once certain allowable costs have been deducted. In most cases this is straightforward because the disposal proceeds are the amount actually received for disposing of the asset. This may include cash payable now or in the future and the value of any asset received in exchange for the asset disposed of. However, in certain circumstances, the disposal proceeds may not accurately reflect the value of the asset and the individual may be treated as disposing of an asset for an amount other than the actual amount (if any) that they received. This applies, in particular, where an asset is transferred as a gift or sold for a price known to be below market value. Disposal proceeds in such transactions are deemed to be equal to the market value of the asset at the time it was disposed of rather than the actual amount (if any) received for it.

Market value represents the price that an asset might reasonably be expected to fetch upon sale in the open market. In the case of unquoted shares or securities, it is assumed that the hypothetical purchaser in the open market would have available all the information that a prudent prospective purchaser of shares or securities might reasonably require if that person were proposing to purchase them from a willing vendor by private treaty and at arm's length. The market value of unquoted shares or securities will often be established following negotiations with the specialist HMRC Shares and Assets Valuation department. The valuation of land and interests in land in the UK is dealt with by the Valuation Office Agency. Special rules apply to determine the market value of shares quoted on the London Stock Exchange.

ALLOWABLE COSTS

When working out a chargeable gain, once the actual or notional disposal proceeds have been determined, certain allowable costs may be deducted. There is a general rule that no costs that could be taken into account when working out income or losses for income tax purposes may be deducted. Subject to this, allowable costs are:

- acquisition costs – the actual amount spent on acquiring the asset or, in certain circumstances, the equivalent market value

- incidental costs of acquiring the asset, such as fees paid for professional advice, valuation costs, stamp duty and advertising costs to find a seller
- enhancement costs – incurred for the purpose of enhancing the value of the asset (not including normal maintenance and repair costs)
- expenditure on defending or establishing a person's rights over the asset
- incidental costs of disposing of the asset, such as fees paid for professional advice, valuation costs, stamp duty and advertising costs to find a buyer

If an individual disposes of part of his or her interest in an asset, or part of a holding of shares of the same class in the same company, or part of a holding of units in the same unit trust, he or she can deduct the relevant part of the allowable costs of the asset or holding when working out the chargeable gain.

ENTREPRENEURS' RELIEF

Entrepreneurs' relief allows individuals in business and some trustees to claim relief on the first £10m of gains made on the disposal of any of the following:

- all or part of a business
- the assets of a business after it has ceased
- certain shares in a company.

The relief is available to taxpayers as individuals if they are in business, for example as a sole trader or as a partner in a trading business, or if they hold shares in their own personal trading company. This relief is not available for companies.

Depending on the type of disposal, certain qualifying conditions need to be met throughout a qualifying one-year period. For example, if an individual is selling all or part of their business, they must have owned the business during a one-year period that ends on the date of the disposal.

Where all gains qualify for entrepreneurs' relief, CGT is charged at 10 per cent. An individual can make claims for this relief on more than one occasion as long as the lifetime total of all their claims does not exceed £10m of gains qualifying for relief.

BUSINESS ASSET ROLLOVER RELIEF

When certain types of business asset are sold or disposed of and the proceeds are reinvested in new qualifying trading assets, business asset rollover relief makes it possible to 'rollover' or postpone the payment of any CGT that would normally be due. The gain is deducted from the base cost of the new asset and only becomes chargeable to CGT on the eventual disposal of that replacement asset, unless a further rollover situation then develops. Full relief is available if all the proceeds from the original asset are reinvested in the qualifying replacement asset.

For example, a trader sells a freehold office for £75,000 and makes a gain of £30,000. All of the proceeds are reinvested in a new freehold business premises costing £90,000. The trader can postpone the whole of the £30,000 gain made on the sale of the old office, as all of the proceeds have been reinvested. When the trader eventually sells the new business premises and the CGT bill becomes payable, the cost of the new premises will be treated as £60,000 (£90,000 less the £30,000 gain).

If only part of the proceeds from the disposal of an old asset is reinvested in a new one, different rules may apply, but it may still be possible to postpone paying tax on part of the gain until the eventual disposal of the new asset.

Relief is only available if the acquisition of the new asset takes place within a period between 12 months before and 36 months after the disposal of the old asset. However, HMRC may extend this time limit at their discretion where there is a clear intention to acquire a replacement asset. The most common types of business asset that qualify for rollover relief are land, buildings occupied and used for the purposes of trade, and fixed plant and machinery. Assets used for the commercial letting of furnished holiday accommodation qualify if certain conditions are satisfied.

GIFT HOLD-OVER RELIEF

The gift of an asset is treated as a disposal made for a consideration equal to market value, with a corresponding acquisition by the transferee at an identical value. In the case of gifts of business assets made by individuals and a limited range of trustees, a form of hold-over relief may be available. This relief, which must be claimed, in effect enables liability for CGT to be deferred and passed to the person to whom the gift is made. Relief is limited to the transfer of certain assets, including the following:

- gifts of assets used for the purposes of a business carried on by the donor or his or her personal company
- gifts of shares in trading companies that are not listed on a stock exchange
- gifts of shares or securities in the donor's personal trading company
- gifts of agricultural land and buildings that would qualify for inheritance tax agricultural property relief
- gifts that are chargeable transfers for inheritance tax purposes
- certain types of gifts that are specifically exempt from inheritance tax

Hold-over relief is automatically due on certain sorts of gifts, including gifts to charities and community amateur sports clubs, and gifts of works of art where certain undertakings have been given. There are certain rules to prevent gifts hold-over relief being used for tax avoidance purposes. For example, restrictions may apply where an individual gifts assets to trustees administering a trust in which the individual retains an interest, or the assets transferred comprise a dwelling-house. Subject to these exceptions, the effect of a valid claim for hold-over relief is similar to a claim for rollover relief on the disposal of business assets.

OTHER CGT RELIEFS

There are certain other CGT reliefs available on the disposal of property, shares and business assets. For detailed information on all CGT reliefs and for more general guidance on CGT, visit W www.gov.uk/personal-tax/capital-gains-tax.

REPORTING AND PAYING CGT

Individuals are responsible for telling HMRC about capital gains on which they have to pay tax, either:

- on their self assessment tax return by filling in the capital gains supplementary pages (the return explains how to obtain these pages if needed), or
- by visiting W www.gov.uk/capital-gains-tax/report-and-pay-capital-gains-tax, which explains what information to gather before following the link on that page to the 'real time' capital gains tax service

There is a time limit for claiming capital losses. The deadline is four years from 31 January after the end of the tax year in which the loss was made.

INHERITANCE TAX

Inheritance tax (IHT) is a tax on the value of a person's estate on death and on certain gifts made by an individual during his or her lifetime, usually payable within six months of death. Broadly speaking, a person's estate is everything he or she owned at the time of death, including property, possessions, money and investments, less his or her debts. Not everyone pays IHT. It only applies if the taxable value of an estate is above the current IHT threshold. If an estate, including any assets held in trust and gifts made within seven years of death, is less than the threshold (in the nil-rate band), no IHT will be due.

A claim can be made to transfer any unused IHT nil-rate band on a person's death to the estate of their surviving spouse or civil partner. This applies where the IHT nil-rate band of the first deceased spouse or civil partner was not fully used in calculating the IHT liability of their estate. When the surviving spouse or civil partner dies, the unused amount may be added to their own nil-rate band (*see* below for details).

IHT used to be something only very wealthy individuals needed to consider. This is no longer the case. The fact that the IHT threshold has not kept pace with house price inflation in recent years means that the estates of some 'ordinary' taxpayers are now liable for IHT purely because of the value of their home. However, there are a number of ways that individuals – while still alive – can legally reduce the IHT bill that will apply to their estates on death. Several valuable IHT exemptions are available (explained further below) which allow individuals to pass on assets during their lifetime or in their will without any IHT being due. Detailed information on IHT is available at W www.gov.uk/inheritance-tax. Further help is also available from the probate and inheritance tax helpline (T 0300-123 1072).

DOMICILE

Liability to IHT depends on an individual's domicile at the time of any gift or on death. Domicile is a complex legal concept and what follows explains some of the main issues. An individual is domiciled in the country where he or she has a permanent home. Domicile is different from nationality or residence, and an individual can only have one domicile at any given time.

A 'domicile of origin' is normally acquired from the individual's father on birth, so this may not be the country in which the individual is born. For example, a child born in Germany to a father who is working there, but whose permanent home is in the UK, will have the UK as his or her domicile of origin. Until a person legally changes his or her domicile, it will be the same as that of the person on whom they are legally dependent.

Individuals can legally acquire a new domicile – a 'domicile of choice' – from the age of 16 by leaving the current country of domicile, settling in another country and providing strong evidence of intention to live there permanently or indefinitely. Women who were married before 1974 acquired their husband's domicile and still retain it until they legally acquire a new domicile.

For IHT purposes, there is a concept of 'deemed domicile'. This means that even if a person is not domiciled in the UK under general law, he or she is treated as domiciled in the UK at the time of a transfer (ie at the time of a lifetime gift or on death) if he or she was:
• domiciled in the UK at any time in the three years immediately before the transfer, or
• 'resident' in the UK in at least 17 of the 20 income tax years of assessment ending with the year in which a transfer is made

Where a person is domiciled, or treated as domiciled, in the UK at the time of a gift or on death, the location of assets is immaterial and full liability to IHT arises. A non-UK domiciled individual is also liable to IHT, but only on chargeable property in the UK.

The assets of spouses and registered civil partners are not merged for IHT purposes, except that the IHT value of assets owned by one spouse or civil partner may be affected if the other also owns similar assets (eg shares in the same company or a share in their jointly owned house). Each spouse or partner is treated as a separate individual entitled to receive the benefit of his or her exemptions, reliefs and rates of tax.

IHT EXEMPTIONS

There are some important exemptions that allow individuals to legally pass assets on to others, both before and after their death – without being subject to IHT.

Exempt Beneficiaries

Assets can be given away to certain people and organisations without any IHT having to be paid. These gifts, which are exempt whether individuals make them during their lifetime or in their will, include gifts to:
• a spouse or civil partner, even if the couple is legally separated (but not if they are divorced or the civil partnership has been dissolved). Note that gifts to an unmarried partner or a partner with whom the donor has not formed a civil partnership are not exempt
• a 'qualifying' charity established in the EU or another specified country
• some national institutions, including national museums, universities and the National Trust
• UK political parties

Annual Exemption

The first £3,000 of gifts made each tax year by each individual is exempt from IHT. If this exemption is not used, or not wholly used in any year, the balance may be carried forward to the following year only. A couple, therefore, may give away a total of £6,000 per tax year between them or £12,000 if they have not used their previous year's annual exemptions.

Wedding Gifts/Civil Partnership Ceremony Gifts

Some gifts are exempt from IHT because of the type of gift or reason for making it. Wedding or civil partnership ceremony gifts made to either of the couple are exempt from IHT up to certain amounts:
• gifts by a parent or step-parent, £5,000
• gifts by a grandparent or great-grandparent, £2,500
• gifts by anyone else, £1,000
The gift must be made on or shortly before the date of the wedding or civil partnership ceremony. If the ceremony is called off but the gift is made, this exemption will not apply.

Small Gifts

An individual can make small gifts, up to the value of £250, to any number of people in any one tax year without them being liable for IHT. However, a larger sum such as £500 cannot be given and exemption claimed for the first £250. Note that this exemption cannot be used with any other exemption when giving to the same person. For example, a parent cannot combine a 'small gifts exemption' with a 'wedding/civil partnership ceremony gift exemption' to give a child £5,250 when he or she gets married or forms a civil partnership. Neither may an individual combine a 'small gifts exemption' with the 'annual exemption' to give someone £3,250. Note that it is possible to use the 'annual exemption' with any other exemption, such as the 'wedding/civil partnership ceremony gift exemption'. For example, if a child marries or forms a civil partnership, the parent who has not made any other taxable transfers in the year can give him or her a total IHT-free gift of £8,000 by combining £5,000 under the wedding/civil partnership gift exemption and £3,000 under the annual exemption.

Normal Expenditure

Any gifts made out of an individual's after-tax income (not capital) are exempt from IHT if they are part of their normal expenditure and do not result in a fall in their standard of living. These can include regular payments to someone, such as an allowance or gifts for Christmas or a birthday, and regular premiums paid on a life insurance policy for someone else.

Maintenance Gifts

An individual can make IHT-free maintenance payments to his or her spouse or registered civil partner, ex-spouse or former civil partner, relatives dependent because of old age or infirmity, and children (including adopted children and step-children) who are under 18 or in full-time education.

POTENTIALLY EXEMPT TRANSFERS

If an individual makes a gift to either another individual or a certain type of trust and it is not covered by one of the above exemptions, it is known as a 'potentially exempt transfer' (PET). A PET is only free of IHT on two strict conditions:
* the gift must be made at least seven years before the donor's death; if the donor does not survive seven years after making the gift, it will be liable for IHT
* the gift must be made as a true gift with no strings attached (technically known as a 'gift with reservation of benefit'). This means that the donor must give up all rights to the gift and stop benefiting from it in any way

If a gift is made and the donor does retain some benefit from it, then it will still count as part of the donor's estate no matter how long he or she lives after making it. For example, a father could make a lifetime gift of his home to his child, on condition that he continue to live in it. HMRC would not accept this as a true gift unless he paid his child a full commercial rent to do so, because he would be considered to still have a material interest in the gifted home. Its value, therefore, would still be liable for IHT.

In some circumstances a gift with strings attached might give rise to an income tax charge on the donor based on the value of the benefit he or she retains. In this case the donor can choose whether to pay the income tax or have the gift treated as a gift with reservation.

CHARGEABLE TRANSFERS

Any remaining lifetime gifts that are not (potentially or otherwise) exempt transfers are chargeable transfers or 'chargeable gifts', meaning that they incur liability to IHT. Chargeable transfers comprise mainly gifts to or from companies and gifts to particular types of trust. There is an immediate charge to IHT on chargeable gifts, and additional tax may be payable if the donor dies within seven years of making a chargeable gift.

DEATH

Immediately before the time of death an individual is deemed to make a transfer of value. This transfer will comprise the value of assets forming part of the deceased's estate after subtracting most liabilities. Any exempt transfers may be excluded, such as transfers for the benefit of a surviving spouse or civil partner and charities. Death may also trigger three additional liabilities:
* on a PET made within the seven years before death, which loses its potential status and becomes chargeable to IHT
* on the value of gifts made with reservation may incur liability if any benefit was enjoyed within the seven years before the death
* additional tax may become payable for chargeable lifetime transfers made within the seven years before the death

The 'personal representative' (the person nominated to handle the affairs of the deceased person) arranges to value the estate and pay any IHT that is due. One or more personal representatives can be nominated in a person's will, in which case they are known as the 'executors'. If a person dies without leaving a will a court can nominate the personal representative, who is then known as the 'administrator'. Valuing the deceased person's estate is one of the first things a personal representative

needs to do. The representative will not normally be able to take over management of the estate (called 'applying for probate') until all or some of any IHT that is due has been paid.

VALUATIONS

When valuing a deceased person's estate, all assets (property, possessions and money) owned at the time of death and certain assets given away during the seven years before death must be included. The valuation must accurately reflect what those assets would reasonably fetch in the open market at the date of death. The value of all of the assets that the deceased owned should include:
* his or her share of any assets owned jointly with someone else, for example a house owned with a partner
* any assets that are held in a trust, from which the deceased had the right to benefit
* any assets given away, but in which he or she kept an interest (gifts with reservation)
* PETs given away within the last seven years

Most estate assets can be valued quite easily, for example money in bank accounts or stocks and shares. In other instances the help of a professional valuer may be needed. Advice on how to value different assets, including joint or trust assets, is available at W www.gov.uk/valuing-estate-of-someone-who-died.

When valuing an estate, special relief is made available for certain assets. The two main reliefs are agricultural property relief and business relief, outlined below. Once all assets have been valued, the next step is to deduct from the total assets everything that the deceased person owed, such as unpaid bills, outstanding mortgages, other loans and their funeral expenses.

The value of all of the assets, less the deductible debts, is their estate. IHT is only payable on any value above the threshold for the tax year. It is payable at the current rate of 40 per cent. This rate is reduced to 36 per cent where 10 per cent or more of a net estate (after deducting IHT exemptions, reliefs and the nil-rate band) is left to charity.

RELIEF FOR SELECTED ASSETS

Agricultural Property

If an individual owns agricultural property and it is part of a working farm, it is possible to pass on some of this property free of IHT, either during that individual's lifetime or on their death. Agricultural property generally includes land or pasture used in the growing of crops or intensive rearing of animals for food consumption. It can also include farmhouses and farm cottages. The agricultural property can be owner-occupied or let. Relief is only due if the transferor has owned the property and it has been occupied for agricultural purposes for a minimum period.

The chargeable value transferred, either in a lifetime gift or on death, must be determined. This value may then be reduced by a percentage. Depending on the type of property, it will normally qualify for relief of 100 per cent.

Business Relief

Business relief is available on transfers of certain types of business and of business assets if they qualify as relevant business property and the transferor has owned them for a minimum period. The relief can be claimed for transfers made during the person's lifetime or on their death. Where the chargeable value transferred is attributable to relevant business property, the business relief reduces that value by either 50 or 100 per cent, depending on the type of asset. Business relief may be claimed on relevant business property, including property and buildings or assets such as unlisted shares or machinery.

It is a general requirement that the property must have been retained for a period of two years before the transfer or death, and restrictions may be necessary if the property has not been used wholly for business purposes. The same property cannot obtain both business property relief and the relief available for agricultural property.

CALCULATION OF TAX PAYABLE

The calculation of IHT payable adopts the use of a cumulative or 'running' total. Each chargeable lifetime transfer is added to the total if it was made within seven years of the donor's death. To the running total this produces is added the total value of the estate at death. If the total exceeds the inheritance tax threshold (the 'nil-rate band') IHT becomes payable. The rate of tax that is paid is determined by the element that causes the estate to exceed the threshold; gifts use up all or part of the nil-rate band first.

Lifetime Chargeable Transfers

The value transferred by total chargeable transfers during the deceased's lifetime must be added to the seven-year running total to calculate whether any IHT is due. If the nil-rate band is exceeded, tax will be imposed on the excess at the rate of 20 per cent. However, if the donor dies within a period of seven years from the date of the chargeable lifetime transfer, additional tax may be due. This is calculated by applying tax at the full rate of 40 per cent (rather than 20 per cent). The amount of tax is then reduced by applying taper relief, which is a percentage of the full rate of 40 per cent. This percentage is governed by the number of years from the date of the lifetime gift to the date of death, as follows:

TAPER RELIEF

Years between transfer and death	Taper relief %
More than 3 but not more than 4	20%
More than 4 but not more than 5	40%
More than 5 but not more than 6	60%
More than 6 but not more than 7	80%

Should this exercise produce liability greater than that previously paid at the 20 per cent rate on the lifetime transfer, the difference must be paid in additional tax. Where the calculation shows an amount falling below tax paid on the lifetime transfer, no additional liability can arise nor will the shortfall become repayable.

Taper relief is only available if the calculation discloses a liability to IHT. There is no liability if the lifetime transfer falls within the nil-rate band.

Potentially Exempt Transfers

Where a PET loses immunity from liability to IHT because the donor dies within seven years of making the transfer, the value transferred enters into the running total. Any liability to IHT will be calculated by applying the full rate of 40 per cent, reduced by taper relief if applicable. Again, liability to IHT can only arise if the nil-rate band is exceeded.

Death

On death, IHT is due on the value of the deceased's estate plus the running total of gifts made in the seven years before death if that comes to more than the nil-rate band. IHT is then charged at the full rate of 40 per cent on the amount in excess of the nil-rate band.

Settled Property and Trusts

Trusts are special legal arrangements that can be used by individuals to control how their assets are distributed to their beneficiaries and minimise their IHT liability. Complex rules apply to establish IHT liability on 'settled property' which includes property held in trust, and individuals are advised to take expert legal advice when setting up trusts.

RATES OF TAX

There are four rates:

- nil-rate
- lifetime rate of 20 per cent
- full rate of 40 per cent
- reduced rate of 36 per cent applicable to taxable estates where 10 per cent of the net estate has been left to charity (see above)

The basic nil-rate band threshold is £325,000 for 2019–20. In 2015 the government announced that the nil-rate band would remain at this figure until April 2021. Any excess over this level is taxable at the relevant rate.

ADDITIONAL THRESHOLD (RNRB)

The additional threshold (or residence nil-rate band) was introduced from April 2017, applying where a residence the deceased owns and has lived in passes on their death to direct descendants. The additional threshold is £150,000 in 2019–20 and £175,000 in 2020–21. It will increase in line with the consumer prices index (CPI) from 2021–22 onwards. Any unused nil-rate band may be transferred to the surviving spouse or civil partner.

The RNRB will also be available when an individual downsizes or ceases to own a home and other assets of an equivalent value are passed on death to direct descendants. These changes apply for deaths on or after 6 April 2017 where the deceased downsized or disposed of a property after 7 July 2015.

There is a tapered withdrawal of the RNRB for estates with a net value of more than £2m. This will be at a rate of £1 for every £2 over the additional threshold. Guidance on the additional threshold can be found at W www.gov.uk/guidance/inheritance-tax-residence-nil-rate-band.

TRANSFER OF NIL-RATE BAND

Transfers of property between spouses or civil partners are generally exempt from IHT. This means that someone who dies leaving some or all of their property to their spouse or civil partner may not have fully used up their nil-rate band. Any nil-rate band unused on the first death can be used when the surviving spouse or civil partner dies. A transfer of unused nil-rate band from a deceased spouse or civil partner may be made to the estate of their surviving spouse or civil partner.

Where a valid claim to transfer unused nil-rate band is made, the nil-rate band that is available when the surviving spouse or civil partner dies is increased by the proportion of the nil-rate band unused on the first death. For example, if on the first death the chargeable estate is £150,000 and the nil-rate band is £300,000, 50 per cent of the nil-rate band would be unused. If the nil-rate band when the survivor dies is £329,000, then that would be increased by 50 per cent to £493,500. The amount of the nil-rate band that can be transferred does not depend on the value of the first spouse or civil partner's estate. Whatever proportion of the nil-rate band is unused on the first death is available for transfer to the survivor.

The amount of additional nil-rate band that can be accumulated by any one surviving spouse or civil partner is limited to the value of the nil-rate band in force at the time of their death. This may be relevant where a person dies having survived more than one spouse or civil partner.

Where these rules have effect, personal representatives do not have to claim for the unused nil-rate band to be transferred at the time of the first death. Any claims for transfer of unused nil-rate band amounts are made by the personal representatives of the estate of the second spouse or civil partner to die when they make an IHT return.

Guidance on how to transfer the nil-rate band can be found at W www.gov.uk/government/publications/claim-the-residence-nil-rate-band-rnrb-iht435.

PAYMENT OF TAX

IHT is normally due six months after the end of the month in which the death occurs or the chargeable transaction takes place. This is referred to as the 'due date'. Tax on some assets, such as business property, certain shares and securities and land and buildings (including the deceased person's home), can be deferred and paid in equal instalments over ten years, though interest will be charged in most cases. If IHT is due on lifetime gifts and transfers, the person who received the gift or assets (the transferee) is normally liable to pay the IHT, though any IHT already paid at the time of a transfer into a trust or company will be taken into account. If tax owed is not paid by the due date, interest is charged on any unpaid IHT, no matter what caused the delay in payment.

HMRC has developed an online service to support the administration of IHT. This does away with the need to complete paper forms and enables individuals to proceed with their application for probate and submit IHT accounts online:

- if you are dealing with the estate of someone who has died, there is some guidance about the basic processes at W www.gov.uk/valuing-estate-of-someone-who-died and this page also gives links to make the relevant return
- to get a payment reference number, go to W www.gov.uk/paying-inheritance-tax/get-a-reference-number at least three weeks before the payment is due
- forms and worksheets for calculating IHT liabilities are available at W www.gov.uk/government/publications/inheritance-tax-inheritance-tax-account-iht100

CORPORATION TAX

Corporation tax is a tax on a company's profits, including all its income and gains. This tax is payable by UK resident companies and by non-resident companies carrying on a trade in the UK through a permanent establishment. The following comments are confined to companies resident in the UK. The word 'company' is also used to include:

- members' clubs, societies and associations
- trade associations
- housing associations
- groups of individuals carrying on a business but not as a partnership (for example, cooperatives)

A company's taxable income is charged by reference to income or gains arising in its 'accounting period', which is normally 12 months long. In some circumstances accounting periods can be shorter than 12 months, but never longer. The accounting period is normally the period for which a company's accounts are drawn up, but the two periods do not have to coincide.

If a company is liable to pay corporation tax on its profits, several things must be done. HMRC must be informed that the company exists and is liable for tax. A self assessment company tax return plus full accounts and calculation of tax liability must be filed by the statutory filing date, normally 12 months after the end of the accounting period. Companies have to work out their own tax liability and have to pay their tax without prior assessment by HMRC. Records of all company expenditure and income must be kept in order to work out the tax liability correctly. Companies are liable to penalties if they fail to carry out these obligations.

There is a radically simpler way for small self-employed businesses, such as sole traders and partnerships, to calculate their tax. Such businesses with receipts of £150,000 or less are able to work out their income on a cash basis and use simplified expenses rules, rather than having to follow the rules for larger businesses. Limited companies and limited liability partnerships can not use the cash basis. If a small business uses cash basis accounting and the business grows during the tax year, it can stay in the scheme up to a total business turnover of £300,000 a year.

Corporation tax information is available at W www.gov.uk/browse/business/business-tax and companies may file their company tax returns online (W www.gov.uk/file-your-company-accounts-and-tax-return).

RATE OF TAX

The rate of corporation tax is fixed for a financial year starting on 1 April and ending on the following 31 March. If a company's accounting period does not coincide with the financial year, its profits must be apportioned between the financial years and the tax rates for each financial year applied to those profits. The corporation tax liability is the total tax for both financial years.

The rate of corporation tax has been 19 per cent since 1 April 2017, but will decrease to 17 per cent for the financial year commencing 1 April 2020.

ALLOWANCES AND RELIEFS

Businesses can claim capital allowances, on certain purchases or investments. This means that a proportion of these costs can be deducted from a business' taxable profits and should its tax bill. Capital allowances are currently available on plant and machinery such as equipment and business vehicles. Reliefs are also available for research and development, profits from patented inventions and certain creative industries. The amount of the allowance or relief depends on what is being claimed for.

Detailed information on allowances and reliefs is available at W www.gov.uk/corporation-tax-rates/allowances-and-reliefs.

PAYMENT OF TAX

Corporation tax liabilities are normally due and payable in a single lump sum not later than nine months and one day after the end of the accounting period. For 'large' companies – those with profits over £1.5m – there is a requirement to pay corporation tax in four quarterly instalments. Where a company is a member of a group, the profits of the entire group must be merged to establish whether the company is 'large'.

HMRC runs a Business Payment Support Service (BPSS) which allows businesses facing temporary financial difficulties more time to pay their tax bills. Traders concerned about their ability to meet corporation tax, VAT or other payments owed to HMRC can call the BPSS Line (T 0300-200 3835) seven days a week. This helpline is for new enquiries only, not for traders who have already been contacted by HMRC about an overdue payment. For details of the service, visit W www.gov.uk/government/organisations/hm-revenue-customs/contact/business-payment-support-service.

CAPITAL GAINS

Chargeable gains arising to a company are calculated in a manner similar to that used for individuals. However, companies are not entitled to the CGT annual exemption. Companies incur liability to corporation tax rather than CGT on chargeable gains. Tax is due on the full chargeable gain of an accounting period after subtracting relief for any losses.

GROUPS OF COMPANIES

Each company within a group is separately charged corporation tax on profits, gains and income. However, where one group member realises a trading loss for which special rules apply, a claim may be made to offset the taxable loss against profits of some other member of the same group. These rules do not apply to capital losses. The transfer of capital assets from one member of a group to a fellow member will usually incur no liability to tax on chargeable gains.

SPORTS CLUBS

Though corporation tax is payable by unincorporated associations (including most sports clubs) on their profits, a substantial exemption from liability to corporation tax is available to qualifying registered community amateur sports clubs (CASCs). Sports clubs that are registered as CASCs are exempt from liability to corporation tax on:

- profits from trading where the turnover of the trade is less than £50,000 in a 12-month period
- income from letting property where the gross rental income is less than £30,000 in a 12-month period
- bank and building society interest received
- chargeable gains
- any Gift Aid donations

All of the exemptions depend upon the club having been a registered CASC for the whole of the relevant accounting period and the income or gains being used only for qualifying purposes. If the club has only been a registered CASC for part of an accounting period the exemption amounts of £50,000 (for trading) and £30,000 (for income from property) are reduced proportionately. Only interest and gains received after the club is registered are exempted. Full details can be found at W www.gov.uk/government/publications/community-amateur-sports-clubs-detailed-guidance-notes.

CHARITIES

Charities do not pay corporation tax on profits from their charitable activities. To minimise their liability, they often operate their trading activities through a subsidiary company.

VALUE ADDED TAX

Value added tax (VAT) is a tax on consumption which is collected at each stage in the supply chain. It is included in the sale price of taxable goods and services and paid at the point of purchase. Each EU country has its own rates of VAT. VAT is charged on most business transactions involving the supply of goods and services by VAT registered traders in the UK and Isle of Man. It is also charged on goods and some services imported from places outside the EU and on goods and some services coming into the UK from the other EU countries. VAT is administered by HMRC. A wide range of information on VAT, including VAT forms, is available online (W www.gov.uk/topic/business-tax/vat) and HMRC also runs a VAT enquiries helpline (T 0300-200 3700).

HMRC have confirmed that the UK will continue to have a VAT system after it leaves the EU. The revenue that VAT provides is vital for funding public services. The VAT rules relating to UK domestic transactions will continue to apply to businesses as they do now.

RATES OF TAX

There are three rates of VAT in the UK:
- the standard rate, payable on most goods and services in the UK, is 20 per cent
- the reduced rate – currently 5 per cent – is payable on certain goods and services, including domestic fuel and power, children's car seats, women's sanitary products, smoking cessation products and the installation of energy-saving materials such as wall insulation and solar panels
- the zero rate applies to certain items, including, children's clothes, books, newspapers, most food and drink, and drugs and aids for disabled people. There are numerous exceptions to the zero-rated categories, including: confectionery, potato crisps, alcoholic drinks, soft drinks and items sold for consumption in a restaurant or café. Takeaway cold items such as sandwiches are zero-rated, but hot foods like fish and chips are not.

REGISTRATION

All traders, including professional persons and companies, must register for VAT if they are making 'taxable supplies' of a value exceeding the registration threshold. All goods and services that are VAT rated are defined as 'taxable supplies'. This includes zero-rated items, which must be included when calculating the total value of a trader's taxable supplies – his or her 'taxable turnover'. The limits that govern mandatory registration are amended periodically.

An unregistered trader must register for VAT if:
- at the end of any month the total value of his or her taxable turnover (not just profit) for the past 12 months or less is more than the current VAT threshold of £85,000
or
- at any time he or she has reasonable grounds to expect that his or her taxable turnover will be more than the current registration threshold of £85,000 in the next 30 days alone

VAT registration must be completed within 30 days. Most businesses register online, but some need to download a form (W www.gov.uk/vat-registration/how-to-register). Traders who do not register at the correct time can be fined. Traders must charge VAT on their taxable supplies from the effective date of registration.

Traders who only supply zero-rated goods may not have to register for VAT even if their taxable turnover goes above the registration threshold. However, a trader in this position must inform HMRC first and apply to be 'exempt from registration'. A trader whose taxable turnover does not reach the mandatory registration limit may choose to register for VAT voluntarily. This step may be thought advisable to recover input tax (*see* below) or to compete with other registered traders.

Registered traders may submit an application for deregistration if their taxable turnover subsequently falls. An application for deregistration can be made if the taxable turnover for the 12 months beginning on the application date is not expected to exceed £83,000.

INPUT TAX

Traders suffer input tax when buying in goods or services for the purposes of their business. It is the VAT that traders pay out to their suppliers on goods and services coming *in* to their business. Relief can usually be obtained for input tax suffered by registered traders, either by setting that tax against output tax due on sales or by repayment. Most items of input tax can be relieved in this manner. Where a registered trader makes both exempt supplies and taxable supplies to his customers or clients, there may be some restriction in the amount of input tax that can be recovered.

OUTPUT TAX

When making a taxable supply of goods or services, registered traders must account for output tax on the value of that supply. Output tax is the term used to describe the VAT on the goods and services that they supply or sell, so the goods or services are going *out* of the business. It is collected from customers on each sale by increasing the price by the VAT. Failure to make the required addition will not remove liability to pay the output tax to HMRC.

The liability to account for output tax, and also relief for input tax, may be affected where a trader is using a special secondhand goods scheme.

EXEMPT SUPPLIES

VAT is not chargeable on certain goods and services because the law deems them 'exempt' from VAT. These include:
- the provision of burial and cremation facilities
- insurance
- loans of money
- certain types of education and training
- most property transactions, unless the owner has opted to tax the property

Exempt supplies do not enter into the calculation of taxable turnover that governs liability to mandatory registration (*see* above). Such supplies made by a registered trader may limit the amount of input tax that can be relieved.

COLLECTION OF TAX

Registered traders submit VAT returns for accounting periods usually of three months in duration, but arrangements can be made to submit returns on a monthly basis. Very large traders – those whose annual VAT liability exceeds £2.3m – must make payments on account on a monthly basis, with the quarterly return used to determine the balancing payment. The return will show the output tax due for supplies made by the trader in the accounting period and the input tax for which relief is claimed. If the output tax exceeds input tax the balance must be remitted at the time of the VAT return. Where input tax suffered exceeds the output tax due, the registered trader may claim the excess from HMRC.

In this way, each trader in the supply chain collects the tax relating to the value added by their business. Where the supply is made to a person who is not a registered trader there can be no recovery of input tax and it is on this person that the final burden of VAT eventually falls.

As part of the Making Tax Digital initiative, most registered traders are required to use the Making Tax Digital service to keep records digitally and use software to submit their VAT returns from 1 April 2019. From 1 October 2019 the following organisations will also need to use the digital service:

- trusts
- not-for-profit organisations that are not set up as a company
- VAT divisions and groups
- public sector entities required to provide additional information on their VAT return (eg government departments and NHS trusts)
- local authorities
- public corporations
- traders based overseas
- those required to make payments on account
- annual accounting scheme users

For further information *see* W www.gov.uk/guidance/making-tax-digital-for-vat.

Exemptions from Making Tax Digital are available to those:

- that can not use computers, software or the internet due to age, disability or where they live
- or whose business are subject to an insolvency procedure
- that object to using computers on religious grounds

Applications for exemptions should be made to: HMRC – VAT Written Enquiries Team, Portcullis House, 21 India Street, Glasgow G2 4PZ or T 0300-200 3700. Applicants must state their VAT registration number, business name and address, details of how they currently file their VAT Return, and the reason they think they're exempt from Making Tax Digital.

Where goods are acquired by a UK trader from a supplier within the EU, the trader must also account for the tax due on acquisition. At the time of writing, the future of these arrangements is uncertain.

There are a number of simplified arrangements to make VAT accounting easier for businesses, particularly small businesses, and there is advice on the HMRC website about how to choose the most appropriate scheme for a business:

Cash Accounting Scheme

This scheme allows businesses to only pay VAT on the basis of payments received from their customers rather than on invoice dates or time of supply. This is useful for businesses with cash flow problems. Businesses may use the cash accounting scheme if estimated taxable turnover is £1.35m or less for the next 12 months. There is no need to apply for the scheme – eligible businesses may start using it at the beginning of a new tax period. If a trader opts to use this scheme, he or she can do so until the taxable turnover reaches £1.6m. For further information *see* W www.gov.uk/vat-cash-accounting-scheme.

Annual Accounting Scheme

If estimated taxable turnover is £1.35m or less in the next 12 months, the trader may join the annual accounting scheme which allows them to make nine monthly or three quarterly instalments during the year based on an estimate of their total annual VAT bill. At the end of the year they submit a single return and any balance due. The advantages of this scheme for businesses are easier budgeting and cash flow planning, because fixed payments are spread regularly throughout the year. Once a trader has joined the annual accounting scheme, membership may continue until the annual taxable turnover reaches £1.6m. This scheme is not helpful where businesses receive a refund of VAT, because it delays receipt of the refund. For more information *see* W www.gov.uk/vat-annual-accounting-scheme.

Flat Rate Scheme

This scheme allows small businesses with an annual taxable turnover of £150,000 or less to save on administration by paying VAT as a set flat percentage of their annual turnover instead of accounting internally for VAT on each individual 'in and out'. The percentage rate used is governed by the trade sector into which the business falls. The scheme can no longer be used once annual income exceeds £230,000.

Under this scheme, it is not possible to reclaim the VAT on purchases, except for certain assets over £2,000. For further information *see* W www.gov.uk/vat-flat-rate-scheme.

A business can not use the Flat Rate Scheme and the Cash Accounting Scheme at the same time.

Retail Schemes

There are special schemes that offer retailers an alternative if it is impractical for them to issue invoices for a large number of supplies direct to the public. These schemes include a provision to claim relief from VAT on bad debts where goods or services are supplied to a customer who does not pay for them. For further information *see* W www.gov.uk/vat-retail-schemes.

VAT FACT SUMMARY *from 1 April 2019*

Standard rate	20%
Reduced rate	5%
Registration (last 12 months or next 30 days)	over £85,000
Deregistration (next 12 months)	under £83,000
Cash accounting scheme	up to £1,350,000
Exit limit	£1,600,000
Annual accounting scheme	up to £1,350,000
Exit limit	£1,600,000
Flat rate scheme	up to £150,000
Exit limit	£230,000

STAMP DUTY

Stamp duty is payable by the buyer based on the purchase price of a property, stocks and shares. For the majority of people, contact with stamp duty arises when they buy a property. This section aims to provide a broad overview of stamp duty as it may affect the average person.

STAMP DUTY LAND TAX

Stamp duty land tax (SDLT) covers the purchase of houses, flats and other land, buildings and certain leases in the UK.

Buyers of property are responsible for completing a land transaction return form, SDLT1, which contains all information regarding the purchase that is relevant to HMRC and paying SDLT, though the solicitor or licensed conveyancer acting for them in a land transaction will normally complete the relevant paperwork. Once HMRC has received the completed land transaction return and the payment of any SDLT due, a certificate, SDLT5, will be issued that enables a solicitor or licensed conveyancer to register the property in the new owner's name at the land registry.

The threshold for notification of residential property is currently £40,000. This means that taxpayers entering into a transaction involving residential or non-residential property where the chargeable consideration is less than £40,000 do not need to notify HMRC about the transaction. Further information can be found online: W www.gov.uk/government/organisations/hm-revenue-customs/contact/stamp-duty-land-tax.

Since 1 April 2015 stamp duty has no longer applied to land transactions in Scotland. These are now subject to land and buildings transaction tax, details of which can be found online (W www.gov.uk/sdlt-scottish-transactions).

RATES OF SDLT

SDLT is charged at different rates and has thresholds for different types of property and different values of transaction. The tax rate and payment threshold can vary according to whether the property is in residential or non-residential use and whether it is freehold or leasehold.

SDLT on purchases of residential property is charged at increasing rates for each portion of the price.

SDLT ON RESIDENTIAL PROPERTY 2018–19

Portion of the transaction value	SDLT is charged at
Up to £125,000	zero
Between £125,001 and £250,000	2 per cent
Between £250,001 and £925,000	5 per cent
Between £925,001 and £1,500,000	10 per cent
Over £1,500,000	12 per cent

For example, on a property bought for £275,000, a total of £3,750 is payable in SDLT. This is made up of: nothing on the first £125,000, £2,500 (2 per cent) on the next £125,000, and £1,250 (5 per cent) on the remaining £25,000.

Higher rates of SDLT apply to purchases of additional residential properties such as second homes and buy-to-let properties. The higher rates are 3 per cent above the standard rates of SDLT. They do not apply to purchases of caravans, mobile homes, houseboats or property under £40,000.

HIGHER RATE SDLT ON ADDITIONAL RESIDENTIAL PROPERTY 2018–19

Portion of the transaction value	SDLT is charged at
Up to £125,000	3 per cent
Between £125,001 and £250,000	5 per cent
Between £250,001 and £925,000	8 per cent
Between £925,001 and £1,500,000	13 per cent
Over £1,500,000	15 per cent

Each of these higher rates again applies to the portion of the consideration that falls within each rate band. For example, on a buy-to-let property bought for £300,000, a total of £14,000 is payable in higher rate SDLT. This is made up of: £3,750 (3 per cent) on the first £125,000, £6,250 (5 per cent) on the next £125,000, and £4,000 (8 per cent) on the remaining £50,000.

The SDLT on purchases of non-residential and mixed-use property is charged at increasing rates for each portion of the price (in the same way that it is charged on purchases of residential property).

SDLT ON NON-RESIDENTIAL AND MIXED USE PROPERTY PURCHASES 2018–19

Portion of the transaction value	SDLT is charged at
Up to £150,000	zero
Between £150,001 and £250,000	2 per cent
Over £250,001	5 per cent

FIRST TIME BUYERS

From November 2017, first time buyers of homes worth between £300,000 and £500,000 will not pay SDLT on the first £300,000. They will pay the normal rates of SDLT on the price above that. This will save £1,660 on the average first-time property. This zero rate does not apply to first time buy-to-let or holiday home purchases, although those that are investing in buy-to-let property as first time buyers, will still get some relief as they will pay the standard residential rates rather than the higher buy-to-let rates. It is estimated that 80 per cent of people buying their first home will pay no SDLT.

This relief does not apply for those buying properties over £500,000.

CALCULATING SDLT

To work out the amount of SDLT payable on residential or non-residential property, a SDLT calculator is available online (W www.tax.service.gov.uk/calculate-stamp-duty-land-tax/#/intro).

STAMP DUTY RESERVE TAX

Stamp duty or stamp duty reserve tax (SDRT) is payable at the rate of 0.5 per cent when shares are purchased. Stamp duty is payable when the shares are transferred using a stock transfer form, whereas SDRT is payable on 'paperless' share transactions where the shares are transferred electronically without using a stock transfer form. Most share transactions nowadays are paperless and settled by stockbrokers through CREST (the electronic settlement and registration system). SDRT therefore now accounts for the majority of taxation collected on share transactions effected through the London Stock Exchange.

The flat rate of 0.5 per cent is based on the amount paid for the shares, not what they are worth. If, for example, shares are bought for £2,000, £10 SDRT is payable, whatever the value of the shares themselves. If shares are transferred for free, no SDRT is payable.

A higher rate of 1.5 per cent is payable where shares are transferred into a 'depositary receipt scheme' or a 'clearance service'. These are special arrangements where the shares are held by a third party.

CREST automatically deducts the SDRT and sends it to HMRC. A stockbroker will settle up with CREST for the cost of the shares and the SDRT and then bill the purchaser for these and the broker's fees. If shares are not purchased through CREST, the stamp duty must be paid by the purchaser to HMRC.

UK stamp duty or SDRT is not payable on the purchase of foreign shares, though there may be foreign taxes to pay. SDRT is already accounted for in the price paid for units in unit trusts or shares in open-ended investment companies.

Further information on SDRT is available via the stamp taxes helpline on T 0300-200 3510 or the government information website (W www.gov.uk/topic/business-tax/stamp-duty-on-shares).

LEGAL NOTES

These notes outline certain aspects of the law as they might affect the average person. They are intended only as a broad guideline and are by no means definitive. The law is constantly changing so expert advice should always be taken. In some cases, sources of further information are given in these notes.

It is always advisable to consult a solicitor without delay. Anyone who does not have a solicitor can contact the following for assistance in finding one: Citizens Advice (W www.citizensadvice.org.uk), the Community Legal Service (W www.gov.uk) or the Law Society of England and Wales. For assistance in Scotland, contact Citizens Advice Scotland (W www.cas.org.uk) or the Law Society of Scotland.

Legal aid schemes exist to make the help of a lawyer available to those who would not otherwise be able to afford one. Entitlement for most types of legal aid depends on an individual's means but a solicitor or Citizens Advice will be able to advise on this.

LAW SOCIETY OF ENGLAND AND WALES, 113 Chancery Lane, London WC2A 1PL T 020-7242 1222
W www.lawsociety.org.uk

LAW SOCIETY OF SCOTLAND, Atria One, 144 Morrison Street, Edinburgh EH8 8EX T 0131-226 7411
W www.lawscot.org.uk

ABORTION

Abortion is governed by the Abortion Act 1967. Under its provisions, a legally induced abortion must be:
- performed by a registered medical practitioner
- carried out in an NHS hospital or other approved premises
- certified by two registered medical practitioners, acting in good faith, on the basis of one or more of the following grounds:
1. that the pregnancy has not exceeded its 24th week and that the continuance of the pregnancy would involve risk, greater than if the pregnancy were terminated, of injury to the physical or mental health of the pregnant woman or any existing children of her family
2. that the termination is necessary to prevent grave permanent injury to the physical or mental health of the pregnant woman
3. that the continuance of the pregnancy would involve risk to the life of the pregnant woman, greater than if the pregnancy were terminated
4. that there is a substantial risk that if the child were born it would suffer from such physical or mental abnormalities as to be seriously handicapped.

In determining whether the continuance of a pregnancy would involve such risk of injury to health as is mentioned in the first and second grounds, account may be taken of the pregnant woman's actual or reasonably foreseeable environment.

The requirements relating to the opinion of two registered medical practitioners and to the performance of the abortion at an NHS hospital or other approved place cease to apply in circumstances where a registered medical practitioner is of the opinion, formed in good faith, that a termination is immediately necessary to save the life, or to prevent grave permanent injury to the physical or mental health, of the pregnant woman.

The Abortion Act 1967 does not apply to Northern Ireland. Despite a 2015 high court ruling that Northern Ireland's law on abortion is inconsistent with the European Convention on Human Rights, abortion is only permitted where there is a serious long-term risk to the health of the mother.

FAMILY PLANNING ASSOCIATION (UK), 23–28 Penn Street, London N1 5DL T 020-7608 5240 W www.fpa.org.uk

BRITISH PREGNANCY ADVISORY SERVICE (BPAS), 20 Timothys Bridge Road, Stratford-upon-Avon CV37 9BF
T 0345-730 4030 W www.bpas.org

ADOPTION OF CHILDREN

The Adoption and Children Act 2002 reformed the framework for domestic and intercountry adoption in England and Wales and some parts of it extend to Scotland and Northern Ireland. The Children and Adoption Act 2006, recently amended by the Children and Families Act 2014, introduced further provisions for adoptions involving a foreign element.

WHO MAY APPLY FOR AN ADOPTION ORDER

A couple (whether married or two people living as partners in an enduring family relationship) may apply for an adoption order where both of them are over 21 or where one is only 18 but the natural parent and the other is 21. An adoption order may be made for one applicant where that person is 21 and: a) the court is satisfied that person is the partner of a parent of the person to be adopted; or b) they are not married and are not civil partners; or c) married or in a civil partnership but they are separated from their spouse or civil partner and living apart with the separation likely to be permanent; or d) their spouse/civil partner is either unable to be found, or their spouse/civil partner is incapable by reason of ill-health of making an application. There are certain qualifying conditions an applicant must meet, eg residency in the British Isles.

ARRANGING AN ADOPTION

Adoptions may generally only be arranged by an adoption agency or by way of an order from the high court; breach of the restrictions on who may arrange an adoption would constitute a criminal offence. When deciding whether a child should be placed for adoption, the court or adoption agency must consider all the factors set out in the 'welfare checklist' – the paramount consideration being the child's welfare, throughout his or her life. These factors include the child's wishes, needs, age, sex, background and any harm which the child has suffered or is likely to suffer. At all times, the court or adoption agency must bear in mind that delay is likely to prejudice a child's welfare.

ADOPTION ORDER

Once an adoption has been arranged, a court order is necessary to make it legal; this may be obtained from the high court, county court or magistrates' court (including the family proceedings court). An adoption order may not be given unless the court is satisfied that the consent of the child's natural parents (or guardians) has been given correctly. Consent can be dispensed with on two grounds: where the parent or guardian cannot be found or is incapable of giving consent, or where the welfare of the child so demands.

An adoption order extinguishes the parental responsibility that a person other than the adopters (or adopter) has for the child. Where an order is made on the application of the partner of the parent, that parent keeps parental responsibility. Once adopted, the child has the same status as a child born to the adoptive parents, but may lose rights to the estates of those losing their parental responsibility.

REGISTRATION AND CERTIFICATES

All adoption orders made in England and Wales are required to be registered in the Adopted Children Register which also contains particulars of children adopted under registrable foreign adoptions. The General Register Office keeps this register from which certificates may be obtained in a similar way to birth certificates. The General Register Office also has equivalents in Scotland and Northern Ireland.

TRACING NATURAL PARENTS OR CHILDREN WHO HAVE BEEN ADOPTED

An adult adopted person may apply to the Registrar-General to obtain a certified copy of his/her birth certificate. Adoption agencies and adoption support agencies should provide services to adopted persons to assist them in obtaining information about their adoption and facilitate contact with their relatives. There is an Adoption Contact Register which provides a safe and confidential way for birth parents and other relatives to assure an adopted person that contact would be welcome. CoramBAAF (see below) can provide addresses of organisations which offer advice, information and counselling to adopted people, adoptive parents and people who have had their children adopted.

CORAMBAAF ADOPTION AND FOSTERING
ACADEMY, 41 Brunswick Square, London WC1N 1AZ
T 020-7520 0300 W https://corambaaf.org.uk

SCOTLAND

The relevant legislation is the Adoption and Children (Scotland) Act 2007 which came into force on 28 September 2009. In addition, adoptions with a foreign element are governed by the Adoptions with a Foreign Element (Scotland) Regulations 2009. Pre-2009 adoptions are governed by Part IV of the Adoption (Scotland) Act 1978. The provisions of the 2007 act are similar to those described above. In Scotland, petitions for adoption are made to the sheriff court or the court of session.

ADOPTION AND FOSTERING ALLIANCE SCOTLAND,
Foxglove Offices/GF2, 14 Links Place, Edinburgh EH6 7EZ
T 0131-322 8490 W www.afascotland.com

BIRTHS (REGISTRATION)

It is the duty of the parents of a child born in England or Wales to register the birth within 42 days of the date of birth at the register office in the district in which the baby was born. If it is inconvenient to go to the district where the birth took place, the information for the registration may be given to a registrar in another district, who will send your details to the appropriate register office. Failure to register the birth within 42 days without reasonable cause may leave the parents liable to a penalty. If a birth has not been registered within 12 months of its occurrence it is possible for the late registration of the birth to be authorised by the Registrar-General, provided documentary evidence of the precise date and place of birth are satisfactory.

Births that take place in England may only be registered in English, but births that take place in Wales may be registered bilingually in Welsh and English. In order to do this, the details must be given in Welsh and the registrar must be able to understand and write in Welsh.

If the parents of the child were married to each other at the time of the birth (or conception), either the mother or the father may register the birth alone. If the parents were not married to each other at the time of the child's birth (or conception), the father's particulars may be entered in the register only where he attends the register office with the mother and they sign the birth register together or the mother can choose to register the child's birth without the father's details. Where an unmarried parent is unable to attend the register office, either parent may submit to the registrar a statutory declaration of acknowledgement of parentage (this form may be obtained from any registrar in England or Wales or online at W www.gro.gov.uk); alternatively a parental responsibility agreement or appropriate court order may be produced to the registrar.

If the father's details are not included in the birth register, it may be possible to re-register the birth at a later date. If the parents can not register the birth of their child the following people may do so:

- an administrative member of staff of the hospital where the child was born
- a person who was present at the birth
- a person who is responsible for the child

Upon registration of the birth a short (containing only the child's details) or full (containing the child's and parents' details) certificate can be issued at a cost of £11.00 each. It may be possible to register the birth while still at hospital. Hospitals will advise individually whether this is possible.

SAME-SEX COUPLES

Male couples must get a parental order from the court before they can be registered as parents. Female couples can include both of their names on the child's birth certificate when registering the birth; however the rules differ depending on whether or not they are in a civil partnership.

In the case of female civil partners, either woman can register the birth on her own if all of the following are true:

- the mother had the child by donor insemination or fertility treatment
- she was married or in a civil partnership at the time of the treatment

When a mother is not in a civil partnership, her partner can be seen as the child's second parent if both women:

- were treated together in the UK by a licensed clinic
- have made a 'parenthood agreement'

However, for both parents' details to be recorded on the birth certificate, the parents must do one of the following:

- register the birth jointly
- complete a 'statutory declaration of acknowledgement of parentage' form and one parent takes the signed form when she registers the birth
- get a document from the court (eg a court order) giving the second female parent parental responsibility and one parent shows the document when she registers the birth

BIRTHS ABROAD

A child's birth abroad must be registered according to the regulations in the country where the child was born. The local authorities will issue a local birth certificate. The local birth certificate should be accepted in the UK, for example when registering a child with a school or doctor, but the certificate may be required to be translated and certified in English.

Once the child's birth has been registered locally, the birth may be registered with the UK authorities (only if the child was born on or after 1 January 1983). There is no obligation to register a child's birth with the UK authority; however, by registering the birth with the UK authority the birth will be recorded with the General Register Offices and a consular birth registration certificate can be ordered.

SCOTLAND

In Scotland the birth of a child must be registered within 21 days at the registration office of any registration district in Scotland.

If the child is born, either in or out of Scotland, on a ship, aircraft or land vehicle that ends its journey at any place in Scotland, the child, in most cases, will be registered as if born in that place.

CERTIFICATES OF BIRTHS, DEATHS OR MARRIAGES

Certificates of births, marriages and deaths that have taken place in England and Wales since 1837 can be obtained from the General Register Office (GRO).

Marriage or death certificates may also be obtained from the minister of the church in which the marriage or funeral took place. Any register office can advise about the best way to obtain certificates.

The fees for certificates are:

Online application:
- full certificate of birth, marriage, death or adoption, £14.00
- full certificate of birth, marriage, death or adoption with GRO reference supplied, £11.00

By postal/phone/fax application:
- full certificate of birth, marriage, death or adoption, £14.00
- full certificate of birth, marriage, death or adoption with GRO reference supplied, £11.00
- extra copies of the same birth, marriage or death certificate issued at the same time, £11.00

A priority service is available for a fee of £35.00 with GRO reference supplied and £38.00 without.

A complete set of the GRO indexes including births, deaths and marriages, civil partnerships, adoptions and provisional indexes for births and deaths are available at the British Library, City of Westminster Archives Centre, Manchester Central Library, Newcastle City Library, Library of Birmingham, Bridgend Reference and Information Library and Plymouth Central Library. Copies of GRO indexes may also be held at some libraries, family history societies, local records offices and The Church of Jesus Christ of Latter Day Saints family history centres. Some organisations may not hold a complete record of indexes and a small fee may be charged by some of them. GRO indexes are also available online.

The Society of Genealogists has many records of baptisms, marriages and deaths prior to 1837.

SCOTLAND

Certificates of births, deaths or marriages that have taken place in Scotland since 1855 can be obtained from the National Records of Scotland (formerly the General Register Office for Scotland) or from the appropriate local registrar.

Applicable fees – local registrar:
- each extract or abbreviated certificate of birth, death, marriage, civil partnership or adoption within a month of registration, £10.00
- each extract or abbreviated certificate of birth, death, marriage, civil partnership or adoption outwith a month of registration, £15.00

A priority service is available for an additional fee.

The National Records of Scotland also keeps the Register of Divorces (including decrees of declaration of nullity of marriage), and holds parish registers dating from before 1855.

Applicable fees – National Records of Scotland:
- personal application, or postal, telephone or fax order: £15.00

A priority service for a response within 24 hours is available for an additional fee of £15.00. Online fees (excluding postage) are £12.00 or £27.00 for a priority service.

A search of birth, death and marriage records including records of Church of Scotland parishes and other statutory records can be done at the Scotland's People Centre. There are also indexes to some of the old parish registers death and burial records in the library at the centre and indexes and images of census records from 1841–1911 are available. The charges for a full or part-day search pass is £15.00. Online searching is also available. For more information, visit W www.scotlandspeople.gov.uk

THE GENERAL REGISTER OFFICE, General Register Office, Certificate Services Section, PO Box 2, Southport PR8 2JD T 0300-123 1837 W www.gro.gov.uk/gro/content/certificates

THE NATIONAL RECORDS OF SCOTLAND, HM General Register House, 2 Princes Street, Edinburgh EH1 3YT T 0131-334 0380 W www.nrscotland.gov.uk

SCOTLAND'S PEOPLE CENTRE, General Register House, 2 Princes Street, Edinburgh EH1 3YY W www.scotlandspeople.gov.uk

THE SOCIETY OF GENEALOGISTS, 14 Charterhouse Buildings, Goswell Road, London EC1M 7BA T 020-7251 8799 W www.sog.org.uk

BRITISH NATIONALITY

There are different types of British nationality status: British citizenship; British overseas citizenship; British national (overseas); British overseas territories citizenship; British protected persons; and British subjects. The most widely held of these is British citizenship. Everyone born in the UK before 1 January 1983 became a British citizen when the British Nationality Act 1981 came into force, with the exception of children born to certain diplomatic staff working in the UK at the time. Individuals born outside the UK before 1 January 1983 but who at that date were citizens of the UK and colonies and had a right of abode in the UK also became British citizens. British citizens have the right to live permanently in the UK and are free to leave and re-enter the UK at any time.

A person born on or after 1 January 1983 in the UK (including, for this purpose, the Channel Islands and the Isle of Man) is entitled to British citizenship if he/she falls into one of the following categories:
- he/she has a parent who is a British citizen
- he/she has a parent who is settled in the UK
- he/she is a newborn infant found abandoned in the UK
- his/her parents subsequently settle in the UK or become British citizens and an application is made before he/she is 18
- he/she lives in the UK for the first ten years of his/her life and is not absent for more than 90 days in each of those years
- he/she is adopted in the UK and one of the adopters is a British citizen
- the home secretary consents to his/her registration while he/she is a minor
- if he/she has always been stateless and lives in the UK for a period of five years before his/her 22nd birthday
- if he/she has been born on or after 13 January 2010 to a parent who is a member of the UK armed forces
- if he/she has been born on or after 13 January 2010 and a parent becomes a member of the UK armed forces, and an application is made before he/she is 18

A person born outside the UK may acquire British citizenship if he/she falls into one of the following categories:
- he/she has a parent who is a British citizen otherwise than by descent, eg a parent who was born in the UK

- he/she has a parent who is a British citizen serving the crown or a European community institution overseas and was recruited to that service in the UK (including qualifying territories for those born on or after 21 May 2002) or in the European Community (for services within an EU institution); or if the applicant himself/herself has at any time been in crown, or similar, service under the government of a British overseas territory
- if he/she has been born on or after 13 January 2010 to a parent who is a member of the UK armed forces serving outside the UK and qualifying territories, is of good character and (if he/she is a minor at the time of application) all parents then alive consent in signed writing
- the home secretary consents to his/her registration while he/she is a minor
- he/she is a British overseas territories citizen, a British overseas citizen, a British subject or a British protected person and has been lawfully resident in the UK for five years
- he/she is a British overseas territories citizen who acquired that citizenship from a connection with Gibraltar
- he/she is adopted or naturalised

Where parents are married, the status of either may confer citizenship on their child. Since July 2006, both parents are able to pass on nationality even if they are not married, provided that there is satisfactory evidence of paternity. For children born before July 2006, it must be shown that there is parental consent and that the child would have an automatic claim to citizenship or entitlement to registration had the parents been married. Where parents are not married, the status of the mother determines the child's citizenship.

Under the 1981 act, Commonwealth citizens and citizens of the Republic of Ireland were entitled to registration as British citizens before 1 January 1983. In 1983, citizens of the Falkland Islands were granted British citizenship.

Renunciation of British citizenship must be registered with the home secretary and will be revoked if no new citizenship or nationality is acquired within six months. If the renunciation was required in order to retain or acquire another citizenship or nationality, the citizenship may be reacquired only once. If the renunciation was for another reason, the home secretary may allow reacquisition more than once, depending on the circumstances. The secretary of state may deprive a person of a citizenship status if he or she is satisfied that the person has done anything seriously prejudicial to the vital interests of the UK, or a British overseas territory, unless making the order would have the effect of rendering such a person stateless. A person may also be deprived of a citizenship status which results from his registration or naturalisation if the secretary of state is satisfied that the registration or naturalisation was obtained by fraud, false representation or concealment of a material fact.

BRITISH DEPENDENT TERRITORIES CITIZENSHIP
Since 26 February 2002, this category of nationality no longer exists and has been replaced by British overseas territory citizenship.

If a person had this class of nationality only by reason of a connection to the territory of Hong Kong, they lost it automatically when Hong Kong was returned to the People's Republic of China. However, if after 30 June 1997, they had no other nationality and would have become stateless, or were born after 30 June 1997 and would have been born stateless (but had a parent who was a British national (overseas) or a British overseas citizen), they became a British overseas citizen.

BRITISH OVERSEAS CITIZENSHIP
Under the 1981 act, as amended by the British Overseas Territories Act 2002, this type of citizenship was conferred on any UK and colonies citizens who did not become either a British citizen or a British overseas territories citizen on 1 January 1983 and as such is now, for most purposes, only acquired by persons who would otherwise be stateless.

BRITISH OVERSEAS TERRITORIES CITIZENSHIP
This category of nationality replaced British dependent territories citizenship. Most commonly, this form of nationality is acquired where, after 31 December 1982, a person was a citizen of the UK and colonies and did not become a British citizen, and that person, and their parents or grandparents, were born, registered or naturalised in the specified British overseas territory. However, on 21 May 2002, people became British citizens if they had British overseas territories citizenship by connection with any British overseas territory, except for the sovereign base areas of Akrotiri and Dhekelia in Cyprus.

RESIDUAL CATEGORIES
British subjects, British protected persons and British nationals (overseas) may be entitled to registration as British citizens on completion of five years' legal residence in the UK.

Citizens of the Republic of Ireland who were also British subjects before 1 January 1949 can retain that status if they fulfil certain conditions.

EUROPEAN UNION CITIZENSHIP
At the time of writing, British citizens (including Gibraltarians who are registered for this purpose) are also EU citizens and are entitled to travel freely to other EU countries to work, study, reside and set up a business. EU citizens have the same rights with respect to the UK. However, on the day the UK leaves the EU, European freedom of movement will end for all EU citizens (including citizens of Switzerland, Norway, Iceland and Liechtenstein) and their family members in the UK, and for all British citizens living in the EU.

The EU and the UK have negotiated the terms of the UK's withdrawal from the EU. Under the withdrawal agreement, EU law, in the main, would continue to apply in the UK from when the UK leaves the EU until 31 December 2020. This means that the freedom of movement would also continue until this date. In the case of no agreement between the UK and the EU, the freedom of movement would end after the withdrawal date.

NATURALISATION
Naturalisation is granted at the discretion of the home secretary. The basic requirements are lawful residence in the UK in the five years immediately preceding application (three years if the applicant is married to, or is the civil partner of a British citizen), good character, adequate knowledge of the English, Welsh or Scottish Gaelic language, passing the UK citizenship test and an intention to reside permanently in the UK.

The good character requirement applies to adults and children over the age of 10 and in assessing this the Home Office will take into account a range of factors, including any convictions, cautions, civil judgements, bankruptcies, financial soundness and any instances of failure to comply with immigration laws. If a person is deemed not to be of good character their naturalisation application will be refused. In January 2019 the Home Office updated its guidance as to how caseworkers should assess whether or not someone meets the good character requirement. The changes to the guidance apply to all applications made after 16 January 2019 and mainly relate to children, certain immigration offences and genuine mistakes made by the applicant.

STATUS OF ALIENS
Aliens, being persons without any of the above forms of British nationality, may not hold public office or vote in

Britain and they may not own a British ship or aircraft. Citizens of the Republic of Ireland and Commonwealth citizens are not deemed to be aliens. Certain provisions of the Immigration and Asylum Act 1999 make provision about immigration and asylum and about procedures in connection with marriage by superintendent registrar's certificate.

CONSUMER LAW

SALE OF GOODS
The law in this area is enacted to protect buyers who deal as 'consumers' (where the seller is selling in the course of a business, the goods are of a type ordinarily bought for private use and the goods are purchased by a buyer who is not a business buyer).

A sale of goods contract is the most common type of contract. These are governed by the Consumer Rights Act 2015 (CRA), which was designed to modernise and simplify the law in this area by codifying consumer legislation, most notably incorporating the Sale of Goods Act 1979.

The CRA provides protection for buyers by implying terms into every business-to-consumer sale of goods contract. These terms include:
- that the goods must be of a standard such that a reasonable person would deem them to be of satisfactory quality, considering, among other relevant factors, any description of the goods given by the seller and their price. The goods should be of satisfactory quality for the purpose for which they are usually intended, as well as in appearance, and they should not pose safety concerns. Should, prior to purchase, any issue affecting the quality of the goods be made clear to the consumer, then the term will not be applied. The same is true if, prior to purchase, the consumer has the opportunity to make a reasonable examination of the goods or a sample of them which would reveal any issue affecting their quality
- that goods must be suitable for the purpose for which the consumer has, expressly or implicitly, stated that they are intended. This term is applicable regardless of whether or not goods of such a nature are usually intended for this purpose, unless the consumer is advised otherwise by the trader and ignores such advice
- that any description of the goods provided by the seller must be accurate. If the seller provides both a description and a sample, the goods must ultimately correspond with the description, irrespective of whether they mostly correspond with the sample. This term is included even when the goods have been exposed for supply prior to purchase and selected by the consumer
- that goods will match any sample or model provided by the seller before purchase. In the case of the provision of a sample or a model, the goods must match the sample or model with the exception of any difference made clear to the consumer prior to purchase. Where a sample is provided, there must be no defect to the goods that a reasonable examination of the sample would not reveal
- that, in the event that the contract includes the installation of the goods, it is the duty of the seller to install or ensure that the goods are installed correctly
- that, in the event that goods include digital content, such digital content must comply with the contract for the provision of such content, or the goods will be considered as breaching the contract; and
- that the seller has the right to sell the goods, and that the goods have and will continue to have no charge or encumbrance that has not been made clear to the consumer prior to purchase. In the case of the hire of goods, the trader must have the right to transfer the goods for such a purpose

Under the CRA, which draws together and slightly amends the pre-existing rules under the Unfair Contract Terms Act 1977 and the Unfair Terms in Consumer Contracts Regulations 1999, these terms can not be excluded from contracts by the seller.

In a sale of secondhand goods by auction (at which individuals have the opportunity of attending the sale in person), a buyer does not deal as a consumer.

HIRE-PURCHASE AGREEMENTS
Terms similar to those implied in contracts of sales of goods are implied into contracts of hire-purchase, under the CRA. The Act limits the exclusion of these implied terms as before.

SUPPLY OF GOODS AND SERVICES
Before the CRA, the Supply of Goods and Services Act 1982 regulated other types of contracts (including for services, contracts under which ownership of goods pass and contracts for hire of goods). This Act has now also been amalgamated into the CRA. Similar terms to those above are implied into such contracts, however there are additional terms including:
- that the supplier will use reasonable care and skill in carrying out the service
- that the supplier will carry out the service in a reasonable time (unless the time has been agreed)
- that the supplier will make a reasonable charge (unless the charge or mechanism for its calculation has already been agreed)
The CRA Act limits the exclusion of these implied terms in a similar manner as before.

DIGITAL CONTENT
The CRA is the first statute to address the sale and supply of digital products, defined as 'data which are produced and supplied in digital form.' The Act applies to any digital content which is purchased or that which comes free alongside purchased services or goods. As above, implied terms for quality, fitness for purpose and adherence to description will be imposed on all consumer contracts. However, there is an extra term for contracts for digital content: that the seller has the right to provide such content.

These terms also apply to any future update or modification of the content. Should such future alterations fail to meet these standards, then the breach will be treated as having occurred at the time of supply rather than the point at which it was adapted.

Where digital content causes damage to other digital content or devices, and this could have been prevented where the seller had exercised reasonable skill and care, then that seller will be required to remedy the breach.

UNFAIR TERMS
The CRA has also consolidated the provisions of the Unfair Terms in Consumer Contracts Regulations 1999 that protected consumers against the imposition of unfair consumer contract terms. Where the terms have not been individually negotiated (ie where the terms were drafted in advance so that the consumer was unable to influence those terms), a term will be deemed unfair if it operates to the detriment of the consumer (ie causes a significant imbalance in the parties' rights and obligations arising under the contract). An unfair term does not bind the consumer but the contract may continue to bind the parties if it is capable of existing without the unfair term. The CRA contains a non-exhaustive list of terms that are regarded as potentially unfair. When a term does not fall into such a category, whether it will be regarded as fair or not will depend on many factors, including the nature of the goods or services, the surrounding circumstances (such as the bargaining strength of both parties) and the other terms in the contract.

CONSUMER PROTECTION

The Consumer Protection from Unfair Trading Regulations 2008 (CPRs) replaced much previous consumer protection regulation, including the majority of the Trade Descriptions Act 1968. The CPRs prohibit 31 specific practices, including pyramid schemes. In addition the CPRs prohibit business sellers from making misleading actions and misleading omissions, which cause, or are likely to cause, the average consumer to take a different transactional decision. There is also a general duty not to trade unfairly. The CPRs were amended by the Consumer Protection (Amendment) Regulations 2014, which entered into force on 1 October 2014 and introduced a new direct civil right of redress for consumers against businesses for misleading and aggressive practices, as well as extending the CPRs to cover misleading and aggressive demands for payment.

Under the Consumer Protection Act 1987, producers of goods are liable for any injury, death or damage to any property exceeding £275 caused by a defect in their product (subject to certain defences).

Consumers are also afforded protection under the Consumer Contracts (Information, Cancellation and Additional Charges) Regulations 2013 (CCRs), which came into force on 13 June 2014 and require certain information to be provided to the consumer.

The Financial Guidance and Claims Act 2018 makes provision to ensure members of the public are able to access free and impartial money guidance, pensions guidance and debt advice, and to ensure that they are able to access high-quality claims handling services by strengthening the regulation of claims management companies.

The CPA, CPRs and CCRs implement EU legislation and will be amended accordingly on the day that the UK exits the EU.

CONSUMER CREDIT

In matters relating to the provision of credit (or the supply of goods on hire or hire-purchase), consumers are also protected by the Consumer Credit Act 1974 (as amended by the Consumer Credit Act 2006). The Act was most recently amended by a number of statutory instruments made under the Financial Services and Markets Act 2000. These came into force on 1 April 2014 and represent a major overhaul of the consumer credit regime which was carried out in order to implement the recent EU Consumer Credit Directive. Under the new regime, responsibility for consumer credit regulation has been transferred from the Office of Fair Trading (OFT), which has ceased to exist, to the Financial Conduct Authority (FCA). Previously, a licence issued by the OFT was required in order to conduct a consumer credit, consumer hire or an ancillary credit business, subject to certain exemptions. The requirement to obtain a licence from the OFT has been replaced by the need to obtain authorisation from the FCA to carry out a consumer credit 'regulated' activity, which is likewise subject to certain exemptions. Provisions of the 1974 Act as amended include:

- in order for a creditor to enforce a regulated agreement, the agreement must comply with certain formalities and must be properly executed. An improperly executed regulated agreement is enforceable only on an order of the court. The debtor must also be given specified information by the creditor or his/her broker or agent during the negotiations which take place before the signing of the agreement. The agreement must also state certain information to ensure that the debtor or hirer is aware of the rights and duties conferred or imposed on him/her and the protection and remedies available to him/her under the Act
- the right to withdraw from or cancel some contracts depending on the circumstances. For example, subject to

certain exceptions, a borrower may withdraw from a regulated credit agreement within 14 days without giving any reason. The exceptions include agreements for credit exceeding £60,260 and agreements secured on land. The right to withdraw applies only to the credit agreement itself and not to goods or services purchased with it. The borrower must also repay the credit and any interest

- if the debtor is in breach of the agreement, the creditor must serve a default notice before taking any action such as repossessing the goods
- if the agreement is a hire purchase or conditional sale agreement, the creditor cannot repossess the goods without a court order if the debtor has paid one third of the total price of the goods
- in agreements where the relationship between the creditor and the debtor is unfair to the debtor, the court may alter or set aside some of the terms of the agreement

It is intended that the statutory basis of consumer credit regulation, under the 1974 Act, will be replaced by a rules-based approach under the new regime. The FCA will be reviewing the statutory framework over the next few years and will develop rule-based alternatives where possible.

Consumer credit legislation will be amended on the day the UK exits the EU.

SCOTLAND

The legislation governing the sale and supply of goods applies to Scotland as follows:
- the Consumer Rights Act 2015 (with the exception of chapter three)
- the Sale of Goods Act 1979 applies with some modifications and it has been amended by the Sale and Supply of Goods Act 1994
- the Supply of Goods (Implied Terms) Act 1973 applies
- the Supply of Goods and Services Act 1982 does not extend to Scotland but some of its provisions were introduced by the Sale and Supply of Goods Act 1994
- only Parts II and III of the Unfair Contract Terms Act 1977 apply
- the Trade Descriptions Act 1968 applies with minor modifications
- the Consumer Credit Act 1974 applies
- the Consumer Credit Act 2006 applies
- the Consumer Protection Act 1987 applies
- the General Product Safety Regulations 2005 apply
- the Unfair Terms in Consumer Contracts (Amendment) Regulations 2001 apply
- the Consumer Protection (Distance Selling) Regulations 2000 apply
- the Consumer Protection from Unfair Trading Regulations 2008 apply

PROCEEDINGS AGAINST THE CROWN

Until 1947, proceedings against the Crown were generally possible only by a procedure known as a petition of right, which put the private litigant at a considerable disadvantage. The Crown Proceedings Act 1947 placed the Crown (not the sovereign in his/her private capacity, but as the embodiment of the state) largely in the same position as a private individual and made proceedings in the high court involving the Crown subject to the same rules as any other case. The act did not, however, extinguish or limit the Crown's prerogative or statutory powers, and it continued the immunity of HM ships and aircraft. It also left certain Crown privileges unaffected. The act largely abolished the special procedures which previously applied to civil proceedings by and against the Crown. Civil proceedings may be initiated against the appropriate government department or, if there is doubt regarding which is the appropriate department, against the attorney-general.

In Scotland proceedings against the Crown founded on breach of contract could be taken before the 1947 act and no special procedures applied. The Crown could, however, claim certain special pleas. The 1947 act applies in part to Scotland and brings the practice of the two countries as closely together as the different legal systems permit. As a result of the Scotland Act 1998, actions against government departments should be raised against the Lord Advocate or the advocate-general. Actions should be raised against the Lord Advocate where the department involved administers a devolved matter. Devolved matters include agriculture, education, housing, local government, health and justice. Actions should be raised against the advocate-general where the department is dealing with a reserved matter. Reserved matters include defence, foreign affairs and social security.

DEATHS

WHEN A DEATH OCCURS

If the death (including stillbirth) was expected, the doctor who attended the deceased during their final illness should be contacted. If the death was sudden or unexpected, the family doctor (if known) and police should be contacted. If the cause of death is quite clear, the doctor will provide:

• a medical certificate that shows the cause of death
• a formal notice that states that the doctor has signed the medical certificate and that explains how to get the death registered
• if the death was known to be caused by a natural illness but the doctor wishes to know more about the cause of death, he/she may ask the relatives for permission to carry out a post-mortem examination

In England and Wales a coroner is responsible for investigating deaths occurring:

• when there is no doctor who can issue a medical certificate of cause of death
• no doctor has treated the deceased during his or her last illness or when the doctor attending the patient did not see him or her within 14 days before death, or after death
• the death occurred during an operation or before recovery from the effect of an anaesthetic
• the death was sudden and unexplained or attended by suspicious circumstances
• the death might be due to an industrial injury, disease or poisoning
• the death might be due to accident, violence, neglect or abortion
• the death occurred in prison or in police custody
• the cause of death is unknown

The doctor will write on the formal notice that the death has been referred to the coroner; if the post-mortem shows that death was due to natural causes, the coroner may issue a notification which gives the cause of death so that the death can be registered. If the cause of death was violent or unnatural, is still undetermined after a post-mortem, or took place in prison or police custody, the coroner must hold an inquest. The coroner must hold an inquest in these circumstances even if the death occurred abroad (and the body has been returned to England or Wales).

In Scotland the office of coroner does not exist. The local procurator fiscal inquires into sudden or suspicious deaths. A fatal accident inquiry will be held before the sheriff where the death has resulted from an accident during the course of the employment of the person who has died, or where the person who has died was in legal custody or a child required to be kept or detained in secure accommodation, or where

the Lord Advocate deems it in the public interest that an inquiry be held.

REGISTERING A DEATH

In England and Wales the death can be registered at any register office, although if it is registered by the registrar of births and deaths for the district in which it occurred, the necessary documents can be obtained on the same day. A death which occurs in Scotland can be registered in any registration district in Scotland. Information concerning a death can be given before any registrar of births and deaths in England and Wales. The registrar will pass the relevant details to the registrar for the district where the death occurred, who will then register the death.

In England and Wales the death must normally be registered within five days (unless the registrar says this period can be extended); in Scotland within eight days. If the death has been referred to the coroner/local procurator fiscal it cannot be registered until the registrar has received authority from the coroner/local procurator fiscal to do so. Failure to register a death involves a penalty in England and Wales and may lead to a court decree being granted by a sheriff in Scotland. A stillbirth normally needs to be registered within 42 days, and at the latest within three months. In many cases this can be done at the hospital or at the local register office. In Scotland this must be done within 21 days.

If the death occurred at a house or hospital, the death may be registered by:

• any relative of the deceased
• any person present at the death
• any person making the funeral arrangements
• an administrator from the hospital
• in Scotland, the deceased's executor or legal representative

For deaths that took place elsewhere, the death may be registered by:

• any relative of the deceased
• someone present at the death
• someone who found the body
• a person in charge of the body
• any person making the funeral arrangements

The majority of deaths are registered by a relative of the deceased. The registrar would normally allow one of the other listed persons to register the death only if there were no relatives available.

The person registering the death should take the medical certificate of the cause of death (signed by a doctor) with them; it is also useful, though not essential, to take the deceased's birth and marriage/civil partnership certificates, council tax bill, driving licence, passport or NHS medical card. The details given to the registrar must be absolutely correct, otherwise it may be difficult to change them later. The person registering the death should check the entry carefully before it is signed. The registrar will issue a certificate for burial or cremation, and a certificate of registration of death (form BD8, commonly known as a 'death certificate' which is issued for social security purposes if the deceased received a state pension or benefits) – both free of charge. A death certificate is a certified copy of the entry in the death register; copies can be provided on payment of a fee and may be required for the following purposes, in particular by the executor or administrator when sorting out the deceased's affairs:

• the will
• bank and building society accounts
• savings bank certificates and premium bonds
• insurance policies
• pension claims

If the death occurred abroad or on a foreign ship or aircraft, the death should be registered according to the local regulations of the relevant country and a death certificate should be obtained. In many countries the death can also be registered with the British consulate in that country and a record will be kept at the General Register Office. This avoids the expense of bringing the body back.

After 12 months (three months in Scotland) of death or the finding of a dead body, no death can be registered without the written authority of the registrar-general.

BURIAL AND CREMATION

In most circumstances in England and Wales a certificate for burial or cremation must be obtained from the registrar before the burial or cremation can take place. If the death has been referred to the coroner, an order for burial or a certificate for cremation must be obtained. In Scotland a death or still birth must be registered in order that the appropriate certificate can be obtained to allow burial or cremation of the body.

Funeral costs can normally be repaid out of the deceased's estate and should be given priority over any other claims. If the deceased has left a will it may contain directions concerning the funeral; however, these directions need not be followed by the executor.

The deceased's papers should also indicate whether a grave space had already been arranged. This information will be contained in a document known as a 'Deed of Grant'. Most town churchyards and many suburban churchyards are no longer open for burial because they are full. Most cemeteries are non-denominational and may be owned by local authorities or private companies; fees vary.

If the body is to be cremated, an application form, two cremation certificates, one signed by the doctor who issued the medical certificate and the other signed by a different doctor confirming the first certificate (for which there is a charge) or a certificate for cremation if the death was referred to the coroner must be completed in addition to the certificate for burial or cremation (the form is not required if the coroner has issued a certificate for cremation). All the forms are available from the funeral director or crematorium. Most crematoria are run by local authorities; the fees can include the medical referee's fee and the use of the chapel. Ashes may be scattered, buried in a churchyard or cemetery, or kept.

The registrar must be notified of the date, place and means of disposal of the body within 96 hours (England and Wales) or three days (Scotland).

If the death occurred abroad or on a foreign ship or aircraft, a local burial or cremation may be arranged. If the body is to be brought back to England or Wales, a death certificate from the relevant country or an authorisation for the removal of the body from the country of death from the coroner or relevant authority, together with a certificate of embalming, will be required. The British consulate can help to arrange this documentation. To arrange a funeral in England or Wales, a certified translation of a foreign death certificate or a death certificate issued in Scotland or Northern Ireland which must show the cause of death, is needed, together with a certificate of no liability to register from the registrar in England and Wales in whose sub-district it is intended to bury or cremate the body. If burial is intended they will issue a certificate for burial. If it is intended to cremate the body, a cremation order will be required from the Home Office or a certificate for cremation. If the body is to be cremated in Scotland, a certificate permitting this must be obtained from the Death Certification Review Service run by Healthcare Improvement Scotland.

THE GENERAL REGISTER OFFICE, General Register Office, PO Box 2, Southport PR8 2JD T 0300-123 1837
W www.gro.gov.uk/gro/content/certificates

THE NATIONAL RECORDS OF SCOTLAND, New Register House, 3 West Register Street, Edinburgh EH1 3YT
T 0131-334 0380 W www.nrscotland.gov.uk

DIVORCE, DISSOLUTION AND RELATED MATTERS

Divorce is the legal process which ends a marriage. The process is the same whether the parties are of the opposite or same sex pursuant to the Marriage (Same Sex Couples) Act 2013. Dissolution is a similar process which ends a civil partnership. Divorce and dissolution should be distinguished from judicial separation which does not legally dissolve the marriage/civil partnership but removes the legal requirement for a married couple to live together.

DIVORCE

There are two bars to divorce and dissolution: the 'one-year rule' and jurisdiction.

An application for a matrimonial order for divorce may only be presented to the court after one year of marriage. The spouse who lodges this document is known as the 'applicant petitioner' throughout the divorce proceedings and the other spouse is the 'respondent'.

Whether the English court may or may not have jurisdiction to deal with any divorce will depend on where the parties spent their married life and whether or not one party has retained their residence or domicile in England (and Wales). If there is a dispute as to which of two jurisdictions should host the divorce, where the two jurisdictions likely to be relevant are EU countries then the usual rule is that the divorce takes place in the country where the petition is filed first. The exception to this rule is Denmark, which opted out of the EU regulation which determines forums in this way.

If the two countries are not within the EU, or one of them is Denmark, then the forum of divorce may be determined by which is the more appropriate or convenient *(forum conveniens)*. In these circumstances, an election of a jurisdiction in a pre-nuptial agreement can be very important in resolving that dispute, although it cannot override the 'first in time' rule between EU countries (except Denmark) referred to above (save in the case of maintenance claims).

Some EU countries have signed up to the Convention on the Recognition of Divorces and Legal Separations which would allow a couple to elect a choice of law even in EU countries whereby one country would be required to apply the law of another. For the time being, England has not signed up to that convention and would apply English law only.

The UK's withdrawal from the EU will undoubtedly have an impact on the law in this area, since various European instruments apply (as outlined above) in determining in which country and jurisdiction a couple get divorced. In the case of a no-deal Brexit, the 'first-in-time' rules will no longer apply between the UK and the remaining EU member states and the UK would revert to the pre-EU *forum conveniens* rules.

There is only one ground for divorce, namely that the marriage has broken down irretrievably. This ground must be 'proved' by one of the five following facts:

- the respondent has committed adultery and the petitioner finds it intolerable to live with the respondent (an applicant can not file for divorce based on their own adultery)
- the respondent has behaved in such a way that the petitioner cannot reasonably be expected to live with the respondent
- the respondent has deserted the petitioner for a continuous period of at least two years immediately prior to the petition
- the applicant and respondent have lived apart for a continuous period of two years immediately prior to the petition and the respondent agrees to a divorce
- the applicant and respondent have lived apart for a continuous period of five years immediately prior to the petition

If the court is satisfied that the petitioner has proved one of those facts then it must grant a decree nisi *(see* below) unless it is satisfied that the marriage has not broken down.

Periods of up to six months' cohabitation are permitted for attempts at reconciliation without prejudicing the matrimonial proceedings. If the parties continue to live together for more than six months following discovery of adultery, the applicant will not be able to rely on the fact of adultery to prove the marriage has irretrievably broken down and may also adversely affect the applicant's chances of establishing arguments of unreasonable behaviour.

NO-FAULT DIVORCE

The majority of people are not prepared to wait two or five years to divorce and so are forced by the current legislation to apportion blame (adultery or unreasonable behaviour). Following the supreme court case of *Owens v Owens* in 2018, the government announced plans to introduce no-fault divorce and, in April 2019, it was confirmed the government will introduce new legislation to implement the planned changes. Removing blame from the divorce process has come as a welcome development to family lawyers. Following reform, a couple (or one party) would need to notify the court that their marriage has irretrievably broken down. The 'five facts' will be removed, a minimum six-month period will be required to enable couples to 'reflect' on their decision and the ability to contest a divorce will be abolished. Parallel changes will be made to the law governing the dissolution of civil partnerships. The proposed legislation will not cover other areas of matrimonial law such as financial provision.

DECREE NISI

If the judge is satisfied that the petitioner has proved the marriage has irretrievably broken down, a date will be set for the pronouncement of the decree nisi in open court. The decree nisi confirms the grounds for divorce have been met; the marriage will not be legally dissolved until the decree absolute. Neither party needs to attend and all the proceedings up to this point are usually carried out on paper.

DECREE ABSOLUTE

The final step in the divorce procedure is to obtain a decree absolute which formally ends the marriage. The petitioner can apply for this six weeks and one day after the date of the decree nisi. If the petitioner does not apply the respondent can apply, but only after three months from the earliest date on which the petitioner could have applied.

A decree absolute will not usually be granted until the parties have agreed, or the court has dealt with, the parties' financial situation (*see* below for details of financial provision).

DISSOLUTION OF CIVIL PARTNERSHIPS

The legal process for dissolution of a civil partnership follows a model closely based on divorce. Irretrievable breakdown of the partnership is the sole ground for dissolution. The facts to be proved to establish this are the same as for divorce, with the exception of adultery which, due to its legal definition, can only apply to opposite sex couples. Sexual activity with a third party can, however, be used as an example of unreasonable behaviour.

FINANCIAL RELIEF ANCILLARY TO DIVORCE, NULLITY AND JUDICIAL SEPARATION

Following a petition for divorce, nullity or judicial separation, it is open to either spouse or former spouse to make a claim for financial provision provided they have not remarried. It is common practice for such an application to be made at the same time, or shortly after, a divorce petition has been issued. Although most are agreed or settled by the parties themselves, where the parties are unable to agree, the courts have wide powers to make financial provision where a marriage breaks down. Orders can be made for:
• spousal maintenance (periodical payments) which can be capitalised into a lump sum
• lump sum payments
• adjustment or transfer of interests in property
• adjustment of interests in trusts and settlements
• orders relating to pensions

EXERCISE OF THE COURT'S POWERS TO ORDER FINANCIAL PROVISION

The court must exercise its powers so as to achieve an outcome which is fair between the parties, although it has a wide discretion in determining what is a fair financial outcome. It will consider the worldwide assets of both parties, whether liquid or illiquid. In exercising its discretion, the court has to consider a range of statutory factors including:
• the income, earning capacity, property and other financial resources which either party has or is likely to have in the foreseeable future, including, in the case of earning capacity, any increase in that capacity which it would in the opinion of the court be reasonable to expect a party to the marriage to take steps to acquire
• the financial needs, obligations and responsibilities which each of the parties to the marriage has or is likely to have in the foreseeable future
• the standard of living enjoyed by the family before the breakdown of the marriage
• the age of each party to the marriage and the duration of the marriage
• any physical or mental disability of either of the parties to the marriage
• the contribution which each of the parties has made or is likely to make in the foreseeable future to the welfare of the family, including any contribution by looking after the home or caring for the family
• the conduct of each of the parties, if that conduct is such that it would in the opinion of the court be inequitable to disregard it
• the value to each of the parties to the marriage of any benefit which, by reason of the dissolution of that marriage, that party will lose the chance of acquiring

When considering the above factors, the court must give first consideration to the welfare of any child of the family.

The court has a duty when exercising its powers to consider whether a 'clean break' would be appropriate. A clean break severs the financial ties between the parties and would provide no continuing capital payments or spousal periodical payments.

The court has a wide discretion in considering these factors in order to achieve an outcome it considers to be fair. The court's approach changed dramatically following the House of Lords decision of *White v White* in October 2000 where it was said that, after providing for the parties' reasonable needs, the remaining assets should be shared. In that case, it was established that the contributions made by both breadwinner and homemaker are to be regarded as equal and the court's main objective must be to achieve a fair outcome. More recent case law has gone further in establishing that the starting point should be an equal division of matrimonial assets. In lower net worth cases, any departure from an equal division is usually justified on the basis of need.

In high net worth cases, however, a departure from equality is frequently justified not just on the basis of need but also of compensation and non-matrimonial property. In the House of Lords cases of Miller and McFarlane the court refined the thinking in the White case to say that the court should strive to achieve a fair result by considering three strands:
• the needs of the parties going forward
• compensation for any economic disparity between the parties (such as where one party has sacrificed their career to become a full-time parent)
• sharing

NUPTIAL AGREEMENTS

Nuptial agreements are legal agreements drawn up prior to (pre-nuptial) or during (post-nuptial) marriage or civil partnership to regulate financial arrangements and division of assets in the event of divorce or dissolution. Such agreements are not currently binding in England and Wales. In October 2010, the supreme court gave judgment in *Radmacher v Granatino* which made it clear that a nuptial agreement can carry considerable weight (and will most likely be binding) provided the spouses freely and fully agree to its terms, are aware of its implications and it is fair to hold the parties to it, given the circumstances at the time of the court hearing. However, the court will still be able to decide as to whether the agreement is fair and whether the terms setting out the financial provision on divorce should be enforced in whole or in part. The supreme court gave some guidelines on when a pre-nuptial agreement would be considered 'fair', but ultimately it depends on the facts of the individual case.

FINANCIAL PROVISION ON DISSOLUTION OF A CIVIL PARTNERSHIP

The Civil Partnership Act 2004 makes provisions for financial relief for civil partners generally and extends the same rights and responsibilities invoked by marriage. Again the court must consider a number of factors when exercising its discretion and must take into account all of the circumstances of the case while giving first consideration to the welfare of any child of the family who is under 18. The list of statutory factors the court must consider resemble those for marriage and it is likely that the interpretation of these factors will be based on the court's interpretation of the factors relating to marriage.

COHABITING COUPLES

There is no such thing as a common law spouse. Unmarried couples do not benefit from the same statutory protection afforded to married couples. Instead, the rights of cohabitees are based on property law and trust interests. Therefore, it is advisable to consider entering into a contract, or 'cohabitation agreement', which establishes how money, property and the care of any children should be divided in the event of a relationship breakdown.

The Cohabitation Rights bill 2017–19 seeks to introduce certain protections for cohabitees during their lifetime and on death, it received its first reading in the House of Lords on 5 July 2017 and second reading on 15 March 2019, but has made no further progress. Thus, cohabitation agreements continue to be governed by the same general principles of property, trust, and contract law.

FINANCIAL PROVISION FOR CHILDREN

Under the Child Support Act 1991, all parents are under a legal obligation to support their children financially. A parent who does not have day-to-day care of a child is under a duty to pay child maintenance to the parent who does.

Parents can arrange child maintenance themselves (a so-called 'family based arrangement') or, where the parties are not able to reach an agreement, one party may apply to the Child Maintenance Service (CMS), (formerly the Child Support Agency (CSA)) to carry out an assessment. Since 31 December 2017, CMS handles all child maintenance arrangements. The CSA no longer takes on new cases but still handles cases opened before 25 November 2013.

There is a £20 application fee for applying to CMS (unless the applicant is under the age of 18, a victim of domestic abuse, or lives in Northern Ireland), which covers the costs for calculating the amount of child maintenance, the provision to both parties of a yearly updated calculation using HMRC data and provision of information about payment services.

There are three different methods of calculating child support under the statutory child maintenance schemes:

- the 'old' scheme (for all applications up until 3 March 2003)
- the net income scheme (for applications from 3 March 2003)
- the gross income scheme (for all new applications since 25 November 2013)

All CMS child maintenance calculations will be dealt with under the gross income scheme. CMS uses the paying parent's gross weekly income (using information obtained from HMRC) as a starting point to work out the rate of child maintenance a non-resident parent should be liable for. Once the gross income information is received, the CMS applies a specific formula to work out the level of child maintenance payable. The child maintenance calculation may only be reassessed annually, unless the income variation is 25 per cent or more or in cases involving long-term illness or redundancy. It is a criminal offence to make a false statement or representation to or withhold information from the CMS and also to fail to notify CMS of a change of address or other change of circumstances.

Under the gross income scheme, it is mandatory for parents to have a conversation with the Child Maintenance Options (CMO) team to discuss their choices and consider alternatives before they proceed with their application. The CMO will discuss the various options available to parents if they cannot agree a 'family-based arrangement' between themselves:

- 'Direct Pay' (previously known as 'Maintenance Direct' under CSA arrangements) which enables parents to keep control of making and receiving payments. The statutory service works out the payment amounts for parents but will not be involved in collection
- 'Collect and Pay' (previously known as the 'full collection service' under CSA arrangements) whereby CMS calculates how much maintenance the paying parent owes. If the Collect and Pay Service is used, parties will be required to pay a fee for use of the service. Paying parents are required to pay a 20 per cent fee on top of their regular child maintenance payment and receiving parents will have 4 per cent of their child maintenance payment deducted from the total they receive

If payments are not made on time there is a spectrum of collection actions and enforcement powers (the range of which was increased in December 2018) available to the CMS to collect arrears, although they can only be used if a case is on the 'Collect and Pay' scheme. CMS will contact the paying parent to seek continuing payments. Where there is persistent non-payment, the CMS is able to take money directly from the paying parent, either from their earnings or bank account, or to take court action. There are CMS fees for pursuing enforcement action, which may affect the eventual amount of child maintenance received by the receiving party. Since December 2018, the government has had the power to write-off arrears that accumulated when a case was administered by the CSA, if no payment towards those arrears has been made for three months, and subject to certain other conditions.

Further changes were introduced in December 2018 including how CMS calculates child maintenance for complex earnings giving CMS the right to make deductions from joint accounts and unlimited partnership accounts and the power to disqualify a payment parents from holding or obtaining a passport if they have consistently avoided paying their child maintenance debt.

Provision is also made under Schedule 1 of the Children Act 1989 for unmarried parents, step-parents and guardians to apply to the court for periodical payments, lump sum and property adjustment orders.

SCOTLAND

Although some provisions are similar to those for England and Wales, there is separate legislation for Scotland covering nullity of marriage, judicial separation, divorce and ancillary matters. The principal legislation in relation to family law in Scotland is the Family Law (Scotland) Act 1985. The Family Law (Scotland) Act 2006 came in to force on 4 May 2006, and introduced reforms to various aspects of Scottish family law. The following is confined to major points on which the law in Scotland differs from that of England and Wales.

An action for judicial separation or divorce may be raised in the court of session; it may also be raised in the sheriff court if either party was resident in the sheriffdom for 40 days immediately before the date of the action or for 40 days ending not more than 40 days before the date of the action and has no known residence in Scotland at that date. The fee for starting a divorce petition in the sheriff court is £156.

The grounds for raising an action of divorce in Scotland are set down in The Divorce (Scotland) Act 1976 and have been subject to reform in terms of the 2006 act. The current grounds for divorce are:

- the defender has committed adultery. When adultery is cited as proof that the marriage has broken down irretrievably, it is not necessary in Scotland to prove that it is also intolerable for the pursuer to live with the defender
- the defender's behaviour is such that the pursuer cannot reasonably be expected to cohabit with the defender
- there has been no cohabitation between the parties for one year prior to the raising of the action for divorce, and the defender consents to the granting of decree of divorce
- there has been no cohabitation between the parties for two years prior to the raising of the action for divorce
- the marriage has broken down irretrievably
- an interim gender recognition certificate under the Gender Recognition Act 2004 has, after the date of marriage, been issued to either party to the marriage. However, as a result of changes under the Marriage and Civil Partnership (Scotland) Act 2014, this ground of divorce will sometimes not be available where a full gender recognition certificate has been issued under the 2004 Act

The previously available ground of desertion was abolished by the 2006 Act.

A simplified procedure for 'do-it-yourself divorce' was introduced in 1983 for certain divorces. If the action is based on one or two years' separation and will not be opposed or because a gender recognition certificate has been issued; there are no children under 16; no financial claims; there is no sign that the applicant's spouse is unable to manage his or her affairs through mental illness or handicap; and there are no other court proceedings underway which might result in the end of the marriage, the applicant can access the appropriate forms to enable him or her to proceed on the Scottish Courts and Tribunals' website. From 25 April 2019 the fee is £125, however the applicant may be exempt from paying the fee if they are in receipt of certain benefits; or if legal advice and assistance is being provided by a solicitor in terms of the Legal Aid (Scotland) Act 1986.

Where a divorce action has been raised, it may be put on hold for a variety of reasons. In all actions for divorce an extract decree, which brings the marriage to an end, will be made available 14 days after the divorce has been granted. Unlike in England, there is no decree nisi, only a final decree of divorce. Parties must ensure that all financial issues have been resolved prior to divorce, as it is not possible to seek further financial provision after divorce has been granted.

FINANCIAL PROVISION

In relation to financial provision on divorce, the first, and most important, principle is fair sharing of the matrimonial property. There is a presumption that fair share means an equal share of the matrimonial property, which can be departed from if justified by special circumstances. In terms of Scots law matrimonial property is defined as all property acquired by either spouse from the date of marriage up to the date of separation. Property acquired before the marriage is not deemed to be matrimonial unless it was acquired for use by the parties as a family home or as furniture for that home. Property acquired after the date of separation is not matrimonial property. Any property acquired by either of the parties by way of gift or inheritance during the marriage is excluded and does not form part of the matrimonial property.

When considering whether to make an award of financial provision a court shall also take account of any economic advantage derived by either party to the marriage as a result of contributions, financial or otherwise, by the other, and of any economic disadvantage suffered by either party for the benefit of the other party. The court must also ensure that the economic burden of caring for a child under the age of 16 is shared fairly between the parties.

A court can also consider making an order requiring one party to pay the other party a periodical allowance for a certain period of time following divorce. Such an order may be appropriate in cases where there is insufficient capital to effect a fair sharing of the matrimonial property. Orders for periodical allowance are uncommon, as courts will favour a 'clean break' where possible.

CHILDREN

The court has the power to award a residence order in respect of any children of the marriage or to make an order regulating the child's contact with the non-resident parent. The court will only make such orders if it is deemed better for the child to do so than to make no order at all, and the welfare of the children is of paramount importance. The fact that a spouse has caused the breakdown of the marriage does not in itself preclude him/her from being awarded residence.

NULLITY

An action for 'declaration of nullity' can be brought if someone with a legitimate interest is able to show that the marriage is void or voidable. Although the grounds on which a marriage may be void or voidable are similar to those on which a marriage can be declared invalid in England, there are some differences. Where a spouse is capable of sexual intercourse but refuses to consummate the marriage, this is not a ground for nullity in Scots law, though it could be a ground for divorce. Where a spouse was suffering from venereal disease at the time of marriage and the other spouse did not know, this is not a ground for nullity in Scots law, neither is the fact that a wife was pregnant by another man at the time of marriage without the knowledge of her husband.

COHABITING COUPLES

The law in Scotland now provides certain financial and property rights for cohabiting couples in terms of the Family Law (Scotland) Act 2006, or 'the 2006 Act'. The relevant 2006 Act provisions do not place cohabitants in Scotland on an equal footing with married couples or civil partners, but provide some rights for cohabitants in the event that the relationship is terminated by separation or death. The provisions relate to couples who cease to cohabit after 4 May 2006.

The legislation provides for a presumption that most contents of the home shared by the cohabitants are owned in equal shares. A former cohabitant can also seek financial provision on termination of the relationship in the form of a capital payment if they can successfully demonstrate that they have been financially disadvantaged, and that conversely the other cohabitant has been financially advantaged, as a consequence of contributions made (financial or otherwise). An order can also be made in respect of the economic burden of caring for a child of whom the cohabitants are the parents. Such a claim must be made no later than one year after the day on which the cohabitants cease to cohabit.

The 2006 Act also provides that a cohabitant may make a claim on their partner's estate in the event of that partner's death, providing that there is no will. A claim of this nature must be made no later than six months after the date of the partner's death.

THE CENTRAL FAMILY COURT, First Avenue House, 42–49 High Holborn, London WC1V 6NP **T** 020-7421 8594

THE COURT OF SESSION, Parliament House, Parliament Square, Edinburgh EH1 1RQ **T** 0131-225 2595
W www.scotcourts.gov.uk

THE CHILD MAINTENANCE SERVICE, **T** 0800-171 2033
W www.gov.uk/child-maintenance

EMPLOYMENT LAW

EMPLOYEES

A fundamental distinction in UK employment law is that drawn between an employee and someone who is self-employed. Further, there is an important, intermediate category introduced by legislation: 'workers' covers all employees but also catches others who do not have full employment status. An 'employee' is someone who has entered into or works under a contract of employment, while a 'worker' has entered into or works under a contract whereby he undertakes to do or perform personally any work or services for another party whose status is not that of a client or customer. Whether or not someone is an employee or a worker as opposed to being genuinely self-employed is an important and complex question, for it determines that person's statutory rights and protections. For certain purposes, such as protection against discrimination, protection extends to some genuinely self-employed people as well as workers and employees.

The greater the level of control that the employer has over the work carried out, the greater the depth of integration of the employee in the employer's business, and the closer the obligations to provide and perform work between the parties, the more likely it is that the parties will be employer and employee.

PAY AND CONDITIONS

The Employment Rights Act 1996 consolidated the statutory provisions relating to employees' rights. Employers must give each employee employed for one month or more a written statement containing the following information:
• names of employer and employee
• date when employment began and the date on which the employee's period of *continuous* employment began (taking into account any employment with a previous employer which counts towards that period)
• the scale, rate or other method of calculating remuneration and intervals at which it will be paid
• job title or description of job
• hours and the permitted place(s) of work and, where there are several such places, the address of the employer
• holiday entitlement and holiday pay
• provisions concerning incapacity for work due to sickness and injury, including provisions for sick pay
• details of pension scheme(s)
• length of notice the employee is obliged to give and entitled to receive in order to terminate the contract of employment
• if the employment is not intended to be permanent, the period for which it is expected to continue or, if it is for a fixed term, the end date of the contract
• details of any collective agreement (including the parties to the agreement) which directly affects the terms of employment
• details of disciplinary and grievance procedures (including the individual to whom a complaint should be made and the process of making that complaint) except those which relate to health and safety at work
• if the employee is to work outside the UK for more than one month, the period of such work and the currency in which

payment is made and any additional remuneration or benefits payable to them
• a note stating whether a contracting-out certificate is in force

This must be given to the employee within two months of the start of their employment.

If the employer does not provide the written statement within two months (or a statement of any changes to these particulars within one month of the changes being made) then the employee can complain to an employment tribunal, which can specify the information that the employer should have given. When, in the context of an employee's successful tribunal claim, the employer is also found to have been in breach of the duty to provide the written statement at the time proceedings were commenced, the tribunal must award the employee two weeks' pay, and may award four weeks' pay, subject to the statutory cap, unless it would be unjust or inequitable to do so.

The Working Time Regulations 1998, the National Minimum Wage Act 1998, Employment Relations Act 1999, the Employment Act 2002 and the Employment Act 2008 now supplement the 1996 Act.

The Employment Rights (Employment Particulars and Paid Annual Leave) (Amendment) Regulations 2018 will come into force on 6 April 2020 and provides that a written statement of terms must be given on or before the first day of employment, rather than within two months of employment starting. In addition, they increase the amount of information that must be included in the statement.

The Employment Rights (Miscellaneous Amendments) Regulations 2019 will also extend the right to a written statement of terms to all workers, rather than just employees, for all new joiners on or after 6 April 2020.

FLEXIBLE WORKING

The Flexible Working Regulations 2014 gives all employees, from 30 June 2014, the right to apply for flexible working after continuously working for the same employer for at least 26 weeks. An employer must consider and decide upon a request within three months and must have a sound business reason for rejecting any request. If an application under the act is not dealt with in accordance with a prescribed procedure, or is rejected on other than specific grounds, the employee may complain to an employment tribunal. In Northern Ireland an employer must hold a meeting with an employee within 28 days of a request for flexible working, and give reasons in writing within a further 14 days.

SICK PAY

Employees absent from work through illness or injury are entitled to receive Statutory Sick Pay (SSP) from the employer from the fourth day of absence for a maximum period of 28 weeks. The right to SSP will cease where an employee has had linked periods of sickness that have spanned a period of three years.

MATERNITY AND PARENTAL RIGHTS

Under the Employment Relations Act 1999, the Employment Act 2002, the Maternity and Parental Leave Regulations 1999 (as amended in 2001, 2002, 2006, 2013 and 2014), the Paternity and Adoption Leave Regulations 2002 and 2003, the Additional Paternity Leave Regulations 2010 and the Shared Parental Leave Regulations 2014, both men and women are entitled to take leave when they become a parent (including by adoption). Women are protected from discrimination, detriment or dismissal by reason of their pregnancy or maternity, including discrimination by association and by perception. Men and adoptive parents are protected from suffering a detriment or dismissal for taking paternity, adoption or parental leave.

Any woman who needs to attend an antenatal appointment on the advice of a registered medical professional is entitled to paid leave from work to attend. All pregnant women are entitled to a maximum period of maternity leave of 52 weeks. This comprises 26 weeks' ordinary maternity leave, followed immediately by 26 weeks' additional maternity leave. A woman who takes ordinary maternity leave normally has the right to return to the job in which she was employed before her absence. If she takes additional maternity leave, she is entitled to return to the same job or, if that is not reasonably practicable, to another job that is suitable and appropriate for her to do. There is a two-week period of compulsory maternity leave, immediately following the birth of the child, wherein the employer is not permitted to allow the mother to work.

A woman will qualify for Statutory Maternity Pay (SMP), which is payable for up to 39 weeks, if she has been continuously employed for not less than 26 weeks by the end of the 15th week before the expected week of childbirth. For further information *see* Social Welfare, Employer Payments.

Employees are entitled to adoption leave and adoption pay (at the same rates as SMP) subject to fulfilment of similar criteria to those in relation to maternity leave and pay. Where a couple is adopting a child, either one (but not both) of the parents may take adoption leave, and the other may take paternity leave.

Certain employees are entitled to paternity leave on the birth or adoption of a child. To be eligible, the employee must be the child's father, or the partner of the mother or adopter, and meet other conditions. These conditions are, firstly, that they must have been continuously employed for not less than 26 weeks prior to the 15th week before the expected week of childbirth (or, in the case of adoptions, 26 weeks ending with the week in which notification of the adoption match is given) and, secondly, that the employee must have or expect to have responsibility for the upbringing of the child. The employee may take either one week's leave, or two consecutive weeks' leave. This leave may be taken at any time between the date of the child's birth (or placement for adoption) and 56 days later. A statutory payment is available during this period.

For births on or after 5 April 2015, eligible parents are entitled to shared parental leave (SPL) whereby they will be able to share a pot of leave of up to 50 weeks and 37 weeks of pay, after the initial two weeks of maternity leave that is compulsory for the mother (or the equivalent two-week period for the adopter in adoption cases). During that 50 week period, parents can decide to be off work at the same time and/or take it in turns to have periods of leave to look after their child. To be eligible, the employee must be the child's mother, father, adopter, or partner of the mother or adopter, and must have worked for the same employer for not less than 26 weeks prior to the end of the 15th week before the expected week of childbirth (or, in case of adoptions, 26 weeks ending with the week in which notification of the adoption match is given). The amount of leave available is calculated using the mother's entitlement to maternity leave. If a mother reduces maternity leave she and/or her partner may opt to take SPL for the remaining weeks. On taking SPL, a woman will be entitled to statutory shared parental pay, which will generally be at the same rate as SMP, except in the first six weeks of maternity leave, during which a cap applies to shared parental pay but not to SMP.

For more information *see* Social Welfare, Employer Payments.

Any employee with at least year's continuous service who has, or expects to have, responsibility for a child may take parental leave to care for the child. Each parent is entitled to a total of 18 weeks unpaid parental leave for each child or adopted child. This leave must be taken (at the rate of no more than four weeks a year, and in blocks of whole weeks only) before the child's 18th birthday.

The Parental Bereavement (Leave and Pay) Act 2018 is expected to come into force in April 2020 and will provide the right for all employed parents to take two weeks' leave if they lose a child under the age of 18, or suffer a stillbirth from 24 weeks of pregnancy, together with the right to statutory parental bereavement pay if certain eligibility criteria are met. It is likely that any such leave will need to be taken within 56 days of the child's death.

SUNDAY TRADING

The Sunday Trading Act 1994 allows shops to open on Sunday. The Employment Rights Act 1996 gives shop workers and betting workers the right not to be dismissed, selected for redundancy or to suffer any detriment (such as the denial of overtime, promotion or training) if they refuse to work only on Sundays. This does not apply to those who, under their contracts, are employed to work on Sundays.

TERMINATION OF EMPLOYMENT

An employee may be dismissed without notice if guilty of gross misconduct but in other cases a period of notice must be given by the employer. The minimum periods of notice specified in the Employment Rights Act 1996 are:

- one week if the employee has been continuously employed for one month or more but for less than two years
- one week for each complete year of continuous employment, if the employee has been employed for two years or more, up to a maximum of 12 weeks' notice
- longer periods apply if these are specified in the contract of employment

If an employee is dismissed with less notice than he/she is entitled to by statute, or under their contract if longer, he/she will have a wrongful dismissal claim (unless the employer paid the employee in lieu of notice in accordance with a contractual provision entitling it to do so). This claim for wrongful dismissal can be brought by the employee either in the civil courts or the employment tribunal, but if brought in the tribunal the maximum amount that can be awarded is £25,000.

REDUNDANCY

An employee dismissed because of redundancy may be entitled to redundancy pay. This applies if:

- the employment commenced before 6 April 2012 and the employee has at least one year's continuous service or the employment commenced on or after 6 April 2012 and the employee has at least two years' continuous service
- the employee is dismissed by the employer by reason of redundancy (this can include cases of voluntary redundancy)

Redundancy can mean closure of the entire business, closure of a particular site of the business, or a reduction in the need for employees to carry out work of a particular kind.

An employee may not be entitled to a redundancy payment if offered a suitable alternative job by the same (or an associated) employer. The amount of statutory redundancy pay depends on the employee's length of service, age, and their earnings, subject to a weekly maximum of (currently) £525 (£547 in Northern Ireland). The maximum payment that can be awarded is £15,750. The redundancy payment is guaranteed by the government in cases where the employer becomes insolvent.

UNFAIR DISMISSAL

Complaints of unfair dismissal are dealt with by an employment tribunal. Any employee whose employment commenced before 6 April 2012 with at least one year's continuous service or any employee whose employment commenced on or after 6 April 2012 with at least two year's continuous service (subject to exceptions, including in relation to whistleblowers – *see* below) can make a complaint to the tribunal. At the tribunal, it is for the employee to show that the employer dismissed them either expressly or constructively and it is for the employer to prove that the dismissal was due to one or more potentially fair reasons: a statutory restriction preventing the continuation of the employee's contract; the employee's capability or qualifications for the job he/she was employed to do; the employee's conduct; redundancy; or some other substantial reason.

If the employer succeeds in showing this, the tribunal must then decide whether the employer acted reasonably in dismissing the employee for that reason. If the employee is found to have been unfairly dismissed, the tribunal can order that he/she be reinstated, re-engaged or compensated. Any person believing that they may have been unfairly dismissed should contact their local Citizens Advice bureau or seek legal advice. A claim must be brought within three months of the date of effective termination of employment.

The normal maximum compensatory award for unfair dismissal is £86,444 as at April 2019 (£86,614 in Northern Ireland). If the dismissal occurred after 6 April 2009 and the employer unreasonably failed to follow the ACAS Code of Practice on Disciplinary and Grievance Procedures in carrying out the dismissal, the tribunal may increase the employee's compensation by up to 25 per cent.

Employees in Northern Ireland can make a complaint to the tribunal if they have at least one year's continuous service.

WHISTLEBLOWING

Under the whistleblowing legislation (Public Interest Disclosure Act 1998, which inserted provisions into the Employment Rights Act 1996) dismissal of an employee is automatically unfair if the reason or principal reason for the dismissal is that the employee has made a protected disclosure. The legislation also makes it unlawful to subject workers (a broad category that includes employees and certain other individuals, such as agency workers) who have made a protected disclosure to any detriment on the ground that they have done so.

For a disclosure to qualify for protection, the claimant must show that he or she has disclosed information, which in his or her reasonable belief tends to show one or more of the following six categories of wrongdoing: criminal offences; breach of any legal obligation; miscarriages of justice; danger to the health and safety of any individual; damage to the environment; or the deliberate concealing of information about any of the other categories. The malpractices can be past, present, prospective or merely alleged.

A qualifying disclosure will only be protected if the manner of the disclosure fulfils certain conditions, which varies according to the type of disclosure. With effect from 25 June 2013, there is no requirement for the disclosure to have been made in 'good faith', although where it appears to the tribunal that the protected disclosure was not made in good faith, the tribunal may reduce any compensatory award it makes by up to 25 per cent if it considers that it is just and equitable to do so in all the circumstances.

Any whistleblower claim in the employment tribunal must normally be brought within three months of the date of dismissal or other act leading to a detriment.

An individual does not need to have been working with the employer for any particular period of time to be able to bring such a claim and compensation is uncapped (and can include an amount for injury to feelings).

DISCRIMINATION

Discrimination in employment on the grounds of sex (including gender reassignment), sexual orientation, being pregnant or on maternity leave, race, colour, nationality, ethnic or national origins, religion or belief, marital or civil partnership status, age or disability is unlawful. Discrimination legislation generally covers direct discrimination, indirect discrimination, harassment and victimisation. Only in limited circumstances can such discrimination be justified (rendering it lawful).

An individual does not need to be employed for any particular period of time to be able to claim discrimination (discrimination can be alleged at the recruitment phase), and discrimination compensation is uncapped (and can include an amount for injury to feelings). These features distinguish the discrimination laws from, for example, the unfair dismissal laws.

The Equality Act 2010 was passed on 8 April 2010 and its main provisions came into force on 1 October 2010. It unifies several pieces of discrimination legislation, providing one definition of direct discrimination, indirect discrimination, harassment and victimisation. The Act applies to those employed in Great Britain but not to employees in Northern Ireland; it is only likely to apply to those predominantly working abroad if there is a strong connection between their work and Great Britain.

The Act provides that:

- it is unlawful to discriminate on the grounds of sex, gender reassignment, being pregnant or on maternity leave, or marital/civil partner status (all but the last of these categories include discrimination by association and by perception). This covers all aspects of employment (including advertising for jobs), but there are some limited exceptions, such as where the essential nature of the job requires it to be given to someone of a particular sex, or where decency and privacy requires it. The act entitles men and women to equality of remuneration for equivalent work or work of the same value
- individuals have the right not to be discriminated against on the grounds of race, colour, nationality, or ethnic or national origins and this applies to all aspects of employment. Employers may also take lawful positive action, including in relation to recruitment and promotion
- discrimination against a disabled person in all aspects of employment is unlawful. This includes protecting carers from discrimination by association with the disabled persons that they look after. The act also imposes a duty on employers to make 'reasonable adjustments' to the arrangements and physical features of the workplace if these place disabled people at a substantial disadvantage compared with those who are not disabled. The definition of a 'disabled person' is wide and includes people diagnosed with HIV, cancer and multiple sclerosis
- discrimination against a person on the grounds of religion or belief (or lack of belief) including discrimination by association and by perception, in all aspects of employment, is unlawful
- discrimination against an individual on the grounds of sexual orientation, including discrimination by association and by perception, in all aspects of employment, is unlawful
- age discrimination in the workplace is unlawful. However, it is lawful to discriminate because of age in relation to benefits based on length of service, redundancy pay (provided that any enhanced redundancy payment scheme operated by the employer is sufficiently similar to the statutory redundancy payment scheme), national minimum wage and insurance benefits.

The responsibility for monitoring equality in society rests with the Equality and Human Rights Commission.

In Northern Ireland similar provisions exist to those that were in force in Great Britain prior to the coming into force of the Equality Act but are contained in separate legislation (although the Disability Discrimination Act 1995 does extend to Northern Ireland).

In Northern Ireland there is one combined body working towards equality and eliminating discrimination, the Equality Commission for Northern Ireland.

WORKING TIME

The Working Time Regulations 1998 impose rules that limit working hours and provide for rest breaks and holidays. The regulations apply to workers and so cover not only employees but also other individuals who undertake to perform personally any work or services (eg freelancers). The regulations are complex and subject to various exceptions and qualifications but the basic provisions relating to adult day workers are as follows:

- No worker is permitted to work more than an average of 48 hours per week (unless they have made a genuine voluntary opt-out of this limit – it is not generally thought to be sufficient to make it a term of the contract that the worker opts out), and a worker is entitled to, but is not required to take, the following breaks:
- 11 consecutive hours' uninterrupted rest in every 24-hour period
- an uninterrupted rest period of 24 hours in each 7-day period or 48 hours in each fortnight (in addition to the daily rest period)
- 20 minutes' rest break provided that the working day is longer than 6 hours
- 5.6 weeks' paid annual leave (28 days full-time). This equates to 4 weeks plus public holidays

There are specific provisions relating to night work, young workers (ie those over school leaving age but under 18) and a variety of workers in specialised sectors (such as off-shore oil rig workers).

HUMAN RIGHTS

On 2 October 2000 the Human Rights Act 1998 came into force in the UK. This act incorporates the European Convention on Human Rights into the law of the UK. The main principles of the act are as follows:

- all legislation must be interpreted and given effect by the courts as compatible with the Convention so far as it is possible to do so. Before the second reading of a new bill the minister responsible for the bill must provide a statement regarding its compatibility with the Human Rights Act
- subordinate legislation (eg statutory instruments) which is incompatible with the Convention can be struck down by the courts
- primary legislation (eg an act of parliament) which is incompatible with the Convention cannot be struck down by a court, but the higher courts can make a declaration of incompatibility which is a signal to parliament to change the law
- all public authorities (including courts and tribunals) must not act in a way which is incompatible with the Convention
- individuals whose Convention rights have been infringed by a public authority may bring proceedings against that authority, but the act is not intended to create new rights as between individuals

The main human rights protected by the Convention are the right to life (article 2); protection from torture and inhuman or degrading treatment (article 3); protection from slavery or forced labour (article 4); the right to liberty and security of the person (article 5); the right to a fair trial (article 6); the right not to be subject to retrospective criminal offences (article 7); the right to respect for private and family life (article 8); freedom of thought, conscience and religion (article 9); freedom of expression (article 10); freedom of association and peaceful assembly (article 11); the right to marry and found a family (article 12); protection from discrimination (article 14); the right to protection of property (article 1 of protocol No.1); the right to education (article 2 of protocol No.1); and the right to free elections (article 3 protocol No.1). Most of the Convention rights are subject to limitations which deem the breach of the right acceptable on the basis it is 'necessary in a democratic society'.

Human rights are also enshrined in the common law (of tort). Although this is of historical significance, the common law (for example the duty of confidentiality) remains especially important regarding violations of human rights that occur between private parties, where the Human Rights Act 1998 does not apply.

PARENTAL RESPONSIBILITY

The Children Act 1989 (as amended by the Children and Families Act 2014) gives both the mother and father parental responsibility for the child if the parents are married to each other at the time of the child's birth. If the parents are not married, only the mother has parental responsibility. The father may acquire it in accordance with the provisions of section 4 of the Children Act 1989. He can do this in one of several ways, including: by being registered as the father on the child's birth certificate with the consent of the mother (only for fathers of children born after 1 December 2003, following changes to the Adoption and Children Act 2002); by applying to the court for a parental responsibility order; by entering into a parental responsibility agreement with the mother which must be in the prescribed form; or by marrying the mother of the child.

Following changes to the Children Act 1989 (introduced by the Children and Families Act 2014), if a court makes a child arrangements order in favour of a father, providing that the child lives with that father, the court must make a parental responsibility order in his favour. If the child arrangements order provides that the child spend time or otherwise have contact with the father, the court must consider whether to make a parental responsibility order (residence orders were replaced by child arrangement orders under the Children and Families Act 2014, but if obtained prior to 22 April 2014 are still valid).

Where a child's parent, who has parental responsibility, marries or enters into a civil partnership with a person who is not the child's parent, the child's parent(s) with parental responsibility can agree for the step-parent to have parental responsibility by entering into a parental responsibility agreement, or the step-parent may acquire parental responsibility by order of the court (section 4A(1) Children Act 1989).

If a child is conceived after 6 April 2009 by female civil partners or female same-sex spouses, under the Human Fertilisation and Embryology Act (HFEA) 2008, both individuals will have parental responsibility for that child. A female, who is not in a civil partnership or same-sex marriage with the mother at the date of the child's birth, but is the child's other parent (by virtue of HFEA 2008), can acquire parental responsibility in the same way as set out above in relation to a father. Parental responsibility will also be acquired if the mother and the child's other parent enter into a civil partnership or (from 13 March 2014) a same-sex marriage after the child's date of birth.

Where the court makes a child arrangements order and a person (who is not the parent or guardian of the child) is named in the order as a person with whom the child is to live, that person will have parental responsibility while the order remains in force. Where the person (who is not the parent or guardian of the child) is named in the order as a person with whom the child is to spend time or otherwise have contact (but not with whom the child is to live), the court may provide in the order for that person to have parental responsibility for the child, while the provisions in the order continue.

An adoption order gives parental responsibility for the child to the adopters. It extinguishes parental responsibility that any person had for the child immediately before the making of the order.

In Scotland, the relevant legislation is the Children (Scotland) Act 1995, which gives the mother parental rights and responsibilities for her child whether or not she is married to the child's father. A father who is married to the mother, either at the time of the child's conception or subsequently, will also have automatic parental rights and responsibilities. Section 3 of the 2006 act provides that an unmarried father will obtain automatic parental responsibilities and rights if he is registered as the father on the child's birth certificate. For unmarried fathers who are not named on the birth certificate, or whose children were born before the 2006 act came into force, it is possible to acquire parental responsibilities and rights by applying to the court or by entering into a parental responsibilities and rights agreement with the mother. The father of any child, regardless of parental rights, has a duty to aliment that child until he/she is 18 (or under 25 if the child is still at an educational establishment or training for employment or for a trade, profession or vocation).

LEGITIMATION
Under the Legitimacy Act 1976, an illegitimate person automatically becomes legitimate when his/her parents marry. This applies even where one of the parents was married to a third person at the time of the birth. In such cases it is necessary to re-register the birth of the child. In Scotland, the status of illegitimacy has been abolished by section 21 of the 2006 act. The Family Law Reform Act 1987 reformed the law so as to remove so far as possible the legal disadvantages of illegitimacy.

JURY SERVICE

In England and Wales, the law concerning juries is largely consolidated in the Juries Act 1974 (as amended by the Criminal Justice and Courts Act 2015). In England and Wales, a person charged with a serious criminal offence is entitled to have their trial heard by a jury in a crown court, except in cases where there is a danger of jury tampering or where jury tampering has taken place.

In civil cases, there is a right to a jury in the Queen's Bench Division of the high court in cases where the person applying for a jury has been accused of fraud, as well as in cases of malicious prosecution or false imprisonment. The same applies to the county court. In all other cases in the Queen's Bench Division only the judge has discretion to order trial with a jury, though such an order is seldom made. In the chancery division of the high court a jury is never used. The same is true in the family division of the high court.

No right to a jury trial exists in Scotland, although more serious offences are heard before a jury. In England and Wales criminal cases and civil cases in the high court are generally heard by a jury of 12 members, but in the county court the jury is smaller, normally consisting of eight members. In the event that a juror is excused the trial can proceed so long as there are at least seven remaining jurors in the county court and nine in the case of the high court or crown court. At an inquest, there must be at least seven and no more than 11 members. In Scotland there are 12 members of a jury in a civil case in the court of session and certain sheriff court cases, and 15 in a criminal trial in the high court of justiciary. Jurors are normally asked to serve for ten working days, during which time they could sit on more than one case. Jurors selected for longer cases are expected to sit for the duration of the trial.

In England and Wales, every 'registered' parliamentary or local government elector between the ages of 18 and 75 who has lived in the UK (including, for this purpose, the Channel Islands and the Isle of Man) for any period of at least five years since reaching the age of 13 is qualified to serve on a jury unless he/she is disqualified.

Those disqualified from jury service include:

- those who have at any time been sentenced by a court in the UK (including, for this purpose, the Channel Islands and the Isle of Man) to a term of imprisonment or youth custody of five years or more
- those who have within the previous ten years served any part of a sentence of imprisonment, youth custody or detention, been detained in a young offenders' institution, received a suspended sentence of imprisonment or order for detention, or received a community order
- those who are on bail in criminal proceedings
- those who have been convicted of a jury misconduct offence
- those who are liable to be detained, who are under guardianship or who are under a community treatment order under the Mental Health Act 1983 or who are in resident in a hospital on account of mental disorder
- Those who lack capacity, as defined under the Mental Capacity Act 2005, to serve as a juror

The court has the discretion to excuse a juror from service, or defer the date of service, if the juror can show there is good reason why he/she should be excused from attending or good reason why his/her attendance should be deferred. It is an offence (punishable by a fine) to fail to attend when summoned, to serve knowing that you are disqualified from service, or to make false representations in an attempt to evade service. If a juror fails to turn up for service, or attends but cannot serve due to being under the influence of drink or drugs, this is punishable as contempt of court. Any party can object to any juror if he/she can show cause to the trial judge.

It may be appropriate for a judge to excuse a juror from a particular case if he is personally concerned in the facts of the particular case, or closely connected with a party to the proceedings or with a prospective witness. The judge may also discharge any juror who, from a mental or physical incapacity, temporary or permanent, or alternatively due to linguistic difficulties, cannot pay proper attention to the evidence.

An individual juror (or the entire jury) can be discharged if it is shown that they or any of their number have, among other things, separated from the rest of the jury without the leave of the court; talked to any person out of court who is not a member of the jury; determined the verdict of the trial by drawing lots; come to a compromise on the verdict; been drunk, or otherwise incapacitated, while carrying out their duties as a juror; exerted improper pressure on the other members of the jury (eg harassment or bullying); declined to take part in the jury's functions; displayed actual or apparent bias (eg racism, sexism or other discriminatory or deliberate hostility); or inadvertently possessed knowledge of the bad character of a party to the proceedings which has not been adduced as evidence in the proceedings. The factual situations that arise are many, and include falling asleep during the trial, asking friends on Facebook for help in making a decision, consulting an ouija board in the course of deliberations, making telephone calls after retirement, and lunching with a barrister not connected with the proceedings.

The Criminal Justice and Courts Act 2015 has introduced four new offences of juror misconduct with a penalty of up to two years in prison. A juror commits an offence if he: (a) intentionally seeks information during a trial where he knows, or ought to reasonably know, that the information sought is or may be relevant to the case; (b) passes on to another juror information obtained through such research; (c) engages in conduct from which it may reasonably be concluded that he intends to try the issue otherwise than on the basis of the evidence presented in the proceedings on the issue; and (d) discloses information about the jury's deliberations, subject to specified exceptions. A person who has been convicted of one of the above offences within the last ten years will be disqualified from jury duty. A judge now has a discretionary power to order members of a jury to surrender their electronic communication devices for a period of time, and a court security officer is authorised to search a juror for a device that a judge has ordered be surrendered.

In England and Wales, the jury's verdict need not be unanimous. In criminal proceedings, and civil proceedings in the high court, the agreement of ten jurors will suffice when there are not fewer than 11 people on the jury (or nine in a jury of ten). In civil proceedings in the county court the agreement of seven or eight jurors will suffice. Where a majority verdict is given, the court must be satisfied that the jury had reasonable time to consider its verdict based on the nature and complexity of the case. In criminal proceedings this must be no less than two hours and ten minutes (allowing time for the jury to settle after retiring).

A juror is immune from prosecution or civil claim in respect of anything said or done by him or her in the discharge of their office. It is an offence for a juror to disclose what happened in the jury room even after the trial is over. A juror may claim travelling expenses, a subsistence allowance and an allowance for other financial loss (eg loss of earnings or benefits, fees paid to carers or child-minders) up to a stated limit. For more information on jury service, visit W www.gov.uk/jury-service/overview

SCOTLAND

Qualification criteria for jury service in Scotland are similar to those in England and Wales, except that members of the judiciary are ineligible for ten years after ceasing to hold their post, and others concerned with the administration of justice are only eligible for service five years after ceasing to hold office. Certain persons have the right to apply to be excused – full-time members of the medical, dental, nursing, veterinary and pharmaceutical professions, full-time members of the armed forces, ministers of religion, persons who have served on a jury within the previous five years, persons who have attended court to serve on a jury but were not selected by ballot within the previous two years, members of the Scottish parliament, members of the Scottish government, junior Scottish ministers and those aged 71 years or over. Those who are incapable by reason of a mental disorder may also be excused. Such an application will be accepted if the application is made within 7 days of the person being notified that they may have to serve. For civil trials there is an age limit of 65 years. Those convicted of a crime and sentenced to a period of imprisonment of 5 years or more are automatically disqualified. The maximum fine for a person serving on a jury while knowing himself/herself to be ineligible is £1,000. The maximum fine for failing to attend without good cause in criminal trials is also £1,000, however in civil proceedings the maximum fine is £200.

HER MAJESTY'S COURTS AND TRIBUNALS SERVICE, 102 Petty France, London SW1H 9AJ T 0845-456 8770

JURY CENTRAL SUMMONING BUREAU, Freepost LON 19669, Pocock Street, London SE1 0YG T 0300-456 1024 E jurysummoning@justice.gov.uk

SCOTTISH COURTS AND TRIBUNALS SERVICE, Saughton House, Broomhouse Drive, Edinburgh EH11 3XD T 0131-444 3300 W www.scotcourts.gov.uk

LANDLORD AND TENANT

RESIDENTIAL LETTINGS

The provisions outlined here apply only where the tenant lives in a separate dwelling from the landlord and where the dwelling is the tenant's only or main home. It does not apply to licensees such as lodgers, guests or service occupiers.

The 1996 Housing Act radically changed certain aspects of the legislation referred to below; in particular, the grant of assured and assured shorthold tenancies under the Housing Act 1988.

ASSURED SHORTHOLD TENANCIES

If a tenancy was granted on or after 15 January 1989 and before 28 February 1997, the tenant would have an assured tenancy unless the landlord served notice under section 20 in the prescribed form prior to the commencement of the tenancy, stating that the tenancy is to be an assured shorthold tenancy and the tenancy is for a minimum fixed term period of six months (see below). An assured tenancy gives that tenant greater security. The tenant could, for example, stay in possession of the dwelling for as long as the tenant observed the terms of the tenancy. The landlord cannot obtain possession from such a tenant unless the landlord can establish a specific ground for possession (set out in the Housing Act 1988) and obtains a court order. The rent payable is that agreed with the landlord at the start of the tenancy. The landlord has the right to increase the rent annually by serving a notice. If that happens the tenant can apply to the Residential Property Tribunal in England (or a rent assessment committee in Wales) to assess the open market rent for the property. The tenant or the landlord may request that the committee sets the rent in line with open market rents for that type of property.

Under the Housing Act 1996, all new lettings (below an annual rent threshold of £100,000 since October 2010 in England or December 2011 in Wales) entered into on or after 28 February 1997 (for whatever term) will be assured shorthold tenancies unless the landlord serves a notice stating that the tenancy is not to be an assured shorthold tenancy. This means that the landlord is entitled to possession at the end of the tenancy provided he serves a notice under section 21 Housing Act 1988 and commences the proceedings in accordance with the correct procedure. The landlord must obtain a court order, however, to obtain possession if the tenant refuses to vacate at the end of the tenancy. If the tenancy is an assured shorthold tenancy, the court must grant the order.

REGULATED TENANCIES

Before the Housing Act 1988 came into force on 15 January 1989 there were regulated tenancies; some are still in existence and are protected by the Rent Act 1977. Under this act it is possible for the landlord or the tenant to apply to the local rent officer to have a 'fair' rent registered. The fair rent is then the maximum rent payable.

SECURE TENANCIES

Secure tenancies are generally given to tenants of local authorities, housing associations (before 15 January 1989) and certain other bodies. This gives the tenant security of tenure unless the terms of the agreement are broken by the tenant and it is reasonable to make an order for possession. Those with secure tenancies may have the right to buy their property. In practice this right is generally only available to council tenants. However, the Housing and Planning Act 2016 enables housing associations voluntarily to extend the right to buy. A roll out of the extended right to buy regime has now taken place as the Department for Communities and Local Government published its guidance in April 2018.

The Prevention of Social Housing Fraud Act came into force in October 2013. It creates criminal offences for unlawful sub-letting by secure and assured tenants of social housing.

AGRICULTURAL PROPERTY

Tenancies in agricultural properties are governed by the Agricultural Holdings Act 1986, the Agricultural Tenancies

Act 1995 (both amended by the Regulatory Reform (Agricultural Tenancies) (England and Wales) Order 2006), the Tribunals, Courts and Enforcement Act 2007, the Legal Services Act 2007 and the Rent (Agriculture) Act 1976, which give similar protections to those described above, eg security of tenure, right to compensation for disturbance, etc. Similar provisions are applied to Scotland by the Agricultural Holdings (Scotland) Act 2003 for those leases entered into on or after 27 November 2003. The Agricultural Holdings (Scotland) Act 1991 continues to apply to those leases in Scotland entered into prior to this date and in certain other circumstances outlined by the 2003 act. However, one distinction to note between the 1991 act and the 2003 act is that those leases governed by the former have full security of tenure, subject to certain exceptions, whereas leases under the 2003 act are fixed term arrangements of various durations.

EVICTION

The Protection from Eviction Act 1977 (as amended by the Housing Act 1988 and Nationality, Immigration and Asylum Act 2002) sets out the procedure a landlord must follow in order to obtain possession of property. It is unlawful for a landlord to evict a tenant otherwise than in accordance with the law. For common law tenancies and for Rent Act tenants a notice to quit in the prescribed form giving 28 days notice is required. For secure and assured tenancies a notice seeking possession must be served. It is unlawful for the landlord to evict a person by putting their belongings on to the street, by changing the locks and so on. It is also unlawful for a landlord to harass a tenant in any way in order to persuade him/her to give up the tenancy. The tenant may be able to obtain an injunction to restrain the actions of the landlord and get back into the property and be awarded damages.

LANDLORD RESPONSIBILITIES

Under the Landlord and Tenant Act 1985, where the term of the lease is less than seven years, the landlord is responsible for maintaining the structure and exterior of the property, for sanitation, for heating and hot water, and all installations for the supply of water, gas and electricity.

While the responsibility of maintaining the premises remains intact, since July 2012 landlords are no longer permitted to enter the rental premises for the purpose of viewing their state and condition. This power of entry was revoked by the Protection of Freedoms Act 2012.

LEASEHOLDERS

Strictly speaking, leaseholders have bought a long lease rather than a property and in certain limited circumstances the landlord can end the tenancy. Under the Leasehold Reform Act 1967 (as amended by the Housing Acts 1969, 1974, 1980 and 1985), leaseholders of houses, as opposed to flats, may have the right to buy the freehold or to take an extended lease for a term of 50 years. This applies to leases where the term of the lease is more than 21 years and where the leaseholder has occupied the house as his/her only or main residence for the last two years, or for a total of two years over the last ten. It was the case that a low rent and rateable value test applied to the right to buy the freehold, this is generally no longer the case, although they do remain applicable to the right to a lease extension. The tenant must give the landlord written notice of his desire to acquire the freehold or extend the leasehold.

The Leasehold Reform, Housing and Urban Development Act came into force in 1993 and allows the leaseholders of flats in certain circumstances to buy the freehold of the building in which they live. Owners of certain long leases of flats may also have the right to take an extended act of 90 years plus the unexpired residue of their current lease: although technically a grant of a new lease, these are commonly called 'lease extensions'.

Responsibility for maintenance of the structure, exterior and interior of the building should be set out in the lease. Usually the upkeep of the interior of his/her part of the property is the responsibility of the leaseholder, and responsibility for the structure, exterior and common interior areas is shared between the freeholder and the leaseholder(s).

If leaseholders are dissatisfied with charges made in respect of lease extensions, they are entitled to have their situation evaluated by the First-tier Tribunal (Property Chamber).

The Commonhold and Leasehold Reform Act 2002 makes provision for the freehold estate in land to be registered as commonhold land and for the legal interest in the land to be vested in a 'commonhold association', ie a private limited company.

BUSINESS LETTINGS

The Landlord and Tenant Acts 1927 and 1954 (as amended) give security of tenure to the tenants of most business premises. The landlord can only evict the tenant on one of the grounds laid down in the 1954 act, and in some cases where the landlord repossesses the property the tenant may be entitled to compensation. However, it is commonplace for landlords and tenants to agree that these provisions will not apply to their lease, meaning that no security of tenure is granted.

SCOTLAND

In Scotland assured and short assured tenancies exist for residential lettings entered into after 2 January 1989 and before December 2017 are similar to assured shorthold tenancies in England and Wales. The relevant legislation for these is the Housing (Scotland) Act 1988. However, under the provisions of the Private Housing (Tenancies) (Scotland) Act 2016 all new tenancies for private residential lettings from 1 December 2017 take the form of a private rental tenancy. They provide more security for tenants as the 'no fault ground of repossession' (the equivalent of recovering possession under section 21 of the Housing Act 1988 in England) has been abolished. The act also introduced a model tenancy agreement, rent controls and move the adjudication of disputes from the sheriff court to the Housing and Property Chamber of the First-tier Tribunal.

Most tenancies created before 2 January 1989 were regulated tenancies and the Rent (Scotland) Act 1984 still applies where these exist. The act defines, among other things, the circumstances in which a landlord can increase the rent when improvements are made to the property. It does not apply to tenancies where the landlord is the Crown, a local authority or a housing corporation.

The Antisocial Behaviour etc (Scotland) Act 2004 provides that all private landlords letting property in Scotland must register with the local authority in which the let property is situated, unless the landlord is a local authority, or a registered social landlord. Exceptions also apply to holiday lets, owner-occupied accommodation and agricultural holdings. The act applies to partnerships, trusts and companies as well as to individuals.

Tenancy Deposit Schemes (Scotland) Regulations 2011 require that a landlord must pay deposits taken from tenants into an approved scheme and ensure that the money is held by an approved scheme for the duration of the tenancy. Evidence of registration with the relevant local authority in terms of the 2004 Act must be provided when the deposit is paid over.

Landlords who provide a private residential tenancy must provide new tenants with a Tenant Information Pack. The Tenant Information Pack includes information on the Repairing Standard, and its provision satisfies the separate obligation of a landlord to provide a tenant with written information about the landlord's duty to repair and maintain in terms of the Housing (Scotland) Act 2006.

The Housing (Scotland) Acts of 1987 and 2001 relate to local authority and registered social landlord responsibilities for housing, the right to buy, and local authority secured tenancies. The Housing (Scotland) Act 2010 reformed right-to-buy provisions, modernised social housing regulation, introduced the Scottish social housing charter and replaced the regulatory framework established by the 2001 act. Right-to-buy provisions were then abolished by the Housing (Scotland) Act 2014.

In Scotland, business premises are not controlled by statute to the same extent as in England and Wales, although the Tenancy of Shops (Scotland) Act 1949 gives some security to tenants of shops. Tenants of shops can apply to the sheriff, within 21 days of being served a notice to quit, for a renewal of tenancy if threatened with eviction. This application may be dismissed on various grounds, including where the landlord has offered to sell the property to the tenant at an agreed price or, in the absence of agreement as to price, at a price fixed by a single arbiter appointed by the parties or the sheriff. The act extends to properties where the Crown or government departments are the landlords or the tenants.

Under the Leases Act 1449 the landlord's successors (either purchasers or creditors) are bound by the agreement made with any tenants so long as the following conditions are met:
- the lease, if for more than one year, must be in writing
- there must be a rent
- there must be a term of expiry
- the tenant must have entered into possession
- the subjects of the lease must be land
- the landlord, if owner, must be the proprietor with a recorded title, ie the title deeds recorded in the Register of Sasines or registered in the Land Register

On 28 November 2013 certain leases which were granted for more than 175 years and under which the rent does not exceed £100 a year, converted to heritable titles. Therefore the tenants under these leases will become the owners of the property. Conversion of the lease will be automatic, provided certain conditions are met, unless the tenant opts out. It is possible for the landlord to claim compensation for their loss of income.

LEGAL AID

The Access to Justice Act 1999 transformed what used to be known as the Legal Aid system. The Legal Aid Board was replaced by the Legal Services Commission, which was responsible for the development and administration of two legal funding schemes in England and Wales, namely the Criminal Defence Service and the Community Legal Service. The Criminal Defence Service assisted people who were under police investigation or facing criminal charges. The Community Legal Service was designed to increase access to legal information and advice by involving a much wider network of funders and providers in giving publicly funded legal services. In Scotland, provision of legal aid is governed by the Legal Aid (Scotland) Act 1986, the Legal Profession and Legal Aid (Scotland) Act 2007 and the Scottish Civil Justice Council and Criminal Legal Assistance Act 2013, and administered by the Scottish Legal Aid Board.

Under the Legal Aid, Sentencing and Punishment of Offenders Act 2012 (LASPO), which came into force on 1 April 2013, the Legal Services Commission was abolished and replaced by the newly created Legal Aid Agency. The act has also limited the areas of law that fall within the scope of legal aid funding, especially those related to civil legal services. However, the act does include provisions for funding in exceptional cases, such as where failure to provide legal aid would result in a violation of an individual's human rights or where providing legal aid would serve a wider public interest. Further, the act allows for areas of law to be added or omitted from the scope of legal aid independently, without subsequent legislation.

LASPO took whole areas of law out of scope for legal aid; some areas only qualify if they meet certain criteria. Broadly, the following categories of cases are now out of such scope: (a) family cases where there is no proof of domestic violence, forced marriage or child abduction; (b) immigration cases that do not involve asylum or detention; (c) housing and debt matters unless they constitute an immediate risk to the home; (d) welfare benefit cases except appeals to the upper tribunal or high court; (e) almost all clinical negligence cases; and (f) employment cases that do not involve human trafficking or a contravention of the Equality Act 2010. Funding for cases that fall outside of the scope of legal aid may be available under the Exceptional Case Funding scheme.

The Ministry of Justice published a review of LASPO in February 2019 and a Legal Support Action Plan which outlines changes the government intends to make and the future direction for legal aid support.

LEGAL AID AGENCY, W www.gov.uk/government/
organisations/legal-aid-agency

CIVIL LEGAL AID

From 1 January 2000, only organisations (such as solicitors or Citizens Advice) with a contract with the Legal Services Commission (now Legal Aid Agency) have been able to give initial help in any civil matter. Moreover, from that date decisions about funding were devolved from the Legal Services Commission to contracted organisations in relation to any level of publicly funded service in family and immigration cases. For other types of case, applications for public funding are made through a solicitor (or other contracted legal services providers) in much the same way as the former Legal Aid.

Under the civil funding scheme there are broadly six levels of service available:
- legal help
- help at court
- family help – either family help (lower) or family help (higher)
- legal representation – either investigative help or full representation
- family mediation
- such other services as authorised by specific orders

ELIGIBILITY
Eligibility for funding from the Legal Aid Agency depends broadly on five factors:
- the level of service sought (see above)
- whether the applicant qualifies financially
- the merits of the applicant's case
- a costs-benefits analysis (if the costs are likely to outweigh any benefit that might be gained from the proceedings, funding may be refused)
- whether there is any public interest in the case being litigated (ie whether the case has a wider public interest beyond that of the parties involved, eg a human rights case)

The limits on capital and income above which a person is not entitled to public funding vary with the type of service sought. As of Spring 2017, there is a consultation on government proposals seeking to amend the legal financial eligibility system to accommodate the expansion of Universal Credit. Nothing in the consultation will affect the scope of or eligibility threshold for legal aid, but instead when claimants are passported and so would not have to undergo a full assessment of their means. The consultation closed on 11 May 2017 and the outcome is pending.

The 2012 act also amended the merits criteria so that legal aid may be refused where the case is suitable for alternative funding, such as Conditional Fee Agreements. Children, and individuals on certain welfare benefits, may be relieved from means testing and from the liability to make contributions. Financial eligibility requirements may be waived for individuals applying for an order for protection from domestic violence or forced marriage (though a contribution may be required). The government intend to extend the relief of means testing to parents opposing applications for placement orders or adoption orders by summer 2019.

CONTRIBUTIONS
Some of those who qualify for Legal Aid Agency funding will have to contribute towards their legal costs. Contributions must be paid by anyone who has a disposable income or disposable capital exceeding a prescribed amount. The rules relating to applicable contributions are complex and detailed information can be obtained from the Legal Aid Agency. Individuals on certain welfare benefits may not have to contribute.

STATUTORY CHARGE
A statutory charge is made if a person keeps or gains money or property in a case for which they have received legal aid. This means that the amount paid by the Legal Aid Agency fund on their behalf is deducted from the amount that the person receives. This does not apply if the court has ordered that the costs be paid by the other party (unless the amount paid by the other party does not cover all of the costs). In certain circumstances, the Legal Aid Agency may waive or postpone payment.

CONTINGENCY OR CONDITIONAL FEES
This system was introduced by the Courts and Legal Services Act 1990. It can offer legal representation on a 'no win, no fee' basis. It provides an alternative form of assistance, especially for those cases which are ineligible for funding by the Legal Aid Agency. The main area for such work is in the field of personal injuries.

Not all solicitors offer such a scheme and different solicitors may well have different terms. The effect of the agreement is that solicitors may not make any charges, or may waive some of their charges, until the case is concluded successfully. If a case is won then the losing party will usually have to pay towards costs, with the winning party contributing around one third.

SCOTLAND
Civil legal aid is available for cases in the following:
- the sheriff courts
- the Court of Session
- the Supreme Court
- the Lands Valuation Appeal Court
- the Scottish Land Court
- the Sheriff Appeal Court
- the Lands Tribunal for Scotland
- the Employment Appeal Tribunal
- the Proscribed Organisations Appeal Commission
- the Upper Tribunal for Scotland
- certain appeals before the Social Security Commissioners

Civil legal aid is not available for election petitions, some simple procedure actions, simplified divorce procedures or petitions by a debtor for his own sequestration. In defamation actions additional criteria must be met in order for legal aid to be available.

Eligibility for civil legal aid is assessed in a similar way to that in England and Wales, though the financial limits differ in some respects. A person shall be eligible for civil legal aid if their disposable income does not exceed £26,239 a year. A person may be refused civil aid if their disposable capital exceeds £13,017 and it appears to the Legal Aid board that they can afford to pay without legal aid. Additionally:
- if disposable capital is between £7,853 and £13,017, the applicant will be required to pay a contribution which will be equal to the difference between £7,853 and their disposable capital
- if disposable income is between £3,522 and £11,540, a contribution of one third of the difference between £3,522 and the disposable income may be payable
- if disposable income is between £11,541 and £15,743, one third of the difference between £3,522 and £11,540 plus half the difference between £11,541 and the disposable income may be payable
- if disposable income is between £15,744 and £26,239, a contribution of the following: one third of the difference between £3,522 and £11,540, plus half the difference between £11,541 and £15,743, plus all the remaining disposable income between £15,744 and £26,239 – will be payable

CRIMINAL LEGAL AID
The Legal Aid Agency provides defendants facing criminal charges with free legal representation if they pass a merits test and a means test although children and individuals on certain welfare benefits may be relieved from means testing.

Criminal legal aid covers the cost of preparing a case and legal representation in criminal proceedings. It is also available for appeals against verdicts or sentences in magistrates' courts, the crown court or the court of appeal. It is not available for bringing a private prosecution in a criminal court.

If granted criminal legal aid, either the person may choose their own solicitor or the court will assign one. Contributions to the legal costs may be required. The rules relating to applicable contributions are complex and detailed information can be obtained from the Legal Aid Agency.

DUTY SOLICITORS
LASPO also provides for free initial advice and initial assistance to anyone questioned by the police (whether under arrest or helping the police with their enquiries). No means test or contributions are required for this.

SCOTLAND
Legal advice and assistance operates in a similar way in Scotland. A person is eligible:
- if disposable income does not exceed £245 a week. If disposable income is between £105 and £245 a week, contributions are payable
- if disposable capital does not exceed £1,716 (if the person has dependent relatives, the savings allowance is higher)
- if receiving income support or income-related job seeker's allowance they qualify automatically provided their disposable capital is not over the limit

The procedure for application for criminal legal aid depends on the circumstances of each case. In solemn cases (more serious cases, such as murder) heard before a jury, a person is automatically entitled to criminal legal aid until they are given bail or placed in custody. Thereafter, it is for the court to decide whether to grant legal aid. The court will do this if the person accused cannot meet the expenses of the case without undue hardship on him or his dependants. In less serious cases the procedure depends on whether the person is in custody:
- anyone taken into custody has the right to free legal aid from the duty solicitor up to and including the first court appearance

- if the person is not in custody and wishes to plead guilty, they are not entitled to criminal legal aid but may be entitled to legal advice and assistance, including assistance by way of representation

However, regardless of whether the person is in custody if they wish to plead not guilty, they can apply for criminal legal aid. This must be done within 14 days of the first court appearance at which they made the plea.

The criteria used to assess whether or not criminal legal aid should be granted is similar to the criteria for England and Wales. When meeting with your solicitor, take evidence of your financial position such as details of savings, bank statements, pay slips, pension book or benefits book.

Under the relevant provisions of the Scottish Civil Justice Council and Criminal Legal Assistance Act 2013, a person in receipt of criminal legal aid or criminal assistance by way of representation will be required, in most circumstances, to make contributions where their weekly disposable income is £82 or above or if their disposable capital is £750 or more. The Scottish government has delayed the implementation of these provisions and no timetable has yet been proposed.

THE SCOTTISH LEGAL AID BOARD, Thistle House, 91 Haymarket Terrace, Edinburgh EH12 5HE T 0131-226 7061 W www.slab.org.uk

MARRIAGE

Any two persons may marry provided that:
- they are at least 16 years old on the day of the marriage (in England and Wales persons under the age of 18 must generally obtain the consent of their parents or guardian; if consent is refused an appeal may be made to the high court or the family court)
- they are not related to one another in a way which would prevent their marrying
- they are unmarried (a person who has already been married must produce documentary evidence that the previous marriage has been ended by death, divorce or annulment)
- they are capable of understanding the nature, duties and responsibilities of a marriage
- they consent to the marriage

It is now lawful for same sex couples to marry by way of civil or religious ceremony following the passing of the Marriage (Same Sex Couples) Act 2013, which came into force in March 2014. In addition, an existing marriage will now be able to continue where one or both parties change their legal gender and both parties wish to remain married. Civil partnerships are also still available for same sex couples, although The Marriage (Same Sex Couples) Act 2013 provides that couples in civil partnerships may convert their relationship to a marriage if they wish.

The parties should check the marriage will be recognised as valid in their home country if either is not a British citizen.

DEGREES OF RELATIONSHIP

A marriage between persons within the prohibited degrees of consanguinity, affinity or adoption is void.

Neither party may marry his or her parent, child, grandparent, grandchild, sibling, parent's sibling, sibling's child, adoptive parent, former adoptive parent, adoptive child or former adoptive child. All references to siblings include half-brothers/sisters.

Under the Marriage (Prohibited Degrees of Relationship) Act 1986, some exceptions to the law permit a person to marry certain step-relatives or in-laws.

In addition to the above, a person may not marry a child of their former civil partner, a child of a former spouse, the former civil partner of a grandparent, the former civil partner of a parent, the former spouse of a grandparent, the former spouse of a parent, the grandchild of a former civil partner or the grandchild of a former spouse, unless that relationship is the only reason they cannot marry and both persons are over 21 and the younger party has not at any time before attaining the age of 18 been a child of the family in relation to the other party.

ENGLAND AND WALES

TYPES OF MARRIAGE CEREMONY

It is possible to marry by either religious or civil ceremony. A religious ceremony can take place at a church or chapel of the Church of England or the Church in Wales, or at any other place of worship which has been formally registered by the Registrar-General. Same-sex marriages can also take place in a religious building, provided that the premises have been registered for the marriage of same-sex couples. Applications to register are made to the superintendent register of the registration district where the building is located and then forwarded to the General Register Office to be recorded. It is not possible, however, for same-sex marriages to take place in an Anglican church (although the Church of England is currently considering proposals to give same-sex marriage blessings).

A civil ceremony can take place at a register office, a venue approved by the local authority or any religious premises where permission has been given by the relevant religious organisation and is approved by the local authority.

An application for an approved premises licence must be made by the owners or trustees of the building concerned; it cannot be made by the prospective marriage couple. Approved premises must be regularly open to the public for marriages and civil partnerships; be a seemly and dignified venue; and the venue must be deemed to be a permanent and immovable structure. Open-air ceremonies are prohibited.

Non-Anglican marriages may also be solemnised following the issue of a Registrar-General's licence in other premises where one of the parties is seriously ill, is not expected to recover, and cannot be moved to premises where the marriage could normally be solemnised. The marriage must be solemnised in the place stated on the relevant notice of marriage, which may be one of the parties' place of residence. Detained and house-bound persons may also be married at their usual place of residence on the authority of a superintendent registrar's certificates with proper notice and consents.

MARRIAGE IN THE CHURCH OF ENGLAND OR THE CHURCH IN WALES

Marriage by banns

The marriage can take place in a parish in which one of the parties lives, or in a church in another parish if it is the usual place of worship of either or both of the parties. Further to measures introduced in October 2008, marriages can also take place in a parish where one of the parties has a 'qualifying connection', ie in: a parish where one of the parties was baptised (but not if it was part of a combined rite) or confirmed (where the confirmation was entered into the register book of confirmation for a church or chapel in that parish); a parish where one of the parties lived or habitually attended worship for six months or more; a parish where one of the parents of either of the parties lived for six months or more in the child's lifetime; a parish where one of the parents of either of the parties has habitually attended public worship for six months or more in the child's lifetime; or a parish where a parent or grandparent of either of the parties was married. The banns (ie the announcement of the marriage ceremony) must be called in the parish in which the marriage is to take place on three Sundays before the day of the ceremony; if either or both of the parties lives in a different parish the banns must also be called there. After three months the banns are no longer valid. The minister will not perform the marriage unless satisfied that the banns have been properly called.

Marriage by common licence
The couple and the member of the church who is to conduct the marriage will arrange for a common licence to be issued by the local diocese; this dispenses with the necessity for banns. One of the parties must reside in the parish, must usually worship at the parish church or authorised chapel of that parish, or otherwise have a 'qualifying connection' to the parish. The party must swear that they believe there is no lawful impediment to hinder the solemnisation of the marriage in accordance with the licence. If either party is under 18 years old, evidence of consent by their parent or guardian will be required. Any further eligibility requirements vary from diocese to diocese. The licence is valid for three months.

Marriage by special licence
A special licence is granted at the discretion of the Archbishop of Canterbury where a party has a genuine connection to a particular church or chapel but does not satisfy the legal requirements to marry there. They are also used where the building is not authorised for marriages, such as a private chapel. The parties are usually required to demonstrate that they have a genuine worshipping connection to the church or chapel. The special licence will usually be issued to the officiating priest approximately three weeks prior to the date of the wedding and expire three months after the date of issue. An application for the special licence must be made in hard copy to the registrar of the Faculty Office: 1 The Sanctuary, London SW1P 3JT T 020-7222 5381.

Marriage by certificate
The marriage can be conducted on the authority of a superintendent registrar's certificate, provided that the consent of the minister of the church or chapel where the celebration of the marriage is to take place is obtained. Since 2 March 2015, the marriage of non-EU nationals in the Church of England must take place by superintendent registrar's certificate (unless a special marriage licence is required or certain transitional arrangements apply to them), and will be allowed in any situation where the couple would otherwise have qualified for marriage by banns. In the case of British/EU nationals, the certificate procedure will be only be available if one of the parties lives in the parish for at least seven days or usually worships at the church/chapel.

Registration of the Marriage
Immediately following the solemnisation of a marriage according to the rites of the Church of England, the marriage must be registered in duplicate in two marriage register books provided by the Registrar-General for England and Wales. The entry must contain the particulars of the marriage in the prescribed form and must be signed by the clergyman, the parties to the marriage and two witnesses.

MARRIAGE BY OTHER RELIGIOUS CEREMONY
The parties will need to give notice to the register office at least 28 days before the ceremony. One of the parties must normally live in the registration district where the marriage is to take place or usually worship in the building where they wish to be married. If the building where the parties wish to be married has not been registered, the couple can still have a religious ceremony there, but this will have to follow a separate civil marriage ceremony for it to be valid. If the building is registered, in addition to giving notice to the superintendent registrar it may also be necessary to book a registrar, or authorised person to be present at the ceremony.

CIVIL MARRIAGE
A marriage may be solemnised at any register office, registered building or approved premises in England and Wales, without either of the parties being resident in the same district. The superintendent registrar of the district should be contacted and given notice, and, if the marriage is to take place at approved premises, the necessary arrangements at the venue must also be made.

NOTICE OF MARRIAGE
Where a marriage is intended to take place on the authority of a superintendent registrar's certificates, a notice of the marriage must be given in person to the superintendent registrar of the relevant district.

Both parties must have lived in a registration district in England or Wales for at least seven days immediately before giving notice personally at the local register office. If they live in different registration districts, notice must be given in both districts by the respective party in person. The marriage can take place in any register office or other approved premises in England and Wales no sooner than 28 days after notice has been given, when the superintendent registrar issues a certificate. The parties must get married or register the civil partnership within one year of giving notice.

When giving notice of the marriage it is necessary to provide evidence of name and surname, date of birth, place of residence and nationality, for example, with a passport or birth certificate and a recent bank statement. It will also be necessary to produce official proof, if relevant, that any previous marriage has ended in divorce or death by producing the original decree absolute or death certificate (or a certified copy). If the divorce or annulment documents were granted outside the UK, Channel Islands or Isle of Man the registrar may need to get in touch with the General Register Office to confirm their validity, which will incur further costs of between £50 and £75.

If either party is under 18 years old, evidence of consent by their parent or guardian is required. There are special procedures for those wishing to get married in the UK that are subject to immigration control; the register office will be able to advise on these.

SOLEMNISATION OF THE MARRIAGE
On the day of the wedding there must be at least two other people present who are prepared to act as witnesses and sign the marriage register. A registrar of marriages must be present at a marriage in a register office or at approved premises, but an authorised person may act in the capacity of registrar in a registered building.

If the marriage takes place at approved premises, the room must be separate from any other activity on the premises at the time of the ceremony, and no food or drink can be sold or consumed in the room during the ceremony or for one hour beforehand. In addition, proceedings conducted on approved premises cannot be religious in nature (although predominantly non-religious music and/or readings with incidental references to deities may be included).

The marriage must be solemnised with open doors. At some time during the ceremony the parties must make a declaration that they know of no legal impediment to the marriage and they must also say the contracting words; the declaratory and contracting words may vary according to the form of service. It may also be possible to embellish the marriage vows taken by the couple.

CIVIL FEES

Notice and registration of Marriage at a Register Office
By superintendent registrar's certificate, £35 per person for the notice of the marriage (which is not refundable if the

marriage does not in fact take place) and £46 for the registration of the marriage.

Marriage at a Register Office/Approved Premises
Fees for marriage at a register office are set by the local authority responsible. An additional fee will also be payable for the registrar's attendance at the marriage on an approved premises. This is also set locally by the local authority responsible. A further charge is likely to be made by the owners of the building for the use of the premises.

For marriages taking place in a registered religious building, an additional fee (determined by the local authority) is payable for the registrar's attendance at the marriage unless an 'authorised person' has agreed to register the marriage. Additional fees may be charged by the trustees and/or proprietors of the building for the wedding and by the person who performs the ceremony.

ECCLESIASTICAL FEES
(Church of England and Church in Wales)

Marriage by banns
For publication of banns, £30*
For certificate of banns issued at time of publication, £14*
For marriage service, £455*
For marriage certificate at time of registration £11 and £11 thereafter
* These fees are revised from 1 January each calendar year. Some may not apply to the Church in Wales

Marriage by common licence
The fee will be specified by each individual diocese
Marriage by special licence £250*
* This fee is revised on 1 April each calendar year

SCOTLAND

REGULAR MARRIAGES
A regular marriage is one which is celebrated by a minister of religion or authorised registrar or other celebrant. Each of the parties must complete a marriage notice form and return it to the district registrar for the area in which they are to be married, irrespective of where they live, within the three month period prior to the date of the marriage and not later than 29 days prior to that date. The district registrar must then enter the date of receipt and certain details in a marriage book kept for this purpose, and must also enter the names of the parties and the proposed date of marriage in a list which is displayed in a conspicuous place at the registration office until the date of the marriage has passed. All persons wishing to enter into a regular marriage in Scotland must follow the same preliminary procedure regardless of whether they intend to have a religious or civil ceremony. Before the marriage ceremony takes place any person may submit an objection in writing to the district registrar.

A marriage schedule, which is prepared by the registrar, will be issued to one or both of the parties in person up to seven days before a religious marriage; for a civil marriage the schedule will be available at the ceremony. The schedule must be handed to the celebrant before the ceremony starts and it must be signed immediately after the wedding. For religious marriages the schedule must be sent within three days by the parties to the district registrar who must register the marriage as soon as possible thereafter. In civil marriages, the district registrar must register the marriage as soon as possible.

The authority to conduct a religious marriage is deemed to be vested in the authorised celebrant rather than the building in which it takes place; open-air religious ceremonies are therefore permissible in Scotland.

From 10 June 2002 it has been possible, under the Marriage (Scotland) Act 2002, for venues or couples to apply to the local council for a licence to allow a civil ceremony to take place at a venue other than a registration office. To obtain further information, a venue or couple should contact the district registrar in the area they wish to marry.

MARRIAGE BY COHABITATION WITH HABIT AND REPUTE
Prior to the enactment of the Family Law (Scotland) Act 2006, if two people had lived together constantly as husband and wife and were generally held to be such by the neighbourhood and among their friends and relations, a presumption could arise from which marriage could be inferred. Before such a marriage could be registered, however, a decree of declarator of marriage had to be obtained from the court of session. Section 3 of the 2006 act provides that it will no longer be possible for a marriage to be constituted by cohabitation with habit and repute, but it will still be possible for couples whose period of cohabitation began before commencement of the 2006 act to seek a declarator under the old rule of law.

SAME-SEX MARRIAGES
On 12 March 2014 the Scottish government passed the Marriage and Civil Partnership (Scotland) Act 2014. This permits same-sex couples to get married, either in a civil ceremony or a 'religious or belief' ceremony where the religious or belief body has opted-in to solemnising same-sex marriage. Also, certain same-sex couples who have entered into a civil partnership have the option under the act to change their civil partnership to a marriage.

It is still possible for same-sex couples to enter into a civil partnership and this may be a 'religious or belief' civil partnership if the religious or belief body has agreed to perform these.

CIVIL FEES
The fee for submitting a notice of marriage to the district registrar is £30.00 per person. Solemnisation of a civil marriage costs £55.00, while the extract of the entry in the register of marriages attracts a fee of £10.00. The costs of religious marriage ceremonies can vary.

THE GENERAL REGISTER OFFICE, PO Box 2, Southport PR8 2JD T 0300-123 1837 W www.gro.gov.uk/gro/content/certificates

THE NATIONAL RECORDS OF SCOTLAND, New Register House, 3 West Register Street, Edinburgh EH1 3YT T 0131-314 0380 W www.nrscotland.gov.uk

TOWN AND COUNTRY PLANNING

There are a number of acts governing the development of land and buildings in England and Wales and advice should always be sought from Citizens Advice or the local planning authority before undertaking building works on any land or property. If development takes place which requires planning permission without permission being given, enforcement action may take place and the situation may need to be rectified. Planning law in Scotland is similar but certain Scotland-specific legislation applies so advice should always be sought.

PLANNING PERMISSION
Planning permission may be needed if the work involves:
- making a material change in use, such as dividing off part of a house for commercial use, eg for a workshop
- subdivision of a residential house into two or more separate homes
- going against the terms of the original planning permission, eg there may be a pre-existing restriction on fences in front gardens within an 'open-plan' estate

- building, engineering or mining works, except for the permitted developments below
- new or wider access to a main road
- additions or extensions to flats or maisonettes
- work which might obstruct the view of road users

Planning permission is not needed to carry out internal alterations or work which does not affect the external appearance of the building, and are not works for making good war damage or works begun after 5 December 1968 for the alteration of a building by providing additional space in it underground.

Under regulations which came into effect on 15 April 2015, there are certain types of development for which the Secretary of State for the Environment, Food and Rural Affairs has granted general permissions (permitted development rights). These include house extensions and additions, outbuildings and garages, other ancillary garden buildings such as swimming pools or ponds, and laying patios, paths or driveways for domestic use. However, all such developments will still be subject to a number of conditions.

Before carrying out any of the above permitted developments you should contact your local planning authority to find out whether the general permission has been modified in your area. For more information, visit W www.gov.uk/planning-permission-england-wales/when-you-dont-need-it

OTHER RESTRICTIONS

It may be necessary to obtain other types of permissions before carrying out any development. These permissions are separate from planning permission and apply regardless of whether or not planning permission is needed, eg:

- building regulations will probably apply if a new building is to be erected, if an existing one is to be altered or extended, or if the work involves building over a drain or sewer. The building control department of the local authority will advise on this
- listed building consent must be obtained from the local authority in order to make any alterations to a listed building. This applies to the main building, as well as possibly other structures within the curtilage of the building and/ or its grounds
- local authority approval is necessary if a building (or, in some circumstances, gates, walls, fences or railings) in a conservation area is to be demolished; each local authority keeps a register of all local buildings that are in conservation areas
- many trees are protected by tree preservation orders and must not be pruned or taken down without local authority consent
- bats and many other species are protected, and so Natural England or Natural Resources Wales must be notified before any work is carried out that will affect the habitat of protected species, eg timber treatment, renovation or extensions of lofts
- developments in areas with special designations, such as National Parks, Areas of Outstanding Natural Beauty, National Scenic Areas or in the Norfolk or Suffolk Broads, are subject to greater restrictions. The local planning authority will advise or refer enquirers to the relevant authority

There may also be restrictions contained in the title to the property which require you to get someone else's agreement before carrying out certain developments, and which should be considered when works are planned.

VOTERS' QUALIFICATIONS

Those entitled to vote at parliamentary and local government elections are those who, at the date of taking the poll, are:

- on the electoral roll
- aged 18 years or older (although for Scottish parliament and local government elections in Scotland those aged 16 and older can vote)
- British citizens, qualifying Commonwealth citizens or citizens of the Irish Republic who are resident in the UK
- those who suffer from no other legal bar to voting (eg prisoners). It should be noted that there is some uncertainty regarding the future of the legal bar on prisoners' voting following a decision taken by the European Court of Human Rights
- citizens of any EU member state may vote in local elections if they meet the criteria listed above (save for the nationality requirements). There is some uncertainty regarding future voting rights of EU citizens in light of Brexit. However, it should be noted that there will be no change to the voting rights of EU citizens living in the UK while the UK remains in the EU
- registered to vote as a Crown Servant
- registered to vote as a service voter

British citizens resident abroad are entitled to vote, provided they have been registered to vote in the UK within the last 15 years, as overseas electors in domestic parliamentary elections in the constituency in which they were last resident if they are on the electoral roll of the relevant constituency. The government released a policy statement in October 2016 proposing to abolish the current 15 year time limit for British citizens registering as overseas electors although it is unclear when this proposal will be legislated for. Members of the armed forces and their spouses or civil partners, Crown servants and employees of the British Council who are overseas, along with their spouses and civil partners, are entitled to vote regardless of how long they have been abroad. British citizens who had never been registered as an elector in the UK are not eligible to register as an overseas voter unless they left the UK before they were 18, providing they left the country no more than 15 years ago. Overseas electors may opt to vote by proxy or by postal vote. Overseas voters may not vote in local government elections.

The main categories of people who are not entitled to vote at general elections are:

- sitting peers in the House of Lords
- convicted persons detained in pursuance of their sentences (though remand prisoners, unconvicted prisoners and civil prisoners can vote if on the electoral register). This is currently subject to review, as detailed above
- those convicted within the previous five years of corrupt or illegal election practices
- EU citizens (who may only vote in EU and local government elections)

Under the Representation of the People Act 2000, several new groups of people are permitted to vote for the first time. These include: people who live on barges; people in mental health hospitals (other than those with criminal convictions) and homeless people who have made a 'declaration of local connection'.

REGISTERING TO VOTE

Voters must be entered on an electoral register. The Electoral Registration Officer (ERO) for each council area is responsible for preparing and publishing the register for his area by 1 December each year. Names may be added to the register to reflect changes in people's circumstances as they occur and each month during December to August, the ERO publishes a list of alterations to the published register.

On 10 May 2012, the government introduced the electoral registration and administration bill, which received royal assent on 31 January 2013. The act replaced household registration with individual elector registration, meaning each elector must apply individually to be registered to vote. Individuals will also be asked for identifying information such as date of birth and national insurance number. The act also introduced a number of changes relating to electoral administration and the conduct of elections. Anyone failing to supply information to the ERO when requested, or supplying false information, may be fined by up to £1,000. Further, the ERO may impose a civil penalty on those who fail to make an application for registration when required to do so by the ERO. Application forms and more information are available from the Electoral Commission (W www.aboutmyvote.co.uk).

VOTING

Voting is not compulsory in the UK. Those who wish to vote do so in person at the allotted polling station. Postal votes are now available to anyone on request and you do not need to give a reason for using a postal vote.

A proxy (whereby the voter nominates someone to vote in person on their behalf) can be appointed to act in a specific election, for a specified period of time or indefinitely. For the appointment of an indefinite or long-term proxy, the voter needs to specify physical employment, study reasons or a disability to explain why they are making an application. With proxy votes where a particular election is specified, the voter needs to provide details of the circumstances by which they cannot reasonably be expected to go to the polling station. Applications for a proxy are normally available up to six working days before an election, but should the voter fall ill on election day, it is possible to appoint a proxy up until polling day.

On 4 April 2019, a new campaign 'Let Us Vote' was launched with the aim of giving everyone living in the UK the right to vote in elections and referendums. The campaign is seeking new legislation which would allow all UK residents, plus British citizens living abroad, to vote in general elections regardless of their citizenship.

WILLS

A will is used to appoint executors (who will administer the estate), give directions as to the disposal of the body, appoint guardians for children and determine how and to whom property is to be passed. A well-drafted will can operate to reduce the level of inheritance tax which the estate pays. It is best to have a will drawn up by a solicitor, but if a solicitor is not employed the following points must be taken into account:

- if possible the will must not be prepared on behalf of another person by someone who is to benefit from it or who is a close relative of a major beneficiary
- the language used must be clear and unambiguous and it is better to avoid the use of legal terms where the same thing can be expressed in plain language
- it is better to rewrite the whole document if a mistake is made. If necessary, alterations can be made by striking through the words with a pen, and the signature or initials of the testator and the witnesses must be put in the margin opposite the alteration. No alteration of any kind should be made after the will has been executed
- if the person later wishes to change the will or part of it, it is better to write a new will revoking the old. The use of codicils (documents written as supplements or containing modifications to the will) should be left to a solicitor

- the will should be typed or printed, or if handwritten be legible and preferably in ink

The form of a will varies to suit different cases, a solicitor will be able to advise as to wording, however, 'DIY' will-writing kits can be purchased from good stationery shops and many banks offer a will-writing service.

LAPSED LEGATEES

If a person who has been left property in a will dies before the person who made the will, the gift fails and will pass to the person entitled to everything not otherwise disposed of (the residuary estate). If the beneficiary of the residuary estate dies before the person who made the will, the gift of the residuary estate also fails and passes to the closest relative(s) of the testator in accordance with the intestacy rules.

It is always better to draw up a new will if a beneficiary predeceases the person who made the will.

EXECUTORS

It is usual to appoint two executors, although one is sufficient. No more than four persons can deal with the estate of the person who has died. The name and address of each executor should be given in full (the addresses are not essential but including them adds clarity to the document). Executors should be 18 years of age or over. An executor may be a beneficiary of the will.

WITNESSES

A person who is a beneficiary of a will, or the spouse or civil partner of a beneficiary at the time the will is signed, must not act as a witness or else he/she will be unable to take his/her gift. There is nothing preventing the spouse or civil partner of the person making the will from acting as a witness, but as it is rare for a spouse or civil partner not to benefit from the will of his/her spouse or civil partner, an independent witness is usually better.

It is also better that a person does not act as an executor and as a witness, as he/she can take no benefit (including remuneration) under a will to which he/she is witness. In relation to deaths on or after 1 February 2001, however, a professional executor who is also a witness can receive payments due to him or her under a term in the will for services provided as executor.

The identity of the witnesses should be made as explicit as possible, such as by stating their names, addresses, and occupations.

EXECUTION OF A WILL

The person making the will should sign his/her name in the presence of the two witnesses. It is advisable to sign at the foot of the document, so as to avoid uncertainty about the testator's intention. The witnesses must then sign their names while the person making the will looks on. If this procedure is not adhered to, the will may be considered invalid. There are certain exceptional circumstances where these rules are relaxed, eg where the person may be too ill to sign.

CAPACITY TO MAKE A WILL

Anyone aged 18 or over can make a will. However, if there is any suspicion that the person making the will is not, through reasons of infirmity or age, fully in command of his/her faculties, it is advisable to arrange for a medical practitioner to examine the person making the will as near to the time that the testator gives instructions for the will and to when the will is executed (to verify his/her mental capacity and to record that medical opinion in writing), and to ask the examining practitioner to act as a witness. If a person is not mentally able to make a will, the court of protection may do this for him/her by virtue of the Mental Capacity Act 2005.

REVOCATION

A will may be revoked or cancelled in a number of ways:

- a later will revokes an earlier one if it says so; otherwise the

earlier will is by implication revoked by the later one to the extent that it contradicts or repeats the earlier one
- a will is revoked if the original physical document on which it is written is destroyed by the person whose will it is. There must be an intention to revoke the will and an act of destruction. It may not be sufficient to obliterate the will with a pen
- a will is revoked by the testator making a written declaration to this effect executed in the same way as a will
- a will is also revoked when the person marries or forms a civil partnership, unless it is clear from the will that the person intended the will to stand after that particular marriage or civil partnership. A will is not revoked, however, by the conversion of a civil partnership to a marriage, or when the testator is treated as having formed a civil partnership on 5 December 2005 because he/she registered a recognised overseas relationship before that date.
- where a marriage or civil partnership ends in divorce or dissolution or is annulled or declared void, gifts to the spouse or civil partner and the appointment of the spouse or civil partner as executor fail unless the will says that this is not to happen. A former spouse or civil partner is treated as having predeceased the testator. A separation does not change the effect of a married person or civil partner's will.

PROBATE AND LETTERS OF ADMINISTRATION
The grant of probate is granted to the executors named in a will and once granted, the executors are obliged to carry out the instructions of the will. Letters of administration are granted where the deceased died intestate or did not leave a valid will. Letters of administration with will annexed are granted when the deceased did not appoint an executor in the will or the appointed executor(s) are not able or willing to act. The letters of administration give a person, often the next of kin, similar powers and duties to those of an executor.

Applications for the grant of probate or for letters of administration can be made to the Principal Registry of the Family Division, to a district probate registry or to a probate sub-registry. Applicants not using a solicitor will need to send the following documents to the main probate registry of choice: the Probate Application Form (PA1A if the deceased did not leave a will or PA1P if the deceased had a will); the original will and codicils (if any) and three copies of the same; an official copy of the death certificate; and the appropriate tax form (an 'IHT 205' if no inheritance tax is owed; otherwise an 'IHT 421' stamped by HMRC confirming payment of inheritance tax), in addition to a cheque for the relevant probate fee. The applicant will then be invited to an interview at the probate registry of choice where they will swear an oath. Where an applicant is using a solicitor, the PA1 is not necessary and the appropriate oath (for executors or administrators) will be included in the documents to be sent to the probate registry; there is no interview. In both cases, where the estate of the deceased is below £5,000, there is no probate fee to pay. Certain property, up to the value of £5,000, may be disposed of without a grant of probate or letters of administration, as can assets that do not pass under the will such as jointly owned assets which pass automatically on the death of one of the joint holders for the survivor, life policies written in trust, or discretionary pension death benefits.

A new probate regime was scheduled to be in force by April 2019, but due to the immediacy of Brexit, the approval process had been delayed, and at the time of writing there had been no indication from the Ministry of Justice as to when it may come into force. Notwithstanding, the new regime will come into force 21 days after the order is made, unless the approval motion is rejected by parliament and the issue has to be debated and voted on. The new regime stipulates that probate fees will maintained at the current level for estates worth below £50,000 and increased to £6,000 for estates worth over £2m, with a sliding scale for estates worth between £50,000 and £2m.

WHERE TO FIND A PROVED WILL
Since 1858 wills which have been proved, that is wills on which probate or letters of administration have been granted, must have been proved at the Principal Registry of the Family Division or at a district probate registry. The Lord Chancellor has power to direct where the original documents are kept but most are filed where they were proved and may be inspected there and a copy obtained. You can search for a probate record online or by post. The Principal Registry also holds copies of all wills proved at district probate registries and these may be inspected at First Avenue House, High Holborn, London. An index of all grants, both of probate and of letters of administration, is compiled by the Principal Registry and may be seen either at the Principal Registry or at a district probate registry.

It is also possible to discover when a grant of probate or letters of administration is issued by requesting a standing search. In response to a request and for a small fee, a district probate registry will supply the names and addresses of executors or administrators and the registry in which the grant was made, of any grant in the estate of a specified person made in the previous six months or following six months.

PRINCIPAL REGISTRY (FAMILY DIVISION), 7th Floor, 42–49 High Holborn, First Avenue House, London WC1V 6NP
T 020-7421 8509

INTESTACY
Intestacy occurs when someone dies without leaving a will or leaves a will which is invalid or which does not take effect for some reason. Intestacy can be partial, for instance, if there is a valid will which disposes of some but not all of the testator's property. In such cases the person's estate (property, possessions, other assets following the payment of debts) passes to certain members of the family. If a will has been written that disposes of only part of a person's property, these rules apply to the part which is undisposed of.

Some types of property do not follow the intestacy rules, for example, property held as joint tenants, insurance policies taken out for specified individuals or assigned into trust during the testator's lifetime and death benefits under a pension scheme.

Following a lengthy review by the Law Commission, the intestacy rules changed on 1 October 2014.

If the person (intestate) leaves a spouse or a civil partner who survives for 28 days and children (legitimate, illegitimate and adopted children and other descendants), the estate is divided as follows:
- if the estate is worth more than £250,000, the spouse or civil partner takes the 'personal chattels' (household articles, including cars, but nothing used for business purposes or held solely as an investment), £250,000 and half of the rest of the estate absolutely
- the rest of the estate goes to the children*

If the intestate leaves a spouse or civil partner who survives for 28 days but no children, the spouse or civil partner will take the estate in its entirety, regardless of its value.

If there is no surviving spouse or civil partner, the estate is distributed among those who survive the intestate as follows (these provisions remained unchanged at 1 October 2014):
- to surviving children*, but if none to
- parents (equally, if both alive), but if none to
- brothers and sisters of the whole blood* (including issue of deceased ones), but if none to
- brothers and sisters of the half blood* (including issue of deceased ones), but if none to
- grandparents (equally, if more than one), but if none to
- aunts and uncles of the whole blood*, but if none to
- aunts and uncles of the half blood*, but if none to

• the Crown, Duchy of Lancaster or the Duke of Cornwall *(bona vacantia)*
* To inherit, a member of these groups must survive the intestate and attain the age of 18, or marry under that age. If they die under the age of 18 (unless married under that age), their share goes to others, if any, in the same group. If any member of these groups predeceases the intestate leaving children, their share is divided equally among their children.

In England and Wales the provisions of the Inheritance (Provision for Family and Dependants) Act 1975 may allow other people to claim provision from the deceased's assets. This act also applies to cases where a will has been made and allows a person to apply to the court if they feel that the will or rules of intestacy (or both) do not make adequate provision for them. The court can order payment from the deceased's assets or the transfer of property from them if the applicant's claim is accepted. The application must be made within six months of the grant of probate or letters of administration and the following people can make an application:

• the spouse or civil partner
• a former spouse or civil partner who has not remarried or formed a subsequent civil partnership
• a child of the deceased
• someone treated as a child of the deceased's family where the deceased stood in the role of a parent to the applicant
• someone maintained wholly or partly by the deceased
• where the deceased died on or after 1 January 1996, someone who has cohabited for two years before the death in the same household as the deceased and was living as the husband or wife or civil partner of the deceased

SCOTLAND

In Scotland any person over 12 and of sound mind can make a will. The person making the will can only freely dispose of the heritage and what is known as the 'dead's part' of the estate because:

• the spouse or civil partner has the right to inherit one-third of the moveable estate if there are children or other descendants, and one-half of it if there are not
• children are entitled to one-third of the moveable estate if there is a surviving spouse or civil partner, and one-half of it if there is not

The remaining portion of the moveable estate is the dead's part, and legacies and bequests are payable from this. Debts are payable out of the whole estate before any division.

From August 1995, wills no longer needed to be 'holographed' and it is now only necessary to have one witness. The person making the will still needs to sign each page. It is better that the will is not witnessed by a beneficiary although the attestation would still be sound and the beneficiary would not have to relinquish the gift.

As a result of the changes brought in by the Succession (Scotland) Act 2016, from 1 November 2016 a divorce, dissolution or annulment (granted by a UK court) will revoke any provision in a will which confers a benefit or power of appointment on the former spouse or civil partner unless the will expressly provides that the benefit or appointment should still apply in the event of a divorce, dissolution or annulment. Subsequent marriage or civil partnership does not revoke a will but the birth of a child who is not provided for may do so. A will may be revoked by a subsequent will, either expressly or by implication, but in so far as the two can be read together both have effect. If a subsequent will is revoked, the earlier will may be revived provided it was not physically destroyed.

Wills may be registered in the sheriff court Books of the Sheriffdom in which the deceased lived or in the Books of Council and Session at the Registers of Scotland.

CONFIRMATION

Confirmation (the Scottish equivalent of probate) is obtained in the sheriff court of the sheriffdom in which the deceased was domiciled at the time of death. Executors are either 'nominate' (named by the deceased in the will) or 'dative' (appointed by the court in cases where no executor is named in a will or in cases of intestacy). Applicants for confirmation must first provide an inventory of the deceased's estate and a schedule of debts, with an affidavit. In estates under £36,000 gross, confirmation can be obtained under a simplified procedure at reduced fees, with no need for a solicitor. The local sheriff clerk's office can provide assistance.

PRINCIPAL REGISTRY (FAMILY DIVISION), First Avenue House, 42–49 High Holborn, London WC1V 6NP
T 020-7947 6000

REGISTERS OF SCOTLAND, Meadowbank House, 153 London Road, Edinburgh EH8 7AU T 0800-169 9391
W www.ros.gov.uk

INTESTACY

The rules of distribution are contained in the Succession (Scotland) Act 1964 and are extended to include civil partners by the Civil Partnership Act 2004.

A surviving spouse or civil partner is entitled to 'prior rights'. Prior rights mean that if certain conditions are met the spouse or civil partner has the right to inherit:

• the matrimonial or family home up to a value of £473,000, or one matrimonial or family home if there is more than one, or, in certain circumstances, the value of the home
• the furnishings and contents of that home, up to the value of £29,000
• a cash sum of £50,000 if the deceased left children or other descendants, or £89,000 if not

These figures are increased from time to time by regulations. Once prior rights have been satisfied legal rights are settled. Legal rights are:

• *Jus relicti(ae) and rights under the section 131 of the Civil Partnership Act 2004* – the right of a surviving spouse or civil partner to one-half of the net moveable estate, after satisfaction of prior rights, if there are no surviving children; if there are surviving children, the spouse or civil partner is entitled to one-third of the net moveable estate
• *Legitim and rights under the section 131 of the Civil Partnership Act 2004* – the right of surviving children to one-half of the net moveable estate if there is no surviving spouse or civil partner; if there is a surviving spouse or civil partner, the children are entitled to one-third of the net moveable estate after the satisfaction of prior rights

Once prior and legal rights have been satisfied, the remaining estate will be distributed in the following order:

• to descendants
• if no descendants, then to collaterals (ie brothers and sisters) and parents with each being entitled to half of the estate, or if only either parents or collaterals survive, the whole of the estate
• surviving spouse or civil partner
• if no collaterals, parents, spouse or civil partner, then to ascendants collaterals (ie aunts and uncles), and so on in an ascending scale
• if all lines of succession fail, the estate passes to the Crown

Relatives of the whole blood are preferred to relatives of the half blood. Also the right of representation, ie the right of the issue of a person who would have succeeded if he/she had survived the intestate, applies.

The Family Law (Scotland) Act 2006 makes provision to allow an unmarried cohabitant to make a financial claim against the estate of a cohabitant who dies intestate. In general a claim must be made within six months of the deceased's death. The court must take into account certain factors when considering such a claim. If the claim is successful the court has the power to order payment of a capital sum and transfer of property.

In February 2019 the Scottish government launched a consultation on changes to the law of intestate succession.

INTELLECTUAL PROPERTY

Intellectual property is a broad term covering a number of legal rights provided by the government to help people protect their creative works and encourage further innovation. By using these legal rights people can own the things they create and control the way in which others use their innovations. Intellectual property owners can take legal action to stop others using their intellectual property, they can license their intellectual property to others or they can sell it on. Different types of intellectual property utilise different forms of protection including copyright, designs, patents and trade marks, which are all covered below in more detail.

CHANGES TO INTELLECTUAL PROPERTY LAW

Reforms to the Copyright, Designs and Patents Act 1988 came into force on 1 June 2014, giving a number of sectors a legal framework suitable for the digital age, removing unnecessary regulations and enabling these sectors to better preserve and use copyright material. Under the reforms, researchers benefit from a text and data mining exception for non-commercial research and schools, colleges and universities can obtain a licence to use copyright material on interactive whiteboards and in presentations without accidentally infringing copyright. An existing preservation exception was expanded to cover all types of copyright work, and now applies to museums and galleries as well as libraries and archives. The reforms also provided exceptions to copyright for the benefit of disabled people, allowing those with any type of disability which affected access to copyright works to make accessible copies of these works (eg music, film, books) when no commercial alternative existed. Under the Marrakesh Treaty, which entered into force on 11 October 2018, the commercial availability restrictions were removed to allow disabled persons to make accessible copies even when the material is commercially available.

The Intellectual Property Act 2014 came into effect on 1 October 2014. The act modernised intellectual property law to help UK businesses better protect their rights. It also implemented reforms to design legislation and introduced a number of changes to patent law, making it cheaper and easier to use and defend patents. Additional patent rule changes came into effect on 1 October 2016 and 6 April 2017. These streamlined the application process, made procedures more flexible and increased the legal certainty of patents that are granted.

The Intellectual Property (Unjustified Threats) Act 2017 came into effect on 1 October 2017. The act serves to protect businesses against unfair threats of legal action, when no infringement of intellectual property has actually taken place, and to help businesses negotiate fairly over intellectual property disputes and avoid costly litigation.

COPYRIGHT

Copyright protects all original literary, dramatic, musical and artistic works, as well as sound and film recordings and broadcasts. Among the works covered by copyright are novels, computer programs, newspaper articles, sculptures, technical drawings, websites, maps and photographs. Under copyright the creators of these works can control the various ways in which their material may be exploited, the rights broadly covering copying, adapting, issuing (including renting and lending) copies to the public, performing in public, and broadcasting the material (including online). The transfer of copyright works to formats accessible to visually impaired persons without infringement of copyright was enacted in 2002.

Copyright protection in the UK is automatic and there is no official registration system. The creator of a work can help to protect it by including the copyright symbol ©, the name of the copyright owner, and the year in which the work was created. In addition, steps can be taken by the work's creator to provide evidence that they had the work at a particular time (eg by depositing a copy with a bank or solicitor). The main legislation is the Copyright, Designs and Patents Act 1988 (as amended). The term of copyright protection for literary, dramatic, musical (including song lyrics and musical compositions) and artistic works lasts for 70 years after the death of the creator. For film, copyright lasts for 70 years after the director, authors of the screenplay and dialogue, or the composer of any music specially created for the film have all died. Sound recordings are protected for 50 years after their publication (or their first performance if they are not published), and broadcasts for 50 years from the end of the year in which the broadcast/transmission was made. The typographical arrangement of published editions remains under copyright protection for 25 years from the end of the year in which the particular edition was published.

The main international treaties protecting copyright are the Berne Convention for the Protection of Literary and Artistic Works (administered by the World Intellectual Property Organization (WIPO)), the Rome Convention for the Protection of Performers, Producers of Phonograms and Broadcasting Organisations (administered by the the International Labour Organisation, UNESCO and WIPO), the Geneva Phonograms Convention (administered by WIPO), and the Universal Copyright Convention (developed by UNESCO); the UK is a signatory to these conventions. Copyright material created by UK nationals or residents is protected in the countries that have signed one of the above-named conventions by the national law of that country. A list of participating countries may be obtained from the UK Intellectual Property Office. The World Trade Organization's Trade-Related Aspects of Intellectual Property Rights (TRIPS) agreement may also provide copyright protection abroad.

In May 2001 the EU passed a new directive (which became law in the UK in 2003) aimed at harmonising copyright law throughout the EU to take account of the internet and other technologies. More information can be found online (W www.ipo.gov.uk).

LICENSING

Use of copyright material without seeking permission in each instance may be permitted under 'blanket' licences available from national copyright licensing agencies. The International Federation of Reproduction Rights Organisations facilitates agreements between its member licensing agencies and on behalf of its members with organisations such as WIPO, UNESCO, the EU and the Council of Europe. More information can be found online (W www.ifrro.org).

DESIGN PROTECTION

Design protection covers the outward appearance of an article, and in the UK it takes two forms: registered design and design right, which are not mutually exclusive. Registered design protects the aesthetic appearance of an article, including shape, configuration, pattern or ornament; artistic works such as sculptures are excluded, being generally protected by copyright. To achieve design protection the owner of the design must apply to the Intellectual Property Office. In order to qualify for protection, a design must be new and materially different from earlier UK published designs. Initial registration lasts for five years and can be extended in five-year increments to a maximum of 25 years. The current legislation is the Registered Designs Act 1949 (as amended).

UK applicants wishing to protect their designs in the EU can do so by applying for a Registered Community Design with the EU Intellectual Property Office. Outside the EU separate applications must be made in each country in which protection is sought.

Design right is an automatic right which applies to the shape or configuration of articles and does not require registration. Unlike registered design, two-dimensional designs do not qualify for protection but designs of electronic circuits are protected by design right. Designs must be original and non-commonplace. The term of design right is ten years from first marketing of the design, or 15 years after the creation of design, whichever is earlier. This right is effective only in the UK. After five years anyone is entitled to apply for a licence of right, which allows others to make and sell products copying the design. The current legislation is Part 3 of the Copyright, Designs and Patents Act 1988.

PATENTS

A patent is a document issued by the UK Intellectual Property Office relating to an invention. It gives the proprietor the right for a limited period to stop others from making, using, importing or selling the invention without the inventor's permission. The patentee pays a fee to cover the costs of processing the patent and must publicly disclose details of the invention.

To qualify for a patent, an invention must be new, must be functional or technical, must exhibit an inventive step, and must be capable of industrial application. The patent is valid for a maximum of 20 years, subject to renewal on the fourth anniversary of when the application was first filed and annually thereafter. The UK Intellectual Property Office, established in 1852, is responsible for ensuring that all stages of an application comply with the Patents Act 1977, and that the invention meets the criteria for a patent. An online patent renewal service is available at: www.gov.uk/renew-patent.

WIPO is responsible for administering many of the international conventions on intellectual property. The Patent Cooperation Treaty allows inventors to file a single application for patent rights in some or all of the contracting states. This application is searched by an International Searching Authority to confirm the invention is novel and that the same concept has not already been made publicly available. The application and search report are then published by the International Bureau of WIPO. It may also be the subject of an (optional) international preliminary examination. Applicants must then deal directly with the patent offices in the countries where they are seeking patent rights. The European Patent Convention allows inventors to obtain patent rights in all the contracting states by filing a single application with the European Patent Office. More information can be found at: W www.ipo.gov.uk.

RESEARCH DISCLOSURES

Research disclosures are publicly disclosed details of inventions. Once published, an invention is considered no longer novel and becomes 'prior art'. Publishing a disclosure is significantly cheaper than applying for a patent; however, unlike a patent, it does not entitle the author to exclusive rights to use or license the invention. Instead, research disclosures are primarily published to ensure the inventor the freedom to use the invention. This works because publishing legally prevents other parties from patenting the disclosed innovation and, in the UK, patent law dictates that by disclosing details of an invention, even the inventor relinquishes their right to a patent.

In theory, publishing details of an invention anywhere should be enough to constitute a research disclosure. However, to be effective, a research disclosure needs to be published in a location which patent examiners will include in their prior art searches. To ensure global legal precedent it must be included in a publication with a recognised date stamp and made publicly available throughout the world.

Research Disclosure, established in 1960 and operated by Questel Ireland Ltd, is the primary publisher of research disclosures. It is the only disclosure service recognised by the Patent Cooperation Treaty as a mandatory search resource which must be consulted by the international search authorities. (W www.researchdisclosure.com).

TRADE MARKS

Trade marks are a means of identification, enabling traders to make their goods and services readily distinguishable from those supplied by others. Trade marks can take the form of words, a logo or a combination of both. Registration prevents other traders using the same or similar trade marks for similar products or services.

In the UK trade marks are registered at the UK Intellectual Property Office. In order to qualify for registration, a trade mark must be capable of distinguishing its proprietor's goods or services from those of other undertakings; it should be non-deceptive, should not describe the goods and services or any characteristics of them, should not be contrary to law or morality and should not be similar or identical to any earlier trade marks for the same or similar goods or services. The owner of a registered trade mark may include an ® symbol next to it, and must renew their registration every ten years to keep it in force. The relevant current legislation is the Trade Marks Act 1994 (as amended).

It is possible to obtain an international trade mark registration, effective in up to 120 countries, under the Madrid system for the international registration of marks, to which the UK is party. British companies can obtain international trade mark registration in those countries party to the system through a single application to WIPO.

EU trade mark regulation is administered by the EU Intellectual Property Office, which registers Community trade marks, valid throughout the EU. The registration of trade marks in individual member states continues in parallel with EU trade marks.

DOMAIN NAMES

An internet domain name (eg www.whitakersalmanack.com) has to be registered separately from a trade mark, and this can be done through a number of registrars which charge varying rates and compete for business. For each top-level domain name (eg uk.com), there is a central registry to store the unique internet names and addresses using that suffix. A list of accredited registrars can be found online (W www.icann.org).

CONTACTS

COPYRIGHT LICENSING AGENCY LTD, 5th Floor, Shackleton House, 4 Battle Bridge Lane, London SE1 2HX T 020-7400 3100 W www.cla.co.uk
EUROPEAN PATENT OFFICE, 80298 Munich, Germany T (+49) 89 2399-0 W www.epo.org
INTELLECTUAL PROPERTY OFFICE, Concept House, Cardiff Road, Newport NP10 8QQ T 0300-300 2000 W www.ipo.gov.uk
WORLD INTELLECTUAL PROPERTY ORGANIZATION, 34 chemin des Colombettes, CH-1211 Geneva 20, Switzerland T (+41) 22 338 9111 W www.wipo.int

THE MEDIA

CROSS-MEDIA OWNERSHIP

The rules surrounding cross-media ownership were overhauled as part of the 2003 Communications Act. The act simplified and relaxed existing rules to encourage dispersion of ownership and new market entry while preventing the most influential media in any community being controlled by too narrow a range of interests. However, transfers and mergers are not solely subject to examination on competition grounds by the competition authorities. The Secretary of State for Digital, Culture, Media and Sport has a broad remit to decide if a transaction is permissible and can intervene on public interest grounds (relating both to newspapers and cross-media criteria, if broadcasting interests are also involved). The Office of Communications (OFCOM) has an advisory role in this context. Government and parliamentary assurances were given that any intervention into local newspaper transfers would be rare and exceptional. Following a request from the Secretary of State for Digital, Culture, Media and Sport in June 2010 for a removal of all restrictions from the ownership of local media, OFCOM recommended the liberalisation of local cross-media regulations to enable a single owner to control newspapers, a TV licence and radio stations in one area.

REGULATION

OFCOM is the regulator for the communication industries in the UK and has responsibility for television, radio, telecommunications and wireless communications services. OFCOM is required to report annually to parliament and exists to further the interests of consumers by balancing choice and competition with the duty to foster plurality; protect viewers and listeners and promote cultural diversity in the media; and to ensure full and fair competition between communications providers.

OFFICE OF COMMUNICATIONS (OFCOM), Riverside House, 2A Southwark Bridge Road, London SE1 9HA T 020-7981 3000 W www.ofcom.org.uk
Chair, Lord Burns, GCB

COMPLAINTS

Under the Communications Act 2003 OFCOM's licensees are obliged to adhere to the provisions of its codes (including advertising, programme standards, fairness, privacy and sponsorship). Complainants should contact the broadcaster in the first instance (details can be found on OFCOM's website); however, if the complainant wishes the complaint to be considered by OFCOM, it will do so. Complaints must be submitted within 20 working days of broadcast, as broadcasters are only required to keep recordings for the following periods: radio, 42 days; television, 90 days; and cable and satellite, 60 days. OFCOM can fine a broadcaster, revoke a licence or take programmes off the air. Since November 2004 complaints relating to individual advertisements on TV or radio have been dealt with by the Advertising Standards Authority.

ADVERTISING STANDARDS AUTHORITY Mid City Place, 71 High Holborn, London WC1V 6QT T 020-7492 2222 W www.asa.org.uk
Chief Executive, Guy Parker

TELEVISION

There are six major television channel owners who are responsible for the biggest audience share. They are the British Broadcasting Corporation (BBC), Independent Television (ITV), Channel 4, Channel 5, Sky and UKTV. Overall there are around 480 channels available to viewers, through free-to-air, free-to-view and subscription-based services. Following the completion of the switchover to a digital format in October 2012, analogue transmissions ended and digital-only content was broadcast through a range of services, including terrestrial, satellite, cable and IP.

Beginning as a radio station in 1922, the BBC is the oldest broadcaster in the world. The corporation began a London-only television service from Alexandra Palace in 1936 and achieved nationwide coverage 15 years later. A second station, BBC Two, was launched in 1964. The BBC's other free-to-air channels available in the UK comprise BBC Four, BBC News, BBC Parliament, the children's channels, CBeebies and CBBC, and regional channels including BBC Alba, a gaelic-language channel in Scotland. Many of the BBC's channels have a corresponding HD (high definition) service and there are additionally several local channels. BBC's iPlayer service was launched on Christmas Day 2007 and allows users to view and listen to content instantly, stream live television and download programmes on to a computer, tablet or mobile device for up to 30 days. An integrated service for radio was launched in June 2008. In 2009, iPlayer was extended to more than 20 devices, including mobile phones and games consoles, and an HD service was launched. The BBC services are funded by the licence fee. The corporation also has a commercial arm, BBC Worldwide, which was formed in 1994 and exists to maximise the value of the BBC's programme and publishing assets for the benefit of the licence payer. Its businesses include international programming distribution, magazines, other licensed products, live events and media monitoring.

The ITV (Independent Television) network began broadcasting in 1955 on Channel 3 in the London area, under the Television Act 1954 which made provision for commercial television in the UK. The ITV network originally comprised a number of independent licensees, the majority of which have now merged to form ITV plc. The network generates funds through broadcasting television advertisements. The ITV network channels now include ITV2, ITV3, ITV4, ITVBe, ITV Encore and CiTV, while the network also owns UTV Ireland. The majority of ITV channels have corresponding HD services. ITV Player, similar to iPlayer, was launched December 2008 and rebranded as ITV Hub in November 2015. ITV Network Centre is wholly owned by the ITV companies and undertakes commissioning and scheduling of programmes shown across the ITV network and, as with the other terrestrial channels, 25 per cent of programmes must come from independent producers.

Channel 4 and S4C (Sianel Pedwar Cymru – Channel Four Wales) were launched in 1982 to provide programmes with a distinctive character that appeal to interests not catered for by ITV. Channel 4 has a remit to be innovative, experimental and distinctive. Although publicly owned, Channel 4 receives no public funding and is financed predominantly through advertising, but unlike ITV, Channel 4 is not shareholder-owned. It has expanded to create the stations E4, More4, Film4, 4Music and, in July 2012, catchup channel 4seven. All 4 is Channel 4's online service which enables viewers to download and revisit programmes from the last 30 days as well as access an older archive of footage. All 4 replaced Channel 4's first online platform 4oD (launched in 2006) in March 2015 and in March 2019 a subscription service was added, All 4+, which removes ads from the platform. S4C, the Welsh language public service broadcaster, receives annual funding, £15m in 2018–19, from the Department for Digital, Culture, Media and Sport (DCMS). In March 2018, the government decided that S4C would be entirely funded through the TV licence from 2022, which currently fulfils 90 per cent of its budget. S4C will remain independent and be entitled to receive UK government funding and generate its own revenue. The on-demand service is called S4C Clic and some S4C programmes are also available through BBC iPlayer.

Channel 5 began broadcasting in 1997. It was rebranded Five in 2002 but reverted to its original name, Channel 5, after the station was acquired by Northern & Shell in July 2010. Digital stations 5USA and 5Star (formerly Five Life, then Fiver) were launched in October 2006. My5 (formerly Demand 5) is an online service, launched in June 2008, where viewers can watch and download content from the last 30 days on various platforms.

BSkyB was formed after the merger in 1990 of Sky Television and British Sky Broadcasting. Now known as Sky plc, the company operates across five countries: Italy, Germany, Austria, the UK and Ireland and serves 22 million customers. Sky is one of the UK's largest pay-TV broadcasters and Its television service includes Sky Sports, Sky Cinema, Sky Arts and Sky Atlantic. In 2007, Freeview overtook Sky as the UK's most popular digital service.

In February 2011, a new version of OFCOM's Broadcasting Code came into force, permitting product placement for the first time in UK-produced television programmes. A large 'P' logo designed by OFCOM and broadcasters is displayed at the beginning and end of each programme containing product placement. The first instance of product placement occurred on 28 February 2011.

THE TELEVISION LICENCE

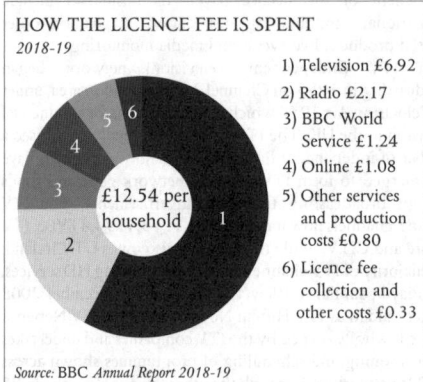

HOW THE LICENCE FEE IS SPENT
2018-19

£12.54 per household

1) Television £6.92
2) Radio £2.17
3) BBC World Service £1.24
4) Online £1.08
5) Other services and production costs £0.80
6) Licence fee collection and other costs £0.33

Source: BBC *Annual Report 2018-19*

In the UK and its dependencies, a television licence is required to receive any publicly broadcast television service, regardless of its source, including commercial, satellite and cable programming. A TV licence registered to a home address allows the viewer to watch television on laptops, tablets and mobile phones outside the place of residence. Since 1 September 2016 a TV licence is required for services such as BBC iPlayer, even if the programme is not being watched live.

The TV licence is classified as a tax, therefore non-payment is a criminal offence. A fine of up to £1,000 can be imposed on those successfully prosecuted. The TV licence is issued on behalf of the BBC as the licensing authority under the

Communications Act 2003. In 2018–19 25,927,000 TV licences were purchased, a 37,000 decrease on the number purchased in 2017–18, resulting in a 3.8 per cent decrease in revenue to £3,690m. As at 1 April 2019, an annual colour television licence costs £154.50 and a black and white licence £52.00. Concessions are available for the elderly and people with disabilities. In June 2019, the BBC announced its intention to end free TV licences for those aged 75 and over from June 2020; only households with someone aged 75 and over who is in receipt of pension credit will remain eligible to apply for a free licence. Further details can be found at W www.tvlicensing.co.uk/information

DIGITAL TELEVISION

The Broadcasting Act 1996 provided for the licensing of 20 or more digital terrestrial television (DTT) channels (on six frequency channels or 'multiplexes'). The first digital services went on air in autumn 1998.

In June 2002, following the collapse of ITV Digital, the digital terrestrial television licence was awarded to a consortium made up of the BBC, BSkyB and transmitter company Crown Castle by the Independent Television Commission. Freeview was launched on 30 October 2002 with 25 free-to-air channels: it now offers over 70 digital channels, up to 15 HD channels and 30 radio stations and requires the one-off purchase of a set-top box, but is subsequently free of charge with no subscription. In Autumn 2005 ITV and Channel 4 officially became shareholders, each taking a 20 per cent stake. As at 2018, around 20 million homes use Freeview on at least one set, amounting to around 30 per cent of UK households. There is an additional Freeview+ service which works in a similar fashion to Sky+, allowing viewers to record programmes. Over 97 per cent of UK homes have access to digital television.

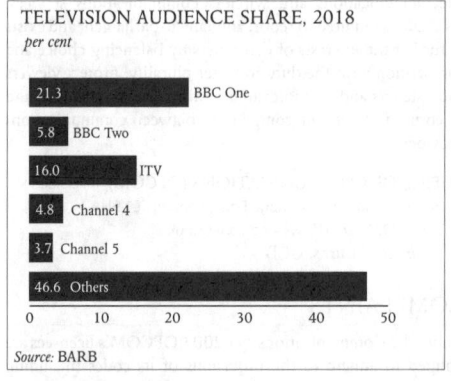

TELEVISION AUDIENCE SHARE, 2018
per cent

	per cent
BBC One	21.3
BBC Two	5.8
ITV	16.0
Channel 4	4.8
Channel 5	3.7
Others	46.6

Source: BARB

RECENT DEVELOPMENTS

The internet has now firmly established itself as an alternative to live and programmed TV, particularly for those aged 16 to 34. Since the launch of 4oD in 2006 and BBC iPlayer in 2007, there has been a noticeable shift in the way viewers can watch their favourite programmes. Technological advancements have also contributed to this phenomenon; more than half of the UK population uses a tablet, over 90 per cent of UK homes and businesses have access to superfast broadband and there are millions of public Wi-Fi hotspots across the UK. There is now a much bigger emphasis on catch-up, and subscription video on demand (SVOD) services then ever before, with BBC iPlayer recording 356 million requests in January 2019, an average of 11.5 million requests a day. SVOD services such as Netflix, Now TV and Amazon Prime Video have experienced a surge in popularity, with subscribers able to stream programmes through computers, mobiles, tablets and games consoles on up to four devices at a time. Both Netflix and Amazon Prime Video commission and distribute their own programmes, available exclusively to their subscribers, contributing to their popularity. UK subscriptions to Netflix surpassed those to Sky for the first time in December 2018. and 47 per cent of all UK households currently have an active subscription to at least one SVOD service. The BBC has provided exclusive content and programmes on iPlayer since 2014 and in 2016 moved BBC Three to an online-only service. ITV and Channel 4 both launched their own SVOD services (ITV Hub+, All 4+) in 2018 and 2019 respectively.

Despite the rise in the popularity of tablets, traditional TV sets are still the most popular way to watch television. HD TV provides more vibrant colours, greater detail and increased picture clarity, along with improved sound quality. An HD television screen uses 1,280 by 720 pixels and up to 1,920 by 1,080 pixels. HD Ready TVs operate at 720p while full HD TVs tend to operate on 1080p or 1080i; the differences between these three settings are down to the number of lines in the resolution and the type of scanning technology. 'HD Ready' simply means the TV will only operate a higher definition once plugged into a decoder, whereas full HD has this built in. In 2017, the average screen size in the UK was 43.7 inches wide and this is expected to increase to 48.9 inches by 2020, indicating a rapidly increasing trend towards bigger screens. Sales of Smart TVs, which can access apps, browse the internet and stream video, are increasing; around 48 per cent of UK households now own a Smart TV.

In April 2010, Samsung released the first consumer 3D TV; in the same month Sky launched the UK's first dedicated 3D channel. Several sporting events were broadcast in 3D, including the Wimbledon Championships. The BBC began a two-year 3D trial in 2011 but announced in July 2013 it would suspend 3D programming for an indefinite period of time due to a lack of public appetite for the technology and the sale of new 3D TV sets and services has now essentially ceased in the UK. In June 2018, the Facebook owned virtual reality (VR) headset company Oculus launched Oculus TV, intended to create a fully immersive experience.

In September 2012, OFCOM awarded its first local TV licences after announcing plans to broadcast 21 channels in total. In November 2013, Estuary TV, based in Grimsby, was the first to be launched. In March 2013, OFCOM stated plans for a further 30 areas to invite bids for local television services. However in April 2018, OFCOM announced its intention to halt the roll out of new local TV stations due several service providers facing financial difficulties and poor audience figures.

CONTACTS

THE BRITISH BROADCASTING CORPORATION (BBC)

BBC Broadcasting House, Portland Place, London W1A 1AA W www.bbc.co.uk
BBC North, Media City UK, Bridge House, Salford Quays, Manchester M50 2BH
Chair, BBC Board, Sir David Clementi
Director-General, Lord Hall of Birkenhead, CBE
BBC Worldwide, 1 Television Centre, Wood Lane, London W12 7FA W www.bbcworldwide.com

INDEPENDENT TELEVISION (ITV)

London Television Centre, 2 Waterhouse Square, 138-142 Holborn, London EC1N 2AE W www.itv.com
Chair, Sir Peter Bazalgette
Chief Executive, Dame Carolyn McCall, DBE

INDEPENDENT TELEVISION (ITV) REGIONS

Anglia (eastern England), W www.itv.com/anglia
Border (Borders and the Isle of Man), W www.itv.com/border
Calendar (Yorkshire), W www.itv.com/calendar
Central (east, west and south Midlands), W www.itv.com/central
Channel (Channel Islands), W www.itv.com/channel
Granada (north-west England), W www.itv.com/granada
London, W www.itv.com/london
Meridian (south and south-east England), W www.itv.com/meridian
STV (Scotland), W www.stv.tv
Tyne Tees (north-east England), W www.itv.com/tynetees
Ulster (Northern Ireland), W www.itv.com/utv
Wales, W www.itv.com/wales
West, W www.itv.com/west

OTHER TELEVISION COMPANIES

Channel 4 Television, 124 Horseferry Road, London SW1P 2TX T 020-7396 4444 W www.channel4.com
Channel 5 Broadcasting Ltd, 10 Lower Thames Street, London EC3R 6EN T 020-8612 7700 W www.channel5.com
Independent Television Network (ITN), 200 Gray's Inn Road, London WC1X 8XZ T 020-7833 3000 W www.itn.co.uk
Provides news programming and services for ITV, Channel 4 and Channel 5, as well as content for international news providers.
Sianel Pedwar Cymru (S4/C), Canolfan S4/C, Yr Egin, Carmarthen SA31 3EQ T 0870-600 4141 W www.s4c.cymru
Freeview, DTV Services Ltd, 27 Mortimer Street, London W1T 3JF W www.freeview.co.uk

DIRECT BROADCASTING BY SATELLITE TELEVISION

Sky plc, Grant Way, Isleworth, Middlesex TW7 5QD T 033-3100 0333 W www.sky.com
Chief Executive, Stephen van Rooyen

RADIO

UK domestic radio services are broadcast across three wavebands: FM, medium wave and long wave (used by BBC Radio 4). In the UK the FM waveband extends in frequency from 87.5MHz to 108MHz and the medium waveband from 531kHz to 1602kHz. A number of radio stations are broadcast in both analogue and digital as well as a growing number in digital alone. As at June 2019, the BBC Radio network controlled around 51.4 per cent of the listening market (*see* BBC Radio section), and the independent sector (*see* Independent Radio section) 45.7 per cent. As at June 2019, a listener tunes into an average of 20.9 hours of radio per week.

ESTIMATED AUDIENCE SHARE

			Percentage
	Apr–Jun 2017	Apr–Jun 2018	Apr–Jun 2019
BBC Radio 1	6.2	5.9	5.7
BBC Radio 2	16.8	17.9	17.4
BBC Radio 3	1.2	1.2	1.2
BBC Radio 4	12.3	11.7	11.9
BBC Radio Five Live	3.4	3.1	3.4
Five Live Sports Extra	0.3	0.3	0.1
BBC 6 Music	1.9	2.4	2.4
BBC Asian Network UK	0.3	0.3	0.2
1Xtra	0.5	0.4	0.4
BBC Local/Regional	7.3	6.7	6.6
BBC World Service	0.9	0.7	0.7
All BBC	52.3	45.0	51.4
All independent	45.0	45.7	45.7
All national independent	16.7	18.1	19.9
All local independent	28.4	27.6	25.9
Other	2.8	2.5	2.8

Source: RAJAR

DIGITAL RADIO

The UK has the world's largest digital radio network, with 103 transmitters, two national Digital Audio Broadcasting (DAB) ensembles and a total of 48 local and regional DAB ensembles, which broadcast around 250 independent and 34 BBC radio stations. The BBC began test transmissions of the DAB Eureka 147 digital radio service in 1990 from the Crystal Palace transmitting station and the service was publicly launched in 1995. As well as DAB, digital televisions, car radios, games consoles, mobile devices and the internet are commonly employed as platforms to listen to radio in the UK. One of the major benefits of DAB is better sound quality than analogue radio, and the availability of a wider choice of stations, in addition to the lack of interference experienced by other broadcast media.

The UK government intends to migrate the majority of AM and FM analogue radio services to digital, based on certain conditions being met such as coverage, listening figures and agreements in relation to funding. In the second quarter of 2018, 50.2 per cent of all radio listening hours in the UK were through digital platforms. From this 50.2 per cent, DAB made up the majority of listenership with 72 per cent. In 2018, over 63 per cent of all UK households were believed to have access to DAB radio.

The BBC's national DAB ensemble has coverage across the UK of around 97 per cent and broadcasts on the frequency 225.648 MHz. Owned and operated by the BBC, the multiplex of broadcasts is transmitted across the UK from a number of sites. Local and regional ensembles, which cover 71.7 per cent of the UK, are transmitted through a number of DAB multiplex operators across the UK, including Digital One and Sound Digital – the two national operators – in addition to local multiplex operators.

There are two criteria that must be met for digital migration to occur:

- at least 50 per cent of radio listening is digital
- national DAB coverage is comparable to FM coverage, and local DAB reaches 90 per cent of the population and all major roads

LICENSING

The Broadcasting Act 1996 provided for the licensing of digital radio services (on multiplexes, where a number of stations share one frequency to transmit their services). To allocate the multiplexes, OFCOM advertises licences for which interested parties can bid. Once the licence has been awarded, the new owner seeks out services to broadcast on the multiplex. The BBC has a separate national multiplex for its services. There are local multiplexes around the country, each broadcasting an average of seven services, plus the local BBC station.

INNOVATIONS

The internet offers a number of advantages compared to other digital platforms such as DAB, including higher sound quality, a greater range of channel availability and flexibility in listening opportunity. Listeners can tune in to the majority of radio stations live on the internet or listen again online generally up to seven days after broadcast. DAB radio does not allow the same interactivity: the data is only able to travel one-way from broadcaster to listener whereas the internet allows a two-way flow of information.

Increases in Wi-Fi hotspots also means listening to radio, podcasts and catch-up programmes is easy to do through tablets and mobile phones; in 2018, over 50 per cent of all reported radio listening was via a digital service. The increase in music streaming services and radio-related apps has had a major effect on music discovery and sharing. In the UK in 2018 the number of streams per week averaged around 550 million. Since 6 July 2014 the UK Official Charts Company has included streaming services in its compilation, with 100 streams the equivalent to one purchase.

Since 2005 most radio stations offer all or part of their programmes as downloadable files, known as podcasts, to listen to on computers, mobiles or tablets. Podcasting technology allows listeners to subscribe in order to automatically receive the latest episodes of regularly transmitted programmes as soon as they become available.

The relationship between radio stations and their audiences is also undergoing change. The quantity and availability of music on the internet has led to the creation of shows dedicated entirely to music sent in by listeners. Another new development in internet-based radio has been personalised radio stations, such as SoundCloud and Spotify. SoundCloud allows users to upload, record, promote and share their music and sounds. Artists who upload their music are given a URL, allowing their music to be embedded anywhere, making it easier to share through social media platforms such as Twitter and Facebook. Users can also create their own playlists and link them to social media platforms. Spotify, available as an app on most smart phones and tablets as well as online, allows listeners access to the track, artist or genre of their choice, or to share and create playlists. It has seen steady growth in popularity since its launch in 2008, with 83 million paying subscribers and 180 million active users globally, as at June 2018. Spotify 'learns as you listen' and makes associated recommendations based on user choices. Radioplayer (W www.radioplayer.co.uk), a not-for-profit company backed by the BBC and commercial radio, allows audiences to listen to live and catch-up radio from one place. Over 6 million people per month use the Radioplayer service. There are over 400 stations available and a 'recommended' service which offers station suggestions depending on location, what is trending and the type of music the user likes. Radioplayer launched as a mobile app in 2012 and a tablet app in 2013. Through the tablet app, users sample an average of 4.6 stations a week in comparison with just 2.1 for analogue users. In November 2018, the BBC launched BBC Sounds (W www.bbc.co.uk/sounds), a digital platform for all BBC radio and podcast output with the intention of streamlining their audio content on to a single platform, personalised to the individual listener's preferences.

BBC RADIO

BBC Radio broadcasts network services to the UK, Isle of Man and the Channel Islands, with around 34.7 million listeners each week. There is also a tier of national services in Wales, Scotland and Northern Ireland and around 40 local radio stations in England and the Channel Islands. In Wales and Scotland there are also dedicated language services in Welsh and Gaelic respectively. The frequency allocated for digital BBC broadcasts is 225.648MHz.

BBC Radio, Broadcasting House, Portland Place, London W1A 1AA
W www.bbc.co.uk/radio

BBC NETWORK RADIO STATIONS

Radio 1 (contemporary pop music and entertainment news) – 24 hours a day, *Frequencies:* 97–99 FM and digital
Radio 1Xtra (contemporary urban and hip-hop music, culture and entertainment) – 24 hours a day, digital only
Radio 2 (popular music, entertainment, comedy and the arts) – 24 hours a day, *Frequencies:* 88–91 FM and digital
Radio 3 (classical music, classic drama, documentaries and features) – 24 hours a day, *Frequencies:* 90–93 FM and digital
Radio 4 (news, documentaries, drama, entertainment and cricket on long wave in season) – 5.20am–1am daily, with BBC World Service overnight, *Frequencies:* 92–95 FM/ 103–105 FM and 198 LW and digital

Radio Five Live (news and sport) – 24 hours a day, *Frequencies:* 909/693 MW and digital*Five Live Sports Extra* (live sport) – schedule varies, digital only

6 Music (contemporary and classic pop and rock music) – 24 hours a day, digital only

Asian Network (news, music and sport) – 5am–1am, with Radio 1Xtra overnight, *Frequencies:* various MW frequencies in Midlands and digital

BBC NATIONAL RADIO STATIONS

Radio Cymru (Welsh-language), *Frequencies:* 92–105 FM and digital

Radio Foyle, Frequencies: 93.1 FM and 792 MW and digital

Radio nan Gaidheal (Gaelic service), *Frequencies:* 103–105 FM and digital

Radio Scotland, Frequencies: 92–95 FM and 810 MW and digital. Local programmes for Orkney, Shetland and Highlands and Islands

Radio Ulster, Frequencies: 1341 MW and 92–95 FM and digital. Local programmes on Radio Foyle

Radio Wales, Frequencies: 657/882 MW and 93–104 FM and digital

BBC WORLD SERVICE

The BBC World Service broadcasts to an estimated weekly audience of 1.5 million people in the UK and 280 million worldwide, in 40 languages including English, and is now available in around 150 capital cities. It no longer broadcasts in Dutch, French for Europe, German, Hebrew, Italian, Japanese or Malay because it was found that most speakers of these languages preferred to listen to the English broadcasts. In 2006 services in ten languages (Bulgarian, Croatian, Czech, Greek, Hungarian, Kazakh, Polish, Slovak, Slovene and Thai) were terminated to provide funding for a new Arabic television channel, which was launched in March 2008. In August 2008 the BBC's Romanian World Service broadcasts were discontinued after 68 years. In January 2011 the BBC announced five more language services would be terminated: Albanian, Caribbean English, Macedonian, Portuguese for Africa and Serbian. The BBC World Service website offers interactive news services in 28 languages including English, Arabic, Chinese, Hindi, Persian, Portuguese for Brazil, Russian, Spanish and Urdu with audiostreaming available.

LANGUAGES

Afaan Oromoo, Amharic, Arabic, Azeri, Bengali, Burmese, Cantonese, English, French, Gujarati, Hausa, Hindi, Igbo, Indonesian, Kinyarwanda, Kirundi, Korean, Kyrgyz, Marathi, Nepali, Nigerian, Nigerian Pidgin, Pashto, Persian, Portuguese, Punjabi, Russian, Sinhala, Somali, Spanish, Swahili, Tamil, Telugu, Tigrinya, Turkish, Ukrainian, Urdu, Uzbek, Yoruba and Vietnamese.

UK frequencies: digital; overnight on BBC Radio 4.

BBC Learning English teaches English worldwide through radio, television and a wide range of published and online courses.

BBC Media Action is a registered charity established in 1999 by BBC World Service, known as the BBC World Service Trust until December 2011. It promotes development through the innovative use of the media in the developing world.

BBC Monitoring tracks the global media for the latest news reports emerging around the world.

BBC WORLD SERVICE, Broadcasting House, Portland Place, London W1A 1AA **W** www.bbc.co.uk/worldservice

INDEPENDENT RADIO

Until 1973, the BBC had a legal monopoly on radio broadcasting in the UK. During this time, the corporation's only competition came from pirate stations located abroad, such as Radio Luxembourg. Christopher Chataway, Minister for Post and Telecommunications, changed this by creating the first licences for commercial radio stations. The Independent Broadcasting Authority (IBA) awarded the first of these licences to the London Broadcasting Company (LBC) to provide London's news and information service. LBC was followed by Capital Radio, to offer the city's entertainment service, Radio Clyde in Glasgow and BRMB in Birmingham.

COMMERCIAL RADIO REVENUE
£ millions

2011	2012	2013	2014	2015	2016	2017	2018
532.5	552.7	536.8	575.4	612.8	645.8	679.1	713.6

Source: RadioCentre Ltd

The IBA was dissolved when the Broadcasting Act of 1990 de-regulated broadcasting, to be succeeded by the less rigid Radio Authority (RA). The RA began advertising new licences for the development of independent radio in January 1991. It awarded national and local radio, satellite and cable services licences, and long-term restricted service licences for stations serving non-commercial establishments such as hospitals and universities. The first national commercial digital multiplex licence was awarded in October 1998 and a number of local digital multiplex licences followed. At the end of 2003 the RA was replaced by OFCOM, which now carries out the licensing administration.

RadioCentre was formed in July 2006 as a result of the merger between the Radio Advertising Bureau (RAB) and the Commercial Radio Companies Association (CRCA), the former non-profit trade body for commercial radio companies in the UK, to operate essentially as a union for commercial radio stations.

RadioCentre, 6th Floor, 55 New Oxford Street, London WC1A 1BS
  T 020-7010 0600 **W** www.radiocentre.org
  Chief Executive, Siobhan Kenny

THE PRESS

The newspaper and periodical press in the UK is large and diverse, catering for a wide variety of views and interests. There is no state control or censorship of the press; however, it is subject to the laws on publication.

The press is not state-subsidised and receives few tax concessions. The income of most newspapers and periodicals is derived largely from sales and from advertising. The Advertising Association reported in July 2018 that national newspaper brands experienced their first increase in advertising spend in seven years in 2017. The UK advertising market in general grew to an estimated £23.5bn in 2018, an increase of 6 per cent.

LEVESON REPORT

The Leveson Inquiry, established under the Inquiries Act 2005, was announced by the prime minister on 13 July 2011 to investigate the role of press and police in the *News of the World* phone-hacking scandal. Lord Justice Leveson was appointed as chair of the inquiry. The hearings began on 14 November 2011 and ended on 24 July 2012 following the testimonies of 650 witnesses.

The Leveson Report was published in late November 2012 and featured several broad and complex recommendations as to how the press should be regulated. The report generally recommended that the press should continue to be self-regulated, with the government allowed no direct power over what is published, and that a new press standards body, with a new code of conduct, should be established by legislation in order to ensure regulation is independent and effective. Lord Justice Leveson concluded that this arrangement should give the public confidence that their complaints would be dealt with seriously and ensure the press would be protected from interference.

SELF-REGULATION

Following the publication of the Leveson Report the Press Complaints Commission (PCC), which had been established in January 1991 as a non-statutory body to operate the press's self-regulation, was closed and replaced by the Independent Press Standards Organisation (IPSO) on 8 September 2014. While the majority of newspapers have signed up to the new regulator, several have not, including *The Guardian*, the *Financial Times* and the *London Evening Standard*.

In 2013 a royal charter on press regulation was granted by the Privy Council to create a watchdog to oversee a new regulator. On 3 November 2014, a fully independent body, the Press Recognition Panel (PRP) was established to consider whether press regulators meet the criteria recommended in the Leveson Report and, if so, to afford these regulators official recognition.

IPSO has not sought recognition from the PRP, but another regulator, IMPRESS, was awarded recognition by the PRP in October 2016.

INDEPENDENT PRESS STANDARDS ORGANISATION,
Gate House, 1 Farringdon Street, London EC4M 7LH
T 0300-123 2220 E inquiries@ipso.co.uk W www.ipso.co.uk
Chair, Rt. Hon. Sir Alan Moses

PRESS RECOGNITION PANEL, Mappin House, 4 Winsley Street, London W1W 8HF
E contact@pressrecognitionpanel.org.uk
W www.pressrecognitionpanel.org.uk
Chair, Dr David Wolfe, QC

NEWSPAPERS

Newspapers are mostly financially independent of any political party, though most adopt a political stance in their editorial comments, usually reflecting proprietorial influence. Ownership of the national and regional daily newspapers is concentrated in the hands of large corporations whose interests cover publishing and communications, although *The Guardian* and *The Observer* are owned by the Scott Trust, formed in 1936 to protect the financial and editorial independence of *The Guardian* in perpetuity. The rules on cross-media ownership, as amended by the Broadcasting Act 1996, which limited the extent to which newspaper organisations may become involved in broadcasting, have been relaxed by the Communications Act 2003: newspapers with over a 20 per cent share of national circulation may own national and/or local radio licences.

In October 2010, *The Independent* launched a concise newspaper, *i*, the first new daily newspaper since 1986 but

the final editions of *The Independent* and *The Independent on Sunday* were published in March 2016 as the paper moved to digital only. In July 2011, *News of the World* was closed by its parent company, News International, following accusations of phone-hacking. In February 2012 News International printed the first edition of *The Sun on Sunday*, a Sunday format of the daily tabloid paper *The Sun*. In November 2014, The Herald and Times Group launched the Scottish daily *The National*, the first newspaper to actively support Scottish independence. In September 2018, *The Sunday National* was launched to replace *The Sunday Herald* which ceased publication on 2 September 2018. In February 2016, Trinity Mirror launched a compact daily newspaper, *The New Day* – the first new standalone paper since *The Independent* in 1986 – but it ceased publication in May 2016 after a sharp drop in circulation. There are 11 daily and Sunday national papers and several hundred local papers that are published daily, weekly or twice-weekly. Scotland, Wales and Northern Ireland all have at least one daily and one Sunday national paper.

National Daily Newspapers	June 2018	June 2019	% +/-
The Sun	1,451,584	1,277,947	-12.72
Daily Mail	1,264,810	1,175,653	-7.31
Daily Mirror	562,523	488,829	-14.02
Daily Star	364,448	310,246	-16.07
The Daily Telegraph	370,613	327,345	-12.40
The Times	428,034	399,672	-6.85
Daily Express	338,527	307,662	-9.57
i	248,234	288,801	-8.14
Financial Times	183,319	175,512	-4.35
The Guardian	138,082	132,821	-3.88
Daily Record	145,724	111,543	-26.57
National Sunday Newspapers			
The Sun on Sunday	1,224,119	1,066,147	-13.80
The Mail on Sunday	1,056,916	986,385	-6.90
The Sunday Times	721,808	686,819	-4.97
Sunday Mirror	475,976	403,350	-16.52
The Sunday Telegraph	288,484	258,394	-11.0
Sunday Express	295,294	268,096	-10.12
Daily Star Sunday	220,684	184,914	-17.63
Sunday People	183,784	151,523	-19.24
The Observer	166,317	159,568	-4.14
Sunday Mail	131,716	113,712	-14.67
Sunday Post	115,973	96,422	-18.41

Source: Audit Bureau of Circulations Ltd

Newspapers are usually published in either broadsheet or smaller, tabloid format. The 'quality' daily papers – ie those providing detailed coverage of a wide range of public matters – have traditionally been broadsheets, the more populist newspapers tabloid. In 2004 this correlation between format and content was redefined when two traditionally broadsheet newspapers, *The Times* and *The Independent*, switched to tabloid-sized editions, while *The Guardian* launched a 'Berliner' format in September 2005. In October 2005 *The Independent on Sunday* became the first Sunday broadsheet to be published in the tabloid (or 'compact') size. *The Observer*, like its daily counterpart *The Guardian*, began publishing in the Berliner format in January 2006 and began publishing in tabloid format in January 2018.

NEWSPAPERS ONLINE
The demand to read news instantly and while on the move has increased the popularity of newspaper websites. Most newspapers now operate their own websites in line with their print editions, often including the same material as seen in daily printed editions but can also include video and audio features. Many articles and columns additionally have the option of reader contributions and debate. Certain newspapers charge a subscription fee to access their websites but the majority are free to browse.

NATIONAL PRESS WEBSITE DAILY AVERAGE BROWSERS

National Press Website	June 2017	June 2018	% +/−
MailOnline	15,406,452	12,622,077	−18.07
metro.co.uk	2,676,403	1,689,148	−36.89
Reach PLC*	10,121,154	8,976,593	−11.31
thesun.co.uk	5,281,981	5,410,691	2.44

* Formerly known as Trinity Mirror Group PLC
Source: Audit Bureau of Circulations Ltd

NATIONAL DAILY NEWSPAPERS

DAILY EXPRESS
Northern & Shell Building, 10 Lower Thames Street, London EC3R 6EN T 020-8612 7000 W www.express.co.uk
Editor, Gary Jones

DAILY MAIL
Northcliffe House, 2 Derry Street, London W8 5TT T 020-7938 6000 W www.dailymail.co.uk
Editor, Geordie Greig

DAILY MIRROR
1 Canada Square, Canary Wharf, London E14 5AP
T 020-7293 3000 W www.mirror.co.uk
Editor, Allison Phillips

DAILY RECORD
1 Central Quay, Glasgow G3 8DA T 0141-309 3000
W www.dailyrecord.co.uk
Editor, David Dick

DAILY STAR
Northern & Shell Building, 10 Lower Thames Street, London EC3R 6EN T 020-8612 7000 W www.dailystar.co.uk
Editor, Jon Clark

THE DAILY TELEGRAPH
111 Buckingham Palace Road, London SW1W 0DT
T 020-7931 2000 W www.telegraph.co.uk
Editor, Chris Evans

FINANCIAL TIMES
Bracken House, 1 Friday Street, London EC4M 9BT
T 020-7873 3000 W www.ft.com
Editor, Lionel Barber

THE GUARDIAN
Kings Place, 90 York Way, London N1 9GU T 020-3353 2000
W www.theguardian.com
Editor-in-Chief, Katharine Viner

THE HERALD
200 Renfield Street, Glasgow G2 3QB T 0141-302 7000
W www.heraldscotland.com
Editor, Graeme Smith

i
2 Derry Street, London W8 5HF T 020-7005 2000
W www.inews.co.uk
Editor, Oliver Duff

MORNING STAR
William Rust House, 52 Beachy Road, London E3 2NS
T 020 8510-0815 W www.morningstaronline.co.uk
Editor, Ben Chacko

THE NATIONAL
200 Renfield Street, Glasgow, G2 3QB T 0141-302 7000
W www.thenational.scot
Editor, Callum Baird

THE SCOTSMAN
Orchard Brae House, 30 Queensferry Road, Edinburgh EH4 2HS
T 0131-311 7311 W www.scotsman.com
Editorial Director, Frank O'Donnell

THE SUN
1 London Bridge Street, London SE1 9GF T 020-7782 4000
W www.thesun.co.uk
Editor, Tony Gallagher

THE TIMES
1 London Bridge Street, London SE1 9GF T 0800-018 5177
W www.thetimes.co.uk
Editor, John Witherow

WEEKLY NEWSPAPERS

DAILY STAR SUNDAY
Northern & Shell Building, 10 Lower Thames Street, London EC3R 6EN T 020-8612 7000 W www.dailystar.co.uk/sunday
Editor, Denis Mann

MAIL ON SUNDAY
Northcliffe House, 2 Derry Street, London W8 HFT T 020-7938 6000 W www.mailonsunday.co.uk
Editor, Ted Verity

THE OBSERVER
Kings Place, 90 York Way, London N1 9GU T 020-3353 2000
W www.theguardian.com/observer
Editor, Paul Webster

THE SUNDAY PEOPLE
1 Canada Square, Canary Wharf, London E14 5AP
T 020-7293 3000 W www.people.co.uk
Editor, Peter Willis

SCOTLAND ON SUNDAY
Orchard Brae House, 30 Queensferry Road, Edinburgh EH4 2HS
T 0131-311 7311 W www.scotlandonsunday.com
Editorial Director, Frank O'Donnell

THE SUN ON SUNDAY
1 London Bridge Street, London SE1 9GF T 020-7782 4000
W www.thesun.co.uk
Editor, Victoria Newton

SUNDAY EXPRESS
Northern & Shell Building, 10 Lower Thames Street, London EC4R 6EN T 020-8612 7000 W www.sundayexpress.co.uk
Editor, Gary Jones

SUNDAY MAIL
1 Central Quay, Glasgow G3 8DA T 0141-309 3000
W www.sundaymail.com
Editor, Brendan McGinty

SUNDAY MIRROR
1 Canada Square, Canary Wharf, London E14 5AP
T 020-7293 3000 W www.sundaymirror.co.uk
Editor, Lloyd Embley

SUNDAY NATIONAL
200 Renfield Street, Glasgow, G2 3QB T 0141 302-7000
W www.thenational.scot
Editor, Richard Walker

SUNDAY POST
Skypark, 8 Elliot Place, Glasgow G3 8EP T 01382-223131
W www.sundaypost.com
Editor, Richard Prest

SUNDAY TELEGRAPH
111 Buckingham Palace Road, London SW1W 0DT
T 020-7931 2000 W www.telegraph.co.uk
Editor, Allister Heath

THE SUNDAY TIMES
1 London Bridge Street, London SE1 9GF T 020-7782 5000
W www.thesundaytimes.co.uk
Editor, Martin Ivens

REGIONAL NEWSPAPERS
EAST ANGLIA
CAMBRIDGE NEWS
Cambridge Research Park, Waterbeach CB25 9PD T 01223-632200
W www.cambridge-news.co.uk
Editor, David Bartlett

EAST ANGLIAN DAILY TIMES
Portman House, 120 Princes Street, Ipswich IP1 1RS
T 01473-230023 W www.eadt.co.uk
Editor, Brad Jones

EASTERN DAILY PRESS
Prospect House, Rouen Road, Norwich NR1 1RE T 01603-628311
W www.edp24.co.uk
Editor, David Powles

IPSWICH STAR
Portman House, 120 Princes Street, Ipswich IP1 1RS
T 01473-230023 W www.ipswichstar.co.uk
Editor, Brad Jones

NORWICH EVENING NEWS
Prospect House, Rouen Road, Norwich NR1 1RE T 01603-628311
W www.eveningnews24.co.uk
Editor, David Powles

EAST MIDLANDS

DERBY TELEGRAPH
2 Siddals Road, Derby DE1 2PB T 01332-411888
W www.derbytelegraph.co.uk
Editor, Julie Bayley

THE LEICESTER MERCURY
16 New Walk, Leicester LE1 6TF T 0116-251 2512
W www.leicestermercury.co.uk
Editor, George Oliver

LINCOLNSHIRE ECHO
Witham Wharf, Brayford Wharf East, Lincoln LN5 7AY
T 01522-804300 W www.lincolnshirelive.co.uk
Editor, Adam Moss

NORTHAMPTON CHRONICLE & ECHO
400 Pavilion Drive, Northants NN4 7PA T 01604-467032
W www.northamptonchron.co.uk
Editor, David Summers

NOTTINGHAM POST
City Gate, Tollhouse Hill, Notts NG1 5FS T 0115-948 2000
W www.nottinghampost.com
Editor, Mike Sassi

LONDON

EVENING STANDARD
Northcliffe House, 2 Derry Street, London W8 5TT T 020-3367 7000
W www.standard.co.uk
Editor, George Osborne

METRO
Northcliffe House, 2 Derry Street, London W8 5TT T 020-3615 3480
W www.metro.co.uk
Editor, Ted Young

NORTH EAST

EVENING CHRONICLE
2nd Floor, Eldon Court, Percy Street, Newcastle upon Tyne NE1 7JB
T 0191-201 6446 W www.chroniclelive.co.uk
Editor-in-Chief, Neil Hodgkinson

HARTLEPOOL MAIL
North East Business & Innovation Centre, Westfield Enterprise Park
East, Sunderland SR5 2TA T 0191-516 6127
W www.hartlepoolmail.co.uk
Editor, Joy Yates

THE JOURNAL
2nd Floor, Eldon Court, Percy Street, Newcastle upon Tyne NE1 7JB
T 0191-201 6446 W www.thejournal.co.uk
Editor, Neil Hodgkinson

THE NORTHERN ECHO
PO Box 14, Priestgate, Darlington, Co. Durham DL1 1NF
T 01325-381313 W www.thenorthernecho.co.uk
Editor, Hannah Chapman

THE SHIELDS GAZETTE
North East Business & Innovation Centre, Westfield Enterprise Park
East, Sunderland SR5 2TA T 0191-516 6127
W www.shieldsgazette.com
Editor, Joy Yates

THE SUNDAY SUN
2nd Floor, Eldon Court, Percy Street, Newcastle upon Tyne NE1 7JB
T 0191-201 6446 W www.sundaysun.co.uk
Editor, Neil Hodgkinson

SUNDERLAND ECHO
North East Business & Innovation Centre, Westfield Enterprise Park
East, Sunderland SR5 2TA T 0191-501 5800
W www.sunderlandecho.com
Editor, Joy Yates

TEESIDE GAZETTE
1st Floor, Hudson Quay, The Halyard, Middlehaven, Middlesbrough
TS3 6RT T 01642-234262 W www.gazettelive.co.uk
Editor, Neil Hodgkinson

NORTH WEST

THE BLACKPOOL GAZETTE
Avroe House, Avroe Crescent, Blackpool FY4 2DP T 01253-400888
W www.blackpoolgazette.co.uk
Editor, Simon Drury

THE BOLTON NEWS
The Wellsprings, Civic Centre, Bolton BL1 1AR T 01204-522345
W www.theboltonnews.co.uk
Editor, Karl Holbrook

CARLISLE NEWS AND STAR
Newspaper House, Dalston Road, Carlisle CA2 5UA
T 01228-612600 W www.newsandstar.co.uk
Editor, Chris Story

LANCASHIRE EVENING POST
Stuart House, 89 Caxton Road, Fulwood, Preston PR2 9ZB
T 01772-254841 W www.lep.co.uk
Editor, Gillian Parkinson

LANCASHIRE TELEGRAPH
50–54 Church Street, Blackburn, Lancs. BB1 5AL T 01254 678678
W www.lancashiretelegraph.co.uk
Editor, Steven Thompson

LIVERPOOL ECHO
5 St Paul's Square, Liverpool L3 9SL T 0151-472 2507
W www.liverpoolecho.co.uk
Editor, Alastair Machray

MANCHESTER EVENING NEWS
Mitchell Henry House, Hollinwood Avenue, Chadderton OL9 8EF
T 0161-832 7200 W www.manchestereveningnews.co.uk
Editor, Darren Thwaites

NORTH-WEST EVENING MAIL
Abbey Road, Barrow-in-Furness, Cumbria LA14 5QS
T 01229-840100 W www.nwemail.co.uk
Editor, Vanessa Sims

SOUTH EAST

THE ARGUS
Dolphin House, 2–5 Manchester Street, Brighton BN2 1TF
T 01273-021400 W www.theargus.co.uk
Editor, vacant

ECHO
Newspaper House, Chester Hall Lane, Basildon, Essex SS14 3BL
T 01268-522792 W www.echo-news.co.uk
Editor, Chris Hatton

MEDWAY MESSENGER
Medway House, Ginsbury Close, Sir Thomas Longley Road,
Rochester, Kent ME2 4DU T 01634-227800
W www.kentonline.co.uk/medway
Editor, Matt Ramsden

THE NEWS, PORTSMOUTH
1000 Lakeside, North Harbour, Portsmouth PO6 3EN
T 023-9266 4488 W www.portsmouth.co.uk
Editor, Mark Waldron

OXFORD MAIL
Newsquest Oxfordshire & Wiltshire, Osney Mead, Oxford OX2 0EJ
T 01865-425262 W www.oxfordmail.co.uk
Managing Editor, Samantha Harmon

READING CHRONICLE
2–10 Bridge Street, Reading, Berks. RG1 2LU T 0118-955 3333
W www.readingchronicle.co.uk
Group Editor, Andrew Colley

THE SOUTHERN DAILY ECHO
Newspaper House, Test Lane, Redbridge, Southampton SO16 9JX
T 023-8042 4777 W www.dailyecho.co.uk
Editor, Gordon Sutter

SOUTH WEST

BRISTOL POST
Temple Way, Bristol BS2 0BY **T** 0117-934 3331
W www.bristolpost.co.uk
Editor, Mike Norton

BOURNEMOUTH ECHO
Richmond Hill, Bournemouth BH2 6HH **T** 01202-554601
W www.bournemouthecho.co.uk
Editor, Andy Martin

CORNISH TIMES
The Tindle Suite, Webbs House, Liskeard PL14 6AH
T 01579-342174 **W** www.cornish-times.co.uk
Editor, Andrew Townsend

DORSET ECHO
Fleet House, Hampshire Road, Weymouth, Dorset DT4 9XD
T 01305-830930 **W** www.dorsetecho.co.uk
Editor, Diarmuid MacDonagh

EXETER EXPRESS & ECHO
Queens House, Little Queen Street, Exeter EX4 3LJ **T** 01392-346763
W www.exeterexpressandecho.co.uk
Editor, Rich Booth

GLOUCESTER CITIZEN
Gloucester Quays, St Ann Way, Gloucester GL1 5SH
T 01452-689320 **W** www.gloucestershirelive.co.uk
Editor, Rachael Sugden

GLOUCESTERSHIRE ECHO
Gloucester Quays, St Ann Way, Gloucester GL1
5SHT 01452 689320 **W** www.gloucestershirelive.co.uk
Editor, Rachael Sugden

THE HERALD
3rd Floor, Millbay Road, Plymouth PL1 3LF **T** 01752-293000
W www.plymouthherald.co.uk
Editor, Edd Moore

SUNDAY INDEPENDENT
Indy House, Lighterage Hill, Truro TR1 2XR **T** 01579-556970
W www.indyonline.co.uk
Editor, John Collings

SWINDON ADVERTISER
Richmond House, Edison Park, Swindon SN3 3RB **T** 01793-528144
W www.swindonadvertiser.co.uk
Editor, Pete Gavan

TORQUAY HERALD EXPRESS
Queens House, Little Queen Street, Exeter EX4 3LJ **T** 01392-346763
W www.devonlive.com
Editor, Rich Booth

WESTERN DAILY PRESS
Temple Way, Bristol BS99 7HD **T** 0117-934 3000
W www.somersetlive.co.uk
Editor, vacant

THE WESTERN MORNING NEWS
3rd Floor, Millbay Road, Plymouth PL1 3LF **T** 01752-293000
W www.thisiswesternmorningnews.co.uk
Editor, Bill Martin

WEST MIDLANDS

BIRMINGHAM MAIL
Embassy House, 60 Church Street, Birmingham B3 2DJ
T 0121-234 5000 **W** www.birminghammail.co.uk
Editor, Anna Jeys

COVENTRY TELEGRAPH
Corporation Street, Coventry CV1 1FP **T** 024-7663 3633
W www.coventrytelegraph.net
Editor, Keith Perry

EXPRESS & STAR
51–53 Queen Street, Wolverhampton WV1 1ES **T** 01902-313131
W www.expressandstar.com
Editor, Martin Wright

THE SENTINEL
Sentinel House, Bethesda Street, Stoke-on-Trent ST1 3GN
T 01782-864100 **W** www.stokesentinel.co.uk
Editor, Martin Tideswell

SHROPSHIRE STAR
Waterloo Road, Ketley, Telford TF1 5HU **T** 01952-242424
W www.shropshirestar.com
Editor, Martin Wright

WORCESTER NEWS
Berrows House, Hylton Road, Worcester WR2 5JX **T** 01905-748200
W www.worcesternews.co.uk
Editor, Michael Purton

YORKSHIRE AND HUMBERSIDE

GRIMSBY TELEGRAPH
Heritage House, Fisherman's Wharf, Grimsby DN31 1SY
T 01472-808000 **W** www.grimsbytelegraph.co.uk
Editor, Jamie Macaskill

HALIFAX COURIER
The Fire Station, Dean Clough Mills, Halifax HX3 5AX
T 01422-260252 **W** www.halifaxcourier.co.uk
Editor, John Kenealy

THE HUDDERSFIELD DAILY EXAMINER
Pennine Business Park, Longbow Close, Bradley Road, Huddersfield
HD2 1GQ **T** 01484-430000 **W** www.examiner.co.uk
Editor, Wayne Ankers

HULL DAILY MAIL
Blundell's Corner, Beverley Road, Hull HU3 1XS **T** 01482-327111
W www.hulldailymail.co.uk
Editor, Neil Hodgkinson

THE PRESS
PO Box 29, 76–86 Walmgate, York YO1 9YN **T** 01904-567131
W www.yorkpress.co.uk
Editor, Nigel Burton

SCARBOROUGH NEWS
17–23 Aberdeen Walk, Scarborough, N. Yorks YO11 1BB
T 01723-60100 **W** www.thescarboroughnews.co.uk
Editor, Jean MacQuarrie

SHEFFIELD STAR
The Balance, 2 Pinfold Street, Sheffield S1 2GU **T** 0114-276 7676
W www.thestar.co.uk
Editor, Nancy Fielder

TELEGRAPH & ARGUS
Hall Ings, Bradford BD1 1JR **T** 01274-729511
W www.thetelegraphandargus.co.uk
Editor, Nigel Burton

YORKSHIRE EVENING POST
26 Whitehall Road, Leeds LS12 1BE **T** 0113-238 8917
W www.yorkshireeveningpost.co.uk
Editor, Hannah Thaxter

YORKSHIRE POST
26 Whitehall Road, Leeds LS12 1BE **T** 0113-238 8427
W www.yorkshirepost.co.uk
Editor, James Mitchinson

SCOTLAND

THE COURIER
2 Albert Square, Dundee DD1 1DD **T** 01382-575291
W www.thecourier.co.uk
Editor, Richard Neville

DUNDEE EVENING TELEGRAPH
2 Albert Square, Dundee DD1 1DD **T** 01382-575950
W www.eveningtelegraph.co.uk
Editor, Dave Lord

EDINBURGH EVENING NEWS
Orchard Brae House, 30 Queensferry Road, Edinburgh EH4 2HS
T 0131-311 7311 **W** www.edinburghnews.scotsman.com
Editor, Euan McGrory

EVENING EXPRESS
1 Marischal Square, Broad Street, Aberdeen AB10 1BL
T 01224-691212 **W** www.eveningexpress.co.uk
Editor, Craig Walker

GLASGOW EVENING TIMES
200 Renfield Street, Glasgow G2 3QB **T** 0141-302 6600
W www.eveningtimes.co.uk
Editor, Donald Martin

INVERNESS COURIER
New Century House, Stadium Road, Inverness IV1 1FF
T 01463-246575 W www.inverness-courier.co.uk
Editor, Andrew Dixon

PAISLEY DAILY EXPRESS
1 Central Quay, Glasgow G3 8DA T 0141-887 7911
W www.paisleydailyexpress.co.uk
Editor, Cheryl McEvoy

THE PRESS AND JOURNAL
1 Marischal Square, Broad Street, Aberdeen AB10 1BL
T 01224-690222 W www.pressandjournal.co.uk
Editor, Alan McCabe

WALES

THE LEADER
Mold Business Park, Mold, Flintshire CH7 1XY T 01352-707707
W www.leaderlive.co.uk
Group Editor, Susan Perry

SOUTH WALES ARGUS
Cardiff Road, Maesglas, Newport NP20 3QN T 01633-810000
W www.southwalesargus.co.uk
Editor, Nicole Garnon

SOUTH WALES ECHO
6 Park Street, Cardiff CF10 1XR T 029-2024 3602
W www.walesonline.co.uk
Editor, Tryst Williams

SOUTH WALES EVENING POST
Urban Village, High Street, Swansea SA1 1NW T 01792-545515
W www.southwales-eveningpost.co.uk
Editor, Jonathan Roberts

WESTERN MAIL
6 Park Street, Cardiff CF10 1XR T 029-2024 3635
W www.walesonline.co.uk
Editor, Catrin Pascoe

NORTHERN IRELAND

BELFAST TELEGRAPH
124–144 Royal Avenue, Belfast BT1 1DN T 028-9026 4000
W www.belfasttelegraph.co.uk
Editor, Gail Walker

IRISH NEWS
113–117 Donegall Street, Belfast BT1 2GE T 028-9032 2226
W www.irishnews.com
Editor, Noel Doran

NEWS LETTER
Arthur House, 41 Arthur Street, Belfast BT1 4GB T 028-3839 5577
W www.newsletter.co.uk
Editor, Alistair Bushe

SUNDAY LIFE
124–144 Royal Avenue, Belfast BT1 1EB T 028-9026 4000
W www.belfasttelegraph.co.uk/sunday-life
Editor, Martin Breen

CHANNEL ISLANDS

GUERNSEY PRESS
PO Box 57, Braye Road, Vale, Guernsey GY1 3BW T 01481-240240
W www.guernseypress.com
Editor, Shaun Green

JERSEY EVENING POST
Guiton House, Five Oaks, St Saviour, Jersey JE4 8XQ
T 01534-611611 W www.jerseyeveningpost.com
Editor, Andy Sibcy

PERIODICALS

ART

AESTHETICA
PO Box 371, York YO23 1WL T 01904-629137
W www.aestheticamagazine.com
Editor, Cherie Federico

APOLLO
22 Old Queen Street, London SW1H 9HP T 020-7961 0150
W www.apollo-magazine.com
Editor, Thomas Marks

ART MONTHLY
12 Carlton House Terrace, London SW1Y 5AH T 020-7240 0389
W www.artmonthly.co.uk
Editor, Patricia Bickers

ARTREVIEW
1 Honduras Street, London EC1Y 0TH T 020-7490 8138
W www.artreview.com
Editor, Mark Rappolt

TATE ETC.
Tate, Millbank, London SW1P 4RG T 020-7887 8724
W www.tate.org.uk/tate-ect
Editor, Simon Grant

BUSINESS AND FINANCE

THE ECONOMIST
20 Cabot Square, London E14 4QW T 020-7576 8000
W www.economist.com
Editor, Zanny Minton Beddoes

MANAGEMENT TODAY
Bridge House, 69 London Road, Twickenham TW1 3SP
T 020-8267 5000 W www.managementtoday.co.uk
Editor, Adam Gale

MARKETING WEEK
79 Wells Street, London W1T 3QN T 020-7292 3711
W www.marketingweek.co.uk
Editor, Russell Parsons

MONEYWEEK
31–32 Alfred Place, London WC1E 7DPT 0330-333 9688
W www.moneyweek.com
Editor-in-Chief, Merryn Somerset Webb

PUBLIC FINANCE
78 Chamber Street, London E1 8BL T 020-7880 6200
W www.publicfinance.co.uk
Managing Editor, John Watkins

CELEBRITY

CLOSER
Endeavour House, 189 Shaftesbury Avenue, London WC2H 8JG
T 020-7295 5000 W www.closeronline.co.uk
Editor, Lisa Burrow

HEAT
Endeavour House, 189 Shaftesbury Avenue, London WC2H 8JG
T 020-7437 9011 W www.heatworld.com
Editor, Suzy Cox

HELLO!
Wellington House, 69–71 Upper Ground, London SE1 9PQ
T 020-7667 8901 W www.hellomagazine.com
Editor, Rosie Nixon

OK!
10 Lower Thames Street, London EC3R 6EN T 020-8612 7000
W www.ok.co.uk
Editor, Kirsty Tyler

CHILDREN'S AND FAMILY

THE BEANO
185 Fleet Street, London EC4A 2HS W www.beano.com
Editor, John Anderson

MOTHER & BABY
Bauer Media Group, Media House, Lynchwood, Peterborough
Business Park, Peterborough PE2 6EA T 01733- 468000
W www.motherandbaby.co.uk
Editor, Sally Saunders

YOUR CAT
Warners Group Publications, The Maltings, West Street, Bourne,
Lincs PE10 9PHT 0177-839 5070 W www.yourcat.co.uk
Editor, Emily Wardle

YOUR DOG
Warners Group Publications, The Maltings, West Street, Bourne,
Lincs PE10 9PH T 0177-839 5070 W www.yourdog.co.uk
Editor, Sarah Wright

CLASSICAL MUSIC AND OPERA

BBC MUSIC
Immediate Media Company Bristol Ltd, Tower House, Colston Avenue, Bristol BS1 4ST T 0117-927 9009
W www.classical-music.com
Editor, Oliver Condy

CLASSICAL MUSIC
Rhinegold House, 20 Rugby Street, London WC1N 3QZ
T 020-7333 1729 W www.classicalmusicmagazine.org
Editor, Lucy Thraves

GRAMOPHONE
c/o Mark Allen Group, St Jude's Church, Dulwich Road, London SE24 0PB T 020-7738 5454 W www.gramophone.co.uk
Editor, Martin Cullingford

OPERA
36 Black Lion Lane, London W6 9BE T 020-8563 8893
W www.opera.co.uk
Editor, John Allison

COMPUTERS AND TECHNOLOGY

PC PRO
31–32 Alfred Place, London WC1E 7DP T 020-3890 3890
W www.alphr.com
Editorial Director, Victoria Woollaston

STUFF
Blackfriars Foundary, 154–156 Blackfriars Road, London SE1 8EN
T 020-8267 5036 W www.stuff.tv
Editor, James Day

T3
T3 magazine, 5 Pinesway Industrial Estate, Bath BA2 3QS
W www.t3.com
Editor, Matt Bolton

WEB USER
Dennis Publishing, 30 Cleveland Street, London W1T 4JD
T 020-7907 6000 W www.webuser.co.uk
Group Editor, Daniel Booth

WIRED
Condé Nast, Vogue House, Hanover Square, London W1S 1JU
T 0844-848 5202 W www.wired.co.uk
Editor-in-Chief, Nicholas Thompson

CRAFT

CARDMAKING & PAPERCRAFT
Immediate Media, Vineyard House, 44 Brook Green, London W6 7BT T 0117-933 8081 W www.cardmakingandpapercraft.com
Editor, Hayley Hawes

SIMPLY KNITTING
Immediate Media, Vineyard House, 44 Brook Green, London W6 7BT T 0117-3008 253 W www.immediate.co.uk/brands/simply-knitting
Commissioning Editor, Kirstie McLeod

THE WORLD OF CROSS STITCHING
Immediate Media, Vineyard House, 44 Brook Green, London W6 7BT T 0117-314 8351 W www.cross-stitching.com
Editor, Hannah Kelly

ENTERTAINMENT

EMPIRE
Endeavour House, 189 Shaftesbury Avenue, London WC2H 8JG
T 020-7437 9011 W www.empireonline.com
Editor-in-Chief, Terri White

RADIO TIMES
Vineyard House, 44 Brook Green, London W6 7BT
T 020-7150 5800 W www.radiotimes.com
Editorial Director, Mark Frith

SIGHT & SOUND
BFI, 21 Stephen Street, London W1T 1LN T 020-7255 1444
W www.bfi.org.uk/sightandsound
Editor, vacant

TIME OUT LONDON
77 Wicklow Street, London WC1X 9JY T 020-7813 3000
W www.timeout.com
Editor, Caroline McGinn

TOTAL FILM
Future Publishing Ltd, 1–10 Praed Mews, London W2 1QY
T 020-7042 4831 W www.gamesradar.com/totalfilm
Editor, Jane Crowther

FASHION AND BEAUTY

COSMOPOLITAN
House of Hearst, 30 Panton Street, London SW1Y 4AJ
T 020-7439 5000 W www.cosmopolitan.co.uk
Editor, Claire Hodgson

ELLE
House of Hearst, 30 Panton Street, London SW1Y 4AJ
T 020-7150 7000 W www.elleuk.com
Editor, Farrah Storr

GLAMOUR
Condé Nast, Vogue House, Hanover Square, London W1S 1JU
T 020-7499 9080 W www.glamourmagazine.co.uk
Editor-in-Chief, Deborah Joseph

GRAZIA
Endeavour House, 189 Shaftesbury Avenue, London WC2H 8JG
T 0845-601 1356 W www.graziadaily.co.uk
Editor, Hattie Brett

HARPER'S BAZAAR
House of Hearst, 30 Panton Street, London SW1Y 4AJ
T 0844-848 5203 W www.harpersbazaar.co.uk
Editor-in-Chief, Justine Picardie

MARIE CLAIRE
161 Marsh Wall, London E14 9AP T 020-3148 5000
W www.marieclaire.co.uk
Editor-in-Chief, Trish Halpin

VOGUE
Condé Nast, Vogue House, Hanover Square, London W1S 1JU
T 0844-848 5202 W www.vogue.co.uk
Editor, Edward Enninful

FOOD AND DRINK

FOOD AND TRAVEL
Suite 51, The Business Centre, Ingate Place, London SW8 3NS
T 020-7501 0511 W www.foodandtravel.com
Editor, Michelle Hather

GOOD FOOD
44 Vineyard House, Brook Green, London W6 7BT
T 020-7150 5022 W www.bbcgoodfood.com
Editor, Christine Hayes

OLIVE
Vineyard House, 44 Brook Green, London W6 7BT
T 020-7150 5024 W www.olivemagazine.com
Editor, Laura Rowe

WHISKY
6 Woolgate Court, St Benedicts Street, Norwich NR2 4AP
T 01603-633 808 W www.whiskymag.com
Editor, Rob Allanson

GENERAL INTEREST

BBC HISTORY
Tower House, Fairfax Street, Bristol BS1 3BN T 0117-927 9009
W www.historyextra.com
Editor, Rob Attar

BOOKSELLER
Floor 10, Westminster Tower, 3 Albert Embankment, London SE1 7SP T 020-3358 0365 W www.thebookseller.com
Editor, Philip Jones

HISTORY TODAY
2nd Floor, 9 Staple Inn, London WC1V 7QH T 020-3219 7810
W www.historytoday.com
Editor, Paul Lay

LITERARY REVIEW
44 Lexington Street, London W1F OLW T 020-7437 9392
W www.literaryreview.co.uk
Editor, Nancy Sladek

NEW STATESMAN
Standard House, 12–13 Essex Street, London WC2R
3AAT 020-7936 6400 W www.newstatesman.com
Editor, Jason Cowley

PRIVATE EYE
6 Carlisle Street, London W1D 3BN T 020-7437 4017
W www.private-eye.co.uk
Editor, Ian Hislop

PROSPECT
5th Floor, 23 Savile Row, London W1S 2ET T 020-7255 1281
W www.prospectmagazine.co.uk
Editor, Tom Clark

READER'S DIGEST
The Maltings, West Street, Bourne BH24 9PH T 0330-333 2220
W www.readersdigest.co.uk
Editor, Fiona Hicks

SAGA
Saga Publishing Ltd, Enbrook Park, Folkestone, Kent CT20 3SE
T 01303-771111 W www.saga.co.uk
Editor, Louise Robinson

THE SPECTATOR
22 Old Queen Street, London SW1H 9HP T 020-7961 0200
W www.spectator.co.uk
Editor, Fraser Nelson

TLS (THE TIMES LITERARY SUPPLEMENT)
1 London Bridge Street, London SE1 9GF T 020-7782 5000
W www.the-tls.co.uk
Editor, Stig Abell

THE WEEK
31–32 Alfred Place, London WC1E 7DP T 020-3890 3890
W www.theweek.co.uk
Editor-in-Chief, Jeremy O'Grady

WHO DO YOU THINK YOU ARE?
Tower House, Fairfax Street, Bristol BS1 3BN T 0117-314 7400
W www.whodoyouthinkyouaremagazine.com
Editor, Sarah Williams

HEALTH AND FITNESS

MEN'S FITNESS
31–32 Alfred Place, London WC1E 7DP T 020-3890 3890
W www.coachmag.co.uk
Editor, Isaac Williams

RUNNER'S WORLD
33 Broadwick Street, London W1F 9EP T 020-7339 4409
W www.runnersworld.co.uk
Editor, Andy Dixon

WW MAGAZINE
The River Group, 1 Neal Street, London WC2H 9QL
T 020-7306 0304 W www.weightwatchers.co.uk
Editor, vacant

WOMEN'S HEALTH
House of Hearst, 30 Panton Street, London SW1Y 4AJ
T 0844-322 1773 W www.womenshealthmag.com/uk
Editor, Claire Sanderson

HOBBIES AND GAMES

AIRFIX MODEL WORLD
Key Publishing Ltd, PO Box 100, Stamford PE9 1XQ
T 01780-755131 W www.airfixmodelworld.com
Editor, Stuart Fone

ANGLING TIMES
Bauer Media Group, Media House, Lynchwood, Peterborough PE2
6EA T 01733-395097 W www.anglingtimes.co.uk
Editor-in-Chief, Steve Fitzpatrick

BRITISH RAILWAY MODELLING
Warners Group Publications, The Maltings, West Street, Bourne,
Lincs PE10 9PH T 01778-391000 W www.world-of-railways.co.uk/
brm
Editor, Steve Cole

BRITISH CHESS MAGAZINE
Albany House, 14 Shute End, Wokingham RG40 1BJ
T 01252-514372 W www.britishchessmagazine.co.uk
Editors, Milan Dinic; Shaun Taulbut

COIN NEWS
Token Publishing Ltd, 40 Southernhay East, Exeter, Devon EX1 1PE
T 01404-46972 W www.tokenpublishing.com
Editor, John Russell

HORNBY
Key Publishing Ltd, PO Box 100, Stamford PE9 1XQ
T 01780-755131 W www.hornbymagazine.com
Editor, Mike Wild

HOME AND GARDEN

BBC GARDENERS' WORLD
Immediate Media, 5th Floor, Vineyard House, 44 Brook Green,
London W6 7BT T 020-7150 5700 W www.gardenersworld.com
Editor, Lucy Hall

GOOD HOUSEKEEPING
House of Hearst, 30 Panton Street, London SW1Y 4AJ
T 020-7439 5000 W www.goodhousekeeping.co.uk
Editor-in-chief, Gaby Huddart

HOUSE & GARDEN
Condé Nast Publications, Vogue House, Hanover Square, London
W1S 1JU T 020-7499 9080 W www.houseandgarden.co.uk
Editor, Hatta Byng

LIVING ETC
TI Media, 161 Marsh Wall, London E14 9SJ T 020-3148 5000
W www.housetohome.co.uk/livingetc
Editor, Sarah Spiteri

MEN'S LIFESTYLE

ESQUIRE
House of Hearst, 30 Panton Street, London SW1Y 4AJ
T 020-7439 5000 W www.esquire.co.uk
Editor, Alex Bilmes

GAY TIMES
Millivres Prowler Group, Spectrum House, 32-34 Gordon House
Road, London NW5 1LP T 020-7424 7400 W www.gaytimes.co.uk
Editor, Tag Warner

GQ
Vogue House, 1 Hanover Square, London W1S 1JU
T 020-7499 9080 W www.gq-magazine.co.uk
Editor, Dylan Jones

MOTORING

BIKE
Bauer Media, Media House, Lynchwood, Peterborough PE2 6EA
T 01733-468000 W www.bikemagazine.co.uk
Editor, Hugo Wilson

CARAVAN
Warners Group Publications, The Maltings, West Street, Bourne,
Lincs PE10 9PH T 01778-392450 W www.outandaboutlive.co.uk
Editor, Daniel Attwood

F1 RACING
Autosport Media, 1 Eton Street, Richmond TW9 1AG
T 020-3405 8100 W www.f1racing.co.uk
Editor, Ben Anderson

PRACTICAL CARAVAN
Haymarket Ltd, Bridge House, 69 London Road, Twickenham TW1
3SP T 020-8267 5712 W www.practicalcaravan.com
Editor, Sarah Wakely

TOP GEAR
Energy Centre, Media Centre, 201 Wood Lane, London W12 7TQ
T 020-7150 5558 W www.topgear.com
Editor, Charlie Turner

PHOTOGRAPHY

AMATEUR PHOTOGRAPHER
Pinehurst 2, Pinehurst Road, Farnborough, Hants. GU14 7BF
T 01252-555213 W www.amateurphotographer.co.uk
Group Editor, Nigel Atherton

DIGITAL CAMERA
Future Publishing Ltd Quay House, The Ambury, Bath BA1 1UA
W www.digitalcameraworld.com
Editor, James Artaius

DIGITAL PHOTOGRAPHER
Future Publishing Ltd, Quay House, The Ambury, Bath BA1 1UA
T 01202-586200 W www.dphotographer.co.uk
Editor-in-Chief, Amy Squibb

POPULAR MUSIC

CLASH
Studio 86, Hackney Downs Studios, 17 Amhurst Terrace, London E8
2BT T 020-7628 2312 W www.clashmusic.com
Editor-in-Chief, Simon Harper

CLASSIC ROCK
Future Publishing Ltd, Quay House, The Ambury, Bath BA1 1UA
W www.loudersound.com/classic-rock
Editor, Siân Llewellyn

DIY
2nd Floor, Unit 23, Tileyard Studios, Tileyard Road, London N7 9AH
W www.diymag.com
Editor, Sarah Jamieson

GUITARIST
Future Publishing Ltd, Beauford Court, 30 Monmouth Street, Bath
BA1 2BW T 01225-442244 W www.musicradar.com/guitarist
Editor, Jamie Dickson

MOJO
Endeavour House, 189 Shaftesbury Avenue, London WC2H 8JG
T 020-7208 3443 W www.mojo4music.com
Editor, John Mulvey

Q
Endeavour House, 189 Shaftesbury Avenue, London WC2H 8JG
T 020-7295 5000 W www.qthemusic.com
Editor-in-Chief, John Mulvey

UNCUT
TI Media, 161 Marsh Wall, London E14 9SJ T 020-3148 5000
W www.uncut.co.uk
Editor, Michael Bonnier

SCIENCE AND NATURE

BBC WILDLIFE
Immediate Media, Eagle House, Colston Avenue, Bristol BS1 4ST
T 0117-927 9009 W www.discoverwildlife.com
Editor, Paul McGuinness

BIRD WATCHING
Bauer Media, Media House, Lynch Wood, Peterborough PE2 6EA
T 01733-468000 W www.birdwatching.co.uk
Editor, Matthew Merritt

COUNTRYFILE
9th Floor, Tower House, Fairfax Street, Bristol BS1 3BN
T 0117-927 9009 W www.countryfile.com
Editor, Fergus Collins

BBC SCIENCE FOCUS
Immediate Media, Eagle House, Colston Avenue, Bristol BS1 4ST
T 0117-927 9009 W www.sciencefocus.com
Editor, Daniel Bennett

HOW IT WORKS
Future Publishing Limited Quay House, The Ambury, Bath BA1 1UA
W www.howitworksdaily.com
Editor-in-Chief, Dave Harfield

NEW SCIENTIST
110 High Holborn, London WC1V 6EU T 020-7611 1206
W www.newscientist.com
Editor-in-Chief, Emily Wilson

BBC SKY AT NIGHT
Immediate Media, Eagle House, Colston Avenue, Bristol BS1
4STT 0117-927 9009 W www.skyatnightmagazine.com
Editor, Chris Bramley

SPORT

BOXING MONTHLY
Kelsey Media, Cudham Tithe Barn, Berry's Hill, Cudham, Kent TN16
3AG T 020-8986 4141 W www.boxingmonthly.com
Editor, Graham Houston

THE CRICKETER
Court House, Cleaver Street, London SE11 4DZ T 020-3198 1359
W www.thecricketer.com
Editor, Simon Hughes

FOURFOURTWO
Future Publishing Ltd, Quay House, The Ambury, Bath BA1 1UA
T 0844-848 2852 W www.fourfourtwo.com
Editor, James Brown

GOLF MONTHLY
TI Media Ltd, Pinehurst 2, Pinehurst Road, Farnborough Business
Park, Farnborough, Hants GU14 7BF T 01252-555197
W www.golf-monthly.co.uk
Editor, Michael Harris

HORSE & HOUND
TI Media Ltd, 161 Marsh Wall, London E14 9SJ T 01252-555029
W www.horseandhound.co.uk
Editor, Pippa Roome

MATCH
Kelsey Media, Cudham Tithe Barn, Berrys Hill, Cudham, Kent, TN16
3AG T 01959-541444 W www.matchfootball.co.uk
Editor, Stephen Fishlock

RUGBY WORLD
TI Media Ltd, 2nd Floor, Pinehurst 2, Pinehurst Road, Farnborough
Business Park, Farnborough, Hants GU14 7BF T 01252-555271
W www.rugbyworld.com
Editor, Sarah Mockford

TENNISHEAD
Advantage Publishing (UK) Ltd,Trinity House, Sculpins Lane,
Braintree, Essex CM7 4AY T 020-8408 7148
W www.tennishead.net
Consultant Editor, Paul Newman

WISDEN CRICKET MONTHLY
PO Box 33, 4th Floor, Kia Oval, Kennington, London, England, SE11
5SS T 01293 312094 W www.wisden.com
Editor, Phil Walker

WORLD SOCCER
TI Media Ltd, 2nd Floor, Pinehurst 2, Pinehurst Road, Farnborough
Business Park, Farnborough, Hants GU14 7BF T 020-3148 4817
W www.worldsoccer.com
Editor, Gavin Hamilton

TRAVEL

CONDÉ NAST TRAVELLER
Vogue House, Hanover Square, London W1S 1JU T 0844-848 2851
W www.cntraveller.com
Editor, Melinda Stevens

FRANCE
Archant House, 3 Oriel Road, Cheltenham GL50 1BB
T 01242-216050 W www.completefrance.com
Editor, Karen Tait

LONELY PLANET
Immediate Media, Eagle House, Colston Avenue, Bristol BS1 4ST
T 0207-150 5000 W www.lonelyplanet.com
Editor, Peter Grunert

NATIONAL GEOGRAPHIC TRAVELLER
Unit 310 Highgate Studios, 53–79 Highgate Road, London NW5 1TL
T 020-7253 9906 W www.natgeotraveller.co.uk
Editor, Pat Riddell

TRADE AND PROFESSIONAL BODIES

The following is a list of employers' and trade associations and other professional bodies in the UK. It does not represent a comprehensive list. For further professional bodies *see* Professional Education.

ASSOCIATIONS

ABTA – THE TRAVEL ASSOCIATION 30 Park Street, London SE1 9EQ T 020-311 70599 W www.abta.com
Chief Executive, Mark Tanzer

ADVERTISING ASSOCIATION 7th Floor North, Artillery House, London SW1P 1RT T 020-7340 1100
E aa@adassoc.org.uk W www.adassoc.org.uk
Chief Executive, Stephen Woodford

AEROSPACE DEFENCE SECURITY Salamanca Square, 9 Albert Embankment, London SE1 7SP T 020-7091 4500
W www.adsgroup.org.uk
Chief Executive, Paul Everitt

AGRICULTURAL ENGINEERS ASSOCIATION Samuelson House, 62 Forder Way, Peterborough PE7 8JB T 0845-644 8748
E ab@aea.uk.com W www.aea.uk.com
Chief Executive, Ruth Bailey

ASBESTOS REMOVAL CONTRACTORS ASSOCIATION Unit 1, Stretton Business Park 2, Brunel Drive, Stretton DE13 0BY
T 01283-566467 E info@arca.org.uk W www.arca.org.uk
Chief Executive, Steve Sadley

ASSOCIATION FOR CONSULTANCY AND ENGINEERING Alliance House, 12 Caxton Street, London SW1H 0QL T 020-7222 6557 E consult@acenet.co.uk
W www.acenet.co.uk
Chief Executive, Hannah Vickers

ASSOCIATION OF ACCOUNTING TECHNICIANS 140 Aldersgate Street, London EC1A 4HY T 020-3735 2468
E aat@aat.org.uk W www.aat.org.uk
Chief Executive, Mark Farrar

ASSOCIATION OF ANAESTHETISTS OF GREAT BRITAIN AND IRELAND 21 Portland Place, London W1B 1PY T 020-7631 1650 E info@aagbi.org W www.aagbi.org
Executive Director, Karin Pappenheim

ASSOCIATION OF BRITISH INSURERS One America Square, London EC3N 2LB T 020-7600 3333 E info@abi.org.uk
W www.abi.org.uk
Director-General, Huw Evans

ASSOCIATION OF BUSINESS RECOVERY PROFESSIONALS 8th Floor, 120 Aldersgate Street, London EC1A 4JQ T 020-7566 4200 E association@r3.org.uk
W www.r3.org.uk
Chief Executive, Emma Lovell

ASSOCIATION OF CONVENIENCE STORES LTD Federation House, 17 Farnborough Street, Farnborough GU14 8AG T 01252-515001 E acs@acs.org.uk
W www.acs.org.uk
Chief Executive, James Lowman

ASSOCIATION OF CORPORATE TREASURERS 69 Leadenhall Street, London EC3A 2BG T 020-7847 2540
W www.treasurers.org
Chief Executive, Caroline Stockmann

ASSOCIATION OF DRAINAGE AUTHORITIES Rural Innovation Centre, Avenue H, Stoneleigh Park CV8 2LG
T 024-7699 2889 E admin@ada.org.uk W www.ada.org.uk
Chief Executive, Innes Thomson, CENG

BOOKSELLERS ASSOCIATION 6 Bell Yard, London WC2A 2JR T 020-7421 4640 E mail@booksellers.org.uk
W www.booksellers.org.uk
Chief Executive, Meryl Halls

BRITISH ANTIQUE DEALERS' ASSOCIATION 14 Dufferin Street, London EC1Y 8PD T 020-7589 4128 E info@bada.org
W www.bada.org
President, Ian Walker (interim)

BRITISH ASSOCIATION OF SOCIAL WORKERS 37 Waterloo Street, Birmingham B2 5PP T 0121-622 3911
W www.basw.co.uk
Chief Executive, Colum Conway

BRITISH BEER & PUB ASSOCIATION Ground Floor, Brewers' Hall, Aldermanbury Square, London EC2V 7HR
T 020-7627 9191 E contact@beerandpub.com
W www.beerandpub.com
Chief Executive, Brigid Simmonds, OBE

BRITISH CHAMBERS OF COMMERCE 65 Petty France, London SW1H 9EU T 020-7654 5800
W www.britishchambers.org.uk
Director-General, Adam Marshall

BRITISH ELECTROTECHNICAL AND ALLIED MANUFACTURERS ASSOCIATION (BEAMA) Rotherwick House, 3 Thomas More Street, London E1W 1YZ
T 020-7793 3000 E info@beama.org.uk W www.beama.org.uk
Chief Executive, Dr Howard Porter

BRITISH HOROLOGICAL INSTITUTE Upton Hall, Upton, Newark NG23 5TE T 01636-813795 E info@bhi.co.uk
W www.bhi.co.uk
Chair, Stella Haward

BRITISH INSTITUTE OF PROFESSIONAL PHOTOGRAPHY The Artistry House, 16 Winckley Square, Preston PR1 3JJ T 01772-367968 E info@bipp.com
W www.bipp.com
Chief Executive, Emily Hancock (interim)

BRITISH INSURANCE BROKERS' ASSOCIATION 8th Floor, John Stow House, 18 Bevis Marks, London EC3A 7JB
T 0344-770 0266 E enquiries@biba.org.uk W www.biba.org.uk
Chief Executive, Steve White

BRITISH MARINE FEDERATION Marine House, Thorpe Lea Road, Egham TW20 8BF T 01784-473377
E info@britishmarine.co.uk W www.britishmarine.co.uk
Chief Executive, Lesley Robinson

BRITISH MEDICAL ASSOCIATION BMA House, Tavistock Square, London WC1H 9JP T 020-7387 4499
W www.bma.org.uk
Chief Executive, Keith Ward

BRITISH OFFICE SUPPLIES AND SERVICES (BOSS) FEDERATION c/o British Printing Industries Federation, 2 Villiers Court, Copse Drive CV5 9RN T 01676-526030
W www.bossfederation.com
Chief Executive, Philip Lawson

BPI (BRITISH PHONOGRAPHIC INDUSTRY) Riverside Building, County Hall, Westminster Bridge Road, London SE1 7JA
T 020-7803 1300 E general@bpi.co.uk W www.bpi.co.uk
Chief Executive, Geoff Taylor

BRITISH PLASTICS FEDERATION 6 Bath Place, London EC2A 3JE T 020-7457 5000 E reception@bpf.co.uk
W www.bpf.co.uk
Director-General, Philip Law

BRITISH PORTS ASSOCIATION 1st Floor, 30 Park Street, London SE1 9EQ T 020-7260 1780 E info@britishports.org.uk W www.britishports.org.uk
Chief Executive, Richard Ballantyne

BRITISH PRINTING INDUSTRIES FEDERATION Unit 2, Villiers Court, Meriden Business Park CV5 9RN T 01676-526030 W www.britishprint.com
Chief Executive, Charles Jarrold

BRITISH PROPERTY FEDERATION 5th Floor, St Albans House, 57–59 Haymarket, London SW1Y 4QX T 020-7802 0110 E info@bpf.org.uk W www.bpf.org.uk
Chief Executive, Melanie Leech

BRITISH RETAIL CONSORTIUM 2 London Bridge, London SE1 9RA T 020-7854 8900 E info@brc.org.uk W www.brc.org.uk
Director-General, Helen Dickinson, OBE

BRITISH TYRE MANUFACTURERS' ASSOCIATION 5 Berewyk Hall Court, White Colne, Colchester CO6 2QB T 01787-226995 W www.btmauk.com
Chief Executive, Graham Willson

BUILDING SOCIETIES ASSOCIATION 6th Floor, York House, London WC2B 6UJ T 020-7520 5900 W www.bsa.org.uk
Chief Executive, Robin Fieth

CHARTERED ASSOCIATION OF BUILDING ENGINEERS Lutyens House, Billing Brook Road, Northampton NN3 8NW T 01604-404121 W www.cbuilde.com
Chief Executive, Dr Gavin Dunn

CHARTERED INSTITUTE FOR ARCHAEOLOGISTS Power Steele Building, Wessex Hall, Whiteknights Road, Reading RG6 6DE T 0118-966 2841 E admin@archaeologists.net W www.archaeologists.net
Chief Executive, Peter Hinton

CHARTERED INSTITUTE OF ENVIRONMENTAL HEALTH Chadwick Court, 15 Hatfields, London SE1 8DJ T 020-7928 6006 E info@cieh.org W www.cieh.org
Chief Executive, Anne Godfrey

CHARTERED INSTITUTE OF JOURNALISTS 2 Dock Offices, Surrey Quays Road, London SE16 2XU T 020-7252 1187 E memberservices@cioj.co.uk W www.cioj.co.uk
General Secretary, Dominic Cooper

CHARTERED INSTITUTE OF PURCHASING AND SUPPLY Easton House, Church Street, Stamford PE9 3NZ T 01780-756777 W www.cips.org
Chief Executive, Malcolm Harrison

CHARTERED INSTITUTE OF TAXATION 30 Monck Street, London SW1P 2AP T 020-7340 0550 E comms@tax.org.uk W www.tax.org.uk
Chief Executive, Peter Fanning

CHARTERED INSURANCE INSTITUTE 42–48 High Road, London E18 2JP T 020-8989 8464 E customer.serv@cii.co.uk W www.cii.co.uk
Chief Executive, Sian Fisher

CHARTERED MANAGEMENT INSTITUTE Management House, Cottingham Road, Corby NN17 1TT T 01536-207360 E cmi@managers.org.uk W www.managers.org.uk
Chief Executive, Anne Francke

CHARTERED QUALITY INSTITUTE 2nd Floor North, Chancery Exchange, London EC4A 1AB T 020-7245 6722 E membership@quality.org W www.quality.org
Chief Executive, Vincent Desmond

CHARTERED TRADING STANDARDS INSTITUTE 1 Sylvan Court, Sylvan Way, Basildon SS15 6TH T 01268-582200 E institute@tsi.org.uk W www.tradingstandards.uk
Chief Executive, Leon Livermore

CHEMICAL INDUSTRIES ASSOCIATION Kings Buildings, Smith Square, London SW1P 3JJ T 020-7834 3399 E enquiries@cia.org.uk W www.cia.org.uk
Chief Executive, Steve Elliott

CONFEDERATION OF PAPER INDUSTRIES 1 Rivenhall Road, Swindon SN5 7BD T 01793-889600 E cpi@paper.org.uk W www.paper.org.uk
Director-General, Andrew Large

CONFEDERATION OF PASSENGER TRANSPORT UK Fifth Floor Offices (South), Chancery House, London WC2A 1QS T 020-7240 3131 E admin@cpt-uk.org W www.cpt-uk.org
Chief Executive, Simon Posner

CONSTRUCTION PRODUCTS ASSOCIATION The Building Centre, 26 Store Street, London WC1E 7BT T 020-7323 3770 W www.constructionproducts.org.uk
Chief Executive, Diana Montgomery

DAIRY UK 6th Floor, London WC1V 7EP T 020-7405 1484 E info@dairyuk.org W www.dairyuk.org
Chief Executive, Dr Judith Bryans

ENERGY UK 26 Finsbury Square, London EC2A 1DS T 020-7930 9390 W www.energy-uk.org.uk
Chief Executive, Lawrence Slade

FEDERATION OF BAKERS 6th Floor, 10 Bloomsbury Way, London WC1A 2SL T 020-7420 7190 E info@fob.uk.com W www.fob.uk.com
Director, Gordon Polson

FEDERATION OF MASTER BUILDERS David Croft House, 25 Ely Place, London EC1N 6TD T 0330-333 7777 W www.fmb.org.uk
Chief Executive, Brian Berry

FSPA (FEDERATION OF SPORTS AND PLAY ASSOCIATIONS) Office 8, Rural Innovation Centre, Unit 169– Avenue H, Kenilworth CV8 2LG T 024-7641 4999 E info@sportsandplay.com W www.sportsandplay.com
Chair, Jack Osborne

FINANCE AND LEASING ASSOCIATION 2nd Floor, Imperial House, 8 Kean Street, London WC2B 4AS T 020-7836 6511 E info@fla.org.uk W www.fla.org.uk
Director-General, Stephen Sklaroff

FOOD AND DRINK FEDERATION 6th Floor, London WC1A 2SL T 020-7836 2460 W www.fdf.org.uk
Chief Executive, Ian Wright

FREIGHT TRANSPORT ASSOCIATION LTD Hermes House, St John's Road, Tunbridge Wells TN4 9UZ T 037-1711 2222 E enquiry@fta.co.uk W www.fta.co.uk
President, Leigh Pomlett

GLASGOW CHAMBER OF COMMERCE 30 George Square, Glasgow G2 1EQ T 0141-204 2121 E chamber@glasgowchamberofcommerce.com W www.glasgowchamberofcommerce.com
Chief Executive, Stuart Patrick

INSTITUTE OF BREWING AND DISTILLING 44A Curlew Street, London SE1 2ND T 020-7499 8144 E enquiries@ibd.org.uk W www.ibd.org.uk
Chief Executive, Dr Jerry Avis

INSTITUTE OF BRITISH ORGAN BUILDING 13 Ryefields, Bury St Edmunds IP31 3TD T 01359-233433 E administrator@ibo.co.uk W www.ibo.co.uk
President, Andrew Moyes

INSTITUTE OF CHARTERED FORESTERS 59 George Street, Edinburgh EH2 2JG T 0131-240 1425 E icf@charteredforesters.org W www.charteredforesters.org
Executive Director, Shireen Chambers

INSTITUTE OF CHARTERED SECRETARIES AND ADMINISTRATORS Saffron House, 6–10 Kirby Street, London EC1N 8TS T 020-7580 4741 E enquiries@icsa.org.uk W www.icsa.org.uk
Chief Executive, Simon Osborne

INSTITUTE OF CHARTERED SHIPBROKERS 30 Park Street, London SE1 9EQ T 020-7357 9722 E enquiries@ics.org.uk W www.ics.org.uk
Director, Julie Lithgow

INSTITUTE OF DIRECTORS 116 Pall Mall, London SW1Y 5ED T 020-7766 8888 E enquiries@iod.com W www.iod.com
Interim Director-Generals, Anna Davoy; Edwin Morgan

INSTITUTE OF EXPORT AND INTERNATIONAL TRADE Export House, Minerva Business Park, Peterborough PE2 6FT T 01733-404400 W www.export.org.uk
Chair, Terry Scuoler, CBE

INSTITUTE OF FINANCIAL ACCOUNTANTS CS111, Clerkenwell Workshops, 27–31 Clerkenwell Close, London EC1R 0AT T 020-3567 5999 E mail@ifa.org.uk W www.ifa.org.uk
Chief Executive, Andrew Conway

INSTITUTE OF HEALTHCARE MANAGEMENT 33 Cavendish Square, London W1G 0PW T 020-7182 4066 E contact@ihm.org.uk W www.ihm.org.uk
Chief Executive, Loretta Outhwaite (interim)

INSTITUTE OF HOSPITALITY 14 Palmerston Road, Surrey SM1 4QL T 020-8661 4900 E info@instituteofhospitality.org W www.instituteofhospitality.org
Chief Executive, Peter Ducker

INSTITUTE OF INTERNAL COMMUNICATION Suite G10, Gemini House, Sunrise Parkway, MK14 6PW T 01908-232168 E enquiries@ioic.org.uk W www.ioic.org.uk
Chief Executive, Jennifer Sproul

INSTITUTE OF MANAGEMENT SERVICES Brooke House, 24 Dam Street, Lichfield WS13 6AA T 01543-266909 E admin@ims-productivity.com W www.ims-productivity.com
Chair, Julian Cutler

INSTITUTE OF QUARRYING McPherson House, 8A Regan Way, Chilwell NG9 6RZ T 0115-972 9995 E mail@quarrying.org W www.quarrying.org
Chief Executive, James Thorne

INSTITUTE OF THE MOTOR INDUSTRY Fanshaws, Hertford SG13 8PQ T 01992-511 521 E comms@theimi.org.uk W www.theimi.org.uk
Chief Executive, Steve Nash

INSTITUTION OF OCCUPATIONAL SAFETY AND HEALTH The Grange, Highfield Drive, Wigston LE18 1NN T 0116-257 3100 E reception@iosh.co.uk W www.iosh.co.uk
Chief Executive, Bev Messinger

IP FEDERATION 60 Gray's Inn Road, London WC1X 8AQ T 020-7242 3923 E admin@ipfederation.com W www.ipfederation.com
President, Belinda Gascoyne

LEATHER UK Leather Trade House, Kings Park Road, Northampton NN3 6JD T 01604-679999 E info@leatheruk.org W www.leatheruk.org
Director, Dr Kerry Senior

MAGISTRATES' ASSOCIATION 10A Flagstaff House, St George Wharf, London SW8 2LE T 020-7387 2353 E information@magistrates-association.org.uk W www.magistrates-association.org.uk
Chief Executive, Jon Collins

MAKE UK, THE MANUFACTURERS' ORGANISATION Broadway House, Tothill Street, London SW1H 9NQ T 0808-168 5874 E enquiries@makeuk.org W www.makeuk.org
Chief Executive, Stephen Phipson, CBE

MANAGEMENT CONSULTANCIES ASSOCIATION 5th Floor, 36–38 Cornhill, London EC3V 3NG T 020-7645 7950 E info@mca.org.uk W www.mca.org.uk
Chief Executive, Tamzen Isacsson

MASTER LOCKSMITHS ASSOCIATION 1 Prospect Park, Rugby CV21 1TF T 01327-262255 E enquiries@locksmiths.co.uk W www.locksmiths.co.uk
Director of Development, Dr Steffan George

NATIONAL ASSOCIATION OF BRITISH MARKET AUTHORITIES The Guildhall, Shrops SY11 1PZ T 01691-680713 E nabma@nabma.com W www.nabma.com
Chief Executive, Graham Wilson, OBE

NATIONAL ASSOCIATION OF ESTATE AGENTS Arbon House, 6 Tournament Court, Warwick CV34 6LG T 01926-496800 E help@propertymark.co.uk W www.naea.co.uk
President, Mark Bentley

NATIONAL FARMERS' UNION (NFU) Agriculture House, Stoneleigh Park, Stoneleigh CV8 2LZ T 024-7685 8500 W www.nfuonline.com
Director-General, Terry Jones

NATIONAL FEDERATION OF RETAIL NEWSAGENTS Yeoman House, Sekforde Street, London EC1R 0HF T 020-7253 4225 E connect@nfrnonline.com W www.nfrnonline.com
Chief Executive, Paul Baxter

NATIONAL LANDLORDS ASSOCIATION 2nd Floor, 200 Union Street, London SE1 0LX T 020-7840 8900 W www.landlords.org.uk
Chief Executive, Richard Lambert

NATIONAL MARKET TRADERS FEDERATION Hampton House, Hawshaw Lane, Barnsley S74 0HA T 01226-749021 E genoffice@nmtf.co.uk W www.nmtf.co.uk
Chief Executive, Joe Harrison

NATIONAL PHARMACY ASSOCIATION Mallinson House, 38–42 St Peter's Street, Herts AL1 3NP T 01727-858687 E npa@npa.co.uk W www.npa.co.uk
Chief Executive, Mark Lyonette

NEWS MEDIA ASSOCIATION 292 Vauxhall Bridge Road, London SW1V 1AE T 020-7963 7480 E nma@newsmediauk.org W www.newsmediauk.org
Chief Executive, David Newell

OIL AND GAS UK 6th Floor East, Portland House, London SW1E 5BH T 020-7802 2400 E info@oilandgasuk.co.uk W www.oilandgasuk.co.uk
Chief Executive, Deirdre Michie

PROPERTY CARE ASSOCIATION 11 Ramsay Court, Kingfisher Way, Huntingdon PE29 6FY T 0844-375 4301 E pca@property-care.org W www.property-care.org
Chief Executive, Stephen Hodgson

PUBLISHERS ASSOCIATION 50 Southwark Street, London SE1 1UN T 020-7378 0504 E mail@publishers.org.uk W www.publishers.org.uk
Chief Executive, Stephen Lotinga

RADIOCENTRE 6th Floor, 55 New Oxford Street, London WC1A 1BS T 020-7010 0600 E info@radiocentre.org W www.radiocentre.org
Chief Executive, Siobhan Kenny

ROAD HAULAGE ASSOCIATION LTD Roadway House, Bretton Way, Bretton PE3 8DD T 01274-863100 W www.rha.uk.net
Chief Executive, Richard Burnett

ROYAL ASSOCIATION OF BRITISH DAIRY FARMERS
Dairy House, Unit 31, Abbey Park, Kenilworth CV8 2LY
T 024-7663 9317 E office@rabdf.co.uk W www.rabdf.co.uk
Managing Director, Matthew Knight

ROYAL FACULTY OF PROCURATORS IN GLASGOW
12 Nelson Mandela Place, Glasgow G2 1BT T 0141-332 3593
E library@rfpg.org W www.rfpg.org
Chief Executive, John McKenzie

SHELLFISH ASSOCIATION OF GREAT BRITAIN
Fishmongers' Hall, London Bridge, London EC4R 9EL
T 020-7283 8305 E projects@shellfish.org.uk
W www.shellfish.org.uk
Director, David Jarrad

SOCIETY OF LOCAL AUTHORITY CHIEF EXECUTIVES
AND SENIOR MANAGERS (SOLACE) Suite 1.3A, 1st
Floor, Millbank Tower, London SW1P 4QP T 0845-652 4010
E info@solace.org.uk W www.solace.org.uk
Directors, Graeme McDonald; Terry McDougall

SOCIETY OF MOTOR MANUFACTURERS AND
TRADERS LTD 71 Great Peter Street, London SW1P 2BN
T 020-7235 7000 E communications@smmt.co.uk
W www.smmt.co.uk
Chief Executive, Mike Hawes

TIMBER TRADE FEDERATION The Building Centre, 26
Store Street, London WC1E 7BT T 020-3205 0067 E ttf@ttf.co.uk
W www.ttf.co.uk
Managing Director, David Hopkins

UK CHAMBER OF SHIPPING 30 Park Street, London
SE1 9EQ T 020-7417 2800 E query@ukchamberofshipping.com
W www.ukchamberofshipping.com
Chief Executive, Bob Sanguinetti

UK FASHION AND TEXTILE ASSOCIATION 3 Queen
Square, London WC1N 3AR T 020-7843 9460 E info@ukft.org
W www.ukft.org
Chief Executive, Adam Mansell

UK FINANCE 5th Floor, 1 Angel Court, London EC2R 7HJ
T 020-7706 3333 W www.ukfinance.org.uk
Chief Executive, Stephen Jones

UKHOSPITALITY 10 Bloomsbury Way, London WC1A 2SL
T 020-7404 7744 W www.ukhospitality.org.uk
Chair, Nick Varney

UK PETROLEUM INDUSTRY ASSOCIATION LTD 37–
39 High Holborn, London WC1V 6AA T 020-7269 7600
E info@ukpia.com W www.ukpia.com
Director-General, Stephen Marcos Jones

ULSTER FARMERS' UNION 475 Antrim Road, Belfast
BT15 3DA T 028-9037 0222 E info@ufuhq.com
W www.ufuni.org
Chief Executive, Wesley Aston

THE WINE AND SPIRIT TRADE ASSOCIATION
International Wine and Spirit Centre, 39–45 Bermondsey Street,
London SE1 3XF T 020-7089 3877 E info@wsta.co.uk
W www.wsta.co.uk
Chief Executive, Miles Beale

CBI

Cannon Place, 78 Cannon Street, London EC4N 6HN
T 020-7379 7400 E enquiries@cbi.org.uk W www.cbi.org.uk

The CBI was founded in 1965 and is an independent non-party political body financed by industry and commerce. It works with the UK government, international legislators and policymakers to help UK businesses compete effectively. It is the recognised spokesman for the business viewpoint and is consulted as such by the government.

The CBI speaks for some 190,000 businesses that together employ approximately one-third of the private sector workforce. Member companies, which decide all policy positions, include FTSE 100 index listed companies, small-and medium-size firms, micro businesses, private and family owned businesses, start-ups and trade associations.

The CBI board is chaired by the president and meets four times a year. It is assisted by 14 expert standing committees which advise on the main aspects of policy. There are nine regional councils for England and three national councils for, Wales, Scotland and Northern Ireland. There are also offices in Beijing, Brussels, New Delhi and Washington DC.

President, John Allan, CBE
Director-General, Dame Carolyn Fairbairn, DBE

WALES, 2 Caspian Point, Caspian Way, Cardiff Bay, Cardiff
CF10 4DQ T 029-2097 7600 E wales.mail@cbi.org.uk
Regional Director, Ian Price
SCOTLAND, 160 West George Street, Glasgow G2 2HQ
T 0141-222 2184 E scotland@cbi.org.uk
Regional Director, Tracy Black
NORTHERN IRELAND, Hamilton House, 3 Joy Street, Belfast
BT2 8LE T 028-9010 1100 E ni.mail@cbi.org.uk
Regional Director, Angela McGowan

TRADE UNIONS

A trade union is an organisation of workers formed for the purpose of collective bargaining over pay and working conditions. Trade unions may also provide legal and financial advice, sickness benefits and education facilities to their members. Legally any employee has the right to join a trade union, but not all employers recognise all or any trade unions. Conversely an employee also has the right not to join a trade union, in particular since the practice of a 'closed shop' system, where all employees have to join the employer's preferred union, is no longer permitted.

THE CENTRAL ARBITRATION COMMITTEE

Fleetbank House, 2–6 Salisbury Square, London EC4Y 8JX
T 0330-109 3610 E enquiries@cac.gov.uk
W www.gov.uk/government/organisations/
central-arbitration-committee

The Central Arbitration Committee's main role is concerned with requests for trade union recognition and de-recognition under the statutory procedures of Schedule A1 of the Employment Rights Act 1999. It also determines disclosure of information complaints under the Trade Union and Labour Relations (Consolidation) Act 1992, considers applications and complaints under the Information and Consultation Regulations 2004, and performs a similar role in relation to European works councils, companies, cooperative societies and cross-border mergers.

Chair, Sir Stephen Redmond
Chief Executive, James Jacob

TRADES UNION CONGRESS (TUC)

Congress House, 23–28 Great Russell Street, London WC1B 3LS
T 020-7636 4030 E info@tuc.org.uk
W www.tuc.org.uk

The Trades Union Congress (TUC), founded in 1868, is an independent association of trade unions. The TUC promotes the rights and welfare of those in work and helps the unemployed. The TUC brings Britain's unions together to draw up common polices; lobbies the government to implement policies that will benefit people at work; campaigns on economic and social issues; represents working people on public bodies and at the UN employment body – the International Labour Organisation; carries out research on employment-related issues; runs training and education programmes for union representatives; helps unions to develop new services for their members and negotiate with each other; and builds links with other trade union bodies worldwide.

The governing body of the TUC is the annual congress which sets policy. Between congresses, business is conducted by a 56-member general council, which meets every two months to oversee the TUC's work programme and sanction new policy initiatives. Each year, at its first post-congress meeting, the general council appoints an executive committee and the TUC president for that congress year. The executive committee meets monthly to implement and develop policy, manage TUC financial affairs and deal with any urgent business. The president chairs general council and executive meetings and is consulted by the General Secretary on all major issues.

President (2018–19), Mark Serwotka
General Secretary, Frances O'Grady

SCOTTISH TRADES UNION CONGRESS (STUC)

333 Woodlands Road, Glasgow G3 6NG T 0141-337 8100
E info@stuc.org.uk W www.stuc.org.uk

The congress was formed in 1897 and acts as a national centre for the trade union movement in Scotland. The STUC promotes the rights to welfare of those in work and helps the unemployed. It helps its member unions to promote membership in new areas and industries, and campaigns for rights at work for all employees, including part-time and temporary workers, whether union members or not. It also makes representations to government and employers. In 2016 the STUC had over 540,000 members from 37 affiliated unions and 20 trade union councils.

The annual congress in April elects a 36-member general council on the basis of six sections.

General Secretary, Grahame Smith

WALES TUC

Wales TUC was established in 1974 to ensure that the role of the TUC was effectively undertaken in Wales. Its structure reflects the four economic regions of Wales and matches the regional committee areas of the National Assembly of Wales. The regional committees oversee the implementation of Wales TUC policy and campaigns in the relevant regions, and liaise with local government, training organisations and regional economic development bodies. The Wales TUC seeks to reduce unemployment, increase the levels of skill and pay, and eliminate discrimination.

The governing body of Wales TUC is the conference, which meets annually in May and elects a general council (usually of around 50 people) that oversees the work of the TUC throughout the year.

There are 49 affiliated unions representing around 400,000 workers.

General Secretary, Martin Mansfield

TUC-AFFILIATED UNIONS
As at June 2019

ACCORD Simmons House, 46 Old Bath Road, Reading RG10 9QR T 0118-934 1808 E info@accordhq.org
W www.accord-myunion.org
General Secretary, Ged Nichols
Membership: 24,815

ADVANCE 2nd Floor, 16–17 High Street, Tring HP23 5AH
T 01442-891122 E info@advance-union.org
W www.advance-union.org
General Secretary, Linda Rolph
Membership: 6,665

AEGIS THE UNION 1–3 Lochside Crescent, Edinburgh EH1 9SE T 0131-549 5474 E members@aegistheunion.co.uk
W www.aegistheunion.co.uk
General Secretary, Brian Linn
Membership: 4,647

AEP (ASSOCIATION OF EDUCATIONAL PSYCHOLOGISTS) 4 The Riverside Centre, Durham DH1 5TA
T 0191-384 9512 E enquiries@aep.org.uk W www.aep.org.uk
General Secretary, Kate Fallon
Membership: 3,453

AFA (ASSOCIATION OF FLIGHT ATTENDANTS) 32
Wingford Road, London SW2 4DS T 0789-1182947
E afalhr@unitedafa.org W www.afacwa.org
General Secretary, Anthony King
Membership: 432

ARTISTS' UNION ENGLAND Old Bakery, Carlow Street,
London NW1 7LH T 07931-774469
E info@artistsunionengland.org.uk
W www.artistsunionengland.org.uk
General Secretary, Martin Sundram and Zita Holborne
Membership: 335

ASLEF (ASSOCIATED SOCIETY OF LOCOMOTIVE
ENGINEERS AND FIREMEN) 77 St John Street, London
EC1M 4NN T 020-7324 2400 E info@aslef.org.uk
W www.aslef.org.uk
General Secretary, Michael Whelan
Membership: 22,424

BALPA (BRITISH AIRLINE PILOTS ASSOCIATION)
BALPA House, 5 Heathrow Boulevard, 278 Bath Road, West
Drayton UB7 0DQ T 020-8476 4000 E balpa@balpa.org
W www.balpa.org
General Secretary, Brian Strutton
Membership: 14,688

BDA (BRITISH DIETETIC ASSOCIATION) 5th Floor,
Charles House, 148–149 Great Charles Street, Birmingham
B3 3HT T 0121-200 8080 W www.bda.uk.com
General Secretary, Andrew Burman
Membership: 9,319

BFAWU (BAKERS, FOOD AND ALLIED WORKERS'
UNION) Stanborough House, Great North Road, Welwyn
Garden City AL8 7TA T 01707-260150 E info@bfawu.org
W www.bfawu.org
General Secretary, Ronnie Draper
Membership: 17,460

BOS TU (BRITISH ORTHOPTIC SOCIETY TRADE
UNION) 5th Floor, Charles House, 148/9 Great Charles Street
Queensway, Birmingham B3 3HT T 0121-728 5633
E bios@orthoptics.org.uk W www.orthoptics.org.uk
Chair, Veronica Greenwood
Membership: 1,081

COMMUNITY 465C Caledonian Road, London N7 9GX
T 0800 389 6332 E servicecentre@community-tu.org
W www.community-tu.org
General Secretary, Roy Rickhuss
Membership: 26,277

COP (COLLEGE OF PODIATRY) Quartz House, London
SE1 2EW T 020-7234 8620 E reception@scpod.org
W www.cop.org.uk
General Secretary, Steve Jamieson
Membership: 9,367

CSP (CHARTERED SOCIETY OF PHYSIOTHERAPY) 14
Bedford Row, London WC1R 4ED T 020-7306 6666
E enquiries@csp.org.uk W www.csp.org.uk
Chief Executive, Karen Middleton
, CBE *Membership*: 57,141

CWU (COMMUNICATION WORKERS UNION) 150 The
Broadway, London SW19 1RX T 020-8971 7200 E info@cwu.org
W www.cwu.org
General Secretary, Dave Ward
Membership: 191,438

EIS (EDUCATIONAL INSTITUTE OF SCOTLAND) 46
Moray Place, Edinburgh EH3 6BH T 0131-225 6244
E enquiries@eis.org.uk W www.eis.org.uk
General Secretary, Larry Flanagan
Membership: 55,251

EQUITY Guild House, Upper St Martin's Lane, London
WC2H 9EG T 020-7379 6000 E info@equity.org.uk
W www.equity.org.uk
General Secretary, Christine Payne
Membership: 45,575

FBU (FIRE BRIGADES UNION) Bradley House, 68 Coombe
Road, Kingston upon Thames KT2 7AE T 020-8541 1765
E office@fbu.org.uk W www.fbu.org.uk
General Secretary, Matthew Wrack
Membership: 33,042

FDA Elizabeth House, 39 York Road, London SE1 7NQ
T 020-7401 5555 E info@fda.org.uk W www.fda.org.uk
General Secretary, Dave Penman
Membership: 16,759

GMB 22 Stephenson Way, London NW1 2HD T 020-7391 6700
E info@gmb.org.uk W www.gmb.org.uk
General Secretary, Tim Roache
Membership: 615,558

HCSA (HOSPITAL CONSULTANTS' AND SPECIALISTS'
ASSOCIATION) 1 Kingsclere Road, Basingstoke RG25 3JA
T 01256-771777 E conspec@hcsa.com W www.hcsa.com
Chief Executive, Joe Chattin (interim)
Membership: 3,368

MU (MUSICIANS' UNION) 60–62 Clapham Road, London
SW9 0JJ T 020-7582 5566 E info@theMU.org
W www.musiciansunion.org.uk
General Secretary, Horace Trubridge
Membership: 30,319

NAHT (NATIONAL ASSOCIATION OF HEAD
TEACHERS) 1 Heath Square, Haywards Heath RH16 1BL
T 0300-303 0333 E info@naht.org.uk W www.naht.org.uk
General Secretary, Paul Whiteman
Membership: 41,612

NAPO (TRADE UNION AND PROFESSIONAL
ASSOCIATION FOR FAMILY COURT AND
PROBATION STAFF) 160 Falcon Road, London SW11 2NY
T 020-7223 4887 E info@napo.org.uk W www.napo.org.uk
General Secretary, Ian Lawrence
Membership: 5,110

NASS (NATIONAL ASSOCIATION OF RACING STAFF)
The Racing Centre, Fred Archer Way, Newmarket CB8 8NT
T 01638-663411 E admin@naors.co.uk W www.naors.co.uk
Chief Executive, George McGrath
Membership: 2,350

NASUWT (NATIONAL ASSOCIATION OF
SCHOOLMASTERS/ UNION OF WOMEN
TEACHERS) Hillscourt Education Centre, Rose Hill, Birmingham
B45 8RS T 0121-453 6150 E nasuwt@mail.nasuwt.org.uk
W www.nasuwt.org.uk
General Secretary, Ms Chris Keates (acting)
Membership: 316,230

NATIONAL HOUSE BUILDING COUNCIL STAFF
ASSOCIATION NHBC House, Davey Avenue, Milton Keynes
MK5 8FP T 0344-644 1000 E cssupport@nhbc.co.uk
W www.nhbc.co.uk
General Secretary, Tom Howard
Membership: 746

NAUTILUS INTERNATIONAL 1–2 The Shrubberies, George
Lane, London E18 1BD T 020-8989 6677
E enquiries@nautilusint.org W www.nautilusint.org
General Secretary, Mark Dickinson
Membership: 20,797

NEU (NATIONAL EDUCATION UNION) Hamilton House,
Mabledon Place, London WC1H 9BD T 0345-811 8111
W www.neu.org.uk
General Secretaries, Dr Mary Bousted; Kevin Courtney
Membership: 450,156

NGSU (NATIONWIDE GROUP STAFF UNION) Middleton Farmhouse, 37 Main Road, Middleton Cheney OX17 2QT T 01295-710767 E ngsu@ngsu.org.uk W www.ngsu.co.uk
General Secretary, Tim Poil
Membership: 12,723

NSEAD (NATIONAL SOCIETY FOR EDUCATION IN ART AND DESIGN) 3 Mason's Wharf, Potley Lane, Corsham SN13 9FY T 01225-810134 E info@nsead.org W www.nsead.org
General Secretary, Michele Gregson
Membership: 1,815

NUJ (NATIONAL UNION OF JOURNALISTS) 72 Acton Street, London WC1X 9NB T 020-7843 3700 E info@nuj.org.uk W www.nuj.org.uk
General Secretary, Michelle Stanistreet
Membership: 26,769

NUM (NATIONAL UNION OF MINEWORKERS) Miners' Offices, 2 Huddersfield Road, Barnsley S70 2LS T 01226-215555 E chris.kitchen@num.org.uk W www.num.org.uk
National Secretary, Chris Kitchen
Membership: 311

PCS (PUBLIC AND COMMERCIAL SERVICES UNION) 160 Falcon Road, London SW11 2LN T 020-7924 2727 W www.pcs.org.uk
General Secretary, Mark Serwotka
Membership: 180,646

PFA (PROFESSIONAL FOOTBALLERS' ASSOCIATION) 20 Oxford Court, Manchester M2 3WQ T 0161-236 0575 E info@thepfa.co.uk W www.thepfa.com
Chief Executive, Gordon Taylor
, OBE *Membership:* 5,360

POA (PROFESSIONAL TRADE UNION FOR PRISON, CORRECTIONAL AND SECURE PSYCHIATRIC WORKERS) Cronin House, 245 Church Street, London N9 9HW T 020-8803 0255 E general@poauk.org.uk W www.poauk.org.uk
General Secretary, Steve Gillan
Membership: 30,901

PROSPECT New Prospect House, 8 Leake Street, London SE1 7NN T 020-7902 6600 E enquiries@prospect.org.uk W www.prospect.org.uk
General Secretary, Mike Clancy
Membership: 142,486

RCM (ROYAL COLLEGE OF MIDWIVES) 15 Mansfield Street, London W1G 9NH T 030-0303 0444 W www.rcm.org.uk
General Secretary, Gill Walton
Membership: 48,231

RMT (NATIONAL UNION OF RAIL, MARITIME AND TRANSPORT WORKERS) Unity House, 39 Chalton Street, London NW1 1JD T 020-7387 4771 E info@rmt.org.uk W www.rmt.org.uk
General Secretary, Mick Cash
Membership: 80,391

SOR (SOCIETY OF RADIOGRAPHERS) 207 Providence Square, Mill Street, London SE1 2EW T 020-7740 7200 W www.sor.org
Chief Executive, Richard Evans
Membership: 30,356

TSSA (TRANSPORT SALARIED STAFFS' ASSOCIATION) 2nd Floor, 17 Devonshire Square, London EC2M 4SQ T 020-7387 2101 E enquiries@tssa.org.uk W www.tssa.org.uk
General Secretary, Manuel Cortes
Membership: 18,169

UCAC (UNDEB CENEDLAETHOL ATHRAWON CYMRU/ NATIONAL UNION OF THE TEACHERS OF WALES) Prif Swyddfa UCAC, Ffordd Penglais, Aberystwyth SY23 3EU T 01970-639950 E ucac@ucac.cymru W www.ucac.cymru
General Secretary, Dilwyn Roberts-Young
Membership: 4,111

UCU (UNIVERSITY AND COLLEGE UNION) Carlow Street, London NW1 7LH T 020-7756 2500 W www.ucu.org.uk
General Secretary, Sally Hunt
Membership: 120,564

UNISON 130 Euston Road, London NW1 2AY T 0800-085 7857 W www.unison.org.uk
General Secretary, Dave Prentis
Membership: 1,369,114

UNITE 128 Theobald's Road, London WC1X 8TN T 020-7611 2500 W www.unitetheunion.org
General Secretary, Len McCluskey
Membership: 1,310,508

URTU (UNITED ROAD TRANSPORT UNION) Almond House, Oak Green, Cheadle, Hulme SK8 6QL T 0800-526 639 E info@urtu.com W www.urtu.com
General Secretary, Robert Monks
Membership: 9,123

USDAW (UNION OF SHOP, DISTRIBUTIVE AND ALLIED WORKERS) 188 Wilmslow Road, Manchester M14 6LJ T 0161-224 2804 E enquiries@usdaw.org.uk W www.usdaw.org.uk
General Secretary, Paddy Lillis
Membership: 431,610

WGGB (WRITERS' GUILD OF GREAT BRITAIN) 134 Tooley Street, London SE1 2TU T 020-7833 0777 E admin@writersguild.org.uk W www.writersguild.org.uk
General Secretary, Ellie Peers
Membership: 2,146

NON-AFFILIATED UNIONS

As at June 2019

ASCL (ASSOCIATION OF SCHOOL AND COLLEGE LEADERS) 130 Regent Road, Leicester LE1 7PG T 0116-299 1122 E info@ascl.org.uk W www.ascl.org.uk
General Secretary, Geoff Barton
Membership: 18,970

BDA (BRITISH DENTAL ASSOCIATION) 64 Wimpole Street, London W1G 8YS T 020-7935 0875 E enquiries@bda.org W www.bda.org
General Secretary, Michael Armstrong
Membership: 17,650

CIOJ (CHARTERED INSTITUTE OF JOURNALISTS) 2 Dock Offices, Surrey Quays Road, London SE16 2XU T 020-7252 1187 E memberservices@cioj.co.uk W www.cioj.co.uk
General Secretary, Dominic Cooper
Membership: 1,009

SOCIETY OF AUTHORS 24 Bedford Row, London WC1R 4EH T 020-7373 6642 E info@societyofauthors.org W www.societyofauthors.org
Chief Executive, Nicola Solomon
Membership: 10,214

SSTA (SCOTTISH SECONDARY TEACHERS' ASSOCIATION) West End House, 14 West End Place, Edinburgh EH11 2ED T 0131-313 7300 E info@ssta.org.uk W www.ssta.org.uk
General Secretary, Seamus Searson
Membership: 6,586

SPORTS BODIES

SPORTS COUNCILS

SPORT AND RECREATION ALLIANCE Holborn Tower, 137–145 High Holborn, London WC1V 6PL **T** 020-7976 3900 **E** info@sportandrecreation.org.uk **W** www.sportandrecreation.org.uk *Chief Executive,* Lisa Wainwright

SPORT ENGLAND 21 Bloomsbury Street, London WC1B 3HF **T** 0345-850 8508 **E** info@sportengland.org **W** www.sportengland.org *Chief Executive,* Tim Hollingsworth

SPORT NORTHERN IRELAND House of Sport, 2A Upper Malone Road, Belfast BT9 5LA **T** 028-9038 1222 **E** info@sportni.net **W** www.sportni.net *Chief Executive,* Antoinette McKeown

SPORTSCOTLAND Doges, Templeton on the Green, 62 Templeton Street, Glasgow G40 1DA **T** 0141-534 6500 **E** sportscotland.enquiries@sportscotland.org.uk **W** www.sportscotland.org.uk *Chief Executive,* Stewart Harris

SPORT WALES Sophia Gardens, Cardiff CF11 9SW **T** 0300-300 3111 **E** info@sport.wales.org.uk **W** www.sport.wales *Chief Executive,* Sarah Powell

UK SPORT 21 Bloomsbury Street, London WC1B 3HF **T** 020-7211 5100 **E** info@uksport.gov.uk **W** www.uksport.gov.uk *Chief Executive,* Liz Nicholl, CBE

AMERICAN FOOTBALL

BRITISH AMERICAN FOOTBALL ASSOCIATION 1 Franchise Street, Kidderminster DY11 6RE **E** human.resources@britishamericanfootball.org **W** www.britishamericanfootball.org *Chair,* Nichole McCulloch

ANGLING

ANGLING TRUST Eastwood House, 6 Rainbow Street, Herefordshire HR6 8DQ **T** 0343-507 7006 **E** admin@anglingtrust.net **W** www.anglingtrust.net *Chief Executive,* Mark Lloyd

ARCHERY

ARCHERY GB Lilleshall National Sports Centre, Newport TF10 9AT **T** 0195-267 7888 **E** enquiries@archerygb.org **W** www.archerygb.org *Chief Executive,* Neil Armitage

ASSOCIATION FOOTBALL

ENGLISH FOOTBALL LEAGUE EFL House, 10-12 West Cliff, Preston PR1 8HU **T** 01772-325800 **E** enquiries@efl.com **W** www.efl.com *Chief Executive,* Shaun Harvey

FOOTBALL ASSOCIATION Wembley Stadium, PO Box 1966, London SW1P 9EQ **T** 0800-169 1863 **E** info@thefa.com **W** www.thefa.com *Chief Executive,* Martin Glenn

FOOTBALL ASSOCIATION OF WALES 11–12 Neptune Court, Vanguard Way, Cardiff CF24 5PJ **T** 029-2043 5830 **E** info@faw.co.uk **W** www.faw.cymru *Chief Executive,* Jonathan Ford

IRISH FOOTBALL ASSOCIATION Donegal Avenue, Belfast BT12 6LU **T** 028-9066 9458 **E** info@irishfa.com **W** www.irishfa.com *Chief Executive,* Patrick Nelson

PREMIER LEAGUE 30 Gloucester Place, London W1U 8PL **T** 020-7864 9000 **E** info@premierleague.com **W** www.premierleague.com *Chief Executive,* vacant

SCOTTISH FOOTBALL ASSOCIATION Hampden Park, Glasgow G42 9AY **T** 0141-616 6000 **E** info@scottishfa.co.uk **W** www.scottishfa.co.uk *Chief Executive,* Ian Maxwell

SCOTTISH PROFESSIONAL FOOTBALL LEAGUE Hampden Park, Glasgow G42 9DE **T** 0141-620 4140 **E** info@spfl.co.uk **W** www.spfl.co.uk *Chief Executive,* Neil Doncaster

ATHLETICS

BRITISH ATHLETICS Athletics House, Alexander Stadium, Birmingham B42 2BE **T** 0121-713 8400 **E** majorevents@britishathletics.org.uk **W** www.britishathletics.org.uk *Chief Executive,* Nigel Holl (interim)

ATHLETICS NORTHERN IRELAND Athletics House, Old Coach Road, Belfast BT9 5PR **T** 028-9060 2707 **E** info@athleticsni.org **W** www.athleticsni.org *General Secretary,* John Allen

SCOTTISH ATHLETICS Caledonia House, Edinburgh EH12 9DQ **T** 0131-539 7320 **E** admin@scottishathletics.org.uk **W** www.scottishathletics.org.uk *Chief Executive,* Mark Munro

WELSH ATHLETICS Cardiff International Sports Stadium, Leckwith Road, Cardiff CF11 8AZ **T** 029-2064 4870 **E** office@welshathletics.org **W** www.welshathletics.org *Chief Executive,* Matt Newman

BADMINTON

BADMINTON ENGLAND National Badminton Centre, Bradwell Road, Milton Keynes MK8 9LA **T** 01908-268400 **E** enquiries@badmintonengland.co.uk **W** www.badmintonengland.co.uk *Chief Executive,* Adrian Christy

BADMINTON SCOTLAND Sir Craig Reedie Badminton Centre, 40 Bogmoor Place, Glasgow G51 4TQ **T** 0141-445 1218 **E** enquiries@badmintonscotland.org.uk **W** www.badmintonscotland.org.uk *Chief Executive,* Keith Russell

BADMINTON WALES Sport Wales National Centre, Sophia Gardens, Cardiff CF11 9SW **T** 029-2033 4938 **E** enquiries@badminton.wales **W** www.badminton.wales *General Manager,* Gareth Hall

BASEBALL

BASEBALLSOFTBALL UK Marathon House, 190 Great Dover Street, London SE1 4YB **T** 020-7453 7055 **W** www.baseballsoftballuk.com *Chief Executive,* John Boyd

BRITISH BASEBALL FEDERATION Marathon House, 190 Great Dane Street, London SE1 4YB **T** 0207-7453 7055 **W** www.britishbaseballfederation.org *President,* Gerry Perez

BASKETBALL

BASKETBALL ENGLAND Etihad Stadium, Rowsley Street, Manchester M11 3FF **T** 0300-600 1170 **E** info@basketballengland.co.uk **W** www.basketballengland.co.uk *Chief Executive,* Stewart Kellett

BASKETBALL SCOTLAND Caledonia House, Edinburgh
EH12 9DQ **T** 0131-317 7260
E enquiries@basketball-scotland.com
W www.basketballscotland.co.uk
Chief Executive, Kevin Pringle

BILLIARDS AND SNOOKER

WORLD SNOOKER 75 Whiteladies Road, Bristol BS8 2NT
T 0117-317 8200 **E** info@worldsnooker.com
W www.worldsnooker.com
Chief Executive, Steve Dawson

BOBSLEIGH

BRITISH BOBSLEIGH & SKELETON ASSOCIATION
University of Bath, Claverton Down, Bath BA2 7AY
T 01225-384343 **E** office@thebbsa.co.uk **W** www.thebbsa.co.uk
Chair, Christopher Rodrigues

BOWLS

BOWLS ENGLAND Riverside House, Milverton Hill, Royal
Leamington Spa CV32 5HZ **T** 01926-334609
E enquiries@bowlsengland.com **W** www.bowlsengland.com
Chief Executive, Tony Allcock, MBE
BRITISH ISLES BOWLS COUNCIL
E bibcsecretary@aol.co.uk **W** www.britishislesbowls.com
President, David Graham, OBE
ENGLISH INDOOR BOWLING ASSOCIATION David
Cornwell House, Bowling Green, Melton Mowbray LE13 0FA
T 01664-481900 **E** enquiries@eiba.co.uk **W** www.eiba.co.uk
Chief Executive, Peter Thompson

BOXING

BRITISH BOXING BOARD OF CONTROL 14 North Road,
Cardiff CF10 3DY **T** 029-2036 7000 **E** admin@bbbofc.com
W www.bbbofc.com
General Secretary, Robert Smith
ENGLAND BOXING English Institute of Sport, Coleridge Road,
Sheffield S9 5DA **T** 0114-223 5654
E enquiries@englandboxing.org **W** www.abae.co.uk
Chief Executive, Gethin Jenkins

CANOEING

BRITISH CANOEING National Water Sport Centre, Adbolton
Lane, Nottingham NG12 2LU **T** 0300-011 9500
E info@britishcanoeing.org.uk **W** www.britishcanoeing.org.uk
Chief Executive, David Joy

CHESS

ENGLISH CHESS FEDERATION The Watch Oak, Chain Lane,
Battle TN33 0YD **T** 01424-775222 **E** office@englishchess.org.uk
W www.englishchess.org.uk
Chief Executive, Mike Truran

CRICKET

ENGLAND AND WALES CRICKET BOARD Lord's Cricket
Ground, St John's Wood Road, London NW8 8QZ
T 020-7432 1200 **W** www.ecb.co.uk
Chief Executive, Tom Harrison
MCC Lord's Cricket Ground, London NW8 8QN **T** 020-7616 8500
E reception@mcc.org.uk **W** www.lords.org
Chief Executive and Secretary, Guy Lavender

CROQUET

CROQUET ASSOCIATION Old Bath Road, Cheltenham
GL53 7DF **T** 01242-242318 **E** caoffice@croquet.org.uk
W www.croquet.org.uk
Manager, Mark Suter

CURLING

BRITISH CURLING c/o The Royal Caledonian Curling Club,
Ochil House, Stirling FK7 7XE **E** info@britishcurling.com
W www.britishcurling.org.uk
Chief Executive, Bruce Crawford
SCOTTISH CURLING Ochil House, Stirling FK7 7XE
T 0131-333 3003 **E** office@scottishcurling.org
W www.scottishcurling.org
Chief Executive, Bruce Crawford

CYCLING

BRITISH CYCLING FEDERATION Stuart Street, Manchester
M11 4DQ **T** 0161-274 2000 **E** info@britishcycling.org.uk
W www.britishcycling.org.uk
Chief Executive, Julie Harrington

DARTS

BRITISH DARTS ORGANISATION Unit 4, Glan-y-Llyn
Industrial Estate, Cardiff CF15 7JD **T** 029-2081 1815
E contact@bdodarts.com **W** www.bdodarts.com
Chairman, Derek Jacklin

EQUESTRIANISM

BRITISH EQUESTRIAN FEDERATION Abbey Park,
Kenilworth CV8 2RH **T** 024-7669 8871 **E** info@bef.co.uk
W www.bef.co.uk
Chief Executive, Nick Fellows
BRITISH EVENTING Abbey Park, Kenilworth CV8 2RN
T 024-7669 8856 **E** info@britisheventing.com
W www.britisheventing.com
Chief Executive, David Holmes

ETON FIVES

ETON FIVES ASSOCIATION 45 Sandhills Crescent, Solihull
B91 3UE **T** 07833-600230 **W** www.etonfives.com
Chair, Chris Davies

FENCING

BRITISH FENCING 1 Baron's Gate, 33 Rothschild Road,
London W4 5HT **T** 020-8742 3032
E headoffice@britishfencing.com **W** www.britishfencing.com
Chief Executive, Georgina Usher

GLIDING

BRITISH GLIDING ASSOCIATION 8 Merus Court, Meridian
Business Park, Leicester LE19 1RJ **T** 0116-289 2956
E office@gliding.co.uk **W** www.gliding.co.uk
Chief Executive, Pete Stratten

GOLF

ENGLAND GOLF The National Golf Centre, Woodhall Spa
LN10 6PU **T** 01526-354500 **E** info@englandgolf.org
W www.englandgolf.org
Chief Executive, Nick Pink
THE ROYAL AND ANCIENT GOLF CLUB Golf Place, St
Andrews KY16 9JD **T** 01334-460000
E thesecretary@randagc.org **W** www.randa.org
Chief Executive and Secretary, Martin Slumbers

GYMNASTICS

BRITISH GYMNASTICS Ford Hall, Lilleshall National Sports
Centre, Newport TF10 9NB **T** 0345-129 7129
E information@british-gymnastics.org
W www.british-gymnastics.org
Chief Executive, Jane Allen

HANDBALL

ENGLAND HANDBALL The Halliwell Jones Stadium, Winwick Road, Warrington WA2 7NE **T** 01925-246482
E office@englandhandball.com **W** www.englandhandball.com
Chief Executive, David Meli

HOCKEY

ENGLAND HOCKEY Bisham Abbey National Sports Centre, Marlow SL7 1RR **T** 01628-897500
E enquiries@englandhockey.co.uk **W** www.englandhockey.co.uk
Chief Executive, Sally Munday
HOCKEY WALES Sport Wales National Centre, Sophia Close, Cardiff CF11 9SW **T** 0300-300 3126 **E** info@hockeywales.org.uk
W www.hockeywales.org.uk
Chief Executive, Ria Male (interim)
SCOTTISH HOCKEY UNION Glasgow National Hockey Centre, 8 King's Drive, Glasgow G40 1HB **T** 0141-550 5999
W www.scottish-hockey.org.uk
Chief Executive, David Sweetman

HORSERACING

BRITISH HORSERACING AUTHORITY 75 High Holborn, London WC1V 6LS **T** 020-7152 0000
E info@britishhorseracing.com **W** www.britishhorseracing.com
Chief Executive, Nick Rust
THE JOCKEY CLUB 75 High Holborn, London WC1V 6LS
T 020-7611 1800 **E** info@thejockeyclub.co.uk
W www.thejockeyclub.co.uk
Chief Executive, Simon Bazalgette

ICE SKATING

NATIONAL ICE SKATING ASSOCIATION English Institute of Sport, Coleridge Road, Sheffield S9 5DA **T** 0115-988 8060
E info@iceskating.org.uk **W** www.iceskating.org.uk
Chair, Rob Jones

LACROSSE

ENGLISH LACROSSE ASSOCIATION National Squash Centre and Regional Arena, Gate 13, Manchester M11 3FF
T 0161-974 7757 **E** info@englandlacrosse.co.uk
W www.englandlacrosse.co.uk
Chief Executive, Mark Coups

LAWN TENNIS

LAWN TENNIS ASSOCIATION National Tennis Centre, 100 Priory Lane, London SW15 5JQ **T** 020-8487 7000
E info@lta.org.uk **W** www.lta.org.uk
Chief Executive, Scott Lloyd

MARTIAL ARTS

BRITISH JUDO ASSOCIATION Floor 1, Kudhail House, 238 Birmingham Road, Great Barr B43 7AH **T** 0121-728 6920
E bja@britishjudo.org.uk **W** www.britishjudo.org.uk
Chief Executive, Andrew Scoular
BRITISH JU JITSU ASSOCIATION 5 Avenue Parade, Accrington BB5 6PN **T** 03333-202039 **E** bjjagb@icloud.com
W www.bjjagb.com
Chairman, Prof. Martin Dixon
BRITISH TAEKWONDO Manchester Regional Arena, Rowsley Street, Manchester M11 3FF **T** 01623-382020
E admin@britishtaekwondo.org.uk
W www.britishtaekwondo.org.uk
Chair, Jonny Cowan (interim)

MODERN PENTATHLON

PENTATHLON GB Sports Training Village, University of Bath, Bath BA2 7AY **T** 01225-386808 **E** admin@pentathlongb.org
W www.pentathlongb.org
Chief Executive, Sara Heath

MOTOR SPORTS

AUTO-CYCLE UNION ACU House, Rugby CV21 2YX
T 01788-566400 **E** admin@acu.org.uk **W** www.acu.org.uk
General Secretary, Gary Thompson, MBE
MOTORSPORT UK Motorsport UK House, Riverside Park, Colnbrook SL3 0HG **T** 01753-765000 **W** www.motorsportuk.org
Chief Executive, Hugh Chambers
SCOTTISH AUTO CYCLE UNION 28 West Main Street, Uphall EH52 5DW **T** 01506-858354 **E** office@sacu.co.uk
W www.sacu.co.uk
Chair, Sandy Mack

MOUNTAINEERING

BRITISH MOUNTAINEERING COUNCIL The Old Church, 177–179 Burton Road, Manchester M20 2BB **T** 0161-445 6111
E office@thebmc.co.uk **W** www.thebmc.co.uk
Chief Executive, Dave Turnbull

MULTI-SPORTS BODIES

ACTIVITY ALLIANCE Loughborough University, 3 Oakwood Drive, LE11 3QF **T** 01509-227750 **W** www.activityalliance.org.uk
Chief Executive, Barry Horne
BRITISH OLYMPIC ASSOCIATION 60 Charlotte Street, London W1T 2NU **T** 020-7842 5700 **E** boa@boa.org.uk
W www.teamgb.com
Chief Executive, Bill Sweeney
BRITISH PARALYMPIC ASSOCIATION 60 Charlotte Street, London W1T 2NU **T** 020-7842 5789 **E** info@paralympics.org.uk
W www.paralympics.org.uk
Chief Executive, Mike Sharrock
BRITISH UNIVERSITIES AND COLLEGES SPORT 20–24 Kings Bench Street, London SE1 0QX **T** 020-7633 5080
E info@bucs.org.uk **W** www.bucs.org.uk
Chief Executive, Vince Mayne
COMMONWEALTH GAMES ENGLAND 5th floor, Holborn Tower, 137–144 High Holborn, London WC1V 6PL
T 020-7831 3444 **E** info@teamengland.org
W www.teamengland.org
Chief Executive, Paul Blanchard
COMMONWEALTH GAMES FEDERATION
Commonwealth House, 55–58 Pall Mall, London SW1Y 5JH
T 020-7747 6427 **E** info@thecgf.com **W** www.thecgf.com
Chief Executive, David Grevemberg, CBE

NETBALL

ENGLAND NETBALL SportPark, 3 Oakwood Drive, Loughborough LE11 3QF **T** 01509-277850
E info@englandnetball.co.uk **W** www.englandnetball.co.uk
Chief Executive, Joanna Adams
NETBALL NI Unit F, Curlew Pavilion, Portside Business Park, Belfast BT3 9ED **T** 028-9073 6320
E bookingsandadmin@netballni.org **W** www.netballni.org
Chair, Geoff Wilson
NETBALL SCOTLAND Emirates Arena, 1000 London Road, Glasgow G40 3HY **T** 0141-428 3460
E membership@netballscotland.com
W www.netballscotland.com
Chief Executive, Claire Nelson
WELSH NETBALL ASSOCIATION Sport Wales National Centre, Sophia Gardens, Cardiff CF11 9SW **T** 029-2033 4950
E welshnetball@welshnetball.com **W** www.welshnetball.com
Chief Executive, Sarah Jones

ORIENTEERING

BRITISH ORIENTEERING Scholes Mill, Old Coach Road, Matlock DE4 5FY **T** 01629-583037
E info@britishorienteering.org.uk
W www.britishorienteering.org.uk
Chief Executive, Peter Hart

POLO

THE HURLINGHAM POLO ASSOCIATION Manor Farm, Little Coxwell, Faringdon SN7 7LW **T** 01367-242828 **E** enquiries@hpa-polo.co.uk **W** www.hpa-polo.co.uk
Chief Executive, David Woodd

RACKETS AND REAL TENNIS

TENNIS AND RACKETS ASSOCIATION c/o The Queen's Club, Palliser Road, London W14 9EQ **T** 020-7835 6937 **E** office@tennisandrackets.com **W** www.tennisandrackets.com
Chief Executive, C. S. Davies

ROWING

BRITISH ROWING 6 Lower Mall, London W6 9DJ **T** 020-8237 6700 **E** info@britishrowing.org **W** www.britishrowing.org
Chief Executive, Andy Parkinson
HENLEY ROYAL REGATTA Regatta Headquarters, Henley-on-Thames RG9 2LY **T** 01491-572153 **W** www.hrr.co.uk
Secretary, Daniel Grist

RUGBY LEAGUE

BRITISH AMATEUR RUGBY LEAGUE ASSOCIATION West Yorkshire House, 4 New North Parade, Huddersfield HD1 5JP **T** 01484-510682 **E** secretary@barla.org.uk **W** www.barla.org.uk
Chair, Sue Taylor
RUGBY FOOTBALL LEAGUE Red Hall, Red Hall Lane, Leeds LS17 8NB **T** 0330-111 1113 **E** enquiries@rfl.uk.co.uk **W** www.rugby-league.com
Chief Executive, Ralph Rimmer

RUGBY UNION

IRISH RUGBY FOOTBALL UNION 10–12 Lansdowne Road, Dublin 4 **T** (+353) 1647 3800 **E** info@irishrugby.ie **W** www.irishrugby.ie
Chief Executive, Philip Browne
RUGBY FOOTBALL UNION Rugby House, Twickenham Stadium, 200 Whitton Road, Twickenham TW2 7BA **T** 0871-222 2120 **E** enquiries@therfu.com **W** www.englandrugby.com
Chief Executive, Bill Sweeney
RUGBY FOOTBALL UNION FOR WOMEN Rugby House, Twickenham Stadium, 200 Whitton Road, Twickenham TW2 7BA **T** 0871-222 2120 **E** enquiries@therfu.com **W** www.englandrugby.com
Managing Director, Rosie Williams
SCOTTISH RUGBY UNION BT Murrayfield, Edinburgh EH12 5PJ **T** 0131-346 5000 **E** feedback@sru.org.uk **W** www.scottishrugby.org
Chief Executive, Mark Dodson
SCOTTISH WOMEN'S RUGBY UNION BT Murrayfield, Edinburgh EH12 5PJ **T** 0131-346 5000 **E** feedback@sru.org.uk **W** www.scottishrugby.org
Chief Executive, Mark Dodson
WELSH RUGBY UNION Principality Stadium, Westgate Street, Cardiff CF10 1NS **T** 0844-249 1999 **E** info@wru.co.uk **W** www.wru.wales
Chief Executive, Martyn Phillips

SHOOTING

BRITISH SHOOTING Bisham Abbey National Sports Centre, Marlow Road, Marlow SL7 1RR **T** 01628-488800 **E** admin@britishshooting.org.uk **W** www.britishshooting.org.uk
Chief Executive, Hamish McInnes
CLAY PIGEON SHOOTING ASSOCIATION Edmonton House, National Shooting Centre, Brookwood, Woking GU24 0NP **T** 01483-485400 **E** info@cpsa.co.uk **W** www.cpsa.co.uk
Chief Executive, Iain Parker

NATIONAL RIFLE ASSOCIATION Bisley Camp, Brookwood GU24 0PB **T** 01483-797777 **E** info@nra.org.uk **W** www.nra.org.uk
Chief Executive, John Webster
NATIONAL SMALL-BORE RIFLE ASSOCIATION Lord Roberts Centre, Bisley Camp, Woking GU24 0NP **T** 01483-485502 **W** www.nsra.co.uk
Chair, Robert Newman

SKIING AND SNOWBOARDING

GB SNOWSPORT 60 Charlotte Street, London W1T 2NU **T** 020-7842 5764 **E** info@gbsnowsport.com **W** www.gbsnowsport.com
Chief Executive, Victoria Gosling, OBE

SPEEDWAY

BRITISH SPEEDWAY ACU Headquarters, Wood Street, Rugby CV21 2YX **T** 01788-560648 **E** office@speedwaygb.co.uk **W** www.speedwaygb.co.uk
Chair, Keith Chapman

SQUASH

ENGLAND SQUASH National Squash Centre, Manchester M11 3FF **T** 0161-231 4499 **W** www.englandsquash.com
Chief Executive, Keir Worth
SCOTTISH SQUASH Oriam, Edinburgh EH14 4AS **T** 0131-451 8525 **E** info@scottishsquash.org **W** www.scottishsquash.org
Chief Executive, Maggie Still
WALES SQUASH AND RACKETBALL Sport Wales National Centre, Sophia Close, Cardiff CF11 9SW **T** 0300-300 3121 **W** www.walessquashandracketball.co.uk
General Manager, Gareth Hall

SUB-AQUA

BRITISH SUB-AQUA CLUB Telford's Quay, South Pier Road, Ellesmere Port CH65 4FL **T** 0151-350 6200 **E** info@bsac.com **W** www.bsac.com
Chief Executive, Mary Tetley

SWIMMING

SWIM ENGLAND Pavilion 3, Sport Park, Loughborough LE11 3QF **T** 01509-618700 **E** customerservices@swimming.org **W** www.swimming.org
Chief Executive, Jane Nickerson
SCOTTISH SWIMMING National Swimming Academy, University of Stirling, FK9 4LA **T** 01786-466520 **E** info@scottishswimming.com **W** www.scottishswimming.com
Chief Executive, Forbes Dunlop
SWIM WALES WNPS, Sketty Lane, Swansea SA2 8QG **T** 01792-513636 **W** www.swimwales.org
Chief Executive, Fergus Feeney

TABLE TENNIS

TABLE TENNIS ENGLAND Bradwell Road, Milton Keynes MK8 9LA **T** 01908-208860 **E** help@tabletennisengland.co.uk **W** www.tabletennisengland.co.uk
Chief Executive, Sara Sutcliffe
TABLE TENNIS SCOTLAND Caledonia House, South Gyle, Edinburgh EH12 9DQ **T** 0131-317 8077 **E** info@tabletennisscotland.co.uk **W** www.tabletennisscotland.co.uk
Chair, Terry McLernon, MBE
TABLE TENNIS WALES Glanrhyd, Ebbw View, Ebbw Vale NP23 5NU **T** 01244-571335 **W** www.tabletennis.wales
Company Secretary, Neil O'Connell

TRIATHLON

BRITISH TRIATHLON PO Box 25, Loughborough LE11 3WX
T 01509-226161 E info@britishtriathlon.org
W www.britishtriathlon.org
Chief Executive, Andy Salmon

VOLLEYBALL

NORTHERN IRELAND VOLLEYBALL ASSOCIATION 7
Greengage Cottages, Ballymoney BT53 6GZ
W www.nivolleyball.com
General Secretary, Paddy Elder
SCOTTISH VOLLEYBALL ASSOCIATION 48 The
Pleasance, Edinburgh EH8 9TJ T 0131-556 4633
E info@scottishvolleyball.org W www.scottishvolleyball.org
Chief Executive, Margaret Ann Fleming
VOLLEYBALL ENGLAND SportPark, Loughborough University,
3 Oakwood Drive, Loughborough LE11 3QF T 01509-227722
E info@volleyballengland.org W www.volleyballengland.org
Chief Executive, Janet Inman
VOLLEYBALL WALES 13 Beckgrove Close, Cardiff CF24 2SE
T 029-2041 6537 E yperkins@cardiffmet.ac.uk
W www.volleyballwales.org
Chair, Yvonne Perkins

WALKING

RACE WALKING ASSOCIATION Hufflers, Heard's Lane,
Brentwood CM15 0SF T 01277-220687
E racewalkingassociation@btinternet.com
W www.racewalkingassociation.com
Hon. General Secretary, Colin Vesty

WATER SKIING

BRITISH WATER SKI AND WAKEBOARD The Forum,
Hanworth Lane, Chertsey KT16 9JX T 01932-560007
E info@bwsf.co.uk W www.bwsw.org.uk
Chief Executive, Patrick Donovan

WEIGHTLIFTING

BRITISH WEIGHT LIFTING St Ann's Mill, Kirkstall Road,
Leeds LS5 3AE T 0113-224 9402
E enquiries@britishweightlifting.org
W www.britishweightlifting.org
Chief Executive, Ashley Metcalfe

WRESTLING

BRITISH WRESTLING ASSOCIATION 41 Great Clowes St,
Salford M7 1RQ T 0161-835 2112 E admin@britishwrestling.org
W www.britishwrestling.org
Chief Executive, Colin Nicholson

YACHTING

ROYAL YACHTING ASSOCIATION RYA House, Ensign
Way, Southampton SO31 4YA T 023-8060 4100
E enquiries@rya.org.uk W www.rya.org.uk
Chief Executive, Sarah Treseder

TIME AND SPACE

ASTRONOMY

The following pages give astronomical data for each month of the year 2020. There are four pages of data for each month. All data are given for 0h Greenwich Mean Time (GMT), ie at midnight at the beginning of the day named. This applies also to data for the months when British Summer Time is in operation (for dates, see below). GMT and Universal Time (UT), the term used by astronomers, are effectively the same, see page 629.

The astronomical data are given in a form suitable for observation with the naked eye or with a small telescope. These data do not attempt to replace the *Astronomical Almanac* for professional astronomers. Positions are given for the equinox of JNow (2019). The difference between JNow and J2000 (used by astronomers) is minimal, typically about one arc minute.

A fuller explanation of how to use the astronomical data is given on pages 626–628.

CALENDAR FOR EACH MONTH

The calendar for each month comprises dates of general interest plus the dates of birth or death of well-known people. The theme for this edition is Astronomy, Space and Physics. For key religious, civil and legal dates see page 9. For details of flag-flying days see page 23. For royal birthdays see pages 23 and 24–5. For public holidays see also pages 10 and 11.

Fuller explanations of the various calendars can be found under Time Measurement and Calendars.

The zodiacal signs through which the Sun is passing each month are illustrated.

JULIAN DATE

The Julian date on 2020 January 0.0 is 2458848.5. To find the Julian date for any other date in 2020 (at 0h GMT), add the day-of-the-year number on the extreme right of the calendar for each month to the Julian date for January 0.0.

BRITISH SUMMER TIME

British Summer Time is the legal time for general purposes during the period in which it is in operation (see also page 631). During this period, clocks are kept one hour ahead of Greenwich Mean Time. The hour of changeover is 01h Greenwich Mean Time. The duration of Summer Time in 2020 is from March 29 01h GMT to October 25 01h GMT.

SEASONS

The seasons are defined astronomically as follows:

Spring from the vernal equinox to the summer solstice
Summer from the summer solstice to the autumnal equinox
Autumn from the autumnal equinox to the winter solstice
Winter from the winter solstice to the vernal equinox

The times when the seasons start in 2020 are:

Northern Hemisphere

Vernal Equinox	March 20d 03h 50m GMT
Summer Solstice	June 20d 21h 44m GMT
Autumnal Equinox	September 22d 13h 31m GMT
Winter Solstice	December 21d 10h 02m GMT

Southern Hemisphere

Autumnal Equinox	March 20d 03h 50m GMT
Winter Solstice	June 20d 21h 44m GMT
Vernal Equinox	September 22d 13h 31m GMT
Summer Solstice	December 21d 10h 02m GMT

The longest day of the year, measured from sunrise to sunset, is at the summer solstice. The longest day in the UK will fall on 20 June in 2020.

The shortest day of the year, measured from sunrise to sunset, is at the winter solstice. The shortest day in the UK will fall on 21 December in 2020.

The equinox is the instant when the Sun's declination is zero, effectively when day and night are of equal length all over the world.

In popular parlance, the seasons in the northern hemisphere comprise the following months:

Spring	March, April, May
Summer	June, July, August
Autumn	September, October, November
Winter	December, January, February

The March equinox can fall as early as 19 March but this has not happened since 1796 and it will not happen again until 2044. This equinox in 2007 was on 21 March, however in 2008 it occurred on 20 March and will not revert to 21 March again until 2102.

In 2008 the June solstice occurred on 20 June, the first time since 1897. The June solstice in 1975 was on 22 June, but it will not occur on this date again until 2203.

January 2020

FIRST MONTH, 31 DAYS. *Janus,* god of the portal, facing two ways, past and future

1	*Wednesday*	Italian astronomer Giuseppe Pazzi discovers the first asteroid, Ceres 1801	day 1
2	*Thursday*	Solar system age set at 4,950,000,000 years by John Reynolds, American physicist 1960	2
3	*Friday*	Oklahoma meteorite visable over large area of US midwest 1970	3
4	*Saturday*	Isaac Newton, physicist and mathematician who discovered the law of gravitation *b.* 1643	4
5	*Sunday*	John Watts Young, commander of first ever space shuttle mission *d.* 2018	5

6	*Monday*	Rotation of the Earth proved by León Foucault 1851	week 1 day 6
7	*Tuesday*	Galileo Galilei makes his first dated telescopic observations of the Moon 1610	7
8	*Wednesday*	Stephen Hawking, theoretical physicist and cosmologist *b.* 1942	8
9	*Thursday*	Heber Curtis, American astronomer who advocated that galaxies other than the Milky Way, exist *d.* 1942	9
10	*Friday*	Robert Woodrow Wilson, winner of 1978 Nobel Prize for Physics *b.* 1936	10
11	*Saturday*	German astronomer William Herschel discovers the first two moons of Uranus 1787	11
12	*Sunday*	Sergey Pavlovich Korolev, Soviet rocket and spacecraft designer *b.* 1907	12

13	*Monday*	NASA selects six women as their first female astronaut candidates for its training programme 1978	week 2 day 13
14	*Tuesday*	Edmond Halley, Astronomer Royal after whom Halley's Comet is named *d.* 1742	14
15	*Wednesday*	Edward Teller, participant in the creation of the first atomic bomb, *b.* 1908	15
16	*Thursday*	William Pickering, who discovered the ninth moon of Saturn *d.* 1938	16
17	*Friday*	Clyde Tombaugh, astronomer who discovered Pluto *d.* 1997	17
18	*Saturday*	An unobserved meteorite strikes a house in Missouri, US 1916	18
19	*Sunday*	Jacobus Kapteyn, Dutch astronomer who determined the movements of stars *b.* 1851	19

20	*Monday*	Edwin 'Buzz' Aldrin, the second man to walk on the Moon *b.* 1930	week 3 day 20
21	*Tuesday*	John Couch Adams, one of two who discovered Neptune *d.* 1892	21
22	*Wednesday*	Roberta Bondar becomes the first Canadian woman in space 1992	22
23	*Thursday*	Georg Bernhard Bilfinger, German author of treatises in astronomy and physics *b.* 1693	23
24	*Friday*	The first motion picture of a total solar eclipse is recorded 1925	24
25	*Saturday*	Robert Boyle, physicist and chemist, known for Boyle's Law *b.* 1627	25
26	*Sunday*	Polykarp Kusch, a German-American quantum physicist *b.* 1911	26

27	*Monday*	A cabin fire during a launch rehearsal of *Apollo 1* results in the deaths of all three crew members 1967	week 4 day 27
28	*Tuesday*	The space shuttle *Challenger* explodes shortly after lift-off, killing all seven crew members 1986	28
29	*Wednesday*	Abdus Salam, Pakistani-British nuclear physicist *b.* 1926	29
30	*Thursday*	John Bardeen, twice winner of the Nobel Prize for physics *d.* 1991	30
31	*Friday*	Ham, a chimp, returns safely to Earth after being sent into space 1961	31

ASTRONOMICAL PHENOMENA

d	h	
4	9	Peak Quadrantid meteor stream
5	8	Earth at perihelion
5	17	Vesta 2° south of the Moon
7	18	Aldebaran 3° south of the Moon
10	19	Penumbral lunar eclipse
12	0	Moon 1° north of the Beehive cluster
12	7	Pluto 1° north of Mercury
18	19	Metis less than 0.5° south of Uranus
27	18	Neptune less than 0.2° north-east of Venus

MINIMA OF ALGOL

d	h	d	h	d	h
2	20.4	14	7.7	25	19.0
5	17.2	17	4.5	28	15.8
8	14.1	20	1.3	31	12.6
11	10.9	22	22.2		

CONSTELLATIONS

The following constellations are near the meridian at

	d	h		d	h
December	1	24	January	16	21
December	16	23	February	1	20
January	1	22	February	15	19

Draco (below the Pole), Ursa Minor (below the Pole), Camelopardalis, Perseus, Auriga, Taurus, Orion, Eridanus and Lepus

THE MOON

Phase, Apsides and Node	d	h	m
◐ First Quarter	3	4	45
○ Full Moon	10	19	21
◑ Last Quarter	17	12	58
● New Moon	24	21	42
Apogee (404,580 km)	2	1	30
Perigee (365,958 km)	13	20	21
Apogee (405,392 km)	29	21	27

Mean longitude of the ascending node on 1st, 98°

THE SUN   Diam. 32.5′

Day	Right Ascension			Dec.	Equation of time		Rise		Transit		Set			Sidereal time			Transit of first point of Aries		
							52°	56°			52°		56°						
	h	m	s	°	m	s	h m	h m	h	m	h m		h m	h	m	s	h	m	s
1	18	43	36	−23.1	−3	08	8 08	8 30	12	03	15 59		15 36	6	40	29	17	16	40
2	18	48	01	−23.0	−3	36	8 08	8 30	12	04	16 00		15 38	6	44	26	17	12	44
3	18	52	25	−22.9	−4	04	8 07	8 30	12	04	16 01		15 39	6	48	22	17	08	49
4	18	56	50	−22.8	−4	32	8 07	8 30	12	05	16 02		15 40	6	52	19	17	04	53
5	19	01	14	−22.7	−4	59	8 07	8 29	12	05	16 04		15 41	6	56	15	17	00	57
6	19	05	37	−22.6	−5	26	8 07	8 29	12	06	16 05		15 43	7	00	12	16	57	01
7	19	10	00	−22.5	−5	53	8 06	8 28	12	06	16 06		15 44	7	04	09	16	53	05
8	19	14	23	−22.3	−6	18	8 06	8 27	12	07	16 07		15 46	7	08	05	16	49	09
9	19	18	45	−22.2	−6	44	8 05	8 27	12	07	16 09		15 47	7	12	02	16	45	13
10	19	23	06	−22.1	−7	09	8 05	8 26	12	07	16 10		15 49	7	15	58	16	41	17
11	19	27	27	−21.9	−7	33	8 04	8 25	12	08	16 12		15 51	7	19	55	16	37	21
12	19	31	47	−21.8	−7	57	8 04	8 24	12	08	16 13		15 52	7	23	51	16	33	25
13	19	36	07	−21.6	−8	20	8 03	8 23	12	09	16 15		15 54	7	27	48	16	29	29
14	19	40	26	−21.4	−8	43	8 02	8 22	12	09	16 16		15 56	7	31	44	16	25	34
15	19	44	45	−21.3	−9	05	8 01	8 21	12	09	16 18		15 58	7	35	41	16	21	38
16	19	49	03	−21.1	−9	26	8 01	8 20	12	10	16 19		15 59	7	39	38	16	17	42
17	19	53	20	−20.9	−9	47	8 00	8 19	12	10	16 21		16 01	7	43	34	16	13	46
18	19	57	36	−20.7	−10	07	7 59	8 18	12	10	16 22		16 03	7	47	31	16	09	50
19	20	01	52	−20.5	−10	26	7 58	8 17	12	11	16 24		16 05	7	51	27	16	05	54
20	20	06	08	−20.3	−10	45	7 57	8 15	12	11	16 26		16 07	7	55	24	16	01	58
21	20	10	22	−20.1	−11	03	7 56	8 14	12	11	16 27		16 09	7	59	20	15	58	02
22	20	14	36	−19.8	−11	20	7 54	8 13	12	11	16 29		16 11	8	03	17	15	54	06
23	20	18	49	−19.6	−11	36	7 53	8 11	12	12	16 31		16 13	8	07	13	15	50	10
24	20	23	01	−19.4	−11	52	7 52	8 10	12	12	16 33		16 15	8	11	10	15	46	14
25	20	27	12	−19.1	−12	07	7 51	8 08	12	12	16 34		16 17	8	15	07	15	42	19
26	20	31	23	−18.9	−12	21	7 49	8 06	12	12	16 36		16 19	8	19	03	15	38	23
27	20	35	33	−18.6	−12	34	7 48	8 05	12	13	16 38		16 21	8	23	00	15	34	27
28	20	39	42	−18.4	−12	47	7 47	8 03	12	13	16 40		16 23	8	26	56	15	30	31
29	20	43	50	−18.1	−12	58	7 45	8 01	12	13	16 41		16 26	8	30	53	15	26	35
30	20	47	58	−17.9	−13	09	7 44	8 00	12	13	16 43		16 28	8	34	49	15	22	39
31	20	52	04	−17.6	−13	19	7 42	7 58	12	13	16 45		16 30	8	38	46	15	18	43

DURATION OF TWILIGHT (in minutes)

Latitude	52°	56°	52°	56°	52°	56°
	1 January		11 January		21 January	
Civil	41	47	40	45	38	43
Nautical	84	96	82	93	80	90
Astronomical	125	141	123	138	120	134

THE NIGHT SKY

Mercury (magnitude −1.0) can be found just above the south-western horizon the last few evenings of January once its elongation improves following superior conjunction on the 10th. A two-day-old Moon is a little to its upper left on the 26th.

Venus (magnitude −4.0) continues a fine evening apparition this winter. It passes 4′ from Neptune (magnitude 7.9) on the 27th but a telescope is required to separate the dimmer world from the glare of Venus. The Moon is 4° away the following evening.

Mars (magnitude 1.5) rises just over three hours before the Sun mid-month. It crosses from Libra into Scorpius on the 8th then Ophiuchus on the 15th, around when Mars is not far from Antares but is dimmer than its stellar rival. The Moon is near Mars on the 20th and 21st.

Jupiter (magnitude −1.8), in Sagittarius, slowly emerges from the solar glare and is low in the southeast before sunrise from the last week. The Moon is in the area on the 22nd but has barely risen as the sky brightens when close to Jupiter on the 23rd.

Saturn (magnitude 0.5), also in Sagittarius, is too close to the Sun all month unfortunately as it moves from the evening sky through superior conjunction on the 13th – the same day as Pluto – and into the morning sky.

The Moon passes north of Earth's shadow during the penumbral lunar eclipse (magnitude 0.886) on the 10th. Some staining of the Moon's southern limb may be noticed mid-eclipse.

THE MOON

Day	R.A.		Dec	Hor Par	Diam	Sun Co-Long	PA of Br. limb	Ph.	Age	Rise 52°		Rise 56°		Transit		Set 52°		Set 56°	
	h	m	°	'	'	°	°	%	d	h	m	h	m	h	m	h	m	h	m
1	23	17	−10.0	54.3	29.6	335	249	30	5.1	11	37	11	44	17	05	22	44	22	39
2	0	01	−5.6	54.2	29.6	348	248	39	6.1	11	53	11	56	17	46	23	51	23	50
3	0	45	−0.9	54.3	29.6	360	247	48	7.1	12	09	12	08	18	27	—	—	—	—
4	1	28	+3.7	54.5	29.8	12	247	58	8.1	12	25	12	20	19	09	0	58	1	01
5	2	13	+8.3	55.0	30.0	24	249	67	9.1	12	43	12	34	19	52	2	06	2	14
6	3	00	+12.7	55.5	30.2	36	251	76	10.1	13	04	12	51	20	39	3	17	3	29
7	3	50	+16.6	56.2	30.6	48	254	84	11.1	13	30	13	12	21	29	4	29	4	46
8	4	42	+19.8	57.0	31.0	60	259	91	12.1	14	05	13	42	22	23	5	41	6	02
9	5	39	+22.1	57.8	31.4	73	265	96	13.1	14	49	14	23	23	21	6	51	7	17
10	6	38	+23.2	58.5	31.8	85	274	99	14.1	15	46	15	20	—	—	7	54	8	21
11	7	39	+22.8	59.1	32.2	97	72	100	15.1	16	57	16	33	0	20	8	48	9	12
12	8	40	+21.0	59.6	32.4	109	96	98	16.1	18	16	17	58	1	20	9	30	9	49
13	9	40	+17.8	59.8	32.6	121	103	94	17.1	19	40	19	26	2	18	10	02	10	17
14	10	38	+13.4	59.9	32.6	133	107	87	18.1	21	04	20	56	3	13	10	29	10	38
15	11	33	+8.4	59.8	32.6	145	110	78	19.1	22	27	22	24	4	06	10	50	10	55
16	12	27	+2.9	59.5	32.4	158	111	68	20.1	23	49	23	51	4	57	11	11	11	11
17	13	19	−2.7	59.2	32.2	170	111	56	21.1	—	—	—	—	5	47	11	30	11	26
18	14	11	−8.1	58.8	32.0	182	110	45	22.1	1	09	1	17	6	37	11	51	11	42
19	15	03	−13.0	58.3	31.8	194	108	34	23.1	2	29	2	42	7	27	12	15	12	02
20	15	57	−17.2	57.8	31.6	206	104	24	24.1	3	47	4	04	8	19	12	43	12	25
21	16	52	−20.3	57.3	31.2	218	99	16	25.1	5	01	5	24	9	13	13	19	12	57
22	17	48	−22.4	56.9	31.0	231	93	09	26.1	6	09	6	34	10	07	14	04	13	37
23	18	45	−23.2	56.4	30.8	243	85	04	27.1	7	06	7	33	11	01	14	57	14	30
24	19	40	−22.8	55.9	30.4	255	73	01	28.1	7	53	8	18	11	54	15	59	15	34
25	20	34	−21.2	55.4	30.2	267	321	00	29.1	8	31	8	51	12	45	17	05	16	45
26	21	26	−18.6	55.0	30.0	279	267	01	0.6	8	59	9	16	13	32	18	14	17	59
27	22	15	−15.3	54.6	29.8	291	258	04	1.6	9	23	9	35	14	18	19	22	19	12
28	23	02	−11.3	54.3	29.6	304	254	09	2.6	9	42	9	50	15	00	20	30	20	23
29	23	46	−7.0	54.1	29.6	316	251	15	3.6	9	58	10	03	15	42	21	37	21	34
30	0	30	−2.4	54.1	29.4	328	250	22	4.6	10	14	10	15	16	22	22	43	22	45
31	1	14	+2.3	54.2	29.6	340	250	31	5.6	10	30	10	26	17	03	23	50	23	56

MERCURY

Day	R.A.		Dec	Mag.	Diam.	Phase	Rise		Transit		Set	
	h	m	°		"	%	h	m	h	m	h	m
1	18	19.3	−24.6	−0.9	5	99	8	09	11	39	15	09
3	18	33.3	−24.7	−0.9	5	99	8	15	11	45	15	15
5	18	47.3	−24.6	−1.0	5	100	8	21	11	51	15	21
7	19	01.3	−24.4	−1.1	5	100	8	25	11	57	15	29
9	19	15.5	−24.2	−1.2	5	100	8	30	12	04	15	38
11	19	29.7	−23.8	−1.2	5	100	8	33	12	10	15	47
13	19	43.9	−23.3	−1.2	5	100	8	36	12	16	15	57
15	19	58.1	−22.8	−1.2	5	100	8	38	12	22	16	08
17	20	12.3	−22.1	−1.2	5	99	8	39	12	29	16	19
19	20	26.5	−21.3	−1.1	5	99	8	39	12	35	16	31
21	20	40.6	−20.5	−1.1	5	98	8	39	12	41	16	44
23	20	54.6	−19.5	−1.1	5	97	8	38	12	47	16	57
25	21	08.4	−18.4	−1.1	5	95	8	37	12	53	17	10
27	21	22.0	−17.3	−1.1	5	93	8	35	12	59	17	24
29	21	35.4	−16.0	−1.0	5	90	8	32	13	04	17	37
31	21	48.3	−14.7	−1.0	6	87	8	29	13	09	17	51

Rising and setting times are for latitude 54°

VENUS

Day	R.A.		Dec	Mag.	Diam.	Phase	Rise		Transit		Set	
	h	m	°		"	%	h	m	h	m	h	m
1	21	09.8	−18.3	−4.0	14	82	10	12	14	28	18	45
6	21	34.1	−16.3	−4.0	14	81	10	03	14	33	19	03
11	21	57.8	−14.2	−4.0	15	80	9	54	14	37	19	20
16	22	20.9	−12.0	−4.0	15	78	9	44	14	40	19	37
21	22	43.5	−9.6	−4.1	15	77	9	33	14	43	19	54
26	23	05.7	−7.1	−4.1	16	75	9	21	14	45	20	11
31	23	27.4	−4.5	−4.1	16	74	9	08	14	47	20	27

MARS

Day	R.A.		Dec	Mag.	Diam.	Phase	Rise		Transit		Set	
	h	m	°		"	%	h	m	h	m	h	m
1	15	44.9	−19.4	+1.6	4	96	4	56	9	03	13	11
6	15	58.9	−20.2	+1.5	4	95	4	55	8	58	13	00
11	16	13.0	−20.9	+1.5	4	95	4	54	8	52	12	50
16	16	27.3	−21.5	+1.5	5	95	4	53	8	47	12	40
21	16	41.7	−22.1	+1.4	5	94	4	52	8	41	12	31
26	16	56.3	−22.5	+1.4	5	94	4	51	8	36	12	22
31	17	10.9	−22.9	+1.4	5	93	4	49	8	31	12	14

SUNRISE AND SUNSET

	London 0° 05′ | 51° 30′		Bristol 2° 35′ | 51° 28′		Birmingham 1° 55′ | 52° 28′		Manchester 2° 15′ | 53° 28′		Newcastle 1° 37′ | 54° 59′		Glasgow 4° 14′ | 55° 52′		Belfast 5° 56′ | 54° 35′	
d	h m	h m	h m	h m	h m	h m	h m	h m	h m	h m	h m	h m	h m	h m
1	8 06	16 02	8 16	16 12	8 18	16 04	8 25	16 00	8 31	15 49	8 47	15 53	8 46	16 08
2	8 06	16 03	8 16	16 13	8 18	16 05	8 25	16 01	8 31	15 50	8 47	15 55	8 46	16 09
3	8 06	16 04	8 16	16 14	8 18	16 06	8 25	16 02	8 31	15 51	8 47	15 56	8 46	16 11
4	8 06	16 05	8 15	16 15	8 18	16 07	8 24	16 03	8 30	15 52	8 46	15 57	8 45	16 12
5	8 05	16 06	8 15	16 16	8 17	16 09	8 24	16 05	8 30	15 54	8 46	15 59	8 45	16 13
6	8 05	16 07	8 15	16 17	8 17	16 10	8 24	16 06	8 30	15 55	8 45	16 00	8 45	16 14
7	8 05	16 08	8 14	16 19	8 17	16 11	8 23	16 07	8 29	15 56	8 45	16 01	8 44	16 16
8	8 04	16 10	8 14	16 20	8 16	16 12	8 23	16 09	8 28	15 58	8 44	16 03	8 43	16 17
9	8 04	16 11	8 13	16 21	8 16	16 14	8 22	16 10	8 28	15 59	8 44	16 05	8 43	16 19
10	8 03	16 12	8 13	16 23	8 15	16 15	8 21	16 12	8 27	16 01	8 43	16 06	8 42	16 20
11	8 03	16 14	8 12	16 24	8 14	16 17	8 21	16 13	8 26	16 02	8 42	16 08	8 41	16 22
12	8 02	16 15	8 12	16 26	8 14	16 18	8 20	16 15	8 25	16 04	8 41	16 09	8 41	16 24
13	8 01	16 17	8 11	16 27	8 13	16 20	8 19	16 16	8 25	16 06	8 40	16 11	8 40	16 25
14	8 00	16 18	8 10	16 28	8 12	16 21	8 18	16 18	8 24	16 07	8 39	16 13	8 39	16 27
15	8 00	16 20	8 10	16 30	8 11	16 23	8 17	16 19	8 23	16 09	8 38	16 15	8 38	16 29
16	7 59	16 21	8 09	16 32	8 10	16 24	8 16	16 21	8 22	16 11	8 37	16 17	8 37	16 30
17	7 58	16 23	8 08	16 33	8 10	16 26	8 15	16 23	8 20	16 13	8 36	16 19	8 36	16 32
18	7 57	16 25	8 07	16 35	8 09	16 28	8 14	16 25	8 19	16 15	8 34	16 20	8 35	16 34
19	7 56	16 26	8 06	16 36	8 07	16 29	8 13	16 26	8 18	16 16	8 33	16 22	8 33	16 36
20	7 55	16 28	8 05	16 38	8 06	16 31	8 12	16 28	8 17	16 18	8 32	16 24	8 32	16 38
21	7 54	16 30	8 04	16 40	8 05	16 33	8 11	16 30	8 16	16 20	8 30	16 26	8 31	16 40
22	7 53	16 31	8 03	16 41	8 04	16 35	8 10	16 32	8 14	16 22	8 29	16 28	8 30	16 41
23	7 52	16 33	8 02	16 43	8 03	16 36	8 08	16 34	8 13	16 24	8 28	16 30	8 28	16 43
24	7 51	16 35	8 00	16 45	8 02	16 38	8 07	16 35	8 11	16 26	8 26	16 32	8 27	16 45
25	7 49	16 36	7 59	16 47	8 00	16 40	8 06	16 37	8 10	16 28	8 24	16 34	8 25	16 47
26	7 48	16 38	7 58	16 48	7 59	16 42	8 04	16 39	8 08	16 30	8 23	16 37	8 24	16 49
27	7 47	16 40	7 57	16 50	7 58	16 44	8 03	16 41	8 07	16 32	8 21	16 39	8 22	16 51
28	7 45	16 42	7 55	16 52	7 56	16 45	8 01	16 43	8 05	16 34	8 19	16 41	8 21	16 53
29	7 44	16 43	7 54	16 54	7 55	16 47	8 00	16 45	8 03	16 36	8 18	16 43	8 19	16 55
30	7 43	16 45	7 52	16 55	7 53	16 49	7 58	16 47	8 02	16 38	8 16	16 45	8 17	16 57
31	7 41	16 47	7 51	16 57	7 52	16 51	7 57	16 49	8 00	16 40	8 14	16 47	8 16	16 59

JUPITER

Day	R.A. h m	Dec °	Mag.	Diam. ″	Rise h m	Transit h m	Set h m
1	18 29.1	−23.2	−1.8	32	8 06	11 47	15 28
11	18 39.1	−23.1	−1.8	32	7 36	11 17	14 59
21	18 48.9	−22.9	−1.9	32	7 05	10 48	14 31
31	18 58.5	−22.7	−1.9	32	6 34	10 18	14 03

Diam. = equatorial; Polar Diam. is 94% of Equatorial Diam.

SATURN

Day	R.A. h m	Dec °	Mag.	Diam. ″	Rise h m	Transit h m	Set h m
1	19 32.5	−21.7	+0.5	15	8 58	12 50	16 42
11	19 37.5	−21.5	+0.5	15	8 22	12 16	16 09
21	19 42.5	−21.3	+0.5	15	7 47	11 41	15 36
31	19 47.5	−21.1	+0.6	15	7 11	11 07	15 03

Diam. = equatorial; Polar Diam. is 90% of Equatorial Diam.
Rings – major axis 34″, minor axis 13″, Tilt 23°

URANUS

Day	R.A. h m	Dec °	Mag.	Diam. ″	Rise h m	Transit h m	Set h m
1	02 02.7	+11.9	+5.7	4	12 08	19 19	2 34
11	02 02.5	+11.9	+5.8	4	11 29	18 40	1 54
21	02 02.7	+12.0	+5.8	4	10 50	18 00	1 15
31	02 03.2	+12.0	+5.8	4	10 11	17 22	0 36

NEPTUNE

Day	R.A. h m	Dec °	Mag.	Diam. ″	Rise h m	Transit h m	Set h m
1	23 11.1	−6.4	+7.9	2	11 00	16 28	21 56
11	23 11.9	−6.3	+7.9	2	10 21	15 49	21 18
21	23 12.8	−6.2	+7.9	2	9 42	15 11	20 40
31	23 14.0	−6.0	+7.9	2	9 03	14 33	20 02

February 2020

SECOND MONTH, 28 or 29 DAYS. *Februa*, Roman festival of Purification

1	*Saturday*	The space shuttle *Columbia* breaks up as it re-enters the Earth's atmosphere 2003	day 32
2	*Sunday*	All eight planets align for the first time in 400 years 1962	33

3	*Monday*	The Soviet Union's *Luna 9* becomes the first controlled spacecraft to land on the Moon 1966	week 5 day 34
4	*Tuesday*	Clyde Tombaugh, astronomer who discovered Pluto *b.* 1906	35
5	*Wednesday*	The Sun, the Moon, Mercury, Venus, Mars, Jupiter and Saturn line up within 16 degrees 1962	36
6	*Thursday*	Alan Shepard, *Apollo 14* astronaut becomes the first and only person to hit a golf ball on the Moon 1971	37
7	*Friday*	Two Challenger spaceshuttle astronauts perform the first untethered spacewalk 1984	38
8	*Saturday*	Meteorite pieces fall in Mexico at 01h 05m 1969	39
9	*Sunday*	*Apollo 14* returns to Earth after the third successful manned Moon landing 1971	40

10	*Monday*	MIT's Lincoln Laboratory announces it has bounced radar waves off Venus 1958	week 6 day 41
11	*Tuesday*	Japan becomes the fourth country to put a satellite, *Osumi*, into orbit 1970	42
12	*Wednesday*	Soviet Union probe, *Venera 1*, is launched towards Venus 1961	43
13	*Thursday*	Galileo Galilei arrives in Rome for the start of his trial for heresy 1633	44
14	*Friday*	Fritz Zwicky, who proposed the existence of dark matter in the universe *b.* 1898	45
15	*Saturday*	Galileo Galilei, mathematician and astronomer *b.* 1564	46
16	*Sunday*	Miranda, famous moon of Uranus, is photographed 1948	47

17	*Monday*	The *Ranger 8* probe launches on a mission to photograph the Moon's Sea of Tranquility 1965	week 7 day 48
18	*Tuesday*	Pluto, then regarded as our solar system's ninth planet, is discovered by Clyde Tombaugh 1930	49
19	*Wednesday*	Nicholas Copernicus, astronomer who proposed the Earth and other planets revolved around the Sun *b.* 1473	50
20	*Thursday*	The Soviet Union launches *Mir*, the world's largest space station 1986	51
21	*Friday*	British physicist and engineer Osborne Reynolds *d.* 1912	52
22	*Saturday*	Heinrich Hertz, physicist after whom the unit of frequency is named *b.* 1857	53
23	*Sunday*	Allan MacLeod Cormack, Nobel laureate and inventor of the CT scanner *b.* 1924	54

24	*Monday*	John Herapath, English physicist known for his early account of the kinetic theory of gases in 1820 *d.* 1868	week 8 day 55
25	*Tuesday*	Thomas Wright, physicist who first proposed the Earth lay in a flat orbit *d.* 1786	56
26	*Wednesday*	Robert Watson-Watt carries out a demonstration that leads to the development of radar technology 1935	57
27	*Thursday*	James Stanley Hey discovers that the Sun radiates radio waves 1942	58
28	*Friday*	Gamma rays strike the Earth and are followed by an afterglow from a galaxy 8.1 billion light years away 1997	59
29	*Saturday*	John Theophilus Desaguliers, French-English experimental assistant to Isaac Newton *d.* 1744	60

ASTRONOMICAL PHENOMENA

d	*h*	
9	22	Regulus 4° south of the Moon
10	14	Mercury greatest elongation east (18°)
12	6	Galilean moons all to the west of Jupiter
13	7	Galilean moons all to the west of Jupiter
19	20	Jupiter 1° north of the Moon
20	14	Saturn 2° north of the Moon
21	13	Ceres 3° south of the Moon
25	5	Galilean moons all to the east of Jupiter
25	6	Mars, Saturn and Jupiter visible

MINIMA OF ALGOL

d	*h*	*d*	*h*	*d*	*h*
3	9.5	14	20.8	26	8.0
6	6.3	17	17.6	29	4.9
9	3.1	20	14.4		
11	23.9	23	11.2		

CONSTELLATIONS

The following constellations are near the meridian at

	d	*h*		*d*	*h*
January	1	24	February	15	21
January	16	23	March	1	20
February	1	22	March	16	19

Draco (below the Pole), Camelopardalis, Auriga, Taurus, Gemini, Orion, Canis Minor, Monoceros, Lepus, Canis Major and Puppis

THE MOON

Phase, Apsides and Node	*d*	*h*	*m*
◐ First Quarter	2	1	42
○ Full Moon	9	7	33
◑ Last Quarter	15	22	17
● New Moon	23	15	32
Perigee (360,461 km)	10	20	28
Apogee (406,278 km)	26	11	34

Mean longitude of the ascending node on 1st, 97°

THE SUN   Diam. 32.5′

Day	Right Ascension			Dec.	Equation of time		Rise		Transit	Set			Sidereal time			Transit of first point of Aries		
							52°	56°		52°		56°						
	h	m	s	°	m	s	h m	h m	h m	h	m	h	m	h	m	s	h	m	s
1	20	56	10	−17.3	−13	28	7 41	7 56	12 14	16	47	16	32	8	42	42	15	14	47
2	21	00	15	−17.0	−13	37	7 39	7 54	12 14	16	49	16	34	8	46	39	15	10	51
3	21	04	19	−16.7	−13	44	7 38	7 52	12 14	16	51	16	36	8	50	36	15	06	55
4	21	08	22	−16.4	−13	51	7 36	7 50	12 14	16	52	16	38	8	54	32	15	03	00
5	21	12	24	−16.1	−13	57	7 34	7 48	12 14	16	54	16	41	8	58	29	14	59	04
6	21	16	26	−15.8	−14	02	7 33	7 46	12 14	16	56	16	43	9	02	25	14	55	08
7	21	20	27	−15.5	−14	06	7 31	7 44	12 14	16	58	16	45	9	06	22	14	51	12
8	21	24	27	−15.2	−14	09	7 29	7 42	12 14	17	00	16	47	9	10	18	14	47	16
9	21	28	26	−14.9	−14	12	7 27	7 40	12 14	17	02	16	49	9	14	15	14	43	20
10	21	32	24	−14.6	−14	14	7 26	7 38	12 14	17	04	16	52	9	18	11	14	39	24
11	21	36	22	−14.3	−14	15	7 24	7 36	12 14	17	05	16	54	9	22	08	14	35	28
12	21	40	18	−13.9	−14	15	7 22	7 33	12 14	17	07	16	56	9	26	05	14	31	32
13	21	44	14	−13.6	−14	14	7 20	7 31	12 14	17	09	16	58	9	30	01	14	27	36
14	21	48	10	−13.3	−14	13	7 18	7 29	12 14	17	11	17	00	9	33	58	14	23	40
15	21	52	04	−12.9	−14	11	7 16	7 27	12 14	17	13	17	03	9	37	54	14	19	45
16	21	55	58	−12.6	−14	08	7 14	7 24	12 14	17	15	17	05	9	41	51	14	15	49
17	21	59	51	−12.2	−14	05	7 12	7 22	12 14	17	17	17	07	9	45	47	14	11	53
18	22	03	44	−11.9	−14	01	7 10	7 20	12 14	17	19	17	09	9	49	44	14	07	57
19	22	07	36	−11.5	−13	56	7 08	7 17	12 14	17	20	17	11	9	53	40	14	04	01
20	22	11	27	−11.2	−13	51	7 06	7 15	12 14	17	22	17	14	9	57	37	14	00	05
21	22	15	17	−10.8	−13	45	7 04	7 13	12 14	17	24	17	16	10	01	34	13	56	09
22	22	19	07	−10.5	−13	38	7 02	7 10	12 14	17	26	17	18	10	05	30	13	52	13
23	22	22	56	−10.1	−13	31	7 00	7 08	12 13	17	28	17	20	10	09	27	13	48	17
24	22	26	45	−9.7	−13	23	6 58	7 05	12 13	17	30	17	22	10	13	23	13	44	21
25	22	30	33	−9.4	−13	14	6 56	7 03	12 13	17	31	17	24	10	17	20	13	40	25
26	22	34	20	−9.0	−13	05	6 54	7 00	12 13	17	33	17	27	10	21	16	13	36	30
27	22	38	07	−8.6	−12	55	6 51	6 58	12 13	17	35	17	29	10	25	13	13	32	34
28	22	41	53	−8.2	−12	45	6 49	6 55	12 13	17	37	17	31	10	29	09	13	28	38
29	22	45	39	−7.9	−12	34	6 47	6 53	12 12	17	39	17	33	10	33	06	13	24	42

DURATION OF TWILIGHT (in minutes)

Latitude	52°	56°	52°	56°	52°	56°
		1 February		11 February		21 February
Civil	37	41	35	39		38
Nautical	77	86	75	83	74	81
Astronomical	117	130	114	126	113	124

THE NIGHT SKY

Mercury gains a little height each evening as the month opens until peaking nearly 10° above the south-western horizon when at greatest elongation east on the 10th and a magnitude −0.6 glint. Thereafter the planet gradually drops lower before slipping back into the solar glare and inferior conjunction on the 26th.

Venus (magnitude −4.2) is setting four hours after the Sun mid-month and dominates the south-western sky. The crescent Moon is near Venus on the 27th.

Mars (magnitude 1.3) moves from Ophiuchus into Sagittarius on the 12th and is now rising more than three hours before the Sun. The planet's course through the Archer takes it quite close to M8, the Lagoon Nebula, on the 18th (when the Moon is nearby too) and within a 0.5° of the rich globular cluster M22 on the 29th.

Jupiter (magnitude −1.9), in Sagittarius, is rising an hour and a half before the Sun. The Moon is near Jupiter on the 19th and lies between it and Saturn on the 20th.

Saturn (magnitude 0.6) should be picked up fairly low in the southeast before dawn during the second week of February. Saturn is not far from Jupiter all year and its rise and set times are presently just under an hour different to those of the bigger planet.

The minor planet (4) Vesta is predicted to occult a magnitude 5.6 star in Aries on the evening of the 11th with the track crossing Scotland and northern England. More detailed information is available at: W www.asteroidoccultations.com.

THE MOON

Day	R.A.		Dec	Hor Par	Diam	Sun Co-Long	PA of Br. limb	Ph.	Age	Rise				Transit		Set			
										52°		56°				52°		56°	
	h	m	°	'	'	°	°	%	d	h	m	h	m	h	m	h	m	h	m
1	1	58	+6.9	54.4	29.6	352	251	40	6.6	10	47	10	39	17	45	—	—	—	—
2	2	43	+11.3	54.9	30.0	5	252	49	7.6	11	06	10	54	18	29	0	58	1	09
3	3	30	+15.3	55.5	30.2	17	255	59	8.6	11	29	11	13	19	17	2	08	2	23
4	4	21	+18.7	56.2	30.6	29	259	69	9.6	11	58	11	37	20	08	3	19	3	39
5	5	15	+21.4	57.1	31.2	41	264	78	10.6	12	36	12	12	21	03	4	30	4	53
6	6	12	+22.9	58.0	31.6	53	271	86	11.6	13	26	13	01	22	01	5	36	6	01
7	7	12	+23.2	58.9	32.0	65	278	93	12.6	14	30	14	06	23	01	6	34	6	58
8	8	14	+22.0	59.7	32.6	77	289	98	13.6	15	47	15	26	—	—	7	22	7	44
9	9	15	+19.2	60.3	32.8	90	323	100	14.6	17	12	16	56	0	01	7	58	8	16
10	10	15	+15.2	60.7	33.0	102	88	99	15.6	18	39	18	28	0	59	8	29	8	41
11	11	13	+10.2	60.8	33.2	114	102	96	16.6	20	06	20	01	1	55	8	53	9	00
12	12	09	+4.6	60.6	33.0	126	107	90	17.6	21	31	21	32	2	49	9	15	9	17
13	13	03	−1.2	60.2	32.8	138	109	81	18.6	22	55	23	01	3	41	9	35	9	32
14	13	57	−6.9	59.6	32.6	150	108	71	19.6	—	—	—	—	4	32	9	56	9	48
15	14	51	−12.0	59.0	32.2	162	106	61	20.6	0	17	0	29	5	24	10	19	10	07
16	15	45	−16.4	58.2	31.8	175	103	50	21.6	1	37	1	53	6	16	10	46	10	28
17	16	40	−19.9	57.5	31.4	187	98	39	22.6	2	53	3	14	7	09	11	19	10	58
18	17	35	−22.2	56.9	31.0	199	93	29	23.6	4	02	4	28	8	03	12	01	11	35
19	18	31	−23.2	56.3	30.6	211	87	20	24.6	5	02	5	30	8	57	12	50	12	24
20	19	26	−23.1	55.7	30.4	223	80	12	25.6	5	52	6	18	9	49	13	49	13	24
21	20	20	−21.8	55.3	30.2	235	73	07	26.6	6	32	6	53	10	40	14	54	14	32
22	21	12	−19.4	54.9	30.0	248	64	03	27.6	7	02	7	21	11	28	16	02	15	44
23	22	01	−16.3	54.5	29.8	260	42	00	28.6	7	27	7	41	12	14	17	10	16	58
24	22	48	−12.4	54.3	29.6	272	297	00	0.4	7	47	7	56	12	57	18	18	18	10
25	23	33	−8.2	54.1	29.4	284	264	02	1.4	8	04	8	10	13	39	19	25	19	22
26	0	17	−3.6	54.0	29.4	296	257	05	2.4	8	20	8	22	14	20	20	32	20	32
27	1	01	+1.1	54.0	29.4	309	254	10	3.4	8	36	8	33	15	00	21	39	21	43
28	1	44	+5.7	54.1	29.4	321	253	16	4.4	8	52	8	45	15	41	22	46	22	55
29	2	29	+10.2	54.4	29.6	333	254	24	5.4	9	09	8	59	16	24	23	54	—	—

MERCURY

Day	R.A.		Dec	Mag.	Diam.	Phase	Rise		Transit		Set	
	h	m	°		"	%	h	m	h	m	h	m
1	21	54.6	−14.0	−1.0	6	85	8	27	13	11	17	57
3	22	06.7	−12.6	−1.0	6	80	8	22	13	15	18	10
5	22	18.0	−11.1	−0.9	6	74	8	17	13	18	18	21
7	22	28.3	−9.7	−0.8	6	67	8	11	13	20	18	31
9	22	37.2	−8.3	−0.7	7	59	8	04	13	21	18	39
11	22	44.4	−7.1	−0.5	7	50	7	56	13	20	18	44
13	22	49.7	−6.0	−0.1	8	41	7	47	13	16	18	46
15	22	52.7	−5.1	+0.3	8	31	7	37	13	11	18	44
17	22	53.2	−4.5	+0.9	9	22	7	26	13	02	18	38
19	22	51.3	−4.2	+1.6	9	14	7	14	12	52	18	28
21	22	47.0	−4.2	+2.5	10	8	7	02	12	39	18	14
23	22	40.8	−4.5	+3.5	10	3	6	50	12	25	17	57
25	22	33.4	−5.1	+4.5	10	1	6	38	12	09	17	38
27	22	25.4	−5.9	+4.6	11	1	6	27	11	53	17	17
29	22	17.7	−6.8	+3.8	11	3	6	16	11	38	16	57

Rising and setting times are for latitude 54°

VENUS

Day	R.A.		Dec	Mag.	Diam.	Phase	Rise		Transit		Set	
	h	m	°		"	%	h	m	h	m	h	m
1	23	31.7	−4.0	−4.1	16	73	9	06	14	48	20	30
6	23	53.0	−1.4	−4.1	17	72	8	53	14	49	20	46
11	00	14.1	+1.2	−4.1	18	70	8	40	14	50	21	02
16	00	34.9	+3.8	−4.2	18	68	8	27	14	52	21	17
21	00	55.6	+6.4	−4.2	19	66	8	13	14	52	21	32
26	01	16.2	+8.9	−4.2	20	64	8	00	14	53	21	47

MARS

Day	R.A.		Dec	Mag.	Diam.	Phase	Rise		Transit		Set	
	h	m	°		"	%	h	m	h	m	h	m
1	17	13.9	−23.0	+1.4	5	93	4	48	8	30	12	13
6	17	28.7	−23.3	+1.3	5	93	4	45	8	25	12	06
11	17	43.6	−23.5	+1.3	5	92	4	42	8	21	11	59
16	17	58.6	−23.6	+1.2	5	92	4	38	8	16	11	54
21	18	13.6	−23.7	+1.2	5	92	4	34	8	11	11	49
26	18	28.7	−23.6	+1.2	5	91	4	29	8	07	11	44

SUNRISE AND SUNSET

	London				Bristol				Birmingham				Manchester				Newcastle				Glasgow				Belfast			
	0°	05'	51°	30'	2°	35'	51°	28'	1°	55'	52°	28'	2°	15'	53°	28'	1°	37'	54°	59'	4°	14'	55°	52'	5°	56'	54°	35'
d	h	m	h	m	h	m	h	m	h	m	h	m	h	m	h	m	h	m	h	m	h	m	h	m	h	m	h	m
1	7	40	16	49	7	49	16	59	7	50	16	53	7	55	16	51	7	58	16	42	8	12	16	49	8	14	17	01
2	7	38	16	51	7	48	17	01	7	49	16	55	7	53	16	53	7	56	16	45	8	10	16	51	8	12	17	03
3	7	36	16	52	7	46	17	03	7	47	16	57	7	52	16	55	7	55	16	47	8	08	16	54	8	10	17	05
4	7	35	16	54	7	45	17	04	7	45	16	59	7	50	16	57	7	53	16	49	8	07	16	56	8	08	17	07
5	7	33	16	56	7	43	17	06	7	44	17	00	7	48	16	59	7	51	16	51	8	05	16	58	8	07	17	09
6	7	32	16	58	7	41	17	08	7	42	17	02	7	46	17	01	7	49	16	53	8	03	17	00	8	05	17	12
7	7	30	17	00	7	40	17	10	7	40	17	04	7	44	17	02	7	47	16	55	8	00	17	02	8	03	17	14
8	7	28	17	02	7	38	17	12	7	38	17	06	7	43	17	04	7	45	16	57	7	58	17	05	8	01	17	16
9	7	26	17	03	7	36	17	13	7	36	17	08	7	41	17	06	7	43	16	59	7	56	17	07	7	59	17	18
10	7	25	17	05	7	35	17	15	7	35	17	10	7	39	17	08	7	41	17	01	7	54	17	09	7	57	17	20
11	7	23	17	07	7	33	17	17	7	33	17	12	7	37	17	10	7	39	17	03	7	52	17	11	7	55	17	22
12	7	21	17	09	7	31	17	19	7	31	17	14	7	35	17	12	7	37	17	06	7	50	17	13	7	53	17	24
13	7	19	17	11	7	29	17	21	7	29	17	16	7	33	17	14	7	35	17	08	7	48	17	15	7	51	17	26
14	7	17	17	13	7	27	17	23	7	27	17	18	7	31	17	16	7	32	17	10	7	45	17	18	7	49	17	28
15	7	15	17	14	7	25	17	24	7	25	17	19	7	29	17	18	7	30	17	12	7	43	17	20	7	46	17	30
16	7	13	17	16	7	23	17	26	7	23	17	21	7	27	17	20	7	28	17	14	7	41	17	22	7	44	17	32
17	7	11	17	18	7	21	17	28	7	21	17	23	7	25	17	22	7	26	17	16	7	39	17	24	7	42	17	34
18	7	10	17	20	7	19	17	30	7	19	17	25	7	23	17	24	7	24	17	18	7	36	17	26	7	40	17	36
19	7	08	17	22	7	17	17	32	7	17	17	27	7	20	17	26	7	21	17	20	7	34	17	29	7	38	17	38
20	7	06	17	23	7	15	17	34	7	15	17	29	7	18	17	28	7	19	17	22	7	32	17	31	7	35	17	41
21	7	04	17	25	7	13	17	35	7	13	17	31	7	16	17	30	7	17	17	24	7	29	17	33	7	33	17	43
22	7	02	17	27	7	11	17	37	7	11	17	33	7	14	17	32	7	14	17	26	7	27	17	35	7	31	17	45
23	6	59	17	29	7	09	17	39	7	08	17	35	7	12	17	34	7	12	17	29	7	24	17	37	7	29	17	47
24	6	57	17	31	7	07	17	41	7	06	17	36	7	09	17	36	7	10	17	31	7	22	17	39	7	26	17	49
25	6	55	17	32	7	05	17	43	7	04	17	38	7	07	17	38	7	07	17	33	7	20	17	42	7	24	17	51
26	6	53	17	34	7	03	17	44	7	02	17	40	7	05	17	40	7	05	17	35	7	17	17	44	7	22	17	53
27	6	51	17	36	7	01	17	46	7	00	17	42	7	03	17	42	7	03	17	37	7	15	17	46	7	19	17	55
28	6	49	17	38	6	59	17	48	6	58	17	44	7	00	17	44	7	00	17	39	7	12	17	48	7	17	17	57
29	6	47	17	40	6	57	17	50	6	55	17	46	6	58	17	46	6	58	17	41	7	10	17	50	7	15	17	59

JUPITER

Day	R.A.		Dec	Mag.	Diam.	Rise		Transit		Set	
	h	m	°		"	h	m	h	m	h	m
1	18	59.4	−22.7	−1.9	32	6	31	10	15	14	00
11	19	08.6	−22.5	−1.9	33	5	59	9	45	13	31
21	19	17.3	−22.2	−1.9	34	5	26	9	14	13	02

Diam. = equatorial; Polar Diam. is 94% of Equatorial Diam.

SATURN

Day	R.A.		Dec	Mag.	Diam.	Rise		Transit		Set	
	h	m	°		"	h	m	h	m	h	m
1	19	48.0	−21.1	+0.6	15	7	07	11	04	15	00
11	19	52.8	−20.9	+0.6	15	6	31	10	29	14	27
21	19	57.3	−20.7	+0.6	15	5	55	9	54	13	53

Diam. = equatorial; Polar Diam. is 90% of Equatorial Diam.
Rings – major axis 35″ minor axis 13″, Tilt 22°

URANUS

Day	R.A.		Dec	Mag.	Diam.	Rise		Transit		Set	
	h	m	°		"	h	m	h	m	h	m
1	02	03.2	+12.0	+5.8	4	10	07	17	18	0	33
11	02	04.1	+12.1	+5.8	4	9	28	16	39	23	51
21	02	05.2	+12.2	+5.8	3	8	49	16	01	23	13

NEPTUNE

Day	R.A.		Dec	Mag.	Diam.	Rise		Transit		Set	
	h	m	°		"	h	m	h	m	h	m
1	23	14.1	−6.0	+7.9	2	8	59	14	29	19	59
11	23	15.3	−5.9	+8.0	2	8	21	13	51	19	21
21	23	16.7	−5.8	+8.0	2	7	42	13	13	18	44

March 2020

THIRD MONTH, 31 DAYS. *Mars,* Roman god of battle

1	*Sunday*	Soviet spacecraft *Venera 3* reaches Venus 1966	day 61
2	*Monday*	*Voyager 1* overtakes *Pioneer 10* to become the farthest human-made object from the Sun 2002	week 9 day 62
3	*Tuesday*	Brian Cox, physicist and science TV presenter *b.* 1968	63
4	*Wednesday*	Robert Henry Dicke, American physicist *d.* 1997	64
5	*Thursday*	*Voyager 1* spacecraft makes its closest approach to Jupiter 1979	65
6	*Friday*	NASA spacecraft *Dawn* enters orbit around the dwarf planet of Ceres 2015	66
7	*Saturday*	First photographs of Pluto released 1996	67
8	*Sunday*	The largest single stone meteorite (1,170kg) falls in Jilin, China 1976	68
9	*Monday*	Yuri Gagarin, cosmonaut and first human to travel into space *b.* 1934	week 10 day 69
10	*Tuesday*	Physicists discover the rings of Uranus 1977	70
11	*Wednesday*	Curt Brown, astronaut known for making six space shuttle flights *b.* 1956	71
12	*Thursday*	John Theophilus Desguliers, French-English experimental assistant to Isaac Newton *b.* 1683	72
13	*Friday*	Uranus is discovered by astronomer William Herschel 1781	73
14	*Saturday*	Albert Einstein, regarded as the father of modern physics *b.* 1879	74
15	*Sunday*	Nicolas Louis de Lacaille, astronomer who catalogued 10,000 southern-hemisphere stars *b.* 1713	75
16	*Monday*	Georg Ohm, physicist after whom the unit of electrical reistance is named *b.* 1789	week 11 day 76
17	*Tuesday*	The US launches the first solar powered satellite 1958	77
18	*Wednesday*	Alexei Leonov completes the first space walk 1965	78
19	*Thursday*	William Rutter Dawes, astronomer who made the first drawings of Mars *b.* 1799	79
20	*Friday*	Isaac Newton, physicist and mathematician who discovered the law of universal gravitation *d.* 1727	80
21	*Saturday*	French physicist Joseph Fourier, credited with the discovery of the Greenhouse Effect *b.* 1768	81
22	*Sunday*	Cosmonaut Valeriy Polyakov sets the record for the most consecutive days in space (437 days) 1995	82
23	*Monday*	Norman Robert Pogson, creator of a scale that measures the brightness of stars *b.* 1829	week 12 day 83
24	*Tuesday*	Josef Stefan, who proposed the 1879 law of radiation *b.* 1835	84
25	*Wednesday*	Astronomer Christaan Huygens discovers the largest of Saturn's moons, Titan 1655	85
26	*Thursday*	John W. Draper takes the first photograph of the Moon 1840	86
27	*Friday*	Douglas Hartree, physicist and mathematician known for his equations on electrons in atoms *b.* 1897	87
28	*Saturday*	The 'Big Bang' name is first mentioned by Fred Hoyle 1949	88
29	*Sunday*	British Summer Time 2020 begins	89
30	*Monday*	First orbit of Halley's comet 240 BC	week 13 day 90
31	*Tuesday*	Isaac Newton, physicist and mathematician who discovered the law of gravitation *d.* 1727	91

ASTRONOMICAL PHENOMENA

d	h	
8	20	Uranus 2° south-east of Venus
18	6	Saturn, Jupiter, Mars, Moon close (within 10°)
18	11	Jupiter 2° north of the Moon
20	4	Spring equinox
20	6	Jupiter 0.7° north of Mars, Saturn to the east
21	6	Mercury just above south-southeast horizon
24	2	Mercury greatest elongation west (28°)
24	15	Moon at furthest apogee (406,692 km)
24	20	Venus greatest elongation east (46°)
26	5	Saturn, Mars and Jupiter form a triangle
29	7	Vesta 0.15° north of the Moon
29	21	Moon occults stars in the Hyades
31	6	Galilean moons all to the east of Jupiter
31	11	Saturn 1° north of Mars

MINIMA OF ALGOL

d	h	d	h	d	h
3	1.7	14	13.0	26	0.3
5	22.5	17	9.8	28	21.1
8	19.3	20	6.6	31	17.9
11	16.2	23	3.4		

CONSTELLATIONS

The following constellations are near the meridian at

d	h		d	h
February	1	24	March	16	21
February	15	23	April	1	20
March	1	22	April	15	19

Cepheus (below the Pole), Camelopardalis, Lynx, Gemini, Cancer, Leo, Canis Minor, Hydra, Monoceros, Canis Major and Puppis

THE MOON

Phase, Apsides and Node	d	h	m
◑ First Quarter	2	19	57
○ Full Moon	9	17	48
◐ Last Quarter	16	9	34
● New Moon	24	9	28
Perigee (357,121 km)	10	6	30
Apogee (406,691 km)*	24	15	23

* Furthest of the year
Mean longitude of the ascending node on 1st, 95°

THE SUN   Diam. 32.3′

Day	Right Ascension			Dec.	Equation of time		Rise 52°		Rise 56°		Transit		Set 52°		Set 56°		Sidereal time			Transit of first point of Aries		
	h	m	s	°	m	s	h	m	h	m	h	m	h	m	h	m	h	m	s	h	m	s
1	22	49	24	−7.5	−12	23	6	45	6	50	12	12	17	40	17	35	10	37	03	13	20	46
2	22	53	09	−7.1	−12	11	6	43	6	48	12	12	17	42	17	37	10	40	59	13	16	50
3	22	56	53	−6.7	−11	58	6	41	6	45	12	12	17	44	17	39	10	44	56	13	12	54
4	23	00	37	−6.3	−11	45	6	38	6	43	12	12	17	46	17	41	10	48	52	13	08	58
5	23	04	20	−6.0	−11	32	6	36	6	40	12	11	17	48	17	44	10	52	49	13	05	02
6	23	08	03	−5.6	−11	18	6	34	6	38	12	11	17	49	17	46	10	56	45	13	01	06
7	23	11	45	−5.2	−11	04	6	32	6	35	12	11	17	51	17	48	11	00	42	12	57	10
8	23	15	27	−4.8	−10	49	6	29	6	33	12	11	17	53	17	50	11	04	38	12	53	15
9	23	19	08	−4.4	−10	34	6	27	6	30	12	10	17	55	17	52	11	08	35	12	49	19
10	23	22	50	−4.0	−10	19	6	25	6	27	12	10	17	56	17	54	11	12	32	12	45	23
11	23	26	30	−3.6	−10	03	6	23	6	25	12	10	17	58	17	56	11	16	28	12	41	27
12	23	30	11	−3.2	−9	47	6	20	6	22	12	10	18	00	17	58	11	20	25	12	37	31
13	23	33	51	−2.8	−9	31	6	18	6	20	12	09	18	02	18	00	11	24	21	12	33	35
14	23	37	31	−2.4	−9	14	6	16	6	17	12	09	18	04	18	02	11	28	18	12	29	39
15	23	41	11	−2.0	−8	58	6	13	6	14	12	09	18	05	18	04	11	32	14	12	25	43
16	23	44	51	−1.6	−8	41	6	11	6	12	12	09	18	07	18	06	11	36	11	12	21	47
17	23	48	30	−1.2	−8	24	6	09	6	09	12	08	18	09	18	09	11	40	07	12	17	51
18	23	52	09	−0.9	−8	06	6	06	6	06	12	08	18	10	18	11	11	44	04	12	13	55
19	23	55	48	−0.5	−7	49	6	04	6	04	12	08	18	12	18	13	11	48	01	12	10	00
20	23	59	27	−0.1	−7	31	6	02	6	01	12	07	18	14	18	15	11	51	57	12	06	04
21	0	03	06	+0.3	−7	13	5	59	5	59	12	07	18	16	18	17	11	55	54	12	02	08
22	0	06	45	+0.7	−6	56	5	57	5	56	12	07	18	17	18	19	11	59	50	11	58	12
23	0	10	23	+1.1	−6	38	5	55	5	53	12	06	18	19	18	21	12	03	47	11	54	16
24	0	14	02	+1.5	−6	20	5	53	5	51	12	06	18	21	18	23	12	07	43	11	50	20
25	0	17	41	+1.9	−6	02	5	50	5	48	12	06	18	23	18	25	12	11	40	11	46	24
26	0	21	19	+2.3	−5	44	5	48	5	45	12	06	18	24	18	27	12	15	36	11	42	28
27	0	24	58	+2.7	−5	26	5	46	5	43	12	05	18	26	18	29	12	19	33	11	38	32
28	0	28	36	+3.1	−5	08	5	43	5	40	12	05	18	28	18	31	12	23	30	11	34	36
29	0	32	15	+3.5	−4	50	5	41	5	38	12	05	18	29	18	33	12	27	26	11	30	40
30	0	35	53	+3.9	−4	32	5	39	5	35	12	04	18	31	18	35	12	31	23	11	26	45
31	0	39	32	+4.3	−4	14	5	36	5	32	12	04	18	33	18	37	12	35	19	11	22	49

DURATION OF TWILIGHT (in minutes)

Latitude	52°	56°	52°	56°	52°	56°
		1 March		11 March		21 March
Civil	34	37	34	37	34	37
Nautical	73	80	73	80	74	81
Astronomical	112	124	113	125	115	128

THE NIGHT SKY

Mercury (magnitude 0.7) is a difficult morning sky prospect reaching at best only 1.5° altitude on the 11th when Civil Twilight begins. Greatest elongation west is on the 24th.

Venus (magnitude −4.4) sets about 4.5 hours after the Sun mid-month. It passes 2° from Uranus (magnitude 5.9) on the 9th with both in the same binocular field for a few days either side of that. Greatest elongation east is on the 24th and Venus shows an exact half phase in a telescope on the 27th with the four-day-old Moon nearby the next night. Venus ends the month about 3° from the Pleiades.

Mars (magnitude 1.0) shares in a remarkable morning sky planetary performance this month. On the 5th, Saturn, Jupiter, and Mars are in a line with 8° separating each. Then on the 18th the Moon, Mars, and Jupiter fit within a 5° circle, with both planets less than 1° apart on the 20th. Mars next passes 1′ from Pluto (magnitude 13.4) on the 23rd but the event is only a curiosity due to the more distant world's faintness. For a finale, Mars gets within 1° of Saturn on the 31st after crossing into Capricornus.

Jupiter (magnitude −2.0), along with Mars, is rising a little more than two hours before the Sun mid-month. On the 26th a slender curve 6.5° long connects Saturn, Mars, and Jupiter.

Saturn (magnitude 0.7) rises two hours before the Sun and crosses into Capricornus on the 22nd. The Moon lies nearby on the 19th.

THE MOON

Day	R.A. h m	Dec °	Hor Par '	Diam '	Sun Co-Long °	PA of Br. limb °	Ph. %	Age d	Rise 52° h m	Rise 56° h m	Transit h m	Set 52° h m	Set 56° h m
1	3 15	+14.3	54.8	29.8	345	256	32	6.4	9 30	9 15	17 10	— —	0 07
2	4 04	+17.9	55.3	30.2	357	259	42	7.4	9 56	9 36	17 58	1 03	1 22
3	4 55	+20.8	56.1	30.6	10	264	52	8.4	10 28	10 06	18 49	2 13	2 36
4	5 50	+22.7	56.9	31.0	22	269	62	9.4	11 12	10 46	19 44	3 20	3 45
5	6 47	+23.4	57.8	31.6	34	275	72	10.4	12 08	11 41	20 42	4 20	4 46
6	7 47	+22.8	58.8	32.0	46	282	81	11.4	13 17	12 54	21 41	5 11	5 36
7	8 47	+20.7	59.8	32.6	58	289	89	12.4	14 37	14 18	22 40	5 52	6 13
8	9 48	+17.3	60.6	33.0	70	298	96	13.4	16 04	15 50	23 37	6 25	6 40
9	10 47	+12.6	61.1	33.4	82	315	99	14.4	17 32	17 25	— —	6 52	7 01
10	11 44	+7.1	61.4	33.4	95	60	100	15.4	19 01	18 59	0 33	7 15	7 19
11	12 41	+1.1	61.3	33.4	107	98	98	16.4	20 29	20 33	1 27	7 36	7 35
12	13 36	−4.9	60.9	33.2	119	104	92	17.4	21 56	22 05	2 21	7 57	7 52
13	14 32	−10.5	60.3	32.8	131	104	85	18.4	23 20	23 35	3 14	8 20	8 09
14	15 28	−15.4	59.4	32.4	143	102	76	19.4	— —	— —	4 08	8 46	8 30
15	16 24	−19.3	58.5	32.0	155	99	65	20.4	0 41	1 00	5 03	9 18	8 57
16	17 21	−21.9	57.6	31.4	168	94	54	21.4	1 55	2 20	5 58	9 57	9 32
17	18 18	−23.3	56.8	31.0	180	88	44	22.4	2 59	3 27	6 53	10 45	10 18
18	19 14	−23.4	56.1	30.6	192	82	34	23.4	3 52	4 19	7 46	11 41	11 16
19	20 08	−22.3	55.4	30.2	204	77	25	24.4	4 35	4 57	8 37	12 45	12 22
20	21 00	−20.2	54.9	30.0	216	71	17	25.4	5 07	5 27	9 26	13 52	13 33
21	21 49	−17.2	54.5	29.8	228	65	10	26.4	5 33	5 48	10 12	15 01	14 46
22	22 37	−13.5	54.2	29.6	241	59	05	27.4	5 53	6 04	10 56	16 09	15 59
23	23 22	−9.3	54.0	29.4	253	50	02	28.4	6 11	6 18	11 38	17 16	17 11
24	0 06	−4.8	53.9	29.4	265	17	00	29.4	6 27	6 30	12 19	18 23	18 22
25	0 50	0.0	53.9	29.4	277	284	00	0.6	6 42	6 41	12 59	19 30	19 33
26	1 33	+4.7	54.0	29.4	290	263	02	1.6	6 58	6 53	13 40	20 37	20 44
27	2 17	+9.2	54.2	29.6	302	259	06	2.6	7 15	7 06	14 22	21 45	21 57
28	3 03	+13.5	54.4	29.6	314	258	11	3.6	7 33	7 20	15 07	22 54	23 11
29	3 50	+17.2	54.8	29.8	326	260	18	4.6	7 57	7 39	15 53	— —	— —
30	4 40	+20.3	55.3	30.2	338	263	26	5.6	8 26	8 05	16 43	0 03	0 25
31	5 33	+22.5	56.0	30.6	351	268	35	6.6	9 05	8 38	17 35	1 10	1 35

MERCURY

Day	R.A. h m	Dec °	Mag.	Diam. "	Phase %	Rise h m	Transit h m	Set h m
1	22 14.1	−7.3	+3.4	11	4	6 12	11 31	16 47
3	22 07.9	−8.2	+2.7	11	8	6 03	11 17	16 29
5	22 03.3	−9.1	+2.0	10	12	5 56	11 05	16 13
7	22 00.5	−9.8	+1.6	10	17	5 49	10 55	15 59
9	21 59.3	−10.4	+1.2	10	22	5 44	10 47	15 47
11	21 59.9	−10.9	+1.0	9	27	5 40	10 40	15 39
13	22 01.9	−11.2	+0.8	9	32	5 36	10 34	15 32
15	22 05.3	−11.3	+0.6	9	36	5 32	10 30	15 27
17	22 09.9	−11.4	+0.5	8	40	5 29	10 27	15 25
19	22 15.6	−11.3	+0.4	8	44	5 26	10 25	15 24
21	22 22.1	−11.0	+0.3	8	48	5 24	10 24	15 25
23	22 29.3	−10.7	+0.3	8	51	5 21	10 24	15 27
25	22 37.3	−10.2	+0.2	7	54	5 18	10 24	15 30
27	22 45.8	−9.6	+0.2	7	57	5 16	10 25	15 34
29	22 54.8	−9.0	+0.2	7	60	5 13	10 26	15 40
31	23 04.3	−8.2	+0.1	7	62	5 10	10 28	15 46

Rising and setting times are for latitude 54°

VENUS

Day	R.A. h m	Dec °	Mag.	Diam. "	Phase %	Rise h m	Transit h m	Set h m
1	01 32.7	+10.9	−4.2	20	63	7 49	14 54	22 00
6	01 53.1	+13.2	−4.3	21	61	7 35	14 55	22 14
11	02 13.6	+15.5	−4.3	22	58	7 22	14 55	22 29
16	02 33.9	+17.6	−4.3	23	56	7 09	14 56	22 43
21	02 54.1	+19.5	−4.3	24	53	6 56	14 56	22 57
26	03 14.0	+21.2	−4.4	26	51	6 43	14 56	23 09
31	03 33.6	+22.8	−4.4	27	48	6 31	14 55	23 21

MARS

Day	R.A. h m	Dec °	Mag.	Diam. "	Phase %	Rise h m	Transit h m	Set h m
1	18 40.7	−23.5	+1.1	5	91	4 24	8 03	11 42
6	18 55.8	−23.3	+1.1	6	91	4 18	7 58	11 38
11	19 10.8	−23.0	+1.0	6	90	4 11	7 54	11 36
16	19 25.7	−22.6	+1.0	6	90	4 04	7 49	11 34
21	19 40.6	−22.2	+0.9	6	89	3 56	7 44	11 33
26	19 55.4	−21.7	+0.9	6	89	3 47	7 39	11 32
31	20 10.1	−21.0	+0.8	6	88	3 37	7 34	11 31

SUNRISE AND SUNSET

	London 0° 05′ 51° 30′				Bristol 2° 35′ 51° 28′				Birmingham 1° 55′ 52° 28′				Manchester 2° 15′ 53° 28′				Newcastle 1° 37′ 54° 59′				Glasgow 4° 14′ 55° 52′				Belfast 5° 56′ 54° 35′			
d	h	m	h	m	h	m	h	m	h	m	h	m	h	m	h	m	h	m	h	m	h	m	h	m	h	m	h	m
1	6	45	17	41	6	55	17	51	6	53	17	47	6	56	17	48	6	55	17	43	7	07	17	52	7	12	18	01
2	6	43	17	43	6	53	17	53	6	51	17	49	6	54	17	49	6	53	17	45	7	05	17	54	7	10	18	03
3	6	40	17	45	6	50	17	55	6	49	17	51	6	51	17	51	6	51	17	47	7	02	17	56	7	07	18	05
4	6	38	17	47	6	48	17	57	6	47	17	53	6	49	17	53	6	48	17	49	7	00	17	58	7	05	18	07
5	6	36	17	48	6	46	17	58	6	44	17	55	6	47	17	55	6	46	17	51	6	57	18	01	7	02	18	09
6	6	34	17	50	6	44	18	00	6	42	17	57	6	44	17	57	6	43	17	53	6	55	18	03	7	00	18	11
7	6	32	17	52	6	42	18	02	6	40	17	58	6	42	17	59	6	41	17	55	6	52	18	05	6	58	18	13
8	6	29	17	54	6	39	18	04	6	37	18	00	6	40	18	01	6	38	17	57	6	49	18	07	6	55	18	15
9	6	27	17	55	6	37	18	05	6	35	18	02	6	37	18	03	6	36	17	59	6	47	18	09	6	53	18	17
10	6	25	17	57	6	35	18	07	6	33	18	04	6	35	18	05	6	33	18	01	6	44	18	11	6	50	18	19
11	6	23	17	59	6	33	18	09	6	31	18	06	6	32	18	06	6	31	18	03	6	42	18	13	6	48	18	21
12	6	20	18	00	6	30	18	10	6	28	18	07	6	30	18	08	6	28	18	05	6	39	18	15	6	45	18	23
13	6	18	18	02	6	28	18	12	6	26	18	09	6	28	18	10	6	26	18	07	6	37	18	17	6	43	18	24
14	6	16	18	04	6	26	18	14	6	24	18	11	6	25	18	12	6	23	18	09	6	34	18	19	6	40	18	26
15	6	14	18	06	6	24	18	16	6	21	18	13	6	23	18	14	6	21	18	11	6	31	18	21	6	38	18	28
16	6	11	18	07	6	21	18	17	6	19	18	15	6	20	18	16	6	18	18	13	6	29	18	23	6	35	18	30
17	6	09	18	09	6	19	18	19	6	17	18	16	6	18	18	18	6	16	18	15	6	26	18	25	6	33	18	32
18	6	07	18	11	6	17	18	21	6	14	18	18	6	16	18	19	6	13	18	17	6	23	18	27	6	30	18	34
19	6	05	18	12	6	15	18	22	6	12	18	20	6	13	18	21	6	10	18	19	6	21	18	29	6	28	18	36
20	6	02	18	14	6	12	18	24	6	09	18	22	6	11	18	23	6	08	18	21	6	18	18	32	6	25	18	38
21	6	00	18	16	6	10	18	26	6	07	18	23	6	08	18	25	6	05	18	23	6	16	18	34	6	23	18	40
22	5	58	18	17	6	08	18	27	6	05	18	25	6	06	18	27	6	03	18	25	6	13	18	36	6	20	18	42
23	5	55	18	19	6	05	18	29	6	02	18	27	6	03	18	29	6	00	18	27	6	10	18	38	6	18	18	44
24	5	53	18	21	6	03	18	31	6	00	18	29	6	01	18	30	5	58	18	29	6	08	18	40	6	15	18	46
25	5	51	18	22	6	01	18	33	5	58	18	30	5	59	18	32	5	55	18	31	6	05	18	42	6	13	18	48
26	5	49	18	24	5	59	18	34	5	55	18	32	5	56	18	34	5	53	18	33	6	02	18	44	6	10	18	50
27	5	46	18	26	5	56	18	36	5	53	18	34	5	54	18	36	5	50	18	35	6	00	18	46	6	08	18	52
28	5	44	18	28	5	54	18	38	5	51	18	36	5	51	18	38	5	48	18	36	5	57	18	48	6	05	18	53
29	5	42	18	29	5	52	18	39	5	48	18	37	5	49	18	40	5	45	18	38	5	55	18	50	6	03	18	55
30	5	40	18	31	5	50	18	41	5	46	18	39	5	46	18	41	5	42	18	40	5	52	18	52	6	00	18	57
31	5	37	18	33	5	47	18	43	5	44	18	41	5	44	18	43	5	40	18	42	5	49	18	54	5	58	18	59

JUPITER

Day	R.A. h	m	Dec °	Mag.	Diam. ″	Rise h	m	Transit h	m	Set h	m
1	19	24.7	−22.0	−2.0	34	4	57	8	46	12	36
11	19	32.2	−21.8	−2.0	35	4	23	8	14	12	06
21	19	38.9	−21.5	−2.1	36	3	49	7	42	11	35
31	19	44.8	−21.3	−2.1	37	3	14	7	08	11	03

Diam. = equatorial; Polar Diam. is 94% of Equatorial Diam.

SATURN

Day	R.A. h	m	Dec °	Mag.	Diam. ″	Rise h	m	Transit h	m	Set h	m
1	20	01.1	−20.5	+0.7	15	5	22	9	23	13	23
11	20	05.0	−20.4	+0.7	16	4	46	8	47	12	49
21	20	08.4	−20.2	+0.7	16	4	09	8	11	12	14
31	20	11.4	−20.1	+0.7	16	3	31	7	35	11	38

Diam. = equatorial; Polar Diam. is 90% of Equatorial Diam.
Rings – major axis 36″ minor axis 13″, Tilt 21°

URANUS

Day	R.A. h	m	Dec °	Mag.	Diam. ″	Rise h	m	Transit h	m	Set h	m
1	02	06.5	+12.3	+5.8	3	8	14	15	27	22	40
11	02	08.1	+12.5	+5.9	3	7	35	14	49	22	03
21	02	10.0	+12.6	+5.9	3	6	57	14	12	21	27
31	02	12.0	+12.8	+5.9	3	6	19	13	34	20	50

NEPTUNE

Day	R.A. h	m	Dec °	Mag.	Diam. ″	Rise h	m	Transit h	m	Set h	m
1	23	17.9	−5.6	+8.0	2	7	07	12	39	18	11
11	23	19.3	−5.5	+8.0	2	6	28	12	01	17	34
21	23	20.7	−5.3	+8.0	2	5	50	11	23	16	56
31	23	22.1	−5.2	+8.0	2	5	11	10	45	16	19

April 2020

FOURTH MONTH, 30 DAYS. *Aperire*, to open; Earth opens to receive seed.

1	*Wednesday*	The first weather observation satellite, *Tiros 1* is launched 1960	day 92
2	*Thursday*	Robert Watson-Watt, Scottish physicist, is granted a patent for radar technology 1935	93
3	*Friday*	Virgil Grissom, astronaut, part of the original 'Mercury Seven' (1959) *b.* 1926	94
4	*Saturday*	*Challenger* space shuttle begins its maiden voyage 1983	95
5	*Sunday*	Vincenzo Viviani, disciple of Galileo Galilei, who first measured the speed of sound *b.* 1622	96

6	*Monday*	*Eary Bird* becomes the first commercial communications satellite to be placed in geosynchronous orbit 1965	week 14 day 97
7	*Tuesday*	Radar signals are bounced off the Sun 1959	98
8	*Wednesday*	David Rittenhouse, who calculated the distance to the Sun *b.* 1732	99
9	*Thursday*	Space shuttle *Endeavour* is launched on an 11-day mission 1994	100
10	*Friday*	Scottish physicist Sir John Leslie, who first created artificial ice *b.* 1766	101
11	*Saturday*	The *Ryan-X-13 Vertijet*, the first jet to take off and land vertically, completes a full flight 1957	102
12	*Sunday*	Yuri Gagarin becomes the first man to travel into space 1961	103

13	*Monday*	Robert Watson-Watt, inventor of radar technology *b.* 1892	week 15 day 104
14	*Tuesday*	Christiaan Huygens, mathematician, astronomer and physicist *d.* 1629	105
15	*Wednesday*	Leonardo da Vinci, polymathic artist, engineer and scientist *b.* 1452	106
16	*Thursday*	Isaac Newton is knighted by Queen Anne at Trinity College, London 1705	107
17	*Friday*	*Apollo 13* lands safely on Earth after suffering a major malfunction while en route to the Moon 1970	108
18	*Saturday*	Albert Einstein is awarded the Nobel Prize for Physics for his theories of relativity *d.* 1955	109
19	*Sunday*	Soviet Union launches the first space station, *Skylab* 1971	110

20	*Monday*	Marie Curie, physicist and chemist, isolates the radioactive element radium 1902	week 16 day 111
21	*Tuesday*	Crew from *Apollo 16* land in the previously unexplored Descartes Highlands area of the Moon 1972	112
22	*Wednesday*	Robert Oppenheimer, theoretical physicist, known as the father of the atomic bomb *b.* 1904	113
23	*Thursday*	Max Planck, physicist who formulated the quantum theory of radiation *b.* 1858	114
24	*Friday*	The Hubble Space Telescope is launched 1990	115
25	*Saturday*	*Pioneer 10* space probe travels beyond Pluto's orbit 1983	116
26	*Sunday*	Heber Curtis and Harlow Shapley debate whether spiral nebulae are part of galaxies separate to ours 1920	117

27	*Monday*	The last telemetry from *Pioneer 10* is received 2002	week 17 day 118
28	*Tuesday*	Denis Tito becomes the first paying passenger to go into space 2001	119
29	*Wednesday*	Harold Urey, scientist and key figure in developing the atomic bomb *b.* 1893	120
30	*Thursday*	J. J. Thomson announces his discovery of the first subatomic particle, the electron 1897	121

ASTRONOMICAL PHENOMENA

d	h	
1	21	Galilean moons all to the west of Jupiter
2		Juno at opposition (Mag. +9.5)
3	3	Galiliean moons all to the west of Jupiter
4	19	Regulus 4° south of the Moon
7	18	Moon at closest perigee (356,906 km)
7	19	Juno 3° north of the Moon
15	9	Saturn 2° north of the Moon
16	5	Mars 2° north of the Moon
24	4	Galilean moons all to the east of Jupiter
26	11	Vesta 0.14° south of the Moon
28		Venus at greatest brilliancy
29	3	Galilean moons all to the east of Jupiter

MINIMA OF ALGOL

d	h	d	h	d	h
3	14.7	15	2.0	26	13.3
6	11.6	17	22.8	29	10.1
9	8.4	20	19.7		
12	5.2	23	16.5		

CONSTELLATIONS

The following constellations are near the meridian at

	d	h		d	h
March	1	24	April	15	21
March	16	23	May	1	20
April	1	22	May	16	19

Cepheus (below the Pole), Cassiopeia (below the Pole), Ursa Major, Leo Minor, Leo., Sextans, Hydra and Crater

THE MOON

Phase, Apsides and Node	d	h	m
◑ First Quarter	1	10	21
○ Full Moon	8	2	35
◑ Last Quarter	14	22	56
● New Moon	23	2	26
◑ First Quarter	30	20	38
Perigee (356,906 km)*	7	18	9
Apogee (406,462 km)	20	19	0

* Closest of the year

Mean longitude of the ascending node on 1st, 93°

THE SUN   Diam. 32.0′

Day	Right Ascension			Dec.	Equation of time		Rise 52°		Rise 56°		Transit		Set 52°		Set 56°		Sidereal time			Transit of first point of Aries		
	h	m	s	°	m	s	h	m	h	m	h	m	h	m	h	m	h	m	s	h	m	s
1	0	43	10	+4.6	−3	56	5	34	5	30	12	04	18	35	18	39	12	39	16	11	18	53
2	0	46	49	+5.0	−3	38	5	32	5	27	12	03	18	36	18	41	12	43	12	11	14	57
3	0	50	28	+5.4	−3	20	5	29	5	24	12	03	18	38	18	43	12	47	09	11	11	01
4	0	54	07	+5.8	−3	03	5	27	5	22	12	03	18	40	18	45	12	51	05	11	07	05
5	0	57	46	+6.2	−2	46	5	25	5	19	12	03	18	41	18	47	12	55	02	11	03	09
6	1	01	26	+6.5	−2	28	5	23	5	17	12	02	18	43	18	49	12	58	59	10	59	13
7	1	05	05	+6.9	−2	11	5	20	5	14	12	02	18	45	18	51	13	02	55	10	55	17
8	1	08	45	+7.3	−1	55	5	18	5	11	12	02	18	47	18	53	13	06	52	10	51	21
9	1	12	25	+7.7	−1	38	5	16	5	09	12	01	18	48	18	55	13	10	48	10	47	25
10	1	16	06	+8.0	−1	22	5	14	5	06	12	01	18	50	18	57	13	14	45	10	43	30
11	1	19	46	+8.4	−1	06	5	11	5	04	12	01	18	52	19	00	13	18	41	10	39	34
12	1	23	27	+8.8	−0	50	5	09	5	01	12	01	18	53	19	02	13	22	38	10	35	38
13	1	27	08	+9.1	−0	35	5	07	4	59	12	00	18	55	19	04	13	26	34	10	31	42
14	1	30	50	+9.5	−0	20	5	05	4	56	12	00	18	57	19	06	13	30	31	10	27	46
15	1	34	32	+9.9	−0	05	5	03	4	54	12	00	18	58	19	08	13	34	28	10	23	50
16	1	38	14	+10.2	+0	09	5	00	4	51	12	00	19	00	19	10	13	38	24	10	19	54
17	1	41	57	+10.6	+0	23	4	58	4	49	11	59	19	02	19	12	13	42	21	10	15	58
18	1	45	40	+10.9	+0	36	4	56	4	46	11	59	19	04	19	14	13	46	17	10	12	02
19	1	49	23	+11.3	+0	49	4	54	4	44	11	59	19	05	19	16	13	50	14	10	08	06
20	1	53	07	+11.6	+1	02	4	52	4	41	11	59	19	07	19	18	13	54	10	10	04	10
21	1	56	52	+11.9	+1	14	4	50	4	39	11	59	19	09	19	20	13	58	07	10	00	15
22	2	00	36	+12.3	+1	26	4	48	4	36	11	58	19	10	19	22	14	02	03	9	56	19
23	2	04	22	+12.6	+1	37	4	46	4	34	11	58	19	12	19	24	14	06	00	9	52	23
24	2	08	07	+12.9	+1	48	4	43	4	31	11	58	19	14	19	26	14	09	57	9	48	27
25	2	11	53	+13.3	+1	58	4	41	4	29	11	58	19	16	19	28	14	13	53	9	44	31
26	2	15	40	+13.6	+2	08	4	39	4	27	11	58	19	17	19	30	14	17	50	9	40	35
27	2	19	27	+13.9	+2	18	4	37	4	24	11	58	19	19	19	32	14	21	46	9	36	39
28	2	23	15	+14.2	+2	27	4	35	4	22	11	57	19	21	19	34	14	25	43	9	32	43
29	2	27	03	+14.5	+2	35	4	34	4	20	11	57	19	22	19	36	14	29	39	9	28	47
30	2	30	52	+14.9	+2	43	4	32	4	18	11	57	19	24	19	38	14	33	36	9	24	51

DURATION OF TWILIGHT (in minutes)

Latitude	52°	56°	52°	56°	52°	56°
		1 April		11 April		21 April
Civil	34	38	35	39	37	42
Nautical	76	84	79	89	83	96
Astronomical	120	136	127	147	137	165

THE NIGHT SKY

Mercury is in the morning sky but too near the Sun to be seen this month.

Venus (magnitude −4.5) reaches greatest brilliancy on the 28th and doesn't set until after midnight with Summer Time in effect. Telescope users see the planet's phase decreasing while also growing in apparent size – it shows a fat crescent when the young Moon is nearby on the 26th. Venus passes a 0.25° from Alcyone, the brightest of the Pleiades, on the 3rd.

Mars (magnitude 0.6) is rising two hours before the Sun and quickly widens the gap from Saturn. A line connects Mars, Saturn, and Jupiter on the 10th with 6° separating each. The Moon is close to Mars on the 16th.

Jupiter (magnitude −2.3) within 1° of Pluto on the 5th is only of passing interest. The Moon lies below Jupiter and Saturn on the morning of the 15th.

Saturn (magnitude 0.6) is at western quadrature on the 21st with the northern aspect of the rings tipped just over 20° earthward that day.

April 26th is the one hundredth anniversary of the Great Debate between Harlow Shapley and Heber Curtis. The former argued for distant 'nebulae' being part of our Milky Way while Curtis believed them to be independent galaxies. Observational evidence acquired by Edwin Hubble in the 1920s proved these ambiguous glows were actually distant galaxies, changing our view of the Universe forever.

THE MOON

Day	R.A.		Dec	Hor Par	Diam	Sun Co-Long	PA of Br. limb	Ph.	Age	Rise				Transit		Set			
										52°		56°				52°		56°	
	h	m	°	'	'	°	°	%	d	h	m	h	m	h	m	h	m	h	m
1	6	29	+23.6	56.7	31.0	3	273	46	7.6	9	54	9	26	18	30	2	11	2	39
2	7	26	+23.5	57.6	31.4	15	279	56	8.6	10	56	10	29	19	27	3	04	3	31
3	8	24	+21.9	58.5	31.8	27	284	67	9.6	12	09	11	47	20	24	3	48	4	11
4	9	23	+19.1	59.4	32.4	39	290	77	10.6	13	30	13	14	21	20	4	23	4	41
5	10	21	+14.9	60.3	32.8	52	296	86	11.6	14	57	14	46	22	15	4	51	5	04
6	11	18	+9.8	60.9	33.2	64	301	93	12.6	16	25	16	20	23	10	5	15	5	22
7	12	14	+3.9	61.3	33.4	76	311	98	13.6	17	54	17	54	—	—	5	36	5	39
8	13	10	−2.2	61.4	33.4	88	4	100	14.6	19	23	19	29	0	04	5	57	5	54
9	14	07	−8.2	61.2	33.4	100	91	99	15.6	20	51	21	03	0	58	6	19	6	11
10	15	04	−13.6	60.6	33.0	112	99	95	16.6	22	17	22	35	1	53	6	43	6	30
11	16	02	−18.1	59.8	32.6	124	98	88	17.6	23	38	—	—	2	50	7	13	6	54
12	17	01	−21.4	58.9	32.0	137	95	80	18.6	—	—	0	00	3	47	7	50	7	26
13	18	00	−23.3	57.9	31.6	149	90	70	19.6	0	50	1	17	4	44	8	35	8	09
14	18	58	−23.8	57.0	31.0	161	85	60	20.6	1	49	2	17	5	40	9	31	9	05
15	19	54	−23.0	56.1	30.6	173	79	50	21.6	2	36	3	00	6	33	10	34	10	10
16	20	47	−21.1	55.4	30.2	185	74	40	22.6	3	12	3	33	7	23	11	41	11	21
17	21	38	−18.2	54.8	29.8	198	69	30	23.6	3	39	3	56	8	10	12	50	12	34
18	22	25	−14.6	54.4	29.6	210	66	22	24.6	4	01	4	14	8	55	13	59	13	47
19	23	11	−10.5	54.1	29.4	222	62	15	25.6	4	19	4	28	9	37	15	06	15	00
20	23	55	−6.0	54.0	29.4	234	59	09	26.6	4	35	4	39	10	18	16	13	16	11
21	0	39	−1.3	53.9	29.4	246	55	04	27.6	4	50	4	50	10	59	17	20	17	22
22	1	22	+3.5	54.0	29.4	259	47	01	28.6	5	05	5	02	11	39	18	28	18	34
23	2	06	+8.2	54.2	29.6	271	355	00	0.0	5	21	5	13	12	21	19	36	19	47
24	2	51	+12.6	54.4	29.6	283	273	01	1.0	5	39	5	27	13	05	20	46	21	00
25	3	39	+16.5	54.7	29.8	295	264	03	2.0	6	01	5	44	13	51	21	55	22	16
26	4	28	+19.8	55.1	30.0	308	264	08	3.0	6	27	6	07	14	39	23	03	23	28
27	5	21	+22.3	55.6	30.4	320	267	14	4.0	7	03	6	37	15	31	—	—		
28	6	15	+23.7	56.2	30.6	332	271	22	5.0	7	47	7	20	16	25	0	07	0	34
29	7	11	+23.9	56.8	31.0	344	276	31	6.0	8	44	8	17	17	20	1	02	1	30
30	8	08	+22.7	57.5	31.4	357	282	41	7.0	9	52	9	28	18	15	1	48	2	13

MERCURY

Day	R.A.		Dec	Mag.	Diam.	Phase	Rise		Transit		Set	
	h	m	°		"	%	h	m	h	m	h	m
1	23	09.2	−7.8	+0.1	7	64	5	09	10	29	15	50
3	23	19.2	−6.9	0.0	6	66	5	06	10	31	15	57
5	23	29.7	−5.9	0.0	6	68	5	03	10	34	16	06
7	23	40.4	−4.8	−0.1	6	71	5	00	10	37	16	15
9	23	51.5	−3.7	−0.1	6	73	4	56	10	40	16	25
11	00	02.9	−2.4	−0.2	6	76	4	53	10	44	16	35
13	00	14.6	−1.1	−0.3	6	78	4	50	10	48	16	46
15	00	26.7	+0.2	−0.4	6	80	4	46	10	52	16	58
17	00	39.1	+1.7	−0.5	6	83	4	43	10	57	17	11
19	00	51.9	+3.2	−0.6	5	85	4	40	11	02	17	25
21	01	05.0	+4.7	−0.7	5	88	4	36	11	07	17	39
23	01	18.7	+6.3	−0.9	5	90	4	33	11	13	17	54
25	01	32.7	+7.9	−1.1	5	93	4	30	11	19	18	10
27	01	47.3	+9.6	−1.2	5	95	4	27	11	26	18	27
29	02	02.4	+11.3	−1.5	5	97	4	24	11	33	18	44

Rising and setting times are for latitude 54°

VENUS

Day	R.A.		Dec	Mag.	Diam.	Phase	Rise		Transit		Set	
	h	m	°		"	%	h	m	h	m	h	m
1	03	37.5	+23.1	−4.4	27	47	6	29	14	55	23	23
6	03	56.4	+24.4	−4.4	29	44	6	17	14	54	23	32
11	04	14.4	+25.5	−4.5	31	41	6	06	14	52	23	39
16	04	31.3	+26.4	−4.5	33	37	5	55	14	49	23	43
21	04	46.6	+27.1	−4.5	36	33	5	45	14	44	23	44
26	05	00.0	+27.5	−4.5	39	29	5	34	14	37	23	41

MARS

Day	R.A.		Dec	Mag.	Diam.	Phase	Rise		Transit		Set	
	h	m	°		"	%	h	m	h	m	h	m
1	20	13.1	−20.9	+0.8	6	88	3	35	7	33	11	31
6	20	27.6	−20.2	+0.7	7	88	3	25	7	28	11	31
11	20	42.0	−19.5	+0.7	7	88	3	15	7	23	11	31
16	20	56.3	−18.6	+0.6	7	87	3	03	7	17	11	32
21	21	10.5	−17.7	+0.5	7	87	2	52	7	12	11	32
26	21	24.4	−16.8	+0.5	7	87	2	40	7	06	11	32

SUNRISE AND SUNSET

	London				Bristol				Birmingham				Manchester				Newcastle				Glasgow				Belfast			
	0°	05'	51°	30'	2°	35'	51°	28'	1°	55'	52°	28'	2°	15'	53°	28'	1°	37'	54°	59'	4°	14'	55°	52'	5°	56'	54°	35'
d	h	m	h	m	h	m	h	m	h	m	h	m	h	m	h	m	h	m	h	m	h	m	h	m	h	m	h	m
1	5	35	18	34	5	45	18	44	5	41	18	43	5	42	18	45	5	37	18	44	5	47	18	56	5	55	19	01
2	5	33	18	36	5	43	18	46	5	39	18	44	5	39	18	47	5	35	18	46	5	44	18	58	5	53	19	03
3	5	30	18	38	5	40	18	48	5	37	18	46	5	37	18	49	5	32	18	48	5	42	19	00	5	50	19	05
4	5	28	18	39	5	38	18	49	5	34	18	48	5	34	18	51	5	30	18	50	5	39	19	02	5	48	19	07
5	5	26	18	41	5	36	18	51	5	32	18	50	5	32	18	52	5	27	18	52	5	36	19	04	5	45	19	09
6	5	24	18	43	5	34	18	53	5	30	18	51	5	30	18	54	5	25	18	54	5	34	19	06	5	43	19	11
7	5	21	18	44	5	32	18	54	5	27	18	53	5	27	18	56	5	22	18	56	5	31	19	08	5	40	19	13
8	5	19	18	46	5	29	18	56	5	25	18	55	5	25	18	58	5	20	18	58	5	29	19	10	5	38	19	14
9	5	17	18	48	5	27	18	58	5	23	18	57	5	23	19	00	5	17	19	00	5	26	19	12	5	35	19	16
10	5	15	18	49	5	25	18	59	5	21	18	58	5	20	19	01	5	15	19	02	5	24	19	14	5	33	19	18
11	5	13	18	51	5	23	19	01	5	18	19	00	5	18	19	03	5	12	19	04	5	21	19	16	5	30	19	20
12	5	10	18	53	5	21	19	03	5	16	19	02	5	15	19	05	5	10	19	06	5	18	19	18	5	28	19	22
13	5	08	18	54	5	18	19	04	5	14	19	04	5	13	19	07	5	07	19	08	5	16	19	20	5	26	19	24
14	5	06	18	56	5	16	19	06	5	12	19	05	5	11	19	09	5	05	19	10	5	13	19	22	5	23	19	26
15	5	04	18	58	5	14	19	08	5	09	19	07	5	09	19	11	5	03	19	11	5	11	19	24	5	21	19	28
16	5	02	18	59	5	12	19	09	5	07	19	09	5	06	19	12	5	00	19	13	5	08	19	26	5	18	19	30
17	5	00	19	01	5	10	19	11	5	05	19	10	5	04	19	14	4	58	19	15	5	06	19	28	5	16	19	32
18	4	58	19	03	5	08	19	13	5	03	19	12	5	02	19	16	4	55	19	17	5	03	19	30	5	14	19	34
19	4	56	19	04	5	06	19	14	5	01	19	14	4	59	19	18	4	53	19	19	5	01	19	32	5	11	19	36
20	4	53	19	06	5	03	19	16	4	58	19	16	4	57	19	20	4	51	19	21	4	59	19	34	5	09	19	37
21	4	51	19	08	5	01	19	18	4	56	19	17	4	55	19	21	4	48	19	23	4	56	19	36	5	07	19	39
22	4	49	19	09	4	59	19	19	4	54	19	19	4	53	19	23	4	46	19	25	4	54	19	38	5	04	19	41
23	4	47	19	11	4	57	19	21	4	52	19	21	4	51	19	25	4	44	19	27	4	51	19	40	5	02	19	43
24	4	45	19	13	4	55	19	23	4	50	19	23	4	48	19	27	4	41	19	29	4	49	19	42	5	00	19	45
25	4	43	19	14	4	53	19	24	4	48	19	24	4	46	19	29	4	39	19	31	4	47	19	44	4	58	19	47
26	4	41	19	16	4	51	19	26	4	46	19	26	4	44	19	31	4	37	19	33	4	44	19	46	4	55	19	49
27	4	39	19	18	4	49	19	28	4	44	19	28	4	42	19	32	4	35	19	35	4	42	19	48	4	53	19	51
28	4	37	19	19	4	47	19	29	4	42	19	30	4	40	19	34	4	32	19	37	4	40	19	50	4	51	19	53
29	4	35	19	21	4	46	19	31	4	40	19	31	4	38	19	36	4	30	19	39	4	37	19	53	4	49	19	55
30	4	34	19	23	4	44	19	32	4	38	19	33	4	36	19	38	4	28	19	41	4	35	19	55	4	47	19	56

JUPITER

Day	R.A.		Dec	Mag.	Diam.	Rise		Transit		Set	
	h	m	°		"	h	m	h	m	h	m
1	19	45.3	−21.3	−2.1	37	3	10	7	05	11	00
11	19	50.0	−21.1	−2.2	38	2	34	6	30	10	27
21	19	53.7	−21.0	−2.3	39	1	58	5	55	9	52

Diam. = equatorial; Polar Diam. is 94% of Equatorial Diam.

SATURN

Day	R.A.		Dec	Mag.	Diam.	Rise		Transit		Set	
	h	m	°		"	h	m	h	m	h	m
1	20	11.6	−20.1	+0.7	16	3	28	7	31	11	35
11	20	13.9	−20.0	+0.6	16	2	50	6	54	10	58
21	20	15.6	−19.9	+0.6	17	2	12	6	16	10	21

Diam. = equatorial; Polar Diam. is 90% of Equatorial Diam.
Rings – major axis 37" minor axis 13", Tilt 21°

URANUS

Day	R.A.		Dec	Mag.	Diam.	Rise		Transit		Set	
	h	m	°		"	h	m	h	m	h	m
1	02	12.2	+12.8	+5.9	3	6	15	13	31	20	47
11	02	14.3	+13.0	+5.9	3	5	36	12	54	20	11
21	02	16.5	+13.2	+5.9	3	4	58	12	16	19	35

NEPTUNE

Day	R.A.		Dec	Mag.	Diam.	Rise		Transit		Set	
	h	m	°		"	h	m	h	m	h	m
1	23	22.2	−5.2	+8.0	2	5	07	10	41	16	15
11	23	23.5	−5.1	+8.0	2	4	28	10	03	15	38
21	23	24.7	−4.9	+7.9	2	3	49	9	25	15	01

May 2020

FIFTH MONTH, 31 DAYS. *Maia*, goddess of growth and increase

1 *Friday*	Pluto is named by Venetia Burney, an 11-year-old girl from Oxford, England 1930		day 122
2 *Saturday*	Johann Palisa, Austrian astronomer known for his discovery of 122 asteroids *d.* 1925		123
3 *Sunday*	Jonathan Homer Lane, American astrophysicist, first to analyse the Sun as a gaseous body *d.* 1880		124
4 *Monday*	Canadian-American physicist D. Allan Bromley, known as the father of modern heavy ion science *d.* 1926	week 18 day 125	
5 *Tuesday*	*Ariel 3*, the first artificial satellite designed and built in Britain, launches from the USA, 1967		126
6 *Wednesday*	Robert H. Dicke, who predicted the existence of the cosmic microwave background *b.* 1916		127
7 *Thursday*	Space shuttle *Endeavour* begins its maiden voyage as the replacement for *Challenger* 1992		128
8 *Friday*	The first transatlantic flight is made as seaplane *NC-4* takes off from the US 1919		129
9 *Saturday*	Albert Michelson, physicist and first American to win a Nobel Prize in the sciences *d.* 1931		130
10 *Sunday*	US nuclear submarine *Triton* becomes the first vessel to circumnavigate the globe underwater 1960		131
11 *Monday*	Richard Feynman, known for his contributions to quantum electrodynamics *b.* 1918	week 19 day 132	
12 *Tuesday*	Soviet probe *Luna 5* crashes onto the Moon 1965		133
13 *Wednesday*	Marie Curie, Nobel Prize winning physicist, becomes the first female professor at the Sorbonne 1906		134
14 *Thursday*	*Skylab* space station launched by NASA 1973		135
15 *Friday*	Pierre Curie, Nobel Prize-winning physicist known for his research on radiation *b.* 1859		136
16 *Saturday*	Nancy Roman, American astronomer and first woman to hold an executive position at NASA *b.* 1925		137
17 *Sunday*	*Venera 6* descends into the atmosphere of Venus before being crushed by air pressure 1969		138
18 *Monday*	*Apollo 10* launches as part of the programme to send humans to the Moon 1969	week 20 day 139	
19 *Tuesday*	Abraham Pais, physicist whose research focused on elementary particle theory *b.* 1918		140
20 *Wednesday*	World Metrology Day		141
21 *Thursday*	Sir Geoffrey de Hallivand, English aircraft designer and pioneer of long-distance jet flying *d.* 1965		142
22 *Friday*	*Apollo 10's* lunar module flies withing 14 miles of the Moon's surface as a rehearsal for *Apollo 11* 1969		143
23 *Saturday*	John Bardeen, twice winner of the Nobel Prize for physics *b.* 1908.		144
24 *Sunday*	Scott Carpenter becomes the second American to orbit the Earth aboard *Aurora 7* 1962		145
25 *Monday*	The unmanned US *Pheonix* spacecraft touches down in the frozen plains of Mars 2008	week 21 day 146	
26 *Tuesday*	Sally Ride, the first American woman to go into space aboard *Challenger* in 1983 *b.* 1951		147
27 *Wednesday*	John Cockcroft, who shared the 1951 Nobel Prize for physics for splitting the atom *b.* 1897		148
28 *Thursday*	Two monkeys, Able and Baker, become the first living creatures to survive space flight 1959		149
29 *Friday*	Johann Heinrich von Mädler, physicist who was the first to map the Moon and Mars *b.* 1794		150
30 *Saturday*	*Surveyor 1*, the first man-made object to land on the Moon, launches 1966		151
31 *Sunday*	Robert Schrieffer, winner of the 1972 Nobel Prize for physics for his work on superconductivity *b* 1931		152

ASTRONOMICAL PHENOMENA

d	h	
2	3	Moon 4.5° north of Regulus
4	19	Eta-Aquarid meteor stream
4	21	Juno 4° north of the Moon
15	4	Mars 3° north of the Moon
20	16	Uranus 4° north of the Moon
24	11	Mercury 3° north of the Moon (care of the Sun)
27	21	Moon 2° north of the Beehive cluster

MINIMA OF ALGOL

d	h	d	h	d	h
2	6.9	13	18.2	25	5.5
5	3.7	16	15.0	28	2.3
8	0.6	19	11.8	30	23.1
10	21.4	22	8.7		

CONSTELLATIONS

The following constellations are near the meridian at

d	h		d	h
April	1	24	May	16	21
April	15	23	June	1	20
May	1	22	June	15	19

Cepheus (below the Pole), Cassiopeia (below the Pole), Ursa Minor, Ursa Major, Canes Venatici, Coma Berenices, Bootes, Leo, Virgo, Crater, Corvus and Hydra

THE MOON

Phase, Apsides and Node	d	h	m
○ Full Moon	7	10	45
◑ Last Quarter	14	14	3
● New Moon	22	17	39
◐ First Quarter	30	3	30

Perigee (359,653 km)	6	3	3
Apogee (405,583 km)	18	7	45

Mean longitude of the ascending node on 1st, 92°

THE SUN   Diam. 31.8′

Day	Right Ascension			Dec.	Equation of time		Rise 52°		Rise 56°		Transit		Set 52°		Set 56°		Sidereal time			Transit of first point of Aries		
	h	m	s	°	m	s	h	m	h	m	h	m	h	m	h	m	h	m	s	h	m	s
1	2	34	41	+15.2	+2	50	4	30	4	15	11	57	19	26	19	40	14	37	32	9	20	55
2	2	38	31	+15.5	+2	57	4	28	4	13	11	57	19	27	19	42	14	41	29	9	17	00
3	2	42	21	+15.8	+3	04	4	26	4	11	11	57	19	29	19	44	14	45	26	9	13	04
4	2	46	12	+16.0	+3	09	4	24	4	09	11	57	19	31	19	46	14	49	22	9	09	08
5	2	50	03	+16.3	+3	15	4	22	4	07	11	57	19	32	19	48	14	53	19	9	05	12
6	2	53	55	+16.6	+3	19	4	20	4	04	11	57	19	34	19	50	14	57	15	9	01	16
7	2	57	47	+16.9	+3	24	4	19	4	02	11	57	19	35	19	52	15	01	12	8	57	20
8	3	01	40	+17.2	+3	27	4	17	4	00	11	57	19	37	19	54	15	05	08	8	53	24
9	3	05	34	+17.4	+3	30	4	15	3	58	11	56	19	39	19	56	15	09	05	8	49	28
10	3	09	28	+17.7	+3	33	4	14	3	56	11	56	19	40	19	58	15	13	01	8	45	32
11	3	13	22	+17.9	+3	35	4	12	3	54	11	56	19	42	20	00	15	16	58	8	41	36
12	3	17	18	+18.2	+3	36	4	10	3	52	11	56	19	43	20	02	15	20	55	8	37	40
13	3	21	13	+18.4	+3	37	4	09	3	50	11	56	19	45	20	03	15	24	51	8	33	45
14	3	25	10	+18.7	+3	37	4	07	3	49	11	56	19	46	20	05	15	28	48	8	29	49
15	3	29	07	+18.9	+3	36	4	06	3	47	11	56	19	48	20	07	15	32	44	8	25	53
16	3	33	05	+19.2	+3	35	4	04	3	45	11	56	19	49	20	09	15	36	41	8	21	57
17	3	37	03	+19.4	+3	33	4	03	3	43	11	56	19	51	20	11	15	40	37	8	18	01
18	3	41	01	+19.6	+3	31	4	01	3	42	11	56	19	52	20	13	15	44	34	8	14	05
19	3	45	01	+19.8	+3	28	4	00	3	40	11	57	19	54	20	14	15	48	30	8	10	09
20	3	49	01	+20.0	+3	25	3	59	3	38	11	57	19	55	20	16	15	52	27	8	06	13
21	3	53	01	+20.2	+3	21	3	57	3	37	11	57	19	57	20	18	15	56	24	8	02	17
22	3	57	02	+20.4	+3	17	3	56	3	35	11	57	19	58	20	19	16	00	20	7	58	21
23	4	01	04	+20.6	+3	12	3	55	3	34	11	57	19	59	20	21	16	04	17	7	54	25
24	4	05	06	+20.8	+3	06	3	54	3	32	11	57	20	01	20	23	16	08	13	7	50	30
25	4	09	08	+21.0	+3	01	3	53	3	31	11	57	20	02	20	24	16	12	10	7	46	34
26	4	13	11	+21.2	+2	54	3	52	3	29	11	57	20	03	20	26	16	16	06	7	42	38
27	4	17	15	+21.3	+2	47	3	51	3	28	11	57	20	05	20	27	16	20	03	7	38	42
28	4	21	19	+21.5	+2	40	3	50	3	27	11	57	20	06	20	29	16	23	59	7	34	46
29	4	25	23	+21.7	+2	32	3	49	3	26	11	58	20	07	20	30	16	27	56	7	30	50
30	4	29	28	+21.8	+2	24	3	48	3	25	11	58	20	08	20	31	16	31	53	7	26	54
31	4	33	33	+22.0	+2	15	3	47	3	24	11	58	20	09	20	33	16	35	49	7	22	58

DURATION OF TWILIGHT (in minutes)

Latitude	52°	56°	52°	56°	52°	56°
		1 May		11 May		21 May
Civil	39	44	41	48	44	53
Nautical	89	106	97	120	106	141
Astronomical	152	204	176	TAN	TAN	TAN

THE NIGHT SKY

Mercury is at superior conjunction on the 4th and then emerges in the evening sky towards the end of the second week of May. It is 3.5° from the Pleiades on the 12th but may then still be too low to be noticed. Gaining in height during the following days, Mercury shines at magnitude −0.7 when around 1° from Venus on the 22nd. After overtaking Venus it climbs to 9° above the western skyline as Civil Twilight ends on the 28th. This is an great opportunity to watch the innermost planets change position daily. The Moon is 4.5° from Mercury on the 24th.

Venus (magnitude −4.6) sets four hours after the Sun on the 1st but those circumstances soon change as it quickly plummets sunward to be lost from view towards the end of May.

Mars (magnitude 0.2) crosses into Aquarius on the 10th and rises just after 01h on the 31st. The Moon is 3° from Mars on the morning of the 15th.

Jupiter (magnitude −2.5) rises around 01h at the beginning of May and a little after 23h on the 31st. The Moon is in the area on the 12th and the planet begins to retrograde on the 14th. Jupiter is without a visible Galilean moon between 11:18 UT and 13:12 UT on the 28th.

Saturn (magnitude 0.5) is also stationary and starts to retrograde on the 11th. Like Jupiter, Saturn is rising before midnight by the end of May with the two planets now about 5° apart.

THE MOON

Day	R.A.		Dec	Hor Par	Diam	Sun Co-Long	PA of Br. limb	Ph.	Age	Rise				Transit		Set			
										52°		56°				52°		56°	
	h	m	°	'	'	°	°	%	d	h	m	h	m	h	m	h	m	h	m
1	9	05	+20.3	58.3	31.8	9	287	52	8.0	11	09	10	50	19	10	2	25	2	45
2	10	02	+16.6	59.0	32.2	21	291	63	9.0	12	30	12	17	20	03	2	54	3	09
3	10	57	+11.9	59.7	32.6	33	295	74	10.0	13	55	13	47	20	56	3	18	3	28
4	11	52	+6.5	60.4	32.8	45	298	83	11.0	15	21	15	19	21	48	3	39	3	44
5	12	46	+0.5	60.8	33.2	57	300	91	12.0	16	48	16	51	22	41	3	59	3	59
6	13	41	−5.6	61.0	33.2	70	303	97	13.0	18	16	18	25	23	36	4	19	4	14
7	14	38	−11.3	60.9	33.2	82	320	100	14.0	19	45	19	59	—	—	4	41	4	30
8	15	36	−16.3	60.5	33.0	94	83	100	15.0	21	10	21	31	0	32	5	08	4	52
9	16	35	−20.3	59.8	32.6	106	94	97	16.0	22	30	22	54	1	30	5	41	5	19
10	17	36	−22.8	59.0	32.2	118	92	91	17.0	23	38	—	—	2	29	6	23	5	58
11	18	36	−24.0	58.1	31.6	131	87	84	18.0	—	—	0	04	3	27	7	16	6	48
12	19	34	−23.6	57.1	31.2	143	82	75	19.0	0	32	0	57	4	23	8	18	7	52
13	20	30	−22.0	56.3	30.6	155	77	66	20.0	1	13	1	36	5	16	9	25	9	04
14	21	23	−19.4	55.5	30.2	167	72	56	21.0	1	44	2	02	6	06	10	36	10	18
15	22	12	−15.9	54.9	30.0	179	69	46	22.0	2	07	2	22	6	52	11	46	11	33
16	22	59	−11.9	54.5	29.6	192	66	37	23.0	2	27	2	37	7	35	12	55	12	46
17	23	44	−7.4	54.2	29.6	204	64	28	24.0	2	43	2	49	8	17	14	02	13	58
18	0	27	−2.7	54.1	29.4	216	63	20	25.0	2	58	3	00	8	57	15	09	15	09
19	1	10	+2.1	54.1	29.4	228	62	13	26.0	3	13	3	11	9	38	16	16	16	21
20	1	54	+6.9	54.2	29.6	240	62	07	27.0	3	28	3	22	10	19	17	25	17	34
21	2	39	+11.4	54.5	29.6	253	61	03	28.0	3	45	3	34	11	02	18	34	18	48
22	3	26	+15.5	54.8	29.8	265	55	01	29.0	4	06	3	50	11	47	19	45	20	03
23	4	15	+19.1	55.2	30.2	277	295	00	0.5	4	30	4	11	12	36	20	55	21	18
24	5	07	+21.8	55.7	30.4	289	269	02	1.5	5	03	4	38	13	27	22	00	22	28
25	6	02	+23.6	56.2	30.6	302	270	05	2.5	5	44	5	17	14	21	22	59	23	28
26	6	58	+24.0	56.7	30.8	314	274	11	3.5	6	37	6	10	15	16	23	49	—	—
27	7	56	+23.2	57.2	31.2	326	279	18	4.5	7	42	7	17	16	12	—	—	0	15
28	8	52	+21.1	57.7	31.4	338	284	27	5.5	8	57	8	35	17	06	0	29	0	50
29	9	48	+17.8	58.3	31.8	351	288	37	6.5	10	15	10	01	17	58	0	58	1	16
30	10	43	+13.4	58.8	32.0	3	292	48	7.5	11	37	11	27	18	50	1	24	1	36
31	11	36	+8.2	59.3	32.4	15	294	60	8.5	13	00	12	55	19	40	1	45	1	51

MERCURY

Day	R.A.		Dec	Mag.	Diam.	Phase	Rise		Transit		Set	
	h	m	°		"	%	h	m	h	m	h	m
1	02	17.9	+13.0	−1.7	5	98	4	22	11	41	19	02
3	02	34.0	+14.6	−2.0	5	100	4	20	11	49	19	21
5	02	50.6	+16.3	−2.3	5	100	4	18	11	58	19	41
7	03	07.6	+17.8	−2.1	5	99	4	16	12	07	20	00
9	03	24.9	+19.3	−1.8	5	98	4	16	12	17	20	20
11	03	42.3	+20.6	−1.6	5	95	4	16	12	26	20	39
13	03	59.8	+21.9	−1.4	5	92	4	16	12	36	20	57
15	04	17.1	+22.9	−1.2	5	88	4	18	12	45	21	14
17	04	34.0	+23.8	−1.1	6	83	4	20	12	54	21	29
19	04	50.5	+24.5	−0.9	6	77	4	23	13	02	21	43
21	05	06.3	+25.0	−0.7	6	72	4	26	13	10	21	55
23	05	21.4	+25.4	−0.5	6	67	4	30	13	17	22	04
25	05	35.7	+25.6	−0.3	7	61	4	35	13	23	22	11
27	05	49.1	+25.7	−0.2	7	56	4	40	13	28	22	17
29	06	01.5	+25.6	0.0	7	52	4	44	13	32	22	20
31	06	12.9	+25.5	+0.2	7	47	4	49	13	35	22	22

Rising and setting times are for latitude 54°

VENUS

Day	R.A.		Dec	Mag.	Diam.	Phase	Rise		Transit		Set	
	h	m	°		"	%	h	m	h	m	h	m
1	05	10.9	+27.8	−4.5	42	25	5	23	14	27	23	33
6	05	18.7	+27.8	−4.5	45	20	5	11	14	14	23	19
11	05	22.8	+27.6	−4.5	49	16	4	57	13	58	22	59
16	05	22.8	+27.1	−4.4	53	11	4	41	13	37	22	33
21	05	18.3	+26.4	−4.3	57	6	4	23	13	12	22	00
26	05	09.8	+25.4	−4.1	60	3	4	04	12	43	21	20
31	04	58.2	+24.0	−3.9	62	1	3	44	12	12	20	36

MARS

Day	R.A.		Dec	Mag.	Diam.	Phase	Rise		Transit		Set	
	h	m	°		"	%	h	m	h	m	h	m
1	21	38.2	−15.8	+0.4	8	86	2	28	7	00	11	33
6	21	51.9	−14.8	+0.3	8	86	2	15	6	54	11	33
11	22	05.3	−13.7	+0.3	8	86	2	03	6	48	11	34
16	22	18.6	−12.6	+0.2	8	85	1	49	6	41	11	34
21	22	31.7	−11.5	+0.1	9	85	1	36	6	35	11	34
26	22	44.6	−10.4	+0.1	9	85	1	23	6	28	11	34
31	22	57.4	−9.2	0.0	9	85	1	09	6	21	11	34

SUNRISE AND SUNSET

	London		Bristol		Birmingham		Manchester		Newcastle		Glasgow		Belfast	
	0°	05′ 51° 30′	2°	35′ 51° 28′	1°	55′ 52° 28′	2°	15′ 53° 28′	1°	37′ 54° 59′	4°	14′ 55° 52′	5°	56′ 54° 35′
d	h m	h m	h m	h m	h m	h m	h m	h m	h m	h m	h m	h m	h m	h m
1	4 32	19 24	4 42	19 34	4 36	19 35	4 34	19 39	4 26	19 43	4 33	19 57	4 45	19 58
2	4 30	19 26	4 40	19 36	4 34	19 36	4 32	19 41	4 24	19 44	4 31	19 59	4 42	20 00
3	4 28	19 27	4 38	19 37	4 32	19 38	4 30	19 43	4 22	19 46	4 28	20 01	4 40	20 02
4	4 26	19 29	4 36	19 39	4 30	19 40	4 28	19 45	4 19	19 48	4 26	20 02	4 38	20 04
5	4 24	19 31	4 34	19 41	4 28	19 42	4 26	19 47	4 17	19 50	4 24	20 04	4 36	20 06
6	4 23	19 32	4 33	19 42	4 26	19 43	4 24	19 48	4 15	19 52	4 22	20 06	4 34	20 08
7	4 21	19 34	4 31	19 44	4 25	19 45	4 22	19 50	4 13	19 54	4 20	20 08	4 32	20 09
8	4 19	19 35	4 29	19 45	4 23	19 46	4 20	19 52	4 11	19 56	4 18	20 10	4 30	20 11
9	4 17	19 37	4 28	19 47	4 21	19 48	4 18	19 54	4 09	19 58	4 16	20 12	4 28	20 13
10	4 16	19 39	4 26	19 49	4 19	19 50	4 17	19 55	4 07	19 59	4 14	20 14	4 27	20 15
11	4 14	19 40	4 24	19 50	4 18	19 51	4 15	19 57	4 06	20 01	4 12	20 16	4 25	20 17
12	4 13	19 42	4 23	19 52	4 16	19 53	4 13	19 59	4 04	20 03	4 10	20 18	4 23	20 19
13	4 11	19 43	4 21	19 53	4 14	19 55	4 11	20 00	4 02	20 05	4 08	20 20	4 21	20 20
14	4 10	19 45	4 20	19 55	4 13	19 56	4 10	20 02	4 00	20 07	4 06	20 22	4 19	20 22
15	4 08	19 46	4 18	19 56	4 11	19 58	4 08	20 04	3 58	20 08	4 04	20 24	4 18	20 24
16	4 07	19 48	4 17	19 58	4 10	19 59	4 07	20 05	3 57	20 10	4 02	20 25	4 16	20 25
17	4 05	19 49	4 15	19 59	4 08	20 01	4 05	20 07	3 55	20 12	4 01	20 27	4 14	20 27
18	4 04	19 51	4 14	20 01	4 07	20 02	4 04	20 08	3 53	20 14	3 59	20 29	4 13	20 29
19	4 02	19 52	4 13	20 02	4 05	20 04	4 02	20 10	3 52	20 15	3 57	20 31	4 11	20 30
20	4 01	19 54	4 11	20 03	4 04	20 05	4 01	20 12	3 50	20 17	3 56	20 33	4 10	20 32
21	4 00	19 55	4 10	20 05	4 03	20 07	3 59	20 13	3 49	20 19	3 54	20 34	4 08	20 34
22	3 59	19 56	4 09	20 06	4 01	20 08	3 58	20 15	3 47	20 20	3 52	20 36	4 07	20 35
23	3 57	19 58	4 08	20 07	4 00	20 10	3 56	20 16	3 46	20 22	3 51	20 38	4 05	20 37
24	3 56	19 59	4 06	20 09	3 59	20 11	3 55	20 17	3 44	20 23	3 49	20 39	4 04	20 38
25	3 55	20 00	4 05	20 10	3 58	20 12	3 54	20 19	3 43	20 25	3 48	20 41	4 03	20 40
26	3 54	20 01	4 04	20 11	3 57	20 14	3 53	20 20	3 42	20 26	3 47	20 42	4 01	20 41
27	3 53	20 03	4 03	20 13	3 56	20 15	3 52	20 22	3 40	20 28	3 45	20 44	4 00	20 43
28	3 52	20 04	4 02	20 14	3 55	20 16	3 51	20 23	3 39	20 29	3 44	20 45	3 59	20 44
29	3 51	20 05	4 01	20 15	3 54	20 17	3 49	20 24	3 38	20 31	3 43	20 47	3 58	20 45
30	3 50	20 06	4 00	20 16	3 53	20 19	3 48	20 25	3 37	20 32	3 42	20 48	3 57	20 47
31	3 49	20 07	4 00	20 17	3 52	20 20	3 48	20 27	3 36	20 33	3 41	20 50	3 56	20 48

JUPITER

Day	R.A.		Dec	Mag.	Diam.	Rise		Transit		Set	
	h	m	°		″	h	m	h	m	h	m
1	19	56.1	−20.9	-2.3	41	1	20	5	18	9	16
11	19	57.2	−20.9	-2.4	42	0	42	4	40	8	38
21	19	57.1	−20.9	-2.5	43	23	59	4	00	7	58
31	19	55.6	−21.0	-2.6	45	23	19	3	19	7	16

Diam. = equatorial; Polar Diam. is 94% of Equatorial Diam.

SATURN

Day	R.A.		Dec	Mag.	Diam.	Rise		Transit		Set	
	h	m	°		″	h	m	h	m	h	m
1	20	16.6	−19.8	+0.6	17	1	33	5	38	9	43
11	20	17.0	−19.8	+0.5	17	0	54	4	59	9	04
21	20	16.7	−19.9	+0.5	18	0	15	4	20	8	25
31	20	15.7	−19.9	+0.4	18	23	31	3	39	7	44

Diam. = equatorial; Polar Diam. is 90% of Equatorial Diam.
Rings – major axis 39″ minor axis 14″, Tilt 21°

URANUS

Day	R.A.		Dec	Mag.	Diam.	Rise		Transit		Set	
	h	m	°		″	h	m	h	m	h	m
1	02	18.7	+13.4	+5.9	3	4	20	11	39	18	59
11	02	20.9	+13.6	+5.9	3	3	42	11	02	18	23
21	02	23.1	+13.7	+5.9	3	3	03	10	25	17	47
31	02	25.2	+13.9	+5.9	3	2	25	9	48	17	11

NEPTUNE

Day	R.A.		Dec	Mag.	Diam.	Rise		Transit		Set	
	h	m	°		″	h	m	h	m	h	m
1	23	25.7	−4.8	+7.9	2	3	10	8	47	14	23
11	23	26.6	−4.7	+7.9	2	2	32	8	08	13	45
21	23	27.4	−4.7	+7.9	2	1	53	7	30	13	07
31	23	27.9	−4.6	+7.9	2	1	14	6	51	12	28

June 2020

SIXTH MONTH, 30 DAYS. *Junius,* Roman *gens* (family)

1 *Monday*	Sir Frank Whittle, pilot and aviation engineer who invented the jet engine *b.* 1907	week 22 day	153
2 *Tuesday*	*Surveyor 1* becomes the first spacecraft to land on an extraterrestrial body when it lands on the Moon 1966		154
3 *Wednesday*	Edward White II becomes the first American astronaut to complete a spacewalk 1965		155
4 *Thursday*	Lloyd Berkner, inventor of the device to measure the height and electron density of the ionosphere *d.* 1967		156
5 *Friday*	John Couch Adams, one of two who discovered Neptune *b.* 1891		157
6 *Saturday*	David Scott, astronaut who was the first to drive a wheeled vehicle on the Moon in 1971 *b.* 1932		158
7 *Sunday*	Philipp Lenard, German physicist and 1905 Nobel laureate for his work on cathode rays *b.* 1862		159

8 *Monday*	A transit of Venus occurs for the first time in 122 years 2004	week 23 day	160
9 *Tuesday*	Johann Gottfried Galle, one of two who discovered Neptune *b.* 1812		161
10 *Wednesday*	NASA launches the *Spirit Rover* towards Mars 2003		162
11 *Thursday*	Johann Palitzsch, astronomer who confirmed the return of Halley's comet on Christmas Day 1758 *b.* 1723		163
12 *Friday*	Sir Oliver Lodge, physicist who contributed to the development of wireless telegraphy *b.* 1851		164
13 *Saturday*	Space probe *Pioneer 10* becomes the first human-made object to exit the solar system 1983		165
14 *Sunday*	The European Space Research Organisation is founded 1962		166

15 *Monday*	Solar eclipse is recorded by the Assyrians 763 BC	week 24 day	167
16 *Tuesday*	Valentina Tereshkova becomes first woman in space (aboard *Vostok 6*) 1963		168
17 *Wednesday*	Soviet probe *Venera 6* transmits data before being crushed by Venus' atmospheric pressure 1969		169
18 *Thursday*	Sally Ride becomes first American woman in Space (aboard the *Challenger*) 1983		170
19 *Friday*	Valentina Tereshkova returns to Earth, three days after becoming the first woman in space 1963		171
20 *Saturday*	Asteroid 5261 Eureka, the first of the *Trojan* asteroids that share an orbit with Mars, is discovered 1990		172
21 *Sunday*	*SpaceShipOne* becomes the first privately funded vessel to reach space 2004		173

22 *Monday*	The Royal Greenwich Observatory is created by royal warrant 1675	week 25 day	174
23 *Tuesday*	Norman Robert Pogson creator of a scale to measure the brightness of stars *d.* 1891		175
24 *Wednesday*	Sir Fred Hoyle, astronomer who formulated a basis for the steady-state theory of the universe *b.* 1915		176
25 *Thursday*	Hermann Oberth, the pioneer of rocket propulsion *b.* 1894		177
26 *Friday*	Charles Messier, astronomer knwon for his catalogue of distant celestial bodies *b.* 1730		178
27 *Saturday*	The world's first atomic power station begins producing electricity in Obninsk, Russia 1954		179
28 *Sunday*	Maria Göppert-Mayer, physicist and second woman to win the Nobel Prize *b.* 1906		180

29 *Monday*	The space shuttle *Atlantis* docks with *Mir* to form the largest man-made satellite to orbit Earth 1995	week 26 day	181
30 *Tuesday*	A meteorite explodes above Siberia releasing energy equivalent to 5–10 megatons of TNT 1908		182

ASTRONOMICAL PHENOMENA

d	h	
1	0	Juno 4° north of the Moon
4	13	Mercury greatest elongation east (24°)
5	19	Penumbral lunar eclipse
9	2	Saturn 3° north of the Moon
12	4	Neptune 2° north of Mars
19	9	Venus 0.7° south of the Moon
19	17	Moon occults Epsilon Tauri for part of the UK
20	22	Summer solstice
25	0	Three Galilean moons close to Jupiter
26	22	Galilean moons all to the east of Jupiter
28	2	Pluto 0.7° south of Jupiter

MINIMA OF ALGOL

d	h	d	h	d	h
2	19.9	14	7.2	25	18.4
5	16.7	17	4.0	28	15.2
8	13.5	20	0.8		
11	10.4	22	21.6		

CONSTELLATIONS

The following constellations are near the meridian at

	d	h		d	h
May	1	24	June	15	21
May	16	23	July	1	20
June	1	22	July	16	19

Cassiopeia (below the Pole), Ursa Minor, Draco, Ursa Major, Canes Venatici, Bootes, Corona, Serpens, Virgo and Libra

THE MOON

Phase, Apsides and Node	d	h	m
○ Full Moon	5	19	12
◑ Last Quarter	13	6	24
● New Moon	21	6	41
◐ First Quarter	28	8	16
Perigee (364,365 km)	3	3	38
Apogee (404,595 km)	15	0	57
Perigee (368,958 km)	30	2	13

Mean longitude of the ascending node on 1st, 90°

THE SUN   Diam. 31.6′

Day	Right Ascension			Dec.	Equation of time		Rise		Transit	Set			Sidereal time			Transit of first point of Aries		
							52°	56°		52°		56°				52°		56°
	h	m	s	°	m	s	h m	h m	h m	h m		h m	h	m	s	h	m	s
1	4	37	38	+22.1	+2	06	3 46	3 23	11 58	20 10		20 34	16	39	46	7	19	02
2	4	41	44	+22.2	+1	57	3 45	3 22	11 58	20 11		20 35	16	43	42	7	15	06
3	4	45	51	+22.3	+1	47	3 45	3 21	11 58	20 12		20 37	16	47	39	7	11	10
4	4	49	57	+22.5	+1	37	3 44	3 20	11 58	20 13		20 38	16	51	35	7	07	15
5	4	54	04	+22.6	+1	27	3 43	3 19	11 59	20 14		20 39	16	55	32	7	03	19
6	4	58	11	+22.7	+1	16	3 43	3 18	11 59	20 15		20 40	16	59	28	6	59	23
7	5	02	19	+22.8	+1	05	3 42	3 18	11 59	20 16		20 41	17	03	25	6	55	27
8	5	06	27	+22.9	+0	54	3 42	3 17	11 59	20 17		20 42	17	07	22	6	51	31
9	5	10	35	+23.0	+0	42	3 42	3 16	11 59	20 18		20 43	17	11	18	6	47	35
10	5	14	43	+23.0	+0	30	3 41	3 16	12 00	20 18		20 44	17	15	15	6	43	39
11	5	18	52	+23.1	+0	18	3 41	3 16	12 00	20 19		20 44	17	19	11	6	39	43
12	5	23	01	+23.2	+0	06	3 41	3 15	12 00	20 20		20 45	17	23	08	6	35	47
13	5	27	10	+23.2	-0	07	3 40	3 15	12 00	20 20		20 46	17	27	04	6	31	51
14	5	31	19	+23.3	-0	19	3 40	3 15	12 00	20 21		20 46	17	31	01	6	27	55
15	5	35	28	+23.3	-0	32	3 40	3 15	12 01	20 21		20 47	17	34	57	6	24	00
16	5	39	38	+23.4	-0	45	3 40	3 14	12 01	20 22		20 47	17	38	54	6	20	04
17	5	43	47	+23.4	-0	58	3 40	3 14	12 01	20 22		20 48	17	42	51	6	16	08
18	5	47	57	+23.4	-1	11	3 40	3 14	12 01	20 22		20 48	17	46	47	6	12	12
19	5	52	07	+23.4	-1	24	3 40	3 14	12 01	20 23		20 49	17	50	44	6	08	16
20	5	56	16	+23.4	-1	37	3 40	3 15	12 02	20 23		20 49	17	54	40	6	04	20
21	6	00	26	+23.4	-1	50	3 41	3 15	12 02	20 23		20 49	17	58	37	6	00	24
22	6	04	36	+23.4	-2	04	3 41	3 15	12 02	20 23		20 49	18	02	33	5	56	28
23	6	08	45	+23.4	-2	17	3 41	3 15	12 02	20 23		20 49	18	06	30	5	52	32
24	6	12	55	+23.4	-2	30	3 42	3 16	12 03	20 23		20 49	18	10	26	5	48	36
25	6	17	04	+23.4	-2	42	3 42	3 16	12 03	20 23		20 49	18	14	23	5	44	41
26	6	21	14	+23.3	-2	55	3 42	3 17	12 03	20 23		20 49	18	18	20	5	40	45
27	6	25	23	+23.3	-3	08	3 43	3 17	12 03	20 23		20 49	18	22	16	5	36	49
28	6	29	32	+23.3	-3	20	3 43	3 18	12 03	20 23		20 49	18	26	13	5	32	53
29	6	33	40	+23.2	-3	32	3 44	3 19	12 04	20 23		20 48	18	30	09	5	28	57
30	6	37	49	+23.2	-3	44	3 45	3 19	12 04	20 23		20 48	18	34	06	5	25	01

DURATION OF TWILIGHT (in minutes)

Latitude	52°	56°	52°	56°	52°	56°
		1 June		11 June		21 June
Civil	46	58	48	61	49	63
Nautical	116	TAN	124	TAN	127	TAN
Astronomical	TAN	TAN	TAN	TAN	TAN	TAN

THE NIGHT SKY

Mercury is a magnitude 0.3 spark when at greatest elongation east on the 4th and remains visible in the evening sky until the middle of June.

Venus passes 0.5° north of the Sun through inferior conjunction on the 3rd and then moves into the morning sky where it should be spotted near the Hyades from the last week. On 19th Venus is occulted by the Moon from 08h 40m until 09h 43m. This is observable from the UK but happens during broad daylight so the Moon (only 27 hours old) and Venus are not visible to the naked eye. Extreme caution is needed to avoid eye damage from the Sun (*see* W www.calsky.com for further information).

Mars (magnitude −0.2) rises shortly after midnight and currently dominates the dim watery constellations in the area. Aptly, it is less than 2° from the sea-god Neptune (magnitude 7.9) on the 13th with the Last Quarter Moon nearby too. Mars crosses into Pisces on the 25th.

Jupiter (magnitude −2.7) is now up late evening and can be found in eastern Sagittarius.

Saturn (magnitude 0.3) is near the Capricornus/Sagittarius border and rises a quarter hour after Jupiter. The Moon is 3.5° away on the night of June 12/13.

A penumbral lunar eclipse (magnitude 0.559) on the 5th will likely not be noticed, although processed images will tease out any contrast effects.

The track of a short duration annular solar eclipse of 38 seconds on the 21st crosses western Africa, the southern Arabian peninsula, Pakistan, northern India, Tibet, southern China, Taiwan, and ends in the Pacific. Parts of Oman experience a second such eclipse just six months after that of 26 December 2019.

THE MOON

Day	R.A. h	R.A. m	Dec °	Hor Par '	Diam '	Sun Co-Long °	PA of Br. limb °	Ph. %	Age d	Rise 52° h	Rise 52° m	Rise 56° h	Rise 56° m	Transit h	Transit m	Set 52° h	Set 52° m	Set 56° h	Set 56° m
1	12	29	+2.6	59.7	32.6	27	296	71	9.5	14	24	14	24	20	31	2	04	2	06
2	13	22	−3.3	60.0	32.8	39	296	81	10.5	15	48	15	55	21	23	2	23	2	20
3	14	16	−9.1	60.2	32.8	52	295	89	11.5	17	14	17	27	22	17	2	43	2	35
4	15	12	−14.4	60.1	32.8	64	293	96	12.5	18	41	18	58	23	13	3	07	2	53
5	16	10	−18.8	59.8	32.6	76	292	99	13.5	20	03	20	27	—	—	3	35	3	16
6	17	10	−22.0	59.3	32.4	88	75	100	14.5	21	18	21	45	0	11	4	13	3	48
7	18	11	−23.7	58.6	32.0	100	90	98	15.5	22	20	22	47	1	10	5	01	4	32
8	19	11	−24.0	57.9	31.6	113	86	94	16.5	23	08	23	33	2	09	6	00	5	31
9	20	09	−22.9	57.1	31.0	125	81	88	17.5	23	44	—	—	3	05	7	06	6	41
10	21	04	−20.5	56.3	30.6	137	76	80	18.5	—	—	0	04	3	57	8	17	7	58
11	21	56	−17.3	55.6	30.2	149	72	71	19.5	0	11	0	28	4	45	9	29	9	14
12	22	44	−13.3	55.0	30.0	161	69	62	20.5	0	32	0	44	5	31	10	39	10	29
13	23	30	−8.9	54.5	29.8	174	67	53	21.5	0	50	0	57	6	13	11	48	11	42
14	0	14	−4.3	54.3	29.6	186	66	43	22.5	1	05	1	09	6	54	12	55	12	54
15	0	57	+0.5	54.2	29.6	198	65	34	23.5	1	20	1	19	7	34	14	02	14	05
16	1	40	+5.3	54.3	29.6	210	66	25	24.5	1	35	1	30	8	15	15	10	15	18
17	2	25	+10.0	54.5	29.6	223	68	17	25.5	1	51	1	42	8	58	16	20	16	32
18	3	11	+14.3	54.8	29.8	235	70	11	26.5	2	10	1	57	9	42	17	30	17	47
19	4	00	+18.1	55.3	30.2	247	74	05	27.5	2	32	2	15	10	30	18	41	19	02
20	4	51	+21.1	55.8	30.4	259	78	02	28.5	3	02	2	39	11	20	19	50	20	16
21	5	46	+23.2	56.4	30.8	272	85	00	29.5	3	40	3	14	12	14	20	53	21	21
22	6	43	+24.1	56.9	31.0	284	268	01	1.0	4	29	4	03	13	10	21	47	22	14
23	7	41	+23.6	57.4	31.4	296	274	03	2.0	5	32	5	06	14	06	22	30	22	52
24	8	39	+21.8	57.9	31.6	308	280	08	3.0	6	45	6	22	15	02	23	03	23	22
25	9	36	+18.7	58.3	31.8	321	285	16	4.0	8	04	7	46	15	55	23	30	23	43
26	10	31	+14.5	58.7	32.0	333	289	25	5.0	9	25	9	14	16	47	23	51	23	59
27	11	24	+9.5	59.0	32.2	345	292	35	6.0	10	47	10	41	17	37	—	—	—	—
28	12	16	+4.0	59.2	32.2	357	293	46	7.0	12	09	12	08	18	27	0	11	0	14
29	13	08	−1.8	59.4	32.4	9	293	58	8.0	13	31	13	36	19	17	0	29	0	28
30	14	01	−7.5	59.4	32.4	22	292	69	9.0	14	54	15	04	20	08	0	48	0	42

MERCURY

Day	R.A. h m	Dec °	Mag.	Diam. "	Phase %	Rise h m	Transit h m	Set h m
1	06 18.3	+25.3	+0.2	8	45	4 52	13 37	22 22
3	06 28.1	+25.0	+0.4	8	40	4 56	13 38	22 20
5	06 36.8	+24.7	+0.6	8	36	5 00	13 39	22 17
7	06 44.4	+24.2	+0.8	9	32	5 03	13 38	22 12
9	06 50.8	+23.7	+1.0	9	28	5 05	13 36	22 06
11	06 55.9	+23.2	+1.2	9	25	5 06	13 33	21 58
13	06 59.7	+22.7	+1.5	10	21	5 06	13 28	21 49
15	07 02.2	+22.1	+1.7	10	18	5 05	13 22	21 39
17	07 03.4	+21.6	+2.0	11	14	5 02	13 15	21 27
19	07 03.3	+21.0	+2.4	11	11	4 58	13 07	21 15
21	07 01.9	+20.5	+2.8	11	8	4 53	12 57	21 01
23	06 59.4	+20.0	+3.3	12	6	4 46	12 46	20 47
25	06 55.8	+19.6	+3.8	12	4	4 37	12 34	20 32
27	06 51.4	+19.2	+4.4	12	2	4 28	12 22	20 17
29	06 46.5	+18.9	+4.8	12	1	4 17	12 09	20 02

Rising and setting times are for latitude 54°

VENUS

Day	R.A. h m	Dec °	Mag.	Diam. "	Phase %	Rise h m	Transit h m	Set h m
1	04 55.7	+23.7	−3.8	62	0	3 40	12 05	20 27
6	04 42.8	+22.2	−3.8	62	0	3 20	11 33	19 43
11	04 31.2	+20.7	−4.0	60	2	3 01	11 03	19 02
16	04 22.4	+19.3	−4.2	58	5	2 42	10 36	18 26
21	04 17.5	+18.3	−4.3	54	9	2 25	10 12	17 57
26	04 16.5	+17.6	−4.4	50	14	2 09	9 53	17 34

MARS

Day	R.A. h m	Dec °	Mag.	Diam. "	Phase %	Rise h m	Transit h m	Set h m
1	22 59.9	−9.0	0.0	9	85	1 06	6 20	11 34
6	23 12.4	−7.8	−0.1	10	85	0 52	6 13	11 33
11	23 24.7	−6.7	−0.2	10	84	0 39	6 05	11 32
16	23 36.8	−5.5	−0.2	10	84	0 24	5 57	11 31
21	23 48.6	−4.4	−0.3	11	84	0 10	5 50	11 30
26	00 00.2	−3.3	−0.4	11	84	23 56	5 42	11 28

SUNRISE AND SUNSET

	London		Bristol		Birmingham		Manchester		Newcastle		Glasgow		Belfast	
	0°	05' 51° 30'	2° 35'	51° 28'	1° 55'	52° 28'	2° 15'	53° 28'	1° 37'	54° 59'	4° 14'	55° 52'	5° 56'	54° 35'
d	h m	h m	h m	h m	h m	h m	h m	h m	h m	h m	h m	h m	h m	h m
1	3 49	20 08	3 59	20 18	3 51	20 21	3 47	20 28	3 35	20 35	3 40	20 51	3 55	20 49
2	3 48	20 09	3 58	20 19	3 50	20 22	3 46	20 29	3 34	20 36	3 39	20 52	3 54	20 51
3	3 47	20 10	3 57	20 20	3 49	20 23	3 45	20 30	3 33	20 37	3 38	20 53	3 53	20 52
4	3 47	20 11	3 57	20 21	3 49	20 24	3 44	20 31	3 32	20 38	3 37	20 55	3 52	20 53
5	3 46	20 12	3 56	20 22	3 48	20 25	3 44	20 32	3 31	20 39	3 36	20 56	3 51	20 54
6	3 45	20 13	3 56	20 23	3 47	20 26	3 43	20 33	3 31	20 40	3 35	20 57	3 51	20 55
7	3 45	20 14	3 55	20 24	3 47	20 27	3 42	20 34	3 30	20 41	3 34	20 58	3 50	20 56
8	3 44	20 15	3 55	20 25	3 46	20 28	3 42	20 35	3 30	20 42	3 34	20 59	3 49	20 57
9	3 44	20 16	3 54	20 26	3 46	20 28	3 41	20 36	3 29	20 43	3 33	21 00	3 49	20 58
10	3 44	20 16	3 54	20 26	3 46	20 29	3 41	20 37	3 28	20 44	3 33	21 01	3 48	20 59
11	3 43	20 17	3 54	20 27	3 45	20 30	3 41	20 37	3 28	20 45	3 32	21 02	3 48	20 59
12	3 43	20 18	3 53	20 28	3 45	20 31	3 40	20 38	3 28	20 45	3 32	21 02	3 48	21 00
13	3 43	20 18	3 53	20 28	3 45	20 31	3 40	20 39	3 27	20 46	3 32	21 03	3 47	21 01
14	3 43	20 19	3 53	20 29	3 45	20 32	3 40	20 39	3 27	20 47	3 31	21 04	3 47	21 01
15	3 43	20 19	3 53	20 29	3 44	20 32	3 40	20 40	3 27	20 47	3 31	21 04	3 47	21 02
16	3 43	20 20	3 53	20 30	3 44	20 33	3 40	20 40	3 27	20 48	3 31	21 05	3 47	21 02
17	3 43	20 20	3 53	20 30	3 44	20 33	3 40	20 41	3 27	20 48	3 31	21 05	3 47	21 03
18	3 43	20 21	3 53	20 30	3 44	20 33	3 40	20 41	3 27	20 49	3 31	21 06	3 47	21 03
19	3 43	20 21	3 53	20 31	3 44	20 34	3 40	20 41	3 27	20 49	3 31	21 06	3 47	21 03
20	3 43	20 21	3 53	20 31	3 45	20 34	3 40	20 42	3 27	20 49	3 31	21 06	3 47	21 04
21	3 43	20 21	3 53	20 31	3 45	20 34	3 40	20 42	3 27	20 49	3 31	21 06	3 47	21 04
22	3 43	20 21	3 54	20 31	3 45	20 34	3 40	20 42	3 28	20 50	3 32	21 06	3 48	21 04
23	3 44	20 22	3 54	20 31	3 45	20 34	3 41	20 42	3 28	20 50	3 32	21 07	3 48	21 04
24	3 44	20 22	3 54	20 31	3 46	20 34	3 41	20 42	3 28	20 50	3 32	21 07	3 48	21 04
25	3 44	20 22	3 55	20 31	3 46	20 34	3 41	20 42	3 29	20 50	3 33	21 06	3 49	21 04
26	3 45	20 22	3 55	20 31	3 47	20 34	3 42	20 42	3 29	20 49	3 33	21 06	3 49	21 04
27	3 45	20 21	3 56	20 31	3 47	20 34	3 42	20 42	3 30	20 49	3 34	21 06	3 50	21 04
28	3 46	20 21	3 56	20 31	3 48	20 34	3 43	20 41	3 30	20 49	3 34	21 06	3 50	21 03
29	3 46	20 21	3 57	20 31	3 48	20 34	3 44	20 41	3 31	20 49	3 35	21 05	3 51	21 03
30	3 47	20 21	3 57	20 31	3 49	20 34	3 44	20 41	3 32	20 48	3 36	21 05	3 52	21 03

JUPITER

Day	R.A.		Dec	Mag.	Diam.	Rise		Transit		Set	
	h	m	°		"	h	m	h	m	h	m
1	19	55.4	−21.0	−2.6	45	23	15	3	15	7	12
11	19	52.5	−21.2	−2.6	46	22	34	2	33	6	29
21	19	48.6	−21.4	−2.7	47	21	52	1	50	5	44

Diam. = equatorial; Polar Diam. is 94% of Equatorial Diam.

SATURN

Day	R.A.		Dec	Mag.	Diam.	Rise		Transit		Set	
	h	m	°		"	h	m	h	m	h	m
1	20	15.6	−19.9	+0.4	18	23	27	3	35	7	40
11	20	13.9	−20.1	+0.4	18	22	47	2	54	6	58
21	20	11.8	−20.2	+0.3	18	22	06	2	13	6	16

Diam. = equatorial; Polar Diam. is 90% of Equatorial Diam.
Rings – major axis 41″ minor axis 15″, Tilt 21°

URANUS

Day	R.A.		Dec	Mag.	Diam.	Rise		Transit		Set	
	h	m	°		"	h	m	h	m	h	m
1	02	25.4	+13.9	+5.9	3	2	21	9	44	17	07
11	02	27.2	+14.1	+5.9	3	1	43	9	07	16	30
21	02	29.0	+14.2	+5.8	3	1	04	8	29	15	54

NEPTUNE

Day	R.A.		Dec	Mag.	Diam.	Rise		Transit		Set	
	h	m	°		"	h	m	h	m	h	m
1	23	28.0	−4.6	+7.9	2	1	10	6	47	12	25
11	23	28.3	−4.6	+7.9	2	0	30	6	08	11	46
21	23	28.5	−4.6	+7.9	2	23	47	5	29	11	07

July 2020

SEVENTH MONTH, 31 DAYS. *Julius* Caesar, formerly *Quintilis*, fifth month of Roman pre-Julian calendar

1	*Wednesday*	Edward Jospeh Hoffman, physicist who helped created the PET scanner *d.* 2004	day 183
2	*Thursday*	Hans Bethe, physicist who contributed to physics, electrodynamics and astrophysics *b.* 1906	184
3	*Friday*	*Contour*, an unmanned NASA satellite, launches on a mission to observe a comet nucleus 2002	185
4	*Saturday*	Marie Curie, famous physicist and chemist *d.* 1934	186
5	*Sunday*	William John Macquorn Rankine, founding contributor to the science of thermodynamics *b.* 1820	187

6	*Monday*	The Sedan Crater is artifically created by a nuclear test in the Nevada desert 1962	week 27 day 188
7	*Tuesday*	Venus occults Regulus, allowing for an accurate reading of Venus' atmosphere 1959	189
8	*Wednesday*	The last mission of NASA's space programme begins with the final launch of *Atlantis* 2011	180
9	*Thursday*	*Voyager 2* encounters Jupiter and observes six active volcanoes on its moons 1979	191
10	*Friday*	The first ever communications satellite, *Telstar*, is launched 1962	192
11	*Saturday*	*Juno* makes the closest ever approach to Jupiter, flying within 4,200 km of Jupiter's clouds 2017	193
12	*Sunday*	Willis Lamb, winner of the Nobel Prize for physics in 1955 *b.* 1913	194

13	*Monday*	Donald Edward Osterbrock, astronomer and historian *b.* 1924	week 28 day 195
14	*Tuesday*	*Mariner 4* takes the first up-close photos of another planet as it passes Mars 1965	196
15	*Wednesday*	*Pioneer 10* becomes the first spacecraft to leave the inner solar system and reach the asteroid belt 1972	197
16	*Thursday*	The first atom bomb is successfully tested in New Mexico, US 1945	198
17	*Friday*	Georges Lemaître, astronomer and cosmologist who proposed the big-bang theory *b.* 1894	199
18	*Saturday*	Hendrik Lorenz, physicist whose work on electromagnetic radiation inspired Albert Einstein *b.* 1853	200
19	*Sunday*	Rosalyn Sussman Yalow, medical physicist and joint winner of the 1977 Nobel Prize *b.* 1921	201

20	*Monday*	*Apollo 11* touches down in the Sea of Tranquility in the first ever Moon landing 1969	week 29 day 202
21	*Tuesday*	Neil Armstrong and Edwin 'Buzz' Aldrin become the first humans to walk on the Moon 1969	203
22	*Wednesday*	Joint winner of the 1925 Nobel Prize, Gustav Ludwig Hertz *b.* 1887	204
23	*Thursday*	Vera Rubin, astronomer known for her research on galaxy rotation rates *b.* 1928	205
24	*Friday*	*Apollo 11* lands in the Pacific Ocean, completing the first ever Moon-landing mission 1969	206
25	*Saturday*	The electric telegraph is used commercially for the first time 1837	207
26	*Sunday*	*Apollo 15* launches, the first US mission to use a lunar rover 1971	208

27	*Monday*	The *de Havilland Comet*, the first jet-propelled airliner, makes its maiden flight 1949	week 30 day 209
28	*Tuesday*	Abraham Pais, physicist whose research focused on elementary particle theory *d.* 2000	210
29	*Wednesday*	The National Aeronautics and Space Administration (NASA) is founded 1958	211
30	*Thursday*	*Apollo 15* lands on the Moon and deploys the first US lunar rover 1971	212
31	*Friday*	Unmanned US spacecraft, *Mariner 6*, makes the first close fly-by of Mars 1971	213

ASTRONOMICAL PHENOMENA

d	h	
4	12	Earth at aphelion
5	22	Jupiter, Moon and Saturn form a triangle
8		Venus at greatest brilliancy
12	4	Aldebaran 1° south of Venus
14	8	Jupiter at opposition (Mag. −2.8)
15	19	Pluto at opposition (Mag. +14.3)
17	5	Aldebaran, Venus and Hyades close
17	7	Venus 3° south of the Moon (care of the Sun)
19	5	Mercury 4° south of the Moon
20	22	Saturn at opposition (Mag. +0.1)
22	15	Mercury greatest elongation west (20°)
26	3	Juno 3° north of the Moon

MINIMA OF ALGOL

d	h	d	h	d	h
1	12.0	12	23.3	24	10.5
4	8.9	15	20.1	27	7.4
7	5.7	18	16.9	30	4.2
10	2.5	21	13.7		

CONSTELLATIONS

The following constellations are near the meridian at

	d	h		d	h
June	1	24	July	16	21
June	15	23	August	1	20
July	1	22	August	16	19

Ursa Minor, Draco, Corona, Hercules, Lyra, Serpens, Ophiuchus, Libra, Scorpius and Sagittarius

THE MOON

Phase, Apsides and Node	d	h	m
○ Full Moon	5	4	44
◑ Last Quarter	12	23	29
● New Moon	20	17	33
◐ First Quarter	27	12	33

	d	h	m
Apogee (404,199 km)	12	19	27
Perigee (368,361 km)	25	5	2

Mean longitude of the ascending node on 1st, 89°

THE SUN   Diam. 31.5′

Day	Right Ascension			Dec.	Equation of time		Rise		Transit	Set			Sidereal time			Transit of first point of Aries		
							52°	56°		52°		56°						
	h	m	s	°	m	s	h m	h m	h m	h m		h m	h	m	s	h	m	s
1	6	41	57	+23.1	-3	56	3 45	3 20	12 04	20 22		20 47	18	38	02	5	21	05
2	6	46	05	+23.0	-4	07	3 46	3 21	12 04	20 22		20 47	18	41	59	5	17	09
3	6	50	12	+22.9	-4	18	3 47	3 22	12 04	20 21		20 46	18	45	55	5	13	13
4	6	54	20	+22.8	-4	29	3 48	3 23	12 05	20 21		20 46	18	49	52	5	09	17
5	6	58	27	+22.8	-4	39	3 48	3 24	12 05	20 20		20 45	18	53	49	5	05	21
6	7	02	33	+22.7	-4	49	3 49	3 25	12 05	20 20		20 44	18	57	45	5	01	26
7	7	06	39	+22.6	-4	59	3 50	3 26	12 05	20 19		20 44	19	01	42	4	57	30
8	7	10	45	+22.4	-5	08	3 51	3 27	12 05	20 19		20 43	19	05	38	4	53	34
9	7	14	51	+22.3	-5	17	3 52	3 28	12 05	20 18		20 42	19	09	35	4	49	38
10	7	18	56	+22.2	-5	26	3 53	3 29	12 05	20 17		20 41	19	13	31	4	45	42
11	7	23	01	+22.1	-5	34	3 54	3 31	12 06	20 16		20 40	19	17	28	4	41	46
12	7	27	05	+21.9	-5	41	3 55	3 32	12 06	20 15		20 39	19	21	24	4	37	50
13	7	31	09	+21.8	-5	49	3 57	3 33	12 06	20 15		20 37	19	25	21	4	33	54
14	7	35	12	+21.6	-5	55	3 58	3 35	12 06	20 14		20 36	19	29	18	4	29	58
15	7	39	15	+21.5	-6	02	3 59	3 36	12 06	20 13		20 35	19	33	14	4	26	02
16	7	43	17	+21.3	-6	07	4 00	3 38	12 06	20 11		20 34	19	37	11	4	22	06
17	7	47	19	+21.1	-6	13	4 01	3 39	12 06	20 10		20 32	19	41	07	4	18	11
18	7	51	20	+21.0	-6	17	4 03	3 41	12 06	20 09		20 31	19	45	04	4	14	15
19	7	55	21	+20.8	-6	22	4 04	3 42	12 06	20 08		20 29	19	49	00	4	10	19
20	7	59	21	+20.6	-6	25	4 05	3 44	12 06	20 07		20 28	19	52	57	4	06	23
21	8	03	21	+20.4	-6	28	4 07	3 46	12 06	20 06		20 26	19	56	53	4	02	27
22	8	07	20	+20.2	-6	31	4 08	3 47	12 07	20 04		20 25	20	00	50	3	58	31
23	8	11	19	+20.0	-6	33	4 09	3 49	12 07	20 03		20 23	20	04	47	3	54	35
24	8	15	16	+19.8	-6	34	4 11	3 51	12 07	20 02		20 21	20	08	43	3	50	39
25	8	19	14	+19.6	-6	35	4 12	3 52	12 07	20 00		20 20	20	12	40	3	46	43
26	8	23	11	+19.4	-6	35	4 14	3 54	12 07	19 59		20 18	20	16	36	3	42	47
27	8	27	07	+19.1	-6	35	4 15	3 56	12 07	19 57		20 16	20	20	33	3	38	51
28	8	31	02	+18.9	-6	34	4 16	3 58	12 07	19 56		20 14	20	24	29	3	34	56
29	8	34	57	+18.7	-6	32	4 18	3 59	12 07	19 54		20 12	20	28	26	3	31	00
30	8	38	51	+18.4	-6	30	4 19	4 01	12 06	19 52		20 10	20	32	22	3	27	04
31	8	42	45	+18.2	-6	27	4 21	4 03	12 06	19 51		20 09	20	36	19	3	23	08

DURATION OF TWILIGHT (in minutes)

Latitude	52°	56°	52°	56°	52°	56°
		1 July		11 July		21 July
Civil	48	61	47	58	44	53
Nautical	124	TAN	117	TAN	107	146
Astronomical	TAN	TAN	TAN	TAN	TAN	TAN

THE NIGHT SKY

Mercury (magnitude 0.3) can be seen in the morning sky during the second half of the month after inferior conjunction on the 1st. It is 6° up at greatest elongation west on the 22nd and brightens to magnitude −0.8 by the end of July while still remaining as high.

Venus (magnitude −4.5) rises 2.5 hours before the Sun and reaches greatest brilliancy on the 8th. It is near the Hyades on the 6th and 1° from Aldebaran on the 12th. The Moon is nearby on the 17th.

Mars (magnitude −0.7) is now a bright ember rising before midnight by the end of July. It moves into Cetus on the 9th and returns to Pisces on the 27th. The Moon is 3° from Mars the night of the 11th.

Jupiter (magnitude −2.7) is at opposition on the 14th and rises mid-evening with Saturn quickly following. The Full Moon is close on the 5th with Saturn nearby.

Saturn (magnitude 0.1) crosses into Sagittarius on the 4th and comes to opposition on the 20th.

Pluto (magnitude 14.3) is at opposition on the 15th in Sagittarius.

All the planets are simultaneously on view mid-month before dawn for observers in the southern UK. Although Mercury is only 3° up on the 19th when the Moon is nearby, while Jupiter is close to setting. Uranus and Neptune along with the dwarf planets Pluto and Ceres can be viewed with a telescope.

A shallow penumbral lunar eclipse (magnitude 0.350) on the 5th will not be noticed.

THE MOON

Day	R.A. h	R.A. m	Dec °	Hor Par '	Diam '	Sun Co-Long °	PA of Br. limb °	Ph. %	Age d	Rise 52° h	Rise 52° m	Rise 56° h	Rise 56° m	Transit h	Transit m	Set 52° h	Set 52° m	Set 56° h	Set 56° m
1	14	54	−12.8	59.4	32.4	34	289	79	10.0	16	18	16	34	21	02	1	10	0	58
2	15	50	−17.4	59.2	32.2	46	285	87	11.0	17	41	18	01	21	58	1	35	1	18
3	16	48	−21.0	58.9	32.2	58	280	94	12.0	18	57	19	24	22	56	2	08	1	45
4	17	48	−23.2	58.5	31.8	70	272	98	13.0	20	05	20	33	23	54	2	49	2	23
5	18	48	−24.1	57.9	31.6	83	242	100	14.0	20	59	21	26	—	—	3	42	3	15
6	19	47	−23.5	57.3	31.2	95	92	99	15.0	21	41	22	03	0	51	4	46	4	20
7	20	43	−21.5	56.7	30.8	107	83	96	16.0	22	12	22	30	1	45	5	57	5	34
8	21	37	−18.6	56.0	30.6	119	77	91	17.0	22	36	22	49	2	36	7	10	6	52
9	22	27	−14.8	55.4	30.2	131	73	85	18.0	22	55	23	04	3	24	8	21	8	09
10	23	14	−10.5	54.9	30.0	144	70	77	19.0	23	11	23	16	4	08	9	32	9	24
11	23	59	−5.8	54.5	29.8	156	69	69	20.0	23	26	23	27	4	50	10	40	10	37
12	0	43	−1.0	54.3	29.6	168	68	59	21.0	23	41	23	38	5	30	11	48	11	49
13	1	26	+3.8	54.2	29.6	180	68	50	22.0	23	56	23	49	6	11	12	55	13	00
14	2	10	+8.5	54.4	29.6	193	69	41	23.0	—	—	—	—	6	52	14	03	14	13
15	2	55	+12.9	54.7	29.8	205	72	31	24.0	0	14	0	02	7	35	15	13	15	28
16	3	43	+16.9	55.1	30.0	217	75	23	25.0	0	34	0	18	8	21	16	24	16	43
17	4	33	+20.2	55.6	30.4	229	80	15	26.0	1	01	0	39	9	11	17	34	17	57
18	5	26	+22.6	56.3	30.6	241	86	08	27.0	1	34	1	10	10	03	18	40	19	06
19	6	23	+23.9	57.0	31.0	254	94	03	28.0	2	19	1	53	10	58	19	38	20	05
20	7	21	+23.9	57.7	31.4	266	109	01	29.0	3	18	2	51	11	56	20	26	20	51
21	8	20	+22.5	58.3	31.8	278	243	00	0.4	4	28	4	05	12	53	21	03	21	24
22	9	19	+19.7	58.8	32.0	290	275	02	1.4	5	47	5	27	13	49	21	33	21	48
23	10	16	+15.7	59.2	32.2	303	283	07	2.4	7	10	6	57	14	42	21	57	22	06
24	11	11	+10.7	59.4	32.4	315	288	13	3.4	8	34	8	26	15	34	22	17	22	22
25	12	04	+5.2	59.5	32.4	327	290	22	4.4	9	57	9	55	16	25	22	36	22	36
26	12	56	−0.6	59.5	32.4	339	291	33	5.4	11	20	11	23	17	15	22	54	22	49
27	13	49	−6.3	59.3	32.4	352	290	44	6.4	12	42	12	51	18	05	23	15	23	05
28	14	42	−11.7	59.1	32.2	4	288	56	7.4	14	05	14	19	18	57	23	38	23	23
29	15	36	−16.4	58.8	32.0	16	285	67	8.4	15	27	15	46	19	51	—	—	23	47
30	16	33	−20.2	58.5	31.8	28	280	77	9.4	16	44	17	08	20	47	0	08	—	—
31	17	31	−22.8	58.1	31.6	41	273	85	10.4	17	53	18	21	21	44	0	45	0	20

MERCURY

Day	R.A. h	R.A. m	Dec °	Mag.	Diam. "	Phase %	Rise h	Rise m	Transit h	Transit m	Set h	Set m
1	06	41.4	+18.7	+5.0	12	1	4	06	11	56	19	48
3	06	36.4	+18.5	+4.8	12	1	3	54	11	44	19	34
5	06	31.8	+18.4	+4.2	12	2	3	42	11	32	19	22
7	06	27.9	+18.5	+3.6	11	4	3	30	11	20	19	11
9	06	25.1	+18.6	+3.0	11	7	3	19	11	10	19	02
11	06	23.5	+18.8	+2.5	10	10	3	08	11	01	18	55
13	06	23.3	+19.0	+2.0	10	13	2	59	10	54	18	50
15	06	24.6	+19.3	+1.6	10	18	2	50	10	48	18	47
17	06	27.4	+19.7	+1.2	9	22	2	43	10	43	18	45
19	06	31.8	+20.1	+0.9	9	27	2	37	10	40	18	45
21	06	37.8	+20.4	+0.5	8	33	2	32	10	39	18	47
23	06	45.4	+20.8	+0.3	8	39	2	29	10	39	18	50
25	06	54.5	+21.1	0.0	7	45	2	29	10	40	18	54
27	07	05.1	+21.3	−0.3	7	52	2	30	10	44	18	59
29	07	17.1	+21.5	−0.5	7	59	2	33	10	48	19	04
31	07	30.4	+21.5	−0.7	6	66	2	38	10	54	19	10

Rising and setting times are for latitude 54°

VENUS

Day	R.A. h	R.A. m	Dec °	Mag.	Diam. "	Phase %	Rise h	Rise m	Transit h	Transit m	Set h	Set m
1	04	19.2	+17.3	−4.5	46	19	1	55	9	37	17	17
6	04	25.3	+17.2	−4.5	43	23	1	41	9	24	17	05
11	04	34.4	+17.4	−4.5	39	28	1	30	9	14	16	57
16	04	45.9	+17.8	−4.5	37	32	1	19	9	06	16	53
21	04	59.5	+18.2	−4.4	34	36	1	10	9	00	16	51
26	05	14.9	+18.7	−4.4	32	39	1	02	8	56	16	51
31	05	31.8	+19.2	−4.4	30	42	0	56	8	54	16	52

MARS

Day	R.A. h	R.A. m	Dec °	Mag.	Diam. "	Phase %	Rise h	Rise m	Transit h	Transit m	Set h	Set m
1	00	11.5	−2.2	−0.5	11	84	23	42	5	33	11	26
6	00	22.5	−1.1	−0.6	12	85	23	27	5	24	11	23
11	00	33.1	−0.1	−0.7	12	85	23	12	5	15	11	19
16	00	43.4	+0.9	−0.8	13	85	22	58	5	06	11	15
21	00	53.3	+1.8	−0.9	13	85	22	43	4	56	11	11
26	01	02.6	+2.6	−1.0	14	86	22	28	4	46	11	05
31	01	11.4	+3.4	−1.1	14	86	22	12	4	35	10	59

SUNRISE AND SUNSET

	London 0° 05′ 51° 30′		Bristol 2° 35′ 51° 28′		Birmingham 1° 55′ 52° 28′		Manchester 2° 15′ 53° 28′		Newcastle 1° 37′ 54° 59′		Glasgow 4° 14′ 55° 52′		Belfast 5° 56′ 54° 35′	
d	h m	h m	h m	h m	h m	h m	h m	h m	h m	h m	h m	h m	h m	h m
1	3 48	20 20	3 58	20 30	3 50	20 33	3 45	20 40	3 33	20 48	3 37	21 05	3 53	21 02
2	3 48	20 20	3 59	20 30	3 50	20 33	3 46	20 40	3 33	20 47	3 38	21 04	3 53	21 02
3	3 49	20 20	3 59	20 29	3 51	20 32	3 47	20 40	3 34	20 47	3 38	21 03	3 54	21 01
4	3 50	20 19	4 00	20 29	3 52	20 32	3 47	20 39	3 35	20 46	3 39	21 03	3 55	21 01
5	3 51	20 19	4 01	20 28	3 53	20 31	3 48	20 38	3 36	20 45	3 40	21 02	3 56	21 00
6	3 52	20 18	4 02	20 28	3 54	20 31	3 49	20 38	3 37	20 45	3 42	21 01	3 57	20 59
7	3 53	20 17	4 03	20 27	3 55	20 30	3 50	20 37	3 38	20 44	3 43	21 00	3 58	20 59
8	3 54	20 17	4 04	20 27	3 56	20 29	3 51	20 36	3 39	20 43	3 44	21 00	3 59	20 58
9	3 55	20 16	4 05	20 26	3 57	20 28	3 52	20 35	3 41	20 42	3 45	20 59	4 00	20 57
10	3 56	20 15	4 06	20 25	3 58	20 28	3 54	20 35	3 42	20 41	3 46	20 58	4 02	20 56
11	3 57	20 14	4 07	20 24	3 59	20 27	3 55	20 34	3 43	20 40	3 48	20 56	4 03	20 55
12	3 58	20 14	4 08	20 23	4 00	20 26	3 56	20 33	3 44	20 39	3 49	20 55	4 04	20 54
13	3 59	20 13	4 09	20 23	4 01	20 25	3 57	20 32	3 46	20 38	3 50	20 54	4 05	20 53
14	4 00	20 12	4 10	20 22	4 02	20 24	3 58	20 31	3 47	20 37	3 52	20 53	4 07	20 52
15	4 01	20 11	4 11	20 21	4 04	20 23	4 00	20 29	3 48	20 36	3 53	20 52	4 08	20 51
16	4 02	20 10	4 13	20 20	4 05	20 22	4 01	20 28	3 50	20 34	3 55	20 50	4 09	20 49
17	4 04	20 09	4 14	20 18	4 06	20 21	4 02	20 27	3 51	20 33	3 56	20 49	4 11	20 48
18	4 05	20 07	4 15	20 17	4 08	20 19	4 04	20 26	3 53	20 32	3 58	20 47	4 12	20 47
19	4 06	20 06	4 16	20 16	4 09	20 18	4 05	20 25	3 54	20 30	3 59	20 46	4 14	20 45
20	4 08	20 05	4 18	20 15	4 10	20 17	4 07	20 23	3 56	20 29	4 01	20 44	4 15	20 44
21	4 09	20 04	4 19	20 14	4 12	20 16	4 08	20 22	3 57	20 27	4 03	20 43	4 17	20 42
22	4 10	20 03	4 20	20 12	4 13	20 14	4 10	20 20	3 59	20 26	4 04	20 41	4 18	20 41
23	4 12	20 01	4 22	20 11	4 15	20 13	4 11	20 19	4 01	20 24	4 06	20 40	4 20	20 39
24	4 13	20 00	4 23	20 10	4 16	20 11	4 13	20 17	4 02	20 23	4 08	20 38	4 22	20 38
25	4 14	19 58	4 25	20 08	4 17	20 10	4 14	20 16	4 04	20 21	4 10	20 36	4 23	20 36
26	4 16	19 57	4 26	20 07	4 19	20 08	4 16	20 14	4 06	20 19	4 11	20 34	4 25	20 34
27	4 17	19 55	4 27	20 05	4 20	20 07	4 17	20 13	4 07	20 17	4 13	20 33	4 27	20 33
28	4 19	19 54	4 29	20 04	4 22	20 05	4 19	20 11	4 09	20 16	4 15	20 31	4 28	20 31
29	4 20	19 52	4 30	20 02	4 23	20 04	4 20	20 09	4 11	20 14	4 17	20 29	4 30	20 29
30	4 22	19 51	4 32	20 01	4 25	20 02	4 22	20 08	4 12	20 12	4 19	20 27	4 32	20 27
31	4 23	19 49	4 33	19 59	4 27	20 00	4 24	20 06	4 14	20 10	4 20	20 25	4 33	20 26

JUPITER

Day	R.A. h m	Dec °	Mag.	Diam. ″	Rise h m	Transit h m	Set h m
1	19 43.8	−21.6	−2.7	47	21 09	1 06	4 58
11	19 38.5	−21.8	−2.7	48	20 27	0 21	4 12
21	19 33.1	−22.1	−2.7	48	19 44	23 33	3 26
31	19 27.9	−22.3	−2.7	47	19 01	22 48	2 39

Diam. = equatorial; Polar Diam. is 94% of Equatorial Diam.

SATURN

Day	R.A. h m	Dec °	Mag.	Diam. ″	Rise h m	Transit h m	Set h m
1	20 09.2	−20.3	+0.2	18	21 25	1 31	5 33
11	20 06.3	−20.5	+0.2	18	20 44	0 49	4 49
21	20 03.2	−20.7	+0.1	18	20 03	0 06	4 06
31	20 00.2	−20.8	+0.1	18	19 22	23 20	3 22

Diam. = equatorial; Polar Diam. is 90% of Equatorial Diam.
Rings – major axis 42″ minor axis 15″, Tilt 22°

URANUS

Day	R.A. h m	Dec °	Mag.	Diam. ″	Rise h m	Transit h m	Set h m
1	02 30.4	+14.3	+5.8	3	0 26	7 51	15 17
11	02 31.7	+14.4	+5.8	4	23 47	7 13	14 39
21	02 32.6	+14.5	+5.8	4	23 08	6 35	14 01
31	02 33.3	+14.6	+5.8	4	22 29	5 56	13 23

NEPTUNE

Day	R.A. h m	Dec °	Mag.	Diam. ″	Rise h m	Transit h m	Set h m
1	23 28.4	−4.6	+7.9	2	23 08	4 50	10 27
11	23 28.2	−4.6	+7.9	2	22 29	4 10	9 48
21	23 27.8	−4.7	+7.8	2	21 49	3 30	9 07
31	23 27.2	−4.7	+7.8	2	21 10	2 50	8 27

August 2020

EIGHTH MONTH, 31 DAYS. *Augustus*, formerly *Sextilis*, sixth month of Roman pre-Julian calendar

1	*Saturday*	Douglas Osheroff, Nobel Prize winner for the discovery of superfluidity in Helium-3 *b.* 1945	day 214
2	*Sunday*	Carl D. Anderson discovers Positron, the antimatter counterpart to the electron 1932	215

3	*Monday*	George Francis Fitzgerald, Irish physicist who helped lay the foundations for wireless telegraphy *b.* 1851	week 31 day 216
4	*Tuesday*	Mathematician and physicist, William Rowan Hamilton, who reformulated Newtonian mechanics *b.* 1805	217
5	*Wednesday*	Neil Armstrong, the first person to set foot on the Moon, *b.* 1930	218
6	*Thursday*	*Curiosity Rover* lands on Mars to explore the Gale Crater 2012	219
7	*Friday*	Alan Hazeltine, inventor of the neutrodyne circuit which made commercial radio possible *b.* 1886	220
8	*Saturday*	Sir Roger Penrose, physicist known for his contributions to cosmology and general relativity *b.* 1931	221
9	*Sunday*	Jonathan Homer Lane, American astrophysicist and first to investigate the Sun as a gaseous body *b.* 1819	222

10	*Monday*	*Magellan*, a space probe tasked with mapping the surface of Venus, arrives at its destination 1990	week 32 day 223
11	*Tuesday*	The last total eclipse of the millenium occurs 1999	224
12	*Wednesday*	Deimos, one of the moons of Mars, is discovered by Asaph Hall 1877	225
13	*Thursday*	Asteroid 433 Eros is the first asteroid to be discovered 1898	226
14	*Friday*	Arthur Jeffrey Dempster, physicist who built the first mass spectrometer in 1918 *b.* 1886	227
15	*Saturday*	Louis de Broglie, Nobel Prize-winning physicist for his work on wave particle duality *b.* 1892	228
16	*Sunday*	Gabriel Lippmann, winner of the 1908 Nobel Prize for reproducing colours in photographs *b.* 1845	229

17	*Monday*	*Venera 7*, the first spacecraft to transmit data from another planet, is launched 1970	week 33 day 230
18	*Tuesday*	Astronomer Pierre Janssen discovers helium in the solar spectrum 1868	231
19	*Wednesday*	The first Astronomer Royal John Flamsteed, who catalogued more than 3,000 stars *b.* 1646	232
20	*Thursday*	NASA spacecraft *Voyager 2* is launched 1977	233
21	*Friday*	A critical indicent occurs with a plutonium core in Los Alamos National Laboratory, US 1945	234
22	*Saturday*	*Voyager 2* discovers Neptune's first complete ring about 27,360km above its atmosphere 1989	235
23	*Sunday*	Osborne Reynolds, physicist recognised for his work in hydraulics and hydrodynamics *b.* 1842	236

24	*Monday*	The International Astronomical Union reclassifies Pluto as a dwarf planet 2006	week 34 day 237
25	*Tuesday*	Galileo Galilei demonstrates his first telescope 1609	238
26	*Wednesday*	James Franck, winner of the 1925 Nobel Prize for his experiments on the Bohr model of the atom *b.* 1882	239
27	*Thursday*	Norman Foster Ramsey, 1989 Nobel laureate for his study of atoms using magnetic fields *b.* 1915	240
28	*Friday*	Vladimir Grigoryevich Shukhov, known for his contributions to structural engineering *b.* 1853	241
29	*Saturday*	Electromagnetic induction is discovered by Michael Faraday 1831	242
30	*Sunday*	Ernest Rutherford, nuclear physics pioneer who achieved the 'splitting' of light atoms *b.*1871	243

31	*Monday*	Guillaume Amontons, who rediscovered Leonardo Da Vinci's laws of friction *b.* 1663	week 35 day 244

ASTRONOMICAL PHENOMENA

d	h	
2	1	Jupiter 2° north of the Moon and Saturn
3	5	Vesta 0.2° north of Mercury
12	13	Perseid meteor swarm
13	0	Venus greatest elongation west (46°)
22	21	Juno 4° north of the Moon
28	12	Ceres at opposition (Mag. +7.7)

MINIMA OF ALGOL

d	h	d	h	d	h
2	1.0	13	12.2	24	23.5
4	21.8	16	9.0	27	20.3
7	18.6	19	5.8	30	17.1
10	15.4	22	2.6		

CONSTELLATIONS

The following constellations are near the meridian at

d	h		d	h
July	1	24	August	16	21
July	16	23	September	1	20
August	1	22	September	15	19

Draco, Hercules, Lyra, Cygnus, Sagitta, Ophiuchus, Serpens, Aquila and Sagittarius

THE MOON

Phase, Apsides and Node	d	h	m
○ Full Moon	3	15	59
◑ Last Quarter	11	16	45
● New Moon	19	2	42
◐ First Quarter	25	17	58
Apogee (404,659 km)	9	13	50
Perigee (363,512 km)	21	10	57
Mean longitude of the ascending node on 1st, 87°			

THE SUN   Diam. 31.5′

Day	Right Ascension h	m	s	Dec. °	Equation of time m	s	Rise 52° h	m	Rise 56° h	m	Transit h	m	Set 52° h	m	Set 56° h	m	Sidereal time h	m	s	Transit of first point of Aries h	m	s
1	8	46	38	+17.9	−6	23	4	23	4	05	12	06	19	49	20	07	20	40	16	3	19	12
2	8	50	30	+17.7	−6	19	4	24	4	07	12	06	19	47	20	05	20	44	12	3	15	16
3	8	54	22	+17.4	−6	14	4	26	4	09	12	06	19	46	20	02	20	48	09	3	11	20
4	8	58	13	+17.2	−6	09	4	27	4	11	12	06	19	44	20	00	20	52	05	3	07	24
5	9	02	04	+16.9	−6	03	4	29	4	12	12	06	19	42	19	58	20	56	02	3	03	28
6	9	05	54	+16.6	−5	56	4	30	4	14	12	06	19	40	19	56	20	59	58	2	59	32
7	9	09	43	+16.3	−5	49	4	32	4	16	12	06	19	39	19	54	21	03	55	2	55	36
8	9	13	32	+16.1	−5	41	4	33	4	18	12	06	19	37	19	52	21	07	51	2	51	41
9	9	17	20	+15.8	−5	33	4	35	4	20	12	05	19	35	19	50	21	11	48	2	47	45
10	9	21	08	+15.5	−5	24	4	37	4	22	12	05	19	33	19	47	21	15	45	2	43	49
11	9	24	55	+15.2	−5	15	4	38	4	24	12	05	19	31	19	45	21	19	41	2	39	53
12	9	28	41	+14.9	−5	05	4	40	4	26	12	05	19	29	19	43	21	23	38	2	35	57
13	9	32	27	+14.6	−4	54	4	41	4	28	12	05	19	27	19	40	21	27	34	2	32	01
14	9	36	13	+14.3	−4	43	4	43	4	30	12	05	19	25	19	38	21	31	31	2	28	05
15	9	39	58	+14.0	−4	31	4	45	4	32	12	04	19	23	19	36	21	35	27	2	24	09
16	9	43	42	+13.7	−4	19	4	46	4	34	12	04	19	21	19	33	21	39	24	2	20	13
17	9	47	26	+13.3	−4	07	4	48	4	36	12	04	19	19	19	31	21	43	20	2	16	17
18	9	51	10	+13.0	−3	53	4	50	4	38	12	04	19	17	19	29	21	47	17	2	12	21
19	9	54	52	+12.7	−3	40	4	51	4	40	12	04	19	15	19	26	21	51	14	2	08	26
20	9	58	35	+12.4	−3	26	4	53	4	42	12	03	19	13	19	24	21	55	10	2	04	30
21	10	02	17	+12.0	−3	11	4	54	4	43	12	03	19	11	19	21	21	59	07	2	00	34
22	10	05	58	+11.7	−2	56	4	56	4	45	12	03	19	08	19	19	22	03	03	1	56	38
23	10	09	39	+11.4	−2	41	4	58	4	47	12	03	19	06	19	16	22	07	00	1	52	42
24	10	13	20	+11.0	−2	25	4	59	4	49	12	02	19	04	19	14	22	10	56	1	48	46
25	10	17	00	+10.7	−2	08	5	01	4	51	12	02	19	02	19	11	22	14	53	1	44	50
26	10	20	40	+10.3	−1	52	5	03	4	53	12	02	19	00	19	09	22	18	49	1	40	54
27	10	24	19	+10.0	−1	34	5	04	4	55	12	01	18	57	19	06	22	22	46	1	36	58
28	10	27	58	+9.6	−1	17	5	06	4	57	12	01	18	55	19	04	22	26	43	1	33	02
29	10	31	37	+9.3	−0	59	5	07	4	59	12	01	18	53	19	01	22	30	39	1	29	06
30	10	35	15	+8.9	−0	40	5	09	5	01	12	00	18	51	18	59	22	34	36	1	25	11
31	10	38	53	+8.5	−0	22	5	11	5	03	12	00	18	49	18	56	22	38	32	1	21	15

DURATION OF TWILIGHT (in minutes)

Latitude	52°	56°	52°	56°	52°	56°
		1 August		11 August		21 August
Civil	41	49	39	45	37	42
Nautical	97	121	90	107	84	97
Astronomical	179	TAN	154	210	139	168

THE NIGHT SKY

Mercury opens the month still nicely placed in the morning sky and reaches magnitude −1.3 at the end of the first week but is a fraction lower. It is lost to view a few days later with superior conjunction coming on the 17th.

Venus (magnitude −4.4) is now rising nearly four hours before the Sun and is at greatest elongation west on the 13th when the disk shows a half phase. The planet lies in the feet of Gemini when the Moon is 5.5° away on the 15th.

Mars (magnitude −1.4) is up just after 23h on the 1st and an hour earlier by the end of August. The Moon and Mars are 3° apart when they rise together on the 8th. By now, separate planned missions from NASA, ESA/Roscosmos, China, and the UAE may be heading to the Red Planet. Schedules have a habit of changing though, so check the respective space agency's website for updates during the year.

Jupiter (magnitude −2.7) graces the south-eastern sky as soon as darkness falls. The Moon is near Jupiter on the 1st and close again on the 28th. Orbiting the giant planet until July 2021 is the Juno spacecraft.

Saturn (magnitude 0.2) can be seen not far from Jupiter as twilight fades. The Moon is near Saturn on the 2nd and 29th.

Perseid maximum on the 13th is two days after Last Quarter Moon so a few hours of dark sky are to be had before moonrise around local midnight.

THE MOON

Day	R.A.		Dec	Hor Par	Diam	Sun Co-Long	PA of Br. limb	Ph.	Age	Rise				Transit		Set			
										52°		56°				52°		56°	
	h	m	°	'	'	°	°	%	d	h	m	h	m	h	m	h	m	h	m
1	18	30	−24.0	57.6	31.4	53	266	92	11.4	18	51	19	19	22	41	1	32	1	06
2	19	28	−23.8	57.1	31.2	65	256	97	12.4	19	37	20	01	23	36	2	31	2	05
3	20	25	−22.3	56.6	30.8	77	236	100	13.4	20	12	20	32	—	—	3	39	3	15
4	21	19	−19.6	56.1	30.6	89	116	100	14.4	20	38	20	53	0	28	4	51	4	32
5	22	10	−16.1	55.5	30.2	101	85	98	15.4	20	58	21	10	1	16	6	04	5	50
6	22	58	−11.9	55.1	30.0	114	77	94	16.4	21	16	21	23	2	02	7	15	7	06
7	23	44	−7.3	54.7	29.8	126	73	89	17.4	21	32	21	34	2	45	8	25	8	20
8	0	28	−2.5	54.4	29.6	138	71	82	18.4	21	46	21	45	3	26	9	33	9	33
9	1	12	+2.4	54.2	29.6	150	70	75	19.4	22	01	21	56	4	07	10	41	10	44
10	1	55	+7.1	54.2	29.6	162	71	66	20.4	22	17	22	08	4	47	11	48	11	56
11	2	40	+11.6	54.4	29.6	175	73	57	21.4	22	36	22	22	5	29	12	56	13	09
12	3	26	+15.7	54.7	29.8	187	75	47	22.4	23	00	22	40	6	14	14	06	14	24
13	4	15	+19.2	55.2	30.0	199	79	38	23.4	23	29	23	06	7	01	15	16	15	38
14	5	06	+21.9	55.8	30.4	211	84	28	24.4	—	—	23	42	7	51	16	24	16	49
15	6	01	+23.7	56.6	30.8	224	90	20	25.4	0	09	—	—	8	44	17	25	17	52
16	6	58	+24.1	57.4	31.2	236	97	12	26.4	1	01	0	32	9	41	18	18	18	44
17	7	57	+23.2	58.2	31.8	248	106	06	27.4	2	06	1	39	10	38	18	59	19	22
18	8	57	+20.9	59.0	32.2	260	119	02	28.4	3	22	3	01	11	36	19	33	19	50
19	9	55	+17.2	59.6	32.4	273	180	00	29.4	4	45	4	29	12	32	19	59	20	11
20	10	52	+12.5	60.1	32.8	285	271	01	0.9	6	12	6	02	13	26	20	21	20	27
21	11	47	+6.9	60.3	32.8	297	283	05	1.9	7	38	7	33	14	18	20	40	20	42
22	12	41	+1.0	60.3	32.8	309	287	12	2.9	9	04	9	05	15	09	20	59	20	56
23	13	35	−5.0	60.1	32.8	322	288	20	3.9	10	29	10	35	16	01	21	19	21	11
24	14	29	−10.7	59.7	32.6	334	287	30	4.9	11	53	12	05	16	53	21	42	21	28
25	15	23	−15.6	59.2	32.2	346	284	42	5.9	13	16	13	34	17	47	22	09	21	50
26	16	20	−19.6	58.6	32.0	358	280	53	6.9	14	36	14	58	18	43	22	44	22	20
27	17	17	−22.5	58.0	31.6	10	274	64	7.9	15	47	16	14	19	39	23	28	23	02
28	18	15	−24.0	57.5	31.4	23	268	74	8.9	16	48	17	16	20	35	—	—	23	56
29	19	13	−24.1	56.9	31.0	35	261	83	9.9	17	37	18	01	21	30	0	23	—	—
30	20	10	−22.9	56.4	30.8	47	254	90	10.9	18	13	18	36	22	22	1	27	1	03
31	21	04	−20.5	55.9	30.4	59	246	95	11.9	18	42	18	58	23	11	2	37	2	16

MERCURY

Day	R.A.		Dec	Mag.	Diam.	Phase	Rise		Transit		Set	
	h	m	°		"	%	h	m	h	m	h	m
1	07	37.5	+21.4	−0.8	6	70	2	42	10	57	19	13
3	07	52.4	+21.2	−1.0	6	76	2	51	11	04	19	18
5	08	08.2	+20.9	−1.2	6	83	3	01	11	13	19	23
7	08	24.6	+20.3	−1.3	5	88	3	14	11	21	19	28
9	08	41.3	+19.6	−1.4	5	92	3	28	11	30	19	31
11	08	58.1	+18.7	−1.6	5	96	3	43	11	39	19	33
13	09	14.8	+17.7	−1.7	5	98	3	59	11	48	19	35
15	09	31.2	+16.5	−1.8	5	99	4	16	11	56	19	35
17	09	47.3	+15.2	−1.9	5	100	4	32	12	04	19	35
19	10	02.8	+13.8	−1.8	5	100	4	49	12	12	19	34
21	10	17.9	+12.4	−1.6	5	99	5	05	12	19	19	32
23	10	32.4	+10.9	−1.4	5	98	5	20	12	26	19	29
25	10	46.5	+9.4	−1.2	5	97	5	36	12	32	19	26
27	11	00.0	+7.9	−1.0	5	96	5	50	12	37	19	23
29	11	13.1	+6.3	−0.8	5	94	6	04	12	42	19	19
31	11	25.8	+4.8	−0.7	5	93	6	18	12	47	19	15

Rising and setting times are for latitude 54°

VENUS

Day	R.A.		Dec	Mag.	Diam.	Phase	Rise		Transit		Set	
	h	m	°		"	%	h	m	h	m	h	m
1	05	35.3	+19.3	−4.4	29	43	0	55	8	53	16	52
6	05	53.7	+19.7	−4.3	27	46	0	51	8	52	16	54
11	06	13.3	+20.0	−4.3	26	49	0	49	8	52	16	56
16	06	33.7	+20.1	−4.3	25	52	0	49	8	53	16	58
21	06	54.9	+20.1	−4.3	23	54	0	50	8	55	16	59
26	07	16.7	+19.9	−4.2	22	57	0	54	8	57	17	00
31	07	38.9	+19.5	−4.2	21	59	0	59	8	59	17	00

MARS

Day	R.A.		Dec	Mag.	Diam.	Phase	Rise		Transit		Set	
	h	m	°		"	%	h	m	h	m	h	m
1	01	13.1	+3.6	−1.1	15	86	22	09	4	33	10	57
6	01	21.1	+4.3	−1.2	15	87	21	54	4	21	10	50
11	01	28.4	+4.9	−1.3	16	88	21	38	4	09	10	41
16	01	34.8	+5.5	−1.4	17	89	21	21	3	56	10	31
21	01	40.3	+5.9	−1.5	17	89	21	05	3	41	10	20
26	01	44.8	+6.3	−1.7	18	91	20	47	3	26	10	07
31	01	48.0	+6.6	−1.8	19	92	20	29	3	10	9	52

SUNRISE AND SUNSET

	London			Bristol			Birmingham			Manchester			Newcastle			Glasgow			Belfast		
	0°	05′	51°	30′	2°	35′	51°	28′	1°	55′	52°	28′	2°	15′	53°	28′	1°	37′	54°	59′	4°	14′	55°	52′	5°	56′	54°	35′
d	h	m	h	m	h	m	h	m	h	m	h	m	h	m	h	m	h	m	h	m	h	m	h	m	h	m	h	m
1	4	25	19	48	4	35	19	58	4	28	19	59	4	25	20	04	4	16	20	08	4	22	20	23	4	35	20	24
2	4	26	19	46	4	36	19	56	4	30	19	57	4	27	20	02	4	18	20	06	4	24	20	21	4	37	20	22
3	4	28	19	44	4	38	19	54	4	31	19	55	4	29	20	00	4	20	20	04	4	26	20	19	4	39	20	20
4	4	29	19	43	4	39	19	52	4	33	19	53	4	30	19	59	4	21	20	02	4	28	20	17	4	40	20	18
5	4	31	19	41	4	41	19	51	4	35	19	52	4	32	19	57	4	23	20	00	4	30	20	15	4	42	20	16
6	4	32	19	39	4	42	19	49	4	36	19	50	4	34	19	55	4	25	19	58	4	32	20	13	4	44	20	14
7	4	34	19	37	4	44	19	47	4	38	19	48	4	35	19	53	4	27	19	56	4	34	20	10	4	46	20	12
8	4	35	19	35	4	46	19	45	4	39	19	46	4	37	19	51	4	29	19	54	4	36	20	08	4	48	20	10
9	4	37	19	34	4	47	19	43	4	41	19	44	4	39	19	49	4	31	19	52	4	37	20	06	4	49	20	08
10	4	39	19	32	4	49	19	42	4	43	19	42	4	41	19	47	4	32	19	50	4	39	20	04	4	51	20	06
11	4	40	19	30	4	50	19	40	4	44	19	40	4	42	19	45	4	34	19	48	4	41	20	01	4	53	20	03
12	4	42	19	28	4	52	19	38	4	46	19	38	4	44	19	43	4	36	19	45	4	43	19	59	4	55	20	01
13	4	43	19	26	4	53	19	36	4	48	19	36	4	46	19	41	4	38	19	43	4	45	19	57	4	57	19	59
14	4	45	19	24	4	55	19	34	4	49	19	34	4	47	19	39	4	40	19	41	4	47	19	55	4	58	19	57
15	4	46	19	22	4	57	19	32	4	51	19	32	4	49	19	36	4	42	19	39	4	49	19	52	5	00	19	55
16	4	48	19	20	4	58	19	30	4	53	19	30	4	51	19	34	4	44	19	36	4	51	19	50	5	02	19	52
17	4	50	19	18	5	00	19	28	4	54	19	28	4	53	19	32	4	45	19	34	4	53	19	48	5	04	19	50
18	4	51	19	16	5	01	19	26	4	56	19	26	4	54	19	30	4	47	19	32	4	55	19	45	5	06	19	48
19	4	53	19	14	5	03	19	24	4	58	19	24	4	56	19	28	4	49	19	30	4	57	19	43	5	08	19	46
20	4	54	19	12	5	04	19	22	4	59	19	21	4	58	19	25	4	51	19	27	4	59	19	40	5	09	19	43
21	4	56	19	10	5	06	19	20	5	01	19	19	5	00	19	23	4	53	19	25	5	01	19	38	5	11	19	41
22	4	58	19	08	5	08	19	17	5	03	19	17	5	01	19	21	4	55	19	22	5	03	19	35	5	13	19	39
23	4	59	19	05	5	09	19	15	5	04	19	15	5	03	19	19	4	57	19	20	5	05	19	33	5	15	19	36
24	5	01	19	03	5	11	19	13	5	06	19	13	5	05	19	16	4	58	19	18	5	07	19	30	5	17	19	34
25	5	02	19	01	5	12	19	11	5	08	19	11	5	07	19	14	5	00	19	15	5	09	19	28	5	19	19	31
26	5	04	18	59	5	14	19	09	5	09	19	08	5	08	19	12	5	02	19	13	5	10	19	25	5	20	19	29
27	5	05	18	57	5	16	19	07	5	11	19	06	5	10	19	09	5	04	19	10	5	12	19	23	5	22	19	27
28	5	07	18	55	5	17	19	05	5	13	19	04	5	12	19	07	5	06	19	08	5	14	19	20	5	24	19	24
29	5	09	18	52	5	19	19	02	5	14	19	02	5	14	19	05	5	08	19	05	5	16	19	18	5	26	19	22
30	5	10	18	50	5	20	19	00	5	16	18	59	5	15	19	02	5	10	19	03	5	18	19	15	5	28	19	19
31	5	12	18	48	5	22	18	58	5	18	18	57	5	17	19	00	5	12	19	00	5	20	19	13	5	30	19	17

JUPITER

Day	R.A.		Dec	Mag.	Diam.	Rise		Transit		Set	
	h	m	°		″	h	m	h	m	h	m
1	19	27.4	−22.3	−2.7	47	18	56	22	44	2	35
11	19	22.9	−22.5	−2.7	46	18	14	22	00	1	50
21	19	19.3	−22.6	−2.6	46	17	32	21	17	1	06
31	19	16.9	−22.7	−2.6	44	16	51	20	35	0	23

Diam. = equatorial; Polar Diam. is 94% of Equatorial Diam.

SATURN

Day	R.A.		Dec	Mag.	Diam.	Rise		Transit		Set	
	h	m	°		″	h	m	h	m	h	m
1	19	59.9	−20.8	+0.1	18	19	18	23	16	3	18
11	19	57.0	−21.0	+0.2	18	18	37	22	34	2	35
21	19	54.4	−21.1	+0.3	18	17	56	21	52	1	52
31	19	52.3	−21.2	+0.3	18	17	15	21	10	1	10

Diam. = equatorial; Polar Diam. is 90% of Equatorial Diam.
Rings – major axis 41″ minor axis 16″, Tilt 22°

URANUS

Day	R.A.		Dec	Mag.	Diam.	Rise		Transit		Set	
	h	m	°		″	h	m	h	m	h	m
1	02	33.4	+14.6	+5.8	4	22	25	5	52	13	19
11	02	33.7	+14.6	+5.8	4	21	46	5	13	12	40
21	02	33.6	+14.6	+5.7	4	21	07	4	34	12	01
31	02	33.3	+14.6	+5.7	4	20	27	3	54	11	21

NEPTUNE

Day	R.A.		Dec	Mag.	Diam.	Rise		Transit		Set	
	h	m	°		″	h	m	h	m	h	m
1	23	27.1	−4.7	+7.8	2	21	06	2	46	8	23
11	23	26.3	−4.8	+7.8	2	20	26	2	06	7	43
21	23	25.5	−4.9	+7.8	2	19	46	1	26	7	02
31	23	24.5	−5.0	+7.8	2	19	07	0	46	6	21

September 2020

NINTH MONTH, 30 DAYS. *Septem* (seven), seventh month of Roman pre-Julian calendar

1	*Tuesday*	A solar flare is observed for the first time by astronomer Richard Carrington 1859	day 245
2	*Wednesday*	Mathematician and physicist, William Rowan Hamilton d. 1865	246
3	*Thursday*	Carl D. Anderson, Nobel prize-winning physicist who discovered the positive electron b.1905	247
4	*Friday*	*Buckminsterfullerene*, a spherical allotrope of carbon, is discovered 1985	248
5	*Saturday*	*Voyager 1* spacecraft is launched 1977	249
6	*Sunday*	John Derry, piloting a de Havilland DH 108, becomes the first Briton to break the sound barrier 1948	250

7	*Monday*	James Van Allen, physicist who discovered Earth's magnetosphere (Van Allen radiation belts) b. 1914	week 36 day 251
8	*Tuesday*	The *Genesis* spacecraft crash lands on Earth whilst trying to deliver solar samples 2004	252
9	*Wednesday*	Luigi Galvani, after whom the metallic coating process 'galvanisation' is named b. 1737	253
10	*Thursday*	The Large Hadron Collider, the largest machine in the world, is switched on 2008	254
11	*Friday*	James Jeans, who formulated the eponymous Rayleigh-Jeans law b. 1877	255
12	*Saturday*	Leo Szilard conceives the idea of nuclear chain reaction 1933	256
13	*Sunday*	Horace Babcock, who proposed the Babcock Model, a theory for the magnetism of sunspots b. 1912	257

14	*Monday*	*Luna 2* becomes the first man-made object to reach the surface of the Moon when it crash lands 1956	week 37 day 258
15	*Tuesday*	Murray Gell-Mann, particle physicist and pioneer of quantum chromodynamics b. 1929	259
16	*Wednesday*	James Jeans, who discovered the critical radius of an interstellar cloud d. 1946	260
17	*Thursday*	NASA unveils the first Space Shuttle 1976	261
18	*Friday*	Léon Foucault, physicist who experimentally proved that the Earth rotates on its axis b. 1819	262
19	*Saturday*	The first photograph of the Earth and Moon together is taken by *Voyager 1* 1977	263
20	*Sunday*	James Dewar, Scottish chemist and physicist b. 1842	264

21	*Monday*	*Galileo's* eight-year mission to Jupiter ends when the probe explodes in the planet's atmosphere 2003	week 38 day 265
22	*Tuesday*	Michael Faraday, physicist who contributed towards the understanding of electromagnetism b. 1791	266
23	*Wednesday*	Johann Galle discovers Neptune after using calculations to predict the planet's location 1846	267
24	*Thursday*	John Young, astronaut who became the first person to make six space flights b. 1930	268
25	*Friday*	Ole Romer, Danish astronomer who made the first quantitative measurements of the speed of light b. 1644	269
26	*Saturday*	Albert Einstein's special theory of relativity is published 1905	270
27	*Sunday*	Martin Ryle, radio astronomer and 1974 Nobel laureate for his work on radio-astrophysics b. 1918	271

28	*Monday*	Paul Ulrich Villard, who discovered gamma rays b. 1860	week 39 day 272
29	*Tuesday*	Enrico Fermi, physicist known for his nuclear research, including on induced radioactivity b. 1901	273
30	*Wednesday*	John Baptise Perrin, who proposed that nuclear reactions provide the source of energy in stars b. 1870	274

ASTRONOMICAL PHENOMENA

d	h	
6	5	Mars 0.5° south of the Moon
7	4	Uranus 3° north of the Moon
11	20	Neptune at opposition (Mag. +7.8)
14	6	Vesta 2° south of the Moon, Beehive cluster to the west
22	9	Spica 0.3° south of Mercury
22	13	Autumnal equinox
23	9	Vesta 2° north of Venus
25	21	Saturn 2° north of the Moon, Jupiter to the west

MINIMA OF ALGOL

d	h	d	h	d	h
2	13.9	14	1.1	25	12.4
5	10.7	16	21.9	28	9.2
8	7.5	19	18.8		
11	4.3	22	15.6		

CONSTELLATIONS

The following constellations are near the meridian at

	d	h		d	h
August	1	24	September	15	21
August	16	23	October	1	20
September	1	22	October	16	19

Draco, Cepheus, Lyra, Cygnus, Vulpecula, Sagitta, Delphinus, Equuleus, Aquila, Aquarius and Capricornus

THE MOON

Phase, Apsides and Node	d	h	m
○ Full Moon	2	5	22
◑ Last Quarter	10	9	26
● New Moon	17	11	0
◐ First Quarter	24	1	55

Apogee (405,606 km)	6	6	29
Perigee (359,081 km)	18	13	48

Mean longitude of the ascending node on 1st, 85°

THE SUN   Diam. 31.7′

Day	Right Ascension			Dec.	Equation of time		Rise 52°		Rise 56°		Transit		Set 52°		Set 56°		Sidereal time			Transit of first point of Aries		
	h	m	s	°	m	s	h	m	h	m	h	m	h	m	h	m	h	m	s	h	m	s
1	10	42	30	+8.2	−0	03	5	12	5	05	12	00	18	46	18	53	22	42	29	1	17	19
2	10	46	08	+7.8	+0	17	5	14	5	07	12	00	18	44	18	51	22	46	25	1	13	23
3	10	49	45	+7.5	+0	36	5	16	5	09	11	59	18	42	18	48	22	50	22	1	09	27
4	10	53	21	+7.1	+0	56	5	17	5	11	11	59	18	39	18	46	22	54	18	1	05	31
5	10	56	58	+6.7	+1	16	5	19	5	13	11	59	18	37	18	43	22	58	15	1	01	35
6	11	00	34	+6.3	+1	37	5	21	5	15	11	58	18	35	18	40	23	02	12	0	57	39
7	11	04	10	+6.0	+1	57	5	22	5	17	11	58	18	33	18	38	23	06	08	0	53	43
8	11	07	46	+5.6	+2	18	5	24	5	19	11	58	18	30	18	35	23	10	05	0	49	47
9	11	11	22	+5.2	+2	38	5	25	5	21	11	57	18	28	18	32	23	14	01	0	45	51
10	11	14	57	+4.8	+2	59	5	27	5	23	11	57	18	26	18	30	23	17	58	0	41	56
11	11	18	33	+4.5	+3	20	5	29	5	24	11	56	18	23	18	27	23	21	54	0	38	00
12	11	22	08	+4.1	+3	42	5	30	5	26	11	56	18	21	18	25	23	25	51	0	34	04
13	11	25	44	+3.7	+4	03	5	32	5	28	11	56	18	19	18	22	23	29	47	0	30	08
14	11	29	19	+3.3	+4	24	5	34	5	30	11	55	18	16	18	19	23	33	44	0	26	12
15	11	32	54	+2.9	+4	45	5	35	5	32	11	55	18	14	18	17	23	37	41	0	22	16
16	11	36	29	+2.5	+5	07	5	37	5	34	11	55	18	12	18	14	23	41	37	0	18	20
17	11	40	04	+2.2	+5	28	5	38	5	36	11	54	18	09	18	11	23	45	34	0	14	24
18	11	43	40	+1.8	+5	50	5	40	5	38	11	54	18	07	18	09	23	49	30	0	10	28
19	11	47	15	+1.4	+6	11	5	42	5	40	11	54	18	05	18	06	23	53	27	0	06	32
20	11	50	50	+1.0	+6	32	5	43	5	42	11	53	18	02	18	03	23	57	23	0	02	36
21	11	54	25	+0.6	+6	53	5	45	5	44	11	53	18	00	18	01	0	01	20	23	54	45
22	11	58	01	+0.2	+7	15	5	47	5	46	11	53	17	57	17	58	0	05	16	23	50	49
23	12	01	36	−0.2	+7	36	5	48	5	48	11	52	17	55	17	55	0	09	13	23	46	53
24	12	05	12	−0.6	+7	57	5	50	5	50	11	52	17	53	17	53	0	13	10	23	42	57
25	12	08	48	−1.0	+8	17	5	52	5	52	11	52	17	50	17	50	0	17	06	23	39	01
26	12	12	24	−1.3	+8	38	5	53	5	54	11	51	17	48	17	47	0	21	03	23	35	05
27	12	16	00	−1.7	+8	59	5	55	5	56	11	51	17	46	17	45	0	24	59	23	31	09
28	12	19	36	−2.1	+9	19	5	57	5	58	11	51	17	44	17	42	0	28	56	23	27	13
29	12	23	12	−2.5	+9	39	5	58	6	00	11	50	17	41	17	39	0	32	52	23	23	17
30	12	26	49	−2.9	+9	59	6	00	6	02	11	50	17	39	17	37	0	36	49	23	19	21

DURATION OF TWILIGHT (in minutes)

Latitude	52°	56°	52°	56°	52°	56°
	1 September		11 September		21 September	
Civil	35	39	34	38	34	37
Nautical	79	89	76	85	74	82
Astronomical	127	147	120	136	116	129

THE NIGHT SKY

Mercury is in the evening sky but is presently too low to be seen from the UK. Observers at more temperate latitudes will see Mercury 0.5° from Spica on the 22nd.

Venus (magnitude −4.2) is a dazzling beacon aloft in the early hours. The Moon and Venus lie either side of the Beehive star cluster in Cancer on the 14th, with Venus just 2.5° from the stellar swarm. Venus then passes 2° from the minor planet Vesta (magnitude 8.3) on the 23rd and ends the month getting close to Regulus.

Mars (magnitude −2.1) is a brilliant amber lamp shining in the eastern sky an hour after sunset. The Moon and Mars rise together the evening of the 5th but huddle closer towards dawn when the planet is occulted from southernmost Europe among other regions. Mars is stationary in Pisces on the 9th when it begins to retrograde and its brightness will surpass that of Jupiter by the end of September.

Jupiter (magnitude −2.5) is stationary on the 13th after which its direct motion resumes. The planet's daily motion on the celestial sphere is a little faster than Saturn's and its slow pursuit of the ringed world picks up again.

Saturn (magnitude 0.4) is stationary on the 29th when it reverses course and goes direct. The Moon and Saturn are 3° apart on the 25th with Jupiter a little to their right.

Neptune (magnitude 7.8) reaches opposition on the 11th when it lies 2° east of the star phi Aquarii.

THE MOON

Day	R.A.		Dec	Hor Par	Diam	Sun Co-Long	PA of Br. limb	Ph.	Age	Rise 52°		Rise 56°		Transit		Set 52°		Set 56°	
	h	m	°	'	'	°	°	%	d	h	m	h	m	h	m	h	m	h	m
1	21	55	−17.2	55.4	15.1	71	233	99	12.9	19	03	19	16	23	57	3	50	3	33
2	22	44	−13.2	55.0	30.0	84	186	100	13.9	19	22	19	30	—	—	5	02	4	50
3	23	30	−8.7	54.7	29.8	96	96	99	14.9	19	37	19	41	0	41	6	12	6	05
4	0	15	−3.8	54.4	29.6	108	80	97	15.9	19	52	19	52	1	23	7	20	7	18
5	0	58	+1.1	54.2	29.6	120	75	93	16.9	20	07	20	02	2	03	8	28	8	31
6	1	42	+5.9	54.1	29.4	132	74	87	17.9	20	22	20	14	2	44	9	36	9	43
7	2	26	+10.5	54.1	29.4	144	74	80	18.9	20	39	20	26	3	25	10	44	10	55
8	3	11	+14.7	54.3	29.6	157	76	72	19.9	21	01	20	43	4	08	11	52	12	08
9	3	58	+18.4	54.6	29.8	169	79	64	20.9	21	26	21	05	4	53	13	01	13	23
10	4	48	+21.4	55.1	30.0	181	83	54	21.9	22	01	21	34	5	41	14	09	14	35
11	5	41	+23.4	55.8	30.4	193	88	44	22.9	22	45	22	17	6	33	15	12	15	40
12	6	36	+24.3	56.5	30.8	205	94	34	23.9	23	43	23	16	7	27	16	07	16	36
13	7	34	+23.9	57.4	31.4	218	100	25	24.9	—	—	—	—	8	23	16	53	17	19
14	8	32	+22.2	58.4	31.8	230	107	16	25.9	0	55	0	30	9	20	17	30	17	50
15	9	30	+19.0	59.3	32.4	242	114	08	26.9	2	15	1	56	10	16	17	58	18	13
16	10	28	+14.6	60.1	32.8	254	124	03	27.9	3	40	3	27	11	11	18	22	18	31
17	11	24	+9.3	60.7	33.0	267	151	00	28.9	5	08	5	01	12	05	18	43	18	46
18	12	20	+3.3	61.0	33.2	279	261	00	0.4	6	36	6	35	12	58	19	02	19	01
19	13	15	−3.0	61.0	33.2	291	281	03	1.4	8	04	8	09	13	51	19	22	19	15
20	14	10	−9.0	60.8	33.2	303	284	09	2.4	9	33	9	43	14	45	19	43	19	31
21	15	06	−14.4	60.3	32.8	315	283	18	3.4	10	59	11	16	15	40	20	10	19	52
22	16	04	−18.9	59.6	32.4	328	280	27	4.4	12	24	12	46	16	36	20	42	20	19
23	17	03	−22.1	58.8	32.0	340	276	38	5.4	13	40	14	06	17	34	21	23	20	58
24	18	02	−24.0	58.0	31.6	352	270	49	6.4	14	46	15	14	18	31	22	16	21	48
25	19	00	−24.4	57.2	31.2	4	264	60	7.4	15	38	16	04	19	26	23	18	22	52
26	19	57	−23.5	56.5	30.8	16	258	70	8.4	16	17	16	41	20	19	—	—	—	—
27	20	52	−21.4	55.9	30.4	29	252	79	9.4	16	47	17	06	21	09	0	27	0	05
28	21	43	−18.2	55.4	30.2	41	246	86	10.4	17	10	17	25	21	55	1	38	1	21
29	22	32	−14.3	54.9	30.0	53	241	92	11.4	17	29	17	39	22	39	2	50	2	37
30	23	18	−9.9	54.6	29.8	65	234	97	12.4	17	45	17	50	23	21	4	01	3	53

MERCURY

Day	R.A.		Dec	Mag.	Diam.	Phase	Rise		Transit		Set	
	h	m	°		"	%	h	m	h	m	h	m
1	11	32.0	+4.0	−0.6	5	92	6	24	12	49	19	13
3	11	44.1	+2.5	−0.5	5	91	6	37	12	53	19	09
5	11	55.9	+1.0	−0.4	5	89	6	49	12	57	19	04
7	12	07.3	−0.6	−0.4	5	87	7	01	13	01	18	59
9	12	18.4	−2.0	−0.3	5	86	7	12	13	04	18	54
11	12	29.3	−3.5	−0.2	5	84	7	23	13	07	18	49
13	12	39.9	−4.9	−0.2	5	82	7	34	13	09	18	44
15	12	50.3	−6.3	−0.1	6	81	7	44	13	12	18	39
17	13	00.4	−7.6	−0.1	6	79	7	53	13	14	18	33
19	13	10.3	−8.9	−0.1	6	77	8	03	13	16	18	28
21	13	19.9	−10.1	0.0	6	75	8	11	13	17	18	22
23	13	29.2	−11.3	0.0	6	72	8	20	13	19	18	17
25	13	38.2	−12.5	0.0	6	70	8	27	13	20	18	11
27	13	46.9	−13.5	0.0	6	67	8	35	13	20	18	05
29	13	55.2	−14.5	0.0	7	64	8	41	13	20	18	00

Rising and setting times are for latitude 54°

VENUS

Day	R.A.		Dec	Mag.	Diam.	Phase	Rise		Transit		Set	
	h	m	°		"	%	h	m	h	m	h	m
1	07	43.4	+19.4	−4.2	21	60	1	01	9	00	17	00
6	08	06.0	+18.7	−4.2	20	62	1	08	9	03	16	58
11	08	28.8	+17.9	−4.2	19	64	1	17	9	06	16	55
16	08	51.8	+16.8	−4.1	19	66	1	27	9	09	16	51
21	09	14.7	+15.5	−4.1	18	68	1	39	9	13	16	46
26	09	37.6	+14.1	−4.1	17	70	1	51	9	16	16	40

MARS

Day	R.A.		Dec	Mag.	Diam.	Phase	Rise		Transit		Set	
	h	m	°		"	%	h	m	h	m	h	m
1	01	48.5	+6.6	−1.8	19	92	20	26	3	06	9	49
6	01	50.3	+6.8	−1.9	20	93	20	07	2	48	9	32
11	01	50.6	+6.9	−2.1	20	94	19	47	2	29	9	13
16	01	49.5	+6.8	−2.2	21	96	19	26	2	08	8	52
21	01	47.0	+6.7	−2.3	22	97	19	03	1	46	8	29
26	01	43.2	+6.5	−2.4	22	98	18	41	1	22	8	05

SUNRISE AND SUNSET

	London		Bristol		Birmingham		Manchester		Newcastle		Glasgow		Belfast	
	0° 05'	51° 30'	2° 35'	51° 28'	1° 55'	52° 28'	2° 15'	53° 28'	1° 37'	54° 59'	4° 14'	55° 52'	5° 56'	54° 35'
d	h m	h m	h m	h m	h m	h m	h m	h m	h m	h m	h m	h m	h m	h m
1	5 13	18 46	5 24	18 56	5 19	18 55	5 19	18 58	5 13	18 58	5 22	19 10	5 31	19 14
2	5 15	18 44	5 25	18 54	5 21	18 52	5 21	18 55	5 15	18 55	5 24	19 07	5 33	19 12
3	5 17	18 41	5 27	18 51	5 23	18 50	5 22	18 53	5 17	18 53	5 26	19 05	5 35	19 09
4	5 18	18 39	5 28	18 49	5 24	18 48	5 24	18 51	5 19	18 50	5 28	19 02	5 37	19 07
5	5 20	18 37	5 30	18 47	5 26	18 45	5 26	18 48	5 21	18 48	5 30	19 00	5 39	19 04
6	5 21	18 35	5 31	18 45	5 28	18 43	5 27	18 46	5 23	18 45	5 32	18 57	5 41	19 02
7	5 23	18 32	5 33	18 42	5 29	18 41	5 29	18 43	5 25	18 43	5 34	18 55	5 42	19 00
8	5 25	18 30	5 35	18 40	5 31	18 38	5 31	18 41	5 26	18 40	5 36	18 52	5 44	18 57
9	5 26	18 28	5 36	18 38	5 32	18 36	5 33	18 39	5 28	18 38	5 38	18 49	5 46	18 55
10	5 28	18 25	5 38	18 35	5 34	18 34	5 34	18 36	5 30	18 35	5 40	18 47	5 48	18 52
11	5 29	18 23	5 39	18 33	5 36	18 31	5 36	18 34	5 32	18 33	5 42	18 44	5 50	18 49
12	5 31	18 21	5 41	18 31	5 37	18 29	5 38	18 31	5 34	18 30	5 43	18 41	5 52	18 47
13	5 33	18 19	5 43	18 29	5 39	18 27	5 40	18 29	5 36	18 27	5 45	18 39	5 53	18 44
14	5 34	18 16	5 44	18 26	5 41	18 24	5 41	18 26	5 38	18 25	5 47	18 36	5 55	18 42
15	5 36	18 14	5 46	18 24	5 42	18 22	5 43	18 24	5 39	18 22	5 49	18 33	5 57	18 39
16	5 37	18 12	5 47	18 22	5 44	18 19	5 45	18 21	5 41	18 20	5 51	18 31	5 59	18 37
17	5 39	18 09	5 49	18 19	5 46	18 17	5 47	18 19	5 43	18 17	5 53	18 28	6 01	18 34
18	5 41	18 07	5 51	18 17	5 47	18 15	5 48	18 16	5 45	18 15	5 55	18 26	6 03	18 32
19	5 42	18 05	5 52	18 15	5 49	18 12	5 50	18 14	5 47	18 12	5 57	18 23	6 04	18 29
20	5 44	18 02	5 54	18 12	5 51	18 10	5 52	18 12	5 49	18 09	5 59	18 20	6 06	18 27
21	5 45	18 00	5 55	18 10	5 52	18 08	5 54	18 09	5 51	18 07	6 01	18 18	6 08	18 24
22	5 47	17 58	5 57	18 08	5 54	18 05	5 55	18 07	5 53	18 04	6 03	18 15	6 10	18 22
23	5 49	17 56	5 59	18 05	5 56	18 03	5 57	18 04	5 54	18 02	6 05	18 12	6 12	18 19
24	5 50	17 53	6 00	18 03	5 57	18 01	5 59	18 02	5 56	17 59	6 07	18 10	6 14	18 16
25	5 52	17 51	6 02	18 01	5 59	17 58	6 01	17 59	5 58	17 57	6 09	18 07	6 15	18 14
26	5 53	17 49	6 03	17 59	6 01	17 56	6 02	17 57	6 00	17 54	6 11	18 04	6 17	18 11
27	5 55	17 46	6 05	17 56	6 03	17 53	6 04	17 55	6 02	17 52	6 13	18 02	6 19	18 09
28	5 57	17 44	6 07	17 54	6 04	17 51	6 06	17 52	6 04	17 49	6 15	17 59	6 21	18 06
29	5 58	17 42	6 08	17 52	6 06	17 49	6 08	17 50	6 06	17 46	6 17	17 57	6 23	18 04
30	6 00	17 40	6 10	17 50	6 08	17 46	6 09	17 47	6 08	17 44	6 19	17 54	6 25	18 01

JUPITER

Day	R.A.		Dec	Mag.	Diam.	Rise		Transit		Set	
	h	m	°		"	h	m	h	m	h	m
1	19	16.7	−22.7	−2.6	44	16	47	20	31	0	19
11	19	15.7	−22.7	−2.5	43	16	07	19	51	23	39
21	19	16.2	−22.7	−2.4	42	15	28	19	12	22	57

Diam. = equatorial; Polar Diam. is 94% of Equatorial Diam.

SATURN

Day	R.A.		Dec	Mag.	Diam.	Rise		Transit		Set	
	h	m	°		"	h	m	h	m	h	m
1	19	52.1	−21.2	+0.3	18	17	11	21	06	1	05
11	19	50.6	−21.3	+0.4	18	16	31	20	25	0	24
21	19	49.7	−21.4	+0.4	17	15	51	19	45	23	43

Diam. = equatorial; Polar Diam. is 90% of Equatorial Diam.
Rings – major axis 40" minor axis 15", Tilt 23°

URANUS

Day	R.A.		Dec	Mag.	Diam.	Rise		Transit		Set	
	h	m	°		"	h	m	h	m	h	m
1	02	33.3	+14.6	+5.7	4	20	23	3	50	11	17
11	02	32.6	+14.5	+5.7	4	19	44	3	10	10	37
21	02	31.6	+14.4	+5.7	4	19	00	2	30	9	56

NEPTUNE

Day	R.A.		Dec	Mag.	Diam.	Rise		Transit		Set	
	h	m	°		"	h	m	h	m	h	m
1	23	24.4	−5.0	+7.8	2	19	03	0	42	6	17
11	23	23.4	−5.2	+7.8	2	18	23	0	01	5	36
21	23	22.4	−5.3	+7.8	2	17	43	23	17	4	55

October 2020

TENTH MONTH, 31 DAYS. *Octo* (eighth), eighth month of Roman pre-Julian calendar

1	*Thursday*	Otto Robert Frisch, known for his work on atomic energy *b.* 1904	day 275
2	*Friday*	German-American engineer Willy Lee, who founded the German Rocket society *b.* 1906	276
3	*Saturday*	The UK tests its first nuclear weapon, named 'Hurricane' in Australia 1952	277
4	*Sunday*	The Soviet Union launches *Sputnik,* the first man-made satellite 1957	278

5	*Monday*	Robert Goddard, inventor and physicist, credited as the father of modern rocketry *b.* 1882	week 40 day 279
6	*Tuesday*	Nobel prize-winning physicist, Ernest Walton, known for splitting the atom with John Cockcroft *b.* 1903	280
7	*Wednesday*	The Soviet space probe *Luna 3* photographs the far side of the Moon for the first time 1959	281
8	*Thursday*	Robert R. Gilruth, aerospace engineer and first director of NASA's Manned Spacecraft Center *b.* 1913	282
9	*Friday*	Max von Laue, 1914 Nobel laureate who discovered the diffraction of X-rays by crystals *b.* 1879	283
10	*Saturday*	Henry Cavendish, physicist known for correctly calculating the density and mass of the Earth *b.* 1731	284
11	*Sunday*	NASA astronaut Kathryn D. Sullivan becomes the first woman to walk in space 1984	285

12	*Monday*	*Voskhod 1* becomes the first spacecraft to launch with a crew of more than one person 1964	week 41 day 286
13	*Tuesday*	At the International Meridian Conference, Greenwich time is adopted as the universal meridian 1884	287
14	*Wednesday*	Martin Ryle, radio astronomer who shared the 1974 Nobel Prize for work in radio-astrophysics *d.* 1984	288
15	*Thursday*	Evangelista Torricelli, physicist credited with inventing the barometer *b.* 1608	289
16	*Friday*	Samuel Franklin Cody completes the first aeroplane flight in the UK 1908	290
17	*Saturday*	Isaak Markovich Khalatnikov, who developed the BKL model of the evolution of the Universe *b.* 1919	291
18	*Sunday*	*Venera 4* becomes the first spacecraft to measure the atmosphere of another planet (Venus) 1967	292

19	*Monday*	Subrahmanyan Chandrasekhar, who contributed to general relativity and stellar evolution *b.* 1910	week 42 day 293
20	*Tuesday*	A metre is classified as the distance light travels in a vacuum in 1/299,792,458 of a second 1983	294
21	*Wednesday*	Ejnar Hertzsprung, chemist and astronomer who developed a classification system for stars *d.* 1967	295
22	*Thursday*	Clinton Davisson, joint winner of the 1937 Nobel Prize for his discovery of electron diffraction *b.* 1881	296
23	*Friday*	William D. Coolidge, known for his contributions to electric lighting and radiology *b.* 1873	297
24	*Saturday*	NASA's *Deep Space 1* probe, dedicated to testing new experimental technologies, launches 1998	298
25	*Sunday*	British Summer Time 2020 ends	299

26	*Monday*	The first electricity generator begins operating at the Hoover Dam 1936	week 43 day 300
27	*Tuesday*	A brown dwarf star is found orbiting the star Gliese 229, paving the way for research on exoplanets 1994	301
28	*Wednesday*	John Wallis, mathematician credited with introducing the symbol for infinity *d.* 1703	302
29	*Thursday*	John Glenn, 77, becomes the oldest person to go into space, aboard the *Discovery* space shuttle 1998	303
30	*Friday*	Joint winner of the 1925 Nobel Prize, Gustav Ludwig Hertz *d.* 1975	304
31	*Saturday*	Michael Collins, astronaut who orbited the Moon in the momentous *Apollo 11* mission *b.*1930	305

ASTRONOMICAL PHENOMENA

d	*h*	
1	16	Mercury greatest elongation east (26°)
3	6	Regulus 0.1° north of Venus
3	3	Mars 0.7° north of the Moon
4	5	Uranus 5° above the Moon
13	23	Mars at opposition (Mag. −2.6)
21	6	Orionid meteor swarm peak
22	19	Jupiter 2° north of Moon, Saturn 6°to east
29	19	Mars 3.5° above the Moon
31	16	Uranus at opposition (Mag. +5.7)

MINIMA OF ALGOL

d	*h*	*d*	*h*	*d*	*h*
1	6.0	12	17.3	24	4.5
4	2.8	15	14.1	27	1.3
6	23.6	18	10.9	29	22.1
9	20.4	21	7.7		

CONSTELLATIONS

The following constellations are near the meridian at

	d	*h*		*d*	*h*
September	1	24	October	16	21
September	15	23	November	1	20
October	1	22	November	15	19

Ursa Major (below the Pole), Cepheus, Cassiopeia, Cygnus, Lacerta, Andromeda, Pegasus, Capricornus, Aquarius and Piscis Austrinus

THE MOON

Phase, Apsides and Node	*d*	*h*	*m*
○ Full Moon	1	21	5
◑ Last Quarter	10	0	40
● New Moon	16	19	31
◐ First Quarter	23	13	23
○ Full Moon	31	14	49

Apogee (406,321 km)	3	17	22
Perigee (356,911 km)	16	23	46
Apogee (406,394 km)	30	18	45

Mean longitude of the ascending node on 1st, 84°

THE SUN   Diam. 31.9′

Day	Right Ascension			Dec.	Equation of time		Rise 52°		Rise 56°		Transit		Set 52°		Set 56°		Sidereal time			Transit of first point of Aries		
	h	m	s	°	m	s	h	m	h	m	h	m	h	m	h	m	h	m	s	h	m	s
1	12	30	26	−3.3	+10	18	6	02	6	04	11	50	17	37	17	34	0	40	45	23	15	26
2	12	34	03	−3.7	+10	38	6	03	6	06	11	49	17	34	17	32	0	44	42	23	11	30
3	12	37	41	−4.1	+10	57	6	05	6	08	11	49	17	32	17	29	0	48	39	23	07	34
4	12	41	19	−4.4	+11	15	6	07	6	10	11	49	17	30	17	26	0	52	35	23	03	38
5	12	44	57	−4.8	+11	33	6	08	6	12	11	48	17	27	17	24	0	56	32	22	59	42
6	12	48	36	−5.2	+11	51	6	10	6	14	11	48	17	25	17	21	1	00	28	22	55	46
7	12	52	15	−5.6	+12	09	6	12	6	16	11	48	17	23	17	19	1	04	25	22	51	50
8	12	55	54	−6.0	+12	26	6	13	6	18	11	47	17	21	17	16	1	08	21	22	47	54
9	12	59	34	−6.4	+12	42	6	15	6	20	11	47	17	18	17	13	1	12	18	22	43	58
10	13	03	15	−6.7	+12	59	6	17	6	22	11	47	17	16	17	11	1	16	14	22	40	02
11	13	06	56	−7.1	+13	14	6	18	6	24	11	47	17	14	17	08	1	20	11	22	36	06
12	13	10	37	−7.5	+13	29	6	20	6	26	11	46	17	12	17	06	1	24	08	22	32	11
13	13	14	19	−7.9	+13	44	6	22	6	28	11	46	17	09	17	03	1	28	04	22	28	15
14	13	18	02	−8.2	+13	58	6	24	6	30	11	46	17	07	17	01	1	32	01	22	24	19
15	13	21	45	−8.6	+14	12	6	25	6	32	11	46	17	05	16	58	1	35	57	22	20	23
16	13	25	28	−9.0	+14	24	6	27	6	34	11	45	17	03	16	56	1	39	54	22	16	27
17	13	29	12	−9.3	+14	37	6	29	6	36	11	45	17	01	16	53	1	43	50	22	12	31
18	13	32	57	−9.7	+14	49	6	31	6	38	11	45	16	59	16	51	1	47	47	22	08	35
19	13	36	43	−10.1	+15	00	6	32	6	40	11	45	16	57	16	48	1	51	43	22	04	39
20	13	40	29	−10.4	+15	10	6	34	6	42	11	45	16	54	16	46	1	55	40	22	00	43
21	13	44	15	−10.8	+15	20	6	36	6	45	11	45	16	52	16	44	1	59	37	21	56	47
22	13	48	03	−11.1	+15	29	6	38	6	47	11	44	16	50	16	41	2	03	33	21	52	51
23	13	51	51	−11.5	+15	38	6	39	6	49	11	44	16	48	16	39	2	07	30	21	48	56
24	13	55	39	−11.8	+15	46	6	41	6	51	11	44	16	46	16	37	2	11	26	21	45	00
25	13	59	28	−12.2	+15	53	6	43	6	53	11	44	16	44	16	34	2	15	23	21	41	04
26	14	03	18	−12.5	+16	00	6	45	6	55	11	44	16	42	16	32	2	19	19	21	37	08
27	14	07	09	−12.9	+16	06	6	47	6	57	11	44	16	40	16	30	2	23	16	21	33	12
28	14	11	01	−13.2	+16	11	6	48	6	59	11	44	16	38	16	27	2	27	12	21	29	16
29	14	14	53	−13.5	+16	15	6	50	7	01	11	44	16	36	16	25	2	31	09	21	25	20
30	14	18	46	−13.9	+16	18	6	52	7	04	11	44	16	35	16	23	2	35	06	21	21	24
31	14	22	40	−14.2	+16	21	6	54	7	06	11	44	16	33	16	21	2	39	02	21	17	28

DURATION OF TWILIGHT (in minutes)

Latitude	52°	56°	52°	56°	52°	56°
		1 October		11 October		21 October
Civil	34	37	34	37	34	38
Nautical	73	80	73	80	74	81
Astronomical	113	125	112	124	113	124

THE NIGHT SKY

Mercury is at greatest elongation east on the 1st but is too low in the twilight to be seen. It then passes through inferior conjunction on the 25th after which it should be picked up the last couple of days of October as a magnitude 2.6 object in the morning sky .

Venus (magnitude −4.0) rises 3.5 hours before the Sun and is 0.25° from Regulus on the 3rd. The crescent Moon is 3.5° away on the 14th.

Mars (magnitude −2.6) comes to opposition on the 13th in Pisces and outshines Jupiter virtually all month. The pumpkin coloured world is better placed for UK observers than in July 2018 with the disk nearly 23 arc-seconds across. The Moon is 3° from Mars on the 2nd but gets much closer the next morning. It's near Mars again on the 29th.

Jupiter (magnitude −2.3) is at eastern quadrature on the 11th and on the meridian after dark to the upper left of the teapot asterism in Sagittarius. The Moon is 2° from Jupiter on the 22nd with Saturn a little to their left.

Saturn (magnitude 0.5) is at eastern quadrature a little later on the 18th. The globe's shadow is seen cast on the rings around this time.

Uranus (magnitude 5.7) reaches opposition on the 31st when it can be found in southern Aries. It is potentially visible to the unaided eye from a dark site but first wait a week or so until the Moon is out of the way.

THE MOON

Day	R.A.		Dec	Hor Par	Diam	Sun Co- Long	PA of Br. limb	Ph.	Age	Rise				Transit		Set			
										52°		56°				52°		56°	
	h	m	°	′	′	°	°	%	d	h	m	h	m	h	m	h	m	h	m
1	0	03	−5.1	54.3	29.6	77	219	99	13.4	17	59	18	00	—	—	5	10	5	06
2	0	46	−0.2	54.1	29.4	90	142	100	14.4	18	13	18	10	0	02	6	18	6	19
3	1	30	+4.7	54.0	29.4	102	88	99	15.4	18	28	18	21	0	42	7	25	7	31
4	2	13	+9.4	54.0	29.4	114	79	96	16.4	18	44	18	33	1	23	8	34	8	43
5	2	58	+13.8	54.0	29.4	126	78	92	17.4	19	04	18	47	2	05	9	42	9	56
6	3	45	+17.7	54.2	29.6	138	79	86	18.4	19	27	19	07	2	49	10	51	11	11
7	4	34	+20.9	54.6	29.8	150	82	78	19.4	19	58	19	32	3	36	11	58	12	24
8	5	25	+23.2	55.0	30.0	163	87	70	20.4	20	37	20	09	4	26	13	03	13	31
9	6	19	+24.4	55.6	30.4	175	92	60	21.4	21	28	21	01	5	18	14	00	14	30
10	7	14	+24.5	56.4	30.8	187	97	50	22.4	22	32	22	06	6	12	14	49	15	16
11	8	11	+23.2	57.2	31.2	199	103	40	23.4	23	46	23	24	7	06	15	28	15	50
12	9	07	+20.6	58.2	31.8	211	109	30	24.4	—	—	—	—	8	01	15	58	16	16
13	10	04	+16.8	59.1	32.2	223	114	20	25.4	1	08	0	52	8	55	16	23	16	35
14	10	59	+11.9	60.0	32.8	236	119	12	26.4	2	33	2	23	9	48	16	44	16	51
15	11	54	+6.1	60.8	33.2	248	124	05	27.4	4	01	3	56	10	41	17	04	17	05
16	12	50	−0.1	61.3	33.4	260	135	01	28.4	5	30	5	31	11	35	17	23	17	19
17	13	45	−6.4	61.4	33.4	272	234	00	29.4	6	59	7	07	12	29	17	43	17	34
18	14	42	−12.4	61.3	33.4	285	277	02	0.8	8	30	8	44	13	25	18	08	17	52
19	15	41	−17.5	60.8	33.2	297	280	07	1.8	9	59	10	20	14	23	18	37	18	16
20	16	42	−21.4	60.0	32.8	309	277	14	2.8	11	24	11	49	15	23	19	16	18	50
21	17	43	−23.8	59.2	32.2	321	272	23	3.8	12	37	13	05	16	22	20	07	19	37
22	18	44	−24.7	58.2	31.8	333	266	34	4.8	13	36	14	03	17	20	21	07	20	38
23	19	43	−24.1	57.3	31.2	346	260	44	5.8	14	20	14	45	18	15	22	15	21	51
24	20	39	−22.2	56.5	30.8	358	255	55	6.8	14	52	15	14	19	06	23	27	23	08
25	21	31	−19.3	55.7	30.4	10	250	65	7.8	15	18	15	34	19	54	—	—	—	—
26	22	21	−15.5	55.1	30.0	22	246	74	8.8	15	37	15	48	20	38	0	40	0	25
27	23	07	−11.1	54.7	29.8	34	243	82	9.8	15	53	16	00	21	20	1	51	1	41
28	23	52	−6.4	54.3	29.6	46	240	89	10.8	16	08	16	10	22	01	3	00	2	55
29	0	36	−1.5	54.1	29.4	59	238	94	11.8	16	22	16	20	22	41	4	08	4	07
30	1	19	+3.4	54.0	29.4	71	234	98	12.8	16	35	16	30	23	22	5	16	5	20
31	2	02	+8.3	54.0	29.4	83	220	100	13.8	16	51	16	41	—	—	6	24	6	32

MERCURY

Day	R.A.		Dec	Mag.	Diam.	Phase	Rise		Transit		Set	
	h	m	°		″	%	h	m	h	m	h	m
1	14	02.9	−15.4	+0.1	7	61	8	46	13	20	17	54
3	14	10.2	−16.3	+0.1	7	58	8	51	13	19	17	48
5	14	16.7	−17.0	+0.1	7	54	8	54	13	17	17	41
7	14	22.4	−17.6	+0.2	7	49	8	55	13	15	17	35
9	14	27.0	−18.1	+0.3	8	44	8	54	13	11	17	29
11	14	30.4	−18.4	+0.4	8	39	8	51	13	06	17	22
13	14	32.3	−18.5	+0.6	8	33	8	46	13	00	17	15
15	14	32.5	−18.4	+0.9	9	27	8	37	12	51	17	08
17	14	30.7	−18.1	+1.2	9	20	8	24	12	41	17	00
19	14	26.8	−17.4	+1.8	10	13	8	07	12	29	16	53
21	14	20.8	−16.5	+2.6	10	7	7	47	12	14	16	45
23	14	13.2	−15.3	+3.7	10	3	7	23	11	59	16	37
25	14	04.5	−13.9	+5.1	10	0	6	58	11	42	16	29
27	13	55.8	−12.4	+4.8	10	1	6	33	11	26	16	22
29	13	48.1	−10.9	+3.3	10	4	6	10	11	11	16	15
31	13	42.3	−9.7	+2.0	9	10	5	50	10	58	16	09

Rising and setting times are for latitude 54°

VENUS

Day	R.A.		Dec	Mag.	Diam.	Phase	Rise		Transit		Set	
	h	m	°		″	%	h	m	h	m	h	m
1	10	00.4	+12.5	−4.1	17	72	2	05	9	19	16	33
6	10	23.1	+10.7	−4.1	16	73	2	18	9	22	16	25
11	10	45.8	+8.8	−4.1	16	75	2	33	9	25	16	17
16	11	08.3	+6.7	−4.0	15	77	2	47	9	28	16	08
21	11	30.7	+4.5	−4.0	15	78	3	02	9	30	15	58
26	11	53.1	+2.3	−4.0	15	80	3	17	9	33	15	48
31	12	15.6	0.0	−4.0	14	81	3	32	9	36	15	39

MARS

Day	R.A.		Dec	Mag.	Diam.	Phase	Rise		Transit		Set	
	h	m	°		″	%	h	m	h	m	h	m
1	01	38.3	+6.2	−2.5	22	99	18	18	0	58	7	39
6	01	32.5	+5.9	−2.6	23	100	17	54	0	32	7	11
11	01	26.2	+5.6	−2.6	22	100	17	30	0	06	6	43
16	01	19.8	+5.3	−2.6	22	100	17	06	23	43	6	15
21	01	13.7	+5.1	−2.5	22	100	16	41	23	17	5	48
26	01	08.3	+4.9	−2.3	21	99	16	17	22	52	5	22
31	01	03.8	+4.8	−2.2	20	98	15	53	22	27	4	57

SUNRISE AND SUNSET

	London		Bristol		Birmingham		Manchester		Newcastle		Glasgow		Belfast	
	0° 05′	51° 30′	2° 35′	51° 28′	1° 55′	52° 28′	2° 15′	53° 28′	1° 37′	54° 59′	4° 14′	55° 52′	5° 56′	54° 35′
d	h m	h m	h m	h m	h m	h m	h m	h m	h m	h m	h m	h m	h m	h m
1	6 02	17 37	6 11	17 47	6 09	17 44	6 11	17 45	6 09	17 41	6 20	17 51	6 27	17 59
2	6 03	17 35	6 13	17 45	6 11	17 42	6 13	17 42	6 11	17 39	6 22	17 49	6 28	17 56
3	6 05	17 33	6 15	17 43	6 13	17 39	6 15	17 40	6 13	17 36	6 24	17 46	6 30	17 54
4	6 06	17 30	6 16	17 40	6 14	17 37	6 17	17 38	6 15	17 34	6 26	17 43	6 32	17 51
5	6 08	17 28	6 18	17 38	6 16	17 35	6 18	17 35	6 17	17 31	6 28	17 41	6 34	17 49
6	6 10	17 26	6 20	17 36	6 18	17 32	6 20	17 33	6 19	17 29	6 30	17 38	6 36	17 46
7	6 11	17 24	6 21	17 34	6 20	17 30	6 22	17 30	6 21	17 26	6 32	17 36	6 38	17 44
8	6 13	17 22	6 23	17 32	6 21	17 28	6 24	17 28	6 23	17 24	6 34	17 33	6 40	17 42
9	6 15	17 19	6 25	17 29	6 23	17 26	6 26	17 26	6 25	17 21	6 36	17 31	6 42	17 39
10	6 16	17 17	6 26	17 27	6 25	17 23	6 27	17 23	6 27	17 19	6 39	17 28	6 44	17 37
11	6 18	17 15	6 28	17 25	6 27	17 21	6 29	17 21	6 29	17 16	6 41	17 26	6 46	17 34
12	6 20	17 13	6 30	17 23	6 28	17 19	6 31	17 19	6 31	17 14	6 43	17 23	6 47	17 32
13	6 21	17 11	6 31	17 21	6 30	17 17	6 33	17 16	6 33	17 12	6 45	17 21	6 49	17 29
14	6 23	17 08	6 33	17 18	6 32	17 14	6 35	17 14	6 35	17 09	6 47	17 18	6 51	17 27
15	6 25	17 06	6 35	17 16	6 34	17 12	6 37	17 12	6 37	17 07	6 49	17 16	6 53	17 25
16	6 27	17 04	6 37	17 14	6 35	17 10	6 38	17 10	6 39	17 04	6 51	17 13	6 55	17 22
17	6 28	17 02	6 38	17 12	6 37	17 08	6 40	17 07	6 41	17 02	6 53	17 11	6 57	17 20
18	6 30	17 00	6 40	17 10	6 39	17 06	6 42	17 05	6 43	17 00	6 55	17 08	6 59	17 18
19	6 32	16 58	6 42	17 08	6 41	17 03	6 44	17 03	6 45	16 57	6 57	17 06	7 01	17 15
20	6 33	16 56	6 43	17 06	6 43	17 01	6 46	17 01	6 47	16 55	6 59	17 03	7 03	17 13
21	6 35	16 54	6 45	17 04	6 44	16 59	6 48	16 58	6 49	16 53	7 01	17 01	7 05	17 11
22	6 37	16 52	6 47	17 02	6 46	16 57	6 50	16 56	6 51	16 50	7 03	16 59	7 07	17 08
23	6 39	16 50	6 49	17 00	6 48	16 55	6 52	16 54	6 53	16 48	7 05	16 56	7 09	17 06
24	6 40	16 48	6 50	16 58	6 50	16 53	6 53	16 52	6 55	16 46	7 07	16 54	7 11	17 04
25	6 42	16 46	6 52	16 56	6 52	16 51	6 55	16 50	6 57	16 44	7 09	16 52	7 13	17 02
26	6 44	16 44	6 54	16 54	6 53	16 49	6 57	16 48	6 59	16 41	7 12	16 49	7 15	17 00
27	6 46	16 42	6 56	16 52	6 55	16 47	6 59	16 46	7 01	16 39	7 14	16 47	7 17	16 57
28	6 47	16 40	6 57	16 50	6 57	16 45	7 01	16 44	7 03	16 37	7 16	16 45	7 19	16 55
29	6 49	16 38	6 59	16 48	6 59	16 43	7 03	16 42	7 05	16 35	7 18	16 43	7 21	16 53
30	6 51	16 36	7 01	16 46	7 01	16 41	7 05	16 40	7 07	16 33	7 20	16 40	7 23	16 51
31	6 53	16 34	7 03	16 45	7 03	16 39	7 07	16 38	7 09	16 31	7 22	16 38	7 25	16 49

JUPITER

Day	R.A.		Dec	Mag.	Diam.	Rise		Transit		Set	
	h	m	°		″	h	m	h	m	h	m
1	19	17.9	−22.7	−2.4	41	14	50	18	34	22	19
11	19	21.0	−22.6	−2.3	39	14	13	17	58	21	44
21	19	25.3	−22.4	−2.2	38	13	37	17	23	21	10
31	19	30.7	−22.3	−2.2	37	13	01	16	49	20	37

Diam. = equatorial; Polar Diam. is 94% of Equatorial Diam.

SATURN

Day	R.A.		Dec	Mag.	Diam.	Rise		Transit		Set	
	h	m	°		″	h	m	h	m	h	m
1	19	49.5	−21.4	+0.5	17	15	12	19	06	23	00
11	19	49.9	−21.4	+0.5	17	14	33	18	27	22	21
21	19	51.1	−21.3	+0.6	17	13	54	17	49	21	43
31	19	53.0	−21.2	+0.6	16	13	16	17	11	21	07

Diam. = equatorial; Polar Diam. is 90% of Equatorial Diam.
Rings – major axis 38″ minor axis 15″, Tilt 23°

URANUS

Day	R.A.		Dec	Mag.	Diam.	Rise		Transit		Set	
	h	m	°		″	h	m	h	m	h	m
1	02	30.4	+14.3	+5.7	4	18	20	1	49	9	15
11	02	29.1	+14.2	+5.7	4	17	40	1	09	8	33
21	02	27.5	+14.1	+5.7	4	17	00	0	28	7	52
31	02	25.9	+14.0	+5.7	4	16	20	23	43	7	10

NEPTUNE

Day	R.A.		Dec	Mag.	Diam.	Rise		Transit		Set	
	h	m	°		″	h	m	h	m	h	m
1	23	21.4	−5.4	+7.8	2	17	04	22	37	4	14
11	23	20.5	−5.5	+7.8	2	16	24	21	57	3	33
21	23	19.7	−5.5	+7.8	2	15	44	21	17	2	53
31	23	19.1	−5.6	+7.8	2	15	05	20	37	2	13

November 2020

ELEVENTH MONTH, 30 DAYS. *Novem* (nine), ninth month of Roman pre-Julian calendar

1 *Sunday*	The US tests the first hydrogen bomb, codenamed 'Ivy Mike', in the Pacific 1952		day 306

2 *Monday*	Howard Hughes flies his eight-engine wooden aeroplane *Spruce Goose* for one minute 1947	week 44 day 307
3 *Tuesday*	The Soviet Union launches its first living creature, a dog named Laika, into space 1957	308
4 *Wednesday*	Norman Foster Ramsey, joint winner of the 1989 Nobel Prize in Physics *d.* 2011	309
5 *Thursday*	Fred Whipple, astronomer who proposed the 'dirty snowball' hypothesis for comets *b.* 1906	310
6 *Friday*	Observations of Jupiter begin while *Pioneer 10* is still 25 million km away 1973	311
7 *Saturday*	Marie Curie, physicist, chemist and winner of two Nobel Prizes *b.* 1867	312
8 *Sunday*	X-Rays are observed for the first time by Wilhelm Conrad Röntgen 1895	313

9 *Monday*	Physicist Gordon Gould records the principles of his invention of the laser, but fails to patent his idea 1957	week 45 day 314
10 *Tuesday*	Igor Dmitriyevich Novikov, theoretical astrophysicist and cosmologist *b.* 1935	315
11 *Wednesday*	Hugh Everett III, who first proposed the 'many worlds' interpretation of quantum physics 1930	316
12 *Thursday*	*Voyager 1* begins sending images of Saturn's rings 1980	317
13 *Friday*	*Mariner 9* enters orbit around Mars, becoming the first spacecraft to orbit another planet 1971	318
14 *Saturday*	Edward H. White II, the first to walk in space during the orbital flight of *Gemini 4 b.* 1930	319
15 *Sunday*	William Herschel, discoverer of Uranus and of infrared raditiation *b.* 1738	320

16 *Monday*	*Venera 3*, the first spacecraft to reach the surface of another planet, launches 1965	week 46 day 321
17 *Tuesday*	*Pioneer 10* passes through Jupiter's magnetopause 1973	322
18 *Wednesday*	Alan Shepard, the first Amerian man in space and one of 12 men to have walked on the Moon *b.* 1923	323
19 *Thursday*	Eileen Collins, astronaut who was the first woman to pilot and later command a US space shuttle *b.* 1956	324
20 *Friday*	Edwin Hubble, astronomer who proved that other galaxies apart from our own exist *b.* 1889	325
21 *Saturday*	Voltaire, French writer and philosopher who popularised the work of Isaac Newton in France *b.* 1694	326
22 *Sunday*	Chad Trujillo, co-discoverer of the dwarf planet Eris in 2003 *b.* 1973	327

23 *Monday*	Johannes Diderik van der Waals, winner of the 1910 Nobel Prize in Physics *b.* 1837	week 47 day 328
24 *Tuesday*	Thomas Dick, astronomer and science teacher *b.* 1774	329
25 *Wednesday*	Julius von Mayer, known for the first law of thermodynamics *b.* 1814	330
26 *Thursday*	The *Curiosity* rover lands on Mars 2012	331
27 *Friday*	Anders Celsius, physicist who developed the eponymous temperature scale *b.* 1701	332
28 *Saturday*	Nathaniel Bliss, the fourth Astronomer Royal (1762–4) *b.* 1700	333
29 *Sunday*	The first US underground atomic bomb test, codenamed 'Uncle', is carried out 1951	334

30 *Monday*	A 4kg meteorite hits Elizabeth Hodges after crashing through her roof in Alabama, USA 1954	week 48 day 335

ASTRONOMICAL PHENOMENA

d	h	
3	7	Moon 5° north of Aldebaran
5	6	South Taurid meteor stream peak
10	17	Mercury greatest elongation west (19°)
12	5	North Taurid meteor stream peak
13	7	Pluto 0.7° south of Jupiter
17	11	Leonid meteor swarm
19	15	Saturn 3° north of the Moon (care of Sun)
25	20	Mars 5° north of the Moon
27	17	Uranus 3° north of the Moon

MINIMA OF ALGOL

d	h	d	h	d	h
1	18.9	13	6.2	24	17.5
4	15.8	16	3.0	27	14.3
7	12.6	18	23.8	30	11.1
10	9.4	21	20.7		

CONSTELLATIONS

The following constellations are near the meridian at

	d	h		d	h
October	1	24	November	15	21
October	16	23	December	1	20
November	1	22	December	16	19

Ursa Major (below the Pole), Cepheus, Cassiopeia, Andromeda, Pegasus, Pisces, Aquarius and Cetus

THE MOON

Phase, Apsides and Node	d	h	m
☽ Last Quarter	8	13	46
● New Moon	15	5	7
☾ First Quarter	22	4	45
○ Full Moon	30	9	30

Perigee (357,836 km)	14	11	43
Apogee (405,893 km)	27	0	29

Mean longitude of the ascending node on 1st, 82°

THE SUN   Diam. 32.2′

Day	Right Ascension			Dec.	Equation of time	Rise		Transit	Set		Sidereal time			Transit of first point of Aries		
						52°	56°		52°	56°						
	h	m	s	°	m s	h m	h m	h m	h m	h m	h	m	s	h	m	s
1	14	26	34	−14.5	+16 23	6 56	7 08	11 44	16 31	16 19	2	42	59	21	13	32
2	14	30	30	−14.8	+16 24	6 57	7 10	11 44	16 29	16 16	2	46	55	21	09	36
3	14	34	26	−15.1	+16 25	6 59	7 12	11 44	16 27	16 14	2	50	52	21	05	41
4	14	38	23	−15.4	+16 24	7 01	7 14	11 44	16 26	16 12	2	54	48	21	01	45
5	14	42	21	−15.7	+16 23	7 03	7 16	11 44	16 24	16 10	2	58	45	20	57	49
6	14	46	19	−16.1	+16 21	7 05	7 18	11 44	16 22	16 08	3	02	41	20	53	53
7	14	50	19	−16.3	+16 18	7 06	7 21	11 44	16 20	16 06	3	06	38	20	49	57
8	14	54	19	−16.6	+16 14	7 08	7 23	11 44	16 19	16 04	3	10	35	20	46	01
9	14	58	20	−16.9	+16 10	7 10	7 25	11 44	16 17	16 02	3	14	31	20	42	05
10	15	02	23	−17.2	+16 04	7 12	7 27	11 44	16 16	16 00	3	18	28	20	38	09
11	15	06	26	−17.5	+15 58	7 13	7 29	11 44	16 14	15 59	3	22	24	20	34	13
12	15	10	29	−17.8	+15 50	7 15	7 31	11 44	16 13	15 57	3	26	21	20	30	17
13	15	14	34	−18.0	+15 42	7 17	7 33	11 44	16 11	15 55	3	30	17	20	26	21
14	15	18	40	−18.3	+15 33	7 19	7 35	11 45	16 10	15 53	3	34	14	20	22	26
15	15	22	46	−18.5	+15 23	7 20	7 37	11 45	16 08	15 52	3	38	10	20	18	30
16	15	26	53	−18.8	+15 12	7 22	7 39	11 45	16 07	15 50	3	42	07	20	14	34
17	15	31	01	−19.0	+15 01	7 24	7 41	11 45	16 06	15 48	3	46	04	20	10	38
18	15	35	10	−19.3	+14 49	7 26	7 43	11 45	16 04	15 47	3	50	00	20	06	42
19	15	39	20	−19.5	+14 35	7 27	7 45	11 46	16 03	15 45	3	53	57	20	02	46
20	15	43	31	−19.7	+14 21	7 29	7 47	11 46	16 02	15 44	3	57	53	19	58	50
21	15	47	42	−20.0	+14 07	7 31	7 49	11 46	16 01	15 42	4	01	50	19	54	54
22	15	51	54	−20.2	+13 51	7 32	7 51	11 46	16 00	15 41	4	05	46	19	50	58
23	15	56	07	−20.4	+13 35	7 34	7 53	11 47	15 59	15 40	4	09	43	19	47	02
24	16	00	21	−20.6	+13 18	7 35	7 55	11 47	15 58	15 38	4	13	39	19	43	07
25	16	04	35	−20.8	+13 00	7 37	7 57	11 47	15 57	15 37	4	17	36	19	39	11
26	16	08	50	−21.0	+12 41	7 39	7 58	11 47	15 56	15 36	4	21	33	19	35	15
27	16	13	06	−21.2	+12 22	7 40	8 00	11 48	15 55	15 35	4	25	29	19	31	19
28	16	17	23	−21.3	+12 02	7 42	8 02	11 48	15 54	15 34	4	29	26	19	27	23
29	16	21	40	−21.5	+11 41	7 43	8 04	11 48	15 54	15 33	4	33	22	19	23	27
30	16	25	58	−21.7	+11 20	7 44	8 05	11 49	15 53	15 32	4	37	19	19	19	31

DURATION OF TWILIGHT (in minutes)

Latitude	52°	56°	52°	56°	52°	56°
	1 November		11 November		21 November	
Civil	36	40	37	41	38	43
Nautical	75	84	78	87	80	90
Astronomical	115	127	117	130	120	134

THE NIGHT SKY

Mercury soars higher in the morning sky until just over 10° up on the 10th when at greatest elongation west and shining at magnitude −0.6. It can be seen all month and only drops below 5° altitude during the last week. Mercury loiters near Spica for a few days at the beginning of November and is 5.5° to the upper right of a very thin Moon on the 14th.

Venus (magnitude −3.9) appears to be heading for another encounter with Mercury but the two get no closer than about 13° on the 12th and hold that gap for about a week before it widens again. The Moon is nearby on the 13th and Venus passes Spica on the 16th.

Mars (magnitude −1.7) fades a whole magnitude during November – the value quoted is mid-month – as it recedes from Earth but still burns bright in Pisces until the early hours. The planet is stationary on the 15th when its direct motion resumes. The Moon is 6.5° from Mars on the 25th.

Jupiter (magnitude −2.1) and Saturn are now just past the meridian as darkness falls.

Saturn (magnitude 0.6) is 3.5° from Jupiter when the Moon is near the two on the 19th.

A penumbral lunar eclipse (magnitude 0.823) on the 30th is at moonset from the UK. This time the Moon passes south of the centre of Earth's shadow. It's also the final penumbral of 2020 – the last time there were four in the same calendar year was 1944.

THE MOON

Day	R.A. h m	Dec °	Hor Par	Diam '	Sun Co-Long °	PA of Br. limb °	Ph. %	Age d	Rise 52° h m	Rise 56° h m	Transit h m	Set 52° h m	Set 56° h m
1	2 47	+12.8	54.0	29.4	95	110	100	14.8	17 09	16 54	0 04	7 33	7 46
2	3 33	+16.9	54.2	29.6	107	84	98	15.8	17 30	17 11	0 47	8 42	8 59
3	4 21	+20.3	54.4	29.6	119	83	95	16.8	17 59	17 34	1 33	9 51	10 14
4	5 12	+22.9	54.7	29.8	131	85	90	17.8	18 34	18 07	2 22	10 56	11 25
5	6 05	+24.4	55.1	30.0	144	90	83	18.8	19 21	18 52	3 13	11 56	12 27
6	7 00	+24.8	55.7	30.4	156	95	75	19.8	20 19	19 52	4 06	12 48	13 16
7	7 55	+23.9	56.3	30.6	168	100	66	20.8	21 28	21 05	4 59	13 29	13 53
8	8 50	+21.8	57.1	31.0	180	105	56	21.8	22 45	22 26	5 52	14 00	14 21
9	9 45	+18.4	57.9	31.6	192	110	45	22.8	— —	23 53	6 45	14 27	14 41
10	10 39	+14.0	58.7	32.0	204	114	35	23.8	0 06	— —	7 36	14 48	14 57
11	11 32	+8.7	59.6	32.4	217	117	24	24.8	1 30	1 22	8 27	15 07	15 11
12	12 26	+2.7	60.3	32.8	229	118	15	25.8	2 55	2 53	9 19	15 25	15 24
13	13 20	−3.5	60.9	33.2	241	119	07	26.8	4 23	4 27	10 11	15 44	15 37
14	14 15	−9.6	61.2	33.4	253	121	02	27.8	5 52	6 02	11 06	16 06	15 53
15	15 13	−15.2	61.2	33.4	265	146	00	28.8	7 24	7 40	12 03	16 31	16 14
16	16 14	−19.8	60.9	33.2	278	273	01	0.3	8 53	9 16	13 03	17 06	16 42
17	17 16	−23.0	60.3	32.8	290	274	05	1.3	10 15	10 43	14 05	17 52	17 23
18	18 19	−24.7	59.5	32.4	302	270	11	2.3	11 24	11 53	15 06	18 49	18 20
19	19 21	−24.6	58.5	31.8	314	264	19	3.3	12 16	12 44	16 05	19 58	19 30
20	20 20	−23.1	57.5	31.4	326	258	28	4.3	12 54	13 18	16 59	21 11	20 49
21	21 16	−20.4	56.6	30.8	339	254	38	5.3	13 23	13 41	17 49	22 25	22 09
22	22 07	−16.8	55.8	30.4	351	250	48	6.3	13 44	13 57	18 36	23 38	23 26
23	22 55	−12.5	55.2	30.0	3	247	58	7.3	14 01	14 10	19 19	— —	— —
24	23 41	−7.8	54.6	29.8	15	245	67	8.3	14 16	14 20	20 00	0 48	0 42
25	0 24	−2.9	54.3	29.6	27	244	76	9.3	14 30	14 30	20 40	1 57	1 55
26	1 07	+2.1	54.1	29.4	39	243	84	10.3	14 44	14 39	21 21	3 05	3 07
27	1 51	+6.9	54.0	29.4	52	244	90	11.3	14 58	14 50	22 02	4 13	4 20
28	2 35	+11.6	54.1	29.4	64	245	95	12.3	15 15	15 02	22 45	5 21	5 33
29	3 21	+15.8	54.2	29.6	76	246	98	13.3	15 35	15 17	23 30	6 31	6 47
30	4 09	+19.5	54.5	29.6	88	241	100	14.3	16 01	15 38	— —	7 41	8 02

MERCURY

Day	R.A. h m	Dec °	Mag.	Diam. "	Phase %	Rise h m	Transit h m	Set h m
1	13 40.4	−9.3	+1.5	9	14	5 42	10 53	16 06
3	13 38.6	−8.6	+0.8	8	23	5 29	10 44	16 00
5	13 39.4	−8.3	+0.2	8	33	5 21	10 38	15 55
7	13 42.7	−8.4	−0.2	8	43	5 17	10 34	15 51
9	13 48.2	−8.7	−0.4	7	52	5 17	10 32	15 46
11	13 55.3	−9.4	−0.6	7	60	5 21	10 31	15 42
13	14 03.7	−10.2	−0.6	6	67	5 26	10 32	15 38
15	14 13.2	−11.1	−0.7	6	73	5 33	10 34	15 34
17	14 23.5	−12.1	−0.7	6	78	5 42	10 37	15 31
19	14 34.3	−13.2	−0.7	6	82	5 51	10 40	15 27
21	14 45.6	−14.2	−0.7	5	86	6 01	10 43	15 24
23	14 57.3	−15.3	−0.7	5	88	6 12	10 47	15 21
25	15 09.3	−16.4	−0.7	5	91	6 23	10 51	15 19
27	15 21.5	−17.4	−0.7	5	93	6 34	10 56	15 16
29	15 33.9	−18.4	−0.7	5	94	6 45	11 00	15 15

Rising and setting times are for latitude 54°

VENUS

Day	R.A. h m	Dec °	Mag.	Diam. "	Phase %	Rise h m	Transit h m	Set h m
1	12 20.1	−0.4	−4.0	14	81	3 36	9 36	15 37
6	12 42.6	−2.7	−4.0	14	83	3 51	9 39	15 27
11	13 05.4	−5.1	−4.0	13	84	4 07	9 42	15 17
16	13 28.3	−7.3	−4.0	13	85	4 23	9 46	15 07
21	13 51.6	−9.6	−4.0	13	86	4 39	9 49	14 58
26	14 15.2	−11.7	−4.0	13	88	4 56	9 53	14 50

MARS

Day	R.A. h m	Dec °	Mag.	Diam. "	Phase %	Rise h m	Transit h m	Set h m
1	01 03.0	+4.8	−2.1	20	98	15 49	22 22	4 52
6	00 59.9	+4.9	−2.0	19	97	15 25	21 59	4 29
11	00 58.0	+5.0	−1.8	18	96	15 03	21 37	4 08
16	00 57.4	+5.3	−1.6	17	95	14 41	21 17	3 49
21	00 58.1	+5.6	−1.5	16	94	14 20	20 57	3 32
26	01 00.0	+6.1	−1.3	15	93	13 59	20 39	3 17

SUNRISE AND SUNSET

	London 0°	05′ 51° 30′	Bristol 2°	35′ 51° 28′	Birmingham 1°	55′ 52° 28′	Manchester 2°	15′ 53° 28′	Newcastle 1°	37′ 54° 59′	Glasgow 4°	14′ 55° 52′	Belfast 5°	56′ 54° 35′
d	h m	h m	h m	h m	h m	h m	h m	h m	h m	h m	h m	h m	h m	h m
1	6 54	16 33	7 04	16 43	7 04	16 37	7 09	16 36	7 11	16 28	7 24	16 36	7 27	16 47
2	6 56	16 31	7 06	16 41	7 06	16 35	7 11	16 34	7 13	16 26	7 26	16 34	7 29	16 45
3	6 58	16 29	7 08	16 39	7 08	16 34	7 13	16 32	7 15	16 24	7 28	16 32	7 31	16 43
4	7 00	16 27	7 10	16 37	7 10	16 32	7 14	16 30	7 17	16 22	7 31	16 30	7 33	16 41
5	7 02	16 26	7 11	16 36	7 12	16 30	7 16	16 28	7 19	16 20	7 33	16 28	7 35	16 39
6	7 03	16 24	7 13	16 34	7 14	16 28	7 18	16 26	7 21	16 18	7 35	16 26	7 37	16 37
7	7 05	16 22	7 15	16 32	7 15	16 27	7 20	16 25	7 23	16 17	7 37	16 24	7 39	16 35
8	7 07	16 21	7 17	16 31	7 17	16 25	7 22	16 23	7 25	16 15	7 39	16 22	7 41	16 33
9	7 09	16 19	7 18	16 29	7 19	16 23	7 24	16 21	7 27	16 13	7 41	16 20	7 43	16 32
10	7 10	16 18	7 20	16 28	7 21	16 22	7 26	16 19	7 29	16 11	7 43	16 18	7 45	16 30
11	7 12	16 16	7 22	16 26	7 23	16 20	7 28	16 18	7 31	16 09	7 45	16 16	7 47	16 28
12	7 14	16 15	7 24	16 25	7 25	16 19	7 30	16 16	7 33	16 08	7 47	16 14	7 49	16 26
13	7 15	16 13	7 25	16 23	7 26	16 17	7 31	16 15	7 35	16 06	7 50	16 12	7 51	16 25
14	7 17	16 12	7 27	16 22	7 28	16 16	7 33	16 13	7 37	16 04	7 52	16 11	7 53	16 23
15	7 19	16 10	7 29	16 21	7 30	16 14	7 35	16 12	7 39	16 03	7 54	16 09	7 55	16 22
16	7 21	16 09	7 31	16 19	7 32	16 13	7 37	16 10	7 41	16 01	7 56	16 07	7 57	16 20
17	7 22	16 08	7 32	16 18	7 33	16 11	7 39	16 09	7 43	15 59	7 58	16 06	7 59	16 19
18	7 24	16 07	7 34	16 17	7 35	16 10	7 41	16 07	7 45	15 58	8 00	16 04	8 00	16 17
19	7 26	16 05	7 36	16 16	7 37	16 09	7 42	16 06	7 47	15 57	8 02	16 03	8 02	16 16
20	7 27	16 04	7 37	16 14	7 39	16 08	7 44	16 05	7 49	15 55	8 04	16 01	8 04	16 14
21	7 29	16 03	7 39	16 13	7 40	16 06	7 46	16 03	7 51	15 54	8 06	16 00	8 06	16 13
22	7 31	16 02	7 40	16 12	7 42	16 05	7 48	16 02	7 52	15 52	8 07	15 58	8 08	16 12
23	7 32	16 01	7 42	16 11	7 44	16 04	7 49	16 01	7 54	15 51	8 09	15 57	8 10	16 10
24	7 34	16 00	7 44	16 10	7 45	16 03	7 51	16 00	7 56	15 50	8 11	15 56	8 11	16 09
25	7 35	15 59	7 45	16 09	7 47	16 02	7 53	15 59	7 58	15 49	8 13	15 55	8 13	16 08
26	7 37	15 58	7 47	16 08	7 48	16 01	7 55	15 58	8 00	15 48	8 15	15 53	8 15	16 07
27	7 38	15 57	7 48	16 08	7 50	16 00	7 56	15 57	8 01	15 47	8 17	15 52	8 16	16 06
28	7 40	15 57	7 50	16 07	7 52	16 00	7 58	15 56	8 03	15 46	8 18	15 51	8 18	16 05
29	7 41	15 56	7 51	16 06	7 53	15 59	7 59	15 55	8 05	15 45	8 20	15 50	8 20	16 04
30	7 43	15 55	7 53	16 05	7 55	15 58	8 01	15 54	8 06	15 44	8 22	15 49	8 21	16 03

JUPITER

Day	R.A. h m	Dec °	Mag.	Diam. ″	Rise h m	Transit h m	Set h m
1	19 31.3	−22.2	−2.2	37	12 58	16 46	20 34
11	19 37.8	−22.0	−2.1	36	12 23	16 13	20 03
21	19 45.0	−21.7	−2.1	35	11 49	15 41	19 33

Diam. = equatorial; Polar Diam. is 94% of Equatorial Diam.

SATURN

Day	R.A. h m	Dec °	Mag.	Diam. ″	Rise h m	Transit h m	Set h m
1	19 53.2	−21.2	+0.6	16	13 12	17 07	21 03
11	19 55.7	−21.1	+0.6	16	12 35	16 31	20 27
21	19 58.8	−21.0	+0.6	16	11 58	15 54	19 52

Diam. = equatorial; Polar Diam. is 90% of Equatorial Diam.
Rings – major axis 36″ minor axis 14″, Tilt 22°

URANUS

Day	R.A. h m	Dec °	Mag.	Diam. ″	Rise h m	Transit h m	Set h m
1	02 25.8	+13.9	+5.7	4	16 16	23 39	7 06
11	02 24.2	+13.8	+5.7	4	15 36	22 58	6 24
21	02 22.7	+13.7	+5.7	4	14 56	22 17	5 42

NEPTUNE

Day	R.A. h m	Dec °	Mag.	Diam. ″	Rise h m	Transit h m	Set h m
1	23 19.0	−5.6	+7.8	2	15 01	20 33	2 08
11	23 18.5	−5.7	+7.9	2	14 21	19 53	1 28
21	23 18.3	−5.7	+7.9	2	13 42	19 13	0 49

December 2020

TWELFTH MONTH, 31 DAYS. *Decem* (ten), tenth month of Roman pre-Julian calendar

1	*Tuesday*	Nicolas-Claude Fabri de Peiresc, who first observed the Orion Nebula in 1610 *b.* 1580	day 336
2	*Wednesday*	The closest known approach to an asteroid is made when *Pioneer 10* passes 307 Nike 1972	337
3	*Thursday*	The first close-up photographs of Jupiter are taken by the *Pioneer 10* space probe 1972	338
4	*Friday*	*Pioneer 10* makes its closest approach to Jupiter, passing within 132,252km of Jupiter's clouds 1972	339
5	*Saturday*	Sheldon Lee Glashow, winner of the 1979 Nobel Prize for his work on electroweak theory, *b.* 1932	340
6	*Sunday*	Johann Palisa, Austrian astronomer known for his discovery of 122 asteroids *b.* 1848	341

7	*Monday*	*Apollo 17,* the sixth and final US mission to land men on the Moon, launches 1972	week 49 day 342
8	*Tuesday*	Harrison Brown, who worked on isolating plutonium for its use in the first atomic bombs *d.* 1986	343
9	*Wednesday*	Astronauts complete repairs on the Hubble Space Telescope by correcting a faulty lens 1993	344
10	*Thursday*	Isaac Newton's derivation of Kepler's laws is read to the Royal Society by Edmund Halley 1684	345
11	*Friday*	*Apollo 17* touches down on the Moon in the last manned Moon-landing missions 1972	346
12	*Saturday*	Radio pioneer Guglielmo Marconi sends the first radio transmission across the Atlantic 1901	347
13	*Sunday*	Gordo, a monkey, is lost in the Atlantic when the recovery parachute of the *Jupiter AM-13* rocket fails 1958	348

14	*Monday*	Rutan Voyager, the first plane to fly non-stop around the world without refuelling, takes off 1986	week 50 day 349
15	*Tuesday*	Henri Becquerel, known for co-discovering radioactivity *b.* 1852	350
16	*Wednesday*	Johann Wilhelm Ritter, who discovered ultraviolet light *b.* 1776	351
17	*Thursday*	*SpaceShipOne* becomes the first privately funded manned spacecraft to travel at supersonic speed 2003	352
18	*Friday*	Sir John Alcock, pilot who made the first non-stop transatlantic flight in 1919 *d.* 1919	353
19	*Saturday*	*Apollo 17* successfully returns to Earth, after completing the final Moon-landing mission 1972	354
20	*Sunday*	A nuclear power plant in Idaho, US becomes the first power plant to generate electricity 1951	355

21	*Monday*	*Apollo 8,* the first manned mission to land on the Moon, is launched 1968	week 51 day 356
22	*Tuesday*	The first TV broadcast from a manned spacecraft is transmitted from *Apollo 8* 1968	357
23	*Wednesday*	*Apollo 8* astronauts become the first to orbit the Moon and escape the influence of Earth's gravity 1968	358
24	*Thursday*	James Prescott Joule, physicist after whom the unit of energy is named *b.* 1818	359
25	*Friday*	Scientists fail to make contact with *Beagle 2,* a British probe which landed on Mars 2003	360
26	*Saturday*	Charles Babbage, pioneer of mechanical computation who proposed the Analytical Engine *b.* 1791	361
27	*Sunday*	*Apollo 8* returns to Earth following the first successful manned Moon-landing 1968	362

28	*Monday*	Hermann Oberth, pioneer of rocket propulsion *d.* 1989	week 52 day 363
29	*Tuesday*	Cosmonaut Yuri Romanenko returns to Earth having spent a record 326 days aboard *Mir* 1987	364
30	*Wednesday*	A second full moon of the month (a 'blue moon') is visable at the same time as a total lunar eclipse 1982	365
31	*Thursday*	John Flamsteed, first Astronomer Royal *d.* 1719	366

ASTRONOMICAL PHENOMENA

d	*h*	
5	1	Moon 2.5° north of Beehive cluster
14	1	Geminid meteor swarm
21	10	Winter solstice
21	16	Saturn 0.1° north of Jupiter
22	9	Ursid meteor swarm
24	23	Uranus 3° north of the Moon
27	20	Moon 5° north of Aldebaran

MINIMA OF ALGOL

d	*h*	*d*	*h*	*d*	*h*
3	7.9	14	19.2	26	6.5
6	4.8	17	16.0	29	3.3
9	1.6	20	12.8		
11	22.4	23	9.7		

CONSTELLATIONS

The following constellations are near the meridian at

	d	*h*		*d*	*h*
November	1	24	December	16	21
November	15	23	January	1	20
December	1	22	January	16	19

Ursa Major (below the Pole), Ursa Minor (below the Pole), Cassiopeia, Andromeda, Perseus, Triangulum, Aries, Taurus, Cetus and Eridarus

THE MOON

Phase, Apsides and Node	*d*	*h*	*m*
◗ Last Quarter	8	0	37
● New Moon	14	16	17
◖ First Quarter	21	23	41
○ Full Moon	30	3	28

Perigee (361,772 km)	12	20	42
Apogee (405,011 km)	24	16	31

Mean longitude of the ascending node on 1st, 81°

THE SUN   Diam. 32.4′

Day	Right Ascension			Dec.	Equation of time		Rise 52°		Rise 56°		Transit		Set 52°		Set 56°		Sidereal time			Transit of first point of Aries		
	h	m	s	°	m	s	h	m	h	m	h	m	h	m	h	m	h	m	s	h	m	s
1	16	30	17	−21.8	+10	58	7	46	8	07	11	49	15	52	15	31	4	41	15	19	15	35
2	16	34	36	−22.0	+10	35	7	47	8	08	11	50	15	52	15	30	4	45	12	19	11	39
3	16	38	56	−22.1	+10	12	7	49	8	10	11	50	15	51	15	30	4	49	08	19	07	43
4	16	43	16	−22.3	+9	48	7	50	8	11	11	50	15	51	15	29	4	53	05	19	03	47
5	16	47	37	−22.4	+9	23	7	51	8	13	11	51	15	50	15	28	4	57	02	18	59	52
6	16	51	59	−22.5	+8	58	7	52	8	14	11	51	15	50	15	28	5	00	58	18	55	56
7	16	56	21	−22.6	+8	33	7	54	8	16	11	52	15	50	15	27	5	04	55	18	52	00
8	17	00	44	−22.7	+8	06	7	55	8	17	11	52	15	49	15	27	5	08	51	18	48	04
9	17	05	07	−22.8	+7	40	7	56	8	18	11	53	15	49	15	27	5	12	48	18	44	08
10	17	09	31	−22.9	+7	13	7	57	8	19	11	53	15	49	15	26	5	16	44	18	40	12
11	17	13	55	−23.0	+6	45	7	58	8	21	11	53	15	49	15	26	5	20	41	18	36	16
12	17	18	19	−23.1	+6	17	7	59	8	22	11	54	15	49	15	26	5	24	37	18	32	20
13	17	22	44	−23.2	+5	49	8	00	8	23	11	54	15	49	15	26	5	28	34	18	28	24
14	17	27	09	−23.2	+5	20	8	01	8	24	11	55	15	49	15	26	5	32	31	18	24	28
15	17	31	34	−23.3	+4	52	8	02	8	25	11	55	15	49	15	26	5	36	27	18	20	32
16	17	36	00	−23.3	+4	22	8	02	8	26	11	56	15	49	15	26	5	40	24	18	16	37
17	17	40	26	−23.4	+3	53	8	03	8	26	11	56	15	50	15	26	5	44	20	18	12	41
18	17	44	52	−23.4	+3	24	8	04	8	27	11	57	15	50	15	27	5	48	17	18	08	45
19	17	49	18	−23.4	+2	54	8	04	8	28	11	57	15	50	15	27	5	52	13	18	04	49
20	17	53	45	−23.4	+2	24	8	05	8	28	11	58	15	51	15	27	5	56	10	18	00	53
21	17	58	11	−23.4	+1	54	8	05	8	29	11	58	15	51	15	28	6	00	06	17	56	57
22	18	02	37	−23.4	+1	24	8	06	8	29	11	59	15	52	15	28	6	04	03	17	53	01
23	18	07	04	−23.4	+0	55	8	06	8	30	11	59	15	52	15	29	6	08	00	17	49	05
24	18	11	30	−23.4	+0	25	8	07	8	30	12	00	15	53	15	30	6	11	56	17	45	09
25	18	15	57	−23.4	−0	05	8	07	8	30	12	00	15	54	15	30	6	15	53	17	41	13
26	18	20	23	−23.4	−0	35	8	07	8	31	12	01	15	54	15	31	6	19	49	17	37	17
27	18	24	49	−23.3	−1	04	8	07	8	31	12	01	15	55	15	32	6	23	46	17	33	22
28	18	29	15	−23.3	−1	33	8	08	8	31	12	02	15	56	15	33	6	27	42	17	29	26
29	18	33	40	−23.2	−2	03	8	08	8	31	12	02	15	57	15	34	6	31	39	17	25	30
30	18	38	06	−23.1	−2	31	8	08	8	31	12	03	15	58	15	35	6	35	35	17	21	34
31	18	42	31	−23.1	−3	00	8	08	8	30	12	03	15	59	15	36	6	39	32	17	17	38

DURATION OF TWILIGHT (in minutes)

Latitude	52°	56°	52°	56°	52°	56°
	1 December		11 December		21 December	
Civil	40	45	41	47	41	47
Nautical	82	93	84	96	85	97
Astronomical	123	138	125	141	126	142

THE NIGHT SKY

Mercury is too low in the morning sky to be seen this month and is at superior conjunction on the 20th. A daylight occultation of Mercury on the 14th will be nigh on impossible to see as it is only 3° from the Sun.

Venus (magnitude −3.9) rises 2.5 hours before the Sun on the 1st but slowly loses height during December. The Moon is nearby on the 12th and 13th. Venus passes 5.5° from Antares on the 24th.

Mars (magnitude −0.7) ends the year in Pisces and doesn't set until the small hours. The Moon is 6.5° away on the 23rd.

Jupiter (magnitude −2.0) crosses into Capricornus on the 19th. The Moon is in the area on the 16th and 17th.

Saturn (magnitude 0.6) moves into Capricornus slightly earlier on the 16th.

Jupiter and Saturn are just six arc-minutes apart on the 21st when they have a once-in-twenty-years Great Conjunction. They set just after 18h that evening and both planets will fit in a 100x eyepiece field with their disks, the Galilean moons, and Saturn's rings all visible. The pair won't have a better conjunction until 2080.

A total solar eclipse on the 14th begins in the southern Pacific and makes landfall in southern Chile before reaching maximum (2m 9s) in central southern Argentina. The path of totality then crosses the southern Atlantic before the eclipse ends at sunset off the coast of Namibia.

The New Moon on the 14th means conditions are perfect for the Geminids maximum that night.

THE MOON

Day	R.A.		Dec	Hor Par	Diam	Sun Co-Long	PA of Br. limb	Ph.	Age	Rise				Transit		Set			
										52°		56°				52°		56°	
	h	m	°	'	'	°	°	%	d	h	m	h	m	h	m	h	m	h	m
1	4	59	+22.3	54.8	29.8	100	87	100	15.3	16	33	16	07	0	19	8	49	9	15
2	5	52	+24.2	55.1	30.0	112	87	98	16.3	17	17	16	48	1	09	9	52	10	21
3	6	47	+24.9	55.6	30.2	124	91	94	17.3	18	12	17	43	2	02	10	46	11	16
4	7	42	+24.3	56.0	30.6	137	97	88	18.3	19	18	18	53	2	55	11	31	11	56
5	8	37	+22.5	56.6	30.8	149	102	80	19.3	20	32	20	12	3	48	12	05	12	27
6	9	32	+19.4	57.1	31.2	161	106	71	20.3	21	51	21	35	4	40	12	32	12	48
7	10	25	+15.3	57.8	31.4	173	110	61	21.3	23	11	23	02	5	31	12	53	13	05
8	11	17	+10.4	58.4	31.8	185	113	50	22.3	—	—	—	—	6	21	13	12	13	19
9	12	08	+4.8	59.1	32.2	197	115	39	23.3	0	32	0	28	7	10	13	30	13	31
10	13	00	−1.2	59.7	32.6	209	115	28	24.3	1	56	1	57	7	59	13	47	13	43
11	13	53	−7.2	60.2	32.8	222	114	18	25.3	3	21	3	28	8	51	14	06	13	57
12	14	48	−12.9	60.5	33.0	234	111	10	26.3	4	49	5	02	9	45	14	29	14	14
13	15	46	−17.9	60.6	33.0	246	107	04	27.3	6	18	6	38	10	43	14	59	14	37
14	16	47	−21.8	60.4	33.0	258	101	01	28.3	7	44	8	09	11	44	15	37	15	11
15	17	50	−24.1	60.0	32.8	270	280	00	29.3	9	00	9	31	12	46	16	28	16	01
16	18	54	−24.9	59.3	32.4	283	271	02	0.8	10	03	10	33	13	47	17	33	17	06
17	19	56	−24.0	58.5	32.0	295	264	07	1.8	10	49	11	15	14	45	18	47	18	22
18	20	54	−21.7	57.7	31.4	307	258	14	2.8	11	23	11	43	15	39	20	04	19	45
19	21	49	−18.2	56.8	31.0	319	254	22	3.8	11	48	12	03	16	29	21	20	21	06
20	22	39	−14.1	56.0	30.6	331	250	31	4.8	12	07	12	18	17	14	22	33	22	24
21	23	26	−9.4	55.3	30.2	343	248	41	5.8	12	23	12	29	17	57	23	43	23	39
22	0	11	−4.5	54.7	29.8	356	246	50	6.8	12	37	12	39	18	38	—	—	—	—
23	0	54	+0.5	54.4	29.6	8	246	60	7.8	12	51	12	48	19	18	0	52	0	52
24	1	38	+5.5	54.2	29.6	20	247	69	8.8	13	05	12	58	19	59	1	59	2	04
25	2	21	+10.2	54.1	29.6	32	249	77	9.8	13	21	13	10	20	41	3	08	3	18
26	3	06	+14.6	54.3	29.6	44	251	84	10.8	13	39	13	23	21	25	4	17	4	32
27	3	54	+18.4	54.5	29.8	56	255	91	11.8	14	03	13	42	22	13	5	27	5	46
28	4	44	+21.6	54.9	29.8	69	261	96	12.8	14	32	14	08	23	03	6	37	7	00
29	5	36	+23.7	55.3	30.2	81	269	99	13.8	15	13	14	44	23	55	7	42	8	10
30	6	31	+24.8	55.8	30.4	93	316	100	14.8	16	05	15	35	—	—	8	41	9	10
31	7	27	+24.6	56.2	30.6	105	84	99	15.8	17	09	16	41	0	49	9	30	9	56

MERCURY

Day	R.A.		Dec	Mag.	Diam.	Phase	Rise	Transit	Set
	h	m	°		"	%	h m	h m	h m
1	15	46.5	−19.3	−0.8	5	96	6 56	11 05	15 13
3	15	59.2	−20.2	−0.8	5	97	7 07	11 10	15 12
5	16	12.1	−21.0	−0.8	5	97	7 18	11 15	15 11
7	16	25.2	−21.8	−0.8	5	98	7 29	11 20	15 11
9	16	38.4	−22.5	−0.9	5	99	7 39	11 25	15 11
11	16	51.7	−23.1	−0.9	5	99	7 49	11 31	15 12
13	17	05.2	−23.6	−1.0	5	99	7 59	11 37	15 14
15	17	18.8	−24.1	−1.0	5	100	8 08	11 42	15 16
17	17	32.5	−24.5	−1.1	5	100	8 17	11 48	15 19
19	17	46.4	−24.8	−1.2	5	100	8 25	11 54	15 23
21	18	00.3	−25.0	−1.2	5	100	8 33	12 00	15 27
23	18	14.3	−25.1	−1.1	5	100	8 40	12 06	15 33
25	18	28.4	−25.1	−1.1	5	100	8 46	12 13	15 39
27	18	42.6	−25.0	−1.0	5	99	8 52	12 19	15 46
29	18	56.7	−24.8	−1.0	5	99	8 56	12 25	15 54
31	19	10.9	−24.5	−1.0	5	98	9 00	12 31	16 03

Rising and setting times are for latitude 54°

VENUS

Day	R.A.		Dec	Mag.	Diam.	Phase	Rise	Transit	Set
	h	m	°		"	%	h m	h m	h m
1	14	39.2	−13.8	−4.0	13	89	5 13	9 57	14 42
6	15	03.7	−15.7	−4.0	12	90	5 29	10 02	14 34
11	15	28.6	−17.4	−4.0	12	91	5 46	10 07	14 28
16	15	54.1	−19.0	−4.0	12	92	6 02	10 13	14 24
21	16	20.0	−20.3	−3.9	12	92	6 18	10 19	14 21
26	16	46.4	−21.5	−3.9	12	93	6 32	10 26	14 20
31	17	13.1	−22.3	−3.9	12	94	6 45	10 33	14 21

MARS

Day	R.A.		Dec	Mag.	Diam.	Phase	Rise	Transit	Set
	h	m	°		"	%	h m	h m	h m
1	01	03.0	+6.7	−1.1	15	92	13 39	20 22	3 03
6	01	06.9	+7.3	−1.0	14	92	13 20	20 06	2 51
11	01	11.8	+8.0	−0.8	13	91	13 01	19 51	2 40
16	01	17.5	+8.7	−0.7	12	90	12 43	19 37	2 30
21	01	23.9	+9.5	−0.5	12	90	12 25	19 23	2 21
26	01	31.0	+10.3	−0.4	11	89	12 08	19 10	2 13
31	01	38.7	+11.2	−0.3	11	89	11 51	18 58	2 06

SUNRISE AND SUNSET

	London 0° 05′	51° 30′	Bristol 2° 35′	51° 28′	Birmingham 1° 55′	52° 28′	Manchester 2° 15′	53° 28′	Newcastle 1° 37′	54° 59′	Glasgow 4° 14′	55° 52′	Belfast 5° 56′	54° 35′
d	h m	h m	h m	h m	h m	h m	h m	h m	h m	h m	h m	h m	h m	h m
1	7 44	15 55	7 54	16 05	7 56	15 57	8 02	15 54	8 08	15 43	8 24	15 48	8 23	16 03
2	7 45	15 54	7 55	16 04	7 57	15 57	8 04	15 53	8 09	15 42	8 25	15 48	8 25	16 02
3	7 47	15 54	7 57	16 04	7 59	15 56	8 05	15 52	8 11	15 42	8 27	15 47	8 26	16 01
4	7 48	15 53	7 58	16 03	8 00	15 56	8 07	15 52	8 12	15 41	8 28	15 46	8 27	16 00
5	7 49	15 53	7 59	16 03	8 01	15 55	8 08	15 51	8 14	15 40	8 30	15 45	8 29	16 00
6	7 51	15 52	8 00	16 02	8 03	15 55	8 09	15 51	8 15	15 40	8 31	15 45	8 30	15 59
7	7 52	15 52	8 02	16 02	8 04	15 54	8 10	15 51	8 17	15 39	8 33	15 44	8 32	15 59
8	7 53	15 52	8 03	16 02	8 05	15 54	8 12	15 50	8 18	15 39	8 34	15 44	8 33	15 59
9	7 54	15 52	8 04	16 02	8 06	15 54	8 13	15 50	8 19	15 39	8 35	15 44	8 34	15 58
10	7 55	15 51	8 05	16 02	8 07	15 54	8 14	15 50	8 20	15 38	8 36	15 43	8 35	15 58
11	7 56	15 51	8 06	16 01	8 08	15 54	8 15	15 50	8 21	15 38	8 38	15 43	8 36	15 58
12	7 57	15 51	8 07	16 01	8 09	15 54	8 16	15 50	8 23	15 38	8 39	15 43	8 37	15 58
13	7 58	15 51	8 08	16 01	8 10	15 54	8 17	15 50	8 24	15 38	8 40	15 43	8 38	15 58
14	7 59	15 51	8 09	16 02	8 11	15 54	8 18	15 50	8 25	15 38	8 41	15 43	8 39	15 58
15	8 00	15 52	8 10	16 02	8 12	15 54	8 19	15 50	8 25	15 38	8 42	15 43	8 40	15 58
16	8 01	15 52	8 10	16 02	8 13	15 54	8 20	15 50	8 26	15 38	8 43	15 43	8 41	15 58
17	8 01	15 52	8 11	16 02	8 14	15 54	8 20	15 50	8 27	15 38	8 43	15 43	8 42	15 58
18	8 02	15 52	8 12	16 02	8 14	15 55	8 21	15 50	8 28	15 39	8 44	15 43	8 43	15 58
19	8 03	15 53	8 12	16 03	8 15	15 55	8 22	15 51	8 28	15 39	8 45	15 44	8 43	15 59
20	8 03	15 53	8 13	16 03	8 16	15 55	8 22	15 51	8 29	15 39	8 45	15 44	8 44	15 59
21	8 04	15 54	8 14	16 04	8 16	15 56	8 23	15 52	8 30	15 40	8 46	15 45	8 44	16 00
22	8 04	15 54	8 14	16 04	8 17	15 56	8 23	15 52	8 30	15 41	8 46	15 45	8 45	16 00
23	8 05	15 55	8 14	16 05	8 17	15 57	8 24	15 53	8 30	15 41	8 47	15 46	8 45	16 01
24	8 05	15 55	8 15	16 05	8 17	15 58	8 24	15 53	8 31	15 42	8 47	15 47	8 46	16 02
25	8 05	15 56	8 15	16 06	8 18	15 58	8 25	15 54	8 31	15 43	8 47	15 47	8 46	16 02
26	8 06	15 57	8 15	16 07	8 18	15 59	8 25	15 55	8 31	15 43	8 48	15 48	8 46	16 03
27	8 06	15 58	8 16	16 08	8 18	16 00	8 25	15 56	8 31	15 44	8 48	15 49	8 46	16 04
28	8 06	15 58	8 16	16 09	8 18	16 01	8 25	15 57	8 32	15 45	8 48	15 50	8 46	16 05
29	8 06	15 59	8 16	16 09	8 18	16 02	8 25	15 58	8 32	15 46	8 48	15 51	8 46	16 06
30	8 06	16 00	8 16	16 10	8 18	16 03	8 25	15 59	8 31	15 47	8 48	15 52	8 46	16 07
31	8 06	16 01	8 16	16 11	8 18	16 04	8 25	16 00	8 31	15 48	8 47	15 53	8 46	16 08

JUPITER

Day	R.A. h m	Dec °	Mag.	Diam. ″	Rise h m	Transit h m	Set h m
1	19 53.0	−21.4	−2.0	34	11 15	15 09	19 04
11	20 01.5	−21.0	−2.0	34	10 42	14 39	18 36
21	20 10.5	−20.5	−2.0	33	10 08	14 08	18 09
31	20 19.8	−20.1	−2.0	33	9 35	13 38	17 42

Diam. = equatorial; Polar Diam. is 94% of Equatorial Diam.

SATURN

Day	R.A. h m	Dec °	Mag.	Diam. ″	Rise h m	Transit h m	Set h m
1	20 02.4	−20.8	+0.6	16	11 21	15 19	19 17
11	20 06.4	−20.6	+0.6	15	10 44	14 43	18 43
21	20 10.8	−20.4	+0.6	15	10 07	14 08	18 10
31	20 15.4	−20.2	+0.6	15	9 31	13 34	17 36

Diam. = equatorial; Polar Diam. is 90% of Equatorial Diam.
Rings – major axis 35″ minor axis 13″, Tilt 22°

URANUS

Day	R.A. h m	Dec °	Mag.	Diam. ″	Rise h m	Transit h m	Set h m
1	02 21.3	+13.6	+5.7	4	14 16	21 36	5 01
11	02 20.1	+13.5	+5.7	4	13 36	20 56	4 20
21	02 19.2	+13.4	+5.7	4	12 56	20 16	3 39
31	02 18.5	+13.4	+5.7	4	12 16	19 36	2 59

NEPTUNE

Day	R.A. h m	Dec °	Mag.	Diam. ″	Rise h m	Transit h m	Set h m
1	23 18.2	−5.7	+7.9	2	13 02	18 34	0 09
11	23 18.3	−5.7	+7.9	2	12 23	17 55	23 26
21	23 18.7	−5.6	+7.9	2	11 44	17 16	22 48
31	23 19.3	−5.6	+7.9	2	11 05	16 37	22 09

ECLIPSES 2020

During 2020 there will be six eclipses, two of the Sun and four of the Moon (all times are in GMT):

1. A penumbral lunar eclipse on 10 January beginning 19h 11m will be visible from Europe, Africa, Asia and Australia.
2. A partial penumbral lunar eclipse on 5 June beginning 17h 45m will be visible from Europe, Africa, Asia and Australia. It will only be visible in Europe and W. Africa after moonrise.
3. An annular solar eclipse on 21 June will be visible from central Africa, south Asia, China and the Pacific and partially visible from Africa, southeast Europe and Asia.
4. A penumbral lunar eclipse on 5 July beginning 3h 07m will be visible from the Americas, south-west Europe and Africa.
5. A penumbral lunar eclipse on 30 November beginning 7h 32m will be visible from Asia, Australia, the Pacific and the Americas. It will only be visible in Asia after moonrise.
6. A total solar eclipse on 14 December will be visible from the south Pacific, Chile, Argentina and the south Atlantic and partially visible from the Pacific, south South America and Antarctica.

Penumbral lunar eclipses result in a dimming of the brightness of the full Moon and can often go unnoticed as the Moon never completely enters the Earth's shadow. Those on the Moon would see a partial solar eclipse.

MEAN AND SIDEREAL TIME

The length of a sidereal day in mean time is 23h 56m 04s.09. Hence 1h MT = 1h+9^s.86 ST and 1h ST = 1h − 9^s.83 MT.

Acceleration						Retardation					
h	m	s	m	s	s	h	m	s	m	s	s
1	0	10	0	00	0	1	0	10	0	00	0
2	0	20	3	02	1	2	0	20	3	03	1
3	0	30	9	07	2	3	0	29	9	09	2
4	0	39	15	13	3	4	0	39	15	15	3
5	0	49	21	18	4	5	0	49	21	21	4
6	0	59	27	23	5	6	0	59	27	28	5
7	1	09	33	28	6	7	1	09	33	34	6
8	1	19	39	34	7	8	1	19	39	40	7
9	1	29	45	39	8	9	1	28	45	46	8
10	1	39	51	44	9	10	1	38	51	53	9
11	1	48	57	49	10	11	1	48	57	59	10
12	1	58	60	00		12	1	58	60	00	
13	2	08				13	2	08			
14	2	18				14	2	18			
15	2	28				15	2	27			
16	2	38				16	2	37			
17	2	48				17	2	47			
18	2	57				18	2	57			
19	3	07				19	3	07			
20	3	17				20	3	17			
21	3	27				21	3	26			
22	3	37				22	3	36			
23	3	47				23	3	46			
24	3	57				24	3	56			

To convert an interval of mean time to the corresponding interval of sidereal time, enter the acceleration table with the given mean time (taking the hours and the minutes and seconds separately) and add the acceleration obtained to the given mean time. To convert an interval of sidereal time to the corresponding interval of mean time, take out the retardation for the given sidereal time and subtract.

The columns for the minutes and seconds of the argument are in the form known as critical tables. To use these tables, find in the appropriate left-hand column the two entries between which the given number of minutes and seconds lies; the quantity in the right-hand column between these two entries is the required acceleration or retardation. Thus the acceleration

for 11m 26s (which lies between the entries 9m 07s and 15m 13s) is 2s. If the given number of minutes and seconds is a tabular entry, the required acceleration or retardation is the entry in the right-hand column above the given tabular entry, eg the retardation for 45m 46s is 7s.

Example – Convert 14h 27m 35s from ST to MT:

	h	m	s
Given ST	14	27	35
Retardation for 14h		2	18
Retardation for 27m 35s			5
Corresponding MT	14	25	12

For further explanation *see* pages 629 and 631.

EXPLANATION OF ASTRONOMICAL DATA

Positions of the heavenly bodies are given only to the degree of accuracy required by amateur astronomers for setting telescopes, or for plotting on celestial globes or star atlases. Where intermediate positions are required, linear interpolation may be employed.

Detailed definitions of the terms used cannot be given here. They must be sought in astronomical literature, the internet or textbooks.

A special feature has been made of the times when the various heavenly bodies are visible in the British Isles. Since two columns, calculated for latitudes 52° and 56°, are devoted to risings and settings, the range 50° to 58° can be covered by interpolation and extrapolation. The times given in these columns are Greenwich Mean Times for the meridian of Greenwich. An observer west of this meridian must add his/her longitude (in time) and vice versa.

In accordance with the usual convention in astronomy, + and − indicate respectively north and south latitudes or declinations.

All data are, unless otherwise stated, for 0h Greenwich Mean Time (GMT), ie at the midnight at the beginning of the day named. Allowance must be made for British Summer Time during the period that this is in operation.

PAGE ONE OF EACH MONTH

The calendar for each month is explained on page 577

Under the heading Astronomical Phenomena will be found particulars of the more important conjunctions of the Sun, Moon and planets with each other, and also the dates of other astronomical phenomena of special interest.

Times of Minima of Algol are approximate times of the middle of the period of diminished light.

The Constellations listed each month are those that are near the meridian at the beginning of the month at 22h local mean time. Allowance must be made for British Summer Time when appropriate. The fact that any star crosses the meridian 4m earlier each night or 2h earlier each month may be used, in conjunction with the lists given each month, to find which constellations are favourably placed at any moment.

The principal phases of the Moon are the GMTs when the difference between the longitude of the Moon and that of the Sun is 0°, 90°, 180° or 270°. The times of perigee and apogee are those when the Moon is nearest to, and farthest from, the Earth, respectively. The nodes or points of intersection of the Moon's orbit and the ecliptic make a complete retrograde circuit of the ecliptic in about 19 years. From a knowledge of the longitude of the ascending node and the inclination, whose value does not vary much from 5°, the path of the Moon among the stars may be plotted on a celestial globe or star atlas.

PAGE TWO OF EACH MONTH

The Sun's diameter, in arc minutes, is given for the 1st of each month.

The right ascension and declination (Dec.) is that of the true Sun. The right ascension of the mean Sun is obtained by applying the equation of time, with the sign given, to the right ascension of the true Sun, or, more easily, by applying 12h to the Sidereal Time. The direction in which the equation of time has to be applied in different problems is a frequent source of confusion and error. Apparent Solar Time is equal to the Mean Solar Time plus the Equation of Time. For example, at 12h GMT on August 8 the Equation of Time is, using linear interpolation, found to be −5m 37s and thus at 12h Mean Time on that day the Apparent Time is 12h − 5m 37s = 11h 54m 23s.

The Greenwich Sidereal Time at 0h and the Transit of the First Point of Aries (which is really the mean time when the sidereal time is 0h) are used for converting mean time to sidereal time and vice versa.

The GMT of transit of the Sun at Greenwich may also be taken as the local mean time (LMT) of transit in any longitude. It is independent of latitude. The GMT of transit in any longitude is obtained by adding the longitude to the time given if west, and vice versa.

LIGHTING-UP TIME

The legal importance of sunrise and sunset is that the Road Vehicles Lighting Regulations 1989 (SI 1989 No. 1796) as amended, make the use of front and rear position lamps on vehicles compulsory during the period between sunset and sunrise. Headlamps on vehicles are required to be used during the hours of darkness on unlit roads, on lit roads with a speed limit exceeding 30mph, or whenever visibility is seriously reduced. The hours of darkness are defined in these regulations as the period between half an hour after sunset and half an hour before sunrise.

In all laws and regulations 'sunset' refers to the local sunset, ie the time at which the Sun sets at the place in question. This common-sense interpretation has been upheld by legal tribunals.

MAGNITUDE

Magnitudes of astronomical objects are measured in what may be considered the reverse to the obvious. Magnitude +3 is brighter than +4, magnitude −2 is brighter than magnitude −1. So from brighter to dimmer: −4, −3, −2, −1, 0, +1, +2, +3 etc, with +6 being the dimmest considered visible with the naked eye in very dark skies. Each magnitude is roughly 2.5 times brighter than the next, so a magnitude +1 object is exactly 100 times brighter than a magnitude +6 object.

SUNRISE AND SUNSET

The times of sunrise and sunset are those when the Sun's upper limb, as affected by refraction, is on the true horizon of an observer at sea-level. Assuming the mean refraction to be 34′, and the Sun's semi-diameter to be 16′, the time given is that when the true zenith distance of the Sun's centre is 90°+34′+16′ or 90° 50′, or, in other words, when the depression of the Sun's centre below the true horizon is 50′. The upper limb is then 34′ below the true horizon, but is brought there by refraction. An observer on a ship might see the Sun for a minute or so longer, because of the dip of the horizon, while another viewing the sunset over hills or mountains would record an earlier time. Nevertheless, the moment when the true zenith distance of the Sun's centre is 90° 50′ is a precise time dependent only on the latitude and longitude of the place, and independent of its altitude above sea-level, the contour of its horizon, the vagaries of refraction

or the small seasonal change in the Sun's diameter; this moment is suitable in every way as a definition of sunset (or sunrise) for all statutory purposes. For further information, see Sunrise, Sunset, Moonrise and Moonset on page 628.

TWILIGHT

Light reaches us before sunrise and continues to reach us for some time after sunset. The interval between darkness and sunrise or sunset and darkness is called twilight. Astronomically speaking, twilight is considered to begin or end when the Sun's centre is 18° below the horizon, as no light from the Sun can then reach the observer. As thus defined twilight may last several hours; in high latitudes at the summer solstice the depression of 18° is not reached, and twilight lasts from sunset to sunrise. The duration of twilight data is given in minutes.

The need for some sub-division of twilight is met by dividing the gathering darkness into four stages.

(1) *Sunrise or Sunset,* defined as above

(2) *Civil twilight,* which begins or ends when the Sun's centre is 6° below the horizon. This marks the time when operations requiring daylight may commence or must cease. In England it varies from about 30 to 60 minutes after sunset and the same interval before sunrise

(3) *Nautical twilight,* which begins or ends when the Sun's centre is 12° below the horizon. This marks the time when it is, to all intents and purposes, completely dark

(4) *Astronomical twilight,* which begins or ends when the Sun's centre is 18° below the horizon. This marks theoretical perfect darkness. It is of little practical importance, especially if nautical twilight is tabulated

To assist observers the durations of civil, nautical and astronomical twilights are given at intervals of ten days. The beginning of a particular twilight is found by subtracting the duration from the time of sunrise, while the end is found by adding the duration to the time of sunset. Thus the beginning of astronomical twilight in latitude 52°, on the Greenwich meridian, on March 11 is found as 06h 23m − 113m = 04h 30m and similarly the end of civil twilight as 17h 58m +34m = 18h 32m. The letters TAN (twilight all night) are printed when twilight lasts all night.

Under the heading The Night Sky will be found notes describing the position and visibility of the planets and other phenomena.

PAGE THREE OF EACH MONTH

Daily tabulation of the Moon's position is given with less precision than for the Sun, because it moves more rapidly among the stars. The precision is appropriate to linear interpolation. The right ascension (RA) and declination (Dec.) are geocentric, ie for an imaginary observer at the centre of the Earth. Observers on the surface of the Earth generally see the Moon at a different position due to parallax. The difference is zero when the Moon is at the zenith and may be as much as 1° when the Moon is on the horizon − 'Hor Par' in the table gives this value.

The lunar terminator is the line separating the bright and dark parts of the Moon's disk. Apart from irregularities of the lunar surface, the terminator is elliptical, because it is a circle seen in projection. It becomes the full circle forming the limb, or edge, of the Moon at New and Full Moon. The selenographic longitude of the terminator is measured from the mean centre of the visible disk, which may differ from the visible centre by as much as 8°, because of libration.

Instead of the longitude of the terminator the Sun's selenographic co-longitude (Sun's co-long.) is tabulated. It is numerically equal to the selenographic longitude of the morning terminator, measured eastwards from the mean centre of the disk. Thus its value is approximately 270° at

New Moon, 360° at First Quarter, 90° at Full Moon and 180° at Last Quarter.

The Position Angle (PA) of the Bright Limb is the position angle of the midpoint of the illuminated limb, measured eastwards from the north point on the disk. The Phase column shows the percentage of the area of the Moon's disk illuminated; this is also the illuminated percentage of the diameter at right angles to the line of cusps. The terminator is a semi-ellipse whose major axis is the line of cusps, and whose semi-minor axis is determined by the tabulated percentage; from New Moon to Full Moon the east limb is dark, and vice versa.

The times given as moonrise and moonset are those when the upper limb of the Moon is on the horizon of an observer at sea-level. The Sun's horizontal parallax is nearly constant at about 9″, and is negligible when considering sunrise and sunset. However, that of the Moon averages about 57′ and varies significantly, and its value is tabulated (Hor Par). Hence the computed time represents the moment when the true zenith distance of the Moon is 90° 50′ (as for the Sun) minus the horizontal parallax. The time required for the Sun or Moon to rise or set is about four minutes (except in high latitudes). See also Sunrise, Sunset, Moonrise and Moonset below.

The GMT of transit of the Moon over the meridian of Greenwich is given; these times are independent of latitude but must be corrected for longitude. For places in the British Isles it suffices to add the longitude if west, and vice versa. For other places a further correction is necessary because of the rapid movement of the Moon relative to the stars. The entire correction is conveniently determined by first finding the west longitude λ of the place. If the place is in west longitude, λ is the ordinary west longitude; if the place is in east longitude, λ is the complement to 24h (or 360°) of the longitude and will be greater than 12h (or 180°). The correction then consists of two positive portions, namely λ and the fraction λ/24 (or λ°/360) multiplied by the difference between consecutive transits. Thus for Christchurch, New Zealand, the longitude is 172° 45′ east, equivalent to 11h 31m east in time, so λ = 12h 29m and the fraction λ/24 is 0.52. The transit on the local date 14 January 2020 is found as follows:

		d	h	m
GMT of transit at Greenwich	January	13	02	18
λ			12	29
0.52 x (3h 13m − 2h 18m)				29
GMT of transit at Christchurch		13	15	16
Corr. to NZ Standard Time			12	00
Local standard time of transit	January	14	03	16

As is evident, for any given place the quantities λ and the correction to local standard time may be combined permanently, being here 24h 29m.

Positions of Mercury are given for every second day, and those of Venus and Mars for every fifth day; linear interpolation can be used to give intermediate values to the same precision. The diameter (Diam.) is given in seconds of arc. The phase is the illuminated percentage of the disk. In the case of the inner planets this approaches 100% at superior conjunction and zero at inferior conjunction. When the phase is less than 50% the planet is crescent-shaped or horned; for greater phases it is gibbous. In the case of the exterior planet Mars, the phase approaches 100% at conjunction and opposition, and is a minimum at the quadratures.

To determine if a planet is visible or not, the transit time should be examined. If the transit time coincides with hours of darkness the planet should be easy to find, provided it is bright enough. If the time of transit is between 00h and 12h

the planet should be visible above the eastern horizon; if between 12h and 24h, above the western horizon. The closer the transit time to midnight (0h) the longer it will be visible.

The inner planets – Mercury and Venus can never transit at midnight because they are, from Earth, seen to be too close to the Sun. If they transit close to noon (12h) then they will be too close to the Sun to be visible except during a total solar eclipse. The rise or set times should be examined to see if either is near sunrise or sunset. If this also coincides with a large positive declination (Dec.) then conditions are favourable for viewing in the northern hemisphere. A negative (southern) declination favours observations in the southern hemisphere.

Consulting The Night Sky paragraphs will also help determine observability.

PAGE FOUR OF EACH MONTH

The GMTs of sunrise and sunset for seven cities, whose positions in longitude (W.) and latitude (N.) are given immediately below the name, may be used not only for these phenomena, but also for lighting-up times. See Sunrise, Sunset, Moonrise and Moonset below for a fuller explanation.

The particulars for the four outer planets resemble those for the planets on Page Three of each month, except that, because of the dimness of Uranus and Neptune, these two planets require an optical aid, such as binoculars or a small telescope, to be seen. The diameters given for the rings of Saturn are those of the major axis (in the plane of the planet's equator) and the minor axis respectively. The former has a small seasonal change due to the slightly varying distance of the Earth from Saturn, but the latter varies from zero when the Earth passes through the ring plane every 15 years to its maximum opening half-way between these periods. The rings were last open at their widest extent (and Saturn at its brightest) in 2017. The Earth passed through the ring plane in 2009.

SUNRISE, SUNSET, MOONRISE AND MOONSET

The tables have been constructed for the meridian of Greenwich and for latitudes 52° and 56°. They give Greenwich Mean Time (GMT) throughout the year. To obtain the GMT of the phenomenon as seen from any other latitude and longitude in the British Isles, first interpolate or extrapolate for latitude by the usual rules of proportion. To the time thus found, the longitude (expressed in time) is to be added if west (as it usually is in Great Britain) or subtracted if east. If the longitude is expressed in degrees and minutes of arc, it must be converted to time at the rate of 1° = 4m and 15′ = 1m.

The GMT at which planets transit the Greenwich meridian is also given. The times of transit may be corrected to local meridians, as described above.

TIME

From the earliest ages, the natural division of time into recurring periods of day and night has provided the practical time-scale for the everyday activities of the human race. Indeed, if any alternative means of time measurement is adopted, it must be capable of adjustment so as to remain in general agreement with the natural time-scale defined by the diurnal rotation of the Earth on its axis. Ideally the rotation should be measured against a fixed frame of reference; in practice it must be measured against the background provided by the celestial bodies. If the Sun is chosen as the reference point, we obtain Apparent Solar Time, which is the time indicated by a sundial. It is not a uniform time but is subject to variations which amount to as much as a quarter of an hour in each direction. Such wide variations cannot be tolerated in a practical time-scale, and this has led to the concept of Mean Solar Time in which all the days are exactly the same length and equal to the average length of the Apparent Solar Day.

The positions of the stars in the sky are specified in relation to a reference point in the sky known as the First Point of Aries (or the Vernal Equinox). It is therefore convenient to adopt this same reference point when considering the rotation of the Earth against the background of the stars. The time-scale so obtained is known as Apparent Sidereal Time.

GREENWICH MEAN TIME

The daily rotation of the Earth on its axis causes the Sun and the other heavenly bodies, which are not circumpolar, to appear to cross the sky from east to west. Circumpolar objects (mostly stars) are close enough to the celestial pole that they never set. It is convenient to represent this relative motion as if the Earth really performed a daily circuit around a fixed Earth. Noon in Apparent Solar Time may then be defined as the time at which the Sun transits across the observer's meridian. In Mean Solar Time, noon is similarly defined by the meridian transit of a fictitious Mean Sun moving uniformly in the sky with the same average speed as the true Sun. Apparent Solar Time used to be observed on the meridian of the transit circle telescope of the Royal Observatory at Greenwich. Modern measurements are made from similar instruments across the world. Greenwich Mean Time (GMT) is derived from these observations. The mean solar day is divided into 24 hours and, for astronomical and other scientific purposes, these are numbered 0 to 23, commencing at midnight. Civil time is usually reckoned in two periods of 12 hours, designated am (*ante meridiem*, ie before noon) and pm (*post meridiem*, ie after noon), although the 24 hour clock is increasingly being used.

UNIVERSAL TIME

Before 1925 January 1, GMT was reckoned in 24 hours commencing at noon; since that date it has been reckoned from midnight. To avoid confusion in the use of the designation GMT before and after 1925, since 1928 astronomers have tended to use the term Universal Time (UT) or Weltzeit (WZ) to denote GMT measured from Greenwich Mean Midnight.

In precision work it is necessary to take account of small variations in Universal Time. These arise from small irregularities in the rotation of the Earth. Observed astronomical time is designated UT0. Observed time corrected for the effects of the motion of the poles (giving rise to a 'wandering' in longitude) is designated UT1. There is also a seasonal fluctuation in the rate of rotation of the Earth arising from meteorological causes, often called the annual fluctuation. UT1 corrected for this effect is designated UT2 and provides a time-scale free from short-period fluctuations. It is still subject to small secular and irregular changes.

APPARENT SOLAR TIME

As mentioned above, the time shown by a sundial is called Apparent Solar Time. It differs from Mean Solar Time by an amount known as the Equation of Time, which is the total effect of two causes which make the length of the apparent solar day non-uniform. One cause of variation is that the orbit of the Earth is not a circle but an ellipse, having the Sun at one focus. As a consequence, the angular speed of the Earth in its orbit is not constant; it is greatest at the beginning of January when the Earth is nearest the Sun.

The other cause is due to the obliquity of the ecliptic; the plane of the equator (which is at right angles to the axis of rotation of the Earth) does not coincide with the ecliptic (the plane defined by the apparent annual motion of the Sun around the celestial sphere) but is inclined to it at an angle of

about 23.4°. As a result, the apparent solar day is shorter than average at the equinoxes and longer at the solstices. From the combined effects of the components due to obliquity and eccentricity, the equation of time reaches its extreme values in February (−14 minutes) and early November (+16 minutes). It has a zero value on four dates during the year, and it is only on these dates (approximately April 15, June 14, September 1 and December 25) that a sundial shows Mean Solar Time.

SIDEREAL TIME

A sidereal day is the duration of a complete rotation of the Earth with reference to the First Point of Aries. The term sidereal (or 'star') time is a little misleading since the time-scale so defined is not exactly the same as that which would be defined by successive transits of a selected star, as there is a small progressive motion between the stars and the First Point of Aries due to the precession of the Earth's axis. This makes the length of the sidereal day shorter than the true period of rotation by 0.008 seconds. Superimposed on this steady precessional motion are small oscillations (nutation), giving rise to fluctuations in apparent sidereal time amounting to as much as 1.2 seconds. It is therefore customary to employ Mean Sidereal Time, from which these fluctuations have been removed. The conversion of GMT to Greenwich sidereal time (GST) may be performed by adding the value of the GST at 0h on the day in question to the GMT converted to sidereal time using the Mean and Sidereal Time table on page 1120.

Example – To find the GST at August 8d 02h 41m 11s GMT:

	h	m	s
GST at 0h	21	07	51
GMT	2	41	11
Acceleration for 2h			20
Acceleration for 41m 11s			7
Sum = GST =	23	49	29

If the observer is not on the Greenwich meridian then their longitude, measured in time, positively westwards from Greenwich, must be subtracted from the GST to obtain Local Sidereal Time (LST). Thus, in the above example, an observer 5h east of Greenwich (ie longitude 75° east), or 19h west, would find the LST as 4h 49m 29s.

EPHEMERIS TIME

An analysis of observations of the positions of the Sun, Moon and planets taken over an extended period is used in preparing ephemerides. (An ephemeris is a table giving the apparent position of a heavenly body at regular intervals of time, eg one day or ten days, and may be used to compare current observations with tabulated positions.) Discrepancies between the positions of heavenly bodies observed over a 300-year period and their predicted positions arose because the time-scale to which the observations were related was based on the assumption that the rate of rotation of the Earth is constant. It is now known that this rate of rotation is variable. A revised time-scale, Ephemeris Time (ET), was devised to bring the ephemerides into agreement with the observations.

The second of ET is defined in terms of the annual motion of the Earth in its orbit around the Sun (1/31,556,925.9747 of the tropical year for 1900 January 0d 12h ET). The precise determination of ET from astronomical observations is a lengthy process as the requisite standard of accuracy can only be achieved by averaging over a number of years.

In 1976 the International Astronomical Union adopted Terrestrial Dynamical Time (TDT), a new dynamical time-scale for general use whose scale unit is the SI second (*see* Atomic Time, below). TDT was renamed Terrestrial Time (TT) in 1991. ET is now of little more than historical interest.

TERRESTRIAL TIME

The uniform time system used in computing the ephemerides of the solar system is Terrestrial Time (TT), which has replaced ET for this purpose. Except for the most rigorous astronomical calculations, it may be assumed to be the same as ET. In June 2020 the difference TT − UT is estimated to be 69.7 seconds. This is known as Delta T.

ATOMIC TIME

The fundamental standards of time and frequency must be defined in terms of a periodic motion which is adequately constant, enduring and measurable. Progress has made it possible to use natural standards, such as atomic or molecular oscillations. Continuous oscillations are generated in an electrical circuit, the frequency of which is then compared or brought into coincidence with the frequency characteristic of the absorption or emission by the atoms or molecules when they change between two selected energy levels. Since the 13th General Conference on Weights and Measures in October 1967, the unit of time, the second, has been defined in the International System of units (SI) as 'the duration of 9,192,631,770 periods of the radiation corresponding to the transition between the two hyperfine levels of the ground state of the caesium-133 atom'.

In the UK, the national time scale is maintained by the National Physical Laboratory (NPL), using an ensemble of atomic clocks based on either caesium or hydrogen atoms. In addition the NPL (along with several other national laboratories) has constructed and operates caesium fountain primary frequency standards, which utilise the cooling of caesium atoms by laser light to determine the duration of the SI second at the highest attainable level of accuracy. Caesium fountain primary standards typically achieve an accuracy of around 2 parts in 10,000,000,000,000,000, which is equivalent to one second in 158 million years.

Timekeeping worldwide is based on two closely related atomic time scales that are established through international collaboration. International Atomic Time (TAI) is formed by combining the readings of more than 400 atomic clocks located in more than 70 institutes and was set close to the astronomically based Universal Time (UT) near the beginning of 1958. It was formally recognised in 1971 and since 1988 January 1 has been maintained by the International Bureau of Weights and Measures (BIPM). Civil time in almost all countries is now based on Coordinated Universal Time (UTC), which differs from TAI by 37 seconds and was designed to make both atomic time and UT available with accuracy appropriate for most users. On 1 January 1972 UTC was set to be exactly 10 seconds behind TAI, and since then the UTC time-scale has been adjusted by the insertion (or, in principle, omission) of leap seconds in order to keep it within ±0.9s of UT. These leap seconds are introduced, when necessary, at the same instant throughout the world, either at the end of December or at the end of June. The last leap second occurred immediately prior to 0h UTC on 2017 January 1, and was the 27th leap second. All leap seconds so far have been positive, with 61 seconds in the final minute of the UTC month. The time 23h 59m 60s UTC is followed one second later by 0h 0m 00s of the first day of the following month. Notices concerning the insertion of leap seconds are issued by the International Earth Rotation and Reference Systems Service (IERS).

The computation of UTC is carried out monthly by the BIPM and takes place in three stages. First, a weighted average known as Echelle Atomique Libre (EAL) is calculated from all of the contributing atomic clocks. In the second stage, TAI is generated by applying small corrections, derived from the results contributed by primary frequency standards, to the scale interval of EAL to maintain its value close to that of the

SI second. Finally, UTC is formed from TAI by the addition of an integer number of seconds. The results are published monthly in the BIPM Circular T in the form of offsets at 5-day intervals between UTC and the time scales of contributing organisations.

RADIO TIME-SIGNALS

UTC is made generally available through time-signals and standard frequency broadcasts such as MSF in the UK, CHU in Canada and WWV and WWVH in the USA. These are based on national time-scales that are maintained in close agreement with UTC and provide traceability to the national time-scale and to UTC. The markers of seconds in the UTC scale coincide with those of TAI.

To disseminate the national time-scale in the UK, special signals (call-sign MSF) are broadcast by the National Physical Laboratory. From April 1, 2007 the MSF service, previously broadcast from British Telecom's radio station at Rugby, has been transmitted from Anthorn radio station in Cumbria. The signals are controlled from a caesium beam atomic frequency standard and consist of a precise frequency carrier of 60 kHz which is switched off, after being on for at least half a second, to mark every second. The first second of the minute begins with a period of 500 ms with the carrier switched off, to serve as a minute marker. In the other seconds the carrier is always off for at least one tenth of a second at the start and then it carries an on-off code giving the British clock time and date, together with information identifying the start of the next minute. Changes to and from summer time are made following government announcements. Leap seconds are inserted as announced by the IERS and information provided by them on the difference between UTC and UT is also signalled. Other broadcast signals in the UK include the BBC six pips signal, the BT Timeline ('speaking clock'), the NPL telephone and internet time services for computers, and a coded time-signal on the BBC 198 kHz transmitters which is used for timing in the electricity supply industry. From 1972 January 1 the six pips on the BBC have consisted of five short pips from second 55 to second 59 (six pips in the case of a leap second) followed by one lengthened pip, the start of which indicates the exact minute. From 1990 February 5 these signals have been controlled by the BBC with seconds markers referenced to the satellite-based US navigation system GPS (Global Positioning System) and time and day referenced to the MSF transmitter. Formerly they were generated by the Royal Greenwich Observatory. The NPL telephone and internet time services are directly connected to the national time-scale.

Due to digital latency, time pips received via Digital Audio Broadcasting (DAB) radio and internet streaming are received late by significant and variable amounts, rendering them inaccurate if received in this way.

Accurate timing may also be obtained from the signals of international navigation systems such as the ground-based eLORAN, or the satellite-based American GPS or Russian GLONASS systems.

STANDARD TIME

Since 1880 the standard time in Britain has been Greenwich Mean Time (GMT); a statute that year enacted that the word 'time' when used in any legal document relating to Britain meant, unless otherwise specifically stated, the mean time of the Greenwich meridian. Greenwich was adopted as the universal meridian on 13 October 1884. A system of standard time by zones is used worldwide, standard time in each zone differing from that of the Greenwich meridian by an integral number of hours or, exceptionally, half-hours or quarter-hours, either fast or slow. The large territories of the USA and

Canada are divided into zones approximately 7.5° on either side of central meridians.

Variations from the standard time of some countries occur during part of the year; they are decided annually and are usually referred to as Summer Time or Daylight Saving Time.

At the 180th meridian the time can be either 12 hours fast on Greenwich Mean Time or 12 hours slow, and a change of date occurs. The internationally recognised date or calendar line is a modification of the 180th meridian, drawn so as to include islands of any one group on the same side of the line, or for political reasons. Changes to the date line would require an international conference.

BRITISH SUMMER TIME

In 1916 an Act ordained that during a defined period of that year the legal time for general purposes in Great Britain should be one hour in advance of Greenwich Mean Time. The Summer Time Acts 1922 and 1925 defined the period during which Summer Time was to be in force, stabilising practice until the Second World War.

During the Second World War (1941–5) and in 1947 Double Summer Time (two hours in advance of Greenwich Mean Time) was used for the period in which ordinary Summer Time would have been in force. During these years clocks were also kept one hour in advance of Greenwich Mean Time in the winter. After the war, ordinary Summer Time was invoked each year from 1948–68.

Between 1968 October 27 and 1971 October 31 clocks were kept one hour ahead of Greenwich Mean Time throughout the year. This was known as British Standard Time.

The most recent legislation is the Summer Time Act 1972, which enacted that 'the period of summer time for the purposes of this Act is the period beginning at two o'clock, Greenwich Mean Time, in the morning of the day after the third Saturday in March or, if that day is Easter Day, the day after the second Saturday in March, and ending at two o'clock, Greenwich Mean Time, in the morning of the day after the fourth Saturday in October.'

The duration of Summer Time can be varied by Order in Council and in recent years alterations have been made to synchronise the period of Summer Time in Britain with that used in Europe. The rule for 1981–94 defined the period of Summer Time in the UK as from the last Sunday in March to the day following the fourth Saturday in October and the hour of changeover was altered to 01h GMT.

There was no rule for the dates of Summer Time between 1995–7. Since 1998 the 9th European Parliament and Council Directive on Summer Time has harmonised the dates on which Summer Time begins and ends across member states as the last Sundays in March and October respectively. Under the directive Summer Time begins and ends at 01hr Greenwich Mean Time in each member state. Amendments to the Summer Time Act to implement the directive came into force on 11 March 2002.

The duration of Summer Time in 2020 is:
March 29 01h GMT to October 25 01h GMT

THE EARTH

The shape of the Earth is that of an oblate spheroid or solid of revolution whose meridian sections are ellipses not differing much from circles, while the sections at right angles are circles. The length of the equatorial axis is about 12,756 km, and that of the polar axis is 12,714 km. The mean density of the Earth is 5.5 times that of water. Density increases from about 3.3g/cc near to the surface to about 17g/cc at the centre. The Earth and Moon revolve about their common centre of gravity in a lunar month; this centre in turn revolves

round the Sun in a plane known as the ecliptic, that passes through the Sun's centre. The Earth's equator is inclined to this plane at an angle of 23.4°. This tilt is the cause of the seasons. In mid-latitudes, and when the Sun is high above the Equator, not only does the high noon altitude make the days longer, but the Sun's rays fall more perpendicularly on Earth's surface; these effects combine to produce summer. In equatorial regions the noon altitude is large throughout the year, and there is little variation in the length of the day. In higher latitudes the noon altitude is lower, and the days in summer are appreciably longer than those in winter.

The average velocity of the Earth in its orbit is 30km/s. It makes a complete rotation on its axis in about 23h 56m of mean time, which is the sidereal day. Because of its annual revolution round the Sun, the rotation with respect to the Sun, or the solar day, is more than this by about four minutes. The extremity of the axis of rotation, or the North Pole of the Earth, is not rigidly fixed, but wanders over an area roughly 20 metres in diameter.

Perihelion is when the Earth is closest to the Sun, and *aphelion* when the Earth is furthest from the Sun:

Perihelion January 2020 5d 07h 48m
(147,091,144km, 0.98324357au)
Aphelion July 2020 4d 11h 35m
(152,095,295km, 1.01669425au)

MEAN REFRACTION

Alt. ° '	Ref. '	Alt. ° '	Ref. '	Alt. ° '	Ref. '
1 20	21	3 12	13	7 54	6
1 30	20	3 34	12	9 27	5
1 41	19	4 00	11	11 39	4
1 52	18	4 30	10	15 00	3
2 05	17	5 06	9	20 42	
2 19	16	5 50	8	32 20	2
2 35	15	6 44	7	62 17	1
2 52	14	7 54		90 00	0
3 12					

This is in the form of a critical table *(see* page 626).

ASTRONOMICAL CONSTANTS

Solar parallax	8.794″
Astronomical unit	149,597,870 km
Annual precession in longitude	50.288″
Precession in right ascension	3.075s
Precession in declination	20.043″
Constant of nutation	9.202″
Constant of aberration	20.496″
Mean obliquity of ecliptic (2018)	23° 26′ 13″
Moon's mean equatorial hor parallax	57′ 02.70″
Velocity of light in vacuo	299,792.5 km/s
Equatorial radius of the Earth	6,378 km
Polar radius of the Earth	6,356 km
North galactic pole	
(IAU standard)	RA 12h 51m (2000.0). Dec + 27.1° N.
Solar apex	RA 18h 04m Dec. + 30°
Solar motion	20.0 km/s

Length of year (in mean solar days)
Tropical	365.24217
Sidereal	365.25636
Anomalistic (perihelion to perihelion)	365.25964
Eclipse	346.62008

Length of month (mean values)	d	h	m	s
Synodic (new Moon to new Moon)	29	12	44	02.8
Sidereal	27	07	43	11.6
Anomalistic (perigee to perigee)	27	13	18	33.2

TERRESTRIAL MAGNETISM

The Earth's main magnetic field corresponds approximately to that of a very strong small bar magnet near the centre of the Earth, but with appreciable smooth spatial departures. The origin of the main field is generally ascribed to electric currents associated with fluid motions in the Earth's core. As a result not only does the main field vary in strength and direction from place to place, but also with time. Superimposed on the main field are local and regional anomalies whose magnitudes may in places approach that of the main field; these are due to the influence of mineral deposits in the Earth's crust. A small proportion of the field is of external origin, mostly associated with electric currents in the ionosphere and magnetosphere. The configuration of the external field and the ionisation of the atmosphere depend on the incident particle and radiation flux from the Sun. There are, therefore, short-term and non-periodic as well as diurnal, 27-day, seasonal and approximate 11-year periodic changes in the magnetic field, dependent upon the position of the Sun, the degree of solar activity and the magnetic field embedded in the solar wind.

A magnetic compass points along the horizontal component of a magnetic line of force. These lines of force converge on the 'magnetic dip-poles', the places where the Earth's magnetic field is vertical. These poles move with time, and their present approximate adopted mean positions are 86.4° N., 169.8° E. and 64.1° S., 135.8° E. Compasses do not point directly, ie via great circle routes, to the dip-poles.

There is also a 'magnetic equator', at all points of which the vertical component of the Earth's magnetic field is zero and a magnetised needle remains horizontal. This line runs between 2° and 12° north of the geographical equator in Asia and Africa, turns sharply south in the Atlantic Ocean and crosses South America south of the geographical equator; it re-crosses the geographical equator in mid-Pacific.

Reference has already been made to secular changes in Earth's field. The following table indicates the changes in magnetic declination (or variation of the compass relative to true north). Magnetic variation or declination is the angle in the horizontal plane between the direction of true north and that in which a magnetic compass points. Similar, though much smaller, changes have occurred in 'dip' or magnetic inclination. Secular changes differ throughout the world.

London (Greenwich)

1580	11°	15′	E.	1900	16°	29′	W.
1622	5°	56′	E.	1925	13°	10′	W.
1665	1°	22′	W.	1950	9°	07′	W.
1730	13°	00′	W.	1975	6°	39′	W.
1773	21°	09′	W.	1998	3°	32′	W.
1850	22°	24′	W.				

In Great Britain, lines of equal declination (isogonics) now run approximately north–northeast to south–southwest. Though there are considerable local deviations due to geological causes, an approximate value of magnetic declination may be obtained by assuming that at 50° N. on the meridian of Greenwich, the value in 2020 is 0° 32′ east. Easterly declination is now being sensed for the first time in over 350 years as the zero isogonic line (the agonic line) passes westwards across the country. Allowing for 10′ west for each degree of latitude northwards and one of 26′ west for each degree of longitude westwards magnetic variation can be computed at other locations. For example, at 53° N., 5° W.,

declination will be about 0° 32′ east + 30′ west + 130′ west, ie 2° 8′ west. The average annual change at the present time is about 13′ to the east. For navigation by compass using maps with the north lines from the British National Grid (as opposed to lines of equal longitude), account has to be taken of the difference between true north and grid north. This angle can be several degrees.

The number of magnetic observatories is about 170, irregularly distributed over the globe. There are three in the UK, run by the British Geological Survey: at Hartland, north Devon; at Eskdalemuir, Dumfries and Galloway; and at Lerwick, Shetland Islands. Some recent annual mean values of the magnetic elements for Hartland:

Year	Declination West		Dip or inclination		Horizontal intensity nT	Vertical intensity nT
	°	′	°	′		
1960	9	58.8	66	43.9	18707	43504
1970	9	06.5	66	26.1	19033	43636
1980	7	43.8	66	10.3	19330	43768
1990	6	15.0	66	09.7	19539	43896
2000	4	43.6	66	06.9	19508	44051
2018	1	43.9	65	58.7	19792	44407

nT = nanoTesla

The magnetic field is also observed by a series of specialised satellites, the latest being a mission called Swarm. Three satellites were successfully launched by the European Space Agency in November 2013, each equipped with magnetometers and star cameras for accurate orientation. With the data from these satellites the Earth's magnetic field and its changes in time continue to be mapped to unprecedented accuracy.

Reliance on the Earth's magnetic field for navigation by compass is not restricted to land, maritime or aeronautical navigation (in the latter two usually as a fail-safe back-up system). It also extends underground with the oil industry using magnetic survey tools when drilling well-bores. Very accurate estimates of the local magnetic field are required for this, taking into account the crustal and external fields.

MAGNETIC STORMS

Occasionally, sometimes with great suddenness, the Earth's magnetic field is subject for several hours to marked disturbance. During a severe storm in October 2003 the declination at Eskdalemuir changed by over 5° in six minutes. In many instances such disturbances are accompanied by widespread displays of auroras, marked changes in the incidence of cosmic rays, an increase in the reception of 'noise' from the Sun at radio frequencies, and rapid changes in the ionosphere and induced electric currents within the Earth. These can adversely affect satellite operations, telecommunications and electric power transmission systems. The disturbances are caused by changes in the stream of ionised particles which emanates from the Sun and through which the Earth is continuously passing. Some of these changes are associated with visible eruptions on the Sun, usually in the region of sun-spots. There is some tendency for disturbances to recur after intervals of about 27 days, the period of rotation of the Sun on its axis as seen from the Earth. But the sources of many disturbances are shorter lived than this. Predicting such disturbances with any useful accuracy remains challenging, but the year 2020 is generally expected to be rather quiet.

ELEMENTS OF THE SOLAR SYSTEM

Orb	Mean distance from Sun (Earth = 1)	km 10⁶	Sidereal period days	Synodic period days	Incl. of orbit to ecliptic ° '	Diameter km	Mass (Earth = 1)	Period of rotation on axis days
Sun	—	—	—	—	—	1,392,000	332,981	25–35*
Mercury	0.39	58	88.0	116	7 00	4,879	0.0553	58.646
Venus	0.72	108	224.7	584	3 24	12,104	0.8150	243.019r
Earth	1.00	150	365.3	—	—	12,756e	1.0000	0.997
Mars	1.52	228	687.0	780	1 51	6,794e	0.1074	1.026
Jupiter	5.20	778	4,331.0	399	1 18	142,984e / 133,708p	317.83	0.410e
Saturn	9.58	1433	10,747	378	2 29	120,536e / 108,728p	95.16	0.446e
Uranus	19.22	2875	30,589	370	0 46	51,118e	14.54	0.718r
Neptune	30.11	4504	56,800	367	1 46	49,528e	17.15	0.671
Pluto †	39.48	5906	90,560	367	17 10	2,390	0.002	6.387r

e equatorial, p polar, r retrograde, * depending on latitude, † reclassified as a dwarf planet since August 2006

THE SATELLITES

Name	Star mag.	Mean distance from primary km	Sidereal period of revolution d	Name	Star mag.	Mean distance from primary km	Sidereal period of revolution d
EARTH				SATURN			
I Moon	—	384,400	27.322	VII Hyperion	14	1,481,000	21.277
				VIII Iapetus	11	3,561,300	79.330
MARS				IX Phoebe	16	12,952,000	550.48r
I Phobos	11	9,378	0.319				
II Deimos	12	23,459	1.262	URANUS			
				VI Cordelia	24	49,770	0.335
JUPITER				VII Ophelia	24	53,790	0.376
XVI Metis	17	127,960	0.295	VIII Bianca	23	59,170	0.435
XV Adrastea	19	128,980	0.298	IX Cressida	22	61,780	0.464
V Amalthea	14	181,300	0.498	X Desdemona	22	62,680	0.474
XIV Thebe	16	221,900	0.675	XI Juliet	21	64,350	0.493
I Io	5	421,600	1.769	XII Portia	21	66,090	0.513
II Europa	5	670,900	3.551	XIII Rosalind	22	69,900	0.558
III Ganymede	5	1,070,000	7.155	XIV Belinda	22	75,260	0.624
IV Callisto	6	1,883,000	16.689	XV Puck	20	86,010	0.762
XIII Leda	20	11,165,000	240.92	V Miranda	16	129,900	1.413
VI Himalia	15	11,460,000	250.57	I Ariel	14	191,020	2.520
X Lysithea	18	11,717,000	259.22	II Umbriel	15	266,300	4.144
VII Elara	17	11,741,000	259.65	III Titania	14	435,910	8.706
XII Ananke	19	21,276,000	629.77r	IV Oberon	14	583,520	13.463
XI Carme	18	23,404,000	734.17r	XVI Caliban	22	7,230,000	579.5r
VIII Pasiphae	17	23,624,000	743.68r	XX Stephano	24	8,002,000	676.5r
IX Sinope	18	23,939,000	758.90r	XVII Sycorax	21	12,179,000	1,283.4r
				XVIII Prospero	23	16,256,000	1,977.3r
SATURN				XIX Setebos	23	17,418,000	2,234.8r
XVIII Pan	20	133,583	0.575				
XV Atlas	18	137,640	0.602	NEPTUNE			
XVI Prometheus	16	139,353	0.613	III Naiad	25	48,230	0.294
XVII Pandora	16	141,700	0.629	IV Thalassa	24	50,080	0.311
XI Epimetheus	15	151,422	0.694	V Despina	23	52,530	0.335
X Janus	14	151,472	0.695	VI Galatea	22	61,950	0.429
I Mimas	13	185,520	0.942	VII Larissa	22	73,550	0.555
II Enceladus	12	238,020	1.370	VIII Proteus	20	117,650	1.122
III Tethys	10	294,660	1.888	I Triton	13	354,760	5.877
XIII Telesto	19	294,660	1.888	II Nereid	19	5,513,400	360.136
XIV Calypso	19	294,660	1.888				
IV Dione	10	377,400	2.737	PLUTO			
XII Helene	18	377,400	2.737	I Charon	17	19,596	6.387
V Rhea	10	527,040	4.518				
VI Titan	8	1,221,850	15.945				

The total number of satellites known so far for the outer planets are: Jupiter 79, Saturn 62, Uranus 27, Neptune 14, Pluto 5.

TIME MEASUREMENT AND CALENDARS

MEASUREMENTS OF TIME

Measurements of time are based on the time taken by the Earth to rotate on its axis (day); by the Moon to revolve around the Earth (month); and by the Earth to revolve around the Sun (year). From these, which are not commensurable, certain average or mean intervals have been adopted for ordinary use.

THE DAY

The day begins at midnight and is divided into 24 hours of 60 minutes, each of 60 seconds. The hours are counted from midnight up to 12 noon (when the Sun crosses the meridian), and these hours are designated am *(ante meridiem)*; and again from noon up to 12 midnight, which hours are designated pm *(post meridiem)*, except when the 24-hour reckoning is employed. The 24-hour reckoning ignores am and pm, numbering the hours 0 to 23 from midnight.

Colloquially the 24 hours are divided into day and night, day being the time while the Sun is above the horizon (including the four stages of twilight defined in the Astronomy chapter). Day is subdivided into morning, ending at noon; afternoon, from noon to about 6pm; and evening, which may be said to extend from 6pm until midnight. Night begins at the close of astronomical twilight (*see* the Astronomy chapter) and extends beyond midnight to sunrise the next day.

The names of the days are derived from Old English translations or adaptations of the Roman titles.

Sunday	Sol	Sun
Monday	Luna	Moon
Tuesday	Tiw/Tyr (god of war)	Mars
Wednesday	Woden/Odin	Mercury
Thursday	Thor	Jupiter
Friday	Frigga/Freyja (goddess of love)	Venus
Saturday	Saeterne	Saturn

THE MONTH

The month in the ordinary calendar is approximately the twelfth part of a year, but the lengths of the different months vary from 28 (or 29) days to 31.

THE YEAR

The equinoctial or tropical year is the time that the Earth takes to revolve around the Sun from equinox to equinox, ie 365.24219 mean solar days, or 365 days 5 hours 48 minutes and 45 seconds.

The calendar year usually consists of 365 days but a year containing 366 days is called a bissextile (*see* Roman calendar) or leap year, one day being added to the month of February so that a date 'leaps over' a day of the week. In the Roman calendar the day that was repeated was the sixth day before the beginning of March, the equivalent of 24 February.

A year is a leap year if the date of the year is divisible by four without remainder, unless it is the last year of the century. The last year of a century is a leap year only if its number is divisible by 400 without remainder, eg the years 1800 and 1900 had only 365 days but the year 2000 had 366 days.

THE SOLSTICE

A solstice is the point in the tropical year at which the Sun attains its greatest distance, north or south, from the Equator. In the northern hemisphere the furthest point north of the Equator marks the summer solstice and the furthest point south marks the winter solstice.

The date of the solstice varies according to locality. For example, if the summer solstice falls on 21 June late in the day

by Greenwich time, that day will be the longest of the year at Greenwich, but it will fall on 22 June, local date, in Japan, and so 22 June will be the longest day there. The date of the solstice is also affected by the length of the tropical year, which is 365 days 6 hours less about 11 minutes 15 seconds. If a solstice happens late on 21 June in one year, it will be nearly 6 hours later in the next (unless the next year is a leap year), ie early on 22 June, and that will be the longest day.

This delay of the solstice does not continue because the extra day in a leap year brings it back a day in the calendar. However, because of the 11 minutes 15 seconds mentioned above, the additional day in a leap year brings the solstice back too far by 45 minutes, and the time of the solstice in the calendar is earlier, in a four-year pattern, as the century progresses. The last year of a century is in most cases not a leap year, and the omission of the extra day puts the date of the solstice later by about 6 hours. Compensation for this is made by the fourth centennial year being a leap year. The solstice became earlier in date throughout the last century and, because the year 2000 was a leap year, the solstice will get earlier still throughout the 21st century. The date of the winter solstice, the shortest day of the year, is affected by same factors as the longest day.

At Greenwich the Sun sets at its earliest by the clock about ten days before the shortest day. The daily change in the time of sunset is due in the first place to the Sun's movement southwards at this time of the year, which diminishes the interval between the Sun's transit and its setting. However, the daily decrease of the Equation of Time causes the time of apparent noon to be continuously later day by day, which to some extent counteracts the first effect. The rates of the change of these two quantities are not equal or uniform; their combination causes the date of earliest sunset to be 12 or 13 December at Greenwich. In more southerly latitudes the effect of the movement of the Sun is less, and the change in the time of sunset depends on that of the Equation of Time to a greater degree, and the date of earliest sunset is earlier than it is at Greenwich, eg on the Equator it is about 1 November.

THE EQUINOX

The equinox is the point at which the Sun crosses the Equator and day and night are of equal length all over the world. This occurs in March and September.

DOG DAYS

The days about the heliacal rising of the Dog Star, noted from ancient times as the hottest period of the year in the northern hemisphere, are called the Dog Days. Their incidence has been variously calculated as depending on the Greater or Lesser Dog Star (Sirius or Procyon) and their duration has been reckoned as from 30 to 54 days. A generally accepted period is from 3 July to 15 August.

CHRISTIAN CALENDAR

In the Christian chronological system the years are distinguished by cardinal numbers before or after the birth of Christ, the period being denoted by the letters BC (Before Christ) or, more rarely, AC *(Ante Christum)*, and AD *(Anno Domini* – In the Year of Our Lord); BCE (Before the Common Era) and CE (Common Era) are now also used instead of BC and AD. The correlative dates of the epoch are the fourth year of the 194th Olympiad, the 753rd year from the foundation of Rome, AM 3761 in Jewish chronology, and the 4,714th year of the Julian period.

The system was introduced into Italy in the sixth century. Though first used in France in the seventh century, it was not universally established there until about the eighth century. It has been said that the system was introduced into England by St Augustine (AD 596), but it was probably not generally used until some centuries later. It was ordered to be used by the bishops at the Council of Chelsea (AD 816).

THE JULIAN CALENDAR

In the Julian calendar (adopted by the Roman Empire in 45 BC) all the centennial years were leap years, and for this reason towards the close of the 16th century there was a difference of ten days between the tropical and calendar years; the equinox fell on 11 March of the calendar, whereas at the time of the Council of Nicaea (AD 325), it had fallen on 21 March. In 1582 Pope Gregory ordained that 5 October should be called 15 October and that of the end-century years only the fourth should be a leap year.

THE GREGORIAN CALENDAR

The Gregorian calendar was adopted by Italy, France, Spain and Portugal in 1582, by Prussia, the Roman Catholic German states, Switzerland, Holland and Flanders on 1 January 1583, by Poland in 1586, Hungary in 1587, the Protestant German and Netherland states and Denmark in 1700, and by Great Britain and its Dominions (including the North American colonies) in 1752, by the omission of 11 days (3 September being reckoned as 14 September). Sweden omitted the leap day in 1700 but observed leap days in 1704 and 1708, and reverted to the Julian calendar by having two leap days in 1712; the Gregorian calendar was adopted in 1753 by the omission of 11 days (18 February being reckoned as 1 March). Japan adopted the calendar in 1872, China in 1912, Bulgaria in 1916, Turkey and Soviet Russia in 1918, Yugoslavia and Romania in 1919, and Greece in 1923.

In the same year that the change was made in England from the Julian to the Gregorian calendar, the start of the new year was also changed from 25 March to 1 January.

THE ORTHODOX CHURCHES

Some Orthodox churches still use the Julian reckoning but the majority of Greek Orthodox churches and the Romanian Orthodox Church have adopted a modified 'New Calendar', observing the Gregorian calendar for fixed feasts and the Julian for movable feasts.

The Orthodox Church year begins on 1 September. There are four fast periods and, in addition to Pascha (Easter), twelve great feasts, as well as numerous commemorations of the saints of the Old and New Testaments throughout the year.

EASTER DAYS AND DOMINICAL LETTERS 1500 TO 2040

Dates up to and including 1752 are according to the Julian calendar. For dominical letters in leap years, *see* note below

		1500–1599	1600–1699	1700–1799	1800–1899	1900–1999	2000–2040
March							
d	22	1573	1668	1761	1818		
e	23	1505/16	1600	1788	1845/56	1913	2008
f	24		1611/95	1706/99		1940	
g	25	1543/54	1627/38/49	1722/33/44	1883/94	1951	2035
A	26	1559/70/81/92	1654/65/76	1749/58/69/80	1815/26/37	1967/78/89	
b	27	1502/13/24/97	1608/87/92	1785/96	1842/53/64	1910/21/32	2005/16
c	28	1529/35/40	1619/24/30	1703/14/25	1869/75/80	1937/48	2027/32
d	29	1551/62	1635/46/57	1719/30/41/52	1807/12/91	1959/64/70	
e	30	1567/78/89	1651/62/73/84	1746/55/66/77	1823/34	1902/75/86/97	
f	31	1510/21/32/83/94	1605/16/78/89	1700/71/82/93	1839/50/61/72	1907/18/29/91	2002/13/24
April							
g	1	1526/37/48	1621/32	1711/16	1804/66/77/88	1923/34/45/56	2018/29/40
A	2	1553/64	1643/48	1727/38	1809/20/93/99	1961/72	
b	3	1575/80/86	1659/70/81	1743/63/68/74	1825/31/36	1904/83/88/94	
c	4	1507/18/91	1602/13/75/86/97	1708/79/90	1847/58	1915/20/26/99	2010/21
d	5	1523/34/45/56	1607/18/29/40	1702/13/24/95	1801/63/74/85/96	1931/42/53	2015/26/37
e	6	1539/50/61/72	1634/45/56	1729/35/40/60	1806/17/28/90	1947/58/69/80	
f	7	1504/77/88	1667/72	1751/65/76	1822/33/44	1901/12/85/96	
g	8	1509/15/20/99	1604/10/83/94	1705/87/92/98	1849/55/60	1917/28	2007/12
A	9	1531/42	1615/26/37/99	1710/21/32	1871/82	1939/44/50	2023/34
b	10	1547/58/69	1631/42/53/64	1726/37/48/57	1803/14/87/98	1955/66/77	2039
c	11	1501/12/63/74/85/96	1658/69/80	1762/73/84	1819/30/41/52	1909/71/82/93	2004
d	12	1506/17/28	1601/12/91/96	1789	1846/57/68	1903/14/25/36/98	2009/20
e	13	1533/44	1623/28	1707/18	1800/73/79/84	1941/52	2031/36
f	14	1555/60/66	1639/50/61	1723/34/45/54	1805/11/16/95	1963/68/74	
g	15	1571/82/93	1655/66/77/88	1750/59/70/81	1827/38	1900/06/79/90	2001
A	16	1503/14/25/36/87/98	1609/20/82/93	1704/75/86/97	1843/54/65/76	1911/22/33/95	2006/17/28
b	17	1530/41/52	1625/36	1715/20	1808/70/81/92	1927/38/49/60	2022/33
c	18	1557/68	1647/52	1731/42/56	1802/13/24/97	1954/65/76	
d	19	1500/79/84/90	1663/74/85	1747/67/72/78	1829/35/40	1908/81/87/92	
e	20	1511/22/95	1606/17/79/90	1701/12/83/94	1851/62	1919/24/30	2003/14/25
f	21	1527/38/49	1622/33/44	1717/28	1867/78/89	1935/46/57	2019/30
g	22	1565/76	1660	1739/53/64	1810/21/32	1962/73/84	
A	23	1508	1671		1848	1905/16	2000
b	24	1519	1603/14/98	1709/91	1859		2011
c	25	1546	1641	1736	1886	1943	2038

No dominical letter is placed against the intercalary day 29 February, but since it is still counted as a weekday and given a name, the series of letters moves back one day every leap year after intercalation. Thus, a leap year beginning with the dominical letter E will change to a year with the dominical letter D on 1 March and it is this letter which is given in the table above.

MOVEABLE FEASTS TO THE YEAR 2040

Year	Ash Wednesday	Easter	Ascension	Pentecost (Whit Sunday)	Advent Sunday
2020	26 February	12 April	21 May	31 May	29 November
2021	17 February	4 April	13 May	23 May	28 November
2022	2 March	17 April	26 May	5 June	27 November
2023	22 February	9 April	18 May	28 May	3 December
2024	14 February	31 March	9 May	19 May	1 December
2025	5 March	20 April	29 May	8 June	30 November
2026	18 February	5 April	14 May	24 May	29 November
2027	10 February	28 March	6 May	16 May	28 November
2028	1 March	16 April	25 May	4 June	3 December
2029	14 February	1 April	10 May	20 May	2 December
2030	6 March	21 April	30 May	9 June	1 December
2031	26 February	13 April	22 May	1 June	30 November
2032	11 February	28 March	6 May	16 May	28 November
2033	2 March	17 April	26 May	5 June	27 November
2034	22 February	9 April	18 May	28 May	3 December
2035	7 February	25 March	3 May	13 May	2 December
2036	27 February	13 April	22 May	1 June	30 November
2037	18 February	5 April	14 May	24 May	29 November
2038	10 March	25 April	3 June	13 June	28 November
2039	23 February	10 April	19 May	29 May	27 November
2040	15 February	1 April	10 May	20 May	2 December

NOTES

Ash Wednesday (first day in Lent) can fall at earliest on 4 February and at latest on 10 March

Mothering Sunday (fourth Sunday in Lent) can fall at earliest on 1 March and at latest on 4 April

Easter Day can fall at earliest on 22 March and at latest on 25 April

Ascension Day is forty days after Easter Day and can fall at earliest on 30 April and at latest on 3 June

Pentecost (Whit Sunday) is seven weeks after Easter and can fall at earliest on 10 May and at latest on 13 June

Trinity Sunday is the Sunday after Whit Sunday

Corpus Christi falls on the Thursday after Trinity Sunday

Sundays after Pentecost – there are not less than 18 and not more than 23

Advent Sunday is the Sunday nearest to 30 November

THE DOMINICAL LETTER

The dominical letter is one of the letters A–G which are used to denote the Sundays in successive years. If the first day of the year is a Sunday the letter is A; if the second, B; the third, C; and so on. A leap year requires two letters, the first for 1 January to 29 February, the second for 1 March to 31 December. The dominical letters for 2020, which is a leap year, are ED (*see also* page 9).

EPIPHANY

The feast of the Epiphany, commemorating the manifestation of Christ, later became associated with the offering of gifts by the Magi. The day was of great importance from the time of the Council of Nicaea (AD 325), as the primate of Alexandria was charged at every Epiphany feast with the announcement in a letter to the churches of the date of the forthcoming Easter. The day was also of importance in Britain as it influenced dates, ecclesiastical and lay, eg Plough Monday, when work was resumed in the fields, fell on the Monday in the first full week after Epiphany.

LENT

The Teutonic word *Lent*, which denotes the fast preceding Easter, originally meant no more than the spring season; but from Anglo-Saxon times, at least, it has been used as the equivalent of the more significant Latin term *Quadragesima*, meaning the 'forty days' or, more literally, the fortieth day. Ash Wednesday is the first day of Lent, which ends at midnight before Easter Day.

PALM SUNDAY

Palm Sunday, the Sunday before Easter and the beginning of Holy Week, commemorates the triumphal entry of Christ into Jerusalem.

MAUNDY THURSDAY

Maundy Thursday is the day before Good Friday, the name itself being a corruption of *dies mandati* (day of the mandate) when Christ washed the feet of the disciples and gave them the mandate to love one another.

EASTER DAY

Easter Day is the first Sunday after the full moon which happens on, or next after, the 21st day of March; if the full moon happens on a Sunday, Easter Day is the Sunday after.

This definition is contained in an Act of Parliament (24 Geo. II ch. 23) and explanation is given in the preamble to the Act that the day of full moon depends on certain tables that have been prepared. These tables are summarised in the early pages of the Book of Common Prayer. The moon referred to is not the real Moon of the heavens, but a hypothetical moon on whose 'full' the date of Easter depends, and the lunations of this 'calendar' moon consist of 29 and 30 days alternately, with certain necessary modifications to make the date of its full agree as nearly as possible with that of the real Moon, which is known as the Paschal Full Moon.

A FIXED EASTER

In 1928 the House of Commons agreed to a motion for the third reading of a bill proposing that Easter Day shall, in the calendar year next but one after the commencement of the Act and in all subsequent years, be the first Sunday after the second Saturday in April. Easter would thus fall on the second or third Sunday in April, ie between 9 and 15 April (inclusive). A clause in the bill provided that before it shall come into operation, regard shall be had to any opinion expressed officially by the various Christian churches. Efforts by the World Council of Churches to secure a unanimous choice of date for Easter by its member churches have so far been unsuccessful.

ROGATION DAYS

Rogation Days are the Monday, Tuesday and Wednesday preceding Ascension Day and from the fifth century were observed as public fasts with solemn processions and supplications. The processions were discontinued as religious observances at the Reformation, but survive in the ceremony known as 'beating the parish bounds'. Rogation Sunday is the Sunday before Ascension Day.

EMBER DAYS

The Ember days occur on the Wednesday, Friday and Saturday of the same week, four times a year. Used for the ordination of clergy, these days are set aside for fasting and prayer. The weeks in which they fall are: (a) after the third Sunday in Advent, (b) before the second Sunday in Lent, (c) before Trinity Sunday and (d) after Holy Cross day.

TRINITY SUNDAY

Trinity Sunday is eight weeks after Easter Day, on the Sunday following Pentecost (Whit Sunday). Subsequent Sundays are reckoned in the Book of Common Prayer calendar of the Church of England as 'after Trinity'.

Thomas Becket (1118–70) was consecrated Archbishop of Canterbury on the Sunday after Whit Sunday and his first act was to ordain that the day of his consecration should be held as a new festival in honour of the Holy Trinity.

HINDU CALENDAR

The Hindu calendar is a luni-solar calendar of 12 months, each containing 29 days, 12 hours. Each month is divided into a light fortnight (Shukla or Shuddha) and a dark fortnight (Krishna or Vadya) based on the waxing and waning of the Moon. In most parts of India the month starts with the light fortnight, ie the day after the new moon, although in some regions it begins with the dark fortnight, ie the day after the full moon.

The new year according to the civil calendar begins on the first day of the month of Chaitra (March/April) and ends in the month of Phalgun (March). The financial new year begins on the first day of Kartik (Diwali day). For most Hindus, the first day of Chaitra and the first day of Kartik are equally important.

The 12 months – Chaitra, Vaishakh, Jyeshtha, Ashadh, Shravan, Bhadrapad, Ashvin, Kartik, Margashirsh, Paush, Magh and Phalgun – have Sanskrit names derived from 12 asterisms (constellations). There are regional variations to the names of the months but the Sanskrit names are understood throughout India.

Every lunar month that has a solar transit is termed pure *(shuddha)*. The lunar month without a solar transit is impure *(mala)* and called an intercalary month. An intercalary month occurs approximately every 32 lunar months, whenever the difference between the Hindu year of 360 lunar days (354 days 8 hours solar time) and the 365 days 6 hours of the solar year reaches the length of one Hindu lunar month (29 days 12 hours).

The leap month, often referred to as Adhik Maas (extra month), may be added at any point in the Hindu year. The name given to the month varies according to when it occurs but is taken from the month immediately following it. The leap month in 2020 is Ashvin.

The days of the week are called Raviwar (Sunday), Somawar (Monday), Mangalwar (Tuesday), Budhawar (Wednesday), Guruwar (Thursday), Shukrawar (Friday) and Shaniwar (Saturday). The names are derived from the Sanskrit names of the Sun, the Moon and five planets, Mars, Mercury, Jupiter, Venus and Saturn.

Most fasts and festivals are based on the lunar calendar but a few are determined by the apparent movement of the Sun, eg

Makar Sankranti and Pongal (in southern India), which are celebrated on 14/15 January to mark the start of the Sun's apparent journey northwards and a change of season.

Festivals celebrated throughout India are Chaitra (the New Year), Raksha Bandhan (the renewal of the kinship bond between brothers and sisters), Navratri (a nine-night festival dedicated to the goddess Parvati), Dussehra (the victory of Rama over the demon army), Diwali (a festival of lights), Makar Sankranti, Shivaratri (dedicated to Shiva), and Holi (a spring festival). British Hindus commonly celebrate the festival of Diwali as the start of the financial new year.

Regional festivals are Durga Puja (dedicated to the goddess Durga (Parvati)), Sarasvati Puja (dedicated to the goddess Sarasvati), Ganesh Chaturthi (worship of Ganesh on the fourth day (Chaturthi) of the light half of Bhadrapad), Ram Navami (the birth festival of the god Rama) and Krishna Janmashtami (the birth festival of the god Krishna).

The main festivals celebrated in the UK are Navratri, Dussehra, Durga Puja, Diwali, Holi, Sarasvati Puja, Ganesh Chaturthi, Raksha Bandhan, Ram Navami and Krishna Janmashtami. For dates in 2020, *see* page 9.

JEWISH CALENDAR

The story of the Flood in the Book of Genesis indicates the use of a calendar of some kind and that the writers recognised 30 days as the length of a lunation. However, after the diaspora, Jewish communities were left in considerable doubt as to the times of fasts and festivals. This led to the formation of the Jewish calendar as used today. It is said that this was done in AD 358 by Rabbi Hillel II, though some assert that it did not happen until much later.

The calendar is luni-solar, and is based on the lengths of the lunation and of the tropical year as found by Hipparchus (*c.*120 BC), which differ little from those adopted at the present day. The year AM 5780 (2019–20) is the 4th year of the 305th Metonic (Minor or Lunar) cycle of 19 years and the 12th year of the 207th Solar (or Major) cycle of 28 years since the Era of the Creation. Jews hold that the Creation occurred at the time of the autumnal equinox in the year known in the Christian calendar as 3760 BC (954 of the Julian period). The epoch or starting point of Jewish chronology corresponds to 7 October 3761 BC. At the beginning of each solar cycle, the Tekufah of Nisan (the vernal equinox) returns to the same day and hour.

The hour is divided into 1,080 minims, and the month between one new moon and the next is reckoned as 29 days 12 hours 793 minims. The normal calendar year, called a regular common year, consists of 12 months of 30 days and 29 days alternately. Since 12 months such as these comprise only 354 days, in order that each of them shall not diverge greatly from an average place in the solar year, a 13th month is occasionally added after the fifth month of the civil year (which commences on the first day of the month Tishri), or as the penultimate month of the ecclesiastical year (which commences on the first day of the month Nisan). The years when this happens are called Embolismic or leap years.

Of the 19 years that form a Metonic cycle, seven are leap years; they occur at places in the cycle indicated by the numbers 3, 6, 8, 11, 14, 17 and 19, these places being chosen so that the accumulated excesses of the solar years should be as small as possible.

A Jewish year is of one of the following six types:

minimal common	353 days
regular common	354 days
full common	355 days
minimal leap	383 days
regular leap	384 days
full leap	385 days

The regular year has alternate months of 30 and 29 days. In a full year, Marcheshvan, the second month of the civil year, has 30 days instead of 29; in minimal years Kislev, the third month, has 29 instead of 30. The additional month in leap years is called Adar Sheni (Adar II) and follows the month called Adar Rishon; the usual Adar festivals are observed in Adar Sheni. In a leap year Adar I has 30 days, in all other years it has 29. None of the variations mentioned are allowed to change the number of days in the other months, which still follow the alternation of the normal 12.

These are the main features of the Jewish calendar, which must be considered permanent because as a Jewish law it cannot be altered except by a Great Sanhedrin.

The Jewish day begins between sunset and nightfall. The time used is that of the meridian of Jerusalem, which is 2h 21m in advance of Greenwich Mean Time. Rules for the beginning of sabbaths and festivals were laid down for the latitude of London in the 18th century and hours for nightfall are fixed annually by the Chief Rabbi.

JEWISH CALENDAR 5780–81
AM 5780 is a full common year of 12 months, 50 sabbaths and 355 days. AM 5781 is a minimal common year of 12 months, 51 sabbaths and 353 days.

Month (length)	AM 5780	AM 5781
Tishri 1 (30)	30 Sep 2019	19 Sep
Marcheshvan 1 (30/29)	30 Oct	19 Oct
Kislev 1 (30/29)	29 Nov	17 Nov
Tebet 1 (29)	29 Dec	16 Dec
Shebat 1 (30)	27 Jan 2020	14 Jan 2021
Adar Rishon 1 (29)	26 Feb	
Nisan 1 (30)	26 Mar	
Iyar 1 (29)	25 April	
Sivan 1 (30)	24 May	
Tammuz 1 (29)	23 Jun	
Ab 1 (30)	22 Jul	
Elul 1 (29)	21 Aug	

JEWISH FASTS AND FESTIVALS
For dates of principal festivals in 2020, *see* page 9.

Tishri 1–2	Rosh Hashanah (New Year)
Tishri 3	*Fast of Gedaliah
Tishri 10	Yom Kippur (Day of Atonement)
Tishri 15–21	Sukkot (Feast of Tabernacles)
Tishri 21	Hoshana Rabba
Tishri 22	Shemini Atseret (Solemn Assembly)
Tishri 23	Simchat Torah (Rejoicing of the Law)
Kislev 25	Hanukkah (Festival of Lights) begins
Tebet 10	Fast of Tebet
†*Adar 13*	§Fast of Esther
†*Adar 14*	Purim
†*Adar 15*	Shushan Purim
Nisan 15–22	Pesach (Passover)
Sivan 6–7	Shavuot (Feast of Weeks)
Tammuz 17	*Fast of Tammuz
Ab 9	*Fast of Ab

* If these dates fall on the sabbath the fast is kept on the following day
† Adar Sheni in leap years
§ This fast is observed on Adar 11 (or Adar Sheni 11 in leap years) if Adar 13 falls on a sabbath

MUSLIM CALENDAR
The Muslim era is dated from the *Hijrah*, or flight of the Prophet Muhammad from Mecca to Medina, the corresponding date of which in the Julian calendar is 16 July AD 622. The lunar *hijri* calendar is used principally in Iran, Egypt, Malaysia, Pakistan, Mauritania, various Arab states and certain parts of India. Iran uses the solar hijri calendar as well as the lunar hijri calendar. The dating system was adopted

about AD 639, commencing with the first day of the month Muharram.

The lunar calendar consists of 12 months of either 30 or 29 days, with the intercalation of one day at the end of the 12th month at stated intervals in each cycle of 30 years. The object of the intercalation is to reconcile the date of the first day of the month with the date of the actual new moon.

Some adherents still take the date of the evening of the first physical sighting of the crescent of the new moon as that of the first of the month. If cloud obscures the Moon the present month may be extended to 30 days, after which the new month will begin automatically regardless of whether the Moon has been seen. (Under religious law a month must have less than 31 days.) This means that the beginning of a new month and the date of religious festivals can vary from the published calendars.

In each cycle of 30 years, 19 years are common and contain 354 days, and 11 years are intercalary (leap years) of 355 days, the latter being called *kabisah*. The mean length of the Hijrah years is 354 days 8 hours 48 minutes and the period of mean lunation is 29 days 12 hours 44 minutes.

To ascertain if a year is common or kabisah, divide it by 30: the quotient gives the number of completed cycles and the remainder shows the place of the year in the current cycle. If the remainder is 2, 5, 7, 10, 13, 16, 18, 21, 24, 26 or 29, the year is kabisah and consists of 355 days.

MUSLIM CALENDAR 1441–42
Hijrah 1441 (remainder one) is a common year and Hijrah 1442 (remainder 2) is kabisah. Calendar dates below are estimates based on calculations of moon phases.

Month (length)	1441 AH	1442 AH
Muharram 1 (30/29)	1 Sep 2019	21 Aug
Safar 1 (29/30)	1 Oct	19 Sep
Rabi'I 1 (30/29)	30 Oct	19 Oct
Rabi'II 1 (29/30)	29 Nov	17 Nov
Jumada I 1 (30/29)	28 Dec	17 Dec
Jumada II 1 (30/29)	27 Jan 2020	15 Jan 2021
Rajab 1 (29)	26 Feb	
Sha'ban 1 (30)	26 Mar	
Ramadan 1 (30)	25 Apr	
Shawwal 1 (29)	25 May	
Dhu'l Qa'da 1 (30)	23 Jun	
Dhu'l Hijjah 1 (29)	23 Jul	

MUSLIM FESTIVALS
Ramadan is a month of fasting for all Muslims because it is the month in which the revelation of the *Qur'an* (Koran) began. During Ramadan, Muslims abstain from food, drink and sexual pleasure from dawn until after sunset.

The two major festivals are *Eid-ul-Fitr* and *Eid-ul-Adha*. Eid-ul-Fitr marks the end of the Ramadan fast and is celebrated on the day after the sighting of the new moon of the following month. Eid-ul-Adha, the festival of sacrifice (also known as the great festival), celebrates the submission of the Prophet Ibrahim (Abraham) to God. Eid-ul-Adha falls on the tenth day of Dhu'l-Hijjah, coinciding with the day when those on *hajj* (pilgrimage to Mecca) sacrifice animals.

Other days accorded special recognition are:

Muharram 1	New Year's Day
Muharram 10	Ashura (the day Prophet Noah left the Ark and Prophet Moses was saved from Pharaoh (Sunni), the death of the Prophet's grandson Husain (Shi'ite))
Rabi'u-l-Awwal (Rabi' I) 12	Mawlid an-Nabi (birthday of the Prophet Muhammad)
Rajab 27	Laylat ul-Isra' wa'l-Mi'raj (The Night of Journey and Ascension)
*Ramadan**	Laylat ul-Qadr (Night of Power)

*Moveable feast

For dates of the major celebrations in 2019–20, *see* page 9.

SIKH CALENDAR

The Sikh calendar is a lunar calendar of 365 days divided into 12 months. The length of the months varies between 29 and 32 days.

There are no prescribed feast days and no fasting periods. The main celebrations are Vaisakhi (the new year and the anniversary of the founding of the Khalsa), Diwali Mela (festival of light), Hola Mohalla Mela (a spring festival held in the Punjab), and the Gurpurbs (anniversaries associated with the ten Gurus).

For dates of the major celebrations in 2020, *see* page 9.

THAI CALENDAR

Thailand adopted the Suriyakati calendar, a modified version of the Gregorian calendar, during the reign of King Rama V in 1888, using 1 April as the first day of the year. In 1940 the date of the new year was changed to 1 January. The years are counted from the beginning of the Buddhist era (BE), which is calculated to have commenced upon the death of the Lord Buddha, taken to have occurred in 543 BC, so AD 2020 is BE 2563. The Chinese system of associating years with one of twelve animals is also in use in Thailand. The Chantarakati lunar calendar is used to determine religious holidays; the new year begins on the first day of the waxing moon in November or, if there is a leap month, in December.

CIVIL AND LEGAL CALENDAR

THE HISTORICAL YEAR
Before 1752, two calendar systems were used in England. The civil or legal year began on 25 March and the historical year on 1 January. Thus the civil or legal date 24 March 1658 was the same day as the historical date 24 March 1659; a date in that portion of the year is written as 24 March 1658/9, the earlier date showing the civil or legal year.

THE NEW YEAR
In England in the seventh century, and as late as the 13th, the year was reckoned from Christmas Day, but in the 12th century the Church in England began the year with the feast of the Annunciation of the Blessed Virgin ('Lady Day') on 25 March, and this practice was adopted generally in the 14th century. The civil or legal year in the British dominions (exclusive of Scotland) began with Lady Day until 1751. But in and since 1752 the civil year has begun with 1 January. New Year's Day in Scotland was changed from 25 March to 1 January in 1600.

Elsewhere in Europe, 1 January was adopted as the first day of the year by Venice in 1522, German states in 1544, Spain, Portugal and the Roman Catholic Netherlands in 1556, Prussia, Denmark and Sweden in 1559, France in 1564, Lorraine in 1579, the Protestant Netherlands in 1583, Russia in 1725, and Tuscany in 1751.

REGNAL YEARS
Regnal years are the years of a sovereign's reign and each begins on the anniversary of his or her accession, eg regnal year 69 of the present queen begins on 6 February 2020.

The system was used for dating Acts of Parliament until 1962. The Summer Time Act 1925, for example, is quoted as 15 and 16 Geo. V ch. 64, because it became law in the parliamentary session which extended over part of both of these regnal years. Acts of a parliamentary session during which a sovereign died were usually given two year numbers, the regnal year of the deceased sovereign and the regnal year of his or her successor, eg those passed in 1952 were dated 16 Geo. VI and 1 Elizabeth II. Since 1962 Acts of Parliament have been dated by the calendar year.

QUARTER AND TERM DAYS
Holy days and saints days were the usual means in early times for setting the dates of future and recurrent appointments. The quarter days in England and Wales are the feast of the Nativity (25 December), the feast of the Annunciation (25 March), the feast of St John the Baptist (24 June) and the feast of St Michael and All Angels (29 September).

The term days in Scotland are Candlemas (the feast of the Purification), Whitsunday, Lammas (Loaf Mass) and Martinmas (St Martin's Day). These fell on 2 February, 15 May, 1 August and 11 November respectively. However, by the Term and Quarter Days (Scotland) Act 1990, the dates of the term days were changed to 28 February (Candlemas), 28 May (Whitsunday), 28 August (Lammas) and 28 November (Martinmas).

RED-LETTER DAYS
Red-letter days were originally the holy days and saints days indicated in early ecclesiastical calendars by letters printed in red ink. The days to be distinguished in this way were approved at the Council of Nicaea in AD 325.

These days still have a legal significance, as judges of the Queen's Bench Division wear scarlet robes on red-letter days falling during the law sittings. The days designated as red-letter days for this purpose are:
Holy and saints days
The Conversion of St Paul, the Purification, Ash Wednesday, the Annunciation, the Ascension, the feasts of St Mark, SS Philip and James, St Matthias, St Barnabas, St John the Baptist, St Peter, St Thomas, St James, St Luke, SS Simon and Jude, All Saints, St Andrew.
Civil calendar (for dates, *see* page 9)
Includes the anniversaries of the Queen's accession, the Queen's birthday and the Queen's coronation, the Queen's official birthday, the birthday of the Duke of Edinburgh, the birthday of the Prince of Wales, St David's Day and Lord Mayor's Day.

PUBLIC HOLIDAYS
Public holidays are divided into two categories, common law and statutory. Common law holidays are holidays 'by habit and custom'; in England, Wales and Northern Ireland these are Good Friday and Christmas Day.

Statutory public holidays, known as bank holidays, were first established by the Bank Holidays Act 1871. They were, literally, days on which the banks (and other public institutions) were closed and financial obligations due on that day were payable the following day. The legislation currently governing public holidays in the UK, which is the Banking and Financial Dealings Act 1971, stipulates the days that are to be public holidays in England, Wales, Scotland and Northern Ireland.

If a public holiday falls on a Saturday or a Sunday then another day will be given in lieu, usually the following Monday. For dates of public holidays in 2020 and 2021, *see* pages 10 and 11.

CHRONOLOGICAL CYCLES AND ERAS

SOLAR (OR MAJOR) CYCLE
The solar cycle is a period of 28 years; in any corresponding year of each cycle the days of the week recur on the same day of the month.

METONIC (LUNAR, OR MINOR) CYCLE
In 432 BC, Meton, an Athenian astronomer, found that 235 lunations are very nearly, though not exactly, equal in duration to 19 solar years and so after 19 years the phases of the Moon recur approximately on the same days of the month. The dates of full moon in a cycle of 19 years were inscribed in figures of

gold on public monuments in Athens, and the number showing the position of a year in the cycle is called the golden number of that year.

JULIAN PERIOD
The Julian period was proposed by Joseph Scaliger in 1582. The period is 7,980 Julian years, and its first year coincides with the year 4713 BC. The figure of 7,980 is the product of the number of years in the solar cycle, the Metonic cycle and the cycle of the Roman indiction (28 x 19 x 15).

ROMAN INDICTION
The Roman indiction is a period of 15 years, instituted for fiscal purposes about AD 300.

EPACT
The epact is the age of the calendar Moon, diminished by one day, on 1 January, in the ecclesiastical lunar calendar.

CHINESE CALENDAR
A lunar calendar was the sole calendar in use in China until 1911, when the government adopted the new (Gregorian) calendar for official and most business activities. The Chinese tend to follow both calendars, the lunar calendar playing an important part in personal life, eg birth celebrations, festivals, marriages; in rural villages the lunar calendar dictates the cycle of activities, denoting the change of weather and farming activities.

The lunar calendar is used in Hong Kong, Singapore, Malaysia, Tibet and elsewhere in south-east Asia. The calendar has a cycle of 60 years. The new year begins at the first new moon after the sun enters the sign of Aquarius, ie the new year falls between 21 January and 19 February in the Gregorian calendar.

Each year in the Chinese calendar is associated with one of 12 animals: the rat, the ox, the tiger, the rabbit, the dragon, the snake, the horse, the sheep, the monkey, the chicken or rooster, the dog, and the pig.

The date of the Chinese new year and the astrological sign for the years 2020–22 are:

2020	25 January	Rat
2021	12 February	Ox
2022	1 February	Tiger

COPTIC CALENDAR
In the Coptic calendar, which is used in parts of Egypt and Ethiopia, the year is made up of 12 months of 30 days each, followed, in general, by five complementary days. Every fourth year is an intercalary or leap year and in these years there are six complementary days. The intercalary year of the Coptic calendar immediately precedes the leap year of the Julian calendar. The era is that of Diocletian or the Martyrs, the origin of which is fixed at 29 August AD 284 (Julian date).

INDIAN ERAS
In addition to the Muslim reckoning, other eras are used in India. The Saka era of southern India, dating from 3 March AD 78, was declared the national calendar of the Republic of India with effect from 22 March 1957, to be used concurrently with the Gregorian calendar. As revised, the year of the new Saka era begins at the spring equinox, with five successive months of 31 days and seven of 30 days in ordinary years, and six months of each length in leap years. The year AD 2020 is 1942 of the revised Saka era.

The year AD 2020 corresponds to the following years in other eras:

Year 2077 of the Vikram Samvat era
Year 1427 of the Bengali San era
Year 1196 of the Kollam era
Year 5121 of the Kaliyuga era

Year 2563 of the Buddha Nirvana era

JAPANESE CALENDAR
The Japanese calendar is essentially the same as the Gregorian calendar, the years, months and weeks being of the same length and beginning on the same days as those of the Gregorian calendar. The numeration of the years is different, based on a system of epochs or periods, each of which begins at the accession of an emperor or other important occurrence. The method is not unlike the British system of regnal years, except that each year of a period closes on 31 December. The Japanese chronology begins about AD 650 and the four latest epochs are defined by the reigns of emperors, whose actual names are not necessarily used:

Epoch
Taisho – 1 August 1912 to 25 December 1926
Showa – 26 December 1926 to 7 January 1989
Heisei – 8 January 1989 to 30 April 2019
Reiwa – 1 May 2019

The year Reiwa 2 begins on 1 January 2020.

The months are known as First Month, Second Month, etc, First Month being equivalent to January. The days of the week are Nichiyobi (Sun-day), Getsuyobi (Moon-day), Kayobi (Fire-day), Suiyobi (Water-day), Mokuyobi (Wood-day), Kinyobi (Metal-day) and Doyobi (Earth-day).

THE MASONIC YEAR
Two dates are quoted in warrants, dispensations, etc, issued by the United Grand Lodge of England, those for the current year being expressed as *Anno Domini* 2020 – *Anno Lucis* 6020. This *Anno Lucis* (year of light) is based on the Book of Genesis 1:3, the 4,000-year difference being derived, in modified form, from *Ussher's Notation,* published in 1654, which places the Creation of the World in 4004 BC.

OLYMPIADS
Ancient Greek chronology was reckoned in Olympiads, cycles of four years corresponding with the Olympic Games held on the plain of Olympia, in Elis. The intervening years were the first, second, etc, of the Olympiad, which received the name of the victor at the Games. The first recorded Olympiad is that of Choroebus, 776 BC.

ZOROASTRIAN CALENDAR
Zoroastrians, followers of the Iranian prophet Zarathushtra (known to the Greeks as Zoroaster) are mostly to be found in Iran and in India, where they are known as Parsees.

The Zoroastrian era dates from the coronation of the last Zoroastrian Sasanian king in AD 631. The Zoroastrian calendar is divided into 12 months, each comprising 30 days, followed by five holy days of the Gathas at the end of each year to make the year consist of 365 days.

In order to synchronise the calendar with the solar year of 365 days, an extra month was intercalated once every 120 years. However, this intercalation ceased in the 12th century and the new year, which had fallen in the spring, slipped back to August. Because intercalation ceased at different times in Iran and India, there was one month's difference between the calendar followed in Iran (Kadmi calendar) and that followed by the Parsees (Shenshai calendar). In 1906 a group of Zoroastrians decided to bring the calendar back in line with the seasons again and restore the new year to 21 March each year (Fasli calendar).

The Shenshai calendar (new year in August) is mainly used by Parsees. The Fasli calendar (new year, 21 March) is mainly used by Zoroastrians living in Iran, in the Indian subcontinent, or elsewhere.

ROMAN CALENDAR

Roman historians adopted as an epoch the foundation of Rome, which is believed to have happened in the year 753 BC. The ordinal number of the years in Roman reckoning is followed by the letters AUC *(ab urbe condita)*, so that the year 2020 is 2773 AUC (MMDCCLXXIII). The calendar that we know has developed from one said to have been established by Romulus using a year of 304 days divided into ten months, beginning with March. To this Numa added January and February, making the year consist of 12 months of 30 and 29 days alternately, with an additional day so that the total was 355. It is also said that Numa ordered an intercalary month of 22 or 23 days in alternate years, making 90 days in eight years, to be inserted after 23 February.

However, there is some doubt as to the origination and the details of the intercalation in the Roman calendar. In the year 46 BC Julius Caesar found that the calendar had been allowed to fall into some confusion. He sought the help of Egyptian astronomer Sosigenes, which led to the construction and adoption (45 BC) of the Julian calendar, and, by a slight alteration, to the Gregorian calendar now in use. The year 46 BC was made to consist of 445 days and is called the Year of Confusion.

In the Roman (Julian) calendar, the days of the month were counted backwards from three fixed points, or days, and an intervening day was said to be so many days before the next coming point, the first and last being counted. These three points were the Kalends, the Nones and the Ides. The year containing 366 days was called *bissextilis annus*, as it had a doubled sixth day *(bissextus dies)* before the March Kalends on 24 February – *ante diem sextum Kalendas Martias,* or a.d. VI Kal. Mart.

Present days of the month	March, May, July, October have thirty-one days		January, August, December have thirty-one days		April, June, September, November have thirty days		February has twenty-eight days, and in leap year twenty-nine	
1	Kalendis		Kalendis		Kalendis		Kalendis	
2	VI		IV	ante	IV	ante	IV	ante
3	V	ante	III	Nonas	III	Nonas	III	Nonas
4	IV	Nonas	pridie Nonas		pridie Nonas		pridie Nonas	
5	III		Nonis		Nonis		Nonis	
6	pridie Nonas		VIII		VIII		VIII	
7	Nonis		VII		VII		VII	
8	VIII		VI	ante	VI	ante	VI	ante
9	VII		V	Idus	V	Idus	V	Idus
10	VI	ante	IV		IV		IV	
11	V	Idus	III		III		III	
12	IV		pridie Idus		pridie Idus		pridie Idus	
13	III		Idibus		Idibus		Idibus	
14	pridie Idus		XIX		XVIII		XVI	
15	Idibus		XVIII		XVII		XV	
16	XVII		XVII		XVI		XIV	
17	XVI		XVI		XV		XIII	
18	XV		XV		XIV		XII	
19	XIV		XIV		XIII		XI	
20	XIII		XIII		XII	ante Kalendas	X	ante Kalendas
21	XII		XII	ante Kalendas	XI	(of the month	IX	Martias
22	XI	ante Kalendas	XI	(of the month	X	following)	VIII	
23	X	(of the month	X	following)	IX		VII	
24	IX	following)	IX		VIII		*VI	
25	VIII		VIII		VII		V	
26	VII		VII		VI		IV	
27	VI		VI		V		III	
28	V		V		IV		pridie Kalendas
29	IV		IV		III		Martias
30	III		III		pridie Kalendas			
31	pridie Kalendas (Aprilis, Iunias, Sextilis, Novembris)		pridie Kalendas (Februarias, Septembris, Ianuarias)		(Maias, Quinctilis, Octobris, Decembris)			

* Repeated in leap year

CALENDAR FOR ANY YEAR 1780–2040

To select the correct calendar for any year between 1780 and 2040, consult the index below
* leap year

1780 N*	1813 K	1846 I	1879 G	1912 D*	1945 C	1978 A	2011 M
1781 C	1814 M	1847 K	1880 J*	1913 G	1946 E	1979 C	2012 B*
1782 E	1815 A	1848 N*	1881 M	1914 I	1947 G	1980 F*	2013 E
1783 G	1816 D*	1849 C	1882 A	1915 K	1948 J*	1981 I	2014 G
1784 J*	1817 G	1850 E	1883 C	1916 N*	1949 M	1982 K	2015 I
1785 M	1818 I	1851 G	1884 F*	1917 C	1950 A	1983 M	2016 L*
1786 A	1819 K	1852 J*	1885 I	1918 E	1951 C	1984 B*	2017 A
1787 C	1820 N*	1853 M	1886 K	1919 G	1952 F*	1985 E	2018 C
1788 F*	1821 C	1854 A	1887 M	1920 J*	1953 I	1986 G	2019 E
1789 I	1822 E	1855 C	1888 B*	1921 M	1954 K	1987 I	2020 H*
1790 K	1823 G	1856 F*	1889 E	1922 A	1955 M	1988 L*	2021 K
1791 M	1824 J*	1857 I	1890 G	1923 C	1956 B*	1989 A	2022 M
1792 B*	1825 M	1858 K	1891 I	1924 F*	1957 E	1990 C	2023 A
1793 E	1826 A	1859 M	1892 L*	1925 I	1958 G	1991 E	2024 D*
1794 G	1827 C	1860 B*	1893 A	1926 K	1959 I	1992 H*	2025 G
1795 I	1828 F*	1861 E	1894 C	1927 M	1960 L*	1993 K	2026 I
1796 L*	1829 I	1862 G	1895 E	1928 B*	1961 A	1994 M	2027 K
1797 A	1830 K	1863 I	1896 H*	1929 E	1962 C	1995 A	2028 N*
1798 C	1831 M	1864 L*	1897 K	1930 G	1963 E	1996 D*	2029 C
1799 E	1832 B*	1865 A	1898 M	1931 I	1964 H*	1997 G	2030 E
1800 G	1833 E	1866 C	1899 A	1932 L*	1965 K	1998 I	2031 G
1801 I	1834 G	1867 E	1900 C	1933 A	1966 M	1999 K	2032 J*
1802 K	1835 I	1868 H*	1901 E	1934 C	1967 A	2000 N*	2033 M
1803 M	1836 L*	1869 K	1902 G	1935 E	1968 D*	2001 C	2034 A
1804 B*	1837 A	1870 M	1903 I	1936 H*	1969 G	2002 E	2035 C
1805 E	1838 C	1871 A	1904 L*	1937 K	1970 I	2003 G	2036 F*
1806 G	1839 E	1872 D*	1905 A	1938 M	1971 K	2004 J*	2037 I
1807 I	1840 H*	1873 G	1906 C	1939 A	1972 N*	2005 M	2038 K
1808 L*	1841 K	1874 I	1907 E	1940 D*	1973 C	2006 A	2039 M
1809 A	1842 M	1875 K	1908 H*	1941 G	1974 E	2007 C	2040 B*
1810 C	1843 A	1876 N*	1909 K	1942 I	1975 G	2008 F*	
1811 E	1844 D*	1877 C	1910 M	1943 K	1976 J*	2009 I	
1812 H*	1845 G	1878 E	1911 A	1944 N*	1977 M	2010 K	

A

	January	February	March
Sun.	1 8 15 22 29	5 12 19 26	5 12 19 26
Mon.	2 9 16 23 30	6 13 20 27	6 13 20 27
Tue.	3 10 17 24 31	7 14 21 28	7 14 21 28
Wed.	4 11 18 25	1 8 15 22	1 8 15 22 29
Thur.	5 12 19 26	2 9 16 23	2 9 16 23 30
Fri.	6 13 20 27	3 10 17 24	3 10 17 24 31
Sat.	7 14 21 28	4 11 18 25	4 11 18 25

	April	May	June
Sun.	2 9 16 23 30	7 14 21 28	4 11 18 25
Mon.	3 10 17 24	1 8 15 22 29	5 12 19 26
Tue.	4 11 18 25	2 9 16 23 30	6 13 20 27
Wed.	5 12 19 26	3 10 17 24 31	7 14 21 28
Thur.	6 13 20 27	4 11 18 25	1 8 15 22 29
Fri.	7 14 21 28	5 12 19 26	2 9 16 23 30
Sat.	1 8 15 22 29	6 13 20 27	3 10 17 24

	July	August	September
Sun.	2 9 16 23 30	6 13 20 27	3 10 17 24
Mon.	3 10 17 24 31	7 14 21 28	4 11 18 25
Tue.	4 11 18 25	1 8 15 22 29	5 12 19 26
Wed.	5 12 19 26	2 9 16 23 30	6 13 20 27
Thur.	6 13 20 27	3 10 17 24 31	7 14 21 28
Fri.	7 14 21 28	4 11 18 25	1 8 15 22 29
Sat.	1 8 15 22 29	5 12 19 26	2 9 16 23 30

	October	November	December
Sun.	1 8 15 22 29	5 12 19 26	3 10 17 24 31
Mon.	2 9 16 23 30	6 13 20 27	4 11 18 25
Tue.	3 10 17 24 31	7 14 21 28	5 12 19 26
Wed.	4 11 18 25	1 8 15 22 29	6 13 20 27
Thur.	5 12 19 26	2 9 16 23	7 14 21 28
Fri.	6 13 20 27	3 10 17 24	1 8 15 22 29
Sat.	7 14 21 28	4 11 18 25	2 9 16 23 30

B (LEAP YEAR)

	January	February	March
Sun.	1 8 15 22 29	5 12 19 26	4 11 18 25
Mon.	2 9 16 23 30	6 13 20 27	5 12 19 26
Tue.	3 10 17 24 31	7 14 21 28	6 13 20 27
Wed.	4 11 18 25	1 8 15 22 29	7 14 21 28
Thur.	5 12 19 26	2 9 16 23	1 8 15 22 29
Fri.	6 13 20 27	3 10 17 24	2 9 16 23 30
Sat.	7 14 21 28	4 11 18 25	3 10 17 24 31

	April	May	June
Sun.	1 8 15 22 29	6 13 20 27	3 10 17 24
Mon.	2 9 16 23 30	7 14 21 28	4 11 18 25
Tue.	3 10 17 24	1 8 15 22 29	5 12 19 26
Wed.	4 11 18 25	2 9 16 23 30	6 13 20 27
Thur.	5 12 19 26	3 10 17 24 31	7 14 21 28
Fri.	6 13 20 27	4 11 18 25	1 8 15 22 29
Sat.	7 14 21 28	5 12 19 26	2 9 16 23 30

	July	August	September
Sun.	1 8 15 22 29	5 12 19 26	2 9 16 23 30
Mon.	2 9 16 23 30	6 13 20 27	3 10 17 24
Tue.	3 10 17 24 31	7 14 21 28	4 11 18 25
Wed.	4 11 18 25	1 8 15 22 29	5 12 19 26
Thur.	5 12 19 26	2 9 16 23 30	6 13 20 27
Fri.	6 13 20 27	3 10 17 24 31	7 14 21 28
Sat.	7 14 21 28	4 11 18 25	1 8 15 22 29

	October	November	December
Sun.	7 14 21 28	4 11 18 25	2 9 16 23 30
Mon.	1 8 15 22 29	5 12 19 26	3 10 17 24 31
Tue.	2 9 16 23 30	6 13 20 27	4 11 18 25
Wed.	3 10 17 24 31	7 14 21 28	5 12 19 26
Thur.	4 11 18 25	1 8 15 22 29	6 13 20 27
Fri.	5 12 19 26	2 9 16 23 30	7 14 21 28
Sat.	6 13 20 27	3 10 17 24	1 8 15 22 29

EASTER DAYS

March 26	1815, 1826, 1837, 1967, 1978, 1989
April 2	1809, 1893, 1899, 1961
April 9	1871, 1882, 1939, 1950, 2023, 2034
April 16	1786, 1797, 1843, 1854, 1865, 1911, 1922, 1933, 1995, 2006, 2017
April 23	1905

EASTER DAYS

April 1	1804, 1888, 1956, 2040
April 8	1792, 1860, 1928, 2012
April 22	1832, 1984

C

	January	February	March
Sun.	7 14 21 28	4 11 18 25	4 11 18 25
Mon.	1 8 15 22 29	5 12 19 26	5 12 19 26
Tue.	2 9 16 23 30	6 13 20 27	6 13 20 27
Wed.	3 10 17 24 31	7 14 21 28	7 14 21 28
Thur.	4 11 18 25	1 8 15 22	1 8 15 22 29
Fri.	5 12 19 26	2 9 16 23	2 9 16 23 30
Sat.	6 13 20 27	3 10 17 24	3 10 17 24 31

	April	May	June
Sun.	1 8 15 22 29	6 13 20 27	3 10 17 24
Mon.	2 9 16 23 30	7 14 21 28	4 11 18 25
Tue.	3 10 17 24	1 8 15 22 29	5 12 19 26
Wed.	4 11 18 25	2 9 16 23 30	6 13 20 27
Thur.	5 12 19 26	3 10 17 24 31	7 14 21 28
Fri.	6 13 20 27	4 11 18 25	1 8 15 22 29
Sat.	7 14 21 28	5 12 19 26	2 9 16 23 30

	July	August	September
Sun.	1 8 15 22 29	5 12 19 26	2 9 16 23 30
Mon.	2 9 16 23 30	6 13 20 27	3 10 17 24
Tue.	3 10 17 24 31	7 14 21 28	4 11 18 25
Wed.	4 11 18 25	1 8 15 22 29	5 12 19 26
Thur.	5 12 19 26	2 9 16 23 30	6 13 20 27
Fri.	6 13 20 27	3 10 17 24 31	7 14 21 28
Sat.	7 14 21 28	4 11 18 25	1 8 15 22 29

	October	November	December
Sun.	7 14 21 28	4 11 18 25	2 9 16 23 30
Mon.	1 8 15 22 29	5 12 19 26	3 10 17 24 31
Tue.	2 9 16 23 30	6 13 20 27	4 11 18 25
Wed.	3 10 17 24 31	7 14 21 28	5 12 19 26
Thur.	4 11 18 25	1 8 15 22 29	6 13 20 27
Fri.	5 12 19 26	2 9 16 23 30	7 14 21 28
Sat.	6 13 20 27	3 10 17 24	1 8 15 22 29

EASTER DAYS
March 25   1883, 1894, 1951, 2035
April 1   1866, 1877, 1923, 1934, 1945, 2018, 2029
April 8   1787, 1798, 1849, 1855, 1917, 2007
April 15   1781, 1827, 1838, 1900, 1906, 1979, 1990, 2001
April 22   1810, 1821, 1962, 1973

E

	January	February	March
Sun.	6 13 20 27	3 10 17 24	3 10 17 24 31
Mon.	7 14 21 28	4 11 18 25	4 11 18 25
Tue.	1 8 15 22 29	5 12 19 26	5 12 19 26
Wed.	2 9 16 23 30	6 13 20 27	6 13 20 27
Thur.	3 10 17 24 31	7 14 21 28	7 14 21 28
Fri.	4 11 18 25	1 8 15 22	1 8 15 22 29
Sat.	5 12 19 26	2 9 16 23	2 9 16 23 30

	April	May	June
Sun.	7 14 21 28	5 12 19 26	2 9 16 23 30
Mon.	1 8 15 22 29	6 13 20 27	3 10 17 24
Tue.	2 9 16 23 30	7 14 21 28	4 11 18 25
Wed.	3 10 17 24	1 8 15 22 29	5 12 19 26
Thur.	4 11 18 25	2 9 16 23 30	6 13 20 27
Fri.	5 12 19 26	3 10 17 24 31	7 14 21 28
Sat.	6 13 20 27	4 11 18 25	1 8 15 22 29

	July	August	September
Sun.	7 14 21 28	4 11 18 25	1 8 15 22 29
Mon.	1 8 15 22 29	5 12 19 26	2 9 16 23 30
Tue.	2 9 16 23 30	6 13 20 27	3 10 17 24
Wed.	3 10 17 24 31	7 14 21 28	4 11 18 25
Thur.	4 11 18 25	1 8 15 22 29	5 12 19 26
Fri.	5 12 19 26	2 9 16 23 30	6 13 20 27
Sat.	6 13 20 27	3 10 17 24 31	7 14 21 28

	October	November	December
Sun.	6 13 20 27	3 10 17 24	1 8 15 22 29
Mon.	7 14 21 28	4 11 18 25	2 9 16 23 30
Tue.	1 8 15 22 29	5 12 19 26	3 10 17 24 31
Wed.	2 9 16 23 30	6 13 20 27	4 11 18 25
Thur.	3 10 17 24 31	7 14 21 28	5 12 19 26
Fri.	4 11 18 25	1 8 15 22 29	6 13 20 27
Sat.	5 12 19 26	2 9 16 23 30	7 14 21 28

EASTER DAYS
March 24   1799
March 31   1782, 1793, 1839, 1850, 1861, 1907, 1918, 1929, 1991, 2002, 2013
April 7   1822, 1833, 1901, 1985
April 14   1805, 1811, 1895, 1963, 1974
April 21   1867, 1878, 1889, 1935, 1946, 1957, 2019, 2030

D (LEAP YEAR)

	January	February	March
Sun.	7 14 21 28	4 11 18 25	3 10 17 24 31
Mon.	1 8 15 22 29	5 12 19 26	4 11 18 25
Tue.	2 9 16 23 30	6 13 20 27	5 12 19 26
Wed.	3 10 17 24 31	7 14 21 28	6 13 20 27
Thur.	4 11 18 25	1 8 15 22 29	7 14 21 28
Fri.	5 12 19 26	2 9 16 23	1 8 15 22 29
Sat.	6 13 20 27	3 10 17 24	2 9 16 23 30

	April	May	June
Sun.	7 14 21 28	5 12 19 26	2 9 16 23 30
Mon.	1 8 15 22 29	6 13 20 27	3 10 17 24
Tue.	2 9 16 23 30	7 14 21 28	4 11 18 25
Wed.	3 10 17 24	1 8 15 22 29	5 12 19 26
Thur.	4 11 18 25	2 9 16 23 30	6 13 20 27
Fri.	5 12 19 26	3 10 17 24 31	7 14 21 28
Sat.	6 13 20 27	4 11 18 25	1 8 15 22 29

	July	August	September
Sun.	7 14 21 28	4 11 18 25	1 8 15 22 29
Mon.	1 8 15 22 29	5 12 19 26	2 9 16 23 30
Tue.	2 9 16 23 30	6 13 20 27	3 10 17 24
Wed.	3 10 17 24 31	7 14 21 28	4 11 18 25
Thur.	4 11 18 25	1 8 15 22 29	5 12 19 26
Fri.	5 12 19 26	2 9 16 23 30	6 13 20 27
Sat.	6 13 20 27	3 10 17 24 31	7 14 21 28

	October	November	December
Sun.	6 13 20 27	3 10 17 24	1 8 15 22 29
Mon.	7 14 21 28	4 11 18 25	2 9 16 23 30
Tue.	1 8 15 22 29	5 12 19 26	3 10 17 24 31
Wed.	2 9 16 23 30	6 13 20 27	4 11 18 25
Thur.	3 10 17 24 31	7 14 21 28	5 12 19 26
Fri.	4 11 18 25	1 8 15 22 29	6 13 20 27
Sat.	5 12 19 26	2 9 16 23 30	7 14 21 28

EASTER DAYS
March 24   1940
March 31   1872, 2024
April 7   1844, 1912, 1996
April 14   1816, 1968

F (LEAP YEAR)

	January	February	March
Sun.	6 13 20 27	3 10 17 24	2 9 16 23 30
Mon.	7 14 21 28	4 11 18 25	3 10 17 24 31
Tue.	1 8 15 22 29	5 12 19 26	4 11 18 25
Wed.	2 9 16 23 30	6 13 20 27	5 12 19 26
Thur.	3 10 17 24 31	7 14 21 28	6 13 20 27
Fri.	4 11 18 25	1 8 15 22 29	7 14 21 28
Sat.	5 12 19 26	2 9 16 23	1 8 15 22 29

	April	May	June
Sun.	6 13 20 27	4 11 18 25	1 8 15 22 29
Mon.	7 14 21 28	5 12 19 26	2 9 16 23 30
Tue.	1 8 15 22 29	6 13 20 27	3 10 17 24
Wed.	2 9 16 23 30	7 14 21 28	4 11 18 25
Thur.	3 10 17 24	1 8 15 22 29	5 12 19 26
Fri.	4 11 18 25	2 9 16 23 30	6 13 20 27
Sat.	5 12 19 26	3 10 17 24 31	7 14 21 28

	July	August	September
Sun.	6 13 20 27	3 10 17 24 31	7 14 21 28
Mon.	7 14 21 28	4 11 18 25	1 8 15 22 29
Tue.	1 8 15 22 29	5 12 19 26	2 9 16 23 30
Wed.	2 9 16 23 30	6 13 20 27	3 10 17 24
Thur.	3 10 17 24 31	7 14 21 28	4 11 18 25
Fri.	4 11 18 25	1 8 15 22 29	5 12 19 26
Sat.	5 12 19 26	2 9 16 23 30	6 13 20 27

	October	November	December
Sun.	5 12 19 26	2 9 16 23 30	7 14 21 28
Mon.	6 13 20 27	3 10 17 24	1 8 15 22 29
Tue.	7 14 21 28	4 11 18 25	2 9 16 23 30
Wed.	1 8 15 22 29	5 12 19 26	3 10 17 24 31
Thur.	2 9 16 23 30	6 13 20 27	4 11 18 25
Fri.	3 10 17 24 31	7 14 21 28	5 12 19 26
Sat.	4 11 18 25	1 8 15 22 29	6 13 20 27

EASTER DAYS
March 23   1788, 1856, 2008
April 6   1828, 1980
April 13   1884, 1952, 2036
April 20   1924

G

	January	February	March
Sun.	5 12 19 26	2 9 16 23	2 9 16 23 30
Mon.	6 13 20 27	3 10 17 24	3 10 17 24 31
Tue.	7 14 21 28	4 11 18 25	4 11 18 25
Wed.	1 8 15 22 29	5 12 19 26	5 12 19 26
Thur.	2 9 16 23 30	6 13 20 27	6 13 20 27
Fri.	3 10 17 24 31	7 14 21 28	7 14 21 28
Sat.	4 11 18 25	1 8 15 22	1 8 15 22 29

	April	May	June
Sun.	6 13 20 27	4 11 18 25	1 8 15 22 29
Mon.	7 14 21 28	5 12 19 26	2 9 16 23 30
Tue.	1 8 15 22 29	6 13 20 27	3 10 17 24
Wed.	2 9 16 23 30	7 14 21 28	4 11 18 25
Thur.	3 10 17 24	1 8 15 22 29	5 12 19 26
Fri.	4 11 18 25	2 9 16 23 30	6 13 20 27
Sat.	5 12 19 26	3 10 17 24 31	7 14 21 28

	July	August	September
Sun.	6 13 20 27	3 10 17 24 31	7 14 21 28
Mon.	7 14 21 28	4 11 18 25	1 8 15 22 29
Tue.	1 8 15 22 29	5 12 19 26	2 9 16 23 30
Wed.	2 9 16 23 30	6 13 20 27	3 10 17 24
Thur.	3 10 17 24 31	7 14 21 28	4 11 18 25
Fri.	4 11 18 25	1 8 15 22 29	5 12 19 26
Sat.	5 12 19 26	2 9 16 23 30	6 13 20 27

	October	November	December
Sun.	5 12 19 26	2 9 16 23 30	7 14 21 28
Mon.	6 13 20 27	3 10 17 24	1 8 15 22 29
Tue.	7 14 21 28	4 11 18 25	2 9 16 23 30
Wed.	1 8 15 22 29	5 12 19 26	3 10 17 24 31
Thur.	2 9 16 23 30	6 13 20 27	4 11 18 25
Fri.	3 10 17 24 31	7 14 21 28	5 12 19 26
Sat.	4 11 18 25	1 8 15 22 29	6 13 20 27

EASTER DAYS

March 23	1845, 1913
March 30	1823, 1834, 1902, 1975, 1986, 1997
April 6	1806, 1817, 1890, 1947, 1958, 1969
April 13	1800, 1873, 1879, 1941, 2031
April 20	1783, 1794, 1851, 1862, 1919, 1930, 2003, 2014, 2025

I

	January	February	March
Sun.	4 11 18 25	1 8 15 22	1 8 15 22 29
Mon.	5 12 19 26	2 9 16 23	2 9 16 23 30
Tue.	6 13 20 27	3 10 17 24	3 10 17 24 31
Wed.	7 14 21 28	4 11 18 25	4 11 18 25
Thur.	1 8 15 22 29	5 12 19 26	5 12 19 26
Fri.	2 9 16 23 30	6 13 20 27	6 13 20 27
Sat.	3 10 17 24 31	7 14 21 28	7 14 21 28

	April	May	June
Sun.	5 12 19 26	3 10 17 24 31	7 14 21 28
Mon.	6 13 20 27	4 11 18 25	1 8 15 22 29
Tue.	7 14 21 28	5 12 19 26	2 9 16 23 30
Wed.	1 8 15 22 29	6 13 20 27	3 10 17 24
Thur.	2 9 16 23 30	7 14 21 28	4 11 18 25
Fri.	3 10 17 24	1 8 15 22 29	5 12 19 26
Sat.	4 11 18 25	2 9 16 23 30	6 13 20 27

	July	August	September
Sun.	5 12 19 26	2 9 16 23 30	6 13 20 27
Mon.	6 13 20 27	3 10 17 24 31	7 14 21 28
Tue.	7 14 21 28	4 11 18 25	1 8 15 22 29
Wed.	1 8 15 22 29	5 12 19 26	2 9 16 23 30
Thur.	2 9 16 23 30	6 13 20 27	3 10 17 24
Fri.	3 10 17 24 31	7 14 21 28	4 11 18 25
Sat.	4 11 18 25	1 8 15 22 29	5 12 19 26

	October	November	December
Sun.	4 11 18 25	1 8 15 22 29	6 13 20 27
Mon.	5 12 19 26	2 9 16 23 30	7 14 21 28
Tue.	6 13 20 27	3 10 17 24	1 8 15 22 29
Wed.	7 14 21 28	4 11 18 25	2 9 16 23 30
Thur.	1 8 15 22 29	5 12 19 26	3 10 17 24 31
Fri.	2 9 16 23 30	6 13 20 27	4 11 18 25
Sat.	3 10 17 24 31	7 14 21 28	5 12 19 26

EASTER DAYS

March 22	1818
March 29	1807, 1891, 1959, 1970
April 5	1795, 1801, 1863, 1874, 1885, 1931, 1942, 1953, 2015, 2026, 2037
April 12	1789, 1846, 1857, 1903, 1914, 1925, 1998, 2009
April 19	1829, 1835, 1981, 1987

H (LEAP YEAR)

	January	February	March
Sun.	5 12 19 26	2 9 16 23	1 8 15 22 29
Mon.	6 13 20 27	3 10 17 24	2 9 16 23 30
Tue.	7 14 21 28	4 11 18 25	3 10 17 24 31
Wed.	1 8 15 22 29	5 12 19 26	4 11 18 25
Thur.	2 9 16 23 30	6 13 20 27	5 12 19 26
Fri.	3 10 17 24 31	7 14 21 28	6 13 20 27
Sat.	4 11 18 25	1 8 15 22 29	7 14 21 28

	April	May	June
Sun.	5 12 19 26	3 10 17 24 31	7 14 21 28
Mon.	6 13 20 27	4 11 18 25	1 8 15 22 29
Tue.	7 14 21 28	5 12 19 26	2 9 16 23 30
Wed.	1 8 15 22 29	6 13 20 27	3 10 17 24
Thur.	2 9 16 23 30	7 14 21 28	4 11 18 25
Fri.	3 10 17 24	1 8 15 22 29	5 12 19 26
Sat.	4 11 18 25	2 9 16 23 30	6 13 20 27

	July	August	September
Sun.	5 12 19 26	2 9 16 23 30	6 13 20 27
Mon.	6 13 20 27	3 10 17 24 31	7 14 21 28
Tue.	7 14 21 28	4 11 18 25	1 8 15 22 29
Wed.	1 8 15 22 29	5 12 19 26	2 9 16 23 30
Thur.	2 9 16 23 30	6 13 20 27	3 10 17 24
Fri.	3 10 17 24 31	7 14 21 28	4 11 18 25
Sat.	4 11 18 25	1 8 15 22 29	5 12 19 26

	October	November	December
Sun.	4 11 18 25	1 8 15 22 29	6 13 20 27
Mon.	5 12 19 26	2 9 16 23 30	7 14 21 28
Tue.	6 13 20 27	3 10 17 24	1 8 15 22 29
Wed.	7 14 21 28	4 11 18 25	2 9 16 23 30
Thur.	1 8 15 22 29	5 12 19 26	3 10 17 24 31
Fri.	2 9 16 23 30	6 13 20 27	4 11 18 25
Sat.	3 10 17 24 31	7 14 21 28	5 12 19 26

EASTER DAYS

March 29	1812, 1964
April 5	1896
April 12	1868, 1936, 2020
April 19	1840, 1908, 1992

J (LEAP YEAR)

	January	February	March
Sun.	4 11 18 25	1 8 15 22 29	7 14 21 28
Mon.	5 12 19 26	2 9 16 23	1 8 15 22 29
Tue.	6 13 20 27	3 10 17 24	2 9 16 23 30
Wed.	7 14 21 28	4 11 18 25	3 10 17 24 31
Thur.	1 8 15 22 29	5 12 19 26	4 11 18 25
Fri.	2 9 16 23 30	6 13 20 27	5 12 19 26
Sat.	3 10 17 24 31	7 14 21 28	6 13 20 27

	April	May	June
Sun.	4 11 18 25	2 9 16 23 30	6 13 20 27
Mon.	5 12 19 26	3 10 17 24 31	7 14 21 28
Tue.	6 13 20 27	4 11 18 25	1 8 15 22 29
Wed.	7 14 21 28	5 12 19 26	2 9 16 23 30
Thur.	1 8 15 22 29	6 13 20 27	3 10 17 24
Fri.	2 9 16 23 30	7 14 21 28	4 11 18 25
Sat.	3 10 17 24	1 8 15 22 29	5 12 19 26

	July	August	September
Sun.	4 11 18 25	1 8 15 22 29	5 12 19 26
Mon.	5 12 19 26	2 9 16 23 30	6 13 20 27
Tue.	6 13 20 27	3 10 17 24 31	7 14 21 28
Wed.	7 14 21 28	4 11 18 25	1 8 15 22 29
Thur.	1 8 15 22 29	5 12 19 26	2 9 16 23 30
Fri.	2 9 16 23 30	6 13 20 27	3 10 17 24
Sat.	3 10 17 24 31	7 14 21 28	4 11 18 25

	October	November	December
Sun.	3 10 17 24 31	7 14 21 28	5 12 19 26
Mon.	4 11 18 25	1 8 15 22 29	6 13 20 27
Tue.	5 12 19 26	2 9 16 23 30	7 14 21 28
Wed.	6 13 20 27	3 10 17 24	1 8 15 22 29
Thur.	7 14 21 28	4 11 18 25	2 9 16 23 30
Fri.	1 8 15 22 29	5 12 19 26	3 10 17 24 31
Sat.	2 9 16 23 30	6 13 20 27	4 11 18 25

EASTER DAYS

March 28	1880, 1948, 2032
April 4	1920
April 11	1784, 1852, 2004
April 18	1824, 1976

K

	January	February	March
Sun.	3 10 17 24 31	7 14 21 28	7 14 21 28
Mon.	4 11 18 25	1 8 15 22	1 8 15 22 29
Tue.	5 12 19 26	2 9 16 23	2 9 16 23 30
Wed.	6 13 20 27	3 10 17 24	3 10 17 24 31
Thur.	7 14 21 28	4 11 18 25	4 11 18 25
Fri.	1 8 15 22 29	5 12 19 26	5 12 19 26
Sat.	2 9 16 23 30	6 13 20 27	6 13 20 27

	April	May	June
Sun.	4 11 18 25	2 9 16 23 30	6 13 20 27
Mon.	5 12 19 26	3 10 17 24 31	7 14 21 28
Tue.	6 13 20 27	4 11 18 25	1 8 15 22 29
Wed.	7 14 21 28	5 12 19 26	2 9 16 23 30
Thur.	1 8 15 22 29	6 13 20 27	3 10 17 24
Fri.	2 9 16 23 30	7 14 21 28	4 11 18 25
Sat.	3 10 17 24	1 8 15 22 29	5 12 19 26

	July	August	September
Sun.	4 11 18 25	1 8 15 22 29	5 12 19 26
Mon.	5 12 19 26	2 9 16 23 30	6 13 20 27
Tue.	6 13 20 27	3 10 17 24 31	7 14 21 28
Wed.	7 14 21 28	4 11 18 25	1 8 15 22 29
Thur.	1 8 15 22 29	5 12 19 26	2 9 16 23 30
Fri.	2 9 16 23 30	6 13 20 27	3 10 17 24
Sat.	3 10 17 24 31	7 14 21 28	4 11 18 25

	October	November	December
Sun.	3 10 17 24 31	7 14 21 28	5 12 19 26
Mon.	4 11 18 25	1 8 15 22 29	6 13 20 27
Tue.	5 12 19 26	2 9 16 23 30	7 14 21 28
Wed.	6 13 20 27	3 10 17 24	1 8 15 22 29
Thur.	7 14 21 28	4 11 18 25	2 9 16 23 30
Fri.	1 8 15 22 29	5 12 19 26	3 10 17 24 31
Sat.	2 9 16 23 30	6 13 20 27	4 11 18 25

EASTER DAYS
March 28   1869, 1875, 1937, 2027
April 4   1790, 1847, 1858, 1915, 1926, 1999, 2010, 2021
April 11   1819, 1830, 1841, 1909, 1971, 1982, 1993
April 18   1802, 1813, 1897, 1954, 1965
April 25   1886, 1943, 2038

M

	January	February	March
Sun.	2 9 16 23 30	6 13 20 27	6 13 20 27
Mon.	3 10 17 24 31	7 14 21 28	7 14 21 28
Tue.	4 11 18 25	1 8 15 22	1 8 15 22 29
Wed.	5 12 19 26	2 9 16 23	2 9 16 23 30
Thur.	6 13 20 27	3 10 17 24	3 10 17 24 31
Fri.	7 14 21 28	4 11 18 25	4 11 18 25
Sat.	1 8 15 22 29	5 12 19 26	5 12 19 26

	April	May	June
Sun.	3 10 17 24	1 8 15 22 29	5 12 19 26
Mon.	4 11 18 25	2 9 16 23 30	6 13 20 27
Tue.	5 12 19 26	3 10 17 24 31	7 14 21 28
Wed.	6 13 20 27	4 11 18 25	1 8 15 22 29
Thur.	7 14 21 28	5 12 19 26	2 9 16 23 30
Fri.	1 8 15 22 29	6 13 20 27	3 10 17 24
Sat.	2 9 16 23 30	7 14 21 28	4 11 18 25

	July	August	September
Sun.	3 10 17 24 31	7 14 21 28	4 11 18 25
Mon.	4 11 18 25	1 8 15 22 29	5 12 19 26
Tue.	5 12 19 26	2 9 16 23 30	6 13 20 27
Wed.	6 13 20 27	3 10 17 24 31	7 14 21 28
Thur.	7 14 21 28	4 11 18 25	1 8 15 22 29
Fri.	1 8 15 22 29	5 12 19 26	2 9 16 23 30
Sat.	2 9 16 23 30	6 13 20 27	3 10 17 24

	October	November	December
Sun.	2 9 16 23 30	6 13 20 27	4 11 18 25
Mon.	3 10 17 24 31	7 14 21 28	5 12 19 26
Tue.	4 11 18 25	1 8 15 22 29	6 13 20 27
Wed.	5 12 19 26	2 9 16 23 30	7 14 21 28
Thur.	6 13 20 27	3 10 17 24	1 8 15 22 29
Fri.	7 14 21 28	4 11 18 25	2 9 16 23 30
Sat.	1 8 15 22 29	5 12 19 26	3 10 17 24 31

EASTER DAYS
March 27   1785, 1842, 1853, 1910, 1921, 2005
April 3   1825, 1831, 1983, 1994
April 10   1803, 1814, 1887, 1898, 1955, 1966, 1977, 2039
April 17   1870, 1881, 1927, 1938, 1949, 2022, 2033
April 24   1791, 1859, 2011

L (LEAP YEAR)

	January	February	March
Sun.	3 10 17 24 31	7 14 21 28	6 13 20 27
Mon.	4 11 18 25	1 8 15 22 29	7 14 21 28
Tue.	5 12 19 26	2 9 16 23	1 8 15 22 29
Wed.	6 13 20 27	3 10 17 24	2 9 16 23 30
Thur.	7 14 21 28	4 11 18 25	3 10 17 24 31
Fri.	1 8 15 22 29	5 12 19 26	4 11 18 25
Sat.	2 9 16 23 30	6 13 20 27	5 12 19 26

	April	May	June
Sun.	3 10 17 24	1 8 15 22 29	5 12 19 26
Mon.	4 11 18 25	2 9 16 23 30	6 13 20 27
Tue.	5 12 19 26	3 10 17 24 31	7 14 21 28
Wed.	6 13 20 27	4 11 18 25	1 8 15 22 29
Thur.	7 14 21 28	5 12 19 26	2 9 16 23 30
Fri.	1 8 15 22 29	6 13 20 27	3 10 17 24
Sat.	2 9 16 23 30	7 14 21 28	4 11 18 25

	July	August	September
Sun.	3 10 17 24 31	7 14 21 28	4 11 18 25
Mon.	4 11 18 25	1 8 15 22 29	5 12 19 26
Tue.	5 12 19 26	2 9 16 23 30	6 13 20 27
Wed.	6 13 20 27	3 10 17 24 31	7 14 21 28
Thur.	7 14 21 28	4 11 18 25	1 8 15 22 29
Fri.	1 8 15 22 29	5 12 19 26	2 9 16 23 30
Sat.	2 9 16 23 30	6 13 20 27	3 10 17 24

	October	November	December
Sun.	2 9 16 23 30	6 13 20 27	4 11 18 25
Mon.	3 10 17 24 31	7 14 21 28	5 12 19 26
Tue.	4 11 18 25	1 8 15 22 29	6 13 20 27
Wed.	5 12 19 26	2 9 16 23 30	7 14 21 28
Thur.	6 13 20 27	3 10 17 24	1 8 15 22 29
Fri.	7 14 21 28	4 11 18 25	2 9 16 23 30
Sat.	1 8 15 22 29	5 12 19 26	3 10 17 24 31

EASTER DAYS
March 27   1796, 1864, 1932, 2016
April 3   1836, 1904, 1988
April 17   1808, 1892, 1960

N (LEAP YEAR)

	January	February	March
Sun.	2 9 16 23 30	6 13 20 27	5 12 19 26
Mon.	3 10 17 24 31	7 14 21 28	6 13 20 27
Tue.	4 11 18 25	1 8 15 22 29	7 14 21 28
Wed.	5 12 19 26	2 9 16 23	1 8 15 22 29
Thur.	6 13 20 27	3 10 17 24	2 9 16 23 30
Fri.	7 14 21 28	4 11 18 25	3 10 17 24 31
Sat.	1 8 15 22 29	5 12 19 26	4 11 18 25

	April	May	June
Sun.	2 9 16 23 30	7 14 21 28	4 11 18 25
Mon.	3 10 17 24	1 8 15 22 29	5 12 19 26
Tue.	4 11 18 25	2 9 16 23 30	6 13 20 27
Wed.	5 12 19 26	3 10 17 24 31	7 14 21 28
Thur.	6 13 20 27	4 11 18 25	1 8 15 22 29
Fri.	7 14 21 28	5 12 19 26	2 9 16 23 30
Sat.	1 8 15 22 29	6 13 20 27	3 10 17 24

	July	August	September
Sun.	2 9 16 23 30	6 13 20 27	3 10 17 24
Mon.	3 10 17 24 31	7 14 21 28	4 11 18 25
Tue.	4 11 18 25	1 8 15 22 29	5 12 19 26
Wed.	5 12 19 26	2 9 16 23 30	6 13 20 27
Thur.	6 13 20 27	3 10 17 24 31	7 14 21 28
Fri.	7 14 21 28	4 11 18 25	1 8 15 22 29
Sat.	1 8 15 22 29	5 12 19 26	2 9 16 23 30

	October	November	December
Sun.	1 8 15 22 29	5 12 19 26	3 10 17 24 31
Mon.	2 9 16 23 30	6 13 20 27	4 11 18 25
Tue.	3 10 17 24 31	7 14 21 28	5 12 19 26
Wed.	4 11 18 25	1 8 15 22 29	6 13 20 27
Thur.	5 12 19 26	2 9 16 23 30	7 14 21 28
Fri.	6 13 20 27	3 10 17 24	1 8 15 22 29
Sat.	7 14 21 28	4 11 18 25	2 9 16 23 30

EASTER DAYS
March 26   1780
April 2   1820, 1972
April 9   1944
April 16   1876, 2028
April 23   1848, 1916, 2000

GEOLOGICAL TIME

Era	Period	Epoch	Dates*	Evolutionary Stages
Cenozoic	Quaternary	Holocene	11,700 BP†–present	
		Pleistocene	2,588,000–11,700 BP	First humans
	Neogene	Pliocene	5.332–2.588 Mya ‡	} Majority of still existing species
		Miocene	23.03–5.332 Mya	
	Palaeogene	Oligocene	33.9–23.03 Mya	} First modern mammals
		Eocene	55.8–33.9 Mya	
		Palaeocene	65.5–55.8 Mya	
Mesozoic	Cretaceous		145.5–65.5 Mya	
	Jurassic		199.6–145.5 Mya	First birds
	Triassic		251–199.6 Mya	First mammals
Palaeozoic	Permian		299–251 Mya	First reptiles
	Carboniferous		359.2–299 Mya	} First traces of land-living creatures
	Devonian		416–359.2 Mya	
	Silurian		443.7–416 Mya	
	Ordovician		488.3–443.7 Mya	First fish
	Cambrian		542–488.3 Mya	First invertebrates
Precambrian	Proterozoic		2,500–542 Mya	First primitive life forms, eg algae and bacteria
	Archaean		3,800–2,500 Mya	} Earth uninhabited
	Hadean		4,600–3,800 Mya	

* approximate † BP = Before Present (1950 = base year) ‡ Mya = million years ago

PALAEOZOIC ('ANCIENT LIFE')

There were two great phases of mountain building in the Palaeozoic era: the Caledonian, characterised in Britain by NE–SW lines of hills and valleys; and the later Hercynian, widespread in west Germany and adjacent areas, and in Britain exemplified in E–W lines of hills and valleys. The end of the era was marked by the extensive glaciations of the Permian period in the southern continents and the decline of amphibians. It was succeeded by an era of warm conditions.

Cambrian – Mainly sandstones, slate and shales; limestones in Scotland. Shelled fossils and invertebrates, eg trilobites and brachiopods, and the earliest known vertebrates (jawless fish) appear

Ordovician – Mainly shales and mudstones, eg in north Wales; limestones in Scotland. First fish

Silurian – Shales, mudstones and some limestones, found mostly in Wales and southern Scotland

Devonian – Old red sandstone, shale, limestone and slate, eg in south Wales and the West Country

Carboniferous – Coal-bearing rocks, millstone grit, limestone and shale. First traces of land-living creatures

Permian – Marls, sandstones and clays. First reptile fossils

MESOZOIC ('MIDDLE FORMS OF LIFE')

Giant reptiles were dominant during the Mesozoic era; marsupial mammals first appeared, as well as *Archaeopteryx lithographica,* the earliest known species of bird. Coniferous trees and flowering plants also developed and, along with the birds and the mammals, were the main species to survive into the Cenozoic era. The giant reptiles became extinct.

Triassic – Mostly sandstone, eg in the W. Midlands; primitive mammals appear

Jurassic – Mainly limestones and clays, typically displayed in the Jura mountains, and in England in a NE–SW belt from Lincolnshire and the Wash to the Severn and the Dorset coast

Cretaceous – Mainly chalk, clay and sands, eg in Kent and Sussex

CENOZOIC ('RECENT LIFE')

From the Miocene through the Pliocene epochs, the Alpine-Himalayan and the circum-Pacific phases of mountain building reached their climax. During the Pleistocene epoch ice-sheets locked up masses of water as land ice, lowering the sea level by 100–200m. The last glacial retreat, merging into the Holocene period, was c.11,700 BP.

Palaeocene/ Eocene – Emergence of new forms of life, including existing species; primates appear

Oligocene – Fossils of a few still existing species

Miocene – Fossils show a balance of existing and extinct species

Piliocene/ Pleistocene – Fossils show a majority of still existing species

Holocene – The present, post-glacial period. Existing species only, except for a few exterminated by humans

HUMAN DEVELOPMENT

All members of the human race belong to one species of animal, *Homo sapiens,* the definition of a species being in biological terms that its members can interbreed and produce viable offspring. As a species of mammal it is possible to group humans with other similar types, known as the primates. Among these is found a sub-group, the apes, which includes, in addition to humans, the chimpanzees, gorillas, orangutans and gibbons. All lack a tail, have shoulder blades at the back, and a Y-shaped chewing pattern on the surface of their molars, as well as showing the more general primate characteristics of four incisors, a thumb which is able to touch the fingers of the same hand, and finger and toe nails instead of claws. However, there once lived creatures, now extinct, which were closer to modern man than the chimpanzees and gorillas and which shared modern man's characteristics: flat faces (ie the absence of a pronounced muzzle), being bipedal, and possessing large brains.

Debate surrounding evidence for the oldest human ancestors is ongoing. The earliest putative hominin for which there is significant fossil evidence is *Ardipithecus ramidus,* for which an almost complete skeleton, dating to at least 4.4 million years ago (Mya), was discovered in the Afar Rift, Ethiopia in 1992. Analysis of the skeleton suggests the creature had both human and ape characteristics; the ability to climb trees and walk on two feet.

The subsequent Australopithecines have left more numerous remains in south and east Africa, among which sub-groups may be detected. Living between about 4.2 and 2.0 Mya, they were relatives of modern humans in the respect that they walked upright, did not have an extensive muzzle and had similar types of pre-molars. The first australopithecine remains were recognised at Taung in South Africa in 1924 and named *Australopithecus africanus,* dating between 3.3 and 2.3 Mya. The most impressive discovery was made at Hadar, Ethiopia, in 1974 when about half a skeleton of *Australopithecus afarensis,* known as 'Lucy', was found. Some 3.2 Mya, 'Lucy' (who is now considered to be male) certainly walked upright. Lomekwi 3, a site in Kenya, has recently produced stone tools that date back to 3.3 Mya. These are judged most likely to have been manufactured by an australopithecine known as *Kenyanthropus platyops,* which had a brain size comparable to a modern chimpanzee. This discovery means that the emergence of modified stone technology can now be associated with hominins in general, rather than being a specifically human trait. It also means that the beginning of the Palaeolithic – or Old Stone Age – which commences with the appearance of stone technology, has also been pushed back to 3.3 Mya.

Homo handiwork can still be discerned in the creation of Oldowan stone tools, which first appeared about 2.6 Mya. The most famous site associated with these implements is Olduvai Gorge in Tanzania. There, and elsewhere in east Africa, lived a hominin group between 2.6 and 1.5 Mya, which walked upright, had a flat face, and a large brain case. Due to their distinctive characteristics, they have been grouped as a separate sub-species, now extinct, of the genus *Homo* and are known as *Homo habilis* or 'handy man'. Also during this period hominins seem to have begun expanding into the world beyond Africa, with stone tools from Shangchen in China recently dated to as far back as 2.1 Mya.

The use of fire is traditionally associated with another group of extinct hominins dating to about 1.8 Mya, whose remains are found in south and east Africa, China, Indonesia, north Africa and Europe. *Homo ergaster* in Africa and *Homo erectus* in Asia are the names given to this group of fossils and they relate to a number of famous individual discoveries, eg Solo Man, Heidelberg Man, and especially Peking Man who lived at the cave site at Choukoutien, which has yielded possible evidence of the controlled use of fire, although its interpretation is contested.

The well-known group the Neanderthals, or *Homo neanderthalensis,* is an extinct human species that appeared over 430,000 years ago and survived until c.40,000 years ago, spanning the last Ice Age and living alongside modern humans. The Neanderthals' ability to adapt to the cold climate on the edge of the ice-sheets is one of their characteristic features, with remains found only in Europe, Asia and the Middle East. Complete Neanderthal skeletons were discovered during excavations at Tabun in Israel, together with evidence of tool-making and the use of fire. Experiments with replica 300,000-year-old spears found in Schöningen, Germany, demonstrated they functioned as effective javelins, with an accurate range of about 20m. Neanderthals were distinguished by very large brains, and it seems that they developed recognisable social customs, including mortuary rites. Why the Neanderthals became extinct is not clear, but it may be connected with climatic change at the end of the Ice Ages, which would have disrupted their food supplies, or finding themselves in direct competition with *Homo sapiens* for such resources. One fascinating discovery is that a piece of bone recovered in Russia in 2012 and dating back about 90,000 years, contains a genome sequence revealing that the mother was a Neanderthal, while the father belonged to a different hominin group: the Denisovans.

As for *Homo sapiens,* current research is moving away from the traditional model of a single ancestor population living somewhere in Africa. Instead, different characteristics and tools appear to have emerged in different regions at different times within Africa. It is possible that this is a product of the dynamic African climate, which would periodically cut off groups, promoting periods of local adaptation. This was followed by opportunities to exchange genetic material when the climate became more amenable and these groups were reunited. Fossils found in Morocco seemingly push the appearance of early *Homo sapiens* back to around 300,000 years ago. In England, the shin bone of Boxgrove Man found in 1993 – *Homo heidelbergensis* – and the Swanscombe skull are the best known early human fossil remains. Some specialists prefer to group Swanscombe Man (or, more probably, woman) together with the Steinheim skull from Germany, seeing both as a separate sub-species.

Anatomically modern humans – *Homo sapiens sapiens* ('doubly wise man') – had evolved to our present physical condition and had colonised much of the world by about 40,000 years ago. There are many previously distinguished individual specimens, eg Cromagnon Man, the first early *Homo sapiens sapiens* of the European Upper Palaeolithic.

Discovery of the structure of DNA in 1953 has come to have a profound effect upon the study of human evolution. For example, it was claimed in 1987 that a common ancestor of all human beings was a person who lived in Africa some 200,000 years ago, thus encouraging the 'out of Africa' theory of migration from east Africa to the Middle East and then throughout the world. Today, DNA analyses are ensuring that the field of human evolution is a fast-moving subject.

CULTURAL DEVELOPMENT

The Three Age system, whereby prehistory was divided into a Stone Age, a Bronze Age and an Iron Age, was devised by Christian Thomsen, curator of the National Museum of Denmark in the early 19th century, to facilitate the classification of the museum's collections. The adjectives referred to the materials from which implements and weapons were made and came to be regarded as the dominant features of the societies to which they related. The Three Age system remains a generally accepted concept in the popular mind. However, it is now seen by archaeologists as an inadequate model for human development. Common sense suggests that there were no complete breaks between one so-called Age and another, although DNA evidence is increasingly pointing to the arrival of Neolithic and Bronze Age technologies in Britain being accompanied by a broader shift in the genetic ancestry of the population, suggesting movement of people on a significant scale. It should also be noted that the Three Age system cannot be applied globally. In some areas it is necessary to insert a Copper Age, while in South Africa there seems to be no Bronze Age at all; in Australia, Old Stone Age societies survived, while in South America, New Stone Age communities exist into modern times.

The concept of the 'Neolithic revolution', associated with the domestication of plants and animals, was a development of particular importance in the human cultural pattern. It reflected a gradual change from hunter-gatherer economies to a more settled agricultural way of life and therefore, so the argument goes, made possible the development of urban civilisation. It appears that the cultivation of wheat and barley was first undertaken, together with the domestication of cattle and goats/sheep, around 10,000 years ago in the Fertile Crescent (the area bounded by the rivers Tigris and Euphrates). There is evidence that sorghum was first domesticated in Africa, rice was first deliberately planted and pigs domesticated in South East Asia, maize first cultivated in Central America and llamas first domesticated in South America. Cultural change took place independently in different parts of the world at different rates and times.

The Neolithic period of cultural development has been difficult to date reliably because it took place long before writing was invented. With the development and refinement of radiocarbon dating and other scientific methods of producing absolute chronologies, it may eventually be possible to obtain a much tighter chronological framework, in terms of years, against which the cultural development of any particular area may be set.

TIDES AND TIDAL PREDICTIONS

Tides are the periodic rise and fall of the sea-level caused mainly by the gravitational pull of the Moon and the Sun. This generates the tide raising force (TRF), of which the Moon accounts for around 70 per cent and the Sun 30 per cent. When the Moon and the Sun are in line with the Earth they are said to be 'in conjunction' or syzygy and their TRFs combine. This produces the largest rise and fall of the tide, known as spring tides; they occur each month just after a full or new Moon. This is amplified, about once every 18 months, when coincident with the Moon at perigee (its closest point to the Earth); giving rise to very high proxigean tides. The opposite effect, just after the Moon's first and last quarters, when the Sun and Moon are at an angle of 90°, produces neap tides, with a relatively small tidal range between high and low water. There is an 18.6-year interval between the astronomical conditions – the Sun and Moon aligning with the Earth at perigee with zero declination – which generates the maximum TRF. Within this cycle there are times when zero solar declination (equinox) and lunar perigee occur almost simultaneously with zero lunar declination. This will next occur on 8 April 2020.

A lunar day is about 24 hours and 50 minutes, giving two complete tidal cycles, with about 12 hours, 25 minutes between successive high waters. These are known as semi-diurnal tides and are applicable in the Atlantic Ocean and around the coasts of north-west Europe. Other parts of the world have diurnal tides, with only one high water and one low water each (lunar) day, or mixed tides which are partly diurnal and partly semi-diurnal.

Land and seabed conditions influence the tides locally. Owing to resonance created by the narrowing funnel of the English Channel as the tide rises, double high waters occur between Swanage and Selsey Bill on the south coast of England and low water is much more sharply defined than high water. Tides can also be greatly affected by the Coriolis force, which is induced by the Earth's rotation and, in the northern hemisphere, tends to deflect any moving object to the right. Thus, the easterly flood tidal stream in the English Channel is deflected towards the French coast causing higher high waters; on the ebb the opposite happens – lower low waters. This, coupled with local geography, means that the mean spring range of the tide at St Malo is nearly 11m while the range on the English coast at Portland, 120 miles to the north, is a mere 2m.

Meteorological conditions such as prolonged strong winds and unusually high (or low) atmospheric pressure can significantly lower (or raise) the height of the tide; the drag of the wind alone (wind stress) can affect the predicted times of high and low water by as much as an hour. Variation of pressure by 34 millibars from the norm can cause a height difference of 0.3m.

STORM SURGES AND SEICHES
On the east and west coasts of the UK there are about 20 events each year when surge levels exceed 0.6m. The semicentennial surge is 1m in the Hebrides and at Land's End and up to 3m in the Thames estuary. Infrequently, surge peaks coincide with high water; the North Sea and Thames estuary experience the most profound effects, often when a deep depression tracks south–easterly across the UK. Negative surges occur when strong southerly winds in the North Sea lower tidal levels by 2m below prediction in these areas and the Dover Strait. Intense minor depressions, line squalls, or other abrupt changes in the weather can cause wave oscillations known as seiches. The wave period of a seiche varies from minutes to two hours,

with heights of up to a metre. Wick on the north-east coast of Scotland and Fishguard in south-west Wales are particularly prone to these.

TIDAL STREAMS
Tidal streams are the horizontal movements of water caused by the rise and fall of the tide. They normally change direction about every six hours. Tidal streams should not be confused with ocean currents, such as the Gulf Stream, which run continuously in the same direction. The rate, or set, of the stream at any particular place is proportional to the range of the tide. Thus, the rate during spring tides is greater than that at neaps. In the central English Channel the maximum spring rate is nearly 5 knots while the neap rate at the same position is just 3 knots. As with tidal heights, local geography plays a significant role in the rate of the tidal stream. In the narrow waters of the Pentland Firth between mainland Scotland and the Orkney Islands, rates of 16 knots have been recorded.

The tidal stream does not necessarily turn at the same time as high or low water. In the English Channel the stream turns at approximately high and low water at Dover. However, high water at Dover is at about the same time as low water at Plymouth, and vice versa.

Around the UK, the main flood tidal stream sets eastward up the English Channel, north-east into the Bristol Channel, and north up the west coasts of Ireland and Scotland. However, the flood sets south-east through the North Channel and south into the Irish Sea, where it meets the northerly flood through St George's Channel at the Isle of Man. Off the east coasts of Scotland and England the stream sets south as far as the Thames estuary before meeting the north-going stream from the eastern part of the Dover Strait.

DEFINITIONS
Highest Astronomical Tide (HAT) and **Lowest Astronomical Tide (LAT)** are the highest and lowest tide levels predicted to occur under average meteorological, and any combination of astronomical, conditions. For a given area, **Chart Datum (CD)** is the level, as close as possible to LAT, below which charted depths are given. It is also the reference for tidal predictions: the total depth at a given time being equal to the charted depth plus the height of the tide. **Ordnance Datum (OD)** at Newlyn is the datum level of land survey on mainland England, Scotland and Wales, from which heights on UK land maps are measured. CD depends on the tidal range and varies around the UK from about 5m above OD to 6.5m below. **Duration** of the tide is the interval between low water and the next high water. It can be used to calculate the approximate time of low water when only the time of high water is known. **Mean Sea Level (MSL or ML)** is the average level of the sea's surface over a long period, normally observed over 18.6 years. The **Range** of the tide is the difference in height between successive high and low waters. It is greatest at spring tides, least at neaps. The range may be indicated by **Tidal Coefficients** which are proportional to, but not the same as, the range on a particular day. A coefficient of 95 indicates an average spring tide; 45 is an average neap tide.

TIDAL PREDICTIONS
The following data gives the daily GMT and height of high water at four ports. When BST applies the one hour time difference should be added. The datum of predictions is the difference of height, in metres, of CD from OD.

Compiled with the assistance of Chris Stevens and Perrin Towler. Tidal predictions © Crown Copyright and/or database rights. Reproduced by permission of the Controller of HM Stationery Office and the UK Hydrographic Office (W www.gov.uk/ukho).

JANUARY 2020 *High Water* GMT

	LONDON BRIDGE Datum of Predictions 3.2m below				LIVERPOOL (Gladstone Dock) Datum of Predictions 4.93 below				GREENOCK Datum of Predictions 1.62 below				LEITH Datum of Predictions 2.90 below			
	hr	ht m	hr	ht m	hr	ht m	hr	ht m	hr	ht m	hr	ht m	hr	ht m	hr	ht m
W 1	05 12	6.3	17 42	6.3	02 36	8.0	14 55	8.3	04 05	3.1	16 16	3.4	06 33	4.8	18 40	4.8
Th 2	05 47	6.1	18 20	6.1	03 21	7.7	15 44	7.9	04 50	3.1	16 59	3.3	07 18	4.6	19 27	4.7
F 3	06 25	6.0	19 04	5.9	04 13	7.3	16 40	7.6	05 38	3.0	17 48	3.1	08 08	4.4	20 22	4.5
Sa 4	07 14	5.8	20 04	5.7	05 14	7.1	17 44	7.5	06 30	2.9	18 45	3.0	09 03	4.4	21 22	4.5
Su 5	08 27	5.6	21 16	5.7	06 23	7.2	18 49	7.5	07 31	2.9	19 50	3.0	10 03	4.4	22 24	4.5
M 6	09 49	5.8	22 22	5.9	07 29	7.4	19 50	7.7	08 38	3.0	21 00	3.0	11 04	4.5	23 26	4.6
Tu 7	10 52	6.1	23 23	6.2	08 25	7.8	20 44	8.1	09 42	3.1	22 02	3.1	12 02	4.7	-	-
W 8	11 49	6.4	-	-	09 13	8.2	21 32	8.4	10 34	3.2	22 56	3.2	00 23	4.8	12 55	5.0
Th 9	00 19	6.5	12 41	6.7	09 56	8.6	22 17	8.8	11 19	3.4	23 44	3.3	01 15	5.0	13 41	5.2
F 10	01 10	6.7	13 29	7.0	10 38	9.0	23 00	9.1	11 59	3.5	-	-	02 00	5.3	14 22	5.4
Sa 11	01 56	6.8	14 15	7.1	11 20	9.3	23 44	9.3	00 31	3.3	12 39	3.6	02 43	5.5	15 02	5.5
Su 12	02 41	6.9	15 00	7.3	12 03	9.5	-	-	01 17	3.4	13 20	3.7	03 25	5.6	15 42	5.6
M 13	03 25	7.0	15 45	7.3	00 29	9.4	12 48	9.5	02 03	3.4	14 02	3.8	04 08	5.7	16 23	5.7
Tu 14	04 07	7.0	16 30	7.3	01 16	9.3	13 34	9.5	02 48	3.4	14 45	3.9	04 53	5.6	17 08	5.6
W 15	04 49	6.9	17 16	7.1	02 03	9.2	14 23	9.3	03 34	3.4	15 30	3.8	05 41	5.5	17 55	5.5
Th 16	05 33	6.8	18 05	6.9	02 53	8.9	15 14	9.0	04 22	3.3	16 16	3.7	06 31	5.3	18 48	5.3
F 17	06 20	6.7	18 59	6.7	03 46	8.5	16 11	8.7	05 11	3.2	17 06	3.6	07 27	5.1	19 49	5.1
Sa 18	07 15	6.5	20 00	6.5	04 46	8.2	17 15	8.3	06 06	3.1	18 02	3.4	08 31	4.9	21 00	5.0
Su 19	08 21	6.4	21 04	6.3	05 54	7.9	18 26	8.1	07 12	3.0	19 08	3.2	09 38	4.8	22 11	4.9
M 20	09 31	6.4	22 11	6.3	07 07	7.9	19 39	8.1	08 31	3.0	20 32	3.1	10 45	4.8	23 20	4.9
Tu 21	10 41	6.4	23 22	6.3	08 16	8.1	20 46	8.2	09 44	3.1	21 54	3.1	11 51	4.9	-	-
W 22	11 49	6.5	-	-	09 15	8.4	21 43	8.5	10 42	3.2	22 58	3.2	00 25	5.0	12 51	5.0
Th 23	00 26	6.5	12 49	6.7	10 05	8.7	22 32	8.7	11 31	3.4	23 51	3.2	01 23	5.1	13 41	5.2
F 24	01 19	6.6	13 39	6.9	10 49	9.0	23 15	8.8	12 15	3.5	-	-	02 11	5.3	14 25	5.3
Sa 25	02 04	6.7	14 23	7.0	11 28	9.1	23 53	8.9	00 37	3.3	12 55	3.6	02 54	5.3	15 06	5.4
Su 26	02 43	6.8	15 03	7.0	12 05	9.2	-	-	01 18	3.2	13 32	3.6	03 34	5.3	15 43	5.4
M 27	03 18	6.8	15 39	6.9	00 27	8.8	12 39	9.2	01 54	3.2	14 06	3.6	04 10	5.3	16 18	5.4
Tu 28	03 50	6.8	16 11	6.8	01 00	8.7	13 12	9.0	02 28	3.2	14 40	3.6	04 45	5.2	16 52	5.3
W 29	04 20	6.7	16 42	6.7	01 32	8.6	13 46	8.8	03 03	3.2	15 14	3.5	05 20	5.1	17 26	5.2
Th 30	04 51	6.6	17 13	6.5	02 05	8.3	14 21	8.6	03 39	3.2	15 49	3.5	05 56	4.9	18 02	5.0
F 31	05 22	6.5	17 45	6.3	02 39	8.1	14 57	8.2	04 16	3.2	16 26	3.3	06 36	4.7	18 42	4.8

FEBRUARY 2020 *High Water* GMT

	LONDON BRIDGE				LIVERPOOL (Gladstone Dock)				GREENOCK				LEITH			
Sa 1	05 55	6.3	18 21	6.1	03 18	7.7	15 39	7.9	04 55	3.1	17 07	3.2	07 18	4.6	19 26	4.6
Su 2	06 33	6.1	19 03	5.9	04 04	7.4	16 32	7.5	05 37	3.0	17 55	3.0	08 08	4.4	20 21	4.5
M 3	07 21	5.9	20 02	5.7	05 05	7.1	17 41	7.3	06 27	2.9	18 53	2.9	09 07	4.3	21 28	4.4
Tu 4	08 30	5.7	21 29	5.7	06 22	7.1	18 58	7.3	07 28	2.8	20 04	2.8	10 13	4.3	22 40	4.4
W 5	10 04	5.8	22 45	5.9	07 39	7.4	20 09	7.6	08 46	2.9	21 25	2.9	11 21	4.5	23 50	4.6
Th 6	11 15	6.2	23 52	6.3	08 42	7.9	21 08	8.1	09 59	3.0	22 35	3.0	12 25	4.8	-	-
F 7	12 16	6.6	-	-	09 34	8.4	22 00	8.6	10 53	3.2	23 31	3.2	00 51	4.9	13 19	5.1
Sa 8	00 50	6.6	13 11	7.0	10 21	9.0	22 47	9.1	11 40	3.4	-	-	01 42	5.2	14 04	5.4
Su 9	01 41	6.9	14 01	7.2	11 06	9.4	23 32	9.5	00 20	3.3	12 23	3.6	02 27	5.5	14 45	5.6
M 10	02 27	7.0	14 47	7.4	11 50	9.7	-	-	01 07	3.3	13 07	3.7	03 09	5.7	15 26	5.8
Tu 11	03 11	7.2	15 32	7.5	00 16	9.7	12 35	9.9	01 53	3.4	13 50	3.8	03 52	5.9	16 07	5.9
W 12	03 53	7.3	16 17	7.5	01 01	9.7	13 19	9.9	02 37	3.4	14 34	3.9	04 36	5.8	16 51	5.9
Th 13	04 35	7.3	17 00	7.3	01 45	9.5	14 04	9.7	03 20	3.4	15 18	3.9	05 21	5.7	17 37	5.8
F 14	05 16	7.2	17 45	7.0	02 30	9.2	14 50	9.3	04 01	3.4	16 02	3.8	06 09	5.4	18 27	5.5
Sa 15	05 59	7.0	18 33	6.7	03 18	8.7	15 41	8.8	04 43	3.3	16 46	3.6	07 00	5.1	19 24	5.2
Su 16	06 48	6.7	19 27	6.4	04 11	8.2	16 41	8.2	05 27	3.1	17 34	3.4	07 59	4.8	20 33	4.9
M 17	07 48	6.5	20 30	6.1	05 17	7.8	17 56	7.7	06 20	2.9	18 29	3.1	09 06	4.6	21 48	4.7
Tu 18	08 59	6.2	21 41	5.9	06 37	7.5	19 21	7.6	07 38	2.8	19 52	2.8	10 18	4.5	23 05	4.6
W 19	10 17	6.1	23 02	6.0	07 57	7.7	20 38	7.8	09 21	2.9	21 53	2.8	11 34	4.6	-	-
Th 20	11 35	6.3	-	-	09 03	8.1	21 37	8.1	10 27	3.1	22 57	3.0	00 20	4.8	12 43	4.8
F 21	00 13	6.3	12 39	6.6	09 54	8.5	22 24	8.5	11 17	3.3	23 47	3.1	01 19	5.0	13 35	5.0
Sa 22	01 07	6.5	13 28	6.8	10 36	8.8	23 02	8.7	12 01	3.4	-	-	02 05	5.1	14 16	5.2
Su 23	01 50	6.7	14 10	6.9	11 13	9.0	23 36	8.8	00 29	3.1	12 41	3.5	02 43	5.2	14 52	5.3
M 24	02 28	6.8	14 47	6.9	11 46	9.2	-	-	01 05	3.2	13 17	3.5	03 16	5.3	15 25	5.4
Tu 25	03 00	6.8	15 19	6.9	00 07	8.9	12 18	9.2	01 36	3.2	13 49	3.5	03 48	5.3	15 56	5.4
W 26	03 29	6.9	15 47	6.8	00 36	8.9	12 48	9.1	02 06	3.2	14 19	3.5	04 18	5.2	16 26	5.3
Th 27	03 57	6.9	16 14	6.8	01 05	8.8	13 18	9.0	02 37	3.2	14 50	3.5	04 50	5.2	16 58	5.3
F 28	04 26	6.8	16 42	6.6	01 34	8.6	13 48	8.8	03 08	3.3	15 22	3.4	05 23	5.0	17 31	5.1
Sa 29	04 55	6.7	17 12	6.4	02 03	8.4	14 19	8.5	03 41	3.3	15 56	3.3	05 58	4.9	18 06	4.9

MARCH 2020 *High Water* GMT

		LONDON BRIDGE Datum of Predictions 3.2m below				LIVERPOOL (Gladstone Dock) Datum of Predictions 4.93 below				GREENOCK Datum of Predictions 1.62 below				LEITH Datum of Predictions 2.90 below			
		hr	ht m	hr	ht m	hr	ht m	hr	ht m	hr	ht m	hr	ht m	hr	ht m	hr	ht m
Su	1	05 26	6.5	17 45	6.2	02 35	8.1	14 54	8.1	04 14	3.2	16 33	3.2	06 36	4.7	18 46	4.7
M	2	06 01	6.3	18 24	6.0	03 13	7.7	15 38	7.7	04 51	3.1	17 16	3.0	07 20	4.5	19 35	4.5
Tu	3	06 45	6.1	19 14	5.7	04 04	7.3	16 42	7.3	05 33	2.9	18 10	2.8	08 14	4.3	20 38	4.3
W	4	07 42	5.8	20 30	5.5	05 23	7.1	18 11	7.1	06 27	2.8	19 21	2.7	09 24	4.2	21 58	4.3
Th	5	09 15	5.8	22 07	5.7	06 55	7.2	19 38	7.4	07 45	2.7	20 56	2.7	10 43	4.3	23 19	4.5
F	6	10 43	6.1	23 24	6.1	08 12	7.7	20 47	8.0	09 20	2.9	22 21	2.9	11 56	4.6	-	-
Sa	7	11 52	6.6	-	-	09 12	8.4	21 42	8.7	10 28	3.1	23 18	3.1	00 28	4.9	12 55	5.0
Su	8	00 27	6.5	12 51	7.0	10 02	9.0	22 30	9.2	11 18	3.3	-	-	01 22	5.3	13 42	5.4
M	9	01 20	6.9	13 42	7.3	10 47	9.6	23 14	9.7	00 06	3.3	12 05	3.5	02 07	5.6	14 24	5.7
Tu	10	02 07	7.2	14 29	7.5	11 31	10.0	23 58	9.9	00 52	3.3	12 50	3.7	02 49	5.8	15 05	5.9
W	11	02 50	7.4	15 13	7.5	12 15	10.1	-	-	01 36	3.4	13 35	3.8	03 31	6.0	15 47	6.1
Th	12	03 32	7.5	15 56	7.5	00 40	9.9	12 58	10.1	02 17	3.4	14 19	3.8	04 14	5.9	16 31	6.0
F	13	04 13	7.5	16 39	7.3	01 23	9.7	13 41	9.8	02 57	3.5	15 02	3.8	04 58	5.7	17 17	5.9
Sa	14	04 54	7.4	17 21	7.0	02 05	9.3	14 25	9.3	03 35	3.4	15 44	3.7	05 44	5.5	18 07	5.5
Su	15	05 36	7.1	18 05	6.6	02 49	8.8	15 13	8.7	04 13	3.3	16 26	3.5	06 33	5.1	19 03	5.2
M	16	06 23	6.8	18 53	6.2	03 40	8.2	16 12	8.0	04 53	3.2	17 10	3.2	07 29	4.8	20 11	4.8
Tu	17	07 19	6.4	19 52	5.9	04 45	7.7	17 30	7.4	05 39	2.9	18 01	2.9	08 36	4.5	21 26	4.5
W	18	08 30	6.0	21 08	5.7	06 08	7.3	19 03	7.2	06 43	2.7	19 14	2.6	09 51	4.3	22 47	4.4
Th	19	09 52	5.9	22 36	5.7	07 34	7.5	20 25	7.5	08 53	2.7	21 48	2.7	11 12	4.4	-	-
F	20	11 16	6.1	23 51	6.1	08 44	7.9	21 23	7.9	10 05	3.0	22 45	2.9	00 08	4.6	12 26	4.7
Sa	21	12 20	6.5	-	-	09 34	8.3	22 06	8.3	10 55	3.2	23 29	3.0	01 06	4.8	13 17	4.9
Su	22	00 44	6.4	13 08	6.8	10 14	8.7	22 41	8.6	11 38	3.3	-	-	01 48	5.0	13 57	5.1
M	23	01 27	6.6	13 48	6.8	10 49	8.9	23 12	8.8	00 07	3.1	12 18	3.4	02 23	5.2	14 31	5.2
Tu	24	02 02	6.8	14 22	6.8	11 20	9.1	23 40	8.9	00 41	3.1	12 53	3.4	02 53	5.2	15 01	5.3
W	25	02 34	6.9	14 51	6.8	11 51	9.1	-	-	01 10	3.2	13 25	3.4	03 21	5.3	15 30	5.3
Th	26	03 02	6.9	15 17	6.8	00 08	8.9	12 21	9.1	01 38	3.2	13 54	3.4	03 50	5.3	16 00	5.3
F	27	03 30	7.0	15 44	6.8	00 36	8.9	12 50	9.0	02 07	3.3	14 23	3.4	04 20	5.2	16 31	5.3
Sa	28	03 59	6.9	16 12	6.7	01 04	8.8	13 19	8.8	02 36	3.3	14 55	3.3	04 52	5.1	17 03	5.1
Su	29	04 29	6.8	16 43	6.5	01 32	8.5	13 49	8.5	03 07	3.4	15 29	3.3	05 26	5.0	17 39	5.0
M	30	05 01	6.6	17 16	6.3	02 03	8.3	14 24	8.2	03 39	3.3	16 06	3.2	06 02	4.8	18 19	4.8
Tu	31	05 36	6.4	17 54	6.1	02 40	8.0	15 09	7.8	04 13	3.2	16 48	3.0	06 43	4.6	19 07	4.6

APRIL 2020 *High Water* GMT

		LONDON BRIDGE				LIVERPOOL (Gladstone Dock)				GREENOCK				LEITH			
W	1	06 19	6.2	18 42	5.8	03 30	7.6	16 11	7.4	04 52	3.0	17 40	2.8	07 34	4.4	20 07	4.4
Th	2	07 16	6.0	19 52	5.6	04 46	7.2	17 39	7.2	05 43	2.9	18 52	2.6	08 43	4.3	21 27	4.4
F	3	08 42	5.9	21 31	5.6	06 22	7.3	19 10	7.4	06 56	2.8	20 35	2.7	10 08	4.3	22 51	4.5
Sa	4	10 13	6.1	22 53	6.1	07 43	7.8	20 23	8.1	08 41	2.8	22 03	2.9	11 25	4.6	-	-
Su	5	11 25	6.6	23 59	6.5	08 45	8.4	21 19	8.7	09 59	3.1	22 58	3.1	00 01	4.9	12 26	5.0
M	6	12 26	7.0	-	-	09 37	9.1	22 07	9.3	10 53	3.3	23 45	3.3	00 57	5.3	13 15	5.4
Tu	7	00 53	6.9	13 18	7.3	10 24	9.6	22 52	9.7	11 41	3.5	-	-	01 42	5.6	13 58	5.8
W	8	01 41	7.2	14 05	7.4	11 08	10.0	23 34	9.9	00 29	3.4	12 29	3.6	02 25	5.8	14 41	6.0
Th	9	02 24	7.5	14 49	7.5	11 52	10.1	-	-	01 12	3.4	13 15	3.7	03 07	5.9	15 25	6.1
F	10	03 07	7.6	15 32	7.4	00 16	9.9	12 36	10.0	01 53	3.5	14 00	3.7	03 51	5.9	16 11	6.0
Sa	11	03 49	7.6	16 14	7.2	00 58	9.7	13 19	9.7	02 31	3.5	14 43	3.7	04 35	5.7	16 59	5.8
Su	12	04 31	7.5	16 56	6.9	01 40	9.3	14 03	9.1	03 08	3.5	15 25	3.6	05 21	5.4	17 50	5.5
M	13	05 14	7.1	17 37	6.5	02 24	8.8	14 51	8.5	03 46	3.4	16 07	3.4	06 09	5.1	18 47	5.1
Tu	14	06 00	6.7	18 22	6.1	03 13	8.2	15 48	7.8	04 25	3.2	16 52	3.1	07 04	4.8	19 51	4.7
W	15	06 53	6.3	19 16	5.7	04 17	7.7	17 04	7.2	05 11	3.0	17 43	2.8	08 09	4.5	21 01	4.4
Th	16	08 02	5.9	20 30	5.5	05 37	7.3	18 35	7.1	06 10	2.8	18 58	2.5	09 22	4.3	22 18	4.4
F	17	09 20	5.8	21 55	5.6	07 00	7.4	19 56	7.3	08 08	2.7	21 19	2.6	10 39	4.4	23 38	4.5
Sa	18	10 40	6.0	23 12	5.9	08 09	7.7	20 53	7.8	09 31	2.9	22 14	2.8	11 52	4.5	-	-
Su	19	11 47	6.3	-	-	09 01	8.1	21 35	8.2	10 23	3.1	22 56	3.0	00 37	4.7	12 46	4.8
M	20	00 09	6.3	12 37	6.6	09 42	8.5	22 10	8.5	11 07	3.2	23 33	3.1	01 19	4.9	13 26	5.0
Tu	21	00 53	6.5	13 16	6.7	10 17	8.7	22 41	8.7	11 46	3.3	-	-	01 53	5.1	14 01	5.1
W	22	01 29	6.7	13 50	6.7	10 50	8.9	23 10	8.8	00 06	3.2	12 23	3.3	02 23	5.2	14 32	5.2
Th	23	02 02	6.9	14 19	6.8	11 21	9.0	23 39	8.9	00 38	3.2	12 55	3.3	02 52	5.2	15 02	5.3
F	24	02 32	7.0	14 47	6.8	11 52	9.0	-	-	01 08	3.3	13 25	3.3	03 21	5.3	15 34	5.3
Sa	25	03 02	7.0	15 15	6.8	00 08	8.9	12 24	8.9	01 37	3.4	13 56	3.3	03 53	5.2	16 06	5.2
Su	26	03 32	7.0	15 47	6.7	00 37	8.8	12 55	8.7	02 06	3.4	14 29	3.3	04 25	5.2	16 41	5.2
M	27	04 05	6.9	16 20	6.5	01 08	8.7	13 29	8.5	02 37	3.5	15 06	3.2	04 59	5.0	17 18	5.0
Tu	28	04 40	6.7	16 55	6.3	01 42	8.4	14 07	8.2	03 10	3.4	15 45	3.1	05 36	4.9	18 00	4.9
W	29	05 19	6.6	17 34	6.1	02 22	8.1	14 55	7.9	03 46	3.3	16 29	3.0	06 18	4.7	18 50	4.7
Th	30	06 05	6.4	18 25	5.9	03 16	7.8	15 58	7.5	04 26	3.2	17 23	2.8	07 10	4.5	19 50	4.6

MAY 2020 *High Water* GMT

		LONDON BRIDGE Datum of Predictions 3.2m below				LIVERPOOL (Gladstone Dock) Datum of Predictions 4.93 below				GREENOCK Datum of Predictions 1.62 below				LEITH Datum of Predictions 2.90 below			
		hr m	ht m	hr m	ht m	hr m	ht m	hr m	ht m	hr m	ht m	hr m	ht m	hr m	ht m	hr m	ht m
F	1	07 03	6.2	19 32	5.7	04 30	7.5	17 20	7.4	05 16	3.0	18 35	2.7	08 16	4.4	21 05	4.5
Sa	2	08 24	6.1	21 02	5.8	05 56	7.6	18 43	7.7	06 26	2.9	20 12	2.7	09 38	4.5	22 23	4.7
Su	3	09 47	6.3	22 21	6.2	07 12	8.0	19 54	8.2	08 07	2.9	21 35	2.9	10 53	4.7	23 32	5.0
M	4	10 56	6.7	23 27	6.6	08 16	8.6	20 52	8.8	09 27	3.1	22 30	3.1	11 54	5.1	-	-
Tu	5	11 58	7.0	-	-	09 10	9.1	21 41	9.2	10 25	3.3	23 18	3.3	00 28	5.3	12 46	5.4
W	6	00 23	7.0	12 52	7.2	09 58	9.5	22 27	9.6	11 16	3.5	-	-	01 16	5.6	13 33	5.7
Th	7	01 13	7.3	13 40	7.3	10 45	9.8	23 10	9.7	00 03	3.4	12 06	3.6	02 00	5.7	14 18	5.9
F	8	01 59	7.5	14 25	7.3	11 30	9.8	23 53	9.7	00 46	3.4	12 54	3.6	02 44	5.8	15 05	6.0
Sa	9	02 43	7.6	15 09	7.2	12 15	9.7	-	-	01 27	3.5	13 40	3.6	03 28	5.8	15 54	5.9
Su	10	03 27	7.6	15 51	7.1	00 36	9.6	13 00	9.3	02 06	3.5	14 25	3.5	04 14	5.6	16 43	5.6
M	11	04 11	7.4	16 33	6.8	01 19	9.2	13 45	8.9	02 44	3.5	15 08	3.4	05 00	5.4	17 35	5.3
Tu	12	04 55	7.0	17 14	6.4	02 03	8.8	14 32	8.3	03 23	3.4	15 51	3.2	05 49	5.1	18 29	5.0
W	13	05 41	6.6	17 56	6.1	02 51	8.3	15 26	7.7	04 03	3.3	16 38	3.0	06 43	4.8	19 28	4.7
Th	14	06 31	6.2	18 44	5.8	03 50	7.8	16 33	7.3	04 49	3.1	17 30	2.8	07 42	4.6	20 29	4.5
F	15	07 31	5.9	19 49	5.6	05 00	7.5	17 49	7.1	05 46	2.9	18 38	2.6	08 47	4.4	21 35	4.4
Sa	16	08 40	5.8	21 05	5.6	06 12	7.4	19 05	7.2	07 09	2.8	20 09	2.6	09 54	4.4	22 46	4.4
Su	17	09 50	5.9	22 16	5.8	07 20	7.6	20 07	7.5	08 40	2.8	21 20	2.7	11 01	4.5	23 49	4.5
M	18	10 55	6.1	23 18	6.1	08 16	7.9	20 53	7.9	09 40	3.0	22 08	2.9	11 59	4.6	-	-
Tu	19	11 51	6.3	-	-	09 02	8.2	21 32	8.2	10 27	3.1	22 50	3.0	00 36	4.7	12 45	4.8
W	20	00 08	6.4	12 36	6.5	09 41	8.5	22 06	8.5	11 09	3.2	23 28	3.2	01 15	4.9	13 24	5.0
Th	21	00 51	6.7	13 13	6.6	10 17	8.6	22 38	8.7	11 46	3.2	-	-	01 48	5.1	14 00	5.1
F	22	01 28	6.8	13 47	6.7	10 52	8.8	23 10	8.8	00 03	3.2	12 21	3.2	02 21	5.2	14 35	5.2
Sa	23	02 03	6.9	14 20	6.8	11 26	8.8	23 42	8.8	00 36	3.3	12 55	3.2	02 54	5.2	15 09	5.2
Su	24	02 37	7.0	14 54	6.8	12 00	8.8	-	-	01 07	3.4	13 30	3.2	03 28	5.2	15 45	5.2
M	25	03 12	7.0	15 29	6.7	00 15	8.8	12 37	8.7	01 39	3.5	14 08	3.2	04 02	5.2	16 22	5.2
Tu	26	03 48	6.9	16 05	6.6	00 51	8.8	13 15	8.6	02 13	3.5	14 48	3.2	04 38	5.1	17 03	5.1
W	27	04 27	6.8	16 44	6.4	01 30	8.6	13 59	8.4	02 49	3.5	15 31	3.1	05 17	5.0	17 47	5.0
Th	28	05 10	6.7	17 27	6.2	02 16	8.4	14 49	8.1	03 28	3.5	16 19	3.0	06 02	4.9	18 38	4.9
F	29	05 59	6.5	18 17	6.1	03 10	8.1	15 50	7.9	04 11	3.3	17 14	2.9	06 53	4.8	19 36	4.8
Sa	30	06 57	6.4	19 19	6.0	04 18	8.0	17 01	7.8	05 02	3.2	18 22	2.8	07 56	4.7	20 44	4.7
Su	31	08 09	6.3	20 37	6.1	05 31	8.0	18 14	7.9	06 08	3.1	19 42	2.9	09 10	4.7	21 55	4.8

JUNE 2020 *High Water* GMT

		LONDON BRIDGE				LIVERPOOL (Gladstone Dock)				GREENOCK				LEITH			
M	1	09 22	6.4	21 51	6.3	06 41	8.2	19 22	8.2	07 34	3.1	20 58	3.0	10 22	4.9	23 01	5.0
Tu	2	10 29	6.6	22 56	6.6	07 45	8.6	20 22	8.6	08 54	3.2	21 58	3.1	11 24	5.1	23 59	5.2
W	3	11 31	6.8	23 55	6.9	08 43	8.9	21 15	9.0	09 57	3.3	22 50	3.2	12 20	5.3	-	-
Th	4	12 28	6.9	-	-	09 35	9.2	22 04	9.3	10 52	3.4	23 38	3.3	00 50	5.4	13 12	5.6
F	5	00 48	7.1	13 19	7.0	10 25	9.4	22 50	9.4	11 44	3.5	-	-	01 38	5.5	14 01	5.7
Sa	6	01 38	7.3	14 06	7.1	11 13	9.4	23 34	9.4	00 22	3.4	12 34	3.4	02 24	5.6	14 51	5.7
Su	7	02 24	7.4	14 50	7.0	11 59	9.3	-	-	01 05	3.5	13 22	3.4	03 10	5.6	15 40	5.6
M	8	03 10	7.4	15 34	6.9	00 18	9.3	12 45	9.0	01 45	3.5	14 08	3.3	03 56	5.5	16 30	5.5
Tu	9	03 55	7.2	16 15	6.7	01 01	9.1	13 29	8.7	02 24	3.5	14 53	3.2	04 43	5.3	17 19	5.3
W	10	04 40	6.9	16 55	6.4	01 44	8.8	14 13	8.3	03 03	3.5	15 37	3.1	05 30	5.2	18 08	5.0
Th	11	05 23	6.6	17 34	6.2	02 29	8.5	15 00	7.9	03 44	3.3	16 22	2.9	06 19	4.9	18 58	4.8
F	12	06 08	6.3	18 16	6.0	03 19	8.1	15 53	7.5	04 27	3.2	17 11	2.8	07 10	4.7	19 50	4.6
Sa	13	06 57	6.0	19 06	5.8	04 16	7.8	16 53	7.2	05 17	3.0	18 04	2.8	08 05	4.6	20 45	4.4
Su	14	07 54	5.8	20 13	5.7	05 18	7.6	17 59	7.2	06 16	2.9	19 02	2.7	09 02	4.5	21 42	4.4
M	15	08 56	5.8	21 22	5.8	06 22	7.5	19 04	7.3	07 27	2.8	20 04	2.8	10 00	4.4	22 40	4.4
Tu	16	09 57	5.9	22 24	6.0	07 26	7.6	20 01	7.5	08 38	2.9	21 06	2.9	10 59	4.5	23 37	4.5
W	17	10 56	6.1	23 21	6.3	08 16	7.9	20 48	7.9	09 37	2.9	22 00	3.0	11 54	4.6	-	-
Th	18	11 50	6.3	-	-	09 03	8.1	21 29	8.2	10 25	3.0	22 47	3.1	00 27	4.7	12 44	4.8
F	19	00 12	6.6	12 38	6.5	09 45	8.3	22 07	8.5	11 08	3.1	23 29	3.2	01 11	4.9	13 28	4.9
Sa	20	00 57	6.8	13 20	6.7	10 24	8.5	22 44	8.7	11 48	3.1	-	-	01 51	5.1	14 09	5.1
Su	21	01 38	6.9	14 01	6.8	11 03	8.7	23 21	8.8	00 06	3.3	12 28	3.1	02 29	5.2	14 48	5.2
M	22	02 18	7.0	14 40	6.8	11 42	8.8	23 59	8.9	00 42	3.4	13 09	3.2	03 07	5.3	15 27	5.3
Tu	23	02 58	7.0	15 20	6.8	12 23	8.8	-	-	01 17	3.5	13 52	3.2	03 44	5.3	16 07	5.3
W	24	03 39	7.1	16 00	6.7	00 39	9.0	13 06	8.7	01 55	3.6	14 36	3.2	04 22	5.3	16 49	5.3
Th	25	04 21	7.0	16 40	6.6	01 23	8.9	13 52	8.7	02 34	3.6	15 22	3.1	05 03	5.3	17 35	5.3
F	26	05 05	6.9	17 23	6.5	02 10	8.8	14 42	8.5	03 16	3.6	16 10	3.1	05 48	5.2	18 24	5.1
Sa	27	05 52	6.8	18 09	6.4	03 02	8.6	15 36	8.3	04 00	3.5	17 03	3.0	06 38	5.1	19 18	5.0
Su	28	06 47	6.6	19 04	6.3	04 00	8.4	16 37	8.1	04 50	3.4	18 01	3.0	07 35	5.0	20 20	4.9
M	29	07 50	6.5	20 12	6.2	05 04	8.3	17 43	8.0	05 48	3.3	19 06	2.9	08 43	4.9	21 27	4.9
Tu	30	08 57	6.4	21 22	6.4	06 10	8.3	18 51	8.1	07 00	3.2	20 17	2.9	09 53	4.9	22 32	4.9

JULY 2020   *High Water* GMT

		LONDON BRIDGE Datum of Predictions 3.2m below				LIVERPOOL (Gladstone Dock) Datum of Predictions 4.93 below				GREENOCK Datum of Predictions 1.62 below				LEITH Datum of Predictions 2.90 below			
		hr	m	hr	m	hr	m	hr	m	hr	m	hr	m	hr	m	hr	m
W	1	10 02	6.5	22 28	6.6	07 18	8.4	19 56	8.3	08 20	3.1	21 26	3.0	10 59	5.0	23 33	5.0
Th	2	11 07	6.6	23 32	6.7	08 21	8.5	20 54	8.6	09 32	3.2	22 25	3.1	12 01	5.2	-	-
F	3	12 09	6.7	-	-	09 20	8.7	21 47	8.9	10 34	3.2	23 18	3.3	00 29	5.2	12 59	5.3
Sa	4	00 31	6.9	13 05	6.8	10 13	8.9	22 36	9.1	11 30	3.3	-	-	01 22	5.3	13 52	5.4
Su	5	01 25	7.1	13 54	6.8	11 03	9.0	23 21	9.2	00 05	3.4	12 23	3.3	02 11	5.4	14 42	5.5
M	6	02 14	7.2	14 40	6.9	11 49	8.9	-	-	00 50	3.4	13 11	3.2	02 57	5.5	15 29	5.5
Tu	7	03 00	7.2	15 22	6.8	00 04	9.2	12 32	8.8	01 30	3.5	13 56	3.1	03 42	5.4	16 15	5.4
W	8	03 44	7.1	16 01	6.7	00 45	9.1	13 12	8.6	02 09	3.5	14 38	3.1	04 26	5.4	16 59	5.3
Th	9	04 25	6.9	16 37	6.6	01 25	8.9	13 50	8.4	02 46	3.5	15 18	3.0	05 08	5.3	17 41	5.1
F	10	05 03	6.7	17 12	6.4	02 04	8.7	14 28	8.1	03 24	3.4	15 59	3.0	05 49	5.1	18 23	4.9
Sa	11	05 41	6.4	17 47	6.3	02 45	8.4	15 10	7.8	04 02	3.3	16 40	3.0	06 32	4.9	19 07	4.7
Su	12	06 18	6.2	18 25	6.1	03 30	8.1	15 57	7.5	04 43	3.2	17 24	2.9	07 17	4.7	19 53	4.5
M	13	07 01	6.0	19 13	5.9	04 21	7.7	16 52	7.3	05 28	3.0	18 11	2.9	08 07	4.6	20 44	4.4
Tu	14	07 55	5.8	20 19	5.8	05 20	7.5	17 55	7.1	06 21	2.9	19 02	2.8	09 02	4.5	21 39	4.4
W	15	08 59	5.7	21 31	5.8	06 23	7.4	19 02	7.2	07 22	2.8	20 00	2.8	10 01	4.4	22 38	4.4
Th	16	10 04	5.8	22 35	6.0	07 27	7.5	20 03	7.5	08 31	2.8	21 05	2.9	11 03	4.5	23 38	4.6
F	17	11 07	6.1	23 35	6.3	08 26	7.7	20 55	7.9	09 39	2.9	22 06	3.0	12 04	4.6	-	-
Sa	18	12 06	6.4	-	-	09 16	8.0	21 40	8.3	10 35	3.0	22 56	3.2	00 35	4.8	12 59	4.8
Su	19	00 28	6.6	12 58	6.6	10 02	8.4	22 22	8.7	11 24	3.0	23 40	3.3	01 24	5.0	13 47	5.1
M	20	01 17	6.9	13 44	6.8	10 45	8.7	23 03	9.0	12 10	3.1	-	-	02 08	5.2	14 29	5.3
Tu	21	02 02	7.0	14 28	6.9	11 27	8.9	23 44	9.2	00 19	3.4	12 55	3.1	02 48	5.4	15 10	5.4
W	22	02 46	7.2	15 10	6.9	12 10	9.1	-	-	00 59	3.5	13 40	3.2	03 27	5.5	15 51	5.6
Th	23	03 29	7.3	15 51	7.0	00 27	9.3	12 54	9.2	01 40	3.6	14 25	3.2	04 06	5.6	16 34	5.6
F	24	04 12	7.3	16 31	6.9	01 11	9.4	13 39	9.1	02 21	3.7	15 11	3.2	04 48	5.6	17 18	5.5
Sa	25	04 55	7.2	17 11	6.9	01 57	9.3	14 26	8.9	03 04	3.7	15 56	3.2	05 32	5.5	18 06	5.4
Su	26	05 39	6.9	17 54	6.8	02 44	9.1	15 15	8.7	03 48	3.7	16 42	3.2	06 20	5.4	18 56	5.2
M	27	06 29	6.7	18 43	6.6	03 36	8.8	16 09	8.3	04 34	3.6	17 31	3.1	07 13	5.2	19 53	5.0
Tu	28	07 25	6.5	19 42	6.5	04 34	8.5	17 12	8.0	05 25	3.4	18 26	3.0	08 16	5.0	20 57	4.8
W	29	08 29	6.3	20 52	6.4	05 42	8.1	18 23	7.9	06 24	3.2	19 33	2.9	09 29	4.9	22 05	4.8
Th	30	09 35	6.2	22 03	6.4	06 56	8.0	19 35	8.0	07 42	3.0	20 56	2.9	10 41	4.9	23 12	4.8
F	31	10 46	6.2	23 15	6.5	08 09	8.1	20 41	8.3	09 14	3.0	22 09	3.0	11 51	4.9	-	-

AUGUST 2020   *High Water* GMT

		LONDON BRIDGE				LIVERPOOL (Gladstone Dock)				GREENOCK				LEITH			
Sa	1	11 57	6.4	-	-	09 14	8.3	21 38	8.6	10 30	3.0	23 06	3.2	00 17	5.0	12 55	5.1
Su	2	00 22	6.7	12 57	6.6	10 09	8.5	22 27	8.9	11 29	3.1	23 54	3.4	01 14	5.1	13 49	5.2
M	3	01 19	6.9	13 46	6.7	10 56	8.7	23 10	9.1	12 19	3.1	-	-	02 03	5.3	14 35	5.4
Tu	4	02 07	7.0	14 30	6.8	11 38	8.8	23 49	9.2	00 37	3.5	13 05	3.1	02 47	5.4	15 17	5.4
W	5	02 50	7.1	15 08	6.9	12 15	8.8	-	-	01 17	3.5	13 44	3.1	03 27	5.5	15 56	5.4
Th	6	03 29	7.0	15 43	6.9	00 26	9.2	12 49	8.7	01 53	3.5	14 19	3.1	04 05	5.6	16 33	5.3
F	7	04 05	6.9	16 15	6.8	01 00	9.1	13 22	8.6	02 27	3.5	14 52	3.1	04 41	5.4	17 09	5.1
Sa	8	04 37	6.8	16 46	6.7	01 34	8.9	13 54	8.4	03 00	3.5	15 27	3.1	05 16	5.2	17 45	5.0
Su	9	05 08	6.6	17 16	6.5	02 08	8.6	14 28	8.1	03 34	3.4	16 03	3.1	05 52	5.1	18 23	4.8
M	10	05 38	6.3	17 48	6.3	02 45	8.3	15 05	7.8	04 09	3.3	16 41	3.1	06 31	4.9	19 05	4.6
Tu	11	06 10	6.1	18 24	6.1	03 25	7.9	15 49	7.5	04 47	3.1	17 22	3.0	07 15	4.7	19 51	4.5
W	12	06 49	5.8	19 09	5.9	04 15	7.5	16 45	7.2	05 33	3.0	18 08	2.9	08 07	4.5	20 47	4.4
Th	13	07 43	5.6	20 14	5.7	05 20	7.2	18 00	7.2	06 29	2.8	19 03	2.9	09 09	4.3	21 49	4.4
F	14	09 07	5.5	21 46	5.7	06 37	7.1	19 18	7.2	07 37	2.7	20 09	2.8	10 18	4.3	22 56	4.4
Sa	15	10 26	5.8	22 58	6.1	07 51	7.4	20 24	7.7	08 58	2.7	21 24	2.9	11 28	4.5	-	-
Su	16	11 36	6.1	-	-	08 52	7.8	21 17	8.2	10 14	2.9	22 27	3.1	00 02	4.7	12 33	4.8
M	17	00 01	6.5	12 34	6.5	09 43	8.3	22 03	8.7	11 10	3.0	23 15	3.3	01 00	5.0	13 26	5.1
Tu	18	00 55	6.9	13 24	6.8	10 28	8.8	22 45	9.2	11 57	3.1	23 59	3.5	01 46	5.2	14 10	5.4
W	19	01 43	7.1	14 09	7.0	11 11	9.2	23 27	9.6	12 42	3.2	-	-	02 27	5.5	14 51	5.6
Th	20	02 28	7.3	14 52	7.1	11 53	9.5	-	-	00 41	3.6	13 27	3.2	03 06	5.7	15 32	5.8
F	21	03 12	7.4	15 33	7.2	00 09	9.8	12 37	9.7	01 24	3.7	14 10	3.3	03 46	5.9	16 14	5.8
Sa	22	03 55	7.4	16 12	7.2	00 53	9.8	13 20	9.5	02 07	3.8	14 52	3.3	04 27	5.9	16 57	5.8
Su	23	04 37	7.3	16 51	7.2	01 36	9.7	14 03	9.3	02 50	3.8	15 33	3.3	05 11	5.8	17 42	5.6
M	24	05 19	7.0	17 33	7.0	02 21	9.4	14 49	8.9	03 32	3.8	16 15	3.3	05 56	5.6	18 31	5.3
Tu	25	06 04	6.7	18 18	6.8	03 09	8.9	15 40	8.4	04 16	3.6	16 57	3.2	06 50	5.4	19 25	5.0
W	26	06 55	6.3	19 13	6.5	04 05	8.4	16 41	7.9	05 02	3.4	17 45	3.0	07 54	5.0	20 29	4.7
Th	27	07 56	6.1	20 24	6.3	05 17	7.8	17 59	7.6	05 54	3.1	18 47	2.9	09 11	4.8	21 42	4.6
F	28	09 08	5.9	21 43	6.2	06 43	7.6	19 21	7.7	07 04	2.8	20 32	2.8	10 29	4.7	22 57	4.6
Sa	29	10 28	5.9	23 03	6.3	08 07	7.7	20 34	8.1	09 21	2.8	21 57	3.0	11 48	4.8	-	-
Su	30	11 45	6.2	-	-	09 13	8.1	21 31	8.5	10 35	3.0	22 53	3.2	00 10	4.8	12 54	5.0
M	31	00 14	6.6	12 45	6.5	10 04	8.4	22 16	8.9	11 26	3.1	23 40	3.4	01 09	5.1	13 44	5.2

SEPTEMBER 2020 *High Water* GMT

		LONDON BRIDGE Datum of Predictions 3.2m below						LIVERPOOL (Gladstone Dock) Datum of Predictions 4.93 below						GREENOCK Datum of Predictions 1.62 below						LEITH Datum of Predictions 2.90 below					
		hr	m	ht m	hr	m	ht m	hr	m	ht m	hr	m	ht m	hr	m	ht m	hr	m	ht m	hr	m	ht m	hr	m	ht m
Tu	1	01	09	6.9	13	33	6.7	10	45	8.7	22	55	9.1	12	11	3.1	-		-	01	54	5.3	14	24	5.3
W	2	01	53	7.0	14	12	6.8	11	20	8.9	23	29	9.2	00	21	3.5	12	50	3.1	02	32	5.4	15	00	5.4
Th	3	02	33	7.0	14	47	6.9	11	52	8.9			-	00	59	3.5	13	22	3.1	03	07	5.5	15	33	5.4
F	4	03	07	7.0	15	18	6.9	00	01	9.2	12	22	8.9	01	33	3.5	13	50	3.1	03	39	5.5	16	04	5.3
Sa	5	03	38	6.9	15	47	6.9	00	32	9.2	12	51	8.8	02	04	3.5	14	20	3.2	04	11	5.4	16	36	5.2
Su	6	04	05	6.8	16	15	6.9	01	03	9.0	13	20	8.6	02	33	3.5	14	51	3.2	04	43	5.3	17	09	5.1
M	7	04	32	6.6	16	44	6.7	01	33	8.8	13	49	8.4	03	05	3.5	15	25	3.3	05	17	5.2	17	44	5.0
Tu	8	05	00	6.4	17	14	6.5	02	05	8.5	14	21	8.1	03	38	3.4	15	59	3.3	05	53	5.0	18	22	4.8
W	9	05	30	6.2	17	47	6.3	02	39	8.1	14	57	7.7	04	14	3.2	16	37	3.2	06	33	4.8	19	05	4.6
Th	10	06	05	5.9	18	28	6.0	03	21	7.6	15	45	7.3	04	55	3.0	17	20	3.0	07	22	4.5	19	57	4.4
F	11	06	49	5.7	19	20	5.7	04	21	7.2	17	00	7.0	05	48	2.8	18	13	2.9	08	23	4.4	21	03	4.3
Sa	12	07	55	5.4	20	44	5.6	05	49	7.0	18	35	7.1	06	58	2.7	19	21	2.8	09	38	4.3	22	18	4.4
Su	13	09	40	5.5	22	19	5.9	07	19	7.2	19	53	7.6	08	29	2.7	20	44	2.9	10	55	4.5	23	31	4.6
M	14	11	02	5.9	23	30	6.4	08	29	7.8	20	52	8.3	10	01	2.9	21	57	3.1	12	06	4.8	-		-
Tu	15	12	05	6.4	-		-	09	22	8.5	21	40	8.9	10	56	3.1	22	50	3.4	00	32	5.0	13	02	5.2
W	16	00	28	6.9	12	58	6.8	10	08	9.1	22	23	9.5	11	41	3.3	23	36	3.5	01	20	5.3	13	47	5.5
Th	17	01	19	7.2	13	44	7.1	10	50	9.5	23	05	9.9	12	24	3.3	-		-	02	02	5.7	14	28	5.8
F	18	02	05	7.4	14	26	7.3	11	32	9.8	23	47	10.1	00	20	3.7	13	06	3.4	02	41	5.9	15	08	6.0
Sa	19	02	49	7.5	15	07	7.4	12	13	9.9	-		-	01	05	3.8	13	47	3.4	03	21	6.1	15	49	6.0
Su	20	03	31	7.4	15	47	7.5	00	29	10.1	12	56	9.8	01	50	3.9	14	27	3.5	04	04	6.1	16	33	5.9
M	21	04	13	7.3	16	28	7.4	01	13	9.9	13	38	9.5	02	33	3.9	15	06	3.5	04	49	6.0	17	17	5.6
Tu	22	04	54	7.0	17	09	7.2	01	57	9.5	14	22	9.0	03	15	3.8	15	45	3.4	05	38	5.7	18	05	5.3
W	23	05	37	6.6	17	55	6.8	02	45	8.9	15	12	8.4	03	57	3.6	16	26	3.3	06	32	5.3	18	59	5.0
Th	24	06	24	6.2	18	48	6.4	03	42	8.2	16	15	7.9	04	41	3.4	17	12	3.1	07	38	4.9	20	05	4.7
F	25	07	22	5.9	20	00	6.1	04	59	7.5	17	38	7.5	05	32	3.0	18	11	2.9	08	56	4.7	21	22	4.5
Sa	26	08	40	5.6	21	23	6.0	06	33	7.3	19	06	7.6	06	42	2.7	20	09	2.9	10	17	4.6	22	41	4.6
Su	27	10	06	5.7	22	46	6.2	08	00	7.6	20	19	8.0	09	26	2.8	21	38	3.1	11	40	4.7	23	56	4.8
M	28	11	25	6.0	23	56	6.6	09	02	8.0	21	14	8.5	10	25	3.0	22	32	3.3	12	43	5.0	-		-
Tu	29	12	23	6.4	-		-	09	47	8.4	21	56	8.8	11	10	3.1	23	17	3.5	00	52	5.1	13	28	5.2
W	30	00	48	6.9	13	09	6.7	10	24	8.7	22	31	9.1	11	48	3.2	23	57	3.6	01	35	5.3	14	04	5.3

OCTOBER 2020 *High Water* GMT

		LONDON BRIDGE						LIVERPOOL (Gladstone Dock)						GREENOCK						LEITH					
Th	1	01	31	7.0	13	47	6.8	10	56	8.9	23	03	9.2	12	22	3.3	-		-	02	10	5.4	14	36	5.4
F	2	02	07	6.9	14	19	6.9	11	24	9.0	23	33	9.3	00	34	3.6	12	51	3.3	02	42	5.4	15	05	5.4
Sa	3	02	38	6.9	14	48	7.0	11	52	9.0	-		-	01	07	3.5	13	18	3.3	03	12	5.5	15	34	5.4
Su	4	03	05	6.9	15	16	7.0	00	03	9.2	12	20	9.0	01	36	3.5	13	47	3.4	03	42	5.4	16	04	5.3
M	5	03	30	6.8	15	44	7.0	00	33	9.1	12	48	8.8	02	05	3.5	14	18	3.4	04	13	5.3	16	35	5.2
Tu	6	03	57	6.7	16	13	6.8	01	03	8.8	13	16	8.6	02	37	3.5	14	50	3.5	04	47	5.2	17	09	5.1
W	7	04	26	6.5	16	44	6.6	01	33	8.5	13	46	8.3	03	10	3.4	15	23	3.5	05	23	5.0	17	45	4.9
Th	8	04	56	6.3	17	18	6.4	02	06	8.2	14	21	8.0	03	47	3.3	15	58	3.4	06	03	4.8	18	26	4.7
F	9	05	30	6.1	17	58	6.2	02	48	7.7	15	08	7.6	04	27	3.1	16	39	3.2	06	50	4.6	19	16	4.5
Sa	10	06	13	5.8	18	50	5.9	03	46	7.3	16	19	7.2	05	18	2.9	17	29	3.0	07	49	4.4	20	21	4.4
Su	11	07	13	5.5	20	03	5.8	05	12	7.0	17	56	7.2	06	29	2.7	18	38	2.9	09	04	4.4	21	41	4.4
M	12	08	48	5.4	21	40	6.0	06	46	7.3	19	19	7.7	08	07	2.7	20	05	3.0	10	24	4.5	22	58	4.6
Tu	13	10	21	5.8	22	55	6.5	08	00	7.9	20	21	8.4	09	40	3.0	21	24	3.2	11	36	4.9	-		-
W	14	11	29	6.3	23	56	6.9	08	56	8.6	21	12	9.1	10	34	3.2	22	22	3.4	00	00	5.0	12	33	5.3
Th	15	12	24	6.8	-		-	09	42	9.2	21	57	9.6	11	18	3.4	23	11	3.6	00	50	5.4	13	19	5.6
F	16	00	49	7.2	13	13	7.2	10	25	9.7	22	40	10.0	11	59	3.5	23	57	3.8	01	33	5.8	14	01	5.9
Sa	17	01	37	7.4	13	57	7.4	11	07	10.0	23	23	10.2	12	41	3.5	-		-	02	15	6.0	14	42	6.0
Su	18	02	22	7.5	14	40	7.6	11	49	10.0	-		-	00	44	3.9	13	22	3.6	02	57	6.2	15	24	6.0
M	19	03	05	7.4	15	22	7.6	00	07	10.1	12	32	9.9	01	30	3.9	14	01	3.6	03	43	6.2	16	08	5.9
Tu	20	03	48	7.2	16	05	7.5	00	51	9.8	13	14	9.5	02	15	3.9	14	41	3.6	04	30	6.0	16	54	5.6
W	21	04	30	6.9	16	48	7.2	01	36	9.3	13	59	9.1	02	58	3.8	15	20	3.6	05	21	5.7	17	42	5.3
Th	22	05	12	6.5	17	35	6.8	02	25	8.7	14	50	8.5	03	41	3.6	16	01	3.4	06	18	5.3	18	37	5.0
F	23	05	57	6.1	18	29	6.4	03	24	8.0	15	53	7.9	04	26	3.3	16	48	3.2	07	23	4.9	19	44	4.7
Sa	24	06	51	5.8	19	36	6.0	04	40	7.4	17	14	7.6	05	19	3.0	17	47	3.0	08	37	4.6	20	59	4.5
Su	25	08	05	5.5	20	55	5.9	06	10	7.2	18	37	7.6	06	40	2.7	19	30	2.9	09	54	4.5	22	15	4.6
M	26	09	30	5.5	22	13	6.0	07	35	7.5	19	49	7.9	09	01	2.8	21	03	3.1	11	13	4.7	23	27	4.7
Tu	27	10	48	5.8	23	24	6.4	08	35	7.9	20	43	8.3	09	57	3.0	22	00	3.3	12	15	4.9	-		-
W	28	11	49	6.2	-		-	09	20	8.3	21	25	8.7	10	39	3.2	22	45	3.5	00	22	5.0	13	00	5.1
Th	29	00	17	6.7	12	35	6.5	09	55	8.6	22	01	8.9	11	15	3.3	23	26	3.5	01	06	5.1	13	36	5.2
F	30	00	59	6.8	13	13	6.7	10	26	8.8	22	34	9.1	11	47	3.4	-		-	01	41	5.3	14	07	5.3
Sa	31	01	35	6.8	13	46	6.9	10	55	9.0	23	05	9.1	00	03	3.5	12	18	3.4	02	14	5.3	14	36	5.4

NOVEMBER 2020 *High Water* GMT

		LONDON BRIDGE Datum of Predictions 3.2m below				LIVERPOOL (Gladstone Dock) Datum of Predictions 4.93 below				GREENOCK Datum of Predictions 1.62 below				LEITH Datum of Predictions 2.90 below			
		hr	ht m	hr	ht m	hr	ht m	hr	ht m	hr	ht m	hr	ht m	hr	ht m	hr	ht m
Su	1	02 05	6.8	14 16	7.0	11 23	9.0	23 36	9.1	00 37	3.5	12 48	3.5	02 44	5.4	15 04	5.4
M	2	02 32	6.8	14 45	7.0	11 52	9.0	-	-	01 08	3.5	13 18	3.6	03 16	5.4	15 35	5.4
Tu	3	02 59	6.8	15 15	7.0	00 07	9.0	12 21	8.9	01 39	3.5	13 48	3.6	03 49	5.3	16 07	5.3
W	4	03 28	6.8	15 47	6.9	00 38	8.8	12 51	8.7	02 12	3.5	14 20	3.6	04 23	5.2	16 40	5.2
Th	5	04 00	6.6	16 21	6.7	01 11	8.6	13 23	8.5	02 48	3.4	14 54	3.6	05 00	5.1	17 16	5.0
F	6	04 32	6.4	16 58	6.6	01 47	8.2	14 01	8.2	03 26	3.3	15 30	3.5	05 42	4.9	17 57	4.8
Sa	7	05 08	6.2	17 40	6.4	02 31	7.9	14 49	7.9	04 08	3.1	16 11	3.4	06 29	4.7	18 46	4.6
Su	8	05 52	5.9	18 32	6.2	03 29	7.5	15 57	7.6	04 59	3.0	16 59	3.2	07 26	4.6	19 47	4.5
M	9	06 49	5.7	19 40	6.0	04 46	7.3	17 23	7.5	06 07	2.8	18 03	3.1	08 35	4.5	21 05	4.5
Tu	10	08 09	5.6	21 07	6.1	06 11	7.5	18 42	7.9	07 38	2.9	19 26	3.1	09 52	4.7	22 22	4.7
W	11	09 41	5.9	22 20	6.5	07 25	8.0	19 47	8.5	09 06	3.0	20 48	3.3	11 02	4.9	23 25	5.1
Th	12	10 51	6.4	23 23	6.9	08 24	8.6	20 41	9.1	10 03	3.3	21 51	3.5	12 00	5.3	-	-
F	13	11 50	6.8	-	-	09 14	9.2	21 30	9.5	10 50	3.4	22 44	3.7	00 18	5.4	12 50	5.6
Sa	14	00 19	7.1	12 42	7.2	10 00	9.6	22 17	9.9	11 33	3.5	23 35	3.8	01 06	5.7	13 34	5.8
Su	15	01 10	7.3	13 30	7.4	10 44	9.8	23 02	10.0	12 16	3.6	-	-	01 51	6.0	14 18	5.9
M	16	01 57	7.3	14 15	7.6	11 27	9.9	23 48	9.9	00 24	3.8	12 58	3.7	02 38	6.1	15 02	5.9
Tu	17	02 42	7.2	15 01	7.6	12 11	9.8	-	-	01 12	3.8	13 39	3.7	03 26	6.0	15 47	5.8
W	18	03 26	7.1	15 46	7.4	00 34	9.6	12 56	9.5	01 59	3.8	14 20	3.7	04 16	5.8	16 34	5.6
Th	19	04 10	6.8	16 32	7.1	01 22	9.1	13 42	9.1	02 44	3.6	15 01	3.7	05 08	5.6	17 23	5.3
F	20	04 53	6.5	17 20	6.8	02 11	8.6	14 32	8.6	03 29	3.4	15 43	3.5	06 04	5.2	18 18	5.1
Sa	21	05 36	6.1	18 11	6.4	03 06	8.0	15 30	8.1	04 16	3.2	16 31	3.4	07 04	4.9	19 20	4.8
Su	22	06 23	5.8	19 10	6.0	04 12	7.5	16 39	7.8	05 11	3.0	17 27	3.2	08 09	4.6	20 27	4.6
M	23	07 25	5.6	20 18	5.9	05 27	7.2	17 52	7.7	06 20	2.8	18 43	3.1	09 16	4.5	21 35	4.6
Tu	24	08 42	5.5	21 26	5.9	06 45	7.3	19 00	7.8	07 54	2.8	20 09	3.1	10 25	4.5	22 41	4.6
W	25	09 53	5.7	22 33	6.1	07 51	7.6	19 59	8.0	09 04	2.9	21 15	3.2	11 29	4.7	23 39	4.8
Th	26	10 57	6.0	23 32	6.3	08 40	8.0	20 47	8.3	09 53	3.1	22 06	3.3	12 20	4.8	-	-
F	27	11 50	6.3	-	-	09 19	8.3	21 27	8.6	10 33	3.3	22 50	3.4	00 28	4.9	13 00	5.0
Sa	28	00 19	6.5	12 35	6.6	09 54	8.6	22 04	8.7	11 11	3.4	23 30	3.4	01 09	5.0	13 35	5.1
Su	29	00 58	6.6	13 13	6.8	10 26	8.8	22 39	8.9	11 46	3.5	-	-	01 45	5.2	14 07	5.3
M	30	01 33	6.7	13 47	6.9	10 57	8.9	23 12	8.9	00 06	3.4	12 20	3.6	02 19	5.2	14 39	5.3

DECEMBER 2020 *High Water* GMT

		LONDON BRIDGE				LIVERPOOL (Gladstone Dock)				GREENOCK				LEITH			
Tu	1	02 05	6.8	14 20	6.9	11 29	8.9	23 46	8.9	00 41	3.4	12 52	3.6	02 54	5.3	15 11	5.3
W	2	02 36	6.8	14 54	6.9	12 01	8.9	-	-	01 16	3.4	13 24	3.7	03 29	5.3	15 45	5.3
Th	3	03 10	6.7	15 29	6.9	00 20	8.8	12 35	8.8	01 52	3.4	13 58	3.7	04 05	5.2	16 19	5.2
F	4	03 44	6.6	16 06	6.8	00 57	8.6	13 11	8.7	02 31	3.4	14 34	3.7	04 44	5.2	16 56	5.1
Sa	5	04 20	6.5	16 46	6.7	01 37	8.4	13 52	8.5	03 12	3.3	15 12	3.7	05 26	5.1	17 37	5.0
Su	6	04 59	6.3	17 31	6.6	02 23	8.2	14 40	8.3	03 56	3.2	15 53	3.6	06 13	4.9	18 25	4.9
M	7	05 44	6.1	18 21	6.4	03 17	7.9	15 40	8.1	04 45	3.1	16 40	3.4	07 06	4.8	19 20	4.8
Tu	8	06 36	6.0	19 22	6.3	04 22	7.8	16 51	8.0	05 45	3.0	17 37	3.3	08 08	4.7	20 29	4.7
W	9	07 42	6.0	20 37	6.3	05 35	7.8	18 03	8.1	07 00	3.0	18 49	3.3	09 19	4.8	21 43	4.8
Th	10	09 03	6.1	21 48	6.5	06 46	8.1	19 10	8.5	08 20	3.0	20 08	3.3	10 27	4.9	22 50	5.1
F	11	10 15	6.4	22 52	6.7	07 50	8.5	20 11	8.8	09 27	3.2	21 19	3.4	11 28	5.2	23 49	5.3
Sa	12	11 18	6.7	23 53	6.8	08 46	8.9	21 07	9.2	10 21	3.3	22 20	3.6	12 22	5.4	-	-
Su	13	12 16	7.0	-	-	09 37	9.2	21 58	9.4	11 10	3.5	23 15	3.6	00 43	5.5	13 11	5.6
M	14	00 48	7.0	13 09	7.2	10 25	9.5	22 48	9.5	11 56	3.6	-	-	01 35	5.7	13 58	5.7
Tu	15	01 39	7.0	13 59	7.3	11 12	9.6	23 37	9.5	00 08	3.7	12 40	3.7	02 25	5.8	14 45	5.7
W	16	02 26	7.0	14 47	7.3	11 57	9.6	-	-	00 59	3.6	13 23	3.7	03 15	5.8	15 32	5.7
Th	17	03 13	7.0	15 35	7.3	00 24	9.3	12 43	9.4	01 47	3.6	14 05	3.7	04 05	5.7	16 19	5.6
F	18	03 57	6.8	16 21	7.1	01 11	9.0	13 28	9.2	02 34	3.5	14 47	3.7	04 55	5.5	17 07	5.4
Sa	19	04 39	6.6	17 06	6.8	01 57	8.6	14 13	8.8	03 19	3.3	15 29	3.6	05 46	5.2	17 57	5.2
Su	20	05 19	6.3	17 52	6.6	02 43	8.2	15 02	8.4	04 04	3.2	16 14	3.5	06 37	5.0	18 49	5.0
M	21	06 00	6.1	18 39	6.2	03 34	7.8	15 55	8.1	04 52	3.0	17 02	3.3	07 31	4.7	19 45	4.8
Tu	22	06 45	5.9	19 32	5.9	04 31	7.4	16 55	7.8	05 44	2.9	17 57	3.2	08 26	4.5	20 43	4.6
W	23	07 45	5.7	20 31	5.8	05 35	7.2	17 59	7.6	06 40	2.9	18 59	3.1	09 24	4.4	21 42	4.5
Th	24	08 54	5.7	21 31	5.8	06 43	7.3	19 03	7.6	07 43	2.9	20 09	3.1	10 23	4.4	22 42	4.5
F	25	09 59	5.8	22 32	6.0	07 46	7.5	20 02	7.8	08 47	3.0	21 14	3.1	11 22	4.5	23 39	4.6
Sa	26	10 59	6.1	23 30	6.2	08 38	7.8	20 52	8.1	09 44	3.1	22 10	3.2	12 15	4.7	-	-
Su	27	11 54	6.3	-	-	09 21	8.1	21 36	8.3	10 34	3.3	22 58	3.2	00 31	4.8	13 00	4.9
M	28	00 21	6.4	12 41	6.6	10 00	8.4	22 16	8.5	11 17	3.4	23 41	3.3	01 17	4.9	13 40	5.1
Tu	29	01 06	6.6	13 23	6.7	10 36	8.7	22 54	8.7	11 56	3.5	-	-	01 58	5.1	14 17	5.2
W	30	01 46	6.7	14 02	6.8	11 11	8.9	23 30	8.8	00 21	3.3	12 31	3.6	02 36	5.2	14 53	5.3
Th	31	02 24	6.7	14 40	6.9	11 46	9.0	-	-	01 00	3.3	13 05	3.7	03 13	5.3	15 29	5.3

ABBREVIATIONS AND ACRONYMS

A

ABA	Amateur Boxing Association
abr	abridged
ac	alternating current
AC	*ante Christum* before Christ
	Companion, Order of Australia
ADC	Aide-de-Camp
ADC (P)	Personal ADC to the Queen
Adj.	Adjutant
Adj. Gen.	Adjutant General
Adm.	Admiral
AE	Air Efficiency award
AEM	Air Efficiency Medal
aet	after extra time
AFC	Air Force Cross
AFM	Air Force Medal
AG	Attorney-General
AH	*anno Hegirae* in the year of the Hegira
AM	Assembly Member (Wales)
ANC	African National Congress
AO	Air Officer
	Officer, Order of Australia
AOC	Air Officer Commanding
apptd	appointed
APR	annual percentage rate
AUC	*ab urbe condita* from the foundation of Rome
	anno urbis conditae from the founding of the city

B

b.	born
	bowled (cricket)
BAFTA	British Academy of Film and Television Arts
BAS	Bachelor in Agricultural Science
	British Antarctic Survey
BBFC	British Board of Film Classification
BCE	Before the Common (or Christian) Era
BCH (D)	Bachelor of (Dental) Surgery
BCL	Bachelor of Civil Law
BCOM	Bachelor of Commerce
BD	Bachelor of Divinity
BDA	British Dental Association
BDS	Bachelor of Dental Surgery
BED	Bachelor of Education
BEM	British Empire Medal
BENG	Bachelor of Engineering
BFPO	British Forces Post Office
BLIT	Bachelor of Literature
BLITT	Bachelor of Letters
BM	Bachelor of Medicine
BMA	British Medical Association
BMUS	Bachelor of Music
Bp	Bishop
BPHARM	Bachelor of Pharmacy
BPHIL	Bachelor of Philosophy
BPS	British Psychological Society
Brig.	Brigadier
BSI	British Standards Institution
BST	British Summer Time
Bt.	Baronet
BTEC	Business and Technology Education Council
BVMS	Bachelor of Veterinary Medicine and Surgery

C

c.	*circa* about
C.	Conservative
Cantuar:	of Canterbury (Archbishop)
Capt.	Captain
Carliol	of Carlisle (Bishop)
CB	Companion, Order of the Bath
CBE	Commander, Order of the British Empire

CC	Companion, Order of Canada
CCHEM	chartered chemist
CD	Civil Defence
	Corps Diplomatique
Cdr	Commander
Cdre	Commodore
CDS	Chief of the Defence Staff
CE	civil engineer
	Common (or Christian) Era
CENG	chartered engineer
Cestr:	of Chester (Bishop)
CET	Central European Time
cf	*confer* compare
CGC	Conspicuous Gallantry Cross
CGEOL	chartered geologist
CGM	Conspicuous Gallantry Medal
CGS	Chief of General Staff
CH	Companion of Honour
CHB/M	Bachelor/Master of Surgery
CI	Channel Islands
Cicestr:	of Chichester (Bishop)
C-in-C	Commander-in-Chief
CILIP	Chartered Institute of Library and Information Professionals
CIPFA	Chartered Institute of Public Finance and Accountancy
CIS	Commonwealth of Independent States
CLJ	Commander, Order of St Lazarus of Jerusalem
CM	*Chirurgiae Magister* Master of Surgery
CMG	Companion, Order of St Michael and St George
CO	Commanding Officer
C of E	Church of England
Col.	Colonel
cons.	consecrated
Cpl.	Corporal
CPS	Crown Prosecution Service
CVO	Commander, Royal Victorian Order

D

d	*denarius* penny
d.	died
DAB	Digital Audio Broadcasting
DBE	Dame Commander, Order of the British Empire
DCB	Dame Commander, Order of the Bath
D CH	*Doctor Chirurgiae* Doctor of Surgery
DCL	Doctor of Civil Law
DCM	Distinguished Conduct Medal
DCMG	Dame Commander, Order of St Michael and St George
DCVO	Dame Commander, Royal Victorian Order
DD	Doctor of Divinity
DDS	Doctor of Dental Surgery
DFC	Distinguished Flying Cross
DFM	Distinguished Flying Medal
DHL	*Doctor Humaniorum Literarum* Doctor of Humane Letters/Literature
DIP ED	Diploma in Education
DIP HE	Diploma in Higher Education
DL	Deputy Lieutenant
DLIT	Doctor of Literature
DLITT	Doctor of Letters
DLR	Docklands Light Railway
DLS	Duckworth–Lewis–Stern method (cricket)
DMUS	Doctor of Music
DNA	deoxyribonucleic acid
DPH *or*	Doctor of Philosophy
DPHIL	
DPP	Director of Public Prosecutions
DSC	Distinguished Service Cross
DSc	Doctor of Science
DSM	Distinguished Service Medal

DSO	Companion, Distinguished Service Order
Dunelm:	of Durham (Bishop)
DUP	Democratic Unionist Party

E

Ebor:	of York (Archbishop)
EC	Elizabeth Cross
	European Community
ECG	electrocardiogram
ED	Efficiency Decoration
EEA	European Economic Area
EEG	electroencephalogram
EIB	European Investment Bank
ER	*Elizabetha Regina* Queen Elizabeth
ERM	exchange rate mechanism
ESA	European Space Agency
et seq	*et sequentia* and the following
Exon:	of Exeter (Bishop)

F

FAQ	frequently asked questions
FBA	Fellow, British Academy
FBS	Fellow, Botanical Society
FBU	Fire Brigades Union
FCA	Fellow, Institute of Chartered Accountants in England and Wales
FCCA	Fellow, Chartered Association of Certified Accountants
FCIB	Fellow, Chartered Institute of Bankers
	Fellow, Corporation of Insurance Brokers
FCII	Fellow, Chartered Insurance Institute
FCIPS	Fellow, Chartered Institute of Purchasing and Supply
FCIS	Fellow, Institute of Chartered Secretaries and Administrators
FCIT	Fellow, Chartered Institute of Transport
FCMA	Fellow, Chartered Institute of Management Accountants
FCP	Fellow, College of Preceptors
FD	*Fidei Defensor* Defender of the Faith
FE	further education
FFA	Fellow, Faculty of Actuaries (Scotland)
	Fellow, Institute of Financial Accountants
FFAS	Fellow, Faculty of Architects and Surveyors
FFCM	Fellow, Faculty of Community Medicine
FFPHM	Fellow, Faculty of Public Health Medicine
FGS	Fellow, Geological Society
FHS	Fellow, Heraldry Society
FHSM	Fellow, Institute of Health Service Management
FIA	Fellow, Institute of Actuaries
FIBIOL	Fellow, Institute of Biology
FICE	Fellow, Institution of Civil Engineers
FICS	Fellow, Institution of Chartered Shipbrokers
FIEE	Fellow, Institution of Electrical Engineers
FIM	Fellow, Institute of Metals
FIMGT	Fellow, Institute of Management
FIMM	Fellow, Institution of Mining and Metallurgy
FLS	Fellow, Linnean Society
FMEDSCI	Fellow, Academy of Medical Sciences
fo	folio
FPHS	Fellow, Philosophical Society
FRAD	Fellow, Royal Academy of Dancing
FRAES	Fellow, Royal Aeronautical Society
FRAGS	Fellow, Royal Agricultural Societies
FRAM	Fellow, Royal Academy of Music
FRAS	Fellow, Royal Asiatic Society
	Fellow, Royal Astronomical Society
FRBS	Fellow, Royal Botanic Society
	Fellow, Royal Society of British Sculptors
FRCA	Fellow, Royal College of Anaesthetists
FRCGP	Fellow, Royal College of General Practitioners
FRCM	Fellow, Royal College of Music
FRCO	Fellow, Royal College of Organists
FRCOG	Fellow, Royal College of Obstetricians and Gynaecologists

FRCP	Fellow, Royal College of Physicians, London
FRCPATH	Fellow, Royal College of Pathologists
FRCPE *or* FRCPED	Fellow, Royal College of Physicians, Edinburgh
FRCPI	Fellow, Royal College of Physicians, Ireland
FRCPSYCH	Fellow, Royal College of Psychiatrists
FRCR	Fellow, Royal College of Radiologists
FRCS	Fellow, Royal College of Surgeons of England
FRCSE *or* FRCSED	Fellow, Royal College of Surgeons of Edinburgh
FRCSGLAS	Fellow, Royal College of Physicians and Surgeons of Glasgow
FRCSI	Fellow, Royal College of Surgeons in Ireland
FRCVS	Fellow, Royal College of Veterinary Surgeons
FRENG	Fellow, Royal Academy of Engineering
FRGS	Fellow, Royal Geographical Society
FRHISTS	Fellow, Royal Historical Society
FRHS	Fellow, Royal Horticultural Society
FRIBA	Fellow, Royal Institute of British Architects
FRICS	Fellow, Royal Institution of Chartered Surveyors
FRMETS	Fellow, Royal Meteorological Society
FRMS	Fellow, Royal Microscopical Society
FRNS	Fellow, Royal Numismatic Society
FRPHARMS	Fellow, Royal Pharmaceutical Society
FRPS	Fellow, Royal Photographic Society
FRS	Fellow, Royal Society
FRSA	Fellow, Royal Society of Arts
FRSC	Fellow, Royal Society of Chemistry
FRSE	Fellow, Royal Society of Edinburgh
FRSH	Fellow, Royal Society of Health
FRSL	Fellow, Royal Society of Literature
FSA	Fellow, Society of Antiquaries
FTII	Fellow, Chartered Institute of Taxation
FZS	Fellow, Zoological Society

G

GBE	Dame/Knight Grand Cross, Order of the British Empire
GC	George Cross
GCB	Dame/Knight Grand Cross, Order of the Bath
GCLJ	Knight Grand Cross, Order of St Lazarus of Jerusalem
GCMG	Dame/Knight Grand Cross, Order of St Michael and St George
GCVO	Dame/Knight Grand Cross, Royal Victorian Order
Gen.	General
GHQ	general headquarters
GLA	Greater London Authority
GM	George Medal
GMB	Britain's General Union
GMT	Greenwich Mean Time
GOC	General Officer Commanding
Gp Capt.	Group Captain
GPS	Global Positioning System
GRU	*Glavnoje Razvedgvatel'noje Upravlenijie* Russian military intelligence agency

H

HB	His Beatitude
HBM	Her/His Britannic Majesty('s)
HE	Her/His Excellency
	higher education
	His Eminence
HH	Her/His Highness
	Her/His Honour
	His Holiness
HIM	Her/His Imperial Majesty
HM	Her/His Majesty('s)
HMAS	Her/His Majesty's Australian Ship
HMC	Headmasters' and Headmistresses' Conference
HMI	Her/His Majesty's Inspector
HMS	Her/His Majesty's Ship
Hon.	Honorary
	Honourable

HRH	Her/His Royal Highness
HRT	hormone replacement therapy
HSE	*hic sepultus est* here is buried
HSH	Her/His Serene Highness

I

IB	International Baccalaureate
ICC	International Cricket Council
	International Criminal Court
ICJ	International Court of Justice
id	*idem* the same
IP	intellectual property
	internet protocol
IPSA	Independent Parliamentary Standards Authority
IRA	Irish Republican Army
IRC	International Rescue Committee
Is	Islands
IS	Islamic State
ISO	Imperial Service Order
	International Organisation for Standardisation
ISP	internet service provider
ISSN	International Standard Serial Number
ITU	International Telecommunication Union

J

JP	Justice of the Peace

K

KBE	Knight Commander, Order of the British Empire
KCB	Knight Commander, Order of the Bath
KCLJ	Knight Commander, Order of St Lazarus of Jerusalem
KCMG	Knight Commander, Order of St Michael and St George
KCVO	Knight Commander, Royal Victorian Order
KG	Knight of the Garter
KLJ	Knight, Order of St Lazarus of Jerusalem
KP	Knight, Order of St Patrick
KStJ	Knight, Order of St John of Jerusalem
Kt.	Knight
KT	Knight of the Thistle

L

Lab.	Labour
Lat.	Latitude
lbw	leg before wicket (cricket)
lc	lower case (printing)
LD	Liberal Democrat
LDS	Licentiate in Dental Surgery
LHD	*Literarum Humaniorum Doctor* Doctor of Humane Letters/Literature
Lib.	Liberal
LITT D	Doctor of Letters
LLB	Bachelor of Laws
LLD	Doctor of Laws
LLM	Master of Laws
loc cit	*loco citato* in the place cited
Londin:	of London (Bishop)
Long.	longitude
lsd	*librae, solidi, denarii* pounds, shillings and pence
Lt.	Lieutenant
LTA	Lawn Tennis Association
LVO	Lieutenant, Royal Victorian Order

M

m.	married
M	Monsieur
Maj.	Major
MB	*Medicinae Baccalaureus* Bachelor of Medicine
MBA	Master of Business Administration
MBE	Member, Order of the British Empire
MC	Master of Ceremonies
	Military Cross
MCB	Muslim Council of Britain

MCC	Marylebone Cricket Club
MCH(D)	Master of (Dental) Surgery
MDS	Master of Dental Surgery
ME	Middle English
	myalgic encephalomyelitis
MED	Master of Education
Mgr	Monsignor
MIT	Massachusetts Institute of Technology
MLA	Member of Legislative Assembly (NI)
MLITT	Master of Letters
Mlle	Mademoiselle
MM	Military Medal
Mme	Madame
MMR	measles, mumps and rubella (vaccine)
MN	Merchant Navy
MPHIL	Master of Philosophy
MR	Master of the Rolls
MRI	magnetic resonance imaging
MRSA	methicillin-resistant staphylococcus aureus
MS	manuscript (*pl* MSS)
	Master of Surgery
	multiple sclerosis
MSP	Member of Scottish Parliament
MUSB/D	Bachelor/Doctor of Music
MVO	Member, Royal Victorian Order

N

NAAFI	Navy, Army and Air Force Institutes
NAFTA	North American Free Trade Agreement
NAO	National Audit Office
NCO	non-commissioned officer
NDPB	non-departmental public body
NFU	National Farmers' Union
non seq	*non sequitur* it does not follow
Norvic:	of Norwich (Bishop)
NP	Notary Public
NSW	New South Wales (Australia)
NUJ	National Union of Journalists
NUS	National Union of Students
NUT	National Union of Teachers

O

Ob *or* obit	died
OBE	Officer, Order of the British Empire
OBR	Office for Budget Responsibility
OE	Old English
OED	*Oxford English Dictionary*
OHMS	On Her/His Majesty's Service
OM	Order of Merit
ono	or near(est) offer
op	*opus* work
op cit	*opere citato* in the work cited
OS	Ordnance Survey
OStJ	Officer, Order of St John of Jerusalem

P

PC	Plaid Cymru
	Police Constable
	Privy Counsellor
Petriburg:	of Peterborough (Bishop)
PG	parental guidance
	postgraduate
PHD	Doctor of Philosophy
pl	plural
PLO	Palestine Liberation Organisation
PM	post mortem
	Prime Minister
PO	Petty Officer
	Pilot Officer
	postal order
PPS	Parliamentary Private Secretary
PR	proportional representation
PRA	President of the Royal Academy
pro tem	*pro tempore* for the time being
prox	*proximo* next month

PRS	President of the Royal Society
PRSE	President of the Royal Society of Edinburgh
Pte.	Private

Q

QBD	Queen's Bench Division
QC	Queen's Counsel
QE	quantitative easing
QED	*quod erat demonstrandum* which was to be proved
QGM	Queen's Gallantry Medal
QHC	Queen's Honorary Chaplain
QHDS	Queen's Honorary Dental Surgeon
QHNS	Queen's Honorary Nursing Sister
QHP	Queen's Honorary Physician
QHS	Queen's Honorary Surgeon
QMG	Quartermaster-General
QPM	Queen's Police Medal
QSO	quasi-stellar object *(quasar)*
	Queen's Service Order
quango	quasi-autonomous non-governmental organisation
qv	*quod vide* which see

R

r.	*recto* on the right-hand page
R	*Regina* Queen
	Rex King
RA	Royal Academy/Academician
	Royal Artillery
RAC	Royal Armoured Corps
RADA	Royal Academy of Dramatic Art
RADC	Royal Army Dental Corps
RAEC	Royal Army Educational Corps
RAES	Royal Aeronautical Society
	Royal Academy of Music
RAMC	Royal Army Medical Corps
RAVC	Royal Army Veterinary Corps
RC	Red Cross
	Roman Catholic
RCN	Royal College of Nursing
RD	Royal Naval and Royal Marine Forces Reserve Decoration
REME	Royal Electrical and Mechanical Engineers
Rep	Republican
Rep.	Republic
Revd	Reverend
RGS	Royal Geographical Society
RHS	Royal Horticultural Society
RI	Royal Institute of Painters in Watercolours
	Royal Institution
RIR	Royal Irish Regiment
RM	Royal Marines
RMA	Royal Military Academy
RMT	National Union of Rail, Maritime and Transport Workers
RNIB	Royal National Institute of Blind People
RNID	Royal National Institute for Deaf People
RNR	Royal Naval Reserve
Roffen:	of Rochester (Bishop)
RPA	Rural Payments Agency
RSA	Royal Scottish Academician
	Royal Society of Arts
RSC	Royal Shakespeare Company
RSE	Royal Society of Edinburgh
Rt. Hon.	Right Honourable
RVS	Royal Voluntary Service

S

s	section (Public Acts)
	solidus shilling
Salop	Shropshire

Sarum:	of Salisbury (Bishop)
SCD	Doctor of Science
SDLP	Social Democratic and Labour Party
SEAQ	Stock Exchange Automated Quotations system
SEN	special educational needs
SF	Sinn Fein
SFO	Serious Fraud Office
SI	statutory instrument
	Système International d'Unités International System of Units
sic	*sic* so written
sig	signature
	Signor
SOE	Special Operations Executive
sp	*sine prole* without issue
Sr	Senior
	Sister (title)
SS	steamship
stet	*stet* let it stand (printing)
Sub Lt.	sub-lieutenant

T

TEFL	teaching English as a foreign language
TNT	trinitrotoluene (explosive)
trans.	translated
TRH	Their Royal Highnesses
trs	transpose (printing)

U

U	Unionist
uc	upper case (printing)
UDA	Ulster Defence Association
UG	undergraduate
UNESCO	United Nations Educational, Scientific, and Cultural Organization
USB	universal serial bus
UTC	*Temps Universel Coordonné* coordinated universal time
UVF	Ulster Volunteer Force

V

v	*versus* against
v.	*verso* on the left-hand page
VC	Victoria Cross
Ven	Venerable
VR	Volunteer Reserves Service Medal
VSO	Voluntary Service Overseas

W

w.	widowed
WBC	World Boxing Council
WBO	World Boxing Organisation
WCC	World Council of Churches
WFTU	World Federation of Trade Unions
Winton:	of Winchester (Bishop)
WO	Warrant Officer
WRAC	Women's Royal Army Corps
WRAF	Women's Royal Air Force
WRNS	Women's Royal Naval Service
WS	Writer to the Signet

Y

YMCA	Young Men's Christian Association
YWCA	Young Women's Christian Association

Z

ZANU-PF	Zimbabwean African National Union-Patriotic Front

INDEX